THE CIVIL WAR

THE FINAL YEAR

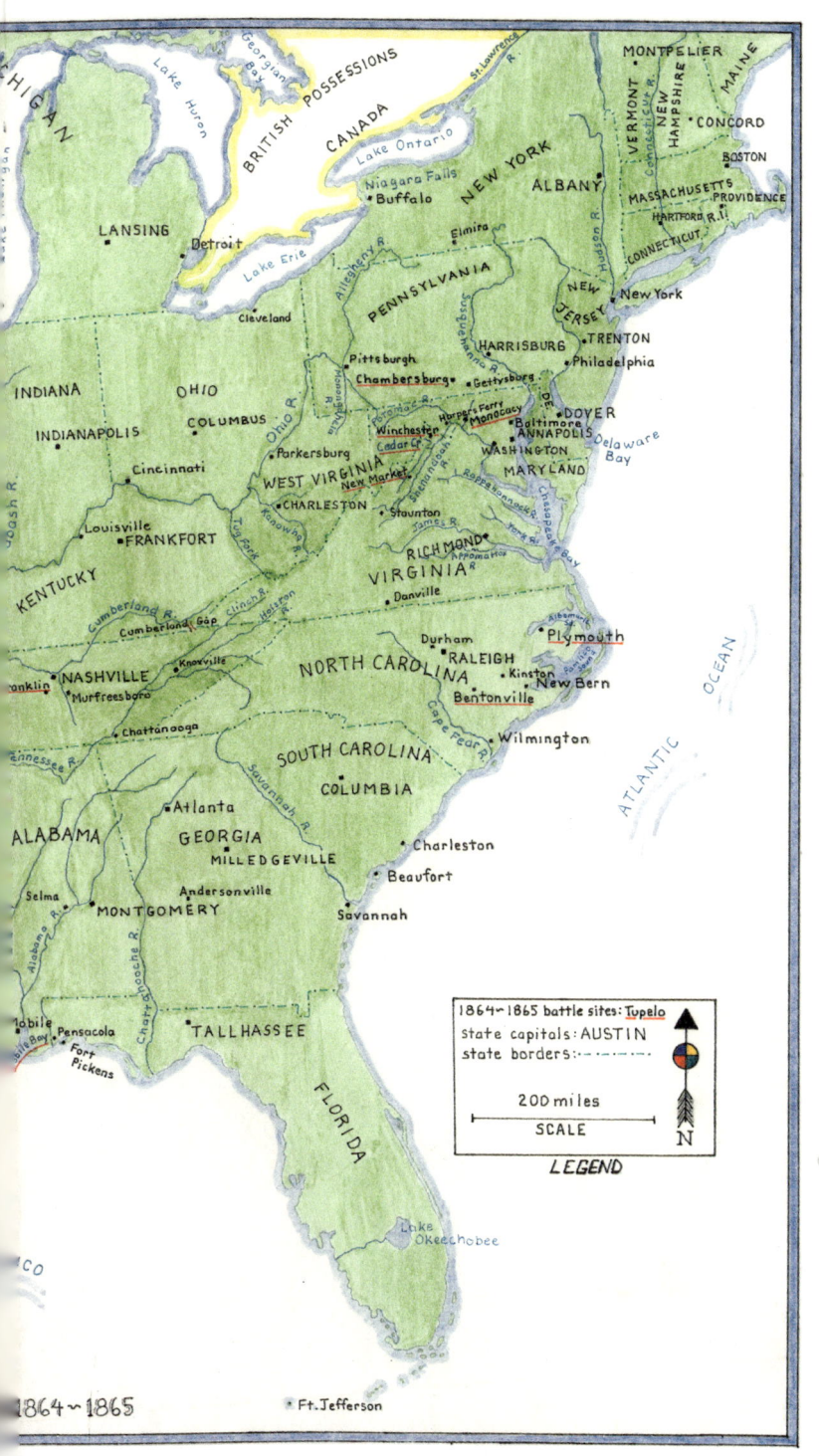

The Civil War

THE FINAL YEAR TOLD BY THOSE WHO LIVED IT

Aaron Sheehan-Dean, editor

THE LIBRARY OF AMERICA

Volume compilation, preface, introduction, notes, and chronology copyright
© 2014 by Literary Classics of the United States, Inc., New York, N.Y.
All rights reserved.
No part of the book may be reproduced commercially
by offset-lithographic or equivalent copying devices without
the permission of the publisher.

Some of the material in this volume is reprinted
by permission of the holders of copyright and publication rights.
Every effort has been made to contact the copyright holders.
If an owner has been unintentionally omitted,
acknowledgment will gladly be made in future printings.
See Note on the Texts on page 791 for further information.

Endpaper maps copyright © 2014 by Earl B. McElfresh,
McElfresh Map Company LLC.

The paper used in this publication meets the
minimum requirements of the American National Standard for
Information Sciences—Permanence of Paper for Printed
Library Materials, ANSI Z39.48—1984.

Distributed to the trade in the United States
by Penguin Random House Inc.
and in Canada by Penguin Random House Canada Ltd.

Library of Congress Control Number: 2013941526
ISBN 978–1–59853–294–4

―――――

Second Printing
The Library of America—250

Manufactured in the United States of America

The Civil War:
The Final Year Told by Those Who Lived It
is published with support from

THE ANDREW W. MELLON FOUNDATION

and

**THE NATIONAL ENDOWMENT
FOR THE HUMANITIES**

The Civil War: The Final Year Told by Those Who Lived It
is kept in print by a gift from

THE BERKLEY FOUNDATION

the Guardians of American Letters Fund,
established by The Library of America
to ensure that every volume in the series
will be permanently available.

Contents

Preface. xxi
Introduction. xxiii

Catherine Edmondston: Diary, March 8, 1864
"Yankee wickedness": North Carolina, March 1864   1

Ellen Renshaw House: Diary, March 9–11, 19, 1864
Occupied Knoxville: Tennessee, March 1864   4

Scientific American: New Rolling Mills in Pittsburgh,
   March 26, 1864
Northern Industry: Pennsylvania, March 1864   9

Harriet Ann Jacobs and Louisa M. Jacobs to Lydia Maria Child,
   March 26, 1864
Opening a Freedmen's School: Virginia, March 1864   11

Jim Heiskell: Statement Regarding His Escape from
   Slavery, March 30, 1864
"My irons were taken off": Tennessee, March 1864   16

Susan C. Woolker to Zebulon B. Vance, April 3, 1864
Hungry Families: North Carolina, April 1864   19

Ulysses S. Grant to William T. Sherman, April 4, 1864
*Planning the Spring Campaign: Washington, D.C.,
   April 1864*   21

William Winters to Harriet Winters, April 4, 1864
"A tear of sorow": Louisiana, April 1864   24

Wilbur Fisk to *The Green Mountain Freeman*, April 7, 1864
Freedom and Slavery: Virginia, April 1864   27

Ellen Renshaw House: Diary, April 8, 1864
An Expulsion Order: Tennessee, April 1864   32

Lois Bryan Adams to the *Detroit Advertiser and Tribune*,
   April 9, 1864
"A proud day": Washington, D.C., April 1864   34

Achilles V. Clark to Judith Porter and Henrietta Ray,
   April 14, 1864
The Fort Pillow Massacre: Tennessee, April 1864   42

Robert E. Lee to Jefferson Davis, April 15, 1864 *Predicting Union Plans: Virginia, April 1864*	45
The New York Times: The Black Flag, April 16, 1864 *"Insatiate as fiends": April 1864*	47
Abraham Lincoln: Address at Baltimore Sanitary Fair, April 18, 1864 *Defining Liberty and Considering Retribution: Maryland, April 1864*	51
R.H.C. to *The Christian Recorder*, April 30, 1864 *"Take no prisoners": April 1864*	54
Gideon Welles: Diary, May 3, 5–6, 1864 *Debating Retaliation: Washington, D.C., May 1864*	57
Petition from the Slaveholders of Randolph County, Alabama, May 6, 1864 *Protesting Slave Impressment: Alabama, May 1864*	60
Samuel W. Fiske to the *Springfield Republican*, May 3, 1864 *"Our right cause": Virginia, May 1864*	63
Theodore Lyman: Journal, May 4–7, 1864 *Battle of the Wilderness: Virginia, May 1864*	68
Wilbur Fisk to *The Green Mountain Freeman*, May 9, 1864 *"The disaster came": Virginia, May 1864*	85
J.F.J. Caldwell: from *The History of a Brigade of South Carolinians* *"Another struggle with death": Virginia, May 1864*	90
Horace Porter: from *Campaigning with Grant* *Grant Turns South: Virginia, May 1864*.	100
Herman Melville: The Armies of the Wilderness *"Strife in the pines": Virginia, May 1864*	102
Ulysses S. Grant to Edwin M. Stanton and to Henry W. Halleck, May 11, 1864 *"If it takes all summer": Virginia, May 1864*	110
Charles Harvey Brewster to Martha Brewster, May 11, 1864; to Mary Brewster, May 13, 1864; and to Martha Brewster, May 15, 1864 *Battle of Spotsylvania: Virginia, May 1864*	112

J.F.J. Caldwell: from *The History of a Brigade of South Carolinians* *The Bloody Angle: Virginia, May 1864*	122
Edward A. Wild to Robert S. Davis, May 12, 1864 *Whipping a Slavemaster: Virginia, May 1864*	130
James A. Connolly to Mary Dunn Connolly, May 15 and 20, 1864 *Battle of Resaca: Georgia, May 1864*	133
Alpheus S. Williams to Mary Williams, May 20, 1864 *"These sad fields": Georgia, May 1864*	137
Samuel T. Foster: Diary, May 23–28, 1864 *Battle of Pickett's Mill: Georgia, May 1864*	140
Richard Taylor: General Orders No. 44, May 23, 1864 *Proclaiming Victory: Louisiana, May 1864*	147
Charles Harvey Brewster to Mary Brewster, May 23, 1864; to Martha Brewster, May 24, 1864; and to Mattie Brewster, May 26, 1864 *"I am scared most to death": Virginia, May 1864*	150
Eugene Forbes: Diary, May 24–27, 1864 *Andersonville Prison: Georgia, May 1864*	160
Charles Francis Adams Jr. to Charles Francis Adams, May 29, 1864 *Appraising Grant: Virginia, May 1864*	163
Lorenzo Thomas to Henry Wilson, May 30, 1864 *Assessing Black Troops: May 1864*	169
Cornelia Hancock to Her Sister, May 28, May 31–June 3, 1864 *Behind the Union Lines: Virginia, May–June 1864*	171
Frank Wilkeson: from *Recollections of a Private Soldier in the Army of the Potomac* *Battle of Cold Harbor: Virginia, May–June 1864*	178
Maria Lydig Daly: Diary, June 8, 1864 *"Born anew in blood and tears": New York, June 1864*	189
Robert Patrick to Alonzo Lewis, June 9, 1864 *"The work of death": Georgia, June 1864*	191
Judith W. McGuire: Diary, June 11, 1864 *Ruined Plantations: Virginia, June 1864*	195

Charles Harvey Brewster to Mattie Brewster, June 11, 1864
"Miserable long dreary days": Virginia, June 1864   199

Charles Francis Adams to Charles Francis Adams Jr.,
June 17, 1864
Completing "the great idea": London, June 1864   202

Charles B. Fisher: Diary, June 19–21, 1864
Fighting the Alabama: The English Channel, June 1864 . . .   205

Wilbur Fisk to *The Green Mountain Freeman*, June 19, 1864
Battle of Petersburg: Virginia, June 1864   211

Stephen Minot Weld to Stephen Minot Weld Sr., June 21, 1864
"Butchered time and again": Virginia, June 1864   216

George E. Chamberlin to Ephraim Chamberlin, June 27, 1864
"A horrid, hellish dream": Virginia, June 1864   218

Eugene Forbes: Diary, June 13–30, 1864
Life at Andersonville: Georgia, June 1864   222

William T. Sherman to Ellen Ewing Sherman, June 30, 1864
The Atlanta Campaign: Georgia, June 1864   232

Horace Greeley to Abraham Lincoln, July 7, 1864
An Appeal for Negotiations: New York, July 1864   235

John White Geary to Mary Geary, July 8, 1864
"An infinity of hills": Georgia, July 1864   238

Abraham Lincoln: Proclamation Concerning Reconstruction,
July 8, 1864
Washington, D.C., July 1864   241

Abraham Lincoln to Horace Greeley, July 9, 1864
Conditions for Peace: Washington, D.C., July 1864   243

Eugene Forbes: Diary, July 11, 1864
Hanging the Andersonville Raiders: Georgia, July 1864 . . .   244

Henry Robinson Berkeley: Diary, July 4–13, 1864
Threatening Washington: Maryland, July 1864   246

Lois Bryan Adams to the *Detroit Advertiser and Tribune*,
July 13 and 15, 1864
The Capital under Attack: Washington, D.C., July 1864 . . .   250

Ulysses S. Grant to Henry W. Halleck, July 14, 1864
Pursuing Early: Virginia, July 1864   256

CONTENTS xiii

Charles A. Dana to Ulysses S. Grant, July 15, 1864
"The deepest shame": Washington, D.C., July 1864 258

Abraham Lincoln: Offer of Safe Conduct for Peace
Negotiators, July 18, 1864
"To Whom it may concern": Washington, D.C., July 1864 . . 259

Clement C. Clay and James P. Holcombe to Horace Greeley,
July 21, 1864
"War to the bitter end": Canada, July 1864 260

James R. Gilmore to the *Boston Evening Transcript*, July 22, 1864
A Meeting with Jefferson Davis: July 1864 264

Henry Robinson Berkeley: Diary, July 14–24, 1864
Fighting in the Shenandoah: Virginia, July 1864 267

Samuel T. Foster: Diary, July 18–23, 1864
Fighting for Atlanta: Georgia, July 1864 271

John Q. A. Dennis to Edwin M. Stanton, July 26, 1864
*"Take my children from those men": Massachusetts,
July 1864* 278

Benjamin F. McIntyre: Diary, July 29, 1864
"A melancholy accident": Texas, July 1864 280

David G. Farragut: General Orders Nos. 10 and 11, July 12
and 29, 1864
Preparing for Battle: Gulf of Mexico, July 1864 283

Stephen Minot Weld: Diary, July 30, 1864, and Memoir
from 1912
The Battle of the Crater: Virginia, July 1864 286

William Pegram to Virginia Johnson Pegram, August 1, 1864
"Murder them in cold blood": Virginia, July 1864 291

C. Chauncey Burr: from *The Old Guard*, August 1864
"This abominable despotism": New York, August 1864 294

Edgeworth Bird to Sallie Bird, August 4, 1864
"Retribution at last": Virginia, August 1864 303

Benjamin F. Wade and Henry Winter Davis: To the Supporters
of the Government, August 5, 1864
"This dictatorial usurpation": August 1864 307

Robert Garlick Hill Kean: Diary, August 7, 1864
"Stern retaliation": Virginia, August 1864 319

CONTENTS

Mathella Page Harrison: Diary, August 17, 1864
"Smoke and flame": Virginia, August 1864 322

Abraham Lincoln: Memorandum on Probable Failure of
Reelection, August 23, 1864
Washington, D.C., August 1864 324

Benjamin F. Butler to Robert Ould, August 27, 1864
Exchanging Prisoners: Virginia, August 1864 325

Robert Toombs to Alexander H. Stephens, August 30, 1864
Defending Atlanta: Georgia, August 1864 333

Platform of the Democratic National Convention, August 30, 1864
"Four years of failure": Illinois, August 1864 336

James R. Gilmore: Our Visit to Richmond, September 1864
"We must conquer": September 1864 338

Robert E. Lee to Jefferson Davis, September 2, 1864
Requesting Reinforcements: Virginia, September 1864 358

Spottswood Rice to His Children and to Kitty Diggs,
September 3, 1864
"My children is my own": Missouri, September 1864 362

Thomas Bramlette to Abraham Lincoln, September 3, 1864
Preserving "our own race": Kentucky, September 1864 365

Gideon Welles: Diary, September 3, 1864
*"Shouting for McClellan": Washington, D.C.,
September 1864* 368

Clement L. Vallandigham to George B. McClellan,
September 4, 1864
Political Advice: Ohio, September 1864 370

Kate Stone: Diary, September 5, 1864
"The wrath to come": Louisiana, September 1864 371

George Templeton Strong: Diary, September 5–8, 1864
"Audacious infamy": New York, September 1864 373

George B. McClellan to the Democratic Nomination
Committee, September 8, 1864
Accepting the Nomination: New Jersey, September 1864 377

James A. Connolly to Mary Dunn Connolly, September 11, 1864
Jonesboro and Atlanta: Georgia, September 1864 380

William T. Sherman to James M. Calhoun and Others, September 12, 1864 *"War is cruelty": Georgia, September 1864*	384
Rachel Ann Wicker to John A. Andrew, September 12, 1864 *Equal Pay for Black Soldiers: Ohio, September 1864*	387
Alexander McKinley to Samuel Francis Du Pont, September 18, 1864 *A Report from Mobile Bay: Alabama, September 1864*	389
Henry Robinson Berkeley: Diary, September 19, 1864 *Battle of Winchester: Virginia, September 1864*	396
Jefferson Davis: Speech at Macon, September 23, 1864 *Georgia, September 1864*	399
Elizabeth Blair Lee to Samuel Phillips Lee, September 24, 1864 *A Cabinet Resignation: Maryland, September 1864*	403
Jefferson Davis: Speech at Columbia, October 4, 1864 *South Carolina, October 1864*	406
Address of the Colored National Convention, October 6, 1864 *A Call for Political Equality: New York, October 1864*	414
William T. Sherman to Ulysses S. Grant, October 9, 1864 *"Make Georgia howl": Georgia, October 1864*	432
Stephen Dodson Ramseur to Ellen Richmond Ramseur, October 10, 1864 *"One great desert": Virginia, October 1864*	434
John B. Jones: Diary, October 10–13, 1864 *Desertion and "despotism": Virginia, October 1864*	437
Samuel Francis Du Pont to William King Hall, October 13, 1864 *England and the Civil War: Delaware, October 1864*	442
Catherine Edmondston: Diary, October 18, 1864 *War News: North Carolina, October 1864*	448
Francis Lieber: Lincoln or McClellan, October 1864 *Unity and Civil Freedom: New York, October 1864*	450
George Templeton Strong: Diary, November 9, 1864 *Election Results: New York, November 1864*	458

John Hay: Diary, November 11, 1864
Reading a Sealed Paper: Washington, D.C., November 1864 460

John S. Mosby to Philip H. Sheridan, November 11, 1864
Retaliatory Executions: Virginia, November 1864 463

Jane Kamper: Statement Regarding Her Emancipation, November 14, 1864
A Slaveowner's Deception: Maryland, November 1864 465

Maria Lydig Daly: Diary, November 15, 1864
"Vox populi, vox dei": New York, November 1864 466

James A. Connolly: Diary, November 17–23, 1864
Sherman's March: Georgia, November 1864 468

John Wilkes Booth: "To whom it may concern," November 1864
"The bitter end": November 1864 479

Henry Adams to Charles Francis Adams Jr., November 25, 1864
Lincoln's Reelection: London, November 1864 483

Joseph Miller: Statement Regarding His Family, November 26, 1864
"My boy was dead": Kentucky, November 1864 486

Samuel T. Foster: Diary, November 30–December 1, 1864
Battle of Franklin: Tennessee, November–December 1864 ... 489

Abraham Lincoln: Annual Message to Congress, December 6, 1864
Washington, D.C., December 1864 493

Henry Nutt to Zebulon B. Vance, December 12, 1864
Reports of a Slave Insurrection: North Carolina, December 1864 510

John Chipman Gray to John C. Ropes, December 14, 1864
Meeting Sherman: Georgia, December 1864 514

John White Geary to Mary Geary, December 17, 1864
Besieging Savannah: Georgia, December 1864 519

Mary S. Mallard: Journal, December 15–21, 1864
Union Looters: Georgia, December 1864 522

Harper's Weekly: Retaliation, January 7, 1865
"The torture of loyal men": New York, January 1865 536

Howell Cobb to James A. Seddon, January 8, 1865
"The most pernicious idea": Georgia, January 1865   538

Catherine Edmondston: Diary, January 9, 1865
*"The birthright of the South": North Carolina,
January 1865*.   541

Petition of the Colored Citizens of Nashville to the Union
   Convention of Tennessee, January 9, 1865
The Right to Vote: Tennessee, January 1865   546

Robert E. Lee to Andrew Hunter, January 11, 1865
Enlisting Slaves "without delay": Virginia, January 1865 . . .   554

Meeting of Colored Ministers with Edwin M. Stanton and
   William T. Sherman, January 12, 1865
"To have land": Georgia, January 1865   558

William T. Sherman: Special Field Orders No. 15, January 16,
   1865
Land for Freedmen: Georgia, January 1865   566

Thirteenth Amendment to the Constitution of the United
   States, January 31, 1865
Washington, D.C., January 1865.   569

George W. Julian: Journal, February 1, 1865
"The greatest event": Washington, D.C., February 1865   570

Robert Garlick Hill Kean: Diary, February 5, 1865
Peace Talks: Virginia, February 1865   572

John H. Stringfellow to Jefferson Davis, February 8, 1865
"We must emancipate": Virginia, February 1865   576

Henry Highland Garnet: A Memorial Discourse, February 12,
   1865
"Let slavery die": Washington, D.C., February 1865   583

Emma LeConte: Diary, February 17–18, 1865
The Burning of Columbia: South Carolina, February 1865 . .   598

Luther Rice Mills to John Mills, March 2, 1865
Confederate Deserters: Virginia, March 1865   609

Abraham Lincoln: Second Inaugural Address, March 4, 1865
Washington, D.C., March 1865.   612

Frederick Douglass: from *Life and Times of Frederick Douglass*
"A sacred effort": Washington, D.C., March 1865   615

Roanoke Island Freedmen to Abraham Lincoln and to Edwin M.
Stanton, March 9, 1865
"We have work faithful": North Carolina, March 1865 618

George Templeton Strong: Diary, March 10, 1865
"The death flurry of a whale": New York, March 1865 623

Alpheus S. Williams to His Daughter, March 12, 1865
*Marching through the Carolinas: North Carolina,
March 1865* 626

Charles Sumner to John Bright, March 13, 1865
Land and Votes: Washington, D.C., March 1865 629

Frances Johnson: Statement Regarding Her Whipping and
Escape, March 25, 1865
"Give me a thousand": Kentucky, March 1865 632

Clarissa Burdett: Statement Regarding Her Whipping and
Escape, March 27, 1865
"A very cruel man": Kentucky, March 1865 635

John B. Jones: Diary, April 2, 1865
"Awaiting my fate": Virginia, April 1865 637

Sallie Brock: from *Richmond During the War*
The Fall of Richmond: Virginia, April 1865 641

George Templeton Strong: Diary, April 3, 1865
"Gloria in excelsis deo": New York, April 1865 650

William Gordon McCabe to Mary Pegram, April 4, 1865
"This peerless comrade": Virginia, April 1865 653

Thomas Morris Chester to the *Philadelphia Press*, April 4
and 6, 1865
Occupying Richmond: Virginia, April 1865 656

Gideon Welles: Diary, April 7, 1865
*Southern "arrogance and folly": Washington, D.C., April
1865* 668

Ulysses S. Grant to Robert E. Lee, April 9, 1865
Surrender Terms: Virginia, April 1865. 671

Robert E. Lee: General Orders No. 9, April 10, 1865
A Commander's Farewell: Virginia, April 1865 673

Elizabeth Keckly: from *Behind the Scenes*
Lincoln's Assassination: Washington, D.C., April 1865 675

George Templeton Strong: Diary, April 15, 1865
"A fearful, gigantic crime": New York, April 1865 684

Gideon Welles: Diary, April 18, 1865
The President's Deathbed: Washington, D.C., April 1865 . . . 688

William T. Sherman to Ulysses S. Grant or Henry W. Halleck, April 18, 1865
A Political Agreement: North Carolina, April 1865 696

Sarah Morgan: Diary, April 19, 1865
"It is all murder": Louisiana, April 1865 700

Robert E. Lee to Jefferson Davis, April 20, 1865
Explaining Surrender: Virginia, April 1865 703

Jefferson Davis to Varina Howell Davis, April 23, 1865
Fleeing Defeat: North Carolina, April 1865 705

Stephen Minot Weld to Hannah Minot Weld, April 24, 1865
"Something that haunted us": Virginia, April 1865 709

Samuel T. Foster: Diary, April 18–May 4, 1865
"What were we fighting for": North Carolina, April–May 1865 711

Ellen Renshaw House: Diary, May 2, 1865
"A thousand rumors": Georgia, May 1865 720

Walt Whitman: from *Specimen Days*
"He behaved so brave": Washington, D.C., May 1865 722

New York Herald: The Grandest Military Display in the World, May 24, 1865
"Heroes of the sublimest conflict": May 1865 725

Lois Bryan Adams to the *Detroit Advertiser and Tribune*, May 24 and 27, 1865
The Grand Review: Washington, D.C., May 1865 728

Gordon Granger: General Orders No. 3, June 19, 1865
"All slaves are free": Texas, June 1865 735

Chronology 739
Biographical Notes 754
Note on the Texts 791
Notes 808
Index 863

Preface

"Has there ever been another historical crisis of the magnitude of 1861–65 in which so many people were so articulate?"
—Edmund Wilson

This Library of America volume is the last in a four-volume series bringing together memorable and significant writing by participants in the American Civil War. Each volume in the series covers approximately one year of the conflict, from the election of Abraham Lincoln in November 1860 to the end of the war in the spring of 1865, and presents a chronological selection of documents from the broadest possible range of authoritative sources—diaries, letters, speeches, military reports, newspaper articles, memoirs, poems, and public papers. Drawing upon an immense and unique body of American writing, the series offers a narrative of the war years that encompasses military and political events and their social and personal reverberations. Created by persons of every class and condition, the writing included here captures the American nation and the American language in the crucial period of their modern formation. Selections have been chosen for their historical significance, their literary quality, and their narrative energy, and are printed from the best available sources. The goal has been to shape a narrative that is both broad and balanced in scope, while at the same time doing justice to the number and diversity of voices and perspectives preserved for us in the writing of the era.

Introduction

On March 8, 1864, Ulysses S. Grant arrived in Washington, D.C., to take command of the armies of the United States, but before he could lead them against the Confederacy, he needed to be introduced to the capital. After meeting President Lincoln for the first time, Grant found himself the center of attention at a White House reception. By the end of the night the modest rumpled man who had been working as a store clerk when the war began was standing on a sofa so that onlookers could catch a glimpse of the general they hoped would save the nation's military fortunes. Grant's victories at Vicksburg and Chattanooga had made him the preeminent Union commander of the war, but he had yet to prove his mettle against Robert E. Lee and his formidable Army of Northern Virginia. Nor was it certain that President Lincoln would be reelected in the fall of 1864, or if he was defeated, that his successor would be willing, or able, to continue the conflict. As the sundered nation began its fourth year of war, both sides could still find reasons to hope that their faith in victory might be rewarded in the months ahead.

The previous year had not begun well for the Union. After its disastrous defeat at Fredericksburg under Ambrose Burnside in December 1862, the Army of the Potomac had suffered from widespread demoralization, alarming desertion rates, and intrigues among its senior generals. Lincoln's decision in January 1863 to replace Burnside with Joseph Hooker helped restore the army's morale, but Hooker's offensive across the Rappahannock River in May ended in a humiliating repulse at Chancellorsville. Confronted by a numerically superior opponent, Lee demonstrated his characteristic audacity by dividing his army and launching a series of counterattacks that drove Hooker back across the river. Although Chancellorsville cost the Confederacy 13,000 men killed, wounded, or missing, the battle bolstered Lee's already high confidence in the ability of his troops. Determined to seize the strategic initiative in the east, Lee invaded Pennsylvania in June in the hope of gaining a third consecutive victory over the Army of the Potomac. When Hooker's successor, George G. Meade, defeated him at Gettysburg in July, Lee managed to escape back across the Potomac into Virginia, where the two opposing commanders maneuvered inconclusively for the remainder of the year. While Lee was aware that the Gettysburg campaign had proved a costly failure, many Southerners considered the battle to have been a draw, while many Northerners—especially President Lincoln—understood that defensive victories alone would not win the war in the east.

By the end of 1863 there was no uncertainty regarding the ability of the Union to win offensive victories in the western theater. After spending the winter engaged in a series of futile attempts to reach the Confederate stronghold at Vicksburg through the rivers and bayous of the Mississippi Delta, Grant had shown a willingness to take risks equal to Lee's. Crossing the Mississippi well below Vicksburg at the beginning of May, Grant had marched his army northeast to Jackson, then turned west to attack his main objective from the rear. Vicksburg's surrender on July 4, the day after the failure of Lee's final assault at Gettysburg, gave the Union control of the entire length of the Mississippi and effectively cut Texas, western Louisiana, and Arkansas off from the rest of the Confederacy. "The Father of Waters," Lincoln gratefully observed, "again goes unvexed to the sea." During the summer of 1863 William S. Rosecrans also succeeded in gaining control of Middle Tennessee for the Union, skillfully maneuvering Braxton Bragg out of a series of defensive positions and forcing him to retreat into northwestern Georgia. Reinforced by Confederate troops from Virginia and Mississippi, Bragg turned on Rosecrans in September and defeated his Army of the Cumberland at Chickamauga. The victory rallied Confederate spirits but proved short-lived. Union forces under Grant broke Bragg's siege of Chattanooga, and in November they drove the Confederates off Missionary Ridge and forced them back into northwestern Georgia.

Union forces faced military, political, and humanitarian challenges as they advanced deeper into southern territory. The need to occupy towns and cities, and to guard railroads and bridges against Confederate guerrillas and cavalry raiders, drew troops away from the main northern armies. In fighting guerrillas, Union soldiers increasingly showed less restraint in exercising the "hard war" policies first adopted in 1862, burning farms, imprisoning or expelling civilians suspected of disloyalty, and often summarily executing captured "bushwhackers," actions that only increased the hatred most white Southerners felt toward the northern occupiers. The question of how civilian governments were to be reconstructed in the South became a potential source of division between President Lincoln and the Radical Republicans in Congress. And both the Union army and the various civilian aid agencies that assisted it found themselves hard-pressed to care for the thousands of former slaves who came into the Union lines each month.

Despite the success of the Union armies, dissension and violence would mark 1863 in the North. When Clement L. Vallandigham, one of the leading Democratic opponents of emancipation and the draft, declared in May that "a wicked, cruel and unnecessary" war was being waged "for the purpose of crushing out liberty and erecting a despotism; a war for the freedom of the blacks, and the enslavement of the whites," Burnside had him arrested and tried by a military commission in Ohio. Burnside's actions stirred up a hornet's nest of controversy over free speech and the permissible boundaries of wartime dissent that continued well after Lincoln banished Vallandigham into Confederate-held territory. In July the enforcement of the draft sent rioters, many of them Irish and German immigrants, rampaging through the streets of New York. Mobs, angry over the draft and emancipation, turned on black New Yorkers, lynching at least eleven African Americans and attacking the homes and businesses of prominent Republicans. The final toll of 105 dead made the New York draft riots the worst act of urban violence in the United States during the nineteenth century. In the meantime, Vallandigham had escaped to Canada, where he campaigned from exile as the Democratic candidate for governor of Ohio. His overwhelming defeat in the fall of 1863 raised Republican hopes for success in the 1864 elections, yet few supporters of the administration expected that it would be reelected if the coming year failed to produce decisive battlefield victories.

Jefferson Davis could take little solace from considering

Lincoln's trials. In the spring of 1863 a series of food riots in southern cities, including the famous Richmond Bread Riot of early April, demonstrated a new militancy on the part of white southern women as they took to the streets to protest rising prices and the Confederate government's failure to organize effective relief. Often identifying themselves as soldiers' wives, these hungry women parlayed their sacrifices in sending sons, husbands, brothers, and fathers off to war to win legislative support for an unprecedented public welfare program that proved only partially successful in alleviating hunger and scarcity in the Confederacy. Confederate conscription efforts also met with violent resistance from armed draft evaders and deserters who took refuge in remote regions of the South.

While white Southerners expressed discontent with the demands of war, black Southerners challenged slavery at every level. Every slaveholder could report evidence of what he considered disrespectful behavior, if not outright rebellion. In rare cases, enslaved people committed acts of violence and destruction against former masters. More often, wherever the opportunity presented itself, slaves fled. Gathering family members, they escaped on foot, on horseback, or by boat to the nearest Union outpost. In the opening months of the war, Union commanders had possessed considerable leeway to return runaway slaves, and Democratic generals, especially George B. McClellan, had drawn the scorn of Republicans in Congress and the press for their willingness to protect slaveholders' rights. But the Emancipation Proclamation, along with legislation passed by Congress in 1862, had turned the Union army into a giant engine for emancipation. In areas such as coastal Georgia and Florida and the Mississippi Valley, the Union army organized expeditions whose main purpose was to free slaves, some of whom were then recruited for service in the rapidly expanding U.S. Colored Troops.

During 1863 the Union army's use of black soldiers began to have a major impact upon the war. The heroic efforts of African American troops at Port Hudson, Milliken's Bend, and Fort Wagner helped change northern attitudes about race. Although many Democrats continued to vigorously oppose black enlistment, a sizable number of skeptical white Northerners came to respect the willingness of black men to die for the Union, while the manpower advantage the North gained by turning slaves (and free black men) into soldiers could not be ignored in the Confederacy. In January 1864 Patrick Cleburne, a Confederate division commander with an outstanding battle record, asked his fellow generals in the Army of Tennessee to consider emancipating slaves and enlisting them in the Confederate forces. A copy of his address was sent to Jefferson Davis, who ordered it suppressed. At the same time, the Davis administration continued to refuse to exchange black prisoners, a policy that had contributed to the breakdown of the exchange cartel during 1863 and increased death and hardship among prisoners of war on both sides.

By the beginning of 1864 mass death and suffering had become a permanent presence in the American psyche. The battle of Gettysburg alone had killed about seven thousand men outright, and several thousand more would eventually die of their wounds or be maimed for life. Northerners and Southerners alike contended with the shock of seeing men without arms or legs, disfigured by shrapnel, or ravaged by disease. Still the war continued, as soldiers and civilians on both sides accepted the necessity of a fourth year of fighting with a mixture of determination and resignation. Many in the North expected that Grant would quickly defeat Lee in the spring and capture Richmond, while Confederate hopes focused on the gradual exhaustion of the northern will to fight and the defeat of the Lincoln administration at the polls. As spring came, both sides would plunge again into the maelstrom of battle.

Aaron Sheehan-Dean

"YANKEE WICKEDNESS":
NORTH CAROLINA, MARCH 1864

Catherine Edmondston:
Diary, March 8, 1864

In July 1862 the Union and Confederate armies negotiated an agreement on prisoner exchanges. The cartel began to collapse in the summer of 1863 because the Confederates refused to treat black soldiers and their officers as prisoners of war. Union officials insisted that black and white prisoners be treated equally under the cartel, and later protested when men paroled at Vicksburg returned to the Confederate ranks without being properly exchanged. By February 1864 some 5,000 Union prisoners were being held in Richmond, where they suffered from hunger, disease, and exposure. Brigadier General Judson Kilpatrick, a division commander in the Army of the Potomac's cavalry corps, gained approval from President Lincoln and Secretary of War Edwin M. Stanton for a raid on the Confederate capital aimed at freeing the prisoners. On February 28 Kilpatrick and 3,500 men crossed the Rapidan River sixty miles north of Richmond, then split up the next day. The main force under Kilpatrick encountered unexpectedly strong resistance when it reached the northern outskirts of the city on March 1, while a smaller body of 460 men led by Colonel Ulric Dahlgren was unable to cross the James River and attack Richmond from the south. While Kilpatrick and most of his command reached the Union lines on the Virginia Peninsula, Dahlgren was killed in an ambush on March 2. In papers found on his body Dahlgren wrote that once the prisoners were released and the city captured, "it must be destroyed and Jeff Davis and Cabinet killed." (Kilpatrick would later deny having given or received orders to burn the city or to kill Confederate leaders.) The papers were given to Jefferson Davis on March 4 and published in the Richmond press the next day. Catherine Edmondston followed reports of the raid from her plantation home in Halifax County, North Carolina.

MARCH 8, 1864
News last night which makes the blood of all true hearted Confederates boil in their veins at this new instance of Yankee

wickedness & meanness. Lieut Pollard Comdg Company H of the 9th Va Cavelry, aided by some Home guards & a small detachment from Lieut Col Robbin's Command, followed a large party of the Yankee Cavalry, harrassing their rear all day Wednesday, crossing the Mattapony after them. The Enemy under Col Dahlgren's command took the fork of the road leading to Walkertown when Lieut Pollard, hastily dividing his force, left a small body in pursuit & taking the other fork succeeding in a circuit, & having been joined by the forces above named, appeared on their front about eleven at night; Dahlgren ordered a charge—& in the act was shot through the head. A fight then ensued in which he took 90 prisoners, 35 negroes, & 150 horses & the rest of the enemy dispersed in the darkness in wild flight through the woods. On Col Dahlgren's person was found memoranda & orders disclosing a most diabolical plan in which, God be praised, he was defeated. He was to cross to the South side of the James about thirty miles above Richmond with one Squadron, keeping the other on the North side, signalling each other as they went. That on the South side was to seize the bridges at Richmond, release the prisoners on Belle Isle, arming them from waggons which they carried loaded with small arms for the purpose & supplying them with oakum balls soaked in tar with which they were all well provided for the purpose of destroying the city by fire.

The North side party was to destroy the Arsenal etc. at Bellona & the two Squadrons making a junction in the city were to seize Mr Davis & his Cabinet, *hang them* immediately, join the prisoners in setting the city on fire, & by daybreak be across the Pamunky in full retreat, leaving murder, rapine, & a city in ashes behind them. But God ordained otherwise. A negroe whom they seized for a guide brought them, doubtless in good faith to them, to a point on the James where he told them they could cross; but the River being higher than he was aware of, when they reached the place, they were unable to do so, whereupon they instantly hanged him. This, however, disconcerted their plans and meeting with a stouter resistance than they thought, they were forced to retreat without so much as entering Richmond. Are our enemies civilized? Do they even *profess* the doctrines of Christ? What sort of a return is this for the way our troops acted towards them in their last summer's campaign into Penn? We respected all private rights, horses only excepted, & not *one* private dwelling in ashes marked the footsteps of our army. One only was molested & that by three men, Mississippians, who had all of them had their own houses burned by the enemy & their wives & children driven out homeless. They dared not *burn* it in retaliation, for they feared the smoke would betray them & that Gen Lee in stern justice would visit on them the penalty of a violated Order, so they only hacked & hewed the furniture to peices, & tell me how many thousand of our Southern homes have been thus and worse treated? Blood thirsty tho it appears, our Government ought to adopt a different course with men captured on such an expedition. It is not regular warfare & they are not entitled to the privileges of prisoners of war. It is mockery to insist that they are. Dahlgren is the son of the Commodore now in command before Charleston. The one aids in the infamous attempt to destroy a whole city & to hurry thousands of non-combattants incapable of resistance to a dreadful death. The other is even worse; at the head of a gang of picked ruffians armed with fire balls, his deliberate purpose is to turn loose upon innocent women a mixed multitude, a mob of prisoners, without even the show of an authority to command them, with orders to pillage, burn, destroy, murder; in short, do all that their evil passions prompt them, whilst he himself a commissioned officer of the U S hangs without trial the heads of a Government whose meanest soldier his Government has admitted to the rights of a belligerant. Talk of Punic Faith no more! hence forth let it be "Yankee faith." Like father like son. Dahlgren and Kilpatrick's paths are marked with desolation, vide some of the particulars marked D.

OCCUPIED KNOXVILLE: TENNESSEE, MARCH 1864

Ellen Renshaw House: Diary, March 9–11, 19, 1864

In a referendum held on June 8, 1861, Tennessee voters had endorsed leaving the Union by 104,913 to 47,238. Secession was opposed by 70 percent of the voters in East Tennessee, a mountainous region with relatively few slaveholders that would remain bitterly divided between secessionists and unionists. Ellen Renshaw House had moved with her family from Marietta, Georgia, to Knoxville shortly before the war. She remained in the city after it was occupied by Union troops on September 2, 1863, and during the subsequent siege by Confederate forces under Lieutenant General James Longstreet from November 17 to December 4. "God grant it is not so. It is so," House wrote in her diary after Longstreet abandoned his attempt to retake Knoxville. By March 1864 one of House's brothers was a prisoner of war on Johnson's Island in Lake Erie, while another brother was serving with the Confederate army at Mobile, Alabama.

March 9. Wednesday. I felt so worried all night about poor Leo, I could not sleep, and got up before daylight, and went down to see him, poor dog. He did not know me, he was dying. Oh! I felt so badly about it got father to go for Dr Rogers. He could not come, then for Will. By the time he got here he was dead. It seems more like a human being had died than a dog. It even bought tears to Will's eyes. I expect it made him think of the baby, & he used to be so fond of him. I have been crying nearly the whole day. I cant help it. My heart aches when I think of his being dead. Will sent a man round to bury him. Dr R. came after he was dead. Said he thought he had probably been shot.

This afternoon father said Lieut Shaw had told him there were sixty prisoners in the jail, and sister & I thought we would go see them. When we went to the office the clerk Jim said there was only one man besides the Indians. I dont know why they have not been sent north with the other prisoners. While I was standing by the door talking, an Officer came up with a Confederate Lieut. I asked Lieut Shaw if I could speak to him. He said certainly. The officers who came with him very pertly said Oh! yes you can look at & talk to him as much as you like. I turned to him and asked in my very pleasantest manner, Where were you captured Lt. He looked slightly sneaking & replied "I was not captured at all." (I know my face was in a blaze. I would liked to see some one slap his face) "You came in" I asked. He said "yes" the contemptable rascal. I turned round as fast and walked off in a hurry. The Yankee Officers laughed. I know Lt Shaw told him that I was the D——t rebel he ever saw.

From there we went to see Mrs French & Mrs McClannahan. Not long after we came home Capt Whitman came with a Capt McAlister to get board for himself, wife & child. Of course mother had to say they could come. I hate the idea of Yankee woman & children in the house. We have whipped them above here at Panther Springs. Letter from Johnnie & I answered it.

March 10. Thursday. It rained heavily last night. Capt McAlister came this morning. He is the nephew of old Col McAlister of Sav. and studied law there. Knows a great many of fathers friends as does his wife, who seems very much of a Lady. They arrived two days since & have been staying at Gen Carters. The Capt & I got at it tonight. He said he heard of me before he came here. Father, he says, is considered a good Union man, Mother a very proper person, but one of the daughters was an outrageous rebel. I told him I was perfectly willing for them to consider me so, and if I thought there was any chance of them sending me South I would cut up some anticks most certainly. I am glad to hear they consider father a good Union man, as long as he has taken the oath, for that being the case they will not make him responsible for any thing I may do, and I expect sometime I will do something devilish—that is just the word, though not a lady like one.

Poor Leo. I miss him so much, turn round expecting to see him every time I hear a noise. I did not think any one could love a dumb animal as much as I did him, and miss him as sadly. Mrs. Currey came over this morning & took tea. I hear that there is a report in town that Mrs Kain went to head Quarters after she had received her orders and begged to be allowed to take the oath. Said she was a northern woman & had always been a Union woman but had never dared to say so. How on earth such a thing could have been started I cant imagine, at least could not till I heard the fountain from which it emanated was Mrs Longward. Of course I wondered no longer. She like her father needs not the slightest foundation for any structure, however elaborate or gigantic. I wonder what Mrs K could say if she could hear it.

March 11. Friday. No news of any importance today. I am told the pickets were run in last night two miles above here. Some say our saints were that near to Knoxville. Capt McAlister told me tonight that he had seen Gen Carter and had quite a long talk with him, during which he (Gen C) had requested him to caution me, as I would certainly be sent South if I were not more prudent. That I had been very active &c, and the military here had from my actions and conversations been led to believe me a very violent rebel, one who would sell her soul and body for the benefit of the Confederates. I told him I certainly would lay down my life willingly did I know by so doing I would do the Confederacy the least good. That I had never done any thing I would not do again or said any thing I would not say over under the same circumstances. The only thing I have ever done was to wave to our poor fellows as they were going north to prison, and there I forgot for the moment I was not free but was living under a despotism. That if they sent me south they would not punish me very much. I'd have been there long ago if father & mother had not been so much opposed to it &c &c. Gen Carter is foolish if he thinks he is going to frighten me. I am not afraid of him or any other Yankee living or dead. The Capt says Capt Whitman told him the same thing about me.

One of his clerks named Price told Lusie he shot my dog, the triffling rascal. Oh! wont I have an opportunity some time to pay off a few of the debts I owe to the miserable wretches, and wont I do it with a good will. Capt McA told mother Gen Carter was very much surprised to hear she was a relation of

Admiral Renshaw. I suppose she should have gone and informed him of the fact on his first arrival in Knoxville. He (Gen C) is an old navy officer.

March 19. Saturday. I felt so badly this morning I did not get up till after breakfast. There has been a fight up the road in which the Yanks did not whip and they have fallen back twenty five miles. Yankee rumor says to that there has been an attack made on the train below in which the Rebels were driven back. Dr. Piggott was in this morning. He says all the sick are getting along very well with one exception. He does not know when he will be sent out, says he is afraid he will take root in East Tenn. Capt McAlister and himself had quite an argument in which the Capt did not get much the best. He is so abominably self-opinionated, so fond of talking about his family being a ruling one for so many years, and about his loving the Southern people so, and his being a christian—and having his hands clean, that he used all his influence to prevent the war and all that kind of stuff—and the next minute says the Southern people must & will be exterminated rather than the Union be destroyed. I do believe it would afford him sincere pleasure to see the whole scale lynching of the rebels which he advocated so strongly carried into execution before his own eyes.

Oh! I do get furious to hear him talk. It seems to me sometimes that I feel perfectly reckless of what I say or do. It is growing on me every day. As long as I could keep out of the way of the vile creatures I did it, and got along very well, but since I cant turn round without seeing one, and have them eternally in our sitting room, always introducing the subject, I cant contain myself. I say all sorts of things about all their officers & men, abuse Carter or any of them, and say every thing impudent that comes into my head. If Gen Longstreet dont come soon goodness only knows where it will end.

I hear that Gen Carter says Col Keith ought to have put Mrs Hamilton in prison because she said she gloried in being a Rebel, and if he had her in his power again he would certainly do it. Maj Gratz says Mrs Hamilton told him the reason she did not want to go south was that Sam H. and herself were to be married as soon as he returned from the North. This afternoon what did Capt & Mrs McA. have to do but go to see Mrs Brownlow—rather reversing the order of things. She told them that she never had done any work in her life and it came very hard now, as she has lost a servant and had to do it. Nothing like telling a good one, and she also said that there were many ladies here who would do themselves the pleasure of calling on her as soon as they knew she was here, was sorry she had not known it sooner. If the tory women come here I'll insult them certain and sure.

NORTHERN INDUSTRY:
PENNSYLVANIA, MARCH 1864

Scientific American:
New Rolling Mills in Pittsburgh

March 26, 1864

A survey of the American iron industry published in 1859 recorded 202 active rolling mills in the United States, only nineteen of which were located in states that later joined the Confederacy. During the war three additional mills went into operation in the Confederate states, while twelve entirely new mills were opened in the North; in addition, many existing northern ironworks expanded their facilities during the conflict. The increased productive capacity of several works in Pittsburgh was detailed by *Scientific American* at a time when the southern iron industry was struggling with shortages of crude iron and skilled workers and the loss of several manufacturing facilities in Tennessee.

―――――――

Quite a number of new rolling mills have been put up by Pittsburgh manufacturers during the past year. Messrs. Lyon & Shorb, of the Sligo Works, have put up a mill two hundred feet in length by one hundred and four feet in width, capable of turning out armor plates of the largest size; the firm has also erected a sheet mill ninety feet long by eighty feet wide. The Messrs. McKnight, of the Birmingham Works, have erected a new sheet-iron and armor-plate mill, the buildings of which are sixty by eighty feet. The plate mill has a capacity of fifty tuns per week, and is constructed with a view to the rolling of sheet-iron, for the production of which it has a capacity of one thousand tuns a year. The Messrs. Jones & Laughlins, of the American Works, have erected a building two hundred by one hundred and twenty-five feet, within which is constructed two sheet mills, and a twelve-inch train for bar, and three eight-inch trains for small iron and hoops; three heating furnaces and two annealing furnaces. The capacity of these mills is thirty tuns per day. Messrs. Reese, Graff & Dull have built a forge, a plate mill and a sheet mill, occupying a building two hundred and five by one hundred and five feet. The plate mill is constructed for rolling armor plates for naval uses, ten feet long and from one to one and a half inches thick, weighing from one thousand six hundred pounds to a tun each. The plate mill has a capacity of one hundred tuns, the sheet mills a capacity of fifteen tuns, and the forge of two hundred and ten tuns a week. They have also erected a hoop mill of two trains with a capacity of eighty tuns per week, the mill building of which is one hundred and twenty by seventy-five feet. Messrs. Kloman & Philipps, and Messrs. Wharton, Brothers & Co. have each put up a new mill.

OPENING A FREEDMEN'S SCHOOL:
VIRGINIA, MARCH 1864

Harriet Ann Jacobs and Louisa M. Jacobs to Lydia Maria Child

In the summer of 1862 Harriet Ann Jacobs, the author of *Incidents in the Life of a Slave Girl*, had begun relief work among the former slaves who had fled to Alexandria, Virginia. She was joined there in November 1863 by her daughter Louisa Matilda Jacobs, and together they established the Jacobs Free School, located at Pitt and Oronoco streets in Alexandria. Harriet and Louisa Jacobs wrote about the school to the abolitionist Lydia Maria Child, who had edited *Incidents*, in a letter that appeared in the *National Anti-Slavery Standard* on April 16, 1864.

———————

ALEXANDRIA, March 26, 1864.

DEAR MRS. CHILD:

When I went to the North, last Fall, the Freedmen here were building a schoolhouse, and I expected it would have been finished by the time I returned. But when we arrived, we found it uncompleted. Their funds had got exhausted, and the work was at a stand-still for several weeks. This was a disappointment; but the time did not hang idle on our hands, I assure you. We went round visiting the new homes of the Freedmen, which now dot the landscape, built with their first earnings as free laborers. Within the last eight months seven hundred little cabins have been built, containing from two to four rooms. The average cost was from one hundred to two hundred and fifty dollars. In building school-houses or shelters for the old and decrepid, they have received but little assistance. They have had to struggle along and help themselves as they could. But though this has been discouraging, at times, it teaches them self reliance; and that is good for them, as it is for everybody. We have over seven thousand colored refugees in this place, and, including the hospitals, less than four hundred rations are given out. This shows that they are willing to earn their own way, and generally capable of it. Indeed, when I look back on the condition in which I first found them, and compare it with their condition now, I am convinced they are not so far behind other races as some people represent them. The two rooms we occupy were given to me by the Military Governor, to be appropriated to the use of decrepid women, when we leave them.

When we went round visiting the homes of these people, we found much to commend them for. Many of them showed marks of industry, neatness, and natural refinement. In others, chaos reigned supreme. There was nothing about them to indicate the presence of a wifely wife, or a motherly mother. They bore abundant marks of the half-barbarous, miserable condition of Slavery, from which the inmates had lately come. It made me sad to see their shiftlessness and discomfort; but I was hopeful for the future. The consciousness of working for themselves, and of having a character to gain, will inspire them with energy and enterprise, and a higher civilization will gradually come.

Children abounded in these cabins. They peeped out from every nook and corner. Many of them were extremely pretty and bright-looking. Some had features and complexions purely Anglo-Saxon; showing plainly enough the slaveholder's horror of amalgamation. Some smiled upon us, and were very ready to be friends. Others regarded us with shy, suspicious looks, as is apt to be the case with children who have had a cramped childhood. But they all wanted to accept our invitation to go to school, and so did all the parents for them.

In the course of our rounds, we visited a settlement which had received no name. We suggested to the settlers that it would be proper to name it for some champion of Liberty. We told them of the Hon. Chas. Sumner, whose large heart and great mind had for years been devoted to the cause of the poor slaves. We told how violent and cruel slaveholders had nearly murdered him for standing up so manfully in defense of Freedom. His claim to their gratitude was at once recognized, and the settlement was called Sumnerville.

Before we came here, a white lady, from Chelsea, Mass., was laboring as a missionary among the Refugees; and a white teacher, sent by the Educational Commission of Boston, accompanied us. One of the freedmen, whose cabin consisted of two rooms, gave it up to us for our school. We soon found that the clamor of little voices begging for admittance far exceeded the narrow limits of this establishment.

Friends at the North had given us some articles left from one of the Fairs. To these we added what we could, and got up a little Fair here, to help them in the completion of the schoolhouse. By this means we raised one hundred and fifty dollars, and they were much gratified by the result. With the completion of the school-house our field of labor widened, and we were joyful over the prospect of extended usefulness. But some difficulties occurred, as there always do in the settlement of such affairs. A question arose whether the white teachers or the colored teachers should be superintendents. The freedmen had built the school-house for their children, and were Trustees of the school. So, after some discussion, it was decided that it would be best for them to hold a meeting, and settle the question for themselves. I wish you could have been at that meeting. Most of the people were slaves, until quite recently, but they talked sensibly, and I assure you that they put the question to vote in quite parliamentary style. The result was a decision that the colored teachers should have charge of the school. We were gratified by this result, because our sympathies are closely linked with our oppressed race. These people, born and bred in slavery, had always been so accustomed to look upon the white race as their natural superiors and masters, that we had some doubts whether they could easily throw off the habit; and the fact of their giving preference to colored teachers, as managers of the establishment, seemed to us to indicate that even their brief possession of freedom had begun to inspire them with respect for their race.

On the 11th of January we opened school in the new schoolhouse, with seventy-five scholars. Now, we have two hundred and twenty-five. Slavery has not crushed out the animal spirits of these children. Fun lurks in the corners of their eyes, dimples their mouths, tingles at their fingers' ends, and is, like a torpedo, ready to explode at the slightest touch. The war-spirit has a powerful hold upon them. No one turns the other cheek for a second blow. But they evince a generous nature. They never allow an older and stronger scholar to impose upon a younger and weaker one; and when they happen to have any little delicacies, they are very ready to share them with others. The task of regulating them is by no means an easy one; but we put heart, mind, and strength freely into the work, and only regret that we have not more physical strength. Their ardent desire to learn is very encouraging, and the improvement they make consoles us for many trials. You would be astonished at the progress many of them have made in this short time. Many who less than three months ago scarcely knew the A.B.C. are now reading and spelling in words of two or three syllables. When I look at these bright little boys, I often wonder whether there is not some Frederick Douglass among them, destined to do honor to his race in the future. No one can predict, now-a-days, how rapidly the wheels of progress will move on.

There is also an evening-school here, chiefly consisting of adults and largely attended; but with that I am not connected.

On the 10th of this month, there was considerable excitement here. The bells were rung in honor of the vote to abolish slavery in Virginia. Many did not know what was the cause of such a demonstration. Some thought it was an alarm of fire; others supposed the rebels had made a raid, and were marching down King st. We were, at first, inclined to the latter opinion; for, looking up that street we saw a company of the most woe-begone looking horsemen. It was raining hard, and some of them had dismounted, leading their poor jaded skeletons of horses. We soon learned that there were a portion of Kilpatrick's cavalry, on their way to Culpepper. Poor fellows! They had had a weary tramp, and must still tramp on, through mud and rain, till they reached their journey's end. What hopeless despondency would take possession of our hearts, if we looked only on the suffering occasioned by this war, and not on the good already accomplished, and the still grander results shadowed forth in the future. The slowly-moving ambulance often passes by, with low beat of the drum, as the soldiers convey some comrade to his last resting-place. Buried on strange soil, far away from mother, wife, and children! Poor fellows! But they die the death of brave men in a noble cause. The Soldier's Burying Ground here is well cared for, and is a beautiful place.

How nobly are the colored soldiers fighting and dying in the cause of freedom! Our hearts are proud of the manhood they evince, in spite of the indignities heaped upon them. They are kept constantly on fatigue duty, digging trenches, and unloading vessels. Look at the Massachusetts Fifty-Fourth! Every man of them a hero! marching so boldly and steadily to victory or death, for the freedom of their race, and the salvation of their country! *Their* country! It makes my blood run warm to think how that country treats her colored sons, even the bravest and the best. If merit deserves reward, surely the 54th regiment is worthy of shoulder-straps. I have lately heard, from a friend in Boston, that the rank of second-lieutenant has been conferred. I am thankful there is a beginning. I am full of hope for the future. A Power mightier than man is guiding this revolution; and though justice moves slowly, it will come at last. The American people will outlive this mean prejudice against complexion. Sooner or later, they will learn that "a man's a man for a' that."

We went to the wharf last Tuesday, to welcome the emigrants returned from Hayti. It was a bitter cold day, the snow was falling, and they were barefooted and bareheaded, with scarcely rags enough to cover them. They were put in wagons and carried to Green Heights. We did what we could for them. I went to see them next day, and found that three had died during the night. I was grieved for their hard lot; but I comforted myself with the idea that this would put an end to colonization projects. They are eight miles from here, but I shall go to see them again to-morrow. I hope to obtain among them some recruits for the Massachusetts Cavalry. I am trying to help Mr. Downing and Mr. Remond; not for money, but because I want to do all I can to strengthen the hands of those who are battling for Freedom.

Thank you for your letter. I wish you could have seen the happy group of faces round me, at our little Fair, while I read it to them. The memory of the grateful hearts I have found among these freed men and women, will cheer me all my life. Yours truly,

H. JACOBS and L. JACOBS.

"MY IRONS WERE TAKEN OFF":
TENNESSEE, MARCH 1864

Jim Heiskell: Statement Regarding His Escape from Slavery

President Lincoln had exempted Tennessee from the states covered by the Emancipation Proclamation in an attempt to strengthen the unionist government established in Nashville by Andrew Johnson in 1862. While the Union army encouraged the slaves of Confederate owners in Tennessee to escape, government policy toward slaves owned by unionists was often ambiguous. Jim Heiskell was owned by William Heiskell, a unionist in Knoxville who served as an agent of the Treasury Department. After running away from a farm outside the city, Jim Heiskell was captured in Knoxville in late March 1864 and then escaped again with the help of his brother Bob. His case aroused controversy when it was alleged by the *New-York Daily Tribune* that Brigadier General Samuel P. Carter, the provost marshal of Knoxville, had sent soldiers to help guard Jim Heiskell after his capture. (Legislation passed by Congress in 1862 prohibited Union officers from returning any fugitive slave, regardless of the loyalty of the owner.) Carter denied the charge and claimed that he had sent the guards to defend the Heiskell house against Bob Heiskell, who reportedly had armed himself with a revolver, threatened William Heiskell's life, and called his wife "a d—d old freckle faced bitch." On March 28, 1864, Major General John M. Schofield, the commander of the Army of the Ohio, ordered that Bob and Jim Heiskell be declared "free from the control of their late master, Mr. William Heiskell," and placed "under the protection of the United States Government." Jim Heiskell gave a statement for the record two days later.

Statement of "Jim" Heiskell

My name is Jim; I have been living on Bull run, with a man by the name of Pierce; they called him Cromwell Pierce. I run off from him nearly two months ago, because he treated me so mean: he half starved and whipped me. I was whipped three or four times a week, sometimes with a cowhide, and sometimes with a hickory. He put so much work on me, I could not do it;

chopping & hauling wood and lumber logs. I am about thirteen years old. I got a pretty good meal at dinner, but he only gave us a half pint of milk for breakfast and supper, with cornbread. I ran away to town; I had a brother "Bob" living in Knoxville, and other boys I knew. I would have staid on the plantation if I had been well used. I wanted also to see some pleasure in town. I hired myself to Capt. Smith as a servant, and went to work as a waiter in Quarter Master Winslow's office as a waiter for the mess. After Capt. Winslow went home, I went to live with Bob, helping him.

Last Friday just after dinner, I saw Pierce Mr. Heiskell's overseer. He caught me on Gay street, he ran after me, and carried me down Cumberland street to Mr. Heiskell's house. Mr. Heiskell, his wife and two sons, and a daughter were in the house. Mr. Heiskell asked me what made me run away; he grabbed me by the back of the ears, and jerked me down on the floor on my face; Mr. Pierce held me & Mr. Heiskell put irons on my legs. Mr. Heiskell took me by the hair of my head, and Mr. Pierce took me around my body, they carried me upstairs, and then Mr. Heiskell dagged me into a room by my hair. They made me stand up, and then they laid me down on my belly & pulled off my breeches as far as they could, and turned my shirt and jacket up over my head. (I heard Mr Heiskell ask for the cowhide before he started with me upstairs.) Mr. Pierce held my legs, and Mr. Heiskell got a straddle of me, and whipped me with the rawhide on my back & legs. Mr. Pierce is a large man, and very strong. Mr. Heiskell rested two or three times, and begun again. I hollowed—"O, Lord" all the time. They whipped me, it seemed to me, half an hour. They then told me to get up and dress, and said if I did'nt behave myself up there they would come up again and whip me again at night. The irons were left on my legs. Mr. Heiskell came up at dark and asked me what that "yallow nigger was talking to me about". He meant my brother Bob, who had been talking to me opposite the house. I was standing up and when he (Mr. Heiskell) asked me about the "yaller nigger", he kicked me with his right foot on my hip and knocked me over on the floor, as the irons were on my feet, I could not catch myself. I knew my brother Bob was around the house trying to get me out. About one hour by sun two soldiers came to the house, one staid & the other went away. I saw them through the window. They had sabres. I thought they had come to guard me to keep Bob from getting me. I heard Bob whisling, and I went to the window and looked through the curtain. Bob told me to hoist the window, put something under it & swing out of the window. I did as my brother told me, and hung by my hands. Bob said "Drop," but I said I was afraid I would hurt myself. Bob said "Wait a minute and I will get a ladder". He brought a ladder and put it against the house, under the window. I got halfway down before they hoisted the window; I fell & Bob caught me and run off with me in his arms. I saw Mr. Pierce sitting at the window, he had a double-barreled gun in his hands. By the time I could count three I heard a gun fired two or three times, quick, I heard Mr. Pierce call "Jim" "Jim" and the guards hollered "halt; halt!" I had no hat or shoes on. We both hid, and laid flat on the ground. I saw the guard, running around there hunting for us. After lying there until the guards had gone away, we got up and Bob carried me to a friend's house. I had the irons on my legs. I got some supper and staid there until next day. My irons were taken off by a colored man, who carried me to the hospital. I am now employed working in the hospital No. 1.

                                              his
–signed–   Jim × Heiskell–
                                    mark

March 30, 1864

HUNGRY FAMILIES: NORTH CAROLINA, APRIL 1864
Susan C. Woolker to Zebulon B. Vance

In February 1863 the North Carolina legislature appropriated $1 million for the relief of indigent wives and families of soldiers and directed the county courts to distribute the aid. Several weeks later food riots broke out in several southern cities, including Salisbury and High Point in North Carolina, as groups of women, many of them soldiers' wives, invaded and looted shops they believed were charging unfair prices. The privations suffered by soldiers' families contributed to the peace movement that emerged in the state during the summer of 1863, when speakers at more than a hundred public meetings called for a negotiated end to the war. Susan C. Woolker, a resident of Davie County, wrote about the food situation in the spring of 1864 to Governor Zebulon B. Vance, a critic of the Davis administration who supported continued prosecution of the war.

Hillsdale N.C.
Apr. the 3 rd /64

Sir I write you a feiw lines to inform you how we are treated about something to eat truly hopeing you will have things changed from what they are now I will inform you what I am alowed per month I am only alowed $10.00 for my self and one child a woman with two childrens only alowed $13.00 per month to get meat and bread with grain is from $20.00 to $30.00 per bushel bacon from $3. to $5.00 per pound and we cant get it for the money the men that has it to sell wont have the money for it and there is aplenty both meat and bread and molases in the country for us all to have plenty but those men that has it wont let the soldiers familys have it they send one load of privisian to the factory after another to get spun cotton and the soldiers familys may suffer while their men are in the army fighting for them and what they have my husband and father has been in the survis over two years Ma is left with three children and is only alowed $13.00 per month and you well know that wont half support her the way evry thing is selling I know some men that has plenty of molases and wont sell them for any thing but grain and that is what soldiers familys has not got I dont know how they can expect the No Ca soldiers to fight and their familys treated as they are. I never have tried to discourage my husband any at all—I try to encourage him all I can I am willing to work for every thing to eat I can but I cant live with my work and what I get from Mr A Reid I sent to him for something to eat yesterday and he sent me word his orders was not to let any of us have any thing untill May court and I have not had any thing at all in over a month and I am very unhealthy not able to do much work and I dont know what I will do and many others that is left in my situation unless you will have this matter attended to in a short time I beg you to have things arranged better for if you dont the soldiers will get disheartened and come home and I dont want them to have to come home without an honerable peace and ef they will find me plenty to eat my husband will fight through this war if he is spaired to live before he will quit and come home but you think yourself of this matter if you was in the army and was to hear your wife and children was suffiring and could not get anything to eat I think you would be very much tempted to start home and you knew there was plenty for them and they was not allowed have it pleas fix this as soon as you can I hope you will send and press this provisions from those men that has it for if you dont I am afraid the women will have it to do and I dont want to press any thing if I can help it they have got spun cotton out our reach it is $80.00 per bunch in Greensborough that will take nearly eight month wages that a soldier gets to get one bunch cotton I will close this by saying pleas provide for us

       yours truly
       SUSAN C WOOLKER

PLANNING THE SPRING CAMPAIGN:
WASHINGTON, D.C., APRIL 1864

Ulysses S. Grant to William T. Sherman

Ulysses S. Grant arrived in Washington, D.C., on March 8, 1864, and was appointed general-in-chief of the Union armies on March 10. That same day he visited Major General George G. Meade in northern Virginia. Grant left Washington the next day, having decided to make his headquarters in the field with the Army of the Potomac while keeping Meade as its commander. He conferred in Nashville and Cincinnati with William T. Sherman, who would succeed him as commander of the Union armies between the Alleghenies and the Mississippi, before returning to Washington on March 22. Grant wrote to Sherman about his plans after presenting them to President Lincoln, who expressed his approval of Grant's intention to use all of the Union forces available by saying, "Those not skinning can hold a leg."

Private & Confidential

Washington, D.C., Apl. 4th *1864.*

MAJ. GEN. W. T. SHERMAN,
COMD.G MIL. DIV. OF THE MISS.
GENERAL,

It is my design, if the enemy keep quiet and allow me to take the initiative in the Spring Campaign to work all parts of the Army to-gether, and, somewhat, towards a common center. For your information I now write you my programme as at present determined upon.

I have sent orders to Banks, by private messenger, to finish up his present expedition against Schrievesport with all dispatch. To turn over the defence of the Red River to Gen. Steele and the Navy and return your troops to you and his own to New Orleans. To abandon all of Texas, except the Rio Grande and to hold that with not to exceed four thousand men. To reduce the number of troops on the Miss. to the lowest number necessary to hold it and to collect from his command not less than twenty-five thousand men. To this I will add five thousand from Mo. With this force he is to commence operations against Mobile as soon as he can. It will be impossible for him to commence too early.

Gilmore joins Butler with ten thousand men and the two operate against Richmond from the south side of James River. This will give Butler thirty-three thousand men to operate with, W. F. Smith commanding the right wing of his forces and Gilmore the left wing. I will stay with the Army of the Potomac increased by Burnsides Corps of not less than 25.000 effective men, and operate directly against Lee's Army wherever it may be found. Sigel collects all his available force in two columns, one under Ord & Averell to start from Beverly Va. and the other under Crook to start from Charleston on the Kanawphy to move against the Va. & Ten. rail-road. Crook will have all Cavalry and will endeavor to get in about Saltville and move East from there to join Ord. His force will be all cavalry whilst Ord will have from ten to twelve thousand men of all arms. You I propose to move against Johnston's Army, to break it up and to get into the interior of the enemy's country as far as you can, inflicting all the damage you can against their War resources.

I do not propose to lay down for you a plan of Campaign but simply to lay down the work it is desirable to have done and leave you free to execute in your own way. Submit to me however as early as you can your plan of operation.

As stated Banks is ordered to commence operations as soon as he can. Gilmore is ordered to report at Fortress Monroe by the 18th inst, or as soon thereafter as practicable. Sigel is concentrating now. None will move from their places of rendezvous until I direct, except Banks. I want to be ready to move by the 25th inst, if possible. But all I can now direct is that you get ready as soon as possible   I know you will have difficulties to encounter getting through the mountains to where supplies are abundant, but I believe you will accomplish it.

From the expedition from the Dept. of West Va. I do not calculate on very great results. But it is the only way I can take troops from there. With the long line of rail-road Sigel has to protect he can spare no troops except to move directly to his front. In this way he must get through to inflict great damage on the enemy, or the enemy must detach from one of his armies a large force to prevent it. In other words if Sigel cant skin himself he can hold a leg whilst some one else skins.

> I am General, very respectfully
> your obt. svt.
> U. S. GRANT
> Lt. Gen.

"A TEAR OF SOROW":
LOUISIANA, APRIL 1864

William Winters to Harriet Winters

In March 1864 about 30,000 Union troops under Major General Nathaniel P. Banks began advancing up the Red River into northwest Louisiana with the objective of capturing Shreveport, the headquarters of the Confederate Trans-Mississippi Department. Although Grant considered the campaign a needless diversion from the goal of seizing Mobile, the Red River expedition was strongly supported by President Lincoln, who hoped that it would extend Union control over all of Louisiana and Arkansas, make possible the occupation of East Texas, and restrain French actions in Mexico. Sergeant William Winters of the 67th Indiana Infantry, a saddle and harness maker from Bartholomew County who had fought in the Vicksburg campaign, was among the soldiers taking part in the expedition. His regiment left Alexandria, Louisiana, on March 28 and marched northwest to Natchitoches. On April 7 Winters reached Pleasant Hill, where his brigade was ordered to reinforce the cavalry leading the advance. The next day Major General Richard Taylor and 8,800 Confederates attacked the head of the Union column near Mansfield, thirty-five miles south of Shreveport, and drove it back to Pleasant Hill. Union losses in the battle of Mansfield (also known as Sabine Crossroads) were reported as 113 killed, 581 wounded, and 1,541 missing. Among the missing was William Winters, who was later declared to have been killed in action on April 8, 1864. His place of burial is unknown.

---

in camp at Nachitoches,
Louisiana, April 4th, 1864
    Mrs. H. J. Winter
    Dear wife, I just received six letters, and I almost jumped up and down when I got them into my hands. I am so glad to hear that you and the children are well, and I hope that you and they will not be visited with either of those fell diseases that is scourgeing the country, and, ma, oh, do take care of our litle girls, for I cant loose them.
    We are in camp here and have been for a couple of days but are ready to be called out at any moment, for we have drove

the enemy before us for several days before we halted, and they are waiting to engage us at Pleasant hill, some thirty five miles above us on the road to shreveport and expect to give us a whiping there, they say, but they have not got the men to do it with. But they will no doubt fight us there.

this place is quite a nice town with a large convent called the Sacred heart of Jesus. There is quite a number of nuns and children that are put here to go to school for fear of the influences of hereticks. I was through a grave yard of theirs with tom Eaton and picked some myrtle flowers, and I will put them in this. The country here and between here and Alexandria is considerably hilley and rolling and covered with pitch pine, and as we marched through it I thought of the pine clad hills of my boyhood home and how oft I had rambled through them in chaseing the nimble squirrill and rabbit, and then I thought of my own litle ones, and a tear of sorow stole down my cheek that I turned aside and wiped away. The country is lovly and rich but mostly catholic. The town of Nachitoches is situated on what they call old river or old red river, the bed of what is red river proper, but the river runs some four miles from here now through a new chanell.

We expect to go forward in a day or two and are liable to be sent at any time. we have not been paid off yet, and I canot tell when we will be paid.

I got a letter from wes. He seems to think that lando might of given more than he did and Jim a litle less, but I guess he is not following a verey honorable calling, or he would not have quite so mutch mony to spend as he apears to have. I got a letter from Bell and one from Mary Jane. Wes wrote that he was agoing to sell out his furniture and move back to the gate and keep house for Aleck. All good enough. vine wrote that she was agoing to the city to keep house for Jim awhile. From what was wrote, Aus and his wife have both joined christy chappell, a blessing to his family if he will only stick to it.

well, hat, we have about a hundred miles more to march to shreveport, and perhaps we may have a couple of fights before we get there, but I hope not, but if we do we will be at Shrevesport before you receive this and it may be in eternity, some of us, but we are all in the best of spirits and health and spirits and ready for all that is our duty to do as soldiers and hope to have the pleasure of seeing our homes, friends, and dear ones after our trials and deprivations are over and this cruel war is at an end.

The weather is butifull, and everything is growing and spreading its buties and oders to all, heeding not the preasence of an invading armey. Some of the fair ones of this country take pleasure in abuseing us in unmeasured terms for comeing into their country and homes and say that we had better stay at home and attend to our business and come to disgrace their homes with our yankey preasence. But we cant help what they think about us. We are all well. My own health is as good as it ever was in my life, and I hope that it may continue to be so for the balance of my term, if I am compeled to serve it out. well, hat, if I had the time I would write you more, if I had time to do so, but will have to conclude with this, as the mail goes out in a few minutes, and it may be the only chance to write before we get to Shreveport, and I would not miss sending this to you, as I know that you want to know where I am. Hopeing that this will find you all well, I remain yours as ever, William Winters

FREEDOM AND SLAVERY: VIRGINIA, APRIL 1864

Wilbur Fisk to The Green Mountain Freeman

Private Wilbur Fisk of the 2nd Vermont Infantry began writing letters in December 1861 to *The Green Mountain Freeman* of Montpelier under the pen name "Anti-Rebel." Fisk fought in the Seven Days' Battles before being hospitalized with chronic diarrhea in September 1862. He returned to his regiment in March 1863, fought in the Chancellorsville campaign, and was posted to a reserve position at Gettysburg. He wrote to the *Freeman* as the Army of the Potomac awaited the opening of its third spring campaign.

Camp near Brandy Station, Va.
April 7, 1864

We have just had what is here known as a general inspection. The inspection occupied but very few minutes, and as it takes the place of our regular drill this afternoon we shall have nothing further to do till night. The pleasantest way that I can think of to spend these idle moments is to pen a few lines to the *Freeman*, though I am afraid it is almost imposing upon good nature to attempt to offer anything for entertainment when the times are as dull as now. I have been tolerated so long that my self-confident assurance has grown immensely, and if I keep on writing I don't know but that my habit of writing for the *Freeman* will by and by become seated and incurable. But I cannot help it. When I know that the readers of the *Freeman* include but very few sneering copperheads if any at all, and that all are interested in the soldier's welfare, and interested in the cause for which we are here, it is very easy and pleasant to write, and I cannot resist the temptation, and I will not try.

The signs of an advance movement begin to thicken. Sutlers have been ordered away, and there is now, I understand, an order at headquarters for the men to pack up, to be sent off, every article that we do not need, such as extra clothing, overcoats, blankets, and the like, as has been our custom every spring. These are only preliminary movements and really indicate nothing immediate, but so far as we know, the army may be ordered to move within a week. We have had considerable wet rainy weather of late, which will doubtless retard operations some. A few that are prone to prophesy say that it is doubtful if we move from here before May. But we soldiers trust this matter is in wiser hands than ours, and when they consider that the proper time has arrived for action, and order us forward, we shall go cheerfully and confidently, whether the time be sooner or later. It seems to be the prevailing opinion here in the army, that we are at last to have a campaign that will for once be really "short, sharp, and decisive," and I will add, victorious. Great confidence is felt in the plans that General Grant will adopt, and the means that he will have to use in crushing the last vestige of this Heaven accursed rebellion. Having authority that extends from the Atlantic to the Mississippi, from Mobile to Washington, we may reasonably expect a concert of action in the coming campaigns that will ensure us success and victory. God grant that we may not be disappointed.

Success and victory! whose heart does not beat quicker at the thought? What consequences will have been achieved when this great rebellion shall have been forever humbled. It is not merely that this terrible war may be ended, and we safely at liberty again, that we hope to conquer our enemies and be once more at peace, but that the great principles of a free government, whose worth no mind short of Infinite Wisdom can estimate, and which even after the world has stood so long is still considered an experiment, may not be overthrown, and the progress of civilization and freedom may not be rolled back for ages, or receive a blow from which they may never recover. We are anxious of course to get out of this war, for we long most earnestly to return to the almost sacred hills and valleys of old Vermont, but we are not so anxious for this, as we are that the faith of the world in the intelligence and virtue of the common people, and their ability to govern themselves and maintain national unity without being rent asunder by internal strife and discord—a faith that despots the world over profess to sneer at, and hold to be a delusion, and which stimulates the noblest energies of the masses of mankind—that this may be maintained, increased and perpetuated. If these principles succeed, Slavery must fall, and fall forever. The two are so antagonistical that, even if both are right, or neither of them, men embracing each could not possibly live together in peace, unless we are to suppose that God has given them a larger spirit of forbearance than is vouchsafed to humanity in general. There never was a real unity between them, and there never can be. Slavery is a relic of the darkest ages, and the poorest government on earth is better in principle than that. If we are going to have a free government at all, let us have it all free, or else we had better give up the name. Slavery has fostered an aristocracy of the rankest kind, and this aristocracy is the bitterest foe that a really free government can have. Slavery and despotism have challenged war with us, and by it she must abide. Slavery was jealous of the comelier strength that Freedom possessed; and maliciously envied her irresistible march onward to a higher destiny. Slavery drew the sword, and would have stabbed Freedom to the heart, had not God denied her the strength. She could not bear that her more righteous neighbor should be prospered, while she herself was accursed, and in her foolish madness she has tried to rend the Union in twain. With that institution it is success or death. Compromise with Slavery, and restore the Union with Slavery in it still! As well might Jehovah compromise with Satan and give him back part of Heaven.

There never before was a rebellion like this one. Generally a rebellion has been the outbreak of the people against the tyranny of a few. Their cause has usually been the cause of liberty, and more or less just. Knit together by the idea of freeing themselves from an odious despotism, and armed with justice, and backed by numbers, they have often succeeded, and history has applauded their bravery. In this war it has been different. The people have not rebelled against the few, but the few have rebelled against the people. Our government is the people's, and against this government the proud slaveholder has rebelled. With Slavery for a corner stone they hope to rob our government of her honor, and erect within our borders a rival government, which every attribute of the Almighty must detest. Can they succeed? Is the glory of our nation to be destroyed forever? Is the great experiment which our forefathers have made, and which has been our pride and boast so long, to be a failure after all? If the North will do her duty, we answer, Never! And the North *will* do her duty. She knows what it is, and she does not fear it. Never in a war before did the rank and file feel a more resolute earnestness for a just cause, and a more invincible determination to succeed, than in this war; and what the rank and file are determined to do everybody knows will surely be done. We mean to be thorough about it too. We are not going to destroy the military power of the dragon Confederacy and not destroy its fangs also. We have as a nation yielded to their rapacious demands times enough. We have cringed before Slavery as long as we will.

> "Far better die in such a strife,
>   Than still to Slavery's claims concede,
> Than crouch beneath her frown for life,
>   Far better in the field to bleed:
> To live thus wage a life-long shame,
>   To die is victory and fame."

I almost lose my temper sometimes (what little I have got) when I hear men that really ought to know better, call this war a mere crusade to free the negroes, "a nigger war" and nothing more. But even if I was fighting to free the negroes simply, I don't know why I should be acting from a motive that I need be ashamed of. I verily believe that He who when He was on the earth healed foul leprosy, gave sight to the blind beggars, and preached the gospel to the poor, would not be ashamed to act from such a motive. And if he would not, why should I? Fighting to free the "niggers!" Why yes, my dear fellow, we are doing just that and a great deal more. But, sir, I am going to tell you, you would not speak of that so contemptuously, if you had not all your life long fed your soul upon motives so small, so mean, and so selfish, that the sublimer motives of sacrificing blood and treasure to elevate a degraded and downtrodden race, is entirely beyond your comprehension. Should such an event, however, rather help than hinder the success of this war, we trust that you will acquiesce in the result, and when the future of this country shall have become by this means more glorious than the past has ever been, we shall hope that you will find that your own liberty and happiness has not been at all infringed upon by giving the same liberty and happiness to a few ignorant and despised sons of Africa.

But I have prolonged this discussion till my space is full, and I have no room for general news, if any had been needed. The weather has been pleasant since the snow and rainstorms of Saturday and Monday, but just now another storm is threatened. We are to have three drills each day till further orders, two in the forenoon, and one in the afternoon, and this with our other duties, getting wood, and the like, will leave us rather a short allowance of time for idleness.

AN EXPULSION ORDER: TENNESSEE, APRIL 1864
Ellen Renshaw House: Diary, April 8, 1864

From January to November 1864 Brigadier General Samuel P. Carter, the provost marshal of Knoxville, ordered the expulsion of more than fifty Confederate sympathizers, the majority of them women. The expulsions were encouraged by Knoxville's leading unionist, the newspaper editor William G. (Parson) Brownlow, who denounced "*she* rebels" as "brazen as the devil" in his *Knoxville Whig and Rebel Ventilator*. Among those banished into Confederate-held territory was Ellen Renshaw House, who was expelled along with Susan Ramsey, the sixteen-year-old daughter of a prominent secessionist. House crossed the lines in northeastern Tennessee and spent the summer in Abingdon, Virginia, before settling in Eatonton, Georgia, in September 1864.

April 8. Friday. Well it has come at last. I am ordered to leave on Monday for the South. My orders came about ten. Mother is perfectly furious about it. At first she said she would come too, but we told her that would never do, so she said sister should come with me. I declare she thinks I am a baby and not fit to take care of myself. She went with sister to ask permission for her to come too. Old Gratz objected, said they did want to send her. She had been very prudent. Said he would have to see Schofield about it &e. Mother told him she would like to know why I had been sent out. He would not tell her for some time. At last he said they had a great many charges against me and they had been thinking of sending me South for some time, but the immediate cause was my insulting Mrs McAlister. It is about the only thing they could accuse me of that I have never done & I never have done that. I almost wish I had now. He said it was reported by a third person, and when Capt McA was asked about it he was a gentleman and was obliged to acknowledge it. Also that Parson Brownlow heard it and urged the matter till Gen Carter ordered me out, that they would have the charges written out by afternoon & I could have them. I wish I could get them but no one would go for them for me. I have a great mind to go after them myself.

Some time after Sister came home, her permission came too. Father takes it very quietly. When I told him all he asked was if I was well supplied with thick shoes. He thinks them essential to my health. When Mr Wilson came home I opened on him. Told him I had received my orders to go South thanks to him. I suppose the charge was my insulting Mrs McA, and reported by a third person, that third person must be him & he had reported what he knew to be false. He said I was very much mistaken. He was very sorry I had been ordered out and had never said anything about me. I replied I was not sorry to go, but glad to find out he was more of a gentleman than I had taken him to be. Cordie Fletcher came over and offered to help me. I have a great many things to get, & am very much afraid I will forget many things I need. One thing is certain. I am going to take my derringer and Johnnies's Uniform &c to a dead most certainty. Reported fight down at Cleveland. The Yankees here say that Joe Johnson is nothing for miles of that place.

"A PROUD DAY": WASHINGTON, D.C., APRIL 1864

Lois Bryan Adams to the Detroit Advertiser and Tribune

Proposals to end slavery by amending the Constitution were introduced in the House of Representatives by Republican congressmen James M. Ashley of Ohio and James F. Wilson of Iowa on December 14, 1863, and in the Senate by Missouri Unionist John B. Henderson on January 11, 1864. Illinois Republican Lyman Trumbull, the chairman of the Senate Judiciary Committee, drew on these proposals to give the Thirteenth Amendment its final form. In a speech in the Senate on March 28, Trumbull admitted that the confiscation acts passed by Congress in 1861 and 1862 and the Emancipation Proclamation were "ineffectual to the destruction of slavery" because their effects did not extend to all slave-owners and to all of the slave states. The proposed amendment, Trumbull said, would ensure that slavery could "never be reestablished by State authority" and would "restore to a whole race that freedom which is theirs by the gift of God, but which we for generations have wickedly denied them." An experienced journalist who had moved from Michigan to Washington in 1863, Lois Bryan Adams worked as a clerk for the recently established Department of Agriculture while contributing regular letters to the *Detroit Advertiser and Tribune*. She wrote about the Senate debate on the amendment in dispatches that appeared on April 15 and 19, 1864.

Letter from Washington
IN THE SENATE | REVERDY JOHNSON | GEORGE
THOMPSON AT THE CAPITOL | AMENDMENT OF THE
CONSTITUTION | SCENE IN THE SENATE
From Our Own Correspondent
Washington, April 9, 1864

The first week of April has been an eventful one at the capital. It was led off in the Senate by the Hon. Reverdy Johnson of Maryland in a noble and thoroughly antislavery speech; followed up in the House by the reception and speech of George

Thompson of England and crowned in the Senate by the passage of a vote to amend the Constitution by inserting a clause abolishing slavery and prohibiting it in the United States henceforth and forever.

Mr. Johnson's speech was one of peculiar interest, and was listened to with more than usual attention by the Senate. It was in explanation and justification of the vote he intended to give on the amendment of the Constitution. He carefully reviewed and refuted the theories advanced by some that the power to abolish slavery lay with the Chief Executive of the nation, or that Congress had the power of enacting laws for the purpose. Neither proclamation nor acts of Congress, he said, could affect slaves not actually under the jurisdiction of the laws of the United States. Except as a war measure, Congress and the President could not move in the matter at all, and the war power conferred upon them could not be exerted against loyal States; therefore, Maryland, Kentucky, and Missouri would be slave states still, though the institution were abolished in all others. He said that whatever his previous opinions had been, he was now convinced that no permanent peace could be established without the utter extinction of slavery. Involuntary servitude and a republican government were totally incompatible; if we would save the one we must destroy the other. It was a clear, calm, logical, and truly patriotic speech, one that it did the hearts of the Republican Senators good to hear, and the stern, incontrovertible truths of which fell heavily on the heads of the few hapless Copperheads present.

Mr. Johnson is an old man with thin white hair, but with a goodly plumpness of body, a freshness of complexion and a depth and strength of voice betokening anything but feebleness, of either mind or body. His face is of an oval cast, guiltless of beard or mustache, and his eyes are remarkably prominent, in fact "pop-eyed" is the only word that can properly describe them. The expression of his face is rather sour and forbidding; he seldom smiles, or appears to let himself down upon a common social level with other mortals, preserving, apparently, a sort of stoical dignity of indifference which seems always to be saying "I am the Honorable Reverdy Johnson, of Maryland." But whether this is only in appearance or not, it is very certain the world can afford to let him look as he pleases, so long as he will give it such hopeful, encouraging words as fell from his lips on Tuesday last.

The announcement that the House of Representatives had voted the use of their hall for Wednesday evening to the noted abolition lecturer, George Thompson of England was a terrible shock to the failing and sensitive nerves of the District slave aristocracy. Alas, they said, what is Washington coming to! Not only are the rail-splitters of the West and the mudsills of the East in our White House, and in our halls of legislation, thronging our Department and swarming our streets, but here they have invited to speak in our capitol, and against our institutions, that, to us, most odious of all human compounds, an Anglo-American Abolitionist. Not many years ago he was mobbed and beaten, and driven from one city to another, and finally from the country; now he is welcomed back, toasted and honored, and taken into the capitol to consummate his triumph.

Yes, it was a triumph, and as such the friends of freedom and free speech felt it. Mr. Thompson's welcome was most enthusiastic. The lecture was given under the auspices of the Washington Young Men's Association, and though the tickets for floor seats were one dollar each, and for the galleries 50 cents, both floor and galleries were early crowded to their utmost capacity. The President and most of his cabinet, as well as many Senators and members, were present. Vice President Hamlin presided, and after a few appropriate words of introduction, presented Mr. Thompson to the audience. The prolonged and hearty cheering which greeted him as he rose, affected him almost to tears. It was some moments before he could control his emotion, or give volume enough to his voice to make it heard across the room.

Washington, the old Washington, has been fairly dazed of late by witnessing events "significant of the times"; it is beginning to understand that there are signs in these times which do not all fail, and events which mark the giant strides of progress in such a way that there can be no retracing them in the future. This event, the mere admission of the speaker to the place where he stood by the invitation of the national Representatives, was one of marked significance; and still more so, if possible, were the shouts of applause and cheers of approval breaking from that great multitude, as from one heart, and raining down from the gilded ceilings like glad omens to the doctrines of universal liberty and human rights. What a change from a few years past, and what a triumph!

Slowly and sullenly the dark clouds of barbarism are rolling away, and quick and bright the sunshine follows. Some of those long dwelling in darkness are sorely hurt and troubled by the light. It blinds and bewilders them: poor creatures, how they struggle and gasp, and stretch out their arms in vain endeavors to bring the cloud back again. Such a spectacle was witnessed in the Senate on Friday, when the resolution to amend the Constitution was before that body. Speeches had been made during the week by Senators Hale and Clark, of New Hampshire, and others, all bearing upon the great question of the amendment, and all in turn snarled, growled, yelped and whined at by Powell, Saulsbury, Davis, and McDougal. Friday, Charles Sumner spoke, and it was understood that the vote was to be taken before the Senate adjourned. Long before Mr. Sumner sat down, it was easy to see how the wrath of Powell, Davis & Co. was working, and the moment his last word was said, Powell was upon his feet, flushed, excited, angry. With all the vehemence of his portly body concentrated in his red face, and quivering, out-stretched hand, he proceeded to denounce the Senators who were so anxious to meddle with what did not belong to them; he sneered at Yankee patriotism as altogether mercenary, and multiplied taunts and invectives on Sumner's head, till his voice grew thick and hoarse, and his arms must have ached from the violence with which it cut the empty air. The honorable Senators, however, at whom he launched his thunderbolts, seemed to feel them as little as the air did his strokes. All were busy attending to little matters of their own, some writing letters, some looking over the piled-up papers on his desk, some with heads bent together, earnestly talking, some glancing over the columns of the newspapers, and not one with the attitude or countenance of a listener. Sumner now and then glanced up from his papers with a quiet smile, as much as to say, "Rave on if it please you; such words are powerless in this chamber now." And he did rave, denounce and protest till, finding he could not disturb the quiet indifference of the Senators, he dropped into his seat, and was succeeded by the mattered growlings of Saulsbury, who wanted to make compromises and peace-offerings; the piping yelps of little old Garrett Davis, who "considered that his niggers belonged to him the same as his horses did, and he wanted compensation for them," and the egotistic, whinings of McDougal, who, while glorifying himself, maintained his perpendicular with some difficulty by holding fast to the two desks between which he stood.

And so, with rage, and whine, and whimper the time wore on, and it was 5 o'clock before the vote was taken. But the Senators knew they could afford to be patient. When the yeas and nays were at last called, the resolution for the amendment passed by a vote of 37 to 6!
L.

Our Washington Letter
A DAY IN THE SENATE | SCENES ON THE FLOOR
AND IN THE GALLERIES | PASSAGE OF THE
AMENDMENT RESOLUTION
From Our Own Correspondent
Washington, April 9, 1864

"'Twere worth whole years of peaceful life, / One glance at their array."

Friday, the 8th of April, was a proud day in the Senate, and a proud one for our country. It was the day on which the vote for the amendment of the Constitution was to be taken, and it was a pleasant sight to look down from the galleries upon the men who had the task in hand, and who were moving on steadily and unitedly to its consummation. The resolution has been referred to the Judiciary committee, by them thoroughly considered, and the demand of millions embodied in words approved by the committee, was now waiting the final action of the Senate before being sent to the House, and from thence to the Legislatures of the several States for their ratification.

Satisfaction, security, triumph, may be seen on almost every face in the Senate chamber today; not the mere triumph of man over man, the security based on numerical strength, or the soulless satisfaction of having gained a point simply for the defeat of an opposition. No; there is something better, nobler, grander in the faces of these men today; something that speaks of purpose based on principle, of deep and earnest thought, and self-reliant action for the right; there is a consciousness of responsibility appropriate to the occasion, and who shall blame them if they blend with this an air of confidence as they compare their position now with what it was in the long, dark, stormy days of southern rule and republican minority. They can speak now like freemen, and there is not a sneaking assassin at hand with knife or bludgeon to strike down the defenders of liberty. So Johnson and Howard and Hale and Clark and others have been speaking during the week that has passed, as so Sumner has been speaking today—speaking for humanity against the legalized tyranny of a slave aristocracy.

Is it to be wondered at that the feeble half dozen defenders of a dead faith, the few lingering relics of a once powerful class of graduates from the institution whose chief cornerstone is barbarism brutalized, should writhe under the truths they are forced to hear, should struggle as with a death agony against the mighty power that is crushing them between the ruins of their own bloody Molock? They do writhe and struggle in the impotence of their rage, and if the calm, confident giants only smile and bend to their task with still more resolute energy, can they be called merciless, unkind?

The world and the future will not call them so. Neither does the great, true heart of the present. With a warm, throbbing amen, in the name of humanity it bids them God speed, till these floors shall no longer be desecrated by the slaveholders' tread, or these walls echo back words that are libels alike on God and Man.

Such words Powell, maddened to desperation, is shouting in the ears of Senators, who hear as if they heard not, or only in the magnanimity of their approaching triumph, permit him to speak unchecked. In the same breath he boasts of what he calls "the staunch, true patriotism of the glorious Old Commonwealth of Kentucky," kills New England with a sneer, buries her with a grimace, accuses the Administration of unprecedented and unlimited corruption, tells us that this war is all for a brute race, who have not in them the elements of manhood, and that, so help him God, he will oppose now and forever every measure that would give them freedom. He raves till his face is like scarlet, and his tongue runs through all the degrees of abuse admissible in Congressional courtesy to find invectives bitter enough to vent his wrath against the Senator from Massachusetts. But sneers, taunts, mockery, and derision, are alike powerless from such a source now. His only attentive listeners are Saulsbury of Delaware who, with hands clenched under his coat tails, walks restlessly up and down his accustomed beat; Garret Davis of Kentucky who, with his little body in one chair, nurses his little feet on the cushions of another, and with a little smile on his little face, drinks in to the extent of his little capacity the wonderful words of his big brother Senator; and McDougal of California who should know better, but who sits open-mouthed to swallow all, that he may dole it out again in his maudlin way, diluted by the nauseous fumes and amber juices that scent his breath and stain his beard. These, after the speaker takes his seat, give back successively a characteristic echo of his words and sentiments.

But stay; there are other listeners, though not many now, in the galleries. A little while ago, when Sumner spoke, all these seats were full, but one by one, and dozens by dozens, the occupants have gone, all but the few scattered here and there, who are resolved to wait till dark, and after, if they must, to hear the vote. These, however, are waiting, rather than listening; for, in little groups, they are softly talking to each other; or, singly, smiling at the futile efforts of the slave-quartette below, to ward off as long as they may the blow that they know must come, and soon. But these are not all. Directly opposite us, and not far from the diplomatic gallery, is a long seat occupied by people who are evidently deeply interested witnesses of every word and act of the Senators upon the floor. They came early, were ushered into that seat by the door-keeper, and, unlike most gallery visitants, have kept their places quietly, and watched with intense and absorbing interest the proceedings of the day. They have attracted some friendly and some angry glances from below. I think Garret Davis would like to pierce them through and through with those little, stiletto-like eyes of his; and I know Saulsbury would be delighted to annihilate them with that terrible frown with which he clouds his brow when his "gentlemanly instincts" are disturbed. See how he scowls over his shoulder and compresses his lips in scorn. Do they see it, or know it, or care for it, those three men and three women in that distant seat? They are the best behaved people in the gallery today; they are handsomely and neatly dressed in black silks and broadcloths, and—their skins are almost black.

But now the pygmies have worried themselves quiet; and the giants are gathering up their strength. For the last hour they have been loitering about, apparently unconscious of the storm they had raised, or of the work yet to be done: now they come up from the corners where they had been gathered in little groups, from the side sofas where they had been stretching their limbs to rest, from anti rooms, from reading of newspapers and from writing at desks—they come, they are ready. Nearly all are standing now. The yeas and nays are called. They are no feeble, half-uttered, half-meant responses that come up and are recorded on that list of names which should be the roll of honor for the present age. There is a heart in every "aye" of the thirty-eight. The six short, sullen "noes" are as soulless as they are powerless.

The work is done, and the giants are men again, smiling and shaking hands amidst the hum and buzz of hearty congratulating voices. So we leave them.

L.

THE FORT PILLOW MASSACRE:
TENNESSEE, APRIL 1864

Achilles V. Clark to Judith Porter and Henrietta Ray

Major General Nathan Bedford Forrest, a wealthy plantation owner and former slave trader who would later become the first Grand Wizard of the Ku Klux Klan, led 2,300 men from his cavalry command in an attack on Fort Pillow, Tennessee, on April 12, 1864. The outpost, located on a bluff overlooking the Mississippi River forty miles north of Memphis, was defended by about 600 Union soldiers, 305 from the 6th U.S. Colored Heavy Artillery and 2nd U.S. Colored Light Artillery and at least 277 from the 13th Tennessee Cavalry, a regiment of white unionists that included deserters from the Confederate army. Sergeant Achilles V. Clark of the Confederate 20th Tennessee Cavalry wrote about the assault on the fort to his sisters, both of whom were married to slaveholding Confederate soldiers (the end of the letter is missing).

Camp near Brownsville
April 14th 1864

My Dear Sisters,
I write you a few hurried lines to inform you that I am quite well and have just passed safely through the most terrible ordeal of my whole life. I guess that you know what I mean as you doubtless have before this heard of the taking of Fort Pillow. In as much as I am a member of Forrest's Cavalry modesty would direct that I should say nothing in our praise nor will I but will tell you in as few words as possible what was done and leave you to judge whether or not we acted well or ill. If you remember we left Paris Wednesday morning from which point we proceeding immediately to Eaton Gibson County where we found Col. Bell's camp. Saturday we prepared five days rations in antisipain of a move to some place we knew not where. Sunday evening directly after supper the bugle sounded to saddle. at twelve o'clock we marched off in the direction of

Brownsville. We camped just at daybreak on the north side and about two miles from South Forked Deer river where we rested one hour. Mounting our horses we crossed the above mentioned stream and one mile this side took the Fort Pillow road. From this time we rightly supposed that we were going to attack that place. At 10 A.M. (Monday) we stopped to feed and were detained about one hour and a half. At 3 P.M. we stopped again and rested until six. From this time on we were in our saddles until we reached a point one and a half miles this side of the Fort where we dismounted to fight (this was about 7 A.M. Tuesday) leaving every fourth man to hold horses, we marched on foot in sight of the fortifications which were said to be manned by about seven hundred renegade Tennesseans and negroes commanded by Major Boothe of the Negro regiment Major Bradford of the 13th Tenn. U.S.V. being second in command. Our brigade filed round to the right of the fort Chalmer's command to the left. Skirmishers were deployed and we advanced very slowly it is true but surely toward the enemy. Just here it would be proper to describe the fort which I shall attempt to do. It is a very strong earthwork situated on a high bluff inside the works erected by Gen. Pillow in 1861. It is formed by an irregular trench being dug somewhat in the shape of a half circle the edge of the bluff being the diameter. The fort is quite small just about large enough to hold a thousand men in two ranks. The ditch is eight feet deep and six wide and the dirt thrown from the ditch on the inside formed a bank five feet high making from the bottom of the ditch to the top of the breast work thirteen feet up which we had to climb. By two o'clock P.M. we had approached within fifty yards of the fort on all sides. A part of our regiment was in twenty steps of it. Strange to say after five hours constant firing the Yankees had not killed a single one of our men and wounded only a very few among whom I am sorry to name the gallant Capt. Wilson of our regiment who fell in twenty steps of the fort shot through the lungs dangerously though tis greatly to be hoped not mortally wounded. At 2 P.M. Gen. Forrest demanded a surrender and gave twenty minutes to consider. The Yankees refused threatening that if we charged their breast works to show no quarter. The bugle sounded the charge and in less than ten minutes we were in the fort hurling the cowardly villains howling down the bluff. Our men were so exasperated by the Yankees' threats of no quarter that they gave but little. The slaughter was awful. Words cannot describe the scene. The poor deluded negroes would run up to our men fall upon their knees and with uplifted hands scream for mercy but they were ordered to their feet and then shot down. The whitte men fared but little better. Their fort turned out to be a great slaughter pen. Blood, human blood stood about in pools and brains could have been gathered up in any quantity. I with several others tried to stop the butchery and at one time had partially succeeded. but Gen. Forrest ordered them shot down like dogs. and the carnage continued. Finally our men became sick of blood and the firing ceased. The result. The report kept in the Post Adjutants office shows that there were seven hundred and ninety men for duty on the morning of the fight. We brought away about one hundred and sixty white men and about seventy five negroes. Two transports came down the morning after the fight and took off the badly wounded Yankees and negroes about thirty or forty in all. The remainder were thrown into the trench before which two hours previous they had stood and bade open defiance to Forrest and all his ragged hounds, and were covered up about two feet deep. We captured seven hundred stands of small arms, six pieces of the finest artillery I ever saw, a large amount of quarter masters and commissary stores. Our loss as compared to that of the enemy were small yet we deeply mourn the loss of ten or fifteen as brave men as ever pulled a trigger. Those from our Regt. John Beard of our company a bright minded moral young man who fell on top of the breast work close to my side. [   ]

PREDICTING UNION PLANS: VIRGINIA, APRIL 1864
Robert E. Lee to Jefferson Davis

The Army of the Potomac and the Army of Northern Virginia had gone into winter quarters on opposite sides of the Rapidan River in December 1863 following the inconclusive Mine Run campaign, which ended without a major battle being fought. During the winter and early spring of 1864 General Robert E. Lee tried to anticipate Union plans while confronting serious shortages of men, food, and forage. "There is nothing to be had in this section for man or animals," he wrote to Jefferson Davis from his headquarters at Orange Court House on April 12. Lee shared his appraisal of the overall military situation with Davis three days later.

Headquarters
April 15, 1864

Mr. President:

The reports of the scouts are still conflicting as to the character of the reinforcements to the Army of the Potomac, & the composition of that at Annapolis under Genl Burnside. I think it probably that the 8th Corps, which embraces the troops who have heretofore guarded the line of the B & O Rr, the entrenchments around Washington, & Alexandria, &c., have been moved up to the Rappahannock, & that an equivalent has been sent to Annapolis from Genl Meade. Lt Col Mosby states that the 11th & 12th Corps, consolidated, have been also sent to Genl Burnside. But whatever doubt there may be on these points, I think it certain that the enemy is organizing a large army on the Rappahannock, & another at Annapolis, & that the former is intended to move directly on Richmond, while the latter is intended to take it in flank or rear. I think we may also reasonably suppose that the Federal troops that have so long besieged Charleston will, with a portion of their iron clad steamers, be transferred to the James River. I consider that the suspension of the attack on that city was virtually declared when Genl Gillmore transferred his operations to the St. John's River. It can only be continued during the summer months by the fleet. The expedition of the enemy up Red River has so diminished his forces about New Orleans & Mobile that I think no attack upon the latter city need be apprehended soon, especially as we have reason to hope that he will return from his expedition in a shattered condition. I have thought therefore that Genl Johnston might draw something from Mobile during the summer to strengthen his hands, & that Genl Beauregard with a portion of his troops might move into North Carolina to oppose Genl Burnside should he resume his old position in that State, or be ready to advance to the James River should that route be taken. I do not know what benefit Genl Buckner can accomplish in his present position. If he is able to advance into Tennessee, reoccupy Knoxville, or unite with Genl Johnston, great good may be accomplished, but if he can only hold Bristol, I think he had better be called for a season to Richmond. We shall have to glean troops from every quarter to oppose the apparent combination of the enemy. If Richmond could be held secure against the attack from the east, I would propose that I draw Longstreet to me & move right against the enemy on the Rappahannock. Should God give us a crowning victory there, all their plans would be dissipated, & their troops now collecting on the waters of the Chesapeake will be recalled to the defence of Washington. But to make this move I must have provisions & forage. I am not yet able to call to me the cavalry or artillery. If I am obliged to retire from this line, either by a flank movement of the enemy or the want of supplies, great injury will befall us. I have ventured to throw out these suggestions to Your Excellency in order that in surveying the whole field of operations you may consider all the circumstances bearing on the question. Should you determine it is better to divide this army & fall back towards Richmond I am ready to do so. I however see no better plan for the defence of Richmond than that I have proposed.

      I am with great respect, your
      obt servt

            R. E. LEE
            Genl

"INSATIATE AS FIENDS": APRIL 1864

The New York Times:
The Black Flag

April 16, 1864

Of the 585 Union soldiers known to have been at Fort Pillow on April 12, 1864, 277 were killed or died from their wounds in Union hospitals—82 from the 13th Tennessee Cavalry and 195 from the 6th U.S. Colored Heavy Artillery and the 2nd U.S. Colored Light Artillery. On April 13 the Confederates paroled several dozen wounded men and allowed them to be evacuated under flag of truce to Memphis and Cairo, Illinois. A report on the massacre from Cairo appeared in *The New York Times* on April 16, the same day stories about Fort Pillow ran in the *New York Herald*, *New-York Tribune*, *Chicago Tribune*, *Cincinnati Gazette*, and *St. Louis Missouri Democrat*.

THE BLACK FLAG.
Horrible Massacre by the Rebels.
Fort Pillow Captured After a Desperate Fight.
Four Hundred of the Garrison Brutally Murdered.
Wounded and Unarmed Men Bayoneted and Their Bodies Burned.
White and Black Indiscriminately Butchered.
Devilish Atrocities of the Insatiate Fiends.

FROM CAIRO.

CAIRO, Thursday, April 14.
On Tuesday morning the rebel Gen. FORREST attacked Fort Pillow. Soon after the attack FORREST sent a flag of truce demanding the surrender of the fort and garrison, meanwhile disposing of his force so as to gain the advantage. Our forces were under command of Major BOOTH, of the Thirteenth Tennessee (U.S.) Heavy Artillery, formerly of the First Alabama Cavalry.

The flag of truce was refused, and fighting resumed. Afterward a second flag came in, which was also refused.

Both flags gave the rebels advantage of gaining new positions.

The battle was kept up until 3 P.M., when Major BOOTH was killed, and Major BRADFORD took command.

The rebels now came in swarms over our troops, compelling them to surrender.

Immediately upon the surrender ensued a scene which utterly baffles description. Up to that time, comparatively few of our men had been killed; but, insatiate as fiends, bloodthirsty as devils incarnate, the Confederates commenced an indiscriminate butchery of the whites and blacks, including those of both colors who had been previously wounded.

The black soldiers, becoming demoralized, rushed to the rear, the white officers having thrown down their arms.

Both white and black were bayoneted, shot or sabred; even dead bodies were horribly mutilated, and children of seven and eight years and several negro women killed in cold blood. Soldiers unable to speak from wounds were shot dead, and their bodies rolled down the banks into the river. The dead and wounded negroes were piled in heaps and burned, and several citizens who had joined our forces for protection were killed or wounded.

Out of the garrison of six hundred, only two hundred remained alive.

Among our dead officers are Capt. BRADFORD, Lieuts. BARR, ACKERSSTROM, WILSON, REVEL and Major BOOTH, all of the Thirteenth Tennessee Cavalry.

Capt. POSTON and Lieut. LYON, Thirteenth Tennessee Cavalry, and Capt. YOUNG, Twenty-fourth Missouri, Acting-Provost-Marshal, were taken prisoners.

Maj. BRADFORD was also captured, but is said to have escaped; it is feared, however, that he has been killed.

The steamer *Platte Valley* came up at about half-past 3 o'clock, and was hailed by the rebels under a flag of truce. Men were sent ashore to bury the dead, and take aboard such of the wounded as the enemy had allowed to live. Fifty-seven were taken aboard, including seven or eight colored. Eight died on the way up. The steamer arrived here this evening, and was immediately sent to the Mound City Hospital, to discharge her suffering cargo.

Among our wounded officers of colored troops are Capt. PORTER, Lieut. LIBBERTS and Adjt. LEMMING.

Six guns were captured by the rebels, and carried off, including two ten-pound Parrotts and two twelve-pound howitzers. A large amount of stores was destroyed or carried away.

The intention of the rebels seemed to be to evacuate the place, and move on toward Memphis.

LATER.

CAIRO, Thursday, April 15.
Two negro soldiers, wounded at Fort Pillow, were buried by the rebels, but afterward worked themselves out of their graves. They were among those brought up in the *Platte Valley*, and are now in hospital at Mound City.

The officers of the *Platte Valley* receive great credit from the military authorities for landing at Fort Pillow, at eminent risk, and taking our wounded on board, and for their kind attentions on the way up.

REPORTS FROM ST. LOUIS.

ST. LOUIS, Friday, April 15.
The correspondent of the *Union*, who was on board the steamer *Platte Valley* at Fort Pillow, gives even a more appalling description of the fiendishness of the rebels than our Cairo dispatches.

Many of our wounded were shot in the hospital. The remainder were driven out, and the hospital was burned.

On the morning after the battle the rebels went over the field, and shot the negroes who had not died from their wounds.

Several of the guns captured by FORREST at Fort Pillow were spiked before falling into his hands. Others were turned upon gunboat No. 7, which, having fired some 300 rounds and exhausted her ammunition, was compelled to withdraw. Although a tinclad, she received but slight injury.

Gen. LEE arrived and assumed the command at the beginning of the battle. Previous to which Gen. CHALMERS directed the movements. FORREST, with the main force, retired after the fight to Brownsville, taking with him the captured funds.

While the steamer *Platte Valley* lay under flag of truce, taking on board our wounded, some of the rebel officers, and among them Gen. CHALMERS, went on board, and some of our officers showed them great deference, drinking with them, and showing them other marks of courtesy.

Many of those who had escaped from the works and hospital, who desired to be treated as prisoners of war, as the rebels said, were ordered to fall into line, and when they had formed, were inhumanly shot down.

Of 350 colored troops not more than 56 escaped the massacre, and not one officer that commanded them survives. Only four officers of the Thirteenth Tennessee escaped death.

The loss of the Thirteenth Tennessee is 800 killed. The remainder were wounded and captured.

Gen. CHALMER told this correspondent that, although it was against the policy of his Government to spare negro soldiers or their officers, he had done all in his power to stop the carnage. At the same time he believed it was right.

Another officer said our white troops would have been protected had they not been found on duty with negroes.

While the rebels endeavored to conceal their loss, it was evident that they suffered severely. Col. REED, commanding a Tennessee regiment, was mortally wounded. There were two or three well filled hospitals at a short distance in the country.

DEFINING LIBERTY AND CONSIDERING
RETRIBUTION: MARYLAND, APRIL 1864

Abraham Lincoln: Address at Baltimore Sanitary Fair

Lincoln spoke at the opening ceremonies of the Baltimore Sanitary Fair, held in the great hall of the Maryland Institute to raise funds for the U.S. Christian and U.S. Sanitary Commissions, the two major relief organizations aiding Union soldiers.

April 18, 1864

Ladies and Gentlemen—Calling to mind that we are in Baltimore, we can not fail to note that the world moves. Looking upon these many people, assembled here, to serve, as they best may, the soldiers of the Union, it occurs at once that three years ago, the same soldiers could not so much as pass through Baltimore. The change from then till now, is both great, and gratifying. Blessings on the brave men who have wrought the change, and the fair women who strive to reward them for it.

But Baltimore suggests more than could happen within Baltimore. The change within Baltimore is part only of a far wider change. When the war began, three years ago, neither party, nor any man, expected it would last till now. Each looked for the end, in some way, long ere to-day. Neither did any anticipate that domestic slavery would be much affected by the war. But here we are; the war has not ended, and slavery has been much affected—how much needs not now to be recounted. So true is it that man proposes, and God disposes.

But we can see the past, though we may not claim to have directed it; and seeing it, in this case, we feel more hopeful and confident for the future.

The world has never had a good definition of the word liberty, and the American people, just now, are much in want of one. We all declare for liberty; but in using the same *word* we do not all mean the same *thing*. With some the word liberty may mean for each man to do as he pleases with himself, and the product of his labor; while with others the same word may mean for some men to do as they please with other men, and the product of other men's labor. Here are two, not only different, but incompatable things, called by the same name—liberty. And it follows that each of the things is, by the respective parties, called by two different and incompatable names—liberty and tyranny.

The shepherd drives the wolf from the sheep's throat, for which the sheep thanks the shepherd as a *liberator*, while the wolf denounces him for the same act as the destroyer of liberty, especially as the sheep was a black one. Plainly the sheep and the wolf are not agreed upon a definition of the word liberty; and precisely the same difference prevails to-day among us human creatures, even in the North, and all professing to love liberty. Hence we behold the processes by which thousands are daily passing from under the yoke of bondage, hailed by some as the advance of liberty, and bewailed by others as the destruction of all liberty. Recently, as it seems, the people of Maryland have been doing something to define liberty; and thanks to them that, in what they have done, the wolf's dictionary, has been repudiated.

It is not very becoming for one in my position to make speeches at great length; but there is another subject upon which I feel that I ought to say a word. A painful rumor, true I fear, has reached us of the massacre, by the rebel forces, at Fort Pillow, in the West end of Tennessee, on the Mississippi river, of some three hundred colored soldiers and white officers, who had just been overpowered by their assailants. There seems to be some anxiety in the public mind whether the government is doing its duty to the colored soldier, and to the service, at this point. At the beginning of the war, and for some time, the use of colored troops was not contemplated; and how the change of purpose was wrought, I will not now take time to explain. Upon a clear conviction of duty I resolved to turn that element of strength to account; and I am responsible for it to the American people, to the christian world, to history, and on my final account to God. Having determined to use the negro as a soldier, there is no way but to give him all the protection given to any other soldier. The difficulty is not in stating the principle, but in practically applying it. It is a mistake to suppose the government is indifferent to this matter, or is not doing the best it can in regard to it. We do not to-day *know* that a colored soldier, or white officer commanding colored soldiers, has been massacred by the rebels when made a prisoner. We fear it, believe it, I may say, but we do not *know* it. To take the life of one of their prisoners, on the assumption that they murder ours, when it is short of certainty that they do murder ours, might be too serious, too cruel a mistake. We are having the Fort-Pillow affair thoroughly investigated; and such investigation will probably show conclusively how the truth is. If, after all that has been said, it shall turn out that there has been no massacre at Fort-Pillow, it will be almost safe to say there has been none, and will be none elsewhere. If there has been the massacre of three hundred there, or even the tenth part of three hundred, it will be conclusively proved; and being so proved, the retribution shall as surely come. It will be matter of grave consideration in what exact course to apply the retribution; but in the supposed case, it must come.

"TAKE NO PRISONERS": APRIL 1864

R.H.C. *to* The Christian Recorder

April 30, 1864

Two weeks after the Fort Pillow massacre *The Christian Recorder*, a weekly newspaper published in Philadelphia by the African Methodist Episcopal Church, printed a letter signed "R.H.C." It may have been written by Richard Harvey Cain, an African Methodist Episcopal minister in Brooklyn, New York, who moved to South Carolina after the war and was elected to Congress during Reconstruction.

FORT PILLOW.

MR. EDITOR:—Still we press forward in the great march of mind and matter: winds still blow; and the southern breezes bring a wail of horror from the devoted "Fort. Pillow." Kentucky, that "virago" in the community of States, whose scoldings have retarded the progress of "civilization," in these war times more than any other, is now drinking the cup of secession wrath, which is a just retribution meted out to her. But, the dying groans of those butchered men, the desolate hearthstones, cry against, and the widowed mothers and orphans, will hold her accountable for their murdered kindred. Yet, through this bloody sea lies the land of liberty; and although we may have to pour out rivers of blood, liberty is not attainable without it. The brutality which prompted the slaughter of that garrison of brave men, is but a preface to the great book of scaled crimes which this abominable system of slavery has been perpetrating upon our race for two hundred and forty-five years. None but the blacks of this land, have heretofore realized the hateful nature of the beast: but now, white men are beginning to feel, and to realize what its beauties are. This fell spirit was the main spring of this rebellion; it has dictated all the movements in the attempt to destroy the government; it moved the schemers to assassinate President Lincoln, on his passage to Washington; it has murdered all colored soldiers captured by the rebels.

While we deplore the loss of these brave men, we feel that, from their ashes will rise thousands to avenge their deaths. We accept the alternative, and believe that the 54th and 55th Mass., 20th and 26th U.S. troops, in connection with the 1st, 4th, and all the other colored men in the service, will receive this news with defiance sparkling in every eye. The terrors of death should not affright them from the resolve to fight the battles of freedom. We all know, that in the destruction of slavery is the safety of the nation, and the hope of the race. We know that, when we enlisted, threats had been made, and we expected them to be fulfilled; and this butchery is not a new thing to us—we have had experiences before to-day. With slaveholders, this is only *an act on a grander scale*, than those thousands of similar ones performed daily by the lords of the lash, before this rebellion—and, instead of daunting our courage, should only nerve us to do and dare more in this struggle for human rights and universal liberty.

We now call on our noble brethren in the army, to swear anew never to cease fighting, until they shall have made a rebel to bite the dust for every hair of those three hundred of our brethren massacred in Fort Pillow; and, whenever you may be called upon to measure arms or bayonets, with the rebel horde, give no quarter; take no prisoners; make it dangerous to take the life of a black soldier by these barbarians; then, they will respect your manhood, and you will be treated as you deserve at the hands of those who have made you outlaws. If there be a complaint that you are savage, you can with justice point to forts Wagoner, Hudson, Pillow, and to Milliken's bend, and remember the deeds of cruelty there inflicted upon the innocent. Warriors! remember that you fight for liberty! Remember the wives and children you have left behind! Remember, you from New York, the *July riots!* You from the South, who are soldiers of the Republic, remember your old gray-haired mothers, who are yet within the lines of rebeldom; remember your wives and little ones, robbed and maltreated by ruffians and "Legrees;" remember your daughters, dishonored by those red-handed murderers of your race! Remember, that for two hundred and fifty years, your people have been sold and bartered like so many beasts, and then bow down before God, and swear anew to uphold your country's cause, and the cause of universal liberty: for, in the maintenance of liberty on this continent is the hope of all European nations. Think not that the blood you shed will avail nothing: if you fall in this mighty struggle; you will leave a name that shall live, after you have passed away; and the generations following will rise up and call you blessed. Your children will, undoubtedly, enjoy more liberty, and, the same spirit which animates you to do and dare in this fearful crisis, will fall upon them in double proportion, and they shall rise up to a position honorable among mankind.

No people can hope to be lifted up entirely by the labors or benevolence of others. We must not look for sympathy; we must not ask for pity; we must rise above this condition. So long as we are pensioners on other people's pity, we will be subject to their insults; but the moment we assume our rights, and maintain them by every lawful means; so soon as it appears to the world that we are not mendicants, but men ready to make any sacrifice for liberty and untrammelled freedom, then, the world will recognize in us more than mere objects of pity.

While our kindred are battling in the field, we who are at home, must not forget that we have duties to perform to those whom they have left behind. We should cheer their hearts by speaking words of comfort; and, if need be, contribute to their wants. Further, the leading minds must look after the interests of the soldiers; see that no injustice be done them by subordinates of the government, for it is by this class they suffer more than any other. And now that there is a great progressive movement on hand, let not any man among us stop, in his efforts to elevate and honor his race. Let those in civil life be on their guard, let them forward the education of the rising generation, and help forward every enterprise which tends to refine, mould, and fashion the future course of our kindred.

R.H.C.

DEBATING RETALIATION:
WASHINGTON, D.C., MAY 1864

Gideon Welles: Diary, May 3, 5–6, 1864

In a proclamation issued in December 1862, Jefferson Davis had ordered that former slaves captured while fighting in the Union army be turned over to state authorities to be tried for the capital offense of insurrection. In May 1863 his policy was extended by the Confederate Congress to apply to free blacks from the North. In practice, captured black soldiers were either summarily executed, returned or sold into slavery, or used for forced labor by the Confederate army. President Lincoln responded on July 30, 1863, issuing an order declaring that "for every soldier of the United States killed in violation of the laws of war, a rebel soldier shall be executed," and that for every one enslaved, "a rebel soldier shall be placed at hard labor on the public works." Despite reports that Confederate troops continued to kill and mistreat black prisoners, no retaliatory measures had been undertaken by the time of the assault on Fort Pillow. Secretary of the Navy Gideon Welles recorded the discussions held by the cabinet in early May as the congressional Joint Committee on the Conduct of the War prepared to release its report on the massacre. The inconclusive deliberations resulted in no further action, and no Confederate officer was ever charged in connection with the killings at Fort Pillow.

Tuesday 3. At the Cabinet meeting the President requested each member to give him an opinion as to what course the Government should pursue in relation to the recent massacre at Fort Pillow. The committee from Congress who have visited the scene returned yesterday and will soon report. All the reported horrors are said to be verified. The President wishes to be prepared to act as soon as the subject is brought to his notice officially, and hence Cabinet advice in advance.

The subject is one of great responsibility and great embarrassment especially before we are in possession of the facts and evidence of the committee. There must be something in these terrible reports, but I distrust Congressional committees. They exaggerate.

Mrs. W. and Edgar left to-day for New York. She is to spend a few days at Irvington—Edgar to complete his college course.

Tom is filled with unrestrained zeal to go to the army. It is much of it boyish fervor but none the less earnest.

Thursday 5. I have written a letter to the President in relation to the Fort Pillow massacre, but it is not satisfactory to me, nor can I make it so without the evidence of what was done, nor am I certain that even then I could come to a conclusion on so grave and important a question. The idea of retaliation—killing man for man which is the popular noisy demand is barbarous, and I cannot assent to or advise it. The leading officers should be held accountable and punished but how. The policy of killing negro soldiers after they have surrendered must not be permitted, and the Rebel leaders should be called upon to avow or disavow it. But how is this to be done? Shall we go to Jeff Davis and his government, or apply to General Lee. If they will give us no answer, or declare they will kill the negroes, or justify Forrest, shall we take innocent Rebel officers as hostages. The whole subject is beset with difficulties. I cannot yield to any inhuman scheme of retaliation. Must wait the publication of the testimony.

Friday 6. At the Cabinet meeting each of the members read his opinion. There had, I think been some concert between Seward and Stanton and probably Chase—that is they had talked on the subject, although there was not coincidence of views on all respects. Although I was dissatisfied with my own, it was as well as most others.

Between Mr. Bates and Mr. Blair a suggestion came out that met my views better than anything that had previously occurred. It is, that the President should, by proclamation declare the officers who had command at the massacre are outlaws, and require any of our officers who may capture them, to detain them in custody and not exchange them, but hold them to punishment. The thought was not very distinctly enunciated. In a conversation that followed the reading of our papers, I expressed myself in favor of this new suggestion which relieved the subject of much of the difficulty. It avoids communication with the Rebel authorities. Takes the matter in our own hands. We get rid of the barbarity of retaliation.

Stanton fell in with my suggestion, so far as to propose that should Forrest, or Chalmers, or any officer conspicuous in this butchery be captured, that he should be turned over for trial for the murders at Fort Pillow. I sat beside Chase and mentioned to him some of the advantages of this course, and he said it made a favorable impression. I urged him to say so, for it appeared to me that the President and Seward did not appreciate it.

We get no tidings from the front. There is an impression that we are on the eve of a great battle and that it may already have commenced.

PROTESTING SLAVE IMPRESSMENT:
ALABAMA, MAY 1864

Petition from the Slaveholders of Randolph County, Alabama

From the beginning of the war the impressment of slaves for military labor by the Confederate army met with widespread resistance from southern slaveholders, who protested the loss of needed labor and feared that their impressed slaves might die, escape, or lose respect for their owners' authority. The Confederate Congress passed legislation in March 1863 intended to make impressment more equitable, but small slaveholders continued to object that the regulations favored large planters. On May 6, 1864, forty-six slaveowners from Randolph County in northeastern Alabama petitioned Jefferson Davis for relief from an assessment levied by Colonel Frederick S. Blount, the impressment agent for the Department of Alabama, Mississippi, and East Louisiana. Blount subsequently wrote on May 14 to Henry M. Gay, the impressment agent for the county, requisitioning fifty slaves for labor service. After Gay responded on June 1 that he would be able to furnish only five slaves, Blount agreed to exempt Randolph County from the impressment.

Wesabulga Randolph Co Ala May 6th 1864 To his Excellency Jefferson Davis The undersigned citizens & Slaveholders of the county of Randolph & State of Alabama would respectfully represent to your Excellency That Col Blount impressing agt of Slaves Stationed at Mobile Ala; has recently ordered an impressment of 33⅓ per cent of the able bodied Slaves of this County; when in adjoining counties where the Slave population is greater only from 5 to 10 per cent have been taken— This we think to be unjust, & *not* in accordance with the intentions of the act. We think that an uniform rate should be levied in the whole State; or so much of it as is now within our lines; So that the burden Should fall uniformly on all; But he appears to order an arbitrary number from each county without refferance to the number of Slaves in the County. He thus levies a percentage which is uniform in the county, but does not bear any proportion to the levies in adjoining Counties— He also counts *in* all the women that are within the ages of 17 to 50 & takes one third of the *total number in men* between the ages of 17 to 50.

Randolph is a poor & mountainous County with the largest population of any in the State. There are only 300 negroes (women & men) within the prescribed ages in the county & he takes one Hundred   Seventy five per cent of the White Males are now in the Service; leaving the great majority of their wives & children to be Supported by the remainder   There are numbers of widows & orphans of the Soldiers who have perished by the casualities of war to be also Supported by public funds—

The County does not in ordinary times produce more than a Sufficiency of food for its population; last year there was a deficit of over 40000 bushels; of corn about one half of which has been provided from the tax in Kind; the ballance has to be purchased in the Canebrake; transported a distance of 125 miles on R.R, & hauled thence in waggons from 30 to 50 miles to reach the various points of distribution in the county—

There are now on the rolls of the Probate court, 1600 indigent families to be Supported; they average 5 to each family; making a grand total of 8000 persons   Deaths from Starvation have absolutely occurred; notwithstanding the utmost efforts that we have been able to make; & now many of the women & children are seeking & feeding upon the bran from the mills

Women riots have taken place in Several parts of the County in which Govt wheat & corn has been seized to prevent Starvation of themselves & families; Where it will end unless relief is afforded we cannot tell

We have entered into these details that your Excellency may See the deplorable condition of things in this County, & aid us if in your power & the exigencies of the Service permit—

To take the Negroes *now* from the fields when the crop is just planted & ready for cultivation would inevitably cause the loss of a portion of the crops So essential to feed the County   we have appealed to Col Blount asking that the impressment be delayed or abandoned; but without effect & we now appeal to your Excellency as our last resource under God to give us Such measure of assistance as you can. If you refuse us—we must Submit & take our chance—do our duty & trust to

Almighty Providence for the result under all the circumstances we therefore pray your Excellency.

That Randolph County be exempt from the operations of the impressment act. If, however the Case is so urgent & the hands are so essential to save Mobile; then we ask that the impressment be delayed until fall when the crops are gathered; In case neither of these prayers can be granted we pray that the rate be made uniform in the Whole State—& that *we* be not punished for our poverty— we would Humbly Suggest to your Excellency that there are large numbers of negroes about our towns & cities (used for the pleasure of their owners; or idling about; a curse to the community—*consumers not producers*) that we think might be exhausted before the agricultural labour of the county is interfered with.

Hoping that your Excellency may favourably consider our humble prayer—we remain as ever your Excellencies devoted Servants

"OUR RIGHT CAUSE": VIRGINIA, MAY 1864

Samuel W. Fiske to the Springfield Republican

A company commander in the 14th Connecticut Infantry, Captain Samuel W. Fiske had joined his regiment in August 1862 and fought at Antietam, Chancellorsville, Gettysburg, and Bristoe Station. On the day before the Army of the Potomac began crossing the Rapidan, he sent one of his regular letters to the *Springfield* (Massachusetts) *Republican*, written under the pen name Dunn Browne. Fiske was shot on the morning of May 6 while fighting along the Orange Plank Road in the Wilderness as part of the Third Brigade, Second Division, Second Corps. Wounded in the right lung, he was taken to a Union army hospital in Fredericksburg, Virginia, where he died on May 22, 1864, the day after this letter appeared in the *Republican*.

Dunn Browne's Parting Grumble and Advice

Camp on the Rapidan, Va.
May 3, 1864

A Tempest In Camp

Dear Republican: Stepping out of my tent yesterday for a moment, I saw a huge red cloud sweeping over Pony mountain with tremendous rapidity and fury, and before we had half done wondering whether it was some stray aurora borealis shooting across Virginia, one of the boys exclaimed, "That's genuine Virginia mud taking to itself wings"; and sure enough, our whole eastern horizon was darkened with a tornado of dust, and we sprang to our houses to keep them from breaking their connection with the hillside on which we are located. What a time we did have, to be sure! The principle of gravitation was nowhere. The "star of empire" never took its way westward with half the velocity with which the barrels from our chimneys, the hats from our heads and the canvas from our huts started on a tour towards the Rocky mountains. We could readily believe that the earth was whirling from west to east as rapidly as the astronomers tell us, and moreover that she evidently meant to leave us behind, this trip at least. The many trees that had been left standing in and about our camp couldn't withstand the blast for a moment, but broke like pipe stems before the first rush of the tempest; and woe to the luckless log hut that happened to be squatted in the path of its fall. A huge pine made kindling wood of the stately mansion of our colonel, grinding to splinters the tender young pines that composed its walls as ruthlessly as the porcine mother sometimes devours her offspring. Well for the colonel that he was out of his hut at the time on a tour of picket duty, or there would have been a likely chance for promotion to somebody in our regiment. I have heard of nobody that was injured, at least seriously, but the "scare" was considerable, and the dust that filled our houses and covered our beds and clothes and food, something like the cloud of ashes that buried Pompeii. Our oldest sailors said they never saw anything like it. The tempest soon blew itself over, however, and the rain that succeeded it was not much more than enough to lay the dust. So we speedily repaired damages and settled into our pristine "quiet along the Rapidan."

A Razee Of Our Houses

To-day, nevertheless, an order from division headquarters has done what the tornado didn't half accomplish, namely, has unroofed all our houses and leveled them to the ground. "Going to move," are we? Oh no, not at all. But the fact is we are getting altogether too effeminate for soldiers. Why should we lie in comfortable dry huts, on bunks raised from the ground, when thousands of acres of sacred Virginia soil lie all around us, on which (with the slight trouble of tearing our houses down) we may extend ourselves? Why indulge in chimneys when it is so much more soldierly to gather round a smoky fire out of doors to cook our food and warm ourselves? Why interfere with the providential design of these searching spring rains and withering winds by remaining behind plastered log barriers and under tight roofs, when so little work will enable us to return to nature's wild simplicity? Some of our foolish boys murmur at these orders emanating from comfortable, luxurious headquarters, and think we might as well have remained in our tight little cabins the few days we have yet to stay, as to catch colds all of us by lying on the ground before we commence our summer's marchings. But it is well known that soldiers will grumble at the kindest provisions made for their comfort, and of course we shall go on with our wholesome sanitary arrangements regardless of any such talk.

The Ration Question

Why, actually, some of these ungrateful boys object to the bill Senator Wilson is introducing, cutting down their ration to the old standard; and declare that with the present ration (marching), they used last summer frequently to eat the ten crackers allowed per day at a single meal, and wonder what they will do if it is reduced. Now it is well known (to all the people that stay at home and read the newspapers) that no man can possibly eat the whole of the bountiful ration that Uncle Sam allows his soldiers; and it is well known to the heads of the war bureaus at Washington (as we see by an order issued on the subject last year) that it is perfectly easy for the soldier to carry 12 days' rations on his person on the march, and even, in case of necessity, where the beef is driven on the hoof, and there is some green corn to be obtained, 24 or 30 days' rations. In face of these well known facts, then, how absurd for a soldier to set up the statement that he does, as a matter of fact, often eat a whole day's marching ration at a single meal and call for more, and that no soldier ever did carry on his back more than what he ate in six days! How preposterous to mention the circumstance that nineteen out of twenty of the enlisted men spend their whole pay in purchasing additions to this same extravagantly liberal allowance of Uncle Sam, and that after a three days' march, on a supply of (it may be) 11 days' rations, the usual price of hard tack is a dime a piece! I have seen hundreds of times a dollar offered for half a dozen hard breads, or for a day's ration, although of course a true soldier will scorn to take money from a comrade for anything to eat that he may happen to have over.

Does it ever occur to anyone who is thinking of the liberal rations of our government, to ask whether the soldier, as a matter of fact, gets that full allowance? It is true that if the soldier had all the beans, rice, molasses, potatoes, dried apples, pickles, hominy, &c., &c., that the regulations allow him, and time and skill to cook them properly, he would be able to satisfy his appetite very reasonably, and even often have something over. But when we come to the marches, the hard work of the soldier, his ration is ten crackers a day (a short pound) and three-fourths of a pound of pork or one and one-quarter pounds of fresh beef of the poorest and boniest kind, and nothing else except a small allowance of sugar and coffee. This hard bread is frequently spoiled by wet, and some part of it unfit to eat by reason of bugs and worms. Now I affirm, in spite of Gen. Wilson, or Gen. Halleck, or anybody else, that this is a short ration for a hearty man on a hard march, and that when the extra of "small rations," as they are called (beans, rice, &c.), are not issued, at least 12 or 14 crackers a day should be issued to make the ration good. If the soldier obtained the money value of these articles to which he is entitled, but which are not issued, as the regulations say he shall, in his company fund, the matter would be better, but in practice he seldom or never does.

THE BOYS LIKE TO BE TALKED TO

There are several things which I could suggest as measures likely to benefit the boys of our army, but as my turn has not yet come to take command of the forces, they may not be at present adopted. I think, for instance, that they ought to be talked to a little more. All the great generals of ancient times, and of modern times, too, have stirred the enthusiasms of their troops on the eve of battle by rousing speeches. Xenophon, Hannibal, Scipio, Caesar, everybody who wanted to get some great exploits out of the troops under his command, has told them what he wanted them to do, appealed to their patriotism, their religion, their love of glory, or whatever motive might most excite them to lofty action. Cromwell stirred up the religious enthusiasm of his troops till no foe of equal numbers could resist their grim onset. Napoleon, with a few fiery sentences, roused his Frenchmen to the most exalted spirit of courage and devotion. Now no soldiers under heaven ever came to war from a more intelligent spirit of patriotism than ours; none with a clearer sense of the principles which lay at the basis of the contest in which they are engaged; none more capable of being encouraged and roused to enthusiasm by the lofty enthusiasms of a generous leader. And our nation, of all others, has been a nation of perpetual public gatherings and speech makings. But our generals have said never a word (I speak in a general way) to encourage the troops, to keep alive their patriotism and regard for the cause, to cherish that living sympathy which should ever exist between a leader and his troops—have seemed desirous, on the whole, to make their men mere machines, going into battle without knowing anything where the pinch of the contest was, or precisely what was required of them—save to go forward at the order "forward" and fire at the order "fire."

I believe a good deal more might be made by a different course of proceeding, that our boys are something more than shooting machines, or if machines, that there are strings and pulleys and wheels in them that mere military orders don't reach, and yet which might have much effect in deciding battles—these great and terrible battles that are to decide this opening campaign, and probably bring the war to an end—these coming successes (as we devoutly hope) that are to atone for the disgraceful reverses our arms have this spring sustained in every quarter where they have been engaged. Oh for power to speak a word that might thrill the breast of every Union soldier and rouse in him that holy enthusiasm for our right cause, which should make every blow struck irresistible, and carry our arms victorious right into the citadel of rebellion, and conquer a right peace. One or two of Meade's modest, earnest orders, published to the army near the Gettysburg times, had a wonderfully happy effect. I trust more may be issued, and that every opportunity may be taken to inspire the patriotism and enthusiasm of our troops, and keep before their minds the great principles which first sent them forth from their peaceful homes to fight for endangered liberty and republican government, for God and freedom throughout the world.

Yours truly,

DUNN BROWNE

BATTLE OF THE WILDERNESS:
VIRGINIA, MAY 1864

Theodore Lyman: Journal, May 4–7, 1864

The Army of the Potomac crossed the Rapidan River on May 4, 1864, the day before Benjamin F. Butler began his waterborne advance up the James River toward Richmond. At the same time, Franz Sigel was leading Union troops south in the Shenandoah Valley, while forces under George Crook and William W. Averell were conducting raids in southwestern Virginia as part of Grant's overall plan to prevent reinforcements from reaching Lee's army. Once across the Rapidan, the Army of the Potomac would have to make its way through the Wilderness of Spotsylvania, an area of scrub woods and dense undergrowth where much of the battle of Chancellorsville had been fought the year before. Grant and Meade hoped their troops would quickly reach more open country, forcing Lee either to retreat or to fight on ground where the Union's numerical superiority in men and artillery could be fully exploited. A wealthy Bostonian, Lieutenant Colonel Theodore Lyman had spent the first two years of the war touring Europe before becoming an aide on Meade's staff in September 1863. Lyman's notebook journal for the period May 3 to June 16, 1864, bears the notation that the "notes in this book were not written herein on the spot, but taken from letters home & from memoranda written at the time and afterwards enlarged when I wrote out the notes of the Campaign for Gen. Meade's Report. This book was not begun till June 1865." In the sketch maps Lyman drew in his notebook, Union corps are indicated by their respective badges: for the Second Corps, commanded by Major General Winfield Scott Hancock, a three-leaf clover; for the Fifth Corps (Major General Gouverneur K. Warren), a Maltese cross; for the Sixth Corps (Major General John Sedgwick), a Greek cross; for the Ninth Corps (Major General Ambrose Burnside), an anchor. The designations "Q," "R," and "S" indicate the order in which the maps appear in Lyman's notebook.

May 4, 1864, Wednesday.
We all were up by star-light; a warm, clear night; had our breakfast by daybreak, and at 5.25 A.M. turned our backs on

our little village of the last six months, and the grove about it, dear even in its desolation! The columns had been moving a good part of the night and we cut a part of the 6th Corps, just at Brandy Station, beyond which point the road was full of waggons and troops. Beyond Stevensburg the road-side was full of violets, and the little leaves of the wood trees were just beginning to unfold, the size of a mouse's ear perhaps. 7 A.M. The General unluckily came up with a cavalry waggon train, out of place; the worst thing for his temper! He sent me after its Quartermaster, Capt. Luddington, whom he gave awful dressing to, and ordered him to get his whole train out of the road and to halt till the other trains had passed. The sun getting well up made the temperature much warmer, as was testified by the castaway packs & blankets with which troops will often at the outset encumber themselves. 8 A.M. Arrived near Germanna Ford and halted just where we had camped the night of the withdrawal from Mine Run. *Sapristi*, it was cold that night! Though here was green grass in place of an half inch of ice, Griffin's division was over and his ammunition was then crossing. 8.30 A.M. News from Hancock that he was crossing, Gregg having had no opposition and having seen only videttes.— Roads everywhere excellent. 9.30. We crossed. There were two pontoons, a wooden & a canvass, the ascent up the opposite high & steep bank was bad, with a difficult turn near the top. We halted just on the other side and Grant & his staff arrived some time after. 12.15 P.M. All the 5th Corps, with its artillery and wheeled vehicles across.— It began at 6.30 A.M. The 6th Corps began to cross at 12.40 and was all over at 5.20 and the canvas pontoon was taken up. A good part of the time, say ½, only one pontoon could be used, because the troops were moving in single column. We may then estimate 15 hours for the passage of 46,000 infantry, with one half of their ambulances and ammunition and intrenching waggons and the whole of their artillery, over a single bridge, with steep, bad approaches on each side; i.e. a little over 3,000 men an hour, with their artillery and wheels. The latter took a good deal of the time because of the delay in getting them up the steep ascent. Sat on the bank and watched the steady stream, as it came over. That eve took a bath in the Rapid Ann and thought that might come sometime to bathe in the James!

Germanna F'd to pike = 5 ml's.
Orange Plank to Todd's = 5 ml's.
Parker's Store to Chancel'V. = 7½ ml's.

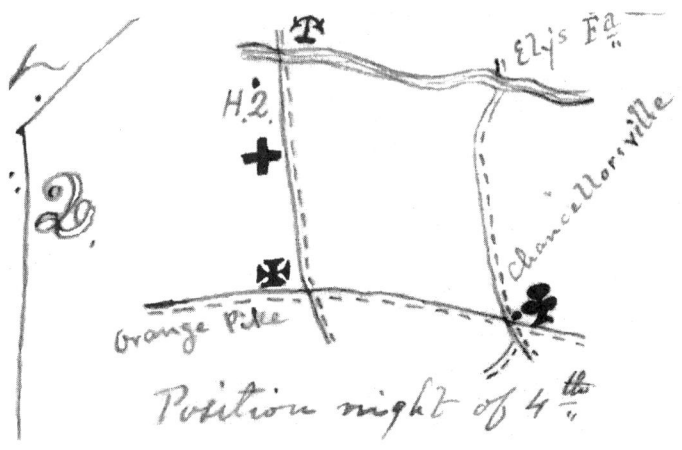

Position night of 4th

Our cook, little M. Mercier, came to grief, having been spirited away by the provost guard of the 2d Corps, as a straggler or spy; so our supper was got up by the waiter boy, Marshall. Our camp was near the river, and Grant's was close to us. Some of his officers; Duff & old Jerry Dent e.g. were very flippant and regarded Grant as already routing Lee and utterly breaking up the rebellion!—not so the more sober.—There arrived Gen. Seymour, the unlucky man of Olustee, dark bearded and over given to talk and write; but of well known valor. He was assigned to a brigade 3d Div. 6th Corps, where his command was destined to be of the shortest.

May 5, Thursday.
The head of the 9th Corps got last night as far as Germanna Ford; but the troops extended thence far back. Order of march (epitome) for May 5. (Of course this was but partially carried out, owing to the battle.) Sheridan, with Gregg's and Torbert's Divisions, to attack enemy's cavalry at Hamilton's crossing (towards Fredericksburg). Wilson's Cav. Div. to move out at 5 A.M. to Craig's Meeting House, on Catharpin road, and to throw out on the Catharpin & Pamunkey roads and on the Orange Plank & Pike, &c. 2d Corps move at 5 to Shady Grove Church, and extend its right towards the 5th Corps at Parker's Store. 5th Corps at 5, to Parker's Store and extend its right to

6th Corps at Wilderness Tavern. 6th Corps to Wilderness Tavern, leaving one Div. at Germanna Fd. till Burnside had got over troops enough to hold it. Reserve Artillery to Corbin's Bridge. Trains to near Todd's Tavern. Headq'rs on Orange Plank near to 5th Corps. When in position the army will be held ready to advance. Right & left flanks to be well watched and pickets thrown well out. (Note. In the first of this order, may be seen already Sheridan's budding ambition for personal and independent distinction. He wanted to do something *separate*, though the interests of the service were plainly against the scattering of forces. The order was countermanded.)— We rode some 4½ miles and arrived at 7.10 A.M. at Old Wilderness Tavern, on the right of the road and near the Orange Pike. Here were Generals Warren & Sedgwick. The 5th Corps was marching past and the 6th was in its rear. Was greeted by Bill Thorndike, Surgeon in the 39th Mass. of Robinson's Div. Told him that Griffin reported the enemy on the Orange Pike, 2 miles west of the Germanna Plank. Wright was ordered to move S.W. from the Germanna Plank and feel for Griffin's right. 10.30 A.M. The 5th New York cavalry, holding the Orange Plank at Parker's store, has been attacked by infantry and driven in, with loss. Enemy reported at Fredericks hall, south of the N. Anna (idle story).— 10.45 Getty's Div. of 6th Corps ordered to proceed at once to junction of the cross-road (continuation of the Brock Road) and the Orange Plank, and hold it. One division of Burnside reported across. All expected over by night. Headq'rs move to a piney knoll on the right of the Orange Pike and opposite the Maj. Lacy house. There was a good space of open country just here extending on both sides of the pike, though chiefly on the left; but, about a mile up the road were pine woods, wherein was Griffin's division going south along the Germanna Plank, the low woods began near the junction of the Brock cross-road with this. 12.10. Ordered to go to Gen. Getty and explain to him the position of the army and direct him to seek roads to the right and join with Crawford's left. At the beginning of the cross-road found Gen. Eustis' brigade going into the woods;—told him the orders, and he said he would send 3 regiments instead of 2, to feel to the right. Found Getty sitting on the ground, near the Plank Road, but on the cross-road. He said the whole of Hill's Corps was coming down the plank, and the skirmishers were within 300 yards. They had been fighting, and two or three bodies lay near us, and a wounded man occasionally passed. Getty told me to tell Gen. Meade that he had but 3 brigades, having been ordered to leave one behind. 12.50. Reported back at Headq'rs. Just at this moment, heavy musketry from Griffin and some apparently from Wright, also from Wadsworth on Griffin's left. It lasted, rising & falling, for about 1½ hours. 1.50. Ordered to go to 5th N.Y. Cav. & direct them, as soon as filled up with ammunition, to proceed down the Brock Road and open communication with Gen. Hancock, who was moving up. Found the regiment to the rear of the Germanna Plank; men distributing cartridges; the Colonel having somewhat cooked. Ordered him to report to Gen. Getty, as above. 2. Sent again to countermand the above order, as Hancock was nearly in junction with Getty's left. Returning to Headq'rs found the pike blocked with ambulances and with wounded on foot, who continually enquired "How far to the 5th Corps Hospital?" They were chiefly from Griffin's Div. and also many from Wadsworth's. Met Joe Hayes, supported by Dalton, and by a servant on his horse. He was talking wildly and the blood streamed down his face! A dangerous wound to look at—shot in the head. There we were three classmates together!— Helped him along till assured he had enough assistance, when left him with Dalton. 2.45. Griffin comes in, followed by his mustering officer, Geo. Barnard. He is stern & angry. Says in a loud voice that he drove back the enemy, Ewell, ¾ of a mile, but got no support on the flanks, and had to retreat—the regulars much cut up. Implies censure on Wright and apparently also on his corps commander, Warren. Wadsworth also driven back.— Rawlins got very angry, considered the language mutinous and wished him put in arrest.— Grant seemed of the same mind and asked Meade; "who is this Gen. *Gregg*? You ought to arrest him!" Meade said "It's Griffin, not Gregg; and it's only his way of talking."— Rawlins asked me what he had done; told him his reputation as an officer was good. In this charge Bartlett's brigade, the first line commanded by Hayes, broke and drove the enemy, handsomely.— Bartlett's horse was killed and he badly hurt in the head by his fall. There is little doubt that Wright made slow work in his advance. 3 P.M. Burnside ordered up. 3.15. Sent with a written order to Getty to attack (& Hancock to go in too); but to attack alone if Hancock was not ready. Delivered it at 3.25. Getty in the same spot—very cool—evidently did not think it good strategy to attack till more of the 2d Corps was up; but promptly sent aides to Eustis & Wheaton directing them to prepare at once to advance. 4.15. Ordered to take with me orderlies; report to Hancock and send back reports of progress from time to time. Reported at 4.45 to Hancock, who sat on his horse at the crossing of the Brock and Plank roads. He told me to write to Gen. Meade that it was hard to bring up troops in this wood—only part of corps up, but would do as well as he could.— All this time heavy musketry in our front and stray balls coming over. The country a "Wilderness" indeed!—a thick cover of sapplings, from 15 to 30 feet high with a close under-growth of bushes. Now rides up an officer—Maj. Mundy—"Sir! Gen. Getty is hard pressed and his ammunition nearly out"—"Tell him to hold on, & Gen. Gibbon will be up to help him!" Another officer, from the left, comes up; "Sir! Gen. Mott's division has broken, and is coming back!"—"Tell him to stop them!" roared Hancock, and galloped towards the left and began rallying the retreating troops in the Brock road. "Maj. Mitchell, go to Gen. Gibbon and tell him to come up on the double-quick!" (The bad conduct of this division of Mott's, once renowned as the 2d Division of the 3d Corps, Hooker's old command, was an instance of demoralization. Commanded successively by the dull Prince, the dancing master Carr, and by Mott, a cool, gallant man but without capacity for a large body of troops, its morale was further shaken by the breaking up of the Third Corps and its transfer to the 2d. In this, and the fights just after, its conduct was doubtless on the whole, disgraceful. When reduced to a brigade, under old McAllister, it did once more, good fighting at the Battle of Hatcher's Run &c.) Hancock rode then off to the left. I was in the "cross-road" (continuation of the Brock) when Carroll's & Hay's brigades came up, the former leading (or Hays perhaps was already there and only sent some regiments to assist.)— At any rate Carroll's men formed in the cross-road, and faced left to the front. They were blown by the double-quick. One of their Colonels said; "Now I don't want any hollering;—that's

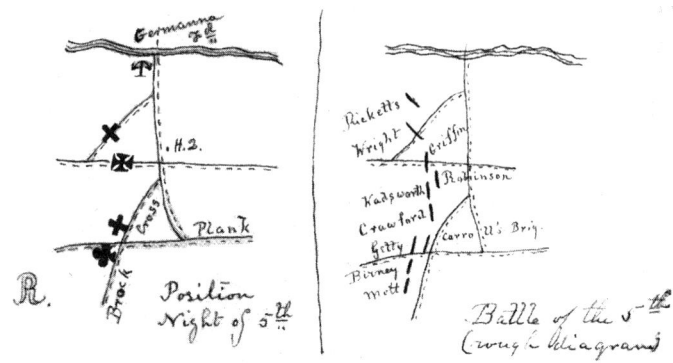

childish!"— Then, prime! Forward!— Soon after heard that Carroll was shot through the arm, and then that Hays was killed. The musketry continued, but the fresh troops had saved the day. Just as the sun was declining Gen. Hays was carried past me, on a stretcher borne on the shoulders of four men. He was shot straight through the head, but still had a mechanical respiration. At dark the fight was a drawn one; the line extending, as before, along the Brock and west of the cross-road. Portions of the 5th, 6th & 2d Corps had been opposed to Hill's & Ewell's Corps. It was after dark when got to Headq'rs, the tents being pitched in a dusty field, east of the Germanna Plank. Had frequently sent reports during the day, as ordered. Wilson's cavalry got cut off today between Parker's Store & Catharpin Road, and had to cut their way through to Sheridan. Grant ordered a general attack tomorrow at 4.30 A.M. but postponed it to 5, because they suggested Burnside would not be up till that time. "He won't be up—I know him well!" said Duane (who hates B.) and so it turned out.

May 6, Friday.
All hands up before daylight. Sunrise was at about 4.50. The General was in the saddle in the gray of the morning. As he sat in the hollow by the Germanna Plank, up comes Capt. Hutton of B's staff and says only one division was up and the road blocked with artillery (part of which was then passing us).— The General uttered some exclamation, and H said: "if you will authorize me sir, I will take the responsibility of ordering

the artillery out of the road, and bring up the infantry at once."—"No Sir" said M flatly. "I have no command over Gen. Burnside." And here was the first mishap—the fight would have been better if Grant had not been there, for Meade knew B well and would have got him on the march at an earlier hour. B had been up the night before and had said "Well then my troops shall break camp by half past two." (I think)—But he had a genius of slowness. 5.15. Ordered to ride to Gen. Hancock, remain there during the day, and report back by orderlies. There was skirmishing already and, as rode down the cross road, the volleys began. Found H at join of the Brock and Plank. "Tell Gen. Meade" he cried, "we are driving them most beautifully. Birney has gone in and he is just cleaning them out beautifully." I said I was ordered to report only one division of Burnside up; but he would attack as soon as he could.—"I knew it! Just what I expected!" cried Hancock. "If he could attack *now*, we could smash A.P. Hill all to pieces!!"— The musketry was receding.—Squads of prisoners were coming in. We had taken the rifle-pits they had made in the night and now we were straightening the line, previous to pushing on. The fire therefore slackened. 6.45. Gen. Getty rode past me, in the cross-road, looking pale; to my enquiry, he said; "I am shot through the shoulder; I don't know how badly"— a man of indomitable courage and coolness!— One of his aides (the fair haired), shot through the arm, the other with his horse shot. Immortal fighting did that valiant 2d Division 6th Corps, on these two bloody days!— About 7 A.M. Webb's brigade moved up the Brock and wheeled into the plank to support Birney. Waved my hand to Abbott, as he rode past at the head of the 20th, smiling gaily. 7.45. Stevenson up with one brigade of his division, sent to reinforce Hancock. The other brigade had lost the road, but was expected soon. There was Charlie Mills, and Stevie Weld, Lt. Col. of the 56th. Told them we were driving them, and they had only to go in & finish up the rebs. 7.50 A.M. One of Barlow's brigades is to go in along the incomplete railroad cut and strike the enemy in flank. 9. Column reported coming up the Brock road and deploying skirmishers. This, in the event, proved only a lot of cavalry, but these demonstrations had a most paralysing effect on our left, and seriously affected the fight. Gibbon was stampeded and

Battle of 6th — Morning
[Rough diagram]

made no vigorous handling of Barlow's division and of Carroll's brigade.— Hancock complained after, that Gibbon's feeble command of the left wing of his corps changed the face of the day. 10. These rebel cavalry were beaten by ours, on the Brock road. It must have been about this time that a prisoner of *Longstreet's Corps* was brought to me! This showed the presence of these troops, who had not before been in the fight, being on the march from Orange C. H. Reported this at once to Gen. Meade.— Macy was shot through the leg about this time, the 20th being heavily engaged on the right of the plank. He told me (after) that Gen. Wadsworth was back & forth there a great deal ordering him to the *left* of the plank, whereas Webb had put him where he was. 11. Abbott mortally wounded. Maj. Angel told me he saw him lying on the line; his eyes fixed. There is a great likeness between Angel & Maj. Norval, both Staff officers of 2d Corps; the former being Engineer at Headq'rs. 11.10. The first grand break—said, by the officer who came, to be first the right of Barlow, but think it was the left of Mott. Longstreet had struck heavily there, diagonally towards the Plank (as would appear from rebel accounts).— For a long time the wounded had been coming back rapidly along the road; at one period 2 light twelves had, by order of Gen. Birney, been placed on the plank and had fired solid shot over our men. Gibbon too had opened a battery on the left, but it ceased firing on information that the shot struck in our own lines. The attack became general on the whole front. Stevenson's brigade of raw "Veterans," broke after being under a severe fire for 10 minutes. Col. Griswold of the 56th was killed. Col. Bartlett, of the 57th, wounded, Gen. Stevenson, nearly surrounded, escaped by the right. A large part of the whole line came back, slowly but mixed up—a hopeless sight! American soldiers, in this condition are enough to sink one's heart! They have no craven terror—they have their arms; but, for the moment, they will not fight, nor even rally. Drew my sword and tried to stop them, but with small success, at the partial rifle-pit that ran along the road. There was no danger, the enemy did not follow. 12. Rode in and reported the state of the case in person to Gen. Meade. Gen. Patrick went out with his brigade, and, as the stream of stragglers came up the cross-road, he stopped them in the open fields & rapidly reorganized them. Artillery had been planted on the ridge near Headq'rs pointing S.W. The General told me to remain a little. Grant, who was smoking stoically under a pine, expressed himself annoyed and surprised that Burnside did not attack, especially as Comstock was with him as engineer & staff officer, to show him the way. 1 P.M. Trains ordered to fall back towards Ely's Ford, as a precautionary measure. 1.15 (about)—Back to Hancock. He alone, in rear of Brock Road; and there he asked me to sit down under the trees, as he was very tired indeed. All his staff were away to set in order the troops. They had now constructed a tolerable rifle-pit extending along the Brock and to the head of the cross-road. He said that his troops were rallied but very tired and mixed up, and not in a condition to advance. He had given orders to have the utmost exertions put forth in putting regiments in order, but many of the field officers were killed & wounded, and it was hard. At 2 P.M. Burnside, after going almost to Parker's Store and again back, made a short attack with loud musketry. Ventured to urge Hancock (who was very pleasant & talkative) to try and attack too, but he said with much regret that it would be to hazard too much, though there was nothing in his immediate front, which had been swept by Stevenson's other brigade, which marched from left to right. He spoke highly of the commander of this brigade. There presently came a note from Gen. Meade that Burnside had attacked and taken a small breastwork, and could Hancock attack also?—Burnside's success was, after all, trifling, if anything. Potter told me (after) that his division like the rest in that corps, was mostly of raw men, that they made a very good rush at first, but were presently driven back as fast as they came. Gen. Wadsworth today was mortally wounded and left in the hands of the enemy, near the Plank Road. The attacks of Griffin and of Sedgwick's two divisions, on the right amounted to nothing. Flint saw (May '65) the place where the 6th Corps charged, and said there were no marks of very hard fighting, but on the left, along the Plank Road, there were places in front of the rebel pits, where the entire growth of sapplings was cut down by musketry. Concerning this fight on the Plank Road there has been the greatest discussion between Webb's brigade, Getty's division and the division of Birney and of Wadsworth, especially the two latter. Wadsworth's people, and Cope, of Gen. Warren's staff, state that they drove back the rebels, and got a footing on the Plank Road (attacking the rebel left in that part of the field) and that one brigade swept the whole front of the 2d Corps and came out on the other side, while the 2d Corps were lying behind breastworks doing nothing! Birney's people *per contra* say that Wadsworth's attack amounted to nothing and he was driven back, though personally he came on the Plank Road and interfered with the order of battle, while they did all the successful fighting! The two accounts are entirely unreconcilable, but are not astonishing in a desperate fight in a thick cover, where no one can see 100 feet, and every one is liable to get turned round. Macy told me that, though he lost over ¼ of his men killed and wounded he *never saw a rebel*! In truth this whole Battle of the Wilderness was a scientific "bushwhack" of 200,000 men! 3.15 P.M. All being quiet got permission of Hancock to go back to 2d Corps Hospital & look after Abbott. (The hospital was some 2 miles back on a cleared farm, approachable only by a winding wood road, south of the plank. It was excellently arranged, particularly for the small means, but a ghastly sight indeed! Arms & legs lay outside the operating tents, and each table had a bleeding man on it, insensible from ether, and with the surgeons at work on him. As I entered a large tent and asked "Is Maj. Abbott here?"—"Here he is, sir," said a servant.— I should not have recognized the white face & uprolled eyes! He was unconscious and dying fast. Lifted Macy up, and we stood there till he was gone—Macy shedding tears. Took his valuables in charge and a lock of his hair, and got the promise that his body should go home, if possible.— In the embalming place (a negro house) there lay already the body of a Captain of Infantry; the assistant had just cut down on the femoral artery.) Abbott died about 4. As was riding again towards the front, about 4.30, the artillery on Gibbon's left suddenly opened heavily, followed by a sharp musketry. Immediately rode up the Germanna Plank to Gen. Meade, reported the fact and asked if he could not get Burnside ordered in to attack and help Hancock. In spite of this Gen. Meade seemed sceptical of the severity of the attack. Burnside did of his own accord, put in a division, with good effect. "The best thing old Burn' did during the day," said the General afterwards. 5.20 P.M. Rode back to join Gen. H but on the road met Maj. Hancock (I think) who said the enemy had broken through at the plank, and there was no communication with the left wing! Found Birney in the cross-road, and he said the same; upon which sent back a note which stampeded the General. All wrong on Birney's part—along came Saunders (I believe) & we rode together down the road & found all open, and that the enemy had only broken through in one small place, but had been driven out, leaving over 50 dead on that spot. Presently found Hancock and remained till about sunset with him. 7 P.M. While at dinner heard a little scattered musketry and presently up gallops Capt. Beaumont, followed by Lt. Col. Kent—in great flurry, saying the 6th Corps was broken and driven back, the enemy on the Germanna Plank & Orange Pike, and that we had better look out not to be captured. They both were quite out of their heads. "And where" said Gen. M calmly, are Upton's & Shaler's brigades, that Sedgwick said he could spare me, this morning?"—"I don't know Sir."— "Do you mean to tell me that the 6th Corps is not to do any more fighting this campaign?"—"I am fearful not Sir!" quoth

Kent. Orders were sent at once for the Pennsylvania Reserves to move to the support, by the Germanna Plank. There were the wildest reports that Gen. Sedgwick was taken &c. &c. Capt. Cadwalader who rode up the plank towards Germanna Ford, was fired on, sure enough, by some rebs! About 7.30 P.M. Ordered to take over a statement of the case to Gen. Grant, in the hollow hard by. He seemed more disturbed than Meade about it, and they afterwards consulted together. In truth they (the enemy) had no idea of their success. They made a dash with Edw. Johnson's division about dusk, or somewhat before, and surprised completely Ricketts' shaky division, which fled at once; but most, or the whole of the first division (and perhaps part of the 3d) stood firm; and the rebels were more than content to get Gens. Seymour & Shaler, and some other prisoners, and a lot of muskets & camp equipage. In consequence of this mishap the right was ordered swung back, so as to slant towards Germanna Plank. That poor 93d N.Y.—the "bloodless," so long the headquarter guard, even from McClellan's day! Today they went in and are bloody enough now; 15 or 16 officers hit in these two days, and men in proportion. Lost my sword today from its scabbard, while galloping in the woods. Some means should be devised to hold in the swords of mounted officers, the number lost is very great. Col. Walker found it & gave it to me; he, by the way, had lost his. Old Washburn, senator & the great friend of Grant, is a companion of the campaign. He came down entirely confident that Grant would at once swallow and annihilate Lee; but he wears another face now! Griffin lost a couple of guns yesterday.— We took some colors today. Grant told Meade that Joe Johnston would have retreated after two such days' punishment. He recognizes the difference of the Western rebel fighting. During this day Sheridan defended our flanks & rear, with considerable fighting.

May 7, Saturday.
When we rose this morn we were pretty uncertain what the enemy was about, whether working on our flanks, or fallen back, or stationary.—All was quiet.— 5 A.M. Ferrero's negro div. of the 9th Corps was up and massed in a hollow in the direction of the Lacy house. It made me sad to see them.—Can

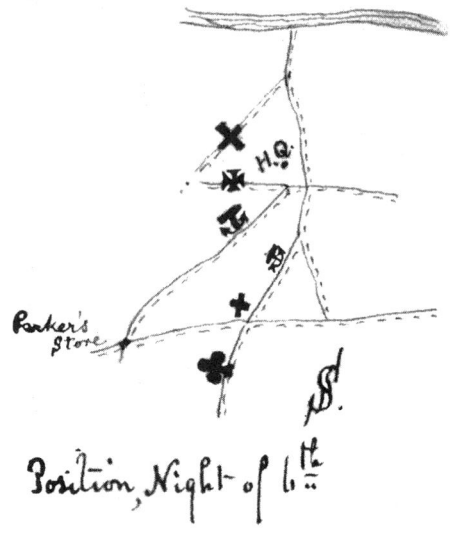

Position, Night of 6th

we not fight our own battles? The General rode through them on his way to Grant. 5.30. Ordered, to write to Gen. Sedgwick and direct him to hold all the ground the enemy would let him; and keep his cavalry & pickets well out. 9. Hancock reports nothing in his immediate front; Wright, from the other wing, reports nothing just in front of him, apparently. Warren reports a force in his front, though perhaps fallen back. 10. Warren sends out a reconnaissance of 1,000 men along the pike, from Griffin.—Heavy skirmish in that direction, and some artillery. 10.45 Ordered to ride out to Griffin and ask the result of the reconnaissance. Rode out to our breastworks on the pike, and found our artillery firing in the road and the enemy firing back, though rather wildly, for the most part. Some shooting in the heavy pine woods in front. There were a good many deep hollows hereabout, quite hilly as compared with the plank-road. Did not find Griffin, but Capt. Martin, his Chief of Artillery, told me the result of the reconnaissance was not yet reported. Rode to the left, then to the rear to Gen. Warren's Headq'rs where stopped and sent a written report to our Headq'rs. Two or three shells fell in the hollow hard by; the place was the Lacy house. 2 P.M. Had returned to

Headq'rs.—Meade in an ill humor, had read what Warren sent—"the enemy's shells fall near my Headquarters."—"Well, can't I see that? What's *that* to do with it?" says the General. Was rejoiced & surprised to find tent-mate "Rosie," who had ridden across country, all the way from Rappahannock Station, in company of Mr. Dana, Assist. Sec. of War, a large man, a combination of scholar and newspaper editor, with a dab of amiability, a large dab of conceit, and another large dab of ultraism. He was to be another civil companion of Grant. Rosie was equipped, from Washington, with what we supposed to be a huge field-glass, but which turned out to be a large casebottle, which banged his ribs whenever he galloped! A scout was now to go through to Rappahannock. Sent (through McGregor, correspondent of the Associated Press) by his hand a telegram to Mimi. 3. The 22d N.Y. Cav., somewhere by Germanna ford, got a shell thrown at them and rushed in wild confusion down the road, led off by the Colonel, an abominable coward and scoundrel. The regiment itself was raw. Meade arrested him and put the Major in his place, remarking tartly, "I don't believe he's a bit better!" Wounded ordered sent to Rappahannock Station. Butler yesterday occupied suddenly City Point. Went into a hollow behind our knoll, where was a field hospital. There were some rebel wounded there lying. They were loading the wounded in ambulances, to go north, only leaving a few very badly hurt. Now however, came notice that the rebel infantry and cavalry were advancing along the river bank, to occupy all the fords, including Ely's. The cavalry officer who sent this in ought to have been shot! The force the enemy sent along there is pretty known now to have been most trifling and nothing prevented us from driving them off. Alas! for the poor wounded! The train of them was already far on its way, when Gen. Meade had to send word to halt, and subsequently to face it towards Fredericksburg. What delay & suffering! How many men whose vital force was just sufficient to have brought them safely to Washington, were killed by this protraction of their trials! This day Sheridan concentrated near Todd's Tavern and attacked and severely beat Stuart's cavalry. The order of march for eve of May 7th. Reserve Artillery at 7 P.M. via Chancellorsville and Aldrich's to crossing of Alsop and Piney Branch Church roads, 5th Corps to Spottsylvania C.H., via Brock road and by Todd's Tavern. 6th Corps by pike & plank to Chancellorsville and escort trains to cross of Piney Branch & Block house roads. 9th Corps follow 6th. 2d follows 5th to Todd's Tavern. As Grant sat under a pine tree, he said, in his short way: "Tonight Lee will be retreating south!" This showed that he did not yet fully take in Lee's obstinacy & the goodness of his army. Although his remark about Johnston showed that he already began to appreciate them. At 8.45 P.M. we left Headquarters. All the afternoon there had been commotion among the baggage waggons, and the heavy artillery were moving too. The dust was in fine clouds as we rode down the cross-road and halted at Hancock's near the junction of the plank. The General bade us ride on and stop for him at Gibbon's whom we found on the Brock, at a little house. It was a picturesque sight the infantry closely huddled asleep, under the breastwork that followed the road. On top it and outside were sentries with their muskets ready. The officers paced up and down; all were prepared for instant action. We got some iced water from Gibbon, and lay down to take a nap in the dust. By & bye came the General, with a following of all that cavalry of Gen. Patrick's, which raised such a dust as well nigh to suffocate us. We rode on by the Brock road; then got wrong, in passing some batteries in position; then got straight again. The General told me to make the cavalry in rear go ahead of us; which did, at expense of tearing my blouse to pieces, for the road was narrow with woods each side and was full of cavalry. Could see nobody, so dark was it. At last we struck a cavalry outpost, and, soon after, got to Todd's Tavern, at the crossing of the roads. It is an ordinary old building, of moderate size. There were some women & negroes there. Gen. Gregg came out to welcome us. They have had successful fighting round here for 3 days.

"THE DISASTER CAME": VIRGINIA, MAY 1864

Wilbur Fisk to The Green Mountain Freeman

Wilbur Fisk served in the 2nd Vermont Infantry, one of five Vermont regiments that made up the Second Brigade, Second Division, Sixth Corps. On May 5 his division, led by Brigadier General George W. Getty, was ordered to occupy and hold the junction of the Brock Road and the Orange Plank Road. In the fighting that followed, the 2nd Vermont, which had crossed the Rapidan with about 700 men in its ranks, lost 297 men killed, wounded, or missing.

———————

On the Battle-Field
May 9, 1864

I presume you have heard, before this, all the incidents worth relating of the present bloody campaign, so that any further account will be only a repetition of the same or similar scenes, such as we all have witnessed. Being one of that fortunate number that lives to "tell the tale," I am inclined, however, to run the risk and do so, though so completely worn out and exhausted as I find myself to-day, I should give a very tame account of what I have seen and experienced, for I have hardly life enough left to tell where I have been or what I have seen. Of course, no one of us can give much of an account of anything that has happened beyond his own range of vision, for it is difficult to get much of an idea beyond that ourselves.

On the morning of the 4th of May we left our old camp at early dawn, and took the war path once more. The morning was bright and clear, the air cool and refreshing, as we bid adieu to our winter's home, and started on what we knew to be the most perilous campaign of the war. We took the same line of march that we did last fall, marching direct to Germanna Ford, and halting for the night two or three miles beyond.

At daylight next morning we took the plank road, and marched out to its junction with the plank road that runs from

Fredericksburg to Gordonsville. We saw nothing of the enemy, and heard nothing of them until just before we reached the latter point, when our column unexpectedly came up on a column of rebel troops coming this way. After a little skirmishing, the rebels fell back. Here was a high point of land where the roads cross at right angles, and it is in the midst of an endless wilderness—"a wilderness of woe," as the boys call it. The troops massed in here in considerable numbers, and after some moments got into working order. Our regiment crossed the Fredericksburg road, and filed into the woods with other troops in line in our rear and front. Pretty soon the order came to advance. We marched in line of battle on the left side of the Fredericksburg road, in the same direction that the road runs, and we soon came upon the enemy. There was one line ahead of us. We followed close to them, and were equally exposed. The rebels gave us a warm reception. They poured their bullets into us so fast that we had to lie down to load and fire. The front line gave way, and we were obliged to take their places. We were under their fire over three hours, before we were relieved. We were close on to them, and their fire was terribly effective. Our regiment lost 264 men in killed and wounded. Just a little to the rear of where our line was formed, where the bullets swept close to the ground, every bush and twig was cut and splintered by the leaden balls. The woods was a dense thicket of small trees about the size of hop poles, and they stood three times as numerous as they are usually set in a hop yard; but along the whole length of the line I doubt if a single tree could have been found that had not been pierced several times with bullets, and all were hit about breast high. Had the rebels fired a little lower, they would have annihilated the whole line; they nearly did it as it was. Our Colonel was killed, our Lieut. Colonel and acting Major wounded, and only three captains were with us after the fight. We all had our hairbreadth escapes to tell of. My propensity for boasting has already been discovered. I could say that I had a bullet pass through my clothes on each side, one of them giving me a pretty smart rap, and one ball split the crown of my cap into two, knocking it off my head as neatly as it could have been done by the most scientific boxer.

Another line marched up to take our places, and we fell back to the road and that night we threw up breastworks the best we could, considering that we had to dig among roots and stumps with but few tools and poor ones at that. The firing stopped at dark without our having gained an inch on the enemy. We were called up in the morning before light. Our hours of sleep were few and brief. At half past four o'clock we were ordered to advance into the same place again. There were pale and anxious faces in our regiment when that order was given. We had had very insufficient rest for the two nights previous, and the terrible nervous exhaustion of fighting had left us in hardly a fit condition to endure another such an ordeal so soon. There was so many men missing from our number that it hardly seemed like the same regiment. But the order was forward, and I do not know that a single man failed to take his place. We advanced directly down to the same place where we fought the day before. Our dead comrades lay on the ground, just as they had fallen, many of whom we recognized. We would gladly have fallen out to give them a decent burial, but we had no time to think of that. We drove the enemy this time and captured some prisoners. The prisoners were mostly North Carolinians, and some of them came into our lines swinging their hats and saying "the tar heels wouldn't stand that morning!" We advanced about a mile and a half, I should think, when our left flank was furiously attacked and a division of the Second Corps miserably gave way, leaving us in a most perilous and exposed position. We were in the point of the letter V, and the rebels were fast closing up the sides. On they came, double quick, elated with the prospect of capturing a fine lot of Yankees. I do not know how well they succeeded. My legs saved me abundantly. We had to leave our dead and wounded, and without much ceremony, or order retreat out of that place, leaving all that we had gained in the hands of the enemy. The front lines became considerably disorganized, but the rear lines held the enemy in check. Oh how discouraging it is to lose ground before the enemy. So much hard fighting, and so many killed and wounded for nothing. We had lost over fifty men in this fight. One of my comrades was shot dead there. I was lying at the time as close to the ground as I could to load and fire, while he, less timid than myself, had raised himself up, and was loading and firing as fast as possible. The ball struck near his heart. He exclaimed, I am killed and attempted to step to the rear, but fell on to me and immediately died. Just then we were obliged to retreat, and leave him where he fell. He was a new recruit but he had shown himself to be a brave soldier. He gave his life for his country, and those of us that have served the longest can do no more.

There was considerable disorder and confusion in our hasty retreat, and the regiment was more or less broken up. There was no chance for us when the left gave away but to run or be taken prisoner. We were between two fires, and the enemy had every advantage. The road was to be the rallying point in case of disaster. The disaster came, and every man that had good legs was in duty bound to use them. I found myself with a squad belonging to the division that broke and caused the defeat—decidedly bad company to be in. Some of their officers drew their swords and revolvers and tried their utmost to rally them again. They might as well have appealed to the winds. When I got back to the road there was considerable excitement. Generals and their aides were giving and carrying orders in all directions. They thought the enemy were coming in overwhelming force. I had got among a lot of stragglers, and I began to consider myself a straggler, too. At any rate I was shamelessly demoralized. I didn't know where my regiment had gone to, and to be candid about it, I didn't care. I was tired almost to death, and as hungry as a wolf. I had been fighting to the best of my ability for Uncle Sam's Constitution, and now I thought it of about as much importance to me individually, to pay a little attention to my own. They tried to halt us at the first line of breastworks, but I saw fresh troops coming that hadn't been in the fight at all, and I thought they might as well hold the line as me. My object was to find a safe place in the rear, and in spite of revolvers, or swords, entreaties, or persuasions, I found it. A Colonel's horse stepped on my foot and crushed off my shoe, and being barefooted, and lame, of course, I had but little difficulty in accomplishing my purpose. I should have been ashamed of such conduct at any other time, but just then all I thought of was a cup of coffee, and a dinner of hard tack. The regiment might have been ordered into another battle, and every man of them been killed, and I shouldn't have been ashamed that I wasn't with them. My patriotism was well nigh used up, and so was I, till I had had some refreshments. I made a deep impression on my haversack, which nourished my fighting qualities so that I could return to my regiment. I found the regiment had moved to the right, a little on the line, and were stationed behind a rude breastwork preparing to defend it against an attack from the enemy, which was momentarily expected. No serious attack, however, was made directly in our front, but to the left, where we advanced in the first place, they tried to break our lines and they tried it hard. They charged clear up to the breastwork, and fairly planted the colors on the top of it, but they did not live to hold them there long. The ground in front of the works was literally covered with the rebel dead after they left. One Colonel lay dead clear up to the breastwork. Two were shot on the top of the breastwork, and fell over on our side. I believe I have never heard such a murderous roar of musketry as was made to repel that charge. The rebels fell back and did not renew the attack.

The next day there was no fighting of any consequence. I was on picket. The picket line was advanced farther out than we had been before. We discovered nothing but a few sharpshooters who retreated as we advanced, until we came upon their line of breastworks. They opened on us with artillery, and having no support we had to fall back. We had been assigned to the second Corps, under General Hancock, during this fighting, and that afternoon we went back to our own Corps.

Such is an off-hand description of what we did during the first few days of this campaign. How much we have accomplished, I cannot tell. You never need to ask a private soldier for general information. He is the last man to get that. His circle of observation is very limited. He sees but little of what is going on, and takes a part in still less. I have told what I saw, which you will please take for what it is worth. If Providence spares my life, and the rebels don't pick me off, I hope before many days to be able to chronicle a decided and glorious victory here.

"ANOTHER STRUGGLE WITH DEATH":
VIRGINIA, MAY 1864

J.F.J. Caldwell: *from* The History of a Brigade of South Carolinians

When Lee learned on May 4 that Grant was crossing the Rapidan, he ordered his infantry corps commanders, Richard Ewell, A. P. Hill, and James Longstreet, to march east from their camps around Orange Court House and Gordonsville. The next morning Lee decided to engage Grant's army before it could move through the Wilderness. He directed Ewell to continue his advance along the Orange Turnpike and Hill to move along the Orange Plank Road three miles to the south, hoping that they would be able to hold the Union forces in position long enough for James Longstreet to attack Grant's open left flank from the south. Lieutenant James F. J. Caldwell served in Company B of the 1st South Carolina Infantry in McGowan's Brigade, which was assigned to Wilcox's Division in A. P. Hill's Third Corps. On the afternoon of May 5 the brigade was posted to the Chewning farm, about a mile from the Orange Plank Road, shortly before Union forces (including Wilbur Fisk and the 2nd Vermont Infantry) counterattacked Hill's advance troops. Caldwell wrote about the fighting that followed in an 1866 brigade history.

About 4 o'clock P. M., when we arrived at Wilderness run, we heard a rambling skirmish fire in front, not far off. We filed to the left and passed through an open field. There were several pieces of artillery here, and near them General Lee and General Stuart, on foot. The battle was evidently not distant, but we flattered ourselves that it was *rather* late in the day for much to be done towards a general engagement. We were carried nearly a mile farther, through a body of woods, and halted on a clear, commanding ridge. Having been marching right in front, we were countermarched by regiments, so as to face the enemy by the front rank. Ewell's corps was engaged at some distance on our left. Rev. Mr. Mullaly, chaplain of Orr's regiment of Rifles, held prayers with his regiment. It was one of the most impressive scenes I ever witnessed. On the left thundered the dull battle; on the right the sharp crack of rifles gradually swelled to equal importance; above was the blue, placid heavens; around us a varied landscape of forest and fields, green with the earliest foliage of spring; and here knelt hirsute and browned veterans shriving for another struggle with death.

In the midst of the prayer, a harsh, rapid fire broke out right on the plank-road we had left; the order was issued to face about and forward; and then we went, sometimes in quick-time, sometimes at the double-quick, towards the constantly increasing battle. The roar of muskets became continuous, augmented occasionally by the report of cannon, and always by the ringing rebel cheer. Heth's division, the only one at this point, was engaged, and we knew that we were going to reinforce them. Just as we reached the plank-road, two or three shell fell among us, but I believe no one was struck in the brigade. The road was crowded with non-combatants, artillery and ordnance wagons. Here and there lay a dead man. The firing in front waxed fiercer, if possible, than ever. The First regiment lead the march. They, with the Rifles, were filed across the road and fronted. The three remaining regiments were formed with their right resting on the road. The following was the order of arrangement, from right to left: First regiment, Orr's Rifles, on the right of the road; Twelfth regiment, Thirteenth regiment, Fourteenth regiment, on the left of the road.

Lane's and Thomas's brigades had been left about the position which I have just described, on the left of and near a mile from the plank-road. We entered the conflict alone. As soon as the line was formed and dressed, the order to advance was given. Balls fired at Heth's division, in front of us, fell among us at the beginning of our advance. We pressed on, guide left, through the thick undergrowth, until we reached Heth's line, now much thinned and exhausted. We had very imprudently begun to cheer before this. We passed over this line cheering. There was no use of this. We should have charged without uttering a word until within a few yards of the Federal line. As it was, we drew upon ourselves a terrific volley of musketry. The advance was greatly impeded by the matted growth of saplings and bushes, and in the delay a scattering fire commenced along our line. The fighting of the brigade cannot be described, as a whole, from this time.

The pressure was greatest on the right of the brigade; for, in addition to the worst conceivable ground for marching, and the demoralizing spectacle of another division lying down, and, after we had passed them, firing through our ranks, the enemy's line extended far to the right of ours. The first regiment was the extreme right regiment on this part of the Confederate line. All idea of a charge had to be abandoned. The First and Rifle regiments halted, and set to firing industriously. The Rifles suffered a peculiar disadvantage in halting upon high ground where the enemy's balls told fearfully. So great indeed was the slaughter that followed the first round or two, that they were forced to retire for a time. The First regiment was now entirely alone. There were no troops, as I said before, on the right of them, on the same line, and on the left was the gap left by at least four hundred men—at least one hundred and fifty yards. The fire of the enemy was not very accurate at first, being much too high; but after a time it became fatally close. Many a life must have been saved by the dense growth of oak saplings. Scarcely a man in that regiment but was struck by a ball during the evening. Lieut. Col. Shooter commanded this regiment with singular gallantry and composure, fighting for an hour everything that could be brought against him.

On the left of the road the advance was carried farther than on the right. It must be admitted, in justice to the regiments on the right, that the fire on the left was not so heavy, at the outset, as that they met. The three regiments pushed forward intrepidly. The Twelfth behaved with their accustomed gallantry. They continued the advance, until they broke the enemy's line, which they followed up, killing large numbers and capturing more. Their charge was too impetuous, if anything. They pushed ahead until they lost the connection with the rest of the brigade, and found themselves almost entirely surrounded by the enemy. They captured, among other prisoners, a brigadier-general, whose sword a friend of mine has to this day. Finding themselves thus outflanked by their own exertions, they faced about, put their prisoners before them, and drove back for our line. They succeeded in cutting out, with a small loss. The two remaining regiments, the Thirteenth and

Fourteenth, continued the advance, though less rapidly, until the fire of the enemy became so severe on their left, (where there were no troops of ours at this time,) that Gen. McGowan deemed it necessary to withdraw the whole brigade a short distance to the rear. Capt. L. C. Haskell and Lieut. G. A. Wardlaw had their horses shot under them. Our loss was heavy.

Orr's regiment of Rifles returned to the attack on the right of the road, but it and the First regiment had to be withdrawn somewhat, for the want of troops on their right. Scales' brigade was sent in to assist them, but they never reached the point of our extreme advance; so that the enemy almost enfiladed the line of these two regiments.

Now the pressure became fearful on both flanks. Our line (I mean the Confederate line) was, as I have once or twice said, miserably short. For a time, we had a front of but a single brigade. I do not judge any one; but I think it was the shortest, most huddled, most ineffective line-of-battle I ever saw. But for the gallantry of our troops, which even surpassed itself, all must have been lost. The balls of the enemy, at one point, crossed the road from each side. Still they pressed on us, filling the air with shouts and the roll of arms, and sweeping the woods with balls. At one time they drove so furiously on the right of the road, that men had to be ranged *along* the road to keep them back, or, rather, to support the meagre line that held them in check. On the extreme left, the pressure was considerably relieved by the putting in of Thomas's brigade. Still a great gap was open on his left, which skirmishers had to be thrown out to protect. It began to look like every man would have to be his own general. The open space on the left, and the presence of artillery on the eminence I before described as the place we met Lee and Stuart, deterred the Federals from any determined advance, otherwise so easily made.

Our whole brigade, after the establishment of Scales' brigade on the right, was moved to the left of the road, where they fought until night. A portion of us went to the extreme left and remained with Thomas's brigade, while the rest occupied a position rather farther back and resting on the road.

Of course, there was some confusion in the command. The difficulties were even greater than I have been able to describe—greater than any one, who has not fought in such a place, can at all understand. Such woods, if you have one line which is to remain stationary and on the defence, are an advantage; but if you attack, (as we always did by countercharge, if not by the first charge,) or if you must relieve one line with another, it is the worst place in the world. It is impossible to keep even a regiment well dressed. Then the enemy open fire on you. Some men will invariably return this fire. Gradually all join in it; and once the whole roar of battle opens, there is an end of unison of action. We did remarkably well. I could not see anything distinctly, on account of the bushes, the smoke of our line and that of the Federal; but other men professed to see the enemy constantly relieving. It has been currently stated, on our side, that two corps and two divisions were engaged on the part of the Federals. We had the two smallest divisions in Lee's army to meet them.

Night came at last, putting an end to actual battle, but, in fact, increasing the confusion and danger of the scene. It was confidently expected that Longstreet, with Kershaw's, Field's, and Anderson's divisions, would relieve us by daylight; and therefore it was not considered necessary to re-form the lines. Besides, the nature of the ground, the intense darkness, and the close proximity of the enemy, rendered it almost impracticable. Moreover, certain persons, high in office, decided that Grant would not renew the attack in the morning!

We lay upon our arms—a portion of the brigade out with Gen. Thomas, on the left and at the extreme front, the larger part with Gen. McGowan, on the plank-road. There was occasional firing among the pickets, but the enemy did not venture upon an attack. Rations of bacon and "hard tack" were issued to us after a fashion.

The night passed and the morning came; still no Blucher. At dawn, General McGowan formed the brigade on the left of the road, about where we had commenced the charge the day before. This was the 6th of May.

Our right rested on the road; Thomas's brigade was immediately on the right of the road. A part of his command had spent the night there, the rest were joined with them at daylight. The line of our brigade struck the road at an acute angle, making a salient with Thomas's brigade. Besides the latter brigade, there were no troops in line on the right of the road, as far as I have been able to learn, except, perhaps, Scales' brigade. Lane's brigade was not disposed, and Heth's division lay— I know not how, but not in line of battle, if all I have heard is correct. *We had reckoned too confidently on the coming of the War Horse!*

Longstreet was early on the way. He had been despatched to execute a grand movement on the left flank of the enemy, as Ewell had done the day before on his right. Longstreet had had to march from Gordonsville, which, of course, delayed him; and then he was recalled when on his way around Grant's left, which must delay his coming to us still more. Indeed, he did well to reach us when he did. But more of this hereafter.

The enemy moved upon us in full force, at sunrise. Our battalion of sharpshooters were deployed as skirmishers, in our front. The Twelfth regiment occupied the right of the brigade, the Fourteenth was next them, the First next them, the Thirteenth next them. Orr's Rifles were disconnected from us and on the extreme left.

The enemy moved up carefully, without noise or disorder. They first engaged our sharpshooters. The latter, though unavoidably, were in the worst position possible, being in a ravine between the elevation over which the enemy approached and the eminence we occupied. They retired slowly on the main line of battle. In the mean time, the Federals advanced along the right side of the road, on Thomas's brigade. For some reason or other, that brigade broke. The enemy may have struck their flank, or overlapped them, or they may not have been well in line. At all events, they gave way, at a distance on the right of the road. The first intimation we had of the state of affairs was the mass of disorganized men who rushed up the road. The enemy, naturally, pushed forward. Soon no troops were left to oppose their advance on that side of the road. The angle made by our lines on each side of the road being a salient, the enemy, by pressing in, came almost square upon the flank of McGowan's brigade. The Twelfth regiment stood firm in spite of the panic on their right, until the Federal line swept up to them, and not only enfiladed them, but threatened to cut them off from the rear. The regiment was even called upon to surrender, but it replied by firing on the confident enemy.

The enemy now advanced in front as well as on the right flank. The pressure was irresistible. The Twelfth regiment doubled back and retired. The movement continued up the line until all the regiments of the brigade, except the Rifles, (who were on the extreme left and disconnected from us,) gave way. There was no panic and no great haste; the men seemed to fall back from a deliberate conviction that it was impossible to hold the ground, and, of course, foolish to attempt it. It was mortifying, but it was only what every veteran has experienced.

We retired upon Poagne's artillery, which was in position, with a low temporary breastwork in front, on the summit of the open hill, about two hundred yards in rear of our original line. Here the brigade was halted at once and reformed along the line of the artillery. General Lee and General Hill were here, evidently excited and chagrined. The former expressed himself rather roughly to us, especially to us unfortunate file-closers; but I am not sure but his anger implied a sort of compliment to our past performances. But let that pass.

We were now informed that Lieutenant-General Longstreet was near at hand, with 25,000 fresh men. This was good matter to rally on. We were marched to the plank-road by special order of General Hill; but, just as we were crossing it, we received an order to return to the left. We saw General Longstreet riding down the road towards us, followed by his column of troops. The fire of the enemy, of late rather scattering, now became fierce and incessant, and we could hear a reply to it from our side. Kershaw's South Carolina brigade, of McLaws', afterwards Kershaw's division, had met them. The fire on both sides of the road increased to a continuous roar. Kershaw's brigade was extended across the road, and received the grand charge of the Federals. Members of that brigade have told me that the enemy rushed upon them at the double-quick, huzzahing loudly. The woods were filled with Confederate fugitives. Three brigades, of Wilcox's division, and all of Heth's, were driven more or less rapidly, crowded together in hopeless disorder, and only to be wondered at, when any of them attempted to make a stand.

Yet Kershaw's brigade bore themselves with illustrious gallantry. Some of the regiments had not only to deploy under fire, but, when they were formed, to force their way through crowds of flying men, and re-establish their line. They met Grant's legions, opened a cool and murderous fire upon them, and continued it so steadily and resolutely that the latter were compelled to give back. Here, I honestly believe, the Army of Northern Virginia was saved! That brigade sustained a heavy loss, beginning with many patient, gallant spirits in the ranks and culminating in Nance, Galliard and Doby.

The bulk of Longstreet's three divisions was now thrown into action. The enemy checked, they charged them, and followed up the advantage, until they drove them far through the wilderness of woods. The principal contest was just along the plank-road. Poagne's artillery, on the left of the road, had a few shots at the enemy, but these soon retired before the well-directed canister. At this place it was that General Lee put himself at the head of a brigade, to lead the charge. He was finally induced to return to the rear, the men imploring him to go back, as they could do all the fighting without him. The charge was gallantly pushed by Longstreet's line, the old ground was retrieved, and the Federals crowded up in most distressing perplexity. General Longstreet was, unfortunately, wounded, just as the tide of victory fairly set in in our favor. Brigadier-General Jenkins, of South Carolina, was killed at the same time.

McGowan's brigade was moved to the left, to the position first occupied by us the evening before, in an open field, about a mile from the road. As we filed out of the woods into this field, our sharpshooters, who were deployed as skirmishers on the right flank, saw and opened upon the skirmishers of the enemy. We were soon fronted and ordered to cross the field and occupy the ridge, some two or three hundred yards distant. We did so, at the double-quick, cheering as we went. The skirmishers of the enemy gave way at once before us. We halted on the ridge designated, expecting to receive the fire of a Federal line of battle, but they did not advance upon us. A scattering fire was kept up by them from the jungle below, and a few casualties resulted in our ranks, but this seemed quite unimportant after the last eighteen hours' work. We were, after a few minutes, retired a hundred or two hundred yards, where we piled up rails for breastworks, and lay during the remainder of the day.

The firing and cheering continued on the right, in the

direction of the plank-road. Both armies were crowding all their energies there. On the left, Ewell was still bending back Grant's right wing, and the firing indicated considerable earnestness on both sides; but the great tumult was along Longstreet's line, and we could see columns of troops moved from Grant's right to re-inforce that point. The artillery posted with us amused themselves by firing into these columns, at long range, and scattering them with shell. We were not disturbed—our position was too strong. It would have been a great relief to chastise somebody in reparation of our morning's misfortune.

We lay quiet for the rest of that day and night. On the afternoon of the next day, the 7th, we were moved to the woods in our front, thereby shortening our line a good deal. There was no fighting, this day, on any part of the line. Fires swept the forests for miles around, obscuring the sun with smoke, and filling the air with stench. We were ordered to erect defences; but we had scarcely begun to collect rails and logs of wood, when we were ordered to desist. At dusk we were ordered to prepare for the march.

We were moved a few hundred yards to the right, and there rested until morning. While we were closing up here, a pace at a time, the grandest vocal exhibition took place that I have ever heard. Far up on the right of the Confederate line a shout was raised. Gradually it was taken up and passed down, until it reached us. We lifted it, as our turn came, and handed it to the left, where it went echoing to the remotest corner of Ewell's corps. This was done once with powerful effect. Then rumors of various things, but always speaking of good fortune that had befallen the Confederates, sped along the line with characteristic swiftness. Again the shout arose on the right—again it rushed down upon us from a distance of perhaps two miles—again we caught it and flung it joyously to the left, where it only ceased when the last post had huzzahed. And yet a third time this mighty wave of sound rang along the Confederate lines. The effect was beyond expression. It seemed to fill every heart with new life, to inspire every nerve with might never known before. Men seemed fairly convulsed with the fierce enthusiasm; and I believe that if at that instant the advance of the whole army upon Grant could have been ordered, we should have swept it into the very Rappahannock. As it was, there was a story prevalent, next day, of the stampeding of a Federal corps. I doubt the entire accuracy of the account; but I know that we gathered an immense amount of private plunder on our front.

GRANT TURNS SOUTH: VIRGINIA, MAY 1864

Horace Porter: from Campaigning with Grant

By nightfall on May 6 the battle of the Wilderness had ended in a stalemate, and on May 7 the opposing armies skirmished while for the most part remaining behind hastily built earthworks. Union losses in the Wilderness were reported as 17,666 men killed, wounded, or missing, while Confederate casualties are estimated to have totaled about 11,000. The Union casualties exceeded those of the battle of Chancellorsville in May 1863, which had ended with the Army of the Potomac under Joseph Hooker retreating across the Rappahannock River. Determined to continue the campaign until Lee was defeated, Grant issued orders on the morning of May 7 for the army to march that night to the crossroads at Spotsylvania Court House, ten miles to the southeast. Lieutenant Colonel Horace Porter was a West Point graduate who had joined Grant's staff in April 1864. He recalled the beginning of the march to Spotsylvania in an 1897 memoir.

All preparations for the night march had now been completed. The wagon-trains were to move at 4 P.M., so as to get a start of the infantry, and then go into park and let the troops pass them. The cavalry had been thrown out in advance; the infantry began the march at 8:30 P.M. Warren was to proceed along the Brock road toward Spottsylvania Court-house, moving by the rear of Hancock, whose corps was to remain in its position during the night to guard against a possible attack by the enemy, and afterward to follow Warren. Sedgwick was to move by way of Chancellorsville and Piney Branch Church. Burnside was to follow Sedgwick, and to cover the trains which moved on the roads that were farthest from the enemy.

Soon after dark, Generals Grant and Meade, accompanied by their staffs, after having given personal supervision to the starting of the march, rode along the Brock road toward Hancock's headquarters, with the intention of waiting there till Warren's troops should reach that point. While moving close to Hancock's line, there occurred an unexpected demonstration on the part of the troops, which created one of the most memorable scenes of the campaign. Notwithstanding the darkness of the night, the form of the commander was recognized, and word was passed rapidly along that the chief who had led them through the mazes of the Wilderness was again moving forward with his horse's head turned toward Richmond. Troops know but little about what is going on in a large army, except the occurrences which take place in their immediate vicinity; but this night ride of the general-in-chief told plainly the story of success, and gave each man to understand that the cry was to be "On to Richmond!" Soldiers weary and sleepy after their long battle, with stiffened limbs and smarting wounds, now sprang to their feet, forgetful of their pains, and rushed forward to the roadside. Wild cheers echoed through the forest, and glad shouts of triumph rent the air. Men swung their hats, tossed up their arms, and pressed forward to within touch of their chief, clapping their hands, and speaking to him with the familiarity of comrades. Pine-knots and leaves were set on fire, and lighted the scene with their weird, flickering glare. The night march had become a triumphal procession for the new commander. The demonstration was the emphatic verdict pronounced by the troops upon his first battle in the East. The excitement had been imparted to the horses, which soon became restive, and even the general's large bay, over which he possessed ordinarily such perfect control, became difficult to manage. Instead of being elated by this significant ovation, the general, thoughtful only of the practical question of the success of the movement, said: "This is most unfortunate. The sound will reach the ears of the enemy, and I fear it may reveal our movement." By his direction, staff-officers rode forward and urged the men to keep quiet so as not to attract the enemy's attention; but the demonstration did not really cease until the general was out of sight.

"STRIFE IN THE PINES": VIRGINIA, MAY 1864

Herman Melville:
The Armies of the Wilderness

"The Armies of the Wilderness" first appeared in *Battle-Pieces and Aspects of the War*, published in August 1866. In an endnote in *Battle-Pieces* to the poem "Chattanooga," Melville described the "enthusiasm" and "elation" with which Union troops had captured Missionary Ridge in November 1863, and then wrote: "General Grant, at Culpepper, a few weeks prior to crossing the Rapidan for the Wilderness, expressed to a visitor his impression of the impulse and the spectacle: Said he, 'I never saw any thing like it:' language which seems curiously undertoned, considering its application; but from the taciturn Commander it was equivalent to a superlative or hyperbole from the talkative." The "visitor" was Melville, who had traveled to Virginia in April 1864 to visit his cousin, Lieutenant Colonel Henry Gansevoort of the 13th New York Cavalry, and then met Grant at his headquarters in Culpeper.

The Armies of the Wilderness.
(1863–4.)

I.

Like snows the camps on Southern hills
    Lay all the winter long,
Our levies there in patience stood—
    They stood in patience strong.
On fronting slopes gleamed other camps
    Where faith as firmly clung:
Ah, froward kin! so brave amiss—
    The zealots of the Wrong.

> *In this strife of brothers*
>   *(God, hear their country call),*
> *However it be, whatever betide,*
>   *Let not the just one fall.*

Through the pointed glass our soldiers saw
   The base-ball bounding sent;
They could have joined them in their sport
   But for the vale's deep rent.
And others turned the reddish soil,
   Like diggers of graves they bent:
The reddish soil and trenching toil
     Begat presentiment.

> *Did the Fathers feel mistrust?*
>   *Can no final good be wrought?*
> *Over and over, again and again*
>   *Must the fight for the Right be fought?*

They lead a Gray-back to the crag:
  "Your earth-works yonder—tell us, man!"
"A prisoner—no deserter, I,
  Nor one of the tell-tale clan."
His rags they mark: "True-blue like you
  Should wear the color—your Country's, man!"
He grinds his teeth: "However that be,
  Yon earth-works have their plan."

> *Such brave ones, foully snared*
>   *By Belial's wily plea,*
> *Were faithful unto the evil end—*
>   *Feudal fidelity.*

"Well, then, your camps—come, tell the names!"
  Freely he leveled his finger then:
"Yonder—see—are our Georgians; on the crest,
  The Carolinians; lower, past the glen,
Virginians—Alabamians—Mississippians—Kentuckians
  (Follow my finger)—Tennesseeans; and the ten
Camps *there*—ask your grave-pits; they'll tell.
  Halloa! I see the picket-hut, the den
Where I last night lay." "Where's Lee?"
  "In the hearts and bayonets of all yon men!"

> *The tribes swarm up to war*
> *As in ages long ago,*
> *Ere the palm of promise leaved*
> *And the lily of Christ did blow.*

Their mounted pickets for miles are spied
    Dotting the lowland plain,
The nearer ones in their veteran-rags—
    Loutish they loll in lazy disdain.
But ours in perilous places bide
    With rifles ready and eyes that strain
Deep through the dim suspected wood
    Where the Rapidan rolls amain.

> *The Indian has passed away,*
>   *But creeping comes another—*
> *Deadlier far. Picket,*
>   *Take heed—take heed of thy brother!*

From a wood-hung height, an outpost lone,
    Crowned with a woodman's fort,
The sentinel looks on a land of dole,
    Like Paran, all amort.
Black chimneys, gigantic in moor-like wastes,
    The scowl of the clouded sky retort;
The hearth is a houseless stone again—
    Ah! where shall the people be sought?

> *Since the venom such blastment deals,*
>   *The South should have paused, and thrice,*
> *Ere with heat of her hate she hatched*
>   *The egg with the cockatrice.*

A path down the mountain winds to the glade
    Where the dead of the Moonlight Fight lie low;
A hand reaches out of the thin-laid mould
    As begging help which none can bestow.
But the field-mouse small and busy ant
    Heap their hillocks, to hide if they may the woe:

By the bubbling spring lies the rusted canteen,
   And the drum which the drummer-boy dying let go.

> *Dust to dust, and blood for blood—*
>   *Passion and pangs! Has Time*
> *Gone back? or is this the Age*
>   *Of the world's great Prime?*

The wagon mired and cannon dragged
   Have trenched their scar; the plain
Tramped like the cindery beach of the damned—
   A site for the city of Cain.
And stumps of forests for dreary leagues
   Like a massacre show. The armies have lain
By fires where gums and balms did burn,
   And the seeds of Summer's reign.

> *Where are the birds and boys?*
>   *Who shall go chestnutting when*
> *October returns? The nuts—*
>   *O, long ere they grow again.*

They snug their huts with the chapel-pews,
   In court-houses stable their steeds—
Kindle their fires with indentures and bonds,
   And old Lord Fairfax's parchment deeds;
And Virginian gentlemen's libraries old—
   Books which only the scholar heeds—
Are flung to his kennel. It is ravage and range,
   And gardens are left to weeds.

> *Turned adrift into war*
>   *Man runs wild on the plain,*
> *Like the jennets let loose*
>   *On the Pampas—zebras again.*

Like the Pleiads dim, see the tents through the storm—
   Aloft by the hill-side hamlet's graves,
On a head-stone used for a hearth-stone there

The water is bubbling for punch for our braves.
What if the night be drear, and the blast
   Ghostly shrieks? their rollicking staves
Make frolic the heart; beating time with their swords,
   What care they if Winter raves?

> *Is life but a dream? and so,*
>   *In the dream do men laugh aloud?*
> *So strange seems mirth in a camp,*
>   *So like a white tent to a shroud.*

II.

The May-weed springs; and comes a Man
   And mounts our Signal Hill;
A quiet Man, and plain in garb—
   Briefly he looks his fill,
Then drops his gray eye on the ground,
   Like a loaded mortar he is still:
Meekness and grimness meet in him—
   The silent General.

> *Were men but strong and wise,*
>   *Honest as Grant, and calm,*
> *War would be left to the red and black ants,*
>   *And the happy world disarm.*

That eve a stir was in the camps,
   Forerunning quiet soon to come
Among the streets of beechen huts
   No more to know the drum.
The weed shall choke the lowly door,
   And foxes peer within the gloom,
Till scared perchance by Mosby's prowling men,
   Who ride in the rear of doom.

> *Far West, and farther South,*
>   *Wherever the sword has been,*
> *Deserted camps are met,*
>   *And desert graves are seen.*

The livelong night they ford the flood;
   With guns held high they silent press,
Till shimmers the grass in their bayonets' sheen—
   On Morning's banks their ranks they dress;
Then by the forests lightly wind,
   Whose waving boughs the pennons seem to bless,
Borne by the cavalry scouting on—
   Sounding the Wilderness.

> *Like shoals of fish in spring*
>   *That visit Crusoe's isle,*
> *The host in the lonesome place—*
>   *The hundred thousand file.*

The foe that held his guarded hills
   Must speed to woods afar;
For the scheme that was nursed by the Culpepper hearth
   With the slowly-smoked cigar—
The scheme that smouldered through winter long
   Now bursts into act—into war—
The resolute scheme of a heart as calm
   As the Cyclone's core.

> *The fight for the city is fought*
>   *In Nature's old domain;*
> *Man goes out to the wilds,*
>   *And Orpheus' charm is vain.*

In glades they meet skull after skull
   Where pine-cones lay—the rusted gun,
Green shoes full of bones, the mouldering coat
   And cuddled-up skeleton;
And scores of such. Some start as in dreams,
   And comrades lost bemoan:
By the edge of those wilds Stonewall had charged—
   But the Year and the Man were gone.

> *At the height of their madness*
>   *The night winds pause,*

> *Recollecting themselves;*
> *But no lull in these wars.*

A gleam!—a volley! And who shall go
    Storming the swarmers in jungles dread?
No cannon-ball answers, no proxies are sent—
    They rush in the shrapnel's stead.
Plume and sash are vanities now—
    Let them deck the pall of the dead;
They go where the shade is, perhaps into Hades,
    Where the brave of all times have led.

> *There's a dust of hurrying feet,*
>   *Bitten lips and bated breath,*
> *And drums that challenge to the grave,*
> *And faces fixed, forefeeling death.*

What husky huzzahs in the hazy groves—
    What flying encounters fell;
Pursuer and pursued like ghosts disappear
    In gloomed shade—their end who shall tell?
The crippled, a ragged-barked stick for a crutch,
    Limp to some elfin dell—
Hobble from the sight of dead faces—white
    As pebbles in a well.

> *Few burial rites shall be;*
>   *No priest with book and band*
> *Shall come to the secret place*
>   *Of the corpse in the foeman's land.*

Watch and fast, march and fight—clutch your gun!
    Day-fights and night-fights; sore is the stress;
Look, through the pines what line comes on?
    Longstreet slants through the hauntedness!
'Tis charge for charge, and shout for yell:
    Such battles on battles oppress—
But Heaven lent strength, the Right strove well,
    And emerged from the Wilderness.

Emerged, for the way was won;
 But the Pillar of Smoke that led
Was brand-like with ghosts that went up
 Ashy and red.

None can narrate that strife in the pines,
 A seal is on it—Sabæan lore!
Obscure as the wood, the entangled rhyme
 But hints at the maze of war—
Vivid glimpses or livid through peopled gloom,
 And fires which creep and char—
A riddle of death, of which the slain
 Sole solvers are.

 Long they withhold the roll
 Of the shroudless dead. It is right;
 Not yet can we bear the flare
 Of the funeral light.

"IF IT TAKES ALL SUMMER": VIRGINIA, MAY 1864

Ulysses S. Grant to Edwin M. Stanton and to Henry W. Halleck

On May 7 Lee anticipated that Grant would leave the Wilderness and ordered Richard Anderson, the new commander of Longstreet's corps, to move to Spotsylvania. Marching overnight, Anderson's men outpaced the southward Union advance and blocked it at Laurel Hill on May 8. The next day both armies extended their lines, skirmished, and entrenched. On May 10 Grant launched a series of attacks that either failed to break through the Confederate lines or had to be abandoned for lack of reinforcements. The following morning he assessed the progress of the campaign in two letters that were carried to Washington by his friend and political patron, Illinois congressman Elihu B. Washburne. Grant's letter to Stanton was widely printed in the northern press and became famous for its closing sentence.

Head Qrs. in the Field, Va
8 AM May 11th 1864.

HON. E. M. STANTON,
SEC. OF WAR. WASHINGTON D. C.

We have now entered the sixth day of very hard fighting. The result to this time is much in our favor. Our losses have been heavy as well as those of the enemy. I think the loss of the enemy must be greater. We have taken over five thousand prisoners, in battle, while he has taken from us but few except stragglers. I propose to fight it out on this line if it takes all summer.

U. S. GRANT
Lieut. Gen. Comdg Armies

Near Spotsylvania C. H. Va.
May 11th 1864. 8.30 A.M.

Maj. Gen. Halleck,
Chief of Staff of Army,
General,

We have now ended the sixth day of very heavy fighting. The result to this time is much in our favor. But our losses have been heavy as well as those of the enemy. We have lost to this time eleven General officers killed, wounded or missing, and probably twenty thousand men. I think the loss of the enemy must be greater we having taken over four thousand prisoners, in battle, whilst he has taken from us but few except stragglers. I am now sending back to Belle Plaines all my wagons for a fresh supply of provisions, and Ammunition, and propose to fight it out on this line if it takes all Summer.

The arrival of reinforcements here will be very encouraging to the men and I hope they will be sent as fast as possible and in as great numbers. My object in having them sent to Belle Plaines was to use them as an escort to our supply train. If it is more convenient to send them out by train to march from the rail-road to Belle Plain or Fredericksburg send them so.

I am satisfied the enemy are very shaky and are only kept up to the mark by the greatest exertion on the part of their officers, and by keeping them entrenched in every position they take.

Up to this time there is no indication of any portion of Lee's Army being detached for the defence of Richmond.

Very respectfully
your obt. svt.
U. S. Grant
Lt. Gen.

BATTLE OF SPOTSYLVANIA: VIRGINIA, MAY 1864

Charles Harvey Brewster to Martha Brewster and to Mary Brewster

Lieutenant Charles Harvey Brewster, the adjutant of the 10th Massachusetts Infantry, had seen action at the siege of Yorktown, Fair Oaks, Oak Grove, Malvern Hill, Chancellorsville, and Rappahannock Station. His regiment was assigned to the Fourth Brigade, Second Division, Sixth Corps, and fought in the Wilderness along the Orange Plank Road before marching to Spotsylvania. He wrote to his mother and his sister Mary about the fighting in the Wilderness, at Laurel Hill on May 8, and at the "Bloody Angle" on May 12.

Head Quarters 10th Mass Vols May 11th 1864

Dear Mother,

I have squatted on the ground in the hot sun to commence a letter to you although whether I shall ever finish it or ever have a chance to send it is more than I can tell. We started from our camp at Brandy Station at 4 o'clock on the morning of May 4th and crossed the Rapidan before night and bivouacked on the heights on this side that night. The next day we moved a short distance into the wilderness where we saw the usual signs of a pending fight. we went into line of battle and waited, or rather moved round from place to place, until about 4 o'clock PM It was thick woods and a man could hardly make his way through. At 4 o'clock we moved forward in line of battle and soon came upon the enemy who opened fire upon us. We fought them in our usual style, and in a very short time the old 10th lost one Officer killed + 4 wounded and 15 men killed + 86 wounded. The names of the Officers are Lt Ashley Co I killed Lt Graves (K) Lt Midgely (H) Lt Eaton (F) Lt Eldridge (E) we were relieved and the fight went on and our forces drove the scamps about half a mile and it then became dark. we went back to the road and replenished our ammunition and went back again. We lay down without blanket and shivered through the night and were aroused about 4 o'clock by the roar of musketry and had to fall in without any breakfast. The battle soon became general and lasted all day neither side gaining much advantage but both losing thousands of men. This day we did not get into the front line and lost but 3 or 4 men and Capt Shurtleff wounded in the arm. Night came on and we lay down and we thought to have a nights rest, but I had only just lain down when an order came to fall in and away we went to join the 1st + 3rd Divisions of our Corps. We had been detached as usual to do some fighting with other Corps. The next day we started at 4 o'clock AM and spent the day maneuvering round and marching in the hot sun but did not get any fighting.

At 8 o'clock PM we started and marched all night, arriving at Chancellorsville in the morning shortly after sunrise. Our Corps had lost up to this time 8000 men. After a halt of about 5 minutes we were started on the Spottsylvania C H road and marched until about 2 o'clock PM when we were halted and expected to sleep all night, but very soon we were ordered to fall in and marched off on to a range of hills where we saw the usual signs of battle in mangled men brought to the rear on stretchers and the woods each side of the road filled with the mingled bodies of dead Rebels and Union soldiers.

We were halted and lay down in the woods a short time when we were assigned our position, first to support a battery and then to form part of a storming party and to take some hills on our front. Our Regt and the 2nd RI formed the left of the line and had to cross a swamp of tangled briers and mud knee deep and before we could reach our position, the first line advanced and we took our places in the 2nd and advanced as well as we could through a dense thicket, but we could not keep up our connection with the rest of the line, and as the attempt failed we being on lower swampy ground did not see when the rest fell back, and consequently were left far in advance of the rest of the Division. We did not hear the orders to fall back and we would not fall back without, and soon found out that we had no communication with the rest of the Army.

It was almost dark and we knew not which way to go, so we concluded to make the best of it and stay where we were all night. It soon became so dark that we could not see a thing and the enemy advanced came down the hill into this hole. We kept quiet until they were under our very noses and then poured a volley into them, when they broke and disapeared like the work of Magic.

We soon became aware of a line of battle approaching in our rear and now the question was whether they were friends or enemies and none could answer. So I went back towards them and as I approached they cocked thier pieces and I began to think it was all over with me and my poor Regiment.

I hailed them, "What troops are those?" "Who be you?" was the reply. I replied United States thinking it best to settle the question at once. Come into the lines then said they. I went in as I knew it was of no use to run as I should bring thier whole fire upon my Regiment if I did. Judge how glad I was to find they were the 77th New York! but I had hard work to convince them that I was not a terrible Rebel in disguise, but I finally succeed and now I saw more trouble, for I knew that if the Rebels advanced again they would open fire and our Regt would catch it both ways. Time was precious, as the Rebs might come again at any moment and we must get our Regiment into the same line with them. When do you think the cowards would not allow it. That is when we proposed the arrangement they insinuated that we were afraid to stay in the front line.

Well it was finally agreed upon that they should uncap thier pieces and we would hold the front. Pretty soon the Rebs did advance again and sure enough a lot of the cowardly devils did blaze away, and there we were between two fires, but we succeeded in stopping them and they probably held thier pieces so high that they did not do us or anybody else any damage, but if we had not got them to uncap thier pieces we should have been destroyed.

As it was we lost 1 killed and 8 wounded, but I cannot tell you the half or tenth part of the terrors of that horrid night. How I got again taken prisoner by the 61st Penn Regt in the same line and lots of other things which I cannot write about that you cannot understand when I tell you.

About six o'clock that morning we were ordered out of that place and came back and joined the rest of the Brigades when the Army began to build breast works, and here we lie in the same place we came to that morning. we are well fortified and the Rebels are all along our front also fortified and fighting is going on all the time. Our losses are enormous and so are the Rebels. We captured in our first fight May 5th we captured 2500 prisoners and yesterday 3400 and every day between more or less. we have been without communication with the rest of the world since we started but I understand that our wounded have finally been carried to Fredericksburg, and communication opened with Washington but we have received no mail nor sent any since we started. Our Division General (Getty) was wounded in the fight May 5th. Gen Hayes + Gen Wadsworth were killed Gen Shaler was captured. And Oh greatest of all losses our beloved Sedgwick was killed by a sharpshooter day before yesterday. His Corps weeps. He was our Uncle John and we shall never see his equal his loss to the country at this time is irreparable. Gen Eustis has gone to command a Brigade in the 1st Division and Col Edwards is commanding ours which is another misery as he does not know anything and we have another fool somebody Neil to command the Division [   ] before we get to Richmond. As an offset to all this we hear that Longstreet is seriously wounded. he was to the Rebel Army what Sedgwick was to ours. It is reported this morning that Gen Augur has arrived with the 8th Corps 27000 strong to reinforce us and I hope it is true.

At the 2nd days fight Burnsides Corps came up and the 57th Veterans of Mass who broke and ran at the very first fire as might be expected the 56th + 58th did not do much better and thier performances together with part of the 2nd Corps came very near finishing the business for the Army. Our Regiment was out all day yesterday and all last night as support for the picket line of our Brigade.

The fighting was terrible all day long on different parts of the line, and thousands must have been killed and wounded on both sides but in our immediate front nothing was done but heavy skirmishing which we had 5 wounded.

I am lying just inside the Breastworks and every little while a sharpshooters bullet from the other side of the line goes humming past my head and smack into a tree or the ground out while out on the skirmish line is the continual popping of the opposing lines which may at any moment break out into the terrible war of the line of battle and the thunder of Artillery but the day is given up to rest on our side if the enemy does not attack and if he attacks us in our fortifications Lord have mercy on him.

It is said that the loss of this Corps is greater than any in the Army and greatest in our Division of the Corps. Our Brigade has lost up to this morning 541 in killed and wounded, the Vt Brigade is almost all used up it is reported this morning that there are but 900 left of it fit for duty. Bill Robinson was wounded twice but not seriously. Our wounded after the 1st + 2nd days battle were brought along in ambulances except such as could walk and there were not enough ambulances + empty wagons for all of them so some had to be left at Chancellorsville which consists of one or two houses and no inhabitants.

It was mighty hard to have to come away and leave them. there were from our Regt and there were lots of wounded Rebels left at the same time many of the Ambulances had wounded Rebels in them and it created great indignation that they were not put out and ours brought off on as many as could be after we got back of Fredericksburg and communication was established the wounded who could walk were started off on foot ahead of the Ambulances and escort of cavalry, and in arriving at Fredericksburg it is reported the citizens armed a lot of boys and marched them off to Richmond as prisoners and yet I do not suppose this blessed government will ever retaliate upon them for it. we are so excessively merciful I have moved about ¾ of a mile since I commenced this letter, and am now sitting under a tree that much farther to the right in the line of battle. the reason is that the Brigade on our right has gone to support another Division which is about to make an assault and we have to extend our front so as to occupy thiers and our own. Just at this moment everything is perfectly still and in a few moments I presume the very air will be rent with the roar of musketry and Artillery.

At Chancellorsville we passed over the battle ground of last year there were lots of human skulls and bones lying top of the ground and we left plenty more dead bodies there to decay and bleach to keep thier grim company. the woods we have fought over both there and here are strewn with the dead bodies of both parties who lay as they fell unburied, but I cannot give you an idea of half the horrors I have witnessed and yet so common have they become that they do not excite a feeling of horror.

Word has just come that letters sent in 5 minutes will go to night so I wind up abruptly. Love to all

Your aff son
Charlie

PS Col P is well.

Head Quarters 10th Mass Vols May 13th 1864

Dear Mary,

I wrote to Mother day before yesterday since which time we had fought another terrible battle. We went in at six o'clock yesterday morning and came out about the same time this morning. I am writing this seated in the mud covered with blood + dirt and powder I have not time to give you the particulars much but yesterday morning some of our troops charged the enemys works in the rain before or at daylight and captured 20 guns and any quantity of prisoners including Maj Gen Johnson + 2 Brig Generals. we went up to hold the enemys rifle pits and redoubts and had not been there long before the enemy charged them. our Regiment was the right of our Brigade and on the right of us was the 2nd Brig of the 1st Div who broke and ran like sheep without firing a gun. the Rebels came into the same rifle pit with us and commenced an enfilading fire before we knew they were there and we had any quantity of men killed and wounded in much less time than it takes to tell of it. Capt Weatherill was hit as were Capt Knight Capt Johnson Capt Gilmore + Geo Bigelow also Major Parker and his horse was riddled with bullets + killed.

Lieut Munyan was also wounded but I think not seriously. Geo Bigelow's wound did not disable him and he is still on duty, a bullet grazed his throat I do not know how many men we have lost yet as we have not got but about 30 muskets with us this morning and some of the Officers are missing yet. both flagstaffs were hit three times and the state flag was cut short off.

We staid there what part of us did not break when the Rebels flanked us and fought until 4 o'clock PM and staid there in the mud without sleep in the mud until about 6 o'clock this morning. I cannot begin to tell you the horrors I have seen, but I must wait to tell you about this campaign when I get home there is to much of it, the incidence crowd upon me so and I have but a little time and it is commencing to rain our men fought the Rebels close to the other side of the breast works and knocked thier guns aside, and jumped up on the work and shot them down. I saw this morning the other side of the pit and the Rebels are piled up in heaps 3 or 4 deep and the pit is filled with them piled up dead and wounded together I saw one completely trodded in the mud so as to look like part of it and yet he was breathing and gasping. it was bad enough on our side of the breast work but on thiers it was awful. some of the wounded were groaning and some praying but I cannot write more this morning. I just wrote a line to let you know that I am safe so far. So is Col P. Have not heard from home yet since the campaign commenced we have had no mails. Love to all

Yours
Charlie.

Head Quarters 10th Mass Vols May 15th 1864

Dear Mother

I wrote to Mary day before yesterday the day after our last battle but when I got it done I directed it to you and as I had but that one envelope I had to let it go so. It is Sunday to day and as we are waiting here in line of battle and throwing up rifle pits, I thought I would commence a letter to you although I do not know that we shall remain here ten minutes. We started yesterday morning about 2 o'c from near our last battle field and marched to the Bowling Green Turnpike striking at some 12 miles from Fredericksburg marching there until about 4 or 5 o'clock PM and then started on and came out into the fields and formed on the left of the 5th Corps preparatory to a grand charge upon the enemy. we have got into a comparatively open country and it was a grand sight to see six lines of battle stretching across the hills and through the vales. we are right upon the banks of the river Po and the men were cautioned to hold up thier cartridge boxes when they crossed the river. some batteries were brought up and threw about 150 shells over onto the opposite hills but got no reply. the Johnies had skeedadled so we were spared one great fight and in the night two which was a great relief to us I can tell you.

But previous to all this in the afternoon a Brigade of the 1st Div of our Corps had crossed alone and the Rebels charged upon them putting them to flight and capturing a large proportion of them. After the performance, we lay down here and had a good nights sleep. it was the most quiet night we have had since we started upon this campaign. Our Regiment suffered terribly in the fight the other day losing 6 Officers wounded and 8 men killed + 34 wounded that we know of besides probably a good many that we do not know of and from 12 to 20 taken prisoners. this makes a grand total of 13 Officers killed + wounded and 24 men killed 135 wounded + 46 missing making 218 Officers + men in 12 days the Regiment is reduced to 150 muskets and at this rate there will be none of us left to see Richmond. Sidney Williams 1st Sergt of Co C is missing since the battle and his company all think he is taken prisoner, although it is possible that he might have been hit and wandered off into the woods. if you tell his people any thing about it you must say that he is taken prisoner without doubt I think he is. Lieut Munyans wound is quite serious and it is feared he will lose his leg. Major Parker also they say will have to lose his right fore arm. Capt Knight was shot in the side, and is in a very critical condition.

We had plenty of rumors yesterday that Richmond was taken but do not place any confidence in them. we have not seen a paper nor recieved any mail since we started. we have had a general order announcing Gen Shermans victories at Tunnell Hill and Dalton and that Gen Butler had captured Petersburgh, also a communication from Gen Sheridan commanding the cavalry, that he has turned the enemys right and got into thier rear, destroyed 10 or 12 miles of the Orange Railroad and expects to fight the enemys cavalry of the South Anna River. They have destroyed a large Depot of supplies of the enemys at Beaver Dam, and recaptured 500 of our men who were taken prisoner by the enemy.

We are being largely reenforced by fresh troops and there is need enough of it, as we should not have any army left by the time we should get to Richmond at the present rate. Our Division started with nearly 9000 men and we have lost about ⅔ of them we seem to get into every fight that takes place. We are tired sleepy and worn out but if we could believe that everything was working out all right we should be satisfied.

We took in the fight of Wednesday 8000 prisoners, 18 guns, 22 colors + 2 General Officers. the field hospitals are full all the time and the Ambulances and empty wagons are kept constantly going with the wounded to Fredericksburgh. I wish it might end soon for it is dreadful to be kept in a constant state of excitement like this. you must remember that we have been 11 days under fire more or less every day and almost every night.

I wish the cowards at home who snear at the noble Army of the Potomac, might be forced out here to take thier share of the luxuries of the Officers Confound them. it is outrageous and abominable that the Army must be slandered and abused by the cowards that stay at home and cannot be coaxed or forced out here at any event. Now that the business seems almost winding up it seems almost as though a government that could not draft its own subjects to fight its battles, is hardly worth volunteering to fight for. I get enraged every time I think of it.

We are encamped on a splendid plantation and the corn and wheat is growing finely or rather was before we came but I am afraid the crops will be very small this year. We have not seen our Wagons since we started, and I am getting sadly delapidated. my rear is entirely unprotected I having worn the seat of my pants and drawers entirely off.

The most terrible sight I ever saw was the Rebel side of the breast work we fought over the other day. there was one point on a ridge where the storm of bullets never ceased for 24 hours and the dead were piled in heaps upon heaps and the wounded men were intermixed with them, held fast by thier dead companions who fell upon them continually adding to the ghastly pile. The breast works were on the edge of a heavy oak woods and large trees 18 inches or more in diameter were worn and cut completely off by the storm of bullets and fell upon the dead and wounded Rebels. those that lay upon our side in the night when the trees fell said that thier howlings were awful when these trees came down upon them. when I looked over in the morning there was one Rebel sat up praying at the top of his voice and others were gibbering in insanity others were groaning and whining at the greatest rate while during the whole of it I did not hear one of our wounded make any fuss other than once in a while one would sing out Oh! when he was hit. but it is a terrible terrible business to make the best of it.

Some of our cavalry the other day took a squad of Rebel prisoners a few days ago and among them was a deserter from our ranks. he was shot without ceremony. that is not much ceremony. I don't know whether he was tried or not but a square was formed and he was to be hung but we were all marching for battle and there was no time to hang him so he was shot. I don't know what Regt he belonged to. we were marching by at the time.

I shall enclose in this a list of names and wounded which you have better have published if there has been none. you can hand it to the Gazzette and they can do as they have a mind to. I don't know when you will get this however as I do not know as any mail is going to day. this is the third letter I have written since I started from camp you must be sure and let me know if you get them. There is a tremendous mail for the Army but nobody can stop to assort consequently we are kept without it I don't know where it is but I suppose at Fredericksburg. Give my respects to all the neighbors, and love to Mary Matt + Thomas reserving a large share for yourself from

Your aff son
Charlie.

THE BLOODY ANGLE: VIRGINIA, MAY 1864
J.F.J. Caldwell: from The History of a Brigade of South Carolinians

On May 8 the South Carolina brigade commanded by Samuel McGowan left the Wilderness and began marching toward Spotsylvania. James F. J. Caldwell later described the battlefield where the brigade had lost 481 men killed, wounded, or missing in two days of fighting: "From a thick wilderness of stunted saplings, unbroken by a hogpath, the place had become a charred, torn, open woods, cut up with numerous narrow wagon-roads. Every tree seemed to be riddled with balls. Small arms, mostly broken or bent, strewed the ground, with every conceivable damaged article of accoutrement or clothing, and graves filled with the dead of both armies, were fearfully frequent. Horses lay unburied. The stench of burning vegetable matter and clothing, and the gases streaming up through the thin covering of the graves, almost suffocated me in the hot, close air of the forest." McGowan's Brigade reached Spotsylvania the next day and was posted to the Confederate right. At dawn on May 12 nearly 20,000 Union soldiers attacked and overran the apex of a large salient near the center of the Confederate line, beginning a close-quarters struggle that lasted for more than twenty-two hours. Although the initial assault captured 3,000 prisoners, the Union troops became disorganized and were soon driven back by Confederate counterattacks. Both sides sent reinforcements to the salient, where the most intense fighting took place on its northwestern side along 200 yards of fieldworks known as the Bloody Angle. The battle for the "Mule Shoe" salient cost the Union about 6,000 men killed, wounded, or missing and the Confederates about 8,000, including 451 men from McGowan's Brigade.

———

THE 12TH OF MAY broke cool and cloudy. Soon after dawn a fine mist set in, which sometimes increased to a hard shower, but never entirely ceased, for twenty-four hours. McGowan's brigade was moved still farther to the left. Firing could be heard on our left, although, on account of the thick growth and irregular surface of the country, we could not determine where or in what force. We could see the enemy moving troops through a cleared space rather northwest of our position. The skirmishers on both sides fired from time to time. After a while, the artillery between us and the Court House opened on the enemy. They replied; and there was a pretty sharp duel for a time. A battery of theirs, considerably on our left, and, apparently, about a salient in our line, almost enfiladed the works we occupied. But we had good traverses, and there were few, if any, casualties in the brigade. I remember seeing only one man (a North Carolinian who had straggled in among us) struck. He made wry faces and not a little noise, but soon recovered.

About ten o'clock, our brigade was suddenly ordered out of the works, detached from the rest of the division, and marched back from the line, but bearing towards the left. The fields were soft and muddy, the rains quite heavy. Nevertheless, we hurried on, often at the double-quick. Before long, shells passed over our heads, and musketry became plainly audible in front. Our pace was increased to a run. Turning to the right, as we struck an interior line of works, we bore directly for the firing.

We were now along Ewell's line. The shell came thicker and nearer, frequently striking close at our feet, and throwing mud and water high into the air. The rain continued. As we panted up the way, Maj. Gen. Rodes, of Ewell's corps, walked up to the road-side, and asked what troops we were. "McGowan's South Carolina brigade," was the reply. "There are no better soldiers in the world than these!" cried he to some officers about him. We hurried on, thinking more of him and more of ourselves than ever before.

Reaching the summit of an open hill, where stood a little old house and its surrounding naked orchard, we were fronted and ordered forward on the left of the road. The Twelfth regiment was on the right of our line, then the First, then the Thirteenth, then the Rifles, then the Fourteenth. Now we entered the battle. There were two lines of works before us: the first, or inner line, from a hundred and fifty to two hundred yards from us, the second, or outer line, perhaps a hundred yards beyond it, and parallel with it. There were troops in the outer line, but in the inner one only what appeared to be masses without organization. The enemy were firing in front of the extreme right of the brigade, and their balls came obliquely down our line; but we could not discover, on account of the woods about the point of firing, under what circumstances the battle was held. There was a good deal of doubt as to how far we should go, or in what direction. At first it was understood that we should throw ourselves into the woods, where the musketry was; but, somehow, this idea changed to the impression that we were to move straight forward—which would bring only about the extreme right regiment to the chief point of attack. The truth is, the road by which we had come was not at all straight, which made the right of the line front much farther north than the rest, and the fire was too hot for us to wait for the long, loose column to close up, so as to make an entirely orderly advance. More than all this, there was a death-struggle ahead, which must be met instantly.

We advanced at the double-quick, cheering loudly, and entered the inner works. Whether by order or tacit understanding, we halted here, except the Twelfth regiment, which was the right of the brigade. That moved at once to the outer line, and threw itself with its wonted impetuosity, into the heart of the battle. Let us pause a moment to describe the state of affairs here.

Major General Edward Johnson's division had held the outer line of works on the night of the 11th. These works, at one point of the line, ran out into a sharp salient. This was on a ridge; but before it was a dense pine thicket, up to the very works. About parallel with the works, and varying from thirty to seventy-five yards from them, was a hollow, which the enemy could crawl up without being perceived, and, by lying down just at the crest of the ridge, have almost as secure a place for firing as was afforded by the Confederate works. An attack was apprehended at this weak point, and a large quantity of artillery was placed there, a strong infantry line was put in, powerful protections against small arms, by means of log-piles in front and traverses on the flank, were erected, and, in fine, perfect preparation, it was thought, made to receive the attack. Just at daylight, however, on the 12th, Grant's massed lines flung themselves against the point, swept over the astonished Confederates, captured about twenty pieces of field-artillery, and near two thousand prisoners, (General Johnson among them,) and broke the very keystone of our arch.

An effort was made, as speedily as possible, to recapture the works. The enemy pressed on to the inner line. What troops were sent against them I do not know, except that among them were some of Anderson's old division. General Abner Perrin charged brilliantly with his brigade, beat away the enemy from the interior line, jumped his horse over the works, and was leading the final charge upon the exterior line, when he was shot through and killed. Here the Confederate movement stopped short. Our brigade was sent to General Ewell to carry it through.

The demoralization of the troops that had been about this point was deplorable. They seemed to feel that Grant had all the hosts of hell in assault upon us.

To resume: the brigade advanced upon the works. About the time we reached the inner line, General McGowan was wounded by a Minie ball, in the right arm, and forced to quit the field. Colonel Brockman, senior colonel present, was also wounded, and Colonel J. N. Brown, of the Fourteenth regiment, assumed command, then or a little later. The four regiments—First, Thirteenth, Fourteenth and Rifles (the Twelfth had passed on to the outer line)—closed up and arranged their lines. Soon the order was given to advance to the outer line. We did so, with a cheer and at the double-quick, plunging through mud knee-deep, and getting in as best we could. Here, however, lay Harris' Mississippi brigade. We were ordered to close to the right. We moved by the flank up the works, under the fatally accurate fire of the enemy, and ranged ourselves along the intrenchment. The sight we encountered was not calculated to encourage us. The trenches, dug on the inner side, were almost filled with water. Dead men lay on the surface of the ground and in the pools of water. The wounded bled and groaned, stretched or huddled in every attitude of pain. The water was crimsoned with blood. Abandoned knapsacks, guns and accoutrements, with ammunition boxes, were scattered all around. In the rear, disabled caissons stood and limbers of guns. The rain poured heavily, and an incessant fire was kept upon us from front and flank. The enemy still held the works on the right of the angle, and fired across the traverses. Nor were these foes easily seen. They barely raised their heads above the logs, at the moment of firing. It was plainly a question of bravery and endurance now.

We entered upon the task with all our might. Some fired at the line lying in front, on the edge of the ridge before described; others kept down the enemy lodged in the traverses on the right. At one or two places, Confederates and Federals were only separated by the works, and the latter not a few times reached their guns over and fired right down upon the heads of the former.

So continued the painfully unvarying battle for perhaps two hours. At the end of that time a rumor arose that the enemy were desirous to come in and surrender. Col. Brown gives the following account of it in his official report:—"About two o'clock, P.M., the firing ceased along the line, and I observed the enemy standing up in our front, their colors flying and arms pointing upward. I called to them to lay down their arms and come in. An officer answered, that he was awaiting our surrender—that we had raised a white flag, whereupon he had ceased firing. I replied that 'I commanded here; and if any flag was raised it was without authority, and unless he came in, firing would be resumed.' He begged a conference, which was granted, and a subordinate officer advanced near the breastwork and informed me that a white flag was flying on my right. He was informed that unless his commander surrendered, the firing would be continued. He started back to his lines, and, failing to exhibit his flag of truce, was shot down midway between the lines, which were not more than twenty yards apart at this point. The firing again commenced with unabated fury."

Farther on the left of the brigade, where nothing was known of this conference, there was an opinion that the light-colored flag (that of Connecticut, I believe) displayed by the enemy was intended for a truce. A Babel of tongues succeeded—officers ordering the resumption of the firing; men calling out to the Federal line, questioning each other, imploring for the fire to be held and the enemy allowed to come in. To those who reflected a moment, it should have been plain that we were deceiving ourselves. The idea of that solid line of men, with arms in their hands, coming in to surrender to us was preposterous. But a general infatuation prevailed—a silly infatuation, if it had not involved so much. So the two lines stood, bawling, gesticulating, arguing, and what not. At length a gun was fired, perhaps the one Colonel Brown mentions. All of both lines joined in, and the roar of battle was renewed, sounding like pleasant music to many of us now.

The Twelfth regiment suffered most heavily. They entered the point of greatest danger—just at the break—and received a concentrated fire of artillery that crashed through the works, and the fusilade of infantry from the front and across the traverses on the right flank. Men just across the works would, in places, thrust over their pieces and discharge them in their faces. They lost fearfully, but they fought nobly. Sometimes, they would have to give way to the left, but they always rallied and fought at the nearest footing.

The firing was astonishingly accurate all along the line. No man could raise his shoulders above the works without danger of immediate death. Some of the enemy lay against our works in front. I saw several of them jump over and surrender during relaxations of firing. An ensign of a Federal regiment came right up to us during the "peace negotiations," and demanded our surrender. Lieutenant Carlisle, of the Thirteenth regiment, replied that we would not surrender. Then the ensign insisted that, as he had come under a false impression, he should be allowed to return to his command. Lieutenant Carlisle, pleased with his composure, consented. But, as he went back, a man, from another part of the line, shot him through the face, and he came and jumped over to us.

This was the place to test individual courage. Some ordinarily good soldiers did next to nothing, others excelled themselves. The question became, pretty plainly, whether one was willing to meet death, not merely to run the chances of it. Two men, particularly, attracted my attention. I regret, exceedingly, that I have not been able to ascertain their names, for I am anxious that they should have what little fame may be derived from distinguished mention in these pages.

The first of these belonged, I think, to the Fourteenth regiment. He was a tall, well-formed man, apparently just arrived at maturity. He was a private. He would load his piece with the greatest care, rise to his full height, (which exposed at least half of his person,) and, after a long, steady aim, deliver his fire. Then he would kneel and reload. Sometimes he would aim, but take down his piece and watch again for his mark, then aim again and fire. The balls flew round him like hail, from front and flank. I saw him fire at least a hundred times between noon and dark. Finally, late in the evening, I saw him rise and single out his man, in the grass in front, and draw down upon him. Then, appearing not to be satisfied, he recovered his piece, remaining erect and watching. After, perhaps, half a minute, he raised his rifle and aimed. Just as his finger touched the trigger, I heard the crash of a ball, and, looking at him, saw a stream of blood gush from his left breast. He fell and died without a struggle.

Another soldier, of probably not more than eighteen years, interested me early in the fight. Although scarcely so deliberate as the other, he fired with great perseverance and coolness, until just after the death of the other. He was a handsome boy, tall and slender, with eyes as tender as a woman's, and a smooth, fair cheek, just darkening with the first downy beard. Seeming to be weary, about sunset, he sat down in the cross-trench to rest. He was hardly down, when a ball glanced from a tree and struck him just behind the right ear. He struggled up and shook with a brief convulsion. Some one caught him in his arms. He raised his eyes, with the sweetest, saddest smile I think I ever saw on earth, and died almost on the instant. It was a strange wound. I could see nothing but a small, red blister where the ball struck him.

A lad in Harris's brigade was shot down among us, early in the fight—a little, smooth-faced fellow, very out of place in this carnage. He fell at once in death agonies, but he cried out to his comrades, "Boys, I'm killed; but tell mother I died a Christian!"

Lieutenant-Colonel Shooter, of the First regiment, was shot as we entered the works. Some of his regiment stopped to assist him. But he bade them go forward and leave him, adding, "I know that I am a dead man; but I die with my eyes fixed on victory!"

We lay five or six deep, closing constantly to the right, and thus losing all distinct organization. A good part of Harris's Mississippians were with us. There was no farther cessation of fire after the pause before described. Every now and then a regular volley would be hurled at us from what we supposed a fresh line of Federals, but it would gradually tone down to the slow, particular, fatal firing of a siege. The prisoners, who ran in to us now and then, informed us that Grant's whole energies were directed against this point. They represented the wood on their side as filled with dead, wounded, fighters and skulkers. A Confederate officer, a prisoner among them at the time, has since told me that he saw many thousand troops, in many successive lines, moving against the bloody angle until night. "Whiskey," he added, "was forwarded by the barrel to the front, and provost-guard drove up, with merciless fidelity, those whom drink failed to bring to the mark." We were told that if we would hold the place till dark we should be relieved. Dark came, but no relief. The water became a deeper crimson; the corpses grew more numerous. Every tree about us, for thirty feet from the ground, was barked by balls. Just before sunset, a tree of six or eight inches diameter, just behind the works, was cut down by the bullets of the enemy. We noticed, at the same time, a large oak hacked and torn in a manner never before seen. Some predicted its fall during the night, but the most of us considered that out of the question. But, about ten o'clock, it did fall forward upon the works, wounding some men and startling a great many more. An officer, who afterwards measured this tree, informed me that it was twenty-two inches in diameter! This was entirely the work of rifle-balls. Midnight came; still no relief, no cessation of the firing. Numbers of the troops sank, overpowered, into the muddy trenches and slept soundly. The rain continued.

Just before daylight, we were ordered, in a whisper, which was passed along the line, to retire slowly and noiselessly from the works. We did so, and either we conducted it so well that the enemy were not aware of the movement, or else, (as I think most likely,) they had become so dispirited by our stubborn resistance of eighteen hours, that they had left only a skirmish line to keep up appearances. At all events, they did not attempt to pursue us. Day dawned as the evacuation was completed. A second line of works, or rather a third, had been thrown up some five hundred yards in our rear, and in this, as we passed over, we found troops of Longstreet's corps, ready for the enemy. They were not called upon to meet him. He entered, but did not hold, the line we had left; much less did he attempt the second one.

WHIPPING A SLAVEMASTER: VIRGINIA, MAY 1864
Edward A. Wild to Robert S. Davis

A homeopathic physician before the war, Edward A. Wild lost an arm while leading the 35th Massachusetts Infantry at South Mountain in September 1862. He returned to duty in 1863 as a brigadier general and in April 1864 was given command of a brigade of black soldiers in the Eighteenth Corps. On May 11 his division commander, Brigadier General Edward W. Hinks, ordered Wild to report on the shooting of a civilian by his troops and the whipping of a civilian prisoner in his custody. Wild refused to reply to Hinks and addressed his response instead to Major Robert S. Davis, assistant adjutant general to Major General Benjamin F. Butler, the commander of the Department of Virginia and North Carolina. Hinks brought charges against Wild in connection with the whipping incident, but they were later withdrawn.

Wilson's Wharf, James River May 12th 64
Sir— Not being in the habit of accepting rebuke for acts not committed, and feeling that I can judge of "the qualities becoming to a man or a Soldier" quite as well as I can be informed by Brig. Genl. Edwd. W. Hinks in *such a letter* as the *above*, I have the honor to forward it, together with this, my protest, through Division Hd. qrs. for the consideration of the Major General Commanding the Department—

I protest against the whole tone of the above letter, as unbecoming and unjust; as being full of harsh rebuke, administered before even making any inquiry; and therefore, as *pre*-judging cases against me, and taking for granted, that "acts perpetrated" by me are necessarily "barbarous and cruel" not admitting the possibility of any justification; nor the probability of any excuse—

I have the honor to submit the following statement of facts—

On Friday May 6th I sent a party to surprise a Rebel Signal Station at Sandy Point. The party at the Station numbered *10* men, on being driven from the house they run into a swamp, directly upon one of my detachments, forming part of the trap— after considerable resistance, the Capture was complete, 5 Rebels were Killed, 3 wounded and 2 Caught, the dead were properly buried on the spot, the wounded and Prisoners were brought into camp and afterwards sent down to Fortress Monroe. The *10* guns were brought into camp, according to the nicest discrimination they were classed thus—*8* Soldiers and *2* citizens of whom *1* citizen was killed and 1 wounded. In this affair great credit is due to Capt. Eagle and Lt. Price 1st U.S.C.T. for skillfully carrying out the Plans.

On Monday Morning May 9th before daylight I sent a party to surprise a Squad of Rebel's who had been playing the *Guerrilla*, and attacked us three times, learning that they were passing the night at a Certain house I sent thither to take them; but being misinformed as to the distance, my party did not arrive till day. The Rebels *11* in number, made a stand, in good order under an officer in uniform, (said to be an adjutant) Our mounted advance party consisting only of *5* charged upon the *11* killed one, wounded another, run them into a bit of a swamp, and then waited for the main body to come up, but the rebels had passed through the swamp, and in two Boats crossed the Chicahominy, The Citizen Killed proved luckily to be Wilcox, the owner of the house, and the Enrolling Officer of the District. He was properly buried in the Yard, His house was burned. In this affair Major Cook 22d U.S.C.T. deserves credit for his boldness, and especially I would mention Henry Harris a Colored Sergeant of Capt. Choate's 2d U.S.C. Baty. for the daring he displayed, I wish it to be distinctly understood by Brig. Genl. Hinks that I shall continue to Kill *Guerrillas*, and Rebels offering armed resistance Whether they style themselves Citizens or Soldiers—

On Tuesday May 10th William H. Clopton, was brought in by the Pickets. He had been actively disloyal so that I held him as Prisoner of War, and have sent him as such to Fortress Monroe. He has acquired a notoriety as the most cruel Slave Master in this region, but in my presence he put on the character of a Snivelling Saint. I found half a dozen *women* among our refugees, whom he had often whipped unmercifully, even baring their whole persons for the purpose in presence of *Whites and Blacks*. I laid him bare and putting the whip into the hands of the Women, three of Whom took turns in settling some old scores on their masters back. A black Man, whom he had abused finished the administration of Poetical justice, and even in this scene the superior humanity of the Blacks over their white master was manifest in their moderation and backwardness. I wish that his back had been as deeply scarred as those of the women, but I abstained and left it to them—I wish it to be distinctly understood by Brig. Genl. Hinks that I shall do the same thing again under similar circumstances. I forgot to state that this Clopton is a high minded Virginia Gentleman, living for many years next door to the late John Tyler ExPresident of the U.S. and then and still intimate with his family.

And now as this is the second time that Brig. Genl. Hinks, has invoked the rules of Civilized warfare, and enjoined upon us the excercise of magnanimity and forbearance, I would respectfully inquire, for my own information and Guidance, whether it has been definitely arranged that Black Troops shall exchange courtesies with Rebel Soldiers? and if so on which side, such courtesies are expected to commence, and whether any guaranties have been offered on the part of the Rebels calculated to prove satisfactory and reassuring to the African Mind? Very Respectfully Your Obt. Sert

(Signed) Edwd. A. Wild

BATTLE OF RESACA: GEORGIA, MAY 1864
James A. Connolly to Mary Dunn Connolly

On May 7 Major General William T. Sherman began his campaign in northern Georgia by advancing toward Dalton along the railroad line from Chattanooga to Atlanta. Sherman commanded about 100,000 men, divided among the Army of the Cumberland (60,000) under Major General George H. Thomas, the Army of the Tennessee (25,000) under Major General James B. McPherson, and the Army of the Ohio (13,000) under Major General John M. Schofield. He was opposed by General Joseph E. Johnston, who commanded about 50,000 men in the Army of Tennessee. While Thomas and Schofield probed the Confederate defenses on Rocky Face Ridge west of Dalton, Sherman sent McPherson on a flanking march to the south toward the railroad at Resaca. When McPherson failed to take the town, Sherman began moving the rest of his army south as well, forcing Johnston to retreat from Dalton to Resaca on the night of May 12. Major James A. Connolly had served with the 123rd Illinois Infantry before joining the staff of Absalom Baird, commander of the Third Division, Fourteenth Corps, in the Army of the Cumberland.

Near Resaca, Ga., May 15, 1864.

Dear wife:

Just as I had written the date above, I said: "Hello, the enemy are shelling us." This exclamation was called out by the fact of a shell from the enemy's battery exploding very near our headquarters. It is now about nine o'clock at night, the moon is shining with a misty light through the battle smoke that is slowly settling down like a curtain, over these hills and valleys; the mournful notes of a whippoorwill, near by, mingle in strange contrast with the exultant shouts of our soldiers— the answering yells of the rebels—the rattling fire of the skirmish line, and the occasional bursting of a shell. To-day we have done nothing but shift positions and keep up a heavy skirmish fire. Yesterday our Division and Judah's Division of Scofield's Corps, had some hard fighting. We drove the enemy about a mile and entirely within his fortifications, several of our regiments planting their colors on his fortifications, but were compelled to withdraw under a terrible fire. We, however, fell back but a short distance to the cover of the woods, where we still are, and the enemy have not ventured outside their works since. A report has just reached us that Hooker drove the enemy about a mile to-day. We will probably be engaged to-morrow, and we may be engaged yet to-night, for the enemy may take a notion to come out of his works under cover of the darkness, and attack us. I hope he wont, for I don't want to be disturbed after I get to sleep, and then I don't like fighting in the night anyhow. We have men enough here to whip Johnston, and if he don't escape pretty soon he never will. I presume "you all," as the Southern people say, feel very much elated over Grant's success. Well, you will hear something from this army, some of these days that will be a full match for anything Grant or any other man can do with the Potomac army, and I begin to have hope that the only large armies of the rebellion will be shattered, if not destroyed, by the 4th of July. We have the railroad in running order to Tilton, which is several miles south of Dalton, and are having no trouble about supplies. The weather is fine, the roads fairly good, our men flushed with success, and I hope we push right on, day and night, though we be ragged, dirty, tired and hungry, until we exterminate these battalions of treason. Good night.

Your husband.

Kingston, Ga., May 20, 1864.

Dear wife:

If you will look at a map you will see that "we all" are still pushing southward, but a look at the map will give you little idea of the country we are passing through—will fail to point out to you the fields that are being reddened by the blood of our soldiers, and the hundreds of little mounds that are rising by the wayside day by day, as if to mark the footprints of the God of War as he stalks along through this beautiful country. This point is where the railroad from Rome forms a junction with the main line from Chattanooga to Atlanta. Rome is in our possession, and such has been the extraordinary rapidity with which the railroad has been repaired, as we have pushed along, that a train from Chattanooga ran into Kingston this morning about daylight, while at the same time a rebel train from Atlanta was whistling on the same road, and only two miles distant, but it is now about 9 o'clock in the morning, and the last whistle of the rebel train, north of the Etowah River, sounded some hours ago, the last rebel has undoubtedly crossed the river, the bridge across the river has been burned, I suppose, and the rebel army is wending its way, weary and dispirited, toward that mythical ditch of which we have heard so much.

Two hours later. Just at this point in this pencilled letter, about two hours ago I was interrupted, and the whole Division startled, by a cavalryman rushing up to headquarters, his horse covered with foam, and reporting that he had just seen the rebels, in line of battle, about one fourth of a mile distant, and advancing on us. In a jiffy this unfinished letter was thrust in my pocket, my horse saddled, and I was ordered by the General to go back with the cavalryman the way he had come, and ascertain the truth of his report, for cavalry reports are much like rebel money—don't pass at their face value. I went out through our pickets and cautiously moved along until I had gone about a mile to the front when I came to a strong line of breastworks, constructed by the rebels last night, but this morning they are deserted. I crossed these breastworks and went on until I came to another line of works, but they too are deserted this morning. I crossed this second line and went on a short distance, when I saw some mounted rebels ahead and they saw me; they fired a couple of shots which fell far short, and seeing I was out of their reach, I stood still with my cavalryman, but the rebs started toward me, and, not wishing to have a difficulty with them, I "fell back in good order" until they fired again, set up a yell and started after me on a run when I accelerated the pace of my "Rosinante" and *advanced to the rear* at a rapid pace and got safely inside our picket line; the cavalryman who accompanied me dodged off to one side and hid in the brush when the chase began. He came in a few moments ago, all right, but is not able to explain why he made his scare report. I reported to the General and all is quiet again, but if you find this letter all crumpled up, remember I had it in its unfinished state in my pocket during that chase, and as I can't get at my desk, paper is scarce, and I can't afford to begin it again. Beautiful country, beautiful weather, and everything going well with the Yankees in Georgia. You may still address me at Ringgold.

Your husband.

"THESE SAD FIELDS": GEORGIA, MAY 1864

Alpheus S. Williams to Mary Williams

The opposing armies skirmished near Resaca on May 13 and then fought inconclusively for the next two days. When Johnston learned that Union troops had crossed the Oostanaula River downstream from Resaca, he abandoned the town and withdrew across the Oostanaula on the night of May 15. The battle of Resaca cost the Union more than 2,700 men killed, wounded, or missing, and the Confederates about 2,800. Johnston's army continued to retreat until May 20, when it crossed the Etowah River thirty miles south of Resaca. Brigadier General Alpheus S. Williams had fought at Cedar Mountain, Second Bull Run, Antietam, Chancellorsville, and Gettysburg before joining the Army of the Cumberland, where he commanded the First Division in the Twentieth Corps. He wrote to his daughter about the fighting at Resaca (the end of the letter is missing).

———————

Camp near Cassville, Georgia,
May 20, 1864.

My Dear Daughter:

For the life of me, I cannot recollect whether I have written you since I left Trickum Post Office or not. I scribbled a short pencil note from that place. Since then my mind has been so full of constant duties, responsibilities, and cares, and events have followed in such rapid and varied succession that my recollections are a jumble. Day and night we may be said to be on duty and under anxieties. No one who has not had the experience can fancy how the mind is fatigued and deranged (as well as the body) by these days and nights of constant labor and care.

We left Trickum Post Office on the night of the 9th after much reconnoitering and skirmishing toward Buzzard's Roost and reached the entrance of Snake Creek Gap in the Chattanooga Mountains in the morning. The whole march, as everywhere, through woods, with hardly a clearing. On the 12th, moved the division through the gap about six miles and encamped. On the 13th moved towards Resaca, under arms always from daylight and lying ready for a fight all night. I carry nothing for myself and staff of a dozen but four tent flies and one wall tent for an office. All private baggage is left behind. The wagon with the tent flies is seldom up and consequently we roll ourselves in overcoats and what we can carry on our horses and take shelter under trees every night. The days are hot and the nights quite cold and foggy. Most of us have been without a change of clothing for nearly three weeks.

On the 14th we moved through thickets and underbrush to the rear and in support of Butterfield's division, and in the afternoon received a hurried order to move rapidly farther to the left to support Stanley's division of the 4th Corps. I reached the ground just in time to deploy one (3rd) brigade and to repulse the Rebels handsomely. They had broken one brigade of Stanley's division and were pressing it with yells and were already near one battery (5th Indiana, Capt. Simonson, Lt. Morrison commanding) when I astonished the exultant rascals by pushing a brigade from the woods directly across the battery, which was in a small "open" in a small valley. They "skedaddled" as fast as they had advanced, hardly exchanging a half-dozen volleys. They were so surprised that they fired wildly and didn't wound a dozen men. I was much complimented for the affair and Gen. Howard, commander of the 4th Corps, came and thanked me.

On the 15th we had a more serious engagement. Butterfield's division attacked their entrenched positions on the hills, short steep hills with narrow ravines. I was supporting. While his attack was in progress, information was brought to me that the Rebels were moving towards our left in force. I changed front and in luck had plenty of time to form my line and place my batteries in position before they attacked. They came on in masses and evidently without expectation of what was before them. All at once, when within fair range, my front line and the batteries (one of which I had with much work got on the ridge of a high hill) opened upon them with a tremendous volley. The rascals were evidently astounded, and they were tremendously punished. They kept up the attack, however, for an hour or so, bringing up fresh troops, but finally gave way in a hurry.

We captured one battle flag and the colonel of the 38th

Alabama, several other officers, and several hundred prisoners. The flag was a gaudy one and covered with the names of battles in which the regiment had been engaged. It was the only flag taken during the day. But that I was not advised of any supports on the left, I could have charged them with great success. As it was, I did a good thing, and the division behaved splendidly. Not a man left the ranks unless wounded. In the language of a private of the 27th Indiana (one of my old regiments) we had a "splendid fight," and he added, "'Old pap' (that is I) was right amongst us."

The fight ended about dusk and in the morning there was no enemy in front. I went out over the field in our front, not out of curiosity but to see what was in advance. There were scores of dead Rebels lying in the woods all along our front, and I confess a feeling of pity as I saw them. One old grey-headed man proved to be a chaplain of the Rebel regiment, and it is rather a singular coincidence that one of our own chaplains (3rd Wisconsin) was seriously wounded directly in front of where he was found dead. Early in the war I had a curiosity to ride over a battlefield. Now I feel nothing but sorrow and compassion, and it is with reluctance that I go over these sad fields. Especially so, when I see a "blue jacket" lying stretched in the attitude that nobody can mistake who has seen the dead on a battlefield. These "boys" have been so long with me that I feel as if a friend had fallen, though I recognize no face that I can recollect to have seen before. But I think of some sorrowful heart at home and oh, Minnie, how sadly my heart sinks with the thought.

I put parties to bury the dead Rebels but was ordered away before half were collected over the mile and a half in our front. I fear many were left unburied, though I left detachments to gather up all they could find. As I marched away, I was obliged to go along the line where my own dead were being collected by their comrades and interred in graves carefully marked with name, rank, and company. It is interesting to see how tenderly and solemnly they gather together their dead comrades in some chosen spot, and with what sorrowful countenances they lay them in their last resting place. There is much that is beautiful as well as sad in these bloody events. I lost in this battle between four and five hundred killed and wounded. [   ]

BATTLE OF PICKETT'S MILL: GEORGIA, MAY 1864
Samuel T. Foster: Diary, May 23–28, 1864

After crossing the Etowah River Johnston withdrew to a strong position at Allatoona Pass. Sherman decided to outflank the Confederate defenses by leaving the railroad, marching to Dallas, fourteen miles southwest of Allatoona, and then heading east toward Marietta. When Union troops began crossing the Etowah on May 23, Johnston anticipated Sherman's maneuver and moved his army toward Dallas. The two sides fought at New Hope Church, four miles northeast of Dallas, on May 25, and then continued to skirmish. Captain Samuel T. Foster led a company in the 24th Texas Cavalry (Dismounted) and had fought at Chickamauga before being wounded at Chattanooga. His regiment was assigned to Brigadier General Hiram B. Granbury's Texas brigade in Major General Patrick R. Cleburne's division. On May 27 Cleburne's division defended the extreme right of the Confederate line against a flanking attack by a division from the Army of the Cumberland. The battle of Pickett's Mill cost the Union 1,600 men killed, wounded, or missing, and the Confederates about 500.

MAY 23—Still here—no move. I had an opportunity to draw a pair of shoes last night but had to take a pair of No 8s because there were none smaller to be had. It was these or none. About 10 OClock this morning the order came to march.

We travel in a south west direction, but none of us have any idea where we are going to. Traveled about 10 miles, and stoped, had a little rain this evening, just enough to lay the dust.

MAY 24th
Last night about 12 O'Clock (midnight) two days rations came to us and were issued, consisting of corn bread and bacon and by 3 O'Clock this morning we are marched off— We kept up the march until about 11 O'Clock AM, having traveled about 15 miles, direction still south west. There are a great many conjectures and guessing as to where we are going

and what we are going for. Some say we are going to Florida and put in a pontoon bridge over to Cuba, and go over there. While others contend that some Yank would put a torpedo under it and blow it up.

May 25th

Remained in our camp last night until 3 O'clock AM, when we were marched back the same road we come along yesterday for about 4 miles— The Yanks are about again. Artillery and small arms, in hearing of us— We are halted here and told to hold ourselves in readiness to move at a moments notice. By 11 O'Clock AM we had all taken a good sleep, when one days rations comes in consisting of bacon and crackers. Later in the evening another days rations are issued. About dusk it commenced raining, and we were ordered to move off. Heavy firing all day in our front— We moved about 2 miles and are halted in the road. After standing in our places in the road for half an hour—an order came to get out one side of the road, make fires and go to sleep.

May 26

Remained in camp by the roadside the rest of the night. This morning we are marched off early, and go in the direction of where the heavy fireing was yesterday— We could hear the skirmish firing from the time we started and as we march, it gets louder and louder nearer and nearer. Now we can hear an occasional bullet whistling past, like it was on the hunt of some one. We are marched up in rear of the line of battle, and then follow the line to the right for about 2 miles where we are put in position as a reserve force— We don't know whether we are on the right left or centre of the army but the heavy firing has been on our left and front all day today. Some of our boys (our Brigade is separated from every body) go to the breastworks in front of us to see what soldiers are there, because they have no confidence in any of them except the Arkansas troops (who are nicknamed "Josh'es" and when ever a Texan meets an Ark. soldier, he says, how are you Josh. Or where are you going Josh &c. It is all the time Josh——). We find Georgia troops in our front; and our boys tell them that if they run that we will shoot them, and no mistake, and as soon as they find out that the Texans are in their rear, they believe we will shoot them sure enough——

May 27

Remained in our place all night, and this morning Genl Granbury called for a scout of 5 men to go around the Yankee Army. Col Wilkes ordered me to send them from my Company. They started out early in the day, and returned in the afternoon, and reported that they were massing their troops on the right of Our Army and would flank us before night if we did not stop them some way— Our Brigad was moved off towards the right of our line following the line of Breast works— until we came to the extreme right of the infantry, and found some dismounted cavalry deployed in the woods still further to the right. We find some Ark. troops on the end of our line, and we form on to their right making our line that much longer and it also puts us just where the scouts said the Yanks were going to try to flank our Army. Our position is in a heavy timbered section with chinquapin bushes as an undergrowth. From the end of the army, where the breastworks stop we followed a small trail or mill path and as soon as our Brigade got its whole length in this place the command is to halt! and at the same instant the cavalry skirmishers came running back to our lines, saying that we had better get away from there, for they were coming by the thousand. These cavalry men had been keeping up a very heavy fire until our arrival, when it got too hot for them. Col. Wilkes ordered me to deploy my men and go forward in the woods. I soon had them all in position and started to move forward, but found the enemy close up to our line on the right, so I advanced the left of the skirmish line by a right wheel until the skirmish line and our line of battle behind us were in the shape of the letter V with our right skirmisher nearly on the line of battle and the left skirmisher was 75 yards from the line. As soon as the skirmish line was put in position our men commenced firing at the enemy skirmishers who were not more than forty to fifty yards from us. One of my men Joe Harrison who never could stop on a line of that kind without seeing the Yanks ran forward through the brush, but came back as fast as he went, saying that they fired a broadside on him, but didn't hit him— He took his place on the skirmish line behind an Oak tree about 14 inches in diameter— The enemy kept advancing through the bushes from tree to tree until they were (some of them) in 30 or 40 feet of our line—nor would they give back. I had three as good men as ever fired a gun killed on this skirmish line—W J Maddox, T L Doran & T F Nolan. The two first named were shot thru the neck and killed instantly, the last one was shot in the bowels and died in about 15 hours after. When the sun was about an hour high in the evening we were ordered back to the line of battle. And it seems that the enemys line of battle was advancing when the order came for the skirmishers to fall back.

The frolick opened in fine style as soon as we got back into our places—instead of two skirmish lines—the two lines of battle open to their fullest extent. No artillery in this fight— nothing but small arms.

Our men have no protection, but they are lying flat on the ground, and shooting as fast as they can. This continues until dark when it gradually stops, until it is very dark, when every thing is very still, so still that the chirp of a cricket could be heard 100 feet away—all hands lying perfectly still, and the enemy not more than 40 feet in front of us.

About 9 O'Clock in the night the order from Genl Granbury is to "Charge in the woods at the sound of the bugle."

Col Wilkes sent his adjutant to me with an order to deploy my Company in front of Our Regt. and go in advance in the charge. While deploying my Company, by the right flank, commencing at the left of the Regt. and stop one man about every 8 or 10 ft. we took some prisoners who had crawled up to 8 or 10 feet of our line of battle. We were finally deployed about 10 ft. in front of the line of battle waiting for the bugle to sound the charge.

While waiting (all this time none had spoke above a whisper) we could hear the Yanks just in front of us moving among the dead leaves on the ground, like hogs rooting for acorns; but not speaking a word above a whisper. To make that charge in the dark, and go in front at that; and knowing that the enemy were just in front of us, was the most trying time I experienced during the whole war.

In about an hour from the time we rec'd Genl Granburys

order to charge, the bugle sounded the charge, and we raised a regular Texas Yell, or an Indian Yell or perhaps both together, and started forward through the brush, and so dark we could not see *anything at all*. We commenced to fire as soon as we started, and the Yanks turned loose, and the flash of their guns would light up the woods like a flash of lightning, and by it we could see a line of blue coats just there in front of us, but the noise we made with our mouths was too much for them. They broke, but not before we were among them with our skirmishers. We were so close that one Yank caught one of my men and told him to "fall in quick as Co. 'C' was gone already"—my man went about 20 steps with them and stoped beside a large tree untill we came up to him again, all of which did not occupy as much time as to write this history of it.

As soon as they broke to run we commenced to take prisoners. We were going down hill, still Yelling like all the devils from the lower regions had been turned loose, and occasionally a tree lying on the ground would have from 5 to 20 Yanks lying down behind the log. We kept finding them as we advanced. All they would say was, *"don't shoot" "don't shoot"*— finally we got down to the bottom of the hill to a little branch and under the banks were just lots of them— But just here at this little branch we lost trail of the enemy, and our men were badly mixed up.

After calling and some loud talking for a little time every man fell into his place when Col Wilkes ordered me to deploy my Company on the hill in front of us and hold the ground until day light, and said the Brigad would go back to where the fight began and make breastworks.

As soon as my Company was put in position I discovered that we were on the top of a ridge and the enemy if near could see us, where we could not see them. So I put my men back about 15 or 20 feet— So we could skylight to the top of the ridge. In the course of half an hour we could see the Yanks lighting their camp fires about a mile or more from us, but immediately in front of us. Their camp appeared to be on a hill side facing towards us. So we could see every fire in the whole camp—and there seemed to be a thousand of them. One of Our Batteries that had been put in position nearly in our rear on the line of the fight in the evening sent word to me that

they were going to shell the enemys camp, over our heads——
Presently "Boom" went a shell which burst right in their
midst. The Artillery kept up the shelling, about an hour, at
which time there was not a fire to be seen—no where— I walk
from one end of my skirmish line to the other all night, and
every man stands on his feet and holds his gun in his hands
until day light— As soon as it gets light we see we have been
standing among dead Yanks all night and did not know it.

I go out in front of the line and I find under a little pine
bush a Yank knapsack with an Oil Cloth and blanket straped to
it and in it is a plug of Tobacco needles thread, pins &c; all of
which except the knapsack, I appropriate to my own use.

I also find scattered here and there tin cups tin plates—
haversacks with knife & fork Bacon and crackers, coffee, *surenough coffee*. Oh I am rich; crackers bacon & coffee.

I also find guns, that seem to have been thrown away last
night—several of them with Bayonets Cartridge Boxes with
plenty of ammunition.

MAY 28th

About sun up this morning we were relieved and ordered
back to the Brigade—and we have to pass over the dead Yanks
of the battle field of yesterday; and here I beheld that which I
cannot discribe; and which I hope never see again, dead men
meet the eye in every direction, and in one place I stoped and
counted 50 dead men in a circle of 30 ft. of me. Men lying in
all sorts of shapes and [   ] just as they had fallen, and it
seems like they have nearly all been shot in the head, and a
great number of them have their skulls bursted open and their
brains running out, quite a number that way. I have seen many
dead men, and seen them wounded and crippled in various
ways, have seen their limbs cut off, but I never saw anything
before that made me sick, like looking at the brains of these men
did. I do believe that if a soldier could be made to faint, that I
would have fainted if I had not passed on and got out of that
place as soon as I did— We learn thru Col Wilkes that we killed
703 dead on the ground, and captured near 350 prisoners.

Genl Joseph E Johnson, and Genl Hardee and Genl Cleburn
and Genl Granbury all ride over the battle ground this morning and Genl Johnson compliments us very highly on the

fight. They all say that the dead are strewn thicker on the ground than at any battle of the war; but it don't seem to be so funny now as it was when it was going on. I feel sick every time I think of those mens brains.

We were not permitted to sit down and reflect over it, but were ordered forw'd about an hour by sun, just our Reg't. We advanced cautiously for about a mile through the wood when we found them again, and open fire upon them and soon have them on the retreat— There is only a skirmish line of them but that is all we have shooting at them, so we drive them back about ½ mile to their breastworks, and here in these woods between their breastworks and where they went to fight us yesterday evening, we find three piles of Oil Clothes, piled up like, a big wagon load at each pile. Every man in our Regt. got one and had several to pick over so he could get a good one— A Lieutenant of Our Regt (from Yorktown Tex) was captured just here while walking about through the chinquapin bushes. He was shot in the leg, and carried into their lines— Late in the evening the 7th Texas relieves us and we go back to our battle ground again.

PROCLAIMING VICTORY: LOUISIANA, MAY 1864

Richard Taylor: General Orders No. 44

The son of President Zachary Taylor, Major General Richard Taylor commanded the Confederate forces opposing the Union advance up the Red River in the spring of 1864. After his victory at Mansfield, Louisiana, on April 8, Taylor pursued the retreating Union forces and attacked them at Pleasant Hill the following day. Although the battle of Pleasant Hill was tactically inconclusive, Major General Nathaniel P. Banks abandoned his offensive and withdrew to Alexandria, where shallow water in the Red River threatened to strand the gunboat flotilla that had accompanied the expedition. Union engineers eventually were able to build a series of dams that raised the water level and allowed the gunboats to escape. Banks abandoned Alexandria on May 13 and after a series of skirmishes retreated across the Atchafalaya Bayou on May 20. The Red River campaign cost the Union about 5,500 men killed, wounded, or missing, the Confederates about 4,300.

HEAD-QUARTERS DISTRICT WESTERN LOUISIANA,
IN THE FIELD, May 23, 1864.
General Orders No. 44.
Soldiers of the Army of Western Louisiana:
  On the 12th of March the enemy, with an army of 30,000 men, accompanied by a fleet of iron-clads mounting 150 guns, moved forward for the conquest of Texas and Louisiana. After 70 days' continuous fighting you stand a band of conquering heroes on the banks of the Mississippi. Fifty pieces of cannon, 7,000 stand of small arms, three gun-boats, and eight transports captured or destroyed, 60 stands of colors, over 10,000 of the enemy killed, wounded or captured—those are the trophies which adorn your victorious banners. Along 300 miles of river you have fought his fleet, and over 200 miles of road you have driven his army. You have matched your bare breasts against his iron-clads, and proved victorious in the contest. You have driven his routed columns beyond the Mississippi, although fed by reinforcements of fresh troops, while many of

your gallant comrades were withdrawn to other fields. The boasted fleet which late sailed triumphant over our waters has fled in dismay, after destroying guns and stripping off armor in its eagerness to escape you. Like recreant knights, the ironclads have fled the field, leaving shield and sword behind.

The devotion and constancy you have displayed in this pursuit have never been surpassed in the annals of war, and you have removed from the Confederate soldier the reproach that he could win battles but could not improve victories.

Along 100 miles of his path, with more than average barbarity, the flying foe burned every house and village within his reach. You extinguished the burning ruins in his base blood, and were nerved afresh to vengeance by the cries of women and children left without shelter or food. Long will the accursed race remember the great river of Texas and Louisiana. The characteristic hue of his turbid waters has a darker tinge from the liberal admixture of Yankee blood. The cruel alligator and ravenous gar-fish wax fat on rich food, and our native vulture holds high revelry o'er many a festering corpse.

If the stern valor of our well-trained infantry was illustrated on the bloody fields of Mansfield and Pleasant Hill, this long pursuit has covered the cavalry with undying renown. Like generous hounds with the game in full view, you have known neither hunger nor fatigue, and the hoarse cannon and ringing rifle have replaced in this stern chase the sonorous horn and joyous halloo. Whether charging on foot, shoulder to shoulder with our noble infantry, or hurling your squadrons on the masses of the foe, or hanging on his flying columns with more than the tenacity of the Cossack, you have been admirable in all. Conquer your own vices, and you can conquer the world.

Our artillery has been the admiration of the army. Boldly advancing without cover against the heavy metal of the hostile fleet, unlimbering often without support, within range of musketry, or remaining last on the field to pour grape and canister into advancing columns, our batteries have been distinguished in exact proportion as opportunity was afforded.

Soldiers! These are great and noble deeds, and they will live in chronicle and in song as long as the Southern race exists to honor the earth. But much remains yet to do. The fairest city of the South languishes in the invader's grasp. Her exiled sons mourn her fate in every land. The cheeks of her fair daughters yet mantle with the blush raised by the tyrant's insult; not a Confederate soldier returns to his colors from this sad Venice of the South, but recounts with throbbing heart and tearful eye how, amidst danger and insult, these noble women—angels upon earth—cheered his confinement and relieved his wants. To view the smiles of these fair dames will be the soldier's proudest boast, the brightest leaf in his chaplet of laurels.

Soldiers! This army marches toward New-Orleans, and though it do not reach the goal, the hearts of her patriot women shall bound high with joy, responsive to the echoes of your guns.

R. TAYLOR, Major-General.

Official: F. R. LABBRET, Lieutenant-Colonel and Assistant Adjutant-General.

"I AM SCARED MOST TO DEATH":
VIRGINIA, MAY 1864

Charles Harvey Brewster to Mary Brewster; to Martha Brewster; and to Mattie Brewster

The fighting in the "Mule Shoe" at Spotsylvania ended in the early hours of May 13 when the Confederates withdrew to a new defensive line across the base of the salient. Grant then tried to turn Lee's right flank on May 14, but called off his planned attack after heavy rain and mud delayed crucial troop movements. On May 18 Union forces assaulted the base of the Mule Shoe and were repulsed. The same day, Grant learned that his secondary offensives in the Shenandoah Valley and along the James River had met with defeat, thereby freeing up reinforcements for Lee's army. He decided to move the Army of the Potomac south to the North Anna River and end the fighting at Spotsylvania, which had cost the Union nearly 18,000 men killed, wounded, or missing, and the Confederates about 12,000. Union troops abandoned their positions at Spotsylvania on May 20–21 and began marching to the southeast. Lee left Spotsylvania at the same time and reached the North Anna before Grant, but was unable to prevent Union forces from crossing the river on May 23. Lieutenant Charles Henry Brewster of the 10th Massachusetts wrote to his mother and to his sisters as his regiment approached and then crossed the North Anna.

Head Quarters 10th Mass Vols Caroline Co VA May 23rd 1864

Dear Mary,

I had just sent my last letter to Mother when we received a mail from home and I got 4 letters and I cannot find words to express the joy it gave me and all the Regiment and you can little imagine the amount of happiness one such mail brings to even one Regt of this great Army. We had two large grain bags full, and I assorted it but alas there was terrible sorrow connected with it which was the many letters for our dead and wounded comrades. I think I found as many as a dozen letters for poor Lt Bartlett who was killed only the day before. We started from near Spottsylvania C H last Saturday night and marched all night long and all day yesterday arriving at this place about 8 o'clock last night. I don't know where we are except that we are some miles south west of Gurneys Station on the Richmond + F'ks'brg R R and in Caroline Co and not a great distance from Bowling Green. We were roused this morning at half past 3 o'clock with orders to get breakfast and be ready to resume the march at 5 o'clock but it is now 8 o'clock and we have not budged an inch.

there is every prospect of a heavy rain storm to day, which will of course add very much to our comfort. The men are entirely out of rations and we know of no chance to get any.

We are travelling through a beautiful country, with lots of splendid plantations but there is nothing growing but corn except an occassional field of wheat.

Just in front of where I am sitting in a sandy cornfield on a side hill is a small swamp full of magnolias in full bloom and thier perfume is very refreshing after the continual stench of the dead bodies of men and horses which we have endured for the last 19 days. One of Co C has just brought in a great boquet of the Magnolias and he has given me two and I will perhaps put one of them in this letter but when it gets to you its white waxen beauty will be all gone though perhaps it may retain some of its fragrance. We are in a country that the Yanks have never been in before and it is not so utterly devastated as the country north of the Rapidan + Rappahannock but it looks good enough here with most of its vast fields, bare and uncultivated, and its want of inhabitants hardly any white men are seen nothing but ragged negroes, and the women of the plantations though many of the latter abandoned everything at our approach and leave thier homes at our disposal. at others they set upon the Portico's and Piazzas of thier homes and stare at the long columns of Cavalry Infantry Artillery Wagons and Ambulances that cross thier fields and tear down thier fences and hedges, in stupid wonder and despair. A report has just come from Division Hd Quarters that the Rebs are all back across the North Anna River so I suppose then we shall have to repeat the desparate fighting of the Wilderness and Spottsylvania C H if so, by the time we get them out of thier strongholds there and on the South Anna we shall have very few men to take the works around Richmond.

We heard heavy firing yesterday which is said to have been Hancock thrashing Gen Ewells Corps at Bowling Green. The 2nd + 5th Corps are in advance of us I find our delay is occasioned by waiting for rations which are expected here every moment. This country is much more open than where we have been, and if it continues so and we come up with them they will get a taste of our Artillery in larger doses than they have had heretofore, as we have not been able to use it but very little as yet. it has succeeded however in killing and wounding of our own men as it is always in the rear and undertakes to throw shell over us and generally manage to burst them right in our own ranks.

There goes the Bugle so I must stop and finish some other time. our Regt leads the Brigade and our Brigade leads the Division, and our Division leads the Corps this morning.

Noon.

We started and our Regiment was immediately ordered out as advanced guard + skirmishers, at which we were greatly elated as it gives us the priviledge of the fields + c and relieves us from the march in the crowded column besides the Artillery + trains. to be sure there is always the prospect of coming upon the enemy or being met by a volley of thier bullets, but to counteract this is the coming first upon the houses before all the chickens are carried off + c. but this morning our hopes soon fell to the ground for after marching a little ways we came upon the rear of the 5th Corps so of course everything eatable was cleaned out from all the houses.

We continued the march to this place where our teams came up and we are now stopping to receive rations. they also brought a mail and in it a letter from Mattie for me dated the 16th by which it appears that you have not got any of my letters of which this makes the sixth I have sent since the campaign commenced. it is most discouraging and it almost seems no use to write. Tell Mattie our Division is the 2nd Division and our Brigade the 4th Brigade. our General was Getty but he was wounded and we are now commanded by Brig Gen Neil who is next thing to a fool if not the thing itself Oh, how hot it is I am seated by the roadside under a rail fence and covered with the dust of the Wagons + Artillery with the hot rays of the sun pressing upon me, and the sweat and dust rolling down my face hurrying to finish this to send back by the Wagons, you must excuse any mistakes Tell Mattie I will write to her as soon as possible meantime she must claim her share in your letters.

The inhabitants inform us that Lee was here yesterday morning 10,000 men and skeedadled out of this place in a hurry. I meant to have made this letter longer but have to seize every chance to send so good by. Love to all. Don't fail to write often, more so than if I recd them regularly for the mail comes through all sorts of channels and some of them will get here if all don't. I was much disappointed in not getting one from home to day. Matt says you have no boarders anything you want at the stores you can have chgd to me and I will pay for it when I come home. don't fail once of writing to

Your aff brother,
Charlie.

Head Quarters 10th Mass Vols South Bank North Anna River
May 24th 1864

Dear Mother,

I sent a letter yesterday while we were on the march to this place to Mary and as we are informed that we are to remain here to day I thought I would commence another although I do not know as the other one has gone any further than the wagon trains which are some where in our rear. I don't know where. You will know by the other letter that we were on the march. about 6 o'clock we began to hear heavy firing and they began to hurry us up and we came about 4 miles almost on a run arriving on the north bank of the river just after dark. We met the stream of wounded coming to the rear, and found that the 5th Corps which was in advance on this road were across the river.

we also met a large squad of Reb prisoners. the firing ceased and we went into line of battle on the other side of the river in the night the Rebels left our front and this morning there have been several hundred Rebel prisoners by us as we lie in line of battle. they are most all North Carolinians and they give themselves up one whole company came in Officers, Non-Commsd Officers and all. they acknowledged themselves whipped. we crossed the river early this morning. another squad of 15 Johnies had just gone by, and they look mighty glad to get in and I don't blame them. I expect they are even more tired and hungry than we are.

Gen Hancock with the 2nd Corps is engaged down the river on our left and it is reported he has not effected a crossing yet. we can hear the thundering of his Cannon and have all day long though it seems a little more distant this afternoon. it was reported by some of the prisoners that he had cut Ewells Corps all to pieces. poor Stewart Campbell I believe you said was in that Corps. I am afraid he may be killed or wounded for they have fared hard.

It is said that poor Munyan is going to die. he is in Fredericksburg. Major Parker has had his arm taken off Lieut Graves is very low also. I see the papers report his name as E. H. Sprague and Munyans as Munger. that is what Artemas Ward calls military glory getting killed and having your name spelled wrong in the newspapers.

We received another mail this morning and I got your letter of the 17th and am glad to hear you have finally received one of my letters. I began to think you never would. I also received Springfield Republicans as late as the 19th. You must not fail to write very often. I do not feel very well to day. I got poisoned in my face yesterday in coming through the woods and my eyes are almost shut up and they are all laughing at me.

There goes another Reb he looks about 7 feet high. he is almost as tall as the Cavalry man on horseback who is guarding him. And there goes some guns in our front so we may get a battle yet to day. Our time begins to look very short only 27 days. I wish we might be spared another battle, but I know we shall not be. the 2nd RI Regts time is out in 12 days and it is reported that they are going Saturday. Regts and parts of Regts are leaving every day now. the 7th Mass has 21 days more to serve. The Rebels are throwing an occasional shell at us but they do not reach the 2nd line where we are yet.

The prisoners who came in report that there are lots of others who want to come but our boys fire at them so they cannot. our men are much opposed to taking prisoners since the Fort Pillow affair, that has cost the Rebels many a life that would otherwise have been spared. I see that the papers are full of the terrible fighting that Burnsides negroes have done, but a few days ago they had not been into a fight at all and I don't believe they have now. I wish I could see them in a battle once, and know for certain whether they would fight or not.

May 25th, 5 o'clock AM.

We moved forward about a quarter of a mile last night and occupied some breast works which the 5th Corps had thrown up and the 5th moved farther to the right.

We had a report last night that the 2nd Corps had captured 15,000 prisoners but we do not know that there is any truth in it.

We heard thier firing all day and up to a late hour last night and it did not seem to move much. We are under marching orders and were ordered to be ready at 5 o'clock. it is now nearly half past but we do not move. I understand that our wagon trains are ordered to the white house. we cannot be far from the VA Central R R and Sextons Junction.

I have thought 50 times of what you spoke of in regard to the Mat Ta Po + the Ny, since we have been on those rivers. There was a house right on the battle line of the 5th Corps when they fought here night before last and the occupants went into the Rebel lines. next morning they came back 2 white women and about 20 Negro women. the soldiers had killed every chicken + pig about the premises and taken all the beds out of the house and slept in them and the chairs were scattered all along the line for the convenience of Uncle Sams nephews. They said when they came back that they thought that the Rebs were going to drive the Yanks all into the river. no doubt thier will was good enough but they found the Yanks a hard party to drive.

We hear no firing anywhere along the line this morning and I presume we shall take up our line of march southward pretty soon but I do not know.

Half past 2 o'clock PM

We finally marched about 8 o'clock this morning and after

marching about a mile we came upon the VA Central RR and the pioneers immediately commenced to tear up the track and burn the ties and bend the rails. we struck the RR at Niels Station according to the sign. we very soon came upon the Rebels and went into line of battle and have been expecting a fight every moment all day. there has been continual skirmishing all day. I suppose we are now near Little River. We have been gradually and carefully crawling along all day. We are protecting the flank to day. Our Corps received 7000 reenforcements yesterday.

Poor Munyan is dead. He died Saturday night he was occasionally out of his head and his brother says he would keep asking for me and inquiring if Adjutant was there. Poor fellow I did not know he was wounded until he was carried from the field and I never saw him afterwards. We have just heard that Capt Weatherells leg has been taken off above the knee. I sat down to finish this as the Q M 2nd RI has come up and offers to take back a mail, so this is right from a prospective battle field which may be one in five minutes from this time. Love to all write often to

Your aff son
Charlie

Hd Quarters 10th Mass Vols 4th Brig 2nd Division 6th Corps Near Sextons Junction VA May 26th 1864
PS I shall have to stop writing letters pretty soon for want of paper + pencils. We have not seen our baggage wagon since we started.

Dear Mattie,

I received your welcome letter of the 15th and was very glad to get it for you cannot in the least imagine what a comfort letters from home are in these trying times. The mail takes rank even before rations with the soldiers, when our first mail came, it came on the same wagons with the supplies and although the men were all out of rations and hungry, and we might have to leave at any moment even before the rations could be issued, yet nobody would pay any attention to the rations until the mail was all distributed and there were two great grain bags full of it, but alas a large proportion of it could be claimed by no owners now with the Regt. as we did not get any mail until over 200 Officer + men were killed, wounded and missing our Lieut who was killed only the day before had as many as a dozen letters. it is very sad.

I sent a letter to Mother yesterday by the Quartermaster of the 2nd RI who took a mail back to the wagon trains.

We crossed the North Anna River day before yesterday morning and remained on the south bank all day and night. yesterday morning we started about 8 o'clock and crossed the VA Central RR and the pioneers immediately commenced tearing it up. they have utterly destroyed several miles of it. immediately after we came upon the pickets of the enemy, and pursued them to the Little River where the enemy were found in force and fortified on the south bank. we formed our lines and threw up breastworks which we have gradually extended nearer and nearer. the pickets are constantly firing at each other and as I write an occasional bullet goes hissing over my head. The enemy have got fourteen pieces of Artillery in front of us which can be seen, but our batteries have banged away at them at intervals ever since we arrived but do not succeed in getting any reply. We have been expecting to attack or be attacked every moment since we got here but have not as yet.

Word just came that the enemy were pressing Gen Griffins front, and we must hold ourselves ready to go to his assistance at a moments notice if required. Gen Griffin commands a Division of the 5th Corps who are on our left.

I have headed my letter so that you can see the number of our Brigade + Division + Corps. The lamented Sedgwick you know was our Corps Commander when we started, and the Corps is now commanded by Gen Wright.

Gen Getty was our Division Commander when we started but he was wounded in the Battle of the Wilderness and Gen Neil now commands the Div. Gen Wright formerly commanded the 1st Division of this Corps, and is an able commander and was much relied on by Gen Sedgwick. Gen Neil is the worst commander it was ever our misfortune to serve under, and I don't think he is fit to command a company. Gen Getty was a most able and gallant General. he had taken command of the Division but a short time before we left Brandy Station and I never saw him to know him. You will think this strange when I tell you that he was wounded not far from where our Regiment was at the time. I saw Gen Wadsworth not ten minutes before he was killed. we were right on the plank road and he told us to pull up the planks and make a breast work. he was an elderly gray headed man and rode his horse on up the road, while the enemy were making a furious attack and forcing our lines back. our Regt was almost the only one left in reserve, and it was just before Burnside came up. The enemies sharp shooters were firing down the road and his fate was certain. Capt Shurtleff was wounded on the same road, and several men.

Our Regt was also close to where Gen Sedgwick was killed and the same party of sharp shooters succeeded in wounding 5 of our men at a very long distance as we lay resting on the edge of a piece of woods. The men where he was cautioned him that there were sharp shooters who commanded that place but he laughed and said they could not hit an elephant at that distance and had hardly said so when he was hit and killed almost instantly.

In the Battle over the Rebel Breastworks (the one I wrote home about where the Rebels were piled up so) I was standing talking to a Capt Shaw of the 2nd RI. I stood partly turned towards him and my elbow just touching his, when a bullet came and struck square in the breast, tearing it open and making an awful sound, but one only too familiar to my ears. He turned round, fell on his face and was dead.

It is very sad to think of the happy party of Officers who spent the winter at Brandy Station. of 28 field line and staff Officers who were with our Regt 4 are dead and 13 wounded besides one (Capt Bishop) who was slightly wounded and returned to duty in 3 or 4 days. One of the others is very slightly wounded a bullet just scratched his face, Lt Cottrell of Pittsfield but he is not at all remarkable for courage and is making the most of it and staying round the Division Field Hospital in the rear. it is not the first time he has played sick to escape dangerous duties. his wound was not half as bad as Capt Bishops, or Geo Bigelows first wound in the throat, or my poisoned face. When we think that we have been on this campaign but 22 days and have got 25 men to stay and that considerably more than half our numbers are taken already, the prospect looks rather dark for the rest of us.

P W K is doing very well for him and keeps up tolerably well now he was in the Battle of the Wilderness, and part of the time at the next battle he disappeared for two or three days but has kept up since.

You are mistaken about thier being nothing cowardly about me. I am scared most to death every battle we have, but I don't think you need be afraid of my sneaking away unhurt. Capt Haydens leg was not shot away nor do I understand that it is taken off although it may have to be. I hear Mr Joel Hayden is in Fredericksburg also Joe + Sid Bridgeman. they say our wounded get but little care, there is but one surgeon for all the wounded Officers in the 6th Corps so you can judge what the enlisted mens chances are. it is a singular fact that two thirds of the killed and wounded in our Regt are Veteran Volunteers.

We get no intimation yet whether the Officers who recd the 35 five days furlough are to go home with the Regt or what is to be done with them. Our line of our breastworks here runs right through a farmers garden and close to his back door through peas in blossom and radishes + tomatoes + c + c I imagine how Mother and Mrs Clarke would look to have 100 blue jackets with musket + bayonette rush into thier gardens stack arms and seize the spade + shovel and go to throwing up a ridge of Earth five foot high. it makes ones prospect for garden sarse very poor indeed.

I have written this letter as it is reported that our Commissary is coming up to night and I may have a chance to send it. You must write often. Give my love to Thomas + Charles and to Mother + Mary, and respects to all

Your affectionate brother
Charlie.

ANDERSONVILLE PRISON: GEORGIA, MAY 1864

Eugene Forbes: Diary, May 24–27, 1864

Concerned about the difficulty of guarding and supplying the thousands of Union prisoners of war held in Richmond, the Confederate War Department decided in the late fall of 1863 to build a new prison camp at Andersonville in southwestern Georgia. Construction of a sixteen-acre stockade designed to hold up to 10,000 men began in January 1864, and the first two hundred prisoners arrived from Richmond on February 24. By the end of May the camp held more than 18,000 men, and nearly 1,500 prisoners had already died. A printer before the war, Sergeant Eugene Forbes had enlisted in the 4th New Jersey Infantry in 1861. Forbes, who was captured in the Wilderness on the evening of May 6 when the Confederates attacked the Union right flank north of the Orange Turnpike, recorded his arrival at Andersonville in a pocket diary.

Tuesday, May 24. Arrived at Macon about daylight; medium sized town, of good appearance; found I was in company with several men of my own regiment, Company H. Arrived at Andersonville, Ga., about noon, and after considerable delay, were turned into a large enclosure, where we found about 15,000 prisoners, many of whom had been prisoners for nine and ten months. Trafficing in tent-poles, salt, corn bread, &c., was soon going on extensively; some of the men are like skeletons, from chronic diarrhea, &c.; some are as black as charcoal men, and have evidently not washed for many days; they seem to have lost all ambition, and of the 15,000 now here, not one-half could march five miles; the camp is about six hundred yards long by four hundred wide, and surrounded by a high board fence, some twelve or fourteen feet high, with two gates on the west side; sentry boxes are placed at regular intervals along the wall. Drew rations of corn bread and bacon at dark.

Wednesday, May 25. Roll-call about 9 A.M.; a heavy shower last night; our squad is Detachment 57, Mess 1; washed ourselves and our clothes the first time since our capture. Gambling is carried on quite extensively; faro, sweat-cloths, dice, &c., are used, and $10 stakes are played for, as if money was as plenty as sand. Six men were carried out on the "dead line" last night from our (the south) side of the camp. A considerable marsh occupies the very center of the pen, which, if not drained, will be apt to create disease among us; the drinking water is very poor; wells are dug, and kept as private property, but the rebel surgeon says the running water is the most wholesome; we use the run water altogether; the well water appears impregnated with sulphur, or some mineral, looks blue, and induces diarrhea. A large squad of prisoners from the western army arrived this P.M.; they report that Gen. Joseph Johnston has been taken prisoner by Sherman. One of the old prisoners states that the deaths here in the last two months will reach 1,800. Trade is carried on with the guards on the outside of the wall, by talking through cracks, and throwing articles over the fence. Rigged up our tent anew, and commenced a regular "skirmish drill;" took no prisoners, but counted about a dozen dead on the field (my shirt). Several negroes are here, captured in Florida; a negro orderly sergeant has charge of a squad of whites and blacks; the negroes are treated in all respects like ourselves; several Indians are also here, so we make a motley crew. Drew rations towards night, corn bread, bacon, and boiled rice. Sentry fired a shot just after dark, but believe no one was hurt; some of our men came in with the squad which arrived this evening, and more are expected tomorrow; they report that only eighty men are left for duty in the regiment, and that Grant's headquarters are twenty-two miles from Richmond.

Thursday, May 26. "Skirmished," as usual. A party of negroes were set at work digging for tunnels, the existence of which is most probably only in the imaginations of the guards; the officer in charge says he will look no more, but give us a ration of grape and canister if an attempt to escape is made. Two men who were with me in the three months' service, came to see me last night (Louis and Kelly); they have been prisoners about four months, but look very well; Louis is now in the cavalry, and Kelly in the gunboat service. Reported that one man was killed and another wounded last night; various rumors afloat in regard to paroling, &c., but none of which the slightest reliance can be placed. Peddling still goes on; a "bunch" (two little onions,) for 25 cents; a 10 cent plug of tobacco, 50 cents and so on. Some of the dirtiest men were ducked and scrubbed today, and some of the "raiders" (thieves), bucked and gagged, and their heads shaved. The weather is warm, with frequent showers. Boxes and letters are received here by the prisoners. Drew pork and mush at dark, but no bread. A squad of prisoners arrived after dark, some of the 4th among them, who report the regiment reduced to eighty effective men.

Friday, May 27. A "raider" caught last night, and kept prisoner till daylight, when he was bucked and gagged, his head shaved, and afterwards marched around the camp; he took it very coolly. A fight occurred between a party of "raiders" and some of the "raidees", in which the latter got the worst of it; one man is said to be pretty badly hurt. Quite an excitement is apparent among the guards outside; the infantry are marching to various points, and horsemen carrying messages from one body to another. One tunnel was discovered yesterday, and the existence of others is probably suspected. Very hot, and the odor from the swamp and sinks by no means pleasant. Three tunnels discovered today, one said to extend sixty feet beyond the stockade. Drew bread, rice and meat about 8 P.M.; the ration appears to be getting smaller by degrees. Tore out the sleeve and back linings of my blouse, cut up our sugar and coffee bags, and cut off the flap of Hoffman's knapsack, sewed them together, and made an end for the tent. A prisoner who came in night before last reports Lieuts. Flannery and Heston captured on the 13th.

APPRAISING GRANT: VIRGINIA, MAY 1864

Charles Francis Adams Jr. to Charles Francis Adams

On May 24 advancing Union troops discovered that Lee's army was strongly entrenched near Hanover Junction just south of the North Anna River. Grant decided to again move to the southeast around Lee's right flank and sent his forces across the Pamunkey River on May 27–28. Captain Charles Francis Adams Jr. commanded a detached company of the 1st Massachusetts Cavalry that served on guard duty at Army of the Potomac headquarters. Adams assessed the ongoing campaign in a misdated letter to his father, the American minister to Great Britain, in which he exaggerated the degree of harmony that existed at the time between Grant and Meade. By the end of May Grant had grown frustrated with Meade's caution, while Meade resented Grant's increasing role in making tactical decisions.

———————

H.Q. Army of Potomac.
Hanover Town Va. 29 April/64.

Hon. C. F. Adams
    London.
My dear Father

I have a leisure day at last, & the means of writing I mean to pay off a little of my heavy arrears to all of you in London. I have no letters from London since I left Brandey Station I don't know what has become of them.—I suppose they were addressed to the regiment & went to it & may turn up; I sent you my present address in a letter to John, which he has probably forwarded. Two days ago I got two papers from Mamma,—please acknowledge them. I have only had two letters from John,—the latest of May 7th,—he speaks as though you were all well.

Meanwhile here we are.—South of the Pamunkey & only 16 miles from Richmond,—that Mecca & Jerusalem of this Army of the Potomac. As I look back over the campaign since the 4th of May, I don't know where to begin to write I feel vexed out of all bounds with myself for neglecting at the start to provide myself with the few writing conveniences which would have enabled me to send you day by day an account of what was saw, felt, & heard. It is lost now, but I think I might have made a contribution to history, besides relieving some of your anxiety. Now I can't tell you much, & that little won't be of much value. The campaign to us here gradually unfolds itself. Grant & Meade discuss & decide, but keep their own counsel & no one knows whether tomorrow the Army is to fight, to march, or to rest. Meanwhile marching now seems to be the order of the day, &, since day before yesterday Head Quarters have moved thirty odd miles,—turning all the exterior lines of Richmond & bringing us down to the interior line of the Chickahominy. Here we rest for to-day. Up to this time Gen. Grant seems to have looked on this campaign in Va as one necessarily to be made up of the hardest kind of fighting, combined with all the Generalship which he could command, &, as we were numerically the strongest, we might as well do the fighting first as last,—pounding & manoevering at the same time. If this was his idea, I think the wisdom of it is becoming apparent. I cannot believe that his operations have been or now are conducted on any fixed plan, he seems to have one end in view,—the capture of Richmond & destruction of Lee's army,—but I imagine his means to that end undergo daily changes & no man in this Army, but Meade perhaps, is even able to give grounds for a guess as to whether we are to approach Richmond from this side or from the other. Meanwhile, though Grant expected hard fighting, I have no idea that he expected anything like the fighting & the slaughter which took place in the Wilderness & at Spotsylvania,—he had never seen anything like it in the West, & the fierce, stubborn resistance we met far surpassed his expectation. Meade knew better what he had to expect, &, in fighting for him those battles, was I imagine of incalculable assistance to Grant. To-day, as near as I can see, results stand as follows,—these two great armies have pounded each other nearly to pieces for many days,—neither has achieved any real success over the other on the field of battle,— our loss has probably been greater than theirs, for ours has been the offensive,—but we have a decided balance of prisoners & captured artillery in our favor,—the enemy, I think, outfight us, but we outnumber them, &, finally, within the last three days one witnesses in this Army as it moves along, all the results of a victory when in fact it has done only barren fighting, for it has done the one thing needful before the enemy,—it has advanced. The result is wonderful,—hammered & pounded as this Army has been,—worked, marched, fought & reduced as it is,—it is in better spirits & better fighting trim to-day than it was on the first days fight in the Wilderness. Strange as it seems to me, it is, I believe, yet the fact, that this Army is now just on its second wind, & is more formidable than it ever was before,—this I see on every march & I attribute it to movement in advance after heavy, though barren, fighting. With the enemy it is otherwise. Heavier fighting, harder marching, & greater privations,—for with them deficiency in numbers was only to be made good by redoubled activity,— two men with them have done the work of three with us,—all these have led only to movements to the rear,—to the abandonment of line after line until now they find themselves with their backs against Richmond. Naturally this discourages troops,—particularly coming after as hard fighting as they know how to do,—& as a result we now get, as I am informed, from all sources but one story & that of discouragement & exhaustion,—the enemy is getting off his fight. What is to come next?—Will Lee try to revive the spirits of his men & the fortunes of his Army by taking the offensive?—Will he try to repeat the story of the Chickahominy & the six days fighting?—What does Grant mean next to do?—I have always noticed that when I try to divine the future of military operations, I am invariably wrong; & so I long ago gave up trying. Of a few things though I feel pretty sure,—Stonewall Jackson is dead,—Grant is not McClellan, nor is Meade McDowell,— Grant will not let his Army be idle, nor will he allow the initiative to be easily taken out of his hands & if Lee can outfight Meade he will do more than he was ever able to do yet when his troops were more numerous, in better heart & much fresher than they now are. Accordingly we find ourselves approaching the climax of the campaign,—under circumstances which certainly seem to me hopeful. The next few days will probably develop Grant's final move,—the line on which he means to approach Richmond & the point at which he means, unless Lee out-generals him, to have the final fight. I don't believe he will allow time to slip away or Lee to repair damages.—I do believe that while the Army is resting to-day, it is drawing breath for the great struggle & on the eve of great movements & decisive results.

Things meanwhile work in the Army charmingly. Grant is certainly a very extraordinary man; he does not look it & might pass well enough for a dumpy & slouchy little subaltern, very fond of smoking,—neither do I know that he shows it in his conversation, for he never spoke to me & doesn't seem to be a very talkative man anyhow;—they say his mouth shows character,—it may, but it is so covered with beard, that no one can vouch for it. The truth is, he is in appearance a very ordinary looking man,—one who would attract attention neither in the one way or the other,—not knowing who it is you would not pronounce him insignificant,—& knowing who it is, it would require some study to find in his appearance material for hero worship, though there is about his face no indication of weakness or lack of force. He has not nearly so strong a head & face as Humphreys for instance, who at once strikes you as a man of force. In figure Grant is comical,—he sits a horse well, but in walking he leans forward & toddles. Such being his appearance however I do not think that any intelligent person could watch him, even from such a distance as mine, without concluding that he is a remarkable man. He handles those around him so quietly & well,—he so evidently has the faculty of disposing of work & managing men,—he is cool & quiet, almost stolid & as if stupid,—in danger & in a crisis he is one against whom all around, whether few in number or a great army as here, would instinctively lean. He is a man of the most exquisite judgment & tact,—see how he has handled this Army,—he took command under the most unfavorable circumstances,—jealousy between East & West, the Army of the Potomac & the Army of the South West,—that general feeling that the officers from the West were going to swagger over those here & finally that universal envy which success creates & which is always ready to carp at it. The moment I came to Head Quarters I saw that; though nothing was said, yet the materials were all ready for an explosion at the first mistake Grant made. All this has passed away & now Grant has this Army as firmly as ever he had that of the S.W. He has effected this simply by the exercise of tact & good taste, he has humored us,—he has given some promotions,—he has made no parade of his authority,—he has given no orders except through Meade & Meade he treats with the utmost confidence & deference,—the result is that even from the most jealously disposed & most indiscreet of Meade's staff not a word is heard against Grant. The result is of inestimable importance,—the Army has a head & confidence in that head;—it has leaders & there is no discord among those leaders;—we seem to have gotten rid of jealousy & all now seem disposed to go in with a will to win.

At last we have gotten out of the Wilderness. That interminable outline of pines of all sizes which it seemed never would end has given way to a clearer & more cultivated country,—& now we come across the old Virginia plantation houses & can now & then see a regular clearing. The Wilderness was a most fearfully discouraging place,—an enemy always in front against whom the fiercest attack we could make made no impression, —incessant fighting day after day,—no progress forward,—& the hospitals cleared out only to be filled again, while the country was becoming peopled with graves. There the Army got very much discouraged & took blue views of life,—the straggling became terrible & you saw men the whole time & officers sometimes living in the woods or wandering round the country. At that time I take it Lee had accomplished his object & the Army of the Potomac was crippled,—it could not effectively have advanced. At that time however it experienced the great advantage of Grants presence & power for he at once re-enforced it by every available man round Washington thus at once restoring its efficiency, while but for his power & name the Administration would, as heretofore, doubtless have defended Washington at the cost of all the fruits of this Army's fighting. Thus Lee found himself again opposed by a fresh army, & every new man who came up from the rear served to revive the spirits of those who had been here before. Now the Army is in capital condition & I feel once more sanguine,—but the telegraphs of the steamer which brings this will tell the whole story.

Meanwhile I hear not a word of your negotiation. What has

become of it?—Is it not too late now?—or is it supposed that disaster or success will bring the rebels to your terms?—I do not even hear that that negotiation has as yet crept into the papers,—but after all, it is of less consequence now, for formerly it might have stopped bloodshed but now it can hardly be in time to do more than pave the way for conciliation,— since this month came in this war seems to have gone so far that now, in this last effort, either we must crush them or leave them so weak that little enough more blood will be left to shed. Pray keep me informed about this, & also do send me books & reading matter,—here at H. Q. I have time & even Shakespeare is getting read out.

As to myself I have little to say,—in this campaign I have been exposed hardly at all, in fact even less than I should wish, but casualties come very easily & no-one knows how or when he & bullets may be round together. Give my love to all, & in future I hope to write more frequently. Affy

C. F. Adams

May 29, 1864

ASSESSING BLACK TROOPS: MAY 1864

Lorenzo Thomas to Henry Wilson

Brigadier General Lorenzo Thomas, the adjutant general of the Union army, began recruiting and organizing black troops in the Mississippi Valley in the spring of 1863. He wrote about their achievements to Henry Wilson, the Massachusetts Republican who headed the Senate Committee on Military Affairs. When Garrett Davis of Kentucky proposed during a debate on June 6 that all black soldiers be disarmed and used as laborers, Wilson had Thomas's letter read into the Senate record.

———————

Washington, May 30, 1864.
Dear Sir: On several occasions when on the Mississippi river I contemplated writing to you respecting the colored troops, and to suggest that as they have been fully tested as soldiers their pay should be raised to that of white troops, and I desire now to give my testimony in their behalf. You are aware that I have been engaged in the organization of freedmen for over a year, and have necessarily been thrown in constant contact with them.

The negro in a state of slavery is brought up by the master from early childhood to strict obedience, and to obey implicitly the dictates of the white man, and they are thus led to believe that they are an inferior race. Now, when organized into troops, they carry this habit of obedience with them; and their officers being entirely white men, the negro promptly obeys his orders. A regiment is thus rapidly brought into a state of discipline. They are a religious people, another high quality for making good soldiers. They are a musical people, and thus readily learn to march and accurately perform their maneuvers. They take pride in being elevated as soldiers, and keep themselves neat and clean, as well as their camp grounds. This I know from personal inspection, and from the reports of my special inspectors, two of my staff being constantly on inspecting duty.

They have proved a most important addition to our forces, enabling the generals in active operations to take a large force of white troops into the field; and now brigades of blacks are placed with the whites. The forts erected at the important points on the river are nearly all garrisoned by blacks—artillery regiments raised for the purpose—say at Paducah and Columbus, Kentucky; Memphis, Tennessee; Vicksburg and Natchez, Mississippi, and most of the works around New Orleans. Experience proves that they manage heavy guns very well. Their fighting qualities have also been fully tested a number of times, and I am yet to hear of the first case where they did not fully stand up to their work. I passed over the ground where the first Louisiana made the gallant charge at Port Hudson, by far the stronger part of the rebel works. The wonder is that so many made their escape. At Milliken's Bend, where I had three incomplete regiments, one without arms until the day previous to the attack; greatly superior numbers of rebels charged furiously up to the very breast-works. The negroes met the enemy on the ramparts, and both sides freely used the bayonet, a most rare occurrence in warfare, as one or other party gives way before coming in contact with the steel. The rebels were defeated with heavy loss. The bridge at Moscow, on the line of railroad from Memphis to Corinth, was defended by one small regiment of blacks. A cavalry attack of three times their number was made, the blacks defeating them in the three charges made by the rebels. They fought them hours, until our cavalry came up, when the defeat was made complete, many of the rebel dead being left on the field. A cavalry force of one hundred and fifty attacked three hundred rebel cavalry near the Big Black with signal success, a number of prisoners being taken and marched to Vicksburg. Forrest attacked Paducah with seven thousand five hundred. The garrison was between five and six hundred; nearly four hundred were colored troops, very recently raised. What troops could have done better? So, too, they fought well at Fort Pillow until overpowered by greatly superior numbers.

The above enumerated cases seem to me sufficient to demonstrate the value of the colored troops. I make no mention of the cases on the Atlantic coast with which you are perfectly familiar. I have the honor to be, Very respectfully, Your obedient servant,

L. Thomas

BEHIND THE UNION LINES:
VIRGINIA, MAY–JUNE 1864

Cornelia Hancock to Her Sister

A Quaker woman from New Jersey, Cornelia Hancock began her service as a volunteer army nurse at Gettysburg in July 1863 and later worked at hospitals in Washington, D.C., and Brandy Station, Virginia. She arrived in Fredericksburg on May 12 to find scenes that "beggared all description" as rain "poured in through the bullet-riddled roofs of the churches until our wounded lay in pools of water made bloody by their seriously wounded condition." Hancock worked at Fredericksburg until the end of May, when her hospital was moved to the new Union supply base at White House on the Pamunkey River.

———————

May 28th, 1864.

MY DEAR SISTER

IT is one of the most beautiful mornings that ever blew. We are just evacuating Fredericksburg, the wounded having been all sent to Washington. We had the pleasure of feeding the wounded who were kept prisoners in the Wilderness for nearly three weeks and almost starved. I met a surg. who asked me why the cavalry had not released them before and wanted to know what was going to be done with them. I told him they most of them had been sent back to the regt. in the front. He filled with tears and said they could not send *him* as he had but eleven men left in his Regt. I never felt more sorry for a man. The men, prepared for march, about 8,000, are all in line with shining bayonets. The cavalry, all mounted officers, riding up and down the line, flags waving, everything around is exhilarating. They go about one hundred yards, then halt. A courier who just brought in a dispatch from Gen. Grant is guarding our wagon. He is an intelligent German and goes out to the farm houses and gets us fresh milk and cakes. He is the most splendid rider I ever saw and is as brave as he can be. He had his horse shot under him yesterday but soon captured another, says he will try to get one for me before we arrive at Port

Royale. We have a battery at the front of the train and Cavalry on all sides, still they say the guerrillas have attacked the rear of the train and captured fourteen men and killed two. Poor soldiers. It is very hard on a march. They are constantly falling by the roadside. I have carried lots of their guns and knapsacks for them today. I felt many times like giving them my seat. I can enjoy myself in a march looking round. There is always something going on interesting and most of the time I can sleep in the most profound manner. They shoot the chickens, calves, pigs, and &c then lay them along the road and every man gets a stick and shoulders a piece. We stopped for dinner and have seen nothing of Grant's messenger since. I guess he has been gobbled by Guerrillas. Every few rods a man sings out: "There is Miss Hancock." Mrs. Lee is a very good singer. It is getting towards night and she is singing as we are wearily nearing Port Royale. In this town we cannot obtain any resting place except in the negro shanties but that does not concern my mind at all. We have a hoe cake for supper and no prospect for breakfast.

May 30th—we stayed in P. Royal all night in some negro quarters and this morning went to the Medical Director's office and heard from time to time that no passes were to be granted to any *ladies* except for them to *return* to *Washington*. I sat upon my trunk perfectly easy. There has always been a way provided and I always expect there will be, so never concern. At length a doctor comes up who volunteers us to go on the transport *without* a pass. That I often do. But I like going in the wagon train better and the Sanitary have offered to carry us thru, so now I am sitting in their wagon. We have plenty of provisions with us and I hope will get thru comfortably. They are making wounded all the time and our services will be needed by the time we get there. I hope you are doing well at home but I have had no tidings that you are as I have never received a letter except one from Ellen. Capt. Harris has just come, volunteers us to be as comfortable as possible.

Direct a letter to Miss Hancock
care of Sanitary Comm.
White House, V.

This morning this place is to be evacuated and the White House is to be the next base. Oh! what a sight. This place was one mass of tired, swearing soldiery, scrambling for a hard tack, killing chickens, pigs, calves &c. Seems like Bedlam let loose. I am always cared for tho'; before we had been in the town half an hour a guard was detailed over the house, so we slept in perfect security. I hope Grant is accomplishing something as he is making terrible suffering for the rear of his army. They never have been used to rapid evacuating and advancing into an enemy's country. The White House sounds nearer to Richmond. I shall always remember with pleasure some Secesh I met in Fredericksburg. I believe we are to have a Johnny cake for breakfast. I have always been well received where I am known and if I could be allowed to stay with them would be content to make few new acquaintances. I do not wish you to give a thought of uneasiness for me. I am always contented with my lot and if *you* will not concern I will promise you *I* will not. I would give lots to see our children especially Eddie. Yesterday during the shelling a child not 3 years old walked across the commons. If thee knows anything of Salem affairs write me. I expect Dr. Potter has lots of letters for me from mother; direct in his care 1st Div. 2nd Corps Hospital. I want a letter awfully, and if you have done your duty there will be some at the front. I have no fear but you have for when I am here I long since have been convinced I have the best sister and mother in the world. If Dr. Aiken returns send my things.

With much love,

I am thy sister—CORNELIA

May 31st, 1864—On March.

MY DEAR SISTER

WE left Port Royale on the Rappahannock 15 miles below Fredericksburg on the 30th of May, Mrs. Lee, Georgy Willets and I having come here from that place in an open wagon the day before. Now we are on our march for the White House— a distance of about 45 miles though the roads are very winding and it may be much farther. It is a very warm day and the guards suffer very much with the dust and heat. There is almost always an alarm along the line about Guerrillas, often just enough to make a pleasant excitement. I cannot feel afraid and strange as it may seem the soldiers want to have a brush with them. I almost worship our faithful soldiers who trudge on and never murmur or complain. I am in a Sanitary spring wagon and it is very comfortable—when I get tired I can lie down and sleep. Mrs. Lee is a very pleasant travelling companion. The army has not passed through this section and there appears to have been some attempt at cultivating the land, but we would not consider that there was anything worth harvesting. We are eating strawberries, peas, &c—Tonight we halted at a village called Newtown, went into a Secesh house, found a nice bed and room to sleep. They told us they have nothing to eat. We sent back to the train for rations and had the colored people to get us a good supper which we ate upon their table. The women are bitter Secessionists—one said her husband is a commisary in the Rebel army. We think he furnishes rations to the guerilla bands and I was not disposed to show them any favours but true to some people's idea of right they wanted to take Sanitary stuff and give those rebels to live on because they said they were starving. There was a splendid side saddle that I wanted to confiscate for I know that has been smuggled from the North. There was not a man in our crowd who had spunk enough to take it. I wish Dr. Dudley had been along, I would have had it then. Protecting Secesh property is entirely played out with me.

June 1st.

At 7 o'clock this morning we left our Secesh enemies and resumed the march which was extremely dusty. After we had gone about a mile on the road the guerrilas made a dash, but our cavalry immediately drove them back into the woods. I never saw anything more promptly accomplished, not a gun was fired, yet the woods have been searched and not a rebel can be found. Our train this morning is 15 miles long and more expected to catch up. Even the colored people are Secesh here and we cannot induce them to go along with us. A few stragglers have joined the teams this morning. In Fredericksburg I never found a disaffected colored person. No one need ever speak against Jersey, it is a paradise compared to Virginia. We rode on about a mile and found a house deserted, the owner of which was said to be a chief of Guerrillas, so the soldiers fired his house and it is now burning. Just beyond us, a line of our cavalry are chasing what appears to us a dozen mounted guerrillas. They have come in, however, finding only some colored people who say that there is a mounted guerrilla band 200 strong. Whether we will overtake them or not is a question. We have halted to water the train which is quite a job. If I ever get through this march safely I shall feel thankful. If not, I shall never regret having made the attempt for I am no better to suffer than the thousands who die. I think that the privates in the army who have nothing before them but hard marching, poor fare and terrible fighting are entitled to all the unemployed muscle of the North and they will get mine with a good will during this summer. Then if Grant does not take Richmond, I am afraid that I shall be discouraged. I can bear all I have witnessed in this campaign if we are only successful. We have, every day, evidences of the most distinguished gallantry of our troops and I know all they want is a leader and I hope that they will find him in Grant. The bridge over the Matapony is broken and we have to remain here about three hours. We hear the cannons dealing them deadly blows near Hanover Court House. I feel quite anxious to get out to the field but have started upon this Campaign possessing my mind with patience, and so I expect to try to continue. We have moved two or three hundred yards nearer the Matapony, over which the bridge is broken. If we cannot go on it is pleasant to rest. We make up our minds to anything that comes and so are not much disappointed. A few hours later finds us one and a half miles beyond the Matapony River around a poor white woman's house. She and her six children live in the most desolate wilderness. They have been plundered of all their eatables and she seemed forlorn indeed. Her husband died about a year ago. She is the nearest approach to a Union woman I have seen in Virginia. She is like the poor of our own neighborhood, only she wishes it settled in order that she may see better times. We left her plenty of supplies. She treated us the best she could and now we have bid her adieu and are just starting out on another day's tramp, expecting to reach Hanover town. There is continued firing both front and rear, but we have been preserved so far. I hope to reach our Division hospital to-day and see who is wounded. There are two young men belonging to the Sanitary Commission, Mr. Clarence Messer and Charles Wycoff, who try to make the trip agreeable. The latter is a brother-in-law to the gentleman who vacated the Chancellor's house and made his escape with his family to the North.

White House, June 3rd—I arrived at this place yesterday having joined a train of wounded coming from the battle field with Dr. Aiken. We got opposite the White House and found no bridge and were obliged to keep our wounded in ambulance 12 hours longer, making two days and nights they have been loaded and on the way. I have turned wound-dresser and cleaner generally. You can hardly imagine the appearance of our wounded men now brought in from the field, after having been under fire for 20 successive days. They hardly look like men but are extremely hopeful that Richmond will be taken. There are lots of women; but I seem to be still in favour in the 2nd Corps and certainly please the wounded men. Dr. Burmeister is in charge here. Dr. Aiken transports the wounded from the field. Dr. Dudley sends me letters but I do not see him. He is at a Division Hospital in the field. Such fighting never was recorded in any history. I hope the people are behaving in a becoming manner at the North for we are wearing sackcloth here, there is so much suffering. We hear the firing night and day, one continued belching forth of artillery. Miss Willets is here, very sick at present. I think it a cause of great thankfulness that I am preserved in health and strength. Mrs. Lee has a cooking shanty up and is therefore happy. I am not cooking, but have a ward and do everything else, which suits me better. I have no more knowledge whether you fare well or ill at home than if I was in my grave, but I hope that I shall receive letters now if they are directed White House, Virginia, care of the Sanitary Commission.

If any body feels an interest to send anything to me in care of the Sanitary Commission, it would be forwarded. I am certain that if the ladies of the North knew how important pads are to us they would send more than we now get. It is impossible to get beds and blankets sufficient and pads afford us great relief. Remember me to everybody. I am afraid I shall be old and gray by the time you see me again, but if I surrender my life it will not be as valuable as thousands of brave men who are falling hereabouts. Send all I write to Mother immediately with the request that she copy it in ink. I want my letters preserved as I keep no other diary. Give my love to the children. I have met with one loss; my photograph album was stolen or lost in the march and I regret the loss.

From thy sister
C. HANCOCK

BATTLE OF COLD HARBOR:
VIRGINIA, MAY–JUNE 1864

Frank Wilkeson: from Recollections of a Private Soldier in the Army of the Potomac

Lee responded to Grant's crossing of the Pamunkey on May 28 by withdrawing to the south and deploying his army along Totopotomoy Creek about ten miles north of Richmond. The two armies fought at Bethesda Church on May 30 as they extended their lines to the east. On May 31 Union troops captured the crossroads at Cold Harbor, about three miles south of Bethesda Church, and held it against a Confederate counterattack the next morning. An attack by two Union corps on the Confederate lines at Cold Harbor on the evening of June 1 was repulsed after heavy fighting. Both sides sent reinforcements, and by nightfall on June 2 Lee's army was strongly entrenched along a seven mile line extending from north of Bethesda Church to south of Cold Harbor. At 4:30 A.M. on June 3 the Army of the Potomac began a series of frontal assaults that failed to break through Lee's defenses and cost the Union about 7,000 men killed, wounded, or missing, and the Confederates about 1,500; most of the Union casualties were suffered in the first hour of fighting. Frank Wilkeson had run away from his family's Hudson Valley farm during the winter of 1863–64 and enlisted in the 11th New York Light Artillery Battery shortly before he turned sixteen. Wilkeson wrote about Cold Harbor, where his battery was assigned to the artillery brigade of the Second Corps, in an 1887 memoir.

―――――

ON the morning of May 28, 1864, the Second Corps crossed the Pamunkey River. Close by the bridge on which we crossed, and to the right of it, under a tree, stood Generals Grant, Meade, and Hancock, and a little back of them was a group of staff officers. Grant looked tired. He was sallow. He held a dead cigar firmly between his teeth. His face was as expressionless as a pine board. He gazed steadily at the enlisted men as they marched by, as though trying to read their thoughts, and they gazed intently at him. He had the power to send us to our deaths, and we were curious to see him. But the men did not evince the slightest enthusiasm. None cheered him, none saluted him. Grant stood silently looking at his troops and listening to Hancock, who was talking and gesticulating earnestly. Meade stood by Grant's side and thoughtfully stroked his own face. I stepped from the column and filled my canteens in the Pamunkey River, and looked my fill at the generals and their staffs, and then ran by the marching troops through a gantlet of chaff, as "Go it, artillery," "The artillery is advancing," "Hurry to your gun, my son, or the battle will be lost," and similar sarcastically good-natured remarks, which were calculated to stimulate my speed.

During the afternoon we heard considerable firing in front of us, and toward evening we marched over ground where dead cavalrymen were plentifully sprinkled. The blue and the gray lay side by side, and their arms by them. With the Confederates lay muzzle-loading carbines, the ramrods of which worked upward on a swivel hinge fastened near the muzzle of the weapon. It was an awkward arm and far inferior to the Spencer carbine with which our cavalry was armed. There were ancient and ferocious-looking horse-pistols, such as used to grace the Bowery stage, lying by the dead Confederates. The poverty of the South was plainly shown by the clothing and equipment of her dead. These dead men were hardly stiff when we saw them. All of their pockets had been turned inside out. That night, while searching for fresh, clean water, I found several dead cavalrymen in the woods, where they had probably crawled after being wounded. I struck a match so as to see one of these men plainly, and was greatly shocked to see large black beetles eating the corpse. I looked at no more dead men that night.

The next day the sound of battle arose again. At distant points it would break out furiously and then die down. In our immediate front heavy skirmishing was going on, and wounded men began to drift to the rear in search of hospitals. They said that there was a stream of water, swamps, and a line of earthworks, behind which lay the Confederate infantry, in our front, and that we could not get to the works. At no time did the fire rise to a battle's volume; it was simply heavy and continuous skirmishing, in which our men fought at great disadvantage, and were severely handled. Finding that these works were too strong to be taken by assault, Grant moved the army to the left. On June 1st we heard heavy fighting to our left, and that night we learned that a portion of the Sixth Corps, aided by ten thousand of Butler's men from Bermuda Hundreds, had forced the Chickahominy River at a loss of three thousand men, and that they held the ground they had taken. The newsgatherers said that the Confederates were strongly intrenched, and evidently had no intention of fighting in the open. We knew that a bloody battle was close at hand, and instead of being elated the enlisted men were depressed in spirits. That night the old soldiers told the story of the campaign under McClellan in 1862. They had fought over some of the ground we were then camped on. Some of the men were sad, some indifferent; some so tired of the strain on their nerves that they wished they were dead and their troubles over. The infantry knew that they were to be called upon to assault perfect earthworks, and though they had resolved to do their best, there was no eagerness for the fray, and the impression among the intelligent soldiers was that the task cut out for them was more than men could accomplish.

On June 2d the Second Corps moved from the right to the left. We saw many wounded men that day. We crossed a swamp or marched around a swamp, and the battery I belonged to parked in a ravine. There were some old houses on our line of march, but not a chicken or a sheep or a cow to be seen. The land was wretchedly poor. The night of June 2d was spent in getting into battle-line. There was considerable confusion as the infantry marched in the darkness. In our front we could see tongues of flames dart forth from Confederate rifles as their pickets fired in the direction of the noise they heard, and their bullets sang high above our heads. My battery went into position just back of a crest of a hill. Behind us was an alder swamp, where good drinking water gushed forth from many springs. Before we slept we talked with some of the Seventh New York Heavy Artillery, and found that they were sad of heart. They knew that they were to go into the fight early in the morning, and they dreaded the work. The whole army seemed to be greatly depressed the night before the battle of Cold Harbor.

Before daybreak of June 3d the light-artillery men were aroused. We ate our scanty breakfast and took our positions around the guns. All of us were loath to go into action. In front of us we could hear the murmurs of infantry, but it was not sufficiently light to see them. We stood leaning against the cool guns, or resting easily on the ponderous wheels, and gazed intently into the darkness in the direction of the Confederate earthworks. How slowly dawn came! Indistinctly we saw moving figures. Some on foot rearward bound, cowards hunting for safety; others on horseback riding to and fro near where we supposed the battle-lines to be; then orderlies and servants came in from out the darkness leading horses, and we knew that the regimental and brigade commanders were going into action on foot. The darkness faded slowly, one by one the stars went out, and then the Confederate pickets opened fire briskly; then we could see the Confederate earthworks, about six hundred yards ahead of us—could just see them and no more. They were apparently deserted, not a man was to be seen behind them; but it was still faint gray light. One of our gunners looked over his piece and said that he could see the sights, but that they blurred. We filled our sponge buckets with water and waited, the Confederate pickets firing briskly at us the while, but doing no damage. Suddenly the Confederate works were manned. We could see a line of slouch hats above the parapet. Smoke in great puffs burst forth from their line, and shell began to howl by us. Their gunners were getting the range. We sprung in and out from the three-inch guns and replied angrily. To our left, to our right, other batteries opened; and along the Confederate line cannon sent forth their balls searching for the range. Then their guns were silent. It was daylight. We, the light-artillery men, were heated with battle. The strain on our nerves was over. In our front were two lines of blue-coated infantry. One well in advance of the other, and both lying down. We were firing over them. The Confederate pickets sprang out of their rifle pits and ran back to their main line of works. Then they turned and warmed the battery with long-range rifle practice, knocking a man over here, killing another there, breaking the leg of a horse yonder, and generally behaving in an exasperating manner. The Confederate infantry was always much more effective than their artillery, and the battery that got under the fire of their cool infantry always suffered severely. The air began to grow hazy with powder smoke. We saw that the line of slouch-hatted heads had disappeared from the Confederate earthworks, leaving heads exposed only at long intervals. Out of the powder smoke came an officer from the battle-lines of infantry. He told us to stop firing, as the soldiers were about to charge. He disappeared to carry the message to other batteries. Our cannon became silent. The smoke drifted off of the field. I noticed that the sun was not yet up. Suddenly the foremost line of our troops, which were lying on the ground in front of us, sprang to their feet and dashed at the Confederate earthworks at a run. Instantly those works were manned. Cannon belched forth a torrent of canister, the works glowed brightly with musketry, a storm of lead and iron struck the blue line, cutting gaps in it. Still they pushed on, and on, and on. But, how many of them fell! They drew near the earthworks, firing as they went, and then, with a cheer, the first line of the Red Division of the Second Corps (Barlow's) swept over it. And there in our front lay, sat, and stood the second line, the supports; why did not they go forward and make good the victory? They did not. Intensely excited, I watched the portion of the Confederate line which our men had captured. I was faintly conscious of terrific firing to our right and of heavy and continuous cheering on that portion of our line which was held by the Fifth and Sixth Corps. For once the several corps had delivered a simultaneous assault, and I knew that it was to be now or never. The powder smoke curled lowly in thin clouds above the captured works. Then the firing became more and more thunderous. The tops of many battle-flags could be seen indistinctly, and then there was a heavy and fierce yell, and the thrilling battle-cry of the Confederate infantry floated to us. "Can our men withstand the charge?" I asked myself. Quickly I was answered. They came into sight clambering over the parapet of the captured works. All organization was lost. They fled wildly for the protection of their second line and the Union guns, and they were shot by scores as they ran. The Confederate infantry appeared behind their works and nimbly climbed over, as though intent on following up their success, and their fire was as the fury of hell. We manned the guns and drove them to cover by bursting shell. How they yelled! How they swung their hats! And how quickly their pickets ran forward to their rifle pits and sank out of sight! The swift, brave assault had been bravely met and most bloodily repulsed. Twenty minutes had not passed since the infantry had sprung to their feet, and ten-thousand of our men lay dead or wounded on the ground. The men of the Seventh New York Heavy Artillery came back without their colonel. The regiment lost heavily in enlisted men and line officers. Men from many commands sought shelter behind the crest of the hill we were behind. They seemed to be dazed and utterly discouraged. They told of the strength of the Confederate earthworks, and asserted that behind the line we could see was another and stronger line, and all the enlisted men insisted that they could not have taken the second line even if their supports had followed them. These battle-dazed visitors drifted off after a while and found their regiments, but some of them drifted to the rear and to coffee pots. We drew the guns back behind the crest of the hill, and lay down in the sand and waited. I noticed that the sun was now about a half an hour high. Soldiers came to the front from the rear, hunting for their regiments, which had been practically annihilated as offensive engines of war. Occasionally a man fell dead, struck by a stray ball from the picket line. By noon the stragglers were mostly gathered up and had rejoined their regiments, and columns of troops began to move to and fro in our rear in the little valley formed by the alder swamp. A column of infantry marching by fours passed to our right. I watched them, listlessly wondering if they were going to get something to eat, as I was hungry. I saw a puff of smoke between the marchers and myself, heard the report of a bursting shell, and twelve men of that column were knocked to the earth. Their officers shouted, "Close up! close up!" The uninjured men hurriedly closed the gap and marched on. The dead and wounded men lay on the ground, with their rifles scattered among them.

Soon some soldiers came out of the woods and carried the wounded men off, but left the dead where they fell. We buried them that night. Then, as the day wore away, and the troops were well in hand again, I saw staff officers ride along the lines, and then I saw the regimental commanders getting their men into line. About four o'clock in the afternoon I heard the charging commands given. With many an oath at the military stupidity which would again send good troops to useless slaughter, I sprang to my feet and watched the doomed infantry. Men, whom I knew well, stood rifle in hand not more than thirty feet from me, and I am happy to state that they continued to so stand. Not a man stirred from his place. The army to a man refused to obey the order, presumably from General Grant, to renew the assault. I heard the order given, and I saw it disobeyed. Many of the enlisted men had been up to and over the Confederate works. They had seen their strength, and they knew that they could not be taken by direct assault, and they refused to make a second attempt. That night we began to intrench.

By daylight we had our earthwork finished and were safe. The Seventh New York Heavy Artillery, armed as infantry, were intrenched about eighty yards in front of us. We were on the crest of a ridge; they were below us. Behind us, for supports, were two Delaware regiments, their combined strength being about one hundred and twenty men. Back of us was the alder swamp, where springs of cool water gushed forth. The men in front of us had to go to these springs for water. They would draw lots to see who should run across the dangerous, bullet-swept ground that intervened between our earthworks and theirs. This settled, the victim would hang fifteen or twenty canteens around him; then, crouching low in the rifle-pits, he would give a great jump, and when he struck the ground he was running at the top of his speed for our earthwork. Every Confederate sharpshooter within range fired at him. Some of these thirsty men were shot dead; but generally they ran into the earthwork with a laugh. After filling their canteens, they would sit by our guns and smoke and talk, nerving themselves for the dangerous return. Adjusting their burden of canteens, they would go around the end of our works on a run and rush back over the bullet-swept course, and again every Confederate sharpshooter who saw them would fire at them. Sometimes these water-carriers would come to us in pairs. One day two Albany men leaped into our battery. After filling their canteens, they sat with us and talked of the beautiful city on the Hudson, and finally started together for their rifle-pits. I watched through an embrasure, and saw one fall. Instantly he began to dig a little hollow with his hands in the sandy soil, and instantly the Confederate sharpshooters went to work at him. The dust flew up on one side of him, and then on the other. The wounded soldier kept scraping his little protective trench in the sand. We called to him. He answered that his leg was broken below the knee by a rifle ball. From the rifle-pits we heard his comrades call to him to take off his burden of canteens, to tie their strings together, and to set them to one side. He did so, and then the thirsty men in the pits drew lots to see who should risk his life for the water. I got keenly interested in this dicing with death, and watched intently. A soldier sprang out of the rifle-pits. Running obliquely, he stooped as he passed the canteens, grasped the strings, turned, and in a flash was safe. Looking through the embrasure, I saw the dust rise in many little puffs around the wounded man, who was still digging his little trench, and, with quickening breath, felt that his minutes were numbered. I noted a conspicuous man, who was marked with a goitre, in the rifle-pits, and recognized him as the comrade of the stricken soldier. He called to his disabled friend, saying that he was coming for him, and that he must rise when he came near and cling to him when he stopped. The hero left the rifle-pits on the run; the wounded man rose up and stood on one foot; the runner clasped him in his arms; the arms of the wounded man twined around his neck, and he was carried into our battery at full speed, and was hurried to the rear and to a hospital. To the honor of the Confederate sharpshooters, be it said, that when they understood what was being done they ceased to shoot.

One day during this protracted Cold Harbor fight, a battery of Cohorn mortars was placed in position in the ravine behind us. The captain of this battery was a tall, handsome, sweet-voiced man. He spent a large portion of his time in our earthworks, watching the fire of his mortars. He would jump on a gun and look over the works, or he would look out through the embrasures. Boy-like, I talked to him. I would have talked to a field-marshal if I had met one. He told me many things relative to mortar practice, and I, in turn, showed him how to get a fair look at the Confederate lines without exposing himself to the fire of the sharpshooters, most of whom we had "marked down." He playfully accused me of being afraid, and insisted that at six hundred yards a sharpshooter could not hit a man. But I had seen too many men killed in our battery to believe that. So he continued to jump on guns and to poke his head into embrasures. One day I went to the spring after water. While walking back I met four men carrying a body in a blanket. "Who is that?" I asked. "The captain of the mortars," was the reply. Stopping, they uncovered his head for me. I saw where the ball had struck him in the eye, and saw the great hole in the back of his head where it had passed out.

The killed and wounded of the first day's fight lay unburied and uncared for between the lines. The stench of the dead men became unbearable, and finally a flag of truce was sent out. There was a cessation of hostilities to bury the dead and to succor the wounded. I went out to the ground in front of our picket line to talk to the Confederate soldiers, and to trade sugar and coffee for tobacco. Every corpse I saw was as black as coal. It was not possible to remove them. They were buried where they fell. Our wounded—I mean those who had fallen on the first day on the ground that lay between the picket lines—were all dead. I saw no live man lying on this ground. The wounded must have suffered horribly before death relieved them, lying there exposed to the blazing southern sun o' days, and being eaten alive by beetles o' nights.

One day four men carrying a pale infantry-man stopped for an instant in my battery. The wounded man suffered intensely from a wound through the foot. My sympathy was excited for the young fellow, and as we at the moment were doing nothing, I asked for half an hour's leave. Getting it, I accompanied him back into the woods to one of the Second Corps' field hospitals. Here, groaning loudly, he awaited his turn, which soon came. We lifted him on the rude table. A surgeon held chloroform to his nostrils, and under its influence he lay as if in death. The boot was removed, then the stocking, and I saw a great ragged hole on the sole of the foot where the ball came out. Then I heard the coatless surgeon who was making the examination cry out, "The cowardly whelp!" So I edged around and looked over the shoulders of an assistant surgeon, and saw that the small wound on the top of the foot, where the ball entered, was blackened with powder! I, too, muttered "The coward" and was really pleased to see the knife and saw put to work and the craven's leg taken off below the knee. He was carried into the shade of a tree, and left there to wake up. I watched the skilful surgeons probe and carve other patients. The little pile of legs and arms grew steadily, while I waited for the object of my misplaced sympathy to recover his senses. With a long breath he opened his eyes. I was with him at once, and looked sharply at him. I will never forget the look of horror that fastened on his face when he found his leg was off. Utter hopelessness and fear that look expressed. I entered into conversation with him; and he, weakened and unnerved by the loss of the leg, and the chloroform, for once told the truth. Lying on his back, he aimed at his great toe, meaning to shoot it off; but being rudely joggled by a comrade at the critical instant, his rifle covered his foot just below the ankle, and an ounce ball went crashing through the bones and sinews. The wound, instead of being a furlough, was a discharge from the army, probably into eternity. Our guns at the front began to howl at the Confederates again, and I was forced to leave the hospital. So I hastened back to my guns. The utter contempt of the surgeons, their change from careful handling to almost brutality, when they discovered the wound was self-inflicted, was bracing to me. I liked it, and rammed home the ammunition in gun No. 1 with vim.

Constantly losing men in our earthwork, shot not in fair fight, but by sharpshooters, we all began to loathe the place. At last, one afternoon the captain ordered us to level the cornhills between the battery and the road, so that we could withdraw the guns without making a noise. At once understanding that a flank movement was at hand, we joyfully gathered up shovels and spades, and went at the obstructions with a will. No. 3 of No. 1 gun, an Albany man, was at my side. I was bent over shovelling. I straightened myself up. He leaned over to sink his shovel, pitched forward in a heap, dead, and an artilleryman beyond him clasped his stomach and howled a death howl. No. 3 was shot from temple to temple. The ball passed through his head and hit the other man in the stomach, fatally wounding him. They were the last men our battery lost at Cold Harbor.

That evening the horses were brought up, and all the guns but mine, No. 1, were taken off. We sat and watched them disappear in the darkness. Soon heavy columns of infantry could be indistinctly seen marching by the alder swamp in our rear. Then all was quiet, excepting the firing of the pickets. We sat and waited for the expected advance of the Confederates; but they did not come. Towards midnight an officer rode into the earthwork and asked lowly who was in command. The sergeant stepped forward and received his orders. Turning to us he whispered, "Limber to the rear." Silently the horses swung around. The gun was limbered, and, with the caisson in the lead, we pulled out of the earthwork, slowly drove across the cornfield, struck into a dusty road in the forest, and marched for the James River and the bloody disasters that awaited us beyond that beautiful stream.

"BORN ANEW IN BLOOD AND TEARS":
NEW YORK, JUNE 1864

Maria Lydig Daly: Diary, June 8, 1864

The daughter of a wealthy New York family of Dutch-German ancestry, Maria Lydig Daly supported the war effort through her contributions to the Women's Central Association for Relief and other charitable activities. Her husband, Charles P. Daly, was an Irish-American Catholic active in Democratic politics who served as chief judge of the New York City Court of Common Pleas (the highest court in the city). She wrote about the news of Grant's campaign in Virginia.

June 8, 1864

I have so much to do and think of that I forget my diary, which, in such momentous times, is a *crime* against myself. Should I live to be an old lady, I shall deeply regret this.

Grant's success has been certain but slow; the enemy has been fighting every inch of the way. I had a letter from Badeau from the front, written in pencil, breathing the utmost confidence in the army, its leader, and the final success which, as he speaks from accurate knowledge, cannot but give us the greatest confidence. Both armies fight with the greatest bravery. Frank Barlow has again greatly distinguished himself, and Grant has recommended him to a major generalship. We have lost some of our best generals—Wadsworth, Sedgwick, Rice, and thousands of heroes whose names are known but to their sorrowing families. Our nationality will be born anew in blood and tears, but we trust it will rise purified and ennobled. On Saturday last, a meeting was called in Union Square in which the Judge took a prominent part to thank and encourage our soldiers and General-in-Chief. It was crowded and enthusiastic. The Judge wrote the resolutions and read them, making very judicious opening remarks, full of point and very practical, counseling moderation and good statesmanship.

I have been very busy lately in the Women's Patriotic League for Diminishing the Use of Imported Luxuries. I think it will succeed, although some of the ladies wish to push it forward much too fast. The manufacturers say they have not enough hands to fill the orders they already have, so we cannot now force people to buy what is not to be had, but must go to work gradually and systematically. I shall have some trouble to subdue the zeal of Miss Mary Hamilton and Miss Schuyler. I plainly see they have made me president but wish to rule themselves. I shall have to give my opinion officially, and I am afraid of Miss Mary. I must try and write out my views upon the subject.

Yesterday the Judge came home after being treated by some Irish gentlemen fresh from home who, it seems, were enthusiastic about him, telling him that no one in Ireland is so popular as himself. The poor Judge was almost abashed by their praises and compliments.

Maggie is at home. We are polite to each other and no more. She is sweet upon the Judge.

"THE WORK OF DEATH": GEORGIA, JUNE 1864

Robert Patrick to Alonzo Lewis

After the Union defeat at Pickett's Mill, Georgia, on May 27 Sherman abandoned his attempt to outflank Johnston at Dallas and began to maneuver his forces back toward the Chattanooga–Atlanta railroad. By June 6 most of Sherman's troops were resting around Acworth, four miles southeast of Allatoona, while Union engineers rebuilt the railroad bridge across the Etowah River and Confederate forces occupied the high ground to the north and west of Marietta. A bookkeeper before the war, Robert Patrick had enlisted in the 4th Louisiana Infantry in 1861, fought at Shiloh, and served under Johnston in the Vicksburg campaign before becoming a quartermaster's clerk in the brigade (later division) commanded by Brigadier General James Cantey. He wrote about the campaign in Georgia to a friend in Clinton, Louisiana.

In Camp near Atlanta, Georgia
June 9, 1864

Dear Friend,

I have frequently heard it said that there is a wide and beaten road leading to an inhospitable region, where fuel is furnished gratis and a man to stir up the chunks in the bargain, that is paved with the best quality of an article denominated "Good Intentions." My intentions to write have been good, but you know that if I do not turn into a road that is macadamized that I will never reach the place that we all desire to find, therefore, the highway of good intentions is here-by ignored and I leave this beaten track for one covered with rocks of "Practice" and "Execution."

I am now and have been ever since last winter, a clerk in the office of Major Woolfolk, Quartermaster in Cantey's Division. I have got along very well with him, though he is very inattentive to business and drinks to excess. This negligence of his and his dissipated habits will, unless he changes his mode of life, certainly lead to ruin.

I think I hear you exclaim—"He sees the beam in the eye of

another, but he does not discern the mote in his own!" But here you are wrong, for I see both, and of the two, the mote is the larger and is to me the most troublesome, and in the future, if I live, I shall use the utmost exertion to eradicate it, and if God is willing with due diligence and watchfullness, I will prevent its ever obstructing my morals ever again.

I have troubles and petty annoyances too numerous to mention with drunken, uncivil, ungentlemanly officers and ignorant, ill-bred and contentious men, who criticize and pass judgment upon matters of which they are totally ignorant and have not the capacity ever to learn. These are small matters, but you know it is the little things which constitute the sum of a man's exactness.

A soldier's life is that of a slave's, or worse, for he must act as the slave does while at the same time he is possessed of greater sensibility than the slave and his toils and sufferings are not confined to the physical man alone.

I hope this war will close soon, and I have made up my mind that this is the last year of the "Reign of Terror." So fully am I convinced of this, that I am even now making my arrangements for the future, as though it were a foregone conclusion. If I am right, it places me in a better position, and if I am wrong, there is no harm done. You will probably wish to know my reasons for being so sanguine.

Well, I do not know that I can give any really good reason for my opinion. Instead of drawing my conclusions as most persons do, by the slow process of deduction, I have discovered a shorter and easier method, to wit:

I *jump at it*. Taking for my stepping-stones, the precarious and critical condition of the financial affairs of the North, which, as sure as fate, will come down with a grand crash, and the aspect of political affairs which are very unsettled and are now being stirred up, as the Dutchman says, "mit a stick." I make a jump into the future, land in the middle of the month of January, 1865, and if at that time I do not have in my pocket a document showing that I have been mustered out of the Confederate Service, or that I shortly will be, then am I no prophet nor a son of a prophet.

I have been no nearer Dalton than Resaca, which is 16 miles south of that point. When the enemy first made his appearance at Resaca, there was only one brigade of Cantey's Division, consisting of three regiments and one battery there, though there were some guns placed in batteries on the heights overlooking the town. This force succeeded in checking the Yankees until reinforcements arrived, which by-the-way, did not come a moment too soon, for I verily believe that Johnston barely missed being caught in a bad box, and whatever may be said to the contrary, I shall always think that it was nothing more than sheer good luck and the lack of enterprise on the part of the Yankees that his communication was not cut off. I know that the wires were cut between Dalton and Resaca and all dispatches were sent by couriers.

On Saturday afternoon and Sunday, the hardest fighting occurred, after which we evacuated the place, burning the bridges after us. We lost some guns and a considerable quantity of stores, and some of the men were forced to swim the river (Oostanaula) to escape capture. The order was well made without a doubt, though I am no military man and not capable of criticizing military movements. I have ventured to give you my ideas of what occurred there.

The order has been well conducted through-out and I do not believe that any General except Johnston could have effected it without serious loss. Sherman's plan seems to be to flank us all the time; although Johnston has offered him battle time and again, he invariably declines it, and sets to work at his wire-pulling gun. The two armies are now confronting each other, each maneuvering for a pass. Sherman is massing his men on our right and has planted his troops on the Altoona Mountains. I presume his intention is to form a new base of operation at the Etowah River.

The citizens all along the line of our march had pulled up root and branch, and removed with all their personnel. Folks farther south say that there is not much falling into the hands of the enemy.

The armies are doing nothing now. I say doing nothing for unless there is a heavy fight, we always say there is nothing going on, but there are many killed and wounded every hour, for even if there is no heavy engagement the skirmish is kept up night and day, and the work of death goes on the while like the current of the flowing river, slow and even sometimes, and at others, as rapid as a catarack. There is not a day passes now that many victims are not offered up at the sacred shrine of Southern Liberty and every breeze brings the roar of the artillery.

The morale of the army was never better than it is now and the men are sanguine of success and their confidence in Johnston is undiminished. I will venture to say that if Bragg had conducted this order, that he would now have had a discontented and demoralized army. It has been remarked by everybody that there is less straggling than ever was known before, and every man is at the post assigned him.

I see that General Pemberton has been promoted down hill. He is now in the regiment, a Lieutenant Colonel of Artillery. If they would give the man that never won a battle (Bragg) the same rank and get him out of the way of better men, I think it very probable that our forces would be more prosperous. I did not know until the other day that the 4th Regiment was up here, my impression being that they were still at Mobile. They have been in a pretty heavy engagement and lost between 20 and 30 men.

General Quarles speaks in very high terms of the regiment and says it is the best in the service.

Give my compliments to Mrs. Lewis. When you write, address your letter to the care of Major Woolfolk, Quarter-Master Cantey Brigade, Polks Corps, Atlanta, Georgia.

Your friend,
s/Rob. D. P.

RUINED PLANTATIONS: VIRGINIA, JUNE 1864
Judith W. McGuire: Diary, June 11, 1864

Judith W. McGuire had fled her home in Alexandria, where her husband was the principal of the Episcopal High School of Virginia, in May 1861 when the town was occupied by Union troops. In February 1862 the McGuires settled in Richmond, where she later found work as a clerk in the Confederate commissary department. She wrote in her diary about the fate of Westwood, the estate of her brother, Dr. William S. R. Brockenbrough, and Summer Hill, the home of her nephew's widow, Mary Newton. Both plantations were located south of the Pamunkey River near Hanovertown, Virginia, and were occupied by Union cavalry on May 27.

11th.—Just heard from W. and S. H. Both places in ruins, except the dwelling-houses. Large portions of the Federal army were on them for eight days. S. H. was used as a hospital for the wounded brought from the battle-fields; this protected the house. At W. several generals had their head-quarters in the grounds near the house, which, of course, protected it. General Warren had his tent in the "shrubbery" for two days, General Burnside for a day or two, and those of lesser rank were there from time to time. General Grant was encamped at S. H. for a time. Dr. B. was at home, with several Confederate wounded from the battle of "Haw's Shop" in the house. Being absent a mile or two from home when they arrived, they so quickly threw out pickets, spread their tents over the surrounding fields and hills, that he could not return to his house, where his wife and only child were alone, until he had obtained a pass from a Yankee officer. As he approached the house, thousands and tens of thousands of horses and cattle were roaming over the fine wheat fields on his and the adjoining estate, (that of his niece, Mrs. N.,) which were now ripe for the sickle. The clover fields and fields of young corn were sharing the same fate. He found his front porch filled with officers. They asked him of his sentiments with regard to the war. He told them frankly that he was an original Secessionist, and ardently hoped to see the North and South separate and distinct nations now and forever. One of them replied that he "honoured his candour," and from that moment he was treated with great courtesy. After some difficulty he was allowed to keep his wounded Confederates, and in one or two instances the Federal surgeons assisted him in dressing their wounds. At S. H. the parlour was used for an amputating room, and Yankee blood streamed through that beautiful apartment and the adjoining passage. Poor M. had her stricken heart sorely lacerated in every way, particularly when her little son came running in and nestled up to her in alarm. A soldier had asked him, "Are you the son of Captain Newton, who was killed in Culpeper?" "Yes," replied the child. "Well, I belong to the Eighth Illinois, and was one of the soldiers that fired at him when he fell," was the barbarous reply.

On these highly cultivated plantations not a fence is left, except mutilated garden enclosures. The fields were as free from vegetation after a few days as the Arabian desert; the very roots seemed eradicated from the earth. A fortification stretched across W., in which were embedded the fence rails of that and the adjoining farms. Ten thousand cavalry were drawn up in line of battle for two days on the two plantations, expecting the approach of the Confederates; bands of music were constantly playing martial airs in all parts of the premises; and whiskey flowed freely. The poor servants could not resist these intoxicating influences, particularly as Abolition preachers were constantly collecting immense crowds, preaching to them the cruelty of the servitude which had been so long imposed upon them, and that Abraham Lincoln was the Moses sent by God to deliver them from the "land of Egypt and the house of bondage," and to lead them to the promised land. After the eight days were accomplished, the army moved off, leaving not a quadruped, except two pigs, which had ensconced themselves under the ruins of a servant's house, and perhaps a dog to one plantation; to the other, by some miraculous oversight, two cows and a few pigs were left. Not a wheeled vehicle of any kind was to be found; all the grain, flour, meat, and other supplies were swept off, except the few things hid in those wonderful places which could not be fathomed even by the "Grand Army." Scarcely a representative of the sons and daughters of

Africa remained in that whole section of country; they had all gone to Canaan, by way of York River, Chesapeake Bay, and the Potomac—not dry-shod, for the waters were not rolled back at the presence of these modern Israelites, but in vessels crowded to suffocation in this excessively warm weather. They have gone to homeless poverty, an unfriendly climate, and hard work; many of them to die without sympathy, for the invalid, the decrepit, and the infant of days have left their houses, beds, and many comforts, the homes of their birth, the masters and mistresses who regarded them not so much as property as humble friends and members of their families. Poor, deluded creatures! I am grieved not so much on account of the loss of their services, though that is excessively inconvenient and annoying, but for their grievous disappointment. Those who have trades, or who are brought up as lady's maids or house servants, may do well, but woe to the masses who have gone with the blissful hope of idleness and free supplies! We have lost several who were great comforts to us, and others who were sources of care, responsibility, and great expense. These particulars from W. and S. H. I have from our nephew, J. P., who is now a scout for General W. H. F. Lee. He called by to rest a few hours at his uncle's house, and says he would scarcely have known the barren wilderness. The Northern officers seemed disposed to be courteous to the ladies, in the little intercourse which they had with them. General Ferrara, who commanded the negro troops, was humane, in having a coffin made for a young Confederate officer who died in Dr B's house, and was kind in other respects. The surgeons, too, assisted in attending to the Confederate wounded. An officer one morning sent for Mrs. N. to ask her where he should place a box of French china for safety; he said that some soldiers had discovered it buried in her garden, dug it up and opened it, but he had come up at this crisis and had placed a guard over it, and desired to know where she wished it put. A place of safety of course was not on the premises, but she had it taken to her chamber. She thanked him for his kindness. He seemed moved, and said, "Mrs. N., I will do what I can for you, for I cannot be too thankful that my wife is not in an invaded country." She then asked him how he could, with his feelings, come to the South. He replied that he was in the regular army, and was obliged to come. Many little acts of kindness were done at both houses, which were received in the spirit in which they were extended. *Per contra:* On one occasion Miss D., a young relative of Mrs. N's, was in one of the tents set aside for the Confederate wounded, writing a letter from a dying soldier to his friends at home. She was interrupted by a young Yankee surgeon, to whom she was a perfect stranger, putting his head in and remarking pertly, "Ah, Miss D., are you writing? Have you friends in Richmond! I shall be there in a few days, and will with pleasure take your communications." She looked up calmly into his face, and replied, "Thank you; *I* have no friends in the Libby!" It was heard by his comrades on the outside of the tent, and shouts and peals of laughter resounded at the expense of the discomfited surgeon. The ladies frequently afterwards heard him bored with the question, "Doctor, when do you go to the Libby?"

"MISERABLE LONG DREARY DAYS":
VIRGINIA, JUNE 1864

Charles Harvey Brewster to Mattie Brewster

The opposing armies remained in close contact at Cold Harbor for more than a week after the failed Union assault on June 3, with skirmishing, sharpshooting, and artillery fire taking its toll of casualties on both sides. Lieutenant Brewster of the 10th Massachusetts Infantry wrote to his sister about the fieldworks built by Union troops and the strain caused by the continual fighting.

Head Quarters 10th Mass Vols In a Bomb Proof
June 11th 1864

Dear Mattie,

I received yesterday your welcome letter of June 7th and am very much obliged to you all for writing so frequently for these are miserable long dreary days for even the bullets now fail to furnish cause for attention or a remark as they go singing by our ears, or whack into the trees around us.

I wish I could furnish you a description that would convey to you any idea of the place where I am now sitting to you but I do not believe I can. it is on top of a ridge or hill and forms part of our line of battle. there is a square place dug out about a foot deep on the sloping side away from the enemy and on the edge of this is built up a double row of pine logs in this form. and the space between is filled with sand. the space between the logs is about 4 feet wide and it is about six feet high over this are placed poles covered with branches of trees to protect us from the sun. across the corner of this runs the rifle pit over the hills and through the ravines. the rifle pit is more properly the breastwork is built of logs laid one above the other to the height of about 4 feet and earth piled up against these upon the side towards the enemy in this lie the men all day and all night with equipments on and musket at hand ready to spring up at any moment and repel any attack of the enemy. in front of us is another breastwork running parallel to this and distant about 30 yards this is the front or first line of battle ours is the 2nd line in front of this about 20 or 30 yards are dug little holes in the ground with the earth thrown up towards the enemy and there lie the sharpshooters and skirmishers. they lie in these little holes, in the sun all day long and can only be relieved after dark and continually crack away at any head they can see across the open field in front at a distance varying from 50 to 200 yards. the enemy return these compliments continually and so we eat sleep and drink with the continual cracking of all sorts of firearms day and night. the bullets come singing whistling or humming some making more, some less noise, patting against the outside of our mimic fort, or whack into the pine and oak trees, and occasionally thug into the body limbs or head of some poor blue coat for the men cannot be kept lying still but get up and move about with a most supreme indifference to these messages of death. we know when one gets hit by an occasional Oh, or a groan. he is picked up and carried off to the hospitals in the rear by stretcher bearers perhaps to die perhaps to have his arm or leg cut off or perhaps to be fixed up and lie round a few days and come back and begin the same life over again.

Along the line is occasionally a heavy fort of earth provided with one two or more guns as its position or the circumstances warrant and in these lie the Cannoniers all day long watching enemys lines and occasionally he jumps up, says fire, and another Cannonier pulls a little string and bang goes the gun followed by the rush of the shot shell or cannister and the crashing through the trees and limbs in the woods on the enemys side and if it is a shell the dull report of its bursting to the damage of numerous grey backs as we fondly hope, but probably do very little damage to anyone. these higher compliments are also returned at intervals by the enemy, and so the work and war goes on. We came up here last night about half past one o'clock taking position considerably to the left of the one we have been holding for 8 or 9 days past, in consequence of the stretching out and thinning of our line. the 6th 18th + 9th Wrights Smiths and Burnsides Corps are now holding the line which has heretofore been held by them and the 2nd + 5th Corps the two latter have been withdrawn and have gone off on some mysterious expedition probably to our left of which you will probably hear sooner than I shall.

Meantime we possess our souls with what patience we can for 10 days longer. I wrote to Mother two or three days ago and told her it would probably be my last letter, I begin to fear that I may have to stay after the Regt goes home. I do not know what to do if I had anything to do when I came home I should try and see if I could not get away anyhow but I do not know as I can get any employment if I came home and I might have to enlist as a private soldier again for my daily bread, which I should dread to do worse than anything but *sawing wood*. But I am very much worried to hear that Mother is so ill both from you and Mary and am now sorry that I signified any willingness to reenter the service. besides if I staid I should have to give up my horse and I feel that I could not stand it a great while as a foot soldier. However, perhaps I shall not be called upon to stay at all I hope not. the 7th Mass Regt goes out in 3 days and I can judge better by what they do with thier Officers. it is impossible to get any information in advance and they keep all the Regiments on the line of battle until thier time is out to the last moment. You ask why they do not put the Negroes in the fights I imagine that they do not amount to any certain sum in a fight and in such tough battles as we have it will not do often times to put in troops which you cannot depend upon. another reason I presume is because the Rebels show them no mercy if captured and our government is too weak to protect them and compel fair usage for them, but if they do not save any lives of white men they add considerably to the strength of the army for they can do many of the duties in the rear which white soldiers once had to do. But though I have seen accounts of thier fighting in the Northern papers I do not believe they have been in any fight at all. still I may be mistaken as they are all in the Burnsides Corps and we see but little of them.

Tell Mary I received her letter at the same time I did yours and will answer it soon. I have written you quite a long letter as I had plenty of time nothing to do but lie around and dodge bullets. Give my love to Mother Mary Thomas and Charlie and my respects to all enquiring friends With much love

Your aff brother
Charlie.

COMPLETING "THE GREAT IDEA":
LONDON, JUNE 1864

Charles Francis Adams to Charles Francis Adams Jr.

The grandson of John Adams and son of John Quincy Adams, Charles Francis Adams had served as U.S. minister to Great Britain since May 1861. He wrote about the historical significance of the war to his son, who was still serving with the cavalry guard at the headquarters of the Army of the Potomac.

Charles F Adams Jr.

London *17 June* 1864

My Dear Charles

As I write the date, my mind very naturally recurs to the time when, as a people, we were first subjected to the baptism of blood, under the necessity of maintaining a great idea. The sufferings of that period, terrible as they proved, were amply compensated for by the blessings enjoyed by the generation succeeding. One slight precaution only was neglected, or its importance undervalued. The consequences we now see and feel in the events that are passing in front of Richmond. As I read the sad accounts of the losses experienced by both sides in the strife, the warning words of Jefferson will ring in my ears— "I tremble for my country, when I reflect that God is just." The moral evil which we consented to tolerate for a season has become a terrific scourge, that brings the life blood at every instant of its application. How long this chastisement is to be continued, it is idle to attempt to predict. Only one thing is clear to me, and that is the paramount duty to future generations of not neglecting again to remove the source of that evil. It is this that completes the great idea for which the first struggle was endured. It is this, and this only that will compensate for the calamities that attend the second. There is not an event that takes place in the slaveholding states that does not confirm me in the conviction that the social system they have fostered has become a standing menace to the peace of America. The very ferocity and endurance with which they fight for their bad principle only contribute to prove the necessity of extirpating it in its very root. This is not simply for the good of America but likewise for that of the civilised world. The sympathy elicited in Europe with this rotten cause, among the aristocratic and privileged classes, is a sufficient proof of the support which wrongful power hopes to obtain from its success. For these reasons, painful as is the alternative, I am reconciled to the continuance of the fearful horror of this strife. Looking back on the progress made since we began, it is plain to my mind that the issue, if persevered in, can terminate only in one way. There is not a moment in which the mere force of gravitation does not incline one scale of the balance more and more at the expense of the other. In resistance to this neither labor nor skill will in the long run avail. The laws of nature are uniform—The question with the South is only of more or less of annihilation by delay. Yet I cannot conceal from myself the nature of the penalty which all of us are equally to pay for our offence before God. If the great trial have the effect of purifying and exalting us in futurity, we as a nation may yet be saved. The labor of extricating us from our perils will devolve upon the young men of the next generation who shall have passed in safety through this fiery furnace. I am now too far advanced to be able to hope to see the day of restoration, if it shall come. But it may be reserved for some of my children—indeed for you if it please God, you survive the dangers of the hour. Great will be the responsibility that devolves upon you! May you acquit yourselves of it with honor and success! The great anniversary has inspired me to write you in this strain. I feel that even at this moment events may be happening in America which will make the memory of it still more dear to the lovers of human liberty and free Institutions all over the world. I accept the omen. May it be verified!

In this old world to which I now turn there is less to stimulate the imagination or to rouse the hopes of the observer. The contention here is now not so much for principle as place. The Conservative-liberal wishes to obtain the office held by the Liberal-conservative. The juggle of names only signifies that neither is in earnest. The day is one of truce between ideas. "Jeshurun has waxed fat"—And the octogenarian leader who represents him, like old Maurepas in anterevolutionary France, thinks to settle every difference with a joke. Such men thrive in periods of transition. But the time is coming when all these frivolities will pass away, and the great national problem of privilege only to the select few will come up and demand a stern solution. Goodbye. God bless you

yr aff father
CFA.

FIGHTING THE ALABAMA:
THE ENGLISH CHANNEL, JUNE 1864

Charles B. Fisher: Diary, June 19–21, 1864

A bark-rigged sailing ship equipped with an auxiliary steam engine, the *Alabama* was built at the Laird shipyard in Liverpool. She left port on July 29, 1862, and was armed with eight guns off the Azores before being commissioned as a Confederate warship on August 24. Over the next twenty-two months the *Alabama* sank a Union gunboat off Texas and captured or burned sixty-four American whalers and merchant ships in the Atlantic, Gulf of Mexico, Indian Ocean, and the East Indies, becoming the most destructive commerce raider in the Confederate navy. On June 11, 1864, she sailed into Cherbourg, France, for much-needed repairs to her hull and engine. News of her arrival quickly reached the U.S.S. *Kearsarge*, a steam sloop armed with seven guns, at the Dutch port of Flushing, and the Union ship reached Cherbourg on June 14. Raphael Semmes, the captain of the *Alabama*, decided to risk battle in order to avoid being blockaded in port, and on June 19 sailed out to fight in international waters. Although the *Kearsarge* had been patrolling European waters and the North Atlantic for Confederate raiders since 1862, her battle with the *Alabama* would be the first time she saw action. Charles B. Fisher had signed onto the *Kearsarge* in February 1862 and served as a novice seaman, officer's cook, and steward. He was one of fifteen black sailors in a crew of about 160 men.

June 19th: 1864: Battle

Off the land twelve miles. The morning is thick and hazy. The shore is scarcely distinguishable. There is all the preparations being made for our Sabbath Day devotions. Inspection at quarters at ten oclock after which we are all waiting to hear the Church bell toll. At ten minutes after ten the fore top man at the mast head sang out—Steamer under the land! Standing out! That's the Alabama, said the quarter master. We all were anxious to catch a glimpse of her before going into battle. The bell sounded fire quarters and the boys were to be seen tumbling down the forecastle ladders—fore rigging Jacobs Ladders & c trying who could be first at their quarters. She was coming straight out for us and we were all ready for the conflict in just three minutes. Decks sanded down. Batteries cast loose and manned. Magazines opened & all reported ready. Go ahead fast, said the Captain. The Alabama was now about two miles distant and coming on fast. Lay down! Every man, said the Captain, and down we all lay flat on the deck. And now as I lay down not knowing how soon I might be killed or maimed for life I thought of home and how I had been neglected by those who should have been all in all to me. My thoughts were bitter, bitter scenes long since forgotten came back to my memory as vividly as if they were being enacted now. Friends and those who were dear to me came before me and I wondered if any of them could know my situation now. Would they feel my sorrow or think kindly of me after I was no more. These and many other thoughts went through my mind swift as lightning. I also thought of Bud and prayed that he might not get hurt in any way. But no time was now given for thoughts or feelings. The Alabama had now opened fire with her starboard battery. Distance one thousand yards. The shell were flying screaming through our rigging and bursting far astern of us. She fired seven times. We keeping head on to her and going full speed. At the seventh shot the 30 pound rifle parrott on our forecastle paid our compliments to her and down came her flag. The gaff was shot away—we still going ahead—she broadside too. She fired five more shot. None of her shot had as yet struck us. We were not quite near her and our helm was put hard a starboard and our noble ship came up beautifully and showed her an awful battery with no men but the Marines on the forecastle. "Ready." "Fire," and our two eleven inch three broadsides & rifle pivot sent death and destruction aboard her. We kept around in a circle and it seemed strange how cooly our men now faced her fire amidst the groans of the dying and cusses of the wounded. Around went the Kearsarge—the Alabama keeping up a hot fire upon us. We could see the shell and solid shot coming and some of them would pass so close that the hot wind from them would puff in our faces. Still nobody hurt aboard of us. One shot had now struck our rudder post and another went through our smoke stack. To those who have never heard the whistle of a shell there is something unearthly and terrible in the sound. One is led to imagine that all the devils in hell are let loose to play around ones ears. The conflict had now lasted half an hour and our boys had commenced to warm to their work. Everytime the Alabama fired a broadside we could see the shot and shell coming at us and everyone of us would drop flat on deck seeking the protection of the water ways. In this way a good many lives were saved from the passing balls. As soon as her shot passed our boys were up in a minute and had our guns loaded & fired before she could again bring her guns to bear. We were steaming fast around her in a circle all the time and they fired two shots to our one, but our boys were cool and took deliberate aim and then fired and we could see the shell pass clean through her and burst on the other side. Our second broadside. Every shell done its work—we could see the splinters and coal dust fly in every direction. The battle had now lasted three quarters of an hour and she commenced to set sail and try to escape to the French coast—seeing which our boys sent up cheer after cheer which made the ship fairly shake—and the battle raged fiercer than ever. One of her shell now struck our engine house and explodings wounded three men two severely and one not. The Chief Engineer Mr. Cushman also had a narrow escape at this time. The Captain also narrowly escaped but was pushed down by Clem Johnson who pushed him down out of the way. A shell from our forward pivot 11 inch now exploded right in her stern carrying away the stern—breaking her fan and killing the men at the wheel also wounding Capt. Semmes and a great number more. She now became perfectly unmanageable and we came around on her port side and pound in a murderous fire of shot and shell and the sight was awful and sublime. The execution was terrible. We came up again intending to rake her decks fore & aft which would have killed or wounded every soul on her. But she fired three *Sea Guns* and haul down her flag. The order passed *Cease Firing*. The battle had been fought and won in one hour and ten minutes. Her boat was not coming toward us but we noticed her settling down and made all haste to lower out boats to save the wounded and survivors. But before our boats could get to her she gave a wild leap forward, threw her bow high in air and went down stern first. It was painful to see her men as they jumped into the sea to meet a watery grave or threw their arms wildly above their heads to cry for help.

We who one moment before would have cut them down to a man, now strained every nerve and made every effort to save them. A perfect sea of heads could now be seen floating on the surface, some clinging to the pieces of wreck or such frail support as they could find. Our boats—that is two of them were picking them up as fast as they could, but numbers of the wounded were sinking fast. The English Yacht *Deerhound* now came up and assisted us in picking up the drowning men, but she did not pick up many. She got Semmes and steamed away to Southampton. We did not follow her but continued to pick up the men. Several French pilots now came up and saved eight men all together. The French iron clad "Corunne" did not lend any assistance. The sight was pitiful to see them dragged half drowned on board the ship with no clothing on and all with the "shivers" from being so long in the water. We gave them dry clothes and rubbed them in blankets to bring them too, and the wounded were carried below and received the same attention from our surgeon that our own did. Her surgeon was killed and her assistant was brought on board us and assisted our surgeon to care for the wounded. We picked up 42 not wounded and eleven wounded and three dead. One of the latter was the carpenter Robinson of New Orleans. Of her crew of one hundred and fifty—only eighty were saved all told. The rest went down with their ship. On our side John W. Dempsey, quarter gunner, lost his right arm. William Gowan, seaman, leg broken in two places. James Macbeth, seaman, wounded in the calf of his leg. None were killed on our ship and except a splitting head ache I was neither frightened nor hurt. We now broke our three flags at the mast heads in token of the great victory we had won. We commenced fighting at the same time people at home were going to church and ended as the minister completed his sermon. We are all too busy now to think of our success but we know the weight of the service we have now rendered our country and will impatiently await the news from home. At two oclock we stood away for the port of Cherbourg and left the Alabama down—down 200 fathoms in her watery home beneath the waves. We came to anchor in the harbor at 3½ oc and sent the wounded ashore to the French hospital. The Kearsarge was struck twenty eight times in her hull and rigging and received no damage but what can be repaired in a few hours. The shore is lined with anxious people and boats are coming off to see us. The French admiral has sent two launches to help convey the wounded men ashore and they are now alongside. The blood from the wounded Pirates covers our berth deck and their groans are awful to hear as they lay dying on our deck. Scarcely five hours have elapsed since they left this port in their noble cruiser hoping to capture the U.S. Sloop Kearsarge and murder her crew. As they said before going into action they would show us no quarter, but the Lord protected us and their fate was sealed.

June 20th: Cherbourg. After the Battle

Up this morning bright and early to remove the blood from our decks and put the ship to rights again. After Holy stones and sand and plenty of fresh water was freely used at 8 ock every vestage of the conflict was removed except the gap in our smoke stack and the dead on the quarter deck. We all feel the effect of the heavy firing being very sore and stiff and head ache. While the battle waged fiercest our little dog *Mose* would run out from under the Forecastle and pick up the splinters in his mouth and run in again. It was evidently good fun for him. The other dogs run away and hid when the firing commenced. Another incident of the fight but more terrible was when our second shell busted aboard of her. It was just in the midst of her rifle guns crew and out of a crew of ten men it killed eight dead. A quick as a flash another rifle shell from us struck a man on her Knight head taking out all of his stomach. He run to the starboard gangway and there fell down on a pile of the wounded and died. The same shell cut two other men completely in two and exploded beyond her. They all say our firing was just as accurate as target practise and did terrible execution and that we may be glad we did not see her decks before she went down as the sight was sickening in the extreme. She was perfectly riddled fore and aft. One shot passed clean through her.

June 21st: After the Battle

Just after she went down Tom Holloway and myself pulled

one poor fellow out of the boat that was very nearly gone. We carried him down below and after rubbing him with towels & blankets brought him too. The first thing he said was. Oh! Boys you showed us no quarter. They told us you would not and you didn't. We did fire into five times after her flag was first struck, but they continued firing after the flag was struck—and as we had shot it away three times and it had been put up again, when the flag was hauled down we did not know it. One thing we knew if we had fell into their hands not one of us would have been left to tell the tale as they had sworn to show us no quarter and the hatred between us previous to the battle was very bitter. But now we have nothing against them and our kindness have quite won their esteem. While our boats were picking them up in our boats three or four jumped out and swam to the Deerhound. They were terror stricken and many would rather have drowned than come on board our ship—to me as they thought a worse fate. One little messenger boy came over the gangway crying bitterly and it was some time before the 1st Lieut. could pacify him. The other was saucy and defiant and didn't care whether he lived or died. Many other incidents occured during the fight.

BATTLE OF PETERSBURG: VIRGINIA, JUNE 1864
Wilbur Fisk to
The Green Mountain Freeman

After the failed assault at Cold Harbor on June 3 Grant decided to cross the James River and attack Petersburg, twenty miles south of Richmond, where three of the four railroads used to supply Lee's army converged. The Army of the Potomac left its positions at Cold Harbor on June 12 and began crossing the James by boat and pontoon bridge two days later. Lee failed to detect the crossing and kept his army north of the river to protect Richmond, leaving the defense of Petersburg to a small garrison commanded by General Pierre G. T. Beauregard. On the evening of June 15 Union troops overran the outer line of defenses east of Petersburg but were unable to capture the city itself. A series of poorly coordinated Union attacks over the three days failed to break through the inner defenses, and on June 18 troops from Lee's army began to reinforce the outnumbered Petersburg garrison. Grant decided not to launch further assaults on the city, and on June 19 Union troops began to entrench around Petersburg. Between the crossing of the Rapidan on May 4 and the movement toward the James on June 12 the Army of the Potomac lost about 55,000 men killed, wounded, or missing, while casualties in the Army of Northern Virginia are estimated at about 33,000 men. Private Wilbur Fisk's regiment, the 2nd Vermont Infantry, lost two-thirds of its men in the Wilderness and at Spotsylvania before escaping the worst of the fighting at Cold Harbor. "I have sometimes hoped that if I must die while I am a soldier," Fisk observed after the battle for the Mule Shoe on May 12, "I should prefer to die on the battlefield, but after looking at such a scene, one cannot help turning away and saying, Any death but that." He wrote to the *Freeman* three days after his regiment crossed the James.

———————

Near Petersburg, Va.
June 19, 1864

Another flank movement has been made by the army, and to-day we find ourselves within a mile of Petersburg with our old enemy in front. For three days there has been pretty severe fighting here, but this time our corps escaped the worst of it.

Our division reached the front night before last. The Second Regiment was sent at once on to the skirmish line, from which we were relieved last night after twenty-four hours hard duty.

We left Cold Harbor the night of the 12th. It was a bright moonlight night, just right for marching, except that the air everywhere was filled with choking dust, which the dampness of evening could not lay. We fell into line at the order, and the most of us guessed where we were going, but our calculations were a little puzzled, when instead of marching off to the left, we started out "right in front" and marched back on to the right flank. It soon became evident that we were sent there only as a rear guard, and after remaining behind good breastworks till midnight, we changed our course towards the Chickahominy. The interval we improved the best we could in catching a little sleep. It was short, and less satisfactory than sweet, scarcely better than none, for it makes a fellow feel more stupid than ever to call him up suddenly from a refreshing sleep just begun. At daylight we halted an hour for breakfast, then pushed on again through the dust and heat till night. We crossed the Chickahominy at Jones' bridge just before sundown, but continued our march a number of miles further before we came to a halt. I don't know exactly how far we marched, it is variously estimated at from twenty to twenty-five miles, but the choking dust and heat and the many crooked turns we made, made the march doubly difficult. We were completely exhausted before we bivouacked for the night. Those last miles were doled out in suffering by inches. If a man wants to know what it is to have every bone in his body ache with fatigue, every muscle sore and exhausted, and his whole body ready to sink to the ground, let him diet on a common soldier's fare till he has only the strength that imparts, and then let him shoulder his knapsack, haversack, gun and equipments, and make one of our forced marches, and I will warrant him to be satisfied that the duties of war are stern and severe, whether we march or face the enemy on the field of battle. A fellow feels very much like grumbling at such times as that, and when we march on and on, expecting every minute to halt but still hurrying forward, when every spark of energy seems about to be extinguished, and the last remnant of strength gone, tired, hungry, sick and sore, who blames a soldier if he finds it hard work to suppress thoughts of a quiet home he has left behind him, with its comforts and endearments, and if he sometime turns his thoughts to himself and wonders if he, as an individual, will ever be compensated for the sacrifice he is making. What if the rebels are whipped, and what if they are not? How does it matter to him? One blunder of General Grant's may make final victory forever impossible and all our lost toil go for nothing. I tell you some of our hard marches put one's patriotism severely to the test. It finds out a fellow's weak points if he has got any, and we don't claim to be without them.

About ten o'clock that night we were ready to lie down for our night's rest, and at four in the morning we were called onto our feet again. We advanced towards the James River, just before Harrison's Landing, where we had a camp two years ago. It would have been quite a treat to have visited that old camp again, but we did not have the opportunity. We crossed the James River the night of the 16th on a pontoon bridge and came directly to this place. The first and third division of this corps, more fortunate than ourselves, were carried to City Point on transports while we made the distance on foot. The whole movement was well planned to save time.

As we were coming on to the ground, we had positive assurance that Petersburg was taken, and of course felt highly elated at the cheering news, but we found when we got here that the news was not quite so good as reported, although we had captured their outer line of fortifications and were almost within musket range of the city. Burnside's negroes claim a large share of credit in taking these works. They made a splendid charge, capturing the whole line of works, thirteen guns, and some prisoners. The negroes were remarkably well pleased with their prowess on this occasion. It was a glorious day for them. They won great favor in the eyes of white soldiers by their courage and bravery. I am sure I never looked upon negroes with more respect than I did upon those soldiers, and I did not hear a word of disrespect towards them from any of the boys. Yesterday they made another charge here, and it was done in excellent style. The best military critic could hardly find fault with it. In a steady straight line they advanced right over the crest of the hill and right up to the enemy's works, under a terrible fire, but without wavering or faltering, compelling the enemy to leave his works in the hands of the blacks. The stream of wounded that came pouring back, some leaning on a comrade and some carried on stretchers, told of the bloody work they had done. Our picket reserve was in the road where they passed by. They captured some prisoners and brought them off. The proud Southerner might have felt a little humbled to be taken prisoner in open fight by a class of people that they refuse to recognize as men, and be conducted off the field in charge of a negro guard. But this they had to submit the best they could. One of the guard, a small, comical looking darkey, rolling up his large white eyes and looking at a tall rebel with a peculiar expression of triumph inquired, "Who rides a horseback now?" The rebel did not deign a reply. He bore the shout that followed with philosophical coolness. Sometimes the negroes treat their prisoners rather roughly in remembrance of Fort Pillow, and similar outrages. I have no doubt, if the truth were known, that many a rebel lost his life at their hands at the taking of the first line fortifications after they had fallen into our hands. Their wrath was especially directed against the officers. The rebels would plead with them, tell them they had no desire to harm them, but the negroes would say, How was it at Fort Pillow? and pay no attention to their entreaties. One of our officers who was a free mason, told of rescuing a rebel brother mason whom the negroes decided to kill. He drew his revolver and peremptorily ordered the negroes who had gathered around him to disperse and had the wounded rebel cared for, otherwise he would have counted as one to pay the terrible bill of retaliation that we have against the enemy. Such a kind of warfare is too horrible to contemplate, though we cannot blame the negroes under the present circumstances.

Notwithstanding the negroes fight so well and show so much bravery, they have hitherto been allowed but the bare pittance of seven dollars a month. Chaplain Hunter, of the 4th U.S. colored troops, a colored man of remarkable ability, denounces with just indignation this rank injustice. He says there are men in his regiment who have left families at home, and seven dollars a month in times like these, is not enough to keep them from actual suffering. In a conversation with a Major

General a short time since, he said he asked him in a case of a battle where all the commissioned officers were killed or wounded in a company or regiment, who would take the command. (Commissioned officers are white but the non-commissioned officers may be black, but a negro is never commissioned—miserable compromise to an unreasonable prejudice.) The General replied that it would devolve upon the ranking non-commissioned officer of course. Then said the chaplain, when the regiment comes to re-organize and new officers be chosen, what will you do with these men that, according to military custom, are entitled to the position they have filled, and who have proved that they are worthy of it. Well, said the General a little puzzled at the annoying question, Congress will have to settle that.

And Congress has wrangled over that question all winter trying to settle it. It seems strange that a question where justice and injustice, right and wrong, are so plainly apparent, should require any wrangling or debate at all. They seem to think that it is degrading to the white soldiers to pay the blacks equally as well. Do they think we are afraid of fair competition with blacks? If negroes can fight as well as we, can we not have magnanimity enough to acknowledge it. Certainly to propose especial legislation to keep our *status* ahead of the blacks is acknowledging them our superiors and in a most humiliating way. Whether it suits our tastes or not, it is doubtless true that the golden rule applies to colored as well as to white people, and Congress as well as everybody else will do well to bear this in mind and act accordingly.

"BUTCHERED TIME AND AGAIN":
VIRGINIA, JUNE 1864

Stephen Minot Weld to Stephen Minot Weld Sr.

Stephen Minot Weld was commissioned as a Union officer in January 1862. He served in the Army of the Potomac as an aide to corps commanders Fitz John Porter, John Reynolds, and John Newton until August 1863, when he became the lieutenant colonel of the newly formed 56th Massachusetts Infantry. Assigned to the First Brigade, First Division of the Ninth Corps, the regiment crossed the Rapidan on May 5, 1864, with about 550 men in its ranks. Weld took command of the 56th Massachusetts the next day when its colonel was killed in the Wilderness, and then led the First Brigade for nearly a week at Spotsylvania after its commander became "sun-struck." The regiment crossed the James on June 15 and assaulted the Petersburg defenses two days later, capturing a line of rifle pits before being driven back by a Confederate counterattack after it ran out of ammunition. (In a memoir written in 1912, Weld blamed the lack of ammunition on his division commander, Brigadier General James H. Ledlie, "a coward" who "took the liquor to try and fortify himself for the fight," and described finding him in "a drunken sleep" after the June 17 attack.) Weld wrote to his father about the course of the Virginia campaign.

HEADQUARTERS 56TH MASS. VOLS., *June* 21, 1864.

DEAR FATHER,—We moved out to the front last evening, relieving General Barlow's division of the Second Corps. The idea is, I believe, to have the Second Corps moved to the left, to prevent a flank movement by the rebels.

There is one thing that I have noticed throughout this campaign. The newspapers have been giving a false and incorrect report of the state of the army and of our battles. They have claimed great victories, where we have been repulsed, and have not stated our losses correctly. It is perhaps necessary to have such reports go abroad in order to prevent our people from being discouraged, but I don't like to see them.

The only time that Grant has got ahead of Lee, was in

crossing the James River, and attacking Petersburg. He did outmanœuvre him there, most certainly, but did not follow up his advantage. The feeling here in the army is that we have been absolutely butchered, that our lives have been periled to no purpose, and wasted. In the Second Corps the feeling is so strong that the men say they will not charge any more works. The cause of the whole trouble, in my opinion, is owing to the carelessness of those high in command, such as corps commanders and higher officers still, who have time and again recklessly and wickedly placed us in slaughter-pens. I can tell you, Father, it is discouraging to see one's men and officers cut down and butchered time and again, and all for nothing.

I don't wish you to think from all this that I am croaking. I feel that we shall take Richmond in time, but hope that some consideration and some regard for life will be shown in doing so. We can't afford to make many more such bloody attacks as we have been doing. The enemy will outnumber us if we do so. We shall have to settle down to a siege of Petersburg and take the place in that way. We have our lines so near the city that it will not be a difficult matter to burn and shell the whole concern out, if necessary.

I have 180 men left for duty in my regiment, and this is a fair-sized regiment.

We are quite fortunate in our position here. We are in woods, with the enemy's line about 300 yards in our front. The woods screen us from them, so that we can walk around with comparative safety, but on our left the line is outside the woods, and woe betide any man who shows his head. The whistling of innumerable bullets around him warns him of the dangerous proximity of the enemy. The camp that we left yesterday was in the middle of a dusty field, where all the dead on both sides, killed during the charge of the 17th, were buried. The effluvia got to be unbearable finally, and we were all glad enough to change to any position, no matter where.

Can you do anything to help recruit this regiment? If you have a chance, I wish you would put some good men in it, as we need them very much.

My health has been remarkably good during the whole campaign. We have been remarkably fortunate in regard to weather, having had pleasant and dry weather almost all the time.

"A HORRID, HELLISH DREAM":
VIRGINIA, JUNE 1864

George E. Chamberlin to Ephraim Chamberlin

The fighting at Petersburg from June 15 to June 18 cost the Union about 8,000 men killed, wounded, or missing, and the Confederates about 3,000, and gave the Union control of the Norfolk & Petersburg, one of the three main railroads that converged on the city. By June 19 the Army of the Potomac was deployed to the east of the Petersburg in an arc extending from the Appomattox River to the Jerusalem Plank Road. On June 21 Grant sent the Second and Sixth Corps west to cut the Weldon & Petersburg Railroad, which connected Richmond and Lee's army with North Carolina and the Deep South. The Confederates counterattacked on June 22, taking 1,800 prisoners from the Second Corps, and then capturing 400 prisoners from the Sixth Corps the next day. On June 24 Union troops retreated from the railroad and took up positions to the west of the Jerusalem Plank Road. George E. Chamberlin had been appointed major of the 11th Vermont Volunteers in the summer of 1862. The regiment was posted to the fortifications defending Washington, D.C., and in December 1862 was designated the 1st Vermont Heavy Artillery. After the battle of the Wilderness the 1st Vermont was one of several heavy artillery regiments sent from the capital to reinforce the Army of the Potomac. It reached Spotsylvania on May 15 and was assigned to the Second Brigade, Second Division of the Sixth Corps. The regiment came under fire for the first time on May 18, lost 119 men killed or wounded in the June 1 fighting at Cold Harbor, and arrived at Petersburg on June 18. A week later Chamberlin wrote to his father about the experience of "trench life."

HEADQUARTERS 1ST ART'Y, 11TH VT. VOLS.,
June 27, 1864.

MY DEAR FATHER:

How often, in the midst of all these dangers and privations, my mind turns back to that delightful *home* where I once lived so joyfully, so peacefully with my father, my mother, and brother and sisters. What blessed days, when the country was at peace; what awful days *these*, of blood, and carnage, and hate. The realities of war, you who have never been on the battlefield can never know or even imagine. To me, who have seen it, it seems more like a horrid, hellish dream, rather than a fact. There will be a fearful reckoning with those who are responsible for all this. Ours is the right side, but we have hard work before us. God will give us the victory sometime, and will surely put our wicked enemies to shame and confusion.

I wish I could write you oftener, but it has been impossible. To Delie I have written very frequently, but beyond this have done no writing, except what was required in my official capacity. I think I have written you only once before since leaving Washington. The campaign has been intensely active and laborious. The night work has been particularly severe, the greater part of the marching having been done by night. At dark, on the evening of June 12th, we left Cold Harbor, and marched all night and all the next day. At evening we rested on the right bank of the Chickahominy, and I was laying my blankets preparing for a good night's sleep, when an order came, detailing me as division officer of the day, and I was on picket line all night without sleep, and marched the greater part of next day. Fatigues, that at home would be thought terrible, entirely too much for flesh and blood to endure, are an every week's occurrence here, and we learn to bear them very naturally.

Delie has written you often, and through her you have been made acquainted with the items of news from time to time. I have been in command of the regiment for about two weeks. Lieutenant-Colonel Benton has resigned and gone home. Colonel Warner is at his home still.

On the 23d, the regiment met with a very great misfortune. We were in line of battle, facing the Garton Branch and Petersburg railroad. A report came in that a party of sharpshooters had pushed forward and taken the road, and wanted support. Two hundred men from our regiment were called for, and immediately sent under charge of Captain M., to be reported to Lieutenant-Colonel P., corps officer of the day. Soon after, I was called on for more men, and sent out Major F. with his battalion. Four hundred of our men were now out. In the afternoon the enemy moved two brigades rapidly down the railroad, formed as a skirmish line, and advanced on our skirmish line, which, not being properly supported, was finally driven back, and a portion of it captured. In that part of the line were our noble boys, and we have lost the greater part of them. Our total loss on that day was twenty-four killed and wounded, and two hundred and seventy-five prisoners. Of these, one officer was killed (Second-Lieutenant Sherman, a fine man and officer) and eighteen captured. My old company, A, is among the unfortunate. Captain M. and Lieutenant R. will know the beauties of a Southern prison. The batteries captured are F, L, K, H and A. A and K were my Totten companies, and L was with me at Lincoln. The greater part of the Fourth Vermont was taken at the same time. The fault was with the corps commander in not ordering proper supports. Our officers and men did their whole duty.

We have had a good deal of trench life during the campaign at Cold Harbor and at Petersburg. We dig up into the very teeth of the enemy, and then watch him. It is not safe to expose one's head above the embankment, as a few sharpshooters keep up their murderous work through little loopholes in the parapet; otherwise there is not much firing. Living under ground is very dirty work, as you can imagine. One night, I remember to have been awakened by something on my neck, which I discovered to be a medium sized toad. Bugs and worms crawl over us promiscuously. What a sad sight, in this enlightened age, to see the sections of this civilized nation fighting each other with such insatiable fury. How much more congenial to our tastes, and how much more consonant with all our christian feelings and impulses, is peace, harmony, brotherly love. God deliver the nation soon from the chastisement of fire and blood which He has seen fit to send upon us.

How soon Carrie will graduate—day after to-morrow. It is probably an occasion of as much interest to her as mine was to me, nearly four years ago. Do any of you go to Troy? Delie wrote that mother would not go. I hope some of you will be there to see her take her honors. I well remember my gratification at seeing you all at Hanover. Delie, I think, has decided to go to Vermont. This I am very glad of, and have advised it all the time. How she will enjoy a visit there! You must drive away her sadness. She is very anxious for me, and I fear it is wearing upon her severely. I hope the Green Mountain air, and the many dear friends she will find there, will cause her to rally, and be as cheerful and healthy as ever. A husband and wife who love each other as we do, have no business to be separated as we are. You will all take good, tender care of her, won't you? Cheer her up and comfort her by every means in your power. If you knew how kind, attentive and devoted she has always been to me, you could not help loving her for my sake. And you do know all about it, and you do love her for my sake, and for herself too. You have seen her, and you know that nobody has a better wife than I. How I wish I might be there with you. All will be there but the "boys." You will miss us. How happy we should be together around that home circle again. I should be happier than ever to be there with my new companion, and you would be happier to see me with her than alone, for I know you joy in my joy. God has blessed me with the kindest of friends always, and I pray for a life long enough to show them that I am grateful. We were very sorry you did not return *via* Washington with Mary. I have had an intimation that you would remove West this fall. Is it so? I want to hear all about it. By the way, why haven't I heard from any of you? I think I have not had a single letter since the campaign commenced. That isn't right. My address is 1st Artillery, 11th Vt. Vols., 2d Brig., 2d Division, 6th Corps, Washington. The weather is very hot. The army is comparatively quiet, and will remain so, probably, until after muster day, the 30th.

Much love to my dear mother and sisters, and also to Edward, when you write. How dear is each and every one to me! Let me hear soon.

Your affectionate son.

LIFE AT ANDERSONVILLE: GEORGIA, JUNE 1864

Eugene Forbes: Diary, June 13–30, 1864

By the end of June 1864 more than 26,000 Union prisoners were crowded into the sixteen-acre stockade at Andersonville. Sergeant Eugene Forbes recorded events and conditions in the camp, including the depredations of the "raiders" who preyed on their fellow prisoners.

Monday, June 13. Rainy all day. Wheat flour has declined to 50c. per pint; salt, to 25c. per five spoonfuls; rice, 25c. per pint, butter, $4.50 per lb. Rumored that Sherman has cut communications, thus putting us on short allowance. No roll call. No medicine for several days. There are quite a number of insane men in camp; one of them has been plundered of everything but his shirt, and while he was asleep, some scoundrel cut off the front tail of that garment, thus leaving him almost without anything to cover his nakedness. Today and yesterday have been so cold that an overcoat would be a comfort, and he must suffer extremely; he was refused admission to the hospital today. Several of the old Belle Island prisoners were vaccinated, before leaving that place, with impure or scrofulous matter; some of these men have since had their arms amputated, while others are walking around with their bones and muscles exposed, the flesh having dropped out piecemeal. Lame men, blind men, deaf men, one-armed men, all alike exposed to the inclemency of the storm, or the blistering rays of the sun; "As ye do unto others it shall be done unto you, and with what measure ye mete, it shall be measured to you again." Drew rice, salt and bacon P.M. Some of the squads drew rice and molasses, but no bacon. Rain continued all night. A few prisoners came in; no news.

Tuesday, June 14. Rain continues. A few prisoners came in. Drew meal, bacon, salt and boiled rice. At about 11 P.M. a terrible row seemed to be taking place about the center of the camp; cries of murder and the sound of blows were heard, alarming the rebs so much that the sentries cried the time every half hour, instead of every hour, as usual. No squads allowed out for wood, two men having escaped yesterday. Last night no response was heard from seven sentry boxes, commencing at No. 17; this morning it was ascertained that fourteen of our men had "tunneled out," and that seven guards had accompanied them, taking their arms and accoutrements. Active skirmishing.

Wednesday, June 15. Saw one man laid out, who died from cold and exposure last night. On the north side they are riding one of the raiders on a rail. A large squad of prisoners came in this A.M., among whom are several from the 4th Regiment; Cooper, of Co. B., is said to be among the number, and to have been captured on the 8th ult. They report that they could hear musketry as they left Libby Prison; they have heard nothing regarding parole or exchange. An individual who was getting a list of names of shoemakers who were willing to go outside and work for the benefit of the Southern Confederacy, was seized by some of the boys on the north side, bucked and gagged, his head shaved, his list taken away from him, and then turned loose, amid the hootings of the crowd. The Captain and Quartermaster told the Sergeant of 57-3 that paroles would be issued tomorrow up to the 20th Detachment. Bet he lies. Drew meal, salt, bacon and raw rice. No one allowed out for wood. Reported that Lincoln has been renominated by the Republicans, and McClellan by the Democrats. Cooper says Grant has 16,000 prisoners in rear of Fredericksburg; First Battalion Veteran Reserve Corps reported ordered to the field. Rainy A.M., but cleared up P.M.

Thursday, June 16. Cloudy all day, with some little rain. Two squads on the north side were deprived of their rations, on account of their connection with the shaving of the shoemaker's head yesterday. (I believe his name is Kearney some of the raiders appear acquainted with him.) Drew meal and bacon. A large squad of prisoners (some 300) came in P.M.; they are mostly from the Army of the Potomac; they report desperate fighting; that Grant moves his picket line every evening close to the rebs, during the night moves his line of battle up to the picket line, throws up earthworks and mounts artillery, in the morning charges, &c. Some of these men were taken at Gaines' Mill, the scene of the Fourth's Capture in 1862. Fifty-seven deaths reported in hospital last night. Letters came for many of the men today. Of course the captain lied yesterday about the parole. One of the sailors lent Atwood a History of America, and it helps to pass time very pleasantly. Used my last chew of tobacco. Rained very hard after dark.

Friday, June 17.   Rainy all day. Gen. Winder reported here. Several men out on wood squads turned on the guard, took their guns, and made their escape. No more allowed out for wood. Drew meal and bacon P.M. Raiding is getting very extensively practiced. Six weeks prisoners today. Wood getting scarce.

Saturday, June 18.   One man slept in the mush box last night; he was surrounded by five or six men during the night, and his pocket cut out; another, walking around with a blanket on his shoulders, was seized by four men, and his blanket taken away.

About 11 o'clock today a man was knocked down and robbed of his watch and $80. "Things is lovely." Rainy by spells. Atwood got tired of his job as commissary sergeant, and threw up the "sit." Some of the men who escaped yesterday were returned today; one of them was shot through the thigh, the other one's forehead was grazed. A squad of prisoners came in about noon, all from hospitals, wounded and sick. Atwood resigned, and Buckley accepted commissary sergeant. "Run." got some vinegar yesterday; it was the color of egg nog, and was made of some acid and water mixed. Potatoes $1.50 per dozen; about 16 fill a quart pot. More parole rumors, but without credibility. Went to see Mat. Hill; he lives near the "raiders." Showery all day, but with a promise of clearing.

Sunday, June 19.   A rainbow this morning. A large black snake was seen by one of the men between the "dead line" and the stockade. He asked permission of the nearest guard to pass the line and kill it, which was given. A sentry on a distant post fired at the man killing the snake, missed him, but struck a tent, wounding two men, one in the head, and the other in the thigh. Some of the prisoners who came in yesterday were wounded as late as May 16th, and their arms, legs, &c. which have been amputated or otherwise acted upon, are perfectly raw. Last night a well, which had been dug very near some tents, caved in, burying three men, who slept in a tent near the edge of the well. Two of them were got out safely, but the third was injured so badly that he was dead by roll call. The camp was more quiet last night than any time since we have been in it. The rebel sergeant says that Gen. Winder is here. Atwood asserts that two of our men were to have been hung, by order of Capt. Wurtz, for over powering the guard, and that Gen. Winder gave orders that no such execution should take place. Some of the men who were in that party are now in camp, the General having forbidden the balls and chains to be put on them. They say that they wandered about that night, but there being no stars to guide their course, they become bewildered, and twice before daylight found themselves close to the stockade. So much for going without a map or compass. A large squad of prisoners came in on the north side this afternoon. Rainy all the afternoon. Our surplus meal has soured from the damp weather. Oak. traded a quart of it for a piece of tobacco. Drew meal, bacon and salt; got a bone for my ration, with more meat on it than on two ordinary rations. Rainy by spells all day. Drew wood.

Monday, June 20. Cloudy and drizzling A.M. No roll call this morning. Blackberries are selling at fifty cents a pint; green apples are in camp, but I did not price them. Washed my shirt, but did not get it dry. Traded two quarts of meal for a pint of beans, and tried to make some bean soup; rained all P.M. putting out our fire, and we had to eat our beans half cooked. Got the diarrhea very bad, may be raw beans will cure it. Had to sleep without my shirt.

Tuesday, June 21. Cleared up this morning. Find I will have to reduce my chirography to its fighting standard, as the book is getting pretty well filled up. Heavy rain P.M. Drew meal, salt and tainted bacon P.M. Went out to the Doctor in the morning, but did not get prescribed for. Saw a large number of men at the dead-house, so many that it would not hold them all, some fifteen or twenty being laid outside. Every one was searched on returning through the gate. Lost nothing. A man was shot on or near the dead-line this P.M. A raider caught stealing a frying pan near 12 P.M. Rumored that Sherman has been defeated, and that Grant has fallen back 14 miles; also, that Fort Darling has been captured for the 999th time. No room in the hospital for more sick, a large number lying outside now. A few prisoners came in. Considerable excitement among the rebs, by a report that Kilpatrick is near here. Rebs drawn up in line of battle all day and night. Hope he will come. No roll call today. Squads still working on the stockade.

Wednesday, June 22.   Clear this morning. All quiet. Brown, of our detachment, has been shamefully treated by some of the men. He has the chronic diarrhea, and having met with an accident, washed his pants and drawers and hung them up to dry. Some scoundrel stole them, leaving him with nothing but a shirt. One of the men gave him a pair of drawers, and he now lies near the runlet, his feet awfully swollen and gradually sinking under disease. Our own men are worse to each other than the rebels are to us. A tunnel was discovered today, and the men ordered to dig it out and then fill it up. The man who was shot last night reported dead today. Saw two men carried out this morning from our side. Louis Traute is very bad with scurvy and diarrhea, and Jagers has the dysentery very bad. Gambling still goes on very extensively, and *hundreds of dollars* are changing hands daily. No roll call again this morning. Made a regular dinner today; soup, dumplings, bread and coffee, all made of Indian meal. Rumored that paroling is to commence between the 7th and 17th July. A few sprinkles of rain in the afternoon, just enough to maintain the reputation of the month. Drew meal, salt and bacon P.M. Cucumbers in market today. Heard a chase after a raider after we had turned in; don't think they caught him.

Thursday, June 23.   Clear this morning, and very warm. Tent next to us had their meat stolen last night; a fight near the sinks, and another near the sailors' tent, early this A.M., but did not amount to much; no roll call; two more tunnels discovered, one on the north side, and the other on the south side, near us. Brown went to the hospital good bye Brown! One man came in from the hospital today, as convalescent. He had been wounded, and *is the first one who has returned from the hospital*; they generally go the other way. A squad of prisoners came in today, mostly from Grant's army; the 7th N.Y. Heavy Artillery seems to own most of the prisoners; they were taken at or near Petersburg; they report Petersburg as now in our possession, and that Richmond is cut off from all railroad communication with the South; that Grant has received reinforcements of 110,000 one hundred day men, and that he will not storm the city, but starve it out. We'll see. Drew meal at night, but nothing else; expect to draw salt and fresh beef in the morning. Not a drop of rain today, being the second day this month. Boys next door think one of their own chums went back on them. No wood today.

Friday, June 24. Clear and warm this morning. Drew salt and fresh beef about 10 A.M., the latter fly-blown; traded a ration of beef for an onion, boiled the rest, and made some soup, which we relished very highly. Atwood sold his tobacco-box for two onions. Took a walk on the north side; it reminds me of Chatham street, New York; it is quite as crowded, and the cries of the peddlers are incessantly heard; "Who wants the wood?" "Come up, now, gentlemen, and give us another bet here's your chance to double your money," &c., &c. Saw a dead man carried out. Seven weeks a prisoner today. Drew meal at night, but no salt or meat. Very warm all day, and no rain. The rumor of the day is, that prisoners who had money taken from them at Richmond are to apply at the gate and receive it back. Jagers is no better, and Mulvaney and Hoffman are both sick; my diarrhea is better. A few prisoners from Sherman came in.

Saturday, June 25. A crazy man is running around naked this morning, some scoundrel having stolen his clothing. Very hot, but a good breeze stirring; clear all day. Drew bacon and salt A.M., and meal, salt and fresh beef P.M.; also a small ration of liver. Fried our liver and some beef, made a gravy thickened with corn meal, scalded our meal and made some improved cakes, and had a "bully" supper. Some 50 prisoners came in from Sherman's army. The rumor that money was to be returned to the prisoners is beginning to take a tangible form; today the sergeants of squads were furnished with blank printed rolls, with columns for name, regiment, company, number of detachment and mess; this looks like business, and has given rise to all sorts of rumors regarding paroling, &c. The work on the new stockade has been discontinued, the men having refused to work. No roll call today. Took a "bully" wash at the spring last night and tonight; the water in the creek is so coated with grease from the cook house, that it is unfit to wash with, much less for drinking.

Sunday, June 26. Drew nothing today, as the drawing commenced on the north side. Saw a regular ring fight today, between two of the old prisoners, near the creek; they fought some fifteen minutes, when one got enough; both were somewhat scratched, but not much injured. No roll call. A party of raiders "cleaned out" Tarbell, McNeese and Nelson, of 57-1; they took boots, blankets, &c. Some few prisoners came in from Sherman, and report him near Atlanta, preparing to attack that place. The latest parole rumors are that 700 barrels of hard tack were unloaded at this depot today; that the rebs are fixing up cars to transport the sick, and that 20,000 reb prisoners are at Fortress Monroe, awaiting shipment. Fried beef for breakfast, and made beef soup for dinner; quite luxurious living for Yankee prisoners. Blackberries are selling at 60 cents a pint; wood is very scarce, as the squads do not get out half the time. Find that scalding our meal saves about one-half of it. We did not eat all our rations before, so now we will have plenty to trade off. Very hot all day. A "raider" was caught and his head shaved this morning; he sold his pint cup for $1.50, and then went at night and stole it back.

Monday, June 27. Two years ago today, I was first taken prisoner; have a mighty good sight of spending another 4th of July in captivity. A "raider" was chased early this morning, but I do not know if he was captured. Drew meal, salt and fresh beef this A.M., and made some beef tea for dinner; drew meal, salt and fresh beef P.M. A fine prospect of a general row this afternoon; the raiders were out in full force; an orderly sergeant was enticed into their tent, and robbed of $50; the raiders near the gate were contemplating an attack on this part of the camp last night; the sailors and raiders in this corner combined their forces, sent out skirmishing parties, and made arrangements to repel the attack, but the fight did not come off. Atwood sold a haversack of meal, and bought an onion and a piece of bacon, so we will live high tomorrow. A squad of prisoners came in today; I heard that a Jerseyman of the 15th regiment was with them, but I did not see him. Petersburg reported taken, also Beauregard and 10,000 prisoners. Clear and hot all day.

Tuesday, June 28. Two years ago I entered Richmond. The night passed without disturbance. Two shots fired last night, but don't know whether any one was hurt. A squad of prisoners came in this P.M., among whom were some from our regiment; Ackerson, of Co. D, reports Jack States as killed at Spottsylvania Court House, Col. Ewing as seriously wounded, and Capt. Gaul in command of the regiment; he says Oakley and myself are reported as taken prisoners; Kinney, Dougherty and Lovett, of Co. D, are wounded. Drew meal P.M. A row was imminent about 11 o'clock tonight, but did not amount to anything. A heavy shower this afternoon, and rainy most of the night. Very sick all night, with chill and fever, diarrhea, and terrible pain in the right breast and side. Grant is reported within 2½ miles of Richmond, and that he has thrown some shells into the city; his army is said to be all on the south side of the James river; Danville is said to be in our hands, and McClellan, with 250,000 one hundred day men, operating at various points. The new comers know nothing about exchange arrangements, and we have no hope of getting away from here before August or September; the veterans of the 1st regiment have been incorporated with the 4th regiment.

Wednesday, June 29. Drew salt and bacon A.M. Cleared up this morning. Feel better today, but still have a violent pain in the right side. The 1st, 2d and 3d regiments started for home on the 4th of June. Drew meal and bacon P.M. About two P.M. two men came along, trying to sell a watch; Dowd asked to look at it, and did so, after which they went away; in short time they returned with reinforcements, and attacked him as he sat in his tent, with clubs, brass knuckles, &c.; he defended himself bravely, and they again departed; he came out of his tent, and put on his pants, when they again attacked him, and finally got him down, took his watch, cut out his money, (which he had sewed in the waistband of his pants,) to the amount of $170; he was badly cut up, but finally got away and reached the gate, and reported to Capt. Wurtz, who came up with him and demanded that the robbers should be given up, under penalty of no rations for one week; in a short time a guard came in, and took eight men from a tent near the dead line on our side; very soon the camp was in an uproar, for the men came into the arrangement, and the raiders were hunted from one end of the camp to the other; by dark the tumult was nearly over, but the raiders are not all caught yet; about 50 were taken outside; the issuing of rations was stopped. Heavy showers P.M. Large quantities of clothing, blankets, &c., were found in some of the raiders' tents. Capt. Wurtz deserves great credit for his prompt action in the matter, and will probably be successful in checking the operations of these thieving scoundrels.

Thursday, June 30. Very warm today. The crusade against the raiders still continues, and several were taken today; three of those who robbed Dowd are reported to be among the number; the fourth and worse one has been caught since the above writing; they are now pretty well cleared out; the sergeants of messes (90) were called up at 9 A.M. and taken to Capt. Wurtz's headquarters, where 24 of them were selected, their names taken, and 12 drawn by lot as a jury for the trial of the principal raiders; this P.M. the trial is progressing; this course is pursued to prevent retaliation on the part of our Government, to whom the whole proceedings are to be sent; it is an act of justice on the part of the Confederate authorities which the men have not expected, they supposing that no notice would be taken of their complaints; but the reverse has been the case, and we can now feel secure from the attacks of daylight assassins or midnight murderers; the issuing of rations was promptly commenced as soon as the men known as ringleaders were captured. We expect to move to the new stockade either today or tomorrow. Oak. went out as a witness; towards night news came in that Sarsfield, one of the principals, who said he "would cut Dowd's heart out and throw it in his face," had been convicted and sentenced to be hung; the trial of the others is to come off tomorrow. Drew fresh meal and meat P.M. I forgot to mention in connection with the raiders, that large amounts of money were discovered in some of the tents today, as well as watches, jewelry, and articles of all descriptions. No rain. Dowd moved his things to the outside today, where he has liberty to the extent of one mile.

THE ATLANTA CAMPAIGN: GEORGIA, JUNE 1864

William T. Sherman to Ellen Ewing Sherman

Sherman resumed his advance in northern Georgia on June 10, moving his troops south from Acworth toward Johnston's positions on the high ground north and west of Marietta. After a week of fighting and maneuvering, on June 18 Johnston withdrew to a defensive line anchored on Kennesaw Mountain. Uncertain of his ability to outflank the position and believing that Johnston had overextended his army across an eight-mile front, Sherman ordered an assault against the Confederate center. On the morning of June 27 about 15,000 Union troops attacked the western end of Kennesaw Mountain and the high ground to the south. The assaults were repulsed with the loss of about 3,000 men killed, wounded, or missing, three times the Confederate casualties. Sherman wrote to his wife three days after the battle.

> Head-Quarters, Military Division
> of the Mississippi,
> In the Field, near Marietta
> June 30, 1864.

Dearest Ellen,

I got Mary Ewings letter, also that of Susan Stambaugh telling me of your serious illness after the birth of the new baby, but I had got Phil's dispatch saying you had been very sick but were much better and on the mend. I have no doubt your anxiety on many accounts has caused your illness but now having a new object of interest I hope your interest will revive & restore you rapidly to health. It is enough to make the whole world start at the awful amount of death & destruction that now stalks abroad. Daily for the past two months has the work progressed and I see no signs of a remission til one or both and all the armies are destroyed when I suppose the balance of the People will tear each other up, as Grant says reenacting the Story of the Kilkenny cats. I begin to regard the death & mangling of a couple thousand men as a small affair, a kind of morning dash—and it may be well that we become so hardened. Each day is killed or wounded some valuable officers and men, the bullets coming from a concealed foe. I suppose the people are impatient why I dont push or move rapidly to Atlanta but those who are here are satisfied with the progress. It is as much as our Railroad can do to Supply us bread meat & corn, and I cannot leave the Railroad to Swing on Johnstons flank or rear without giving him the Railroad which I cannot do without having a good supply on hand. I am moving heaven and earth to accomplish this, in which event I shall leave the Railroad & move to the Chattahoochee, threatening to cross which will I think force him to do that very thing when I will swing round on the road again. In that Event we may be all ready and attempt to hold both Road & river, but my opinion is he has not force enough to do both. In that Event you will be without news of us for ten days. I think we can whip his army in fair battle, but behind the hills and trunks our loss of life & limb on the first assault would reduce us too much, in other words at this distance from home we cannot afford the losses of such terrible assaults as Grant has made. I have only one source of supply, Grant had several in Succession. One of my chief objects was to prevent Joe Johnston from detaching against Grant till he got below Richmond & that I have done. I have no idea of besieging Atlanta, but may cross the Chattahoochee & circle round Atlanta breaking up its Roads. As you begin to get well I fear you will begin to fret again about changing your abode. If you are not comfortable at home try and rent some house, not the Small one of Martins you bespoke, but get Martin or Phil to find some other, & live as quietly & comfortably as possible. The worst of the war is not yet begun, the civil strife at the North has to come yet, and the tendency to Anarchy to be cured. Look at matters in Kentucky & Missouri and down the Mississipi & Arkansas where Shallow People have been taught to believe the war is over & you will see troubles enough to convince you I was right in my view of the case from the first. Stay as quietly as you can at Lancaster till Grant & I have our downfall, or are disposed of & then if we can do better, will be time enough to change. In such a quiet place as Lancaster you can hardly realize the truth that is so plain & palpable to me.

I hardly think Johnston will give us a chance to fight a decisive Battle, unless at such a disadvantage that I ought not to accept, and he is so situated that when threatened or pressed too hard he draws off leaving us a barren victory. He will thus act all summer unless he gives a great advantage in position or succeeds in breaking our Roads.

My love to all the children & folks and believe me always Yrs.

W. T. Sherman

AN APPEAL FOR NEGOTIATIONS:
NEW YORK CITY, JULY 1864

Horace Greeley to Abraham Lincoln

In January 1863 Horace Greeley, the influential founder and editor of the *New-York Daily Tribune*, had become involved with the Colorado mining promoter William Cornell Jewett in an unsuccessful attempt to gain support for European mediation of the war. On July 5, 1864, Jewett wrote to Greeley from Niagara Falls that "*two Ambassaders—of Davis & Co. are now in Canada—with full & complete powers for a peace*" and that the Confederate envoys wished to meet with Greeley and President Lincoln. The next day Jewett telegraphed to ask if Greeley would come to Niagara Falls. Greeley forwarded Jewett's messages to Lincoln on July 7 with an accompanying letter.

New York, July 7th, 1864.

My Dear Sir:

I venture to inclose you a letter and telegraphic dispatch that I received yesterday from our irrepressible friend, Colorado Jewett, at Niagara Falls. I think they deserve attention. Of course, I do not indorse Jewett's positive averment that his friends at the Falls have "full powers" from J. D., though I do not doubt that *he* thinks they have. I let that statement stand as simply evidencing the anxiety of the Confederates everywhere for peace. So much is beyond doubt.

And thereupon I venture to remind you that our bleeding, bankrupt, almost dying country also longs for peace—shudders at the prospect of fresh conscriptions, of further wholesale devastations, and of new rivers of human blood. And a widespread conviction that the Government and its prominent supporters are not anxious for Peace, and do not improve proffered opportunities to achieve it, is doing great harm now, and is morally certain, unless removed, to do far greater in the approaching Elections.

It is not enough that we anxiously *desire* a true and lasting peace; we ought to demonstrate and establish the truth beyond cavil. The fact that A. H. Stephens was not permitted, a year ago, to visit and confer with the authorities at Washington, has done harms, which the tone of the late National Convention at Baltimore is not calculated to counteract.

I entreat you, in your own time and manner, to submit overtures for pacification to the Southern insurgents which the impartial must pronounce frank and generous. If only with a view to the momentous Election soon to occur in North Carolina, and of the Draft to be enforced in the Free States, this should be done at once.

I would give the safe conduct required by the Rebel envoys at Niagara, upon their parole to avoid observation and to refrain from all communication with their sympathizers in the loyal States; but *you* may see reasons for declining it. But, whether through them or otherwise, do not, I entreat you, fail to make the Southern people comprehend that you and all of us are anxious for peace, and prepared to grant liberal terms. I venture to suggest the following

Plan of Adjustment.

1. The Union is restored and declared perpetual.
2. Slavery is utterly and forever abolished throughout the same.
3. A complete Amnesty for all political offenses, with a restoration of all the inhabitants of each State to all the privileges of citizens of the United States.
4. The Union to pay $400,000,000 in five per cent. U. S. Stock to the late Slave States, loyal and Secession alike, to be apportioned *pro rata* according to their Slave population respectively, by the Census of 1860, in compensation for the losses of their loyal citizens by the Abolition of Slavery. Each State to be entitled to its quota upon the ratification, by its Legislature, of this adjustment. The bonds to be at the absolute disposal of the Legislature aforesaid.
5. The said Slave States to be entitled henceforth to representation in the House on the basis of their *total* instead of their *Federal* population—the whole being now Free.
6. A National Convention, to be assembled so soon as may be, to ratify this adjustment and make such changes in the Constitution as shall be deemed advisable.

Mr. President, I fear you do not realize how intently the People desire any Peace consistent with the National integrity and honor, and how joyously they would hail its achievement and bless its authors. With U. S. Stocks worth but forty cents, in gold, per dollars, and drafting about to commence on the third million of Union soldiers, can this be wondered at?

I do not say that a just Peace is now attainable, though I believe it to be so. But I *do* say that a frank *offer* by you to the insurgents of terms which the impartial will say *ought* to be accepted, will, at the worst, prove an immense and sorely-needed advantage to the National cause: it *may* save us from a Northern insurrection.

Yours truly,
Horace Greeley

P. S. Even though it should be deemed unadvisable to *make* an offer of terms to the Rebels, I insist that, in any possible way it is desirable that any offer *they* may be disposed to make should be *received* and either accepted or rejected. I beg you to write those now at Niagara to exhibit their credentials and submit their ultimatum. H. G.

"AN INFINITY OF HILLS": GEORGIA, JULY 1864

John White Geary to Mary Geary

On July 2 Sherman succeeded in turning the southern end of Johnston's defensive line and forcing the evacuation of Kennesaw Mountain and Marietta. By July 5 Johnston had withdrawn to a fortified position extending for several miles along the west bank of the Chattahoochee River about six miles from Atlanta. A lawyer from Pennsylvania who had fought at Cedar Mountain, Chancellorsville, Gettysburg, and Chattanooga, Brigadier General John White Geary commanded the Second Division, Twentieth Corps, in the Army of the Cumberland. Geary wrote to his wife about the campaign in northern Georgia.

Hd. Qrs. 2nd Div. 20th Army Corps
Near Chattahoochie River, Ga.   July 8th 1864

My Dearest Mary

I am the recipient of three letters from you bearing date at Germantown, and I assure you it afford me no ordinary pleasure to know that you have had the enjoyment of a congenial visit among friends and true hearted people. I sincerely trust that you will also enjoy your return home among the household jewels. I exceedingly regret that I have not yet been paid, (no paymaster having arrived) or I would have furnished sufficient funds for procuring furniture sufficient for the house. This was my intention had the P.M. done his duty. I am astonished to find there is nine hundred dollars to my credit in the Harrisburg Bank. Either Snodgrass or Mrs Brown has not collected the money due them and it still remains there on deposit, subject to my drafts which they hold. This is the only way in which I can account for that at present. If I could remit to you I would do so at once in sufficient amount to pay all our debts and furnish the house. I wish it was done.

We have had much hard fighting in Northern Georgia. The enemy has stubbornly contested every inch of ground. As fast as we drive him from one fortified position he simply falls back to another perhaps stronger, better, and more easy of defence aided by natural as well as artificial defences. The surface of the country is broken into an infinity of hills of the most irregular shapes and running in every possible direction. No two of them parallel. The valleys are deep ravines, and very marshy, being difficult to pass our artillery & waggons across them. It is almost universally covered with heavy timber with a dense undergrowth, and here and there *only* a field forms the exception. The country is well watered, and here in the vicinity of the river we find some cool springs which afford most delicious beverage. The inhabitants with but few exceptions have fled from before us as we have advanced in our victorious career. There is scarcely a man, woman, or child, or negro to be seen, not a horse (except the dead ones our cannon forced the enemy to leave behind) nor a cow, hog, or sheep is to be seen, even the very chickens, geese, and turkeys are driven before us as the enemy recedes, and not a living thing is left to tell the tale. Talking of turkeys reminds me of an incident a day or two ago. We were driving the enemy before us at a furious rate when near the head of my column a fine turkey mounted into the top of a hickory tree. It was very tempting, to think of the delicious meal it would make, so I drew my trusty revolver, and fired with deadly aim, down came the bird, and subsequently our agreeable anticipations were fully realized with a sumptuous repast.

The enemy are encamped partly on this side and partly on the south side. They are very strongly fortified and have an immense amount of artillery in position. They will undoubtedly make a stubborn resistance in this position. This Camp is about 1½ miles from the river, with the enemy between us and them. The only way to beat them here will be to outflank them as we have done heretofore.

The weather is excruciatingly warm, and it is almost impossible to perform more than half a day's labor in 24 hours. There is much remittant fever among the soldiers in consequence of the malarious influences arising from the decaying vegetable matter around us.

My own health, admist all my exposures, wettings, burnings, and dangers, is unusually good, and although death and sickness and every evil to which humanity is heir dwells around me, I am still by the mercy and goodness of Our Heavenly

Father, a spared monument of His mercy. Let us devoutly and sincerely thank and praise Him for His manifold mercy to us.

We are now in full view of Atlanta (8 miles). Like Moses, we can find a high toped Pisgah, and from it view the promised land. *Geographically* speaking it is only 8 miles from us, but *militarily* it may be much further.

Kenesaw Mountain and the city of Marietta were taken on the 3rd inst. and since then we have fought our way here.

I am pleased that the Philadelphia fair was so grand a success, and that you and Willie Geary had the satisfaction of visiting it. Such an occurrence may never happen again in a lifetime.

I long to see you and our dear ones at home once more. May God bless us and preserve us from every evil and soon restore our country to peace. Ever your true & loving husband

Jno W Geary

WASHINGTON, D.C., JULY 1864

Abraham Lincoln:
Proclamation Concerning Reconstruction

In December 1863 President Lincoln used his annual message to Congress and an accompanying proclamation to outline a plan for restoring loyal governments in the insurrectionary states. Under his proposal, a new state government committed to the abolition of slavery could be established after 10 percent of the state's voters had sworn future allegiance to the Union. Although his plan was initially well received by most Republicans, it came under increasing criticism by Radicals for being too lenient and for failing to guarantee the rights of the freed people. On July 2 Congress passed a reconstruction bill, sponsored by Ohio senator Benjamin F. Wade and Maryland congressman Henry Winter Davis, that required a majority of a state's white male voters to swear allegiance before elections could be held for a new state constitutional convention. Suffrage in the new elections would be restricted to voters who took the "Ironclad Oath" swearing that they had never voluntarily supported or aided the Confederacy. The Wade-Davis bill also abolished slavery in all of the Confederate states. (It was passed after the Thirteenth Amendment failed, 93–65, to win passage in the House of Representatives on June 15.) Lincoln pocket vetoed the bill and then issued a proclamation on reconstruction.

July 8, 1864
By the President of the United States.
A Proclamation.

Whereas, at the late Session, Congress passed a Bill, "To guarantee to certain States, whose governments have been usurped or overthrown, a republican form of Government," a copy of which is hereunto annexed:

And whereas, the said Bill was presented to the President of the United States, for his approval, less than one hour before the *sine die* adjournment of said Session, and was not signed by him:

And whereas, the said Bill contains, among other things, a plan for restoring the States in rebellion to their proper practical relation in the Union, which plan expresses the sense of Congress upon that subject, and which plan it is now thought fit to lay before the people for their consideration:

Now, therefore, I, Abraham Lincoln, President of the United States, do proclaim, declare, and make known, that, while I am, (as I was in December last, when by proclamation I propounded a plan for restoration) unprepared, by a formal approval of this Bill, to be inflexibly committed to any single plan of restoration; and, while I am also unprepared to declare, that the free-state constitutions and governments, already adopted and installed in Arkansas and Louisiana, shall be set aside and held for nought, thereby repelling and discouraging the loyal citizens who have set up the same, as to further effort; or to declare a constitutional competency in Congress to abolish slavery in States, but am at the same time sincerely hoping and expecting that a constitutional amendment, abolishing slavery throughout the nation, may be adopted, nevertheless, I am fully satisfied with the system for restoration contained in the Bill, as one very proper plan for the loyal people of any State choosing to adopt it; and that I am, and at all times shall be, prepared to give the Executive aid and assistance to any such people, so soon as the military resistance to the United States shall have been suppressed in any such State, and the people thereof shall have sufficiently returned to their obedience to the Constitution and the laws of the United States,—in which cases, military Governors will be appointed, with directions to proceed according to the Bill.

In testimony whereof, I have hereunto set my hand and caused the Seal of the United States to be affixed.

Done at the City of Washington this eighth day of July, in the year of Our Lord, one thousand eight hundred and sixty-four, and of the Independence of the United States the eighty-ninth.

ABRAHAM LINCOLN.

By the President:

WILLIAM H. SEWARD, Secretary of State.

CONDITIONS FOR PEACE:
WASHINGTON, D.C., JULY 1864

Abraham Lincoln to Horace Greeley

President Lincoln replied on July 9 to Horace Greeley's letter concerning possible peace negotiations. Greeley responded the following day that "I have neither purpose nor desire to be made a confidant, far less an agent in such negotiations." He continued: "Meantime, I wish you would consider the propriety of *somehow* apprising the People of the South, especially those of North Carolina, that *no* overture or advance looking to Peace and Reunion has ever been repelled by you, but that such a one would at any time have been cordially received and favorably regarded—and would still be."

Hon. Horace Greely Washington, D.C.
Dear Sir July 9. 1864

Your letter of the 7th., with inclosures, received. If you can find, any person anywhere professing to have any proposition of Jefferson Davis in writing, for peace, embracing the restoration of the Union and abandonment of slavery, what ever else it embraces, say to him he may come to me with you, and that if he really brings such proposition, he shall, at the least, have safe conduct, with the paper (and without publicity, if he choose) to the point where you shall have met him. The same, if there be two or more persons. Yours truly

A LINCOLN

HANGING THE ANDERSONVILLE RAIDERS: GEORGIA, JULY 1864

Eugene Forbes: Diary, July 11, 1864

Six of the Andersonville "raiders" were tried and condemned by their fellow prisoners and publicly executed after their sentences were approved by the Confederate authorities in Richmond. Sergeant Eugene Forbes watched as they were hanged by the "regulators" who had banded together and defeated the raiders in late June. In September Forbes was transferred to the prison camp at Florence, South Carolina, where he would die on February 7, 1865.

Monday, July 11. Cloudy A.M. Atlanta reported in flames, and Johnston gone to reinforce Lee. A Charleston prisoner, captured yesterday week, told me Foster had been repulsed in an attack on Fort Johnston, on James Island. A slight shower came up about 4 P.M., cooling the air considerably. About 5 o'clock P.M. a rebel guard was seen marching toward the stockade, preceded by a drum corps, playing the "Dead March," and conducting six prisoners. They entered the gate at the southeast part of the stockade, when Capt. Wurtz (commanding the camp) delivered the prisoners over to a body of the Regulators, headed by "Limber Jim." A gallows had been previously erected in the street leading from the southwest gate. The prisoners names were given as follows: "Moseby," "Murray," "Terry," "Sarsfield," "Delainy," and "Curtis." They were all of Irish birth or extraction, except "Moseby," who was English. "Limber Jim," with his assistants, proceeded to bind the prisoners' hands, the Captain having withdrawn the guard to the outside, leaving the condemned to be disposed of by our men. When Curtis was about to be bound, he exclaimed, "This cannot be," and made a dash through the crowd and toward the creek; he succeeded in reaching the other side, but was arrested and brought back. Shortly after five o'clock, the whole six were swung off, but "Moseby's" rope broke, bringing him to the ground, but he was soon swung up again. After having hung about fifteen minutes they were cut down, when the crowd quietly dispersed. So endeth the raid on Dowd, three of his principal assailants being among those executed. And it is to be hoped that it will also end the system of organized robbery and ruffianism which has so long ruled this camp. "Limber Jim" and his assistants were taken out of the stockade after the execution, and it is supposed they will be employed outside. A squad (1700?) of prisoners came in today from Grant's Army; they bring a report that the Exchange Commissioners have agreed on terms for exchange and parole, to commence on the 16th inst. Drew pork, salt and meal P.M. Changed our sergeant, appointing Emmett in place of Buckley.

THREATENING WASHINGTON:
MARYLAND, JULY 1864

Henry Robinson Berkeley: Diary, July 4–13, 1864

Major General Franz Sigel had advanced up the Shenandoah Valley with a force of 9,000 men in early May as part of Grant's plan for a coordinated Union offensive in Virginia. Sigel was defeated at New Market on May 15 by 5,000 Confederates under Major General John C. Breckinridge, and was replaced by Major General David Hunter. After reorganizing his forces, Hunter defeated Brigadier General William E. Jones at Piedmont on June 5, occupied Lexington, and then began advancing on Lynchburg, an important rail junction that linked Petersburg and Richmond with the Shenandoah Valley. On June 13 Lee sent his Second Corps, now commanded by Lieutenant General Jubal A. Early, to help defend Lynchburg. Early's troops began to arrive on June 17, and after two days of skirmishing Hunter abandoned his offensive and retreated into the mountains of West Virginia. His withdrawal allowed Early to march north through the Shenandoah Valley and launch a raid into Maryland intended to draw Union troops away from Petersburg. A veteran of Yorktown, Glendale, Fredericksburg, Gettysburg, the Wilderness, Spotsylvania, and Cold Harbor, Private Henry Robinson Berkeley served in an artillery battalion in the Confederate Second Corps.

July 4. Taking the right-hand road, we passed through Smithfield and Charlestown, Jefferson County, Virginia and encamped on the Harpers Ferry Pike four miles south of Harpers Ferry. Here we remained all night. The Yanks who were in Harpers Ferry have retired to the Maryland Heights, leaving a good deal of plunder in the Ferry. Some of our boys went into the town to plunder. They got quite a lot of sugar, coffee, hardtack, molasses, etc. John McCorkle went in on a mule and undertook to bring out a water bucket of molasses on his mule. The Yanks were amusing themselves by throwing among our plundering boys a lot of shell. They did no harm and no one was hurt; but a lamp post (i.e. a nine-inch shell) whizzing from the Maryland Heights, "busted" about three yards in rear of John's mule's tail, while John was on his way back to camp with his water bucket of molasses. This shell lighted up all the surroundings for a few seconds, and John's mule lighted out for camp; that mule made two-forty time to camp. John, however, clung bravely to his molasses, knowing full well that "lasses" was "lasses" in Dixie in those days, and finally arrived in camp covered completely with molasses, having about two quarts left in his bucket. He spent the rest of the night washing his clothes and his mule. Thus ended for us, The Glorious Fourth of July, 1864.

July 5. In the afternoon we marched over to Shepherdstown and encamped near the town for the night.

July 6. Left camp near Shepherdstown and, after crossing the Potomac River, which came a little above our waist, we encamped near Sharpsburg, Maryland. Had to examine my caisson boxes to see if the water had gotten into any of them, while crossing the Potomac. I found them O.K.

July 7. Remained in camp near Sharpsburg all day.

July 8. Marched to Frederick City, Maryland, and encamped near the town.

July 9. Passed through Frederick City and took the Washington, D. C., Pike and came upon the Yanks in line of battle on Washington side of the Monocacy River; the latter is a small stream flowing into the Potomac. We first took a position on the left of the Washington Pike and afterwards crossed over to right and put our battery on a hill fronting a still higher hill held by the Yanks. We got here about 1 P.M. We were ordered to open on the Yankees, as soon as we heard Gen. Gordon's Division open on our right. Gordon was flanking the Yanks on our right. About 3:45 P.M. we heard, on our right, some heavy fighting in a big field of big corn. We immediately opened on the Yanks in our front. I was acting as gunner, which position I had filled since R. B. Winston was wounded on June 3, 1864. We were hotly engaged only for about twenty minutes, the Yanks in our front giving away very soon; but, alas! We had three splendid men killed: viz., Gardner and Page were killed instantly by a shell and Lieut. George Hobson was killed by a sharpshooter after the enemy had been routed, and was retreating rapidly from the field. Hobson had had a wheel on his gun knocked to pieces by a cannon shot and could not go with us as we moved rapidly down the pike after the Yanks. While his men were putting a new wheel on his gun, he and J. H. Berkeley, being on their horses, rode to the brow of the hill in front of them (which hill overlooked the river), and halted their horses. Just at the moment they halted, two Minié balls whizzed over from beyond the river, one of which struck Lieut. Hobson on the right shoulder and, passing diagonally downward, stopped on his left hip. He sank from his horse and was caught by my brother and laid on the grass. He never spoke after being struck and breathed his last in about ten minutes. Just as he was shot, he was talking to my brother (J. H. Berkeley) of Gardner and Page, who had been killed a few moments before and whose bodies had been left unburied a short way behind us. And these were the last words on his lips, "Those poor boys must be buried and their graves marked, if I have to go back." As he reached the word, "back," the fatal ball struck him and he sank from his horse. Our chaplain, Mr. Gilmer, carried his body and those of Gardner and Page back to Frederick City and had them all three put into coffins, neatly buried and their graves marked. Lieut. Woodruff is missing tonight and has not been seen or heard of since one o'clock today. A cannon ball came very near taking my head off today. I think it was the same ball which killed Gardner and Page. I was leaning over aiming my cannon and it passed just over my head. If I had been standing up it would have struck me full in the face. We crossed the Monocacy River and after having followed the enemy for three miles we went into camp in a wheat field, which had just been cut. We found a wounded Yank in the fence corner near our campfire and carried him to our fire, gave him some water and after dressing his wound (he had been shot through the leg) and giving him some supper and a cup of coffee we fixed him a bed with some bundles of wheat and put him on it. He was very grateful and told us that he was a Marylander and was only about ten miles from his home. He said he was only eighteen. He looked very young. He said that he had been told that we were very cruel to our prisoners, and that when we first came to him, he thought we were going to kill him immediately.

July 10. The Yanks are falling back on Baltimore. We took

the Washington Pike, and after a long and hot day's march encamped for the night twenty miles from that city. We gave our wounded Yankee some breakfast this morning and fixed up his blanket on four stakes to keep off the sun. We left him to his friends. I have no doubt that by this time he is at home. Lieut. Woodruff still missing. He is supposed to have been killed or captured. He was last seen in Capt. Carpenter's Battery, asking for us and left there to find us. Some of our boys think he has deserted to the Yanks. I have very little confidence in him. I have just found, on going to bed, that it is Sunday. In times of marching and fighting, a soldier frequently forgets the days of the week, all being just alike.

July 11. We marched to within two miles of the corporate limits of Washington City and encamped at "Silver Spring," the home of Postmaster General Blair. We can see the dome of the capitol and a large part of the city. There has been some heavy picket fighting this evening. There is a rumor that we are to try and storm the fortifications at daybreak tomorrow.

July 12. Remained near Washington, D. C., all day on the farm of Francis P. Blair. It is called "Silver Spring." Is a beautiful place with a large lawn running down to a beautiful and cold spring fixed up with marble basins, etc. There was very heavy skirmishing this evening, but no attempt to take the strong fortifications in our front. We retreated after dark and marched all night towards Leesburg, Virginia.

July 13. Continued to march towards Leesburg, marching all night, only stopping at 4 P.M. long enough for the men to cook and eat and for our horses to be fed. We reached the Potomac River, at Edwards' Ferry about day.

THE CAPITAL UNDER ATTACK:
WASHINGTON, D.C., JULY 1864

Lois Bryan Adams to the Detroit Advertiser and Tribune

Although Washington was surrounded in July 1864 by a ring of strongly built fortifications, most of the capital's garrison had been sent on Grant's orders to Virginia to reinforce the Army of the Potomac, leaving about 10,000 semi-invalid veterans and inexperienced militiamen to defend the city. Jubal Early crossed the Potomac into Maryland on July 5–6 and advanced with 14,000 men to the Monocacy River near Frederick, where he defeated 6,000 Union troops under Major General Lew Wallace on July 9. The battle of Monocacy delayed Early's arrival at Washington by one day, allowing time for reinforcements sent by Grant from Petersburg to reach the capital. Early sent skirmishers toward Fort Stevens north of the city on July 11 as troops from the Sixth Corps began arriving by boat along the Potomac. The next day President Lincoln came under fire as he watched the fighting from the fort's parapet. Convinced that he could not break through the strengthened Union defenses, Early withdrew on the night of July 12. Lois Bryan Adams wrote about the Confederate attack in letters that appeared in the *Detroit Advertiser and Tribune* on July 20 and July 21, 1864.

Washington During the Siege
EXPERIENCES OF A RESIDENT
From Our Own Correspondent
Washington, July 13, 1864

I write you today from the center of the besieged capital, not knowing how or when my letter may reach you. Communication with the rest of world by rail or telegraph, is, as Michigan doubtless knows before this date, entirely cut off. The Potomac, however, is still running, and, as far as we know, its connection with the Chesapeake and Atlantic coast is still unbroken. So there is hope that in the course of time the waves may wash this waif on its northward way.

After the adjournment of Congress and the "noise and confusion" consequent upon a proper observation of the Fourth were past, the old Federal city, having assured itself that between Christian and Sanitary Commissions and State Relief Associations its sick and wounded defenders would be decently cared for, quietly addressed itself to preparations for its usual summer siesta. Confident of Grant's ability to whittle, smoke, and burrow himself into Richmond, and devoutly believing that the rebels would kindly stay there to witness his *entree* and grace his triumph, Washington stretched itself beside its slimy canal in the shadow of its unfinished monument, and said, "Now for a 'little more slumber, a little more folding of the hands to sleep,'" and was dreamily dozing off when startled by Maryland's cry of alarm and the smoke and flame of her burning dwellings. Hardly yet awake, she sprang to her feet barely in time to turn the key of her own door against the invader who already had his hand upon the latch. His coming was sudden, but still not altogether unprepared for.

This is the third day of our isolation from the civilized world, yet but for the lack of outside news, the addition of more stir among the inside military, and the distant roll of drums and roar of cannon around the borders, there is little to remind us that we are not one with the rest of the world as ever. Business seems progressing about the same as before, with the exception perhaps of a little rise in the prices of wares and goods. The workmen at the north front of the Patent Office still keep up their steady, monotonous pecking at the great marble blocks; laborers are quietly relaying and repairing street pavements; shop and tradespeople are going on with their business as usual; the tinsmith over the alley makes more noise than ever with the inevitable clattering hammer of his, and the dozens of rattle-brained children on the pavement rattle on, happily oblivious of the change.

It seems strange to be sitting here so quietly listening to the measured tread of armies and the ceaseless roll of their heavy trains through our streets. We know that "the front" now is no mythical or distant place far down the Rapidan, the Rappahannock, or the James; but, for the present at least, a reality terribly near, a dark horizon shutting us in, flashing with fire and streaming with blood. The neighing of the war horse in on our very ears—"the thunder of Captains and the noise of the shouting."

Yesterday and the day before there was considerable cannonading along our northern boundaries, only three or four miles from the city. Today we have but little; as yet there has been only skirmishing, and the throwing of shot and shell from the forts to prevent the rebels from concentrating in favorable positions. Surmises, conjectures, and rumors of every sort are in circulation, as to the number and object of the enemy, and as many differences of opinions probably, in regard to the result of this dashing venture. It will all very likely end in a little more than a great scare, some loss of life, the devastation of Maryland, the abstraction of millions of valuable property, and final escape of the daring raiders with it to Dixie. Even while I write, a rumor comes that they are across the Potomac again with their booty. Whether they will be intercepted or not remains to be seen.

Quite an engagement took place last evening, and it is said that the rebels have left some three or four hundred wounded on the field. They made Postmaster General Blair's house their headquarters, and did not burn it as they did the residences of known Union men. This fact is considered significant. It is reported that Sheridan will meet these plunderers on their way back to Richmond. Union people here will be terribly exasperated if they are allowed to escape.

L.

Letter from Washington
THE SIEGE RAISED | DEVELOPMENTS BY THE LATE
EXCITEMENT | WEEDS IN UNCLE SAM'S GARDEN |
DISLOYALTY IN DEPARTMENTS | THE SPIRIT MANIFEST |
BRIGHT TINTS | AN INCIDENT OF THE SEVENTH
STREET BATTLE
From Our Own Correspondent
Washington, July 15, 1864

The two days' siege of the capital is raised, cars are again running on the road that never was torn up, the valorous government clerks after enduring the hardships of war for several hours, returned yesterday, covered with dust and glory, to do duty at their desks and ledgers once more; secessionists, who in the moment of government alarm had become jubilant at the prospect of the fall of the capitol, and were shut in prison for safe keeping, are released and restored to favor—in short Washington is itself again, with all the symptoms of summer noontide somnolence creeping over its heart and brain.

The recent stir and excitement have had the effect to develop to a fuller extent than has heretofore been shown, the strong pro-slavery and Southern sympathetic elements existing here. People in distant States and cities have no knowledge of the prevalence and strength of these elements, or what inevitable, and it would seem irremediable, clogs they are upon the energies of the government.

The truth is, Uncle Sam's house, garden, and, for that matter, some of his large fields, too, have become weedy and foul beyond description. He has hesitated about pulling up the tares lest he might root up the wheat also; and now not only tares in the fields at large, but rank pigweeds, purslane, couchgrass and nettles, in his very conservatory and dooryard, claim his protection, and get it too, as it were in spite of himself and his most vigilant gardeners. It is easy to say, "pull them up and throw them to the dogs," but the doing of it is another thing. Still it does seem to some of us who stand peeping through the fence, that better use might be made of the rich ground occupied by those pompous pigweeds, sneaking couch-grass and purslane, and vindictive nettles.

It is a fact shamefully notorious here that there is scarcely one, indeed, I think it may be said with certainty, not one, of the government departments where the pro-slavery sentiment and the enemies of the Administration are not strongly represented. The representatives of rebeldom have secured appointments through the favor and influence of Copperhead Congressmen, or have bought them of tinctured or temporizing officials, and hold them probably because Government has more important matters to attend to than ferreting out "little foxes." Yet they are the very ones that are spoiling the grapes in the heart of the vineyard.

A case is publicly known and talked of where a woman

employed in one of the departments, at a salary of $50 per month, had a brother in the Union army who was wounded and brought to one of the hospitals in the city, but whom she never visited or took the least notice of, though she went daily with a government pass to carry comforts and luxuries to a rebel uncle who was confined in prison in the Old Capitol. Many other instances of the same nature transpire everyday, and many of these lady employees of government have relatives and friends in the rebel army, with whom they are in constant correspondence, and to whom it is said portions of their salaries are often transmitted. Is not this a delicate and unselfish way of aiding and comforting traitors?

But the women are far from being alone in this business; indeed they would not be in it at all if men were what they ought to be; for if all heads of Departments and Bureaus were what they should be in times like these, no such traitoresses would find their way into them under such flimsy pretenses as they do, to plunder and betray. This last raid seemed for a while to promise certain success to the rebels; sympathizers here appeared confident of it, and were quite open and insolent in the avowal of their sentiments. In no way perhaps did they better manifest the true spirit of their principles than in their insolent behavior towards the colored population. Even little misses spread themselves across the pavement when one of that luckless race was seen coming, and signified that "nigger might take their place in the gutter again."

These things are humiliating to national pride, but they go to show that there is a great deal of human nature, with a strong cross of Southern blood in it, still to be found in this good city of Washington. What the President and his trusty advisers have to contend with in the manifestation of this mongrel nature among officials, civil and military, no pen need undertake to tell. Happy will it be for us if, in spite of all, the old ship of State is at last brought safely through the storm.

A woman living near the battleground north of the city, has a brother in the rebel army who took the opportunity of being near to make her a visit, hoping also to get much needed supplies of food and clothing; but she indignantly drove him from her house, and threatened to shoot him for a traitor, as he is, if he ever attempted to appeal to her or call her sister again.

Union soldiers, though strangers, she fed and gave drink to with blessings and God speed, but the brother who had betrayed his country and sought its ruin, she cast from her as a wretch worthy only of the traitor's doom—the scorn and detestation of all loyal hearts.

L.

PURSUING EARLY: VIRGINIA, JULY 1864
Ulysses S. Grant to Henry W. Halleck

Throughout the war the Shenandoah Valley had served as a crucial source of food, fodder, and livestock for the Confederate forces in Virginia. As Early withdrew from Maryland, Grant issued directions for the pursuit of the retreating Confederates and the devastation of the valley.

City Point, Va, July 14th *1864*

MAJ. GEN. H. W. HALLECK,
CHIEF OF STAFF OF THE ARMY,
GENERAL,

It would seem from dispatches just received from Mr. Dana, Asst. Sec. of War, that the enemy are leaving Maryland. If so Hunter should follow him as rapidly as the jaded condition of his men and horses will admit. The 6th & 19th Corps should be got here without any delay so that they may be used before the return of the troops sent into the valley by the enemy. Hunter moving up the valley will either hold a large force of the enemy or he will be enabled to reach Gordonsville & Charlottesville. The utter destruction of the road at, and between, these two points will be of immense value to us.

I do not intend this as an order to bring Wright back whilst he is in pursuit of the enemy with any prospect of punishing him, but to secure his return at the earliest possible moment after he ceases to be absolutely necessary where he is.

Col. Comstock who takes this can explain to you fully the situation here. The enemy have the Weldon road completed but are very cautious about bringing cars through on it. I shall endeavor to have it badly destroyed, and for a long distance, within a few days. I understand from a refugee that they have twenty-five miles of track yet to lay to complete the Danville road.

If the enemy has left Maryland, as I suppose he has, he should have upon his heels, veterans, Militiamen, men on horseback and everything that can be got to follow, to eat out Virginia clear and clean as far as they go, so that Crows flying over it for the balance of this season will have to carry their provender with them.

> I am Gen. very respectfully
> your obt. svt.
> U. S. GRANT
> Lt. Gen.

"THE DEEPEST SHAME":
WASHINGTON, D.C., JULY 1864

Charles A. Dana to Ulysses S. Grant

Assistant Secretary of War Charles A. Dana wrote to Grant after it had become clear that Early, like Lee after Antietam in 1862 and Gettysburg in 1863, had escaped across the Potomac into Virginia. A former newspaper editor, Dana had become Grant's confidant during the Vicksburg campaign while serving at his headquarters as a special emissary of the War Department.

WASHINGTON, D. C., *July* 15, 1864—11.30 A.M.
Lieut. Gen. U. S. GRANT:

Our latest advices indicate that the head of the retreating rebel column has reached Ashby's Gap. Wright is not yet at Edwards Ferry. The enemy will doubtless escape with all his plunder and recruits, leaving us nothing but the deepest shame that has yet befallen us.

C. A. DANA.

"TO WHOM IT MAY CONCERN":
WASHINGTON, D.C., JULY 1864

Abraham Lincoln: Offer of Safe Conduct for Peace Negotiators

On July 13 Horace Greeley assured Lincoln "that two persons, duly commissioned and empowered to negotiate for peace, are at this moment not far from Niagara Falls, in Canada." Lincoln responded two days later that "I was not expecting you to *send* me a letter, but to *bring* me a man, or men." In a separate letter sent the same day, the President told Greeley, "I not only intend a sincere effort for peace, but I intend that you shall be a personal witness that it is made." Greeley then went to Niagara Falls with a safe conduct pass, issued on Lincoln's orders, allowing four Confederate agents to travel to Washington. On July 18 Lincoln issued a proclamation calling for 500,000 volunteers and ordering a draft for September 5 to fill the quota for new troops. That day, Greeley telegraphed from Niagara Falls that while the Confederate envoys presently in Canada lacked the authority to negotiate, they or other representatives would be authorized to do so if Lincoln expressed interest. The President wrote a new offer of safe conduct, addressed "To Whom it may concern," and gave it to his secretary John Hay to take with him to Niagara Falls.

To Whom It May Concern
Executive Mansion,
Washington, July 18, 1864.

To Whom it may concern:

Any proposition which embraces the restoration of peace, the integrity of the whole Union, and the abandonment of slavery, and which comes by and with an authority that can control the armies now at war against the United States will be received and considered by the Executive government of the United States, and will be met by liberal terms on other substantial and collateral points; and the bearer, or bearers thereof shall have safe-conduct both ways.

ABRAHAM LINCOLN

"WAR TO THE BITTER END": CANADA, JULY 1864
Clement C. Clay and James P. Holcombe to Horace Greeley

John Hay crossed into Canada with Horace Greeley on July 20 and gave Lincoln's offer of safe conduct to James P. Holcombe, one of the Confederate agents who had been corresponding with Greeley. Instead of replying to Hay, Holcombe and his colleague Clement C. Clay addressed a letter to Greeley and released it on July 21 to the Associated Press. The letter was widely printed in the northern press the following day, along with earlier correspondence between Greeley and the Confederate agents that did not mention the conditions for peace Lincoln had set forth on July 9 (see p. 243 in this volume). Greeley asked the President on August 4 to publish their correspondence regarding the Niagara Falls episode. Lincoln agreed, but requested that Greeley suppress passages in his letters the President believed "give too gloomy an aspect to our cause, and those which present the carrying of elections as a motive of action." Greeley refused, and their correspondence remained unpublished. Clay, Holcombe, and their colleagues continued to meet with Peace Democrats in an effort to influence the platform and nomination of the Democratic national convention, which was scheduled to meet in Chicago on August 29.

NIAGARA FALLS, CLIFTON HOUSE, July 21.
To Hon. Horace Greeley:

SIR: The paper handed to Mr. HOLCOMBE on yesterday, in your presence, by Maj. HAY, A.A.G., as an answer to the application in our note of the 18th inst., is couched in the following terms:

EXECUTIVE MANSION, WASHINGTON, D.C.,
July 18, 1864.

To whom it may Concern:

Any proposition which embraces the restoration of peace, the integrity of the whole Union, and the abandonment of Slavery, and which comes by and with an authority that can control the armies now at war against the United States, will be received and considered by the Executive Government of the United States, and will be met by liberal terms, on other substantial and collateral points, and the bearer or bearers thereof shall have safe conduct both ways.

ABRAHAM LINCOLN.

The application to which we refer was elicited by your letter of the 17th instant, in which you inform Mr. JACOB THOMPSON and ourselves that you were authorized by the President of the United States to tender us his safe conduct on the hypothesis that we were "duly accredited from Richmond as bearers of propositions looking to the establishment of peace," and desired a visit to Washington in the fulfillment of this mission. This assertion, to which we then gave, and still do, entire credence, was accepted by us as the evidence of an unexpected but most gratifying change in the policy of the President, a change which we felt authorized to hope might terminate in the conclusion of a peace mutually just, honorable and advantageous to the North and to the South, exacting no condition but that we should be "duly accredited from Richmond as bearers of propositions looking to the establishment of peace." Thus proffering a basis for conference as comprehensive as we could desire, it seemed to us that the President opened a door which had previously been closed against the Confederate States for a full interchange of sentiments, free discussion of conflicting opinions and untrammeled effort to remove all causes of controversy by liberal negotiations. We, indeed, could not claim the benefit of a safe conduct which had been extended to us in a character we had no right to assume and had never affected to possess; but the uniform declarations of our Executive and Congress, and their thrice repeated, and as often repulsed, attempts to open negotiations, furnish a sufficient pledge to assure us that this conciliatory manifestation on the part of the President of the United States would be met by them in a temper of equal magnanimity. We had, therefore, no hesitation in declaring that if this correspondence was communicated to the President of the Confederate States, he would promptly embrace the opportunity presented for seeking a peaceful solution of this unhappy strife. We feel confident that you must share our profound regret that the spirit which dictated the first step toward peace had not continued to animate the counsels of your President. Had the representatives of the two Governments met to consider this question, the most momentous ever submitted to human statesmanship, in a temper of becoming moderation and equity, followed as their deliberations would have been by the prayers and benedictions of every patriot and Christian on the habitable globe, who is there so bold as to pronounce that the frightful waste of individual happiness and public prosperity which is daily saddening the universal heart, might not have been terminated; or if the desolation and carnage of war must still be endured through weary years of blood and suffering, that there might not at least have been infused into its conduct something more of the spirit which softens and partially redeems its brutalities. Instead of the safe conduct which we solicited, and which your first letter gave us every reason to suppose would be extended for the purpose of initiating a negotiation in which neither Government would compromise its rights or its dignity, a document has been presented which provokes as much indignation as surprise. It bears no feature of resemblance to that which was originally offered, and is unlike any paper which ever before emanated from the constitutional Executive of a free people. Addressed "to whom it may concern," it precludes negotiation, and prescribes in advance the terms and conditions of peace. It returns to the original policy of "No bargaining, no negotiations, no truces with rebels except to bury their dead, until every man shall have laid down his arms, submitted to the Government, and sued for mercy." What may be the explanation of this sudden and entire change in the views of the President, of this rude withdrawal of a courteous overture for negotiation at the moment it was likely to be accepted, of this emphatic recall of words of peace just uttered, and fresh blasts of war to the bitter end, we leave for the speculation of those who have the means or inclination to penetrate the mysteries of his Cabinet, or fathom the caprice of his imperial will. It is enough for us to say that we have no use whatever for the paper which has been placed in our hands. We could not transmit it to the President of the Confederate States without offering him an indignity, dishonoring ourselves and incurring the well-merited scorn of our countrymen.

Whilst an ardent desire for peace pervades the people of the

Confederate States, we rejoice to believe that there are few, if any among them, who would purchase it at the expense of liberty, honor and self-respect. If it can be secured only by their submission to terms of conquest, the generation is yet unborn which will witness its restitution. If there be any military autocrat in the North who is entitled to proffer the conditions of this manifesto, there is none in the South authorized to entertain them. Those who control our armies are the servants of the people, not their masters; and they have no more inclination, than they have right, to subvert the social institutions of the sovereign States, to overthrow their established Constitutions, and to barter away their priceless heritage of self-government. This correspondence will not, however, we trust, prove wholly barren of good results.

If there is any citizen of the Confederate States who has clung to a hope that peace was possible with this Administration of the Federal Government, it will strip from his eyes the last film of such a delusion. Or, if there be any whose hearts have grown faint under the suffering and agony of this bloody struggle, it will inspire them with fresh energy to endure and brave whatever may yet be requisite to preserve to themselves and their children all that gives dignity and value to life or hope and consolation to death. And if there be any patriots or Christians in your land, who shrink appalled from the illimitable virtue of private misery and public calamity which stretches before them, we pray that in their bosoms a resolution may be quickened to recall the abused authority and vindicate the outraged civilization of their country. For the solicitude you have manifested to inaugurate a movement which contemplates results the most noble and humane, we return our sincere thanks; and are, most respectfully and truly, your obedient servants,

C. C. CLAY, Jr.
JAMES P. HOLCOMBE.

A MEETING WITH JEFFERSON DAVIS: JULY 1864

James R. Gilmore to the Boston Evening Transcript

July 22, 1864

In early July President Lincoln gave Colonel James F. Jaquess, a Methodist minister on leave from the 73rd Illinois Infantry, and James R. Gilmore, an author of books and sketches under the pen name Edmund Kirke, permission to travel to Richmond and hold unofficial talks on peace terms with Confederate leaders. Jaquess and Gilmore crossed into Confederate-held territory on July 16 and met with Jefferson Davis the following day. They returned to the Union lines on July 18, having obtained, as Lincoln hoped, an unyielding statement from Davis regarding the Confederacy's war aims. Gilmore published a letter about his trip with Jaquess in the *Boston Evening Transcipt* on July 22 that was reprinted in *The New York Times* and other northern newspapers. He wrote a longer account of his mission, "Our Trip to Richmond," which appeared in the *Atlantic Monthly* in September 1864 (see pp. 338–357 in this volume).

A CARD FROM EDMUND KIRKE

Editor of the Transcript: As the small amount of printer's ink which you used upon me in last evening's Transcript somewhat affects my friend Col. Jaquess—for whom you charge me with having "a weakness"—you will, I know, allow me a small space in reply.

I confess to a "weakness" for Colonel Jaquess, and I hope the day may never come when I have not a weakness for him, and for all men like him. I consider him a brave, true, patriotic, Christian gentleman. He is widely known and esteemed at the West. Before the war he was for fourteen years President of Quincy College, Illinois, and at the breaking out of the rebellion was selected by Gov. Yates to raise a three years' regiment.

He did so, and with that regiment was in the front of the assault at Fort Donelson; did effective service at Pittsburg Landing; saved our left wing at Perryville; "fought as *I* never saw man fight before" (those were General Rosecrans's exact words to me) at Stone river; stood his ground till three horses were shot under him, and three fourths of his men lay dead or wounded about him, at Chickamauga, and was the *first* man to enter the rebel intrenchments on the heights of Mission Ridge. Such a record, I think, should justify any weakness I have for him.

With his supposed "mission," I have nothing to do. I went with him—or rather he went with me, for my pass directed General Grant to "allow J. R. Gilmore and *friend* to pass our lines and go South,"—to Richmond, on Saturday last, and I can say, unequivocally, that the President knew nothing of his accompanying me.

Mr. Lincoln, though an old-time friend and acquaintance of Col. Jaquess, has not even *seen* him for now nearly three years.

How the newspaper statements in reference to our visit to Mr. Davis, originated, I do not know. Until twelve o'clock last night—when I returned to my home in this city—I had communicated to no human being, except Generals Butler and Grant and the President, the fact of having been in the rebel capital at all.

So much for your paragraph. Now, allow me a few words in reference to a telegram in this morning's Advertiser, which charges me with being an *attache* of the New York Tribune, and with having some connection with the Sanders-Greeley negotiation that is said to be going on at Niagara Falls.

I am *not*, and *never have been*, connected with the New York Tribune. At the urgent solicitation of Mr. Sidney Howard Gay, the managing editor of that journal (who is a very dear and intimate friend of mine,) I *did* consent, nearly two years ago, to the *Tribune Association* publishing a cheap edition of my books, (but that arrangement was long since discontinued,) and I did, in July last, write half a dozen sketches for that paper.

I have not, however, exchanged a word with Mr. Greeley, or even seen him, for fully three months, and I have no connection with, in fact I know nothing of, his "negotiations."

This much, however, in reference to that much-talked-of matter, being a Yankee, I can *guess. It will result in nothing.* Jefferson Davis said to me last Sunday (and with all his faults I believe him a man of truth) "This war must go on till the last of this generation falls in his tracks, and his children seize his musket and fight our battle, *unless you acknowledge our right to self government*. We are not fighting for slavery. We are fighting for INDEPENDENCE, and that, or extermination, we *will* have."

If Messrs. Sanders, Holcomb, Thompson & Co. have "pulled the wool" over the eyes of Mr. Greeley, they have not pulled it over the eyes of Mr. Lincoln. He, I know, fully understands and appreciates their overtures, and you can safely assure your readers that the interests and honor of the country are safe in his hands. If every man, woman and child in this nation knew him as I do, they would believe this, and would say, as I do, GOD BLESS HIM.

I have returned from the South much prostrated by disease contracted there, but if my strength allows, I shall tell you, and your readers, "how and why I went to Richmond," in the next (September) number of the Atlantic Monthly. You have alluded to me as "Edmund Kirke," and the reading public know me by that cognomen, but as I desire to be considered "personally responsible" for the statements herein, I subscribe my true name hereto.

JAMES R. GILMORE,
37 West Cedar street, Boston.

Friday Morning.

FIGHTING IN THE SHENANDOAH:
VIRGINIA, JULY 1864

Henry Robinson Berkeley: Diary, July 14–24, 1864

Jubal Early crossed the Potomac on July 14 and returned to the northern Shenandoah Valley two days later. After fighting with Union forces near Berryville on July 18, he began retreating south toward Strasburg the next day. Convinced that Early was about to rejoin Lee's army, Major General Horatio G. Wright, the commander of the pursuing Union forces, ordered most of his troops to return to the Petersburg front by way of Washington. Instead, Early marched north with 14,000 men and attacked 9,000 Union troops under Brigadier General George R. Crook at Kernstown on July 24. Confederate artilleryman Henry Robinson Berkeley wrote about the fighting at Kernstown and the earlier battle of Rutherford's Farm (or Stephenson's Depot), fought near Winchester on July 20.

July 14. Crossed the Potomac about 7 A.M. and encamped at the Big Spring two miles north of Leesburg. The march from Washington to this place has been the most severe I have ever experienced. We marched two nights and two days consecutively and during that time only halted our march the second afternoon long enough for men and horses to get something to eat. This heavy marching was made necessary because three Yankee armies were after us, any one of which was as large as our army under Gen. Early. These Yankee armies were Canby's at Washington, D. C., Gen. Wallace's at Baltimore and Gen. Hunter's now at Frederick City, Maryland. We marched out from between their converging lines. We got to the Big Spring about 9 A.M. I never had been so sleepy and tired before in all my life. I threw off my knapsack and blanket, crawled under an Osage orange hedge and in two minutes was fast asleep. We slept until 5 P.M. and then woke up and cooked and ate a hearty supper, feeling much refreshed after a bath.

July 15. Remained near Big Spring and washed our clothes.

July 16. We pulled out this morning and taking the Winchester Pike marched to Snickersville and encamped for the night. The Yankee cavalry made a dash on our wagon train about 3 P.M. and burnt a few wagons. We fired a few rounds at them. Two Yankees were killed and a few captured.

July 17. Sunday. We crossed the mountains by Snicker's Gap and continued our march towards Winchester and encamped near Berryville.

July 18. Remained near Berryville. Received six letters from home. Some of these letters had been following us ever since we left Richmond.

July 20. Moved last night from Berryville and marched three miles north of Winchester and there halted to get breakfast for men and horses. We remained in this place until 4 P.M. when we were ordered to follow Ramseur's Division down the pike towards Martinsburg. The Yanks in the meanwhile had driven back our cavalry. After going about a mile down the pike, Ramseur ran into an ambush the Yanks had set for us. Just as we reached the farther edge of a piece of woods, and while our men were still in line of march; the Yanks opened on us from behind a stone fence at close quarters before our line of battle could be formed, or our men load their guns which were empty. Our men gave way and, the Yanks charging when they saw our confusion, the whole thing soon became a panic. We lost our entire battery, bringing out only one limber and a caisson. We had twenty-five horses killed and four men killed in our battery. The following men were wounded, viz., Lieut. Basye, lost right foot, Lieut. Latham, believed to be mortally wounded, left at his aunt's in Winchester, Bolling Hewitt, John Hawkins, Frank Miller, Billy Good. The last two were left on the battle field and fell into the hands of the Yankees. Several other men were slightly hurt. Lieut. Basye's foot was cut off late tonight after we got back to Newtown, where we encamped for the night. Today's loss takes from our battery all four of our lieutenants, who started from winter quarters the first of April. Our sergeants are acting as lieutenants, and privates as corporals and sergeants.

July 21. We marched three miles towards Strasburg and then stopped and cooked, and fed the few horses we had left. We then went on to Strasburg and encamped there for the night.

July 22. Marched just beyond Strasburg and took the right-hand road; went out towards North Mountain for a mile and encamped there for the night.

July 23. Saturday. Remained here all day and washed our clothes.

July 24. We moved back towards Winchester early this morning and came on the Yanks at Kernstown. It is Sunday and I am riding Frank Kinckle's horse, Frank being sick and riding in our ambulance. Having lost our guns, and not having gotten others, we (I and my company) had the pleasure of looking on at this hot and successful little fight without taking part in it. After a short and hot fight our men drove the Yankees from all parts of the field, killing and capturing a good many. The Yankee cavalry at one time during the battle, charged the 61st and 2nd Virginia Regiments in an apple orchard. It was a very daring charge, and they did it to save their wagon train, but their loss was very heavy. It seemed to me, looking on from a distant hill, that every man was killed or captured and few horses went back, but most were without riders. I went to the spot when the fight was over. The wounded had been removed, but dead Yankees lay thick. Oh! How horrid is war. We ran the Yanks through Winchester and followed them, until night stopped us near Bunker Hill. We found in Winchester this evening Lieut. Latham, and Frank Miller. William Good had died of his wounds and been buried by the good people of Winchester. I visited the place where we lost our battery and am fully convinced if Gen. Ramseur had not interfered with us, we would never have lost our guns or the battle. We had taken position on the right and were ready to fire, when Gen. Ramseur ordered us to limber up and come over on the left of the pike. We did limber up and started over and it was while we were crossing the pike that the Yankees charged us and our infantry gave way. We could have fired at least a dozen rounds of canister into the crowded ranks of the Yanks while we were limbering up and I believe the canister would have saved the day, because I have never seen them fail to run when you went for them with canister at close quarters. It is sad to think of that mistake which cost us at least a hundred men killed and two hundred wounded. I would not like to be a general having men killed by my errors and mistakes.

Frank Miller's right leg has been amputated above the knee; this puts an end to his soldier life. He joined our company in March. He is only sixteen years old. He behaved in the fight like an old soldier. No doubt his mother will be glad to have her boy back home minus his leg. Alas! How many boys we have buried since we left our winter quarters in Orange. Who will be the next to fall?

FIGHTING FOR ATLANTA: GEORGIA, JULY 1864

Samuel T. Foster: Diary, July 18–23, 1864

On July 8 Sherman began sending troops across the Chattahoochee River to the north of the fortified position Johnston had retreated into after evacuating Kennesaw Mountain. Johnston withdrew from the west bank of the Chattahoochee on the night of July 9 and deployed his army of 60,000 men along Peachtree Creek, about three miles north of Atlanta. During the week that followed Sherman moved most of his 90,000 men across the Chattahoochee while sending cavalry to attack the railroad connecting Atlanta with Montgomery, Alabama. On July 17 Jefferson Davis relieved Johnston and replaced him with Lieutenant General John B. Hood, a corps commander in the Army of Tennessee who had previously led a division in the Army of Northern Virginia and been seriously wounded at Gettysburg and Chickamauga. Hood saw an opportunity to seize the initiative on July 19 when Sherman divided his forces, sending the Army of the Cumberland south across Peachtree Creek while the Army of the Tennessee occupied Decatur, six miles east of Atlanta. The next day, Hood attacked the Army of the Cumberland without success in fighting that cost the Confederates 2,500 men killed, wounded, or missing, and the Union 1,900. Captain Samuel T. Foster, a company commander in the dismounted 24th Texas Cavalry, served in Cleburne's Division in the corps commanded by Lieutenant General William J. Hardee. After being held in reserve during the battle on July 20, Cleburne's Division was posted to the east of Atlanta. On July 22 Hood launched another counterattack, sending Hardee's corps around the southern flank of the Army of the Tennessee. The resulting battle cost the Confederates 5,500 men killed, wounded, or missing, and the Union 3,700.

JULY 18

No move today— A circular from Genl Johnson announces that he has been removed from the command of this Army, and that Gen Hood succeeds him.

In less than an hour after this fact becomes known, groups of three, five, seven, ten or fifteen men could be seen all over camp discussing the situation— Gen. Johnson has so endeared himself to his soldiers, that no man can take his place. We have never made a fight under him that we did not get the best of it. And the whole army had become so attached to him, and to put such implicit faith in him, that whenever he said for us to fight at any particular place, we went in feeling like Gen Johnson knew all about it and we were certain to whip.

He never deceived us once. It is true we have had hard fighting and hard marching, but we always had something to eat, and in bad weather, or after an extra hard march we would have a little whiskey issued.

He was always looking after our comfort and safety. He would investigate our breastworks in person, make suggestions as to any little addition or improvement that would make them safer or more comfortable.

Gen Johnson could not have issued an order that these men would not have undertaken to accomplish—

For the first time, we hear men openly talk about going home, by tens (10) and by fifties (50). They refuse to stand guard, or do any other camp duty, and talk open rebellion against all Military authority— All over camp, (not only among Texas troops) can be seen this demoralization—and at all hours in the afternoon can be heard Hurrah for Joe Johnson and God D——n Jeff Davis.

July 19th

The noise and confusion was kept up all night. Genl Johnson was serenaded, and if Jeff Davis had made his appearance in this army during the excitement he would not have lived an hour.

This morning, in order (I suppose) to quiet the men, It is reported that Hood refuses to take command, and that Johnson will remain in command until after the fight at Atlanta.

In the afternoon we are put in position, build breastworks, and by night we are ready for the Yanks.

July 20

I am Brigade-officer-of-the-day today. And as it has been my luck heretofore to have trouble with the Yanks every time I am officer of the day—I suppose we will have a Muss of some sort. The Yanks have crossed the river above us and are coming, in fact they are shooting away to our right now, and have been since yesterday—

They are extending their line around Atlanta to the east, and now reaches from the river north of the rail road to the Augusta R.R. and cut us off from that direction—and they are still extending their lines in that direction. About 3 O'Clock PM Cheathams Div. in front of our Div. advanced through the woods until we found the Yanks, behind breastworks— We opened a tremendous fire with artillery and small arms, which is kept up until it is dark—*very dark*.

This was a little east of north from Atlanta— As soon as it gets dark our Brigade is withdrawn very quietly and marched to the city. Thence down the Augusta RR until we reach our line of breastworks running south.

We take along the breastwork to the south for about 1½ miles when we find the end of them. We then turn more to the west and stop and commence to build works—connecting with the main line.

July 21st

Made breastworks of logs, and by nine Oclock A.M. the Yanks artillery open on us from our left, their shell enfalading our lines. They have heard us chopping down trees and building our works and have our range—and the woods are so thick we can't see them. Their artillery are killing our men very fast— One company just to my left after finishing their works sat down to rest in a little ditch they had dug, when a shell came and took them at one end and killed and crippled every man in the ditch. Knocked one man in a hundred pieces—one hand and arm went over the works and his cartridge box was ten feet up in a tree.

My Company had completed their works when as I was lying down resting on my elbow—and another man in about the same position with our heads about two feet apart and our feet in opposite directions, a shell (schrapnell) exploded just between us—blowing me one way and him the other hurting neither one of us but killing three men about 10 ft. from us eating their breakfast.

About the middle of the day the small arms open on us in

front of us and as soon as our pickets came in a general fire opens along our line.

There are some dismounted cavalry to our right making our line longer and when the Yanks make the charge the cavalry shoot their guns off as fast as possible, while our pickets are getting in front of them. The pickets could do nothing but lie down and be captured by the Yanks—I lost three thus. As soon as the cavalry discharge their guns they all break and run like good fellows which leaves our right exposed and the Yanks following the cavalry pass by the right end of our line while those in front of us are held back by us.

Our Regt. which is on the right are taken out of the works and form a line at a double quick behind our works and perpendicular to it, which puts the left of the regt at the works— while the right is the length of the regt. off— We go forward quick time and drive the Yanks out in short order, and swing around and occupy our line again—then we are put in single file so as to cover the ground that had been occupied by the cavalry.

Here is where Lt Boerner of Capt Flys Co and Bud Martin same company were killed—both shot in the head, and while we were driving the Yanks out from our rear, one man (Joe Harrison) of my Co. ran up to a Yank, that was cursing a wounded Confed, put the muzzle of his gun to his back and blew him up.

I lost today out of my Company Sergt [   ] Chas Pepper and John Sutton killed— Thos Fisher wounded; and three captured on the picket line.

I am put in charge of the Picket line today to bring off the Pickets tonight— Our whole corps (Hardees) will move tonight some where, and the Yanks are so close to us in front that it is a dangerous maneuver—and requires considerable skill.

July 22nd

Last night about midnight the command moved off and left me out with the Pickets. I soon had all the pickets to move cautiously back to the breastworks and had them so scattered that they occupied the whole line, built little fires, and would knock with sticks on the log breastworks and talk pretty loud.

Kept this up until nearly day light when I had them all assemble about the centre and move off in a pretty fast walk.

We followed the command, passing through Atlanta again, turning south. Kept turning to the left. Caught up with the command about 12 O'clock M. and by 2 PM we are opposite to where we left this morning, in the rear of the Yanks. Hardees whole Corpse is here and form line-of-battle facing towards Atlanta with the Yanks in front of us with their backs to us. A skirmish line is put out to cover the whole front—and by 2½ PM we go forward. I and my whole Company are on the skirmish line. The enemy are about 2½ miles from us—as we go forward we go through fields, woods, briars &c with order for the skirmishers to go to the enemys line without firing a gun.

About 2 miles we see a Yank in front of us, when two or three men fire at him and kill him dead on the spot.

A little further on we find QuarterMasters wagons and tents, find a table set ready for dinner for 4 men—two wagons loaded with spades and picks &c a battery of artillery—but the skirmish line pass right on—woods very thick consisting of Oak Chestnut poplar and undergrowth— A Yankee General was back here and a man in my Co. (Cowan) shot at him and wounded him very badly—but did not know who it was only that he was an officer.

Cowan ran back from the skirmish line to get the litter bearers, so they could carry him back into our lines; but before he got back he had been taken in to *their* lines— The skirmishers push on until we find their works which they are preparing to leave.

The skirmishers stop in about 150 yards of the Yanks line-of-battle, to wait our own line to come up with us.

It appears that Genl Walker of a Georgia Brigade got killed about this time and the enemys line being crooked some parts of our line struck them before other parts.

All these or something else broke our line behind us, so they never came to us, but were fighting to our right and left.

I remained here for half an hour or more during which time the Yanks had discovered that there was only a skirmish line of us, they began to get over their scare and get together again, and began to shoot at us— They also turned their Artillery on us and began shelling the woods.

Soon they began sending out bodies of men into the woods where we are, and Occasionally, there is a terrible shooting to our right or left, and sometimes nearly behind us, but the woods are so thick that we can't see but a short distance.

After taking in the situation I assemble my own Company, and start back to find the line-of-battle that should have been close in our rear. Just here we capture three teamsters in the bushes. We start back through the wood, but had not got more than fifty yards before a Yank appeared before us. I ordered him to throw his gun down. Instead of doing so he cocked his gun, and aimed it at me not more than 20 feet away, and in an instant would have fired, but one of my men (Jake Eastman) was too quick for him and shot him down, the ball passing in the lower part of his bowels and out at the small of his back, which droped him in his tracks. Eastman then went up to the Yank, gave him some water and they made friends, the Yank forgiving him saying, that he done wrong, in not throwing his gun down when I told him to.

While they were talking, I with the rest of the Company and prisoners moved on and was soon out of sight of them.

While they were still there (only a few moments) a squad of Yanks came close to them, when the wounded Yank told my man to squat down by the tree, or they would see him, and take him prisoner. He did so, but they saw him and came and captured him surenough.

They took his gun from him, and put him in charge of one man to take him back to their lines— All this time I was getting further from him at every step, not dreaming of his trouble—

These two men (the Yank and his prisoner) soon got lost and my man kept telling him to go a little further this way else he would come into our line, until he saw there was no chance to get Mr Yank to come voluntarily into our line, when he concluded he would try to take the Yanks gun from him. So he picked a favorable spot and sprang upon him and caught the gun. Then they had it there all alone in the woods, each one wanting that gun but neither could get it. They soon began to get wearied out when Eastmans eye happened to catch sight of the Yanks bayonett still in his scabbard.

He grabbed it and put the point of it to the Yanks breast, when the Yank let loose the gun and surrendered.

Eastman of course brought him in to our lines. We soon found the command, reforming, and soon went in where I had just come out.

The fight is kept up all the evening. Jr. Harrison is severely wounded also Sam Fisher Alf Neil and Ogle Love— Three killed one wounded and three captured yesterday. Today four wounded is cutting the Company down very fast. We look loansome.

The fighting is kept up til night, very heavy. We charged in the woods then fall back—repeated it several times until night puts an end to the conflict.

July 23

All quiet this morning, after a terrible day yesterday all along the lines.

Our men are getting boots hats &c watches knives &c off of the dead Yanks near us in the woods—lots of them.

Alf Neil and Ogle Love come back this morning, having been over heated yesterday, and retired. Our dead have all been buried, and the Yanks will be as soon as they can do so.

We cook and eat, talk and laugh with the enemys dead lying all about us as though they were so many logs.

"TAKE MY CHILDREN FROM THOSE MEN":
MASSACHUSETTS, JULY 1864

John Q. A. Dennis to Edwin M. Stanton

In July 1863 Colonel William Birney, son of the abolitionist leader James G. Birney, began recruiting black soldiers in eastern Maryland. Although his instructions limited his recruiting to free blacks and the slaves of disloyal owners, Birney used his position to free slaves regardless of the loyalty of their masters. It is likely that John Q. A. Dennis was freed by an expedition Birney ("Cornel borne") sent in the fall of 1863 to Worcester County. No record has been found in the War Department archives of a response to the appeal Dennis made to Secretary of War Stanton for help in freeing his family. On October 12–13, 1864, Maryland voters approved, 30,174–29,799, a new constitution that abolished slavery in the state on November 1.

Boston July 26th 1864
Dear Sir   I am Glad that I have the Honour to Write you afew line   I have been in troble for about four yars   my Dear wife was taken from me Nov 19th 1859 and left me with three Children and I being a Slave At the time Could Not do Anny thing for the poor little Children for my master it was took me Carry me some forty mile from them So I Could Not do for them and the man that they live with half feed them and half Cloth them & beat them like dogs & when I was admited to go to see them it use to brake my heart & Now I say agian I am Glad to have the honour to write to you to see if you Can Do Anny thing for me or for my poor little Children   I was keap in Slavy untell last Novr 1863. then the Good lord sent the Cornel borne Down their in Marland in worsester Co   So as I have been recently freed I have but letle to live on but I am Striveing Dear Sir   but what I went too know of you Sir is is it possible for me to go & take my Children from those men that keep them in Savery   if it is possible will you pleas give me a permit from your hand then I think they would let them go   I Do Not know what better to Do but I am sure that you know what is best for me to Do

my two son I left with Mr Josep Ennese & my litle daughter I left with Mr Iven Spence in worsister Co [ ] of Snow hill

Hon sir will you please excuse my Miserable writeing & answer me as soon as you can I want get the little Children out of Slavery, I being Criple would like to know of you also if I Cant be permited to rase a Shool Down there & on what turm I Could be admited to Do so No more At present Dear Hon Sir

John Q A Dennis

Hon Sir will you please direct your letter to No 4½ Milton St Boston mass

"A MELANCHOLY ACCIDENT": TEXAS, JULY 1864

Benjamin F. McIntyre: Diary, July 29, 1864

A Union expeditionary force of 6,000 men landed on Brazos Island at the mouth of the Rio Grande on November 2, 1863, and occupied Brownsville, Texas, four days later in an attempt to block Confederate trade with Europe through Mexican ports. Although the garrison at Brownsville was able to control the lower Rio Grande valley, the Confederates continued to export cotton and import supplies across the river west of the town. In the summer of 1864 the Union troops along the Rio Grande, now numbering 2,700, came under attack by a force of 1,300 irregular Confederate cavalry. After a series of skirmishes the Union forces evacuated Brownsville on July 29 and withdrew to the coast, where a small garrison would continue to hold Brazos Island. Second Lieutenant Benjamin F. McIntyre of the 19th Iowa Infantry had fought at Prairie Grove, in the siege of Vicksburg, and at Stirling's Plantation before being sent to Brownsville.

White House Ranch July 29th 1864

The Illinois 94th boys were favored with a ride from here on the Mustang, while the 91st Ill., 38th 20th & 19th Iowa under the command of Col Day of the 91st took up the line of march and by the judicious management in marching of Col Day we made this point at an early hour.

I Know not from what this place derives its name—if however a little white house the size of a hen coop is a white house and patches of cactus and chapperal on a barren sandy plain is a ranch this place must be rightly named. The 91st Ill. 20th Wis. have gone on to Brazos. I noticed on the steamer this morning the wives of Maj Pettybone, Capt Drake, & Lieut Yorke who has been on a visit to their husbands at Brownsville for several weeks past. At present we seem to form an Iowa Brigade our Colonel Com'dg.

In review of the past two days march of our troops It was as pleasant as could have been expected under circumstance. The Rio Grande was high and the country was flooded to a great extent and very many places the troops were compelled to pass through water two and three feet deep. The roads were very muddy and the days excessively hot with occasional rain and in passing through the closely matted chapperal upon either side excluding every breath of air and yet not sufficient in height to afford a shade.

A provost guard, left at Brownsville after our departure to watch unobserved a few Strong Union men left behind, captured some half dozen who as soon as we had left raised the Confederate flag & took formal possession of the place in the name of Godly "Jeff"—they were brought along as the guards did not think Brownsville a healthy place for them.

A melancholy accident happened this morning. The 20th Wis. & 94th Ill. were in camp with the Division last night at Union Ranch and for which two steamers were sent up last evening on which they were to embark. The boats were lying side by side in the stream. The two regiments were ordered upon them at an early hour—it was very dark and no lights were placed on the boats so that the troops could desern their way distinctly over piles of freight of every variety. The 20th Wis. Reg. were to take the outside boat—necessitating them of course to pass over the inside one. The river was full banks, the current very swift. Each man had his Knapsack strapped to his back and of course had also a full set of equipments beside his cartridge box containing forty rounds. One of the soldiers of the 20th thus equipped in passing over boxes, coils of rope, barrels, wood, tents &c made a misstep and fell into the river. As I Stated the river was high & swift and it was very dark. The unfortunate man Sustained himself upon the water for some time and had floated quite a half a mile. A yawl was put after him which in the confusion took minits to unloosen and got to within a few feet of the drowning man when he sank.

It would be folly in me to say anything regarding this matter—it is but a reiteration of many similar cases and was occasioned merely by officers not properly attending to their duties and not attending to the care of their men—a single lantern upon the bow of the Steamer would have Spared this meloncholy accident. He will soon be forgotten and the incidents attending his death be lost among the things of the past so far as his regiment is concerned, and the country will forget such a man ever existed—Yet far distant in the Badger

State near a little glassy lake are hearts who will preserve his memory green. It was a happy home and joy and happiness has lingered in the little domicil with its shades of vine—Sorrow henceforth will be its companion and that little glassy lake will mirror back the pale tearful faces of that once happy household desolated by the lack of care by the officer who was over him who today would be amoung us had ordinary precaution been taken and usual care exercised. The two days march has been a hot one—the 2d day while under the command of Col Day was rendered comfortable as far as marching is concerned for he understands how to march men—which not one out of a dozen of our Commanders do understand.

Gen Herron complimented his men on the dispatch with which they accomplished this march. Compliments are very good but when a man has been compelled to do his utmost & can do no more, compliments—even from a Major General—proves no balm—rather let our Generals use discretion and a little sense and his men will prove hereafter of benefit to him. Under the circumstances his compliments are in bad grace.

Gen Herron and his immortal Staff left this evening by steamer for Brazos. Two steamers—the James Hale and Mustang—remain here.

Col Bruce will receive orders from the General tomorrow probably regarding our future.

Col Dye is at the Island where his wife lies dangerously ill—it is a happiness for the husband to meet with his family after a long absence, yet here to some it has brought a great sorrow—the Surgeon of the 20th Wis. buried his wife at Brownsville—Lieut Yorke a staff officer left an interesting little child. Others were quite sick and came near their end and now they are left in a strangers land—a land soon to which no Union man holds any claim—but amid the chapperal and cactus they will rest—the mockingbird will carroll for them his morning anthem while gentle breezes will waft over them its orange ladened breeze. O how oft will the Kindred heart of loved ones yearn for this sacred Spot and wish their dead could repose in their own native soil. Over them sad memories might call up pleasing recollections and in their sorrow find a melancholy joy which is now forever denied them.

PREPARING FOR BATTLE:
GULF OF MEXICO, JULY 1864

David G. Farragut:
General Orders Nos. 10 and 11

A veteran of the War of 1812 and the U.S.-Mexican War, Rear Admiral David G. Farragut had led the Union squadron that forced a passage between Forts Jackson and St. Philip on the lower Mississippi in April 1862 and captured New Orleans. In July 1864 Farragut issued tactical instructions to his ship captains as his squadron prepared to fight its way past Forts Gaines and Morgan at the entrance to Mobile Bay. The texts of General Orders Nos. 10 and 11 printed here are taken from the *Official Records of the Union and Confederate Navies in the War of the Rebellion* (1894–1922). In *The Life of David Glasgow Farragut, First Admiral of the United States Navy, Embodying His Journal and Letters* (1879), Loyall Farragut, the admiral's son, published a somewhat different version of General Orders No. 11 that is probably based on a manuscript draft; the substantive differences between the two texts are presented in the endnotes to this volume.

U. S. FLAGSHIP HARTFORD,
Off Mobile Bay, July 12, 1864.

GENERAL ORDERS,
NO. 10.

Strip your vessels and prepare for the conflict. Send down all your superfluous spars and rigging. Trice up or remove the whiskers. Put up the splinter nets on the starboard side, and barricade the wheel and steersmen with sails and hammocks. Lay chains or sand bags on the deck over the machinery, to resist a plunging fire. Hang the sheet chains over the side, or make any other arrangement for security that your ingenuity may suggest. Land your starboard boats or lower and tow them on the port side, and lower the port boats down to the water's edge. Place a leadsman and the pilot in the port quarter boat, or the one most convenient to the commander.

The vessels will run past the forts in couples, lashed side by side, as hereinafter designated. The flagship will lead and steer from Sand Island N. by E. by compass, until abreast of Fort Morgan; then N. W. half N. until past the Middle Ground; then N. by W., and the others, as designated in the drawing, will follow in due order until ordered to anchor; but the bow and quarter line must be preserved to give the chase guns a fair range, and each vessel must be kept astern of the broadside of the next ahead; each vessel will keep a very little on the starboard quarter of his next ahead, and when abreast of the fort, will keep directly astern, and as we pass the fort will take the same distance on the port quarter of the next ahead, to enable the stern guns to fire clear of the next vessel astern.

It will be the object of the admiral to get as close to the fort as possible before opening fire. The ships, however, will open fire the moment the enemy opens upon us, with their chase and other guns, as fast as they can be brought to bear. Use short fuzes for the shell and shrapnel, and as soon as within 300 or 400 yards give them grape. It is understood that heretofore we have fired too high, but with grapeshot it is necessary to elevate a little above the object, as grape will dribble from the muzzle of the gun.

If one or more of the vessels be disabled, their partners must carry them through, if possible; but if they can not then the next astern must render the required assistance; but as the admiral contemplates moving with the flood tide, it will only require sufficient power to keep the crippled vessels in the channel.

Vessels that can must place guns upon the poop and topgallant forecastle and in the tops on the starboard side. Should the enemy fire grape, they will remove the men from the topgallant forecastle and poop to the guns below until out of grape range.

The howitzers must keep up a constant fire from the time they can reach with shrapnel until out of its range.

D. G. FARRAGUT,
Rear-Admiral, Commanding West Gulf Blockading Squadron.

FLAGSHIP HARTFORD,
Mobile Bay, July 29, 1864.

GENERAL ORDERS,
No. 11.

Should any vessel be disabled to such a degree that her consort is unable to keep her in her station, she will drop out of line to the westward and not embarrass the vessels next astern by attempting to regain her station. Should she repair damages, so as to be able to reenter the line of battle, she will take her station in the rear as close to the last vessel as possible.

So soon as the vessels have passed the fort and kept away N. W., they can cast off the gunboats at the discretion of the senior officer of the two vessels, and allow them to proceed up the bay to cut off the enemy's gunboats that may be attempting to escape up to Mobile. There are certain black buoys placed by the enemy from the piles on the west side of the channel across it toward Fort Morgan. It being understood that there are torpedoes and other obstructions between the buoys, the vessels will take care to pass to the eastward of the easternmost buoy, which is clear of all obstructions.

So soon as the vessels arrive opposite the end of the piles, it will be best to stop the propeller of the ship and let her drift the distance past by her headway and the tide, and those having side-wheel gunboats will continue on by the aid of their paddle wheels, which are not likely to foul with the enemy's drag ropes.

D. G. FARRAGUT,
Rear-Admiral.

THE BATTLE OF THE CRATER:
VIRGINIA, JULY 1864

Stephen Minot Weld: Diary, July 30, 1864, and Memoir from 1912

Lieutenant Colonel Henry Pleasants, the commander of the 48th Pennsylvania Infantry outside of Petersburg, was a mining engineer, and many of his men were coal miners. With the approval of Major General Ambrose Burnside, the commander of the Ninth Corps, Pleasants and his men began digging a tunnel on June 25 that eventually extended more than 500 feet and ended beneath a strongpoint overlooking the Union siege lines. When completed, the mine would be loaded with gunpowder and exploded, creating a breach in the center of the Confederate defenses that the Ninth Corps would attack through. Of the four divisions in the corps, three were badly understrength after suffering heavy losses in the spring campaign, while the Fourth Division, made up of nine regiments of the U.S. Colored Troops, had previously been used only to guard bridges and wagon trains. Impressed by the morale of his black troops, Burnside chose them to lead the assault, and had the division practice the maneuvers that would be needed to advance around the crater formed by the blast. On July 28 Meade ordered Burnside to place the Fourth Division in reserve, citing its inexperience in battle, and to use white troops in the initial assault. His decision was supported by Grant, who feared the political repercussions if it appeared that black troops had been deliberately sacrificed in a costly attack. Burnside had his three other division commanders draw lots to determine who would lead the assault. The task fell to the First Division, while the two other white divisions would protect its flanks. At 4:45 A.M. on July 30 the battle began as a lit fuse detonated 8,000 pounds of gunpowder. Lieutenant Colonel Stephen Minot Weld of the 56th Massachusetts Infantry advanced with the First Brigade of the First Division. He wrote about the battle in his diary and in reminiscences published in *War Diary and Letters of Stephen Minot Weld, 1861–1865* (1912).

Saturday, July 30.—We were formed in column of brigade wings, the 2d Brigade leading, under Colonel Marshall. General Bartlett commanded our brigade, Colonel Gould having the right wing, and I the left, consisting of the 21st Massachusetts on the right, the 56th Massachusetts in the centre, and the 100th Pennsylvania on the left. We were in position about three quarters of an hour before the mine was blown up, and while waiting my feelings were anything but pleasant. The officers and men were disappointed and discouraged at having to lead, as we had heard all along that the negroes were to do this, and we had no confidence in Ledlie. He had failed us on several occasions, notably on June 17. At 4.30 A.M. the mine was blown up. It was just early dawn, light enough to distinguish a person a few yards off. The explosion was the grandest spectacle I ever saw. The first I knew of it, was feeling the earth shaking. I looked up and saw a huge mass of earth and flame rising some 50 or 60 feet in the air, almost slowly and majestically, as if a volcano had just opened, followed by an immense volume of smoke rolling out in every direction. The noise was very slight indeed, considering that there were nine tons of powder exploded. The men of the division were stampeded at first, but were soon rallied. We charged, having to go by the flank, as we could only get over in one or two places, and entered the enemy's pits under a moderately heavy fire. We found an immense hole here, formed by the explosion, some 30 feet deep by 100 long and 40 wide. We were ordered to go to the right of the crater, and here I endeavored to re-form my regiments. The scene inside was horrible. Men were found half buried; some dead, some alive, some with their legs kicking in the air, some with the arms only exposed, and some with every bone in their bodies apparently broken. We held the enemy's line about three or four hours, capturing some 500 prisoners. When we had been there about four hours, the negro troops charged over, filling our pits and crowding us so that our men could not use their muskets. They made a charge on the enemy in our front, which was repulsed and followed by a countercharge, driving the negroes head over heels on to us, trampling down every one, and adding still more to the confusion. Several negroes were shot down close by me. I was taken prisoner and sent to the rear, where I found several of my men, together with Captain Fay. While on the way, I had to climb a breastwork exposed to our men's fire. I saw the rebs run up and shoot negro prisoners in front of me. One was shot four times.

We were taken to a place about half a mile from Petersburg, and kept there until evening. General Bartlett, Colonel Marshall and Captain Amory arrived about 4 P.M., in a squad that was captured later. We were moved still nearer the city, and camped in an open lot there. Charlie Amory had his boots stolen from under his head while asleep. He was using them as a pillow.

[These notes are written fifty years after the event, but it seems to me as if the whole matter was as vivid and clear as if it had happened yesterday. We started down late that evening and got into the covered way, which was a zigzag trench leading up to our rifle-pits. The rifle-pits had strong abattis trenches and wires and everything else, including chevaux-de-frise, to impede any of the enemy who were charging us. Orders had been given that the trenches were to be filled up with sandbags, and the abattis removed for a space of 200 yards, so that a regiment could march forward practically in line of battle. This was not done, for when we charged we had to go by the flank, not more than four men at a time, a space only about eight or ten feet having been filled up, and none of the abattis removed. This delayed the advance very much and undoubtedly had a great deal to do with losing us the battle this day. The mine was planned to be blown up at half-past four, but the fuse went out and they had to send men in to unpack the stuff which had been put around the fuse to prevent the force of the powder blowing out the tunnel, which took some time, so that it finally blew up at about half-past six or seven. The minute the mine exploded, a hundred and forty of our guns opened fire from the lines in the rear, shelling the Confederate lines all around on both sides of us. It was a magnificent sight and one never to be forgotten. I never shall forget my mortification while waiting for this mine to blow up. The troops were all standing in line, ready to charge, and bullets fired by sharpshooters and pickets kept zipping over us all the time and the men kept ducking. They were not to blame for this, as the orders were, when we were in the rifle-pits, invariably to duck if they saw a puff of smoke from the other side. This was absolutely necessary, as we lost men every day from their curiosity in peeking up to see what was going on. The minute a cap appeared it was the target for a dozen sharpshooters. Of course we were all nervous, standing there waiting for a charge which we were very uncomfortable about, owing to reasons which I have explained later on, and the men kept ducking as a bullet passed by. I said, "Steady, men, that bullet has gone by you by the time you hear it." Just then a bullet, which I am convinced was specially meant for me, went whizzing by me and I at once ducked. Every one laughed and I did not blame them, but a more mortified man than I was never lived.

When the mine did go up, it looked as if this immense cloud of timber, dirt and stones and everything was going to fall right down on us and we involuntarily shrank back. We at once got over this and started to make the charge. When we got to the pits, as I have said, there was no getting over except by a flank. Instead of going over about in line of battle, we moved by the flank through this narrow space, and before I could get over, the firing had become very hot and the dust was knocked up all around my feet all the time as I went over. The neglect to fix the works in our front also had another very bad effect. It broke the regiments all up. The men went over by the flank, scattered along as they could get through, and with almost no organization. As soon as we got into the crater, I did all I could to get my men together, and in some sort of shape for a fight. By that time it was almost impossible to do anything. We were as badly off then as we were in our own pits. There was no head. Our division commander was off on the other side and did not come over with us. General Bartlett was a cripple and had his wooden leg broken, and it was almost impossible to get anything done. I came near having my head knocked off by grape-shot two or three times. Finally the rebels charged on both our flanks. I was packed in there in the midst of the negroes. It was a perfect pandemonium. The negroes charged into the mine, and we were packed in there like sardines in a box. I literally could not raise my arms from my side. Finally, when the Confederates charged, those of the men nearest the rifle-pits next our line got over the line and got away. Luckily most of my men I had formed there, so that they were able to get away and protect our colors.

I got cut off and took refuge in a bomb-proof, as I could not run away, being surrounded on all sides. Pretty soon the rebels yelled, "Come out of there, you Yanks." I walked out, and the negro who had gone in there with me, and Captain Fay came out also. The negro was touching my side. The rebels were about eight feet from me. They yelled out, "Shoot the nigger, but don't kill the white man"; and the negro was promptly shot down by my side. They then grabbed my sword and my hat. "Come out of that hat, you Yank!" they yelled; and one of them cried, "What do you 'uns come down here and fight we 'uns for?" Then they told me to get over our embankment in their rear, which formed their second line, and I scrambled up, the bullets from our own men striking the dirt on all sides of me. I got over the embankment all right, and was walking to the rear, when I saw a negro soldier ahead of me. Three rebels rushed up to him in succession and shot him through the body. He dropped dead finally at the third shot. It was altogether the most miserable and meanest experience I ever had in my life. You could not fight, you could not give an order, you could not get anything done. Out of the nine regiments in my brigade I was the only regimental commander left alive. The others were all killed outright or mortally wounded. We were sent back about a mile to the rear and camped on a hill that night.

My diary for the year 1864, during the Wilderness Campaign, was carried in my boot-leg and so escaped seizure when I was captured at the mine.]

"MURDER THEM IN COLD BLOOD":
VIRGINIA, JULY 1864

William Pegram to Virginia Johnson Pegram

In the assault following the mine explosion many men from the First Division became trapped when they took shelter inside the crater instead of moving around it. As the attack became increasingly disorganized, the black troops of the Fourth Division were sent forward. They succeeded in capturing a Confederate defense line beyond the crater before being driven back by a counterattack launched around 9 A.M. Fighting continued into the afternoon as the Confederates eventually regained the ground they had lost in the morning. Union losses totaled about 3,800 men killed, wounded, or missing, including 1,300 from the Fourth Division, while the Confederates lost about 1,500 men. Brigadier General James H. Ledlie, who had spent much of the battle drinking liquor in a bombproof shelter, was relieved of command of the First Division, while Burnside was sent home on leave for the remainder of the war. Lieutenant Colonel William Pegram, a veteran artillery officer in the Army of Northern Virginia, wrote to his sister about the battle and the killing of black prisoners by Confederate troops.

Petersburg, Aug: 1st 1864.
My dear Jenny
I believe that you owe me a letter, but of this I am not certain; and even if I was, it would not prevent my writing to you, as I wish to set you a good example as a correspondent.

I supose you all have gotten, before this, a correct account of the affair on Saturday. It was an exceedingly brilliant one for us.

The enemy avoided our mine, & ran theirs under Cousin Dick's Batty. They blew it up about daylight, & taking advantage of the temporary confusion & demoralization of our troops at that point, rushed a large body of whites & blacks into the breach. This turned out much worse for them in the end. The ever ready Mahone was carried down to retake the line with his fine troops, which he did, with comparatively small loss to himself, & great loss to the enemy. I never saw such a sight as I saw on that portion of the line—for a good distance in the trenches, the Yankees, white & black, principally the latter, were piled two or three or four deep. A few of our men were wounded by the negroes, which exasperated them very much. There were hardly less than six hundred dead—four hundred of whom were negroes. As soon as we got upon them, they threw down their arms to surrender, but were not allowed to do so. Every bomb proof I saw, had one or two dead negroes in it, who had skulked out the fight, & been found & killed by our men. This was perfectly right, as a matter of policy. I think over two hundred negroes got into our lines, by surrendering & running in, along with the whites, while the fighting was going on. I don't believe that much over half of these ever reached the rear. You could see them lying dead all along the route to the rear. While there was a temporary lull in the fighting, after we had recaptured the first portion of the line, & before we recaptured the second, I was down there, & saw a fight between a negro & one of our men in the trench. I suppose that the Confederate told the negro he was going to kill him, after he had surrendered. This made the negro desperate, & he grabbed up a musket, & they fought quite desperately for a little while with bayonets, until a bystander shot the negro dead.

It seems cruel to murder them in cold blood, but I think the men who did it had very good cause for doing so. Gen. Mahone told me of one man who had a bayonet run through his cheek, which instead of making him throw down his musket & run to the rear, as men usually do when they are wounded, exasperated him so much that he killed the negro, although in that condition. I have always said that I wished the enemy would bring some negroes against this army. I am convinced, since Saturday's fight, that it has a splendid effect on our men.

I did not fire any guns on Saturday, but got some in position, where they were exposed to some shelling & musketry. My hat was struck by a Minie ball just over the place I was wounded at Sharpsburg, which was quite a singular coincidence. I saw Cousin Dick Pegram after the fight. Fortunately, he had been relieved, & was not in the trenches when the mine was sprung.

On the whole, Saturday was, through the merciful kindness

of an all & ever-merciful God, a very brilliant day to us. The enemy's loss was, at the lowest figures, three to our one—but the moral effect to our arms was very great. For it shews that he cannot blow us out of our works; or, at least, that he cannot hold a breach after making it. Saturday's fight shewed also the superiority of veterans to new troops—i.e. of Lee's to Beauregard's troops. They had to take Mahone's Division from this portion of the line, to that point, near the centre, to retake & reestablish the line, because those troops failed, although, as I was told by one of Beauregard's staff, they had a very fine opportunity for doing so immediately after the explosion.

Uncle William will probably go over with his family about the middle of the week. In case they do, I will write to Mother by them. Uncle William is now laid up with the gout, & it is somewhat doubtful.

Uncle Duke told me that he saw all at home, but yourself—that you had gone out.

I suppose you are all grieving today at Brother's proposed departure tomorrow. I wish very much that I could be with him & you all, but this is impossible. God has been so merciful to us, that I trust implicitly that we will be reunited again on this earth. If not, then certainly in a far better home. Have Uncle Robert & Jimmy determined yet about going abroad? Tell Jimmy to remember that he owes me a letter, which I hope to receive soon.

Tell Mother & Sister, with much love, that they had better go with you to the country somewhere, as you will all be benefitted by the change. How are Aunt Lelia & Mattie? Tell Aunt Lelia that I was at Aunt Martha's yesterday, & all were well. Aunt Martha told me that Aunt Lelia had written over, with an invitation from Mother for Nannie to come over to Richmond. I was glad to hear this. She is a very sweet child, & will be a very pretty woman; but lacks grace.

Is there any news from Atlanta? I am looking daily for its fall. If Maj Bradford is still with you, give him my love—& Ask him why he does not run over. Excuse haste. Your devoted brother

W. J. Pegram

Col. McIntosh was slightly wounded on Saturday—not sufficiently however to go off duty.

"THIS ABOMINABLE DESPOTISM":
NEW YORK, AUGUST 1864

C. Chauncey Burr: *from* The Old Guard

August 1864

A friend of Edgar Allan Poe, Charles Chauncey Burr had edited an anti-slavery reform magazine in the late 1840s, but later became a pro-Southern Democrat. In 1862 Burr founded *The Old Guard*, a monthly magazine published in New York City "devoted to the principles of 1776 and 1787." Burr used its pages to defend slavery and secession, relentlessly attack President Lincoln, and support Peace Democrats who advocated negotiating an armistice with the Confederacy. He began his August 1864 "Editor's Table" by criticizing Grant's campaign in Virginia.

EDITOR'S TABLE.

—We are informed by a member of Congress (not a Democrat) that for the first three weeks of Gen. Grant's campaign against Richmond, Mr. Lincoln and the Cabinet had no idea that all was not progressing well. But, at the end of that period, they came to comprehend the fact, which had all the time been perfectly understood by all who are not demented by passion, that every one of Grant's so-called flank movements was a most ruinous and mortifying defeat of the Abolition army. Now, all who are not willing to lie outright, confess that Gen. Grant has not obtained a single victory in battle since he crossed the Rapidan. But this failure in battle is really the least of Grant's misfortunes. He has destroyed the best part of his veteran army, and has fearfully demoralized what is remaining of it. An army as badly shattered as Gen. Grant's has been in these conflicts with Lee, must be necessarily, to a greater or lesser extent, demoralized. But the soldiers under Grant believe that their comrades in arms have been recklessly and foolishly slaughtered. A gallant officer, wounded in one of the last of Grant's disastrous defeats, in speaking of the useless and horrible waste of life, said in our hearing, "If this is generalship, I have misunderstood the meaning of the word." The feeling shown by this officer pervades Gen. Grant's army to-day. It pervades the country. Of all the unfortunate commanders who have fallen in the public estimation since we began this war, Gen. Grant is the most unfortunate and the most to be pitied. Curses will follow his head to his grave. Of the seven Generals who have commanded the Army of the Potomac, only two, McClellan and Mead, have escaped public contempt; but poor Grant, from the highest, has fallen to the lowest niche of fame. McDowell will be pitied, Pope laughed at, Burnside and Hooker jeered, but Grant will be despised. With better means than all the rest put together, he has wasted all in such a manner as to plunge the most sanguine hope into despair. Never more can he go into a town or village in the whole North where his name will not excite horror in the breasts of numberless widows and orphans. He is the death's head of a whole people. Thus lies prostrate the seventh and last idol of the Potomac. Where is the next victim?

—Are we not tired of hearing so much about "supporting the government," "resisting the government," "destroying the government," and a great deal of like nonsense? Who resists the government? Before we can answer that question, it is important to settle the matter as to who is the government. Mr. Lincoln is not the government. Congress is not the government. The Supreme Court is not the government. All these united do not form the governing power of our country. Under our system *The People* is the government; and the President, the Congress, and the Supreme Court, are only official agents to execute the will of the *sovereign* people, or to administer their laws under carefully guarded Constitutional limitations. All of Mr. Lincoln's usurpations are assaults upon the government. He is the guilty party, who is opposing and seeking to *destroy the government!* In England, the governing power, instead of being the *people*, is the *aristocracy*. Suppress the aristocracy in England, and there is no political organization left—the government of that country would be overthrown, just as Lincoln is seeking to overthrow the government of this country by suppressing the rights and powers of the *people*. Said Napoleon: "If religion had been taken away from Rome, nothing would have been left." The reason was that the government of Rome was the priesthood. If we take *sovereignty* from the people of America, there is nothing left of our government. It would be as effectually destroyed as the government of Great Britain would be by the overthrow of the *aristocracy*, or as the government of Austria would be by ignoring the crown. So if it be true, as these noisy imbeciles declare, that those who are opposing, and trying to destroy our government, ought to be hanged, Mr. Lincoln's neck is the one to which they must fit their halter. He is the *traitor* who is opposing the government established by the *people* of the United States.

—A foolish editor, the organ of Mr. Lincoln's abominations, says: "The greatest mistake we have made is that we did not crush out the last vital spot of Copperhead Democracy at the start." No, poor fool, the greatest mistake you made was to compel the people of the South to fight for their liberty, which also compelled all good people in the North to denounce your despotism. The greatest good of a people is their liberty. Liberty is to the collective body what health is to the individual. Without health no pleasure can be tasted by man. Without liberty no happiness can be enjoyed by society. The obligation, therefore, to defend liberty is greater than all others; and he is a traitor to a free country who will not gladly devote his life to preserve its freedom. Mr. Lincoln has forced upon Gen. Lee the honor, which we should gladly have withheld from him, of fighting the battle of defensive liberty on this continent, while Lincoln and his party carry on a war of offensive despotism. Lincoln's war is not upon the South alone; it is upon the North also. It is a war against a great principle—the principle of liberty and self-government. It is a war against Democracy—against the party that made the Constitution, and conducted the country through every step of its progressive glory, up to the hour when it fell by falling into the hands of a clan of despots and desperadoes. It is possible that we have only entered the field of blood—that the terrible struggle is but just commenced. If, as is more than intimated by the leading Republican papers, the despotism inaugurated over the North is to be continued, then, indeed, the sword is as yet but just started from its scabbard. If we have not a right to our thoughts, our sympathies, our hopes and faith, then shall the battle rage until we have vindicated our liberties and our manhood. We are coming to a point where the fight must be with those who are attempting to rob us of our freedom. The delusion of fighting for the skeleton of a Union, after we have ourselves crushed the soul out of it, is nearly over. For one, we do not hesitate to declare that we a thousand times prefer death in an honorable conflict to preserve our liberties, than a life of servitude and submission to the bloated despotism which hourly threatens us. If we are not free, let us make ourselves so! We know what we say. We hear, but we despise the threats! We may individually fall, but we know that we leave those behind us who are sworn to execute our last will and testament, which is that of death to the assassins. We are weary of hearing and reading the threats of Mr. Lincoln's satraps. If they stop where they are, all is well—all that is demanded is peace, liberty, and justice; but this we will have, or, failing, we will take our foes along with us, to be tried at that high court from which there is no appeal. Shall we longer walk the street to be threatened with "arrest," or "hanging," every time we exercise the freeman's sacred right of thinking and speaking the honest thought that is in us? Shall we longer owe our peace or safety to the whim or passion of slavering ignorance, or brutal prejudice and fanaticism? In God's name, *no!* For instance, if we believe that Jeff. Davis is a wise man, and that Abraham Lincoln is a fool, we shall take the liberty to say so, just whenever and wherever we please. If we have not the same right to respect the intellect of Jefferson Davis that another has to admire the ignorance and the trifling obscenity of Abraham Lincoln, let us set ourselves to work to regain that right. If we have not the right to prefer the Government and the Union that were formed by our fathers to this abominable despotism which Lincoln and his party are attempting to fasten upon us, let us strike for that right, and strike as our fathers did! This, then, is what we have to say to the besotted wretches who talk of "*crushing out Democrats.*"

Better stop where you are, and learn to carry a civil tongue, or you will be convinced that you are nearer the judgment day than your delusion has permitted you to imagine!

—The "Rebel Invasion" turns out to have been only a raid of the larger dimensions, to retaliate for our numerous plundering and burning expeditions in the South. Never before has Lee allowed his army to wantonly destroy private property; and, to his credit be it spoken, that he did not permit the late devastating raid as a means of civilized warfare, but placed it upon the ground of retaliation for barbarisms the Abolition soldiery have inflicted upon his people. For three years he has protested against the unsoldierly and uncivilized fashion of Lincoln's warfare. So has all Europe done the same; but nothing has been able to check the thieving and burning proclivities of the Abolitionists. In this instance Gen. Lee has resorted to the painful expedient of visiting upon the Abolitionists a taste of their own style of war; but he did not, like Lincoln, allow his soldiers to burn and plunder all private houses indiscriminately, for it seems that an individual, perfectly acquainted with the locality, accompanied his army to point out the dwellings of the Abolition leaders, who are considered the authors of the war. If the war continues as long as Lincoln lays out for it, there will, no doubt, be plenty more of opportunities for the invasion of the North; and if we would save ourselves from a repetition of this terrible raid, we have only to stop plundering and burning private property in the South. The Maryland victims may thank Lincoln and his generals for all they have suffered. The raiders, it is said, took away six millions of property, besides what they destroyed. And Gen. Lee could safely spare the large force to do this, even while Grant's army was making all the thunder in its power at the gates of Richmond. This looks very much like treating Grant with contempt. Gen. Lee himself says that he considers that Grant's campaign was virtually ended at the battle of Spottsylvania. And it is true that there has been no general engagement of all the forces of the two armies since that battle. From that spot Lee swung him round into McClellan's old shoes in the deadly swamp, where he, too, is practicing the sublime art of digging, so much despised by the Abolitionists. From a blazing *King of Diamonds*,

Grant has fallen down into a sombre *Jack of Spades*. All in six weeks! Where will he be at the end of the next six weeks?

—The Newburyport *Herald*, (Mass.,) an influential Republican paper, says:

> "We never did knowingly, and never intend to infringe upon the Constitution, and trample down the laws and usages, and compromises upon which the nation stands, for the emancipation of slaves in the southern States. Holding to State rights—the right of each community to legislate upon and control its local affairs, which idea is at the bottom of American freedom—the very keel of our ship of state, we do now and have always repudiated all interference with local matters in States to which we do not belong. It was never necessary or justifiable. We have no slavery in Massachusetts, and we would resist to the death its imposition upon us; but if we had slavery here, established by the free will of the people, as just, right and expedient for us, though we might differ from the majority, we would resent and resist any interference on the part of Maine or Vermont, or any other community or government under heaven, to forcibly or unlawfully abolish that slavery.
>
> "When even slavery is abolished by violence, at the expense of the Constitution and Union, it will not make the negroes free, but it certainly will destroy the liberties of thirty millions of whites. There can be no other result."

This is, indeed, light in the darkness. It is a voice of reason and truth from Massachusetts! Let not the world despair. What is to become of Mr. Lincoln and his war, when Republican newspapers begin to talk in that fashion?

—A lady writing in the Macon *Telegraph*, of Georgia, makes this noble appeal:

> "A word or two to my own sex. How many of you have passed through this terrible war unscathed? Oh, God, how many of us have lost our all, homes, comforts, and friends! Yet where is the southern woman who would be willing to yield to Yankee despotism? If such there be, let me say to you, death were preferable. I have felt their power; I know their meanness. They have deprived me of every worldly possession. Heart strings have been severed. Yet I would say to those loved ones still baring their breasts—Conquer or die. Many of us may go

through life with crushed and bleeding hearts; but liberty has ever been purchased at a costly sacrifice."

We envy not the wretch whose heart kindles not with a glow of admiration at these thrilling words from the pen of a woman. We pity the soldier who would not rather himself die than wage barbarous war to deprive such a people of their liberty.

—A Republican contemporary complains of the language we apply to Mr. Lincoln. It is not our fault. No other language would suit the occasion. Shall we speak of a blackguard as a gentleman? Of an ignoramus as a scholar? Of an obscene joker and clown as a well-bred man of refinement and taste? All this would be out of character, and in bad taste. *Oderint dum metuant*, came properly out of the mouth of a tyrant; but Euripides would never have put that execrable sentence into the mouth of Minos or Æacus, any more than we would put decent language into the mouth of Abraham Lincoln. To say that we shall not speak of Lincoln *coarsely* is to forbid us to mention his name.

—We present the patrons of THE OLD GUARD this month with an excellent likeness of the Hon. Gideon J. Tucker, of whom it can be truly said, but rarely said, that he has never been known to be politically wrong in his life. Among all the divisions and subdivisions and factions that have so often demoralized the Democratic party of this city and State, Mr. Tucker is one of the few men who have faithfully followed one line of principle. He has often found himself in small minorities, but has, we believe, never yielded to the pressure of that *policy* which would immolate *principle* upon the selfish altars of personal ambition or mere party success. We know of no man who has a more consistent or a more honorable political record.

When Mr. Tucker was elected Surrogate two years ago, it was demanded that he, and the officers under him, should take the oath of allegiance which Elijah F. Purdy, a so-called Democrat, had caused to be adopted by the Board of Supervisors. This extra Lincoln oath, imposed upon all the county officials, Mr. Tucker refused to take, nor would he allow it to be administered to any officer in his department, notwithstanding the Supervisors had ordered that no county officers refusing to take the Lincoln oath should receive their salaries. This act of defiance of the unconstitutional orders of a corrupt and foolish Board of Supervisors, was characteristic of Mr. Tucker's whole political life. When this war was commenced by Mr. Lincoln, he was one of the very first to denounce it as alike unconstitutional, impolitic and unjust. He was one of the very few public men who had the integrity and courage to denounce the damning usurpation and despotism in the terms they deserved. He never shrunk from the extreme peace ground for a moment. As an unflinching advocate of peace, he went before the voters of this city a candidate for the very honorable and responsible office of Surrogate, and was elected by a far larger majority than any other official in that canvass. The "War Democrats" were pained at the "indiscretion" of Mr. Tucker in so boldly proclaiming his peace principles, and yet he was elected by nearly double the majority received by any "War Democrat" in that election.

Mr. Tucker is a man of ability, and is considered one of the best political writers in the United States. In 1857 he was Secretary of the State of New York, an office in which he acquitted himself so ably and faithfully as to command the respect of even his political opponents.

—It is often asked what the Democrats mean to do. They mean, as a first step, to fill the executive chair with patriotism, and to banish faction and despotism from the administration of the Federal Government. What next they will do depends upon what they can do to restore peace and prosperity to our country. They are in the condition of a skillful surgeon who is called to a man who fell into the hands of assassins. If his wounds are not mortal he will restore him. If Abolition has not killed the Union, the Democrats will restore it. But, at any rate, they will save liberty from going entirely down in the whirlpool of blood.

—The New York *World*, in trying to comfort the poor, says, there are five hundred dollars of bounty money between every poor man and extreme poverty. That is, he can go into the army and throw away his life for negroes. That is a remedy, indeed! The $500 bounty is really only about $200. It would serve his family, possibly, two months, when they would become paupers, and he, probably, dead, or mutilated, crippled and helpless for life. The *World* gives the poor strange advice—such advice as ought not to come from a human heart or brain. The poor man, of all others, should not go into the army; he owes it to his family not to expose his life to such deadly peril. It is advising him to throw away his life for two months' subsistence, and to leave his wife and children paupers.

"RETRIBUTION AT LAST": VIRGINIA, AUGUST 1864
Edgeworth Bird to Sallie Bird

A cotton planter from Hancock County, Edgeworth Bird served as a company commander in the 15th Georgia Infantry until he was wounded at Second Manassas. In the spring of 1863 he returned to duty with the Army of Northern Virginia as quartermaster of Benning's Brigade in Hood's (later Field's) Division. Bird wrote home to his wife shortly after a raid on Macon, Georgia, by 2,000 Union cavalry ended on July 31 with the capture of Major General George Stoneman and 700 of his men.

Near Richmond Va
Aug 4th 1864

Yesterday's mail brought me Sallie's letter and your "leaves from the blank book"—written whilst you all were in such excitement & dread of a raiding visit from our hated foes—My own best loved darling, whilst I read I was fully aware that you had escaped the danger, that their route was not immediately in our neighbourhood, and that elsewhere they had been routed and dispersed—but yet my innermost heart was moved, and my very soul troubled to learn of the deep anxiety and distress you had been subjected to—I sorrow for all our people, darling, that such times have come upon us—that the merciless din of war has reached our very homesteads that we thought so remote from its cruel ravages—but that my dear, dear children and more than loved wife should be so near the reach of these accursed vandals is a trial not to be quietly borne, and a ceaseless pain to my soul—Revolution in all its horrors is indeed upon us, and there is but one trust, one arm on which to lean—that *can save* us—and to its unfailing support I commit you & my dear ones at home—Your brave hopefullness & self reliance fill me with pleasure, and are a double assurance of your improving health—God grant that all our Ladies may be alike calm & resolute—a firm front always goes far to intimidate a cowardly foe—but dearest darling, if possible I never wish you to be in their power—At this distance I cannot advise what course of action would be wisest under circumstances transpiring at so great a distance—under sudden emergencies the advice of friends is best—Should they come on our little town suddenly be with some tried friends—I do not think they would harm a few resolute Ladies who stood by each other—Should they overrun our immediate country, I don't know where you'd go unless to your Cousin Mrs. Springs—Augusta will be a prominent point of interest to them—So much for the gloomy side—but, precious darling, I don't believe they will reach Hancock—They have already made their outer circle—Hood's army is strengthening every week—our people are arming & organizing—the defence of Macon has taught them these itinerant horse thieves can be checked and beaten—and Iverson has shown how they may be torn to pieces—Lieut Genl S. D. Lee now commands our Cavalry and he has acquired a *habit* of victory—So cheer up, dearest, all will yet go well—Hood is an able man, and his industry and perseverance are endless—tho much inferior to Johnston I have great faith in him—and he is so ably supported—then the Govt will give *him* every support—the enemies Cavalry were never dashing around the Army after this style while Johnston commanded—But I earnestly and truly believe we have seen the worst—S. D. Lee brought reinforcements to Hood—others *must* be coming—the *fable* that Forrest is to be turned loose on Sherman's rear, must one day become a fact—And, darling, there seems a general, accepted idea that the rout of that Army would ensure peace—the North seems almost ripe for it—it's a growing sentiment there—we are nowhere unsuccessful except in Georgia—Here Grant is at a deadlock—his last well planned and desperate move of blowing up a way into Petersburg is a total and to him disastrous failure—he will be foiled in every effort—his gunboats and position on the river is all that has saved him so far—Early's main force has not crossed the Potomac yet—but his Cavalry has taken a little turn—Pennsylvania has burning homesteads and desolate wives—The beautiful town of Chambersburg is a black, charred mass—there is retribution at last—We all recall the defiant & scornful faces of its ladies as we marched through a year ago—I then and still respect them for their spirit—but their scorn has been turned into wailing—Each month's continuance of this war will witness an increased ferocity—but the very violence of the contest will sooner bring peace—Precious old fellow—how troubled you must have been—you and daughter alone—and all those terrible rumours coming in on you thick & fast—you do right to supply any demand that may be made upon you under such circumstances—and do so promptly & cheerfully—bless your cheerful, brave heart—It strengthens me away off here to read your letters—May you never be subjected to such another trial—tho our loved state is welcome to the last horse we have in her sore need, I must confess I was glad our men took the cars, and Lucille and Blandy came back—cars ride better than horses and go faster—What do our black people think of the hubbub and near approach of the Yankees—when they come, if ever, such as wish to go with them are welcome—those of the men who do not should take to the woods—for they will seize every one of them and enroll them in their army to meet such fates as the poor creatures at Ft Pillow and the other day at Petersburg—They force every negro man they get hold of into their Army. The negro women I do not think they'll interfere with—It is not worth while for your Mother to persist in staying in Athens in case of a Raid there—she could do no good and seems to me you should all be together to mutually sustain each other—I wish Mrs Waddell would come to you— I feel quite sure the Col will bring her down before he returns— he'll be dogmean not to do so, that he may tell me how you are—I readily understand how dreadfully anxious you were about your dear Mother when you thought they were coming towards Athens—I feel with you through it all, my darling, fully and truly—would to God I could take the burden from you—and that I could be there to assist in defending our own homes—Bud would be a comfort to you now—but I suppose it best for him to be with his Grandma—Alone as she is she surely needs him—but I wish both were with you—I know now that the enemy did not go to Athens and that all there is safe—including that very necessary factory—Twould indeed be a blow to us to lose that—But Twould take a pretty strong raiding party to take Athens if they are fortifying it—Sallie's expresses undying confidence in Cook's batallion, and there is considerable local force—Ah, dearest, could we only be near each other in such times—but it has not been given us—Dr Jervey Robinson paid me a visit a day or so since—he is on duty with 1st S. Carolina—McGowan's Brigade—has been a prisoner since we saw him—he desired very particular remembrances to you—he is not very far off and I promised to ride by and see him—says he wrote you as soon as he heard I was wounded—did you get the letter—I couldn't remember to have heard you speak of it—He sought out my company to learn the extent of the wound—very kind wasn't it—Doc Pierce has a letter from home telling of the excitement there—he is quite well as is also Sammie, Pete & Dud A—Ben A—has been quite sick with dyspepsia—is now about well—Everything here quiet just now—Field's division, and several other Brigades are on North side of James—our troops here are having a comparative time of rest after their severe hardships in Trenches around Petersburg—Dearest, I'm afraid you've lost ground this time—do make it up by extra care—tell me how your contrabands all behaved—neither you or Sallie speak of having had a rain yet—I am so profoundly thankful the hateful Yankees have not fed upon our cribs or polluted our grounds with their presence—Darling present my congratulations to Mrs Lucy upon her contribution of strength to the Confederacy—I am very glad for her & Edgar—and I hope Mrs Terrell is in health again—Thank dear Sallie for her letter only I don't look for half sheets from a young & healthy damsel—Will her school be interrupted—Love to Father—How does he bear our adversity—Bob is well and sends love to all our people—Says he wishes he was at home about these times of trouble there—Remembrances to all our negroes—

My own darling—May God bless and care for you in these days of trial—look to him for strength & guidance—Let me hear often—A thousand loves and kisses to dear daughter and yourself from your own loving—

Edge.

"THIS DICTATORIAL USURPATION": AUGUST 1864

Benjamin F. Wade and Henry Winter Davis: To the Supporters of the Government

August 5, 1864

Ohio senator Benjamin F. Wade and Maryland congressman Henry Winter Davis published their response to President Lincoln's pocket veto of their reconstruction bill in the *New-York Daily Tribune* on August 5. Their radical denunciation of the President's policies, drafted by Davis, was described by the Democratic *New York World* as "an impeachment" and by the Republican *New York Times* as "by far the most effective Copperhead campaign document thus far issued." Lincoln did not publicly respond to the Wade-Davis manifesto, telling Gideon Welles that he "could himself take no part in such a controversy as they seemed to wish to provoke." In a memoir published in 1895, the journalist Noah Brooks would recall Lincoln saying: "To be wounded in the house of one's friends is perhaps the most grievous affliction that can befall a man."

TO THE SUPPORTERS OF THE GOVERNMENT.

We have read without surprise, but not without indignation, the Proclamation of the President of the 8th of July, 1864.

The supporters of the Administration are responsible to the country for its conduct: and it is their right and duty to check the encroachments of the Executive on the authority of Congress, and to require it to confine itself to its proper sphere.

It is impossible to pass in silence this Proclamation without neglecting that duty; and, having taken as much responsibility as any others in supporting the Administration, we are not disposed to fail in the other duty of asserting the rights of Congress.

The President did not sign the bill "to guarantee to certain States whose Governments have been usurped, a Republican form of Government"—passed by the supporters of his Administration in both Houses of Congress after mature deliberation.

The bill did not therefore become *a law*: and it is therefore *nothing*.

The Proclamation is neither an approval nor a veto of the bill; it is therefore a document unknown to the laws and Constitution of the United States.

So far as it contains an apology for not signing the bill, it is a political manifesto against the friends of the Government.

So far as it proposes to execute the bill which is not a law, it is a grave Executive usurpation.

It is fitting that the facts necessary to enable the friends of the Administration to appreciate the apology and the usurpation be spread before them.

The Proclamation says:

> "And whereas the said bill was presented to the President of the United States for his approval less than one hour before the *sine die* adjournment of said session, and was not signed by him—"

If that be accurate, still this bill was presented with other bills which were signed.

Within that hour, the time for the sine die adjournment was three times postponed by the votes of both Houses; and the least intimation of a desire for more time by the President to consider this bill would have secured a further postponement.

Yet the Committee sent to ascertain if the President had any further communication for the House of Representatives reported that he had none; and the friends of the bill, who had anxiously waited on him to ascertain its fate, had already been informed that the President had resolved not to sign it.

The time of presentation, therefore, had nothing to do with his failure to approve it.

The bill had been discussed and considered for more than a month in the House of Representatives, which it passed on the 4th of May; it was reported to the Senate on the 27th of May without material amendment, and passed the Senate absolutely as it came from the House on the 2d of July.

Ignorance of its contents is out of the question.

Indeed, at his request, a draft of a bill substantially the same in all material points, and identical in the points objected to by the Proclamation, had been laid before him for his consideration in the Winter of 1862–1863.

There is, therefore, no reason to suppose the provisions of the bill took the President by surprise.

On the contrary, we have reason to believe them to have been so well known that this method of preventing the bill from becoming a law without the constitutional responsibility of a veto, had been resolved on long before the bill passed the Senate.

We are informed by a gentleman entitled to entire confidence, that before the 22d of June in New-Orleans it was stated by a member of Gen. Banks's staff, in the presence of other gentlemen in official position, that Senator Doolittle had written a letter to the department that the House Reconstruction bill would be staved off in the Senate to a period too late in the session to require the President to veto it in order to defeat it, and that Mr. Lincoln would retain the bill, if necessary, and thereby defeat it.

The experience of Senator Wade, in his various efforts to get the bill considered in the Senate, was quite in accordance with that plan; and the fate of the bill was accurately predicted by letters received from New-Orleans before it had passed the Senate.

Had the Proclamation stopped there, it would have been only one other defeat of the will of the people by an Executive perversion of the Constitution.

But it goes further. The President says:

> "And whereas the said bill contains, among other things, a plan for restoring the States in rebellion to their proper practical relation in the Union, which plan expresses the sense of Congress upon that subject, and which plan it is now thought fit to lay before the people for their consideration—"

By what authority of the Constitution? In what forms? The result to be declared by whom? With what effect when ascertained?

Is it to be a law by the approval of the people without the approval of Congress at the will of the President?

Will the President, on his opinion of the popular approval, execute it as law?

Or is this merely a device to avoid the serious responsibility of defeating a law on which so many loyal hearts reposed for security?

But the reasons now assigned for not approving the bill are full of ominous significance.

The President proceeds:

> "Now, therefore, I, ABRAHAM LINCOLN, President of the United States, do proclaim, declare and make known, that, while I am (as I was in December last, when by proclamation I propounded a plan for restoration) unprepared, by a formal approval of this bill, to be inflexibly committed to any single plan of restoration—"

That is to say, the President is resolved that the people shall not *by law* take any securities from the Rebel States against a renewal of the Rebellion, before restoring their power to govern us.

His wisdom and prudence are to be our sufficient guarantees! He further says:

> "And, while I am also unprepared to declare that the Free-State Constitutions and Governments already adopted and installed in Arkansas and Louisiana shall be set aside and held for naught, thereby repelling and discouraging the loyal citizens who have set up the same as to further effort—"

That is to say, the President persists in recognizing those shadows of Governments in Arkansas and Louisiana, which Congress formally declared should not be recognized—whose Representatives and Senators were repelled by formal votes of both Houses of Congress—which it was declared formally should have no electoral vote for President and Vice-President.

They are mere creatures of his will. They cannot live a day without his support. They are mere oligarchies, imposed on the people by military orders under the forms of election, at which generals, provost-marshals, soldiers and camp-followers were the chief actors, assisted by a handful of resident citizens, and urged on to premature action by private letters from the President.

In neither Louisiana nor Arkansas, before Banks's defeat, did the United States control half the territory or half the population. In Louisiana, Gen. Banks's proclamation candidly declared: "*The fundamental law of the State is martial law.*"

On that foundation of freedom, he erected what the President calls "the free Constitution and Government of Louisiana."

But of this State, whose fundamental law was martial law, only sixteen parishes out of forty-eight parishes were held by the United States; and in five of the sixteen we held only our camps.

The eleven parishes we substantially held had 233,185 inhabitants; the residue of the State not held by us, 575,617.

At the farce called an election, the officers of Gen. Banks returned that 11,346 ballots were cast; but whether any or by whom the people of the United States have no legal assurance; but it is probable that 4,000 were cast by soldiers or employees of the United States military or municipal, but none according to any law, State or National, and 7,000 ballots represent the State of Louisiana.

Such is the free Constitution and Government of Louisiana; and like it is that of Arkansas. Nothing but the failure of a military expedition deprived us of a like one in the swamps of Florida; and before the Presidential election, like ones may be organized in every Rebel State where the United States have a camp.

The President, by preventing this bill from becoming a law, holds the electoral votes of the Rebel States at the dictation of his personal ambition.

If these votes turn the balance in his favor, is it to be supposed that his competitor, defeated by such means, will acquiesce?

If the Rebel majority assert their supremacy in those States, and send votes which elect an enemy of the Government, will we not repel his claims?

And is not that civil war for the Presidency, inaugurated by the votes of Rebel States?

Seriously impressed with these dangers, Congress, "*the proper constitutional authority*," formally declared that there are no State Governments in the Rebel States, and provided for their erection at a proper time; and both the Senate and the House of Representatives rejected the Senators and Representatives chosen under the authority of what the President calls the free Constitution and Government of Arkansas.

The President's Proclamation "*holds for naught*" this judgment, and discards the authority of the Supreme Court, and strides headlong toward the anarchy his Proclamation of the 8th of December inaugurated.

If electors for President be allowed to be chosen in either of those States, a sinister light will be cast on the motives which induced the President to "hold for naught" the will of Congress rather than his Government in Louisiana and Arkansas.

That judgment of Congress which the President defies was the exercise of an authority exclusively vested in Congress by the Constitution to determine what is the established Government in a State, and in its own nature and by the highest judicial authority binding on all other departments of the Government.

The Supreme Court has formally declared that under the 4th section of the IVth article of the Constitution, requiring the United States to guarantee to every State a republican form of government, "*it rests with Congress to decide what Government is the established one in a State;*" and "*when Senators and Representatives of a State are admitted into* the councils of the Union, the *authority* of the *Government under which they are appointed*, as well as its republican character, *is recognized by the proper constitutional authority, and its decision is binding on every other department of the Government*, and could not be questioned in a judicial tribunal. It is true that the contest in this case did not last long enough to bring the matter to this issue; and, as no Senators or Representatives were elected under the authority of the Government of which Mr. Dorr was the head, Congress was not called upon to decide the controversy. Yet the right to decide is placed *there*."

Even the President's proclamation of the 8th of December, formally declares that "Whether members sent to Congress from any State shall be admitted to seats, constitutionally rests exclusively with the respective Houses, and not to any extent with the Executive."

And that is not the less true because wholly inconsistent with the President's assumption in that proclamation of a right to institute and recognize State Governments in the Rebel States, nor because the President is unable to perceive that his recognition is a nullity if it be not conclusive on Congress.

Under the Constitution, the right to Senators and Representatives is inseparable from a State Government.

If there be a State Government, the right is absolute.

If there be no State Government, there can be no Senators or Representatives chosen.

The two Houses of Congress are expressly declared to be the sole judges of their own members.

When, therefore, Senators and Representatives are admitted, the State Government, under whose authority they were chosen, is conclusively established; when they are rejected, its existence is as conclusively rejected and denied; and to this judgment the President is bound to submit.

The President proceeds to express his unwillingness "to declare a constitutional competency in Congress to abolish Slavery in States" as another reason for not signing the bill.

But the bill nowhere proposes to abolish Slavery in States.

The bill did provide that all *slaves* in the Rebel States should be *manumitted*.

But as the President had already signed three bills manumitting several classes of slaves in States, it is not conceived possible that he entertained any scruples touching *that* provision of the bill respecting which he is silent.

He had already himself assumed a right by proclamation to free much the larger number of slaves in the Rebel States, under the authority given him by Congress to use military power to suppress the Rebellion; and it is quite inconceivable that the President should think Congress could vest in him a discretion it could not exercise itself.

It is the more unintelligible from the fact that, except in respect to a small part of Virginia and Louisiana, the bill covered only what the Proclamation covered—added a Congressional title and judicial remedies by law to the disputed title under the Proclamation, and perfected the work the President professed to be so anxious to accomplish.

Slavery as an institution can be abolished only by a change of the Constitution of the United States or of the law of the State; and this is the principle of the bill.

It required the new Constitution of the State to provide for that prohibition; and the President, in the face of his own proclamation, does not venture to object to insisting on *that* condition. Nor will the country tolerate its abandonment—yet he defeated the only provision imposing it!!

But when he describes himself, in spite of this great blow at emancipation, as "sincerely hoping and expecting that a constitutional amendment abolishing Slavery throughout the nation may be adopted," we curiously inquire on what his expectation rests, after the vote of the House of Representatives at the recent session, and in the face of the political complexion of more than enough of the States to prevent the possibility of its adoption within any reasonable time; and why he did not indulge his sincere hopes with so large an installment of the blessing as his approval of the bill would have secured.

After this assignment of his reasons for preventing the bill from becoming a law, the President proceeds to declare his purpose *to execute it as a law by his plenary dictatorial power.*

He says:

"Nevertheless, I am fully satisfied with the system for restoration contained in the bill as one very proper plan for the loyal people of any State choosing to adopt it; and that I am, and at all times shall be, prepared to give the Executive aid and assistance to any such people so soon as the military resistance to the United States shall have been suppressed in any such State, and the people thereof shall have sufficiently returned to their obedience to the Constitution and the laws of the United States; in which cases Military Governors will be appointed, with directions to proceed according to the bill."

A more studied outrage on the legislative authority of the people has never been perpetrated.

Congress passed a bill; the President refused to approve it, and then by proclamation puts as much of it in force as he sees fit, and proposes to execute those parts by officers unknown to the laws of the United States and not subject to the confirmation of the Senate!

The bill directed the appointment of Provisional Governors by and with the advice and consent of the Senate.

The President, after defeating the law, proposes to appoint without law, and without the advice and consent of the Senate, *Military* Governors for the Rebel States!

He has already exercised this dictatorial usurpation in Louisiana, and he defeated the bill to prevent its limitation.

Henceforth we must regard the following precedent as the Presidential law of the Rebel States:

> "EXECUTIVE MANSION,
> "WASHINGTON, March 15, 1864.
> "*His Excellency* MICHAEL HAHN, *Governor of Louisiana*,
> "Until further orders, you are hereby invested with the powers exercised hitherto by the Military Governor of Louisiana.
> Yours, "ABRAHAM LINCOLN."

This Michael Hahn is no officer of the United States; the President, without law, without the advice and consent of the Senate, by a private note not even countersigned by the Secretary of State, makes him Dictator of Louisiana!

The bill provided for the civil administration of the laws of the State—till it should be in a fit temper to govern itself—repealing all laws recognizing Slavery, and making all men equal before the law.

These beneficent provisions the President has annulled. People will die, and marry and transfer property, and buy and sell: and to these acts of civil life courts and officers of the law are necessary. Congress legislated for these necessary things, and the President deprives them of the protection of the law!

The President's purpose to instruct his Military Governors "to proceed according to the bill"—a makeshift to calm the disappointment its defeat has occasioned—is not merely a grave usurpation but a transparent delusion.

He cannot "proceed according to the bill" after preventing it from becoming a law.

Whatever is done will be at his will and pleasure, by persons responsible to no law, and more interested to secure the interests and execute the will of the President than of the people; and the will of Congress is to be "*held for naught*," "unless the loyal people of the Rebel States choose to adopt it."

If they should graciously prefer the stringent bill to the easy proclamation, still the registration will be made under no legal sanction; it will give no assurance that a majority of the people of the States have taken the oath; if administered, it will be without legal authority, and void; no indictment will lie for false swearing at the election, or for admitting bad or rejecting good votes; it will be the farce of Louisiana and Arkansas acted over again, under the forms of this bill, but not by authority of *law*.

But when we come to the guarantees of future peace which Congress meant to exact, the forms, as well as the substance of the bill, must yield to the President's will that *none* should be *imposed*.

It was the solemn resolve of Congress to protect the loyal men of the nation against three great dangers, (1) the return to power of the guilty leaders of the Rebellion, (2) the continuance of Slavery, and (3) the burden of the Rebel debt.

Congress *required* assent to those provisions by the Convention of the State; and if refused, it was to be dissolved.

The President "holds for naught" that resolve of Congress, because he is unwilling "to be inflexibly committed to any one plan of restoration," and the people of the United States are not to be allowed to protect themselves unless their enemies agree to it.

The order to proceed according to the bill is therefore merely at the will of the Rebel States; and they have the option to reject it, accept the proclamation of the 8th of December, and demand the President's recognition!

Mark the contrast! The bill requires a majority, the proclamation is satisfied with one-tenth; the bill requires one oath, the proclamation another; the bill ascertains voters by registering; the proclamation by guess; the bill exacts adherence to existing territorial limits, the proclamation admits of others; the bill governs the Rebel States *by law*, equalizing all before it, the proclamation commits them to the lawless discretion of military Governors and Provost-Marshals; the bill forbids electors for President, the proclamation and defeat of the bill threaten us with civil war for the admission or exclusion of such votes; the bill exacted exclusion of dangerous enemies from power and the relief of the nation from the Rebel debt, and the prohibition of Slavery forever, so that the suppression of the Rebellion will double our resources to bear or pay the national debt, free the masses from the old domination of the Rebel leaders, and eradicate the cause of the war; the proclamation secures neither of these guaranties.

It is silent respecting the Rebel debt and the political exclusion of Rebel leaders; leaving *Slavery* exactly where it was by law at the outbreak of the rebellion, and adds no guaranty even of the freedom of the slaves he undertook to manumit.

It is summed up in an illegal oath, without a sanction, and therefore void.

The oath is to support all proclamations of the President, during the Rebellion having reference to slaves.

Any Government is to be accepted at the hands of one-tenth of the people not contravening *that oath*.

Now that oath neither secures the abolition of Slavery, nor adds any security to the freedom of the slaves the President declared free.

It does not secure the abolition of Slavery; for the proclamation of freedom merely professed to free certain slaves while it recognized the institution.

Every Constitution of the Rebel States at the outbreak of the Rebellion may be adopted without the change of a letter; for none of them contravene that Proclamation; none of them establish Slavery.

It adds no security to the freedom of the slaves.

For their title is the Proclamation of Freedom.

If it be unconstitutional, an oath to support it is void. Whether constitutional or not, the oath is without authority of law, and therefore void.

If it be valid and observed, it exacts no enactment by the State, either in law or Constitution, to add a State guaranty to the proclamation title; and the right of a slave to freedom is an open question before the State courts on the relative authority of the State law and the Proclamation.

If the oath binds the one-tenth who take it, it is not exacted of the other nine-tenths who succeed to the control of the State Government; so that it is annulled instantly by the act of recognition.

What the State courts would say of the Proclamation, who can doubt?

But the master would not go into court—he would seize his slave.

What the Supreme Court would say, who can tell?

When and how is the question to get there?

No habeas corpus lies for him in a United States Court; and

the President defeated with this bill its extension of that writ to this case.

Such are the fruits of this rash and fatal act of the President—a blow at the friends of his Administration, at the rights of humanity, and at the principles of republican government.

The President has greatly presumed on the forbearance which the supporters of his Administration have so long practiced, in view of the arduous conflict in which we are engaged, and the reckless ferocity of our political opponents.

But he must understand that our support is of a cause and not of a man; that the authority of Congress is paramount and must be respected; that the whole body of the Union men of Congress will not submit to be impeached by him of rash and unconstitutional legislation; and if he wishes our support, he must confine himself to his executive duties—to obey and execute, not make the laws—to suppress by arms armed Rebellion, and leave political reorganization to Congress.

If the supporters of the Government fail to insist on this, they become responsible for the usurpations which they fail to rebuke, and are justly liable to the indignation of the people whose rights and security, committed to their keeping, they sacrifice.

Let them consider the remedy for these usurpations, and, having found it, fearlessly execute it.

B. F. WADE, Chairman Senate Committee.
H. WINTER DAVIS, Chairman Committee
House of Representatives on the Rebellious States.

"STERN RETALIATION": VIRGINIA, AUGUST 1864

Robert Garlick Hill Kean: *Diary, August 7, 1864*

A lawyer from Lynchburg, Virginia, Robert Garlick Hill Kean had served since April 1862 as head of the Bureau of War, an administrative division of the Confederate War Department. Kean wrote in his diary about the war's increasing harshness.

———————

Aug. 7. From the 16th to the 21st ult. I was sick and on the 22nd left Richmond for a fortnight in Albemarle to recruit, returned on the 4th inst. Mr. G. A. Trenholm was appointed secretary of the treasury, when he came to Richmond as indicated in last entry, which was the end of that imbroglio. Bragg has been absent nearly a month in the South; hence no further trouble with him. Hood has held his own at Atlanta pretty well and has delivered some good blows.

On the 5th inst. the Yankee fleet passed the forts at the entrance of Mobile Bay, 14 ships and 3 ironclads getting in Fort Morgan; sank one monitor. Our fleet was then destroyed, the *Tennessee* captured, the *Selma* sunk, the *Gaines* run aground. The *Morgan* alone escaped.

Yesterday a week ago Grant sprang his great mine at Petersburg and Meade his grand assault, which was prognosticated with much flourishing of trumpets by the Yankee press. The disastrous defeat he met with in the assault has manifestly struck a chill to the Northern heart, as is indicated by their newspapers. The *World* declaims his whole campaign a disastrous failure and declares the opinion that Richmond and Petersburg cannot be taken. The Democratic and anti-administration papers suggest that their army had better be moved to a position in which it will protect 'loyal' territory from invasion. The *Times* (N.Y.) argues at great length that the failure at Petersburg should not produce such excessive discouragement, that Sebastopol was ineffectually assaulted several times, etc. Recent Northern papers intimate that there is to be a change in the command of the army below Petersburg and indicated Hooker as Meade's successor. Meade being as near a gentleman as a Yankee comes, he's probably become distasteful to the Washington concern.

The war is taking on features of exaggerated harshness. Hunter when he re-entered the Valley caused a number of private residences of the finest character to be burned, e. g. Mr. Andrew Hunter's, McCaig's, etc. Early has burned Chambersburg to enforce a refractory town into paying a requisition. The Yankees have had the unutterable meanness to make an expedition up the Rappahannock for the purpose of burning the house of Mrs. May Seddon, the widow of Major John Seddon, the brother of the Secretary. Her condition was perfectly well known to them, and the fact of her connection with the Secretary of War was avowed as the reason!! Somebody over the border will smoke for this outrage. I am satisfied that this thing which they have been doing now for three years in Florida (Jacksonville), Mississippi (Jackson), South Carolina on the Combahee, and all through Virginia on the northern border, can be stopped by deliberate and stern retaliation. They are in more of our territory but their people live so much more in towns that one expedition can burn more houses than they can destroy in a campaign. That they are amenable to the influences of retaliation is plain for the well known fact that when they have to deal with a man who they know will be as good as his word they are awed.

The whole Yankee army harks to Jack Mosby. He caught a fellow who had burned a home near or in New Market, Shenandoah County, and shot him. The officer in command swore he would burn the village; Mosby sent him word if he did he would execute prisoners of whom he held a number. A party was sent to burn the village but receiving the message in time did nothing, and New Market is yet safe.

Captain Brooke of Fauquier, delegate in the Virginia Legislature, told me (he has a son in Mosby's command) that one of Mosby's men, a captive, was murdered in Upperville by a Yankee. Mosby sent a citizen to investigate the facts, and sent the commanding officer word that unless the case was satisfactorily explained or the murderer punished he would take ample vengeance. The message produced great consternation, the case was inquired into, no explanation could be made—it was a brutal murder—and he promised that the offender should be punished. He failed to keep faith, which Mosby discovered, and he executed *ten*. Of the substantial truth of this I have no doubt.

It is a curious fact that precisely coincident with his tendency to aggravation in the character of the war, a great development of a disposition towards peace is making in public sentiment in the North. With their conscription in September and their election in November, this sentiment may be fairly expected to increase to a head that will be influential, though it will probably not suffice to defeat Lincoln. It may get control of the next U. S. Congress. Gold 252.

"SMOKE AND FLAME": VIRGINIA, AUGUST 1864

Mathella Page Harrison: Diary, August 17, 1864

The Union defeat at Kernstown, Virginia, on July 24 and the burning of Chambersburg, Pennsylvania, by Jubal Early's cavalry on July 30 led Lincoln and Grant to reorganize the forces opposing Early in the Shenandoah Valley. Major General Philip H. Sheridan, the commander of the Army of the Potomac's Cavalry Corps, took command of the new Army of the Shenandoah on August 7 and began advancing south from Harpers Ferry three days later. When his cavalry encountered infantry reinforcements from Lee's army near Front Royal on August 16, Sheridan decided to withdraw to the north and guard the Potomac River crossings. From her farm in Millwood, Mathella Page Harrison watched as Union soldiers carried out Grant's orders to confiscate or destroy the Valley's provisions, forage, and livestock.

Wednesday, August 17th—Night has closed at last on this day of horrors. Years almost seem to have rolled since I opened my eyes this morning. The first sound that greeted my ears was the rumbling of Yankee waggons passing onward with their troops to swell the hosts of those who passed last week and who were assembled in and around Winchester waiting for Early's return. At nine o'clock Yankee pickets were stationed in every hill. Fires of barns, stockyards etc. soon burst forth and by eleven, from a high elevation, fifty could be seen blazing forth. The whole country was enveloped with smoke and flame. The sky was lurid and but for the green trees one might have decided the shades of Hades had descended suddenly. The shouts, ribald jokes, awful oaths, demoniacal laughter of the fiends added to the horrors of the day. They demanded feed when they had just applied the torch to the provisions of the year, and indeed years, for now the seed which would have been sown has been destroyed. In almost every instance every head of stock was driven off. Those young animals that refused to go were shot down. Near a farm where eight fires were blazing, Custer and his staff sat exulting over the ruin they had wrought. Large families of children were left without one cow. In many of the barns were stowed in and around carriages, all kinds of farming implements, waggons, plows etc., and in no instance did they allow anything to be saved. The loss is inestimable and unpardonable in these times, situated as we are, communications with our lines so difficult, and no trade with the enemy even if we wished it. Hay, oats and straw were burnt with the wheat. I cannot imagine what the poor cattle are to live on this winter. Owing to the great drought the field grass burnt like tinder. About half of the county was in flames. Some of the dwellings were sacked, clothing, provisions, male and female taken indiscriminately. Remember Chambersburg was their watch word. Thoroughly did they enjoy their days work. When one fire was at its hottest, the dwelling in peril of being added to the number, one turned to the other, "Haven't we had a nice day?" Retaliation may be glorious for the interior of Dixie but to those in this poor debatable land its fires are almost beyond endurance.

WASHINGTON, D.C., AUGUST 1864

Abraham Lincoln: Memorandum on Probable Failure of Reelection

Lincoln became the first president since 1840 to be nominated for a second term when he received the nearly unanimous vote of the National Union convention, a coalition of Republicans and War Democrats on June 8. By August the President feared that he would lose the election to George B. McClellan, his likely Democratic opponent. His pessimism was shared by many Republican leaders. On August 22 Thurlow Weed wrote to Secretary of State William H. Seward, his close political ally, that Lincoln's reelection was an impossibility because the "People are wild for Peace." The same day Henry J. Raymond, the editor of *The New York Times* and chairman of the National Union executive committee, wrote to Lincoln that he would probably lose Illinois, Pennsylvania, and New York. Raymond attributed "this great reaction in public sentiment" to "the want of military successes, and the impression in some minds, the fear and suspicion in others, that we are not to have peace *in any event* under this Administration until Slavery is abandoned. In some way or other the suspicion is widely diffused that we *can* have peace with Union if we would." Lincoln wrote his memorandum on a sheet of paper, folded it, and then had the members of his cabinet sign the paper without reading its contents.

Executive Mansion
Washington, Aug. 23, 1864.
This morning, as for some days past, it seems exceedingly probable that this Administration will not be re-elected. Then it will be my duty to so co-operate with the President elect, as to save the Union between the election and the inauguration; as he will have secured his election on such ground that he can not possibly save it afterwards. A. LINCOLN

EXCHANGING PRISONERS: VIRGINIA, AUGUST 1864

Benjamin F. Butler to Robert Ould

By the summer of 1864 both the Union and the Confederacy held tens of thousands of prisoners in overcrowded camps as a result of the breakdown of the exchange cartel during the previous year. Colonel Robert Ould, the Confederate commissioner of exchange, signaled on August 10 his government's willingness to resume general exchanges using a formula previously proposed by the Union authorities. Grant advised against resuming exchanges in a letter to Major General Benjamin F. Butler, the Union exchange commissioner. "It is hard on our men held in Southern prisons not to exchange them but it is humanity to those left in the ranks to fight our battles," he wrote on August 18. "Every man released, on parole or otherwise, becomes an active soldier against us at once either directly or indirectly. If we commence a system of exchanges which liberates all prisoners taken we will have to fight on until the whole South is exterminated." Butler responded to Ould by restating the Union position that black and white prisoners be treated equally in exchanges. Ould did not respond to Butler's letter, which was published in the northern press on September 6.

HDQRS. DEPT. OF VIRGINIA AND NORTH CAROLINA,
In the Field, August 27, 1864.
Hon. ROBERT OULD, *Commissioner for Exchange:*

SIR: Your note to Major Mulford, assistant agent of exchange, under date of 10th of August, has been referred to me.

You therein state that Major Mulford has several times proposed to exchange prisoners respectively held by the two belligerents, officer for officer, and man for man, and that "the offer has also been made by other officials having charge of matters connected with the exchange of prisoners," and that "this proposal has been heretofore declined by the Confederate authorities;" that you now consent to the above proposition, and agree to deliver to you (Major Mulford) the prisoners held in captivity by the Confederate authorities, provided you agree to deliver an equal number of officers and men. As equal numbers are delivered from time to time they will be declared exchanged. This proposal is made with the understanding that the officers and men on both sides who have been longest in captivity will be first delivered, where it is practicable.

From a slight ambiguity in your phraseology, but more, perhaps, from the antecedent action of your authorities, and because of your acceptance of it, I am in doubt whether you have stated the proposition with entire accuracy.

It is true, a proposition was made both by Major Mulford and myself, as agent of exchange, to exchange all prisoners of war taken by either belligerent party, man for man, officer for officer, of equal rank, or their equivalents. It was made by me as early as the first of the winter of 1863–64, and has not been accepted. In May last I forwarded to you a note desiring to know whether the Confederate authorities intended to treat colored soldiers of the U. S. Army as prisoners of war. To that inquiry no answer has yet been made. To avoid all possible misapprehension or mistake hereafter as to your offer now, will you say now whether you mean by "prisoners held in captivity" colored men, duly enrolled and mustered into the service of the United States, who have been captured by the Confederate forces, and if your authorities are willing to exchange all soldiers so mustered into the U. S. Army, whether colored or otherwise, and the officers commanding them, man for man, officer for officer?

At an interview which was held between yourself and the agent of exchange on the part of the United States, at Fort Monroe, in March last, you will do me the favor to remember the principal discussion turned upon this very point, you, on behalf of the Confederate Government, claiming the right to hold all negroes who had heretofore been slaves and not emancipated by their masters, enrolled and mustered into the service of the United States, when captured by your forces, not as prisoners of war, but, upon capture, to be turned over to their supposed masters or claimants, whoever they might be, to be held by them as slaves.

By the advertisements in your newspapers, calling upon masters to come forward and claim these men so captured, I suppose that your authorities still adhere to that claim; that is to say, that whenever a colored soldier of the United States is captured by you, upon whom any claim can be made by any person residing within the States now in insurrection, such soldier is not to be treated as a prisoner of war, but is to be turned over to his supposed owner or claimant, and put at such labor or service as that owner or claimant may choose; and the officers in command of such soldiers, in the language of a supposed act of the Confederate States, are to be turned over to the Governors of States, upon requisitions, for the purpose of being punished by the laws of such States for acts done in war in the armies of the United States.

You must be aware that there is still a proclamation by Jefferson Davis, claiming to be Chief Executive of the Confederate States, declaring in substance that all officers of colored troops mustered into the service of the United States were not to be treated as prisoners of war, but were to be turned over for punishment to the Governors of States.

I am reciting these public acts from memory, and will be pardoned for not giving the exact words, although I believe I do not vary the substance and effect. These declarations on the part of those whom you represent yet remain unrepealed, unannulled, unrevoked, and must therefore be still supposed to be authoritative. By your acceptance of our proposition, is the Government of the United States to understand that these several claims, enactments, and proclaimed declarations are to be given up, set aside, revoked, and held for naught by the Confederate authorities, and that you are ready and willing to exchange, man for man, those colored soldiers of the United States, duly mustered and enrolled as such, who have heretofore been claimed as slaves by the Confederate States, as well as white soldiers?

If this be so, and you are so willing to exchange these colored men claimed as slaves, and you will so officially inform the Government of the United States, then, as I am instructed, a principal difficulty in effecting exchanges will be removed.

As I informed you personally, in my judgment, it is neither consistent with the policy, dignity, nor honor of the United States, upon any consideration, to allow those who, by our laws solemnly enacted, are made soldiers of the Union, and who have been duly enlisted, enrolled, and mustered as such soldiers—who have borne arms in behalf of this country, and who have been captured while fighting in vindication of the rights of that country—not to be treated as prisoners of war, and remain unexchanged and in the service of those who claim them as masters; and I cannot believe that the Government of the United States will ever be found to consent to so gross a wrong.

Pardon me if I misunderstood you in supposing that your acceptance of our proposition does not in good faith mean to include all the soldiers of the Union, and that you still intend, if your acceptance is agreed to, to hold the colored soldiers of the Union unexchanged, and at labor or service, because I am informed that very lately, almost cotemporaneously with this offer on your part to exchange prisoners, and which seems to include all prisoners of war, the Confederate authorities have made a declaration that the negroes heretofore held to service by owners in the States of Delaware, Maryland, and Missouri, are to be treated as prisoners of war when captured in arms in the service of the United States. Such declaration, that a part of the colored soldiers of the United States were to be prisoners of war, would seem most strongly to imply that others were not to be so treated; or, in other words, that colored men from the insurrectionary States are to be held to labor and returned to their masters, if captured by the Confederate forces while duly enrolled and mustered into and actually in the armies of the United States.

In the view which the Government of the United States takes of the claim made by you to the persons and services of these negroes, it is not to be supported upon any principle of national or municipal law.

Looking upon these men only as property, upon your theory of property in them, we do not see how this claim can be made; certainly not how it can be yielded. It is believed to be a well-settled rule of public international law, and a custom and part of the laws of war, that the capture of movable property vests the title to that property in the captor, and therefore, when one belligerent gets into full possession of property belonging to the subjects or citizens of the other belligerent, the owner of that property is at once divested of his title, which rests in the belligerent government capturing and holding such possession. Upon this rule of international law all civilized nations have acted, and by it both belligerents have dealt with all property, save slaves, taken from each other during the present war.

If the Confederate forces capture a number of horses from the United States, the animals are immediately claimed to be, and, as we understand it, become the property of the Confederate authorities.

If the United States capture any movable property in the rebellion, by our regulations and laws, in conformity with the international law and the laws of war; such property is turned over to our Government as its property. Therefore, if we obtain possession of that species of property known to the laws of the insurrectionary States as slaves, why should there be any doubt that that property, like any other, vests in the United States?

If the property in the slave does so vest, the *jus disponendi*, the right of disposing of that property, rests in the United States.

Now, the United States have disposed of the property which they have acquired by capture in slaves taken by them, by giving that right of property to the man himself, to the slave— *i. e.*, by emancipating him and declaring him free forever; so that if we have not mistaken the principles of international law and the laws of war, we have no slaves in the armies of the United States. All are free men, being made so in such manner as we have chosen to dispose of our property in them which we acquire by capture.

Slaves being captured by us, and the right of property in them thereby vested in us, that right of property has been disposed of by us by manumitting them, as has always been the acknowledged right of the owner to do to his slave. The manner in which we dispose of our property while it is in our possession certainly cannot be questioned by you.

Nor is the case altered if the property is not actually captured in battle, but comes either voluntarily or involuntarily from the belligerent owner into the possession of the other belligerent.

I take it no one would doubt the right of the United States to a drove of Confederate mules, or a herd of Confederate cattle, which should wander or rush across the Confederate lines into the lines of the U.S. Army. So it seems to me, treating the negro as property merely, if that piece of property passes the Confederate lines and comes into the lines of the United States, that property is as much lost to its owner in the Confederate States as would be the mule or ox, the property of the resident of the Confederate States, which should fall into our hands.

If, therefore, the principles of international law and the laws of war used in this discussion are correctly stated, then it would seem that the deduction logically flows therefrom, in natural sequence, that the Confederate States can have no claim upon the negro soldiers captured by them from the armies of the United States, because of the former ownership of them by their citizens or subjects, and only claim such as result, under the laws of war, from their capture merely.

Do the Confederate authorities claim the right to reduce to a state of slavery freemen, prisoners of war, captured by them? This claim our fathers fought against under Bainbridge and Decatur when set up by the Barbary powers on the northern shore of Africa, about the year 1800, and in 1864 their children will hardly yield it upon their own soil.

This point I will not pursue further, because I understand you to repudiate the idea that you will reduce freemen to slaves because of capture in war, and that you base the claim of the Confederate authorities to re-enslave our negro soldiers when captured by you upon the *jus postlimini*, or that principle of the law of nations which rehabilitates the former owner with his property taken by an enemy when such property is recovered by the forces of his own country. Or, in other words, you claim that, by the laws of nations and of war, when property of the subjects of one belligerent power captured by the forces of the other belligerent is recaptured by the armies of the former owner, then such property is to be restored to its prior possessor, as if it had never been captured; and therefore under this principle your authorities propose to restore to their masters the slaves which heretofore belonged to them which you may capture from us.

But this postliminary right under which you claim to act, as understood and defined by all writers of national law, is applicable simply to immovable property, and that, too, only after the complete subjugation of that portion of the country in which the property is situated upon which this right fastens itself. By the laws and customs of war this right has never been applied to movable property.

True it is, I believe, that the Romans attempted to apply it in the case of slaves, but for 2,000 years no other nation has attempted to set up this right as ground for treating slaves differently from other property.

But the Romans even refused to re-enslave men captured from opposing belligerents in a civil war, such as ours unhappily is.

Consistently, then, with any principle of the law of nations, treating slaves as property merely, it would seem impossible for the Government of the United States to permit the negroes in their ranks to be re-enslaved when captured, or treated otherwise than as prisoners of war.

I have forborne, sir, in this discussion to argue the question upon any other or different grounds of right than those adopted by your authorities in claiming the negro as property, because I understand that your fabric of opposition to the Government of the United States has the right of property in man as its corner stone. Of course it would not be profitable in settling a question of exchange of prisoners of war to attempt to argue the question of abandonment of the very corner stone of their attempted political edifice. Therefore I have omitted all the considerations which should apply to the negro soldier as a man, and dealt with him upon the Confederate theory of property only.

I unite with you most cordially, sir, in desiring a speedy settlement of all these questions, in view of the great suffering endured by our prisoners in the hands of your authorities, of which you so feelingly speak. Let me ask, in view of that suffering, why you have delayed eight months to answer a proposition which, by now accepting, you admit to be right, just, and humane, allowing that suffering to continue so long? One cannot help thinking, even at the risk of being deemed uncharitable, that the benevolent sympathies of the Confederate authorities have been lately stirred by the depleted condition of their armies, and a desire to get into the field, to affect the present campaign, the hale, hearty, and well-fed prisoners held by the United States, in exchange for the half-starved, sick, emaciated, and unserviceable soldiers of the United States now languishing in your prisons. The events of this war, if we did not know it before, have taught us that it is not the Northern portion of the American people alone who know how to drive sharp bargains.

The wrongs, indignities, and privations suffered by our soldiers would move me to consent to anything to procure their exchange, except to barter away the honor and faith of the Government of the United States, which has been so solemnly pledged to the colored soldiers in its ranks.

Consistently with national faith and justice we cannot relinquish this position. With your authorities it is a question of property merely. It seems to address itself to you in this form: Will you suffer your soldier, captured in fighting your battles, to be in confinement for months rather than release him by giving for him that which you call a piece of property, and which we are willing to accept as a man?

You certainly appear to place less value upon your soldier than you do upon your negro. I assure you, much as we of the North are accused of loving property, our citizens would have no difficulty in yielding up any piece of property they have in exchange for one of their brothers or sons languishing in your prisons. Certainly there could be no doubt that they would do so were that piece of property less in value than $5,000 in Confederate money, which is believed to be the price of an able-bodied negro in the insurrectionary States.

Trusting that I may receive such a reply to the questions propounded in this note as will lead to a speedy resumption of the negotiations for a full exchange of all prisoners and a delivery of them to their respective authorities,

I have the honor to be, very respectfully,
your obedient servant,
BENJ. F. BUTLER,
Major-General and Commissioner for Exchange.

DEFENDING ATLANTA: GEORGIA, AUGUST 1864

Robert Toombs to Alexander H. Stephens

After the battle of July 22 the opposing armies at Atlanta entrenched along three sides of the city. While Union artillery shelled Atlanta, Sherman launched a series of cavalry raids that failed to cut the two railroads that supplied the city from the south. On August 25 Sherman withdrew his troops from their trenches east and north of Atlanta and began moving his forces south of the city. Robert Toombs was a former U.S. senator from Georgia who had briefly served as the Confederate secretary of state in 1861 and commanded a brigade in the Army of Northern Virginia in 1862. He wrote about the situation at Atlanta to his fellow Georgian, Confederate vice president Alexander H. Stephens.

ATLANTA, GEO., *30th Aug., 1864.*

DEAR STEPHENS, I wrote you some fortnight ago but hearing thro' a letter from Linton to Genl. Smith that he had heard nothing from either of us and my letter to him being of same date I think it probable from not hearing from you that yours also miscarried. I have been very closely engaged here since the enemy began shelling the city. He hauled off a few days ago and the army seemed as much elated as tho' we had gained a great victory, whereas it was simply changing his mode of attack. Our works were formidable; he felt of them half a dozen times; his men could not be got to charge them. He then wisely fell back, massed himself 6 or 7 miles west so. west of the town on the West Point R. Road, entrenched, and is gradually moving, entrenching as he goes, until he straddles the Macon road, cuts off our supplies, and compels us to fight him in his works or evacuate the place as soon as our rations are out. In the mean time he places a corps on the Chattahoochee defending his line from Vining's Station to Sand Town in his rear and thus protecting his line of communications. In fact, allowing for the topography of the country, it is precisely the Vicksburg movement acted over again, except we can get out when we want to and Pemberton could not. But we shall be equally unable to hold the place. The enemy care nothing for Wheeler and his seven thousand cavalry in the rear. They did not obstruct his trains more than four days, if that; and Wheeler avoided all depots where there were as much as armed sutlers. He has been gone for three weeks. I cannot say he has done no good, for he has relieved the poor people of this part of the country temporarily from his plundering marauding bands of cowardly robbers. It is said he is in Tennessee. I hope to God he will never get back into Georgia. We have a question of famine upon us. His band consumes more than the whole army besides and will accelerate the evil day. This army of Tennessee is in a deplorable condition. Hood is getting ridd of Bragg's worthless pets as fast as he can, but Davis supports a great number of them, and many other incompts. are sent from other places to take their commands. Hood I think the very best of the generals of his school; but like all the rest of them he knows no more of business than a ten year old boy, and don't know who does know anything about it. The longer the war lasts the more and more important it becomes to husband the resources of the country; but ours are wasted with a wild recklessness that would disgrace the Choctaw Indians. One third of the white population in Georgia are in the enemy's lines or so close to them as to make them or their industry unavailable to us. About a fourth of the residue is devastated by our armies and the villains around posts. Behold the prospect! This army has less than thirty thousand musketts present for duty, leaving out the militia who have under four thousand. Sherman I do not think has over 45 thousand musketts, and the possession of empire depends on this small force. Kirby Smith and Dick Taylor have over thirty thousand musketts in La. They have not fired a gun or perhaps marched ten miles since Banks left Alexandria last spring. I have a strong opinion that this force was promised to Hood. I saw Gov. Lubbock of Texas last night, who came direct thro' Dick Taylor's camp and therefore spoke on his personal knowledge of these important events. Therefore upon the whole our affairs here are gloomy enough. A good victory would change them much for the better.

I have been interrupted more than a dozen times in writing this letter and have not written you one tenth part that I want to. I will write you again tomorrow or next. Hood has sent me a request to send out people to collect and send him bacon in waggons to Social Circle en route for this place and a whole crowd of them are now in my tent waiting orders.

I hope if Linton gets well he will come back. Urge him to do so if his health will allow. There are many reasons for it.

"FOUR YEARS OF FAILURE":
ILLINOIS, AUGUST 1864

Platform of the Democratic National Convention

August 30, 1864

Originally scheduled to meet in Chicago on July 4, the Democratic national convention was postponed until August 29 due to the uncertain military situation. The plank in the platform calling for "a cessation of hostilities" was drafted by former Ohio congressman Clement L. Vallandigham, who had been left undisturbed by the Lincoln administration after returning from his exile in Canada in June 1864.

RESOLUTIONS:

Resolved, That in the future, as in the past, we will adhere with unswerving fidelity to the Union under the Constitution as the only solid foundation of our strength, security and happiness as a people, and as a framework of government equally conducive to the welfare and prosperity of all the States, both northern and southern.

Resolved, That this convention does explicitly declare, as the sense of the American people, that after four years of failure to restore the Union by the experiment of war, during which, under the pretence of a military necessity, or war power higher than the Constitution, the Constitution itself has been disregarded in every part, and public liberty and private right alike trodden down and the material prosperity of the country essentially impaired,—justice, humanity, liberty and the public welfare demand that immediate efforts be made for a cessation of hostilities, with a view to an ultimate convention of the States, or other peaceable means, to the end that at the earliest practicable moment peace may be restored on the basis of the Federal Union of the States.

Resolved, That the direct interference of the military authorities of the United States in the recent elections held in

Kentucky, Maryland, Missouri, and Delaware, was a shameful violation of the Constitution; and a repetition of such acts in the approaching election, will be held as revolutionary, and resisted with all the means and power under our control.

Resolved, That the aim and object of the Democratic party is to preserve the Federal Union and the rights of the States unimpaired; and they hereby declare that they consider that the administrative usurpation of extraordinary and dangerous powers not granted by the constitution; the subversion of the civil by military law in States not in insurrection; the arbitrary military arrest, imprisonment, trial and sentence of American citizens in States where civil law exists in full force; the suppression of freedom of speech and of the press; the denial of the right of asylum; the open and avowed disregard of State rights; the employment of unusual test oaths; and the interference with and denial of the right of the people to bear arms in their defence, is calculated to prevent a restoration of the Union and the perpetuation of a government deriving its just powers from the consent of the governed.

Resolved, That the shameful disregard of the administration to its duty in respect to our fellow citizens who now are, and long have been, prisoners of war in a suffering condition, deserves the severest reprobation on the score alike of public policy and common humanity.

Resolved, That the sympathy of the Democratic party is heartily and earnestly extended to the soldiery of our army and sailors of our navy, who are, and have been in the field and on the sea, under the flag of their country; and in the event of its attaining power, they will receive all the care, protection and regard that the brave soldiers and sailors of the Republic have so nobly earned.

"WE MUST CONQUER": SEPTEMBER 1864

James R. Gilmore: Our Visit to Richmond

September 1864

Gilmore published this account of the trip he had made to Richmond in July with James F. Jaquess in *The Atlantic Monthly* under his pen name Edmund Kirke.

WHY WE WENT THERE.

WHY my companion, the Rev. Dr. Jaquess, Colonel of the Seventy-Third Regiment of Illinois Volunteers, recently went to Richmond, and the circumstances attending his previous visit within the Rebel lines,—when he wore his uniform, and mixed openly with scores of leading Confederates,—I shall shortly make known to the public in a volume called "Down in Tennessee." It may now, however, be asked why I, a "civil" individual, and not in the pay of Government, became his travelling-companion, and, at a time when all the world was rushing North to the mountains and the watering-places, journeyed South for a conference with the arch-Rebel, in the hot and dangerous latitude of Virginia.

Did it never occur to you, reader, when you have undertaken to account for some of the simplest of your own actions, how many good reasons have arisen in your mind, every one of which has justified you in concluding that you were of "sound and disposing understanding"? So, now, in looking inward for the why and the wherefore which I know will be demanded of me at the threshold of this article, I find half a dozen reasons for my visit to Richmond, any one of which ought to prove that I am a sensible man, altogether too sensible to go on so long a journey, in the heat of midsummer, for the mere pleasure of the thing. Some of these reasons I will enumerate.

First: Very many honest people at the North sincerely believe that the revolted States will return to the Union, if assured of protection to their peculiar institution. The Government having declared that no State shall be readmitted which has not first abolished Slavery, these people hold it responsible for the continuance of the war. It is, therefore, important to know whether the Rebel States will or will not return, if allowed to retain Slavery. Mr. Jefferson Davis could, undoubtedly, answer that question; and that may have been a reason why I went to see him.

Second: On the second of July last, C. C. Clay, of Alabama, J. P. Holcombe, of Virginia, and G. N. Sanders, of nowhere in particular, appeared at Niagara Falls, and publicly announced that they were there to confer with the Democratic leaders in reference to the Chicago nomination. Very soon thereafter, a few friends of the Administration received intimations from those gentlemen that they were Commissioners from the Rebel Government, with authority to negotiate preliminaries of peace on something like the following basis, namely: A restoration of the Union as it was; all negroes actually freed by the war to be declared free, and all negroes not actually freed by the war to be declared slaves.

These overtures were not considered sincere. They seemed concocted to embarrass the Government, to throw upon it the odium of continuing the war, and thus to secure the triumph of the peace-traitors at the November election. The scheme, if well managed, threatened to be dangerous, by uniting the Peace-men, the Copperheads, and such of the Republicans as love peace better than principle, in one opposition, willing to make a peace that would be inconsistent with the safety and dignity of the country. It was, therefore, important to discover—what was then in doubt—whether the Rebel envoys really had, or had not, any official authority.

Within fifteen days of the appearance of these "Peace Commissioners," Jefferson Davis had said to an eminent Secession divine, who, late in June, came through the Union lines by the Maryland back-door, that he would make peace on no other terms than a recognition of Southern Independence. (He might, however, agree to two governments, bound together by a league offensive and defensive,—for all external purposes *one*, for all internal purposes *two*; but he would agree to nothing better.)

There was reason to consider this information trustworthy, and to believe Mr Davis (who was supposed to be a clear-minded man) altogether ignorant of the doings of his Niagara satellites. If this were true, and were proven to be true,—if the *great* Rebel should reiterate this declaration in the presence of a trustworthy witness, at the very time when the *small* Rebels were opening their Quaker guns on the country,—would not the Niagara negotiators be stripped of their false colors, and their low schemes be exposed to the scorn of all honest men, North and South?

I may have thought so; and that may have been another reason why I went to Richmond.

Third: I had been acquainted with Colonel Jaquess's peace-movements from their inception. Early in June last he wrote me from a battle-field in Georgia, announcing his intention of again visiting the Rebels, and asking an interview with me at a designated place. We met, and went to Washington together. Arriving there, I became aware that obstacles were in the way of his further progress. Those obstacles could be removed by my accompanying him; and that, to those who know the man and his "mission," which is to preach peace on earth and good-will among men, would seem a very good reason why I went to Richmond.

Fourth,—and this to very many may appear as potent as any of the preceding reasons,—I had in my boyhood a strange fancy for church-belfries and liberty-poles. This fancy led me, in school-vacations, to perch my small self for hours on the cross-beams in the old belfry, and to climb to the very top of the tall pole which still surmounts the little village-green. In my youth, this feeling was simply a spirit of adventure; but as I grew older it deepened into a reverence for what those old bells said, and a love for the principle of which that old liberty-pole is now only a crumbling symbol.

Had not events shown that Jeff. Davis had never seen that old liberty-pole, and never heard the chimes which still ring out from that old belfry? Who knew, in these days when every wood-sawyer has a "mission," but *I* had a "mission," and it was to tell the Rebel President that Northern liberty-poles still stand for Freedom, and that Northern church-bells still peal out, "Liberty throughout the land, to *all* the inhabitants thereof"?

If that *was* my mission, will anybody blame me for fanning Mr. Davis with a "blast" of cool Northern "wind" in this hot weather?

But enough of mystification. The straightforward reader wants a straightforward reason, and he shall have it.

We went to Richmond because we hoped to pave the way for negotiations that would result in peace.

If we should succeed, the consciousness of having served the country would, we thought, pay our expenses. If we should fail, but return safely, we might still serve the country by making public the cause of our failure. If we should fail, and *not* return safely, but be shot or hanged as spies,—as we might be, for we could have no protection from our Government, and no safe-conduct from the Rebels,—two lives would be added to the thousands already sacrificed to this Rebellion, but they would as effectually serve the country as if lost on the battle-field.

These are the reasons, and the only reasons, why we went to Richmond.

HOW WE WENT THERE.

WE went there in an ambulance, and we went together,— the Colonel and I; and though two men were never more unlike, we worked together like two brothers, or like two halves of a pair of shears. That we got *in* was owing, perhaps, to me; that we got *out* was due altogether to him; and a man more cool, more brave, more self-reliant, and more self-devoted than that quiet "Western parson" it never was my fortune to encounter.

When the far-away Boston bells were sounding nine, on the morning of Saturday, the sixteenth of July, we took our glorious Massachusetts General by the hand, and said to him,—

"Good bye. If you do not see us within ten days, you will know we have 'gone up.'"

"If I do not see you within that time," he replied, "I'll demand you; and if they don't produce you, body and soul, I'll take two for one,—better men than you are,—and hang them higher than Haman. My hand on that. Good bye."

At three o'clock on the afternoon of the same day, mounted on two raw-boned relics of Sheridan's great raid, and armed with a letter to Jeff. Davis, a white cambric handkerchief tied to a short stick, and an honest face,—this last was the Colonel's,—we rode up to the Rebel lines. A ragged, yellow-faced boy, with a carbine in one hand, and another white handkerchief tied to another short stick in the other, came out to meet us.

"Can you tell us, my man, where to find Judge Ould, the Exchange Commissioner?"

"Yas. Him and t' other 'Change officers is over ter the plantation beyont Miss Grover's. Ye 'll know it by its hevin' nary door nur winder [the mansion, he meant]. They 's all busted in. Foller the bridle-path through the timber, and keep your rag a-flyin', fur our boys is thicker 'n huckelberries in them woods, and they mought pop ye, ef they did n't seed it."

Thanking him, we turned our horses into the "timber," and, galloping rapidly on, soon came in sight of the deserted plantation. Lolling on the grass, in the shade of the windowless mansion, we found the Confederate officials. They rose as we approached; and one of us said to the Judge,—a courteous, middle-aged gentleman, in a Panama hat, and a suit of spotless white drillings,—

"We are late, but it 's your fault. Your people fired at us down the river, and we had to turn back and come overland."

"You don't suppose they saw your flag?"

"No. It was hidden by the trees; but a shot came uncomfortably near us. It struck the water, and ricochetted not three yards off. A little nearer, and it would have shortened me by a head, and the Colonel by two feet."

"That would have been a sad thing for you; but a miss, you know, is as good as a mile," said the Judge, evidently enjoying the "joke."

"We hear Grant was in the boat that followed yours, and was struck while at dinner," remarked Captain Hatch, the Judge's Adjutant,—a gentleman, and about the best-looking man in the Confederacy.

"Indeed! Do you believe it?"

"I don't know, of course"; and his looks asked for an answer. We gave none, for all such information is contraband. We might have told him that Grant, Butler, and Foster examined their position from Mrs. Grover's house,—about four hundred yards distant,—two hours after the Rebel cannon-ball danced a break-down on the Lieutenant-General's dinner-table.

We were then introduced to the other officials,—Major

Henniken of the War Department, a young man formerly of New York, but now scorning the imputation of being a Yankee, and Mr. Charles Javins, of the Provost-Guard of Richmond. This latter individual was our shadow in Dixie. He was of medium height, stoutly built, with a short, thick neck, and arms and shoulders denoting great strength. He looked a natural-born jailer, and much such a character as a timid man would not care to encounter, except at long range of a rifle warranted to fire twenty shots a minute, and to hit every time.

To give us a *moonlight view* of the Richmond fortifications, the Judge proposed to start after sundown; and as it wanted some hours of that time, we seated ourselves on the ground, and entered into conversation. The treatment of our prisoners, the *status* of black troops, and non-combatants, and all the questions which have led to the suspension of exchanges, had been good-naturedly discussed, when the Captain, looking up from one of the Northern papers we had brought him, said,—

"Do you know, it mortifies me that you don't hate us as we hate you? You kill us as Agassiz kills a fly,—because you love us."

"Of course we do. The North is being crucified for love of the South."

"If you love us so, why don't you let us go?" asked the Judge, rather curtly.

"For that very reason,—because we love you. If we let you go, with slavery, and your notions of 'empire,' you'd run straight to barbarism and the Devil."

"We'd take the risk of that. But let me tell you, if you are going to Mr. Davis with any such ideas, you might as well turn back at once. He can make peace on no other basis than Independence. Recognition must be the beginning, middle, and ending of all negotiations. Our people will accept peace on no other terms."

"I think you are wrong there," said the Colonel. "When I was here a year ago, I met many of your leading men, and they all assured me they wanted peace and reunion, even at the sacrifice of slavery. Within a week, a man you venerate and love has met me at Baltimore, and besought me to come here, and offer Mr. Davis peace on such conditions."

"That may be. Some of our old men, who are weak in the knees, may want peace on any terms; but the Southern people will not have it without Independence. Mr. Davis knows them, and you will find he will insist upon that. Concede that, and we 'll not quarrel about minor matters."

"We 'll not quarrel at all. But it 's sundown, and time we were 'on to Richmond.'"

"That 's the 'Tribune' cry," said the Captain, rising; "and I hurrah for the 'Tribune,' for it 's honest, and—I want my supper."

We all laughed, and the Judge ordered the horses. As we were about to start, I said to him,—

"You 've forgotten our parole."

"Oh, never mind that. We 'll attend to that at Richmond."

Stepping into his carriage, and unfurling the flag of truce, he then led the way, by a "short cut," across the corn-field which divided the mansion from the high-road. We followed in an ambulance drawn by a pair of mules, our shadow—Mr. Javins—sitting between us and the twilight, and Jack, a "likely darky," almost the sole survivor of his master's twelve hundred slaves, ("De ress all stole, Massa,—stole by you Yankees,") occupying the front-seat, and with a stout whip "working our passage" to Richmond.

Much that was amusing and interesting occurred during our three-hours' journey, but regard for our word forbids my relating it. Suffice it to say, we saw the "frowning fortifications," we "flanked" the "invincible army," and, at ten o'clock that night, planted our flag (against a lamp-post) in the very heart of the hostile city. As we alighted at the doorway of the Spotswood Hotel, the Judge said to the Colonel,—

"Button your outside-coat up closely. Your uniform must not be seen here."

The Colonel did as he was bidden; and, without stopping to register our names at the office, we followed the Judge and the Captain up to No. 60. It was a large, square room in the fourth story, with an unswept, ragged carpet, and bare, white walls, smeared with soot and tobacco-juice. Several chairs, a marble-top table, and a pine wash-stand and clothes-press straggled about the floor, and in the corners were three beds, garnished with tattered pillow-cases, and covered with white counterpanes, grown gray with longing for soapsuds and a wash-tub. The plainer and humbler of these beds was designed for the burly Mr. Javins; the others had been made ready for the extraordinary envoys (not envoys extraordinary) who, in defiance of all precedent and the "law of nations," had just then "taken Richmond."

A single gas-jet was burning over the mantel-piece, and above it I saw a "writing on the wall" which implied that Jane Jackson had run up a washing-score of fifty dollars!

I was congratulating myself on not having to pay that woman's laundry-bills, when the Judge said,—

"You want supper. What shall we order?"

"A slice of hot corn-bread would make *me* the happiest man in Richmond."

The Captain thereupon left the room, and shortly returning, remarked,—

"The landlord swears you 're from Georgia. He says none but a Georgian would call for corn-bread at this time of night."

On that hint we acted, and when our sooty attendant came in with the supper-things, we discussed Georgia mines, Georgia banks, and Georgia mosquitoes, in a way that showed we had been bitten by all of them. In half an hour it was noised all about the hotel that the two gentlemen the Confederacy was taking such excellent care of were from Georgia.

The meal ended, and a quiet smoke over, our entertainers rose to go. As the Judge bade us good-night, he said to us,—

"In the morning you had better address a note to Mr. Benjamin, asking the interview with the President. I will call at ten o'clock, and take it to him."

"Very well. But will Mr. Davis see us on Sunday?"

"Oh, that will make no difference."

WHAT WE DID THERE.

THE next morning, after breakfast, which we took in our room with Mr. Javins, we indited a note—of which the following is a copy—to the Confederate Secretary of State.

"Spotswood House, Richmond, Va.
"July 17th, 1864.

"Hon. J. P. Benjamin,
"Secretary of State, etc.

"DEAR SIR,—The undersigned respectfully solicit an interview with President Davis.

"They visit Richmond only as private citizens, and have no official character or authority; but they are acquainted with the views of the United States Government, and with the sentiments of the Northern people relative to an adjustment of the differences existing between the North and the South, and earnestly hope that a free interchange of views between President Davis and themselves may open the way to such *official* negotiations as will result in restoring PEACE to the two sections of our distracted country.

"They, therefore, ask an interview with the President, and awaiting your reply, are

"Truly and respectfully yours."

This was signed by both of us; and when the Judge called, as he had appointed, we sent it—together with a commendatory letter I had received, on setting out, from a near relative of Mr. Davis—to the Rebel Secretary. In half an hour Judge Ould returned, saying,—"Mr. Benjamin sends you his compliments, and will be happy to see you at the State Department."

We found the Secretary—a short, plump, oily little man in black, with a keen black eye, a Jew face, a yellow skin, curly black hair, closely trimmed black whiskers, and a ponderous gold watch-chain—in the northwest room of the "United States" Custom-House. Over the door of this room were the words, "State Department," and round its walls were hung a few maps and battle-plans. In one corner was a tier of shelves filled with books,—among which I noticed Headley's "History," Lossing's "Pictorial," Parton's "Butler," Greeley's "American Conflict," a complete set of the "Rebellion Record," and a dozen numbers and several bound volumes of the "Atlantic Monthly,"—and in the centre of the apartment was a black-walnut table, covered with green cloth, and filled with a multitude of "state-papers." At this table sat the Secretary. He rose as we entered, and, as Judge Ould introduced us, took our hands, and said,—

"I am glad, very glad, to meet you, Gentlemen. I have read your note, and"—bowing to me—"the open letter you bring from ———. Your errand commands my respect and sympathy. Pray be seated."

As we took the proffered seats, the Colonel, drawing off his "duster," and displaying his uniform, said,—

"We thank you for this cordial reception, Mr. Benjamin. We trust you will be as glad to hear us as you are to see us."

"No doubt I shall be, for you come to talk of peace. Peace is what we all want."

"It is, indeed; and for that reason we are here to see Mr. Davis. Can we see him, Sir?"

"Do you bring any overtures to him from your Government?"

"No, Sir. We bring no overtures and have no authority from our Government. We state that in our note. We would be glad, however, to know what terms will be acceptable to Mr. Davis. If they at all harmonize with Mr. Lincoln's views, we will report them to him, and so open the door for official negotiations."

"Are you acquainted with Mr. Lincoln's views?"

"One of us is, fully."

"Did Mr. Lincoln, *in any way*, authorize you to come here?"

"No, Sir. We came with his pass, but not by his request. We say, distinctly, we have no official, or unofficial, authority. We come as men and Christians, not as diplomatists, hoping, in a frank talk with Mr. Davis, to discover some way by which this war may be stopped."

"Well, Gentlemen, I will repeat what you say to the President, and if he follows my advice,—and I think he will,—he will meet you. He will be at church this afternoon; so, suppose you call here at nine this evening. If anything should occur in the mean time to prevent his seeing you, I will let you know through Judge Ould."

Throughout this interview the manner of the Secretary was cordial; but with this cordiality was a strange constraint and diffidence, almost amounting to timidity, which struck both my companion and myself. Contrasting his manner with the quiet dignity of the Colonel, I almost fancied our positions reversed,—that, instead of our being in his power, the Secretary was in ours, and momently expecting to hear some unwelcome sentence from our lips. There is something, after all, in moral power. Mr. Benjamin does not possess it, nor is he a great man. He has a keen, shrewd, ready intellect, but not the *stamina* to originate, or even to execute, any great good or great wickedness.

After a day spent in our room, conversing with the Judge, or watching the passers-by in the street,—I should like to tell who they were and how they looked, but such information is just now contraband,—we called again, at nine o'clock, at the State Department.

Mr. Benjamin occupied his previous seat at the table, and at his right sat a spare, thin-featured man, with iron-gray hair and beard, and a clear, gray eye full of life and vigor. He had a broad, massive forehead, and a mouth and chin denoting great energy and strength of will. His face was emaciated, and much wrinkled, but his features were good, especially his eyes,— though one of them bore a scar, apparently made by some sharp instrument. He wore a suit of grayish-brown, evidently of foreign manufacture, and, as he rose, I saw that he was about five feet ten inches high, with a slight stoop in the shoulders. His manners were simple, easy, and quite fascinating; and he threw an indescribable charm into his voice, as he extended his hand, and said to us,—

"I am glad to see you, Gentlemen. You are very welcome to Richmond."

And this was the man who was President of the United States under Franklin Pierce, and who is now the heart, soul, and brains of the Southern Confederacy!

His manner put me entirely at my ease,—the Colonel would be at his, if he stood before Cæsar,—and I replied,—

"We thank you, Mr. Davis. It is not often you meet men of our clothes, and our principles, in Richmond."

"Not often,—not so often as I could wish; and I trust your coming may lead to a more frequent and a more friendly intercourse between the North and the South."

"We sincerely hope it may."

"Mr. Benjamin tells me you have asked to see me, to"——

And he paused, as if desiring we should finish the sentence. The Colonel replied,—

"Yes, Sir. We have asked this interview in the hope that you may suggest some way by which this war can be stopped. Our people want peace,—your people do, and your Congress has recently said that *you* do. We have come to ask how it can be brought about."

"In a very simple way. Withdraw your armies from our territory, and peace will come of itself. We do not seek to subjugate you. We are not waging an offensive war, except so far as it is offensive-defensive,—that is, so far as we are forced to invade you to prevent your invading us. Let us alone, and peace will come at once."

"But we cannot let you alone so long as you repudiate the Union. That is the one thing the Northern people will not surrender."

"I know. You would deny to us what you exact for yourselves,—the right of self-government."

"No, Sir," I remarked. "We would deny you no natural right. But we think Union essential to peace; and, Mr. Davis, *could* two people, with the same language, separated by only an imaginary line, live at peace with each other? Would not disputes constantly arise, and cause almost constant war between them?"

"Undoubtedly,—with this generation. You have sown such bitterness at the South, you have put such an ocean of blood between the two sections, that I despair of seeing any harmony in my time. Our children may forget this war, but *we* cannot."

"I think the bitterness you speak of, Sir," said the Colonel, "does not really exist. *We* meet and talk here as friends; our soldiers meet and fraternize with each other; and I feel sure, that, if the Union were restored, a more friendly feeling would arise between us than has ever existed. The war has made us know and respect each other better than before. This is the view of very many Southern men; I have had it from many of them,—your leading citizens."

"They are mistaken," replied Mr. Davis. "They do not understand Southern sentiment. How can we feel anything but bitterness towards men who deny us our rights? If you enter my house and drive me out of it, am I not your natural enemy?"

"You put the case too strongly. But we cannot fight forever; the war must end at some time; we must finally agree upon something; can we not agree now, and stop this frightful carnage? We are both Christian men, Mr. Davis. Can *you*, as a Christian man, leave untried any means that may lead to peace?"

"No, I cannot. I desire peace as much as you do. I deplore bloodshed as much as you do; but I feel that not one drop of the blood shed in this war is on *my* hands,—I can look up to my God and say this. I tried all in my power to avert this war.

I saw it coming, and for twelve years I worked night and day to prevent it, but I could not. The North was mad and blind; it would not let us govern ourselves; and so the war came, and now it must go on till the last man of this generation falls in his tracks, and his children seize his musket and fight his battle, *unless you acknowledge our right to self-government.* We are not fighting for slavery. We are fighting for Independence,—and that, or extermination, we *will* have."

"And there are, at least, four and a half millions of us left; so you see you have a work before you," said Mr. Benjamin, with a decided sneer.

"We have no wish to exterminate you," answered the Colonel. "I believe what I have said,—that there is no bitterness between the Northern and Southern *people*. The North, I know, loves the South. When peace comes, it will pour money and means into your hands to repair the waste caused by the war; and it would now welcome you back, and forgive you all the loss and bloodshed you have caused. But we *must* crush your armies, and exterminate your Government. And is not that already nearly done? You are wholly without money, and at the end of your resources. Grant has shut you up in Richmond. Sherman is before Atlanta. Had you not, then, better accept honorable terms while you can retain your prestige, and save the pride of the Southern people?"

Mr. Davis smiled.

"I respect your earnestness, Colonel, but you do not seem to understand the situation. We are not exactly shut up in Richmond. If your papers tell the truth, it is your capital that is in danger, not ours. Some weeks ago, Grant crossed the Rapidan to whip Lee, and take Richmond. Lee drove him in the first battle, and then Grant executed what your people call a 'brilliant flank-movement,' and fought Lee again. Lee drove him a second time, and then Grant made another 'flank-movement'; and so they kept on,—Lee whipping, and Grant flanking,—until Grant got where he is now. And what is the net result? Grant has lost seventy-five or eighty thousand men,—*more than Lee had at the outset,*—and is no nearer taking Richmond than at first; and Lee, whose front has never been broken, holds him completely in check, and has men enough to spare to invade Maryland, and threaten Washington! Sherman, to be sure, *is* before Atlanta; but suppose he is, and suppose he takes it? You know, that, the farther he goes from his base of supplies, the weaker he grows, and the more disastrous defeat will be to him. And defeat *may* come. So, in a military view, I should certainly say our position was better than yours.

"As to money: we are richer than you are. You smile; but admit that our paper is worth nothing,—it answers as a circulating-medium; and we hold it all ourselves. If every dollar of it were lost, we should, as we have no foreign debt, be none the poorer. But it *is* worth something; it has the solid basis of a large cotton-crop, while yours rests on nothing, and you owe all the world. As to resources: we do not lack for arms or ammunition, and we have still a wide territory from which to gather supplies. So, you see, we are not in extremities. But if we were,—if we were without money, without food, without weapons,—if our whole country were devastated, and our armies crushed and disbanded,—could we, without giving up our manhood, give up our right to govern ourselves? Would *you* not rather die, and feel yourself a man, than live, and be subject to a foreign power?"

"From your stand-point there is force in what you say," replied the Colonel. "But we did not come here to argue with you, Mr. Davis. We came, hoping to find some honorable way to peace; and I am grieved to hear you say what you do. When I have seen your young men dying on the battle-field, and your old men, women, and children starving in their homes, I have felt I could risk my life to save them. For that reason I am here; and I am grieved, grieved, that there is no hope."

"I know your motives, Colonel Jaquess, and I honor you for them; but what can I do more than I am doing? I would give my poor life, gladly, if it would bring peace and good-will to the two countries; but it would not. It is with your own people you should labor. It is they who desolate our homes, burn our wheat-fields, break the wheels of wagons carrying away our women and children, and destroy supplies meant for our sick and wounded. At your door lies all the misery and the crime of this war,—and it is a fearful, fearful account."

"Not all of it, Mr. Davis. I admit a fearful account, but it is not *all* at our door. The passions of both sides are aroused.

Unarmed men are hanged, prisoners are shot down in cold blood, by yourselves. Elements of barbarism are entering the war on both sides, that should make us—you and me, as Christian men—shudder to think of. In God's name, then, let us stop it. Let us do something, concede something, to bring about peace. You cannot expect, with only four and a half millions, as Mr. Benjamin says you have, to hold out forever against twenty millions."

Again Mr. Davis smiled.

"Do you suppose there are twenty millions at the North determined to crush us?"

"I do,—to crush your *government*. A small number of our people, a very small number, are your friends,—Secessionists. The rest differ about measures and candidates, but are united in the determination to sustain the Union. Whoever is elected in November, he *must be* committed to a vigorous prosecution of the war."

Mr. Davis still looking incredulous, I remarked,—

"It is so, Sir. Whoever tells you otherwise deceives you. I think I know Northern sentiment, and I assure you it is so. You know we have a system of lyceum-lecturing in our large towns. At the close of these lectures, it is the custom of the people to come upon the platform and talk with the lecturer. This gives him an excellent opportunity of learning public sentiment. Last winter I lectured before nearly a hundred of such associations, all over the North,—from Dubuque to Bangor,— and I took pains to ascertain the feeling of the people. I found a unanimous determination to crush the Rebellion and save the Union at every sacrifice. The majority are in favor of Mr. Lincoln, and nearly all of those opposed to him are opposed to him because they think he does not fight you with enough vigor. The radical Republicans, who go for slave-suffrage and thorough confiscation, are those who will defeat him, if he is defeated. But if he is defeated before the people, the House will elect a worse man,—I mean, worse for you. It is more radical than he is,—you can see that from Mr. Ashley's Reconstruction Bill,—and the people are more radical than the House. Mr. Lincoln, I know, is about to call out five hundred thousand more men, and I can't see how you *can* resist much longer; but if you do, you will only deepen the radical feeling of the Northern people. They will now give you fair, honorable, *generous* terms; but let them suffer much more, let there be a dead man in every house, as there is now in every village, and they will give you *no* terms,—they will insist on hanging every Rebel south of —— Pardon my terms. I mean no offence."

"You give no offence," he replied, smiling very pleasantly. "I would n't have you pick your words. This is a frank, free talk, and I like you the better for saying what you think. Go on."

"I was merely going to say, that, let the Northern people once really feel the war,—they do not feel it yet,—and they will insist on hanging every one of your leaders."

"Well, admitting all you say, I can't see how it affects our position. There are some things worse than hanging or extermination. We reckon giving up the right of self-government one of those things."

"By self-government you mean disunion,—Southern Independence?"

"Yes."

"And slavery, you say, is no longer an element in the contest."

"No, it is not, it never was an *essential* element. It was only a means of bringing other conflicting elements to an earlier culmination. It fired the musket which was already capped and loaded. There are essential differences between the North and the South that will, however this war may end, make them two nations."

"You ask me to say what I think. Will you allow me to say that I know the South pretty well, and never observed those differences?"

"Then you have not used your eyes. My sight is poorer than yours, but I have seen them for years."

The laugh was upon me, and Mr. Benjamin enjoyed it.

"Well, Sir, be that as it may, if I understand you, the dispute between your government and ours is narrowed down to this: Union or Disunion."

"Yes; or to put it in other words: Independence or Subjugation."

"Then the two governments are irreconcilably apart. They have no alternative but to fight it out. But it is not so with the people. They are tired of fighting, and want peace; and as they bear all the burden and suffering of the war, is it not right they should have peace, and have it on such terms as they like?"

"I don't understand you. Be a little more explicit."

"Well, suppose the two governments should agree to something like this: To go to the people with two propositions: say, Peace, with Disunion and Southern Independence, as your proposition,—and Peace, with Union, Emancipation, No Confiscation, and Universal Amnesty, as ours. Let the citizens of all the United States (as they existed before the war) vote 'Yes,' or 'No,' on these two propositions, at a special election within sixty days. If a majority votes Disunion, our government to be bound by it, and to let you go in peace. If a majority votes Union, yours to be bound by it, and to stay in peace. The two governments can contract in this way, and the people, though constitutionally unable to decide on peace or war, can elect which of the two propositions shall govern their rulers. Let Lee and Grant, meanwhile, agree to an armistice. This would sheathe the sword; and if once sheathed, it would never again be drawn by this generation."

"The plan is altogether impracticable. If the South were only one State, it might work; but as it is, if one Southern State objected to emancipation, it would nullify the whole thing; for you are aware the people of Virginia cannot vote slavery out of South Carolina, nor the people of South Carolina vote it out of Virginia."

"But three-fourths of the States can amend the Constitution. Let it be done in that way,—in any way, so that it be done by the people. I am not a statesman or a politician, and I do not know just how such a plan could be carried out; but you get the idea,—that the PEOPLE shall decide the question."

"That the *majority* shall decide it, you mean. We seceded to rid ourselves of the rule of the majority, and this would subject us to it again."

"But the majority must rule finally, either with bullets or ballots."

"I am not so sure of that. Neither current events nor history shows that the majority rules, or ever did rule. The contrary, I think, is true. Why, Sir, the man who should go before the Southern people with such a proposition, with *any* proposition which implied that the North was to have a voice in determining the domestic relations of the South, could not live here a day. He would be hanged to the first tree, without judge or jury."

"Allow me to doubt that. I think it more likely he would be hanged, if he let the Southern people know the majority could n't rule," I replied, smiling.

"I have no fear of that," rejoined Mr. Davis, also smiling most good-humoredly. "I give you leave to proclaim it from every house-top in the South."

"But, seriously, Sir, you let the majority rule in a single State; why not let it rule in the whole country?"

"Because the States are independent and sovereign. The country is not. It is only a confederation of States; or rather it *was*: it is now *two* confederations."

"Then we are not a *people*,—we are only a political partnership?"

"That is all."

"Your very name, Sir, '*United* States,' implies that," said Mr. Benjamin. "But, tell me, are the terms you have named—Emancipation, No Confiscation, and Universal Amnesty—the terms which Mr. Lincoln authorized you to offer us?"

"No, Sir, Mr. Lincoln did not authorize me to offer you any terms. But I *think* both he and the Northern people, for the sake of peace, would assent to some such conditions."

"They are *very* generous," replied Mr. Davis, for the first time during the interview showing some angry feeling. "But Amnesty, Sir, applies to criminals. We have committed no crime. Confiscation is of no account, unless you can enforce it. And Emancipation! You have already emancipated nearly two millions of our slaves,—and if you will take care of them, you may emancipate the rest. I had a few when the war began. I was of some use to them; they never were of any to me. Against their will you 'emancipated' them; and you may 'emancipate' every negro in the Confederacy, but *we will be free*! We will govern ourselves. We *will* do it, if we have to see every Southern plantation sacked, and every Southern city in flames."

"I see, Mr. Davis, it is useless to continue this conversation," I replied; "and you will pardon us, if we have seemed to press our views with too much pertinacity. We love the old flag, and that must be our apology for intruding upon you at all."

"You have not intruded upon me," he replied, resuming his usual manner. "I am glad to have met you, both. I once loved the old flag as well as you do; I would have died for it; but now it is to me only the emblem of oppression."

"I hope the day may never come, Mr. Davis, when *I* say that," said the Colonel.

A half-hour's conversation on other topics—not of public interest—ensued, and then we rose to go. As we did so, the Rebel President gave me his hand, and, bidding me a kindly good-bye, expressed the hope of seeing me again in Richmond in happier times,—when peace should have returned; but with the Colonel his parting was particularly cordial. Taking his hand in both of his, he said to him,—

"Colonel, I respect your character and your motives, and I wish you well,—I wish you every good I can wish you consistently with the interests of the Confederacy."

The quiet, straightforward bearing and magnificent moral courage of our "fighting parson" had evidently impressed Mr. Davis very favorably.

As we were leaving the room, he added,—

"Say to Mr. Lincoln from me, that I shall at any time be pleased to receive proposals for peace on the basis of our Independence. It will be useless to approach me with any other."

When we went out, Mr. Benjamin called Judge Ould, who had been waiting during the whole interview—two hours—at the other end of the hall, and we passed down the stairway together. As I put my arm within that of the Judge, he said to me,—

"Well, what is the result?"

"Nothing but war,—war to the knife."

"Ephraim is joined to his idols,—let him alone," added the Colonel, solemnly.

I should like to relate the incidents of the next day, when we visited Castle Thunder, Libby Prison, and the hospitals occupied by our wounded; but the limits of a magazine-article will not permit. I can only say that at sundown we passed out of the Rebel lines, and at ten o'clock that night stretched our tired limbs on the "downy" cots in General Butler's tent, thankful, devoutly thankful, that we were once again under the folds of the old flag.

Thus ended our visit to Richmond. I have endeavored to sketch it faithfully. The conversation with Mr. Davis I took down shortly after entering the Union lines, and I have tried to report his exact language, extenuating nothing, and coloring nothing that he said. Some of his sentences, as I read them over, appear stilted and high-flown, but they did not sound so when uttered. As listened to, they seemed the simple, natural language of his thought. He spoke deliberately, apparently weighing every word, and knowing well that all he said would be given to the public.

He is a man of peculiar ability. Our interview with him explained to me why, with no money and no commerce, with nearly every one of their important cities in our hands, and with an army greatly inferior in numbers and equipment to ours, the Rebels have held out so long. It is because of the sagacity, energy, and indomitable will of Jefferson Davis. Without him the Rebellion would crumble to pieces in a day; with him it may continue to be, even in disaster, a power that will tax the whole energy and resources of the nation.

The Southern masses want peace. Many of the Southern leaders want it,—both my companion and I, by correspondence and intercourse with them, know this; but there can be no peace so long as Mr. Davis controls the South. Ignoring slavery, he himself states the issue,—the only issue with him,— Union, or Disunion. That is it. We must conquer, or be conquered. We can negotiate only with the bayonet. We can have peace and union only by putting forth all our strength, crushing the Southern armies, and overthrowing the Southern government.

REQUESTING REINFORCEMENTS:
VIRGINIA, SEPTEMBER 1864

Robert E. Lee to Jefferson Davis

Grant began his second attempt to cut the Weldon & Petersburg Railroad on August 14 by attacking north of the James River at Deep Bottom, ten miles southeast of Richmond. In fighting that continued until August 20 the Union forces failed to gain ground, but succeeded in drawing Confederate troops away from the Petersburg front. Union troops were then able to cut the Weldon Railroad six miles south of Petersburg in the battle of Globe Tavern, August 18–21. A subsequent Union expedition sent to destroy the railroad to a point twenty miles south of Petersburg ended in defeat at Reams Station on August 25. Together, the three battles cost the Union about 10,000 men killed, wounded, or missing, and the Confederates about 4,000. The defeat at Globe Tavern forced the Confederates to stop trains on the Weldon Railroad sixteen miles south of Petersburg and then transport supplies by wagon over thirty miles of road. Lee wrote to Davis a week after the offensive ended.

Headquarters, Army of Northern Virginia
September 2, 1864

Mr. President:

I beg leave to call your attention to the importance of immediate and vigorous measures to increase the strength of our armies, and to some suggestions as to the mode of doing it. The necessity is now great, and will soon be augmented by the results of the coming draft in the United States. As matters now stand, we have no troops disposable to meet movements of the enemy or strike where opportunity presents, without taking them from the trenches and exposing some important point. The enemy's position enables him to move his troops to the right or left without our knowledge, until he has reached the point at which he aims, and we are then compelled to hurry our men to meet him, incurring the risk of being too late to check his progress and the additional risk of the advantage he may derive from their absence. This was fully illustrated in the late demonstration north of James River, which called troops from our lines here, who if present might have prevented the occupation of the Weldon Railroad. These rapid and distant movements also fatigue and exhaust our men, greatly impairing their efficiency in battle. It is not necessary, however, to enumerate all the reasons for recruiting our ranks. The necessity is as well known to Your Excellency as to myself and as much the object of your solicitude. The means of obtaining men for field duty, as far as I can see, are only three.

A considerable number could be placed in the ranks by relieving all able bodied white men employed as teamsters, cooks, mechanics, and laborers, and supplying their places with negroes. I think measures should be taken at once to substitute negroes for whites in every place in the army, or connected with it, where the former can be used. It seems to me that we must choose between employing negroes ourselves, and having them employed against us.

A thorough and vigorous inspection of the rolls of exempted and detailed men is in my opinion of immediate importance. I think you will agree with me that no man should be excused from service for any reason not deemed sufficient to entitle one already in service to his discharge.

I do not think that the decision of such questions can be made so well by any as by those whose experience with troops has made them acquainted with those urgent claims to relief, which are constantly brought to the attention of commanding officers, but which they are forced to deny. For this reason I would recommend that the rolls of exempts and details in each State be inspected by officers of character and influence who have had experience in the field and have had nothing to do with the exemptions and details. If all that I have heard be true, I think it will be found that very different rules of action have been pursued towards men in service and those liable to it in the matter of exemptions and details, and I respectfully recommend that Your Excellency cause reports to be made by the Enrolling Bureau of the number of men enrolled in each State, the number sent to the field, and the number exempted or detailed. I regard this matter as of the utmost moment. Our ranks are constantly diminishing by battle and disease, and few recruits are received. The consequences are inevitable, and I feel confident that the time has come when no man capable of bearing arms should be excused, unless it be for some controlling reason of public necessity. The safety of the country requires this in my judgment, and hardship to individuals must be disregarded in view of the calamity that would follow to the whole people if our armies meet with disaster. No detail of an arms bearing man should be continued or granted, except for the performance of duty that is indispensable to the army, and that cannot be performed by one not liable to or fit for service. Agricultural details take numbers from the army without any corresponding advantage. I think that the interest of land owners and cultivators may be relied upon to induce them to provide means for saving their crops, if they be sent to the field. If they remain at home their produce will only benefit the enemy, as our armies will be insufficient to defend them. If the officers and men detailed in the Conscript Bureau have performed their duties faithfully, they must have already brought out the chief part of those liable to duty, and have nothing to do now except to get such as from time to time reach military age. If this be true many of these officers and men can now be spared for the army. If not, they have been derelict, and should be sent back to the ranks, & their places supplied by others who will be more active. Such a policy will stimulate the energy of this class of men. The last resource is the reserve force. Men of this class can render great service in connection with regular troops, by taking their places in trenches, forts, &c., and leaving them free for active operations.

I think no time should be lost in bringing out the entire strength of this class, particularly in Virginia & North Carolina. If I had the reserves of Virginia to hold the trenches here, or even enough to man those below Richmond on the north side of the river, they would render greater service than they can in any other way. They would give me a force to act with on the defensive or offensive, as might be necessary, without weakening any part of our lines. Their mere presence in the works below Richmond would prevent the enemy from making feints in that quarter to draw troops from here, except in such force as to endanger his own lines around Petersburg. But I feel confident that with vigorous effort, and an understanding on the part of the people of the necessity of the case, we could get more of this class than enough for the purpose last indicated. We could make our regular troops here available in the field.

The same remarks are applicable to the reserves of North Carolina, who could render similar services at Wilmington, and allow the regular troops to take the field against any force that might land there. I need not remind Your Excellency that the reserves are of great value in connection with our regular troops to prevent disaster, but would be of little avail to retrieve it. For this reason they should be put in service before the numerical superiority of the enemy enables him to inflict a damaging blow upon the regular forces opposed to him. In my opinion the necessity for them will never be more urgent, or their services of greater value than now. And I entertain the same views as to the importance of immediately bringing into the regular service every man liable to military duty. It will be too late to do so after our armies meet with disaster, should such unfortunately be the case.

I trust Your Excellency will excuse the length and earnestness of this letter, in view of the vital importance of its subject, and am confident that you will do all in your power to accomplish the objects I have in view.

With great respect, your obt servt
R. E. Lee
Genl

"MY CHILDREN IS MY OWN":
MISSOURI, SEPTEMBER 1864

Spottswood Rice to His Children and to Kitty Diggs

Spottswood Rice escaped from a Missouri tobacco plantation and enlisted in the 67th U.S. Colored Infantry in February 1864. He wrote to his children and to Kitty Diggs, the owner of his daughter Mary, from Benton Barracks in St. Louis. F. W. Diggs, Kitty Diggs's brother and the owner of Rice's daughter Cora, sent both of his letters to Major General William S. Rosecrans, the Union commander in Missouri, on September 10. In an accompanying note Diggs professed his loyalty to the Union and wrote that "to be thus insulted by such a black scoundrel is more than I can stand." Rice was eventually reunited with his daughters.

My Children   I take my pen in hand to rite you A few lines to let you know that I have not forgot you and that I want to see you as bad as ever   now my Dear Children I want you to be contented with whatever may be your lots   be assured that I will have you if it cost me my life   on the 28th of the mounth. 8 hundred White and 8 hundred blacke solders expects to start up the rivore to Glasgow and above there thats to be jeneraled by a jeneral that will give me both of you   when they Come I expect to be with, them and expect to get you both in return. Dont be uneasy my children   I expect to have you. If Diggs dont give you up this Government will and I feel confident that I will get you   Your Miss Kaitty said that I tried to steal you   But I'll let her know that god never intended for man to steal his own flesh and blood. If I had no cofidence in God I could have confidence in her   But as it is If I ever had any Confidence in her I have none now and never expect to have   And I want her to remember if she meets me with ten thousand soldiers she will meet her enemy   I once thought that I had some respect for them but now my respects is worn out and have no sympathy for Slaveholders. And as for her cristianantty I expect the Devil has Such in hell   You tell her from me that She is the frist Christian that I ever hard say that aman could Steal his own child especially out of human bondage

You can tell her that She can hold to you as long as she can   I never would expect to ask her again to let you come to me because I know that the devil has got her hot set againsts that that is write   now my Dear children I am a going to close my letter to you   Give my love to all enquiring friends   tell them all that we are well and want to see them very much and Corra and Mary receive the greater part of it you sefves   and dont think hard of us not sending you any thing   I you father have a plenty for you when I see you   Spott & Noah sends their love to both of you   Oh! My Dear children how I do want to see you

September 3, 1864

I received a leteter from Cariline telling me that you say I tried to steal to plunder my child away from you   now I want you to understand that mary is my Child and she is a God given rite of my own and you may hold on to hear as long as you can but I want you to remembor this one thing that the longor you keep my Child from me the longor you will have to burn in hell and the qwicer youll get their   for we are now makeing up a bout one thoughsand blacke troops to Come up tharough and wont to come through Glasgow and when we come wo be to Copperhood rabbels and to the Slaveholding rebbels for we dont expect to leave them there root neor branch   but we thinke how ever that we that have Children in the hands of you devels we will trie your vertues the day that we enter Glasgow   I want you to understand kittey diggs that where ever you and I meets we are enmays to each orthere   I offered once to pay you forty dollers for my own Child but I am glad now that you did not accept it   Just hold on now as long as you can and the worse it will be for you   you never in you life befor I came down hear did you give Children any thing not eny thing whatever not even a dollers worth of expencs   now you call my children your property   not so with me   my Children is my own and I expect to get them and when I get ready to come after mary I will have bout a powrer and autherity to bring hear away and to exacute vengencens on them that holds my Child   you will then know how to talke to me   I will assure that and you will know how to talk rite too   I want you now to just hold on to hear if you want to   iff your conchosence tells thats the road go that road and what it will brig you to kittey diggs   I have no fears about geting mary out of your hands   this whole Government gives chear to me and you cannot help your self

Spottswood Rice

September 3, 1864

PRESERVING "OUR OWN RACE":
KENTUCKY, SEPTEMBER 1864

Thomas Bramlette to Abraham Lincoln

Thomas Bramlette commanded a Union regiment and served as U.S. district attorney for Kentucky before being nominated for governor by the Union Democrats in the spring of 1863. In August he overwhelmingly defeated Charles A. Wickliffe, a Peace Democrat, in an election marked by Union military interference. As governor, Bramlette supported the war but strongly opposed the recruitment of black troops in Kentucky. The continued guerrilla warfare in Kentucky caused Lincoln to issue a proclamation on July 5, 1864, suspending the writ of habeas corpus and declaring martial law in the state. Lincoln did not reply to the governor's letter.

Frankfort Sept 3rd 1864
Sir: Kentucky is and ever has been loyal as a State and people. Her people have triumphantly passed through the severest ordeal, and borne without yielding the severest tests ever applied to the loyalty of any people. Yet we are dealt with as though Kentucky was a rebellious and conquered province, instead of being as they are a brave and loyal people.—

Without any occasion for such measures the State has by special Executive edict been declared under Martial law; and this just preceding the elections.

Without rebuke the Military Commandant issued an order directly interfering with the most important election then depending; and in open Conflict with the Constitution and laws of the State, and in dereliction of the most sacred rights of a free and loyal people.

The ordinary and necessary trade of the State is now by Military trade regulations subjected to restrictions, which harrass the citizen without any compensating public good; and which wear more the phase of subjecting the citizens to odious political tests, than looking to the public good. I send herewith a copy of a permit, with the test questions as appended, the original I retain as a specimen and memorial of the military follies and harrassments to which Kentuckians are subjected.

The citizens of Western Kentucky have for a long while been the subjects of insult, oppression, and plunder by officers who have been placed to defend and protect them.

Having on yesterday stated the conduct of Genl Payne & his accomplices & heretofore Communicated in reference to Cunningham who is now overshadowed by Genl Payne, I will not again state it.—

The Military Authorities throughout the State assume at pleasure to make assessments upon the citizens and enforce the payment of heavy fines without a hearing. And yet the laws of Kentucky are ample and the Courts open for redress of every just grievance, without any such military judgements.

I send herewith a copy of one of those orders assessing a citizen—merely as a specimen of what is of daily occurrence.

That these measures with others of kindred nature have been urged by the Counsels of a class of men who represent the *evil genius* of loyalty, I am well assured.

No one who has a love for our Country and a desire to preserve our Government, if possessed of ordinary intellect and a common inteligence with a knowledge of our people, would advise such measures. My hope is that in the multifarious affairs of State, your attention has not been caught to these matters, and that by my drawing your attention to them your sense of justice and what is due to a loyal people will prompt you to order a revocation of those orders and a correction of these evils. The course pursued by many of those entrusted with Federal authority in Kentucky, has made to your Administration and re-election, thousands of bitter and irreconcileable opponents, where a wise and just policy and action would more easily have made friends.

Extreme measures by which they sought to break the just pride and subdue the free spirit of the people; and which would only have fitted them for enslavement, have aroused the determined opposition to your re-election of at least three fourths of the people of Kentucky; when a different and just policy might have made them friends. You will pardon me for speaking thus plainly, for I assure you it is done in the kindest spirit;

although I am opposed to your re-election, and regard a change of policy as essential to the salvation of our Country.

In common with the loyal masses of Kentucky *my Unionism is unconditional*. We are for preserving the rights and liberties of our own race—and upholding the character and dignity of our position. We are not willing to sacrifice a single life, or imperil the smallest right of free white men for the sake of the negro. We repudiate the Counsels of those who say the Government must be restored *with Slavery*, or that it must be restored *without Slavery, as a condition of their Unionism*. We are for the restoration of our Government throughout our entire limits regardless of what may happen to the negro. We reject as spurious, the Unionism of all who make the Status of the negro a sine qua non to peace and unity. We are not willing to imperil the life liberty and happiness of our own race and people for the freedom or enslavement of the negro. To permit the question of the freedom or slavery of the negro, to obstruct the restoration of National authority and unity is a blood stained sin. Those whose sons are involved in this strife demand, as they have the right to do, *that the negro be ignored in all questions of settlement, and not make his condition*—whether it shall be free or slave, *an obstacle to the restoration of national unity & peace*. Such are the sentiments of the loyal masses of Kentucky. Why therefore are unequal burdens laid upon the people of Kentucky? Is it not unwise, not to say unjust that this is done. Surely the appealing blood of her sons, which crimsons the battlefields, sufficiently attests the loyalty of Kentucky and her people, to entitle the State to be freed from those Military manacles, which fetter her noble limbs, and chafe the free spirit of her loyal people.

It cannot surely be the purpose of any to ascertain by actual experiment how much a brave and manly people will bear rather than revolt against their Government.

And yet some of the measures adopted wear much the aspect of such an experiment.

May the God of our Fathers speedily give to us deliverance, by a restoration of our Government in unity and peace
      Respectfully
        Thos E Bramlette

"SHOUTING FOR MCCLELLAN":
WASHINGTON, D.C., SEPTEMBER 1864

Gideon Welles: Diary, September 3, 1864

On August 31 the Democratic national convention nominated Major General George B. McClellan for president and Ohio congressman George H. Pendleton, a leading Peace Democrat, for vice president. Secretary of the Navy Gideon Welles wrote about McClellan's nomination and reports that Sherman had taken Atlanta.

September 3, *Saturday.* New York City is shouting for McClellan, and there is a forced effort elsewhere to get a favorable response to the proceeding at Chicago. As usual some timid men are alarmed, and there are some like Raymond, Chairman of the National Committee who have no fixed and reliable principles that are without confidence and another set, like Greeley, who have a lingering hope that they can yet have an opportunity to make a new candidate. But this will soon be over. The issue is made up. It is whether a war shall be made against Lincoln to get peace with Jeff Davis. Those who met at Chicago prefer hostility to Lincoln rather than to Davis. Such is extreme partisanism.

We have to-day word that Atlanta is in our possession, but we have yet no particulars. It has been a long hard struggle, continued through weary months. This intelligence will not be gratifying to the zealous partisans who have just sent out a peace platform. But it is a melancholy and sorrowful reflection that there are among us so many who do not rejoice in the success of the Union arms. They feel a conscious guilt, and affect not to be dejected, but discomfort is in their countenances, deportment and tone. While the true Unionists are cheerful and hilarious, greeting all whom they meet, the Rebel sympathizers shun company and are dolorous. This is the demon of party,—the days of its worst form,—a terrible spirit, which in its excess leads men to rejoice in the calamities of their country and to mourn its triumphs. Strange, and wayward, and unaccountable are men. While the facts are as I have stated, I cannot think these men are destitute of love of country; but they permit party prejudices and party antagonisms to absorb their better natures. The leaders want power. All men crave it. Few, comparatively, expect to attain high position, but each hopes to be benefited within a certain circle which limits perhaps his present ambition. There is fatuity in nominating a general and warrior on a peace platform.

POLITICAL ADVICE: OHIO, SEPTEMBER 1864
Clement L. Vallandigham to George B. McClellan

Vallandigham wrote to McClellan while the general was still drafting a letter accepting the nomination. The "Eastern friends" Vallandigham refers to included the banker August Belmont, chairman of the Democratic national committee, and Samuel L. M. Barlow, an attorney and railroad executive active in Democratic politics. As Vallandigham anticipated, both men advised McClellan to reject the peace plank in the Democratic platform.

Dayton, Ohio
Sept. 4, 1864

Strictly Private
Maj. Gen. Geo. B. McClellan, Orange, N.J.

My Dear Sir:—Pardon the liberty I take, but for Heaven's Sake, hear the words of one who has now nothing so much at heart as your success. Do not listen to any of your Eastern friends who in an evil hour, may advise you to *insinuate* even, a little war into your letter of acceptance. We have difficulty in preventing trouble now, tho all will come right; but if any thing implying war is presented, two hundred thousand men in the West will withold their support, & many go further still. Accept the word, on this subject of one who knows, & whose heart's desire is that nothing may be done to take away his power to aid you with his whole might in this campaign.

Very truly
C. L. Vallandigham

P.S. I shall be in Trenton on the 14th or 15th of this month.

"THE WRATH TO COME":
LOUISIANA, SEPTEMBER 1864

Kate Stone: Diary, September 5, 1864

Kate Stone and her family had fled their cotton plantation near the Mississippi in Madison Parish, Louisiana, in March 1863 to escape Union foraging parties. After spending a year in eastern Texas, Stone returned to northeastern Louisiana in the summer of 1864 to stay with family friends near Oak Ridge in Morehouse Parish. She wrote about reports of a Union retaliatory raid in the area.

Sept. 5: Intense excitement in the neighborhood. Yankees reported advancing in large force—destroying, burning, and murdering as they come!! Capt. Lea with his small band of guerrillas contesting every mile of the way but being steadily forced back by superior numbers! Praying Col. Parsons, who has the only troops near, for reinforcements, but who refuses to send them as he is under stringent orders and making forced marches! Blank consternation among the citizens who hear that the Federals have vowed vengeance against this section on account of Capt. Lea and his guerrillas. Everyone is preparing to flee the wrath to come.

Such were the startling reports brought to Col. Templeton by terrified Mr. Philips this morning, frightening us nearly to death, for great is our horror of the vandal hordes since their ruthless destruction of Floyd and Pin Hook and their outrageous conduct at those doomed places. Mrs. Templeton soon had everything arranged for our rapid flight through the swamp across the Ouachita to the safe haven of Col. Wadley's home, should the reports prove true, leaving Mrs. Templeton and Mrs. Savage here to brave the storm, Col. Templeton going with us. We were on the *qui vive* all day looking for a mounted messenger galloping up through the wooded lawn shouting, "Flee, Flee." But about sunset the tension relaxed. We heard that the Yankees came out only as far as Floyd on a reconnaisance and are retiring to the river, and so we breathe freely once more.

The Yankee raids are no joke, though we laugh at each other for being frightened. Last week 200 of the Corps D'Afrique, officered by six big white men (wretches they are), came out and laid the two little villages of Floyd and Pin Hook in ashes, not allowing the people to remove any of their possessions from their houses and thus leaving them utterly destitute. They were very rough and insulting in their language to the ladies, tore the pockets from their dresses and the rings from their fingers, cursing and swearing, and frightening the helpless folks nearly into fits. This was done in revenge for a guerrilla raid a few days before, in which a good many government stores were destroyed and eighty or ninety Negroes brought out. The Yankees know they make it ten times worse for us by sending Negroes to commit these atrocities. The Paternal Government at Washington has done all in its power to incite a general insurrection throughout the South, in the hopes of thus getting rid of the women and children in one grand holocaust. We would be practically helpless should the Negroes rise, since there are so few men left at home. It is only because the Negroes do not want to kill us that we are still alive. The Negroes have behaved well, far better than anyone anticipated. They have not shown themselves revengeful, have been most biddable, and in many cases have been the only mainstay of their owners.

Five or six citizens, unarmed, were murdered by the Yankees in that Floyd raid. How thankful I am we left home when we did. To lose everything is bad, but constant terror and insult are worse.

The guerrillas report that the cotton crop on the river is a complete failure, entirely eaten up by the worms. The fields are swept of every vestige of green and there is hardly a matured boll to a stalk. This news rejoices our very hearts. Those are true "Confederate worms," working for the good of the Cause.

Emmie and I are practising singing. Neither of us is gifted with the voice of a siren, but enough to amuse the noncritical. Am making a calico dress which promises to be a love, if I can only get it long enough.

"AUDACIOUS INFAMY":
NEW YORK, SEPTEMBER 1864

George Templeton Strong: Diary, September 5–8, 1864

A successful New York lawyer, George Templeton Strong served as treasurer of the U.S. Sanitary Commission and was a founder of the Union League Club. In his diary he reflected on the fall of Atlanta and the Democratic convention.

September 5. Two days of cold easterly storm. Thank God the fall of Atlanta is fully confirmed. We hardly dared believe it till today. Its importance, both moral and military, is immense. Hardee is said to be killed, and two less notorious rebel generals. He is no great loss to Secessia. Hood seems to have destroyed much rolling stock and stores, which he could not carry off. We have news that the rebel privateer, *Georgia*, has been bagged by the *Niagara* (her name makes the event a coincidence, for I suppose Sherman's success gives us mastery of nearly all that state) and there is some reason to fear a complication with England, as the *Georgia* was sailing under British colors.

Dined with Agnew after a busy day. He is overworked and may be in danger of breaking down, which would be a grave misfortune.

The general howl against the base policy offered for our endorsement at Chicago is refreshing. Bitter opponents of Lincoln join in it heartily, and denounce the proposition that the country should take its hands off the throat of half-strangled treason, go down on its knees before its prostrate but insolent enemy, and beg it to do a little friendly negotiating. The audacious infamy of the Chicago traitors seems likely to produce a reaction and make the Administration party vigorous and united once more. Friends of the government have been somewhat languid and disheartened for a couple of months, always on the defensive, and apologetic in the tone of their talk. Chicago has put new life into them.

> Is all our travail turned to this effect?
> After the slaughter of so many peers,
> So many captains, gentlemen, and soldiers,
> That in this quarrel have been overthrown,
> And sold their bodies for their country's benefit,
> Shall we at last conclude effeminate peace?

Lord help us and save us from ourselves, our own deadliest enemy!

September 6. . . . Belmont tells Charley, who returned from Newport this morning, that McClellan's letter of acceptance will be most satisfactory even to the most resolute "War Democrats," and will secure his election. He may succeed in mystifying people with plausible generalities and commonplaces. If he take his stand on the Chicago platform, without some attempt at a protest, my faith in his honesty and loyalty will be shattered. Major Halpine (Miles O'Reilly) tells —— that he and Jem Brady and others are urging "little Mac" to say in substance: "I accept the nomination, and I adopt the platform. I want negotiation, armistice, and peace as badly as anybody. My policy will be to expedite them by a very vigorous prosecution of the war, which must soon put us in a position to negotiate with advantage for settlement, reconstruction, and pacification." Halpine is a very shrewd fellow, and on the fence till McClellan shall distinctly define his ground. He wants to support him, which he can do most efficiently—provided McClellan set himself right and repudiate the Vallandigham wing of his party. He thinks the defeat of Lincoln would give the rebels "a canoe to come ashore in"; that we cannot hope they will consent to scuttle their own ship and founder at sea, even after many calamities like the loss of Atlanta; that they are tired of war and will come back if we do something that looks like compromise. Perhaps. It would be a most hazardous experiment.

A new danger looms up, larger and darker every day. It is nothing less than civil war in the Northwest States! They are honeycombed by secret societies, working in aid of the rebellion, and controlled by reckless, desperate traitors for whom the gallows is far too good. The navigation of the Mississippi is still closed to ordinary trade, and that fact enables these "Knights of the Golden Circle" (more properly caitiffs of the Hempen Circle) to spread disaffection among western farmers and tradesmen. Both parties seem to be arming.

The great experiment of democracy may be destined to fail a century sooner than I expected in disastrous explosion and general chaos, and this our grand republic over which we have bragged so offensively may be cast down as a great milestone into the sea and perish utterly—and all this within sixty days from the date of these presents. So much for traitors, demagogues, and lunatics! All the South and half the North are absolutely demented. Neither Lincoln nor McClellan is strong enough to manage so large and populous an asylum. Who is? Satan seems superintendent *de facto* just now. Old Fuller wrote two hundred years ago, when civil war was ravaging English homes: "Our sins were ripe. God could no longer be just if we were prosperous."

September 8. Political indications furnished by our Quogue family are encouraging. A fortnight ago Blake and Charley Lawrence expected to stump the state for McClellan. But the Chicago platform has changed their views. They cannot support McClellan, no matter what he says in his letter of acceptance. If he accept the nomination, he is bound by the resolutions that define the policy he is nominated to represent; and how can his co-nominee for the Vice-Presidency (George H. Pendleton, an avowed peacemonger), and members of Congress and governors of states nominated by the same party convention or by affiliated conventions, be disposed of? Must they each and all write letters denouncing their own party principles, or explaining them away? Blake insists that Lincoln possesses neither ability nor honesty, but he cannot oppose him *now*. He undervalues Lincoln, but no matter. Lincoln is an honest man, of considerable ability (far below the first grade), but made odious by the vagaries and the arbitrary temper of Mr. Secretary Stanton. As for McClellan, approved by Vallandigham and the London *Times* and the asylum-burning rioters, who hurrahed for him in July, 1863, *noscitur a sociis qui non noscitur ab ipso*. His name generates what old Fuller calls (in his *Worthies of England*) a most "valiant and offensive" stench. But there are men among us base enough to support him and to

> Sue for bondage, yielding to demands
> As impious as they're insolent and base.

ACCEPTING THE NOMINATION:
NEW JERSEY, SEPTEMBER 1864

George B. McClellan to the Democratic Nomination Committee

McClellan had been instructed to await "further orders" after Lincoln relieved him as commander of the Army of the Potomac in November 1862. Despite his hopes for reinstatement McClellan received no further command assignments, although he retained his commission as a major general in the regular army. In October 1863 he had endorsed George W. Woodward, the unsuccessful Democratic candidate for governor of Pennsylvania, and began to make his willingness to accept the 1864 presidential nomination known to influential party leaders. McClellan wrote six drafts of his letter of acceptance and completed the final version with the help of his friend Samuel L. M. Barlow. In a private message to the financier William H. Aspinwall, McClellan wrote that "my letter will be acceptable to all true patriots, & will only drive off the real adherents of Jeff Davis this side of the line."

Gentlemen   Orange New Jersey Sept 8 1864

I have the honor to acknowledge the receipt of your letter informing me of my nomination by the Democratic National Convention, recently assembled at Chicago, as their candidate, at the next election, for President of the United States.

It is unnecessary for me to say to you that this nomination comes to me unsought. I am happy to know that when the nomination was made the record of my public life was kept in view. The effect of long and varied service in the Army, during war and peace, has been to strengthen and make indelible in my mind and heart the love and reverence for the Union, Constitution, Laws and Flag of our country impressed upon me in early youth.

These feelings have thus far guided the course of my life, and must continue to do so to its end.

The existence of more than one Government over the region which once owned our flag is incompatible with the peace, the power, and the happiness of the people.

The preservation of our Union was the sole avowed object for which the war was commenced.

It should have been conducted for that object only, and in accordance with those principles which I took occasion to declare when in active service. Thus conducted, the work of reconciliation would have been easy, and we might have reaped the benefits of our many victories on land and sea.

The Union was originally formed by the exercise of a spirit of conciliation and compromise.

To restore and preserve it the same spirit must prevail in our Councils, and in the hearts of the people. The reestablishment of the Union in all its integrity is, and must continue to be, the indispensable condition in any settlement. So soon as it is clear, or even possible, that our present adversaries are ready for peace upon the basis of the Union, we should exhaust all the resources of statesmanship practiced by civilized nations, and taught by the traditions of the American people, consistent with the honor and interests of the country, to secure such peace, reestablish the Union, and guarantee for the future the Constitutional rights of every State. The Union is the one condition of peace. We ask no more.

Let me add what I doubt not was, although unexpressed, the sentiment of the Convention, as it is of the people they represent, that when any one State is willing to return to the Union, it should be received at once, with a full guarantee of all its Constitutional rights.

But if a frank, earnest and persistent effort to achieve these objects should fail, the responsibility for ulterior consequences will fall upon those who remain in arms against the Union. But the Union must be preserved at all hazards. I could not look in the face of my gallant comrades of the Army and Navy, who have survived so many bloody battles, and tell them that their labors, and the sacrifice of so many of our slain and wounded brethren had been in vain—that we had abandoned that Union for which we have so often perilled our lives.

A vast majority of our people, whether in the Army and Navy or at home, would, as I would, hail with unbounded joy the permanent restoration of peace, on the basis of the Union under the Constitution, without the effusion of another drop of blood. But no peace can be permanent without Union.

As to the other subjects presented in the resolutions of the Convention, I need only say that I should seek in the Constitution of the United States, and the laws framed in accordance therewith, the rule of my duty and the limitations of executive power,—endeavor to restore economy in public expenditure, reestablish the supremacy of law, & by the assertion of a more vigorous nationality reserve our commanding position among the nations of the Earth. The condition of our finances, the depreciation of the paper currency, and the burdens thus imposed on labor & capital show the necessity of a return to a sound financial system; while the rights of citizens and the rights of States, and the binding authority of law over President, Army and people are subjects of not less vital importance in war than in peace. Believing that the views here expressed are those of the Convention and the people you represent, I accept the nomination.

I realize the weight of the responsibility to be borne should the people ratify your choice.

Conscious of my own weakness, I can only seek fervently the guidance of the Ruler of the Universe, and, relying on His all-powerful aid, do my best to restore Union and Peace to a suffering people, and to establish and guard their liberties and rights.

 I am, Gentlemen very respectfully your obedient servant
              Geo B McClellan

Hon Horatio Seymour
and others, Committee etc.

JONESBORO AND ATLANTA:
GEORGIA, SEPTEMBER 1864

James A. Connolly to Mary Dunn Connolly

Sherman's turning movement south of Atlanta achieved its objective on August 31 when Union troops reached the Macon & Western Railroad near Rough and Ready. The same day, entrenched Union troops repulsed a Confederate counterattack farther south at Jonesboro. With his main supply line cut, Hood ordered the evacuation of Atlanta on September 1, and Union forces entered the city the following day. The four-month-long Atlanta campaign cost the Union about 37,000 men killed, wounded, or missing, and the Confederates about 32,000. Major James A. Connolly served in the Army of the Cumberland as an aide to Brigadier General Absalom Baird, the commander of the Third Division, Fourteenth Corps. He wrote to his wife about the second day of fighting at Jonesboro.

Atlanta, Sunday, September 11, 1864.

Dear wife:

It is a pleasant, breezy afternoon in September, and as I sit here in my tent, on a beautiful grassy hill in the suburbs of the fallen city, and watch our National colors floating gaily from its spires, I feel profoundly thankful that God has permitted me to pass safely through all the stern struggles of this long campaign, and that mine eyes are permitted to see the old flag floating over still another stronghold of the enemy. I knew we would triumph; in the darkest hours of this campaign my faith in our ultimate success was strong; I did not expect the city would fall into our hands without terrible fighting, but I knew we could do the fighting, and had no fears of the result. Our Corps had the honor of giving the grand finishing stroke to the campaign, on the first day of this month, at Jonesboro, on the Macon railroad, about 20 miles south of Atlanta, where we met the enemy, charged his works and carried them with the bayonet, capturing 8 pieces of artillery, instead of 4 as I wrote you before, several stands of colors, over 1,000 prisoners, instead of 500, among them Brig. Gen. Govan, and utterly routing and scattering the rest of the army confronting us. Oh, it was a glorious battle! But this Division suffered terribly. There was no chance for flinching there. Generals, Colonels, Majors, Captains and privates, all had to go forward together over that open field, facing and drawing nearer to death at every step we took, our horses crazy, frantic with the howling of shells, the rattling of canister and the whistling of bullets, ourselves delirious with the wild excitement of the moment, and thinking only of getting over those breast works—great volleys of canister shot sweeping through our lines making huge gaps, but the blue coated boys filled the gaps and still rushed forward right into the jaws of death—we left hundreds of bleeding comrades behind us at every step, but not one instant did that line hesitate—it moved steadily forward to the enemy's works—over the works with a shout—over the cannon —over the rebels, and then commenced stern work with the bayonet, but the despairing cries of surrender soon stopped it, the firing ceased, and 1,000 rebels were hurried to the rear as prisoners of war. The General rode forward with the front line despite our protests and had two horses shot under him during the charge, my tent mate, Capt. A——— was shot in the right arm, why the other five of us escaped is one of the strange things found in a battle, when we were all similarly exposed to the fire. When the cheer of victory went up I recollect finding myself in a tangled lot of soldiers, on my horse, just against the enemy's log breast-works, my hat off, and tears streaming from my eyes, but as happy as a mortal is ever permitted to be. I could have lain down on that blood stained grass, amid the dying and the dead and wept with excess of joy. I have no language to express the rapture one feels in the moment of victory, but I do know that at such a moment one feels as if the joy were worth risking a hundred lives to attain it. Men at home will read of that battle and be glad of our success, but they can never feel as we felt, standing there quivering with excitement, amid the smoke and blood, and fresh horrors and grand trophies of that battle field. That night, as we lay on the ground without blankets or tents, we were aroused by sound of distant explosions away off to the North, in the direction of Atlanta, and many were the conjectures as to the cause, but the afternoon brought us the intelligence that the enemy had "evacuated Atlanta last night, blowing up 86 car loads of ammunition, and destroying large amounts of public stores." Then went up more lusty cheers than were ever heard in that part of Georgia before. Atlanta was ours; the object of our campaign was accomplished, and *of course*, we were happy. I expect the newspaper correspondents will tell you all about the various movements by which Hood was deceived, his army divided, and Atlanta won; it would take me too long to do it here, and besides I want to reserve it until I get home, and then I'll tell you all about it, and puzzle your head over military maps, plans, diagrams, &c., until I make quite a soldier of you. Now I suppose you want to know something about the great "Golden Apple," Atlanta, for the possession of which these two armies have been struggling so long. It is situated on high rolling land; two or three small streams run through the city in irregular courses, breaking the continuity of streets, and giving those parts of the city a very ragged appearance; the population is variously estimated at from 15,000 to 70,000; a good many citizens remain in the city, but the majority of them have gone to other Southern cities to escape from "the vandals." I have noticed some fine residences in the city, but the business buildings, so far as I have observed, are of mediocre quality, not comparable with business buildings in a Northern city of similar size. Atlanta looks more like a new, thriving Western city than any place I have seen in the South.

It has none of that built-up, finished, moss grown, venerable, aristocratic air, so noticeable in Southern cities; and in days of peace, I have no doubt Atlanta throbbed with the pulsations of that kind of enterprise that is converting our Western prairies into gardens, and dotting them with cities that rise up with the magic and suddenness of the coral isles. I notice that many of the buildings in the region of the depot have been struck by our shells, but I have only been in the city once since we returned from Jonesboro, and have only seen a small part of it, so that I do not know the full extent of damage our artillery did. As soon as I can get time I shall explore it thoroughly, and can give you a full report when I get home. I presume everybody at home is so deeply immersed in politics as to scarcely give a thought to the armies in the field. One party seems to want peace. That suits us here. We want peace too, *honorable* peace, won in the full light of day, at the cannon's mouth and the bayonet's point, with our grand old flag flying over us as we negotiate it, instead of cowardly peace purchased at the price of national dishonor. I received your letter of August 30th today.   xxxx

I don't know how it will be about leaves of absence from here now, but will soon know, and if there is an opportunity I will get a leave, but I think our stay here will be brief, Hood has *some* army left, and we must destroy it, and I want to be "in at the death." You have not yet told me about that poetical quotation I wrote you about. Please don't forget it.

Your husband.

"WAR IS CRUELTY": GEORGIA, SEPTEMBER 1864

William T. Sherman to James M. Calhoun and Others

On September 7 Sherman ordered the expulsion of the remaining civilian population of Atlanta. His decision was protested by the mayor and city council, who warned that it would cause "consequences appalling and heartrending." Sherman's response was widely printed in the northern press, along with a heated exchange of letters between Sherman and Hood regarding the expulsion order and the laws of war. About 1,600 Atlanta residents were sent south across the Confederate lines, while perhaps an equal number chose to go north.

Headquarters, Military Division of the Mississippi,
In the Field, Atlanta Sept. 12 1864.
James M. Calhoun, Mayor, E. E. Rawson, and S. C. Wells, representing City Council of Atlanta.
Gentlemen,

I have your letter of the 11th in the nature of a Petition to revoke my orders removing all the inhabitants from Atlanta. I have read it carefully and give full credit to your statements of the distress that will be occasioned by it, and yet shall not revoke my orders, simply because my orders are not designed to meet the humanities of the case, but to prepare for the future struggles in which millions yea hundreds of millions of Good People outside of Atlanta have a deep interest. We must have *Peace*, not only at Atlanta, but in All America. To secure this we must stop the war that now desolates our once Happy and Favored country. To stop war we must defeat the Rebel Armies, that are arrayed against the Laws and Constitution which all must respect and obey. To defeat those armies we must prepare the way to reach them in their recesses provided with the arms and instruments which enable us to accomplish our purpose. Now, I know the vindictive nature of our enemy, and that we may have many years of military operations from this Quarter, and therefore deem it wise and prudent to prepare in time.

The use of Atlanta for warlike purposes is inconsistent with its character as a home for families. There will be no manufactures, commerce, or agriculture here for the maintenance of families and Sooner or later want will compel the Inhabitants to go. Why not go *now*, when all the arrangements are completed for the transfer instead of waiting till the plunging shot of contending armies will renew the scenes of the past month? Of course I do not apprehend any such thing at this moment, but you do not suppose this army will be here till the war is over. I cannot discuss this subject with you fairly, because I cannot impart to you what I propose to do, but I assert that my military plans make it necessary for the Inhabitants to go away, and I can only renew my offer of services to make their exodus in any direction as easy and comfortable as possible. You cannot qualify war in harsher terms than I will. War is cruelty, and you cannot refine it: and those who brought war into our Country deserve all the curses and maledictions a people can pour out. I know I had no hand in making this war, and I know I will make more sacrifices today than any of you to Secure Peace. But you cannot have Peace and a Division of our Country. If the United States submits to a Division now it will not stop, but will go on till we reap the Fate of Mexico, which is Eternal War. The United States does and must assert its authority wherever it once had power, if it relaxes one bit to pressure it is gone, and I know that Such is the National Feeling. This Feeling assumes various shapes, but always comes back to that of *Union.* Once admit the Union, once more acknowledge the Authority of the National Government, and instead of devoting your houses, and Streets and Roads to the dread uses of War. I & this army become at once your protectors & supporters, shielding you from danger let it come from what quarter it may. I know that a few individuals cannot resist a torrent of error and passion such as swept the South into rebellion, but you can part out, so that we may know those who desire a Government, and those who insist on war & its desolation.

You might as well appeal against the thunder storm as against these terrible hardships of war. They are inevitable and the only way the People of Atlanta can hope once more to live in peace & quiet at home is to Stop the war, which can alone be done by admitting that it began in Error and is perpetuated in pride. We don't want your negros or your horses, or your houses or your Lands, or any thing you have, but we do want and will have a just obedience to the Laws of the United States. That we will have and if it involves the destruction of your improvements we cannot help it. You have heretofore read public sentiment in your newspapers that live by falsehood & excitement and the quicker you seek for truth in other quarters the better for you.

I repeat then that by the original compact of Government the United States had certain Rights in Georgia which have never been relinquished, and never will be: that the South began the war by seizing Forts, Arsenals Mints Custom Houses &c. &c. long before Mr. Lincoln was installed, & before the South had one jot or tittle of provocation. I myself have seen in Missouri, Kentucky Tennessee and Mississipi hundreds and thousands of women & children fleeing from your armies & desperadoes, hungry and with bleeding feet. In Memphis Vicksburg and Mississipi we fed thousands upon thousands of the families of Rebel Soldiers left on our hands and whom we could not see starve. Now that war comes home to you you feel very different. You deprecate its horrors, but did not feel them when you sent car-loads of soldiers and ammunition, moulded shells & shot to carry on war into Kentucky & Tennessee, & desolate the homes of hundreds & thousands of good People who only asked to live in Peace at their old homes, and under the Government of their inheritance. But these comparisons are idle. I want peace, and believe it can now only be reached through union and war, and I will ever conduct war partly with a view to perfect & early success.

But my dear sirs when that Peace do come you may call on me for anything—Then will I share with you the last cracker, and watch with you to shield your homes & families against danger from every quarter.

Now you must go, & take with you the old & feeble, feed & nurse them, & build for them in more quiet places proper habitations, to shield them against the weather till the mad passions of men cool down, and allow the Union and peace once more settle over your old homes at Atlanta. Yrs., in haste,

W. T. Sherman

EQUAL PAY FOR BLACK SOLDIERS:
OHIO, SEPTEMBER 1864

Rachel Ann Wicker to John A. Andrew

The men who enlisted in the 54th and 55th Massachusetts Regiments in the winter and spring of 1863 were promised equal pay with white soldiers. However, in June 1863 the War Department ruled that black soldiers would receive the pay authorized by the Militia Act of July 17, 1862, which had envisioned that blacks would serve mainly as military laborers. Privates and noncommissioned officers would both be paid $10 a month minus a $3 clothing allowance, at a time when white privates received $13 (later $16) a month plus $3.50 for clothing. The men of the 54th and 55th Massachusetts refused to accept unequal pay, and rejected as well the attempt by the Massachusetts legislature to make up the difference using state funds. In June 1864, Congress equalized pay and authorized back pay for all black soldiers to January 1, 1864, and to their date of enlistment for soldiers who swore an oath that they had been free men on April 19, 1861. John A. Andrew, the Republican governor of Massachusetts, forwarded Rachel Ann Wicker's letter to the War Department, which was in the process of implementing the new legislation. The 55th Massachusetts would be paid in full on October 7, 1864, and in March 1865, Congress authorized back pay for freed slaves who had enlisted early in the war.

Piqua Miama Co ohio   Sep 12 1864
Sir   i write to you to know the reason why our husbands and sons who enlisted in the 55 Massichusette regiment have not Bin paid off   i speak for my self and Mother and i know of a great many others as well as ourselve are suffering for the want of money to live on   when provision and Clotheing wer Cheap we might have got a long   But Every thing now is thribbl and over what it was some thre year Back   But it matters not if Every thing was at the old Price   i think it a Piece of injustice to have those soldiers there 15 months with out a cent of Money   for my part i Cannot see why they have not th same rite to their 16 dollars per month as th Whites or Even th Coulord Soldiers that went from ohio   i think if Massichusette had

left off Comeing to other States for Soldiers th Soldirs would have bin Better off and Massichusette saved her Credit i wish you if you pleas to Answer this Letter and tell me Why it is that you Still insist upon them takeing 7 dollars a month when you give the Poorest White Regiment that has went out 16 dollars Answer this if you Pleas and oblige Your humble Servant
Rachel Ann Wicker

A REPORT FROM MOBILE BAY:
ALABAMA, SEPTEMBER 1864

Alexander McKinley to Samuel Francis Du Pont

Alexander McKinley served on the staff of Rear Admiral David Farragut as his secretary and on August 5 had witnessed the battle of Mobile Bay from the Union flagship *Hartford*. McKinley had previously been secretary to Rear Admiral Samuel Francis Du Pont, the former commander of the South Atlantic Blockading Squadron, and wrote to him about the battle.

———————

Hartford, Mobile Bay, 18 Sept. 1864

Dear Admiral,

Your letter mailed on the 10th of August was a long time on its passage, as I never received it until the 14th of this month, just four days ago. Where it has been delayed I cannot imagine. However I was very glad to receive it. Until Captain Drayton heard from you I was uncertain whether my letter had ever reached you, fearing that it might have gone down in the *Locust Point* or fallen into rebel hands. The pirates seem to be more active of late, despite of Fox's fast *Eutaw* class of vessels. Corbin paid us a visit with the *Augusta* as a convoy to the ill-fated *Tecumseh* but did not get nearer us than Pensacola. Fearing that such would probably be the case, I got leave of absence for a few days and ran over to Pensacola and remained as his guest for that time. Old times were discussed with mutual pleasure—it did my heart good to meet with an old South Atlantic Blockading Squadron officer and particularly one who may be said to have been on your staff. He has however gone away disgusted with sundry grievances against our squadron, which doubtless he has mentioned to you, and I am afraid that Admiral Farragut has not found favor in his eyes. His criticisms in connection with the fight of August 5th, so far as the Admiral is concerned, are I think unjust, based probably upon one-sided statements, and I have very plainly told him so in a few lines I wrote to him a few days ago, but I will refer to this matter again in another part of my letter. Captain Jenkins has fallen particularly under his displeasure for taking from his ship his executive officer and bringing him over to Mobile to join in the attack on the forts, thus, as he says, preventing him from being present himself. The *Augusta* needed repairs and after a month's detention at Pensacola sailed on the 3d of this month for the North Atlantic Blockading Squadron. Corbin's description of the character of the blockade off Wilmington would be amusing, were it not so disgraceful to the government. We are almost openly defied by the blockade runners, who run in and out at all hours of the day and night and laugh at the Department's fast cruisers. Of course I know full well the difficulties of blockading any port, but I should think much more could be done in checking the evil at Wilmington than has been done heretofore. The Charleston and Mobile blockades were frequently broken by the rebels but in no instance that I am aware of in broad daylight. However there may be some excuses unknown to me.

Long ere this you have read full accounts of the engagement of the 5 of August last, and I am not sure that I could give you any additional information. Of course many of the reports are ridiculous, as always will be the case when attempts are made to glorify particular individuals or particular ships. The Admiral's brief report, written hurriedly on the evening of the attack, contained however all the material facts, though inadvertently it was not stated that the ram *Tennessee* attacked the fleet instead of the fleet attacking the ram. The Admiral's detailed report, mailed on the 12th instant, corrected this oversight and gave an accurate and clear account of the whole engagement. I do not know whether this has been published, though I have seen extracts from it in the *Army and Navy Journal.* The best report, up to a certain point, which has yet been published is contained in the New York *Herald* of the 27th of August. The description of the topography of the bay, the description of the channels and the advance of the fleet until they had passed the fort, is not only graphic but truthful. Here however the value of the report ceases—the account of the *second* fight, viz., with the ram, is full of error and absurdities. The ironclads had been ordered to take up their position on the starboard side of the fleet or between the advanced wooden vessels and Fort Morgan, for the double purpose of keeping down the enemy's fire from their *water battery* and to interpose between them and the rebel ironclads after we had passed the fort. I say *fort* because "Gaines" never did and never could have molested us, the distance being too great for any effective fire from her guns. These monitors, as you are aware, are not very easily handled and on the morning of the 5th could not get into their proper position very readily—so that when the advance of our wooden line of vessels was well up with Fort Morgan, one of them, the *Manhattan*, I believe, was in the way of the *Brooklyn* and our progress was stopped. The *Brooklyn*, which was the leading vessel, actually ceased going ahead and was in fact backing. At this critical moment the *Tecumseh*, which was in advance of all and heading directly for the rebel ram *Tennessee*, was blown up by a torpedo and sunk in less than a minute. Our line was getting crowded and very soon we should all have been huddled together, a splendid mark for the enemy's guns. The Admiral immediately gave the word to go ahead with the *Hartford* and pass the *Brooklyn*. We sheered to port, passing the *Brooklyn* on our starboard side and, as we cleared her bows, fired shell and shrapnel into the water battery like hail. We passed directly over the line of torpedoes planted by the enemy, and we could hear the snapping of the submerged devilish contrivances as our hull drove through the water—but it was neck or nothing and that risk must be taken. All the other vessels followed in our wake and providentially all escaped. Why more of the torpedoes did not explode is a mystery, for though doubtless many of them by long submersion may have been rendered harmless, yet we have learned since, to our cost, that some at least retained their vitality. The only part of the channel free from obstructions was immediately adjacent to the fort and directly under all its guns. The *Tecumseh* was just on the edge of this channel, and had she passed fifty feet further to the eastward she would have escaped. After passing the fort the *Hartford* steamed up the bay, where she was attacked by the whole rebel fleet, consisting of the ram, the gunboats *Selma*, *Morgan*, and *Gaines*. The first named, however, did not continue long in chase of us but turned to attack the rest of the vessels as they emerged from under the fire of the forts.

The other gunboats devoted themselves almost exclusively to us. The *Selma* got into a raking position directly ahead of us where none of our guns could bear upon her—one heavy shell came on our forecastle, disabled the gun carriage of one of our two 100-pounders and killed over one half of the gun's crew. To get rid of him the *Metacomet* was cast off and sent in pursuit when she hauled off and tried to escape. Our broadside guns had in the meantime done effective execution on the *Gaines*, compelling her to turn back and seek shelter under the guns of Fort Morgan, and the *Morgan* followed her example. We continued on our course, followed by the other ships, until we had passed perhaps three miles beyond Fort Morgan, when the vessels were told to anchor. The *Tennessee* was observed in our rear not far from the fort where it was supposed she would remain, but to our astonishment it was soon observed that she was heading directly for the flagship with the evident determination of fighting the whole of us, and considering that *we* had three monitors (though two only carried 11-inch guns), it really was one of the most daring and gallant attacks that any officer of any navy ever attempted before. Orders were at once given to all the larger ships to weigh anchor and attack the foe, not only with their guns but by ramming her at full speed— then began one of the most exciting contests mortal eye ever witnessed. Unfortunately, for some reason which I cannot explain, our monitors were not in their right place, and the wooden vessels were compelled to do the work. The *Monongahela* was the first that struck her as she was making for our flagship, but after the collision and an exchange of shots the ram steadily continued her course. The *Lackawanna* then dashed at full speed against her side, but she still kept on, and then at each other the two flagships went. It so happened that in weighing anchor the last time we could not get our anchor up; it therefore hung dangling over our port bow, and as the two ships came together the ram's bow struck against the anchor, forcing her off from the ship's side so that we struck her only a slanting blow and the two vessels ground against each other as we rushed in opposite directions. Just before or at the time of striking us, however, she sent one of her 7-inch rifled shells into our berth deck which did fearful execution, and as she was passing us we could hear the priming of another gun snap just as she was abreast of our boilers—if this gun had gone off we might have been disabled. Our port battery was fired scarcely ten feet from her casemate, but we might as well have thrown loaves of bread at her. As soon as we cleared each other, orders were given to turn again and ram her. We had succeeded in this and was once more bearing down upon her when the *Lackawanna*, bound on the same errand, unfortunately struck us just forward of the mizzenmast, crashing in the bulwarks, capsizing one of our 11-inch guns and, as we then thought, cutting us down to the water's edge. In a moment however it was discovered that we had two feet to spare above the water line, and orders were given to dash on. But before we reached the enemy the contest was over, the white flag was flying from the *Tennessee*, and the fight was closed. Her smokestack had been shot away and her steering gear jammed and one of the Mississippi monitors had gotten a position under her stern and poured in shot after shot against that part of her casemate, jamming the port shutters, wounding Admiral Buchanan, and bidding fair in a short time to dash in her armor and rake the ship. Our old friend Captain Le Roy in the *Ossipee* was just about trying the virtue of his vessel against the ram's iron ribs when she surrendered, but his heading was such that though he backed his engine and sheered off he could not avoid giving her a glancing blow.

You have doubtless read the report of the board of survey ordered to examine the *Tennessee*'s hull, etc., after the fight, and to that I must refer you to show what actual damage was done to her. What might have been the result, had she not lost her smokestack and had her steering gear injured, it is difficult to say. She might have run the gantlet and got back to Fort Morgan, for certainly she was, until these misfortunes happened, much more manageable and much quicker in her movements than our monitors. I believe myself that Admiral Buchanan made a great mistake in rushing into the combat as he did. Had he waited until night he might have come upon us and done us terrible injury, for as it was even difficult for us in broad daylight to keep out of each other's way in attacking her, at night the danger of running into each other would have been increased tenfold. However, as he has since said, so much reproach had been cast upon the navy (rebel) that he was determined to remove it if possible from his shoulders. I am also of the opinion that if Admiral Buchanan had not been placed hors de combat, the *Tennessee* would have been fought for some time longer. Commander Johnston is not, I think, remarkable for pluck and certainly has none of the "die in the last ditch valor." Prudence suggested, "Surrender," and he listened to her warning voice when other men would have said, "Get thee behind me, Satan." The Marine officer of the *Hartford*, Captain Heywood, was on the *Cumberland* when Buchanan in the *Merrimack* rammed her, and it so happened that Heywood was ordered with some of his guard on board the *Tennessee* to take charge and look after the police of the ship. He had a conversation with the Admiral and, on some allusion being made to the *Cumberland*, Buchanan said, "Well it must be confessed, to give the devil his due, you never surrendered." "No," replied Heywood, "we had no thought of surrendering."

But I am afraid that you are already tired of reading this long epistle, and as the mail will shortly leave I will only add a few lines more. On the afternoon of the 5th the *Chickasaw* was sent towards Fort Powell, the fort which from the outside of the bay had defied all our attacks. This monitor, only drawing between six and seven feet, was able to approach within a few hundred yards and throw her 11-inch shell, grape, canister, and everything else without fear of response. The result was that when night came on the fort was abandoned, the garrison escaping to the mainland by wading—previously, however, blowing up the magazine. On the afternoon of the next day this same vessel approached Fort Gaines and tried the same experiment. The colonel commanding (Anderson) soon perceived that between the Navy on one side and the Army on the other the case was hopeless. The next morning he sent off a boat to our ship with a proposal to surrender to the fleet, but Admiral Farragut would not thus ignore the Army. He therefore sent for General Granger, and the surrender was made to the Army and Navy. When the ceremony of giving up swords took place, the officers (having previously asked whether *they* had any option to surrender their side arms to Army or Navy and having been told such choice was theirs) with only one exception surrendered to the Navy! The surrender took place in the morning, and by the dawn of the next day the Army's force were in the rear of *Morgan*. General Page shortly after fired all his outlying buildings and retired to the fort. The result is well known and has been generally truthfully told. On the day our batteries opened fire, the rebels never *answered once*. In truth made only a passive resistance which did not continue over twenty-four hours. There was no *pluck* shown by either Page or his officers. Very little has been done since. General Canby has withdrawn all his forces except such as are necessary to garrison the forts elsewhere, but whether he can spare them again is yet uncertain. Of course without an army Mobile cannot be taken. *Water* will not admit the approach of our vessels. The enemy still have the *Nashville*, which is a side-wheel ironclad and said to be very formidable, but she is watched by the two Mississippi monitors. The *Brooklyn* has gone North; whether any other vessel will follow is not yet determined on.

I regret to hear that you have had a renewal of your old complaint, but I trust that you have entirely recovered. Please give my best regards to Mrs. Du Pont and all my friends in your family. Captain Drayton desires to be remembered to you and Mrs. Du Pont.

I wish Duvall and Stimers had their deserts but hope in this case is, I fear, hopeless.

The ram *Tennessee* has been appraised at $883,000. The *Selma* has not yet been appraised. I could write much more but I am afraid of wearing your patience out. Yours most truly,

A. McKinley

BATTLE OF WINCHESTER:
VIRGINIA, SEPTEMBER 1864

Henry Robinson Berkeley: Diary, September 19, 1864

By the middle of September Sheridan had concentrated about 35,000 Union troops around Berryville in the northern Shenandoah Valley, while Early held Winchester ten miles to the west with 12,500 men. Early then divided his forces, sending two of his four infantry divisions north to disrupt the Baltimore & Ohio Railroad at Martinsburg while the other two divisions remained near Winchester. On the morning of September 19 Sheridan attacked toward Winchester as Early moved to reunite his troops. Although a Confederate counterattack in the late morning almost succeeded in breaking the Union line, Sheridan was able to turn Early's left flank in the afternoon and force the Confederates to flee south toward Strasburg. The battle cost the Union about 5,000 men killed, wounded, or missing, and the Confederates about 3,600. Private Berkeley recorded his experiences after the fighting ended.

September 19. Monday. This has been one the longest and hardest day's fighting that I have done since this awful war began. The Yankees attacked us before sunrise this morning on the Berryville Pike. Our battery has been engaged all day. We had, it seemed to me, not less than five or six to one against us. We kept them back the entire day, until about 5 P.M. when their cavalry, breaking into our wagon train, caused our left, composed of Vaughan's cavalry, to give way, and our army was compelled to fall back. We came back in good order, even stopping to water our horses, and retreated towards Strasburg and going into camp for the night near Kernstown. We had some ten or twelve men wounded in my company. Capt. Massie, of our battalion, had four or five men killed and some ten or twelve wounded. Capt. Milledge, of our battalion, lost two men killed and some eight or ten wounded. This was a great artillery fight, and the artillery covered itself with honor and glory; but its loss has been very heavy. My battery was engaged from sunrise until 9 P.M. with short intervals of cessation between fierce engagements at close quarters. The Yanks would come at us frequently, with three heavy lines of infantry. When we would concentrate on the first a very heavy artillery fire, which never failed to break it, and this falling back on their second line made that line give way, and the two routed lines going back on their third line made that line also give way. The Yankee loss must have been very heavy in killed. Bluecoats, our infantry say, never laid thicker than they did today in front of Rodes's Division; but, alas, Gen. Rodes was killed. We, in our company, fired about sixteen hundred rounds of ammunition, about four times as much as we have ever used in a fight before. All our wounded were left in Winchester and consequently are in Yankee hands. Little George Ware acted bravely and gallantly today. He is our ambulance driver and he carried his ambulance frequently between the lines of battle, and under heavy fire, to bring out our wounded as bravely and as gallantly as anyone could possibly do, although he is a boy of only sixteen. I acted today as gunner, sergeant and lieutenant. Col. Nelson acted as chief of artillery, and our Capt. Kirkpatrick was commanding our battalion. This left us with only one commissioned officer, Bill Harris, recently acting as lieutenant. This shows our heavy loss since leaving winter quarters. We started out with four lieutenants; three of these have been killed and the fourth has not been seen or heard of for two months. At one time today there came a Yankee shell, which struck the middle horse of my limber right between its eyes, and bursting, took off the middle horse's head, cut off the hind legs of the saddle horse in front of him and the front legs of the horse just behind him, cut the pole of the limber in two pieces, passed through the limber box, which fortunately was nearly empty, and knocked Bill McDaniel down, who was standing just behind the limber box. Bill was acting as Number 6. None of the drivers were hurt and Bill soon picked himself up, being more frightened than hurt. I don't see how Charley Taliaferro, who was the driver of the horse that had its head carried away, could possibly have escaped, but he did most wonderfully. He was holding his horse close up near the bit, when the shell struck it, and, after the bursting of the shell, Charley was left unhurt, holding the reins and bit in his right hand, but covered from his face to his knees with the brains and blood of the horse. I could not help being amused at his appearance, yet it was an awful gruesome place to be amused. But Charles quietly went to the limber, gathered up a handful of cotton, dipped it into the sponge bucket and proceeded to wipe his face and clothes off. Soldiers are never made cooler, or braver, than Charles Taliaferro. It is sad to think that such men are falling around us every day. When will this cruel war be over? It happened on another part of the field today that at my gun, three men, one after the other, were shot down at my right hand: viz., Jim Pleasants, John Graves and James Monroe. Jim Pleasants lost his right foot, by a musket ball burying itself in his ankle; John Graves was knocked over, but the strap on his belt saved his life. Jim Monroe was wounded in the fleshy part of his right leg and will get well. These three men, with several others at our other guns, were wounded by Yankee shooters who had gotten up into trees and whom we could not bring our guns to bear on. I thought my time would certainly come next. A sharpshooter's ball went through my gaiter and scraped my ankle. Gen. Ramseur came up about this time, and I told him that if he kept us there much longer that every one of my men would be picked off by the Yankee sharpshooters. He then ordered me to retire to the hill just behind where we then were, and which we did very handsomely and without loss of men or horses.

GEORGIA, SEPTEMBER 1864

Jefferson Davis: Speech at Macon

September 23, 1864

On September 20 Jefferson Davis left Richmond to meet with Hood and try to rally support for his administration. Georgia was home to some of his most outspoken critics, including Robert Toombs, Governor Joseph E. Brown, and the Confederate vice president, Alexander H. Stephens. Although all three men supported the war, they strongly opposed conscription and the suspension of habeas corpus and questioned Davis's competence and character. Davis arrived in Macon on September 23 and spoke at a public meeting held to raise funds for Atlanta refugees. His speech was printed in the *Macon Telegraph* the next day and widely reported in both the southern and northern press. Davis went on to Palmetto, twenty-four miles southwest of Atlanta, where he conferred with Hood and his corps commanders for two days.

LADIES AND GENTLEMEN, FRIENDS AND FELLOW-CITIZENS:—

It would have gladdened my heart to have met you in prosperity instead of adversity—But friends are drawn together in adversity. The son of a Georgian, who fought through the first Revolution, I would be untrue to myself if I should forget the State in her day of peril.

What, though misfortune has befallen our arms from Decatur to Jonesboro', our cause is not lost. Sherman cannot keep up his long line of communication, and retreat sooner or later, he must. And when that day comes, the fate that befel the army of the French Empire and its retreat from Moscow will be reacted. Our cavalry and our people will harrass and destroy his army as did the Cossacks that of Napoleon, and the Yankee General, like him will escape with only a body guard.

How can this be the most speedily effected? By the absentees of Hood's army returning to their posts And will they not? Can they see the banished exiles, can they hear the wail of their suffering country-women and children, and not come. By what influences they are made to stay away, it is not necessary to speak. If there is one who will stay away at this hour, he is unworthy of the name of a Georgian. To the women no appeal is necessary. They are like the Spartan mothers of old. I know of one who had lost all her sons, except one of eight years. She wrote me that she wanted me to reserve a place for him in the ranks. The venerable Gen. Polk, to whom I read the letter, knew that woman well, and said that it was characteristic of her. But I will not weary you by turning aside to relate the various incidents of giving up the last son to the cause of our country known to me. Wherever we go we find the heart and hands of our noble women enlisted. They are seen wherever the eye may fall, or step turn. They have one duty to perform—to buoy up the hearts of our people.

I know the deep disgrace felt by Georgia at our army falling back from Dalton to the interior of the State, but I was not of those who considered Atlanta lost when our army crossed the Chattahoochee. I resolved that it should not, and I then put a man in command who I knew would strike an honest and manly blow for the city, and many a Yankee's blood was made to nourish the soil before the prize was won.

It does not become us to revert to disaster. "Let the dead bury the dead." Let us with one arm and one effort endeavor to crush Sherman. I am going to the army to confer with our Generals. The end must be the defeat of our enemy. It has been said that I had abandoned Georgia to her fate. Shame upon such a falsehood. Where could the author have been when Walker, when Polk, and when Gen. Stephen D. Lee was sent to her assistance. Miserable man. The man who uttered this was a scoundrel. He was not a man to save our country.

If I knew that a General did not possess the right qualities to command, would I not be wrong if he was not removed? Why, when our army was falling back from Northern Georgia, I even heard that I had sent Bragg with pontoons to cross into Cuba. But we must be charitable.

The man who can speculate ought to be made to take up his musket When the war is over and our independence won, (*and we will establish our independence,*) who will be our aristocracy? I hope the limping soldier. To the young ladies I would say when choosing between an empty sleeve and the man who had remained at home and grown rich, always take the empty sleeve. Let the old men remain at home and make bread. But should they know of any young men keeping away from the service who cannot be made to go any other way, let them write to the Executive. I read all letters sent me from the people, but have not the time to reply to them.

You have not many men between 18 and 45 left. The boys— God bless the boys—are as rapidly as they become old enough going to the field. The city of Macon is filled with stores, sick and wounded. It must not be abandoned, when threatened, but when the enemy come, instead of calling upon Hood's army for defence, the old men must fight, and when the enemy is driven beyond Chattanooga, they too can join in the general rejoicing.

Your prisoners are kept as a sort of Yankee capital. I have heard that one of their Generals said that their exchange would defeat Sherman. I have tried every means, conceded everything to effect an exchange to no purpose. Butler the Beast, with whom no Commissioner of Exchange, would hold intercourse, had published in the newspapers that: that if we would consent to the exchange of negroes, all difficulties might be removed. This is reported as an effort of his to get himself whitewashed by holding intercourse with gentlemen. If an exchange could be effected, I dont know but that I might be induced to recognise Butler. But in the future every effort will be given as far as possible to effect the end. We want our soldiers in the field, and we want the sick and wounded to return home.

It is not proper for me to speak of the number of men in the field. But this I will say, that two-thirds of our men are absent— some sick, some wounded, but most of them absent without leave. The man who repents and goes back to his commander voluntarily, at once appeals strongly to executive clemency. But suppose he stays away until the war is over and his comrades return home, when every man's history will be told, where will he shield himself? It is upon these reflections that I rely to make men return to their duty, but after conferring with our Generals at headquarters, if there be any other remedy it shall be applied.

I love my friends and I forgive my enemies. I have been asked to send reinforcements from Virginia to Georgia. In

Virginia the disparity in numbers is just as great as it is in Georgia. Then I have been asked why the army sent to the Shenandoah Valley was not sent here? It was because an army of the enemy had penetrated that Valley to the very gates of Lynchburg, and Gen. Early was sent to drive them back. This he not only successfully did, but, crossing the Potomac, came wellnigh capturing Washington itself, and forced Grant to send two corps of his army to protect it. This the enemy denominated a raid. If so, Sherman's march into Georgia is a raid. What would prevent them now, if Early was withdrawn, penetrating down the valley and putting a complete cordon of men around Richmond? I counselled with that great and grave soldier, Gen. Lee, upon all these points. My mind roamed over the whole field.

With this we can succeed. If one-half the men now absent without leave will return to duty, we can defeat the enemy. With that hope I am going to the front. I may not realize this hope, but I know there are men there who have looked death in the face too often to despond now. Let no one despond. Let no one distrust, and remember that if genius is the beau ideal, hope is the reality.

The President then alluded to the objects for which the meeting had assembled, and expressed the hope that the refugees and exiles would be well provided for.

A CABINET RESIGNATION:
MARYLAND, SEPTEMBER 1864

Elizabeth Blair Lee to Samuel Phillips Lee

A coalition of abolitionists, radical German Americans, and War Democrats had gathered in Cleveland on May 31 and nominated Major General John C. Frémont for president. Although the Frémont candidacy failed to attract significant Republican support, Lincoln worried that it might draw enough votes to swing key states to the Democrats. At the same time, many Radical Republicans sought the removal from the cabinet of the conservative postmaster general Montgomery Blair, whose father, Francis Preston Blair, served as an adviser to Lincoln. On September 22 Frémont announced his withdrawal from the race. Elizabeth Blair Lee, Montgomery Blair's sister, wrote about political developments to her husband, the commander of the North Atlantic Blockading Squadron. She enclosed a copy of a letter from her father to her brother Frank Blair, a former Missouri congressman who now commanded a corps in the Army of the Tennessee.

———————

Silver Spring   September 24
Dear Phil   Brother resigned his place in the Cabinet yesterday & last night when Father was going to bed he handed me the following addressed to Frank who is on leave of 30 days at St Louis now— saying you will please copy that for Phil & send it to him from me— He may want to know my views of *the position* "My Dear Frank

Your brother resigned today and in consequence of a conversation I had with the President when your Brother was at Portsmouth— I called one night on the P. at the Soldiers Home to talk with him about the election— things looking then very gloomy and he had been very much depressed I told him that he might rely on my sons to do all they could for him & suggested that he ought recall you from the army to heal party divisions in Missouri & Stump the States that Montgomery would go the rounds also— and would very willingly be a martyr to the Radical phrenzy or jealousy, that would feed on the Blairs, if that would help He said nobody but enemies wanted Montgy out of the Cabinet with one exception & this man was your friend in the Frémont controversy & was also Montgomerys friend. He told me that he replied to this gentleman that he did not think it good policy to sacrifice a true friend to a false one or an avowed enemy— though he remarked "Montgomery had himself told him that he would cheerfully resign to conciliate the class of men who had made their war on the Blairs because they were his friends— and sought to injure him among the ignorant partizans of those seeking to supplant him

When Montg returned some weeks ago, he broached the conversation I had reported to him again to the President & made the same suggestion, & in some conversations & I believe letters to some of Frémonts associates intimated that he would quit the Cabinet in case Frémont would retire from the Canvass— Some of those who thought this a good suggestion & were glad to get rid of Montgy pressed this matter, I have no doubt on Frémont & got him to resign on this condition & urged the President to avail himself of Montgomerys overture— & he is out—

In my opinion it is all for the best— In the first place if it tends to give a greater certainty of the defeat of McClellan, which I look upon as the salvation of the Republic, it is well The Blairs prefer a restoration of the Union to all their earthly personal interests— Again you know my greatest solicitude for M's advancement is in the line of his profession in which I would have his old age crowned with its highest honor— I know he would wear it with greatest advantage to his Country— This is my ambition for him— Lincoln I know entertains unbounded confidence in his probity, patriotism & judicial capacities— And this act of self sacrifice to him will secure his gratitude & he will be glad to shew it, especially as it will mortify those common enemies of himself & myself who worked this martyrdom—

I hope you will concur with the views I have taken The true interests of the Country require the reelection of Lincoln— McClellan whose depths I sounded lately as I wrote you in my last letter will, if elected by the Copperheads, will close with the enemy on something short of the integrity of the Union— Whatever compromise they may hatch up will end in the dissolution of the great nation of the Western Hemisphere— If Lincoln triumphs the vile Harpies that surround him will be killed off by public opinion If they remain with him to the end it will result in building up a new party of reform & the war which delivers us from Negro slavery, will be followed by a new political era which will establish a popular power in our commonalty— which will preserve our white laboring class from the fangs of a corrupt aristocracy The Shoddy Aristocracy of the War will perish with the slave aristocracy— All well— Your affectionate father FPB

There you have the whole as it looks to us— I think I am more hurt than anybody else Betty laughs at my "bruised feelings sticking out" but I confess to a proclivity for Mr. Lincolns first view— of the poor policy of sacrificing his friends to his enemies— but I can feel— rather— *think*— it is for the best & *feel*— uncomfortable at the same time Brother went to Frederick today to make a speech— he shows a fine manly bearing & I believe it hurts only his wife & me—

Blair still suffers from a severe cold— but it would be a small matter save that it keeps me haunted with fear of croup— I received a letter from Horace & one from Sara— both urging me to go to Aunt Becky who is still feeble— My duties are all here now— Sarah says William Preston & his family are now in Montreal & she sees a great deal of them Susan Preston a widow the second time was also with them— They are debating about staying there or going to New York to stay Kentucky is too much in the strife for them to live there comfortably We were robbed of about 300 bushels of perserving peaches this week & this morning there is scarce one left to eat— & one of our neighbors sold his off of 60 trees for $300— so our hundred trees were a great loss— but we are a helpless set of people as you ever saw & yet I see no way of helping to a better condition— Ever your own Lizzie

SOUTH CAROLINA, OCTOBER 1864

Jefferson Davis: Speech at Columbia

Davis left Hood's headquarters at Palmetto on September 27. During his return to Richmond he spoke in Montgomery, Columbus, and Augusta before arriving in Columbia, South Carolina, where he addressed a large crowd from the home of James and Mary Chesnut. His speech was printed in the *South Carolinian* on October 6.

October 4, 1864

LADIES AND GENTLEMEN OF THE METROPOLIS OF SOUTH CAROLINA:

Your Mayor has welcomed me to your home. I receive his greeting with that gratitude which one only feels when he hears expressed the language of commendation from those whose silence would have made him realize that his conduct had been bad indeed. If in this great struggle for the rights of the States and the liberties of the people, to secure the possession of which and to transmit which to us, our fathers of the revolution shed their blood, South Carolina, who has stood for thirty years in the vanguard, should give him who asserted those rights, no word of well done, he might turn convinced that he had failed as a public servant to perform his mission, and as a man had proven unable to cope with the responsibilities of his position. Therefore it is, Mr. Mayor, and fellow-citizens of Columbia, that I feel heartily grateful for the welcome received at your hands.

South Carolina has struggled nobly in the war and suffered many sacrifices. There is, indeed, no portion of our land where the pall of mourning has not been spread; but I thank the Giver of all Good that our people still remain firm there, above all other places. I am told there have been none to waver and none to doubt. It often happens that at a distance from a scene of action, men, who if present would easily measure it, magnify danger, until at last those become despondent whose hearts, if actually stirred by perils, would no sooner think of shrinking from the prompt performance of duty, than the gallant sons of Carolina, whose blood has so generously flowed on the many battle-fields of this war. But if there be any who feel that our cause is in danger; that final success may not crown our efforts; that we are not stronger to-day than when we began this struggle; that we are not able to continue the supplies to our armies and to our people, let all such read a contradiction in the smiling face of our land, and the teaming evidences of plenty which every where greet the eye; let them go to those places where brave men are standing in front of the foe, and there receive the assurance that we *shall* have final success, and that every man who does not live to see his country free, will see a freeman's grave. (Applause.)

There are those who, like the Israelites of old, are longing to turn back to the flesh pots they have left; who have thought there may still be some feasible mode of reconciliation, and would even be willing to rush into a reconstruction of the Union. Such, I am glad to know, do not flourish on the soil of South Carolina. Such cannot be the sentiment of any man in the Confederate States, if he will only recollect that from the beginning down to the present hour, your Government has made every effort within its power, to avoid a collision of arms in the first instance, and since then to obtain every possible means of settlement honorable to ourselves, based on a recognition of our independence. First, we sent commissioners to ask on what terms the quarrel could be adjusted, and since that time we have proclaimed in every public paper our desire for peace. Insolently, our every effort has been met. The Vice-President of the Confederate States was refused a passport to the North, when his object was negotiation—that means by which all wars must be terminated. The door was rudely shut in our faces. Intervention and recognition by foreign States, so long anticipated, has proved an *ignis fatuus*. There is, then, but one means by which you can hope to gain independence and an honorable peace, and that is by uniting with harmony, energy and determination in fighting those great battles and achieving those great victories, which will teach the world that we can defend our rights, and the Yankee nation that it is death to invade them. (Applause.)

With every Confederate victory, our stocks rise in the

foreign market—that touch stone of European sentiment. With every noble achievement that influences the public mind abroad, you are taking one step forward, and bringing foreign nations one step nearer your aid in recognizing and lending you friendly intervention, whenever they are satisfied that, intervention or no intervention, the Confederacy can sustain itself.

Does any one believe that Yankees are to be conciliated by terms of concession? Does any man imagine that we can conquer the Yankees by retreating before them, or do you not all know that the only way to make spaniels civil is to whip them? And you *can* whip them, if all the men capable of bearing arms will do their duty by taking their places under the standard of their country, before the veteran troops of the North receive the fresh increment which is being gathered in the Northern States. Now is the good and accepted time for every man to rally to the standard of his country and crush the invader upon her soil; and this, I believe, is in your power. If every man fit to bear arms will place himself in the ranks with those who are already there, we shall not battle in vain, and our achievement will be grand, final and complete. Is this a time to ask what the law demands of you—to inquire whether or not you are exempt under the law, or to ask if the magistrate will take you out of the enrolling office by a writ of *habeas corpus*? Rather is it not the time for every man capable of bearing arms to say: "My country needs my services, and my country shall have them!" When your heroic fathers, the Whigs of the Revolution, fought in that war which secured your birth-right, their armies were not gathered by asking who can be forced into the field? but "who are able to fight?" No man was too old and no boy too young, if he had the physical capacity to enter the ranks of the army. In the days of the Revolution, the boy left his paternal roof only to return to its blackened ruins. He grew to manhood among its struggles; and may not your country claim similar services from the youth of the present day? Like them, you must emulate the glory of your sires. Say not that you are unequal to the task, for I believe that our people are even better than were our honored ancestors. They have fought more and bloodier battles, and there are fewer who are luke-warm in the cause now, than existed in the days of the Revolution. What a glorious reflection it is, that wherever the tide of war has rolled its devastating wave over the land, just then do you find every heart beating true to the Confederacy, strengthened, as it were, by vicissitudes, and every woman ready to share her last loaf with the soldier who is fighting for our rights.

A plan of negociation has been offered for consideration—a plan of negociation by States. Well, it is easy to see on what terms the States can negotiate. In the first place, they have no constitutional power to do so. In the second place, Mr. Lincoln has said that he will not negotiate with them unless they can control the army, and they can only obtain the power to control the army by traitorously attempting to enter into a treaty contrary to the Government they have instituted. But suppose this were possible, what are the terms offered? If you will acknowledge your crime, lay down your arms, emancipate your slaves and turn over your leaders—as they call your humble servant—to be punished, then you will have permission to vote together with your negroes upon the terms under which Mr. Lincoln will be graciously pleased to allow you to live as a part of the nation over which he presides. If there be a man within the sound of my voice who contemplates such a proposition, I pity him from the bottom of my heart. My only wish is that he was North of the dividing line. His is not the spirit that animated our fathers, and he is not fit to exist among the men who are now periling their lives in the cause in which we are engaged, for he who is so slavish cannot be trusted with the sacred guardianship of the widows and orphans of the soldiers who have died in battle.

I have just returned from that army from which we have had the saddest accounts—the army of Tennessee; and I am able to bear to you words of good cheer. That army has increased in strength since the fall of Atlanta. It has risen in tone; its march is onward; its face looking to the front. So far as I am able to judge, General Hood's strategy has been good and his conduct has been gallant. His eye is now fixed upon a point far beyond that where he was assailed by the enemy. He hopes soon to have his hand upon Sherman's line of communications, and to fix it where he can hold it. And if but a half, nay, one-fourth, of the men to whom the service has a right, will give him their strength, I see no chance for Sherman to escape from a defeat or a disgraceful retreat. I therefore hope, in view of all the contingencies of war, with all the confidence which I found in the army, that within thirty days that army, which has so boastfully taken up its winter quarters in the heart of the Confederacy, will be in search of a crossing on the Tennessee River.

That our army retreated far, was but a natural precursor of that despondency which spread itself over the country; but as I approached the region occupied by our troops the hope increased, until at last I found in the army the *acme* of confidence itself. Gen. Beauregard, so well known to you all, is going there with a general command, which will enable him to concentrate all the troops that can be made available for the public defence. I therefore say, be of good cheer, for I hope that brighter intelligence will soon reach you. (Applause.)

But, my friends, if it be otherwise—if we suffer reverses, it is what is to be expected from the fortunes of war. It is the fate of all human designs. In that event, we shall have reason to anticipate from all brave men a conduct becoming the occasion, and shall look to you to redress your misfortunes, to rise in the face of disaster, and resolve to succeed, determined that you will live or die free. (Applause.)

Your brave sons are battling for the cause of the country everywhere; your Fort Sumter, where was first given to the breeze the flag of the Confederacy, still stands. The honor of the State has not been dimmed in the struggle, and her soldiers will be sustained by the thought that when they are no more, South Carolina will still retain that honor with which she commenced the war, and have accumulated that greatness and glory which will make her an exemplar of all that is chivalric and manly in a nation struggling for existence. You who have so long been the advocates of State Rights have never raised a clamor against the laws which seem to invade them, and I think, for obvious reasons, you are not like those new-born lights who, perhaps, are just beginning to appreciate the great principles of that creed. You saw laws passed which were necessary to make those States which are in co-operation effective for the good of the whole. You understood the nature of the compact entered into by the sovereign States, and you have not been fearful that the agent created by yourselves was likely to turn against that Government for which he and you had been so long struggling. Understanding the means of preserving your State Governments, you have not been frightened by the clamor of those who do not breathe the pure air of State sovereignty. Then you have had no difficulty in the organization of the three forces incident to military service. You are in that condition in which your defence must depend upon what does not belong to the active force of the country. Your battles are fought on other fields. You have on the coast some necessity for what is termed an active army, and should it be incumbent upon you to furnish troops from your reserves, you have no constitutional scruples, like Gov. Strong, of Massachusetts, against marching your militia from the borders of the State, to fight the battles of the cause in which you are engaged. I honor you for it. It is needless for me to argue questions here which have been discussed elsewhere, for here I am among the disciples of him from whom I learned my lessons of State Rights—the great, the immortal John C. Calhoun.

Among those to whom we are indebted in South Carolina, I have not yet alluded to that peculiar claim of gratitude which is due to the fair countrywomen of the Palmetto State—they who have gone to the hospital to watch by the side of the sick—those who throng your way-side homes—who have nursed as if nursing was a profession—who have used their needle with the industry of sewing women—who have borne privation without a murmur and who have given up fathers, sons and husbands with more than Spartan virtue, because they called no one to witness and record the deed. Silently, with all the dignity and grandeur of patriotism, they have made their sacrifices—sacrifices which, if written, would be surpassed by nothing in history. If all the acts of heroism and virtue of the women of the South could be transmitted to the future, it would present such a record as the world has never seen. All honor, then, I say, to the ladies of the Palmetto State. Their gallantry is only different from that of her sons in this, that they deem it unfeminine to strike; and yet such is the heroism they have displayed—such the noble demeanor they have exhibited—that at the last moment, when trampled upon and it became a necessity, they would not hesitate to strike the invader a corpse at their feet. (Applause.)

It is scarcely necessary for me, at a time like this, to argue grave questions, respecting policy past, present or prospective.

I only ask you to have faith and confidence, and to believe that every faculty of my head and my heart is devoted to your cause, and to that I shall, if necessary, give my life. Let every one in his own sphere and according to his own capacity, devote himself to the single purpose of filling up and sustaining our armies in the field. If required to stay at home, let him devote himself, not to the acquisition of wealth, but to the advancement of the common cause. If there is to be any aristocracy in the land after this war, I hope that it will be an aristocracy of those men who have become poor while bleeding to secure our liberty. (Applause.) If there are to be any peculiarly favored by public opinion hereafter, I trust it will be those men who have longest borne a musket and oftenest bled upon the battle fields. If there is to be any man shunned by the young ladies when he seeks their favor, I trust it will be the man who has grown rich by skulking.

And with all sincerity, I say to my young friends here, if you want the right man for a husband, take him whose armless sleeve and noble heart betokens the duties that he has rendered to his country, rather than he who has never shared the toils, or borne the dangers of the field. If there still be left any of those military critics who have never spoken of our generals but to show how much better things could have been managed, or of our Government, but to find fault with it, because it never took their advice—in mercy's name, let these wise men go to the front and aid us in achieving our independence. With their wisdom and strength swelling our armies, I should have some hopes that I will not be a corpse before our cause is secured, and that our flag would never trail in dishonor, but would wave victoriously above the roar and smoke of battle.

I believe it is in the power of the men of the Confederacy to plant our banners on the banks of the Ohio, where we may say to the Yankee, "be quiet, or we shall teach you another lesson." Within the next thirty days much is to be done, for upon our success much depends. Within the next thirty days, therefore, let all who are absentees, or who ought to be in the army, go promptly to their ranks. Let fresh victories crown our arms, and the peace party, if there be such at the North, can elect its candidate. But whether a peace candidate is elected or not,

Yankee instinct will teach him that it is better to end the war and leave us to the enjoyment of our own rights.

Prayerful for your welfare, confiding in the army of the Confederate States to do that which soft words can never achieve, and in the hope that God will preserve the little ones of all brave men who are in the field, or who are going to it, and trusting that in the future, under brighter auspices, it may be my fortune to meet the good people of Columbia, I wish you all for the present farewell. (Applause.)

A CALL FOR POLITICAL EQUALITY:
NEW YORK, OCTOBER 1864

Address of the Colored National Convention

October 6, 1864

Frederick Douglass, William Wells Brown, Henry Highland Garnet, and John Mercer Langston were among the 145 delegates from eighteen states who attended the National Convention of Colored Men held in Syracuse, New York, from October 4 to October 7. The convention established the National Equal Rights League and adopted an address to the public written by Douglass.

ADDRESS
OF THE
COLORED NATIONAL CONVENTION
TO THE
PEOPLE OF THE UNITED STATES.

FELLOW-CITIZENS,—

The members of the Colored National Convention, assembled in Syracuse, State of New York, October the 4th, 1864, to confer with each other as to the complete emancipation, enfranchisement, and elevation of our race, in essaying to address you on these subjects, warmly embrace the occasion to congratulate you upon the success of your arms, and upon the prospect of the speedy suppression of the slaveholders' rebellion. Baptized in the best blood of your noblest sons, torn and rent by a strife full of horrors,—a strife undertaken and prosecuted for aims and objects the guiltiest that can enter the wicked hearts of men long in the practice of crime,—we ardently hope with you that our country will come out of this tremendous conflict, purer, stronger, nobler, and happier than ever before. Having shared with you, in some measure, the hardships, perils, and sacrifices of this war for the maintenance of the Union and Government, we rejoice with you also in every sign which gives promise of its approaching termination, and of the return of our common country again to those peaceful, progressive, and humanizing activities of true national life, from which she has been so wantonly diverted by the insurrection of slaveholders.

In view of the general cheerfulness of the national situation, growing brighter every day; the rapid dispersement of the heavy clouds of dismal terror, which only a few weeks ago mantled our land with the gloomiest forebodings of national disaster and ruin,—we venture to hope that the present is a favorable moment to commend to your consideration the subject of our wrongs, and to obtain your earnest and hearty co-operation in all wise and just measures for their full redress.

When great and terrible calamities are abroad in the land, men are said to learn righteousness. It would be a mark of unspeakable national depravity, if neither the horrors of this war, nor the dawning prospect of peace, should soften the heart, and dispose the American people to renounce and forsake their evil policy towards the colored race. Assuming the contrary, we deem this a happily chosen hour for calling your attention to our cause. We know that the human mind is so constituted, that all postponement of duty, all refusal to go forward when the right path is once made plain, is dangerous.

After such neglect of, and disobedience to, the voice of reason and conscience, a nation becomes harder and less alive than before to high moral considerations. If won to the path of rectitude at all, thereafter, it must be by means of a purer light than that which first brought right convictions and inclinations to the national mind and heart. We speak, then, fellow-citizens, at an auspicious moment. Conviction has already seized the public mind. Little argument is needed. We shall appeal rather than argue; and we may well implore an attentive hearing for our appeal. The nation is still in tears. The warm blood of your brave and patriotic sons is still fresh upon the green fields of the Shenandoah. Mourning mingles everywhere with the national shout of victory; and though the smoke and noise of battle are rolling away behind the southern horizon, our brave armies are still confronted in Georgia and Virginia by a stern foe, whose haughtiness and cruelty have sprung naturally from his long and undisputed mastery over men. The point attained in the progress of this war is one from which you can if you will view to advantage the calamities which inevitably follow upon long and persistent violation of manifest duty; and on the other hand, the signs of final triumph enable you to anticipate the happy results which must always flow from just and honorable conduct. The fear of continued war, and the hope of speedy peace, alike mark this as the time for America to choose her destiny. Another such opportunity as is now furnished in the state of the country, and in the state of the national heart, may not come again in a century. Come, then, and let us reason together.

We shall speak, it is true, for our race,—a race long oppressed, enslaved, ignored, despised, slandered, and degraded; but we speak not the less for our country, whose welfare and permanent peace can only result from the adoption of wise and just measures towards our whole race, North and South.

Considering the number and the grievous character of the wrongs and disabilities endured by our race in this country, you will bear witness that we have borne with patience our lot, and have seldom troubled the national ear with the burden of complaint. It is true that individuals among us have constantly testified their abhorrence of this injustice; but as a people, we have seldom uttered, as we do this day, our protest and remonstrance against the manifold and needless injustice with which we are upon all sides afflicted. We have suffered in silence, trusting that, though long delayed, and perhaps through terrible commotions, the hour would come when justice, honor, and magnanimity would assert their power over the mind and heart of the American people, and restore us to the full exercise and enjoyment of the rights inseparable from human nature. Never having despaired of this consummation so devoutly wished, even in the darkest hours of our history, we are farther than ever from despairing now. Nowhere in the annals of mankind is there recorded an instance of an oppressed people rising more rapidly than ourselves in the favorable estimation of their oppressors. The change is great, and increasing, and is viewed with astonishment and dread by all those who had hoped to stand forever with their heels upon our necks.

Nevertheless, while joyfully recognizing the vast advances made by our people in popular consideration, and the apparent tendency of events in our favor, we cannot conceal from ourselves, and would not conceal from you, the fact that there are many and powerful influences, constantly operating, intended and calculated to defeat our just hopes, prolong the existence of the source of all our ills,—the system of slavery,—strengthen the slave power, darken the conscience of the North, intensify popular prejudice against color, multiply unequal and discriminating laws, augment the burdens long borne by our race, consign to oblivion the deeds of heroism which have distinguished the colored soldier, deny and despise his claims to the gratitude of his country, scout his pretensions to American citizenship, establish the selfish idea that this is exclusively the white man's country, pass unheeded all the lessons taught by these four years of fire and sword, undo all that has been done towards our freedom and elevation, take the musket from the shoulders of our brave black soldiers, deny them the constitutional right to keep and bear arms, exclude them from the ballot-box where they now possess that right, prohibit the extension of it to those who do not possess it, overawe free speech in and out of Congress, obstruct the right of peaceably assembling, re-enact the Fugitive-slave Bill, revive the internal slave-trade, break up all diplomatic relations with Hayti and Liberia, reopen our broad territories to the introduction of slavery, reverse the entire order and tendency of the events of the last three years, and postpone indefinitely that glorious deliverance from bondage, which for our sake, and for the sake of the future unity, permanent peace, and highest welfare of all concerned, we had fondly hoped and believed was even now at the door.

In surveying our possible future, so full of interest at this moment, since it may bring to us all the blessings of equal liberty, or all the woes of slavery and continued social degradation, you will not blame us if we manifest anxiety in regard to the position of our recognized friends, as well as that of our open and declared enemies; for our cause may suffer even more from the injudicious concessions and weakness of our friends, than from the machinations and power of our enemies. The weakness of our friends is strength to our foes. When the "Antislavery Standard," representing the American Anti-slavery Society, denies that that society asks for the enfranchisement of colored men, and the "Liberator" apologizes for excluding the colored men of Louisiana from the ballot-box, they injure us more vitally than all the ribald jests of the whole proslavery press.

Again: had, for instance, the present Administration, at the beginning of the war, boldly planted itself upon the doctrine of human equality as taught in the Declaration of Independence; proclaimed liberty to all the slaves in all the Slave States; armed every colored man, previously a slave or a freeman, who would or could fight under the loyal flag; recognized black men as soldiers of the Republic; avenged the first act of violence upon colored prisoners, in contravention of the laws of war; sided with the radical emancipation party in Maryland and Missouri; stood by its antislavery generals, instead of casting them aside,—history would never have had to record the scandalous platform adopted at Chicago, nor the immeasurable horrors of Fort Pillow. The weakness and hesitation of our friends, where promptness and vigor were required, have invited the contempt and rigor of our enemies. Seeing that, while perilling every thing for the protection and security of our country, our country did not think itself bound to protect and secure us, the rebels felt a license to treat us as outlaws. Seeing that our Government did not treat us as men, they did not feel bound to treat us as soldiers. It is, therefore, not the malignity of enemies alone we have to fear, but the deflection from the straight line of principle by those who are known throughout the world as our special friends. We may survive the arrows of the known negro-haters of our country; but woe to the colored race when their champions fail to demand, from any reason, equal liberty in every respect!

We have spoken of the existence of powerful re-actionary forces arrayed against us, and of the objects to which they tend. What are these mighty forces? and through what agencies do they operate and reach us? They are many; but we shall detain by no tedious enumeration. The first and most powerful is slavery; and the second, which may be said to be the shadow of slavery, is prejudice against men on account of their color. The one controls the South, and the other controls the North. Both are original sources of power, and generate peculiar sentiments, ideas, and laws concerning us. The agents of these two evil influences are various: but the chief are, first, the Democratic party; and, second, the Republican party. The Democratic party belongs to slavery; and the Republican party is largely under the power of prejudice against color. While gratefully recognizing a vast difference in our favor in the character and composition of the Republican party, and regarding the accession to power of the Democratic party as the heaviest calamity that could befall us in the present juncture of affairs, it cannot be disguised, that, while that party is our bitterest enemy, and is positively and actively re-actionary, the Republican party is negatively and passively so in its tendency. What we have to fear from these two parties,—looking to the future, and especially to the settlement of our present national troubles,—is, alas! only too obvious. The intentions, principles, and policy of both organizations, through their platforms, and the antecedents and the recorded utterances of the men who stand upon their respective platforms, teach us what to expect at their hands, and what kind of a future they are carving out for us, and for the country which they propose to govern. Without using the word "*slavery*," or "*slaves*," or "*slaveholders*," the Democratic party has none the less declared, in its platform, its purpose to be the endless perpetuation of slavery. Under the apparently harmless verbiage, "*private rights*," "*basis of the Federal Union*," and under the language employed in denouncing the Federal Administration for "*disregarding the Constitution in every part*," "*pretence of military necessity*," we see the purpose of the Democratic party to restore slavery to all its ancient power, and to make this Government just what it was before the rebellion,—simply an instrument of the slave-power. "The basis of the Federal Union" only means the alleged compromises and stipulations, as interpreted by Judge Taney, by which black men are supposed to have no rights which white men are bound to respect; and by which the whole Northern people are bound to protect the cruel masters against the justly deserved violence of the slave, and to do the fiendish work of hell-hounds when slaves make their escape from thraldom. The candidates of that party take their stand upon its platform; and will, if elected,—which Heaven forbid!—carry it out to the letter. From this party we must look only for fierce, malignant, and unmitigated hostility. Our continued oppression and degradation is the law of its life, and its sure passport to power. In the ranks of the Democratic party, all the worst elements of American society fraternize; and we need not expect a single voice from that quarter for justice, mercy, or even decency. To it we are nothing; the slave-holders every thing. We have but to consult its press to know that it would willingly enslave the free colored people in the South; and also that it would gladly stir up against us mob-violence at the North,—re-enacting the sanguinary scenes of one year ago in New York and other large cities. We therefore pray, that whatever wrath, curse, or calamity, the future may have in store for us, the accession of the Democratic party to the reins of power may not be one of them; for this to us would comprise the sum of all social woes.

How stands the case with the great Republican party in question? We have already alluded to it as being largely under the influence of the prevailing contempt for the character and rights of the colored race. This is seen by the slowness of our Government to employ the strong arm of the black man in the work of putting down the rebellion: and in its unwillingness, after thus employing him, to invest him with the same incitements to deeds of daring, as white soldiers; neither giving him the same pay, rations, and protection, nor any hope of rising in the service by meritorious conduct. It is also seen in the fact, that in neither of the plans emanating from this party for reconstructing the institutions of the Southern States, are colored men, not even those who had *fought* for the country, recognized as having any political existence or rights whatever.

Even in the matter of the abolition of slavery,—to which, by its platform, the Republican party is strongly committed, as well by President Lincoln's celebrated Proclamation of the first of January, 1863, and by his recent letter "To whom it may concern,"—there is still room for painful doubt and apprehension. It is very evident, that the Republican party, though a party composed of the best men of the country, is not prepared to make the abolition of slavery, in all the Rebel States, a consideration precedent to the re-establishment of the Union. However antislavery in sentiment the President may be, and however disposed he may be to continue the war till slavery is abolished, it is plain that in this he would not be sustained by his party. A single reverse to our arms, in such a war, would raise the hands of the party in opposition to their chief. The hope of the speedy and complete abolition of slavery, hangs, therefore, not upon the disposition of the Republican party, not upon the disposition of President Lincoln; but upon the slender thread of Rebel power, pride, and persistence. In returning to the Union, slavery has a fair chance to live; out of the Union, it has a still better chance to live: but, fighting against the Union, it has no chance for any thing but destruction. Thus the freedom of our race and the welfare of our country tremble together in the balance of events.

This somewhat gloomy view of the condition of affairs— which to the enthusiastic, who have already convinced themselves that slavery is dead, may not only seem gloomy, but untruthful—is nevertheless amply supported, not only by the well-known sentiment of the country, the controlling pressure of which is seriously felt by the Administration; but it is sustained by the many attempts lately made by the Republican press to explain away the natural import of the President's recent address "To whom it may concern," in which he makes the abolition of Slavery a primary condition to the restoration of the Union; and especially is this gloomy view supported by the remarkable speech delivered only a few weeks ago at Auburn, by Hon. William H. Seward, Secretary of State. Standing next to the President in the administration of the government, and fully in the confidence of the Chief Magistrate, no member of the National Cabinet is better qualified than Mr. Seward to utter the mind and policy of the Administration upon this momentous subject, when it shall come up at the close of the war. Just what it will do in the matter of slavery, Mr. Seward says,—

"When the insurgents shall have disbanded their armies, and laid down their arms, the war will instantly cease; and all the war measures then existing, including those which affect slavery, will cease also; and all the moral, economical, and political questions, as well affecting slavery as others, which shall then be existing between individuals and States and the Federal Government, whether they arose before the civil war began, or whether they grew out of it, will, by force of the Constitution, pass over to the arbitrament of courts of law, and the counsels of legislation."

These, fellow-citizens, are studied words, full of solemn and fearful import. They mean that our Republican Administration is not only ready to make peace with the Rebels, but to make peace with slavery also; that all executive and legislative action launched against the slave-system, whether of proclamation or confiscation, will cease the instant the Rebels shall disband their armies; and lay down their arms. The hope that the war will put an end to slavery, has, according to this exposition, only one foundation; and that is, that the courts and Congress will so decree. But what ground have we here? Congress has already spoken, and has refused to alter the Constitution so as to abolish Slavery. The Supreme Court has yet to speak; but what it will say, if this question shall come before it, is very easily divined. We will not assert positively what it will say; but indications of its judgment are clearly against us. What then have we? Only this, as our surest and best ground of hope; namely, that the Rebels, in their madness, will continue to make war upon the Government, until they shall not only become destitute of men, money, and the munitions of war, but utterly divested of their slaves also.

But, fellow-citizens, the object of this Address is not merely to state facts, and point out sources of danger. We would distinctly place our whole cause before you, and earnestly appeal to you to make that cause practically your cause; as we believe it is the cause of justice and of our whole country. We come before you altogether in new relations. Hitherto we have addressed you in the generic character of a common humanity; only as men: but to-day, owing to the events of the last three years, we bring with us an additional claim to consideration. By the qualities displayed, by the hardships endured, and by the services rendered the country, during these years of war and peril, we can now speak with the confidence of men who have deserved well of their country. While conscious of your power and of our comparative weakness, we may still claim for our race those rights which are not less ours by our services to the country than by the laws of human nature. All, therefore, that justice can demand, and honor grant, we can now ask, without presumption and without arrogance, of the American people.

Do you, then, ask us to state, in plain terms, just what we

want of you, and just what we think we ought to receive at your hands? We answer: First of all, the complete abolition of the slavery of our race in the United States. We shall not stop to argue. We feel the terrible sting of this stupendous wrong, and that we cannot be free while our brothers are slaves. The enslavement of a vast majority of our people extends its baleful influence over every member of our race; and makes freedom, even to the free, a mockery and a delusion: we therefore, in our own name, and in the name of the whipped and branded millions, whose silent suffering has pleaded to the humane sentiment of mankind, but in vain, during more than two hundred years for deliverance, we implore you to abolish slavery. In the name of your country, torn, distracted, bleeding, and while you are weeping over the bloody graves of more than two hundred thousand of your noblest sons, many of whom have been cut down, in the midst of youthful vigor and beauty, we implore you to abolish slavery. In the name of peace, which experience has shown cannot be other than false and delusive while the rebellious spirit of Slavery has an existence in the land, we implore you to abolish slavery. In the name of universal justice, to whose laws great States not less than individuals are bound to conform, and the terrible consequences of whose violation are as fixed and certain as the universe itself, we implore you to abolish slavery; and thus place your peace and national welfare upon immutable and everlasting foundations.

Why would you let slavery continue? What good thing has it done, what evil thing has it left undone, that you should allow it to survive this dreadful war, the natural fruit of its existence? Can you want a second war from the same cause? Are you so rich in men, money, and material, that you must provide for future depletion? Or do you hope to escape the consequences of wrong-doing? Can you expect any better results from compromises in the future, than from compromises with slavery in the past? If the South fights desperately and savagely to-day for the possession of four millions of slaves, will she fight less savagely and desperately when the prize for which she fights shall become eight instead of four millions? and when her ability to war upon freedom and free institutions shall have increased twofold?

Do you answer, that you have no longer any thing to fear? that slavery has already received its death-blow? that it can only have a transient existence, even if permitted to live after the termination of the war? We answer, So thought your Revolutionary fathers when they framed the Federal Constitution; and to-day, the bloody fruits of their mistake are all around us. Shall we avoid or shall we repeat their stupendous error? Be not deceived. Slavery is still the vital and animating breath of Southern society. The men who have fought for it on the battle-field will not love it less for having shed their blood in its defence. Once let them get Slavery safely under the protection of the Federal Government, and ally themselves, as they will be sure to do, to the Democratic party of the North; let Jefferson Davis and his Confederate associates, either in person or by their representatives, return once more to their seats in the halls of Congress,—and you will then see your dead slavery the most living and powerful thing in the country. To make peace, therefore, on such a basis as shall admit slavery back again into the Union, would only be sowing the seeds of war; sure to bring at last a bitter harvest of blood! The sun in the heavens at noonday is not more manifest, than the fact that slavery is the prolific source of war and division among you; and that its abolition is essential to your national peace and unity. Once more, then, we entreat you—for you have the power—to put away this monstrous abomination. You have repeatedly during this wanton slaveholding and wicked Rebellion, in the darkest hours of the struggle, appealed to the Supreme Ruler of the universe to smile upon your armies, and give them victory: surely you will not now stain your souls with the crime of ingratitude by making a wicked compact and a deceitful peace with your enemies. You have called mankind to witness that the struggle on your part was not for empire merely; that the charge that it was such was a gross slander: will you now make a peace which will justify what you have repeatedly denounced as a calumny? Your antislavery professions have drawn to you the sympathy of liberal and generous minded men throughout the world, and have restrained all Europe from recognizing the Southern Confederacy, and breaking up your blockade of Southern ports. Will you now proclaim your own baseness and hypocrisy by making a peace which shall give the lie to all such professions? You have over and over again, and very justly, branded slavery as the inciting cause of this Rebellion; denounced it as the fruitful source of pride and selfishness and mad ambition; you have blushed before all Europe for its existence among you; and have shielded yourselves from the execrations of mankind, by denying your constitutional ability to interfere with it. Will you now, when the evil in question has placed itself within your constitutional grasp, and invited its own destruction by its persistent attempts to destroy the Government, relax your grasp, release your hold, and to the disappointment of the slaves deceived by your proclamations, to the sacrifice of the Union white men of the South who have sided with you in this contest with slavery, and to the dishonor of yourselves and the amazement of mankind, give new and stronger lease of life to slavery? We will not and cannot believe it.

There is still one other subject, fellow-citizens,—one other want,—looking to the peace and welfare of our common country, as well as to the interests of our race; and that is, political equality. We want the elective franchise in all the States now in the Union, and the same in all such States as may come into the Union hereafter. We believe that the highest welfare of this great country will be found in erasing from its statute-books all enactments discriminating in favor or against any class of its people, and by establishing one law for the white and colored people alike. Whatever prejudice and taste may be innocently allowed to do or to dictate in social and domestic relations, it is plain, that in the matter of government, the object of which is the protection and security of human rights, prejudice should be allowed no voice whatever. In this department of human relations, no notice should be taken of the color of men; but justice, wisdom, and humanity should weigh alone, and be all-controlling.

Formerly our petitions for the elective franchise were met and denied upon the ground, that, while colored men were protected in person and property, they were not required to perform military duty. Of course this was only a plausible excuse; for we were subject to any call the Government was pleased to make upon us, and we could not properly be made to suffer because the Government did not see fit to impose military duty upon us. The fault was with the Government, not with us.

But now even this frivolous though somewhat decent apology for excluding us from the ballot-box is entirely swept away. Two hundred thousand colored men, according to a recent statement of President Lincoln, are now in the service, upon field and flood, in the army and the navy of the United States; and every day adds to their number. They are there as volunteers, coming forward with other patriotic men at the call of their imperilled country; they are there also as substitutes filling up the quotas which would otherwise have to be filled up by white men who now remain at home; they are also there as drafted men, by a certain law of Congress, which, for once, makes no difference on account of color: and whether they are there as volunteers, as substitutes, or as drafted men, neither ourselves, our cause, nor our country, need be ashamed of their appearance or their action upon the battle-field. Friends and enemies, rebels and loyal men,—each, after their kind,—have borne conscious and unconscious testimony to the gallantry and other noble qualities of the colored troops.

Your fathers laid down the principle, long ago, that universal suffrage is the best foundation of Government. We believe as your fathers believed, and as they practised; for, in eleven States out of the original thirteen, colored men exercised the right to vote at the time of the adoption of the Federal Constitution. The Divine-right Governments of Europe, with their aristocratic and privileged classes of *priests* and *nobles*, are little better than cunningly devised conspiracies against the natural rights of the people to govern themselves.

Whether the right to vote is a natural right or not, we are not here to determine. Natural or conventional, in either case we are amply supported in our appeal for its extension to us. If it is, as all the teachings of your Declaration of Independence imply, a *natural right*, to deny to us its exercise is a wrong done to our human nature. If, on the other hand, the right to vote is simply a conventional right, having no other foundation or significance than a mere conventional arrangement, which may be extended or contracted, given or taken away, upon reasonable grounds, we insist, that, even basing the right upon this uncertain foundation, we may reasonably claim a right to a voice in the election of the men who are to have at their command our time, our services, our property, our persons, and our lives. This command of our persons and lives is no longer theory, but now the positive practice of our Government. We say, therefore, that having required, demanded, and in some instances compelled, us to serve with our time, our property, and our lives, coupling us in all the obligations and duties imposed upon the more highly favored of our fellow-citizens in this war to protect and defend your country from threatened destruction, and having fully established the precedent by which, in all similar and dissimilar cases of need, we may be compelled to respond to a like requisition,—we claim to have fully earned the elective franchise; and that you, the American people, have virtually contracted an obligation to grant it, which has all the sanctions of justice, honor, and magnanimity, in favor of its prompt fulfilment. Are we good enough to use bullets, and not good enough to use ballots? May we defend rights in time of war, and yet be denied the exercise of those rights in time of peace? Are we citizens when the nation is in peril, and aliens when the nation is in safety? May we shed our blood under the star-spangled banner on the battle-field, and yet be debarred from marching under it to the ballot-box? Will the brave white soldiers, bronzed by the hardships and exposures of repeated campaigns, men who have fought by the side of black men, be ashamed to cast their ballots by the side of their companions-in-arms? May we give our lives, but not our votes, for the good of the republic? Shall we toil with you to win the prize of free government, while you alone shall monopolize all its valued privileges? Against such a conclusion, every sentiment of honor and manly fraternity utters an indignant protest.

It is quite true, that some part of the American people may, with a show of plausibility, evade the force of this appeal and deny this claim. There are men in all countries who can evade any duty or obligation which is not enforced by the strong arm of the law. Our country is no exception to the rule. They can say in this case, "Colored men, we have done you no wrong. We have purchased nothing at your hands, and owe you nothing. From first to last, we have objected to the measure of employing you to help put down this rebellion; foreseeing the very claim you now set up. Were we to-day invested with the power and authority of this Government, we would instantly disband every colored regiment now in front of Richmond, and everywhere else in the Southern States. We do not believe in making soldiers of black men." To all that, we reply, There need be no doubt whatever. No doubt they would disband the black troops if they had the power; and equally plain is it that they would disband the white troops also if they had the power.

They do not believe in making black men soldiers; but they equally do not believe in making white men soldiers to fight slaveholding rebels. But we do not address ourselves here to particular parties and classes of our country-men: we would appeal directly to the moral sense, honor, and magnanimity of the whole nation; and, with a cause so good, cannot believe that we shall appeal in vain. Parties and classes rise and fall, combine and dissolve: but the national conscience remains forever; and it is that to which our cause is addressed. It may, however, be said that the colored people enlisted in the service of the country without any promise or stipulation that they would be rewarded with political equality at the end of the war; but all the more, on this very account, do we hold the American people bound in honor thus to reward them. By the measure of confidence reposed in the national honor and generosity, we have the right to measure the obligation of fulfilment. The fact, that, when called into the service of the country, we went forward without exacting terms or conditions, to the mind of the generous man enhances our claims.

But, again, why are we so urgent for the possession of this particular right? We are asked, even by some Abolitionists, why we cannot be satisfied, for the present at least, with personal freedom; the right to testify in courts of law; the right to own, buy, and sell real estate; the right to sue and be sued. We answer, Because in a republican country, where general suffrage is the rule, personal liberty, the right to testify in courts of law, the right to hold, buy, and sell property, and all other rights, become mere privileges, held at the option of others, where we are excepted from the general political liberty. What gives to the newly arrived emigrants, fresh from lands governed by kingcraft and priestcraft, special consequence in the eyes of the American people? It is not their virtue, for they are often depraved; it is not their knowledge, for they are often ignorant; it is not their wealth, for they are often very poor: why, then, are they courted by the leaders of all parties? The answer is, that our institutions clothe them with the elective franchise, and they have a voice in making the laws of the country. Give the colored men of this country the elective franchise, and you will see no violent mobs driving the black laborer from the wharves of large cities, and from the toil elsewhere by which he honestly gains his bread. You will see no influential priest, like the late Bishop Hughes, addressing mobocrats and murderers as "gentlemen;" and no influential politician, like Governor Seymour, addressing the "misguided" rowdies of New York as his "friends." The possession of that right is the keystone to the arch of human liberty: and, without that, the whole may at any moment fall to the ground; while, with it, that liberty may stand forever,—a blessing to us, and no possible injury to you. If you still ask why we want to vote, we answer, Because we don't want to be mobbed from our work, or insulted with impunity at every corner. We are men, and want to be as free in our native country as other men.

Fellow-citizens, let us entreat you, have faith in your own principles. If freedom is good for any, it is good for all. If you need the elective franchise, we need it even more. You are strong, we are weak; you are many, we are few; you are protected, we are exposed. Clothe us with this safeguard of our liberty, and give us an interest in the country to which, in common with you, we have given our lives and poured out our best blood. You cannot need special protection. Our degradation is not essential to your elevation, nor our peril essential to your safety. You are not likely to be outstripped in the race of improvement by persons of African descent; and hence you have no need of superior advantages, nor to burden them with disabilities of any kind. Let your Government be what all governments should be,—a copy of the eternal laws of the universe; before which all men stand equal as to rewards and punishments, life and death, without regard to country, kindred, tongue, or people.

But what we have now said, in appeal for the elective franchise, applies to our people generally. A special reason may be urged in favor of granting colored men the right in all the rebellious States.

Whatever may be the case with monarchical governments;

however they may despise the crowd, and rely upon their *prestige*, armaments, and standing armies, to support them,—a republican government like ours depends largely upon the friendship of the people over whom it is established, for its harmonious and happy operation. This kind of government must have its foundation in the affections of the people: otherwise the people will hinder, circumvent, and destroy it. Up to a few years of the rebellion, our government lived in the friendship of the masses of the Southern people. Its enemies were, however, numerous and active; and these at last prevailed, poisoned the minds of the masses, broke up the government, brought on the war. Now, whoever lives to see this rebellion suppressed at the South, as we believe we all shall, will also see the South characterized by a sullen hatred towards the National Government. It will be transmitted from father to son, and will be held by them "as sacred animosity." The treason, mowed down by the armies of Grant and Sherman, will be followed by a strong undergrowth of treason which will go far to disturb the peaceful operation of the hated Government.

Every United-States mail-carrier, every custom-house officer, every Northern man, and every representive of the United-States Government, in the Southern States, will be held in abhorrence; and for a long time that country is to be governed with difficulty. We may conquer Southern armies by the sword; but it is another thing to conquer Southern hate. Now what is the natural counterpoise against this Southern malign hostility? This it is: give the elective franchise to every colored man of the South who is of sane mind, and has arrived at the age of twenty-one years, and you have at once four millions of friends who will guard with their vigilance, and, if need be, defend with their arms, the ark of Federal Liberty from the treason and pollution of her enemies. You are sure of the enmity of the masters,—make sure of the friendship of the slaves; for, depend upon it, your Government cannot afford to encounter the enmity of both.

If the arguments addressed to your sense of honor, in these pages, in favor of extending the elective franchise to the colored people of the whole country, be strong, that which we are prepared to present to you in behalf of the colored people of rebellious States can be made tenfold stronger. By calling them to take part with you in the war to subdue their rebellious masters, and the fact that thousands of them have done so, and thousands more would gladly do so, you have exposed them to special resentment and wrath; which, without the elective franchise, will descend upon them in unmitigated fury. To break with your friends, and make peace with your enemies; to weaken your friends, and strengthen your enemies; to abase your friends, and exalt your enemies; to disarm your friends, and arm your enemies; to disfranchise your loyal friends, and enfranchise your disloyal enemies,—is not the policy of honor, but of infamy.

But we will not weary you. Our cause is in some measure before you. The power to redress our wrongs, and to grant us our just rights, is in your hands. You can determine our destiny,—blast us by continued degradation, or bless us with the means of gradual elevation. We are among you, and must remain among you; and it is for you to say, whether our presence shall conduce to the general peace and welfare of the country, or be a constant cause of discussion and of irritation,—troubles in the State, troubles in the Church, troubles everywhere.

To avert these troubles, and to place your great country in safety from them, only one word from you, the American people, is needed, and that is JUSTICE: let that magic word once be sounded, and become all-controlling in all your courts of law, subordinate and supreme; let the halls of legislation, state and national, spurn all statesmanship as mischievous and ruinous that has not justice for its foundation; let justice without compromise, without curtailment, and without partiality, be observed with respect to all men, no class of men claiming for themselves any right which they will not grant to another,—then strife and discord will cease; peace will be placed upon enduring foundations; and the American people, now divided and hostile, will dwell together in power and unity.

"MAKE GEORGIA HOWL":
GEORGIA, OCTOBER 1864

William T. Sherman to Ulysses S. Grant

During his visit to Georgia, Jefferson Davis had approved Hood's plan to force Sherman to retreat from Atlanta by cutting his railroad supply line. Hood crossed the Chattahoochee River southwest of Atlanta, September 28–29, and began advancing toward the Chattanooga–Atlanta railroad. Leaving one corps to guard the city, Sherman set off in pursuit of Hood with the remainder of his troops on October 3. After destroying eight miles of track between Big Shanty and Acworth, Confederate forces were repulsed when they tried to capture the Union supply depot at Allatoona on October 5. When Sherman telegraphed Grant from Allatoona on October 9, Hood was twenty miles to the southwest preparing to advance on Resaca. Sherman previously proposed a march on Savannah in a telegram sent to Grant on October 1.

Allatoona 7.30 P.M.
Oct. 9th 1864

Lt. Gen. Grant
City Point

It will be a physical impossibility to protect this road now that Hood, Forrest, Wheeler and the whole batch of Devils are turned loose without home or habitation. I think Hoods movements indicate a direction to the end of the Selma and Talladega road to Blue Mountain about sixty miles south west of Rome from which he will threaten Kingston, Bridgeport and Decatur and I propose we break up the road from Chattanooga and strike out with wagons for Milledgeville Millen and Savannah.

Until we can repopulate Georgia it is useless to occupy it, but the utter destruction of its roads, houses, and people will cripple their military resources. By attempting to hold the roads we will lose a thousand men monthly and will gain no result. I can make the march and make Georgia howl. We have

over 8000 cattle and 3,000,000 pounds of bread but no corn, but we can forage in the interior of the state.
                    W. T. Sherman
                    M. Genl.

"ONE GREAT DESERT": VIRGINIA, OCTOBER 1864

Stephen Dodson Ramseur to Ellen Richmond Ramseur

Following his victory at Winchester, Sheridan pursued Early's retreating army and defeated it at Fisher's Hill near Strasburg on September 22. Sheridan then advanced as far south as Staunton before withdrawing to the north. As they fell back, Union troops carried out Grant's instructions to turn the Shenandoah Valley into "a barren waste." An 1860 graduate of West Point, Major General Stephen Dodson Ramseur led a division in Early's army at the age of twenty-seven. He wrote to his wife nine days before he was fatally wounded during the Confederate defeat at Cedar Creek on October 19.

Camp near New Market Va.
Oct. 10th 1864

My Own Darling Wife

Yesterday my Courier handed me a letter from Mr. S, one from Charley and *three* from your dear Self. Yours were dated respectively 23rd 26th Sept. and 30th ditto.

Do you know how much better I feel after getting these letters from you. I have been questioning Mr. Harding too, and he tells me you are perfectly well and "sweet accordin." Oh me! how I want to be with you. Every day I think more and more about you. I cant help feeling the most intense anxiety and solicitude on your behalf. Since our disasters over here in the Valley, my prospects for a furlough are greatly diminished. I think my duty is plain. I ought not to leave *now* even if I could do so.

So my Beloved Darling you must be brave and cheerful without me for a while, a short while I hope. I do earnestly pray that your life may not be endangered. That you may be soon restored to health. And that both of our hearts may be gladdened and our natures improved by the issue of your confinement. Oh! My beautiful Darling Wife! I can not begin to write what I feel now that you need so much my presence and sympathy. I do so long to be with you! 'Tis the greatest trial of my life to be separated from you *now*! But these trials do us good, even as gold is refined by the fire. When in God's good Providence we are permitted again to meet and live together in Peace, we can look back to these dark days as the time when we were tried and not found wanting. I hope and pray that we may be benefited spiritually as well as mentally by the trials to which we are now subjected.

Mr. S. writes me that all are well at home, that Father tho' much discouraged by the late disasters to our army, is still hopeful as to the final result. I agree with you in your remarks about the Croakers. I must confess, I would be willing to take a musket and fight to the bitter end, rather than submit to these miserable Yankees. I think they have placed themselves outside of the pale of civilization by the course they have pursued in this Campaign. This beautiful and fertile Valley has been totally destroyed. Sheridan has had *some* houses, *all* the mills & barns, every straw & wheat stack burned. This Valley is one great desert. I do not see how these poor people are to live. We have to haul our supplies from away up the Valley. It is rumoured that the Yankees are rebuilding the Manassa Gap Rail Road. If this is so, Sheridan will not give up his hold upon the Valley and we will probably remain here for the Winter, unless Gen'l. Lee becomes so hard pressed that we will have to go to him. It is (or rather was, before our disasters) more pleasant campaigning in the Valley than in those terrible trenches before Richmond.

My hope now is from Hood. I do hope he may be enabled to overwhelm Sherman and send reinforcements to our great Gen'l. Lee. When Providence smiled on us here, one always had bad news from the West. May we not hope now for cheer and support from that Quarter?

The last private advices I had from Georgia were very encouraging. Time is an important element. I believe Hood will whip Sherman. I hope he'll do it quickly.

I rec'd. a long, kind letter from Col. Frank Huger a few days ago. He is full of hope and sprightliness. Says his sister Mrs. Preston has the finest boy (so she says) in the Confederacy. May be we will have something to say about that some of these days. Nous verrons!

I have not been writing to you so often recently My Darling Wife, because I have been either so constantly occupied or (I must acknowledge it) so much mortified at the recent disasters to our Army of the Valley that I could not write with any pleasure. There is something now to write about. Dr. David has just come in & sends love to you. He is very well and is doing well. Caleb sends love & will write soon. Mr. H was with me sometime today. He is very homesick, talks about his babies all the time. Do give my love to all! Write as often as you can. Telegraph anything that happens to you. If you need me I'll try to get home. Telegraph to Maj Gen'l. R. army of the Valley. Near Harrisonburg. Give my very best love to dear Mama. I know she will take the very best care of you. Accept my heart full of love my Beloved Wife. God bless you and keep you and may He in Mercy speedily grant us peace. Yr devoted Husband

DESERTION AND "DESPOTISM":
VIRGINIA, OCTOBER 1864

John B. Jones: Diary, October 10–13, 1864

On September 29, Union troops attacked north of the James River and succeeded in capturing New Market Heights and Fort Harrison but were unable to break through the inner defensive line protecting Richmond. The next day a Confederate attempt to retake the fort was repulsed. With Confederate reserves committed north of the James, Grant again attacked south of Petersburg with the goal of cutting the Southside Railroad. In three days of fighting around Peebles Farm, September 30–October 2, Union forces failed to reach the railroad but were able to extend their trench line closer to the Boydton Plank Road, which was used to supply Petersburg by wagon train. On October 7 a Confederate attempt to turn the Union right flank north of the James was defeated in fighting along the Darbytown and New Market roads. The three engagements cost the Union about 6,700 men killed, wounded, or missing, and the Confederates about 4,300. During the battle for Fort Harrison, John B. Jones had watched white smoke from artillery fire "floating along the horizon over the woods and down the river" from the Confederate War Department, where he worked as a clerk. He wrote about the measures taken to reinforce the ranks of Richmond's defenders.

―――――――

OCTOBER 10TH.—*A white frost*; first frost of the season. All quiet below.

Gen. W. M. Gardner (in Gen. Winder's place) reports that of the exempts and citizens taken from the streets to the front, last week, *a majority have deserted* This proves that even a despotic military act cannot be committed with impunity.

Gen. Beauregard telegraphs from Opeleka, Ala., that he has arranged matters satisfactorily between Gov. Brown of Georgia and Gen. Cobb, regarding exempts and State militia.

The President directs the Secretary to ascertain if this has been done in accordance with law and the interests of the service.

Gen. R. Taylor telegraphs that Gen. E. K. Smith has proclaimed pardon to deserters, from trans-Mississippi Department, after he had arrested most of them and sent them to their regiments, and now he recommends that no more troops be brought over the river or they will be sure to desert. The President directs the Secretary to correspond with Gen. Smith on the subject. Gen. Taylor is the President's kinsman—by his first marriage.

Gen. Beauregard left Opeleka on the 7th inst. for Hood's army, so in a few days we may expect a battle.

OCTOBER 11TH.—Bright and pleasant. All is quiet below.

From Georgia we have many rumors. It is reported that a battle has been fought (second time) at Altoona, which we captured, with 4000 prisoners; that Rome has been taken, with 3000 negro prisoners; and, finally, that we have Atlanta again. I have seen no such dispatches. But the gentleman who assured me it was all true, has a son a clerk at the President's office, and a relative in the telegraph office. Dispatches may have come to the President; and, if so, it may be our policy to forbid their publication for the present, as the enemy would derive the first intelligence of their disaster from our newspapers.

Well, Gen. Gardner reports, officially, that of the number of exempts, and of the mixed class of citizens arrested in the streets, and summarily marched to the "front," "a majority have deserted!" Men, with exemptions in their pockets, going to or returning from market, have been seized by the Adjutant-General's orders, and despotically hurried off without being permitted even to send a message to their families. Thousands were entrapped, by being directed to call at Gen. Barton's headquarters, an immense warehouse, and receive passes; but no Gen. Barton was there—or if there, not visible; and all the anxious seekers found themselves in prison, only to be liberated as they were incorporated into companies, and marched "to the front." From the age of fifteen to fifty-five, all were seized by that order—no matter what papers they bore, or what the condition of their families—and hurried to the field, where there was no battle. No wonder there are many deserters—no wonder men become indifferent as to which side shall prevail, nor that the administration is falling into disrepute at the capital.

OCTOBER 12TH.—Bright and beautiful. All quiet below, save an occasional booming from the fleet.

Nothing from Georgia in the papers, save the conjectures of the Northern press. No doubt we have gained advantages there, which it is good policy to conceal as long as possible from the enemy.

Squads of able-bodied *detailed* men are arriving *at last*, from the interior. Lee's army, in this way, will get efficient reinforcements.

The Secretary of the Treasury sends a note over to the Secretary of War to-day, saying the Commissary-General, in his estimates, allows but $31,000,000 for tax in kind—whereas the tax collectors show an actual amount, credited to farmers and planters, of $145,000,000. He says this will no doubt attract the notice of Congress.

Mr. Peck, our agent to purchase supplies in North Carolina, has delivered no wheat yet. He bought supplies for his family; 400 bushels of wheat for 200 clerks, and 100 for Assistant Secretary of War, Judge Campbell, and Mr. Kean, the young Chief of the Bureau. This he says he bought with private funds; but he brought it at the government's expense. The clerks are resolved not to submit to his action.

I hear of more desertions. Mr. Seddon and Mr. Stanton at Washington are engaged in a singular game of chance. The harsh orders of both cause mutual abandonments, and now we have the spectacle of men deserting our regiments, and quite as many coming over from the enemy's regiments near the city.

Meantime Gen. Bragg is striving to get the able-bodied men out of the bureaus and to place them in the field.

The despotic order, arresting every man in the streets, and hurrying them to "the front," without delay, and regardless of the condition of their families—some were taken off when getting medicine for their sick wives—is still the theme of execration, even among men who have been the most ultra and uncompromising secessionists. The terror caused many to hide themselves, and doubtless turned them against the government. They say now such a despotism is quite as bad as a Stanton despotism, and there is not a toss-up between the rule of the United States and the Confederate States. Such are some of the effects of bad measures in such critical times as these. Mr. Seddon has no physique to sustain him. He has intellect, and has read much; but, nevertheless, such great men are sometimes more likely to imitate some predecessor at a critical moment, or to adopt some bold yet inefficient suggestion from another, than to originate an adequate one themselves. He is a scholar, an invalid, refined and philosophical—but effeminate.

OCTOBER 13TH.—Rained all night; clear and cool this morning.

The government publishes nothing from Georgia yet; but it is supposed there is intelligence of an important character in the city, which it would be impolitic to communicate to the enemy.

All still remains quiet below the city. But the curtain is expected to rise on the next act of the tragedy every moment. Gen. Grant probably furloughed many of his men to vote in Pennsylvania and Ohio, on Tuesday last—elections preliminary to the Presidential election—and they have had time to return to their regiments.

If this pause should continue a week or two longer, Gen. Lee would be much strengthened. Every day the farmers, whose details have been revoked, are coming in from the counties; and many of these were in the war in '61 and '62—being experienced veterans. Whereas Grant's recruits, though greater in number, are raw and unskilled.

The Medical Boards have been instructed to put in all men that come before them, capable of bearing arms *ten days*. One died in the trenches, on the eleventh day, of consumption!

There is a rumor of a fight on our extreme left. It is said Field's division (C. S.) repulsed three assaults of the enemy. If the battle be still continued (4 P.M.—the wind from the west prevents us from hearing guns), no doubt it is the beginning of a general engagement—decisive, perhaps, of the fate of Richmond.

We have many accounts of evasions of military service, occasioned by the alleged bad faith of the government, and the despotic orders from the Adjutant-General's office.

And yet Gov. Smith's certificates for exemption of rich young Justices of the Peace, Commissioners of the (county) Revenue, Deputy Sheriffs, clerks, constables, officers and clerks of banks, still come in daily; and they are "allowed" by the Assistant Secretary of War. Will the poor and friendless fight their battles, and win their independence for them? It may be so; but let not rulers in future wars follow the example! Nothing but the conviction that they are fighting for their families, their sacred altars, and their little property induces thousands of brave Southerners to remain in arms against such fearful odds as are now arrayed against them.

Mr. Kean, the young Chief of the Bureau of War, has come in from "the front," with a boil on his thigh. He missed the sport of the battle to-day.

Mr. Peck, the agent to purchase supplies for his starving fellow-clerks, confesses that he bought 10 barrels of flour and 400 pounds of bacon for himself; 4 barrels of flour for Judge Campbell, Assistant Secretary of War; 4 barrels for Mr. Kean, 1 for Mr. Cohen, and 1 for Mr. Shepherd. This has produced great indignation among the 200 clerks who sent him, and who got but 73½ pounds each, and they got 13 pounds of bacon each; while Mr. P. bought for himself 400 pounds.

ENGLAND AND THE CIVIL WAR:
DELAWARE, OCTOBER 1864

Samuel Francis Du Pont to William King Hall

A career naval officer, Samuel Francis Du Pont had commanded the South Atlantic Blockading Squadron at the capture of Port Royal Sound, South Carolina, in November 1861 and was promoted to rear admiral the following year. In April 1863 Du Pont led an unsuccessful attack on the fortifications guarding Charleston Harbor and was relieved of command of the South Atlantic squadron three months later. He wrote about the war to his friend Sir William King Hall, a captain in the Royal Navy he met while serving in China in 1858.

Near Wilmington, 13 Oct. 1864

My dear Hall,

I received a few days since your most kind letter of the 13th ultimo from Dover. You put coals of fire on my head by this second evidence of friendly remembrance, and the coals burned none the less that you had the delicacy not to allude to my delinquency.

Your letter after my return from the Southern coast was directed to Washington and was a long time reaching me. It found me much absorbed in my own affairs, and the reaction from two and a half years of intense war work, where the *pen* labor as you know is more than the sword, gave me a repugnance to taking up the former and threw me into procrastination, thus letting the accepted time go by. I sent you an especial message by Goodenough—it was a great pleasure to me to meet him; we talked over China affairs and you occupied a conspicuous place in our reminiscences.

Our friend Foote had scarcely passed away when his wife followed him; fortunately his children will be well cared for. He was a great loss to his country and to his profession. To myself he was a true friend to the last as you saw. For these reasons I greatly regretted him, but I had also an additional one, perhaps a selfish one. It would have been greatly to my professional interest had I been relieved in my command by him as first intended—things could not have gone differently at Charleston even with his skill, pluck, and prestige, and the question would have been more *quickly* settled with a small portion of our public and press. Time however has done this most effectually. I am proud to say the Navy never doubted. How could it? When did an admiral ever come out of an unsuccessful engagement with each and all of his commanding officers in *perfect accord* with *every* act from the beginning to end of the affair? These officers too had been selected with especial care for their professional cleverness, tried men under fire, and in all emergencies—yet differing much from each other. Never committed by me to any opinion, never consulted, and perfectly free to dissent and catch a popular breath. You saw a sample of them in Rodgers, and they were eleven in number—all have clung to me with hooks of steel. Unworthy ambition or an ugly temper among them might have entailed a controversy for life upon me, such as your service and ours have many examples. The controversy here has been kept up by ironmongers and their sympathizers, and I have not deigned to notice them. Strange as it may seem I have been simply the victim of *menials* in office, and I have been too proud to appeal to their superiors, who are too absorbed in this terrible rebellion to look themselves into individual cases. But, my dear Hall, I did not intend to go so much into my personal affairs, and you must ascribe my doing so to the kind remarks and inquiries in your two much prized letters.

You refer to our terrible civil war. I wish so much we could talk it over together—the subject is too vast to attempt even to allude to it in the brief space of a letter. We feel here how little the subject is understood in Europe, because our political institutions have never been comprehended there. One sentiment across the water seems quite pervasive and I perceive you share in it, viz., that we cannot be a united people again. Why should we be an exception to the world's history and to your own history in this respect? Is there bad blood between England and Scotland now? Is not Ireland united with you? How is it across the Channel? Has Louis Napoleon more devoted adherents than in Brittany? Your historians tell us there was a dead body or wounded man in every hamlet in La Vendée during the civil war in that desolated country—where the forests were burned in order to extinguish the last haunts of the opposition, smoked and burnt out, after the manner of Pélissier in Algeria.

All right-minded Christian men must be shocked at the atrocities of civil war—it entails countless woes, and its ramifications of evil are infinite—and ours is a gigantic one, having no parallel in history. But who made it and who fired the first gun? The patience and forbearance of the North only brought on arrogance and insult to add to the injury done—those silly duelists and bowie-knife knights thought the North would not fight. But what has caused me most surprise has been the course pursued by England in these our troubles. During previous years when slavery, the whole and sole cause of our rebellion, began to excite our land, England aided and abetted in every way the extremists in the North on this vexed question. Enthusiasts, including members of Parliament, traveled over the land exhorting and reproaching us for having an institution so repugnant to our political organization. Dukes and duchesses threw open their gilded mansions to the authoress of a clever antislavery novel—she was feted throughout the kingdom. Lord Brougham insulted our minister in London, Mr. Dallas, by the tone, manner, and occasion on which he called the latter's attention to the presence of a Negro admitted as a member of a society where the nobility and gentry of the land were assembled. In short all that brought upon us the taunts of England for the last quarter of a century were of Southern origin and growth—slavery, repudiation, filibustering, lynch law! What then was the surprise of the nation to find that England not only immediately recognized the Southern Confederacy as belligerents but gave her sympathy to their cause, backed by material aid. As if aware of the inconsistency involved, the British press represented that it was a tariff quarrel—it had nothing to do with slavery, etc. Why! Jefferson Davis has recently stated that they have lost two millions of the four millions of slaves, doubtless a great exaggeration to suit the purpose in hand. Still we have already 100,000 of them in the ranks of the Army, and as the latter march South those not "run off" are practically liberated, amounting now I should think to about one million. Be the process what it may, slavery was sure to fall with the first gun.

To the general *sore* produced by the withdrawal of all sympathy with the North have been added special acts calculated to irritate a nation—such as the destruction of our commerce by privateers, built, equipped, and manned in the United Kingdom; rejoicing at our defeats; making that poor creature Semmes a hero, and British naval officers of high rank and position getting up subscriptions to replace his sword. When Buchanan surrendered in the *Tennessee* after the most wonderful of naval combats and was lying wounded, he *sent* his sword to Farragut by his aide. All these matters to my deep regret have reopened the wounds of the wars of the Revolution and of 1812–15. These had become healed and forgotten, and replaced by most cordial sentiments of regard and admiration—even the Fourth of July orations were less and less vaunting on the olden times, and the country looked upon England as the great bulwark of liberty and Protestantism in the old world, as we hoped to be in the new.

The war has lasted longer than most persons believed. We have blundered dreadfully, as all free people and popular governments do at the first. The pervading radical error has been to permit the contest to become an equal one—this equilibrium has lasted now three and a half years but is fortunately disappearing; our superior numbers are telling everywhere as they should have done in the beginning. When those foolish Carolinians fired the first gun on Sumter, which sounded the death knell of slavery, the North rose *en masse* and we could have had a half million of men in a week as we had 75,000 in a day—and in that case the rebellion would have been crushed out in a year.

In June last we had raised 1,800,000 men (official records), for our people never flinched. In September 300,000 more were called for and are all enlisted at this date, volunteers mostly. These great masses have been better paid, fed, clothed, and armed, the wounded more cared for, and the system of sanitary appliances more complete than ever known before in the history of armies. Among the causes of delay in closing up this ugly work, I ought to have mentioned that when the rebellion broke out, it had four full months the start of us. The government was in the hands of Southern sympathizers, to use a mild expression. The Secretary of War, the Secretary of the Treasury, and of the Interior were all three traitors, the two first now in arms. Our small Army had been sent to Texas and to Utah among the Mormons—and our Southern forts, arsenals, and depots were purposely left without garrisons and fell without a show of resistance. Our few ships in commission had also been scattered and were kept away. We soon had 3,500 miles of coast to blockade. Four squadrons were organized—in my section of the coast I had sixty-odd vessels; Farragut has now ninety. Very great efforts were made to create this immense navy, for we always apprehended intervention—not on the part of England, for I always believe the word of a British minister, but that Gallic gentleman is a very freaky personage.

I have not spoken of the blockade running—that must be charged to the cupidity of man and is irrespective of country; our injuries from it were greatly aggravated by having your colonies, the Bermudas and Bahamas, on our flanks for depots and entrepots, and the Havana as the fitting-out place for the Gulf coast. The last port now run into to any extent will soon be effectually closed. Have you ever reflected how steam has changed, indeed inverted almost, the old system of blockades— the advantages are nine tenths in favor of the *runner*. In olden times of sailing ships, a frigate and her boats were sufficient to cover almost any one port. I wrote a paper on this subject while on the coast to satisfy our people—if I could put my hands on it I would send it to you. Notwithstanding the difficulties, the captures have amounted to twenty-six millions of dollars—one half goes to the officers and men.

But, my dear Hall, I must bring this letter to a close. I doubt if you ever ask me again to write you a long one. I have been compelled to scribble in haste for I leave my home today to be absent some weeks, to attend to my church matters, for I am president and member of various societies which meet in Boston this year. You of course hear of and see occasionally your former chief, Sir Michael Seymour—if he has not forgotten me, will you make my best regards; I have always spoken of him as a model admiral and gentleman.

Also whenever you may meet any of my old China friends please mention me—Sir Robert McClure, Shadwell, Hand,

Osborn, Dew, Saumarez, Hoskins, etc. I saw much of Captain Hancock of the *Immortalité* and fancied him prodigiously. He brought Barnard of the *Nile* to see me while I was in New York last year—their ships were in magnificent order, and I think I have never seen even in former days so fine a crew as the *Nile*'s. You do wonders in keeping up your sailors in spite of steam and iron pots. I missed Sir Alexander Milne but had a kind note from him, from Halifax.

You asked me about our spirit ration. It worked well with me for some ten months, until I left—the sailors were perfectly satisfied; drunken mechanics who ship as landsmen complain the most. Congress have no intention of repealing the law.

Until I can find the report of my monitor captains which you ask for, I enclose a letter of mine which covers most of my affairs—and which may afford you some interest.

I also enclose a "carte de visite" which perhaps Mrs. Hall will do me the honor to accept. Mrs. Du Pont bids me ask for yours if you have one. Mine, my relations and friends pronounce the only good one that has been taken of me.

I sent your message to Mr. Reed and I suppose he got Goodenough to give you one in return—he requested me to do so at the time, saying he had frequently inquired after you.

When this war closes I hope to go to Europe with Mrs. DP—it may not be a great while, though everyone has stopped predicting except the newspapers. The rebels now seem sorely pressed, if we take their own *accounts*, more than ever before; they admit a want of men and their armies are greatly thinned by desertions.

I hope your children are quite recovered and that Mrs. Hall is now well—please present me respectfully and cordially to her, and believe me, my dear Hall, Yours most sincerely,

S. F. Du Pont

WAR NEWS: NORTH CAROLINA, OCTOBER 1864
Catherine Edmondston: Diary, October 18, 1864

Catherine Edmondston followed news of the war and the northern elections from her plantation in North Carolina. The congressional elections held in Indiana, Ohio, and Pennsylvania on October 11 had resulted in Republican gains in all three states.

OCTOBER 18, 1864

On Sunday the 16th Father & Mama left us for their own home, the early frost having rendered such a step safe a full month earlier than usual. I all day yesterday with Mr E at the plantation; his molasses mills being out of order he was kept busy all day. Have just gathered my tea nuts, nearly a peck of them & clipped my Tea plants a second time. How I wish we had plants enough to supply us; we would laugh at Yankee Blockaders.

The war news is good. We repulsed a heavy attack on the North side of the James on the Darby town road on Tuesday the 11th. Our loss small; that of the enemy heavy. In the Valley our cavalry have met with a repulse from pressing too far ahead of their infantry supports annoying Sheridan's rear. We lost five guns & many prisoners, but Early coming up, Sheridan continued to fall back. Grant has issued an order which, for barbarity, equals anything yet done in this most barbarous of all wars. He directs the Valley of Va to be laid entirely waste, everything which can support life to be destroyed and all the stock of all kind to be driven off or killed. His Lieutenants are carrying it out to the letter! In one day Sheridan reports he burned [ ] Mills, [ ] Barns filled to the roof with wheat, oats, & corn enough to maintain Early for three months, all the farming implements, the seed wheat, has fed 3000 sheep to his army & driven off stock & horses in such quantity that there has been as yet no account taken of them! Grant tells him "to leave the Valley such a waste that next year a crow flying across will have to carry his own rations with him." What a monster! Fit associate for Butler & Sherman! He is a disgrace to humanity! His cheif engineer was killed by a band of guerrillas & as retaliation he ordered every dwelling within an area of five miles to be burnt! I preserve Grants order & Sheridans report, both official, & such conduct is tolerated by a nation who *calls itself Christian*!

From Georgia we get but little news, the War Depart surpressing all details for fear of giving information to the enemy. Hood is well in Sherman's rear & has possession of the RR. We beleive we were victorious at Alatoona & that we captured 3000 Yankees altho Stanton reports officially that we were beaten with heavy loss. Rome is in our hands, but Stanton publishes a dispatch from that point. Atlanta we beleive to be evacuated but of that have no confirmation, mere rumours. One thing is certain, Stanton & Lincoln are terribly alarmed & lie more than ever to hide their fears & to prevent their reverses having an unfavourable effect on the coming election. By their falsities they have influenced in their favor the Penn & Ohio State Elections & if they can continue keep the public mind in the dark until the 8th of next month, it may be well for them. Grant us overwhelming victories at all points ere then! But why should I wish to disappoint them? Lincolns election, if there is a choice, is better for us than McClellan's, because he is the greater fool. I honestly beleive McClellan will be a better President for the Yankees & a more formidable antagonist to us than Lincoln; so therefore, Hurrah for Lincoln, the greatest and most corrupt fool of the age! He has attempted to buy off McClellan from the Presidential contest by an offer of the command of the army, flattering him with the assurance that a man of his patriotism will, he is sure, choose that post in which he can render the greatest service to his country & that his (McClellan's) military are greater than his diplomatic talents, but little Mac is "too old a bird to be caught by such chaff."

UNITY AND CIVIL FREEDOM:
NEW YORK, OCTOBER 1864

Francis Lieber: Lincoln or McClellan

October 1864

A German immigrant who taught history and political science at Columbia College, Francis Lieber had drafted General Orders No. 100, an influential code of the laws of war issued by the Union army in April 1863. Lieber also served as the president of the Loyal Publication Society, which published dozens of pamphlets and broadsides supporting the Union cause. In September 1864 Lieber wrote *Lincoln oder McClellan? Aufruf an die Deutschen in Amerika* for circulation among German-American voters. The Loyal Publication Society published an English translation of the pamphlet in October, as well as a Dutch version. Before receiving his professorship at Columbia, Lieber had taught at South Carolina College for twenty years. His eldest son had joined the Confederate army and been mortally wounded in 1862, while his other two sons served as Union officers and would survive the war.

LINCOLN OR McCLELLAN.
APPEAL TO THE GERMANS IN AMERICA.
TRANSLATED FROM THE GERMAN BY T. C.*

COUNTRYMEN AND FELLOW-CITIZENS:

The presidential election is rapidly approaching, and it is time for every citizen to reflect and decide conscientiously for whom he shall give his ballot. At an election of such impor-

---

* This appeal was written several weeks before the letter of Alexander H. Stephens to some friends in Georgia, and the report of Judge Advocate Holt, on the conspiracy in this country, for the subversion of its government in favor of the rebels, were published. These two documents, the first speaking of "the ultimate and absolute sovereignty of the states," the other showing many prominent men of the Chicago Convention loaded with crimes of the deepest dye—these documents would have furnished the writer of the appeal with many sad illustrations.—*Translator.*

tance, when everything dear to us, as citizens, is staked on the issue, it is unworthy—it is cowardly—to throw away the right of voting. No patriot will choose political impotency at this crisis. The entire political existence of this country, of which we became citizens by the choice of our mature years, and not by the accident of birth, rests upon the free ballot; and he who has the right, has also the duty to vote. If sensible and honest voters stay away from the polls, they may be sure that those whose votes have been bought, and those who have no right to vote at all, will be ready there to appear in their stead.

The great majority of those who come from Germany to America are Democrats in the true sense, and when they find in this country a large party, which for years has been called the Democratic party, many allow themselves to be deceived by the mere name. The assemblage which gathered at Chicago, and nominated General McClellan for the Presidency, also calls itself the Democratic party—and of what sort of people was this mixed-up convention composed? In the first place, a great proportion consisted of old "Know-nothings." They openly proclaimed themselves such. Can you, Germans, vote on the same side with these men, whose only principle has been to shut in your faces the gates of this wide continent, to which their own fathers came from Europe, or else, as you are here already, to take from you the right of citizenship? Will you vote with those who, like their friends, the rebels, would load you with infamy, and who speak of you as the offscouring of the earth? The Know-nothings plot in secret. They have their lodges, and form a secret society. Is that, in a free country, democratic? Freedom, above all, rests on publicity.

Another portion of the Chicago convention consisted of those who set State-Rights, as they call it, above everything else; who openly say that Americans have not a country! and that the sovereignty of the single state stands high above everything else—is absolute; that each state has the right to tear itself away, and be a separate dominion; that there is therefore no right anywhere to compel such a state to remain in the Union. They utter untruths, and they know it! What would these same people have done if Ohio or Massachusetts had suddenly broken away and declared itself a monarchy? What do the rulers in Richmond at this very instant say of those men in North Carolina, who desire to withdraw their own state from the so-called confederacy? They call them rebels. How comes it that, up to this very day, there are men sitting in the congress at Richmond, as delegates from Missouri and Kentucky? Have these states seceded? Why have the rebels all along claimed Maryland as belonging to them? The delegates from Kentucky and Missouri sit in their congress; Maryland troops fight in their ranks, because Kentucky, Missouri, and Maryland are, or were, slaveholding states. With these enemies of the Union, therefore, slavery is the principle of cohesion of a new country, and state-sovereignty is not the basis of the right of secession. Why did these gentlemen all support General Jackson, when the old hero told South Carolina she should be compelled, by force of arms, to stay in the Union? And is the doctrine of state-sovereignty democratic? I feel almost ashamed to ask such a question of a German. The Democracy has always, and everywhere, been for the unity of the country; it will have but one country, worthy of a great nation. All Pumpernickel sovereignties, all the "Algerine states," as in Germany they are now called, have always been objects of loathing and execration to the Democracy.

Unquestionably each state in the United States has its rights, and ought to have them. But so, too, each man has his rights, and the rights of the individual which belong to every person in a free country are far more valuable, and are more important, taken on the whole, than the rights of states are. But the individual man is not for this reason a sovereign. Do you know that the word "sovereignty" does not once occur in that great instrument, the Constitution of the United States? The word "sovereignty" was smuggled into our political dictionary when this Constitution had already been adopted. Who then is sovereign in America if the states are not? Nobody! No man, no corporation, no congress, no president, no officer, no body of men, is sovereign in a free country. The United States are sovereign in respect to all other sovereign nations. We are sovereign when we treat with France and England, or when we engage in war; but within the country itself no one is sovereign.

This is no new theory, nor is it any theory at all. It is a fact.

Two hundred years ago, when the famous Bill of Rights was under consideration in the English Parliament, the greatest lawyer in England declared that the word "sovereign" was not known to English law. He said this because the dynasty which had just then been expelled had constantly talked of the king's sovereign power.

But can it be necessary to argue with Germans against a hankering after petty state domination and provincial pomposity. State sovereignty, indeed! Have we not had enough of that sort of thing in the land from which we came? If a German wants to have a stew of states, he never need come for it to America. Has he not got enough of sovereign states, big, little, and minute, at home?

What are the ideas which most animate the German in Germany? They are the unity of Germany and civil freedom. And shall he here give his vote for those who would see the country torn asunder in fragments while the cause of human slavery should triumph?

German working men! why did you leave home, family, the friends of your youth, and seek this distant America? It was because you had heard that in the United States you would find a country wherein you and your children would enjoy all the rights of the free citizen; where skill and industry would surely find their reward, and where your children would never find themselves debarred from any merited attainment by the privileges of others. If then you would not have, in place of this Union, a land where the working man should be delivered over to a grinding tyranny far worse than any endured in the oppressed countries of Europe, do not lend your aid to the party which would give up the Union to the dominion of the Southern landholders.

For do you know what this slave-owning, would-be oligarchy pretends to aim at? Perhaps you suppose they struggle only to retain possession of their negro slaves. The Southern slaveholders are fighting for that which was for so long a time the prerogative of the owners of the soil, the privilege of using the working man, whether white or black, as the instrument of their power, their pleasure, and their arrogance. The working man is to bear all the burdens of the state, but he is to have no rights in it. It is for him to obey, and for the rich man alone to rule. Hear what the secession leaders have said:

> "No state can endure in which the laboring class has political rights. Those alone who own the soil and the capital must govern and be the masters of those who labor."

And they say this, remember it well:

> "Capital has an inherent right to own labor."

If you would have masters set up over you, on this principle, vote for McClellan. Would you retain your equal rights as the citizens of a free country, vote for Lincoln, who has been an honest working man like yourselves.

Another part of the Chicago Convention consisted of those who seem to believe that all can be made right if people will only keep on shouting "the Constitution, the Constitution," as loud as they can.

We think we understand the Constitution quite as well as these gentlemen, and respect it more. For it should be noticed that the so-called Democratic party has of late years always set the Constitution aside whenever it seemed to be for their advantage. Was Nullification constitutional? Was it constitutional when Mr. Douglas, shortly before the last Presidential election, promised the South to advocate a law subjecting to heavy punishment the mere discussion of the slavery question? Was it constitutional, when, for twenty years, and probably longer, the letterbags in the South were opened to see whether they contained abolition documents? Was it constitutional to deny the right of petition? Is Secession constitutional? Is it consistent with the Constitution to say with those Chicago people that it is the President's right and duty to release any State that may desire to leave the Union? Is it constitutional to speak of secession as "one of the reserved rights of the State"? Is it constitutional to declare that our whole political State-structure exists only to benefit a single class of men—a class known by the complexion of the skin? Even the ancient heathen had a higher view of the State and of the objects of civil government. Is it constitutional to represent one whole government as a mere Confederation or League—that poorest of all governments for a modern and free people? Was it in the spirit of the Constitution when Mr. Calhoun and all his followers proclaimed that the Senate should always be equally divided between slave states and free states, thus making for the first time in our history slavery an immutable institution? Was the precious Ostend proclamation conceived in a constitutional spirit?

We too honor the Constitution, but the Constitution is not a deity. We love our country, the nation, freedom; and these things are superior even to the Constitution; and it should never be forgotten that by this Southern Rebellion a state of things is brought upon us for which the Constitution never was, and never could be calculated. Shall we fold our hands, as did Mr. Buchanan, and declare that nothing can be done on our part to save the country because the Constitution does not prescribe what we are to do in such a case? Such was the opinion which his Attorney-General of the United States gave to Mr. Buchanan. God forbid! We are one nation; we mean to remain one people, and our country must not be suffered to perish. The life of the patient must be saved whether the case is mentioned in the recipe book or not. The Constitution did not make the people, for the people made the Constitution. But has the Constitution been violated at all? We have not space for an examination of the question. But, my countrymen, admitting that some things may have occurred which could not be justified by existing laws, I am, as I think I may safely say, as well acquainted with the history of the past as any of these Chicago gentlemen, and I can advisedly affirm that never yet has there been any civil war, nor even any ordinary war in which the government has tolerated the thousandth part of that liberty which the enemies of the Government and the friends of those enemies enjoy among us—infinitely more, than the latter would allow us in a reversed case.

It is the so-called Democratic party which has brought this civil war upon us, and now they say that they only can end it. Why so? Does a man in America acquire some mysterious power or wisdom as soon as he calls himself a Democrat? They want to make up a peace, to give still greater guarantees to the South— everything to the rebels; in short, they belong to those in the North who have always been the obsequious servants of the

South, and who seem to think themselves honored by fulfilling the behests of an arrogant slaveholder. Is that Democracy?

My friends, let us vote for Lincoln. Many of you doubtless say that he has done some things which you do not like, or that sometimes he has not acted with sufficient promptitude. But the simple question before the people now is, shall Lincoln or McClellan be the next President? No other man can be elected; and now is there a German who can hesitate, or one who can be so indifferent as not to vote for either. The one candidate is *national*, the other is not. The one is for freedom and for the removal of that which is the disgrace of this century—he is opposed to slavery, which has brought upon us the demon of civil war. The other would preserve slavery. The one is out-spoken and candid; is the other so? The one is for all the citizens of this great country, whether they were born here or not; the other owes his nomination in a great degree to the Know-Nothings. The one is truly a Democrat—he is a man of the people; the other is no real Democrat—at least those who have set him up before the people are anything but democratic in feeling. The one, though surrounded by unparalleled difficulties, has at least so guided the ship of state that we are now in sight of the desired haven; the other, when he was at the head of one of the grandest armies that had been seen in a century, did little more than hesitate, when he might, as the enemy now admits, have put an end to the war.

It is easy to understand why some very rich and some very poor Germans, who want to get into office, exert themselves for McClellan. But of every German who has no such views, who simply gives his vote for the honor, the unity, and the freedom of his adopted country, and who does not allow himself to be deluded by the mere name of "Democrat," we may naturally expect that when he has calmly reflected on the vast importance of the occasion, and the character of the candidates, he will vote for Lincoln.

Every citizen ought to exert himself to the utmost in this remarkable election, when a great nation is called upon at the very crisis of a gigantic civil war, to elect a ruler by the popular and untrammelled ballot. It is not sufficient to carry the election of Mr. Lincoln by a bare overplus of numbers. A sweeping national majority is required to prove to Europe, to the South, and to its friends here in the midst of us, that this people is resolved to maintain this country in its integrity, a great and unimpaired commonwealth. The result of this election should be like a great national harvest, garnering its full sheaves from every portion of the land.

ELECTION RESULTS: NEW YORK, NOVEMBER 1864

George Templeton Strong: Diary, November 9, 1864

Sherman's capture of Atlanta, Sheridan's victories in the Shenandoah Valley, and McClellan's rejection of the peace plank in the Democratic platform brought about a reversal in Lincoln's political fortunes. On November 8 he became the first president to be reelected since Andrew Jackson in 1832, winning 55 percent of the popular vote and 212 of 233 electoral votes. George Templeton Strong followed the results in New York City.

VICTORIA! Te Deum laudamus. Te Dominum confitemur.
November 9. Laus Deo! The crisis has been past, and the most momentous popular election ever held since ballots were invented has decided against treason and disunion. My contempt for democracy and extended suffrage is mitigated. The American people can be trusted to take care of the national honor. Lincoln is reëlected by an overwhelming vote. The only states that seem to have McClellanized are Missouri, Kentucky, Delaware, and New Jersey. New York, about which we have been uneasy all day, is reported safe at the Club tonight. The Copperheads are routed—*Subversi sunt quasi plumbum in aequis vehementibus.* Poor "little Mac" will never be heard of any more, I think. No man of his moderate calibre ever had such an opportunity of becoming illustrious and threw it away so rapidly. Notwithstanding a certain lukewarmness in the national cause, his instincts and impulses were, on the whole, right and loyal. Had he acted on them honestly and manfully, he would have been elected. But his friends insisted on his being *politic*, and he had not the strength to resist them. He allowed Belmont and Barlow to strike out of his letter of acceptance a vigorous sentence declaring an armistice with armed rebels out of the question, and to append to it its unmeaning finale (which imposed on no man) stating that he assumed the views he had expressed to be what the Chicago

Convention really meant to say in its treasonous resolutions. *Fuit* McClellan, Napoleoniculus. Five years hence people will wonder how such a fuss ever came to be made about him.

A very wet, warm day. Copperheads talk meekly and well. "It's a terrible mistake, but we have got to make the best of it and support the government." The serene impudence of this morning's *World* can hardly be matched. It says the mission of the Democratic Party for the next four years will be to keep A. Lincoln from making a dishonorable disunion peace with the South. So a gentleman who has just received a sentence of four years in the State Prison might (if cheeky enough) inform the court and jury that their unjust decision would oblige him to be especially careful during his term that law and order were maintained throughout the state and that no crime failed to meet prompt punishment. The *World* is, moreover, uncommonly proud of the "Democratic masses" (Governor Seymour's "friends," the liquor dealers, roughs, and brutal Irishry of the city) because they committed no disorders yesterday, *though* so easily tempted to make a general row by the offensive and insulting presence of General Butler with sundry regiments to back him. . . .

George Anthon dined here, and we proceeded to the Union League Club, where was much folk. Discoursed with General Banks among others. It would seem that William E. Dodge is defeated by James Brooks, that most coprophagous of Copperheads, in this congressional district. A great pity, but Dodge's election was hardly hoped for. Would we were quite sure that Seymour is beaten! John Astor says he thinks Seymour's election would be more mischievous than McClellan's, and he may be right. Seymour and McClellan are weak men, but the latter means well. Seymour's instincts are all evil. He is quite as bad as Fernando Wood.

READING A SEALED PAPER:
WASHINGTON, D.C., NOVEMBER 1864

John Hay: Diary, November 11, 1864

Lincoln's secretary John Hay was present when the President read to his cabinet the memorandum he had written eleven weeks before the election.

———————

11 NOVEMBER 1864, FRIDAY

This morning Nicolay sent a dispatch from Illinois giving us 25000 majority and 10 Congressmen which we take to mean Wentworth Farnsworth Washburne Cook Ingersoll Harding Cullom Bromwell Kuykendall, and Moulton at Large, leaving the Copperheads Thornton Morrison Ross and Marshall.

At the meeting of the Cabinet today, the President took out a paper from his desk and said, "Gentlemen do you remember last summer I asked you all to sign your names to the back of a paper of which I did not show you the inside? This is it. Now, Mr Hay, see if you can get this open without tearing it!" He had pasted it up in so singular style that it required some cutting to get it open. He then read as follows:

> Executive Mansion
> Washington
> Aug. 23, 1864.

This morning, as for some days past, it seems exceedingly probable that this Administration will not be re-elected. Then it will be my duty to so cooperate with the President elect, as to save the Union between the election and the inauguration; as he will have secured his election on such ground that he cannot possibly save it afterwards.

A Lincoln.

This was indorsed:

William H. Seward
W. P. Fessenden
Edwin M Stanton
Gideon Welles

Edw. Bates
M Blair
JP Usher
August 23, 1864

The President said "you will remember that this was written at a time (6 days before the Chicago nominating convention) when as yet we had no adversary, and seemed to have no friends. I then solemnly resolved on the course of action indicated above. I resolved, in case of the election of General McClellan being certain that he would be the Candidate, that I would see him and talk matters over with him. I would say, 'General, the election has demonstrated that you are stronger, have more influence with the American people than I. Now let us together, you with your influence and I with all the executive power of the Government, try to save the country. You raise as many troops as you possibly can for this final trial, and I will devote all my energies to assisting and finishing the war.'"

Seward said, "And the General would answer you '*Yes, Yes*'; and the next day when you saw him again & pressed these views upon him he would say 'Yes—yes' & so on forever and would have done nothing at all."

"At least" added Lincoln "I should have done my duty and have stood clear before my own conscience."

Seward was abusing Forney today for a report of his (S's) remarks last night at the serenade, which appeared horribly butchered in the Chronicle, in which S.s Biblical lore is sadly out at the elbows.

The speech of the President at the two last Serenades are very highly spoken of. The first I wrote after the fact, to prevent the "loyal Pennsylvanians" getting a swing at it themselves. The second one, last night, the President himself wrote late in the evening and read it from the window. "Not very graceful" he said "but I am growing old enough not to care much for the manner of doing things."

Today I got a letter from Raymond breathing fire and vengeance against the Custom House which came so near destroying him in his District. I read it to the President. He answered that it was the spirit of such letters as that that created the faction and malignity of which Raymond complained.

It seems utterly impossible for the President to conceive of the possibility of any good resulting from a rigorous and exemplary course of punishing political dereliction. His favorite expression is "I am in favor of short statutes of limitations in politics."

RETALIATORY EXECUTIONS:
VIRGINIA, NOVEMBER 1864

John S. Mosby to Philip H. Sheridan

A lawyer from southwest Virginia, John S. Mosby had served in the 1st Virginia Cavalry and as a scout for Major General J.E.B. Stuart before being given command of a small detachment of partisan rangers in northern Virginia in January 1863. Using guerrilla tactics, Mosby raided Union outposts and supply wagons in Fairfax, Prince William, Fauquier, and Loudoun counties, sometimes striking within fifteen miles of Washington. By the summer of 1864 Mosby commanded about 300 men in the 43rd Battalion Virginia Cavalry, and in August he began attacking Sheridan's supply lines in the Shenandoah Valley. While the Confederate authorities considered members of the 43rd Battalion to be lawful combatants, most Union soldiers believed them to be no different from civilian guerrillas. On September 23 six of his men were captured near Front Royal during a skirmish in which a Union cavalry officer was mortally wounded while allegedly trying to surrender. Major General Alfred Torbert, Sheridan's cavalry commander, had two of the prisoners hanged, while the other four were shot by Union soldiers. Another one of Mosby's men was hanged on October 14 by Colonel William H. Powell in response to the killing of a Union soldier by two Confederate civilians. After receiving approval from Robert E. Lee, Mosby had seven Union prisoners selected on November 6 for retaliatory execution. The next day three of the prisoners were hanged, two were shot but survived after being left for dead, and two escaped unharmed. No further executions were authorized by either Sheridan or Mosby, but in late November Sheridan sent a cavalry division into Fauquier and Loudoun counties with orders to seize or destroy all food, forage, and livestock.

NOVEMBER 11, 1864.

Maj. Gen. P. H. SHERIDAN,
Commanding U. S. Forces in the Valley:

GENERAL: Some time in the month of September, during my absence from my command, six of my men who had been captured by your forces were hung and shot in the streets of Front Royal, by the order and in the immediate presence of

Brigadier-General Custer. Since then another, captured by a Colonel Powell on a plundering expedition into Rappahannock, was also hung. A label affixed to the coat of one of the murdered men declared that "this would be the fate of Mosby and all his men." Since the murder of my men not less than 700 prisoners, including many officers of high rank, captured from your army by this command, have been forwarded to Richmond, but the execution of my purpose of retaliation was deferred in order, as far as possible, to confine its operation to the men of Custer and Powell. Accordingly on the 6th instant seven of your men were, by my order, executed on the Valley pike, your highway of travel. Hereafter any prisoners falling into my hands will be treated with the kindness due to their condition, unless some new act of barbarity shall compel me reluctantly to adopt a course of policy repulsive to humanity.

Very respectfully, your obedient servant,

JNO. S. MOSBY,
Lieutenant-Colonel.

A SLAVEOWNER'S DECEPTION:
MARYLAND, NOVEMBER 1864

Jane Kamper: Statement Regarding Her Emancipation

The constitutional convention that met in Annapolis, Maryland, on April 27, 1864, voted in favor of the immediate abolition of slavery and rejected proposals to compensate slaveowners and to apprentice the minor children of freed slaves to their masters. After being approved by the voters in October, the new constitution went into effect on November 1, 1864. Two weeks later, a newly freed woman from the eastern shore of Maryland told the military authorities in Baltimore how her former master had tried to deceive her regarding the legal status of her children.

Balto. Novr 14"/64
Statement of Jane Kamper
Slave of Wm Townsend of Talbot County Md.

I was the slave of Wm Townsend of Talbot county & told Mr. Townsend of my having become free & desired my master to give my children & my bedclothes he told me that I was free but that my Children Should be bound to him. he locked my Children up so that I could not find them I afterwards got my children by stealth & brought them to Baltimore. I desire to regain possession of my bed clothes & furniture.

My Master pursued me to the Boat to get possession of my children but I hid them on the boat

her
Jane X Kamper (fn)
mark

"VOX POPULI, VOX DEI":
NEW YORK, NOVEMBER 1864

Maria Lydig Daly: Diary, November 15, 1864

In the November 8 election Lincoln lost New York City to McClellan by about 37,000 votes, but managed to carry the state by a margin of 6,749. Maria Lydig Daly reflected on the election results.

November 15, 1864

The election has taken place. Lincoln has been reelected. *Vox Populi, vox Dei*. So it must be for the best. All now left us is to put the shoulder to the wheel and do our best to draw the governmental machine out of the slough. There was some ill feeling about General Butler's being sent here to overawe the election. However, there seems to be little ill feeling on either side—a hopeful sign for the country. It is well that Lincoln has so large a majority, as now there will be no one to lay the blame upon.

I wish our political parsons could be done away with together with slavery. What autocrats they are! Beecher, a few Sundays since, before he began to preach, announced: "I am going to preach a political sermon, and if anyone does not like it, he can leave the church." A man rose up and gave three cheers for McClellan.

Poor McClellan! What a lesson he has had of the instability of popular favor and of fair-weather friends. None of his old companions-in-arms, hardly, have voted for him, and the reason is clear—it would not be the way to promotion. A lady said to me a few days since, "What, your husband votes for McClellan and you have a brother in the army?"

Yesterday, Mr. Theodore Fay from Bremen, our former minister to Prussia, came in. He is for Lincoln and quoted what he called "Mr. Lincoln's very appropriate though homely saying that a countryman in crossing a dangerous stream or ford would not willingly change horses." I answered very mildly that Mr. Lincoln was very happy in these little sayings, that like in Scripture, you could always find a story or text to suit the occasion. Now those who, like my husband, voted for McClellan, could quote another of his aphorisms as their excuse. When removing some General (Rosecrans, I believe), he said, "They that made the mess are not exactly the ones to finish it." Mr. Fay, however, is a perfectly sincere and conscientious man.

Butler has been serenaded and feted as though he had saved the country, whereas he did nothing. It was the policy of the Democrats to keep the peace, as they wanted to poll as many votes as possible, whereas the policy of the others was to institute, if possible, martial law. The Judge was asked to meet him on Saturday, but he did not go. Beecher, at the Loyal League Club, proposed him as the next President. In Butler's speech, he adopts McClellan's ideas and thinks everything should now be done to make peace.

Darley and his wife spent the evening with us. The Judge got out his theatrical portraits, I brought forward some doppelkümmel and cake, and we had quite a pleasant time around the blazing woodfire until twelve o'clock. Sunday likewise we had company: Mr. Hackett, Mr. Young, and Mr. Dykes. Tonight I am alone. The Judge has gone out with a great friend of his, a bookworm like himself, to see another of their species, and I shall write up all my letters. His "Chancellor Kent," I think, will be a great success. He has been much complimented on the opening chapters.

I have been writing an article explaining the reasons that we cannot find American goods and exposing the tricks of the manufacturers and shopkeepers, which Mr. Field has promised to publish.

Mrs. Dana came in to bid me good-by, and very kindly invited us to come and stay with her in Washington. Her husband is Assistant Secretary of War. I thought it very kind of her but declined. If I go at all, it will be only as the guest of Baron Gerolt. The dear old gentleman has just left us after a stay of a fortnight. I like him every day more and more. He is so good a Christian, so wise and observing, and so amiable and generous.

SHERMAN'S MARCH: GEORGIA, NOVEMBER 1864

James A. Connolly:
Diary, November 17–23, 1864

Hood continued his offensive against the Chattanooga–Atlanta railroad on October 13, capturing the Union garrison at Dalton and destroying twenty-five miles of track between Resaca and Tunnel Hill. He then moved his army into northern Alabama and advanced along the south bank of the Tennessee River until he reached Tuscumbia on October 31. Sherman pursued Hood as far as Gaylesville, Alabama, before returning to northwest Georgia. While Hood gathered supplies and prepared to invade Middle Tennessee, Sherman received Grant's approval on November 2 for his proposed march on Savannah. After sending 25,000 of his men north to help George H. Thomas defend Tennessee against Hood, Sherman burned much of Atlanta and began his march to the sea on November 15 with 62,000 troops. Major Connolly recorded the progress of the Union forces, which were opposed by about 13,000 Confederates, many of them Georgia militia.

———————

Thursday, Nov. 17th.
Division marched at daylight. Passed through Lithonia, on the R. R., at 9 A.M., where I noticed Gen. Sherman standing on the R. R. track giving directions as to how he wanted the track torn up and destroyed. Several buildings were burning as we passed through. We arrived at Conyers at noon, and as our Division had four miles of R. R. to destroy before moving any further, Capt. Acheson, who plays the piano finely, and myself started out to walk around through the town and find a piano, so that we could have some music while our soldiers were destroying the track. Meeting a little girl on the street who told us where there was a piano, we went to the house and on knocking at the door a grey headed, meek, ministerial looking old rebel opened the door and asked what we wanted. I had agreed to do the talking so I told him "we wanted" to destroy the R. R. first, and asked him what he thought of it. The old gent looked wise and said nothing; I then asked him if he had

a piano in the house; the old man looked worried and replied that his daughter had one. All right, said I, that's just what we want, we want some music; the old man said he didn't think his daughter could play, and looked incredulous when we pushed by him into the room, and the Captain sat down at the piano; but the Captain's fingers soon made the keys dance to the air of the Star Spangled Banner, and the old man sat there astonished at the thought that a rough, vulgar, brutal Yankee should be able to play so skillfully. Then the Captain played "Dixie" in excellent style; this made the old man talkative, brought in the daughter and some other young ladies, and we soon had them playing for us, while the Captain and I sat back and quietly enjoyed the discomfiture of the old man, and laughed at the efforts of the rebel damsels to appear composed. Finally, to cap the climax, we induced these Southern ladies to sing us the "Confederate Toast", which they told us was their favorite song, and one verse of it I remember, viz:

> "Here's to old Butler and his crew,
>   Drink it down!
> Here's to old Butler and his crew,
>   Drink it down!
> Here's to old Butler and his crew,
> May the devil get his due,
> Drink it down! Drink it down! Drink it down!"

We left them, though, notwithstanding their elegant and patriotic songs—they, no doubt, hoping we might be shot before night. Our troops having finished their work on the R. R. we moved forward 4 miles, and encamped on Mr. Zachry's plantation having marched 15 miles today, and utterly destroyed 4 miles of R. R. Old Zachry has a son who is a Colonel in the rebel army in Virginia, and the negroes, i. e. his own negroes tell us tonight that the old sinner has a federal flag hid away in his house which his son captured and sent home from Virginia a year ago. We have searched the house all over for it, but can't find it yet, and the old man and old woman deny having it, but one of their house servants told me most positively tonight that it *is* in the house, and that they know where it is. If we don't get it before we leave tomorrow morning the old fellow's house will surely be burnt, for the soldiers have all heard of it. They *did* burn the old fellow's cotton gin, filled with cotton, tonight. Passed through fine country today. Conyers is a village of about 500 inhabitants, and Lithonia about 300, both stations on the R. R.; a good many negroes came into camp with us tonight; they are of all shades and sizes; and are apparently happy if they can be permitted to go along with us.

Friday, Nov. 18th.

After striking tents this morning I took old Zachry out one side, and with an air of great concern, and in the greatest confidence told him that unless he produced that flag, the soldiers were determined to burn his house as soon as General Baird got out of sight. The old sinner was alarmed and asked me to leave him a guard until the soldiers all passed, at the same time protesting that he knew nothing about the flag. I, of course, told him that we never left guards, and parted from him, expressing deep sympathy, for I assured him that the soldiers would in all probability burn his house. In less than ten minutes the old rascal brought the flag out and delivered it up. I don't know whether his house was burned or not. I know he owns about 40 niggers less tonight than he did last night. We crossed "Yellow River" about noon, and commenced destroying R. R. just after crossing. We destroyed about 4 miles. Yellow River, where we crossed, is quite a deep clear stream, about 6 rods wide and with high bluff banks. I stopped at a dwelling on the east side of the river, which the occupants (Merriwether's) dignified with the name of "Airy Mount." Had quite a discussion here with a strong minded elderly woman, on Abolition and Amalgamation; the old lady forced it on me, and as there were three or four very light colored mulatto children running around the house, they furnished me an admirable weapon to use against the old lady's remark that the Northern people were Amalgamationists. She didn't explain to my entire satisfaction how her slaves came to be so much whiter than African Slaves are usually supposed to be. Marched on through Covington and encamped a short distance east of it. Covington is a place of some pretension, and on the whole is rather a pretty place. The houses are very neat, built in modern Southern style, and painted white. The good people of Covington only heard of our advance yesterday so they are all at home, not having had time to run away. The "leading citizens" were affable when we entered the place, and everybody invited officers to stay all night at their house. I was in the Court Room and Masonic Lodge, the door of which was open.

Saturday, Nov. 19th.

Division moved at daybreak and crossed the Ulcofauhatchee River. This stream is not very deep, rapid, without any well defined banks, the water spreading out and making a swamp on either side of the stream for a considerable distance. The name of this stream is pronounced by the inhabitants "Alcovy." Land in its vicinity looks very poor; the ears of corn only grow about 6 inches long, and the stalks are very light. An old man told us today that some of his land averaged 6 bushels of corn to the acre and some of it "don't average anything." There are no wealthy planters in the immediate vicinity of the "Ulcofauhatchee" along our line of march. The farms are all in hundred acre lots, but their owners call them "Plantations"; the citizens look at our troops as they pass, with the utmost astonishment; they have no idea where we are going, and the negroes stare at us with open eyes and mouths, but generally, before the whole column has passed they pack up their bundles and march along, going, they know not whither, but apparently satisfied they are going somewhere toward freedom; but these wretched creatures, or a majority of them, don't know what freedom is. Ask them where they are going as they trudge along with their bundles on their heads, and the almost invariable reply is: "Don't know Massa; gwine along wid you all." Our men are foraging on the country with the greatest liberality. Foraging parties start out in the morning; they go where they please, seize wagons, mules, horses, and harness; make the negroes of the plantation hitch up, load the wagons with sweet potatoes, flour, meal, hogs, sheep, chickens, turkeys, barrels of molasses, and in fact everything good to eat, and sometimes considerable that's good to drink. Our men are living as well as they could at home and are in excellent health. Rain falling all the forenoon, roads heavy and marching difficult. Passed through Sand Town today about 2 o'clock. It is a little weather beaten village of about 250 or 300 inhabitants. The citizens were not much expecting us, but they heard of our approach day before yesterday and have spent the time since in carrying off and hiding in the swamp their valuables, but the negroes told the soldiers of these hiding places and most of these hidden valuables found their way into our camp tonight. Went into camp at dark. We have neither seen nor heard of any armed rebels yet, and we march along with as much unconcern as if we were marching through Ohio. We are beginning to talk about Milledgeville, and speculate on the probabilities of a battle there. There can't be much of a battle there though, for we have troops enough to eat up all the army Georgia's capital can muster.

Sunday, Nov. 20th.

Division moved at daylight, and at 9 A.M. passed through "Shady Dale." I have known for the past 3 days that our line of march led through "Shady Dale", and judging from the name I had fancied to myself that Shady Dale was probably a nice, clean, quiet, aristocratic country town, situated in some romantic, shaded valley, and as we started this morning I retouched my mental picture of "Shady Dale", so that I might have it entirely finished to my taste before seeing the place itself, and then have the satisfaction of determining whether "there's anything in a name" by comparing my ideal "Shady Dale" with the real "Shady Dale." I am now satisfied that "there is something in a name", but it was proven to me this morning in a manner that totally surprised me. As we rode along we came to a beautiful plantation, and by the roadside was a cluster of about 50 whitewashed negro houses, and in the midst of them an old fashioned frame house with porch all around it and dormor windows. The negro houses were filled with nice cleanly looking negroes of all ages and sizes, and as the head of our column came up with band playing, such a nest of negroes I never saw before; they poured out of those cabins to the road side in such numbers as to lead me to suppose they had been packed away inside like mackerel in a barrel. The music of the band started the young niggers at dancing, and they capered around like little imps; the old ones stood with uncovered heads, hands raised, mouths open and eyes turned up; the young negresses stood bowing and curtseying, trying to bow to every soldier that passed; while each negro in his or her own style kept uttering ejaculations of wonder such as "Lawd, jest look at em"; "whar'd dey cum from"; "looks like de whole wuld was comin" &c, &c. Each one expressing his wonder in some original and quaint style. I sat on my horse and listened to and watched them, while I laughed at their comicalities until tears rolled down my cheeks. There is as much difference between the negroes we see in the North and the plantation negroes of the South, as there is between a cultivated gentleman and a clown in the circus ring.

Presently I asked a venerable old African patriarch where "Shady Dale" was, and he told me: "Dis is it massa"; why, said I, is it called "Shady Dale"? "Cos" said he grinning, "deres so many of us black uns here." Whereupon I laughed too, and rode on, satisfied that there *is* something in a name, when a plantation can figure on the maps as "Shady Dale", on account of the number of "Shades" living there. This plantation is owned by a man named "Whitfield", and it is the finest one I ever saw, but by the time our column has all passed Mr. Whitfield won't have a sweet potato, a pig, chicken, turkey, horse, mule, cow, and scarcely a nigger left. The negroes on all these plantations tell us their masters have given them no meat to eat during the past two years, and as a consequence the negroes have been in the habit of prowling about the country at night, foraging, as they call it; that is stealing chickens, hogs, &c, and killing them in the swamps. They raise turnips extensively through Georgia so far as we have been, and every turnip patch we pass is thoroughly stripped by the soldiers and negroes, who, by the way, make excellent foragers. Our stock of negroes is increasing rapidly; many of them travel on horseback now; they furnish their own, i. e., their masters, horses, saddles and bridles, so they are no expense to Uncle Sam; a great many of our privates are getting negro servants for themselves; the negro walks along beside the soldier, with his knapsack and cooking utensils strapped upon his back, thus relieving the soldier of his load, and helping him along. What soldier *wouldn't* be an abolitionist under such circumstances. We have marched through beautiful country today. Halted one hour for dinner. We made 18 miles today, and encamped 6 miles from Eatonton, and 27 from Milledgeville.

Monday, Novr. 21st.

Division moved at daylight. Crossed "Murder Creek" at noon, and went into camp 4 miles beyond, having marched only 9 miles today, and being, tonight within 18 miles of Milledgeville. Rain falling heavily all day. Roads in a horrible condition. Things have not looked promising today. What would become of us if this weather should continue two weeks? We couldn't march; would be compelled to halt here in the midst of a hostile country, and thus let the enemy have time to recover from his surprise and concentrate against us. Well, let the worst come, will get to the capital of Georgia anyhow, and my long desire to see it will at length be gratified. We are all wet through and covered with mud, and our horses jaded, but our supper of coffee, fried chickens, sweet potatoes, &c, and a good sleep will bring us out all right in the morning, and if our horses give out, the stable of some wealthy Georgian must furnish us a remount. Citizens everywhere look paralyzed and as if stricken dumb as we pass them. Columns of smoke by day, and "pillars of fire" by night, for miles and miles on our right and left indicate to us daily and nightly the route and location of the other columns of our army. Every "Gin House" we pass is burned; every stack of fodder we can't carry along is burned; every barn filled with grain is destroyed; in fact everything that can be of any use to the rebels is either carried off by our foragers or set on fire and burned.

Tuesday, Nov. 22d.

Division moved at daylight, crossing Cedar Creek at 9 A.M., passing through the camp of Morgan's Division, and taking the advance for Milledgeville. Rather cold today. I spent most of the day in advance of the column searching for roads to the capital and picking up such items of information as I could get from negroes and white citizens in regard to the enemy, but I have not been able to ascertain that there are any rebel soldiers in the city. The negroes and others say that all the soldiers that were in Milledgeville have gone to Macon, under command of General Howell Cobb. We are encamped tonight on a plantation belonging to "General Cobb," and the 23d Missouri has received permission to burn all the rails and buildings on the plantation tonight. General Sherman has his tents pitched in the dooryard of the overseer's house on this plantation tonight. About 3 P.M. while the column was halted I rode ahead in the direction of Milledgeville, in company with General Baird, Colonel Poe, chief topographical engineer on General Sherman's staff, and Captain Buttrick of our staff. After we had ridden about a mile ahead of the column, admiring the beautiful country and speculating on the probability of taking Milledgeville without fighting, we suddenly discovered a mounted man in the middle of the road coming toward us. He was then about one-half mile from us and just on the crest of a little hill in the road. He discovered us at the same time we did him and we halted at the same time. Glasses were out in a minute and we discovered that his uniform was gray. Ah, ha! This, then, is the outer picket watching our approach to the capital. This settles the question; we'll have to fight for Milledgeville. The solitary horseman in rebel uniform turned his horse toward the city and disappeared behind the crest of the hill. There were some negro houses by the roadside about half way between where we were and where the gray clad horseman appeared. The negroes were out in the road looking at us. We were very anxious to get as far down the road as the negro houses, but didn't think it safe. In a few moments two gray clad horsemen appeared on the hill. They looked at us—were counting us evidently; they turned their horses around uneasily. Presently another horseman appeared, then another and another, until at least twenty were in sight on the crest of the hill. They were evidently too strong for us, even if we had been well armed, which we were not. But they were at least half a mile from us and our column was only about a mile from us—the road behind us was good, we were well mounted and we felt that if they *did* make a dash at us we could run the mile back to our troops before they could overtake us. But what if one of our horses should stumble and fall in the chase? Oh, well! Let the rider jump over a fence and run as fast as he can somewhere, anywhere, to gain a few minutes time. But look! The gray clad horsemen are starting forward and now they are waving a white handkerchief. It must be a deputation of citizens coming out to surrender the capital to us. So the General thought; so we all thought. The General directed Colonel Poe to go forward and meet the party and see what they wanted and who they were. Forward dashed Poe, and there we sat watching the scene with intense anxiety. Can it be possible that we are to meet with such good fortune as to receive the formal surrender of Georgia's capital? Poe meets the horsemen, they halt a few moments, then Poe turns, and they all come on to where the General, Captain Buttrick and myself are waiting in the road. We ask each other what this means. Can there be treachery here? Do they mean to deceive us with a white flag and capture us all? They approach within 200 yards and we plainly see their rebel uniforms. Shall we run or stand? Moments are precious. They come steadily on. The General looks pale. I *feel* pale and nervous, but the General stands, and therefore I *must*. They reach us, rein up their horses and the gray clad officer riding at the head of the party salutes the General and announces himself and party as Kilpatrick's scouts just from Milledgeville; they say there is not a rebel soldier there. Hurrah! Milledgeville is ours, and our sensations are now quite different from what they were ten minutes ago. The scouts go on to report to General Sherman and we ride on to the negro houses ahead, which the negroes tell us belong to "Ginral Cobb." In the dooryard of the overseer's house stand three large new iron kettles for boiling sorghum. Poe picked up an axe and with a few blows shivered one of them into atoms. Buttrick took the axe and shivered the second one. I then took the axe and paid my respects to "Ginral Cobb" by shattering the third one. The General sent back and ordered the troops forward and placed them in camp on the arch rebel's plantation. General Sherman coming up in about an hour, placed his headquarters in the yard where we broke the sorghum kettles. About dark this evening, it is said, the old negro who is the commissary of the plantation told some of General Sherman's staff officers that he wanted to see the great General, just to see how he looked. He was taken to the door of Sherman's tent, and the old man took off his hat, looked at the General a few moments, then bowing respectfully turned and walked off, saying to himself as he walked off shaking his head: "He's got the Linkum head, the Linkum head, he's got the Linkum head." We are only ten miles from Milledgeville tonight.

Wednesday, Nov. 23d.

Division moved at daylight. A bright, beautiful day; roads excellent and surrounding country magnificent. We reached the capital at about 9 A.M., but our troops didn't get up until noon on account of the 20th Corps, which came in from Eatonton, entering the city on the same road with us and in advance of us, as they struck the road first. Our troops encamped just outside the city limits on the west side. Our headquarters in the city in a dwelling house of some runaway citizen. General Davis' headquarters in the city near the Governor's mansion. General Sherman's in the mansion and General Slocum's at the Milledgeville Hotel, opposite the capitol square. Here I am, finally, at Milledgeville. My boyish desire is gratified, and I find that my boyish fancy in regard to the appearance of the city was quite correct. The dwellings are scattered and surrounded by large and tastefully decorated grounds. As one rides along its sandy streets, even at this season of the year, the faint perfume from every variety of tree and shrub, bud, blossom and flower fills the air with delicious fragrance. The exterior of the residences bespeak refinement within, and everything about the city serves to impress one with the idea that he is in an old, aristocratic city, where the worth of a man is computed in dollars and cents. The streets are regularly laid out and the capitol stands on a slight elevation rather east of the center of the city and overlooking the Oconee River. It is built of reddish looking sandstone and is a large square building, with rather a superabundance of fancy cornice outside. It has entrances on the north, south, east and west, each having a broad flight of stone steps. The offices and State library are on the first floor, the legislative halls on the second floor, and also the committee rooms. Each chamber has life size oil paintings of the prominent old men of Georgia hung around its walls in plain gilt frames. I should have thought "Oglethorpe" would have appeared in this State picture gallery, but he does not. General Jackson does, though, tricked out in a line officer's coat with a general's epaulettes on his shoulders, a line officer's sash around his waist, and a sort of cross between a Turkish scimeter and an artillery sabre by his side. Our soldiers and even some officers have been plundering the State library today and carrying off law and miscellaneous works in armfuls. It is a downright shame. Public libraries should be sacredly respected by all belligerents, and I am sure General Sherman will, some day, regret that he permitted this library to be destroyed and plundered. I could get a thousand dollars worth of valuable law books there if I would just go and take them, but I wouldn't touch them. I should feel ashamed of myself every time I saw one of them in my book case at home. I don't object to stealing horses, mules, niggers and all such *little things*, but I will not engage in plundering and destroying public libraries. Let them alone, to enlarge and increase for the benefit of the loyal generations that are to people this country long after we shall have fought our last battle and gone into our eternal camp. The State penitentiary was burned last night. There are but few business buildings here, and the population never could have been more than ten thousand. I shall devote myself to looking around town tomorrow, as I understand we will not march in the morning.

"THE BITTER END": NOVEMBER 1864

John Wilkes Booth: "To whom it may concern"

In August 1864 the actor John Wilkes Booth, a fervent Confederate sympathizer, began recruiting potential co-conspirators in a plot to abduct President Lincoln, take him to Richmond, and use him as a hostage in order to force the resumption of prisoner exchanges. Booth visited his sister, Asia, in Philadelphia in the latter part of November while on his way to New York, where he would appear with his brothers Edwin and Junius in a benefit performance of *Julius Caesar* on November 25. During this visit Booth gave his sister a packet for safekeeping that contained two letters. One was addressed to Booth's mother, while the other was probably intended for Asia's husband, John Sleeper Clarke, a successful comic actor and theater manager whom Booth had quarreled with over politics. Addressed "To whom it may concern," it would be published in the *Philadelphia Inquirer* on April 19, 1865, the day after Clarke turned it over to the U.S. marshal in Philadelphia.

1864

My Dear Sir

You may use this, as you think best, but as *some*, may wish to know *when*, *who*, and *why*, and as I know not, *how*, to direct, I give it (in the words of your Master)

"To whom it may concern"

Right, or wrong, God, judge me, not man. For be my motive good or bad, of one thing I am sure the lasting condemnation of the north.

I love peace more than life. Have loved the Union beyond expression. For four years have I waited, hoped and prayed for the dark clouds to break And for a restoration of our former sunshine, to wait longer would be a crime. All hope for peace is dead, my prayers have proved as idle as my hopes. 'God's will be done.' I go to see, and share the bitter end.

I have ever held the South were right. The very nomination of Abraham Lincoln four years ago, spoke plainly—war—war upon Southern rights and institutions, his election proved it. "Await an overt act" yes till you are bound and plundered, what folly, the South were wise, who thinks of argument or patience when the finger of his enemy presses on the trigger. In a *foreign war*, I too could say "Country right or wrong," but in a struggle *such as ours* (where the brother tries to pierce the brothers heart.) for God's sake choose the right. When a country like this spurns *justice* from her side, She forfeits the allegiance of every honest freeman, and should leave him untrammeled by any fealty soever, to act, as his conscience may approve.

People of the north, to hate tyranny to love liberty and justice, to strike at wrong and oppression, was the teaching of our fathers. The study of our early history will not let *me* forget it, and may it never.

This country was formed for the *white* not for the black man. And looking upon *African slavery* from the same standpoint, held by those noble framers of our Constitution. I for one, have ever considered *it*, one of the greatest blessings (both for themselves and us,) that God ever bestowed upon a favored nation. Witness heretofore our wealth and power, witness their elevation in happiness and enlightment above their race, elsewhere, I have lived among it most of my life and have seen *less* harsh treatment from Master to Man, than I have beheld in the North from father to son. Yet Heaven knows *no one* would be willing to do, *more* for the negro race than I, could I but see a way to still better their condition. But Lincoln's policy is only preparing the way, for their total annihilation, The South *are not. nor have they been fighting* for the continuance of slavery, the first battle of Bull-run did away with that idea. Their causes *since* for *war*, have been as *noble*, and *greater far than those that* urged our *fathers on, Even* should we allow, they were *wrong* at the beginning of this contest, *cruelty and injustice*, have made the wrong become the *right*. And they stand *now*, (before the wonder and admiration of the *world*,) as a noble band of patriotic heroes. Hereafter, reading of *their deeds*, Thermopylae will be forgotten.

When I aided in the capture and execution of John Brown, (Who was a murderer on our Western Border, and who was fairly *tried* and *convicted*,—before an impartial judge & jury—of treason,—And who by the way has since been made a

God—I was proud of my little share in the transaction, for I deemed it my duty And that I was helping our common country to perform an act of justice. But what was a crime in poor John Brown, is now considered (by themselves) as the greatest and only virtue, of the whole Republican party. Strange transmigration, *vice* to become a *virtue*. Simply because *more* indulge in it. I thought then, *as now*, that the abolitionists, *were the only traitors* in the Land, And that the entire party, deserved the fate of poor old Brown, not because they wish to abolish slavery, but on account of the means they have ever endeavored to use, to effect that abolition. If Brown were living, I doubt if he *himself*, would set slavery, against the Union. Most, or many, in the North do, and openly curse the Union, if the South are to return and retain a *single right* guaranteed them by every tie which we once *revered as sacred*. The south can make no choice, It is either extermination, or slavery for *themselves*, (worse than death) to draw from, I would know *my* choice.

I have, also, studied hard to discover upon what grounds, the rights of a state to Secede have been denied, when our very name (United States) and our Declaration of Independence, *both* provide for secession. But there is no time for words. I write in haste, I know how foolish I shall be deemed, for undertaking such a step, as this, where on the one side, I have many friends, and everything to make me happy. Where my profession *alone* has gained me an income of *more than* Twenty thousand dollars a year. And where my great personal ambition in my profession has such a great field for labor. On the other hand—the south have never bestowed upon me one kind word, A place now, where I have no friends, except beneath the sod. A place where I must either become a private soldier, or a beggar. To give up all of the *former* for the *latter*, besides my mother and sisters whom I love so dearly, (although they so widely differ with me in opinion) seems insane, But God is my judge I love *justice*, more, than I do a country, that disowns it. More than fame and wealth, more—(Heaven pardon me if wrong) more than a happy home. I have never been upon a battlefield, but O my countrymen, could you all but see the *reality* or effects of this horrid war, as I have seen them (in *every State*, save Virginia) I know you would think like me,

And would pray the Almighty to create in the northern mind a sense of *right* and *justice*, (even should it possess no seasoning of mercy.) and that he would dry up this Sea of blood between us,—which is daily growing wider, Alas—poor country, Is she to meet her threatend doom; Four years ago, I would have given a thousand lives, to see her remain, (as I had always known her) powerful and unbroken. And even now I would hold my life as naught, to see her what she was. O my friends if the fearful scenes of the past four years had never been enacted, or if what has been, had been but a frightful dream, from which we could now awake, with what overflowing hearts could we bless our God and pray for his continued favor, How I have loved the *old flag* can never, now, be known. A few years since and the entire world could boast of *none*, so pure and spotless, But I have of late been seeing and hearing of the *bloody deeds* of which She has *been made, the emblem*, and would shudder to think how changed she had grown, O How I have longed to see her break from the mist of blood and death that circles round her folds, spoiling her beauty and tarnishing her honor. But no, day by day has she been draged deeper and deeper into cruelty and oppression, till now (in my eyes) her once bright red stripes, look like *bloody gashes* on the face of Heaven. I look now upon my early admiration of her glories as a dream. My love, (as things stand to-day)—is for the South alone. Nor, do I deem it a dishonor, in attempting to make for her a prisoner of this man, to whom she owes so much of misery. If success attends me, I go penniless to her side, They say she has found *that* "last ditch" which the north have so long derided, and been endeavoring to force her in, forgetting they are our brothers, and that its impolitic to goad an enemy to madness. Should I reach her in safety and find it true, I will proudly beg permission to triumph or die in that same "ditch" by her side, *A Confederate*, doing duty *upon his own responsibility*.

J Wilkes Booth
November 1864

LINCOLN'S REELECTION:
LONDON, NOVEMBER 1864

Henry Adams to Charles Francis Adams Jr.

Henry Adams had accompanied his father, Charles Francis Adams, to London in 1861 and served as his confidential secretary. He wrote about the recent American election to his brother, who in July had been appointed lieutenant colonel of the 5th Massachusetts Cavalry, a black regiment.

No. 29. London. 25 Nov. 1864.
My dear Colonel:

Our last advices announce your arrival at home. I hope you will not return to camp until you have got wholly rid of your dysentery.

The election is over then, and after all that excitement, worry and danger, behold all goes on as before! It was one of those cases in which life and death seemed to hang on the issue, and the result is so decisive as to answer all our wishes and hopes. It is a curious commentary upon theoretical reasoning as to forms of Government, that this election which ought by all rights to be a defect in the system, and which is universally considered by the admirers of "strong Governments" to be a proof of the advantage of their own model, should yet turn out in practice a great and positive gain and a fruitful source of national strength. After all, systems of Government are secondary matters, if you've only got your people behind them. I never yet have felt so proud as now of the great qualities of our race, or so confident of the capacity of men to develop their faculties in the mass. I believe that a new era of the movement of the world will date from that day, which will drag nations up still another step, and carry us out of a quantity of old fogs. Europe has a long way to go yet to catch us up.

Anything that produces a great effect in our favor on this side, usually produces a sort of general silence as the first proof of its force. So this election has been met on this side by a species of blindness. People remark the fact with wonder and anger, but they have only just such a vague idea of what are to be its consequences, as shuts their mouths without changing their opinions. Only the most clear-headed see indistinctly what bearing it is likely to have on English politics, and I expect that it will be years yet before its full action gets into play. Meanwhile the Government is now stronger than ever and our only weak point is the financial one. May our name not have to stand guard on that!

You can imagine with what enthusiasm we received the news, and drank to the success of the new Administration. For the time, all interest has centered in the election, and even the incomprehensible state of things in Georgia has been overlooked. How many more campaigns we shall have to make, seems very doubtful, but thus far our rate of progression has been regular, and if continued, ought to bring us to Augusta at the next round. We can afford to be patient however, now, for all we have to fear is pecuniary ruin, and that is tolerably certain.

I don't know that I've anything to tell you that's new or original on this side. Loo Brooks came through this week on her way home after five weeks of most harrassing contact with her mamma-in-law, who appears to have been superbly herself. Poor Loo was happy to escape, and we cheered her and little Fanny amazingly by a few hours at Ealing. I sent by her a cargo of books to the young 'uns, our nephews which ought to keep them in literature till they're old men. By the way, should you go to Washington, try and have a talk with Seward about our affairs. The Chief, by this steamer, sends *privately* a request to be relieved. You can intimate to S. that if compelled to stay, he means at any rate to send his family home and break up the establishment, remaining himself as a temporary occupant till a successor is appointed. He even talks of doing so at once, and sending the women to Italy in January preparatory to their going home in June. Seward must see that a change, if necessary at all, had best be made quickly for the public good. Don't quote me however. On no account let what I say, come back. You will probably get at first hand all the information you want. Best say nothing at all, yet, of the idea of retirement except to S. if you see him. Let me know what he says.

You see we are in a "transition state." But I do not see a chance of release before March—unless for worse chains.

"MY BOY WAS DEAD": KENTUCKY, NOVEMBER 1864

Joseph Miller: Statement Regarding His Family

Located twenty miles south of Lexington, Kentucky, the Union supply depot at Camp Nelson became a major recruitment center for the U.S. Colored Troops in June 1864, and almost 4,000 black soldiers had enlisted there by the end of October. Some of the soldiers were accompanied to the camp by their families, who were either fleeing slavery or had been driven from their homes by whites bitterly opposed to black enlistment. In an effort to conciliate slaveholding Kentucky unionists who objected to the military giving refuge to slaves, Adjutant-General Lorenzo Thomas issued orders in July barring the families of black soldiers from Camp Nelson. Despite his instructions, families continued to live in the camp. On November 22 Brigadier General Speed S. Fry, the Kentucky unionist who commanded Camp Nelson, ordered the expulsion in freezing weather of some 400 women and children and the destruction of their huts and cabins. Captain Theron E. Hall, a quartermaster who had served at the camp, protested Fry's action to Brigadier General Stephen G. Burbridge, the Union commander in Kentucky. Writing as "Humanitas," Hall published an account of the expulsions in the *New-York Daily Tribune* that was accompanied by Joseph Miller's affidavit. Burbridge countermanded Fry's order, and on November 29 gave Hall authority over the refugees. Hall and the Reverend John G. Fee established a refugee home at Camp Nelson in January 1865, but were unable to save many of those who had been driven out in November. On February 21, 1865, Fee wrote that of the 400 expelled, about 250 had returned to the camp, and that 102 of those who returned had died "in consequence of being exposed to cold & then herded together in Barracks" where "noise, disease & death rage." Among the dead were the Miller family. Joseph Miller's sons, Joseph Jr. and Calvin; his daughter, Maria; and his wife, Isabella, all died at Camp Nelson between December 17, 1864, and January 2, 1865. They were followed on January 6 by Joseph Miller himself.

———————

Camp Nelson Ky   November 26, 1864
Personally appered before me E. B W Restieaux Capt. and

Asst. Quartermaster Joseph Miller a man of color who being duly sworn upon oath says

I was a slave of George Miller of Lincoln County Ky. I have always resided in Kentucky and am now a Soldier in the service of the United States. I belong to Company I 124 U.S.C. Inft now Stationed at Camp Nelson Ky. When I came to Camp for the purpose of enlisting about the middle of October 1864 my wife and children came with me because my master said that if I enlisted he would not maintain them and I knew they would be abused by him when I left. I had then four children ages respectively ten nine seven and four years. On my presenting myself as a recruit I was told by the Lieut. in command to take my family into a tent within the limits of the Camp. My wife and family occupied this tent by the express permission of the aforementioned Officer and never received any notice to leave until Tuesday November 22" when a mounted guard gave my wife notice that she and her children must leave Camp before early morning. This was about six O'clock at night. My little boy about seven years of age had been very sick and was slowly recovering   My wife had no place to go and so remained until morning. About eight Oclock Wednesday morning November 23" a mounted guard came to my tent and ordered my wife and children out of Camp   The morning was bitter cold. It was freezing hard. I was certain that it would kill my sick child to take him out in the cold. I told the man in charge of the guard that it would be the death of my boy   I told him that my wife and children had no place to go and I told him that I was a soldier of the United States. He told me that it did not make any difference. he had orders to take all out of Camp. He told my wife and family that if they did not get up into the wagon which he had he would shoot the last one of them. On being thus threatened my wife and children went into the wagon   My wife carried her sick child in her arms. When they left the tent the wind was blowing hard and cold and having had to leave much of our clothing when we left our master, my wife with her little one was poorly clad. I followed them as far as the lines. I had no Knowledge where they were taking them. At night I went in search of my family. I found them at Nicholasville about six miles from Camp. They were in an old meeting house belonging to the colored people. The building was very cold having only one fire. My wife and children could not get near the fire, because of the number of colored people huddled together by the soldiers. I found my wife and children shivering with cold and famished with hunger   They had not recieved a morsel of food during the whole day. My boy was dead. He died directly after getting down from the wagon. I Know he was Killed by exposure to the inclement weather   I had to return to camp that night so I left my family in the meeting house and walked back. I had walked there. I travelled in all twelve miles   Next morning I walked to Nicholasville. I dug a grave myself and buried my own child. I left my family in the Meeting house—where they still remain   And further this deponent saith not

                                            his
(Signed) Joseph   Miller
                                         mark

BATTLE OF FRANKLIN: TENNESSEE,
NOVEMBER–DECEMBER 1864

Samuel T. Foster:
Diary, November 30–December 1, 1864

John B. Hood began his invasion of Middle Tennessee on November 21, advancing from Florence, Alabama, with 38,000 men. The Union troops opposing Hood's offensive were divided between Pulaski, Tennessee, where John M. Schofield commanded 30,000 men, and Nashville, seventy miles to the north, where George H. Thomas had assembled a force of 25,000 men. As Hood attempted to maneuver between the two Union armies, Schofield withdrew north to Columbia on the Duck River. On November 29 Hood succeeded in turning Schofield's flank by crossing the Duck, but was unable to overcome Union resistance near Spring Hill and block the Columbia–Franklin turnpike before dusk. During the night Schofield retreated past Hood's army and reached Franklin. Angered by the Union escape and determined to prevent Schofield from joining Thomas at Nashville, Hood ordered a series of frontal assaults on the entrenchments outside Franklin late in the afternoon of November 30. (In his postwar memoir *Advance and Retreat*, Hood would partially blame his failure at Spring Hill on the unwillingness of his army "to accept battle unless under the protection of breastworks," a reluctance he attributed to the "ruinous" and "timid" defensive policy followed by his predecessor Joseph E. Johnston during the Confederate retreat from Dalton to Atlanta.) Captain Foster of the dismounted 24th Texas Cavalry wrote about the battle, which cost the Confederates 6,200 men killed, wounded, or missing, and the Union 2,300. After the fighting ended, Schofield withdrew across the Harpeth River and joined Thomas at Nashville.

———————

Nov 30th

Our Corpse were sent across Duck river yesterday above the town with orders to go around and strike the Pike at Spring Hill. The Yanks seem to have found out that we were flanking them and they left in the night last night and went to Franklin.

This morning I leave Columbia at 9½ O'Clock AM and reach Spring Hill at 12.

I overtake the command three (3) miles from Franklin.

The line of battle is formed, with our Brigade near the centre and just on the right of the Turn Pike. Our regiment being on the left of the Brigd. put our Regt. next the Pike, and my Company being on the left of the regiment—it puts us on the Pike— A skirmish line is put out two or three hundred yards in advance of the main line. Here we have something new in the way of fighting. At the command forward the Bands begin to play and we march off to the music, in a few minutes our skirmishers commenced firing.

We soon came up to the skirmishers fighting the Yanks in line of battle behind breastworks. We make no halt, but keep strait on without firing a gun, and they fire a few shots and break to run, and as soon as they break to run our men break after them. They have nearly ½ mile to run to get back to their next line—so here we go right after them and yelling like fury and shooting at them at the same time. Kill some of them before they reach their works, and those that are in the second line of works are not able to shoot us because their own men are in front of us—and between us and them. So here we go, Yanks runing for life and we for the fun of it, but the difference in the objects are so great that they out run us, but loose quite a number of their men before they get there.

By the time they get to their 2nd line of works the men that were in them are out and on the run, and they all run back to the 3rd line of breastworks, while we stop at the 2nd line. The 3rd line was not over 40 yds from us— We take position out side of their works, and they come out and charge us in return.

They come up and meet us at this 2nd line and stop on one side and we on the other—with a bank of dirt between us. By this time it was getting dark and the firing was stoping gradually.

We are just in the edge of the town, and the dead and wounded are all around us, and Yank and Confed. lie dead near each other— The firing by an hour after night has nearly ceased, except when one man will hold his gun up as high as he can and shoot over the bank of dirt.

They throw clods of dirt over and sticks or anything they can get hold of.

We hear that Gen Pat Cleburn, and Gen Granbury are both dead. We hear that Hood has ordered all of our artillery (112 pieces) to be put in position to open on the town at daylight.

About 1 O'Clock in the night we find that the Yanks have all left, actually sliped off and we did not know it. As soon as Hood hears of it he ordered all the Artillery to shell the road on the other side of the river. This was about 2 O'Clock in the morning.

When every thing is still (in the night) and one hundred and twelve pieces of artilery all open at once, it makes no little noise, but it did not last long. They were all gone, out of reach towards Nashville— Now we strike a light and make fires and begin to look around, and count noses.

I find that eight of my men are wounded—two killed and two missing, supposed to be captured.

DEC 1st   At Daylight this morning we can see the terrible results of the fight on yesterday and last night— The dead of both armies are lying together all over the ground—sometimes they are together.

There is great destruction of human life here— I have seen places where the blood run off in a stream, and also to stand in pools in places— Eighteen men dead on the ground out of our Regt.

Col. Young killed Maj Taylor captured and our Brigade is left without a field officer. Hickox of my Co. that was captured last night made his escape and came to us this morning. He is wounded also.

All the army follow the Yanks this morning on to Nashville. Our Brigd and the Ark. Brigd are so badly cut up that we can't move. Some officers have no men, and some companies have no officers— So we have to reorganize and consolidate, a Captain has to command the Brigade.

Gen. Hood has betrayed us (The Army of Tenn). This is not the kind of fighting he promised us at Tuscumbia and Florence Ala. when we started into Tenn.

This was not a "fight with equal numbers and choice of the ground" by no means.

And the wails and cries of widows and orphans made at Franklin Tenn Nov 30th 1864 will heat up the fires of the bottomless pit to burn the soul of Gen J B Hood for Murdering their husbands and fathers at that place that day. It can't be called anything else but cold blooded Murder.

He sacrificed those men to make the name of Hood famous; when if the History of it is ever written it will make him *infamous*.

He had near 10,000 men murdered around Atlanta trying to prove to the world that he was a greater man than Genl Johnson— Because Johnson said that Atlanta was untenable, and could not be held with the men he had against the men that Sherman had. And how small he must have felt when he had to leave there in the night to keep from being captured.

And now in order to recover from the merited disgrace of that transaction he brings this Army here into middle Tenn. and by making them false promises and false statements get these men killed— Put them into a fight where the Yanks have three lines of breastworks; the second or middle line being lined with artillery.

The men have a right to believe he told the truth and go forward to certain and sure destructions; but "Vengeance is mine Sayeth the Lord" and it will surely overtake him.

WASHINGTON, D.C., DECEMBER 1864

Abraham Lincoln:
Annual Message to Congress

President Lincoln sent his annual message to Congress four weeks after his reelection. The voting figures for the 1864 presidential election that accompanied it were supplied by the governors of the Union states after Lincoln sent telegrams requesting them on November 15 and November 29. His prediction that the 39th Congress, which was scheduled to meet in December 1865, would "almost certainly" pass a constitutional amendment abolishing slavery was based on the Republican gain of forty-three House seats in the 1864 elections.

December 6, 1864
Fellow-citizens of the Senate and House of Representatives:

Again the blessings of health and abundant harvests claim our profoundest gratitude to Almighty God.

The condition of our foreign affairs is reasonably satisfactory.

Mexico continues to be a theatre of civil war. While our political relations with that country have undergone no change, we have, at the same time, strictly maintained neutrality between the belligerents.

At the request of the states of Costa Rica and Nicaragua, a competent engineer has been authorized to make a survey of the river San Juan and the port of San Juan. It is a source of much satisfaction that the difficulties which for a moment excited some political apprehensions, and caused a closing of the inter-oceanic transit route, have been amicably adjusted, and that there is a good prospect that the route will soon be reopened with an increase of capacity and adaptation. We could not exaggerate either the commercial or the political importance of that great improvement.

It would be doing injustice to an important South American state not to acknowledge the directness, frankness, and cordiality with which the United States of Colombia have entered into intimate relations with this government. A claims convention has been constituted to complete the unfinished work of the one which closed its session in 1861.

The new liberal constitution of Venezuela having gone into effect with the universal acquiescence of the people, the government under it has been recognized, and diplomatic intercourse with it has opened in a cordial and friendly spirit. The long-deferred Aves Island claim has been satisfactorily paid and discharged.

Mutual payments have been made of the claims awarded by the late joint commission for the settlement of claims between the United States and Peru. An earnest and cordial friendship continues to exist between the two countries, and such efforts as were in my power have been used to remove misunderstanding and avert a threatened war between Peru and Spain.

Our relations are of the most friendly nature with Chile, the Argentine Republic, Bolivia, Costa Rica, Paraguay, San Salvador, and Hayti.

During the past year no differences of any kind have arisen with any of those republics, and, on the other hand, their sympathies with the United States are constantly expressed with cordiality and earnestness.

The claim arising from the seizure of the cargo of the brig Macedonian in 1821 has been paid in full by the government of Chile.

Civil war continues in the Spanish part of San Domingo, apparently without prospect of an early close.

Official correspondence has been freely opened with Liberia, and it gives us a pleasing view of social and political progress in that Republic. It may be expected to derive new vigor from American influence, improved by the rapid disappearance of slavery in the United States.

I solicit your authority to furnish to the republic a gunboat at moderate cost, to be reimbursed to the United States by instalments. Such a vessel is needed for the safety of that state against the native African races; and in Liberian hands it would be more effective in arresting the African slave trade than a squadron in our own hands. The possession of the least organized naval force would stimulate a generous ambition in the republic, and the confidence which we should manifest by furnishing it would win forbearance and favor towards the colony from all civilized nations.

The proposed overland telegraph between America and Europe, by the way of Behring's Straits and Asiatic Russia, which was sanctioned by Congress at the last session, has been undertaken, under very favorable circumstances, by an association of American citizens, with the cordial good-will and support as well of this government as of those of Great Britain and Russia. Assurances have been received from most of the South American States of their high appreciation of the enterprise, and their readiness to co-operate in constructing lines tributary to that world-encircling communication. I learn, with much satisfaction, that the noble design of a telegraphic communication between the eastern coast of America and Great Britain has been renewed with full expectation of its early accomplishment.

Thus it is hoped that with the return of domestic peace the country will be able to resume with energy and advantage its former high career of commerce and civilization.

Our very popular and estimable representative in Egypt died in April last. An unpleasant altercation which arose between the temporary incumbent of the office and the government of the Pacha resulted in a suspension of intercourse. The evil was promptly corrected on the arrival of the successor in the consulate, and our relations with Egypt, as well as our relations with the Barbary powers, are entirely satisfactory.

The rebellion which has so long been flagrant in China, has at last been suppressed, with the co-operating good offices of this government, and of the other western commercial states. The judicial consular establishment there has become very difficult and onerous, and it will need legislative revision to adapt it to the extension of our commerce, and to the more intimate intercourse which has been instituted with the government and people of that vast empire. China seems to be accepting with hearty good-will the conventional laws which regulate commercial and social intercourse among the western nations.

Owing to the peculiar situation of Japan, and the anomalous form of its government, the action of that empire in performing treaty stipulations is inconstant and capricious. Nevertheless, good progress has been effected by the western powers, moving with enlightened concert. Our own pecuniary claims have been allowed, or put in course of settlement, and the inland sea has been reopened to commerce. There is reason also to believe that these proceedings have increased rather than diminished the friendship of Japan towards the United States.

The ports of Norfolk, Fernandina, and Pensacola have been opened by proclamation. It is hoped that foreign merchants will now consider whether it is not safer and more profitable to themselves, as well as just to the United States, to resort to these and other open ports, than it is to pursue, through many hazards, and at vast cost, a contraband trade with other ports which are closed, if not by actual military occupation, at least by a lawful and effective blockade.

For myself, I have no doubt of the power and duty of the Executive, under the law of nations, to exclude enemies of the human race from an asylum in the United States. If Congress should think that proceedings in such cases lack the authority of law, or ought to be further regulated by it, I recommend that provision be made for effectually preventing foreign slave traders from acquiring domicile and facilities for their criminal occupation in our country.

It is possible that, if it were a new and open question, the maritime powers, with the lights they now enjoy, would not concede the privileges of a naval belligerent to the insurgents of the United States, destitute, as they are, and always have been, equally of ships-of-war and of ports and harbors. Disloyal emissaries have been neither less assiduous nor more successful during the last year than they were before that time in their efforts, under favor of that privilege, to embroil our country in foreign wars. The desire and determination of the governments of the maritime states to defeat that design are believed to be as sincere as, and cannot be more earnest than our own. Nevertheless, unforeseen political difficulties have arisen, especially in Brazilian and British ports, and on the northern boundary of the United States, which have required, and are likely to continue to require, the practice of constant vigilance, and a just and conciliatory spirit on the part of the United States as well as of the nations concerned and their governments.

Commissioners have been appointed under the treaty with

Great Britain on the adjustment of the claims of the Hudson's Bay and Puget's Sound Agricultural Companies, in Oregon, and are now proceeding to the execution of the trust assigned to them.

In view of the insecurity of life and property in the region adjacent to the Canadian border, by reason of recent assaults and depredations committed by inimical and desperate persons, who are harbored there, it has been thought proper to give notice that after the expiration of six months, the period conditionally stipulated in the existing arrangement with Great Britain, the United States must hold themselves at liberty to increase their naval armament upon the lakes, if they shall find that proceeding necessary. The condition of the border will necessarily come into consideration in connection with the question of continuing or modifying the rights of transit from Canada through the United States, as well as the regulation of imposts, which were temporarily established by the reciprocity treaty of the 5th of June, 1854.

I desire, however, to be understood, while making this statement, that the Colonial authorities of Canada are not deemed to be intentionally unjust or unfriendly towards the United States; but, on the contrary, there is every reason to expect that, with the approval of the imperial government, they will take the necessary measures to prevent new incursions across the border.

The act passed at the last session for the encouragement of emigration has, so far as was possible, been put into operation. It seems to need amendment which will enable the officers of the government to prevent the practice of frauds against the immigrants while on their way and on their arrival in the ports, so as to secure them here a free choice of avocations and places of settlement. A liberal disposition towards this great national policy is manifested by most of the European States, and ought to be reciprocated on our part by giving the immigrants effective national protection. I regard our emigrants as one of the principal replenishing streams which are appointed by Providence to repair the ravages of internal war, and its wastes of national strength and health. All that is necessary is to secure the flow of that stream in its present fullness, and to that end the government must, in every way, make it manifest that it neither needs nor designs to impose involuntary military service upon those who come from other lands to cast their lot in our country.

The financial affairs of the government have been successfully administered during the last year. The legislation of the last session of Congress has beneficially affected the revenues, although sufficient time has not yet elapsed to experience the full effect of several of the provisions of the acts of Congress imposing increased taxation.

The receipts during the year, from all sources, upon the basis of warrants signed by the Secretary of the Treasury, including loans and the balance in the treasury on the first day of July, 1863, were $1,394,796,007 62; and the aggregate disbursements, upon the same basis, were $1,298,056,101 89, leaving a balance in the treasury, as shown by warrants, of $96,739,905 73.

Deduct from these amounts the amount of the principal of the public debt redeemed, and the amount of issues in substitution therefor, and the actual cash operations of the treasury were: receipts, $884,076,646 57; disbursements $865,234,087 86; which leaves a cash balance in the treasury of $18,842,558 71.

Of the receipts, there were derived from customs, $102,316,152 99; from lands, $588,333 29; from direct taxes, $475,648 96; from internal revenue, $109,741,134 10; from miscellaneous sources, $47,511,448 10; and from loans applied to actual expenditures, including former balance, $623,443,929 13.

There were disbursed, for the civil service, $27,505,599 46; for pensions and Indians, $7,517,930 97; for the War Department $690,791,842 97; for the Navy Department $85,733,292 77; for interest of the public debt $53,685,421 69;—making an aggregate of $865,234,087.86, and leaving a balance in the treasury of $18,842,558.71, as before stated.

For the actual receipts and disbursements for the first quarter, and the estimated receipts and disbursements for the three remaining quarters of the current fiscal year, and the general operations of the treasury in detail, I refer you to the report of the Secretary of the Treasury. I concur with him in the opinion that the proportion of moneys required to meet the expenses consequent upon the war derived from taxation should be still further increased; and I earnestly invite your attention to this subject, to the end that there may be such additional legislation as shall be required to meet the just expectations of the Secretary.

The public debt on the first day of July last, as appears by the books of the treasury, amounted to $1,740,690,489 49. Probably, should the war continue for another year, that amount may be increased by not far from five hundred millions. Held as it is, for the most part, by our own people, it has become a substantial branch of national, though private, property. For obvious reasons, the more nearly this property can be distributed among all the people the better. To favor such general distribution, greater inducements to become owners might, perhaps, with good effect, and without injury, be presented to persons of limited means. With this view, I suggest whether it might not be both competent and expedient for Congress to provide that a limited amount of some future issue of public securities might be held by any bona fide purchaser exempt from taxation, and from seizure for debt, under such restrictions and limitations as might be necessary to guard against abuse of so important a privilege. This would enable every prudent person to set aside a small annuity against a possible day of want.

Privileges like these would render the possession of such securities, to the amount limited, most desirable to every person of small means who might be able to save enough for the purpose. The great advantage of citizens being creditors as well as debtors, with relation to the public debt, is obvious. Men readily perceive that they cannot be much oppressed by a debt which they owe to themselves.

The public debt on the first day of July last, although somewhat exceeding the estimate of the Secretary of the Treasury made to Congress at the commencement of the last session, falls short of the estimate of that officer made in the preceding December, as to its probable amount at the beginning of this year, by the sum of $3,995,097 31. This fact exhibits a satisfactory condition and conduct of the operations of the Treasury.

The national banking system is proving to be acceptable to capitalists and to the people. On the twenty-fifth day of November five hundred and eighty-four national banks had been organized, a considerable number of which were conversions from State banks. Changes from State systems to the national system are rapidly taking place, and it is hoped that, very soon, there will be in the United States, no banks of issue not authorized by Congress, and no bank-note circulation not secured by the government. That the government and the people will derive great benefit from this change in the banking systems of the country can hardly be questioned. The national system will create a reliable and permanent influence in support of the national credit, and protect the people against losses in the use of paper money. Whether or not any further legislation is advisable for the suppression of State bank issues, it will be for Congress to determine. It seems quite clear that the treasury cannot be satisfactorily conducted unless the government can exercise a restraining power over the bank-note circulation of the country.

The report of the Secretary of War and the accompanying documents will detail the campaigns of the armies in the field since the date of the last annual message, and also the operations of the several administrative bureaus of the War Department during the last year. It will also specify the measures deemed essential for the national defence, and to keep up and supply the requisite military force.

The report of the Secretary of the Navy presents a comprehensive and satisfactory exhibit of the affairs of that Department and of the naval service. It is a subject of congratulation and laudable pride to our countrymen that a navy of such vast proportions has been organized in so brief a period, and conducted with so much efficiency and success.

The general exhibit of the navy, including vessels under construction on the 1st. of December, 1864, shows a total of 671 vessels, carrying 4,610 guns, and of 510,396 tons, being an actual increase during the year, over and above all losses by shipwreck or in battle, of 83 vessels, 167 guns, and 42,427 tons.

The total number of men at this time in the naval service, including officers, is about 51,000.

There have been captured by the navy during the year 324 vessels, and the whole number of naval captures since hostilities commenced is 1,379, of which 267 are steamers.

The gross proceeds arising from the sale of condemned

prize property, thus far reported, amount to $14,396,250 51. A large amount of such proceeds is still under adjudication and yet to be reported.

The total expenditures of the Navy Department of every description, including the cost of the immense squadrons that have been called into existence from the 4th of March, 1861, to the 1st. of November, 1864, are $238,647,262 35.

Your favorable consideration is invited to the various recommendations of the Secretary of the Navy, especially in regard to a navy yard and suitable establishment for the construction and repair of iron vessels, and the machinery and armature for our ships, to which reference was made in my last annual message.

Your attention is also invited to the views expressed in the report in relation to the legislation of Congress at its last session in respect to prize on our inland waters.

I cordially concur in the recommendation of the Secretary as to the propriety of creating the new rank of vice-admiral in our naval service.

Your attention is invited to the report of the Postmaster General for a detailed account of the operations and financial condition of the Post Office Department.

The postal revenues for the year ending June 30, 1864, amounted to $12,438,253.78 and the expenditures to $12,644,786.20; the excess of expenditures over receipts being $206,652.42.

The views presented by the Postmaster General on the subject of special grants by the government in aid of the establishment of new lines of ocean mail steamships and the policy he recommends for the development of increased commercial intercourse with adjacent and neighboring countries, should receive the careful consideration of Congress.

It is of noteworthy interest that the steady expansion of population, improvement and governmental institutions over the new and unoccupied portions of our country have scarcely been checked, much less impeded or destroyed, by our great civil war, which at first glance would seem to have absorbed almost the entire energies of the nation.

The organization and admission of the State of Nevada has been completed in conformity with law, and thus our excellent system is firmly established in the mountains, which once seemed a barren and uninhabitable waste between the Atlantic States and those which have grown up on the coast of the Pacific ocean.

The territories of the Union are generally in a condition of prosperity and rapid growth. Idaho and Montana, by reason of their great distance and the interruption of communication with them by Indian hostilities, have been only partially organized; but it is understood that these difficulties are about to disappear, which will permit their governments, like those of the others, to go into speedy and full operation.

As intimately connected with, and promotive of, this material growth of the nation, I ask the attention of Congress to the valuable information and important recommendations relating to the public lands, Indian affairs, the Pacific railroad, and mineral discoveries contained in the report of the Secretary of the Interior, which is herewith transmitted, and which report also embraces the subjects of patents, pensions and other topics of public interest pertaining to his department.

The quantity of public land disposed of during the five quarters ending on the 30th of September last was 4,221,342 acres, of which 1,538,614 acres were entered under the homestead law. The remainder was located with military land warrants, agricultural scrip certified to States for railroads, and sold for cash. The cash received from sales and location fees was $1,019,446.

The income from sales during the fiscal year, ending June 30, 1864, was $678,007,21, against $136,077,95 received during the preceding year. The aggregate number of acres surveyed during the year has been equal to the quantity disposed of; and there is open to settlement about 133,000,000 acres of surveyed land.

The great enterprise of connecting the Atlantic with the Pacific States by railways and telegraph lines has been entered upon with a vigor that gives assurance of success, notwithstanding the embarrassments arising from the prevailing high prices of materials and labor. The route of the main line of the road has been definitely located for one hundred miles westward from the initial point at Omaha City, Nebraska, and a preliminary location of the Pacific railroad of California has been made from Sacramento eastward to the great bend of the Truckee river in Nevada.

Numerous discoveries of gold, silver and cinnabar mines have been added to the many heretofore known and the country occupied by the Sierra Nevada and Rocky mountains, and the subordinate ranges, now teems with enterprising labor, which is richly remunerative. It is believed that the product of the mines of precious metals in that region has, during the year, reached, if not exceeded, one hundred millions in value.

It was recommended in my last annual message that our Indian system be remodelled. Congress, at its last session, acting upon the recommendation, did provide for reorganizing the system in California, and it is believed that under the present organization the management of the Indians there will be attended with reasonable success. Much yet remains to be done to provide for the proper government of the Indians in other parts of the country to render it secure for the advancing settler, and to provide for the welfare of the Indian. The Secretary reiterates his recommendations, and to them the attention of Congress is invited.

The liberal provisions made by Congress for paying pensions to invalid soldiers and sailors of the republic, and to the widows, orphans, and dependent mothers of those who have fallen in battle, or died of disease contracted, or of wounds received in the service of their country, have been diligently administered. There have been added to the pension rolls, during the year ending the 30th day of June last, the names of 16,770 invalid soldiers, and of 271 disabled seamen, making the present number of army invalid pensioners 22,767, and of navy invalid pensioners 712.

Of widows, orphans and mothers, 22 198 have been placed on the army pension rolls, and 248 on the navy rolls. The present number of army pensioners of this class is 25,433, and of navy pensioners 793. At the beginning of the year the number of revolutionary pensioners was 1,430; only twelve of them were soldiers, of whom seven have since died. The remainder are those who, under the law, receive pensions because of relationship to revolutionary soldiers. During the year ending the

30th of June, 1864, $4,504,616.92 have been paid to pensioners of all classes.

I cheerfully commend to your continued patronage the benevolent institutions of the District of Columbia which have hitherto been established or fostered by Congress, and respectfully refer, for information concerning them, and in relation to the Washington aqueduct, the Capitol and other matters of local interest, to the report of the Secretary.

The Agricultural Department, under the supervision of its present energetic and faithful head, is rapidly commending itself to the great and vital interest it was created to advance. It is peculiarly the people's department, in which they feel more directly concerned than in any other. I commend it to the continued attention and fostering care of Congress.

The war continues. Since the last annual message all the important lines and positions then occupied by our forces have been maintained, and our arms have steadily advanced; thus liberating the regions left in rear, so that Missouri, Kentucky, Tennessee and parts of other States have again produced reasonably fair crops.

The most remarkable feature in the military operations of the year is General Sherman's attempted march of three hundred miles directly through the insurgent region. It tends to show a great increase of our relative strength that our General-in-Chief should feel able to confront and hold in check every active force of the enemy, and yet to detach a well-appointed large army to move on such an expedition. The result not yet being known, conjecture in regard to it is not here indulged.

Important movements have also occurred during the year to the effect of moulding society for durability in the Union. Although short of complete success, it is much in the right direction, that twelve thousand citizens in each of the States of Arkansas and Louisiana have organized loyal State governments with free constitutions, and are earnestly struggling to maintain and administer them. The movements in the same direction, more extensive, though less definite in Missouri, Kentucky and Tennessee, should not be overlooked. But Maryland presents the example of complete success. Maryland is secure to Liberty and Union for all the future. The genius of rebellion will no more claim Maryland. Like another foul spirit, being driven out, it may seek to tear her, but it will woo her no more.

At the last session of Congress a proposed amendment of the Constitution abolishing slavery throughout the United States, passed the Senate, but failed for lack of the requisite two-thirds vote in the House of Representatives. Although the present is the same Congress, and nearly the same members, and without questioning the wisdom or patriotism of those who stood in opposition, I venture to recommend the reconsideration and passage of the measure at the present session. Of course the abstract question is not changed; but an intervening election shows, almost certainly, that the next Congress will pass the measure if this does not. Hence there is only a question of *time* as to when the proposed amendment will go to the States for their action. And as it is to so go, at all events, may we not agree that the sooner the better? It is not claimed that the election has imposed a duty on members to change their views or their votes, any further than, as an additional element to be considered, their judgment may be affected by it. It is the voice of the people now, for the first time, heard upon the question. In a great national crisis, like ours, unanimity of action among those seeking a common end is very desirable—almost indispensable. And yet no approach to such unanimity is attainable, unless some deference shall be paid to the will of the majority, simply because it is the will of the majority. In this case the common end is the maintenance of the Union; and, among the means to secure that end, such will, through the election, is most clearly declared in favor of such constitutional amendment.

The most reliable indication of public purpose in this country is derived through our popular elections. Judging by the recent canvass and its result, the purpose of the people, within the loyal States, to maintain the integrity of the Union, was never more firm, nor more nearly unanimous, than now. The extraordinary calmness and good order with which the millions of voters met and mingled at the polls, give strong assurance of this. Not only all those who supported the Union ticket, so called, but a great majority of the opposing party also, may be fairly claimed to entertain, and to be actuated by, the same purpose. It is an unanswerable argument to this effect, that no candidate for any office whatever, high or low, has ventured to seek votes on the avowal that he was for giving up the Union. There have been much impugning of motives, and much heated controversy as to the proper means and best mode of advancing the Union cause; but on the distinct issue of Union or no Union, the politicians have shown their instinctive knowledge that there is no diversity among the people. In affording the people the fair opportunity of showing, one to another and to the world, this firmness and unanimity of purpose, the election has been of vast value to the national cause.

The election has exhibited another fact not less valuable to be known—the fact that we do not approach exhaustion in the most important branch of national resources—that of living men. While it is melancholy to reflect that the war has filled so many graves, and carried mourning to so many hearts, it is some relief to know that, compared with the surviving, the fallen have been so few. While corps, and divisions, and brigades, and regiments have formed, and fought, and dwindled, and gone out of existence, a great majority of the men who composed them are still living. The same is true of the naval service. The election returns prove this. So many voters could not else be found. The States regularly holding elections, both now and four years ago, to wit, California, Connecticut, Delaware, Illinois, Indiana, Iowa, Kentucky, Maine, Maryland, Massachusetts, Michigan, Minnesota, Missouri, New Hampshire, New Jersey, New York, Ohio, Oregon, Pennsylvania, Rhode Island, Vermont, West Virginia, and Wisconsin cast 3.982.011 votes now, against 3.870.222 cast then, showing an aggregate now of 3.982.011. To this is to be added 33.762 cast now in the new States of Kansas and Nevada, which States did not vote in 1860, thus swelling the aggregate to 4.015.773 and the net increase during the three years and a half of war to 145.551. A table is appended showing particulars. To this again should be added the number of all soldiers in the field from Massachusetts, Rhode Island, New Jersey, Delaware, Indiana, Illinois, and California, who, by the laws of those States, could not vote away from their homes, and which number cannot be less than 90.000. Nor yet is this all. The number in organized Territories is triple now what it was four years ago, while thousands, white and black, join us as the national arms press back the insurgent lines. So much is shown, affirmatively and negatively, by the election. It is not material to inquire *how* the increase has been produced, or to show that it would have been *greater* but for the war, which is probably true. The important fact remains demonstrated, that we have *more* men *now* than we had when the war *began*; that we are not exhausted, nor in process of exhaustion; that we are *gaining* strength, and may, if need be, maintain the contest indefinitely. This as to men. Material resources are now more complete and abundant than ever.

The national resources, then, are unexhausted, and, as we believe, inexhaustible. The public purpose to re-establish and maintain the national authority is unchanged, and, as we believe, unchangeable. The manner of continuing the effort remains to choose. On careful consideration of all the evidence accessible it seems to me that no attempt at negotiation with the insurgent leader could result in any good. He would accept nothing short of severance of the Union—precisely what we will not and cannot give. His declarations to this effect are explicit and oft-repeated. He does not attempt to deceive us. He affords us no excuse to deceive ourselves. He cannot voluntarily reaccept the Union; we cannot voluntarily yield it. Between him and us the issue is distinct, simple, and inflexible. It is an issue which can only be tried by war, and decided by victory. If we yield, we are beaten; if the Southern people fail him, he is beaten. Either way, it would be the victory and defeat following war. What is true, however, of him who heads the insurgent cause, is not necessarily true of those who follow. Although he cannot reaccept the Union, they can. Some of them, we know, already desire peace and reunion. The number of such may increase. They can, at any moment, have peace simply by laying down their arms and submitting to the national authority under the Constitution. After so much, the government could not, if it would, maintain war against them. The loyal people would not sustain or allow it. If questions should remain, we would adjust them by the peaceful means of legislation, conference, courts, and votes, operating only in constitutional and lawful channels. Some certain, and other possible, questions are, and would be, beyond the Executive power to adjust; as, for instance, the admission of members into Congress, and whatever might require the appropriation of money. The Executive power itself would be greatly diminished by the cessation of actual war. Pardons and remissions of forfeitures, however, would still be within Executive control. In what spirit and temper this control would be exercised can be fairly judged of by the past.

A year ago general pardon and amnesty, upon specified terms, were offered to all, except certain designated classes; and, it was, at the same time, made known that the excepted classes were still within contemplation of special clemency. During the year many availed themselves of the general provision, and many more would, only that the signs of bad faith in some led to such precautionary measures as rendered the practical process less easy and certain. During the same time also special pardons have been granted to individuals of the excepted classes, and no voluntary application has been denied. Thus, practically, the door has been, for a full year, open to all, except such as were not in condition to make free choice—that is, such as were in custody or under constraint. It is still so open to all. But the time may come—probably will come—when public duty shall demand that it be closed; and that, in lieu, more rigorous measures than heretofore shall be adopted.

In presenting the abandonment of armed resistance to the national authority on the part of the insurgents, as the only indispensable condition to ending the war on the part of the government, I retract nothing heretofore said as to slavery. I repeat the declaration made a year ago, that "while I remain in my present position I shall not attempt to retract or modify the emancipation proclamation, nor shall I return to slavery any person who is free by the terms of that proclamation, or by any of the Acts of Congress." If the people should, by whatever mode or means, make it an Executive duty to re-enslave such persons, another, and not I, must be their instrument to perform it.

In stating a single condition of peace, I mean simply to say that the war will cease on the part of the government, whenever it shall have ceased on the part of those who began it.

December 6. 1864.   ABRAHAM LINCOLN

Table showing the aggregate votes in the States named, at the presidential election respectively in 1860 and 1864.

	1860.	1864.
California	118,840	*110,000
Connecticut	77,246	86,616
Delaware	16,039	16,924
Illinois	339,693	348,235
Indiana	272,143	280,645
Iowa	128,331	143,331
Kentucky	146,216	*91,300
Maine	97,918	115,141
Maryland	92,502	72,703
Massachusetts	169,533	175,487
Michigan	154,747	162,413
Minnesota	34,799	42,534
Missouri	165,538	*90,000
New Hampshire	65,953	69,111
New Jersey	121,125	128,680
New York	675,156	730,664
Ohio	442,441	470,745
Oregon	14,410	†14,410
Pennsylvania	476,442	572,697
Rhode Island	19,931	22,187
Vermont	42,844	55,811
West Virginia	46,195	33,874
Wisconsin	152,180	148,513
	3,870,222	3,982,011
Kansas		17,234
Nevada		16,528
		33,762
		3,982,011
Total		4,015,773
		3,870,222
Net increase		145,551

*Nearly   †Estimated.

REPORTS OF A SLAVE INSURRECTION:
NORTH CAROLINA, DECEMBER 1864

Henry Nutt to Zebulon B. Vance

Henry Nutt, a prominent Wilmington merchant, wrote to Governor Zebulon B. Vance about reports of a planned slave insurrection in southeastern North Carolina and the measures taken to suppress it. By 1864 the shortage of white men available to enforce slavery had become a widespread problem for the Confederacy, where in some counties as many as 90 percent of white males of military age had been taken into the army. With so few white men at home, it became increasingly difficult to sustain the patrols that had helped maintain slavery in the antebellum South by monitoring roads and capturing runaways. Authorities in North Carolina and elsewhere were further alarmed by cases in which escaped slaves joined bands of Confederate deserters. The number of persons who were executed for their involvement with the slave rebellion allegedly planned in North Carolina in December 1864 is not known. Captain Lewis H. Webb, an artillery officer from Richmond County serving near Weldon, would write in his diary on December 22 that "numerous arrests of slaves have been made & several hung by the incensed citizens" after the discovery of an insurrection planned for Christmas night. In what may have been a reference to the same incident, David P. Conyngham of the *New York Herald* reported in a dispatch sent from Fayetteville on March 12, 1865, that Confederate authorities had discovered a plot by slaves from nearby Laurinburg to "force their way" toward Sherman's army as it marched through the Carolinas, and that "after a kind of a mock trial, twenty-five were hung."

Prospect Hall P.O. Bladen Cty. N.C.
12th Decr 1864

To his Excellency
Z. B. Vance Governor N.C.
Raleigh N.C.
 Governor
  I presume, on this, you have heard all the particulars, from parties on the spot, but as it is possible you may not have been so informed, I feel it my duty to avail myself of this, the earliest

opportunity to inform you of the discovery of a well planned, formidable, & most diabolical scheme of Insurrection among the negroes of this section of the state, extending from Troy, in Montgomery County to Society Hill in So Carolina, how far it extends on either side of the line between these points is not known. Their courier was arrested on his way into Robeson County, his confessions led to the arrest of some forty or fifty others on the above line, a list of one hundred & ten names were found. The country is aroused & every one on the alert & parties are now out in search of as many of the culprits as can be found, but the country is very deficient in men to arrest & convey them to a safe prison. The negroes all tell the same story. That there are some white men (deserters) concerned. That they were regularly organized, by the election of a Chief, Captains, Lieutenants, couriers &c. rules & regulations were adopted for their government & action, one of their rules was that all negroes who refused to participate were to be murdered, & about Christmas the general massacre was to commence of all white persons, regardless of age, sex or condition, except such as they might choose & select for wives or concubines. One of the negroes was hung in Richmond County on friday last & some four or five others were to be hung to day, some forty others would be sent to prison for safety & trial, but their is no jail in Robeson, or this county & there are no spare men to send them by, it is considered unsafe to keep or to send them away. Consequently I think it is more than probable the whole of them will be hung by the enraged populace without the form or sanction of the civil Law.

Under such circumstances, I submit, whether it would not be well to call the attention of the Legislature now in session to the subject of local defence & protection against such enemies, & if there is no existing law for summary punishment and execution, whether it would not be well for them to enquire into the practicability of authorizing three or more Magistrates to try & adjudge under proper restrictions all such, & similar cases, & to dispose of them summarily, without the delays, risk of escapes, expence, & demoralizing effects of a long course of law through the courts, for such offences as Insurrection, Rape, Murder, Rebellion &c by negroes upon whites. Summary punishment is required, & such punishment, is & will be sustained by public opinion, with or without the sanction of the Civil Law, & if public opinion sanctions the violation of one Law, the precedent is laid for other violations, & where the Civil Law is set aside, where will you look for the limit of excesses, & what protection will remain to the people for life, liberty or property.

While at Lumberton to day, I was told of a most aggravated case of rape by a negro upon the person of a young Lady daughter of a most respectable & wealthy farmer, the negro had been sent off to be sold, the agrieved party followed him to Lumberton, & would have shot him down on sight.

Our Country (this region particularly) is so thoroughly drained of white males from 13 years old upwards, that it is impossible to sustain a patrol, or any police regulations whatever, there is hardly any government of negroes at all, the few old men & women who own negroes tell them what to do & that is all, they have no power whatever, to enforce any order, & you know what the result of such a state of things must lead to, & you know further, enough of the negro character to know, "*that he will exist in no community, in any other Capacity, than as Slave or Master.*" In connection with this subject I beg leave to suggest, most respectfully to your Excellency, the propriety of instituting, or organizing some systematic plan of preserving, under practicable restrictions & limitations, a sufficient number of men, uniformly scattered over the country, to help make provisions for the people & for the families of those who are in the army, & to serve in some degree as a protection to their homes & families, if it is not done, I fear that it will be difficult to keep our soldiers in the field, & desertions in the army will increase. The scenes being enacted around us at this time, is calculated to increase them. To give you some idea of the condition of the families of soldiers in this county. The court last year appropriated $40,000 to buy bread for them, it was found insufficient, & at last November term $100,000 was appropriated for that purpose, which is now thought to be inadequate. There is, in this whole district (Hollow District) (a large one too) but four white males slave holders that I know of, above the age of 50. & exempt from military service, so thoroughly has been the drain for the army.

And I may here add, that in addition to all the other grievances men calling themselves 'Impressing officers' are travelling through the country stripping farmers of (in some cases) all their work animals Horses & mules, & in no case as I learn, has a sufficient number been left to cultivate the farm. Cattle have been impressed as I learn, at the rate of one eighth, counting work oxen, cows, calves, yearlings & all.

What is to be done, are the people to be stripped of not only their own support, but of the means of supporting the government & the war? And then, the assessing & collecting of taxes & impressing of property is so unequal & unjust in its operation, & from which no appeal can be taken, the agents have it in their power, & not unfrequently exercise it, of punishing private enemies, & rewarding friends, thus taxpayers are entirely at the mercy of collectors, who interpret the law as it pleases them, owing to the ambiguity of the law, & the law itself makes them the judges of it & from which there is no appeal. No body complains of the amount of taxes, the people would pay with cheerfulness five times the amt. if the wants of the Government required it, but its ambiguity, which makes it unequal & unjust in its operations, is what makes it onerous & I may say even odious.

I trust Governor you will pardon this long & perhaps uninteresting communication, & hope you will not consider it impertinent. You are the father of us all, living away yonder in Raleigh & it is not presumed you can know the wants & grievances of all your people, unless they tell you of them, hence this liberty

> I am Governor
> Very Respectfully & truly
> Your friend & Obt Servt
> H. Nutt

MEETING SHERMAN: GEORGIA, DECEMBER 1864
John Chipman Gray to John C. Ropes

Before Sherman's army left Atlanta it destroyed the railroad and telegraph lines connecting the city with the North. As the Union forces marched across Georgia to the coast, few people outside the region knew much about their progress beyond what they read in the often contradictory reports printed in the southern press. President Lincoln noted in his annual message to Congress that the result of Sherman's venture "not yet being known, conjecture in regard to it is not here indulged," and told a crowd of well-wishers on December 6: "We all know where he went in at, but I can't tell where he will come out at." Sherman's troops reached the outer defenses of Savannah on December 10 and captured Fort McAllister south of the city three days later, opening a supply line down the Ogeechee River to Union ships in Ossabaw Sound. Major John Chipman Gray joined the Union army in 1862 and had served as an aide to George H. Gordon, a division commander in several theaters, before becoming judge advocate general of the Department of the South, commanded by Major General John G. Foster, in the fall of 1864. He wrote about meeting Sherman to his friend John C. Ropes, a Boston lawyer.

STR. NEMALA, *December* 14, 1864

DEAR JOHN,—I have just passed a whole morning in the company of the greatest military genius of the country in the height of his success. If I were to write a dozen pages I could not tell you a tenth part of what he said, for he talked incessantly and more rapidly than any man I ever saw. A despatch boat goes North immediately on our arrival at Hilton Head with the glorious news of Sherman's success, but I will try to scribble a word or two as we go along in this shaky boat.

A line first about preliminary movements; about the 25th of November General Foster received orders to make demonstrations against the Charleston and Savannah Road and cut it, if possible, with the view of helping General Sherman, and on the 27th I started with General Foster on board the steamer *Nemala*, together with 5000 troops, who after they were landed were to be under the command of General Hatch. General Foster's wound makes him unable either to walk or ride so that he remained on the steamer, and directed operations therefrom. We first attempted to reach the Railroad near Grahamville, but met a battery which barred our progress and we retired after considerable loss. Other demonstrations were made in different directions, and finally a force was landed at Tallifinny Creek and pushing forward after a sharp skirmish gained a position about three-fourths of a mile from the R.R. which we still occupy and from which with our artillery we can prevent the passage of trains at least in the day time. When this force landed I accompanied General Potter who was in command, and the fight which ensued was the first time I was ever under musketry fire or indeed any fire of consequence. It is singular that I should have been two years an aide-de-camp on the staff of a fighting brigadier without hearing a bullet whistle, and within two months after becoming the legal adviser of a supposed sleeping department, I should be in the midst of a hot fire, for it was brisk work and looked badly for a few minutes. I suppose you may by this time have seen Colonel Hartwell who was slightly wounded in the fight at Grahamville while landing his regiment in a most gallant manner. All this, which I would like to dwell on, must give place to the great news. I had a long talk with General Foster about Fort Sumter, but this also I must reserve for a future time. On the morning of the 11th news came that a scout of General Howard's had come through and reported all well and last night after General Foster had once attempted in vain to open communication with General Sherman, he again started on the *Nemala* for Ossabaw Sound, and throwing all business aside, I was bound to go with him. We started about half past seven P.M., and reached Ossabaw Sound at two A.M., where we were boarded by a signal officer who informed us that Fort McAllister had been captured by General Hazen's division in an assault at five o'clock the night before, and that he (the signal officer) had seen General Sherman. We steamed up the Ogeechee as near to Fort McAllister as the obstructions and supposed torpedoes would allow us, and sending a boat on shore General Sherman with a captain of his staff came off, arriving about half past seven o'clock and remaining till half past one.

First about Fort McAllister, the 'all important capture' of which as General S. terms it, secures an excellent base for such supplies as may be needed. The Fort is very strong mounting twenty-one guns, some of which are field pieces, and many months ago beat off three heavy ironclads, inflicting considerable damage; the assault was made by three columns each of three regiments, and twenty-five minutes by the watch, as General Sherman says, after the first order was given the fort was in our possession. The garrison fought desperately, and several refusing to surrender were killed inside of the Fort. Our loss was about eighty, of whom half were killed and wounded by the explosion of torpedoes buried in the ground which were exploded by our men walking over the works after they were captured. General Sherman set the prisoners to work digging them up and informed the commander of the fort that he had it in consideration to shut him up with a number of his men equal to the number of our men who were killed by torpedoes and blow them up by gunpowder.

General Sherman is the most American looking man I ever saw, tall and lank, not very erect, with hair like thatch, which he rubs up with his hands, a rusty beard trimmed close, a wrinkled face, sharp, prominent red nose, small, bright eyes, coarse red hands; black felt hat slouched over the eyes (he says when he wears anything else the soldiers cry out, as he rides along, 'Hallo, the old man has got a new hat'), dirty dickey with the points wilted down, black, old-fashioned stock, brown field officer's coat with high collar and no shoulder straps, muddy trowsers and one spur. He carries his hands in his pocket, is very awkward in his gait and motions, talks continually and with immense rapidity, and might sit to *Punch* for the portrait of an ideal Yankee. He was of course in the highest spirits and talked with an openness which was too natural not to be something more than apparent. In striving to recall his talk, I find it impossible to recall his language or indeed what he talked about, indeed it would be easier to say what he did not talk about than what he did. I never passed a more amusing or instructive day, but at his departure I felt it a relief and experienced almost an exhaustion after the excitement of his vigorous presence.

He has Savannah securely invested, his left rests securely on the Savannah River, his right at Fort McAllister, his line is within the three mile post from the city, he intends to throw a division across the Savannah to prevent the escape of Hardie from the city, and says he shall take his own time about reducing the city, unless he is hurried by despatches from General Grant, he has 60,000 men with him and only wishes there were more men in Savannah; he says the city is his sure game and stretches out his arm and claws his bony fingers in the air to illustrate how he has his grip on it. There is a 'whip the creation' and an almost boastful confidence in himself which in an untried man would be very disgusting, but in him is intensely comic. I wish you could see him, he is a man after your own heart. Like Grant he smokes constantly, and producing six cigars from his pocket said they were his daily allowance, but judging at the rate at which he travelled through them while he was on our boat, he must often exceed it. He scouted the idea of his going on ships and said he would rather march to Richmond than go there by water, he said he expected to turn north toward the latter end of December, at the same time the sun did, and that if he went through South Carolina, as he in all probability should, that his march through that state would be one of the most horrible things in the history of the world, that the devil himself could not restrain his men in that state, and I do not think that he (that is Sherman, not the devil) would try to restrain them much; he evidently purposes to make the South feel the horrors of war as much as he legitimately can, and if the men trespass beyond the strict limits of his orders he does not inquire into their cases too curiously. He told with evident delight how on his march he could look forty miles in each direction and see the smoke rolling up as from one great bonfire.

His army has been and is in perfect health and spirits, with everything they want, in much better condition than if they had remained at Atlanta, they are all ready to march anywhere with the 'old man' in five minutes. The army has not been on diminished rations a day since they left Chattanooga, and since they started on this last march General Sherman says that they have had turkeys every morning for breakfast, and won't condescend to eat hogs. His better disciplined regiments have now in their knapsacks seven of eight days' bread with which they started and the army brought in great droves of cattle, mules and negroes, the latter of whom he wants to turn over to General Saxton, and evidently does not believe in the African as a soldier; he says he has destroyed $50,000,000.00 worth of property and saved the Government $3,000,000.00 for the expenses of his army.

The steamer is going and I have to close without beginning to say what I wish; General Sherman says the opposition to him was puerile and his infantry was never attacked.

Please show this to my father, and let him take it home, or better take it yourself.

J. C. GRAY, JR.

BESIEGING SAVANNAH: GEORGIA, DECEMBER 1864

John White Geary to Mary Geary

Brigadier General John White Geary commanded the Second Division in the Twentieth Corps, which formed part of the left wing of Sherman's army as it marched through Georgia. Geary wrote to his wife after Lieutenant General William J. Hardee, who held Savannah with 10,000 men, refused Sherman's demand for the surrender of the city.

———————

Near Savannah Ga.   Dec 1864

My Dearest Mary

Yesterday was a day racy and rare, and under all the circumstances long to be remembered. We had been thirty-one days cut off from the world and "the rest of mankind," during which period we had not received a single word concerning the affairs of the North, except occasionally through the unreliable and lying *sheets* of the South, but yesterday we had a carnival of letters and newspapers. From you I acknowledge favors of Nov 10th, 13th, 15th & 17th. Also two from Willie G. and one from Mary Lee. Of course I proceed to write to you first, and at a more convenient season I will reply to theirs. The news of the presidential election was all fresh to us, although we had learned, through rebel sources, of Mr. Lincoln's election. I hope the friends of "little Mac" are satisfied now. They certainly understand by this time that they are making a very large sized error and that their dogmas are not in keeping with the progress of the age, in which our lots have been cast, away up in the noon of the nineteenth century. They seem to be antiquated fossils, and like the Jews in the Christian era, cannot discern the signs of the times. It is now certain that the United States must be all *free* or all *slave*, and the momentous question has been decided in favor of freedom by the edict of the people in November. The rebellion is certainly much crippled by the result, and as Mr. Lincoln has had so great a triumph, he can afford to make *peace* by the offer of most generous terms.

This last campaign of Sherman's has almost disembowelled the rebellion. The state of Georgia is about as badly destroyed as some of the tribes of the land of Canaan were by the Israelitish army, according to Biblical record. One hundred millions of dollars would not restore it to its former condition. But I will come at once to our present condition. We are in sight of the "promised land," after a pilgrimage of three hundred miles, and we are also once more beseiging a city of huge proportions, and a huge and defiant army, with whom we have to contend for its possession by force of arms, which seems to be the only arbitrament left, as they have just refused Sherman's demand for the surrender of the city. The place is a great prize, and like all things of great value, very difficult to obtain.

There will therefore be some hard fighting, but I think it must yield. My troops are now engaged throwing up immense batteries from which we expect to commence the bombardment of the city on next Tuesday. Being in good shelling range we will soon knock it to pieces. As I intend to write you frequently, I will not anticipate results, but will wait to chronicle each in its turn as it occurs. The climate is very warm here now, and every insect is creeping about. Butter flies are dallying in the sunshine, and even snakes of every kind are creeping about. Shad are most abundant in the rivers, but the luxury of fish or oysters has not yet been tasted by us, as the fishing waters are covered by the enemy's cannon. Almost every breeze bears the hostile blast of the trumpet, and the thunder of the enemy's guns answers loudly to the thunder of our own. But I think our success is certain.

Although our "Cracker Line" is open, still through the laziness of some party our fresh supplies have not yet reached us. Though we look for the first installment almost hourly. We are now on very short allowance.

I do not recollect whether I told you, in my last, about the death of my famous black horse, "Charly." He died near the city of Milledgeville, *full of honor*. He was a noble *charger* and carried me safely through a score of battles. I miss the old fellow very much, and I hope ere long to find one as good, but probably never will find one with so much nobleness of character.

John Brooks (my servant) while out foraging was captured a few days ago. He was in company with a Captain Geary of one of my batteries who was also captured.

Give my love to all the children. Remember me most kindly to Captain Lee and Mrs Church and Comfort, and be particular not to forget my good friend Eberly.

Hoping that God will stand by me during this struggle and preserve me from wound and death, and restore me again in health to my family to enjoy repose in its loved society. I am as ever

Your loving husband
J. W. Geary
December 17, 1864

UNION LOOTERS: GEORGIA, DECEMBER 1864

Mary S. Mallard:
Journal, December 15–21, 1864

A week before his army left Atlanta, Sherman issued orders directing his troops to "forage liberally on the country" during their march through Georgia. His orders prohibited foraging parties from entering dwellings and placed restrictions on the destruction of property. During the march Sherman's infantry moved in four large columns roughly twenty miles apart, while his cavalry maneuvered along the front and flanks of the advance. As a result, Georgia residents were sometimes visited by different parties of Union "bummers" (foragers), as well as by groups of stragglers and Confederate deserters. At the end of the march Sherman estimated that his troops had consumed or destroyed resources worth $100 million, of which $20 million was used by the army, while the rest was "simple waste and destruction." Union troops engaged in very few acts of physical violence against white civilians, while violence against African Americans was more common. In December 1864 Mary S. Mallard was staying with her widowed mother Mary Jones at Montevideo, a rice and cotton plantation on the North Newport River in Liberty County south of Savannah. She wrote about her encounters with Union soldiers.

―――――――――

Thursday, December 15th. About ten o'clock Mother walked out upon the lawn, leaving me in the dining room. In a few moments Elsie came running in to say the Yankees were coming. I went to the front door and saw three dismounting at the stable, where they found Mother and rudely demanded of her: "Where are your horses and mules? Bring them out!"—at the same instant rushing by her as she stood in the door. I debated whether to go to her or remain in the house. The question was soon settled, for in a moment a stalwart Kentucky Irishman stood before me, having come through the pantry door. I scarcely knew what to do. His salutation was: "Have you any whiskey in the house?"

I replied: "None that I know of."

"You ought to know," he said in a very rough voice.

I replied: "This is not my house, so I do not know what is in it."

Said he: "I mean to search this house for arms, but I'll not hurt you." He then commenced shaking and pushing the folding door and calling for the key.

Said I: "If you will turn the handle and slide the door you will find it open."

The following interrogatories took place:

"What's in that box?"

"Books."

"What's in that room beyond?"

"Search for yourself."

"What's in that press?"

"I do not know."

"Why don't you know?"

"Because this is my mother's house, and I have recently come here."

"What's in that box?"

"Books and pictures."

"What's that, and where's the key?"

"My sewing machine. I'll get the key."

He then opened the side door and discovered the door leading into the old parlor. "I want to get into that room."

"If you will come around, I will get the key for you."

As we passed through the parlor into the entry he ran upstairs and commenced searching my bedroom. "Where have you hid your arms?"

"There are none in the house. You can search for yourself."

He ordered me to get the keys immediately to all my trunks and bureaus. I did so, and he put his hands into everything, even a little trunk containing needle books, boxes of hair, and other small things. All this was under cover of searching for arms and ammunition. He called loudly for *all* the keys; I told him my mother would soon be in the house and she would get her keys for him.

While he was searching my bureau he turned to me and asked: "Where is your watch?"

I told him my husband had worn my watch, and he had been captured the day before at Walthourville.

Shaking his fist at me, he said: "Don't you lie to me! You have got a watch!"

I felt he could have struck me to the floor; but looking steadily at him, I replied: "I have a watch and chain, and my husband has them with him."

"Well, were they taken from him when he was captured?"

"That I do not know, for I was not present."

Just at this moment I heard another Yankee coming up the stair steps and saw a young Tennessean going into Mother's room, where he commenced his search. Mother came in soon after and got her keys; and there we were, following these two men around the house, handing them keys (as they would order us to do in the most insolent manner), and seeing almost everything opened and searched and tumbled about.

The Tennessean found an old workbox, and hearing something rattling in it, he thought it was coin and would have broken it open. But Dick, the Kentuckian, prevented him until Mother got the key, and his longing eyes beheld a bunch of keys.

In looking through the bureaus, to Mother's surprise, Dick pulled out a sword that had belonged to her deceased brother and had been in her possession for thirty-one years. Finding it so rusty, they could scarcely draw it from the scabbard, and concluded it would not kill many men in this war and did not take it away.

The Tennessean found a large spyglass which had belonged to Mr. Mallard's father, and brought it out as quite a prize.

I said to him: "You won't take that!"

"No," said he, "I only want to look through it. It's of no use to me."

Dick went into the attic, but did not call for the keys to the two locked rooms. He took up the spyglass, and winking at me said: "I mean to take this to Colonel Jones." (Susan had told him Mary Ruth was Colonel Jones's child.)

Mother said to him: "Is your commanding officer named Jones?"

He laughed and said he meant to take the glass to Colonel Jones.

I said: "You won't take that, for I value it very much, as it belonged to my father."

Said he: "It's of no use to you."

"No, none whatever beyond the association, and you have much finer in your army."

He did not take it, though we thought he would have done so if we had not been present. He turned to Mother and said: "Old lady, haven't you got some whiskey?"

She replied: "I don't know that I have."

"Well," said he, "I don't know who ought to know if you don't!"

Mother asked him if he would like to see his mother and wife treated in this way—their house invaded and searched.

"Oh," said he, "none of us have wives!"

Whilst Mother walked from the stable with one of the Yankees from Kentucky he had a great deal to say about the South bringing on the war. On more than one occasion they were anxious to argue political questions with her. Knowing it was perfectly useless, she would reply: "This is neither the time nor place for these subjects. My countrymen have decided that it was just and right to withdraw from the Union. We wished to do it peaceably; you would not allow it. We have now appealed to arms; and I have nothing more to say with you upon the subject."

Mother asked him if he would like to see his mother and sisters treated as they were doing us.

"No," said he, "I would not. And I never do enter houses, and shall not enter yours."

And he remained without while the other two men searched. They took none of the horses or mules, as they were too old.

A little before dinner we were again alarmed by the presence of five Yankees dressed as marines. One came into the house— a very mild sort of a man. We told him the house had already been searched. He asked if the soldiers had torn up anything. One of the marines (as they called themselves) came into the pantry and asked if they could get anything to eat. Mother told them she had only what was prepared for our own dinner, and if they chose they could take it where it was—in the kitchen. They said they preferred to take it there, and going to the kitchen, they cursed the servants awfully, ordered milk, potatoes, and other things. They called for knives and forks, and having no others Mother sent out those we used; but they ordered Milton to take them immediately back and to tell his mistress to put them away in a safe place, as "a parcel of damned Yankees" would soon be along, and they would take every one from her.

We hoped they would not intrude upon the dwelling; but as soon as they finished eating, the four came in, and one commenced a thorough search, ordering us to get him all the keys. He found some difficulty in fitting the keys, and I told him I would show them to him if he would hand me the bunch.

He replied: "I will give them to you when I am ready to leave the house."

He went into the attic and instituted a thorough search into every hole and corner. He opened a large trunk containing the private papers of my dear father, and finding a tin canister, he tried to open it. Mother could not immediately find the key, and as he spoke insolently to her about getting the key, she told him he had better break it, but she could assure him it contained only the private papers of her husband, who was a minister of the gospel.

"Damn it," he said, "if you don't get the key I will break it. I don't care!"

In looking through the trunk he found a beautiful silver goblet which had been given to Mother by her dear little granddaughter Julia, and which she had valued as a keepsake. His eyes sparkled as he held it up and called out: "Here's something pretty, boys!"

Mother looked at him scornfully and said: "And would you take it?"

He said no, and put it quickly down, although we believe only our presence kept him from pocketing it.

One of the party came in with a secession rosette which Brother Charlie had worn at the great meeting in Savannah when he was mayor of the city. Mother had given it to Jack with a few letters to put away. As they were riding up he took it from Jack, and we were quite amused to see him come in with it pinned on the lapel of his jacket. This one was quite inclined to argue about the origin of the struggle.

One of them had an old cap—the helmet-shaped cap with horsehair plume belonging to the Liberty Independent Troop, and the jacket also, as we afterwards understood were those formerly used by the troop. Being blue with bell buttons, they could very well pass for sailors' jackets. They had rigged themselves from some house they had searched before coming here.

After spending a long time in the search, they prepared to leave with all the horses. Mother told them they were over seventeen years old and would do them no service. They took away one mule, but in a short time we saw it at the gate: they had turned it back.

After they left I found that my writing desk had been most thoroughly searched and everything scattered, and all my little articles of jewelry, pencils, etc., scattered. A gold pen was taken from my workbox.

Mother felt so anxious about Kate King that she sent Charles and Niger in the afternoon to urge her coming over to us, and told them if she was too unwell to walk or ride, they must take her up in their arms and let someone help to bring the little children. But they did not reach South Hampton, as they met a Yankee picket which turned Niger back and took Charles with them to assist in carrying horses to Midway, promising to let him return.

Friday, December 16th. Much to our relief, Prophet came over this morning with a note from Kate to know if we thought she could come to us. Mother wrote her to come immediately, which she did in great fear and trembling, not knowing but that she would meet the enemy on the road. We all felt truly grateful she had been preserved by the way.

About four in the afternoon we heard the clash of arms and noise of horsemen, and by the time Mother and I could get downstairs we saw forty or fifty men in the pantry, flying hither and thither, ripping open the safe with their swords and breaking open the crockery cupboards. Fearing we might not have a chance to cook, Mother had some chickens and ducks roasted and put in the safe for our family. These the men seized whole, tearing them to pieces with their teeth like ravenous beasts. They were clamorous for whiskey, and ordered us to get our keys. One came to Mother to know where her meal and flour were, insisted upon opening her locked pantry, and took every particle. They threw the sacks across their horses. Mother remonstrated and pointed to her helpless family; their only reply was: "We'll take it!"

They flew around the house, tearing open boxes and everything that was closed. They broke open Mother's little worktable with an andiron, hoping to find money or jewelry; it contained principally little mementos that were valuable only to herself. Failing to find treasure, they took the sweet little locks of golden hair that her mother had cut from the heads of her angel children near a half century ago, and scattering them upon the floor trampled them under their feet. A number of them rifled the sideboard, taking away knives, spoons, forks, tin cups, coffeepots, and everything they wished. They broke open Grandfather's old liquor case and carried off two of the large square gallon bottles, and drank up all the blackberry wine and vinegar which was in the case. It was vain to utter a word, for we were completely paralyzed by the fury of these ruffians.

A number of them went into the attic into a little storeroom and carried off twelve bushels of meal Mother had stored there for our necessities. She told them they were taking all she had to support herself and daughter, a friend, and five little children. Scarcely one regarded even the sound of her voice; those who did laughed and said they would leave one sack to keep us from starving. But they only left some rice which they did not want, and poured out a quart or so of meal upon the floor. At other times they said they meant to starve us to death. They searched trunks and bureaus and wardrobes, calling for shirts and men's clothes.

We asked for their officer, hoping to make some appeal to him; they said they were all officers and would do as they pleased. We finally found one man who seemed to make a little show of authority, which was indicated by a whip which he carried. Mother appealed to him, and he came up and ordered the men out. They instantly commenced cursing him, and we thought they would fight one another. They brought a wagon and took another from the place to carry off their plunder.

It is impossible to imagine the horrible uproar and stampede through the house, every room of which was occupied by them, all yelling, cursing, quarreling, and running from one room to another in wild confusion. Such was their blasphemous language, their horrible countenances and appearance, that we realized what must be the association of the lost in the world of eternal woe. Their throats were open sepulchres, their mouths filled with cursing and bitterness and lies. These men belonged to Kilpatrick's cavalry. We look back upon their conduct in the house as a horrible nightmare, too terrible to be true.

When leaving they ordered all the oxen to be gotten up early next morning.

Montevideo, *Saturday*, December 17th, 1864

As soon as it was light Kate discovered an officer near the house, which was a great relief to our feelings. Mother and I went down immediately, when she said to him: "Sir, I see that you are an officer; and I come to entreat your protection for my family, and that you will not allow your soldiers to enter my dwelling, as it has been already three times searched and every particle of food and whatever they wanted taken." He replied it was contrary to orders for the men to be found in houses, and the penalty was death; and so far as his authority extended with his own men, none of them should enter the house. He said he and his squad (there were many others present) had come on a foraging expedition, and intended to take only provisions.

Upon Mother's inviting him to see some of the work of the previous evening he came in and sat awhile in the parlor. Before leaving he discovered a portable desk on a table and walked up and opened it. She said: "That is my private property; it is here for my own use, and has only a little paper in it." He closed it immediately. (It had previously escaped observation and removal.)

The Yankees made the Negroes bring up the oxen and carts, and took off all the chickens and turkeys they could find. They carried off all the syrup from the smokehouse. We had one small pig, which was all the meat we had left; they took the whole of it. Mother saw everything like food stripped from her premises, without the power of uttering one word. Finally they rolled out the carriage and took that to carry off a load of chickens. They took everything they possibly could.

The soldier who acted as our volunteer guard was from Ohio, and older than anyone we had seen; for generally they were young men and so active that Mother called them "fiery flying serpents." As he was going Mother went out of the house and said to him: "I cannot allow you to leave without thanking you for your kindness to myself and family; and if I had anything to offer I would gladly make you some return."

He replied: "I could not receive anything, and only wish I was here to guard you always."

It was not enough that they should insult us by converting our carriage into a chicken-cart and take it away drawn by our own carriage horses; but they sent in to tell Mother if she wanted her carriage to send for it, and when they were done with it she might have it. We afterwards learned it was broken to pieces and left beyond Midway Church.

They took off today June, Martin, George, Ebenezer, Little Pulaski, our house servant Jack, and Carpenter Pulaski. Seeing the two last-named going away, Mother called to the soldier who had them in charge: "Why are you taking my young men away?"

He said: "They need not go if they do not want to."

She then asked: "Boys, do you wish to go or stay?"

They immediately replied: "We wish to stay."

She then said: "Do you hear that? Now, by what right do you force them away?"

They had Pulaski laden down with our turkeys, and wanted Jack to drive one of the carts. So they were all carried off—carriages, wagons, carts, horses and mules and servants, with food and provisions of every kind—and, so far as they were concerned, leaving us to starvation.

A little while after this party started, Mother walked to the smokehouse and found an officer taking sugar that had been put to drip. He was filling a bag with all that was dry. He seemed a little ashamed of being caught in the act, but did not return the sugar, but carried it off on his horse. He was mounted on Mr. Audley King's pet horse, a splendid animal which he had just stolen, and as he rode off said: "How the man who *owns* this horse will curse the Yankee who took him when he goes home and finds him gone!" He had Mr. King's servant mounted on another of his horses, and no doubt knew Mrs. King was with us and would hear the remark.

Immediately we went to work moving some salt and the little remaining sugar into the house; and while we were doing it a Missourian came up and advised us to get everything into the house as quickly as possible, and he would protect us while doing so. He offered to show Mother how to hide her things. She said: "We need instruction from Yankees, for we have never been accustomed to any such mean business." He said he had enlisted to fight for the *Constitution*; but since then the war had been turned into another thing, and he did not approve this abolitionism, for his wife's people all owned slaves. He told us what afterwards proved false—that ten thousand infantry would soon pass through Riceboro on their way to Thomasville.

Soon after this some twenty rode up and caught me having a barrel rolled toward the house. They were gentlemanly. A few only dismounted; said they were from various of our Confederate States. They said the war would soon be over, for they would have Savannah in a few days.

I replied: "Savannah is not the Confederacy."

They spoke of the number of places they had taken.

I said: "Yes, and do you hold them?"

One of them replied: "Well, I do admire your spunk."

They inquired for all the large plantations.

Squads came all day until near dark. We had no time to eat a mouthful. The remaining ox-wagons were taken to the cornhouse and filled with corn.

Sabbath, December 18th. We passed this day with many fears, but no Yankees came to the lot; though many went to Carlawter and were engaged carrying off corn, the key of the cornhouse having been taken from Cato the day before and the door ordered to be left open. A day comparatively free from interruptions was very grateful to us, though the constant state of apprehension in which we were was distressing.

In the afternoon, while we were engaged in religious services, reading and seeking protection of our Heavenly Father, Captain Winn's Isaiah came bringing a note from Mr. Mallard to me and one from Mr. John Stevens to Mother, sending my watch. This was our first intelligence from Mr. Mallard, and oh, how welcome to us all; though the note brought no hope of his release, as the charge against him was taking up arms against the U.S. Captain Winn had been captured but released. We were all in such distress that Mother wrote begging Mr.

Stevens to come to us. We felt so utterly alone that it would be a comfort to have him with us.

Monday, December 19th. Squads of Yankees came all day, so that the servants scarcely had a moment to do anything for us out of the house. The women, finding it entirely unsafe for them to be out of the house at all, would run in and conceal themselves in our dwelling. The few remaining chickens and some sheep were killed. These men were so outrageous at the Negro houses that the Negro men were obliged to stay at their houses for the protection of their wives; and in some instances they rescued them from the hands of these infamous creatures.

Tuesday, December 20th. A squad of Yankees came soon after breakfast. Hearing there was one yoke of oxen left, they rode into the pasture and drove them up, and went into the woods and brought out the horse-wagon, to which they attached the oxen. Needing a chain for the purpose, they went to the well and took it from the well bucket. Mother went out and entreated them not to take it from the well, as it was our means of getting water. They replied: "You have no right to have even wood or water," and immediately took it away.

Wednesday, December 21st. 10 A.M. Six of Kilpatrick's cavalry rode up, one of them mounted on Mr. Mallard's valuable gray named Jim. They looked into the dairy and empty smokehouse, every lock having been broken and doors wide open day and night. They searched the servants' houses; then they thundered at the door of the dwelling. Mother opened it, when one of them presented a pistol to her breast and demanded why she dared to keep her house closed, and that "he be damned if he would not come into it."

She replied: "I prefer to keep my house closed because we are a helpless and defenseless family of women and little children. And one of your officers informed me that the men were not to enter private dwellings. And it is also contrary to the published orders of your general."

He replied: "I'll be damned if I don't come in and take just what I want. Some of the men got wine here, and we must have some."

She told them her house had been four times searched in every part, and everything taken from it. And recognizing one who had been of the party that had robbed us, she said: "You know my meal and everything has been taken."

He said: "We left you a sack of meal and that rice."

Mother said: "You left us some rice; but out of twelve bushels of meal you poured out a quart or so upon the floor—as you said, to keep us from starving."

She then entreated them, on account of the health of her daughter, not to enter the house. With horrible oaths they rode off, shooting two ducks in the yard.

About half an hour after, three came. One knocked in the piazza and asked if Mother always kept her doors locked. She said she had recently done so by the advice of an officer; and Kate King said: "We have been compelled to do so since the house has been so repeatedly ransacked."

He said: "Well, I never do that and did not come for that." Asked if we knew Mrs. S—— of Dorchester, for he had turned some men out of her house who were ransacking it. He demeaned himself with respect, and did not insist upon coming in.

Upon one occasion one of the men as he sat on the bench in the piazza had his coat buttoned top and bottom, and inside we could plainly see a long row of stolen breast pins and jewelry—gallant trophies, won from defenseless women and children at the South to adorn the persons of their mothers, wives, sisters, and friends in Yankeeland!

One hour after, five came. Mother and Kate trembled from head to feet. It appeared as if this day's trials were more than they could bear. They knelt and asked strength from God; went down and found that three had already entered the pantry with false keys brought for the purpose. They immediately proceeded to cut open the wires of the safe and took all they wanted, amongst other things a tin kettle of eggs we had managed to get.

Mother said to them: "Why, you have entered my house with false keys!"

With demoniacal leer they said: "We want none of your keys," and tried to put in one of those they brought into the pantry door.

She told them: "Your soldiers have already broken the key in that lock, and it cannot be opened; but everything has already been taken." When they insultingly insisted the door should be opened, Mother told them: "Very well, break it open just as soon as you please."

She remonstrated against their coming over the house, and told them of the order of the officers. They replied none of their officers prohibited them from coming in, and they would be damned if they would mind any such orders, would be damned if they did not go where they pleased, and would be damned if they did not take what they pleased. Mother remonstrated, and in her earnest entreaty placed her hand upon the shoulder of one of them, saying: "You must not go over my house." Strange to say, they did not go beyond the pantry, and appeared restrained, as we afterwards believed, by the hand of God. They said they wanted pots and buckets, for they were in camp and had nothing to cook in. One asked for whiskey. To our amusement the man who stole the eggs stumbled and fell as he went down the steps and broke them all—but carried off the bucket. (Psalm 27:2—"When the wicked, even mine enemies and my foes, came upon me to eat up my flesh, they stumbled and fell.")

At dinner time twelve more came—six or seven to the door asking for flour and meal. Mother told them she was a defenseless widow with an only daughter on the eve of again becoming a mother, a young friend, and five little children dependent on her for food and protection. They laughed and said: "Oh, we have heard just such tales before!" They wanted to know why the house was kept locked; said it would only make it worse for us. (This had proven false, for when the doors were open it was impossible to keep them out.) Kate observed a large cravat upon the neck of one made of a black silk dress of hers which had been taken by one of them a few days before. Every species of men's clothing in our trunks and bureaus and portmanteaus was taken, but none of our personal apparel, for we generally stood by when they were searching our wardrobes. They took every piece of jewelry they could find. Twelve sheep were found shot and left in the pasture—an act of wanton wickedness.

Late in the afternoon more came and carried off the few remaining ducks. Going to the Negro houses, they called Cato, the driver, and told him they knew he was feeding "that damned old heifer in the house," and they would "blow out his damned brains" if he gave her another morsel to eat, for they meant to starve her to death. Pointing to the chapel, they asked what house that was. Cato answered: "A church which my master had built for the colored people on the place to hold prayers in the week and preach in on Sunday." They said: "Yes, there he told all his damned lies and called it preaching." And with dreadful oaths they cursed him. To Patience, when they were taking good and valuable books from his library (as they said, to send their old fathers at home), they said, when she spoke with honor of her master and his labors for the good of the colored people: "He was a damned infernal villain, and we only wish he was now alive; we would blow his brains out." To Sue they said, when she spoke of his goodness to the people: "We wish he was now here; we would cut his throat." They stole two blankets from July, and attempted to steal his hat. They took a piggin of boiled potatoes from Sue, and threw the piggin in the marsh when they had eaten them.

After all the day's trials, late at night came Kate's servant Prophet bringing her some clothing and chickens. We were rejoiced to see anyone. He reported South Hampton had been visited by a hundred and fifty men, who had taken all the corn given to the Negroes (three months' allowance), killed forty or fifty hogs and taken seven beef cattle, stolen all the syrup and sugar from the Negroes, and taken their clothing, crawling under their houses and beds searching for buried articles.

"THE TORTURE OF LOYAL MEN":
NEW YORK, JANUARY 1865

Harper's Weekly: *Retaliation*

January 7, 1865

In May 1864 the congressional Joint Committee on the Conduct of the War published testimony from recently paroled Union soldiers recounting their suffering from cold and hunger in the Belle Isle prison camp in Richmond, along with lithographic images of several emaciated former prisoners. As reports of the horrific conditions at Andersonville and other southern prison camps reached the North in the summer and fall of 1864, there were increasing calls for retaliation. *Harper's Weekly*, an illustrated journal with a circulation of more than 100,000 copies, addressed the question early in the New Year. Retaliation was an accepted practice under the laws of war, but one that the Lincoln administration was reluctant to engage in, as shown by its response to the Fort Pillow massacre (see pp. 57–59 in this volume). Beginning on January 16, 1865, the Senate would debate a resolution calling for captured Confederate officers to be given the same food, clothing, and shelter as Union prisoners, and on January 31 adopt an amended version that "directed" the executive to retaliate on Confederate prisoners in an "effective" manner. The resolution was never considered by the House of Representatives. On January 24 Robert Ould, the Confederate commissioner for exchange, would write to Grant offering to exchange "all" Union prisoners. His letter was understood to signal a willingness to treat black and white prisoners equally, and general exchanges would resume in February 1865. During the war at least 30,000 Union and 26,000 Confederate soldiers died while being held as prisoners.

IF we were at war with cannibals who ate alive the prisoners whom they took from our armies, we could not retaliate in kind. If we were fighting Indians who burned their captives at the stake, we could not retaliate in kind. We are at war with men whom the long habit of enslaving other men has imbruted and barbarized, and who starve and freeze to death the prisoners who fall into their hands. Of the fact there can be no reasonable doubt. The testimony is conclusive. Nor is there any reason why men who do not hesitate in time of peace to force other men to work for them without wages, that they may live in idleness and call themselves "gentlemen," should be reluctant to expose their prisoners to starvation. It is not so barbarous to starve a prisoner who has been fighting against you as it is to whip a man to death because he will not work for you for nothing.

What ought to be done? It is a question which is constantly asked and is not easy to answer. It is estimated that we have some sixty thousand rebel prisoners, and that the rebels have about forty-five thousand loyal men in their hands. If we exchange them man for man we give the staggering rebellion a fresh army. That is one of the purposes of the rebel starvation of our men. Yet how can we relieve their unhappy condition if they are not exchanged?

Retaliation is a policy authorized by the customs of all nations. It has its limits of course. With us the object of retaliation would be to put an end to the torture of loyal men. But it could not use torture as a means. Northern men would not tolerate it. They are not used to seeing women whipped for so loving their children as to try to save them from being sold at the shambles, and they could not starve helpless men to death.

But if retaliation does not admit torture it does allow death. Retaliation need not necessarily be in kind. If it be wise to resort to it at all in the present instance—and of that there must always be a question—then for the Union prisoners put to death by the slow agony of starvation and exposure, certain designated rebel prisoners should be shot to death. When two Union officers were to be hung in Richmond the prompt order of the Government that two rebel officers in our hands should suffer the same fate saved our men. So when the rebel officers were placed in the trenches before Charleston, it procured the release of Union officers who had been put under fire. And when retaliation on either side has been carried to extremity it has not occasioned a general massacre, as some unwise persons predicted.

The question at best is very difficult. No Government ought to be severely censured either for refusing to reinforce its enemy's army, or for declining to destroy prisoners of war. To justify retaliation in the abstract is very easy: to advise it in a specific instance is to assume a very solemn responsibility.

"THE MOST PERNICIOUS IDEA":
GEORGIA, JANUARY 1865

Howell Cobb to James A. Seddon

In January 1864 Major General Patrick R. Cleburne presented a memorandum to the senior commanders of the Army of Tennessee proposing that the Confederacy emancipate slaves and enlist them as soldiers. A copy was sent to Jefferson Davis, who ordered the suppression of the memorandum and of discussion about it. By the autumn of 1864 the Confederate need for manpower had forced Davis to revisit the question. In his message to the Confederate Congress on November 7, Davis called for enlisting 40,000 slaves as military laborers and emancipating them once their service was completed. While rejecting the arming of slaves at the present time, he wrote that "should the alternative ever be presented of subjugation or of the employment of the slave as a soldier, there seems no reason to doubt what should then be our decision." At about the same time, Robert E. Lee endorsed using slaves as soldiers in a private letter to Confederate congressman William Porcher Miles. As the use of black soldiers was debated in the Confederate Congress and the southern press, Howell Cobb, a prominent Georgia politician who now commanded the state's local defense troops, wrote to the Confederate secretary of war.

HDQRS. GEORGIA RESERVES AND MIL. DIST. OF GEORGIA,
Macon, Ga., January 8, 1865.

Hon. JAMES A. SEDDON,
Secretary of War, Richmond, Va.:

SIR: Your letter of the 30th of December received by yesterday's mail. I beg to assure you that I have spared no efforts or pains to prosecute vigorously the recruiting of our Army through the conscript camp. It is true, as you say, there are many liable to conscription who have not been reached, and for reasons I have heretofore given I fear never will be reached. Rest assured, however, that I will not cease my efforts in that regard. In response to your inquiries, how our Army is to be recruited, I refer with strength and confidence to the policy of opening the door for volunteers. I have so long and so urgently pressed this matter that I feel reluctant even to allude to it, and yet I should not be true to my strong convictions of duty if I permitted any opportunity to pass without urging and pressing it upon the proper authorities. It is in my opinion not only the best but the only mode of saving the Army, and every day it is postponed weakens its strength and diminishes the number that could be had by it. The freest, broadest, and most unrestricted system of volunteering is the true policy, and cannot be too soon resorted to. I think that the proposition to make soldiers of our slaves is the most pernicious idea that has been suggested since the war began. It is to me a source of deep mortification and regret to see the name of that good and great man and soldier, General R. E. Lee, given as authority for such a policy. My first hour of despondency will be the one in which that policy shall be adopted. You cannot make soldiers of slaves, nor slaves of soldiers. The moment you resort to negro soldiers your white soldiers will be lost to you; and one secret of the favor with which the proposition is received in portions of the Army is the hope that when negroes go into the Army they will be permitted to retire. It is simply a proposition to fight the balance of the war with negro troops. You can't keep white and black troops together, and you can't trust negroes by themselves. It is difficult to get negroes enough for the purpose indicated in the President's message, much less enough for an Army. Use all the negroes you can get, for all the purposes for which you need them, but don't arm them. The day you make soldiers of them is the beginning of the end of the revolution. If slaves will make good soldiers our whole theory of slavery is wrong—but they won't make soldiers. As a class they are wanting in every qualification of a soldier. Better by far to yield to the demands of England and France and abolish slavery, and thereby purchase their aid, than to resort to this policy, which leads as certainly to ruin and subjugation as it is adopted; you want more soldiers, and hence the proposition to take negroes into the Army. Before resorting to it, at least try every reasonable mode of getting white soldiers. I do not entertain a doubt that you can by the volunteering policy get more men into the service than you can arm. I have more fears about arms than about men. For heaven's sake try it before you fill with gloom and despondency the hearts of many of our truest and most devoted men by resorting to the suicidal policy of arming our slaves.

Having answered the inquiries of your letter, let me volunteer in a few words a suggestion. Popularize your administration by some just concessions to the strong convictions of public opinion. Mark you, I do not say yield to popular clamor, but concede something to the earnest convictions of an overwhelming, and, I will say, an enlightened public opinion. First, yield your opposition to volunteering in the form and manner which I have heretofore urged; second, restore General Johnston to the command of the Army of Tennessee, and return General Beauregard to South Carolina.

With Lee in Virginia, Johnston here, and Beauregard in South Carolina you restore confidence and at once revive the hopes of the people. At present I regret to say that gloom and despondency rule the hour, and bitter opposition to the Administration, mingled with disaffection and disloyalty, is manifesting itself. With a dash of the pen the President can revolutionize this state of things, and I earnestly beseech him to do it.

Sincerely, yours,

HOWELL COBB,
Major-General.

"THE BIRTHRIGHT OF THE SOUTH":
NORTH CAROLINA, JANUARY 1865

Catherine Edmondston: Diary, January 9, 1865

From her home in Halifax County, North Carolina, Catherine Edmondston followed the debate over arming slaves while drawing encouragement from the repulse of the Union expedition that attempted to capture Fort Fisher on December 24–25, 1864. The fort guarded the entrance to Wilmington, North Carolina, the last major port still in Confederate hands.

JANUARY 9, 1865

"Out of the abundance of the heart the mouth speaketh," but the hand writeth not. Never were we more absorbed in outward matters, never have we looked on them so anxiously as now, & yet it is days since I have written aught of them. This negro question, this vexed negro question, will if much longer discussed do us more injury than the loss of a battle. Gen Lee advises the Conscription & ultimate Emancipation of 200,000 Slaves to be used as soldiers. One or two rabid partizan papers, Democratic, I might almost say Agrarian to the core, seize on the proposal, hold it up to the people, to the army, in the most attractive lights. They promise the white soldier that if the negro is put in the army, for every negro soldier fifteen white ones will be allowed to return home. They use it as an engine to inflame the passions of one class against another, tell the poor man that the War is but for his rich neighbor's slaves, that his blood is poured out to secure additional riches to the rich, etc., etc., nay one paper, to its shame be it said, the Richmond Enquirer, openly advocates a general Emancipation! as the price for fancied benefits to be obtained by an alliance with England & France. Actually it offers to sell the birthright of the South, not for a mess of pottage, but only for the hope of obtaining one. The Traitor, recreant to principle, lost to every sense of national honour, & blind to what constitutes a true national prosperity—the wonder is that he finds anyone either to read or think seriously of his monstrous proposition. But so it is. Coming as it does on the evacuation of Savannah when we are almost ready to sink under the accumulation of Yankee lies & Yankee bragg, over their boasted Victory over Hood, our money depreciated & depreciating daily more & more, deafened on one side by loud mouthed politicians who advocate "Reconstruction to save Annihilation," "Reconstruction as a choice of Evils," & on the other by the opponents of the Government who expatiate with alass too much truth upon the mismanagement, the waste, the oppression which, cast our eyes which way we will we see around us, threatened again with a new suspension of Habeas Corpus, the Constitution daily trampled under foot by Impressment Laws & Government Schedules, what wonder that many unthinking people catch at this straw as at hope of salvation & delivery from present misery without pausing to ask themselves what will be their condition when they have accepted it. But sounder & better councils will prevail. This beaten and crushed Abolitionist, the Enquirer, will find that the body of the people are against him, that the foxes who have lost their tails are too few in number to govern those who still retain theirs. Slaveholders on principle, & those who hope one day to become slaveholders in their time, will not tacitly yeild their property & their hopes & allow a degraded race to be placed at one stroke on a level with them. But these discussions & these thoughts have occupied us for the past fortnight & such a deluge of gloomy forebodings have been penned out upon us that I almost hailed the frequent mail failures as a blessing.

The tide now seems turning. God has blessed us with a signal victory over the Yankee fleet. God's blessing & God's hand alone it is, for we had but little to do with it. Yankee accounts of the doings of their great Armada have reached us, which make our hearts rise in gratitude to Him who exalteth & who casteth down. In the first place there was no cooperation between the land & naval forces. Then came the gale which drove them out to sea, then the bombardment of Ft Fisher, when the bursting of six six-hundred-pound Parrot Guns on six different Vessels destroyed the confidence of the men who saw their comrades torn, mangled, & bleeding amongst the ruins of their own offensive engines. Then a barge with two hundred & *fifteen tons* of Powder was floated to within a short distance of Ft Fisher & exploded without the slightest result. "The Rebels were not even paralized by it," but why continue the tale of their disaster? Suffice it that God's hand is apparent in it all & the fleet has returned to Hampton Roads discomforted, defeated, dejected, & out of repair & quarrelling miserably amongst themselves. To God alone be the Glory.

Better news but still not authentic reaches us from Tenn. We hear that in a second battle we regained some of the prestige lost before Nashville, of which however we have still only Yankee accounts, but I will refrain all but passing mention of them until they are confirmed. Still they influence our spirits wonderfully. What cheers our very hearts is an intimation that Mr Davis has reinstated Gen Joe Johnston in command. The whole nation hails it with acclamation. Gen D H Hill too is ordered to report to Gen Beauregard, so our old dogs of War are unleashed again.

Sherman is reposing himself in Savannah after his leisurely saunter through Geo & bloodless conquest of that city. He makes a magnificent Christmas gift to Mr Lincoln of the City of Savannah with arms, munitions of war, cotton, Rice, seige guns, etc., too tedious for me to enumerate. He even includes the 25,000 inhabitants in his munificent donation; so, as other autocrats do, he has now only to enslave & deport them. God help them! The evacuation took them entirely by surprise we hear. Few of them escaped & they with the loss of all their effects. Sherman has a right to his self glorification. Let him indulge it whilst we cherish the hope that Beauregard will yet pluck the Laurel crown from his brow & trample it in the dust. His programme, as announced, is the capture of Branchville and advance along the lines of R R into Va. Nous verrons! No news from Petersburg or Richmond for days. All quiet since the defeat of the demonstration on Gordonsville.

As for ourselves, since the negroes holiday at Christmas, for Christmas shone no holiday to any but them, we have been engaged with our year's supply of meat. Frying up Lard, squeezing out cracklins, & all the, to me, disagreeable et ceteras of "a hog killing" are I beleive a perfect happiness to Cuffee! The excitement & interest over the weight of their favorites, the feasting on chitterlings & haslets, the dabbling in grease, seems to constitute a negro paradise, whilst the possession of a "bladder to blow" or better still a hog tail is all a negro child needs of earth's enjoyments. Well we "killed Hogs" here, then we went to Hascosea & did the same thing there.

As usual we were weatherbound & detained 24 hours longer than we intended to remain. Mr E ordered a large box of books, principally farming periodicals (which we had bound the winter before the commencement of the war & which came home whilst we were in great excitement about Ft Sumter & which we have since refrained from opening on account of our unsettled state & the determination we from time to time take to pack up all our books) to be opened, & we passed the time most pleasantly & profitable, rubbing up our old knoledge, forming new plans, agricultural, horticultural, & domestic which this spring & summer we hope to put in execution. I lent an especial eye to the Poultry yard—am armed with several infalible receipts to cure & to prevent "the gapes," all of which I shall try on my spring chickens. In Vinegar receipts too I have come home quite learned & I now sigh for a peice of genuine Vinegar plant! I have some very fine Vinegar made from the skimmings of last year's Sorghhum, but alas, it is too little for my many uses. I used to be famous for Pickles, but my cunning has departed, as the price of whisky and Apple Brandy has risen, for on them did I rely to give my Vinegar body. I am now making yeast by the pailful and even contemplate malting some corn to supply the deficiency. This war is teaching us many things. Dying, spinning, and weaving are no longer unknown mysteries to me. I think of making a compilation of all my practical knoledge on the subject and I intend for the future Peace or war to let *homespun* be my ordinary dress. The object of my ambition is to have a black watered silk trimmed with black thread lace. Think of it! How shall I feel when I pull off my russet yarn spun & woven on the Plantation & bedeck myself in that style! It seems so long since I wore a silk dress that I begin to doubt if I ever owned one.

I have been reading Motley's "United Netherlands" & have derived great comfort from it. We are not so divided, lean not so much on foreign aid, & are not reduced near so low as they were, & yet by perseverance they triumphed. Their advantage lay in a command of the Sea, however, an ability to export and import as they liked, an assistance we too would have did foreign nations uphold their own international Law on the subject of Blockades! International Law, a humbug & a sham, designed only by the strong as a police code to keep order amongst themselves but ignored & forgotten when a weak power suffers from its infringement. This it is which has changed our once strong love to England into Gall! this & the manner in which her boasted *Neutrality* is maintained. Her *Neutrality*, heaven save the mark, is only another word for *deceit*, for mean low petty trickery, for cringing to the U S, saying to us "Am I not in Peace my brother" & stabbing as Joab-like under the fifth rib. Neutrality, faugh! I am reading, too, Ld Bacon's Essays regularly through, one every day, & what a mine of thought they are! The foundation, nay the superstructure, of almost all modern moral Essays is found in them. It is sorrowful in the extreme to see how the human mind but reproduces itself, how the same gem appears generation after generation, modified only in the setting. Sometimes I come on a thought or an idea that I fancied I had thought out of myself, which I had hugged to my heart as my own, when hey presto! I recognize it again stamped by the hand of a master in a form at once so terse, so complete, so chisled, & so chaste that tho two hundred years old, it stands forth as clear, sharp, & distinct as tho just from the mint; & with a sigh I relinquish my proprietorship and take refuge with Solomon in the declaration that "there is nothing new under the sun."

THE RIGHT TO VOTE: TENNESSEE, JANUARY 1865
Petition of the Colored Citizens of Nashville to the Union Convention of Tennessee

After the battle of Franklin, John B. Hood followed the retreating Union army north and reached the outskirts of Nashville on December 2, 1864. Unable to assault the strongly defended city, Hood chose to entrench his army a few miles to the south and await a Union offensive. On December 15–16 George H. Thomas launched a series of attacks that routed Hood's army and forced it to retreat to northern Mississippi. Thomas's decisive victory sealed the fate of the Confederacy in Tennessee and allowed a "Liberty and Union" convention to meet in Nashville on January 9, 1865. Under the leadership of Andrew Johnson, a conservative War Democrat who had served as the military governor of Tennessee since 1862, the convention established a loyal civilian government and proposed amendments to the state constitution. Although the convention adopted an amendment abolishing slavery, it did nothing to extend civil or political rights to black Tennesseans. On February 22, 1865, the abolition amendment would be approved 25,293–48 in a referendum in which only white unionists were permitted to vote. The Tennessee legislature would pass legislation in 1866 allowing blacks to testify against whites and would extend the franchise to black men in 1867.

Nashville, January 9th, 1865:
PETITION OF THE COLORED CITIZENS OF NASHVILLE.

We the undersigned petitioners, American citizens of African descent, natives and residents of Tennessee, and devoted friends of the great National cause, do most respectfully ask a patient hearing of your honorable body in regard to matters deeply affecting the future condition of our unfortunate and long suffering race.

First of all, however, we would say that words are too weak to tell how profoundly grateful we are to the Federal Government for the good work of freedom which it is gradually carrying forward; and for the Emancipation Proclamation which has set free all the slaves in some of the rebellious States, as well as many of the slaves in Tennessee.

After two hundred years of bondage and suffering a returning sense of justice has awakened the great body of the American people to make amends for the unprovoked wrongs committed against us for over two hundred years.

Your petitioners would ask you to complete the work begun by the nation at large, and abolish the last vestige of slavery by the express words of your organic law.

Many masters in Tennessee whose slaves have left them, will certainly make every effort to bring them back to bondage after the reorganization of the State government, unless slavery be expressly abolished by the Constitution.

We hold that freedom is the natural right of all men, which they themselves have no more right to give or barter away, than they have to sell their honor, their wives, or their children.

We claim to be men belonging to the great human family, descended from one great God, who is the common Father of all, and who bestowed on all races and tribes the priceless right of freedom. Of this right, for no offence of ours, we have long been cruelly deprived, and the common voice of the wise and good of all countries, has remonstrated against our enslavement, as one of the greatest crimes in all history.

We claim freedom, as our natural right, and ask that in harmony and co-operation with the nation at large, you should cut up by the roots the system of slavery, which is not only a wrong to us, but the source of all the evil which at present afflicts the State. For slavery, corrupt itself, corrupted nearly all, also, around it, so that it has influenced nearly all the slave States to rebel against the Federal Government, in order to set up a government of pirates under which slavery might be perpetrated.

In the contest between the nation and slavery, our unfortunate people have sided, by instinct, with the former. We have little fortune to devote to the national cause, for a hard fate has hitherto forced us to live in poverty, but we do devote to its success, our hopes, our toils, our whole heart, our sacred honor, and our lives. We will work, pray, live, and, if need be, die for the Union, as cheerfully as ever a white patriot died for his country. The color of our skin does not lesson in the least degree, our love either for God or for the land of our birth.

We are proud to point your honorable body to the fact, that so far as our knowledge extends, not a negro traitor has made his appearance since the begining of this wicked rebellion.

Whether freeman or slaves the colored race in this country have always looked upon the United States as the Promised Land of Universal freedom, and no earthly temptation has been strong enough to induce us to rebel against it. We love the Union by an instinct which is stronger than any argument or appeal which can be used against it. It is the attachment of a child to its parrent.

Devoted as we are to the principles of justice, of love to all men, and of equal rights on which our Government is based, and which make it the hope of the world. We know the burdens of citizenship, and are ready to bear them. We know the duties of the good citizen, and are ready to perform them cheerfully, and would ask to be put in a position in which we can discharge them more effectually. We do not ask for the privilege of citizenship, wishing to shun the obligations imposed by it.

Near 200,000 of our brethren are to-day performing military duty in the ranks of the Union army. Thousands of them have already died in battle, or perished by a cruel martyrdom for the sake of the Union, and we are ready and willing to sacrifice more. But what higher order of citizen is there than the soldier? or who has a greater trust confided to his hands? If we are called on to do military duty against the rebel armies in the field, why should we be denied the privilege of voting against rebel citizens at the ballot-box? The latter is as necessary to save the Government as the former.

The colored man will vote by instinct with the Union party, just as uniformly as he fights with the Union army.

This is not a new question in Tennessee. From 1796 to 1835, a period of thirty-nine years, free colored men voted at all her elections without question. Her leading politicians and statesmen asked for and obtained the suffrages of colored voters, and were not ashamed of it. Such men as *Andrew Jackson*, President of the United States, Hon. *Felix Grundy*, John Bell, Hon. *Hugh L. White, Cave Johnson*, and *Ephraim H. Fos-*

ter, members of the United States Senate and of the Cabinet, *Gen. William Carroll, Samuel Houston*, Aaron V. Brown, and, in fact, all the politicians and candidates of all parties in Tennessee solicited colored free men for their votes at every election.

Nor was Tennessee alone in this respect, for the same privileges was granted to colored free men in North Carolina, to-day the most loyal of all the rebellious States, without ever producing any evil consequences.

If colored men have been faithful and true to the Government of the United States in spite of the Fugitive Slave Law, and the cruel policy often pursued toward them, will they not be more devoted to it now than ever, since it has granted them that liberty which they desired above all things? Surely, if colored men voted without harm to the State, while their brethren were in bondage, they will be much more devoted and watchful over her interests when elevated to the rank of freemen and voters. If they are good law-abiding citizens, praying for its prosperity, rejoicing in its progress, paying its taxes, fighting its battles, making its farms, mines, work-shops and commerce more productive, why deny them the right to have a voice in the election of its rulers?

This is a democracy—a government of the people. It should aim to make every man, without regard to the color of his skin, the amount of his wealth, or the character of his religious faith, feel personally interested in its welfare. Every man who lives under the Government should feel that it is his property, his treasure, the bulwark and defence of himself and his family, his pearl of great price, which he must preserve, protect, and defend faithfully at all times, on all occasions, in every possible manner.

This is not a Democratic Government if a numerous, law-abiding, industrious, and useful class of citizens, born and bred on the soil, are to be treated as aliens and enemies, as an inferior degraded class, who must have no voice in the Government which they support, protect and defend, with all their heart, soul, mind, and body, both in peace and war.

This Government is based on the teachings of the Bible, which prescribes the same rules of action for all members of the human family, whether their complexion be white, yellow, red or black. God no where in his revealed word, makes an invidious and degrading distinction against his children, because of their color. And happy is that nation which makes the Bible its rule of action, and obeys principle, not prejudice.

Let no man oppose this doctrine because it is opposed to his old prejudices. The nation is fighting for its life, and cannot afford to be controlled by prejudice. Had prejudice prevailed instead of principle, not a single colored soldier would have been in the Union army to-day. But principle and justice triumphed, and now near 200,000 colored patriots stand under the folds of the national flag, and brave their breasts to the bullets of the rebels. As we are in the battlefield, so we swear before heaven, by all that is dear to men, to be at the ballot-box faithful and true to the Union.

The possibility that the negro suffrage proposition may shock popular prejudice at first sight, is not a conclusive argument against its wisdom and policy. No proposition ever met with more furious or general opposition than the one to enlist colored soldiers in the United States army. The opponents of the measure exclaimed on all hands that the negro was a coward; that he would not fight; that one white man, with a whip in his hand could put to flight a regiment of them; that the experiment would end in the utter rout and ruin of the Federal army. Yet the colored man has fought so well, on almost every occasion, that the rebel government is prevented, only by its fears and distrust of being able to force him to fight for slavery as well as he fights against it, from putting half a million of negroes into its ranks.

The Government has asked the colored man to fight for its preservation and gladly has he done it. It can afford to trust him with a vote as safely as it trusted him with a bayonet.

How boundless would be the love of the colored citizen, how intense and passionate his zeal and devotion to the government, how enthusiastic and how lasting would be his gratitude, if his white brethren were to take him by the hand and say, "You have been ever loyal to our government; henceforward be voters." Again, the granting of this privilege would stimulate the colored man to greater exertion to make himself an intelligent, respected, useful citizen. His pride of character would be appealed to this way most successfully; he would send his children to school, that they might become educated and intelligent members of society. It used to be thought that ignorant negroes were the most valuable, but this belief probably originated from the fact that it is almost impossible to retain an educated, intelligent man in bondage. Certainly, if the free colored man be educated, and his morals enlightened and improved, he will be a far better member of society, and less liable to transgress its laws. It is the brutal, degraded, ignorant man who is usually the criminal.

One other matter we would urge on your honorable body. At present we can have only partial protection from the courts. The testimony of twenty of the most intelligent, honorable, colored loyalists cannot convict a white traitor of a treasonable action. A white rebel might sell powder and lead to a rebel soldier in the presence of twenty colored soldiers, and yet their evidence would be worthless so far as the courts are concerned, and the rebel would escape. A colored man may have served for years faithfully in the army, and yet his testimony in court would be rejected, while that of a white man who had served in the rebel army would be received.

If this order of things continue, our people are destined to a malignant persecution at the hands of rebels and their former rebellious masters, whose hatred they may have incurred, without precedent even in the South. Every rebel soldier or citizen whose arrest in the perpetration of crime they may have effected, every white traitor whom they may have brought to justice, will torment and persecute them and set justice at defiance, because the courts will not receive negro testimony, which will generally be the only possible testimony in such cases. A rebel may murder his former slave and defy justice, because he committed the deed in the presence of half a dozen respectable colored citizens. He may have the dwelling of his former slave burned over his head, and turn his wife and children out of doors, and defy the law, for no colored man can appear against him. Is this the fruit of freeedom, and the reward of our services in the field? Was it for this that colored soldiers fell by hundreds before Nashville, fighting under the flag of the Union? Is it for this that we have guided Union officers and soldiers, when escaping from the cruel and deadly prisons of the South through forests and swamps, at the risk of our own lives, for we knew that to us detection would be death? Is it for this that we have concealed multitudes of Union refugees in caves and cane-brakes, when flying from the conscription officers and tracked by bloodhounds, and divided with them our last morsal of food? Will you declare in your revised constitution that a pardoned traitor may appear in court and his testimony be heard, but that no colored loyalist shall be believed even upon oath? If this should be so, then will our last state be worse than our first, and we can look for no relief on this side of the grave? Has not the colored man fought, bled and died for the Union, under a thousand great disadvantages and discouragements? Has his fidelity ever had a shadow of suspicion cast upon it, in any matter of responsibility confided to his hands?

There have been white traitors in multitudes in Tennessee, but where, we ask, is the black traitor? Can you forget how the colored man has fought at Fort Morgan, at Milliken's Bend, at Fort Pillow, before Petersburg, and your own city of Nashville?

When has the colored citizen, in this rebellion been tried and found wanting?

In conclusion, we would point to the fact that the States where the largest measure of justice and civil rights has been granted to the colored man, both as to suffrage and his oath in court, are among the most rich, intelligent, enlightened and prosperous. Massachusetts, illustrious for her statesmen and her commercial and manufacturing enterprises and thrift, whose noble liberality has relieved so many loyal refugees and other sufferers of Tennessee, allows her colored citizens to vote, and is ever jealous of their rights. She has never had reason to repent the day when she gave them the right of voting.

Had the southern states followed her example the present rebellion never would have desolated their borders.

Several other Northern States permit negro suffrage, nor have bad effects ever resulted from it. It may be safely affirmed that Tennessee was quite as safe and prosperous during the 39 years while she allowed negro suffrage, as she has been since she abolished it.

In this great and fearful struggle of the nation with a wicked rebellion, we are anxious to perform the full measure of our duty both as citizens and soldiers to the Union cause we consecrate ourselves, and our families, with all that we have on earth. Our souls burn with love for the great government of freedom and equal rights. Our white brethren have no cause for distrust as regards our fidelity, for neither death nor life, nor angels, nor principalities, nor powers, nor things present, nor things to come, nor height, nor depth, nor any other creature, shall be able to separate us from the love of the Union.

Praying that the great God, who is the common Father of us all, by whose help the land must be delivered from present evil, and before whom we must all stand at last to be judged by the rule of eternal justice, and not by passion and prejudice, may enlighten your minds and enable you to act with wisdom, justice, and magnanimity, we remain your faithful friends in all the perils and dangers which threaten our beloved country.

ENLISTING SLAVES "WITHOUT DELAY":
VIRGINIA, JANUARY 1865

Robert E. Lee to Andrew Hunter, January 11, 1865

Lee expressed his opinion on arming slaves in response to a letter soliciting his views from Andrew Hunter, a Virginia state senator whose house in Charlestown had been burned by the Union army in July 1864. While Lee's letter was not published until after the war, his recommendation that the Confederacy should enlist slaves was reported in the Richmond press. At the urging of Judah P. Benjamin, the Confederate secretary of state, Lee would write a letter intended for publication to Confederate congressman Ethelbert Barksdale on February 18. In his letter to Barksdale, Lee argued that arming slaves was "not only expedient but necessary" and that "those who are employed should be freed."

HEADQUARTERS ARMY OF NORTHERN VIRGINIA,
January 11, 1865.

Hon. ANDREW HUNTER,
Richmond, Va.:

DEAR SIR: I have received your letter of the 7th instant, and without confining myself to the order of your interrogatories, will endeavor to answer them by a statement of my views on the subject. I shall be most happy if I can contribute to the solution of a question in which I feel an interest commensurate with my desire for the welfare and happiness of our people.

Considering the relation of master and slave, controlled by humane laws and influenced by Christianity and an enlightened public sentiment, as the best that can exist between the white and black races while intermingled as at present in this country, I would deprecate any sudden disturbance of that relation unless it be necessary to avert a greater calamity to both. I should therefore prefer to rely upon our white population to preserve the ratio between our forces and those of the enemy, which experience has shown to be safe. But in view of the preparations of our enemies, it is our duty to provide for continued war and not for a battle or a campaign, and I fear that we cannot accomplish this without overtaxing the capacity of our white population.

Should the war continue under existing circumstances, the enemy may in course of time penetrate our country and get access to a large part of our negro population. It is his avowed policy to convert the able-bodied men among them into soldiers, and to emancipate all. The success of the Federal arms in the South was followed by a proclamation of President Lincoln for 280,000 men, the effect of which will be to stimulate the Northern States to procure as substitutes for their own people the negroes thus brought within their reach. Many have already been obtained in Virginia, and should the fortune of war expose more of her territory, the enemy would gain a large accession to his strength. His progress will thus add to his numbers, and at the same time destroy slavery in a manner most pernicious to the welfare of our people. Their negroes will be used to hold them in subjection, leaving the remaining force of the enemy free to extend his conquest. Whatever may be the effect of our employing negro troops, it cannot be as mischievous as this. If it end in subverting slavery it will be accomplished by ourselves, and we can devise the means of alleviating the evil consequences to both races. I think, therefore, we must decide whether slavery shall be extinguished by our enemies and the slaves be used against us, or use them ourselves at the risk of the effects which may be produced upon our social institutions. My own opinion is that we should employ them without delay. I believe that with proper regulations they can be made efficient soldiers. They possess the physical qualifications in an eminent degree. Long habits of obedience and subordination, coupled with the moral influence which in our country the white man possesses over the black, furnish an excellent foundation for that discipline which is the best guaranty of military efficiency. Our chief aim should be to secure their fidelity.

There have been formidable armies composed of men having no interest in the cause for which they fought beyond their pay or the hope of plunder. But it is certain that the surest foundation upon which the fidelity of an army can rest, especially in a service which imposes peculiar hardships and privations, is the personal interest of the soldier in the issue of the contest. Such an interest we can give our negroes by giving immediate freedom to all who enlist, and freedom at the end of the war to the families of those who discharge their duties faithfully (whether they survive or not), together with the privilege of residing at the South. To this might be added a bounty for faithful service.

We should not expect slaves to fight for prospective freedom when they can secure it at once by going to the enemy, in whose service they will incur no greater risk than in ours. The reasons that induce me to recommend the employment of negro troops at all render the effect of the measures I have suggested upon slavery immaterial, and in my opinion the best means of securing the efficiency and fidelity of this auxiliary force would be to accompany the measure with a well-digested plan of gradual and general emancipation. As that will be the result of the continuance of the war, and will certainly occur if the enemy succeed, it seems to me most advisable to adopt it at once, and thereby obtain all the benefits that will accrue to our cause.

The employment of negro troops under regulations similar in principle to those above indicated would, in my opinion, greatly increase our military strength and enable us to relieve our white population to some extent. I think we could dispense with the reserve forces except in cases of necessity.

It would disappoint the hopes which our enemies base upon our exhaustion, deprive them in a great measure of the aid they now derive from black troops, and thus throw the burden of the war upon their own people. In addition to the great political advantages that would result to our cause from the adoption of a system of emancipation, it would exercise a salutary influence upon our whole negro population, by rendering more secure the fidelity of those who become soldiers, and diminishing the inducements to the rest to abscond.

I can only say in conclusion that whatever measures are to be adopted should be adopted at once. Every day's delay increases the difficulty. Much time will be required to organize and discipline the men, and action may be deferred until it is too late.

Very respectfully, your obedient servant,

R. E. LEE,
General.

"TO HAVE LAND": GEORGIA, JANUARY 1865

Meeting of Colored Ministers with Edwin M. Stanton and William T. Sherman

When Sherman's army reached Savannah it was accompanied by as many as 20,000 freed people who had liberated themselves by following the Union forces as they marched through Georgia. Although Sherman understood the debilitating effect the loss of slave labor had on the ability of the Confederacy to wage war, once he reached the coast he planned to "clear the army of surplus negros." On January 11 Secretary of War Stanton arrived in Savannah to confer with Sherman and to investigate allegations that his army had treated black refugees cruelly. Reports had reached the North that an unknown number of freed people had drowned in early December while trying to escape Confederate cavalry after Union Brigadier General Jefferson C. Davis ordered his troops to remove a pontoon bridge across Ebenezer Creek, a decision Sherman defended as militarily necessary. At Stanton's urging, Sherman then convened a meeting with local black leaders to solicit their views on emancipation. The minutes of their conference were published in the *New-York Daily Tribune* on February 13, 1865.

MINUTES OF AN INTERVIEW BETWEEN THE COLORED MINISTERS AND CHURCH OFFICERS AT SAVANNAH WITH THE SECRETARY OF WAR AND MAJOR-GEN. SHERMAN.
HEADQUARTERS OF MAJ.-GEN. SHERMAN,
CITY OF SAVANNAH, GA., Jan. 12, 1865—8 P.M.

On the evening of Thursday, the 12th day of January, 1865, the following persons of African descent met by appointment to hold an interview with Edwin M. Stanton, Secretary of War, and Major-Gen. Sherman, to have a conference upon matters relating to the freedmen of the State of Georgia, to-wit:

One: William J. Campbell, aged 51 years, born in Savannah, slave until 1849, and then liberated by will of his mistress, Mrs. May Maxwell. For ten years pastor of the 1st Baptist Church of Savannah, numbering about 1,800 members. Average congregation, 1,900. The church property belonging to the congregation. Trustees white. Worth $18,000.

Two: John Cox, aged fifty-eight years, born in Savannah; slave until 1849, when he bought his freedom for $1,100. Pastor of the 2d African Baptist Church. In the ministry fifteen years. Congregation 1,222 persons. Church property worth $10,000, belonging to the congregation.

Three: Ulysses L. Houston, aged forty-one years, born in Grahamsville, S.C.; slave until the Union army entered Savannah. Owned by Moses Henderson, Savannah, and pastor of Third African Baptist Church. Congregation numbering 400. Church property worth $5,000; belongs to congregation. In the ministry about eight years.

Four: William Bentley, aged 72 years, born in Savannah, slave until 25 years of age, when his master, John Waters, emancipated him by will. Pastor of Andrew's Chapel, Methodist Episcopal Church—only one of that denomination in Savannah; congregation numbering 360 members; church property worth about $20,000, and is owned by the congregation; been in the ministry about twenty years; a member of Georgia Conference.

Five: Charles Bradwell, aged 40 years, born in Liberty County, Ga.; slave until 1851; emancipated by will of his master, J. L. Bradwell. Local preacher in charge of the Methodist Episcopal congregation (Andrew's Chapel) in the absence of the minister; in the ministry 10 years.

Six: William Gaines, aged 41 years; born in Wills Co., Ga. Slave until the Union forces freed me. Owned by Robert Toombs, formerly United States Senator, and his brother, Gabriel Toombs, local preacher of the M.E. Church (Andrew's Chapel.) In the ministry 16 years.

Seven: James Hill, aged 52 years; born in Bryan Co., Ga. Slave up to the time the Union army came in. Owned by H. F. Willings, of Savannah. In the ministry 16 years.

Eight: Glasgon Taylor, aged 72 years, born in Wilkes County, Ga. Slave until the Union army came; owned by A. P. Wetter. Is a local preacher of the M.E. Church (Andrew's Chapel.) In the ministry 35 years.

Nine: Garrison Frazier, aged 67 years, born in Granville

County, N.C. Slave until eight years ago, when he bought himself and wife, paying $1,000 in gold and silver. Is an ordained minister in the Baptist Church, but, his health failing, has now charge of no congregation. Has been in the ministry 35 years.

Ten: James Mills, aged 56 years, born in Savannah; free-born, and is a licensed preacher of the first Baptist Church. Has been eight years in the ministry.

Eleven: Abraham Burke, aged 48 years, born in Bryan County, Ga. Slave until 20 years ago, when he bought himself for $800. Has been in the ministry about 10 years.

Twelve: Arthur Wardell, aged 44 years, born in Liberty County, Ga. Slave until freed by the Union army. Owned by A. A. Solomons, Savannah, and is a licensed minister in the Baptist Church. Has been in the ministry 6 years.

Thirteen: Alexander Harris, aged 47 years, born in Savannah; free born. Licensed minister of Third African Baptist Church. Licensed about one month ago.

Fourteen: Andrew Neal, aged 61 years, born in Savannah, slave until the Union army liberated him. Owned by Mr. Wm. Gibbons, and has been deacon in the Third Baptist Church for 10 years.

Fifteen: Jas. Porter, aged 39 years, born in Charleston, South Carolina; free-born, his mother having purchased her freedom. Is lay-reader and president of the board of wardens and vestry of St. Stephen's Protestant Episcopal Colored Church in Savannah. Has been in communion 9 years. The congregation numbers about 200 persons. The church property is worth about $10,000, and is owned by the congregation.

Sixteen: Adolphus Delmotte, aged 28 years, born in Savannah; free born. Is a licensed minister of the Missionary Baptist Church of Milledgeville. Congregation numbering about 300 or 400 persons. Has been in the ministry about two years.

Seventeen: Jacob Godfrey, aged 57 years, born in Marion, S.C. Slave until the Union army freed me; owned by James E. Godfrey—Methodist preacher now in the Rebel army. Is a class-leader and steward of Andrew's Chapel since 1836.

Eighteen: John Johnson, aged 51 years, born in Bryan County, Georgia. Slave up to the time the Union army came here; owned by W. W. Lincoln of Savannah. Is class-leader and treasurer of Andrew's Chapel for sixteen years.

Nineteen: Robt. N. Taylor, aged 51 years, born in Wilkes Co., Ga. Slave to the time the Union army came. Was owned by Augustus P. Welter, Savannah, and is class-leader in Andrew's Chapel for nine years.

Twenty: Jas. Lynch, aged 26 years, born in Baltimore, Md.; free-born. Is presiding elder of the M.E. Church and missionary to the department of the South. Has been seven years in the ministry and two years in the South.

Garrison Frazier being chosen by the persons present to express their common sentiments upon the matters of inquiry, makes answers to inquiries as follows:

First: State what your understanding is in regard to the acts of Congress and President Lincoln's proclamation, touching the condition of the colored people in the Rebel States.

Answer—So far as I understand President Lincoln's proclamation to the Rebellious States, it is, that if they would lay down their arms and submit to the laws of the United States before the first of January, 1863, all should be well; but if they did not, then all the slaves in the Rebel States should be free henceforth and forever. That is what I understood.

Second—State what you understand by Slavery and the freedom that was to be given by the President's proclamation.

Answer—Slavery is, receiving by *irresistible power* the work of another man, and not by his *consent*. The freedom, as I understand it, promised by the proclamation, is taking us from under the yoke of bondage, and placing us where we could reap the fruit of our own labor, take care of ourselves and assist the Government in maintaining our freedom.

Third: State in what manner you think you can take care of yourselves, and how can you best assist the Government in maintaining your freedom.

Answer: The way we can best take care of ourselves is to have land, and turn it and till it by our own labor—that is, by the labor of the women and children and old men; and we can soon maintain ourselves and have something to spare. And to assist the Government, the young men should enlist in the service of the Government, and serve in such manner as they may be wanted. (The Rebels told us that they piled them up and made batteries of them, and sold them to Cuba; but we don't believe that.) We want to be placed on land until we are able to buy it and make it our own.

Fourth: State in what manner you would rather live—whether scattered among the whites or in colonies by yourselves.

Answer: I would prefer to live by ourselves, for there is a prejudice against us in the South that will take years to get over; but I do not know that I can answer for my brethren. (Mr. Lynch says he thinks they should not be separated, but live together. All the other persons present, being questioned one by one, answer that they agree with Brother Frazier.)

Fifth: Do you think that there is intelligence enough among the slaves of the South to maintain themselves under the Government of the United States and the equal protection of its laws, and maintain good and peaceable relations among yourselves and with your neighbors?

Answer—I think there is sufficient intelligence among us to do so.

Sixth—State what is the feeling of the black population of the South toward the Government of the United States; what is the understanding in respect to the present war—its causes and object, and their disposition to aid either side. State fully your views.

Answer—I think you will find there are thousands that are willing to make any sacrifice to assist the Government of the United States, while there are also many that are not willing to take up arms. I do not suppose there are a dozen men that are opposed to the Government. I understand, as to the war, that the South is the aggressor. President Lincoln was elected President by a majority of the United States, which guaranteed him the right of holding the office and exercising that right over the whole United States. The South, without knowing what he would do, rebelled. The war was commenced by the Rebels before he came into office. The object of the war was not at first to give the slaves their freedom, but the sole object of the war was at first to bring the rebellious States back into the Union and their loyalty to the laws of the United States. Afterward, knowing the value set on the slaves by the Rebels, the President thought that his proclamation would stimulate them to lay down their arms, reduce them to obedience, and help to bring back the Rebel States; and their not doing so has now made the freedom of the slaves a part of the war. It is my opinion that there is not a man in this city that could be started to help the Rebels one inch, for that would be suicide. There were two black men left with the Rebels because they had taken an active part for the Rebels, and thought something might befall them if they stayed behind; but there is not another man. If the prayers that have gone up for the Union army could be read out, you would not get through them these two weeks.

Seventh: State whether the sentiments you now express are those only of the colored people in the city; or do they extend to the colored population through the country? and what are your means of knowing the sentiments of those living in the country?

Answer: I think the sentiments are the same among the colored people of the State. My opinion is formed by personal communication in the course of my ministry, and also from the thousands that followed the Union army, leaving their homes and undergoing suffering. I did not think there would be so many; the number surpassed my expectation.

Eighth: If the Rebel leaders were to arm the slaves, what would be its effect?

Answer: I think they would fight as long as they were before the bayonet, and just as soon as they could get away, they would desert, in my opinion.

Ninth: What, in your opinion, is the feeling of the colored people about enlisting and serving as soldiers of the United States? and what kind of military service do they prefer?

Answer: A large number have gone as soldiers to Port Royal to be drilled and put in the service; and I think there are thousands of the young men that would enlist. There is something about them that perhaps is wrong. They have suffered so long from the Rebels that they want to shoulder the musket. Others want to go into the Quartermaster's or Commissary's service.

Tenth: Do you understand the mode of enlistments of colored persons in the Rebel States by State agents under the Act of Congress? If yea, state what your understanding is.

Answer: My understanding is, that colored persons enlisted by State agents are enlisted as substitutes, and give credit to the States, and do not swell the army, because every black man enlisted by a State agent leaves a white man at home; and, also, that larger bounties are given or promised by State agents than are given by the States. The great object should be to push through this Rebellion the shortest way, and there seems to be something wanting in the enlistment by State agents, for it don't strengthen the army, but takes one away for every colored man enlisted.

Eleventh: State what, in your opinion, is the best way to enlist colored men for soldiers.

Answer: I think, sir, that all compulsory operations should be put a stop to. The ministers would talk to them, and the young men would enlist. It is my opinion that it would be far better for the State agents to stay at home, and the enlistments to be made for the United States under the direction of Gen. Sherman.

In the absence of Gen. Sherman, the following question was asked:

Twelfth: State what is the feeling of the colored people in regard to Gen. Sherman; and how far do they regard his sentiments and actions as friendly to their rights and interests, or otherwise?

Answer: We looked upon Gen. Sherman prior to his arrival as a man in the Providence of God specially set apart to accomplish this work, and we unanimously feel inexpressible gratitude to him, looking upon him as a man that should be honored for the faithful performance of his duty. Some of us called upon him immediately upon his arrival, and it is probable he would not meet the Secretary with more courtesy than he met us. His conduct and deportment toward us characterized him as a friend and a gentleman. We have confidence in Gen. Sherman, and think that what concerns us could not be under better hands. This is our opinion now from the short acquaintance and interest we have had. (Mr. Lynch states that with his limited acquaintance with Gen. Sherman, he is unwilling to express an opinion. All others present declare their agreement with Mr. Frazier about Gen. Sherman.)

Some conversation upon general subjects relating to Gen. Sherman's march then ensued, of which no note was taken.

War Dept. Adjt. Gen.'s Office
Washington, Feb. 1, 1865.

I do hereby certify that the foregoing is a true and faithful report of the questions and answers made by the colored ministers and church members of Savannah in my presence and hearing, at the chambers of Major-Gen. Sherman, on the evening of Thursday, Jan. 12, 1865. The questions of Gen. Sherman and the Secretary of War were reduced to writing and read to the persons present. The answers were made by the Rev. Garrison Frazier, who was selected by the other ministers and church members to answer for them. The answers were written down in his exact words, and read over to the others, who one by one expressed his concurrence or dissent as above set forth.

E. D. TOWNSEND, Asst.-Adjt.-Gen.

LAND FOR FREEDMEN: GEORGIA, JANUARY 1865

William T. Sherman:
Special Field Orders No. 15

Following their meeting with Garrison Frazier and other black leaders in Savannah, Sherman and Stanton collaborated in drafting Special Field Orders No. 15, possibly in consultation with Brigadier General Rufus Saxton, the Union commander in the South Carolina Sea Islands. Special Field Orders No. 15 sought to provide land both for the refugees who had followed Sherman's army through Georgia and for the freed people who lived in the coastal region of South Carolina and Georgia. Before the war the cultivation of extra-long staple cotton had made the Sea Islands one of the wealthiest regions of the United States. Beginning with Union capture of Port Royal in November 1861, the plantation owners of the Sea Islands had fled inland. Some of the abandoned plantations in the islands were seized during the war by the U.S. treasury department and sold to northern investors, who experimented with raising cotton using paid labor. Their efforts were resisted by many of the freed people, who preferred to own their own land and grow food crops. By the summer of 1865 about 40,000 former slaves were living on the 400,000 acres of land set apart by Sherman's order. (Some of the settlers worked their forty-acre plots with surplus mules provided by the Union army, possibly giving rise to the phrase "forty acres and a mule.") In August 1865 President Andrew Johnson revoked Special Field Orders No. 15 by directing that abandoned southern lands be returned to owners who were willing to swear allegiance to the Union.

IN THE FIELD, SAVANNAH, GA., January 16th, 1865.
SPECIAL FIELD ORDERS,
No. 15.

I. The islands from Charleston, south, the abandoned rice fields along the rivers for thirty miles back from the sea, and the country bordering the St. Johns river, Florida, are reserved and set apart for the settlement of the negroes now made free by the acts of war and the proclamation of the President of the United States.

II. At Beaufort, Hilton Head, Savannah, Fernandina, St. Augustine and Jacksonville, the blacks may remain in their chosen or accustomed vocations—but on the islands, and in the settlements hereafter to be established, no white person whatever, unless military officers and soldiers detailed for duty, will be permitted to reside; and the sole and exclusive management of affairs will be left to the freed people themselves, subject only to the United States military authority and the acts of Congress. By the laws of war, and orders of the President of the United States, the negro is free and must be dealt with as such. He cannot be subjected to conscription or forced military service, save by the written orders of the highest military authority of the Department, under such regulations as the President or Congress may prescribe. Domestic servants, blacksmiths, carpenters and other mechanics, will be free to select their own work and residence, but the young and able-bodied negroes must be encouraged to enlist as soldiers in the service of the United States, to contribute their share towards maintaining their own freedom, and securing their rights as citizens of the United States.

Negroes so enlisted will be organized into companies, battalions and regiments, under the orders of the United States military authorities, and will be paid, fed and clothed according to law. The bounties paid on enlistment may, with the consent of the recruit, go to assist his family and settlement in procuring agricultural implements, seed, tools, boots, clothing, and other articles necessary for their livelihood.

III. Whenever three respectable negroes, heads of families, shall desire to settle on land, and shall have selected for that purpose an island or a locality clearly defined, within the limits above designated, the Inspector of Settlements and Plantations will himself, or by such subordinate officer as he may appoint, give them a license to settle such island or district, and afford them such assistance as he can to enable them to establish a peaceable agricultural settlement. The three parties named will subdivide the land, under the supervision of the Inspector, among themselves and such others as may choose to settle near them, so that each family shall have a plot of not more than (40) forty acres of tillable ground, and when it borders on some water channel, with not more than 800 feet water front, in the possession of which land the military authorities will afford them protection, until such time as they can protect themselves, or until Congress shall regulate their title. The Quartermaster may, on the requisition of the Inspector of Settlements and Plantations, place at the disposal of the Inspector, one or more of the captured steamers, to ply between the settlements and one or more of the commercial points heretofore named in orders, to afford the settlers the opportunity to supply their necessary wants, and to sell the products of their land and labor.

IV. Whenever a negro has enlisted in the military service of the United States, he may locate his family in any one of the settlements at pleasure, and acquire a homestead, and all other rights and privileges of a settler, as though present in person. In like manner, negroes may settle their families and engage on board the gunboats, or in fishing, or in the navigation of the inland waters, without losing any claim to land or other advantages derived from this system. But no one, unless an actual settler as above defined, or unless absent on Government service, will be entitled to claim any right to land or property in any settlement by virtue of these orders.

V. In order to carry out this system of settlement, a general officer will be detailed as Inspector of Settlements and Plantations, whose duty it shall be to visit the settlements, to regulate their police and general management, and who will furnish personally to each head of a family, subject to the approval of the President of the United States, a possessory title in writing, giving as near as possible the description of boundaries; and who shall adjust all claims or conflicts that may arise under the same, subject to the like approval, treating such titles altogether as possessory. The same general officer will also be charged with the enlistment and organization of the negro recruits, and protecting their interests while absent from their settlements; and will be governed by the rules and regulations prescribed by the War Department for such purposes.

VI. Brigadier General R. SAXTON is hereby appointed Inspector of Settlements and Plantations, and will at once enter on the performance of his duties. No change is intended or desired in the settlement now on Beaufort Island, nor will any rights to property heretofore acquired be affected thereby.

BY ORDER OF MAJOR GENERAL W. T. SHERMAN

WASHINGTON, D.C., JANUARY 1865

Thirteenth Amendment to the Constitution of the United States

Drafted in its final form by Senator Lyman Trumbull, an Illinois Republican, the Thirteenth Amendment was approved by the Senate, 38–6, on April 8, 1864. In a 93–65 vote in the House of Representatives on June 15, opposition from Democrats and conservative border state unionists prevented the amendment from winning the two-thirds majority necessary for passage. President Lincoln used his annual message in December to urge the 38th Congress to adopt the amendment in its final session, and, along with Secretary of State Seward, began to lobby vigorously for its passage. (Lincoln had previously hoped that slavery would be legally abolished in the border states and in the reconstructed South by amending the various state constitutions.) On January 31, 1865, the House of Representatives approved the amendment, 119–56, and it was submitted to the states for ratification. The following evening Lincoln told a crowd that the amendment was "a King's cure for all the evils" left unaddressed by the Emancipation Proclamation. Although Delaware, Kentucky, New Jersey, and Mississippi would vote against ratification, the Thirteenth Amendment would be approved by twenty-seven states, including eight former members of the Confederacy, by December 6, and on December 18, 1865, Seward declared that its ratification had been completed.

Article XIII.

SECTION 1. Neither slavery nor involuntary servitude, except as a punishment for crime whereof the party shall have been duly convicted, shall exist within the United States, or any place subject to their jurisdiction.

SECTION 2. Congress shall have power to enforce this article by appropriate legislation.

January 31, 1865

"THE GREATEST EVENT":
WASHINGTON, D.C., FEBRUARY 1865

George W. Julian: Journal, February 1, 1865

An active abolitionist since the 1840s, George W. Julian was a Radical Republican congressman from Indiana whose commitment to racial equality was unusual for an officeholder from the antebellum Midwest. In 1831 Indiana had followed the example of Ohio and Illinois by adopting legislation forbidding black people from moving into the state without first posting a bond for good behavior, and in 1851 the state constitution was amended to include an outright prohibition on black migration into Indiana. (The constitutional prohibition would be overturned in 1866 by the Indiana supreme court in a decision based in part on the enforcement clause of the Thirteenth Amendment.) Speaking in support of the Second Confiscation Act in May 1862, Julian told Congress that slavery was ultimately responsible for "all the unutterable agonies of our many battle-fields, all the terrible sorrows which rend so many thousands of loving hearts, all the ravages and desolation of this stupendous conflict." Nearly three years later, he wrote in his journal about the passage of the Thirteenth Amendment.

WEDNESDAY NIGHT, February 1.

Just returned from Mr. Chase's reception, where I went with Mrs. Cheesman. Mrs. Sprague appeared grandly and so did the Chief Justice.

The greatest event of this century occurred yesterday in the passage of the Constitutional Amendment in the House. The spectacle during the vote was the most solemn and impressive I ever witnessed. The result for a good while remained in doubt, and the suspense produced perfect stillness. When it was certainly known that the measure had carried, the cheering in the hall and densely packed galleries exceeded anything I ever before saw and beggared description. Members joined in the shouting, and kept it up for some minutes. Some embraced one another, others wept like children. I never before felt as I then did, and thanked God for the blessed opportunity of recording my name where it will be as honored as those of the signers of the Declaration of Independence. What a grand jubilee for the old battle-scarred Abolitionists. Glorious fruit of the war. I have felt, ever since the vote, as if I were in a new country. I seem to breathe better, and feel comforted and refreshed.

Another event, following close after this, was the admission of Doctor Rock, of Boston, a colored lawyer and scholar, to practice in the Supreme Court. No objection was made, even by the old Dred Scott judges.

Have my bill ready to offer.

PEACE TALKS: VIRGINIA, FEBRUARY 1865

Robert Garlick Hill Kean: Diary, February 5, 1865

In January 1865, Francis Preston Blair, a former adviser to Andrew Jackson who served as an unofficial counselor to President Lincoln, traveled to Richmond twice to meet with Jefferson Davis. Blair proposed to Davis that the Union and Confederate armies should jointly expel the French from Mexico as a prelude to national reunion. Neither Davis nor Lincoln believed in Blair's proposal, but they were both willing to use him as an intermediary. On January 12 Davis asked Blair to tell Lincoln that he was willing to "enter into conference with a view to secure peace to the two countries." Lincoln responded on January 18 that he would accept an emissary "with the view of securing peace to the people of our one common country." Despite Lincoln's refusal to acknowledge Confederate independence, Davis appointed as commissioners Confederate vice president Alexander H. Stephens, Confederate senator Robert M. T. Hunter, and John A. Campbell, the Confederate assistant secretary of war. The three men met with Lincoln and Secretary of State Seward on February 3 onboard the Union steamboat *River Queen* at Hampton Roads, Virginia. No notes were taken during the meeting, but the various accounts written afterward by the participants agree that Lincoln insisted on a complete cessation of hostilities and the full restoration of the union while refusing to retreat from his emancipation policies. Robert Garlick Hill Kean, an administrator in the Confederate War Department who worked closely with Campbell, wrote about the Hampton Roads conference in his diary on February 5. The next day Davis attributed the meeting's failure in a message to the Confederate Congress to northern insistence on "unconditional submission."

Feb. 5. Last night at about 8 o'clock, Messrs. Stephens, Hunter and Campbell got back. After they were admitted into Grant's lines, they were carried down to City Point where they were taken in hand by Major Eckert, the censor of the telegraph, who was the person to have charge of their going forward. Some notes passed on the subject of the character and objects of their mission, and delay was produced by which they were kept at City Point till Thursday morning from Monday night. Judge Campbell thinks this was in order to give time for the announcement of the vote in the Yankee House of Representatives on the emancipation amendment to the Constitution and the action of the Eastern states legislatures on it—all of which Seward, who was all the while at Old Point, was waiting for, and brought out in the conference. Finally on Thursday they were taken down on Grant's steamboat, getting into the Roads. Lincoln arrived from Washington that evening and sent them word that he was tired with travel, but would see them the next day. So next morning they were taken on board the steamer where Lincoln and Seward were, and had a conference of about three hours, in which a great deal was talked over.

Mr. Stephens reminded Lincoln of their intimacy in the time when they served on the secret committee together, which engineered the election of General Taylor. Lincoln remembered the acquaintance but appeared oblivious of the 'sleeping together' after the manner of Botts and Tyler. Mr. Stephens then went into a long discussion of the 'Monroe Doctrine' in its relations to this quarrel. After he had proceeded for some time (this cue having been taken from Blair) Lincoln appeared to have become impatient and interrupted with the remark that there was but one ground on which propositions could be made or received, and that was the restoration of the national authority over all places in the states. This diverted the discussion, but Mr. Seward said he desired to hear Mr. Stephens out; his view was one in which he was interested.

Mr. Stephens cited historical instances of nations at war laying aside their quarrel to take up other matters of mutual interest to both. Mr. Lincoln replied that he knew nothing about history, 'You must talk history to Seward.' It having become distinctly understood that no terms short of reconstruction were to be considered, Judge Campbell took up the discussion and inquired searchingly into their ideas of the manner of it. It was brought out distinctly that submission was contemplated pure and simple, though they called our envoys to witness that they never used the word 'submission.' Their phrase was 'restoration of the national authority.' The terms of Lincoln's message in December last were all they had to offer.

On the subject of their penal legislation, Lincoln said that we must accept all the consequences of the application of the law, that he would be disposed to use liberally the power confided to him for the remission of pains and penalties. In this connection Judge Campbell remarked that he had never regarded his neck as in danger. Lincoln replied that there were a good many oak trees about the place where he lived, the limbs of which afforded many convenient points from which he might have dangled. This was said with temper, and was the only exhibition of it at all. They said there could be no convention on this subject with us either as a national government or as states, as to make such a convention would be a 'recognition.' Mr. Hunter replied that this did not follow; there were frequent instances of such conventions, as between Charles I and the parliament. Lincoln answered, 'And Charles I lost his head; that's all I know about that; you must talk history to Seward.' Judge Campbell stated the difference between the law of conquest and a pacification by convention. They left no opening for any convention. Everything was to be settled by the laws of Congress and the decisions of the courts.

The slavery question was mentioned. That, Lincoln said, would be decided by the courts. Some said his proclamations had no effect whatever; others, that they operated only in particular places; others, that they were of general operation. He supposed this would be tested by some one taking a negro, and the question of his freedom being brought before the courts.

(In this connection and in reply to Mr. Hunter's suggestion as to negro women and children in exposed places, like Eastern Virginia where productive labor had all absconded, Lincoln told his *story* of the pigs.)

In this connection Seward produced the vote in the House of Representatives on the amendment to the Constitution. He said this country was in a revolutionary condition, and as always was the case, the most extreme party succeeds. He cited Maryland. The first proposition was to get rid of slavery in 50 years. This would have been satisfactory, but a more extreme party arose for emancipation in seven years, then a more violent one for immediate emancipation, and this one succeeded. So in New York, the *Tribune* which a few years ago was the *only* abolition political paper supported by the country, was now the most conservative of the Northern press while the *Herald* leads the abolition party.

The conditions of a truce were also discussed, equally unsatisfactory. The only governments which could be recognized in states where there are two would be the bogus Yankee government. Judge Campbell also asked if Virginia went back whether it would be with her ancient limits. The reply was that it would be a question for the courts. West Virginia would be regarded as a state. The gentlemen prepared their answer to the President this morning, which I presume will be published. This ends this peace *fiasco* which must satisfy the most sceptical that we have nothing whatever to hope or expect short of the exaction of all the rights of conquest, whether we are overrun by force, or submit.

"WE MUST EMANCIPATE":
VIRGINIA, FEBRUARY 1865

John H. Stringfellow to Jefferson Davis

Born in Virginia, John H. Stringfellow studied medicine in Philadelphia before moving to Missouri. In 1854 he helped found the town of Atchison, Kansas, and became a leader of the proslavery settlers in the territory. The speaker of the first territorial house of representatives, Stringfellow coedited the *Squatter Sovereign*, a weekly newspaper that urged its readers to "scourge the country of abolitionism, free soilism, and every other damnable ism that exists." Discouraged by the prospects of making Kansas a slave state, he returned to Virginia in 1858 and during the war served as a surgeon in Confederate army hospitals. Stringfellow wrote to Davis from his home outside Richmond as the Confederate Congress debated whether to arm slaves. On February 20 the Confederate house of representatives would approve, 40–37, a bill that authorized the Confederate army to enlist slaves with the permission of their masters, but without providing for their emancipation. The bill would pass the Confederate senate 9–8 on March 8 and was signed by Davis five days later. General Orders No. 14, issued by the Confederate adjutant general on March 23, would require that masters free their slaves before enlistment. The Confederate army would recruit only a few hundred black soldiers before the end of the war.

Glenn Allen Henrico   Feby 8th 1865
My dear Sir   Impelled by the perils of our country, and the thousand conflicting theories as to the cause, and cure; to continually have these things before me; I have been amazed to see, that no one thus far has concieved, or if concieved, had the boldness to present in my judgment, the only solution of all these perils and difficulties. I address you because you have already taken a long stride in the right direction & because I believe your mind has already reached the true solution, but owing to peculiar circumstances has hesitated to enunciate it. The history of this war demonstrates the wonderfull fact, that the Confederate states mainly subsists both of the immense

armies engaged in the conflict, and actually after furnishing *all* the soldiers to our army, contributes about one half of those making the army of its enemies, and should the war continue for annother year, the south will probably furnish *two thirds* of the army of her foes. These facts which cannot be controverted show certainly any thing but *weakness, or inferiority* on the part of the south; but it does show that a change of policy in relation to the conduct of the war, and that a radical one must be adopted, or we shall be destroyed. Let us look at a few facts. The Yankees have now in their service 200 000 of our ex-slaves, and under their next draft, will probably have half as many more. We have not *one* soldier from that source in our ranks. It is held by us that *slaves* will not make soldiers, therefore we refuse to put them in the service & I think are correct in so doing. But while we thus think, and thus act, our enemies are creating, in addition to their *white force which we have found to our cost in the last year, to be quite as large as we could manage*, an auxiliary army of our own escaped slaves, of three or four hundred thousand men. Now however we may decry the negro as a soldier every one knows that if the white troops of the yankees are numerous enough to hold all ours in check, then this negro army can, at will, ravage and destroy our whole country, and we will be absolutely conquered by our own slaves. We allege that *slaves* will not fight in our armies, escaped slaves fight & fight bravely for our enemies, therefore a freed Slave will fight. If at the begining of this war, all our negroes had been free, does any one believe the Yankees would have been able to recruit an army amongst them, does any one know of a solitary free negro escaping to them and joining their army. If our slaves were *now* to be freed would the Yankees be able to raise another recruit amongst them? If freedom and amnesty were declared in favour of those already in the Yankee lines, would they not almost to a man desert to their old homes? Would not our *freed* negroes make us as good soldiers as they make for our enemies? Again suppose we free a portion of our slaves & put them in the army, we leave *all the rest* as a recruiting field for the enemy, from which we cannot get a single soldier and thus we see one half of our *entire* population of no avail to us, but on the contrary ready at every oportunity to join the ranks of our enemies. Now sir Southern soldiers are the best that ever drew a blade in the cause of liberty, but there are some things which *they* cannot do; they cannot fight our battles against overwhelming numbers, and raise the necessary supplies for the army and the women and children at home, and yet sir this is what they will be called upon to do if this war is protracted for two years longer. I ask sir then in view of these *facts* if the prompt abolition of slavery, will not prove a remedy sufficient to arrest this tide of disaster? The Yankee army will be diminished by it, our own army can be increased by it & our labour retained by it. Without it, if the war continues, we shall in the end be subjugated, our negroes emancipated, our lands parcelled out amongst them, and if any of it be left to us, only an equal portion with our own negroes, and ourselves given only equal (if any) social and political rights and privileges. If we emancipate, our independence is secured, the white man only will have any, and all political rights, retain all his real and personal property, exclusive of his property in his slave, make the laws to controll the freed negro, who having no land, must labor for the land owner; and being an adequate *supply of labor*, must work for the land owner on terms about as economical as tho owned by him.

We cannot consent to reconstruction even if they repeal all their laws, and withdraw all their proclamations in regard to us, our Lands & our Negroes, because they now have, or at any session of their congress can make the necessary number of states, to alter the Constitution, in a constitutional manner, and thus abolish slavery, and interfere in any other way they think proper. But even if the present administration should pledge any thing we may ask, it binds no one but themselves, during their own term of service, which you of course understand better than I do and suppose they should even promise and stand by their promise to pay us for our negroes, lost or to be emancipated, how will they pay us. They cannot by direct taxation, but only in levying an export duty on our products, Cotton, Tobacco & Naval stores: and this war has shown them & the world, if not us, how much they will bear, Cotton commanding one dollar pr pound, Tobacco three dollars, Tar two hundred dollars pr Barrel &c &c. To pay their war debt & for our negroes would make a debt of six (thousand) millions or probably eight the interest of which at five pr ct, would take four hundred millions of revenue to pay, and to raise something additional to extinguish the principal, would require an additional hundred million, thus you see an export duty to this extent would be levied & could easily be raised upon our own products; twenty cents upon cotton which would make the price about 32 or 33 cts, the world would pay, because they must have it & have bought it for much more, would bring an annual income of about four hundred million without countg the duty on Tobacco & Naval Stores but even with this most favorable view of the case we should loose the whole of our own war debt which is or will be say two thousand million of course this would be repudiated & justly by our enemies if we consent to reconstruction Whereas if *we* emancipate we save the two thousand million, & we can pay for the negroes four thousand million more, and the export duty on cotton alone (which we should have levied if we go back into the Union) will pay the interest upon this at 5 pr ct and leave a hundred million as a sinking fund to extinguish the principal in some 30 or 40 years & the slave owner have all his labour on his farm that he had before; (for having no home & no property to buy one with, he must live with & work for his old owner for such wages as said owner may choose to give, to be regulated by law hereafter as may suit the change of relation) And this six thousand million is not a debt we tax ourselves to pay, but the world pays it. The speculator who buys the cotton & pays the duty, makes the manufacturer pay him his ten or fifteen pr ct nett profit on his gross outlay, the manufacturer makes the merchant pay him his ten or fifteen pr ct on his gross outlay, the merchant charges the retail dealer his ten or fifteen pr ct on his gross outlay, and so on till the *shirt* is made *and he who wears it out pays the duty & all the diferent pr centages upon it.* Thus *we* will pay to the extent of our consumption of the exported article when manufactured & returned to us, a mere nothing when compared to the immense gratuity, six thousand million which the World makes to us, & which they so justly should be made to hand over to us, for the cold blooded, heartless indifferance with which thay have contemplated the bloody, inhuman, barbarous, and apparently hopeless contest in which we have been engaged, and which they at any moment could have arrested by a word.

By emancipation I think we would not only render our triumph secure as I have attempted to prove, in & of itself but in all future time the negro in place of being useless in time of war as a soldier, & really dangerous as we have seen to our cost, continues to be an element of strength. And I think we may *reasonably* hope that the nations of the earth would no longer be unwilling to recognise us, for surely no people ever before strugled so long, and under so many dificulties, and endured so many privations so uncomplainingly as we have without finding some friendly hand outstretched to encourage or to help; and there can be no other reason than that we are exclusively & peculiarly a nation of slaveholders. I think that even amongst our enemies numbers would be added to those who are already willing to let us go in peace, for we should thus give the lie at once & forever to the charge that we are waging a war only for negro slavery, and the heart of ever honest lover of human liberty throughout the world would sumpathise with the men who for their cherished rights as freemen, would wage such an unequal contest as we have waged & besides sacrefising all their earnest convictions as to the humanity & righteousness of slavery were willing to sacrefice their property interest of four thousand millions to secure their independence, which might all be saved so far as the *promises* of our enemies are concerned, by reconstruction. In my judgement, the only question for us to decide, is whether we shall gain our independence by freeing the negro, we retaining all the power to regulate them by law when so freed, or permit our enemies through our own slaves to compel us to submit to Emancipation with equal or superior political rights for our negroes and partial or complete confiscation of our property for the use & benefit of the negro   And sir if the war continues as it is now waged, and we are forced, by the overwhelming odds of the Yankees and our own slaves in arms against us, into submission it would be but an act of simple justice for the Yankee Govt to see to it that their negro allies are at least as *well* provided for in the way of homes, as those who have been arrayed in arms against them.

I have always believed & still believe that slavery is an institution sanctioned if not established by the Almighty and the most humane & beneficial relation that can exist between Labor & Capital, still I think that this contest has proven that in a military sense it is an element of weakness & the teachings of providence as exhibited in this war dictates conclusively & imperitively that *to secure & perpetuate our independence we must emancipate the negro.*

P.S. We should then get rid of the only impediment in the way of an exchange of prisoners thus getting 30 or 40 thousand more men in the field

I have given you what I conceive to be the only solution to our dificulties. How to effect this is a serious difficulty. Men are reluctant, in fact it might be imprudent, to discuss this thing publickly; but we know that in great crises men think & act rapidly, or at least should do so. If congress could be convinced of the correctness of this course they could in Convention with the Governors of the States devise some method, by which conventions of the states could be held and the necessary measures adopted; first by law of Congress if necessary provide for paying the owners for them I have not found a single slave holder with whom I have conversed but is willing to submit to the measure if deemed necessary by the proper Authorities Indeed I have no doubt of the power of Congress as a military necessity, to impress all of the able bodied male negroes & pay for them giving them their freedom & providing for paying for the rest upon the condition of manumission, but the other course would be least objectionable We burn an individuals cotton, corn or meat to keep it from the enemy so we can take his negro man & set him free to keep him from recruiting the enemys army.

I have written you this much, hoping it may aid you in some way. I have shown what I have written to no one, nor communicated my intentions to any one. If you think what I have written worth anything, make what use of it you chose, if not just stick it between the bars of your grate. What I have written is with an honest endeavour to aid you in guiding our ship through the perils & darkness which surround her & from no feeling of dissatisfaction or distrust as to yourself, for you have all my sympathies & all of my trust & confidence With diffidence & the warmest admiration & Respect I remain Your friend

J H Stringfellow

Written very hurriedly & with no effort at arrangement but only as "food for thought"   JHS

I opened the envelope to say that my communication was written before I heard of the return of our commissioners, & that I am more than sustained by their report, and the action of the Yankee Congress on the slavery question, & now we have only to decide on or between *Emancipation for our independence*, or Subjugation & Emancipation coupled with negro equality or superiority, as our enemies may elect   JHS

"LET SLAVERY DIE":
WASHINGTON, D.C., FEBRUARY 1865

Henry Highland Garnet: A Memorial Discourse

February 12, 1865

Born into slavery in Maryland, Henry Highland Garnet escaped with his parents and settled in New York, where Garnet became a Presbyterian minister and a prominent abolitionist. During the war he helped recruit black troops and aided victims of the New York City draft riots. At the invitation of William Henry Channing, the chaplain of the House of Representatives, Garnet preached a sermon in the House chamber on Sunday, February 12, becoming the first African American to speak before Congress.

> MATTHEW XXIII. 4: "For they bind heavy burdens, and grievous to be borne, and lay them on men's shoulders, but they themselves will not move them with one of their fingers."

IN this chapter, of which my text is a sentence, the Lord Jesus addressed his disciples, and the multitude that hung spell-bound upon the words that fell from his lips. He admonished them to beware of the religion of the Scribes and Pharisees, which was distinguished for great professions, while it succeeded in urging them to do but a little, or nothing that accorded with the law of righteousness.

In theory they were right; but their practices were inconsistent and wrong. They were learned in the law of Moses, and in the traditions of their fathers, but the principles of righteousness failed to affect their hearts. They knew their duty, but did it not. The demands which they made upon others proved that they themselves knew what things men ought to do. In condemning others they pronounced themselves guilty. They demanded that others should be just, merciful, pure, peaceable, and righteous. But they were unjust, impure, unmerciful—they hated and wronged a portion of their fellow-men, and waged continual war against the government of God.

On other men's shoulders they bound heavy and grievous burdens of duties and obligations. The people groaned beneath the loads which were imposed upon them, and in bitterness of spirit cried out, and filled the land with lamentations. But, with their eyes closed, and their hearts hardened, they heeded not, neither did they care. They regarded it to be but little less than intolerable insult to be asked to bear a small portion of the burdens which they were swift to bind on the shoulders of their fellow-men. With loud voice, and proud and defiant mien, they said these burdens are for them, and not for us. Behold how patiently they bear them. Their shoulders are broad, and adapted to the condition to which we have doomed them. But as for us, it is irksome, even to adjust their burdens, though we see them stagger beneath them.

Such was their conduct in the Church and in the State. We have modern Scribes and Pharisees, who are faithful to their prototypes of ancient times.

With sincere respect and reverence for the instruction, and the warning given by our Lord, and in humble dependence upon him for his assistance, I shall speak this morning of the Scribes and Pharisees of our times who rule the State. In discharging this duty, I shall keep my eyes upon the picture which is painted so faithfully and life-like by the hand of the Saviour.

Allow me to describe them. They are intelligent and well-informed, and can never say, either before an earthly tribunal or at the bar of God, "*We knew not of ourselves what was right.*" They are acquainted with the principles of the law of nations. They are proficient in the knowledge of Constitutional law. They are teachers of common law, and frame and execute statute law. They acknowledge that there is a just and impartial God, and are not altogether unacquainted with the law of Christian love and kindness. They claim for themselves the broadest freedom. Boastfully they tell us that they have received from the court of heaven the MAGNA CHARTA of human rights that was handed down through the clouds, and amid the lightnings of Sinai, and given again by the Son of God on the Mount of Beatitudes, while the glory of the Father shone around him. They tell us that from the Declaration of Independence and the Constitution they have obtained a guaranty of their political freedom, and from the Bible they derive their claim to all the blessings of religious liberty. With just pride they tell us that they are descended from the Pilgrims, who threw themselves upon the bosom of the treacherous sea, and braved storms and tempests, that they might find in a strange land, and among savages, free homes, where they might build their altars that should blaze with acceptable sacrifice unto God. Yes! they boast that their fathers heroically turned away from the precious light of Eastern civilization, and taking their lamps with oil in their vessels, joyfully went forth to illuminate this land, that then dwelt in the darkness of the valley of the shadow of death. With hearts strengthened by faith they spread out their standard to the winds of heaven, near Plymouth rock; and whether it was stiffened in the sleet and frosts of winter, or floated on the breeze of summer, it ever bore the motto, "*Freedom to worship God.*"

But others, their fellow-men, equal before the Almighty, and made by him of the same blood, and glowing with immortality, they doom to life-long servitude and chains. Yes, they stand in the most sacred places on earth, and beneath the gaze of the piercing eye of Jehovah, the universal Father of all men, and declare, "*that the best possible condition of the negro is slavery.*"*

> "Thus man devotes his brother and destroys;
> And more than all, and most to be deplored,
> As human nature's broadest, foulest blot,
> Chains him, and tasks him, and exacts his sweat
> With stripes, that Mercy with bleeding heart,
> Weeps to see inflicted on a beast."

In the name of the TRIUNE GOD I denounce the sentiment as unrighteous beyond measure, and the holy and the just of the whole earth say in regard to it, Anathema-maranatha.

What is slavery? Too well do I know what it is. I will present to you a bird's-eye view of it; and it shall be no fancy picture, but one that is sketched by painful experience. I was born among the cherished institutions of slavery. My earliest recollections of parents, friends, and the home of my childhood are clouded with its wrongs. The first sight that met my eyes was a

---

*Speech of FERNANDO WOOD, of New York, in Congress, 1864.

Christian mother enslaved by professed Christians, but, thank God, now a saint in heaven. The first sounds that startled my ear, and sent a shudder through my soul, were the cracking of the whip, and the clanking of chains. These sad memories mar the beauties of my native shores, and darken all the slave-land, which, but for the reign of despotism, had been a paradise. But those shores are fairer now. The mists have left my native valleys, and the clouds have rolled away from the hills, and Maryland, the unhonored grave of my fathers, is now the free home of their liberated and happier children.

Let us view this demon, which the people have worshiped as a God. Come forth, thou grim monster, that thou mayest be critically examined! There he stands. Behold him, one and all. Its work is to chattleize man; to hold property in human beings. Great God! I would as soon attempt to enslave GABRIEL or MICHAEL as to enslave a man made in the image of God, and for whom Christ died. Slavery is snatching man from the high place to which he was lifted by the hand of God, and dragging him down to the level of the brute creation, where he is made to be the companion of the horse and the fellow of the ox.

It tears the crown of glory from his head, and as far as possible obliterates the image of God that is in him. Slavery preys upon man, and man only. A brute cannot be made a slave. Why? Because a brute has not reason, faith, nor an undying spirit, nor conscience. It does not look forward to the future with joy or fear, nor reflect upon the past with satisfaction or regret. But who in this vast assembly, who in all this broad land, will say that the poorest and most unhappy brother in chains and servitude has not every one of these high endowments? Who denies it? Is there one? If so, let him speak. There is not one; no, not one.

But slavery attempts to make a man a brute. It treats him as a beast. Its terrible work is not finished until the ruined victim of its lusts, and pride, and avarice, and hatred, is reduced so low that with tearful eyes and feeble voice he faintly cries, "*I am happy and contented—I love this condition.*"

> "Proud Nimrod first the bloody chase began,
> A mighty hunter he; his prey was man."

The caged lion may cease to roar, and try no longer the

strength of the bars of his prison, and lie with his head between his mighty paws and snuff the polluted air as though he heeded not. But is he contented? Does he not instinctively long for the freedom of the forest and the plain? Yes, he is a lion still. Our poor and forlorn brother whom thou hast labelled "*slave*," is also a man. He may be unfortunate, weak, helpless, and despised, and hated, nevertheless he is a man. His God and thine has stamped on his forehead his title to his inalienable rights in characters that can be read by every intelligent being. Pitiless storms of outrage may have beaten upon his defenceless head, and he may have descended through ages of oppression, yet he is a man. God made him such, and his brother cannot unmake him. Woe, woe to him who attempts to commit the accursed crime.

Slavery commenced its dreadful work in kidnapping unoffending men in a foreign and distant land, and in piracy on the seas. The plunderers were not the followers of Mahomet, nor the devotees of Hindooism, nor benighted pagans, nor idolaters, but people called Christians, and thus the ruthless traders in the souls and bodies of men fastened upon Christianity a crime and stain at the sight of which it shudders and shrieks.

It is guilty of the most heinous iniquities ever perpetrated upon helpless women and innocent children. Go to the shores of the land of my forefathers, poor bleeding Africa, which, although she has been bereaved, and robbed for centuries, is nevertheless beloved by all her worthy descendants wherever dispersed. Behold a single scene that there meets your eyes. Turn not away neither from shame, pity, nor indifference, but look and see the beginning of this cherished and petted institution. Behold a hundred youthful mothers seated on the ground, dropping their tears upon the hot sands, and filling the air with their lamentations.

Why do they weep? Ah, Lord God, thou knowest! Their babes have been torn from their bosoms and cast upon the plains to die of hunger, or to be devoured by hyenas or jackals. The little innocents would die on the "Middle Passage," or suffocate between the decks of the floating slave-pen, freighted and packed with unparalleled human woe, and the slavers in mercy have cast them out to perish on their native shores. Such is the beginning, and no less wicked is the end of that system which the Scribes and Pharisees in the Church and the State pronounce to be just, humane, benevolent and Christian. If such are the deeds of mercy wrought by angels, then tell me what works of iniquity there remain for devils to do?

This commerce in human beings has been carried on until three hundred thousand have been dragged from their native land in a single year. While this foreign trade has been pursued, who can calculate the enormities and extent of the domestic traffic which has flourished in every slave State, while the whole country has been open to the hunters of men.

It is the highly concentrated essence of all conceivable wickedness. Theft, robbery, pollution, unbridled passion, incest, cruelty, cold-blooded murder, blasphemy, and defiance of the laws of God. It teaches children to disregard parental authority. It tears down the marriage altar, and tramples its sacred ashes under its feet. It creates and nourishes polygamy. It feeds and pampers its hateful handmaid, prejudice.

It has divided our national councils. It has engendered deadly strife between brethren. It has wasted the treasure of the Commonwealth, and the lives of thousands of brave men, and driven troops of helpless women and children into yawning tombs. It has caused the bloodiest civil war recorded in the book of time. It has shorn this nation of its locks of strength that was rising as a young lion in the Western world. It has offered us as a sacrifice to the jealousy and cupidity of tyrants, despots, and adventurers of foreign countries. It has opened a door through which a usurper, a perjured, but a powerful prince, might stealthily enter and build an empire on the golden borders of our southwestern frontier, and which is but a stepping-stone to further and unlimited conquests on this continent. It has desolated the fairest portions of our land, "until the wolf long since driven back by the march of civilization returns after the lapse of a hundred years and howls amidst its ruins."

It seals up the Bible, and mutilates its sacred truths, and flies into the face of the Almighty, and impiously asks, "*Who art thou that I should obey thee?*" Such are the outlines of this fearful national sin; and yet the condition to which it reduces man, it is affirmed, is the best that can possibly be devised for him.

When inconsistencies similar in character, and no more

glaring, passed beneath the eye of the Son of God, no wonder he broke forth in language of vehement denunciation. Ye Scribes, Pharisees, and hypocrites! Ye blind guides! Ye compass sea and land to make one proselyte, and when he is made ye make him twofold more the child of hell than yourselves. Ye are like unto whited sepulchres, which indeed appear beautiful without, but within are full of dead men's bones, and all uncleanness!

Let us here take up the golden rule, and adopt the self-application mode of reasoning to those who hold these erroneous views. Come, gird up thy loins and answer like a man, if thou canst. Is slavery, as it is seen in its origin, continuance, and end the best possible condition for thee? Oh, no! Wilt thou bear that burden on thy shoulders, which thou wouldest lay upon thy fellow-man? No. Wilt thou bear a part of it, or remove a little of its weight with one of thy fingers? The sharp and indignant answer is no, no! Then how, and when, and where, shall we apply to thee the golden rule, which says, "*Therefore all things that ye would that others should do to you, do ye even so unto them, for this is the law and the prophets.*"

Let us have the testimony of the wise and great of ancient and modern times:

> "Sages who wrote and warriors who bled."

PLATO declared that "Slavery is a system of complete injustice."

SOCRATES wrote that "Slavery is a system of outrage and robbery."

CYRUS said, "To fight in order not to be a slave is noble."

If Cyrus had lived in our land a few years ago he would have been arrested for using incendiary language, and for inciting servile insurrection, and the royal fanatic would have been hanged on a gallows higher than Haman. But every man is fanatical when his soul is warmed by the generous fires of liberty. Is it then truly noble to fight in order not to be a slave? The Chief Magistrate of the nation, and our rulers, and all truly patriotic men think so; and so think legions of black men, who for a season were scorned and rejected, but who came quickly and cheerfully when they were at last invited, bearing a heavy burden of proscriptions upon their shoulders, and having faith in God, and in their generous fellow-countrymen, they went forth to fight a double battle. The foes of their country were before them, while the enemies of freedom and of their race surrounded them.

AUGUSTINE, CONSTANTINE, IGNATIUS, POLYCARP, MAXIMUS, and the most illustrious lights of the ancient church denounced the sin of slave-holding.

THOMAS JEFFERSON said at a period of his life, when his judgment was matured, and his experience was ripe, "There is preparing, I hope, under the auspices of heaven, a way for a total emancipation."

The sainted WASHINGTON said, near the close of his mortal career, and when the light of eternity was beaming upon him, "It is among my first wishes to see some plan adopted by which slavery in this country shall be abolished by law. I know of but one way by which this can be done, and that is by legislative action, and so far as my vote can go, it shall not be wanting."

The other day, when the light of Liberty streamed through this marble pile, and the hearts of the noble band of patriotic statesmen leaped for joy, and this our national capital shook from foundation to dome with the shouts of a ransomed people, then methinks the spirits of Washington, Jefferson, the Jays, the Adamses, and Franklin, and Lafayette, and Giddings, and Lovejoy, and those of all the mighty, and glorious dead, remembered by history, because they were faithful to truth, justice, and liberty, were hovering over the august assembly. Though unseen by mortal eyes, doubtless they joined the angelic choir, and said, Amen.

POPE LEO X. testifies, "That not only does the Christian religion, but nature herself, cry out against a state of slavery."

PATRICK HENRY said, "We should transmit to posterity our abhorrence of slavery." So also thought the Thirty-Eighth Congress.

LAFAYETTE proclaimed these words: "Slavery is a dark spot on the face of the nation." God be praised, that stain will soon be wiped out.

JONATHAN EDWARDS declared "that to hold a man in slavery is to be every day guilty of robbery, or of man stealing."

Rev. Dr. WILLIAM ELLERY CHANNING, in a *Letter on the Annexation of Texas in 1837*, writes as follows:

"The evil of slavery speaks for itself. To state is to condemn the institution. The choice which every freeman makes of death for his child and for every thing he loves in preference to slavery, shows what it is. The single consideration that by slavery one human being is placed powerless and defenceless in the hands of another to be driven to whatever labor that other may impose, to suffer whatever punishment he may inflict, to live as his tool, the instrument of his pleasure, this is all that is needed to satisfy such as know the human heart and its unfitness for irresponsible power, that of all conditions slavery is the most hostile to the dignity, self-respect, improvement, rights, and happiness of human beings. * * * Every principle of our government and religion condemns slavery. The spirit of our age condemns it. The decree of the civilized world has gone out against it. * * * Is there an age in which a free and Christian people shall deliberately resolve to extend and perpetuate the evil? In so doing we cut ourselves off from the communion of nations; we sink below the civilization of our age; we invite the scorn, indignation, and abhorrence of the world."

MOSES, the greatest of all lawgivers and legislators, said, while his face was yet radiant with the light of Sinai: "Whoso stealeth a man, and selleth him, or if he be found in his hand, he shall surely be put to death." The destroying angel has gone forth through this land to execute the fearful penalties of God's broken law.

The Representatives of the nation have bowed with reverence to the Divine edict, and laid the axe at the root of the tree, and thus saved succeeding generations from the guilt of oppression, and from the wrath of God.

Statesmen, Jurists, and Philosophers, most renowned for learning, and most profound in every department of science and literature, have testified against slavery. While oratory has brought its costliest, golden treasures, and laid them on the altar of God and of freedom, it has aimed its fiercest lightning and loudest thunder at the strongholds of tyranny, injustice, and despotism.

From the days of Balak to those of Isaiah and Jeremiah, up to the times of Paul, and through every age of the Christian Church, the sons of thunder have denounced the abominable thing. The heroes who stood in the shining ranks of the hosts of the friends of human progress, from Cicero to Chatham, and Burke, Sharp, Wilberforce, and Thomas Clarkson, and Curran, assaulted the citadel of despotism. The orators and statesmen of our own land, whether they belong to the past, or to the present age, will live and shine in the annals of history, in proportion as they have dedicated their genius and talents to the defence of Justice and man's God-given rights.

All the poets who live in sacred and profane history have charmed the world with their most enchanting strains, when they have tuned their lyres to the praise of Liberty. When the Muses can no longer decorate her altars with their garlands, then they hang their harps upon the willows and weep.

From Moses to Terence and Homer, from thence to Milton and Cowper, Thomson and Thomas Campbell, and on to the days of our own bards, our Bryants, Longfellows, Whittiers, Morrises, and Bokers, all have presented their best gifts to the interests and rights of man.

Every good principle, and every great and noble power, have been made the subjects of the inspired verse, and the songs of poets. But who of them has attempted to immortalize slavery? You will search in vain the annals of the world to find an instance. Should any attempt the sacrilegious work, his genius would fall to the earth as if smitten by the lightning of heaven. Should he lift his hand to write a line in its praise, or defence, the ink would freeze on the point of his pen.

Could we array in one line, representatives of all the families of men, beginning with those lowest in the scale of being, and should we put to them the question, Is it right and desirable that you should be reduced to the condition of slaves, to be registered with chattels, to have your persons, and your lives, and the products of your labor, subjected to the will and the interests of others? Is it right and just that the persons of your wives and children should be at the disposal of others, and be yielded to them for the purpose of pampering their lusts and greed of gain? Is it right to lay heavy burdens on other men's shoulders which you would not remove with one of your fingers? From the rude savage and barbarian the negative response would come, increasing in power and significance as it rolled up the line. And when those should reply, whose minds and hearts are illuminated with the highest civilization and with the spirit of Christianity, the answer deep-toned and prolonged would thunder forth, no, no!

With all the moral attributes of God on our side, cheered as we are by the voices of universal human nature,—in view of the best interests of the present and future generations—animated with the noble desire to furnish the nations of the earth with a worthy example, let the verdict of death which has been brought in against slavery, by the THIRTY-EIGHTH CONGRESS, be affirmed and executed by the people. Let the gigantic monster perish. Yes, perish now, and perish forever!

> "Down let the shrine of Moloch sink,
>   And leave no traces where it stood;
> No longer let its idol drink,
>   His daily cup of human blood.
> But rear another altar there,
>   To truth, and love, and mercy given,
> And freedom's gift and freedom's prayer,
>   Shall call an answer down from heaven."

It is often asked when and where will the demands of the reformers of this and coming ages end? It is a fair question, and I will answer.

When all unjust and heavy burdens shall be removed from every man in the land. When all invidious and proscriptive distinctions shall be blotted out from our laws, whether they be constitutional, statute, or municipal laws. When emancipation shall be followed by enfranchisement, and all men holding allegiance to the government shall enjoy every right of American citizenship. When our brave and gallant soldiers shall have justice done unto them. When the men who endure the sufferings and perils of the battle-field in the defence of their country, and in order to keep our rulers in their places, shall enjoy the well-earned privilege of voting for them. When in the army and navy, and in every legitimate and honorable occupation, promotion shall smile upon merit without the slightest regard to the complexion of a man's face. When there shall be no more class-legislation, and no more trouble concerning the black man and his rights, than there is in regard to other American citizens. When, in every respect, he shall be equal before the law, and shall be left to make his own way in the social walks of life.

We ask, and only ask, that when our poor frail barks are launched on life's ocean—

> "Bound on a voyage of awful length
> And dangers little known,"

that, in common with others, we may be furnished with rudder, helm, and sails, and charts, and compass. Give us good pilots to conduct us to the open seas; lift no false lights along the dangerous coasts, and if it shall please God to send us propitious winds, or fearful gales, we shall survive or perish as our energies or neglect shall determine. We ask no special favors, but we plead for justice. While we scorn unmanly dependence; in the name of God, the universal Father, we demand the right to live, and labor, and to enjoy the fruits of our toil. The good work which God has assigned for the ages to come, will be finished, when our national literature shall be so purified as to reflect a faithful and a just light upon the character and social habits of our race, and the brush, and pencil, and chisel, and Lyre of Art, shall refuse to lend their aid to scoff at the afflictions of the poor, or to caricature, or ridicule a long-suffering people. When caste and prejudice in Christian churches shall be utterly destroyed, and shall be regarded as totally unworthy of Christians, and at variance with the principles of the gospel. When the blessings of the Christian religion, and of sound, religious education, shall be freely offered to all, then, and not till then, shall the effectual labors of God's people and God's instruments cease.

If slavery has been destroyed merely from *necessity*, let every class be enfranchised at the dictation of *justice*. Then we shall have a Constitution that shall be reverenced by all: rulers who shall be honored, and revered, and a Union that shall be sincerely loved by a brave and patriotic people, and which can never be severed.

Great sacrifices have been made by the people; yet, greater still are demanded ere atonement can be made for our national sins. Eternal justice holds heavy mortgages against us, and will require the payment of the last farthing. We have involved ourselves in the sin of unrighteous gain, stimulated by luxury, and pride, and the love of power and oppression; and prosperity and peace can be purchased only by blood, and with tears of repentance. We have paid some of the fearful installments, but there are other heavy obligations to be met.

The great day of the nation's judgment has come, and who shall be able to stand? Even we, whose ancestors have suffered the afflictions which are inseparable from a condition of slavery, for the period of two centuries and a half, now pity our land and weep with those who weep.

Upon the total and complete destruction of this accursed sin depends the safety and perpetuity of our Republic and its excellent institutions.

Let slavery die. It has had a long and fair trial. God himself has pleaded against it. The enlightened nations of the earth have condemned it. Its death warrant is signed by God and man. Do not commute its sentence. Give it no respite, but let it be ignominiously executed.

Honorable Senators and Representatives! illustrious rulers of this great nation! I cannot refrain this day from invoking upon you, in God's name, the blessings of millions who were ready to perish, but to whom a new and better life has been opened by your humanity, justice, and patriotism. You have said, "Let the Constitution of the country be so amended that slavery and involuntary servitude shall no longer exist in the United States, except in punishment for crime." Surely, an act so sublime could not escape Divine notice; and doubtless the deed has been recorded in the archives of heaven. Volumes may be appropriated to your praise and renown in the history of the world. Genius and art may perpetuate the glorious act on canvass and in marble, but certain and more lasting monuments in commemoration of your decision are already erected in the hearts and memories of a grateful people.

The nation has begun its exodus from worse than Egyptian bondage; and I beseech you that you say to the people, "*that they go forward*." With the assurance of God's favor in all things done in obedience to his righteous will, and guided by day and by night by the pillars of cloud and fire, let us not pause until we have reached the other and safe side of the stormy and crimson sea. Let freemen and patriots mete out complete and equal justice to all men, and thus prove to mankind the superiority of our Democratic, Republican Government.

Favored men, and honored of God as his instruments,

speedily finish the work which he has given you to do. *Emancipate, Enfranchise, Educate, and give the blessings of the gospel to every American citizen.*

> "Hear ye not how, from all high points of Time,—
> From peak to peak adown the mighty chain
> That links the ages—echoing sublime
> A Voice Almighty—leaps one grand refrain,
> Wakening the generations with a shout,
> And trumpet-call of thunder—Come ye out!
>
> "Out from old forms and dead idolatries;
> From fading myths and superstitious dreams:
> From Pharisaic rituals and lies,
> And all the bondage of the life that seems!
> Out—on the pilgrim path, of heroes trod,
> Over earth's wastes, to reach forth after God!
>
> "The Lord hath bowed his heaven, and come down!
> Now, in this latter century of time,
> Once more his tent is pitched on Sinai's crown!
> Once more in clouds must Faith to meet him climb!
> Once more his thunder crashes on our doubt
> And fear and sin—'My people! come ye out!'
>
> "From false ambitions and base luxuries;
> From puny aims and indolent self-ends;
> From cant of faith, and shams of liberties,
> And mist of ill that Truth's pure day-beam bends:
> Out, from all darkness of the Egypt-land,
> Into my sun-blaze on the desert sand!
>
> * * * * * *
>
> "Show us our Aaron, with his rod in flower!
> Our Miriam, with her timbrel-soul in tune!
> And call some Joshua, in the Spirit's power,
> To poise our sun of strength at point of noon!
> God of our fathers! over sand and sea,
> Still keep our struggling footsteps close to thee!"*

Then before us a path of prosperity will open, and upon us will descend the mercies and favors of God. Then shall the

*Atlantic Monthly, 1862.

people of other countries, who are standing tip-toe on the shores of every ocean, earnestly looking to see the end of this amazing conflict, behold a Republic that is sufficiently strong to outlive the ruin and desolations of civil war, having the magnanimity to do justice to the poorest and weakest of her citizens. Thus shall we give to the world the form of a model Republic, founded on the principles of justice, and humanity, and Christianity, in which the burdens of war and the blessings of peace are equally borne and enjoyed by all.

THE BURNING OF COLUMBIA:
SOUTH CAROLINA, FEBRUARY 1865

Emma LeConte: Diary, February 17–18, 1865

After learning of Hood's defeat at Nashville, Grant approved on January 2, 1865, Sherman's proposal to march his army north from Savannah through the Carolinas and, if needed, join in a campaign against Lee. "The truth is the whole army is burning with an insatiable desire to wreak vengeance upon South Carolina," Sherman wrote about the state northerners most blamed for starting the war. "I almost tremble at her fate, but feel that she deserves all that seems in store for her." On February 1 Sherman began his advance, feinting toward Charleston and Augusta in order to conceal his intention to move on Columbia. Many Confederates hoped in vain that heavy winter rain and flooded rivers would slow the Union advance through the swampy South Carolina low country. General Joseph E. Johnston would later recall that "when I learned that Sherman's army was marching through the Salkehatchie swamps, making its own corduroy road at the rate of a dozen miles a day or more, and bringing its artillery and wagons with it, I made up my mind that there had been no such army in existence since the days of Julius Cæsar." On February 16 General Pierre G. T. Beauregard decided to evacuate his badly outnumbered forces from Columbia. Union troops entered the city the following morning as residents looted stores and warehouses and fires began among the bales of cotton stockpiled in the streets. Some Union soldiers fought the fires, while others lit new ones. Spread by high winds, the flames eventually burned almost half the city. When a woman seeking a guard for her house denounced the Union for waging war on women and children, Lieutenant Colonel Jeremiah W. Jenkins, the commander of the 31st Iowa Infantry, told her: "The women of the South kept the war alive—and it is only by making them suffer that we can subdue the men." Seventeen-year-old Emma LeConte was the daughter of Joseph LeConte, a professor of chemistry and geology at South Carolina College who had operated a laboratory on campus for the Confederate Niter and Mining Bureau.

Friday 17th Feb. How long is this distress of mind to continue! It is now about 11 o'clock and the longest morning I ever lived through. I threw myself on the bed late last night or rather early this morning without undressing, feeling if I did not take some rest I would be sick. I lay awake a long time, in spite of heavy eyelids listening to the occasional cannon reports, wondering if the shelling would be renewed and thinking of the tumult there was reigning up town. At last I fell into a heavy sleep. At about six o'clock while it was still quite dark and all in the room were buried in profound slumber, we were suddenly awakened by a terrific explosion,—The house shook, broken window panes clattered down and we all sat up in bed, for a few seconds mute with terror. My first impression on waking was that a shell had struck the house, but as soon as I could collect my senses I knew that no shell could make such a noise. We lit the candle and mother sent Jane to enquire of Henry the cause. Of course he did not know. I went out of doors— the day was beginning to break murkily and the air was still heavy with smoke. All continuing quiet we concluded that the authorities had blown up some stores before evacuating. Whatever the cause, the effect was to scare us very effectually and to drive away all thought of sleep. We got up an hour later, almost fainting, for we had eaten almost nothing the preceding day. I forced myself to eat a little and to drink a half a cup of coffee. After breakfast the cannon opened again and so near that every report shook the house. I think it must have been a cannonade to cover our retreat. It did not continue very long. The negroes all went up town to see what they could get in the general pillage, for all the shops had been opened and provisions were scattered in all directions. Henry says in some parts of Main St corn and flour and sugar cover the ground. An hour or two ago they came running back declaring the Yankees were in town and that our troops were fighting them in the streets. This was not true, for at that time every soldier nearly had left town but we did not know it then. I had been feeling wretchedly faint, and nauseated with every mouthful of food I swallowed. And now I trembled all over and thought I should faint. I knew this would not do. So I lay down awhile and by dint of a little determination got quiet again. Mother is down right sick. She had been quite collected and calm until this news but now she suddenly lost all self control and exhibited the most lively terror—indeed I thought she would grow hysterical. As for Sallie her fright may be more easily imagined than described. This condition of affairs only lasted about half an hour but it was dreadful while it did last. As soon as I could I put on my pockets and nerved my self to meet them, but by and by the firing ceased and all was quiet again. It was denied that the Yankees had yet crossed the river or even completed their pontoon bridge and most of the servants returned up town. They have brought back a considerable quantity of provisions—The negroes are very kind and faithful—they have supplied us with meat and Jane brought mother some rice and crushed sugar for Carrie knowing that she had none. How times change! Those whom we have so long fed and cared for now help us + + We are intensely eager for every item of news, but of course can only hear through the negroes. A gentleman told us just now that the mayor had gone forward to surrender the town.

1 o'clock P.M. Well they are here! I was sitting in the back parlour, when I heard the shouting of the troops. I was at the front door in a moment. Jane came running and crying, "O Miss Emma, they've come at last!" She said they were then marching down Main Street, before them flying a panic stricken crowd of women and children, who seemed crazy. As she came along by Aunt Josie's, Miss Mary was at the gate about to run out. "For God's sake Miss Mary" she cried "stay where you are!" I suppose she (Miss M.) thought of running to the convent. I ran up stairs to my bed room window, just in time to see the U.S. flag run up over the State House. O what a horrid sight! what a degradation—to see it over the capital of South Carolina. After four long bitter years of bloodshed and hatred —now to float there at last—that hateful symbol of despotism! I do not think I could possibly describe my feelings. I know I could not look at it. I left the window and went back downstairs to mother. In a little while a guard arrived to protect the hospital. They have already fixed a shelter of boards against the wall near the gate. Sentinels are stationed and they are cooking their dinner. The wind is very high today and blows their hats around. This is the first sight we have had of these fiends except as prisoners—the sight does not stir up very pleasant feelings in our hearts—we cannot look at them with any thing but horror and hatred—loathing and disgust.

The troops now in town is a brigade commanded by Col Stone. Everything is quiet and orderly. Guards have been placed to protect houses and Sherman has promised not to disturb private property. How relieved and thankful we feel after all our anxiety & distress! *Later*—Gen Sherman has *assured* the mayor "that he and all the citizens may sleep as securely and quietly tonight as if under *Confederate rule*. Private property shall be carefully respected. Some public buildings have to be destroyed, but he will wait until tomorrow, when the wind shall have entirely subsided." It is said that one or two stragglers from Wheeler's command fired on the flag as it was borne down Main St on the carriage containing the Mayor Col Stone and other officers.

Saturday Afternoon, 18th. What a night of horror misery and agony! It is so useless to try to put on paper any idea of it. The recollection of it is so fearful—yet any attempt to describe it seems so useless—it even makes one sick to think of writing down such scenes. And yet as I have written thus far, I ought, while it is still fresh, try even imperfectly to give some account of last night. Every incident is now so vividly before me and yet it does not seem real—rather like a fearful dream, or nightmare that still oppresses.

Until dinner time we saw little of the Yankees, except the guard about the Campus and the officers and men galloping up and down the street. It is true, as I have since learned, that as soon as the bulk of the army entered, the work of pillage began. But we are so far off and so secluded from the rest of the town that we were happily ignorant of it all. I do not know exactly when Sherman entered, but I should judge about two or between one & two P.M. We could hear their shouts as they surged down Main St and through the State House but were too far off to see much of the tumult nor did we dream what a scene of pillage and terror was being enacted. I hear they found a picture of President Davis in the Capitol, which was set up as a target and shot at amid the jeers of the soldiery. From three o'clock till seven their Army was passing down the street by the Campus, to encamp back of us in the woods. Two Corps entered town—Howards and Logans. One, the diabolical 15th which Sherman has hitherto never permitted to enter a city on account of their vile and desperate character. Slocum's Corps remained over the river and I suppose Davis' also. The devils as they marched by looked strong, and well clad in dark dirty-looking blue. The wagon trains were immense.

Night drew on—Of course we did not expect to sleep but we looked forward to a tolerably tranquil night. Strange as it may seem we were actually idiotic enough to believe Sherman would keep his word!—A *Yankee*—and *Sherman*! It does seem incredible, such credulity—but I suppose we were so anxious to believe him—The lying fiend! I hope retributive justice will find him out one day. At about 7 o'clock I was standing on the back piazza in the third story. Before me the whole southern horizon was lit up by camp-fires which dotted the woods. On one side the sky was illuminated by the burning of Gen Hampton's residence a few miles off in the country, on the other by some blazing buildings near the river. I had scarcely gone down stairs again when Henry told us there was a fire on Main Street. Sumter Street was brightly lighted by a burning house so near our piazza that we could feel the heat. By the red glare, we could watch the wretches walking—generally staggering—back and forth from the camp to the town. Shouting hurrahing cursing South Carolina swearing blaspheming, singing ribald songs and using such obscene language that we were forced to go indoors. The fire on Main Street was now raging and we anxiously watched its progress from the upper front windows. In a little while however the flames broke forth in every direction. The Drunken devils roamed about setting fire to every house the flames seemed likely to spare. They were fully equipped for the noble work they had in hand—each soldier was furnished with combustibles compactly put up—they would enter houses and in the presence of helpless women and children pour turpentine on the beds and set them on fire. Guards were rarely of any assistance—most generally they assisted in the pillaging and firing. The wretched people rushing from their burning homes were not allowed to keep even the few necessaries they gathered up in their flight—even blankets and food were taken from them and destroyed. The Firemen attempted to use their engines but the hose were cut to pieces and their lives threatened. The wind blew a fearful gale wafting the flames from house to house with frightful rapidity. By midnight the whole town (except the outskirts) was wrapt in one huge blaze. Still the flames had not approached sufficiently near us to threaten our immediate safety and for some reason not a single Yankee soldier had entered our house. And now the fire instead of approaching us seemed to recede. Henry said the danger was over and sick of the dreadful scene worn out with fatigue and excitement we went down stairs to our room and tried to rest. I fell into a heavy kind of stupor from which I was presently aroused by the bustle about me. Our neighbour Mrs. Caldwell and her two younger sisters stood before the fire wrapped in blankets and weeping—their home was on fire and the great sea of flame had again swept down our way to the very campus walls. I felt a kind of sickening despair and did not even stir to go and look out. After awhile Jane came in to say that Aunt Josies house was in flames—then we all went up to the front door—My God! what a scene! It was about four o'clock and the State House was one grand conflagration. Imagine night turned to noonday only with a blazing, scorching glare that was horrible—a copper coloured sky across which swept columns of black rolling smoke glittering with sparks and flying embers, while all around us were falling thickly showers of burning flakes. Everywhere the palpitating blaze walling the streets with solid masses of flame as far as the eye could reach—filling the air with its horrible roar—on every side the crackling and devouring fire while every instant came the crashing of timbers and the thunder of the falling buildings. A quivering molten ocean seemed to fill the air and sky. The library building opposite us seemed framed by the gushing flames & smoke while through the windows gleamed the liquid fire. This we thought must be Aunt Josie's house. It was the next one for although hers caught frequently it was saved. The college buildings caught all along that side, and had the incendiary work continued one half hour longer than it did they must have gone. All the physicians and nurses were on the roof trying to save the buildings and the poor inmates left to themselves such as could crawled out while those who could not move waited to be burned to death. The Common opposite the gate was crowded with homeless women & children—a few wrapped in blankets and many shivering in the night air. Such a scene as this with the drunken fiendish soldiery in their dark uniforms, infuriated cursing, screaming, exulting in their work, came nearer realizing the material ideal of hell than any thing I ever expect to see again. They call themselves Sherman's "hell hounds."

Mother collected together some bedding, clothing and food which Henry carried to the back of the garden and covered them with a hastily ripped up carpet to protect them from the sparks and flakes of fire. He worked so hard, so faithfully and tried to comfort mother as best he could while she was sobbing and crying at the thought of being left shelterless with a delicate baby. While this was going on I stood with Mary Ann at the kitchen door. She tried to speak hopefully—I could not cry—it was all too horrible—Yet I felt the house must burn. By what miracle it was saved I cannot think. No effort could be made—no one was on the roof which was old and dry and all the while the sparks and burning timbers were flying over it like rain. When the few things she tried to save were moved, mother took up little Carrie who was sleeping unconsciously, and wrapping ourselves in shawls and blankets we went to the front door and waited for the house to catch. There we stood watching and listening to the roaring and crashing. It seemed inevitable—they said they would not leave a house—and what would become of us! I suppose we owe our final escape to the presence of the Yankee wounded in the hospital. When all seemed in vain Dr Thomson went to an officer and asked if he would see his own soldiers burnt alive. He said he would save the hospital and he and his men came to Dr T's assistance. Then too about this time even the Yankees seemed to have grown weary of their horrible work. The signal for the cessation of the fire—a blast on the bugle was given—and in fifteen minutes the flames ceased to spread. By seven o'clock the last flame had expired. About six o'clock a crowd of drunken soldiers assaulted the campus gate and threatened to overpower the guard—swearing the buildings should not be spared. By great exertions Dr Thomson found Sherman and secured a strong guard in time to rescue the hospital.

Mrs C. who had been to see after her house now returned and sitting down sobbed convulsively as she told us of the insults she had received from the soldiery engaged in pillaging her home. An officer riding by ordered the men to stop. So broken down and humbled by the terrible experience of the night was she that she cried out—"O, sir! please make them stop—You do'n't know what I suffered this night!" "I don't care a damn for your sufferings" he replied, "but my men have no right to pillage against orders." Fortunately—oh, so fortunately for us the hospital is so strictly guarded that we are unmolested within the walls.

O that long twelve hours! Never surely again will I live through such a night of horrors—the memory of it will haunt me as long as I shall live! It seemed as if the day would never come. The sun rose at last, dim and red through the thick murky atmosphere. It set last night on a beautiful town full of women and children—it shone dully down this morning on smoking ruins and abject misery. I do not know how the others felt after the strain of the fearful excitement but I seemed to sink into a dull apathy. We none seemed to have the energy to talk. After awhile breakfast came in—a sort of mockery for no one could eat. After taking a cup of coffee and bathing my face begrimed with smoke I felt better and the memory of the night seemed like a frightful dream. I have scarcely slept for three nights yet my eyes are not heavy.

During the forenoon Aunt Josie and Aunt Jane came over to see how we had fared. We met as after a long separation and for some seconds no one could speak—then we exchanged experiences. They were nearer the flames than we, but they had Dr Carter with them—Some one to look to and to help them. Aunt Josie says the northern side of their house became so heated that no one could remain on that side. The house caught fire three times. Being outside the hospital buildings they were more exposed than we. Once a number of Yankees rushed in saying the roof was on fire. Andrew the negro boy, followed them up, saw them tear up the tin roofing and place lighted combustibles and after they went down he succeeded in extinguishing them. A tolerably faithful guard was some protection to them. The view from their attic windows commands the whole town and Aunt Jane said it was like one surging ocean of flame. She thought with us that it was more like the mediæval pictures of hell than any thing she had ever imagined. We do not know the extent of the destruction but we are told that the greater portion of the town is in ashes—perhaps the lovliest town in all our Southern country. This is civilized warfare! This is the way in which the "cultured" Yankee nation wars upon women and children. Failing with our men in the field *this* is the way they must conquer! I suppose there was scarcely an able bodied man except the hospital physicians in the whole 20000 people. It is so easy to burn the homes over the heads of the helpless women and children and turn them with insults & sneers into the streets. One expects these people to lie and steal but it does seem such an outrage even upon degraded humanity that those who practise such wanton and useless cruelty should call themselves men. It seems to us even a contamination to look at these devils. Think of the degradation of being conquered and ruled by such a people! It seems to me now as if we would choose extermination first. I have only had to speak once to one of the blue coated fiends. I went to the front door to bid Francena & Nellie C. goodbye early this morning when a soldier came up the steps and asked me who was the Mayor. "Dr Goodwyn," I answered shortly and turned away. "Do you know his initials?" "No" and I shut the door quickly behind me.

The State House of course is burned and they talk of blowing up the new uncompleted granite one, but I do not know if it can be done in its unfinished unroofed condition. We dread tonight. Mother asked Dr Thomson (who has been very kind about coming in and in keeping us posted) for a guard but he says it is unnecessary as double guards will be placed throughout the city. Dr T. says some of the officers feel very much ashamed of last night's work. Their compunctions must have visited them since daylight. The men openly acknowledge that they received orders to burn & plunder before they crossed the river. The drunken scoundrels who tried to force their way into the Campus this morning have been under guard at the gate. Several hundred of them—fighting and quarrelling among themselves for two or three hours.

Poor father! What will be his state of mind when he hears of all this—the first reports that reach him will be even exaggerated. It is some comfort to us in our uncertainty & anxiety to hope that he may be safe. The explosion last night was the accidental blowing up of the Charleston freight depot. There had been powder stored there and it was scattered thickly over the floor. The poor people and negroes went in with torches to search for provisions.

When will these Yankees go that we may breathe freely again! The past three days are more like three weeks. And yet when they are gone we may be worse off with the whole country laid waste—the railroads out in every direction, starvation seems to stare us in the face. Our two families have between them a few bushels of corn and a little musty flour. We have no meat but the negroes give us a little bacon every day.

8 P.M. There has been no firing as yet. All is comparatively quiet. These buildings are surrounded by a heavy guard and we are told they are distributed throughout the city. All day the devils have been completing their work of plunder but in the hospital here we have been exempt from this. When I remember how blest we have been I cannot be too thankful. We have the promise of a quiet night but I dare not trust our hopes—there is no telling what diabolical intentions they may have. O if they were only gone—even to the last straggler. What a load would be lifted from our hearts. We are anxious to learn the fate of our friends but the little we can gather (except from Aunt Josie and Mrs. Green) is through the negroes, and ours scarcely dare venture up town. The Yankees plunder the negroes as well as the whites and I think they are becoming somewhat disgusted with their *friends*. Although the servants seem quite willing, it is difficult to get any work out of them on account of the wild excitement. Ah, the dreadful excitement. I seem to stand it very well, but it seems to me we must all be ill when it is over. Anxiety, distress, want of rest and food must tell upon us. Mrs Wilson (Mr Shand's daughter) with a babe one week old, was moved last night from her father's burning house. The Burroughs escaped with only the clothing they wore. Many many fared similarly. Some tried to save a little food—even this was torn from their hands. I have heard a number of distressing incidents but have not time to write them down. O the sorrow and misery of this unhappy town!

From what I hear their chief aim while taunting helpless women has been to "humble their pride"—"Southern pride." "Where now" they would hiss "is all your pride" "See what we have brought you to!" "This is what you get for setting yourselves up as better than other folks." The women acted with quiet dignity and refused to lower themselves by any retort. Some one told me the following: Some soldiers were pillaging the house of a lady. One asked her if they had not humbled her pride *now*. "No indeed" she said "nor can you ever." "You *fear* us anyway"—"No" she said. "By G— but you *shall* fear me." And he cocked his pistol and put it to her head. "Are you afraid now?" She folded her arms and looking him steadily in the eye, said contemptuously: "No." He dropped his pistol and with an exclamation of admiration left her.

CONFEDERATE DESERTERS: VIRGINIA, MARCH 1865

Luther Rice Mills to John Mills

On October 27–28, 1864, Grant had launched another offensive against Lee's flanks, attacking without success southwest of Petersburg at Hatcher's Run and east of Richmond at the Darbytown Road and Fair Oaks. Both armies went into winter quarters in November as bad weather brought a halt to major operations. A second Union offensive at Hatcher's Run, February 5–7, failed to cut the Boydton Plank Road but succeeded in further stretching the overextended Confederate lines. During the winter inadequate food, clothing, and shelter; cancelled leaves; and letters from home telling of increased privation and insecurity increasingly undermined morale in the Army of Northern Virginia and caused thousands of men to leave its ranks. On February 28 Lee reported to the Confederate War Department that nearly 1,100 men had deserted from his army in a single ten-day period (February 15–25), and that some of them had left in armed groups. "I regret to say that the greatest number of these desertions have occurred among the North Carolina troops," he wrote, "who have fought as gallantly as any soldiers in the army." Lieutenant Luther Rice Mills, a company commander in the 26th Virginia Infantry, wrote to his brother about the situation at Petersburg.

―――――――――――

Trenches Near Crater
March 2nd, 1865.

BROTHER JOHN:

Something is about to happen. I know not what. Nearly every one who will express an opinion says Gen'l Lee is about to evacuate Petersburg. The authorities are having all the cotton, tobacco &c. moved out of the place as rapidly as possible. This was commenced about the 22nd of February. Two thirds of the Artillery of our Division has been moved out. The Reserved Ordnance Train has been loaded up and is ready to move at any time. I think Gen'l Lee expects a hard fight on the right and has ordered all this simply as a precautionary measure. Since my visit to the right I have changed my opinion about the necessity for the evacuation of Petersburg. If it is evacuated Johnson's Division will be in a bad situation for getting out. Unless we are so fortunate as to give the Yankees the slip many of us will be captured. I would regret very much to have to give up the old place. The soiled and tattered Colors borne by our skeleton Regiments is sacred and dear to the hearts of every man, No one would exchange it for a new flag. So it is with us. I go down the lines, I see the marks of shot and shell, I see where fell my comrades, the Crater, the grave of fifteen hundred Yankees, when I go to the rear I see little mounds of dirt some with headboards, some with none, some with shoes protruding, some with a small pile of bones on one side near the end showing where a hand was left uncovered, in fact everything near shows desperate fighting. And here I would rather "fight it out." If Petersburg and Richmond is evacuated —from what I have seen & heard in the army—our cause will be hopeless. It is useless to conceal the truth any longer. Many of our people at home have become so demoralized that they write to their husbands, sons and brothers that desertion *now* is not *dishonorable*. It would be impossible to keep the army from straggling to a ruinous extent if we evacuate. I have just received an order from Wise to carry out on picket tonight a rifle and ten rounds of Cartridges to shoot men when they desert. The men seem to think desertion no crime & hence never shoot a deserter when he goes over—they always shoot but never hit. I am glad to say that we have not had but four desertions from our Reg't to the enemy. I enjoyed my trip to the right very much indeed. Saw Royall, Cooke, Satterwhite, Dr. & John Cannady, Prof. Wingate & the "immortal T. H. P." Cooke's Brig can scarcely be said to be in service. They are in the pride, pomp & circumstance of a glorious war. Had no idea that any of the army of N. V. was doing so well. Saw 12th Regt Va. Infantry yesterday. It had only about two hundred men & I feel sure that you could not two hundred officers—no not one hundred—out of Johnson's Division who would look as neat & as clean. I felt ashamed to go among such a neat bandbox crowd as Cooke's Brig was. Prof. W. & T. H. P. assisted by Dr. Cannady were trying to "fland" some sliding elders. Sliding Elders had decided advantage in position. Sorry I did not see Baldy Williams. Did not see the Parson. I sent you this morning "Five months in a Yankee prison" by a Petersburg Militiaman.

Write soon.

Yours truly

L. R. MILLS

WASHINGTON, D.C., MARCH 1865

Abraham Lincoln: Second Inaugural Address

President Lincoln delivered his Second Inaugural Address from the East Portico of the Capitol to an audience of thirty to forty thousand people, including thousands of African Americans. After Chief Justice Salmon P. Chase administered the oath of office, Lincoln leaned forward and kissed the Bible, which was opened to Isaiah 5:27–28. In a letter to New York Republican leader Thurlow Weed on March 15, Lincoln would write that he expected the address "to wear as well as—perhaps better than—any thing I have produced; but I believe it is not immediately popular. Men are not flattered by being shown that there has been a difference of purpose between the Almighty and them. To deny it, however, in this case, is to deny that there is a God governing the world. It is a truth which I thought needed to be told; and as whatever of humiliation there is in it, falls most directly on myself, I thought others might afford for me to tell it."

Fellow Countrymen: March 4, 1865

At this second appearing to take the oath of the presidential office, there is less occasion for an extended address than there was at the first. Then a statement, somewhat in detail, of a course to be pursued, seemed fitting and proper. Now, at the expiration of four years, during which public declarations have been constantly called forth on every point and phase of the great contest which still absorbs the attention, and engrosses the energies of the nation, little that is new could be presented. The progress of our arms, upon which all else chiefly depends, is as well known to the public as to myself; and it is, I trust, reasonably satisfactory and encouraging to all. With high hope for the future, no prediction in regard to it is ventured.

On the occasion corresponding to this four years ago, all thoughts were anxiously directed to an impending civil-war. All dreaded it—all sought to avert it. While the inaugeral address was being delivered from this place, devoted altogether to *saving* the Union without war, insurgent agents were in the city seeking to *destroy* it without war—seeking to dissolve the Union, and divide effects, by negotiation. Both parties deprecated war; but one of them would *make* war rather than let the nation survive; and the other would *accept* war rather than let it perish. And the war came.

One eighth of the whole population were colored slaves, not distributed generally over the Union, but localized in the Southern part of it. These slaves constituted a peculiar and powerful interest. All knew that this interest was, somehow, the cause of the war. To strengthen, perpetuate, and extend this interest was the object for which the insurgents would rend the Union, even by war; while the government claimed no right to do more than to restrict the territorial enlargement of it. Neither party expected for the war, the magnitude, or the duration, which it has already attained. Neither anticipated that the *cause* of the conflict might cease with, or even before, the conflict itself should cease. Each looked for an easier triumph, and a result less fundamental and astounding. Both read the same Bible, and pray to the same God; and each invokes His aid against the other. It may seem strange that any men should dare to ask a just God's assistance in wringing their bread from the sweat of other men's faces; but let us judge not that we be not judged. The prayers of both could not be answered; that of neither has been answered fully. The Almighty has His own purposes. "Woe unto the world because of offences! for it must needs be that offences come; but woe to that man by whom the offence cometh!" If we shall suppose that American Slavery is one of those offences which, in the providence of God, must needs come, but which, having continued through His appointed time, He now wills to remove, and that He gives to both North and South, this terrible war, as the woe due to those by whom the offence came, shall we discern therein any departure from those divine attributes which the believers in a Living God always ascribe to Him? Fondly do we hope—fervently do we pray—that this mighty scourge of war may speedily pass away. Yet, if God wills that it continue, until all the wealth piled by the bond-man's two hundred and fifty years of unrequited toil shall be sunk, and until every drop of blood drawn with the lash, shall be paid by another drawn with the sword, as was said three thousand years ago, so still it must be said "the judgments of the Lord, are true and righteous altogether."

With malice toward none; with charity for all; with firmness in the right, as God gives us to see the right, let us strive on to finish the work we are in; to bind up the nation's wounds; to care for him who shall have borne the battle, and for his widow, and his orphan—to do all which may achieve and cherish a just, and a lasting peace, among ourselves, and with all nations.

"A SACRED EFFORT":
WASHINGTON, D.C., MARCH 1865

Frederick Douglass: from Life and Times of Frederick Douglass

Frederick Douglass, America's leading black abolitionist, was among those who heard Lincoln give his Second Inaugural Address. In his autobiography *Life and Times of Frederick Douglass* (1881), he would write that it "sounded more like a sermon than a state paper." From the beginning of the war, Douglass had called for immediate emancipation and the arming of black troops, and had denounced Lincoln for his attempts to conciliate southern and border state slaveowners and for advocating the colonization of freed slaves. He later praised the Emancipation Proclamation and helped recruit for the Massachusetts 54th Infantry (in which two of his sons served), but criticized the President for failing to provide black soldiers with equal pay and protection from Confederate retribution. After meeting with Lincoln at the White House in August 1863 and August 1864, Douglass began to respect the President for his steadfastness on emancipation and willingness to rethink his positions. In *Life and Times* he would praise Lincoln for having "conducted the affairs of the nation with singular wisdom, and with absolute fidelity to the great trust confided in him. A country redeemed and regenerated from the foulest crime against human nature that ever saw the sun!" In his autobiography Douglass remembered his attempt to defy tradition and attend the inaugural reception in 1865.

In the evening of the day of the inauguration, another new experience awaited me. The usual reception was given at the executive mansion, and though no colored persons had ever ventured to present themselves on such occasions, it seemed now that freedom had become the law of the republic, now that colored men were on the battle-field mingling their blood with that of white men in one common effort to save the country, it was not too great an assumption for a colored man to offer his congratulations to the President with those of other citizens. I decided to go, and sought in vain for some one of my own color to accompany me. It is never an agreeable experience to go where there can be any doubt of welcome, and my colored friends had too often realized discomfiture from this cause to be willing to subject themselves to such unhappiness; they wished me to go, as my New England colored friends in the long-ago liked very well to have me take passage on the first-class cars, and be hauled out and pounded by rough-handed brakemen, to make way for them. It was plain, then, that some one must lead the way, and that if the colored man would have his rights, he must take them; and now, though it was plainly quite the thing for me to attend President Lincoln's reception, "they all with one accord began to make excuse." It was finally arranged that Mrs. Dorsey should bear me company, so together we joined in the grand procession of citizens from all parts of the country, and moved slowly towards the executive mansion. I had for some time looked upon myself as a man, but now in this multitude of the élite of the land, I felt myself a man among men. I regret to be obliged to say, however, that this comfortable assurance was not of long duration, for on reaching the door, two policemen stationed there took me rudely by the arm and ordered me to stand back, for their directions were to admit no persons of my color. The reader need not be told that this was a disagreeable set-back. But once in the battle, I did not think it well to submit to repulse. I told the officers I was quite sure there must be some mistake, for no such order could have emanated from President Lincoln; and if he knew I was at the door he would desire my admission. They then, to put an end to the parley, as I suppose, for we were obstructing the doorway, and were not easily pushed aside, assumed an air of politeness, and offered to conduct me in. We followed their lead, and soon found ourselves walking some planks out of a window, which had been arranged as a temporary passage for the exit of visitors. We halted so soon as we saw the trick, and I said to the officers: "You have deceived me. I shall not go out of this building till I see President Lincoln." At this moment a gentleman who was passing in recognized me, and I said to him: "Be so kind as to say to Mr. Lincoln that Frederick Douglass is detained by officers at the door." It was not long before Mrs. Dorsey and I walked into the spacious East Room, amid a scene of elegance such as in this country I had never witnessed before. Like a mountain pine high above all others, Mr. Lincoln stood, in his grand simplicity, and *home-like beauty*. Recognizing me, even before I reached him, he exclaimed, so that all around could hear him, "Here comes my friend Douglass." Taking me by the hand, he said, "I am glad to see you. I saw you in the crowd to-day, listening to my inaugural address; how did you like it?" I said, "Mr. Lincoln, I must not detain you with my poor opinion, when there are thousands waiting to shake hands with you." "No, no," he said, "you must stop a little, Douglass; there is no man in the country whose opinion I value more than yours. I want to know what you think of it?" I replied, "Mr. Lincoln, that was a sacred effort." "I am glad you liked it!" he said; and I passed on, feeling that any man, however distinguished, might well regard himself honored by such expressions, from such a man.

It came out that the officers at the White House had received no orders from Mr. Lincoln, or from any one else. They were simply complying with an old custom, the outgrowth of slavery, as dogs will sometimes rub their necks, long after their collars are removed, thinking they are still there. My colored friends were well pleased with what had seemed to them a doubtful experiment, and I believe were encouraged by its success to follow my example. I have found in my experience that the way to break down an unreasonable custom, is to contradict it in practice. To be sure in pursuing this course I have had to contend not merely with the white race, but with the black. The one has condemned me for my presumption in daring to associate with them, and the other for pushing myself where they take it for granted I am not wanted. I am pained to think that the latter objection springs largely from a consciousness of inferiority, for as colors alone can have nothing against each other, and the conditions of human association are founded upon character rather than color, and character depends upon mind and morals, there can be nothing blameworthy in people thus equal in meeting each other on the plane of civil or social rights.

"WE HAVE WORK FAITHFUL":
NORTH CAROLINA, MARCH 1865

Roanoke Island Freedmen to Abraham Lincoln and to Edwin M. Stanton

In February 1862 the Union army captured Roanoke Island in North Carolina. Hundreds of slaves fled to the island during the following year, and in May 1863 the military established a freedmen's colony on the northern end of the island designed to "train and educate" the former slaves "for a free and independent community." By 1865 the settlement had a church, several schools, a sawmill, and about 3,900 residents, who grew food on one-acre family plots. Despite the hopes of Captain Horace James, the Congregational army chaplain from Massachusetts who served as its superintendent, the colony was unable to become self-sufficient. Most of the adult freedmen either served in the U.S. Colored Troops or worked away from the island as military laborers, leaving the women and children in the settlement dependent on army rations for food. The protests addressed to Lincoln and Stanton on March 9, 1865, were presented to the War Department in Washington on April 6 by Richard Boyle, a black schoolteacher on the island, and were probably drafted by him. They were forwarded to Horace James, who, in a letter sent to an officer of the Freedmen's Bureau on July 10, 1865, denied there was any danger of starvation in the colony. "The truth is *they have had too much* given them," James wrote. He described the freed people who protested their treatment as "persons to be treated like children, who do not know when they are well used, and whose complaints should influence us but a little, while we do for them that which we know will promote their best good. Those who come most in contact with the negros in the work of doing them good, *seldom win their gratitude—*" Over the next two years most of the freed people would leave Roanoke Island, and in 1867 the colony was formally decommissioned.

Roanoke Island N.C   march 9th 1865.
Mr President Dear Sir   We Colored men of this Island held a meeting to consult over the affairs of our present conditions and our rights and we find that our arms are so Short that we cant doe any thing with in our Selves So we Concluded the

best thing we could do was to apply to you or Some of your cabinets we are told and also we have read that you have declared all the Colored people free bothe men and woman that is in the Union lines and if that be so we want to know where our wrights is or are we to be Stamp down or troden under feet by our Superintendent which he is the very man that we look to for assistents, in the first place his Proclamation was that no able boded man was to draw any rations except he was at work for the Government we all agreed to that and was willing to doe as we had done for $10,oo per month and our rations though we Seldom ever get the mony

the next thing he said that he wanted us to work and get our living as White men and not apply to the Government and that is vry thing we want to doe, but after we do this we cant satisfie him Soon as he Sees we are trying to Support our Selves without the aid of the Government he comes and make a Call for the men, that is not working for the Government to Goe away and if we are not willing to Goe he orders the Guards to take us by the point of the bayonet, and we have no power to help it we know it is wright and are willing to doe any thing that the President or our head Commanders want us to doe but we are not willing to be pull and haul a bout so much by those head men as we have been for the last two years and we may say Get nothing for it, last fall a large number of we men was Conscript and sent up to the front and all of them has never return Some Got Kill Some died and When they taken them they treated us mean and our owners ever did they taken us just like we had been dum beast

We Colored people on Roanok Island are willing to Submit to any thing that we know the President or his cabinet Say because we have Got since enough to believe it is our duty to doe every thing we Can doe to aid Mr Lyncoln and the Government but we are not willing to work as we have done for Chaplain James and be Troden under foot and Get nothing for it we have work faithful Since we have been on the Island we have built our log houses we have Cultivate our acre of Ground and have Tried to be less exspence to the Government as we Possible Could be and we are yet Trying to help the Government all we Can for our lives those head men have done every thing to us that our masters have done except by and Sell us and now they are Trying to Starve the woman & children to death cutting off they ration they have Got so now that they wont Give them no meat to eat, every ration day beef & a little fish and befor the Ten days is out they are going from one to another Trying to borrow a little meal to last until ration day Mr Streeter will just order one barrell of meet for his fish men and the others he Gives nothing but beaf but we thank the Lord for that if we no it is the President or the Secretarys orders this is what want to know whoes orders it is, one of our minister children was fool to ration house and Sent off and his father working three days in every week for his ration

Roanoke Island N.C march 9th 1865

we have appeal to General Butler and Genl Butler wrote to Capt James to do Better and Capt James has promies to do Better and instead of doing better he has done worst and now we appeal to you which is the last resort and only help we have got, feeling that we are entily friendless, on the Island there numrous of Soldiers wives and they Can hardly get any rations and some of them are almost starving

we dont exspect to have the same wrights as white men doe we know that are in a millitary country and we exspect to obey the rules and orders of our authories and doe as they say doe, any thing in reason we thank God and thank our President all of his aids for what has been done for us but we are not satisfide with our Supertendent nor the treatement we receives now we want you to send us answer what to depen upon let it be good or bad and we will be Satisfide Respectifully yours

Roanoke Island N.C.

Roanoke Island N.C March 9th 1865

we want to know from the Secretary of War has the Rev Chaplain James which is our Superintendent of negros affairs has any wright to take our boy Children from us and from the School and Send them to newbern to work to pay for they ration without they parent Consint if he has we thinks it very hard indeed he essued a Proclamation that no boys Should have any rations at 14 years old well we thought was very hard that we had to find our boy Children to Goe to School hard as times are, but rather then they Should Goe without learning we thought we would try and doe it and say no more a bout it and the first thing we knowed Mr Stereeter the Gentlemen that ration the Contrabands had Gone a round to all the White School-Teachers and told them to Give the boys orders to goe and get they ration on a Cirtain day so the negros as we are Call are use to the Cesesh plots Suspicion the Game they was Going to play and a Greate many never Sent they Children. So Some twenty or twenty-five went and Mr Streeter Give them they rations and the Guard march them down to the head quarters and put them on board the boat and carried them to newbern here is woman here on the Island which their husbands are in the army just had one little boy to help them to cut & lug wood & to Goe arrand for them Chaplain James has taken them and sent them away Some of these little ones he sent off wasen oer 12 years olds. the mothers of Some went to Chaplain and Grieved and beg for the little boys but he would not let them have them we want to know if the Prisident done essued any ration for School boys if he dont then we are satisfide we have men on the Island that Can Support the boys to Goe to School but here are Poor woman are not able to do it So the orphans must Goe without they learning that all we can say a bout the matter

the next is Concerning of our White Soldiers they Come to our Church and we treat them with all the Politeness that we can and Some of them treats us as though we were beast and we cant help our Selves Some of them brings Pop Crackers and Christmas devils and throws a mong the woman and if we Say any thing to them they will talk about mobin us. we report them to the Capt he will Say you must find out Which ones it was and that we cant do but we think very hard it they put the pistols to our ministers breast because he Spoke to them about they behavour in the Church, the next is Capt James told us When he got the mill built he would let us have plank to buil our houses we negroes went to work and cut and hewd the timber and built the mill under the northern men derection and now he Charges us 3 and 4 dollars a hundred for plank and if we Carry 3 logs to the mill he takes 2 and

Gives us one. that is he has the logs haul and takes one for hauling and one for Sawing and we thinks that is to much Without he paid us better then he does. and the next thing is he wont allow a man any ration While he is trying to buil him Self a house. to live in and how are negroes to live at that rate we Cant See no way to live under Such laws, Without Some Altiration

                             Roanoke Island N.C. March 9th 1865
here is men here that has been working for the last three year and has not been paid for it. they, work on the forts and Cut spiles and drove them and done any thing that they was told to do Capt James Came on the Island Jan. 1864 and told they men that he had made all the matters wright a bout they back pay and now says he I want all of you men that has due bills to carry them to Mr Bonnell at head quarters and all them has not got no paper to show for they work I will make them Swear and kiss the Bibel and the men done just as he told them and he told us that he had made out the rolls and sent them up to Washington City and now he says that money is all dead So we are very well Satisfide just So we know that he has never received it for our head men has fool us so much just because they think that we are igorant we have lost all Confidince in them. so all we wants is a Chance and we can Get a living like White men we are praying to God every day for the war to Stop So we wont be beholding to the Government for Something to Eat Yours Respectfully

                                                Roanoke Island.

"THE DEATH FLURRY OF A WHALE":
NEW YORK, MARCH 1865

George Templeton Strong: Diary, March 10, 1865

On March 6 Strong wrote that "all New York seemed in the streets, at the windows, or on the housetops" as the city held a seven-mile-long procession to celebrate recent Union victories. "All this extravagant, exuberant rejoicing frightens me," he noted. "It seems a manifest omen of mishap." Four days later Strong was encouraged by reports of desertions from Lee's army and by the Confederate debate over arming slaves.

———————

March 10. . . . Richmond newspapers are in a special spasm of fury beyond any fit they have yet suffered. We must not attach too much weight to what these sensitive, excitable, high-toned, chivalric creatures rave when in nervous exaltation, whether arising from patriotic or from alcoholic stimulus. But this particular paroxysm certainly resembles the death flurry of a whale. The editorial utterances are violent, desperate, incoherent, hurried, and objectless. They amount in substance to this, that there is somewhere a class of "whipped seceders" and "whipped croakers" who desire subjugation and have an appetite for infamy—that these caitiffs want Davis to abdicate, and their pressure is sufficient to make it worthwhile to expend much bad language on them—that they will not succeed in these base designs, because Southerners never, never, *never* will be slaves, and because "our women" ought to take up their broomsticks and drive these wretches into the James River, and so on. There are certainly signs in Secessia of incipient decomposition. The rebellion has, at the very least, another year's fight in it, but it may die of inward disease within thirty days. I trust it will not die too soon and that it will be killed, not merely "kilt." I long for peace, but only for a durable peace, of material that will wear. John Bright writes

F. M. Edge that he hopes our war will not end till its work is done, and he sees the case aright.

The rebel hosts continue to be seriously drained by desertion. Not less than fifty deserters have taken refuge within Grant's lines every day for many weeks past, and their average number is probably nearer one hundred than fifty. Companies come in, led by their company officers. All tell the same story of compulsory service, hardships, failure of pay and of clothing and of rations, and of general despondency. The Confederacy has "gone up," they say. "We all know it, and we know it is useless to fight any longer." Lee's soldiers would throw away their arms and disband tomorrow if they dared, and so on. Such statements made by deserters are worth much "less than their face." But when made by hundreds, and corroborated by the actual desertion of thousands, at imminent risk of life and with certain and conscious loss of honor, they are worth a great deal. It is likely, moreover, that for every rebel who flees within our lines, two flee the other way and take sanctuary in the hill country or the "piney woods," supporting themselves by levying contributions on all and sundry as sovereign powers so far as their own personal sovereignty can be made practically available, and thus carrying out the doctrine of secession to its ultimate results. Many counties of Virginia, the Carolinas, and the Gulf States are said to swarm with these banditti, and they are admitted to be even more savage and reckless than the vandal hordes of the North.

The Rebel Congress seems to have reconsidered its refusal to arm the slaves and to have decided, reluctantly, and by a very close vote, that there is no help for it and that Cuffee must be conscripted and made to fight for his chivalric master. So much for the visions of glory the South saw in 1860. This sacrifice of the first principles of the Southern social system is a confession of utter exhaustion; a desperate remedy and a most dangerous experiment. And the experiment is tried at least a year too late. It will take six months to drill and equip any considerable *corps d'Afrique*, and Sherman, Sheridan, Thomas, and Grant are likely, with God's blessing, to give rebellion its death blow within that time.

But the measure has its immediate effects. It disgusts and alienates many slaveholders and many fanatical theorists about slavery, and it is received as an affront by the rebel rank and file—an affront that justifies desertion. They will feel it not only as an affront, but as a disheartening surrender of the principle for which they have fought. They learn that niggers are now to be armed and put into the field as the allies of Southern gentlemen; "that it will depend on the nigger's pluck and muscle and endurance how far he is to share with white men the glory of upholding the Southern cause. It will depend on that and nothing else. Moreover, he is to be rewarded for good service by freedom." But the first of all Southern axioms has been for thirty years past that freedom was a punishment to the slave, servitude his normal condition, and that he loved and looked up to and depended on his owner as a good dog does on his master, and that he despised and rejected emancipation just as a good dog would dislike being discharged from his duty of guardianship and kicked into the street to get his own living as best he could.

MARCHING THROUGH THE CAROLINAS:
NORTH CAROLINA, MARCH 1865

Alpheus S. Williams to His Daughter

After the destruction of Columbia, Sherman's army of 60,000 men moved north again and reached Laurel Hill, North Carolina, on March 8. Its objective was Goldsboro, where Sherman planned to join up with 30,000 Union troops advancing from the North Carolina coast under John M. Schofield. Sherman's march into North Carolina was opposed by about 20,000 Confederates led by Joseph E. Johnston, whom Jefferson Davis had reluctantly restored to command on February 25. Union Brigadier General Alpheus S. Williams, the commander of the Twentieth Corps, wrote to his daughter about the campaign in the Carolinas.

Fayetteville, North Carolina, Mar. 12, 1865.
My Dear Daughter:
After long and weary marches we entered this town yesterday. A gunboat came up this morning by which I am enabled to send you a line in pencil. As soon as we get our "base," or if we linger here long enough, I will copy my journal to this point.

Our campaign has been more arduous, weather worse, and roads infamously worse than on the Georgia campaign. We have had but little fighting, however, so far, the enemy always easily driven away from the strongest positions. He has evidently been confounded by the audacity of our movements. We swept through South Carolina, the fountain-head of rebellion, in a broad, semi-circular belt, sixty miles wide, the arch of which was the capital of the state, Columbia. Our people, impressed with the idea that every South Carolinian was an arrant Rebel, spared nothing but the old men, women, and children. All materials, all vacant houses, factories, cotton-gins and presses, everything that makes the wealth of a people, everything edible and wearable, was swept away. The soldiers quietly took the matter into their own hands. Orders to respect houses and private property not necessary for the subsistence of the army were not greatly heeded. Indeed, not heeded at all. Our "bummers," the dare-devils and reckless of the army, put the flames to everything and we marched with thousands of columns of smoke marking the line of each corps. The sights at times, as seen from elevated ground, were often terribly sublime and grand; often intensely painful from the distressed and frightened condition of the old men and women and children left behind.

We saw no young men, save the deformed, the sick or wounded, and deserters (pretty numerous). Everybody else had been forced into the service, even to decrepit old men of sixty and upwards, lots of whom came to us to be paroled or to be sent home. Boys deserted to us, not over thirteen years old. The "Confederacy" has literally gathered its infancy and aged, its first and second childhood. If it fails now, all material for reinforcing its armies is gone, unless, indeed, they can make fighting men out of the Negroes.

Our line of march has been across the largest rivers, the broadest swamps, and the muddiest creeks of the state. I think I am within bounds in saying that this corps has corduroyed over a hundred miles of road. For the last fifty miles we have traveled over a shell of quicksand which would not bear up a horse, and through which a wagon would cut to the box. The country was much poorer than I expected to find. Even respectable houses are very rare, and superior ones rarer. The soil, never very fertile, is worn out. The people left at home, mainly sickly-looking and grossly ignorant. How even the politicians of South Carolina can boast a superiority over our hardy and industrious Northern people is more than I can imagine. Everything in that state presents evidence of decay and retrogradation. There is nothing new, nothing that looks flourishing, and the people look like "fossil remains."

So far into North Carolina the country, if possible, is worse and the people worser! This town, you know, is at the navigable headwaters of the Cape Fear River, and is second only to Wilmington in population. One of the largest U.S. Arsenals is here, which the Rebs. have used as their largest. Only one U.S. Arsenal stolen by Rebeldom now remains to them, that at Augusta. Our march in the rear of Charleston made necessary the evacuation of the first fort upon which the Rebels fired, and Wilmington and all their seaports follow as we interpose between them and their interior communications. How much more effectual this has proved than all the costly attempts to take these places from the sea front!

I suppose we shall move on tomorrow or next day. Gen. Sherman announces that we have new duties before us. I have no doubt that his great objective point is Richmond, but we shall probably halt this side to replenish and refit our army on the Charleston and Savannah Railroad. I received a letter from Rene of January 24th and Minnie's journal to January 17th. This is the last I have had from home. It was a pleasant surprise, brought to us from a rear corps.

I will write you again if I have time. We are sixty miles from Goldsboro and shall probably halt there for some days, if we get it, as I doubt not. Love to uncles and aunts and cousins, and believe me as ever,

Your Affectionate Father,
A.S.W.

P.S. My health has been and is excellent. No exposure seems to affect me.

LAND AND VOTES:
WASHINGTON, D.C., MARCH 1865

Charles Sumner to John Bright

A leading Radical Republican, Massachusetts senator Charles Sumner led a filibuster in late February 1865 that prevented the seating of senators representing the Louisiana state government supported by President Lincoln. Sumner, who believed that Congress should play the leading role in reconstruction, opposed restoring representation to southern states that denied black men the vote and failed to guarantee the equality of all persons before the law. He wrote about the challenges of reconstruction to his English friend John Bright, a prominent reformer, orator, and member of parliament who was one of the staunchest supporters of the Union cause in Great Britain.

---

private

Washington 13th March '65

Dear Mr Bright,

I have yr good & most suggestive letter. I concur in it substantially. A practical difficulty is this; can Emancipation be carried out without using the lands of the slave-masters. We must see that the freedmen are established on the soil & that they may become proprietors.

From the beginning I have regarded confiscation only as ancillary to Emancipation. The great plantations, which have been so many nurseries of the rebellion, must be broken up, & the freedmen must share the pieces.

It looks as if we were on the eve of another agitation. I insist that the rebel States shall not come back except on the footing of the Decltn of Indep. with all persons equal before the law, & govt. founded on the consent of the governed. In other words there shall be no discrimination on account of color. If *all* whites vote, then must all blacks; but there shall be no limitation of suffrage for one more than the other.

It is sometimes said "what—let the freedmen yesterday a slave vote?" I am inclined to think that there is more harm in refusing than in conceding the franchise. It is said that they are as intelligent as the Irish just arrived.

But the question has become immensely practical in this respect. Without their votes, we cannot establish stable govts. in the rebel states. Their votes are as necessary as their musquets. Of this I am satisfied. Without them, the old enemy will reappear &, under the forms of law, take possession of the govts.—choose magistrates & officers—&, in alliance with the Northern democracy, put us all in peril again, postpone the day of tranquility, & menace the national credit by assailing the national debt. To my mind, the nation is now bound by self-interest—aye, *self-defence*—to be thoroughly just.

The Declaration of Indep. has pledges which have never been redeemed. We must redeem them, at least as regards the rebel states which have fallen under our jurisdiction.

Mr Lincoln is slow in accepting truths. I have reminded him that if he would say the word we might settle this question promptly & rightly. He hesitates.

Meanwhile I felt it my duty to oppose his scheme of govt. in Louisiana, which for the present is defeated in Congress. Chief Justice Chase yesterday pronounced an opinion of the Sup. Ct declaring the whole scheme "illegal & void" from the beginning; so that it fares no better in court than in Congress. Mr Chase & myself have always concurred in opinion on this question. With the habit of deference here to the Sup. Ct. I anticipate much from this opinion. Substantially it affirms the conclusion which I adopted three years ago, sometimes called "the territorial theory."

That has been much misunderstood in Europe. It has been supposed sometimes as a menace of subjugation. Nothing further from my mind—at least in any offensive sense. I felt that the rebel region must for a while pass under the *jurisdiction of Congress*, in order to set up the necessary safeguards for the future; & I have labored to this end.

Nothing has been heard of Sherman for weeks,—but Mr Stanton has no anxiety about him. He will re-appear in North Carolina. Grant is very cheerful. But for the moment the curtain is down. It may lift any day.

I send you the Resolutions on Reciprocity & Lake Armaments,

as they passed the House, & as amended by me. The Italics are mine; & that is the form adopted.

You will see from the date of the House Resolution on Armaments how long I held it back. I was unwilling to take the step, until the outrages on the Lakes seemed to shew its necessity.

I came into the proposition to give the notice to terminate the Reciprocity Treaty, because I was satisfied that we could not negotiate for its modification, on a footing of equality unless our hands were untied. You will see this in my speech. I make this remark in reply to yr suggestion on the subject.

Congress has separated in good humor, without anxiety for the future, & indeed confident that we are on the verge of peace. My desire is that England should do something to take out the bitterness from the American heart—before the war closes. Help. I owe Cobden, & shall write him next.

Ever Yours,   Charles Sumner

"GIVE ME A THOUSAND": KENTUCKY, MARCH 1865

Frances Johnson: Statement Regarding Her Whipping and Escape

Public outrage in the North over the expulsion of black refugees from Camp Nelson, Kentucky, in November 1864 (see pp. 486–88 in this volume) led Congress to pass a joint resolution on March 3, 1865, that emancipated the wives and children of black soldiers. The law was widely ignored by slaveowners in Kentucky, where the legislature had rejected ratification of the Thirteenth Amendment on February 24. In late March, Frances Johnson, the wife of a Union soldier, testified in a sworn statement about her attempt to secure freedom for herself and her children.

Camp Nelson   Ky   25th March 1865
Personally appeared before me J M Kelley Notary Public in and for the County of Jessamine State of Kentucky Frances Johnson a woman of color who being duly sworn according to law doth depose and say—

I am the wife of Nathan Johnson a soldier in Company F. 116th U.S.C. Infty. I have three children and with them I belonged to Matthias Outon Fayette County Ky. My husband who belonged to Mary Outon Woodford Co. Ky enlisted in the United States service at Camp Nelson Ky. in May 1864. The day after my husband enlisted my master knew it and said that he (my husband) and all the "niggers" did mighty wrong in joining the Army. Subsequent to May 1864 I remained with my master until forced to leave on account of the cruel treatment to which I was subjected. On Wednesday March 8th 1865, my masters son Thomas Outon whipped me severely on my refusing to do some work which I was not in a condition to perform. He beat me in the presence of his father who told him (Thos Outon) to "buck me and give me a thousand" meaning thereby a thousand lashes. While beating me he threw me on the floor and as I was in this prostrate and helpless condition he continued to whip me endeavoring at one time to tie my hands and at another time to make an indecent exposure of my person before those present. I resisted as much as I could and to some extent thwarted his malignant designs. In consequence of this whipping suffered much pain in my head and sides. The scar now visible on my neck was inflicted at that time. After such treatment I determined to leave my master and early on the following morning—Thursday March 9″ 1865 I stealthly started for Lexington about seven miles distant where my sister resided. On my arrival there I was confined on account of sickness produced by the abuse I had received from my masters son as aforementioned.

During Friday March 10″ 1865 I sought a lodging for myself and children— Towards evening I found one and about 7 o'clock at night I left for my masters intending to take my children away. About 9. O'clock I arrived there much fatigued, went to the Cabin where my children were, no one but the colored folks knowing that I was present, got my children with the exception of one that was too sick to move, and about 10″ o'clock P.M. started for a neighboring Cabin where we remained during the night. At day break next morning I started for Lexington. My youngest child was in my arms, the other walked by my side. When on the Pike about a mile from home I was accosted by Theophilus Bracey my masters son-in-law who told me that if I did not go back with him he would shoot me. He drew a pistol on me as he made this threat. I could offer no resistance as he constantly kept the pistol pointed at me. I returned with him to his (Bracys) house carrying my children as before. I remained at Bracys all day. My sick child was moved there during the day. I tried to find some chance of running away but Bracey was watching me. He took my eldest child (about seven years of age) and kept her as an Hostage. I found I could not get away from Bracey's with my children, and determined to get away myself hoping by this means to obtain possession of them afterwards. I knew Bracey would not give me my children or allow me to go away myself so at daybreak on the following morning Sunday March 12″ I secretly left Bracey's, took to the woods in order to elude pursuit, reached Lexington and subsequently arrived at Camp Nelson. My children are still held by Bracey. I am anxious to have them but I am afraid to go near them knowing that Bracey would not let me have them and fearing least he would carry out his threat to shoot me. And further the deponent saith not

her
(Signed) Frances × Johnson
mark

"A VERY CRUEL MAN": KENTUCKY, MARCH 1865

Clarissa Burdett: Statement Regarding Her Whipping and Escape

Like Frances Johnson, Clarissa Burdett was the wife of a Union soldier who suffered violence at the hands of a Kentucky slaveowner. Slavery would remain legal in Kentucky and in Delaware until the ratification of the Thirteenth Amendment was completed in December 1865.

Camp Nelson   Ky   27th of March 1865
Personally appeared before me J M Kelley Notary Public in and for the County of Jessamine State of Kentucky Clarissa Burdett a woman of color who being duly sworn according to law doth despose and say

I am a married woman and have four children. My husband Elijah Burdett is a soldier in the 12″ U.S.C.H. Arty. I and my children belonged to Smith Alford Garrard County Ky. When my husband enlisted my master beat me over the head with an axe handle saying as he did so that he beat me for letting Ely Burdett go off. He bruised my head so that I could not lay it against a pillow without the greatest pain. Last week my niece who lived with me went to Camp Nelson. This made my master very angry and last monday March 20″ 1865 he asked me where the girl had gone. I could not tell him   He then whipped me over the head and said he would give me two hundred lashes if I did not get the girl back before the next day. On Wednesday last March 22″ he said that he had not time to beat me on Tuesday but now he had time and he would give it to me. He then tied my hands threw the rope over a joist stripped me entirely naked and gave me about three hundred lashes. I cried out. He then caught me by the throat and almost choked me then continued to lash me with switches until my back was all cut up. The marks of the switches are now very visible and my back is still very sore. My master was a very cruel man and strongly sympathizes with the rebels.

He went with the Rebel General Bragg when the latter retreated from the State. He took me and my children to Beans Station and send the parents and two sisters of my niece to Knoxville where he sold them. After he whipped me on Wednesday last he said he would give me until next morning to bring the girl back, and if I did not get her back by that time he would give me as much more. I knew that I would be whipped so I ran away. My master frequently said that he would be jailed before one of his niggers would go to Camp. I therefore knew he would not permit any of my children to come with me. So when I ran away I had to leave my children with my master. I have four children there at present and I want to get them but I cannot go there for them knowing that master who would whip me would not let any of my children go nor would he suffer me to get away

her
(Signed) Clarissa   Burdett
mark

"AWAITING MY FATE": VIRGINIA, APRIL 1865

John B. Jones: Diary, April 2, 1865

By the spring of 1865 Lee's army of about 60,000 men held a line that extended for thirty-seven miles from east of Richmond to southwest of Petersburg. Lee knew that he could not defend his position indefinitely against the 100,000 Union troops opposing him, and made plans to join Johnston in North Carolina and undertake an offensive against Sherman. In an attempt to open an escape route to the west for his army, Lee attacked Fort Stedman, a Union strongpoint east of Petersburg, on March 25, hoping that its loss would force Grant to shorten his lines west of the city. The attack failed, costing the Confederates about 3,000 men killed, wounded, or captured. Grant then directed Major General Philip H. Sheridan to turn Lee's western flank. After heavy fighting at Dinwiddie Court House and White Oak Road on March 31, Sheridan advanced with 22,000 men on Five Forks, a crossroads about twelve miles southwest of Petersburg. The junction was defended by a force of 10,000 under Major General George E. Pickett, who had been ordered by Lee to hold the position "at all hazards." On the afternoon of April 1 Sheridan's troops broke the Confederate lines at Five Forks and captured 2,500 prisoners. Grant then ordered a general assault on the Petersburg defenses at dawn on April 2. Within hours Lee had telegraphed the Confederate War Department that both Petersburg and Richmond would have to be abandoned that night. John B. Jones wrote in his diary about the evacuation of the Confederate capital.

APRIL 2D.—Bright and beautiful. The tocsin was sounded this morning at daybreak, and the militia ordered to the fortifications, to relieve some regiments of Longstreet's corps, posted on this side of the river. These latter were hurried off to Petersburg, where a battle is impending, I suppose, if not in progress.

A street rumor says there was bloody fighting yesterday a little beyond Petersburg, near the South Side Road, in which Gen. Pickett's division met with fearful loss, being engaged with superior numbers. It is said the enemy's line of intrenchments was carried once or twice, but was retaken, and remained in their hands.

I hear nothing of all this at the department; but the absence of dispatches there is now interpreted as bad news! Certain it is, the marching of veteran troops from the defenses of Richmond, and replacing them hurriedly with militia, can only indicate an emergency of alarming importance. A decisive struggle is probably at hand—and may possibly be in progress while I write. Or there may be nothing in it—more than a precautionary concentration to preserve our communications.

Mrs. Davis sold nearly all her movables—including presents —before leaving the city. She sent them to different stores.

An intense excitement prevails, at 2 P.M. It pervaded the churches. Dr. Hoge intermitted his services. Gen. Cooper and the President left their respective churches, St. James's and St. Paul's. Dr. Minnegerode, before dismissing his congregation, gave notice that Gen. Ewell desired the local forces to assemble at 3 P.M.—and afternoon services will not be held. The excited women in this neighborhood say they have learned the city is to be evacuated to-night.

No doubt our army sustained a serious blow yesterday; and Gen. Lee may not have troops sufficient to defend both the city and the Danville Road at the same time.

It is true! The enemy have broken through our lines and attained the South Side Road. Gen. Lee has dispatched the Secretary to have everything in readiness to *evacuate the city to-night*. The President told a lady that Lieut.-Gen. Hardee was only twelve miles distant, and might get up in time to save the day. But then Sherman must be in *his* rear. There is no wild excitement—*yet*. Gen. Kemper was at the department looking for Gen. Ewell, and told me he could find no one to apply to for orders. The banks will move to-night. Eight trains are provided for the transportation of the archives, etc. No provision for civil employees and their families.

At 6 P.M. I saw the Hon. James Lyons, and asked him what he intended to do. He said many of his friends advised him to leave, while his inclination was to remain with his sick family. He said, being an original secessionist, his friends apprehended that the Federals would arrest him the first man, and hang him. I told him I differed with them, and believed his presence here might result in benefit to the population.

Passing down Ninth Street to the department, I observed quite a number of men—some in uniform, and some of them officers—hurrying away with their trunks. I believe they are not allowed to put them in the cars.

The Secretary of War intends to leave at 8 P.M. this evening. The President and the rest of the functionaries, I suppose, will leave at the same time.

I met Judge Campbell in Ninth Street, talking rapidly to himself, with two books under his arm, which he had been using in his office. He told me that the chiefs of bureaus determined which clerks would have transportation—embracing only a small proportion of them, which I found to be correct.

At the department I learned that all who had families were advised to remain. No compulsion is seen anywhere; even the artisans and mechanics of the government shops are left free to choose—to go or to stay.

A few squads of local troops and reserves—guards—may be seen marching here and there. Perhaps they are to burn the tobacco, cotton, etc., if indeed anything is to be burned.

Lee must have met with an awful calamity. The President said to several ladies to-day he had hopes of Hardee coming up in time to save Lee—else Richmond must succumb. He said he had done his best, etc. to save it. Hardee is distant two or three days' march.

The negroes stand about mostly silent, as if wondering what will be their fate. They make no demonstrations of joy.

Several hundred prisoners were brought into the city this afternoon—captured yesterday. Why they were brought here I am at a loss to conjecture. Why were they not paroled and sent into the enemy's lines?

At night. All is yet quiet. No explosion, no conflagration, no riots, etc. How long will this continue? When will the enemy come?

It was after 2 o'clock P.M. before the purpose to evacuate the city was announced; and the government had gone at 8 P.M.! Short notice! and small railroad facilities to get away. All horses were impressed.

There is a report that Lieut.-Gen. A. P. Hill was killed, and that Gen. Lee was wounded. Doubtless it was a battle of great magnitude, wherein both sides had all their forces engaged.

I remain here, broken in health and bankrupt in fortune, awaiting my fate, whatever it may be. I can do no more. If I could, I would.

THE FALL OF RICHMOND: VIRGINIA, APRIL 1865

Sallie Brock: from
Richmond During the War

Widespread looting broke out in Richmond on the night of April 2 as hungry residents broke into warehouses in search of food. "The most revolting revelation," LaSalle Pickett (George E. Pickett's wife) later wrote, "was the amount of provisions, shoes and clothing which had been accumulated by the speculators who hovered like vultures over the scene of death and desolation." Amid the chaos Lieutenant General Richard S. Ewell, Richmond's military commander, ordered the destruction of the city's stockpiles of tobacco and cotton to prevent them from falling into Union hands. Sallie Brock, a Virginia native whose father owned a hotel in Richmond, described the fall of the city in a memoir published in 1867 under the pseudonym "a Richmond Lady." Brock's narrative of the evacuation draws heavily on the account presented in *The Last Year of the War* (1866) by Edward A. Pollard, the associate editor of the *Richmond Examiner*.

EVACUATION OF RICHMOND—BURNING OF THE CITY.

THE MORNING of the 2d of April, 1865, dawned brightly over the capital of the Southern Confederacy. A soft haze rested over the city, but above that, the sun shone with the warm pleasant radiance of early spring. The sky was cloudless. No sound disturbed the stillness of the Sabbath morn, save the subdued murmur of the river, and the cheerful music of the church bells. The long familiar tumult of war broke not upon the sacred calmness of the day. Around the War Department, and the Post Office, news gatherers were assembled for the latest tidings, but nothing was bruited that deterred the masses from seeking their accustomed places in the temples of the living God. At St. Paul's church the usual congregation was in attendance. President Davis occupied his pew.

It was again the regular monthly return for the celebration of the sacrament of the Lord's Supper. The services were progressing as usual, no agitation nor disturbance withdrew the thoughts from holy contemplation, when a messenger was observed to make his way up the aisle, and to place in the hands of the President a sealed package. Mr. Davis arose, and was noticed to walk rather unsteadily out of the church. An uneasy whisper ran through the congregation, and intuitively they seemed possessed of the dreadful secret of the sealed dispatch—the unhappy condition of General Lee's army and the necessity for evacuating Richmond. The dispatch stated that this was inevitable unless his lines could be reformed before eight o'clock that evening.

At the Second Presbyterian Church, Dr. Hoge, who had received information of the dire calamity impending over us, told his congregation of our situation, and the probability that never again would they meet there for worship, and in the thrilling eloquence of which he is so truly the master, bade them farewell.

The direful tidings spread with the swiftness of electricity. From lip to lip, from men, women, children and servants, the news was bandied, but many received it at first, as only a "Sunday sensation rumor." Friend looked into the face of friend to meet only an expression of incredulity; but later in the day, as the truth, stark and appalling, confronted us, the answering look was that of stony, calm despair. Late in the afternoon the signs of evacuation became obvious to even the most incredulous. Wagons were driven furiously through the streets, to the different departments, where they received as freight, the archives of the government, and carried them to the Danville Depot, to be there conveyed away by railroad.

Thousands of the citizens determined to evacuate the city with the government. Vehicles commanded any price in any currency possessed by the individual desiring to escape from the doomed capital. The streets were filled with excited crowds hurrying to the different avenues for transportation, intermingled with porters carrying huge loads, and wagons piled up with incongruous heaps of baggage, of all sorts and descriptions. The banks were all open, and depositors were busily and anxiously collecting their specie deposits, and directors were as busily engaged in getting off their bullion. Millions of dollars of paper money, both State and Confederate, were carried to the Capitol Square and buried.

Night came on, but with it no sleep for human eyes in Richmond. Confusion worse confounded reigned, and grim terror spread in wild contagion. The City Council met, and ordered the destruction of all spirituous liquors, fearing lest, in the excitement, there would be temptation to drink, and thus render our situation still more terrible. In the gutters ran a stream of whiskey, and its fumes filled and impregnated the air. After night-fall Richmond was ruled by the mob. In the principal business section of the city they surged in one black mass from store to store, breaking them open, robbing them, and in some instances (it is said) applying the torch to them.

In the alarm and terror, the guards of the State Penitentiary fled from their posts, and numbers of the lawless and desperate villains incarcerated there, for crimes of every grade and hue, after setting fire to the workshops, made good the opportunity for escape, and donning garments stolen wherever they could get them, in exchange for their prison livery, roamed over the city like fierce, ferocious beasts. No human tongue, no pen, however gifted, can give an adequate description of the events of that awful night.

While these fearful scenes were being enacted on the streets, in-doors there was scarcely less excitement and confusion. Into every house terror penetrated. Ladies were busily engaged in collecting and secreting all the valuables possessed by them, together with cherished correspondence, yet they found time and presence of mind to prepare a few comforts for friends forced to depart with the army or the government. Few tears were shed; there was no time for weakness or sentiment. The grief was too deep, the agony too terrible to find vent through the ordinary channels of distress. Fathers, husbands, brothers and friends clasped their loved ones to their bosoms in convulsive and agonized embraces, and bade an adieu, oh, how heart-rending!*—perhaps, thought many of them, forever.

At midnight the train on the Danville Railroad bore off the officers of the Government, and at the same hour many

---

*At eleven o'clock on that night, Colonel ——, on General ——'s staff, came into the city and was married. In a few moments he left his bride, in the terrible uncertainty of ever again meeting.

persons made their escape on the canal packets, and fled in the direction of Lynchburg.

But a still more terrible element was destined to appear and add to the horrors of the scene. From some authority—it seems uncertain what—an order had been issued to fire the four principal tobacco warehouses. They were so situated as to jeopardize the entire commercial portion of Richmond. At a late hour of the night, Mayor Mayo had dispatched, by a committee of citizens, a remonstrance against this reckless military order. But in the mad excitement of the moment the protest was unheeded. The torch was applied, and the helpless citizens were left to witness the destruction of their property. The rams in the James River were blown up. The "Richmond," the "Virginia" No. 2 and the "Beaufort" were all scattered in fiery fragments to the four winds of heaven. The noise of these explosions, which occurred as the first grey streaks of dawn broke over Richmond, was like that of a hundred cannon at one time. The very foundations of the city were shaken; windows were shattered more than two miles from where these gunboats were exploded, and the frightened inhabitants imagined that the place was being furiously bombarded. The "Patrick Henry," a receiving-ship, was scuttled, and all the shipping at the wharves was fired except the flag-of-truce steamer "Allison."

As the sun rose on Richmond, such a spectacle was presented as can never be forgotten by those who witnessed it. To speed destruction, some malicious and foolish individuals had cut the hose in the city. The fire was progressing with fearful rapidity. The roaring, the hissing, and the crackling of the flames were heard above the shouting and confusion of the immense crowd of plunderers who were moving amid the dense smoke like demons, pushing, rioting and swaying with their burdens to make a passage to the open air. From the lower portion of the city, near the river, dense black clouds of smoke arose as a pall of crape to hide the ravages of the devouring flames, which lifted their red tongues and leaped from building to building as if possessed of demoniac instinct, and intent upon wholesale destruction. All the railroad bridges, and Mayo's Bridge, that crossed the James River and connected with Manchester, on the opposite side, were in flames.

The most remarkable scenes, however, were said to have occurred at the commissary depot. Hundreds of Government wagons were loaded with bacon, flour and whiskey, and driven off in hot haste to join the retreating army. In a dense throng around the depot stood hundreds of men, women and children, black and white, provided with anything in which they could carry away provisions, awaiting the opening of the doors to rush in and help themselves. A cascade of whiskey streamed from the windows. About sunrise the doors were thrown open to the populace, and with a rush that seemed almost sufficient to bear off the building itself, they soon swept away all that remained of the Confederate commissariat of Richmond.

By this time the flames had been applied to or had reached the arsenal, in which several hundred car loads of loaded shell were left. At every moment the most terrific explosions were sending forth their awful reverberations, and gave us the idea of a general bombardment. All the horrors of the final conflagration, when the earth shall be wrapped in flames and melt with fervent heat, were, it seemed to us, prefigured in our capital.

At an early hour in the morning, the Mayor of the city, to whom it had been resigned by the military commander, proceeded to the lines of the enemy and surrendered it to General Godfrey Weitzel, who had been left by General Ord, when he withdrew one-half of his division to the lines investing Petersburg, to receive the surrender of Richmond.

As early as eight o'clock in the morning, while the mob held possession of Main street, and were busily helping themselves to the contents of the dry goods stores and other shops in that portion of the city, and while a few of our cavalry were still to be seen here and there in the upper portions, a cry was raised: "The Yankees! The Yankees are coming!" Major A. H. Stevens, of the Fourth Massachusetts Cavalry, and Major E. E. Graves, of his staff, with forty cavalry, rode steadily into the city, proceeded directly to the Capitol, and planted once more the "Stars and Stripes"—the ensign of our subjugation—on that ancient edifice. As its folds were given to the breeze, while still we heard the roaring, hissing, crackling flames, the explosions of the shells and the shouting of the multitude, the strains of an old, familiar tune floated upon the air—a tune that, in days gone by, was wont to awaken a thrill of patriotism. But now only the most bitter and crushing recollections awoke within us, as upon our quickened hearing fell the strains of "The Star Spangled Banner." For us it was a requiem for buried hopes.

As the day advanced, Weitzel's troops poured through the city. Long lines of negro cavalry swept by the Exchange Hotel, brandishing their swords and uttering savage cheers, replied to by the shouts of those of their own color, who were trudging along under loads of plunder, laughing and exulting over the prizes they had secured from the wreck of the stores, rather than rejoicing at the more precious prize of freedom which had been won for them. On passed the colored troops, singing, "John Brown's body is mouldering in the grave," etc.

By one o'clock in the day, the confusion reached its height. As soon as the Federal troops reached the city they were set to work by the officers to arrest the progress of the fire. By this time a wind had risen from the south, and seemed likely to carry the surging flames all over the northwestern portion of the city. The most strenuous efforts were made to prevent this, and the grateful thanks of the people of Richmond are due to General Weitzel and other officers for their energetic measures to save the city from entire destruction.

The Capitol Square now presented a novel appearance. On the south, east, and west of its lower half, it was bounded by burning buildings. The flames bursting from the windows, and rising from the roofs, were proclaiming in one wild roar their work of destruction. Myriads of sparks, borne upward by the current of hot air, were brightening and breaking in the dense smoke above. On the sward of the Square, fresh with the emerald green of early spring, thousands of wretched creatures, who had been driven from their dwellings by the devouring flames, were congregated. Fathers and mothers, and weeping, frightened children sought this open space for a breath of fresh air. But here, even, it was almost as hot as a furnace. Intermingled with these miserable beings were the Federal troops in their garish uniform, representing almost every nation on the continent of Europe, and thousands of the *Corps d'Afrique*.

All along on the north side of the Square were tethered the horses of the Federal cavalry, while, dotted about, were seen the white tents of the sutlers, in which there were temptingly displayed canned fruits and meats, crackers, cheese, etc.

The roaring, crackling and hissing of the flames, the bursting of shells at the Confederate Arsenal, the sounds of instruments of martial music, the neighing of the horses, the shoutings of the multitude, in which could be distinctly distinguished the coarse, wild voices of the negroes, gave an idea of all the horrors of Pandemonium. Above all this scene of terror, hung a black shroud of smoke through which the sun shone with a lurid angry glare like an immense ball of blood that emitted sullen rays of light, as if loth to shine over a scene so appalling.

Remembering the unhappy fate of the citizens of Columbia and other cities of the South, and momentarily expecting pillage, and other evils incidental to the sacking of a city, great numbers of ladies sought the proper military authorities and were furnished with safeguards for the protection of themselves and their homes. These were willingly and generously furnished, and no scene of violence is remembered to have been committed by the troops which occupied Richmond.

Throughout the entire day, those who had enriched themselves by plundering the stores were busy in conveying off their goods. Laughing and jesting negroes tugged along with every conceivable description of merchandise, and many an astute shopkeeper from questionable quarters of Richmond thus added greatly to his former stock.

The sun had set upon this terrible day before the awful reverberations of exploding shells at the arsenal ceased to be heard over Richmond. The evening came on. A deathlike quiet pervaded the late heaving and tumultuous city, broken only by the murmuring waters of the river. Night drew her sable mantle over the mutilated remains of our beautiful capital, and we locked, and bolted, and barred our doors; but sleep had fled our eyelids. All night long we kept a fearful vigil, and listened with beating heart and quickened ears for the faintest sound that might indicate the development of other and more terrible phases of horror. But from all these we were mercifully and providentially spared.

We will just here notice the range and extent of the fire which had in the afternoon literally burned itself out. From an authentic account we copy at length:

> "It had consumed the very heart of the city. A surveyor could scarcely have designated the business portion of the city more exactly than did the boundaries of the fire. Commencing at the Shockoe warehouse the fire radiated front and rear, and on two wings, burning down to, but not destroying, the store No. 77 Main street, south side, halfway between Fourteenth and Fifteenth Streets, and back to the river through Cary and all the intermediate streets. Westward on Main the fire was stayed on Ninth Street, sweeping back to the river. On the north side of Main, the flames were stayed between Thirteenth and Fourteenth streets. From this point the flames raged on the north side of Main up to Eighth Street, and back to Bank Street.
>
> "Among some of the most prominent of the buildings destroyed were the Bank of Richmond, Traders' Bank, Bank of the Commonwealth, Bank of Virginia, Farmers' Bank, all of the banking houses, the American Hotel, the Columbian Hotel, the Enquirer building, on Twelfth Street, the Dispatch office and job-rooms, corner of Thirteenth and Main Streets, all that block of buildings known as Belvin's Block, the Examiner office, engine and machinery rooms, the Confederate Post Office Department building, the State Court House, a fine old building on the Capitol Square at its Franklin Street entrance, the Mechanics' Institute, vacated by the Confederate War Department, and all the buildings on that Square up to Eighth Street, and back to Main Street, the Confederate Arsenal, and the Laboratory on Seventh Street.
>
> "The streets were crowded with furniture and every description of wares, dashed down and trampled in the mud, or burned where it lay. All the government stores were thrown open, and what could not be gotten off by the government was left to the people.
>
> "Next to the river the destruction of property was fearfully complete. The Danville and Petersburg Railroad depots, and the buildings and shedding attached, for the distance of half-a-mile from the north side of Main Street to the river, and between Eighth and Fifteenth Streets, embracing upwards of twenty blocks, presented one waste of smoking ruins, blackened walls, and solitary chimneys."

Except the great fire in New York, in 1837, there is said never to have been so extensive a conflagration on this continent as the burning of Richmond on that memorable day.

Upon reaching the city, General Weitzel established his headquarters in the Hall of the State Capitol, previously occupied by the Virginia House of Delegates. He immediately issued an order for the restoration of quiet, and intended to allay the fears and restore confidence and tranquillity to the minds of the inhabitants. General Shepley was appointed Military Commander of Richmond, and Lieutenant-Colonel Fred L. Manning was made acting Provost Marshal.

General Shepley issued an order which protected the citizens from insult and depredation by the Federal soldiers, and which also included a morbidly sensitive clause in deprecation of insult to the "flag," calculated rather to excite the derision than the indignation of the conquered inhabitants.

The scenes of this day give rise to many reflections, the most of which are too deeply painful to dwell upon. The spirit of extortion, the wicked and inordinate greed of mammon which sometimes overclouds and overrules all the nobler instincts of humanity, are strikingly illustrated by a single incident in this connection. A lady passed up Franklin Street early on the morning of the 3d of April, and held in her hand a small phial in which there was about a table spoonful of paregoric. "This," said she, "I have just purchased on Main Street, at ——'s drug store. Richmond is in flames, and yet for this spoonful of medicine for a sick servant I had to pay five dollars."

An hour had not passed when the fire consumed the establishment of the extortionate vender of drugs. This incident points a moral which all can apply. Riches take to themselves wings, and in a moment least expected elude our grasp. Many who shirked the conscription, who made unworthy use of exemption bills, for the purpose of heaping up and watching their ill-gotten treasures, saw them in a single hour reduced to ashes and made the sport of the winds of heaven. Truly man knoweth not what a day may bring forth.

"GLORIA IN EXCELSIS DEO":
NEW YORK, APRIL 1865

George Templeton Strong: Diary, April 3, 1865

George Templeton Strong recorded the jubilation that greeted the news of the fall of Richmond in New York City. Strong would travel to the former Confederate capital three weeks later on behalf of the U.S. Sanitary Commission, which had opened an office in Richmond. After walking through the "burned district, a wide area of ruin still smoking," he visited the commission's office and found it "crowded with applicants, mostly women in black, with baskets. They were receiving Northern charity with little shew of gratitude, much as a hungry, sulky, ill-conditioned hound accepts a bone—uncertain whether to gnaw the donation or to bite the fingers of the donor. The women were arrogant and sour, but there were poor little children with wan faces and pitiful stories of sick mothers and of privation and misery endured for months. We decided to stop these issues pursuant to the resolutions adopted last week. It seems hard and cruel, but providing tea and sugar for sick rebels is no part of our legitimate work, and it strengthens Southerners in their delusions about their own supreme dignity and the duty of Yankees to take care of them."

April 3. Petersburg and Richmond! *Gloria in excelsis Deo.* New York has seen no such day in our time nor in the old time before us. The jubilations of the Revolutionary War and the War of 1812 were those of a second-rate seaport town. This has been metropolitan and worthy an event of the first national importance to a continental nation and a cosmopolitan city.

The morning papers disclosed nothing decisive. There were two short despatches from City Point giving later news of yesterday's great battle, which looked well, but I omnibussed downtown expecting only to learn during the day more positively that the South Side Railroad was cut; that Lee had returned to his entrenchments badly punished, and that it was confidently expected that he would have to evacuate them at some future period.

Walking down Wall Street, I saw something on the *Com-*

mercial Advertiser bulletin board at the corner of Pine and William Streets and turned off to investigate. I read the announcement "Petersburg is taken" and went into the office in quest of particulars. The man behind the counter was slowly painting in large letters on a large sheet of brown paper another annunciation for the board outside: "Richmond is"— "What's that about Richmond?" said I. "Anything more?" He was too busy for speech, but he went on with a capital C, and a capital A, and so on, till I read the word *CAPTURED*!!! Finding that this was official, I posted up to Trinity Church to tell the sexton to suggest to Vinton to ask the Rector's permission to set the chimes going (which was duly done). When I came back, all William Street in front of the *Advertiser* office was impenetrably crowded, and people were rushing together in front of the Custom House (the *ci-devant* Merchants' Exchange), where Prosper M. Wetmore and Simeon Draper were getting up a meeting on the spur of the moment.

An enormous crowd soon blocked that part of Wall Street, and speeches began. Draper and the Hon. Moses Odell and Evarts and Dean (a proselyte from Copperheadism) and the inevitable Wetmore, and others, severally had their say, and the meeting, organized at about twelve, did not break up, I hear, till four P.M. Never before did I hear cheering that came straight from the heart, that was given because people felt relieved by cheering and hallooing. All the cheers I ever listened to were tame in comparison, because seemingly inspired only by a design to shew enthusiasm. These were spontaneous and involuntary and of vast "magnetizing" power. They sang "Old Hundred," the Doxology, "John Brown," and "The Star-Spangled Banner," repeating the last two lines of Key's song over and over, with a massive roar from the crowd and a unanimous wave of hats at the end of each repetition. I think I shall never lose the impression made by this rude, many-voiced chorale. It seemed a revelation of profound national feeling, underlying all our vulgarisms and corruptions, and vouchsafed to us in their very focus and centre, in Wall Street itself.

I walked about on the outskirts of the crowd, shaking hands with everybody, congratulating and being congratulated by scores of men I hardly know even by sight. Men embraced and hugged each other, *kissed* each other, retreated into doorways to dry their eyes and came out again to flourish their hats and hurrah. There will be many sore throats in New York tomorrow. My only experience of a people stirred up to like intensity of feeling was at the great Union meeting at Union Square in April, 1861. But the feeling of today's crowd was not at all identical with that of the memorable mass-meeting four years ago. It was no less earnest and serious, but it was founded on memories of years of failure, all but hopeless, and on the consciousness that national victory was at last secured, through much tribulation. . . .

After dinner to the Union League Club. Vast crowd, enthusiasm, and excitement. Meeting organized upstairs, Captain Marshall in the chair, and "a few remarks" made by a score of people. Honest, downright old Judge Vanderpoel was very good. "Gentlemen," said the judge, "I tell you that for years before this rebellion, we at the North lived under the tyranny of the slaveholders. I see now that when I was in Congress, almost every important vote I gave was dictated by them and given under the plantation lash. I confess it with shame, and humbly ask pardon of this meeting and of all my fellow-countrymen."

Hamilton Fish was at the Club—I never saw him there before —beaming and gushing, and shaking everybody's hands with fervor. Two years ago he talked nothing but discouragement and practical disloyalty. But (as Sydney Smith irreverently said of bishops), "If you want to know which way the wind blows, throw up Hamilton Fish."

It seems like a Fourth of July night—such a fusillade and cannonade is going on. Thus ends a day *sui generis* in my life. We shall long remember that the first troops to enter Richmond were niggers of Weitzel's corps. It is a most suggestive fact. It's said there were abundant signs of Union feeling in the city. Lee, Davis, & Co. are supposed to be making for Burke's Junction. Lynchburg or Danville is doubtless their proposed harbor of refuge. May Sheridan's cavalry be fresh enough to deal with them according to the example of Blücher after Waterloo. The government of the "Confederate States" has become nomadic. Its capitol and its departments of state and of war are probably in a dirty, damaged, worn-out railroad car, and its "seat of government" probably rests on the saddle which Jeff Davis bestrides.

"THIS PEERLESS COMRADE":
VIRGINIA, APRIL 1865

William Gordon McCabe to Mary Pegram

William Pegram left the University of Virginia law school in 1861 to join the Confederate army and became the commander of the Purcell artillery battery in March 1862. Assigned to the Light Division led by A. P. Hill, he distinguished himself at Mechanicsville by keeping his battery in action after losing two-thirds of his guns and half of his men and horses. Pegram fought in every major engagement of the Army of Northern Virginia and became one of its most famous artillery officers, in part because his severe near-sightedness made him wear gold-rimmed spectacles even in battle. Promoted to battalion command in 1863, he remained hopeful about the Confederacy's prospects even after his older brother, Brigadier General John Pegram, was killed at Hatcher's Run on February 6, 1865. Writing to his sister Mary on March 14, he contrasted the "fine spirits & condition" of Lee's army with the "croakers & cowards" in Richmond who spread harmful rumors "conceived in their craven hearts." On April 1 Pegram and his close friend and adjutant, Captain William Gordon McCabe, were at Five Forks with six guns from their battalion. McCabe wrote to Mary Pegram about her brother's fate.

―――――――――

Bivouac in Amelia County. April 4th. 1865. Tuesday morning.
My dear Miss Mary,

I wrote two letters to Major Pegram in regard to the death of our dearest Colonel, but I fear neither will reach you, as Richmond has been evacuated. Unfortunately I sent in the last one a piece of his hair, as the opportunity seemed such a sure one. Mr Taylor, of Amelia promised to take it, & they all knew you & your mother so well & manifested such interest about it, that I reckoned very surely on its reaching you. Life is so uncertain now that I wish to tell you every circumstance concerning the death of our precious boy, as I was the only person with him when he put on immortality. On Saturday morning last at the Five (5) Forks near Mrs. Gillem's the enemy commenced pressing us, & our guns became engaged. He & I, as usual, were together, & our forces soon repelled the feeble demonstration of the enemy. We laid down together at the foot of a tree & he was sleeping, when a fierce assault was made on our centre where we had three (3) guns. I awakened him & we both mounted our horses & rode down among the guns, which were posted on the infantry line of battle. The enemy were now within 30 yds. of the guns & the fire terrific beyond description. I remember distinctly the sweet serenity of his face as he rode calmly to the very front. His last order was "Fire your canister low" & in a minute afterwards he fell from his saddle, shot through the left arm & side. He cried out, "Oh! Gordon I'm mortally wounded, take me off the field." I called the ambulance corps, sent him off, gave his last order to the Batteries, & then ran to where he was. At that time the enemy had gotten in our rear & our men were rapidly falling back. They cried out to me that we would be taken, but I put him in the ambulance & we drove through two parallel lines-of-battle of the enemy. Happily night put an end to the pursuit. Oh! dear Miss Mary, I am so thankful that I was with him then. I made him put his head on my arm & put the other one under his body to prevent the jolting of the ambulance, & we rode so for ten miles. When we were bringing him off the field, he took my hand & said, "Tell my mother & sisters that I commend them to God's protection." He was in great pain, & the Dr. gave him morphine. While in the ambulance I held him in my arms & prayed for him & kissed him over & over again. Once when I prayed that his life might be spared, he said, "If it is God's will to take me, I am perfectly resigned. I only wish life for my mother's & sisters' sake." He said several times—"Give my love to mother & both sisters & tell them I thought of them in my last moments." Once when in my agony I cried out—"My God, my God, why hast Thou forsaken me," he said quickly—"Don't say that, Gordon, it is'nt right." One thing I love to dwell upon. I bent over him & kissed him & said, calling him by his name for the first time in my life, "Willie, I never knew how much I loved you until now." He pressed my hand & answered, "But I did." Without ceasing, except when I lost my voice in tears, I prayed for him, for comfort for body & soul, & he would simply say "*Amen*." I carried him to Ford's Depot, on the S. S. R.R. to a Mr.

Pegram's & procured a bed for him. We got there about 10 o'clock at night & about 12 the Yankees advanced & I was left alone with him. I sent off our horses, sabres, & spurs, as I did n't want them to fall into the hands of the enemy. He had been suffering very greatly & begged me for more morphine. I made the Dr give me some, with directions about using it, & he soon told me that he was better. I fixed his head easily & he fell asleep, never more to speak to me. Oh! that terrible night. All alone with him & another Col. mortally wounded, feeling utterly wretched in my impotence to help him, tho' I dressed his wound as well as I knew how, cut off from our own forces, & momentarily expecting the enemy to come & perhaps to remain deaf to my entreaties to remain with him. Dear Miss Mary, I could only watch & pray. He fell into a stupour about 2 o'clock. I could only sit by him & moisten his lips & smooth his hair & kiss him & call him a thousand fond names though he never heard me. At A.M. Sunday morning, he died without a struggle. I helped myself to dig his grave, so fearful was I that the Yankees would get his body. I buried him at Mr Pegram's in the back yard & read the service over him, as I knew he would have desired it. After he was dead, I cut off a piece of his hair for you & one for myself, & laid him out in uniform. Oh! what a splendid soldier he looked. Mr. Pegram promised me faithfully that he wd. have a fence built around the grave. He & his wife were very kind. I threw myself on their charity as I had n't a cent in the world. As soon as I had buried him, I jumped on a horse I found there & made my escape, after being fired on three or four times by their picket. And now my heart, as yours, is left unto me desolate. I will never admit that anybody loved him more than I did. This peerless comrade, my darling Willie, who was with me always, who read with me, prayed with me, slept with me, is at rest. On this terrible retreat I have talked with his spirit hour after hour, & the men, who always saw us riding together, have been very kind to me in my grief. God help us all. Remember that I will always do you any service to the measure of my life.

      Your friend,
       W. Gordon McCabe

OCCUPYING RICHMOND: VIRGINIA, APRIL 1865

Thomas Morris Chester
to the Philadelphia Press

On the morning of April 3 Major General Godfrey Weitzel, the commander of the Twenty-fifth in the Army of the James, occupied Richmond with a regiment of black cavalry and two infantry divisions, one made up of white soldiers and the other of U.S. Colored Troops. Weitzel's men spent the day fighting fires and restoring order in the city. The following day they were surprised by the unexpected arrival of President Lincoln, who had been visiting Grant's headquarters at City Point, Virginia, since March 24. Despite Stanton's fears for his safety, Lincoln resolved to go to the captured city and telegraphed the Secretary of War: "I will take care of myself." Thomas Morris Chester had been sending dispatches to the *Philadelphia Press* from the Army of the James since August 1864. He was the only black correspondent to report on the war for a major daily newspaper.

HALL OF CONGRESS
RICHMOND, APRIL 4, 1865.

Seated in the Speaker's chair, so long dedicated to treason, but in the future to be consecrated to loyalty, I hasten to give a rapid sketch of the incidents which have occurred since my last despatch.

To Major General Godfrey Weitzel was assigned the duty of capturing Richmond. Last evening he had determined upon storming the rebel works in front of Fort Burnham. The proper dispositions were all made, and the knowing ones retired with dim visions of this stronghold of treason floating before them. Nothing occurred in the first part of the evening to awaken suspicion, though for the past few days it has been known to the authorities that the rebels, as I informed you, were evacuating the city. After midnight explosions began to occur so frequently as to confirm the evidence already in possession of the General-in-chief, that the last acts of an outgeneralled army were in course of progress. The immense flames curling up throughout the rebel camps indicated that they were destroying all that could not be taken away.

The soldiers along the line gathered upon the breastworks to witness the scene and exchange congratulations. While thus silently gazing upon the columns of fire one of the monster rams was exploded, which made the very earth tremble. If there was any doubt about the evacuation of Richmond that report banished them all. In a very few moments, though still dark, the Army of the James, or rather that part of it under General Weitzel, was put in motion.

It did not require much time to get the men in light-marching order. Every regiment tried to be first. All cheerfully moved off with accelerated speed. The pickets which were on the line during the night were in the advance.

Brevet Brigadier General Draper's brigade of colored troops, Brevet Major General Kautz's division, were the first infantry to enter Richmond. The gallant 36th U. S. Colored Troops, under Lieutenant Colonel B. F. Pratt, has the honor of being the first regiment. Captain Bicnnef's company has the pride of leading the advance.

The column having passed through Fort Burnham, over the rebel works, where they were moving heavy and light pieces of artillery, which the enemy in his haste was obliged to leave behind, moved into the Osborn road, which leads directly into the city.

In passing over the rebel works, we moved very cautiously in single file, for fear of exploding the innumerable torpedoes which were planted in front. So far as I can learn none has been exploded, and no one has been injured by those infernal machines. The soldiers were soon, under engineers, carefully digging them up and making the passage way beyond the fear of casualties.

Along the road which the troops marched, or rather double quicked, batches of negroes were gathered together testifying by unmistakable signs their delight at our coming. Rebel soldiers who had hid themselves when their army moved came out of the bushes, and gave themselves up as disgusted with the service. The haste of the rebels was evident in guns, camp equipage, telegraph wires, and other army property which they did not have time to burn.

When the column was about two miles from Richmond General Weitzel and staff passed by at a rapid speed, and was hailed by loud cheering. He soon reached the city, which was surrendered to him informally at the State House by Mr. Joseph Mayo, the mayor. The General and staff rode up Main street amid the hearty congratulations of a very large crowd of colored persons and poor whites, who were gathered together upon the sidewalks manifesting every demonstration of joy.

There were many persons in the better-class houses who were peeping out of the windows, and whose movements indicated that they would need watching in the future. There was no mistaking the curl of their lips and the flash of their eyes. The new military Governor of Richmond will, no doubt, prove equal to such emergencies.

When General Draper's brigade entered the outskirts of the city it was halted, and a brigade of Devin's division, 24th Corps, passed in to constitute the provost guard. A scene was here witnessed which was not only grand, but sublime. Officers rushed into each other's arms, congratulating them upon the peaceful occupation of this citadel. Tears of joy ran down the faces of the more aged. The soldiers cheered lustily, which were mingled with every kind of expression of delight. The citizens stood gaping in wonder at the splendidly-equipped army marching along under the graceful folds of the old flag. Some waved their hats and women their hands in token of gladness. The pious old negroes, male and female, indulged in such expressions: "You've come at last"; "We've been looking for you these many days"; "Jesus has opened the way"; "God bless you"; "I've not seen that old flag for four years"; "It does my eyes good"; "Have you come to stay?"; "Thank God", and similar expressions of exultation. The soldiers, black and white, received these assurances of loyalty as evidences of the latent patriotism of an oppressed people, which a military despotism has not been able to crush.

Riding up to a group of fine looking men, whose appearance indicated that they would hardly have influence enough to keep them out of the army, I inquired how it was they were not taken away with the force of Lee. They replied that they had hid themselves when the rebel army had evacuated the city, and that many more had done likewise, who would soon appear when assured that there was no longer any danger of falling into the power of the traitorous army.

These scenes all occurred at the terminus of Osborn road, which connects with the streets of the city, and is within the municipal limits. There General Draper's brigade, with the gallant 36th U.S.C.T.'s drum corps, played "Yankee Doodle" and "Shouting the Battle Cry of Freedom," amid the cheers of the boys and the white soldiers who filed by them. It ought to be stated that the officers of the white troops were anxious to be the first to enter the city with their organizations, and so far succeeded as to procure an order when about three miles, distant, that General Draper's brigade should take the left of the road, in order to allow those of the 24th Corps, under General Devin, to pass by. General Draper obeyed the order, and took the left of the road in order to let the troops of Devin go by, but at the same time ordered his brigade on a double-quick, well knowing that his men would not likely be over taken on the road by any soldiers in the army. For marching or fighting Draper's 1st Brigade, 1st Division, 25th Corps, is not to be surpassed in the service, and the General honors it with a pride and a consciousness which inspire him to undertake cheerfully whatever may be committed to his execution. It was his brigade that nipped the flower of the Southern army, the Texas Brigade, under Gary, which never before last September knew defeat. There may be others who may claim the distinction of being the first to enter the city, but as I was ahead of every part of the force but the cavalry, which of necessity must lead the advance, I know whereof I affirm when I announce that General Draper's brigade was the first organization to enter the city limits. According to custom, it should constitute the provost guard of Richmond.

Kautz's division, consisting of Draper's and Wild's brigades, with troops of the 24th Corps, were placed in the trenches around the city, and Thomas' brigade was assigned to garrison Manchester. Proper dispositions have been made of the force to give security, and, soldier-like, placed the defences of the city beyond the possibility of a surprise.

As we entered all the Government buildings were in flames, having been fired by order of the rebel General Ewell. The flames soon communicated themselves to the business part of the city; and continued to rage furiously throughout the day. All efforts to arrest this destructive element seemed for the best part of the day of no avail. The fire department of Richmond rendered every aid, and to them and the co-operate labors of our soldiers belongs the credit of having saved Richmond from the devastating flames. As it is, all that part of the city lying between Ninth and Fourteenth streets, between Main street and the river inclusive, is in ruins. Among the most prominent buildings destroyed are the rebel War Department, Quartermaster General's Department, all the buildings with commissary stores, Shockoe's and Dibbrel's warehouses, well stored with tobacco, *Dispatch* and *Enquirer* newspaper buildings, the court house, (Guy) House, Farmers' Bank, Bank of Virginia, Exchange Bank, Tracers' Bank, American and Columbia hotels, and the Mayo bridge which unites Richmond with Manchester. The buildings of the largest merchants are among those which have been reduced to ashes.

The flames, in spreading, soon communicated to poor and rich houses alike. All classes were soon rushing, into the streets with their goods, to save them. They hardly laid them down before they were picked up by those who openly were plundering everyplace where anything of value was to be obtained. It was retributive justice upon the aiders and abettors of treason to see their property fired by the rebel chiefs and plundered by the people whom they meant to forever enslave. As soon as the torch was applied to the rebel storehouses, the negroes and poor whites began to appropriate all property, without respect to locks or bolts. About the time our advance entered the city the tide of this inadmissible confiscation was at its highest ebb. Men would rush to the principal stores, break open the doors, and carry off the contents by the armful.

The leader of this system of public plundering was a colored man who carried upon his shoulder an iron crow-bar, and as a mark of distinguishment had a red piece of goods around his waist which reached down to his knees. The mob, for it could not with propriety be called anything else, followed him as their leader; moved on when he advanced, and rushed into every passage which was made by the leader with his crow-bar. Goods of every description were seized under these circumstances and personally appropriated by the supporters of an equal distribution of property. Cotton goods in abundance, tobacco in untold quantities, shoes, rebel military clothing, and goods and furniture generally were carried away by the people as long as any thing of value was to be obtained. As soon as Gen. Ripley was assigned to provost duty, all plundering immediately ceased, the flames were arrested, and an appearance of recognized authority fully sustained. Order once more reigns in Richmond. The streets were as quiet last night as they possibly could be. An effective patrolling and provost guard keeps everything as quiet as can be expected.

The F. F. V.'s have not ventured out of their houses yet, except in a few cases, to apply for a guard to protect their property. In some cases negroes have been sent to protect the interest of these would-be man sellers. It is pleasant to witness the measured pace of some dark sentinel before the houses of persons who, without doubt, were outspoken rebels until the Union army entered the city, owing the security which they feel to the vigilance of the negro guard.

When the army occupied the city there were innumerable inquiries for Jeff Davis, but to all of which the answer was made that he went off in great haste night before last, with all the bag and baggage which he could carry. The future capital of the Confederacy will probably be in a wagon for the facilities which it affords to travel. Jeff's mansion, where he lived in state, is now the headquarters of Gen. Weitzel.

Brigadier General Shepley has been appointed Governor of Richmond, and has entered upon the arduous duties of the office. A better selection could not have been made.

It is due to Major Stevens, of the 4th Massachusetts Cavalry, provost marshal, on the staff of Gen. Weitzel, to give him credit for raising the first colors over the State House. He hoisted a couple of guidons, in the absence of a flag, which excited prolonged cheering. Soon after General Shepley's A. D. C. raised the first storm flag over the Capitol. It is the acme standard which General Shepley laid a wager would wave over the St. Charles Hotel in the beginning of the rebellion, and he also laid another that it would be hoisted over Richmond, both of which he has had the satisfaction of winning.

During the early part of the day a number of rebel officers were captured at the Spottswood House, where they were drinking freely. They belonged to the navy, the last of which disappeared in smoke, excepting a few straggling officers and men. These fellows, when arrested, did not wish to walk through the street under a guard, but solicited the favor of being permitted to go to the provost marshal in a carriage. Their impudence was received as it deserved, with suppressed contempt.

On Sunday evening, strange to say, the jails in this place were thrown open, and all runaway negroes, those for sale and those for safe keeping were told to hop out and enjoy their freedom. You may rely upon it that they did not need a second invitation. Many of these persons will have no difficulty in convincing themselves that they were always on the side of the Union and the freedom of the slave. Great events have a wonderful influence upon the minds of guilty, trembling wretches.

When the rebels blew up the magazine in the vicinity of French Garden Hill, the people were not informed of the fact. Some of them knew it, but the great body of those in the vicinity were ignorant of what was taking place. The result was that quite a number were killed. Nearly if not quite all the paupers in the poor house—the numbers not being large—which was very near the magazine, were instantly killed also.

The fire is still burning, but not too much damage.

HALL OF CONGRESS

RICHMOND, APRIL 6, 1865.

The exultation of the loyal people of this city, who, amid the infamy by which they have been surrounded, and the foul misrepresentations to allure them from their allegiance, have remained true to the old flag, is still being expressed by the most extravagant demonstrations of joy. The Union element in this city consists of negroes and poor whites, including all that have deserted from the army, or have survived the terrible exigencies which brought starvation to so many homes. As to the negroes, one thing is certain, that amid every disaster to our arms, amid the wrongs which they daily suffered for their known love for the Union, and amid the scourging which they received for trying to reach our army and enlist under our flag, they have ever prayed for the right cause, and testified their devotion to it in ten thousand instances, and especially in aiding our escaped prisoners to find our lines when to do so placed their own lives in peril.

The great event after the capture of the city was the arrival of President Lincoln in it. He came up to Rocket's wharf in one of Admiral Porter's vessels of war, and, with a file of sailors for a guard of honor, he walked up to Jeff Davis' house, the headquarters of General Weitzel. As soon as he landed the news sped, as if upon the wings of lightning, that "Old Abe," for it was treason in this city to give him a more respectful address, had come. Some of the negroes, feeling themselves free to act like men, shouted that the President had arrived. This name having always been applied to Jeff, the inhabitants, coupling it with the prevailing rumor that he had been captured, reported that the arch-traitor was being brought into the city. As the people pressed near they cried "Hang him!" "Hang him!" "Show him no quarter!" and other similar expressions, which indicated their sentiments as to what should be his fate. But when they learned that it was President Lincoln their joy knew no bounds. By the time he reached General Weitzel's headquarters, thousands of persons had followed him to catch a sight of the Chief Magistrate of the United States. When he ascended the steps he faced the crowd and bowed his thanks for the prolonged exultation which was going up from that great concourse. The people seemed inspired by this acknowledgment, and with renewed vigor shouted louder and louder, until it seemed as if the echoes would reach the abode of those patriot spirits who had died without witnessing the sight.

General Weitzel received the President upon the pavement, and conducted him up the steps. General Shepley, after a good deal of trouble, got the crowd quiet and introduced Admiral Porter, who bowed his acknowledgments for the cheering with which his name was greeted. The President and party entered the mansion, where they remained for half an hour, the crowd still accumulating around it, when a headquarters' carriage was brought in front, drawn by four horses, and Mr. Lincoln, with his youngest son, Admiral Porter, General Kautz, and General Devin entered. The carriage drove through the principal streets, followed by General Weitzel and staff on horseback, and a cavalry guard. There is no describing the scene along the route. The colored population was wild with enthusiasm. Old men thanked God in a very boisterous manner, and old women shouted upon the pavement as high as they had ever done at a religious revival. But when the President passed through the Capitol yard it was filled with people. Washington's monument and the Capitol steps were one mass of humanity to catch a glimpse of him.

It should be recorded that the Malvern, Admiral Porter's flag-ship, upon which the President came; the Bat, Monticello, Frolic, and the Symbol, the torpedo-boat which led the advance and exploded these infernal machines, were the first vessels to arrive in Richmond.

Nothing can exceed the courtesy and politeness which the whites everywhere manifest to the negroes. Not even the familiarity peculiar to Americans is indulged in, calling the blacks by their first or Christian names, but even masters are addressing their slaves as "Mr. Johnson," "Mrs. Brown," and "Miss Smith." A cordial shake of the hand and a gentle inclination of the body, approaching to respectful consideration, are evident in the greetings which now take place between the oppressed and the oppressor.

Masters are looking through the camps of our colored troops to find some of their former slaves to give them a good character. The first night our troops quartered in the city this scene was enacted in Gen. Draper's brigade limits, his being the first organization to enter the city. His troops now hold the inner lines of works. The rapid occupation of the city cut off the retreat of many rebels, who are daily being picked up by the provost guard.

Every one declares that Richmond never before presented such a spectacle of jubilee. It must be confessed that those who participated in this informal reception of the President were mainly negroes. There were many whites in the crowd, but they were lost in the great concourse of American citizens of African descent. Those who lived in the finest houses either stood motionless upon their steps or merely peeped through the window-blinds, with a very few exceptions. The Secesh-inhabitants still have some hope for their tumbling cause.

The scenes at the Capitol during the day are of a very exciting character. The offices of General Shepley, the Military

Governor, and Colonel Morning, the Provost Marshal General, are besieged by crowds, mostly poor people, with a small sprinkling of respectability, upon every kind of pretext. They want protection papers, a guard over their property, to assure the authorities of their allegiance, to take the oath, to announce that they are paroled prisoners and never have been exchanged, and don't desire to be, and innumerable other circumstances to insure the protection of the military authorities.

The people of Richmond, white and black, had been led to believe that when the Yankee army came its mission was one of plunder. But the orderly manner in which the soldiers have acted has undeceived them. The excitement is great, but nothing could be more orderly and decorous than the united crowds of soldiers and citizens.

The Capitol building all day yesterday from the moment we took possession was surrounded by a crowd of hungry men and women clamoring for something to eat. The earnestness of their entreaties and looks showed that they were in a destitute condition. It was deemed necessary to station a special guard at the bottom of the steps to keep them from filling the building. These suffering people will probably be attended to in a day or so in that bountiful manner which has marked the advance of the Union armies.

I visited yesterday (Tuesday) several of the slave jails, where men, women, and children were confined, or herded, for the examination of purchasers. The jailors were in all cases slaves, and had been left in undisputed possession of the buildings. The owners, as soon as they were aware that we were coming, opened wide the doors and told the confined inmates they were free. The poor souls could not realize it until they saw the Union army. Even then they thought it must be a pleasant dream, but when they saw Abraham Lincoln they were satisfied that their freedom was perpetual. One enthusiastic old negro woman exclaimed: "I know that I am free, for I have seen Father Abraham and felt him."

When the President returned to the flag-ship of Admiral Porter, in the evening, he was taken from the wharf in a cutter. Just as he pushed off, amid the cheering of the crowd, another good old colored female shouted out, "Don't drown, Massa Abe, for God's sake!"

The fire, which was nearly extinguished when I closed my last despatch, is entirely so now. Thousands of persons are gazing hourly with indignation upon the ruins. Gen. Lee ordered the evacuation of the city at an hour known to the remaining leaders of the rebellion, when Gens. Ewell and Breckinridge, and others, absconded, leaving orders with menials, robbers, and plunderers, kept together during the war by the "cohesive power of public plunder," to apply the torch to the different tobacco warehouses, public buildings, arsenals, stores, flour mills, powder magazines, and every important place of deposit. A south wind prevailed, and the flames spread with devastating effect. The offices of the newspapers, whose columns have been charged with the foulest vituperation against our Government, were on fire; two of them have been reduced to ashes, another one injured beyond repair, while the remaining two are not much damaged. Every bank which had emitted the spurious notes of the rebels was consumed to ruins. Churches no longer gave audience to empty prayers, but burst forth in furious flames. Magazines exploded, killing the poor inhabitants. In short, Secession was burnt out, and the city purified as far as fire could accomplish it.

As I informed you in a previous despatch, the Union soldiers united with the citizens to stay the progress of the fire, and at last succeeded, but not until all the business part of the town was destroyed.

About three o'clock on Monday morning the political prisoners who were confined in Castle Thunder, and the Union prisoners who were in Libby, were marched out and driven off. Some of our officers escaped and were kindly cared for by the good Union folks of this city. The rebels also gathered together as many colored persons as possible, and were forcing them ahead with drawn sabres, but before they were out of the city Spear's cavalry came down upon them, rescued the negroes, and captured seventeen of the Johnnies, with their horses.

Yesterday afternoon I strolled through Castle Thunder, where so many Union men have suffered every species of meanness and tyranny which the rebels could invent. The only thing that attracted especial attention was the large number of manacles which were for the benefit of the prisoners. This place has been so often described, that it would be unnecessary to weary the reader again. The Castle is empty at present, and is in charge of Capt. Mattison, 81st New York Volunteers, who, by the way, is a very accommodating officer. The Hotel de Libby is now doing a rushing business in the way of accommodating a class of persons who have not heretofore patronized that establishment. It is being rapidly filled with rebel soldiers, detectives, spies, robbers, and every grade of infamy in the calendar of crime. The stars and stripes now wave gracefully over it, and traitors look through the same bars behind which loyal men were so long confined.

Quite a large number of rebels were brought into the city last night. I did not for a certainty learn whether they were captured, or deserted from a bad cause—most probably the latter.

Lieut. Gen. Grant will arrive in this city tomorrow, and will doubtless receive an ovation equal to President Lincoln's.

SOUTHERN "ARROGANCE AND FOLLY":
WASHINGTON, D.C., APRIL 1865

Gideon Welles: Diary, April 7, 1865

After abandoning Richmond and Petersburg, Lee marched west with about 40,000 men, hoping to evade his Union pursuers and reach Johnston's army in North Carolina. His army reached Amelia Court House, about thirty-five miles northwest of Petersburg, on April 4, having lost thousands of hungry, exhausted, and demoralized men along the way to straggling and desertion. When Lee discovered that Sheridan had blocked his planned route into North Carolina, he was forced to continue heading west toward Lynchburg. On April 6, Union troops led by Sheridan closed in on the rear of the Confederate column at Sailor's Creek and captured more than 6,000 prisoners, including eight generals. Watching the fighting from a nearby hill, Lee exclaimed, "My God! Has the army been dissolved?" In his message reporting the victory, Sheridan wrote, "If the thing is pressed I think Lee will surrender." Lincoln then telegraphed Grant: "Let the *thing* be pressed." With the end of the war seemingly close, Secretary of the Navy Gideon Welles reflected on its origins.

April 7, Friday. We have word that Sheridan has had a battle with a part of Lee's army, has captured six Rebel generals and several thousand prisoners. His dispatch intimates the almost certain capture of Lee.

In the closing up of this Rebellion, General Grant has [ ] proved himself a man of undoubted military talent and genius. Those who have doubted and hesitated must concede him great capacity as a general. His demonstrations and movements have been masterly. The persistency which he has exhibited is as much to be admired as any quality in his character. He is regardless of life.

It is desirable that Lee should be captured. He, more than any one else has the confidence of the Rebels, and can, if he escapes, and is weak enough to try to continue hostilities, rally for a time a brigand force in the interior. I can hardly suppose he would do this, but he has shown great weakness, and his infidelity to the country which educated, and employed, and paid him betrays gross ingratitude. His true course would be to desert the country he has betrayed, and never return.

Memo. This Rebellion which has convulsed the nation for four years, threatened the Union and caused such sacrifice of blood and treasure may be traced in a great degree to the diseased imagination of certain South Carolina gentlemen, who some thirty and forty years since studied Scott's novels, and fancied themselves cavaliers, imbued with chivalry, a superior class, not born to labor but to command, brave beyond mankind generally, more intellectual, more generous, more hospitable, more liberal than others. Others of their countrymen who did not own slaves, and who labored with their own hands, who depended on their own exertions for a livelihood, who were mechanics, traders and tillers of the soil were, in their estimate, inferiors who would not fight, were religious and would not gamble, moral and would not countenance duelling, were serious and minded their own business, economical and thrifty, which was denounced as mean and miserly. Hence the chivalrous Carolinian affected to, and actually did, hold the Yankee in contempt.

The women caught the contagion. They were to be patriotic, Revolutionary matrons and maidens. They admired the bold, dashing, swaggering, licentious, boasting, chivalrous slave-master who told them he wanted to fight the Yankee but could not kick and insult him into a quarrel. And they disdained and despised the pious, peddling, plodding, persevering Yankee who would not drink, and swear, and fight duels.

The speeches and letters of James Hamilton and his associates from 1825 forward will be found impregnated with the romance and poetry of Scott, and they came ultimately to believe themselves a superior and better race.

Only a war could wipe out this arrogance and folly which had through party and sectional instrumentalities been disseminated through a large portion of the South. Face to face in battle and in field, they learned their own weakness and misconception of the Yankee character. Without self-assumption of superiority, the Yankee was proved to be as brave, as generous, as humane, as chivalric as the vaunting and superficial Carolinian to say the least. Their ideal, however in Scott's pages of Marmion, Ivanhoe, etc., no more belonged to the Sunny South the punky Palmetto than to other sections less arrogant and presuming but more industrious and frugal.

SURRENDER TERMS: VIRGINIA, APRIL 1865

Ulysses S. Grant to Robert E. Lee

Grant's aggressive pursuit of Lee neared its end on April 8 when Union cavalry blocked the road to Lynchburg near Appomattox Court House. The next morning the Army of Northern Virginia soon found itself surrounded on three sides. When Lee realized that his army was trapped, he told his aides "there is nothing left for me to do but to go and see General Grant, and I would rather die a thousand deaths." The two generals met on the afternoon of April 9 in the parlor of the McLean House, Lee wearing a full dress uniform with sword and Grant a private's uniform with a lieutenant general's shoulder straps. On March 3 Lincoln had responded sternly to an overture from Lee about negotiating peace "by means of a military convention," ordering Grant "not to decide, discuss, or confer upon any political question" with the Confederate commander. Subsequently, when Grant, Sherman, and Lincoln had conferred at City Point on March 28, the President expressed a desire to have the Confederate armies receive lenient terms of capitulation. With these indications in mind, Grant wrote out his surrender terms.

Appomattox C. H. Va.
Apl. 9th 1865

GEN. R. E. LEE,
COMD.G C. S. A.
GEN.

In accordance with the substance of my letter to you of the 8th inst. I propose to receive the surrender of the Army of N. Va. on the following terms: towit:

Rolls of all the officers and men to be made in duplicate One copy to be given to an officer designated by me, the other to be retained by such officer or officers as you may designate. The officers to give their individual paroles not to take up arms against the Government of the United States until properly exchanged and each company or regimental commander sign a like parole for the men of their commands.

The Arms, Artillery and public property to be parked and

stacked and turned over to the officer appointed by me to receive them. This will not embrace the side Arms of the officers nor their private horses or baggage.—This done each officer and man will be allowed to return to their homes not to be disturbed by United States Authority so long as they observe their parole and the laws in force where they may reside.
      Very respectfully
      U. S. GRANT Lt. Gn

A COMMANDER'S FAREWELL: VIRGINIA, APRIL 1865

Robert E. Lee: General Orders No. 9

Lee read Grant's terms and remarked that in the Confederate army soldiers serving in the cavalry and the artillery owned their own horses. Grant did not revise his written terms, which addressed only horses owned by officers, but told Lee that he would permit paroled soldiers to take their own horses and mules home with them. He also gave orders for the surrendered Confederates to be fed from Union army rations. Lee signed a letter accepting Grant's terms, and the two men parted. As news of the surrender spread, the Union artillery began firing a one-hundred-gun salute that Grant immediately ordered silenced. "The Confederates were now our prisoners," he would write in his memoirs, "and we did not want to exult over their downfall." Thousands of men cheered Lee and reached out to touch him as he rode through the Confederate ranks on his horse Traveller. The next day Lee issued a farewell message to his army that was initially drafted by one of his senior aides, Lieutenant Colonel Charles Marshall. Having given his parole, Lee left Appomattox Court House on April 11 and returned to his home in Richmond.

GENERAL ORDER, NO. 9

Headquarters, Army of Northern Virginia
April 10, 1865

After four years of arduous service, marked by unsurpassed courage and fortitude, the Army of Northern Virginia has been compelled to yield to overwhelming numbers and resources.

I need not tell the brave survivors of so many hard fought battles, who have remained steadfast to the last, that I have consented to the result from no distrust of them.

But feeling that valor and devotion could accomplish nothing that would compensate for the loss that must have attended the continuance of the contest, I determined to avoid the useless sacrifice of those whose past services have endeared them to their countrymen.

By the terms of the agreement officers and men can return to their homes and remain until exchanged. You will take with you the satisfaction that proceeds from the consciousness of duty faithfully performed, and I earnestly pray that a Merciful God will extend to you His blessing and protection.

With an increasing admiration of your constancy and devotion to your country, and a grateful remembrance of your kind and generous considerations for myself, I bid you all an affectionate farewell.

R. E. LEE
Genl

LINCOLN'S ASSASSINATION:
WASHINGTON, D.C., APRIL 1865

Elizabeth Keckly: from Behind the Scenes

Lincoln returned to Washington from City Point on April 9, Palm Sunday, the day Lee surrendered to Grant. Two days later the President spoke to a large crowd from a window in the White House. After saying that "the surrender of the principal insurgent army" gave "hope of a righteous and speedy peace," Lincoln devoted most of his speech to the problems of reconstruction. Defending at length his support for the new government in Louisiana, which was opposed by Charles Sumner and other Radical Republicans (see pp. 629–31 in this volume), he cited its adoption of a free-state constitution, ratification of the Thirteenth Amendment, and creation of public schools for black and white children. Regarding the failure of the Louisiana government to extend the franchise to black men, Lincoln stated that "I would myself prefer that it were now conferred on the very intelligent, and on those who serve our cause as soldiers." It was his first public endorsement of black suffrage. Listening in the audience was John Wilkes Booth. "This means nigger citizenship," Booth said. "Now, my God, I'll put him through." Elizabeth Keckly was a former slave who had become a successful Washington dressmaker and a confidante of Mary Todd Lincoln. She wrote about the President's speech on April 11 and the days that followed in her 1868 memoir, *Behind the Scenes, or, Thirty Years a Slave, and Four Years in the White House*.

I HAD never heard Mr. Lincoln make a public speech, and, knowing the man so well, was very anxious to hear him. On the morning of the Tuesday after our return from City Point, Mrs. Lincoln came to my apartments, and before she drove away I asked permission to come to the White House that night and hear Mr. Lincoln speak.

"Certainly, Lizabeth; if you take any interest in political speeches, come and listen in welcome."

"Thank you, Mrs. Lincoln. May I trespass further on your kindness by asking permission to bring a friend with me?"

"Yes, bring your friend also. By the way, come in time to dress me before the speaking commences."

"I will be in time. You may rely upon that. Good morning," I added, as she swept from my room, and, passing out into the street, entered her carriage and drove away.

About 7 o'clock that evening I entered the White House. As I went up-stairs I glanced into Mr. Lincoln's room through the half-open door, and seated by a desk was the President, looking over his notes and muttering to himself. His face was thoughtful, his manner abstracted, and I knew, as I paused a moment to watch him, that he was rehearsing the part that he was to play in the great drama soon to commence.

Proceeding to Mrs. Lincoln's apartment, I worked with busy fingers, and in a short time her toilette was completed.

Great crowds began to gather in front of the White House, and loud calls were made for the President. The band stopped playing, and as he advanced to the centre window over the door to make his address, I looked out, and never saw such a mass of heads before. It was like a black, gently swelling sea. The swaying motion of the crowd, in the dim uncertain light, was like the rising and falling of billows—like the ebb and flow of the tide upon the stranded shore of the ocean. Close to the house the faces were plainly discernible, but they faded into mere ghostly outlines on the outskirts of the assembly; and what added to the weird, spectral beauty of the scene, was the confused hum of voices that rose above the sea of forms, sounding like the subdued, sullen roar of an ocean storm, or the wind soughing through the dark lonely forest. It was a grand and imposing scene, and when the President, with pale face and his soul flashing through his eyes, advanced to speak, he looked more like a demi-god than a man crowned with the fleeting days of mortality.

The moment the President appeared at the window he was greeted with a storm of applause, and voices re-echoed the cry, "A light! a light!"

A lamp was brought, and little Tad at once rushed to his father's side, exclaiming:

"Let me hold the light, Papa! let me hold the light!"

Mrs. Lincoln directed that the wish of her son be gratified, and the lamp was transferred to his hands. The father and son standing there in the presence of thousands of free citizens, the one lost in a chain of eloquent ideas, the other looking up into the speaking face with a proud, manly look, formed a beautiful and striking tableau.

There were a number of distinguished gentlemen, as well as ladies, in the room, nearly all of whom remarked the picture.

I stood a short distance from Mr. Lincoln, and as the light from the lamp fell full upon him, making him stand out boldly in the darkness, a sudden thought struck me, and I whispered to the friend at my side:

"What an easy matter would it be to kill the President, as he stands there! He could be shot down from the crowd, and no one be able to tell who fired the shot."

I do not know what put such an idea into my head, unless it was the sudden remembrance of the many warnings that Mr. Lincoln had received.

The next day, I made mention to Mrs. Lincoln of the idea that had impressed me so strangely the night before, and she replied with a sigh:

"Yes, yes, Mr. Lincoln's life is always exposed. Ah, no one knows what it is to live in constant dread of some fearful tragedy. The President has been warned so often, that I tremble for him on every public occasion. I have a presentiment that he will meet with a sudden and violent end. I pray God to protect my beloved husband from the hands of the assassin."

Mr. Lincoln was fond of pets. He had two goats that knew the sound of his voice, and when he called them they would come bounding to his side. In the warm bright days, he and Tad would sometimes play in the yard with these goats, for an hour at a time. One Saturday afternoon I went to the White House to dress Mrs. Lincoln. I had nearly completed my task when the President came in. It was a bright day, and walking to the window, he looked down into the yard, smiled, and, turning to me, asked:

"Madam Elizabeth, you are fond of pets, are you not?"

"O yes, sir," I answered.

"Well, come here and look at my two goats. I believe they are the kindest and best goats in the world. See how they sniff the clear air, and skip and play in the sunshine. Whew! what a jump," he exclaimed as one of the goats made a lofty spring.

"Madam Elizabeth, did you ever before see such an active goat?" Musing a moment, he continued: "He feeds on my bounty, and jumps with joy. Do you think we could call him a bounty-jumper? But I flatter the bounty-jumper. My goat is far above him. I would rather wear his horns and hairy coat through life, than demean myself to the level of the man who plunders the national treasury in the name of patriotism. The man who enlists into the service for a consideration, and deserts the moment he receives his money but to repeat the play, is bad enough; but the men who manipulate the grand machine and who simply make the bounty-jumper their agent in an outrageous fraud are far worse. They are beneath the worms that crawl in the dark hidden places of earth."

His lips curled with haughty scorn, and a cloud was gathering on his brow. Only a moment the shadow rested on his face. Just then both goats looked up at the window and shook their heads as if they would say "How d'ye do, old friend?"

"See, Madam Elizabeth," exclaimed the President in a tone of enthusiasm, "my pets recognize me. How earnestly they look! There they go again; what jolly fun!" and he laughed outright as the goats bounded swiftly to the other side of the yard. Just then Mrs. Lincoln called out, "Come, Lizabeth; if I get ready to go down this evening I must finish dressing myself, or you must stop staring at those silly goats."

Mrs. Lincoln was not fond of pets, and she could not understand how Mr. Lincoln could take so much delight in his goats. After Willie's death, she could not bear the sight of anything he loved, not even a flower. Costly bouquets were presented to her, but she turned from them with a shudder, and either placed them in a room where she could not see them, or threw them out of the window. She gave all of Willie's toys—everything connected with him—away, as she said she could not look upon them without thinking of her poor dead boy, and to think of him, in his white shroud and cold grave, was maddening. I never in my life saw a more peculiarly constituted woman. Search the world over, and you will not find her counterpart. After Mr. Lincoln's death, the goats that he loved so well were given away—I believe to Mrs. Lee, *née* Miss Blair, one of the few ladies with whom Mrs. Lincoln was on intimate terms in Washington.

During my residence in the Capital I made my home with Mr. and Mrs. Walker Lewis, people of my own race, and friends in the truest sense of the word.

The days passed without any incident of particular note disturbing the current of life. On Friday morning, April 14th—alas! what American does not remember the day—I saw Mrs. Lincoln but for a moment. She told me that she was to attend the theatre that night with the President, but I was not summoned to assist her in making her toilette. Sherman had swept from the northern border of Georgia through the heart of the Confederacy down to the sea, striking the death-blow to the rebellion. Grant had pursued General Lee beyond Richmond, and the army of Virginia, that had made such stubborn resistance, was crumbling to pieces. Fort Sumter had fallen;—the stronghold first wrenched from the Union, and which had braved the fury of Federal guns for so many years, was restored to the Union; the end of the war was near at hand, and the great pulse of the loyal North thrilled with joy. The dark war-cloud was fading, and a white-robed angel seemed to hover in the sky, whispering "Peace—peace on earth, good-will toward men!" Sons, brothers, fathers, friends, sweethearts were coming home. Soon the white tents would be folded, the volunteer army be disbanded, and tranquillity again reign. Happy, happy day!—happy at least to those who fought under the banner of the Union. There was great rejoicing throughout the North. From the Atlantic to the Pacific, flags were gayly thrown to the breeze, and at night every city blazed with its tens of thousand lights. But scarcely had the fireworks ceased to play, and the lights been taken down from the windows, when the lightning flashed the most appalling news over the magnetic wires. "The President has been murdered!" spoke the swift-winged messenger, and the loud huzza died upon the lips. A nation suddenly paused in the midst of festivity, and stood paralyzed with horror—transfixed with awe.

Oh, memorable day! Oh, memorable night! Never before was joy so violently contrasted with sorrow.

At 11 o'clock at night I was awakened by an old friend and neighbor, Miss M. Brown, with the startling intelligence that the entire Cabinet had been assassinated, and Mr. Lincoln shot, but not mortally wounded. When I heard the words I felt as if the blood had been frozen in my veins, and that my lungs must collapse for the want of air. Mr. Lincoln shot! the Cabinet assassinated! What could it mean? The streets were alive with wondering, awe-stricken people. Rumors flew thick and fast, and the wildest reports came with every new arrival. The words were repeated with blanched cheeks and quivering lips. I waked Mr. and Mrs. Lewis, and told them that the President was shot, and that I must go to the White House. I could not remain in a state of uncertainty. I felt that the house would not hold me. They tried to quiet me, but gentle words could not calm the wild tempest. They quickly dressed themselves, and we sallied out into the street to drift with the excited throng. We walked rapidly towards the White House, and on our way passed the residence of Secretary Seward, which was surrounded by armed soldiers, keeping back all intruders with the point of the bayonet. We hurried on, and as we approached the White House, saw that it too was surrounded with soldiers. Every entrance was strongly guarded, and no one was permitted to pass. The guard at the gate told us that Mr. Lincoln had not been brought home, but refused to give any other information. More excited than ever, we wandered down the street. Grief and anxiety were making me weak, and as we joined the outskirts of a large crowd, I began to feel as meek and humble as a penitent child. A gray-haired old man was passing. I caught a glimpse of his face, and it seemed so full of kindness and sorrow that I gently touched his arm, and imploringly asked:

"Will you please, sir, to tell me whether Mr. Lincoln is dead or not?"

"Not dead," he replied, "but dying. God help us!" and with a heavy step he passed on.

"Not dead, but dying! then indeed God help us!"

We learned that the President was mortally wounded—that he had been shot down in his box at the theatre, and that he was not expected to live till morning; when we returned home with heavy hearts. I could not sleep. I wanted to go to Mrs. Lincoln, as I pictured her wild with grief; but then I did not know where to find her, and I must wait till morning. Never did the hours drag so slowly. Every moment seemed an age, and I could do nothing but walk about and hold my arms in mental agony.

Morning came at last, and a sad morning was it. The flags that floated so gayly yesterday now were draped in black, and hung in silent folds at half-mast. The President was dead, and a nation was mourning for him. Every house was draped in black, and every face wore a solemn look. People spoke in subdued tones, and glided whisperingly, wonderingly, silently about the streets.

About eleven o'clock on Saturday morning a carriage drove up to the door, and a messenger asked for "Elizabeth Keckley."

"Who wants her?" I asked.

"I come from Mrs. Lincoln. If you are Mrs. Keckley, come with me immediately to the White House."

I hastily put on my shawl and bonnet, and was driven at a rapid rate to the White House. Everything about the building was sad and solemn. I was quickly shown to Mrs. Lincoln's room, and on entering, saw Mrs. L. tossing uneasily about upon a bed. The room was darkened, and the only person in it besides the widow of the President was Mrs. Secretary Welles, who had spent the night with her. Bowing to Mrs. Welles, I went to the bedside.

"Why did you not come to me last night, Elizabeth—I sent for you?" Mrs. Lincoln asked in a low whisper.

"I did try to come to you, but I could not find you," I answered, as I laid my hand upon her hot brow.

I afterwards learned, that when she had partially recovered from the first shock of the terrible tragedy in the theatre, Mrs. Welles asked:

"Is there no one, Mrs. Lincoln, that you desire to have with you in this terrible affliction?"

"Yes, send for Elizabeth Keckley. I want her just as soon as she can be brought here."

Three messengers, it appears, were successively despatched for me, but all of them mistook the number and failed to find me.

Shortly after entering the room on Saturday morning, Mrs. Welles excused herself, as she said she must go to her own family, and I was left alone with Mrs. Lincoln.

She was nearly exhausted with grief, and when she became a little quiet, I asked and received permission to go into the Guests' Room, where the body of the President lay in state.

When I crossed the threshold of the room, I could not help recalling the day on which I had seen little Willie lying in his coffin where the body of his father now lay. I remembered how the President had wept over the pale beautiful face of his gifted boy, and now the President himself was dead. The last time I saw him he spoke kindly to me, but alas! the lips would never move again. The light had faded from his eyes, and when the light went out the soul went with it. What a noble soul was his—noble in all the noble attributes of God! Never did I enter the solemn chamber of death with such palpitating heart and trembling footsteps as I entered it that day. No common mortal had died. The Moses of my people had fallen in the hour of his triumph. Fame had woven her choicest chaplet for his brow. Though the brow was cold and pale in death, the chaplet should not fade, for God had studded it with the glory of the eternal stars.

When I entered the room, the members of the Cabinet and many distinguished officers of the army were grouped around the body of their fallen chief. They made room for me, and, approaching the body, I lifted the white cloth from the white face of the man that I had worshipped as an idol—looked upon as a demi-god. Notwithstanding the violence of the death of the President, there was something beautiful as well as grandly solemn in the expression of the placid face. There lurked the sweetness and gentleness of childhood, and the stately grandeur of god-like intellect. I gazed long at the face, and turned away with tears in my eyes and a choking sensation in my throat. Ah! never was man so widely mourned before. The whole world bowed their heads in grief when Abraham Lincoln died.

Returning to Mrs. Lincoln's room, I found her in a new paroxysm of grief. Robert was bending over his mother with tender affection, and little Tad was crouched at the foot of the bed with a world of agony in his young face. I shall never forget the scene—the wails of a broken heart, the unearthly shrieks, the terrible convulsions, the wild, tempestuous outbursts of grief from the soul. I bathed Mrs. Lincoln's head with cold water, and soothed the terrible tornado as best I could. Tad's grief at his father's death was as great as the grief of his mother, but her terrible outbursts awed the boy into silence.

Sometimes he would throw his arms around her neck, and exclaim, between his broken sobs, "Don't cry so, Mamma! don't cry, or you will make me cry, too! You will break my heart."

Mrs. Lincoln could not bear to hear Tad cry, and when he would plead to her not to break his heart, she would calm herself with a great effort, and clasp her child in her arms.

Every room in the White House was darkened, and every one spoke in subdued tones, and moved about with muffled tread. The very atmosphere breathed of the great sorrow which weighed heavily upon each heart. Mrs. Lincoln never left her room, and while the body of her husband was being borne in solemn state from the Atlantic to the broad prairies of the West, she was weeping with her fatherless children in her private chamber. She denied admittance to almost every one, and I was her only companion, except her children, in the days of her great sorrow.

"A FEARFUL, GIGANTIC CRIME":
NEW YORK, APRIL 1865

George Templeton Strong: Diary, April 15, 1865

After the fall of Richmond, John Wilkes Booth abandoned his plan to abduct Lincoln and resolved instead to simultaneously assassinate the president, vice president, and secretary of state. On the night of April 14, Good Friday, as Lincoln watched *Our American Cousin* in Ford's Theatre, Booth shot him in the head, then jumped down onto the stage, shouted "Sic semper tyrannis," and escaped. At the same time Booth's fellow conspirator Lewis Powell, a former Confederate soldier, used a ruse to enter the house of Secretary of State William H. Seward, who was recovering from a serious carriage accident on April 5. Powell severely beat Seward's son Frederick with a revolver that broke apart, then used a bowie knife to slash Seward, his son Augustus, a male army nurse, and a state department messenger before fleeing. Seward's life was saved by a heavy neck brace that protected him when Powell tried to cut his throat. The plot to assassinate Vice President Andrew Johnson at his hotel failed when George Atzerodt, another conspirator, lost his nerve and fled. George Templeton Strong recorded the reaction in New York to the attacks in Washington.

April 15, SATURDAY.   Nine o'clock in the morning. *LINCOLN AND SEWARD ASSASSINATED LAST NIGHT!!!!*
The South has nearly filled up the measure of her iniquities at last! Lincoln's death not yet certainly announced, but the one o'clock despatch states that he was then dying. Seward's side room was entered by the same or another assassin, and his throat cut. It is unlikely he will survive, for he was suffering from a broken arm and other injuries, the consequence of a fall, and is advanced in life. Ellie brought this news two hours ago, but I can hardly *take it in* even yet. *Eheu* A. Lincoln!

I have been expecting this. I predicted an attempt would be made on Lincoln's life when he went into Richmond; but just now, after his generous dealings with Lee, I should have said the danger was past. But the ferocious malignity of Southerners is infinite and inexhaustible. I am stunned, as by a fearful personal calamity, though I can see that this thing, occurring just at this time, may be overruled to our great good. Poor Ellie is heartbroken, though never an admirer of Lincoln's. We shall appreciate him at last.

Up with the Black Flag now!

Ten P.M. What a day it has been! Excitement and suspension of business even more general than on the 3rd instant. Tone of feeling very like that of four years ago when the news came of Sumter. This atrocity has invigorated national feeling in the same way, almost in the same degree. People who pitied our misguided brethren yesterday, and thought they had been punished enough already, and hoped there would be a general amnesty, including J. Davis himself, talk approvingly today of vindictive justice and favor the introduction of judges, juries, gaolers, and hangmen among the dramatis personae. Above all, there is a profound, awe-stricken feeling that we are, as it were, in immediate presence of a fearful, gigantic crime, such as has not been committed in our day and can hardly be matched in history.

Faulkner, one of our Kenzua directors, called for me by appointment at half-past nine, and we drove to the foot of Jane Street to inspect apparatus for the reduction of gold ore by amalgamation, which he considers a great improvement on the machinery generally used for that purpose. Returned uptown and saw Bellows to advise about adjournment of our Sanitary Commission meeting next week. Thence to Wall Street. Immense crowd. Bulletins and extras following each other in quick, contradictory succession. Seward and his Fred had died and had not. Booth (one of the assassins, a Marylander, brother of Edwin Booth) had been taken and had not. So it has gone on all day. Tonight the case stands thus:

Abraham Lincoln died at twenty-two minutes after seven this morning. He never regained consciousness after the pistol ball fired at him from behind, over his wife's shoulder, entered his brain. Seward is living and may recover. The gentleman assigned to the duty of murdering him did his butchery badly. The throat is severely lacerated by his knife, but it's believed that no arteries are injured. Fred Seward's situation is less hopeful, his skull being fractured by a bludgeon or sling shot used by the same gentleman. The attendant who was stabbed, is dead. (Is not.)

The temper of the great meeting I found assembled in front of the Custom House (the old Exchange) was grim. A Southerner would compare it with that of the first session of the Jacobins after Marat's death. I thought it healthy and virile. It was the first great patriotic meeting since the war began at which there was no talk of concession and conciliation. It would have endured no such talk. Its sentiment seemed like this: "Now it is plain at last to everybody that there can be no terms with the woman-flogging aristocracy. Grant's generous dealing with Lee was a blunder. The *Tribune's* talk for the last fortnight was folly. Let us henceforth deal with rebels as they deserve. The rose-water treatment does not meet their case." I have heard it said fifty times today: "These madmen have murdered the two best friends they had in the world!" I heard of three or four men in Wall Street and near the Post Office who spoke lightly of the tragedy, and were instantly set upon by the bystanders and pummelled. One of them narrowly escaped death. It was Charles E. Anderson, brother of our friend Professor Henry James Anderson, father of pretty Miss Louisa. Moses H. Grinnell and the police had hard work to save him. I never supposed him a secessionist.

To Trinity Church vestry meeting, specially called, at half-past three at the rebuilt vestry office, corner Fulton and Church. A series of resolutions was read, drawn by the Rector. They were masculine and good, and they were passed *nem. con.*, though Verplanck and Tillou were in their seats—Copperheads both. I looked at the record of our action when Washington died sixty-six years ago. It was a mere resolution that the church and chapels be put in mourning. Our resolutions of today went, naturally, much further. I record to the credit of Gouverneur Ogden, whom I have always held cold-hearted and selfish, that he broke down in trying to read these resolutions, could not get beyond the first sentence, and had to hand them back to the Rector. There was a little diversity of opinion whether we should put our chancel into mourning tomorrow, being Easter Sunday, or postpone it a day longer. We left it to the Rector's discretion. No business was done today. Most shops are closed and draped with black and white muslin. Broadway is clad in "weepers" from Wall Street to Union Square. At 823 with Agnew, Bellows, and Gibbs. George Anthon dined here; with him to Union League Club. Special meeting and dense, asphyxiating crowd. Orations by George Bancroft and by the Rev. (Presbyterian) Thompson of the Tabernacle. Both good; Thompson's very good. "When A. Johnson was sworn in as President today," said the Rev. Thompson, "the Statue of Liberty that surmounts the dome of the Capitol and was put there by Lincoln, looked down on the city and on the nation and said, 'Our Government is unchanged—it has merely passed from the hands of one man into those of another. Let the dead bury their dead. Follow thou Me.'" Burnside tells me this morning that he ranks Johnson very high.

Jeff Davis has at last issued a manifesto. It is from Danville, before Lee's surrender and is full of fight.

THE PRESIDENT'S DEATHBED:
WASHINGTON, D.C., APRIL 1865

Gideon Welles: Diary, April 18, 1865

By 1865 Seward and Gideon Welles were the only members of Lincoln's original cabinet still serving in the administration. Sometimes called "Father Neptune" by Lincoln, Welles had successfully presided over the wartime expansion and modernization of the U.S. Navy. He recorded his recollections of the assassination and its immediate aftermath on April 18, the day before funeral services were held for the President in the White House. John Wilkes Booth would be fatally wounded by Union troops near Port Royal, Virginia, on April 26. Eight defendants were convicted by a military commission for conspiring with Booth, and four of them—Lewis Powell, George Atzerodt, David Herold, and Mary Surratt—were hanged on July 7, 1865. Although the prosecution alleged that Jefferson Davis and several Confederate agents in Canada had conspired in the assassination, they presented no evidence beyond the testimony of three unreliable witnesses. While Booth may have told Confederate agents about his plan to abduct Lincoln, most historians believe he was the sole instigator of the assassination plot.

I had retired to bed about half-past ten on the evening of the 14th of April, and was just getting asleep when my wife said some one was at our door. Sitting up in bed I heard some one twice call to John, my son whose sleeping room was directly over the front. I arose at once and raised a window, when my messenger James called to me that Mr. Lincoln the President had been shot, and that Secretary Seward and his son, Assistant Secretary Frederick Seward, were assassinated. James was much alarmed and excited. I told him his story was very incoherent and improbable, that he was associating men who were not together and liable to attack at the same time. Where, I inquired, was the President when shot? James said he was at Ford's Theatre on 10th Street. Well, said I Secretary Seward is an invalid in bed in his house on 15th Street. James said he had been there, stopped in at the house to make inquiry before alarming me.

I immediately dressed myself, and against the earnest remonstrance and appeals of my wife went directly to Mr. Seward's. James accompanied me. As we were crossing 15th Street, I saw four or five men in earnest consultation under the lamp on the corner by St. John's Church. Before I had got half across the street, the lamp was suddenly extinguished and the knot of persons rapidly dispersed. For a moment and but a moment I was disconcerted to find myself in darkness but recollecting that it was late and about time for the moon to rise, I proceeded on, not having lost five steps, merely making a pause without stopping. Hurrying forward into 15th Street I found it pretty full of people especially near the residence of Secretary Seward, where there were many soldiers as well as citizens already gathered.

Entering the house I found the lower hall and office full of persons, and among them most of the foreign legations, all anxiously inquiring what truth there was in the horrible rumors afloat. I replied that my object in calling was to ascertain the facts. Proceeding through the hall to the stairs, I found one, and I think two of the servants there checking the crowd. They were frightened and appeared relieved to see me. I hastily asked what truth there was in the story that an assassin or assassins had entered the house and assaulted the Secretary. I was assured that it was true, and that Mr. Frederick was also badly injured. They wished me to go up, but no others. At the head of the first stairs I met the elder Mrs. Seward or her sister I think who desired me to proceed up. On reaching the third story I met Mrs. Frederick Seward who, although evidently distressed, was, under the circumstances exceedingly composed. I inquired for the Secretary's room which she pointed out—the southwest room. As I entered, I met Miss Fanny Seward with whom I exchanged a single word, and proceeded to the foot of the bed. Dr. Verdi and I think two others were there. The bed was saturated with blood. The Secretary was lying on his back, the upper part of his head covered by a cloth, which extended down over his eyes. His mouth was open, the lower jaw dropping down. I exchanged a few whispered words with Dr. V. Secretary Stanton who came almost simultaneously with me spoke in a louder tone. We almost immediately withdrew and went into the adjoining front room, where lay Frederick Seward on his right side. His eyes were open but he did not move them, nor a limb, nor did he speak. Doctor White told me he was unconscious and more dangerously injured than his father.

As we descended the stairs, I asked Stanton what he had heard in regard to the President that was reliable. He said the President was shot at Ford's Theatre, that he had seen a man who was present and witnessed the occurrence. I remarked that I would go immediately to the White House. Stanton told me the President was not there but was down at the theatre. Then, said I let us go immediately there. He said that was his intention, and asked me, if I had not a carriage, to go with him.

In the lower hall we met General Meigs, whom he requested to take charge of the house, and to clear out all who did not belong there. General Meigs requested Stanton not to go down to 10th Street, others remonstrated against his going. Stanton I thought hesitated. I remarked that I should go immediately, and I thought it his duty also. He said he should certainly go, but the remonstrants increased and gathered round him. I remarked that we were wasting time, and pressing through the crowd entered the carriage and urged Stanton, who was detained after he had placed his foot on the step. I was impatient. Stanton, as soon as he had seated himself, said the carriage was not his. I said that was no objection. He invited Meigs to go with us, and Judge Cartter of the Supreme Court mounted with the driver. At this moment Major Eckert rode up on horseback and protested vehemently against Stanton's going to 10th Street—said he had just come from there, that there were thousands of people of all sorts there and he considered it very unsafe for the Secretary of War to expose himself. I replied that I knew not where he would be safe, and the duty of both of us was to attend the President immediately. Stanton concurred. Meigs called to some soldiers to go with us, and there was one on each side of the carriage. The streets were full of people. Not only the sidewalk but the carriage-way was to some extent occupied, all or nearly all hurrying towards 10th Street. When we entered that street we found it pretty closely packed.

The President had been carried across the street from the

theatre, to the house of a Mr. Peterson. We entered by ascending a flight of steps above the basement and passing through a long hall to the rear the President lay extended on a bed breathing heavily. Several surgeons were present, at least six, I should think more. Among them I was glad to observe Dr. Hall, who, however soon left. I inquired of one of the Surgeons Dr. H., I think, the true condition of the President and was told he was dead to all intents, although he might live three hours or perhaps longer.

The giant sufferer lay extended diagonally across the bed which was not long enough for him. He had been stripped of his clothes. His large arms, which were occasionally exposed were of a size which one would scarce have expected from his spare appearance. His slow, full respiration lifted the clothes. His features were calm and striking. I had never seen them appear to better advantage than for the first hour, perhaps, that I was there. After that his right eye began to swell and became discolored.

Senator Sumner was there, I think, when I entered. If not he came in soon after, as did Speaker Colfax, Mr. Secretary McCulloch and the other members of the Cabinet, with the exception of Mr. Seward. A double guard was stationed at the door and on the sidewalk, to repress the crowd which was excited and anxious.

The room was small and overcrowded. The surgeons and members of the Cabinet were as many as should have been in the room, but there were many more, and the hall and other rooms in the front or main house were full. One of them was occupied by Mrs. Lincoln and her attendants. Mrs. Dixon and Mrs. Kinney came about twelve o'clock. About once an hour Mrs. Lincoln would repair to the bedside of her dying husband and remain until overcome by her emotion.

A door which opened upon a porch or gallery, and the windows were kept open for fresh air. The night was dark, cloudy and damp, and about six it began to rain. I remained until then without sitting or leaving, when, there being a vacant chair at the foot of the bed, I occupied for nearly two hours, listening to the heavy groans, and witnessing the wasting life of the good and great man who was expiring before me.

About 6 A.M. a fainting sickness came over me and for the

first time since entering the room, a little past eleven, I left it and the house, and took a short walk in the open air. It was a dark and gloomy morning, and rain set in before I returned to the house, some fifteen minutes. Large groups of people were gathered every few rods, all anxious and solicitous. Some one stepped forward as I passed, to inquire into the condition of the President, and to ask if there was no hope. Intense grief exhibited itself on every countenance when I replied that the President could survive but a short time. The colored people especially—and there were at this time more of them perhaps than of whites—were painfully affected.

Returning to the house, I seated myself in the back parlor where the Attorney-General and others had been engaged in taking evidence concerning the assassination. Stanton, and Speed, and Usher were there, the latter asleep on the bed— there were three or four others also in the room. While I did not feel inclined to sleep as did many, I was somewhat indisposed and had been for several days—the excitement and atmosphere from the crowded rooms oppressed me physically.

A little before seven, I went into the room where the dying President was rapidly drawing near the closing moments. His wife soon after made her last visit to him. The death struggle had begun. Robert, his son stood at the head of the bed and bore himself well, but on two occasions gave way to overpowering grief and sobbed aloud, turning his head and leaning on the shoulder of Senator Sumner. The respiration became suspended at intervals, and at length entirely ceased at twenty-two minutes past seven.

A prayer followed from Dr. Gurley; and the Cabinet, with the exception of Mr. Seward and Mr. McCulloch immediately thereafter assembled in the back parlor, from which all other persons were excluded, and signed a letter which had been prepared by Attorney-General Speed to the Vice President, informing him of the event, and that the government devolved upon him.

Mr. Stanton proposed that Mr. Speed, as the law officer, should communicate the letter to Mr. Johnson with some other member of the Cabinet. Mr. Dennison named me. I saw that it disconcerted Stanton, who had expected and intended to be the man and to have Speed associated with him. As I was disinclined personally to any effort for myself I therefore named Mr. McCulloch as the first in order after the Secretary of State.

I arranged with Speed with whom I rode home for a Cabinet meeting at twelve meridian at the room of the Secretary of the Treasury, in order that the government should experience no detriment, and that prompt and necessary action might be taken to assist the new Chief Magistrate in promoting the public tranquillity. We accordingly met at noon. Mr. Speed reported that the President had taken the oath which was administered by the Chief Justice, and had expressed a desire that affairs should proceed without interruption. Some discussion took place as to the propriety of an inaugural address, but the general impression was that it would be inexpedient. I was most decidedly of that opinion.

President Johnson, who was invited to be present, deported himself with gentlemanly and dignified courtesy, and on the subject of an inaugural was of the opinion that his acts would best disclose his policy. In all essentials it would be the same as that of the late President. He desired the members of the Cabinet to go forward with their duties without any interruption. Mr. Hunter, Chief Clerk of the State Department was designated to act *ad interim* as Secretary of State. I suggested Mr. Speed, but I saw it was not acceptable in certain quarters. Stanton especially expressed a hope that Hunter should be assigned.

A room for the President as an office was proposed, and Mr. McCulloch offered the adjoining room. I named the State Department as appropriate and proper until there was a Secretary of State, or so long as the President wished, but objections arose at once. The papers of Mr. Seward would be disturbed— it would be better here, etc., etc. Stanton I saw had a purpose.

On returning to my house the morning of Saturday, I found Mrs. Welles who had been confined to the house from indisposition for a week had been twice sent for by Mrs. Lincoln and had yielded, and imprudently gone, although the weather was inclement. She remained at the Executive Mansion through the day.

For myself, wearied, shocked, exhausted but not inclined to sleep, the day passed off strangely.

On Sunday the 16th the President and Cabinet met by agreement at 10 A.M. at the Treasury. The President was half an hour behind time. Stanton was more than an hour later and brought with him papers, and had many suggestions relative to our measures before the Cabinet at our last meeting with President Lincoln. The general policy of the treating the Rebels and the Rebel States was fully discussed. President Johnson is not disposed to treat treason lightly, and the chief Rebels he would punish with exemplary severity.

Stanton has divided his original plan and made the reestablishing of State government applicable to North Carolina, leaving Virginia which has a loyal government and governor, to arrange that matter of election to which I had excepted, but elaborating it for North Carolina and the other States.

Being at the War Department Sunday evening, I was detained conversing with [   ] and finally Senator Sumner came in. He was soon followed by Gooch and Dawes of Massachusetts and some two or three other general officers also came in. Stanton took from his table in answer to an inquiry from some one, his document which had been submitted to the Cabinet and which was still a Cabinet measure.

It was evident the gentlemen were there by appointment and that I came as an intruder. Stanton did not know how to get rid of me and supposed I was there by arrangement; I felt embarrassed and was very glad after he had read to them his first programme for Virginia, and had got about half through with the other, when a line was brought me at this time by the messenger, giving me an opportunity to leave.

On Monday the 17th I was actively engaged in bringing forward business issuing orders, and arranging for the funeral solemnities of President Lincoln. Secretary Seward and his son continue in a low condition, and Mr. Fred Seward's life is precarious.

Tuesday, 18. Details in regard to the funeral, which takes place on the 19th, occupied general attention and little else was done at the Cabinet meeting. From every part of the country comes lamentation. Every house, almost, has some drapery, especially the homes of the poor. Profuse exhibition is displayed on the public buildings and the houses of the wealthy, but the little black ribbon or strip of black cloth from the hovel of the poor negro or the impoverished white is more touching.

I have tried to write something consecutively since the horrid transactions of Friday night, but I have no heart for it, and the jottings down are mere mementos of a period, which I will try to fill up when more composed, and I have some leisure or time for the task.

Sad and painful, wearied and irksome, the few preceding incoherent pages have been written for future use, for they are fresh in my mind and may pass away with me but cannot ever be forgotten by me.

A POLITICAL AGREEMENT:
NORTH CAROLINA, APRIL 1865

William T. Sherman to Ulysses S. Grant or Henry W. Halleck

After fighting an inconclusive battle with Joseph E. Johnston at Bentonville, North Carolina, on March 19–21, Sherman had reached Goldsboro on March 23, establishing a supply line to the coast and joining up with Union forces under John M. Schofield. His army remained at Goldsboro for nearly three weeks, resting and resupplying, while Johnston held Smithfield twenty-five miles to the northwest. Sherman resumed the offensive on April 10, advancing toward Raleigh with 89,000 men while Johnston withdrew with about 20,000 troops toward Greensboro. By the time Union forces occupied Raleigh on April 13, both commanders had learned of Lee's surrender at Appomattox. Convinced that continued fighting would be futile, Johnston wrote to Sherman proposing a cease-fire and the opening of peace negotiations. The two commanders met near Durham Station on April 17, shortly after Sherman learned of Lincoln's assassination. Although Sherman had telegraphed Grant that he would offer Johnston the same terms given to Lee and "be careful not to complicate any points of civil policy," he changed his position once the talks began. Concerned about the prospect of prolonged guerrilla warfare, Sherman offered political concessions in return for the surrender of all the remaining Confederate armies. On April 18 the opposing commanders signed their "basis of agreement," which Sherman sent to Washington by courier along with an accompanying letter.

Headquarters, Military Division
of the Mississippi,
In the Field, Raleigh N.C.,
April 18, 1865.

Lt. Genl. U. S. Grant, or Maj. Gen. Halleck,
Washington D.C.
General,

I enclose herewith a copy of an agreement made this day between Gen. Joseph E. Johnston and myself which if approved by the President of the United States will produce Peace from the Potomac and the Rio Grande. Mr. Breckinridge was present at our conference in his capacity as Major General, and satisfied me of the ability of General Johnston to carry out to the full extent the terms of this agreement, and if you will get the President to simply endorse the copy, and commission me to carry out the terms I will follow them to the conclusion.

You will observe that it is an absolute submission of the Enemy to the lawful authority of the United States, and disperses his armies absolutely, and the point to which I attach most importance is that the dispersion and disbandment of these armies is done in Such a manner as to prevent their breaking up into Guerilla Bands. On the other hand we can retain just as much of an army as we please. I agreed to the mode and manner of the surrender of arms set forth, as it gives the States the means of repressing Guerrillas which we could not expect them to do if we stript them of all arms.

Both Generals Johnston & Breckinridge admitted that Slavery was dead and I could not insist on embracing it in such a paper, because it can be made with the states in detail. I know that all the men of substance south sincerely want Peace and I do not believe they will resort to war again during this century. I have no doubt that they will in the future be perfectly subordinate to the Laws of the United States.

The moment my action in this matter is approved, I can spare five Corps and will ask for orders to leave Gen. Schofield here with the 10th Corps and to march myself with the 14, 15, 17, 20 and 23d Corps, via Banksville, and Gordonsville to Frederick or Hagerstown there to be paid and mustered out. The question of Finance is now the chief one and every soldier & officer not needed should be got home at work. I would like to be able to begin the march north by May 1. I urge on the part of the President speedy action as it is important to get the Confederate Armies to their homes as well as our own. I am with great respect yr. obt. Servant

      William T. Sherman
      Maj. Gen. Comdg.
      (Copy)

Memorandum or basis of agreement, made this 18th day of April, A.D. 1865, near Durham's Station in the State of

North Carolina, by and between General Joseph E. Johnston, commanding the Confederate army, and Major General William T. Sherman, commanding the Army of the United States in North Carolina, both present:

First: The contending armies now in the field to maintain the "*status quo*," until notice is given by the commanding General of any one to its opponent, and reasonable time, say forty-eight hours, allowed.

Second: The Confederate armies now in existence to be disbanded and conducted to their several State capitals, then to deposit their arms and public property in the State Arsenal: and each officer and man to execute and file an agreement to cease from acts of war, and to abide the action of both State and Federal authority. The number of arms and munitions of war to be reported to the Chief of Ordnance at Washington City, subject to the future action of the Congress of the United States, and in the meantime to be used solely to maintain peace and order within the borders of the States respectively.

Third: The recognition by the Executive of the United States of the several State Governments, on their officers and Legislatures taking the oaths prescribed by the Constitution of the United States: and where conflicting State Governments have resulted from the war, the legitimacy of all shall be submitted to the Supreme Court of the United States.

Fourth: The re-establishment of all the Federal Courts in the several States, with powers as defined by the Constitution and laws of Congress.

Fifth: The people and inhabitants of all the States to be guaranteed, so far as the Executive can, their political rights and franchises, as well as their rights of person and property as defined by the Constitution of the United States and of the States respectively.

Sixth: The Executive authority of the Government of the United States not to disturb any of the people by reason of the late war, so long as they live in peace and quiet, abstain from acts of armed hostility, and obey the laws in existence at the place of their residence.

Seventh: In general terms, the war to cease: a general

amnesty so far as the Executive of the United States can command, on condition of the disbandment of the Confederate armies, the distribution of the arms, and the resumption of peaceful pursuits by the officers and men hitherto composing said armies.

Not being fully empowered by our respective principals to fulfil these terms, we individually and officially pledge ourselves to promptly obtain the necessary authority and to carry out the above programme.

 (signed) W. T. Sherman (signed) J. E. Johnston
   Maj. Genl. Com'd'g   General Comg.
   Army U.S. in N.C.   C.S. Army in N.C.

compared with the original in my possession and hereby certified.

     W. T. Sherman
     Maj. Gen. Comdg.

"IT IS ALL MURDER": LOUISIANA, APRIL 1865
Sarah Morgan: Diary, April 19, 1865

Reactions to Lincoln's assassination varied widely among white Southerners. Sherman wrote that when Joseph E. Johnston learned of the President's death during their meeting on April 17, he "admitted that the act was calculated to stain his cause with a dark hue, and he contended that the loss was most serious to the People of the South, who had begun to realize that Mr. Lincoln was the best friend the South had." Amid the ruins of Columbia, South Carolina, Emma LeConte responded differently, writing on April 21: "Hurrah! Old Abe Lincoln has been assassinated! It may be abstractly wrong to be so jubilant, but I just can't help it. After all the heaviness and gloom of yesterday this blow to our enemies comes like a gleam of light. We have suffered till we feel savage. There seems no reason to exult, for this will make no change in our position—will only infuriate them against us. Never mind, our hated enemy has met the just reward of his life." The daughter of a prominent Baton Rouge lawyer, Sarah Morgan had reluctantly moved with her sister and widowed mother to Union-occupied New Orleans in April 1863. Two of her brothers had died in January 1864, one while serving with Lee's army in Virginia and the other in a Union prison camp in Ohio.

April 19th. 1865. No. 211. Camp St.

"All things are taken from us, and become portions and parcels of the dreadful past."

My life change, changes. I let it change as God will, feeling he doeth all things well. Sister has gone to Germany with Charlotte, Nellie, and Lavinia to place them at school, probably at Brussels. Mother and I have taken her place with the five remaining children. I am nominally housekeeper; that is to say I keep the keys in my pocket, and my eyes on the children, and sit at the head of the table. But I dont order dinner, for which I am thankful; for I would not be able to name a single article, if my reputation depended on the test. Of course I have a general idea that soup, roast, baked and boiled meats are eaten, but whether all the same day, or which to be chosen, I could not decide, nor as to the kind of animal or fish. So the cook does that, though I am trying to observe every day what he provides, in order to perfect myself in the mystery.

In five days, I have twice been heart-broken about making Brother's coffee too strong. He will not complain, and I would still be ignorant of the error if I had not accidently observed the untouched cup after he left the table, and discovering the mistake by tasting punished myself by drinking every drop of the bitter draught. Mem. To-morrow if I fail, drink it until I learn the exact proportion.

Thursday the 13th, came the dreadful tidings of the surrender of Lee and his army on the 9th. Every body cried, but I would not, satisfied that God will still save us, even though all should apparently be lost. Followed at intervals of two or three hours by the announcement of the capture of Richmond, Selma, Mobile, and Johnson's army, even the staunchest Southerners were hopeless. Every one proclaimed Peace, and the only matter under consideration was whether Jeff. Davis, all politicians, every man above the rank of Captain in the army, and above that of Lieutenant in the navy, should be hanged immediately, or *some* graciously pardoned. Henry Ward Beecher humanely pleaded mercy for us, supported by a small minority. Davis and all leading men *must* be executed; the blood of the others would serve to irrigate the country. Under this lively prospect, Peace! blessed Peace! was the cry. I whispered "Never! let a great earthquake swallow us up first! Let us leave our land and emigrate to any desert spot of the earth, rather than return to the Union, even as it Was!"

Six days this has lasted. Blessed with the silently obstinate disposition, I would not dispute, but felt my heart swell repeating "God is our refuge and our strength, a very present help in time of trouble," and could not for an instant believe this could end in our overthrow.

This morning when I went down to breakfast at seven, Brother read the announcement of the assassination of Lincoln and Secretary Seward. "Vengence is mine; I will repay, saith the Lord." This is murder! God have mercy on those who did it! A while ago, Lincoln's chief occupation was thinking what death, thousands who ruled like lords when he was cutting logs, should die. A moment more, and the man who was progressing to murder countless human beings, is interrupted in his work by the shot of an assassin. Do I justify this murder? No! I shudder with horror, wonder, pity and fear, and then feeling that it is the salvation of all I love that has been purchased by this man's crime, I long to thank God for those spared, and shudder to think that that is rejoicing against our enemy, being grateful for a fellow-creature's death. I am not! Seward was ill—dying—helpless. This was dastard murder. His throat was cut in bed. Horrible!

Charlotte Corday killed Marat in his bath, and is held up in history as one of Liberty's martyrs, and one of the heroines of her country. To me, it is all Murder. Let historians extol blood shedding; it is woman's place to abhor it. And because I know that they would have apotheosized any man who had crucified Jeff Davis, I abhor this, and call it foul murder, unworthy of our cause—and God grant it was only the temporary insanity of a desperate man that committed this crime! Let not his blood be visited on our nation, Lord!

Across the way, a large building undoubtedly inhabited by officers is being draped in black. Immense streamers of black and white hang from the balcony. Down town, I understand all shops are closed, and all wrapped in mourning. And I hardly dare pray God to bless us, with the crape hanging over the way. It would have been banners, if our president had been killed, though! Now the struggle will be desperate, awful, short. Spare Jimmy, dear Lord! Have mercy on us as a people!

And yet what was the song of Deborah, when she hammered a nail in the head of the sleeping Sisera? Was she not extolled for the treacherous deed? What was Miriam's song over the drowning Egyptian? "Our enemies are fallen, fallen!" Was not Judith immortalized for delivering her people from the hands of a tyrant? "Pour le salut de ma patree—!"

Where does patriotism end, and murder begin? And considering that every one is closely watched, and that five men have been killed this day for expressing their indifference on the death of Mr Lincoln, it would be best to postpone this discussion.

EXPLAINING SURRENDER: VIRGINIA, APRIL 1865

Robert E. Lee to Jefferson Davis

Ten days after attributing the surrender of his army to "overwhelming numbers and resources" in General Orders No. 9 (pp. 673–74 in this volume), Lee offered a different explanation for his defeat in a letter to Jefferson Davis. Writing to the Confederate president, now in Charlotte, North Carolina, Lee reflected on the "moral condition" of his troops while arguing against a resort to partisan warfare. In a memoir drafted in 1897–99, Edward Porter Alexander, the longtime artillery commander in Longstreet's corps, recounted a conversation he had with Lee at Appomattox on the morning of April 9, 1865. Alexander recalled urging Lee to order his men to "scatter in the woods & bushes" and then carry on the war, either with Johnston in North Carolina or in their home states. Lee responded that the "men would have no rations & they would be under no discipline. They are already demoralized by four years of war. They would have to plunder & rob to procure subsistence. The country would be full of lawless bands in every part, & a state of society would ensue from which it would take the country years to recover." Lee told Alexander that "as for myself, while you young men might afford to go to bushwhacking, the only proper & dignified course for me would be to surrender myself & take the consequences of my actions." Deeply moved by his commander's arguments, Alexander had surrendered with the rest of the army. (While it is unlikely that he remembered his conversation with Lee verbatim, it is probable that Alexander's account reflects Lee's views at the time.)

———————

Richmond, Virginia
April 20, 1865

Mr. President:

The apprehensions I expressed during the winter, of the moral condition of the Army of Northern Virginia, have been realized. The operations which occurred while the troops were in the entrenchments in front of Richmond and Petersburg were not marked by the boldness and decision which formerly characterized them. Except in particular instances, they were feeble; and a want of confidence seemed to possess officers and men. This condition, I think, was produced by the state of feeling in the country, and the communications received by the men from their homes, urging their return and the abandonment of the field. The movement of the enemy on the 30th March to Dinwiddie Court House was consequently not as strongly met as similar ones had been. Advantages were gained by him which discouraged the troops, so that on the morning of the 2d April, when our lines between the Appomattox and Hatcher's Run were assaulted, the resistance was not effectual: several points were penetrated and large captures made. At the commencement of the withdrawal of the army from the lines on the night of the 2d, it began to disintegrate, and straggling from the ranks increased up to the surrender on the 9th. On that day, as previously reported, there were only seven thousand eight hundred and ninety-two (7892) effective infantry. During the night, when the surrender became known, more than ten thousand men came in, as reported to me by the Chief Commissary of the Army. During the succeeding days stragglers continued to give themselves up, so that on the 12th April, according to the rolls of those paroled, twenty-six thousand and eighteen (26,018) officers and men had surrendered. Men who had left the ranks on the march, and crossed James River, returned and gave themselves up, and many have since come to Richmond and surrendered. I have given these details that Your Excellency might know the state of feeling which existed in the army, and judge of that in the country. From what I have seen and learned, I believe an army cannot be organized or supported in Virginia, and as far as I know the condition of affairs, the country east of the Mississippi is morally and physically unable to maintain the contest unaided with any hope of ultimate success. A partisan war may be continued, and hostilities protracted, causing individual suffering and the devastation of the country, but I see no prospect by that means of achieving a separate independence. It is for Your Excellency to decide, should you agree with me in opinion, what is proper to be done. To save useless effusion of blood, I would recommend measures be taken for suspension of hostilities and the restoration of peace.

I am with great respect, yr obdt svt
R. E. Lee
Genl

FLEEING DEFEAT: NORTH CAROLINA, APRIL 1865
Jefferson Davis to Varina Howell Davis

Jefferson Davis and his cabinet had left Richmond by train on the night of April 2 and arrived in Danville, Virginia, along the North Carolina border the following day. On April 4 he issued an address to "the People of the Confederate States of America" asserting that the fall of Richmond left the Army of Northern Virginia "free to move from point to point and strike in detail the detachments and garrisons of the enemy, operating on the interior of our own country, where supplies are more accessible, and where the foe will be far removed from his own base and cut off from all succor in case of reverse, nothing is now needed to render our triumph certain but the exhibition of our own unquenchable resolve. Let us but will it, and we are free." Davis left Danville on April 10 and went by train to Greensboro, North Carolina, where he reluctantly agreed to let Johnston open negotiations with Sherman before departing for Charlotte on April 15. Traveling by horseback because of Union cavalry raids against the railroad, he reached his destination four days later. When he wrote to his wife, who had left Richmond with their four children on March 30, Davis was uncertain as to her whereabouts, but correctly surmised that she was staying in Abbeville, South Carolina.

———————

Charlotte N. C 23 April 65

My dear Winnie

I have been detained here longer than was expected when the last telegram was sent to you. I am uncertain where you are and deeply felt the necessity of being with you if even for a brief time, under our altered circumstances. Gov. Vance and Genl. Hampton propose to meet me here and Genl. Johnston sent me a request to remain at some point where he could readily communicate with me. Under these circumstances I have asked Mr. Harrison to go in search of you and to render you such assistance as he may. Your Brother William telegraphed in reply to my inquiry that you were at Abbeville and that he would go to see you. My last despatch was sent to that place and to the care of Mr. Burt. Your own feelings will convey to you an idea of my solicitude for you and our family, and I will not distress by describing it.

The dispersion of Lee's army and the surrender of the remnant which remained with him destroyed the hopes I entertained when we parted. Had that army held together I am now confident we could have successfully executed the plan which I sketched to you and would have been to-day on the high road to independence. Even after that disaster if the men who "straggled" say thirty or forty thousand in number, had come back with their arms and with a disposition to fight we might have repaired the damage; but all was sadly the reverse of that. They threw away theirs and were uncontrollably resolved to go home. The small guards along the road have sometimes been unable to prevent the pillage of trains and depots.

Panic has seized the country. J. E. Johnston and Beauregard were hopeless as to recruiting their forces from the dispersed men of Lee's army and equally so as to their ability to check Sherman with the forces they had. Their only idea was to retreat of the power to do so they were doubtful and subsequent desertions from their troops have materially diminished their strength and I learn still more weakend their confidence.

The loss of arms has been so great that should the spirit of the people rise to the occasion it would not be at this time possible adequately to supply them with the weapons of War.

Genl. Johnston had several interviews with Sherman and agreed on a suspension of hostilities, and the reference of terms of pacification. They are secret and may be rejected by the Yankee govt.—to us they are hard enough, though freed from wanton humiliation and expressly recognizing the state governments, and the rights of person and property as secured by the Constitutions of the U. S. and the several states. Genl. Breckenridge was a party to the last consultation and to the agreement. Judge Reagan went with him and approved the agreement though not present at the conference.

Each member of the Cabinet is to give his opinion in writing to day, 1st upon the acceptance of the terms, 2d upon the mode of proceeding if accepted. The issue is one which it is very painful for me to meet. On one hand is the long night of oppression which will follow the return of our people to the "Union"; on the other the suffering of the women and children, and courage among the few brave patriots who would still oppose the invader, and who unless the people would rise en masse to sustain them, would struggle but to die in vain.

I think my judgement is undisturbed by any pride of opinion or of place, I have prayed to our heavenly Father to give me wisdom and fortitude equal to the demands of the position in which Providence has placed me. I have sacrificed so much for the cause of the Confederacy that I can measure my ability to make any further sacrifice required, and am assured there is but one to which I am not equal, my Wife and my Children. How are they to be saved from degradation or want is now my care. During the suspension of hostilities you may have the best opportunity to go to Missi. and thence either to sail from Mobile for a foreign port or to cross the river and proceed to Texas, as the one or the other may be more practicable. The little sterling you have will be a very scanty store and under other circumstances would not be counted, but if our land can be sold that will secure you from absolute want. For myself it may be that our Enemy will prefer to banish me, it may be that a devoted band of Cavalry will cling to me and that I can force my way across the Missi. and if nothing can be done there which it will be proper to do, then I can go to Mexico and have the world from which to choose a location. Dear Wife this is not the fate to which I invited when the future was rose-colored to us both; but I know you will bear it even better than myself and that of us two I alone will ever look back reproachfully on my past career.

I have thus entered on the questions involved in the future to guard against contingencies, my stay will not be prolonged a day beyond the prospect of useful labor here and there is every reason to suppose that I will be with you a few days after Mr. Harrison arrives.

Mrs Omelia behaved very strangely about putting the things you directed—Robt says she would not permit to pack, that she even took groceries out of the mess chest when he had put a small quantity there. Little Maggie's saddle was concealed and I learned after we left Richmond was not with the saddles and bridles which I directed to be all put together. At the same time I was informed that your saddle had been sent to the Saddlers and left there. Every body seemed afraid of connexion with our property and your carriage was sent to the Depot to be brought with me. a plea was made that it could not go on the cars of that train but should follow in the next, specific charge and promise was given but the carriage was left. The notice to leave was given on Sunday, but few hours were allowed and my public duties compelled to rely on others, count on nothing as saved which you valued except the bust and that had to be left behind.

Mrs. Omelia said she was charged in the event of our having to leave, to place the valuables with the Sisters and that she would distribute every thing. I told her to sell what she could, and after feeling distrust asked Mrs. Grant to observe her; and after that became convinced that she too probably under the influence of her husband was afraid to be known as having close relations with us.

Kiss Maggie and the children many times for me. The only yearning heart in the final hour was poor old Sara wishing for "Pie cake", and thus I left our late home. No bad preparation for a search for another. Dear children I can say nothing to them, but for you and them my heart is full my prayers constant and my hopes are the trust I feel in the mercy of God.

Farewell my Dear; there may be better things in store for us than are now in view, but my love is all I have to offer and that has the value of a thing long possessed and sure not to be lost. Once more, and with God's favor for a short time only, farewell—

YOUR HUSBAND

"SOMETHING THAT HAUNTED US":
VIRGINIA, APRIL 1865
Stephen Minot Weld to Hannah Minot Weld

For many of the young men who came of age during the war, soldiering came to seem their only way of life. "We expect to make this our trade for we have become fitted for nothing else now," wrote Samuel Selden Brooke, a company commander in the 47th Virginia Infantry, in March 1864. Lieutenant Colonel Stephen Minot Weld had been captured at the battle of the Crater in Petersburg on July 30, 1864, while leading the 56th Massachusetts Infantry. Weld was imprisoned in Columbia, South Carolina, until December, when he was paroled and sent north. Exchanged in March 1865, he rejoined his regiment in Virginia on April 4. He wrote to his older sister about Lee's surrender.

CITY POINT, *April* 24, 1865.

DEAR HANNAH,—I received several letters from you last night, several of them complaining of my short letters and my want of enthusiasm for Lee's surrender. To tell the truth, we none of us realize even yet that he has actually surrendered. I had a sort of impression that we should fight him all our lives. He was like a ghost to children, something that haunted us so long that we could not realize that he and his army were really out of existence to us. It will take me some months to be conscious of this fact.

In regard to the brevity of my epistle, I can only say that I have nothing to tell about.

I have got a splendid mule, which I am going to take home with me, if I can. He is the finest animal I have ever seen.

Last Thursday we received orders to move to City Point, and from there to Washington. Part of our corps has already moved and we are waiting for transportation. We shall probably move to-morrow, having reached here yesterday afternoon. Last Wednesday, the day before we moved, I went up to General Miles's headquarters. First I went to Second Corps headquarters and then with Charlie Whittier to General Miles's. While there, about forty negroes came in from Danville. General Miles ordered the band out, and told the negroes that he would hang every one who would not dance. About seven refused to dance, saying they were church members. The rest went at it tooth and nail, gray-headed old men and young boys. I never laughed so hard in my life. From General M.'s we went to General Barlow's, who commands the 2d Division. We amused ourselves with a galvanic battery which General B. has for his health. From there we went to General Meade's headquarters, where I had a very pleasant talk with General M. Saw Theodore Lyman, who is probably home by this time. He was very kind to me indeed, and gave me several articles of clothing which were very acceptable. Had a very nice time there indeed, and had a very pleasant reception from the staff. When my men saw me on my arrival, they gave me 9 cheers and then 9 more, etc., etc. I tell you this because you asked me.

We had quite hard marching, making 63 miles in a little over 3 days. The story is that we are going to Texas, that we are to be sent home for 6 months to be disbanded by that time, in case we are not wanted, etc., etc. No one seems to know what we are going to do. If we have a good camp in or near Washington, perhaps I will let you come down there.

"WHAT WERE WE FIGHTING FOR":
NORTH CAROLINA, APRIL–MAY 1865

Samuel T. Foster: Diary, April 18–May 4, 1865

Following the costly battle of Franklin, Captain Samuel T. Foster of the 24th Texas Cavalry (dismounted) had advanced with the Army of Tennessee to the outskirts of Nashville, where the Confederates were decisively defeated on December 15–16, 1864. Foster and his men had then retreated through bitter cold, freezing rain, and snow into northern Mississippi, where in January 1865 General John B. Hood resigned his command. At the end of January the remnants of the Army of Tennessee began moving to the Carolinas, and on March 20 Foster joined Johnston's forces at Smithfield, North Carolina. Foster's company was camped near Greensboro when Johnston and Sherman signed their agreement on April 18. He recorded in his diary the hopes, fears, and bizarre rumors that swept through their camp as Johnston's army confronted "the new order of things," which in many respects would not be as severe as Foster and his fellow soldiers feared. Despite their apprehensions, Confederate veterans would not have their lands confiscated, nor would they endure lifelong disenfranchisement.

APRIL 18

Still in camp. More clothing issued today, but still not enough. Had Battalion drill today just to see if the men would drill.

Various reports afloat in camp. Some say the surrender is already made— But there is so much news that there is no importance attached to anything we hear— Late this evening an order comes from Genl Johnson which is read out to all the troops announcing that an Armistice has been agreed upon by the commanders of the two armies, but not for the purpose of surrendering this army— This seems to satisfy everybody. Lees men from Va. are passing us every day—one at the time— Every man for himself. It is also reported that Genl [   ] is south of us with 10,000 mounted infantry—which have been sent down there by Genl Grant from his Army since Lees surrender—

April 19,

Moved ½ mile today and camp in regular order to remain until the armistice ends. We hear it reported on very good authority that the President of the U S Mr Lincoln was killed a few nights ago in Washington, and that about the same time Seward was shot at and mortally wounded.

It is also reported that the United States has recognized the Confederacy, and agrees to give us all our rights (and slavery) if we will help them to fight all their enemies whatsoever.

Another report is we go back into the Union and free all the slaves in —— years—some fill up the blank with 5 years some 10 and some 20 and so on. All hands talking politics and making peace.

Soon after we arrive at our new camp today some of our men found two barrels of Old Apple brandy burried under the root of an old pine tree that had blown down. One barrel of it was brought to Our Brigade and tapped— Every one helped themselves, and of course some get funny, some get tight some get gentlemanly drunk and some get dog drunk, of this latter class are all the officers from our Maj up. Kept up a noise nearly all night, but no one gets mad—all in a good humor.

April 20th

We are still in camp passing rumors from one Brigade to another all day— Some say that the thing is settled and some say that the difficulty has hardly begun yet—so it goes.

April 21st 1865

Rumor today says we are to go back into the Union, but as that is not the kind of news we want to hear, we don't believe a word of it. What have we been fighting all these years for? Oh no—no more Union for us.

April 22

Rumor says (this morning) that we will start for home in course of the next 10 days, and the rumor comes or purports to come from those that ought to know.

Later in the day the report is that we go to fighting again, that Genl Johnson can't make any terms but submission re-union free negroes &c, and we have been fighting too long for that.

I have not seen a man today but says fight on rather than submit.

April 23 *Sunday*

We have moved camp today 6 or 7 miles, and are nearer Greensboro.

I have been out Visiting this evening and find that we are in a quaker settlement. Considerable talk about the peace question— Rumor says the Yankee Army is being fed from our Comissary to keep them from living off the citizens.

Plenty rumors of the French and the U.S.' going to war. If that is true then we will have recognition or nothing.

Apr 24

All very quiet today. No rumors from any source that can be relied upon.

Some think that the big war is about to commence, a war of some Magnitude. France Austria Mexico and the Confederacy on one side, against England Russia and the U S' on the other, and the great battle ground will be in the Confederacy. One plan is for the Confederacy to go back into the Union, then France will declare war with the U S' and land her troops on the C S' Coast where they will have no opposition, and as the French Army advances through the C S' the people will take the oath of Allegiance to France, and our soldiers will enlist under French colors & so on.

April 25

This morning an order is read to the command from Genl Cheatham saying "that Sherman has notified Johnson that the armistice will end and hostilities begin tomorrow 26th inst. at 11 Oclock A.M." At this announcement every body seems gloomy and despondent.

The supposition is that as we can't run out of this place we must fight out. We had talked peace so long in camp and had made so many calculations how we were going home &c that it is up hill business to go to fighting again. We have been very loose in discipline here of late, but that will all come out right in a few days of hard marching and some fighting.

Late in the evening the rumor is that another flag-of-truce has gone to Genl. Sherman, and our fate depends upon the answer. Should it come back before 11 Oclock tomorrow, we may not move yet awhile or we may go double quick.

APRIL 26th

Ordered to be ready to move at 11 O'Clock today, but whether we move or not depends upon the answer to the new propositions sent by the flag-of-truce yesterday.

Andy Johnson the *now* President of the U S' (no kin to the General) sent back the peace papers sent by Sherman as agreed upon between him and Genl Johnson. Not signed by him nor accepted, as a settlement of the war questions at all. —Saying "that the rebellion must be crushed by the force of Arms, and all the prominent men concerned put to death, and the rest banished or made slaves."

At 12 Noon we move out and travel 10 or 12 miles in a westerly direction and camp. Some say we are to remain here tomorrow.

APRIL 27

No move today. This evening Muster Rolls are made out and all hands including officers and men draw 1.25 in silver— the first silver larger than a dime I have seen in a long while.

Just before night the following order from Head Qurs is read

> Hd Qurs Army of Tenn
> near Greensboro N C
> April 27 1865

Genl order
NO 18

By the terms of a military convention made on the 26th inst. by Maj. Gen. W. T. Sherman U S A. and Gen. J. E. Johnson C. S. A. the officers and men of this army are to bind themselves not to take up arms against the U. S.' until properly relieved from that obligation, and shall receive guarantees from the U. S.' officers against molestation by the U. S.' authorities, so long as they observe that obligation, and the laws in force where they reside.

For these objects a duplicate muster roll will be immediately made, and after distribution of the necessary papers, the troops will march under their officers to their respective States, and there be disbanded, all retaining their personal property. The object of this convention is pacification to the extent of the authority of the commanders who made it.

Events in Va. which broke every hope of success by war imposed on its General the duty of sparing the blood of this gallant army, and saving the country from further desolation and the people from ruin.

J E Johnson
General

April 28th

We had a dreadful night, all hands up and talking over the situation. They go over the war again, count up the killed and wounded, then the results obtained— It is too bad! If crying would have done any good, we could have cried all night.

Just to think back at the beginning of this war—and see the young men in the bloom of life—the flower of the country— Volunteering to defend their country from the Yankee hosts, who were coming to desolate their homes. Men who shut their stores and warehouses, stoped their plows, droped the axe, left their machinery lying idle, closed their law offices, churches banks and workshops; and all fall into line to defend the country.

Now where are they. As for our own Company, Regt. and Brgd.—they can be found at Ark. Post, at the prison cemetery of Camp Springfield Ill. at Chickamauga—at Missionary Ridge—at New Hope Church 27 May 64 at Atlanta Aug 22/64 at Jonesboro Ga at Franklin and Nashville Tenn. Dec/64 and there find the remains of as noble men, and as kind hearted faithful friends as ever trod the face of the earth.

And those men who fell in 1864 even in Dec. 64 sacrificed their lives as freely as did the very first that fell in the war. There was no cooling down, no tapering off, no lukewarmness in those men, but they would brave danger when ordered as fearless of Yankee bullets as if they no power to hurt them. At Franklin Tenn. Dec 1st or Nov 30/64 was the most wholesale butchery of human lives ever witness by us. Those brave men had been taught by Genl Johnson to fear nothing when he made a fight, and expecting the same thing of Hood, were betrayed into a perfect slaughter pen.

Who is to blame for all this waste of human life? It is too bad to talk about. And what does it amount to? Has there been anything gained by all this sacrifice? What were we fighting for, the principles of slavery?

And now the slaves are all freed, and the Confederacy has to be dissolved. We have to go back into the Union. Ah! there is the point. Will there ever be any more Union, as there once was?

April 29th

Men still talking politics, but it is over and over the same thing, with the same regrets for our loss, and end with the same "What does it amount to?"

Later in the day the talk is about going home, by what route, and whether we will have to walk all the way &c &c.

Men are beginning to realize their situation, and are talking about going home to Texas. Our guns have all been turned in, to our own Ordnance officers. And we suppose to save us from further humiliation there has not been a Yank in sight of us yet.

Our Muster rolls went up yesterday for paroles, which will be here tomorrow or next day.

April 30th

It seems curious that mens minds can change so sudden, from opinions of life long, to new ones a week old.

I mean that men who have not only been taught from their infancy that the institution of slavery was right; but men who actually owned and held slaves up to this time,—have now changed in their opinions regarding slavery, so as to be able to see the other side of the question,—to see that for man to have property in man was wrong, and that the "Declaration of Independence meant more than they had ever been able to see before. That all men are, and of right ought to be free" has a meaning different from the definition they had been taught from their infancy up,—and to see that the institution (though perhaps wise) had been abused, and perhaps for that abuse this terrible war with its results, was brought upon us as a punishment.

These ideas come not from the Yanks or northern people but come from reflection, and reasoning among ourselves.

This evening a circular from Head Qurs. announce that Rev. J B McFerrin Our Army Chaplain will preach his farewell sermon to the Texas and Ark. troops tomorrow at 10 O'Clock AM.

MAY 1st 1865

Have just heard the best sermon that it has ever been our good fortune to hear before. Rev. J B McFerrin preached to us out in the open woods, the men sitting on the ground, and the preacher holding one book while the other is on the ground.

His text is Revelations 11th Chapter, and the latter part of the 10th verse "Be thou faithful unto death, and I will give thee a Crown of life—" The congregation joined in the singing with their whole souls and for prayer all without an exception knelt down, and for the sermon it held those rough weatherbeaten soldiers spell bound for more than an hour by the eloquence of the preacher— It was a time long to be remembered.

In the evening we receive our parols, which read as follows—

Greensborough
North Carolina
May 2nd 1865

In accordance with the terms of the military convention entered into on the twenty-sixth day of April 1865 between General Joseph E. Johnson Commanding the Confederate Army: and Major General W. T. Sherman, Commanding the United States Army in North Carolina, S T Foster Company "I" Granburys Brigade Consolidated, has given his solemn obligation not to take up arms against the Government of the United States until properly released from this obligation; and is permitted to return to his home, not to be disturbed by the United States Authorities so long as he observes this obligation and obey the laws in force where he may reside

S M Litchee	W. A. Ryan
Maj & CM U.S.A.	Lieut Col. C S A
Special Commission	Commanding

MAY 3rd

After turning in our guns, and getting our parols, we feel relieved. No more picket duty, no more guard duty, no more fighting, no more war. It is all over, and we are going home. HOME after an absence of four years from our families and friends.

Actually going to start home tomorrow or perhaps this morning.

Left our camp surenough at 9 A.M. Came 10 miles, crossed the R.R. at Thomasville, and came 12 miles further towards Salisbury making 22 miles today, and all hands very tired.

MAY 4th

Came to Salisbury today—traveled 20 miles. The Confederate Army will go to pieces here. The South Carolina and Georgia Alabama and Missippi troops will march on foot directly home. The Tennessee Arkansas and Texas troops will turn west from here and cross over the Blue Ridge into East Tennessee, and there take the R.R. for Chattanooga and to Nashville where *we* will take a steamboat for N. O. provided the Yanks will give us transportation.

We are getting accostomed to the new order of things, but there is considerable speculation as to what will be done with us.

Some think that all the officers will be courtmartialed. Some think they will be banished out of the country.

Nearly every one deplores the death of Lincoln and believes that he would have been the best man for us now.

That things would have been different if he had lived. Some go so far as to say that perhaps we were wrong, and that the negroes ought to have been freed at the start off. While others are still not whiped and evince a determination to fight it out some way, or leave the country, rather than go back into the Union, and be ruled by them; and have to be ground to death by being robbed of all our negroes, and lands and other property—not allowed to Vote nor hold office any more.

We do not suppose, nor expect to be allowed to vote any more, as long as we live. We also expect that all the lands in the Confederacy, will be taken away from the white people to pay their war expenses then given in small 160 acre lots to the negroes.

"A THOUSAND RUMORS": GEORGIA, MAY 1865

Ellen Renshaw House: Diary, May 2, 1865

Ellen Renshaw House had settled in Eatonton in central Georgia several months after the Union army expelled her from Knoxville for her Confederate sympathies. A visitor from nearby Milledgeville told House on April 21 that Lee had surrendered, a report she initially refused to believe. Two days later she conceded its validity, writing, "We have depended too much on Gen Lee too little on God, & I believe God has suffered his surrender to show us he can use other means than Gen Lee to affect his ends." By May 2 she had still not received definitive news regarding Johnston's surrender. When the Johnston-Sherman agreement reached Washington on April 21, President Johnson and the cabinet had immediately rejected it and sent Grant to North Carolina to obtain Johnston's capitulation on terms similar to those given to Lee. Johnston complied, and on April 26 surrendered all Confederate forces in the Carolinas, Georgia, and Florida. In the summer of 1865, House returned to Tennessee and was reunited with her beloved younger brother, John Moore House, after his release from the Union prison camp on Johnson's Island in Lake Erie. Her happiness at his return was cut short in November when "Johnnie" was killed by robbers near Nashville, a victim of the widespread lawlessness that would afflict much of the South in the aftermath of the war.

May 2. Tuesday. I have been in such a state for the last week I could not write. We have heard a thousand rumors. First that we would be recognized, then that we were going back into the Union. I would not believe the last for a long time, but I am obliged to. Oh! how humiliating. Gen Johnston has surrendered, or rather Gen Sherman and himself have had a conference in which it was agreed that Gen Johnston's men should be marched to their respective states and disbanded. We to go back into the Union with all our former rights &c. Gen Johnston was so completely surrounded that he was compelled to succumb. We have heard so many reports. First that the French have taken New Orleans. That we are to have armed intervention. That Kirby Smith has been reenforced by one hundred thousand French. That there is a French fleet off New York, and I dont know what else.

Lieut Thomas and Capt Robinson called this afternoon, both very blue. How can a true Southerner be any thing else. Yesterday there was a large picnic at Jenkins Mill, neither of us went. I do not think this is any time for picnics &e. Tonight there is to be a dance at Mr Buddins—a Union man. What the young men and girls can be thinking of to go there at such a time I cannot imagine. Almost all the young men have returned. I never saw so many in as small a place.

"HE BEHAVED SO BRAVE":
WASHINGTON, D.C., MAY 1865

Walt Whitman: from Specimen Days

Walt Whitman left Brooklyn and traveled to northern Virginia in December 1862 when he learned that his brother George, a captain in the 51st New York Infantry, had been wounded at Fredericksburg. After discovering that his brother's wound was slight, Whitman accompanied a group of wounded soldiers to Washington. He stayed in the capital for most of the remainder of the war, visiting military hospitals while working as a government clerk. In his book of prose remembrance, *Specimen Days* (1882), Whitman included a letter he sent to the mother of a Union soldier who had been wounded near Petersburg in the last weeks of the war. In an earlier passage in *Specimen Days* he wrote about the fatally wounded soldiers who never reached hospitals and were never buried in marked graves: "No history ever—no poem sings, no music sounds, those bravest men of all—those deeds. No formal general's report, nor book in the library, nor column in the paper, embalms the bravest, north or south, east or west. Unnamed, unknown, remain, and still remain, the bravest soldiers. Our manliest—our boys—our hardy darlings; no picture gives them. Likely, the typic one of them (standing, no doubt, for hundreds, thousands,) crawls aside to some bush-clump, or ferny tuft, on receiving his death-shot—there sheltering a little while, soaking roots, grass and soil, with red blood—the battle advances, retreats, flits from the scene, sweeps by—and there, haply with pain and suffering (yet less, far less, than is supposed,) the last lethargy winds like a serpent round him—the eyes glaze in death—none recks—perhaps the burial-squads, in truce, a week afterwards, search not the secluded spot—and there, at last, the Bravest Soldier crumbles in mother earth, unburied and unknown."

DEATH OF A PENNSYLVANIA SOLDIER.

Frank H. Irwin, company E, 93d Pennsylvania—died May 1, '65—My letter to his mother.—Dear madam: No doubt you and Frank's friends have heard the sad fact of his death in hospital here, through his uncle, or the lady from Baltimore, who took his things. (I have not seen them, only heard of them visiting

Frank.) I will write you a few lines—as a casual friend that sat by his death-bed. Your son, corporal Frank H. Irwin, was wounded near fort Fisher, Virginia, March 25th, 1865—the wound was in the left knee, pretty bad. He was sent up to Washington, was receiv'd in ward C, Armory-square hospital, March 28th—the wound became worse, and on the 4th of April the leg was amputated a little above the knee—the operation was perform'd by Dr. Bliss, one of the best surgeons in the army—he did the whole operation himself—there was a good deal of bad matter gather'd—the bullet was found in the knee. For a couple of weeks afterwards he was doing pretty well. I visited and sat by him frequently, as he was fond of having me. The last ten or twelve days of April I saw that his case was critical. He previously had some fever, with cold spells. The last week in April he was much of the time flighty—but always mild and gentle. He died first of May. The actual cause of death was pyæmia, (the absorption of the matter in the system instead of its discharge.) Frank, as far as I saw, had everything requisite in surgical treatment, nursing, &c. He had watches much of the time. He was so good and well-behaved and affectionate, I myself liked him very much. I was in the habit of coming in afternoons and sitting by him, and soothing him, and he liked to have me—liked to put his arm out and lay his hand on my knee—would keep it so a long while. Toward the last he was more restless and flighty at night—often fancied himself with his regiment—by his talk sometimes seem'd as if his feelings were hurt by being blamed by his officers for something he was entirely innocent of—said, "I never in my life was thought capable of such a thing, and never was." At other times he would fancy himself talking as it seem'd to children or such like, his relatives I suppose, and giving them good advice; would talk to them a long while. All the time he was out of his head not one single bad word or idea escaped him. It was remark'd that many a man's conversation in his senses was not half as good as Frank's delirium. He seem'd quite willing to die—he had become very weak and had suffer'd a good deal, and was perfectly resign'd, poor boy. I do not know his past life, but I feel as if it must have been good. At any rate what I saw of him here, under the most trying circumstances, with a painful wound, and among strangers, I can say that he behaved so brave, so composed, and so sweet and affectionate, it could not be surpass'd. And now like many other noble and good men, after serving his country as a soldier, he has yielded up his young life at the very outset in her service. Such things are gloomy—yet there is a text, "God doeth all things well"—the meaning of which, after due time, appears to the soul.

I thought perhaps a few words, though from a stranger, about your son, from one who was with him at the last, might be worth while—for I loved the young man, though I but saw him immediately to lose him. I am merely a friend visiting the hospitals occasionally to cheer the wounded and sick.

W. W.

"HEROES OF THE SUBLIMEST CONFLICT":
MAY 1865

New York Herald: *The Grandest Military Display in the World*

May 24, 1865

On May 4 Lieutenant General Richard Taylor surrendered all Confederate forces in Alabama, Mississippi, and eastern Louisiana. Jefferson Davis was captured by Union cavalry near Irwinville, Georgia, on May 10, ending his hopes of reaching Texas. With the war almost over, the Union celebrated its victory by staging a Grand Review of the Armies in Washington on May 23 and 24. Over the course of two days about 150,000 men from the Army of the Potomac and the Armies of the Tennessee and Georgia marched along Pennsylvania Avenue from the Capitol to the White House. At the start of the procession they passed a large banner hung across the northwest corner of the Capitol that read: "The Only National Debt We Can Never Pay, Is The Debt We Owe To The Victorious Soldiers." Tens of thousands of citizens watched and cheered. "God Bless them all," wrote Benjamin Brown French, the commissioner of public buildings for the District of Columbia, "I saw them depart for the war, and my eyes moistened with grief, as I thought how many of them would never return! I have seen many of them come back—brave veterans who have fought and bled to defend the liberties for which their fathers fought so well, and my eyes moistened with joy to think that they were on their way *home*." The *New York Herald* had become one of the most widely circulated newspapers in the country under its founding editor James Gordon Bennett. Although the *Herald* had criticized Lincoln for much of his administration, the newspaper had remained neutral in the 1864 election. On May 24 the *Herald* hailed the triumph of the Union armies and commented on the international significance of their victory.

Yesterday the magnificent review at Washington began. The vast army of two hundred thousand American soldiers commenced to pass before the President and the Lieutenant General. The scenes and incidents will be found fully described in our news columns. Washington was of course crowded with strangers from all parts of the Union, and their cheers expressed to the brave veterans the gratitude which the country feels toward them for its preservation. There have been many grand military displays in the past; but never before has there been one as grand as this. The number of soldiers in line is immense. Neither Napoleon nor Wellington ever saw so many veterans in one army at one time. When Napoleon reviewed his army of two hundred thousand men, at the opening of his first Russian campaign, many of his soldiers were young conscripts, fresh from the farm and the counter. The great Russian army, reviewed by the Duke of Wellington after the capitulation of Paris in 1814, numbered only one hundred and sixty thousand. But our army—which is, in fact but part of our force, since the commands of Thomas, Schofield, Curtis, Ord, Canby, Foster and others are not represented—is composed entirely of veterans, and is quite two hundred thousand strong.

It is not mere numbers, however, which make this display at Washington so grand. The immensity of the numbers has its effect, because we have never seen anything like it in this country before. General Grant gives us a faint idea of this immensity when he says that it will take this army two days to cross the Long Bridge. McClellan's reviews were small compared to this, and the long processions which we get up here in the metropolis in honor of distinguished visitors sink into insignificance. But this review is a review of triumph. The troops which file before the thousands of spectators at Washington are not going into a war, and are not preparing for battle. They have come out of the war triumphant, and all their battles are over. Leading them we see Peace and Victory hand in hand. The gallant conquerors of many a hard fought field are going home to share the blessings they have won for the nation. They are not only heroes, but they are the heroes of the sublimest conflict in all history. They have been battling for that great principle of democracy for which so many valiant martyrs in former times have fallen in vain, and they have secured the perpetuity of that Union upon which the hopes of all oppressed of all climes and countries depend. They are the champions of free governments throughout the world. The applause which greets them comes not from the Washington crowds alone, nor from the millions of their fellow citizens in all the States; but we can hear it ringing across the Atlantic, echoed alike from the Alps and the Andes, and swelled by the majestic chorus of republican voices from Mexico to Denmark. From one end of the world to the other the people thank our soldiers for having conquered in the people's cause.

Two hundred thousand American soldiers are marching on through Washington to-day. Every regiment, brigade and division has its proud record, which spectators eagerly recall. Those fine fellows fought at Antietam, and those at Atlanta. Here are the men who held Lee in a vice, and yonder come Sherman's legions, who passed like a sword through the vitals of the rebellion. We leave to our correspondents the grateful task of noting the achievements of the troops in line, and pause to ask ourselves where their march is to end? They are going home; but will they stay there long? With one-quarter of the number Scott captured Mexico. With one-half of that tremendous army Canada would be ours. With such a body of veterans our generals could humble the pride of combined Europe. Where will their grand march end? This is a question which no one can answer now. One thing is, nevertheless, sure. These thousands of soldiers may fight no more; their remaining years may be passed in quiet usefulness, at their homes; one by one they may pass away, honored and beloved by all, like the patriots of the Revolution; scattered far and wide, their bodies may rest sweetly beneath the flowers and the grasses; but all this while their souls and those of their slain comrades will be marching on. On—till thrones shake and crumble at the sound of their coming, and are crushed beneath their steady tramp. On—till the people everywhere rise and demand their liberties with invincible voices. On—till no despot tyrannizes over his fellow men, and no aristocracy lords it over the down-trodden masses. On—till every nation is a republic, and every man a freeman. On—till the soldiers of Grant, Sherman and Sheridan have saved the world as they have saved the Union. On, and on, and on!

THE GRAND REVIEW:
WASHINGTON, D.C., MAY 1865

Lois Bryan Adams to the Detroit Advertiser and Tribune

Lois Bryan Adams described the Grand Review for her readers in Michigan in dispatches that appeared on May 29 and 31. In her second letter Adams observed that the only black troops who marched on either day of the celebration were pioneers attached to Sherman's army. Although some abolitionists protested that the U.S. Colored Troops had been excluded from the Grand Review as the result of a deliberate slight, there were no black regiments assigned to the Army of the Potomac or to the Armies of the Tennessee and Georgia, and the black troops from the Army of the James were about to embark for Texas. Black soldiers had participated in the inaugural parade in March and in Lincoln's funeral procession on April 20, and the presence in the review of black pioneers who had built roads and bridges for Sherman's army was celebrated by the abolitionist newspaper *The Liberator*.

Letter from Washington
REVIEW OF THE ARMIES MARCHING HOME
Washington, May 24, 1865

For two days past Washington has done nothing but watch our national heroes marching home. The display, though embracing but comparatively a small portion of the entire army of the Union, has been a very grand one indeed. The manner of the review was not such as would permit of military evolutions by the troops; it was simply a street parade, and as such only limited numbers of the immense masses passing by could be seen from any one point. The best view was from the head of Pennsylvania Avenue, where it bends to the north past the Treasury building. Standing there and looking towards the Capitol, the scene was a most grand and imposing one. As far as the eye could reach on either hand, the sidewalks were densely crowded with spectators, and every window and balcony and even the roofs and the trees along the way were full. As brigade after brigade swept up the noble avenue with their war-worn flags and inspiring music, they were welcomed with cheers and songs, the waving of flags and handkerchiefs, and now and then a showering of bouquets and wreaths of evergreens and beautiful flowers. Many of the Generals had their horses' necks wreathed with garlands, the gifts of grateful hands along the way.

The children of the public schools dressed in uniform white, with black sashes, assembled at the Capitol and greeted the troops with songs and flowers. Everywhere, through all the grand pageant, blended with the symbols of rejoicing were to be seen also the emblems of mourning for the dead President—he who so longed to see this day, and was caught up out of our sight before it came. All the National flags about the city were at half-mast and heavily draped with black, and every ensign, banner and battle-flag in the passing regiments had crape upon it, while mourning badges were worn by all the officers and very many of the soldiers.

Immense temporary pavilions built in front of the White House and occupying all the broad pavements on either side of the avenue, were handsomely decorated, and filled by Government dignitaries and officials, from the President down, together with Foreign Ministers, attaches, etc., and here also was stationed Lieut. Gen. Grant, before whom these two grand armies passed in review. Standing back of these, almost hidden by the dense foliage of the great trees around it, the White House with its tall pillars still shrouded in black, was desolate and silent as a tomb. It was as if life and death, joy and sorrow had met, and hope had crowned them together with victory and peace and the bloom of spring.

The entire of yesterday was occupied with the passage of Sheridan's cavalry and the 9th, 5th, and 2d Army Corps, together with artillery and engineer corps. Sheridan of course was not here, as he has gone to crush out the one head of the hydra yet alive, in Texas; but his gallant troopers, under command of our own brave Custer, were wildly cheered as they swept up the avenue. Indeed, all were cheered, as they well deserved to be; but, oh, how poor, how empty does all this pageantry and cheering seem, compared with what we owe to these bronzed and war-torn veterans. Shouts and songs and fading flowers seem almost like mockery when offered to such men who have accomplished a work so grand, and yet what else had these gratified crowds to offer?

Sherman's magnificent army passed through the city today. It was worth a lifetime of common events to witness a sight like this. If your Northern doughfaces and copperheads could but look in the iron faces of these men, as they come up in their mighty strength, they would easily understand why chivalry begged for peace and then took to its heels, in petticoats, at their approach. Grinding between the upper and nether millstone wouldn't have been a circumstance to the pulverizing all secession would have got, if it had not crumbled in pieces and scattered just as it did. No one can look at troops like these without feeling sure that an enemy's country, through which they have once marched, must be pretty thoroughly conquered. They are not the men to march without a purpose, and certainly not the ones to leave till that purpose is accomplished.

There were some particulars about this army, and some little incidents, which I will try to gather up this afternoon, and give you in my next.

L.

Letters from Washington
The Grand Review | An Englishman's Opinion | Citizen Soldiers | South Carolina's Punishment | Sherman's Men | Grant's Irish Brigade | Serenade to Gov. Crapo and Senator Chandler | Michigan's Record, etc.

From Our Own Correspondent
Washington, May 27, 1865

For twelve hours, from 9 till 3 o'clock on Tuesday, and the same on Wednesday, we stood at the head of Pennsylvania Avenue and watched the moving masses of men crowned with glittering steel as they came pouring around and down the slopes of Capitol Hill and went rolling on like a mighty river past the stand where the great review took place. It was, without doubt, the grandest military pageant ever witnessed upon the American continent. I overheard an Englishman speaking of it, and he said, "I have witnessed military reviews in England and France, and other parts of Europe, but never saw anything that could equal this. I only wish John Bull at home could see what we see here today." There was an emphasis in the tone that gave a peculiar force to the words; coming from English lips, too, it seemed to mean something, especially when it was added, "And to think that this is not more than one-third of the Union army! and the grandeur of it all is that these men are citizens."

Yes; there is where foreigners see the grandeur, if we do not. These are all citizens who know the value of their country and their Government; they saw the danger menacing both, they made heroes of themselves, they have averted the danger, have given a progressive interpretation to the old Constitution, and are now quietly disbanding to go home and be citizens again. The heroes made by Kings and Emperors are not to be compared with these.

I remember in the early part of the war there was a great anxiety on the part of many as to what should be done with the soldiers after the war was over. But even the most anxious need have no uneasiness on that score; the soldiers will take care of themselves just as well as they did before the war, and better too, many of them. I have talked with hundreds of them, and the universal expression is one of joy at the prospect of going home—home to their families, their farms, and their workshops. Home is the first word they speak in connection with their discharge from service. Our soldiers don't know what "demoralization" means. They had something dearer than life to fight for; they fought, and won, and are now going home to enjoy the peaceful fruits of their victory.

Some of Sherman's men who had fallen out of the ranks from weariness yesterday, came and stood beside us and told us of the hollowness of the Confederate shell through which they had been marching. They said that if ever there was a thoroughly whipped and conquered people it was the Southern rebels; and, said one, "South Carolina is, as it deserves to be, the most completely humbled and desolated spot in all rebeldom. We had no friends there, and we made the country support us. I think it will be some time before that State will want to set up for herself against the Union again!"

It is impossible to describe the feeling of these men towards their commander. They speak of Sherman as a beloved and indulgent father. "There's no place this side of Tophet," said one, "that Sherman's boys wouldn't take if he asked them to; and I reckon they'd go clean that out if he said so!"

The troops came up the broad avenue in splendid marching order, 26 abreast, each corps of infantry followed by its artillery, the shining brass pieces and wicked steel rifled guns, each drawn by eight stout horses, and their accompanying caissons the same. These cannon, which have been talking thunder to the rebels so long, looked peaceful and innocent enough now, and many of them were wreathed with evergreens and garlands of flowers.

One peculiarity of Sherman's army was the great numbers of heavily packed mules between the divisions, and the long train of loaded army wagons, and the promiscuous masses following in the rear. Most of those leading or riding the mules were contrabands of all ages, from little boys to old men; one black woman was among them. But what created great amusement among the thousands of spectators were the roosters perched on tops of the mule-packs and seeming to enjoy the display as much as anybody. They looked around with great apparent satisfaction on the laughing, clapping, shouting crowd, and every now and then answered the cheers by flapping their wings and crowing triumphantly as they "went marching on." They evidently understood that there was victory to be celebrated and that they were expected to do their part; and they did it. In one instance there was a beautiful white goat, a pet of some good soldier boy, standing on one of the mule-packs eating from a pannier as contentedly as if born to ride horseback and live on rations.

No colored troops were on review either day, except the few with Sherman's army who were attached to the Pioneer corps and armed with picks and shovels. The black soldiers are still in the field, in the army of the James, or at the West and Southwest.

The Irish Brigade, under Grant, the first day made a fine appearance, every soldier in it having a sprig of green box in his cap. Looking over and down the long columns, the effect was very pleasing. The green flag of Erin was carried beside the national colors, and the tattered battle flags give token of the hard service they had seen.

The weather for the grand review could not have been finer. For a week or more past there had been a constant succession of thunderstorms, day and night; so that when it did clear off the atmosphere was pure and fresh and cool. Both days were perfectly delightful, with clear blue skies, bright sunshine, and sweet invigorating airs.

Hundreds of Michigan people have been here to witness the spectacle. It was chronicled on Monday that Gov. Crapo and staff, Senator Chandler, and others were in town, and on the evening of that day they were serenaded by the band of the Michigan Cavalry Brigade. The Governor was called out and made a patriotic speech. Senator Chandler also spoke, and the band were handsomely entertained at the Governor's rooms.

This cavalry brigade, comprising the 6th, 7th, 1st, and 5th Michigan cavalry, was commanded by Col. Peter Stagg, of Trenton, Mich. He was a Colonel day before yesterday, but is a Brigadier General now, having been promoted since the review.

It was amusing yesterday to hear the little boys as they ran up and down among the crowds on the side-walks, crying "Photographs of Jeff. Davis trying to escape in his wife's clothes."

Here, if ever, from the scene in the avenue on one hand, to the pictured masquerade on the other, the oft talked-of "step from the sublime to the ridiculous" was a visible, tangible reality.

But the splendid pageant of the day passed on, and as the sun went down the armies of the Union spread their tents on the hills and along the valleys, around about the capital they have guarded so long and so well. The city, with its 70,000 visitors, seemed as quiet as ordinarily, save the serenading bands, with their pleasant music at the hotels, where their Generals were quartered.

Today the boys in blue have taken the city by storm. They are everywhere, seeing the sights and making the most of Washington while the opportunity lasts.

L.

"ALL SLAVES ARE FREE": TEXAS, JUNE 1865
Gordon Granger: General Orders No. 3

On May 26 General Edmund Kirby Smith surrendered all Confederate forces west of the Mississippi. Major General Gordon Granger arrived in Galveston on June 18 and issued General Orders No. 3 the following day. His order enforcing the Emancipation Proclamation brought freedom to about 250,000 slaves in Texas and became the basis for the African American holiday of Juneteenth.

HEADQUARTERS DISTRICT OF TEXAS,
Galveston, Tex., June 19, 1865.

GENERAL ORDERS,
No. 3.

The people of Texas are informed that, in accordance with a proclamation from the Executive of the United States, all slaves are free. This involves an absolute equality of personal rights and rights of property between former masters and slaves, and the connection heretofore existing between them becomes that between employer and hired labor. The freedmen are advised to remain quietly at their present homes and work for wages. They are informed that they will not be allowed to collect at military posts and that they will not be supported in idleness either there or elsewhere.

By order of Major-General Granger:

F. W. EMERY,
Major and Assistant Adjutant-General.

CHRONOLOGY

BIOGRAPHICAL NOTES

NOTE ON THE TEXTS

NOTES

INDEX

Chronology
March 1864–June 1865

1864   Union Brigadier General Judson Kilpatrick abandons cavalry raid aimed at freeing prisoners of war held in Richmond, Virginia, on March 1 and retreats toward Union lines. Richmond newspapers publish documents found during the Kilpatrick raid on the body of Union Colonel Ulric Dahlgren outlining plans to kill Jefferson Davis and burn Richmond, March 5 (Kilpatrick will deny any knowledge of alleged plot). The same day, Secretary of the Treasury Salmon P. Chase ends his undeclared challenge to the renomination of President Abraham Lincoln by announcing that he is not a candidate for president. Major General Ulysses S. Grant and President Lincoln meet for the first time on March 8 at the White House. Grant receives his commission as lieutenant general the next day, and is named general-in-chief of the armies of the United States on March 10. Union expedition in Louisiana led by Major General Nathaniel P. Banks and Rear Admiral David P. Porter begins advance up the Red River toward Shreveport, March 12, and occupies Alexandria, March 15. Arkansas unionists vote 12,177–266 in favor of a constitutional amendment abolishing slavery in the state, March 14–16. Confederate cavalry commander Major General Nathan Bedford Forrest leads raid from northern Mississippi into West Tennessee and southwestern Kentucky, March 15–May 5. Grant discusses plans for the spring campaign with Major General William T. Sherman, his successor as overall Union commander in the western theater, in Nashville and Cincinnati, March 17–20. Major General Frederick Steele leaves Little Rock, Arkansas, with 6,800 Union troops on March 23 and begins advance on Shreveport from the north. Altercation between Union soldiers on furlough and antiwar Copperheads in Charleston, Illinois, on March 28 results in riot in which six soldiers and three civilians are killed.

    In letter to Sherman on April 4, Grant outlines plan for spring campaign involving simultaneous Union offensives with the objective of decisively defeating the two main

Confederate armies. Sherman will move against the Army of Tennessee in northern Georgia, led by General Joseph E. Johnston, while Grant will make his headquarters in the field with the Army of the Potomac, commanded by Major General George G. Meade, and direct its operations against the Army of Northern Virginia, led by General Robert E. Lee. The Army of the Potomac's offensive against Lee will be supported by Major General Benjamin F. Butler, who will move up the James River toward Richmond, and Major General Franz Sigel, who will advance south through the Shenandoah Valley. (Grant's plan for Banks to lead an expedition in the spring against Mobile, Alabama, will be abandoned due to the Red River campaign.) Convention in Louisiana approves on April 6 a new state constitution abolishing slavery. U.S. Senate approves Thirteenth Amendment to the Constitution abolishing slavery by 38–6 vote on April 8. The same day, Major General Richard Taylor defeats the vanguard of Banks's army at Sabine Crossroads near Mansfield, Louisiana, and drives it back several miles to Pleasant Hill. Although fighting at Pleasant Hill on April 9 is tactically inconclusive, Banks abandons advance on Shreveport and begins retreat to Alexandria. Confederate troops led by Forrest capture Union outpost at Fort Pillow, Tennessee, on April 12 and kill hundreds of black soldiers who are trying to surrender. News of the massacre causes widespread outrage in the North. Steele's expedition in southern Arkansas occupies Camden on April 13. Grant orders general prisoner exchanges suspended on April 17 until the Confederates treat black and white prisoners equally and recognize the validity of the surrender terms given to the Confederate garrisons at Vicksburg and Port Hudson in July 1863. Confederates capture Plymouth, North Carolina, and take 2,500 Union prisoners, April 17–20. Corps commanded by Lieutenant General James Longstreet rejoins Lee's army near Gordonsville, Virginia, on April 22 after serving in East Tennessee since September 1863. Retreating forces under Banks reach Alexandria, April 25–26, where low water in the Red River threatens to strand the Union gunboat flotilla. Confederate destruction of Union supply columns at Poison Spring, April 18, and Marks's Mill, April 25, forces Steele to abandon expedition against Shreveport. Union forces evacuate Camden on April 26 and fight rear-guard action at Jenkins's Ferry, April 30, as they retreat across the Saline River toward Little Rock. (Evidence indicates that some black troops killed Confederate prisoners at Jenkins's Ferry in retaliation for the murder of black soldiers and fugitive slaves at Poison Spring and Marks's Mill.)

On May 4 the Army of the Potomac begins crossing the Rapidan River in Virginia east of Lee's camps and advances into the Wilderness of Spotsylvania, an area of scrub woods and dense undergrowth. Butler sails up the James River on May 5 with 30,000 men and begins landing at Bermuda Hundred, a peninsula between the James and Appomattox rivers south of Richmond and north of Petersburg. Lee moves his army of 66,000 men into the Wilderness to engage the Union forces, which total about 120,000. Two days of intense fighting in the Wilderness, May 5–6, end in a stalemate after the Union loses more than 17,000 men killed, wounded, or missing, and the Confederates 11,000. Both armies move southeast toward Spotsylvania Court House on May 7. Sherman begins his campaign in northern Georgia on May 7 by advancing toward Dalton along the railroad line from Chattanooga to Atlanta. His command of about 100,000 men, divided among the Army of the Cumberland (Major General George H. Thomas), the Army of the Tennessee (Major General James B. McPherson), and the Army of the Ohio (Major General John M. Schofield), is opposed by General Joseph E. Johnston, who commands about 50,000 men (later reinforced to 60,000) in the Army of Tennessee. While Thomas and Schofield probe the Confederate defenses on Rocky Face Ridge west of Dalton, Sherman sends McPherson on a flanking march to the south toward the railroad at Resaca. Lee's troops reach crossroads at Spotsylvania Court House ahead of Union forces on May 8 and the two armies begin fighting there. Butler advances toward Petersburg on May 9, but then withdraws to prepare for movement toward Richmond. Union assault at Spotsylvania on May 10 fails to break the Confederate line. Major General J.E.B. Stuart, the commander of Lee's cavalry since 1862, is fatally wounded on May 11 at Yellow Tavern near Richmond while fighting a cavalry raid led by Major General Philip H. Sheridan. Union assault on "Mule Shoe" salient at Spotsylvania, May 12, captures several thousand Confederate prisoners but fails to achieve a decisive break in Lee's lines. The same day, Butler begins advance from Bermuda Hundred toward the southern defenses of Richmond at Drewry's Bluff. Johnston abandons Dalton, Georgia, on the night of May 12 and retreats to Resaca. Banks evacuates Alexandria, Louisiana, on May 13 after the Union gunboat flotilla escapes down the Red River. Johnston retreats from Resaca on May 15 after two days of fighting around the town. Union army of 9,000 men led by Franz Sigel is defeated at New Market in the Shenandoah Valley on May 15 by force of 5,000 Confederates led by Major General John C. Breckinridge that includes local militia and more than two hundred Virginia Military Institute cadets. General Pierre G. T. Beauregard defeats Union forces at Drewry's Bluff on May 16, causing Butler to retreat to Bermuda Hundred and entrench his position. Failure of Sigel's and Butler's offensives allows reinforcements to reach Lee. Union assault against the base of the "Mule Shoe" salient is repulsed on May 18. Johnston retreats to strong defensive position at Allatoona Pass, Georgia, May 19–20. Banks retreats across Atchafalaya Bayou in southern Louisiana on May 20, ending Red River campaign. Grant abandons Union positions at Spotsylvania, May 20–21, and moves southeast toward the North Anna River, ending battle in which about 18,000 Union and 12,000 Confederate soldiers are killed, wounded, or missing. Lee reaches North Anna before Grant but is unable to prevent Union troops from crossing the river on May 23. Sherman moves away from the Chattanooga–Atlanta railroad on May 23 in attempt to turn Johnston's southern flank. Union forces encounter strongly entrenched Confederate position south of the North Anna River on May 24. Sherman's flanking maneuver results in heavy fighting at New Hope Church, May 25, and Pickett's Mill, May 27. Grant's troops cross the Pamunkey River, May 27–28, and occupy crossroads at Cold Harbor nine miles east of Richmond on May 31. Coalition of abolitionists and War Democrats hold Radical Democracy convention in Cleveland on May 31 and nominate Major General John C. Frémont for president.

Fighting at Cold Harbor on June 1 is inconclusive. Grant orders general assault against Lee's defensive line on June 3 that is repulsed with the loss of 7,000 Union soldiers killed, wounded, or missing, while Confederate casualties total about 1,500. National Union convention, coalition of Republicans and War Democrats meeting in

Baltimore, nominates Lincoln for president on nearly unanimous first ballot on June 8 and chooses Democrat Andrew Johnson, the military governor of Tennessee, as its vice presidential candidate. After maneuvering back to the Chattanooga–Atlanta railroad line, Sherman resumes his advance on June 10. With a force of 3,500 men, Forrest defeats 8,500 Union troops led by Brigadier General Samuel G. Curtis at Brice's Crossroads in northern Mississippi, June 10. Major General David Hunter, Sigel's replacement as Union commander in the Shenandoah Valley, occupies Lexington on June 11 and burns Virginia Military Institute the following day. Grant withdraws from Cold Harbor on June 12 and begins moving the Army of the Potomac toward the James River. (From May 4 to June 12 the Army of the Potomac lost about 55,000 men killed, wounded, or missing, while losses in the Army of Northern Virginia are estimated at about 33,000 men.) Union troops begin crossing the James on June 14. Lincoln signs legislation on June 15 that partially redresses grievances of black soldiers regarding their unequal pay. The same day, the House of Representatives defeats passage of the Thirteenth Amendment, 93–65. Union troops assault Petersburg, June 15–18, capturing several defensive positions but failing to take the city itself despite their superior numbers. Grant decides not to launch any further frontal assaults on the city, and Union troops begin to entrench east and southeast of Petersburg. Hunter advances on railroad junction at Lynchburg, Virginia, June 17–18, then retreats into West Virginia when he encounters reinforcements sent by Lee from the Army of Northern Virginia. After a week of skirmishing and maneuvering in northern Georgia, Johnston retreats to defensive line anchored on Kennesaw Mountain, June 18. U.S.S. *Kearsarge* sinks the Confederate commerce raider C.S.S. *Alabama* off Cherbourg, France, on June 19. Union forces make unsuccessful attempt to cut Weldon Railroad linking North Carolina with Petersburg, June 21–24. Confederate troops under Lieutenant General Jubal A. Early begin advancing north through the Shenandoah Valley toward Maryland. Sherman orders unsuccessful frontal assault on Confederate positions at Kennesaw Mountain, June 27. Congress repeals Fugitive Slave Act on June 28 (legislation passed in March 1862 had already prohibited the Union military from returning fugitive slaves). Lincoln accepts Chase's resignation as secretary of the treasury on June 30 and names William P. Fessenden as his replacement.

Sherman turns southern flank of the Confederate position at Kennesaw Mountain on July 2, forcing Johnston to retreat to the Chattahoochee River. Congress passes Wade-Davis reconstruction bill, July 2. Lincoln pocket-vetoes the bill on July 4 and recommits himself to the "Ten Percent Plan" for reconstruction he first put forward in December 1863. The same day, Lincoln signs bill abolishing the $300 commutation fee paid by drafted men to avoid military service (the legislation allows the fee to be paid by conscientious objectors, and continues to permit the hiring of substitutes). Early crosses the Potomac in western Maryland with 14,000 men, July 5–6, and moves toward Washington. Sherman sends troops across the Chattahoochee upriver from Johnston's defensive position, July 8. Johnston abandons the western bank of the Chattahoochee, July 9, and falls back to Peachtree Creek on the north side of Atlanta. Early defeats Major General Lew Wallace at the battle of Monocacy, July 9. As reinforcements from the Army of the Potomac arrive by water in Washington, Early's troops skirmish with Union defenders at Fort Stevens on the northern outskirts of Washington, July 11–12. Early withdraws from the capital and retreats across the Potomac on July 14. Union force of 14,000 men led by Major General Andrew J. Smith defeats 9,500 Confederates under the command of Lieutenant General Stephen D. Lee and Forrest at Tupelo, Mississippi, July 14–15. (Fighting at Brice's Crossroads and Tupelo helps prevent Forrest from raiding the Nashville–Chattanooga railroad that supplies Sherman's army in Georgia.) Davis removes Johnston from command of the Army of Tennessee on July 17 and replaces him with Lieutenant General John B. Hood. (From May 4 to July 17 Sherman's troops lose about 22,000 men killed, wounded, or missing, and Johnston's about 14,000.) Jefferson Davis meets in Richmond with two unofficial Union envoys on July 17 and tells them that the Confederacy will only negotiate peace once its independence is recognized. Lincoln issues call for 500,000 volunteers on July 18, with unfulfilled quotas to be met by a draft held on September 5. The same day, Lincoln writes a safe-conduct for Confederate agents in Canada in which he states his willingness to negotiate peace on the basis of reunion and emancipation. Hood unsuccessfully attacks Sherman's forces south of Peachtree Creek on July 20. Confederate agents in Canada release letter to the press on July 21 denouncing Lincoln's peace terms. Hood orders assault on Union forces east of Atlanta, July 22, that is repulsed with the loss of 5,500 Confederate and 3,700 Union soldiers killed, wounded, or missing. Union forces are defeated at Kernstown in the Shenandoah Valley, July 24. Hood attacks Union positions west of Atlanta at Ezra Church on July 28 and is again repulsed. Sherman entrenches his army to the east, north, and west of Atlanta and begins shelling Hood's positions. Grant sends Union troops across the James River at Deep Bottom, July 27–29, to draw Confederate reserves away from Petersburg by threatening attack on Richmond from the southeast. Union engineers explode mine beneath strongpoint at Petersburg on July 30, creating breach in Confederate line that Union troops are unable to exploit. Battle of the Crater costs the Union 3,800 men killed, wounded, or missing, including about 1,300 men from the U.S. Colored Troops, while Confederate losses total about 1,500. Cavalry from Early's command raid Chambersburg, Pennsylvania, on July 30 and demand $100,000 in gold as compensation for destruction of property in the Shenandoah Valley carried out on Hunter's orders. They then burn much of the town when its residents fail to pay.

In North Carolina, Governor Zebulon B. Vance, a critic of the Davis administration who supports continued fighting for Confederate independence, wins reelection on August 4, defeating peace candidate William W. Holden, 57,873–14,432. Union squadron led by Rear Admiral David G. Farragut forces passage between Forts Morgan and Gaines and defeats Confederate flotilla in Mobile Bay, August 5, closing off the main Confederate port on the Gulf of Mexico. Grant appoints Sheridan to command Union forces in the Shenandoah Valley, August 7. Second Union offensive at Deep Bottom, August 14–20, draws Confederate reserves away from Petersburg and allows Union forces to cut the Weldon Railroad at Globe Tavern, August 18–21. Forrest raids Memphis on August 21. Lincoln writes private memorandum on August 23 acknowledging that he will probably not win reelection. Union attempt to destroy the Weldon Railroad below Globe Tavern is defeated at Reams Station on August 25. The same day, Sherman begins moving his army south of Atlanta in order to cut the railroad line to Macon. Democratic national convention in Chicago adopts platform calling for an immediate armistice, August 30, and nominates Major General George B. McClellan for president, August 31. Sherman's forces cut the Atlanta–Macon railroad, August 31, and repulse a Confederate counterattack at Jonesboro, August 31–September 1.

Hood abandons Atlanta on September 1 and retreats to Lovejoy's Station twenty miles south of the city. Union troops enter Atlanta September 2. (From July 18 to September 2 Sherman's troops lose about 15,000 men killed, wounded, or missing, and Hood's about 17,000.) Confederate cavalry raider Brigadier General John Hunt Morgan is killed by Union troops at Greeneville, Tennessee, September 4. Unionist voters approve the new Louisiana state constitution abolishing slavery, 6,836–1,566, on September 5. Sherman orders the evacuation of the remaining civilian population of Atlanta, September 7, causing outrage in the Confederacy. McClellan accepts Democratic nomination, September 8, but repudiates platform plank calling for immediate armistice. Confederate Major General Sterling Price invades southeastern Missouri on September 19 with 12,000 men and advances toward St. Louis. Sheridan defeats Early at Winchester, September 19, and Fisher's Hill, September 22. Union troops seize livestock and burn barns, mills, and warehouses in the Shenandoah Valley, a major source of food and fodder for the Confederate armies. Frémont announces his withdrawal from the presidential contest on September 22. Lincoln replaces conservative Montgomery Blair as postmaster general with William Dennison as conciliatory gesture to Radical Republicans, September 23. Forrest raids Union outposts and railroads in northern Alabama and Middle Tennessee, September 24–October 6, but fails to reach the Nashville–Chattanooga rail line. Price unsuccessfully attacks Union outpost at Pilot Knob, Missouri, September 27. The same day, Confederate guerrillas led by William (Bloody Bill) Anderson kill and mutilate 146 Union soldiers, some of them unarmed, at Centralia, Missouri. Hood crosses Chattahoochee River southwest of Atlanta, September 28–29, and advances toward Atlanta–Chattanooga railroad in attempt to cut Sherman's supply line and force him to retreat from Georgia. In the battle of New Market Heights,

September 29–30, Union troops attacking north of the James River capture Fort Harrison but are unable to break through the inner Richmond defenses. At Peebles Farm, September 30–October 2, Union forces extend their trench line south of Petersburg closer to the Boydton Plank Road, a major Confederate supply route into the city.

Price occupies Union, Missouri, forty miles from St. Louis, October 1–3, then abandons plans to take the city and turns westward. Hood destroys several miles of track along the Chattanooga–Atlanta railroad, October 2–4, but is repulsed by the Union garrison at Allatoona Pass, October 5, as Sherman pursues him with most of his army. In battle of the Darbytown Road, October 7, Union troops repulse Lee's attempt to regain the ground lost outside Richmond in late September. U.S.S. *Wachusett* captures Confederate commerce raider *Florida* in port of Salvador, Brazil, October 7. Chief Justice of the U.S. Supreme Court Roger B. Taney, the author of the *Dred Scott* decision, dies October 12. Maryland voters approve constitution abolishing slavery, 30,174–29,799, October 12–13. Union assault on new Confederate defensive line near the Darbytown Road is repulsed on October 13. Hood continues offensive against the Chattanooga–Atlanta railroad, capturing Dalton, Georgia, on October 13 and destroying more track before moving his army west toward northern Alabama. Forrest begins raid into West Tennessee, October 16. Early mounts a successful surprise attack with 21,000 men on Sheridan's army of 32,000 at Cedar Creek on October 19. Sheridan rides to the battlefield from Winchester, rallies his troops, and directs counterattack that routs Early's forces and gives the Union control of the northern Shenandoah Valley. Confederate commerce raider *Shenandoah*, purchased as merchant ship in Great Britain, is commissioned off Madeira in the North Atlantic, October 19. Band of Confederate raiders rob three banks in St. Albans, Vermont, of $200,000 on October 19 before escaping back into Canada. Sherman halts his pursuit of Hood at Gaylesville, Alabama, on October 21. Price is defeated by Union forces at Westport, Missouri, October 23, and Mine Creek, Kansas, October 25. Confederate guerrilla leader "Bloody Bill" Anderson is killed by Union cavalry near Albany, Missouri, October 27. Union offensives east of Richmond at the Darbytown Road and Fair

Oaks and southwest of Petersburg at Hatcher's Run fail to gain ground, October 27–28. Sherman leaves Gaylesville, October 28, and returns to Georgia. Hood reaches Tuscumbia, Alabama, October 31, and begins gathering supplies for invasion of Middle Tennessee. Union forces retake Plymouth, North Carolina, October 31.

Sherman sends 25,000 troops north to help Major General George H. Thomas defend Tennessee against Hood's anticipated invasion. Price escapes into Indian Territory, November 7. In message to the Confederate Congress on November 7, Jefferson Davis suggests that arming slaves may become necessary if the Confederacy is to survive. Lincoln is reelected on November 8, winning 55 percent of popular vote and 212 of 233 electoral votes. Republicans also gain forty-three seats in the House of Representatives and defeat the reelection bid of New York governor Horatio Seymour, a leading anti-administration Democrat. Forrest returns from West Tennessee raid and joins Hood's army at Florence, Alabama, on November 14. Sherman leaves Atlanta on November 16 after destroying railroads, factories, and part of the city, and with army of 60,000 men begins march across Georgia that advances along front 50–60 miles wide. Hood leaves Florence, Alabama, with 38,000 men on November 21 and begins invasion of Tennessee. Sherman's troops capture Milledgeville, the Georgia state capital, on November 23. U.S. attorney general Edward Bates resigns on November 24 and is replaced by James Speed. After several months of escalating violence between whites and Indians in Colorado and western Kansas, Union Colonel John M. Chivington leads Colorado militia in attack on Indian village at Sand Creek in eastern Colorado on November 29, in which more than 150 Southern Cheyenne and Arapaho men, women, and children are killed and mutilated. Hood outflanks Union position at Columbia, Tennessee, on November 29, but fails to prevent Major General John M. Schofield from retreating past his army at Spring Hill and reaching Franklin. On November 30 Hood orders series of frontal assaults on the Union lines at Franklin that cost the Confederates 6,200 men killed, wounded, or missing, and the Union 2,300. Schofield withdraws after the battle and joins Thomas at Nashville.

Hood reaches vicinity of Nashville on December 2 and entrenches south of the city. In his annual message to Congress, December 6, Lincoln urges the House to promptly pass the Thirteenth Amendment. The same day, he nominates, and the Senate confirms, Salmon P. Chase as chief justice of the Supreme Court. Sherman reaches outskirts of Savannah, Georgia, on December 10 and captures Fort McAllister on December 13, opening supply line to naval vessels offshore. In battle of Nashville, December 15–16, Union force of 55,000 men under Thomas defeats Hood's army and forces it to retreat into northern Mississippi. Confederate losses in the fighting are about 6,000 men killed, wounded, or missing, while Union losses total about 3,000. Confederate troops evacuate Savannah, December 20, and Union forces occupy the city the next day. Expedition led by Major General Benjamin F. Butler and Rear Admiral David D. Porter unsuccessfully attacks Fort Fisher, North Carolina, December 24–25. (The fort commands the entrance to Wilmington, the last remaining Confederate deep-water port on the Atlantic coast.)

1865 At Grant's request, Lincoln relieves Butler on January 8. Grant names Brigadier General Alfred H. Terry as army commander of renewed attack on Fort Fisher. State convention in Missouri votes 60–4 in favor of the immediate abolition of slavery, January 11. Tennessee convention approves constitutional amendment abolishing slavery, January 13. Second Union expedition captures Fort Fisher, January 13–15. After consulting with Secretary of War Stanton, Sherman issues Special Field Orders No. 15 on January 16, reserving coastal strip thirty miles wide from Charleston, South Carolina, to the St. John's River in Florida for the settlement of freed people. Confederate Congress passes bill on January 23 creating position of general-in-chief of the Confederate armies. U.S. House of Representatives approves the Thirteenth Amendment, 119–56, on January 31. (Although Delaware, Kentucky, New Jersey, and Mississippi will vote against ratification, the Thirteenth Amendment is approved by twenty-seven states, included eight former members of the Confederacy, by December 6, 1865, and on December 18 Secretary of State Seward will declare its ratification complete.)

On February 1 Boston lawyer John S. Rock becomes the first black man admitted to the bar before the U.S. Supreme Court. Sherman leaves Savannah and begins advance into South Carolina, February 1, inflicting greater destruction on private homes and property than in Georgia. Lincoln and Seward hold unsuccessful negotiations with Confederate peace commissioners Alexander H. Stephens, Robert M. T. Hunter, and John A. Campbell on the *River Queen* in Hampton Roads, February 3. Renewed Union offensive at Hatcher's Run southwest of Petersburg, February 5–7, forces Lee to further extend his already overstretched lines. James A. Seddon resigns as Confederate secretary of war on February 6 and is replaced by John C. Breckinridge. The same day, Davis appoints Lee as general-in-chief (Lee remains commander of the Army of Northern Virginia). Sherman's army enters Columbia, South Carolina, February 17. On the night of February 17 fire destroys much of the city while Union soldiers engage in widespread looting. Confederates evacuate Charleston on February 18 (among the Union troops who occupy the city are former slaves from the region now serving in the 21st U.S. Colored Infantry). On February 20 the Confederate House of Representatives approves bill, 40–37, authorizing the Confederate army to enlist slaves with the permission of their masters, but without providing for their emancipation. Tennessee unionists approve, 25,293–48, amendment to the state constitution abolishing slavery, February 22. The same day, Union troops capture Wilmington. Davis reluctantly restores Joseph E. Johnston to command of the Army of Tennessee, which is being sent to the Carolinas to oppose Sherman, February 24.

Sheridan's cavalry routs the remnants of Early's command at Waynesboro, Virginia, March 2, ending organized fighting in the Shenandoah Valley. On March 3 Lincoln signs bill creating the Bureau of Refugees, Freedmen, and Abandoned Lands, as well as legislation emancipating enslaved family members of black soldiers and giving black troops full back pay. Lincoln is inaugurated for his second term on March 4. Hugh McCulloch replaces William P. Fessenden as U.S. secretary of the treasury. Confederate Senate approves bill for arming slaves, 9–8, March 8. Sherman occupies Fayetteville, North Carolina, on March 11. Johnston attacks the left wing of Sherman's army near Bentonville on March 19 with force of 21,000 men and is repulsed. After withdrawing behind entrenchments on March 20, Johnston retreats to Smithfield on the night of March 21. Sherman enters Goldsboro on March 23 and joins up with Union forces under Schofield that had advanced from the coast. Lee launches unsuccessful assault on Fort Stedman, Union strongpoint east of Petersburg, on March 25. Major General Edward R. S. Canby begins siege of Spanish Fort, Confederate strongpoint on the eastern side of Mobile Bay, March 27. Grant orders Sheridan to lead major offensive west of Petersburg, resulting in heavy fighting at Dinwiddie Court House and White Oak Road on March 31.

Sheridan overruns the Confederate positions at Five Forks west of Petersburg on April 1, capturing 2,500 prisoners. Grant orders general assault on the Petersburg defenses at dawn on April 2. Attack breaks Confederate lines and forces Lee to evacuate Petersburg and Richmond on the night of April 2. (Fighting at Petersburg and Richmond costs the Union about 42,000 men killed, wounded, or missing from June 1864 to April 1865, and the Confederates about 28,000.) Davis and his cabinet flee by train to Danville, Virginia, as fires set by retreating Confederate troops cause extensive destruction in the city. Union cavalry captures Selma, Alabama, on April 2. Lincoln tours Richmond on April 4. Lee's army retreats westward to Amelia Court House on April 4. Unable to secure needed supplies and finding his planned route to North Carolina blocked by Union troops, Lee continues retreating to the west. Pursuing Union forces capture more than 6,000 prisoners at Sailer's Creek, Virginia, on April 6. After his retreat is blocked by Union troops at Appomattox Court House, Lee surrenders to Grant on April 9. The same day, Union troops storm Fort Blakely near Mobile. Sherman resumes offensive in North Carolina, April 10. Union cavalry captures Montgomery, Alabama, on April 12, the same day that Confederate forces abandon Mobile. Sherman occupies Raleigh on April 13. While watching a performance of *Our American Cousin* at Ford's Theatre in Washington on April 14, Lincoln is shot by actor John Wilkes Booth, who flees the theater. At the same time, Secretary of State Seward is seriously wounded by Booth's co-conspirator Lewis Powell. Lincoln dies on the morning of April 15 and Andrew Johnson is sworn in as president. Sherman and Johnston meet near Durham Station, North Carolina, on April 18 and sign agreement providing military and political terms for the surrender of the remaining Confederate armies. Lincoln funeral train leaves Washington on April 21 and is viewed by millions as it makes its way to Illinois. The same day, Johnson and the cabinet reject the Sherman-Johnston agreement. Johnston surrenders Confederate forces in the Carolinas, Georgia, and Florida on April 26 on terms similar to those given to Lee. The same day, Booth is killed by Union troops near Port Royal, Virginia. (Powell and three other convicted conspirators are hanged on July 7.) Steamship *Sultana* explodes and burns in the Mississippi near Memphis, April 27, killing 1,600–1,800 people, mostly released Union prisoners of war.

Lincoln is buried in Springfield, Illinois, on May 4. The same day, Lieutenant General Richard Taylor surrenders Confederate forces in Alabama, Mississippi, and eastern Louisiana to Major General Edward R. S. Canby on May 4. Union cavalry capture Jefferson Davis near Irwinville, Georgia, on May 10 and take him as a prisoner to Fort Monroe, Virginia. The same day, Confederate guerrilla leader William Quantrill is fatally wounded by Union troops near Bloomfield, Kentucky. In the Grand Review of the Union Armies, May 23–24, about 150,000 men from the Army of the Potomac and Sherman's armies march through Washington. Surrender terms for the Confederate Trans-Mississippi department are negotiated in New Orleans on May 26. Unaware of the Confederate surrenders, the commerce raider *Shenandoah* begins capturing and burning American whaling ships in the Sea of Okhotsk on May 29. (After making its final capture in the Bering Sea on June 28, the *Shenandoah* ceases hostilities and sails into Liverpool, England, on November 7.) Johnson issues proclamation on amnesty and pardon on May 29 and begins establishing new state governments in the South on terms Radical Republicans consider too lenient.

Confederate General Edmund Kirby Smith signs Trans-Mississippi surrender agreement on June 2. Major General Gordon Granger arrives in Galveston and issues General Orders No. 3 on June 19, proclaiming the end of slavery in Texas.

The official records of the U.S. War Department recorded the deaths of 360,000 Union soldiers during the war, including 110,000 in battle or from battle wounds and 250,000 from disease and other non-battle causes. Confederate deaths were estimated in the late nineteenth century at 258,000, including 94,000 battle deaths and 164,000 non-battle deaths. Many records of Confederate battle losses are missing or incomplete, and the assumption underlying the estimate for Confederate non-battle deaths—that Confederate soldiers died from disease at the same rate as Union soldiers—has been challenged. In the late twentieth century, total civilian deaths in the war, primarily from disease and malnutrition, were estimated at 50,000. A new study of census records published in 2011 by the demographic historian J. David Hacker estimated that the war caused the death of 752,000 American men from 1861 to 1870.

Biographical Notes

Charles Francis Adams (August 18, 1807–November 21, 1886) Born in Boston, Massachusetts, the son of John Quincy Adams and Louisa Johnson Adams and grandson of John and Abigail Adams. Graduated from Harvard in 1825. Admitted to the bar in 1829. Married Abigail Brown Brooks the same year. Served as a Whig in the Massachusetts house of representatives, 1841–43, and in the state senate, 1844–45. Vice-presidential candidate of the Free Soil Party in 1848. Edited *The Works of John Adams* (1850–56). Served in Congress as a Republican, 1859–61. As U.S. minister to Great Britain, 1861–68, helped maintain British neutrality in the Civil War. Served as the U.S. representative on the international arbitration tribunal that settled American claims against Great Britain for losses caused by Confederate commerce raiders built in British shipyards, 1871–72. Edited the *Memoirs of John Quincy Adams* (1874–77). Died in Boston.

Charles Francis Adams Jr. (May 27, 1835–March 20, 1915) Born in Boston, Massachusetts, brother of Henry Adams, son of lawyer Charles Francis Adams and Abigail Brooks Adams, grandson of John Quincy Adams, great-grandson of John Adams. Graduated Harvard College, 1856. Read law in Boston and passed bar, 1858. Commissioned first lieutenant, 1st Massachusetts Cavalry, December 1861. Served at Hilton Head, South Carolina, 1862, and with the Army of the Potomac, 1862–63, including Antietam and Gettysburg campaigns; promoted to captain, October 1862. Commanded detached company on guard service at Army of the Potomac headquarters, spring 1864. Commissioned as lieutenant colonel of the 5th Massachusetts Cavalry, a black regiment, in July 1864, and as its colonel, February 1865; the regiment guarded Confederate prisoners at Point Lookout, Maryland, until March 1865, when it was sent to Virginia. Left army and married Mary Ogden in November 1865. Served on Massachusetts Railroad Commission, 1869–79. President of Union Pacific Railroad, 1884–90. Published series of historical works, including *Three Episodes of Massachusetts History* (1892) and biographies of Richard Henry Dana (1890) and Charles Francis Adams (1900). Died in Washington, D.C.

Henry Adams (February 16, 1838–March 27, 1918) Born in Boston, Massachusetts. Brother of Charles Francis Adams Jr., son of lawyer Charles Francis Adams and Abigail Brooks Adams, grandson of John Quincy Adams, great-grandson of John Adams. Graduated Harvard

1858; studied law in Berlin and Dresden until 1860. Served as secretary to father while Charles Francis Adams served in Congress, 1860–61, and as U.S. minister to Great Britain, 1861–68. Reported British reaction to the American Civil War as anonymous London correspondent of *The New York Times*, 1861–62. Returned to Washington, D.C., in 1868 to work as journalist. Appointed assistant professor of history at Harvard (1870–77); assumed editorship of *North American Review* (1870–76). Married Marion Hooper in 1872. Published *The Life of Albert Gallatin* (1879), biography; *Democracy* (1880), a novel that appeared anonymously; *John Randolph* (1882), a biography; *Esther* (1884), a novel that appeared pseudonymously; *History of the United States during the Administrations of Thomas Jefferson and James Madison* (1889–91); *Mont-Saint-Michel and Chartres: A Study of Thirteenth-Century Unity* (1904); *The Education of Henry Adams* (1907). Died in Washington.

Lois Bryan Adams (October 14, 1817–June 28, 1870) Born in Whitestown, New York, the daughter of a carpenter. Family moved in 1823 to Michigan Territory and settled near Ypsilanti, then moved to the Constantine area in 1835. Attended White Pigeon Academy, branch of the University of Michigan, in 1839. Married James R. Adams, a newspaper editor, in 1841. Moved to Kentucky after her husband died of consumption in 1848, and taught school for three years before returning to Michigan in 1851. Began writing for the monthly (later weekly) *Michigan Farmer* and for the *Detroit Advertiser and Tribune*. Moved to Detroit in 1853 to work on the *Michigan Farmer*, and became its copublisher in 1854 and household editor in 1856. Sold her interest in the publication in 1861. Published *Sybelle and Other Poems* (1862). Moved to Washington, D.C., in 1863 to take post as clerk in the recently formed Department of Agriculture and became assistant to the director of the agricultural museum. Volunteered during the war for the Michigan Soldiers' Relief Association while contributing columns to the *Detroit Advertiser and Tribune*. Continued work at the Department of Agriculture after the war. Died in Washington, D.C.

Henry Robinson Berkeley (March 27, 1840–January 16, 1918) Born in Hanover County, Virginia, the son of a farmer. Studied at the Hanover Academy, 1859–61. Enlisted in the Hanover artillery company in May 1861. Sent home in October 1861 to recover from typhoid fever. Returned to duty in March 1862. Saw action in the siege of Yorktown and at Glendale. Joined Kirkpatrick's Battery in Nelson's Battalion after the Hanover company disbanded in October 1862. Fought at Fredericksburg, Gettysburg, the Wilderness, Spotsylvania, Cold Harbor, Monocacy, Kernstown, Winchester, Fisher's Hill, and Cedar

Creek. Captured at Waynesboro, Virginia, March 2, 1865. Held as prisoner of war at Fort Delaware until June 20, 1865, when he was released after taking oath of allegiance. Became tutor and schoolteacher in Loudoun County, Virginia. Moved to Orange County, Virginia, in 1882. Married his cousin Anna Louisa Berkeley in 1883. Bought farm near Orange Court House in 1886 and operated school there until 1900. Retired from teaching in 1904. Died in Orange County, Virginia.

Edgeworth Bird (July 21, 1825–January 11, 1867) Born William Edgeworth Bird in Hancock County, Georgia, the son of a planter. Graduated from Georgetown College in 1844. Married Sarah Baxter in 1848. Lived on Granite Farm, a cotton plantation four miles east of Sparta, Georgia. Ran unsuccessfully as secessionist for the Georgia convention held in January 1861. Became captain of Company E, 15th Georgia Infantry, in the summer of 1861. Seriously wounded at Second Manassas on August 30, 1862. Returned to duty in March 1863 as quartermaster of Benning's Brigade in Hood's (later Field's) Division. Served at Gettysburg, Chickamauga, Knoxville, the Wilderness, Cold Harbor, and in the defense of Richmond. Appointed in September 1864 to board handling claims made for the loss of slaves used as laborers by the Confederate army. Returned to Granite Farm in early 1865. Died in Hancock County, Georgia.

John Wilkes Booth (May 10, 1838–April 26, 1865) Born on a farm near Bel Air, Maryland, the son of well-known actor Junius Booth. Raised on farm and in Baltimore. Educated at Milton Academy in Cockeysville and St. Timothy's Hall in Catonsville. Began acting career in Baltimore in 1855. Became a member of the nativist Know-Nothing movement. Continued acting in Philadelphia and Richmond. A strong supporter of slavery, Booth joined Virginia militia company that helped guard the execution of John Brown at Charles Town in December 1859. Began touring the country as a leading man in 1860. Ended professional acting career in May 1864, although he would later appear in benefit performance of *Julius Caesar* with his brothers Edwin and Junius. Began enlisting conspirators in plot to abduct President Lincoln and exchange him for Confederate prisoners of war. Met with Confederate agents in Montreal in October 1864 and may have taken money from them. (Booth told his sister Asia in November 1864 that he smuggled quinine into the Confederacy.) Decided after the fall of Richmond to assassinate Lincoln, Secretary of State Seward, and Vice President Johnson. Shot Lincoln in Washington on April 14 and escaped through Maryland into Virginia, where he was killed by Union soldiers at the Garrett farm near Port Royal on April 26, 1865.

Thomas Bramlette (January 3, 1817–January 12, 1875) Born in Cumberland County, Kentucky. Studied law and was admitted to the Kentucky bar in 1837. Married Sallie Travis in 1837. Elected as Whig to the state house of representatives and served one term, 1841–42. Appointed commonwealth's attorney for the eighth district, 1849–51. Moved to Adair County in 1852. Elected judge for the sixth district and served 1856–61. At the outbreak of the war Bramlette opposed both secession and the neutrality policy of Governor Beriah Magoffin. Raised and led the 3rd Kentucky Infantry, August 1861–July 1862. Appointed as U.S. district attorney for Kentucky by Lincoln in February 1863. Elected governor as a Union Democrat in August 1863 and served from September 1863 until September 1867. Opposed enlistment of black troops and suspension of the writ of habeas corpus in Kentucky. Practiced law in Louisville after leaving office. Married Mary Adams in 1874 after the death of his first wife. Died in Louisville.

Charles Harvey Brewster (October 10, 1833–October 7, 1893) Born in Northampton, Massachusetts. Educated in Northampton public schools. Worked as a store clerk. Voted for Lincoln in the 1860 election. Enlisted in 10th Massachusetts Infantry in April 1861 and commissioned as second lieutenant in December 1861. Served at Camp Brightwood outside Washington, D.C., until April 1862, when his regiment was sent to the Peninsula. Saw action in the siege of Yorktown, Fair Oaks, Oak Grove, and Malvern Hill. Promoted to first lieutenant in September 1862 and made regimental adjutant in December 1862. Saw action at Chancellorsville, Rappahannock Station, the Wilderness, Spotsylvania, North Anna, and Cold Harbor. Mustered out in June 1864 when his regiment completed its three-year term of service. Commissioned as captain and served as recruiter of black troops in Norfolk, Virginia, from July to November 1864, when he resigned from the army and returned to Northampton. Married Anna Williams in 1868. Opened sash, door, and paint store, then began successful florist business. Died onboard ship in New York harbor.

Sallie Brock (March 18, 1831–March 22, 1911) Born Sarah Ann Brock in Madison County, Virginia, the daughter of a hotel owner. Moved with her family to Richmond in 1858. Began working as a tutor in King and Queen County, Virginia, in 1860, but returned to Richmond in 1861 and remained there for the duration of the war. Moved to New York City in 1865. Published *Richmond During the War: Four Years of Personal Observations* (1867). Edited *The Southern Amaranth* (1869), a collection of poetry about the Confederacy and the war, and published a novel, *Kenneth, My King* (1873). Married Richard F. Putnam in 1882. Died in Brooklyn.

Clarissa Burdett A slave from Garrard County, Kentucky, who escaped to Camp Nelson in March 1865 and sought help in freeing her four children. Her husband, Elijah Burdett, was a soldier in the 12th U.S. Colored Heavy Artillery.

C. Chauncey Burr (1815–May 1, 1883) Born Charles Chauncey Burr in Maine. Studied law and passed bar. Edited quarterly magazine *The Nineteenth Century* in Philadelphia, 1848–52, which included reform and antislavery material. Helped care for Edgar Allan Poe when Poe collapsed in Philadelphia in 1849, and wrote article defending his reputation in 1852. Married Celia Kellum in 1851. Edited and published newspaper *Daily National Democrat* in New York, 1851–54. Managed lecture tours of Lola Montez in the United States, Ireland, and Great Britain, 1857–60 (the claim that he ghosted her lectures and autobiography is disputed). Edited *The Old Guard*, 1862–69, monthly magazine published in New York that defended slavery and secession and supported the Peace Democrats. Published *The History of the Union and the Constitution* (1862) and *Notes on the Constitution of the United States* (1864). Remained active in Democratic politics and journalism after the war. Died in West Hoboken, New Jersey.

Benjamin F. Butler (November 5, 1818–January 11, 1893) Born in Deerfield, New Hampshire, the son of a merchant. Graduated from Waterville (now Colby) College in 1838. Admitted to the bar in 1840 and began practicing law in Lowell, Massachusetts. Married Sarah Hildreth in 1844. Served as a Democrat in the Massachusetts house of representatives, 1853, and in the Massachusetts senate, 1859. Commissioned as brigadier general of Massachusetts militia in April 1861 and as major general of U.S. volunteers in May 1861. Led occupation of Baltimore in May 1861 before becoming commander at Fort Monroe, Virginia. Commanded troops that captured Fort Hatteras, North Carolina, in August 1861. Military governor of New Orleans, May–December 1862. Commanded the Army of the James in Virginia, 1864. Relieved of command by Ulysses S. Grant after his failed assault on Fort Fisher, North Carolina, in December 1864. Served in Congress as a Republican, 1867–75 and 1877–79, and was one of the House managers at the impeachment trial of Andrew Johnson in 1868. Elected governor of Massachusetts as a Democrat and served one-year term in 1883. Presidential candidate of the Greenback and Anti-Monopolist parties in 1884. Died in Washington, D.C.

J.F.J. Caldwell (September 19, 1837–February 3, 1925) Born in Newberry, South Carolina, the son of a lawyer, and later named James Fitz James Caldwell. Graduated from South Carolina College in 1857. Studied law in Charleston and was admitted to bar. Spent two years traveling in Europe before returning to South Carolina in early 1861. Enlisted as private in 3rd South Carolina Infantry and served until after the First Manassas campaign, when he was discharged because of illness. Joined Company B, 1st South Carolina Infantry, in April 1862 and became aide to its commander, Colonel Daniel H. Hamilton. Saw action at Mechanicsville, Gaines's Mill, Second Manassas, Antietam, and Fredericksburg. Served as brigade ordnance officer before returning to duty as lieutenant in 1st South Carolina in early 1863. Fought at Chancellorsville and was wounded at Gettysburg on July 1, 1863. Saw action at the Wilderness, Spotsylvania, North Anna, Cold Harbor, the first battle of Weldon Railroad, First Deep Bottom, and Second Deep Bottom, where he was wounded on August 16, 1864. Returned to duty in late November 1864 and served as brigade staff officer. Fought at White Oak Road and Sutherland's Station before surrendering at Appomattox. Published *The History of a Brigade of South Carolinians, known first as "Gregg's," and subsequently as "McGowan's Brigade"* (1866). Practiced law in Newberry and served as bank director and as trustee of the University of South Carolina. Married Rebecca Connor in 1875. Published *The Stranger* (1907), novel set in South Carolina during Reconstruction. Died in Newberry.

George E. Chamberlin (June 30, 1838–August 22, 1864) Born in Lyndon, Vermont. Graduated from Dartmouth College in 1860, studied law in St. Louis, and graduated from Harvard Law School in 1862. Commissioned as major in the 11th Vermont Infantry in August 1862. Served in fortifications defending Washington, D.C. Regiment renamed the 1st Vermont Heavy Artillery in December 1862. Married Adelia Gardiner in October 1863. After his regiment was sent to fight as infantry with the Army of the Potomac, saw action at Spotsylvania, Cold Harbor, and in the first battle of Weldon Railroad. Promoted to lieutenant colonel. Returned to Washington, D.C., in July when regiment was sent to help defend the capital against raid led by Lieutenant General Jubal A. Early. Wounded in skirmish at Charles Town, West Virginia, on August 21, 1864, and died at Sandy Hook, Maryland, the following day.

Salmon P. Chase (January 13, 1808–May 7, 1873) Born in Cornish, New Hampshire, the son of a farmer. After the death of his father in 1817, he was raised in Worthington, Ohio, by his uncle, Philander Chase, an Episcopal bishop. Graduated from Dartmouth College in 1826. Read law in Washington with Attorney General William Wirt and was admitted to the bar in 1829. Established law practice in Cincinnati, Ohio, in 1830. Married Catherine Jane Garniss, 1834; after her death, Eliza Ann Smith, 1839; and after Smith's death, Sarah Bella Dunlop Ludlow, 1846. Began defending fugitive slaves and those who aided them in 1837. Became a leader in the antislavery Liberty Party and campaigned for the Free Soil ticket in 1848. Served in the U.S. Senate as a Free Soil Democrat, 1849–55. Republican governor of Ohio, 1856–60. Candidate for the Republican presidential nomination in 1860. Won election to the U.S. Senate in 1860, but resigned in March 1861 to become secretary of the treasury. Helped found national banking system and successfully financed Union war effort. Resigned June 29, 1864, after making unsuccessful attempt to challenge Lincoln for the Republican nomination. Appointed chief justice of the U.S. Supreme Court on December 6, 1864, and served until his death. Upheld Radical Reconstruction measures and presided over the 1868 Senate impeachment trial of President Andrew Johnson. Died in New York City.

Thomas Morris Chester (May 11, 1834–September 30, 1892) Born in Harrisburg, Pennsylvania, the son of a restaurant owner. Parents were abolitionists active in the local black community. Attended Allegheny Institute, 1850–52. Became advocate for African American emigration to Liberia. Attended Alexander High School in Monrovia, Liberia, 1853–54. Returned to United States and attended Thetford Academy in Vermont, 1854–56. Visited Liberia 1856–58, 1858–59, and 1860–62, teaching school in Robertsport and Monrovia and publishing newspaper *Star of Liberia*. Recruited in Pennsylvania in 1863 for the 54th and 55th Massachusetts regiments. Made lecture tour in Britain in support of the Union cause, 1863–64. Began reporting on U.S. Colored Troops serving with the Army of the James for the *Philadelphia Press* in August 1864, becoming the first black war correspondent for a major American daily newspaper. Covered the fall of Richmond and Lincoln's visit to the city. Returned to Harrisburg in the summer of 1865 and joined the Equal Rights League, which campaigned against racial discrimination in the North. Made lecture tour of Britain and Europe, 1866–67, and visited Russia. Studied law in London, 1867–70, and was called to the English bar. Returned to the United States and went to Louisiana in 1871. Wounded during altercation between Republican factions in New Orleans, January 1, 1872. Admitted to the Louisiana bar in 1873. Served as brigadier general of Louisiana militia, 1873–76, and superintendent of public education for a district outside New Orleans, 1875–76. Married Florence Johnson. Practiced law in Louisiana and Pennsylvania. Settled in New Orleans in 1888. Died in Harrisburg.

Achilles V. Clark (March 13, 1842–July 29, 1874) Born in Henry County, Tennessee. College student and slaveowner at the start of the war. Enlisted in the Confederate 20th Tennessee Cavalry in early 1864. Promoted to sergeant and then lieutenant. Returned to Henry

County after the war and settled in Paris. Married Mary Elizabeth Wilson in 1866. Died in Nashville.

Clement C. Clay (December 13, 1816–January 3, 1882) Born in Huntsville, Alabama, the son of a lawyer who later served as governor of Alabama and as a U.S. senator. Graduated from the University of Alabama, 1834. Received law degree from the University of Virginia, 1839. Began legal practice in Huntsville in 1840. Married Virginia Tunstall in 1843. Served in state legislature, 1842, 1844, and 1845. Judge of the Madison County court, 1846–48. Served in the U.S. Senate as a Democrat, 1853–61, and in the Confederate senate, 1862–64. Confederate agent in Canada, May 1864–January 1865. Surrendered at Macon, Georgia, on May 11, 1865, after being accused of complicity in the assassination of President Lincoln. Imprisoned without trial at Fort Monroe until his release in April 1866. Returned to Alabama and practiced law in Jackson County. Died in Madison County, Alabama.

Howell Cobb (September 7, 1815–October 9, 1868) Born in Jefferson County, Georgia, the son of a wealthy cotton planter. Graduated from The University of Georgia and married Mary Ann Lamar in 1834. Admitted to the bar in 1836. Served as solicitor general of the western judicial district of Georgia, 1837–41. Elected to Congress as a Democrat and served 1843–51 and 1855–57. Supported Compromise of 1850 as Speaker of the House, 1849–51. Governor of Georgia, 1851–53. Secretary of the treasury in the Buchanan administration from March 1857 until December 1860, when he resigned and called for the immediate secession of Georgia. President of the Provisional Confederate Congress, February 1861–February 1862. Commissioned as brigadier general in February 1862. Led brigade in Seven Days' Battles and at Crampton's Gap. Promoted to major general in 1863. Commanded Georgia state troops, 1863–65. Practiced law in Macon after the war. Died in New York City.

James A. Connolly (March 8, 1838–December 15, 1914) Born in Newark, New Jersey, the son of a tanner. Moved with family around 1850 to Chesterville, Ohio. Graduated from Selby Academy in Chesterville and studied law. Admitted to the bar in 1859 and served as assistant clerk of the Ohio state senate, 1859–60. Moved to Charleston, Illinois, in 1860. Mustered into service as major of the newly formed 123rd Illinois Infantry in September 1862. Fought at Perryville. Married Mary Dunn, sister of the judge with whom he had read law, in February 1863. Fought at Milton (Vaught's Hill) and Chickamauga. Joined staff of the Third Division, Fourteenth Corps, commanded by Brigadier General Absalom Baird. Served at Chattanooga, in the

Atlanta campaign, and in Sherman's marches through Georgia and the Carolinas. Helped escort Abraham Lincoln's body to Springfield. Returned to law practice in Charleston before moving to Springfield in 1886. Served in Illinois house of representatives, 1872–76, as U.S. attorney for the Southern District of Illinois, 1876–85 and 1889–94, and as a Republican congressman, 1895–99. Died in Springfield.

Maria Lydig Daly (September 12, 1824–August 21, 1894) Born Maria Lydig in New York City, the daughter of a wealthy grain merchant and landowner. Married Judge Charles P. Daly of the New York Court of Common Pleas, the son of poor Irish immigrants, in 1856 despite opposition from many members of her family who objected to his Catholicism and family background. Supported the Woman's Central Association of Relief during the Civil War and visited sick and wounded soldiers. Died at her country home in North Haven, New York.

Charles A. Dana (August 8, 1819–October 17, 1897) Born in Hinsdale, New Hampshire, the son of a merchant. Worked as clerk in uncle's store in Buffalo, New York, 1831–39. Studied at Harvard, 1839–41. Lived at Brook Farm, utopian community in West Roxbury, Massachusetts, 1841–46. Wrote for the *Boston Daily Chronotype*, 1844–46. Married Eunice MacDaniel in 1846. Hired by Horace Greeley as city editor of the *New-York Daily Tribune* in 1847. Reported for the *Tribune* from France and Germany, 1848–49. Served as managing editor of the *Tribune*, 1849–62, and helped make it one of the most widely circulated antislavery newspapers in the country. Began working for the War Department, and was sent to Grant's headquarters in the spring of 1863 to report on his conduct to Lincoln and Secretary of War Stanton. Gained Grant's confidence and wrote reports that reassured the administration. Served as assistant secretary of war, January 1864–July 1865. Editor of the *Chicago Daily Republican*, 1865–67. Wrote campaign biography *The Life of Ulysses S. Grant* (1868) with James H. Wilson. Editor of the *New York Sun*, 1868–97. Supported Horace Greeley, the Liberal Republican candidate, against Grant in 1872 and followed independent course in politics afterward. Published *The Art of Newspaper Making* (1895). Memoir *Recollections of the Civil War* (1898), published posthumously, was based in part on interviews journalist Ida M. Tarbell conducted with Dana in 1896. Died in Glen Cove, New York.

Henry Winter Davis (August 16, 1817–December 30, 1865) Born in Annapolis, Maryland, the son of an Episcopal minister. Graduated from Kenyon College in 1837. Studied law at the University of Virginia. Began legal practice in Alexandria, Virginia, 1840. Married

Constance Gardiner in 1845. Moved to Baltimore, 1850. Elected to Congress as an American (Know-Nothing) and served 1855–61. Married Nancy Morris in 1857 after the death of his first wife. Opposed secession in Maryland. Defeated for reelection but returned to Congress as an Unconditional Unionist, 1863–65. Served on the Select Committee on Rebellious States and coauthored the Wade-Davis reconstruction bill in 1864. Defeated for reelection. Died in Baltimore.

Jefferson Davis (June 3, 1808–December 6, 1889) Born in Christian (now Todd) County, Kentucky, the son of a farmer. Moved with his family to Mississippi. Graduated from West Point in 1828 and served in the Black Hawk War. Resigned his commission in 1835 and married Sarah Knox Taylor, who died later in the year. Became a cotton planter in Warren County, Mississippi. Married Varina Howell in 1845. Elected to Congress as a Democrat and served 1845–46, then resigned to command a Mississippi volunteer regiment in Mexico, 1846–47, where he fought at Monterrey and was wounded at Buena Vista. Elected to the Senate and served from 1847 to 1851, when he resigned to run unsuccessfully for governor. Secretary of war in the cabinet of Franklin Pierce, 1853–57. Elected to the Senate and served from 1857 to January 21, 1861, when he withdrew following the secession of Mississippi. Inaugurated as provisional president of the Confederate States of America on February 18, 1861. Elected without opposition to six-year term in November 1861 and inaugurated on February 22, 1862. Captured by Union cavalry near Irwinville, Georgia, on May 10, 1865. Imprisoned at Fort Monroe, Virginia, and indicted for treason. Released on bail on May 13, 1867; the indictment was dropped in 1869 without trial. Published *The Rise and Fall of the Confederate Government* in 1881. Died in New Orleans.

John Q. A. Dennis A freed slave from Worcester County, Maryland, who was living in Boston in 1864 when he wrote to Secretary of War Stanton seeking help in freeing his three children.

Frederick Douglass (February 1818–February 20, 1895) Born Frederick Bailey in Talbot County, Maryland, the son of a slave mother and an unknown white man. Worked on farms and in Baltimore shipyards. Escaped to Philadelphia in 1838. Married Anna Murray, a free woman from Maryland, and settled in New Bedford, Massachusetts, where he took the name Douglass. Became a lecturer for the American Anti-Slavery Society, led by William Lloyd Garrison, in 1841. Published *Narrative of the Life of Frederick Douglass, An American Slave* (1845). Began publishing *North Star*, first in a series of antislavery newspapers, in Rochester, New York, in 1847. Broke with Garrison and became an ally of Gerrit Smith, who advocated an antislavery interpretation of the Constitution and participation in electoral politics. Published *My Bondage and My Freedom* (1855). Advocated emancipation and the enlistment of black soldiers at the outbreak of the Civil War. Met with Abraham Lincoln in Washington in August 1863 and August 1864, and wrote public letter supporting his reelection in September 1864. Continued his advocacy of racial equality and women's rights after the Civil War. Served as U.S. marshal for the District of Columbia, 1877–81, and as its recorder of deeds, 1881–86. Published *Life and Times of Frederick Douglass* (1881). After the death of his wife Anna, married Helen Pitts in 1884. Served as minister to Haiti, 1889–91. Died in Washington, D.C.

Samuel Francis Du Pont (September 27, 1803–June 23, 1865) Born in Bergen Point, New Jersey, the son of a former French diplomat. Moved with family to Delaware, where his uncle had founded the Du Pont gunpowder works. Appointed a midshipman in the U.S. Navy in 1815. Promoted to lieutenant, 1826. Married first cousin Sophie Madeleine du Pont in 1833. Promoted to commander, 1842. Commanded sloop *Cyane* along the Pacific coast during the Mexican War. Promoted to captain, 1855, and flag officer, September 1861. Led South Atlantic blockading squadron in capture of Port Royal, South Carolina, in November 1861. Appointed rear admiral, 1862. Failed to capture Charleston in April 1863 while leading fleet of seven ironclad monitors. Relieved of command in July 1863 at his request. Died in Philadelphia.

Catherine Edmondston (October 10, 1823–January 3, 1875) Born Catherine Ann Devereux in Halifax County, North Carolina, the daughter of a plantation owner. Married Patrick Edmondston in 1846. Lived on Looking Glass plantation in Halifax County. Published pamphlet *The Morte d'Arthur: Its Influence on the Spirit and Manners of the Nineteenth Century* (1872), in which she accused the Union army of barbarism. Died in Raleigh.

David G. Farragut (July 5, 1801–August 14, 1870) Born James Glasgow Farragut at Campbell's Station, near Knoxville, Tennessee, the son of a naval officer. After his mother's death in 1808 he was adopted by David Porter, a naval officer, and became foster brother to his son David D. Porter (later a Union rear admiral). Appointed midshipman in the U.S. Navy, 1810. Changed his name to David. Served in the War of 1812 under Porter's command on frigate *Essex* until the ship's capture off Chile in March 1814. Married Susan C. Marchant in 1823 and settled in Norfolk, Virginia. Promoted to lieutenant, 1825, and commander, 1843. After the death of his first wife, married Virginia Loyall in 1843. Assigned to blockade duty during the

U.S.-Mexican War. Promoted to captain in 1855 while serving as commander of the Mare Island navy yard in Vallejo, California. Remained loyal to the Union when Virginia seceded, and was appointed commander of the West Gulf Blockading Squadron in January 1862. Forced passage of the lower Mississippi and captured New Orleans, April 24–25, 1862. Promoted to newly created rank of rear admiral, July 1862. Commanded squadron in the Union victory at Mobile Bay, August 5, 1864. Promoted to vice admiral in 1864 and admiral in 1866. Remained on active duty until his death in Portsmouth, New Hampshire.

Charles B. Fisher (c. 1839–January 27, 1903) Born in Alexandria, Virginia. Worked as a bookbinder. Enlisted in U.S. Navy in Boston, January 1862. Served on the steam sloop U.S.S. *Kearsarge* as landsman (apprentice seaman), officers' cook, and steward. Discharged November 1864. After the war, formed and led "Butler's Zouaves," the first black militia in the District of Columbia. Died in Washington, D.C.

Wilbur Fisk (June 7, 1839–March 12, 1914) Born in Sharon, Vermont, the son of a farmer. Family moved to Lowell, Massachusetts, in 1852 to work in woolen mills, then returned to Vermont in 1854 and settled on farm in Tunbridge. Worked as hired farm laborer and taught in local schools. Enlisted in September 1861 in Company E, 2nd Vermont Infantry. Contributed regular letters under the name "Anti-Rebel" to *The Green Mountain Freeman* of Montpelier from December 11, 1861, to July 26, 1865. Saw action in the siege of Yorktown and in the Seven Days' Battles. Hospitalized with severe diarrhea in Washington, D.C., in early September 1862. Recovered in convalescent camp in Fairfax, Virginia, then went absent without leave and married Angelina Drew of Lawrence, Massachusetts, in February 1863. Returned to regiment in March 1863 and served at Chancellorsville, Gettysburg, Rappahannock Station, Mine Run, the Wilderness, Spotsylvania, North Anna, Cold Harbor, and Petersburg. Sent with regiment in July 1864 to help defend the capital against Jubal Early's Washington raid. Served in the Shenandoah Valley at Winchester, Fisher's Hill, and Cedar Creek before returning to Petersburg siege lines in December 1864. Detached for guard duty at Sixth Corps hospital at City Point, Virginia, in January 1865, and served there for remainder of the war. Rejoined family, who had moved to Geneva, Kansas, and worked on farm. Licensed as Congregational preacher in 1874, and the following year became pastor of a church in Freeborn, Minnesota, where he served until his retirement in 1909. Following the death of his first wife in 1898, married Amanda Dickerson Dickey in 1909. Died in Geneva, Kansas.

Samuel W. Fiske (July 23, 1828–May 22, 1864) Born in Shelburne, Massachusetts. Graduated from Amherst College in 1848. Taught school, studied for three years at Andover Theological Seminary, then returned to Amherst in 1853 as a tutor. Traveled in Europe and the Middle East. Published *Dunn Browne's Experiences in Foreign Parts* (1857), travel letters written to the *Springfield Republican* under a nom de plume. Became pastor of the Congregational church in Madison, Connecticut, in 1857. Married Elizabeth Foster in 1858. Became second lieutenant in the 14th Connecticut Infantry in August 1862. Signing himself Dunn Browne, wrote weekly letters to the *Springfield Republican* describing campaigns and camp life (collected in 1866 under the title *Mr. Dunn Browne's Experiences in the Army*). Served at Antietam and Fredericksburg. Promoted to captain in early 1863. Captured at Chancellorsville on May 3, 1863, was paroled in late May and exchanged in June. Served at Gettysburg. Wounded in the battle of the Wilderness on May 6, 1864, and died in Fredericksburg, Virginia.

Eugene Forbes (May 14, 1833–February 7, 1865) Born in Trenton, New Jersey. Worked as a printer. Served in the 3rd New Jersey Militia, April–August 1861. Enlisted for three years in Company B, 4th New Jersey Infantry, in fall 1861. Captured along with most of his regiment at Gaines's Mill. Held at the Libby prison and Belle Isle camp in Richmond before being exchanged in August 1862. Saw action at Second Bull Run, Crampton's Gap, and Fredericksburg, and guarded supply trains at Chancellorsville and Gettysburg. Reenlisted in 1864 and promoted to sergeant. Captured in the Wilderness on May 6, 1864. Imprisoned in stockades at Andersonville, Georgia, May 24–September 12, and Florence, South Carolina, from September 15 until his death on February 7, 1865. His diary was saved by a fellow prisoner and printed at Trenton in 1865.

Samuel T. Foster (November 9, 1829–January 8, 1919) Born in Union District (county), South Carolina. Moved with family to Hallettsville, Lacava County, Texas, in 1847. Married Mary Ham in 1855 and began practicing law. Moved in 1859 to Oakville and was appointed chief justice of the Live Oak County court in 1860. Mustered into Confederate service in April 1862 as first lieutenant, Company H, 24th Texas Cavalry. Regiment was sent to Arkansas in summer of 1862 and dismounted. Captured at surrender of Fort Hindman, Arkansas, January 11, 1863. Imprisoned at Camp Chase, Columbus, Ohio. Exchanged in May 1863. Posted with his regiment to the Army of Tennessee. Promoted to captain. Commanded company in the Tullahoma campaign and at Chickamauga. Wounded at Chattanooga. Returned to duty in March 1864 and led company during the Atlanta campaign and the invasion of Tennessee. Fought at Franklin before being wounded outside Nashville on December 13, 1864. Retreated into northern Mississippi. Joined Joseph E. Johnston's army in North Carolina in March 1865, and surrendered with Johnston's forces on April 26, 1865. Returned to Oakville. Served in Texas house of representatives in 1866. Moved to Corpus Christi in 1868 and became manager for a general merchandising and banking house. Moved to Laredo in 1880. Served as commissioner for the U.S. District Court for the Western (later Southern) District of Texas. After the death of his first wife, married Bettie Moore in 1897. Died in Laredo.

Garrison Frazier (1797–?) Born into slavery in Granville County, North Carolina. Became a Baptist minister around 1830. Bought his and his wife's freedom for $1,000 in 1856. Lived in Savannah, Georgia, in 1865.

Henry Highland Garnet (December 23, 1815–February 13, 1882) Born in Kent County, Maryland, the son of slaves. Family escaped in 1824 and settled in New York City, taking the name Garnet. Graduated from the Oneida Institute in Whitesboro, New York, in 1839. Served as pastor of the Liberty Street Presbyterian Church in Troy, New York, 1840–48. Underwent leg amputation in 1840 as the result of an earlier injury. Became active in the antislavery Liberty Party and a leading advocate of abolishing the property qualification that prevented most black men from voting in New York State. Attended National Negro Convention held in Buffalo in 1843, where his call for violent resistance to slavery was opposed by Frederick Douglass. Taught school in Geneva, New York, 1848–49. Toured Great Britain and Ireland as an antislavery speaker, 1850–53. Served as a Presbyterian missionary in Jamaica, 1853–56, and as pastor of the Shiloh Presbyterian Church in New York City, 1856–64. Founded African Civilization Society in 1858 to promote cotton cultivation by African American colonists in the Niger valley. Helped recruit black troops and aided victims of the New York draft riots in 1863. Became pastor of the Fifteenth Street Presbyterian Church in Washington, D.C., in 1864. Delivered sermon in the House of Representatives in 1865 to celebrate congressional approval of the Thirteenth Amendment. President of Avery College in Allegheny, Pennsylvania, 1868–70, then returned to Shiloh Church. Appointed U.S. minister to Liberia in 1881 and died there shortly after his arrival.

John White Geary (December 30, 1819–February 8, 1873) Born near Mount Pleasant, Pennsylvania, the son of a schoolmaster. Studied at Jefferson College. Taught school and worked as surveyor and railroad engineer. Studied law and was admitted to the Pennsylvania bar.

Married Margaret Logan in 1843. Appointed lieutenant colonel of the 2nd Pennsylvania Infantry in January 1847 and fought at La Hoya, Chapultepec, and Garita de Belen. Promoted to colonel, November 1847. Served as postmaster of San Francisco, 1849, and as its mayor, 1850–51. Returned to Pennsylvania in 1852 to practice law. Appointed governor of Kansas Territory in July 1856. Resigned in March 1857 after coming into conflict with proslavery settlers. After the death of his first wife, married Mary Henderson in 1858. Appointed colonel of the 28th Pennsylvania Infantry in June 1861. Became commander of a brigade posted on the upper Potomac in September 1861, and was wounded in skirmishes at Bolivar Heights, October 1861, and Leesburg, March 1862. Commissioned as a brigadier general, April 1862. Seriously wounded at Cedar Mountain, August 1862. Returned to duty in late September 1862 and was given command of the Second Division, Twelfth Corps. Led division at Chancellorsville, where he was again wounded, and at Gettysburg. Sent with his division to Tennessee in October 1863. Fought at Wauhatchie, where his eighteen-year-old son Edward, an officer in the division, was killed, and at Chattanooga. Division became part of the Twentieth Corps, April 1864. Served in the Atlanta campaign, the march to Savannah, and the march through the Carolinas. Elected governor of Pennsylvania as a Republican, 1866, and served two terms, 1867–73. Died in Harrisburg, Pennsylvania.

James R. Gilmore (September 10, 1822–November 16, 1903) Born in Boston, Massachusetts. Established successful cotton and shipping business in New York City. Proprietor of *Continental Monthly*, 1862–64. Under the penname Edmund Kirke, published *Among the Pines, or South in Secession-time* (1862) and *My Southern Friends* (1863). Accompanied Colonel James F. Jaquess on unofficial peace mission to Richmond in July 1864. Writing as Edmund Kirke, published *Down in Tennessee, and back by way of Richmond* (1864), *Among the Guerillas* (1866), *Patriot Boys and Prison Pictures* (1866), and *On the Border* (1867). Married Laura Edmonds. Resumed business career in 1873. Under his own name, published *The Life of James A. Garfield* (1880). Retired from business in 1883. Published *The Rear-Guard of the Revolution* (1886), *John Sevier as a Commonwealth-Builder* (1887), *The Advance-Guard of Western Civilization* (1888), *A Mountain-White Heroine* (1889), *The Last of the Thorndikes* (1889), and *Personal Recollections of Abraham Lincoln and the Civil War* (1898). Died in Glen Falls, New York.

Gordon Granger (November 6, 1822–January 10, 1876) Born in Joy, Wayne County, New York. Graduated from West Point in 1845 and commissioned as second lieutenant. Fought at Cerro Gordo, Contreras, Churubusco, and Chapultepec in the war with Mexico. Served in

Washington and Oregon, 1849–51, and Texas and New Mexico, 1852–60. Promoted to first lieutenant, 1852, and captain, 1861. Fought at Wilson's Creek as a brigade staff aide. Commissioned as colonel of the 2nd Michigan Cavalry in September 1861. Promoted to brigadier general, March 1862, and led cavalry division in John Pope's Army of the Mississippi at New Madrid, Island No. 10, and the advance on Corinth. Promoted to major general. Commanded Union troops in Kentucky and Middle Tennessee, October 1862–June 1863, and defended Franklin, Tennessee, against Confederate cavalry raids. Led Reserve Corps of the Army of the Cumberland in the Tullahoma campaign and at Chickamauga, where he reinforced George H. Thomas and helped hold the Union left. Commanded Fourth Corps of the Army of the Cumberland at Chattanooga and in the relief of Knoxville. Led army detachment that captured Forts Gaines and Morgan in Mobile Bay, August 1864. Commanded Union forces in western Florida and southern Alabama, September 1864–February 1865. Led Thirteenth Corps in Mobile campaign, March–April 1865. Commanded District of Texas, June–August 1865. Mustered out of volunteer service in 1866 and served as colonel in the postwar army. Married Maria Letcher in 1867. Commanded District of New Mexico, 1871–73 and 1875–76. Died in Santa Fe, New Mexico Territory.

Ulysses S. Grant (April 22, 1822–July 23, 1885) Born in Point Pleasant, Ohio, the son of a tanner. Graduated from West Point in 1843. Served in the U.S.-Mexican War, 1846–48, and promoted to first lieutenant in 1847. Married Julia Dent in 1848. Promoted to captain, 1854, and resigned commission. Worked as a farmer, real estate agent, and general store clerk, 1854–61. Commissioned colonel, 21st Illinois Volunteers, June 1861, and brigadier general of volunteers, August 1861. Promoted to major general of volunteers, February 1862, after victories at Forts Henry and Donelson. Defeated Confederates at Shiloh, April 1862, and captured Vicksburg, Mississippi, July 1863. Promoted to major general in the regular army, July 1863, and assigned to command of Military Division of the Mississippi, covering territory between the Alleghenies and the Mississippi, October 1863. Won battle of Chattanooga, November 1863. Promoted to lieutenant general, March 1864, and named general-in-chief of the Union armies. Accepted surrender of Robert E. Lee at Appomattox Court House, April 9, 1865. Promoted to general, July 1866. Served as secretary of war ad interim, August 1867–January 1868. Nominated for president by the Republican Party in 1868. Defeated Democrat Horatio Seymour, and won reelection in 1872 by defeating Liberal Republican Horace Greeley. President of the United States, 1869–77. Made world tour, 1877–79. Failed to win Republican presidential nomination, 1880. Worked on Wall Street, 1881–84, and was financially ruined when private banking firm of Grant & Ward collapsed. Wrote *Personal Memoirs of U.S. Grant*, 1884–85, while suffering from throat cancer, and completed them days before his death at Mount McGregor, New York.

John Chipman Gray (July 14, 1839–February 25, 1915) Born in Brighton, Massachusetts, the son of a merchant and iron manufacturer. Educated at Boston Latin School. Graduated from Harvard College in 1859 and from Harvard Law School in 1862. Commissioned as second lieutenant in the 41st Massachusetts Infantry, October 1862. Served as an aide to Brigadier General George H. Gordon in Virginia, South Carolina, Florida, and Arkansas, 1862–64. Appointed judge advocate for the Department of the South in the fall of 1864 and served until the end of the war. Founded successful law practice with John Codman Ropes in 1865. Married Anna Lyman Mason, 1873. Lecturer at Harvard Law School, 1870–75, Story Professor of Law, 1875–83, and Royall Professor of Law, 1883–1913. Published *Restraints on the Alienation of Property* (1883), *The Rule against Perpetuities* (1886), and *The Nature and Sources of the Law* (1909). Died in Boston.

Horace Greeley (February 3, 1811–November 29, 1872) Born in Amherst, New Hampshire, the son of a farmer. Learned printing trade in Vermont, upstate New York, and Pennsylvania. Moved to New York City in 1831. Founded and edited weekly *New Yorker*, 1834–41. Married Mary Cheney in 1836. Edited Whig campaign newspapers *Jeffersonian*, 1838, and *Log Cabin*, 1840. Founded *New York Tribune*, 1841, and used it to advocate for social reforms and antislavery positions. Served in Congress, 1848–49. Active in Whig and Republican politics. Nominated for president by the Liberal Republicans and the Democrats in 1872, but was defeated by Ulysses S. Grant. Died in New York City.

Cornelia Hancock (February 8, 1840–December 31, 1927) Born in Hancock's Bridge, near Salem, New Jersey, the daughter of a Quaker fisherman. Educated in Salem schools. Brother and several cousins enlisted in Union army in 1862. Traveled to Gettysburg with her brother-in-law Dr. Henry T. Child in July 1863 and served as volunteer nurse in Second Corps and general army hospitals until September. Volunteered as nurse at the Contraband Hospital for escaped slaves in Washington, D.C., October 1863–February 1864, and at army hospitals in Virginia at Brandy Station, February–April 1864; Fredericksburg and White House, May–June 1864; and City Point, June 1864–May 1865. Founded the Laing School for freed slaves in

Pleasantville, South Carolina, in 1866 with funds from the Freedmen's Bureau and donations from the Philadelphia Yearly Meeting of the Society of Friends. Resigned as principal in 1875 and returned to Philadelphia. Visited England and studied efforts to help the poor in London. Helped found the Philadelphia Society for Organizing Charitable Relief in 1878 and the Children's Aid Society of Philadelphia in 1882. Engaged in philanthropic work in the Sixth Ward and in "Wrightsville," a slum neighborhood in South Philadelphia. Retired in 1914 to Atlantic City, New Jersey, where she died.

Mathella Page Harrison A resident of Clarke County, Virginia, in 1864. Her husband was a slaveholding physician and farmer.

John Hay (October 8, 1838–July 1, 1905) Born in Salem, Indiana, the son of a doctor. Family moved to Warsaw, Illinois. Graduated from Brown University in 1858. Studied law in office of his uncle in Springfield, Illinois. Traveled to Washington in 1861 as assistant private secretary to Abraham Lincoln, serving until early in 1865. First secretary to American legation in Paris, 1865–67; chargé d'affaires in Vienna, 1867–68; and legation secretary in Madrid, 1868–70. Published *Castilian Days* (1871) and *Pike County Ballads and Other Pieces* (1871). Married Clara Louise Stone in 1874. Served as assistant secretary of state, 1879–81. Political novel *The Bread-Winners*, an attack on labor unions, published anonymously in 1884. In collaboration with John G. Nicolay, wrote *Abraham Lincoln: A History* (10 volumes, 1890) and edited *Complete Works of Abraham Lincoln* (2 volumes, 1894). Ambassador to Great Britain, 1897–98. Served as secretary of state in the administrations of William McKinley and Theodore Roosevelt, 1898–1905. Among first seven members elected to American Academy of Arts and Letters in 1904. Died in Newbury, New Hampshire.

Jim Heiskell (1848–June 14, 1886) A slave who escaped from his loyalist owner in Knoxville in March 1864 and was freed by the Union army. Later worked as a barber in Knoxville, where he died.

James P. Holcombe (September 20, 1820–August 22, 1873) Born in Powhatan County, Virginia, the son of a physician. Attended Yale and the University of Virginia. Married Anne Watts, 1841. Practiced law for several years in Cincinnati, Ohio, and published several books on legal subjects. Professor of law at the University of Virginia, 1851–61. Prominent advocate of secession in the Virginia convention. Member of the Confederate house of representatives, 1862–64. Served as Confederate agent in Canada, March–September 1864. Opened private school in Bedford County, Virginia, in 1866. Died in Capon Springs, West Virginia.

Ellen Renshaw House (August 10, 1843–May 19, 1907) Born in Savannah, Georgia, the daughter of a customs collector. Moved with family to Marietta in 1848 and to Knoxville around 1860. Expelled from Knoxville by the Union army in April 1864 as a Confederate sympathizer. Lived in Abingdon, Virginia, and Eatonton, Georgia, before returning to Knoxville in June 1865. Married James Fletcher in 1867. Died while visiting family in South Carolina.

Harriet Ann Jacobs (1813–March 7, 1897) Born in Edenton, North Carolina, the daughter of slaves. After the death of her mother in 1819, she was raised by her grandmother and her white mistress, Margaret Horniblow, who taught her to read, write, and sew. In 1825 Horniblow died, and Jacobs was sent to the household of Dr. James Norcom. At sixteen, to escape Norcom's repeated sexual advances, Jacobs began a relationship with a white lawyer, Samuel Tredwell Sawyer (later a member of the U.S. House of Representatives), with whom she had two children, Joseph (b. 1829) and Louisa Matilda (b. 1833). In 1835, Jacobs ran away and spent the next seven years hiding in a crawl space above her freed grandmother's storeroom. In 1842, she escaped to New York City, where she was reunited with her children. Worked as a nurse for the family of Nathaniel Parker Willis; moved to Boston in 1843 to avoid recapture by Norcom. Moved to Rochester in 1849, where she became part of a circle of abolitionists surrounding Frederick Douglass. In 1852, Cornelia Grinnell Willis, second wife of Nathaniel Parker Willis, purchased Jacobs's manumission. Published *Incidents in the Life of a Slave Girl, Written by Herself* pseudonymously in 1861. From 1862 to 1868 engaged in Quaker-sponsored relief work among former slaves in Washington, D.C.; Alexandria, Virginia; and Savannah, Georgia. She then lived with her daughter in Cambridge, Massachusetts, and in Washington, D.C., where she died.

Louisa M. Jacobs (1833–April 5, 1917) Born in Edenton, North Carolina, the daughter of Harriet Jacobs and Samuel Tredwell Sawyer. In 1835 she was sold by Dr. James Norcom to her father, who took her to Washington, D.C., and then sent her to Brooklyn to work as a maid for his cousins. Rescued in 1844 by her mother and lived with her in Boston. Attended Young Ladies' Domestic Seminary in Clinton, New York. Lived with her mother at Idlewild, the home of Nathaniel Parker Willis in Cornwall-on-Hudson, New York, and in Brooklyn and Boston. With her mother, established schools for freed people in Alexandria, Virginia, in 1864 and Savannah, Georgia, in 1865. Toured upstate New York as speaker for the Equal Rights Association. Taught school in Washington, D.C. Lived in Cambridge, Massachusetts, 1868–77. Returned to Washington in 1877. Taught in the Industrial School at Howard University and later worked at the National Home for the Relief of Destitute Colored Women and Children. Died in Cambridge, Massachusetts.

Frances Johnson A slave from Fayette County, Kentucky, who escaped to Camp Nelson in March 1865 and sought help in freeing her three children. Her husband, Nathan Johnson, was a soldier in the 116th U.S. Colored Infantry.

John B. Jones (March 6, 1810–February 4, 1866) Born in Baltimore, Maryland. Lived in Kentucky and Missouri as a boy. Married Frances Custis in 1840. Became editor of the *Saturday Visitor* in Baltimore, 1841. Published several novels, including *Wild Western Scenes* (1841), *The War Path* (1858), and *Wild Southern Scenes* (1859). Established weekly newspaper *Southern Monitor* in Philadelphia, 1857. Fearing arrest as a Confederate sympathizer, Jones moved in 1861 to Richmond, Virginia, where he worked as a clerk in the Confederate War Department. Died in Burlington, New Jersey, shortly before the publication of *A Rebel War Clerk's Diary*.

George W. Julian (May 5, 1817–July 7, 1899) Born near Centreville, Indiana, the son of a farmer. Attended common schools, studied law, and was admitted to the Indiana bar in 1840. Married Anne Elizabeth Finch in 1845. Elected as a Whig to the Indiana house of representatives and served 1845–46. Attended convention in Buffalo, New York, that founded Free Soil party in 1848. Elected to Congress as a Free Soiler and served 1849–51. Free Soil candidate for vice president in 1852. Attended first Republican national convention in Philadelphia, 1856. Served in Congress as a Republican, 1861–71. A member of the Joint Committee on the Conduct of the War, Julian later helped prepare the articles of impeachment against President Johnson. After the death of his first wife, married Laura Giddings, daughter of abolitionist congressman Joshua Giddings, in 1863. Supported Horace Greeley, the Liberal Republican nominee, against Grant in 1872 and later became a Democrat. Advocated woman suffrage. Practiced law in Washington, D.C., 1879–84, and served as surveyor general of New Mexico Territory, 1885–89. Published *Political Recollections, 1840 to 1872* (1884) and *The Life of Joshua R. Giddings* (1892). Died in Irvington, Indiana.

Jane Kamper A slave from Talbot County, Maryland, who fled with her children to Baltimore in November 1864.

Robert Garlick Hill Kean (October 7, 1828–June 13, 1898) Born in Caroline County, Virginia, the son of a schoolmaster and farmer. Graduated from the University of Virginia in 1850 and studied law. Began legal practice in Lynchburg in 1853. Married Jane Randolph in

1854. Enlisted in 11th Virginia Infantry and fought at First Manassas. Commissioned as captain in February 1862 and assigned to the staff of Brigadier General George W. Randolph, his wife's uncle. Randolph was appointed Confederate secretary of war in March 1862, and in April Kean became the head of the Bureau of War, where he served for the remainder of the war. Retreated with other members of the Confederate War Department to Charlotte, North Carolina, after the fall of Richmond. Left Charlotte on April 26, 1865, and returned to Virginia. Resumed his law practice in Lynchburg. After the death of his first wife, married Adelaide Prescott in 1874. Died in Lynchburg.

Elizabeth Keckly (February 1818–May 26, 1907) Born Elizabeth Hobbs in Dinwiddie County, Virginia, the daughter of Agnes Hobbs, a slave, and her owner, Armistead Burwell. Worked from an early age as a house servant. Moved to Hillsborough, North Carolina, in 1835 with family of Robert Burwell, Armistead's son. Forced into a sexual relationship by Alexander Kirkland, a white neighbor, and gave birth to a son, George, in 1839. Returned to Dinwiddie County in 1842 and worked in household of Hugh Garland, Armistead Burwell's son-in-law. Moved to St. Louis with the Garland family in 1847. Became successful dressmaker. Married James Keckly, a black man from Virginia, in 1852. Using $1,200 borrowed from her clients, bought her and her son's freedom in 1855. Separated from her husband and moved to Washington, D.C., in 1860. Began making dresses for Mary Lincoln in 1861 and became her close friend and confidante. Her son, George Kirkland, enlisted as a white man in the 1st Missouri Light Artillery and was killed at Wilson's Creek in August 1861. Founded the Contraband Relief Association in 1862 to assist former slaves in Washington. Published memoir *Behind the Scenes, or, Thirty Years a Slave and Four Years in the White House* (1868); its appearance caused Mary Lincoln to break off their friendship. Moved to Xenia, Ohio, in 1892 to teach in the Department of Sewing and Domestic Science Arts at Wilberforce University. Returned to Washington and lived in the National Home for the Relief of Destitute Colored Women and Children. Died in Washington, D.C.

Emma LeConte (December 10, 1847–March 2, 1932) Born in Liberty County, Georgia, the daughter of a chemist and geologist. Lived in Athens, 1852–56, while father taught at The University of Georgia. Family moved to Columbia, South Carolina, when father became professor at South Carolina College. Educated at home in Greek, Latin, French, German, and mathematics. Witnessed burning of Columbia in February 1865. Married Farish Furman in 1869 and moved to farm near Milledgeville, Georgia. Assumed management of the farm after her husband died in 1883. Moved to Macon early in the twentieth century. Died in Macon, Georgia.

Elizabeth Blair Lee (June 20, 1818–September 13, 1906) Born in Frankfort, Kentucky, daughter of journalist Francis Preston Blair and Elizabeth Gist Blair, sister of Montgomery Blair (postmaster general, 1861–64) and Frank Blair (a Union major general, 1862–65). Moved with family in 1830 to Washington, D.C., where her father edited the *Globe* and advised Andrew Jackson. Educated at boarding school in Philadelphia. Married naval officer Samuel Phillips Lee, a cousin of Robert E. Lee, in 1843. Became board member and active patron of the Washington City Orphan Asylum in 1849. Lived in Washington and at the Blair estate in Silver Spring, Maryland. Died in Washington.

Robert E. Lee (January 19, 1807–October 12, 1870) Born in Westmoreland County, Virginia, the son of Revolutionary War hero Henry "Light-Horse Harry" Lee and Ann Carter Lee. Graduated from West Point in 1829. Married Mary Custis, great-granddaughter of Martha Washington, in 1831. Served in the U.S.-Mexican War, and as superintendent of West Point, 1852–55. Promoted to colonel in March 1861. Resigned commission on April 20, 1861, after declining offer of field command of the Federal army. Served as commander of Virginia military forces, April–July 1861; commander in western Virginia, August–October 1861; commander of the southern Atlantic coast, November 1861–March 1862; and military advisor to Jefferson Davis, March–May 1862. Assumed command of the Army of Northern Virginia on June 1, 1862, and led it until April 9, 1865, when he surrendered to Ulysses S. Grant at Appomattox. Named general-in-chief of all Confederate forces, February 1865. Became president of Washington College (now Washington and Lee), September 1865. Died in Lexington, Virginia.

Francis Lieber (March 18, 1798–October 2, 1872) Born Franz Lieber in Berlin, Prussia. Fought in the Prussian army in the Waterloo campaign and was seriously wounded at Namur. Imprisoned for four months for antigovernment activities in 1819. Received degree in mathematics from Jena in 1820. Studied at Dresden, then served briefly as volunteer in the Greek War of Independence in 1822. Left Greece and traveled to Rome, where the Prussian ambassador, the historian Barthold Niebuhr, encouraged him to publish a book on his experiences in Greece (it appeared in 1823). Returned to Berlin in 1823 and continued his study of mathematics. Arrested in 1824 and imprisoned for six months for alleged subversion. Fled to England in 1826. Immigrated to Boston in 1827, where he served as director of a newly established gymnasium and swimming school. After the gymnasium venture failed, edited the *Encyclopaedia Americana*, published successfully in thirteen volumes, 1829–33. Married Mathilda Oppenheimer in 1829. Moved to Philadelphia in 1834 and published a constitution and plan of education for Girard College. Accepted a chair in history and political economy at South Carolina College (later University of South Carolina) in Columbia in 1835. Published numerous books and essays on law, government, and politics, including *Legal and Political Hermeneutics* (1837), *Manual of Political Ethics* (1838–39), and *On Civil Liberty and Self-Government* (1853). Resigned position in South Carolina in 1855. Appointed professor of history and political science at Columbia College in New York in 1857. During the Civil War one of his sons was killed fighting for the Confederacy in 1862, while his other two sons fought for the Union, one of them losing an arm at Fort Donelson. Became adviser to Henry W. Halleck on the laws of war. Wrote *A Code for the Government of Armies*, issued in revised form by the Union War Department as General Orders No. 100 in April 1863. Became professor at Columbia Law School in 1865. Helped gather and preserve the records of the Confederate government. Appointed in 1870 to commission settling claims arising from the U.S.-Mexican War. Died in New York City.

Abraham Lincoln (February 12, 1809–April 15, 1865) Born near Hodgenville, Kentucky, the son of a farmer and carpenter. Family moved to Indiana in 1816 and to Illinois in 1830. Settled in New Salem, Illinois, and worked as a storekeeper, surveyor, and postmaster. Served as a Whig in the state legislature, 1834–41. Began law practice in 1836 and moved to Springfield in 1837. Married Mary Todd in 1842. Elected to Congress as a Whig and served from 1847 to 1849. Became a public opponent of the extension of slavery after the passage of the Kansas-Nebraska Act in 1854. Helped found the Republican Party of Illinois in 1856. Campaigned in 1858 for Senate seat held by Stephen A. Douglas and debated him seven times on the slavery issue; although the Illinois legislature reelected Douglas, the campaign brought Lincoln national prominence. Received Republican presidential nomination in 1860 and won election in a four-way contest; his victory led to the secession of seven southern states. Responded to the Confederate bombardment of Fort Sumter by calling up militia, proclaiming the blockade of southern ports, and suspending habeas corpus. Issued preliminary and final emancipation proclamations on September 22, 1862, and January 1, 1863. Appointed Ulysses S. Grant commander of all Union forces in March 1864. Won reelection in 1864 by defeating Democrat George B. McClellan. Died in Washington, D.C., after being shot by John Wilkes Booth.

Theodore Lyman (August 23, 1833–September 9, 1897) Born in

Waltham, Massachusetts, the son of a wealthy merchant and textile manufacturer. Graduated from Harvard in 1855. Studied natural history with Louis Agassiz after graduation. Traveled to Florida in 1856 to collect marine specimens for the Harvard Museum of Comparative Zoology. Graduated from Lawrence Scientific School at Harvard in 1858. Married Elizabeth Russell, a cousin of Robert Gould Shaw, in 1858. Traveled in Europe, 1861–63. Joined staff of George G. Meade in September 1863 with rank of lieutenant colonel and served until Lee's surrender. Returned to home in Brookline, Massachusetts, and resumed work at Museum of Comparative Zoology. Served in Congress as an independent, 1883–85. Retired from scientific work in 1887 due to failing health. Died in Brookline.

William Gordon McCabe (August 4, 1841–June 1, 1920) Born in Richmond, Virginia, the son of an Episcopal minister. Educated at Hampton Academy. Entered University of Virginia in 1860. Contributed poems, essays, and stories to the *Southern Literary Messenger*. Enlisted as private in the 3rd Company, Richmond Howitzer Battalion in May 1861. Commissioned as first lieutenant of artillery, May 1862. Served in Richmond defenses with the 19th Battalion, Virginia Heavy Artillery (Atkinson's), and as adjutant of Lightfoot's Artillery Battalion, 1862–63. Assigned to staff of Brigadier General Roswell S. Ripley during the siege of Charleston Harbor, August–October 1863. Returned to Richmond defenses in the fall of 1863. Became ordnance officer, and later adjutant, of field artillery battalion commanded by William Pegram and saw action at the Wilderness, Spotsylvania, Cold Harbor, and in the Petersburg campaign. Founded University School preparatory academy in Petersburg in 1865. Married Jane Osborne in 1867. Contributed poems, essays, and historical articles to newspapers and magazines in the United States and Britain. Published *A Grammar of the Latin Language* (1884), *Caesar's Gallic War* (1886), and *Virginia Schools Before and After the Revolution* (1890). Moved school to Richmond in 1895 and closed it when he retired as headmaster in 1901. After the death of his first wife, married Gallena Cary in 1915. Died in Richmond.

George B. McClellan (December 3, 1826–October 29, 1885) Born in Philadelphia, the son of a surgeon. Graduated from West Point in 1846. Served in the U.S.-Mexican War. Resigned from the army in 1857 to become chief engineer of the Illinois Central Railroad. Became president of the Ohio & Mississippi Railroad in 1860. Married Ellen Marcy, 1860. Appointed major general in the regular army, May 1861. Commanded offensive that drove Confederate troops from western Virginia, July 1861. Assumed command of the Military Division of the Potomac on July 25, 1861, following the Union defeat at First Bull

Run. Served as general-in-chief of the Union armies, November 1861–March 1862. Commanded the Army of the Potomac on the Peninsula, in the Second Bull Run campaign, and at Antietam. Relieved of command by President Lincoln on November 7, 1862. Nominated for president by the Democratic Party in 1864, but was defeated by Lincoln. Governor of New Jersey, 1878–81. Died in Orange, New Jersey.

Judith W. McGuire (March 19, 1813–March 21, 1897) Born Judith White Brockenbrough near Richmond, Virginia, the daughter of a judge. Married John P. McGuire, an Episcopalian rector, in 1846. Moved to Alexandria in 1852 when husband became principal of the Episcopal High School of Virginia. Fled Alexandria in May 1861 and settled in Richmond in February 1862. Worked as a clerk in the Confederate commissary department, November 1863–April 1864. Published *Diary of a Southern Refugee, During the War* (1867). Kept a school with her husband in Essex County in the 1870s. Published *General Robert E. Lee: The Christian Soldier* (1873). Died in Richmond.

Benjamin F. McIntyre (September 15, 1827–November 7, 1910) Born in Adams County, Ohio. Educated in public schools. Moved to Maysville, Kentucky, in 1849. Married Emeline Williams in 1850. Moved to Keokuk, Iowa, in 1856. Worked as a carpenter and undertaker. Enlisted in the 19th Iowa Infantry in August 1862 as first sergeant. Served in southern Missouri and northern Arkansas, September 1862–May 1863, and fought at Prairie Grove. Promoted to second lieutenant in January 1863. Sent with regiment to Vicksburg in mid-June and served in siege until Confederate surrender on July 4, 1863. Remained in Mississippi until late July, when the 19th Iowa was posted to Louisiana. Escaped capture at battle of Sterling's Plantation, where more than 200 men from his regiment were taken prisoner on September 29, 1863. Served in force that occupied Brownsville, Texas, November 1863–July 1864. Promoted to first lieutenant in August 1864. Posted to Fort Barrancas near Pensacola, Florida, August–December 1864. Served at Fort Gaines at the entrance to Mobile Bay and in southeastern Mississippi, December 1864–March 1865. Saw action in the siege of Spanish Fort near Mobile, March 27–April 8, 1865. Remained at Mobile after the Confederate surrender until July 1865, when his regiment was mustered out. Returned to Keokuk and worked as carpenter and builder. Died in Lee County, Iowa.

Alexander McKinley (September 10, 1817–August 24, 1874) Born in Philadelphia, Pennsylvania. Graduated from the University of

Pennsylvania in 1835. Admitted to Philadelphia bar in 1844. Practiced law with William B. Reed and served as his secretary when Reed was U.S. minister to China, 1857–58. Served as civilian secretary to Samuel Francis Du Pont, commander of the South Atlantic Blockading Squadron, 1861–63, and to David G. Farragut, 1864–65. Died in Philadelphia.

Mary S. Mallard (June 12, 1835–August 31, 1889) Born in Liberty County, Georgia, the daughter of the Rev. Charles C. Jones, a Presbyterian clergyman and plantation owner. Attended seminary in Philadelphia, 1850–52. Married Robert Q. Mallard, a Presbyterian clergyman, in 1857. Lived in Walthourville, Georgia, 1857–63, and Atlanta, 1863–64. Moved to New Orleans in 1866. Died in Marietta, Georgia.

Herman Melville (August 1, 1819–September 28, 1891) Born in New York City, the son of a merchant. Educated at schools in New York City and in upstate New York. Worked as bank clerk, bookkeeper, and schoolteacher. Sailed for Pacific on whaling ship in 1841 and returned in 1844 on frigate *United States*. Published *Typee* (1846) and *Omoo* (1847), fictionalized accounts of his experiences in the South Seas. Married Elizabeth Shaw in 1847. Published *Mardi* (1849), *Redburn* (1849), *White-Jacket* (1850), *Moby-Dick* (1851), *Pierre; or, The Ambiguities* (1852), *Israel Potter* (1855), *The Piazza Tales* (1856), and *The Confidence-Man* (1857). Visited Union troops in Virginia in spring 1864. Published poetry collection *Battle-Pieces and Aspects of the War* (1866). Worked as customs inspector in New York City, 1866–85. Published long poem *Clarel* (1876) and two small books of poetry, *John Marr and Other Sailors* (1888) and *Timoleon* (1891). Died in New York City, leaving *Billy Budd, Sailor*, in manuscript.

Joseph Miller (1819–January 6, 1865) A slave from Lincoln County, Kentucky, who enlisted in the 124th U.S. Colored Infantry in October 1864. His wife, Isabella, and their four children accompanied him to Camp Nelson. Died at Camp Nelson, Kentucky.

Luther Rice Mills (August 17, 1840–August 18, 1920) Born in Halifax County, Virginia, the son of a Baptist minister and plantation owner. Graduated from Wake Forest College in 1861. Enlisted in the 26th Virginia Infantry and was eventually commissioned as second lieutenant. Served at Gloucester Point, Virginia, during winter of 1861–62. Posted with regiment to Chaffin's Bluff on the James River near Richmond in May 1862, and remained there through the summer of 1863, seeing no action. Sent with regiment to Charleston, South Carolina, in September 1863. Returned to Virginia in May 1864 and fought at Bermuda Hundred and in the defense of

Petersburg. Wounded in the battle of the Crater. Returned to duty and commanded a company of sharpshooters. Captured during retreat to Appomattox. Released on June 19, 1865, after taking oath of allegiance. Professor of mathematics at Wake Forest College, 1867–1907, and bursar of the college, 1876–1907. Married Anna Lewis in 1869. Died in Wake Forest, North Carolina.

Sarah Morgan (February 28, 1842–May 5, 1909) Born in New Orleans, the daughter of a lawyer. Family moved in 1850 to Baton Rouge, where father served as a judge. Spent war with widowed mother and sisters in Baton Rouge, in the countryside near Port Hudson, and in Union-occupied New Orleans. Two of her brothers died of illness in January 1864 while serving in the Confederate army. Moved with mother to brother's plantation near Columbia, South Carolina, in 1872. Began writing editorials for the Charleston *News and Courier* in 1873 as "Mr. Fowler." Married Francis Warrington Dawson, editor of the *News and Courier*, in 1874. Husband killed in 1889 by doctor who had been paying unwanted attentions to family's governess. Moved in 1899 to Paris, where her son lived. Published *Les Aventures de Jeannot Lap*, version of Brer Rabbit stories, in 1903. Died in Paris.

John S. Mosby (December 6, 1833–May 30, 1916) Born in Powhatan County, Virginia, the son of slave-owning farmer. Family moved in 1841 to large farm near Charlottesville. Entered the University of Virginia in 1850. Dismissed in 1853 after shooting a fellow student who was trying to beat him. Convicted of unlawful shooting and served seven months of one-year sentence before being pardoned in December 1853. Studied law and was admitted to the Virginia bar in 1855. Established practice in Howardsville, Virginia, and married Pauline Clarke in 1856. Moved to Bristol, Tennessee, in 1858. Voted for Stephen A. Douglas in the 1860 presidential election. Enlisted in the 1st Virginia Cavalry in 1861. Served as a scout for Confederate cavalry commander J.E.B. Stuart, 1861–62. With the support of Stuart, organized a small detachment of partisan rangers in northern Virginia in January 1863 and began raiding Union outposts and supply wagons in Fairfax, Prince William, Fauquier, and Loudoun counties. Commissioned as major in March 1863. Command designated as 43rd Battalion, Virginia Cavalry, in June 1863. Scouted for Stuart during the Gettysburg campaign and raided Union supply lines during the 1864 Shenandoah Valley campaign. Wounded in August 1863, September 1864, and December 1864. Promoted to lieutenant colonel, January 1864, and to colonel, December 1864. Disbanded his command on April 21, 1865. Practiced law in Warrenton, Virginia, 1865–76. Angered many former Confederates by supporting Ulysses S.

Grant in the 1872 presidential election. Served as U.S. consul in Hong Kong, 1878–85. Attorney for the Southern Pacific Railroad in San Francisco, 1885–1901. Investigated land fraud for the Department of the Interior in Colorado, Nebraska, and Alabama, 1901–4. Assistant attorney at the Department of Justice in Washington, D.C., 1904–10. Published *Mosby's War Reminiscences and Stuart's Cavalry Campaigns* (1887) and *Stuart's Cavalry in the Gettysburg Campaign* (1908). Died in Washington, D.C.

Henry Nutt (June 25, 1811–December 18, 1881) A successful merchant and distillery owner in New Hanover County, North Carolina, who owned thirty-eight slaves in 1850. Promoted the clearing and dredging of the Cape Fear River at Wilmington. Served as director of the Wilmington and Manchester Railroad after the war.

Robert Patrick (December 24, 1835–December 8, 1866) Born in East Feliciana Parish, Louisiana. Family moved in 1842 to Clinton, Louisiana, where father worked as a court clerk. Attended local schools. Worked as bookkeeper before becoming a deputy sheriff in 1860. Enlisted in the 4th Louisiana Infantry in May 1861. Served as quartermaster and commissary clerk. Saw action at Shiloh. Posted to Port Hudson, October 1862–April 1863. Served with Joseph E. Johnston's army during the Vicksburg campaign. Posted to garrison in Mobile, then served as brigade quartermaster clerk during the Atlanta campaign. Accompanied the Army of Tennessee through northern Georgia and Alabama, October–November 1864, then remained in northern Mississippi when Hood invaded Tennessee. Served in South Carolina at the end of the war. Returned to his position as deputy sheriff. Died in East Feliciana Parish.

William Pegram (June 29, 1841–April 2, 1865) Born in Richmond, Virginia, the son of a banker. Studied law at the University of Virginia, 1840–41. Appointed second lieutenant in the Purcell artillery battery, May 1861. Saw action at First Manassas. Promoted to captain in March 1862 and appointed battery commander. Fought at Mechanicsville, Gaines's Mill, Malvern Hill, Cedar Mountain, Second Manassas, Antietam, Fredericksburg, and Chancellorsville in A. P. Hill's Light Division. Promoted to major and became commander of an artillery battalion commander in Hill's Third Corps. Fought at Gettysburg. Promoted to lieutenant colonel in February 1864. Led battalion in the Wilderness, Spotsylvania, Cold Harbor, and in the battles near Petersburg. Promoted to colonel in February 1865. Fatally wounded at the battle of Five Forks, April 1, 1865. Died in Dinwiddie County, Virginia.

Horace Porter (April 15, 1837–May 29, 1921) Born in Huntingdon,

Pennsylvania, the son of an iron manufacturer who served as governor, 1839–45. Attended Lawrence Scientific School at Harvard. Graduated from West Point in 1860. Commissioned as first lieutenant in May 1861. Served as ordnance officer in the Sea Islands, October 1861–July 1862, and saw action at Fort Pulaski and Secessionville. Posted to the Army of the Potomac, July–September 1862. Served as chief ordnance officer of the Army of the Ohio, September 1862–January 1863, and of the Army of the Cumberland, January–November 1863. Assigned to ordnance bureau in Washington, D.C., November 1863–April 1864. Appointed as aide to Ulysses S. Grant in April 1864 with rank of lieutenant colonel, and remained with him for the rest of the war. Served as aide to Grant in the postwar army, 1865–69, and as his personal secretary in the White House, 1869–73. Moved to New York City, became vice president of the Pullman Car Company, and invested in several other railroad ventures, 1873–97. Published *Campaigning with Grant* (1897). U.S. ambassador to France, 1897–1905, and delegate to the Hague peace conference, 1907. Died in New York City.

Stephen Dodson Ramseur (May 31, 1837–October 20, 1864) Born in Lincolnton, North Carolina, the son of a merchant. Attended Davidson College, 1853–55. Graduated West Point in 1860. Resigned from the U.S. Army in April 1861. Commissioned as major and served with 1st North Carolina Artillery near Norfolk, Virginia. Appointed colonel of the 49th North Carolina Infantry in April 1862. Led regiment at Malvern Hill, where he was severely wounded. Promoted to brigadier general in November 1862. Returned to duty in January 1863 as brigade commander. Led North Carolina brigade in Rodes's Division, Second Corps, Army of Northern Virginia, at Chancellorsville and Gettysburg. Married Ellen Richmond in October 1863. Commanded brigade at the Wilderness, Spotsylvania, and North Anna. Promoted to major general and assigned command of Early's Division in the Second Corps. Led division at Cold Harbor, Monocacy, Winchester, Fisher's Creek, and Cedar Creek, where he was mortally wounded and captured on October 19, 1864. Died the following day at Union headquarters near Meadow Mills, Virginia.

Spottswood Rice (November 20, 1819–October 31, 1907) Born into slavery in Madison County, Missouri, Sold in 1843 to Benjamin Lewis, a tobacco farmer in Howard County, Missouri. Married Arry Ferguson in 1844 (marriage was officially recorded in 1864). Separated from his wife and children, who lived on another plantation. Escaped in February 1864 and enlisted in the 67th U.S. Colored Infantry. Reunited with his family, he lived in St. Louis after the war. Became a minister in the African Methodist Episcopal Church in 1874. Founded

Grant Chapel in Albuquerque, New Mexico, in 1882. After his first wife died, married Eliza Lightner in 1888. Moved to Colorado Springs, where he founded Payne Chapel. Died in Colorado Springs, Colorado.

William T. Sherman (February 8, 1820–February 14, 1891) Born in Lancaster, Ohio, the son of an attorney. Graduated from West Point in 1840. Served in Florida and California, but did not see action in the U.S.-Mexican War. Married Ellen Ewing in 1850. Promoted to captain; resigned his commission in 1853. Managed bank branch in San Francisco, 1853–57. Moved in 1858 to Leavenworth, Kansas, where he worked in real estate and was admitted to the bar. Named first superintendent of the Louisiana State Seminary of Learning and Military Academy at Alexandria (now Louisiana State University) in 1859. Resigned position when Louisiana seceded in January 1861. Commissioned colonel, 13th U.S. Infantry, May 1861. Commanded brigade at First Bull Run, July 1861. Appointed brigadier general of volunteers, August 1861, and ordered to Kentucky. Assumed command of the Department of the Cumberland, October 1861, but was relieved in November at his own request. Returned to field in March 1862 and commanded division under Ulysses S. Grant at Shiloh. Promoted major general of volunteers, May 1862. Commanded corps under Grant during Vicksburg campaign, and succeeded him as commander of the Army of the Tennessee, October 1863, and as commander of the Military Division of the Mississippi, March 1864. Captured Atlanta, September 1864, and led march through Georgia, November–December 1864. Marched army through the Carolinas and accepted the surrender of Confederate General Joseph E. Johnston at Durham Station, North Carolina, April 26, 1865. Promoted to lieutenant general, 1866, and general, 1869, when he became commander of the army. Published controversial *Memoirs of General W. T. Sherman* (1875, revised 1886). Retired from army in 1884 and moved to New York City. Rejected possible Republican presidential nomination, 1884. Died in New York City.

Kate Stone (May 8, 1841–December 28, 1907) Born Sarah Katherine Stone in Hinds County, Mississippi, the daughter of a plantation owner. Family moved to plantation in Madison Parish, Louisiana, thirty miles northwest of Vicksburg. Educated at boarding school in Nashville. Two of her five brothers died while serving in the Confederate army in 1863. Family fled plantation in March 1863 during the Vicksburg campaign and went to eastern Texas. Returned to plantation in November 1865. Married Henry Bry Holmes in 1869. Founded local chapter of the United Daughters of the Confederacy. Died in Tallulah, Louisiana.

John H. Stringfellow (November 14, 1819–July 24, 1905) Born in Culpeper County, Virginia. Educated at Columbian College, Washington, D.C. Received medical degree from the University of Pennsylvania in 1845. Moved to Carrollton, Missouri, that same year and married Ophelia Simmons. Practiced in Platte City and Brunswick, Missouri. Moved to Kansas Territory in 1854 and helped found town of Atchison. Founded the proslavery *Atchison Squatter Sovereign* and served as speaker of the house of representatives in the first Kansas territorial legislature. Led proslavery militia in the sack of Lawrence, Kansas, in May 1856. Returned to Virginia in 1858. Served as surgeon in Confederate army hospitals throughout the war. Practiced medicine in Atchison, Kansas, 1871–76, before moving to St. Joseph, Missouri, where he died.

George Templeton Strong (January 26, 1820–July 21, 1875) Born in New York City, the son of an attorney. Graduated from Columbia College in 1838. Read law in his father's office and was admitted to the bar in 1841. Joined father's firm. Married Ellen Ruggles in 1848. Served on Columbia board of trustees and as vestryman of Trinity Episcopal Church. Helped found the U.S. Sanitary Commission, June 1861, and served as its treasurer through the end of the war; also helped found the Union League Club of New York in 1863. Died in New York City.

Charles Sumner (January 6, 1811–March 11, 1874) Born in Boston, Massachusetts, the son of a lawyer. Graduated from Harvard College in 1830 and from Harvard Law School in 1833. Practiced law in Boston and became active in social reform movements. Unsuccessful Free Soil candidate for Congress in 1848. Elected to the U.S. Senate as a Free Soiler in 1851. Badly beaten with a cane on the Senate floor by South Carolina congressman Preston Brooks on May 22, 1856, two days after delivering his antislavery speech "The Crime Against Kansas." Reelected as a Republican in 1857, but did not regularly return to his seat in the Senate until December 1859; reelected in 1863 and 1869. Chairman of the Senate Foreign Relations Committee, 1861–71. Supported Radical Reconstruction and the rights of blacks after the war. Married Alice Mason Hooper in 1866. Joined Liberal Republicans in opposing reelection of President Grant in 1872. Died in Washington, D.C.

Richard Taylor (January 27, 1826–April 12, 1879) Born near Louisville, Kentucky, the son of army officer and future president Zachary Taylor. Graduated from Yale College in 1845. Managed father's cotton plantation in Jefferson County, Mississippi, 1848–49. Inherited sugar plantation in St. Charles Parish, Louisiana, after President

Taylor's death in 1850. Married Louise Marie Myrthé Bringier, 1851. Served in the Louisiana senate, 1856–61. Commissioned as colonel of the 9th Louisiana Infantry, July 1861. Promoted to brigadier general, October 1861. Commanded the Louisiana Brigade in the Shenandoah Valley campaign of 1862. Promoted to major general, July 1862, and assigned command of the District of Western Louisiana, August 1862. Defeated General Nathaniel P. Banks in the Red River campaign in Louisiana, March–May 1864. Promoted to lieutenant general, May 1864. Commanded the Department of Alabama, Mississippi, and Eastern Louisiana from September 1864 to May 4, 1865, when he surrendered at Citronelle, Alabama. Active in the postwar Democratic Party in Louisiana. *Destruction and Reconstruction: Personal Experiences of the Late War* published posthumously in 1879. Died in New York City.

Lorenzo Thomas (October 26, 1804–March 2, 1875) Born in New Castle, Delaware. Graduated from West Point in 1823. Served as quartermaster in the Second Seminole War, 1836–37, and as staff officer in the U.S.-Mexican War. Chief of staff to General-in-Chief Winfield Scott, 1853–61. Served as adjutant-general of U.S. Army, March 1861–March 1863. Promoted to brigadier general in August 1861. Assigned by Secretary of War Stanton to recruit and organize black troops in the Mississippi Valley, March 1863–October 1865. Returned to duty as adjutant-general and made inspection tour of national cemeteries. Appointed secretary of war by President Andrew Johnson on February 21, 1868, but was unable to serve because Stanton refused to surrender the office. Retired from the army in February 1869. Died in Washington, D.C.

Robert Toombs (July 2, 1810–December 15, 1885) Born in Wilkes County, Georgia, the son of a cotton planter. Studied at The University of Georgia. Graduated from Union College in Schenectady, New York, in 1828. Studied law at the University of Virginia. Began legal practice in Washington, Georgia, in 1830, and married Julia DuBose in the same year. Led company of Georgia militia in 1836 during the Creek War, but saw no action. Served in the Georgia house of representatives, 1837–40 and 1842–43. Elected to Congress as a Whig and served 1845–53. Supported the Compromise of 1850. Elected to the U.S. Senate as member of the Constitutional Union party and served 1853–61. Supported immediate secession at the Georgia convention in 1861. Member of the Provisional Confederate Congress, February 1861–February 1862. Confederate secretary of state, February–June 1861. Commissioned as brigadier general, July 1861. Led brigade in the Seven Days and at Antietam, where he was wounded. Resigned commission in March 1863 and became a leading public critic of the Davis administration. Served as inspector general of the Georgia militia, 1864. Fled his home in May 1865 to avoid arrest and made his way to Cuba and then France. Returned to the United States in 1867 and reestablished law practice. Delegate to the 1877 Georgia constitutional convention. Died in Washington, Georgia.

Clement L. Vallandigham (July 29, 1820–June 17, 1871) Born in New Lisbon, Ohio, the son of a Presbyterian minister. Attended New Lisbon Academy and Jefferson College in Washington, Pennsylvania. Served as principal of Union Academy in Snow Hill, Maryland, 1838–40. Returned to Ohio in 1840 to study law. Admitted to bar in 1842. Served as a Democrat in the Ohio house of representatives, 1845–46. Married Louisa Anna McMahon in 1846. Moved in 1847 to Dayton, where he practiced law and edited the *Dayton Western Empire*, 1847–49. Served in Congress, 1858–63, and became a leading "Peace Democrat" opposed to emancipation and the continued prosecution of the war. Arrested in Dayton on May 5, 1863, and tried before military commission for expressing "disloyal sentiments and opinions." Expelled across lines into Confederate-held territory in Tennessee. Made his way to Canada in June 1863 after receiving Democratic nomination for governor of Ohio and campaigned from exile, but was defeated in October 1863. Returned to United States in June 1864 and helped draft peace platform adopted by Democratic national convention in August. Resumed law practice. Accidentally shot himself on June 16, 1871, while demonstrating to other attorneys how his client's alleged victim could have accidentally shot himself during an altercation (his client was later acquitted). Died the following day in Lebanon, Ohio.

Benjamin F. Wade (October 27, 1800–March 2, 1878) Born in Feeding Hills, Massachusetts, the son of a farmer. Moved with family to Andover, Ohio, in 1821. Worked as a laborer on the Erie Canal, taught school, and studied medicine in Albany, New York, before being admitted to the Ohio bar in 1828. Served in Ohio senate as a Whig, 1837–38 and 1841–42. Married Caroline Rosekrans, 1841. Judge of circuit court of common pleas, 1847–51. Served in the U.S. Senate as a Whig and then as a Republican, 1851–69. Chairman of the Joint Committee on the Conduct of the War, 1861–65. Co-sponsored the Wade-Davis Bill on Reconstruction, 1864, which was pocket-vetoed by President Lincoln. Elected president pro tempore of the Senate in 1867, he would have succeeded Andrew Johnson as president had Johnson been convicted during his impeachment trial. Unsuccessful candidate for Republican vice-presidential nomination in 1868. Died in Jefferson, Ohio.

Stephen Minot Weld (January 4, 1842–March 16, 1920) Born in

Jamaica Plain, Massachusetts, the son of a schoolmaster. Graduated from Harvard in 1860. Served as civilian aide in Port Royal expedition in 1861. Commissioned as second lieutenant in the 18th Massachusetts Infantry in January 1862. Served on staff of Brigadier General Fitz John Porter, commander of the Fifth Corps, during the Peninsula campaign. Captured at Gaines's Mill and exchanged in early August. Served as aide to Porter at Second Bull Run and Antietam. Testified at Porter's court-martial in December 1862. Served on staff of the Engineer Brigade of the Army of the Potomac at Chancellorsville. Joined staff of Major General John Reynolds, commander of the First Corps, in May 1863. Served at Gettysburg on July 1, 1863, before accompanying Reynolds's body to Philadelphia. Appointed lieutenant colonel of the 56th Massachusetts Infantry in August 1863. Led regiment at the Wilderness, Spotsylvania, North Anna, Cold Harbor, and Petersburg. Promoted to colonel. Captured in the battle of the Crater, paroled in December 1864, and exchanged in March 1865. Returned to Massachusetts and became a successful cotton broker and horticulturalist. Married Eloise Rodman in 1869 and, after her death, Susan Waterbury in 1904. Privately published *War Diary and Letters of Stephen M. Weld* (1912). Died in Boca Grande, Florida.

Gideon Welles (July 1, 1802–February 11, 1878) Born in Glastonbury, Connecticut, the son of a merchant. Educated in Vermont at the American Literary, Scientific, and Military Academy (now Norwich University). Editor of the *Hartford Times*, 1826–36. Served as a Democrat in the Connecticut house of representatives, 1827–35. Married Mary Hale in 1835. Postmaster of Hartford, 1836–41. Served as chief of the bureau of provisions and clothing in the navy department, 1846–49. Helped organize Republican Party in Connecticut. Wrote for the *Hartford Evening Press*, the *New York Evening Post*, and other Republican newspapers. Secretary of the navy in the Lincoln and Andrew Johnson administrations, 1861–69. Died in Hartford.

Walt Whitman (May 31, 1819–March 26, 1892) Born in Huntington Township, New York, the son of a farmer and carpenter. Moved with family to Brooklyn in 1823. Learned printing trade at Brooklyn newspapers. Taught school on Long Island, 1836–38. Became freelance journalist and printer in New York and Brooklyn. Published first edition of *Leaves of Grass* in 1855 (revised editions appeared in 1856, 1860, 1867, 1870, 1881, and 1891). Traveled to northern Virginia in December 1862 after learning that his brother George had been wounded at Fredericksburg. Became volunteer nurse in Washington, D.C., army hospitals. Published *Drum-Taps* and *Sequel to Drum-Taps* in 1865. Worked as clerk at the Interior Department, 1865, and the office of the attorney general, 1865–73. Published prose recollections of his war experiences in *Memoranda During the War* (1875) and *Specimen Days and Collect* (1882). Died in Camden, New Jersey.

Rachel Ann Wicker (August 1840–1910) Born in Urbana, Ohio. Married William Leroy Walker in 1858. Her husband enlisted in the 55th Massachusetts Infantry in June 1863 and survived the war. Died in Piqua, Ohio.

Edward A. Wild (November 25, 1825–August 28, 1891) Born in Brookline, Massachusetts, the son of a physician. Graduated from Harvard in 1844 and from Jefferson Medical College in Philadelphia in 1846. Began homeopathic practice in Brookline, 1847. Traveled in Europe, 1849–50. Married Frances Ellen Sullivan in 1855. Volunteered as surgeon with the Turkish army during the Crimean War, 1855–56, and served in the Caucasus. Returned to Brookline in 1857 and resumed practice. Mustered in as captain of Company A, 1st Massachusetts Volunteers, in May 1861. Fought at Blackburn's Ford, First Bull Run, Yorktown, and Williamsburg, and was wounded at Oak Grove. Appointed colonel of the 35th Massachusetts Infantry, August 1862. Wounded at South Mountain, September 14, 1862, and lost his left arm. Commissioned brigadier general in April 1863 and spent the remainder of the war recruiting and commanding black troops. Began recruiting "African Brigade" at New Bern, North Carolina, May 1863. Led brigade during siege of Charleston Harbor, August–October 1863. Assigned command of the U.S. Colored Troops at Norfolk, Virginia, and led them on raid into eastern North Carolina, December 1863. Commanded First Brigade, Third Division, Eighteenth Corps, Army of the James, April–June 1864, holding outposts along the James River and then fighting at Petersburg. Found guilty at court-martial of disobeying orders, but verdict was overturned. Recruited at Fort Monroe, July–October 1864. Commanded First Division in the Twenty-fifth Corps, January–March 1865, and the Second Brigade of the First Division, March–April 1865. Helped occupy Richmond. Supervisor of the Freedmen's Bureau in Macon, Georgia, June–September 1865. Became involved in silver-mining ventures in Nevada, Colorado, and Canada. Traveled to Colombia in 1891 to help survey railroad route. Died in Medellín, Colombia.

Frank Wilkeson (March 8, 1848–April 22, 1913) Born in Buffalo, New York, the son of a lawyer and iron manufacturer who later reported on the Civil War for the *New-York Daily Tribune* and the *New York Times*. After his older brother Bayard was killed at Gettysburg, he enlisted in the 11th New York Light Artillery Battery during the winter of 1863–64. Saw action at the Wilderness, Spotsylvania, North Anna, Cold Harbor, and Petersburg. Commissioned as second lieutenant in the 4th U.S. Artillery in June 1864. Served in Washington defenses during Early's raid, and helped guard Confederate prisoners in Elmira, New York, before being posted to northern Alabama and East Tennessee in the spring of 1865. Worked as mining engineer in Pennsylvania. Married Mary Crouse in 1869. Moved to cattle ranch and wheat farm in Gypsum, Kansas, in 1871. Helped survey possible railroad route through the North Cascades. Wrote for newspapers and magazines about hunting, fishing, and ranching. Published *Recollections of a Private in the Army of the Potomac* (1887). Lived in Washington and Kansas. Died in Chelan, Washington.

Alpheus S. Williams (September 20, 1810–December 21, 1878) Born in Deep River, Connecticut, the son of a manufacturer. Graduated from Yale College in 1831. Admitted to the bar in 1834. Moved to Detroit in 1836, where he practiced law and joined the local militia company. Married Jane Hereford Pierson in 1839; she died in 1848. Served as probate judge of Wayne County, 1840–44, and published the *Detroit Daily Advertiser*, 1843–48. Commissioned as brigadier general of volunteers in August 1861. Commanded brigade in the Army of the Potomac, October 1861–March 1862. Led a division in the Shenandoah Valley campaign and at Cedar Mountain and Second Bull Run. Assumed temporary command of Twelfth Corps at Antietam following the death of General Mansfield. Commanded division at Chancellorsville and was temporary commander of the Twelfth Corps at Gettysburg. Sent with his division in September 1863 to Tennessee, where they guarded railroads. Served in the Atlanta campaign and commanded the Twentieth Corps in the march through Georgia and the Carolinas. Mustered out on January 15, 1866. Served as U.S. minister to San Salvador, 1866–69. Returned to Detroit. Married Martha Ann Tillman in 1873. Elected to Congress as a Democrat and served from 1875 until his death in Washington, D.C.

William Winters (1830–April 8, 1864?) Born in Connecticut. Married Harriet J. Smith in Cincinnati, Ohio, in 1853. Moved to Hawes Creek Township in Bartholomew County, Indiana, where he worked as a saddle and harness maker. Enlisted in Company I, 67th Indiana Infantry, in August 1862. Taken prisoner along with his regiment when the Union garrison at Munfordville, Kentucky, surrendered on September 17, 1862. Returned to Indiana after being paroled the day after his capture. Exchanged in late November 1862. Regiment joined Sherman's expedition against Vicksburg. Saw action at Chickasaw Bayou. Served as hospital attendant during expedition to capture Arkansas Post and in army camps near Vicksburg. Saw action at Port Gibson, Champion Hill, Big Black River, and in the siege of Vicksburg. Sent with regiment to southern Louisiana in August 1863 and to Matagorda Bay, Texas, in December. Returned to southern Louisiana in February 1864 and served in Red River campaign. Missing in action and presumed killed in the battle of Sabine Crossroads.

Susan C. Woolker Lived in Hillsdale, North Carolina, in 1864. Her husband served in the Confederate army.

Note on the Texts

This volume collects nineteenth- and early twentieth-century writing about the Civil War, bringing together public and private letters, newspaper and magazine articles, pamphlets, memoranda, speeches, journal and diary entries, proclamations, messages, addresses, military orders, legal statements, poems, sermons, and excerpts from memoirs written by participants and observers and dealing with events in the period from March 1864 to June 1865. Most of these documents were not written for publication, and most of them existed only in manuscript form during the lifetimes of the persons who wrote them. With seven exceptions, the texts presented in this volume are taken from printed sources. In cases where there is only one printed source for a document, the text offered here comes from that source. Where there is more than one printed source for a document, the text printed in this volume is taken from the source that appears to contain the fewest editorial alterations in the spelling, capitalization, paragraphing, and punctuation of the original. In seven instances where no printed sources (or no complete printed sources) were available, the texts in this volume are printed from manuscripts.

This volume prints texts as they appear in the sources listed below, but with a few alterations in editorial procedure. The bracketed conjectural readings of editors, in cases where original manuscripts or printed texts were damaged or difficult to read, are accepted without brackets in this volume when those readings seem to be the only possible ones; but when they do not, or when the editor made no conjecture, the missing word or words are indicated by a bracketed two-em space, i.e., [   ]. In cases where a typographical error or obvious misspelling in manuscript was marked by earlier editors with "[*sic*]," the present volume omits the "[*sic*]" and corrects the typographical error or slip of the pen. In some cases, obvious errors were not marked by earlier editors with "[*sic*]" but were printed and then followed by a bracketed correction; in these instances, this volume removes the brackets and accepts the editorial emendation. Bracketed editorial insertions used in the source texts to identify persons or places, to expand contractions and abbreviations, or to clarify meaning, have been deleted in this volume. In instances where canceled, but still legible, words were printed in the source texts with lines through the deleted material, or where canceled words were printed and indicated with an asterisk, this volume omits the canceled words.

In *The Papers of Jefferson Davis*, material that was written in interlined form in manuscript is printed within diagonal marks; this volume prints the interlined words and omits the diagonals. *The Papers of Jefferson Davis* prints two portions of a sentence in the letter written by Davis to Varina Howell Davis on April 23, 1865, as canceled material because they were crossed out in the manuscript. This volume prints "and after" and "bly under the the influence of her husband was afraid to be known as having close relations with us" (see page 708.12–15 in this volume) without cancellation marks because they were crossed out by someone other than Davis. Similarly, *Inside Lincoln's White House: The Complete Civil War Diary of John Hay* (1997), edited by Michael Burlingame and John R. Turner Ettlinger, prints as canceled material a paragraph that was crossed out in the manuscript of the November 11, 1864, entry, describing William H. Seward's anger at the newspaper editor John W. Forney (page 461.26–29 in this volume). This volume prints the paragraph without cancellation marks because it is likely that it was crossed out by someone other than Hay, possibly after his death.

The selections from the diary of Gideon Welles, the secretary of the navy in the Lincoln administration, are taken from *Diary of Gideon Welles* (1960), edited by Howard K. Beale. Welles kept a diary during the Civil War that he extensively revised from 1869 to his death in 1878. The revised text was published in 1911 as *Diary of Gideon Welles*, edited by his son Edgar T. Welles with the assistance of John Morse Jr. and Frederick Bancroft. In the 1960 edition, Beale presented the text of the 1911 edition while printing deleted material from the original diary in the margins and using brackets, italics, strike-through lines, and other editorial markings to indicate the differences between the original version of the diary and the revised text. The texts of the selections from the Welles diary printed in this volume are taken from the 1960 edition and incorporate the changes indicated by Beale in order to present a clear text of the diary as originally written by Welles during the Civil War. In two instances, emendations made by Welles while revising his diary have been accepted in this volume as corrections of slips of the pen: at 690.30, "that there thousands" becomes "that there were thousands," and at 691.27, "but there many more" becomes "but there were many more."

An error in the letter written by John H. Stringfellow to Jefferson Davis on February 8, 1865, is treated as a slip of the pen and corrected in this volume, even though it was not corrected in *Freedom: A Documentary History of Emancipation, 1861–1867, Series II: The Black Military Experience*: at 577.1, "furnishishing" becomes "furnishing." Six slips of the pen in documents printed from manuscript sources are also corrected: at 303.19, "my innermost heat" becomes "my innermost heart"; at 304.5–6, "they would they would harm" becomes "they would harm"; at 304.12, "Hood's army is stregthening" becomes "Hood's army is strengthening"; at 304.37–38, "there is retribution atlast" becomes "there is retribution at last"; at 306.1, "but I has not been given us" becomes "but it has not been given us"; at 512.31, "is calculated to to increase them" becomes "is calculated to increase them."

The following is a list of the documents included in this volume, in the order of their appearance, giving the source of each text. The most common sources are indicated by these abbreviations:

CWAL *The Collected Works of Abraham Lincoln*, ed. Roy P. Basler (8 vols., New Brunswick, N.J.: Rutgers University Press, 1953). Copyright © 1953 by the Abraham Lincoln Association. Used by permission of the Abraham Lincoln Association.

Foster *One of Cleburne's Command: The Civil War Reminiscences and Diary of Capt. Samuel T. Foster, Granbury's Texas Brigade, CSA*, ed. Norman D. Brown (Austin: University of Texas Press, 1980). Copyright © 1980 by the University of Texas Press.

Freedom: *Freedom: A Documentary History of Emancipation,*
Destruction *1861–1867. Series I, Volume I: The Destruction of Slavery*, ed. Ira Berlin, Barbara J. Fields, Thavolia Glymph, Joseph P. Reidy, Leslie S. Rowland (New York: Cambridge University Press, 1985.) Copyright © 2010 by Cambridge University Press. Used by permission of Cambridge University Press.

Freedom: *Freedom: A Documentary History of Emancipation,*
Lower South *1861–1867. Series I, Volume III: The Wartime Genesis of Free Labor: The Lower South*, ed. Ira Berlin, Thavolia Glymph, Steven F. Miller, Joseph P. Reidy, Leslie S. Rowland, Julie Saville (New York: Cambridge University Press, 1993). Copyright © 1993 by Cambridge University Press. Used by permission of Cambridge University Press.

Freedom: *Freedom: A Documentary History of Emancipation,*
Military *1861–1867. Series II: The Black Military Experience*, ed. Ira Berlin (Cambridge and New York: Cambridge University Press, 1982). Copyright © 2010 by Cambridge University Press. Used by permission of Cambridge University Press.

Freedom: *Freedom: A Documentary History of Emancipation,*
Upper South *1861–1867. Series I, Volume II: The Wartime Genesis of Free Labor: The Upper South*, ed. Ira Berlin, Steven F. Miller, Joseph P. Reidy, Leslie S. Rowland (New York:

	Cambridge University Press, 1993). Copyright © 1993 by Cambridge University Press. Used by permission of Cambridge University Press.
OR	*The War of the Rebellion: A Compilation of the Official Records of the Union and Confederate Armies* (128 vols., Washington, D.C.: Government Printing Office, 1880–1901).
PUSG	*The Papers of Ulysses S. Grant*, ed. John Y. Simon (31 vols. to date, Carbondale: Southern Illinois University Press, 1967–2009). Volume 10 (1982), Volume 11 (1984), Volume 14 (1985). Copyright © 1982, 1984, 1985 by The Ulysses S. Grant Association. Used by permission of The Ulysses S. Grant Association.
SCW	*Sherman's Civil War: Selected Correspondence of William T. Sherman, 1860–1865*, ed. Brooks D. Simpson and Jean V. Berlin (Chapel Hill: The University of North Carolina Press, 1999). Copyright © 1999 by The University of North Carolina Press. Used by permission of the publisher, www.uncpress.unc.edu.
Strong	George Templeton Strong, *Diary of the Civil War, 1860–1865*, ed. Allan Nevins (New York: The Macmillan Publishing Company, 1962). Reprinted with permission of Scribner, a Division of Simon & Schuster, Inc., from *The Diary of George Templeton Strong* edited by Allan Nevins and Milton Halsey Thomas. Copyright © 1952 by The Macmillan Publishing Company; copyright renewed © 1980 by Milton Halsey Thomas. All rights reserved.
Welles	*Diary of Gideon Welles*, volume II, ed. Howard K. Beale (New York: W. W. Norton & Company, Inc., 1960). Copyright © 1960 by W. W. Norton & Company, Inc.
WPREL	*The Wartime Papers of Robert E. Lee*, ed. Clifford Dowdey and Louis H. Manarin (Boston: Little, Brown, 1961). Copyright © 1961 by Commonwealth of Virginia. Used by permission of Little, Brown and Company. All rights reserved.

Catherine Edmondston: Diary, March 8, 1864. *"Journal of a Secesh Lady": The Diary of Catherine Ann Devereux Edmondston, 1860–1866*, ed. Beth G. Crabtree and James W. Patton (Raleigh: North Carolina Division of Archives and History, 1979), 536–38. Copyright © 1979 by the North Carolina Division of Archives and History. Used by permission.

Ellen Renshaw House: Diary, March 9–11, March 19, 1864. *A Very Violent Rebel: The Civil War Diary of Ellen Renshaw House*, ed. Daniel E. Sutherland (Knoxville: University of Tennessee Press, 1996), 112–14, 117–18. Copyright © 1996 by The University of Tennessee Press/Knoxville. Ellen Renshaw House's diary, Copyright © 1996 by Ellen Allran and Victoria Guthrie. Used by permission of the University of Tennessee Press.
Scientific American: New Rolling Mills in Pittsburgh. *Scientific American*, March 26, 1864.
Harriet Ann Jacobs and Louisa M. Jacobs to Lydia Maria Child, March 26, 1864. *The Harriet Jacobs Family Papers*, vol. II, ed. Jean Fagan Yellin (Chapel Hill: The University of North Carolina Press, 2008), 558–61. Copyright © 2008 Jean Fagan Yellin. Used by permission of the publisher.
Jim Heiskell: Statement Regarding His Escape from Slavery, March 30, 1864. *Freedom: Destruction*, 320–22.
Susan C. Woolker to Zebulon B. Vance, April 3, 1864. *North Carolina Civil War Documentary*, ed. W. Buck Yearns and John G. Barrett (Chapel Hill: The University of North Carolina Press, 1980), 262–63. Copyright © 1980 by The University of North Carolina Press. Used by permission of the publisher, www.uncpress.unc.edu.
Ulysses S. Grant to William T. Sherman, April 4, 1864. *PUSG*, vol. 10, 251–53.
William Winters to Harriet Winters, April 4, 1864. *The Musick of the Mocking Birds, the Roar of the Cannon: The Civil War Diary and Letters of William Winters*, ed. Steven E. Bloodworth (Lincoln: University of Nebraska Press, 1998), 121–22. Copyright © 1998 by University of Nebraska Press. Used by permission of the publisher.
Wilbur Fisk to *The Green Mountain Freeman*, April 7, 1864. *Hard Marching Every Day: The Civil War Letters of Private Wilbur Fisk, 1861–1865*, ed. Emil and Ruth Rosenblatt (Lawrence: University Press of Kansas, 1992), 205–8. Copyright © 1983, 1992 by Emil Rosenblatt. Used by permission of the University Press of Kansas.
Ellen Renshaw House: Diary, April 8, 1864. *A Very Violent Rebel: The Civil War Diary of Ellen Renshaw House*, ed. Daniel E. Sutherland (Knoxville: University of Tennessee Press, 1996), 127–28. Copyright © 1996 by The University of Tennessee Press/Knoxville. Ellen Renshaw House's diary, Copyright © 1996 by Ellen Allran and Victoria Guthrie. Used by permission of the University of Tennessee Press.
Lois Bryan Adams to the *Detroit Advertiser and Tribune*, April 9, 1864. Lois Bryan Adams, *Letter from Washington, 1863–1865*, ed. Evelyn Leasher (Detroit: Wayne State University Press, 1999), 102–7. Copyright © 1999 by Wayne State University Press.

Achilles V. Clark to Judith Porter and Henrietta Ray, April 14, 1864. John Cimprich and Robert C. Mainfort Jr., "Fort Pillow Revisited: New Evidence About an Old Controversy," *Civil War History*, vol. 28, no. 4, December 1982, 297–99. Copyright © 1982 by Kent State University Press.

Robert E. Lee to Jefferson Davis, April 15, 1864. *WPREL*, 699–700.

The New York Times: The Black Flag. *The New York Times*, April 16, 1864.

Abraham Lincoln: Address at Baltimore Sanitary Fair, April 18, 1864. *CWAL*, vol. VII, 301–3.

R.H.C. to *The Christian Recorder*. *The Christian Recorder*, April 30, 1864.

Gideon Welles: Diary, May 3, 5–6, 1864. *Welles*, vol. 2, 23–24, 24–25.

Petition from the Slaveholders of Randolph County, Alabama, May 6, 1864. *Freedom: Destruction*, 756–58.

Samuel W. Fiske to the *Springfield Republican*, May 3, 1864. *Mr. Dunn Browne's Experiences in the Army: The Civil War Letters of Samuel W. Fiske*, ed. Stephen W. Sears (New York: Fordham University Press, 1998), 245–49. Copyright © 1998 by Stephen W. Sears. Used by permission of Fordham University Press.

Theodore Lyman: Journal, May 4–7, 1864. *Meade's Army: The Private Notebooks of Lt. Col. Theodore Lyman*, ed. David W. Lowe (Kent, Ohio: Kent State University Press, 2007), 130–44. Copyright © 2007 by Kent State University Press. Used by permission of the publisher.

Wilbur Fisk to *The Green Mountain Freeman*, May 9, 1864. *Hard Marching Every Day: The Civil War Letters of Private Wilbur Fisk, 1861–1865*, ed. Emil and Ruth Rosenblatt (Lawrence: University Press of Kansas, 1992), 214–18. Copyright © 1983, 1992 by Emil Rosenblatt. Used by permission of the University Press of Kansas.

J.F.J. Caldwell: from *The History of a Brigade of South Carolinians*. J.F.J. Caldwell, *The History of a Brigade of South Carolinians, known first as "Gregg's," and subsequently as "McGowan's Brigade"* (Philadelphia: King & Baird, 1866), 127–36.

Horace Porter: from *Campaigning with Grant*. Horace Porter, *Campaigning with Grant* (New York: The Century Co., 1897), 78–79.

Herman Melville: The Armies of the Wilderness. (1863-4.) Herman Melville, *Battle-Pieces and Aspects of the War* (New York: Harper & Brothers, 1866), 93–104.

Ulysses S. Grant to Edwin M. Stanton and Henry W. Halleck, May 11, 1864. *PUSG*, vol. 10, 422–23.

Charles Harvey Brewster to Martha Brewster, May 11, 1864; to Mary Brewster, May 13, 1864; and to Martha Brewster, May 15, 1864. *When This Cruel War Is Over: The Civil War Letters of Charles*

Harvey Brewster, ed. David W. Blight (Amherst: The University of Massachusetts Press, 1992), 292–300. Copyright © 1992 by Historic Northampton.

J.F.J. Caldwell: from *The History of a Brigade of South Carolinians*. J.F.J. Caldwell, *The History of a Brigade of South Carolinians, known first as "Gregg's," and subsequently as "McGowan's Brigade"* (Philadelphia: King & Baird, 1866), 140–47.

Edward A. Wild to Robert S. Davis, May 12, 1864. *Freedom: Destruction*, 95–97.

James A. Connolly to Mary Dunn Connolly, May 15, 20, 1864. "Major James Austin Connolly," *Transactions of the Illinois State Historical Society for the Year 1928* (Springfield: Illinois State Historical Library, 1928), 331–32. Used by permission of the Abraham Lincoln Presidential Library and Museum.

Alpheus S. Williams to Mary Williams, May 20, 1864. *From the Cannon's Mouth: The Civil War Letters of Alpheus S. Williams*, ed. Milo M. Quaife (Detroit: Wayne State University Press, 1959), 307–9.

Richard Taylor: General Orders No. 44, May 23, 1864. *The New York Times*, May 20, 1879.

Samuel T. Foster: Diary, May 23–28, 1864. *Foster*, 80–89.

Charles Harvey Brewster to Mary Brewster, May 23, 1864; to Martha Brewster, May 24, 1864; and to Mattie Brewster, May 26, 1864. *When This Cruel War Is Over: The Civil War Letters of Charles Harvey Brewster*, ed. David W. Blight (Amherst: The University of Massachusetts Press, 1992), 300–8. Copyright © 1992 by Historic Northampton.

Eugene Forbes: Diary, May 24–27, 1864. *Death Before Dishonor: The Andersonville Diary of Eugene Forbes, 4th New Jersey Infantry*, ed. William B. Styple (Kearny, N.J.: Belle Grove Publishing Company, 1995), 53–56.

Charles Francis Adams Jr. to Charles Francis Adams, May 29, 1864. Manuscript, Adams Family Papers, Massachusetts Historical Society. Used by permission.

Lorenzo Thomas to Henry Wilson, May 30, 1864. *Freedom: Military*, 530–31.

Cornelia Hancock to Ellen Hancock Child, May 28, May 31–June 3, 1864. *Letters of a Civil War Nurse: Cornelia Hancock, 1863–1865*, ed. Henrietta Stratton Jaquette (Lincoln: University of Nebraska Press, 1998), 91–97.

Frank Wilkeson: from *Recollections of a Private Soldier in the Army of the Potomac*. Frank Wilkeson, *Recollections of a Private Soldier in the Army of the Potomac* (New York: G. P. Putnam's Son, 1887), 128–39, 149–52.

Maria Lydig Daly: Diary, June 8, 1864. Maria Lydig Daly, *Diary of a Union Lady, 1861–1865*, ed. Harold Earl Hammond (New York: Funk & Wagnalls, 1962), 298–300. Copyright © 1962 by Funk and Wagnalls Company, Inc.

Robert Patrick to Alonzo Lewis, June 9, 1864. *Reluctant Rebel: The Secret Diary of Robert Patrick, 1861–1865*, ed. F. Jay Taylor (Baton Rouge: Louisiana State University Press, 1959), 180–82. Copyright © 1959 by Louisiana State University Press. Used by permission of the publisher.

Judith W. McGuire: Diary, June 11, 1864. Judith W. McGuire, *Diary of a Southern Refugee, during the war*, 3rd edition (Richmond, Va.: J. W. Randolph & English, Publishers, 1889), 276–80.

Charles Harvey Brewster to Mattie Brewster, June 11, 1864. *When This Cruel War Is Over: The Civil War Letters of Charles Harvey Brewster*, ed. David W. Blight (Amherst: The University of Massachusetts Press, 1992), 314–16. Copyright © 1992 by Historic Northampton.

Charles Francis Adams to Charles Francis Adams Jr., June 17, 1864. Manuscript, Adams Family Papers, Massachusetts Historical Society. Used by permission.

Charles B. Fisher: Diary, June 19–21, 1864. *Diary of Charles B. Fisher*, ed. Paul E. Sluby, Sr., and Stanton L. Wormley (Washington, D.C.: Columbian Harmony Society, 1983), 83–91. Copyright © 1983 by Charles B. Fisher III and the Columbian Harmony Society.

Wilbur Fisk to *The Green Mountain Freeman*, June 19, 1864. *Hard Marching Every Day: The Civil War Letters of Private Wilbur Fisk, 1861–1865*, ed. Emil and Ruth Rosenblatt (Lawrence: University Press of Kansas, 1992), 229–32. Copyright © 1983, 1992 by Emil Rosenblatt. Used by permission of the University Press of Kansas.

Stephen Minot Weld to Stephen Minot Weld Sr., June 21, 1864. *War Diary and Letters of Stephen Minot Weld, 1861–1865* (Cambridge, Mass.: The Riverside Press, 1912), 317–19.

George E. Chamberlin to Ephraim Chamberlin, June 27, 1864. *Letters of George E. Chamberlin, Who Fell in the Service of His Country near Charlestown, Va., August 21st, 1864*, ed. Caroline Chamberlin Lutz (Springfield, Ill.: H. W. Rokker, 1883), 338–42.

Eugene Forbes: Diary, June 13–30, 1864. *Death Before Dishonor: The Andersonville Diary of Eugene Forbes, 4th New Jersey Infantry*, ed. William B. Styple (Kearny, N.J.: Belle Grove Publishing Company, 1995), 69–80.

William T. Sherman to Ellen Ewing Sherman, June 30, 1864. *SCW*, 659–61.

Horace Greeley to Abraham Lincoln, July 7, 1864. Manuscript, Abraham Lincoln Papers, Library of Congress.

John White Geary to Mary Geary, July 8, 1864. *A Politician Goes to War: The Civil War Letters of John White Geary*, ed. William Alan Blair (University Park, Pa.: The Pennsylvania State University Press, 1995), 184–86. Copyright © 1995 by The Pennsylvania State University. Used by permission of The Pennsylvania State University Press.

Abraham Lincoln: Proclamation Concerning Reconstruction, July 8, 1864. *CWAL*, vol. VII, 433–34.

Abraham Lincoln to Horace Greeley, July 9, 1864. *CWAL*, vol. VII, 435.

Eugene Forbes: Diary, July 11, 1864. *Death Before Dishonor: The Andersonville Diary of Eugene Forbes, 4th New Jersey Infantry*, ed. William B. Styple (Kearny, N.J.: Belle Grove Publishing Company, 1995), 85–87.

Henry Robinson Berkeley: Diary, July 4–13, 1864. *Four Years in the Confederate Artillery: The Diary of Private Henry Robinson Berkeley*, ed. William H. Runge (Chapel Hill: The University of North Carolina Press, 1961), 85–88. Copyright © 1961 by The Virginia Historical Society. Used by permission of The Virginia Historical Society.

Lois Bryan Adams to the *Detroit Advertiser and Tribune*, July 13, 15, 1864. Lois Bryan Adams, *Letter from Washington, 1863–1865*, ed. Evelyn Leasher (Detroit: Wayne State University Press, 1999), 174–77. Copyright © 1999 by Wayne State University Press.

Ulysses S. Grant to Henry W. Halleck, July 14, 1864. *PUSG*, vol. 11, 242–43.

Charles A. Dana to Ulysses S. Grant, July 15, 1864. *OR*, series 1, vol. 37, part 2, 332.

Abraham Lincoln, Offer of Safe Conduct for Peace Commissioners, July 18, 1864. *CWAL*, vol. VII, 451.

Clement C. Clay and James P. Holcombe to Horace Greeley, July 21, 1864. *The New York Times*, July 22, 1864.

James R. Gilmore to the *Boston Evening Transcript. Boston Evening Transcript*, July 22, 1864.

Henry Robinson Berkeley: Diary, July 14–24, 1864. *Four Years in the Confederate Artillery: The Diary of Private Henry Robinson Berkeley*, ed. William H. Runge (Chapel Hill: The University of North Carolina Press, 1961), 85–88. Copyright © 1961 by The Virginia Historical Society. Used by permission of The Virginia Historical Society.

Samuel T. Foster: Diary, July 18–23, 1864. *Foster*, 105–15.

John Q. A. Dennis to Edwin M. Stanton, July 26, 1864. *Freedom: Destruction*, 386.

Benjamin McIntyre: Diary, July 29, 1864. *Federals on the Frontier: The Diary of Benjamin F. McIntyre, 1862–1864*, ed. Nannie M. Tilley

(Austin: University of Texas Press, 1963), 380–82. Copyright © 1963, renewed 1991 by Nannie M. Tilley. Used by permission of the University of Texas Press.

David G. Farragut, General Orders Nos. 10 and 11, July 12 and 29, 1864. *Official Records of the Union and Confederate Navies in the War of the Rebellion*, series 1, vol. 21 (Washington: Government Printing Office, 1906), 397–98.

Stephen Minot Weld: Diary, July 30, 1864, and Memoir from 1912. *War Diary and Letters of Stephen Minot Weld, 1861–1865* (Cambridge, Mass.: The Riverside Press, 1912), 352–57.

William Pegram to Virginia Johnson Pegram, August 1, 1864. "'The Boy Artillerist': Letters of Colonel William Pegram, C.S.A.," ed. James I. Robertson Jr., *The Virginia Magazine of History and Biography*, vol. 98, no. 2, April 1990, 242–45. Copyright © 1990 by The Virginia Historical Society. Used by permission of The Virginia Historical Society.

C. Chauncey Burr: Editor's Table. *The Old Guard*, August 1864.

Edgeworth Bird to Sallie Bird, August 4, 1864. Manuscript, Hargrett Rare Book and Manuscript Library, University of Georgia.

Benjamin F. Wade and Henry Winter Davis: To the Supporters of the Government. *New-York Daily Tribune*, August 5, 1864.

Robert Garlick Hill Kean: Diary, August 7, 1864. *Inside the Confederate Government: The Diary of Robert Garlick Hill Kean*, ed. Edward Younger (New York: Oxford University Press, 1957), 168–70. Copyright © 1957 by Oxford University Press. Used by permission of Oxford University Press, USA.

Mathella Page Harrison: Diary, August 17, 1864. Typescript, Albert and Shirley Small Special Collections Library, University of Virginia.

Abraham Lincoln: Memorandum on Probable Failure of Reelection, August 23, 1864. *CWAL*, vol. VII, 514.

Benjamin F. Butler to Robert Ould, August 27, 1864. *OR*, series 2, vol. 7, 687–91.

Robert Toombs to Alexander H. Stephens, August 30, 1864. *The Correspondence of Robert Toombs, Alexander H. Stephens, and Howell Cobb*, ed. Ulrich B. Phillips (Washington, D.C.: American Historical Association, 1913), 651–52.

Platform of the Democratic National Convention, August 30, 1864. *Official Proceedings of the Democratic National Convention, held in 1864 at Chicago* (Chicago: The Times Steam Book and Job Printing House, 1864), 27.

James R. Gilmore: Our Visit to Richmond. *The Atlantic Monthly*, September 1864.

Robert E. Lee to Jefferson Davis, September 2, 1864. *WPREL*, 847–50.

Spottswood Rice to His Children and to Kitty Diggs, September 3, 1864. *Freedom: Military*, 689–90.
Gideon Welles: Diary, September 3, 1864. *Welles*, vol. 2, 135–36.
Thomas Bramlette to Abraham Lincoln, September 3, 1864. *Freedom: Destruction*, 604–6.
Clement L. Vallandigham to George B. McClellan, September 4, 1864. Manuscript, George B. McClellan Papers, Library of Congress.
Kate Stone: Diary, September 5, 1864. *Brokenburn: The Journal of Kate Stone, 1861–1868*, ed. John Q. Anderson (Baton Rouge: Louisiana State University Press, 1955), 194–99. Copyright © 1989 by Louisiana State University Press. Used by permission of Louisiana State University Press.
George Templeton Strong: Diary, September 5–8, 1864. *Strong*, 481–83.
George B. McClellan to the Democratic Nomination Committee, September 8, 1864. *The Civil War Papers of George B. McClellan: Selected Correspondence, 1860–1865*, ed. Stephen W. Sears (New York: Ticknor & Fields, 1989), 595–96. Copyright © 1989 by Stephen W. Sears. Used by permission of the Houghton Mifflin Harcourt Publishing Company. All rights reserved.
James A. Connolly to Mary Dunn Connolly, September 11, 1864. "Major James Austin Connolly," *Transactions of the Illinois State Historical Society for the Year 1928* (Springfield: Illinois State Historical Library, 1928), 360–62. Used by permission of the Abraham Lincoln Presidential Library.
William T. Sherman to James M. Calhoun and Others, September 12, 1864. *SCW*, 707–9.
Rachel Ann Wicker to John A. Andrew, September 12, 1864. *Freedom: Military*, 402–3.
Alexander McKinley to Samuel Du Pont, September 18, 1864. *Samuel Francis Du Pont: A Selection from His Civil War Letters*, vol. III, ed. John D. Hayes (Ithaca, N.Y.: Cornell University Press, 1969), 381–87. Copyright © 1969 by Eleutherian Mills-Hagley Foundation. Reprinted courtesy of Hagley Museum and Library.
Henry Robinson Berkeley: Diary, September 19, 1864. *Four Years in the Confederate Artillery: The Diary of Private Henry Robinson Berkeley* (Chapel Hill: The University of North Carolina Press, 1961), 96–99. Copyright © 1961 by The Virginia Historical Society. Used by permission of The Virginia Historical Society.
Jefferson Davis, Speech at Macon, September 23, 1864. *The Papers of Jefferson Davis, Volume 11: September 1864–May 1865*, ed. Lynda Lasswell Crist, Barbara J. Rozek, and Kenneth H. Williams (Baton Rouge: Louisiana State University Press, 2003), 61–63. Copyright

© 2003 by Louisiana State University Press. Used by permission of the publisher.

Elizabeth Blair Lee to Samuel Phillips Lee, September 24, 1864. *Wartime Washington: The Civil War Letters of Elizabeth Blair Lee*, ed. Virginia Laas (Urbana: University of Illinois Press, 1990), 281–83. Copyright © 1991 by the Board of Trustees of the University of Illinois. Used by permission from the Blair and Lee Family Papers, Manuscripts Division, Department of Rare Books and Special Collections, Princeton University Library.

Jefferson Davis, Speech at Columbia, October 4, 1864. *The Papers of Jefferson Davis, Volume 11: September 1864–May 1865*, ed. Lynda Lasswell Crist, Barbara J. Rozek, and Kenneth H. Williams (Baton Rouge: Louisiana State University Press, 2003), 82–88. Copyright © 2003 by Louisiana State University Press. Used by permission of the publisher.

Address of the Colored National Convention, October 6, 1864. *Proceedings of the National Convention of Colored Men, Held in the City of Syracuse, N.Y., October 4, 5, 6 and 7, 1864* (Boston: Geo. C. Rand & Avery, 1864), 44–62.

William T. Sherman to Ulysses S. Grant, October 9, 1864. *SCW*, 731.

Stephen Dodson Ramseur to Ellen Richmond Ramseur, October 10, 1864. *The Bravest of the Brave: The Correspondence of Stephen Dodson Ramseur*, ed. George G. Kundahl, 286–88. Copyright © 2010 by The University of North Carolina Press. Used by permission of the publisher, www.uncpress.unc.edu.

John B. Jones: Diary, October 10–13, 1864. J. B. Jones, *A Rebel War Clerk's Diary at the Confederate States Capital*, vol. II (Philadelphia: J. B. Lippincott & Co., 1866), 302–6.

Samuel Francis Du Pont to William King Hall, October 13, 1864. *Samuel Francis Du Pont: A Selection from His Civil War Letters*, vol. III, ed. John D. Hayes (Ithaca, N.Y.: Cornell University Press, 1969), 401–6. Copyright © 1969 by Eleutherian Mills-Hagley Foundation. Reprinted courtesy of Hagley Museum and Library.

Catherine Ann Devereux Edmondston: Diary, October 18, 1864. *"Journal of a Secesh Lady," The Diary of Catherine Ann Devereux Edmondston*, ed. Beth G. Crabtree and James W. Patton (Raleigh: North Carolina Division of Archives and History, 1979), 623–24. Copyright © 1979 by the North Carolina Division of Archives and History. Used by permission.

Francis Lieber: Lincoln or McClellan. Francis Lieber, *Lincoln or McClellan, Appeal to the Germans in America* (New York: Loyal Publication Society, 1864), 1–8.

George Templeton Strong: Diary, November 9, 1864. *Strong*, 511–12.

John Hay: Diary, November 11, 1864. *Inside Lincoln's White House: The Complete Civil War Diary of John Hay*, ed. Michael Burlingame and John R. Turner Ettlinger (Carbondale and Edwardsville: Southern Illinois University Press, 1997), 247–49. Copyright © 1997 by the Board of Trustees, Southern Illinois University. Used by permission of Southern Illinois University Press.

John S. Mosby to Philip H. Sheridan, November 11, 1864. *OR*, series I, vol. 43, pt. 2, 920.

Jane Kamper: Statement Regarding Her Emancipation, November 14, 1864. *Freedom: Upper South*, 519.

Maria Lydig Daly: Diary, November 15, 1864. *Diary of a Union Lady, 1861–1865*, ed. Harold Earl Hammond (New York: Funk & Wagnalls, 1962), 312–14. Copyright © 1962 by Funk and Wagnalls Company, Inc.

James A. Connolly: Diary, November 17–23, 1864. "Major James Austin Connolly," *Transactions of the Illinois State Historical Society for the Year 1928* (Springfield: Illinois State Historical Library, 1928), 401–8. Used by permission of the Abraham Lincoln Presidential Library.

Henry Adams to Charles Francis Adams Jr., November 25, 1864. *The Letters of Henry Adams*, vol. I, ed. J. C. Levenson, Ernest Samuels, Charles Vandersee, Viola Hopkins Winner (Cambridge: The Belknap Press of Harvard University Press, 1982), 458–59. Copyright © 1982 by the Massachusetts Historical Society. Reprinted courtesy of the Adams Family Papers, Massachusetts Historical Society. Used by permission.

John Wilkes Booth: "To whom it may concern," November 1864. Papers Relating to John Wilkes Booth, 1864–1865, General Records of the Department of Justice, 1790–2002, Record Group 60, National Archives at College Park, MD. [Online version, *research.archives.gov/description/6783029*, February 13, 2014.]

Joseph Miller: Statement Regarding His Family, November 26, 1864. *Freedom: Military*, 269–71.

Samuel T. Foster: Diary, November 30–December 1, 1864. *Foster*, 147–51.

Abraham Lincoln, Annual Message to Congress, December 6, 1864. *CWAL*, vol. VIII, 136–53.

Henry Nutt to Zebulon B. Vance, December 12, 1864. Manuscript, Zebulon B. Vance Papers, State Archives of North Carolina, Raleigh, North Carolina. Used by permission of the State Archives of North Carolina.

John Chipman Gray to John C. Ropes, December 14, 1864. *War Letters, 1862–1865, of John Chipman Gray and John Codman Ropes*, ed.

Worthington Chauncey Ford (Boston: Houghton Mifflin Company, 1927), 425–29.

John White Geary to Mary Geary, December 17, 1864. *A Politician Goes to War: The Civil War Letters of John White Geary*, ed. William Alan Blair (University Park, Pa.: The Pennsylvania State University Press, 1995), 217–18. Copyright © 1995 by The Pennsylvania State University. Used by permission of The Pennsylvania State University Press.

Mary S. Mallard: Journal, December 17–21, 1864. *The Children of Pride: A True Story of Georgia and the Civil War*, abridged edition, ed. Robert Manson Myers (New Haven, Conn.: Yale University Press, 1984), 510–15. Copyright © 1972, 1984 by Robert Manson Myers.

Harper's Weekly: Retaliation. *Harper's Weekly*, January 7, 1865.

Howell T. Cobb to James A. Seddon, January 8, 1865. *OR*, series 4, vol. 3, 1009–10.

Catherine Ann Devereux Edmondston: Diary, January 9, 1865. *"Journal of a Secesh Lady": The Diary of Catherine Ann Devereux Edmondston*, ed. Beth G. Crabtree and James W. Patton (Raleigh: North Carolina Division of Archives and History, 1979), 652–55. Copyright © 1979 by the North Carolina Division of Archives and History. Used by permission.

Petition of the Colored Citizens of Nashville to the Union Convention of Tennessee, January 9, 1865. *Freedom: Military*, 811–16.

Robert E. Lee to Andrew Hunter, January 11, 1865. *OR*, series 4, vol. 3, 1012–13.

Meeting of Colored Ministers with Edwin M. Stanton and William T. Sherman, January 12, 1865. *Freedom: Lower South*, 332–37.

William T. Sherman: Special Field Orders No. 15, January 16, 1865. *Freedom: Lower South*, 338–40.

Thirteenth Amendment to the Constitution of the United States, January 31, 1865. *The Debate on the Constitution: Part Two: January to August 1788*, ed. Bernard Bailyn (New York: The Library of America, 1993), 957.

George Julian: Journal, February 1, 1865. "George Julian's Journal—The Assassination of Lincoln," *Indiana Magazine of History*, vol. XI, no. 4, December 1915, 327.

Robert Garlick Hill Kean: Diary, February 5, 1865. *Inside the Confederate Government: The Diary of Robert Garlick Hill Kean*, ed. Edward Younger (New York: Oxford University Press, 1957), 194–98. Copyright © 1957 by Oxford University Press. Used by permission of Oxford University Press, USA.

John H. Stringfellow to Jefferson Davis, February 8, 1865. *Freedom: Military*, 291–95.

Henry Highland Garnet: A Memorial Discourse, February 12, 1865. *A Memorial Discourse by Rev. Henry Highland Garnet, delivered in the hall of the House of representatives, Washington City, D.C. on Sabbath, February 12, 1865* (Philadelphia: Joseph M. Wilson, 1865), 69–91.
Emma LeConte: Diary, February 17–18, 1865. Manuscript, Emma LeConte Diary, #420-z, Southern Historical Collection, The Wilson Library, The University of North Carolina at Chapel Hill.
Luther Rice Mills to John Mills, March 2, 1865. George D. Harmon, "Letters of Luther Rice Mills—A Confederate Soldier," *The North Carolina Historical Review*, vol. IV, no. 3, July 1927, 307–8. Published by the North Carolina Historical Commission. Used by permission of the North Carolina Office of Archives and History.
Abraham Lincoln, Second Inaugural Address, March 4, 1865. *CWAL*, vol. VIII, 332–33.
Frederick Douglass: from *Life and Times of Frederick Douglass. Life and Times of Frederick Douglass* (Hartford, Conn.: Park Publishing Co., 1882), 443–45.
Roanoke Island Freedmen to Abraham Lincoln, March 9, 1865. *Freedom: Upper South*, 231–35.
George Templeton Strong: Diary, March 10, 1865. *Strong*, 563–64.
Alpheus S. Williams to His Daughter, March 12, 1865. *From the Cannon's Mouth: The Civil War Letters of Alpheus S. Williams*, ed. Milo M. Quaife (Detroit: Wayne State University Press, 1959), 373–75.
Charles Sumner to John Bright, March 13, 1865. *The Selected Letters of Charles Sumner*, vol. II, ed. Beverly Wilson Palmer (Boston: Northeastern University Press, 1990), 273–74. Copyright © 1990 by Beverly Wilson Palmer; copyright © 1990 by University Press of New England, Lebanon, N.H. Used by permission.
Frances Johnson: Statement Regarding Her Whipping and Escape, March 25, 1865. *Freedom: Military*, 694–95.
Clarissa Burdett: Statement Regarding Her Whipping and Escape, March 27, 1865. *Freedom: Destruction*, 615–16.
John B. Jones: Diary, April 2, 1865. J. B. Jones, *A Rebel War Clerk's Diary at the Confederate States Capital*, vol. II (Philadelphia: J. B. Lippincott & Co., 1866), 465–67.
Sallie Brock: from *Richmond During the War*. Sallie Brock Putnam, *Richmond During the War: Four Years of Personal Observation* (New York: G. W. Carleton & Co., 1867), 362–71.
George Templeton Strong: Diary, April 3, 1865. *Strong*, 573–76.
William Gordon McCabe to Mary Pegram, April 4, 1865. *Ham Chamberlayne—Virginian: Letters and Papers of an Artillery Officer in the War for Southern Independence 1861–1865*, ed. C. G. Chamberlayne (Richmond, Va.: Dietz Printing Co., 1932), 317–19. Copyright © 1932 by C. G. Chamberlayne.

Thomas Morris Chester to the *Philadelphia Press*, April 4 and 6, 1865. *Thomas Morris Chester, Black Civil War Correspondent: His Dispatches from the Virginia Front*, ed. R.J.M. Blackett (Baton Rouge: Louisiana State University Press, 1989), 288–99. Copyright © 1989 by Louisiana State University Press. Used by permission of the publisher.

Gideon Welles: Diary, April 7, 1865. *Welles*, vol. 2, 276–78.

Ulysses S. Grant to Robert E. Lee, April 9, 1865. *PUSG*, vol. 14, 373–74.

Robert E. Lee, April 10, 1865. *WPREL*, 934–35.

Elizabeth Keckly: from *Behind the Scenes*. Elizabeth Keckly, *Behind the Scenes, or, Thirty Years a Slave, and Four Years in the White House* (New York: G. W. Carleton & Co., 1868), 174–93.

George Templeton Strong: Diary, April 15, 1865. *Strong*, 582–84.

Gideon Welles: Diary, April 18, 1865. *Welles*, vol. 2, 283–92.

William T. Sherman to Ulysses S. Grant or Henry Halleck, April 18, 1865. *SCW*, 863–65.

Sarah Morgan: Diary, April 19, 1865. *The Civil War Diary of Sarah Morgan*, ed. Charles East (Athens: The University of Georgia Press, 1991), 605–8. Copyright © 1991 by The University of Georgia Press. Used by permission of The University of Georgia Press.

Robert E. Lee to Jefferson Davis, April 20, 1865. *WPREL*, 938–39.

Jefferson Davis to Varina Howell Davis, April 23, 1865. *The Papers of Jefferson Davis, Volume 11: September 1864–May 1865*, eds. Lynda Lasswell Crist, Barbara J. Rozek, and Kenneth H. Williams (Baton Rouge: Louisiana State University Press, 2003), 557–60. Copyright © 2003 by Louisiana State University Press. Used by permission of the publisher.

Stephen Minot Weld to Hannah Weld, April 24, 1865. *War Diary and Letters of Stephen Minot Weld, 1861–1865* (Cambridge, Mass.: The Riverside Press, 1912), 396–98.

Samuel T. Foster: Diary, April 17–May 4, 1865. *Foster*, 164–74.

Ellen Renshaw House: Diary, May 2, 1865. *A Very Violent Rebel: The Civil War Diary of Ellen Renshaw House*, ed. Daniel E. Sutherland (Knoxville: The University of Tennessee Press, 1996), 163. Copyright © 1996 by The University of Tennessee Press/Knoxville. Ellen Renshaw House's diary, Copyright © 1996 by Ellen Allran and Victoria Guthrie. Used by permission of The University of Tennessee Press.

Walt Whitman: from *Specimen Days*. Walt Whitman, *Specimen Days & Collect* (Philadelphia: Rees Walsh & Co., 1882–83), 71–72.

New York Herald: The Grandest Military Display in the World. *New York Herald*, May 24, 1865.

NOTE ON THE TEXTS

Lois Bryan Adams to the *Detroit Advertiser and Tribune*, May 24, 27, 1865. Lois Bryan Adams, *Letter from Washington, 1863–1865*, ed. Evelyn Leasher (Detroit: Wayne State University Press, 1999), 263–68. Copyright © 1999 by Wayne State University Press.

Gordon Granger, General Orders No. 3, June 19, 1865. *OR*, series 1, vol. 48, pt. 2, 929.

This volume presents the texts of the printings and manuscripts chosen as sources here but does not attempt to reproduce features of their typographic design or physical layout. In the texts that have been printed from manuscript, the beginnings of sentences have been capitalized and punctuation at the end of sentences and closing quotation marks have been supplied. The texts are printed without other alteration except for the changes previously discussed and for the correction of typographical errors. Spelling, punctuation, and capitalization are often expressive features, and they are not altered, even when inconsistent or irregular. The following is a list of typographical errors corrected, cited by page and line number: 4.6, Dahlgreen's; 52.30, it's; 54.17, thu; 54.18, butched; 111.1, Spotylvania; 114.12, it as; 147.27, arms. three; 153.1, presssing; 169.30, graounds; 170.31, trops; 170.35–36, demonstate; 172.19, staied; 174.40, dosen; 197.13, that it; 199.28, rife; 206.22–23, fore castle; 207.27, perfactly; 213.36, work of; 227.15, their one; 273.14, runing; 300.7, cotemporary; 322.23, in every; 323.1, Caster; 337.29, well; 364.10, Spotswood; 366.19, assured; 400.25, enemy It; 404.38 Cooperheads,; 405.15, enemies—"; 408.17, power If; 461.34, things.; 491.7, and and; 499.5, $1,740,690 489 49.; 491.7, and and; 503.27, pension, rolls,; 504.1, $4,505,616,92; 516.33, be to; 549.20, whey; 552.9, grave.; 558.25, Jan., 12,; 563.24, as soon as soon; 579.30, outly,; 581.31, of if; 614.2, altogether"; 617.4, exclaimed. so; 633.25, mad; 633.28, before I; 646.7, calvary; 654.24, protection. He; 654.28, resigned." I; 654.29, sake. He; 662.22, to much; 694.37, al most,; 697.27, 17 20; 707.32, arrives; 708.14, know; 713.33, A.M. At; 713.34, despondent.; 720.28, humilating; 722.36, seem.

Notes

In the notes below, the reference numbers denote page and line of this volume (the line count includes headings, but not rule lines). No note is made for material included in the eleventh edition of *Merriam-Webster's Collegiate Dictionary*. Biblical references are keyed to the King James Version. Quotations from Shakespeare are keyed to *The Riverside Shakespeare*, ed. G. Blakemore Evans (Boston: Houghton Mifflin, 1974). Footnotes and bracketed editorial notes within the text were in the originals. For further historical and biographical background, references to other studies, and more detailed maps, see James McPherson, *Battle Cry of Freedom: The Civil War Era* (New York: Oxford University Press, 1988); *Encyclopedia of the American Civil War: A Political, Social, and Military History*, edited by David S. Heidler and Jeanne T. Heidler (New York: W. W. Norton, 2002); *The Library of Congress Civil War Desk Reference*, edited by Margaret E. Wagner, Gary W. Gallagher, and Paul Finkelman (New York: Simon & Schuster, 2002); and Aaron Sheehan-Dean, *Concise Historical Atlas of the U.S. Civil War* (New York: Oxford University Press, 2008).

2.1 Lieut. Pollard] First Lieutenant James Pollard of New Kent County, whose military service ended when he lost a leg in the fighting at Nance's Shop southeast of Richmond on June 24, 1864.

3.15–16 Dahlgren . . . the Commodore] Ulric Dahlgren (1842–1864) was the son of Rear Admiral John A. Dahlgren (1809–1870), commander of the South Atlantic Blockading Squadron, 1863–65.

3.17 infamous attempt . . . whole city] Union artillery based on the islands of Charleston Harbor had been intermittently shelling the city of Charleston since August 1863.

3.27–28 Punic Faith] Proverbially, an untrustworthy oath, having the character of treachery attributed to the Carthaginians by the Romans.

3.30 marked D] Edmondston placed newspaper clippings regarding the Kilpatrick-Dahlgren raid in another part of her journal.

4.22 Will] House's brother William McLean House (1834–1884).

4.31 sister] Frances Renshaw House (1832–1923).

5.19 Johnnie] House's brother John Moore House (1844–1865), a prisoner on Johnson's Island who had been captured at Chattanooga in November 1863.

NOTES 809

5.25   Gen Carters] Brigadier General Samuel P. Carter (1819–1891) was the Union provost marshal at Knoxville.

7.1   Admiral Renshaw] House's uncle, Francis B. Renshaw (1815–1867), a commander in the Confederate navy, had resigned his commission as a lieutenant in the U.S. Navy in 1861.

7.3   (Gen C) is an old navy officer] Carter had joined the navy in 1840 and held a commission as a lieutenant commander while serving in the Union army.

7.31   Gen Longstreet] After his failure to capture Knoxville in November 1863, Lieutenant General James Longstreet (1821–1904) had retreated into northeast Tennessee.

8.2–3   Mrs Brownlow] Eliza O'Brien Brownlow (1819–1914), the wife of William G. Brownlow (1805–1877), a prominent Knoxville unionist.

12.32   Chas. Sumner] See Biographical Notes.

14.19–20   vote to abolish slavery in Virginia] A constitutional convention called by the unionist "Restored Government" of Virginia met in Alexandria on February 13, 1864, and voted to abolish slavery on March 10.

15.12–13   rank of second-lieutenant . . . conferred] Massachusetts governor John A. Andrew (1818–1867) commissioned Sergeant Stephen A. Swails (1832–1900) of the 54th Massachusetts Infantry as a second lieutenant on March 11, 1864. Because of opposition from the War Department, Swails was not mustered in as an officer until January 17, 1865.

15.17–18   "a man's a man for a' that."] See Robert Burns, "For A' That and A' That" (1795).

15.19–20   emigrants returned from Hayti] President Lincoln had signed a contract on December 31, 1862, with Bernard Kock, a cotton trader who proposed to transport 5,000 freed slaves to Île à Vache, a small uninhabited island off the southwest coast of Haiti. In April 1863 a ship carried 453 former slaves from Fort Monroe, Virginia, to the island, where attempts to establish a cotton plantation failed. Of the colonists, 88 died of hunger and disease, 73 fled to the Haitian mainland, and 292 returned to the United States on the relief ship *Marcia Day*, which docked at Alexandria on March 20, 1864.

15.29   the Massachusetts Cavalry] The 5th Massachusetts Cavalry, a black regiment.

15.30   Mr. Downing . . . Mr. Remond] Black abolitionists George T. Downing (1819–1903) of Rhode Island and Charles L. Remond (1810–1873) of Massachusetts.

21.26–29   Banks . . . Steele] Major General Nathaniel P. Banks (1816–1894) commanded the Department of the Gulf, December 1862–May 1864. Major General Frederick Steele (1819–1868) commanded the Department of Arkansas, January–December 1864. For the Red River campaign, see the headnote on page 24 of this volume, and the Chronology, March–May 1864.

22.4–7 Gilmore . . . W. F. Smith] Major General Quincy A. Gillmore (1825–1888), commander of the Tenth Corps in South Carolina, who would join the Army of the James for the spring offensive; Major General Benjamin F. Butler (1818–1893), commander of the Army of the James; Major General William F. Smith (1824–1903), who would lead the Eighteenth Corps in the Army of the James.

22.9 Burnsides Corps] The Ninth Corps, commanded by Major General Ambrose Burnside (1824–1881).

22.11–13 Sigel . . . Crook] Major General Franz Sigel (1824–1902), commander of the Department of West Virginia; Major General Edward O. C. Ord (1818–1883); Brigadier General William W. Averell (1832–1900); Brigadier General George Crook (1828–1890).

30.14–19 "Far better die . . . and fame."] Cf. the final stanza of "The Call of Kansas" by the Reverend John Pierpont (1785–1866), published in the *New-York Daily Tribune* on July 30, 1856: "Far better fall, in such a strife, / Than still to Slavery's claims concede: / Than crouch beneath her frown, for life, / Far better on the field to bleed. / To live thus is a life-long shame! / To die thus, victory and fame!"

32.23 Schofield] Major General John M. Schofield (1831–1906), commander of the Army of the Ohio.

34.32 Reverdy Johnson] Johnson (1796–1876) repesented Maryland in the Senate as a Whig, 1845–49, and as a Democrat, 1863–68.

34.34–35.1 George Thompson] Thompson, a prominent British abolitionist (1804–1878), was on his third and final lecture tour of the United States.

37.14 Senators Hale and Clark] John P. Hale (1806–1873) represented New Hampshire in the Senate as a Free Soiler, 1847–53, and as a Republican, 1855–65; Daniel Clark (1809–1891) was a Republican senator from New Hampshire, 1857–66.

37.17–18 Powell . . . McDougal] Lazarus W. Powell (1812–1867), Democratic senator from Kentucky, 1859–65; Willard Saulsbury Sr. (1820–1892), Democratic senator from Delaware, 1859–71; James Alexander McDougall (1817–1867), Democratic senator from California, 1861–67; Garrett Davis (1801–1872), Unionist and later Democratic senator from Kentucky, 1861–65, 1865–72.

38.15 vote of 37 to 6!] The vote was 38–6.

38.22–23 "'Twere worth . . . at their array."] Cf. Sir Walter Scott, *The Lady of the Lake* (1810), canto 6, stanza 15: "'Twere worth ten years of peaceful life, / One glance at their array!"

39.13 Howard] Jacob M. Howard (1805–1871), Republican senator from Michigan, 1862–71.

42.31 Col. Bell] Tyree H. Bell (1815–1902) commanded a brigade in Forrest's Cavalry Corps.

43.14–15 Major Boothe . . . Major Bradford] Lionel F. Booth (1838–1864) commanded the 1st Battalion of the Sixth U.S. Colored Heavy Artillery; William F. Bradford (c. 1832–1864) commanded the 13th Tennessee Cavalry, which he had organized at Union City in the fall of 1863.

43.34 Capt. Wilson] J. Cardwell Wilson (c. 1839–1864) led Company F of the Confederate 20th Tennessee Cavalry.

45.19–22 the 8th Corps . . . Rappahannock] The Eighth Corps had not been moved to the Rappahannock front.

45.23 Lt Col Mosby] John S. Mosby (1833–1916); see Biographical Notes.

45.24–25 11th & 12th Corps, consolidated . . . Burnside] The Eleventh and Twelfth Corps of the Army of the Cumberland were consolidated into the Twentieth Corps in April 1864 and remained in the western theater.

46.8 Beauregard] General Pierre G. T. Beauregard (1818–1893) commanded the troops defending Charleston, South Carolina.

46.12 Genl Buckner] Major General Simon B. Buckner (1823–1914) commanded the Department of East Tennessee. His headquarters were at Bristol on the Tennessee-Virginia border.

48.27–28 Capt. BRADFORD . . . REVEL] Captain Theodorick F. Bradford, Major Bradford's brother, and Second Lieutenant John C. Barr (1837–1864) of Company D were killed during the attack on the fort. Lieutenant Wilson of Company A, Lieutenant Cordy B. Revelle of Company E, and Lieutenant John C. Akerstrom, the post quartermaster, were killed after surrendering.

48.30 Capt. POSTON and Lieut. LYON] Captain John L. Poston of Company E was captured but escaped in November 1864. There is no record of a Lieutenant Lyon in the 13th Tennessee Cavalry; the dispatch may be referring to First Lieutenant Nicholas Logan of Company C, who was taken prisoner and died on June 6, 1864.

48.31 Capt. YOUNG] While a Confederate prisoner, Captain John T. Young (d. 1915) of the 24th Missouri signed an affidavit stating that he had seen "no ill-treatment of the wounded on the evening of the battle or the next morning," though he later recanted, saying the statement had been "extorted from me while under duress."

48.33 Maj. BRADFORD . . . has been killed] Bradford was murdered by Confederate soldiers near Brownsville, Tennessee, on April 14, 1864.

49.3–4 Capt. PORTER . . . Adjt. LEMMING] Captain John H. Porter (or Potter) was shot in the head and died on June 21, 1864. Lieutenant Henry Lippett died on April 18, 1864. Adjutant Mack J. Leming, or Lemming, survived.

49.6   Parrotts] Muzzle-loading artillery with rifled barrels, named after their designer, Robert Parker Parrott (1804–1877), superintendent of the West Point Iron and Cannon Foundry.

49.36   Gen. LEE] Major General Stephen D. Lee (1833–1908), the Confederate cavalry commander in Mississippi, was not at Fort Pillow.

50.1   Gen. CHALMERS] Brigadier General James Ronald Chalmers (1831–1898) commanded the First Division of Forrest's Cavalry Corps.

50.25   Col. REED] Lieutenant Colonel Wyly M. Reed of the 5th Mississippi Cavalry.

51.13–14   soldiers . . . pass through Baltimore] Four soldiers from the 6th Massachusetts Infantry were killed by a pro-secessionist mob while passing through Baltimore on April 19, 1861.

55.30   Wagoner . . . Milliken's bend] Black soldiers had fought at Fort Wagner, South Carolina, July 18, 1863; Port Hudson, Louisiana, May 27, 1863; and at Milliken's Bend, Louisiana, June 7, 1863.

55.34   New York, the *July riots!*] At least eleven African American men were lynched during the draft riots in New York City, July 13–17, 1863.

55.38   "Legrees;"] Simon Legree, cruel slave owner in *Uncle Tom's Cabin* (1852) by Harriet Beecher Stowe.

57.26–27   committee from Congress . . . soon report.] The Joint Committee reported to Congress on May 5, 1864, that the Confederates had massacred three hundred Union soldiers at Fort Pillow after the garrison had surrendered.

58.1   Mrs. W and Edgar] Mary Jane Hale Welles (1817–1886) and Edgar Thaddeus Welles (1843–1914).

58.3   Tom] Thomas Gideon Welles (1846–1892).

58.24   Seward . . . Chase] William H. Seward (1801–1872), secretary of state, 1861–69; Edwin M. Stanton (1814–1869), secretary of war, 1862–68; Salmon P. Chase (1808–1873), secretary of the treasury, 1861–64.

58.28   Mr. Bates and Mr. Blair] Edward Bates (1793–1869), attorney general, 1861–64; Montgomery Blair (1813–1883), postmaster general, 1861–64.

65.11   Senator Wilson] Henry Wilson (1812–1875), Republican senator from Massachusetts, 1855–73, was chairman of the Committee on Military Affairs.

66.13   Gen. Halleck] Major Henry W. Halleck (1814–1872), chief of staff of the Union army, 1864–65.

NOTES   813

67.29   Meade's]   Major General George G. Meade (1815–1872), commander of the Army of the Potomac, 1863–65.

69.8   the General]   Meade.

69.17   withdrawal from Mine Run. *Sapristi*]   Meade had crossed the Rapidan on November 26, 1863, in an attempt to turn Lee's right flank. After deciding not to attack the Confederate positions along Mine Run on November 30, Meade withdrew the Army of the Potomac back across the Rapidan on December 1. *Sapristi*: French: Good heavens!

69.19   Griffin]   Brigadier General Charles Griffin (1825–1867), commander of the First Division of the Fifth Corps.

69.21   Gregg]   Brigadier General David M. Gregg (1833–1916) led the Second Division of the Army of the Potomac's Cavalry Corps, commanded by Major General Philip H. Sheridan.

71.5   Duff & old Jerry Dent]   Lieutenant Colonel William L. Duff (1822–1894) and Lieutenant Colonel Frederick T. Dent (1820–1892) were aides to Grant. Dent was a West Point classmate of Grant's and his brother-in-law.

71.7–8   Gen. Seymour . . . Olustee]   Brigadier General Truman Seymour (1824–1891) commanded the Second Brigade, Third Division, Sixth Corps. While commanding Union forces in northern Florida, Seymour had been defeated at the battle of Olustee, February 20, 1864.

71.16–18 Torbert . . . Wilson]   The three divisions of Sheridan's cavalry corps were commanded by Brigadier General Alfred T. A. Torbert (1833–1880), Brigadier General David M. Gregg (see note 69.21), and Brigadier General James H. Wilson (1837–1925).

72.15–16 Bill Thorndike . . . Robinson]   William Thorndike (1835–1887), who had graduated from Harvard a year before Lyman, had served as the surgeon of the 39th Massachusetts Infantry since November 1863. Brigadier General John C. Robinson (1817–1897) commanded the Second Division of the Fifth Corps.

72.18   Wright]   Brigadier General Horatio G. Wright (1820–1899) commanded the First Division of the Sixth Corps.

72.23   Getty]   Brigadier General George W. Getty (1819–1901) led the Second Division of the Sixth Corps.

72.36–37 Crawford's . . . Gen. Eustis]   Brigadier General Samuel W. Crawford (1829–1892) commanded the Third Division of the Fifth Corps; Brigadier General Henry L. Eustis (1819–1911) led the Fourth Brigade, Second Division, Sixth Corps.

72.40   Hill]   Lieutenant General Ambrose Powell Hill (1825–1865) commanded the Third Corps in the Army of Northern Virginia.

73.7 Wadsworth] Brigadier General James S. Wadsworth (1807–1864) commanded the Fourth Division of the Fifth Corps.

73.20 Joe Hayes . . . Dalton] Colonel Joseph Hayes (1835–1912), commander of the 18th Massachusetts Infantry, and Surgeon Edward Dalton (1834–1872), medical inspector of the Army of the Potomac, were both Harvard classmates of Lyman.

73.25–26 mustering officer, Geo. Barnard] Captain George M. Barnard Jr. (1835–1898), the officer responsible for maintaining the muster rolls (personnel records) in Griffin's division.

73.27 Ewell] Lieutenant General Richard S. Ewell (1817–1872) led the Second Corps of the Army of Northern Virginia until May 27, 1864, when he fell seriously ill with dysentery. He was replaced by Major General Jubal A. Early (1816–1894).

73.31 Rawlins] Brigadier General John A. Rawlins (1831–1869), Grant's chief of staff.

73.37 Bartlett] Brigadier General Joseph J. Bartlett (1834–1893) led the Third Brigade, First Division, Fifth Corps.

74.6 Wheaton] Brigadier General Frank Wheaton (1833–1903) led the First Brigade, Second Division, Sixth Corps.

74.16 Maj. Mundy] Major Charles Mundee (1826–1871), assistant adjutant general on Getty's staff.

74.18–19 Gen. Gibbon . . . Gen. Mott] Brigadier General John Gibbon (1827–1896) commanded the Second Division of the Second Corps; Brigadier General Gershom Mott (1822–1884) led the Fourth Division of the Second Corps.

74.22–23 Maj. Mitchell] Major William Mitchell (1836–1883), an aide on Hancock's staff.

74.27 Prince . . . Carr] Brigadier General Henry Prince (1811–1892) commanded the division from July 1863 to March 1864. He was succeeded by Brigadier General Joseph B. Carr (1828–1895), who held the position for a little more than a month owing to procedural difficulties with his promotion to brigadier general.

74.29–30 breaking up of the Third Corps] The First and Third Corps were broken up in March 1864 when the Army of the Potomac was reorganized into three infantry corps.

74.32–33 reduced to a brigade . . . Battle of Hatcher's Run] On May 13 the two infantry brigades that composed Mott's division were assigned to the Third Division, Second Corps. They were later consolidated into a single brigade, commanded by Colonel Robert McAllister (1813–1891), that fought with distinction at the battle of Hatcher's Run, February 5–7, 1865.

74.35   Carroll's & Hays's]   Colonel Samuel S. Carroll (1832–1893) led the Third Brigade, Second Division, Second Corps, and Brigadier General Alexander Hays (1819–1864) commanded the Second Brigade, Third Division, Second Corps.

75.18   Duane]   Major James C. Duane (1824–1897), chief engineer on Meade's staff.

75.22–23   Capt. Hutton of B's staff]   Captain Charles G. Hutton (d. 1900) was an aide on the staff of Ambrose Burnside, the commander of the Ninth Corps.

76.2–3   no command over Gen. Burnside]   Burnside, who outranked Meade, reported directly to Grant until May 23, 1864, when he was placed under Meade's command.

76.13   Birney]   Major General David B. Birney (1825–1864) led the Third Division of the Second Corps.

76.27   Webb's brigade]   Brigadier General Alexander S. Webb (1835–1911) led the First Brigade, Second Division, Second Corps.

76.29   Abbott]   Major Henry Livermore Abbott (1842–1864) of the 20th Massachusetts Infantry.

76.30   Stevenson]   Brigadier General Thomas G. Stevenson (1836–1864) led the First Division of the Ninth Corps.

76.33   Charlie Mills . . . Stevie Weld]   Lieutenant Charles J. Mills (1841–1865), an adjutant general on Stevenson's staff; Lieutenant Colonel Stephen M. Weld, see Biographical Notes.

76.35   Barlow's]   Brigadier General Francis C. Barlow (1834–1896) led the First Division of the Second Corps.

77.6   *Longstreet's Corps*]   James Longstreet, commander of the First Corps of the Army of Northern Virginia, had rejoined Lee's army in April 1864 after serving in northern Georgia and East Tennessee since September 1863.

77.9   Macy]   Colonel George N. Macy (1837–1875), who had lost his left hand at Gettysburg, was the commander of the 20th Massachusetts Infantry.

77.14   Maj. Angel]   Major Ashbel W. Angel (c. 1838–1884), a topographical engineer with the Second Corps.

77.15   Maj. Norval]   Major John M. Norvell (1834–1922).

78.7   brigade of raw "Veterans"]   The First Brigade of Stevenson's division contained three Massachusetts infantry regiments, the 56th, 57th, and 59th, that had been organized in early 1864. Their soldiers were a mixture of reenlisted veterans, mostly from nine-month service regiments, and conscripts.

78.8   Col. Griswold]   Colonel Charles E. Griswold (1834–1864), commander of the 56th Massachusetts Infantry.

78.9 Col. Bartlett] Colonel William F. Bartlett (1840–1876), commander of the 57th Massachusetts Infantry.

78.18 Gen. Patrick] Brigadier General Marsena R. Patrick (1811–1888) was provost marshal of the Army of the Potomac, commanding a brigade of three infantry and one cavalry regiments.

78.25 Comstock] Lieutenant Colonel Cyrus B. Comstock (1831–1910), a member of Grant's staff.

79.7 Potter] Brigadier General Robert B. Potter (1829–1887) led the Second Division of the Ninth Corps.

79.13 Flint] Captain Edward A. Flint (1832–1886) of the 1st Massachusetts Cavalry returned to the Wilderness in May 1865 and later shared with Lyman his impressions of the battlefield.

79.21 Cope] Captain Emmor B. Cope (1834–1927), a topographical engineer.

79.32 Macy] See note 77.9.

80.20 Major Hancock] Major John Hancock (1830–1912) was an aide to Brigadier General Francis Barlow and brother of Second Corps commander Winfield Scott Hancock.

80.25 Saunders] Captain William W. Sanders (1839–1883), a mustering officer on Meade's staff.

80.32 Capt. Beaumont . . . Lt. Col. Kent] Captain Eugene B. Beaumont (1837–1916) was an aide on the staff of Major General John Sedgwick. Lieutenant Colonel Jacob Kent (1835–1918) was Sedgwick's inspector general.

80.36 Gen. M] Meade.

80.37 Upton . . . Shaler] Colonel Emory Upton (1839–1881) commanded the Second Brigade, First Division, Sixth Corps, and Brigadier General Alexander Shaler (1827–1911) led the Fourth Brigade, First Division, Sixth Corps.

81.4 Capt. Cadwalader] Captain Charles E. Cadwalader (1839–1907), a member of Meade's staff.

81.10 Edw. Johnson's division] The engagement was fought with the Confederate brigade commanded by Brigadier General Robert D. Johnston (1837–1919), part of the division led by Major General Jubal Early in the Second Corps of the Army of Northern Virginia.

81.11 Ricketts] Brigadier General James B. Ricketts (1817–1887) was commander of the Third Division of the Sixth Corps.

81.23 Col. Walker] Lieutenant Colonel Francis A. Walker (1840–1897) was Hancock's chief of staff.

81.25 Washburn] Elihu B. Washburne (1816–1887), Grant's political patron

NOTES 817

since 1861, was a Whig, and then a Republican, congressman from northwestern Illinois, 1853–69. He later served as U.S. minister to France, 1869–77.

81.37–38 Ferrero's negro div.] Brigadier General Edward Ferrero (1831–1899) was commander of the Fourth Division of the Ninth Corps; both of its infantry brigades were composed entirely of black troops.

82.16 Capt. Martin] Captain Augustus P. Martin (1835–1902).

83.4 "Rosie"] Lieutenant Frederick Rosenkrantz, a courier on General Meade's staff.

83.6 Mr. Dana, Asst. Sec. of War] Charles A. Dana; see Biographical Notes.

83.13–14 McGregor . . . Associated Press] William D. McGregor (1826–1907).

83.15 Mimi] Lyman's wife, Elizabeth Russell Lyman (1836–1911).

84.20 the General] Meade.

86.25 hop poles] Tall poles, usually fifteen feet or more in height, on which hop plants are trained.

90.33 Rev. Mr. Mullaly . . . Orr] Francis P. Mulally was chaplain of the 1st (Orr's) Regiment, South Carolina Rifles, commanded by Lieutenant Colonel George Miller.

91.13 Heth's division] Major General Henry Heth (1825–1899) led one of the four divisions in A. P. Hill's Third Corps.

91.23–25 First regiment . . . Fourteenth Regiment] All of the regiments were from South Carolina.

91.27 Lane's and Thomas's brigades] Brigadier General James H. Lane (1833–1907) led a brigade of five North Carolina infantry regiments, and Brigadier General Edward L. Thomas (1825–1898) commanded a brigade of four Georgia regiments; both brigades served in Major General Cadmus M. Wilcox's division.

92.22 Lieut. Col. Shooter] Lieutenant Colonel Washington P. Shooter (1837–1864).

93.3 Gen. McGowan] Brigadier General Samuel McGowan (1819–1897).

93.5–6 Capt. L. C. Haskell . . . Lieut. G. A. Wardlaw] Alexander C. Haskell (1839–1910) and George A. Wardlaw, quartermaster of the 1st South Carolina Infantry.

93.9–10 Scales' brigade] Brigadier General Alfred M. Scales (1827–1892) led a brigade composed of five North Carolina regiments in Wilcox's Division.

94.18–19 Kershaw's . . . Anderson's divisions] Brigadier General Joseph B. Kershaw (1822–1894) and Major General Charles W. Field (1828–1892) led divisions in Longstreet's First Corps. Brigadier General Richard H. Anderson (1821–1879) commanded a division in Hill's Third Corps.

94.31 still no Blucher] The timely arrival of Field Marshal Gebhard von Blücher's Prussian army at Waterloo on the evening of June 18, 1815, resulted in the defeat of Napoleon's army.

95.4–5 *the War Horse!*] Longstreet was sometimes referred to as "Lee's War Horse."

96.10 Poague's artillery] Lieutenant Colonel William T. Poague (1835–1914) commanded an artillery battalion in Hill's Third Corps.

96.27 McLaws', afterwards Kershaw's division] Major General Lafayette McLaws (1821–1897) had fallen out with Longstreet in December 1863 and been replaced as division commander by Kershaw.

97.7 Nance . . . Doby] Colonel James D. Nance (1837–1864), commander of the 3rd South Carolina Infantry; Lieutenant Colonel Franklin Gaillard (1829–1864), commander of the 2nd South Carolina Infantry; and Captain Alfred E. Doby, an aide to Kershaw, were killed in the fighting on May 6, 1864.

97.20–22 Longstreet . . . Brigadier-General Jenkins] Both Longstreet and Micah Jenkins (1835–1864), a brigade commander in Field's Division, were accidentally shot by Confederate soldiers.

104.20 Paran] In Genesis 21:21, the wilderness dwelling place of the outcast Ishmael.

105.22 Lord Fairfax's parchment deeds] In 1719, Thomas, sixth Lord Fairfax of Cameron (1693–1781), had inherited title to more than five million acres of land in Virginia, including the Northern Neck, the land between the Rappahannock and Potomac Rivers.

106.29 Mosby's prowling men] See headnote, page 463 of this volume.

107.31 Stonewall had charged] Confederate Lieutenant General Thomas J. (Stonewall) Jackson led a successful attack against the Union right flank on May 2, 1863, during the battle of Chancellorsville. He was mortally wounded that night when his own men accidentally opened fire on his returning scouting party.

109.2 *Pillar of Smoke*] See Exodus 13:21.

109.6 Sabæan lore] The surviving inscriptions of the Sabæans of Yemen, the biblical Sheba, have proved difficult to read and interpret.

112.28–30 Lt Ashley . . . Lt Eldridge] First Lieutenant William A. Ashley (1828–1864) of Company I; First Lieutenant Edward H. Graves (c. 1839–1880) of Company K, who was severely wounded in the abdomen; Lieutenant Alfred W. Midgley (1838–1864) of Company H, who died from his wounds on May 12; First Lieutenant L. Oscar Eaton of Company F was severely wounded in the leg; Second Lieutenant Simeon N. Eldridge of Company E was wounded in the arm. Graves, Eaton, and Eldridge were mustered out on July 1, 1864.

113.5   Capt Shurtleff] Captain Flavel Shurtleff (1829–1910) commanded Company H of the 10th Massachusetts Infantry.

113.26   the 2nd RI] The 2nd Rhode Island Infantry.

115.12   Sedgwick was killed] Major General John Sedgwick (1813–1864) was killed by a sharpshooter at Spotsylvania on May 9, 1864. He was succeeded as Sixth Corps commander by Horatio G. Wright.

115.17   Colonel Edwards] Colonel Oliver Edwards (1835–1904) had previously commanded the 37th Massachusetts Infantry.

115.18   Neil] Brigadier General Thomas H. Neill (1826–1885) had replaced Getty as commander of the Second Division, Sixth Corps.

115.22   Gen Augur] Major General Christopher C. Augur (1821–1898) commanded the Twenty-second Corps at Washington, D.C. The report of his arrival was unfounded.

115.25–26   the 57th Veterans of Mass] See note 78.7.

116.9   Bill Robinson] Captain William B. Robinson of the 5th Vermont Infantry Regiment was wounded twice at the Wilderness, and discharged in August 1864.

117.7   Col P] Lieutenant Colonel Joseph B. Parsons (1828–1906) of Northampton commanded the 10th Massachusetts Infantry.

117.17–18   Maj Gen Johnson + 2 Brig Generals] Major General Edward Johnson (1816–1873), a division commander in the Second Corps, and Brigadier General George H. Steuart (1828–1903), one of Johnson's brigade commanders. Both men were exchanged on August 3, 1864.

117.26–29   Capt Weatherill . . . Lieut Munyan] Captain James H. Weatherell (1826–1864) of Company C died from his wounds on June 20; Captain Edwin L. Knight of Company E was wounded in the left side, but lived until 1909; Captain Eben M. Johnson of Company K was slightly wounded in the hand; Captain Homer G. Gilmore of Company D was severely wounded in the leg, but lived until 1908; Captain George W. Bigelow of Company F was wounded on the side of the head, but survived and was still living in 1909; Major Dexter F. Parker (1828–1864) was shot in the right arm and died from complications after amputation on May 30, 1864; Alanson E. Munyan, a first lieutenant in Company H from Northampton, died from his wounds on May 21, 1864.

119.22   Sidney Williams] First Sergeant Sydney S. Williams (1837–1916), another Northampton resident, was taken prisoner on May 12 and was held at Andersonville, Georgia, and Florence, South Carolina, before escaping on September 19. He was recaptured but then made a successful escape in February 1865. Brewster married his sister, Anna B. Williams, in 1868.

119.35   Gen Shermans . . . Gen Butler] Union forces captured Tunnel Hill and Dalton in northern Georgia, May 7–11, 1864. The report that Butler had captured Petersburg, Virginia, was incorrect.

121.23   the Gazzette] The Northampton, Massachusetts, *Daily Hampshire Gazette*.

121.31   Thomas] Brewster's brother-in-law, Thomas Boland.

123.22   Maj. Gen. Rodes] Major General Robert E. Rodes (1829–1864) commanded a division in the Second Corps of the Army of Northern Virginia.

125.3–4   General Abner Perrin] Brigadier General Abner M. Perrin (1827–1864) commanded an Alabama brigade in Anderson's Division, Third Corps.

125.16–17   Colonel Brockman . . . Colonel J. N. Brown] Colonel Benjamin T. Brockman (1831–1864), commander of the 13th South Carolina Infantry, died of his wounds on June 8, 1864; Colonel Joseph N. Brown (1832–1921).

125.24   Harris] Nathaniel H. Harris (1834–1900) commanded a brigade in Anderson's Division, Third Corps.

127.18   Lieutenant Carlisle] First Lieutenant John W. Carlisle (1827–1914) commanded Company C of the 13th South Carolina Infantry.

129.21–22   this tree, . . . twenty-two inches in diameter!] The stump of this tree is in the collection of the National Museum of American History of the Smithsonian Institution in Washington, D.C.

129.36   Longstreet's corps] The First Corps had been led by Richard H. Anderson since May 7.

131.10   Capt. Eagle] Captain Clifford F. Eagle (1845–1938) commanded Company B of the 1st U.S. Colored Infantry.

131.26–28   Major Cook . . . Capt. Choate] Major John B. Cook (c. 1839–?), Sergeant Henry Harris (c. 1843–?), Captain Francis C. Choate (1832–1881).

133.33   Judah] Brigadier General Henry Moses Judah (1821–1866) commanded the Second Division, Twenty-third Corps, Army of the Ohio.

134.6   Hooker] Major General Joseph Hooker (1814–1879) commanded the Twentieth Corps, Army of the Cumberland.

135.34   "Rosinante"] In *Don Quixote* (1605–15), Rocinante, a worn-out workhorse, is the hero's steed.

138.10   Butterfield] Major General Daniel Butterfield (1831–1901) commanded the Third Division of the Twentieth Corps, Army of the Cumberland.

138.12   Stanley] Major General David S. Stanley (1828–1902) commanded the First Division of the Fourth Corps, Army of the Cumberland.

138.16–17   Capt. Simonson, Lt. Morrison] Captain Peter Simonson (1804–

1864), commander of the 5th Indiana Light Artillery, known as Simonson's Battery, was killed at Pine Mountain, Georgia, on June 16; First Lieutenant Alfred Morrison (1836–1901).

138.23   Gen. Howard]   Major General Oliver Otis Howard (1830–1909).

142.6–7   Genl Granbury]   Brigadier General Hiram B. Granbury (1831–1864).

142.7   Col Wilkes]   Colonel Franklin C. Wilkes (c. 1822–1881) commanded the 24th Texas Cavalry Regiment (Dismounted) in Granbury's Brigade.

145.37   Genl Hardee]   Lieutenant General William J. Hardee (1815–1873) commanded the First Corps of the Army of Tennessee.

150.34   Lt. Bartlett]   First Lieutenant Edwin B. Bartlett (1839–1864) of Company B in the 10th Massachusetts Infantry was shot through the head and killed on May 22.

154.13   Stewart Campbell]   Stuart Campbell, Brewster's first cousin, lived in western Virginia and served in the Confederate army.

154.17–18   Major Parker . . . Lieut Graves]   See notes 117.26–29 and 112.28–30.

154.20–22   Artemas Ward . . . wrong in the newspapers.]   Artemas Ward was the pen name of American humorist Charles Farrar Browne (1834–1867). The quip has also been ascribed to Lord Byron.

158.25   Capt Shaw of the 2nd RI]   Captain John P. Shaw (1834–1864).

158.33   Capt Bishop]   Captain Willard I. Bishop (1837–1911), commanding Company A of the 10th Massachusetts Infantry, had been injured in the eye by a pine tree limb and was mustered out on July 1, 1864.

158.35   Lt Cottrell]   Mark H. Cottrell was first lieutenant in Company D of the 10th Massachusetts Infantry.

159.11–13   Captain Haydens leg . . . Mr. Joel Hayden]   Captain Joseph L. Hayden, the commander of Company H of the 37th Massachusetts Infantry, was discharged for disability on September 22, 1864. Joel Hayden (1798–1873) of Williamsburg, Massachusetts, just north of Northampton, was lieutenant governor of Massachusetts, 1863–66, and the proprietor of a large brass works factory in Haydenville. The reference may be to him, or to his son of the same name.

159.14   Joe + Sid Bridgeman]   Brothers Joseph C. Bridgman (1831–1910) and Sidney E. Bridgman (1827–1906) were booksellers in Northampton who traveled to Fredericksburg as representatives of the U.S. Christian Commission, an organization that provided supplies, medical services, and religious material to Union soldiers.

159.18   Veteran Volunteers]   Veterans who had reenlisted.

162.30 Lieuts. Flannery and Heston] Lieutenants David Flannery and Joseph S. Heston of the 4th New Jersey Infantry were exchanged in March 1865.

163.26 John] Adams's brother John Quincy Adams II (1833–1894), who was serving on the staff of Massachusetts governor John A. Andrew.

165.31 McClellan . . . McDowell] Brigadier General Irvin McDowell (1818–1885) had been defeated at the first battle of Bull Run, July 21, 1861, and replaced as commander of what became the Army of the Potomac by Major General George B. McClellan (see Biographical Notes). Promoted to major general the following year, McDowell was defeated at Second Bull Run, August 28–30, 1862, while commanding the Third Corps of the Army of Virginia. He was relieved of command and held no further field assignments during the war.

166.20 Humphreys] Major General Andrew A. Humphreys (1810–1883), chief of staff of the Army of the Potomac, July 1863–November 1864.

167.40 your negotiation] In the spring of 1864, Charles Francis Adams Sr. had become involved in an abortive effort to explore possible peace terms with the Confederate government through an intermediary, American businessman Thomas Yeatman (1828–1880). The attempt ended when Yeatman failed to make his way to Richmond.

170.20–22 bridge at Moscow . . . regiment of blacks] The 61st U.S. Colored Infantry defended the bridge at Moscow, Tennessee, against a raid by Forrest's cavalry on December 4, 1863.

170.29 Forrest attacked Paducah] Forrest raided the town of Paducah, Kentucky, on March 25–26, 1864, but was unable to capture Fort Anderson, an outpost defended by 665 Union soldiers, including 274 men from the 8th U.S. Colored Heavy Artillery.

172.14 Mrs. Lee] Mary W. Lee (c. 1819–?), nurse with the Army of the Potomac.

172.33 Capt. Harris] Captain Isaac Harris (1838–1907) of Brooklyn, New York, an assistant superintendent with the U.S. Sanitary Commission.

173.29 Georgy Willets] Georgiana Willets (1840–1912), nurse with the Army of the Potomac.

174.21 Dr. Dudley] Dr. Frederick Dudley (1842–1923), a Union army surgeon with whom Hancock may have been romantically involved during the war.

176.6 Dr. Aiken] Dr. John Aiken (1838–1866), surgeon attached to the 71st Pennsylvania Infantry. His death was attributed to a disease contracted while serving with the army in August 1864.

179.20 Spencer carbine] A lever-action repeating rifle that held seven rounds in a tube magazine.

182.18 the Red Division] The First Division, Second Corps, commanded

NOTES   823

by Brigadier General Francis C. Barlow (1834–1895). Its standard featured a red three-leaf clover on a white field.

183.4–6   Twenty minutes . . . ten-thousand of our men] Union losses at Cold Harbor on June 3, 1864, totaled about 7,000 men killed, wounded, or missing.

184.7–8   The army . . . refused to obey] The claim that Union soldiers refused en masse to advance at Cold Harbor on the afternoon of June 3 was first made by William Swinton (1833–1892), a war correspondent for *The New York Times*, in his book *Campaigns of the Army of the Potomac* (1866). It is not known to be supported by contemporaneous letters, diaries, or narratives.

189.17   Badeau] Colonel Adam Badeau (1831–1895) was military secretary on Grant's staff. He wrote several books after the war, including *Military History of Ulysses S. Grant* (1881) and *Grant in Peace: From Appomattox to Mount McGregor* (1887), and assisted Grant in the preparation of his memoirs until the two men had a falling-out in May 1885.

189.24   Wadsworth, Sedgwick, Rice] Brigadier General James Wadsworth, commanding the Fourth Division, Fifth Corps, was fatally wounded in the Wilderness on May 6 and died in a Confederate field hospital on May 8; Major General John Sedgwick was killed by a sharpshooter at Spotsylvania on May 9; Brigadier General James C. Rice (1828–1864), commanding the Second Brigade, Fourth Division, Fifth Corps, was wounded at Spotsylvania on May 10 and died later that day after his leg was amputated.

189.28   Saturday last] June 4, 1864.

189.29   the Judge] Daly's husband, Charles P. Daly.

189.34–190.1   Women's Patriotic League . . . Luxuries] Daly was president of the Women's Patriotic Association for Diminishing the Use of Imported Luxuries, which was organized in New York on May 16, 1864. The organization was dedicated to stemming the drain of specie overseas by curtailing imports of "silks, satins, velvets, laces, jewelry, ribbons, trimmings, carpets, mirrors, and other imported luxuries."

190.7   Miss Mary Hamilton . . . Miss Schuyler] Mary M. Hamilton (1828–1877), granddaughter of Alexander Hamilton, served on the association's committee on manufactures. Louisa Lee Schuyler (1837–1926), Mary M. Hamilton's niece and later stepdaughter, was a key figure in the Woman's Central Association of Relief, an auxiliary of the U.S. Sanitary Commission.

191.35–192.1   sees the beam . . . mote in his own!"] Cf. Matthew 7:3–5.

194.11   General Pemberton] Captured at Vicksburg when he surrendered the city on July 4, 1863, and exchanged on October 13, Major General John C. Pemberton (1814–1881) had resigned as a general officer on May 9, 1864, and offered to serve as a private. Jefferson Davis instead recommissioned him as a lieutenant colonel on May 12.

194.20   General Quarles] Brigadier General William A. Quarles (1825–1893) commanded a brigade in Walthall's Division, Third Corps, Army of Tennessee.

195.19   General Warren] Major General Gouverneur K. Warren (1830–1882) commanded the Fifth Corps, Army of the Potomac.

195.23   "Haw's Shop"] Confederate and Union cavalry had fought for eight hours near Haw's Shop in Hanover County, Virginia, on May 28, 1864. The battle, in which the Union lost 365 men killed, wounded, or missing, and the Confederates 378, ended in a Confederate retreat.

196.11   her little son] Willoughby Newton (1856–1923).

196.13   Captain Newton] Captain William Brockenbrough Newton (1832–1863) of the 4th Virginia Cavalry was killed at Raccoon Ford, Virginia, on October 11, 1863.

197.20–21   our nephew, J. P., . . . General W. H. F. Lee] Jefferson Phelps (1834–?) of the 9th Virginia Cavalry; Major General William Henry Fitzhugh Lee (1837–1891), Robert E. Lee's son, commanded a cavalry division in the Army of Northern Virginia.

197.25   General Ferrara] See note 81.37–38.

198.12   the Libby] Prison for Union officers established in a Richmond warehouse formerly used by Libby & Sons, a ship-provisioning company.

200.35–36   18th . . . Smiths] On Grant's orders, the Eighteenth Corps, led by Major General William F. Smith (1824–1903), had been detached from the Army of the James and transported by water to reinforce the Army of the Potomac. The corps began disembarking at White House Landing on the Pamunkey on May 30 and had fought at Cold Harbor.

202.13   write the date] Adams wrote to his son on the eighty-ninth anniversary of the battle of Bunker Hill, June 17, 1775.

202.23   "I tremble for my country . . . God is just."] From *Notes on the State of Virginia* (1785), query XVIII.

204.1   "Jesurun has waxed fat"] See Deuteronomy 32:15.

204.1–2   octogenarian leader . . . Maurepas] Henry John Temple, third Viscount Palmerston (1784–1865), prime minister of Great Britain, 1859–65; Jean-Frédéric Phélypeaux, Comte de Maurepas (1701–1781), adviser to Louis XV and Louis XVI.

206.4   the Captain] Captain John A. Winslow (1811–1873).

206.26–27   wounding Capt. Semmes] Semmes (1809–1877) was not wounded during the battle.

208.38   down 200 fathoms] In 1984 the French navy discovered the wreck of the *Alabama* in about 200 feet of water seven miles off the coast.

NOTES

213.28 Burnside's negroes] The black troops who fought at Petersburg in mid-June 1864 were from the Third Division of Smith's Eighteenth Corps.

214.35 Chaplain Hunter] The Reverend William H. Hunter, a Methodist minister from Baltimore, was born into slavery in Raleigh, North Carolina, in 1831.

219.28 Lieutenant-Colonel Benton] Lieutenant Colonel Reuben C. Benton (1830–1895) had resigned after contracting a malarial fever.

219.29 Colonel Warner] Colonel James M. Warner (1836–1897) had been wounded at Spotsylvania on May 18 and sent home to convalesce. He returned to duty on July 8 as a brigade commander.

219.31–32 Garton Branch and Petersburg Railroad] More commonly known as the Weldon Railroad.

219.35 Captain M.] Captain Edwin J. Morrill (1834–1864) of St. Johnsbury had enlisted in August 1862.

219.36 Lieutenant-Colonel P.] Lieutenant Colonel Samuel E. Pingree (1832–1922) of the 3rd Vermont Infantry. As the corps officer of the day, Pingree commanded the advance detachments from the 4th Vermont and 11th Vermont that formed the brigade skirmish line on June 23. Pingree escaped capture and was mustered out on July 27, 1864. He later served as governor of Vermont, 1884–86.

219.37 Major F] Major Charles K. Fleming (1831–1919) was captured on June 23, 1864, and held in a military prison in Columbia, South Carolina, before being paroled on February 28, 1865.

220.5 two hundred and seventy-five prisoners] A total of 407 officers and enlisted men from the Vermont Brigade were captured on June 23, 1864, including 267 men from the 11th Vermont Infantry and 140 from the 4th Vermont Infantry. Of the 407, two officers were killed trying to escape, while 224 of the enlisted men died either while being held as prisoners of war or shortly after their release.

220.6 Second-Lieutenant Sherman] Merritt H. Sherman (1842–1864) of Company C.

220.8 Captain M. and Lieutenant R.] Morrill was wounded while trying to escape on June 29 and died the following day. Lieutenant Lester S. Richards (1825–1910) was paroled on March 1, 1865.

220.10–11 Totten . . . Lincoln] Forts in the Washington, D.C., fortifications.

220.31 Carrie] Chamberlin's younger sister, Caroline.

222.19 Belle Island] Belle Isle, in the James River at Richmond, Virginia, was used as a prison camp for Union enlisted men, June–September 1862 and May 1863–October 1864.

222.25–27   "As ye do . . . to you again."]   Cf. Matthew 7:2 and 7:12 and Luke 6:31.

223.23   57-3]   Beginning in April 1864, camp administrators divided Andersonville's prisoners into detachments of 270 men each for the purpose of calling the roll and distributing rations. Each detachment was divided into three ninety-man squads, and each squad into five eighteen-man messes.

224.3–4   Gaines' Mill]   Most the 4th New Jersey Infantry was surrounded and captured at the battle of Gaines's Mill on June 27, 1862. The battle of Cold Harbor was fought near the Gaines's Mill battlefield.

224.10   Gen. Winder]   Brigadier General John H. Winder (1800–1865) had administered the Libby and Belle Isle prisons as provost marshal of Richmond, 1861–64. He arrived at Andersonville on June 16 and personally supervised the camp until July 26, when he was given responsibility for all prison camps in Georgia and Alabama. In November 1864, Winder was placed in charge of all prison camps east of the Mississippi, a position he held until his death from a heart attack on February 7, 1865.

225.12   Capt. Wurtz]   Swiss-born Captain Henry H. Wirz (1823–1865) was commandant of Andersonville from April 1864 until his arrest by Union forces in May 1865. He stood trial on multiple charges relating to his administration of the camp, including murder, and was hanged on November 10, 1865, the only Confederate officer executed for war crimes committed during the Civil War.

226.7   Fort Darling]   Union name for the Confederate fortifications on Drewry's Bluff overlooking the James River south of Richmond.

226.10   Kilpatrick]   Brigadier General Hugh Kilpatrick (1836–1881) had been wounded at Resaca on May 13, 1864, while leading a cavalry division in the Army of the Cumberland. He returned to his command in late July 1864.

229.17   Col. Ewing . . . wounded]   Lieutenant Colonel Charles Ewing (1841–1872), the commander of the 4th New Jersey Infantry, was discharged as a result of his wound.

232.22   Mary Ewing]   Mary Gillespie Ewing (1832–1880) was the wife of Philomen Ewing (1820–1896), Sherman's brother-in-law.

232.23   the new baby]   Charles Sherman, born on June 11, would die on December 4, 1864.

232.34   the Kilkenny Cats]   Cats who according to an Irish tradition fought each other so fiercely that in the end nothing but their tails was left of either of them.

233.37   Lancaster]   In Ohio.

235.35   A. H. Stephens]   Confederate vice president Alexander H. Stephens (1812–1883) had approached Fort Monroe in Virginia on a Confederate flag of truce boat on July 4, 1863, and requested safe passage to Washington in an attempt to open peace negotiations. Lincoln and his cabinet refused to receive him, and Stephens returned to Richmond.

236.7–8 momentous election . . . North Carolina] See Chronology, August 4, 1864.

240.4 Pisgah] See Deuteronomy 3:27.

244.13–14 Foster . . . James Island] The assault ordered by Major General John G. Foster (1823–1874), commander of the Department of the South, was repulsed on July 3, 1864. James Island was one of many low-lying islands near Charleston, South Carolina.

247.29–30 Gen Gordon's Division] Major General John B. Gordon (1832–1904) commanded a division in the Second Corps of the Army of Northern Virginia.

248.18–19 Mr. Gilmer] Thomas W. Gilmer (1834–1869), a Presbyterian, was chaplain in Lieutenant Colonel William Nelson's artillery battalion.

249.7–8 Capt. Carpenter's Battery] Captain John C. Carpenter (1839–1912) led the artillery battery attached to the 27th Virginia Infantry.

251.12–13 'a little more slumber . . . hands to sleep,'] Cf. Proverbs 6:10.

252.1–2 "the thunder . . . the shouting."] Cf. Job 39:25.

253.37–38 "little foxes.". . . spoiling the grapes] Cf. Song of Solomon 2:15.

256.12 Mr. Dana] See Biographical Notes.

256.14 Hunter] Major General David Hunter (1802–1886), commander of the Department of West Virginia.

256.15 19th Corps] A detachment from the Nineteenth Corps in the Gulf that was originally intended to reinforce the Army of the James was sent to Washington during Early's raid.

256.20 the road] The railroad.

256.22 Wright] Major General Horatio Wright, commander of the Sixth Corps.

256.26 Col. Comstock] See note 78.25.

261.8 JACOB THOMPSON] Jacob Thompson (1810–1885) was the senior Confederate agent in Canada, 1864–65. He had served as a Democratic congressman from North Carolina, 1839–51, and as secretary of the interior, 1857–61.

262.24–27 "No bargaining . . . sued for mercy."] A close paraphrase of a passage from a speech given in Congress on August 2, 1861, by Pennsylvania Republican Thaddeus Stevens (1792–1868).

264.31 Gov. Yates] Richard Yates (1815–1873), Republican governor of Illinois, 1861–65.

264.33–34 Pittsburg Landing] A northern name for the battle of Shiloh.

265.1 General Rosecrans's] Major General William S. Rosecrans (1819–1898) commanded the Army of the Cumberland, October 1862–October 1863.

265.25–26 Sanders-Greeley negotiation] George N. Sanders (1812–1873) of Kentucky, one of the Confederate agents in Canada, had served as U.S. consul-general in London, 1853–54.

265.28 Sidney Howard Gay] Gay (1814–1888) was managing editor of the *New-York Daily Tribune*, 1862–67.

267.26–27 Canby's . . . Gen. Hunter's] In addition to his own Sixth Corps, which had been sent from the Army of the Potomac, the force that Wright led from Washington in pursuit of Early included a detachment from the Nineteenth Corps led by Brigadier General William H. Emory (1811–1887). Emory's detachment had originally been sent from the Military Division of West Mississippi, commanded by Major General Edward R. S. Canby (1811–1873), to reinforce the Army of the James, but had been diverted to the defense of Washington. Major General Lew Wallace commanded the Eighth Corps, and Major General David Hunter (1802–1886) led the Army of West Virginia.

268.15 Ramseur] Brigadier General Stephen D. Ramseur (1837–1864). See Biographical Notes.

273.7 Cheatham] On July 19, Major General Benjamin F. Cheatham (1820–1886) had assumed command of Second Corps when Hood was elevated to replace Johnston. Command of Cheatham's Division was assigned to Brigadier General George E. Maney (1826–1901).

275.31 Genl Walker] Major General William H. T. Walker (1816–1864) led a division in the First Corps of the Army of Tennessee.

280.19 the Mustang] A coastal steamer that had been commandeered by Union forces when they occupied Brownsville.

280.20 Col Day] Colonel Henry M. Day (1827–1900).

282.13 Gen Herron] Major General Francis J. Herron (1837–1902), commander of the Union forces in Texas.

282.23 Col Bruce] Lieutenant Colonel John Bruce (1832–1901) led the 19th Iowa Infantry.

282.25 Col Dye] Colonel William M. Dye (1831–1899) of the 20th Iowa Infantry.

285.20 all obstructions.] After this sentence, the text printed in *The Life of David Glasgow Farragut* includes the following sentence: "The Admiral will endeavor to remove the others before the day of attack, as he thinks they support that which will otherwise sink, and at least to destroy them for guides to the demons who hope to explode them."

285.25 the enemy's] In *The Life of David Glasgow Farragut*, "their." The text printed in *The Life of David Glasgow Farragut* also included a postscript: "P.S.— Carry low steam. D. G. F."

286.35–36 Colonel Marshall . . . Colonel Gould] Colonel Elisha G. Marshall (1829–1883) was wounded and captured during the battle of the Crater; Brigadier General William F. Bartlett (1840–1876), leading the First Brigade, had lost his left leg at Yorktown in April 1862, and would lose his cork prosthesis at the Crater; Colonel Jacob P. Gould (1822–1864), leading the 59th Massachusetts Infantry, was wounded and died on August 22.

287.8 Ledlie] Brigadier General James H. Ledlie (1832–1882), commander of the First Division, Ninth Corps.

287.38 Captain Fay] Captain Wilson W. Fay (d. 1922), of Company D, 56th Massachusetts Infantry.

288.3 Captain Amory] Captain Charles B. Amory (1841–1919) of the 24th Massachusetts Regiment was Bartlett's adjutant. He was captured with Bartlett, whom he had helped off the field after his cork leg was shattered. Amory described his experience of the "great disaster" of the battle of the Crater in *A Brief Record of the Army Life of Charles B. Amory, Written for His Children* (1902).

290.18–20 nine regiments . . . left alive.] Four out of the six regimental commanders in Weld's brigade were killed or mortally wounded in the battle of the Crater.

291.28–29 Cousin Dick's batty] Captain Richard G. Pegram (1829–1896) led an artillery battery in Branch's artillery battalion.

291.33 Mahone] On May 7, 1864, Brigadier General William Mahone (1826–1895) had assumed command of Anderson's Division of the Third Corps.

292.36 Sharpsburg] A southern name for the battle of Antietam.

293.6–7 Beauregard's] Beauregard had defended Petersburg against the initial Union assaults in mid-June 1864 with forces not assigned to the Army of Northern Virginia.

293.39 Col. McIntosh] Lieutenant Colonel David G. McIntosh (1836–1919). He married Virginia Pegram on November 8, 1865.

295.12 Pope . . . Hooker] Major General John Pope (1822–1892), commander of the Army of Virginia, was defeated at Second Bull Run in August 1862; Burnside led the Army of the Potomac to defeat at Fredericksburg in December 1862; Hooker lost the battle of Chancellorsville in May 1863.

296.2–3 Said Napoleon . . . left."] As recorded by his nephew, Charles-Louis Napoleon Bonaparte, the future Napoleon III, in *Des Idées Napoléoniennes. On the Opinions and Policy of Napoleon* (1840).

300.12–13 *Oderint dum metuant*] Latin: Let them hate, so long as they fear. The phrase, attributed to the poet Lucius Accius, was said to be a favorite of the emperor Caligula.

300.15 Minos or Æacus] Legendary kings who in Greek mythology were judges in the underworld.

300.20 Gideon J. Tucker] Tucker (1826–1899) was secretary of state of New York, 1858–59, and surrogate of New York County, 1863–69. He co-founded the *New York Daily News* in 1855.

300.34 Elijah F. Purdy] Purdy (1796–1866) was a banker and member of the Tammany Hall political organization.

303.13 Sallie's letter] Bird's daughter Saida (Sallie) Bird (1848–1922) regularly corresponded with her father.

304.15–16 Iverson . . . Lieut Genl S. D. Lee] Brigadier General Alfred Iverson (1829–1911) commanded the Confederate cavalry force that captured Stoneman near Hillsboro, Georgia, on July 31, 1864. Lieutenant General Stephen D. Lee (1833–1908) commanded the Second Corps, Army of Tennessee.

304.37 Chambersburg] See Chronology, July 30, 1864.

305.39 Cook's battalion] Major Ferdinand W. C. Cook, a firearms manufacturer in Athens, led the battalion of the Georgia State Guard charged with protecting the city. He was killed in action on December 11, 1864.

309.12–13 Gen. Banks . . . Senator Doolittle] Nathaniel P. Banks was commander of the Department of the Gulf, headquartered in New Orleans; James R. Doolittle (1815–1897), Republican senator from Wisconsin, 1857–69.

310.36 Banks's defeat] In the Red River campaign.

310.38 Gen. Banks's proclamation] Addressed to "The People of Louisiana," the proclamation, issued on January 11, 1864, announced that elections for governor and other state offices would be held on February 22.

311.17–18 failure of a military . . . Florida] The Union defeat at Olustee, Florida, on February 20, 1864.

312.13 The Supreme Court has formally declared] In *Luther v. Borden* (1849), a case that grew out of an 1841–42 rebellion against the government of Rhode Island led by Thomas W. Dorr (1805–1854). Stymied in his efforts to reform Rhode Island's government as a legislator, Dorr organized the People's Party, which held a convention and drafted a new constitution that instituted universal male suffrage. When Dorr was elected governor under the new constitution, the established state government declared martial law and jailed Dorr and many of his supporters, including Martin Luther. Luther appealed his arrest by state official Luther M. Borden on the grounds that the original, or charter, government of Rhode Island had been rendered illegal by the new constitution. Called upon to decide which government was legitimate, the

NOTES 831

Court ruled it was a political question to be decided by Congress and not the judiciary.

315.5 MICHAEL HAHN] Hahn (1830–1886) was elected governor of Louisiana on February 22, 1864, and served until March 4, 1865, when he resigned.

319.10–12 Mr. G. A. Trenholm . . . imbroglio] Citing irreconcilable differences with the Confederate Congress, Treasury Secretary Christopher G. Memminger (1803–1888) resigned on June 15, 1864. Wealthy cotton broker George A. Trenholm (1807–1876) and two other individuals declined Jefferson Davis's offer of the post, before Trenholm finally accepted it on July 18.

319.12–13 Bragg . . . in the South] Jefferson Davis's military advisor at Richmond since February 1864, Major General Braxton Bragg (1817–1876) had been sent by Davis to Atlanta on July 9 to assess the military situation in Georgia and evaluate the candidates to replace Johnston.

320.12 the Secretary] James Seddon (1815–1880) was the Confederate secretary of war, 1862–65.

320.26 Jack Mosby] See Biographical Notes.

321.2–3 Mosby . . . executed *ten*] There is no record of Mosby engaging in the retaliatory executions described by Kean here. Mosby did order the hanging of seven Union prisoners on November 6, 1864, in retaliation for the killing of seven of his men (see pp. 463–64 in this volume).

321.5 his] The enemy's.

321.12 Gold 252] That is, on the New York gold exchange $252 of paper money (greenbacks) would buy $100 in gold. (In the first four months after the passage of the Legal Tender Act in February 1862, the highest greenback price for $100 in gold was $106.)

323.1 Custer] Brigadier General George Armstrong Custer (1839–1876) commanded a cavalry brigade in Sheridan's Army of the Shenandoah.

325.24 Major Mulford] Major John E. Mulford (1829–1908).

333.16 Linton] Lieutenant Colonel Linton Stephens (1823–1872), commander of the 15th Georgia Infantry, was Stephens's half brother.

334.2 Wheeler] Major General Joseph Wheeler (1836–1906), commander of the cavalry corps in the Army of Tennessee.

334.13 Bragg's worthless pets] General Braxton Bragg (1817–1876) had commanded the Army of Tennessee, November 1862–December 1863.

334.30 Kirby Smith . . . Dick Taylor] Lieutenant General Edmund Kirby Smith (1824–1893) commanded the Trans-Mississippi Department; Lieutenant General Richard Taylor (1826–1879) commanded the Department of Alabama and East Mississippi.

334.34 Gov. Lubbock] Francis Lubbock (1815–1905), governor of Texas, 1861–63.

338.13–14 "Down in Tennessee."] *Down in Tennessee, and Back By Way of Richmond* (1864).

341.27–28 our glorious Massachusetts General] Benjamin F. Butler.

341.33–34 hang them higher than Haman] See Esther 7:9.

342.36 Foster] Brigadier General Robert S. Foster (1834–1903) led the Third Brigade of the First Division, Tenth Corps, Army of the James.

345.32 J. P. Benjamin] Judah P. Benjamin (1811–1884) served as Confederate secretary of state, 1862–65.

346.23–25 Headley's "History," . . . a complete set of the "Rebellion Record,"] J. T. Headley, *The Great Rebellion: A History of the Civil War in the United States* (2 vols., 1863); Benson J. Lossing, *Pictorial Field Book of the American Revolution* (2 vols., 1855); James Parton, *General Butler in New Orleans* (1864); Horace Greeley, *The American Conflict: A History of the Great Rebellion in the United States of America, 1860–'64* (1864); Frank Moore, editor, *The Rebellion Record: A Diary of American Events* (12 vols., 1861–68), of which seven volumes had been published by July 1864.

348.19–20 President of the . . . Franklin Pierce] Davis was secretary of war in the Pierce administration, 1853–57.

352.36–37 Mr. Ashley's Reconstruction Bill] James M. Ashley (1824–1896) was a Republican congressman from Ohio, 1859–69. Ashley introduced a reconstruction bill in December 1863 that authorized the president to appoint provisional military governors in the rebelling states. The governors would organize elections for state constitutional conventions in which suffrage would be extended to black men but denied to those who had fought against the Union or held office in a secessionist government. The bill was tabled in February 1864.

356.31 "Ephraim is joined . . . alone,"] See Hosea 4:17.

356.34 Castle Thunder] Confederate prison in Richmond used to house political prisoners and suspected spies.

360.24 the reserve force] The Confederate reserve force was made up of white males aged 17–18 and 45–50.

363.18 mary] Born in 1852, Mary Rice married a man named Bell in 1882. In 1937, at the age of 85, Mary Bell was interviewed in St. Louis by the Federal Writers' Project of the Works Progress Administration for their collection of narratives by former slaves. Bell concluded her life story by saying: "I love a man who will fight for his rights, and any person who wants to be something."

365.24–25 Military Commandant . . . important election] An election

NOTES   833

was held in the second appellate district of Kentucky on August 1, 1864, for judge of the state court of appeals. In an attempt to secure the seat for the Unconditional Unionist candidate, Brigadier General Stephen G. Burbridge (1831–1894), the Union commander in Kentucky, ordered county sheriffs on July 29 to remove the name of Alvin Duvall (1813–1891), the incumbent since 1856, from the poll books. Union Democrats in the district then rallied behind George Robertson (1790–1874), a former chief justice of the court of appeals, who was elected on August 1.

365.29–30   necessary trade . . . restrictions]   On August 12, 1864, Burbridge required all persons shipping goods or produce in Kentucky to obtain special permits and take loyalty oaths.

366.6   Genl Payne]   Brigadier General Eleazer A. Paine (1815–1882) had assumed command of the District of Western Kentucky on July 19, 1864. After levying a $100,000 tax on suspected Confederate sympathizers in his district, Paine expelled twenty-three prominent citizens from Paducah and confiscated their property. Brigadier General Henry Prince (1811–1892), the Union commander at Columbus, Kentucky, wrote to Grant on August 16 about the expulsions, and detailed two instances "well and thoroughly known to me" in which Paine had men publicly killed "in semblance of an execution, without authority of law or any proper justification." On September 4, Grant ordered Halleck to remove Paine from western Kentucky. "He is not fit to have a command where there is a single solitary family within reach favorable to the Government," Grant wrote. "He will do to put in an intensely disloyal district to scourge the people but even then it is doubtful whether it comes within the bounds of civilized warfare to use him." Paine was replaced on September 11, 1864, and received no other command before resigning his commission in 1865.

366.7–8   Genl Payne . . . Cunningham]   Lieutenant Colonel Richard D. Cunningham of the 8th U.S. Colored Heavy Artillery had led his troops on a raid from Paducah up the Ohio River to Union County on June 7, 1864, and seized a steamboat carrying 158 slaves. Le Roy Fitch, a Union naval officer serving on the Ohio, wrote to his superior on June 11 that Cunningham's troops had "gone on shore to conscript every negro they could find. These negroes, it is reported, were sent on shore armed and without an officer with them, entered private houses, broke open the doors, and entered ladies' bedrooms before they were up, insulted women, and plundered and searched generally."

368.12   Raymond]   See headnote on page 324 of this volume.

371.12   Capt. Lea]   Joseph C. Lea (1841–1904), Confederate guerrilla leader in Louisiana who had previously fought with William Quantrill in Missouri and participated in the August 1863 raid on Lawrence, Kansas.

371.14   Col. Parsons]   Colonel William H. Parsons (1826–1907) led a Texas cavalry brigade that fought in Louisiana and Arkansas.

371.24 ruthless destruction of Floyd and Pin Hook] In retaliation for raids made by Lea's guerrillas on Union-held plantations, a detachment of 230 men from the 3rd U.S. Colored Cavalry burned the villages of Pin Hook and Floyd on August 30, 1864.

372.4 Corps D'Afrique] In May 1863, Major General Nathaniel P. Banks had announced plans to organize a "Corps d'Afrique" of eighteen black regiments in Louisiana. The name was later used by both northerners and southerners to refer to black troops in general.

373.12 Hardee is said to be killed] An incorrect report.

373.15–20 *Georgia* . . . British colors.] Confederate agents had purchased the British steamer *Japan* in 1863 and commissioned it at sea as the commerce raider *Georgia*. After capturing nine American ships, the *Georgia* was decommissioned as a warship in Liverpool on May 10, 1864, and subsequently sold to a British merchant. The ship was seized off the coast of Portugal on August 15, 1864, by the U.S.S. *Niagara* and taken to Boston, where a federal court condemned it as a lawful prize on account of its previous belligerent status.

373.21 Agnew] Cornelius R. Agnew (1830–1888), an ophthalmologist, was surgeon general of New York state, 1859–62, and served on the executive committee of the Sanitary Commission.

374.3–8 Is all our travail . . . effeminate peace?] *1 Henry VI*, V.v.102–7.

374.11 Belmont tells Charley] New York financier August Belmont (1813–1890) was chairman of the Democratic National Committee; Charles E. Strong (1824–1897) was Strong's cousin and law partner.

374.18 Major Halpine (Miles O'Reilly)] Charles G. Halpine (1829–1868), Irish-born journalist and poet who while serving on Halleck's staff published humorous topical articles under the name of "Miles O'Reilly," a purported private in the 47th New York Infantry.

374.19 Jem Brady] James Topham Brady (1815–1869), a prominent New York trial lawyer.

375.3 "Knights of the Golden Circle"] A secret society founded in the 1850s to promote the creation of a "golden circle" of slaveholding states surrounding the Gulf of Mexico and the Caribbean. During the Civil War, Union authorities alleged that it was a predecessor of various Copperhead secret societies, including the Organization of American Knights and the Sons of Liberty.

375.15–18 Fuller . . . we were prosperous."] Thomas Fuller, *Mixt Contemplations in Better Times* (1660), xvi.

375.20 Blake] Charles F. Blake (1834–1881), a New York patent lawyer.

375.26–27 George H. Pendleton] Pendleton (1825–1889) was a Democratic congressman from Ohio, 1857–65.

375.38–39 *noscitur . . . ab ipso*] Latin: He who is not known in himself is known by the company he keeps.

375.40 *Worthies of England*] By Thomas Fuller (1608–1661), published posthumously in 1662.

376.3–4 Sue for bondage, yielding . . . as they're insolent and base.] See William Cartwright (1611–1643), *The Siege, or Love's Convert*, I.i.

379.30 Horatio Seymour] Seymour (1810–1886) was the Democratic governor of New York, 1853–54 and 1863–64.

380.35 Brig. Gen. Govan] Daniel C. Govan (1829–1911) commanded a brigade in Patrick Cleburne's Division in the First Corps of the Army of Tennessee.

381.21 Capt. A——] John W. Acheson (1837–1872), a cousin of Baird from Washington, Pennsylvania, served as an assistant adjutant general on Baird's staff.

389.16 Captain Drayton] Captain Percival Drayton (1812–1865) commanded Farragut's flagship, the U.S.S. *Hartford*.

389.18–19 gone down in the *Locus Point*] The Union steamship *Locust Point* collided with the steamship *Matanzas* and sank off Absecon, New Jersey, on July 3, 1864, with the loss of seventeen lives.

389.20 Fox's fast *Eutaw* class] Gustavas V. Fox (1821–1883) was first assistant secretary of the navy. Commissioned on July 2, 1863, the U.S.S. *Eutaw* was a steam gunboat capable of making ten knots.

389.21 Corbin] Captain Thomas G. Corbin (1820–?) of the U.S.S. *Augusta* had departed Hampton Roads on July 5, 1864, to escort the monitor *Tecumseh* to the Gulf of Mexico where it was to join Farragut's squadron. The *Augusta* experienced engine trouble and only made it as far as Pensacola.

390.2 Captain Jenkins] Captain Thornton A. Jenkins (1811–1893), commanding the U.S.S. *Richmond*, was fleet captain of Farragut's squadron.

391.14–16 *Tecumseh . . .* sunk] The explosion and sinking killed 94 members of the ship's crew.

393.16 Mississippi monitors] The monitors *Chickasaw* and *Winnebago* had been built in Missouri for service on the Mississippi River.

393.19 Admiral Buchanan] Admiral Franklin Buchanan (1800–1874) commanded the Confederate squadron at Mobile from his flagship, the ironclad *Tennessee*, and suffered a fractured right leg before surrendering. He was exchanged on March 7, 1865.

393.20 Captain Le Roy] William E. LeRoy (1818–1888), commander of the 11-gun steam sloop *Ossipee*.

394.4 Commander Johnston] James D. Johnston (c. 1817–1896) was commander of the *Tennessee*.

394.7–8 "Get thee behind me, Satan."] Matthew 16:23.

394.8–10 Captain Heywood . . . *Merrimack* rammed her] Buchanan had commanded the Confederate ironclad *Virginia* (formerly the U.S.S. *Merrimack*) when it rammed and sank the U.S.S. *Cumberland* at Hampton Roads on March 8, 1862. Captain Charles Heywood (1839–1915) served aboard the *Cumberland* as the commander of its marine detachment.

394.29–32 (Anderson) . . . surrender] Colonel Charles D. Anderson (c. 1827–1901) surrendered over 800 men and 26 guns.

394.34 General Granger] Major General Gordon Granger (1822–1876), the commander of the Reserve Corps of the Department of the Gulf, led the Union land forces in the battle of Mobile Bay.

395.1 General Page] Brigadier General Richard L. Page (1807–1901).

395.2 The result] Fort Morgan surrendered on August 23.

395.7 General Canby] Major General Edward Richard S. Canby (1817–1873), commander of the Military Division of West Mississippi.

396.26 Vaughan] Brigadier General John C. Vaughan (1824–1875) led a brigade in Breckenridge's Division, Second Corps, Army of Northern Virginia.

396.30–31 Capt. Massie] Captain John L. Massie (1838–1864) led a company of Virginia Light Artillery in Nelson's battalion. He was fatally wounded on September 23.

396.32 Capt. Milledge] Captain John Milledge Jr. led a company of Georgia Light Artillery in Nelson's battalion.

397.10 Rodes] See note 123.22. Rodes was struck in the back of the head by a shell fragment.

397.20–21 Capt. Kirkpatrick] Captain Thomas J. Kirkpatrick (1829–1897) led a company of Virginia Light Artillery in Nelson's battalion.

398.20 Gen. Ramseur] Brigadier General Stephen D. Ramseur. See Biographical Notes.

400.7 Gen. Polk] Lieutenant General Leonidas Polk (1806–1864) had been killed by an artillery projectile at Pine Mountain, Georgia, on June 14, 1864, while commanding the Third Corps of the Army of Tennessee. Polk had joined Johnston in northern Georgia in May, bringing three infantry divisions with him from Alabama.

400.22–23 "Let the dead bury the dead."] Matthew 8:22.

400.26 said that I had abandoned Georgia] Joseph E. Brown (1821–1894), governor of Georgia, 1857–65, and a bitter political opponent of Davis, had issued an address to the state militia on July 9 that began: "A late correspondence with the President of the Confederate States satisfies my mind that Georgia is to be left to her own resources."

400.28 Walker . . . Gen. Stephen D. Lee] Major General William H. T. Walker (1816–1864), commander of a division that was transferred to Hardee's First Corps of the Army of Tennessee in December 1863, was killed during the battle east of Atlanta on July 22. Lieutenant General Stephen D. Lee was transferred from Mississippi to lead the Second Corps of the Army of Tennessee on July 26.

401.18 Butler the Beast] Davis had issued a proclamation on December 23, 1862, outlawing Benjamin F. Butler as "a felon, deserving of capital punishment," for his actions as the Union commander of occupied New Orleans.

404.2 the Frémont controversy] The Blair family had initially supported the appointment of Major General John C. Frémont as Union commander in Missouri in July 1861, but then became highly critical of his leadership and sought his removal. After Lincoln relieved Frémont on November 2, 1861, many Radical Republicans in Congress sought his exoneration and restoration to command. When Frank and Montgomery Blair testified against Frémont before the Joint Committee on the Conduct of the War in February 1862, Frémont responded by giving the *New-York Daily Tribune* a letter Montgomery Blair had written to him on August 24, 1861, in which the postmaster general criticized Lincoln for being inclined "to the feeble policy of Whigs." Blair offered his resignation from the cabinet, but Lincoln refused to accept it. Frank Blair then denounced "the paralyzing influence" of Frémont's "imbecility" in a speech to Congress on March 7. Despite the opposition of the Blairs, Lincoln chose to conciliate the Radicals by appointing Frémont to command in western Virginia on March 11, 1862.

404.27–29 its highest honor . . . my ambition for him] Francis Preston Blair hoped that his son Montgomery would be chosen to replace Chief Justice Roger B. Taney, who was known to be in declining health. (Taney died on October 12, 1864.)

405.12 Betty] Elizabeth Blair (1841–1872), Montgomery Blair's daughter.

405.19 Blair] Francis Preston Blair Lee (1857–1944), the only child of Elizabeth Blair Lee and Samuel Phillips Lee.

406.11 Your Mayor] Thomas Jefferson Goodwyn (1800–1877), a physician who had served in the 1860 secession convention, was elected mayor of Columbia in 1863.

407.14–15 Israelites . . . flesh pots] See Exodus 16:3.

407.25 we sent commissioners] Davis had sent three commissioners to

Washington on February 27, 1861, in an attempt to gain recognition of southern independence. They were never officially received by the Lincoln administration, but did exchange messages with Secretary of State Seward through intermediaries. The commissioners left Washington on April 11 after it became clear that the administration would attempt to resupply Fort Sumter.

407.28–29   Vice-President . . . refused a passport] See note 235.35.

407.40–408.1   our stocks . . . foreign market] Confederate cotton bonds were traded in the European financial markets.

409.6   plan of negociation by States] The idea that peace could be negotiated by a convention of the states had been endorsed by Alexander H. Stephens in a public letter written on September 22, 1864.

411.10   Gov. Strong, of Massachusetts] During the War of 1812, Massachusetts governor Caleb Strong, a Federalist who opposed the war, refused to order the Massachusetts militia into federal service, arguing that only the governor of a state, and not the president, had the authority to call out its militia.

417.38–418.1   "Anti-slavery Standard," . . . "Liberator"] *The National Anti-Slavery Standard* (1840–70), official weekly newspaper of the National Anti-Slavery Society, and *The Liberator* (1831–65), abolitionist newspaper founded and edited by William Lloyd Garrison.

419.31–32   interpreted by Judge Taney] Chief Justice Roger B. Taney (1777–1864), in the opinion for the Court in the *Dred Scott* case in 1857.

421.25   a few weeks ago . . . Seward] Seward spoke in Auburn, New York, on September 3.

429.7–10   the late Bishop Hughes . . . Governor Seymour] John Joseph Hughes (1797–1864), Roman Catholic archbishop of New York, 1850–64, was a supporter of the war and opponent of abolitionism. On July 17, 1863, the last day of the New York draft riots, Hughes spoke from the balcony of his residence to a crowd of several thousand people and appealed for the restoration of peace and order. As reported in the *New York Herald*, he began his speech by saying: "Men of New York: They call you rioters but I cannot see a rioter's face among you [applause]. I call you men of New York, not gentlemen, because gentlemen is so threadbare a term that it means nothing positive [applause]." Horatio Seymour (1810–1886), the Democratic governor of New York, 1863–64, who had repeatedly criticized the draft as unconstitutional, addressed as "My friends" a crowd gathered outside of City Hall on the morning of July 14, the second day of the riots.

434.16   Mr. S.] Ramseur's lifelong friend David Schenck (1835–1902), who had married Ramseur's sister Sarah (Sallie) in 1859. He edited and published *Sketches of Maj.-Gen. Stephen Dodson Ramseur*, a collection of tributes in prose and verse, in 1892.

434.17   Charley] Ramseur's brother, Charles R. Ramseur (1847–?).

NOTES 839

434.32–33 the issue of your confinement] Ramseur had married his cousin Ellen Richmond (1840–1900) on October 28, 1863, and their only child, Mary Dodson Ramseur (1864–1935), was born on October 11, 1864. Before his death on October 20, Ramseur learned that his wife had given birth, but did not know the name or the sex of the baby.

435.35 Colonel Frank Huger] Lieutenant Colonel Frank Huger (1837–1897) led Huger's Artillery Battalion in the First Corps of the Army of Northern Virginia in the 1864 spring campaign and the siege of Petersburg.

435.40 Nous verrons!] French: We shall see!

436.5 Dr. David] Ramseur's brother, Dr. David P. Ramseur (1839–1905), a surgeon who served with the 14th North Carolina Infantry.

436.7 Caleb . . . Mr. H.] Lieutenant Caleb Richmond, one of Ramseur's cousins, whom Ramseur had placed on his staff as an aide. The Reverend Ephraim H. Harding (1832–1923), chaplain of the 45th North Carolina Infantry, was Ramseur's confidant and frequent courier.

437.25 Gen. W. M. Gardner . . . Gen. Winder's place] Brigadier General William M. Gardner (1824–1901) had replaced Winder (see note 224.10) as superintendent of Richmond prisons.

437.26 exempts] Men who had been exempted from conscription on account of their occupation.

437.30–31 Gov. Brown . . . State militia] Joseph E. Brown (1821–1894), governor of Georgia, 1857–65; Major General Howell Cobb (1815–1868) was the commander of the Georgia state troops.

438.5 Gen. Taylor is the President's kinsman] Jefferson Davis had married Sarah Knox Taylor (1813/14–1835), Richard Taylor's sister, on June 17, 1835. Sarah Davis died of malaria on September 15, 1835, at Brierfield, Davis's plantation on the Mississippi forty miles south of Vicksburg.

438.27 Gen. Barton] Brigadier General Seth M. Barton (1829–1900) commanded a brigade that served in the southern Richmond defenses as part of the division led by Brigadier General George Washington Custis Lee (1832–1913), Robert E. Lee's son.

439.5 *detailed* men] Soldiers who had been detailed to noncombat positions.

439.17 Judge Campbell, and Mr. Kean] John A. Campbell (1811–1889) was the Confederate assistant secretary of war, 1862–65. He had previously served as an associate justice of the U.S. Supreme Court, 1853–61. For Robert Garlick Hill Kean, see Biographical Notes.

440.27 Field's] See note 94.18–19.

440.35 Gov. Smith] William Smith (1797–1887) was governor of Virginia,

1846–49 and 1864–65. He had led a regiment, and then a brigade, in the Army of Northern Virginia, 1862–63, and saw action at the Seven Days, Antietam, Chancellorsville, and Gettysburg before resigning his commission as a major general.

442.27 Goodenough] James G. Goodenough (1830–1875), a gunnery expert and captain in the Royal Navy, had served on the China station with Du Pont and Hall. He was sent to America in 1863 to observe the war.

442.30 Foote] Rear Admiral Andrew H. Foote (1806–1863) had died on his way to take command of the South Atlantic Blockading Squadron. The command went instead to Rear Admiral John A. Dahlgren (see note 3.15–16).

443.16 Rodgers] John Rodgers II (1812–1882) had served as Du Pont's aide at Port Royal Sound in 1861. Promoted to captain, he commanded the ironclad monitor U.S.S. *Weehawken* during Du Pont's unsuccessful attack on the fortifications guarding Charleston Harbor on April 7, 1863.

444.1 La Vendée] Region of west-central France, scene of a revolt against the French revolutionary government, 1793–96, that resulted in 60,000 to 200,000 deaths.

444.4–5 Pélissier in Algeria] Colonel Amable Jean-Jacques Pélissier (1794–1864), a French commander in Algeria, gave orders on June 18, 1845, to set fires that suffocated more than five hundred Kabyle men, women, and children who had taken refuge in a series of caves near Mostaganem. The incident stirred indignation in Europe, but the French government rewarded Pélissier with successive promotions, later conferring on him the title Duke of Malakoff for his military accomplishments in the Crimean War.

444.21–22 a clever antislavery novel] Harriet Beecher Stowe's *Uncle Tom's Cabin* (1852).

444.23–27 Lord Brougham . . . land were assembled.] At the opening session of the International Statistical Congress in London in 1860, with Prince Albert in attendance, Lord Brougham, the presiding officer, publicly drew the attention of George Dallas (1792–1864), the U.S. minister to Great Britain, to the presence of abolitionist Martin Delany (1812–1885). When Dallas refrained from acknowledging him, Delany reportedly responded: "I pray your Royal Highness will allow me to thank his lordship, who is always a most unflinching friend of the negro, for the observation he has made, and I assure your Royal Highness and his lordship that I also am a man."

445.7 poor creature Semmes] See headnote, page 205 of this volume.

446.2–4 The Secretary of War . . . now in arms] John Buchanan Floyd (1806–1863), secretary of war, 1857–60, became a brigadier general in the Confederate army, 1861–62, and later a major general of the Virginia militia, before he succumbed to illness in 1863; Howell Cobb (see note 437.30–31), secretary of the treasury, 1857–60, became president of the provisional

Confederate Congress, 1861–62, before being commissioned a brigadier general in the Confederate army; and Jacob Thompson (see note 261.8).

446.14   Gallic gentleman . . . freaky personage.] Possibly a reference to Henri Mercier (1816–1886), the French minister to the United States from July 1860 to December 1863, who was considered by many northerners to be sympathetic to the Confederacy.

446.36   Sir Michael Seymour] Admiral Sir Michael Seymour (1802–1887) was commander-in-chief of the East Indies and China Station, 1856–59.

447.12   landsmen] Novice seamen.

449.3   cheif engineer] Lieutenant John R. Meigs (1841–1864), the son of Quartermaster General Montgomery C. Meigs, was killed near Dayton, Virginia, on October 3 after he encountered three Confederate cavalry scouts. His death was attributed to guerrilla "bushwhacking," and more than twenty houses were burned in retaliation.

449.34   "too old a bird . . . such chaff."] Variant of a proverb dating at least to the fifteenth century.

450.26–27   letter of Alexander H. Stephens . . . Judge Advocate Holt] Stephens's public letter was written on September 22, 1864, and reprinted in *The New York Times* on October 16. Joseph Holt (1807–1894), the judge advocate general of the Union army, submitted a lengthy report to Stanton on October 8 regarding the subversive activities of the Organization of American Knights, the Sons of Liberty, and other Copperhead secret societies.

452.13   old hero told South Carolina] In his Nullification Proclamation, issued on December 10, 1832.

452.18–19   Pumpernickel sovereignties . . . "Algerine states,"] Allusions to Germany's division into many autonomous petty states. Although nominally under the authority of the Ottoman Sultan, the regencies of Algiers, Tunis, and Tripolitania were in fact each ruled independently by a pasha or dey.

455.5   Ostend proclamation] The result of a meeting in 1854 at Ostend, Belgium, attended by the U.S. ministers to Spain, Great Britain, and France, the Ostend Manifesto argued for the purchase of Cuba from Spain and proposed annexation by force if Spain refused. It was widely understood as an attempt to acquire slaveholding territory beyond the continental United States.

455.16   the opinion which his Attorney-General . . . gave] Attorney General Jeremiah S. Black (1810–1883) submitted his opinion on secession and coercion to Buchanan on November 20, 1860, for the President's use in drafting his annual message to Congress. In his conclusion, Black argued that the "right of the General Government to preserve itself in its whole constitutional vigor by repelling a direct and positive aggression upon its property or its officers, cannot be denied. But this is a totally different thing from an offensive war to punish the people for the political misdeeds of their State Government, or to prevent a threatened violation of the Constitution or to enforce an acknowledgment that the Government of the United States is supreme. The States are colleagues of one another, and if some of them shall conquer the rest and hold them as subjugated provinces, it would totally destroy the whole theory upon which they are now connected."

458.11–12   *VICTORIA! Te Deum . . . Deo!*]   Latin: Victory! We praise thee, O God; we acknowledge thee to be God . . . Praise God!

458.18–19   McClellanized are Missouri, . . . New Jersey.]   Lincoln won in Missouri.

458.21–22   *Subversi sunt . . . vehementibus*]   Exodus 15:10: "They sank as lead in the mighty waters."

458.30   Belmont . . . Barlow]   August Belmont (see note 374.11); New York lawyer Samuel L. M. Barlow (1826–1889).

459.2   *Fuit* McClellan, Napoleoniculus]   Latin: This was McClellan, the Little Napoleon.

459.20   presence of General Butler]   Butler was sent to New York City with 5,000 troops to maintain order on election day. His soldiers remained on their transport ships during the voting.

459.22   George Anthon]   Schoolmaster George C. Anthon (1821–1870), a close friend of the Strongs.

459.24–25   William E. Dodge . . . James Brooks]   Republican William E. Dodge (1805–1883) and Democrat James Brooks (1810–1873), candidates in the New York Eighth Congressional District. Dodge successfully challenged the election results and was seated in Congress in April 1866.

459.28   sure that Seymour is beaten!]   Seymour lost to the Union candidate, Reuben E. Fenton (1819–1885), by 8,293 votes.

460.8   Nicolay]   John G. Nicolay (1832–1901), secretary to Abraham Lincoln, 1860–65.

460.10–11   Wentworth . . . and Moulton at Large]   Republicans John Wentworth (1815–1888), John F. Farnsworth (1820–1897), Elihu Washburne (see note 81.25), Burton C. Cook (1819–1894), Ebon C. Ingersoll (1831–1879), Abner C. Harding (1807–1874), Shelby M. Cullom (1829–1914), Henry P. H. Bromwell (1823–1903), Andrew J. Kuykendall (1815–1891), and Samuel W. Moulton (1821–1905).

460.12   Thornton . . . and Marshall]   Democrats Anthony Thornton (1814–1904), William R. Morrison (1824–1909), Lewis W. Ross (1812–1895), and Samuel S. Marshall (1821–1890).

461.24   Forney]   John W. Forney (1817–1881), editor of the *Philadelphia Press* and the *Washington Chronicle*.

NOTES   843

461.28   President . . . two last Serenades]   Lincoln had spoken to well-wishers at the White House on November 8 and 10.

461.35   Raymond]   Henry J. Raymond (see headnote, page 324 of this volume) had narrowly won election to Congress as the Union candidate in the New York Sixth District. Raymond believed that members of rival Republican factions employed in patronage jobs at the New York Custom House had worked to defeat him.

466.9   *Vox Populi, vox Dei*]   Latin: The voice of the people is the voice of God.

466.18   Beecher]   Henry Ward Beecher (1813–1887), prominent pastor of Plymouth Congregational Church in Brooklyn, New York.

466.29   Theodore Fay]   Fay (1807–1898) was secretary of the U.S. legation in Berlin, 1837–53, and the U.S. minister to Switzerland, 1853–61. He was a prolific author whose novels included *Norman Leslie* (1835) and *Hoboken: A Romance* (1843).

467.12   the Judge]   Daly's husband, Charles P. Daly.

467.17   Darley and his wife]   Artist and book illustrator Felix O. C. Darley (1822–1888) and his wife, Jenny Colburn Darley.

467.18–19   doppelkümmel]   A liqueur made with caraway, cumin, or fennel.

467.24   "Chancellor Kent,"]   Charles P. Daly was writing a biography (never completed) of jurist and legal scholar James Kent (1763–1847), New York state chancellor, 1814–23.

467.29   Mr. Field]   The Reverend Henry M. Field (1822–1907), publisher of *The Evangelist*, a "religious and family paper."

467.34   Baron Gerolt]   Friedrich von Gerolt (1797–1879), Prussian minister to the United States, 1844–71.

468.25   Capt. Acheson]   See note 381.21.

469.30   a son who is a colonel]   Colonel Charles T. Zachry (1828–1906), the son of James B. Zachry, led the 27th Georgia Infantry.

475.5–6   Colonel Poe . . . Captain Buttrick]   Colonel Orlando M. Poe (1832–1895) and Captain Edward K. Buttrick of the 31st Wisconsin Infantry.

476.16   Kilpatrick]   See note 226.10.

477.11–13   Davis' . . . Slocum's]   Brigadier General Jefferson C. Davis (1828–1879) led the Fourteenth Corps. During the march through Georgia and the Carolinas, Major General Henry W. Slocum (1827–1894) commanded the left wing of Sherman's army, which consisted of the Fourteenth and Twentieth Corps.

477.33 "Oglethorpe"] James Oglethorpe (1696–1785), social reformer and investigator of prison abuses who was granted a royal charter in 1732 to establish the colony of Georgia.

479.21–22 (In the words of your Master.)] See page 259 in this volume.

484.30–31 The Chief . . . be relieved.] Charles Francis Adams (1807–1886) would serve as U.S. minister to Great Britain until May 1868.

491.3 Gen Pat Cleburn . . . Gen Granbury] Both Major General Patrick R. Cleburne (1828–1864), Foster's division commander, and Brigadier General Hiram Granbury (1831–1864), his brigade commander, were killed at Franklin.

491.27–28 Col. Young . . . Hickox] Lieutenant Colonel Robert B. Young (1828–1864) of the 10th Texas Infantry was Granbury's chief of staff. Major William A. Taylor (1832–1891) was held in an officers' prison at Johnson's Island, Ohio, until June 1, 1865. Like Foster, Lieutenant Alfred Hickox was an officer in Company H of the 24th Texas Cavalry.

492.22–23 "Vengeance is mine . . . the Lord"] Cf. Romans 12:19.

493.17 Mexico continues . . . civil war] Between the imperialist forces of Maximilian (1832–1867), who had been installed by the French as emperor of Mexico in June 1864, and the republican supporters of President Benito Juárez (1806–1872).

493.24–26 the difficulties . . . inter-oceanic transit route] General Máximo Jerez (1818–1881) staged a revolt in 1863 against the Nicaraguan government of Tomás Martínez (1820–1873) that was suppressed in 1864.

493.34–494.1 a claims convention] Addressing long-standing U.S. claims arising out of an 1856 riot in Panama, then a province of Colombia.

494.7 Aves Island claim] The claim was made by a group of Boston merchants for losses suffered when their guano mining operation on Aves Island in the Caribbean was confiscated by the Venezuelan navy in 1854. The Venezuelan government agreed in 1859 to pay $130,000 over a six-year period in return for the merchants dropping their claim to the uninhabited island.

494.14–15 threatened war between Peru and Spain] A fatal altercation between Peruvian landowners and Spanish immigrants at Talambo in August 1863 led to the Spanish navy seizing the Chinchas Islands off Peru in April 1864. Under a treaty signed in January 1865, Peru agreed to pay three million pesos in compensation for the return of the islands. Public outrage in Peru caused the agreement to be rejected, and in 1866, Peru and Chile fought a brief naval war with Spain.

494.23–24 seizure of the cargo . . . in 1821] During the Chilean War of Independence, Chilean forces seized $70,400 in silver from an American merchant ship captain in southern Peru, claiming that it was Spanish property. Acting as an international arbiter, King Leopold I of Belgium settled the

NOTES   845

dispute on May 15, 1863, by awarding the American claimants $42,400, which was paid by the Chilean government in April 1864.

495.20–24   representative in Egypt . . . the successor] William S. Thayer (1830–1864), the American consul general in Egypt since 1861, died in April 1864. Francis Dainese, the acting consul, then became involved in a dispute with the Egyptian authorities over damage to a water aqueduct allegedly caused by an American citizen, and eventually broke off relations with the government in Cairo. Relations were restored when Thayer's replacement, Charles Hale (1831–1888), took up his post in the fall of 1864.

495.27   The rebellion . . . has at last been suppressed] The Taiping Rebellion ended with the fall of the rebel capital Nanking (Nanjing) in July 1864.

496.32–33   political difficulties . . . Brazilian and British ports] The U.S.S. *Wachusett* had captured the Confederate commerce raider *Florida* in the neutral port of Salvador, Brazil, on October 7, 1864, causing a protest by the Brazilian government. British authorities had protested when the U.S.S. *Tioga* anchored in the Bimini roadstead in the Bahamas without official permission on April 12, 1864.

497.1–2   the claims . . . in Oregon] These claims by British companies were first recognized by the United States in the 1846 treaty with Great Britain that resolved the Oregon boundary dispute. The claims were settled when the United States made payments of $325,000 in 1870 and 1871.

497.6–7   recent assaults and depredations] Confederate raiders based in Canada attempted on September 19, 1864, to capture the gunboat U.S.S. *Michigan* and use it to free the Confederate prisoners held on Johnson's Island in Lake Erie. The Confederates were able to seize two ferryboats, but abandoned their plan to board the *Michigan* after realizing that its crew had been alerted. On October 19, 1864, a band of Confederate raiders crossed the Canadian border and robbed three banks in St. Albans, Vermont, killing one citizen and escaping back into Canada with $200,000.

497.26–27   The act passed . . . encouragement of emigration] Passed on July 4, 1864, the act established a commissioner of immigration within the State Department and authorized labor contracts under which emigrants could pledge up to twelve months of their future wages to pay for transportation.

501.18   creating the new rank of vice-admiral] Congress established the rank on December 21, 1864.

504.9–10   Agricultural Department . . . energetic and faithful head] Isaac Newton (1800–1867), commissioner of agriculture, 1862–67. (The first secretary of agriculture with cabinet rank was appointed in 1889.)

504.15   The war continues.] Surviving autograph fragments indicate that the message from this point on was Lincoln's own composition. The preceding parts were probably written by the various members of the cabinet, with the likely exception of the opening paragraph.

514.2 *John C. Ropes*] Ropes (1836–1899) was unable to serve in the army because of a childhood spinal injury. He later formed a law partnership with John Chipman Gray and published several works of military history, including *The Army under Pope* (1881) and *The Story of the Civil War* (2 vols., 1894–98). His brother, First Lieutenant Henry Ropes (1839–1863), fought with the 20th Massachusetts Infantry at Fair Oaks, the Seven Days' Battles, Antietam, Fredericksburg (December 1862 and May 1863), and Gettysburg, where he was killed by the premature explosion of a Union shell.

515.1 General Hatch] Brigadier General John P. Hatch (1822–1901) commanded the Coast Division in the Department of the South.

515.2 General Foster's wound] Foster had been wounded in the leg in the battle of Molino del Ray, on September 8, 1847. The same leg was seriously injured when his horse fell in East Tennessee on December 23, 1863.

515.5–6 Grahamville, . . . considerable loss] Union casualties in the fighting near Grahamville, South Carolina, on November 30, 1864, were reported as 88 men killed, 623 wounded, and 43 missing.

515.12 General Potter] Formerly Foster's chief of staff, Brigadier General Edward E. Potter (1823–1889) had assumed command of the First Brigade of the Coast Division on November 28, 1864.

515.20 Colonel Hartwell] Colonel Alfred S. Hartwell (1836–1912) of the 55th Massachusetts Infantry led the Second Brigade of the Coast Division.

515.25 General Howard's] During the march through Georgia and the Carolinas, Major General Oliver Otis Howard (1830–1909) commanded the right wing of Sherman's army, which consisted of the Fifteenth and Seventeenth Corps.

515.34 General Hazen] Major General William B. Hazen (1830–1887) led the Second Division, Fifteenth Corps.

516.30 *Punch*] Weekly English humor magazine founded in 1841.

517.3 Hardie] Lieutenant General William J. Hardee.

518.3 General Saxton] Brigadier General Rufus Saxton (1824–1908) commanded the District of Beaufort in the Department of the South.

519.19 discern the signs of the times] See Matthew 16:3.

521.1 John Brooks] A black man from Georgia, Brooks escaped and made his way north to Pennsylvania in March 1865.

524.33–34 Colonel Jones." . . . Mary Ruth] Mallard's brother, Lieutenant Colonel Charles C. Jones (1831–1893), a Confederate artillery officer, and Mallard's niece, Mary Ruth Jones (1861–1934).

NOTES 847

526.32–33   Brother Charlie . . . mayor]   Charles C. Jones was mayor of Savannah, 1860–61.

526.39   Liberty Independent Troop]   Mounted militia organized in Liberty County, Georgia, in 1778.

537.28–30   two Union officers . . . two rebel officers]   On July 6, 1863, Confederate authorities selected by lot Henry Sawyer and John Flinn, two Union captains held in Libby Prison in Richmond, and announced that they would be executed in retaliation for the deaths of Captain William Francis Corbin and Lieutenant Thomas Jefferson McGraw, who had been shot as spies on May 15, 1863, after being captured within the Union lines in northern Kentucky while secretly recruiting for the Confederate army. President Lincoln responded on July 15 by declaring that if Sawyer and Flinn were executed, the Union would retaliate by hanging Brigadier General William Henry Fitzhugh Lee (1837–1891), Robert E. Lee's son, who had been captured by Union cavalry in Virginia on June 26. The threatened executions were not carried out, and on March 14, 1864, Sawyer, Flinn, and Brigadier General Neal Dow were exchanged for Lee and another Confederate officer who had been held as a hostage, Captain Robert H. Tyler.

537.32–33   trenches before Charleston . . . release of Union officers]   In June 1864, Major General Samuel Jones (1819–1887), the Confederate commander in South Carolina, attempted to deter the further shelling of Charleston by having fifty Union officers imprisoned in an area of the city within the range of Union artillery. Major General John G. Foster retaliated by having fifty Confederate officers sent from Fort Delaware and held on Morris Island in Charleston Harbor. During the summer of 1864 another 900 Union prisoners were sent to Charleston as Confederate authorities tried to reduce the number of prisoners who could potentially be freed by Union cavalry raids in Georgia. Foster then responded by having another 600 Confederate officers sent to Morris Island, where they were imprisoned in an open-air stockade near Fort Wagner. When the Union prisoners at Charleston were moved inland in October 1864, Foster sent the Confederate officers on Morris Island to Fort Pulaski in Georgia.

541.12   "Out of the abundance . . . mouth speaketh,"]   Cf. Luke 6:45.

543.2–3   short distance of Ft Fisher]   The sidewheel steamer *Louisiana* was loaded with 215 tons of gunpowder and detonated about 600 yards from the fort at 1:46 A.M. on December 24, 1864.

543.16   Gen D H Hill]   Major General Daniel H. Hill (1821–1889) was placed in command of the Confederate forces at Augusta, Georgia, on January 21, 1865. Hill (no relation to A. P. Hill) had commanded a division in the Seven Days' Battles and Antietam and a corps at Chickamauga.

543.21   Christmas gift to Mr. Lincoln]   Sherman had sent a telegram to President Lincoln from Savannah on December 22, 1864, that read: "I beg to present you as a Christmas gift the City of Savannah with 150 heavy guns & plenty of ammunition & also about 25,000 bales of cotton."

543.34 demonstration on Gordonsville] Union cavalry advanced on the rail junction at Gordonsville, Virginia, on December 23, 1864, but then retreated after discovering that the town was defended by two infantry brigades.

544.1 haslets] Hog viscera.

544.37 Motley's "United Netherlands"] John Lothrop Motley (1814–1877), *History of the United Netherlands* (2 vols. 1860). The final two volumes were published in 1867.

545.12 stabbing as Joab] See 2 Samuel 3:27.

545.13 Ld Bacon's Essays] Francis Bacon, *The Essays, or Counsels, Civill and Morall* (1597–1625).

545.26–27 "there is nothing . . . sun."] Ecclesiastes 1:9.

548.39–549.1 *Felix Grundy . . . Foster*] Felix Grundy (1777–1840) served in the Senate, 1829–38 and 1839–40, and as attorney general, 1838–39; John Bell (1796–1869) served in the Senate, 1847–59; Hugh L. White (1773–1840) served in the Senate, 1825–40; Cave Johnson (1793–1866) was postmaster general, 1845–49; Ephraim H. Foster (1794–1854) served in the Senate, 1838–39 and 1843–45.

549.2 *Gen. William Carroll . . . Aaron V. Brown*] William Carroll (1788–1844), governor of Tennessee, 1821–27 and 1829–35; Samuel Houston (1793–1863), governor of Tennessee, 1827–29; and Aaron V. Brown (1795–1859), governor of Tennessee, 1845–47.

563.36–37 the Act of Congress] An act adopted on July 4, 1864, permitting Union agents to recruit black men in the South and credit their numbers against northern draft quotas.

570.22–23 Mr. Chase . . . Mrs. Sprague] Salmon P. Chase had been nominated and confirmed as chief justice of the U.S. Supreme Court on December 6, 1864. Kate Chase Sprague (1840–1899), the wife of Rhode Island senator William Sprague, was the chief justice's daughter.

571.8 Doctor Rock] Boston abolitionist, physician, and lawyer John S. Rock (1825–1866) was the first black man to be admitted to the bar of the Supreme Court. His admission was sponsored by Senator Charles Sumner.

571.10 the old Dred Scott judges] James M. Wayne (1790–1867), associate justice, 1835–67; John Catron (1786–1865), associate justice, 1837–65; Samuel Nelson (1792–1873), associate justice, 1845–73; and Robert C. Grier (1794–1870), associate justice, 1846–70, had all voted in the majority in *Dred Scott v. Sandford* (1857).

572.33 Major Eckert] Major Thomas T. Eckert (1825–1910), superintendent of the War Department telegraph office, 1862–66.

573.16 the secret committee] While serving in Congress together in 1847–48, Lincoln and Stephens had been members of a committee that worked to secure the Whig nomination for Zachary Taylor.

573.18–19 'sleeping together' . . . Botts and Tyler] John Minor Botts (1802–1869), a Whig congressman from Virginia, 1839–43 and 1847–49, and vice president–elect John Tyler had shared a bed in an overcrowded hotel in Washington, D.C., while attending the inauguration of President William Henry Harrison in 1841.

574.28–31 Mr. Hunter's . . . *story* of the pigs.)] On June 7, 1865, the Augusta, Georgia, *Chronicle and Sentinel* printed what it described as "the history" of the Hampton Roads conference "as nearly as we can remember it from the statement of Mr. STEPHENS to us, directly after his return." The *Chronicle and Sentinel* reported that when Robert M. T. Hunter "said something about the inhumanity of leaving so many poor old negroes and young children destitute, by encouraging the able-bodied negroes to run away, and asked what are they— the helpless—to do?" Lincoln responded by saying, "that reminded him of an old friend in Illinois, who had a crop of potatoes and did not want to dig them. So he told a neighbor that he would turn in his hogs and let them dig them for themselves. But, said the neighbor, the frost will soon be in the ground, and when the soil is hard frozen, what will they do then? To which the worthy farmer replied, '*let 'em root!*'" In his memoir *Six Months at the White House with Abraham Lincoln* (1866), the painter Francis B. Carpenter recorded how the President had retold the story of the hogs to him shortly after the conference. In Carpenter's version, Lincoln told the story after Hunter warned that "both blacks and whites would starve" throughout the South if slavery were ended.

575.10–11 the President] Jefferson Davis.

585.23–28 "Thus man devotes . . . inflicted on a beast."] See William Cowper (1731–1800), *The Task* (1785), book 2, lines 20–25.

585.31 Anathema-maranatha.] See I Corinthians 16:22, where these words, one Greek, often used in excommunications, the other Syriac, meaning "the Lord cometh" (i.e., to take vengeance), are invoked as a curse.

586.37–38 "Proud Nimrod . . . his prey was man."] Alexander Pope, "Windsor Forest" (1713), lines 61–62.

587.17 Mahomet] Muhammad.

589.19–20 "*Therefore all things . . . the prophets.*"] Matthew 7:12.

589.23 "Sages who wrote . . . bled."] William Marsden (1754–1836), "What Is Time?" line 6.

589.31 higher than Haman] See Esther 7:9.

590.8–10 "There is preparing . . . a total emancipation."] See *Notes on the State of Virginia*, Query XVIII: "The spirit of the master is abating, that of the slave rising from the dust, his condition mollifying, the way I hope preparing, under the auspices of heaven, for a total emancipation, and that this is disposed, in the order of events, to be with the consent of the masters, rather than by their extirpation."

590.13–16 "It is among . . . not be wanting."] Cf. Washington's August 4, 1797, letter to Lawrence Lewis: "I wish from my Soul that the Legislature of this State could see the policy of a gradual abolition of Slavery; It might prevt much future mischief."

590.22–23 Giddings . . . Lovejoy] Joshua R. Giddings (1795–1864), congressman from Ohio, 1838–42 and 1842–59, was an outspoken opponent of slavery; Owen Lovejoy (1811–1864), abolitionist who served as a Republican congressman from Illinois, 1857–64. His brother, Elijah Lovejoy (1802–37), a newspaper editor, was killed by a proslavery mob in Alton, Illinois.

590.28 POPE LEO X testifies] Leo X issued a papal bull criticizing the enslavement of American Indians in 1514.

590.30 PATRICK HENRY said] Cf. Henry's January 13, 1773, letter to John Alsop: "I believe a time will come when an opportunity will be afforded to abolish this lamentable evil. Everything we can do, is to improve it, if it happens in our day; if not, let us transmit to our descendants, together with our slaves, a pity for their unhappy lot, and an abhorrence of Slavery."

590.33 LAFAYETTE proclaimed] In the second number of *The Liberator*, January 8, 1831, William Lloyd Garrison quoted Lafayette as having said: "While I am indulging in my views of American prospects, and American liberty, it is mortifying to be told that in that very country, a large portion of the people are slaves! It is a dark spot on the face of the nation. Such a state of things cannot always exist."

590.36 JONATHAN EDWARDS declared] Jonathan Edwards the Younger (1745–1801), son of the famous theologian, was himself a theologian and minister. In *The Injustice and Impolicy of the Slave Trade*, a sermon preached in New Haven on September 15, 1791, before the annual meeting of the Connecticut Society for the Promotion of Freedom, Edwards said that "to hold a man in a state of slavery, who has a right to his liberty, is to be every day guilty of robbing him of his liberty, or of manstealing."

591.21–23 "Whoso stealeth . . . be put to death."] See Exodus 21:16.

591.37 Balak] King of Moab; see Numbers 22–24.

592.1–2 Chatham, . . . Curran,] William Pitt, Earl of Chatham (1708–1778), British statesman; Edmund Burke (1729–1797), British orator and essayist; Granville Sharp (1735–1813), William Wilberforce (1759–1833), and Thomas Clarkson (1760–1846), leaders of the British antislavery movement; John Philpot Curran (1750–1817), Irish lawyer and statesman.

NOTES

592.16 Morrises, and Bokers] George Pope Morris (1802–1864), newspaper publisher and popular poet; George Henry Boker (1823–1890), author of *Poems of the War* (1864) and a founder of the Union League Club.

593.11–18 "Down let the shrine . . . from heaven."] John Greenleaf Whittier, "Expostulation" (1834), lines 105–112.

594.3–4 "Bound on . . . little known,"] William Cowper, "Human Frailty," lines 17–18.

595.32–33 "*that they go forward.*"] See Exodus 14:15.

596.4–33 "Hear ye not . . . close to thee!"] "Exodus," by Adeline Dutton Train Whitney (1824–1906), first published anonymously in the April 1862 number of the *Atlantic Monthly*.

598.3 *Emma LeConte: Diary*] LeConte wrote her diary in pencil on "pieces of brownish Confederate letter paper," and later copied it into a notebook at the time of her marriage in 1869. The text printed here is taken from the 1869 notebook. Some of the sheets of the original diary have survived, and a collation of the two texts shows that LeConte made significant revisions in wording while copying the original. An example of these changes is presented in the note below.

598.37–599.6 How long is . . . reigning up town.] In the original diary, this appears as: "How long is this distress of mind to continue? It is now about 11 o'clock and it is the longest morning I ever passed. I threw myself on the bed without undressing, late last night—or rather early this morning feeling that if I did not take some rest I would be sick. It was some time before I could sleep as every now and then a cannon report would break the stillness. So in spite of my heavy eyelids I lay awake thinking of the dreadful possibility of the town being shelled in the night and also of the tumult I knew was reigning up town."

599.14 Jane . . . Henry] Slaves who worked as servants in the LeConte household.

600.1 Sallie] Sarah Elizabeth LeConte (1850–1915), Emma LeConte's younger sister.

600.11 Carrie] Caroline Eaton LeConte (1863–1946), Emma LeConte's youngest sister.

600.15 the mayor] See note 406.11.

600.23 Aunt Josie's, Miss Mary] Eleanor Josephine Graham LeConte (1824–1894), the wife of John LeConte (1818–1891), and her sister, Mary A. Graham (d. 1890).

601.1–2 Col Stone] Colonel George A. Stone (1833–1901) commanded the Third Brigade, First Division, Fifteenth Corps.

601.11   Wheeler's command]   Major General Joseph Wheeler (1836–1906) led a Confederate cavalry corps during Sherman's march through the Carolinas.

601.38   Howards and Logans]   Major General Oliver Otis Howard (1830–1909) commanded the right wing of Sherman's army, which consisted of the Fifteenth and Seventeenth Corps. Major General John A. Logan (1826–1886) commanded the Fifteenth Corps.

602.1–2   Slocum's . . . Davis']   See note 477.11–13.

602.14–15   Gen Hampton]   Lieutenant General Wade Hampton (1818–1902), a wealthy South Carolina plantation owner, had recently been appointed commander of Confederate cavalry in South Carolina. Hampton had previously led the cavalry corps of the Army of Northern Virginia, May 1864–January 1865.

604.11   Mary Ann]   A slave who worked as a servant in the LeConte household. She and Henry were married.

604.25   Dr Thomson]   Andrew W. Thomson (1827–1881) was the surgeon in charge of the Second North Carolina Hospital, which was housed on the South Carolina College campus.

606.35   Poor father! . . . he hears]   Joseph LeConte (1823–1901) and his brother John left Columbia on February 16 with several wagons carrying household belongings and Niter Bureau property. They encountered soldiers from the left wing of Sherman's army, who took their food and destroyed the wagons. Joseph LeConte returned to Columbia and was reunited with his family on February 24, 1865.

609.30   our Division]   Johnson's Division, led by Major General Bushrod R. Johnson (1817–1880), part of the Fourth Corps of the Army of Northern Virginia, commanded by Lieutenant General Richard H. Anderson (1821–1879).

610.22   Wise]   Mills served in a brigade commanded by Brigadier General Henry A. Wise (1806–1876), the former governor of Virginia, 1856–60.

610.28   Cooke]   First Lieutenant Charles M. Cooke (1844–1920), the adjutant of the 55th North Carolina Infantry, had attended Wake Forest College with Mills.

610.29   Dr. & John Cannady]   Isaac G. Cannady, assistant surgeon of the 55th North Carolina Infantry, and Sergeant John P. Cannady, who served in Company K. Both men surrendered at Appomattox.

610.30   Cooke's Brig]   The 55th was one of five North Carolina regiments in an infantry brigade commanded by Brigadier General John R. Cooke (1833–1891). It was assigned to the division led by Major General Henry Heth (1825–1899), part of the Third Corps of the Army of Northern Virginia.

613.22–23   let us . . . judged.]   Cf. Matthew 7:1; Luke 6:37.

613.25–27   "Woe unto . . . the offence cometh!"]   Matthew 18:7.

NOTES 853

614.1–2 "the judgments . . . altogether!"] See Psalms 19:9.

616.12–13 "they all with . . . make excuse."] See Luke 14:18.

616.13 Mrs. Dorsey] Louise Tobias Dorsey, the free-born wife of Thomas J. Dorsey, a former slave who had established a successful catering business in Philadelphia.

620.6 Mr Streeter] Holland Streeter, a former butcher from Lowell, Massachusetts, who had originally been hired by Horace James to oversee shad fisheries on the island, became the assistant superintendent of the colony in October 1864. He was accused in June 1865 of profiting from the illegal sale of rations intended for distribution to the colonists. On July 24, 1865, a military commission convicted Streeter of embezzlement and fraud and sentenced him to three months' hard labor and a $500 fine (the prison sentence was later remitted).

620.14 General Butler] Major General Benjamin F. Butler (1818–1893) commanded the Department of Virginia and North Carolina, November 1863–January 1865.

623.33 John Bright] A prominent orator and reformer who served in the House of Commons, 1843–89, John Bright (1811–1889) was a leading British advocate of the Union cause.

624.1 F. M. Edge] Frederick Milnes Edge (1830–?), a British journalist, pamphleteer, and supporter of the Union cause. In 1862, Edge had accompanied the Army of the Potomac in the Peninsula campaign as a correspondent for the London *Morning Star*.

627.2 "bummers,"] Soldiers detailed to foraging parties.

628.10 Rene . . . Minnie's] Williams's daughters, Irene Williams (1843–1907) and Mary Williams (1846–1935).

629.17 yr good & most suggestive letter] In a letter written on February 17, 1865, Bright advised that reconstruction should be based on the abolition of slavery, a generous amnesty policy, limited confiscation of southern land, the exclusion of Confederate leaders from federal or state office, and the nullification of Confederate debts.

630.19–20 govt. in Louisiana . . . defeated in Congress] On February 24, 1865, the Senate began debating a resolution recognizing the legitimacy of the reconstruction government in Louisiana. Sumner engaged in a successful filibuster against the measure, and on February 27 the Senate voted, 34–12, to postpone further consideration of the resolution.

630.20–22 Chief Justice Chase . . . "illegal & void"] In a letter to Bright written on March 18, 1865, Sumner explained that he had initially misunderstood Chase's ruling in *United States v. Alexander*, a case arising from the seizure of cotton by the Union navy during the 1864 Red River campaign.

The chief justice had subsequently explained to him that the Court had not ruled on "the validity of the La. govt., but only on the validity of proceedings in certain parts of the state."

630.28 "the territorial theory."] Sumner had argued in 1862 that the seceding states should be treated as federal territories over which Congress had complete jurisdiction.

630.39 Resolutions on Reciprocity & Lake Armaments,] The Senate had voted on January 12, 1865, to terminate the Reciprocity Treaty of 1854, liberalizing trade between the United States and Canada, and on January 18 to terminate the Rush-Bagot Treaty of 1817, limiting naval armaments on the Great Lakes and Lake Champlain.

631.3–4 the date . . . held it back] Concerned about the activities of Confederate agents in Canada, the House of Representatives voted on June 20, 1864, to end the Great Lakes naval agreement. As chairman of the Foreign Relations Committee, Sumner had delayed Senate consideration of the measure.

631.5 outrages on the Lakes] See note 497.6–7.

631.16 Cobden] Richard Cobden (1804–1865), a British reformer who served in Parliament, 1841–57 and 1859–65, was a supporter of the Union and a friend and political ally of John Bright.

635.15 U.S.C.H. Arty.] United States Colored Heavy Artillery.

636.1–2 Rebel General Bragg . . . the State] After the inconclusive battle of Perryville, October 8, 1862, General Braxton Bragg abandoned his invasion of Kentucky and retreated into Tennessee.

637.32 the South Side Road] The Southside Railroad, which connected Petersburg with Lynchburg in western Virginia.

638.9–10 Mrs. Davis . . . leaving the city] Varina Howell Davis left Richmond on March 30, 1865.

638.12 Dr. Hoge . . . Gen. Cooper] Moses Hoge (1818–1889), pastor of the Second Presbyterian Church of Richmond; General Samuel Cooper (1798–1876), adjutant general of the Confederate army.

638.14 Dr. Minnegerode] Charles Minnegerode (1814–1894), rector of St. Paul's Episcopal Church in Richmond.

638.15 Gen. Ewell] Lieutenant General Richard S. Ewell (1817–1872) had commanded the Department of Richmond since June 13, 1864.

638.21 Danville Road] The Richmond & Danville Railroad.

638.23–24 the Secretary] Confederate Secretary of War John C. Breckinridge (1821–1875).

638.25 Lieut.-Gen. Hardee] Lieutenant General William J. Hardee

NOTES 855

(1815–1873) commanded a corps in the Army of Tennessee. At the beginning of April 1865 his corps was camped near Smithfield, North Carolina.

638.28   Gen. Kemper] Major General James L. Kemper (1823–1895) commanded the Reserve Forces of Virginia, made up of men aged 17–18 and 45–50, as well as men aged 18–46 who had been exempted from army service to work in munitions manufacture.

638.33   Hon. James Lyons] James Lyons (1801–1882), a Richmond attorney who served in the Confederate Congress, 1862–64.

639.8   Judge Campbell] John A. Campbell (1811–1889), associate justice of the U.S. Supreme Court, 1853–61, and Confederate assistant secretary of war, 1862–65.

639.38–39   A. P. Hill . . . Lee] Hill was killed on the morning of April 2, 1865, but Lee was not wounded.

643.37–38   Colonel —— . . . his bride] Lieutenant Colonel Walter H. Taylor (1838–1916), an assistant adjutant general on Robert E. Lee's staff, married Ellen Selden Saunders (1840–1916).

644.8   Mayor Mayo] Joseph C. Mayo (1795–1872), mayor of Richmond, 1853–65 and 1866–68.

644.22   receiving-ship] A vessel where new recruits were sent to await their service assignments.

645.23–24   General Godfrey Weitzel . . . General Ord] Major General Godfrey Weitzel (1835–1884) commanded the Twenty-fifth Corps in the Army of the James; Major General Edward O. C. Ord (1818–1883) had replaced Benjamin F. Butler as commander of the Army of the James on January 8, 1865.

645.25   one-half of his division] Ord had sent the Twenty-fourth Corps, i.e, one half of the Army of the James, to the Petersburg front.

645.32–33   Major A. H. Stevens . . . Major E. E. Graves] Atherton H. Stevens Jr. (1824–1872); Emmons E. Graves (1843–1891).

646.7   Long lines of negro cavalry] From the 5th Massachusetts Cavalry, commanded by Colonel Charles Francis Adams Jr.

648.2–3   an authentic account] Edward A. Pollard, *The Last Year of the War* (1866).

649.8–9   General Shepley . . . Lieutenant-Colonel Fred L. Manning] Brigadier General George F. Shepley (1819–1878), chief of staff of the Twenty-fifth Corps, Army of the James; Frederick L. Manning (1837–?), provost marshal of the Army of the James.

649.13–14   morbidly sensitive clause . . . "flag,"] In his order of April 3, 1865, Shepley stated: "No treasonable or offensive expressions insulting the flag, the cause or the armies of the Union will hereafter be allowed."

649.34–35 man knoweth not . . . bring forth.] Cf. Proverbs 27:1.

650.28 City Point] City Point, Virginia, a port on the James River where Grant had made his headquarters during the siege of Petersburg.

651.11 Vinton] Francis Vinton (1809–1872), assistant minister of Trinity Church.

651.16 Prosper M. Wetmore . . . Simeon Draper] Wetmore (1798–1876) was a merchant active in Democratic politics; Draper (1804–1866) was collector of customs at New York, 1864–65, and had served as chairman of the state Republican Party, 1860–62.

651.19–20 Hon. Moses Odell and Evarts] Odell (1818–1866) was a Democratic congressman from New York, 1861–65; William Evarts (1818–1901), a New York attorney who later served as U.S. attorney general, 1868–69, as secretary of state, 1877–81, and as a Republican senator from New York, 1885–91.

652.12–14 Captain Marshall . . . Judge Vanderpoel] Charles Henry Marshall (1792–1865), a merchant and retired sea captain; Aaron Vanderpoel (1799–1870), a judge of the New York Superior Court, 1842–50, had served in Congress as a Jacksonian Democrat, 1833–37 and 1839–41.

652.22 Hamilton Fish] Fish (1808–1893) had been a Whig congressman, 1843–45, governor of New York, 1849–50, and a U.S. senator, 1851–57. He later served as secretary of state, 1869–77.

652.25 Sydney Smith] English essayist (1771–1845).

653.24 Major Pegram] William Pegram's surviving brother, Major James West Pegram (1839–1881), who served on Ewell's staff.

654.32–33 "My God, . . . forsaken me,"] Matthew 27:46.

655.9 another Col. mortally wounded] Colonel Joshua H. Hudson (1832–1909), commander of the 26th South Carolina Infantry, survived the wound he received at Five Forks.

656.26 Fort Burnham] After capturing Fort Harrison on September 29, 1864, the Union army renamed the strongpoint after Brigadier General Hiram Burnham (1814–1864), who had been killed during the assault. The fort was about seven miles southeast of Richmond.

657.15–19 Brevet Brigadier General Draper . . . Captain Bicnnef] Colonel Alonzo Draper (1835–1865) commanded the First Brigade, First Division, Twenty-fifth Corps; Brigadier General August Kautz (1828–1895) commanded the First Division, Twenty-fifth Corps; Benjamin F. Pratt (1824–1890) led the 36th U.S. Colored Infantry in the First Brigade; Captain Francis A. Bicknell (1844–?) commanded Company A of the 36th U.S. Colored Infantry.

658.16 Devin's] Brigadier General Charles Devens (1820–1891) commanded the Third Division, Twenty-fourth Corps, Army of the James. The

Third Division had remained north of the James River when the remainder of the Twenty-fourth Corps was sent to the Petersburg front in late March 1865.

659.23–24 Texas Brigade, under Gary] In the battle of New Market Heights (or Chaffin's Farm), September 29, 1864, Draper's brigade of U.S. Colored Troops captured a position held by Gregg's Brigade, composed of the 1st, 4th, and 5th Texas and 3rd Arkansas infantry regiments. The Texas Brigade, which had been one of the most renowned formations in the Army of Northern Virginia since the Seven Days' Battles, was led during the battle by Colonel Frederick S. Bass (1831–1897) of the 1st Texas Infantry. Brigadier General John Gregg (1828–1864), the brigade's commander, was in overall command of the Confederate forces defending New Market Heights, which also included a brigade of dismounted cavalry led by Brigadier General Martin W. Gary (1831–1881). At the time of New Market Heights, Draper's brigade was designated the Second Brigade, Third Division, Eighteenth Corps. It lost 477 men killed, wounded, or missing in the battle.

659.32 Wild's] Brigadier General Edward A. Wild (1825–1891) led the Second Brigade, First Division, Twenty-fifth Corps.

659.34 Thomas' brigade] Brigadier General Henry G. Thomas (1837–1897) led the Third Brigade, First Division, Twenty-fifth Corps.

661.5 Gen. Ripley] Colonel Edward H. Ripley (1839–1915) led the First Brigade, Third Division, Twenty-fourth Corps.

661.11 F.F.V.' s] First Families of Virginia.

663.6 Admiral Porter's] Rear Admiral David D. Porter (1813–1891) commanded the North Atlantic Blockading Squadron, 1864–65.

663.37 his youngest son] Thomas (Tad) Lincoln (1853–1871).

663.38 General Devin] Devens (see note 658.16).

665.1 Colonel Morning] Manning (see note 649.8–9).

665.24 yesterday (Tuesday)] April 4, 1865.

666.7–8 "cohesive power of public plunder"] The origin of this phrase is attributed to a speech in the Senate by John C. Calhoun on May 27, 1836: "A power has risen up in the government greater than the people themselves, consisting of many and various and powerful interests, combined into one mass, and held together by the cohesive power of the vast surplus in the banks."

666.33 Spear's cavalry] Colonel Samuel P. Spear (1815–1875) commanded the Second Brigade, Cavalry Division, Army of the James.

667.2 Capt. Mattison] Lucius V. S. Mattison (1842–1910).

667.15 Lieut. Gen. Grant . . . tomorrow] Grant was in the field with the Army of the Potomac on April 7, 1865, as it pursued Lee's retreating army.

669.30   James Hamilton] James Hamilton Jr. (1786–1857), governor of South Carolina, 1830–32, and a leading proponent of nullification.

670.2–3   Marmion, Ivanhoe] *Marmion: A Tale of Flodden Field* (1808), *Ivanhoe: A Romance* (1819).

678.27   Willie's death] William Wallace (Willie) Lincoln (1850–1862), the Lincolns' third son, had died in the White House on February 20, 1862, probably from typhoid fever.

678.38   Mrs. Lee, *née* Miss Blair] Elizabeth Blair Lee (1818–1906); see Biographical Notes.

679.2   Mr. and Mrs. Walker Lewis] Walker Lewis worked for the government as a messenger and steward; Virginia Lewis was a seamstress.

681.18   Mrs. Secretary Welles] Mary Jane Hale Welles (1817–1886).

682.32   Robert] Robert Todd Lincoln (1843–1926), the Lincolns' oldest son.

684.29   Ellie] Ellen Ruggles Strong (1825–1888), Strong's wife.

684.30   *Eheu*] Latin: Alas.

685.19   Faulkner . . . Kenzua] Hiram D. Faulkner, who served with Strong on the board of directors of the Kenzua Petroleum Company.

685.24   Bellows] Henry Bellows (1814–1882), a Unitarian pastor from New York City, helped found the U.S. Sanitary Commission in 1861 and served as its president throughout the war.

685.27   his Fred] Frederick W. Seward (1830–1915), assistant secretary of state, 1861–69, recovered from his wounds.

686.19–20   Professor Henry James Anderson . . . Moses H. Grinnell] Anderson (1799–1875) was professor of mathematics and astronomy at Columbia, 1825–43, and a trustee of the college, 1851–75; Grinnell (1803–1877), a merchant and banker, had served in Congress as a Whig, 1839–41.

686.26   Verplanck and Tillou] Gulian Verplanck (1786–1870), a lawyer who had served in Congress, 1825–33, and in the state senate, 1838–41; Francis R. Tillou (c. 1795–1865), an attorney who served as recorder of New York City, 1852–54.

686.31   Gouverneur Ogden] Ogden (1809–1884) was an attorney and trustee of Columbia College.

686.40   823 . . . Gibbs] 823 Broadway, the headquarters of the U.S. Sanitary Commission; Oliver Wolcott Gibbs (1822–1908), professor of chemistry at the Free Academy (later City College of New York), 1849–63, and at Harvard, 1863–87, and a member of the executive committee of the Sanitary Commission.

687.2–3   George Bancroft . . . Rev. (Presbyterian) Thompson] Bancroft

(1800–1891), author of *History of the United States* (1854–78); Joseph Parrish Thompson (1819–1879), pastor of the Broadway Tabernacle, 1845–71.

687.10   Let the dead bury their dead.]   Cf. Matthew 8:22.

687.11   Burnside]   Ambrose Burnside, who had been sent on indefinite leave in August 1864 following the Union defeat in the battle of the Crater.

687.13   Jeff Davis . . . Danville]   See headnote, page 705 in this volume.

688.24   John, my son]   John Arthur Welles (1849–1883).

689.26   elder Mrs. Seward or her sister]   Frances Miller Seward (1805–1865), who died on June 21, 1865, after years of poor health; Lazette Miller Worden (1803–1875).

689.28   Mrs. Frederick Seward]   Anna Wharton Seward (1836–1919).

689.31–32   Miss Fanny Seward]   Frances Adeline Seward (1844–1866), the daughter of William H. Seward and Frances Miller Seward.

689.33   Dr. Verdi]   Tullio Verdi (1829–1902).

690.14   General Meigs]   Brigadier General Montgomery C. Meigs (1816–1892), quartermaster general of the U.S. Army, 1861–82.

690.26   Judge Cartter]   David Cartter (1812–1887), chief justice of the Supreme Court of the District of Columbia, 1863–87.

690.27   Major Eckert]   See note 572.33.

691.1   Mr. Peterson]   William Petersen (1816–1871), a tailor, lived in the house with his family and several boarders.

691.5–6   Dr. Hall]   James Crowdhill Hall (1805–1880).

691.19   Senator Sumner]   See Biographical Notes.

691.20–21   Speaker Colfax, Mr. Secretary McCulloch]   Schuyler Colfax (1823–1885), Republican congressman from Indiana, 1855–69, Speaker of the House, 1863–69, and vice president of the United States, 1869–73; Hugh McCulloch (1808–1895), secretary of the treasury, 1865–69 and 1884–85.

691.29–30   Mrs. Dixon . . . Mrs. Kinney]   Elizabeth Cogswell Dixon (1819–1871) and her sister Mary Cogswell Kinney (1814–1877). Elizabeth Dixon was a friend of Mary Lincoln and the wife of James Dixon, a Republican senator from Connecticut.

692.13   the Attorney General]   James Speed (1812–1887) served as attorney general, 1864–66.

692.15   Usher]   John Palmer Usher (1816–1889), secretary of the interior, 1863–65.

692.29 Dr. Gurley] Phineas Gurley (1816–1868), pastor of the New York Avenue Presbyterian Church in Washington, D.C.

692.38 Mr. Dennison] William Dennison Jr. (1815–1882), postmaster general, 1864–66.

693.22 Mr. Hunter] William Hunter (1805–1886), chief clerk of the Department of State, 1852–66, and second assistant secretary of state, 1866–86.

694.12 Virginia which has a loyal government] The unionist "Restored Government" of Virginia was established in Wheeling in June 1861. When West Virginia was admitted as a state on June 20, 1863, Governor Francis H. Pierpont (1814–1899) had relocated his government to Alexandria, where it exercised authority over areas occupied by Union forces.

694.17 Gooch and Dawes] Daniel Wheelwright Gooch (1820–1891), Republican congressman from Massachusetts, 1858–65 and 1873–75; Henry L. Dawes (1816–1903), Republican congressman from Massachusetts, 1857–75, and U.S. senator, 1875–93.

694.30 his son] Major Augustus Seward (1826–1876) had been wounded during the assassination attempt.

697.1–2 Mr. Breckinridge] Major General John C. Breckinridge (1821–1875) served as Confederate secretary of war, February 6–May 10, 1865. Sherman would only meet with him in his capacity as a Confederate officer because of the Union policy prohibiting any recognition of the Confederate government.

697.25 Gen. Schofield] Brigadier General John M. Schofield (1831–1906), commanding general, Army of the Ohio, 1864–65, and of the Department of North Carolina, 1865.

700.23–24 "All things . . . the dreadful past."] See Alfred Tennyson, "Choric Song of the Lotos-Eaters" (1832), lines 46–47.

700.26–27 Sister . . . Lavinia] Morgan's sister-in-law, Beatrice Ford Morgan (1826–1905), and her three oldest children, Charlotte (1853–1884), Nellie (1855–?), and Lavinia (1857–?).

700.28–29 five remaining children] The five youngest children of Beatrice Ford Morgan and Philip Hickey Morgan (1825–1900), Morgan's half brother.

701.31–32 "God is our refuge . . . trouble,"] See Psalm 46:1.

701.36–37 "Vengence . . . the Lord."] Cf. Romans 12:19.

702.26 Spare Jimmy] Morgan's brother, James Morris Morgan (1845–1928), served as midshipman in the Confederate navy, 1861–65, and later published a memoir, *Recollections of a Rebel Reefer* (1917).

702.27–28 Deborah . . . Sisera] See Judges 4:2–3.

702.29–30 Miriam . . . fallen, fallen!"] See Exodus 15:20–21.

702.31   Judith]   See the Book of Judith.

702.32   "Pour le salut de ma patree—!"]   French: To save my country.

705.27   Gov. Vance]   Zebulon B. Vance (1830–1894), governor of North Carolina, 1862–65 and 1877–79, and a Democratic U.S. senator, 1879–94.

705.31   Mr. Harrison]   Burton Harrison (1838–1904), private secretary of Jefferson Davis, 1862–65.

705.35   Mr. Burt]   Armistead Burt (1802–1883), Democratic congressman from South Carolina, 1843–53.

706.6   executed the plan]   For Lee's army to join Johnston's forces in North Carolina and defeat Sherman.

706.15   Beauregard]   General Pierre G. T. Beauregard (1818–1893) was serving as Johnston's second in command.

706.33   Judge Reagan]   John H. Reagan (1818–1905), a former Texas district court judge, served as Confederate postmaster general, 1861–65.

706.35   member of the Cabinet . . . opinion]   The Confederate cabinet unanimously recommended that Davis accept the terms negotiated by Johnston and Sherman. Davis agreed to do so, although he correctly anticipated that President Johnson would reject the agreement.

707.33   Mrs Omelia]   Mary O'Melia (c. 1822–1907) was the Davises' housekeeper in Richmond.

707.36   Little Maggie's]   Davis's daughter, Margaret Howell Davis (1855–1909).

708.12   Mrs. Grant]   Ann Elizabeth Crenshaw Grant (1826–1901), a close friend and neighbor of Varina Howell Davis in Richmond.

708.15   Maggie]   Margaret Howell (1842–1930), younger sister of Varina Howell Davis.

709.32   General Miles]   Brigadier General Nelson Miles (1839–1925) commanded the First Division, Second Corps.

709.34   Charlie Whittier]   Lieutenant Colonel Charles A. Whittier (1840–1908), a Harvard classmate of Weld's, served on the staff of the Sixth Corps, 1863–64, and the Second Corps, 1865.

710.5   Barlow's]   Brigadier General Francis C. Barlow (1834–1896) had commanded the First Division, Second Corps, until August 17, 1864, when he went on sick leave. Barlow rejoined the Army of the Potomac on April 6, 1865, and was assigned command of the Second Division, Second Corps.

710.9   Theodore Lyman]   See Biographical Notes.

713.30–31   Genl Cheatham]   Major General Benjamin F. Cheatham commanded a division in the Army of Tennessee at the time of its surrender.

715.32 Atlanta Aug 22/64] The battle east of Atlanta was fought on July 22, 1864.

717.10 Rev. J B McFerrin] John B. McFerrin (1807–1887), a Methodist minister from Nashville, served as a chaplain with the Army of Tennessee, 1863–65.

717.18–19 Revelations IIth . . . 10th verse] Revelation 2:10.

718.25 N. O.] New Orleans.

720.37 Kirby Smith] See note 334.30.

723.3 fort Fisher, Virginia] A large Union earthwork south of Petersburg built after the battle of Peebles Farm, September 30–October 2, 1864.

723.8 Dr. Bliss] D. Willard Bliss (1825–1889), chief surgeon of Armory Square Hospital, 1862–65.

729.38 our own brave Custer] Brigadier General George Armstrong Custer had spent part of his youth in Michigan, and had led a brigade composed of the 1st, 5th, 6th, and 7th Michigan cavalry regiments, June 1863–September 1864.

733.3 The Irish Brigade] The Second Brigade, First Division, Second Corps, commanded by Colonel Robert Nugent (1824–1901).

733.16–17 Gov. Crapo . . . Senator Chandler] Henry H. Crapo (1804–1869), Republican governor of Michigan, 1865–69; Zachariah Chandler (1813–1879), Republican senator from Michigan, 1857–75.

733.23 Col. Peter Stagg] Stagg (1836–1884) commanded the Michigan cavalry brigade in the Shenandoah Valley and the Appomattox campaign, October 1864–May 1865.

733.29–30 Jeff. Davis . . . wife's clothes."] Jefferson Davis was wearing his wife's cloak and shawl when he was captured by Union cavalry near Irwinville, Georgia, on May 10, 1865.

733.32–33 "step from . . . ridiculous"] In *Histoire de l'Ambassade dans le Grand-Duché de Varsovie en 1812* (1815), Dominique de Pradt (1759–1837) quotes Napoleon as saying after his retreat from Moscow: "Du sublime au ridicule, il n'y a qu'un pas" (There is only one step from the sublime to the ridiculous).

Index

Abbeville, S.C., 705
Abbott, Henry Livermore, 76–77, 79–80
Abolition of slavery, 34–41, 236, 241–43, 299, 313–15, 317, 324, 339, 420–23, 465, 481, 493, 505, 539, 541, 546–47, 569–71, 578
Abolitionism, 14, 36, 196, 278, 294, 298, 301, 403, 428, 454, 481, 531, 570–71, 575–76, 583, 615, 728
Acheson, John W., 468–69
Ackerson (Union prisoner), 229
Acworth, Ga., 191, 232
Adams, Charles Francis, 163, 202–4, 483–84
Adams, Charles Francis, Jr., 163–68, 202, 483
Adams, Henry, 483–85
Adams, John, 202, 590
Adams, John Quincy, 202
Adams, Lois Bryan, 34–41, 250–55, 728–34
Address of the Colored National Convention, 414–31
Africa, 31, 132, 197, 330, 429, 480, 494–95, 587
African Methodist Episcopal Church, 54, 559–66
Agnew, Cornelius R., 373, 686
Agriculture Department, U.S., 504
Aiken, John, 173, 176
Akerstrom, John C., 48
Alabama, 22, 46, 339, 468, 718, 725; battle of Mobile Bay, 319, 389–95; impressment of slaves in, 60–62
Alabama, C.S.S., 205–10, 445
Alabama 38th Regiment, 138–39
Albany, N.Y., 184, 187
Alexander, Edward Porter, 703
Alexandria, La., 24, 147, 334
Alexandria, Va., 11–15, 45, 195
Alford, Smith, 635–36
Algiers, 330, 444, 452, 495
Allatoona, Ga., 140, 191, 193, 432, 438, 449

Amelia, Va., 668
American Anti-Slavery Society, 417
Amnesty, 354–55, 508, 685, 699, 701
Amory, Charles B., 288
Anderson, Charles D., 394
Anderson, Henry James, 686
Anderson, Richard H., 91, 110, 125
Andersonville Prison, 160–62, 222–31, 244–45
Andrew, John A., 387
Angel, Ashbel W., 77
Annapolis, Md., 45, 465
Anthon, George C., 459, 686–87
Antietam, battle of, 63, 137, 258, 292, 727
Appomattox, Va., 671–75, 679, 696, 701, 703–4, 706, 709, 711–12, 720
Appomattox River, 218
Argentina, 494
Arkansas, 24, 141, 233, 242, 310–12, 316, 504, 717–18
Arkansas Post, 715
Army, C.S., 19–20, 319, 394, 401, 450, 468, 725, 735; Atlanta campaign, 232–34, 238–40, 271–77, 333–35, 380–85, 432, 449; attack on Washington, 246–55; battle of Cold Harbor, 178–88; battle of Franklin, 489–92, 546; battle of Petersburg, 211–21, 286–93; battle of Pickett's Mill, 140–46; battle of Resaca, 133–39; battle of Sabine Crossroads, 24; battle of Spotsylvania, 110–29; battle of the Wilderness, 68–109; battle of Winchester, 396–98; conscription, 359–60, 399, 541, 552, 624, 649; defense of Savannah, 514–17, 519; deserters, 437–39, 510–11, 609–11, 623–25, 627, 668, 704; exchange of prisoners, 325–32; fall of Richmond, 637–39, 650, 653–55, 668, 705; fighting in Shenandoah Valley, 267–70, 320, 322, 434–36, 448, 463–64; Fort Pillow massacre, 42–44, 47–50, 52–59; General Orders No. 9, 673–

74, 703; General Orders No. 14, 576; in Georgia, 191–94, 303–6; impressment of slaves, 60–62, 359, 542; Lee's assessment of Union plans, 45–46; in Louisiana, 24, 147–49, 371–72; in North Carolina, 626–28, 696, 703, 711–19; raid on St. Albans, Vermont, 497; siege of Knoxville, 4, 7; slave enlistment in, 538–42, 554–57, 563, 576–82, 623, 627; surrender at Appomattox, 671–75, 703–4, 706; surrender at Durham Station, 696–99; in Texas, 280–82, 735; and Union raid on Richmond, 1–3; in Virginia, 22–23, 45–46, 150–59, 163–67, 197–98, 246, 248, 256–58, 298, 306, 358–61, 437–41

Army, U.S., 237, 301–2, 337, 377–78, 445–46, 500, 506, 688; in Andersonville Prison, 160–62, 222–31, 244–45; Atlanta campaign, 232–34, 238–40, 271–77, 333–34, 373, 380–86, 432, 449; battle of Cold Harbor, 178–88; battle of Franklin, 489–92, 546; battle of Mobile Bay, 394–95; battle of Petersburg, 211–21, 286–93, 319–20; battle of Pickett's Mill, 140–46; battle of Resaca, 133–39; battle of Sabine Crossroads, 24; battle of Spotsylvania, 110–29; battle of the Wilderness, 68–109; battle of Winchester, 396–98; in Belle Isle Prison Camp, 536–37; black soldiers in, 1, 15, 42–44, 47–50, 52–59, 81, 131–32, 155, 169–70, 197, 201, 213–15, 278–79, 286–87, 290–92, 305, 325–32, 343, 362–65, 372, 387–88, 417–18, 426–28, 438, 444, 483, 486–88, 518, 536, 548, 550–52, 563–64, 568, 577, 583, 615, 618, 632, 635, 646, 656–59, 661, 675, 728, 732–33; burning of Columbia, 598–608; conscription, 236, 259, 321; defense of Washington, 246–55; exchange of prisoners, 325–32; fall of Richmond, 637–39, 645–47, 649, 652–68; fighting in Shenandoah Valley, 267–70, 320, 322–23, 434–36, 448, 463–64; Fort Pillow massacre, 42–44, 47–50, 52–59; and fugitive slaves, 16–18; General Orders No. 3, 735; General Orders No. 100, 450; in Georgia, 191, 193, 303–6; Grand Review of, 725–34; hospitals, 171–76, 722–24; in Kentucky, 486–88; Lee's assessment of plans by, 45–46; in Libby Prison, 160, 198, 223, 356, 666–67; looting by, 522–35, 626–27; in Louisiana, 21, 24–26, 46, 147, 371–72; march across Carolinas, 626–28, 696; march across Georgia, 432–33, 468–78, 504, 510, 514–20, 522–35, 558, 563, 626; occupation of Knoxville, 4–8, 16–18, 32–33, 46; pensions, 503; raid on Richmond, 1–3; rations for, 65–66; siege of Savannah, 514–20; Special Field Orders No. 15, 566–68; spring 1864 initiatives, 21–23; and surrender at Appomattox, 671–75, 704; and surrender at Durham Station, 696–99; in Texas, 280–82, 735; treatment of civilians, 130–32; in Virginia, 21–23, 27–31, 45–46, 63–67, 130–32, 150–59, 163–67, 171–77, 189, 195–97, 199–201, 246, 256–58, 294–95, 298, 358–61, 437–41, 609, 709–10

Army and Navy Journal, 390
Ashley, James M., 34, 352
Ashley, William A., 112
Aspinwall, William H., 377
Associated Press, 83, 260
Astor, John, 459
Athens, Ga., 305
Atlanta, Ga., 133–35, 191, 194, 228, 233, 238, 240, 244, 271–77, 293, 319, 333–35, 350–51, 368, 373–74, 380–86, 399–400, 409, 432, 438, 449, 458, 468, 489, 492, 514, 517, 715, 727
Atlantic Monthly, 264, 266, 338, 346, 596
Atwood (Union prisoner), 224–25, 227
Atzerodt, George, 684, 688
Auburn, N.Y., 421
Augur, Christopher C., 115
Augusta, Ga., 304, 406, 598, 627
Augusta, U.S.S., 389–90
Augusta Railroad, 273
Austria, 296
Averell, William W., 22, 68

Badeau, Adam, 189
Bahamas, 446, 496
Bainbridge, William, 330
Baird, Absalom, 133, 135, 380, 470, 475
Baltimore, Md., 51, 236, 248, 267, 343, 465
Baltimore and Ohio Railroad, 45, 396
Baltimore Sanitary Fair, 51
Bancroft, George, 687
Banks, Nathaniel P., 21–22, 24, 147, 309–11, 334, 459
Banksville, N.C., 697
Baptists, 558–60
Barbary powers, 330, 452, 495
Barksdale, Ethelbert, 554
Barlow, Francis C., 76–77, 182, 189, 216, 710
Barlow, Samuel L. M., 370, 377, 458
Barnard, George M., 73
Barr, John C., 48
Bartlett, Edwin B., 150
Bartlett, Joseph J., 73
Bartlett, William F., 286, 288–89
Barton, Seth M., 438
Basye, Lieutenant, 268
Bates, Edward, 58, 461
Beard, John, 44
Beaufort, S.C., 567
Beaufort (C.S. ram ship), 644
Beaumont, Eugene B., 80
Beauregard, Pierre G. T., 46, 211, 229, 293, 410, 437–38, 540, 543, 598, 706
Beecher, Henry Ward, 466–67, 701
Bell, John, 548
Bell, Tyree H., 42
Belle Isle Prison Camp, 222, 536–37
Bellows, Henry W., 685–86
Belmont, Augustus, 370, 374, 458
Benjamin, Judah P., 345–48, 350, 352–53, 355–56, 554
Bennett, James Gordon, 725
Benning (Confederate officer), 303
Bentley, William, 559
Benton, Reuben C., 219
Bentonville, N.C., 696
Berkeley, Henry Robinson, 246–49, 267–70, 396–98
Berkeley, J. H., 248
Bermuda, 446
Berryville, Va., 267–68, 396

Bible, 467, 520, 549–50, 583–84, 588, 591, 612–13, 717
Bicknell, Francis A., 657
Big Black River, 170
Bigelow, George, 117, 158
Bill of Rights (English), 453
Bird, Edgeworth, 303–6
Bird, Sallie, 303
Birney, David B., 76, 78–80
Birney, James G., 278
Birney, William, 278
Bishop, Willard I., 158
Black, Jeremiah S., 455
Blair, Francis Preston, 249, 403, 405, 572–73
Blair, Frank, 403
Blair, Montgomery, 58, 249, 252, 403–5, 461
Blake, Mr., 375
Bliss, Willard, 723
Blockade, 205, 284, 389–90, 403, 424, 442, 446, 496, 543
Bloody Angle, battle of, 112, 122–29
Blount, Frederick S., 60–61
Blue Ridge Mountains, 718
Boerner, Lieutenant, 274
Boker, George H., 592
Bolivia, 494
Bolling (Confederate soldier), 268
Booth, Edwin, 479, 685
Booth, John Wilkes, 479–82, 675, 684–85, 688, 702
Booth, Junius, 479
Booth, Lionel F., 43, 47–48
Boston, Mass., 12, 15, 68, 266, 278–79
Boston Evening Transcript, 264
Bowling Green, Va., 151–52
Boyle, Richard, 618
Bracey, Theophilus, 633–34
Bradford, Theodorick F., 48
Bradford, William F., 43, 48
Bradwell, Charles, 559
Brady, James T., 374
Bragg, Braxton, 194, 319, 334, 400, 439, 636
Bramlette, Thomas, 365–67
Branchville, Va., 543
Brandy Station, Va., 27, 69, 112, 158, 171
Brazil, 496
Brazos Island, 280, 282

Breckinridge, John C., 246, 638, 666, 697, 706
Brewster, Charles Harvey, 112–21, 150–59, 199–201
Brewster, Martha, 112, 118, 153
Brewster, Mary, 112, 117, 150
Brewster, Mattie, 156, 199
Bridgeport, Ga., 432
Bridgman, Joseph C., 159
Bridgman, Sidney E., 159
Bright, John, 623, 629
Bristoe Station, battle of, 63
Bristol, Tenn., 46
Britain, 35–36, 163, 202–4, 295–96, 375, 443, 446, 452–53, 483–84, 629, 631, 731; *Georgia* affair, 373; relations with, 495–97; ships for Confederate navy, 205; support for Confederacy, 444–45, 539, 541, 545
Brock, Sallie, 641–49
Brockenbrough, William S. R., 195
Brockman, Benjamin T., 125
Bromwell, Henry P. H., 460
Brooke, James V., 320
Brooke, Samuel Selden, 709
Brooklyn, N.Y., 54
Brooklyn, U.S.S., 391, 395
Brooks, James, 459
Brooks, John, 521
Brooks, Noah, 307
Brougham, Henry Peter, 444
Brown, Aaron V., 549
Brown, John, 480–81
Brown, Joseph E., 399, 437
Brown, Joseph N., 125–26
Brown, William Wells, 414
Brown (Union prisoner), 226–27
Brownlow, William G., 32
Brownsville, Tenn., 42–43, 50
Brownsville, Texas, 280–82
Bruce, John, 282
Bryant, William Cullen, 592
Buchanan, Franklin, 393–94, 445
Buchanan, James, 455
Buckley (Union prisoner), 224, 245
Buckner, Simon B., 46
Bull Run, battle of (First Bull Run), 480
Bull Run, battle of (Second Bull Run), 137, 303
Burbridge, Stephen G., 486

Burdett, Clarissa, 635–36
Burdett, Elijah, 635
Burke, Abraham, 560
Burke, Edmund, 592
Burmeister, Dr., 176
Burnside, Ambrose, 22, 45–46, 68, 72–73, 75–76, 78–80, 100, 115, 155, 195, 200–1, 213, 286, 291, 295
Burr, Charles Chauncey, 294–302
Burt, Armistead, 705
Butler, Benjamin F., 22, 68, 83, 119, 130, 180, 265, 325–32, 341–42, 356, 401, 449, 459, 466–67, 469, 620
Butterfield, Daniel, 138
Buttrick, Edward K., 475–76

Cabinet (Davis administration), 1–2, 705–6
Cabinet (Johnson administration), 720
Cabinet (Lincoln administration), 57–59, 262, 294, 324, 403–4, 421, 460–61, 619, 679–80, 682, 688, 691–94
Cadwalader, Charles E., 81
Cain, Richard Harvey, 54
Cairo, Ill., 47, 49
Caldwell, James F. J., 90–99, 122–29
Calhoun, James M., 384
Calhoun, John C., 411, 455
California, 40, 503
Cameron, Simon, 446
Camp Nelson, 486–88, 632–33, 635–36
Camp Springfield, 715
Camp Sumter. *See* Andersonville Prison
Campbell, John A., 439, 441, 572–75, 639
Campbell, Stuart, 154
Campbell, William J., 558–59
Canada, 235, 259–60, 336, 497, 630–31, 688, 727
Canby, Edward R. S., 267, 395, 726
Cannady, Isaac G., 610
Cannady, John P., 610
Cantey, James, 191, 193–94
Cape Fear River, 627
Carlisle, John W., 127
Caroline County, Va., 150–51
Carpenter, John C., 249
Carr, Joseph B., 74
Carroll, Samuel S., 74–75
Carroll, William, 549

Carter, Samuel P., 5–7, 16, 32
Cartter, David K., 690
Cassville, Ga., 137
Castle Thunder (Richmond prison), 356, 666–67
Catholics, 429
Cato (slave), 531, 534–35
Catron, John, 571
Cedar Creek, battle of, 434
Cedar Mountain, battle of, 137, 238
Census of 1860, 236
Chalmers, James R., 43, 50, 59
Chamberlain, Ephraim, 218
Chamberlain, George E., 218–21
Chambersburg, Pa., 304, 320, 322–23
Chancellorsville, Va., 27, 63, 68, 83–84, 100, 112–13, 116, 137, 238
Chandler, Zachariah, 733
Channing, William Ellery, 590–91
Channing, William Henry, 583
Charles (slave), 527
Charleston, S.C., 3, 45, 390, 442–43, 537, 566, 598, 627
Charleston and Savannah Railroad, 628
Charlotte, N.C., 703, 705
Charlottesville, Va., 256
Chase, Salmon P., 58–59, 446, 570, 612, 630, 693
Chattahoochee River, 233, 238, 271, 333, 400, 432
Chattanooga, Tenn., 133–35, 137, 140, 238, 401, 517, 718
Chattanooga and Atlanta Railroad, 191, 432, 468
Cheatham, Benjamin F., 273
Chelsea, Mass., 12
Cherbourg, France, 205, 208–9
Chesapeake Bay, 46, 197
Chesnut, James, 406
Chesnut, Mary, 406
Chester, Thomas Morris, 656–67
Chicago, Ill., 260, 336, 339, 368, 373–75, 377, 418, 450–51, 454–55, 458, 461
Chicago Tribune, 47
Chickahominy River, 131, 164–65, 180, 212, 219
Chickamauga, battle of, 140, 265, 271, 715
Chickasaw, U.S.S., 394
Child, Lydia Maria, 11
Chile, 494
China, 495
Choate, Francis C., 131
Choctaws, 334
Christian Recorder, 54
Christianity, 2, 262–64, 347, 349, 352, 362–63, 444, 449, 554, 584, 586–88, 590–91, 593–94, 597
Cincinnati, Ohio, 21
Cincinnati Gazette, 47
City Point, Va., 83, 213, 256, 432, 572–73, 650, 656, 671, 675, 709
Clark, Achilles V., 42–44
Clark, Daniel, 37, 39
Clarke, Asia Booth, 479
Clarke, John Sleeper, 479
Clarkson, Thomas, 592
Clay, Clement C., 260–63, 339
Cleburne, Patrick R., 140, 145, 271, 491, 538
Cleveland, Ohio, 403
Cleveland, Tenn., 33
Clopton, William H., 130–32
Cobb, Howell, 437, 446, 474, 476, 538–40
Cobden, Richard, 631
Cold Harbor, battle of, 178–88, 199, 211–12, 218–20, 246
Colfax, Schuyler, 691
Colombia, 493–94
Colonization, 562, 615
Columbia, S.C., 406, 413, 598–608, 626, 647, 700, 709
Columbia, Tenn., 489–90
Columbia College, 450
Columbus, Ga., 406
Columbus, Ky., 170
Comstock, Cyrus B., 78, 256
Confiscation Acts (1861, 1862), 34, 570
Confiscation of property, 354–55, 422
Congregationalists, 618
Congress, C.S., 57, 60, 261, 439, 538, 572, 576, 581, 624
Congress, U.S., 16, 169, 215, 251, 253, 294–95, 321, 348, 417, 422, 424, 426, 447, 455, 561, 567–68, 570, 574, 582, 631–32, 652, 698; equal pay for black soldiers, 387; Garnet's sermon before, 583–97; Lincoln's message to, 493–509, 514, 569; and reconstruction, 241–42, 307–18,

352, 629–30, 675; and Thirteenth Amendment, 34–41, 241–42, 569–71, 573–74
Connecticut, 126
Connecticut 14th Regiment, 63
Connolly, James A., 133–36, 380–83, 468–78
Connolly, Mary Dunn, 133, 380
Conscription, 236, 259, 321, 359–60, 399, 541, 552, 624, 649
Constitution, C.S., 542
Constitution, U.S., 88, 236, 295–96, 299, 424, 426, 452, 454–55, 480, 507, 531, 584, 594–95, 698, 706, 731; Democratic Party view of, 336–37, 377–79; and Wade-Davis bill, 308–9, 312–14. *See also* Thirteenth Amendment
Constitution (Arkansas), 311
Constitution (Indiana), 570
Constitution (Kentucky), 365
Constitution (Louisiana), 311, 675
Constitution (Maryland), 465
Constitution (Tennessee), 546–47
Contraband of war, 621
Conyers, Ga., 468–70
Conyngham, David P., 510
Cook, Burton C., 460
Cook, Frederick W. C., 305
Cook, John B., 131
Cooke, Charles M., 610
Cooke, John R., 610
Cooper, Samuel, 638
Cooper, Thomas, 223
Cope, Emmor B., 79
Copperheads, 253, 296, 307, 339, 363, 404, 458–60, 651, 686, 730
Corbin, Thomas G., 389–90
Corinth, Miss., 170
Costa Rica, 493–94
Cotrell, Mark H., 158
Cotton, 19–20, 351, 522, 543, 566, 578–79, 598, 641, 661
Covington, Ga., 470–71
Cowan (Confederate soldier), 275
Cox, John, 559
Crapo, Henry H., 733
Crater, battle of the, 286–93, 709
Crawford, Samuel W., 72
Cromwell, Oliver, 66
Crook, George R., 22, 68, 267

Cuba, 141, 400, 446, 561
Cullom, Shelby M., 460
Culpeper, Va., 14, 102, 107, 196
Cumberland, U.S.S., 394
Cunningham, Richard D., 366
Curran, John P., 592
Curtis, Samuel R., 726
Curtis (Union prisoner), 244
Cushman, William H., 207
Custer, George Armstrong, 323, 464, 729

Dahlgren, John A., 3
Dahlgren, Ulric, 1–3
Dainese, Francis, 495
Dallas, Ga., 140, 191
Dallas, George Mifflin, 444
Dalton, Edward, 73
Dalton, Ga., 133–34, 192–93, 400, 468, 489
Daly, Charles P., 189–90, 467
Daly, Maria Lydig, 189–90, 466–67
Dana, Charles A., 83, 256, 258, 467
Danville, Va., 229, 256, 643, 652, 687, 705, 709
Darbytown, Va., 437
Darley, Felix O. C., 467
Darley, Jenny Colburn, 467
Davis, Garrett, 37–38, 40, 169
Davis, Henry Winter, 241, 307–18
Davis, Jefferson, 1–2, 19, 57–58, 235, 243, 261–62, 271–72, 281, 297, 327, 334, 368, 377, 424, 432, 437–38, 444, 507, 543, 572, 623, 626, 663, 685, 687–88, 701–2, 733; capture of, 725; and enlistment of slaves in Confederate army, 538–40, 576; and fall of Richmond, 638–39, 641–42, 652, 661; Lee's explanation of surrender to, 703–4; Lee's memoranda on Union army to, 45–46, 358–61; letter to Varina Davis, 705–8; meeting with James Gilmore, 264–66, 338–41, 343, 345–57; and petition protesting impressment of slaves, 60–62; speech at Columbia, 406–13; speech at Macon, 399–402
Davis, Jefferson C., 477, 558, 602
Davis, Margaret Howell, 707
Davis, Robert S., 130

Davis, Varina Howell, 638, 705
Dawes, Henry L., 694
Day, Henry M., 280, 282
Dayton, Ohio, 370
Dean, Mr., 651
Debt: Confederate, 316; Union, 630
Decatur, Ga., 271, 399, 432
Decatur, Stephen, 330
Declaration of Independence, 418, 426, 481, 571, 584, 629–30, 716
Deep Bottom, battle of, 358
Delainy (Union prisoner), 244
Delaware, 40, 184, 328, 337, 458, 569, 635
Delmotte, Adolphus, 560
Democracy, 375, 549
Democratic Party, 189, 223, 253, 260, 294, 296, 300–1, 307, 319, 324, 336–37, 339, 365, 368–70, 373–79, 403, 419–20, 424, 451–52, 454–56, 458–60, 467, 505, 546, 569, 630
Dempsey, John W., 208
Denmark, 727
Dennis, John Q. A., 278–79
Dennison, William, 692
Dent, Frederick T., 71
Deserters, 437–39, 510–11, 609–11, 623–25, 627, 668, 704
Detroit Advertiser and Tribune, 34, 250, 728
Devens, Thomas C., 658–59, 663
Diggs, F. W., 362
Diggs, Kitty, 362–64
Dinwiddie, Va., 637, 704
Discrimination, 629
District of Columbia. *See* Washington, D.C.
Dixon, Elizabeth C., 691
Doby, Alfred E., 97
Dodge, William E., 459
Doolittle, James R., 309
Doran, T. L., 143
Dorr, Thomas W., 312
Dorsey, Louise T., 616
Dougherty (Union prisoner), 229
Douglas, Stephen A., 454
Douglass, Frederick, 14, 414, 615–17
Dowd (Union prisoner), 229–31, 245
Downing, George Thomas, 15
Draft riots, 55, 420, 583
Drake, Captain, 280

Draper, Alonzo, 657–59, 664
Draper, Simeon, 651
Drayton, Percival, 389, 395
Dred Scott decision, 571
Du Pont, Samuel Francis, 389, 442–47
Duane, James C., 75
Duck River, 489
Dudley, Frederick, 174, 176
Duff, William L., 71
Durham Station, N.C., 696–99, 705–6, 711, 713–14, 717, 720
Dye, William M., 282

Eagle, Clifford F., 131
Early, Jubal A., 246, 250, 256, 258, 267, 304, 320, 322, 396, 402, 434
Eastman, Jake, 276–77
Eaton, Oscar, 112
Eaton, Tom, 25
Eatonton, Ga., 473, 477, 720
Ebenezer Creek, 558
Eckert, Thomas T., 572, 690
Edge, Frederick M., 624
Edmondston, Catherine, 1–3, 448–49, 541–45
Education, 11–15, 675
Edwards, Jonathan, 590
Edwards, Oliver, 115
Egypt, 495
El Salvador, 494
Eldridge, Simeon N., 112
Election of 1864, 321, 324, 336–37, 339, 352, 366–70, 403–4, 412–13, 440, 448–60, 466, 483–85, 493, 505–7, 509, 519, 562, 725
Emancipation, 30–31, 313–14, 317, 354–55, 414, 465, 538–41, 554–56, 558, 572–74, 576–82, 596, 615, 625, 629, 632, 712, 716, 718, 735
Emancipation Proclamation, 16, 34, 420, 508, 546, 561–62, 566, 569, 615, 735
Emery, F. W., 735
Emmett (Union prisoner), 245
Emory, William H., 267
Equality, 418, 429, 570, 582, 629, 735
Etowah River, 135, 137, 140, 191, 193
Euripides, 300
Eustis, Henry L., 72, 74, 115
Eutaw (U.S. naval vessel), 389
Evarts, William M., 651

Ewell, Richard S., 73, 75, 90, 95, 98, 123, 125, 152, 154, 638, 641, 649, 666
Ewing, Charles, 229

Fair Oaks, battle of, 112
Fairfax County, Va., 463
Farnsworth, John F., 460
Farragut, David G., 283–85, 389–90, 394, 445–46
Faulkner, Hiram D., 685
Fauquier County, Va., 463
Fay, Theodore, 466–67
Fay, Wilson W., 287, 290
Fayetteville, N.C., 510, 626–27
Fee, John G., 486
Fernandina, Fla., 496, 567
Ferrero, Edward, 81, 197
Fessenden, William P., 460
Field, Charles W., 94, 303, 306, 440
Field, Henry M., 467
Fish, Hamilton, 652
Fisher, Charles B., 205–10
Fisher, Sam, 277
Fisher, Thomas, 274
Fisher's Hill, battle of, 434
Fisk, Wilbur, 27–31, 85–90, 211–15
Fiske, Samuel W., 63–67
Flag, American, 645, 649, 658, 667, 679, 729
Flannery, David, 162
Fleming, Charles K., 219
Flint, Edward A., 79
Florence, Ala., 489, 491
Florence, S.C., 244
Florida, 141, 161, 311, 320, 496, 566–67, 720
Floyd, John B., 446
Floyd, La., 371–72
Fly, Captain, 274
Food riots, 19–20, 61
Foote, Andrew H., 442
Forbes, Eugene, 160–62, 222–31, 244–45
Ford's Theatre, 684, 688, 690–91
Forney, John W., 461
Forrest, Nathan B., 42–44, 47, 49–50, 58–59, 170, 304, 432
Fort Burnham, 656–57
Fort Darling, 226
Fort Donelson, battle of, 264

Fort Fisher, 541–43, 723
Fort Gaines, 283, 391, 394–95
Fort Harrison, 437
Fort Jackson, 283
Fort Johnston, 244
Fort McAllister, 514–17
Fort (Fortress) Monroe, 22, 131, 228, 326
Fort Morgan, 283–85, 319, 391–93, 552
Fort Pillow massacre, 42–44, 47–50, 52–59, 155, 170, 214, 305, 418, 536, 552
Fort Powell, 394
Fort St. Philip, 283
Fort Stedman, 637
Fort Stevens, 250
Fort Sumter, 410, 445, 515, 544, 679, 685
Fort Wagner, 55
Foster, Ephraim H., 548–49
Foster, John G., 244, 514–15, 726
Foster, Robert S., 342
Foster, Samuel T., 140–46, 244, 271–77, 489–92, 711–19
Fox, Gustavus V., 389
France, 204, 399, 443–44, 446, 452, 539, 541, 720–21, 731; involvement in Mexico, 24, 572; *Kearsarge-Alabama* battle off coast of, 205–10
Frankfort, Ky., 365
Franklin, Benjamin, 590
Franklin, Tenn., 489–92, 546, 711, 715–16
Franklin, William A., 491
Frazier, Garrison, 559–62, 564–66
Frederick, Md., 247–48, 250, 267, 405, 697
Fredericksburg, Va., 63, 83, 111, 115–16, 118, 120–21, 154, 159, 171, 173–74, 223, 246, 722
Free persons of color, 548–49
Freedmen: education of, 11–15, 675; land for, 566–68, 629, 719; on Roanoke Island, 618–22
Freedmen's Bureau, 618
Frémont, John C., 403–4
French, Benjamin Brown, 725
Front Royal, Va., 322, 463
Fry, Speed S., 486
Fugitive Slave Law, 417, 549

Fugitive slaves, 16, 196–97, 362, 444, 510, 661
Fuller, Thomas, 375–76

Gaillard, Franklin, 97
Gaines, C.S.S., 319, 391–92
Gaines, William, 559
Gaines's Mill, battle of, 224
Galveston, Texas, 735
Gansevoort, Henry, 102
Gardner, William M., 437–38
Gardner (Confederate soldier), 247–48
Garnet, Henry Highland, 414, 583–97
Garton Branch and Petersburg Railroad, 219
Gary, Martin W., 659
Gaul, Captain, 229
Gay, Henry M., 60
Gay, Sidney Howard, 265
Gaylesville, Ala., 468
Geary, John White, 238–40, 519–21
Geary, Mary, 238, 519
Geary, William, 521
Georgia, 340, 345, 399–402, 415, 435, 437–40, 449–50, 484, 538, 540, 718, 720; Andersonville Prison, 160–62, 222–31, 244–45; Atlanta campaign, 232–34, 238–40, 271–77, 333–35, 350–51, 368, 373–74, 380–86, 409, 432, 458; battle of Pickett's Mill, 140–46; battle of Resaca, 133–39; Confederate army in, 191–94, 303–6; Savannah campaign, 514–20, 522, 531, 542–43, 558, 564–65; Sherman's march across, 432–33, 468–78, 504, 514–20, 522–35, 543, 558, 563, 626, 679; Union army in, 191, 193, 303–6
Georgia (Confederate raider), 373
Georgia 15th Regiment, 303
German immigrants, 403, 450–53, 456
Germany, 452–53, 466
Gerolt, Friedrich von, 467
Getty, George W., 72–74, 76, 79, 85, 115, 152, 157–58
Gettysburg, Pa., 3, 27, 63, 67, 137, 171, 238, 246, 258, 271
Gibbon, John, 74, 76–78, 80, 84
Gibbs, Oliver Wolcott, 686
Giddings, Joshua R., 590
Gilmer, Thomas W., 248
Gilmore, Homer G., 117

Gilmore, James R., 264–66, 338–57
Gilmore, Quincy A., 22, 45
Glendale, Va., 246
Globe Tavern, battle of, 358
Godfrey, Jacob, 560
Goldsboro, N.C., 626, 628, 696
Gooch, Daniel W., 694
Good, William, 268–69
Goodenough, James G., 442
Goodwyn, Thomas Jefferson, 600
Gordon, George H., 514
Gordon, John B., 247
Gordonsville, Va., 90, 95, 256, 543, 697
Gould, Jacob P., 286
Govan, Daniel C., 380
Gowan, William, 208
Grahamville, Ga., 515
Granbury, Hiram B., 140, 142–45, 491, 717
Grand Review of the Armies, 725–34
Granger, Gordon, 394, 735
Grant, Ann Elizabeth Crenshaw, 708
Grant, Ulysses S., 24, 28, 124, 129, 134, 150, 161, 163–67, 171–73, 175, 178–80, 184, 189, 195, 232–33, 245–46, 250–51, 258, 265, 286, 294–95, 298–99, 304, 322, 325, 342, 350, 354, 358, 402, 430, 432, 434, 437, 440, 448–49, 468, 504, 517, 536, 572–73, 598, 609, 624, 630, 696, 720, 725–27, 729, 733; at battle of Petersburg, 211, 213, 216–18, 223, 226–27, 319; at battle of the Wilderness, 68–69, 71, 73, 75–76, 78, 81–84, 90, 94–95, 97–98, 100–2, 106, 110; fall of Richmond, 637, 656, 667–68; letter to Edwin Stanton, 110–11; letter to Henry Halleck, 256–57; spring 1864 campaign plans, 21–23; and surrender at Appomattox, 671–75, 679, 686, 712
Gratz, Major, 7, 32
Graves, Edward H., 112, 154
Graves, Emmons E., 645
Graves, John, 398
Gray, John Chipman, 514–18
Greece, ancient, 400, 411
Greeley, Horace, 235–37, 259–60, 265–66, 368; *The American Conflict*, 346
Green Mountain Freeman, 27, 85, 211
Greensboro, N.C., 696, 705, 711, 714

Gregg, David M., 69, 71, 73, 84
Grier, Robert C., 571
Griffin, Charles, 69, 72–73, 79, 81–82, 157
Grinnell, Moses H., 686
Griswold, Charles E., 78
Grundy, Felix, 548
Gunboats, 147–48, 285, 389, 494
Gurley, Phineas, 692

Habeas corpus, writ of, 317, 365, 399, 408, 542
Hagerstown, Md., 697
Hahn, Michael, 315
Haiti, 15, 417, 494
Hale, John P., 37, 39
Halifax County, N.C., 1, 541
Hall, James C., 691
Hall, Theron E., 486
Hall, William King, 442
Halleck, Henry W., 66, 111, 256, 696
Halpine, Charles G., 374
Hamilton, James, 669
Hamilton, Mary, 190
Hamlin, Hannibal, 36
Hampton, Wade, 705
Hampton Roads, Va., 572–73
Hancock, Cornelia, 171–77
Hancock, John, 80
Hancock, Winfield S., 68–69, 73–80, 82, 84, 89, 100, 152, 154, 178–79
Hancock County, Va., 303–4
Hannibal, 66
Hanover, Va., 163, 175
Hanovertown, Va., 195
Hardee, William J., 145, 271, 274–75, 373, 517, 519, 638–39
Harding, Abner C., 460
Harding, Ephraim H., 436
Harpers Ferry, W.Va., 246, 322
Harper's Weekly, 536–37
Harpeth River, 489
Harris, Alexander, 560
Harris, Bill, 397
Harris, Henry, 131
Harris, Isaac, 172
Harris, Nathaniel H., 125, 128
Harrison, Burton, 705
Harrison, Joe, 142, 274, 277
Harrison, Mathella Page, 322–23
Hartford, U.S.S., 283–85, 389, 391, 394

Hartwell, Alfred S., 515
Haskell, Alexander C., 93
Hatch, Captain, 342–45
Hatch, John P., 515
Havana, Cuba, 446
Hawkins, John, 268
Haw's Shop, battle of, 195
Hay, John, 259–60, 460–62
Hayden, Joel, 159
Hayden, Joseph, 159
Hayes, Joseph, 73, 115
Hays, Alexander, 74–75
Hazen, William B., 515
Headley, J. T.: *The Great Rebellion*, 346
Heiskell, Bob, 16–18
Heiskell, Jim, 16–18
Heiskell, William, 16–17
Henderson, John B., 34
Henniken, Major, 343
Henry, Patrick, 590
Herold, David, 688
Herron, Francis J., 282
Heston, Joseph S., 162
Heth, Henry, 91, 95–96
Hewitt (Confederate soldier), 268
Heywood, Charles, 394
Hickox, Alfred, 491
High Point, N.C., 19
Hill, Ambrose P., 72, 75–76, 90, 96, 639, 653
Hill, Daniel H., 543
Hill, James, 559
Hill, Matthew, 224
Hillsdale, N.C., 19
Hilton Head Island, 567
Hindus, 587
Hinks, Edward W., 130–32
Hobson, George, 247–48
Hoffman (Union prisoner), 227
Hoge, Moses D., 638, 642
Holcombe, James P., 260–63, 266, 339
Holloway, Tom, 209
Holt, Joseph, 450
Hood, John B., 271–72, 303–4, 319, 334–35, 373, 380, 382–84, 399, 406, 409, 432, 435, 438, 449, 468, 489, 491–92, 542, 546, 598, 711, 716
Hooker, Joseph, 74, 100, 134, 295, 320
Hospitals, 11, 18, 49, 79–80, 120, 159, 171–76, 186–87, 195–96, 356, 604, 722–24

House, Ellen Renshaw, 4–8, 32–33, 720–21
House, John Moore, 720
House of Representatives, C.S., 576
House of Representatives, U.S., 34, 36, 38, 241, 308–13, 318, 493, 505, 536, 569–70, 573–74, 583, 595, 631. *See also* Congress, U.S.
Houston, Samuel, 549
Houston, Ulysses L., 559
Howard, Jacob M., 39
Howard, Oliver O., 138, 515, 601
Hudson, Joshua H., 655
Huger, Frank, 435
Hughes, John Joseph, 429
Humphreys, Andrew A., 166
Hunter, Andrew, 554
Hunter, David, 246, 256, 267, 320
Hunter, Robert M. T., 572, 574
Hunter, William, 693
Hunter, William H., 214
Hutton, Charles G., 75

Idaho Territory, 502
Illinois, 34, 110, 324, 460, 569–70
Illinois 8th Regiment, 196
Illinois 73rd Regiment, 264, 338
Illinois 91st Regiment, 280
Illinois 94th Regiment, 280–81
Illinois 123rd Regiment, 133
Immigrants, 403, 428, 450–53, 456, 459, 497–98, 630
Impressment of slaves, 60–62, 359, 542
Indiana, 448, 570
Indiana 5th Regiment, 138
Indiana 27th Regiment, 139
Indiana 67th Regiment, 24–26
Indians, 4, 161, 334, 498, 502–3, 536
Ingersoll, Ebon C., 460
Interior Department, U.S., 502–3
Iowa, 34, 281–82
Iowa 19th Regiment, 280
Iowa 20th Regiment, 280
Iowa 31st Regiment, 598
Iowa 38th Regiment, 280
Ireland, 190, 733
Irish immigrants, 189–90, 459, 630, 733
Iron industry, 9–10
Irwin, Frank H., 722–24
Irwinville, Ga., 725

Isaiah (slave), 531
Israelites, ancient, 196–97, 407, 520

Jackson, Andrew, 452, 458, 477, 548, 572
Jackson, Miss., 320
Jackson, Thomas J. (Stonewall), 107, 165
Jacksonville, Fla., 320, 567
Jacobs, Harriet Ann, 11–15
Jacobs, Louisa M., 11–15
Jacobs Free School, 11–15
Jagers (Union prisoner), 226–27
James, Horace, 618–22
James Hale (U.S. naval vessel), 282
James River, 1–2, 22, 45–46, 68–69, 130, 150, 188, 211, 213, 216–17, 229, 251, 306, 358–59, 437, 448, 623, 644, 704
Japan, 495–96
Jaquess, James F., 264–65, 338, 340, 343–44, 346–51, 356–57
Javins, Charles, 343–45
Jay, John, 590
Jefferson, Thomas, 202, 590
Jenkins, Jeremiah W., 598
Jenkins, Micah, 97
Jenkins, Thornton A., 390
Jewett, William Cornell, 235
Johnson, Andrew, 16, 546, 566, 684, 687, 692–94, 696–97, 714, 720, 725, 729
Johnson, Bushrod R., 609
Johnson, Cave, 548
Johnson, Clem, 207
Johnson, Eben M., 117
Johnson, Edward, 81, 117, 124
Johnson, Frances, 632–34
Johnson, John, 560
Johnson, Nathan, 632
Johnson, Reverdy, 34–36, 39
Johnson's Island Prison Camp, 720
Johnston, James D., 394
Johnston, Joseph E., 22, 33, 46, 81, 84, 133–34, 137, 140, 145, 161, 271–72, 304, 489, 492, 540, 543, 598, 626, 637, 668, 696–701, 703, 705–6, 711, 713–17, 720
Johnston, Robert D., 81
Joint Committee on the Conduct of the War, 57, 536–37
Jones, John B., 437–41, 637–40

Jones, Mary, 522–35
Jones, William E., 246
Jonesboro, Ga., 380, 382, 399, 715
Judah, Henry M., 133
Julian, George W., 570–71
Julius Caesar, 66, 598

Kamper, Jane, 465
Kansas, 506, 576
Kautz, August V., 657, 659, 663
Kean, Robert Garlick Hill, 319–21, 439, 441, 572–75
Kearney (Union prisoner), 223
Kearsarge, U.S.S., 205–10
Keckly, Elizabeth, 675–83
Keith, Colonel, 7
Kelly (Union prisoner), 161
Kemper, James L., 638
Kennesaw Mountain, battle of, 232–34, 238–40, 271
Kent, Jacob, 80–81
Kent, James, 467
Kentucky, 35, 39–40, 54, 169, 233, 337, 365–67, 386, 405, 452, 458, 486–88, 504, 524–25, 569, 632–36
Kernstown, Va., 267, 269, 322, 396
Kershaw, Joseph B., 94, 96
Kilpatrick, Judson, 1, 3, 14, 226, 529, 532
Kinckle, Frank, 269
King, Kate, 527, 529, 533–35
Kingston, Ga., 134–35, 432
Kinney, Mary C., 691
Kinney (Union prisoner), 229
Kirkpatrick, Thomas J., 397
Knight, Edwin L., 117, 119
Knights of the Golden Circle, 375
Know-Nothing Party, 451, 456
Knoxville, Tenn., 4–8, 16–18, 32–33, 46, 636, 720
Knoxville Whig and Rebel Ventilator, 32
Ku Klux Klan, 42
Kuykendall, Andrew J., 460

Labbret, F. R., 149
Laborers, 11–12, 60, 429, 453–54
Lackawanna, U.S.S., 392–93
Lafayette, Marie-Joseph du Motier de, 590
Laird, John and Henry H. (shipbuilders), 205

Land, for freedmen, 566–68, 629, 719
Lane, James H., 91, 95
Langston, John Mercer, 414
Latham, Lieutenant, 268–69
Laurel Hill, N.C., 626
Laurel Hill, Va., 110, 112
Law of nations, 496, 545
Lawrence, Charles, 375
Lea, Joseph C., 371
Leaming, Mack J., 49
LeConte, Emma, 598–608, 700
LeConte, Joseph, 606
Ledlie, James H., 216, 287, 291
Lee, Elizabeth Blair, 403–5, 678
Lee, Mary W., 172–74, 176
Lee, Robert E., 3, 22, 45–46, 58, 111, 150, 163–67, 178, 197, 244, 258, 267, 293–94, 296, 298, 322, 350, 354, 402, 435, 439–40, 463, 598, 609, 623–24, 700, 727; at battle of Petersburg, 211, 216–18; at battle of the Wilderness, 68, 71, 81, 84, 90, 93–94, 96–97, 100, 110; on enlistment of slaves in Confederate army, 538–41, 554–57; explanation of surrender to President Davis, 703–4; fall of Richmond, 637–39, 642, 650, 652–53, 658, 666, 668–69; General Orders No. 9, 673–74, 703; memoranda to President Davis, 45–46, 358–61; surrender at Appomattox, 671–75, 679, 684, 686–87, 696, 701, 703–4, 706, 709, 711–12, 720
Lee, Samuel Phillips, 403–5
Lee, Stephen D., 49, 304, 400
Lee, William Henry Fitzhugh, 197
Leesburg, Va., 249, 267
Leo X, 590
LeRoy, William E., 393
Lewis, Alonzo, 191
Lewis, Walker, 679–80
Lexington, Ky., 486, 633
Lexington, Va., 246
Libby Prison, 160, 198, 223, 356, 666–67
Liberator, 418, 728
Liberia, 417, 494–95
Liberty County, Ga., 522
Lieber, Francis, 450–57
Limber Jim (Union prisoner), 244–45

INDEX 875

Lincoln, Abraham, 1, 21, 24, 54–55, 57–59, 196, 223, 250, 254, 260–62, 264–66, 321–22, 336, 347, 352, 355–56, 365, 368, 373–75, 377, 386, 405, 409, 421, 426, 454, 456, 462, 479–80, 536, 543, 555, 567–68, 618–20, 629–30, 725, 729; address at Baltimore Sanitary Fair, 51–53; assassination of, 675–96, 700–2, 712, 718; correspondence with Horace Greeley, 235–37, 243; Emancipation Proclamation, 16, 420, 561–62, 566, 569; funeral of, 694, 728; inaugural reception, 615–17; meeting with Confederate peace negotiators, 572–75; memorandum on reelection, 324, 460–61; message to Congress (December 1864), 493–509, 514, 569; opposition to, 294–301, 403–4; proclamation concerning reconstruction, 241–42; reelection, 458–59, 466, 493, 505–7, 509, 519, 562; in Richmond, 656, 663–65, 667, 684; safe conduct pass offer, 259; Second Inaugural Address, 612–15, 617; and surrender at Appomattox, 668, 671, 675; veto of Wade-Davis reconstruction bill, 307–18
Lincoln, Mary Todd, 675–83, 691, 693
Lincoln, Robert Todd, 682–83, 692
Lincoln, Thomas (Tad), 663, 676, 682–83
Lincoln, William Wallace (Willie), 678, 682
Lincoln County, Ky., 487
Lippett, Henry, 49
Litchee, S. M., 718
Lithonia, Ga., 468, 470
Little River, 156–57
Liverpool, England, 205
Locust Point (U.S. naval vessel), 389
Logan, John A., 601
London, England, 163, 202, 483
Longfellow, Henry Wadsworth, 592
Longstreet, James, 4, 7, 77, 90, 94–98, 108, 110, 115, 129, 637, 703
Looting, 522–35, 598, 626–27, 641, 643–47, 660–61, 666
Lossing, Benson J., 346
Loudoun County, Va., 463
Louis (Union prisoner), 161

Louisiana, 242, 310–16, 334, 418, 504, 700, 725; Confederate army in, 24, 147–49, 371–72; Lincoln's reconstruction plan for, 629–30, 675; Union army in, 21, 24–26, 46, 147, 371–72
Louisiana 1st (Colored) Regiment, 170
Louisiana 4th Regiment, 191, 194
Love, Ogle, 277
Lovejoy, Owen, 590
Lovett (Union prisoner), 229
Loyal Publication Society, 450
Lubbock, Francis R., 334
Ludington, Marshall, 69
Lumberton, N.C., 512
Lyman, Theodore, 68–84, 710
Lynch, James, 561–62, 564
Lynchburg, Va., 246, 402, 644, 652, 668, 671
Lyon, Lieutenant, 48
Lyons, James, 638

Macbeth, James, 208
Macedonian (merchant ship), 494
Macon, Ga., 160, 303–4, 399, 401, 474, 538
Macon and Western Railroad, 380
Macon Telegraph, 299–300, 399
Macy, George N., 77, 80
Maddox, W. J., 143
Madison Parish, La., 371
Magna Carta, 584
Mahone, William, 291–93
Maine, 299
Mallard, Mary S., 522–35
Malvern, U.S.S., 663–64
Malvern Hill, battle of, 112
Manassas Gap Railroad, 435
Manchester, Va., 644, 659–60
Maney, George E., 273
Manhattan, U.S.S., 391
Manning, Frederick L., 649, 665
Mansfield, La., 24, 147–48
Marietta, Ga., 140, 191, 232, 238, 240
Marshall, Charles, 673–74
Marshall, Charles Henry, 652
Marshall, Elisha G., 286, 288
Marshall, Samuel S., 460
Marshall (cook), 71
Martial law, 310–11, 365–67, 467
Martin, Augustus P., 82

Martin, Bud, 274
Martinsburg, W.Va., 268, 396
Maryland, 34–35, 52, 241, 278–79, 298, 307, 328, 337, 339, 350, 403–5, 418, 452, 465, 504–5, 574, 685; and Confederate attack on Washington, 246–55
Massachusetts, 40, 169, 299, 387–88, 411, 451, 552, 629, 694
Massachusetts 1st Regiment, 163
Massachusetts 4th Regiment, 645, 661
Massachusetts 5th Regiment, 483
Massachusetts 7th Regiment, 154, 201
Massachusetts 10th Regiment, 112–19, 150–59, 199–201
Massachusetts 21st Regiment, 287
Massachusetts 35th Regiment, 130
Massachusetts 39th Regiment, 72
Massachusetts 54th Regiment, 15, 55, 387, 615
Massachusetts 55th Regiment, 55, 387
Massachusetts 56th Regiment, 76, 78, 115, 216–17, 286–87, 709
Massachusetts 57th Regiment, 78, 115
Massachusetts 58th Regiment, 115
Massie, John L., 396
Mattaponi River, 175
Mattison, Lucius V. S., 667
Maurepas, Jean-Frédéric Phélypeaux de, 204
Mayo, Joseph C., 644–45, 658
McAlister, Robert, 5–8, 32, 74
McCabe, William Gordon, 653–55
McClellan, George B., 81, 165, 180, 223, 229, 295, 298, 324, 368–70, 374–75, 377–79, 404, 449–51, 454, 456, 458–59, 461, 466–67, 519, 726
McCorkle, John, 246–47
McCulloch, Hugh, 691–93
McDaniel, Bill, 397
McDougall, James A., 37–38, 40
McDowell, Irvin, 165, 295
McFerrin, John B., 717
McGowan, Samuel, 90, 93–95, 97, 122–23, 125, 306
McGregor, William D., 83
McGuire, Judith W., 195–98
McIntosh, David G., 293
McIntyre, Benjamin F., 280–82
McKinley, Alexander, 389–95
McLaws, Lafayette, 96

McNeese (Union prisoner), 228
McPherson, James B., 133
Meade, George G., 21, 45, 67–68, 73–74, 76–81, 83–84, 100, 163–65, 167, 178–79, 286, 295, 319–20, 710
Mechanicsville, Va., 653
Meigs, Montgomery C., 690
Melville, Herman: "The Armies of the Wilderness," 102–9; *Battle-Pieces and Aspects of the War*, 102; "Chattanooga," 102
Memphis, Tenn., 42, 47, 49, 170, 386
Mercier (cook), 71
Merrimack, U.S.S., 394
Messer, Clarence, 175
Metacomet, U.S.S., 392
Methodists, 264
Mexico, 24, 280, 385, 493, 572, 707, 727
Michigan, 250, 733
Michigan, U.S.S., 631
Michigan 1st Regiment, 733
Michigan 5th Regiment, 733
Michigan 6th Regiment, 733
Michigan 7th Regiment, 733
Middle Passage, 587
Midgely, Alfred W., 112
Miles, Nelson A., 709–10
Miles, William P., 538
Military governors, 314–16
Militia, 411, 437, 468, 638
Militia Act, 387
Milledge, John, 396
Milledgeville, Ga., 432, 472–78, 520, 720
Millen, Ga., 432
Miller, Calvin, 486–88
Miller, Frank, 268–70
Miller, George, 487
Miller, Isabella, 486–88
Miller, Joseph, 486–88
Miller, Joseph, Jr., 486–88
Miller, Maria, 486–88
Milliken's Bend, battle of, 55, 170, 552
Mills, Charles, 76
Mills, James, 560
Mills, John, 609
Mills, Luther Rice, 609–11
Millwood, Va., 322
Milton, John, 592
Mine Run campaign, 45

Minnegerode, Charles, 638
Missionaries, 12
Mississippi, 3, 125, 128, 320, 386, 546, 569, 707, 711, 718, 725
Mississippi River, 21, 42, 52, 147, 169–70, 233, 283, 375, 393, 395, 704, 707, 735
Missouri, 22, 34–35, 233, 328, 337, 362, 386, 403, 418, 452, 458, 504, 531
Missouri 23rd Regiment, 474
Missouri 24th Regiment, 48
Mitchell, William, 74
Mobile, Ala., 22, 24, 46, 60, 62, 194, 390, 395, 701, 707
Mobile Bay, 283–85, 319, 389–95, 445
Monocacy River, 247–48, 250
Monongahela, U.S.S., 392
Monroe, James (Confederate soldier), 398
Monroe Doctrine, 573
Montana Territory, 502
Montevideo plantation, 522–35
Montgomery, Ala., 271, 406
Moore, Frank: *The Rebellion Record*, 346
Morehouse Parish, La., 371
Morgan, C.S.S., 319, 391–92, 395
Morgan, James M., 702
Morgan, John Hunt, 474
Morgan, Sarah, 700–2
Mormons, 446
Morocco, 330, 452, 495
Morrill, Edwin J., 219–20
Morris, George P., 592
Morrison, Alfred, 138
Morrison, William R., 460
Mosby, John S., 45, 106, 320–21, 463–64
Moscow, Tenn., 170
Moseby (Union prisoner), 244
Motley, John Lothrop, 544
Mott, Gershom, 74, 77
Moulton, Samuel W., 460
Mulally, Francis P., 90
Mulford, John E., 325–26
Mulraney (Union prisoner), 227
Mundee, Charles, 74
Munyan, Alanson E., 117, 119, 154, 156
Murray (Union prisoner), 244

Muslims, 587
Mustang (U.S. transport vessel), 282

Nachitoches, La., 24–25
Nance, James D., 97
Napoléon I (Napoléon Bonaparte), 66, 296, 399, 726, 733
Napoléon III (Louis Napoléon), 443, 446
Nashville, C.S.S., 395
Nashville, Tenn., 16, 21, 489, 491, 543, 546–53, 598, 711, 715, 718, 720
Natchez, Miss., 170
National Anti-Slavery Standard, 11, 417
National banks, 499–500
National Convention of Colored Men, 414–31
National debt, 630
National Union convention, 324
Natural rights, 426
Navy, C.S., 542–43, 662; *Alabama–Kearsarge* battle, 205–10; battle of Mobile Bay, 319, 389–96
Navy, U.S., 21, 45–46, 147–48, 337, 378, 442–43, 445–46, 500–1, 688; battle of Mobile Bay, 283–85, 319, 389–95; black sailors in, 205–10, 426; *Kearsarge–Alabama* battle, 205–10; and Lincoln's visit to Richmond, 663–64; pensions, 503; siege of Savannah, 514–18; siege of Wilmington, 542–43
Navy Department, U.S., 390, 498, 500–1
Neal, Andrew, 560
Nebraska Territory, 502
Negroes, 299, 301, 339, 444, 480, 692, 709–10; in Andersonville Prison, 161; education of, 11–15; land for freedmen, 566–68, 629, 719; mistreatment by Union soldiers, 522, 532, 535, 558, 563, 621; suffrage, 414, 417–18, 426–29, 446–53, 596, 629–30, 675; in Union army, 1, 15, 42–44, 47–50, 52–59, 81, 131–32, 155, 169–70, 197, 201, 213–15, 278–79, 286–87, 290–92, 305, 325–32, 343, 362–65, 372, 387–88, 417–18, 438, 444, 483, 486–88, 518, 536, 548, 550–52, 563–64, 568, 577, 583, 615, 618, 632, 635,

646, 656–59, 661, 675, 728, 732–33; in Union navy, 205–10, 426
Neil, Alf, 277
Neill, Thomas H., 115, 152, 157
Nelson, Samuel, 571
Nelson, William, 397
Nelson (Union prisoner), 228
Nemala, U.S.S., 514–15
Neutrality, 545
Nevada, 501, 506
New Hampshire, 37
New Jersey, 171, 458, 569
New Jersey 4th Regiment, 160, 162, 223, 229
New Jersey 15th Regiment, 229
New Market, Va., 246, 320, 434, 437
New Orleans, La., 21, 46, 148–49, 283, 309, 700, 702, 718, 720
New York, 300–1, 324, 405, 458, 466
New York 5th Regiment, 72
New York 7th Regiment, 180, 183–84, 227
New York 11th Regiment, 178
New York 13th Regiment, 102
New York 22nd Regiment, 83
New York 51st Regiment, 722
New York 77th Regiment, 114
New York 81st Regiment, 667
New York 93rd Regiment, 81
New York City, 189–90, 227, 368, 459, 479, 623, 648, 650–52, 721; and assassination of Lincoln, 684–87; draft riots in, 55, 420, 583; opposition to Lincoln in, 294, 300, 466
New York Commercial Advertiser, 650–51
New York Herald, 47, 390, 510, 575, 725
New York Times, 47, 264, 307, 319, 324
New York Tribune, 16, 47, 235, 265, 307, 344, 486, 558, 574, 686
New York World, 301–2, 307, 319, 459
Newburyport Herald, 299
Newton, Captain, 196
Newton, John, 216
Newton, Mary, 195–96
Newtown, Va., 268
Niagara, U.S.S., 373
Niagara Falls peace negotiations, 235–37, 259–63, 265–66, 339–40
Nicaragua, 493

Nicholasville, Ky., 488
Nicolay, John G., 460
Niger (slave), 527
Nolan, T. F., 143
Norfolk, Va., 496
Norfolk and Petersburg Railroad, 218
North Anna River, 150–51, 153, 157, 163
North Carolina, 19–20, 46, 87, 123, 154, 218, 236, 243, 360–61, 390, 439, 448, 452, 609, 637, 668, 694, 703; Roanoke Island Freedmen's Colony, 618–22; Sherman's march across, 626–28, 630, 696; slave unrest in, 510–13; surrender at Durham Station, 696–99, 705–6, 711, 713–14, 717, 720
Norvell, John M., 77
Nutt, Henry, 510–13

Oak Grove, battle of, 112
Oakley (Union prisoner), 229–30
Oconee River, 477
Odell, Moses, 651
Ogden, Gouverneur, 686
Ogeechee River, 514–15
Oglethorpe, James, 477
Ohio, 34, 241, 307, 440, 448–49, 451, 472, 529, 570
Ohio River, 412
Old Guard, 294, 300
Olustee, battle of, 71
Omaha, Nebraska Territory, 502
O'Melia, Mary, 707
Oostanaula River, 137, 193
Opelika, Ala., 437–38
Orange, N.J., 370, 377
Orange, Va., 45, 77, 90, 270
Orange and Alexandria Railroad, 119
Ord, Edward O. C., 22, 645, 726
Oregon, 497
Orr, James L., 90–93, 95–96, 123, 125
Ossabaw Sound, 514–15
Ossipee, U.S.S., 393
Ostend Manifesto, 455
Ould, Robert, 325, 342–47, 356, 536
Outon, Thomas, 632

Paducah, Ky., 170
Page, Richard L., 395
Page (Confederate soldier), 247–48
Paine, Eleazer A., 366

Palmetto, Ga., 399, 406
Pamunkey River, 2, 163, 171, 178–79, 195
Panther Springs, battle of, 5
Paraguay, 494
Parker, Dexter F., 117, 119, 154
Parliament (British), 444, 453, 629
Parsons, Joseph B., 118
Parsons, William H., 371
Parton, James: *General Butler in New Orleans*, 346
Patrick, Marsena R., 78, 84
Patrick, Robert, 191–94
Patriotism, 66–67, 89, 149, 213, 262–64, 377, 404, 411, 415, 426, 449, 451, 480, 505, 550, 623, 646, 669, 678, 702, 707, 727, 733
Peace Democrats, 260, 294, 365, 368, 412–13
Peace negotiations, 235–37, 243, 259–60, 321, 326, 339–41, 347, 368, 370, 374–75, 378–79, 409, 458, 507, 572–75
Peck (Confederate supply agent), 439, 441
Peebles Farm, battle of, 437
Pegram, James W., 653
Pegram, John, 653
Pegram, Mary, 653
Pegram, Richard G., 291–92
Pegram, Virginia Johnson, 291
Pegram, William, 291–93, 653–55
Pélissier, Aimable, 444
Pemberton, John C., 194, 333
Pendleton, George H., 368, 375
Pennsylvania, 3, 81, 304, 320, 322–24, 377, 440, 448–49, 461
Pennsylvania 48th Regiment, 286
Pennsylvania 61st Regiment, 114
Pennsylvania 93rd Regiment, 722
Pennsylvania 100th Regiment, 287
Pensacola, Fla., 389–90, 496
Pensions, 498, 503–4
Pepper, Charles, 274
Perrin, Abner M., 125
Perryville, Ky., 264
Peru, 494
Petersburg, Va., 119, 211–21, 227, 229, 246, 250, 267, 286–93, 304–6, 319–20, 358, 360, 437, 543, 552, 609–11, 637, 645, 650–51, 668, 703, 709, 722

Petersburg and Richmond Railroad, 246, 648
Petersen, William and Anna, 691
Petition of the Colored Citizens of Nashville to the Union Convention of Tennessee, 546–53
Pettybone, Major, 280
Phelps, Jefferson, 197
Philadelphia, Pa., 54, 240, 479
Philadelphia Inquirer, 479
Philadelphia Press, 656
Pickett, George E., 637, 641
Pickett, LaSalle, 641
Pickett's Mill, battle of, 140–46, 191
Pierce, Dr., 306
Pierce, Franklin, 348
Pierce (overseer), 17–18
Pierpont, John: "The Call of Kansas," 30
Pilgrims (Separatists), 585
Pillow, Gideon J., 43
Pin Hook, La., 371–72
Pingree, Samuel E., 219
Piqua, Ohio, 387
Pitt, William, 592
Pittsburg Landing, Tenn., 264
Pittsburgh, Pa., 9–10
Platte Valley (U.S. naval vessel), 48–50
Pleasant Hill, La., 24–25, 147–48
Pleasants, Henry, 286
Pleasants, Jim, 398
Poagne, William T., 96–97
Poe, Orlando M., 475–76
Polk, Leonidas, 194, 400
Pollard, Edward A., 648
Pollard, James, 2
Pope, John, 295
Port Hudson, La., 55, 170
Port Royal, S.C., 442, 563, 566
Port Royal, Va., 688
Porter, David D., 663–65
Porter, Fitz-John, 216
Porter, Horace, 100–1
Porter, James, 560
Porter, John H., 49
Porter, Judith, 42
Post Office Department, U.S., 501
Poston, John L., 48
Potomac River, 197, 247, 249–50, 252, 267, 322, 402
Potter, Dr., 173

Potter, Edward E., 515
Potter, Robert B., 79
Powell, Lazarus W., 37, 39
Powell, Lewis, 684–85, 688
Powell, William H., 463–64
Prairie Grove, Ark., 280
Pratt, Benjamin F., 657
Presbyterians, 583, 642, 687
Preston, Caroline, 435
Price, Lieutenant, 131
Prince, Henry, 74
Prince William County, Va., 463
Prisoner exchanges, 325–32, 479, 536
Prisoners of war, 1–6, 48, 50, 87, 116–17, 120, 131, 139, 153–55, 287–88, 291–92, 325–32, 343, 401, 418, 438, 463–64, 536–37, 666–68, 673
Prisons, 160–62, 222–31, 325, 356, 536–37, 666–67, 700, 715, 720
Protestants, 445
Prussia, 466
Public land, 502
Pulaski, Tenn., 489
Purdy, Elijah F., 300

Quakers, 171
Quarles, William A., 194

Radical Republicans, 241, 352, 403, 570, 629, 675
Railroads, 22, 45, 119, 133–35, 155–57, 191, 218–19, 227, 233, 246, 256, 271, 273, 333–34, 358–59, 380, 396, 432, 435, 437, 449, 468–70, 502–3, 514–15, 543, 628, 637, 642–43, 648, 650, 705, 718
Raleigh, N.C., 513, 696
Ramseur, Charles R., 434
Ramseur, David P., 436
Ramseur, Ellen Richmond, 434
Ramseur, Stephen D., 268–69, 398, 434–36
Ramsey, Susan, 32
Randolph County, Ala., 60–62
Rapidan River, 1, 45, 63, 68–69, 85, 90, 102, 104, 112, 151, 211, 216, 251, 294, 350
Rappahannock River, 45–46, 99–100, 151, 173, 251, 320, 464
Rappahannock Station, Va., 83, 112
Rawlins, John A., 73

Rawson, E. E., 384
Ray, Henrietta, 42
Raymond, Henry J., 324, 368, 461
Reagan, John H., 706
Reams Station, battle of, 358
Reconstruction, 241–42, 307–18, 352, 374, 407, 421, 542, 569, 573, 578–79, 629–30, 675
Red River, 21, 24–25, 46, 147
Reed, Colonel, 50
Refugees, 11–12, 399, 402, 486, 558, 563, 566, 632
Remond, Charles Lenox, 15
Renshaw, Francis B., 7
Republican Party, 34–35, 169, 223, 241, 297, 299–300, 307, 324, 339, 352, 387, 403, 419–22, 448, 458–60, 481, 493, 505, 569–70, 612, 629–30, 675
Resaca, Ga., 133–39, 192–93, 432, 468
Restieaux, E. B. W., 486
Revelle, Cordy B., 48
Revolutionary War, 399, 406, 408, 424, 445, 650, 727
Reynolds, John, 216
Rhode Island 2nd Regiment, 113, 154, 157–58
Rice, 522, 543
Rice, Cora, 362–63
Rice, James C., 189
Rice, Mary, 362–63
Rice, Spottswood, 362–64
Richards, Lester S., 220
Richmond, Caleb, 436
Richmond, Va., 68, 101, 115–16, 119–20, 151, 161, 163–65, 173, 176, 178, 195, 202, 217–18, 227, 229, 244, 251–52, 261, 264–66, 268, 293–94, 303, 319, 338, 340–41, 343–45, 348, 350, 356–58, 399, 402, 406, 428, 435, 451–52, 479, 517, 543, 554, 572, 609–10, 623, 628, 673, 679; Belle Isle Prison Camp, 536–37; defense of, 45–46, 111, 211, 360, 437, 440; fall of, 637–38, 684, 701, 703–5; Libby Prison, 160, 198, 223, 356, 666–67; Lincoln's visit to, 656, 663–65, 667, 684; slaves in, 639, 646–47, 657–58, 660, 663–66; Union raid on, 1–3
Richmond (C.S. ram ship), 644
Richmond and Danville Railroad, 642–43, 648

INDEX

Richmond and Fredericksburg Railroad, 150
Richmond County, N.C., 510–11
Richmond Dispatch, 660
Richmond Enquirer, 541–42, 660
Ricketts, James B., 81
Rio Grande, 21, 280–81
Ripley, Edward H., 661, 665
River Queen (steamboat), 572–73
Roanoke Island Freedmen's Colony, 618–22
Robbins, Lieutenant Colonel, 2
Robeson County, N.C., 511
Robinson, Captain, 721
Robinson, Jervey, 306
Robinson, William B., 116
Robinson (Confederate sailor), 208
Robinson (Union officer), 72
Rock, John S., 571
Rodes, Robert E., 123, 397
Rodgers, John, 443
Rome, ancient, 331
Rome, Ga., 134, 432, 438, 449
Ropes, John C., 514
Rosecrans, William S., 265, 362, 467
Rosenkrantz, Frederick, 83
Ross, Lewis W., 460
Russia, 399, 495
Rutherford's Farm, battle of, 267–68
Ryan, W. A., 718

Sabine Crossroads, battle of, 24
Sacramento, Calif., 503
Sailor's Creek, 668
St. Albans, Vt., 497
St. Augustine, Fla., 567
St. Johns River, 45, 566
St. Louis, Mo., 49, 362, 403
St. Louis Democrat, 47
Salisbury, N.C., 19, 718
Sanders, George N., 265–66, 339
Sanitary fairs, 13, 15, 51–53, 240, 251
Santo Domingo, 494
Sarsfield (Union prisoner), 231, 244
Saulsbury, Willard, 37, 40–41
Saunders (Union officer), 80
Savannah, Ga., 432, 468, 514–20, 522, 531, 542–43, 558–67, 598
Savannah River, 517
Saxton, Rufus, 518, 566, 568
Scales, Alfred M., 93, 95

Schenck, David, 434
Schofield, John M., 16, 32, 133, 489, 626, 696–97, 726
Schuyler, Louisa, 190
Scientific American, 9
Scipio Africanus, 66
Scott, Dred, 571
Scott, Walter, 669–70
Scott, Winfield, 727
Secession, 4, 32, 195, 236, 352, 354, 452, 454, 481
Seddon, James A., 320, 437–40, 538, 639
Seddon, John, 320
Seddon, Mary, 320
Sedgwick, John, 68, 72, 79–82, 100, 115, 157–58, 189
Selma, Ala., 701
Selma, C.S.S., 319, 391–92, 395
Selma and Talladega Railroad, 432
Semme, Raphael, 205, 207–8, 445
Senate, C.S., 576
Senate, U.S., 34–41, 169, 308–15, 455, 493, 505, 536, 569, 595. *See also* Congress, U.S.
Seven Days' Battles, 27
Seward, Augustus, 684
Seward, Frederick W., 684–85, 688–90, 694
Seward, William H., 58–59, 242, 324, 421, 460–61, 484, 569, 572–74, 680, 684–85, 688–89, 691–94, 701–2, 712
Sextons Junction, Va., 155–56
Seymour, Horatio, 379, 429, 459
Seymour, Michael, 446
Seymour, Truman B., 71, 81
Shady Dale, Ga., 472–73
Shakespeare, William, 168
Shaler, Alexander, 80–81, 115
Sharp, Granville, 592
Sharpsburg, Md., 247, 292
Shaw, John P., 158
Shaw, Lieutenant, 4–5
Shenandoah Valley, 68, 150, 246, 256, 267–70, 320, 322–23, 396–98, 402, 415, 434–36, 448–49, 458, 463–64
Shepherdstown, Md., 247
Shepley, George F., 649, 661, 663–64

Sheridan, Philip H., 71–72, 75, 81, 83, 119, 252, 322, 341, 396, 434–35, 448, 458, 463, 624, 637, 668, 727, 729
Sherman, Ellen Ewing, 232
Sherman, Merritt H., 220
Sherman, William T., 21–22, 119, 133, 140, 161, 191, 193, 222, 226, 228, 304, 430, 435, 449, 624, 637–38, 671, 700, 727–28, 730–32; Atlanta campaign, 232–34, 238, 271, 333–34, 350–51, 368, 373, 380, 384–86, 399–402, 409, 432, 458; march across Carolinas, 598, 601–2, 604, 626, 628, 630, 696; march across Georgia, 432–33, 468–78, 492, 504, 510, 514–20, 522, 543, 558, 626, 679; Savannah campaign, 514–20, 522, 543, 558, 564–68; Special Field Orders No. 15, 566–68; and surrender at Durham Station, 696–99, 705–6, 711, 713–14, 717, 720
Shiloh, battle of, 191
Shooter, Washington P., 92, 128
Shreveport, La., 21, 24–26
Shurtleff, Flavel, 113, 158
Sigel, Franz, 22–23, 68, 246
Simonson, Peter, 138
Slave revolts, 510–13
Slave trade (domestic), 417, 588
Slave trade (foreign), 494, 587–88
Slavery, 12–14, 29–30, 51, 169, 202, 260, 343, 354, 367, 417, 419, 424–25, 444–45, 452, 455–56, 480, 494, 508, 613, 625, 697, 712, 716–17; abolition of, 34–41, 236, 241–43, 299, 313–15, 317, 324, 339, 420–23, 465, 481, 493, 505, 539, 541, 546–47, 569–71, 578; defense of, 294; Garnet's sermon about, 583–97
Slaves, 305, 339, 470, 613; black prisoners of war treated as, 325–32; emancipation of, 30–31, 313–14, 317, 354–55, 414, 465, 539–41, 554–56, 558, 576–82, 596, 615, 625, 629, 632, 712, 716, 718, 735; encountered in march across Georgia, 469–73, 478, 522, 532, 535, 558; enlistment in Confederate army, 538–42, 554–57, 563, 576–82, 623, 627; fugitive, 16, 196–97, 362, 444, 510, 661; impressment of, 60–62, 359, 542; as refugees, 11–12, 558, 563, 566, 632; in Richmond, 639, 646–47, 657–58, 660, 663–66
Slocum, Henry W., 477, 602
Smith, Caleb B., 446
Smith, Edmund Kirby, 334, 437–38, 720, 735
Smith, Sydney, 652
Smith, Thomas B., 333
Smith, William, 440
Smith, William F., 22, 200
Smithfield, N.C., 696, 711
Snickersville, Va., 268
South Anna River, 151
South Carolina, 320, 354, 406–7, 410–11, 445, 452, 511, 517, 540, 566–67, 627, 669–70, 718, 720, 732; burning of Columbia, 598–608, 626
South Carolina 1st Regiment, 90–93, 95, 123, 125, 128, 306
South Carolina 12th Regiment, 91–92, 95–96, 123–25, 127
South Carolina 13th Regiment, 91–92, 95, 123, 125, 127
South Carolina 14th Regiment, 91–93, 95, 123, 125, 127
South Carolinian, 406
Southside Railroad, 437, 637, 650
Spain, 494
Sparta, ancient, 400, 411
Spear, Samuel P., 666
Speed, James, 692–93
Spotsylvania, Va., 68, 100, 110–29, 150–51, 164, 211, 218, 229, 246, 298
Sprague, Kate Chase, 570
Spring Hill, Tenn., 489–90
Springfield Republican, 63, 154
Stagg, Peter, 733
Stanley, David S., 138
Stanton, Edwin M., 1, 58–59, 110, 278, 375, 439, 449, 460, 558, 564–66, 618, 620, 630, 656, 689–90, 692–94
"Star-Spangled Banner, The," 646, 651
State banks, 500
State constitutions, 242, 569
State Department, C.S., 346, 348
State Department, U.S., 497, 693
States, Jack, 229
States' rights, 410–11, 451–53
Staunton, Va., 434
Steele, Frederick, 21

INDEX

Stephens, Alexander H., 235, 333, 399, 407, 450, 572–73
Stephens, Linton, 333, 335
Stephenson's Depot, battle of, 267–68
Stevens, Atherton H., 645, 661
Stevens, John, 531–32
Stevenson, Thomas G., 76, 78–79
Stirling's Plantation, battle of, 280
Stone, George A., 601
Stone, Kate, 371–72
Stoneman, George, 303
Stowe, Harriet Beecher: *Uncle Tom's Cabin*, 444
Strasburg, Va., 267–69, 396, 434
Streeter, Holland, 620
Stringfellow, John H., 576–82
Strong, Caleb, 411
Strong, Charles E., 374
Strong, Ellen Ruggles, 684
Strong, George Templeton, 373–76, 458–59, 623–25, 650–52, 684–87
Stuart, J.E.B., 83, 90, 93, 463
Suffrage, 414, 417–18, 426–29, 546–53, 596, 629–30, 675, 711, 719
Summer Hill plantation, 195–97
Sumner, Charles, 12, 37, 40, 629–31, 675, 691–92, 694
Supreme Court, U.S., 295, 311–12, 317, 422, 630, 698
Surratt, Mary, 688
Sutton, John, 274
Symbol (U.S. torpedo boat), 664
Syracuse, N.Y., 414

Taiping rebellion, 495
Talbot County, Md., 465
Taliaferro, Charles, 397–98
Taney, Roger B., 419
Tarbell (Union prisoner), 228
Taxation, 498–99, 578–79
Taylor, Glasgon, 559
Taylor, Richard, 24, 147–49, 334, 437–38, 725
Taylor, Robert N., 561
Taylor, Walter H., 643
Taylor, William A., 491
Taylor, Zachary, 147, 573
Tecumseh, U.S.S., 389, 391
Telegraph, transatlantic, 495
Templeton, Colonel, 371

Tennessee, 9, 334, 338, 386, 468, 504, 524, 543, 718, 720; battle of Franklin, 489–92, 546; black suffrage in, 546–53; Fort Pillow massacre, 42–44, 47–50, 52–59; Union occupation of Knoxville, 4–8, 16–18, 32–33, 46
Tennessee, C.S.S., 319, 390–95, 445
Tennessee 13th Regiment (Union), 42–44, 47–50
Tennessee 20th Regiment (Confederate), 42–44, 47–50
Tennessee River, 410, 468
Territories, 502, 506
Terry (Union prisoner), 244
Texas, 21, 24, 141–42, 147–48, 334, 371, 446, 590, 659, 707, 710, 716–18, 725, 728–29; fighting in, 280–82; surrender in, 735
Texas 7th Regiment, 146
Texas 24th Regiment, 140–46, 271–77, 489–91, 711–19
Thirteenth Amendment, 34–41, 236, 241–43, 314, 493, 505, 569–71, 573–74, 578, 632, 635, 675
Thomas, Edward, 91, 93–95
Thomas, George H., 133, 468, 489, 546, 624, 726
Thomas, Henry G., 659
Thomas, Lieutenant, 721
Thomas, Lorenzo, 169–70, 486
Thomasville, N.C., 718
Thompson, George, 34–36
Thompson, Jacob, 261, 266
Thompson, Joseph P., 687
Thomson, Andrew W., 604, 606
Thorndike, William, 72
Thornton, Anthony, 460
Tillou, Francis R., 686
Times (London), 375
Tobacco, 362, 578–79, 641, 660–61
Toombs, Robert, 333–35, 399, 559
Torbert, Alfred, 71, 463
Townsend, E. D., 565
Townsend, William, 465
Transatlantic telegraph, 495
Transcontinental railroad, 502–3
Traute, Louis, 226
Treasury, U.S., 498–99
Treasury Department, U.S., 498–99, 566

Trenholm, George A., 319, 439
Trumbull, Lyman, 34, 569
Tucker, Gideon J., 300–1
Tunis, 330, 452, 495
Tuscumbia, Ala., 468, 491
Tyler, John, 132

U.S. 1st Colored Regiment, 131
U.S. 2nd Colored Regiment, 42–44, 47–50, 52–59, 131
U.S. 4th Colored Regiment, 214
U.S. 6th Colored Regiment, 42–44, 47–50, 52–59
U.S. 12th Colored Regiment, 635
U.S. 20th Colored Regiment, 55
U.S. 22nd Colored Regiment, 131
U.S. 26th Colored Regiment, 55
U.S. 36th Colored Regiment, 657, 659
U.S. 67th Colored Regiment, 362
U.S. 124th Colored Regiment, 487
U.S. Christian Commission, 51–53, 159, 251
U.S.-Mexican War, 283, 727
U.S. Sanitary Commission, 13, 15, 51–53, 172, 175–76, 251, 373, 650, 685
Union Democrats, 365
Union League Club, 652, 687
Unionism, 16, 32, 34, 367, 378–79, 404, 486, 546, 548, 569
Upton, Emory, 80
Usher, John P., 461, 692
Utah Territory, 446

Vallandigham, Clement L., 336, 370, 374–75
Vance, Zebulon B., 19, 510, 705
Vanderpoel, Aaron, 652
Vaughan, John Crawford, 396
Venezuela, 494
Verdi, Tullio, 689
Vermont, 28, 220–21, 299; Confederate raid on St. Albans, 497
Vermont 1st Regiment, 218
Vermont 2nd Regiment, 27, 85–90, 211–15
Vermont 11th Regiment, 218–21
Verplanck, Gulian C., 686
Vicksburg, Miss., 1, 24, 70, 191, 258, 280, 333, 386
Vinton, Francis, 651
Virginia, 313, 338–39, 354, 401–2, 469, 481, 540, 543, 554–55, 574–76, 694; battle of Cold Harbor, 178–80; battle of Petersburg, 211–21, 286–93, 319–20; battle of Spotsylvania, 110–29; battle of the Wilderness, 68–109; battle of Winchester, 396–98; Confederate army in, 22–23, 45–46, 150–59, 163–67, 197–98, 246, 248, 256–58, 298, 306, 358–61, 437–41; fall of Richmond, 637–38, 703–5; fighting in Shenandoah Valley, 267–70, 320, 322–23, 415, 434–36, 448–49, 463–64; freedmen's school in, 11–15; impressment of slaves, 359; Lincoln's visit to Richmond, 656, 663–65, 667, 684; plantations, 195–97; surrender at Appomattox, 671–75, 679, 696, 701, 703–4, 706, 709, 711–12, 720; Union army in, 21–23, 27–31, 63–67, 130–32, 150–59, 163–67, 171–77, 189, 195–97, 199–201, 246, 256–58, 294–95, 298, 358–61, 437–41; Union raid on Richmond, 1–3
Virginia 1st Regiment, 463
Virginia 2nd Regiment, 269
Virginia 9th Regiment, 2
Virginia 26th Regiment, 609
Virginia 47th Regiment, 709
Virginia 61st Regiment, 269
Virginia (C.S. ram ship), 644
Virginia and Tennessee Railroad, 22
Virginia Central Railroad, 155–57

Waddell, Colonel, 305
Wade, Benjamin F., 241, 307–18
Wade-Davis bill, 241–42, 307–18
Wadsworth, James S., 73, 77, 79, 115, 158, 189
Walker, Francis A., 81
Walker, William H. T., 275, 400
Wallace, Lew, 250, 267
War Democrats, 301, 324, 374, 403, 546
War Department, C.S., 160, 319, 343, 437, 449, 609, 638–39, 641, 660
War Department, U.S., 258, 387, 498, 500, 567, 618, 694
War of 1812, 283, 445, 650
Ward, Artemus, 154
Wardell, Arthur, 560
Wardlaw, George A., 93

Ware, George, 397
Warner, James M., 219
Warren, Gouverneur K., 68, 72–73, 79, 82–83, 100, 195
Washburne, Elihu B., 81, 110, 460
Washington, D.C., 21, 34, 35, 45–46, 55, 57, 65, 83, 115, 167, 169, 171, 218, 221, 236, 241–43, 258–61, 267, 320, 324, 340, 350–51, 372, 460, 463, 467, 484, 504, 573, 612, 618, 622, 629, 698, 709–10, 712, 720, 722–24; assassination of Lincoln, 675–85, 688–96; Confederate attack on, 246–55, 402; Grand Review of the Armies, 725–34
Washington, George, 590, 686
Wayne, James M., 571
Weatherell, James H., 117, 156
Webb, Alexander S., 76, 79
Webb, Lewis H., 510
Weed, Thurlow, 324, 612
Weitzel, Godfrey, 645–46, 649, 652, 656–58, 661, 663
Weld, Hannah Minot, 709
Weld, Stephen Minot, 216
Weld, Stephen Minot, Jr., 76, 216–17, 286–90, 709–10
Weldon, N.C., 510
Weldon and Petersburg Railroad, 218, 256, 358–59
Welles, Gideon, 57–59, 307, 368–69, 460, 668–70, 688–95
Welles, Mary, 681, 693
Wellington, Duke of (Arthur Wellesley), 726
Wells, S. C., 384
Wentworth, John, 460
West Virginia, 575
Westwood plantation, 195–97
Wetmore, Prosper M., 651
Wheaton, Frank, 74
Wheeler, Joseph, 334, 432
White, Hugh L., 548
White House, Va., 171–72, 176
Whitfield (plantation owner), 473
Whitman, Captain, 5–6
Whitman, George, 722
Whitman, Walt: *Specimen Days*, 722–24
Whittier, Charles A., 709
Whittier, John Greenleaf, 592–93

Wicker, Rachel Ann, 387–88
Wickliffe, Charles A., 365
Wilberforce, William, 592
Wilcox, Cadmus M., 90, 96
Wild, Edward A., 130–32, 659
Wilderness, battle of the, 63, 68–110, 112, 122, 151, 157, 159–60, 164–65, 167, 171, 211, 216, 218, 246, 290
Wilkes, Franklin C., 142–45
Wilkeson, Frank, 178–88
Willets, Georgiana, 173
Williams, Alpheus S., 137–39, 626–28
Williams, Mary, 137
Williams, Sidney, 119
Wilmington, Del., 442
Wilmington, N.C., 390, 510, 541–43, 627–28
Wilson, Henry, 65, 169
Wilson, J. Cardwell, 43
Wilson, James F., 34
Wilson, James H., 66, 71, 75
Wilson, Julius, 48
Winchester, Va., 267–70, 322, 396–98, 434
Winder, John H., 224–25, 437
Winn, Captain, 531
Winslow, John A., 206–7
Winston, R. B., 247
Winters, Harriet, 24
Winters, William, 24–26
Wirz, Henry H., 225, 230, 244
Wisconsin 3rd Regiment, 139
Wisconsin 20th Regiment, 280–82
Wise, Henry A., 610
Women's Central Association for Relief, 189
Women's Patriotic Association for Diminishing the Use of Imported Luxuries, 189–90
Wood, Fernando, 459, 585
Woodruff, Lieutenant, 248–49
Woodward, George W., 377
Woolfolk, Pichegru, 191, 194
Woolker, Susan C., 19–20
Worcester County, Md., 278–79
Wright, Horatio G., 72–73, 82, 157, 200, 256, 258, 267
Wycoff, Charles, 175–76

Xenophon, 66

Yates, Richard, 264
Yellow River, 470
York River, 197
Yorke, Lieutenant, 280, 282
Yorktown, Va., 112, 246

Young, John T., 48
Young, Robert B., 491

Zachry, James B., 469–70

*This book is set in 10 point ITC Galliard Pro, a
face designed for digital composition by Matthew Carter
and based on the sixteenth-century face Granjon. The paper
is acid-free lightweight opaque and meets the requirements
for permanence of the American National Standards Institute.
The binding material is Brillianta, a woven rayon cloth made
by Van Heek–Scholco Textielfabrieken, Holland.
Composition by Dedicated Book Services. Printing and
binding by Edwards Brothers Malloy, Ann Arbor.
Designed by Bruce Campbell.*

THE LIBRARY OF AMERICA SERIES

The Library of America fosters appreciation and pride in America's literary heritage by publishing, and keeping permanently in print, authoritative editions of America's best and most significant writing. An independent nonprofit organization, it was founded in 1979 with seed funding from the National Endowment for the Humanities and the Ford Foundation.

1. Herman Melville: *Typee, Omoo, Mardi*
2. Nathaniel Hawthorne: *Tales and Sketches*
3. Walt Whitman: *Poetry and Prose*
4. Harriet Beecher Stowe: *Three Novels*
5. Mark Twain: *Mississippi Writings*
6. Jack London: *Novels and Stories*
7. Jack London: *Novels and Social Writings*
8. William Dean Howells: *Novels 1875–1886*
9. Herman Melville: *Redburn, White-Jacket, Moby-Dick*
10. Nathaniel Hawthorne: *Collected Novels*
11. Francis Parkman: *France and England in North America*, vol. I
12. Francis Parkman: *France and England in North America*, vol. II
13. Henry James: *Novels 1871–1880*
14. Henry Adams: *Novels, Mont Saint Michel, The Education*
15. Ralph Waldo Emerson: *Essays and Lectures*
16. Washington Irving: *History, Tales and Sketches*
17. Thomas Jefferson: *Writings*
18. Stephen Crane: *Prose and Poetry*
19. Edgar Allan Poe: *Poetry and Tales*
20. Edgar Allan Poe: *Essays and Reviews*
21. Mark Twain: *The Innocents Abroad, Roughing It*
22. Henry James: *Literary Criticism: Essays, American & English Writers*
23. Henry James: *Literary Criticism: European Writers & The Prefaces*
24. Herman Melville: *Pierre, Israel Potter, The Confidence-Man, Tales & Billy Budd*
25. William Faulkner: *Novels 1930–1935*
26. James Fenimore Cooper: *The Leatherstocking Tales*, vol. I
27. James Fenimore Cooper: *The Leatherstocking Tales*, vol. II
28. Henry David Thoreau: *A Week, Walden, The Maine Woods, Cape Cod*
29. Henry James: *Novels 1881–1886*
30. Edith Wharton: *Novels*
31. Henry Adams: *History of the U.S. during the Administrations of Jefferson*
32. Henry Adams: *History of the U.S. during the Administrations of Madison*
33. Frank Norris: *Novels and Essays*
34. W.E.B. Du Bois: *Writings*
35. Willa Cather: *Early Novels and Stories*
36. Theodore Dreiser: *Sister Carrie, Jennie Gerhardt, Twelve Men*
37a. Benjamin Franklin: *Silence Dogood, The Busy-Body, & Early Writings*
37b. Benjamin Franklin: *Autobiography, Poor Richard, & Later Writings*
38. William James: *Writings 1902–1910*
39. Flannery O'Connor: *Collected Works*
40. Eugene O'Neill: *Complete Plays 1913–1920*
41. Eugene O'Neill: *Complete Plays 1920–1931*
42. Eugene O'Neill: *Complete Plays 1932–1943*
43. Henry James: *Novels 1886–1890*
44. William Dean Howells: *Novels 1886–1888*
45. Abraham Lincoln: *Speeches and Writings 1832–1858*
46. Abraham Lincoln: *Speeches and Writings 1859–1865*
47. Edith Wharton: *Novellas and Other Writings*
48. William Faulkner: *Novels 1936–1940*
49. Willa Cather: *Later Novels*
50. Ulysses S. Grant: *Memoirs and Selected Letters*
51. William Tecumseh Sherman: *Memoirs*
52. Washington Irving: *Bracebridge Hall, Tales of a Traveller, The Alhambra*
53. Francis Parkman: *The Oregon Trail, The Conspiracy of Pontiac*
54. James Fenimore Cooper: *Sea Tales: The Pilot, The Red Rover*
55. Richard Wright: *Early Works*
56. Richard Wright: *Later Works*
57. Willa Cather: *Stories, Poems, and Other Writings*
58. William James: *Writings 1878–1899*
59. Sinclair Lewis: *Main Street & Babbitt*
60. Mark Twain: *Collected Tales, Sketches, Speeches, & Essays 1852–1890*
61. Mark Twain: *Collected Tales, Sketches, Speeches, & Essays 1891–1910*
62. *The Debate on the Constitution: Part One*
63. *The Debate on the Constitution: Part Two*
64. Henry James: *Collected Travel Writings: Great Britain & America*
65. Henry James: *Collected Travel Writings: The Continent*

66. *American Poetry: The Nineteenth Century*, Vol. 1
67. *American Poetry: The Nineteenth Century*, Vol. 2
68. Frederick Douglass: *Autobiographies*
69. Sarah Orne Jewett: *Novels and Stories*
70. Ralph Waldo Emerson: *Collected Poems and Translations*
71. Mark Twain: *Historical Romances*
72. John Steinbeck: *Novels and Stories 1932–1937*
73. William Faulkner: *Novels 1942–1954*
74. Zora Neale Hurston: *Novels and Stories*
75. Zora Neale Hurston: *Folklore, Memoirs, and Other Writings*
76. Thomas Paine: *Collected Writings*
77. *Reporting World War II: American Journalism 1938–1944*
78. *Reporting World War II: American Journalism 1944–1946*
79. Raymond Chandler: *Stories and Early Novels*
80. Raymond Chandler: *Later Novels and Other Writings*
81. Robert Frost: *Collected Poems, Prose, & Plays*
82. Henry James: *Complete Stories 1892–1898*
83. Henry James: *Complete Stories 1898–1910*
84. William Bartram: *Travels and Other Writings*
85. John Dos Passos: *U.S.A.*
86. John Steinbeck: *The Grapes of Wrath and Other Writings 1936–1941*
87. Vladimir Nabokov: *Novels and Memoirs 1941–1951*
88. Vladimir Nabokov: *Novels 1955–1962*
89. Vladimir Nabokov: *Novels 1969–1974*
90. James Thurber: *Writings and Drawings*
91. George Washington: *Writings*
92. John Muir: *Nature Writings*
93. Nathanael West: *Novels and Other Writings*
94. *Crime Novels: American Noir of the 1930s and 40s*
95. *Crime Novels: American Noir of the 1950s*
96. Wallace Stevens: *Collected Poetry and Prose*
97. James Baldwin: *Early Novels and Stories*
98. James Baldwin: *Collected Essays*
99. Gertrude Stein: *Writings 1903–1932*
100. Gertrude Stein: *Writings 1932–1946*
101. Eudora Welty: *Complete Novels*
102. Eudora Welty: *Stories, Essays, & Memoir*
103. Charles Brockden Brown: *Three Gothic Novels*
104. *Reporting Vietnam: American Journalism 1959–1969*
105. *Reporting Vietnam: American Journalism 1969–1975*
106. Henry James: *Complete Stories 1874–1884*
107. Henry James: *Complete Stories 1884–1891*
108. *American Sermons: The Pilgrims to Martin Luther King Jr.*
109. James Madison: *Writings*
110. Dashiell Hammett: *Complete Novels*
111. Henry James: *Complete Stories 1864–1874*
112. William Faulkner: *Novels 1957–1962*
113. John James Audubon: *Writings & Drawings*
114. *Slave Narratives*
115. *American Poetry: The Twentieth Century*, Vol. 1
116. *American Poetry: The Twentieth Century*, Vol. 2
117. F. Scott Fitzgerald: *Novels and Stories 1920–1922*
118. Henry Wadsworth Longfellow: *Poems and Other Writings*
119. Tennessee Williams: *Plays 1937–1955*
120. Tennessee Williams: *Plays 1957–1980*
121. Edith Wharton: *Collected Stories 1891–1910*
122. Edith Wharton: *Collected Stories 1911–1937*
123. *The American Revolution: Writings from the War of Independence*
124. Henry David Thoreau: *Collected Essays and Poems*
125. Dashiell Hammett: *Crime Stories and Other Writings*
126. Dawn Powell: *Novels 1930–1942*
127. Dawn Powell: *Novels 1944–1962*
128. Carson McCullers: *Complete Novels*
129. Alexander Hamilton: *Writings*
130. Mark Twain: *The Gilded Age and Later Novels*
131. Charles W. Chesnutt: *Stories, Novels, and Essays*
132. John Steinbeck: *Novels 1942–1952*
133. Sinclair Lewis: *Arrowsmith, Elmer Gantry, Dodsworth*
134. Paul Bowles: *The Sheltering Sky, Let It Come Down, The Spider's House*
135. Paul Bowles: *Collected Stories & Later Writings*
136. Kate Chopin: *Complete Novels & Stories*
137. *Reporting Civil Rights: American Journalism 1941–1963*
138. *Reporting Civil Rights: American Journalism 1963–1973*
139. Henry James: *Novels 1896–1899*
140. Theodore Dreiser: *An American Tragedy*
141. Saul Bellow: *Novels 1944–1953*
142. John Dos Passos: *Novels 1920–1925*

143. John Dos Passos: *Travel Books and Other Writings*
144. Ezra Pound: *Poems and Translations*
145. James Weldon Johnson: *Writings*
146. Washington Irving: *Three Western Narratives*
147. Alexis de Tocqueville: *Democracy in America*
148. James T. Farrell: *Studs Lonigan: A Trilogy*
149. Isaac Bashevis Singer: *Collected Stories I*
150. Isaac Bashevis Singer: *Collected Stories II*
151. Isaac Bashevis Singer: *Collected Stories III*
152. Kaufman & Co.: *Broadway Comedies*
153. Theodore Roosevelt: *The Rough Riders, An Autobiography*
154. Theodore Roosevelt: *Letters and Speeches*
155. H. P. Lovecraft: *Tales*
156. Louisa May Alcott: *Little Women, Little Men, Jo's Boys*
157. Philip Roth: *Novels & Stories 1959–1962*
158. Philip Roth: *Novels 1967–1972*
159. James Agee: *Let Us Now Praise Famous Men, A Death in the Family*
160. James Agee: *Film Writing & Selected Journalism*
161. Richard Henry Dana, Jr.: *Two Years Before the Mast & Other Voyages*
162. Henry James: *Novels 1901–1902*
163. Arthur Miller: *Collected Plays 1944–1961*
164. William Faulkner: *Novels 1926–1929*
165. Philip Roth: *Novels 1973–1977*
166. *American Speeches: Part One*
167. *American Speeches: Part Two*
168. Hart Crane: *Complete Poems & Selected Letters*
169. Saul Bellow: *Novels 1956–1964*
170. John Steinbeck: *Travels with Charley and Later Novels*
171. Capt. John Smith: *Writings with Other Narratives*
172. Thornton Wilder: *Collected Plays & Writings on Theater*
173. Philip K. Dick: *Four Novels of the 1960s*
174. Jack Kerouac: *Road Novels 1957–1960*
175. Philip Roth: *Zuckerman Bound*
176. Edmund Wilson: *Literary Essays & Reviews of the 1920s & 30s*
177. Edmund Wilson: *Literary Essays & Reviews of the 1930s & 40s*
178. *American Poetry: The 17th & 18th Centuries*
179. William Maxwell: *Early Novels & Stories*
180. Elizabeth Bishop: *Poems, Prose, & Letters*
181. A. J. Liebling: *World War II Writings*
182s. *American Earth: Environmental Writing Since Thoreau*
183. Philip K. Dick: *Five Novels of the 1960s & 70s*
184. William Maxwell: *Later Novels & Stories*
185. Philip Roth: *Novels & Other Narratives 1986–1991*
186. Katherine Anne Porter: *Collected Stories & Other Writings*
187. John Ashbery: *Collected Poems 1956–1987*
188. John Cheever: *Collected Stories & Other Writings*
189. John Cheever: *Complete Novels*
190. Lafcadio Hearn: *American Writings*
191. A. J. Liebling: *The Sweet Science & Other Writings*
192s. *The Lincoln Anthology: Great Writers on His Life and Legacy from 1860 to Now*
193. Philip K. Dick: *VALIS & Later Novels*
194. Thornton Wilder: *The Bridge of San Luis Rey and Other Novels 1926–1948*
195. Raymond Carver: *Collected Stories*
196. *American Fantastic Tales: Terror and the Uncanny from Poe to the Pulps*
197. *American Fantastic Tales: Terror and the Uncanny from the 1940s to Now*
198. John Marshall: *Writings*
199s. *The Mark Twain Anthology: Great Writers on His Life and Works*
200. Mark Twain: *A Tramp Abroad, Following the Equator, Other Travels*
201. Ralph Waldo Emerson: *Selected Journals 1820–1842*
202. Ralph Waldo Emerson: *Selected Journals 1841–1877*
203. *The American Stage: Writing on Theater from Washington Irving to Tony Kushner*
204. Shirley Jackson: *Novels & Stories*
205. Philip Roth: *Novels 1993–1995*
206. H. L. Mencken: *Prejudices: First, Second, and Third Series*
207. H. L. Mencken: *Prejudices: Fourth, Fifth, and Sixth Series*
208. John Kenneth Galbraith: *The Affluent Society and Other Writings 1952–1967*
209. Saul Bellow: *Novels 1970–1982*
210. Lynd Ward: *Gods' Man, Madman's Drum, Wild Pilgrimage*
211. Lynd Ward: *Prelude to a Million Years, Song Without Words, Vertigo*
212. *The Civil War: The First Year Told by Those Who Lived It*
213. John Adams: *Revolutionary Writings 1755–1775*
214. John Adams: *Revolutionary Writings 1775–1783*
215. Henry James: *Novels 1903–1911*
216. Kurt Vonnegut: *Novels & Stories 1963–1973*

217. *Harlem Renaissance: Five Novels of the 1920s*
218. *Harlem Renaissance: Four Novels of the 1930s*
219. Ambrose Bierce: *The Devil's Dictionary, Tales, & Memoirs*
220. Philip Roth: *The American Trilogy 1997–2000*
221. *The Civil War: The Second Year Told by Those Who Lived It*
222. Barbara W. Tuchman: *The Guns of August & The Proud Tower*
223. Arthur Miller: *Collected Plays 1964–1982*
224. Thornton Wilder: *The Eighth Day, Theophilus North, Autobiographical Writings*
225. David Goodis: *Five Noir Novels of the 1940s & 50s*
226. Kurt Vonnegut: *Novels & Stories 1950–1962*
227. *American Science Fiction: Four Classic Novels 1953–1956*
228. *American Science Fiction: Five Classic Novels 1956–1958*
229. Laura Ingalls Wilder: *The Little House Books, Volume One*
230. Laura Ingalls Wilder: *The Little House Books, Volume Two*
231. Jack Kerouac: *Collected Poems*
232. *The War of 1812: Writings from America's Second War of Independence*
233. *American Antislavery Writings: Colonial Beginnings to Emancipation*
234. *The Civil War: The Third Year Told by Those Who Lived It*
235. Sherwood Anderson: *Collected Stories*
236. Philip Roth: *Novels 2001–2007*
237. Philip Roth: *Nemeses*
238. Aldo Leopold: *A Sand County Almanac & Other Writings on Ecology and Conservation*
239. May Swenson: *Collected Poems*
240. W. S. Merwin: *Collected Poems 1952–1993*
241. W. S. Merwin: *Collected Poems 1996–2011*
242. John Updike: *Collected Early Stories*
243. John Updike: *Collected Later Stories*
244. Ring Lardner: *Stories & Other Writings*
245. Jonathan Edwards: *Writings from the Great Awakening*
246. Susan Sontag: *Essays of the 1960s & 70s*
247. William Wells Brown: *Clotel & Other Writings*
248. Bernard Malamud: *Novels and Stories of the 1940s & 50s*
249. Bernard Malamud: *Novels and Stories of the 1960s*
250. *The Civil War: The Final Year Told by Those Who lived It*
251. *Shakespeare in America: An Anthology from the Revolution to Now*
252. Kurt Vonnegut: *Novels 1976–1985*
253. *American Musicals 1927–1949: The Complete Books & Lyrics of Eight Broadway Classics*
254. *American Musicals 1950–1969: The Complete Books & Lyrics of Eight Broadway Classics*
255. Elmore Leonard: *Four Novels of the 1970s*
256. Louisa May Alcott: *Work, Eight Cousins, Rose in Bloom, Stories & Other Writings*
257. H. L. Mencken: *The Days Trilogy, Expanded Edition*
258. Virgil Thomson: *Music Chronicles 1940–1954*
259. *Art in America 1945–1970: Writings from the Age of Abstract Expressionism, Pop Art, and Minimalism*

To subscribe to the series or to order individual copies, please visit www.loa.org or call (800) 964-5778.

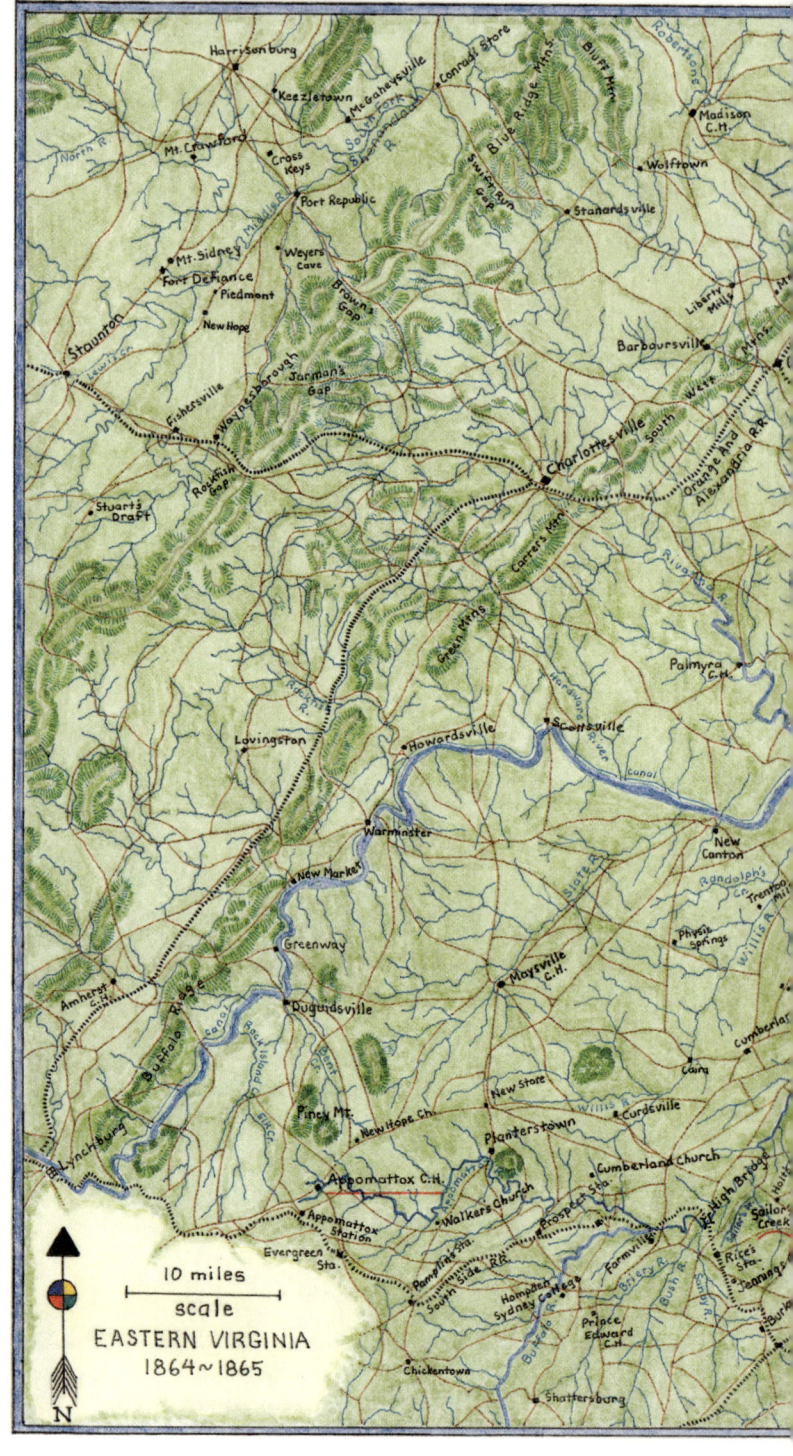

THE CIVIL WAR

THE THIRD YEAR

THE CIVIL WAR

THE THIRD YEAR TOLD BY THOSE WHO LIVED IT

Brooks D. Simpson, editor

THE LIBRARY OF AMERICA

Volume compilation, preface, introduction, notes, and chronology copyright
© 2013 by Literary Classics of the United States, Inc., New York, N.Y.
All rights reserved.
No part of the book may be reproduced commercially
by offset-lithographic or equivalent copying devices without
the permission of the publisher.

Some of the material in this volume is reprinted
by permission of the holders of copyright and publication rights.
Every effort has been made to contact the copyright holders.
If an owner has been unintentionally omitted,
acknowledgment will gladly be made in future printings.
See Note on the Texts on page 792 for further information.

Endpaper maps copyright © 2013 by Earl B. McElfresh,
McElfresh Map Company LLC.

The paper used in this publication meets the
minimum requirements of the American National Standard for
Information Sciences–Permanence of Paper for Printed
Library Materials, ANSI Z39.48–1984.

Distributed to the trade in the United States
by Penguin Random House Inc.
and in Canada by Penguin Random House Canada Ltd.

Library of Congress Control Number: 2012935176
ISBN 978–1–59853–197–8

Second Printing
The Library of America—234

Manufactured in the United States of America

The Civil War:
The Third Year Told by Those Who Lived It
is published with support from

THE ANDREW W. MELLON FOUNDATION

and

**THE NATIONAL ENDOWMENT
FOR THE HUMANITIES**

The Civil War: The Third Year Told by Those Who Lived It
is kept in print in memory of

WILLIAM BRADFORD WARREN
(1934–2010)
for his years of dedicated service to the foundation

with a gift from

The Arthur F. and Alice E. Adams Charitable Foundation

to
the Guardians of American Letters Fund,
established by The Library of America
to ensure that every volume in the series
will be permanently available.

Contents

Preface	xxiii
Introduction	xxv

Edmund DeWitt Patterson: Journal, January 20, 1863
Picket Duty and Snowballs: Virginia, January 1863 1

Theodore A. Dodge: Journal, January 21–24, 1863
The Mud March: Virginia, January 1863 3

Henry Adams to Charles Francis Adams Jr., January 23, 1863
Emancipation and Public Opinion: London, January 1863 . . 9

George G. Meade to Margaret Meade, January 23, 26, and 28, 1863
A Change in Command: Virginia, January 1863 11

Abraham Lincoln to Joseph Hooker, January 26, 1863
Advising a New Commander: Washington, D.C., January 1863 18

John A. Andrew to Francis Shaw, January 30, 1863
Raising a Black Regiment: Massachusetts, January 1863 . . . 20

William Parker Cutler: Diary, February 2 and 9, 1863
Debating Black Soldiers: Washington, D.C., February 1863 . . 23

George Templeton Strong: Diary, February 3–5, 1863
"These be dark blue days": New York, February 1863 25

Oliver W. Norton to Edwin Norton, February 6, 1863
"The soldier's pest": Virginia, February 1863 28

Robert E. Lee to Mary Lee, February 8, 1863
Short Rations: Virginia, February 1863 32

Robert Gould Shaw to Annie Haggerty, February 8, 1863
Accepting a Colonelcy: Virginia, February 1863 34

Richard Cobden to Charles Sumner, February 13, 1863
Emancipation and Intervention: London, February 1863 . . . 36

Isaac Funk: Speech in the Illinois State Senate, February 14, 1863
"These traitors right here": Springfield, February 1863 39

Taylor Peirce to Catharine Peirce, February 16, 1863
"His wife crying over him": Missouri, February 1863 44

William T. Sherman to Thomas Ewing Sr., February 17, 1863,
and to John Sherman, February 18, 1863
The Menace of the Press: Louisiana, February 1863 47

Clement L. Vallandigham: Speech in Congress,
February 23, 1863
Opposing Conscription: Washington, D.C., February 1863 . . . 57

Samuel W. Fiske to the *Springfield Republican*,
February 25, 1863
"Vile and traitorous resolutions": Virginia, February 1863 . . 90

Charles C. Jones Jr. to Charles C. Jones Sr. and Mary Jones,
March 3, 1863
Defending Fort McAllister: Georgia, March 1863 93

Charles C. Jones Sr. to Charles C. Jones Jr., March 4, 1863
"Fight more manfully than ever": Georgia, March 1863 96

Harriet Jacobs to Lydia Maria Child, March 18, 1863
Black Refugees: Virginia, March 1863 98

William Henry Harrison Clayton to Nide and Rachel Pugh,
March 26, 1863
Unionist Refugees: Missouri, March 1863 101

Henry W. Halleck to Ulysses S. Grant, March 31, 1863
*Withdrawing Slaves from the Enemy: Washington, D.C.,
March 1863* 105

Frederick Law Olmsted to John Olmsted, April 1, 1863
The Army before Vicksburg: Louisiana, March 1863 108

Frederick Douglass: Why Should a Colored Man Enlist?,
April 1863
"A war for Emancipation": April 1863 117

Jefferson Davis to William M. Brooks, April 2, 1863
Defending General Pemberton: Virginia, April 1863 122

John B. Jones: Diary, April 2–4, 1863
The Richmond Bread Riot: Virginia, April 1863 124

Whitelaw Reid to the *Cincinnati Gazette*, April 4, 1863
The Necessity of Fighting: April 1863 127

Charles S. Wainwright: Diary, April 5–12, 1863
Lincoln Reviews the Army: Virginia, April 1863. 129

Francis Lieber: No Party Now, But All for Our Country,
April 11, 1863
Loyalty to the Nation: New York, April 1863. 134

Catharine Peirce to Taylor Peirce, April 12, 1863
Home and Family News: Iowa, April 1863. 146

James A. Connolly to Mary Dunn Connolly, April 20, 1863
"Fighting goes like fortunes": Tennessee, April 1863 148

Ulysses S. Grant to Jesse Root Grant, April 21, 1863
"I am doing my best": Louisiana, April 1863 151

David Hunter to Jefferson Davis, April 23, 1863
Threatening Retaliation: South Carolina, April 1863 153

Kate Stone: Journal, April 25, 1863
"A night and day of terror": Louisiana, March–April 1863 . . 155

Wilbur Fisk to *The Green Mountain Freeman*, April 26, 1863
Waiting to March: Virginia, April 1863 161

John Hampden Chamberlayne to Martha Burwell
Chamberlayne, April 30, 1863
"Rain, mud, & night": Virginia, April 1863 166

Sarah Morgan: Diary, April 30, 1863
Expelling "enemies": Louisiana, April 1863 169

Samuel Pickens: Diary, May 1–3, 1863
Battle of Chancellorsville: Virginia, May 1863 172

Jedediah Hotchkiss: Journal, May 2–6, 1863
"Disorder reigned supreme": Virginia, May 1863 178

Taylor Peirce to Catharine Peirce, May 4, 1863
Battle of Port Gibson: Mississippi, May 1863 184

Catherine Edmondston: Diary, May 5–7, 9, and 11–12, 1863
"The nation's idol": North Carolina, May 1863 189

Charles F. Morse to His Family, May 7, 1863
"The great Joe Hooker": Virginia, May 1863. 195

Samuel W. Fiske to the *Springfield Republican*, May 9
and 11, 1863
"Disgraceful and disastrous defeat": Virginia, May 1863 . . . 205

Charles B. Wilder: Testimony before the American Freedmen's
   Inquiry Commission, May 9, 1863
Escaping Slavery: Virginia, May 1863   213

Thomas Wentworth Higginson: Journal, May 10, 1863
Commanding a Black Regiment: South Carolina, May 1863 .   216

Edward O. Guerrant: Diary, May 15, 1863
Mourning Stonewall Jackson: Kentucky, May 1863   219

George Richard Browder: Diary, May 17–26, 1863
Swearing Allegiance: Kentucky, May 1863   222

Harper's Weekly: The Arrest of Vallandigham, May 30, 1863
"The people can be trusted": New York, May 1863   226

Oliver W. Norton to Elizabeth Norton Poss, June 8, 1863
Meeting "Secesh" Civilians: Virginia, June 1863   229

Robert Gould Shaw to Annie Haggerty Shaw, June 9–13, 1863
The Burning of Darien: Georgia, June 1863   232

William Winters to Harriet Winters, June 9, 1863
Siege of Vicksburg: Mississippi, June 1863   238

Matthew M. Miller to His Aunt, June 10, 1863
Battle of Milliken's Bend: Louisiana, June 1863   240

Robert E. Lee to Jefferson Davis, June 10, 1863
"Dividing and weakening" the North: Virginia, June 1863 . .   243

William T. Sherman to John T. Swayne, June 11, 1863
"The hand of destruction": Mississippi, June 1863   246

Henry C. Whelan to Mary Whelan, June 11, 1863
Battle of Brandy Station: Virginia, June 1863   249

Abraham Lincoln to Erastus Corning and Others,
   June 12, 1863
*The Constitution in Wartime: Washington, D.C.,
   June 1863*   254

William Henry Harrison Clayton to Amos and Grace Clayton,
   June 18, 1863, and to George Washington Clayton and John
   Quincy Adams Clayton, June 28, 1863
The Vicksburg Siege Continues: Mississippi, June 1863   264

Charles B. Haydon: Journal, June 20, 1863
"A soldier never knows": Mississippi, June 1863.   270

William T. Sherman to Ellen Ewing Sherman, June 27, 1863 *"They have sowed the wind": Mississippi, June 1863*	273
Edmund DeWitt Patterson: Journal, June 24–30, 1863 *Invading the North: Maryland and Pennsylvania, June 1863.*	278
Lafayette McLaws to Emily McLaws, June 28, 1863 *"A very different race": Pennsylvania, June 1863*	281
Alpheus S. Williams to Irene and Mary Williams, June 29, 1863 *Changing Commanders: Maryland, June 1863*	285
Samuel W. Fiske to the *Springfield Republican*, June 30, 1863 *"This business of war": Maryland, June 1863*	288
Arthur James Lyon Fremantle: Diary, July 1–4, 1863 *Battle of Gettysburg: Pennsylvania, July 1863*	292
Samuel Pickens: Diary, July 1–3, 1863 *"What terrible work": Pennsylvania, July 1863.*	308
Francis Adams Donaldson: Narrative of Gettysburg, July 2–3, 1863 *"This trial of the nerves": Pennsylvania, July 1863.*	312
Elizabeth Blair Lee to Samuel Phillips Lee, July 3 and 4–5, 1863 *News of Gettysburg: Washington, D.C., July 1863*	325
Joshua Lawrence Chamberlain to George B. Herendeen, July 6, 1863 *Defending Little Round Top: Pennsylvania, July 1863.*	328
Henry Livermore Abbott to Josiah Gardner Abbott, July 6, 1863 *Defeating Pickett's Charge: Pennsylvania, July 1863.*	333
Lafayette McLaws to Emily McLaws, July 7, 1863 *"A series of terrible engagements": Pennsylvania, July 1863* . .	338
Cornelia Hancock to Her Cousin, July 7, 1863, and to Ellen Hancock Child, July 8, 1863 *A Nurse at Gettysburg: Pennsylvania, July 1863*	341
Catharine Peirce to Taylor Peirce, July 5, 1863 *Celebrating the Fourth: Iowa, July 1863*	346

William Henry Harrison Clayton to Amos and Grace Clayton,
July 5, 1863
Vicksburg Surrenders: Mississippi, July 1863   348

William T. Sherman to Ellen Ewing Sherman, July 5, 1863
"The event of the war": Mississippi, July 1863.   352

William Winters to Harriet Winters, July 6, 1863
A "forlorn and forsaken" place: Mississippi, July 1863   357

Benjamin B. French: Journal, July 8, 1863
"The glorious result": Washington, D.C., July 1863.   360

Catherine Edmondston: Diary, July 8–11, 1863
War News and Rumors: North Carolina, July 1863   362

George Hamilton Perkins to Susan G. Perkins, July 29, 1863
Fighting on the Mississippi: Louisiana, July 1863   368

Charles B. Haydon: Journal, July 11, 1863
"I must die very soon": Mississippi, July 1863   372

John Hay: Diary, July 11–15, 1863
*"The Prest was deeply grieved": Washington, D.C.,
July 1863*   375

Abraham Lincoln to Ulysses S. Grant, July 13, 1863
Acknowledging a Victory: Washington, D.C., July 1863   377

Abraham Lincoln to George G. Meade, July 14, 1863
*"Your golden opportunity is gone": Washington, D.C.,
July 1863*   378

Samuel Pickens: Diary, July 14, 1863
*Crossing the Potomac: Maryland and West Virginia,
July 1863*   380

George Templeton Strong: Diary, July 13–17, 1863
The Draft Riots: New York, July 1863   382

Emma Holmes: Diary, July 16–19, 1863
Battle of Charleston Harbor: South Carolina, July 1863   390

Walter H. Taylor to Richard Taylor, July 17, 1863
"We crippled them severely": Virginia, July 1863   397

James Henry Gooding to the *New Bedford Mercury*,
July 20, 1863
Battle of Fort Wagner: South Carolina, July 1863   402

Lewis Douglass to Amelia Loguen, July 20, 1863
"Not a man flinched": South Carolina, July 1863 405

Charlotte Forten: Journal, July 20–24, 1863
Mourning Colonel Shaw: South Carolina, July 1863 407

Maria Lydig Daly: Diary, July 23, 1863
"Four days of great anxiety": New York, July 1863. 411

Herman Melville: The House-top
"The Atheist roar of riot": New York, July 1863 414

Henry Adams to Charles Francis Adams Jr., July 23, 1863
News of Victory: London, July 1863. 416

George G. Meade to Henry W. Halleck, July 31, 1863
Justifying a Decision: Virginia, July 1863 420

Robert E. Lee to Jefferson Davis, July 31, 1863
"I am alone to blame": Virginia, July 1863 423

Hannah Johnson to Abraham Lincoln, July 31, 1863
"What is right": New York, July 1863. 425

Frederick Douglass to George L. Stearns, August 1, 1863
Refusing to Recruit: New York, August 1863 427

Frederick Douglass: The Commander-in-Chief and His Black Soldiers, August 1863
Demanding Retaliation: New York, August 1863 431

Walt Whitman to Lewis Kirk Brown, August 1, 11, and 15, 1863
Visiting the Wounded: Washington, D.C., August 1863 435

George E. Stephens to the *Weekly Anglo-African*, August 7, 1863
Demanding Equal Pay: South Carolina, August 1863. 441

Robert E. Lee to Jefferson Davis, August 8, 1863
An Offer to Resign: Virginia, August 1863. 447

Jefferson Davis to Robert E. Lee, August 11, 1863
Refusing a Resignation: Virginia, August 1863 450

Wilbur Fisk to *The Green Mountain Freeman*, August 10, 1863
Pillaging Wood: Virginia, August 1863 452

Frederick Douglass to George L. Stearns, August 12, 1863
Meeting the President: Washington, D.C., August 1863   457

William H. Neblett to Elizabeth Scott Neblett,
August 18, 1863
Demoralization at Galveston: Texas, August 1863   461

Richard Cordley: Narrative of the Lawrence Massacre
"Such a scene of horror": Kansas, August 1863   465

Ulysses S. Grant to Abraham Lincoln, August 23, 1863
The Impact of Black Troops: Illinois, August 1863   488

Jonathan Worth to Jesse G. Henshaw, August 24, 1863
Peace Meetings: North Carolina, August 1863.   490

John M. Schofield to Thomas Ewing Jr., August 25, 1863
"The most radical remedy": Missouri, August 1863   492

Abraham Lincoln to James C. Conkling, August 26, 1863
*Emancipation and Black Soldiers: Washington, D.C.,
August 1863*   495

Ulysses S. Grant to Elihu B. Washburne, August 30, 1863
"Slavery is already dead": Mississippi, August 1863   500

Charles Francis Adams to Lord Russell, September 5, 1863
The Laird Rams: London, September 1863   502

Charles C. Jones Jr. to Mary Jones, September 6 and 9, 1863
The Siege of Charleston: South Carolina, September 1863 . . .   505

Raphael Semmes: Journal, September 16–24, 1863
The Raider Alabama: Cape Colony, September 1863.   508

William T. Sherman to Henry W. Halleck, September 17, 1863
Reconstruction: Mississippi, September 1863   512

William W. Heartsill: Journal, September 17–28, 1863
Battle of Chickamauga: Georgia, September 1863   521

John S. Jackman: Diary, September 18–21, 1863
"Lying so thick over the field": Georgia, September 1863   531

Kate Cumming: Journal, September 28–October 1, 1863
"The nameless dead": Georgia, September–October 1863   535

Jefferson Davis: Speech at Missionary Ridge, October 10, 1863
Tennessee, October 1863   546

Oliver W. Norton to Elizabeth Norton Poss, October 15, 1863
Becoming an Officer: Washington, D.C., October 1863 548

Jefferson Davis: Speech at Wilmington, November 5, 1863
North Carolina, November 1863 551

Walter H. Taylor to Bettie Saunders, November 15, 1863
"We have no fears": Virginia, November 1863 555

Cornelia Hancock to an Unknown Correspondent,
   November 15, 1863
Contraband Hospital: Washington, D.C., November 1863. . . 560

John Hay: Diary, November 18–19, 1863
A Trip to Gettysburg: Pennsylvania, November 1863. 562

Abraham Lincoln: Address at Gettysburg, November 19, 1863
Pennsylvania, November 1863 566

Petition from the Colored Citizens of Beaufort,
   November 20, 1863
Protesting Impressment: North Carolina, November 1863 . . . 568

William Wrenshall Smith: Journal, November 13–25, 1863
Battle of Chattanooga: Tennessee, November 1863 569

Montgomery C. Meigs: Journal, November 23–25, 1863
"Wild with excitement": Tennessee, November 1863 582

James A. Connolly to Mary Dunn Connolly, November 26
   and December 7, 1863
*"The grandest sight I ever saw": Tennessee and Georgia,
   November 1863* 590

Theodore Lyman: Journal, November 26–December 2, 1863
*The Mine Run Campaign: Virginia,
   November–December 1863* 601

Wilbur Fisk to *The Green Mountain Freeman*, November 29
   and December 8, 1863
*A Soldier at Mine Run: Virginia,
   November–December 1863* 611

George G. Meade to Margaret Meade, December 2 and 7, 1863
"My conscience is clear": Virginia, December 1863 622

Frederick Douglass: Our Work Is Not Done, December 4, 1863
"Every free man a voter": Pennsylvania, December 1863 . . . 627

Abraham Lincoln: Annual Message to Congress,
December 8, 1863
Washington, D.C., December 1863 637

Abraham Lincoln: Proclamation of Amnesty and Reconstruction,
December 8, 1863
Washington, D.C., December 1863 654

George Templeton Strong: Diary, December 11–13, 1863
Subduing the South: New York, December 1863 658

Catherine Edmondston: Diary, December 11, 1863
*"One misfortune follows another": North Carolina,
December 1863* 661

Mary Chesnut: Diary, January 1, 1864
"God help my country": Virginia, January 1864. 664

Judith W. McGuire: Diary, January 1, 1864
"And yet we must go on": Virginia, January 1864. 674

Patrick R. Cleburne: Memorandum on Emancipation and
Enlisting Black Soldiers, January 2, 1864
Sacrificing Slavery: Georgia, January 1864 677

William T. Sherman to Roswell M. Sawyer, January 31, 1864
"They have appealed to War": Mississippi, January 1864 . . . 687

Lois Bryan Adams to the *Detroit Advertiser and Tribune*,
February 8 and 23, 1864
*Meeting "Father Abraham": Washington, D.C.,
February 1864* 693

Francis J. Higginson to John A. Dahlgren, February 18, 1864
Sinking of the Housatonic: South Carolina, February 1864 . . 701

James H. Tomb: Notes on the *H. L. Hunley*, January 1865
*A Submarine Torpedo Boat: South Carolina, October 1863–
February 1864* 703

Judith W. McGuire: Diary, February 28, 1864
A Soldier's Widow: Virginia, February 1864. 705

John Paris: Sermon Preached at Kinston, February 28, 1864
Hanging Deserters: North Carolina, February 1864 708

Oliver W. Norton to Elizabeth Norton Poss,
February 29, 1864
Battle of Olustee: Florida, February 1864 723

John B. Jones: Diary, March 1–2 and 5, 1864
The Kilpatrick-Dahlgren Raid: Virginia, March 1864 728

Ulysses S. Grant to William T. Sherman, March 4, 1864
Summoned to Washington: Tennessee, March 1864. 733

William T. Sherman to Ulysses S. Grant, March 10, 1864
"Come out West": Tennessee, March 1864 735

Chronology 739
Biographical Notes 755
Note on the Texts 792
Notes 809
Index 883

Preface

"Has there ever been another historical crisis of the magnitude of 1861–65 in which so many people were so articulate?"
—Edmund Wilson

THIS Library of America volume is the third in a four-volume series bringing together memorable and significant writing by participants in the American Civil War. Each volume in the series covers approximately one year of the conflict, from the election of Abraham Lincoln in November 1860 to the end of the war in the spring of 1865, and presents a chronological selection of documents from the broadest possible range of authoritative sources—diaries, letters, speeches, military reports, newspaper articles, memoirs, poems, and public papers. Drawing upon an immense and unique body of American writing, the series offers a narrative of the war years that encompasses military and political events and their social and personal reverberations. Created by persons of every class and condition, the writing included here captures the American nation and the American language in the crucial period of their modern formation. Selections have been chosen for their historical significance, their literary quality, and their narrative energy, and are printed from the best available sources. The goal has been to shape a narrative that is both broad and balanced in scope, while at the same time doing justice to the number and diversity of voices and perspectives preserved for us in the writing of the era.

Introduction

On January 1, 1863, President Abraham Lincoln, weary from a day of greeting well-wishers and shaking hands, slowly put pen to paper and signed the Emancipation Proclamation. His signature declared free more than three million people, but the fulfillment of the proclamation's promise was highly contingent upon the course of events. Lincoln's action might be declared unconstitutional by the Supreme Court or be revoked by his successor if the Democrats won the 1864 presidential election. Above all, the success of emancipation depended on the Union winning the war, an outcome that was far from certain as the new year began.

The previous year had shown how uncertain the course of the conflict could be. After a winter and spring marked by northern victories in Kentucky, western Tennessee, northern Arkansas, coastal North Carolina, and southern Louisiana, the Union retreat during the Seven Days' Battles outside Richmond in late June sharply curtailed northern hopes that the war might be won before the end of the year. Union expectations that support for southern independence might erode in the face of battlefield reverses or the experience of occupation proved wistful. Lincoln found his faith in southern unionism misplaced, as many tepid loyalists declined to assert themselves forcefully. In turn, Confederate hopes for decisive victory in 1862 faded after late summer counteroffensives in Kentucky and Maryland ended in retreat. Both of these abortive incursions into the border states failed to rally large numbers of supporters to the secessionist cause, and in their wake expectations diminished that the British and French governments would recognize Confederate independence or offer to mediate a settlement to the conflict.

Despite these setbacks, many Confederates began 1863 confident of continued battlefield success in the east. Robert E. Lee had proved himself to be an audacious and determined commander when he drove George B. McClellan away from Richmond and routed John Pope at Manassas. Determined to retain the strategic initiative, Lee then invaded Maryland, where he barely fended off McClellan at Antietam before escaping back across the Potomac. In December he had defeated the Army of the Potomac when its new commander, Ambrose Burnside, launched an offensive across the Rappahannock at Fredericksburg. After fighting four campaigns against numerically superior opponents and besting three Union generals, Lee believed the Army of Northern Virginia was nearly invincible. Many white southerners shared his conviction, as well as Lee's deep confidence in his three principal subordinates, Thomas J. (Stonewall) Jackson, James Longstreet, and J.E.B. Stuart. But few observers could be oblivious to the human cost of Lee's four campaigns in 1862. While the Union had lost more than 70,000 men killed, wounded, captured, or missing fighting Lee, casualties in the Army of Northern Virginia under his command totaled 48,000. This was a rate of attrition that the Confederacy, with three-tenths the white male population of the free states, could not sustain indefinitely. And despite its bloody repulse at Fredericksburg, the Army of the Potomac began the new year still encamped on the northern bank of the Rappahannock, only sixty miles from Richmond.

No Union commander in 1862 had matched Lee's success. Once hailed as the "Young Napoleon" by his supporters in the press, George B. McClellan had failed to take Richmond and was judged by Lincoln to be too lethargic in the wake of Antietam. Relieved of the command of his beloved Army of the Potomac, McClellan was awaiting "further orders" at year's end. John Pope had been sent to Minnesota to fight the Dakota after his defeat at Manassas, while the disaster at Fredericksburg appeared to confirm Ambrose Burnside's own doubts about his ability to lead an army. In the west, the nearly unknown Ulysses S. Grant had emerged to national prominence with his stunning victory at Fort Donelson in February 1862, but his subsequent narrow escape from defeat at Shiloh had drawn intense criticism. Grant spent the summer and fall defending Union gains in western Tennessee and northern Mississippi before making a failed attempt to take Vicksburg at year's end that renewed doubts about his leadership. In the upper South, Don Carlos Buell, the commander of the Army of the Ohio, had turned back the Confederate invasion of

Kentucky but was then relieved by Lincoln for failing to pursue Braxton Bragg's retreating Army of Tennessee. At the turn of the year William S. Rosecrans, Buell's replacement, won a narrow victory at Stones River that forced Bragg to fall back into southern Tennessee. While the Confederacy succeeded in 1862 in retaining control of the Mississippi between Vicksburg and Port Hudson, its commanders failed at Pea Ridge, Shiloh, Iuka, Corinth, Perryville, Prairie Grove, and Stones River to win victories that would give it the strategic initiative in the west and allow it to reclaim territory lost to the Union in the first half of the year.

Support for the conflict wavered in 1862 on both sides as its cost in blood and treasure mounted, and it became increasingly hard to recruit volunteers motivated by patriotism or the desire for adventure. In the spring the Confederate Congress passed a conscription act that provoked widespread evasion and resistance throughout the South, especially in upland regions. By midyear Union authorities were also considering introducing conscription, although for the moment federal and state officials relied upon bounties and the threat of a nine-month militia draft to encourage enlistment. In the fall, Democrats capitalized on war weariness and opposition to emancipation to win state elections in Illinois, Indiana, New Jersey, and New York, and reduce the Republican majority in the House of Representatives by thirty-four seats. Although some Democrats favored continued prosecution of the war while others advocated reunion through negotiation, the party was united in its hostility to emancipation and its willingness to ask voters why white men should die so black people could be free.

It was only after months of cautious deliberation that Lincoln decided in the summer of 1862 that the immediate emancipation of the slaves in Confederate-controlled territory was necessary to save the Union. In March he had proposed using federal funds to compensate slave-owners in states that adopted plans for gradual emancipation. Determined to prevent any "radical change of our social system," representatives from the border states refused to support this proposal. At the same time, Lincoln angered many blacks and Radical Republicans by repeatedly calling for the voluntary colonization of former slaves abroad, which he earnestly believed would protect the freed people from the racial backlash he expected to follow emancipation. While Lincoln had sought support for gradual emancipation, he also signed into law a series of antislavery measures initiated by Republicans in Congress. In the spring and summer of 1862, Congress prohibited the military from returning runaway slaves, abolished slavery in the District of Columbia and the federal territories, and passed a confiscation act that created an unwieldy legal mechanism for freeing slaves held by disloyal masters. As Congress, the President, and the cabinet debated alternative courses of action, thousands of slaves had sought freedom by fleeing into Union-held territory, while thousands more were liberated by the advance of the Union armies, eroding the foundations of the "peculiar institution" from below. By year's end the prospect of enlisting blacks in the Union forces offered the promise not only of augmenting northern military power, but also of laying the foundation for claims of citizenship on behalf of those who would now help to preserve the nation.

As 1863 opened, the course of the war was as uncertain as ever. Would Lee continue his mastery over the commanders of the Army of the Potomac, and at what human cost? Would Grant take Vicksburg? Could Bragg regain central Tennessee, or would Rosecrans seize Chattanooga and open the way for a Union invasion of Georgia? Would the Union navy continue to tighten its hold on the southern coastline, or was there some way for the Confederates to break the blockade? Was the possibility of foreign intervention indeed at an end, or could it be revived in the wake of new Confederate successes? What measures would each side have to embrace to maintain their armies, and how would they affect public support for the conflict? In particular, how would the Confederacy be able to reconcile the principle of states' rights with a central government that enforced conscription and asserted the power to impose martial law? Would slaves in Confederate-controlled areas rebel or flee en masse? Would emancipation help the Union war effort, or would it only intensify opposition among Democrats to the policies of the Lincoln administration? How would Confederates, and white Union soldiers, react to the sight of black men in blue uniforms?

By the beginning of 1863 both sides had reluctantly accepted the reality that only long and hard fighting could bring the conflict to an end, although there was still a lingering hope that one great battle, an American Austerlitz or Waterloo, might go far to achieve that result. What was even more uncertain than the war's end was what would follow. If, as Lincoln said, "broken eggs can not be mended," it seemed increasingly likely that the old union was so broken by war that whatever nation—or nations—emerged from the conflict would take on radical new forms that no one could envision.

Brooks D. Simpson

PICKET DUTY AND SNOWBALLS:
VIRGINIA, JANUARY 1863

Edmund DeWitt Patterson: Journal, January 20, 1863

Following the Union defeat at Fredericksburg on December 13, 1862, the opposing armies in northern Virginia faced each other across the Rappahannock River. With the Confederate Army of Northern Virginia on the southern bank was Edmund DeWitt Patterson, a native of Lorain County, Ohio, who had moved to northern Alabama shortly before the war and enlisted in the 9th Alabama Infantry in 1861. He first saw action in the Peninsula campaign during the spring of 1862, was seriously wounded at Glendale on June 30, and rejoined his regiment in late November as a lieutenant.

January 20th 1863. I have almost given up writing in my journal for the fact that I have nothing in the world to record. There is too much sameness about this kind of soldier life. One day is the repetition of the duties of the day before, and I can always tell what (in all probability) I will be doing on the same day one month ahead. Capt. Crow is often on other duty, Cannon and Chandler on detached service, and I am generally in command of the Company. Every fifth day at three o'clock P.M. I go on picket and remain twenty four hours. We stand on our side of the river and look at the Yanks. They stand on their side and look at us. Sometimes we exchange papers, though in violation of orders, and sometimes the boys trade them tobacco for coffee. Just below the dam the water is not more than three feet deep, and the boys wade out to a little shoal of rocks in the middle of the stream and meet and take a drink together, make such trades as they wish, then each returns to his own side again. I have to visit some other post in the meantime, or make it convenient to have business in another direction, for it would not do for me to see these violations of orders. And yet I like to read a New York or Philadelphia newspaper.

The principal amusement of the troops now-a-days is snowballing. A great many of them never saw any snow, or at least not enough to cover the ground, until last winter, and many of the Florida troops have never seen any at all. Sometimes whole brigades and even divisions, with their officers in command, get into a battle with snowballs. Then the sport becomes exciting, and the balls fly so thick that the opposing forces scarcely distinguish each other. I think this imitation battle is decidedly more pleasant than the real. The health of the company and regiment is much better than it was last winter. The men have become acclimated and accustomed to exposure, and it would be almost impossible to kill one of them now, by anything except a bullet. About this time last winter, quite a number of our company was sick, several of whom died. McKelvey, Fowler, Irion, Webb, and several others. Thus far our death from disease has been more than from battle. And I believe that the same thing is true with every command in the army, at least with those from the Gulf States.

THE MUD MARCH: VIRGINIA, JANUARY 1863

Theodore A. Dodge: Journal, January 21–24, 1863

In November 1862 President Lincoln had chosen Major General Ambrose Burnside to replace George B. McClellan as the commander of the Army of the Potomac. Burnside's failed attack at Fredericksburg in December cost the Union more than 12,600 men killed, wounded, or missing, and caused much of the army to lose confidence in his leadership. Determined to take the offensive again, Burnside decided to cross the Rappahannock four miles upriver from Fredericksburg and outflank Robert E. Lee's defensive positions from the west. One of the regiments participating in the maneuver was the 119th New York Infantry, part of the Third Division of the Eleventh Corps. Its adjutant, Theodore A. Dodge, had been commissioned as a lieutenant in the 101st New York in 1862 and had fought in the Seven Days' Battles and the Second Bull Run campaign before being wounded at Chantilly on September 1. In November 1862 he joined the 119th New York, where he served alongside his father, Nathaniel S. Dodge, the regimental quartermaster ("Q.M.").

Camp near Berea, 4 miles N.W. of Falmouth
January 21st 1863

At last, after our numerous scares of being under orders to march at a moment's notice, we received day before yesterday orders to move "at 7 A.M. tomorrow. Further particulars will be sent," said the order, and we accordingly went to bed at 9 P.M., ready to start at any moment to carry out the provisions of any further orders that might arrive. About an hour after I had gone to sleep, an order did arrive, giving the order of march and directing our Brigade to fall in behind the 1st Brigade, which would pass our camp about 8 A.M.

This gave us a clue as to the direction in which we were to march, viz. towards Falmouth. We thought we should go to Brooke's Station, and that the Corps would be stationed along the line of communications between Aquia Creek

Landing and Burnside's Army. We were partly right. Just as we were breakfasting at 6¼ o'clock A.M. yesterday (20th), Lt. Stoldt, the Acting Assistant Adjutant General of our Brigade, came over with orders not to wait for the 1st Brigade but to fall into line and march at once. So, we hurried our things together and got off at 7 o'clock.

We took the road towards Falmouth, and came over the road which Stahel's Division had taken for Aquia Creek Landing and Brooke's Station; and further we found that we were destined for Hartwood Church. This point we reached about 3 P.M. and our present position about 5. The roads were good and we had a very prosperous march. Berea is on the direct road from Warrenton to Falmouth, 4 miles from the latter and consists of a fine farm house and accompanying buildings. Near this house we met Burnside's Army passing on to Banks's Ford, 4 miles from here, where a pontoon bridge is to be thrown across and the Army to pass the river. They expected to have done this last night but the wind was so high and the rain in such torrents that it was not possible. We got a little supper and then retired for the night about 8 o'clock.

The Q. M. had brought his trains along the good road at a fast pace, getting here almost as soon as we did, so that we were able to put up two tents—one for the Colonel and Lieutenant Col., and one for the Q. M. and myself. We tried to make a fire in the tent, but the stove would not draw on account of the wind, and the smoke nearly drove us wild; so we at length gave it up as a bad job, and took refuge in our cots. Towards morning, I woke up and found the wind had loosened the pins of the tent, and that it was on the point of falling. So I determined to get up and fix it. I groped about for my specs, which having found, I was trying in the dark to distinguish between the Q. M.'s boots and mine, when a sudden gust of wind raised the unfortunate tent from over our heads, and carried it several yards to leeward of its original position, when it suddenly collapsed, leaving us at the mercy of the elements. "Quarter Master!" shouted I to the cot opposite. No answer. "Quarter Master!" "What's the matter?" said he, coolly uncovering his head which had to that moment been buried in blankets. When he saw the desolation around him and the wild waving branches of the tree above him, he was filled with astonishment. It was a mercy the tent pole did not fall upon him. We roused teamsters & servants and finally got the tent pitched again. It was now nearly 6 o'clock, so we concluded to stay up and make a fire, which we accordingly did. Now (towards noon) the wind has gradually abated and there is a chance for getting fixed.

Batteries and troops are pouring on towards the river incessantly. We have just got notice that we shall stop here some time, so before night we hope to be all right again.

January 22nd 1863

Much to our surprise & gratification, a mail came this morning bringing us three letters from you. One which had been delayed since the 6th, one of the 16th and one of the 17th inst. We did not expect a mail so soon after our arrival here, and were in high glee to find our postal communications again established. We were very sorry to hear that your chilly, damp weather and east wind was afoot again and commencing his annoying attacks on your throat. What an inveterate throttler he is to be sure! He never seizes you anywhere else, but always straight at your throat. I hope, dear Mother, that his grip may be less powerful this time than his last attack.

We seem to be here to guard the communications between Aquia Landing and Burnside's Army. Stahel's Division is posted at the former place and along the R. R. to Brooke's Station, from whence to Falmouth I believe Von Steinwehr guards the R. R.; from Falmouth to Burnside his own Division along the Warrenton Turnpike. At all events, we have the post nearest the main Army, tho' if the weather should now prove so bad as to oblige us to go into winter quarters I should much prefer Aquia Landing; for a more desolate place you never saw than the one we are now occupying, rendered doubly so by rain and wind. Troops are continually passing on to the river below, and really when I see the poor wretched fellows tramping through the ankle deep mud, and remember from many sad experiences how hard such marching is, I feel as if our position were to be envied.

You have no idea of how soon the roads turn from good to bad here in Virginia. A clayey soil is hard and the very best for marching on in favorable weather, but let it rain but an hour and troops and wagons march over the road, and the mud is worse than anyone who has not been in Virginia can conceive of. The wagon train passing down to the river got stuck last night and could not move for many hours. If Burnside gets far away from the R. R. there will be the devil to pay, for the wagon trains can scarce move over the roads. You watch a train a little while and you will see horses dropping dead from sheer exhaustion every now and then. A four-horse team cannot possibly drag more than 1,000 lbs. over these roads and scarcely that.

Trains are a very different thing to manage here from what they are in Europe, where the roads are good. A turnpike here is what would be a shocking bad country lane in England. The rain ceased about 10 this evening, but the wind has not yet entirely subsided. These N. E. storms generally last 36 hours at least.

January 23, 1863

As expected, so it has come to pass. The batteries, which moved down to Banks's Ford 3 days ago, are now moving back again. It seems that Mud is really King. He sets down his foot and says, "Ye shall not pass," and lo and behold we cannot. But Mud wields more despotic sway these last two days than ever I saw him wield before. The horses sank into mud up to their bellies, and it is said down near the river you sometimes have to put sticks under the mules' necks to prevent their being engulfed in the very slough of despond. How inspirited and confident the men feel in their leaders you can well imagine. The Genl. Commanding announces to the Army of the Potomac "that they are about to meet the enemy face to face once more," says General Order No. 7, January 20th. "Go back from where you came," says order of today.

This Corps will probably wait till the Grand Divisions of Hooker and Franklin have once more waded their weary way through the mud to their old positions near Falmouth; then we shall do the same. At all events we shall have drier roads by that time, I hope. How it happens that Burnside did not make calculations upon the possibility of its raining whilst he made his move, I cannot imagine. It would seem that plans ought not to be made which rest on the favor of the elements.

The Q. M. and I pitched a new tent yesterday, and gave the one which blew from over us on the 21st to the Commissary Sergt. Owing to a scarcity of tents, the Q. M. and I have our Departments together. It is rather crowded on account of his having one clerk and I having the Sergt. Major and another clerk in the tent most of the time, but we get along tolerably well. The weather is still very damp, and as we have no flooring to our tent, cold feet are prevalent. This is however one of the minor evils. We have got out of wood today, on account of most of the rails round the farms here have been taken to corduroy the roads, and we cut down an immense oak tree close by our tents. It was a tree several hundred years old probably, & very large. We got a corporal of Co. K, who is a woodman by trade, to cut it down, and we watched with great interest to see whether he would fell it clear of the Colonel's tent and ours, which he succeeded in doing. The old tree fell with a terrible crash and thousands of branches flew up into the air like spray from a waterfall.

The other night, when the tent blew over, it broke my camp cot, and I have to set it up every night now with the greatest care, and lie still on my back all night for fear of its giving way and my coming down on to the ground. It is one of those complicated cots that pack up very small and is exceedingly difficult to mend. We have been wishing to ride down to the river these past two days, but the mud is so deep it is much too serious an undertaking.

Berea Church, January 24th 1863

A singular circumstance occurred today. The pontoons, the horses to which had been used in bringing the artillery up from the river along these excruciating roads, were being dragged up by Regiments, about 50 to each pontoon, fire engine style. This, though hard work, rather pleases the boys, & they were cheering as they came to good bits of road and running races with each other. We sat in our tents watching them on the road, about 150 yards off, when the Lieut. Col. proposed to go nearer and see what Regiments were there. As we reached the road the Lieut. Col. spoke to a young Lieutenant, who was trudging along through the mud. He turned out to be Willie Hyslop, whose family we know so well and whom we had thus singularly met. He got leave of his Colonel to come over to our tent & stay for dinner. We found him a very intelligent fellow and had a pleasant talk with him.

We asked him what the troops in his Division thought of this move. He said they quoted the proclamation, "If the Almighty is willing," and had come to the conclusion that the Almighty was not willing; that they all thoroughly laughed at Burnside, & were of the opinion that if McClellan was known to have been reinstated, not only would such cheers go up from the Army of the Potomac as were never heard, but that they would march with such a will and confidence upon Fredericksburg, either to storm the heights or to outflank the town, as would inevitably insure success. Col. P. is an inveterate opponent of McClellan, and was pumping Hyslop for his opinion, when he got the above, which *rather* took him down.

Poor Hyslop has been in active service since June '61, and is now only Lieutenant, never having been home at all. It is curious how different the chances of promotion are in different Regiments. Here is Hyslop, for example, who has been 2 years in the service, has been in almost every battle, and has served well and faithfully, and has only risen one step in all that time. Then take George Pomeroy, who has, in much less time, risen from Lieut. to Lieut. Col., and is now paymaster in the Regular Army. Some of the very best of the old Regiments are slowest in promotions.

EMANCIPATION AND PUBLIC OPINION:
LONDON, JANUARY 1863

Henry Adams to Charles Francis Adams Jr.

Henry Adams was confidential secretary to his father, Charles Francis Adams, the American minister to Great Britain. He wrote to his brother Charles, a captain in the 1st Massachusetts Cavalry serving in northern Virginia with the Army of the Potomac.

London. 23 January. 1863.

My dear Charles:

I have but a moment till it grows dark and the bag closes, but I don't think I've much to say, so it don't matter. I've had a hard day's work too, as we generally do on Fridays, and am tired. We are in the dark as to movements at home since the 8th, no steamer being yet in owing I suppose to the awful gales.

We are as usual very quiet, having been dragged the rounds of the Christmas pantomimes and bored to death with them. I wish you or John were here to be funny and amuse people; you know I never could do it, and now I grow stupider and stupider every year as my hair grows thinner. I haven't even the wit left to talk to girls. I wish I were fifty years old at once, and then I should feel at home.

The Emancipation Proclamation has done more for us here than all our former victories and all our diplomacy. It is creating an almost convulsive reaction in our favor all over this country. The London Times is furious and scolds like a drunken drab. Certain it is, however, that public opinion is very deeply stirred here and finds expression in meetings; addresses to Pres. Lincoln; deputations to us; standing committees to agitate the subject and to affect opinion; and all the other symptoms of a great popular movement peculiarly unpleasant to the upper classes here because it rests altogether on the spontaneous action of the laboring classes and has a pestilent squint at sympathy with republicanism. But the Times is on its last legs and has lost its temper. They say it always does lose its temper when it finds such a feeling too strong for it, and its next step will be to come round and try to guide it. We are much encouraged and in high spirits. If only you at home don't have disasters, we will give such a checkmate to the foreign hopes of the rebels as they never yet have had.

We are all well and happy. I am at last on the point of buying a little mare and expect to have to hand her over to Mary, as her own horse is rather too much for her. Also having had my watch, hat and purse stolen at my celebrated Turkish baths, I have succeeded in obtaining a compensation of £15.0.0. with which I propose immediately to invest in a new watch. The exchange would be an inducement to invest at home, where I do not hear that my income has materially increased in spite of the superfluity of money. The mare costs £40.0.0 and will cost me at least £5.0.0 a month in keep.

Lebe wohl. Time is up and the Chief is a cussin and swearin like anythink for my letters.

Ever Yrs.

A CHANGE IN COMMAND:
VIRGINIA, JANUARY 1863

George G. Meade to Margaret Meade

A career army officer, Major General George G. Meade had led a brigade in the Seven Days' Battles and at Second Bull Run, and a division at Antietam and Fredericksburg, before becoming commander of the Fifth Corps in late December 1862. He wrote to his wife about the "Mud March" and its consequences for the Army of the Potomac.

Camp near Falmouth Va.
Jany. 23d. 1863

Dear Margaret—

I have not written to you for several days (my last being on the 18th) for the reasons that I have had no opportunity & that I was aware all letters from the camp were stopped, in Washington, so that there was no use in writing.—On the 19th in the night we received orders to move the next day. On the 20th the whole army moved from the camp to a position 4 miles up the river, where crossing places had been previously selected. Every thing went off very well up to about 8 P.M. of the 20th. The army reached its position—the pontoons, artillery & all other accessories were up in time, & we all thought the next morning the bridges would be thrown over and we should be at it. But man proposes & God disposes. About 9 P.M. a terrific storm of wind & rain set in, and continued all night. At once I saw the game was up. The next day the roads were almost impassable. The pontoons, in attempting to get them to the waters edge stuck on the bank and 100 men could not budge them. Instead of 6 bridges being thrown over by *8 A.M.*, it was found late in the day that the materials of *one* only could be got to the waters-edge. Burnside visited us, and soon saw the state of the case. Still in hopes something might happen, he directed we should remain in position. All that night 21st. & the next day 22d. it continued to rain & the roads to get in such a condition, that early yesterday the 22d. I had to turn out the *whole* of my corps 15,000 men, and go to work and bridge with logs, or corduroy as it is called nearly the whole road from our camp to the crossing place 8 miles. The men worked cheerfully at this which was accomplished by early this morning, and Burnside having recalled the army to its old camp we have been all day getting our artillery back & tomorrow the infantry will return thus consuming two days to get back what it took only a few hours to get there.

I never felt so disappointed & sorry for any one in my life as I did for Burnside. He really seems to have all the elements against him. I told him warmly when I saw him how sorry I felt, and that I had almost rather have lost a limb than that the storm should have occurred. He seemed quite philosophical. Said he could not resist the elements and perhaps it was as well, for that his movement had been most strongly opposed, & some of his Generals had told him he was leading the men to a *slaughter pen*. And I am sorry to say there were many men & among them Generals high in command who openly rejoiced at the storm & the obstacle it presented.—We were very much amused to see in the papers today flaming accounts of our crossing, of the battle & Hooker's being mortally wounded. I hope you did not attach any importance to these absurd reports—which when I saw I feared you might have been anxious. I presumed the truth had been telegraphed and that you would know the storm had frustrated our plans. The plan was based on the presumption, that we would take the enemy unawares at least so far as the place of crossing was concerned and I believe but for the storm we should have succeeded in this.—What will be done now, I can not imagine. The mud is at present several feet thick wherever any wagons pass over a road, and if the weather from this time should at all resemble that of last year, it will effectively stop all operations for two months to come.—

On my return I found your letter of the 20th and two written by Markoe. I had written to Markoe, telling him it was useless for me to write to Halleck, and that my letter nominating him, was as strong an expression of my desire to have him, as any I could make, and that any further effort, would not only be unsuccessful but might bring from H— an answer that

I should not like to receive.—I am very sorry for Markoes disappointment, and would have been very glad to have him, but the thing it seems can not be effected, and there is no use, in struggling against fixed facts, besides Markoe knows I *doubted* from the first the practicality of success, and gave him distinctly to understand, that *he* must overcome in Washington the difficulties I anticipated. I can not & will not write to Halleck, because I do not believe it would be of the slightest use & I do not choose to lay myself in the power of that gentleman when I feel so confident I should fail. You can tell this to Markoe on my part, and advise him to be resigned to what can not be helped. I did not see George during our *fiasco*, tho I was at one time bivouacked near a part of his regiment but his company was not with that part. ——

Doubleday has been assigned to the *Reserves*, which is a good thing for me, for now they will think a great deal more of me than before. ——

I am very glad to hear Mr. Meredith heard such good reports of me in Washington. I see my name has gone to the Senate, all the papers say the Senate will not repeal their limiting resolution in which case my nomination can not be confirmed. I presume however the President will reappoint me after Congress adjourns, as he has done in other cases, where the Senate have tried to hand him off. ——

It is very late & I am tired so I will bid you Good bye.

Ever yours, *Geo. G. Meade*

———————

Camp near Falmouth Va
Jany. 26./63—9 P.M.

Dear Margaret—

I wrote you a long letter today little thinking while I was quietly employed writing to you what momentous events were going on immediately around me. After writing to you I went out to ride for exercise & on my return at 6 P.M., found an order awaiting me announcing Maj. Genl. Hooker is in command of the Army of the Potomac & Maj. Genl. Meade in command of the Centre Grand Division. I then learned for the first time that this news arrived this morning Burnside having brought it down from Washington last night that he Burnside & all his staff had gone off this morning, and that Genls. *Sumner* & *Franklin* had both been relieved & ordered to Washington. You can readily imagine my surprise at all this, altho some such step had been talked about for some time back.—As to my commanding a Grand Division I consider it a mere temporary arrangement, as either some one of more rank will be sent or what is more likely the Grand Division organisation broken up altogether, as it was purely an invention of Burnsides, and has not I think been considered a good one. The removal of so many officers of rank however makes it certain I shall not go lower than a corps, and that is really all I particularly care for & is as much as I want.

You will doubtless be anxious to know what I think of these changes. With all my respect & I may almost say affection for Burnside, for he has been most kind & considerate towards me—I can not shut my eyes to the fact, that he was not equal to the command of so large an army. He had some very positive qualifications such as determination & nerve, but he wanted knowledge & judgement, and was deficient in that enlarged mental capacity which is essential in a commander. Another drawback, was a very general opinion among officers & men, brought about by his own assertions, that the command was too much for him. This greatly weakened his position.

As to Hooker you know my opinion of him frequently expressed. I believe my opinion is more favorable than any other of the old regular officers, most of whom are decided in their hostility to him. I believe Hooker is a good soldier. The danger he runs, is of subjecting himself to bad influences, such as *Dan Butterfield* & *Dan Sickles* who being intellectually more clever than Hooker & leading him to believe they are very influential, will obtain an injurious ascendancy over him & insensibly affect his conduct. I may however in this be wrong—time will prove. What we are now going to do remains to be seen. I have not seen Hooker since the news came & only write to tell you what is thus far known. Ever yours

Geo. G. Meade

Camp near Falmouth Va
Jany. 28. 1863

Dear Margaret—

Last evening yours of the 24th reached me. I am sorry to hear you have been sick, and still more sorry to know it has arisen from uncertainty & agitation, which it was not in my power to prevent. In the first place after the movement was determined on, I ascertained orders had been given to stop *all letters* at Acquia Creek. 2dly even if letters had been permitted to pass, it was impossible for me with my occupation & without materials to write. Again I relied on the agents of the Press to communicate the *truth*, at least sufficient to allay any unnecessary apprehensions, and never supposed *Washington canards* would be so greedily swallowed as the truth. Next time I will try & smuggle to you definite information.

Your anxiety lest I should be placed in command of the Army causes me Dearest to smile. Still I must confess when such men as Gibbons say it is talked about, it really does look serious & alarming. Yet when I look back on the good fortune which has thus attended my career I can not believe so sudden a change for the worse, can occur as would happen if I were placed in command. I think therefore we may for the present dismiss our fears on that score.—Genl. Hooker has been two days in Washington. I am looking anxiously for his return to hear what will be the result.—Before he was placed in command he was open-mouthed and constant, in his *assertions* that he did not want to command and that he *would not* command unless he was perfectly un-trammelled and allowed in every respect to do exactly as he pleased.—Now I am quite confident no such conditions will be acceded to in Washington—hence either "Fighting Joe" will have to back down, or some one else will be sent to take the command. From my knowledge of friend Hooker, I am inclined to surmise the former will be the case.—But even supposing they give him *carte-blanche* his position is any thing but enviable. This army is in a *false position* both as regards the enemy, and the public. With respect to the enemy we can literally do nothing, and our numbers are inadequate to the accomplishment of any result even if we go to the James river. On the other hand, the wise public, are under the delusion, that we are omnipotent, and that it is only necessary to go ahead to achieve unheard of success. Of course under such circumstances neither Cæsar, Napoleon, or any other mighty *genius* could fail to meet with condemnation, never mind what he did, and Hooker I fancy will find in time, his fate, in the fate of his predecessors—in, *undue* & *exaggerated praise before* he does any thing, and a total absence of reason & intelligence in the discussion of his acts, when he does attempt any thing and a denial of even ordinary military qualifications unless he achieves impossibilities.—Such being the case, he certainly is not to be envied, and we may well be satisfied that there is no chance of my being his successor.—I think when his head is cut off the admn. will try a General of their own kidney, either Fremont, Hunter &c

Of course so long as Hooker is absent I continue in command of the Centre Grand Division, but I am more & more inclined to believe that his visit to Washington will result in the abolition of the Grand Division system altogether, and the return to corps alone. In this case I infer I am bound to have a corps for since the departure of Sumner & Franklin there are at present only Six (6) generals ranking me viz Hooker, Couch Sigel Slocum Smith W. F. & Sedgewick. As Hooker is in command of all & there are *8 corps*, it will make me the 6th corps commdr. Should Reynolds be confirmed & appointed, I suppose he will rank me which would give me the 7th corps rank. The only danger of my being reduced lower would be the promotion of *Stoneman* on the same date as myself (Nov. 29).

This is not likely, his name not being on the list sent in, but he has gone to Washington to try & have it done, and he will undoubtedly have Hooker's influence in his behalf. Per contra there is another probability, which is that Sigel will decline serving under Hooker particularly if the Grand Divisions are broken up, of which he has now one. So—should he leave & both Stoneman & Reynolds be put over me I would still have a corps. I therefore look with confidence to my not getting lower than this. And I hope I shall retain the 5th corps as it is one of the best including as it does the Regulars.—Humphreys has gone to Washn to try & be made a Maj. Genl swearing he will resign if they do not accede to his *claim*.

I believe I wrote you, he behaved with distinguished gallantry at Fredericksburg. It appears soon after the battle Burnside told him both the President & Secy. assured him solemnly that Humphreys should be immediately promoted. He now finds a long list sent to the senate including such names as *Butterfield Sickles, Berry* & others who have really done nothing, while his name is omitted, and he can not hear that there is any record in the Dept. going to shew he has ever, even been thought of. Under these circumstances he is naturally very indignant and swears he will quit the service altogether if justice is not done him. This is all *entre-nous.* Just as I had gotten this far I heard Hooker had returned, and notwithstanding it is storming & snowing violently, I rode 3 miles to his Hd. Qtrs. to see him, and have just returned.—He seemed in excellent spirits, said they had treated him en Prince in Washn. & told him he had only to ask & he should have what he wanted. He did not tell me his plans but intimated that as soon as the weather & the roads permitted he was prepared to try something. He did tell me however, as I suspected that he had *Stonemans* name put on the list of Maj. Genls thus putting another one over my head. At the same time he said my commission ought to be antedated to South Mountain tho' he said nothing about asking this for me. Well I am satisfied to take things as they are. There seems to be no justice and I am really tired of scrambling & pushing for it.

I have received your delightful letter of the 26th describing your happy relatives in the BG. & other members of your family. Pon my word I am glad I am here altho I stand a chance of being shot, than in such a position as you describe yours. Seriously why do you pay any attention to such weaknesses. Woodruff I trust in a few days will send you a soothing check, and as soon as my Decr. acct. can be paid you will be all right. Love to all. Keep up your spirits & take care of your health. Ever yours

G. G. Meade

ADVISING A NEW COMMANDER:
WASHINGTON, D.C., JANUARY 1863

Abraham Lincoln to Joseph Hooker

Frustrated by insubordination among his senior generals, Burnside drafted an order on January 23 transferring William B. Franklin and William F. Smith, who sought to have McClellan restored to command of the Army of the Potomac, and cashiering Joseph Hooker, who sought to command the army himself. The next day Burnside met with Lincoln at the White House and gave the President the choice of either endorsing his order or accepting his resignation. Lincoln replaced Burnside with Hooker on January 25, and then wrote to his new commander.

Executive Mansion,
Washington, January 26, 1863.

Major General Hooker:
General.

I have placed you at the head of the Army of the Potomac. Of course I have done this upon what appear to me to be sufficient reasons. And yet I think it best for you to know that there are some things in regard to which, I am not quite satisfied with you. I believe you to be a brave and a skilful soldier, which, of course, I like. I also believe you do not mix politics with your profession, in which you are right. You have confidence in yourself, which is a valuable, if not an indispensable quality. You are ambitious, which, within reasonable bounds, does good rather than harm. But I think that during Gen. Burnside's command of the Army, you have taken counsel of your ambition, and thwarted him as much as you could, in which you did a great wrong to the country, and to a most meritorious and honorable brother officer. I have heard, in such way as to believe it, of your recently saying that both the Army and the Government needed a Dictator. Of course it was not *for* this, but in spite of it, that I have given you the command. Only those generals who gain successes, can set up dictators. What I now ask of you is military success, and I will risk the dictatorship. The government will support you to the utmost of it's ability, which is neither more nor less than it has done and will do for all commanders. I much fear that the spirit which you have aided to infuse into the Army, of criticising their Commander, and withholding confidence from him, will now turn upon you. I shall assist you as far as I can, to put it down. Neither you, nor Napoleon, if he were alive again, could get any good out of an army, while such a spirit prevails in it.

And now, beware of rashness. Beware of rashness, but with energy, and sleepless vigilance, go forward, and give us victories. Yours very truly

A. LINCOLN

RAISING A BLACK REGIMENT:
MASSACHUSETTS, JANUARY 1863

John A. Andrew to Francis Shaw

From the beginning of the war Frederick Douglass and other abolitionists had advocated the raising of black troops to fight for the Union. Despite opposition from the border states and northern Democrats, Congress authorized the president in July 1862 to enroll blacks as soldiers, and by the end of the year five black regiments had been formed at the initiative of Union commanders in South Carolina, Louisiana, and Kansas. After resisting calls for enlistment of blacks, President Lincoln declared in the Emancipation Proclamation that they would be "received into the armed service of the United States to garrison forts, positions, stations, and other places." Encouraged by the proclamation, John A. Andrew, the Republican governor of Massachusetts, sought and received authorization from Secretary of War Edwin M. Stanton to recruit a black regiment from among the freemen of the northern states. Andrew solicited the assistance of Francis Shaw, an abolitionist and social reformer from a wealthy and socially prominent Massachusetts family.

Commonwealth of Massachusetts.
Executive Department.
Boston, Jan. 30th 1863

Francis G. Shaw, Esq. Staten Island. N.Y.
Dear Sir:
    As you may have seen by the newspapers, I am about to raise a Colored Regiment in Massachusetts. This I cannot but regard as perhaps the most important corps to be organized during the whole war, in view of what must be the composition of our new levies; and therefore I am very anxious to organize it judiciously in order that it may be a model for all future Colored Regiments. I am desirous to have for its officers —particularly for its field officers—young men of military experience, of firm Anti Slavery principles, ambitious, superior to a vulgar contempt for color, and having faith in the capacity of

Colored men for military service. Such officers must be necessarily gentlemen of the highest tone and honor; and I shall look for them in those circles of Educated Anti Slavery Society, which next to the colored race itself has the greatest interest in the success of this experiment.

Reviewing the young men of the character I have described, now in the Massachusetts service it occurs to me to offer the Colonelcy of such a Regiment to your son, Capt Shaw of the 2nd Mass. Infantry, and the Lt. Colonelcy to Capt. Hallowell of the 20th Mass. Infantry, the son of Mr. Morris L. Hallowell of Philadelphia. With my deep conviction of the importance of this undertaking in view of the fact that it will be the first Colored Regiment to be raised in the Free States, and that its success or its failure will go far to elevate or to depress the estimation in which the character of the Colored Americans will be held throughout the World, the command of such a Regiment seems to me to be a high object of ambition for any officer. How much your son may have reflected upon such a subject I do not know, nor have I any information of his disposition for such a task except what I have derived from his general character and reputation, nor should I wish him to undertake it unless he could enter upon it with a full sense of its importance, with an earnest determination for its success; and with the assent and sympathy and support of the opinion of his immediate family. I therefore beg to enclose to you the letter in which I make him the offer of this commission, and I will be obliged to you, if you will forward it to him accompanying it with any expression to him of your own views, and if you will also write to me upon the subject.

My mind is drawn towards Capt. Shaw by many considerations. I am sure that he would attract the support, sympathy and active co-operation of many besides his immediate family and relatives. The more ardent, faithful, true Republicans and friends of Liberty would recognize in him, a scion of a tree whose fruit and leaves have alike contributed to the strength and healing of our generation. So also it is with Capt. Hallowell. His father is a quaker gentleman of Philadelphia, two of whose sons are officers in our regiments and another is a Merchant in Boston. Their house in Philadelphia is a hospital almost for Mass. officers, and the family are full of good works;

Mr. H. being my constant adviser in the interest of our soldiers, when sick or in distress in that city. I need not add that young Capt. H. is a gallant and fine fellow, true as steel to the cause of Human Nature, as well as to the flag of the Country.

I wish to engage the field officers and then get their aid in selecting those of the line. I have offers from "Oliver T. Beard of Brooklyn, N.Y. late Lt. Col. 48th N. Y. V." who says he can already furnish 600 men, and from others wishing to furnish men from New York, and from Conn., but I do not wish to start the regiment under a stranger to Massachusetts. Still I have written to Col. H. E. Howe to learn about Col. Beard, since he may be useful in some contingency hereafter. If in any way, by suggestion or otherwise, you can aid the purpose which is the burden of this letter, I shall receive your cooperation with the heartiest gratitude.—

I dont want the office to go begging; & if this offer is refused I wd. prefer its being kept reasonably private. Hoping to hear from you immediately on yr receiving this note, I am, with high regard, Your obt. servant & friend,

       John A. Andrew.

DEBATING BLACK SOLDIERS:
WASHINGTON, D.C., FEBRUARY 1863

William Parker Cutler: Diary, February 2 and 9, 1863

Congressman Thaddeus Stevens of Pennsylvania, a leading Radical Republican, introduced a bill on January 12, 1863, authorizing the enlistment of 150,000 black soldiers. After a debate in which opponents denounced the measure as "suicidal and seditious" and designed to "exterminate and drive out the white people" of the cotton states, the bill passed and was sent to the Senate. William Parker Cutler, a Republican congressman from Ohio, witnessed the final vote in the House and later discussed the issue of black soldiers with President Lincoln. The Stevens bill was withdrawn from consideration in the Senate after Henry Wilson, the Massachusetts Republican who chaired the Committee on Military Affairs, reported on February 13 that the president already had authority to enlist blacks under the Militia Act passed in July 1862.

Feb 2   After a long contest over Mr Stevens bill to raise Negro regiments—it finally passed to day 83 to 54. The Democrats seemed determined to make capital out of the idea of putting a Negro on an equality with the white man—by making him a soldier. They have made every effort to rouse up the worst prejudices of the army & the people—& seem to glory & exult in the opportunity presented to degrade & tread down *Gods image* in the person of the Negro. Surely there is no solution to terrible complications of our situation except in power & strong arm of God himself. The Democrats claim a strong reaction in their favor—& seem intent only upon increasing the universal dissatisfaction & turning it all to their own account in building up a peace party. Political demagogues rule the hour—The people are bewildered & in the fog. The true friends of the govt & of the great principles which underlie this contest are groping around without a *leader*—absolutely no one to command entire confidence—& yet progress is being made daily. This vote is a recognition of the Negros *manhood*—such as has never before been made by this nation. We say in the hour of peril—come save us. "*Our God is marching on.*"

Feb 9th   Called this morning on Pres. Lincoln to present him a petition signed by—say 30 members of Congress asking him to appoint Capt Carpenter of the famous Jessie Scouts as Col. of one of the Negro regiments—in case the bill passes the Senate. He said the great difficulty he feared was the treatment these Negroes would receive at first from the rebels in case they were captured. I remarked that it was the more important that the regiments should be of good material & well officered so as to take care of themselves in a fight. He assented quickly to this—But remarked that he was troubled to know what we should do with these people—Negroes—after peace came—I remarked that I supposed the same plantations that now required their labor would then need them just as much. He said that "Whatever you and me may think on these matters peoples opinions were every thing"—He seemed to be sticking in the bank because of the popular delusion that nothing can be done with the Negro if he is *free*. Interest will settle these questions—If land owners cant get the Negroes labor for nothing—he will pay him for it—that is all. Washburne of Ill. was in the room at the same time & read a letter from Grant at Vicksburg dated Jan 29th—in which he said the canal cut there was only 9 feet wide at the top & of course was of no account. He was trying a larger one—But thought he could take the place by getting a channel through into the Yazoo & operating from the Mississippi side. The Mississippi was then bank full. Lincoln said that Richmond papers stated that the gun boat which run the Vicksburg blockade was doing mischief below.

"THESE BE DARK BLUE DAYS":
NEW YORK, FEBRUARY 1863

George Templeton Strong: Diary, February 3–5, 1863

A successful New York lawyer, Strong served as treasurer of the U.S. Sanitary Commission, a civilian organization dedicated to caring for sick and wounded soldiers and improving conditions in army camps. In his diary he considered the prospects for the Union cause.

February 3. Life and Trust Company meeting this morning. To a poor man like me the talk of these wholesale moneyers, like old Joe Kernochan and Aspinwall and others, is sublime. With what irreverent familiarity do they talk of millions! At 823 afterwards.

Murray Hoffman dined here and I went at eight to Executive Committee meeting at Dr. Bellows's, where were also Gibbs and Agnew. Among other little matters that came before us was a draft for some $1,100, the third article of the sort received from Honolulu. Agnew says he expects the next big aerolite that arrives will bring us a contribution from American citizens in the moon. The success of this Sanitary Commission has been a marvel. Our receipts in cash up to this time are nearly $700,000 at the central office alone, beside what has been received and spent by auxiliaries, and the three or four millions' worth of stores of every sort contributed at our depots. It has become a "big thing," has the Sanitary Commission, and a considerable fact in the history of this people and of this war. Our work at Washington and at Louisville, our two chief nervous centres, is on a big scale, employs some two hundred agents of every sort, and costs not much less than $40,000 a month.

National affairs seem stagnant, but I suppose we shall very soon hear news of the first importance from Vicksburg and possibly from Rosecrans. I think the national destiny will be decided in the Southwest, not in Virginia. Richmond is an *ignis fatuus.* We have mired ourselves badly in trying to reach it, twice at least, and can apply our strength more advantageously at other points. I am more and more satisfied, as I have been from the first, that our true policy is to occupy every Southern port, to open the Mississippi, to keep a couple of armies in strong and comfortable and healthy positions on the rebel frontier, and then to say to Jefferson Davis, "We are not going to advance into your jungle over your muddy roads. If you want a fight, you must come to us. If you don't want it, stay where you are and let us see which party will first be starved and wearied into submission." We do not need enterprise and dash near so much as resolution and steadiness, perseverance and pluck; the passive pluck that can suffer a little and wait quietly for the inevitable result. Therein this people seems wanting. Perhaps I do it injustice, but all the symptoms of the last four months indicate a fearful absence of vital power and constitutional stamina to resist disease and pain. The way the Dirt-Eaters and Copperheads and sympathizers and compromisers are coming out on the surface of society, like ugly petechiæ and vibices, shows that the nation is suffering from a most putrescent state of the national blood, and that we are a very typhoid community here at the North.

Thank God for the rancorous, vindictive, ferocious, hysterical utterances that reach us from the South—for the speeches and the Richmond *Enquirer* editorials declaring compromise and reconstruction impossible, that "Southrons" would not take back "Yankees" even as their slaves, that Northern Democrats who talk about restoring the Union are fools and blind. Were the South only a little less furious, savage, and spiteful, it could in three months so strengthen our "Peace Democracy" as to paralyze the nation and destroy all hope of ever restoring its territorial integrity. It is strange Jefferson Davis & Co. fail to see their best move. With a few unmeaning, insincere professions of desire for reconstruction, additional Constitutional guaranties, and so forth, they could bring us grovelling to their feet and secure an armistice most profitable to them, most dishonorable and disastrous to us.

February 5. These be dark blue days. Of course, every man's duty is to keep a stiff upper lip—*fortem in arduis rebus servare mentem*—"to talk turkey" about the moral certainty of triumph at last. I do so very valiantly. It's fearful and wonderful the way I blow and brag about our national invincibility, the extent of our conquests during the last twenty months, and our steady progress toward subjugation of the South. It is the right kind of talk for the times, and is more than half true, and has materially relieved the moral and political *adynamia* of at least one man, Bidwell, already. But (between me and my journal) things do in fact look darker and more dark every day. We are in a fearful scrape, and I see no way out of it. Recognition of the "Confederacy" is impossible. So is vigorous prosecution of the war twelve months longer. This proposition is self-evident "if this court understand herself, and she think she do." How can these two contradictions be reconciled? Rabelais furnishes a case equally difficult. Jupiter created a fox that was destined never to be caught, and afterwards, by inadvertence, a dog destined to catch all foxes, so that the Olympian Ledger of Destiny could not be made to balance. If I rightly remember my learned and pious author, Jupiter got rid of the embarrassment by turning dog and fox into two stars, or two constellations, or two stones, which was a mere evasion, and no solution of the great problem he had to deal with. We are in a similar deadlock of contradiction, I fear; North cannot be defeated and South cannot be conquered. (Of course, this is taking the worst view of the case.)

"THE SOLDIER'S PEST":
VIRGINIA, FEBRUARY 1863

Oliver W. Norton to Edwin Norton

The bugle call "Taps" was first played in July 1862 by Oliver W. Norton, who served as brigade bugler for the tune's composer, Brigadier General Daniel Butterfield. A private in the 83rd Pennsylvania Infantry, Norton had enlisted in 1861 and seen action in the Peninsula campaign and at Second Bull Run and Fredericksburg. He wrote to his brother from an army camp near the north bank of the Rappahannock.

———————

Stoneman Station, Va.,
Friday, Feb. 6, 1863.

Dear E.:—

Wicks' golden opinions of "Little Norton" may do very well to repeat at home. Perhaps he thinks, as he has said so much for me, I should return the compliment and praise him up to the skies. I can't see the point. I don't thank anybody to say that I have done more than I agreed to do, more than a soldier's duty, and if any one says I have not done my duty, send him to me to say it. I don't know what Wicks saw me do at Malvern Hill. I didn't see him at all in the fight. I was under the impression that he was "taken with a sunstroke" just before the fight commenced. At Bull Run the boys say he did "fight like the devil."

I don't care anything about what he told you of my smoking. I could have told you that long ago if I had thought you cared anything about it. You all knew when I left home that I used tobacco some, and Mother and L. particularly urged me to quit it. I wouldn't make any promises about it and continued to smoke, but a year ago last Christmas I did quit, and then I wrote home and told all about it. Well, not the first one said so much as "I'm glad," or advised me to stick to it. I waited a month or so and heard nothing, and then I thought if that was all you cared about it, if it made no difference to any of you, it didn't to me, so I went at it again. If Wicks had told you that I chewed two pounds of plug a week and a pound of opium, drank gin and gambled, would you have believed him? Well, if it makes any difference to you I will just say for your comfort that I don't.

I am glad to hear that Wicks is looking so well. The boys who saw him in Alexandria said there was nothing left of him but his mustache. If I get down so low as that, I would not be much to load down an ambulance or a hog-car, would I?

No, siree, I wouldn't take a discharge now if I could get it. You need not trouble yourself about that. If I did want one, I fancy (pardon my vanity) I could play off on the doctors and get it, but I don't want it, and I would kick a man that would offer me one. As to being the "captain's friend" I don't see the point. I despise him too much for that. Personally I have no fault to find. He has always treated me well, perhaps favored me some, but I am not the friend of the man who always has the piles or something of the sort when a fight is coming off. At Hanover Court House he couldn't keep up, at Gaines' Mill he lay behind a tree and laughed while the men fell all round him. At Malvern he shouted retreat and ran like a greyhound, and got shot in the back with a three-cornered something. Last summer at Fredericksburg when we expected a fight he was too weak to march, and we didn't see him again till after Antietam. At this last at Fredericksburg he did go in and acted something like a man, the first and last time he has done so. When we moved last, expecting another battle, he couldn't go, he had the piles. Should I be the "captain's friend"? I don't know that he has but one in the company, and he is a sort of sucker. Mrs. A. is a woman, a true woman. I respect her very much, and so does every man in the company. Nothing but that respect for her feelings prevents the company from complaining of him and having him cashiered for cowardice.

I think some of my letters must have been lost. Did you never get the one that told of Henry's watch being lost? I felt so bad about that. I would have bought a dozen rather than lost that. I kept it till we got to Antietam, waiting for a chance to send it by express, but finally after getting Mary's permission, sent it by mail, and it was never heard from. I took all the precautions I could to make it safe, did it up in a little box like an ambrotype, but the last I heard it had not arrived, and if it had, they would have told me.

I wrote you in my last how our march terminated. Did Wicks tell you anything about camp lice? I do not know that I have ever said a word about them in all my letters, but they are so plenty here that they are the subject of half the standing jokes and *bons mots* in camp. I presume you never saw one. They are the soldier's pest. I never saw one till we got to Yorktown. They resemble head lice in appearance, but not in habits. They don't go near the hair, but stay in the clothes, shirt and drawers. There is no way to get rid of them, but to scald them out. They will hide in the seams and nit in every hiding place possible. Cold water won't faze them. They multiply like locusts and they will fat on "onguentum." At the time we left the Peninsula they were plenty, and until we got to Antietam, more than a month, no one had a chance to wash his clothes in hot water. I do not believe there was a man in our brigade, officer, private or nigger, but was lousy. They grow to enormous size and are the most cunning and most impudent of all things that live. During the late snow storm the boys, for want of something else to do, made sleds of their jaw bones, and slid down the bank of the railroad. The other night after supper I was sitting by the fire smoking a cigar, when I felt something twitch at my pants' leg. I looked down and there was one of the "crumbs" with a straw in his mouth, standing on his hind legs and working his claws round like a crab on a fish line. I gave a kick at him, but he dodged it and sticking up his cigar squeaked out, "Give me a light."

I woke up the other night and found a regiment of them going through the manual of arms on my back. Just as I woke the colonel gave the command "charge bayonets," and the way they let drive at my sirloin was a proof of their capacity. Any one of them can throw himself into a hollow square and bite at the four corners. I would be willing to let them have what blood and meat they wanted to eat, but the devils amuse themselves nights by biting out chunks and throwing them away. Well, this is a pretty lousy leaf, ain't it? Most likely the next one will be something different if it is not.

Joe (my housemaid) is sitting by the fire picking his teeth

with a bayonet and swearing at the beef. He says it is a pity it was killed, it was tough enough to stand many a long march yet. Well, it is tough. When Burnside got stuck in the mud, the artillery harness all broke, and the only way they could get the guns out was for the men to cut their rations of beef into strips, and make tugs out of them.

SHORT RATIONS: VIRGINIA, FEBRUARY 1863
Robert E. Lee to Mary Lee

After the battle of Fredericksburg the Army of Northern Virginia held a defensive line along the south bank of the Rappahannock extending from Bank's Ford, four miles above the town, to Port Royal, eighteen miles downriver. Forced to rely on the single-track Richmond & Fredericksburg railroad for its supplies, the army suffered from a shortage of food and clothing for its soldiers and forage for its animals. "Our horses & mules suffer the most," General Robert E. Lee wrote to his daughter Agnes on February 6. "They have to bear the cold & rain, tug through the mud, & suffer all the time with hunger." Lee wrote to his wife from Fredericksburg two days later.

Camp
February 8, 1863

I have just received dear Mary your letter of the 7th. I am distressed to hear of your suffering. I fear you are very imprudent, & that unless you are careful, you will reduce yourself to confinement altogether. You ought not to go out in bad weather, or to expose yourself at any time. I beg you will be careful. I send the passport for Mrs. Murdock, &c. I presume they intend returning the way they came, by Leesburg. Inform them they cannot pass through Fredericksburg. Genl Hooker has refused to permit passage through his lines here. I see in the Washington papers orders from Genl Halleck forbidding transportation of any citizens on the steamers plying between that city & Aquia Creek. All the boats &c. are reserved for the military. There is therefore no chance for them by this route. They can take the cars to Culpeper Court House & must thence find their way to Warrenton & Leesburg by private conveyance. Their best route is by flag of truce boat from City Point to Baltimore if that is permitted. But when they get home, my advice is to stay there & to let their sons & brothers alone. The men can do very well & soldiers must learn to take care of themselves. I have done however all I can. If this passport does not answer, it is useless to apply to me for another. It will take them anywhere through my lines. I know the yankees will get out of them all they know. I hope they know nothing to injure us. Not that I believe they will intentionally say or do ought to injure us, but the yankees have a very coaxing & insidious manner, that our Southern women in their artlessness cannot resist, no matter how favourable they may be to our cause or how full of good works for our men. I have not seen any of your gloves on the men, & therefore cannot say how they answer. I should think well, if they fit, & you know all your garments are warranted to do that. I advise you however to send up all you have made at once & then stop for this winter. After about a month they will be of no use. The men cannot preserve them & will throw them away. Remember me kindly to the Caskies. I cannot get down to R now. Nor can I expect any pleasure, during this war. We are in a liquid state at present. Up to our knees in mud & what is worse on short rations for men & beasts. This keeps me miserable. I am willing to starve myself, but cannot bear my men or horses to be pinched. I fear many of the latter will die. Give my love to Agnes. I wrote to her the other day. Where is she staying? As you both seem to prefer Richmond to anywhere else, you had better take a house there. Be careful of the small pox & other diseases. Tell Miss N that I told Major Talcott, after he had seen his sweetheart, he must go up & look at her for me. So she must give him a sweet look. Present me very kindly to Mrs. Jones. I sympathize with her deeply in the death of her husband. He was always a great favorite with me. Fitzhugh is still low down the Rappahannock, I believe Charlotte is with him still. But have not heard. He is 40 miles from me.

With great affection, yours
R. E. Lee

P.S. I have George as cook now. He is quite subdued but has only been here a day. I give him & Perry each 8.20 per month. I hope they will be able to lay up something for themselves.

R. E. L.

ACCEPTING A COLONELCY:
VIRGINIA, FEBRUARY 1863

Robert Gould Shaw to Annie Haggerty

Commissioned as a second lieutenant in the 2nd Massachusetts Infantry in 1861, Captain Robert Gould Shaw saw action at Front Royal, Cedar Mountain, and Antietam. On February 3, 1863, he was visited at his camp in northern Virginia by his father Francis, who brought with him Governor John A. Andrew's offer of the colonelcy of a Massachusetts black regiment (see pp. 20–22 in this volume). Shaw initially rejected the position, then changed his mind. He wrote to his fiancée about his decision.

Stafford C. H., Va.
Feb. 8, 1863
Dear Annie,

You know by this time, perhaps, that I have changed my mind about the black regiment. After Father left, I began to think I had made a mistake in refusing Governor Andrew's offer. Mother has telegraphed to me that you would not disapprove of it, and that makes me feel much more easy about having taken it. Going for another three years is not nearly so bad a thing for a colonel as a captain; as the former can much more easily get a furlough. Then, after I have undertaken this work, I shall feel that what I have to do is to prove that a negro can be made a good soldier, and, that being established, it will not be a point of honour with me to see the war through, unless I really occupied a position of importance in the army. Hundreds of men might leave the army, you know, without injuring the service in the slightest degree.

Last night I received your letter of last Sunday, February 1st. You must be at Susie's house now,—at least I judge so from Mother's telegram. As I may not receive my order to leave here for some days, do promise to stay there until I get to New York. You do not know how I shall feel if I find you are gone.

It is needless for me to overwhelm you with a quantity of arguments in favour of the negro troops; because you are with

Mother, the warmest advocate the cause can have. I am inclined to think that the undertaking will not meet with so much opposition as was at first supposed. All sensible men in the army, of all parties, after a little thought, say that it is the best thing that can be done; and surely those at home, who are not brave or patriotic enough to enlist, should not ridicule, or throw obstacles in the way of men who are going to fight for them. There is a great prejudice against it; but now that it has become a government matter, that will probably wear away. At any rate, I shan't be frightened out of it by its unpopularity; and I hope you won't care if it is made fun of.

Dear Annie, the first thing I thought of, in connection with it, was how you would feel, and I trust, now I have taken hold of it, I shall find you agree with me and all of our family, in thinking I was right. You know how many eminent men consider a negro army of the greatest importance to our country at this time. If it turns out to be so, how fully repaid the pioneers in the movement will be, for what they may have to go through! And at any rate I feel convinced I shall never regret having taken this step, as far as I myself am concerned; for while I was undecided I felt ashamed of myself, as if I were cowardly.

Good bye, dear Annie. I hope that when I arrive at Sue's door you will not be very far off.

With a great deal of love, (more every day) your
Rob

EMANCIPATION AND INTERVENTION:
LONDON, FEBRUARY 1863

Richard Cobden to Charles Sumner

Along with his friend and parliamentary colleague John Bright, the reformer Richard Cobden was one of the leading British supporters of the Union cause. In the fall of 1862 the Liberal government led by Lord Palmerston had considered attempting to mediate an end to the American Civil War, but had decided to wait until the military situation was clearer. Cobden wrote about the impact of the Emancipation Proclamation to his friend Charles Sumner, the Massachusetts Radical Republican who chaired the Senate Committee on Foreign Relations.

———————

ATHENÆUM CLUB
LONDON, 13 Feby., 1863

Private

My dear Sumner.

If I have not written to you before it is not because I have been indifferent to what is passing in your midst. I may say sincerely that my thoughts have run almost as much on American as English politics. But I could do you no service, and shrunk from occupying your overtaxed attention even for a moment. My object in now writing is to speak of a matter which has a practical bearing on your affairs.

You know how much alarmed I was from the first lest our government should interpose in your affairs. The disposition of our ruling class, and the necessities of our cotton trade, pointed to some act of intervention and the indifference of the great mass of our population to your struggle, the object of which they did not foresee and understand, would have made intervention easy indeed popular if you had been a weaker naval power. This state of feeling existed up to the announcement of the President's emancipation policy. From that moment our old anti-slavery feeling began to arouse itself, and it has been gathering strength ever since. The great rush of the public to all the public meetings called on the subject shows how wide and deep the sympathy for personal freedom still is in the hearts of our people. I know nothing in my political experience so striking as a display of spontaneous public action as that of the vast gathering at Exeter Hall when without one attraction in the form of a popular orator the vast building, its minor rooms and passages and the streets adjoining were crowded with an enthusiastic audience. That meeting has had a powerful effect on our newspapers and politicians. It has closed the mouths of those who have been advocating the side of the South. And I now write to assure you that any unfriendly act on the part of our government, no matter which of our aristocratic parties is in power, towards your cause is not to be apprehended. If an attempt were made by the government in any way to commit us to the South, a spirit would be instantly aroused which would drive our government from power. This I suppose will be known and felt by the Southern agents in Europe and if communicated to their government must I should think operate as a great discouragement to them. For *I know* that those agents have been incessantly urging in every quarter where they could hope to influence the French and English governments the absolute necessity of *recognition* as a means of putting an end to the war. Recognition of the South, by England, whilst it bases itself on negro slavery, is an impossibility, unless indeed after the Federal government have recognized the Confederates as a nation.

So much for the influence which your emancipation policy has had on the public opinion of England. But judging from the tone of your press in America it does not seem to have gained the support of your masses. About this however I do not feel competent to offer an opinion. Nor, to confess the truth, do I feel much satisfaction in treating of your politics at all. There appears to me great mismanagement I had almost said incapacity in the management of your affairs, and you seem to be hastening towards financial and economical evils in a manner which fills me with apprehension for the future.

When I met Frémont in Paris two years ago just as you commenced this terrible war I remarked to him that the total abolition of slavery in your northern Continent was the only issue which could justify the war to the civilized world. Every symptom seems to point to this result. But at what a price is the negro to be emancipated! I confess that if then I had been the arbiter of his fate I should have refused him freedom at the cost of so much white men's blood and women's tears. I do not however blame the North. The South fired the first shot, and on them righteously falls the malediction that "they who take the sword shall perish by the sword." And it seems unlikely that after all the much despised "nigger," and not the potentates and statesmen of Europe will be the final arbitrator in the great struggle.

Let me have a line from you when your Senatorial duties have ceased on the 4th, and afford you a little leisure.

Believe me,
Yours very truly
R. COBDEN.

"THESE TRAITORS RIGHT HERE":
SPRINGFIELD, FEBRUARY 1863

Isaac Funk: Speech in the Illinois State Senate

February 14, 1863

In the fall 1862 elections the Democrats won the governorships of New Jersey and New York, legislative majorities in Illinois, Indiana, and New Jersey, and gained thirty-four seats in the House of Representatives. When the new Illinois general assembly met in Springfield on January 5, 1863, the house of representatives began adopting a series of resolutions that condemned the Emancipation Proclamation, the suspension of habeas corpus, and the administration's conduct of the war, and called for an armistice and a national convention to negotiate terms of reunion. Richard Yates, the Republican governor of Illinois, described the legislature in a letter as "a wild, rampant, revolutionary body" seeking to deprive him of executive power. President Lincoln told Senator Charles Sumner that he now feared "'the fire in the rear'—meaning the Democracy, especially at the Northwest—more than our own military chances." The fatal illness of a Democratic member prevented the anti-administration resolutions from being adopted by the closely divided state senate before the general assembly adjourned on February 14. The text of Republican senator Isaac Funk's speech from the final day of the legislative session is taken from a New York pamphlet printing titled *Copperheads under the Heel of an Illinois Farmer.*

———————

ON THE last day of the Illinois Legislature, in February, 1863, Mr. Funk, a Senator from McLean County, delivered a speech, which is thus described and reported by the Springfield correspondent of the Chicago *Tribune*:

A great sensation was created by a speech by Mr. Funk, one of the richest farmers in the State, a man who pays over three thousand dollars per annum taxes towards the support of the Government. The lobby and gallery were crowded with spectators. Mr. Funk rose to object to trifling resolutions, which had been introduced by the Democrats to kill time and stave off a vote upon the appropriations for the support of the State Government. He said:

Mr. Speaker, I can sit in my seat no longer and see such by-play going on. These men are trifling with the best interests of the country. They should have asses' ears to set off their heads, or they are traitors and secessionists at heart.

I say that there are traitors and secessionists at heart in this Senate. Their actions prove it. Their speeches prove it. Their gibes and laughter and cheers here nightly, when their speakers get up to denounce the war and the administration, prove it.

I can sit here no longer and not tell these traitors what I think of them. And while so telling them, I am responsible, myself, for what I say. I stand upon my own bottom. I am ready to meet any man on this floor in any manner, from a pin's point to the mouth of a cannon, upon this charge against these traitors. [Tremendous applause from the galleries.]

I am an old man of sixty-five; I came to Illinois a poor boy; I have made a little something for myself and family. I pay three thousand dollars a year in taxes. I am willing to pay six thousand, aye, twelve thousand, [great cheering, the old gentleman striking the desk with a blow that would knock down a bullock, and causing the inkstand to fly in the air,] aye, I am willing to pay my whole fortune, and then give my life, to save my country from these traitors that are seeking to destroy it. [Tremendous applause, which the Speaker could not control.]

Mr. Speaker, you must please excuse me; I could not sit longer in my seat and calmly listen to these traitors. My heart, that feels for my poor country, would not let me. My heart, that cries out for the lives of our brave volunteers in the field, that these traitors at home are destroying by thousands, would not let me. My heart, that bleeds for the widows and orphans at home, would not let me. Yes, these traitors and villains in this Senate [striking his clenched fist on the desk with a blow that made the Senate ring again] are killing my neighbors' boys now fighting in the field. I dare to say this to these traitors right here, and I am responsible for what I say to any one or all of them. [Cheers.] Let them come on now, right here. I am sixty-five years old, and I have made up my mind to risk my life right here, on this floor, for my country. [Mr. Funk's seat is near the lobby railing, and a crowd collected around him, evidently with the intention of protecting him from violence, if necessary. The last announcement was received with great cheering, and I saw many an eye flash and many a countenance grow radiant with the light of defiance.]

These men sneered at Colonel Mack a few days since.* He is a small man, but I am a large man. I am ready to meet any of them in place of Colonel Mack. I am large enough for them, and I hold myself ready for them now and at any time. [Cheers from the galleries.]

Mr. Speaker, these traitors on this floor should be provided with hempen collars. They deserve them. They deserve hanging, I say, [raising his voice, and violently striking the desk;] the country would be the better of swinging them up. I go for hanging them, and I dare to tell them so, right here to their traitorous faces. Traitors should be hung. It would be the salvation of the country to hang them. For that reason I must rejoice at it. [Tremendous cheering.]

Mr. Speaker, I beg pardon of the gentlemen in this Senate who are not traitors, but true loyal men, for what I have said. I only intend it and mean it for secessionists at heart. They are here in this Senate. I see them gibe, and smirk, and grin at the true Union men. Must I defy them? I stand here ready for them, and dare them to come on. [Great cheering.] What man, with the heart of a patriot, could stand this treason any longer? I have stood it long enough. I will stand it no more. [Cheers.] I denounce these men and their aiders and abettors as rank traitors and secessionists. Hell itself could not spew out a more traitorous crew than some of the men that disgrace this Legislature, this State, and this country. For myself, I protest against and denounce their treasonable acts. I have voted against their measures; I will do so to the end. I will denounce them as long as God gives me breath; and I am ready to meet the traitors themselves, here or any where, and fight them to the death. [Prolonged cheers and shouts.]

I said I paid three thousand dollars a year taxes. I do not say

---

*Hon. A. W. Mack delivered a powerful speech in the Senate of Illinois, on the thirteenth of February, in opposition to the Armistice Resolutions of the "Copperheads."

it to brag of it. It is my duty, yes, Mr. Speaker, my privilege, to do it. But some of these traitors here, who are working night and day to put their miserable little bills and claims through the Legislature, to take money out of the pockets of the people, are talking about high taxes. They are hypocrites as well as traitors. I heard some of them talking about high taxes in this way, who do not pay five dollars to the support of the Government. I denounce them as hypocrites as well as traitors. [Cheers.]

The reason they pretend to be afraid of high taxes is, that they do not want to vote money for the relief of the soldiers. They want to embarrass the Government and stop the war. They want to aid the secessionists to conquer our boys in the field. They care about high taxes! They are picayune men, any how, and pay no taxes at all, and never did, and never hope or expect to. This is an excuse of traitors. [Cheers.]

Mr. Speaker, excuse me. I feel for my country, in this her hour of danger, from the tips of my toes to the ends of my hair. That is the reason I speak as I do. I can not help it. I am bound to tell these men to their teeth what they are, and what the people, the true loyal people, think of them. [Tremendous cheering. The Speaker rapped upon his desk, apparently to stop it, but really to add to its volume, for I could see by his flushed cheek and flashing eye that his heart was with the brave and loyal old gentleman.]

Mr. Speaker, I have said my say. I am no speaker. This is the only speech I have made, and I do not know that it deserves to be called a speech. I could not sit still any longer and see these scoundrels and traitors work out their hellish schemes to destroy the Union. They have my sentiments; let them, one and all, make the most of them. I am ready to back up all I say, and I repeat it, to meet these traitors in any manner they may choose, from a pin's point to the mouth of a cannon. [Tremendous applause, during which the old gentleman sat down, after he had given the desk a parting whack, which sounded loud above the din of cheers and clapping of hands.]

I never before witnessed so much excitement in an assembly. Mr. Funk spoke with a force of natural eloquence, with a conviction and truthfulness, with a fervor and pathos which wrought up the galleries, and even members on the floor, to the highest pitch of excitement. His voice was heard in the stores that surround the square, and the people came flocking in from all quarters. In five minutes he had an audience that packed the hall to its utmost capacity. After he had concluded, the Republican members and spectators rushed up and took him by the hand to congratulate him. The Democrats said nothing, but evidently felt the castigation they were receiving most keenly, as might be seen from their blanched cheeks and restless and uneasy glances.

"HIS WIFE CRYING OVER HIM":
MISSOURI, FEBRUARY 1863

Taylor Peirce to Catharine Peirce

Union forces were able to prevent Missouri from seceding in 1861, but the state remained bitterly divided between unionists and secessionists and became the scene of the fiercest guerrilla conflict of the war. Although the Union victory at Pea Ridge, Arkansas, in March 1862 halted Confederate attempts to invade the state, Confederate irregulars in Missouri continued to harass Union troops with ambushes and raids. Taylor Peirce mustered into the 22nd Iowa Infantry as a sergeant in August 1862 and was soon sent to southern Missouri, where his regiment guarded railroad lines, supply depots, and wagon trains. He wrote to his wife from the Ozarks describing the summary treatment often meted out to suspected guerrillas.

Eminince, Mo Feby 16 1863
Dear Catharine
I again set down to write you all again. I wrote you last week but the mails are so irregular in this region that I do not know how long it will take this to reach you but Col Stone and the Chaplain leaves this for Rolla to-morrow and I think you will get it in about 6 or 7 days. I am well and in good heart. We have been on the move for 3 weeks except 3 or 4 days that we lay at West Plains. We are now about 60 miles from Rolla and will Either go to Rolla or to Pilot Knob. One Division of the army started this morning to the Knob and we will either start for that place or Rolla to morrow. The rebles are all gone from this country except some few Gurrillas and them we gather up as we go along and shoot them. They are a set of murderers and are not fit to live to encumber society. Some of the cavalry took one yesterday morning who has shot at Gen Bentons Courier the night before not knowing that the cavalry was about. So yesterday morning they caught him in his house and took him out about a mile and shot him. When we came along he was lying by the side of the road and his wife crying over him but she was no better than he for she kept on swearing

vengence against the Federals and said she would make them kiss his blood and so we left her. It looks hard to me to see a man shot and his wife and children left alone but these men are the ones that keep up the cruelties that are continually being practiced in this part of Missouri.

We have been traveling through the Ozark mountain ever since the 1st of this month and a rough country it is. There is some pretty vallies in through them and now and then a very good settlement along some stream but the land is generally stony and poor covered with oak and yellow Pine. Some of the timber is very good and some day will be valuable. We are now on the Currant River some 25 miles from the Arkansas line and 3 miles from Eminence a town with one house and a court house and jail in it and an old mill which constitutes the whole town. I have been running a mile for two or three days grinding corn for the brigade as our rations have run short and the roads are so bad that our supplies can not reach us and we have been on ½ rations for some time. But I have enough to eat all the time and more than I need but some of the large eaters grow terribly about it. I expect that we will have short allowances until we get to the Rail Road for the trains can not reach us through this god forsaken country.

Lieutenant Murray starts home in the morning and has promised to call and see you and tell you how I get along and what I am doing. And if it is possible for you to get your pictures taken I mean Cyrus & Mary & thine and the babys I would like you to send it by him. The paymaster has come and has paid me my money and as soon as I get to the Express office I will express it home.

I would send it by Murray but the Col thinks that it will be safer to keep it until we get to the office as they might be attacked by a forrageing party and robed as they will only have a small escort with them. So I concluded to keep it with me untill we get to the Rail Road. Cap Ault and I have fell out and I do not hold any communication with him any more than just what is nessessary for me to have to do my duty. He has shown himself just as damned a dog as lives and if he was not afraid of me he would be overbearing as the devil himself but I have the upper hand and he has to keep mum. The Lt can tell you about it and so you need not fear for me but I will get along all right.

I must now close for we will have to march in the morning and of course the time is precious with me. Give my love to all. Tell the children to be good and Pap will try and get home to see them this spring. Give Cyrus my best respects and tell him he could make some money following the army and buying up the worn out horses and mules and if I get my commission to raise the negroes I will come home and put him on the track.

I remain affect your husband father and brother.

Taylor Peirce

THE MENACE OF THE PRESS:
LOUISIANA, FEBRUARY 1863

William T. Sherman to Thomas Ewing Sr. and to John Sherman

Major General William T. Sherman became the commander of the Fifteenth Corps in Ulysses S. Grant's Army of the Tennessee in January 1863. From his camp across the Mississippi River from Vicksburg, Sherman wrote to his father-in-law, Thomas Ewing Sr., and to his brother John, a Republican senator from Ohio, about the dangers posed by the press. In December 1861 the *Cincinnati Commercial* had reported Sherman to be "insane" after he was relieved from commands in Kentucky and Missouri, and in the spring of 1862 Sherman had been infuriated by sensational newspaper stories falsely claiming that his men had been bayoneted in their tents during the initial Confederate attack at Shiloh. His antagonism toward the press reached a new level after his failed assault at Chickasaw Bayou near Vicksburg on December 29, 1862. When the *New York Herald* printed a story highly critical of his leadership in the battle, Sherman had its author, correspondent Thomas W. Knox, court-martialed on charges of giving intelligence to the enemy, being a spy, and disobedience of orders. On February 18, 1863, the court-martial convicted Knox of the third charge and ordered him to be expelled from the Army of the Tennessee's lines. When Knox sought Sherman's consent to return to the army in April, Sherman wrote that he would welcome him as a soldier, but as a reporter, "my answer is Never."

Camp before Vicksburg, Feb. 17, 1863.
Hon. Thomas Ewing
Dear Sir,

Ellen has sent me the enclosed slips from the Cincinnati Commercial. The Editor evidently seems disposed to deal fairly by me, and as I have more leisure than usual now I will illustrate by examples fresh in the memory of all, why I regard newspaper correspondents as spies, & why as a Servant of an enlightened Government I feel bound in honor and in common honesty to shape my official conduct accordingly. A spy is one who furnishes an enemy with knowledge useful to him & dangerous to us. One who bears into a Fortress or Camp a baneful influence that encourages sedition or weakens us. He need not be an enemy, is often a trader woman or Servant. Such characters are by all belligerents punished Summarily & with the extremest penalties, not because they are of themselves filled with the guilty thought & intent that makes the Madman the Burglar the Thief the Felon in civil affairs, but because he or she endangers the safety of an army a nation or the cause for which it is contending. Andre carried no intelligence back to Genl. Clinton but was the mere instrument used to corrupt the fidelity of an Officer holding an important command. Washington admitted the high & pure character of Andre but the safety of the cause demanded his punishment. It is hard to illustrate my point by reference to our past history, but I wish to convey the full idea that a nation & an army must defend its safety & existence by making acts militating against it criminal regardless of the mere interest of the instrument. We find a scout surveying our camp from a distance in noways threatening us but seeking information of the location strength & composition of our forces, we shoot him of course without asking a question. We find a stranger in our camp seeking a stray horse & find afterwards he has been to the enemy: we hang him as a spy because the safety of the army & the cause it fights is too important to be risked by any pretext or chance. Now in these modern times a class of men has been begotten & attend our camps & armies gathering minute information of our strength plans & purposes & publish them so as to reach the enemy in time to serve his purposes. Such publications do not add a man to our strength, in no ways benefit us but are invaluable to the enemy. You know that this class published in advance all the plans of the Manassas movement enabled Johnston to reinforce Beauregard whereby McDowell was defeated & the enemy gained tremendous strength & we lost in comparison. I know the enemy received from the same source some similar notice of our intended attack on Vicksburg & thwarted our well laid scheme. I know that Beauregard at Corinth received from the same source full details of all troops ascending the Tennessee & acted accordingly. I know that it was by absolute reticence only that Halleck succeeded in striking Forts Henry & Donaldson & prevented their reinforcements in time to thwart that most brilliant movement. And it was only by the absence of newspapers that we succeeded in reaching the post of Arkansas before it could be reinforced.

I *know* that the principal northern papers reach the enemy regularly & promptly & I *know* that all the vigilance of our Army cannot prevent it & I know that by this means the enemy can defeat us to the end of time. I could instance other examples but these suffice to illustrate this branch of the subject.

Another view of the case. The Northern Press either make public opinion or reflect it. By gradual steps public opinion instead of being governed governs our country. All bow to it, & even military men who are sworn officers of the Executive Branch of the Government go behind & look to public opinion. The consequence is & has been that officers instead of keeping the Executive Branch advised of all movements events or circumstances that would enable it to act advisedly & with vigor communicate with the public direct through the Press so that the Government authorities are operated on by public opinion formed too often on false or interested information. This has weakened our Executive and has created jealousies mistrust & actual Sedition. Officers find it easier to attain rank known fame and notoriety by the cheap proces of newspapers. This cause has paralized several fine armies & by making the people at home mistrust the ability of Leaders Surgeons & Quarter Masters has even excited the fears of parents so far that many advise their sons & brothers to desert until desertion & mutiny have lost their odious character. I'll undertake to say that the army of the Potomac has not today for battle one half the men whom the U.S. pays as Soldiers & this is partially the case with the army in Tennessee & here. In all armies there must be wide differences of opinion & partial causes of disaffection—*want of pay*, bad clothing dismal camps crowded transports hospitals rudely formed & all the incidents of war. These cannot be entirely avoided & newspapers can easily change them to negligence of commanders & thereby create disaffection. I do not say that the Press intends this but they have done this and are doing it all the time now I know that I made the most minute and careful preperation for the sick & wounded on the Yazoo, plenty of ambulances & men detailed in advance *to remove* the wounded—four (4) of the largest transports prepared & set aside before a shot was fired, & that every wounded man was taken from the field dressed & carefully attended immediately & yet I know that the Press has succeeded in making the very reverse impression & that many good people think there was criminal negligence. The same naked representations were made at Shiloh & I saw hundreds of Physicians come down & when our Surgeons begged & implored their help they preferred to gather up trophies & consume the dainties provided for the wounded & go back & represent the cruelty of the Army Surgeons & boast of their own disinterested humanity. I know this & that they nearly ruined Dr. Hewit one of the hardest working Surgeons in any army. I see similar attempts less successful however against Dr. McMillan not a word of truth not even a pretence of truth but it is a popular & successful theme & they avail themselves of it. What is the consequence? All officers of industry who stand by at all times through storm & sunshine find their reputations blasted & others usually the most lazy & indolent reaping cheap glory & fame through the correspondents of the Press. I say in giving intelligence to the enemy, in sowing discord & discontent in an army these men fulfil all the conditions of spies. Shall we succumb or shall we meet & overcome the evil? I am satisfied they have cost the country hundreds of millions of dollars, & brought our country to the brink of ruin & that unless the nuisance is abated we are lost. Here we are in front of Vicksburg. The attack direct in front would in our frail transports be marked by the sinking of Steamers loaded with troops, a fearful assault against hills fortified with great care by a cunning enemy. Every commander who has looked at it says it cannot be done in front it must be turned. I tried it but newspaper correspondents had sent word in advance & ample preperations were made & reinforcements to double my number had reached Vicksburg.

McClernand was unwilling to attack in front. Grant do. Then how turn the position? We cannot ascend the Yazoo to where our men can get a footing. We cannot run our frail transports past the Vicksburg Batteries then we resolve to cut a channel into Yazoo at the old pass near Delta above & into the Tensas by way of Lake Providence. Secrecy & dispatch are the chief elements of success. The forces here are kept to occupy the attention of the enemy two steamers are floated past the Batteries to control the River below & men are drawn secretly from Helena & Memphis to cut the canals & levies & remove all the inhabitants so that the enemy could not have notice till the floods of the Missippi could finish the work of man. But what avail? Known spies accompany each expedition & we now read in the northern papers (the same are in Vicksburg now) that our forces here are unequal to the direct assault but are cutting the two canals above: all our plans revealed & thwarted, the levies are cut & our plans work to a charm but the enemy now knows our purposes & hastens above, fells trees into the narrow head streams, cuts the side levies disperses the waters & defeats our well conceived plans. Who can carry on war thus? It is terrible to contemplate; & I say it that no intelligent officer in this or any American army now in the field but would prefer to have his opponent increased twenty—yea fifty per cent if the internal informers & spies could be excluded from our camps. I know our people are full of anxiety to hear from our armies but every soldier can & does write home, his family can at all times hear of his welfare & if the people could only see as I see the baneful effects of this mischeivous practise they would cry aloud in indignant tones. We may in self defense be compelled to take the law into our own hands for our safety or we may bend to the storm and seek a position where others may take the consequences of this cause. I early foresaw this result & have borne the malignity of the Press but a day will come & that far distant when the Press must surrender some portion of its freedom to save the rest else it too will perish in the general wreck. I think the *Commercial* misjudges my character somewhat. I certainly am not proud or haughty. Every soldier of my command comes into my presence as easy as the highest officer. Their beds & rations are as good as mine & certainly no General officer moves about with as little pomp as I. They see me daily nightly hourly, along the picket line afoot alone or with a Single orderly or officer whilst others have their mighty escorts & retinue. Indeed I am usually laughed at for my simplicity in this respect. Abrupt I am & all military men are. The mind jumps to its conclusions & is emphatic, & I can usually divine the motive of the insidious cotton Speculator camp follower & hypercritical humanity seeker before he discloses his plans & designs & an officer who must attend to the thousand & one wants of thirty thousand men besides the importunities of thousands of mischeivous camp followers must need be abrupt unless the day can be made more than twenty four hours long. A citizen cannot understand that an officer who has to see to the wants and necessities of an army has no time to listen to their usual long perorations & I must confess I have little patience with this class of men. To be sure policy would dictate a different course, & I know I could easily have acheived popularity by yeilding to these outside influences but I could not do what I see other popular officers do furnish transportation at Government expense to newspaper agents & supply them with public horses Seat them at my table to hear conversations of public matter give access to official papers which I am commanded to withhold to the world till my Employer has the benefit of them. I could not do these things & feel that I was an honest man & faithful servant of the Government for my memory still runs back to the time when Peter Hagner was Auditor of the Treasury, & when an officer would not take a Government nail out of a keg on which to hang his coat or feed his horse out of the public crib without charging its cost against his pay. That time is past, but must again return before the United States can regain its lost good name among the nations of the earth.

Again the habit of indiscriminate praise & flattery has done us harm. Let a stranger read our official reports & he would blush at the praise bespattered over who Regiments Divisions and Corps for skirmishes & actions where the dead & wounded mark no Serious conflict. When I praise I mean it & when troops fall into disorder I must notice it but you may read my reports in vain for an instance where troops have kept their ranks & done even moderately well but I have encouraged them to a better future. There is an unwritten history that will come out when the real soldiers come home. At the Post of Arkansas I wanted to storm the rifle pits by a Hurrah! One of my divisions faltered and in reply to my aid "How are things with you"? "Why Damn it my men are only wasting ammunition", I cautioned him to patience. "Be kind & coax along & notify me the moment you think your men are equal to the work"—hundreds heard me & yet this same officer would indulge now in extravagant boasts. I know that in trouble in danger in emergencies the men know I have patience a keen appreciation of the truth of facts & ground equalled by few and one day they will tell the truth. Many a solitary picket has seen me creeping by night examining ground before I ordered them to cross it & yet other lazy rascals ignorant of the truth would hang behind sleep or crouch around the distant camp fire till danger was passed, & then write "how Sherman with insane rashness had pushed his brave soldiers into the jaws of death."

I have departed from my theme. My argument is that newspaper correspondents & camp followers, writing with a purpose & with no data communicate facts useful to an enemy and useless to our cause & calculated to impair the discipline of the army & that the practise must cease We cannot appeal to Patriotism because news are a saleable commodity & the more valuable as it is the more pithy & damaging to our cause I am satisfied the enemy encourages this as the cheapest & most effectual weapon of war either by direct contribution of money or by becoming large purchasers of its numbers. The law gives us the means to stop it & as an army we fail in our duty to the Government to our cause & to ourselves if we do not use them.

To shew how the Press is used I will tell of another recent instance. The Captain of the Gun Boat *New Era* behaved badly, cowardly at Arkansas Post. Admiral Porter, a gallant officer sent him to Cairo in banishment. It was necessary for him to cover up his disgrace. Getting into safety nearly up to the Ohio he pretended he saw an army of 3,000 men near Island No. 10, & he shelled them away at a cost of many thousands of dollars. He alarmed the whole country & wrote his own account but not a man here believes he saw a single Guerilla. This is true of many glorious battles in the newspapers.

Our camp is about flooded & consequent idleness must form my apology for this long letter. If you think proper I have no objection to the Editor of the Commericial seeing this but I confess myself too "haughty" to allow it or anything else of mine to be printed. Affectionately
       W. T. Sherman

Camp before Vicksburg,
February 18, 1863

My Dear Brother,

I have seen your speeches on the subject of absentees, filling up the army with conscripts, and the necessity of standing by the President for the sake of unity of action. So at last I see you and the Country begin to realize what we ought to have known two years ago, that individual opinions however sincere, real & honest are too various to Secure unity of action, and at last that men must forego their individual notions and follow some one Leader, the Legitimate & Constitutional one if possible. Two years of war, costly & bloody have been endured and we have arrived by sad experience at a Result that all the world knew before. If the People of the North will not learn from the experience of the world, but must go on groping in the dark for experience to develop and demonstrate the Truth of established principles of Government, why of course there is no help for it, but as a people we must pay the price.

We have reproached the South for arbitrary conduct in coercing her People—at last we find we must imitate their example—we have denounced their tyranny in filling their armies with conscripts—and now we must follow her example—We have denounced their tyranny in suppressing freedom of speech and the press, and here too in time we must follow her Example. The longer it is deferred the worse it becomes.

Who gave notice of McDowell's movement on Manassas, & enabled Johnston so to reinforce Beauregard that our army was defeated?

The Press.

Who gave notice of the movement on Vicksburg?

The Press.

Who has prevented all secret combinations and movements against our enemy?

The Press.

Who has sown the seeds of hatred so deep, that Reason, Religion and Self interest cannot eradicate them?

The Press.

What is the real moving cause in this Rebellion? Mutual hatred & misrepresentations made by a venal Press.

In the South this powerful machine was at once scotched and used by the Rebel Government, but at the North was allowed to go free. What are the results. After arousing the passions of the people till the two great sections hate each other with a hate hardly parallelled in history, it now begins to Stir up sedition at home, and even to encourage mutiny in our armies. What has paralyzed the Army of the Potomac? Mutual jealousies kept alive by the Press. What has enabled the enemy to combine so as to hold Tennessee after we have twice crossed it with victorious armies. What defeats and will continue to defeat our best plans here and elsewhere? The Press.

I cannot pick up a paper but tells of our situation here, in the mud, sickness, and digging a canal in which we have little faith. But our officers attempt secretly to cut two other channels one into Yazoo by an old Pass, and one through Lake Providence into Tensas, Black Red &c., whereby we could turn not only Vicksburg Port Hudson, but also Grand Gulf, Natchez, Ellis Cliff, Fort Adams and all the strategic points on the Main River, and the busy agents of the Press follow up and proclaim to the world the whole thing, and instead of surprising our enemy we find him felling trees & blocking passages that would without this have been in our possession, and all the real effects of surprise are lost. I say with the Press unfettered as now we are defeated to the end of time. Tis folly to say the people must have news. Every soldier can and does write to his family & friends & all have ample opportunities for so doing, and this pretext forms no good reasons why agents of the Press should reveal prematurely all our plans & designs. We cannot prevent it. Clerks of steamboats, correspondents in disguise or openly attend each army & detachment, and presto appears in Memphis & St. Louis minute accounts of our plans & designs. These reach Vicksburg by telegraph from Hernando & Holly Springs before we know of it.

The only two really successful military strokes out here have succeeded because of the absence of newspapers or by throwing them off the trail—Halleck had to make a simulated attack on Columbus to prevent the Press giving notice of his intended move against Forts Henry & Donelson. We succeeded in reaching the Post of Arkansas before the Correspondents could reach their Papers. Now in war it is bad enough to have a bold daring enemy in great strength to our front without having an equally dangerous & treacherous foe within. I know if the People of the United States could see & realize the Truth of this matter they would agree to wait a few days for their accustomed batch of exciting news rather than expose their sons, brothers & friends as they inevitably do to failure and death. Of course I know the President & Congress are powerless in this matter & we must go on till perpetual defeat & disaster point out one of the Chief Causes. Instead of being governed by Reason, our people prefer to grope their way through personal Experience and must pay its cost. I only await a good time to Slide out & let the experiment go on at the expense of others. I have had my share & wish no more. I still have unlimited faith in Halleck & prefer that he should command the whole army than McClellan. Still I would like to have him come West. Affectionately

       Sherman

OPPOSING CONSCRIPTION:
WASHINGTON, D.C., FEBRUARY 1863

Clement L. Vallandigham: Speech in Congress

February 23, 1863

Ohio congressman Clement L. Vallandigham attended the final session of the 37th Congress as a lame duck after having been defeated for reelection in October 1862. A leader of the "Peace Democrats" who opposed emancipation and the continued prosecution of the war, Vallandigham gave a lengthy speech in the House on January 14 calling for an armistice, the withdrawal of Union troops from the seceded states, and negotiations aimed at peaceful reunion. He spoke again in February as the House debated the recently introduced conscription bill. Under its terms, male citizens (and immigrants applying for citizenship) between twenty and forty-five were subject to conscription if voluntary enlistments failed to fill the recruitment quota for their district. Men who were selected by lottery to be drafted could avoid service by hiring a substitute or by paying a $300 commutation fee. The bill passed the Senate, 35–11, and the House, 115–48, and was enacted on March 3, 1863.

Mr. VALLANDIGHAM said:

Mr. SPEAKER: I do not propose to discuss this bill at any great length in this House. I am satisfied that there is a settled purpose to enact it into a law, so far as it is possible for the action of the Senate and House and the President to make it such. I appeal, therefore, from you, from them, directly to the country; to a forum where there is no military committee, no previous question, no hour rule, and where the people themselves are the masters. I commend the spirit in which this discussion was commenced by the chairman of the Military Committee, [Mr. OLIN,] and I do it the more cheerfully because, unfortunately, he is not always in so good a temper as he was to-day: and I trust that throughout the debate, and on its close, he will exhibit that same disposition which characterized his opening remarks. Only let me caution him that he cannot dictate to the minority here what course they shall pursue. But, sir, I regret that I cannot extend the commendation to the gentleman from Pennsylvania, [Mr. CAMPBELL,] who addressed the House a little while ago. His speech was extremely offensive, and calculated to stir up a spirit of bitterness and strife, not at all consistent with that in which debates in this House should be conducted. If he or any other gentleman of the majority imagines that any one here is to be deterred by threats from the expression of his opinions, or from giving such votes as he may see fit to give, he has utterly misapprehended the temper and determination of those who sit on this side of the Chamber. His threat I hurl back with defiance into his teeth. I spurn it. I spit upon it. That is not the argument to be addressed to equals here: and I therefore most respectfully suggest that hereafter all such be dispensed with, and that we shall be spared personal denunciation and insinuations against the loyalty of men who sit with me here; men whose devotion to the Constitution and attachment to the Union of these States is as ardent and immovable as yours, and who only differ from you as to the mode of securing the great object nearest their hearts.

Mr. CAMPBELL. The gentleman will allow me—

Mr. VALLANDIGHAM. I yield for explanation.

Mr. CAMPBELL. Mr. Speaker, it is a significant fact that the gentleman from Ohio has applied my remarks to himself and others on his side of the House. Why was this done? I was denouncing *traitors* here, and I will denounce them while I have a place upon this floor. It is my duty and my privilege to do so. And if the gentleman from Ohio chooses to give my remarks a personal application, he can so apply them.

Mr. VALLANDIGHAM. That is enough.

Mr. CAMPBELL. One moment.

Mr. VALLANDIGHAM. Not another moment after that. I yielded the floor in the spirit of a gentleman, and not to be met in the manner of a blackguard. [Applause and hisses in the galleries.]

Mr. CAMPBELL. The member from Ohio is a blackguard. [Renewed hisses and applause in the galleries.]

Mr. ROBINSON. I rise to a question of order. I demand

that the galleries be cleared. We have been insulted time and again by contractors and plunderers of the Government, in these galleries, and I ask that they be now cleared.

Mr. COX. I hope my friend from Illinois will not insist on that. Only a very small portion of those in the galleries take part in these disturbances. The fool-killer will take care of them.

The SPEAKER *pro tempore*. The Chair will have to submit the question to the House.

Mr. COX. I hope the demand will be withdrawn.

The SPEAKER *pro tempore*. The Chair will state, that if disorder is repeated, whether by applause or expressions of disapprobation, he will feel called upon himself to order the galleries to be cleared, trusting that the House will sustain him in so doing.

Mr. ROBINSON. I desire the order to be enforced now, and the galleries to be cleared, excepting the ladies' gallery.

Mr. ROSCOE CONKLING. I was going to say that I hoped the order would not be extended to that portion of the galleries.

Mr. ROBINSON. The galleries were cautioned this afternoon.

Mr. JOHNSON. And it is the same men who have been making this disturbance now. I know their faces well.

Mr. VALLANDIGHAM. I think, Mr. Speaker, that this lesson has not been lost; and that it is sufficiently impressed now upon the minds of the audience that this is a legislative, and is supposed to be a deliberative, assembly, and that no breach of decorum or order should occur among them, whatever may be the conduct of any of us on the floor. I trust, therefore, that my friends on this side will withdraw the demand for the enforcement of the rule of the House.

Mr. ROBINSON. I withdraw the demand.

Mr. VERREE. I raise the point of order that members here, in debating questions before the House, are not at liberty to use language that is unparliamentary, and unworthy of a member.

The SPEAKER. That is the rule of the House.

Mr. VERREE. I hope it will be enforced.

Mr. VALLANDIGHAM. And I hope that it will be enforced, also, against members on the other side of the Chamber.

We have borne enough, more than enough of such language, for two years past.

The SPEAKER. The gentleman from Illinois withdraws his demand to have the galleries cleared. The Chair desires to say to gentlemen in the galleries, that this being a deliberative body, it is not becoming this House, or the character of American citizens, to disturb its deliberations by any expression of approval or disapproval.

Mr. VALLANDIGHAM. The member from Pennsylvania [Mr. CAMPBELL] alluded to-day, generally, to gentlemen on this side of the House. There was no mistaking the application. The language and gesture were both plain enough. He ventured also, approvingly, to call our attention to the opinions and course of conduct of some Democrats in the State of New York, as if we were to learn our lessons in Democracy, or in anything else, from that quarter. I do not know, certainly, to whom he alluded. Perhaps it was to a gentleman who spoke not long since in the city of New York, and advocated on that occasion, what is called in stereotype phrase "the vigorous prosecution of the war," and who, but two months previously, addressed assemblages in the same State and city, in which he proposed only to take Richmond, and then let the "wayward sisters depart in peace." Now, I know of no one on this side of the Chamber occupying such a position; and I, certainly, will not go to that quarter to learn lessons in patriotism or Democracy.

I have already said that it is not my purpose to debate the general merits of this bill at large, and for the reason that I am satisfied that argument is of no avail here. I appeal, therefore, to the people. Before them I propose to try this great question —the question of constitutional power, and of the unwise and injudicious exercise of it in this bill. We have been compelled, repeatedly, since the 4th of March, 1861, to appeal to the same tribunal. We appealed to it at the recent election. And the people did pronounce judgment upon our appeal. The member from Pennsylvania ought to have heard their sentence, and I venture to say that he did hear it, on the night of the election. In Ohio they spoke as with the voice of many waters. The very question of summary and arbitrary arrests, now sanctioned in this bill, was submitted, as a direct issue, to the people of that

State, as also of other States, and their verdict was rendered upon it. The Democratic convention of Ohio assembled on the 4th of July, in the city of Columbus, the largest and best ever held in the State, among other resolutions of the same temper and spirit, adopted this without a dissenting voice:

> "And we utterly condemn and denounce the repeated and gross violation, by the Executive of the United States, of the rights thus secured by the Constitution; and we also utterly repudiate and condemn the monstrous dogma, that in time of war the Constitution is suspended, or its power in any respect enlarged beyond the letter and true meaning of that instrument.
> "And we view, also, with indignation and alarm, the illegal and unconstitutional seizure and imprisonment, for alleged political offenses, of our citizens, without judicial process, in States where such process is unobstructed, but by executive order by telegraph, or otherwise, and call upon all who uphold the Union, the Constitution, and the laws, to unite with us in denouncing and repelling such flagrant violation of the State and Federal Constitutions, and tyrannical infraction of the rights and liberties of American citizens; and that the people of this State CANNOT SAFELY AND WILL NOT SUBMIT to have the freedom of speech and freedom of the press, the two great and essential bulwarks of civil liberty, put down by unwarranted and despotic exertion of power."

On that the judgment of the people was given at the October elections, and the party candidates nominated by the convention which adopted that resolution, were triumphantly elected. So, too, with the candidates of the same party in the States of Wisconsin, Illinois, Indiana, Pennsylvania, New Jersey, and New York. And, sir, that "healthy reaction," recently, of which the member from Pennsylvania [Mr. CAMPBELL] affected to boast, has escaped my keenest sense of vision. I see only that handwriting on the wall which the fingers of the people wrote against him and his party and this whole Administration, at the ballot-box, in October and November last. Talk to me, indeed, of the leniency of the Executive! too few arrests! too much forbearance by those in power! Sir, it is the people who have been too lenient. They have submitted to your oppressions and wrongs as no free people ought ever to submit. But the day of patient endurance has gone by at last. Mistake them not. They will be lenient no longer. Abide by the Constitution, stand by the laws, restore the Union if *you* can restore it—not by force; you have tried that and failed. Try some other method now—the ancient, the approved, the reasonable way—the way in which the Union was first made. Surrender it not now—not yet—never. But unity is not Union; and attempt not, at your peril—I warn you—to coerce unity by the utter destruction of the Constitution and of the rights of the States and the liberties of the people. Union is liberty and consent; unity is despotism and force. For what was the Union ordained? As a splendid edifice, to attract the gaze and admiration of the world? As a magnificent temple—a stupendous superstructure of marble and iron, like this Capitol, upon whose lofty dome the bronzed image—hollow and inanimate —of freedom is soon to stand erect in colossal mockery, while the true spirit, the living goddess of liberty, veils her eyes and turns away her face in sorrow, because, upon the altar established here, and dedicated by our fathers to her worship, you, a false and most disloyal priesthood, offer up, night and morning, the mingled sacrifices of servitude and despotism? No, sir. It was for the sake of the altar, the service, the religion, the devotees, that the temple of the Union was first erected; and when these are all gone, let the edifice itself perish. Never—never— never—will the people consent to lose their own personal and political rights and liberties, to the end that you may delude and mock them with the splendid unity of despotism.

Sir, what are the bills which have passed, or are still before the House? The bill to give the President entire control of the currency—the purse—of the country. A tax bill to clothe him with power over the whole property of the country. A bill to put all power in his hands over the personal liberties of the people. A bill to indemnify him, and all under him, for every act of oppression and outrage already consummated. A bill to enable him to suspend the writ of *habeas corpus*, in order to justify or protect him, and every minion of his, in the arrests which he or they may choose to make—arrests, too, for mere opinions' sake. Sir, some two hundred years ago, men were burned at the stake, subjected to the horrors of the Inquisition, to all the tortures that the devilish ingenuity of man could invent—for what? For opinions on questions of religion —of man's duty and relation to his God. And now, to-day, for opinions on questions political, under a free Government, in a country whose liberties were purchased by our fathers by seven years' outpouring of blood, and expenditure of treasure—we have lived to see men, the born heirs of this precious inheritance, subjected to arrest and cruel imprisonment at the caprice of a President or a Secretary or a constable. And, as if that were not enough, a bill is introduced here to-day, and pressed forward to a vote, with the right of debate, indeed—extorted from you by the minority—but without the right to amend, with no more than the mere privilege of protest—a bill which enables the President to bring under his power, as Commander-in-Chief, every man in the United States between the ages of twenty and forty-five—three millions of men. And, as if not satisfied with that, this bill provides, further, that every other citizen, man, woman, and child, under twenty years of age and over forty-five, including those that may be exempt between these ages, shall be also at the mercy—so far as his personal liberty is concerned—of some miserable "provost marshal" with the rank of a captain of cavalry, who is never to see service in the field; and every congressional district in the United States is to be governed—yes, governed—by this petty satrap —this military eunuch—this Baba—and he even may be black —who is to do the bidding of your Sultan, or his Grand Vizier. Sir, you have but one step further to go—give him the symbols of his office—the Turkish bow-string and the sack.

What is it, sir, but a bill to abrogate the Constitution, to repeal all existing laws, to destroy all rights, to strike down the judiciary, and erect upon the ruins of civil and political liberty a stupendous superstructure of despotism. And for what? To enforce law? No, sir. It is admitted now by the legislation of Congress, and by the two proclamations of the President, it is admitted by common consent, that the war is for the abolition of negro slavery, to secure freedom to the black man. You tell me, some of you, I know, that it is so prosecuted because this is the only way to restore the Union; but others openly and candidly confess that the purpose of the prosecution of the war is to abolish slavery. And thus, sir, it is that the freedom of the negro is to be purchased, under this bill, at the sacrifice of every right of the white men of the United States.

Sir, I am opposed, earnestly, inexorably opposed, to this

measure. If there were not another man in this House to vote against it, if there were none to raise his voice against it, I, at least, dare stand here alone in my place, as a Representative, undismayed, unseduced, unterrified, and heedless of the miserable cry of "disloyalty," of sympathy with the rebellion and with rebels, to denounce it as the very consummation of the conspiracy against the Constitution and the liberties of my country.

Sir, I yield to no man in devotion to the Union. I am for maintaining it upon the principles on which it was first formed; and I would have it, at every sacrifice, except of honor, which is "the life of the nation." I have stood by it in boyhood and in manhood, to this hour; and I will not now consent to yield it up; nor am I to be driven from an earnest and persistent support of the only means by which it can be restored, either by the threats of the party of the Administration here, or because of affected sneers and contemptuous refusals to listen, now, to reunion, by the party of the administration at Richmond. I never was weak enough to cower before the reign of terror inaugurated by the men in power here, nor vain enough to expect favorable responses now, or terms of settlement, from the men in power, or the presses under their control, in the South. Neither will ever compromise this great quarrel, nor agree to peace on the basis of reunion; but, I repeat it—stop fighting, and let time and natural causes operate—uncontrolled by military influences—and the ballot there, as the ballot here, will do its work. I am for the Union of these States; and but for my profound conviction that it can never be restored by force and arms; or, if so restored, could not be maintained, and would not be worth maintaining, I would have united, at first —even now would unite, cordially—in giving, as I have acquiesced, silently, in your taking, all the men and all the money you have demanded. But I did not believe, and do not now believe, that the war could end in anything but final defeat; and if it should last long enough, then in disunion; or, if successful upon the principles now proclaimed, that it must and would end in the establishment of an imperial military despotism— not only in the South—but in the North and West. And to that I never will submit. No, rather, first I am ready to yield up property, and liberty—nay, life itself.

Sir, I do not propose to discuss now the question of the constitutionality of this measure. The gentleman from Ohio who preceded me, [Mr. WHITE,] has spared me the necessity of an argument on that point. He has shown that between the Army of the United States, of which, by the Constitution, the President of the United States is the Commander-in-Chief, and the militia, belonging to the States, there is a wide and clearly marked line of distinction. The distinction is fully and strongly defined in the Constitution, and has been recognized in the entire legislation and practice of the Government from the beginning. The States have the right, and have always exercised it, of appointing the officers of their militia, and you have no power to take it away. Sir, this bill was originally introduced in the Senate as a militia bill, and as such it recognized the right of the States to appoint the officers; but finding it impossible, upon that basis, to give to the Executive of the United States the entire control of the millions thus organized into a military force, as the conspirators against State rights and popular liberty desire, the original bill was abandoned; and to-day behold here a stupendous conscription bill for a standing army of more than three million men, forced from their homes, their families, their fields, and their workshops; an army organized, officered, and commanded by the servant President, now the master dictator of the United States. And for what? Foreign war? Home defense? No; but for coercion, invasion, and the abolition of negro slavery by force. Sir, the conscription of Russia is mild and merciful and just compared with this. And yet the enforcement of that conscription has just stirred again the slumbering spirit of insurrection in Poland, though the heel of despotic power has trodden upon the necks of her people for a century.

Where, now, are your taunts and denunciations, heaped upon the confederate government for its conscription, when you, yourselves, become the humble imitators of that government, and bring in here a conscription act, more odious even than that passed by the confederate congress at Richmond? Sir, the chairman of the Military Committee rejoiced that for the last two years the Army had been filled up by voluntary enlistments. Yes, your Army has hitherto been thus filled up by the men of the North and West. One million two hundred and thirty-seven thousand men—for most of the drafted men enlisted, or procured substitutes—have voluntarily surrendered their civil rights, subjected themselves to military law, and thus passed under the command and within the control of the President of the United States. It is not for me to complain of that. It was their own act—done of their own free will and accord—unless bounties, promises, and persuasion may be regarded as coercion. The work you proposed was gigantic, and your means proportionate to it. And what has been the result? What do you propose now? What is this bill? A confession that the people are no longer ready to enlist; that they are not willing to carry on this war longer, until some effort has been made to settle this great controversy in some other way than by the sword. And yet, in addition to the one million two hundred and thirty-seven thousand men who have voluntarily enlisted, you propose now to force the entire body of the people, between the ages of twenty and forty-five, under military law, and within the control of the President as Commander-in-Chief of the Army, for three years, or during the war—which is to say "for life;" ay, sir, for life, and half your Army has already found, or will yet find, that their enlistment was for life too.

I repeat it, sir, this bill is a confession that the people of the country are against this war. It is a solemn admission upon the record in the legislation of Congress that they will not voluntarily consent to wage it any longer. And yet, ignoring every principle upon which the Government was founded, this measure is an attempt by compulsion to carry it on against the will of the people. Sir, what does all this mean? You were a majority at first; the people were almost unanimously with you, and they were generous and enthusiastic in your support. You abused your power and your trust, and you failed to do the work which you promised. You have lost the confidence, lost the hearts of the people. You are now in a minority at home. And yet, what a spectacle is exhibited here to-night! You, an accidental, temporary majority, condemned and repudiated by the people, are exhausting the few remaining hours of your political life in attempting to defeat the popular will, and to compel, by the most desperate and despotic of expedients ever resorted to, the submission of the majority of the people, at home, to the minority, their servants here. Sir, this experiment has been tried before in other ages and countries, and its issue always, among a people born free, or fit to be free, has been expulsion or death to the conspirators and tyrants.

I make no threats. They are not arguments fit to be addressed to equals in a legislative assembly; but there is truth—solemn, alarming truth—in what has been said to-day by gentlemen on this side of the Chamber. Have a care, have a care, I entreat you, that you do not press these measures too far. I shall do nothing to stir up an already excited people—not because of any fear of your contemptible petty provost marshals, but because I desire to see no violence or revolution in the North or West. But I warn you now, that whenever, against the will of the people, and to perpetuate power and office in a popular Government which they have taken from you, you undertake to enforce this bill, and, like the destroying angel in Egypt, enter every house for the first-born sons of the people—remember Poland. You cannot and will not be permitted to establish a military despotism. Be not encouraged by the submission of other nations. The people of Austria, of Russia, of Spain, of Italy have never known the independence and liberty of freemen. France, in seventy years, has witnessed seven principal revolutions—the last brought about in a single day by the arbitrary attempt of the king to suppress freedom of speech and of the press, and next the free assembling of the people; and when he would have retraced his steps and restored these liberties, a voice from the galleries—not filled with clerks and plunderers and placemen—uttered the sentiments and will of the people of France, in words now historic: "It is too late." The people of England never submitted, and would not now submit, for a moment, to the despotism which you propose to inaugurate in America. England cannot, to-day, fill up her standing armies by conscription. Even the "press gang," unknown to her laws, but for a time acquiesced in, has long since been declared illegal; and a sweeping conscription like this, now, would hurl not only the ministry from power, but the queen from her throne.

Sir, so far as this bill is a mere military measure, I might have been content to have given a silent vote against it; but there are two provisions in it hostile, both to the letter and spirit of the Constitution, and inconsistent with the avowed scope and purpose of the bill itself; and, certainly, as I read them in the light of events which have occurred in the past two years, of a character which demands that the majority of this House shall strike them out. There is nothing in the argument that we have no time to send the bill back to the Senate, lest it should be lost. The Presiding Officers of both Houses are friends of the bill, and will constitute committees of conference of men favorable to it. They will agree at once, and can at any moment, between this and the 4th of March, present their report as a question of the highest privilege; and you have a two thirds majority in both branches to adopt it.

With these provisions of the bill stricken out, leaving it simply as a military measure, to be tested by the great question of peace or war, I would be willing that the majority of the House should take the responsibility of passing it without further debate; although, even then, you would place every man in the United States, between the ages of twenty and forty-five, under military law, and within the control, everywhere, of the President, except the very few who are exempt; but you would leave the shadow, at least, of liberty to all men not between these ages, or not subject to draft under this bill, and to the women and children of the country too.

Sir, these two provisions propose to go a step further, and include every one, man, woman, and child, and to place him or her under the arbitrary power not only of the President and his Cabinet, but of some two hundred and fifty other petty officers, captains of cavalry, appointed by him. There is no distinction of sex, and none of age. These provisions, sir, are contained in the seventh and twenty-fifth sections of the bill. What are they? I comment not on the appointment of a general provost marshal of the United States, and provost marshals in every congressional district. Let that pass. But what do you propose to make the duty of each provost marshal in carrying out the draft? Among other things, that he shall "inquire into and report to the Provost Marshal General"—what? Treason? No. Felony? No. Breach of the peace, or violation of law of any kind? No; but "treasonable practices;" yes, TREASONABLE PRACTICES. What mean you by these strange, ominous words? Whence come they? Sir, they are no more new or original than any other of the cast-off rags filched by this Administration from the lumber-house of other and more antiquated despotisms. The history of European tyranny has taught us somewhat of this doctrine of constructive treason. Treasonable practices! Sir, the very language is borrowed from the old proclamations of the British monarchs some hundreds of years ago. It brings up the old, identical quarrel of the fourteenth century. Treasonable practices? It was this that called forth that English act of Parliament of twenty-fifth Edward III, from which we have borrowed the noble provision against constructive treason in the Constitution of the United States. Arbitrary arrests for no crime known, defined or limited by law, but for pretended offenses, herded together under the general and most comprehensive name of "treasonable practices," had been so frequent, in the worst periods of English history that, in the language of the act of Henry IV, "no man knew how to behave himself or what to do or say for doubt of the pains of treason." The statute of Edward III had cut all these fungous, toadstool treasons up by the root; and yet, so prompt is arbitrary power to denounce all opposition to it as treasonable that, as Lord Hale observes—

"Things were so carried by parties and factions in the succeeding reign of Richard II, that this statute was but little observed but as this or that party got the better. So the crime of high treason was, in a manner, arbitrarily imposed and adjudged *to the disadvantage of the party which was to be judged*; which, by various vicissitudes and revolutions, mischiefed all parties first and last, and left a great unsettledness and unquietness in the minds of the people, and was one of the occasions of the unhappiness of the king."

And he adds that—

"It came to pass that almost every offense that was *or seemed to be* a breach of the faith and allegiance due to the king, was, by *construction, consequence, and interpretation*, raised into the offense of high treason."

Richard II procured an act of Parliament—even he did not pretend to have power to do it by proclamation—declaring that the bare purpose to depose the king and to place another in his stead, without any overt act, was treason; and yet, as Blackstone remarks, so little effect have over-violent laws to prevent crime, that within two years afterwards this very prince was both deposed and put to death. Still the struggle for arbitrary and despotic power continued; and up to the time of Charles I, at various periods, almost every conceivable offense relating to the government, and every form of opposition to the king, was declared high treason. Among these were execrations against the king; calling him opprobrious names by public writing; refusing to abjure the Pope; marrying, without license, certain of the king's near relatives; derogating from his royal style or title; impugning his supremacy; or assembling riotously to the number of twelve, and refusing to disperse on proclamation. But steadily, in better times, the people and the Parliament of England returned to the spirit and letter of the act of Edward III, passed by a Parliament which now, for five hundred years, has been known and honored as *Parliamentum benedictum*, the "blessed Parliament"—just as this Congress will be known, for ages to come, as "the accursed Congress"— and among many other acts, it was declared by a statute, in the first year of the fourth Henry's reign, that "*in no time to come* any treason be judged, otherwise than as ordained by the statute of King Edward III." And for nearly two hundred years, it has been the aim of the lawyers and judges of England to adhere to the plain letter, spirit, and intent of that act, "to be extended," in the language of Erskine in his noble defense of Hardy, "by no new or occasional constructions—to be strained by no fancied analogies—to be measured by no rules of political expediency—to be judged of by no theory—to be determined by the wisdom of no individual, however wise—but to be expounded by the simple, genuine letter of the law."

Such, sir, is the law of treason in England to-day; and so much of the just and admirable statute of Edward as is applicable to our form of government was embodied in the Constitution of the United States. The men of 1787 were well read in history and in English constitutional law. They knew that monarchs and Governments, in all ages, had struggled to extend the limits of treason, so as to include all opposition to those in power. They had learned the maxim that, miserable is the servitude where the law is either uncertain or unknown, and had studied and valued the profound declaration of Montesquieu, that, "if the crime of treason be indeterminate, that alone is sufficient to make any Government degenerate into arbitrary power." Hear Madison, in the Federalist:

"As *new-fangled and artificial treasons* have been the great engines by which violent factions, the natural offspring of free governments, have usually *wreaked their alternate malignity on each other*, the convention have, with great judgment, opposed a barrier to this peculiar danger, by inserting a constitutional definition of the crime, fixing the proof necessary for conviction of it, and restraining the Congress, even in punishing it, from extending the consequences of guilt beyond the person of its author."

And Story, not foreseeing the possibility of such a party or Administration as is now in power, declared it "*an impassable barrier* against arbitrary constructions, either by the courts or by Congress, upon the crime of treason." "Congress;" that, sir, is the word, for he never dreamed that the President, or, still less, his clerks, the Cabinet ministers, would attempt to declare and punish treasons. And yet what have we lived to hear in America daily, not in political harangues or the press only, but in official proclamations and in bills in Congress! Yes, your high officials talk now of "treasonable practices" as glibly "as girls of thirteen do of puppy dogs." Treasonable practices! Disloyalty! Who imported these precious phrases, and gave them a legal settlement here? Your Secretary of War. He it was who by command of our most noble President authorized every marshal, every sheriff, every township constable, or city policeman, in every State in the Union, to fix, in his own imagination, what he might choose to call a treasonable or disloyal practice, and then to arrest any citizen at his discretion, without any accusing oath, and without due process or any process of law. And now, sir, all this monstrous tyranny, against the whole spirit and the very letter of the Constitution, is to be deliberately embodied in an act of Congress! Your petty provost marshals are to determine what treasonable practices are, and "inquire into," detect, spy out, eaves-drop, insnare, and then inform, report to the chief spy at Washington. These, sir, are now to be our American liberties under your Administration. There is not a crowned head in Europe who dare venture on such an experiment. How long think you this people will submit? But words, too—conversation or public speech—are to be adjudged "treasonable practices." Men, women, and children are to be haled to prison for free speech. Whoever shall denounce or oppose this Administration; whoever may affirm that war will not restore the Union, and teach men the gospel of peace, may be reported and arrested upon some old grudge, and by some ancient enemy, it may be, and imprisoned as guilty of a treasonable practice.

Sir, there can be but one treasonable practice under the Constitution in the United States. Admonished by the lessons of English history, the framers of that instrument defined what treason is. It is the only offense defined in the Constitution. We know what it is. Every man can tell whether he has committed treason. He has only to look into the Constitution, and he knows whether he has been guilty of the offense. But neither the Executive nor Congress, nor both combined, nor the courts, have a right to declare, either by pretended law or by construction, that any other offense shall be treason, except that defined and limited in this instrument. What is treason? It is the highest offense known to the law, the most execrable crime known to the human heart—the crime of *læsæ majestatis*; of the parricide who lifts his hand against the country of his birth or his adoption. "Treason against the United States," says the Constitution, "shall consist ONLY in levying war against them, or in adhering to their enemies, giving them aid and comfort." [Here a Republican member nodded several times and smiled.] Ah, sir, I understand you. But was Lord Chatham guilty of legal treason, treasonable aid and comfort, when he denounced the war against the colonies, and rejoiced that America had resisted? Was Burke, or Fox, or Barré guilty, when defending the Americans in the British Parliament, and demanding conciliation and peace? Were even the Federalists guilty of treason, as defined in the Constitution, for "giving aid and comfort" to the enemy in the war of 1812? Were the Whigs in 1846? Was the Ohio Senator liable to punishment, under the Constitution, and by law, who said, sixteen years ago, in the Senate Chamber, when we were at war in Mexico, "if I were a Mexican as I am an American, I would greet your volunteers with bloody hands, and welcome them to hospitable graves?" Was Abraham Lincoln guilty, because he denounced that same war, while a Representative on the floor of this House? Was all this "adhering to the enemy, giving him aid and comfort" within the meaning of this provision?

A MEMBER.   The Democratic papers said so.

Mr. VALLANDIGHAM.   Sir, I am speaking now as a lawyer and as a legislator to legislators and lawyers acting under oath and the other special and solemn sanctions of this Chamber, and not in the loose language of the political canvass. And I repeat, sir, that if such had been the intent of the Constitution, the whole Federal party and the whole Whig party and their representatives in this and the other Chamber might have been indicted and punished as traitors. Yet, not one of them was ever arrested. And shall they or their descendants undertake now to denounce and to punish, as guilty of treason, every man who opposes the policy of this Administration, or is against this civil war, and for peace upon honorable terms? I hope, in spite of the hundreds of your provost marshals, and all your threats, that there will be so much of opposition to the war as will compel the Administration to show a decent respect for and yield some sort of obedience to the Constitution and laws, and to the rights and liberties of the States and of the people.

But to return; the Constitution not only defines the crime of treason, but in its jealous care to guard against the abuses of tyrannic power, it expressly ascertains the character of the proof, and the number of witnesses necessary for conviction, and limits the punishment to the person of the offender; thus going beyond both the statute of Edward, and the common law. And yet every one of these provisions is ignored or violated by this bill.

"No person"—

Says the Constitution—

"shall be convicted of treason"—

As just defined—

"unless on the testimony of two witnesses."

Where and when, and by whom, sir, are the two witnesses to be examined, and under what oath? By your provost marshals, your captains of cavalry? By the jailors of your military bastiles, and inside of Forts Warren and La Fayette? Before arrest, upon arrest, while in prison, when discharged, or at any time at all? Has any witness ever been examined in any case heretofore? What means the Constitution by declaring that no person shall be *convicted* of treason "unless on the *testimony of two witnesses?*" Clearly, conviction in a judicial court, upon testimony openly given under oath, with all the sanctions and safe-guards of a judicial trial to the party accused. And if any doubt there could be upon this point, it is removed by the sixth article of the amendments.

But the Constitution proceeds:

"Unless on the testimony of two witnesses *to the same overt act.*"

But words, and still less, thoughts or opinions, sir, are not acts; and yet nearly every case of arbitrary arrest and imprisonment, in the wholly loyal States, at least, has been for words spoken or written, or for thoughts or opinions supposed to be entertained by the party arrested. And that, too, sir, is precisely what is intended by this bill.

But further:

"The testimony of two witnesses to the same overt act, *or confession in open court.*"

What court? The court of some deputy provost marshal at home, or of your Provost Marshal General or Judge Advocate General here in Washington? The court of a military bastile, whose gates are shut day and night against every officer of the law, and whose very casemates are closed to the light and air of heaven? Call you that "open court?" Not so the Constitution. It means judicial court, law court, with judge and jury and witnesses and counsel; and to speak of it as anything else is a confusion of language, and an insult to intelligence and common sense. Yet, to-night, you deliberately propose to enact the illegal and unconstitutional executive orders, or proclamations of last summer, into the semblance and form of law.

"To inquire into treasonable practices," says the bill. So, then, your provost marshals are to be deputy spies to the grand spy, holding his secret inquisitions here in Washington, upon secret reports, sent by telegraph, perhaps, or through the mails, both under the control of the Executive. What right has he to arrest and hold me without a hearing, because some deputy spy of his chooses to report me guilty of "disloyalty," or of "treasonable practices?" Is this the liberty secured by the Constitution? Sir, let me tell you that if the purpose of this bill be to crush out all opposition to the Administration and the party in power, you have no constitutional right to enact it, and not force enough to compel the people, your masters, to submit.

But the enormity of the measure does not stop here. Says the Constitution:

"Congress shall make no law abridging the freedom of speech or of the press."

And yet speech—mere words, derogatory to the President, or in opposition to his administration and his party and policy, have, over and over again, been reported by the spies and informers and shadows, or other minions, of the men in power, to be "disloyal practices," for which hundreds of free American citizens, of American, not African descent, have been arrested and imprisoned for months, without public accusation, and without trial by jury, or trial at all. Even upon pretense of guilt of that most vague and indefinite, but most comprehensive of all offenses, "discouraging enlistments," men have been seized at midnight, and dragged from their beds, their homes, and their families, to be shut up in the stone casemates of your military fortresses, as felons. And now, by this bill, you propose to declare, in the form and semblance of law, that whoever "counsels or dissuades" any one from the performance of the military duty required under this conscription, shall be summarily arrested by your provost marshals, and held without trial till the draft shall have been completed. Sir, even the "sedition law" of '98 was constitutional, merciful, and just, compared with this execrable enactment. Wisely did Hamilton ask, in the Federalist, "What signifies a declaration that the liberty of the press (or of speech) shall be inviolably preserved, when its security must altogether depend on public opinion, *and on the general spirit of the people*, and of the Government?"

But this extraordinary bill does not stop here.

"No person,"

Says the Constitution,

"*No* person shall be held to answer for a capital or otherwise infamous crime, unless on a presentment or indictment of a grand jury, except in cases arising in the land and naval force, or in the militia when in actual service in time of war or public danger; nor be deprived of life, liberty, or property, without due process of law."

Note the exception. Every man not in the military service is exempt from arrest except by due process of law; or, being arrested without it, is entitled to demand immediate inquiry and discharge, or bail; and if held, then presentment or indictment by a grand jury in a civil court, and according to the law of the land. And yet you now propose by this bill, in addition to the one million two hundred and thirty-seven thousand men who have voluntarily surrendered that great right of freemen, second only to the ballot—and, indeed, essential to it—to take it away forcibly and against their consent, from three millions more, whose only crime is that they happen to have been so born as to be now between the ages of twenty and forty-five. Do it, if you can, under the Constitution; and when you have thus forced them into the military service they will be subject to military law, and not entitled to arrest only upon due process of law, nor to indictment by a grand jury in a civil court. But you cannot, you shall not—because the Constitution forbids it—deprive the whole people, also, of the United States of these rights, "inestimable to them and formidable to tyrants only," under the "war power," or upon pretense of "military necessity," and by virtue of an act of Congress creating and defining new treasons, new offenses, not only unknown to the Constitution, but expressly excluded by it.

But again:

"In all criminal prosecutions"—

And wherever a penalty is to be imposed, imprisonment or fine inflicted, it is a criminal prosecution—

"In all criminal prosecutions"—

Says the Constitution—

"the accused shall enjoy the right to a speedy and public trial, by an impartial jury of the State and district wherein the crime shall have been committed, which district shall have been previously ascertained by law; and to be informed of the nature and cause of the accusation; to be confronted with the witnesses against him; to have compulsory process for obtaining witnesses in his favor, and to have the assistance of counsel for his defense."

Do you propose to allow any of these rights? No, sir; none —not one; but, in the twenty-fifth section, you empower these provost marshals of yours to arrest any man—men not under military law—whom he may charge, or any one else may charge before him, with "counseling or dissuading" from military service, and to hold him in confinement indefinitely, until the draft has been completed. Sir, has it been completed in Connecticut yet? Is it complete in New York? Has it been given up? If so now, nevertheless it was in process of pretended execution for months. In any event, you propose now to leave to the discretion of the Executive the time during which all persons arrested under the provisions of this bill, shall be held in confinement upon that summary and arbitrary arrest; and when he sees fit, and then only, shall the accused be delivered over to the civil authorities for trial. And is this the speedy and public trial by jury which the Constitution secures to every citizen not in the military service?

"The State and district wherein the crime"—

Yes, crime, for crime it must be, known to and defined by law, to justify the arrest—

"shall have been committed, which district shall have been previously ascertained by law."

Do you mean to obey that, and to observe State lines or district lines in arrests and imprisonments? Has it ever been done? Were not Keyes and Olds and Mahoney and Sheward, and my friend here to the left, [Mr. ALLEN, of Illinois,] and my other friend from Maryland, [Mr. MAY,] dragged from their several States and districts to New York or Massachusetts or to this city? The pirate, the murderer, the counterfeiter, the thief—you would have seized by due and sworn process of law, and tried forthwith, by jury, at home; but honorable and guiltless citizens, members of this House, your peers upon this floor, were thrust, and may again, under this bill, be thrust into distant dungeons and bastiles, upon the pretense of some crawling, verminous spy and informer that they have "dissuaded" some one from obedience to the draft, or are otherwise guilty of some "treasonable practice."

"And to be informed of the nature and cause of the accusation."

How? By presentment or indictment of a grand jury. When? "Speedily," says the Constitution. "When the draft is completed," says this bill; and the President shall determine that. But who is to limit and define "counseling or dissuading" from military service? Who shall ascertain and inform the accused of the "nature and cause" of a "treasonable practice?" Who, of all the thousand victims of arbitrary arrests, within the last twenty-two months, even to this day, has been informed of the charge against him, although long since released? Yet even a Roman pro-consul, in a conquered province, refused to send up a prisoner without signifying the crimes with which he was charged.

"To be confronted with the witnesses against him."

Witnesses, indeed! Fortunate will be the accused if there be any witnesses against him. But is your deputy provost marshal to call them? Oh, no; he is only to "inquire into, and report." Is your Provost Marshal General? What! call witnesses from the remotest parts of the Union to a secret inquisition here in Washington. Has any "prisoner of State" hitherto been confronted with witnesses at any time? Has he even been allowed to know so much as the names of his accusers? Yet Festus could boast that it was not the manner of the Romans to punish any man "before that he, which is accused, have the accusers face to face."

"To have compulsory process for obtaining witnesses in his favor."

Sir, the compulsory process will be, under this bill, as it has been from the first, to compel the absence, rather, of not only the witnesses, but the friends and nearest relatives of the accused; even the wife of his bosom and his children—the inmates of his own household. Newspapers, the Bible, letters from home, except under surveillance, a breath of air, a sight of the waves of the sea, or of the mild, blue sky, the song of birds, whatever was denied to the prisoner of Chillon, and more, too; yes, even a solitary lamp in the casemate, where a dying prisoner struggled with death, all have been refused to the American citizen accused of disloyal speech or opinions, by this most just and merciful Administration.

And, finally, says the Constitution:

"To have the assistance of counsel for his defense."

And yet your Secretary of State, the "conservative" Seward—the confederate of Weed, that treacherous, dissembling foe to constitutional liberty and the true interests of his country—forbade his prisoners to employ counsel, under penalty of prolonged imprisonment. Yes, charged with treasonable practices, yet the demand for counsel was to be dealt with as equal to treason itself. Here is an order, signed by a minion of Mr. Seward, and read to the prisoners at Fort La Fayette, on the 3d of December, 1861:

"I am instructed by the Secretary of State to inform you that the Department of State of the United States *will not recognize anyone as an attorney for political prisoners*, and will look with distrust upon all applications for release through such channels; and that such applications *will be regarded as additional reasons for declining to release the prisoners.*"

And here is another order to the same effect, dated "Department of State, Washington, November 27, 1861," signed by William H. Seward himself, and read to the prisoners at Fort Warren on the 29th of November, 1861:

"Discountenancing and repudiating all such practices"—

The disloyal practice, forsooth, of employing counsel—

"the Secretary of State desires that all the State prisoners may understand *that they are expected to revoke all such engagements now existing and avoid any hereafter*, as they can only lead to new complications and embarrassments to the cases of prisoners on whose behalf *the Government might be disposed to act with liberality.*"

Most magnanimous Secretary! Liberality toward men guilty of no crime, but who, though they had been murderers or pirates, were entitled by the plain letter of the Constitution to have "the assistance of counsel for their defense." Sir, there was but one step further possible, and that short step was taken some months later, when the prisoners of State were required to make oath, as the condition of their discharge, that they would not seek their constitutional and legal remedy in court for the wrongs and outrages inflicted upon them.

Sir, incredible as all this will seem some years hence, it has happened, all of it, and more yet untold, within the last twenty months, in the United States. Under Executive usurpation, and by virtue of presidential proclamations and cabinet orders, it has been done without law and against Constitution; and now it is proposed, I repeat, to sanction and authorize it all by an equally unconstitutional and void act of Congress. Sir, legislative tyranny is no more tolerable than Executive tyranny. It is a vain thing to seek to cloak all this under the false semblance of law. Liberty is no more guarded or secured, and arbitrary power no more hedged in and limited here than under the Executive orders of last summer. We know what has already been done, and we will submit to it no longer. Away, then, with your vain clamor about disloyalty, your miserable mockery of treasonable practices. We have read with virtuous indignation in history ages ago of an Englishman executed for treason, in saying that he would make his son heir to the crown, meaning of his own tavern-house, which bore the sign of the crown; and of that other Englishman, whose favorite buck the king had killed, and who suffered death as a traitor, for wishing, in a fit of vexation, that the buck, horns and all, were emboweled in the body of the king. But what have we not lived to see in our own time? Sir, not many months ago, this Administration in its great and tender mercy toward the six hundred and forty prisoners of State, confined for treasonable practices, at Camp Chase near the capital of Ohio, appointed a commissioner, an extra judicial functionary, unknown to the Constitution and laws, to hear and determine the cases of the several parties accused, and with power to discharge at his discretion, or to banish to Bull's Island, in Lake Erie. Among the political prisoners called before him was a lad of fifteen, a newsboy upon the Ohio river, whose only offense proved, upon inquiry, to be that he owed fifteen cents the unpaid balance of a debt due to his washer-woman—possibly a woman of color—who had him arrested by the provost marshal as guilty of "disloyal practices." And yet, for four weary months the lad had lain in that foul and most loathsome prison, under military charge, lest, peradventure, he should overturn the Government of the United States; or, at least, the administration of Abraham Lincoln!

Several MEMBERS on the Democratic side of the House. Oh no; the case cannot be possible.

Mr. VALLANDIGHAM.   It is absolutely true, and it is one only among many such cases. Why, sir, was not the hump-back carrier of the New York Daily News, a paper edited by a member of this House, arrested in Connecticut, for selling that paper, and hurried off out of the State, and imprisoned in Fort La Fayette? And yet, Senators and Representatives, catching up the brutal cry of a bloodthirsty but infatuated partisan press, exclaim "the Government has been too lenient, there ought to have been more arrests!"

Well did Hamilton remark that "arbitrary imprisonments have been in all ages the favorite and most formidable instruments of tyranny;" and, not less truly, Blackstone declares that they are "a less public, a less striking, and therefore *a more dangerous engine* of arbitrary government" than executions upon the scaffold. And yet, to-night, you seek here, under cloak of an act of Congress, to authorize these arrests and imprisonments, and thus to renew again that reign of terror which smote the hearts of the stoutest among us, last summer, as "the pestilence which walketh in darkness."

But the Constitution provides further, that

"The right of the people to be secure in their persons, houses, papers, and effects, against unreasonable searches and seizures, shall not be violated, and no warrants shall issue but upon probable cause, supported by oath or affirmation, and particularly describing the place to be searched and the persons or things to be seized."

Sir, every line, letter, and syllable of this provision has been repeatedly violated, under pretense of securing evidence of disloyal or treasonable practices; and now you propose by this bill to sanction the past violations, and authorize new and continued infractions in future. Your provost marshals, your captains of cavalry are to "inquire into treasonable practices."

How? In any way, sir, that they may see fit; and of course by search and seizure of person, house, papers, or effects; for, sworn and appointed spies and informers as they are, they will be and can be of no higher character, and no more scrupulous of law or right or decency than their predecessors of last summer, appointed under Executive proclamations of no more or less validity than this bill which you seek now to pass into a law. Sir, there is but one step further to take. Put down the peaceable assembling of the people; the right of petition for redress of grievances; the "right of the people to keep and bear arms;" and finally the right of suffrage and elections, and then these United States, this Republic of ours, will have ceased to exist. And that short step you will soon take, if the States and the people do not firmly and speedily check you in your headlong plunge into despotism. What yet remains? The Constitution declares that—

"The enumeration in the Constitution of certain rights shall not be construed to deny or disparage others retained by the people."

And again:

"The powers not delegated to the United States by the Constitution, nor prohibited by it to the States, are reserved to the States respectively or to the people."

And yet, under the monstrous doctrine that in war the Constitution is suspended, and that the President as Commander-in-Chief, not of the military forces only, but of the whole people of the United States, may, under "the war power," do whatever he shall think necessary and proper to be done, in any State or part of any State, however remote from the scene of warfare, every right of the people is violated or threatened, and every power of the States usurped. Their last bulwark, the militia, belonging solely to the States when not called as such into the actual service of the United States, you now deliberately propose, by this bill, to sweep away, and to constitute the President supreme military dictator, with a standing army of three millions and more at his command. And for what purpose are the militia to be thus taken from the power and custody of the States? Sir, the opponents of the Constitution anticipated all this, and were denounced as raving incendiaries or distempered enthusiasts.

"The Federal Government"—

Said Patrick Henry, in the Virginia Convention,

"squints towards monarchy. Your President may easily become a king. If ever he violates the laws, *will not the recollection of his crimes teach him to make one bold push for the American throne?* Will not the immense difference between being master of everything and being ignominiously tried and punished powerfully excite him to make this bold push? But, sir, where is the existing force to punish him? Can he not, at the head of his army, beat down all opposition? What, then, will become of you and your rights? Will not absolute despotism ensue?"*

And yet, for these apprehensions, Henry has been the subject of laughter and pity for seventy years. Sir, the instinctive love of liberty is wiser and more far-seeing than any philosophy.

Hear, now, Alexander Hamilton, in the Federalist. Summing up what he calls the exaggerated and improbable suggestions respecting the power of calling for the services of the militia, urged by the opponents of the Constitution, whose writings he compares to some ill-written tale, or romance full of frightful and distorted shapes, he says:

"The militia of New Hampshire, they allege, is to be marched to Georgia; of Georgia to New Hampshire; of New York to Kentucky; and of Kentucky to Lake Champlain. Nay, the debts due to the French and Dutch are to be paid in militia men, instead of Louis d'ors and ducats. At one moment, there is to be a large army to lay prostrate the liberties of the people; at another moment, the militia of Virginia are to be dragged from their homes, five or six hundred miles, to tame the republican contumacy of Massachusetts; *and that of Massachusetts is to be transported an equal distance to subdue the refractory haughtiness of the aristocratic Virginians.* Do persons who

---

*And the reporter, unable to follow the vehement orator of the Revolution, adds:

"Here, Mr. Henry strongly and pathetically expatiated on the probability of the President's enslaving America, and the horrid consequences that must result."

rave at this rate imagine that their eloquence can impose any conceits or absurdities upon the people of America for infallible truths?"

And yet, sir, just three quarters of a century later we have lived to see these ravings, conceits, and absurdities practiced, or attempted, as calmly and deliberately as though the power and the right had been expressly conferred.

And now, sir, listen to the answer of Hamilton to all this—himself the friend of a strong Government, a Senate for life, and an Executive for life, with the sole and exclusive power over the militia, to be held by the national Government; and the Executive of each State to be appointed by that Government:

> "If there should be an army to be made use of as the engine of despotism, what need of the militia? If there should be no army, *whither would the militia, irritated at being required to undertake a distant and distressing expedition, for the purpose of riveting the chains of slavery upon a part of their countrymen, direct their course*, BUT TO THE SEATS OF THE TYRANTS WHO HAD MEDITATED SO FOOLISH AS WELL AS SO WICKED A PROJECT; TO CRUSH THEM IN THEIR IMAGINED INTRENCHMENTS OF POWER, AND MAKE THEM AN EXAMPLE OF THE VENGEANCE OF AN ABUSED AND INCENSED PEOPLE? Is this the way in which usurpers stride to dominion over a numerous and enlightened nation?"

Sir, Mr. Hamilton was an earnest, sincere man, and, doubtless, wrote what he believed: he was an able man also, and a philosopher; and yet how little did he foresee, that just seventy-five years later, that same Government, which he was striving to establish, would, in desperate hands, attempt to seize the whole militia of the Union, and convert them into a standing army, indefinite as to the time of its service, and for the very purpose of not only beating down State sovereignties, but of abolishing even the domestic and social institutions of the States.

Sir, if your objects are constitutional, you have power abundantly under the Constitution, without infraction or usurpation. The men who framed that instrument made it both for war and peace. Nay, more, they expressly provide for the cases of insurrection and rebellion. You have ample power to do all that of right you ought to do—all that the people, your masters, permit under their supreme will, the Constitution. Confine, then, yourselves within these limits, and the rising storm of popular discontent will be hushed.

But I return, now, again, to the arbitrary arrests sanctioned by this bill, and by that other consummation of despotism, the indemnity and suspension bill, now in the Senate. Sir, this is the very question which, as I said a little while ago, we made a chief issue before the people in the late elections. You did, then, distinctly claim—and you found an Attorney General and a few other venal or very venerable lawyers to defend the monstrous claim—that the President had the right to suspend the writ of *habeas corpus*; and that every one of these arrests was legal and justifiable. We went before the people with the Constitution and the laws in our hands, and the love of liberty in our hearts; and the verdict of the people was rendered against you. We insisted that Congress alone could suspend the writ of *habeas corpus* when, in cases of rebellion or invasion, the public safety might require it. And today, sir, that is beginning to be again the acknowledged doctrine. The Chief Justice of the Supreme Court of the United States so ruled in the Merryman case; and the supreme court of Wisconsin, I rejoice to say, has rendered a like decision; and if the question be ever brought before the Supreme Court of the United States, undoubtedly it will be so decided, finally and forever. You yourselves now admit it; and at this moment, your "indemnity bill," a measure more execrable than even this conscription, and liable to every objection which I have urged against it, undertakes to authorize the President to suspend the writ all over or in any part of the United States. Sir, I deny that you can thus delegate your right to the Executive. Even your own power is conditional. You cannot suspend the writ except where the public safety requires it, and then only in cases of rebellion or invasion. A foreign war, not brought home by invasion, to our own soil, does not authorize the suspension, in any case. And who is to judge whether and where there is rebellion or invasion, and whether and when the public safety requires that the writ be suspended? Congress alone, and they cannot substitute the judgment of the President for their own. Such, too, is the opinion of Story: "The right to judge," says he, "whether exigency has arisen, must *exclusively* belong to that body." But not so under the bill which passed this House the other day.

Nor is this all. Congress alone can suspend the writ. When and where? In cases of rebellion or invasion. Where rebellion? Where invasion? Am I to be told that because there is rebellion in South Carolina the writ of *habeas corpus* can be suspended in Pennsylvania and Massachusetts where there is none? Is that the meaning of the Constitution? No, sir; the writ can be suspended only where the rebellion or invasion exists—in States, or parts of States, alone, where the enemy, foreign or domestic, is found in arms; and moreover, the public safety can require its suspension only where there is rebellion or invasion. Outside of these conditions, Congress has no more authority to suspend the writ than the President, and, least of all, to suspend it without limitation as to time, and generally all over the Union, and in States not invaded or in rebellion. Such an act of Congress is of no more validity, and no more entitled to obedience, than an executive proclamation; and in any just and impartial court I venture to affirm that it will be so decided.

But again, sir, even though the writ be constitutionally suspended, there is no more power in the President to make arbitrary arrests than without it. The gentleman from Rhode Island [Mr. SHEFFIELD] said, very justly—and I am sorry to see him lend any support to this bill—that the suspension of the writ of *habeas corpus* does not authorize arrests except upon sworn warrant, charging some offense known to the law and dangerous to the public safety. He is right. It does not; and this was so admitted in the bill which passed the Senate in 1807. The suspension only denies release upon bail, or a discharge without trial, to parties thus arrested. It suspends no other right or privilege under the Constitution—certainly not the right to a speedy public trial by jury in a civil court. It dispenses with no "due process of law," except only that particular writ. It does not take away the claim for damages to which a party illegally arrested, or legally arrested, but without probable cause, is entitled.

And yet, everywhere, it has been assumed that a suspension of the writ of *habeas corpus* is a suspension of the entire Constitution and of all laws, so far as the personal rights of the citizen are concerned, and that, therefore, the moment it is suspended, either by the President, as heretofore asserted, or by Congress, as now about to be authorized, arbitrary arrests, without sworn warrant or other due process of law, may be made at the sole pleasure or discretion of the Executive. I tell you no; and that, although we may not be able to take the body of the party arrested from the provost marshal by writ of *habeas corpus*, every other right and privilege of the Constitution and of the common law remains intact, including the right to resist the wrong-doer or trespasser, who, without due authority, would violate your person, or enter your house, which is your castle; and, after all this, the right also to prosecute on indictment or for damages, as the nature or aggravation of the case may demand. And yet, as claimed by you of the party in power, the suspension of this writ is a total abrogation of the Constitution and of the liberties of the citizen and the rights of the States. Why, then, sir, stop with arbitrary arrests and imprisonments? Does any man believe that it will end here? Not so have I learned history. The guillotine! the guillotine! the guillotine follows next.

Sir, when one of those earliest confined in Fort La Fayette— I had it from his own lips—made complaint to the Secretary of State of the injustice of his arrest, and the severity of the treatment to which he had been subjected in the exercise of arbitrary power, no offense being alleged against him, "why," said the Secretary, with a smile of most significant complacency, "my dear sir, you ought not to complain; *we might have gone further*." Light flashed upon the mind of the gentleman, and he replied: "Ah! that is true, sir; you had just the same right to behead as to arrest and imprison me." And shall it come to this? Then, sir, let us see who is beheaded first. It is horrible enough to be imprisoned without crime, but when it becomes a question of life or death, remember the words of the book of Job—"All that a man hath will he give for his life."

Sir, it is this which makes revolutions. A gentleman upon the other side asked this afternoon which party was to rise now in revolution. The answer of the able and gallant gentleman from Pennsylvania [Mr. BIDDLE] was pertinent and just—"No party, but an outraged people." It is not, let me tell you, the leaders of parties who begin revolutions. Never. Did any one of the distinguished characters of the Revolution of 1776 participate in the throwing of the tea into Boston harbor? Who was it? Who, to-day, can name the actors in that now historic scene? It was not Hancock, nor Samuel Adams, nor John Adams, nor Patrick Henry, nor Washington; but men unknown to fame. Good men agitate; obscure men begin real revolutions; great men finally direct and control them. And if, indeed, we are about to pass through the usual stages of revolution, it will not be the leaders of the Democratic party—not I, not the men with me here to-night—but some man among the people, now unknown and unnoted, who will hurl your tea into the harbor; and it may even be in Boston once again; for the love of liberty, I would fain believe, lingers still under the shadow of the monument on Bunker Hill. But, sir, we seek no revolution —except through the ballot-box. The conflict to which we challenge you, is not of arms but of argument. Do you believe in the virtue and intelligence of the people? Do you admit their capacity for self-government? Have they not intelligence enough to understand the right, and virtue enough to pursue it? Come then: meet us through the press, and with free speech, and before the assemblages of the people, and we will argue these questions, as we and our fathers have done from the beginning of the Government—"Are we right or you right, we wrong or you wrong?" And by the judgment of the people we will, one and all, abide.

Sir, I have done now with my objections to this bill. I have spoken as though the Constitution survived, and was still the supreme law of the land. But if, indeed, there be no Constitution any longer, limiting and restraining the men in power, then there is none binding upon the States or the people. God forbid. We have a Constitution yet, and laws yet. To them I appeal. Give us our rights; give us known and fixed laws; give us the judiciary; arrest us only upon due process of law; give us presentment or indictment by grand juries; speedy and public trial; trial by jury, and at home; tell us the nature and cause of the accusation; confront us with witnesses; allow us witnesses in our behalf, and the assistance of counsel for our defense; secure us in our persons, our houses, our papers, and our effects; leave us arms, not for resistance to law or against rightful authority, but to defend ourselves from outrage and violence;

give us free speech and a free press; the right peaceably to assemble; and above all, free and undisturbed elections and the ballot; take our sons, take our money, our property, take all else; and we will wait a little, till at the time and in the manner appointed by Constitution and law we shall eject you from the trusts you have abused, and the seats of power you have dishonored, and other and better men shall reign in your stead.

"VILE AND TRAITOROUS RESOLUTIONS":
VIRGINIA, FEBRUARY 1863

Samuel W. Fiske to the Springfield Republican

The Democratic state convention that met in Hartford, Connecticut, on February 18, 1863, nominated Thomas H. Seymour for governor. It adopted a platform denouncing "the 'monstrous fallacy' that the Union can be restored by the armed hand" and calling for a negotiated peace. Lieutenant Samuel W. Fiske of the 14th Connecticut Infantry responded in one of his regular letters to the *Springfield* (Massachusetts) *Republican*, written under the pen name Dunn Browne. Several Connecticut regiments, including Fiske's, subsequently adopted statements opposing Seymour's candidacy and the Hartford platform. The resolutions of the 14th Connecticut, possibly drafted by Fiske, called for "the earnest, thorough and rapid prosecution of the war" and declared that the regiment's sacrifices had been made "in the cause of republican government, of democracy against aristocracy, of freedom against slavery." In the election held on April 6, Governor William A. Buckingham, the Republican incumbent running on a Union ticket, defeated Seymour with 51.6 percent of the vote.

On the Connecticut Copperheads

Camp near Falmouth, Va.
February 25

Oh Republican! Give me a Hartford Times or some other appropriate receptacle, for I am about to vomit. I am sick, nauseated, poisoned; have taken something that, most emphatically, doesn't agree with me; have swallowed the vile and traitorous resolutions of the recent Democratic convention at Hartford, and have read in connection some of the speeches on the same occasion, filled with ribaldry and profanity just about in keeping with the whole spirit of the meeting. And I am ashamed and confounded, disgusted and grieved, to see what proportions treason has attained even in dear old New England. I knew that such things were talked in the darker sections of our western Egypt. I wouldn't have been surprised to read of proceedings a little like those at Hartford as having taken place in some very ignorant district in southern Indiana. But in Connecticut, faugh! I can't begin to express my feelings, and yet I am obliged to confess that I am one of her citizens. If the dear old state doesn't spew out of her mouth this ill-savoring Tom Seymour Democracy at the coming April election, we of the army will march North instead of South to get at the heart of the rebellion.

Talk about demoralization of the army! Well, we have fallen pretty low. We haven't the same strain of lofty patriotism in our talk as when we first came out. We have been knocked round and starved and frozen till we have some of us forgotten the distinction between a good government and its sometimes corrupt agents, and in our personal indignation we lost sight, for the moment, of our correct principles. We have said many things that were not complimentary to our lawful civil and military leaders; yes, we have said many things that we shall be ashamed of, if we ever get home; but I do still fully believe and hope that if any man should talk such foul stuff as that of this modern Hartford convention in any of our camps, we should have principle and decency enough left to roll him in one of our Virginia gutters and drum him out of camp. Thank God we are not so demoralized yet as to suffer downright, earnest treason to be talked in our presence.

But enough of such a disgusting subject. Let us roll some more pleasantly flavored morsel under our tongue to get that taste out of our mouth. Spring is coming, our time of hope, of fresh life and vigor, our time of accustomed triumph. The winter is almost over. Let us hope that the "winter of our discontent," of our discouragement, reverses and distress, shall pass away with it, and that when the mud dries up, and the grass grows green, we may also "dry up" our murmuring, and our laurels grow green. I look for a great series of spring victories like those of last year—of grand, crushing, final victories—victories that shall shut off all question of foreign intervention, make such a performance as this Hartford convention a thing for even Connecticut Seymour Democrats to be ashamed of, and take away every shadow of hope from their fellow traitors at the South. I say I am *looking* for such victories. I shall continue to *look* for them very attentively and anxiously. Oh how happy we shall all be if we only find them. Yours, as ever,

DUNN BROWNE

February 25, 1863

DEFENDING FORT MCALLISTER:
GEORGIA, MARCH 1863

Charles C. Jones Jr. to Charles C. Jones Sr. and Mary Jones

Lieutenant Colonel Charles C. Jones Jr., a Confederate artillery officer serving at Savannah, wrote to his parents about the Union bombardment of Fort McAllister, which guarded the entrance to the Ogeechee River south of the city. Contrary to Jones's expectation, the Union attack on the fort was not renewed on the following day. It had been ordered by Rear Admiral Samuel F. Du Pont, who was planning an assault on Charleston Harbor, as a test of the ability of his ironclads to damage earthwork fortifications.

Savannah, *Tuesday*, March 3rd, 1863

My very dear Father and Mother,

The abolitionists, with three ironclads, four gunboats, and several mortar boats, attacked Fort McAllister this morning. They opened fire about half-past eight, and the engagement continued without intermission until near half-past four o'clock P.M. The last dispatch, which left the fort after the firing had ceased, reports that only two of our men were wounded during the whole of this protracted bombardment, and they only slightly. The carriage of the eight-inch columbiad was disabled by a shot from the enemy. A new one has been sent out; and the gun itself, which was not injured, will be remounted during the night and be all ready for action in the morning. The injury to the parapet of the fort is slight, and will be repaired during the night. The garrison is in fine spirits, and are determined to hold the fort to the last extremity. It is truly wonderful how mercifully and abundantly the good and great God of Battles has encircled our brave men with the protection of His all-powerful arm, shielding them from harm amid dangers imminent and protracted. To Him our hearts ascend in humble, fervent gratitude for the past; from Him we earnestly implore like favor in the future. If the Lord is on our side, as we honestly trust and believe He is, we will not fear what our enemies, with all their boasted strength, can do unto us.

The enemy seems determined to reduce this fort if practicable, probably with a view to the destruction of the railroad bridge. That little fort has thus far so successfully and so bravely resisted every effort on their part for its reduction that they will doubtless use every endeavor, as a matter of pride, to compass its destruction. There is no question of the fact that it is a remarkably well-constructed earthwork—well traversed. The lessons of the past and of the present so demonstrate. It is almost a miniature edition of Vicksburg. In like manner must all our defenses be conducted.

The dispatch to which I alluded above states further that the ironclads, etc., retired, apparently with a view to obtaining an additional supply of ammunition. They dropped down the river only a little way, and a store ship soon joined them and appeared to be serving out ammunition. The attack will doubtless be renewed in the morning; in fact, while I write from my office in the barracks at this 9½ P.M., I hear guns in the direction of Genesis Point. The enemy will probably continue the bombardment at intervals during the night, with a view to wearying our men and preventing the necessary repairs to the fort; and when the morning light again cleverly dawns, the attack will be renewed with vigor. We are supplying the deficiencies in ammunition caused by the expenditures of the day. It is thought that one ironclad was seriously injured. This may be, however, only *conjecture*; we hope such is the *fact*.

The land force on our side, now in the vicinity of the fort and prepared to resist any effort of the enemy to land, consists of the 29th Georgia Regiment, the sharpshooter battalion, two companies in the fort, our light battery, and some seven or more cavalry companies. With the natural advantages of the country these men, if they do their duty, ought to accomplish a great deal.

We have been reinforced at this point by the arrival of the brave General Walker. General Clingman reached the city today with his brigade of three regiments, and General Taliaferro is expected with his brigade. General Beauregard announces himself prepared to come over at any moment that his services are needed. I trust and confidently believe that we will, with the blessing of Heaven, be able successfully to defend the city from the expected attack, and to teach the enemy a fearful lesson which will not be speedily forgotten.

I am getting my light artillery in capital condition, and hope, when the opportunity presents itself, to render efficient service.

The Doctor came in this afternoon and is staying with us. Mr. Ward also returned by the Charleston train. Many, many thanks, my very dear mother, for your kind and most acceptable remembrance of us.

I am very much pained, my dear father, to hear that you are still so weak. All I can do is to hope and pray that you may soon be better, and that it would please God in tender mercy to us all to prolong your days, so precious to us all. . . . Do, my dear parents, let me know if I can do anything for you at any time, or for my dear little daughter. I wish very much to see you all, but at present it is impossible for me to leave the post of duty, for it is emphatically the fact that we know not what an hour may bring forth. . . . With warmest love to you both, my dear father and mother, and many tender kisses for my dear little daughter, I am ever

> Your affectionate son,
> Charles C. Jones, Jr.

"FIGHT MORE MANFULLY THAN EVER": GEORGIA, MARCH 1863

Charles C. Jones Sr. to Charles C. Jones Jr.

A retired Presbyterian minister, Jones wrote to his son from one of the three plantations his family owned in Liberty County, Georgia. After suffering for years from the "wasting palsy," Jones would die peacefully at Arcadia plantation on March 16, 1863.

Arcadia, *Wednesday*, March 4th, 1863

My dear Son,

Your kind favor of last evening reached us this morning, and afforded us the very information which we were anxious to receive—circumstantial and reliable. No paper from Savannah came.

Surely we have reason to bless God and take courage and fight more manfully than ever. The bombardment of Genesis Point is one of *the events* of this most eventful war. The failure of the vaunted ironclads will have a great moral effect. The enemy will have less confidence, and we stronger assurance, of being able with properly constructed fortifications and good armament, and above all with *brave men*, to repulse them. I look upon it as a special providence—an answer to prayer. Eight hours' bombardment with three ironclads and some six or seven mortar and gunboats, and only two men slightly wounded, one gun carriage injured, and the damage to the breastworks repaired in the night! We learn that the enemy has renewed the attack this morning. May it please God to help us through to the end, that they may be finally repulsed!

The effect of this affair will be most salutary upon our troops in Savannah and Charleston. Right glad am I to learn that you are still receiving reinforcements for the defense of the city, and that an excellent spirit prevails, and that our outposts are to be defended to the last extremity and the enemy fought inch by inch. That is the plan. We heard yesterday that the enemy were to be permitted to land, and the outposts were to be given up, and our forces retired within the line of the city defenses! What an idea! What would be the consequence? A regular siege approach, an accumulation of men and matériel, and the city in all probability captured! Never retire and confine ourselves within our defenses until we are forced to do it.

Am happy to know also that you are so much better, and exerting yourself with energy and judgment and with so much success in putting your batteries in the best order for service. They will no doubt play an important part if the conflict comes, and may determine the fortunes of the day—in which event I trust, my dear son, and pray that God would shield your life and your person and enable you to discharge your duty as a Christian man and as a true soldier and patriot. General Walker is a great accession. Do you observe the *mercy* in the Genesis affair? *Not a man killed*; not one *dangerously* wounded!

The presence of your dear brother with you at this time gives great comfort to Mother and myself, and must be so to you both. The Doctor would not delay, but went down to be with you and on hand with the staff of surgeons if there should be a necessity. I looked at all his fine cases of instruments, and told him I wished they might always be kept in the same capital order, but he never be called to use them on the field of battle. His visit has greatly refreshed us.

Your dear baby is quite well all to the eruption. *She walked alone for the first time Sunday, March 1st, 1863.* Mother, Daughter, Robert, and Miss Kitty Stiles all unite in love and respects to you both. The Lord bless and keep you both!

Your ever affectionate father (with a tired hand),

C. C. Jones.

BLACK REFUGEES: VIRGINIA, MARCH 1863
Harriet Jacobs to Lydia Maria Child

Harriet Jacobs, the author of *Incidents in the Life of a Slave Girl*, had gone to the District of Columbia in the summer of 1862 and begun relief work among the former slaves who had fled there. She wrote about conditions in northern Virginia to the abolitionist Lydia Maria Child, who had edited *Incidents*, in a letter that appeared in William Lloyd Garrison's antislavery newspaper *The Liberator* on April 10, 1863.

COLORED REFUGEES IN OUR CAMPS.

The following letter is from a very worthy, intelligent woman, who was herself a slave during twenty-five years, and who is now manifesting sympathy with her long-oppressed people by nursing them in the vicinity of our camps. To do this, she not only relinquishes good wages in a family for many years strongly attached to her, but also liberally imparts from her own earnings to the destitute around her.

L. M. CHILD.

ALEXANDRIA, March 18.

Since I last wrote to you, the condition of the poor refugees has improved. During the winter months, the small pox carried them off by hundreds; but now it has somewhat abated. At present, we have one hundred and forty patients in the hospital. The misery I have witnessed must be seen to be believed. The Quakers of Philadelphia, who sent me here, have done nobly for my people. They have indeed proved themselves a Society of Friends. Had it not been for their timely relief, many more must have died. They have sent thousands and tens of thousands of dollars to different sections of the country, wherever these poor sufferers came within our lines. But, notwithstanding all that has been done, very many have died from destitution. It is impossible to reach them all. Government has erected here barracks for the accommodations of five hundred. We have fifteen hundred on the list.

Many have found employment, and are supporting themselves and their families. It would do your heart good to talk with some of these people. They are quick, intelligent, and full of the spirit of freedom. Some of them say to me, "The white men of the North have helped us thus far, and we want to help *them*. We would like to fight for them, if they would only treat us like men."

The colored people could not do enough for the first regiments that came here. They had entire faith in them as the deliverers of their race. The sight of the U.S. uniform took all fear out of their hearts, and inspired them with hope and confidence. Many of them freely fed the soldiers at their own tables, and lodged them as comfortably as possible in their humble dwellings. The change is very sad. In return for their kindness and ever-ready service, they often receive insults, and sometimes beatings, and so they have learned to distrust those who wear the uniform of the U.S. You know how warmly I have sympathized with the Northern army; all the more does it grieve me to see so many of them false to the principles of freedom. But I am proud and happy to know that the black man is to strike a blow for liberty. I am rejoiced that Col. Shaw heads the Massachusetts regiment, for I know he has a noble heart.

How pitiful it is that members of any religious sect should come here, and return home to report their observations, without one word of sympathy for God's suffering poor! This is suggested to me by reading the New York *Evangelist*. These poor refugees undoubtedly have faults, as all human beings would have, under similar circumstances. I agree with that noble man, Gen. Saxton, who says they appear to him to be "extremely human." As to drunkenness, I have seen but one case. As to stealing, I wish the writer in the New York *Evangelist* had made himself acquainted with the old slave-pen here, now used for a prison. When I last went there, I found seventy whites and one colored man. The marriage law has been disregarded, from old habits formed in slavery, and from want of true friends to encourage them in the observance of it now. I wish the writer of that article could have been where I was last night, in our rough, little, poorly-built church.

It was densely crowded; and although some alarm was

excited by the rafters giving way overhead, quiet was soon restored, and the people were deeply attentive. Eight couples were married on this occasion. We have a day-school of eighty scholars, and a large number attend our evening school—mostly adults. A large sewing-circle, composed of young and old, meet every Saturday afternoon. Three colored men teach a school in this city for those who can afford to pay somewhat for instruction. They have a large number of pupils, mostly children of colored citizens; but a few of the "little contrabands" attend their school.

We are now collecting together the orphan children, of whom there are a great number, owing to the many deaths that have occurred of late. In justice to the refugee women, I am bound to testify that I have never known them, in any one instance, refuse to shelter an orphan. In many cases, mothers who have five or six children of their own, without enough to feed and cover them, will readily receive these helpless little ones into their own poor hovels.

O, when will the white man learn to know the hearts of my abused and suffering people!

HARRIET JACOBS.

UNIONIST REFUGEES: MISSOURI, MARCH 1863

William Henry Harrison Clayton to Nide and Rachel Pugh

By 1863 disaffection with the war and resistance to conscription had become widespread in many upland areas of the Confederacy, including western Virginia, eastern Tennessee, western North Carolina, northwestern Georgia, and northern Alabama. William Henry Harrison Clayton, a company clerk in the 19th Iowa Infantry, wrote from southwestern Missouri about Arkansas Unionists.

Forsyth MO.
March 26th, 1863
Dear Uncle & Aunt:
I take up my pen this evening for the purpose of writing a few lines to you. I have been thinking of writing for some time past, but not having anything of importance to communicate I neglected doing so.

You will see by the heading of my letter that we are still in the same old place, where we have been for the past two months. We have been holding the "*post*" here during the time mentioned, but once or twice have thought of "driving it in the ground" and leaving but have not done so as yet. In one of my letters home a short time ago I mentioned that our forage train was attacked by the rebels and although three times as many in number as our men, they retreated after our men gave them one volley.

The commander at Springfield hearing that there was a force marching upon this place sent down a reinforcement of about 200 men of the 13th Kansas infantry & 4 field pieces. They remained here a few days and then returned to Springfield, forage being so scarce in this part of the world that it is impossible to keep a battery here. Things quieted down until a few days ago, when a couple of suspicious looking fellows came around examining things and were caught in trying to get through the pickets after dark. They immediately were put under guard, and one of our *Union* butternuts with them. During the night this fellow by playing secesh got out of them, that they were *spies* and were to get $300 apiece for coming here to find out our numbers and position and report them to the rebel commander at Yellville on the morning of the 24th and then it was their intention to attack us with 5000 men and some artillery. Nearly the whole regiment was set to work erecting breastworks. A number of log houses were torn down and the logs piled up and a long line of breastworks was put up in short order. We worked at them yesterday and the day before. Today the usual quiet reigns in camp, there being only a few men at work putting on the *finishing touch*.

I apprehend no attack here at the present time anyhow for we have reinforcements within a day or two's march, and they will never attack us unless they have five or six times as many as we have.

A large number of Union refugees are here or have passed through here going north. Last Sunday 20 Union men came in. They are recruits for an Arkansas regiment being made up at Fayetteville, one of them an old man 57 years of age had been shot through the left shoulder by the bushwhackers a short time before they came away. The most of them had been lying out in mountains for a good while to escape being taken to the Confederate army. Several of them were *conscripts* and were with Hindman at Prairie Grove. Hindman's army was completely demoralized at that fight. One of these men said that all in the regiment he belongs to deserted, except 3 men. They also say that Hindman had 32 regiments in that engagement. We fought them in that long-to-be-remembered fight from 10 o'clock A.M. until 4 P.M. with only 6 regiments. Blunt then came in with 3 or 4 more regiments and we cleaned them out.

We have witnessed some painful things here. Members of families have passed through going north. They generally have cattle yoked to their old ricketty wagons, and often they are driven by women or very small boys, the father being either in some of the Missouri regiments, killed by the bushwhackers, or conscripted into the rebel army. To see women trudging along through the mud, poorly clad, and driving ox teams or as I saw in one instance when five women came from Arkansas all walking, two or three of them carrying infants in their arms and several children beside about "knee high to a duck" (they were hardly old enough to walk). Some of the women carried a few articles such as tin buckets etc. and the balance of their property was packed on an old grey horse. The "secesh" had taken everything from these women because their husbands had enlisted in the Union Arkansas regiment. Such sights make the blood boil and to make a person come to the conclusion that there is no punishment severe enough for those scoundrels who have brought about the present state of affairs by their taking up arms against the best government that this world has ever seen. There is another thing that "kinder gits" us, that is the action of a set of men in the North who are blind to their own interests and are endeavoring to *kick up a fuss* in even our own state of Iowa. Would to God that some of the leading copperheads were compelled to come down to this region and if they had to live here six months I think it would cure them and they would be content to go home and stay there and let the government take its own course in putting down the rebellion. One consolation is that they find little sympathy in the army and I assure you that some of them would be roughly used if they were where the soldiers could get hold of them.

The 19th adopted a series of resolutions a short time ago assuring the people of Iowa and all others that we give the government our undivided support. We enlisted for the purpose of aiding in putting down this infernal rebellion and we intend to do so. I have heard a number of the regiment express their views in regard to these northern *traitors* for they are nothing else and always there is ten times the hatred towards the northern traitors there is to those who are in arms against us.

We have two new recruits in our company who came from Texas. They came in and desired to enlist and were taken in our company.

Today 5 more came in and have enlisted in another company. Part of them have been in the rebel service. The rebels are conscripting in Arkansas, and numbers will doubtless be compelled to go who would rather be on our side.

We have had excellent weather for 3 weeks past. Part of the time it was nearly warm enough for summertime, the ground was dry and in good order for plowing but there is none of that kind of work going on in this vicinity. The grass is coming along nicely, and the woods are beginning to put on their coat of green.

Peach trees are out in blossom. There has been a few cold mornings lately but I think not cold enough to kill the peaches.

The past winter has been very favorable as far as cold weather is concerned, to us soldiers. I have not seen the ground froze more than 2 or 3 inches during the winter. I believe I have scribbled enough for one time and will bring my letter to a close.

Uncle Nide, I know your dislike of writing but I want you to write me a letter if it is ever so short. If Uncle Sammy Clayton is at your house tell him to write also. I send my best respects to him. Tell the folks at home that I am all right. "Nincy" and Ab. Buckles are well.

Hoping this will find you as it leaves me, in the enjoyment of good health.

I remain ever your affectionate nephew,
Wm. H. H. Clayton

P.S. I suppose that Lt. Ferguson has reached home before this time. Tell him that Lt. Sommerville has been and is yet very sick. Disease typhoid fever. He was taken to a private residence about 3 miles up the river a week or two ago. Also that our devil Bill Hartson has come to the company. All quiet on White River at the present.

WITHDRAWING SLAVES FROM THE ENEMY:
WASHINGTON, D.C., MARCH 1863

Henry W. Halleck to Ulysses S. Grant

Believing that his army could neither provide for nor safely transport black refugees, Major General Ulysses S. Grant issued orders in February 1863 forbidding them from coming into the Union camps near Vicksburg. Major General Henry W. Halleck had been Grant's commanding officer in the western theater before being appointed general-in-chief of the Union army in July 1862. Halleck wrote to Grant about the government's policy regarding freed slaves in advance of the arrival in early April of Brigadier General Lorenzo Thomas, the army's adjutant general, who had been sent to recruit black soldiers in the Mississippi Valley. Grant would energetically assist Thomas in his recruiting efforts, and on April 11 ordered one of his division commanders to "encourage all negroes, particularly middle aged males to come within our lines."

HEADQUARTERS OF THE ARMY,
Washington, March 31, 1863.

Maj. Gen. U. S. GRANT,
Commanding Department of the Tennessee, near Vicksburg:

GENERAL: It is the policy of the Government to withdraw from the enemy as much productive labor as possible. So long as the rebels retain and employ their slaves in producing grains, &c., they can employ all the whites in the field. Every slave withdrawn from the enemy is equivalent to a white man put *hors de combat.*

Again, it is the policy of the Government to use the negroes of the South, as far as practicable, as a military force, for the defense of forts, depots, &c. If the experience of General Banks near New Orleans should be satisfactory, a much larger force will be organized during the coming summer; and if they can be used to hold points on the Mississippi during the sickly season, it will afford much relief to our armies. They certainly can be used with advantage as laborers, teamsters, cooks, &c., and it is the opinion of many who have examined the question without passion or prejudice, that they can also be used as a military force. It certainly is good policy to use them to the very best advantage we can. Like almost anything else, they may be made instruments of good or evil. In the hands of the enemy, they are used with much effect against us; in our hands, we must try to use them with the best possible effect against the rebels.

It has been reported to the Secretary of War that many of the officers of your command not only discourage the negroes from coming under our protection, but by ill-treatment force them to return to their masters. This is not only bad policy in itself, but is directly opposed to the policy adopted by the Government. Whatever may be the individual opinion of an officer in regard to the wisdom of measures adopted and announced by the Government, it is the duty of every one to cheerfully and honestly endeavor to carry out the measures so adopted. Their good or bad policy is a matter of opinion before they are tried; their real character can only be determined by a fair trial. When adopted by the Government, it is the duty of every officer to give them such a trial, and to do everything in his power to carry the orders of his Government into execution.

It is expected that you will use your official and personal influence to remove prejudices on this subject, and to fully and thoroughly carry out the policy now adopted and ordered by the Government. That policy is to withdraw from the use of the enemy all the slaves you can, and to employ those so withdrawn to the best possible advantage against the enemy.

The character of the war has very much changed within the last year. There is now no possible hope of reconciliation with the rebels. The Union party in the South is virtually destroyed. There can be no peace but that which is forced by the sword. We must conquer the rebels or be conquered by them. The North must conquer the slave oligarchy or become slaves themselves—the manufacturers mere "hewers of wood and drawers of water" to Southern aristocrats.

This is the phase which the rebellion has now assumed. We must take things as they are. The Government, looking at the subject in all its aspects, has adopted a policy, and we must cheerfully and faithfully carry out that policy.

I write you this unofficial letter simply as a personal friend and as a matter of friendly advice. From my position here, where I can survey the entire field, perhaps I may be better able to understand the tone of public opinion and the intentions of the Government than you can from merely consulting the officers of your own army.

Very respectfully, your obedient servant,

H. W. HALLECK.

THE ARMY BEFORE VICKSBURG:
LOUISIANA, MARCH 1863

Frederick Law Olmsted to John Olmsted

In December 1862 Grant had made his first attempt to capture Vicksburg, advancing south from Oxford, Mississippi, while Sherman led a river expedition down from Memphis to the Yazoo River north of the city. The plan failed when Confederate cavalry destroyed the Union supply depot at Holly Springs, forcing Grant to retreat, and Sherman was repulsed at Chickasaw Bayou on the Yazoo. After abandoning plans for a renewed overland offensive through northern Mississippi, Grant assumed command of the river expedition on January 30. Hoping to bypass the Confederate batteries at Vicksburg, he had his troops work on a canal across a peninsula opposite the city, and tried to open a water route through a series of Louisiana lakes, rivers, and bayous to the Mississippi below the city. Grant also made two attempts to reach the Yazoo River above Vicksburg by sending expeditions to open passages through the rivers and bayous of the Mississippi Delta. The landscape architect Frederick Law Olmsted, a founder of the U.S. Sanitary Commission who served as its general secretary, visited Grant's army in late March.

Sanitary Store Boat, "Dunleith",
on the Mississippi, above Memphis;
April 1st 1863.

Dear Father,

We are returning from a visit to the army before Vicksburg, which we reached on the 22d. General Grant's command consists of four army corps: one under Gen'l Hurlbert is in Tennessee; there being detachments at Columbus; Isd No 10; New Madrid, Jackson, Helena, and considerable bodies at Corinth and Memphis. A second corps is amphibious between Helena and New Providence, under Gen'l McPherson; a third, having been recently drowned out of camp at Young's Point, near the canal across the neck, is now at Milliken's bend, ten miles above; Sherman's corps alone remains in direct observation of Vicksburg. It is camped on a series of plantations, from one to two miles above the canal. Head quarters is on the steamboat Magnolia, which lies, nose up, on the only ground which I saw, above water, outside the levee below Milliken's bend. There were a dozen large steamboats at the same place, two being quarters of Col. Bissell's Western Engineer Regiment; two ordnance boats, (loaded with ammunition) one medical store-boat; one hospital boat, several transports and forage boats, and one immense floating ware-house containing Commissary stores; also a score or two of flatboats loaded with coal. The space of ground out of water is about 1000 feet in length. At the other end of Sherman's encampment, there are half a dozen more Commissary boats. There are near here also three or four iron-clads and rams, and in the mouth of the Yazoo, which is just opposite Hd. Q., the flag boat of Admiral Porter, half a dozen mortar boats, another iron-clad, and some more rams and a naval hospital boat. Most of the Squadron, and considerable force from each army-corps were absent on the Sunflower and Blackwater expeditions, from which they were getting back as we left; the sternwheel transports, wonderfully knocked to pieces; their smoke-stacks all down, so that the black coal-smoke was thrown directly upon the hurricane decks, which were necessarily crowded with men, who must have been nearly suffocated by it.

The day after our arrival Gen'l Grant sent an aid on board our boat to take us near to Vicksburg as it would be safe to go. It was near enough to set our watches by the town-clock and to see negroes shovelling earth upon the breast-works. Bissell was building a case-mate battery for two 30 lbr Parrotts, concealed from the enemy by the levee, at the point nearest the town; from which it was intended to open fire upon their R.R. station and Commissary storehouse, the morning after we left. The next day we went with Medical Director Hewit, to look at the camps, riding on the levee, and across one plantation on a corduroy road. The ground inside the levee even, is elsewhere impassible, the ground being all soaked, where it is not flooded, with the "seepage-water" straining through and under the levees. The camps are near the levee; the tents being furnished with bedsteads made of saplings, lifting the men a few inches off the ground; the men of one battery, having been flooded out elsewhere, had pitched their tents on terraces cut in the slope of the levee; forming a very picturesque camp; the levee is here about 14 ft. high. A part of McPherson's men whom we visited opposite Yazoo pass were camped on a strip of the forest left above water, not more than fifty feet wide; the water so nearly over it, that the swell caused by our boat rolled into one of the tents. The water had risen an inch and a half during the night, and you would say it was about the most dismal place and the most dismal prospect upon which an army could be put. So here of Sherman's corps: the ground all asoak and water backing up on them in every direction except where the levee restrained it. The levee itself was lined with graves; there being no other place where the dead could be buried, on account of the water, which at once fills every cavity. These graves, which must be seen by everyone, there being no other road to travel near the camps, have helped, I suppose, to give the impression that Grant's army was in a terribly diseased state. I suppose country people would get the impression that a fearful epidemic was prevailing if they should see the burials daily occurring in any town of 40,000 inhabitants, or if they should see all the graves made within a month placed in two lines, head to foot, as they are for this army, on the levee.

In fact the health of the army, tho' not quite as good as that of the army in general, is amazingly good. You can not conceive how well and happy the men in general looked. They are mostly now well broken in, and know how to take care of themselves. Considering that they were living athletically and robustly, with plentiful air; I don't know anything that they wanted. I have enough of the Bedouin nature in my composition to envy them. I never saw men looking healthier or happier. The food is abundant, varied and most excellent in quality. I don't believe that one in fifty ever lived as well before. They were well-clothed and well-shod. If I were young and sound, I would like nothing so well as to be one of them.

We dined at Sherman's Head Quarters, which are in a planter's house in a little grove of willow oaks and Pride of China, just greened out, but dinner was served in a tent. Here I met Captain Janney, Sherman's staff-engineer, with whom I rode a couple of hours in the afternoon and whose talk I enjoyed greatly. He has had a half artist education in Paris and was warm on parks, pictures, architects, engineers and artists.

Reminiscences of Cranch and Fontainbleau; of student-life at the Politechnique and Centrale, discussions of the decoration of the Louvre, had a peculiar zest in the midst of raw upper Louisiana plantation, where nature's usual work is but half-done; looking across the River into tree-tops hung with the weird Spanish-moss, vultures floating above; shouts and turmoil of a gang of contrabands tearing down the gin-house of the plantation—Captain Janney wants the material for bridges—the drums beating and bugles sounding for evening parade behind and the distant boom of Farragut's big guns on the Hartford, pitching shells at intervals into my quondam host's, Dick Taylor's, rebel batteries at Warrenton. Another excellent fellow here was Sherman's Medical Director, McMillan, whom I have known before; indeed have met often since the war began. He was Stoneman's Medical Director on the Peninsula. He was grossly abused by the Herald's correspondent, for "entire neglect to make any provision for the wounded" at the battle of Chickasaw bluffs, whereas his arrangements were really the most complete that have ever been formed before a battle, with perhaps a single exception, and he is one of the most humane, industrious, enlightened and efficient surgeons in the Army. It is oftener than otherwise that the really good surgeons are maligned and held up to public execration, and the surgeons who always fail in an emergency pass for the best.

McMillan & Janney rode with us to call on Gen'l Steele, living in a large room of a planter's house, which had been half finished years ago, and since inhabited in its unfinished state. There were school-classics left behind on the mantel-piece. From Gen'l Steele's we rode to Gen'l Blair's also quartered in a planter's house. (The boat shakes so, it is scarcely possible to write legibly—but a pencil can be better managed).

Janney, by the way, who has charge of the Young's Point Canal and employs several hundred contrabands, and who also employed a large number while Sherman's corps was at Memphis, speaks well of the negroes as industrious, disciplinable, grateful and docile. They have less vigor and endurance than whites, can not do as much hard work and seem generally to be of weak constitution. A remarkable proportion of them are deformed or mutilated, apparently from injuries in childhood.

Nearly all bear the marks of injuries which they are unable to explain. You know that I have contended that the negro race in slavery was constantly growing in the mass less and less qualified for self dependence; the instinct of self-preservation being more and more worked out, and the habit of letting "master take care of his nigger" bred in to the race. Janney believes that slave children while more precocious than white, suffer more from accidents than the children of the poor with us. The most valuable negroes, who are also, as a rule, the cleverest, have generally been taken away from the plantations by their owners, the least enterprising and those who would be most bewildered in trying to look out for themselves, and who are worth least for army purposes, being left as they are always told to "look after things" on the plantations. Wonderfully little it is they have to look after, however. A good many who are taken away, however, contrive to escape and return to the plantation or to their relatives and friends who follow the Union army. They often show strong attachments in this way, not to their owners but to localities and to their families. Among the company which was working under him at Memphis, Captain Janney said that there was one very active, sharp, industrious and faithful fellow, who had left a plantation about twenty miles off. Soon after his good qualities had attracted Janney's attention, his owner—a rank rebel, came as they often do, with complete assurance, to ask that he should be given up to him. Janney assured him that the country needed his services and it could not be thought of at present. Some weeks after this the same negro came one morning to Janney's tent and said: "Here's a right good fowling-piece, Captain, and I want to gib it to you."

"Where did you get it?"

"Got him ob my old massa, Sah."

"How is that? What did he give you his fowling piece for?"

"Did'n gib'm me, Sah; I took 'em."

"When?"

"Last night."

"Has your master been here again?"

"No Sah, I been down dar, to de old place, myself lass night, and I see de gun, dah, and I tort he was a rebel and he ortn't to be let hab a gun, and I ort to take 'em away, tort dat wus right, Captain, wusn't it? He ain't no business wid a gun, has he? Only to shoot our teamsters wid it."

"What sent you out there?"

"Well, I went dah, Sah, for to get my wife and chile dat was dah. I tried to get 'em nodder way but I was cheated, and I had to go myself."

"What other way did you try?"

"I'll tell ou, Sah; I want my wife and chile: dey was down dah on de ole plantation. Last Sunday when we'd got our pay, I seen a white man dat libs ober dah, and he tell me if I gib him my money he get my wife for me. I had thirty dollars Sah, and I gib it to him, but my wife did'n come. So I went myself. My wife, house servant, Sah, and I creep up to de house and look into de windah: de windah was open and I heah de ole man and de ole woman dere snorin in de corner, and I put my head in and dah I see de gun standing by de fi' place. I jumped right in and cotch up de gun, and turn roun' and hold em so. Says I, 'Master, I want my wife.' 'You can take her,' says he, and he didn say another word, nor move a bit, nor Missis eider. My wife she heerd me, and she come down wid de chile and we just walk out ob de door; but I tort, I'd take de gun. He ain't no Union man and he ortn't to hab a gun, Captain. You'll take it, Sah, won't you?"

"Yes, I'll turn it in for you."

Returning to the Magnolia, we took tea with Gen'l Grant. He told me of the return of Admiral Porter and the failure of the "Sunflower" expedition. He said there seemed to be no way open to attack Vicksburg but by direct assault in front and an attempt to take it in this way would involve a frightful loss of life. He was obviously full of grave thought and concern and I avoided keeping his attention at all. He lives in the ladies' cabin of the boat, there is a sentry, or an apology for one, at the boat's gangway, but he stops no one from going on board, and there is free range in the cabin for anyone to and beyond the table, which the General, with others, writes upon, near the stern. He is more approachable and liable to interruptions than a merchant or lawyer generally allows himself to be in his office, and in my observation, citizens who had been allowed to come to the army to remove bodies of the dead for their friends; or on other pretexts, several times came in and introduced themselves to him; one man saying, "I hain't got no business with you, General, but I just wanted to have a little talk with you because folks will ask me if I did." The General had just received a number of Vicksburg papers by a deserter, which he invited me to look over. He was reading these and writing during most of the evening, while I was conversing with the gentlemen of the staff; when I rose to go, he got up and said: "I wish you would be in as much as convenient while you stay, I am not always as much occupied, as I am tonight, and whenever you see that I am not, understand that I shall be glad to talk with you." The next night I went in and had an hour's conversation with him. He is one of the most engaging men I ever saw. Small, quiet, gentle, modest—extremely, even uncomfortably, modest—frank, confiding and of an exceedingly kind disposition. He gives you the impression of a man of strong will, however, and of capacity, underlying these feminine traits. As a general, I should think his quality was that of quick common-sense judgments, unobstructed by prejudices, and deep abiding quiet resolution. He confided to me in a comic, plaintive, half humorous, half indignant way, the annoyances, obstructions, embarrassments and hindrances to which the Governors of the various Western states constantly subjected him, and keenly reviewed their various methods. The Governors of Iowa and Wisconsin were moderate in their inflictions and seemed to have some appreciation of his situation. He must do them the credit to say that they were forbearing and thoroughly patriotic. The Governor of Illinois was an amiable and weak man. He seemed to think it his business to help any citizen of Illinois to anything he wanted. "He must be in the habit of signing papers without reading them, and the quantities of letters he writes me urging me to grant favors to people who come here with them, is appalling. Favors too, which he ought to know that I have no right to grant—no more than you would have. It's very hard on me, especially when he sends women here, to get favors for their sons. It's a pastime to face a battery compared with facing a woman begging for her son, you know. These letters from the Governor of Illinois being all open letters, are written in the most earnest tone of personal and official anxiety. "He could not be more in earnest if he were pleading for his own son. And yet there are so many of them, they can't mean anything. I've been expecting a letter from him to tell me that he did not want me to pay any attention to them. It's different with the Governor of Indiana. He is perfectly cold-hearted. He seems to think, because I have some Indiana regiments, that he has a right to demand my assistance in any way he chooses, to carry out his state political arrangments. By the way, doctor, there's a lady from _____ on the _____ which arrived this afternoon, who has a great many favors to ask. I've seen her; I can't see her again. You must answer her. It's easier for you to say no to a woman than 'tis for me. Some things she wants, can be granted; some can't; you'll see how it is, when you talk with her. But don't leave it necessary for me to see her again."

I had some suggestions to make to the General; he heard me patiently, met me quickly, almost eagerly, adopted and advanced upon my views, allowed me to prepare a draft for an order in accordance with them, which next day he adopted adding one clinching sentence, and handed over to his adjutant General, who at once gave it the form of an order, signed, copied, printed and issued it. The openness of mind, directness, simplicity and rapidity of reasoning and clearness, with consequent confidence, of conclusion, of Genl Grant is very delightful. Those about him become deeply attached to him. Towards Sherman there is more than attachment, something of veneration, universally expressed, most by those who know him most intimately, from which I suspect that he has more genius than Grant.

We spent one day chiefly among the iron-clads and gunboats. Admiral Porter is a gentlemanly, straight forward and resolute sort of man. Breese his flag-captain a smiling, cheerful and most obliging and agreeable man. He assumes friendship from the start, but, with all this, one gets an impression of strong will & great certainty that when the time comes for boarding or cutting out, he will bear his part with the same ingenuous ease and grace. Some of the new men of the navy whom we saw did not strike us so favorably. Scurvy was threatening the squadron and we put on 200 barrels of potatoes and onions on the flag-boat.

April 3d Cairo.

We have just arrived here, all quite well.
Expect to go to St. Louis this evening.
Your affectionate Son,

                Fred. Law Olmsted.

John Olmsted, Esqr
Hartford, Ct

(Please send this to Washington.)

"A WAR FOR EMANCIPATION": APRIL 1863

Frederick Douglass: Why Should a Colored Man Enlist?

April 1863

Frederick Douglass joined William Wells Brown, Martin Delany, Henry Highland Garnet, and other black abolitionists in recruiting men for the 54th Massachusetts Infantry. After his sons Charles and Lewis enlisted in the regiment, Douglass canvassed western and upstate New York, then spoke at public meetings in New York City and Philadelphia. By the middle of April he had sent more than one hundred recruits to the regiment's training camp at Readville, Massachusetts. This article appeared in his newspaper, *Douglass' Monthly*.

WHY SHOULD A COLORED MAN ENLIST?

THIS QUESTION has been repeatedly put to us while raising men for the 54th Massachusetts regiment during the past five weeks, and perhaps we cannot at present do a better service to the cause of our people or to the cause of the country than by giving a few of the many reasons why a colored man should enlist.

First. You are a man, although a colored man. If you were only a horse or an ox, incapable of deciding whether the rebels are right or wrong, you would have no responsibility, and might like the horse or the ox go on eating your corn or grass, in total indifference, as to which side is victorious or vanquished in this conflict. You are however no horse, and no ox, but a man, and whatever concerns man should interest you. He who looks upon a conflict between right and wrong, and does not help the right against the wrong, despises and insults his own nature, and invites the contempt of mankind. As between the North and South, the North is clearly in the right and the South is flagrantly in the wrong. You should therefore, simply as a matter of right and wrong, give your utmost aid to the North. In presence of such a contest there is no neutrality for any man. You are either for the Government or against the Government. Manhood requires you to take sides, and you are mean or noble according to how you choose between action and inaction.—If you are sound in body and mind, there is nothing in your *color* to excuse you from enlisting in the service of the republic against its enemies. If *color* should not be a criterion of rights, neither should it be a standard of duty. The whole duty of a man, belongs alike to white and black.

"A man's a man for a' that."

Second. You are however, not only a man, but an American citizen, so declared by the highest legal adviser of the Government, and you have hitherto expressed in various ways, not only your willingness but your earnest desire to fulfil any and every obligation which the relation of citizenship imposes. Indeed, you have hitherto felt wronged and slighted, because while white men of all other nations have been freely enrolled to serve the country, you a native born citizen have been coldly denied the honor of aiding in defense of the land of your birth. The injustice thus done you is now repented of by the Government and you are welcomed to a place in the army of the nation. Should you refuse to enlist *now*, you will justify the past contempt of the Government towards you and lead it to regret having honored you with a call to take up arms in its defense. You cannot but see that here is a good reason why you should promptly enlist.

Third. A third reason why a colored man should enlist is found in the fact that every Negro-hater and slavery-lover in the land regards the arming of Negroes as a calamity and is doing his best to prevent it. Even now all the weapons of malice, in the shape of slander and ridicule, are used to defeat the filling up of the 54th Massachusetts (colored) regiment. In nine cases out of ten, you will find it safe to do just what your enemy would gladly have you leave undone. What helps you hurts him. Find out what he does not want and give him a plenty of it.

Fourth. You should enlist to learn the use of arms, to become familiar with the means of securing, protecting and defending your own liberty. A day may come when men shall learn war no more, when justice shall be so clearly apprehended, so universally practiced, and humanity shall be so profoundly loved and respected, that war and bloodshed shall be confined only to beasts of prey. Manifestly however, that time has not yet come, and while all men should labor to hasten its coming, by the cultivation of all the elements conducive to peace, it is plain that for the present no race of men can depend wholly upon moral means for the maintenance of their rights. Men must either be governed by love or by fear. They must love to do right or fear to do wrong. The only way open to any race to make their rights respected is to learn how to defend them. When it is seen that black men no more than white men can be enslaved with impunity, men will be less inclined to enslave and oppress them. Enlist therefore, that you may learn the art and assert the ability to defend yourself and your race.

Fifth. You are a member of a long enslaved and despised race. Men have set down your submission to Slavery and insult, to a lack of manly courage. They point to this fact as demonstrating your fitness only to be a servile class. You should enlist and disprove the slander, and wipe out the reproach. When you shall be seen nobly defending the liberties of your own country against rebels and traitors—brass itself will blush to use such arguments imputing cowardice against you.

Sixth. Whether you are or are not, entitled to all the rights of citizenship in this country has long been a matter of dispute to your prejudice. By enlisting in the service of your country at this trial hour, and upholding the National Flag, you stop the mouths of traducers and win applause even from the iron lips of ingratitude. Enlist and you make this your country in common with all other men born in the country or out of it.

Seventh. Enlist for your own sake. Decried and derided as you have been and still are, you need an act of this kind by which to recover your own self-respect. You have to some extent rated your value by the estimate of your enemies and hence have counted yourself less than you are. You owe it to yourself and your race to rise from your social debasement and take your place among the soldiers of your country, a man among men. Depend upon it, the subjective effect of this one act of enlisting will be immense and highly beneficial. You will stand more erect, walk more assured, feel more at ease, and be less liable to insult than you ever were before. He who fights the battles of America may claim America as his country—and have that claim respected. Thus in defending your country now against rebels and traitors you are defending your own liberty, honor, manhood and self-respect.

Eighth. You should enlist because your doing so will be one of the most certain means of preventing the country from drifting back into the whirlpool of Pro-Slavery Compromise at the end of the war, which is now our greatest danger. He who shall witness another Compromise with Slavery in this country will see the free colored man of the North more than ever a victim of the pride, lust, scorn and violence of all classes of white men. The whole North will be but another Detroit, where every white fiend may with impunity revel in unrestrained beastliness towards people of color; they may burn their houses, insult their wives and daughters, and kill indiscriminately. If you mean to live in this country now is the time for you to do your full share in making it a country where you and your children after you can live in comparative safety. Prevent a compromise with the traitors, compel them to come back to the Union whipped and humbled into obedience and all will be well. But let them come back as masters and all their hate and hellish ingenuity will be exerted to stir up the ignorant masses of the North to hate, hinder and persecute the free colored people of the North. That most inhuman of all modern enactments, with its bribed judges, and summary process, the Fugitive Slave Law, with all its infernal train of canting divines, preaching the gospel of kidnapping, as twelve years ago, will be revived against the free colored people of the North. One or two black brigades will do much to prevent all this.

Ninth. You should enlist because the war for the Union, whether men so call it or not, is a war for Emancipation. The salvation of the country, by the inexorable relation of cause and effect, can be secured only by the complete abolition of Slavery. The President has already proclaimed emancipation to the Slaves in the rebel States which is tantamount to declaring Emancipation in all the States, for Slavery must exist everywhere in the South in order to exist anywhere in the South.

Can you ask for a more inviting, ennobling and soul enlarging work, than that of making one of the glorious Band who shall carry Liberty to your enslaved people? Remember that identified with the Slave in color, you will have a power that white soldiers have not, to attract them to your lines and induce them to take up arms in a common cause. One black Brigade will, for this work, be worth more than two white ones. Enlist, therefore, enlist without delay, enlist now, and forever put an end to the human barter and butchery which have stained the whole South with the warm blood of your people, and loaded its air with their groans. Enlist, and deserve not only well of your country, and win for yourselves, a name and a place among men, but secure to yourself what is infinitely more precious, the fast dropping tears of gratitude of your kith and kin marked out for destruction, and who are but now ready to perish.

When time's ample curtain shall fall upon our national tragedy, and our hillsides and valleys shall neither redden with the blood nor whiten with the bones of kinsmen and countrymen who have fallen in the sanguinary and wicked strife; when grim visaged war has smoothed his wrinkled front and our country shall have regained its normal condition as a leader of nations in the occupation and blessings of peace—and history shall record the names of heroes and martyrs—who bravely answered the call of patriotism and Liberty—against traitors, thieves and assassins—let it not be said that in the long list of glory, composed of men of all nations—there appears the name of no colored man.

DEFENDING GENERAL PEMBERTON:
VIRGINIA, APRIL 1863

Jefferson Davis to William M. Brooks

The Confederate president wrote to William M. Brooks, an Alabama lawyer who had presided over his state's secession convention, defending his choice of John C. Pemberton to lead the army defending Vicksburg. A West Point graduate from Philadelphia married to a Virginian, Pemberton had commanded the Atlantic coast defenses of South Carolina, Georgia, and Florida before being sent to Mississippi in October 1862.

Richmond, April 2 1863

My dear Sir.

Your letter of the 20th ulto, reached me in due course; and has received careful attention. Your friendly assurance of the extent to which I am honored by the confidence and esteem of my fellow-citizens is a source of sincere gratification, the more acceptable coming from one so well qualified to judge as yourself.

I was not prepared to learn the dissatisfaction which you represent as existing in regard to the assignment of Lt. Genl. Pemberton, and I hope that the distrust in his fidelity & ability to which you allude is not as great as you have been led to believe.

I selected Genl. Pemberton for the very important command which he now holds from a conviction that he was the best qualified officer for that post then available, and have since found no reason to change the opinion I then entertained of him.

If success which is generally regarded in popular estimation as evidence of qualification be so regarded in his case, I am surprised that Genl. Pemberton's merits should still be doubted. With a force far inferior in numbers to the enemy, menaced by attack at several points widely distant from each other, with no naval force to meet the enemy's fleets on the Mississippi and its tributaries by his judicious disposition of his forces and skilful selection of the best points of defense he has repulsed the enemy at Vicksburg, Port Hudson, on the Tallahatchie and at Deer Creek, and has thus far foiled his every attempt to get possession of the Mississippi river and the vast section of country which it controls.

I think that he has also demonstrated great administrative as well as military ability. He has been enabled to subsist and clothe his army without going out of his own Dept., and though within a recent period some difficulty may have arisen in the transportation of supplies, or some scarcity may have been apprehended which circumstance is, I regret to say, not confined to his command, I think he is not the less commendable for his former success in this regard & that he is entitled to confidence in his ability to overcome the difficulty and procure the requisite provisions for his troops, if indeed such may be practicable.

I still hope that "the suspicions and distrust" which you mention do not exist to any considerable extent; but however this may be, I feel assured that they are "groundless".

With reference to the fact that General Pemberton was born at the North being alleged as a justification of distrust in his fidelity to our cause, I can imagine nothing more unjust and ungenerous.

General Pemberton resigned his commission in the U.S. army on the secession of Virginia—his adopted State.—He came at once to Richmond and was one of the first officers of the U.S. army who offered his services to Governor Letcher, by whom he was immediately appointed to a field commission. He afterwards entered the service of the Confederate States in which he has risen from step to step to his present position. In addition to the other proofs which he has afforded of his devotion to the cause of the Confederate States, I may add that by coming South he forfeited a considerable fortune.

Your suggestions as to Col. I. W. Garrett shall receive due attention. I recollect him very favorably and have no doubt that your estimate of him is just. With assurances of regard and esteem I remain very respl. & truly yours

JEFFN. DAVIS.

THE RICHMOND BREAD RIOT:
VIRGINIA, APRIL 1863

John B. Jones: Diary, April 2–4, 1863

Food riots broke out in the spring of 1863 in Atlanta, Georgia; Salisbury, North Carolina; Mobile, Alabama; Petersburg, Virginia; and other southern cities as groups of women, many of them soldiers' wives, invaded and looted shops they believed were charging unfair prices. The largest disturbance occurred in Richmond on April 2. John B. Jones, a clerk in the Confederate War Department who witnessed the riot, had recorded in his diary three days earlier the rising cost of cornmeal and potatoes while observing that meat had almost disappeared and "none but the opulent can afford to pay $3.50 per pound for butter."

APRIL 2D.—This morning early a few hundred women and boys met as by concert in the Capitol Square, saying they were hungry, and must have food. The number continued to swell until there were more than a thousand. But few men were among them, and these were mostly foreign residents, with exemptions in their pockets. About nine A.M. the mob emerged from the western gates of the square, and proceeded down Ninth Street, passing the War Department, and crossing Main Street, increasing in magnitude at every step, but preserving silence and (so far) good order. Not knowing the meaning of such a procession, I asked a pale boy where they were going. A young woman, seemingly emaciated, but yet with a smile, answered that they were going to find something to eat. I could not, for the life of me, refrain from expressing the hope that they might be successful; and I remarked they were going in the right direction to find plenty in the hands of the extortioners. I did not follow, to see what they did; but I learned an hour after that they marched through Cary Street, and entered diverse stores of the speculators, which they proceeded to empty of their contents. They impressed all the carts and drays in the street, which were speedily laden with meal, flour, shoes, etc. I did not learn whither these were driven; but probably they were rescued from those in charge of them. Nevertheless, an immense amount of provisions, and other articles, were borne by the mob, which continued to increase in numbers. An eye-witness says he saw a boy come out of a store with a hat full of money (notes); and I learned that when the mob turned up into Main Street, when all the shops were by this time closed, they broke in the plate-glass windows, demanding silks, jewelry, etc. Here they were incited to pillage valuables, not necessary for subsistence, by the class of residents (aliens) exempted from military duty by Judge Campbell, Assistant Secretary of War, in contravention of Judge Meredith's decision. Thus the work of spoliation went on, until the military appeared upon the scene, summoned by Gov. Letcher, whose term of service is near its close. He had the Riot Act read (by the mayor), and then threatened to fire on the mob. He gave them five minutes' time to disperse in, threatening to use military force (the city battalion being present) if they did not comply with the demand. The timid women fell back, and a pause was put to the devastation, though but few believed he would venture to put his threat in execution. If he had done so, he would have been hung, no doubt.

About this time the President appeared, and ascending a dray, spoke to the people. He urged them to return to their homes, so that the bayonets there menacing them might be sent against the common enemy. He told them that such acts would bring *famine* upon them in the only form which could not be provided against, as it would deter people from bringing food to the city. He said he was willing to share his last loaf with the suffering people (his best horse had been stolen the night before), and he trusted we would all bear our privations with fortitude, and continue united against the Northern invaders, who were the authors of all our sufferings. He seemed deeply moved; and indeed it was a frightful spectacle, and perhaps an ominous one, if the government does not remove some of the quartermasters who have contributed very much to bring about the evil of scarcity. I mean those who have allowed transportation to forestallers and extortioners.

Gen. Elzey and Gen. Winder waited upon the Secretary of War in the morning, asking permission to call the troops from the camps near the city, to suppress the women and children by a summary process. But Mr. Seddon hesitated, and then declined authorizing any such absurdity. He said it was a municipal or State duty, and therefore he would not take the responsibility of interfering in the matter. Even in the moment of aspen consternation, he was still the politician.

I have not heard of any injuries sustained by the women and children. Nor have I heard how many stores the mob visited; and it must have been many.

All is quiet now (three P.M.); and I understand the government is issuing rice to the people.

APRIL 3D.—Gen. D. H. Hill writes from North Carolina that the business of conscription is miserably mismanaged in that State. The whole business, it seems, has resolved itself into a machine for making money and putting pets in office.

No account of yesterday's riot appeared in the papers to-day, for obvious reasons. The mob visited most of the shops, and the pillage was pretty extensive.

Crowds of women, Marylanders and foreigners, were standing at the street corners to-day, still demanding food; which, it is said, the government issued to them. About midday the City Battalion was marched down Main Street to disperse the crowd.

Congress has resolved to adjourn on the 20th April. The tax bill has not passed both Houses yet.

Gen. Blanchard has been relieved of his command in Louisiana. He was another general from Massachusetts.

APRIL 4TH.—It is the belief of some that the riot was a premeditated affair, stimulated from the North, and executed through the instrumentality of emissaries. Some of the women, and others, have been arrested.

We have news of the capture of another of the enemy's gunboats, in Berwick Bay, Louisiana, with five guns. It is said to have been done by *cavalry*.

A dispatch just received from Charleston states that the enemy's monitors were approaching the forts, seven in number, and that the attack was commencing. This is *joyful* news to our people, so confident are they that Gen. Beauregard will beat them.

THE NECESSITY OF FIGHTING: APRIL 1863
Whitelaw Reid to the Cincinnati Gazette

Writing under the pen name "Agate," Reid was the Washington correspondent for the *Cincinnati Gazette*, a Republican newspaper aligned with the party's Radical faction. Amid reports of widespread food shortages in the South, Reid considered the prospects for an early victory over the Confederacy.

1863, April 4

Now, with opening buds and stiffening roads, we are ready again, and such another spring and summer's work will bear our banners to the Gulf.

But, like the victim of lunatic periods, we begin to return to the old delusion. In bulletins from the army headquarters, speculations of the army correspondents, reasonings of the editors, speeches of Generals, declarations at Union meetings we have the old madness revived: "The rebels are nearly exhausted. Millionaires are having dealt out to them the rations of the private soldier. Four months yet must pass before they can have a new crop—before that time they must succumb."

Let us be warned in time by the experiences of eighteen months ago. The starvation theory proved folly then; it can be no less foolish now. The rebels have improved the intervening time by developing their agricultural resources. If, taken at every disadvantage, with fields sown in cotton instead of corn, and without accumulated supplies, they were able to go through the first year, each succeeding one must grow easier and easier. It is not impossible that the lack of labor has produced some inconvenience on Southern plantations and has somewhat decreased their production. Lax discipline among the slaves, consequent on the absence of their masters in the army, has doubtless tended to the same result. But on the other hand, a much greater breadth of cereals must have been sown, and much more general attention paid to the growing of live stock.

It cannot, therefore, but be as fatal a delusion now as it was in 1861, to base hopes upon the miseries produced by the blockade instead of the bayonet; or to depend upon subduing the rebels by starving them in their homes instead of routing them on the battlefield. There can be no more dangerous symptom than the recurring expressions of belief that if we "can now only hold our own a few months longer," the rebellion must fall of its own weight. A People that has accomplished what the South has in the last two years, is not to be starved out—is not likely to succumb merely from being severely let alone—*is not to be subdued, in short, save by equal pluck and superior endurance on the battlefield.* Fighting, not starving, is to win the battle and end the war, if the victory and the end are to come at all.

LINCOLN REVIEWS THE ARMY:
VIRGINIA, APRIL 1863

Charles S. Wainwright: Diary, April 5–12, 1863

After taking command of the Army of the Potomac on January 26, Joseph Hooker reorganized its command structure and raised its morale by improving camp conditions, providing better food, and granting furloughs. President Lincoln traveled to Virginia in early April to inspect the reinvigorated army and to discuss plans for the spring campaign with Hooker. Among the troops who passed in review was the artillery of the First Corps, commanded by Colonel Charles S. Wainwright. A former officer of the New York militia, Wainwright had served in Hooker's division in the early battles of the Peninsula campaign.

CAMP THREE MILES FROM BELLE PLAINE, APRIL 5, SUNDAY. We are still undisturbed in our winter quarters and several reasons are plain for our remaining so for at least a week to come. First the weather which is very uncertain and stormy; all day yesterday and extending through last night, we had one of the most severe storms of the season, wind, rain and snow. It was much like the one we had last year during the time I was loading my batteries at Liverpool Point, except that one was longer and more severe. Then General Hooker has just commenced to review the different corps of the army, and cannot well get through under a week: while the War Department has ordered a general muster of all the troops on the 10th, for the use of the provost-marshal in making drafts to fill up the regiments, and so forth. . . .

This corps was reviewed by General Hooker on Thursday. The troops are so scattered, and the ground hereabouts so broken that we could not get the whole corps out together, so it was reviewed by divisions. The Third Division was formed about half a mile from our headquarters here. Doubleday made bad work of it, for the ground was very much cramped

even for his little command of only some 3,000 men. . . .
The next day, Friday, I went over to see the Sixth Corps reviewed. The whole of it was out together, though the ground it formed on was very rough. It is a larger corps than ours, and certainly made a much better appearance, but I hear that General Hunt says my batteries looked decidedly the best. There is no doubt that the Fifth and Sixth Corps under Porter and Franklin were much better instructed and disciplined than any of the others. Another cause for its superiority over this corps lies in the great proportion of Pennsylvania regiments that we have; which as a rule are, without doubt, worse officered than any others in this army. Major DePeyster is now on duty with Howe's division of the Sixth Corps; and made himself very ridiculous at the review by his strutting manner, which called attention to him, while he not only did not mount his cannoneers, but also commanded "present sabres" when he passed in review. Every officer of my acquaintance whom I met after the review congratulated me on my major. The Twentieth New York met General Hooker about half a mile from the review grounds and marched up with us as a sort of escort; for the purpose of shewing the excellence of their drill. It is said (and I believe truly) to be the best drilled regiment in the army; their marching, and changes from company front to the flank, and their wheeling into line on Friday were certainly wonderful. It is a German regiment, raised in New York City, and commanded by Colonel Von Vegesack (I don't know how to spell the name) an officer of standing in the Swedish service, and a very nice fellow in every way.

I hear that the President is expected down today. In case he comes, we may very likely have all our reviewing to go over again on a grander scale. Hooker has considerable liking for that sort of thing when he can make it pay; and is said to have boasted a good deal while at Washington; declaring that he "had the finest army on this planet" and that "he could march it straight to New Orleans." Whether or no he will prove capable of taking it as far as Richmond remains to be seen, to say nothing of going to New Orleans. By the bye, Farragut's success on the Mississippi does not turn out to be quite so great as at first reported. The news looks anything but very brilliant from both west and south. Consequently, the expected capture of Charleston, Port Hudson, and Vicksburg is again postponed; and gold is once more on the rise.

APRIL 8, WEDNESDAY. President Lincoln came down on Saturday afternoon instead of on Sunday, and arrived at headquarters quite unexpectedly. It is said that their arrival created quite a commotion on Hooker's back stairs, hustling off some of his female acquaintances in a most undignified way. Mrs. Lincoln and one of his sons came down with the President. The object of his visit seems to be to review the army, which according to present appearances will keep him here all this week. The Cavalry Corps under General Stoneman was reviewed first, on Monday. It was probably the largest body of cavalry ever seen together on this continent, there being 11,000 out, it is said. Some of the regiments looked quite well, but many were little better than ridiculous. The country here is not calculated to make fine cavalry. Our men are far too slouchy, the "setting up" and bearing of the real soldier showing much more on horseback than on foot; and the plain, simple uniform now worn in our army prevents any attempt at style, especially on such wretched horses as we have here. The horse batteries were much more creditable, and looked really finely. They are all regular batteries, except one, and in most cases are commanded by old light artillery officers. The one volunteer battery is the Sixth New York which was with me on the Peninsula. Bramhall has resigned, and Martin is now the captain. Even in the midst of the old regular batteries they keep up their reputation, in camp as well as in the field. I have been to see them several times on my way to Army Headquarters, the shortest road leading almost through their camp, and always meet with the warmest welcome.

Today the Second, Third, Fifth, and Sixth Corps were reviewed together, and made really a splendid show. There must have been 50,000 men out; the ground was fair, and the arrangements capital. It would be hard to say which of the four corps made the best appearance: the Third has, if any, turned out in a little the best style, and Sickles deserves credit for getting so good a line formed; and for the manner in which the whole corps saluted at one time by bugle command. I rode around with General Hooker and the reviewing party, as did several ladies, of whom there were a large number present. . . .

APRIL 12, SUNDAY. The reviewing is over, the President gone back to Washington, and all once more quietly waiting for orders to move which will probably be the next excitement. On Thursday the whole of this corps was marched down to the plain on which the First Division was drawn up last week, and was there reviewed by the President. The day was fine, the view of the Potomac beautiful, the ground most capital. Reynolds and everybody worked hard, so the troops looked and marched well; and our efforts were repaid by the generally expressed opinion that it went off altogether better than any of the other reviews. There was one new feature in it, at any rate. The whole of the artillery was massed, and passed in review as one body, so that I appeared in my proper place, as an actual commander. It was General Reynolds's own proposition, without any request on my part; whether it arose from his really approving the brigade organization, or was only done for convenience and effect, I do not know. The ten batteries made quite a display, marching battery front, and looked well, although some being six and others four-gun batteries rather broke the column. Hunt was much pleased with it. After the review, the President, most of the general officers present, and their ladies had a lunch at our headquarters, which Sanderson got up, and capped the satisfaction already felt with our review. . . .

We do not yet get any direct accounts of the attempt on Charleston: the reports through rebel sources are that Dupont's fleet was repulsed and the monitor *Keokuk* sunk. I fear it may be true, as Charleston is almost as precious to them as Richmond, and every effort will be made to save it; while on our side we have anything but a desirable commander of the land forces in old Hunter.

Everybody is reading the first report of the Congressional Committee on the Conduct of the War. It is quite voluminous, and comes down to the close of last year. I am trying to get through it, but its unfairness, partiality, and in very many cases absolute falseness make me so nervous that I can make but little progress. The radical party, who have complete control over the Cabinet and do pretty much what they please with our weak President, seem to be determined to stick at nothing in order to punish every official who does not go all lengths with them. A small instance of this has just come out in a War Department order dismissing a volunteer lieutenant for what they call treasonable sentiments expressed in a private letter to his uncle in China!

LOYALTY TO THE NATION:
NEW YORK, APRIL 1863

Francis Lieber: No Party Now, But All for Our Country

April 11, 1863

A professor of history and political science at Columbia College, Francis Lieber drafted General Orders No. 100, an influential code of the laws of war issued by the Union army on April 24, 1863. Lieber gave this address at a mass meeting held in New York City to mark the anniversary of the attack on Fort Sumter. It was circulated as a pamphlet by the Loyal Publication Society, which Lieber helped organize in February 1863. Before receiving his appointment at Columbia, Lieber had taught at South Carolina College for twenty years. His eldest son had joined the Confederate army and been mortally wounded in 1862, while his other two sons served as Union officers and would survive the war.

ADDRESS
READ AT THE INAUGURAL MEETING OF THE LOYAL NATIONAL LEAGUE, BY THE REQUEST OF THE LEAGUE, IN UNION SQUARE, NEW YORK, ON THE 11TH OF APRIL, 1863.

IT is just and wise that men engaged in a great and arduous cause should profess anew, from time to time, their faith, and pledge themselves to one another, to stand by their cause to the last extremity, even at the sacrifice of all they have and all that God has given them—their wealth, their blood, and their children's blood. We solemnly pledge all this to our cause, for it is the cause of our Country and her noble history, of freedom, and justice, and truth—it is the cause of all we hold dearest on this earth: we profess and pledge this—plainly, broadly, openly in the cheering time of success, and most fervently in the day of trial and reverses.

We recollect how, two years ago, when reckless arrogance attacked Fort Sumter, the response to that boom of treasonable cannon was read, in our city, in the flag of our country—waving from every steeple and school-house, from City Hall and Court House, from every shop window and market stall, and fluttering in the hand of every child, and on the head-gear of every horse in the busy street. Two years have passed; uncounted sacrifices have been made—sacrifices of wealth, of blood, and limb, and life—of friendship and brotherhood, of endeared and hallowed pursuits and sacred ties—and still the civil war is raging in bitterness and heart-burning—still we make the same profession, and still we pledge ourselves firmly to hold on to our cause, and persevere in the struggle into which unrighteous men, bewildered by pride, and stimulated by bitter hatred, have plunged us.

We profess ourselves to be loyal citizens of these United States; and by loyalty we mean a candid and loving devotion to the object to which a loyal man—a loyal husband, a loyal friend, a loyal citizen—devotes himself. We eschew the attenuated arguments derived by trifling scholars from meagre etymology. We take the core and substance of this weighty word, and pledge ourselves that we will loyally—not merely outwardly and formally, according to the letter, but frankly, fervently and according to the spirit—adhere to our country, to her institutions, to freedom, and her power, and to that great institution called the government of our country, founded by our fathers, and loved by their sons, and by all right-minded men who have become citizens of this land by choice and not by birth—who have wedded this country in the maturity of their age as verily their own. We pledge ourselves as National men devoted to the Nationality of this great people. No government can wholly dispense with loyalty, except the fiercest despotism ruling by naked intimidation; but a republic stands in greater need of it than any other government, and most of all a republic beset by open rebellion and insidious treason. Loyalty is pre-eminently a civic virtue in a free country. It is patriotism cast in the graceful mould of candid devotion to the harmless government of an unshackled nation.

In pledging ourselves thus, we know of no party. Parties are unavoidable in free countries, and may be useful if they acknowledge the country far above themselves, and remain within the sanctity of the fundamental law which protects the enjoyment of liberty prepared for all within its sacred domain. But Party has no meaning in far the greater number of the highest and the common relations of human life. When we are ailing, we do not take medicine by party prescription. We do not build ships by party measurement; we do not pray for our daily bread by party distinctions; we do not take our chosen ones to our bosoms by party demarcations, nor do we eat or drink, sleep or wake, as partisans. We do not enjoy the flowers of spring, nor do we harvest the grain, by party lines. We do not incur punishments for infractions of the commandments according to party creeds. We do not pursue truth, or cultivate science, by party dogmas; and we do not, we must not, love and defend our country and our liberty, dear to us as part and portion of our very selves, according to party rules. Woe to him who does. When a house is on fire, and a mother with her child cries for help at the window above, shall the firemen at the engine be allowed to trifle away the precious time in party bickerings, or is then the only word—"Water! pump away; up with the ladder!"

Let us not be like the Byzantines, those wretches who quarrelled about contemptible party refinements, theological though they were, while the truculent Mussulman was steadily drawing nearer—nay, some of whom would even go to the lord of the crescent, and with a craven heart would beg for a pittance of the spoil, so that they would be spared, and could vent their party spleen against their kin in blood, and fellows in religion.

We know of no party in our present troubles; the word is here an empty word. The only line which divides the people of the North, runs between the mass of loyal men who stand by their country, no matter to what place of political meeting they were used to resort, or with what accent they utter the language of the land, or what religion they profess, or what sentiments they may have uttered in the excitement of former discussions, on the one hand, and those on the other hand, who keep outside of that line—traitors to their country in the hour of need—or those who allow themselves to be misled by shallow names, and by reminiscences which cling around those names from by-gone days, finding no application in a time which asks for things more sterling than names, theories, or platforms.

If an alien enemy were to land his hosts on your shores, would you fly to your arms and ring the tocsin because your country is in danger, or would you meditatively look at your sword and gun, and spend your time in pondering whether the administration in power, which must and can alone direct the defence of your hearths, has a right to be styled by this or that party name, or whether it came into power with your assistance, and will appoint some of your party to posts of honor or comfortable emoluments? And will any one now lose his time and fair name as an honest and brave citizen, when no foreigner, indeed, threatens your country, at least not directly, but far more, when a reckless host of law-defying men, heaping upon you the vilest vituperation that men who do not leave behind them the ingenuity of civilization when they relapse into barbarism, can invent—when this host threatens to sunder your country and cleave your very history in twain, to deprive you of your rivers which God has given you, to extinguish your nationality, to break down your liberty and to make that land, which the Distributor of our sphere's geography has placed between the old and older world as the greatest link of that civilization which is destined to encircle the globe—to make that land the hot-bed of angry petty powers, sinking deeper and deeper as they quarrel and fight, and quarrelling and fighting more angrily as they sink deeper? It is the very thing your foreign enemies desire, and have long desired. When nullification threatened to bring about secession—and the term secession was used at that early period—foreign journals stated in distinct words that England was deeply interested in the contest; for nullification might bring on secession, and secession would cause a general disruption—an occurrence which would redound to the essential benefit of Great Britain.

But the traitors of the North, who have been so aptly called adders or copperheads—striking, as these reptiles do, more secretly and deadly even than the rattlesnake, which has some chivalry, at least in its tail—believe, or pretend to believe, that no fragmentary disruption would follow a division of our country into North and South, and advocate a compromise, by which they affect to believe that the two portions may possibly be reunited after a provisional division, as our pedlers putty a broken china cup.

As to the first, that we might pleasantly divide into two comfortable portions, we prefer being guided by the experience of all history, to following the traitors in their teachings. We will not hear of it. We live in an age when the word is Nationalization, not De-nationalization; when fair Italy has risen, like a new-born goddess, out of the foaming waves of the Mediterranean. All destruction is quick and easy; all growth and formation is slow and toilsome. Nations break up, like splendid mirrors dashed to the ground. They do not break into a number of well-shaped, neatly framed little looking-glasses. But a far more solemn truth even than this comes here into play. It is with nations as with families and with individuals. Those destined by nature to live in the bonds of friendship and mutual kindliness, become the bitterest and most irreconcilable enemies, when once fairly separated in angry enmity; in precisely the same degree in which affection and good-will were intended to subsist between them. We must have back the South, or else those who will not reunite with us must leave the country; we must have the country at any price. If, however, a plain division between the North and the South could take place, who will deny that those very traitors would instantly begin to manœuvre for a gradual annexation of the North to the South? It is known to be so. Some of them, void of all shame, have avowed it. They are ready to petition on their knees for annexation to the South, and to let the condescending grantor, "holding the while his nose," introduce slavery, that blessed "corner-stone of" the newest "civilization," into the North, which has been happily purged from this evil. Let us put the heel on this adder, and bruise all treason out of its head.

As to the compromise which they propose, we know of no compromise with crime that is not criminal itself, and senseless in addition to its being wicked. New guarantees, indeed, may be asked for at the proper time, but it is now our turn to ask for them. They will be guarantees of peace, of the undisturbed integrity of our country, of law, and liberty, and security, asked for and insisted upon by the Union men, who now pledge themselves not to listen to the words, compromise, new guarantees for the South, armistice, or convention of delegates from the South and North—as long as this war shall last, until the North is victorious, and shall have established again the national authority over the length and breadth of the country as it was; over the United States dominion as it was before the breaking out of the crime, which is now ruining our fair land—ruining it in point of wealth, but, with God's help, elevating it in character, strength, and dignity.

We believe that the question of the issue, which must attend the present contest, according to the character it has now acquired, is reduced to these simple words—Either the North conquers the South, or the South conquers the North. Make up your minds for this alternative. Either the North conquers the South and re-establishes law, freedom, and the integrity of our country, or the South conquers the North by arms, or by treason at home, and covers our portion of the country with disgrace and slavery.

Let us not shrink from facts or mince the truth, but rather plainly present to our minds the essential character of the struggle in which hundreds of thousands, that ought to be brothers, are now engaged. What has brought us to these grave straits?

Are we two different races, as the new ethnologists of the South, with profound knowledge of history and of their own skins, names, and language, proclaim? Have they produced the names which Europe mentions when American literature is spoken of? Have they produced our Crawfords? Have they advanced science? Have they the great schools of the age? Do they speak the choice idiom of the cultivated man? Have the thinkers and inventors of the age their homes in that region? Is their standard of comfort exalted above that of ours? What has this wondrous race produced? what new idea has it added to the great stock of civilization? It has produced cotton, and added the idea that slavery is divine. Does this establish a superior race?

The French, ourselves, the English, the Germans, the Italians, none of whom are destitute of national self-gratulation, have ever made a preposterous claim of constituting a different race. Even the new idea of a Latin Race—a Bonaparte anachronism—is founded upon an error less revolting to common sense and common knowledge.

There is no fact or movement of greater significance in all

history of the human race, than the settlement of this great continent by European people at a period when, in their portion of the globe, great nations had been formed, and the national polity had finally become the normal type of government; and it is a fact equally pregnant with momentous results, that the northern portion of this hemisphere came to be colonized chiefly by men who brought along with them the seeds of self-government, and a living common law, instinct with the principles of manly self-dependence and civil freedom.

The charters under which they settled, and which divided the American territory into colonies, were of little more importance than the vessels and their names in which the settlers crossed the Atlantic; nor had the origin of these charters a deep meaning, nor was their source always pure. The people in this country always felt themselves to be one people, and unitedly they proclaimed and achieved their independence. The country as a whole was called by Washington and his compeers America, for want of a more individual name. Still, there was no outward and legal bond between the colonies, except the crown of England; and when our people abjured their allegiance to that crown, each colony stood formally for itself. The Articles of Confederation were adopted, by which our forefathers attempted to establish a confederacy, uniting all that felt themselves to be of one nation, but were not one by outward legal form. It was the best united government our forefathers could think of, or of which, perhaps, the combination of circumstances admitted. Each colony came gradually to be called a State, and called itself sovereign, although none of them had ever exercised any of the highest attributes of sovereignty; nor did ever after the States do so.

Wherever political societies are leagued together, be it by the frail bonds of a pure confederacy, or by the consciousness of the people that they are intrinsically one people, and form one nation, without, however, a positive National Government, then the most powerful of these ill-united portions needs must rule and, as always more than one portion wishes to be the leader, intestine struggles ensue in all such incoherent governments. It has been so in antiquity; it has been so in the middle ages; it has been so, and is so in modern times.

Athens and Sparta, Castile and Aragon, Austria and Prussia, are always jealous companions, readily turned into bitter enemies. Those of our forefathers who later became the framers of our Constitution, saw this approaching evil, and they observed many other ills which had already overtaken the confederacy. Even Washington, the strong and tenacious patriot, nearly desponded. It was a dark period in our history; and it was then that our fathers most boldly, yet most considerately, performed the greatest act that our annals record—they engrafted a national, complete and representative government on our insufficient confederacy; a government with an exclusively National executive, in which the Senate, though still representing the States as States, became Nationalized in a great measure, and in which the House of Representatives became purely National like the Executive. Virginia, which, under the Articles of Confederation, was approaching the leadership over all (in the actual assumption of which she would have been resisted by other rapidly growing states, which would inevitably have led to her Peloponnesian war)—Virginia was now represented according to her population, like every other portion of the country; not as a unit, but by a number of representatives who were bound to vote individually, according to their consciences, as National men. The danger of internal struggle and provincial bitterness had passed, and our country now fairly entered as an equal among the leading nations in the course, where nations, like Olympic chariot-horses, draw abreast the car of civilization. We advanced rapidly; the task assigned to us by Providence was performed with a rapidity which had not been known before; for we had a National Government commensurate to our land and, it seemed, adequate to our destiny.

But while thus united and freed from provincial retardation and entanglements, a new portent appeared.

Slavery, which had been planted here in the colonial times, and which had been increased in this country, by the parent government, against the urgent protestations of the colonists, and especially of the Virginians, existed in all the colonies at the time when they declared themselves independent. It was felt by all to be an evil which must be dealt with as best it might be, and the gradual extinction of which must be wisely yet surely provided for. Even Mr. Calhoun, in his earlier days, called slavery a scaffolding erected to rear the mansion of civilization, which must be taken down when the fabric is finished.

This institution gave way gradually as civilization advanced. It has done so in all periods of history, and especially of Christian history. Slavery melts away like snow before the rays of rising civilization. The South envied the North for getting rid of slavery so easily, and often expressed her envy. But a combination of untoward circumstances led the South to change her mind. First, it was maintained that if slavery is an evil, it was their affair and no one else had a right to discuss it or to interfere with it; then it came to be maintained that it was no evil; then slavery came to be declared an important national element, which required its own distinct representation and especial protection; then it was said—we feel ashamed to mention it— that slavery is a divine institution. To use the words of the great South-Carolinian, whose death we deeply mourn—of James Louis Petigru—they placed, like the templars, Christ and Baphomet on the same altar, worshipping God and Satan simultaneously. But though slavery were divine, they choked the wells of common knowledge with sand and stones, and enacted perpetual ignorance for the slave. Then the renewal of that traffic, the records of which fills far the darkest pages of European history, and which the most strenuous and protracted efforts of civilized nations have not yet wholly succeeded in abolishing, was loudly called for; and our national laws, making that unhallowed trade piracy, were declared unconstitutional. Yet still another step was to be taken. It was proclaimed that slavery is a necessary element of a new and glorious civilization; and those who call themselves conservatives plunged recklessly into a new-fangled theory of politics and civilization.

Some thirty years ago we first heard of Southern Rights. Some twenty years since we were first made familiar with the expression, Southern Principles. Within the present lustre, Southern Civilization has been proclaimed. What else remained but to invent Southern Mathematics and to decree a Southern God? And what does *Southern* mean in this connection? *South* is a word which indicates relative position in geography. Yet, in these combinations, it refers neither to geography, nor to climate, nor to product, but singly and exclusively to Slavery. Southern Rights, Southern Principles, Southern Civilization, and Southern Honor or "Chivalry," are novel phrases, to express the new idea of principles and civilization characterized and tested by the dependence of one class of people as chattel upon another. A more appalling confusion of ideas is not recorded in the history of any tribe or nation that has made any use of the terms—Rights, Principles, or Civilization.

Thus slavery came to group the different portions of our country; outside of, and indeed in hostility to, the National Government and National Constitution. The struggle for the leadership was upon us. The South declared openly that it must rule; we, in the meantime, declaring that the Nation must rule, and if an issue is forced upon us, between the South and the North, then, indeed, the North must rule and shall rule. *This* is the war in which we are now engaged—in which, at the moment this is read to you, the precious blood of your sons, and brothers, and fathers, is flowing.

Whenever men are led, in the downward course of error and passion, ultimately to declare themselves, with immoral courage, in favor of a thing or principle which for centuries and thousands of years their own race has declared, by a united voice, an evil or a crime, the mischief does not stop with this single declaration. It naturally, and by a well-established law, unhinges the whole morality of man; it warps his intellect, and inflames his soul, with bewildering passions, with defiance to the simplest truth and plainest fact, and with vindictive hatred toward those who cannot agree with him. It is a fearful thing to become the defiant idolater of wrong. Slavery, and the consequent separation from the rest of men, begot pride in the leading men of the South—absurdly even pretending to be of a different and better race. Pride begot bitter and venomous hatred, and this bitter hatred, coupled with the love of owning men as things, begot at last a hatred of that which distinguishes the whole race to which we belong, more than aught else—the striving for and love of liberty.

There is no room, then, for pacifying arguments with such men in arms against us, against their duty, their country, their civilization. All that remains for the present is the question, Who shall be the victor?

It is for all these reasons which have been stated, that we pledge ourselves anew, in unwavering loyalty, to stand by and support the Government in all its efforts to suppress the rebellion, and to spare no endeavor to maintain, unimpaired, the national unity, both in principle and territorial boundary.

We will support the Government, and call on it with a united voice to use greater and greater energy, as the contest may seem to draw to a close; so that whatever advantages we may gain, we may pursue them with increasing efficiency, and bring every one in the military or civil service, that may be slow in the performance of his duty, to a quick and efficient account.

We approve of the Conscription Act, and will give our loyal aid in its being carried out, whenever the Government shall consider the increase of our army necessary; and we believe that the energy of the Government should be plainly shown by retaliatory measures, in checking the savage brutalities committed by the enemy against our men in arms, or against unarmed citizens, when they fall into their hands.

We declare that slavery, the poisonous root of this war, ought to be compressed within its narrowest feasible limits, with a view to its speedy extinction.

We declare that this is no question of politics, but one of patriotism; and we hold every one to be a traitor to his country, that works or speaks in favor of our criminal enemies, directly or indirectly, whether his offence be such that the law can overtake him or not.

We declare our inmost abhorrence of the secret societies which exist among us in favor of the rebellious enemy, and that we will denounce every participator in these nefarious conventicles, whenever known to us. We believe publicity the very basis of liberty.

We pledge our fullest support of the government in every measure which it shall deem fit to adopt against unfriendly and mischievous neutrality; and we call upon it, as citizens that have the right and duty to call for protection on their own government, to adopt the speediest possible measures to that important end.

We loyally support our government in its declarations and measures against all and every attempt of mediation, or armed or unarmed interference in our civil war.

We solemnly declare that we will resist every partition of any portion of our country to the last extremity, whether this partition should be brought about by rebellious or treasonable citizens of our own, or by foreign powers, in the way that Poland was torn to pieces.

We pronounce every foreign minister accredited to our government, who tampers with our enemies, and holds covert intercourse with disloyal men among us, as failing in his duty toward us and toward his own people, and we await with attention the action of our government regarding the recent and surprising breach of this duty.

And we call upon every American, be he such by birth or choice, to join the loyal movement of these National Leagues, which is naught else than to join and follow our beckoning flag, and to adopt for his device—

OUR COUNTRY!

HOME AND FAMILY NEWS: IOWA, APRIL 1863

Catharine Peirce to Taylor Peirce

While her husband Taylor served with the 22nd Iowa Infantry, Catharine Peirce managed several farm and town properties, handled the family finances, and raised three young children. After his enlistment Catharine and the children had moved in with her brother, Cyrus, and his wife, Mary, who was Taylor's sister.

Des Moines April/12/63
Dear Taylor
I have not got much to communicate this morning but it is sunday and I write to let thee know how we all are. We are all well to day. Cyrus is better than he has been for some time at least better than he was this time last year and I hope he will get better as the spring advances.

Dear one I sit down to write to thee not knowing what I may find to say to thee. We get no war news at this time. I suppose that the heads of affairs are trying to keep thing quiet for the present so the rebles will not know what thair at. All I have to say about it is that I hope they will do something soon that will tell and that pritty loudly too for I think that now is the time to strike a blow that will make them squirm. From what I can hear the rebles are nearly starved out and if it is true they will have to give up before long. We heard last week that there had been a bread riot among the woman and Children in Savanna and that they were in a starveing Steate and would set fire to the city if they did not get bread. It seems to me that is a big threat for woman to make but then a woman will do and dair a great deal for her starveing children. I think a pity of the poor little children but the just must suffer with the unjust. If the parents had not been such foul traitors they might still of enjoyed peace and plenty unless they belong to the class of men that are pressed into the war against their principals which I learned there are hundreds of such among the reble forces.

I can not help but feel thankful to the giver of all good that we have pleny here at the North and a fine prospect for more. The spring is opend but not as earley or as forward as it had the apperence of two or three weeks ago. But still the framework gos on gloriously. We have had no rain for some time and it is geting pritty dry so the grass is backward this season. We have had no boats up this spring and that has made teaming a good business here and wages are good generaly. The river was full enought at one time for boats to run up but I suppose that government has them all in her services to carrie provisions for the soldiers. It must take an awfull amount to supply the army that lay around Vicksburg with enough to eat.

Thee wanted me to send thy book account on Ault and a note. The note I inclose to thee. The book account I hope thee has receved before this time as I sent it some three weeks ago and also Mary's and Franks pictures. I would get little Ellis picure if I thought I could get any thing like a good one to send to thee but the artists do not like to take the picture of a baby and it is a hard matter to get them still long enough to get any like a picture. So I will wait a while and hope that thee will get home soon to see the little thing. I think he looks very much like the old hoss himself. The other Children say they want thee to come home so that they can kiss and hugg thee. They both have to kiss thair Aunt and uncle every night before they go to bed and wish one for thee. I believe I must close now. With heart felt love I remain thine Catharine. Give my respects to all that I know that thee think are deserveing of such.

        Catharine A Peirce Des Moines Iowa Polk County

"FIGHTING GOES LIKE FORTUNES":
TENNESSEE, APRIL 1863

James A. Connolly to Mary Dunn Connolly

Following its costly victory in the battle of Stones River, December 31, 1862–January 2, 1863, the Union Army of the Cumberland had remained at Murfreesboro, Tennessee, while the Confederate Army of Tennessee occupied Tullahoma, thirty-five miles to the south. On March 20 a Union reconnaissance force of 1,300 men repulsed 3,500 Confederates near Milton, about twelve miles northeast of Murfreesboro. Major James A. Connolly of the 123rd Illinois Infantry recounted the action.

Murfreesboro, Tenn., April 20, 1863.
Dear wife:
 I am alone in my tent to-night, I have a good solid floor in it, an excellent fire place in one end, graced by a pair of andirons, a cheerful fire is glowing on the hearth for though the days are warm the nights are a little cool; my good *feather bed*, with *feather* pillow is waiting for me; the excellent brass band of the 19th regulars, who are encamped near us, fills the soft night air with splendid music, and while I am content as it is yet if you were here with me I should be happy. You remember when I was at home I was almost entirely out of the notion of soldiering much longer, and I really expected that by this time I should be out of the service. But I was not well then, I was petulant, ill humored, weak from my long illness, I know I was. Military rules and orders were interfering with my freedom of action and that engendered in me a rebellious spirit toward everything military, but as time has passed and my general health improved that spirit has passed away and I begin to feel somewhat the spirit of a soldier. I am a better soldier than I was before we were married, not that I am any more rash, or want to fight any more, but somehow I enter into the spirit of things here more, my experience has given me more confidence in myself, but I am in no hurry to get into any more battles, for I think we have done our full share so far. We

have been under fire 15 times, we are cut down in 8 months service from 962 men to about 460, 200 of that loss being in battle and skirmish, so that all things considered I don't care to fight any more, at least until regiments in service longer than we have tried their mettle once or twice. Still I know the fighting can't be divided out that way. Fighting goes like fortunes. Some get more than their equal share while many get less. The other day when I sent you that little money package, I wrote you a short note, the first for many days; I had been unfit to do anything for ten days but grumble, although I was compelled by circumstances to be on duty. I saw your brother Jerry the day before he left his boarding place to go to his regiment. I was quite unwell then, had just got in from a hard trip of 9 days, and intended to write you next day and send it by him, but on returning to camp found an order from Division headquarters appointing me officer in charge of the Division picket for next day; I wouldn't send up an excuse of sickness but worried it through, and when I got off that duty and my report forwarded, I went back to camp, took to bed and called for calomel and jalap as the only consolation. The order for marching which the regiment had received the day I sent you that package was countermanded but issued again last evening, and at 9 o'clock this morning our whole Division started with 6 days rations in the direction of Woodbury, east of here, from there they will probably go to McMinnville and may possibly encounter the combined force of Morgan, Wheeler, Wharton and Forrest, supposed to be about 20 regiments of cavalry and mounted infantry with 6 or 8 pieces of artillery.

Our force is not more than 9 regiments of infantry, 4 pieces of artillery and 2 regiments of cavalry, but they won't dare to fight us if they can help it by running away. Since the Milton fight our men have no more fear of Morgan and his crew than they would for that many boys with guns. It is "grape vine" that Grant's and Burnsides' armies will unite with us within the next month, and then Bragg must find new camps for we will have business at Tullahoma and Chattanooga. In your last letter you say I said something about "bullet holes". I certainly did. I wrote you a long letter describing our Milton fight and telling you how and when I got my "bullet holes", one tearing away part of my saddle holster and shattering the pommel of

my saddle, the other tearing away the collar of my overcoat and knocking me down slightly, all of which caused me no pain and very little uneasiness, but many of the men and officers saw me fall and the word passed along the line: "the Major is shot", but when the fighting was over and they all saw I was unhurt we had a jolly time hand shaking for a few minutes. I knew it was a mistake all the time but they didn't. I was some distance in front of the regiment when my saddle was hit, and happened to be the only officer on horseback visible to the enemy. They were in a cedar thicket and I couldn't see them but they could see me. On looking around I saw that all the other field officers were dismounted so I got out of there in a hurry, dismounted and had my horse led back by an orderly; a few minutes later while standing behind our line of men lying down, some "Johnnie" in the cedars who was a tolerably good shot sent a bullet through my overcoat collar and down I went. I expect he thought he shot me but he was badly mistaken. I was conscious all the time, knew I had fallen, but knew I was not wounded, although I was shocked as if by a galvanic battery; in three minutes I was all right again; it seems much worse in writing than the actual experience. Oh yes my clothing in the trunk; you can send it to father's if you choose, but I want it kept for myself as I hope to wear it again some day.
xxxxxxxxx

      Your husband.

"I AM DOING MY BEST":
LOUISIANA, APRIL 1863

Ulysses S. Grant to Jesse Root Grant

At the end of March Grant abandoned his attempts to open a water route around Vicksburg and began making preparations to move his army down the west bank of the Mississippi and cross the river below the city. His plan was opposed by Sherman, who favored withdrawing to Memphis and making a renewed overland advance on Vicksburg through central Mississippi. Grant persisted, and on the night of April 16 a flotilla of Union gunboats and transports successfully ran past the Vicksburg shore batteries and headed downriver in preparation for the army's crossing. Grant wrote to his father as he prepared to move south.

Millikins Bend La
April 21st 1863.

DEAR FATHER,

Your letter of the 7th of April has just this day reached me. I hasten to answer your interrogitories.

When I left Memphis with my past experiance I prohibited trade below Helena. Trade to that point had previously been opened by the Treasury Department. I give no permits to buy Cotton and if I find any one engaged in the business I send them out of the Department and seize their Cotton for the Government. I have given a few families permission to leave the country and to take with them as far as Memphis their Cotton. In doing this I have been decieved by unprincipled speculators who have smuggled themselves along with the Army in spite of orders prohibiting them and have been compelled to suspend this favor to persons anxious to get out of Dixie.

I understand that Govt has adopted some plan to regulate geting the Cotton out of the country. I do not know what plan they have adopted but am satisfied that any that can be adopted, except for Government to take the Cotton themselves, and rule out speculators altogether will be a bad one. I feel all Army followers who are engaged in speculating off the misfortunes of their country, and really aiding the enemy more than they possibly could do by open treason, should be drafted at once and put in the first forlorn hope.

I move my Head Quarters to New Carthage to-morrow. This whole country is under water except strips of land behind the levees along the river and bayous and makes opperations almost impossible. I struck upon a plan which I thought would give me a foot hold on the East bank of the Miss. before the enemy could offer any great resistance. But the difficulty of the last one & a half miles next to Carthage makes it so tedious that the enemy cannot fail to discover my plans. I am doing my best and am full of hope for complete success. Time has been consumed but it was absolutely impossible to avoid it. An attack upon the rebel works at any time since I arrived here must inevitably resulted in the loss of a large portion of my Army if not in an entire defeat. There was but two points of land, Hains Bluff & Vicksburg itself, out of water any place from which troops could march. These are thoroughly fortified and it would be folly to attack them as long as there is a prospect of turning their position. I never expect to have an army under my command whipped unless it is very badly whipped and cant help it but I have no idea of being driven to do a desperate or foolish act by the howlings of the press. It is painful to me as a matter of course to see the course pursued by some of the papers. But there is no one less disturbed by them than myself. I have never saught a large command and have no ambitious ends to accomplish. Was it not for the very natural desire of proving myself equal to anything expected of me, and the evidence my removal would afford that I was not thought equal to it, I would gladly accept a less responsible position. I have no desire to be an object of envy or jealousy, nor to have this war continue. I want, and will do my part towards it, to put down the rebellion in the shortest possible time without expecting or desiring any other recognition than a quiet approval of my course. I beg that you will destroy this letter. At least do not show it.

Julia and the children are here but will go up by the first good boat. I sent for her to come down and get instructions about some business I want attended to and see no immediate prospect of being able to attend to myself.

Ulysses

THREATENING RETALIATION:
SOUTH CAROLINA, APRIL 1863

David Hunter to Jefferson Davis

Major General David Hunter, the commander of the Union-held enclaves along the South Carolina and Georgia coasts, began on his own initiative to organize a regiment of freed slaves in May 1862. At the direction of Jefferson Davis, the Confederate War Department issued orders in August 1862 outlawing Hunter and declaring that any captured Union officer involved in organizing or training slaves for military service would be held for "execution as a felon." Hunter wrote to Davis without authorization from the Lincoln administration and did not carry out any acts of retaliation before being relieved of his command (for unrelated reasons) in June 1863. His letter to the Confederate leader was printed in the northern press.

HILTON HEAD, Port Royal, S. C., April 23rd. 1863.
The United States flag must protect all its defenders, white, black or yellow. Several negroes in the employ of the Government, in the Western Department, have been cruelly murdered by your authorities, and others sold into slavery. Every outrage of this kind against the laws of war and humanity, which may take place in this Department, shall be followed by the immediate execution of the Rebel of highest rank in my possession; man for man, these executions will certainly take place, for every one murdered, or sold into a slavery worse than death. On your authorities will rest the responsibility of having inaugurated this barbarous policy, and you will be held responsible, in this world and in the world to come, for all the blood thus shed.

In the month of August last you declared all those engaged in arming the negroes to fight for their country, to be felons, and directed the immediate execution of all such, as should be captured. I have given you long enough to reflect on your folly. I now give you notice, that unless this order is immediately revoked, I will at once cause the execution of every rebel officer, and every rebel slaveholder in my possession. This sad state of things may be kindly ordered by an all wise Providence, to induce the good people of the North to act earnestly, and to realize that they are at war. Thousands of lives may thus be saved.

The poor negro is fighting for liberty in its truest sense; and Mr. Jefferson has beautifully said,—"in such a war, there is no attribute of the Almighty, which will induce him to fight on the side of the oppressor."

You say you are fighting for liberty. Yes you are fighting for liberty: liberty to keep four millions of your fellow-beings in ignorance and degradation;—liberty to separate parents and children, husband and wife, brother and sister;—liberty to steal the products of their labor, exacted with many a cruel lash and bitter tear,—liberty to seduce their wives and daughters, and to sell your own children into bondage;—liberty to kill these children with impunity, when the murder cannot be proven by one of pure white blood. This is the kind of liberty —the liberty to do wrong—which Satan, Chief of the fallen Angels, was contending for when he was cast into Hell. I have the honor to be, very respectfully, Your mo. ob. serv.

D. HUNTER,
Major Gen.
Com.

"A NIGHT AND DAY OF TERROR":
LOUISIANA, MARCH–APRIL 1863

Kate Stone: Journal, April 25, 1863

Kate Stone lived with her family at Brokenburn, a cotton plantation in what is now Madison Parish, Louisiana, about thirty miles northwest of Vicksburg. Foraging parties from the Union army camps along the Mississippi moved through the area in early 1863, seizing food and horses and encouraging slaves to leave their plantations. On March 22 Stone recorded how "two most villainous-looking Yankees" had taken her horse at gunpoint. The following day, alarmed by reports that armed former slaves were helping Union soldiers plunder neighboring plantations, she wrote: "The sword of Damocles in a hundred forms is suspended over us, and there is no escape." A month later, Stone and her family were refugees staying near Monroe, Louisiana, eighty miles west of the Mississippi. She described the incident that caused them to flee.

April 25: We see that Van Dorn has had another fight and been repulsed. We can only hope Brother Coley and Dr. Buckner are safe. We will not hear for many days. Affairs look dark for our Confederacy just now.

This country is filled with refugees. Nearly all our friends are back here or on their way to Texas, where we hope to be before long. Out here the prices asked for everything are enormous. The people of Monroe seem determined to fleece the refugees. It cost us $3,000 to get a four-horse hack to bring us from Monroe here—four miles."

Having no other way of amusing myself, I may as well write the account of our flight from home and our subsequent adventures.

On Thursday, March 26, hearing that Mr. Hardison had returned from Monroe, Sister and I walked up in the afternoon to hear what news he had brought. As we approached the house, it struck me that something was wrong. As we were going through the garden George Richards came out and told us a party of Yankees and armed Negroes had just left, carrying with them every Negro on the place, most of Mrs. Hardison's and the children's clothes, and all the provisions they could manage. They were led by Charles, Mr. Hardison's most trusted servant, and they were all vowing vengeance against Mr. Hardison. They said they would shoot him on sight for moving two of his Negroes a few days before. Mr. Hardison had fortunately seen them coming and, knowing he would be arrested or perhaps killed as a conscript officer, had escaped to the woods.

We walked in and found Mrs. Hardison and the children all much excited and very angry, with flaming cheeks and flashing eyes. The Negroes had been very impertinent. The first armed Negroes they had ever seen. Just as we were seated someone called out the Yankees were coming again. It was too late to run. All we could do was to shut ourselves up together in one room, hoping they would not come in. George Richards was on the gallery. In a minute we heard the gate open and shut, rough hoarse voices, a volley of oaths, and then a cry, "Shoot him, curse him! Shoot him! Get out of the way so I can get him." Looking out of the window, we saw three fiendish-looking, black Negroes standing around George Richards, two with their guns leveled and almost touching his breast. He was deathly pale but did not move. We thought he would be killed instantly, and I shut my eyes that I might not see it. But after a few words from George, which we could not hear, and another volley of curses, they lowered their guns and rushed into the house "to look for guns" they said, but only to rob and terrorize us. The Negroes were completely armed and there was no white man with them. We heard them ranging all through the house, cursing and laughing, and breaking things open.

Directly one came bursting into our room, a big black wretch, with the most insolent swagger, talking all the time in a most insulting manner. He went through all the drawers and wardrobe taking anything he fancied, all the time with a cocked pistol in his hand. Cursing and making the most awful threats against Mr. Hardison if they ever caught him, he lounged up to the bed where the baby was sleeping. Raising the bar, he started to take the child, saying as he waved the pistol, "I ought to kill him. He may grow up to be a jarilla. Kill him." Mrs. Hardison sprang to his side, snatched the baby up, and shrieked, "Don't kill my baby. Don't kill him." The Negro turned away with a laugh and came over where I was sitting with Little Sister crouched close to me holding my hand. He came right up to us standing on the hem of my dress while he looked me slowly over, gesticulating and snapping his pistol. He stood there about a minute, I suppose. It seemed to me an age. I felt like I would die should he touch me. I did not look up or move, and Little Sister was as still as if petrified. In an instant more he turned away with a most diabolical laugh, gathered up his plunder, and went out. I was never so frightened in my life. Mrs. Hardison said we were both as white as marble, and she was sure I would faint. What a wave of thankfulness swept over us when he went out and slammed the door. In the meanwhile, the other Negroes were rummaging the house, ransacking it from top to bottom, destroying all the provisions they could not carry away, and sprinkling a white powder into the cisterns and over everything they left. We never knew whether it was poison or not.

The Negroes called and stormed and cursed through the house, calling each other "Captain" and "Lieutenant" until it nearly froze the blood in our veins, and every minute we expected them to break into our room again. I was completely unnerved. I did not think I could feel so frightened.

Mrs. Alexander went into her room hoping to prevent their robbing her bed, when one of them pointed his pistol at her and said, "I told you once before, old woman, to keep out of here and stop your jaw." Mr. McPherson and George were all the time on the gallery with Negroes guarding them with leveled guns.

After carrying on this way about two hours they lit matches, stuck them about the hall, and then leisurely took themselves off, loaded down with booty. We rushed around, put out all the matches, gathered up the few little articles left, and started at once for home. Since the Negroes declared as they moved off that they were coming back in a little while and burn every house on the place, I took the baby and Mrs. Hardison, Mrs. Alexander, and the children with George and Mr. McPherson gathered up everything of any value left, and we hurried home, reaching there spent with excitement. Mrs. Hardison was almost crazy.

As we passed through our quarters, there were numbers of strange Negro men standing around. They had gathered from the neighboring places. They did not say anything, but they looked at us and grinned and that terrified us more and more. It held such a promise of evil. Jimmy went out at once to where Mr. Hardison was in hiding to tell him his family were with us. Jimmy just escaped being shot by Mr. Hardison, who, in the dusk, took him for a Yankee. Mr. and Mrs. Hardison and the small children went off as soon as possible, not thinking it safe to remain so near home. During the night a party came to the yard looking for them, but on the house servants' assuring them that the Hardisons were gone, they did not come to the house.

We made preparations that night to move at daybreak, but something deterred us. Mamma thought she would go out and get letters of protection but later abandoned the idea. It was then too late for us to get off, and we spent a night and day of terror. The next evening the Negroes from all the inhabited places around commenced flocking to Mr. Hardison's, and they completely sacked the place in broad daylight, passing our gate loaded down with plunder until twelve at night. That more than anything else frightened Mamma and determined her to leave, though at the sacrifice of everything we owned.

We made arrangements to get Dr. Carson's skiffs and sent Webster around collecting saddles and bridles. On account of the water we could go only on horseback to take the skiffs. With much difficulty we got everything ready for the start at midnight. Aunt Laura was the only one who did not want to go. She begged Mamma to let her and Beverly stay, saying that she would get old Mr. Valentine to stay with her, but of course Mamma could not allow that. The boys brought in everything we had buried out, except Aunt Laura's silver. That had to be left packed in a barrel and buried in the yard. The boys had done it one very dark night, when they hoped all the Negroes were in their cabins as it was raining. All the servants behaved well enough except Webster, but you could see it was only because they knew we would soon be gone. We were only on sufferance.

Two days longer and we think they would all have gone to the Yankees, most probably robbing and insulting us before they left. About eleven the boys went off with their guns to have the horses saddled and brought up. After a good deal of trouble, they came. The boys carried their guns all the time. Without them I think we would never have gotten off. Webster tried every artifice to get hold of one of them, but the boys never relaxed their watch. The night was cloudy and dark with occasional claps of thunder, but we had to go then or never. We knew the news would be carried to camp, and the Yankees had forbidden citizens to leave their places. Aunt Laura, protesting all the time she could not ride, was at last after much coaxing and fixing mounted on poor Little Jack Fisher, the family pony, old and gentle, with Annie perched behind her. I took Beverly in my lap. All the others mounted, and with the baggage cart with Uncle Bob driving and Jimmy guarding it in the extreme rear, the procession moved off.

It was too dark to see the road but Johnny led off, and each one followed the shadow in front. At first Aunt Laura was loud in exclamation and complaint, until someone suggested that she would bring the Negroes down on us. That acted as a quietus, and thereafter she groaned only in spirit. Several times as the clouds lifted and it grew something lighter, I saw her pony struggling in a mud hole and Aunt Laura reeling in the saddle, but not a scream disturbed the stillness of the night. As we opened gates and rode through place after place in perfect silence, not a light was visible anywhere. After passing Out Post, the road was so bad and it was so dark that we were forced to wait for daylight. We dismounted in the middle of the road, and to Aunt Laura's surprise and amazement Mamma lay her head down in Johnny's lap and went sound asleep. Riding in the dark made her sick, and she was worn out with excitement and loss of sleep.

As soon as it was light enough to see, the sleepers were awakened, and we mounted and went on over the very worst road it was possible for ladies to travel—just a long bog from one end to the other. The morning air was pleasantly cool, and as the red light crept up the sky we heard all kinds of wildwoods sounds—squirrels chattering in the trees, birds waking with a song, the calls of the wild ducks and turkeys, and three or four deer bounding into the woods just before us.

When we reached within a mile of our place of debarkation,

the road became impassable, and we struck off into the woods. The cart had to be left there and the baggage carried on by mules. After much trouble, getting lost and riding through water up to our saddle skirts—I actually swam a bayou with Beverly in my arms—we succeeded in getting all of our party and a little of our baggage to the landing place below Mrs. Stevens'. We sent Webster back to the cart for the baggage, and no sooner was he out of sight than he mounted a horse and set off for home. He told Charles that he knew he was not going to Bayou Macon with Miss Manda and that Charles had better come on with him. Thus by his treachery we lost almost everything we brought away with us, for when we heard it, it was already too late to send back for the things. We knew the Yankees would certainly be where we were by 8 o'clock, and it was nearly that hour. We knew that we must get off at once if at all, for when the Yankees came they would turn us back. They never allow anyone to leave if they can help it. Finish this another day.

WAITING TO MARCH: VIRGINIA, APRIL 1863

Wilbur Fisk to The Green Mountain Freeman

Private Wilbur Fisk of the 2nd Vermont Infantry began writing letters in December 1861 to *The Green Mountain Freeman* of Montpelier under the pen name "Anti-Rebel." Fisk fought in the Seven Days' Battles before being hospitalized with chronic diarrhea in September 1862. He returned to his regiment near Fredericksburg in March 1863 and wrote to the *Freeman* as the Army of the Potomac awaited the opening of the spring campaign. At the end of April Hooker had 134,000 men under his command, while Lee defended his lines along the Rappahannock with about 60,000 men.

Camp near White Oak Church, Va.
April 26, 1863

We have not moved from our old camp yet, although we came so near it once that we considered it a foregone conclusion. Last week every possible preparation was made for such an event; the usual orders were read, some more stringent and particular than ever before. The order in regard to straggling was read by the adjutant to each company separately, besides being read, according to usual custom, on dress parade, twice. Great stress was laid upon the importance of preventing a practice so demoralizing and weakening to the army. Regimental and Company officers were to be held responsible and, besides other punishments threatened, leaves of absence and furloughs would be withheld from those regiments where straggling was permitted.

The order in regard to rations informed us that we must each of us carry eight days' rations of bread, coffee and sugar, three days' rations of meat—the remaining five days' rations of meat were to be taken along on the hoof. This was making far greater provision for ourselves than had ever before been required of us, and seemed to bode heavy, fatiguing loads for our backs, or else extreme destitution in the matter of blankets and extra clothing. We were not exactly ordered, but very strongly advised, to take only our rubber blankets, and leave our woollen ones in the care of the Quartermaster. Everything else, except a change of underclothing, must be left. Once before we had been ordered to send off to Washington everything worth saving that could possibly be dispensed with in a summer campaign. We thought we had been remarkably self-sacrificing and had stinted ourselves to the lowest possible extreme, but this order pressed us down another notch. Some sent off their woollen blankets and even their dress coats,— their overcoats had been sent off before. They saved nothing but their rubber blankets and their blouse coats, or fatigue jackets. Others determined to keep their woollen blankets at all hazards, and if sorely weighed down on the march, they could throw them away. Inasmuch as we didn't move, these saw the wisdom of their decision. Those that sent off all their things consoled themselves with the philosophy that they are as well off in camp without them, as they would be on the march.

But all of our preparations were nothing, as present appearances indicate. It is quite amusing, though, to be in a camp like ours on the eve of a march, and hear the debates, suggestions, and decisions in regard to a thousand little valuables,—whether they should be left behind or carried. Things of no special merit, but which had contributed to our comfort or convenience, were heedlessly thrown aside or destroyed. Many an article that a few days before would have been gladly bought at a high price, were at once valueless and could not be given away. Often a knapsack would have to be unpacked and its contents sorted over and over again, and other articles selected out and doomed to stay behind, to the no small regret of the wistful owner. No bigger article than a can for butter, or a frying-pan, would be made the subject of earnest debate, but the question, "how can we get along without them?" was confronted by one still more inexorable, "How can we carry them?" If we only knew where we were going? but we did not know that, and it was wisdom to prepare for the worst. That night it rained like a deluge, and marching the next day was rendered impracticable. It would be the merest guesswork, to undertake to tell when we shall be called upon to get ready for marching again.

The boys were never in better spirits or in better health than now, and they were never in better condition to endure the fatigues of a march than at the present time. But very few of the men are on the sick list, and those that are are mostly recruits who are not yet fully acclimated. The boys "feel their oats," as the saying is, immensely. I have never seen the time when the boys would engage in all manner of athletic sports with such eager relish as now. There is none of that thin, gloomy, woebegone expression to be seen in the faces of the men that was visible upon almost every countenance at the end of last summer's campaign. The boys never felt more *boyish* than they do now, and they never enjoyed themselves better. We can get up a sham fight that might look a little rough to some of our milder acquaintances at home, perhaps, but it passes with us as good, earnest boy's play. Rough as the Second boys have the name of being—and rough customers we certainly are, to those who are foolish enough to proclaim themselves our adversaries—a quarrel among ourselves is an unheard of thing and "difficulties" quite unknown. Almost perfect equanimity and good feeling exist throughout the entire regiment. Our guard-house remains empty, or in fact we have no guard-house at all, the apology of a thing we once had having become totally ruined and demoralized for want of use and care. The whole institution is nearly obsolete, and putting men under arrest is well nigh played out.

The 26th New Jersey regiment belongs to this brigade—a regiment of nine months men who came out here with big bounties, and, of course, has seen more hardships, endured more privations, and suffered more generally than any of the old soldiers ever dreamed of. The boys call them "two hundred dollar men," and they take wicked delight in playing their pranks on them whenever they have a chance. Our boys have no particular grudge against the Jerseys, but their mischief loving propensities must find vent somewhere and the Jersey regiment furnishes them abundant victims. It will be a long time before the boys will allow them to forget the dog scrape we got them into when we tempted them to steal a nicely dressed dog, which was duly served up to their officers in fine style. They stole it out of pure mischief and a desire not to be outstripped in that line of business by our boys; and doubtless it tasted remarkably sweet in consequence, as stolen articles proverbially do, but the joke leaked out, and it will be a long time before they will hear the last of it. It must be very provoking to them to hear the *barking* that springs spontaneously, as it would seem, from our regiment, whenever we pass the Jerseys, but nobody can tell who does it, and the Jerseys have to "grin and bear it." Our boys love to make them visits occasionally, after roll-call at night, and, as they generally come back in high glee, with a mouthful of stories to tell, it may be safely considered that the visit was a pleasant one to at least one of the parties. In one of these nocturnal visits some of our boys, for some reason or other, probably a misunderstanding, got caught, and were put into the guard-house. But the guard-house didn't hold them long. They run the guard and outrun the guard's bullets, and, though the Jerseys did their best, they couldn't imprison them again, nor tell who they were. After that our boys generously offered to stand guard for them, but our services were declined. Some time ago some officers of the Fifth advised the Jerseys to let the Second boys alone or they would find more than they could handle, and the Jerseys are beginning to think it best to accept this advice.

The paymaster made us a visit about a fortnight ago, and this has contributed not a little to keep the boys in good spirits, for there is nothing in the world that will make the boys feel so good-natured as it will to get their pockets lined with Uncle Sam's greenbacks. We received four months' pay. It made quite a little sum for us, but it is easily spent here. Some are beginning to borrow already. While every luxury (we call them luxuries, though any one but soldiers would consider the term "necessaries" more appropriate) that we have to buy rules so high, as here in the army, money is of but little account. For instance: butter is 60 cents a pound, cheese 50 cents a pound, apples 5 cents apiece, papers tobacco at the rate of nearly $3.00 a pound, whiskey $1.00 a drink or $3.00 a bottle, and so on to the end of the chapter. For five dollars a fellow could get a pretty good dinner at the sutler's. It is unnecessary, in order to tell a big story, to quote prices in Jeff's dominions; here in the Union army we can beat the rebs all hollow even in that.

The weather to-day and yesterday, has been remarkably fine. The sun shines clear and pleasant with scarcely a cloud to intervene. A stiff northwest wind has been blowing steadily, in regular April style. In Vermont it would be considered excellent weather to make sugar, as well as to dry the land and prepare it for the plow. Here it is still quite cool, and a sunny side is preferable to a shade for comfort. With this weather Virginia mud must soon disappear. Something besides mud will have to be our excuse for remaining here much longer. There has been some curious rumors afloat to account for our not moving. In the first place Gen. Hooker had broken his leg, by being thrown from a horse, and therefore could not be with the army. Then it was said that he ordered a movement to be made, but the President countermanded the order. Upon this, it is said, Hooker resigned and Fremont was now in command. They are all about equally true, probably. But whether we move or stay, as the boys say "it is all inside of the three years."

Quite a disgraceful affair occurred the other day with the 5th regiment which perhaps I ought to mention. Five or six from Co. D, of that regiment went out to a house near the picket line, for purposes too foul to mention. The guard stationed at the house was relieved, who reported his suspicions of something wrong at the nearest picket reserve. A squad of pickets was immediately sent to arrest the guilty party. They succeeded, but were fired upon and two of their number hit. I do not know the extent of the injuries received. The affair will soon undergo an investigation, and some think the death penalty will be inflicted upon one or more of the culprits.

"RAIN, MUD, & NIGHT": VIRGINIA, APRIL 1863

John Hampden Chamberlayne to Martha Burwell Chamberlayne

On April 27 Hooker began an offensive designed to drive Lee out of his entrenched positions and force him either to retreat toward Richmond or fight on open ground. While Union troops prepared to cross the Rappahannock at Fredericksburg, Hooker sent three corps on a rapid march upriver. By April 30 his flanking force had crossed the Rappahannock and Rapidan rivers and reached Chancellorsville, a crossroads clearing ten miles west of Fredericksburg in the midst of an area of scrub woods and dense undergrowth known as the Wilderness. Lieutenant John Hampden Chamberlayne was a veteran Confederate artillery officer whose battery, like many in Lee's army, had been bivouacked south of Fredericksburg so as to be nearer supplies of food and forage. By the time his unit reached the front on April 30, Union troops had crossed the river just below the city and taken up positions in front of the high ground held by the Confederates.

Camp near Fredericksbg
April 30th 1863 (within 300
yards of that of Dec 12th 1862)

My dear Mother

Yesterday we received very suddenly an order to the front, distance 25 miles; starting with all the inevitable entanglements & delays about 11½ A.M. we marched some till 3 A.M. this morning, some till long after day; my Battery, as it was in the rear of the column, came in last about sunrise; our provisions followed us into camp about 12 M. today—The march was through mud, mud, mud, & cold north east rain, no sleep, no food—You who naturally think much of my hardships should only have seen the boys of my Battery almost falling asleep as they stumbled through the dark clinging mist, yet falling in at the word into knee-deep slush & mud to play at horses and push the guns up on the fagged out brutes—Some oaths and some grumbling but at bottom a will *to do it*—These men, the privates marched the 25 miles through rain, mud, & night, carrying on their backs all their worldly goods & about half the time helping the horses along—The continued embarrassment such as I mention is hardly to be avoided in bad roads filled with long drawn columns of Artillery, every pause in front makes a stop in the whole line & every carriage makes the road worse until the horses to the rear carriages become cold from stopping when warm then grow restive & uncertain & finally often "baulk" (or balk), as we say, at nothing at all.

Does this begin to explain how 100 men can be of use with 4 guns? Add that each gun is drawn by six horses, driven by three drivers postilion fashion & is followed by its caisson or carriage for ammunition with three more drivers, then there are several wagoners for the Battery, a forge driver, two or three mechanics as harness makers, smiths &c, then add for each gun a sergeant & a corporal (a bugler & a flag bearer for the battery), thrown in the chances of 10 per cent being always wounded or sick & you find that 25 to a gun does not more than furnish 10 to 13 actual cannoneers, of which class one brings ammunition from the chest to the gun, one sponges & rams, one keeps the vent or touchhole closed when sponged, one primes, one fires, one aims & all assist to run the piece back when it recoils from the place of fire &c &c.

Your welcome letter reached me yesterday just as we were moving; I wrote you a scrawled line in pencil by Harrison Col. W's servant & sent by him my trunk & key; I have with me all that it is desirable or proper to carry—Please have the things aired &c from time to time—I asked that you would send by Hn the coat &c—, if not it makes little difference Yesterday I did not starve; going by to bid the Woolfolks farewell I was I might say constrained to accept a couple of huge slices of nice bread holding between them ditto meat.

We are all in the utmost spirits & confidence of success— I do not know what to think, whether we will have a battle here or not I hope we will but I am afraid not Yesterday Rhodes' formerly D. H. Hill's Divn was skirmishing; today there has been artillery at long intervals, I do not believe we have fired at all—A. P. Hill is in 1st line of reserve supporting (I believe but am not certain) both Trimble & Early, tomorrow he may be in front, if so we will be with him—I rather believe we will move up tonight or tomorrow toward the left flank toward

Orange Co Ho—My time is short to write now as you may well believe & I find I must hurry.

I have not seen V. or Mann—Hope to do so shortly—I wrote to Sister on Sunday or Monday—Love to her & to bro— Ed— & Hart—John is well, got a letter from his Mother lately, proud of it—

Give my love to all friends, I have not time to name them And I am & always will be

Your devoted son
J H Chamberlayne

Address (except by Hn) Care Col. Crutchfield Chief Arty Jackson's Corps Army N. Va

EXPELLING "ENEMIES": LOUISIANA, APRIL 1863

Sarah Morgan: Diary, April 30, 1863

Sarah Morgan had fled her home in Baton Rouge, Louisiana, in August 1862 when Confederate forces unsuccessfully attempted to retake the city. She lived for eight months with relatives at Linwood, a plantation five miles northeast of Port Hudson, while her widowed mother stayed in the nearby town of Clinton. Severe food shortages and the prospect of a Union attack on Port Hudson eventually drove Morgan, her sister Miriam, and their mother from northern Louisiana in April 1863. After fruitlessly trying to find refuge in Georgia, Alabama, and Mississippi, they reluctantly decided to move in with Morgan's half brother in Union-occupied New Orleans. In September 1862 Major General Benjamin F. Butler, the Union commander at New Orleans, had ordered that any person who failed to take the oath of allegiance be registered as "an enemy of the United States." Shortly after Morgan arrived in New Orleans, Major General Nathaniel P. Banks, Butler's successor, ordered the expulsion of all registered enemies who remained within Union lines. Morgan wrote about the order on the anniversary of the death of her brother Henry, who had been killed in a duel in New Orleans in 1861.

Thursday April 30th.

Was not the recollection of this day bitter enough to me already? I did not think it could be more so. Yet behold me crying as I have not cried for many and many a day. Not for Harry; I dare not cry for him. I feel a deathlike quiet when I think of him; a fear that even a deep drawn breath would wake him in his grave. And as dearly as I love you, O Hal I dont want you in this dreary world again! Not here, O Hal! Not here! Stay where you can look down on these pitiful mortals and smile at their littleness. But I would not have you among them, Hal! Stay there, where maybe one day God will call me. I will go to you, but dont wish to be back here, Harry. Long long ago I learned to say "Thy will be done," and almost to be thankful you were in your grave. Two years ago to day Hal, you folded your hands and died so quietly and meekly. Two years of trials and hardships have been spared you. Say thank

God, Harry! O safe, safe, in the heaven above pray for us, pity us, miserable creatures that we are!

To day came to us the proclamation which should link the name of Yankee to those of the inhabitants of the lower regions. Talk of the Revocation of the Edict of Nantes! Talk of Louis XIV! Of— Pshaw! my head is in such a whirl that history gets all mixed up, and all paralels seem weak and moderate in comparison to this infamous outrage. To day, thousands of families, from the most respectable down to the least, all who have had the firmness to register themselves enemies to the United States, are ordered to leave the city before the fifteenth of May. Think of the thousands, perfectly destitute, who can hardly afford to buy their daily bread even here, sent to the Confederacy, where it is neither to be earned, nor bought, without money, friends, or a home. Hundreds have comfortable homes here, which will be confiscated to enrich those who drive them out. "It is an ill wind that blows no one good."

Such dismal faces as one meets every where! Each looks heart broken. Homeless, friendless, beggars, is written in every eye. Brother's face is too unhappy to make it pleasant to look at him. True, he is safe; but hundreds of his friends are going forth destitute, leaving happy homes behind, not knowing where the crust of bread for famishing children is to come from to-morrow. He went to Gen. Bowen and asked if it were possible that women and children were included in the order. Yes, he said; they should all go, and go in the Confederacy. They should not be allowed to go elsewhere.

Penned up like sheep to starve! That's the idea! With the addition of forty thousand mouths to feed, they think they can invoke famine to their aid, seeing that their negro brothers dont help them much in the task of subjugating us. And these are the men who cry Liberty, Equality, Fraternity! These are the men who hope to conquer us! Ever unite with them? Never, never! Defenders of Charleston, Savannah, Mobile! *These* are the foes who are striving to overcome you! Deliver your cities in their hands? Die first!

O that from the Atlantic to the Rio Grande their vile footsteps should have been allowed to press our soil! Give up to them? Rather than submit, I would that, all gathered together, we should light our own funeral pyre, and old men, brave soldiers, fair women and tender children should all perish hand in hand in the bright flames we would send up to Heaven as a memorial of our toil, sorrow, and suffering.

If I was a man! O if I was only a man! For two years that has been my only cry, and to day I fairly rave about it. Blood, fire, desolation, I feel ready to invoke all, on these Yankees. Miriam and I are both desperate. If we could only get back, even to Clinton! It seems base treason to remain apparently under the protection of this hateful flag, while all of our own creed and country are sent out to starve. We would endure any thing, if we could only get mother's consent. If she would only stay with Brother, and let us go back to Clinton! For she cannot endure the privations we would have to undergo, while we could stand anything, just to get out of sight of these Yankees again. But she wont listen to it. So we will have to remain patiently here, and consequently labor under the suspicion of belonging to a side we abhor with all our souls. George and Gibbes will be frantic about it. If we could only, only get away!

Evidently, Banks had been whipped in the Attakapas. In spite of his fanfaronade of trumpets, I believe he has been outrageously beaten (as usual) and turns round to punish women and children for his defeat. The "Union" is certainly on its last legs when its generals resort to such means as getting negroes to fight its battles seeing how white men fail, and take to running women and children out of the land. You have roused the Devil in us, Banks! We women will tear you to pieces yet!

Dont care who knows I smuggled in a dozen letters! Wish I had had more!

BATTLE OF CHANCELLORSVILLE:
VIRGINIA, MAY 1863

Samuel Pickens: Diary, May 1–3, 1863

Lee responded to Hooker's flanking maneuver by dividing his already outnumbered army. Leaving 10,000 men to defend Fredericksburg, he sent Jackson and the remainder of his troops to oppose the Union forces advancing from the west. On May 1 the two sides fought at the edge of the Wilderness three miles east of Chancellorsville. When Hooker withdrew his men to defensive positions around the Chancellorsville clearing, Lee and Jackson decided to again divide their forces and seize the initiative. While Lee kept 14,000 men to face the 70,000 Union troops at Chancellorsville, Jackson marched 33,000 troops twelve miles through the Wilderness on May 2 and struck at Hooker's exposed right flank. Private Samuel Pickens had joined the 5th Alabama Infantry in the fall of 1862 and served in Jackson's corps in the division led by Brigadier General Robert E. Rodes. After writing his diary entry for May 3, Pickens was taken prisoner in the fighting around Chancellorsville.

May 1, Friday

It was Bob Price & myself who were sent fr. our Co. as guards to brstwks last eveng. at dark. We were divid. to 3 reliefs & B & I stood 1st—fr. 8 till 11. Had fire in Ditch where a place was cut out for cannon. In eveng. Yanks. threw shell over it & 1 burst just in front of it & piece passd. very near Knowland's head & struck in bank wh. K. got & showed us. We could see our signal lights on eminences on our right & faraway to left— waving occasionally. Bob & I then spread our blankets & lay front of fire expecting to sleep 6 hrs—; but just after lying a little over 3 hrs. we were waked & all the guard orderd to join Regt. wh. we found in line of battle in edge of woods, & then ('bout 2½ or 3 A.M.) movd by left flank & marchd. up the river. Roads were very wet & slippery & bad for mchg. At Hamilton's Crossing we were detained some time by a continuous & it seemed to me then an endless line of troops passing on up river by road into wh. we were then coming. There was the densest fog this morng I ever saw. We made very slow time during the morng. on acct. of the wagons in front stopping frequently. Passed many deserted camps wh. had been occup. during Winter by parts of our army. Halted between 11 & 12 near a house intended for hospital & rested, ate something & filled Canteens. I was very much exhausted & felt sick & faint fr. mching so hard thro' hot sun. Then fell in & loaded & Regts of Brig. moved on. As Col. Sam. B. Pickens of 12 Ala. passed we shook hands—& wished each other a safe passage thro' the impending battle. We then moved on down the road & came into the plank road leading fr. Culpeper C.H.? to Frdksbg. The cannon could be heard all the time firing slowly. Today for 1st time noticed trees budding & putting out new leaves. Stopped on Plank R. & piled up knap sacks & at same time our noble old Genl Robt. E. Lee passed followed by a troop of aids & couriers. He is a well set venerable looking man with white hair & beard. He passed so rapidly that I had not a good chance to see his countenance. Whether it was that he was not generally known by the troops or our silent advance towds scene of action that caused it I dont know, but he passed in silence—no cheering. All who knew him was inspired with the utmost confidence & gazed attentively upon him. We then went on further & stopped little while [   ] right flank in line of battle thro a very thick piece woods [   ] confusion not possible to preserve any thing of a line in such a thick [   ] & soon came to another road nearby [   ] with plank—as hot as could be & nearly broken down. Went by left flank along the road, passed house where there were some of 12 Va who told us they had opened the fight on Wed. & there were some wounded men on litters in yard [   ] Were orderd back a little distance & stopped—I then turned round & went still further up road [   ] wounded & prisoners. In eveng. we made a large circuit thro' woods (Brig.) passg several lines of battle lying in woods & then stopped on brstwks at edge of woods—where we washed & lay down an hour or so & [   ] mch. refreshed. Afterwds stacked arms & went bak for knap-sax —troops & artillery passing fast—men who went bak said saw 1000 troops moving. Jackson we began to see was about makg one of his favorite flank movements. We marchd on up Plank road till betwen. 9 & 10 & halted in field & orchrd. completely broke down. Had eaten very little but as had only a biscuit left & no prospect of getg. more concluded to keep it for Brkfst. Carey brot us biscuits Thurs. morng. at day light & we had a little smoked beef wh. we had lived on 2 days.

May 2, Saturday

Put down blankets. Jack, Bill Lenier & I slept together *Sat 2nd* [   ] had on the go 18 hrs. yesterday. Allowed to sleep later than expected after day light. went to branch & took good wash & made feel fresh. Resumed the march passing good many troops lying along the road. Stopped to rest a few min. & gave Matt. Jones ½ biscuit & ate the other & scrap meat & afterwds 2 or 3 little butter crackers—whole not more than 1 biscuit. We heard Commiss. wagons had been orderd up & hoped wd. overtake us but in this we were disappointed. We heard Yanks. cheering in their formal stiff way & some boys wished Jackson would come along that we might raise a cheer. In a little while the word was passed up lines to give way to left—& there came Glorious old Stonewall at a sweeping gallop—hat in hand on his sorrel horse followed by aids & couriers. All long line troops waved hats & cheered long & loud. I cant describe my feelings at thus seeing him suddenly for 1st time—but my breast swelled with emotions of pride & gratification, & all must have felt confident of success when we shd. meet enemy. Could only see he was a younger lookg man than I expected to see & not so stout but apparently well made—blk hair & beard & a little bald spot on back head that showed plainly after passing. But saw him again when we had passed enemy's right flank & were getting round in their rear—he gave some directions in remark. mild & cool manner as to where he wished our Divis. to go. His hair curls round edges of his military cap—regular features & very good looking & pleasant countenance.

(Sat. 2nd Cont) We moved on down Plank Road towds river I think then to the right & were in the rear of Yankees Right, & from being on Right of our lines—below Fredbg. on Thurs. we had moved to extreme Left-flanked Yankees & got in rear of Right of their lines. We formd line battle in woods as front line & lay down to rest (betwn 3 & 4 P.M.) while 2 other lines formed in rear of us to support us. When everything was ready about 6 P.M. wh. was so late that some began to think we might not make the attack till mornig, but we were ordered forwd & had very rough time getting thro' the thick woods. By & by we heard the sharp shooters firing & we started double quick—& most terrific volleys of musketry opened on our right & such was the excitement & the desire to be doing something too, that they commencd firing in our Co. & Regt. & as they were firing around me—altho' I could not see anything & still I thought the Yanks must be there & imagined I saw blue line on opposite hillside in pines & blazed away too. Capt. Williams immediately orderd firing to be stopped that there was nothing to shoot at, & I determd not to be guilty of such folly again & did not shoot unless I had a fair mark. We loaded & started in run yelling & soon saw the blue rascals running like turkeys & our men—shooting, cheering, & pursuing as fast as they could. When Yanks got behind hill or breastwk they would stop & shoot & minute or two—but as our men would come charging upon them they'd be off again. Saw a Y. shot down & as we approached, he jumped up & started again when he was again shot down. One fell standing by tree with but of gun up to signify he surrendered. Col. Hobson called to him to drop his gun & lie down or he'd be killed—he did so & Col. H. told him to go to rear. I soon got separated from entire Co. & looking round could not see one I knew but Col. Hob. & I kept with him—he was waving sword and gallantly leading the men on. Never saw such confusion in my life—men scattered & mixed up every way. It was a running fight & difficulty was to keep near enough to Y. to shoot them. They shot at us very little—only when they'd half a little behind breast wks. (redoubts) Our men from marching all day before & that day & having nothing to eat scarcely—were so much exhausted that great many were scattered along behind a long distance & some excited fellows were firing wildly over the heads of us who were ahead & really there seemed at times as great danger of being killed by our men as by Yks. & several times we'd stop & wait for them to get up in line with us. Some fired without takg. sight up in air & I notices ball strike grd. just in front of us. Some of our men were wounded by our own side. Grt. pity theres so much confusion & men get scattered so badly—several times men were stopped from firing into friends & I recollect joining in & screaming to them not to do it—several times I knockd up gun 1ce of fellow in act of doing it. 1st redoubt we advanced on the artillery stuck out pretty well & threw grape & canister like hail—a good many of us in edge of pine thicket lay down a minute or 2 but on went our men & a shout told Yanks. were driven on. Parts of 3 Batteries were captured that eveng. Noticed a large N. Foundland dog—in agonies of death with a ball hole thro' him. Some of Y. officers on horsebk. rode along lines & tried to rally troops but all in vain. we drove them a mile & ½ or 2—till night closed in on the scene. At one time noticed flags of 2 Regts. close together & mass of men around & fired 1ce or 2ce into them. Passed on down slope & rose another & in edge of pines there was a horse standing. Hobson started to it—calling to some men to catch it for him & learned afterwds he was shot down before getting to it—he was struck in leg above the knee—fortun. only a flesh wound. I kept on & a wounded Yank. beckoned & called to me—shook canteen & offered water, wh. he drank—& askd name & Regt & said he would be ever mindful of me or somethg of sort—he was a Lieut, & said wanted to see a Surg. that imposs. & I passed on keeping as near Thomson with our Colors as could. He had become separated fr. Regt. or greater part of it. Finally fell in with Ed. Hutchinson & afterwds with Ch. Hafner & John Cowin & Jim Arrington. We kept together & went on till near dark when so exhausted we sat down in pines. Pretty soon Yanks. opened with battery & shelled woods, & threw grape everywhere. We could not go forwd or back without greatest risk & so lay close to ground. It was terrific cannonading— shell burst & grape cut trees all around & above us. When it ceased a squad of men came by with some Prisoners & we started on back to go over field & get some rations as were very hungry. I had one crack. that had taken fr. Yank. Havresak, going on & divided it with J. Arrington. As we went on men fr. various Regts. of diff. states were calling the name of Regt. trying to get together. Never saw such confus. & scattering. Occas. 1 or 2 & sometimes small squad of 5th Ala. fell in with us, & went on but did n't find any plunder or rations—the troops behind had swept them. Saw one fellow who. had 3 watches. finally we found out where Col. O'Neal was collecting the Brigade & joined them. Everyone felt so grateful at coming out safely that he would shake each acquaintance warmly by hand & express delight at seeing him come out safely. 5 of our Co. were wounded—Matt Jones, Hausman, Youngblood Sr, S. Jackson & B. Price, also Col. Hobson. Stacked arms, made fires & ate supper wh. was taken fr. Yanks. the best had some time. Crackers, ham & Coffee. Yanks had 8 da. rations with them 5 in kn.sk. & 3 in Haver sk. It seems Rodes Brig. was halted late in eveng. & tried to collect & form it, but I with others had gotten separated way to right & kept on till dark—Met. Col. Pickens of 12th safe. All the boys had trophys fr. Bat. field & well supplied with oil cloths, Blankets, canteens & havresacks &c. Gave me 2 or 3 Yank. letters. Aft. sup. movd up road & to line brst wks, near Hospital. Good deal our artil going fowd. (Cannonading in front & heavy volleys musketry bright pretty night. fightg kept up as men on guard said till 12 or 1 o'clk)

May 3, Sunday

Sprd. blankts & lay on edge entrenchmts with gun & accoutremts. ready to don at moments warng. didn't even pull off boots. Up pretty early & went to spring & washd. wh. refreshg. We were waiting for Cop. Hutchinson to come up with Provision wh. he soon did but bef. could give out enemy began to shell us pretty severely & all took to trench as it wd slacken some fellows wd go up & draw for 2 or 3 around him. Then moved front in piece pines & lay few minutes when orderd forwd.

"DISORDER REIGNED SUPREME":
VIRGINIA, MAY 1863

Jedediah Hotchkiss: Journal, May 2–6, 1863

Major Jedediah Hotchkiss had served on Jackson's staff since March 1862 and become the leading mapmaker in the Army of Northern Virginia. At Jackson's direction, Hotchkiss spent April 30 making maps of the Wilderness and scouting marching routes west of Fredericksburg. The following day he rode to the battlefield near Chancellorsville and distributed his maps to the Confederate division commanders.

Saturday, May 2nd. The Generals were up at an early hour and had a consultation, in the pines on the top of the hill where the Catherine Furnace road turns from the Plank Road, sitting on Yankee Cracker boxes which the enemy had left there. I went down to Mr. Welford's, where General Stuart had his quarters, and ascertained the roads that led around to the enemy's rear and came back and reported to Generals Lee and Jackson, who consulted and examined the map and then started the Second Corps down by the furnace, Rodes' division in front, and went on to the Brock road, and then up it a piece and into a private road, and so on to the Plank Road and across both Plank Roads to the Old Turnpike and formed our line of battle at the   house and with three lines of battle fell on the enemy's rear at Talley's, at precisely 6 o'clock, and after an infantry fight on our side, of 32 minutes, the enemy using infantry and artillery, we routed them and drove them completely from the field and some three miles beyond, driving them out of two lines of entrenchments and on to some breastworks when it had become dark and by accident our men fired into each other and by that fire General Jackson was wounded, having three balls through his left arm and one through his right hand, having held up both hands to urge our men to desist. The enemy had but a moment before breaking our advance and throwing it into confusion but General J. had rallied it by telling the flying men "Jackson himself calls on you to halt." The enemy took advantage of our mistake and opened a terrific volley of musketry and artillery, sweeping the roads in which our forces had become massed by the dense growth on either side and the swampy nature of the ground. Disorder reigned supreme for a few moments, the "Great Chief" being struck down; but General A. P. Hill, who had rushed to the General's side saying, "I have been trying to make the men cease firing," himself met the advance of the yankee skirmishers then formed a line of men and repulsed them, so saving General J. from capture and he was borne off in a litter by Smith and   . One of those bearing him was struck by a shell in the furious cannonade and the General received a fall. I hastened back for an ambulance and some spirits and found Dr. McGuire and sent him forward. I rode a long ways back, but could find no spirits. Mr. Lacey had left me at Tally's, at dark, and I looked for him in vain. Late at night I found my way back to the Wilderness Tavern, where General Jackson had been taken, and where he was yet in a state of stuper from the shock he had received—, not having rallied enough to have his wounds dressed. At 12, midnight, I started for General Lee's, with young Chancellor as a guide, to inform him of the state of our affairs, making a wide detour, as the enemy had penetrated our lines. I went around and struck the Catharpen road and went on and found General Lee, at his old camp, at 4 A.M., and informed him of what had occurred. Wilbourn had preceded me an hour and informed him of the General's wounds. He was much distressed and said he would rather a thousand times it had been himself. He did not wish to converse about it. I informed him of the situation of the troops and he and Colonel Long consulted and arranged for the morrow. I lay down and slept awhile. He ordered General Stuart, who had taken Jackson's command (General A. P. Hill having been struck on the leg by a shell and disabled for the time), to move around to the right and connect with the left of Anderson who was on General Lee's right and would move to the left of McLaws who was in his front, and so make a connection behind Chancellorsville which the enemy held. I spent a part of the day at General Lee's headquarters copying map, and when the enemy advanced towards the front of General Lee and made a demonstration on the rear of General Jackson's ordnance train and artillery, near the furnace, Mr. Lacy and myself went down the Catharpen road and made our way by the Brock Road to General Jackson's position in time to be present at the fight. The enemy thought we were retreating towards Richmond when they fell on our train. They were repulsed by some of the artillery that turned back, but they soon came on again and were held in check by the 23rd. Georgia and the Irish Battalion until they surrounded and captured them after an obstinate struggle, but our train escaped. After General Jackson was wounded General Hill restored order, aided by the gallant efforts of Major A. S. Pendleton, and several fierce encounters took place in the night, in all of which the enemy was repulsed. The day was quite warm and pleasant —the night clear. The trees are becoming quite green and the apple and pear trees are in full bloom. Hooker commanded in person on the yankee side. The musketry was incessant from 6 to 6½ P.M. and as heavy as I ever heard. Our loss was considerable. There was a slight shower in the P.M. and a thunder storm towards the Blue Ridge during the battle.

Sunday, May 3rd. After breakfasting with General Lee he sent me back with a message to General Stuart to press the enemy vigorously and make the junction of our wings. The enemy had withdrawn from the furnace so I went that way. Our men were capturing and bringing in the yankee pickets which had been left out. Anderson was forming his line of battle near the furnace to make the junction of the two wings, as I passed. Gen. Lee told me to tell General Stuart that he would soon come there in person. I went on around and down to near Tally's, and there rested a while, being so sleepy that I could hardly keep my eyes open. Our forces were pressing forward and fighting severely. After resting awhile I started on to look for my friend Boswell, whom I had not seen or heard of since the fight. I went to where the General was wounded and there I found him, some 20 steps in advance, by the road-side, dead, pierced through the heart by two balls and wounded in the leg. I was completely overcome, although I had expected it from the state of his mind before, expecting him to be killed in this fight. His body had been riffled of hat, glass, pistol daguerreotype, & c., but his look in death was as peaceful and pleasant as in life.—I procured an ambulance and took him to where the General was, at Wilderness Tavern, and with many tears buried him in a grave which I had dug in the family burying ground at Elwood, the home of Major J. Horace Lacey, by the side of General Jackson's arm which had been amputated and buried there. We buried him just as the moon rose, wrapped in his martial coat, Rev. B. T. Lacy making a feeling prayer. Brown, who assisted me, the two men I had employed to dig the grave, Mr. Lacy and myself were all that were present. I wept for him as for a brother; he was kind and gentle and with as few faults as most men. Peace to his memory.

We united the two wings of our army and drove the enemy, by a vigorous and bloody onset, out of his strong works at Chancellorsville and took possession of that place, the loss being very heavy on both sides. Hooker was in the Chancellor house until it was struck by a shell, he then retired to a safer place.

Brown and I slept in the yard at Elwood, on the rich and soft green carpet of its verdant slopes and our weary horses cropped the choice grass. The sight of the dead and wounded today is horrible. Warm and pleasant. A heavy dew in the morning. The woods were on fire in many places and some of the wounded must have been burnt up. Morrison was sent for Mrs. Jackson.

Monday, May 4th. Mr. Lacy aroused me up at an early hour to guide the ambulance with General Jackson and Colonel Crutchfield to Guiney's Station. I saddled up and we soon got off, going by the Brock Road to Todd's Tavern and then to Spotsylvania C. H. and on to Guiney Station. The General stood the ride very well. We passed crowds of wounded men going the same way, all cheerful and each one wishing himself the badly wounded one instead of General Jackson.—The day was quite pleasant but we had a thunder storm late in the evening. Our forces fell on the enemy today and drove them from Marye's Hill which they had taken from us, and drove them up the River; so we now have the old town again. We found the cavalry camp at Spotsylvania C. H. and the country full of wild rumors about the Yankee cavalry raids to Richmond, cutting our communications, etc. I found that our wagons at Guiney's had been sent away to avoid capture and were back again in alarm. Found Col. French at Guiney's, he having been on the train that was captured near Ashland. He said the enemy was at Chickahominy Bridge and there was nothing to keep them from Richmond & c. That the enemy had destroyed much of the Virginia Central Railroad and that Stoneman was behaving very well. Col. F. slept with me. General Jackson stood the ride very well. I washed and cleaned up and got some sleep. General Jackson came to Guiney's by General Lee's advice.

Tuesday, May 5th. We were roused up before day by a report that the enemy was coming—, that is—his cavalry, and the wagons were hitched up to depart; so I got on my horse and went over to see the General; found him cheerful, although he had not rested much; bade him good-by. He said he hoped to be soon in the field again and sent his regards to General Lee. I went by Mr. Alsop's and breakfasted with him, then on to near Fredericksburg and across to the plank road and thence on to General Lee's headquarters near Chancellorsville. I ascertained that he wanted the roads to the United States Ford, so went back by the furnace to get them and on to Mr. Stevens', where, in the P.M., there was a heavy thunder storm. After which I went on to Mr. Bullock's, a mile beyond Wilderness Run and learned from him about the roads, & c. Some young men came after him for a guide. We went to bed for a short time.

We fought the enemy near Salem Church yesterday. It was cool in the morning; the rain made the mud very deep. We have many thousand Yankee prisoners at Guiney's.

Wednesday, May 6th. We were up at 3 A.M. and off to camp. I found Gen. Stuart near Chancellorsville, asleep, the division of Gen. Rodes about moving to the enemy's right flank to dislodge him from his strong position between Chancellorsville and United States Ford. General Stuart sent me on to General Lee and told me to tell him he was satisfied the enemy was retreating. I found General Lee at his old camp and just dressing. He did not much credit the report of the enemy's retreat, and, after a cup of coffee, sent me back to tell General Stuart to press on the movement to our left. General Lee soon came up and he and General Stuart had a consultation, with the map, about the roads I had ascertained. General A. P. Hill soon came up and joined them. It rained nearly all of last night, hard, and most of to-day. It was soon ascertained that the enemy had retreated, leaving five lines of strong entrenchments which they had just thrown up. We followed them closely but they had availed themselves of the rain and darkness to make good their escape, and the mud, and the immense advantage secured to them by the other bank for artillery, prevented our doing them much damage, though we took a good many prisoners.

We spent most of the day near Chancellorsville. Orders were given for the forces to go back to their old camps. General Lee directed me to make a map of the battlefield, then General Stuart and then General A. P. Hill to whom I had reported. Late in the evening General A. P. Hill's wagons started back towards our old quarters. I went on and waited for them, but they did not come, so I started to go to Colonel Smith's quarters, but the rain, mud and darkness made me halt in a Miss. camp, where I was kindly entertained by the Sergeant of the 12th., and got a good night's rest. It has rained heavily and is quite cold.

BATTLE OF PORT GIBSON:
MISSISSIPPI, MAY 1863

Taylor Peirce to Catharine Peirce

Grant crossed the Mississippi with more than 20,000 men at Bruinsburg, thirty miles southwest of Vicksburg, on April 30. The following day his advancing forces engaged 6,000 Confederates under Brigadier General John S. Bowen at Port Gibson in a battle that cost each side about 800 men killed, wounded, or missing. One of the Union soldiers who fought at Port Gibson was Taylor Peirce of the 22nd Iowa Infantry, whose regiment had been sent in March from Missouri to Louisiana to serve in the Thirteenth Corps of the Army of the Tennessee.

Head Quarters 22 Iowa Inftry
Port Gibson Mississippi May 4th 1863
    Dear Catharine & all of you,
I have set down to write to you knowing that you would hear of our battle and would be very anxious about me and as soon as I found that I could send a letter I concluded to do so. On the 29th day of April we tried the experiment of bombarding the fort at Grand Gulf with the view of landing our forces at that place but the fort was impregnable being hewn out of the rock and after six hours cannonading it was found impossible to silence their guns. So the Genl concluded to run the blockade with the Transports and as they kept along side of the Steamboats and kept up such a continual roar of cannon that they did not get to injure one of them and there was not a life lost. So we were then marched down the river on the La side three miles below where we encamped for the night. Early the next morning we were then on board. There was 3 divisions one under Genl Carr one under Genl Hovey and one under Genl Ousterhouse. The whole under Comd of Genl McClernand. The whole number of men amounted to about 20 or 25 thousand men and said to be the finest army that has ever been together. We were taken down the river on the 30th of April about 10 miles to Rodney where after feeling for the

rebles and finding none we landed and drew 3 day rations and left about 3 oclock P.M. for this place. We marched out about 6 miles and halted and eat supper. In about an hour we started again. Our brigade being in advance we moved along sloly expecting every minute to hear our advance Guard fire on the reble pickets. About one oclock at night the long expected sound was heard. After some pretty sharp firing we were opened on by the reble battery which they had placed to rake us as we come up a lane but oweing to our caution and silence we had passed our whole brigade along the lane before they were aware of it. As soon as the battery opened on us we halted and laid down untill Harry Griffith come up with his six pieces of cannon. As soon as he got them fixed we were moved on the double quick around behind it into the head of a ravine where we all laid down and at it they went and kept it up untill near daylight when the rebles ceased to fire and we laid and slept on our arms untill sunrise. We were all tired and anxious when the morning came knowing that the rebles would contest the ground to the utmost. Our regiment was ordered to support the battery through the night and of course we lay right where the ball and shell flew and if a man has weak nerves then is the time he will be likely to feel it haveing to stand inactive. And the roar of the guns and this whissing of ball and bursting of shell is terrible but thank fortune I am not of the weak nerved kind and did not suffer from that sickning failing called fear and am very thankfull that I am so constituted that I do not.

Well after about an hours suspence waiting to see where the attack was to come from as the rebles were concealed in the cane breaks and gullies we sent a challange to them in the shape of a shell and imediately they opened on us in earnest the ball for the May party was opened. Our forces was in three divisions. Our regt under Carr with 21 & 23 Iowa the 8th & 18 Indiana & 11 Wisconsin formed the right wing of the army. Genl Hovey the centre. I do not know what troops he had. Genl Osterhouse was on the left. I suppose our lines were 3 miles in extent and the rebles under Genl Green Stacy & Bowen all under Genl Baldwin attacked all three of our divisions at once about 7 oclock in the morning and attempted to surround us. The Battle became general abot 9 oclock and continued without intermission untill about 1 pm when our division made charge and the rebles gave way and retreated across the Bayou burning the bridge. That left us at liberty to go in on the Centre which we did and after some pretty hard fighting the rebles broke and run and Osterhaus had got through with his work and by sunset the whole reble army was in full flight and our victory complete. This is said to be the most unfortunate battle of the war for them. They came down in the morning with about 13,000 fresh troops boasting that they would just capture the d—d Yankee and make slaves of them. They retreated in the evening a defeated and dispairing rabble without order leaving about 3,500 of their men behind them. The slaughter on their side was dreadful for the number engaged although they had the advantage of knowing the ground and kept hid in the cane breaks all the time just standing far enough in to keep out of sight so that they could fire out at us. But our English rifles sent their Leaden messengers in and thinned their ranks as if the plague was amongst them. Harry Griffith with his first Iowa battery tore their ranks from end to end. He is as brave as Ney. All night long we could hear him giving his commands with a clear loud voice and urging his men to give it to them while he sat or moved round amongst the guns on his horse amid a perfect shower of grape canister and shell as though it was but a May shower of rain instead of a shower of iron and seemed as unconcious of danger as when he used to walk the streets of Des Moines. Indeed our Officers all showed a bravery that was sublime. Not one of them but seemed that on his coolness and example before the men depended the fate of the battle.

Our loss is small. Our regiment was more exposed than any other but it come of the best except the 23. Our regt lost 3 killed and 12 wounded. 2 of the wounded are mortally. The rest will all get well. The 23d met the 23d Alabama and after about an hours hard fighting put them to flight. What the loss is in the 23 Iowa I have not learned certain but not much. I suppose 30 killed & wounded will cover the loss. The 23 Alabama left 360 Dead in the field or rather in the cane breaks and I suppose a number that was not discovered. We took some thing over 500 prisoners and been gathering them up ever since. I guess we will not have far short of 7 hundred. I heard we got 12 of their guns but I do not know whether it is correct or not. I do not know what the official report is but you will see it and the comments on it before you get this. We had one man wounded and none killed. Cap Ault showed considerable courage and behaved much better than I expected he would. Our Lts are good men and true and Col Stone showed us what he was as brave as he is good by the way they talk of making him governer of Iowa. Although I do not want to lose him from our regt yet I would like to see him at the head of the affairs of the State for he would give the copperheads hell and I want you to do all you can for him to get him in there. If there is a man in the world deserving it is him. Lt Col Glasgow is another here. Although I was a quarter of a mile from him I could hear him shouting to his men and telling them to give to the damd rebles and well his men obeyed him. Genl McClernand remained on the field all the time of the battle and actually sighted some of the guns himself. Old Grant heard us fighting and come on to the field about 11 oclock and when the victory was complete you ought to have heard the shout that rung out on the evening air. It was enough to pay us for all our fatigue and dangers. I am well and stouter than I have been for years although I had gone 48 hours without sleep and had to eat my meat raw with hard crackers and water and twice a little tea and marched with 40 pounds and my gun and 80 rounds of cartrige. I was able to fight the whole day among the cane breaks and ravines with the thermomater up to 90 without anything to eat. I walked 2 miles for my supper and back again on to the battle field when we lay and you had better believe I slept sound that night. After we got a little breakfast we all started after the retreating rebles but they had burned the bridges. And so we had to stop and make a bridge across bayou peirie when Genl Quinbys brigade started after them at 3 oclock P.M. of the 2 and Osterhaus and Smiths Divisions started at one oclock in the morning.

At 7 oclock we started for Grand Gulf to take the forces there and capture the battery by land but the rebs were to smart for us for they evacuated. And so we are laying now about 2 miles west SW of Port Gibson and 6 miles from Grand Gulf awaiting orders. I understand the rebs will make a stand at willow springs 18 miles from here. But I think they have either been whipped or they have not stopped there or else we would have been ordered up to assist in the fight. If they do not make a stand there they will evacuate Vicksburgh without a fight. I have just learned that the 23d lost 7 men killed and 24 wounded. Smith is safe and all the rest that you are acquainted with. Our forces engaged was abot 7,000. The rebs about 10,000. Our whole force could not get up in time to help us. I must quit as my paper is done.

Your afft Taylor

"THE NATION'S IDOL":
NORTH CAROLINA, MAY 1863

Catherine Edmondston:
Diary, May 5–7, 9, and 11–12, 1863

On May 3 Lee's army drove Union forces from the Chancellorsville clearing after several hours of intense fighting. As Hooker withdrew to a new defensive position close to the Rappahannock, Lee learned that Union troops under Major General John Sedgwick had captured Marye's Heights at Fredericksburg and were advancing on Chancellorsville. Leaving about 20,000 men to face Hooker, Lee attacked Sedgwick on May 4 at Salem Church, four miles west of Fredericksburg. After an inconclusive battle, Sedgwick withdrew across the Rappahannock on the night of May 4–5. Hooker retreated across the river the following night, ending a campaign in which the Union lost about 17,000 men killed, wounded, or missing, and the Confederates about 13,000. Catherine Edmondston followed reports of the fighting from her plantation home in Halifax County, North Carolina.

———————

MAY 5, 1863

News last night principally rumours. The enemy under General Stoneman have made a dash into our lines and emulous of Stuart have penetrated into the heart of Va, cutting Telegraph wires, tearing up R R tracks, but as I do not know whether the particulars are authentic I will wait until they are confirmed. Rumour has it that we fought on Sunday the 3d & repulsed the enemy at every point save one & took five thousand prisoners. Stonewall Jackson and A P Hill both wounded, the first slightly, the latter severely, but we do not know whether it be true or not; in fact we do not know that there has been a fight—not even a Telegram. Matters in the West more confused than ever. I cannot keep up with them—a skirmish here at some unpronounceable unheard of before name in which we are successful & another there at some equally unknown place from which we retire. Morgan, Van Dorn, and Forrest destroy R R Bridges & tear up tracks until one would think there were none left to be destroyed. They capture one waggon train only to make room for another, but our eyes are bent now on Fredericksburg & Gen Lee. God grant him the victory. Rachel Jones came to make us a visit last night.

May 6, 1863

News of a Victory at Fredericksburg! Hooker is repulsed & is in retreat. More than that we cannot tell, but that fills our hearts with grateful praise. Lee telegraphs that by "the blessing of God we have gained a great Victory"—10,000 prisoners are captured, no details of our loss in either killed or Wounded. The Cavalry expedition sent out to beat up our quarters carry dismay and surprise to an unexpectant country. They have torn up the R R track between Gordonsville & Richmond, stolen horses, & captured an old engine. Beyond that they have effected nothing, but the insult is great & a burning shame which must be wiped out in blood ere it can be atoned. One of the Col's, one Davis, boasts that he is a Virginian, is familiar with the country over which he has often fox hunted! More shame to him a traitor & a renegade! Their movements are wrapped in obscurity, & they have cut the Telegraph wires so that our intercourse with the Army is destroyed for the present. The next news we hear of them will, I hope, be that they are all in the Libby Prison, but it is the most daring thing the Yankees have as yet attempted & should put us on our guard against despising our enemy.

Where is Stuart? "One blast upon his bugle horn were worth ten thousand men." Where is he that he allows the Abolitionists thus to careen through our lines & pluck his Laurels unwithered from his brow?

May 7, 1863

News from the Rappahanock! A victory, tho dearly bought! The Abolitionists crossed, as I before stated, about 15 miles above Fredericksburg after making a feint at that point. He strongly entrenched that wing of his army which rested upon the River, but Jackson making a rapid march got into his rear beyond Chancellorsville whilst Lee made an attack in point at that point. Thus pressed, his left Flank was doubled up upon his right which lay on the River (the Rapid Ann) which he crossed in great confusion, the slaughter being terrific. In the mean time Early who had been left in command of Fredericksburg & the intrenchments there was attacked by over whelming odds under Gen Sedgwick (I wonder if he is any kin of mine) & driven from the post, Sedgwick even gaining Marye's Hill. But let me tell the rest in Lee's own words—"At the close of the battle of Chancellorsville on Sunday the enemy was reported as advancing from Fredericksburg in our rear. General McLaws was sent back to arrest his progress & repulsed him handsomly that afternoon. Learning that this corps consisted of his corps under General Sedgwick I determined to attack it & marched back yesterday with General Anderson & uniting with McLaws & Early in the afternoon, succeeded by the blessing of Heaven in driving Gen Sedgewick over the River. We have reoccupied Fredericksburg, & no enemy remains south of the Rappahanock in its vicinity." Dated May 5th.

Hooker is on the South bank of the Rappahanock, reported as entrenching & receiving reinforcements, but he is a beaten man. His prestige is gone and to God are our praises due. "With His own right hand and His holy arm hath He gotten Himself the victory." Fill our hearts with grateful praise, and may we as a nation ascribe unto God the praise due unto His name.

Jackson's wound was in this wise. At midnight on Saturday night, his troops being drawn up in line of battle, a body of men were seen a short distance in advance of our line. It being doubtful whether they were friends or enemies, Gen Jackson & staff rode forward to reconnoitre. Whilst thus engaged, his own men being unaware of his movements, mistook himself & staff for enemies & fired a volley into them instantly killing one & severely wounding Gen Jackson & Major Crutchfield. One ball struck his left arm below the elbow & ranging upwards shattered the bone near the shoulder. Another passed through his right hand. He instantly fell to the ground. His brother in Law laid down by his side to ascertain what were his wounds. In a moment the unknown troops in front who proved to be the enemy advancing captured two of his staff who were standing over him without, however, perceiving him. A stretcher was procured & four of his men were bearing him to the rear when they were all shot down. His arm has been amputated above the elbow, and the injury to his right hand is severe, one of the bones having been shot away, but it is beleived that he will recover the use of it. He is reported as doing well & Mrs Jackson—who was in Richmond has joined him. He is a heavy loss to us & the Yankees will think their defeat cheaply purchased with his life. Of course they will say that his men did it purposely & that they were demoralized—but who will beleive them?

The Cavalry raid in the vicinity of Richmond is most annoying & insulting, but they have done but little real damage besides destroying a span of the R R Bridge over the Chickahominy & delaying our communication with Fredericksburg. The damage will soon be repaired, but the additional suffering to our wounded is a serious consideration. They captured an ambulance train, destroyed the engine & paroled the wounded. A young lady having heard of their advance informed Col Duke of Wise's Legion who was, with a small detachment of men—infantry, fortunately within reach. He placed his men on the train & reached Tunstall's at the very moment that they did. Taking them thus by surprise, he killed several & captured fifteen of the marauders. They came within two miles of Richmond, stealing Mr John Young's horse from before his door in his sight. He, poor man, offered no resistance thinking Gen Lee was beaten and that this was the advance of Hooker's army. He had no time for "an abstraction" then, fond as he used to be of them.

May 9, 1863

Gen Lee's dispatch to the President dated Chancellorsville May 7th tells us that "After driving Sedgewick across the Rappahanock on the night of the 4th I (he) returned on the 5th to Chancellorsville. The march was delayed by a storm which continued all night and the following day. In placing the troops in position on the morning of the 6th to attack Gen Hooker, it was ascertained that he had abandoned his fortified position. The line of skirmishers was pressed forward until they came in range of the enemies batteries planted on the north of the Rappahanock which from the configuration of the ground completely commanded this side. His army, therefore, escaped with the loss of a few additional prisoners." Signed R E Lee, General. So he is gone, driven back, beaten ignominiously by a far inferior force, for we had but 80,000 (eighty thousand) men all told, whilst he has 158,000 (one hundred and fifty eight). Our loss is stated on the best authority now attainable at nine hundred killed & six thousand wounded many of them slightly so. We lost some prisoners, but all told killed, wounded, prisoners, and missing—eight thousand covers it. Theirs is estimated at thirty thousand. We have nine thousand prisoners! We took fifty three canon & lost five on Marye's Hill, belonging to the Washington Artillery. The no of muskets captured & picked up on the battlefield is enormous. Were Lee now to advance, a large part of Hooker's Army could not fight for want of a weapon. They are piled by the side of the R R track—a wonder to the beholder. The enemies loss in generals is heavy, including the infamous Sickles. Six are enumerated, but they are not of consequence enough to interest me. We lose one—Gen Paxton—in command of the old Stonewall Brigade. We have lost several Colonels, but as yet the details are not published. Stoneman is reported as encamped in heavy force near Gordonsville. Ah that we could capture him! No news of importance from the West. Van Dorn is dead, but how we hear not. Forrest, Wheeler, & Morgan continue to annoy Rosencrans & capture his marauding parties. In Louisianna we have had a repulse. At Grand Gulf Gen Taylor was forced to retreat, which he did fighting, after two days battle. He had 3000, the enemy 20,000 men, yet he came off in good order, bringing guns & stores. One waggon (whose mule gave out) only was captured. Our loss not heavy. All quiet before Vicksburg.

MAY 11, 1863

Went out Hascosea after dinner with Mr E on horseback. Everything is terribly backward there. The garden wants work & the flowers resent the neglect by refusing to bloom. A little girl ran out from the house of one of our neighbours & stopped us to ask for some flowers for their May party next

Friday. Promised to send them, much to her gratification. Ah! me what happiness have May Queen's conferred on me in times gone by & what a contrast to the times does a Queen of May now present.

The mail came in after tea & heavy news it brought us. A chill went through my heart as Mr Edmondston unfolded the paper & I saw that it was in mourning. I felt that Jackson was dead! & so it proved! He died of pneumonia on Sunday the 10th, eight days after the amputation of his arm, died in the fulness of his reputation, the brightness of his glory, a Christian patriot, unselfish, untiring, with no thought but for his country, no aim but for her advancement. I have no heart to write more, tho the paper is full of news. I care for nothing but him. It is as tho a Divine voice has said again "Little children keep yourselves from idols." He was the nation's idol, not a breath even from a foe has ever been breathed against his fame. His very enemies reverenced him. God has taken him from us that we may lean more upon *Him*, feel that He can raise up to Himself instruments to work His Divine Will.

MAY 12, 1863

Woke up this morning with a sense of a heavy misfortune. Asked myself what had happened & remembered that Jackson was dead! Omitted to write yesterday that my nephew Thomas Jones had brought his wife to fathers. We go up to see her this morning. I shall offer her a home until the war is ended—for she cannot return into the lines of the hated enemy & since Hill's repulse at Washington, they have grown more stringent & oppressive. The papers are full of McClellan's & Burnside testimony respecting the command & conduct of the Army of the Potomac. I take little interest in any of them, or anything they say. They only offer an additional proof, if proof were wanting, that neither Lincoln, Halleck, Stanton, McClellan, Burnside, or Hooker understand the first principles of a gentleman. Deficient alike in self respect & respect for each other, they know not what is due themselves from their subordinates, or their subordinates from their own hands. Faugh! they disgust me, a set of cold blooded quill drivers. They have neither the instincts or the impulses of gentlemen.

"THE GREAT JOE HOOKER": VIRGINIA, MAY 1863
Charles F. Morse to His Family

Captain Charles F. Morse joined the 2nd Massachusetts Infantry in 1861 and became a close friend of Robert Gould Shaw. He fought at Front Royal, Cedar Mountain, and Antietam before being appointed provost marshal of the Twelfth Corps in February 1863. During the Chancellorsville campaign Morse served as an aide to Major General Henry W. Slocum, the commander of the Twelfth Corps.

STAFFORD C. H., May 7, 1863.

I am going to give you, without any introduction, a history of this last campaign against Richmond by the army under the great Joe Hooker. I believe I have seen it and judged it fairly.

On Monday, April 27th, our corps broke camp early in the morning and marched to Hartwood Church, ten miles; there it went into camp for the night. The Eleventh and Fifth Corps also came up there and camped in our vicinity; next morning, we all moved and camped that night near Kelly's Ford. A pontoon bridge was thrown across and the Eleventh was over before daylight Wednesday; the other corps followed rapidly and the advance began towards the Rapidan. The Eleventh and Twelfth marched on the road to Germana Ford, the Fifth on the road to Ely's Ford; all three of the corps were under command of General Slocum. I was detailed, the morning of the advance, as Aide to General Slocum, and another officer was made Acting Provost Marshal. All the companies of the Second Massachusetts were sent to the Regiment. We skirmished all the way to Germana Ford; there we met quite a determined resistance; our cavalry was drawn in and the Second Massachusetts and the Third Wisconsin sent forward to clear the way; they drove everything before them and, by their heavy fire, forced the rebels at the Ford to surrender (about one hundred officers and men). We lost in this skirmish about a dozen killed and wounded.

General Slocum now determined to cross the Rapidan,

though there was no bridge and the ford was almost impassable. He sent the First and Third Brigade, (First Division, Twelfth Corps), through the water although it was more than waist deep, also five batteries of artillery, which took position on the other side of the river. A bridge was then constructed, and before daylight Thursday morning, the remainder of the Twelfth and Eleventh Corps were across the river. By eight o'clock, A.M., we were moving again. The rebels kept attacking us on our flank with cavalry and artillery, and any less bold officer than General Slocum would have halted his column and delayed the march; but he kept along steadily, detaching a small force at intervals to repel the enemy. I had the pleasure of superintending, at one of these skirmishes, having in charge the Twenty-ninth Pennsylvania Regiment; we drove the rebels before us for nearly a mile, almost capturing their artillery, taking a large number of prisoners. At about noon, we arrived at Chancellorsville, and found the Fifth Corps already there. We had a small cavalry skirmish, in which Colonel McVicars was killed with about a dozen of his men, but besides that, nothing of importance occurred that day; the troops were formed in line of battle, but were not attacked. Up to this time you see everything had gone well and success seemed certain.

Towards night, General Hooker arrived with his staff, and we heard of the crossing at the U. S. Ford of the Second, Third and First Corps. All the headquarters were in the vicinity of the Chancellor House, a large, fine brick mansion. General Hooker took supper with General Slocum; he didn't seem to be able to express his gratification at the success of General Slocum in bringing the three corps up so rapidly. Then, in the most extravagant, vehement terms, he went on to say how he had got the rebels, how he was going to crush them, annihilate them, etc.

The next morning at ten, the Fifth and Twelfth Corps advanced in order of battle on two parallel roads; we soon met the enemy and skirmished for about two miles, when they appeared in considerable force and the battle began. We were in a splendid position and were driving the enemy when an order came to General Slocum to retire his command to its former position. No one could believe that the order was genuine, but almost immediately, another of General Hooker's staff brought the same order again. Now, perhaps, you don't know that to retire an army in the face of an enemy when you are engaged, is one of the most difficult operations in war; this we had to do. I carried the order to General Geary to retire his division in echelon by brigades, and stayed with him till the movement was nearly completed. It was a delicate job; each brigade would successively bear the brunt of the enemy's attack. Before the last brigades of the Fifth and Twelfth Corps were in position, the enemy made a furious attack on the Chancellor House; luckily, we had considerable artillery concentrated there and they were driven back. The next attack was on our corps, but the enemy were severely repulsed. This about ended the fighting on Friday; we lost, I suppose, about five hundred men.

During the night, the men were kept at work digging trenches and throwing up breastworks of logs. Our headquarters were at Fairview, an open piece of ground rising into quite a crest in the centre. Skirmishing began at daylight next morning and continued without much result to either side, till afternoon, when the enemy began to move, in large force, towards our right, opposite General Howard, Eleventh Corps. This corps was in a fine position in intrenchments, with almost open country in front of them, the right resting on Hunting creek. At about four P.M., the Third Corps, General Sickles, was moved out to the right of the Twelfth and advanced towards Fredericksburgh. The order then came to General Slocum that the enemy were in full retreat, and to advance his whole line to capture all he could of prisoners, wagons, etc. Our right, General Williams' Division, advanced without much trouble, driving the enemy before it, but the Second Division had hardly got out of the trenches before it was attacked with great determination, yet it steadily retained its position. At about five P.M., a tremendous and unceasing musketry fire began in the direction of the Eleventh Corps. As it was necessary to know what was going on there in order to regulate the movements of the Twelfth Corps, General Slocum and the rest of us rode for our lives towards this new scene of action. What was our surprise when we found, that instead of a fight, it was a complete Bull Run rout. Men, horses, mules, rebel prisoners, wagons, guns, etc., etc., were coming down the road in terrible confusion, behind them an unceasing roar of musketry. We rode until we got into a mighty hot fire, and found that no one was attempting to make a stand, but every one running for his life. Then General Slocum dispatched me to General Hooker to explain the state of affairs, and three other staff officers to find General Williams and order him back to his trenches with all haste.

I found General Hooker sitting alone on his horse in front of the Chancellor House, and delivered my message; he merely said, "Very good, sir." I rode back and found the Eleventh Corps still surging up the road and still this terrible roar behind them. Up to this time, the rebels had received no check, but now troops began to march out on the plank road and form across it, and Captain Best, Chief of Artillery of our corps, had on his own responsibility gathered together all the batteries he could get hold of, had put them in position (forty-six guns in all) on Fairview, and had begun firing at the rate of about one hundred guns a minute, into the rebels. This, in my opinion, saved our army from destruction. After delivering my message to General Hooker, I went back and tried to find General Slocum, but it was now after eight o'clock and I was unsuccessful in my search, so I took hold and tried to rally some of the cowardly Dutchmen. With the help of one cavalry orderly, I succeeded in forming a good many of them on the left of the new line, but an unusually heavy volley coming, they broke and ran like sheep. After this little episode, I again searched after the General. Towards ten, I found the rest of the staff, and soon after, we came across the General. At about eleven, the fighting stopped, but we were all hard at work getting the men of our corps into position. You see, while our First Division was advancing, the rebels had routed the Teutons and were now occupying our trenches. The Second and Third Brigades got into their former position, but the First made out only to cut through the rebels, losing a large part of its men and taking a position considerably in the rear of its former one. General Sickles fought his way through with the exception of one division and one battery, which were left out in front of our lines that night. The artillery men were hard at work all night, throwing up traverses to protect their guns, and about two in the morning we all lay down on the ground and slept until about four, when daylight began to appear. Our right was now formed by the Third, Fifth and First Corps, about five hundred yards in the rear of our first position. The rebels began the attack, as soon as there was light enough, from the left of our First Division to about the right of the Third Corps. General Birney's Division of the Third Corps was out in front of General Williams; his men behaved badly, and after a slight resistance, fell back into our lines, losing a battery.

The rebels now charged down our First Division, but were met with such a deadly fire that they were almost annihilated. Their second line was then sent in, but met the same fate, and their third and last line advanced. Our men now had fired more than forty rounds of cartridges and were getting exhausted. General Slocum sent almost every one of his staff officers to General Hooker, stating his position and begging for support; Hooker's answer was, "I can't make men or ammunition for General Slocum." Meantime, Sickles' Corps was holding its own on the right of ours, but it was rapidly getting into the same condition as the Twelfth. The rebels were driven back every time they advanced, and we were taking large numbers of prisoners and colors. All this time while our infantry was fighting so gallantly in front, our battery of forty-six guns was firing incessantly. The rebels had used no artillery till they captured the battery from Birney, when they turned that on us, making terrible destruction in General Geary's line. General Meade, Fifth Corps, now went to Hooker and entreated that he might be allowed to throw his corps on the rebel flank, but General Hooker said, "No, he was wanted in his own position." On his own responsibility, General Meade sent out one brigade, which passed out in rear of the enemy's right, recaptured a battery, three hundred of our men who were prisoners, and four hundred of the rebels, and took them safely back to their corps.

It was now after seven o'clock. Our men had fired their sixty rounds of cartridges and were still holding their position; everything that brave men could do, these men had done, but now nothing was left but to order them to fall back and give up their position to the enemy. This was done in good order and they marched off under a heavy fire to the rear of our batteries. The rebels, seeing us retreating, rushed forward their artillery and began a fearful fire. I found I could be useful to

Captain Best, commanding our artillery, so I stayed with him. I never before saw anything so fine as the attack on that battery; the air was full of missiles, solid shot, shells, and musket balls. I saw one solid shot kill three horses and a man, another took a leg off one of the captains of the batteries. Lieutenant Crosby of the Fourth Artillery was shot through the heart with a musket ball; he was a particular friend of Bob Shaw and myself; he lived just long enough to say to Captain Best, "Tell father I die happy."

The rebels came up to the attack in solid masses and got within three hundred yards, but they were slaughtered by the hundreds by the case-shot and canister, and were driven back to the woods. Still not an infantry man was sent to the support of the guns. More than half the horses were killed or wounded; one caisson had blown up, another had been knocked to pieces; in ten minutes more, the guns would have been isolated. They, too, therefore, were ordered to retire, which they did without losing a gun. You see, now, our centre was broken, everything was being retired to our second line, the rebel artillery was in position, their line of battle steadily advancing across our old ground. This fire of the batteries was concentrated on the Chancellor House, Hooker's original headquarters, and it was torn almost to pieces by solid shot and was finally set on fire by a shell.

The army was now put in position in the second line; the centre was on a rising piece of ground and protected by a battery of forty or fifty guns. The Fifth Corps was on the right and was the last to fall back out of the woods and it was closely followed by the rebel masses, but these were met by such a tremendous artillery fire that they were actually rolled back into the woods. Our corps was ordered to support first the Third, afterwards the Second and Eleventh. Towards night the enemy made another desperate assault on our centre, but they were again repulsed. Our corps was now ordered to the extreme left to form behind the Eleventh. I believe that General Slocum remonstrated with General Hooker so firmly that he finally got permission to put the Twelfth Corps on the extreme left and to have only one division of the Eleventh in the trenches on his right.

You can easily see that, if the enemy once forced our right or left, our communications would at once be cut and all possibility of retreat prevented. Late that night, we lay down close beside the Rappahannock. By three o'clock next morning, we were awakened by a heavy artillery fire and shells bursting over us. Our guns replied and kept at it for about an hour, when the enemy's batteries were silenced. We now mounted our horses and rode along the lines to look at our position; we found that it was a very strong one and capable of being made very much more so.

We found that the sharpshooters were getting altogether too attentive to our party, so we moved back to our line and had hardly turned away, when a sergeant was shot dead almost on the spot where the general had been standing. All that day, our men were hard at work throwing up breastworks, cutting abattis, etc. No attack was made on us, but throughout that day and night, we heard Sedgwick fighting in the direction of Fredericksburgh.

Tuesday morning, I knew by appearances that a retreat was to be effected, as a large part of the artillery, all the ambulances, etc., were removed across the river, although the men were kept at work making line after line of trenches and breastworks. Just before dark, the order of retreat came, the Fifth and Twelfth Corps being the last to cross. About four o'clock that afternoon it began to rain in torrents. There were originally three pontoon bridges, but before most of the crossing had been effected, the river became so swollen that one of the bridges had to be taken up to piece out the other two; this caused a great delay. At about twelve, I was sent down to the ford to examine into the condition of things; it was a terrible night, the wind blowing a gale and the rain pouring, the road for a mile full of artillery. I found, at the bridge, that not a thing was moving, and learned from General Patrick that the order for retreat had been suspended and everything was to move back to its former position. This order came, remember, when half of the artillery was on the north side of the Rappahannock, the soldiers without a ration and the supply trains ten miles the other side of the river. I ran my horse back to headquarters and made my report; the telegraph was down between U. S. Ford and Falmouth, *where General Hooker was.* General Slocum wrote a dispatch, saying, that unless the movement was continued, our army would have to be surrendered within twenty-four hours; this was sent by an orderly who was ordered to kill his horse carrying it. Then to prepare for the worst, General Slocum sent one of his aides and myself back to the Ford to get our artillery ready to move back into position, that our corps might, at least, be ready to make a desperate fight in the morning; but at about two-thirty A.M., the messenger returned from General Hooker with orders for the movement to continue.

At about five, one of our divisions began to cross. The two or three succeeding hours were the most anxious I ever passed in my life. A large part of our army was massed on the south side of the river, only two bridges for the whole of it to cross, the river full to the edge of its banks; a very little extra strain would have carried away the upper bridge, and this would have swept away the lower one and all retreat would have been cut off. The rebel artillery began to fire on our troops and bridges, but was silenced by our guns; we had sixty in position on the north side.

It soon became evident that the enemy were not in force in our vicinity, but for all that, it was one of the happiest moments of my life when I saw the last of our corps over the bridge. We all started then for Stafford C. H., where our corps was ordered to its old camp. We arrived at our old headquarters at about two P.M., and found, to our joy, that our wagons had arrived and tents were being pitched. It was not until after we were in comfortable quarters that the terrible fatigue of the last ten days began to tell on us. Since we had left Stafford, we had been without wagons or blankets, with nothing to eat except pork and hard bread, and half the time not even that, and we had averaged each day at least twelve or sixteen hours in the saddle. The moment we touched a seat, we sunk into the most profound sleep and stayed in this condition for several hours. It may seem strange to you that I speak of being happy to get back into our old quarters, but you must remember that we had been through danger and hardship for ten days and had met with constant disappointment and were now safe back again where we were going to have sleep, rest, and food.

Now, let us see what this campaign shows. It seems to me that the plan was a very good one, with the exception of separating Sedgwick with thirty thousand men from the army, and that it was carried out with great success till General Hooker arrived at Chancellorsville. The next thing shown is that the commander of our army gained his position by merely brag and blow, and that when the time came to show himself, he was found without the qualities necessary for a general. If another battle had been fought on Monday, it would have been by the combined corps commanders, and the battle would have been won.

I doubt if, ever in the history of this war, another chance will be given us to fight the enemy with such odds in our favor as we had last Sunday, and that chance has been worse than lost to us. I don't believe any men ever fought better than our Twelfth Corps, especially the First Division; for two hours, they held their ground without any support, against the repeated assaults of the enemy; they fired their sixty rounds of cartridges and held their line with empty muskets till ordered to fall back. The old Second, of course, did splendidly, and lost heavily, twenty-two killed, one hundred and four wounded, ten missing; my company had five killed and eleven wounded. Lieutenant Fitzgerald was killed, Coggswell, Grafton, Perkins, and Powers, wounded. George Thompson had a narrow escape; a grape shot tore one leg of his trousers and his coat almost off and grazed his leg. Our colors got thirty new holes in them and the staff (the third one), was smashed to pieces.*

You cannot imagine the amount of admiration I have for General Slocum, for the gallant way in which he conducted himself throughout the campaign, and his skillful management of his command; then besides all that, we have been so together, that he has seemed almost like my old friends in the regiment.

I have written in this letter a pretty full account of the operations as I have seen them, and I don't believe any one has had a better chance, for during the fighting, I was at different times at every part of our lines, and in communication with General Hooker and other generals.

Our staff casualties were as follows:—Lieutenant Tracy,

---

*Actual loss: 31 killed and mortally wounded, 91 wounded, 7 prisoners. Total loss, 129.

badly wounded in right arm, his horse shot in four places; one of our orderlies shot and two more horses. I feel thankful to have come out unharmed from so much danger. Tracy was carrying an order to General Williams, when he was hit; somehow, he got outside our lines and was ordered to surrender; he said he thought he wouldn't, turned his horse and ran for it, while the rebels put two volleys after him.

I telegraphed, last Monday, that I was all right; I hope you received the message.

"DISGRACEFUL AND DISASTROUS DEFEAT":
VIRGINIA, MAY 1863

Samuel W. Fiske to the Springfield Republican

In the spring of 1863 Fiske was promoted to captain and assigned to the staff of a brigade in the Second Corps. The letters he wrote about Chancellorsville from prison in Richmond were sent to the *Springfield Republican* after Fiske was paroled to Annapolis, Maryland. They were published on May 30, two weeks after the newspaper had erroneously reported that Fiske had been killed during the fighting on May 3 and printed an obituary.

DUNN BROWNE IN DIXIE:
HOW HE HAPPENED TO GO THERE

Libby Prison, Richmond, Va.
May 9

Dear Republican: There is nothing so likely to secure an observer from prejudice and false views and representations of things as to take a fair look at both sides before giving his final opinion upon any question. Your correspondent accordingly, having already made a survey of the great rebellion from the northern side, has now crossed the frontier and is making observations, with his usual philosophic imperturbability, upon the southern aspect of the secesh monster. His opportunity for this unbiased and impartial view of things came to him in this wise.

He was acting on the staff of a general of brigade last Sabbath morning in the thick of the battle about Chancellorsville. Things were in a decidedly mixed condition. The splendid semi-circular line of battle of Gen. Hooker had been broken the night before (Saturday, May 2d) by the disgraceful failure of the 11th and 12th army corps to maintain their entrenched position, although attacked by a greatly inferior force of the enemy. Our brigade, the 1st in French's division, in the early

Sabbath morning was ordered to leave its position, in rifle-pits pretty well over to the left of our line, and cross over the plank-road towards the right to recover the ground, a portion of it, lost the night before. Our boys charged in splendid style through a thicket of tangled wood for half a mile or more, driving the enemy before them like chaff, slaying many, taking some prisoners and fairly running over some and leaving them in their rear. Indeed, they charged with too much impetuosity and advanced so far that they were not properly supported on the flanks and were exposed to an enfilading fire of artillery as well as musketry. To halt our line and form it anew a little further to the rear in the woods, I was sent forward by the general, together with a fine young friend, one of his aides, both on foot, as our horses were left behind as utterly impracticable in that thicket of undergrowth. We had separated, he to the right and I to the left, delivered our orders to the colonels and assisted in executing it in the midst of a fire, the most diabolical that my eyes have yet witnessed, from front and rear (our own artillery from behind the wood occasionally dropped a shell among us) and both flanks, from at least 64 different points of the compass, I should say, and then I hastened to retrace my steps to report progress to the general.

I was hindered some little time in picking up prisoners (whom I didn't like to leave with arms in their hands in the rear of our line). I would disarm and put them in squads of 3 or 4 in the charge of some one of our slightly wounded men, first seeing that his gun was loaded and capped, and then on again till I had picked up some 20 or more of the "butternuts." Had a couple of the fellows on my hands and none of my own men in sight and was hurrying them forward by the persuasion of a cocked revolver, expecting every moment to come upon our general, when all at once pressing through a terribly dense portion of the undergrowth, I found myself face to face, at not twelve feet distance, with at least a whole regiment of the brownest and most ill-looking vagabonds that I ever set eyes on, every one of them with a gun in his hand, who were that moment rising up from behind a long line of rifle-pits they had taken from us the night before.

Here was a fix for an amiable and well disposed correspondent of yours, who had traveled some and ought to have known better, to get himself into. Here was a big mouthful to swallow for a belligerent patriot, intent on squelching the rebellion, who had just gotten his blood up, hadn't been fighting more than an hour, and was bound to distinguish himself before night. Here was a capital chance for a man, who had just gotten his hand in at the business of capturing prisoners, to put a thousand or fifteen hundred more in his bag—if they would only let him. The undersigned is compelled to acknowledge that in this one instance he found the situation too much for him. He had drawn a mighty big elephant in a lottery and didn't know what to do with him. One of the impudent wretches he had captured a few minutes before turned round with a grin and says, "Cap'en, I reckon things is different from the way they was, and you'll hev to 'low you're our prisoner now." A very sensible remark of the young man, and timely, though he hadn't a shirt to his back and only a part of a pair of pantaloons. Things *was* different from the way they were, with a vengeance. I gracefully lowered my pistol to an officer who stepped out from the ranks and presented it to him, apologizing for so doing by the remark that, "doubtless it would be more disagreeable to a whole regiment to surrender to one man, than to one man to surrender to a whole regiment." The hard-hearted fellows didn't seem to care at all for my misfortune, and only laughed when I told them my story. I was courteously treated and sent at once to the rear, minus my pistol and trusty sword (the loss of which I the more regretted, as it was not the purchase of money but the gift of a friend), and so hath ended ingloriously, for the present, my military service.

The transition from the fierce excitement of battle to the quiet stillness of my walk of near a mile through the woods with my guard, was so great that I could hardly realize it. It seemed the flitting of a vision before my mind's eye. The roar of the cannonade and rattle of the musketry sounded far away to me, and I was like a boy rambling with a friend in the forest of a summer morning. Not for long though could the horrid sights and sounds of battle be put away from one's thoughts. We soon came upon other portions of the bloody field and had to pick our steps among mangled corpses of friend and foe, past men without limbs and limbs without men, now seeing a group of surgeons and assistants operating on the wounded under a tree, and now passing a group of ambulance men carrying on a stretcher some groaning sufferer. Occasionally a wounded horse struggling in his death-agony would kick at us, and occasionally a wounded secesh would mutter a curse as he saw the "d—d Yankee" pass. And in a little time we were far in the rear, and I was turned over to the care of the provost marshal, into a crowd of 1,700 captured "Yankees" about to be marched in the broiling sun, without a mouthful to eat, save the few who had their haversacks and rations with them, to Spottsylvania Court House, about 10 miles distant. Never did that nice black horse I drew a few weeks ago from provident Uncle Sam seem a more desirable underpinning to my weary fleshly tabernacle than now that I could only remember him left in the edge of that fatal forest, with my blankets and provisions on his back.

Yours, forlornly and in bonds, but yet a "prisoner of hope,"

DUNN BROWNE
May 9, 1863

PRISON REFLECTIONS ON THE CHANCELLORSVILLE FIGHT

Libby Prison, Richmond, Va.
May 11

Dear Republican: Richmond is jubilant over the great victory that the South has gained, the tremendous thrashing the chivalry has given "the best army on the planet," though to be sure their joy is fringed with mourning to-day over the funeral ceremonies of their hero, Jackson. Doubtless a great many reasons are given for our most disgraceful and disastrous defeat. There is only one real reason, and that the simplest possible. Our army didn't fight as well as that of our enemies. We had every possible advantage. Our numbers more than doubled their's till Longstreet's reinforcements came up, which didn't then bring their forces up to 100,000 to oppose our 130,000. Indeed, it would now seem that Longstreet didn't come up at all. We had the advantage of position, and no inconsiderable amount of entrenchment. Gen. Hooker's plan was admirably arranged and excellently carried out, until the fighting took place. He exposed himself in the hottest places of danger, and set an electrifying example of heroism to the whole army. The terrible loss of life among our generals shows that on the whole they were not found wanting at their posts of duty. We had men enough, well enough equipped, and well enough posted, to have devoured the ragged, imperfectly armed and equipped host of our enemies from off the face of the earth. Their artillery horses are poor, starved frames of beasts, tied on to their carriages and caissons with odds and ends of rope and strips of rawhide. Their supply and ammunition trains look like a congregation of all the crippled California emigrant trains that ever escaped off the desert out of the clutches of the rampaging Comanche Indians. The men are ill-dressed, ill-equipped and ill-provided, a set of ragamuffins that a man is ashamed to be seen among, even when he is a prisoner and can't help it. And yet they have beaten us fairly, beaten us all to pieces, beaten us so easily that we are objects of contempt even to their commonest private soldiers, with no shirts to hang out of the holes in their pantaloons, and cartridge boxes tied round their waists with strands of ropes.

I say they beat us easily, for there hasn't been much of a fight up here on the bank of the Rappahannock after all, the newspapers to the contrary notwithstanding. There was an awful noise, for I heard it. There was a tremendous amount of powder exploded, for I saw the smoke of it ascend up to heaven. There was a vast amount of running done "faced by the rear rank," but I cannot learn that there was in any part of the field very much real fighting. I have seen men from every part of the ground fought over, men from almost every division of the army, and have inquired diligently after every vestige of conflict, and not one of them all had *seen* a great deal of spirited fighting, though a good many had *heard* a vast amount of it. The particular brigade or regiment or company of each man was captured because the enemy appeared in vast numbers on their flank or in their rear. They didn't fight much because they were so unfortunately situated or surrounded that there wasn't much use in resisting. I never heard of so much cross firing and enfilading fire, and fire in the rear, in all the history of battles with which I am acquainted. Do you point to the big lists of the killed and wounded, 15,000 or 20,000 on our side, as evidence of the desperateness of the encounter? I tell you that when men get up and run out of their rifle-pits and breastworks like a flock of sheep, instead of staying in and defending them, not only they deserve to be shot, but as an actual matter of fact they do get hit and killed about four-fold what would be hurt if they did their soldierly duty like men.

Am I saying things that oughtn't to be spoken of out of school? That had better be smoothed over and explained away? I'm not certain about that. I think people ought to understand somewhere about where the truth lies, and I do not think soldiers ought to be eulogized and told that men never fought more gallantly on the face of the earth and the victory would have been theirs if their officers hadn't mismanaged, when as a matter of fact their officers gallantly did their duty and were left to be killed or captured on the field because their men turned tail and ran away from them. Mind, I don't mean to say that this was very generally the case in the late battle. But I do mean to say that according to my best information and belief the great 11th corps of our army, attacked by an inferior force of the enemy, gave way with only a shadow of resistance and ran out of their entrenchments like a parcel of frightened deer, thus making a great gap in our grand line of battle and disconcerting all our good arrangements, and opening the way for the disasters that followed. And from all I can learn the 12th corps didn't do much better, and though a very large portion of the army did their duty very fairly, I have yet to learn of any considerable body of troops that displayed that real gallantry and determination to win which only can restore a losing battle and atone for the disgraceful flight of the cowards and panic-stricken. I know of whole regiments and brigades, long and heavy lines of battle, that gave way before lines of the enemy so thin and straggling as hardly to be considered more than skirmishers. I saw regiment after regiment and brigade after brigade of those corps I have mentioned come pouring back through our reserves till they covered acres and acres of ground, enough to have made a stand against all the rebels in Virginia, and only breaking our lines and telling such cock and bull stories of being cut to pieces in front and surrounded and attacked in the rear as carried evidence of their absurdity on the very face of them, till I could have cried for shame and grief to be obliged to acknowledge myself as belonging to the same army.

Still in spite of all I have said, it is by no means the truth that our men are a parcel of cowards and poltroons. They are as brave as the average of people—quite as brave as our enemies are. But we don't fight in such a common-sense way as they do. Shall I tell you how one of our lines of battle engages? They go in fine style, steadily, in a good line and without any flinching, halt at what is held to be a desirable point, and at the command commence firing, standing, kneeling or lying down, as may be ordered. Then, as in all their previous training they have been told to load and fire as rapidly as possible, three or four times a minute, they go into the business with all fury, every man vying with his neighbor as to the number of cartridges he can ram into his piece and spit out of it. The smoke arises in a minute or two so you can see nothing where to aim. The noise is deafening and confusing to the last degree. The impression gets around of a tremendous conflict going on. The trees in the vicinity suffer sorely and the clouds a good deal. By-and-by the guns get heated and won't go off and the cartridges begin to give out. The men have become tired with their furious exertions and the excitement and din of their own firing, and without knowing anything about the effect produced upon the enemy, very likely having scarcely had one glimpse of the enemy at all, begin to think they have fought about enough and it is nearly time to retire.

Meanwhile the enemy, lying quietly a hundred or two hundred yards in front, crouching on the ground or behind trees, answer our fire very leisurely, as they get a chance for a good aim, about one shot to our 300, hitting about as many as we do, and waiting for the wild tornado of ammunition to pass over their heads, and when our burst of fighting is pretty much over they have only commenced. They probably rise and advance upon us with one of their unearthly yells as they see our fire slacken. Our boys, finding that the enemy has survived such an avalanche of fire as we have rolled in upon him, conclude he must be invincible, and being pretty much out of ammunition, retire. Now, if I had charge of a regiment or brigade, I'd put every man in the guardhouse who could be proved to have fired more than twenty rounds in any one battle; I wouldn't let them carry more than their cartridge box full (40 rounds), and have them understand that that was meant to last them pretty much through a campaign, and in every possible way would endeavor to banish the Chinese style of fighting with a big noise and smoke, and imitate rather the backwoods style of our opponents.

Whenever we choose to defeat the armies of the rebels, we can do so, and we don't need 500,000 more men to do it with either. There are men enough in Hooker's army now to march straight through to Richmond. Too many men are only an encumbrance. There isn't the general living who has shown his ability to manage properly, certainly, more than 100,000 men. All we have to do is to make up our minds not to run before an equal number of the enemy, to keep cool and save our ammunition to shoot something besides trees with, and when the butternuts find we don't run away, they will. Meanwhile, till I am able to return and effect in our army this change in their method of fighting, I have the honor to assure you that these brown-coated fellows are not so bad as they might be, only they don't furnish us any sugar to put in our coffee, nor yet any coffee to put sugar in. Yours affably,

DUNN BROWNE

May 11, 1863

ESCAPING SLAVERY: VIRGINIA, MAY 1863

Charles B. Wilder: Testimony before the American Freedmen's Inquiry Commission

May 9, 1863

The American Freedmen's Inquiry Commission, appointed by Secretary of War Edwin M. Stanton on March 16, 1863, was charged with investigating and reporting measures that would contribute to the "protection and improvement" of the newly emancipated "so that they may defend and support themselves." Its three members, Robert Dale Owen, James McKaye, and Samuel Gridley Howe, were antislavery advocates active in various social reform movements. In May the commissioners traveled to Fort Monroe in Virginia and heard testimony from Captain Charles B. Wilder, the superintendent of contrabands at the post.

May 9, 1863.

Question How many of the people called contrabands, have come under your observation?

Answer Some 10,000 have come under our control, to be fed in part, and clothed in part, but I cannot speak accurately in regard to the number. This is the rendezvous. They come here from all about, from Richmond and 200 miles off in North Carolina. There was one gang that started from Richmond 23 strong and only 3 got through.

Q In your opinion, is there any communication between the refugees and the black men still in slavery?

A Yes Sir, we have had men here who have gone back 200 miles.

Q In your opinion would a change in our policy which would cause them to be treated with fairness, their wages punctually paid and employment furnished them in the army, become known and would it have any effect upon others in slavery?

A Yes—Thousands upon Thousands. I went to Suffolk a short time ago to enquire into the state of things there—for I found I could not get any foot hold to make things work there, through the Commanding General, and I went to the Provost Marshall and all hands—and the colored people actually sent a deputation to me one morning before I was up to know if we put black men in irons and sent them off to Cuba to be sold or set them at work and put balls on their legs and whipped them, just as in slavery; because that was the story up there, and they were frightened and didn't know what to do. When I got at the feelings of these people I found they were not afraid of the slaveholders. They said there was nobody on the plantations but women and they were not afraid of them. One woman came through 200 miles in Men's clothes. The most valuable information we received in regard to the Merrimack and the operations of the rebels came from the colored people and they got no credit for it. I found hundreds who had left their wives and families behind. I asked them "Why did you come away and leave them there?" and I found they had heard these stories, and wanted to come and see how it was. "I am going back again after my wife" some of them have said "When I have earned a little money" What as far as that?" "Yes" and I have had them come to me to borrow money, or to get their pay, if they had earned a months wages, and to get passes. "I am going for my family" they say. "Are you not afraid to risk it?" "No I know the Way" Colored men will help colored men and they will work along the by paths and get through. In that way I have known quite a number who have gone up from time to time in the neighborhood of Richmond and several have brought back their families; some I have never heard from. As I was saying they do not feel afraid now. The white people have nearly all gone, the blood hounds are not there now to hunt them and they are not afraid, before they were afraid to stir. There are hundreds of negroes at Williamsburgh with their families working for nothing. They would not get pay here and they had rather stay where they are. "We are not afraid of being carried back" a great many have told us and "if we are, we can get away again" Now that they are getting their eyes open they are coming in. Fifty came this morning from Yorktown who followed Stoneman's Cavalry when they returned from their raid. The officers reported to their Quartermaster that they had so many horses and fifty or sixty negroes. "What did you bring them for" "Why they followed us and we could not stop them." I asked one of the men about it and he said they would leave their work in the field as soon as they found the Soldiers were Union men and follow them sometimes without hat or coat. They would take best horse they could get and every where they rode they would take fresh horses, leave the old ones and follow on and so they came in. I have questioned a great many of them and they do not feel much afraid; and there are a great many courageous fellows who have come from long distances in rebeldom. Some men who came here from North Carolina, knew all about the Proclammation and they started on the belief in it; but they had heard these stories and they wanted to know how it was. Well, I gave them the evidence and I have no doubt their friends will hear of it. Within the last two or three months the rebel guards have been doubled on the line and the officers and privates of the 99th New York between Norfolk and Suffolk have caught hundreds of fugitives and got pay for them.

Q   Do I understand you to say that a great many who have escaped have been sent back?

A   Yes Sir, The masters will come in to Suffolk in the day time and with the help of some of the 99th carry off their fugitives and by and by smuggle them across the lines and the soldier will get his $20. or $50.

COMMANDING A BLACK REGIMENT: SOUTH
CAROLINA, MAY 1863

Thomas Wentworth Higginson: Journal, May 10, 1863

A writer, minister, social reformer, and radical abolitionist who had helped finance John Brown's raid on Harpers Ferry, Thomas Wentworth Higginson joined the newly organized 51st Massachusetts Infantry as a captain in September 1862. He was preparing to leave for New Bern, North Carolina, in November when Brigadier General Rufus Saxton, the Union military governor of South Carolina, offered him the command of the 1st South Carolina Volunteers, a recently formed regiment recruited from freed slaves. Higginson accepted, and in January 1863 led the regiment on a successful expedition into southern Georgia and northern Florida during which his troops gathered supplies, liberated slaves, and skirmished with Confederate forces. During a second expedition in March the 1st South Carolina briefly occupied Jacksonville, Florida, before returning to its base at Port Royal.

MAY 10

Such fun as we have had over the newspaper accounts of us. I just told Dr Rogers it was fortunate that novels were still published, that there might be truth found somewhere, since history certainly affords none; but he says if things go on so much longer we c'ant even put faith in novels. We have just seen the scrap about our picket firing—two negroes wounded—two butternuts biting the dust—all sheer fabrication. Occasionally they fire a little, at very long range & my men fire back, & that's all about it—except Gen. Hunter's pithy endorsement on the back of Gen. Saxton's letter—"Give them as good as they send —D. Hunter, Maj. Genl. Commanding"—that was to the point.

The great drawback of these Southern col'd regt's will always be the severe burden of writing they throw on officers, both field & line. I spend hours daily, & much vitality needed for other things, in doing writing which every Col. of a white reg't has one or more clerks detailed to do; the same with my Quartermaster, the same with my adjutant. This is inevitable; in addition in this particular case, the Lt. col. & the Major are not naturally bookkeepers, any more than drillmasters (neither of them could drill either the reg't or a company ten minutes without some serious mistake—& if we were in battle & I were injured, a Captain would have to take command); The Sergeant Major, the only other person I can ever call on for aid in writing, is sick, & not efficient when well, & has his own work beside. If col'd regt's were not easier to drill & discipline than white ones, all their officers would die, except those who had happily never learned to write.

I d'ont wish to be severe on my field officers—Maj Strong I should be very sorry to lose; he has no turn for drill & his health is delicate, but he is the soul of courage, full of enterprise & resources, always amiable always ready to work. Lt. Col. Billings is absolutely worthless.

It is Sunday noon & a wedding party is sitting under the trees, awaiting the Chaplain. One soldier a good looking youth in uniform coat & festive white pants & gloves; & two young girls, jet black, in low necked white muslin dresses, shirt sleeves, straw colored sashes, with good figures, not too stout which they are apt to be & of the handsome shade of black. Many have a *grimy* black, which is repulsive looking as if it would come off—but with many the color is a very deep wine colour which to my eye is very handsome in its way; the skin being smoother & finer grained than ours, (Dr Rogers observes) both in the men & the women; their arms are particularly handsome, because labor seems to develop them without making them wiry or hairy or sunburnt. We have had many recruits lately & Dr Rogers often calls me in to admire their fine physique or to see the common marks of the lash.

Last Sunday there was a funeral on this plantation & during the whole sunny day a great prayer meeting of women sat under the great live oaks before my window & sang hymn upon hymn—an old Deborah leading off, gesticulating and beating time with her whole body & calling on each woman present by name. In the afternoon old men came from the various plantations & I let the soldiers march there, instead of to our usual meeting. The women all looked neat, with handkerchiefs round their heads.

As for the wedding, this is one of the days in the quarter when they go to be married "by de book" as they call it; often letting a mere social ceremony suffice for a time.

My poor Lieuts. O'Neil & Stockdale have fared hard. After 48 days imprisonment they were tried by court martial—convicted not of desertion but of absence without leave & set at liberty as punished enough. This Gen. S. attributes to my being too mild on them in my evidence & saying too much in their favor; but he made them resign & Gen. Hunter dismisses them from service as incompetent & worthless and they forfeit all their pay, & all this because two women, who had been soldiers wives for years, couldn't make up their minds to go to New York alone! At any rate they will not return to the reg't of which I was at one time afraid.

The rapid multiplication of colored regiments is of more *personal* importance to me than to all the rest of the nation, for it is taking a load of personal responsibility off my shoulders. There is no doubt that for many months the fate of the whole movement for colored soldiers rested on the behavior of this one regiment. A mutiny, an extensive desertion, an act of severe discipline, a Bull Run panic, a simple defeat, might have blasted the whole movement for arming the blacks—& through it the prospects of the war & of a race. Now the thing is so far advanced that Africa holds many shares in the lottery of war & should the 1st S.C.V. prove a blank, others will not. The Tribune correspondent said to me the other day, "This is the only *regiment* with which the public has become familiar; in all other cases they have known at most the Division or the Brigade. (It is amusing to see, even now, how they all call my 850 a Brigade.) I have had enough of this notoriety & am very willing to be merged in an army of such regiments!

MOURNING STONEWALL JACKSON:
KENTUCKY, MAY 1863

Edward O. Guerrant: Diary, May 15, 1863

Captain Edward O. Guerrant was a native Kentuckian who served as an adjutant to Brigadier General Humphrey Marshall, the commander of Confederate forces in the mountains of southwestern Virginia and eastern Kentucky. Guerrant had just returned to southeastern Kentucky from a visit to Richmond, Virginia, when he learned of Jackson's death.

Friday 15h. May 1863.
Today returned to Col. Hawkins' camps on Rock House. Williams of the battery just returned from Abingdon—Says

General Jackson is Dead!
General Jackson is Dead!

Was a nation's woe ever condensed in so few words—or a people's calamity so far beyond language to express!? O Fate "That is the unkindest stroke of all"! All other losses we have ever sustained are light in comparison with this great calamity. So mighty a warrior,—so dauntless a spirit, so pure a patriot & so devoted a Christian!—A nations homage lay at his feet—its honors crown his brow. We have not another Jackson to die! Centuries are slow in the birth of such men. The Christian Napoleon! A greater than Alexander is dead. If a nation's prayers & tears could have availed anything at a Throne of Mercy then "Stonewall" Jackson had not died! But God called him up higher—& in the ranks of a mightier army, & almost peerless in that innumerable host—stands our great Warrior.

The fire of his genius will no longer lead his invincible legions to certain victory,—& the scream of his exultant Eagles will no more echo along the bloody banks of the Rappahannock, or by the bosom of the Potomac or in the beautiful Valley of the Shenandoah—his own sweet "Valley of Virginia". But the memory of his deeds—his immortal deeds still lives—& will live while genius has an admirer—liberty a devotee—Christ a follower—or Nobility a friend & patron. If human sacrifices could have shielded his life from death's fatal stroke—a thousand—yea ten thousand lives would have been offered up on War's bloody altar that "Stonewall" Jackson might live.

But God's Eternal & wise decree has gone forth & called from the head of his veteran warriors the great commander—& He will provide another whose arm he will strengthen to drive the invaders from our soil. In Jackson's beautiful, christian resignation let us bow to the Divine decree & say "Thy will be done". From the ashes of the immortal Jackson the Genius of Liberty will rise triumphant over death and place a nation & its Great Benefactor beyond the malice or power of enemies—on the tablet of an enduring fame.

We weep over our loss—& rejoice we had such a man to die. Jackson dead is worth 10000 Hookers living. We cannot estimate our loss—It is great beyond degree. The Richmond Enquirer says we had better lost a Corps of our Army. Northern journals pay him the highest honors—acknowledging the terror of his very name—his great genius—his invincibility—& the meekness & purity of his christian character. He is styled the Modern Bonaparte. McClellan grieved over his loss—& acknowledged him to have been our greatest Executive General. He possessed more than any of our Generals, the love & confidence of our people. They idolized "Stonewall" Jackson. God's purposes are wise to have removed him. "*He gave & hath taken away*".

While reconnoitering—with Gen. A. P. Hill & both their staffs &c. in the night of Saturday 2 May Genl. Jackson was wounded by one of his own Regiments (a N.C. Regt) on Picket—& not 50 yards from the Enemy. He received two wounds in his left arm & one in his right hand. He came near bleeding to death on the field. While being borne off by four men one of them was killed & he fell from the other's shoulders & was severely hurt. His arm was amputated—but Pneumonia setting in terminated his life at Guinnea's Station on the Rappahannock R.R. on   at 3¼ P.M.

Before his death he was cheerful—. Expressed the opinion that if he had been permitted another hour of light or life on that great battle day he would have cut off Hooker's retreat by

U.S. Ford. He died delirious—his last words referring to his army. "Tell Gen Hill", said he "to prepare his division for action, & tell Major Hawkes to send forward provisions for the men."—

His remains were brought to Richmond on   where they received every honor an admiring & sorrowful people could bestow on all that was mortal of the illustrious dead. It is estimated that at least twenty thousand people crowded the avenues of the National Capitol—where he was laid in state—to behold the pallid, serene, & thoughtful countenance of the mighty, dead chieftain. He expressed a desire to be buried at "Lexington—in the Valley of Virginia"; his place of residence.

Gen Ewell, who commanded a Division under him & lost his leg at the battle of   was Genl. Jacksons choice as his successor.

It is proposed to have a bronze statue of Jackson placed in the Capitol at Richmond—that all may see the likeness of the man whose "fame is more enduring than brass"—upon whose living form they never looked. It will be a Mecca for generations to come.

As usual after some terrible defeat Mr. Lincoln has taken to his usual resort—*more men*. This time he caps the climax by calling all the armbearing population of the North into the field to "suppress the rebellion".

A grand rise from 75,000 to 4,000,000 of men!

If Thirteen Hundred & Eighty Five Thousand armed warriors are incompetent for our subjugation—what virtue is there in numbers such as his! Xerxes stands in awe at Lincoln's Abolition host 4,000,000 He never boasted half of that.

Poor Mr. Lincoln.—When will the scales of his judicial blindness fall from his eye as he beats his *obstinate, Balaams numerical horse*, & reveal the angel warrior with his retributive sword standing to stay him!? Poor man!

SWEARING ALLEGIANCE: KENTUCKY, MAY 1863

George Richard Browder: Diary, May 17–26, 1863

Union troops occupied Logan County, Kentucky, in February 1862 and held it for the remainder of the war. A Methodist preacher and slave-owning farmer, George Richard Browder lived in the southern part of the county less than ten miles from the Tennessee border. Although he sympathized with the secessionist cause and believed the war to be the result of "the mad schemes of an abolition fanaticism," Browder did not join the Confederate army. "I am positively a *peace man*," he wrote in his diary in March 1863.

———————

May 15—Papers to day report Genl Vandorn & T. J. Jackson both dead—federal loss at Fredericksburg immense—say 20,000 killed & wounded. Lo the horrors of the war still crowd upon us. There is now a military order requiring all male citizens 21 years old & upward to report at Russellville & take the oath or be arrested & sent beyond the federal lines to remain until the close of the war under penalty of being shot if they return! This is a cruel & merciless order of Brig Genl Shackleford—a Cumberland Presbyterian Bro. & may give him trouble to enforce it. Who ever takes this oath under such duress is not acting of his own free will & accord. I do not know what I shall do. I am willing to do right & submit to the lawful authorities—but military men have no just right to control peaceable citizens.

May 17—There is much excitement in the country & hundreds are flocking in to take the oath of allegiance—grumbling as they go & yet swearing that they "do it of their own free will, without any mental reservation whatever." I do not see how I can conscientiously swear that I do "of my own free will" what if left to myself I should not do—& yet I must or be banished from my home & my property confiscated. Ought a Christian man to swear against his conscience to avoid suffering any more than to obtain any desired good? Is the duress sufficient to force a man so to swear or is the injunction of scripture "submit to the powers that be" a law of conscience requiring obedience to the civil or military power right or wrong! I confess that I am in some trouble about it & do not know what to do, but suppose I must submit to what I cannot avoid considering that the action is not mine—just as if I should compel my son or servant to break the sabbath, against his will. *I* should be the sabbath breaker & not he. If I were compelled to lose my hand or my head, I should of my free will give my hand to save my head—but of my *free* will would lose neither. My Hogan neighbors, arrested some weeks ago accused of harboring guerillas have been released on oath & bond. As good a man as Thos Gilbert is put under 5000 bond —accused of disloyalty! Almeda, daughter of K. C. Mason— deceased—arrested for writing to her brother in rebel army has been detained for a week or more in Russellville & now sent on to Genl Burnside for further orders. Some are wearing ball & chain & many crowded up in Russellville courthouse— charged with aiding rebellion. Oh Russellville! Little did thy people think of such scenes when they shouted & rejoiced over the entering forces of Buckner from camps Boone & Burnett a year ago last September.

The federal loss at Fredericksburg is now estimated at 30,000 & rebel loss, papers say not less—& rebels claim 50,000 stands of arms & immense supplies, clothing &c. Jackson Miss is reported captured by feds—& other federal successes. These are times of peril & trial such as I never expected to witness. C. L. Vallandigham the great statesman and orator of Ohio is condemned to close confinement in Fort Lafayette during the war for publicly denouncing the policy of the administration & warning the people that they were in danger of a military despotism. In Ky a man was arrested—taken to Louisville & imprisoned by military for speaking disrespectfully of the President! but was released. Spies & detectives are roaming the country in disguise listening for some disloyal utterance to report —& seeking by stratagem to get men to avow Southern sympathies that they may arrest them & require oath & bond— consequently men are suspicious of their servants, neighbors, & even kindred blood if they disagree in politics. Confidence is withheld—& general mistrust prevails. The papers boast of raiders burning houses—haystacks—& carrying off booty & negroes, as if they had done virtuous acts & rebels do likewise—except burning houses & taking negroes. Swearing—drunkenness & thriftless indolence are vastly increasing in the land. Altogether the picture is a gloomy one. This summer must witness an immensity of suffering—blood & death.

May 22—Went to Keysburg—was halted by some little boys on stick horses & carrying switch sabres. They said they were Morgans cavalry & would require me to go to the school house & take the oath! Even the children are full of war manoeuvres. I had a small audience, preached on Pauls prayer—Eph 3.14–21. Felt sad about the state of the country & the oath we are bound to take.

May 24—This is the great gathering day at Pleasant Grove—where all the young folks are apt to collect & dress out. It is vulgarly called "Showday." At 4—the negroes had a fine time & I preached a short sermon—Rev 14.13.

May 25—I dined with my father & others at Uncle Dicks where Lizzie was gone when I got home. We decided to go to Russellville tomorrow to comply with "order No. 18" compelling us under penalty of banishment to go to Russellville & take the oath of Allegiance—& to aid in putting down rebellion. If there be any evil in this oath let it be upon those who impose it upon us. It is not our act when forced upon us.

May 26—Bro Alexander & I went to town and took the oath & as for me I shall give no one an opportunity to convict me of violating it. The dictates of humanity I cannot disregard. I never did & will not now encourage the rebellion but as a Christian I must be humane even if I have to feed an enemy when hungry. Most of my old friends in town seemed very glad to see me & treated me most cordially.

For several days past the papers have been rejoicing over great Federal victories & the capture of great numbers of prisoners & cannon & military stores & it is believed that Vicksburg has fallen or must fall & also the greater part of the rebel army. If this is true, it is a severe blow to the rebellion & they have probably lost more at Vicksburg than they gained at Fredericksburg. I feel like withdrawing my thoughts from all public matters & trying more to be an humble Christian & get safely out of this wicked world.

"THE PEOPLE CAN BE TRUSTED":
NEW YORK, MAY 1863

Harper's Weekly:
The Arrest of Vallandigham

May 30, 1863

Speaking at a Democratic rally in Mount Vernon, Ohio, on May 1, former congressman Clement L. Vallandigham declared that "a wicked, cruel and unnecessary" war was being waged "for the purpose of crushing out liberty and erecting a despotism; a war for the freedom of the blacks, and the enslavement of the whites." He also denounced General Orders No. 38, issued on April 13 by Major General Ambrose Burnside, which warned that "declaring sympathies for the enemy will not be allowed" in the Department of the Ohio. Burnside had Vallandigham arrested at his home in Dayton on May 5 and tried by a military commission. Charged with violating General Orders No. 38 by publicly expressing "sympathy for those in arms against the United States, and declaring disloyal sentiments and opinions, with the object and purpose of weakening the power of the Government in its efforts to suppress an unlawful rebellion," Vallandigham was convicted on May 7 and sentenced to imprisonment for the duration of the war. His application for a writ of habeas corpus was rejected by the U.S. circuit court in Cincinnati, which declined to issue a writ for a prisoner in military custody. The controversy drew the attention of *Harper's Weekly*, an illustrated journal with a circulation of more than 100,000 copies. Its editorial went to press before it became known that President Lincoln had ordered Vallandigham expelled into Confederate-held territory.

IT IS known that Clement C. Vallandigham, late member of Congress from Dayton, Ohio, was lately arrested at his house by order of General Burnside, tried by court-martial, and convicted of inciting resistance to the Government in the prosecution of the war. And it is reported that he has been sentenced to imprisonment in a fortress during the war. The President enjoys the power of commuting or remitting this sentence altogether; and it is the unanimous hope of the loyal North that he will remit it.

For, whether the arrest of Vallandigham was or was not a wise step, there can be very little question but his imprisonment for months, and perhaps years, in a military fortress would make a martyr of him, and would rally to his side, for the sake of liberty and free speech, an immense number of sympathizers. It would probably make him Governor of Ohio, and would impart great strength to the rapidly-decaying Copperhead sentiment of the Northwest. Notwithstanding the new lessons taught by the war, and the new duties which it has devolved upon us, we have not yet learned to look with complacency on the methods which are familiar to Old World despotisms; and the spectacle of a man immured in a prison for opinion's or words' sake shocks our feelings and arouses our anger.

It is all very well to say, as General Burnside says in his noble and patriotic reply to the Cincinnati Court, that war involves a sacrifice of liberty, and that this man Vallandigham was a pernicious and malignant enemy of his country. This we all know, and if Vallandigham would go out of the country to the rebels or any where else, loyal people would heartily rejoice. But the question is not whether Vallandigham be a traitor, or whether war involve a suspension of individual rights; it is—shall we better ourselves and help the country by locking this man up in a fortress, instead of letting him prate his seditious trash to every one who will listen? To that question the reply must be in the negative.

The mistake which has all along been made in this war by the Government and many of its agents has been not trusting the people sufficiently. Arresting seditious talkers implies a fear that the people have not sense or strength of mind enough to resist the appeals of sedition; just as the suppression or retention for a time of intelligence of a defeat implies a doubt whether the people have courage enough to bear bad news. Let us assure Mr. Lincoln, and all in authority under him, that the people of the United States have quite courage enough to bear any amount of misfortunes, and quite sense enough to withstand any amount of seditious nonsense, be it uttered ever so glibly. The only effect thus far produced by such talkers as Vallandigham has been to kill off the Copperhead sentiment in the Northwest, to reduce Fernando Wood's party to a mere corporal's guard, and to render the names of the Copperhead leaders a by-word and a reproach among honest men. Vallandigham was fast talking himself into the deepest political grave ever dug when Burnside resurrected him.

The people can be trusted to deal with traitors without any help from Washington, and those who suffer the penalty they inflict—ignominy and disgrace—never find sympathy any where. At the meeting held in this city on 18th to protest against Vallandigham's arrest not one leading man, not a single man who commands general esteem, or who carries the least weight, ventured to be present, and the performance was, on the whole, the most wretched of all the wretched fizzles that have ever been enacted in this city in the way of political meetings. Not but that every body, including the leaders of all parties, and the editors of all leading journals, regret the arrest. But Copperheadism has become so odious, and the doom of every sympathizer with treason so obvious, that not a single man who has any future to risk will jeopard it by placing himself on the record as even indirectly sympathizing with a Copperhead. So long as the people are thus firm in their loyalty it is surely superfluous for Government to interpose for their protection against traitors.

MEETING "SECESH" CIVILIANS:
VIRGINIA, JUNE 1863

Oliver W. Norton to Elizabeth Norton Poss

Private Norton fought at Chancellorsville with the 83rd Pennsylvania Infantry under Colonel Strong Vincent. In late May Vincent became the new brigade commander, and Norton was assigned to brigade headquarters.

Headquarters, Third Brigade, First Division,
Fifth Army Corps,
Crittenden's Mill, Va., June 8, 1863.

Dear Sister L.:—

I have no letter of yours to answer, but having nothing to do and knowing that you are always glad to hear from me, perhaps I can't do better than to spend an hour jotting down for your amusement a few incidents by the way. Life at headquarters is pleasant on one account—it gives me a better opportunity to see and talk with the people of the country than I had in the regiment.

You will see by this that we have again moved. Since the 27th ult. we have been engaged in guarding the river at different points above Fredericksburg. Crittenden's Mill is some twenty miles above town and two miles back of the river. Ellis' Ford and Kempel's Ford are near, and our brigade is ordered to guard these crossings and watch the enemy on the other side. Reports of the observations have to be sent to Division headquarters every four hours of the day and night. Headquarters are at the house of a certain widow James. She has three sons in the rebel army and is a pretty loud *secesh* herself. My bivouac is in one of the old lady's tobacco houses, and there I am writing this at present, so if it smells of tobacco don't charge it to my habits. On the road up here we stopped one night at the house of a Mr. Imbray. He was a cripple and at home, but made no secret of his being *secesh* to the backbone. "I belong to the South," said he, "and my heart is with the South. If I was with the army I should shoot at you with all the power I had, but, meeting as we do, I shall not allow any difference of opinion to influence my treatment of you." (Very considerate, wasn't he, when we had the force there to enforce respect?) But it wasn't of him I meant to speak, but of his daughters. There were two, one a lady of "uncertain age," and the other not. The "not" was about eighteen, and the bitterest, rabidest, outspokenest, cantankerous-est specimen of *secesh* femininity I've come across yet. She had no objection to talk, and she commenced at me when she saw my flag, with, "Is that a Yankee flag?" "Well, the Yankees use it," said I, "but here's the Yankee flag," and I unrolled a new silk "star spangled" and waved it over her head. "Don't you think," said I, "that that's a prettier flag than the 'stars and bars?'" "No, indeed! I can't see it, sir—no, sir—give me the Confederate flag. I don't want none o' yer gridirons about me." Finally after some bantering we dropped the subject and I induced her after a chaffer to sell me two quarts of milk for half a dollar, and she offered me half a loaf of rye bread for the same price, but I preferred hard tack. "We're no way particular about prices with you all," she said. "So I see," meekly replied I. Next morning we were going, and I was bound to have some fun first, so I opened by asking her if she didn't sometimes feel lonesome with none of the young men about. "Well, sir, not lonesome enough to care to see you Yankees about." (Repulse.) "Have you any relatives in the rebel army?" "I have two brothers and a lover in the Confederate army." (Cool—that about the lover.) "Then Yankee boys stand no chance in your good graces?" "No, sir, I hate the sight of them." (Cooler yet.) "Why, I don't think you are a secessionist." (Tactics.) "Well, I am, sir, I am true to the South." (I wish I could write their pronunciation of South; it beats all the down-east you ever heard of.) "No, you are a Yankee, at least a Yankee *secesh*." "No, indeed, sir, nary drop o' Yankee blood in my veins, I tell you, sir." "Oh, but you are, begging your pardon, and I'll prove it to you." "No, sir, you can't do that, sir; better tell that to some one else. If I had any Yankee blood in me I'd let it out. Yes, indeed, I would." "Well, you acknowledge that a Yankee thinks more of property and money than anything else, don't you?" "Yes, sir, I've heard they do, and I believe it." "Yes, well, you're a Yankee then. If you were a *secesh* you would go with the South and help them. True *secesh* women do that, but your family have some property here and you stay to take care of it and let the South get along the best she can. You are a genuine Yankee, say what you please. You wouldn't go and share the fortunes of your 'Sunny South,' but you must stay to keep the Yankees from destroying the property." Oh, how she did sputter! "To think that she should be called a Yankee!" I guess she'll get over it.

Down on the bank of the river I went into a house and met a young married woman with a baby in her arms. She had been pretty once and it was not age that spoiled her beauty, but care. "Can you sell me a pie, or something good for my dinner?" said I. "A pie! sir," said she. "Well, now, sir, if I was to tell you that I have not tasted or seen a piece of pie for more than a year, would you believe me?" "I certainly should if you said so. Of course I couldn't doubt a lady's word." "Sir, 'fore God it is the truth. I have only been married 'bout a year, and my husband, who was an overseer, came on to this place after the fruit was all gone, and I've had no fruit. I haven't seen a bit of sugar, nor coffee, nor tea for nigh eight months, I reckon," and she went on and gave me such a story of struggles to keep alive, to get enough to keep from starving, as made all the hard times I have ever seen seem like a life of luxury. I did pity her. On such as she, the poor whites of the South, the burden of this war is heaviest. She had but little sympathy for the South or North either. She cared but little how the war ended, so it ended soon. Poor woman, she understood but little of the nature of the contest. She sent a little darky girl to bring in a pan of milk. The girl came with it balanced on her head, not touching her hands. I remarked how strange it seemed to me to see everybody in the south carry pails on their heads. "Why," said she, "how do you-all carry 'em?" "In our hands." She laughed. "I have to tote all my water up a steep bank, and, if I toted it in my hand, it would pull me over." She gave me some milk, and by the time I had eaten my dinner the colonel came back from the lines, and I mounted my horse and came back to camp.

Strawberries are ripe and I get a few. No more news from Fredericksburg.

THE BURNING OF DARIEN: GEORGIA, JUNE 1863

Robert Gould Shaw to
Annie Haggerty Shaw

The 54th Massachusetts Infantry left its training camp at Readville on May 28 and marched through the streets of Boston before sailing for Beaufort, South Carolina. Its departure was cheered by thousands of spectators, including Frederick Douglass, Harriet Jacobs, and William Lloyd Garrison, in what Shaw described as a "perfect triumph." When Shaw arrived in Beaufort he met Colonel James Montgomery, the commander of the 2nd South Carolina Volunteers, a regiment of freed slaves formed in early 1863. A friend of John Brown, Montgomery had led a free-state militia in Kansas before the war and commanded Union troops fighting guerrillas in Missouri. In a letter to his father, Shaw wrote: "He is an Indian in his mode of warfare, and though I am glad to see something of it, I can't say I admire it. It isn't like a fair stand up such as our Potomac Army is accustomed to." On June 8 the 54th Massachusetts was sent to join Montgomery's regiment on St. Simon's Island, Georgia.

St. Simon's Island, Ga.
Tuesday, June 9, 1863
My Dearest Annie,

We arrived at the southern point of this island at six this morning. I went ashore to report to Colonel Montgomery, and was ordered to proceed with my regiment to a place called "Pike's Bluff," on the inner coast of the island, and encamp. We came up here in another steamer, the "Sentinel," as the "De Molay" is too large for the inner waters,—and took possession to-day of a plantation formerly owned by Mr. Gould. We have a very nice camping-ground for the regiment, and I have my quarters in "*the house*"; very pleasantly situated, and surrounded by fine large trees. The island is beautiful, as far as I have seen it. You would be enchanted with the scenery here; the foliage is wonderfully thick, and the trees covered with hanging moss, making beautiful avenues wherever there is a road or path; it is more like the tropics than anything I have seen. Mr. Butler King's plantation, where I first went ashore, must have been a beautiful place, and well kept. It is entirely neglected now, of course; and as the growth is very rapid, two years' neglect almost covers all traces of former care.

12th.—If I could have gone on describing to you the beauties of this region, who knows but I might have made a fine addition to the literature of our age? But since I wrote the above, I have been looking at something very different.

On Wednesday, a steamboat appeared off our wharf, and Colonel Montgomery hailed me from the deck with, "How soon can you get ready to start on an expedition?" I said, "In half an hour," and it was not long before we were on board with eight companies, leaving two for camp-guard.

We steamed down by his camp, where two other steamers with five companies from his regiment, and two sections of Rhode Island artillery, joined us. A little below there we ran aground, and had to wait until midnight for flood-tide, when we got away once more.

At 8 A.M., we were at the mouth of the Altamaha River, and immediately made for Darien. We wound in and out through the creeks, twisting and turning continually, often heading in directly the opposite direction from that which we intended to go, and often running aground, thereby losing much time. Besides our three vessels, we were followed by the gunboat "Paul Jones."

On the way up, Montgomery threw several shells among the plantation buildings, in what seemed to me a very brutal way; for he didn't know how many women and children there might be.

About noon we came in sight of Darien, a beautiful little town. Our artillery peppered it a little, as we came up, and then our three boats made fast to the wharves, and we landed the troops. The town was deserted, with the exception of two white women and two negroes.

Montgomery ordered all the furniture and movable property to be taken on board the boats. This occupied some time; and after the town was pretty thoroughly disembowelled, he said to me, "I shall burn this town." He speaks always in a very low tone, and has quite a sweet smile when addressing you. I told him, "I did not want the responsibility of it," and he was only too happy to take it all on his shoulders; so the pretty little place was burnt to the ground, and not a shed remains standing; Montgomery firing the last buildings with his own hand. One of my companies assisted in it, because he ordered them out, and I had to obey. You must bear in mind, that not a shot had been fired at us from this place, and that there were evidently very few men left in it. All the inhabitants (principally women and children) had fled on our approach, and were no doubt watching the scene from a distance. Some of our grapeshot tore the skirt of one of the women whom I saw. Montgomery told her that her house and property should be spared; but it went down with the rest.

The reasons he gave me for destroying Darien were, that the Southerners must be made to feel that this was a real war, and that they were to be swept away by the hand of God, like the Jews of old. In theory it may seem all right to some, but when it comes to being made the instrument of the Lord's vengeance, I myself don't like it. Then he says, "We are outlawed, and therefore not bound by the rules of regular warfare"; but that makes it none the less revolting to wreak our vengeance on the innocent and defenceless.

By the time we had finished this dirty piece of business, it was too dark to go far down the narrow river, where our boat sometimes touched both banks at once; so we lay at anchor until daylight, occasionally dropping a shell at a stray house. The "Paul Jones" fired a few guns as well as we.

I reached camp at about 2 P.M. to-day, after as abominable a job as I ever had a share in.

We found a mail waiting for us, and I received your dear letter, and several from Father, Mother, Effie, and some business correspondence. This is the first news we have had since our departure, and I rather regained my good spirits.

Now, dear Annie, remember not to breathe a word of what I have written about this raid, to any one out of our two families, for I have not yet made up my mind what I ought to do. Besides my own distaste for this barbarous sort of warfare, I am not sure that it will not harm very much the reputation of black troops and of those connected with them. For myself, I have gone through the war so far without dishonour, and I do not like to degenerate into a plunderer and robber,—and the same applies to every officer in my regiment. There was not a deed performed, from beginning to end, which required any pluck or courage. If we had fought for possession of the place, and it had been found necessary to hold or destroy it, or if the inhabitants had done anything which deserved such punishment, or if it were a place of refuge for the enemy, there might have been some reason for Montgomery's acting as he did; but as the case stands, I can't see any justification. If it were the order of our government to overrun the South with fire and sword, I might look at it in a different light; for then we should be carrying out what had been decided upon as a necessary policy. As the case stands, we are no better than "Semmes," who attacks and destroys defenceless vessels, and haven't even the poor excuse of gaining anything by it; for the property is of no use to us, excepting that we can now sit on chairs instead of camp-stools.

But all I complain of, is wanton destruction. After going through the hard campaigning and hard fighting in Virginia, this makes me very much ashamed of myself.

Montgomery, from what I have seen of him, is a conscientious man, and really believes what he says,—"that he is doing his duty to the best of his knowledge and ability."

. . . There are two courses only for me to pursue: to obey orders and say nothing; or to refuse to go on any more such expeditions, and be put under arrest, probably court-martialled, which is a serious thing.

June 13th.—This letter I am afraid will be behindhand, for a boat went to Hilton Head this morning from the lower end of the island, and I knew nothing about it. Colonel Montgomery has gone up himself, and will not be back until Tuesday probably.

. . . To-day I rode over to Pierce Butler's plantation. It is an immense place, and parts of it very beautiful. The house is small, and badly built, like almost all I have seen here. There are about ten of his slaves left there, all of them sixty or seventy years old. He sold three hundred slaves about three years ago.

I talked with some, whose children and grandchildren were sold then, and though they said that was a "weeping day," they maintained that "Massa Butler was a good massa," and they would give anything to see him again. When I told them I had known Miss Fanny, they looked very much pleased, and one named John wanted me to tell her I had seen him. They said all the house-servants had been taken inland by the overseer at the beginning of the war; and they asked if we couldn't get their children back to the island again. These were all born and bred on the place, and even selling away their families could not entirely efface their love for their master. Isn't it horrible to think of a man being able to treat such faithful creatures in such a manner?

The island is traversed from end to end by what they call a shell-road; which is hard and flat, excellent for driving. On each side there are either very large and overhanging trees, with thick underbrush, or open country covered with sago-palm, the sharp-pointed leaves making the country impassable. Occasionally we meet with a few fields of very poor grass; when there is no swamp, the soil is very sandy.

There are a good many of these oyster-shell roads, for in many places there are great beds of them, deposited nobody knows when, I suppose. The walls of many of the buildings are built of cement mixed with oyster-shells, which make it very durable.

I forgot to tell you that the negroes at Mr. Butler's remembered Mrs. Kemble very well, and said she was a very fine lady. They hadn't seen her since the young ladies were very small, they said. My visit there was very interesting and touching.

A deserted homestead is always a sad sight, but here in the South we must look a little deeper than the surface, and then we see that every such overgrown plantation, and empty house, is a harbinger of freedom to the slaves, and every lover of his country, even if he have no feeling for the slaves themselves, should rejoice.

Next to Mr. Butler's is the house of Mr. James E. Cooper. It must have been a lovely spot; the garden is well laid out, and the perfume of the flowers is delicious. The house is the finest on the island. The men from our gunboats have been there, and all the floors are strewed with books and magazines of every kind. There is no furniture in any of these houses.

Please send this to Father, for I want him and Mother to read it, and I don't care about writing it over.

Colonel Montgomery's original plan, on this last expedition, was to land about fifteen miles above Darien, and march down on two different roads to the town, taking all the negroes to be found, and burning every planter's house on the passage. I should have commanded our detachment, in that case. The above are the orders he gave me.

Good bye for to-day, dearest Annie.

Your loving Rob

9 P.M. June 13th . . . To-morrow is Sunday, and perhaps you will be at Staten Island; at any rate, I suppose, not at Lenox; but wherever you are, I wish I could go to church with you, and saunter about in some pretty garden afterwards.

. . . There is a beautiful little church near here, almost buried in trees and moss. I have had it put to rights (it was damaged by some sailors and soldiers), and the Chaplain of the Second South Carolina Regiment is to preach there for us tomorrow.

I shall always have a service of some kind on Sunday; and if we can't always get a chaplain, I shall have one of the officers officiate. I don't feel good enough myself to undertake to teach others, as you suggest. Perhaps I shall some time. I have read some of Robertson's sermons, and think them very beautiful.

. . . I shall never let Mr. Ritchie go, if I can prevent it. He is a perfect jewel, and has been of incalculable service to us, in managing the regimental quartermaster's department. . . .

Your loving Husband

SIEGE OF VICKSBURG: MISSISSIPPI, JUNE 1863

William Winters to Harriet Winters

After his victory at Port Gibson on May 1 Grant advanced northeast toward Jackson, forty miles east of Vicksburg, while his troops supplied themselves by foraging on the countryside. His forces defeated the Confederates at Raymond, May 12, and captured Jackson, May 14, frustrating attempts by General Joseph Johnston to assemble reinforcements there. While Sherman's men destroyed factories and railroads in Jackson, Grant turned most of his army west toward Vicksburg. Union victories at Champion Hill, May 16, and Big Black River Bridge, May 17, forced the Confederates to retreat inside the Vicksburg fortifications. Grant ordered assaults on the Vicksburg defenses, May 19 and May 22, both of which failed, and then began siege operations. Sergeant William Winters had enlisted in the 67th Indiana Regiment in August 1862 and fought in the Vicksburg campaign as part of the Thirteenth Corps, commanded by Major General John A. McClernand. His regiment saw action at Port Gibson, Champion Hill, Big Black River, and the May 22 assault, and lost about forty-five men killed and wounded in these engagements.

In Camp, Seige of
Vicksburg, June 9, 1863
Dear wife,
We are still tunneling away at the rebel works around the city and in same position as we were when I last wrote to you, with a fair prospect of remaining so for several days to come, but we will go into the city of Vicksburgh after awhile, that is shure, for we can live outside of their works longer than they can inside of them, that is certain, for we can get everything we want, and they can get nothing atall. We hear all kinds of rumors of how they are suffering for the want of water and provisions, but we cant tell which tale is the true one, and so we lett them pass for what they will fitch.

The only thing we have here that we can rely on for certain is the roar of cannon and the rattle of musketry, but we have been taking it perfectly cool and easely since the day of the charge. if you where here some time you would not think that we were face to face with an enemy, the men whistling and singing, sutlers selling their wares, and everything looks as if we were in camp for a big rest instead of beseigeing a rebell city.

The worst thing here is the water does not agree with the men. A good many of them are complaining with the diareah. Jacob Shut, Emanuel Sawers, and Levi Snyder are here in our hospt. they are trying to get Shut and Sawers furloughs for twenty days, but I dont know how they will succeed, but I hope they will get them as they ought to have them.

The weather for the last three days has been most intolrably hot. It looks a litle like rain to day. I hope that it will as we need it. Tom Eaton, Charly Bannes, and the rest of the boys that we left back at the river sick have all got well and are here with the regiment. I believe that the boys are all well but the three that we have here in the Hospt.

the boys are all verey mutch put out with Captain Eaton. They say that he promised to write to the most of them but he's never wrote a word to the company attall. We all hope that he is doing well. Letters from home are a scarce thing here now. We get the news from the cincinnati, st. Louis, Memphis, and Chicago papers every few days, but this is all. We got a mail the other day that had three letters in it for the 67th Reg. And that was all. Three letters in three weeks for three hundred and fifty men is a heavey mail I think.

I am not verey well and dont expect to be untill I get away from this watter. I have written this makes seven letters since I have received one from any person, but I reckon the next mail will be full of them. I hoope that we will be in Vicksburgh before I have to write again. give my love to all. Tell them I eat as many ripe blackberreys as I wanted on day before yesterday. Write soon. From your Afect Husband

Wm. Winters

BATTLE OF MILLIKEN'S BEND:
LOUISIANA, JUNE 1863

Matthew M. Miller to His Aunt

One of the first battles of the war to involve significant numbers of black troops was fought on June 7 when 1,500 Confederates attacked the Union supply depot at Milliken's Bend, Louisiana, in an attempt to disrupt the siege of Vicksburg. The position was defended by about 1,000 men from the 23rd Iowa Infantry and four recently recruited black regiments, the 1st Mississippi Infantry and the 9th, 11th, and 13th Louisiana Infantry (African Descent), that had not completed their musket training. Although the Confederates succeeded in driving the defenders back to the riverbank, they broke off their attack after several hours and retreated under fire from two Union gunboats. The Confederates lost 175 men killed or wounded, the Union forces 386. Captain Matthew M. Miller of Galena, Illinois, described the fighting in a letter that was published in the *Galena Advertiser*, reprinted in other newspapers, and included in a preliminary report issued by the American Freedmen's Inquiry Commission on June 30, 1863.

MILLIKEN'S BEND, *June 10, 1863.*
DEAR AUNT: We were attacked here on June 7, about 3 o'clock in the morning, by a brigade of Texas troops, about 2,500 in number. We had about 600 men to withstand them, 500 of them negroes. I commanded Company I, Ninth Louisiana. We went into the fight with 33 men. I had 16 killed and 11 badly wounded, 4 slightly. I was wounded slightly on the head, near the right eye, with a bayonet, and had a bayonet run through my right hand near the forefinger; that will account for this miserable style of penmanship.

Our regiment had about 300 men in the fight. We had 1 colonel wounded, 4 captains wounded, 2 first and 2 second lieutenants killed, 5 lieutenants wounded, and 3 white orderlies killed and 1 wounded in the hand and two fingers taken off. The list of killed and wounded officers comprises nearly all the officers present with the regiment, a majority of the rest being absent recruiting.

We had about 50 men killed in the regiment and 80 wounded, so you can judge of what part of the fight my company sustained. I never felt more grieved and sick at heart than when I saw how my brave soldiers had been slaughtered, one with six wounds, all the rest with two or three, none less than two wounds. Two of my colored sergeants were killed, both brave, noble men; always prompt, vigilant, and ready for the fray. I never more wish to hear the expression, "The niggers wont fight." Come with me 100 yards from where I sit and I can show you the wounds that cover the bodies of 16 as brave, loyal, and patriotic soldiers as ever drew bead on a rebel.

The enemy charged us so close that we fought with our bayonets hand to hand. I have six broken bayonets to show how bravely my men fought. The Twenty-third Iowa joined my company on the right, and I declare truthfully that they had all fled before our regiment fell back, as we were all compelled to do.

Under command of Colonel Page I led the Ninth and Eleventh Louisiana when the rifle-pits were retaken and held by our troops, our two regiments doing the work.

I narrowly escaped death once. A rebel took deliberate aim at me with both barrels of his gun, and the bullets passed so close to me that the powder that remained on them burned my cheek. Three of my men who saw him aim and fire thought that he wounded me each fire. One of them was killed by my side, and he fell on me, covering my clothes with his blood, and before the rebel could fire again I blew his brains out with my gun.

It was a horrible fight, the worst I was ever engaged in, not even excepting Shiloh. The enemy cried, "No quarters," but some of them were very glad to take it when made prisoners.

Colonel Allen, of the Seventeenth Texas, was killed in front of our regiment, and Brigadier-General Walker was wounded. We killed about 180 of the enemy. The gun-boat Choctaw did good service shelling them. I stood on the breast-works after we took them, and gave the elevations and direction for the gun-boat by pointing my sword, and they sent a shell right into their midst, which sent them in all directions. Three shells fell there, and 62 rebels lay there when the fight was over.

My wound is not serious, but troublesome. What few men I have left seem to think much of me because I stood up with them in the fight. I can say for them that I never saw a braver company of men in my life.

Not one of them offered to leave his place until ordered to fall back; in fact, very few ever did fall back. I went down to the hospital three miles to-day to see the wounded. Nine of them were there, two having died of their wounds. A boy I had cooking for me came and begged a gun when the rebels were advancing, and took his place with the company, and when we retook the breast-works I found him badly wounded with one gunshot and two bayonet wounds. A new recruit I had issued a gun to the day before the fight was found dead, with a firm grasp on his gun, the bayonet of which was broken in three pieces. So they fought and died defending the cause that we revere. They met death coolly, bravely; not rashly did they expose themselves, but all were steady and obedient to orders.

So God has spared me again through many dangers. I cannot tell how it was I escaped.

Your affectionate nephew,

M. M. MILLER.

"DIVIDING AND WEAKENING" THE NORTH: VIRGINIA, JUNE 1863

Robert E. Lee to Jefferson Davis

Despite victories at Fredericksburg and Chancellorsville, Lee worried that these triumphs did not markedly change the strategic situation. He proposed to Jefferson Davis that the Confederacy seize the initiative in the eastern theater by invading Pennsylvania, allowing the Army of Northern Virginia to gather food and forage in enemy territory and giving Lee an opportunity to weaken northern morale by winning a third consecutive victory over the Army of the Potomac. Davis agreed, and after reorganizing his army, Lee started his troops toward the Shenandoah Valley on June 3. He wrote to Davis a week later from his temporary headquarters at Culpeper Court House, thirty miles northwest of Fredericksburg.

Headquarters, Army of Northern Virginia
June 10, 1863

Mr. President:

I beg leave to bring to your attention a subject with reference to which I have thought that the course pursued by writers and speakers among us has had a tendency to interfere with our success. I refer to the manner in which the demonstration of a desire for peace at the North has been received in our country.

I think there can be no doubt that journalists and others at the South, to whom the Northern people naturally look for a reflection of our opinions, have met these indications in such wise as to weaken the hands of the advocates of a pacific policy on the part of the Federal Government, and give much encouragement to those who urge a continuance of the war.

Recent political movements in the United States, and the comments of influential newspapers upon them, have attracted my attention particularly to this subject, which I deem not unworthy of the consideration of Your Excellency, nor inappropriate to be adverted to by me in view of its connection with the situation of military affairs.

Conceding to our enemies the superiority claimed by them in numbers, resources, and all the means and appliances for carrying on the war, we have no right to look for exemptions from the military consequences of a vigorous use of these advantages, excepting by such deliverance as the mercy of Heaven may accord to the courage of our soldiers, the justice of our cause, and the constancy and prayers of our people. While making the most we can of the means of resistance we possess, and gratefully accepting the measure of success with which God has blessed our efforts as an earnest of His approval and favor, it is nevertheless the part of wisdom to carefully measure and husband our strength, and not to expect from it more than in the ordinary course of affairs it is capable of accomplishing. We should not therefore conceal from ourselves that our resources in men are constantly diminishing, and the disproportion in this respect between us and our enemies, if they continue united in their efforts to subjugate us, is steadily augmenting. The decrease of the aggregate of this army as disclosed by the returns affords an illustration of this fact. Its effective strength varies from time to time, but the falling off in its aggregate shows that its ranks are growing weaker and that its losses are not supplied by recruits.

Under these circumstances we should neglect no honorable means of dividing and weakening our enemies that they may feel some of the difficulties experienced by ourselves. It seems to me that the most effectual mode of accomplishing this object, now within our reach, is to give all the encouragement we can, consistently with truth, to the rising peace party of the North.

Nor do I think we should in this connection make nice distinctions between those who declare for peace unconditionally and those who advocate it as a means of restoring the Union however much we may prefer the former.

We should bear in mind that the friends of peace at the North must make concessions to the earnest desire that exists in the minds of their countrymen for a restoration of the Union, and that to hold out such a result as an inducement is essential to the success of their party.

Should the belief that peace will bring back the Union become general, the war would no longer be supported, and that after all is what we are interested in bringing about. When peace is proposed to us it will be time enough to discuss its terms, and it is not the part of prudence to spurn the proposition in advance, merely because those who wish to make it believe, or affect to believe, that it will result in bringing us back to the Union. We entertain no such apprehensions, nor doubt that the desire of our people for a distinct and independent national existence will prove as steadfast under the influence of peaceful measures as it has shown itself in the midst of war.

If the views I have indicated meet the approval of Your Excellency you will best know how to give effect to them. Should you deem them inexpedient or impracticable, I think you will nevertheless agree with me that we should at least carefully abstain from measures or expressions that tend to discourage any party whose purpose is peace.

With the statement of my own opinion on the subject, the length of which you will excuse, I leave to your better judgment to determine the proper course to be pursued.

> I am with great respect, your obt servt
>
> R. E. Lee
> Genl

"THE HAND OF DESTRUCTION":
MISSISSIPPI, JUNE 1863

William T. Sherman to John T. Swayne

John T. Swayne, the judge of the Memphis criminal court, wrote to Sherman to protest a recent military order expelling from the city persons who refused to swear allegiance to the United States. Sherman responded to Swayne from his headquarters near Vicksburg, enclosing a letter to Major General Stephen A. Hurlbut, the Union commander at Memphis, in which Sherman endorsed the power of the military to punish spying and sedition among an occupied population but expressed doubts about the "efficiency and policy" of exacting "a 'naked oath.'"

Hd. Qrs. 15th. Army Corps.
Camp on Walnut Hills, June 11, 1863

Judge Swayne, Memphis
Dear Sir,

As you can readily understand, I have about as much local business, as should engage the attention of one man, desirous of following the great revolution, which is sweeping as with whirlwind speed to destruction or Safety, I enclose you a letter, I have hastily written to General Hurlbut, which is as Specific as I ought to write. The General is a Southerner born and educated Lawyer, as well as Politician and it looks like an absurdity in one, who professes nothing of the kind to suggest to him any course of policy founded in a state of facts, of which I must be ignorant. If God himself smote Sodom and Gomorra, for departing from the law, and setting up their blind prejudice instead, surely I could not plead forbearance on the part of the U.S. if the people of Memphis are known to be conspiring against our law and safety.

But on the other hand, if the people of Memphis are acting in good faith, I will plead for them, that they be dealt with fairly honestly and even with kindness.

I fear me, that politicians and news mongers have so stirred up the vile passions of our People, and so poisoned their minds, that a government founded on public opinion, will for years to come be too unstable to curb these passions, and restrain the excesses, to which they lead, and that the U.S. Government assume the strong and dictatorial form, which alone can protect life and property.

The value of theoretical political notions, must I fear yield to that of more substantial interest. The sooner the people of the South discover this truth, and act upon it, the more will they save from the wrack of matter, that now threatens their universal ruin.

They may display heroic courage, they may elicit the admiration of the world, by the display of military genius, but they cannot stay the hand of destruction, that is now setting adrift their Slaves, occupying with fruitless muskets their adult whites, consuming and wasting their fields and improvements, destroying their roads, bridges, and the labor and fruits of near a century of undisturbed prosperity.

Men of extreme opinion and action cannot reason together and calm this tumult. It is the task allotted to such as you, and the time will come, and that soon, that even you, if you fail to act will be swept aside, helpless as a wisp of straw in the gale of wind.

Instead of appealing to Genl. Hurlbut to assist you, to escape a dangerous remote contingency, I say: think—act. Take your part and see, that some power is raised in America, that can stay the hand of strife, and substitute the rule of justice and mercy for that of force, violence and destruction.

If such men as you sit idle now, you are barred in all future Tribunals to plead for mercy and forbearance. What is a court without Power and a Sheriff? What is a Government, without Power and an Executive? Restore to our old Government its wonted power, and soon will cease this strife, and the Rights, you once prized, but now fast sinking into insignificance amidst new issues, will return and assume their natural weight.

But prolong the strife, and you may safely burn your library and turn your thoughts to some more lucrative trade than the Law.

I believe, you will receive from me in good part thoughts so crude, and it may be unreasonable. I surely wish you well. With Respect

       W. T. Sherman
       Maj. Genl.

BATTLE OF BRANDY STATION:
VIRGINIA, JUNE 1863

Henry C. Whelan to Mary Whelan

The largest cavalry battle of the war was fought on June 9 when 11,000 Union troops crossed the Rappahannock and attacked 10,000 Confederate cavalrymen deployed around Brandy Station, five miles northeast of Culpeper Court House. Although they were taken by surprise, the Confederates eventually drove the Union forces from the field. The Confederates lost about 500 men killed, wounded, or missing, and the Union about 900. Major Henry C. Whelan of the 6th Pennsylvania Cavalry described the battle to his sister.

Thursday Morning, June 11/63.
Old Camp under the Oaks near
Catletts Station, Va.

On Monday the 8th we marched from here at 3 P.M. and halted near the ford for the night—no fires—and all kept perfectly quiet. At 3 in the morning we were again in the saddle and our Regiment, at the head of the Regular Brigade, crossed the river, when fighting immediately began. The Rebels fell back slowly, until they gained a good position, when they made a stand. Whilst I was by the side of Haseltine, talking with him, a number of shots hissed close by us, and a minute after, Harry's magnificent horse "Medor" fell, shot through the flank. About 15 minutes later we were ordered to advance on the woods from which the enemy were annoying us with sharp shooters. We had with us then five, Captain Treichel's Company A; Company D, Lieut. White; Company F, Captain Davis; Company K, Lieut Colliday; and Company L, Captain Leiper—the other five Companies were on duty on the north side of the river and joined us later in the day. Leiper's Company advanced as skirmishers, and Major Morris led the two squadrons, he at the head of the first, I of the second. We passed through the woods, being heavily shelled on our left by the enemy's batteries. When we came through to the open, we found a whole brigade of Stuart's Cavalry drawn up to receive us. We dashed at them, squadron front with drawn sabres, and as we flew along—our men yelling like demons—grape and cannister were poured into our left flank and a storm of rifle bullets on our front. We had to leap three wide deep ditches, and many of our horses and men piled up in a writhing mass in those ditches and were ridden over. It was here that Major Morris' horse fell badly with him, and broke away from him when he got up, thus leaving him dismounted and bruised by the fall. I didn't know that Morris was not with us, and we dashed on, driving the Rebels into and through the woods, our men fighting with the sabre alone, whilst they used principally pistols. Our brave fellows cut them out of the saddle and fought like tigers, until I discovered they were on both flanks, pouring a cross fire of carbines and pistols on us, and then tried to rally my men and make them return the fire with their carbines.

I found we were rapidly getting hemmed in, so I, as rapidly as possible, gathered together the remnant of our Regiment and dashed out of the woods, only to find that hundreds of grey devils occupied both sides of the open;—and because we had not been supported, we were completely surrounded. Then came a *race for life*—I shook the reins on poor little "Lancer's" neck, and he dashed off with the speed of a deer, passed by scores of yelling demons, who devoted most of their attention and shots to me. How many were fired at once I am afraid to guess, as it would look like exaggeration. I had to dash to the right and to the left to avoid and get between them, and a dozen of them fired so close to me that I almost felt the hot breath of their pieces—one officer rode close up on my right side and levelled his pistol. I stooped under his arm on "Lancer's" neck as he fired, and gave him a hissing right cut with my sabre as I flew by—I then dropped my sabre on my wrist and drew my pistol and fired at all who came too close—I passed a dismounted Rebel officer so close that I could have cut his head off. An Irishman, of Company K, who was splendidly mounted, stuck to me like a leech, and called out from behind: "Major, there's an officer—shall I cut him down?" I saw his horse was killed and he himself stood defenceless, so I told the man to let him alone. That Irishman cried out, when I cut the rebel who fired his pistol at me: "Good for you, Major", and gave a regular Irish whoop.

Oh! What a fearful ride, full two miles of ground covered with dead and wounded men and horses, wide ditches, which my dear sorrel cleared like an antelope, and all the time pursued and fired at by those grey blood-hounds, who kept yelling for me to surrender. To get rid of some of them, I made a desperate dash at a stone wall about 5 feet high, which "Lancer" topped like a bird. After that, only four or five continued the chase, until I caught sight of some of our Cavalry and rode for them across the country, over a deep creek and two wide ditches and one more stone wall. I found they were a Company of the 2nd Regulars, Captain Rodenbaugh, of Easton. As soon as I joined them, the Rebels broke out of the woods, five times the number of Rodenbaugh's men, so he wheeled about and started his men back by fours at a gallop. I rode along with them, and going through a narrow gate their horses got jambed and piled up in a horrid kicking mass—poor "Lancer" was almost crushed—I could only see part of his head, some grey horse's legs were right over his neck, and I was crushed in so tight, with horses on both sides, that I could not move. Strange to say, after much kicking, groaning and rolling about, I managed to get "Lancer" partly free; and then he struggled out with me, considerably bruised, and his hind leg bleeding. It was only a minute perhaps, but it seemed hours of horror, to be pinioned and fettered by a writhing mass of heavy horses, and the murderous Rebels coming up to shoot or stab us in the back.

"Lancer" was no sooner free than away he sped like an arrow from the bow, and bore me back safe, though covered with dust and bruised and weary. The men I got together, who made their way back from the charge, only numbered about one small squadron. I was reinforced by Frazier's squadron, from the other side of the river, and sent to take possession of a stone wall which the Rebels were trying to get with their skirmishers.

The enemy, in about an hour, brought so strong a force against the place that they ordered me to take the balance of my Company and to garrison this wall. I had to take them over an open field, about six hundred yards, through a perfect tempest of shell, grape, canister, solid shot and rifle bullets. I took them at a full run, but before we reached the wall, poor Captain Davis was shot dead with a grape shot; two of Frazier's men, together with their horses, were literally smashed by a solid shot; a large number of men were wounded, and horses killed. Going to and down at that wall was decidedly the hottest place I was ever in. A man could not show his head or a finger without a hundred rifle shots whistling about you. We saw negroes with white teeth grinning firing at us with long rifles. I was obliged to ride three times up and down that fearful place with the air almost solid with lead.

At last, when the 5th Cavalry men, who were out of ammunition, left to return, the Rebels charged in number 3 to 1 of us; and we were forced to fall back. I had just sprung on poor "Lancer's" back when there came a rifle ball right through his flank, and the noble little fellow could move no more. He fell with and although in that hail storm of iron and lead I could have sat down and cried. I own that my eyes filled with tears as I walked slowly away. In a moment my orderly, Ward, of Company C, rode up to me, sprung to the ground, and said, "Major, take my horse—I have a carbine, and can get back safe on foot". I mounted and rode back, whilst Ward turned and shot a Rebel who was robbing "Lancer" of his saddle blanket. Lieut. Lennig was lost at that place, whether killed, wounded or taken prisoner, we don't know. How I escaped through all I can't imagine. I was only grazed on the left wrist, and didn't know it till I saw my wrist bathed in blood. The shot which killed "Lancer" passed close to my thigh through the saddle bag and piercing Bulwer's "What will he do with it", which was strapped to the saddle bag. I will send the book to you by mail. It has some of "Lancer's" blood upon it. All the rest of that day we were engaged constantly under severe fire from artillery and small arms, until we fired away all our ammunition, and about five in the afternoon the regular brigade, exhausted by 14 hours hard fighting, retired to the other side of the river.

The conduct of officers and men of the 6th Penna. Cavalry is spoken of in the highest terms by all. General Buford says the regiment has covered itself with glory, but at a fearful expense. We lost six officers and over one hundred men killed, wounded and missing, and took 347 men and 18 officers into the fight. Our loss is thus one third of the whole command engaged.

Our charge on the Rebel brigade is said by all to have been the finest feature of the fight and leaving us unsupported to cut our own way back is severely blamed on—"somebody".

I have tried to give you as faithful account as I could, but such a crowd of terrible incidents is almost impossible to describe. Charley Leiper was cut across the forehead by a sabre, but he fought like a Turk with pistol and sabre, was surrounded and disarmed, but still stuck to his horse and striking with his fists finally broke away and escaped. Haseltine was twice struck by spent balls, one hurting him quite severely. Eight of our officers had their horses shot away under them. Lennig had two horses shot, and so had White. Colliday was lost in the charge—Rudolph Ellis was shot in the leg during the afternoon. He was quite close to me—he and Leiper were sent to Washington. I recovered the body of Capt. Davis and sent it to Washington with the Chaplain there to be embalmed and sent home. He is a great loss to the Regiment and is deeply mourned.

THE CONSTITUTION IN WARTIME:
WASHINGTON, D.C., JUNE 1863

Abraham Lincoln to Erastus Corning and Others

The arrest and trial of former congressman Clement L. Vallandigham were widely criticized by Democrats and by some Republicans. In private President Lincoln and his cabinet regretted General Burnside's actions, but, as Lincoln wrote Burnside, "being done, all were for seeing you through with it." After commuting his prison sentence to banishment, the President wrote a public letter responding to resolutions protesting Vallandigham's arrest adopted at a public meeting in Albany, New York. (The meeting was presided over by Erastus Corning, a Democratic congressman and president of the New York Central Railroad.) Lincoln's letter appeared in the press on June 15, four days after the Ohio Democratic convention nominated Vallandigham for governor.

EXECUTIVE MANSION
Washington.
June 12, 1863.

Hon. ERASTUS CORNING *and others:*

GENTLEMEN: Your letter of May 19, inclosing the resolutions of a public meeting held at Albany, N. Y., on the 16th of the same month, was received several days ago.

The resolutions, as I understand them, are resolvable into two propositions—first, the expression of a purpose to sustain the cause of the Union, to secure peace through victory, and to support the Administration in every constitutional and lawful measure to suppress the Rebellion; and secondly, a declaration of censure upon the Administration for supposed unconstitutional action, such as the making of military arrests. And, from the two propositions, a third is deduced, which is that the gentlemen composing the meeting are resolved on doing their part to maintain our common government and country, despite the folly or wickedness, as they may conceive, of any Administration. This position is eminently patriotic, and as such I thank the meeting and congratulate the nation for it. My own purpose is the same; so that the meeting and myself have a common object, and can have no difference, except in the choice of means or measures for effecting that object.

And here I ought to close this paper, and would close it, if there were no apprehension that more injurious consequences than any merely personal to myself might follow the censures systematically cast upon me for doing what, in my view of duty, I could not forbear. The resolutions promise to support me in every constitutional and lawful measure to suppress the Rebellion; and I have not knowingly employed, nor shall knowingly employ, any other. But the meeting, by their resolutions, assert and argue that certain military arrests, and proceedings following them, for which I am ultimately responsible, are unconstitutional. I think they are not. The resolutions quote from the Constitution the definition of treason, and also the limiting safeguards and guarantees therein provided for the citizen on trials for treason, and on his being held to answer for capital or otherwise infamous crimes, and, in criminal prosecutions, his right to a speedy and public trial by an impartial jury. They proceed to resolve "that these safe-guards of the rights of the citizen against the pretensions of arbitrary power were intended more *especially* for his protection in times of civil commotion." And, apparently to demonstrate the proposition, the resolutions proceed: "They were secured substantially to the English people *after* years of protracted civil war, and were adopted into our Constitution at the *close* of the Revolution." Would not the demonstration have been better if it could have been truly said that these safeguards had been adopted and applied *during* the civil wars and *during* our Revolution, instead of *after* the one and at the *close* of the other? I, too, am devotedly for them *after* civil war, and *before* civil war, and at all times, "except when, in cases of rebellion or invasion, the public safety may require" their suspension. The resolutions proceed to tell us that these safeguards "have stood the test of seventy-six years of trial, under our republican system, under circumstances which show that, while they constitute the foundation of all free government, they are the elements of the enduring stability of the Republic." No one denies that they have so stood the test up to the beginning of the present Rebellion, if we except a certain occurrence at New-Orleans; nor does any one question that they will stand the same test much longer after the Rebellion closes. But these provisions of the Constitution have no application to the case we have in hand, because the arrests complained of were not made for treason—that is, not for *the* treason defined in the Constitution, and upon conviction of which the punishment is death—nor yet were they made to hold persons to answer for any capital or otherwise infamous crimes; nor were the proceedings following, in any constitutional or legal sense, "criminal prosecutions." The arrests were made on totally different grounds, and the proceedings following accorded with the grounds of the arrests. Let us consider the real case with which we are dealing, and apply to it the parts of the Constitution plainly made for such cases.

Prior to my installation here, it had been inculcated that any State had a lawful right to secede from the national Union, and that it would be expedient to exercise the right whenever the devotees of the doctrine should fail to elect a President to their own liking. I was elected contrary to their liking; and, accordingly, so far as it was legally possible, they had taken seven States out of the Union, had seized many of the United States forts, and had fired upon the United States flag, all before I was inaugurated, and, of course, before I had done any official act whatever. The Rebellion thus began soon ran into the present Civil War; and, in certain respects, it began on very unequal terms between the parties. The insurgents had been preparing for it more than thirty years, while the Government had taken no steps to resist them. The former had carefully considered all the means which could be turned to their account. It undoubtedly was a well-pondered reliance with them that, in their own unrestricted efforts to destroy Union, Constitution, and law, all together, the Government would, in great degree, be restrained by the same Constitution and law from arresting their progress. Their sympathizers pervaded all departments of the Government and nearly all communities of the people. From this material, under cover of "liberty of speech," "liberty of the press," and "habeas corpus," they hoped to keep on foot among us a most efficient corps of spies, informers, suppliers, and aiders and abettors of their cause in a thousand ways. They knew that in times such as they were inaugurating, by the Constitution itself, the "habeas corpus" might be suspended; but they also knew they had friends who would make a question as to *who* was to suspend it; meanwhile, their spies and others might remain at large to help on their cause. Or, if, as has happened, the Executive should suspend the writ, without ruinous waste of time, instances of arresting innocent persons might occur, as are always likely to occur in such cases; and then a clamor could be raised in regard to this, which might be, at least, of some service to the insurgent cause. It needed no very keen perception to discover this part of the enemy's programme, so soon as, by open hostilities, their machinery was fairly put in motion. Yet, thoroughly imbued with a reverence for the guaranteed rights of individuals, I was slow to adopt the strong measures which by degrees I have been forced to regard as being within the exceptions of the Constitution, and as indispensable to the public safety. Nothing is better known to history than that courts of justice are utterly incompetent to such cases. Civil courts are organized chiefly for trials of individuals, or, at most, a few individuals acting in concert; and this in quiet times, and on charges of crimes well defined in the law. Even in times of peace, bands of horse-thieves and robbers frequently grow too numerous and powerful for the ordinary courts of justice. But what comparison, in numbers have such bands ever borne to the insurgent sympathizers, even in many of the loyal States? Again: a jury too frequently has at least one member more ready to hang the panel than to hang the traitor. And yet, again, he who dissuades one man from volunteering, or induces one soldier to desert, weakens the Union cause as much as he who kills a Union soldier in battle. Yet this dissuasion or inducement may be so conducted as to be no defined crime of which any civil court would take cognizance.

Ours is a case of rebellion—so called by the resolutions before me—in fact, a clear, flagrant, and gigantic case of rebellion; and the provision of the Constitution that "the privilege of the writ of habeas corpus shall not be suspended, unless when, in cases of rebellion or invasion, the public safety may require it," is *the* provision which specially applies to our present case. This provision plainly attests the understanding of those who made the Constitution, that ordinary courts of justice are inadequate to "cases of rebellion"—attests their purpose that, in such cases, men may be held in custody whom the courts, acting on ordinary rules, would discharge. Habeas corpus does not discharge men who are proved to be guilty of defined crime; and its suspension is allowed by the Constitution on purpose that men may be arrested and held who cannot be proved to be guilty of defined crime, "when, in cases of rebellion or invasion, the public safety may require it." This is precisely our present case—a case of rebellion, wherein the public safety *does* require the suspension. Indeed, arrests by process of courts, and arrests in cases of rebellion, do not proceed altogether upon the same basis. The former is directed at the small per centage of ordinary and continuous perpetration of crime; while the latter is directed at sudden and extensive uprisings against the Government, which at most, will succeed or fail in no great length of time. In the latter case, arrests are made, not so much for what has been done, as for what probably would be done. The latter is more for the preventive and less for the vindictive than the former. In such cases, the purposes of men are much more easily understood than in cases of ordinary crime. The man who stands by and says nothing when the peril of his Government is discussed, cannot be misunderstood. If not hindered, he is sure to help the enemy; much more, if he talks ambiguously—talks for his country with "buts" and "ifs" and "ands." Of how little value the constitutional provisions I have quoted will be rendered, if arrests shall never be made until defined crimes shall have been committed, may be illustrated by a few notable examples. Gen. John C. Breckinridge, Gen. Robert E. Lee, Gen. Joseph E. Johnston, Gen. John B. Magruder, Gen. William B. Preston, Gen. Simon B. Buckner, and Commodore Franklin Buchanan, now occupying the very highest places in the Rebel war service, were all within the power of the Government since the Rebellion began, and were nearly as well known to be traitors then as now. Unquestionably if we had seized and held them, the insurgent cause would be much weaker. But no one of them had then committed any crime defined in the law. Every one of them, if arrested, would have been discharged on *habeas corpus* were the writ allowed to operate. In view of these and similar cases, I think the time not unlikely to come when I shall be blamed for having made too few arrests rather than too many.

By the third resolution, the meeting indicate their opinion that military arrests may be constitutional in localities where rebellion actually exists, but that such arrests are unconstitutional in localities where rebellion or insurrection does *not* actually exist. They insist that such arrests shall not be made "outside of the lines of necessary military occupation, and the scenes of insurrection." Inasmuch, however, as the Constitution itself makes no such distinction, I am unable to believe that there *is* any such constitutional distinction. I concede that the class of arrests complained of can be constitutional only when, in cases of rebellion or invasion, the public safety may require them; and I insist that in such cases they are constitutional *wherever* the public safety does require them; as well in places to which they may prevent the Rebellion extending as in those where it may be already prevailing; as well where they may restrain mischievous interference with the raising and supplying of armies to suppress the Rebellion, as where the Rebellion may actually be; as well where they may restrain the enticing men out of the army, as where they would prevent mutiny in the army; equally constitutional at all places where they will conduce to the public safety, as against the dangers of rebellion or invasion. Take the particular case mentioned by the meeting. It is asserted, in substance, that Mr. Vallandigham was, by a military commander, seized and tried "for no other reason than words addressed to a public meeting, in criticism of the course of the Administration, and in condemnation of the Military orders of the General." Now, if there be no mistake about this; if this assertion is the truth and the whole truth; if there was no other reason for the arrest, then I concede that the arrest was wrong. But the arrest, as I understand, was made for a very different reason. Mr. Vallandigham avows his hostility to the War on the part of the Union; and his arrest was made because he was laboring, with some effect, to prevent the raising of troops; to encourage desertions from the army; and to leave the Rebellion without an adequate military force to suppress it. He was not arrested because he was damaging the political prospects of the Administration, or the personal interests of the Commanding General, but because he was damaging the Army, upon the existence and vigor of which the life of the Nation depends. He was warring upon the Military, and this gave the Military constitutional jurisdiction to lay hands upon him. If Mr. Vallandigham was not damaging the military power of the country, then his arrest was made on mistake of fact, which I would be glad to correct on reasonably satisfactory evidence.

I understand the meeting, whose resolutions I am considering, to be in favor of suppressing the Rebellion by military force—by armies. Long experience has shown that armies cannot be maintained unless desertions shall be punished by the severe penalty of death. The case requires, and the law and the Constitution sanction, this punishment. Must I shoot a simple-minded soldier boy who deserts, while I must not touch a hair of a wily agitator who induces him to desert? This is none the less injurious when effected by getting a father, or brother, or friend, into a public meeting, and there working upon his feelings till he is persuaded to write the soldier boy that he is fighting in a bad cause, for a wicked Administration of a contemptible Government, too weak to arrest and punish him if he shall desert. I think that in such a case to silence the agitator, and save the boy is not only constitutional, but withal a great mercy.

If I be wrong on this question of constitutional power, my error lies in believing that certain proceedings are constitutional when, in cases of rebellion or invasion, the public safety requires them, which would not be constitutional when, in the absence of rebellion or invasion, the public safety does *not* require them: in other words, that the Constitution is not, in its application, in all respects the same, in cases of rebellion or invasion involving the public safety, as it is in time of profound peace and public security. The Constitution itself makes the distinction; and I can no more be persuaded that the Government can constitutionally take no strong measures in time of rebellion, because it can be shown that the same could not be lawfully taken in time of peace, than I can be persuaded that a particular drug is not good medicine for a sick man, because it can be shown not to be good food for a well one. Nor am I able to appreciate the danger apprehended by the meeting that the American people will, by means of military arrests during the Rebellion, lose the right of Public Discussion, the Liberty of Speech and the Press, the Law of Evidence, Trial by Jury, and Habeas Corpus, throughout the indefinite peaceful future, which I trust lies before them, any more than I am able to believe that a man could contract so strong an appetite for emetics during temporary illness as to persist in feeding upon them during the remainder of his healthful life.

In giving the resolutions that earnest consideration which you request of me, I cannot overlook the fact that the meeting speak as "Democrats." Nor can I, with full respect for their known intelligence, and the fairly presumed deliberation with which they prepared their resolutions, be permitted to suppose that this occurred by accident, or in any way other than that they preferred to designate themselves "Democrats" rather than "American citizens." In this time of national peril, I would have preferred to meet you upon a level one step higher than any party platform; because I am sure that, from such more elevated position, we could do better battle for the country we all love than we possibly can from those lower ones where, from the force of habit, the prejudices of the past, and selfish hopes of the future, we are sure to expend much of our ingenuity and strength in finding fault with, and aiming blows at each other. But, since you have denied me this, I will yet be thankful, for the country's sake, that not all Democrats have done so. He on whose discretionary judgment Mr. Vallandigham was arrested and tried is a Democrat, having no old party affinity with me; and the judge who rejected the constitutional view expressed in these resolutions, by refusing to discharge Mr. Vallandigham on habeas corpus, is a Democrat of better days than these, having received his judicial mantle at the hands of President Jackson. And still more, of all those Democrats who are nobly exposing their lives and shedding their blood on the battle-field, I have learned that many approve the course taken with Mr. Vallandigham, while I have not heard of a single one condemning it. I cannot assert that there are none such. And the name of President Jackson recalls an instance of pertinent history: After the battle of New-Orleans, and while the fact that the treaty of peace had been concluded was well known in the city, but before official knowledge of it had arrived, Gen. Jackson still maintained martial or military law.

Now, that it could be said the war was over, the clamor against martial law, which had existed from the first, grew more furious. Among other things, a Mr. Louiallier published a denunciatory newspaper article. Gen. Jackson arrested him. A lawyer by the name of Morel procured the United States Judge Hall to issue a writ of habeas corpus to release Mr. Louiallier. Gen. Jackson arrested both the lawyer and the judge. A Mr. Hollander ventured to say of some part of the matter that "it was a dirty trick." Gen. Jackson arrested him. When the officer undertook to serve the writ of habeas corpus, Gen. Jackson took it from him, and sent him away with a copy. Holding the judge in custody a few days, the General sent him beyond the limits of his encampment, and set him at liberty, with an order to remain till the ratification of peace should be regularly announced, or until the British should have left the Southern coast. A day or two more elapsed, the ratification of a treaty of peace was regularly announced, and the judge and others were fully liberated. A few days more, and the judge called Gen. Jackson into court and fined him $1,000 for having arrested him and the others named. The General paid the fine, and there the matter rested for nearly thirty years, when Congress refunded principal and interest. The late Senator Douglas, then in the House of Representatives, took a leading part in the debates, in which the constitutional question was much discussed. I am not prepared to say whom the journals would show to have voted for the measure.

It may be remarked: First, that we had the same Constitution then as now; secondly, that we then had a case of invasion, and now we have a case of rebellion; and, thirdly, that the permanent right of the People to Public Discussion, the Liberty of Speech and the Press, the Trial by Jury, the Law of Evidence, and the Habeas Corpus, suffered no detriment whatever by that conduct of Gen. Jackson, or its subsequent approval by the American Congress.

And yet, let me say that, in my own discretion, I do not know whether I would have ordered the arrest of Mr. Vallandigham. While I cannot shift the responsibility from myself, I hold that, as a general rule, the commander in the field is the better judge of the necessity in any particular case. Of course, I must practice a general directory and revisory power in the matter.

One of the resolutions expresses the opinion of the meeting that arbitrary arrests will have the effect to divide and distract those who should be united in suppressing the Rebellion, and I am specifically called on to discharge Mr. Vallandigham. I regard this as, at least, a fair appeal to me on the expediency of exercising a Constitutional power which I think exists. In response to such appeal, I have to say, it gave me pain when I learned that Mr. Vallandigham had been arrested—that is, I was pained that there should have seemed to be a necessity for arresting him—and that it will afford me great pleasure to discharge him so soon as I can, by any means, believe the public safety will not suffer by it. I further say that, as the war progresses, it appears to me, opinion, and action, which were in great confusion at first, take shape, and fall into more regular channels, so that the necessity for strong dealing with them gradually decreases. I have every reason to desire that it should cease altogether, and far from the least is my regard for the opinions and wishes of those who, like the meeting at Albany, declare their purpose to sustain the Government in every constitutional and lawful measure to suppress the Rebellion. Still, I must continue to do so much as may seem to be required by the public safety.

A. LINCOLN

THE VICKSBURG SIEGE CONTINUES:
MISSISSIPPI, JUNE 1863

William Henry Harrison Clayton to Amos and Grace Clayton and to George Washington Clayton and John Quincy Adams Clayton

The 19th Iowa Infantry was sent downriver from Missouri in June 1863 to join the Union forces investing Vicksburg and assigned to the Seventeenth Corps, commanded by Major General James B. McPherson. William Henry Harrison Clayton, the clerk of Company H, described the siege to his parents and to his younger brothers.

Camp of 19th Iowa Infantry
In the rear of Vicksburg
June 18th, 1863

Dear Father & Mother:

Having a few spare moments, I thought that I would improve them by writing and give you an account of our movements since leaving Young's Point, LA. at which point I last wrote.

We left there on the 12th, marching across the bend, and reached the river 3 or 4 miles below Vicksburg and in full view of the town.

We have 5 or 6 steamboats below Vicksburg that are used for carrying troops, supplies, etc. across to Warrenton. Some of these run the blockade and are pretty well used up. The *Forest Queen* is a nice sidewheel boat, the others are stern-wheelers. The ram *Switzerland* was there and is as good as ever. When running the blockade a ball passed into one of her boilers and let the steam out in a hurry but did no other damage. Several gunboats are stationed there to watch the river. The *Tuscumbia* is a large boat and looks like a large turtle with its back out of water.

We crossed to Warrenton 6 or 8 miles below Vicksburg, on

the *Silver Wave*. Her guards had been nearly all torn off some how and was a hard looking boat.

At Warrenton we remained over night. Here I saw 3 large guns that were captured by our forces at Grand Gulf. They are having them brought up and will soon have them planted opposite some of the Rebel forts here. The Rebels had a pretty strong earthwork at Warrenton & places fixed with railroad iron and logs to protect the men. All is destroyed now.

We first used our shelter tents at Warrenton. They do well enough to keep off the sun but will not turn much rain. Each tent is composed of two pieces about 3 yards square and is for two men each of whom carries his piece and one pole each about 4 ft. long, when the two pieces composing it are put together. When we pitch tents we button the two pieces together, fix the "sticks" in the center and stake down two ends. The sides are open and permit the air to circulate freely!

On the 13th we marched 3 or 4 miles towards our lines and camped that night. On the 14th we took our present position, to the left of the center. We are camped *under* a hill side, to shelter us from the Rebel shells which come over occasionally. It is not a mile straight across to the Rebel line. We, that is Co. "H" and 5 other companies of the 19th were on picket yesterday & last night.

We acted more as skirmishers than anything else. We were strung along behind logs and stumps and kept popping away whenever we would see a shadow of a Rebel, our guns with the sights raised to 300 yards would strike their outer works every time, some of their pickets were not more than 150 yards from us, but they had holes in the ground so that we would not see them and could only tell where they were by the smoke when they discharged their guns. The discharge of small arms is almost constant along the line, but they don't do much damage on either side. A fellow has to keep his head pretty low though, for some ball would whistle by, very close. Occasionally the heavy artillery takes a turn and makes things "git."

I and one of our boys yesterday, saw 5 or 6 "Rebs" on their works some distance off, and thought that we would see how close we could shoot to them. We raised the gun sights to 800 yards. He shot and we could notice that one got out of that place in a hurry. I then shot at them standing all together in an embrasure of a fort, the dust flew up close by them. It was not more than 2 minutes before *boom* went a gun and a shell came crashing over us. They fired three times but hit no one.

Our forces along this part of the line have advanced several hundred yards, and will be apt to go farther, not however without digging in on the right and center. Our boys are close under their guns, so close that they cannot fire them. Some of the 15th Iowa boys have been down to see their friends. They said that they had worked in the trenches not more than 20 yds. from their forts.

I expect the people of the North are getting impatient because Grant does not take Vicksburg, but if they were here for themselves they would not wonder at the delay. It is certainly the roughest country I ever seen. The hills are not so very high, but the whole country is nothing but a succession of hills and hollows about like some places on the Buckles farm.

The Rebels have forts thrown up about 200 or 300 yds. apart all along their line, with heavy guns mounted and forts in the rear of these, making the place almost impregnable. I do not believe that another place in the country could be found that is so naturally fortified. They had forts outside of our present lines that they evacuated, that would have been hard to take. The hills in places rise abruptly, and look almost as though they had been drawn up purposefully for a fort. The boys who have been here since the siege began appear to be in good spirits. They say that it will be almost impossible for Johnston to get in with reinforcements. The timber has been cut down for miles and we have a large force on Big Black watching him. I don't see what Pemberton is holding out so long for. It looks almost impossible for reinforcements to reach him. I suppose he will hold out until his provisions give out, and that may be sometime longer. Deserters say that they are living on quarter rations. The weather here is right warm. The magnolia trees are in full bloom. There is lots of them in the woods. I saw some green figs a day or two ago. Peaches are nearly full size. The blackberries are ripe in this part of the world. Corn is out in tassel in places. I have not seen much around here but I suppose there is plenty of it growing further back.

I was a good deal surprised to see the cane here grow where

it does. I always thought that grew in swamps or in the low grounds, but here it grows on the hills. Where we are camped it is thick, some of it 25 or 30 feet long.

The boys are all well at present. I had an idea that the change would make us sick, but it has not made much of a difference in the sick list yet. John Stone is one of our company cooks. The cooks do nothing but get our "grub" ready for eating, have no other duty to perform. Mooney is cooking for the col. and captain. He is a very good hand at the business. There is a little insect that bothers us a great deal. They are called "jiggers," "chickers," or something like it. They are little red things not bigger than a pin point. They stick like a tick and raise little places like muskuits bites. As I expected the furlough business has *played out*, I suppose no more will be granted until after Vicksburg is taken.

Give my respects to all friends.
I remain your affectionate son,
W. H. H. Clayton

Camp of the 19th Iowa
In the rear of Vicksburg
June 28, 1863

Dear Brothers:

I received John's letter of the 7th a few days ago and was glad to hear from you again.

I have nothing of interest to write, but thought that I would send a few lines to let you know that I am well and getting along finely.

We have been here two weeks. Nothing of especial importance has transpired along our part of the line.

We have mounted several siege guns since we came here. They fire on the Rebels occasionally and make them hunt their holes. The Rebels fired at us considerably for a few days after our arrival here but since then have not fired much, only when our guns opened upon them, and for some days past they fired none at all.

Yesterday however they opened on our battery from a mortar that they had planted under a hill so that our guns could not reach them. Our camp is in range of their shells and some that came over the battery made us lay "kinder" close. The pieces flew around considerably but luckily no one was hurt.

There has been no firing on either side today. It is said that our gun boats got range of the mortar that disturbed us and silenced it. I hope it is so for it is not pleasant to hear shells buzzing around. The blamed things are apt to burst and the pieces go every direction. We have been on picket 4 times since we came here. The last two times we were up or awake all night. One night it rained the whole night slowly. I tell you, I would not have taken a good deal for my gum blanket that night. We laid within a few hundred yards of a brigade of Rebels, so we have learned since from prisoners. There was nearly two companies of us, we were there to prevent a movement on our guns. The 94th Ill. and 20th Wis. have taken 20 or 30 prisoners since we came here by charging upon their (the Rebels) rifle pits. But such work don't pay. The last *sortie* of this kind was by a company of the 94th. They took 8 men, and had one mortally wounded, he died an hour or two later, and another wounded so that it will render him unfit for service. The Rebels could have the rifle-pit defended by eight more men, right away, for it was not held by our men. Thus by the operation we lost two men and the Rebels got rid of feeding 8. I think the more men we can keep in there, the sooner will it surrender. There is no telling anything about how long it will hold out. Some prisoners & deserters say that they have not got much provision and others that they have enough to last 2 or 3 months. There has been no mail received here for several days. It is reported in camp that letters from here do not go further than Memphis. I think if such was the case we would not be allowed to send them from camp. I would like very much to hear how the Rebel raid into Pennsylvania terminated. We have no news later than June 17th. It takes a letter at least 10 days to come from Iowa here. We are in as bad a position to get news as we were when at Forsyth away down in Missouri. It is 10 or 12 miles around our line and we know no more what is going on at the other end of the line than you do. Sometimes it is reported that they have had a big fight on the right or in the center, and they have heard that we have had a battle here when there was nothing of the kind. We would like to get the St. Louis daily papers so that we could get news from Vicksburg!

The weather is very warm especially so in the sun. We lay around in the shade the most of the time when not on duty. The boys stand the change much better than I expected, but of course the sick list is larger than it was at Salem. Co. "H" has 47 men for duty, and 7 or 8 sick. The water here is not very good. We get it by digging 10 ft. It goes rather hard after being used to good spring water. The Chequest boys stand it "Bully" all being able for their rations.

There has been an oven erected here, and all our flour is baked and issued in loaves by the quartermaster. I like it much better than the biscuits our cooks make. I never did like hot or warm bread, but have had to get used to it, and sometimes glad to get anything in the bread line. We get half our bread rations in hard crackers.

Col. Kent was honored today by a visit from Mrs. Wittemeyer, U.S. Sanitary Commission agent, from Iowa. I suppose she is on a tour of inspection. Gen. Herron was also here today.

Well I must quit writing for the present. I want you to write whenever you can.

I remain your affectionate brother,
W. H. H. Clayton

"A SOLDIER NEVER KNOWS":
MISSISSIPPI, JUNE 1863

Charles B. Haydon: Journal, June 20, 1863

A veteran of the Peninsula campaign, Second Bull Run, and Fredericksburg, Captain Charles B. Haydon was a company commander in the 2nd Michigan Infantry. In March 1863 his regiment was transferred from Virginia to Kentucky, and in mid-June it was sent up the Yazoo River fifteen miles from Vicksburg to help guard against a possible Confederate attempt to relieve the city. Haydon recorded his impressions the day after his arrival at his new post.

JUNE 20, 1863   We are really down South—Latitude 32° 20′, a degree south of Charleston, on a line with the great desert of Africa. Everything looks new and at this point not very pleasing. The hills are not high but the ground is in all conceivable shapes & so full of ravines as to be almost impassable. The water is brackish & bad, very bad. The woods are oak, basswood, sycamore, cottonwood, magnolia, palmetto &c. They are so full of underbrush, briars, nettles, poisonous weeds and such like that it is very unpleasant & difficult to get through them. The trees are loaded with the long grey Southern moss which hangs from the limbs in clusters & sheets from 2 to 10 feet in length (perpendicular) and swings loose in the wind. This gives to everything a sort of dull sombre appearance. It looks old, very old, as though everything was on the decline.

Canebrakes such as we buy at home for fish poles are very abundant & are used by the men for almost everything. There are some *alligators*, a good many snakes, lizards everywhere, plenty of mosquitoes, flies, bugs, tarantulas, horned frogs & other infernal machines too numerous to mention. I have not been far into the woods. I went up to the edge once to day & very cautiously looked in a little way then walked off. I am not much afraid of snakes but I do not wish to provoke any unnecessary collision. They say that in the woods snakes & lizards tumble down on your head every few steps but could not swear to that. There are blackberries & wild plums in abundance, ripe & inviting.

There was terrific firing at Vicksburgh this m'g commencing before daylight. How I wish we could go down to the front where there is something doing. I saw Lt. Col. May and several other acquaintances from Michigan.

Our Regt. got very drunk on the way here. Moore and Montague had their hands full with Co. E. I have had experience enough in loading drunken soldiers onto boats & cars. They act like devils. If they should act so when sober it would not take long to adjust matters but in this case you have to tolerate some things which you would not at any other time. The men know perfectly well that as a rule the officers want to get drunk as bad as they do & that if it were not for the responsibility & their presence they would.

Still I do not believe that many of them would drink much after they had been out of the army a few days. A soldier never knows one day where he may be the next & his hold on the future being so uncertain he crowds the present to the utmost. "Eat drink & be merry for to morrow you die." I know by experience how powerfully those words appeal to the desires & if I do not indulge in wine as others do I presume it is only because other things please me more.

After some months of hard fare you arrive in a city. There is no one there who knows you except comrades who never tell tales. You have money & opportunity. Everything within you says there is no law or restraint here. Do as you please. "Let joy be unconfined." It may be your last chance. Everyone seems to think you are doing exactly right & to be anxious to help you in all your undertakings. Be careful & you will meet your Chaplain or hear his voice in the next room. But enough of this. Those who have tried it know all about it & those who have not can never learn from mere description.

There must be an increase of sickness if we remain here long. I am not much afraid of disease but can see the possibility of hard times ahead. The darkies are jubilant. "God bless Massa Lincum" say they all. They do nothing now but gather blackberries & plums to sell together with their master's property to soldiers. I saw a planter try to stop one who threw down his hoe & was walking off. He called out to him "where are you going?" "Oh I'se gwine to 'list—yah, yah, yah" was the reply & off he went & three others after him.

Their employment as soldiers is looked upon here with much more favor than in the Army of the Potomac. They are pretty well posted & are nearly all anxious to fight. It is thought here that they will make good soldiers. I find that my late journey amounts to about 2000 miles & that of the Regt. to about 1200 miles. There is no further need of troops in this vicinity.

"THEY HAVE SOWED THE WIND":
MISSISSIPPI, JUNE 1863

William T. Sherman to Ellen Ewing Sherman

Sherman wrote to his wife several days after Grant assigned him command of the forces guarding against a possible Confederate attempt to relieve Vicksburg.

Camp on Bear Creek,
20 miles N.W. of Vicksburg.
June 27, 1863.

Dearest Ellen,

I am out here studying a most complicated Geography and preparing for Joe Johnston if he comes to the relief of Vicksburg. As usual I have to leave my old companions & troops in the trenches of Vicksburg, and deal with strange men, but I find all willing & enthusiastic. Although the weather is intensely hot, I have ridden a great deal, and think I know pretty well the weak and strong points of this extended Line of Circumvallation, and if Johnston comes I think he will have a pretty hard task to reach Vicksburg, although from the broken nature of the country he may feign at many points and attack but on one. Black River the real Line is now so low it can be forded at almost any point and I prefer to fight him at the Ridges along which all the Roads lead. Of these there are several some of which I have blocked with fallen trees and others left open for our own purposes, and which will be open to him if he crosses over—Our accounts of his strength & purposes are [   ] as the [   ] of fact of deserters & spies [   ] are. I [   ] to be governed by what I suppose he will do, under the pressure of opinion that must be brought to bear on him to relieve a brave & beleaguered Garrison. I suppose he made large calculations on obstructing the River at some point above us, and it seems the Boats coming down & going up receive shots at various points along the River, but thus far reinforcements and supplies have reached us without serious check. My Line extends from the Railroad Bridge on Black River, around to Haines Bluff, both of which are entrenched. I have some works at intermediate points, but if Johnston crosses the fight will be mostly by detachments along the narrow Ridges with which the country abounds, and along which alone Roads can be made.

The siege of Vicksburg progresses. From my camp I hear the booming of cannon, telling of continued battering. My trenches had connected with the main ditch before I left, and had I remained I think by this time we should have made a push for the Bastion in my front. I hear every day, that things remain status quo. I left Charley at Head Qrs. to continue his inspections and Hugh in command of his Brigade which is on the main approach. He say he writes often to his wife and to you all. [   ] I have [   ]—He is very stubborn & opinionated, but has his Brigade in good order, which is the only test to which I refer in official & military matters. I must not favor him or Charley unfairly, as it would do them no good & me much harm. You will feel sure that each has as much of my thoughts and affections as can be spared for the thousands subject to my orders & care. My military family numbers by the tens of thousands and all must know that they enjoy a part of my thoughts and attention. With officers & soldiers I know how to deal but am willing to admit ignorance as to the People who make opinion according to their contracted Knowledge & biassed prejudices, but I know the time is coming when the opinion of men "not in arms at the countrys crisis, when her calamities call for every man capable of bearing arms" will be light as to that of men who first, last & all the time were in the war. I enclose a slip which came to me by accident, describing our Leaders here. Were I to erase the names you would not recognize one, although the narrative meant to be fair & impartial.

I meet daily incidents which would interest you but these you will have to draw out on cross examination when we meet —I find here a Mrs. Klein only child of Mrs. Day of New Orleans & niece of Tom Bartley [   ] and will continue to befriend them. They have a son in the Confederate Army now in Vicksburg, a lad some 18 years of age. The day I approached Vicksburg, my advance Guard caught a Confederate soldier and a negro, servant to George Klein, carrying a letter to the father at his Country refuge near here. Of course the negro was sent north and the letter read. It contained much useful information, and among other things he described the loss of the Battery of Guns at Champion Hill in which he used the Expression, "We lost our Guns, but they will do the Yankees no good, for we broke up the carriages and hid the Guns in a Ravine" so this boy of Ohio birth is not very loyal, though he was with John Sherman during his Electioneering Canvas which resulted in Lincolns Election. Mr. Klein father continually exclaims, "they cant hold out much longer—their provisions must be out &c." but the enemy in Vicksburg in my judgment shows no abatement of vigorous resistance or short food—with every house in sight of our lines marked with the Hospital Flag—Orange Yellow. We cant show a hand or cap above our rifle pits without attracting a volley. But of course there must be an end to all things & I think if Johnston do not make a mighty effort to relieve Vicksburg in a week they will cave in.

I would at this moment be in the saddle, but have sent a Brigade down to Black River to examine a certain Ford where one of our Pickets was fired on last night by Cavalry. I rather think two of our patrols came together & mistook. Nobody was hurt but I must watch closely, as I know Joe Johnston will give me little time to combine after he moves. He may approach from the North North East or East, all of which routes I am watching closely, but it will be necessary to draw from two quarters to reinforce one, and it will be exceedingly difficult to judge from signs the Real point from the Feints. Their cavalry is so much better than ours, that in all quick movements they have a decided advantage.

As I am now on my second sheet, and as I am listening for signs of action at a Ford in the bottom 3 miles off, I might as well go on and punish you with a surfeit after the manner of your affectionate son & uncle, and bosom friend, Lt. Col. Charley Ewing. My Head Qrs. here are in a tent by the Road side, where one forks down to Bear Creek & the other goes along down to Black River direct. I have with me the invariable Hill who still puts me on a damned allowance of segars & whiskey & insists on blacking my boots & brushing my clothes in & out of season. Boyer my orderly is also here, with my horses Dolly, Abner, Sam and a new one recently presented me by General Steele called Duke. Dolly carries me when I explore —Sam & Duke when I expect to be shot at. Yesterday morning with Dolly, Boyer, McCoy & Hill aids and a small escort I started on a circuit visiting outposts & pickets—At a Mrs. Fox's I found as is the case of all farms here a bevy of women waiting patiently the fate of husbands & sons penned up in Vicksburg—one of them a Mrs. Eggleston, whose pretty children I noticed asked me if I were the Genl. Sherman of New Orleans—of course not—She asked because a Mrs. Wilkinson was a great friend of his—What Mrs. Wilkinson? a Mrs. Wilkinson of New Orleans. Where was she? spending the day at another Mrs. Fox, Parson Fox about a mile further on—As my route lay that way I rode up the yard of Parson Fox. A company of Iowa men lay in the shade on picket, and about a dozen ladies sat on the broad balcony. I rode up close saluted the ladies & inquired for Mrs. Wilkinson a small old lady answered— I asked if she were of Plaquemine Parish—Yes—Where was her husband the General? Killed on the Plains of Manassas, fighting for his Country," with a paroxism of tears at tearing open the old wound, and all the women looking at me as though I had slain him with my own hand—I knew him well, he was a direct descendant of the General Wilkinson of the old wars, and was once a client of your father, I think in the famous Land case of Penrose St. Louis. He had a son at Alexandria about whom we corresponded a good deal. When I left Louisiana I regarded him as an Union man and had forgotten that he was killed at Manassas at the first Battle—After the old lady had cooled down a little I inquired for the Son. He is in Vicksburg, and the mother has got this near to watch his fate. Do, oh do General Sherman spare my son, in one breath and in another, that Lincoln was a tyrant and we only Murderers, Robbers, plunderers and defilers of the houses and altars of an innocent & outraged People. She and all the women were real secesh, bitter as gall & yet Oh do General Sherman protect my son. The scene set all the women crying, and Dolly & I concluded to go into the more genial atmosphere out in the Fields & Woods. I doubt if History affords a parallel of the deep & bitter enmity of the women of the South. No one who sees them & hears them but must feel the intensity of their hate. Not a man is seen—nothing but women, with houses plundered, fields open to the cattle & horses, pickets lounging on every porch, and desolation sown broadcast—Servants all gone and women & children bred in luxury, beautiful & accomplished begging with one breath for the soldiers Ration and in another praying that the Almighty or Joe Johnston will come & kill us, the despoilers of their houses and all that is sacred—Why cannot they look back to the day & the hour when I a stranger in Louisiana begged & implored them to pause in their course, that secession was death, was everything fatal, and that their seizure of the public arsenals was an insult that the most abject nation must resent or pass down to future ages an object of pity & scorn. Vicksburg contains many of my old pupils & friends. Should it fall into our hands I will treat them with kindness, but they have sowed the wind & must reap the whirlwind. Until they lay down their arms, and submit to the rightful authority of their Government, they must not appeal to me for mercy or favors—The weather is very hot, though the nights are cool—wild plums abounded, have ripened and are gone. Blackberries are now as abundant as ever an army could ask, and are most excellent—Apples & peaches & figs are ripening, and of all these there will be an abundance even for our host. Corn too is in silk & tassel and soon Roasting ears will give our soldiers an additional tendency to sickness—advice, orders & remonstrance are all idle. Soldiers are like children, and eat, eat all the time. Water is very poor & scarce on the hills but is found in moving brooks down in the chasms and hollows of Clear & Bear Creeks near which all my Camps are—I have written Minnie & Willy & sent the latter some fishing poles from the "Battle Field"—Tell Tom & Lizzy they must write me also. Tell them all that actually I have hardly time to write to you and I get tired of writing more than I used to—Love to all yrs. ever

       Sherman

INVADING THE NORTH:
MARYLAND AND PENNSYLVANIA, JUNE 1863

Edmund DeWitt Patterson:
Journal, June 24–30, 1863

Lieutenant Edmund DeWitt Patterson of the 9th Alabama Infantry had fought at Marye's Heights and Salem Church during the Chancellorsville campaign. He marched north in June as part of the Third Corps of the Army of Northern Virginia, commanded by Lieutenant General A. P. Hill. The advance forces of Lee's army defeated the Union garrison at Winchester in the Shenandoah Valley on June 15 and crossed into Pennsylvania on June 22.

Near Boonesboro, Md. Wednesday the 24th. This morning bright and early we crossed the Potomac at Mill Ford one mile below Shepherdtown. The water from three to four feet deep. It was a little cool but we were all in such fine spirits that we didn't mind it. We came up on the hill near Sharpesburg and halted for an hour or two; while there General Wright and staff rode into town and all came near being captured. All escaped but the General's son, who could not ride fast on account of the loss of a leg which he parted with at Manassas. The squad who made the charge escaped before our infantry could reach them. Passed through Sharpesburg which is a hard looking dilapidated old town, and which still shows the marks of the battle fought there. The battle of Sharpsburg, or Antietam as the Yankees have it, will long be remembered. We have had an easy march today, and are now camping in a pretty meadow, in a valley three miles from Boonesboro.

Hagerstown, Md. Thurs. 25th. Passed through Boonesboro this morning just as the sun was rising bright and glorious over the South Mountain. Everything on the road looks strange to us coming as we do from the desolate fields of Virginia. Here we see houses, barns filled with grain, fine stock etc. Today we met a fine large drove of beef cattle going to the rear. Some of the boys who have fully realized the effects of the war at their own houses are fairly itching to retaliate, but Gen'l. Lee's order issued the morning we crossed into Md. is too strict. The majority of the people seem to be "loyal" tho we find quite a number who are with us heart and soul, though not bodily. Fungston seems to contain quite a number of families who are Southern sympathizers. We reached this place at one o'clock this evening, and quite a number of the boys have been in the city. I preferred to remain in camp.

Two miles from Green Castle, Penn. Friday the 26th of June. This morning Capt. Harry Lee, Jim Crow and I left camps about daylight and came into the city of Hagerstown. Had an old fashioned time. Patronized the barber shop, hotel, and saloon, and as it bade fair to rain all day we laid in a supply of the "needful." About 8 o'clock our command passed through Middlebury. Crossed the Pennsylvania and Maryland line at 11 o'clock precisely. Jim Crow, Van Whitehead and I persuaded an old gentleman to show us exactly where the line ran and then standing with one foot in Maryland and the other in Pennsylvania, we finished the contents of a canteen, drinking some pretty heavy toasts. Green Castle seems to be a pretty little town but intensely "loyal." It would probably be more so, if it had passed through what many of the towns in the South have, tried with fire. Gen'l. A. P. Hill passed us on the march looking ready for a fight.

Saturday the 27th. On the march again. Passed through Marion and Chambersburg. While passing through the latter place Gen'l. Lee rode up the column speaking kindly to acquaintances and passed on. The boys never cheer him, but pull off their hats and worship. The females of Chambersburg seem to be very spiteful, make faces, sing "Rally round the flag," wave their little banners etc. I think if they had a hole burned out in their town about the size and extent of that which the Yankees burned in Florence or Athens, Alabama, these patriotic females would not be quite so saucy. A widow in the place discovered the knapsack of her deceased husband in the command, she wished it and the soldier gave it to her. He had picked it up on the battlefield of "Gaine's Mills," where we fought the "squirrel tail rifles." I suppose that her husband has gone to that home from whence etc., such is war. We reached this place, Fayetteville, a little before sun down, and Jim and I went out and took supper with a good old Pennsylvania farmer; plenty of everything, especially apple butter, the first I have tasted since I left Ohio.

Fayetteville, Sunday Evening, 28th. I have been down town nearly all day sauntering about up and down the streets. No preaching either in camps or in town. Some of the boys have been "capturing" chickens. It is against positive orders, but I would not punish one of them, for as Joe McMurray says, it's not half as bad as they did, to his mother and sisters in Alabama, for they not only took such things, but took the rings from his sisters' fingers, and earrings from their ears, besides cursing and abusing them. It is well that Joe isn't General in Chief for he would try what virtue there is in fire, as well as the sword.

Tues. 30th. Still at Fayetteville, but there is something on the tapis, for yesterday Heath's and Pender's divisions left, and have gone in the direction of Gettysburg. I took dinner yesterday at the hotel, and at night Jim Crow, Dick Hobbs and I went out about two miles into the country to get supper, and had a most magnificent time. The young lady was Union but called herself a "copperhead." I would not mind being bitten by her a few times. On our way back as we were coming through the town we serenaded the citizens with "The Bonnie Blue Flag," "The Sunny South Forever," etc. Don't think it was appreciated though. Hood's and McLaws' divisions passed through town late this evening. Met several of my old friends in the 4th Alabama. Also saw Cousin Frank. Had but little time to talk to him. Was on brigade guard today, and kept things *straight* around the hotel, took dinner there, and so won the heart of the old landlord that he filled my canteen with cherry brandy. I pronounce him a "gentleman and scholar and a judge of the article."

"A VERY DIFFERENT RACE":
PENNSYLVANIA, JUNE 1863

Lafayette McLaws to Emily McLaws

A West Point graduate who joined the Confederate army in 1861 and fought in the Seven Days' Battles, Antietam, Fredericksburg, and Chancellorsville, Major General Lafayette McLaws commanded one of the three divisions in the First Corps of the Army of Northern Virginia, led by Lieutenant General James Longstreet. When McLaws wrote to his wife on June 28, Longstreet's and A. P. Hill's corps were camped around Chambersburg, while the Second Corps, commanded by Lieutenant General Richard Ewell, was divided between Carlisle and York. After learning on the night of June 28 that the Army of the Potomac had left northern Virginia and reached Frederick, Maryland, Lee issued orders for his army to reunite at either Cashtown, seventeen miles east of Chambersburg, or at Gettysburg, another eight miles farther to the east.

Head Quarters Division
June 28'/63
Camp near Chambersburg, Pa

My Dear Emily
My command arrived at this place, this morning at 10 oclock, and joined the rest of the Corps camped near this place.

We left Martinsburg in Virginia on the 26th at five oclock in the morning, and fording the river, camped three Brigades near Wmsport and one brigade with my artillery near Hagerstown. I camped in an open lot in the town. The ford at Wmsport is a very good one the men crossing without difficulty. The Chesapeake and Ohio Canal which runs along the river bank on the north side, was dry, the aquaduct having been blown up. The track of the Baltimore and Ohio Canal running along the canal was also destroyed—from Martinsburg to the river, eleven miles, the houses were all closed, the curtains drawn and the people either absent or invisible—showing an evident dislike to our cause. It was remarked as we went into Martinsburg that the magnificent farm of the Honl. Charles J

Faulkner who was the Adjutant General of General Jackson was in a beautiful state of cultivation, not a stone of his fences injured and the laborers at work with their teams, collecting the clover which has been cut and cured. While on the other side of the road, the fences were down, the crops destroyed, the grounds trampled and everything wearing the appearance of places which had long ago been deserted and devastated. The secret was out, when we visited the town and was told that Mrs Faulkner had not long since returned from Washington, and on the evening our troops first entered the town she had issued tickets for a large party to be given to the Yankee officers. Her daughters were also constantly visiting the Yankee families and were being visited by them and the Yankee officers generally, and that the greatest cordiality existed between them.

The farms we saw lying in waste were those of southern families who were not so devoted to Yankeedom. There was no welcome given us in Martinsburg, except by a very few and those of the ladies who exhibited any cordiality I noticed were clothed in silks, and de lames & muslins, and all the finery of a thriving Yankee town. Many women & children made faces at us as we marched along, and although we could not hear them, we could see their mouths moving, and from their expressions knew they were giving us their maledictions. As we crossed into Williamsport, the people were more friendly but yet all the shops were closed and the houses generally deserted or exhibiting no signs of being inhabited. One lady said she was delighted to see us. Shook hands very cordially. Said she expected to be sent over the river if the enemy should ever return but did not care. Shortly after I went to the window to get some water and seeing a boy of nine or ten in the room with the blue blouse of a Yankee. I Said "You are a Yankee Sir"; the boy said nothing but held down his head. The young lady before mentioned said to him "Speak up buddy and tell him you are no Yankee." "Yes but I am one" asserted the boy. And I remarked "Children take their opinions from their older sisters and brothers & they always tell the truth" and rode away. The family within looking as if they had been caught in a falsehood.

I camped three Brigades near Wmsport and one near Hagerstown with four batteries and camped in the town myself

(Hagerstown) where a good many persons called to see me and I was invited to supper and breakfast. I went to supper and had nothing better than I usually have at home; in camp, did not mention the breakfast. Was introduced to Mr Roman formerly Member of Congress from Maryland, and went to his house for a few minutes. Found him a very polished gentleman, and his wife and niece good specimens of southern ladies. I was very glad to meet them as I thus had in my mind to contrast between the southern gentleman and ladies and the very different species I soon encountered. As I crossed the line into Pennsylvania. At Green Castle on the road to Chambersburg. Several young ladies were assembled engaged in scoffing at our men as they passed, but they were treated with contempt or derision. I heard of nothing witty said by any of them. It was made evident however that they were not ladies in the southern acceptations of the word. The men I spoke to acknowledged that the brutalities practiced by their troops, upon the southern people, fully justified our retaliating and were surprised at our moderation—the poorer classes told me that our troops behaved better to them than their own did. Arrived at & marched through Chambersburg on 28th, a town of five thousand inhabitants perhaps more. And camped two miles east of it on the Harrisburg Road. Then arrived in camp on the 29th & destroyed about four miles of the rail road leading then to Harrisburg. The people of Chambersburg are decidedly. The men dare not show it but by their looks, the women tried to be sarcastic on various occasions but succeeded in being vulgar only. They are a very different race from the southern. There is a coarsness in their manners and looks and a twang in their voices—which grates harshly on the senses of our men; the distinction of class, the poor & sick is very marked. Every one speaks for peace at any price, and since war has been brought to their own homes, they look desponding to the last degree, and begin to believe that they have been vastly deceived by engaging in it— I have found no one to speak of Lincoln as a man of either capacity or patriotism, every one even the women think he is under abolition influence entirely, and they assert boldly that freedom should not be the lot of the negro. To day I moved camp seven miles on the Gettysburg Road, to Greenwood a small village, sending one brigade two miles on to Caledonia, where Thadeus Stevens, the abolition Member of Congress from Penna who introduced the bill for the employment of negro troops, had large iron works. They were burned by our troops however, and are now in ashes & total ruin—

My division mail rider was caught by the enemy, in Hagerstown on his way here with letters.

When you write, therefore you must be cautious and particular. This may be captured also & I am particularly cautious as you may observe.

You may send this letter to WmR to be returned to you.

Give much love to the children, and ask them to write me, also to sister Laura & Bet. —Good night and much love from your devoted husband L.

CHANGING COMMANDERS:
MARYLAND, JUNE 1863

Alpheus S. Williams to Irene and Mary Williams

When Lee began to move his army away from Fredericksburg, Hooker proposed crossing the Rappahannock and advancing on Richmond, but Lincoln directed him to instead make Lee's army his objective. Hooker started moving his army north on June 13 along a route that kept it between Lee's forces and Washington and began crossing the Potomac on June 25. By then, the President had become frustrated by Hooker's requests for reinforcements and his inability to work with General-in-Chief Henry W. Halleck. When a dispute with Halleck led Hooker to submit his resignation, Lincoln accepted it and named Major General George G. Meade to replace him. Brigadier General Alpheus S. Williams, a former officer in the Michigan militia who commanded a division in the Twelfth Corps, wrote to his daughters about the change in command.

Frederick, Md., June 29, 1863.
My Dear Daughters:

I have a moment in the office of Dr. Steiner of the Sanitary Commission to tell you where I am. We left Leesburg on Friday last, the 26th inst., and marched across the river at Edwards Ferry on pontoons and encamped that night at the mouth of the Monocacy. The next day we marched to within a mile of Knoxville, which Rene will remember is within two miles of the Longbridges on the Baltimore & Ohio Railroad, where we generally took the railroad for Baltimore. The Saturday's march was too tedious and fatiguing for me to go to the Longbridges. Besides, I did not get my brigades in camp until after dark. The whole line of march was crowded by baggage wagons and trains. I expected to march through Sandy Hook towards Williamsport but during the night was ordered to march my division towards Frederick. I reached this place yesterday afternoon, when a change of commanders was announced, Meade superceding Hooker.

It was intimated that we should remain at this place a day or so, but at 2.30 this morning I was awakened by a messenger ordering my division to march towards Taneytown at 5 A.M. I was camped in a fine grove and had a great desire for sleep after three days' fatiguing marches, but there is no help under orders. Besides, we are filled with an idea that the Rebels are getting into Pennsylvania, and of course we are bound to go on, cost what of human flesh it may. For myself, I am rejoiced at the change of commanders. I have said very little in my letters, but enough for you to guess that I had no confidence in Hooker after Chancellorsville. I can say now, that if we had had a commander of even ordinary merit at that place the army of Jackson would have been annihilated. I cannot conceive of greater imbecility and weakness than characterized that campaign from the moment Hooker reached Chancellorsville and took command.

I am not much of a military genius, but if I could have commanded the Army of the Potomac at Chancellorsville I would have wagered my life on being in Richmond in ten days! All we are suffering now in shame and mortification and in the great risk of losing the whole fortunes of the war is the legitimate result of the weakness which characterized that campaign. Since then, and as the results of that campaign, our army has been reduced over 50,000 men, two-thirds by expiration of term of service of three-months' and two-years' troops, and yet not one soldier has been added to our forces. All winter, by the natural disintegration of armies, we have been running down at the rate of 20 per cent per annum; add to this 35 to 40,000 men discharged by expiration of service and 25,000 killed and wounded in battle and you have at least 85,000 men in this army less now than last December, and this, too, at the season when active field duties commence. I have in my division less than half the men I had in January last, when I reached Stafford Court House. I think my division is a fair sample of the Army of the Potomac.

You see we have a great task before us to preserve the Republic. It is reported that the Rebels are 110,000 strong in infantry, with 20,000 cavalry. I think the report is greatly exaggerated, but they have been all winter recruiting by conscription, while we have been all winter running down. Still, I don't despair. On the contrary, now with a gentleman and a soldier in command I have renewed confidence that we shall at least do enough to preserve our honor and the safety of the Republic. But we run a fearful risk, because upon this small army everything depends. If we are badly defeated the Capital is gone and all our principal cities and our national honor. That this dilemma could have been suffered by men deputed to care for the safety of the Republic is indeed disheartening. That our northern people could sit down in search of the almighty dollar, when their all is depending upon this conflict, is indeed passing strange. If we fail in this war, be assured there is an end of northern prosperity. The Rebels in Baltimore and Washington will dictate terms and these terms will humiliate and destroy us. I would I had an archangel's voice to appeal to the patriotism (if there be any left) in the North!

I sent you a sort of journal of a few days we were in Leesburg, excepting two or three of the last. Those were devoted to putting the forts in good condition for the Rebels and making several miles of rifle pits and breast works.

Love to all; my column has passed and I must follow. This is a hasty scrawl, but I know with you better than none. Keep writing me. I am full of faith and yet fearfully anxious. There must be a decisive battle, I think, soon, but you will hear of it before this reaches you, probably. Possibly the enemy may withdraw, and I am not without hope that we may strike them on a weak flank exposure.

Whatever may happen, be contented and resigned, and believe it is all for the best. In nations, as in individuals, we must believe there is a "Divinity which shapes our ends, rough hew them as we will."

Your Affectionate Father,
A.S.W.

"THIS BUSINESS OF WAR":
MARYLAND, JUNE 1863

Samuel W. Fiske to the Springfield Republican

Following his parole to Annapolis, Fiske was exchanged, allowing him to return to duty as a brigade staff officer in the Second Corps. He wrote his dispatch as the Army of the Potomac continued to march northward.

Toward Gettysburg

Uniontown, Md.
June 30

Dear Republican: There is a deal of romance about this business of war. We lay us down at night under heaven's glorious canopy, not knowing if at any moment the call to arms may not disturb our slumbers. We wake at reveille, cook and eat our scanty breakfast, thankful if we have any to dispose of in that way. At the bugle-call we strike tents, put on our harness and packs, and start off, not knowing our direction, the object of our march, or its extent; taking everything on trust, and enjoying as much as possible the varied experience of each passing hour; and ready for a picnic or a fray, a bivouac, a skirmish, a picket, a reconnaissance, or a movement in retreat. There is no life in which there is more room for the exercise of faith than in this same soldierly life of ours—faith in our own good right arms, and in the joint strength and confidence of military discipline; faith in the experience and watchfulness of our tried commanders (happy if they be not tried and found wanting); faith in the ultimate success of our country's good and holy cause; faith in the overruling care and protection of Almighty Jehovah, who holdeth the movements of armies and nations, as also the smallest concerns of private individuals, in His hand.

Our marches for the last few days have been through the

most lovely country, across the state of Maryland to the east of Frederick City. There is not a finer cultivated scenery in the whole world, it seems to me; and it was almost like going to Paradise from—another place; the getting-out of abominable, barren, ravaged Old Virginia into fertile, smiling Maryland. It is a cruel thing to roll the terrible wave of war over such a scene of peace, plenty, and fruitfulness; but it may be that here on our own soil, and in these last sacrifices and efforts, the great struggle for the salvation of our country and our Union may successfully terminate. Poor Old Virginia is so bare and desolate as to be only fit for a battle-ground; but it seems that we must take our turn too, in the Northern states, of invasion, and learn something of the practical meaning of war in our own peaceful communities. I sincerely hope that the scare up in Pennsylvania isn't going to drive all the people's wits away, and prevent them from making a brave defense of homes, altars, and hearths. When I read in a paper to-day of the "chief burgess" of York pushing out eight or ten miles into the country to find somebody to surrender the city to, I own to have entertained some doubts as to the worthiness and valor of that representative of the dignity of the city. It would be well for the citizens of Pennsylvania to remember that Lee's soldiers are only men, after all, and that their number is not absolutely limitless, and that they have not really the power of being in a great many places at the same time.

Also, that, if they wish to enable the proper military authorities to defend them understandingly, it will be just as well to see to the accuracy of the information they carry, and not magnify a half-dozen cavalrymen into a huge invading army. It is the very best time in the world now for everybody to keep cool, and use a little common sense. When there isn't any danger near, it doesn't matter much about that. The simple truth is, that the enemy cannot by any possibility, leaving many of his men behind to keep his long line of communications open, carry into Pennsylvania anything like the number of forces we can bring to meet him; and it is only the circumstance of our being frightened to death at the audacity of his movement that can save him from repenting most ruefully the audacity of his crossing the Potomac northward. We of the unfortunate "grand army," to be sure, haven't much reason to make large promises; but we are going to put ourselves again in the way of the butternuts, and have great hopes of retrieving, on our own ground, our ill fortune in the last two engagements, and, by another and still more successful Antietam conflict, deserve well of our country.

Our troops are making tremendous marches some of these days just past; and, if the enemy is anywhere, we shall be likely to find him and feel of him pretty soon. For sixteen days we have been on the move, and endure the fatigues of the march well. There is much less straggling, and much less pillaging, than in any march of the troops that I have yet accompanied. Our men are now veterans, and acquainted with the ways and resources of campaigning. There are very few sick among us. The efficient strength, in proportion to our numbers, is vastly greater than when we were green volunteers. So the Potomac Army, reduced greatly in numbers as it has been by the expiration of the term of service of so many regiments, is still a very numerous and formidable army. An innocent "Dunker" (if you know that religious denomination), at whose house we staid last night, thought that he had seen pretty much all the people of the world when a corps or two of our forces had passed his house.

We passed, in our march up the Potomac, the field of the two Bull Run battles; and I was much shocked to find such great numbers of the bodies of Union soldiers lying still unburied. Their skeletons, with the tattered and decaying uniforms still hanging upon them, lie in many parts of last year's battle field, in long ranks, just as they fell; and in one place, under a tree, was a whole circle of the remains of wounded soldiers, who had been evidently left to die under the shade of which they had crawled, some of them with bandages round their skeleton limbs, one with a battered canteen clasped in his skeleton hand, and some with evidence, as our boys fancied, of having starved to death. On one old broken cart lies what is left of eight Union soldiers, left to decay as they were laid to be borne off the field, and the vehicle struck, probably, by a cannon ball. In many instances the bodies which were partially or hastily buried are now much uncovered; and a grinning skull meets our gaze as you pass, or a fleshless arm stretches out its ghastly welcome.

Still it is wonderful to notice how quickly and how kindly Nature covers up the traces of murderous conflict on her face. The scars are mostly healed, verdure reigns, and beauty smiles over the bloody field; and save in a lonely chimney here and there, and the ghastly sights I have above referred to, which result from human neglect and barbarity, and are not to be charged at all to Nature, you would not suspect your feet were pressing the sod that one year and two years ago was reddened in human gore.

Enough of moralizing for the present, and "a little more sleep and a little more slumber" for the heavy eyelids of one who was in the saddle fifteen hours out of the last twenty-four, and expects to be as many more in the next twenty-four. No news except that which can be gathered from the date of this epistle. Yours truly,

DUNN BROWNE

June 30, 1863

BATTLE OF GETTYSBURG:
PENNSYLVANIA, JULY 1863

Arthur James Lyon Fremantle: Diary, July 1–4, 1863

Fighting broke out northwest of Gettysburg on the morning of July 1 when a Confederate infantry division advancing from Cashtown encountered two dismounted Union cavalry brigades defending the town. Both sides brought up reinforcements, and by the end of the day Lee and Meade had committed their armies to a battle that would eventually involve 83,000 Union and 75,000 Confederate troops. Arthur James Lyon Fremantle was a lieutenant colonel in the British army who took six months leave in early 1863 in order to visit the Confederacy. Fremantle entered Texas from Mexico on April 2, and met with Joseph E. Johnston in Mississippi, Braxton Bragg in Tennessee, and Jefferson Davis in Richmond before joining the Army of Northern Virginia in the Shenandoah Valley on June 22. Shortly after the battle of Gettysburg Fremantle crossed the lines in western Maryland and traveled to New York City, where he witnessed the draft riots before sailing for England on July 15. His diary was published in London shortly before Christmas as *Three Months in the Southern States: April–June 1863*, and was reprinted in both New York and Mobile in 1864.

1st July (Wednesday).—We did not leave our camp till noon, as nearly all General Hill's corps had to pass our quarters on its march towards Gettysburg. One division of Ewell's also had to join in a little beyond Greenwood, and Longstreet's corps had to bring up the rear. During the morning I made the acquaintance of Colonel Walton, who used to command the well-known Washington Artillery, but he is now chief of artillery to Longstreet's *corps d'armée*. He is a big man, *ci-devant* auctioneer in New Orleans, and I understand he pines to return to his hammer.

Soon after starting we got into a pass in the South Mountain, a continuation, I believe, of the Blue Ridge range, which is broken by the Potomac at Harper's Ferry. The scenery through the pass is very fine. The first troops, alongside of whom we rode, belonged to Johnson's division of Ewell's corps. Among them I saw, for the first time, the celebrated "Stonewall" Brigade, formerly commanded by Jackson. In appearance the men differ little from other Confederate soldiers, except, perhaps, that the brigade contains more elderly men and fewer boys. All (except, I think, one regiment) are Virginians. As they have nearly always been on detached duty, few of them knew General Longstreet, except by reputation. Numbers of them asked me whether the General in front was Longstreet; and when I answered in the affirmative, many would run on a hundred yards in order to take a good look at him. This I take to be an immense compliment from any soldier on a long march.

At 2 P.M. firing became distinctly audible in our front, but although it increased as we progressed, it did not seem to be very heavy.

A spy who was with us insisted upon there being "a pretty tidy bunch of *blue-bellies* in or near Gettysburg," and he declared that he was in their society three days ago.

After passing Johnson's division, we came up to a Florida brigade, which is now in Hill's corps; but as it had formerly served under Longstreet, the men knew him well. Some of them (after the General had passed) called out to their comrades, "Look out for work now, boys, for here's the old bulldog again."

At 3 P.M. we began to meet wounded men coming to the rear, and the number of these soon increased most rapidly, some hobbling alone, others on stretchers carried by the ambulance corps, and others in the ambulance wagons. Many of the latter were stripped nearly naked, and displayed very bad wounds. This spectacle, so revolting to a person unaccustomed to such sights, produced no impression whatever upon the advancing troops, who certainly go under fire with the most perfect nonchalance. They show no enthusiasm or excitement, but the most complete indifference. This is the effect of two years' almost uninterrupted fighting.

We now began to meet Yankee prisoners coming to the rear in considerable numbers. Many of them were wounded, but they seemed already to be on excellent terms with their captors, with whom they had commenced swapping canteens, tobacco, &c. Among them was a Pennsylvanian colonel, a miserable object from a wound in his face. In answer to a question, I heard one of them remark, with a laugh, "We're pretty nigh whipped already." We next came to a Confederate soldier carrying a Yankee color, belonging, I think, to a Pennsylvania regiment, which he told us he had just captured.

At 4.30 P.M. we came in sight of Gettysburg, and joined General Lee and General Hill, who were on the top of one of the ridges which form the peculiar feature of the country round Gettysburg. We could see the enemy retreating up one of the opposite ridges, pursued by the Confederates with loud yells. The position into which the enemy had been driven was evidently a strong one. His right appeared to rest on a cemetery, on the top of a high ridge to the right of Gettysburg, as we looked at it.

General Hill now came up and told me he had been very unwell all day, and in fact he looks very delicate. He said he had had two of his divisions engaged, and had driven the enemy four miles into his present position, capturing a great many prisoners, some cannon, and some colors. He said, however, that the Yankees had fought with a determination unusual to them. He pointed out a railway cutting, in which they had made a good stand; also, a field in the centre of which he had seen a man plant the regimental color, round which the regiment had fought for some time with much obstinacy, and when at last it was obliged to retreat, the color-bearer retired last of all, turning round every now and then to shake his fist at the advancing rebels. General Hill said he felt quite sorry when he saw this gallant Yankee meet his doom.

General Ewell had come up at 3.30, on the enemy's right (with part of his corps), and completed his discomfiture. General Reynolds, one of the best Yankee generals, was reported killed. Whilst we were talking, a message arrived from General Ewell, requesting Hill to press the enemy in the front, whilst he performed the same operation on his right. The pressure was accordingly applied in a mild degree, but the enemy were too strongly posted, and it was too late in the evening for a regular attack. The town of Gettysburg was now occupied by Ewell, and was full of Yankee dead and wounded. I climbed up a tree in the most commanding place I could find, and could form a pretty good general idea of the enemy's position, although the tops of the ridges being covered with pine-woods, it was very difficult to see anything of the troops concealed in them. The firing ceased about dark, at which time I rode back with General Longstreet and his Staff to his headquarters at Cashtown, a little village eight miles from Gettysburg. At that time troops were pouring along the road, and were being marched towards the position they are to occupy to-morrow.

In the fight to-day nearly 6,000 prisoners had been taken, and 10 guns. About 20,000 men must have been on the field on the Confederate side. The enemy had two *corps d'armée* engaged. All the prisoners belong, I think, to the 1st and 11th corps. This day's work is called a "brisk little scurry," and all anticipate a "big battle" to-morrow.

I observed that the artillerymen in charge of the horses dig themselves little holes like graves, throwing up the earth at the upper end. They ensconce themselves in these holes when under fire.

At supper this evening, General Longstreet spoke of the enemy's position as being "very formidable." He also said that they would doubtless intrench themselves strongly during the night.* The Staff officers spoke of the battle as a certainty, and the universal feeling in the army was one of profound contempt for an enemy whom they have beaten so constantly, and under so many disadvantages.

2d July (Thursday).—We all got up at 3.30 A.M., and breakfasted a little before daylight. Lawley insisted on riding, notwithstanding his illness. Captain —— and I were in a dilemma for horses; but I was accommodated by Major Clark (of this Staff), whilst the stout Austrian was mounted by Major Walton. The Austrian, in spite of the early hour, had shaved his cheeks and *ciréd* his mustaches as beautifully as if he was on parade at Vienna.

Colonel Sorrell, the Austrian, and I arrived at 5 A.M. at the

---

*I have the best reason for supposing that the fight came off prematurely, and that neither Lee nor Longstreet intended that it should have begun that day. I also think that their plans were deranged by the events of the first.

same commanding position we were on yesterday, and I climbed up a tree in company with Captain Schreibert of the Prussian army. Just below us were seated Generals Lee, Hill, Longstreet, and Hood, in consultation—the two latter assisting their deliberations by the truly American custom of *whittling* sticks. General Heth was also present; he was wounded in the head yesterday, and although not allowed to command his brigade, he insists upon coming to the field.

At 7 A.M. I rode over part of the ground with General Longstreet, and saw him disposing of M'Laws's division for to-day's fight. The enemy occupied a series of high ridges, the tops of which were covered with trees, but the intervening valleys between their ridges and ours were mostly open, and partly under cultivation. The cemetery was on their right, and their left appeared to rest upon a high rocky hill. The enemy's forces, which were now supposed to comprise nearly the whole Potomac army, were concentrated into a space apparently not more than a couple of miles in length. The Confederates inclosed them in a sort of semicircle, and the extreme extent of our position must have been from five to six miles at least. Ewell was on our left; his headquarters in a church (with a high cupola) at Gettysburg; Hill in the centre; and Longstreet on the right. Our ridges were also covered with pine-woods at the tops, and generally on the rear slopes. The artillery of both sides confronted each other at the edges of these belts of trees, the troops being completely hidden. The enemy was evidently intrenched, but the Southerners had not broken ground at all. A dead silence reigned till 4.45 P.M., and no one would have imagined that such masses of men and such a powerful artillery were about to commence the work of destruction at that hour.

Only two divisions of Longstreet were present to-day—viz., M'Laws's and Hood's—Pickett being still in the rear. As the whole morning was evidently to be occupied in disposing the troops for the attack, I rode to the extreme right with Colonel Manning and Major Walton, where we ate quantities of cherries, and got a feed of corn for our horses. We also bathed in a small stream, but not without some trepidation on my part, for we were almost beyond the lines, and were exposed to the enemy's cavalry.

At 1 P.M. I met a quantity of Yankee prisoners who had been

picked up straggling. They told me they belonged to Sickles's corps (3d, I think), and had arrived from Emmetsburg during the night. About this time skirmishing began along part of the line, but not heavily.

At 2 P.M. General Longstreet advised me, if I wished to have a good view of the battle, to return to my tree of yesterday. I did so, and remained there with Lawley and Captain Schreibert during the rest of the afternoon. But until 4.45 P.M. all was profoundly still, and we began to doubt whether a fight was coming off to-day at all. At that time, however, Longstreet suddenly commenced a heavy cannonade on the right. Ewell immediately took it up on the left. The enemy replied with at least equal fury, and in a few moments the firing along the whole line was as heavy as it is possible to conceive. A dense smoke arose for six miles; there was little wind to drive it away, and the air seemed full of shells—each of which appeared to have a different style of going, and to make a different noise from the others. The ordnance on both sides is of a very varied description. Every now and then a caisson would blow up—if a Federal one, a Confederate yell would immediately follow. The Southern troops, when charging, or to express their delight, always yell in a manner peculiar to themselves. The Yankee cheer is much more like ours; but the Confederate officers declare that the rebel yell has a particular merit, and always produces a salutary and useful effect upon their adversaries. A corps is sometimes spoken of as a "good yelling regiment."

So soon as the firing began, General Lee joined Hill just below our tree, and he remained there nearly all the time, looking through his field-glass—sometimes talking to Hill and sometimes to Colonel Long of his Staff. But generally he sat quite alone on the stump of a tree. What I remarked especially was, that during the whole time the firing continued, he only sent one message, and only received one report. It is evidently his system to arrange the plan thoroughly with the three corps commanders, and then leave to them the duty of modifying and carrying it out to the best of their abilities.

When the cannonade was at its height, a Confederate band of music, between the cemetery and ourselves, began to play polkas and waltzes, which sounded very curious, accompanied by the hissing and bursting of the shells.

At 5.45 all became comparatively quiet on our left and in the cemetery; but volleys of musketry on the right told us that Longstreet's infantry were advancing, and the onward progress of the smoke showed that he was progressing favorably; but about 6.30 there seemed to be a check, and even a slight retrograde movement. Soon after 7, General Lee got a report by signal from Longstreet to say "*we are doing well*." A little before dark the firing dropped off in every direction, and soon ceased altogether. We then received intelligence that Longstreet had carried every thing before him for some time, capturing several batteries, and driving the enemy from his positions; but when Hill's Florida brigade and some other troops gave way, he was forced to abandon a small portion of the ground he had won, together with all the captured guns, except three. His troops, however, bivouacked during the night on ground occupied by the enemy this morning.

Every one deplores that Longstreet *will* expose himself in such a reckless manner. To-day he led a Georgian regiment in a charge against a battery, hat in hand, and in front of everybody. General Barksdale was killed and Semmes mortally wounded; but the most serious loss was that of General Hood, who was badly wounded in the arm early in the day. I heard that his Texans are in despair. Lawley and I rode back to the General's camp, which had been moved to within a mile of the scene of action. Longstreet, however, with most of his Staff, bivouacked on the field.

Major Fairfax arrived at about 10 P.M. in a very bad humor. He had under his charge about 1,000 to 1,500 Yankee prisoners who had been taken to-day; among them a general, whom I heard one of his men accusing of having been "so G—d d—d drunk that he had turned his guns upon his own men." But, on the other hand, the accuser was such a thundering blackguard, and proposed taking such a variety of oaths in order to escape from the U.S. army, that he is not worthy of much credit. A large train of horses and mules, &c., arrived to-day, sent in by General Stuart, and captured, it is understood, by his cavalry, which had penetrated to within 6 miles of Washington.

3d July (Friday).—At 6 A.M. I rode to the field with Colonel Manning, and went over that portion of the ground which, after a fierce contest, had been won from the enemy yesterday evening. The dead were being buried, but great numbers were still lying about; also many mortally wounded, for whom nothing could be done. Amongst the latter were a number of Yankees dressed in bad imitations of the Zouave costume. They opened their glazed eyes as I rode past in a painfully imploring manner.

We joined Generals Lee and Longstreet's Staff: they were reconnoitring and making preparations for renewing the attack. As we formed a pretty large party, we often drew upon ourselves the attention of the hostile sharpshooters, and were two or three times favored with a shell. One of these shells set a brick building on fire which was situated between the lines. This building was filled with wounded, principally Yankees, who, I am afraid, must have perished miserably in the flames. Colonel Sorrell had been slightly wounded yesterday, but still did duty. Major Walton's horse was killed, but there were no other casualties amongst my particular friends.

The plan of yesterday's attack seems to have been very simple —first a heavy cannonade all along the line, followed by an advance of Longstreet's two divisions and part of Hill's corps. In consequence of the enemy's having been driven back some distance, Longstreet's corps (part of it) was in a much more forward situation than yesterday. But the range of heights to be gained was still most formidable, and evidently strongly intrenched.

The distance between the Confederate guns and the Yankee position—*i. e.*, between the woods crowning the opposite ridges —was at least a mile—quite open, gently undulating, and exposed to artillery the whole distance. This was the ground which had to be crossed in to-day's attack. Pickett's division, which had just come up, was to bear the brunt in Longstreet's attack, together with Heth and Pettigrew in Hill's corps. Pickett's division was a weak one (under 5,000), owing to the absence of two brigades.

At noon all Longstreet's dispositions were made; his troops for attack were deployed into line, and lying down in the woods; his batteries were ready to open. The general then dismounted and went to sleep for a short time. The Austrian officer and I now rode off to get, if possible, into some commanding position from whence we could see the whole thing without being exposed to the tremendous fire which was about to commence. After riding about for half an hour without being able to discover so desirable a situation, we determined to make for the cupola, near Gettysburg, Ewell's headquarters. Just before we reached the entrance to the town, the cannonade opened with a fury which surpassed even that of yesterday.

Soon after passing through the toll-gate at the entrance of Gettysburg, we found that we had got into a heavy cross-fire; shells both Federal and Confederate passing over our heads with great frequency. At length two shrapnel shells burst quite close to us, and a ball from one of them hit the officer who was conducting us. We then turned round and changed our views with regard to the cupola—the fire of one side being bad enough, but preferable to that of both sides. A small boy of twelve years was riding with us at the time: this urchin took a diabolical interest in the bursting of the shells, and screamed with delight when he saw them take effect. I never saw this boy again, or found out who he was.

The road at Gettysburg was lined with Yankee dead, and as they had been killed on the 1st, the poor fellows had already begun to be very offensive. We then returned to the hill I was on yesterday. But finding that, to see the actual fighting, it was absolutely necessary to go into the thick of the thing, I determined to make my way to General Longstreet. It was then about 2.30. After passing General Lee and his Staff, I rode on through the woods in the direction in which I had left Longstreet. I soon began to meet many wounded men returning from the front; many of them asked in piteous tones the way to a doctor or an ambulance. The further I got, the greater became the number of the wounded. At last I came to a perfect stream of them flocking through the woods in numbers as great as the crowd in Oxford-street in the middle of the day. Some were walking alone on crutches composed of two rifles, others were supported by men less badly wounded than themselves, and others were carried on stretchers by the ambulance corps; but in no case did I see a sound man helping the wounded to the rear, unless he carried the red badge of the ambulance corps. They were still under a heavy fire; the shells were continually bringing down great limbs of trees, and carrying further destruction amongst this melancholy procession. I saw all this in much less time than it takes to write it, and although astonished to meet such vast numbers of wounded, I had not seen *enough* to give me any idea of the real extent of the mischief.

When I got close up to General Longstreet, I saw one of his regiments advancing through the woods in good order; so, thinking I was just in time to see the attack, I remarked to the General that "*I wouldn't have missed this for any thing.*" Longstreet was seated at the top of a snake fence at the edge of the wood, and looking perfectly calm and imperturbed. He replied, laughing, "*The devil you wouldn't! I would like to have missed it very much; we've attacked and been repulsed: look there!*"

For the first time I then had a view of the open space between the two positions, and saw it covered with Confederates slowly and sulkily returning towards us in small broken parties, under a heavy fire of artillery. But the fire where we were was not so bad as further to the rear; for although the air seemed alive with shell, yet the greater number burst behind us.

The General told me that Pickett's division had succeeded in carrying the enemy's position and capturing his guns, but after remaining there twenty minutes, it had been forced to retire, on the retreat of Heth and Pettigrew on its left. No person could have been more calm or self-possessed than General Longstreet under these trying circumstances, aggravated as they now were by the movements of the enemy, who began to show a strong disposition to advance. I could now thoroughly appreciate the term bulldog, which I had heard applied to him by the soldiers. Difficulties seem to make no other impression upon him than to make him a little more savage.

Major Walton was the only officer with him when I came up—all the rest had been put into the charge. In a few minutes Major Latrobe arrived on foot, carrying his saddle, having just had his horse killed. Colonel Sorrell was also in the same predicament, and Captain Goree's horse was wounded in the mouth.

The General was making the best arrangements in his power

to resist the threatened advance, by advancing some artillery, rallying the stragglers, &c. I remember seeing a General (Pettigrew, I think it was)* come up to him, and report that "he was unable to bring his men up again." Longstreet turned upon him and replied with some sarcasm: "*Very well; never mind, then, General; just let them remain where they are: the enemy's going to advance, and will spare you the trouble.*"

He asked for something to drink: I gave him some rum out of my silver flask, which I begged he would keep in remembrance of the occasion; he smiled, and, to my great satisfaction, accepted the memorial. He then went off to give some orders to M'Laws's division. Soon afterwards I joined General Lee, who had in the mean while come to that part of the field on becoming aware of the disaster. If Longstreet's conduct was admirable, that of General Lee was perfectly sublime. He was engaged in rallying and in encouraging the broken troops, and was riding about a little in front of the wood, quite alone—the whole of his Staff being engaged in a similar manner further to the rear. His face, which is always placid and cheerful, did not show signs of the slightest disappointment, care, or annoyance; and he was addressing to every soldier he met a few words of encouragement, such as, "All this will come right in the end: we'll talk it over afterwards; but, in the mean time, all good men must rally. We want all good and true men just now," &c. He spoke to all the wounded men that passed him, and the slightly wounded he exhorted "to bind up their hurts and take up a musket" in this emergency. Very few failed to answer his appeal, and I saw many badly wounded men take off their hats and cheer him. He said to me, "This has been a sad day for us, Colonel—a sad day; but we can't expect always to gain victories." He was also kind enough to advise me to get into some more sheltered position, as the shells were bursting round us with considerable frequency.

Notwithstanding the misfortune which had so suddenly befallen him, General Lee seemed to observe every thing, however trivial. When a mounted officer began licking his horse for shying at the bursting of a shell, he called out, "Don't whip

---

*This officer was afterwards killed at the passage of the Potomac.

him, Captain; don't whip him. I've got just such another foolish horse myself, and whipping does no good."

I happened to see a man lying flat on his face in a small ditch, and I remarked that I didn't think he seemed dead; this drew General Lee's attention to the man, who commenced groaning dismally. Finding appeals to his patriotism of no avail, General Lee had him ignominiously set on his legs by some neighboring gunners.

I saw General Willcox (an officer who wears a short round jacket and a battered straw hat) come up to him, and explain, almost crying, the state of his brigade. General Lee immediately shook hands with him and said cheerfully, "Never mind, General, *all this has been* MY *fault*—it is *I* that have lost this fight, and you must help me out of it in the best way you can." In this manner I saw General Lee encourage and reanimate his somewhat dispirited troops, and magnanimously take upon his own shoulders the whole weight of the repulse. It was impossible to look at him or to listen to him without feeling the strongest admiration, and I never saw any man fail him except the man in the ditch.

It is difficult to exaggerate the critical state of affairs as they appeared about this time. If the enemy or their general had shown any enterprise, there is no saying what might have happened. General Lee and his officers were evidently fully impressed with a sense of the situation; yet there was much less noise, fuss, or confusion of orders than at an ordinary field-day; the men, as they were rallied in the wood, were brought up in detachments, and lay down quietly and coolly in the positions assigned to them.

We heard that Generals Garnett and Armistead were killed, and General Kemper mortally wounded; also, that Pickett's division had only one field-officer unhurt. Nearly all this slaughter took place in an open space about one mile square, and within one hour.

At 6 P.M. we heard a long and continuous Yankee cheer, which we at first imagined was an indication of an advance; but it turned out to be their reception of a general officer, whom we saw riding down the line, followed by about thirty horsemen. Soon afterwards I rode to the extreme front, where there were four pieces of rifled cannon almost without any infantry support. To the non-withdrawal of these guns is to be attributed the otherwise surprising inactivity of the enemy. I was immediately surrounded by a sergeant and about half-a-dozen gunners, who seemed in excellent spirits and full of confidence, in spite of their exposed situation. The sergeant expressed his ardent hope that the Yankees might have spirit enough to advance and receive the dose he had in readiness for them. They spoke in admiration of the advance of Pickett's division, and of the manner in which Pickett himself had led it. When they observed General Lee they said, "We've not lost confidence in the old man: this day's work won't do him no harm. 'Uncle Robert' will get us into Washington yet; you bet he will!" &c. Whilst we were talking, the enemy's skirmishers began to advance slowly, and several ominous sounds in quick succession told us that we were attracting their attention, and that it was necessary to break up the conclave. I therefore turned round and took leave of these cheery and plucky gunners.

At 7 P.M., General Lee received a report that Johnson's division of Ewell's corps had been successful on the left, and had gained important advantages there. Firing entirely ceased in our front about this time; but we now heard some brisk musketry on our right, which I afterwards learned proceeded from Hood's Texans, who had managed to surround some enterprising Yankee cavalry, and were slaughtering them with great satisfaction. Only eighteen out of four hundred are said to have escaped.

At 7.30, all idea of a Yankee attack being over, I rode back to Moses's tent, and found that worthy commissary in very low spirits, all sorts of exaggerated rumors having reached him. On my way I met a great many wounded men, most anxious to inquire after Longstreet, who was reported killed; when I assured them he was quite well, they seemed to forget their own pain in the evident pleasure they felt in the safety of their chief. No words that I can use will adequately express the extraordinary patience and fortitude with which the wounded Confederates bore their sufferings.

I got something to eat with the doctors at 10 P.M., the first for fifteen hours.

I gave up my horse to-day to his owner, as from death and exhaustion the Staff are almost without horses.

4th July (Saturday).—I was awoke at daylight by Moses complaining that his valuable trunk, containing much public money, had been stolen from our tent whilst we slept. After a search it was found in a wood hard by, broken open and minus the money. Dr. Barksdale had been robbed in the same manner exactly. This is evidently the work of those rascally stragglers, who shirk going under fire, plunder the natives, and will hereafter swagger as the heroes of Gettysburg.

Lawley, the Austrian, and I, walked up to the front about eight o'clock, and on our way we met General Longstreet, who was in a high state of amusement and good humor. A flag of truce had just come over from the enemy, and its bearer announced among other things that "General Longstreet was wounded, and a prisoner, but would be taken care of." General Longstreet sent back word that he was extremely grateful, but that, being neither wounded nor a prisoner, he was quite able to take care of himself. The iron endurance of General Longstreet is most extraordinary: he seems to require neither food nor sleep. Most of his Staff now fall fast asleep directly they get off their horses, they are so exhausted from the last three days' work.

Whilst Lawley went to headquarters on business, I sat down and had a long talk with General Pendleton (the parson), chief of artillery. He told me the exact number of guns in action yesterday. He said that the universal opinion is in favor of the 12-pounder Napoleon guns as the best and simplest sort of ordnance for field purposes.* Nearly all the artillery with this army has either been captured from the enemy or cast from old 6-pounders taken at the early part of the war.

At 10 A.M. Lawley returned from headquarters, bringing the news that the army is to commence moving in the direction of Virginia this evening. This step is imperative from want

---

*The Napoleon 12-pounders are smooth-bore brass guns, with chambers, very light, and with long range. They were invented or recommended by Louis Napoleon years ago. A large number are being cast at Augusta and elsewhere.

of ammunition. But it was hoped that the enemy might attack during the day, especially as this is the 4th of July, and it was calculated that there was still ammunition for one day's fighting. The ordnance train had already commenced moving back towards Cashtown, and Ewell's immense train of plunder had been proceeding towards Hagerstown by the Fairfield road ever since an early hour this morning.

Johnson's division had evacuated during the night the position it had gained yesterday. It appears that for a time it was actually in possession of the cemetery, but had been forced to retire from thence from want of support by Pender's division, which had been retarded by that officer's wound. The whole of our left was therefore thrown back considerably.

At 1 P.M. the rain began to descend in torrents, and we took refuge in the hovel of an ignorant Pennsylvanian boor. The cottage was full of soldiers, none of whom had the slightest idea of the contemplated retreat, and all were talking of Washington and Baltimore with the greatest confidence.

At 2 P.M. we walked to General Longstreet's camp, which had been removed to a place three miles distant, on the Fairfield road. General Longstreet talked to me for a long time about the battle. He said the mistake they had made was in not concentrating the army more, and making the attack yesterday with 30,000 men instead of 15,000. The advance had been in three lines, and the troops of Hill's corps who gave way were young soldiers, who had never been under fire before. He thought the enemy would have attacked had the guns been withdrawn. Had they done so at that particular moment immediately after the repulse, it would have been awkward; but in that case he had given orders for the advance of Hood's division and M'Laws's on the right. I think, after all, that General Meade was right not to advance—his men would never have stood the tremendous fire of artillery they would have been exposed to.

Rather over 7,000 Yankees were captured during the three days; 3,500 took the parole; the remainder were now being marched to Richmond, escorted by the remains of Pickett's division. It is impossible to avoid seeing that the cause of this check to the Confederates lies in the utter contempt felt for the enemy by all ranks.

Wagons, horses, mules, and cattle captured in Pennsylvania, the solid advantages of this campaign, have been passing slowly along this road (Fairfield) all day: those taken by Ewell are particularly admired. So interminable was this train that it soon became evident that we should not be able to start till late at night. As soon as it became dark we all lay round a big fire, and I heard reports coming in from the different generals that the enemy was *retiring*, and had been doing so all day long. M'Laws reported nothing in his front but cavalry videttes. But this, of course, could make no difference to General Lee's plans: ammunition he must have—he had failed to capture it from the enemy (according to precedent); and as his communications with Virginia were intercepted, he was compelled to fall back towards Winchester, and draw his supplies from thence. General Milroy had kindly left an ample stock at that town when he made his precipitate exit some weeks ago. The army was also incumbered with an enormous wagon-train, the spoils of Pennsylvania, which it is highly desirable to get safely over the Potomac.

Shortly after 9 P.M. the rain began to descend in torrents. Lawley and I luckily got into the doctors' covered buggy, and began to get slowly under way a little after midnight.

"WHAT TERRIBLE WORK":
PENNSYLVANIA, JULY 1863

Samuel Pickens: Diary, July 1–3, 1863

On the morning of July 1 two divisions of the Army of Northern Virginia's Second Corps began marching from Heidlersburg to Cashtown, but then changed direction after Lieutenant General Richard Ewell, the corps commander, learned of the Confederate advance on Gettysburg. Serving with the 5th Alabama Infantry, one of the regiments in the division commanded by Robert E. Rodes, was Private Samuel Pickens, who had been quickly exchanged after his capture at Chancellorsville. Pickens recorded his regiment's part in the fighting on July 1 and in the subsequent Confederate attempts to capture Cemetery Hill, which, along with the adjoining Culp's Hill, anchored the northern end of the Union defensive line.

July 1, Wednesday

Left camp this morning at 6:30 A.M. & marched 7 miles on the Chambersburg road to Middletown, where we turned to the left on the Gettysburg road. As we approached the town we heard the cannonading & formed a line of battle about 2 miles off & advanced upon the Yankees. Our Regt. was on the left of the Brigade & as it moved forward it made a partial right wheel & thus kept us at a double quick march all the time; & as it was an excessively hot day & we were going through wheat fields & ploughed ground & over fences, it almost killed us. I was perfectly exhausted & never suffered so from heat & fatigue in my life. A good many fell out of ranks being completely broken down & some fainted. We halted & lay down for some time at a fence & witnessed an artillery duel between one of our batteries stationed about 150 yds. in front of us & a Yankee battery away to our left. 5 or 6 dead horses & 1 or 2 broken caissons or gun carriages were left by our battery when it moved off. Our Regt. then went forward, for the rest of the Brigade had gone on while we had been left to guard the space between our Brigade & Doles' which was on our left & prevent either from being flanked. We came up with the

Brig., however, at a fence where it had halted and there our Company was sent forward to a barn to act as sharp-shooters. There were some N.C. sharp-shooters there who had shot away all their cartridge. Wm. Stokes was wounded before getting to the barn, & Joe Brown while in it. We kept up pretty brisk firing at the Yankees, but it seemed as if we could do very little execution as they were so far off & behind a fence in the woods, though they made the bullets whistle over us. After the Brig. passed on we ran out of the barn & through an open field where the bullets were flying thick & went down on the left to a lane where the Regt. was. I never saw troops so scattered & in such confusion. We were under a heavy fire from the front & a cross fire from the left & pretty soon had to fall back to a fence where the Brig. was rallied by Col. O'Neal & Genl Rodes. Paul Lavender was coming off wounded & asked Lt. Jones (in commd. of Co.) to let me help him. I got three of the ambulance corps of the 26th Regt. & a litter & had to carry Paul about a mile to get to a Surgeon. Mr. Mushat extracted the ball & after waiting in vain all the evening for an ambulance to take the wounded to the Hospital, I set out to find the H. & get ambulances, which I succeeded in doing after a long walk & a deal of difficulty. The scenes about the Hospital were the most horrible I ever beheld. There were the poor wounded men lying all over the yard, moaning & groaning, while in the barn the terrible work of amputating limbs was going on, and the pallid limbs lying around presented a most disagreeable sight. As soon as I could get 2 ambulances we set out & had to go a very roundabout way, so by time we got to the wounded it was some time after night & they had been put in a house & were so comfortable they did not want to be moved, so the ambulances were dismissed to return in the morning. In the mean time our troops had driven the Yankees and were in possession of the town of Gettysburg. When our Brig. was reformed it moved up & took position along the Rail-road to the right of town. Oh! what terrible work has been done to-day. The loss in our Brig. was very heavy—particularly in our Regt. I was much affected on learning that my warm friend & mess-mate Tean Nutting had been mortally wounded & died in a short time on the field. He was at his post with the colors. A nobler, more generous or braver boy never lived. He was a great favorite & will be much missed. Marched 14 ms. before getting in fight.

July 2, Thursday

The ambulances came this morning and conveyed the wounded to the Hospitals, & I, with Cruse Coleman returned to the Regiment. The town is full of the enemy's wounded & every large building has been made a hospital. David Barnum brought from town a havresack of candy, plenty of lemons & other nice things which were a great treat. It was pretty quiet during the morning while we were placing our artillery in position. Gilliam J. told us that 80 pieces were being massed on a hill to our right. After a while they opened all around & the cannonading was terrific: almost as rapid as musketry. Late in the evening our Divis. was moved forward in line of battle & as we advanced upon the hill where the Yankees had all their artillery & troops massed we expected to have to charge it, but it was then after dark & we lay a while in a wheat field & then went back in town. The loss in our Regt. in killed, wounded & missing is 226. The no. that left camp was 380; but a great many fell out of ranks, & Col. Hall thinks that not many over 300 went into the fight—so our loss was very heavy, & nearly all killed or wounded, for there are only———missing. In our Co. ("D") the loss is:—

Killed — George Nutting
Wounded — P. H. Lavender—thigh.
J. L. Wright—shoulder.
J. M. Brown—foot.
Wm Stokes—leg—& Prisoner.
Wm A. Lenier—hand—& Prisoner.
Prisoners — Jas. Burton.
J. T. Knowlan.
J. C. Ray

July 3, Friday

We lay in line along one of the streets last night & this morning our Brigade with the exception of our Regt. was sent down on the left with Johnson's Divis. & participated in the fight. Our Regt. was attached to Doles' Brig. & stayed in town during the morning—while our Co. was sent to the edge of town as sharp-shooters. We built breast works and remained there till evening. An occasional minnie ball whizzed over us & a shell passed through a stable or crib beside us & exploded immediately after. The Regt. then moved up with Doles' Brig. & lay in line of battle in a lane. There was no shade, & the heat of the sun was almost insupportable. A heavy cannonading was kept up—a great many shells passing over us—and some from our own batteries exploded over our line & killed men in Doles', Ramseur's &, I think, Iversons Brigades. It was either very inferior ammunition or great carelessness on the part of the gunners. Saw Tom Biscoe in town to-day. His looks shewed plainly that he had seen hard service. His Brigade (Hays') made a desperate charge upon *the Hill* last night & took a battery, but were not supported & had to fall back. Tom is now in command of the 5th La. Regt.

"THIS TRIAL OF THE NERVES":
PENNSYLVANIA, JULY 1863

Francis Adams Donaldson: Narrative of Gettysburg, July 2–3, 1863

A company commander in the 118th Pennsylvania Infantry, Captain Francis Adams Donaldson had fought at Ball's Bluff, Fair Oaks, Shepherdstown, Fredericksburg, and Chancellorsville. His regiment was assigned to the Fifth Corps, which advanced from Union Mills, Maryland, to Hanover, Pennsylvania, on July 1, then turned west and marched until 3:30 A.M. on July 2, when it halted four miles east of Gettysburg. On the afternoon of July 2 Meade learned that Major General Daniel E. Sickles, the commander of the Union Third Corps, had moved his men forward from the low-lying southern part of Cemetery Ridge toward slightly higher ground along the Emmitsburg Road, forming a salient with its apex at a peach orchard and opening a large gap in the Union lines. As Longstreet's corps began its attack on the exposed Third Corps, Donaldson's brigade was sent to help defend a stony hill south of the peach orchard against an assault by Lafayette McLaw's division. (The hill adjoined farmer John Rose's wheat field, which would become the scene of some of the day's fiercest fighting.) The next day Donaldson was posted on the northeast slope of Big Round Top, at the southern end of the Union defensive line. He recorded his experiences on July 2–3 as part of a long letter to his aunt, Eliza Ann Nice, written on July 21.

July 2nd. I slept about an hour then arose, brushed the dew from my hair and looked around me. The woods were a scene of busy stir, here and there the blue smoke was curling up in playful wreaths from our bivouac fires, while the men were cooking coffee or otherwise preparing to take the road again. About 5 A.M. our division moved out into the open ground beyond the woods and commenced to deploy for action, the regiments being formed at deploying distance in close column. It was a beautiful sight to see, as far as the eye could reach, regiment after regiment in mass, with colors unfurled, upon a line as straight as a die, while the death like silence pervading all made the senses keen to note every trifling incident.

It took some time to satisfactorily arrange us, but finally the order came to move forward, and with a firm tread and muskets at the right shoulder, the movement commenced. Over fields and fences went the silent moving mass, while nothing was heard save an occasional caution from our Colonel as to the guide, and the singular noise made by the tramping of so many thousands of feet thro' the crushing leaves and grass, while the atmosphere was heavy with the pennyroyal smell so peculiar to all battlefields. As we gradually approached the rising ground in front, from beyond which musketry firing could be distinctly heard, a change of direction to the right was made, which after continuing for some time was changed again to the front.

We halted in a piece of woods to the front of which our army was then engaged, and from the length of time we remained here, I presume were upon the reserve. After listening for a long time to the intermittent firing, the battle suddenly became very animated, the deafening and unceasing roar of artillery making the earth fairly quake. By its long continuance and regularity, all felt that if not pushing the enemy they were certainly not getting the advantage of our people, and as we had received no orders to load, our help was evidently not needed. Drawing this inference I determined to avail myself of an opportunity to indulge in a bath, a pond of inviting water being but a short distance to the rear of our regiment. I stripped myself, rushed eagerly into the water and was soon splashing and dashing about like a dolphin, when noticing some very curious weeds sticking to my person, I hastened out to rid myself of them, when to my astonishment I found them to be leeches. I postponed further bathing. After this little episode nothing was to be done but to sit down and listen to the firing, which was now becoming terrible, the shells whistling above us and plunging away beyond our ammunition trains which were directly to the rear of us.

My feelings at this time can be readily described, as but one thought was paramount, a hope that the troops in front would be able to thrash the confederates without our aid, for with rest comes a dislike for bloody encounters. With this thought uppermost and while considering our probable chances for continuing this *soft* thing, even then, amid the thunder of the artillery bursting upon my ear, the missiles flying and the sound of musketry piercing the air, I, before I was aware of it, grew drowsy, my eyelids grew heavy and shut, thus closing out the warlike scene, and I was asleep. I know not how long I had been sleeping when suddenly I was awakened by the cry of "fall in," which was quickly responded to by all. As the men took their places in line, still laughing and jesting among themselves, the order to load was given, which at once put a stop to all trifling, and by its peculiar significance made the blood leap suddenly in the veins, and the choking sensation to rise in the throat, as each realized that we were about to take an active part in the battle going on in front. The enemy were shelling our lines furiously which seemed to indicate a general assault.

At 3:30 P.M. we moved by the left flank, and our regiment, being on the left of the brigade, of course now became the advance. Already the battle was raging fearfully ahead, and strings of ambulances with the wounded and mangled fellows were passing to the rear. As nearer and nearer we approached the field, shells could be seen bursting in vast quantities, while ammunition wagons and limber boxes were being hurried forward, and the usual confusion, noise and bustle of the rear of an immense army during a battle met our eye, and, I may add, left an unpleasant feeling upon us.

We now entered the woods which appeared to crown an eminence whose sides, full of rocks and boulders, sloped away towards the enemy, and were at once amid the dreadful bursting shells, which, however, flew past us and did no harm. At this point I saw an orderly leading a splendid black horse which was limping along on three legs, the other having been shot off at the hoof. Inquiring to whom it belonged, I learned that Capt. John Fassitte of General Birney's staff, its owner, fearing harm would come to this fine animal, had mounted another and sent it to the rear for safety, but just as our column was reached, a shell had struck the poor beast and he would now have to be killed. At this moment Captain Crocker came to me and asked my opinion of the present movement. I replied that judging from the heavy musketry fire going on to the front, I had no doubt our movement was intended to support a threatened point, or to retrieve a disaster which had already happened; certainly the peculiar rebel cheer now heard above every other sound would indicate that they had been successful somewhere.

A few minutes after, we formed in line immediately to the rear of a very thin line of battle that looked to me like a skirmish line, which retired as soon as we were posted. Our brigade was now rapidly drawn up in the following order: 118th P.V. on the right, 22nd Massachusetts on the left, 1st Michigan in rear of the 22nd Mass., and the 18th Mass. in rear of the right of the 1st Michigan and left of our regiment. We had in our brigade all told but 425 men, the balance, having straggled during the night before, had been collected, formed into a stragglers brigade, and taken into a different part of the field. The reason the 1st Mich., and 18th Mass. were not in line was because the 2nd brigade crowded us to such an extent there was no room for them, and they therefore acted as supports. . . . Our position was in all respects a good one. We were on the edge of a heavy growth of timber, with rocks and huge boulders scattered about forming ample protection, and just beyond, the hill fell off to quite a slope, up which the enemy would have to reach us. Upon our immediate right a battery of brass guns was posted which was, even now, being served with wonderful rapidity. Shortly before the engagement commenced on our part we were moved slightly to the rear, which allowed the 1st Mich. to get into line. . . . Nearly one half of our regiment was refused on the right in order to prevent flanking. The skirmishers were but a short distance to the front, and I greatly feared many of them would be unable to get back, owing to the extreme eagerness of the men to open fire, and I particularly cautioned my company to be extremely careful and allow our people to get in before firing.

At this moment Private Jas. Godfrey, the man I had forced into the company the day before, came to me with his watch and pocket book, also a letter to his wife saying, "Here, Captain, take these things and if I get killed send them to my wife, I am going to show the boys how to fight today, I have been called coward long enough." I could not help smiling at what this action implied, altho' of course not so intended, as I was as likely to be killed as he, but taking him by the hand and giving it a good honest squeeze and a terrible shake, I said, "Well done Godfrey, I knew you were sound at heart and I will write to your wife of your conduct this day, here, take a pull at this," and stepping behind a tree I let him have my canteen. Well, I really thought the poor fellow would certainly choke in his eagerness to get the rum down him. When I thought he had enough I sent him back to the company, and shortly after saw him standing, in advance of all with sleeves rolled up, musket aport, and foot firmly planted awaiting the development of events. I now felt very badly for the skirmishers as I was sure Godfrey was certainly one of them.

During all this time the enemy were making their charge, and from the rapid firing of the battery on our right, I judged, were drawing closer and closer to our line, altho' as yet unseen by us. The roar of the artillery was deafening, and from the excited manner of the gunners all efforts had evidently failed to check the onset. The voice of the officer commanding the guns could be heard loudly calling for "canister," while the surrounding objects were becoming less and less distinct from the sulphurous smoke occasioned by such rapid firing. Soon was heard a startling volley of musketry towards the left of our brigade, another and another followed in a wild and continuous rattle as the enemy's column came within range. The scene now beggars description. The deafening shouts of the combatants, the crash of artillery, the trembling ground beneath us, the silent and stricken countenances of the men, the curtain of smoke over all and its peculiar smell, made up a picture never to be forgotten by any who witnessed it.

As the enemy's columns came nearer, the artillery was served with shell with short fuse, which burst at once upon leaving the gun, scattering destruction broadcast. Our skirmishers now came running rapidly towards us, and a moment after, the enemy's column was seen moving at a quick pace obliquely along our front, very many of them in their shirt sleeves, and all appearing to be loading and firing as they came steadily up the hillside in the face of the battery, which seemed to be their objective point. Our regiment now opened and in a few minutes were at it pell mell loading and firing as rapidly as possible.

So eager were the men to fight that I did not notice one of them taking advantage of the trees and rocks, but all standing bravely up to the work and doing good execution.

As I passed up and down in rear of the company speaking to the men and directing their firing, I noticed one of them like a blazing Vesuvius, standing a yard to two in front of all, begrimed with powder, hatless and shouting as he fired his piece, "Give them hell boys," and by his extraordinary behavior making himself the most conspicuous object in our whole line. It was Godfrey, who by his determined bravery had actually assumed a leadership among his hitherto jeering comrades, and now had several of them loading his and their own muskets for him to discharge. Passing thro' the line I took my place beside him to observe more closely the movements of the enemy, who were now so near that the countenances of many of them were quite distinct. I noticed one man in particular on the right of a division, as it seemed to me, with big broad brimmed hat on the back of his head, large black whiskers and eyes directed towards our regiment, as in evident fear of danger from that quarter, he looked the personification of physical daring as he rammed a cartridge into the musket he held at a trail. Altho' I know he was the object of several shots specially directed at him, yet I saw him gradually move away apparently unhurt, and finally with his comrades disappear altogether in the dense smoke of the guns.

Our line now became somewhat broken and open as the men, after firing, would step back to load, but this is generally the case in all stationary lines of battle. A cheer now broke forth, the smoke was rent, and the rebels dashed in upon the battery with a savage yell. The artillery men retreated somewhat to the rear dragging their guns with them by ropes, which in anticipation of a catastrophe had been fastened to them.

Running to the rear of my company to prevent any movement looking towards a retreat, for all saw that our position was now untenable as the cannon were virtually in the hands of the enemy, I was met by Capt. Richd. W. Davids, who was slowly walking towards me. Upon stopping to see what was wanted, he said, "Capt., I am hit." "Where?," said I. "Thro' the stomach and bowels," said he, at the same time placing his hand upon his waist belt. "You had better go to the rear," cried I, and he started to do so, but had not gone more than twenty steps before he fell, and I knew that death had come upon him. I was the last person he ever spoke to upon this earth, and mine the ears to hear the last utterance of as brave and noble a gentleman as ever trod God's green footstool.

Nothing could now stop the rebel onset, and the shouts of rage and defiance rose up amid the roar of musketry as they swarmed upon the cannon. In a moment our guns were lost and the enemy in fierce numbers were crowding upon our right and rear. Our line wavered, trembled and commenced to give ground, when Maj. Herring, in a clear and distinct voice heard by the whole command above the din and roar of battle, cried, "Change front to rear on 10th company," and as upon parade the men performed the movement of swinging round to right angles with the line previously held, thus compelling the enemy to continue on a longer circle in order to outflank and get to our rear. This, however, they continued to do, and at last we were compelled reluctantly to fall back. Our retreat was as follows—1st Mich. and 118th P.V. immediately to the rear, the 18th and 22d Mass. by the left flank to the 3rd brigade. Our regiment was pushed back directly among the ammunition trains, but the men still kept up a straggling fire as they retreated.

Soon after we commenced to give way Maj. Biddle, of Genl. Meade's staff, and I am not sure but the general himself, appeared and entreated, prayed and called upon the men for God sake to halt, not to give way, that this was the only portion of the line broken, to think of the safety of the ammunition train, that the whole army would have to retreat—but to no purpose, for with dogged silence the men retired slowly and without apparent panic or hurry, for they were perfectly well satisfied of the impossibility of longer holding their ground.

While this was happening, observing Capt. Crocker lingering behind, I allowed the men to pass me and went back to see what could possibly detain him amid such extreme danger. With a manner perfectly cool and collected he said it was too bad our boys had not stood their ground longer, and that he wanted to see how many the enemy numbered and what they would do next. It was a strange sight to look upon. The rebels were crowding up in great numbers but appeared unable to realize the extent of their success, and were standing cheering and yelling without attempting to pursue or even to fire upon our retreating line. Turning to me Crocker seized the pistol I held in my hand and discharged the two remaining barrels at the mass in front of us, then suddenly taking to his heels beat a rapid retreat quickly followed by me.

Our regiment continued to fall slowly back for a few minutes longer, when all at once it was brought to a stand still by a yell so fierce and terrible that the very blood seemed to curdle in our veins, while a sound as of a hurricane was swept towards us. It was the crushing of leaves and twigs made by the Pennsylvania Reserves coming up in mass, at the double quick, arms at the right shoulder, bayonets fixed and with Genl. Crawford on horseback at their head, hat in hand, waving it excitedly as he led the most terrific charge I ever witnessed. With diabolical screeches and shouts they pressed forward, struck the bewildered enemy and by very force of the onset sweeping every living thing before them, retaking the cannon, crushing under foot and bayonetting all who for a moment attempted a resistance and finally pushing back the whole rebel line up over and beyond a hill of considerable height upon our left which had evidently been occupied by them. In the meantime the 2nd and 3rd brigade had been performing a movement rarely occuring in battle, resisting a bayonet charge; and it was give and take with them, no quarter being shown on either side. The 16th Mich. of the 2nd brigade was nearly annihilated, their colonel being bayonetted several times thro' the stomach and bowels as he sat on horseback, and died at his post, not having yielded an inch of ground. This bloody work could not last long and the 2nd brigade gave ground slowly, and was about to retire altogether when a cheer arose, and a line of glistening steel was seen approaching. It was the 20th Maine, 83rd and 10th Penna. of the 3rd brigade, together with the Penna. Reserves, who, having just cleared our front, now did the same for the hard pressed 2nd. I have been told that the 16th Mich. bayonetted every living rebel, wounded or unhurt, that fell into their hands, in retaliation for the loss of their Colonel. Such was the ending of this conflict from out of which our command so narrowly escaped annihilation or capture. We remained at the spot where we had halted and adjusted our line, while the 6th Corps, just arrived, formed line to our rear, and Penna. Reserves continuing to the front. After these dispositions we prepared for the night.

I must mention more prisoners had been taken than we had men in the brigade, these unfortunates being caught between us and the charging Reserves. I went among them eagerly questioning right and left for news of the 22nd Virginia Regt., and from what I could learn, that regiment is with Bradley Johnson and was not engaged today. The prisoners, one and all, seemed rejoiced to have passed safely thro' such a "blazing Hell" as they termed the fire we poured upon them. They say we have no idea of the tremendous slaughter made among their people and are unable to explain how it was they escaped unhurt. One man told me they thought it was militia they were to encounter and rather took comfort from being beaten by old soldiers. About 8 o'clock P.M. the ammunition wagons unloaded at our regiment enough cartridges to have supplied a whole division. Surely this seemed to me a most uncalled for waste, as we really did not need more than an additional thirty rounds per man, and these boxes would therefore be abandoned when most probably some other portion of the field would need them.

At last the battle was hushed and all was still, night veiled the earth. Its gloomy shades were thickened by a sulphurous cloud that like a pall hung sadly over the field. The woods and fields were strewn with the wounded and dying, and with the ghastly forms of the dead. It is indeed remarkable that men can lie down and sleep so tranquilly when they know the danger that awaits them on the morrow, when they hear the cries of the already mangled, when they know that the dead lie strewn around and that with the early dawn of the coming day, the work of death will be resumed as all felt it would surely be, now that the whole army was up and the enemy had been repulsed.

July 3rd. At day break we were moved to the left and took position on the summit of quite a high hill from which the Reserves had driven the enemy last evening, and we had now a commanding view of the whole field. The ground in front was heavily wooded and the enemy occupied the base of the hill, while our skirmishers were unable to push forward but a short distance from the line . . . and vast numbers of dead and wounded encumbered the ground, and to make the sight more horrifying, wild hogs were seen feeding on some of the badly torn bodies. The troops who had occupied this place last night had erected a substantial stone breastwork from the loose boulders and broken fragments that covered the mountains.

Just after we had been established in our new position a rebel officer was seen leisurely walking towards our line, with his hands in pockets, segar in mouth and without sword or weapon of any kind, while his jacket was thrown open in careless abandon. The skirmishers allowed him to walk into their line, and he was greatly astonished and mortified to learn he was a prisoner. He said he was Genl. Heth's Adjutant General, had left his command but a few minutes before and strolled along not supposing for a moment the "Yanks" were so near. He betrayed considerable feeling as he was led to the rear by two privates who were instructed to deliver him to Genl. Meade.

During the morning nothing of moment was done on either side and with the exception of a cannon shot now and then, everything remained perfectly quiet. Availing myself of the presence of the chaplain, who had come up in order to talk seriously to the men and distribute tracts among them, I wrote home that I had thus far escaped unhurt, the chaplain promising to forward any letters given him. Our men, wherever they could, gathered up the wounded enemy and carried them to the rear. I talked to one poor fellow who was shot thru' the breast, the lungs most probably, and who had been placed upon a stretcher and left to await the return of the ambulance men. He was suffering great anguish from thirst and was scarcely able to articulate his gratitude for the kindness shown by those from whom he had expected other treatment. The poor fellow was not as sanguine as he would liked to have been as to the final result of the battle, as our men looked to him so healthy, well fed and clothed, and yet capable of making a stout fight behind such splendid breastworks. He was an intelligent attractive man of about 45 years, and was exceedingly gentlemanly in his speech, always thanking us for any attention. I gave him some water and whiskey which appeared to help him considerably, and was sorry when compelled to leave him so helpless and alone.

About 1 o'clock, there suddenly burst forth the deafening crash of what appeared to me to be the whole of the enemy's artillery. I went to my post to see what was the occasion of this sudden concentration of the enemy fire that was making the ground rock as in the throes of an earthquake. The air was soon filled with a hissing, bursting torrent, while the men crouched low along the line. Standing on a rock I could see the smoke rising up along the whole of the enemy's position, and supposed they were about to try and beat us out by the weight of their artillery. The sun shone gloriously, making objects quite distinct in the distance, and I could see puffs of smoke from our own guns which were now replying. Retiring to the rear of our line, I sought shelter from the screaming and exploding shells, but could find none, so was compelled, along with many others, to sit still and endure this trial of the nerves for at least two hours. There was scarcely a second that we were free from shot or shell, and I never remembered to have seen so many solid shot thrown before. The missiles were sent one after the other so rapidly that a constant, prolonged and connected whizzing was maintained. Shells were exploded in front, now in the rear of us and frequently over our heads, solid shot came rushing madly, crashing and tearing among the trees, while the air was filled with fragments and the suspense was horrible to endure. During this time Capt. O'Neill and myself were sitting together on a piece of shelter tent which protected us from the damp ground. We had very little to say to one another and were very close together for protection, as it were. A shell bursting rather nearer than usual over our heads caused us to huddle still closer, while our very hearts ceased to beat as we listened to the singing of a fragment that seemed to be coming rapidly towards us. With one look we read in each others faces the alarm both felt, and saw the impossibility of avoiding the terrible death dealing missile. As we sat motionless—breathless,—it dashed furiously between my knees, and with a thud and splash of dirt, buried itself deep into the ground. I dug up the ragged piece of metal, felt its sharp edges, and put it into my haversack as a memento of the narrow escape I had made.

After enduring the fire of the rebels for at least two hours there was again a lull in the storm of battle, the artillery gradually slackened and finally ceased altogether. We could observe the field to be free from troops, the rebel infantry being within the woods. I now ran back to see after the poor wounded reb we had left on the stretcher, and found him torn to atoms and the stretcher to shreds. Poor fellow, he had been killed by his own friends, how terrible that must be, and what agony it must have been to him to have lain there fearful, not of his enemies, but lest he should be killed by his own people. Well, he was mortally wounded in the first place, and is now better off.

For a time everything continued to remain perfectly calm and quiet. Such quiet is always ominous; it betokens preparation for something of vital importance. Our own men we could not see owing to the woods, but the line could be easily traced as it stretched away to the right in the shape of an exceedingly shallow semicircle. We could clearly observe the movements of the enemy should they make any, and, I can add, all eyes were eagerly rivetted on their line to see what they would do next. About 4 P.M. they began to show themselves at the edge of the woods and to manifest signs of an intended attack. Our batteries again opened, but the rebs appeared firm and proceeded in two lines to advance in splendid order. There seemed to be a heavy body upon their rear and flank, apparently as supports, all forming a mass, I should say, of at least eight or ten thousand men, who were being pushed forward in the face of our whole army upon some point considerably to the right of our position. There was nothing to hinder anyone in our whole line from witnessing their advance, and the eagerness with which each man gazed upon this magnificent spectacle was evidence that all felt a terrible crisis was approaching. On every side could be heard men questioning the capability of our line resisting so tremendous an onset. After proceeding some distance to the front, the enemy appeared to move obliquely to the left, owing, no doubt, to the severe fire from the batteries near us. They again changed to the front, however, after proceeding a short distance, and came up in the face of all our artillery. They continued to move on unflinchingly, and it was a grand sight to see them, their splendid behavior calling forth bursts of admiration from us all. A piece of woods considerably to our right and beyond which the enemy's column soon passed shut out from our sight the finale of this desperate charge, but our ears were soon greeted by the tremendous roar of musketry, whilst a curtain of smoke ascended to the tops of the trees and remained there to tell us that a desperate fight was in progress. This state of things continued for some time and we were uncertain as to the result, when presently a few men were seen running from beyond the woods, followed by others, and at last whole clusters of the enemy were seen scampering to the rear as fast as possible, but it was also noticed that not one third of those who, but a few moments before had gone forward so bravely, returned; they had all been killed or wounded and the charge was unsuccessful. This latter fact we knew, as the enemy soon opened again their artillery fire to cover the retreat of their men, and we accepted the sign by giving a fearful shout for the victory gained.

NEWS OF GETTYSBURG:
WASHINGTON, D.C., JULY 1863

Elizabeth Blair Lee to Samuel Phillips Lee

Elizabeth Blair Lee wrote to her husband, a Union naval officer commanding the squadron blockading the North Carolina coast, from the Maryland estate of her politically prominent family. Her father, Francis Preston Blair, was an adviser to Andrew Jackson who now counseled President Lincoln; her brother Montgomery was postmaster general; and her brother Frank was a former Republican congressman from Missouri who now commanded a division at Vicksburg.

———————

Silver Spring
My Dear Phil   We are here still on tiptoe with all eyes turned towards the north West where I have felt all day that a mortal combat was going on for our Country's life & I think our troops are more alive to the exigencies of the country ever before— besides Meade has just done what the Rebels did two years ago— ordered the instant death of the recreant— if this had been done by Grant we would have had Vicksburg. & saved many brave men by punishing the Cowards & preventing their Contagion from spreading— & that is one reason why the Rebels fight well Our political Generals are afraid to deal with our Army according to Military discipline— I have great hopes of Mead   the whole family are people of talent & energy & as he was born in Spain he can never be President— thus will not be warred upon by Politicians or get a tete monte himself

Letters today from Frank who writes confidently They know that Bragg's army are coming on them. but says they have now means to cope with them— but Grant hopes to be in Vicksburg before they turn to fight Joe Johnston— Frank encloses a letter to him from Sherman giving the history of Genl McClellands dismissal by Grant

A letter today from Meade to the P says yesterday at 3 olk— he had all his Army concentrated but 2 corps were so prostrated for an immense march that he would not attack until today— Our Army lay in full view of the enemy I think Lee will retreat if it is possible— Our two corps 1st & 11th got the best of the fight with Longstreet & Hill until they were reinforced by Ewell— when it became a drawn battle— Mead says they got our field of battle & the wounded which gives them therin the Victory in all else the battle was a drawn one— I send you a poster which is cast on every wall in New York— Your devoted Lizzie No news from Silver Spring today— Father rides to the Fort in a few minutes— Mother is very content here—

July 3, 1863

Washington   July 4, 1863
Dear Phil   Mother Blair & I have just returned from the Country where we went after a 7 olk breakfast— We found everything in good order & as quietly beautiful as ever— birds were joyous & dogs gave Blair a riotous welcome and I think all three of us were heartily sorry to come back to the City— altho entirely comfortable here

The news from the Armies is favorable but scarcely decisive enough for my appetite but I confess to some relief about things for our Army was *not* concentrated as rapidly as the enemy & I feared bad results from the fatigue & *scramble* with which it was collected— but Meade has only had it in hand 6 days— & in that time has fought three of them— he is in good position & on the defensive to get his men rested & in hand for an assault— Betty says there was an artillery train by this door today which took three quarters of an hour to pass— I have just asked Brother for the news & he says nothing especial—

Blair is firing of his small artillery in the alley under the window where he first realized that his Country had a birthday— & this one will long be remembered by the Nation & Lee's retreat will sanctify it anew in the feelings of the people— He commenced his Retreat at 3 olk this morning— Now I hope Meade will show his energy of which none of his family I've known lack— that is *the* trait of the race— especially in a quarrel or fight— but George & Robt— who was my friend always kept themselves out of the family feuds—

I recieved a letter from Apo inviting me most cordially to come stay with her says it will be a comfort to her as well as of service to Blair & me— the journey is too long to go alone besides I am loth to leave my mother who said to me I cannot last long under such trials— & yet a little while after she was amused by Blair   I feel I am a comfort to her & it is a great one to your own affecate Lizzie

Sunday July 5/63 I was too late getting in town to have this mailed yesterday, I went next door with it & there met your Secy with a dispatch in his hand— he said it was a matter of business— Dalhgren son a Capt. intercepted a letter of Jeff Davis' to Robt. Lee which developes their plan of this perilous campaign out of which he is trying now to extricate himself— the plan was for Lee to lead off Hooker just as he has done— take Harrisburg & then strike for Phila & Baltimore & Cut off all our Railroad resources— when Beauregard was to strike in at the rear of Washington led by Stuart— but when Cooper came to ordering off Beauregard— Jeff objected it seems that he had not been taken in confidence by Cooper & Lee— & his intercepted letter shows this fact— & he explains how impossible it is to part with Beauregard— that the Yankees are at the White House & threatening Charleston from which place he has had to reinforce Johnston & through the mercy of God we are saved by Jeff fears— for if Beauregard had accompanied Stuart last Saturday this day a week ago— Washington would now have been in the hands of the Rebels— that you & I know—

Meade would pursue Lee instantly but has to stop to get food for his men!! this I heard the President say when we met him at the White House door— where we took Blair to see the fireworks in which he was disappointed— And he also said that Meade said he was not yet certain whether Lee was beating a retreat— or in search of a good stronghold— at which to have another fight— You see the details of the battles so I need not dwell upon them I shall return home tomorrow— but Nothing is sure in this world. Your own   Lizzie

DEFENDING LITTLE ROUND TOP:
PENNSYLVANIA, JULY 1863

Joshua Lawrence Chamberlain to George B. Herendeen

On the afternoon of July 2 Brigadier General Gouverneur K. Warren, the chief engineer of the Army of the Potomac, discovered that, aside from a detachment of signalmen, there were no Union troops on Little Round Top, a hill at the southern end of the battlefield that dominated the Union defensive positions along Cemetery Ridge. Warren's urgent request for troops reached Colonel Strong Vincent, a brigade commander in the Fifth Corps, who hurried his men onto the hill as it came under Confederate assault. A professor of rhetoric and modern languages at Bowdoin College, Joshua Lawrence Chamberlain joined the 20th Maine Infantry in August 1862 and saw action at Shepherdstown and Fredericksburg before becoming the regiment's commander in late May 1863. He described his part in the battle for Little Round Top in a report sent to a brigade staff officer. Eventually regiments from two Union brigades secured the position, although both brigade commanders—Vincent and Brigadier General Stephen H. Weed—as well as artillery battery commander First Lieutenant Charles Hazlett were killed. (A longer version of Chamberlain's report to Lieutenant Herendeen was published in 1889 in *The War of the Rebellion: a Compilation of the Official Records of the Union and Confederate Armies.* Although it was dated July 6, 1863, it was actually written by Chamberlain in 1884 after the War Department told him that his original report had been lost.)

Head Quarters 20th Maine Vols.
Field near Gettysburg, Pa.
July 6th 1863

Lieut,

In compliance with orders from Brigade Hd. Qrs. I have the honor to submit the following Report of the part taken by the 20th Regt. Maine Vols, in the action of July 2d and 3d near Gettysburg, Pa.

On reaching the field at about 4 P.M. July 2d, Col. Vincent

commanding the Brigade, placing me on the left of the Brigade and consequently on the extreme left of our entire line of battle, instructed me that the enemy were expected shortly to make a desperate attempt to turn our left flank, and that the position assigned to me must be held at every hazard.

I established my line on the crest of a small spur of a rocky and wooded hill, and sent out at once a company of skirmishers on my left to guard against surprise on that unprotected flank.

These dispositions were scarcely made when the attack commenced, and the right of the Regt. found itself at once hotly engaged. Almost at the same moment, from a high rock which gave me a full view of the enemy, I perceived a heavy force in rear of their principal line, moving rapidly but stealthily toward our left, with the intention, as I judged, of gaining our rear unperceived. Without betraying our peril to any but one or two officers, I had the right wing move by the left flank, taking intervals of a pace or two, according to the shelter afforded by rocks or trees, extending so as to cover the whole front then engaged; and at the same time moved the left wing to the left and rear, making a large angle at the color, which was now brought to the point where our left had first rested.

This hazardous maneuvre was so admirably executed by my men that our fire was not materially slackened in front, and the enemy gained no advantage there, while the left wing in the mean time had formed a solid and steady line in a direction to meet the expected assault. We were not a moment too soon; for the enemy having gained their desired point of attack came to a front, and rushed forward with an impetuosity which showed their sanguine expectations. Their astonishment however was evident, when emerging from their cover, they met instead of an unsuspecting flank, a firm and ready front. A strong fire opened at once from both sides, and with great effect—the enemy still advancing until they came within *ten paces* of our line, where our steady and telling volleys brought them to a stand. From that moment began a struggle fierce and bloody beyond any that I have witnessed, and which lasted in all its fury, a full hour. The two lines met, and broke and mingled in the shock. At times I saw around me more of the enemy than of my own men. The edge of conflict swayed to and fro—now one and now the other party holding the contested ground. Three times our line was forced back, but only to rally and repulse the enemy. As often as the enemy's line was broken and routed, a new line was unmasked, which advanced with fresh vigor. Our "sixty rounds" were rapidly reduced: I sent several messengers to the rear for ammunition, and also for reinforcements. In the mean time we seized the opportunity of a momentary lull, to gather ammunition and more serviceable arms, from the dead and dying on the field. With these we met the enemy's last and fiercest assault. Their own rifles and their own bullets were turned against them. In the midst of this struggle, our ammunition *utterly failed*. The enemy were close upon us with a fresh line, pouring on us a terrible fire. Half the left wing already lay on the field. Although I had brought two companies from the right to its support, it was now scarcely more than a skirmish line. The heroic energy of my officers could avail no more. Our gallant line writhed & shrunk before the fire it could not repel. It was too evident that we could maintain the *defensive* no longer. As a last, desperate resort, I ordered a *charge*. The word "fix bayonets" flew from man to man. The click of the steel seemed to give new zeal to all. The men dashed forward with a shout. The two wings came into one line again, and extending to the left, and at the same time wheeling to the right, the whole Regiment described nearly a half circle, the left passing over the space of half a mile, while the right kept within the support of the 83d Penna. thus leaving no chance of escape to the enemy except to climb the steep side of the mountain or to pass by the whole front of the 83d Penna. The enemy's first line scarcely tried to run—they stood amazed, threw down their loaded arms and surrendered in whole companies. Those in their rear had more time and gave us more trouble. My skirmishing company threw itself upon the enemy's flank behind a stone wall, and their effective fire added to the enemy's confusion. In this charge we captured three hundred & sixty eight prisoners, many of them officers, and took three hundred stand of arms. The prisoners were from four different regiments, and admitted that they had attacked with a Brigade.

At this time Col. Rice commanding the Brigade (Col. Vincent having been mortally wounded) brought up a strong support from Genl. Crawford's command, and 3000 rounds of ammunition. The wounded and the prisoners were now sent to the rear, and our dead gathered and laid side by side.

Shortly after Col. Rice desired me to advance and take the high steep hill, called "Wolf Hill" or "Round Top" half a mile or more to our left and front, where the enemy had assembled on their repulse—a position which commanded ours in case the assault should be renewed.

It was then dusk. The men were worn out, and heated and thirsty almost beyond endurance. Many had sunk down and fallen asleep the instant the halt was ordered. But at the command they cheerfully formed their line once more, and the little handful of men went up the hill, scarcely expecting ever to return. In order not to disclose our numbers—as I had now but two hundred guns—and to avoid bringing on an engagement in which I was sure to be overpowered, I forbid my men to fire, and trusted to the bayonet alone. Throwing out two small detachments on each flank, we pushed straight up the hill. The darkness favored us, concealing our force and preventing the enemy from getting range so that their volleys went over our heads, while they deemed it prudent to retire before us. Just at the crest we found more serious difficulty and were obliged to fall back for a short time. We advanced again with new energy, which the knowledge of our isolated and perilous position rendered perhaps desperate, and carried the desired point. We took twenty five prisoners in this movement, among them some of the staff of Genl. Laws. From these officers I learned that Hoods whole Division was massed but a short distance in front, that he had just prepared to advance and take possession of the heights, and was only waiting to ascertain the number and position of our force. I posted my command among the rocks along the crest in line of battle, and sent two companies in charge of judicious officers to reconnoitre the ground in front. They reported a large body of the enemy in a ravine not more than two or three hundred yards distant. I therefore kept these two companies out, with orders to watch the enemy, while our main line, kept on the alert by occasional volleys from below, held its position among the rocks throughout the night. In the meantime the 83d

Penna. and the 5th & 12th Penna Reserves came up and formed as a support. The next day at noon we were relieved by the 1st Brigade.

We were engaged with Laws' Brigade, Hood's Div. The prisoners represented themselves as from the 15th and 47th Alabama and the 4th and 5th Texas Regts. The whole number of prisoners taken by us is three hundred & ninety three—of arms captured three hundred stand. At least one hundred and fifty of the enemy's killed and wounded were found in front of our first line of battle.

We went into the fight with three hundred & fifty eight guns. Every pioneer and musician who could carry a musket was armed and engaged. Our loss is one hundred & thirty six —thirty killed, one hundred & five wounded—many mortally —and one taken prisoner in the night advance. Often as our line was broken and pierced by the enemy, there is not a man to be reported "missing."

I have to regret the loss of a most gallant young officer, Lt. W. L. Kendall, who fell in the charge also Capt. C. W. Billings mortally wounded early in the action, and Lieut. A. N. Linscott mortally wounded on the crest of "Wolf Hill." Our advantage was dearly bought with the loss of such admirable officers as these.

As for the conduct of my officers and men, I will let the result speak for them. If I were to mention any, I might do injustice by omitting some equally deserving. Our roll of Honor is the three hundred & eighty officers and men who *fought at Gettysburg.*

My thanks are due the 83d Penna, Capt Woodward comdg. for their steady and gallant support, and I would particularly acknowledge the services of Adjt. Gifford of that Regt. who exposed himself to the severest fire to render me aid.

Very respectfully
Your obdt. servt.
J. L. Chamberlain
Col. 20th Maine Vols.

Lt. Geo. B. Herendeen,
Act. Asst. Adjt. Genl.
3d Brigade 1st Div. 5th Corps.

DEFEATING PICKETT'S CHARGE:
PENNSYLVANIA, JULY 1863

Henry Livermore Abbott to Josiah Gardner Abbott

A veteran of Ball's Bluff, Fair Oaks, the Seven Days, Fredericksburg, and Chancellorsville, Captain Henry Livermore Abbott commanded a company in the 20th Massachusetts Infantry. His regiment reached the Gettysburg battlefield early on July 2 and was posted along with the rest of the Second Corps at the center of the Union line on Cemetery Ridge. On the afternoon of July 3, as Lee sent about 13,000 men against the Union center, the section of Cemetery Ridge defended by the 20th Massachusetts came under attack by two brigades from the division commanded by Major General George E. Pickett.

July 6 / 1863
Near Gettysburg Pa

My dear Papa,

When our great victory was just over, the exultation of victory was so great that one didn't think of our fearful losses, but now I cant help feeling a great weight at my heart. Poor Henry Ropes was one of the dearest friends I ever had or expect to have. He was one of the purest-minded, noblest, most generous men I ever knew. His loss is terrible. His men actually wept when they showed me his body, even under the tremendous cannonade, a time when most soldiers see their comrades dying around them with indifference. Col. Hall, I believe, means to mention him in his report. He says that of every body in the army, Henry was the only one he knew that was fighting simply from patriotism, & that he would himself almost have given his life to have had Ropes lived to see the splendid victory he always so earnestly hoped for. I cant cease to think of him, whenever I am alone, which is pretty frequent now that we have only 3 left. All our pique against Revere too had long ceased, since we saw him on the march struggling so nobly with his physical weakness, & he is regretted as such a man should be. Then there is poor Macy with a hand gone. Herbert Mason hit too, with Ropes my most intimate friend here, two of the finest & bravest officers that ever fought in this war. Just as he was going off from the hospital, with a consideration that wounded men going home very rarely feel for those left, he send me his brandy, tobacco, &c a perfect God-Send at the time. Patten too, who is going to be mentioned by Col. Hall for the gallantry, with which he held his outpost, when the skirmishers on both flanks had run, & our whole fire in the direst confusion had gone over him. In deed with only two officers besides myself remaining, I cant help feeling a little spooney when I am thinking, & you know I am not at all a lachrymose individual in general. However I think we can run the machine. Our losses are—of 13 officers, 3 killed, 7 wounded. Of 231 enlisted men, 30 killed, 84 wounded, 3 missing, total 117, with officers, aggregate 127. I haven't time to give you an account as I have to write to Mr. Ropes, & John Revere, also to Paines father. (Paine was one of the finest officers I have ever seen though only 17 years of age). The enemy, after a morning of quiet on our part of the line, (a little to the right of the left center) began the most terrific cannonade with a converging fire of 150 pieces that I ever heard in my life & kept it up for 2 hours, almost entirely disabling our batteries, killing & wounding over half the officers & men & silencing most of the guns. The thin line of our division against which it was directed was very well sheilded by a little rut they lay in & in front of our brigade by a little pit, just one foot deep & one foot high, thrown up hastily by one shovel, but principally by the fact that it is very difficult to hit a single line of troops, so that the enemy chiefly threw over us with the intention of disabling the batteries & the reserves which they supposed to be massed in rear of the batteries in the depression of the hill. In the former object they were successful, in the latter they were better than successful. The one brigade brought up in support had to be retired 2 miles, & no other reserves could be brought up, for any massing of troops would under that fire would have proved their own destruction, without their being of any service to us. No infantry in the world could have been massed under that fire for half an hour. The rebels thus left us entirely unsupported & advanced with perfect confidence, after ceasing their artillery, our artillery being so well knocked up that only one or two shots were fired into them which however were very well aimed & we could see tumble over squads in the rebel lines. Had our batteries been intact, the rebels would never have got up to our musketry, for they were obliged to come out of the woods & advance from a half to 3/4 of a mile over an open field & in plain sight. A magnificent sight it was too. Two brigades in two lines, their skirmishers driving in ours. The moment I saw them, I knew we should give them Fredericksburg. So did every body. We let the regiment in front of us get within 100 feet of us, & then bowled them over like nine pins, picking out the colors first. In two minutes there were only groups of two or three men running round wildly, like chickens with their heads off. We were cheering like mad, when Macy directed my attention to a spot 3 or 4 rods on our right where there were no pits, only, a rail fence. Baxter's Pennsylvania men had most disgracefully broken, & the rebels were within our line. The order was immediately given to fall back far enough to form another line & prevent us being flanked. Without however waiting for that, the danger was so imminent that I had rushed my company immediately up to the gap, & the regiment & the rest of the brigade, being there some before & the rest as quick as they could. The rail fence checked the main advance of the enemy & they stood, both sides, pegging away into each other. The rows of dead after the battle, I found to be within 15 and 20 feet apart, as near hand to hand fighting as I ever care to see. The rebels behaved with as much pluck as any men in the world could, they stood there against the fence, until they were nearly all shot down. The rebels batteries, seeing how the thing was going, pitched shell into us, all the time, with great disregard of their own friends who were so disagreeably near us. Gen Webb who commands the Philadelphia brigade in his official report has given Hall's brigade the credit of saving the day, after his own men had run away. A miserable rowdy named Hays comdg. the 3rd div. of our corps, who was not engaged at all in the musketry fire, claims I believe all the credit of the thing. So look out for false stories in papers. Dont confound this fellow with Hays comdg the corps, who is said to be a good officer, & who got up just after the fight, Hancock commanding the corps & Gibbon comdg the div, a splendid officer, being both wounded. Our lines were something of this form.

The field was mostly open where we all were with scarcely a perceptible rise, comanded by the rebel side, on the centre a little wooded still better commanded by the rebel side, on the right, I am told, wooded & rocky, both parties contending for the slopes towards us. The mountains facing our left were out of cannon range. On the right they were not, but I am told, of such a nature that the rebels could have only got so little artillery into position, that our superior number of batteries would soon have knocked them into pie, notwithstanding their commanding hight, which accounts for what at first was very strange to me, why the rebs didn't shell us out, since the hights near the right center commanded the entire field around the centre, where it is very narrow. Moreover our line of retreat was so narrow that it was easy, if our left was turned to cut us off from it. Had the rebels driven in our left (they twice tried it & I have told you how near they came to it,) it would have been all up with us. The advantages of our position were that the comdg. general could over look almost the whole line, a rare thing in this country, & that moving on the chord of the circle while the enemy moved on the arc, we could reinforce any part of the line from any other part much quicker than they could, an advantage which Meade availed himself of admirably in the first day's rebel attack, but which their shell fire prevented him from doing in the second day's. In person, Meade is a tall, thin lantern-jawed respectable covey, wearing spectacles, looking a good sort of a family doctor. Uncle John Sedgewick, as have most other of our good officers, long ago told us that McClellan was the first choice, Franklin the 2nd,

& Meade the 3rd. An extremely good officer you see, with no vanity or nonsense of any kind, knowing just exactly what he could do & what he couldn't. Our troops were so elated by the removal of Hooker, both Generals, line officers & men, & by the feeling that they were on their own soil, that perhaps they deserve fully as much credit as the generalship of Meade. I dont know however. I am afraid Meade would hardly have conducted an invasion into Va. as well.

I find I am getting a good deal longer than I meant to be, so I will conclude with asking you to thank mama for the things she sent. Wm Kelly was delighted & the tobacco for me came just when I was starting on the march without any. You can imagine what a godsend it was.

I suppose you have all been suffering a great deal of anxiety, but how thankful you must be now that certainty doesn't bring you the same grief that the Ropes family have. God grant we may have no bad news from Fletcher. My love of course to all the family including George & Mary Welch. Tell them to be sure & write how John is. We miss him terribly.

Your aff. son,
H. L. Abbott

I have had no mail since leaving Falmouth.

"A SERIES OF TERRIBLE ENGAGEMENTS":
PENNSYLVANIA, JULY 1863

Lafayette McLaws to Emily McLaws

As the Army of Northern Virginia retreated through Maryland, Major General Lafayette McLaws wrote about his division's actions at Gettysburg. The unexpected resistance his troops encountered around the peach orchard was caused by the advance of the Union Third Corps toward the Emmitsburg road in the early afternoon of July 2.

Headquarters Division
July 7th/63

My Dear Wife

Since I wrote you last we have had a series of terrible engagements out of which God has permitted me to come unscathed again. On the 1st of July we left Chambersburg and went across the mountains by Fayetteville and Greenwood to Cashtown and camped within five miles of Gettysburg. Where we heard that there had been a considerable battle fought between the forces of the enemy and the Corps of Genls Ewell and Hill, resulting in the route of the enemy with a loss of several thousand prisoners. The next morning we moved around Gettysburg towards the Emmitsburg road, to arrive at the *Peach orchard*, a small settlement with a very large Peach Orchard attached. The intention was to get in rear of the enemy who were supposed to be stationed principally in rear of Gettysburg or near it. The report being that the enemy had but two regiments of infantry and one battery at the Peach orchard. On arriving at the vicinity of the Orchard, the enemy were discovered in greater force than was supposed, and two of my Brigades were deployed to face the enemy, and the other two in the rear as reserve; ten or twelve pieces were put in position, and fire opened— General Longstreet sent word that he was satisfied there was but a small force of the enemy in front and that I must proceed at once to the assault. On examination it was discovered that the enemy were in much greater force than was expected, and the assualt was delayed, but again delayed and finally I was directed not to assault until General Hood was in position. Gen H had gone around above me to the right, and found that the enemy were very strongly posted on two rocky hills, with artillery and infantry and before he could aid me it was necessary to carry one of the hills—the one nearest to him—which was done by his troops after a desperate encounter, and my division was then ordered in readiness, and as Genl Hoods success became apparent, the Brigades of Kershaw and Semmes were ordered to advance and then those of Barksdale and Wofford, gallantly our men swept the enemy before them, away from the Peach orchard and on to the woods and hills beyond with great slaughter. The enemy in crowds running to our lines. The right Brigades attempted to storm the second hill which was very steep and rocky and bare of trees towards the top, their efforts were however vain and we were obliged to desist. We however occupied the woods beneath the hills, and remained during the night. Genl Barksdale, commanding the Mississippi Brigade was killed, Genl Semmes badly wounded. Colonel Carter of the 13th Miss killed, Colonel Griffin of the 18th Miss & Col Holder 17th Miss. badly wounded, Col de Saussure 15th S.C. killed, Lt. Col. Fiser 17th Miss. Wounded, &c &c. —The loss in my Division was near twenty four hundred, the heaviest of the war, and many of the most valuable officers in the whole service have been killed. Thus ended the battle of the Peach orchard. In place of there being but two regiments of infantry and one battery, the enemy were in very great force, very strongly posted and aided by very numerous arty. I think the attack was unnecessary and the whole plan of battle a very bad one. Genl Longstreet is to blame for not reconnoitering the ground and for persisting in ordering the assault when his errors were discovered. During the engagement he was very excited, giving contrary orders to every one, and was exceedingly overbearing. I consider him a humbug—a man of small capacity, very obstinate, not at all chivalrous, exceedingly conceited, and totally selfish. If I can it is my intention to get away from his command. We want Beauregard very much indeed, his presence is imperatively called for. On the 3d inst, all our available arty was put in position along our lines, and commenced the most tremendous artillery fire I expect ever heard on our continent. We had several hundred cannon and the enemy as many more; finally our troops assaulted the centre, and gained the enemies batteries but were compelled to relinquish our hold and retire to our lines of the day previous to the assualt—where we remained until the next day, when were retired at dark without molestation and reached this place 2 miles from Hagerstown last night about ten oclock. Our men very much fatigued and foot sore, but not disheartened.

The retirement was necessary because it became important to re-establish our communications with the government.

Give a thousand kisses to my dear children, and my dear wife a thousand kisses to you also, and much love indeed. The mail is waiting & I write in a hurry.

Your devoted husband
LM

Be careful in writing as the last mails were captured by the enemy and were of course read by all, & may be published.

A NURSE AT GETTYSBURG:
PENNSYLVANIA, JULY 1863

Cornelia Hancock to Her Cousin and to Ellen Hancock Child

The battle of Gettysburg cost the Confederates about 28,000 men killed, wounded, or missing, while Union losses totaled about 23,000. Cornelia Hancock, a young Quaker woman from New Jersey, went to Gettysburg with her brother-in-law, Dr. Henry T. Child, to help care for the wounded. (She was not related to Major General Winfield Scott Hancock, the commander of the Union Second Corps.) Hancock arrived at Gettysburg on the evening of July 6 and began working in an army field hospital the next day.

Gettysburg, Pa. July 7th, 1863.

My dear cousin

I AM very tired tonight; have been on the field all day—went to the 3rd Division 2nd Army Corps. I suppose there are about five hundred wounded belonging to it. They have one patch of woods devoted to each army corps for a hospital. I being interested in the 2nd, because Will had been in it, got into one of its ambulances, and went out at eight this morning and came back at six this evening. There are no words in the English language to express the sufferings I witnessed today. The men lie on the ground; their clothes have been cut off them to dress their wounds; they are half naked, have nothing but hard-tack to eat only as Sanitary Commissions, Christian Associations, and so forth give them. I was the first woman who reached the 2nd Corps after the three days fight at Gettysburg. I was in that Corps all day, not another woman within a half mile. Mrs. Harris was in first division of 2nd Corps. I was introduced to the surgeon of the post, went anywhere through the Corps, and received nothing but the greatest politeness from even the lowest private. You can tell Aunt that there is every opportunity for "secesh" sympathizers to do a good work among the butternuts; we have lots of them here suffering fearfully. To give you some idea of the extent and numbers of the wounds, four surgeons, none of whom were idle fifteen minutes at a time, were busy all day amputating legs and arms. I gave to every man that had a leg or arm off a gill of wine, to every wounded in Third Division, one glass of lemonade, some bread and preserves and tobacco—as much as I am opposed to the latter, for they need it very much, they are so exhausted.

I feel very thankful that this was a successful battle; the spirit of the men is so high that many of the poor fellows said today, "What is an arm or leg to whipping Lee out of Penn." I would get on first rate if they would not ask me to write to their wives; *that* I cannot do without crying, which is not pleasant to either party. I do not mind the sight of blood, have seen limbs taken off and was not sick at all.

It is a very beautiful, rolling country here; under favorable circumstances I should think healthy, but now for five miles around, there is an awful smell of putrefaction. Women are needed here very badly, anyone who is willing to go to field hospitals, but nothing short of an order from Secretary Stanton or General Halleck will let you through the lines. Major General Schenk's order for us was not regarded as anything; if we had not met Miss Dix at Baltimore Depot, we should not have gotten through. It seems a strange taste but I am glad we did. We stay at Doctor Horner's house at night—direct letters care of Dr. Horner, Gettysburg, Pa. If you could mail me a newspaper, it would be a great satisfaction, as we do not get the news here and the soldiers are so anxious to hear; things will be different here in a short time.

CORNELIA

Gettysburg—July 8th, 1863.

My dear sister

WE have been two days on the field; go out about eight and come in about six—go in ambulances or army buggies. The surgeons of the Second Corps had one put at our disposal. I feel assured I shall never feel horrified at anything that may happen to me hereafter. There is a great want of surgeons here; there are hundreds of brave fellows, who have not had their wounds dressed since the battle. Brave is not the word; more, more Christian fortitude never was witnessed than they exhibit, always say—"Help my neighbor first he is worse." The Second Corps did the heaviest fighting, and, of course, all who were badly wounded, were in the thickest of the fight, and, therefore, we deal with the very best class of the men—that is the bravest. My name is particularly grateful to them because it is Hancock. General Hancock is very popular with his men. The reason why they suffer more in this battle is because our army is victorious and marching *on* after Lee, leaving the wounded for citizens and a very few surgeons. The citizens are stripped of everything they have, so you must see the exhausting state of affairs. The Second Army Corps alone had two thousand men wounded, this I had from the Surgeon's head quarters. I cannot write more. There is no mail that comes in, we send letters out: I believe the Government has possession of the road. I hope you will write. It would be very pleasant to have letters to read in the evening, for I am so tired I cannot write them. Get the Penn Relief to send clothing here; there are many men without anything but a shirt lying in poor shelter tents, calling on God to take them from this world of suffering; in fact the air is rent with petitions to deliver them from their sufferings.

C. HANCOCK

Direct boxes—E. W. Farnham, care of Dr. Horner, Gettysburg, Penna. for Second Corps Hospital. Do not neglect this; clothing is shockingly needed. We fare pretty well for delicacies sent up by men from Baltimore.

If you direct your letters Miss Hancock, Second Corps, Third Division Hospital, do not scruple to put the Miss to it, and leave out Cornelia, as I am known only by that cognomen. I do not know when I shall go home—it will be according to how long this hospital stays here and whether another battle comes soon. I can go right in an ambulance without being any expense to myself. The Christian Committee support us and when they get tired the Sanitary is on hand. Uncle Sam is very rich, but very slow, and if it was not for the Sanitary, much suffering would ensue. We give the men toast and eggs for breakfast, beef tea at ten o'clock, ham and bread for dinner, and jelly and bread for supper. Dried rusk would be nice if they were only here. Old sheets we would give much for. Bandages are plenty but sheets very scarce. We have plenty of woolen blankets now, in fact the hospital is well supplied, but for about five days after the battle, the men had no blankets nor scarce any shelter.

It took nearly five days for some three hundred surgeons to perform the amputations that occurred here, during which time the rebels lay in a dying condition without their wounds being dressed or scarcely any food. If the rebels did not get severely punished for this battle, then I am no judge. We have but one rebel in our camp now; he says he never fired his gun if he could help it, and, therefore, we treat him first rate. One man died this morning. I fixed him up as nicely as the place will allow; he will be buried this afternoon. We are becoming somewhat civilized here now and the men are cared for well.

On reading the news of the copperhead performance, in a tent where eight men lay with nothing but stumps (they call a leg cut off above the knee a "stump") they said if they held on a little longer they would form a stump brigade and go and fight them. We have some plucky boys in the hospital, but they suffer awfully. One had his leg cut off yesterday, and some of the ladies, newcomers, were up to see him. I told them if they had seen as many as I had they would not go far to see the sight again. I could stand by and see a man's head taken off I believe—you get so used to it here. I should be perfectly contented if I could receive my letters. I have the cooking all on my mind pretty much. I have torn almost all my clothes off of me, and Uncle Sam has given me a new suit. William says I am very popular here as I am such a contrast to some of the office-seeking women who swarm around hospitals. I am black as an Indian and dirty as a pig and as well as I ever was in my life—have a nice bunk and tent about twelve feet square. I have a bed that is made of four crotch sticks and some sticks laid across and pine boughs laid on that with blankets on top. It is equal to any mattress ever made. The tent is open at night and sometimes I have laid in the damp all night long, and got up all right in the morning.

The suffering we get used to and the nurses and doctors, stewards, etc., are very jolly and sometimes we have a good time. It is very pleasant weather now. There is all in getting to do what you *want* to do and I am doing that.

The First Minnesota Regiment bears the first honors here for loss in the late battle. The Colonel was wounded—Lieutenant Colonel, Major, and Adjutant. They had four captains killed outright and when they came out of battle, the command devolved on the First Lieutenant. Three hundred and eighty-four men went into battle, one hundred and eighty were wounded and fifty-four killed. The Colonel I know well; he is a very fine man. He has three bullets in him; has had two taken out by Dr. Child, the other he got in at Antietam and it is there yet. I do hope he will recover. Most of the men are from New York here now; they are very intelligent and talk good politics. McClellan is their man mostly. Meade they think sympathizes with McClellan and therefore they like him. Hooker is at a very low ebb except as they think he fed them well—a circumstance that soldiers make great account of. Such feeders you never saw.

Pads are terribly needed here. Bandages and lint are plenty. I would like to see seven barrels of dried rusk here. I do not know the day of the week or anything else. Business is slackening a little though—order is beginning to reign in the hospital and soon things will be right. One poor fellow is hollowing fearfully now while his wounds are being dressed.

There is no more impropriety in a *young* person being here provided they are sensible than a sexagenarian. Most polite and obliging are all the soldiers to me.

It is a very good place to meet celebrities; they come here from all parts of the United States to see their wounded. Senator Wilson, Mr. Washburn, and one of the Minnesota Senators have been here. I get beef tenderloin for dinner.—Ladies who work are favored but the dress-up palaverers are passed by on the other side. I tell you I have lost my memory almost entirely, but it is gradually returning. Dr. Child has done very good service here. All is well with me; we do not know much war news, but I know I am doing all I can, so I do not concern further. Kill the copperheads. Write everything, however trifling, it is all interest here.

From thy affectionate
C. HANCOCK

CELEBRATING THE FOURTH:
IOWA, JULY 1863

Catharine Peirce to Taylor Peirce

Catharine Peirce wrote with news of home to her husband, a soldier with the 22nd Iowa Infantry at Vicksburg. She would later receive a letter Taylor had written to her on July 4 announcing that the "Gibralter of America has fallen."

Des Moines City July 5th 1863
I sit down to write feeling a little bad again not having had a letter for two weeks but I will try and be patient hoping thee is well and that I will get one in a few days more. We are all well to day. Cyrus seems to be in a better condition this two weeks than he has been for a long time. I do not know whather it is Ayers medicine that is helping him or not. We have had a very pleasant summer so far with the exception of a few very warm days but our fourth was not near so hot as it was last year I do not think. We had a very nice celebration on the fair ground and a real good addres by a Mr Palmer in favour of the war the Union and the Soldeirs and death to all Copperheads and rebel sympathisers. It was a good thing and just suited my stile. The speaker went on to say that Goverment must be sustained and the soldiers cared for at all hazards but Dear me I can not write half of the good that was spoken in behalf of our Country and our Countrys cause. Mary received a letter from Rachel day before yesterday. R writes they are all well but Aunt Hannah she is no better and there appears very little prospect of her ever being any better. Rachel writes very gloomily of the times. The Rebels have got up into Penn and are doing a great amount of damage. But if thee has a chance to see the Union papers thee will know more about what they are doing than I can write, but it seem as our army in the east has not or can not attane much some how or other. What is the reason I am shour I can not tell. It seemed to me if they let the rebles overrun them there that there is very little hope

for our beloved Country. But I still hope and trust there is still a just God in heaven that will set the Nation right one of these days, wheather we live to see it or not Dear Taylor. I can not write to do any good or that will be interesting to thee for the simple reason that I do not know of any thing of interest to write of.

I have not had any news from Jasper Co for a week or more. Mr Vowel and his wife was up here about two weeks ago and gave me the full news. There is nothing of importance except deaths. Preston Caloson was killed at the Battle of Black river Bridge and Willis Greens son also but I expect thee has seen the account of the killed before this time. Vowel says that there is no thing doing in Newton this summer to a mount to any thing. He thinks if the railroad should mis it a few miles that it will die a naturel death and that right soon they have got the cars runing to Grenell now and are working on this side. They say thair are going to grade Skunk bottom this fall but it may not be done if the Draft gos on. The baby is siting on the floor by side me and is beginig to fuss and I will have to close.

With love I remain thy wife Catharine

VICKSBURG SURRENDERS:
MISSISSIPPI, JULY 1863

William Henry Harrison Clayton to Amos and Grace Clayton

With no hope of relief or resupply, Lieutenant General John C. Pemberton opened surrender negotiations at Vicksburg on July 3. Grant initially demanded an unconditional surrender, but then agreed to parole the garrison in order to avoid having to transport 30,000 prisoners to Illinois; he also hoped that many of the paroled Confederates would return home and spread disaffection with the war. Pemberton's army capitulated on July 4, ending a nine-week campaign that had cost the Union about 9,000 men killed, wounded, or missing. William Henry Harrison Clayton of the 19th Iowa Infantry witnessed the surrender.

Vicksburg, Miss.
July 5th, 1863
Dear Father & Mother:
It is with great pleasure that I pen the following lines. Yesterday, the *"glorious* Fourth of July" was made doubly so, by the *surrender*, and *occupation* of this, the strongest rebel position in their Confederacy.

It was an event that we, and I suppose the whole Northern people, have been patiently waiting for, for months past, and what is better than all it fell without the necessity of storming the works and thus losing numbers of valuable lives.

We have *starved* them out, they held out until they could do so no longer, and they were compelled to come to terms.

I saw from the Keosaqua papers that there was to be celebrations on the Fourth at a number of places in the county, one being at Lebanon. I would have given anything almost if I could by some means, have been conveyed from here, there and given the joyful news. What a celebration there would have been had you only known the situation here. I imagine that copperheads would have looked down their noses and wish themselves hid from the gaze of exultant loyal people. My sincere wish now is, that Lee and his army may get the *devil* from Hooker or someone else. I think that the Rebs would be about *played out*.

Hostilities ceased here on the 3rd before noon, they had hoisted a flag of truce. Negotiations were pending until the morning of the Fourth, when they surrendered.

I have not yet learned the terms. The prisoners are still in places they occupied yesterday morning. On the 3rd when firing ceased, our boys laid down their guns and went over to their rifle pits and forts and had quite a chat with them. It looked singular to see men, who but a few minutes previously were shooting at each other, mingle together and shake hands, and be as friendly, apparently, as brothers, but such is among the incidents of war.

Our batteries had been well supplied with ammunition and it was the intention to celebrate the Fourth on a *grand* scale, by shelling the town's 7 fortifications, but owing to the surrender only the National salute was fired, with blank cartridges.

We received orders, and at 9½ o'clock Ormes' brigade started for the inside of the fortifications. It was very hot and dusty and the march was very fatiguing. It is but a short distance from here to our old camp, but by the wagon road it is 2 or 3 miles. We are a mile or two from the town but as we are inside the works, considered that we are in Vicksburg, and began my letter accordingly. We received orders before we started in to *not cheer* or make any demonstration upon coming in. The Rebs were surprised at our conduct, and were as friendly as could be expected under the circumstances. Some of them are fine looking fellows, and some are very reasonable and admit that they are defending a bad cause. I have talked with a number that say they will fight no more if they can possibly help it. I was talking to one awhile ago close by an earthwork where our regimental flag was waving to the breeze. He said it looked better to him yet, than any other flag. I have looked in vain for the Rebel flag (the stars & bars) but have not seen it *yet*. I have seen their battery flags flying at the different forts. That of Georgia is a red flag with two black stripes diagonally across it, another flag was white with a large spot in the center. I asked a fellow this morning what kind of flag they had, but he could not tell me, he said they had several kinds but could describe none.

If we had charged these works there would have been great loss of life, for they have an abundance of ammunition and the works command each other so that if one should be taken there is two or three others ready to open upon it. They say that we never could have taken the place if they had plenty of provision, but I think it would have been taken anyhow.

They acknowledge that we did as much work in a nights time building forts and digging rifle-pits as they could do in a week. They say that we are western troops or the place never would have been taken. They seem to think that eastern troops do not possess the valor of western troops. After we entered the works the gunboats above steamed down and each fired the National salute as she rounded to. A number of boats came down during the day, screaming and blowing around as though glad to once more pass the spot so long barricaded.

Numbers of the prisoners say that they have had but one biscuit a day, and a piece of meat about the size of a persons finger, twice a day for two weeks past. The meat gave out toward the last, and I have it from a number of them that they actually eat mule-meat. They say that if the place had not been surrendered when it was they would not have stood it much longer, but laid down their arms and refused to fight longer. We have made a *big* haul, from 20 to 30,000 prisoners, the same number stands of arms and *lots* of field artillery & heavy guns, and any quantity of ammunition for them. It has been the most glorious event of the war. I would not have missed being here for a good deal. Herron's command occupies the right of their defenses or the left of our army, being below town. I received a letter from Lizzie Cooper yesterday. All were well excepting Aunt Agness who was no better. She said that there was considerable excitement there in regard to the Rebel invasion, but that preparations were being made to give them a warm reception if they should make their appearance there. The boys are all well and are pleased to be present at the fall of Vicksburg.

Give my respects to all my friends.

Your affectionate son,

W. H. H. Clayton

P.S. As I write the poor devils are running around trading tobacco for bread or anything to eat. There is so many that it takes a long time to issue provisions to them. Our boys have given them all that we could spare. They have drawn tobacco since they came here & have plenty.

The 19th had but one man wounded during our three weeks stay here. We have been lucky, were as much exposed as the other regiments that had some killed and wounded but we passed through without loss.

"THE EVENT OF THE WAR":
MISSISSIPPI, JULY 1863

William T. Sherman to Ellen Ewing Sherman

Sherman wrote to his wife on July 5, four days before the Confederate garrison at Port Hudson, Louisiana, surrendered to Major General Nathaniel P. Banks. The fall of Port Hudson, which had been under siege since May 22, would give the Union control of the entire length of the Mississippi River.

Camp near Black River,
20 miles east of Vicksburg,
July 5, 63

Dearest Ellen,

You will have heard all about the capitulation of Vicksburg on the 4th of July, and I Suppose duly appreciate it. It is the event of the war thus far. Davis placed it in the scale of Richmond, and pledged his honor that it should be held even if he had to abandon Tennessee. But it was of no use, and we are now in full possession. I am out and have not gone in to See, as even before its surrender Grant was disposing to send me forth to meet Johnston who is and has been since June 15 collecting a force about Jackson to raise the siege. I will have Ords corps, the 13th (McClernands) Shermans 15th and Parkes 9th. All were to have been out last night but Vicksburg & the 4th of July were too much for one day and they are not yet come. I expect them hourly. I am busy making 3 bridges to cross Black River and Shall converge on Bolton and Clinton and if not held back by Johnston shall enter Jackson, and then finish what was so well begun last month and break up all the Railroads & bridges in the Interior so that it will be impossible for armies to assemble again to threaten the River.

The capture of Vicksburg is to me the first gleam of daylight in this war—It was strong by nature, and had been strengthened by immense labor & stores—Grant telegraphs me 27,000 prisoners, 128 Field Guns and 100 siege pieces—add to these, 13 Guns, & 5000 Prisoners at Arkansas Post, 18 Guns & 250 prisoners at Jackson, 5 Guns & 2000 prisoners at Port Gibson —10 heavy Guns at Grand Gulf, 60 field Guns & 3500 prisoners at Champion Hill, and 14 heavy Guns at Haines Bluff, beside the immense amounts of ammunition, shot shells, horses, wagons &c. make the most extraordinary fruits of our six months campaign. Here is Glory enough for all the Heros of the West, but I content myself with Knowing & feeling that our enemy is weakened so much, and more yet by failing to hold a point deemed by them as essential to their empire in the South West. We have ravaged the Land, and have sent away half a million of negros so that this country is paralyzed and cannot recover its lost strength in twenty years.

Had the Eastern armies done half as much war would be substantially entered upon. But I read of Washington, Baltimore & Philadelphia being threatened & Rosecrans sitting idly by, writing for personal favor in the newspapers, and our Government at Washington chiefly engaged in pulling down its leaders. Hooker now consigned to retirement. Well I thank God, we are far from Washington and that we have in Grant not a Great man or a hero—but a good, plain sensible kindhearted fellow. Here are Grant, & Sherman & McPherson, three sons of Ohio, have achieved more actual success than all else combined and I have yet to see the first kindly notice of us in the State, but on the contrary a system of abuse designed & calculated to destroy us with the People & the Army: but the army of the Tennessee, those who follow their colors & do not skulk behind in the North, at the Hospitals & depots far to the Rear, Know who think & act, and if Life is spared us our Countrymen will realize the Truth. I shall go on through heat & dust till the Mississipi is clear, till the large armies of the enemy in this quarter seek a more secure base, and then I will renew my hopes of getting a quiet hour when we can grow up among our children & prepare them for the dangers which may environ their later life. I did hope Grant would have given me Vicksburg and let some one else follow up the enemy inland, but I never suggest anything to myself personal, and only what I deem necessary to fulfil the purposes of war. I know that the capture of Vicksburg will make an impression the world over, and expect loud acclamations in the North West, but I heed more its effects on Louisiana & Arkansas. If Banks succeed as he now must at Port Hudson, and the army in Missouri push to Little Rock, the Region west of the Mississipi will cease to be the Theater of war save to the Bands of Robbers created by war who now prefer to live by pillage than honest labor. Rosecrans army & this could also, acting in concert, drive all opposing masses into the recesses of Georgia & Alabama, leaving the Atlantic slopes the great Theater of War.

I wish Halleck would put a Guard on the White House to keep out the Committees of preachers Grannies & Dutchmen that absorb Lincolns time & thoughts, fill up our thinned Ranks with conscripts, and then handle these vast armies with the Single thought of success regardless of who shall get the personal credit and Glory.

I am pleased to hear from you that occasionally you receive Kindness from men out of regard to me. I know full well there must be a large class of honest people north who are sick of the wrangling of officers for power and notoriety and are sick of the silly flattery piled by interested parties on their favorites. McClernand the only sample of that List with us played himself out, and there is not an officer or soldier here but rejoices he is gone away. With an intense selfishness and lust of notoriety he could not let his mind get beyond the limits of his vision and therefore all was brilliant about him and dark & suspicious beyond. My style is the reverse. I am somewhat blind to what occurs near me, but have a clear perception of things & events remote. Grant possesses the happy medium and it is for this reason I admire him. I have a much quicker perception of things than he, but he balances the present & remote so evenly that results follow in natural course. I would not have risked the passing the Batteries at Vicksburg & trusting to the long route by Grand Gulf & Jackson to reach what we both knew were the key points to Vicksburg, but I would have aimed to reach the same points by Grenada—But both arrived at the same points and though both of us Knew little of the actual ground, it is wonderful how well they have realized our military calculations.

As we sat in Oxford last November we saw in the future what we now realize and like the architect who sees developed the beautiful vision of his Brain, we feel an intense satisfaction at the realization of our military plans. Thank God no president was near to thwart our plans, and that the short sighted Public could not drive us from our object till the plan was fully realized.

Well the campaign of Vicksburg is ended, and I am either to begin anew or simply make complete the natural sequences of a finished Job. I regard my movement as the latter, though you and others may be distressed at the guesses of our newspaper correspondent on the Spot (Cairo) and made to believe I am marching on Mobile, or Chattanooga or Atlanta. The weather is intensely hot, and dust terrible I may have to march far & long, but unless Johnston fight at Clinton or Jackson I will not expect more than affairs of Cavalry till my return.

Dayton brought me the clothes, but the truth is I never undress now except semioccasionally to put on clean under clothes. For near two months I have slept in my clothes ready to jump to the saddle, for I have been close upon an enemy since we crossed the Mississipi near two months ago. I have just written to Brooks Bros. New York to send me two Coats & two pants—Sweat & dust have made my clothes shabby, and the bushes have made me ragged below the Knee. Hill takes admirable care of things and I can always get clean drawers, socks & shirts by asking for them. Indeed I distress him sometimes by wearing shirts & socks too long. Still we manage to get along most admirably. He is the most faithful fellow I ever saw—and my nigger Carter keeps my horses seat fat. So I am well off—Hammond is with me as cranky as ever, but as long as he can find buttermilk he lives. He has found some secesh relations and at this moment has gone to Bovina to See a cousin, a handsome widow? whose husband is in Vicksburg. Oh the wail of these secesh Girls when Vicksburg surrendered. They cried and tore their hair, but I told them they had better not—they would survive the humiliating thought and eat whatever bread with as much relish as they ever did the corn dodgers of Aunt Dinah—now Gone to the Land of Linkum. It is hard to see as I do here an old preacher Mr. Fox, 40 years resident on this spot, with 17 children born to him lawfully & 11 still alive—carrying wood and milking cows. Two months ago he had a dozen house servants & 40 field hands, but now all gone, fences open & corn eaten up—garden pillaged by soldiers, house gutted of all furniture &c., indeed desolation, and he & his family compelled to appeal to us for the Soldier's Ration. This you will say is the judgment of God, but stiff necked he dont see it.

Yesterday I expected to cross Black River today but the troops have not come out from the siege, but I hope to cross Black tomorrow and see who are behind the saucy pickets that sit their horses so jauntily in the Cornfield beyond.

Charley has written you, we are all well—Love to all the folks. Yrs. Ever

W. T. Sherman

A "FORLORN AND FORSAKEN" PLACE:
MISSISSIPPI, JULY 1863

William Winters to Harriet Winters

Sergeant William Winters of the 67th Indiana Infantry had described the ongoing bombardment of Vicksburg to his wife on June 21: "For six hours our artilery opened on the rebel works at six oclock and poured it into them untill thenn, and such a roar of canon as was never heard in this neck of the woods before." After the surrender Winters surveyed the result of weeks of shelling.

Division Hospital, rear of Vicksburgh, July 6th, 1863
 Dear Wife,
 Vicksburgh is ours!
 Pemberton surendered on the 4th, and such a day was never known in this country, I know, for we had got tired of laying here in these hollows and pounding without doing verey mutch aparent good, but the rebs had to come to it at last, but they held out as long as they had any thing to eat and actuly eat mule beef before they surendered.
 I was down to the city on yesterday afternoon and took a stroll through the town looking at the work of destruction which is visable on every hand. The effects of our mortor shell is frightfull to look at, for where ever they struck they lef a frightful mark. I saw houses that shells from our mortor had struck and went straight down through from the roof to the cellar and the hole was large enough to drop a bushell basket through and some would take out nearly one whole side [   ]. When they struck the ground before bursting, they left a queer looking hole. Some of them left a place resembling a potatoe hill where the potatoes had cracked the hill all open, only in size they looked as if a cow was buried on the top of the ground. Others again would throw the dirt about and leave a hole that would hid a hogshead, and the efect of the shot and shell in some places is terible to look at. I saw one house that had 27 round shot holes in it and I dont know how many from musket balls and fragments of shell, but it was an awfull sight.

And then the greatest curiosity was the caves in the hill side that the citisens have dug to protect themselves from the deadly misels that our guns were constatly hurling into their midst. They cut them with the roof arched and the side of them trimmed down very smooth, and there was this rush carpet laid down to walk upon and nicly tacked around over the walls and ceiling so as to keep their clothes clean; and from the looks, every family in the city must of had one or more as the hills are perfectly full of them. I counted 20 in one roe in one place and sixteen in another, and I had not time to take particular notice. I only saw those that I walked pased.

This city looks dirty and disgraceful, a great many of the residents having left for safer quarters some 2 months ago, and the dust is so deep and dry that it has setled all over everything and gives the place a forlorn and forsaken apearance. And then to see those poor sick rebels lying about dirty and raged! Everything around them looks filthy and greasey and the atmosphere is full of a nasty, sickening, humid smell ariseing from the decaying animal matter and ofals of one kind and another that is laying around in every direction. The quarters where their men stay are perfectly filthy, and their hospitals are but verey litle better. those in the field are no better. I should like to have you see the diferenace between where I have my men quartered at and one of those rebel hospitals, as they choose to call them. I have my men all upon cots and with bed sacks filled with cotton, a clean white sheet spread over that, and then I made them all put on clen white shirts and red flanel drawers, and they look realey comfortable. And then I keep the tents and quarters swept up clean, and I think if some of those rebel surgeons would come out and look at our division Hospital they would think that our sanitary societies at home were doeing a noble work and they would go back and make their men keep themselves more clean and tidy. We have not nearly the amount of sickness that they have, notwithstanding they are in their own climate and we are not. I saw a great maney that were nearly eat up with the scurvey, something we have not been troubled with as yet, having had only a few cases and those were not bad.

I took a strole down along the levey, and it was perfectly crowded with rebs looking at our gun boats and steam boats.

The wharf was crowded for a mile with boats, something that plenty of the rebels had never saw, having lived away back in the interior. And it was amusing to hear the remarks that some of them would make as the sailors from the gun boats would come off from their boats to see what damage their firing had done to the rebel town and fortifacations. Whenever the rebels would see a black sailor with his white pants and blue shirt they would swear at an awful rate.

But the most of them dont want to be paroled at all. They say they want to go north untill this war is over as they are tired of it, or if they cant do that they want to take the oath of alegiance and then go north untill the war is over, as they are satisfied of how the thing is going. Some of them, however, swear that they will fight us as long as they live or have a foot of ground to fight upon, but they are only the fewest [   ].

We are going to send Joe gambold up the river to Memphis or some other place, as there is no chance for him to get well down here.

the Regiment left yesterday in morning for to try old Joe Johnson a fight if he will stop for them to do it. we heard to day noon that they had him surounded some where between here and Jackson, but I dont know how true it is.

Well, I guess I have written enough for this time. this is rebel paper that come from Vicksburgh. Give my love to all and write oftener. I haven't received but one letter in three weeks, and there was from wes the [   ].

Wm. Winter

tell the folks that I am well.

P.S. I wish you had some peaches like I paid a dime for a half a dozen of yesterday—if I had only had some cream.

Bill

Joe gamboled leaves for the river this afternoon.

Bill

What do you think of rebel letter paper? And then what is the matter with Mat Beavers? Is she mareed yet to Jotham Sleare?

"THE GLORIOUS RESULT":
WASHINGTON, D.C., JULY 1863

Benjamin B. French: Journal, July 8, 1863

A longtime Washington resident and former clerk of the House of Representatives, Benjamin B. French was appointed commissioner of public buildings for the capital in September 1861.

Wednesday, July 8. "*Vicksburg has fallen!*" Since 2 o'clock yesterday I suppose I have heard that said a thousand times. "It is a glorious victory," and I trust we shall soon have more of the same sort. Rumor already has it that Port Hudson is captured, and I believe if our army does all its duty Lee's army will scarcely ever see old Virginia soil again *as an army*. It is already awfully used up and is fast being pushed to annihilation. Richmond must soon go, and then poor Jeff will be driven to his wits end. My guess is that the Rebs. will soon find themselves a set of poor, miserable wretches, and they will cry to come back into our glorious Union! I see National glory in the future such as the past has never seen. Slavery forever abolished! The South populated and thriving under Free labor & Free rule! No more Cotton lords, but plenty of Cotton Commons, and all the land pouring out its productions & becoming immensely rich! Industry, Wealth, Happiness, Virtue, all marching hand in hand, and millions of voices raising their thanks to God for His goodness in doing good to all. Oh how manifest it is to my mind that *He* is now working out the future goodness and greatness of this, his chosen people, by the sore affliction and sacrifice of War! My Faith in the glorious result has not wavered a single instant since the Rebel cannon opened on Fort Sumter, and I think now I have a perfectly realizing sense of what our future is to be; and to the goodness and honesty of Abraham Lincoln, who has acted, in my beliefs, as the servant of the Most High God in all that he has done, do we owe all that we are to be.

The weather was very dry nearly all June. The Potomac was very low and easily fordable. Lee's army crossed as easily as the Israelites crossed the Red Sea, but no sooner were they well away from its Northern bank than the rain began to fall, and it has been raining almost continually till the river has risen so much as not to be fordable at any point, & Lee & his whole army are caught, & must be captured! Is not the finger of Providence as clear in this as it was to the Israelites of old when they escaped so miraculously from Pharaoh & his Hosts? I think it is. Then—

> Sound the loud timbrel o'er Egypt's dark sea,
> *JEHOVAH* hath triumphed! *His* people are *FREE*!

WAR NEWS AND RUMORS:
NORTH CAROLINA, JULY 1863

Catherine Edmondston:
Diary, July 8–11, 1863

On her North Carolina plantation Catherine Edmondston struggled to make sense of conflicting reports regarding events in Pennsylvania and Mississippi.

———————

JULY 8, 1863

News! News! News!—so much of it that I do not know how to begin to tell it! There has been a battle, a terrible battle at Gettysburg in Penn. We get Yankee accounts alone of it, but from their gasconade, bluster, & boasting, we pick the grain of wheat & are sure that the modest telegram which announces to us that Meade is falling back to Baltimore & Lee pursuing him is true. We lose three Brigadier's, Garnett, Barksdale, & Kemper killed—Pender & Scales wounded. I know none of the Col's so do not enumerate them. On their side the loss is heavier, including Reynolds, said to be the best General they have. He commanded the 3d army corps. Sickles, the infamous, loses his leg, so he will assassinate no more men because the world had discovered what he had long known & winked at. They have taken 2,000 (two thousand), we twelve thousand prisoners! The slaughter terrific both sides admit. The bridge over the Susquehanna at Wrightsville has been destroyed, whether by us or them I cannot understand. Gen Lee has issued orders for the government of his army in the enemy's country so widely different from those that emanate from the pens of their Generals that I preserve it for contrast. Read it & then turn to Pope's and Steinwehr's! A no 20.

These twelve thousand prisoners of ours refuse their parole, in order I suppose to embarras us & weaken Lee by the guard which they will force him to send with them. They deserve to be shot but we are, fortunately for them, too much under the law of Knightly honour & chivalry to give them their deserts.

The Yankee papers report that Johnson has cut Grant to peices & that Vicksburg is releived, but it does not elate us in the least, for we do not beleive it. The accounts from Louisiana are very fine but too good & a little contradictory. Brashear city has been taken by Gen. Dick Taylor. Magruder threatens New Orleans. Banks has fallen back from Port Hudson with only five thousand men & more to the same effect. It does not affect us much. We know not how much to beleive & Gettysburg eclipses all else. The news from Tennessee & Bragg is bad, *very* bad. He has fallen back from Tallahoma & virtually abandoned Tenn and part of North Ala, but we must not yet blame him. He may have been weakened by reinforcing Johnson in order to rescue Vicksburg. Let us wait before we condemn him. The damage done to the R R at Magnolia is slight, but a handful of miscreants have scoured the country burning & destroying everything before them, under Gen Martins very nose too! Murad the Unlucky I call him.

Went with Father and Mama to call on Mrs Clark & Miss Hines. Mrs James Smith poor thing did not make her appearance, being too much distressed about her brother, Col Evans, of whose fate they are yet in ignorance. How I pity those poor people who have friends at Gettysburg! What agony they must endure. From Mr Smith we learned that the enemy under the German Gen Weitzel had advanced to Williamston which they occupied & burned a few more houses. Col Martin holds Rainbow Banks where he is strongly entrenched. Brisk firing has been heard there today. The Yankees may intend only a diversion or they may be coming up to destroy the Gunboat now building. A few hours will determine. Gettysburg, however, absorbs every thought, so that we almost forget our own fate in that of our Army.

July 9, 1863

Glorious news, too good to be true! We hear unofficially that the fight was renewed on Sunday. Gen Hill made a feint of falling back. Meade pressed on when the two wings commanded by Ewell & Longstreet swept round & enclosed the entire Yankee Army; 40,000 men laid down their arms. Now this cannot be true. So large a number of men would not surrender in an open plain & in their own country. The Telegraph has played pranks with its message. I will not transcribe the flying rumours, the reports brought by "reliable gentlemen" & "wounded officers." There has been a fight & victory seems to incline to our side. We *hope* but we dare not beleive as yet.

Came brother yesterday afternoon, like "Widrington" in "*doleful dumps*," beleives a wild rumour gotten up I fancy by speculation to the effect that Vicksburg has capitulated. We laugh at it in spite of what we hear Com Barron says about its want of provisions & Johnston's weakness. Mr E & himself armed themselves & went down to the store with the intention if need was of keeping on & volunteering under Col Martin at Rainbow but met the good news on the road that we had ambushed the enemy at Gardner's bridge & that they had retired leaving ten of their number dead on the field, for which God be praised! Ah! for news from Penn! God keep Gen Lee. Give him wisdom & to his men endurance, obedience, & moderation.

JULY 10, 1863

Grant me patience with the news! I know not what to beleive! I hate to fill my Journal with rumours & yet it will be no truthful expositor of our lives if I fail to relate the state into which these uncertain Telegrams have brought us. One tells us that the fight was not renewed on Sunday, consequently the 40,000 men whom it reported as refusing parole were *not* captured & Lee is not pressing Meade who is not falling back to Baltimore, but per contra *Lee* it is who is falling back to Hagerstown. Now which is true? But our perplexities do not end here. A Dispatch which freezes the marrow in our bones, signed, too, Joseph E Johnston, tells Mr Seddon that Vicksburg has capitulated, that the garrison march out with the honours of war, officers wearing their side arms. This no one seems to beleive tho it is countersigned by one of Johnson's staff. The impression is that the wires have been tampered with by sugar speculators.

The news from the North Via Fortress Monroe inform us that Grant is retiring, that Vicksburg is releived, that Banks has been driven from Port Hudson, cries aloud for succour for N O & says Louisiana is slipping from the grasp. Then, too, another telegram from Loring dated Jackson tells us of his successes on the 'Big Black,' news of Dick Taylor's & Magruder's victories, one at Port Hudson the other in the Teche, whilst another has it that they have joined forces. I take refuge in utter unbeleif. I wish I could convince myself that the war is a myth, a hideous dream, but alaas! it presses too heavily to be thrown off like an incubus. There is but one comfort left—that our *Government* unlike the Yankee despotism does not lie. Its official Dispatches are all true, for they come from Gentlemen & through Gentlemen's hands do they pass until they reach us. So when we see 'R E Lee' signed to a dispatch we can rely on it, as there is no Telegraph to be tampered with by unprincipled speculators, as we hope and beleive is the case with Johnston's reported Dispatch. Vicksburg cannot have fallen! Not ten days ago they drove 300 mules out of the city. Surely, Yankee tho he is, Pemberton is not a traitor! He must have been able to inform Johnston of his situation. I cannot beleive it. As for the news from Penn, I never expected so much as they gave us, so am not depressed when they take the surplusage away. Give me the bare fact of a *Victory* & I am content without a "*rout.*" I have been so occupied with public that I have omitted all mention of private matters.

Last week we had a freshet in the River, a heavy one which drowned a large portion of our corn. We hoped, however, to save much of it, as the water remained up but a short time. These hopes, however, are all crushed, for a second rise higher & slower than the first is now in progress. The crop is all resubmerged & much that escaped last week is destroyed this. It is a heavy blow. The loss to Father and Mr Edmondston is heavy, heavier to Father than to Patrick, for the Low grounds proper at Looking Glass are not in cultivation this year. But God has sent it. We must not repine.

I have been very unwell for some days & the suspense about public matters, the wearing anxiety about Vicksburg, & the uneasiness about the river do not help to make me better. Hannah More's ill "*bile*"—oppresses me. I leave our killed & wounded until they are authenticated. I hope they are exagerated. Petigru again wounded!

JULY 11, 1863

I have no heart to write. Vicksburg has fallen! It is all true. No lying speculator has imposed upon us. Pemberton has surrendered! As yet it is all dark. We are told that they were reduced to the verge of starvation & yet 200 mounted men of the garrison have been paroled & have reached Jackson, the officers allowed to march out with their side arms, retain their *horses* & private property. Now who ever heard of a beleagured city starving with horses & mules in it? Pemberton drove 500 mules out of his lines not ten days since & now lo, he is starving. The garrison surrendered on the 4th of July. I would have waited until the 5th & not have sullied our national anniversary with such an act. My doubts of Pemberton return. He is a Pennsylvanian & his heart cannot be in the cause as ours is. Can he be a traitor? I am not willing to trust him. I could have born the disaster better had it come to us through a Southern hand.

Ah! Mr Davis, Mr Davis, have we not suffered enough from Northern Generals. Remember Lovel & New Orleans & now comes Pemberton & Vicksburg to crown that first disaster! Just at the moment of triumph too. Banks driven from Port Hudson and Johnston nearly ready to fall on Grant. We remember Pemberton's blunders before he was shut up in Vicksburg, blunders which his defence of it had almost made us forget, & then his bluster about holding out whilst there was a "pound of Mule's flesh" left. Think of Londonderry, think of Antwerp, & then think of marching out with 200 mounted men besides officers, horses & citizen's "stock," which now they are "in haste to remove." We remember all this I say, & thoughts too bitter for words rise in our hearts against *this Northerner, this Pemberton*! The truth will never be known, smothered in a court of Inquiry, as was Lovels conduct at New Orleans. Grant me patience O Lord! grant me patience. Let me see Thy hand in it & make me cease to repine at the instruments Thou hast chosen to chastise us with!

From Lee's army we get only Northern accounts through lying newspapers in Yankee pay & tho they are depressing enough, we do not credit them. They have it that Lee is beaten & in full retreat, demoralized & scattered & that Meade's victorious army presses on him whilst French & Milroy's late command & a host of other generals in Buckram bar his retreat across the Potomac. They will "fight him eight hours" by "Shrewsbury clock" no doubt. We know from our operator at Martinsburg that he is at Hagerstown, a retreat certainly but rendered necessary on account of his wounded & thirteen Thousand prisoners with whom he is encumbered. The Yankees say he left his wounded on the field, not one word of which we beleive. In the face of their victory Keyes & his marauders are ordered immediately to Washington. Eastern Va is deserted by them & if Lee had been beaten surely they are not such fools as not to reinforce him & send him before he recover from the shock in a triumphant "On to Richmond" march. I have not said so much of Keyes as I ought perhaps. Latterly, he has long since ceased to give us uneasiness & has merely been ravaging the country, burning & destroying with the usual Yankee wickedness, barbarity, and wantonness.

D H Hill has been more than a match for him & he is now gone back to his master Lincoln. I do not tell all the Yankees say of our pretended defeat. I shall have the truth soon from our own side. We are sad enough today without their lies to madden us in addition. What with the loss of Vicksburg & our crop, well may we say—"The King does not dine today." At present prices we lose $30,000 worth of corn by this rise (Father, brother, & Patrick I mean), a heavy blow, but we are in God's hands. We see Him in it & do not murmur, but when a human instrument like Pemberton peirces us, we feel it deeply & keenly, tho' it is God still who allows it. We should remember that.

Suffolk has been evacuated, not a Yankee left in it after thirteen months occupation. An order was issued to burn it, but before it could be carried into execution Lee was over the border & fearing retaliation, Dix countermanded his barbarous edict. So, we go. Grant's army is marching on Jackson, "burning every dwelling that they come to on their route," women & helpless children turned without food or shelter into the woods & fields. How long O Lord? how long?

FIGHTING ON THE MISSISSIPPI:
LOUISIANA, JULY 1863

George Hamilton Perkins to
Susan G. Perkins

Confederate forces attacked Donaldsonville, Louisiana, on June 28 as part of an offensive designed to relieve Port Hudson by disrupting Union river traffic along the Mississippi and threatening to recapture New Orleans. After the Union garrison repelled the assault, the Confederates set up artillery batteries along the levee about ten miles below the town. Lieutenant Commander George Hamilton Perkins, a Union naval officer, commanded the *New London*, a wooden screw steamer armed with five guns. When Port Hudson fell on July 9, the *New London* was sent downriver carrying dispatches reporting the surrender. Perkins described his encounter with the shore batteries to his sister. The capture of Port Hudson caused the Confederates to withdraw from the river bank, and on July 16 an unescorted cargo ship from St. Louis safely arrived in New Orleans.

JULY 29, 1863.

Since I wrote you last I have been through more excitement, and it seems to me as if I had been in more danger, than ever before in my life; and I am going to try and describe to you my last trip in the New London.

I had passed the Whitehall Point batteries in her successfully five times, but on the sixth trip, when the New London was returning to New Orleans, just as she was passing those batteries, at about quarter past one, on the morning of the 10th of July, the enemy discovered her, and opened with artillery and sharpshooters. One shot struck the New London's boiler, which exploded, severely scalding six men, and another shot penetrated the steam drum. This disabled the vessel, and I ordered her to be run towards the eastern bank, but the escaping steam made it impossible for the helmsman to remain at the wheel, and the ship grounded within range of the battery. The gunboat Winona, which had been ordered to escort the New

London, past Whitehall Point, ran away, at the first shot, and was out of sight by this time. I fired rockets to inform her of my danger and to summon her to my assistance, but received no response.

We were at the mercy of the sharpshooters, and every shot dealt death and destruction. My first lieutenant was shot through the head, and the men now became so terrified that they began to leap overboard. I then ordered a boat to be manned and kedged off the ship astern, till she drifted down stream out of the way of the upper battery. But the most powerful fortification of the battery was still below us; so I towed the ship to the eastern bank and made her fast; but danger pursued me here, and it was soon plain that I had only gained a respite from the murderous fire, for I could see the enemy cutting embrasures to move their guns down for a better range, and I knew that daylight would seal the fate of my ship and crew.

I determined to save them if I could. I sent the ship's company ashore under the protection of the levee, where they could use their muskets to repel an attack, and stationed pickets along the road. I then despatched messengers by land to Donaldsonville, where General Weitzel was, for assistance, and sent a boat by the river to the Monongahela and Essex with the same request. These two ships were stationed some miles below on the river to protect an encampment of our troops on the eastern bank.

The messengers returned from Donaldsonville saying no assistance could be rendered; while, with regard to the success of those I sent by the river, I felt very doubtful, so much was the passage of the Whitehall Point batteries dreaded. Just at this time information was brought me that a force of rebel cavalry—five hundred strong—was only a few miles in the interior. I felt desperate, for I realized the whole peril of the situation, and I was determined that my ship and crew should not fall into the hands of the enemy. I resolved to follow the dictates of my own judgment. I knew that upon a personal application Weitzel would at once grant me anything I wanted. I went ashore and, capturing a horse that was tied to a fence, I rode back to Donaldsonville. Arrived opposite I signaled to the Princess Royal to send a boat for me, and, to save time, I first demanded assistance from her senior officer; this he thought fit to refuse.

The Princess Royal was one of our gunboats stationed at Donaldsonville to protect and help Weitzel. I immediately hastened to him, and without delay he started a body of troops down the river for my assistance. But when I returned to the spot where I had left the New London, I found her gone, and I concluded—rightly, as it afterwards proved—that the boat I had sent early in the morning had succeeded in reaching our ships, and that they had come up and taken her off. I found afterwards that it was the ironclad Essex, and it towed her directly to New Orleans.

This was a great relief to me, for now the lives of my men were safe, and the ship was still under its own flag; but I began to realize that my own position was now one of considerable danger. I fastened the horse I had so unceremoniously borrowed, to the spot I first found him, and then hired a negro to drive me, in any sort of vehicle he could get, down the levee road to our lines. This proved to be a carry-all harnessed to a mule; but it was the best he could do. I took the back seat and laid my loaded pistols by my side close under my hand. At the negro's earnest entreaty, I put on my uniform coat wrong-side out, that it might not attract attention, and so I started—a Union officer, miles from our troops—on my passage through the enemy's country, along a road where rebel troops, bands of guerillas, and sharpshooters were usually in constant movement. Yet by some rare fortune it happened, just at this time, that my chief danger—except the overhanging peril of the whole situation—was not incurred until I approached our lines, except that around a grocery shop, which I passed, there were lounging a group of armed rebels. My driver was terribly frightened at this, and kept saying, "Set back, massa, for God's sake, set back! Mebbe dey won't see you!" And then whipped up his mule till we were safe beyond their reach.

But I had been seen and suspected by the rebel troops on the other side of the river, and they had sent a boat and some soldiers across to capture me. They reached the bank on my side, landed, and came up the road to intercept me, just as I was nearing our lines. Fortunately all this was perceived by our troops, and a body of cavalry was sent out, which captured the rebels, and conducted me in safety to the camp by one and the same proceeding. Here I found one of our ships—the Monongahela—and I went on board of her in a perfectly exhausted condition. Flinging myself in a bunk I slept soundly for hours, undisturbed by the fact that a short time before, while lying in that very same place, the Captain of the Monongahela —Abner Read—had been killed by a rebel shot which penetrated the ship's side and struck him, and that his dead body was then on board, being conveyed to New Orleans.

I roused myself very early next morning in order to continue my journey to New Orleans in a commissary wagon, but when daylight dawned, I saw a gunboat coming down the river in command of my friend Captain Cooke, and I went on board of her, and made the rest of my trip by water.

"I MUST DIE VERY SOON":
MISSISSIPPI, JULY 1863

Charles B. Haydon: Journal, July 11, 1863

On July 4 Grant ordered Sherman to move east and drive Joseph E. Johnston's forces away from Jackson. Captain Charles B. Haydon of the 2nd Michigan Infantry described a skirmish fought on July 11, five days before the Confederates evacuated the city.

JULY 11 We were up at 3 A.M. I had very little supper & no breakfast. Our clothes are constantly wet with sweat & having no water to wash we are suffering terribly from sores, eruptions & a breaking out of the skin which makes one almost raw & feels as though he were in the fire.

A little before sunrise the 2d was deployed as skirmishers covering the front of our brigade and connecting with others on the right & we all slowly advanced. The skirmishers had orders to advance till they drew the fire of the rebel batteries if possible. We had gone but a little way when some Regts. to the right of us which seemed to be resting carelessly received a brisk fire which appeared to be pretty effective. They moved to the rear in very quick time, sent out skirmishers & advanced again. A few shots fell near but no one was struck. We moved forward across a very difficult ravine & gained good cover under a fence with an open field beyond.

Here we encountered a moderate but well directed fire from skirmishers at long range. The whistling of the balls animated the men greatly. Chas. Smith of my Co. recd a severe shot in the leg & some others of the Regt. were struck. We lay here abt an hour when an order came to advance at double quick. We had before us abt 100 rods of open field, then a narrow steep ravine through which runs a brook, then a hill, thick bushes, further on a corn field fence with rifle pits at a short distance. Between us & the fence there were as we have since learned three Regts. of Infantry.

We crossed the open at a run & without much loss, the men

full of fire, yelling like devils, Kearney's name being uppermost in their cry. I never felt more eager. Their skirmishers flew before us. We sprang down into the ravine & up the other bank. I tumbled back once & did not get up as quick as most of the others. When I did I found a narrow terrace & another steep bank. The Co. had all halted at the bank & seemed waiting to see who should go up first. I swore a most substantial oath (being indignant at them for stopping) & then we all made a dash at the hill.

It was so steep that only three or four got up at first. The Rebs were about three rods off. I made abt half the distance to them when I was whirled around & laid on my back suddenly, very suddenly & in a manner which left no doubt in my mind that I was hit. All who came up with me shared the same fate.

When I first became conscious, which was very soon, I lay on my back wondering what was to come next. I tried to get up but could not stir so much as a finger, nor could I speak although I could see & hear all that was doing, the trees above & the bullets around. Our men had halted at the brink of the hill so that I lay between the fires. I tried two or three times to rise but finding I could not move I began to reflect on other matters. I now observed that my hands were laid across my breast & in fact that my whole position was that of the greater part of those killed in battle. I then began to question myself as to whether I were not really dead.

I soon discarded this idea but still felt certain that I must die very soon. My whole feeling became one of wonder & curiosity as to the change which I believed I was about to experience. I was in no pain bodily & no mental anxiety. After abt 2 minutes I heard Sergt. Keyser of my Co. cry out to the men "G-d d--n your souls are you going to leave the Capt. lying there?" A second after he with eminent danger to himself sprang forward & caught me by the arm. The instant he touched me I sprang to my feet. Just then the Regt. went past on a charge driving the enemy before them. I tried to give my Co. a word of encouragement but my throat was so full of blood that I strangled when I attempted to speak.

With the aid of the Sergt. I walked back to the brook & lay down partly in it. He gave me water to drink & poured it over me in large quantities. I soon got up again & with his aid walked back 50 to 60 rods & lay down again. I could speak pretty well now but still threw up large quantities of blood from the lungs. I was soon able to walk again & started but met some men with a stretcher who carried me to the field hospital. But for the aid of the Sergt. I should have fallen into the hands of the enemy as the Regt. being wholly unsupported was very soon compelled to fall back.

My Co. numbered for the fight 18 men & 2 officers. One man was killed & four wounded. Both officers were wounded, Lt. Montague receiving a severe flesh wound below the knee. The Regt. lost 58 killed & wounded. I never saw better fighting done but the want of support rendered it of little avail beyond the mere number of the enemy killed which was however very considerable.

On arriving at the Hospt. my wound was dressed, my chances of recovery discussed, some encouragement was given by the Surgeons & I resolved to get well. I was laid on a blanket under a tree & soon after ate a good dinner to make up for the want of breakfast. No very severe pain to day. The ball struck me in the right shoulder abt an inch below the collar bone & passed out just at the lower edge of the shoulder blade.

"THE PREST WAS DEEPLY GRIEVED":
WASHINGTON, D.C., JULY 1863

John Hay: Diary, July 11–15, 1863

Lee began his retreat from Gettysburg on July 4, the same day a Union cavalry raid destroyed the Confederate pontoon bridge at Falling Waters, West Virginia. Meade started his pursuit the next day. The movements of both armies were slowed by heavy rain that made the Potomac unfordable. By July 12 Meade's army reached the defensive lines Lee established to protect the crossing at Williamsport, Maryland, six miles upriver from Falling Waters. John Hay had lived in the White House since 1861 while serving as one of Lincoln's principal secretaries. He recorded the President's response to subsequent events.

———————

11 JULY 1863, SATURDAY

The President seemed in a specially good humor today, as he had pretty good evidence that the enemy were still on the North side of the Potomac and Meade had announced his intention of attacking them in the morning. The Prest. seemed very happy in the prospect of a brilliant success. He had been rather impatient with Gen Meade's slow movements since Gettysburg, but concluded today that Meade would yet show sufficient activity to inflict the Coup de grace upon the flying rebels.

12 JULY 1863, SUNDAY

Rained all the afternoon, have not yet heard of Meade's expected attack.

13 JULY 1863, MONDAY

The President begins to grow anxious and impatient about Meade's silence. I thought and told him there was nothing to prevent the enemy from getting away by the Falling Waters, if they were not vigorously attacked. Eckert says Kelly is up on their rear. Nothing can save them, if Meade does his duty. I doubt him. He is an engineer.

14 July 1863, Tuesday

This morning the Prest. seemed depressed by Meade's despatches of last night. They were so cautiously & almost timidly worded—talking about reconnoitering to find the enemy's weak place and other such. He said he feared he would do nothing.

About noon came the despatch stating that our worst fears were true. The enemy had gotten away unhurt. The Prest was deeply grieved. We had them within our grasp" he said. "We had only to stretch forth our hands & they were ours. And nothing I could say or do could make the Army move."

Several days ago he sent a despatch to Meade which must have cut like a scourge but Meade returned so reasonable and earnest a reply that the Prest concluded he knew best what he was doing & was reconciled to the apparent inaction which he hoped was merely apparent.

Every day he has watched the progress of the Army with agonizing impatience, hopes struggling with fear. He has never been easy in his own mind about Gen Meade since Meades General Order in which he called on his troops to drive the invader from our soil. The Prest. says "This is a dreadful reminiscence of McClellan. The same spirit that moved McC. to claim a great victory because Pa & Md were safe. The hearts of 10 million people sank within them when McClellan raised that shout last fall. Will our Generals never get that idea out of their heads? The whole country is *our* soil."

15 July 1863, Wednesday

Went with R.T.L. around town to concert saloons. Saw some very queer dancing and singing at one place and some very tolerable singing at a great hall where mann sauft and trinkt and raucht.

R. T. L. says the Tycoon is grieved silently but deeply about the escape of Lee. He said "If I had gone up there I could have whipped them myself." I know he had that idea.

ACKNOWLEDGING A VICTORY:
WASHINGTON, D.C., JULY 1863

Abraham Lincoln to Ulysses S. Grant

Although Lincoln praised Grant's Vicksburg campaign as "one of the most brilliant in the world" in a letter to a congressman on May 26, the President had had doubts about his leadership. Concerned by allegations that Grant was incompetent, opposed to emancipation, and frequently drunk, Lincoln and Secretary of War Stanton had sent Charles A. Dana as a special emissary to Grant's headquarters in the spring of 1863. Aware of the nature of Dana's mission, Grant took him into his confidence, and Dana's favorable reports helped reassure the President. Lincoln received definitive news of the surrender of Vicksburg on July 7 and wrote his first personal note to Grant six days later.

Executive Mansion,
Washington, July 13, 1863.

Major General Grant
My dear General

I do not remember that you and I ever met personally. I write this now as a grateful acknowledgment for the almost inestimable service you have done the country. I wish to say a word further. When you first reached the vicinity of Vicksburg, I thought you should do, what you finally did—march the troops across the neck, run the batteries with the transports, and thus go below; and I never had any faith, except a general hope that you knew better than I, that the Yazoo Pass expedition, and the like, could succeed. When you got below, and took Port-Gibson, Grand Gulf, and vicinity, I thought you should go down the river and join Gen. Banks; and when you turned Northward East of the Big Black, I feared it was a mistake. I now wish to make the personal acknowledgment that you were right, and I was wrong.

Yours very truly
A. LINCOLN

"YOUR GOLDEN OPPORTUNITY IS GONE":
WASHINGTON, D.C., JULY 1863

Abraham Lincoln to George G. Meade

On the afternoon of July 14 Halleck telegraphed Meade that "the escape of Lee's army without another battle has created great dissatisfaction in the mind of the President." Meade replied within ninety minutes, describing Lincoln's "censure" as "undeserved" and asking to be relieved of his command. The President wrote this letter in response, but never signed or sent it, and Meade remained the commander of the Army of the Potomac.

———

Executive Mansion,
Washington, July 14, 1863.

Major General Meade

I have just seen your despatch to Gen. Halleck, asking to be relieved of your command, because of a supposed censure of mine. I am very—*very*—grateful to you for the magnificent success you gave the cause of the country at Gettysburg; and I am sorry now to be the author of the slightest pain to you. But I was in such deep distress myself that I could not restrain some expression of it. I had been oppressed nearly ever since the battles at Gettysburg, by what appeared to be evidences that yourself, and Gen. Couch, and Gen. Smith, were not seeking a collision with the enemy, but were trying to get him across the river without another battle. What these evidences were, if you please, I hope to tell you at some time, when we shall both feel better. The case, summarily stated is this. You fought and beat the enemy at Gettysburg; and, of course, to say the least, his loss was as great as yours. He retreated; and you did not, as it seemed to me, pressingly pursue him; but a flood in the river detained him, till, by slow degrees, you were again upon him. You had at least twenty thousand veteran troops directly with you, and as many more raw ones within supporting distance, all in addition to those who fought with you at Gettysburg; while it was not possible that he had received a single recruit; and yet you stood and let the flood run down, bridges be built, and the enemy move away at his leisure, without attacking him. And Couch and Smith! The latter left Carlisle in time, upon all ordinary calculation, to have aided you in the last battle at Gettysburg; but he did not arrive. At the end of more than ten days, I believe twelve, under constant urging, he reached Hagerstown from Carlisle, which is not an inch over fiftyfive miles, if so much. And Couch's movement was very little different.

Again, my dear general, I do not believe you appreciate the magnitude of the misfortune involved in Lee's escape. He was within your easy grasp, and to have closed upon him would, in connection with our other late successes, have ended the war. As it is, the war will be prolonged indefinitely. If you could not safely attack Lee last monday, how can you possibly do so South of the river, when you can take with you very few more than two thirds of the force you then had in hand? It would be unreasonable to expect, and I do not expect you can now effect much. Your golden opportunity is gone, and I am distressed immeasureably because of it.

I beg you will not consider this a prossecution, or persecution of yourself. As you had learned that I was dissatisfied, I have thought it best to kindly tell you why.

CROSSING THE POTOMAC:
MARYLAND AND WEST VIRGINIA, JULY 1863

Samuel Pickens: Diary, July 14, 1863

Samuel Pickens of the 5th Alabama Infantry described his crossing of the Potomac at Williamsport. The pontoon bridge at Falling Waters used by Longstreet's and A. P. Hill's corps had been rebuilt by Confederate engineers after the July 4 cavalry raid that destroyed its predecessor.

———————

July 14, Tuesday

Late yesterday evening the troops left the breastworks quietly & commenced falling back, leaving one Regt. from each Brig. to fill the space occupied by the Brig. Our Regt. was one of the no. that remained. The Yankees soon found that most of our troops were gone & commenced a brisk skirmishing & on the left charged with a double line of skirmishers, & a line-of-battle; but Ramseur's sharpshooters fought splendidly & 3 or 4 pieces of artillery at the breastworks where we were, opened on them & they charged back again. About 8 or 9 O'clock the remaining Regts. fell back, while only our sharpshooters and a few Cavalry were left along the lines. We marched about two miles along behind the ridge on which are our fortifications, & where fires were left burning. What a splendid position we occupied! I think if the Yankees had attacked Genl Lee he would have whipped them badly. We had very rough, muddy, & bad marching before reaching the pike, which was itself perfectly sloppy; & to make it still more disagreeable there was a light rain falling for a while. The road was so blocked up with troops that we did not get on very fast, & when we got to Williamsport we found it crowded with soldiers. Here we had to *stand* & wait an hour or more, for there was no place to sit down as the streets were ankle deep with mud & water. Finally we moved on down towards the River, but every few yards the column would halt—so that we were just creeping along at a most fatiguing pace. We went to a ford several hundred yards higher up the river than where we crossed before—going up the aqueduct through water that smelt very offensively. As soon as we got near the river we knew the men were wading, by the yelling & hallooing that we heard. The Potomac being swollen, was very wide & was over waist deep. The water felt cool when we first entered it, but afterwards very pleasant. We waded two & two side by side, holding on to each other in order to resist the current better & be more steady. There were orders for the men to hang their cartridge-boxes around their necks, but a great many failed to do it & there was a considerable amount of ammunition damaged & destroyed by getting wet. Our clothes, blankets (partly) & havresacks all got wet, which increased our load & made it very disagreeable marching after crossing. The banks were muddy & on this side so steep & slippery that it was difficult to scuffle up it. We were very tired & confidently expected to stop directly after getting over the river, but on we went without stopping. Although the distance from Hagerstown was only about six miles, & we were on our feet from 8 or nine O'clock last night, it was daybreak when we got across the Potomac. We passed by "Falling Water" where our Pontoon bridge spanned the river, on which Longstreet's & A. P. Hill's Corps were crossing & also the artillery & wagon trains. At 6 or 7 O'clock this morning we came to a halt. After being on our feet the whole night—marching on a sloppy pike, & stopped to rest only once (5 or 10 mins.) during the whole trip. Oh! it was a killing march. It beggars description. We waded into a little pond where we stopped and washed the mud off our pants, socks and shoes, then made fires and dried our clothes—after which we lay down and slept. At 11½ A.M., though we were called up & marched on 3 or 4 miles & camped in a nice piece of woods. As we had gotten our rations wet—what little we had—David Barnum & several others went out & killed two hogs. We broiled the meat at the fire & ate one for supper. I had the pleasure of hearing from home to-day by a letter from Jamie. Happy to hear Mama has, at last gotten rid of the Standenmeyers—having dismissed them. Our Mess was up till 10 or 11 O'clock P.M. cooking. Marched 8 or 9 miles from Williamsport.

THE DRAFT RIOTS: NEW YORK, JULY 1863

George Templeton Strong:
Diary, July 13–17, 1863

The first draft lottery conducted in New York City under the 1863 conscription act was held on July 11. Two days later a mob attacked the draft office at Third Avenue and 46th Street, beginning five days of violence in which at least 105 people were killed. The riots were eventually suppressed by several regiments of Union troops, some of which had fought at Gettysburg. Strong recorded his attempts to persuade the authorities to take early and decisive action against the rioters.

July 13, MONDAY. A notable day. Stopped at the Sanitary Commission office on my way downtown to endorse a lot of checks that had accumulated during my absence, and heard there of rioting in the upper part of the city. As Charley is at Newport and Bidwell in Berkshire County, I went to Wall Street nevertheless; but the rumors grew more and more unpleasant, so I left it at once and took a Third Avenue car for uptown. At the Park were groups and small crowds in more or less excitement (which found relief afterwards, I hear, in hunting down and maltreating sundry unoffending niggers), but there was nothing to indicate serious trouble. The crowded car went slowly on its way, with its perspiring passengers, for the weather was still of this deadly muggy sort with a muddy sky and lifeless air. At Thirteenth Street the track was blocked by a long line of stationary cars that stretched indefinitely up the Avenue, and I took to the sidewalk. Above Twentieth Street all shops were closed, and many people standing and staring or strolling uptown, not riotously disposed but eager and curious. Here and there a rough could be heard damning the draft. No policemen to be seen anywhere. Reached the seat of war at last, Forty-sixth Street and Third Avenue. Three houses on the Avenue and two or three on the street were burned down: engines playing on the ruins—more energetically, I'm told, than they did when their efforts would have been useful.

The crowd seemed just what one commonly sees at any fire, but its nucleus of riot was concealed by an outside layer of ordinary peaceable lookers-on. Was told they had beat off a squad of police and another of "regulars" (probably the Twelfth Militia). At last, it opened and out streamed a posse of perhaps five hundred, certainly less than one thousand, of the lowest Irish day laborers. The rabble was perfectly homogeneous. Every brute in the drove was pure Celtic—hod-carrier or loafer. They were unarmed. A few carried pieces of fence-paling and the like. They turned off west into Forty-fifth Street and gradually collected in front of two three-story dwelling houses on Lexington Avenue, just below that street, that stand alone together on a nearly vacant block. Nobody could tell why these houses were singled out. Some said a drafting officer lived in one of them, others that a damaged policeman had taken refuge there. The mob was in no hurry; they had no need to be; there was no one to molest them or make them afraid. The beastly ruffians were masters of the situation and of the city. After a while sporadic paving-stones began to fly at the windows, ladies and children emerged from the rear and had a rather hard scramble over a high board fence, and then scudded off across the open, Heaven knows whither. Then men and small boys appeared at rear windows and began smashing the sashes and the blinds and shied out light articles, such as books and crockery, and dropped chairs and mirrors into the back yard; the rear fence was demolished and loafers were seen marching off with portable articles of furniture. And at last a light smoke began to float out of the windows and I came away. I could endure the disgraceful, sickening sight no longer, and what could I *do*?

The fury of the low Irish women in that region was noteworthy. Stalwart young vixens and withered old hags were swarming everywhere, all cursing the "bloody draft" and egging on their men to mischief.

Omnibussed down to No. 823, where is news that the Colored Half Orphan Asylum on Fifth Avenue, just above the reservoir, is burned. "*Tribune* office to be burned tonight."

Railroad rails torn up, telegraph wires cut, and so on. If a quarter one hears be true, this is an organized insurrection in the interest of the rebellion and Jefferson Davis rules New York today.

Attended to business. Then with Wolcott Gibbs to dinner at Maison Dorée. During our symposium, there was an alarm of a coming mob, and we went to the window to see. The "mob" was moving down Fourteenth Street and consisted of just thirty-four lousy, blackguardly Irishmen with a tail of small boys. Whither they went, I cannot say, nor can I guess what mischief the handful of *canaille* chose to do. A dozen policemen would have been more than a match for the whole crew, but there were no policemen in sight.

Walked uptown with Wolcott Gibbs. Large fire on Broadway and Twenty-eighth Street. Signs of another to the east, said to be on Second Avenue. Stopped awhile at Gibbs's in Twenty-ninth Street, where was madame, frightened nearly to death, and then to St. Nicholas Hotel to see the mayor and General Wool. We found a lot of people with them. There were John Jay and George W. Blunt and Colonel Howe and John Austin Stevens, Jr., all urging strong measures. But the substantial and weighty and influential men were not represented; out of town, I suppose. Their absence emboldened Gibbs and myself to make pressure for instant action, but it was vain. We begged that martial law might be declared. Opdyke said that was Wool's business, and Wool said it was Opdyke's, and neither would act. "Then, Mr. Mayor, issue a proclamation calling on all loyal and law-abiding citizens to enroll themselves as a volunteer force for defense of life and property." "Why," quoth Opdyke, "that is *civil war* at once." Long talk with Colonel Cram, Wool's chief of staff, who professes to believe that everything is as it should be and sufficient force on the ground to prevent further mischief. Don't believe it. Neither Opdyke nor General Wool is nearly equal to this crisis. Came off disgusted. Went to Union League Club awhile. No comfort there. Much talk, but no one ready to do anything whatever, not even to telegraph to Washington.

We telegraphed, two or three of us, from General Wool's rooms, to the President, begging that troops be sent on and stringent measures taken. The great misfortune is that nearly all our militia regiments have been despatched to Pennsylvania. All the military force I have seen or heard of today were in Fifth Avenue at about seven P.M. There were two or three feeble companies of infantry, a couple of howitzers, and a squadron or two of unhappy-looking "dragoons."

These wretched rioters have been plundering freely, I hear. Their outbreak will either destroy the city or damage the Copperhead cause fatally. Could we but catch the scoundrels who have stirred them up, what a blessing it would be! God knows what tonight or tomorrow may bring forth. We may be thankful that it is now (quarter past twelve) raining briskly. Mobs have no taste for the effusion of cold water. I'm thankful, moreover, that Ellie and the children are out of town. I sent Johnny off to Cornwall this afternoon in charge of John the waiter.

July 14. Eleven P.M. Fire bells clanking, as they have clanked at intervals through the evening. Plenty of rumors throughout the day and evening, but nothing very precise or authentic. There have been sundry collisions between the rabble and the authorities, civil and military. Mob fired upon. It generally runs, but on one occasion appears to have rallied, charged the police and militia, and forced them back in disorder. The people are waking up, and by tomorrow there will be adequate organization to protect property and life. Many details come in of yesterday's brutal, cowardly ruffianism and plunder. Shops were cleaned out and a black man hanged in Carmine Street, for no offence but that of Nigritude. Opdyke's house again attacked this morning by a roaming handful of Irish blackguards. Two or three gentlemen who chanced to be passing saved it from sack by a vigorous charge and dispersed the popular uprising (as the *Herald*, *World*, and *News* call it), with their walking sticks and their fists.

Walked uptown perforce, for no cars and few omnibi were running. They are suppressed by threats of burning railroad and omnibus stables, the drivers being wanted to reinforce the mob. Tiffany's shop, Ball & Black's, and a few other Broadway establishments are closed. (Here I am interrupted by report of a fire near at hand, and a great glare on the houses across the Park. Sally forth, and find the Eighteenth Ward station house, Twenty-second Street, near First Avenue, in full blaze. A splendid blaze it made, but I did not venture below Second Avenue, finding myself in a crowd of Celtic spectators disgorged by the circumjacent tenement houses. They were exulting over the damage to "them bloody police," and so on. I thought discretion the better part of curiosity. Distance lent enchantment to that view.)

At 823 with Bellows four to six; then home. At eight to Union League Club. Rumor it's to be attacked tonight. Some say there is to be great mischief tonight and that the rabble is getting the upper hand. Home at ten and sent for by Dudley Field, Jr., to confer about an expected attack on his house and his father's, which adjoin each other in this street just below Lexington Avenue. He has a party there with muskets and talks of fearful trouble before morning, but he is always a blower and a very poor devil. Fire bells again at twelve-fifteen. No light of conflagration is visible.

Bellows's report from Gettysburg and from Meade's headquarters very interesting. Thinks highly of Meade. Thinks the battle around Williamsport will be tolerably evenly matched, Lee having been decidedly beaten a week ago, but not at all demoralized. But there's a despatch at the Union League Club tonight that Lee has moved his whole army safely across, except his rear guard, which we captured.

A good deal of yelling to the eastward just now. The Fields and their near neighbour, Colonel Frank Howe, are as likely to be attacked by this traitor-guided mob as any people I know. If they *are*, we shall see trouble in this quarter, and Gramercy Park will acquire historical associations. O, how tired I am! But I feel reluctant to go to bed. I believe I dozed off a minute or two. There came something like two reports of artillery, perhaps only falling walls. There go two jolly Celts along the street, singing a genuine Celtic howl, something about "Tim O'Laggerty," with a refrain of pure Erse. Long live the sovereigns of New York, Brian Boroo *redivivus* and multiplied. Paddy has left his Egypt—Connaught—and reigns in this promised land of milk and honey and perfect freedom. Hurrah, there goes a strong squad of police marching eastward down this street, followed by a company of infantry with gleaming bayonets. One A.M. Fire bells again, southeastward,

"Swinging slow with sullen roar." Now they are silent, and I shall go to bed, at least for a season.

July 15. Wednesday begins with heavy showers, and now (ten A.M.) cloudy, hot, and steaming. Morning papers report nothing specially grave as occurring since midnight. But there will be much trouble today. Rabbledom is not yet dethroned any more than its ally and instigator, Rebeldom.

News from the South is consolatory. Port Hudson surrendered. Sherman said to have beaten Joseph Johnston somewhere near Vicksburg. Operations commencing against Charleston. Bragg seems to be abandoning Chattanooga and retiring on Atlanta. *Per contra*, Lee has got safely off. I thought he would. . . . Lots of talk and rumors about attacks on the New York Custom-house (*ci-devant* Merchants' Exchange) and the Treasury (late Custom-house). Went to see Cisco and found his establishment in military occupation—sentinels pacing, windows barricaded, and so on. He was as serene and bland as the loveliest May morning ("so cool, so calm, so bright") and showed me the live shell ready to throw out of the window and the "battery" to project Assay Office oil-of-vitriol and the like. He's all right. Then called on Collector Barney and had another long talk with him. Find him well prepared with shells, grenades, muskets, and men, but a little timid and anxious, "wanting counsel," doubtful about his right to fire on the mob, and generally flaccid and tremulous—poor devil!

Walked uptown with Charley Strong and Hoppin, and after my cup of coffee, went to Union League Club. A delegation returned from police headquarters, having vainly asked for a squad of men to garrison the clubhouse. *None can be spared.* What is worse, we were badly repulsed in an attack on the mob in First Avenue, near Nineteenth Street, at about six P.M. Fired upon from houses, and had to leave sixteen wounded men and a Lieutenant Colonel Jardine in the hands of these brutes and devils. This is very bad indeed. But tonight is quieter than the last, though there seems to be a large fire downtown, and we hear occasional gun-shots.

At the club was George Biggs, full of the loudest and most emphatic jawing. "General Frémont's house and Craven's to be attacked tonight, Croton mains to be cut, and gas works destroyed," and so on. By way of precaution, I had had the bathtubs filled, and also all the pots, kettles, and pails in the house. . . . Twelve-thirty: Light as of a large fire to the south.

July 16. Rather quiet downtown. No trustworthy accounts of riot on any large scale during the day. General talk downtown is that the trouble is over. We shall see. It will be as it pleases the scoundrels who are privily engineering the outbreak —agents of Jefferson Davis, permitted to work here in New York.

Omnibusses and railroad cars in full career again. Coming uptown tonight I find Gramercy Park in military occupation. Strong parties drawn up across Twentieth Street and Twenty-first Streets at the east end of the Square, by the G House, each with a flanking squad, forming an L. Occasional shots fired at them from the region of Second or First Avenue, which were replied to by volleys that seem to have done little execution. An unlucky cart-horse was knocked over, I hear. This force was relieved at seven by a company of regulars and a party of the Seventh with a couple of howitzers, and there has been but a stray shot or two since dark. The regulars do not look like steady men. I have just gone over to the hotel with John Robertson and ordered a pail of strong coffee to put a little life into them.

Never knew exasperation so intense, unqualified, and general as that which prevails against these rioters and the politic knaves who are supposed to have set them going, Governor Seymour not excepted. Men who voted for him mention the fact with contrition and self-abasement, and the Democratic Party is at a discount with all the people I meet. (Apropos of discount, gold fell to one hundred and twenty-six today, with the city in insurrection, a gunboat at the foot of Wall Street, the Custom-house and Treasury full of soldiers and live shells, and two howitzers in position to rake Nassau Street from Wall to Fulton!!!!)

Every impression that's made on our people passes away so soon, almost as if stamped on the sand of the sea-beach. Were our moods a little less fleeting, I should have great hope of permanent good from the general wrath these outrages have provoked, and should put some faith in people's prophesyings that Fernando Wood and McCunn, and the New York *Herald*, and the Brookses and others, are doomed henceforth to obscurity and contempt. But we shall forget all about it before next November. Perhaps the lesson of the last four days is to be taught us still more emphatically, and we have got to be worse before we are better. It is not clear that the resources of the conspiracy are yet exhausted. The rioters of yesterday were better armed and organized than those of Monday, and their inaction today may possibly be meant to throw us off our guard, or their time may be employed perfecting plans for a campaign of plundering and brutality in yet greater force. They are in full possession of the western and the eastern sides of the city, from Tenth Street upward, and of a good many districts beside. I could not walk four blocks eastward from this house this minute without peril. The outbreak is spreading by concerted action in many quarters. Albany, Troy, Yonkers, Hartford, Boston, and other cities have each their Irish anti-conscription Nigger-murdering mob, of the same type with ours. It is a grave business, a *jacquerie* that must be put down by heroic doses of lead and steel.

Dr. Peters and Charley Strong called at eleven P.M. They have been exploring and report things quiet except on First Avenue from Nineteenth to Thirtieth Street, where there is said to be trouble. A detachment of the Seventh Regiment, five hundred or six hundred strong, marched to that quarter from their armory an hour ago.

July 17. The Army of Gramercy Park has advanced its headquarters to Third Avenue, leaving only a picket guard in sight. Rain will keep the rabble quiet tonight. We are said to have fifteen thousand men under arms, and I incline to hope that this movement in aid of the rebellion is played out.

BATTLE OF CHARLESTON HARBOR:
SOUTH CAROLINA, JULY 1863

Emma Holmes: Diary, July 16–19, 1863

Nine Union ironclads attempted to enter Charleston Harbor on April 7, 1863, but were repulsed by artillery fire from Fort Sumter and several shore batteries. Following the failure of the naval expedition, Brigadier General Quincy A. Gillmore made plans to capture Morris Island at the southern entrance to the harbor and use it to bombard Fort Sumter. Union troops landed on the southern end of Morris Island on July 10 and made an unsuccessful assault the following day on Battery Wagner (also known as Fort Wagner) on the northern end. Emma Holmes, the daughter of a plantation owner, followed the battle for the harbor from the city of Charleston.

Thursday 16 Our troops on James I. made a reconnaissance & found negro troops to oppose them—scarcely a white officer among them—at the first discharge they fled, pursued by our men, who mowed them down, & would have cut them to pieces, but one of our officers, put a stop to it, saying he wished some captured to be hung as an example & 16 were taken—most of the gentlemen think it decidedly a wrong step, as many nice questions will now be involved—if we hang them, will not the Yankees retaliate upon our men—they are fiendish enough to delight in the idea—yet it is revolting to our feelings to have them treated as prisoners of war as well as injurious in its effects upon our negroes—however they were brought to the city, barefoot, hatless & coatless & tied in a gang, like common runaways—

Friday morning I was much surprised to receive a message from Carrie saying Mary Jane & Hattie & herself had "run the blockade" but expected to leave next day for Summerville & begging me to go to see her—just as I was starting determined to make a great effort to walk so far, "our good Dr." came in to visit his patients, & said he would drive me up—he is almost the only person who fully understands & appreciates my weakness & debility—the girls arrived soon after I did, & most happy were we to meet once more—Dr. White & Sims also came in at different times, so I had quite a pleasant day seeing old friends—Isaac driving me down after tea—by the bye, he has sold his pet horse Prince, a beautiful animal, $2000 having been offered him for it & he now drives a remarkably fine large pair of mules, for which he has already been offered $1600—

Lee has recrossed the Potomac, in admirable order, and the army in splendid trim and spirits, without loss, though continual skirmishing took place, in which the gallant Gen. J. J. Pettigrew was mortally wounded & has since died—this time his death is certain, as Henry Young, his aid, telegraphed the fact—Lee's move has surprised one half the community, & pleased the other—the latter thinking he had gone too far from his base of supplies and communication, particularly as the still frequent heavy rains, which by the bye are now ruining the fine crops everywhere made the Potomac almost impassable—It is said, that the President ordered the recrossing of the river, much to Lee's anger & mortification & that he said if it were not for his country he would resign—His retreat from Gettysburg was strategic, to draw Meade's army from the high hills behind which they took refuge—President Davis has called out all *male residents* of the Confederacy, capable of bearing arms, between 18 & 45. The New York Herald of the 14th gives an account of a tremendous riot which took place there in the attempt to enforce the Conscription Act—it is headed—"The Draft. Tremendous Excitement in the City. Popular Opposition to enforcement of the Conscription—Enrolling Offices in Eight Districts Demolished. Two whole blocks of houses in Third Avenue, near Broadway burned. Military ordered out. Several Citizens & Soldiers killed, Arrival of the Police; and their attack, on the Crowd, Police Dispersed, some killed, others badly beaten—Superintendent Kennedy severely wounded. An Armory destroyed, Raid on negroes, Colored Orphan Asylum laid in ashes Hotels burnt, two mansions sacked, Tribune office attacked, as negro hanged—etc—etc—Everybody and every thing was in a state of excitement, cannon planted in the streets & troops guarding the Post office, & Newspaper offices & hotels—every negro seen by the mob was either murdered or cruelly beaten, and altogether a most demoniac scene—I am glad the Yankees are suffering a touch, even though such a faint one, of the horrors they have committed or tried to incite in our midst—

They have just made another raid on Pon Pon carrying off hundreds of negroes & burning & destroying the most elegant residences & barns etc. of Messrs. Heyward Manigault, Edward Barnwell & Col. Morris, Mrs. Hayne & others—

Saturday 18th. From daylight this morning the enemy was bombarding Battery Wagner furiously; they have over 70 guns concentrated from their various batteries & Monitors, & they fired at the rate of 20 shots a minute—it was intended to demoralize our troops, preparatory to the assault which commenced at dark—I spent a good part of the day with an excellent spy glass watching the Ironsides and four Monitors; I could see almost every discharge, & when the Yankee shells struck the earth, sending up a tall column of sand; I did not feel at all alarmed or excited; I had become so accustomed to the cannonading—but watched everything with intense interest. The Ironsides lay like a huge leviathan, long, low & black, discharging broadsides, while at her side, but nearer to Morris Island, lying between herself & land was a Monitor, whose peculiar black turrets were instantly recognizable, so distinctly defined against the sky are their huge black forms—Our batteries on Morris I. & Sumter slowly replied, but with excellent effect; during the morning the Yankee columns were formed for an attack, but our grape & canister drove them back with considerable loss. I could with a glass, see not only the signalling from our various forts and batteries, but from the Yankee observatory on Folly Island, which is high above the trees I was wishing so much I could read their dispatches & found later that Mr. Westervelt had done so, & intercepted Gilmore's orders for a general attack on our batteries Saturday night, so our men were ready for them—

Just as we were going to dinner cousin John's Baltimorean friend from the Marion Artillery, Mr. Jenkins (who had like himself, come to the city sick, & gone to the Roper Hospital, where he had received great attention from various ladies including cousin Beck & aunt Amelia) came to get a view of the bombardment; he is a delicate looking, very gentlemanly young man, who quite interested us—cousin Christopher & others came later, for the same purpose, and the Battery was thronged with spectators; during the afternoon I received a note from Carrie, saying the Summerville plan had been necessarily given up, as Mr. Hughes might be ordered off with the Bank to Columbia at any time, so Carrie intended remaining here till obliged to leave, then go to Camden, & wished me to come and stay with her—At such a time when everything of interest was concentrated on the Battery, & I am not able to walk down there, it really is a sacrifice to friendship to come up into the interior of the town; however, I determined to enjoy a last walk on the Battery & with Miss Ellen, promenaded till dark, watching the beautiful effect of the broad flashes of light at every discharge, which illuminated the sky; on our return found Gen. Gonzales, who had been on the housetop for a long time, in cousin Beck's piazza, & I could not help being amused to think how war had leveled ceremony all were obliged to pass through her chamber, where she was busily writing by a bright gas light the room was of course neatly arranged, but the pavilion down, etc. & as he was halfway through, some question was asked, and a long & interesting conversation ensued, which decidedly cheered all parties—He said the reason those lower batteries on Morris I. had not been completed was, that instead of sending their negroes, the planters preferred paying the fines, consequently instead of the three or four thousand laborers needed, there were only twenty odd at one time, & we did not even have troops enough to build them, for we had sent 10,000 men to Miss—& had only about three regiments here & if the Yankees had dared, they could have taken the city before, but now there was no cause for apprehension, at present, at least, & he had written for his wife, (he married Miss Elliott of Savannah) to come to the city if she wished & he promised to tell cousin B. when he thought it time for her to leave—Men were not what we wanted on Morris I. we had plenty now, but heavier guns, which were being rapidly supplied there, & on Sullivan's I. If Battery Wagner were taken, the Yankees' troubles would only commence, he said, for it would be a work of time to erect batteries to reduce Sumter & every day was gain to us. he had recommended Beauregard to strengthen the officer's quarter's there, the weakest side, by taking away the floors & making a wall of compressed cotton on a flooring of wet sand & Battery

Bee, on Sullivan's I. is as strong as Sumter & heavier guns are being put on Moultrie, so even if Sumter were taken, the city was not necessarily lost. I was really glad I had seen him, & was very much pleased with him—Just after Isaac called for me, & everything seemed so quiet up in Beaufain St. that we all slept as quietly as possible, little dreaming of what a sanguinary engagement was going on almost at our doors—

Sunday morning we learned what a tremendous assault had been made & how gloriously repulsed—about eight Saturday evening the Yankees advanced in six columns, as Willie Ramsey has since described to me, in perfect line of battle—our men waited till within 800 yards, then opened on them with grape & canister, which mowed huge gaps in their ranks; they would waver for a moment, then close up and move steadily on, again to be cut down—again and again were assaults made, & in the darkness & melie two or three hundred gained a position on the magazine, where they planted their flag & held it for more than an hour, it being some little time before they were discovered—a call for volunteers to dislodge them was made & numbers instantly stood forth—and in doing so, we lost the majority of our killed & wounded, among them Capt. Ryan of the Irish Volunteers, a very brave man killed & Maj. David Ramsey severely wounded—After having made other desperate assaults, they were finally driven off—They had expected our men to be completely demoralized by the incessant cannonading, & William White who was down there with Ramsey, assisting in erecting a mortar battery, says nothing can be more demoralizing, for the men to be cooped up all day in the close bomb proofs, with this awful never-ending roaring & whistling—the nerves kept in such a state of intense excitement—Our loss is about 24 killed & 70 wounded—sad to say, Lieut. Col. Simpkins, commanding the fort, a most gallant & excellent officer was killed, & Capt. William S. Stone dangerously wounded by our own men. Clingman's North Carolinians having fired into them by mistake, & Yankee prisoners say their troops did the same—it is fearful to think of such a battle in the darkness, with the roar of artillery mingled with the rattle of musketry. Capt. Warren Adams & William Sinkler wounded slightly, also Lieut. Wm. Clarkson, & William Macbeth very badly in the leg Willie Ramsey says may lose both it & his life—my old acquaintance Lieut. James Powe, whose gallantry is highly spoken, is also wounded—

William W. & William R. have both given us accounts of the fight & say they had heard of "piles of dead Yankees" & "bodies three deep" but never saw it till now, when they actually would be four deep, one on the other, as they fell forward, in every conceivable attitude—it was an awful sight in the ditch below the parapet—The Yankees sent a flag of truce, seeking the body of Col. Putnam, acting Brigadier a splendid looking man, grandson of Gen. Israel Putnam, & requesting to bury their dead—the first request was granted, the latter refused, as it was thought they only wanted an opportunity of close inspection, & the answer was we would bury their dead & take care of their wounded, many of whom however must have been carried off—we buried 600 among them numerous field officers, as well as captains & lieutenants, & beyond our lines the enemy buried over 200; among them about 150 negroes, and a good many of them were among the 230 wounded brought to the city, many so severely they will certainly die—and a negro has been put alternately with a Yankee in the hospital, much to their disgust, but our surgeons told them as they had put them on an equality they must abide the consequences—Their loss in killed, wounded & prisoners must 1500—Col. Shaw of Massachusetts was buried with eleven negroes over him—among the wounded prisoners is a remarkable intelligent negro from Bermuda, educated in the military school there—having no employment at home & needing support for his mother, he went to New York & Boston to seek it, & found large bounties being offered to volunteers, & as he had nothing else to provide his mother with, he joined the army & was made a sergeant—he says, when the column to assault was formed, the general rode up to the negro regiment commanded by Shaw, & told them to charge bravely, remembering if they faltered, 10,000 bayonets were behind them, & he says they marched with the bayonets almost in their backs. He curses the Yankees fearfully, for a set of vile cowards & wretches—

Sunday morning Carrie & I went to Grace Church & heard Rev. Mr. Seabrook; Sims & the girls & Edward dined with us, & in the evening Hanna & Mr. H. came down, having heard a report of W. Ramsey's death & feeling anxious about their brother—they said they heard a telegram had just been received from Louis Stark, saying Tom Ferguson was better—constant heavy skirmishing has been taking place between Grant's & Johnson's army, in which we repulsed them handsomely two or three times, but we finally evacuated Jackson again, Bragg seems to be quiet again, while Morgan is "*raiding*" in Indiana & scaring Hoosierdom out of its senses—

"WE CRIPPLED THEM SEVERELY":
VIRGINIA, JULY 1863

Walter H. Taylor to Richard Taylor

A member of Robert E. Lee's personal staff since 1861, Major Walter H. Taylor served as his adjutant during the Gettysburg campaign. He wrote to his brother from the Shenandoah Valley about the recent battle in Pennsylvania and its consequences. (Walter H. Taylor was not related to the Confederate general Richard Taylor.)

Camp near Winchester
17 July 1863

Presuming that Mary Lou may have left Richmond before this I will address myself to you and get you to forward this letter after reading it to our people wherever they may be.

I have written twice and telegraphed once since the late battle in Pennsyla giving assurance of the safety of Rob and myself and, as far as I know, of all our immediate friends. I hope these advices have been received & that all anxiety on our account has been allayed.

I was rejoiced to hear that John was unhurt up to the 24th of last month and trust that ere this you have received later tidings from him and that he is well. But for the loss of prisoners & the morale effect I would not much regret the fall of Vicksburg. Our people make a sad mistake when they attempt to hold such isolated points & attach so much importance to their being held successfully. After the enemy had obtained possession of the reach between Vicksburg & Pt. Hudson and held the same with their gunboats, I regarded the two points as of no more importance than any other two points on the Miss river. We could have prevented the free navigation of the stream by means of light and moveable batteries, and by concentrating our forces been enabled perhaps to have successfully resisted Grant's advance into the interior. Even now it seems to me affairs are terribly deranged out west. If Genl Johnston feels too weak to attack Grant, or rather felt too weak to attempt to relieve Pemberton, why so weaken Bragg to such an extent to make him powerless to resist Rosecrans? Division and not concentration seems to be the order of the day out there. But it is not proper to criticise yet, nor do I blame anyone particularly; only it looks to me as if there was some lack of judgment or some mismanagement.

As regards our own affairs, I wish I could write you an account in full of all that has transpired since we left the Rappahannock but I cannot now do this. Indeed you are already aware of all that happened up to our arrival at Gettysburg and engagements at that place. On the first day we were eminently successful. We fought two corps of their army with two divisions & a fraction of ours and drove them handsomely, capturing a number of prisoners & reducing the two corps to less than half their strength. The Northern papers admit a loss in one corps of 66 per cent.

On the second day we were also successful & drove them from a very strong position, capturing some cannons & many prisoners. But now we came to a position that was a sort of Gibraltar. Their two flanks were protected by two insurmountable, impracticable rocky mountains. It was out of the question to turn them. We reached the very base of the stronghold only to find almost perpendicular walls of rock. Besides the natural advantages of the place the enemy had strengthened themselves very much by artificial works. There was no opportunity whatever for a successful flank movement and on the third day two divisions assaulted a position a little to the left of their centre. Pickett's division of Virginians here immortalized itself. Its charge was the handsomest of the war as far as my experience goes and though it carried the works and captured a number of guns, it was not well supported by the division on its left, which failed to carry the works in its front & retired without any sufficient cause, thereby exposing Pickett's flank. The enemy then moved on Pickett's left & forced him to retire. The loss I suppose in killed, wounded & missing was about half of his command, which however was very small, consisting of only 3 reduced brigades.

Tho not much affected by this repulse, it was deemed inexpedient to make any more attempts to carry this place by assault. It was beyond our strength, simply this. If we had have had say 10,000 more men, we would have forced them back. As it was they did not resist Pickett but fled before him & had the supporting or second division performed its part as well, the result would have been different. On the next day we waited patiently for the enemy to attack us. This they did not do nor have they at any time since either attacked or manifested any desire to attack us. They retired from Gettysburg before we did and only claimed a victory after they had discovered our departure.

They only followed us with a little cavalry & horse artillery & their attempts to annoy our rear were ridiculous and insignificant. We took our time to Hagerstown, though to tell the truth we could not have moved rapidly had we desired it, for it rained in torrents incessantly, as indeed it did the whole month we were north of the Potomac. We arrived at Hagerstown & did not even hear of the enemy in our vicinity. Why he did not attempt to intercept us must appear remarkable to those who believe his lies about his *grand victory*. After four or five days he made his appearance. This time we had selected the ground and were most anxious for an attack. Our ordnance wagons had been replenished, we had enough to eat & the high waters of the Potomac gave no concern, if the enemy would only attack us.

We could not wait there for weeks & do nothing, nor could we afford to attack him in position, but if he would attack us, we would rejoice exceedingly. This the rascals dared not do, and their army, as they say, anxious to meet us again & flushed (as they say) with victory, did meet us & what next? They went to work fortifying as hard as they could and as I have discovered from their papers since, anticipated an attack from us. As they manifested no intention of fighting us, it was necessary or at least proper for us to leave our position and go where we could subsist. We threw a bridge over the Potomac & in face of this tremendous Yankee army flushed with victory (?) came into Virginia without the slightest annoyance from the enemy, but the elements were certainly against us. I never saw it rain so hard and our poor fellows had a hard time of it, I can tell you. The Yankees must organize a new army before they can again enjoy an "On to Richmond." We crippled them severely & they cannot now make any formidable aggressive movement.

We are again restive & ready for work. I will not hide one truth—that our men are better satisfied on this side of the Potomac. They are not accustomed to operating in a country where the people are inimical to them & certainly every one of them is today worth twice as much as he was three days ago. I am persuaded that we cannot without heavy acquisitions to our strength invade successfully for any length of time. Indeed had we been eminently successful at Gettysburg, in all probability we would have been obliged to make the same movements we have. Posterity will be astonished when the *facts* of this war are made known to see against what *odds* this little army contended. Even you would be surprised if I were to give you the figures of the Yankee army and our own.

I have just received Sister's letter of the 13th and am grieved to see that she has not received my letter. I wrote immediately after the fight & hoped she certainly would have rec'd it as soon as the Dept did the Genl's dispatches, which it accompanied. I did not know before that Mother had returned to Norfolk, tho I had received a letter stating she was detained in Annapolis. I try to be resigned & imagine that tho it now seems hard to us, some good will result from their cruel treatment of our household. God ordains all things well & I am assured we have only to wait patiently to see the good in this instance. We must get her some money if possible, or else she must borrow from the banks on some of her stocks or her real estate. I will send a draft to you by first safe opportunity for her half year's interest on her Virginia stock.

I expect Mrs Parks will write to Norfolk & advise of the safety of all of us.

Unlike most people I think Peace is near at hand & more probable now than when we entered Pennsylvania, that is, provided Genls Grant & Rosecrans are not allowed to overrun the whole west & do as they please. If they are confined to the fall of Vicksburg & that of Pt Hudson all will be well, but if allowed to go where & when they please without any genuine show of resistance, why then we can't say what the result will be. What the North is to be taught in order to secure peace is that a few military successes do not at all affect the ultimate result. Let them know that a success here and one there only prolongs the war without rendering our conquest by any means probable & they will not be able to resist the propositions of the Peace party in the North. Europe too may now think that we are weak in the knees & about to collapse and as sure as they do for fear of a reunion they will certainly recognize the independence of the South. The last thing they desire is to see us restored to the Union & if they see any apparent probability of it, they will move Heaven & Earth to prevent it.

Give my love to all at home when you write to Sally or Marcia and to all in Richmond. Aff yr bro

Walter

BATTLE OF FORT WAGNER:
SOUTH CAROLINA, JULY 1863

James Henry Gooding to the
New Bedford Mercury

The 54th Massachusetts Infantry returned to Hilton Head, South Carolina, from coastal Georgia in late June and was assigned to the force attacking Charleston. On July 11 the regiment landed on James Island, located between Morris Island and the mainland. (The low-lying, marshy islands south of the harbor were separated from each other by a series of tidal creeks and inlets.) After skirmishing with Confederate troops on James Island, the 54th Massachusetts was sent to Morris Island on July 18 to take part in a second attack on Fort Wagner. When his brigade commander offered Colonel Shaw the honor of having his regiment lead the assault, Shaw accepted. That evening the 54th Massachusetts led 5,000 men in an advance that at one point had to move forward along a strip of sand less than one hundred feet wide. Private James Henry Gooding was a sailor from New Bedford who enlisted in the 54th Massachusetts in February 1863. The following month he began writing regular letters to the *New Bedford Mercury*, where his account of the battle of Fort Wagner appeared on August 1.

Morris Island, July 20, 1863

Messrs. Editors:—At last we have something stirring to record. The 54th, the past week, has proved itself twice in battle. The first was on James Island on the morning of the 16th. There were four companies of the 54th on picket duty at the time; our picket lines extending to the right of the rebel battery, which commands the approach to Charleston through the Edisto river. About 3 o'clock in the morning, the rebels began harassing our pickets on the right, intending, no doubt, to drive them in, so that by daylight the coast would be clear to rush their main force down on us, and take us by surprise. They did not suppose we had any considerable force to the rear of our pickets on the right, as Gen. Stevenson's brigade was plain in sight on the left; and their plan, I suppose, was to rush down and cut Gen. Stevenson off. They made a mistake—instead of returning fire, the officer in charge of the pickets directed the men to lie down under cover of a hedge, rightly expecting the rebels to advance by degrees toward our lines. As he expected, at daylight they were within 600 yards of the picket line, when our men rose and poured a volley into them. That was something the rebels didn't expect—their line of skirmishers was completely broken; our men then began to fall back gradually on our line of battle, as the rebels were advancing their main force on to them. On they came, with six pieces of artillery and four thousand infantry, leaving a heavy force to drive Gen. Stevenson on the left. As their force advanced on our right, the boys held them in check like veterans; but of course they were falling back all the time, and fighting too. After the officers saw there was no chance for their men, they ordered them to move on to a creek under cover of the gunboats. When the rebels got within 900 yards of our line of battle, the right wing of Gen. Terry's brigade gave them three volleys, which checked their advance. They then made a stand with their artillery and began shelling us, but it had no effect on our forces, as the rebels fired too high. The 6th Connecticut battery then opened fire on them from the right, the John Adams and May Flower from the creek between James and Cole Islands, and the Pawnee and a mortar schooner from the Edisto, when the rebels began a hasty retreat. It was a warmer reception than they had expected. Our loss in the skirmishing before the battle, so far as we can ascertain, was nine killed, 13 wounded, and 17 missing, either killed or taken prisoners; but more probably they were driven into the creek and drowned. Sergeant Wilson, of Co. H, was called upon to surrender, but would not; he shot four men before he was taken. After he was taken they ordered him to give up his pistol which he refused to do, when he was shot through the head.

The men of the 54th behaved gallantly on the occasion—so the Generals say. It is not for us to blow our horn; but when a regiment of white men gave us three cheers as we were passing them, it shows that we did our duty as men should.

I shall pass over the incidents of that day, as regards individuals, to speak of a greater and more terrible ordeal the 54th regiment has passed through. I shall say nothing now of how we came from James to Morris Island; suffice it to say, on Saturday afternoon we were marched up past our batteries, amid the cheers of the officers and soldiers. We wondered what they were all cheering for, but we soon found out. Gen. Strong rode up, and we halted. Well, you had better believe there was some guessing what we were to do. Gen. Strong asked us if we would follow him into Fort Wagner. Every man said, yes—we were ready to follow wherever we were led. You may all know Fort Wagner is the Sebastopol of the rebels; but we went at it, over the ditch and on to the parapet through a deadly fire; but we could not get into the fort. We met the foe on the parapet of Wagner with the bayonet—we were exposed to a murderous fire from the batteries of the fort, from our Monitors and our land batteries, as they did not cease firing soon enough. Mortal men could not stand such a fire, and the assault on Wagner was a failure. The 9th Me., 10th Conn., 63d Ohio, 48th and 100th N.Y. were to support us in the assault; but after we made the first charge, everything was in such confusion that we could hardly tell where the reserve was. At the first charge the 54th rushed to within twenty yards of the ditches, and, as might be expected of raw recruits, wavered—but at the second advance they gained the parapet. The color bearer of the State colors was killed on the parapet. Col. Shaw seized the staff when the standard bearer fell, and in less than a minute after, the Colonel fell himself. When the men saw their gallant leader fall, they made a desperate effort to get him out, but they were either shot down, or reeled in the ditch below. One man succeeded in getting hold of the State color staff, but the color was completely torn to pieces.

I have no more paper here at present, as all our baggage is at St. Helena yet; so I cannot further particularize in this letter. Lieut. Grace was knocked down by a piece of shell, but he is not injured. He showed himself a great deal braver and cooler than any line officer.

J. H. G.

Our correspondent gives a list of killed, wounded and missing. It is the same that we have already published.

"NOT A MAN FLINCHED":
SOUTH CAROLINA, JULY 1863
Lewis Douglass to Amelia Loguen

The July 18 assault on Fort Wagner cost the Union 1,515 men killed, wounded, or captured, while the 1,800 Confederate defenders lost 222 men. Casualties in the 54th Massachusetts were 272 men killed, wounded, or captured, more than two-fifths of the regiment. Among the survivors was Sergeant Major Lewis Douglass, Frederick Douglass's eldest son, who wrote about the battle to Amelia Loguen, his future wife.

MORRIS ISLAND. S. C. July 20
MY DEAR AMELIA: I have been in two fights, and am unhurt. I am about to go in another I believe to-night. Our men fought well on both occasions. The last was desperate we charged that terrible battery on Morris Island known as Fort Wagoner, and were repulsed with a loss of 300 killed and wounded. I escaped unhurt from amidst that perfect hail of shot and shell. It was terrible. I need not particularize the papers will give a better than I have time to give. My thoughts are with you often, you are as dear as ever, be good enough to remember it as I no doubt you will. As I said before we are on the eve of another fight and I am very busy and have just snatched a moment to write you. I must necessarily be brief. Should I fall in the next fight killed or wounded I hope to fall with my face to the foe.

If I survive I shall write you a long letter. DeForrest of your city is wounded George Washington is missing, Jacob Carter is missing, Chas Reason wounded Chas Whiting, Chas Creamer all wounded. The above are in hospital.

This regiment has established its reputation as a fighting regiment not a man flinched, though it was a trying time. Men fell all around me. A shell would explode and clear a space of twenty feet, our men would close up again, but it was no use we had to retreat, which was a very hazardous undertaking. How I got out of that fight alive I cannot tell, but I am here.

My Dear girl I hope again to see you. I must bid you farewell should I be killed. Remember if I die I die in a good cause. I wish we had a hundred thousand colored troops we would put an end to this war. Good Bye to all Your own loving

Write soon
LEWIS

MOURNING COLONEL SHAW:
SOUTH CAROLINA, JULY 1863

Charlotte Forten: Journal, July 20–24, 1863

The daughter of a prominent Philadelphia black family and an active abolitionist, Charlotte Forten became one of the first black schoolteachers in the Sea Islands when she arrived on St. Helena Island, South Carolina, in October 1862. Forten met Robert Gould Shaw in early July when the 54th Massachusetts was posted to St. Helena, and wrote in her journal: "What purity what nobleness of soul, what exquisite gentleness in that beautiful face!"

Monday, July 20. For nearly two weeks we have waited, oh how anxiously for news of our regt. which went, we know, to Morris Is. to take part in the attack on Charleston. To-night comes news oh, so sad, so heart sickening. It is too terrible, too terrible to write. We can only hope it may not all be true. That our noble, beautiful young Colonel is killed, and the regt. cut to pieces! I cannot, cannot believe it. And yet I know it may be so. But oh, I am stunned, sick at heart. I can scarcely write. There was an attack on Fort Wagner. The 54th put in advance; fought bravely, desperately, but was finally overpowered and driven back after getting into the Fort. Thank Heaven! they fought bravely! And oh, I still must hope that our colonel, *ours* especially he seems to me, is not killed. But I can write no more to-night.

Beaufort, July 21. Came to town to-day hearing that nurses were sadly needed. Went to Mrs. L.'s. Found Col. H. and Dr. R. there. Mrs. L. was sure I sh'ld not be able to endure the fatigues of hospital life even for a few days, but I thought differently, and the Col. and Dr. were both on my side. So at last Mrs. L. consented and made arrangements for my entering one of the hospitals to-morrow.

It is sad to see the Col. at all feeble. He is usually so very strong and vigorous. He is going North next week. The Dr. is looking very ill. He is quite exhausted. I shall not feel at peace until he is safe in his northern home. The attachment between these two is beautiful, both are so thoroughly good and noble. And both have the rarest charm of manner.

Wednesday, July 22. My hospital life began to-day. Went early this morning with Mrs. L. and Mrs. G., the surgeon's wife, saw that the Dr. had not finished dressing the wounds, and while I waited below Mrs. S. gave me some sewing to do—mending the pantaloons and jackets of the poor fellows. (They are all of the 54th.) It was with a full heart that I sewed up bullet holes and bayonet cuts. Sometimes I found a jacket that told a sad tale—so torn to pieces that it was far past mending. After awhile I went through the wards. As I passed along I thought "Many and low are the pallets, but each is the face of a friend." And I was surprised to see such cheerful faces looking up from the beds. Talked a little with some of the patients and assisted Mrs. G. in distributing medicines. Mrs. L. kindly sent her carriage for me and I returned home, weary, but far more pleasantly impressed than I had thought possible, with hospital life.

Thursday, July 23. Said farewell to Col. H. who goes North in the "Arago" today. Am very sorry that Dr. R. c'ld not go with him, not having been able to get his papers. He is looking so ill. It makes me very anxious. He goes to Seaside for a few days. I hope the change, and Mrs. H.'s kind care will do him good. Took a more thorough survey of the hospital to-day. It is a large new brick building—quite close to the water,—two-storied, many windowed, and very airy—in every way well adapted for a hospital. Yesterday I was employed part of the time in writing letters for the men. It was pleasant to see the brave, cheerful, uncomplaining spirit which they all breathed. Some of the poor fellows had come from the far west—even so far as Michigan. Talked with them much to-day. Told them that we had heard that their noble Colonel was not dead, but had been taken prisoner by the rebels. How joyfully their wan faces lighted up! They almost started from their couches as the hope entered their souls. Their attachment to their gallant young colonel is beautiful to see. How warmly, how enthusiastically they speak of him. "He was one of the best little men in the world," they said. "No one c'ld be kinder to a set of men than he was to us." Brave grateful hearts! I hope they will ever prove worthy of such a leader. And God grant that he may indeed be living. But I fear, I greatly fear it may be but a false report. One poor fellow here interests me greatly. He is very young, only nineteen, comes from Michigan. He is very badly wounded—in both legs, and there is a ball—in the stomach—it is thought that cannot be extracted. This poor fellow suffers terribly. His groans are pitiful to hear. But he utters no complaint, and it is touching to see his gratitude for the least kindness that one does him. Mrs. G. asked him if he w'ld like her to write to his home. But he said no. He was an only son, and had come away against his mother's will. He w'ld not have her written to until he was better. Poor fellow! that will never be in this world.*

Another, a Sergeant, suffers great pain, being badly wounded in the leg. But he too lies perfectly patient and uncomplaining. He has such a good, honest face. It is pleasant to look at it—although it is black. He is said to be one of the best and bravest men in the regiment.

When I went in this morning and found my patients so cheerful some of them even quite merry, I tho't it c'ld not be possible that they were badly wounded. Many, indeed have only flesh wounds. But there are others—and they among the most uncomplaining—who are severely wounded;—some dangerously so. Brave fellows! I feel it a happiness, an honor, to do the slightest service for them. True they were unsuccessful in the attack of Fort Wagner. But that was no fault of theirs. It is the testimony of all that they fought bravely as men can fight, and that it was only when completely overwhelmed by superior numbers that they were driven back.

Friday, July 24. To-day the news of Col. Shaw's death is confirmed. There can no longer be any doubt. It makes me sad, sad at heart. They say he sprang from the parapet of the fort and cried "Onward, my brave boys, onward"; then fell, pierced with wounds. I know it was a glorious death. But oh, it is hard, very hard for the young wife, so late a bride, for the invalid mother, whose only and most dearly loved son he was, —that heroic mother who rejoiced in the position which he occupied as colonel of a colored regiment. My heart bleeds for her. His death is a very sad loss to us. I recall him as a much

---

*He has since recovered. I am surprised to hear.

loved friend. Yet I saw him but a few times. Oh what must it be to the wife and the mother. Oh it is terrible. It seems very, very hard that the best and the noblest must be the earliest called away. Especially has it been so throughout this dreadful war.

Mr. P. who has been unremitting in his attention to the wounded—called at our building to-day, and took me to the Officers Hospital, which is but a very short distance from here. It is in one of the finest residences in Beaufort, and is surrounded by beautiful grounds. Saw Major Hallowell, who, though badly wounded—in three places—is hoped to be slowly improving. A little more than a week ago I parted with him, after an exciting horseback ride, how strong, how well, how vigorous he was then! And now thoroughly prostrated! But he with all the other officers of the 54th, like the privates, are brave, patient—cheerful. With deep sadness he spoke of Col. Shaw and then told me something that greatly surprised me;—that the Col. before that fatal attack had told him that in case he fell he wished me to have one of his horses—He had three very fine spirited ones that he had brought from the North. (I afterward found this to be a mistake. He only wished me to take charge of the horses until they c'ld be sent North to his wife.—) How very, very kind it was! And to me, almost a perfect stranger. I shall treasure this gift most sacredly, all my life long.

"FOUR DAYS OF GREAT ANXIETY":
NEW YORK, JULY 1863

Maria Lydig Daly: Diary, July 23, 1863

The daughter of a wealthy New York family of Dutch-German ancestry, Maria Lydig Daly supported the war effort through contributions to the Women's Central Association for Relief and other charitable activities. Her husband, Charles P. Daly, was an Irish-American Catholic active in Democratic politics who served as chief judge of the New York City Court of Common Pleas (the highest court in the city). She wrote about the draft riots shortly after their suppression. In early August Horatio Seymour, the Democratic governor of New York, would ask that the draft be suspended in his state. Lincoln refused, and on August 19 conscription resumed in New York City under a heavy military guard.

July 23, 1863

At last the riot is quelled, but we had four days of great anxiety. Fighting went on constantly in the streets between the military and police and the mob, which was partially armed. The greatest atrocities have been perpetrated. Colonel O'Brian was murdered by the mob in such a brutal manner that nothing in the French Revolution exceeded it. Three or four Negroes were hung and burned; the women assisted and acted like furies by stimulating the men to greater ferocity. Father came into the city on Friday, being warned about his house, and found fifteen Negroes secreted in it by Rachel. They came from York Street, which the mob had attacked, with all their goods and chattels. Father had to order them out. We feared for our own block on account of the Negro tenements below MacDougal Street, where the Negroes were on the roof, singing psalms and having firearms.

One night, seeing a fire before the house, I thought the time had come, but it proved to be only a bonfire. The Judge sallied out with his pistol, telling me that if he were not at home in five minutes to call up the servants. This mob seems to have a curious sense of justice. They attacked and destroyed many disreputable houses and did not always spare secessionists. On Saturday (the fifth day) we went up to see Judge Hilton, who thought me very courageous, but I felt sorry for Mrs. Hilton upon hearing that she had been so terribly frightened. She gave me such details that I came home too nervous to sleep. In Lexington Avenue, houses were destroyed. One lady before whose house the mob paused with the intention of sacking it, saved her house by raising her window, smiling, and waving her handkerchief. Mr. Bosie's brother was seized by a rioter who asked him if he had $300.

"No," said he.

"Then come along with us," said the rioter, and they kept him two hours. Mrs. Hilton said she never saw such creatures, such gaunt-looking savage men and women and even little children armed with brickbats, stones, pokers, shovels and tongs, coal-scuttles, and even tin pans and bits of iron. They passed her house about four o'clock on Monday morning and continued on in a constant stream until nine o'clock. They looked to her, she said, like Germans, and her first thought was that it was some German festival. Whilst we sat there, we heard occasional pistol shots, and I was very glad that I had ordered a carriage to take us home. The carriage, it seems, was very unwillingly sent since the livery-stable keeper was so much afraid.

Every evening the Judge *would* go out near eleven o'clock, to my great distress. But he threatened to send me into the country if I objected (which I dreaded still more), so I kept quiet. Leonard, the Superintendent of Police in our neighborhood, said the draft could not be enforced; the firemen are against it, as well as all the working classes.

Among those killed or wounded have been found men with delicate hands and feet, and under their outward laborers' clothes were fine cambric shirts and costly underclothing. A dressmaker says she saw from her window a gentleman whom she knows and has seen with young ladies, but whose name she could not remember, disguised in this way in the mob on Sixth Avenue.

On Sunday we went to see Mrs. Jarvis and Mr. James T. Brady, who had just arrived from Washington. I saw Susanna Brady, who talked in the most violent manner against the Irish and in favor of the blacks. I feel quite differently, although very sorry and much outraged at the cruelties inflicted. I hope it will give the Negroes a lesson, for since the war commenced, they have been so insolent as to be unbearable. I cannot endure free blacks. They are immoral, with all their piety.

The principal actors in this mob were boys, and I think they were Americans. Catherine, my seamstress, tells me that the plundering was done by the people in the neighborhood who were looking on and who, as the mob broke the houses open, went in to steal. The police this morning found beds, bedding, and furniture in the house of a Scotch Presbyterian who was well off and owned two cows and two horses. The Catholic priests have done their duty as Christians ministers in denouncing these riotous proceedings. One of them remonstrated with a woman in the crowd who wanted to cut off the ears of a Negro who was hung. The priest told her that Negroes had souls. "Sure, your reverence," said she, "I thought they only had gizzards."

On Sunday evening, Mr. Dykes came in. He had seen Judge Pierrepont, who had gone to Washington with others to see what can be done. Mr. Dykes thinks that New York, being a Democratic city, may expect little indulgence from the Administration. The Judge went up to see General Dix, now in command here, who says that the government is determined to carry the draft measure through at all costs. Yesterday we went to the wedding of Lydia Watson in Westchester County. Mr. Adie told the Judge that there was a secessionist plot to burn all the houses in the neighborhood on Thursday night, that he had heard that his had been exempted by vote, and that the principal instigator and mover in it was one of the richest and most influential men in the neighborhood. The purpose of the plot was to intimidate the government and prevent conscription. Mrs. Harry Morris, who I hear has been very violent in her invectives against the North, wished to know if the soldiers could be relied upon. I told her entirely so, that they declared they would rather fight these traitors at home who made this fire in their rear whilst they were risking their life to preserve order and the laws than the rebels. For her comfort, I told her that the mob had destroyed the houses of secessionists. I frightened her, I think, not a little.

"THE ATHEIST ROAR OF RIOT":
NEW YORK, JULY 1863
Herman Melville: The House-top

Although Herman Melville was living in Pittsfield, Massachusetts, during the draft riots, some of his family and friends experienced the violence firsthand, among them his cousin Henry Gansevoort, a Union cavalry officer who helped restore order in the city. "The House-top" first appeared in *Battle-Pieces and Aspects of the War*, published in August 1866. (The footnote to the poem in this volume originally appeared as an endnote in *Battle-Pieces*.)

The House-top.
A Night Piece.
(JULY, 1863.)

No sleep. The sultriness pervades the air
And binds the brain—a dense oppression, such
As tawny tigers feel in matted shades,
Vexing their blood and making apt for ravage.
Beneath the stars the roofy desert spreads
Vacant as Libya. All is hushed near by.
Yet fitfully from far breaks a mixed surf
Of muffled sound, the Atheist roar of riot.
Yonder, where parching Sirius set in drought,
Balefully glares red Arson—there—and there.
The Town is taken by its rats—ship-rats
And rats of the wharves. All civil charms
And priestly spells which late held hearts in awe—
Fear-bound, subjected to a better sway
Than sway of self; these like a dream dissolve,
And man rebounds whole æons back in nature.[i]

NOTE [i]
"I dare not write the horrible and inconceivable atrocities committed," says Froissart, in alluding to the remarkable sedition in France during his time. The like may be hinted of some proceedings of the draft-rioters.

Hail to the low dull rumble, dull and dead,
And ponderous drag that shakes the wall.
Wise Draco comes, deep in the midnight roll
Of black artillery; he comes, though late;
In code corroborating Calvin's creed
And cynic tyrannies of honest kings;
He comes, nor parlies; and the Town, redeemed,
Gives thanks devout; nor, being thankful, heeds
The grimy slur on the Republic's faith implied,
Which holds that Man is naturally good,
And—more—is Nature's Roman, never to be scourged.

NEWS OF VICTORY: LONDON, JULY 1863

Henry Adams to
Charles Francis Adams Jr.

News of Lee's defeat and the surrender of Vicksburg reached London on July 19. Henry Adams shared his reaction with his brother, who had fought with the 1st Massachusetts Cavalry in the Gettysburg campaign.

---

23 July. 1863.

I positively tremble to think of receiving any more news from America since the batch that we received last Sunday. Why can't we sink the steamers till some more good news comes? It is like an easterly storm after a glorious June day, this returning to the gloomy chronicle of varying successes and disasters, after exulting in the grand excitement of such triumphs as you sent us on the 4th. For once, there was *no* drawback, unless I except anxiety about you. I wanted to hug the army of the Potomac. I wanted to get the whole of the army of Vicksburg drunk at my own expense. I wanted to fight some small man and lick him. Had I had a single friend in London capable of rising to the dignity of the occasion, I don't know what mightn't have happened. But mediocrity prevailed and I passed the day in base repose.

It was on Sunday morning as I came down to breakfast that I saw a telegram from the Department announcing the fall of Vicksburg. Now, to appreciate the value of this, you must know that the one thing upon which the London press and the English people have been so positive as not to tolerate contradiction, was the impossibility of capturing Vicksburg. Nothing could induce them to believe that Grant's army was not in extreme danger of having itself to capitulate. The Times of Saturday, down to the last moment, declared that the siege of Vicksburg grew more and more hopeless every day. Even now, it refuses, after receiving all the details, to admit the fact, and only says that Northern advices report it, but it is not yet confirmed. Nothing could exceed the energy with which everybody in England has reprobated the wicked waste of life that must be caused by the siege of this place during the sickly season, and ridiculed the idea of its capture. And now, the announcement was just as though a bucket of iced-water were thrown into their faces. They couldn't and wouldn't believe it. All their settled opinions were overthrown, and they were left dangling in the air. You never heard such a cackling as was kept up here on Sunday and Monday, and you can't imagine how spiteful and vicious they all were. Sunday evening I was asked round to Monckton Milnes's to meet a few people. Milnes himself is one of the warmest Americans in the world, and received me with a hug before the astonished company, crowing like a fighting cock. But the rest of the company were very cold. W. H. Russell was there, and I had a good deal of talk with him. He at least did not attempt to disguise the gravity of the occasion, nor to turn Lee's defeat into a victory. I went with Mr Milnes to the Cosmopolitan Club afterwards, where the people all looked at me as though I were objectionable. Of course I avoided the subject in conversation, but I saw very clearly how unpleasant the news was which I brought. So it has been everywhere. This is a sort of thing that can be neither denied, palliated, nor evaded; the disasters of the rebels are unredeemed by even any hope of success. Accordingly the emergency has produced here a mere access of spite; preparatory (if we suffer no reverse) to a revolution in tone.

It is now conceded at once that all idea of intervention is at an end. The war is to continue indefinitely, so far as Europe is concerned, and the only remaining chance of collision is in the case of the iron-clads. We are looking after them with considerable energy, and I think we shall settle them.

It is utterly impossible to describe to you the delight that we all felt here and that has not diminished even now. I can imagine the temporary insanity that must have prevailed over the North on the night of the 7th. Here our demonstrations were quiet, but ye Gods! how we felt! Whether to laugh or to cry, one hardly knew. Some men preferred the one, some the other. The Chief was the picture of placid delight. As for me, as my effort has always been here to suppress all expression of feeling, I preserved sobriety in public, but for four days I've been internally singing Hosannahs and running riot in exultation. The future being doubtful, we are all the more determined to drink this one cup of success out. Our friends at home, Dana, John, and so on, are always so devilish afraid that we may see things in too rosy colors. They think it necessary to be correspondingly sombre in their advices. This time, luckily, we had no one to be so cruel as to knock us down from behind, when we were having all we could do to fight our English upas influences in front. We sat on the top of the ladder and didn't care a copper who passed underneath. Your old friend Judge Goodrich was here on Monday, and you never saw a man in such a state. Even for him it was wonderful. He lunched with us and kept us in a perfect riot all the time, telling stories without limit and laughing till he almost screamed.

I am sorry to say however that all this is not likely to make our position here any pleasanter socially. All our experience has shown that as our success was great, so rose equally the spirit of hatred on this side. Never before since the Trent affair has it shown itself so universal and spiteful as now. I am myself more surprised at it than I have any right to be, and philosopher though I aspire to be, I do feel strongly impressed with a desire to see the time come when our success will compel silence and our prosperity will complete the revolution. As for war, it would be folly in us to go to war with this country. We have the means of destroying her without hurting ourselves.

In other respects the week has been a very quiet one. The season is over. The streets are full of Pickford's vans carting furniture from the houses, and Belgravia and May Fair are the scene of dirt and littered straw, as you know them from the accounts of Pendennis. One night we went to the opera, but otherwise we have enjoyed peace, and I have been engaged in looking up routes and sights in the guide book of Scotland. Thither, if nothing prevents and no bad news or rebel's plot interferes, we shall wend our way on the first of August. The rest of the family will probably make a visit or two, and I propose to make use of the opportunity to go on with Brooks and visit the Isle of Skye and the Hebrides, if we can. This is in imitation of Dr Johnson, and I've no doubt, if we had good weather, it would be very jolly. But as for visiting people, the truth is I feel such a dislike for the whole nation, and so keen a sensitiveness to the least suspicion of being thought to pay court to any of them, and so abject a dread of ever giving anyone the chance to put a slight upon me, that I avoid them and neither wish them to be my friends nor wish to be theirs. I haven't the strength of character to retain resentments long, and some day in America I may astonish myself by defending these people for whom I entertain at present only a profound and lively contempt. But at present I am glad that my acquaintances are so few and I do not intend to increase the number.

You will no doubt be curious to know, if, as I say, I have no acquaintances, how the devil I pass my time. Certainly I do pass it, however, and never have an unoccupied moment. My candles are seldom out before two o'clock in the morning, and my table is piled with half-read books and unfinished writing. For weeks together I only leave the house to mount my horse and after my ride, come back as I went. If it were not for your position and my own uneasy conscience, I should be as happy as a Virginia oyster, and as it is, I believe I never was so well off physically, morally and intellectually as this last year.

I send you another shirt, and a copy of the Index, the southern organ, which I thought you would find more interesting this week than any other newspaper I can send. It seems to me to look to a cessation of *organised* armed resistance and an ultimate resort to the Polish fashion. I think we shall not stand much in their way there, if they like to live in a den of thieves.

Ever

JUSTIFYING A DECISION:
VIRGINIA, JULY 1863

George G. Meade to Henry W. Halleck

Meade remained sensitive to criticism of his pursuit of Lee's army after Gettysburg. On July 28 Halleck wrote to Meade, praising him for handling his troops during the battle "as well, if not better, than any general has handled his army during the war," and expressing continued confidence in his leadership. Halleck also told Meade that he "should not have been surprised or vexed at the President's disappointment at the escape of Lee's army," adding that Lincoln "felt no little impatience" at Lee's "unexpected escape." Meade replied from his headquarters at Warrenton in northern Virginia.

UNOFFICIAL.]

HEADQUARTERS ARMY OF THE POTOMAC,
July 31, 1863.

Major-General HALLECK,
General-in-Chief:

MY DEAR GENERAL: I thank you most sincerely and heartily for your kind and generous letter of the 28th instant, received last evening. It would be wrong in me to deny that I feared there existed in the minds of both the President and yourself an idea that I had failed to do what another would and could have done in the withdrawal of Lee's army. The expression you have been pleased to use in your letter, to wit, "a feeling of disappointment," is one that I cheerfully accept and readily admit was as keenly felt by myself as any one. But permit me, dear general, to call your attention to the distinction between disappointment and dissatisfaction. The one was a natural feeling, in view of the momentous consequences that would have resulted from a successful attack, but does not necessarily convey with it any censure. I could not view the use of the latter expression in any other light than as intending to convey an expression of opinion on the part of the President that I had failed to do what I might and should have done. Now, let me say, in the frankness which characterizes your letter, that perhaps the President was right; if such was the case, it was my duty to give him an opportunity to replace me by one better fitted for the command of the army. It was, I assure you, with such feelings that I applied to be relieved. It was not from any personal considerations, for I have tried in this whole war to forget all personal considerations, and have always maintained they should not for an instant influence any one's actions.

Of course you will understand that I do not agree that the President was right, and I feel sure when the true state of the case comes to be known, that however natural and great may be the feeling of disappointment, no blame will be attached to any one.

Had I attacked Lee the day I proposed to do so, and in the ignorance that then existed of his position, I have every reason to believe the attack would have been unsuccessful, and would have resulted disastrously. This opinion is founded on the judgment of numerous distinguished officers, after inspecting Lee's vacated works and position. Among these officers I could name Generals Sedgwick, Wright, Slocum, Hays, Sykes, and others.

The idea that Lee had abandoned his lines early in the day that he withdrew, I have positive intelligence is not correct, and that not a man was withdrawn till after dark. I mention these facts to remove the impression, which newspaper correspondents have given the public, that it was only necessary to advance to secure an easy victory. I had great responsibility thrown on me. On one side were the known and important fruits of victory, and, on the other, the equally important and terrible consequences of a defeat. I considered my position at Williamsport very different from that at Gettysburg. When I left Frederick, it was with the firm determination to attack and fight Lee, without regard to time or place, as soon as I could come in contact with him; but after defeating him, and requiring him to abandon his schemes of invasion, I did not think myself justified in making a blind attack simply to prevent his escape, and running all the risks attending such a venture. Now, as I said before, in this, perhaps, I erred in judgment, for I take this occasion to say to you, and through you to the President, that I have no pretensions to any superior capacity for the post he has assigned me to; that all I can do is to exert my utmost efforts and do the best I can; but that the moment those who have a right to judge my actions think, or feel satisfied, either that I am wanting or that another would do better, that moment I earnestly desire to be relieved, not on my own account, but on account of the country and the cause.

You must excuse so much egotism, but your kind letter in a measure renders it necessary. I feel, general, very proud of your good opinion, and assure you I shall endeavor in the future to continue to merit it.

Reciprocating the kind feeling you have expressed, I remain, general, most truly and respectfully, yours,

GEO. G. MEADE,
Major-General.

"I AM ALONE TO BLAME":
VIRGINIA, JULY 1863

Robert E. Lee to Jefferson Davis

Lee wrote to Davis in response to a July 27 note from the Confederate president that has not been found. It enclosed a clipping from the *Charleston Mercury*, possibly a dispatch from Richmond on July 18 that referred to "the ill-timed Northern campaign, which cost us Vicksburg, with the States of Mississippi and Tennessee, and endangered Charleston." The *Mercury* was owned by Robert Barnwell Rhett and edited by his son, Robert Barnwell Rhett Jr., both bitter political opponents of the Davis administration.

Camp, Culpeper
July 31, 1863

Mr. President:

Your note of the 27 enclosing a slip from the *Charleston Mercury* relative to the battle of Gettysburg is received. I much regret its general censure upon the operations of the army, as it is calculated to do us no good either at home or abroad. But I am prepared for similar criticism & as far as I am concerned the remarks fall harmless. I am particularly sorry however that from partial information & mere assumption of facts that injustice should be done any officer, & that occasion should be taken to asperse your conduct, who of all others are most free of blame. I do not fear that your position in the confidence of the people, can be injured by such attacks, & I hope the official reports will protect the reputation of every officer. These cannot be made at once, & in the meantime as you state much falsehood may be promulgated. But truth is mighty & will eventually prevail. As regards the article in question I think it contains its own contradiction. Although charging Heth with the failure of the battle, it expressly states he was absent wounded. The object of the writer & publisher is evidently to cast discredit upon the operations of the Government & those connected with it & thus gratify feelings more to be pitied than envied. To take notice of such attacks would I think do more harm than good, & would be just what is desired. The delay that will necessarily occur in receiving official reports has induced me to make for the information of the Department a brief outline of operations of the army, in which however I have been unable to state the conduct of troops or officers. It is sufficient to show what was done & what was not done. No blame can be attached to the army for its failure to accomplish what was projected by me, nor should it be censured for the unreasonable expectations of the public. I am alone to blame, in perhaps expecting too much of its prowess & valour. It however in my opinion achieved under the guidance of the Most High a general success, though it did not win a victory. I thought at the time that the latter was practicable. I still think if all things could have worked together it would have been accomplished. But with the knowledge I then had, & in the circumstances I was then placed, I do not know what better course I could have pursued. With my present knowledge, & could I have foreseen that the attack on the last day would have failed to drive the enemy from his position, I should certainly have tried some other course. What the ultimate result would have been is not so clear to me. Our loss has been very heavy, that of the enemy's is proportionally so. His crippled condition enabled us to retire from the country comparatively unmolested. The unexpected state of the Potomac was our only embarrassment. I will not trespass upon Your Excellency's time more. With prayers for your health & happiness, & the recognition by your grateful country of your great services

I remain truly & sincerely yours
R. E. LEE

"WHAT IS RIGHT": NEW YORK, JULY 1863
Hannah Johnson to Abraham Lincoln

It is not known if President Lincoln ever saw this letter, which is preserved in the National Archives in the records of the adjutant general's office.

Buffalo July 31 1863

Excellent Sir My good friend says I must write to you and she will send it My son went in the 54th regiment. I am a colored woman and my son was strong and able as any to fight for his country and the colored people have as much to fight for as any. My father was a Slave and escaped from Louisiana before I was born morn forty years agone I have but poor edication but I never went to schol, but I know just as well as any what is right between man and man. Now I know it is right that a colored man should go and fight for his country, and so ought to a white man. I know that a colored man ought to run no greater risques than a white, his pay is no greater his obligation to fight is the same. So why should not our enemies be compelled to treat him the same, Made to do it.

My son fought at Fort Wagoner but thank God he was not taken prisoner, as many were I thought of this thing before I let my boy go but then they said Mr. Lincoln will never let them sell our colored soldiers for slaves, if they do he will get them back quck he will rettallyate and stop it. Now Mr Lincoln dont you think you oght to stop this thing and make them do the same by the colored men they have lived in idleness all their lives on stolen labor and made savages of the colored people, but they now are so furious because they are proving themselves to be men, such as have come away and got some edication. It must not be so. You must put the rebels to work in State prisons to making shoes and things, if they sell our colored soldiers, till they let them all go. And give their wounded the same treatment. it would seem cruel, but their no other way, and a just man must do hard things sometimes, that shew him to be a great man. They tell me some do you will take back the Proclamation, don't do it. When you are dead and in Heaven, in a thousand years that action of yours will make the Angels sing your praises I know it. Ought one man to own another, law for or not, who made the law, surely the poor slave did not. so it is wicked, and a horrible Outrage, there is no sense in it, because a man has lived by robbing all his life and his father before him, should he complain because the stolen things found on him are taken. Robbing the colored people of their labor is but a small part of the robbery   their souls are almost taken, they are made bruits of often. You know all about this

Will you see that the colored men fighting now, are fairly treated. You ought to do this, and do it at once, Not let the thing run along   meet it quickly and manfully, and stop this, mean cowardly cruelty. We poor oppressed ones, appeal to you, and ask fair play. Yours for Christs sake

Hannah Johnson.

Hon. Mr. Lincoln   The above speaks for itself   Carrie Coburn

REFUSING TO RECRUIT:
NEW YORK, AUGUST 1863

Frederick Douglass to George L. Stearns

In a proclamation issued on December 23, 1862, Jefferson Davis ordered that former slaves captured while fighting for the Union be turned over to state authorities to be tried for the capital offense of insurrection. His policy was extended by a joint resolution of the Confederate Congress, adopted on May 1, 1863, to apply to free blacks from the North. In practice, captured black soldiers were either summarily executed, returned or sold into slavery, or used for forced labor by the Confederate army. Angered by the Lincoln administration's apparent unwillingness to retaliate, Douglass announced his refusal to continue recruiting black soldiers in a public letter to George L. Stearns that appeared in *Douglass' Monthly*. (A wealthy Boston abolitionist who had financially supported John Brown, Stearns had been commissioned by Governor Andrew to recruit for the 54th Massachusetts and in turn had enlisted Douglass and other black abolitionists in the effort.) In fact, Lincoln had issued an order on July 30 declaring that to "sell or enslave any captured person, on account of his color, and for no offence against the laws of war, is a relapse into barbarism and a crime against the civilization of the age." The order specified that "for every soldier of the United States killed in violation of the laws of war, a rebel soldier shall be executed," and that for every one enslaved, "a rebel soldier shall be placed at hard labor on the public works."

Rochester, August 1st, 1863

My Dear Sir:

Having declined to attend the meeting to promote enlistments, appointed for me at Pittsburgh, in present circumstances, I owe you a word of explanation. I have hitherto deemed it a duty, as it certainly has been a pleasure, to cooperate with you in the work of raising colored troops in the free states, to fight the battles of the Republic against the slaveholding rebels and traitors. Upon the first call you gave me to this work, I responded with alacrity. I saw, or thought I saw a ray of light, brightening the future of my whole race as well as that of our war troubled country, in arousing colored men to fight for the nation's life, I continue to believe in the black man's arm, and still have some hope in the integrity of our rulers. Nevertheless, I must for the present leave to others the work of persuading colored men to join the Union Army. I owe it to my long abused people, and especially of them already in the army, to expose their wrongs and plead their cause. I cannot do that in connection with recruiting. When I plead for recruits I want to do it with all my heart, without qualification. I cannot do that now. The impression settles upon me that colored men have much overrated the enlightenment, justice and generosity of our rulers at Washington. In my humble way I have contributed somewhat to that false estimate. You know, that when the idea of raising colored troops was first suggested, the special duty to be assigned them, was the garrisoning of forts and arsenals in certain warm, unhealthy and miasmatic localities in the South. They were thought to be better adapted to that service than white troops. White troops, trained to war, brave and daring, were to take fortifications, and the blacks were to hold them and keep them from falling again into the hands of the rebels.—Three advantages were to arise out of this wise division of labor. 1st. The spirit and pride of white troops was not to waste itself in dull and monotonous inactivity in fort-life. Their arms were to be kept bright by constant use. 2dly. The health of the white troops was to be preserved. 3dly. Black troops were to have the advantage of sound military training, and be otherwise useful at the same time that they should be tolerably secure from capture by the rebels, who early avowed their determination to enslave and slaughter them in defiance of the laws of war. Two out of the three advantages, were to accrue to the white troops. Thus far however, I believe that no such duty as holding fortifications has been committed to colored troops. They have done far other and more important work than holding fortifications. I have no special complaint to make at this point, and I simply mention it to strengthen the statement that from the beginning of this business it was the confident belief among both the colored and white friends of colored enlistments that President Lincoln as Commander-in-Chief of the army and navy would certainly see to it, that his colored troops should be so handled and disposed of as to be but little exposed to capture by the rebels, and that—if so exposed—as they have repeatedly been from the first, the President possessed both the disposition and the means for compelling the rebels to respect the rights of such as might fall in their hands. The piratical proclamation of President Davis announcing Slavery and assassination to colored prisoners was before the country and the world. But men had faith in Mr. Lincoln and his advisers. He was silent, to be sure, but charity suggested that being a man of action rather than words, he only waited for a case in which he should be required to act. This faith in the man enabled us to speak with warmth and effect in urging enlistments among colored men. That faith, my dear Sir, is now nearly gone. Various occasions have arisen during the last six months for the exercise of his power in behalf of the colored men in his service. But no word comes from Mr. Lincoln or from the War Department, sternly assuring the Rebel Chief that inquisitions shall yet be made for innocent blood. No word of retaliation when a black man is slain by a rebel in cold blood. No word was said when free men from Massachusetts were caught and sold into slavery in Texas. No word is said when brave black men who according to the testimony of both friend and foe, fought like heroes to plant the star spangled banner on the blazing parapets of Fort Wagner, and in doing so were captured, some mutilated and killed, and others sold into slavery. The same crushing silence reigns over this scandalous outrage as over that of the slaughtered teamsters at Murfreesboro.— The same as over that at Millikens Bend and Vicksburg. I am free to say, my dear sir, that the case looks as if the confiding colored soldiers had been betrayed into bloody hands by the very Government in whose defense they were heroically fighting. I know what you will say to this; you will say; "wait a little longer, and after all, the best way to have justice done to your people is to get them into the army as fast as possible." You may be right in this; my argument has been the same, but have we not already waited, and have we not already shown the highest qualities of soldiers and on this account deserve the protection of the Government for which we are fighting? Can any case stronger than that before Charleston ever arise? If the President is ever to demand justice and humanity for black soldiers, is not this the time for him to do it? How many 54ths must be cut to pieces, its mutilated prisoners killed and its living sold into Slavery, to be tortured to death by inches before Mr. Lincoln shall say: "Hold, enough!"

You know the 54th. To you, more than any one man belongs the credit of raising that Regiment. Think of its noble and brave officers literally hacked to pieces while many of its rank and file have been sold into a slavery worse than death, and pardon me if I hesitate about assisting in raising a fourth Regiment until the President shall give the same protection to them as to white soldiers. With warm and sincere regards,

Frederick Douglass

Since writing the foregoing letter, which we have now put upon record, we have received assurance from Major Stearns, that the Government of the United States is already taking measures which will secure for the captured colored soldiers, at Charleston and elsewhere, the same protection against slavery and cruelty, extended to white soldiers. What ought to have been done at the beginning, comes late, but it comes. The poor colored soldiers have purchased this interference dearly. It really seems that nothing of justice, liberty, or humanity can come to us except through tears and blood.

DEMANDING RETALIATION:
NEW YORK, AUGUST 1863

Frederick Douglass:
The Commander-in-Chief and His Black Soldiers

August 1863

This article appeared in *Douglass' Monthly* along with the letter to Stearns.

Whatever else may be said of President Lincoln, the most malignant Copperhead in the country cannot reproach him with any undue solicitude for the lives and liberties of the brave black men, who are now giving their arms and hearts to the support of his Government. When a boy, on a slave plantation the saying was common: "Half a cent to kill a Negro and half a cent to bury him."—The luxury of killing and burying could be enjoyed by the poorest members of Southern society, and no strong temptation was required to induce white men thus to kill and bury the black victims of their lust and cruelty. —With a Bible and pulpit affirming that the Negro is accursed of God, it is not strange that men should curse him, and that all over the South there should be manifested for the life and liberty of this description of man, the utterest indifference and contempt. Unhappily the same indifference and contempt for the lives of colored men is found wherever slavery has an advocate or treason an apologist. In the late terrible mobs in New York and elsewhere, the grim features of this malice towards colored men was everywhere present. Beat, shoot, hang, stab, kill, burn and destroy the Negro, was the cry of the crowd. Religion has cursed him and the law has enslaved him, and why may not the mob kill him?—Such has been our national education on this subject, and that it still has power over Mr. Lincoln seems evident from the fact, that no measures have been openly taken by him to cause the laws of civilized warfare to be observed towards his colored soldiers. The slaughter of blacks taken as captives, seems to affect him as little as the slaughter of beeves for the use of his army. More than six months ago Mr. Jefferson Davis told Mr. Lincoln and the world that he meant to treat blacks not as soldiers but as felons. The threat was openly made, and has been faithfully executed by the rebel chief. At Murfreesboro twenty colored teamsters in the Federal service, were taken by the rebels, and though not soldiers, and only servants, they were in cold blood—every man of them—shot down. At Milliken's Bend, the same black flag with its death's head and cross-bones was raised. When Banks entered Port Hudson he found white federal prisoners, but no black ones. Those of the latter taken, were no doubt, in cold blood put to the sword. Today, news from Charleston tells us that Negro soldiers taken as prisoners will not be exchanged, but sold into slavery—that some twenty of such prisoners are now in their hands. Thousands of Negroes are now being enrolled in the service of the Federal Government. The Government calls them, and they come. They freely and joyously rally around the flag of the Union, and take all the risks, ordinary and extraordinary, involved in this war. They do it not for office, for thus far, they get none; they do it not for money, for thus far, their pay is less than that of white men. They go into this war to affirm their manhood, to strike for liberty and country.—If any class of men in this war can claim the honor of fighting for principle, and not from passion, for ideas, not from brutal malice, the colored soldier can make that claim preeminently. He strikes for manhood and freedom, under the forms of law and the usages of civilized warfare. He does not go forth as a savage with tomahawk and scalping knife, but in strict accordance with the rules of honorable warfare. Yet he is now openly threatened with slavery and assassination by the rebel Government—and the threat has been savagely executed.

What has Mr. Lincoln to say about this slavery and murder? What has he said?—Not one word. In the hearing of the nation he is as silent as an oyster on the whole subject. If two white men are threatened with assassination, the Richmond Rebels are promptly informed that the Federal Government will retaliate sternly and severely. But when colored soldiers are so threatened, no word comes from the Capitol. What does this silence mean? Is there any explanation short of base and scandalous contempt for the just rights of colored soldiers?

For a time we tried to think that there might be solid reasons of state against answering the threats of Jefferson Davis—but the Government has knocked this favorable judgment from under us, by its prompt threat of retaliation in the case of the two white officers at Richmond who are under sentence of death. Men will ask, the world will ask, why interference should be made for those young white officers thus selected for murder, and not for the brave black soldiers who may be flung by the fortunes of war into the hands of the rebels? Is the right to "life, liberty and the pursuit of happiness" less sacred in the case of the one than the other?

It may be said that the black soldiers have enlisted with the threat of Jefferson Davis before them, and they have assumed their position intelligently, with a full knowledge of the consequences incurred. If they have, they have by that act shown themselves all the more worthy of protection. It is noble in the Negro to brave unusual danger for the life of the Republic, but it is mean and base in the Republic if it rewards such generous and unselfish devotion by assassination, when a word would suffice to make the laws of war respected, and to prevent the crime. Shocking enough are the ordinary horrors of war, but the war of the rebels toward the colored men is marked by deeds which well might "shame extremest hell." And until Mr. Lincoln shall interpose his power to prevent these atrocious assassinations of Negro soldiers, the civilized world will hold him equally with Jefferson Davis responsible for them. The question is already being asked: Why is it that colored soldiers which were first enlisted with a view to "garrison forts and arsenals, on the Southern coast"—where white men suffer from climate, should never be heard of in any such forts and arsenals? Was that a trick? Why is it that they who were enlisted to fight the fevers of the South, while white soldiers fight the rebels are now only heard of in "forlorn hopes," in desperate charges always in the van, as at Port Hudson, Milliken's Bend, James Island and Fort Wagner? Green colored recruits are called upon to assume the position of veterans. They have performed their part gallantly and gloriously, but by all the proofs they have given of their patriotism and bravery we protest against the meanness, ingratitude and cruelty of the Government, in whose behalf they fight, if that Government remains longer a silent witness of their enslavement and assassination. Having had patience and forbearance with the silence of Mr. Lincoln a few months ago, we could at least imagine some excuses for his silence as to the fate of colored troops falling by the fortunes of war into the hands of the rebels, but the time for this is past. It is now for every man who has any sense of right and decency, to say nothing of gratitude, to speak out trumpet-tongued in the ears of Mr. Lincoln and his Government and demand from him a declaration of purpose, to hold the rebels to a strict account for every black federal soldier taken as a prisoner. For every black prisoner slain in cold blood, Mr. Jefferson Davis should be made to understand that one rebel officer shall suffer death, and for every colored soldier sold into slavery, a rebel shall be held as a hostage. For our Government to do less than this, is to deserve the indignation and the execration of mankind.

VISITING THE WOUNDED:
WASHINGTON, D.C., AUGUST 1863

Walt Whitman to Lewis Kirk Brown

Walt Whitman was living in Brooklyn and working as a freelance journalist when he learned in December 1862 that his brother George had been wounded at Fredericksburg. Whitman traveled to northern Virginia, where he learned that his brother's wound was slight. After visiting army hospitals and camps around Falmouth, he accompanied a group of wounded soldiers to Washington. Whitman would remain in the capital until June 1864, visiting military hospitals while working part-time as a government clerk. One of the soldiers he befriended in the Armory Square Hospital was Lewis Kirk Brown of Elkton, Maryland. Wounded in the leg by a shell at Rappahannock Station, Virginia, on August 19, 1862, Brown lay in the open for four days before being brought to Washington. His wound did not heal, and in January 1864 his left leg would be amputated below the knee. The operation was successful, and Brown lived until 1926.

———————

Washington, August 1, 1863.
Both your letters have been received Lewy—the second one came this morning, & was welcome, as any thing from you will always be, & the sight of your face welcomer than all, my darling—I see you write in good spirits, & appear to have first rate times—Lew you must not go around too much, nor eat & drink too promiscuous, but be careful & moderate, & not let the kindness of friends carry you away, lest you break down again, dear son—I was at the hospital yesterday four or five hours, was in Ward K—Taber has been down sick, so he had to lay abed, but he is better now, & goes around as usual—Curly is the same as usual—most of the others are the same—there have been quite a good many deaths—the young man who lay in bed 2 with a very bad leg is dead—I saw Johnny Mahay in ward E,—poor fellow, he is very poorly, he is very thin, & his face is like wax—Lew I must tell you what a curious thing happened in the Chaplain's house night before last—there has been a man in Ward I, named Lane, with two fingers amputated,

very bad with gangrene, so they removed him to a tent by himself—last Thursday his wife came to see him. She seemed a nice woman but very poor. She stopt at the Chaplain's—about 3 o'clock in the morning she got up & went to the sink, & there she gave birth to a child, which fell down the sink into the sewer runs beneath, fortunately the water was not turned on—the Chaplain got up, carried Mrs. Lane out, & then roused up a lot of men from the hospital, with spades &c. dug a trench outside, & got into the sink, & took out the poor little child, it lay there on its back, in about two inches of water—well, strange as it may seem, the child was alive, (it fell about five feet through the sink)—& is now living & likely to live, is quite bright, has a head of thick black hair—the Chaplain took me in yesterday, showed me the child, & Mrs. Jackson, his wife, told me the whole story, with a good deal I haven't told you—& then she treated me to a good plate of ice cream—so I staid there nearly an hour & had quite a pleasant visit. Mrs. Lane lay in an adjoining room. Lew, as to me & my affairs there is nothing very new or important—I have not succeeded in getting any employment here yet, except that I write a little, (newspaper correspondence &c) barely enough to pay my expenses—but it is my fault, for I have not tried hard enough for anything—the last three weeks I have not felt very well—for two or three days I was down sick, for the first time in my life, (as I have never before been sick)—I feel pretty fair to-day—I go round most every day, the same as usual—I have some idea of giving myself a furlough of three or four weeks, & going home to Brooklyn, N Y but I should return again to Washington, probably. Lew, it is pretty hot weather here, & the sun affects me—(I had a sort of sun stroke about five years ago.)—You speak of being here in Washington again about the last of August—O Lewy how glad I should be to see you, to have you with me—I have thought if it could be so that you & one other person & myself could be where we could work & live together, & have each other's society, we three, I should like it so much—but it is probably a dream—Well, Lew they had the great battle of Gettysburgh, but it does not seem to have settled anything, except to have killed & wounded a great many thousand men—It seems as though the two armies were falling back again to near their old positions on the Rappahannock—it is hard to tell what will be the next move—Yet Lewy I think we shall conquer yet—I don't believe it is destined that this glorious Union is to be broken up by all the Sesech South, or Copheads north either—Well my darling I have scribbled you off something to show you where I am & that I have rec'd your welcome letters—but my letter is not of much interest, for I don't feel very bright to-day—Dear son you must write me whenever you can—take opportunity—when you have nothing to do, & write me a good long letter—Your letters & your love for me are very precious to me, for I appreciate it all Lew, & give you the like in return. It is now about 3 o'clock & I will go out & mail this letter, & then go & get my dinner—So good bye Lewy—good bye my dear son & comrade & I hope it will prove God's will that you get well & sound yet, & have many good years yet—.

WALT

Address my letters care Major Hapgood paymaster U S A at cor. 15th & F st Washington D C

Washington
August 11 1863

Dear Lewy,

I thought I would write you a few lines to day—I suppose you rec'd a letter from me eight or nine days ago—I hope this will find you in good health & spirits—I wrote to you not to go about too much, & eat & drink too freely, & I must repeat the caution—a fellow can keep himself in good condition by a little care & prudence—

Well Lewy the presentation to Dr. Bliss came off last Saturday evening—it was in Ward F—the beds were all cleared out, the sick put in other wards—the room cleaned, hung with greens &c. looked very nice—the instruments were there on exhibition the afternoon. I took a view of them, they were in four cases, & looked very fine—in the evening they were presented —speeches were made by one & another—there was a band of music &c—I stopt about 20 minutes, but got tired, and went off among the boys that were confined to their beds—the room was crowded, and everything passed off right I heard—

Lewy, we had the hottest weather here I ever experienced— it has been now about ten days, & no let up yet—Yesterday & last night was the hottest, no rain for sometime & the air prickly & burning—Still I am enjoying very good health, thank God,—better this last week than I have had for two or three months—I have some thought of going on to New York for a short time, as I have not been home now in eight months, but if I do, I shall pretty surely return here before long—Lewy the draft has been put through here in Washington the past week—they drafted lots of Seccessionists & quite a good many darks—(I wonder if it wouldn't be a good plan to draft all of both them kinds)—I don't hear any particular war news,—the Army of the Potomac is down around Warrenton—there are conscripts arriving there to fill up the regts. more or less every day—it will be a great & sudden change of life to many, especially such weather as this.—I believe I told you in my last letter about the strange way the baby was born in the Chaplain's —Well the baby is alive and growing like a pig, & the father Mr. Lane is getting well, Mrs. Lane ditto—Dr. Bliss is just going off on a furlough—the Chaplain & wife have left on a furlough—Taber & the rest in Ward K are all right—there have been quite a good many deaths in hospital the past week or so, the heat is bad for the poor wounded men—Well Lewy I must now wind up—I send you my love my darling son & comrade, & request you to write me soon as convenient, how you are getting along & all about things—I will write again before very long, till then good bye & God bless you dear son.

WALT WHITMAN

Address care Major Hapgood paymaster U S A cor 15th St & F st Washington D C

Washington
August 15 1863

Lewy, your letter of August 10 came safe, & was glad to hear all about you, & the way you are spending the time—Lew you must be having first rate times out there,—Well you need something to make up what you have suffered—You speak of being used well out there—Lewy I feel as if I could love any one that uses you well, & does you a kindness—but what kind of heart must that man have that would treat otherwise, or say anything insulting to a crippled young soldier, hurt in fighting for this union & flag? (well—I should say damned little man or heart in the business)—Should you meet any such you must not mind them, dear comrade, & not allow your feelings to be hurt by such loafers—(I agree with you that a rebel in the Southern army is much more respectable than a Northern Copperhead.) Dear son, when I read about your agreeable visit of a week, & how much you enjoyed yourself, I felt as much gratified as though I had enjoyed it myself—& I was truly thankful to hear that your leg is still doing well, & on the gain—you must not mind its being slowly, dear son, if it only goes forward instead of backward, & you must try to be very careful of your eating and drinking &c. not indulge in any excesses & not eat too much flummery, but generally plain food, for that is always best, & it helps along so much.—Lewy I believe I wrote you an acc't of the presentation to Dr. Bliss—he is now off North for three weeks—Dr. Butler, (ward D) is in charge—some of the doctors & wardmasters have been drafted —poor Johnny Mahay is not in very good spirits—he was to have an operation performed before Bliss went, but he went off and did not do it—Johnny is pretty low some days—Things in Ward K are pretty much the same—they had some improvements in the Hospital, new sinks, much better, & the grounds in front & between the wards nicely laid out in flowers & grass plots &c.—but Lew it has been awful hot in the wards the past two weeks, the roofs burnt like fire—There is no particular war news,—they are having batches of conscripts now every day in the Army—Meade is down on the Upper Rappahannock & fords & around Warrenton—Lee stretches down toward Gordonsville, they say his headquarters is there—folks are all looking toward Charleston,—if we could only succeed there, I don't know what Secesh would do—the ground seems to be slipping more & more from under their feet—Lew, the *Union* & the *American Flag* must conquer, it is destiny—it may be long, or it may be short, but that will be the result—but O what precious lives have been lost by tens of thousands in the struggle already—Lew you speak in your letter how you would like to see me—well my darling I wonder if there is not somebody who would be gratified to see you, & always will be wherever he is—Dear comrade, I was highly pleased at your telling me in your letter about your folks' place, the house & land & all the items—you say I must excuse you for writing so much foolishness,—nothing of the kind—my darling boy when you write to me, you must write without ceremony. I like to hear every little thing about yourself & your affairs,—you need never care how you write to me Lewy, if you will only—I never think about literary perfection in letters either, it is the *man* & the *feeling*—Lew, I am feeling pretty well but the sun affects me a little, aching & fulness on the head—a good many have been sun-struck here the last two weeks—I keep shady through the middle of the day lately—Well my dear boy I have scribbled away any thing for I wanted to write you to-day & now I must switch off—good by my darling comrade, for the present, & I pray God to bless you now & always. Write when you feel like it, Lewy. Don't hurry.

WALT.

Address still care Major Hapgood, paymaster U S A at cor 15th & F st Washington D C

DEMANDING EQUAL PAY:
SOUTH CAROLINA, AUGUST 1863

George E. Stephens to the Weekly Anglo-African

Although enlistees in the 54th Massachusetts had been promised equal pay with white soldiers, in June 1863 the War Department decided otherwise. It ruled that black soldiers would receive the pay authorized by the Militia Act of July 17, 1862, which had envisioned that blacks would serve mainly as military laborers. Privates and noncommissioned officers would both be paid $10 a month minus a $3 clothing allowance, at a time when white privates received $13 a month plus $3.50 for clothing. Among the soldiers who protested against this discrimination was Sergeant George E. Stephens, a Philadelphia native who had fought at Fort Wagner. Stephens wrote about the 54th Massachusetts in one of his regular letters to the *Weekly Anglo-African*, an influential black newspaper in New York. The regiment would remain on Morris Island until January 1864, when it was sent to Florida.

In Camp,
Morris Island, S.C.,
Aug. 7, 1863.

Mr. Editor: Since I wrote my last letter the startling news of the mobs, riots, incendiarism, pillage and slaughter, recently so rife in the North, particularly in New York City, has reached here. You may judge what our thoughts and feelings were as we read bulletin after bulletin depicting to the life the scenes of violence and bloodshed which rivaled and even surpassed in their horrors, those which were perpetrated in Paris, during the bloody French Revolution, for we are yet to find an instance there where the orphan was ruthlessly assailed, or women and children murdered and maltreated without cause or provocation, simply for belonging to another race or class of people.

What cause or provocation have the New York rabble for disloyalty to their country, and for their bloody, atrocious assaults on my countrymen? Are we their enemies? Have we tyrannized over them? Have we maltreated them? Have we robbed them? Are we alien enemies? And are we traitors? Has not the unrequited labor of nearly four million of our brethren added to the country's wealth? Have we not been loyal to the country, in season and out of season, through good report and evil? And even while your mob-fiends upheld the assassin knife, and brandished the incendiary torch over the heads of our wives and children and to burn their homes, we were doing our utmost to sustain the honor of our country's flag, to perpetuate, if possible, those civil, social, and political liberties, they, who so malignantly hate us, have so fully enjoyed. Oh! how causeless, senseless, outrageous, brutal, and violative of every sentiment of manhood, courage and humanity these attacks on our defenseless brethren have been!

Fearful as these mobs have been, I trust they may prove to be lessons, though fearful ones, to guide the popular and loyal masses in the country, in all times of national emergency and peril, for when the services of every citizen or denizen of the country are imperatively required to defend it against powerful and determined foes, either foreign or domestic, and there can be found a strong minority ready and willing to subvert the government by popular violence and tumult or a base submission unworthy the meanest varlet of some monarchy; much less the boasted citizens of this great and magnificent country, it will bring still more forcibly to their minds the truism that "eternal vigilance is the price of liberty."

These mobs are the stepping-stones upon which base traitors and demagogues hope to mount into arbitrary power, and to overawe and subvert liberty and law. They seek anarchy; and despotism, they think, must succeed. First anarchy, then despotism. They make the negro the catspaw or victim; but the loyalist and the friend of law and order cannot fail to see that every blow directed against the negro is directed against them. Our relation to the government is and has been that of unflinching, unswerving loyalty. Even when the government, by its every precept and practice, conserved the interests of slavery, and slaves were hunted down by United States soldiers and surrendered to traitorous slave-masters, the conduct of the negro was marked with distinguished loyalty. The instances are too numerous to cite of their braving the most fearful dangers to convey valuable information to the Union armies, and for this, the half yet untold, such has been our reward. Does not Milliken's Bend and Port Hudson furnish a chapter of valor and faithful loyalty? Is there no justice in America—or are we doomed to general massacre, as Mr. Blair said we would be, in the event of the issue of the President's Emancipation proclamation? If this be our doom let us prepare for the worst.

The siege of Charleston has not yet commenced. The preparations of Gen. Gillmore are very ample. There is no doubt that this citadel of treason will fall. Every one is impatient at the delay; but the siege of a stronghold upon which all of the engineering skill of the rebel Confederacy has been lavished, cannot be planned and matured in a day. They harass our fatigue parties considerably with their shells, but they only succeed in killing and wounding one or two men a day. These shells are very disagreeable at first, but after one is under them a while he can learn to become accustomed to them. The men sing, dance, and play cards and sleep as carelessly within range of them as if they were no more harmful than so many soap bubbles.

This Morris Island is the most desolate heap of sand-hills I ever saw. It is so barren that you cannot find so much as a gypsum weed growing. Our situation is almost unbearable. During the day the sun is intensely hot, and this makes the sand hot; so we are sandwiched between the hot sun and the hot sand. Happily, the evenings are cool and bracing—so much so, that woolen blankets are not uncomfortable. The bathing is most delightful. I think Morris Island beach the most magnificent on the whole Atlantic coast. Had we in the North such a bathing shore, it would soon eclipse Newport, Atlantic City or Long Branch, and the other bathing resorts. The beach at some points is at least one-third of a mile in width, descending at an almost imperceptible angle into the more refreshing breakers.

There is quite a stir in the camp of the 54th just at this moment, created by an attempt on the part of the Paymaster and Col. Littlefield of the 4th Connecticut volunteers (who has been temporarily assigned to the command of our regiment since the death of Col. Shaw, our lamented commander) to pay us off with the paltry sum of $10 per month, the amount paid to contrabands. Col. Littlefield had the men drawn up in their company streets, and addressed them in a style something like this: "Gentlemen, I know that you are in want of money. Many of you have families who are dependent on you for support. The Paymaster refuses to pay any of the colored troops more than $10 per month. I have no doubt that Congress, when it meets next December, will pay you the balance of your pay. The government, in paying you this sum, only advances you this amount—it is not considered paying you off." Only one company consented to take this sum. The rest of the regiment are highly incensed at the idea that after they have been enlisted as Massachusetts soldiers, and been put into the active service of the United States government, they should be paid off as the drafted ex-slaves are. The non-commissioned officers are to be paid the same as the privates.

There is to be, according to the Colonel's and Paymaster's arrangement, no distinction. Our First Sergeants, Sergeant-Major, and other Sergeants are to be paid only $10 per month. Now, if this $10 per month is advanced by the Paymaster, and he is so confident or certain that the next Congress will vote us the pay that regularly enlisted soldiers, like the 54th, generally receive, why does he not advance the privates and non-commissioned officers their full pay? Or does he not fear that the next Congress may refuse to have anything to do with it, and conclude that if we could receive $10 and make out until then, we could make out with that amount to the end of our term? To offer our non-commissioned officers the same pay and reducing them to the level of privates, is, to say the least, insulting and degrading to them.

Then, again, if we are not placed on the same footing with other Massachusetts soldiers, we have been enlisted under false pretenses. Our enlistment itself is fraudulent. When Gov. Andrew addressed us at Readville on the presentation of our colors, he claimed us as Massachusetts soldiers. Frederick Douglass, in his address to the colored people to recruit the 54th, and who penned it by the authority of Gov. Andrew, declares that we form part of the quota of troops furnished by the State of Massachusetts. If this be the case, why make this invidious distinction? We perform the same duties of other

Massachusetts troops, and even now we have to perform fatigue duty night and day, and stand in line of battle from 3 to 5 A.M. with white soldiers, and for all this, not to say anything of the many perils we necessarily encounter, we are offered $10 per month or nothing until next December or January! Why, in the name of William H. Seward, are we treated thus? Does the refusal to pay us our due pander to the pro-slavery Cerberus? Negroes in the navy receive the same pay that the Irish, English, German, Spanish or Yankee race do, and take it as a matter of course. Why, sir, the State of Massachusetts has been rebuked and insulted through her colored soldiers, and she should protect us, as Gov. Andrew has pledged his word she would. Since our regiment has been in this department, an attempt has been made to substitute the dark for the light-blue pantaloons of the U. S. army. This was at St. Helena. Col. Shaw rejected them, and we continue to wear the uniform of the U.S. Infantry corps.

The ever-memorable anniversary of British West India Emancipation was observed by the non-commissioned officers of the 54th, by calling, on the 1st instant, a meeting, and passing a series of resolutions. This meeting was organized by the appointment of Sergeant-Major Douglass, Chairman, and Sergt. Fletcher, Co. A, Secretary. A long list of Vice-Presidents were appointed, representing nearly every State. Commissary-Sergeant Lee represented South Carolina; Sergt. Grey, Massachusetts; Sergt. Swails, Pennsylvania. A Committee, consisting of Sergts. Francis, Stephens, Barquet, Johnson and Gambier, presented the following resolutions, which were passed:

1. Resolved, That we look with joy upon the example set by Great Britain twenty-nine years ago in liberating the slaves in her West India Islands, thereby making a long stride in the pathway of civilization, and eliciting the gratitude of enthralled millions everywhere—contributing largely to influence the people of this country to seek the overthrow of that system which has brought the nation to the verge of dissolution. We hail with more than gratification the determination of our government to follow her great and good example as evinced by that glorious instrument of January 1st, 1863, proclaiming freedom to slaves of rebels in Southern States—the desire to purchase those in loyal States—the decision of Attorney-General Bates, and the

calling to its aid the strong arms and loyal hearts of its black citizens.

2. Resolved, That we have another day added to our small family of holidays; we hail the 1st of January as twin-sister to the 1st of August; and as we have met together within six miles of the birthplace of secession to commemorate this day, we trust that on the 1st day of January next, by the blessing of God on our arms, the city of Charleston will ring with the voices of free men, women and children shouting, "Truly, the day of Jubilee has come."

3. Resolved, That while we look forward with sanguine hope for that day, and have the arms in our hands to help bring it about, we will use them, and put forth all our energies, and never cease until our ears shall hear the jubilant bell that rings the knell of slavery.

4. Resolved, That in our humble opinion the force of circumstances has compelled the loyal portion of this nation to acknowledge that man is physically the same, differing only in the circumstances under which he lives, and that action—true, manly action, only—is necessary to secure to us a full recognition of our rights as men by the controlling masses of this nation; and we see in the army, fighting for liberty and Union, the proper field for colored men, where they may win by their valor the esteem of all loyal men and women—believing that "Who would be free, themselves must strike the blow."

5. Resolved, That we recognize in the brilliant successes of the Union armies the proofs that Providence is on our side; that His attributes cannot take sides with the oppressor.

Private John Peer, Co. B, died at 6 o'clock P.M. this instant.

G. E. S.

AN OFFER TO RESIGN:
VIRGINIA, AUGUST 1863

Robert E. Lee to Jefferson Davis

As the controversy over the Pennsylvania campaign continued in the southern press, several Richmond newspapers defended Lee, while the *Charleston Mercury* declared that it "is impossible for an invasion to have been more foolish and disastrous." A widely reprinted dispatch by Peter W. Alexander, a war correspondent for the *Savannah Republican*, questioned Lee's decision to continue attacking at Gettysburg after the first day of the battle. Lee wrote to the Confederate president from his headquarters near Orange Court House, about thirty miles west of Fredericksburg.

                                                  Camp Orange
                                                  8 Aug 1863

MR PRESIDENT

Your letters of 28 July & 2 Aug have been recd., & I have waited for a leisure hour to reply, but I fear that will never come. I am extremely obliged to you for the attention given to the wants of this Army & the efforts made to supply them. Our absentees are returning, & I hope the earnest & beautiful appeal made to the country in your proclamation, may stir up the virtue of the whole people & that they may see their duty & perform it. Nothing is wanted but that their fortitude should equal their bravery to ensure the success of our cause. We must expect reverses, even defeats. They are sent to teach us wisdom & prudence, to call forth greater energies & to prevent our falling into greater disasters. Our people have only to be true & united, to bear manfully the misfortunes incident to war & all will come right in the end. I know how prone we are to censure, & how ready to blame others for the nonfulfilment of our expectations. This is unbecoming in a generous people & I grieve to see its expression. The general remedy for the want of success in a military commander is his removal. This is natural & in many instances proper. For no matter what may be the ability of the officer if he loses the confidence of his troops, disaster must sooner or later ensue. I have been prompted by these reflections more than once since my return from Penna. to propose to your Excy the propriety of selecting another commander for this army. I have seen & heard of expression of discontent in the public journals at the result of the expedition. I do not know how far this feeling extends in the army. My brother officers have been too kind to report it, & so far the troops have been too generous to exhibit it. It is fair however to suppose that it does exist, & success is so necessary to us that nothing should be risked to secure it. I therefore in all sincerity request your Excy to take measures to supply my place. I do this with the more earnestness because no one is more aware than myself of my inability for the duties of my position. I cannot even accomplish what I myself desire. How can I fulfil the expectations of others? In addition, I sensibly feel the growing failure of my bodily strength. I have not yet recovered from the attack I experienced the past spring. I am becoming more & more incapable of exertion, & am thus prevented from making the personal examinations & giving the personal supervision to the operations in the field which I feel to be necessary. I am so dull that in making use of the eyes of others I am frequently misled. Every thing therefore points to the advantages to be derived from a new commander, & I the more anxiously urge the matter upon your Excy from my belief that a younger & abler man than myself can readily be attained. I know that he will have as gallant & brave an army as ever existed to second his efforts, & it would be the happiest day of my life to see at its head a worthy leader; one that would accomplish more than I could perform & all that I have wished. I hope your Excy will attribute my request to the true reason. The desire to serve my country & to do all in my power to ensure the success of her righteous cause. I have no complaints to make of any one but myself. I have recd. nothing but kindness from those above me & the most considerate attention from my comrades & companions in arms. To your Excy I am specially indebted for uniform kindness & consideration. You have done every thing in your power to aid me in the work committed to my charge, without omitting anything to promote the general welfare. I pray that your efforts may at length be crowned with success & that you may long live to enjoy the thanks of a grateful people— With sentiments of great esteem I am very respectfully & truly yours

R E Lee
Genl

REFUSING A RESIGNATION:
VIRGINIA, AUGUST 1863

Jefferson Davis to Robert E. Lee

Lee would reply to this letter on August 22 by asking Davis to accept his resignation "whenever in your opinion the public service will be advanced" by a change in command. In conclusion, he wrote: "Beyond such assistance as I can give to an invalid wife and three houseless daughters I have no object in life but to devote myself to the defense of our violated country's rights."

Richmond, Va., Augt. 11, 1863.
Yours of the 8th. inst. has been received. I am glad to find that you concur so entirely with me as to the want of our country in this trying hour, and am happy to add that after the first depression consequent upon our disasters in the West, indications have appeared that our people will exhibit that fortitude which we agree in believing is alone needful to secure ultimate success.

It well became Sydney Johnston when overwhelmed by a senseless clamor to admit the rule that success is the test of merit, and yet there has been nothing which I have found to require a greater effort of patience than to bear the criticisms of the ignorant, who pronounce everything a failure which does not equal their expectations or desires, and can see no good result which is not in the line of their own imaginings. I admit the propriety of your conclusions, that an officer who loses the confidence of his troops should have his position changed, whatever may be his ability; but when I read the sentence, I was not at all prepared for the application you were about to make. Expressions of discontent in the public journals furnish but little evidence of the sentiment of an army. I wish it were otherwise even tho' all the abuse of myself should be accepted as the results of honest observation. I say, I wish I could feel that the public journals were not generally partisan nor venal.

Were you capable of stooping to it, you could easily surround yourself with those who would fill the press with your laudations, and seek to exalt you for what you had not done rather than detract from the achievements which will make you and your army the subject of history and object of the worlds admiration for generations to come.

I am truly sorry to know that you still feel the effects of the illness you suffered last Spring, and can readily understand, the embarrassments you experience in using the eyes of others, having been so much accustomed to make your own reconnaissances. Practice will however do much to relieve that embarrassment, and the minute knowledge of the country which you have acquired will render you less dependent for topographical information.

But suppose, my dear friend, that I were to admit, with all their implications, the points which you present, where am I to find that new commander who is to possess the greater ability which you believe to be required. I do not doubt the readiness with which you would give way to one who could accomplish all that you have wished, and you will do me the justice to believe that if Providence would kindly offer such a person for our use, I would not hesitate to avail of his services.

My sight is not sufficiently penetrating to discover such hidden merit if it exists, and I have but used to you the language of sober earnestness, when I have impressed upon you the propriety of avoiding all unnecessary exposure to danger because I felt our country could not bear to lose you. To ask me to substitute you by some one in my judgment more fit to command, or who would possess more of the confidence of the army, or of the reflecting men in the country is to demand an impossibility.

It only remains for me to hope that you will take all possible care of yourself, that your health and strength may be entirely restored, and that the Lord will preserve you for the important duties devolved upon you in the struggle of our suffering country, for the independence which we have engaged in war to maintain. As ever very respectfully & truly yrs.

JEFFN. DAVIS

PILLAGING WOOD: VIRGINIA, AUGUST 1863

Wilbur Fisk to
The Green Mountain Freeman

Private Fisk of the 2nd Vermont Infantry had fought with the Sixth Corps at Marye's Heights and Salem Church during the Chancellorsville campaign and been posted to a reserve position at Gettysburg. He wrote from northern Virginia about the routines of camp life and their impact on the civilians living nearby.

Camp near Warrenton, Va.
Aug. 10, 1863

This camp is, I believe, without an official name at present. We are within about five miles of Warrenton, and about two from what was once the village of Waterloo. Warrenton is on your left, and Waterloo on your right as we face the enemy. You will perceive since writing my last we have moved our camp once more. This remarkable event occurred last Wednesday. I cannot say whether it was a military necessity, or a military convenience, or some other motive that prompted the change, but so far as my humble opinion can judge, I think the move a wise and judicious one. We went almost directly back to where we were encamped at first, only swinging in a half a mile or so nearer the Rappahannock. This may not be quite so good a camping place as that, but it is better than the last one, and makes a very acceptable compromise between the two. So, having become somewhat domesticated in our new position, I see no better way of employing one of the fairest mornings here that Virginia ever saw than by writing a line or so to my always welcome visitor, the *Freeman*. To be sure, nothing has transpired worth noticing, and there is nothing to write about; but incessant talkers and scribblers can generally manage to make themselves sufficiently troublesome without the aid of these superfluous auxiliaries.

Living in camp is a peculiar kind of life, but like every other situation one may become so accustomed to it that the evil and the good bear a relation to each other very nearly approaching to what may be found in almost any other pursuit. It may often seem dull and irksome, imposing burdensome restraints and duties not at all agreeable, but only the croaker will say the days are all dark and cheerless. We certainly have had hardships and privations to endure, and sometimes pretty severe ones, too; but we have also, now and then, a time for sport, joyous, health-inspiring, and full of fun. We have our games of chess, backgammon, draughts, cards, and others, to make merry many a dull, listless hour. We get occasionally a book to read, sometimes a paper, or what is often better than either, a letter from home. These last are the chinks that fill up many a useless, if not burdensome, hour, presenting to the soldier's mind something tangible that his thoughts will love to dwell upon. Many hours are pleasantly spent in answering these letters, many in visiting our friends in other portions of the camp, many more in fishing and foraging; and thus the day often closes before we are aware or wish to have it.

Since we formed our new camp we have been employed principally in making our tents comfortable and convenient. I would like to introduce the reader in to our camp this morning that he might see what pleasant houses we can improvise at short notice and very little expense. If you can imagine a pole or rail, whichever happens to be the handiest, elevated a little higher than one's head and held horizontally by two crotches, or by being strapped to two other rails that are perpendicular, which are inserted in the ground, one at each end, you have an idea of the first starting point in putting up a tent. The principal difficulty in all this is to get an ax or hatchet to cut a pole or sharpen the stake that is to be driven into the ground; but sometimes a big jack-knife will answer the purpose. The next thing is to throw our tent, which is nothing more nor less than two pieces of cotton or linen cloth, about five feet square buttoned together, over this ridge-pole and fasten the lower edge, or eaves, to small stakes as near the ground as we have calculated to have the tent come. The boys generally prefer from two to three feet. Here then is a tent for two men. Others can join on to the ends indefinitely, thus making a continual line of tents and have it all one. Along the centre of this we can build our bunks, running lengthwise, if we have tents sufficient, at a convenient height from the ground, making us a good seat or lounge in the day-time, and a bed for the night, or we can build them crosswise, if we prefer, and thus economize the room. Being open all around, the tent has the freest circulation of air, and we escape the unhealthy damp of living on the ground. Some of the boys fix themselves up stands for writing-desks, and cupboards for their cups, plates, and fragments of rations. Many other conveniences are constructed as necessity demands, or ingenuity invents. Generally we provide ourselves with all the proudest aristocrat needs to ask for, while the whole establishment would be costly at five dollars.

But in order to tell the whole story, which seeing I have begun I might as well continue, it will be necessary to speak of the manner in which the boys often procure the boards to build and ornament their singular habitations. The rapid disappearance however of barns and sometimes houses in the vicinity of where a new camp is being formed disclosed the secret. In our last camp the boys had begun to render their location quite pleasant and tasteful, supposing that the promise to stay there was made in good faith, and were quite loth to leave in consequence. Boards were plenty there as the Village had been vacated but not entirely destroyed. Every building there, of whatever description that was not occupied was speedily sacrificed to the boys' greediness for comfortable tents. They had been polluted with the heresy of secession, and the boys could not be made to feel any compunction for their downfall. As soon as a building was struck it was doomed. The first blow became a signal for a general attack, and soon all that was left would be a few scattering timbers and fragments of boards, while the road to camp would be lined with soldiers sweating under their loads of plunder.

There was one old miller left in the village of Waterloo, and I believe he is the last of his race in that spot. The village was burnt last summer or destroyed when we came, except one negro shanty. It used to contain two stores, a woollen factory besides the grist mill and blacksmith shop. Waterloo is on the Hedgeman river or Rappahannock proper, which stream is the southern boundary of Fauquier County of which Warrenton is the capitol. It is about sixty miles from Washington in a direction a little south of west. It is represented as having been a very thrifty place but like many of her sister towns it has become totally crushed out by this desolating war.

The camp of the 2nd regiment since moving from Waterloo, is on a small ridge crowned with a grove of bushes which unfortunately was not so extensive but that both ends of the regiment extended out into open sunlight. The 3rd, 4th and 6th are camped near by; the 5th are guarding Thompson's Ford. We have found lumber much more difficult to obtain here than at Waterloo. "But where there is a will there is a way" and where there is plenty of boards only two miles distant, who would be willing to lie in the dirt and go without them? Certainly not Vermonters, if we may judge from the throng that has been continually streaming back to that place over the hills and brooks and coming again with a load such as no lazy man would ever put on his shoulders. The officers had teams to bring their boards, but the men being more independent brought theirs on their backs. By dint of much perseverance and industry we have again established ourselves in camp pretty much to our satisfaction. Next week I may be able to chronicle another move.

Perhaps some one will question the constitutionality of our confiscating secesh boards and buildings in the manner I have described. I can only say it is a way we have of managing affairs here, and our officers had much rather help than hinder us. This morbid tenderness towards secesh property has been stifled by the rebels themselves, in their uncivilized conduct toward Union people when the power has been with them. Still I must confess it looks a little barbarous to go into a man's door yard, almost, as we did the miller's at Waterloo and tear down his barn and shed under his very eyes. This "erring brother" could only look demurely on and witness the progress of the destruction; he was powerless to prevent it. But they not only tore down his buildings they carried away his garden fence and ransacked and spoiled his garden. Excuse me reader, but I too went into that garden to help harvest the immature crop, and should have carried out my intentions, perhaps, but when I saw the woman and one of her children looking in sorrowful submission from the window at the wasteful destruction going on in their own garden—and it was a pretty one—my courage failed me, and I withdrew without taking so much as a pod of peas or a handful of potatoes. I never was caught stealing sheep or any thing of that sort, but I fancied I then had a very realizing sense of such a culprit's self-importance. It is impossible I suppose in war time but that such offences will come, and doubtless, in most cases they are well enough deserved, but when they are to happen to women and children that appear innocent in this case, I thought it would be as safe for me in the end to shirk the responsibility, and let them come through some one else; and certainly it was as consistent with my inclination on this particular occasion. Generally I am not behind when secession sinners are being punished after this fashion.

MEETING THE PRESIDENT:
WASHINGTON, D.C., AUGUST 1863

Frederick Douglass to George L. Stearns

On August 10 Douglass visited the capital, where, with the help of Senator Samuel C. Pomeroy, a Radical Republican from Kansas, he was able to meet with Secretary Stanton and President Lincoln. In his conversation with Stanton, Douglass agreed to help recruit black troops in Mississippi with the understanding that he would be commissioned as an officer. When the War Department failed to send the commission, Douglass would refuse to go south as a civilian.

Head Quars 1210 Chestnut St
Phila Aug 12th 1863

Maj Geo. L Stearns.
A.A.G. USV &c
Dear Sir.

According to your request I paid a flying visit to Washington. I spent the entire day (Monday) in calling upon the Heads of Depts there and other influential persons. I had the good fortune, early in the morning after reaching there, of meeting with Senator Pomeroy who at once offered to accompany me and facilitate my mission. First I called on Secty Stanton at the War Department who kindly granted me an interview of about thirty minutes which must be considered a special privilege in view of the many pressing demands upon his time and attention. His manner was cold and business like throughout but earnest.

I at once gave him in brief my theory of the elements of negro character which should be had in view in all measures for raising colored troops. I told him that the negro was the victim of two extreme opinions. One claimed for him too much and the other too little. That it was a mistake to regard him either as an angel or a demon. He is simply a man and should be dealt with purely as such. That a certain percentage of negroes were brave and others cowardly. That a part were ambitious and aspiring and another part quite otherwise and that the theory in practice of the Government in raising colored troops should conform to these essential facts. The Secty instantly inquired in what respect the present conditions of colored enlistments conflicted with the views I had expressed. I answered "In the unequal pay accorded to colored soldiers and in the fact that no incentive was given to the ambition of colored soldiers and that the regulations confined them to the dead level of privates or non-commissioned officers." In answer the Secty went into an interesting history of the whole subject of the employment of Colored Troops briefly mentioning some of the difficulties and prejudices to be surmounted. Gave a history of the bill drawn up by himself, giving equal pay, the same rations, the same uniforms, and equipments, to colored troops as to White, and spoke with much apparent regret that his bill, though passed in the House was defeated in the Senate on what he considered quite an insufficient reason alleging that the President already possessed necessary powers to employ colored troops.

I told Mr Stanton that I held it to be the duty of Colored men to fight for the Government even though they should be offered but subsistance and arms considering that we had a cause quite independent of pay or place. But he quickly responded, "That he was in favor of giving the same pay to black as to white soldiers and also of making merit the criterion of promotion further stating his readiness to grant commissions to any reported to him by their superior officers for their capacity or bravery." The conclusion of our conversation was, that Gen Thomas was now vigorously engaged in organizing colored troops on the Mississippi and that he (the Secty) wished me to report to Gen Thomas and cooperate with him in raising said troops. I told the Secty that I was already at work under the direction of Major Stearns and that I thought that he would still need my services. But the Secty thought I had better report as aforesaid, adding that he would send me sufficient papers immediately. Thus you see, My dear Sir, that you have sent me to Washington to some purpose. Mr Stanton was very imperative in his manner, and I did not know but that you had suggested this prompt employment of me, from the fact that you inquired as to my willingness to go South in this work. My interview with Mr Stanton was free from compliments of every kind. There was nothing from him to me, nor from me to him, but I felt myself stopped in regard to your own efficient services not so much from his manner as from what I knew to be your own wishes.

From the War Office I went directly to the White House. Saw for the first time the President of the United States. Was received cordially and saw at a glance the justice of the popular estimate of his qualities expressed in the prefix "*Honest*" to the name of Abraham Lincoln. I have never seen a more transparent countenance. There was not the slightest shadow of embarrassment after the first moment. The drift of my communication to the President, except that I thanked him for extending equal protection to Colored Prisoners of War, was much the same as that to the Secty of War. I desired only to say so much as to furnish a text for a discourse from Mr Lincoln himself. In this I was quite successful for the President instantly upon my ceasing to speak proceeded with an earnestness and fluency of which I had not suspected him, to vindicate his policy respecting the whole slavery question and especially that in reference to employing colored troops. I need not here repeat his views. One remark, however, of his was of much significance. He said he had frequently been charged with tardiness, hesitation and the like, especially in regard to issuing his retaliatory proclamation. But had he sooner issued that proclamation such was the state of public popular prejudice that an outcry would have been raised against the measure. It would be said "Ah! We thought it would come to this. White men were to be killed for negroes. His general view was that the battles in which negroes had distinguished themselves for bravery and general good conduct was the necessary preparation of the public mind for his proclamation. But the best thing said by the President was "I have been charged with vacillation even by so good a man as Jno. Sherman of Ohio, but" said he "I think the charge cannot be sustained. No man can say that having once taken the position I have contradicted it or retreated from it." This remark of the President I took as our assurance that whoever else might abandon his anti slavery policy President Lincoln would stand firm to his. My whole interview with the President was gratifying and did much to assure me that slavery would not survive the War and that the

Country would survive both Slavery and the War. I am very sorry my Dear Sir, not to see you before leaving. I should be glad to have a line from you if convenient before I leave Rochester.

With Great Respect and Regard

        Your Obt Servant
        (Signed) Fredk Douglass

DEMORALIZATION AT GALVESTON:
TEXAS, AUGUST 1863

William H. Neblett to Elizabeth Scott Neblett

Galveston, Texas, had been captured by a Union expeditionary force on October 4, 1862, then retaken by the Confederates on New Year's Day in 1863. Among the soldiers posted there was William H. Neblett, a lawyer and farmer from Grimes County who had enlisted in March 1863 as a private in the 20th Texas Infantry. Neblett wrote from Harrisburg (now part of Houston) to his wife, Elizabeth, who was managing their farm while raising five children. The mutiny he described among some of the troops of the Galveston garrison ended when their commanders promised to improve their food and grant limited furloughs.

Harrisburg Texas
Aug 18th/63
Dear Lizzie

Yours of the 11th inst was recd a few days since. It is really astonishing how much pleasure it gives me to receive a letter from home and although there is no news related still the fact that all are well is sufficient to make the heart thrill with joy. There is a member of Capt. Dickie's Co here who says he left Orange yesterday week. He says John Scott was well & the Co well pleased with their situation. Two letters came to John after he left both of which I forwarded to him at Orange. We arrived here on the 16th and will remain here until 1st of Sept unless some unexpected order moves us. There has been considerable insubordination among the troops in Galveston lately. Col Lucketts Reg recently from the Rio Grande were furnished it seems with corn meal with worms in it. They refused to drill unless flour was furnished. Debray ordered all the troops on the Island including Lucketts out to the parade ground. All supposed it was for General Inspection but when the troops arrived Lucketts men still not suspecting anything were ordered to stack their arms, which they did. Their guns were taken away and the parade dismissed to their respective quarters. Since then Cooks Reg have demanded furlough and are in a state of insubordination have or did in one instance turn the guns of one of the Forts on the city declaring that they would fire on the town and troops if any attempt was made to disarm them. Yesterday Lucketts Reg was sent from the Island and are near here now and Browns Battallion sent down. This Co received orders also to go back to Galveston yesterday but the Bayou City being out of order the order was countermanded. I fear there will be some trouble if not bloodshed before the matter is settled. Gen Magruder passed here on the way to Galveston yesterday.

There is a great deal of demoralization in the Regiments here. From what I can hear such is not the case with the troops East of the Mississippi or those who have been in active service from Texas. I notice that you are quite despondend in your last letter and am sorry to see it. For my own part I have never lost hope even for a moment and moreover I do not think it probable that Texas will be invaded within the next six months by any force formidable enough to make head against the forces in Texas and moreover I think that within the next six months France will recognize our Independence & be followed soon by England & other powers. You ask what are you to do in case the yankees get to Grimes. This is like providing for a remote contingency but still one in the limits of possibility. In such a case all the advise I can give is to harness up your horses and have the wagon & oxen to help haul what provisions &c with all the wagons. The direction you go will have to be determined by the direction the yanks come from. I do not think an attempt will be made to subjugate Texas until East of the Mis is subjugated & at least until our great armies are whiped & dispersed. I do not anticipate any such direful result as this, and although the fall of Vicksburg was a sad reverse of fortune & the capture of Morgan one of less magnitude still I do not think such things should alarm the country into inaction or submission. You ask me what should be done on the farm. I cannot well answer the question. I want the hogs taken care of, and the pork hogs kept growing so that when the mast falls they will grow fast and fatter. I also wish that piece of new ground cleared up this month if possible. I suppose you have heard something of the bagging rope twine & salt which I was to get from Houston. I want the cotton hauled to the Gin & as soon as Ginned sent to [   ] of Houston who pay the Rail Road freight on the cotton while I am to pay the freight on the Bagging Rope Twine and salt. I also wish the cotton weighed and the weights kept so that I may know how much there is. As soon as the cotton is sold buy what you wish of flour and any other things. Calico is $4.00 per yard but it is best to buy & if I am where I can get it I will buy you some. Confederate money is going down fast & I believe as soon as the war ends it will be perfectly worthless and it may be so before then. Bonds may be worth something but there will be an effort made after the war to repudiate them unless they are in the hands of foreigners and the fear of a war prevents repudiating of such as are held by them. For this reason the money you get for the cotton had best be spent in paying debts contracted since the war and for such things as you wish. Have the seed saved from the cotton sent to McCune I shall want at least half of it for planting next year. The balance can be used for feeding the oxen this Winter & next Spring. I agreed to let McCune have a few bushels to plant (say 4 or 5 bus).

I am glad to hear that Bettie is getting well of her cholic. I hear that there is prevailing east of Lake Creek putrid soar throat or Diptheria and has been quite fatal. I feel uneasy sometimes about our children on that account. Tell Mary to write me another letter when you write again. I expect you had better try and get old Keifer to come and curry your leather about the first of Sept. You can get him to do so I expect for $10. or 12.00. Get him also to blacken the calf and coon skins. I expect you had better look out for some person to make your shoes and Marys & Walters. If you could get McDonald's negro to do so at $2 or 3.00 per day it will be about as cheap as you may expect, & you may have to pay $4 or 5.00 to get shoes for yourself made fit to wear. Perhaps you had better write to Mrs Mc Donald on the subject. I am in good health.

       yours affectionately
       Wm H Neblett

P.S. The following is used by the soldiers here for flux very sucessfully. Tea spoon full of salt and Table spoon full of vinegar with a little water to be repeated after every operation.

"SUCH A SCENE OF HORROR":
KANSAS, AUGUST 1863

Richard Cordley:
Narrative of the Lawrence Massacre

Born in Ohio in 1837, William C. Quantrill taught school in Illinois and worked a farm in eastern Kansas before turning to rustling and slave-catching shortly before the war. In 1862 he became the leader of a guerrilla band based in Jackson County, Missouri. Commissioned by the Confederacy as a captain of partisan rangers, Quantrill engaged in an increasingly bitter conflict with the Union army and "Jayhawker" raiders from Kansas. On August 21, 1863, he led more than 400 men (among them the future bank robbers Cole Younger and Frank James) across the border in an attack on Lawrence. After killing more than 180 men and teenage boys, the raiders eluded pursuing Union cavalry and escaped into the wooded hills of western Missouri. Richard Cordley was the minister of the Plymouth Congregational Church in Lawrence and editor of *The Congregational Record*. Despite the destruction of his office during the raid, Cordley was able to write a narrative of the massacre for the September–October 1863 number of his church publication.

THE LAWRENCE MASSACRE.

The destruction of Lawrence had no doubt been long contemplated by the rebels of the border. Ever since the war commenced, rumors have been constantly reaching us of the maturing of such a purpose. Each rumor called forth efforts for defense. The people had become so accustomed to alarms as to be almost unaffected by them. At several times the prospect had been absolutely threatening. This was especially the case after the battle of Springfield, and again after the capture of Lexington by the rebels. The people had never felt more secure than for a few months preceding the raid of last August. The power of the rebellion was broken in Missouri, and the Federal force on the Border, while it could not prevent depredations by small gangs, seemed to be sufficiently vigilant to prevent the gathering of any large force. No rumors of danger had been received for several months.

Still many of the citizens did not feel that the place was entirely safe. Mayor Collamore, early in the summer, prevailed upon the military authorities to station a squad of soldiers in Lawrence. These soldiers were under command of Lieut. Hadley, a very efficient officer. Lieut. Hadley had a brother on Gen. Ewing's staff. About the first of August this brother wrote him that his spies had been in Quantrell's camp—had mingled freely with his men—and had learned from Quantrell's clerk, that they purposed to make a raid on Lawrence about the full of the moon, which would be three weeks before the actual raid. He told his brother to do all he could for the defense of the town, to fight them to the last, and never be taken prisoner, for Quantrell killed all his prisoners. Lieut. Hadley showed this letter to Mayor Collamore, who at once set about the work of putting the town in a state of defense. The militia was called out, pickets detailed, the cannon got in readiness, and the country warned. Had Quantrell's gang come according to promise, they would have been "welcomed with bloody hands to hospitable graves." Some one asked Quantrell, when in Lawrence, why he did not come before when he said he would. He replied, "You were expecting me then—but I have caught you napping, now."

It may be asked, why the people of Lawrence relaxed their vigilance so soon after receiving such authentic evidence of Quantrell's intentions? The city and military authorities made the fatal mistake of keeping the *grounds of their apprehensions a profound secret*. Nobody knew the reason of the preparation. Rumors were afloat, but they could not be traced to any reliable source. Companies came in from the country, but could not ascertain why they were sent for, and went home to be laughed at by their neighbors. Unable to find any reliable ground of alarm, people soon began to think that the rumors were like the other false alarms by which they had been periodically disturbed for the last two years. The course of the military authorities tended to strengthen this view.

Mayor Collamore sent to Fort Leavenworth for cannon and troops. They were at once sent over, but were met at Lawrence by a dispatch from Headquarters at Kansas City, ordering them back. A few days after, the squad of soldiers under Lieut. Hadley were ordered away. It was evident, therefore, that the military authorities at Kansas City, who ought to know, did not consider the place in danger. The usual sense of security soon returned. Citizens were assured that Quantrell could not penetrate the military line on the border without detection. They felt sure, too, that he could not travel fifty miles through a loyal country without their being informed of the approach of danger. The people never felt more secure, and never were less prepared, than the night before the raid.

REBEL SPIES.

There is no doubt Quantrell had spies in Lawrence for weeks before the raid, who kept him constantly informed of the condition of things. The sense of security felt by the people was so great, that everybody was permitted to go and come as he pleased. The familiarity of the rebels with the place and the people, abundantly proved this. Several of them, in all probability, came up the night before. One, asking where Jim. Lane was, was told that he was out of town. "No, he is not," replied the rebel, "did n't I see him at the railroad meeting last night?" Some ladies and gentlemen returning late the night before, saw horsemen stationed at the outskirts of the town. Supposing them to be citizen pickets they took no notice of the fact. So the town was guarded that night by rebel pickets. The design was doubtless to notice if any messenger came in to warn of danger, and to be sure that no alarm was given. They showed that they were familiar with the common expressions of the town. As they were riding round and doing their work of death, one cries to another—"Quantrell is coming!" "No he 'aint," says another, "he can't get here!"

THE APPROACH.

Quantrell assembled his gang about noon on the day before the raid, and started towards Kansas about two o'clock. They crossed the border between five and six o'clock, and struck directly across the prairie toward Lawrence. He passed through Gardner, on the Santa Fe road, about eleven o'clock at night.

Here they burned a few houses and killed one or two citizens. They passed through Hesper, ten miles southeast of Lawrence, between two and three o'clock. The moon was now down and the night was very dark and the road doubtful. They took a little boy from a house on Captain's Creek near by, and compelled him to guide them into Lawrence. They kept the boy during their work in Lawrence, and then Quantrell dressed him in a new suit of clothes, gave him a horse and sent him home. They entered Franklin about the first glimmer of day. They passed quietly through, lying upon their horses, so as to attract as little attention as possible. The command, however, was distinctly heard—"Rush on, boys, it will be daylight before we are there. We ought to have been there an hour ago." From here it began to grow light, and they traveled faster. When they first came in sight of the town they stopped. Many were inclined to waver. They said "they would be cut to pieces and it was madness to go on." Quantrell finally declared that *he* was going in, and they might follow who would. Two horsemen were sent in ahead to see that all was quiet in town. Those horsemen rode through the town and back without attracting attention. They were seen going through the Main street, but their appearance there at that hour was nothing unusual. At the house of Rev. S. S. Snyder a gang turned aside from the main body, entered his yard and shot him. Mr. Snyder was a prominent minister among the United Brethren. He held a commission as lieutenant in the Second Colored Regiment, which probably accounts for their malignity.

Their progress from here was quite rapid, but cautious. Every now and then they checked up their horses as if fearful to proceed. They were seen approaching by several persons in the outskirts of town, but in the dimness of the morning and the distance, they were supposed to be Union troops. As they passed the house of Mr. Joseph Savage, half a mile from town, one of them entered the yard and called at the door. Mr. Savage was just up and was washing himself. Having weak eyes, he was longer washing them, and was delayed thereby in going to the door. When he opened the door the rebel was just going out of the gate. His weak eyes doubtless saved his life, as he did not suspect the character of his visitor. They passed on in a body till they come to the high ground facing the Main street, when the command was given—"Rush on to the town!" Instantly they rushed forward with the yells of demons. The attack was perfectly planned. Every man knew his place. Detachments scattered to every section of the town, and it was done with such promptness and speed that before people could gather the meaning of their first yell, every part of the town was full of them. They flowed into every street and lane like water dashed upon a rock. Eleven rushed up to Mount Oread, from which all the roads leading into the town could be seen for several miles out. These were to keep watch of the country round about, lest the people should gather and come in upon them unawares. Another and larger squad, struck for the west part of the town, while the main body, by two or three converging streets, made for the hotel. The first came upon a camp of recruits for the Kansas Fourteenth. On these they fired as they passed, killing seventeen out of twenty two. This attack did not in the least check the speed of the general-advance. A few turned aside to run down and shoot fugitive soldiers, but the company rushed on at the command—"To the hotel!" which could be heard all over the town. In all the bloody scenes which followed, nothing equalled, in wildness and terror, that which now presented itself. The horsemanship of the guerrillas was perfect. They rode with that ease and abandon which are acquired only by a life spent in the saddle amid desperate scenes. Their horses scarcely seemed to touch the ground, and the riders sat with bodies and arms perfectly free, with revolvers on full cock, shooting at every house and man they passed, and yelling like demons at every bound. On each side of this stream of fire, as it poured in towards the street, were men falling dead and wounded, and women and children half dressed, running and screaming—some trying to escape from danger and some rushing to the side of their murdered friends.

THE CAPTURE OF THE HOTEL.

They dashed along the main street, shooting at every straggler on the sidewalk, and into almost every window. They halted in front of the Eldridge House. The firing had ceased and all was silence for a few minutes. They evidently expected resistance here, and sat gazing at the rows of windows above them, apparently in fearful suspense. In a few moments, Captain Banks, Provost Marshal of the State, opened a window and displayed a white flag, and called for Quantrell. Quantrell rode forward, and Banks, as Provost Marshal, surrendered the house, stipulating for the safety of the inmates. At this moment the big gong of the hotel began to sound through the halls to arouse the sleepers. At this the whole column fell back, evidently thinking this signal for an attack from the hotel. In a few moments, meeting with no resistance, they pressed forward again, and commenced the work of plunder and destruction. They ransacked the hotel, robbing the rooms and their inmates. These inmates they gathered together at the head of the stairs, and when the plundering was done, marched them across the street on to Winthrop street under a guard. When they had proceeded a little distance, a ruffian rode up, and ordered a young man out the ranks, and fired two shots at him, but with no effect. One of the guard at once interposed, and threatened to kill the ruffian if one of the prisoners was molested. Quantrell now rode up and told them the City Hotel, on the river bank, would be protected, because he had boarded there some years ago and was well treated. He ordered the prisoners to go in there, and *stay in*, and they would be safe. The prisoners were as obedient to orders as any of Quantrell's own men, and lost no time in gaining the house of refuge. This treatment of the prisoners of the Eldridge House shows that they expected resistance from that point, and were relieved by the offer of surrender. They not only promised protection, but were as good as their word. Other hotels received no such favors, and had no such experience of rebel honor.

At the Johnson House they shot at all that showed themselves, and the prisoners that were finally taken and marched off, were shot a few rods from the house, some of them among the fires of the burning buildings. Such was the common fate of those who surrendered themselves as prisoners. Mr. R. C. Dix was one of these. His house was next door to the Johnson House, and being fired at in his own house, he escaped to the Johnson House. All the men were ordered to surrender. "All we want," said a rebel, "is for the men to give themselves up, and we will spare them and burn the house." Mr. Dix and others gave themselves up. They marched them towards town, and when they had gone about two hundred feet, the guard shot them all, one after another. Mr. Hampson, one of the number, fell wounded, and lay as if dead till he could escape unseen. A brother of Mr. Dix remained in the shop, and was shot four times through the window, and fell almost helpless. The building was burning over his head, and he was compelled to drag himself out into the next building, which fortunately was not burned. The air was so still that one building did not catch fire from another.

After the Eldridge House surrendered, and all fears of resistance were removed, the ruffians scattered in small gangs to all parts of the town in search of plunder and blood. The order was "to burn every house and kill every man." Almost every house was visited and robbed, and the men found in them killed or left, according to the character or whim of the captors. Some of these seemed completely brutalized, while others showed some signs of remaining humanity. One lady said that as gang after gang came to her house, she always met them herself, and tried to get them to talking. If she only got them to talking, she could get at what little humanity was left in them. Those ladies who faced them boldly, fared the best.

SCENE IN TOWN.

It is doubtful whether the world has ever witnessed such a scene of horror—certainly not outside the annals of savage warfare. History gives no parallel, where an equal number of such desperate men, so heavily armed, were let perfectly loose in an unsuspecting community. The carnage was much worse from the fact that the citizens could not believe that men could be such fiends. No one expected an indiscriminate slaughter. When it was known that the town was in their possession, everybody expected they would rob and burn the town, kill all military men they could find, and a few marked characters. But few expected a wholesale murder. Many who could have escaped, therefore, remained and were slain. For this reason the colored people fared better than the whites. They knew the men which slavery had made, and they ran to the brush at the first alarm. A gentleman who was concealed where he could see the whole, said the scene presented was the most perfect realization of the slang phrase, "Hell let loose," that ever could be imagined. Most of the men had the look of wild beasts; they were dressed roughly and swore terribly. They were mostly armed with a carbine and with from two to six revolvers strapped around them. It is doubtful whether three hundred such men were ever let perfectly loose before.

INSTANCES OF RESISTANCE.

The surprise was so complete that no organized resistance was possible. Before people could fully comprehend the real state of the case, every part of the town was full of rebels, and there was no possibility of rallying. Even the recruits in camp were so taken by surprise that they were not in their places. The attack could scarcely have been made at a worse hour. The soldiers had just taken in their camp guard, and people were just waking from sleep. By some fatal mistake, the authorities had kept the arms of the city in the public armory, instead of in each man's house. There could be no general resistance therefore from the houses. When the rebels gained possession of the main street, the armory was inaccessible to the citizens, and the judicious disposition of squads of rebels in other parts of the town, prevented even a partial rally at any point. There was no time nor opportunity for consultation or concert of action, and every man had to do the best he could for himself. A large number, however, did actually start with what arms they had towards the street. Most saw at once that the street could not be reached, and turned back. Some went forward and perished. Mr. Levi Gates lived about a mile in the country, in the opposite direction from that by which the rebels entered. As soon as he heard the firing in town, he started with his rifle, supposing that a stand would be made by the citizens. When he got to town he saw at once that the rebels had possession. He was an excellent marksman and could not leave without trying his rifle. The first shot made the rebel jump in his saddle, but did not kill him. He loaded again and fired one more shot, when the rebels came on him and killed him; and after he was dead, brutally beat his head in pieces.

Mr. G. W. Bell, County Clerk, lived on the side hill overlooking the town. He saw the rebels before they made their charge. He seized his musket and cartridge box with the hope of reaching the main street before them. His family endeavored to dissuade him, telling him he would certainly be killed. "They may kill *me*, but they cannot kill the principles I fight for. If they take Lawrence they must do it over my dead body." With a prayer for courage and help he started. But he was too late. The street was occupied before he could reach it. He endeavored then to get round by a back way, and come to the ravine west of the street. Here he met other citizens. He asked, "Where shall we meet?" They assured him it was too late to meet anywhere, and urged him to save himself. He turned back, apparently intending to get home again. The rebels were now scattered in all directions, and he was in the midst of them. A friend urged him to throw his musket away, which he did. Finding escape impossible, he went into an unfinished brick house, and got up on the joists above, together with another man. A rebel came in and began shooting at them. He interceded for his friend, and soon found that the rebel was an old acquaintance who had often eaten at his table. He appealed to him in such a way that he promised to save both their lives for old acquaintance sake, if they would come down. They came down, and the rebel took him out to about twenty of his companions outside. "Shoot him! Shoot him!" was the cry at once. He asked for a moment to pray, which they granted, and then shot him with four balls. His companion was wounded and lay for dead, but afterwards recovered. The treacherous rebel who deceived and murdered him, afterwards went to his house, and said to his wife, who was ignorant of her husband's fate: "We have killed your husband and we have come to burn his house." They fired it, but the family saved it. Mr. Bell was a man of excellent character, and leaves a wife and six children to miss and mourn him.

REBELS COWARDLY AS WELL AS BRUTAL.

What little resistance was offered to the rebels, developed their cowardice as much as the general license given them developed their brutality. On the opposite bank of the river twelve soldiers were stationed. When the rebels first came into town, they filled Massachusetts street clear to the river bank, firing into every house, and robbing every stable. They even attempted to cut the rope of the ferry. But these brave boys on the opposite side made free use of their rifles, firing at every butternut that came in sight. Their minnie balls went screaming up the street, and it was not many minutes before that section of the town was pretty much deserted; and if one of the ruffians by chance passed along that way, he was very careful not to expose himself to the bullets from across the river. The result was, all that section of the town which stretched along the river bank was saved. In this section stood Gov. Robinson's house, which was the first inquired for. Here was the armory, which they took possession of early, but left it with the most of its guns unharmed.

Another evidence of their cowardice was shown in the fact, that very few stone houses were molested. They shunned almost all houses which were closed tightly, so that they could not see in, when the inmates did not show themselves. There is a deep ravine, wooded but narrow, which runs almost through the centre of the town. Into this many citizens escaped. They often chased men into this ravine, shooting at them all the way. But *they never followed one into the ravine itself*, and seldom followed up to the brink. Whenever they came near to it, they would shy off as if expecting a stray shot. The cornfield west of the town was full of refugees. The rebels rode up to the edge often, as if longing to go in and butcher those who had escaped them, but a wholesome fear that it might be a double game, restrained them. A Mrs. Hindman lives on the edge of this cornfield. They came repeatedly to her house for water. The gang insisted on knowing what "was in that cornfield?" She, brave woman, replied, "Go in and see. You will find it the hottest place you have been in to-day." Having been in to carry drink to the refugees, she could testify to the heat. The rebels took her word and left. So every little ravine and thicket round the outskirts of the town were shunned as if a viper had been in it. Thus scores of lives were saved that would otherwise have been destroyed.

In almost every case where a determined resistance was offered, the rebels withdrew. Mr. A. K. Allen lives in a large brick house. A gang came to his door and ordered him out. "No!" replied the old gentleman, "if you want anything of me, come where I am—I am good for five of you." They took his word for it, and he and his house were thenceforth unmolested. The two Messrs. Rankin were out in the street trying to gain a certain house, when they were overtaken by six of the ruffians. They at once turned and faced their foes, drew their revolvers, and began to fire, when the whole six broke and fled. The cowards evidently did not come to fight, but to murder and steal.

INCIDENTS.

We can only give a few of the incidents of the massacre as specimens of the whole. The scenes of horror we describe must be multiplied till the amount reaches one hundred and eighty, the number of killed and wounded.

Gen. Collamore, Mayor of the city, was awakened by their shouts around his house. His house was evidently well known, and they struck for it first to prevent his taking measures for defense. When he looked out, the house was surrounded. Escape was impossible. There was but one hiding place—the well. He at once went into the well. The enemy entered the house and searched for the owner, swearing and threatening all the while. Failing to find him, they fired the house and waited round to see it burn. Mrs. Collamore went out and spoke to her husband while the fire was burning. But the house was so near the well that when the flames burst out they shot over the well, and the fire fell in. When the flame subsided, so that the well could be approached, nothing could be seen of Mr. Collamore or the man who descended into the well with him. After the rebels had gone, Mr. Lowe, an intimate friend of Gen. Collamore, went at once down the well to seek for him. The rope supporting him broke, and he also died in the well, and three bodies were drawn from its cold waters.

At Dr. Griswold's there were four families. The doctor and his lady had just returned the evening before from a visit east. Hon. S. M. Thorp, State Senator, Mr. J. C. Trask, Editor of the State Journal, Mr. G. W. Baker, Grocer, with their ladies, were boarding in Dr. Griswold's family. The house was attacked about the same time as Gen. Collamore's. They called for the men to come out. When they did not obey very readily, they assured them "they should not be harmed—if the citizens quietly surrendered, it might save the town." This idea brought them out at once. Mr. Trask said, "If it will help save the town, let us go." They went down stairs and out of doors. The ruffians ordered them to get into line, and to march before them towards town. They had scarcely gone twenty feet from the yard before the whole four were shot down. Dr. Griswold and Mr. Trask were killed at once. Mr. Thorp and Mr. Baker wounded, but apparently dead. The ladies attempted to come to their husbands from the house, but were driven back. A guard was stationed just below, and every time any of the ladies attempted to go from the house to their dying friends, this guard would dash up at full speed, and with oaths and threats drive them back. After the bodies had lain about half an hour, a gang rode up, rolled them over and shot them again. Mr. Baker received his only dangerous wound at this shot. After shooting the men, the ruffians went in and robbed the house. They demanded even the personal jewelry of the ladies. Mrs. Trask begged for the privilege of retaining her wedding ring. "You have killed my husband, let me keep his ring." "No matter," replied the heartless fiend, and snatched the relic from her hand. Dr. Griswold was one of the principal druggists of the place; Mr. Thorp was State Senator; Mr. Trask, Editor of the State Journal, and Mr. Baker one of the leading grocers of the place. Mr. Thorp lingered in great pain till the next day, when he died. Mr. Baker, after long suspense, recovered. He was shot through the neck, through the arm, and through the lungs.

The most brutal murder was that of Judge Carpenter. Several gangs called at his house and robbed him of all he had—but his genial manner was too much for them, and they all left him alive and his house standing. Toward the last, another gang came more brutal than the rest. They asked him where he was from. He replied, "New York." "It is you New York fellows that are doing the mischief in Missouri," one replied, and drew his revolver to shoot him. Mr. Carpenter ran into the house, up stairs, then down again, the ruffian after him and firing at him at every turn. He finally eluded them and slipped into the cellar. He was already badly wounded, so that the blood lay in pools in the cellar where he stood for a few minutes. His hiding place was soon discovered, and he was driven out of the cellar into the yard and shot again. He fell mortally wounded. His wife threw herself on to him and covered him with her person to shield him from further violence. The ruffian deliberately walked round her to find a place to shoot under her, and finally raised her arm and put his revolver under it, and fired so that she could see the ball enter his head. They then fired the house, but through the energy of the wife's sister, the fire was extinguished. This sister is the wife of Rev. G. C. Morse, of Emporia, who was making her first visit to her sister's house. The Judge had been married less than a year. He was a young man, but had already won considerable distinction in his profession. He had held the office of Probate Judge for Douglas county, and a year ago was candidate for Attorney General of the State.

Mr. Fitch was called down stairs and instantly shot. Although the second ball was probably fatal, they continued to fire until they lodged six or eight balls in his lifeless body. They then began to fire the house. Mrs. Fitch endeavored to drag the remains of her husband from the house, but was forbidden. She then endeavored to save his miniature, but was forbidden to do this. Stupified by the scene, and the brutality exhibited towards her, she stood there gazing at the strange work going on around her, utterly unconscious of her position or her danger. Finally one of the ruffians compelled her to leave the house, or she would probably have been consumed with the rest. Driven out, she went and sat down with her three little ones in front, and watched the house consumed over the remains of her husband. Mr. Fitch was a young man of excellent character and spirit. He was one of the "first settlers" of Lawrence, and taught the first school in the place. He was a member of the Congregational Church, and very active in both Church and Sabbath School. He was the man always to stand in the "gap." If there was anything which others had left undone, he was the man to see it and do it. If a subscription for library, papers or any other object in Church or Sabbath School, fell short of the needed amount, he always made up the deficiency. All these things were done so quietly, that few ever knew of them. He was a firm but quiet man, taking little part in public affairs, and it seems strange that the rebels should have exhibited towards him such malignity. The only explanation is, that they were enraged by the Union flag which the children had set up on the wood pile.

Mr. Sargent, another member of the same Church, and a most excellent Christian man, was shot with his wife clinging to him. The revolver was placed so near as to burn his wife's neck. He lingered some ten days and then died.

James Perine and James Eldridge were clerks in the "Country Store." They were sleeping in the store when the attack was made and could not escape. The rebels came into the store and ordered them to open the safe, promising to spare their lives. The moment the safe door flew open, they shot both of them dead and left them on the floor. They were both very promising young men, about seventeen years of age.

Mr. Burt was standing by a fence, when one of the rebels rode up to him and demanded his money. He handed up his pocket-book, and as the rebel took the pocket-book with one hand, he shot Mr. Burt with the other. Mr. Murphy, a short distance up the same street, was asked for a drink of water. He brought out the water, and as the fiend took the cup with his left hand he shot his benefactor with his right hand. Mr. Murphy was over sixty years of age. Mr. Ellis, a German blacksmith, ran into the corn in the Park, taking his little child with him. For some time he remained concealed, but the child growing weary began to cry. The rebels outside, hearing the cries, ran in and killed the father, leaving the child in its dead father's arms. Mr. Allbranch, a German, was sick in bed. They ordered the house cleared that they might burn it. The family carried out the sick man on the mattrass, and laid him in the yard, when the rebels came out and killed him on his bed, unable to rise. These are a species of cruelty to which savages have never yet attained.

But even the fiendishness of these deeds was surpassed. Mr. D. W. Palmer, formerly of Andover, Mass., but one of the early settlers of Kansas, kept a gun shop just south of the business part of the town, on the main street. His position prevented escape, but he and his shop were spared till near the last. As a large gang of drunken rebels were going out, they came upon his shop. Mr. Palmer and another man were standing by the door. They fired upon them, wounding both, and then set fire to the shop. The shop being old and all of wood, without plastering, burned rapidly. While it was burning, the rebels took up the wounded men, bound their hands together and threw them into the burning shop. A woman who was standing on the opposite sidewalk, says she saw the poor men get up among the flames and endeavor to come out, but were pushed back by the guns of the torturers. The fire having consumed the bandages from their hands, she saw Mr. Palmer throw up his hands, and cry, "O God, save us!" and then fall lifeless among the embers. The fiends all this time stood around the building shouting and cheering, and when the poor men fell dead, they gave one shout of triumph and passed on. We have been slow to believe this terrible story; but two reliable persons, in full sight, witnessed the scene, and a score of circumstances corroborate it. It comes the nearest to the old description of the fiends around the pit of anything we have ever heard.

The most severely wounded man was Mr. Thornton. After being awakened by the firing in the street and around him, he remained up stairs till the house was burning. He then came down and ran. The rebels fired at him, inflicting three wounds in his hip. As he was attempting to get over some bars into a yard, another shot struck him back of the shoulder and passed down through the whole length of the back and out at the hip. His wife followed him and clung to him to shield him from further violence. The rebel sat on his horse over them, and finally got his pistol between the two and fired again, the ball going through his hat, grazing his eye and passing through his cheek. The fellow then cried out—"I can kill you," and began beating him over the head with the butt of his revolver, till the poor man fell senseless from exhaustion. The brute, not yet satisfied, leveled his revolver to shoot him again, but the wife flew at him, exclaiming, "You are not going to shoot him again," and pushed the revolver aside. The fellow soon left, supposing his victim dead. Mr. Thornton still lives, but both his legs are helpless. He will probably be a cripple for life.

Age was no protection. Many of the oldest people in town were the most brutally murdered. It was said Quantrell ordered his men to burn no churches and kill no ministers. Still they burned the Colored Church in Lawrence, and the Congregational Church of Wakarusa. They did not set fire to the Colored Church, but they set fire to a little wood shanty right under its walls, and must have designed to burn the Church, as they must have known the Church would catch from the shanty, and there could be little object in burning the one except for the sake of burning the other. The Church at Wakarusa was just finished. It was five miles from Lawrence (south), and they took it on their way out. While it was burning, the whole band gathered around, cheering and yelling, as if they were doing some specially congenial work. The first and the last man killed were preachers—Rev. Mr. Snyder was the first, and Mr. Rothrock—a Dunkard preacher—the last. Mr. Rothrock was an old man of very excellent character. He lived ten miles south of the town, and on their way out several rebels stopped at his house and ordered breakfast. His wife cooked them a good breakfast which they ate with good relish. After rising, they inquired about the old gentleman, and some one told them "he was a preacher." "We intend to kill all the d—d preachers," and at once shot him and left him for dead. He lived, however, and may recover. Rev. H. D. Fisher, they hunted like a wild beast, and it was almost a miracle that he was not burned in his house. Rev. Mr. Paddock they inquired for repeatedly, shot into his house and shot at him. Rev. R. Cordley they asked for in a number of places, as "that negro preacher," "negro harborer," and as "that abolition preacher who had been preaching at Kansas City." A lady, hoping to save his house, told one of them to whom it belonged, supposing they would spare a minister's house. He immediately whirled his horse round and rode up to the house and set it on fire. However others might have fared, there can be no doubt but these three would have been killed if they had been found.

As we said before, age was no protection. Mr. Longley lived about a mile from town. He was about sixty years of age. He was a very quiet, peaceable man, taking no part in public affairs, any further than to perform the duties of a private citizen and a Christian. He and his wife were living quietly on their farm. Two of the pickets stationed outside the town, while their bloody work was being done in town, come to his house.

His wife begged them to be merciful. "They were old people and could not live long at best." They heeded none of her entreaties, but shot the old gentleman in his yard. The first shot not doing its work, they shot again and again, and then proceeded to burn the house. Through the energy of the old lady, the fire was put out and the house saved.

THE COLORED PEOPLE.

The colored people were pursued with special malignity, but they knew the character of their old masters so well that they all ran who could, at the first alarm. Few, comparatively, were killed, therefore. Most of the killed were the old and decrepid, who could not run. Old Uncle Frank, as he was called, was about ninety years old. He was born in "Old Virginia." He said when he first came to Lawrence, "When I was a slave I pray de Lord to let me go some whar so as I could tend meetins all I wanted to. And now de Lord has answered my prayer." He was a short, heavy set man, lame with "rheumatiz," and compelled to hobble round on his cane. Still he would work, getting a job of chopping at one place and a job of hoeing at another. In this way, he earned what little his simple habits required. He always worked faithfully and did his work well, though slow. When the rebels came he was unable to escape. He was seen and shot. He fell and was left for dead. After a while, when he thought himself unobserved, he got up and endeavored to escape. Some of the rebels seeing him, dashed upon him and killed him.

"Uncle Henry" was another decrepid old negro. He hid in a barn, and was killed, and burned up in the building. Old man Stonestreet was a Baptist preacher among the colored people. He was about sixty. He also was killed, as was Mr. Ellis, another old man of about sixty. Anthony Oldham was another preacher and a man of fine character and of great influence. He was shot in his own door in the presence of his daughter.

ESCAPES.

There were many hair-breadth escapes. Many escaped to the cornfields near to town; others escaped to the "friendly brush" by the river bank. The ravine which runs almost through the centre of the town, proved a safe refuge to scores. The cornfield west of town and the woods east, were all alive with refugees. Many hid in the "Park" which was planted with corn. Many others, who could get no further, hid among the weeds and plants in their gardens. Mr. Strode, colored blacksmith, had a little patch of tomatoes, not more than ten feet square. He took his money and buried himself among the vines. The rebels came up and burned his shop, not more than ten feet off, but did not discover him.

Mr. Hampson, of whom we spoke before, lay wounded close by a burning building. It would be certain death to show signs of life. His wife, therefore, who stood by him, asked one of the rebels to help her carry her husband's body away from the flames. He took hold of Hampson and carried him out of reach of the fire without discovering that he was alive. As soon as she could, his wife helped him on to a hand-cart, and covered him up with rags, and then drew the whole away out of danger. The rebels she passed thought her crazy for "drawing off that load of old rags."

One of the most wonderful escapes was that of Rev. H. D. Fisher. We give an account of it in his own words, in a letter to a friend in Pittsburg:

"When Quantrell and his gang came into our town, almost all were yet in their beds. My wife and second boy were up, and I in bed, because I had been sick of quinsy. The enemy yelled and fired a signal. I sprang out, and my other children, and we clothed ourselves as quick as it was possible.

I took the two oldest boys and started to run for the hill, as we were completely defenceless and unguarded. I ran a short distance, and felt I would be killed. I returned to my house, where I had left my wife with Joel, seven years old, and Frank, six months old, and thought to hide in our cellar. I told Willie, twelve years old, and Eddie, ten years old, to run for life, and I would hide. I had scarcely found a spot in which to secrete myself, when four murderers entered my house and demanded of my wife, with horrid oaths, where that husband of hers was, who was hid in the cellar. She replied, "The cellar is open; you can go and see for yourselves. My husband started over the hill with the children." They demanded a light to search. My wife gave them a lighted lamp, and they came, light and revolvers in hand, swearing to kill me at first sight. They came within eight feet of where I lay, but my wife's self-possession in giving the light had disconcerted them, and they left without seeing me. They fired our house in four places; but my wife by almost superhuman efforts, and with baby in arms, extinguished the fire. Soon after, three others came and asked for me. But she said, 'Do you think he is such a fool as to stay here? They have already hunted for him, but, thank God! they did not find him.' They then completed their work of pillage and robbery, and fired the house in five places, threatening to kill her if she attempted to extinguish it again. One stood, revolver in hand, to execute the threat if it was attempted. The fire burned furiously. The roof fell in, then the upper story, and then the lower floor; but a space about six by twelve feet was by great effort kept perfectly deluged with water by my wife to save me from burning alive. I remained thus concealed as long as I could live in such peril. At length, and while the murderers were still at my front door and all around my lot, watching for their prey, my wife succeeded, thank God, in covering me with an old dress and a piece of carpet, and thus getting me out into the garden and to the refuge of a little weeping willow covered with 'morning-glory' vines, where I was secured from their fiendish gaze and saved from their hellish thirst for my blood. I still expected to be discovered and shot dead. But a neighbor woman who had come to our help, aided my wife in throwing a few things saved from the fire over and around the little tree where I lay, so as to cover me more securely."

Mr. Riggs, District Attorney, was set upon by the vilest ruffian in the lot. His wife rushed to his side at once. After a short parley the man drew his revolver and took aim. Mr. Riggs pushed the revolver aside and ran. The man started after him, but Mrs. Riggs seized hold of the bridle rein and clung to it till she was dragged round a house, over a wood pile, and through the yard back on to the street again. Mr. Riggs was still in sight, and the man was taking aim at him again, when Mrs. Riggs seized the other rein and timed his horse round, and Mr. Riggs was beyond reach. All this time the man was swearing and striking at her with his revolver, and threatening to shoot her.

Old Mr. Miner hid among the corn in the Park. Hearing the racket around Mr. Fisher's house near by, he ventured to the edge of the corn to gratify his curiosity. He was seen and immediately shot at. He ran back into the corn, but had not proceeded far before he heard them breaking down the fence. The corn was evidently to be searched. He ran, therefore, *through* the corn, and lay down among the weeds beyond. The weeds only partially covered him, but it was the best he could do. He had scarcely lain down, when the rebels came dashing through the corn, and stationing a picket at each corner of the field to prevent escape, they searched the field through but found no one. They did not happen to look among the grass almost at their very feet.

Near the centre of the town was a sort of out-door cellar with a very obscure entrance. A woman, whose name we have been unable to obtain, but who ought to be put on record as one of the heroines of that day, took her station at a convenient distance from this cellar. Every poor fugitive that came into that region, she directed into this hidden cellar. Thus eight or ten escaped from the murderers. Finally, the rebels noticing that their victims always disappeared when they came into this locality, suspected this woman of aiding in their escape. They demanded of her that she should show their hiding place. She refused. One of them drew his revolver, and pointing it at her, said, "Tell us or I will shoot you." "You may shoot me," answered the brave woman, "but you will not find the men." Finding they could not intimidate her, they left.

Mr. Bergen was wounded and then taken off with six or eight other prisoners. After taking them a short distance, their captors shot all of them dead but Mr. Bergen. He was lying down exhausted from loss of blood, and for some reason they passed him by. There he lay among the dead, feigning death. After lying a short time, a rebel rode up, and discovering he was not dead, took aim at his head and fired. He felt the ball pass and instinctively dropped his head, and the rebel supposing he had completed his work, rode off. His head was now brought under the body of a young man who had been killed with the rest. There he lay, the living under the dead, till the rebels left town. At one time, the young man's mother came to wash the blood from the face of her murdered son. Mr. Bergen begged her not to move her son's body, as his only hope of life was in lying still with his head under the lifeless corpse.

Several saved themselves by their ready wit. An officer in the camp of recruits, when the attack was made, ran away at full speed. He was followed by several horsemen, who were firing at him continually. Finding escape impossible, he dashed into the house of a colored family, and in the twinkling of an eye, slipped on a dress and a shaker bonnet, passed out of the back door and walked deliberately away. The rebels surrounded the house, and then some of them entered and searched, but found no prey.

A son of John Speer hid for some time under the side-walk. The fire soon drove him into the street, which was full of rebels. He went boldly up to them and offered his services in holding horses. They asked his name, and thinking that the name Speer would be his death warrant, he answered "John Smith," and he remained among them unharmed to the last.

One man was shot as he was running away, and fell into a gutter. His wife, thinking him killed, began to wring her hands and scream. The rebel thinking from this her husband was dead, left. As soon as he was gone, the man said, "Don't take on so, wife, I don't know as I am hit at all." And so it proved.

Mr. Winchell, being hard pressed, ran into Mr. Reynolds' house (Episcopal Minister's). Mrs. Reynolds at once arrayed him in female attire, and shaved off his whiskers with a pen knife, and set him in a rocking chair with a baby in his arms, and christened him "Aunt Betsie." The rebels searched the house, but did not disturb "Aunt Betsie."

THE SCENE AFTER THE MASSACRE.

As the scene at their entrance was one of the wildest, the scene after their departure was one of the saddest that ever met mortal gaze. Massachusetts street was one bed of embers. On this one street, seventy-five buildings, containing at least twice that number of places of business and offices, were destroyed. The dead lay all along the side-walk, many of them so burned that they could not be recognized, and could scarcely be taken up. Here and there among the embers, could be seen the bones of those who had perished in the buildings and been consumed. On two sides of another block, lay seventeen bodies. Almost the first sight that met our gaze, was a father, almost frantic, looking for the remains of his son among the embers of his office. The work of gathering and burying the dead soon began. From every quarter they were being brought in, until the floor of the Methodist Church, which was taken as a sort of hospital, was covered with dead and wounded. In almost every house could be heard the wail of the widow and orphan. The work of burial was sad and wearying. Coffins could not be procured. Many carpenters were killed and most of the living had lost their tools. But they rallied nobly and worked night and day, making pine and walnut boxes, fastening them together with the burnt nails gathered from the ruins of the stores. It sounded rather harsh to the ear of the mourner, to have the lid *nailed* over the bodies of their loved ones; but it was the best that could be done. Thus the work went on for three days, till one hundred and twenty-two were deposited in the Cemetery, and many others in their own yards. Fifty-three were buried in one long grave. Early on the morning after the massacre, our attention was attracted by loud wailings. We went in the direction of the sound, and among the ashes of a large building, sat a woman, holding in her hands the blackened skull of her husband, who was shot and burned in that place. Her cries could be heard over the whole desolated town, and added much to the feeling of sadness and horror which filled every heart.

THE RESULT.

The whole number of persons known to be killed, or who died from wounds, was one hundred and forty-three. It is probable some others were killed and burned and never found. There were about twenty-five wounded, most of them severely. Only two of the wounded have since died—the rest are recovering. Several men are now walking our streets who had balls through their heads or lungs.

The loss of property has been variously estimated; some putting it as low as $750,000, and others as high as $2,500,000. We think it cannot fall below $1,500,000.

The business of the place was mainly on Massachusetts

street, between Winthrop and Warren—a space of about 1,800 feet. This was one continued line of stores on both sides. In this space about seventy-five buildings were destroyed. Only one block, containing two stores, remained, and those two stores were robbed. On the lower end of the street there also remain two or three small buildings and one grocery store. In other parts of the town there were about seventy-five dwelling houses burned. As many more were fired, but saved by the women. The loss in buildings and goods could be very nearly estimated. But these by no means constitute the whole. All the rooms over the stores were occupied as offices or by families. The loss in the Eldridge House alone was beyond all the estimates yet made. The original cost of the house is said to have been $70,000. In the lower story were five stores and a law office. In these stores were doubtless $60,000 in goods. There were sixty inmates in the hotel, with their personal baggage. Many of these were families boarding permanently, with all their personal and household goods there. Estimating the building at its original cost, the loss in that house would not fall much short of $150,000. Then almost every house in town was robbed, and every man, woman and child that could be found.

On their way out of town, also, the rebels burned a large share of the farm houses along their route for about ten miles, when they were overtaken by citizens in pursuit.

In this narrative we have not pretended to give all the details, but only a part of those that have come to our knowledge in the regular performance of duty. Every house has a story almost as thrilling as any to which we have referred.

Lawrence has been stunned by the blow, but not killed. We feel confident she will rise from her ashes stronger than ever.

THE IMPACT OF BLACK TROOPS:
ILLINOIS, AUGUST 1863

Ulysses S. Grant to Abraham Lincoln

After the fall of Vicksburg Grant wrote to Halleck and proposed mounting a campaign against Mobile, Alabama. On August 9 President Lincoln wrote to Grant that while an expedition against Mobile was "tempting," the ongoing French intervention in Mexico made him "greatly impressed with the importance of re-establishing the national authority in Western Texas as soon as possible." Lincoln added that Brigadier General Lorenzo Thomas was returning to the Mississippi Valley to raise more black troops, and observed that recruiting blacks "works doubly, weakening the enemy and strengthening us." In closing, the President asked if Grant had received his letter of July 13 (p. 377 in this volume). Grant replied from Cairo, Illinois, where he had been visiting with his family.

Cairo Illinois
August 23d 1863,

HIS EXCELLENCY A. LINCOLN
PRESIDENT OF THE UNITED STATES,
SIR:

Your letter of the 9th inst. reached me at Vicksburg just as I was about starting for this place. Your letter of the 13th of July was also duly received.

After the fall of Vicksburg I did incline very much to an immediate move on Mobile. I believed then the place could be taken with but little effort, and with the rivers debouching there, in our possession, we would have such a base to opperate from on the very center of the Confederacy as would make them abandon entirely the states bound West by the Miss. I see however the importance of a movement into Texas just at this time.

I have reinforced Gen. Banks with the 13th Army Corps comprising ten Brigades of Infantry with a full proportion of Artillery.

I have given the subject of arming the negro my hearty support. This, with the emancipation of the negro, is the heavyest blow yet given the Confederacy. The South rave a greatdeel about it and profess to be very angry. But they were united in their action before and with the negro under subjection could spare their entire white population for the field. Now they complain that nothing can be got out of their negroes.

There has been great difficulty in getting able bodied negroes to fill up the colored regiments in consequence of the rebel cavalry runing off all that class to Georgia and Texas. This is especially the case for a distance of fifteen or twenty miles on each side of the river. I am now however sending two expeditions into Louisiana, one from Natchez to Harrisonburg and one from Goodriche's Landing to Monroe, that I expect will bring back a large number. I have ordered recruiting officers to accompany these expeditions. I am also moving a Brigade of Cavalry from Tennessee to Vicksburg which will enable me to move troops to a greater distance into the interior and will facilitate materially the *recruiting service*.

Gen. Thomas is now with me and you may rely on it I will give him all the aid in my power. I would do this whether the arming the negro seemed to me a wise policy or not, because it is an order that I am bound to obey and do not feel that in my position I have a right to question any policy of the Government. In this particular instance there is no objection however to my expressing an honest conviction. That is, by arming the negro we have added a powerful ally. They will make good soldiers and taking them from the enemy weaken him in the same proportion they strengthen us. I am therefore most decidedly in favor of pushing this policy to the enlistment of a force sufficient to hold all the South falling into our hands and to aid in capturing more.

Thanking you very kindly for the great favors you have ever shown me I remain, very truly and respectfully

your obt. svt.
U. S. GRANT
Maj. Gn.

PEACE MEETINGS:
NORTH CAROLINA, AUGUST 1863

Jonathan Worth to Jesse G. Henshaw

Between July and September 1863 about one hundred "peace meetings" were held in North Carolina, most of them in the central Piedmont region of the state. Some of the speakers at the rallies called for negotiations with the North resulting in Confederate independence, while others advocated reunion on terms that would preserve slavery. William H. Holden, the editor of the Raleigh *North Carolina Standard* and an opponent of secession in 1861, became the leader of the "Peace Party." His support for an "honorable peace" caused a breach with his political ally, Governor Zebulon B. Vance, a critic of the Davis administration who supported continued prosecution of the war. A successful lawyer from the Piedmont region who had opposed secession, Jonathan Worth was elected state treasurer in 1862. He wrote about the peace movement to Jesse G. Henshaw, a farmer and mill owner in Randolph County. The peace meetings ended in early September after Confederate soldiers ransacked Holden's newspaper offices and Governor Vance issued a proclamation denouncing the movement. Nevertheless, candidates who advocated seeking an "honorable peace" would win six out of ten seats when the state voted in the fall for representatives to the Second Confederate Congress.

RALEIGH *Aug. 24, 1863.*

* * * * * * *

I hardly know whether I am in favor of the peace meetings or not. On the one hand, it is very certain that the President and his advisers will not make peace, if not forced into it by the masses and the privates in the army. Their cry echoed by almost every press is: "Independence, or the last man and the last dollar." The North will not make peace on the basis of Independence. The real question which nobody—not even Holden—will squarely present is, shall we fight on with certain desolation and impoverishment and probable ultimate defeat; or make peace on the basis of reconstruction? Nearly every public man—every journal, political and religious, and every politician, in the fervor of their patriotism, has vociferously declared in favor of "the last man and the last dollar" cry. These classes cannot be consistent unless they still cry war. Many believe the masses in their saner hours, never approved the war and would rather compromise on the basis of the Constitution of the U. S. with such additional securities against any future rupture as could be agreed on. If there be any sense in peace meetings they mean reconstruction. They may rather do mischief if they are not so imposing as to force the administration to reconstruction. They will be impotent and mischievous if the *army* is still for war to the last man and the last dollar. I do not know the sentiments of the rank and file of the army.

I am for peace on *almost any terms* and fear we shall never have it until the Yankees dictate it. Upon the whole I would not go into a peace meeting now or advise others to go into one, particularly in Randolph—but I have no repugnance to them in other places and see no other chance to get to an early end of this wicked war, but by the action of the masses who have the fighting to do. If an open rupture occur between Gov. V. and Mr. Holden, it will be ruinous to us. There ought to be none and I trust there will be none. There is no difference between them that justifies a breach. The Governor concedes the right of the people to hold meetings and express their wishes, but he deems such meetings inexpedient and tending to dissatisfaction and disorganization in the army and that no honorable peace can be made, after we cease to present a strong military front. The Gov. acts consistently and in the eminent difficult position he occupied, I doubt whether any pilot could manage the crippled ship in such a storm with more skill. Repress all expressions of dissatisfaction against him. He values the extravagant eulogiums of the fire-eaters at their worth. They are playing an adroit game. They would get up dissention between the Gov. and Holden and then break up the Conservative party and seize the helm of Government.

NEW SALEM.

"THE MOST RADICAL REMEDY":
MISSOURI, AUGUST 1863

John M. Schofield to Thomas Ewing Jr.

Four days after the Lawrence massacre Major General John M. Schofield, the Union commander in Missouri, proposed draconian measures against the border counties that sheltered Quantrill. By the time he received Schofield's letter, Brigadier General Thomas Ewing Jr., the commander of the Missouri border district (and William T. Sherman's brother-in-law), had already taken action. On August 25 Ewing ordered the expulsion within fifteen days of the entire population of Jackson, Cass, Bates, and northern Vernon counties, except for the residents of five garrisoned towns. Ewing's General Orders No. 11 would be enforced mainly by Union troops from Kansas, who expelled between 10,000 and 20,000 persons from the border district and burned most of its houses, barns, and crops. Quantrill's men would remain in western Missouri until early October, when they killed more than eighty Union soldiers at Baxter Springs in southeastern Kansas before escaping to Texas.

HEADQUARTERS DEPARTMENT OF THE MISSOURI,
Saint Louis, August 25, 1863.

Brigadier-General EWING,
Commanding District of the Border, Kansas City, Mo.:

GENERAL: I inclose a draught of an order which I propose to issue in due time. I send it to you in order that you may make the necessary preparations for it. Such a measure will, of course, produce retaliation upon such loyal people as may be exposed to it, and they should, as far as possible, be removed to places of safety before the execution of the order is commenced or the purpose to execute it is made public. Also, it is necessary to be quite certain that you have the power to put down the rebel bands and prevent retaliation like that recently inflicted upon Lawrence, if, indeed, that can be regarded or was intended as an act of retaliation. My information relative to that distressing affair is too imperfect to enable me to judge accurately on this point. But it occurs to me as at least probable that the massacre and burning at Lawrence was the immediate consequence of the inauguration of the policy of removing from the border counties the slaves of rebels and the families of bushwhackers. If this is true, it would seem a strong argument against the wisdom of such policy. You are in position to judge of all this better than I can. At all events, I am pretty much convinced that the mode of carrying on the war on the border during the past two years has produced such a state of feeling that nothing short of total devastation of the districts which are made the haunts of guerrillas will be sufficient to put a stop to the evil. Please consider the matter fully and carefully, and give me your views in regard to the necessity for the application of such severe remedy, and of the wisdom of the method proposed. I will be guided mainly by your judgment in regard to it. If you desire the order to be issued as I have written it, or with any modifications which you may suggest, please inform me when you are ready for it.

Very respectfully, your obedient servant,

J. M. SCHOFIELD,
Major-General.

A band of robbers and murderers, under the notorious Quantrill, has been for a long time harbored and fed by the disloyal people of Jackson, Cass, and Bates Counties, Missouri, and have driven out or murdered nearly all the loyal people of those counties; and, finally, on the —— of the present month these brigands, issuing suddenly from their hiding-places, made a descent upon the town of Lawrence, in Kansas, and in the most inhuman manner sacked and burned the town, and murdered in cold blood a large number of loyal and unoffending citizens. It is manifest that all ordinary means have failed to subdue the rebellious spirit of the people of the counties named, and that they are determined to harbor and encourage a band of scoundrels whose every object is plunder and murder. This state of things cannot be permitted longer to exist, and nothing less than the most radical remedy will be sufficient to remove the evil. It is therefore ordered that the disloyal people of Jackson, Cass, and Bates Counties will be given until the —— day of ——— to remove from those counties, with such of their personal property as they may choose to carry away. At the end of the time named all houses, barns, provisions, and other property belonging to such disloyal persons, and which can be used to shelter, protect, or support the bands of robbers and murderers which infest those counties, will be destroyed or seized and appropriated to the use of the Government. Property situated at or near military posts, and in or near towns which can be protected by troops so as not to be used by the bands of robbers will not be destroyed, but will be appropriated to the use of such loyal or innocent persons as may be made homeless by the acts of guerrillas or by the execution of this order. The commanding general is aware that some innocent persons must suffer from these extreme measures, but such suffering is unavoidable, and will be made as light as possible. A district of country inhabited almost solely by rebels cannot be permitted to be made a hiding-place for robbers and murderers, from which to sally forth on their errands of rapine and death. It is sincerely hoped that it will not be necessary to apply this remedy to any other portion of Missouri. But if the people of disloyal districts wish to avoid it, they must unite to prevent its necessity, which is clearly in their power to do.

This order will be executed by Brigadier-General Ewing, commanding District of the Border, and such officers as he may specially detail for the purpose.

EMANCIPATION AND BLACK SOLDIERS:
WASHINGTON, D.C., AUGUST 1863

Abraham Lincoln to James C. Conkling

Lincoln was invited by his old friend James C. Conkling to address a mass meeting in Springfield, Illinois, on September 3. Unable to attend, he sent Conkling a public letter accompanied by a personal note: "I can not leave here now. Herewith is a letter instead. You are one of the best public readers. I have but one suggestion. Read it very slowly." On August 31 Lincoln would send a telegram adding a passage ("I know as fully . . . good faith," pp. 497.29–498.3 in this volume) that alluded to a letter he had recently received from Ulysses S. Grant (pp. 488–489 in this volume). The Conkling letter was widely printed in the northern press.

———————

Executive Mansion,
Washington, August 26, 1863.

Hon. James C. Conkling
My Dear Sir.

Your letter inviting me to attend a mass-meeting of unconditional Union-men, to be held at the Capital of Illinois, on the 3d day of September, has been received.

It would be very agreeable to me, to thus meet my old friends, at my own home; but I can not, just now, be absent from here, so long as a visit there, would require.

The meeting is to be of all those who maintain unconditional devotion to the Union; and I am sure my old political friends will thank me for tendering, as I do, the nation's gratitude to those other noble men, whom no partizan malice, or partizan hope, can make false to the nation's life.

There are those who are dissatisfied with me. To such I would say: You desire peace; and you blame me that we do not have it. But how can we attain it? There are but three conceivable ways. First, to suppress the rebellion by force of arms. This, I am trying to do. Are you for it? If you are, so far we are agreed. If you are not for it, a second way is, to give up the Union. I am against this. Are you for it? If you are, you should say so plainly. If you are not for *force*, nor yet for *dissolution*, there only remains some imaginable *compromise*. I do not believe any compromise, embracing the maintenance of the Union, is now possible. All I learn, leads to a directly opposite belief. The strength of the rebellion, is its military—its army. That army dominates all the country, and all the people, within its range. Any offer of terms made by any man or men within that range, in opposition to that army, is simply nothing for the present; because such man or men, have no power whatever to enforce their side of a compromise, if one were made with them. To illustrate—Suppose refugees from the South, and peace men of the North, get together in convention, and frame and proclaim a compromise embracing a restoration of the Union; in what way can that compromise be used to keep Lee's army out of Pennsylvania? Meade's army can keep Lee's army out of Pennsylvania; and, I think, can ultimately drive it out of existence. But no paper compromise, to which the controllers of Lee's army are not agreed, can, at all, affect that army. In an effort at such compromise we should waste time, which the enemy would improve to our disadvantage; and that would be all. A compromise, to be effective, must be made either with those who control the rebel army, or with the people first liberated from the domination of that army, by the success of our own army. Now allow me to assure you, that no word or intimation, from that rebel army, or from any of the men controlling it, in relation to any peace compromise, has ever come to my knowledge or belief. All charges and insinuations to the contrary, are deceptive and groundless. And I promise you, that if any such proposition shall hereafter come, it shall not be rejected, and kept a secret from you. I freely acknowledge myself the servant of the people, according to the bond of service—the United States constitution; and that, as such, I am responsible to them.

But, to be plain, you are dissatisfied with me about the negro. Quite likely there is a difference of opinion between you and myself upon that subject. I certainly wish that all men could be free, while I suppose you do not. Yet I have neither adopted, nor proposed any measure, which is not consistent with even your view, provided you are for the Union. I suggested compensated emancipation; to which you replied you wished not to be taxed to buy negroes. But I had not asked you to be taxed to buy negroes, except in such way, as to save you from greater taxation to save the Union exclusively by other means.

You dislike the emancipation proclamation; and, perhaps, would have it retracted. You say it is unconstitutional—I think differently. I think the constitution invests its commander-in-chief, with the law of war, in time of war. The most that can be said, if so much, is, that slaves are property. Is there—has there ever been—any question that by the law of war, property, both of enemies and friends, may be taken when needed? And is it not needed whenever taking it, helps us, or hurts the enemy? Armies, the world over, destroy enemies' property when they can not use it; and even destroy their own to keep it from the enemy. Civilized belligerents do all in their power to help themselves, or hurt the enemy, except a few things regarded as barbarous or cruel. Among the exceptions are the massacre of vanquished foes, and non-combatants, male and female.

But the proclamation, as law, either is valid, or is not valid. If it is not valid, it needs no retraction. If it is valid, it can not be retracted, any more than the dead can be brought to life. Some of you profess to think its retraction would operate favorably for the Union. Why better *after* the retraction, than *before* the issue? There was more than a year and a half of trial to suppress the rebellion before the proclamation issued, the last one hundred days of which passed under an explicit notice that it was coming, unless averted by those in revolt, returning to their allegiance. The war has certainly progressed as favorably for us, since the issue of the proclamation as before. I know as fully as one can know the opinions of others, that some of the commanders of our armies in the field who have given us our most important successes, believe the emancipation policy, and the use of colored troops, constitute the heaviest blow yet dealt to the rebellion; and that, at least one of those important successes, could not have been achieved when it was, but for the aid of black soldiers. Among the commanders holding these views are some who have never had any affinity with what is called abolitionism, or with republican party politics; but who hold them purely as military opinions. I submit these opinions as being entitled to some weight against the objections, often urged, that emancipation, and arming the blacks, are unwise as military measures, and were not adopted, as such, in good faith.

You say you will not fight to free negroes. Some of them seem willing to fight for you; but, no matter. Fight you, then, exclusively to save the Union. I issued the proclamation on purpose to aid you in saving the Union. Whenever you shall have conquered all resistance to the Union, if I shall urge you to continue fighting, it will be an apt time, then, for you to declare you will not fight to free negroes.

I thought that in your struggle for the Union, to whatever extent the negroes should cease helping the enemy, to that extent it weakened the enemy in his resistance to you. Do you think differently? I thought that whatever negroes can be got to do as soldiers, leaves just so much less for white soldiers to do, in saving the Union. Does it appear otherwise to you? But negroes, like other people, act upon motives. Why should they do any thing for us, if we will do nothing for them? If they stake their lives for us, they must be prompted by the strongest motive—even the promise of freedom. And the promise being made, must be kept.

The signs look better. The Father of Waters again goes unvexed to the sea. Thanks to the great North-West for it. Nor yet wholly to them. Three hundred miles up, they met New-England, Empire, Key-Stone, and Jersey, hewing their way right and left. The Sunny South too, in more colors than one, also lent a hand. On the spot, their part of the history was jotted down in black and white. The job was a great national one; and let none be banned who bore an honorable part in it. And while those who have cleared the great river may well be proud, even that is not all. It is hard to say that anything has been more bravely, and well done, than at Antietam, Murfreesboro, Gettysburg, and on many fields of lesser note. Nor must Uncle Sam's Web-feet be forgotten. At all the watery margins they have been present. Not only on the deep sea, the broad bay, and the rapid river, but also up the narrow muddy bayou, and wherever the ground was a little damp, they have been, and made their tracks. Thanks to all. For the great republic—for the principle it lives by, and keeps alive—for man's vast future,—thanks to all.

Peace does not appear so distant as it did. I hope it will come soon, and come to stay; and so come as to be worth the keeping in all future time. It will then have been proved that, among free men, there can be no successful appeal from the ballot to the bullet; and that they who take such appeal are sure to lose their case, and pay the cost. And then, there will be some black men who can remember that, with silent tongue, and clenched teeth, and steady eye, and well-poised bayonet, they have helped mankind on to this great consummation; while, I fear, there will be some white ones, unable to forget that, with malignant heart, and deceitful speech, they have strove to hinder it.

Still let us not be over-sanguine of a speedy final triumph. Let us be quite sober. Let us diligently apply the means, never doubting that a just God, in his own good time, will give us the rightful result. Yours very truly

A. LINCOLN.

"SLAVERY IS ALREADY DEAD":
MISSISSIPPI, AUGUST 1863

Ulysses S. Grant to Elihu B. Washburne

Henry Wilson, a Republican from Massachusetts, was the chairman of the Senate Committee on Military Affairs. On July 25 he wrote to Illinois Republican congressman Elihu B. Washburne, Grant's political patron since 1861, praising Grant for favoring the overthrow of slavery. Wilson added that he hoped Grant would remain with the Army of the Tennessee and not accept a reported offer of the command of the Army of the Potomac, where, he warned, Grant would be "ruined" by envious men "in and out of that army." Washburne sent Wilson's letter to Grant, who responded from his headquarters at Vicksburg.

Vicksburg Mississippi
August 30th 1863.

HON. E. B. WASHBURN,
DEAR SIR;

Your letter of the 8th of August, enclosing one from Senator Wilson to you, reached here during my temporary absence to the Northern part of my command; hence my apparent delay in answering. I fully appreciate all Senator Wilson says. Had it not been for Gen. Halleck & Dana I think it altogether likely I would have been ordered to the Potomac. My going could do no possible good. They have there able officers who have been brought up with that army and to import a commander to place over them certainly could produce no good. Whilst I would not possitively disobey an order I would have objected most vehemently to taking that command, or any other except the one I have. I can do more with this army than it would be possible for me to do with any other without time to make the same acquaintance with others I have with this. I know that the soldiers of the Army of the Ten. can be relied on to the fullest extent. I believe I know the exact capacity of every General in my command to command troops, and just where to place them to get from them their best services. This is a matter of no small importance.

Your letter to Gen. Thomas has been delivered to him. I will make an effort to secure a Brigadiership for Col. Chetlain with the colored troops   Before such a position will be open however more of these troops will have to be raised. This work will progress rapidly.

The people of the North need not quarrel over the institution of Slavery. What Vice President Stevens acknowledges the corner stone of the Confederacy is already knocked out. Slavery is already dead and cannot be resurrected. It would take a standing Army to maintain slavery in the South if we were to make peace to-day guaranteeing to the South all their former constitutional privileges.

I never was an Abolitionest, not even what could be called anti slavery, but I try to judge farely & honestly and it become patent to my mind early in the rebellion that the North & South could never live at peace with each other except as one nation, and that without Slavery. As anxious as I am to see peace reestablished I would not therefore be willing to see any settlement until this question is forever settled.

Rawlins & Maltby have been appointed Brigadier Generals. These are richly deserved promotions. Rawlins especially is no ordinary man. The fact is had he started in this war in the Line instead of in the Staff there is every probability he would be to-day one of our shining lights. As it is he is better and more favorably know than probably any other officer in the Army who has filled only staff appointments. Some men, to many of them, are only made by their Staff appointments whilst others give respectability to the position. Rawlins is of the latter class.

My kind regards to the citizens of Galena.

Your sincere friend
U. S. GRANT

THE LAIRD RAMS: LONDON, SEPTEMBER 1863
Charles Francis Adams to Lord Russell

Under the Foreign Enlistment Act of 1819, British subjects were forbidden to arm or equip ships to be used by foreign belligerents at war with a power friendly with Great Britain. The Confederate naval agent James D. Bulloch circumvented the law by having unarmed warships built in English shipyards and then arranging for them to be equipped with guns and ammunition outside of British territory. Despite repeated protests by Charles Francis Adams, the U.S. minister to Great Britain, the Palmerston government failed to prevent the construction and sailing of the commerce raiders *Florida*, *Alabama*, and *Georgia*. Bulloch had also contracted with the Laird shipyard in Liverpool for the building of two large ironclad rams, and then devised the stratagem of selling them to a French broker purportedly acting for the Egyptian government. On July 11, 1863, Adams sent the first of a series of letters to the British foreign secretary, Lord Russell, protesting the construction of the rams and providing evidence of their true destination. In his reply of September 1 Russell described most of the evidence as hearsay and said the government had no legal grounds to interfere. Adams responded in this letter with a warning that became famous after it was published in January 1864. In fact, Russell had given orders on September 3 for the rams to be detained in port. The British government seized the ships in October, and they were purchased by the Royal Navy in May 1864.

LEGATION OF THE UNITED STATES,
London, September 5, 1863.

MY LORD: At this moment, when one of the iron-clad vessels is on the point of departure from this kingdom, on its hostile errand against the United States, I am honored with the reply of your lordship to my notes of the 11th, 16th and 25th of July, and of the 14th of August. I trust I need not express how profound is my regret at the conclusion to which her Majesty's government have arrived. I can regard it no otherwise than as practically opening to the insurgents free liberty in this kingdom to execute a policy described in one of their late publications in the following language:

"In the present state of the harbor defences of New York, Boston, Portland, and smaller northern cities, such a vessel as the Warrior would have little difficulty in entering any of these ports and inflicting a vital blow upon the enemy. The destruction of Boston alone would be worth a hundred victories in the field. It would bring such a terror to the 'blue-noses' as to cause them to wish eagerly for peace, despite their overweening love of gain, which has been so freely administered to since the opening of this war. Vessels of the Warrior class would promptly raise the blockade of our ports, and would even, in this respect, confer advantages which would soon repay the cost of their construction."

It would be superfluous in me to point out to your lordship that this is war. No matter what may be the theory adopted of neutrality in a struggle, when this process is carried on in the manner indicated, from a territory and with the aid of the subjects of a third party, that third party to all intents and purposes ceases to be neutral. Neither is it necessary to show that any government which suffers it to be done fails in enforcing the essential conditions of international amity towards the country against whom the hostility is directed. In my belief it is impossible that any nation, retaining a proper degree of self-respect, could tamely submit to a continuance of relations so utterly deficient in reciprocity. I have no idea that Great Britain would do so for a moment.

After a careful examination of the full instructions with which I have been furnished, in preparation for such an emergency, I deem it inexpedient for me to attempt any recurrence to arguments for effective interposition in the present case. Under these circumstances, I prefer to desist from communicating to your lordship even such further portions of my existing instructions as are suited to the case, lest I should contribute to aggravate difficulties already far too serious. I therefore content myself with informing your lordship that I transmit, by the present steamer, a copy of your note for the consideration of my government, and shall await the more specific directions that will be contained in the reply.

I seize this opportunity to pray permission of your lordship to correct a clerical error inadvertently made in my note of the 3d instant, in inserting the date of two notes of mine as having received the express approbation of my government. The intention was to specify only one, that of the 11th of July. The correction is not material, excepting as it conforms more strictly to the truth.

I pray your lordship to accept the assurances of the highest consideration with which I have the honor to be, my lord, your most obedient servant,

CHARLES FRANCIS ADAMS.

Right Honorable EARL RUSSELL, *&c., &c., &c.*

THE SIEGE OF CHARLESTON: SOUTH CAROLINA, SEPTEMBER 1863

Charles C. Jones Jr. to Mary Jones

Lieutenant Colonel Jones, a Confederate artillery officer, wrote to his mother in Georgia about the ongoing siege of Charleston. While Union artillery fire forced the evacuation of Fort Wagner on September 7 and demolished much of Fort Sumter, the siege would continue until February 1865.

James Island, *Sunday*, September 6th, 1863

It is Sabbath morning, my dear mother, but it is a very difficult matter to realize the fact. All day yesterday, all last night, and all day up to this hour, Battery Wagner has been subjected to a most terrific bombardment. Over one hundred were killed and wounded within its walls yesterday. No human being could have lived for one moment upon its walls or upon its parade. Against it were hurled the combined projectiles fired from the ironsides and the various mortar and Parrott batteries of the enemy located at different points on Morris Island. As their shells in numbers would explode in the parapet and within the fort, Wagner would seem converted into a volcano. Never was any battery called upon to resist such a bombardment, and I fear that it is now held more as a matter of military pride than anything else. It is very questionable whether this should be done.

In full view of everything on yesterday afternoon, from Battery Haskell, which was firing upon the enemy, I witnessed the progress of the siege. The gunnery of the Federals was wonderful. Wagner could not answer a single shot. The enemy last night assaulted Battery Gregg, which is located on the extreme north point of Morris Island, and were repulsed. God be praised for that; for had Gregg been carried, the entire garrison at Wagner would have been captured. I would not be surprised if the enemy assaulted Wagner tonight. That portion of the parapet looking towards the south of Morris Island has been knocked very much to pieces, and the sand crumbled into the ditch. In the very nature of things it cannot be held very much longer.

As a port of commercial ingress and egress Charleston is gone; but my impression at present is that the enemy will never be able to obtain possession of the city itself. It may be destroyed in whole or in part by the shells of the enemy, but it is questionable whether they can ever hold it as a site. The inner defenses are as yet intact, and the large Blakely gun is nearly mounted. Three ironclad gunboats are in the harbor, ready to attack the enemy in the event of their endeavoring to enter with their fleet.

We know not what a day may bring forth, but I trust that we may all be enabled, by God's blessing, to do our heroic duty under any and every circumstance. This life is a terrible one, but must be endured. Do, my dear mother, kiss my precious little daughter for me. Assure all at home of my sincerest love. And believe me ever

Your affectionate son,
Charles C. Jones, Jr.

James Island, *Wednesday*, September 9th, 1863
My very dear Mother,

I write simply to assure you and my dear little daughter and all at home of my constant remembrance and truest love.

The enemy yesterday attacked, with the ironsides and four monitors, Fort Moultrie, and were repulsed after a severe and prolonged bombardment. Last night an assault was made by them in barges upon Fort Sumter. The assault was signally repelled. We captured nineteen commissioned officers, one hundred and two noncommissioned officers and privates, and six barges. It is supposed that we killed and wounded and drowned between two and three hundred of the rascals. Our ironclads performed signal service. We captured also the flag which floated from Sumter when that fort was surrendered by Anderson, and which the enemy had brought in the expectation of again planting it upon the walls of that fort.

Day before yesterday I proceeded to the Stono with three

light batteries to engage the sloop of war *Pawnee*; but she would not come within range, and after firing a few random shots retired.

Through God's great mercy I am still quite well. I think matters are assuming a rather more favorable aspect, and if the enemy will only delay a little longer any contemplated attack by the way of James Island, we will have completed a new and formidable line of defenses. The enemy will find it a very difficult matter to enter the harbor. What I most fear is the partial destruction of the city by the long-range Parrott batteries of the Federals located on Morris Island. The scoundrels are busy as bees placing them in position, and apparently are training them upon the city and our James Island batteries. Our batteries are always firing, night and day.

Do, my dear mother, kiss my precious little daughter for me. Give best love to all at home. And remember me ever as

Your affectionate son,
Charles C. Jones, Jr.

I have had no letter from home yet.

THE RAIDER ALABAMA:
CAPE COLONY, SEPTEMBER 1863

Raphael Semmes: Journal, September 16–24, 1863

A bark-rigged sailing ship equipped with an auxiliary steam engine, the *Alabama* was built at the Laird shipyard in Liverpool. She left port on July 29, 1862, and was armed with eight guns off the Azores before being commissioned as a Confederate warship on August 24. Her captain was Raphael Semmes, who had entered the U.S. Navy in 1826 and risen to the rank of commander before resigning his commission in 1861. As captain of the Confederate raider *Sumter*, he had captured eighteen American merchant ships between July 1861 and January 1862 before seeking refuge at Gibraltar. Unable to repair his ship, Semmes went to England and was given command of the new raider. While almost all of the ship's officers were Confederates, the crew of the *Alabama* had been recruited in Liverpool and served for double their normal wages and the promise of prize money. By the time she reached Simon's Town in British South Africa, the *Alabama* had sunk a Union gunboat, captured or burned fifty-four American whalers and merchant ships, and was being pursued by the U.S.S. *Vanderbilt*. After leaving Simon's Town, the Confederacy's most destructive raider would sail through the East Indies and into the South China Sea before returning to the Indian Ocean in the new year.

Wednesday, September 16.—Weather very fine. At daylight lighted fires and at 8 A.M. went ahead under steam. Saw nothing during nearly a whole day's steaming, except a bark (neutral) toward evening. At 3 P.M. doubled the Cape of Good Hope and steamed into the anchorage at Simon's Town, where we came to at about 4:30 P.M. The *Vanderbilt* had left on Friday last and was reported to have hovered near the cape for a day or two. Greatly discouraged by the news from home—Vicksburg and Port Hudson fallen, Rosecrans's army marching southward, and Lee having recrossed the Potomac. Our poor people seem to be terribly pressed by the Northern hordes of

Goths and Vandals, but we shall fight it out to the end, and the end will be what an all-wise Providence shall decree.

Thursday, September 17.—Weather good. Called on the admiral and received a visit from the captain of the *Narcissus*, Bickford. Various misrepresentations had been made to the admiral as to my proceedings since I left, etc., by the U. S. consul, which I explained away. Spent an agreeable half hour with the admiral and his lady. There being no coal here—the *Vanderbilt* having taken it all—I made arrangements for it to be sent to me from Cape Town. Visited the Dutch transport.

Friday, September 18.—Weather pleasant. Took a long stroll up the hills, permitting the men to visit the shore on liberty, and they are behaving badly, as usual.

Saturday, September 19.—The steamer *Kadie* arrived with coals for me from Cape Town. Hauled her alongside and commenced coaling. Walked on shore and lunched with Captain Bickford. Dispatched letters for the mail steamer for England. Liberty men drunk and few returning. Dined with the admiral. A very pleasant party, composed entirely of naval officers—the captains of the ships present, the captain superintendent of the dockyard, etc. After dinner the young ladies made their appearance in the drawing-room and we had some music.

Sunday, September 20.—Weather very fine. Heeled ship over to get at the copper around the blowpipe, which was worn off. Visited the shore at half past 9, took a long walk, dropped in upon the port captain, and went to church, Father Kiernan saying mass. He is an earnest, simple-minded Irish priest, with a picturesque little church on the hillside, and a small congregation, composed chiefly of soldiers and sailors, a seaman serving mass, Captain J. H. Coxon and a couple of the lieutenants of the squadron being present. Liberty men returning in greater numbers to-day; the money is giving out and the drunk wearing off.

Monday, September 21.—Morning cloudy. At daylight hauled the steamer alongside again, and recommenced coaling. Called to see the ladies at the admiral's after the dinner, and walked through their quite extensive garden, winding up a ravine, with a rapid little stream of water passing through it. Afternoon rainy.

Tuesday, September 22.—Morning cloudy, with showers of rain; wind hauling to the S. E., and the weather clearing toward noon. Coaling. A large number of liberty men on shore yet. The Yankee consul, with usual unscrupulousness, is trying to persuade them to desert, and the drunken and faithless rascals will, many of them, no doubt, sell themselves to him. With one or two exceptions the whole crew have broken their liberty—petty officers and all. With many improvements in the character of the seaman of the present day in regard to intelligence, he is as big a drunkard and as great a villain as ever. Finished coaling this afternoon. Equinoctial weather, blustering and rainy.

Wednesday, September 23.—Refitting the fore-topmast. Some twenty men still absent. A few are picked up by the Simon's Town police for the sake of the reward; and the sailor landlords, those pests of all seaports, are coming on board and presenting bills against the drunken rascals for board, etc. Of course these claims are not listened to. It is a common contrivance with Jack and these sharks to endeavor to extort money out of their ships. The process is simple enough. The landlord gives Jack a glass or two of bad liquor, and, it may be, a meal or two, and it is agreed between them that a bill of twenty times the value received shall be acknowledged. The land shark charges in this exorbitant way for the risk he runs of not being able to get anything. Knowing the villains well, I did not permit them to impose upon me.

Thursday, September 24.—Blowing a gale from the S. E. Waiting for the chance of getting over my deserters from Cape Town. Informed by telegraph in the afternoon that it was useless to wait longer, as the police declined to act. It thus appearing that the authorities declined to enable me to recover my men, 14 in number, enough to cripple my crew, I received on board 11 vagabonds, hungry and nearly shirtless, to take passage with me out to my own dominions, the high seas; thus very nearly setting off the number I had lost. Having a high respect for her Majesty, I made no contract with these fellows in her dominions. Informed by telegrams from Cape Town that vessels had arrived reporting the *Vanderbilt* on two successive days off Cape Agulhas and Point Danger. The moon being near its full, I preferred not to have her blockade me in

Simon's Bay, as it might detain me until I should have a dark moon, and being all ready for sea, this would have been irksome, and so, the gale having lulled somewhat toward 9 P.M., I ordered steam got up, and at half past 11 we moved out from our anchors. The lull only deceived us, as we had scarcely gotten underway before the gale raged with increased violence, and we were obliged to buffet it with all the force of our four boilers. The wind blew fiercely, but still we drove her between 5 and 6 knots per hour in the very teeth of it. Nothing could exceed the peculiar, weird-like aspect of the scene, as we struggled under the full moonlight with this midnight gale. The surrounding mountains and highlands, seemingly at a great distance in the hazy atmosphere, had their tops piled with banks of fleecy clouds remaining as motionless as snow banks, which they very much resembled, the cold south wind assisting the illusion; the angry waters of the bay breaking in every direction and occasionally dashing on board of us; the perfectly clear sky, with no sign of a cloud anywhere to be seen, except those piled on the mountains already mentioned; and the bright full moon shedding her mysterious rays on all surrounding objects, illuminating, yet distancing objects; all these were things to be remembered. And last, the revolving light on the cape at regular intervals lighting up the renowned old headland. We passed the cape at about 3 A.M., and bearing away gave her the trysails reduced by their bonnets and close-reefed topsails; and I turned in to snatch a brief repose before the toils of another day should begin.

RECONSTRUCTION:
MISSISSIPPI, SEPTEMBER 1863

William T. Sherman to Henry W. Halleck

In a private letter of August 29, Halleck told Sherman that the "question of reconstruction in Louisiana, Mississippi, and Arkansas will soon come up for decision of the government." Hoping that the President would "consult opinions of cool and discreet men," Halleck wished to solicit the views of generals who knew the region. Sherman replied from his headquarters on the Big Black River, where his corps had been resting during the extreme heat and drought of summer. Halleck later told him that Lincoln had read his letter carefully.

---

private and confidential

Head Qrs. 15 Army Corps.
Camp on Big Black Miss. Sept. 17. 63
Maj. Genl. Halleck, Comdr. in Chief, Washington, D.C.
Dear General,

I have received your letter of Aug. 29, and with pleasure confide to you fully my thoughts on the important matter you suggest, with absolute confidence that you will use what is valuable, and reject the useless or superfluous.

That part of the Continent of North America Known as Louisiana, Mississipi, and Arkansas is in my judgment the Key to the Whole Interior. The valley of the Mississipi is America, and although Railroads have changed the scenery of intercommunication, yet the water channels still mark the Lines of fertile land, and afford carriage to the heavy products of it. The inhabitants of the country on the Monongehela, the Illinois, the Minnesota, the Yellowstone and Osage are as directly concerned in the security of the Lower Mississipi as are those who dwell on its very banks in Louisiana, and now that the nation has recovered its possessions, this Generation of men would make a fearful mistake if we again commit its charge to a People liable to mistake their title, and assert as was recently done that because they dwelt by sufferance on the Banks of this mighty stream they had a right to control its navigation. I would deem it very unwise at this time, or for years to come, to revive the State Governments of Louisiana &c. or to institute in this Quarter any Civil Government in which the local People have much to say. They had a Government, and so mild & paternal that they gradually forgot they had any at all, save what they themselves controlled; they asserted an absolute right to seize public monies, Forts, arms, and even to Shut up the national avenues of travel & commerce. They chose War. They ignored & denied all the obligations of the Solemn Contract of Government and appealed to force.

We accepted the issue, and now they begin to realize that War is a two edged sword, and it may be that many of the Inhabitants cry for Peace. I know them well, and the very impulses of their nature, and to deal with the Inhabitants of that part of the South which borders the Great River, we must recognise the classes into which they have naturally divided themselves.

1st The Large Planters, owning Lands, slaves and all kinds of personal property. These are on the whole the ruling Class. They are educated, wealthy, and easily approached. In some districts they are bitter as gall, and have given up, slaves, plantations & all, serving in the armies of the Confederacy, whereas in others they are conservative. None dare admit a friendship to us, though they Say freely that they were opposed to disunion and war. I *know* we can manage this class, but only by *action*. Argument is exhausted, and words have not their usual meaning. Nothing but the Logic of events touches their understanding, but of late this has worked a wonderful change. If our Country were like Europe, crowded with people, I would say it would be easier to replace this population than to reconstruct it subordinate to the Policy of the Nation, but as this is not the case it is better to allow them with individual exceptions gradually to recover their plantations to hire any species of labor and adapt themselves to the new order of things. Still their friendship and assistance to reconstruct order out of the present Ruin cannot be depended on. They watch the operations of our Armies, and hope still for a Southern Confederacy that will restore to them the slaves and privileges which they feel are otherwise lost forever. In my judgment we have two more battles to win before we should even bother our minds with the idea of restoring civil order, viz. one near Meridian in November, and one near Shreveport in February and March where Red River is navigable by our Gunboats. When these are done, then & not till then will the Planters of Louisiana, Arkansas & Mississipi submit. Slavery is already gone, and to cultivate the Land, negro or other labor must be hired. This of itself is a vast revolution and time must be afforded to allow men to adjust their minds and habits to the new order of things. A civil Government of the Representative type would suit this class far less than a pure Military Rule, one readily adapting itself to actual occurrences, and able to enforce its laws & orders promptly and emphatically.

2nd. The smaller farmers, mechanics, merchants and laborers:

This class will probably number ¾ of the whole, have in fact no real interest in the establishment of a Southern Confederacy, and have been led or driven into war, on the false theory that they were to be benefitted somehow, they Knew not how. They are essentially tired of the War, & would slink back home if they could. These are the real Tiers-etat of the South and are hardly worthy a thought for they swerve to & fro according to events they do not comprehend or attempt to shape. When the time for reconstruction comes, they will want the old political system, of caucuses, Legislatures &c. something to amuse them, and make them believe they are achieving wonders, but in all things they will follow blindly the lead of the Planter. The Southern Politicians who understand this class use them as the French do their masses. Seemingly consulting their prejudices they make their orders and enforce them. We should do the same.

3rd. The Union men of the South. I must confess I have little respect for this class. They allowed a clamorous set of demagogues to muzzle & drive them as a pack of curs. Afraid of shadows, they submit tamely to squads of dragoons and permit them without a murmur to burn their cotton, take their horses, corn and everything; and when we reach them, they are full of complaints, if our men take a few fence rails for firewood, or corn to feed our horses. They give us no assistance or information, and are loudest in their complaints at the smallest excess of our Soldiers. Their sons, horses arms and everything useful are in the army against us, and they stay at home claiming all the exemptions of peaceful citizens. I account them as nothing in this Great Game.

4th. The young Bloods of the South, sons of Planters, Lawyers about Town, good billiard players & sportsmen. Men who never did work, or never will. War suits them: and the rascals are brave, fine riders, bold to rashness, and dangerous subjects in every sense. They care not a "sous" for niggers, land or anything. They hate Yankees "per se" and don't bother their brains about the Past, present or Future. As long as they have a good horse, plenty of Forage and an open Country they are happy. This is a larger class than most men suppose, and are the most dangerous set of men which this war has turned loose upon the world. They are splendid riders, shots, and utterly reckless. Stuart, John Morgan, Forrest, and Jackson are the types & leaders of this class. They must all be killed, or employed by us before we can hope for Peace. They have no property or future & therefore cannot be influenced by anything except personal considerations. I have two Brigades of these fellows to my Front, commanded by Cosby of the old army and Whitfield of Texas, Stephen D. Lee in command of the whole. I have frequent interviews with the officers, and a good understanding; and am inclined to think when the resources of their country are exhausted we must employ them. They are the best Cavalry in the world, but it will tax Mr. Chase's Genius of Finance to supply them with horses. At present horses cost them nothing for they take where they find, and dont bother their brains, who is to pay for them. Same of the corn fields which have, as they believe been cultivated by a good natured people for their special benefit. We propose to share with them the free use of these cornfields planted by willing hands that will never gather them.

Now, that I have sketched the People who inhabit the District of Country under consideration, I will proceed to discuss the Future. A Civil Government for any part of it would be simply ridiculous. The People would not regard it, and even the Military Commanders of the antagonistic party would treat it lightly. Governors would be simply petitioners for military assistance to protect supposed friendly interests, and Military

Commanders would refuse to disperse & weaken their armies for military reasons. Jealousies would arise between the two conflicting powers, and instead of contributing to the end we all have in view, would actually defer it. Therefore I contend that the interest of the United States, and of the real parties concerned, demand the continuance of the simple military Rule till long after *all* the organized armies of the South are dispersed, conquered and subjugated. All this Region is represented in the Army of Virginia, Charleston, Mobile and Chattanooga. They have sons & relations in each and naturally interested in their fate. Though we hold military possession of the Key Points of this country, still they contend & naturally that should Lee succeed in Virginia, or Bragg at Chattanooga, that a change would occur here also. We cannot for this reason attempt to reconstruct parts of the South as we conquer it, till all idea of the establishment of a Southern Confederacy is abandonned. We should avail ourselves of the lull here, to secure the Geographical points that give us advantage in future military movements, and Should treat the idea of Civil Government as one in which we as a nation have a Minor or subordinate interest. The opportunity is good to impress on the population the Truth that they are more interested in Civil Government than we are, and that to enjoy the protection of Laws, they must not be passive observers of events, but must aid and Sustain the constituted authorities in enforcing the Laws: they must not only submit themselves, but pay their taxes, and render personal services when called on.

It seems to me in contemplating the past two years history, all the people of our country north, south, east & west have been undergoing a Salutary Political Schooling, learning lessons which might have been taught by the History of other People; but we had all become so wise in our own conceit, that we would only learn by actual experience of our own.

The people even of small & unimportant localities north as well as south, had reasoned themselves into the belief that their opinions were superior to the aggregated interest of the whole nation. Half our territorial nation rebelled on a doctrine of secession that they themselves now scorn, and a real numerical majority actually believed, that a little state was endowed with such sovereignty, that it could defeat the Policy of the Great Whole. I think the present war has exploded that notion, and were this war to cease now, the experience gained though dear would be worth the expense.

Another Great & important natural Truth is still in contest and can only be solved by War. Numerical majorities by vote is our Great Arbiter. Heretofore all have submitted to it in questions left open, but numerical majorities are not necessarily physical majorities. The South though numerically inferior, contend they can whip the Northern superiority of numbers, and therefore by natural Law are not bound to submit. This issue is the only real one, and in my judgement all else should be deferred to it. War alone can decide it, and it is the only question left to us as a People.

Can we whip the South? If we can, our numerical majority has both the natural and constitutional right to govern. If we cannot whip them they contend for the natural right to Select their own Government, and they have the argument. Our Armies must prevail over theirs, our officers, marshals and courts must penetrate into the innermost recesses of their Land before we have the natural right to demand their submission. I would banish all minor questions, and assert the broad doctrine that as a nation the United States has the Right and also the Physical Power to penetrate to every part of the National domain, and that we will do it—that we will do it in our own time and in our own way, that it makes no difference whether it be in one year, or two, or ten or twenty: that we will remove & destroy every obstacle, if need be take every life, every acre of land, every particle of property, every thing that to us seems proper, that we will not cease till the end is attained, that all who do not aid are enemies, and we will not account to them for our acts. If the People of the South oppose they do so at their peril, and if they stand by mere lookers on the domestic tragedy, they have no right to immunity, protection or share in the final Result.

I even believe and contend further, that in the North every member of the Nation is bound by both natural & constitutional Law to "maintain and defend the Government against all its opposers whomsoever." If they fail to do it, they are derelict, and can be punished, or deprived of all advantage arising from the labors of those who do—If any man north or south withholds his share of taxes, or physical assistance in this crisis of our History, he could and should be deprived of all voice in the future Elections of this country and might be banished or reduced to the condition of a Denizen of the Land.

War is upon us. None can deny it. It is not the act of the Government of the United States but of a Faction. The Government was forced to accept the issue or submit to a degradation fatal & disgraceful to all the Inhabitants. In accepting war it should be pure & simple as applied to the Belligerents. I would Keep it so, till all traces of war are effaced, till those who appealed to it are sick & tired of it, and come to the emblem of our Nation and Sue for Peace. I would not coax them, or even meet them half way, but make them so sick of war that Generations would pass before they would again appeal to it.

I know what I say, when I repeat that the insurgents of the South sneer at all overtures looking to their interest. They Scorn the alliance with Copperheads: they tell me to my face that they respect Grant, McPherson and our brave associates who fight manfully & well for a principle, but despise the Copperheads & sneaks, who profess friendship for the South, and opposition to the War, as mere covers to their Knavery & poltroonery.

God knows that I deplored this fratricidal war as much as any man living, but it is upon us a physical fact; and there is only one honorable issue from it. We must fight it out, army against army, and man against man, and I know and you Know, and civilians begin to realize the fact, that reconciliation and reconstruction will be easier through and by means of strong, well equipped & organised armies than through any species of conventions that can be framed. The issues are made & all discussion is out of place and ridiculous.

The Section of 30 pounder Parrott Rifles now drilling before my tent is a more convincing argument than the largest Democratic or Union meeting the State of New York could assemble at Albany: and a simple order of the War Department to draft enough men to fill our Skeleton Regiments would be more convincing as to our national perpetuity, than an humble pardon to Jeff Davis and all his misled host.

The only Government now needed or deserved by the States

of Louisiana, Arkansas and Mississipi now exists in Grants Army. It needs simply enough privates to fill its Ranks, all else will follow in due season. This army has its well defined code of Laws and Practice, and can adapt itself to the wants and necessities of a city, the country, the Rivers, the Sea, indeed to all parts of this Land. It better subserves the interest and Policy of the General Government and the People prefer it to any weak or servile combination, that would at once from force of habit revive & perpetuate local prejudices and passions. The People of this country have forfeited all Right to a voice in the Councils of the Nation. They Know it and feel it, and in after years they will be the better citizens from the dear bought experience of the present Crisis. Let them learn now, and learn it well that good citizens must obey as well as command. Obedience to law, absolute yea even abject is the lesson that this war under Providence will teach the Free & enlightened American Citizen. As a Nation we will be the better for it.

I never have apprehended Foreign Interference in our family quarrel. Of course Governments founded on a different & it may be antagonistic principle with ours, would naturally feel a pleasure at our complications: but in the end England & France will join with us in jubilation in the triumph of a Constitutional Government over Faction: even now the English manifest this. I do not profess to understand Napoleons design in Mexico, but I do not see that his taking military possession of Mexico concerns us. We have as much territory as we want. The Mexicans have failed in self Government and it was a question to what nation she would fall a prey. That is solved, and I dont see that we are damaged. We have the finest part of the North American Continent, all we can people & take care of, and if we can suppress rebellion in our Land and compose the strife generated by it, we will have people, resources & wealth which if well combined can defy interference from any and every quarter. I therefore hope the Government of the U.S. will continue as heretofore in collecting in well organized armies the physical strength of the nation, apply it as heretofore in asserting the national authority, persevering without relaxation to the end. This whether near or far off is not for us to say, but fortunately we have no choice. We *must* succeed. No other choice is left us but degradation.

The South must be ruled or will rule. We must conquer them or ourselves be conquered. There is no middle course.

They ask and will have nothing else, and all this talk of compromise is bosh, for we know they would even now scorn and despise the offer.

I wish this war could have been deferred for twenty years, till the superabundant population of the North could flow in and replace the losses sustained by War, but this could not be, and we are forced to take things as they arise.

All therefore I can now venture to advise is the pushing the draft to its maximum, fill the present Regiments to as large a standard as possible, and push this War, "pure and simple."

Great attention should be paid to the discipline of our armies, for on them will be founded the future stability of our Government. The Cost of the War is of course to be considered, but finances will adjust themselves to the actual state of affairs, and even if we would, we could not change the cost. Indeed, the larger the cost now, the less will it be in the end, for the End must be attained somehow regardless of cost of Life and Treasure, and is merely a question of Time. Excuse so long a letter. With great respect your friend & servant

      W. T. Sherman
      Maj. Genl.

BATTLE OF CHICKAMAUGA:
GEORGIA, SEPTEMBER 1863

William W. Heartsill:
Journal, September 17–28, 1863

The opposing armies in the battle of Stones River, December 31, 1862–January 2, 1863, had each lost about one-third of their men killed, wounded, or missing. In the six months that followed, the Union Army of the Cumberland under Major General William S. Rosecrans had remained at Murfreesboro, Tennessee, while the Confederate Army of Tennessee under General Braxton Bragg occupied Tullahoma, thirty-five miles to the south. Rosecrans began advancing on June 23 and executed a series of flanking maneuvers that forced Bragg to retreat across the Tennessee River on July 6. After pausing to repair bridges and build up supplies, Rosecrans resumed his offensive on August 16. By crossing the Tennessee downriver from Chattanooga, he again outflanked Bragg and forced him to evacuate the town, a strategic railroad junction, on September 8. As Rosecrans advanced into the mountains of northwest Georgia, Bragg received reinforcements from Mississippi, eastern Tennessee, and Virginia. The two armies skirmished on September 18, then began fighting the next day in the dense woods along the western side of West Chickamauga Creek, about eight miles south of Chattanooga. William W. Heartsill had enlisted in 1861 in the W. P. Lane Rangers, a Texas cavalry company that was captured at Arkansas Post in January 1863. Exchanged in April, the men of the Lane Rangers joined an infantry brigade led by Brigadier General James Deshler. As part of the division commanded by Major General Patrick Cleburne, Deshler's Brigade fought on the Confederate right wing at Chickamauga, attacking the Union lines south of Winfrey Field at dusk on September 19 and at the southern end of Kelly Field the following morning.

———————

Whartons Cavalry is passing down the mountain and in 15 minutes firing of small arms commences and now as the sun is rising the fire is quite lively only one shot from the Big guns up to this time. The firing with Whartons men is waxing warm. 7 oclock our Cavalry has just charged the enemy and compelled him to fall back with a loss of one killed (a Geo Captain) and 8 wounded. 8 oclock our Batterries are keeping up the music on the right verry lively the enemy remains quiet except his sharp shooters. ½ past 8 all is now quiet General orders No 108 from Gen Bragg announcing the check of the enemy twice in his attempt at flanking and that now this army would press forward and compell him to fight even on his own ground. Gen B. calls upon his men to stand as true as in the days of Murfreesboro Shiloh Perryville & victory will crown our arms. To the world wee can say from what wee have seen that the Army of Tennessee is enthusiastic & will come out victorious if the Enemy will give us any thing like a fair showing. Either Ewell or Longstreet is here with troops from Va. at 1 oclock Adams Brigade comes up our Brigade goes to the foot of the Pass at 3. our Batterys open again on the enemy without a reply, at 4 oclock the small arms are rattling lively again, at 5 our Brigade is thrown forward on the right and now at sunset our Company is thrown forward along the fence of a cornfield with orders to hold the Woods in our rear at all hazzards and while I am writing the enemy is not idle They are some 1½ miles in front of us & The Smokey sides of Look out mountain looms up still beyon them while clouds of smoke and dust plainly indicates that they are preparing as well as wee for the deadly work of tomorrow. If wee are not greatly mistaken this time tomorrow will see many a throbing heart cease many that will be cold and stiff in death that little think twill be him. wee know not our fate and would not if wee could but leave all to him who governs the world as well as the lives of mortal man

Sept 18 The pickets kep up a slow but continious rattle of musketry all night, but our lines was not molested. At daybreak wee were called in an now at sunup are resting at the foot of the pass. 7 oclock all the infantry is gone and our Co is ordered to bring up the rear Some Cavalry are left to guard the Gap. Wee Soon wind up the mountain and at 10 oclock wee pass within two miles of Lafayett. Two miles farther on the road and now wee can plainly hear connonnading in the direction of Lee & Gordons mills, on the road wee meet Capt Nutt from the Hospital also Lawrence & McCain They thinking it too hazardous to cross the Mississippi river come back to share our fate for Good or bad. 12 oclock wee have been ordered to our Brigade and are now resting in a meadow This is the first fall day and by the by a fine one for fighting Fall in Fall in comes ringing down the Brigade and of course I stop writing and fall in. one mile on the road and the cannonnading is geting loud thick and fast and the prospects are magnificent for us to get into a brush this evening one ock and wee are now in line of Battle on the right of the road and in verry good trim for a fight The evening wears away evry moment we expected to start and now at Sunset all is quiet From what I can see wee have plenty of troops and if Rosy will give us an opportunity he will see that the ocupation of East Tennessee is dearly bought. The clouds are flying from North to South and as wee are all siting around our Camp fires chating over the pending fight the first chilly winds of Autumn is blowing about our ears. A great many of the men have not even one Blanket and now as I am just rolling up in my old Green army coat to roll down on a pile of leaves to think and dream of comeing events or of loved ones at home oh how many aching hearts would be ore our country did they but know wha a few days will bring forth Cruel Cruel war and thrice cruel invaders that come to drench our sunny south in blood and drag us to worse than slavery Up southrons and strike for God and our native land may the God of the right hover ore our Battle flag and may our independance be dated, from the begining of this pending contest that it is to be one of the most sanguinary and decisive battles of the war no one doubts. Wee close for the night while at evry camp fire nothing but the coming struggle is discused

Sept 19 This morning is still cool but the day promises to be verry pleasant. at 7 oclock cannonading is ringing some three miles toward Chattanooga and now at 8 all is quiet Courrirs are dashing to and fro all in perfect motion. our position here is at present the reserve of the extreme left Gen Hills HcQts are some two hundred yards down the road on the right at the forks of the road one leading to Chattanooga the other west toward Lookout mountain 10 oclk the roar of Battle is pealing forth on the right. The cannonnading is terrific wee cannot hear the small arms on account of the distance and hills on our right 11 oclk The battle still rages we have rumors that Breckenridge & Longstreet have crossed the Chicamauga driving the enemy before them The rattle of musketry is now geting close at ½ past 11 wee are called into lines and expect to moove at any moment. ¼ to 12 wee moove to the right other troops are pooring down the valley. at 12 the fight is raging verry heavy. This fight decides whether this shall be a long or a short war our Boys are confidend. Wee march quick and double quick for 5 miles and have the pleasure of wading the chicamauga below Lee & Gordons mills. The fireing is now on our left and is quite lively wee pass 150 prisoners in one group and several smaller squads some are wounded. At 5 oclock wee are now about the center of the army the firing is verry heavy on our left for the past 4 hours The fight has raged with unceasing furry our boys at sunset have driven them some two miles. wee have just passed annother squad of prisoners. Our wounded are scatered around in large numbers at dark Deshlers Brigade is on the front and the fight is increasing on our right and continues until 8 oclock our Brigade participated on the right and Col Wilkes Regt. took 250 prisons and now at 9 oclock all is quiet we are the front line. Wee have seen 7 yankee stand of collors and some 4 or 5 hundred prisoners from the fight on our extreme left at L & Gs mills wee have no news. The 7th Texas is heare some of the Boys saw Capt Talley of Marshall who is now nobly braving dangers for his native state. Nearly all the Texans are here and will give a good account of The Lone Star State. Wee manuver all night do not get a particle of sleep wee pass over a large number of Dead Yankes

Sept 20 Annother sunday and evry prospect of a fierce conflict between mighty armies at day break wee advance in line of Battle wee are waiting paitiently for the dread conflict of to day. The woods wee are now show evidence of the fierce fight of yesterday There is an abundance of Dead Yankees scatered around. our Litter corps have carried all the enemys wounded to the rear that can be found. 7 oclock skirmishing has commenced in front. 8 oclock the artillery has just opened Cheathams men are opening the Ball fineley. Gens Brag & Hill have just passed to the front at 9 oclock Deshlers brigade is ordered forward. wee front forward about face right & left flank quick and double quick for about 3 miles and take our position in the center on a ridge amidst a perfect storm of Grape stoom solid shot and minie balls which are pooring in on us from the valley beyond. Wee lay down and thus escape destruction at 9 oclock Gen Deshler is killed by shell it is usless to pass eulogies upon Gen D. for to know him was to love him and evry man in his Brigade regrets his death. Col Wilks is wounded therefore the Command fall upon Col Mills—our Brigade holds the position althou the enemy try evry means to disloge us at 3 oclock the fight became general and until sun set never did the roar of Battle peal louder it seemed that the verry heavens and earth shook and then the triumphant shout that went up at sun set our Boys are driving them back in fact they are in full retreat our victory is completed and now at 9 oclock I am writing by a federal Camp fire wee have captured a good number of Prisoners and several Battery wee must wait for particulars. our Brigade lost about 200 killed & wounded. Our Company* two wounded and four missing none of the W P L Rs were wounded. Wee have to night passed over part of the Battle ground and find the Yanks in perfect heaps. wee have work before us for Rosey will certainly hold us a lively string for the next few days it is bed time I must sleep for our work is fairly begun

Sept 21 This is a lovely morning and a perfect calm succeeds yesterdays Battle, wee can get no particulars of yesterdays work but it is satisfactory all our missing are in except Alvin Anderson but think he is not hurt. Deshlers Brigade held a position that two other brigades failed in. The Enemy has splendid brest works in our front & on the right Their works were made of large logs notched and fited close. They were stongly fortified but our Boys were too determined for them Clebourns Division suffered severly expecially Woods Brigade 8 oclock Anderson comes in all right. The loss of our Brigade is heavier than wee at first thought it will run up to near 400 killed and wounded. Sunset and wee are still at our last nights camp and from what wee can learn, Meinhier Rosecrance is in full retreat to chattanooga wee can form nothing like an acurate list of killed wounded & prisoners Wee have orders to be ready to march at a moments notice. our army is in motion Northward and day light may see us several miles from this camp. a stroll over part of the Battle field this evening was any thing els but

---

*Benge slightly wounded

pleasant wee can but forgive an Enemy even as savage a foe as the Federal Soldiers is when wee see him stiff in death or suffering from wounds. The sight was truly hart rending The enemys dead greatly outnumber ours The woods caught fire last night and a number of the dead are badly burned but it was unavoidable at dark wee fall in and march toward Chattanooga for two miles then take a right hand road Company C & Nutts Co were flankers on the left and a sweet time wee had through corn fields meadows over hills & hollows across ravines and up cliffs & Bluffs & at 2 oclock wee camp but dont ask us where at for wee do not know but think wee are in the neighbourhood of Graysville or Chicamauga Depot

Sept 22 This morning wee are awakened by the welcome words come and draw your rations which command is obeyed verry punctually by evry man. Upon looking around wee are camped on the south bank of the Chicamauga and about 3 miles from the Depo. as to what is up by this moovment none of us have the least idea but I guess Rosy will find that Corpl Bragg is wide awake. Wee marched two miles and camp once more in old Tennessee. Maj Van Zandt of the 7th Tex came over to see us this evening from him wee learn that Lieutenant L R Bayless of our Co died at Pine Bluff Ark some months ago also that several others of the Company are dead but he had forgoten their names. This camp is about 5 miles East of Chattanooga.

Sept 23 At 7 oclock wee march and 3 miles wee reach the top of Missionary Ridge here The view of Lookout Valley is verry fine while the fortifications and suburbs of Chattanooga is to our right along the river in front of us looms up Lookout mountain. at the fork of the Ridge wee file to the left and cross our line of Battle and from along the ridge near two miles from the foot of Lookout mountain The enemy is verry active and it is believed he is evacuating the place as Smoke is bursting forth from different parts of the Town and clouds of dust indicate such a moovment. at 2 oclock wee march in colum and in 1 mile of Town are again thrown into line our Brigade is on the right of Gen Breckenridges Division. The Enemy have evry few minutes made known his presents by shelling us from the fortifications—at sunset orders from Gen Bragg announcing a complete victory and rout of the enemy on the field of

Chicamauga and that too over superior numbers He however reminds us that while wee drop a tear to our brave comrades who fell by our sides on the hard fought Battle of the 18th 19 & 20 of Sept wee must now press forward to new victorys and drive the invaders from our land So Gen Bragg has named the Battle field and the thrilling victory of Chicamauga will send a throb of joy and thanksgiving throughout our land. Wee hardly think the enemy will give us battle on this side of the river but to morrow will tell what his intentions are

Sept 24 At day break this morning the Feds commenced shelling our lines and kepp it up quite brisk for an hour and now at 8 oclock skirmishing is going on to our left & near the foot of the mountain Longstreet is on the left at 8 oclock all is quiet. At 9 wee fall back and form a line along the foot of the ridge our artillery is in position 50 yards in front. here wee remain until Sunset The enemy keeping up a continuous but slow cannonading all day. our artillery has advanced some 200 yards There is a little sharp shooting going on and from the direction of the cannonading on the right & left our forces must bee surrounding the Enemy. It is now growing dark the valley is full of smoke & dust which prooves activity of troops below. To morrow old Lookout mountain will I think shake to its foundation with the roar of Battle. Wee dread the nights as they are so verry cool and the days are verry warm. The common expression of the Boys is freeze in the night & thaw in the day. While I am writeing Longstreets artillery is thundering away to the left near Lookout and in fact it seems to be even beyon the mountain. Lawrence & McCain have gone to the rear verry sick Leaving of the Rangers present Lt. Smith Sergt Heartsill & Elgin—Privates A H M Vanderson—Bence Beard & Watson. Hamlett is at his post as the Boys call him 3rd doctor In our line of Artillery in front of us is 36 pieces, forty yards apart making 678 artillery horses in one line look out Rosey or somebody will get hurt.

Sept 25 Wee rested finely until midnight when the rapid fire of musketry in front of us soon aroused us and by the time wee were in line cannon was belching forth and at the dead calm hour of midnight the moon shining lovely a sharp little battle is rageing in Lookout Valley. wee are thrown forth in front of our artillery and in an hour all is quiet Can you guess what commenced the fight to night twas this the Federal pickets had their super brought out to them and was just gathering around to eat when our boys who are allways wide a wake made a dash upon them and after a slight resistance they took to their heels and left their super to the Rebs Two Boxes passed by us while in line containing Bread &cc so much for bringing Eatiables in sight of starving Rebles after all was quiet wee are ordered back to our old position and pass the remainder of the night without molestation—and at day light this morning wee are thrown forward again and are some ¼ mile in front of our line of artillery nothing but an occasional shot from the pickets to remind us that Roseys men are near us and to keep a sharp look-out. 8 oclock The yanks are busy building brest works while their Bands keep up one continuous strain of music. At 11 oclock wee back again to the ridge and at 12 wee forward and take a position 600 yards from the foot of the ridge and by sunset wee have first rate brest works made of rails Rocks and Logs. Slow cannonadeing is going on to our left, wee are verry well fixed for minie balls and grape but wont do for 12 pounders wee will do the best wee can four of the Co return from the Hospital in the number is Snediker and wee are glad to see him improving so finely. Wee are verry much in hopes wee may get to rest to night but it is doubtful. and now for a snack and then down in the dirt for a nights rest behind brest works

Sept 26. This morning at daybreak our Pickets advance and drove the enemy to his intrenchments now at 8 oclock all is quiet except our Boys strengthing their works. It is reported that only about 5000 Federals are now in Chattanooga. Longstreet has possesion of the Rail Road below town thereby forcing the enemy to evacuate the place by crossing the mountina oposite. It is also reported that Forrest has captured a large number of wagons loaded with commissary stores verry good if true Some wounded men by this mornings skirmish have just passed. They say they killed several yankees Wee spent the remainder of the day without molestation and now preparing for another nights rest behind our works

Sept 27. All is quiet even the Pickets appear to have reaverance for the sabath for scarcly a shot has been fired to this time 9 oclock. Wee receiv orders to strengthen our works as our artilleryists will give us a bit of fun on to morrow. Wee all work finely in fact I blistered my hands I hardly think twould have been the case at any other work. But men will work at brest works when they will work at nothing els. Capt Nutt called at Gen Braggs HcQts and is satisfied that wee will get to cross the river after this campaign is over. Weaver returned & ready for the fun

Sept 28 The morning wears away and wee learn that the order to open fire this morning was countermanded at any rate there has been no firing up to this time 12 oclock. at 10 oclock wee witnessed the shooting of a deserter he left his command at Tullahoma July 1st and was caught after the fight on the Chickamaga having joined the Federals he had on the Federal Uniform After prayer by an aged minister the guilty man kneeling the command was given Aim Fire and Henry Roberts of Co K 26th Tenn paid the penalty of his crime Wee have had the pleasure of seeing a large *number of Harrison County Boys sience the late Battle in the Number Lieutenants Allen Woodson & Lipscombe also Charley & Jno Bedell Jno Smith Dan Dapplemyer Jno Weebb Jim Bradfield Ringold Hynson. Wee are sorry to learn that several were wounded in the number is Felix Johnson Henry Mills Lee Sanders & Joe Alford & Howell Lewis. but hope to meet all the Boys one more in Marshall when the trials and privations of camp life is over and the war at an end then wee can talk over our strugle for independance and laugh at our hairbreadth escapes long marches through mud dust Rain hail storm winter & Summer In after days wee will think of the Rapidan Raphanoc Patomac Chicahomini Big Black Peal Tennessee Yazzoo Chicamauga and other waters by whose sides our camp fires have glittered and when the Battles of Raymond Jackson Fort Doneldson Ark Post Richmond Gettysburg 2nd Manasses Shepherdstown Chickamauga and scores of other are mentioned wee will remember that Texans bled upon that day and sealed our caus with patriots Blood Those are days to come the present wee are now enjoying in Brest works ½ mile in front of the enemy works. our rations are brought to us evry day cooked and they are of verry short allowance in fact rather too much so I am

---

*H Rains Engine Mundon Curry Atkins Lee Ward Blalack Lieut Perry.

sure wee could eat as much more. Wee must not however complain as it is some distance to our nearest Depot station and then wee have the consolation of knowing if Rosey get any thing to eat he must haul it over cumberlane mountains as our forces have possession of the Railroads above and below the Town This condition of affairs will certainly force a fight or retreat from the enemy in a few days. If a fight is the result I think wee are fully prepared

"LYING SO THICK OVER THE FIELD":
GEORGIA, SEPTEMBER 1863

John S. Jackman:
Diary, September 18–21, 1863

John S. Jackman had enlisted in 1861 in the Confederate 5th Kentucky Infantry (later redesignated the 9th Kentucky) and saw action at Shiloh and Stones River. His regiment formed part of the 1st Kentucky Brigade, commanded at Chickamauga by Brigadier General Ben Hardin Helm, the husband of Mary Todd Lincoln's half-sister Emilie. On the morning of September 20 the brigade was posted to the Confederate right flank where, as part of the division commanded by Major General John C. Breckinridge, it repeatedly assaulted Union troops fighting from behind log breastworks at the northern end of Kelly Field. At midday James Longstreet (who was on detachment with two divisions from Lee's army) launched an attack that discovered a quarter-mile gap in the Union center and split Rosecrans's army in two. While Rosecrans and the Union right wing fled toward Chattanooga, Major General George H. Thomas withdrew his troops on the left onto a ridge and held the position for several hours before withdrawing at nightfall. Dismayed by his heavy losses in men and artillery horses, Bragg did not occupy the heights overlooking Chattanooga until September 23 and chose to besiege the town rather than assault it.

———————

Sept. 18th.—About noon came to the road leading off to where the wagon train is encamped, we left the wagon, and started for the regiment. Part of the time our road led over steep hills, and had a very tiresome walk. In the evening, a party of us left the main road to make a "near cut." There were 4 of us—Capt. N., 1st Seg't, J. F. of his company, Dr. S., our Ass't Surg., and myself. We could hear the cannon booming occasionally. At night we stopped at a cabin on the roadside, and got a good supper. Then adjourned to a neighboring pine-thicket, where we passed the night, nearly freezing, as blankets were scarce.

Sept. 19th.—On the road early. Stopped at a well to wash and breakfast. A lady seeing us, sent out some butter and milk. Five miles brought us to the regiment near Glass' Mills. The brigade had just crossed Chicamauga River at Glass' Ford to support Cobbs' and Slocums' batteries, & the wickedest artillery duel ensued, I ever saw. Slocum and Cobb had to "limber to the rear" and move their batteries back across the river. There were several of our regiment wounded—three afterward, died of their wounds. About the middle of the afternoon moved a mile or two further to the right and halted in line of battle sending out skirmish line. While here we could hear the battle raging further to the right. But before sundown, our division again commenced moving to the right. At sundown, and a little after dark, the musketry rattled incessantly. I don't believe I ever heard heavier volleys of small arms. The word came back that Cleburn was driving the enemy on the right. Having to move 5 or 6 miles, we continued our march until sometime after dark and the night being black, we had a deal of trouble. We at last crossed the Chicamauga at Alexander's Bridge, and not far from the bridge we stopped in an old field for the night. We built a large fire, yet not having any blankets with me, I did not sleep any. The night was very cold and my large overcoat came in good place.

Sept. 20th.—Before daylight, the division moved to take position in line of battle. After we had stopped for the night, the field band had been sent to the rear with the horses of the field and staff, and were not back in time; so the Col., etc., had to "foot it." The Col. left me at the fire to tell the musicians where to bring the horses. Daylight came and a heavy frost was on the ground. I waited until long after sunup, yet the drummers did not come; so I shouldered a long bundle of blankets intended to be put on the horses, and started for the regiment. I had to pass over the ground where Cleburn had fought the evening before. The dead of both sides were lying thick over the ground. I saw where six Federal soldiers had been killed from behind one small tree, and where eight horses were lying dead, harnessed to a Napoleon gun. Men and horses were lying so thick over the field, one could hardly walk for them. I even saw a large black dog lying mangled by a grape. In the rear of the brigade, I found our ambulance, and put the blankets in it, then went on to the regiment. The boys were lying in line of battle, and cracking jokes as usual. Many of them I noticed to be in the finest spirits were in a few minutes afterwards numbered with the slain. All the time the skirmishers about two hundred yards on advance, were very noisy. About 10 o'clock A.M. Maj. Wilson rode up to Gen'l Helm, who was sitting against a tree in "rear" of our regiment, talking to Col. C., and gave him the verbal order from Breckinridge to advance in fifteen minutes, and adjust his movements to the brigade on the right. The General got up and mounted his horse, laughing and talking as though he was going on parade. I had intended to go along with the infirmary corps, but as the drummers had not come up with the horses, Col. C., ordered me to go back and see if I could find them. I had not gone far, before I came to several of our boys that had been wounded on the skirmish line and as the shells were tearing up the ground about them, which makes a helpless man feel very uncomfortable, I helped put them in an ambulance and sent them to a hospital. I went a little farther, in hopes of finding the drummers, but they were nowhere to be found. I then started back for the regiment. The rattle of musketry was kept up pretty lively. As I passed along over the field, could see all the little gullies were packed full of straggling soldiers, (but I saw none of our Brigade among them) avoiding the shells. When I got to the regiment it was just falling back under a heavy fire, having charged three times unsuccessfully. The regiment was greatly reduced—by half at least—Col. C. had been wounded. Out of our company, my old friend J. H. had fallen with others and many had been wounded. Gen'l Helm had received a mortal wound and had to be borne to the hospital on a litter. Lt. Col. W., in command of the regiment, had me to ride the general's horse back to the hospital. Our brigade hospital was more than a mile from the field, across the Chicamauga. The wounded, I found, scattered over a half acre of ground—all out of our brigade too. Here I found one of the refugee drummers on Col. H's horse, which I immediately rode to the regiment, piloting Maj. Hope and others to the brigade. The sun was then getting low and Col. W. immediately despatched me on his horse to the wagon train, or cook wagons, to hurry up the rations, the boys, not having had much to eat for two or three days. I had not been long gone, when our troops advanced again on the extreme right, and this time our brigade went over the enemy's works. The loss though, was nothing, compared to that of the morning fighting. When I got to the cook train, our wagon had gone to the regiment with rations, which I had accidentally passed in the darkness. I then rode back to the hospital, and stayed until morning.

Sept. 21st.—As soon as it was light enough to see how to ride, I started for the regiment. I found them lying around loose, in line of battle, waiting orders. A skirmish line was soon after sent forward to find the enemy, but he had withdrawn during the night. The Army of Tennessee, *for once* had beaten the enemy in an open field fight. Gen'l Bragg rode along the lines, and everywhere was loudly cheered. We tried to get tools to bury our boys, but could not. Late in the evening, was sent with orders to the hospital, and remained there all night. After I had left, the brigade started towards Chattanooga. A detail was left to bury the dead.

"THE NAMELESS DEAD":
GEORGIA, SEPTEMBER–OCTOBER 1863

Kate Cumming:
Journal, September 28–October 1, 1863

Kate Cumming had begun her nursing service with the Confederate army in April 1862 when she volunteered after the battle of Shiloh. After spending two months caring for sick and wounded soldiers at Corinth and Okolona in northern Mississippi, she returned home to Mobile, Alabama. She then began serving as a hospital matron in Chattanooga in September 1862, the same month the Confederate Congress authorized paid positions for women in the army medical department. Evacuated from Chattanooga in July 1863, Cumming was working at a hospital in Newnan, Georgia, when she learned of the fighting at Chickamauga. On September 26 she recorded news of the death of several Confederate officers and wrote: "Alas! what scenes of horror does not even the word victory bring up before us!" Out of an army of about 65,000, the Confederates lost more than 18,000 men killed, wounded, or missing in the battle, while Union losses totaled more than 16,000 men out of about 60,000.

September 28.—Last evening, Rev. Dr. Husten made a speech at the depot, calling on the people to send up provisions and nurses to Chickamauga, for the purpose of feeding and nursing the wounded, as General Bragg has gone with his whole army to take Chattanooga, and requires the services of every man who is able to travel, and there are not enough left to take care of the sufferers. Our cooks have been up all night long, cooking food to send up. The same has been done in all the other hospitals.

This morning Mrs. Johnston called, and I went with her to a meeting, which was held in town, about the wounded.

Dr. Heustis addressed us, and presented a picture of suffering that would have wrung the heart of the most hardened, and said he had only told us about our own men; that if they were in such distress we could guess in what state the prisoners were.

He told us the principal thing needed was something to eat, and he believed that in one place where the men were lying, that if a basket full of biscuits was put down in the midst of them, they would let out a shout of joy that would rend the air. He had worked day and night while there, dressing wounds and giving the men water to drink, and said he believed many persons could be kept busy doing nothing but the latter. He urged all the men to go that could possibly do so; said that ladies could not go yet, as there is no place for them to stay. The enemy had destroyed a portion of the railroad, and the wounded had to be taken to a place called the "Burnt Shed," some twenty miles distant from the battlefield, there to await transportation on the cars.

Colonel Colyer of Tennessee made a very stirring speech, and was ready himself to go. A collection was then taken up, and many hundreds of dollars given. Mrs. J. introduced me to Dr. Heustis. I told him I was very anxious to go; I knew I could get some place to stay, as I was well acquainted in that neighborhood; the Burnt Shed being only a short distance from Cherokee Springs. He tried to persuade me not to think of it. On my way home I met our chaplain, Mr. Green, who told me he was going, and that if I wished I could go with him, and stay with a very nice lady, a friend of his. I intend leaving this afternoon, and am busy collecting what I can to take with me. Dr. Devine has just received a box full of delicacies from Mississippi, for troops from that state. It is impossible to send any thing to the army at present. He has given me some nice wine and other things.

Some of the ladies of the place intend going up in a few days, but none are ready to go at present. Mrs. Colonel Griffin gave me a black man for a servant.

October 6.—Left here on the 28th ult., about 3 o'clock A. M. The cars were densely crowded with soldiers returning to their commands. When we arrived at the Burnt Shed, found that the rail track had been finished to Ringgold; so we passed on to that place. As I was familiar with it, I went to the nearest building, which had been the Bragg Hospital.

There was no light to be seen any place, excepting that which came from a fire outside, around which stood a crowd of shivering soldiers.

Wounded men, wrapped in their blankets, were lying on the balcony. I went into a room which was filled with others in the same state; some of whom were suffering for want of water. They all seemed perfectly resigned; the more so as we had been victorious. How they seemed to glory in it!

After finding a vacant room to put my baggage in, I went to our old friend, Mrs. Evans. She was delighted to see me, said she had often wondered what had become of Mrs. W. and myself.

She had passed through the fearful ordeal of having been under the fire of the enemy; and she was obliged to live in the woods for some days.

I remained there until after breakfast; then I went down to the main hospital, where I was introduced to the surgeon in charge, Dr. Ussery. He gave me bandages to roll; I was assisted by a young man by the name of Dearing, from Kentucky, who was disabled by being wounded in one of his arms. Mr. Green and the colored man were kept busy all day dressing wounds.

Mr. D. and myself sat on the up-stairs gallery, where we could see the wagon trains come in with their precious burdens. As many as fifty came in at one time. We rolled bandages until the afternoon, and could scarcely supply the demand. The surgeons were getting the wounded men ready to send off on the train. I was rejoiced when we were told we had rolled enough for that day. This work had been quite a trial for me, as I had been compelled to see our poor fellows brought in as they were taken from the field hospital, and I had no chance of doing any thing for them.

There had been no rain for some time, and the wagons raised the dust in clouds, and when the men were taken out of them they were almost as black as negroes.

I took the blackberry wine which Dr. D. had given me and put it in a bucket of water, which made a nice drink. With it and something to eat, Mr. D. and I went down and waited on the men; I never saw any thing relished as much as it was. When we came to Mississippians, and told them it was from Mississippi, they relished it still more. I wondered if the ladies of Mississippi who made it had the least idea by whom and where it would be used.

While in one of the rooms a gentleman came up to me and said he was rejoiced to see me, and that I was the first lady he had seen there. He told me these men were Kentuckians, and that he was leaving on the train with some wounded. He said any attention I paid to these sufferers he would take as a personal favor.

After he left I asked one of the men who he was, and was informed he was Professor Pickett, a Baptist minister, and chaplain of a Kentucky brigade, and that he was a true Christian and zealous patriot, and had done much good in the cause.

We went into the cars which were filled with the wounded. Mr. D., while waiting on the patients, ran the risk of having his arm again broken, as he had the use of but one hand.

About dark I took some cloth for bandages and went to Mrs. Evans's to remain all night. On reaching there I met a widow lady, Mrs. ——. I asked Mrs. E. what the ladies of the place were doing, as not one of them had visited the hospital that day; and I said, if they would all roll bandages, that would be all I would ask of them. Mrs. —— did not seem to like my remarks, and said the surgeons had never asked them, and that the Federals had taken all the cloth they had to make bandages with. I answered her that I supposed the surgeons thought the ladies did not need asking, and that there was plenty of cloth at the hospitals. She said she would work at them to-morrow. She then assisted me with what I had.

Colonels Walter and Hays, who were stopping at Mrs. E.'s, came in. Colonel W. said, word for word, what I had about the ladies; only added that such neglect pained him very much. To this Mrs. —— said nothing.

I think these two gentlemen were there for the purpose of seeing that the wounded were properly cared for. I believe they are on General Bragg's staff. Colonel W. was very talkative. He spoke highly of the Mobile ladies and their beauty; said it was a dangerous place for any one who was at all susceptible of the tender passion, and that, fortified as he was by age and a wife, he nearly lost his heart. Both of these men seemed high-toned gentlemen; such as most all our educated southerners are.

Next morning, the 30th, I arose early, and took a hurried

breakfast, and when leaving asked Mrs. —— if she intended coming for the bandages. She answered, with emphasis, "I never go to hospitals, but will send for them."

On reaching the hospital, to my joy and surprise, I found that Dr. Stout had arrived early in the morning, and with him a hospital corps of surgeons and nurses; among them my kind friends, Dr. Burt and Mrs. Ellis. I knew that now the wounded would be well cared for.

Dr. Stout and his corps had been at the "Burnt Shed" for some days. He told me that when he went there, he found quite a number of regimental surgeons, and, to his sorrow, nearly all were intoxicated. He had done what he could to have every thing put in as good order as the place would admit of. He also said that no words could tell the amount of good which had been done by the Georgia Relief Committees; that had it not been for them, many of our men would have died of starvation. Part of the Atlanta Committee (I think it was) was then with him. He introduced me to some of the members; among them was Neal Brown, ex-governor of Tennessee, who was a Unionist when the war broke out; but after seeing how badly the Federal government acted, joined our side.

I had made up my mind, on seeing so many there to take care of the wounded, that I would go right back to Newnan, as I had left Mrs. W. quite sick, and much work to do.

I have always had a great desire to go on a battle-field. I can not call it idle curiosity; but a wish to see and know the most of every thing, so that I might judge for myself, and know how I may be of service.

There was a Mrs. Weir, from Griffin, Georgia, who had come to nurse her son. He had lost a leg, and was at a private house near the battle-field. This lady told me she had a young friend, whose corpse she had heard was still on the battle-field unburied. She kindly asked me to go with her.

The field was some fifteen miles distant; so we had to watch our chances of getting a conveyance. There were wagons coming in all the time with the wounded, but none going back that day; so an opportunity for getting out seemed slender. Mr. Dearing was on the watch for us. A very nice-looking covered private wagon came, and after depositing its load, Mr. D. requested the owner to take us; but he stoutly refused, saying his horses were completely worn out. Mr. D. then told him that there was one of the ladies who had nursed at least one thousand Confederates, and was very anxious to go out to the field. He immediately drew up and invited us all in, Mr. D. going with us.

We found our kind driver quite intelligent and very talkative. He related to us many anecdotes of the late battle. His name was Tedford. The first line of battle was formed on his farm, but I believe was moved before there was any fighting. His wife's pantry had suffered from our own men. She was ordered out of the house, and took shelter in the woods. After the battle, when the men found the house deserted, they went in and took every thing they could get; even taking some preserves which Mrs. T. had hid away in an attic. They also took her clothes and tore them up; the latter might have been done for the benefit of the wounded, which Mr. T. seemed to think. He did not grumble, for he was too happy about our having gained the victory for that.

The battle was partly fought at Tedford's Ford, on his brother's farm, and he said that the havoc made there was very great.

He related an incident to us about his brother, or one of his neighbor's sons, who had been in the service during the war. He had been on duty at a post far south, and had been sent to Bragg's army when it was reinforced. He was killed on or near his father's farm.

We traveled over the roughest roads I ever was on. I thought, if this was the road our wounded had to come, they must indeed suffer; and, sure enough, we met what seemed to me hundreds of wagons, with their loads, going to Ringgold. We also saw many wounded men wending their way on foot, looking wearied enough. We stopped and spoke to them; all were cheerful.

On arriving at Mr. Strickland's house, where Mrs. Weir's son was, Mr. T. begged me to go on to Mr. Hunt's, where part of Hindman's Division Hospital was. He told me that there was a nice young lady there, Miss H., who was doing a great deal for the wounded, and he was certain she would be delighted to have my help. The temptation was a great one. I was anxious to see what a field hospital was like, and to know if I could be of any service; and another thing, I had heard nothing certain regarding my brother. He was in Hindman's division; so I thought by going there I might hear from him.

On our way we met Dr. Ray, who had just heard of a brother being badly wounded, and was on his way to see him. He and the other surgeons had had a hard time since leaving us. They had wandered two days on foot in search of head-quarters, or any one who could tell them where to go. They had been all that time without food, but had come across a pig, which they had *pressed*. They had quite a number of nurses with them. I think he said they were at Claiborne's Division Hospital, and if I recollect the number rightly, he told me the first day they went there, there were no less than twelve hundred men to attend. This seems almost incredible, but we have had many more wounded than killed. He also told me that at first they had neither food to give the men or cloth to dress their wounds, and that at present rags were very scarce. I promised to send them some, and go and see them.

Mr. Hunt's house was a small cottage, surrounded by a garden. In the latter were tents, flies, and sheds, which were filled with wounded.

I went to the house with Mr. T., who introduced me to one of the surgeons. He informed me that this was Managault's Brigade Hospital, and also that Captain Chamberlain and Lieutenant Cooper of the Twenty-fourth Alabama Regiment were lying badly wounded in the house. I went in to see them; found them lying on the floor, but on mattresses. They were old friends, and glad to see me. Captain C. looked very badly, as besides his being wounded his health was delicate.

I was introduced to Miss Hunt, a very nice-looking young girl, and as I had already heard much of her kindness to the soldiers, knew she was a true southern woman.

My wounded friends informed me that Lieutenant Bond of the company of which my brother is a member had been to see them, and but one man had been killed in the company.

Captain C. introduced me to the surgeons—Drs. Cochran of the Twenty-fourth Alabama Regiment, Gibbs, and Gourie, who had charge of the hospital; the latter I had met before in Chattanooga. Dr. C. took me around to see the Mobilians—an old man by the name of Chillion, Mr. New, and Mr. Brown—neither of whom I had seen before. Mr. Chillion is a brother of Mr. C., a well-known Roman Catholic priest. He is now in his seventieth year, and has been in the service since the commencement of the war. He went through the Kentucky campaign, and every other in which the Twenty-fourth Alabama Regiment has been, and kept up as well as the youngest man. The poor old man actually cried when he found out who I was. He is a Frenchman, and I could scarcely make him understand me. He requested me to write to Mrs. Chaudron and Mrs. Perey Walker of Mobile, and let them know where he was. The men were lying on bunks made out of branches of trees.

I visited the room where Mr. Hunt and his family were. They had been driven from every corner of their house, which was filled with wounded, and had taken shelter in a small kitchen. I don't know how many there were, but this room was sleeping-room, dining-room, kitchen, and every thing else for the whole family. In it were two bedsteads, and some of the family were then lying sick. I heard no grumbling or complaint from any of them, with the exception of the old man, who sat by the fire, and it is not much to be wondered that he murmured a little.

Before the battle his farm was stocked and his barn filled with grain, and now he has nothing left but the house over his head. Winter is coming on, and with it want and starvation for him and his family; as all the neighbors for miles around had shared the same fate, he could expect no aid from them.

Before the battle the enemy had full possession of that country, and helped themselves to what they wanted. After the battle our troops took what was left, the houses being empty, as the inmates were forced to fly from the bullets. There had been fighting in Mr. H.'s yard, and many killed there.

It was in this house that Captain O'Brien had breathed his last. He lived two days after he was wounded.

When Miss H. and I retired for the night, we went up into a loft in the house, which had no flooring. We had to be careful for fear of falling through the plastering. It was filled with furniture, which had been taken out of the rooms. We had a mattress, with which we made a comfortable bed.

The next morning when Miss H. got up, as there were no windows, it was as dark as night. The ceiling was so low we could not stand upright. On coming down-stairs we found it raining in torrents, and as there were so many persons crowded together, it was any thing else but comfortable. The surgeons ate in the hall, and very kindly asked me to take breakfast with them, but I declined; I felt as if I never should eat again. The scenes with which I was surrounded had taken away all my appetite. They sent me a cup of pure coffee, which did me more good than any thing I ever took in my life. I think if Cowper had drank coffee instead of tea, he would have found it a still more cheering beverage.

I found my two friends much better than they were the evening previous. I had a small basket with me, into which I had put a few articles on leaving Ringgold, thinking I might meet some one on the road who would need them. I had no idea when leaving Ringgold of visiting any of the hospitals, as I had been told I could be of no service in them, or I should have taken plenty of every thing with me. I had a few biscuits and a box of sardines; the latter I received from the Mobile Hebrew Military Aid Society while I was in Chattanooga. I divided them around, and they seemed to be relished.

The Georgia Aid Society had as yet done nothing for this hospital. There seemed to be no food of any kind, excepting corn-bread and bacon, provided by the government; any thing else was private property. What cooking was done for the patients was done outside in the rain.

I found I could be of little service there, and became very anxious to get back to where I had left Mrs. Weir, as I knew I could very readily get a conveyance from there to Ringgold. Mr. D. tried everywhere to get some kind of a wagon, but his efforts were of no avail. He went to Mr. Tedford's to ask him for his, but our men had broken into his barn the evening before, and taken what little corn he had left to feed his mules, and he had gone in search of provender.

It rained so hard that I found it impossible to visit the patients. I was gratified to see how much solicitude the surgeons exhibited for them. They were out in the rain nearly all the morning, trying to make the patients as comfortable as possible. They said that the rain was pouring down on some of them, but it could not be avoided. They informed me that from what they had heard of many of the other brigade hospitals, the men were in a much worse plight than theirs. They blamed Dr. Foard for not attending to their wants, or appointing a deputy. They had a number of patients who were ready for transportation, but there were no wagons.

I asked what Drs. Foard and Flewellyn were doing, and said that I thought these hospitals their especial care. Was answered, "They were watching General Bragg look at the army."

There was a man there who had had his arm cut off on the late battle-field, and he was not only walking about, but nursing the others, and apparently quite well.

I assisted Miss Hunt in making some arrow-root, and showed how she could prepare it without milk, as that article was scarce. Captain C. had a little wine, which made it very nice. There were no chickens or eggs to be had for miles around.

I have always found eggnog the best thing ever given to wounded men. It is not only nourishing, but a stimulant.

Miss H. is very pleasant, well educated, and intelligent. She was assiduous in her attention to the suffering.

Captain C. was expecting his wife, and Lieutenant C. his mother. I should like to have remained until these ladies came, but I could not.

Deus's Brigade Hospital I wished to visit, but the rain prevented me. I heard there were some Mobilians wounded there, among them Mr. Murray, adjutant Thirty-sixth Alabama Regiment.

As we found it impossible to get a wagon, Drs. Gourie and Gibbs kindly offered the use of their horses, which was gratefully accepted. Miss H. loaned me her saddle and skirt.

I took leave of my two Mobile friends with many regrets. I had seen numbers die from such wounds as theirs, and did not know but this might be the last time we would meet on earth.

As we rode out of the yard I tried to look neither to the right or left, for I knew there were many pairs of eyes looking sadly at us from the sheds and tents. I could do nothing for them, and when that is the case I try to steel my heart against their sorrows.

I saw men cooking out in the rain; it seemed like hard work keeping the fire up; a perfect war between the two elements; all around had a most cheerless aspect.

As we rode out the tents of the different field hospitals came in view; when we thought of the inmates and their sufferings, it only served to add to the gloom.

I looked in the direction of the battle-field, and thought of the nameless dead who were there. A nation weeps for them, and that day nature, like Rachel, was shedding tears for her children, because they were not.

I thought of the awful conflict which had so recently raged between brother and brother. "O, what a field of fratricide was there!" it makes one cry out in anguish, as did brave Faulkland of old. "Peace! peace! when will it come? Alas! who can tell?"

TENNESSEE, OCTOBER 1863

Jefferson Davis: Speech at Missionary Ridge

October 10, 1863

After laying siege to Chattanooga, Bragg sought to replace two of his corps commanders, Leonidas Polk and D. H. Hill (no relation to A. P. Hill), for their alleged poor performance and disobedience before and during the battle of Chickamauga. At the same time, many of Bragg's generals blamed him for having failed to pursue aggressively Rosecrans's defeated army and capture Chattanooga, and twelve of them had written to Jefferson Davis asking that Bragg be relieved. On October 9 Davis arrived at Bragg's headquarters on Missionary Ridge and tried to resolve the conflict. In a meeting with Bragg and his senior generals, four of his corps commanders—James Longstreet, Simon Bolivar Buckner, Benjamin F. Cheatham, and Hill—called for Bragg's replacement. The next day Davis addressed the army's senior officers and about one hundred soldiers from the porch of a farmhouse. His remarks were reported in the Marietta, Georgia, *Confederate* and later reprinted in other newspapers. Before leaving the Army of Tennessee on October 14, Davis would decide to retain Bragg as its commander and transfer Polk and Hill to other posts.

He began by paying a warm tribute to their gallantry, displayed on the bloody field of Chickamauga, defeating the largely superior force of the enemy, who had boasted of their ability to penetrate to the heart of Georgia, and driving them back, like sheep, into a pen, and protected by strong entrenchments, from which naught but an indisposition to sacrifice, unnecessarily, the precious lives of our brave and patriotic soldiers, prevented us from driving them. But, he said, they had given still higher evidence of courage, patriotism, and resolute determination to live freemen, or die freemen, by their patient endurance and buoyant, cheerful spirits, amid privations and suffering from half-rations, thin blankets, ragged clothes, and shoeless feet, than given by baring their breasts to the enemy.

He reminded them that obedience was the first duty of a soldier, remarking that when he was a youth a veteran officer said to him: "My son, remember that obedience is the soldier's first duty. If your commanding officer orders you to burn your neighbor's house down, and to sit on the ridge-pole till it falls in, do it." The President said, this is an exaggerated statement of the duty, but prompt, unquestioning obedience of subordinates to their superiors could not be too highly commended. If the subordinate stops to consider the propriety of an order, the delay may derange the superior's whole plan, and the opportune moment for achieving a success or averting a defeat may be irretrievably lost.

He alluded to the boast of our enemy that, on the occupation of East Tennessee, they would heavily recruit their army and subjugate us with the aid of our own people; but the boast had not been fulfilled. He said the proper course to pursue towards the misguided people of East Tennessee was, not to deride and abuse them, but to employ reason and conciliation to disabuse them of their error; that all of us had once loved and revered the old flag of the Union; that he had fought under its folds, and, for fifteen years, had striven to maintain the Constitution of our fathers in its purity, but in vain. It could not be saved from the grasping ambition for power and greed of gain of the Yankees, and he had to relinquish it. The error of the misguided among us was, that they clung longer than we to what was once a common sentiment and feeling of us all, and, he repeated, they must be reasoned with and conciliated.

In closing, he expressed his deep conviction of our eventual success under the blessing of Providence, and expected the army of Tennessee, when they should resume active operations, not to pause on the banks of the Cumberland, but to plant our banners permanently on the banks of the Ohio.— This, he believed, would be done. As the humble representative of the people he returned their grateful thanks to the army of Tennessee for what they had already accomplished, and fervently invoked the blessing of Almighty God upon all officers and men comprising it.

BECOMING AN OFFICER:
WASHINGTON, D.C., OCTOBER 1863

Oliver W. Norton to Elizabeth Norton Poss

At Gettysburg Norton's brigade had played a crucial role in holding Little Round Top for the Union at the cost of more than 120 men killed or mortally wounded, including the brigade commander, Colonel Strong Vincent. "There is no one to fill his place," wrote Norton, who had served as Vincent's brigade bugler. "Oh, how we loved him!" Norton served at brigade headquarters for another three months before seeking a new position in the army.

Home of the Sanitary Commission,
Washington, D. C., Oct. 15, 1863.

Dear Sister L:—.

My mind has been in such a muddle since I came to Washington that I cannot remember whether I have written to you since I came here or not. I know I have answered your last letter, but I believe I did that in camp, and though I have not heard from you since, it seems time to write again, so here it is.

First, what I am doing here. If you have not heard, you are wondering if I have at last got into a hospital. Not very, at least I am not under medical treatment.

You know that, with my restless disposition, I could not be contented as brigade bugler while there was a possibility of doing better. As long ago as last May I began to work for a commission in a colored regiment. I wrote to Galusha A. Grow for advice. (I presume you noticed the record of that in my diary and wondered what that was about.) I heard nothing from him till this fall, when I received a letter recommending me to the notice of C. W. Foster, Major and Assistant Adjutant General, Chief of Colored Bureau, and requesting that I might be examined. It was dated September 21st. I immediately made an application to Major Foster, enclosing this letter, and in due time received an order from the War Department permitting me to appear for examination before the board of which Major General Casey is president. I reported to the board on the 1st of October and was informed that I could not be examined for a week or two yet, and was sent to this place to stay in the meantime.

Second, my prospects. When I first came here I had a very poor idea of the qualifications requisite to pass a successful examination. I knew I was as well qualified as half the officers of my regiment and I hoped to get through. Now I find that none are commissioned who are not qualified to hold the same rank in the regular army, and I begin to feel very small indeed. A man is required to show, first, a thorough knowledge of Casey's Tactics (and the examination is very severe in this), then a good knowledge of geography and history, arithmetic, algebra and geometry. Then the "Army Regulations," "Articles of War," muster and pay rolls, etc., etc., in fact be fully as well posted for second lieutenant as colonel of volunteers. Since I have been here two lieutenant colonels and many line officers have been rejected as unfit for second lieutenants.

After all this comes a searching physical examination, and no matter how well a person is posted, if the surgeon does not pronounce him sound in every respect, he is rejected. Knowing all this you may believe that my hopes of success are very small indeed. However, I shall try, and if I succeed shall be very agreeably disappointed, and I shall consider it no small honor, either. I am studying all I can, but I cannot fix my mind to study as I once could. Two years and a half in the army vetoes that.

I left the army at Culpeper. To-day they are reported at Bull Run, and the air is full of rumors of another great battle on that already famous field. For the first time, if so, the "Third Brigade" has been in a fight without me. I confess to no little anxiety for the result. Our army, I know, is weakened. The Eleventh and Twelfth corps have been sent to Rosecrans, and the First, Second, Third, Fifth and Sixth comprise the whole of our army. The papers say that "Meade is only falling back to seek a field," but I don't believe it. If he had the force, the fields at Culpeper are just as good as those at Bull Run, where the rebels have the memory of two victories. However, I will not croak, but hope for the best.

From Pennsylvania and Ohio we have glorious news. Curtin is re-elected by 30,000 majority and Brough has beat

Vallandigham 100,000. That is a greater victory for Pennsylvania than the battle of Gettysburg. It is a victory for the country. Copperheads are nowhere and the elections speak in unmistakable terms the determination of the people to support the administration. It cannot but have its influence on the South and on the war.

NORTH CAROLINA, NOVEMBER 1863

Jefferson Davis: Speech at Wilmington

After leaving the Army of Tennessee, Davis toured through Alabama, eastern Mississippi, Georgia, and South Carolina before arriving in Wilmington on November 5. His speech, delivered from a balcony on Market Street, was reported in the *Wilmington Journal* the following day.

November 5, 1863

The President in reply returned his thanks to the people of Wilmington and to Mr. Wright as their organ, for the cordial welcome they had given him. He was proud to be welcomed by such an enthusiastic concourse of North Carolinians to the soil of the ancient and honored town of Wilmington. He hoped that Wilmington, although frequently menaced, might be forever free from the tread of an invading foe. He knew well the importance of her harbor, now the only one through which foreign trade was carried on, and he trusted that the valor of her people, assisted by the means which the government would send to her defence would be fully adequate for that purpose. He had given for the defence of Wilmington one of the best soldiers in the Confederate army—one whom he had seen tried in battle and who had risen higher and higher as dangers accumulated around him. What other means the government could command had been sent here, and in case of attack such additions would be made to the garrison in men and arms as would, he believed, enable Wilmington to repulse the foe, however he might come, by land or by sea.

The President urged upon all their duty to do a full part in the present great struggle, the issues of which were on the one hand freedom, independence, prosperity—on the other hand, subjugation, degredation and absolute ruin.—The man who could bear arms should do so. The man who could not bear arms, but had wealth, should devote it freely to the support of the soldiers and to taking care of their widows and orphans.

Those who for the necessities of civil government, or for the carrying on of industrial pursuits deemed essential to the country, were exempt from the general service, were still bound to take part in the local defence; even the old man who was unable to bear arms, must, in the course of long years have acquired an influence, which should be exerted to arouse those in his neighbourhood to fresh zeal and renewed exertions in support of the cause in which all are so deeply interested. If we were unanimous, if all did their duty manfully, bravely disinterestedly, then our subjugation would be impossible; but if, neglecting the interests of the country, and only anxious to heap up sordid gain, each man attended only to his own private interests, then would it be found that such gains were accumulated only to fall into the hands of the plundering Yankees. The soldier who had fought bravely for his country, although he could leave his children no other fortune, would leave them rich in an inheritance of honor, while the wealth gathered and heaped up in the spirit of Shylock, in the midst of a bleeding country, would go down with a branding and a curse.

Since the President had last passed through Wilmington he had travelled far and visited many portions of the country, and in some he had found ruin and devastation marking the track of the vandal foe. Blackened chimneys alone remained to mark the spot where happy homes once stood, and smouldering ashes replaced the roofs that had sheltered the widow and the orphan. Wherever the invader had passed the last spark of Union feeling had been extinguished, and the people of the districts which the Yankees had supposed subjugated were the warmest and most devoted friends of the Confederacy.

He had visited the army of the West, had gone over the bloody battle field of Chickamauga, and a survey of the ground had heightened his admiration for that valor and devotion, which, with inferior numbers, had overcome difficulties so formidable, and after two days' fighting had achieved a glorious victory, the routed foe only finding shelter under the cover of night.

He had visited Charleston, where the thunder of the enemy's guns is heard day and night hurling their fiercest fire against Sumter, and still the grand old fortress stands grim, dark and silent, bidding defiance to the utmost efforts of the foe. He had visited the other points about Charleston, and had found the spirit of the people and of the troops alike resolute and determined. The Yankees were anxious to crush what they called the nest of the rebellion. He believed that it would stand, spite of their utmost efforts for its capture. It had his best prayers for its safety. God bless the noble old city!

The President said that in North Carolina, as elsewhere, the contact of the Yankees had thoroughly extinguished every spark of Union feeling wherever they had come. The Eastern portion of the State which had suffered most from the enemy was perhaps the most loyal and devoted portion of the whole State; and North Carolina as a State had not been behind any other in the number of troops she had given to the armies of the Confederacy. In every field, from great Bethel, the first, to Chickamauga, the last, the blood of North Carolinians had been shed and their valor illustrated, and if she had fewer trumpeters than some others to sound her fame, the list of killed and wounded from every battle-field attested her devotion and bore witness to her sacrifices. North Carolina might well be proud of her soldiers in the armies of the Confederacy.

We are all engaged in the same cause. We must all make sacrifices. We must use forbearance with each other.—We are all liable to err. Your Generals may commit mistakes; your President may commit mistakes; *you* yourselves may commit mistakes. This is human and for this proper allowance must be made. We must cultivate harmony, unanimity, concert of action. We must, said the President, beware of croakers—beware of the man who would instil the poison of division and disaffection because this section or that section had not got its full share of the spoils and the plunder, the honors and the emoluments of office. Did we go into this war for offices or for plunder?—did we expect to make money by it? If so, then he and others, who, like him, had lost all—had seen the product of years swept away, had been woefully mistaken. But we had not gone into this war from any such ignoble motives, and no such narrow considerations ought to control appointments. Merit and merit alone should be the criterion. And merit *had* been found, and North Carolinians had received and now held a full proportion of the high positions in the army. He here alluded to General Bragg, a native son of North Carolina.

If, there were those who yielded to despondency, who despaired of the Republic, who were willing to submit to degradation, they were not to be found in the ranks of the army, where all was confidence and determination. Those who complained most, were those who had made the fewest sacrifices, not the soldiers who had made the most.

In the changing fortunes of war, we may for a time be driven back, but with a resolute purpose and united effort we would regain all that we had lost, and accomplish all that we had proposed. Freed from the shackles imposed upon us by our uncongenial association with a people who had proved themselves to be ten times worse than even he had supposed them to be, the Confederate States would spring forward in a career of happiness and prosperity surpassing the dreams of the most sanguine.

The President again returned thanks for his kind and enthusiastic reception, and withdrew.

"WE HAVE NO FEARS":
VIRGINIA, NOVEMBER 1863

Walter H. Taylor to Bettie Saunders

In the last week of September two corps from the Army of the Potomac were sent west to reinforce Rosecrans, leaving Meade with about 75,000 men camped around Culpeper, Virginia. Although the detachment of Longstreet and his two divisions had left him with only 45,000 men, Lee decided to take the offensive. Starting on October 9, Lee's army marched west and then north, turning Meade's right flank and causing him to withdraw along the Orange & Alexandria railroad to Centreville, forty miles to the north of Culpeper. On October 14 A. P. Hill lost more than 1,300 men killed, wounded, or captured in a battle with the Union rear guard at Bristoe Station, ending Confederate hopes of cutting off the Union retreat. Unable to supply his army near Centreville, Lee turned south on October 18 and withdrew behind the Rappahannock. On November 7 a Union night attack overran the Confederate bridgehead at Rappahannock Station, capturing 1,600 prisoners. Lee then retreated across the Rapidan, and by November 10 the two armies had returned to their previous positions. Major Walter H. Taylor, Lee's adjutant, wrote to his fiancée after the campaign ended.

Camp near Orange CHo
15 November 1863

For the first time I think since the commencement of the war Sunday has come upon me unawares. I had persuaded myself that it was to come on the 16th of the month and all day yesterday and this morning I have imagined that this was Saturday & contemplated writing you a letter tonight as usual. When George Peterkin came in just now and asked me if there was any objection to his going to attend service in Orange, I was highly entertained at his having, as I thought, gained a day. How I made such a mistake I cannot tell. As the roar of artillery is again heard this morning, I hasten whilst time is left me to acknowledge the receipt of yours of last Sunday and to thank you my dear Bettie, for all that it contains. I cannot tell you how anxiously I watch the mails when the time arrives when I think I may reasonably expect a letter. When there is none, I bear my disappointment like a Trojan and patiently await another day. And when the earnestly longed for favor makes its appearance I almost tremble with delight. Oh Bettie, my precious one, your letters are very dear to me. When I read them, I am almost transported with joy to see that you are my own truly my own. My happiness is almost too great when I perceive that you too look forward to our future with anticipations of a happy life together. When we shall be all in all to each other. When I shall study and labor, oh! so earnestly and faithfully to secure your comfort and happiness. Hitherto, dear Bettie, my devotion for you has struggled alone under most adverse circumstances, it could not develop itself because it was unrequited: 'twas not encouraged; but now that it meets with reciprocal sentiment on your part, now that I can properly remove the restraint which I always imposed upon it, it assumes mammoth proportions, it absorbs my whole being. Did I not feel very secure, yes, did I not recognize the kind hand of Providence in bringing us thus together finally after my many hopes, fears and prayers, I should tremble indeed when I realize how entirely dependent I am upon you; when I have to confess that you are all to me, light, life, everything. . . .

But little of importance has occurred in the army since my letter or note of last Saturday. From the papers, you have no doubt learned of our movement to the south side of the Rapidan. Contrary to my expectations the enemy was very tardy in pushing his advantage, after our misfortune at Rappanhannock Station. Soon after my note to you was dispatched, we struck tents, packed the wagons and sent them to the rear—only moving ourselves about twelve o'clock. Before leaving our camp we built the most immense fires in all our new chimneys, to show how nicely they would draw; and wrapped in my overcoat, I stretched out in front of mine upon a pile of straw and soon lost consciousness in a sweet sleep. I was presently awakened by an exclamation from the General addressed to those around to the effect that Major Taylor was a happy fellow, meaning that I could sleep, whether circumstances were propitious or the reverse, at any time. After the chimneys themselves, as well as the wood in the fire places, were consumed, for we were determined the Yankees should not reap the profits of our industry and skill, we commenced our march for the point where it had been arranged HdQtrs should be established for the anticipated engagement. So soon as we arrived there, it being yet some hours before day, the "happy fellow" again composed himself to sleep and awoke about day with a thought of his absent dear one and ready for Meade or "the newest fashions"—(Pray excuse the slang).

But the Yankees were apparently satisfied; at all events evinced no desire to bring on a general engagement and permitted us to remain in line of battle all day Sunday without any serious molestation. Sunday night, in pursuance of the original design of the General, we resumed our march for the Rapidan and encamped on the south side of that river that night. A day or two afterwards we changed camp to our present location— one much nearer Orange CHo. more central to the army and more convenient to all parties. It is a camp of my selection and I am pleased to see it gives general satisfaction. I hope we may have as nice a one for the winter, if we do not remain where we are.

When the thundering of the artillery commenced this morning, a message was received that the enemy was attempting a passage of the river at one of the lower fords; the whole army was at once signaled to be under arms and ready for battle and the General, with all the Staff save me, started for the front. I was left to attend to whatever should arrive in the General's absence, and was to follow when convinced there was really to be a battle and when there was no longer any necessity for my remaining at HeadQtrs. So I have had a nice quiet time to write and what is the best part of it, I have been relieved of all anxiety about the threatened battle, by the receipt of a signal message informing Genl. Lee that the movement was only a cavalry demonstration. So there will be no fight today. When it does come we have no fears as to the result. Don't you mind what you hear in Richmond, wait for my letters, I will always, when it is possible, keep you promptly advised of what is transpiring here. It is needless for me to admonish you as I did Mother yesterday, not to follow and put faith in Dame Rumor, and to deviate from the fashion in the capital, always wear a cheerful, hopeful countenance. Above all, don't wound our pride by feeling any apprehension on our account. Don't imagine that the enemy are to have it all their own way. Our confidence in God and our own strong arms is by no means impaired, and it is not flattering to see our good people doubtful of our ability to manage our old enemy, so often fairly beaten by this army. You ask if there is any prospect of our falling back to Richmond. I see none now. The enemy, I trust, will never force us back so far. I cannot say what we may be compelled to do through a want of forage for our animals; this depends on the departments in Richmond. Personally I would be gratified to be so near you; but with you I think of the country which would be laid open to the enemy and the people who would be exposed to their tyranny and I pray we may never relinquish again so much of the Old Commonwealth. I only wish the General had good Lieutenants. We miss Jackson & Longstreet terribly. Poor Ewell—a cripple—is now laid up and not able to be in the field. . . .

I was very sorry to hear of Mayhew Hobson's death. Poor Mrs. H.—she looked so comfortable and happy when I saw her at home. When I thought how happily fixed the three brothers were, with their beautiful homes, I little dreamed how soon one would be taken away. I received a letter for Mr. John H. a few days ago, enclosed to my care from Pemberton. It was post marked 9th & reached here on the 12th. I presumed it was about his brother and sent it over by a special courier. Mr. Hobson had just been to Stuart's HdQ. to try and get a leave of absence and there learned of his brother's death. I am sorry that he cannot go home now, but Genl. Stuart tells me there is but one Lieut. with his Co. Apart from this, which would preclude any merriment at the Neck so soon as Christmas, I very much fear that my chances for a leave so recently after my last are quite poor. But I can ride to Goochland in a day and when you go there, I shall certainly do likewise if practicable, and if my stay must be limited to one day. Our Staff is very small now and is growing smaller. Two of them, I know, will expect to visit their families next month. This leaves but one other besides me. I expect to lose my tent mate Venable. He is the only congenial spirit I have here, and I shall miss him very much. He is a great friend of Col Preston's and the latter wished him to take a place with increased rank in the

Conscription Bureau. I think he will take it. He has a wife and two children & has seen 3 years field service. He consulted me and I advised him to go. The truth is Genl. Lee doesn't make *our time pleasant here* & when promotion is offered his staff elsewhere, it is not to be wondered at if they accept the offer. Don't say anything of this as Venable has told no one else. As for my promotion, please don't expect it; for I shall feel badly if you think I should advance and I do not. I only care for it on your account but Genl. Lee will not push us up tho every body else goes. I have given over all expectation of being more than a Major—certainly as long as his say governs the matter.

I heard from Frank Huger a few days since. He had just received a letter from Fanny Kerr. Said she was well but not in good spirits. I don't wonder at it, she must have written about the time of Dr. Wright's execution. He tells me Fanny wishes to know if certain rumors regarding you and me are true. He seconded her in her request for information. I think my reply should have satisfied you. Tell Mrs. Jack Preston (that is if you choose) that when her husband applies for leave of absence I will be faithful to my promise & help him. His application the other day was to join Genl. Hampton under orders—that is on duty, & as Genl. H. was then en route to the army, it was not proper that *the Major* should go. My love to all at the Neck; to Pattie & Maria & Mrs Petty. Are my letters too long? Goodbye. God bless you. All is quiet now. Your W. I am glad to say there has been a change of opinion, as regards the person most responsible for the Bristoe Station misfortune. Genl. Heth is not so much blamed. I intended mentioning this before.

Walter

CONTRABAND HOSPITAL: WASHINGTON, D.C.,
NOVEMBER 1863

Cornelia Hancock to an Unknown Correspondent

Cornelia Hancock served as a nurse in army hospitals near Gettysburg until early September. After visiting family in Philadelphia and New Jersey, she went to Washington in late October and began working at the Contraband Hospital in northwest Washington.

———————

Contraband Hospital, Washington.
Nov. 15th, 1863.

I shall depict our wants in true but ardent words, hoping to affect you to some action. Here are gathered the sick from the contraband camps in the northern part of Washington. If I were to describe this hospital it would not be believed. North of Washington, in an open, muddy mire, are gathered all the colored people who have been made free by the progress of our Army. Sickness is inevitable, and to meet it these rude hospitals, only rough wooden barracks, are in use—a place where there is so much to be done you need not remain idle. We average here one birth per day, and have no baby clothes except as we wrap them up in an old piece of muslin, *that* even being scarce. Now the Army is advancing it is not uncommon to see from 40 to 50 arrivals in one day. They go at first to the Camp but many of them being *sick* from exhaustion soon come to us. They have nothing that any one in the North would call clothing. I always see them as soon as they arrive, as they come here to be vaccinated; about 25 a day are vaccinated. This hospital is the reservoir for all cripples, diseased, aged, wounded, infirm, from whatsoever cause; all accidents happening to colored people in all employs around Washington are brought here. It is not uncommon for a colored driver to be pounded nearly to death by some of the white soldiers. We had a dreadful case of Hernia brought in today. A woman was brought here with three children by her side; said she had been on the road for some time; a more forlorn, wornout looking creature I never beheld. Her four eldest children are still in Slavery, her husband is dead. When I first saw her she laid on the floor, leaning against a bed, her children crying around her. One child died almost immediately, the other two are still sick. She seemed to need most, food and rest, and those two comforts we gave her, but clothes she still wants. I think the women are more trouble than the men. One of the white guards called to me today and asked me if I got any pay. I told him no. He said he was going to be paid soon and he would give me 5 dollars. I do not know what was running through his mind as he made no other remark. I ask for clothing for women and children, both boys and girls. Two little boys, one 3 years old, had his leg amputated above the knee the cause being his mother not being allowed to ride inside, became dizzy and dropped him. The other had his leg broken from the same cause. This hospital consists of all the lame, halt, and blind escaped from slavery. We have a man & woman here without any feet theirs being frozen so they had to be amputated. Almost all have scars of some description and many have very weak eyes. There were two very fine looking slaves arrived here from Louisiana, one of them had his master's name branded on his forehead, and with him he brought all the instruments of torture that he wore at different times during 39 years of very hard slavery. I will try to send you a Photograph of him he wore an iron collar with 3 prongs standing up so he could not lay down his head; then a contrivance to render one leg entirely stiff and a chain clanking behind him with a bar weighing 50 lbs. This he wore and worked all the time hard. At night they hung a little bell upon the prongs above his head so that if he hid in any bushes it would tinkle and tell his whereabouts. The baton that was used to whip them he also had. It is so constructed that a little child could whip them till the blood streamed down their backs. This system of proceeding has been stopped in New Orleans and may God grant that it may cease all over this boasted free land, but you may readily imagine what development such a system of treatment would bring them to. With *this* class of beings, those who wish to do good to the contrabands must labor. Their standard of morality is very low.

A TRIP TO GETTYSBURG: PENNSYLVANIA,
NOVEMBER 1863

John Hay: Diary, November 18–19, 1863

In the immediate aftermath of the battle of Gettysburg, Union soldiers and local civilians hastily buried the bodies of about 7,000 men and burned the carcasses of more than 3,000 horses and mules. David Wills, a prominent Gettysburg lawyer, was appointed by Governor Andrew G. Curtin to arrange for the proper reburial of Pennsylvania's soldiers. In late July Wills proposed to Curtin that the Union dead be reburied in a new national cemetery at Gettysburg, a plan eventually supported by the seventeen northern states that had lost men in the battle. On November 2, Wills officially invited President Lincoln to the dedication ceremony and asked him to "formally set apart these grounds to their Sacred use by a few appropriate remarks." Lincoln was accompanied to Gettysburg by his secretary John Hay.

---

18 NOVEMBER 1863, WEDNESDAY

We started from Washington to go to the Consecration of the Soldiers' Cemetery at Gettysburg. On our train were the President Seward Usher & Blair: Nicolay & Myself: Mercier & Admiral Reynaud; Bertinatti & Capt. Isola & Lt. Martinez & Cora: Mrs Wise: Wayne McVeagh: McDougal of Canada and one or two others. We had a pleasant sort of a trip. At Baltimore Schenck's staff joined us.

Just before we arrived at Gettysburg the President got into a little talk with McVeagh about Missouri affairs. McV. talked radicalism until he learned that he was talking recklessly. The President disavowed any knowledge of the Edwards case, said that Bates said to him, as indeed he said to me, that Edwards was inefficient and must be removed for that reason.

At Gettysburg the President went to Mr. Wills who expected him and our party broke like a drop of quicksilver spilt. McVeagh young Stanton & I foraged around for a while—walked out to the College got a chafing dish of oysters then some supper and finally loafing around to the Court House where Lamon was holding a meeting of Marshals, we found

Forney and went around to his place Mr. Fahnestocks and drank a little whiskey with him. He had been drinking a good deal during the day and was getting to feel a little ugly and dangerous. He was particularly bitter on Montgomery Blair. McVeagh was telling him that he pitched into the Tycoon coming up and told him some truths. He said the President got a good deal of that from time to time and needed it.

He says "Hay you are a fortunate man. You have kept yourself aloof from your office. I know an old fellow now seventy who was Private Secretary to Madison. He has lived ever since on its recollection. He thought there was something solemn and memorable in it. Hay has laughed through his term."

He talked very strangely referring to the affectionate and loyal support which he and Curtin had given to the President in Pennsylvania: with references from himself and others to the favors that had been shown the Cameron party whom they regard as their natural enemies. Forney seems identified fully now with the Curtin interest, though when Curtin was nominated he called him a heavy weight to carry and said that Cameron's foolish attack nominated him.

We went out after a while following the music to hear the serenades. The President appeared at the door said half a dozen words meaning nothing & went in. Seward who was staying around the corner at Harper's was called out and spoke so indistinctly that I did not hear a word of what he was saying. Forney and McVeagh were still growling about Blair.

We went back to Forney's room having picked up Nicolay and drank more whiskey. Nicolay sung his little song of the "Three Thieves" and we then sung John Brown. At last we proposed that Forney should make a speech and two or three started out Shannon and Behan and Nicolay to get a band to serenade him. I staid with him. So did Stanton and McVeagh. He still growled quietly and I thought he was going to do something imprudent. He said if I speak, I will speak my mind. The music sounded in the street and the fuglers came rushing up imploring him to come down. He smiled quietly told them to keep cool and asked "are the recorders there." "I suppose so of course" shouted the fugler. "Ascertain" said the imperturbable Forney. "Hay, we'll take a drink." They shouted and begged him to come down The thing would be a failure—it would be his fault &c. "Are the recorders congenial?" he calmly insisted on knowing. Somebody commended prudence He said sternly "I am always prudent." I walked down stairs with him.

The crowd was large and clamorous. The fuglers stood by the door in an agony. The reporters squatted at a little stand in the entry. Forney stood on the Threshold, John Young & I by him. The crowd shouted as the door opened. Forney said "My friends, these are the first hearty cheers I have heard tonight. You gave no such cheers to your President down the street. Do you know what you owe to that Great man? You owe your country—you owe your name as American citizens."

He went on blackguarding the crowd for their apathy & then diverged to his own record saying he had been for Lincoln in his heart in 1860—that open advocacy was not as effectual as the course he took—dividing the most corrupt organization that ever existed—the proslavery Dem. Party. He dwelt at length on this question and then went back to the eulogy of the President that great, wonderful mysterious inexplicable man: who holds in his single hands the reins of the republic: who keeps his own counsels: who does his own purpose in his own way no matter what temporizing minister in his cabinet sets himself up in opposition to the progress of the age.

And very much of this.

After him Wayne McVeagh made a most touching and beautiful speech of five minutes and Judge Shannon of Pittsburg spoke effectively and acceptably to the people.

"That speech must not be written out yet" says Young. He will see further about it, when he gets sober," as we went up stairs. We sang John Brown and went home

In the morning I got a beast and rode out with the President's suite to the Cemetery in the procession. The procession formed itself in an orphanly sort of way & moved out with very little help from anybody & after a little delay Mr. Everett took his place on the stand—And Mr Stockton made a prayer which thought it was an oration—and Mr Everett spoke as he always does perfectly—and the President in a firm free way, with more grace than is his wont said his half dozen lines of consecration and the music wailed and we went home through crowded and cheering streets. And all the particulars are in the daily papers.

I met Genl. Cameron after coming in and he McV. and I went down to dinner on board the railroad U. C. R. R. car. I was more than usually struck by the intimate, jovial relations that exist between men that hate and detest each other as cordially as do those Pennsylvania politicians.

We came home the night of the 19th.

PENNSYLVANIA, NOVEMBER 1863

Abraham Lincoln: Address at Gettysburg

November 19, 1863

Lincoln delivered his dedicatory address to an audience of 15,000 to 20,000 people, following a two-hour oration by Edward Everett. The text printed here is his final version, prepared in the spring of 1864 for facsimile reproduction in *Autograph Leaves of Our Country's Authors*, a book published in Baltimore to raise funds for the U.S. Sanitary Commission. A report by the Associated Press, which may be closer to what Lincoln actually said at Gettysburg, is printed in the endnotes to this volume.

FOUR SCORE and seven years ago our fathers brought forth on this continent, a new nation, conceived in Liberty, and dedicated to the proposition that all men are created equal.

Now we are engaged in a great civil war, testing whether that nation, or any nation so conceived and so dedicated, can long endure. We are met on a great battle-field of that war. We have come to dedicate a portion of that field, as a final resting place for those who here gave their lives that that nation might live. It is altogether fitting and proper that we should do this.

But, in a larger sense, we can not dedicate—we can not consecrate—we can not hallow—this ground. The brave men, living and dead, who struggled here, have consecrated it, far above our poor power to add or detract. The world will little note, nor long remember what we say here, but it can never forget what they did here. It is for us the living, rather, to be dedicated here to the unfinished work which they who fought here have thus far so nobly advanced. It is rather for us to be here dedicated to the great task remaining before us—that from these honored dead we take increased devotion to that cause for which they gave the last full measure of devotion—that we here highly resolve that these dead shall not have died in vain—that this nation, under God, shall have a new birth of freedom—and that government of the people, by the people, for the people, shall not perish from the earth.

PROTESTING IMPRESSMENT: NORTH CAROLINA,
NOVEMBER 1863

Petition from the Colored Citizens of Beaufort

Former slaves living within the Union lines were often forced by the military to work for little or no pay. This petition was addressed to Major General Benjamin F. Butler, the commander of the Department of Virginia and North Carolina. It was signed by seventeen individuals whose names were followed by the notation "and fifty outher." There is no record that it ever received a reply.

Beaufort N. Carolina Nov 20th 1863

the undersigned Colored Citizens of the town of Beaufort in behaf of the Colord population of this Commuinty in view of the manner in which their Brotheren on oppressed by the military authurities in this Vicenity Respeckfuley pitision you are at the Head of this military Department for a redress of grievunces

Your politiness disire to make known to you that they and there brothern to the President of the United States are undiscriminatly inpressed by the authorities to labor upon the Public woorks without compensation   that in Consequence of this System of fource labor they Have no means of paying Rents and otherwise Providing for ther families

Your pitisioners disire futher to Express ther Entire Willingness to Contribute to the Cause of the union in anyway consistant with there cause as Freemen and the Rights of their families

Anything that can Be don By You to relieve us from the Burden which wee are nou Labooring will Be Highly appriciated By Your Pitistiorers

And your pititioners Will Ever pray   Yours Respeckfully & Soforth

BATTLE OF CHATTANOOGA: TENNESSEE,
NOVEMBER 1863

William Wrenshall Smith: Journal, November 13–25, 1863

On October 18 Grant met with Secretary of War Stanton in Indianapolis and received orders appointing him commander of the new Military Division of the Mississippi, covering almost all of the territory from the Allegheny Mountains to the Mississippi. Grant promptly replaced Rosecrans as commander of the Army of the Cumberland with George H. Thomas, named Sherman as the new commander of the Army of the Tennessee, and then headed for Chattanooga. He arrived there on October 23 after riding over the only route still open into the besieged town, a narrow, muddy wagon road through the mountains north of the Tennessee River. By October 30 Union troops had opened the "Cracker Line," a new supply route that cut across a sharp bend in the river west of Chattanooga. In early November Bragg sent 15,000 men under Longstreet to attack Ambrose Burnside's Army of the Ohio at Knoxville. While Longstreet besieged Knoxville, Grant awaited the arrival at Chattanooga of Sherman and four divisions of the Army of the Tennessee. William Wrenshall Smith, a successful businessman from Washington, Pennsylvania, was a first cousin of Grant's wife, Julia Dent Grant. Wishing to "see a *battle*," Smith traveled by train to Bridgeport, Alabama, then took a steamer up the Tennessee to Kelley's Ferry at the western end of the "Cracker Line."

Friday, Nov. 13 When we awake about 4 oclock this morning (a little before daylight) find we are as far as the Boat goes—Kellie's Ferry—as the enemy have possession of the river above. Get baggage out on bank about daylight and by the kindness of the Mate—(a Pittsburgh Irishman, and a relation of Quails) and the Captain of the Boat—I find a place to wash—and get a tin of Coffee, and some bread and meat—Gen Starkweather says he will take my baggage with his to Chattanooga and, as the Gen's Horses dont come, we all start on foot.

Camps now become plentyer—all I beleave, of Hookers troops. The road was now one continuous stream of wagons. We soon got under the famous Look out moutain and within range of thire cannon and every moment expected a shot from the enemy, but we passed clear to Chattanooga, and over two pon-toon bridges, without any interuption. We all sat down on the bank at this (South) end of the Pontoon Bridge, and waited for some time—From the immense quantity of wagons on the other side, awaiting their turns to pass over, ours would have to be delayed some time—so we seperated—Starkweather and his party going down the river to their camps, and I—north to the town, alone—

When on the principal street I asked an officer for Grant's Head Quarters, and following his direction I soon found it in a neat little white frame house overlooking the river. No one at home but servants, and I wash myself in "the Doctors" room. After waiting some time (½ hour) on the porch Gen Rawlins comes in—recognises me—and gives me a hearty welcome. While talking on the front porch, Lagow dismounts & immediately takes possession of me, and insists on my taking up my quarter in his room—which is opposite the General's.

In a short time the General arrives. He greets me cordially, and takes me into his room. He puts his quarters and horses at my disposal and makes me feel altogether comfortable.

We have a long talk. He tells me all about his children, about his purchases since he has been in the army—his saving all the money he could for the future, not knowing when his fortunes might change, and he be thrown out of his office—Besides buying the ground and beautiful English Villa in which he lived when I was visiting him 5 years ago in Missouri, from Fred Dent,—he has invested five thousand Dollars in U.S. 5/20's; He now wants to buy five thousand Dollars worth of Chicago city Passenger Rail Way Stock, and concludes to send his note for that amount—with the U.S. 5/20's as collateral—for discount, to secure the stock. We have a long pleasant talk till Dinner—which is at 6 oclock. The dinner is very plain—consisting of Roast Beef, Boiled Potatoes, Bread and Butter. The mess consists of the General Dr. Kittoe, Col Lagow, Capt Hudson and (now is added) myself. The General at the head of the table does the carving. None of my baggage has yet arrived. Gen Starkweather promised to send it as soon as his wagons should get to his camp. I am fearful the Gen's bottle of wine will be confiscated.

After Dinner, a little after dark, Col. Lagow, Capt. Hudson and myself start on horse back and see some of Lagow's friends —Dr. & Capt. somebody—who are pretty lively larks. Poker and Cold punch fills in the time. I don't join in the play. Get home about eleven oclock and get to playing Eucre. The General comes in and looks over my hand for half an hour and remarks on my playing.

Saturday Nov. 14. 1863. There was a little rain this morning which made the road too slippery for horses; so we stay at home all day. I send an orderly with a note to Gen Starkweather for my baggage this afternoon. He sends it all but my shawl and a box of segars, both of which were stolen from the wagons, when they crossed the ferry last night. The Gen is pleased to get his bottle of wine. A good many General officers with the General. The Head Quarters are very quiet, as much so as a private house. Quite a disgraceful party—friends of Col Lagow, stay up nearly all night playing &c. The Gen breaks up the party himself about 4 oclock in the morning.

Sunday Nov. 15. The horses are to-day sent to Kellie's ferry for General Hunter—who has been ordered here from Washington to inspect the army. An inspection, Grant, says is imposseble as the men are on more important duty—principally making roads. Dead horses and mules are very plenty. Gen Rawlins gives us readings this afternoon—among other things the evening service. He has a fine strong voice.

Lt. Col. Duff, and Lt.s Towner and Dunn are churchmen. Dr. Kittoe also is a Churchman. But all religion is lost in the army. Lagow don't come to table to-day. He is greatly mortified at his conduct last night. Grant is much offended at him and I am fearful it will result in his removal.

Gen Hunter is the guest of the General, and is to stay in his room. Capt. Ross' cot is moved in for him. The cot breaks down and sets him onto the floor—and the Gen. gives up his bed to him & is compelled to "bunk" with Dr Kittoe

Monday Nov. 16. This morning quite a number of General officers at Head quarters. I was standing in front of quarters as they come out to mount and Grant called to me to get Capt

Hudson's horse and ride with him. Hudson's horse was soon out and I follow just in time to get to the boat (rope ferry) as it was about pushing off. Grant stopped it till I got my horse on. The Boat was crowded and we had some dificulty in making the northern shore. The party was Gen's. Grant, Thomas, Sherman, Smith, Hunter, Reynolds, Branen, Rawlins, Lt. Col. Duff and myself, with three orderlies. After riding up the river less than a mile we turned up the hill to the left into the woods perhaps a mile more where our horses were left behind the hill & we all walked to the edge of the woods overlooking the river and the country beyond all of which was held by the enemy. The field glasses of the Generals closely examined Missionary Ridge & the country this side After about half an hour remounted and went up the river still further to the place selected for the Pontoon bridge to be built. Gens Sherman and Smith went out to examine with their glasses while the balance of the party remained behind the woods. Grant was in a fine humor, and as he leaned against the fence, was telling us about the former great speculations in Real Estate in Chicago and Millwaukee When Gens Smith and Sherman came back, Smith asked Grant if he would walk down and see the spot they had selected for the bridge. We could see them as they picked their way over the rather wide bottom between the wooded hill and the river bank, and thought they were getting too near the rifles of the pickets on the other side.

They come back in about half an hour, when Grant immediately mounts and I with him & we ride rapidly back leaving the others behind. After riding for some time I find that Gen Hunter & Col Duff are the only ones of the party who are in sight. Grant told me about his boys at school—he is very proud of them and fond of talking of them. He also tells me of Col. Hillyer, who after leaving him went to N.Y. and is now doing finely at his profession—the Law The hills we have been traveling over to-day appear to be composed of a porous, (like pomice stone) rock which make the roads over it excellent. I say to Grant I think the hill country is worthless for agricultural purposes, but he says it is the finest country for grapes he has seen.

Gen Hunter and Col Duff overtake us at a farm house on top of the hill, where we commence to descend to the river bottom, and we all stop and get a drink of water without dismounting. As we pass the ferry, find the Boat on the other side and we ride very rapidly to the Pontoon Bridge, but find it broken—by a raft—so we ride back more slowly to the ferry again,—where we find the balance of our party. The enemy are continually sending down large rafts to destroy the Pontoon bridges. But most of them are caught and hauled in by the troops for fire-wood, which is exceedingly scarce. While riding back to the ferry Grant & Hunter were telling stories of old army acquaintenses some of which were very rich and were hugely enjoyed. Grant is in high spirits—and tells a story admirably. In general he is extreemly reserved, but with one or two friends he is very entertaining and agreeable.

As we are coming over on the Boat my horse (Hudsons) insists on drinking a great deal of the clear, cold water of the river. As we get off the boat he rears with me, running me against a pile of amunition boxes and almost against the wheel of a big army waggon. I get off however with only some slight scrapes on my leg.—We have lunch at about 3 oclock, after which go out on Rosses horse with Gen Grant, Hunter, Capt Hudson and others to see the fortifications on this side of the river—From fort Wood we go to an eminence south west of the town, under Lookout Mountain. While there the enemy must have been attracted by so large a party on horseback, for a shell from Lookout no doubt fired at us, exploded midway in the air.

Get back in time for a good dinner. After dark go with Lagow to a meeting of Indiana officers. A large room is crowded by them and as I soon see it is a business meeting I go out on the porch and listen to a fine band playing in the yard. After the meeting every body fell to playing Eucre &c. (I noticed four Generals who had monopolised one table.) We did not stay long, but after a few games with some very clever fellows, went home.

Tuesday Nov. 17, 1863. There is such a dense fog today that we cannot go out. Think of home—and the little Church, which is being consecrated to-day, and console myself by reading the consecration service. Amuse myself by writing and talking to some of the Staff officers. The General has a great many General officers and others to see him on business. At dinner Gen Hunter who is a great Puritan remarked that Card playing was very prevelent in the camps. Grant says he thinks it the best possible amusement the troops can have.

Wednesday Nov. 18, 1863. The 79th Penna Band serenade the General this evening. He comes out on the porch, and when they are through, takes off his hat to them, and without saying a word, walks into his room again.

He is very anxious about Burnsides, and is up every night till 12 and 2 o'clock—writing and sending off dispatches.

Thursday Nov. 19. The General had ordered the horses and we were about mounting when despatches are received from Burnsides—so the General can't go, and we order the horses back—and I spend the morning on the knob or promentory overhaging the river and about the ruined Iron works— reading and throwing stones into the river. The mouth of a great cave is said to be just under me. When I first came here this hill was covered with very large cedar trees—they have now disappeared—stumps and all—for fire wood. There is a good deal of stir about Head Quarter to-day It sounds like business. Gen John E. Smith of Sherman's Army here this afternoon. He looks rough and tired. Capts. Hudson and Ross ride with me about the works and camps. Every thing about them looks very clean and comfortable.

Friday Nov. 20. Cloudy to-day. The General has a good many in this room to-day among whom I notice Gen's Hooker, Howard &c. Business is lively about Head Quarters. The Steamer "Dunbar" which is being fast completed just under the bank below our quarters has her boilers protected by piles of cotton bales. Numbers of pontoon boats are being made every day under cover of the bank and disappear during the night.

Capt. Ross, who to-day, takes charge of the mess—("runing the mess" they call it) expects to have a grand dinner and has invited several guests. As the lunch don't come on at the usual hour we commence complaining, and he informs us he don't intend to have any as Dinner to-day is to be at 4 o'clock. As the hunger of the party increases their complaints grow louder, till Ross, at last, has to order lunch at 3 oclock

At 5 oclock we have Dinner. Besides our own party we have Gen's Meigs, Gen Wilson and Mr. Dana (of the warr office).

Ross don't provide enough plates, and Lagow and Hudson have to retire to curse Ross in private. The General adds further to Ross' discomfort by saying that he had lunch so late and dinner so early that he has no appetite. The guests however enjoy there dinner and we do the talking.

Among other things the General says Bragg sent him word by flag of truce this afternoon, advising him to remove all noncombatants from Chattanooga within forty-eight hours. The Gen. says he did not answer it, but will when Sherman gets up. We have several jokes and laughs over it.

Gen Hooker and Howard here agan to-day

Saturday Nov. 21. As it is a pretty day I ask Gen Hunter to ride with me to Gen A Baird's quarters. He is a Washington man and Gen Hunter is acquainted with him. So after lunch Hunter on the Gen's Celebrated Yellow Stallion, "Jack" (which horse he has monopolized) and myself on Capt Ross' horse, start for a short ride. We find Baird's quarters in a pretty little one-story cottage in the south western part of the town. I introduce myself to the General who immediately recognises me, and asks about our family, and his relations and acquantenses in "little" Washington. He had quite a talk with Gen Hunter explaining with a chart his part in the unfortunate battle of Chikamauga. He is also very attentive to me, and when we are going away repeatedly presses me to come and see him often. I speak to him about getting John Acheson transferred to his staff.

Sunday Nov. 22. Capt. Ross and I ride to Fort Wood and have a look at the enemy. The picket line is about a quarter of a mile in front of us and we can planly see their pickets. This side of Missionary ridge is white with the tents of the Confederates. We hold but a little space on the south side of the river about Chattanooga. In the fort I meet and shake hands with Gen. Baird who again asks me to call on him. Lt's Towner and Duff are doing a great deal of riding on duty—Gen Wilson is also very active, being nearly always on horseback—

Read the Church service in our room. Shermans men are being hurried to their concealed camps on the other side of the river.

Monday Nov. 23. 1863 This morning is cloudy. The heavy guns at Fort Wood keep up quite a regular fire on the

Confederate camps. The battle was to have commenced this morning; but Sherman is not quite ready. Spend the Morning at Fort Wood looking at the fireing. At one o'clock the General tells me to take the elegant brown horse presented to him by Gen. Meigs and ride with him. We go in company with Gen Hunter and others, to fort Wood. Gen Thomas and quite a number of General and Staff officers are there, and it looks very much like business. We sit about on the sand bags, smoking and amuse ourselves looking at the bursting of our shells— when they *do* burst.

About half past two Gen Thomas' troops move out in front of us, as if in review. "By Heaven, tis a splendid sight to see, For one who hath no friend, no brother there." The enemy from Missionary-ridge and the near rifle pits look at the show—supposing no doubt it is a review. At about 2½ oclock a long line of battle is formed more than a mile in length and just in front of us. The skirmishers move forward, and then, the whole line advances. As our skirmishers come near the enemys pickets, we see, distinctly, their rifles aimed, and the smoke, followed by the reports. It is like a piece of machenary —Then, in a few minutes, the long line become engaged in the woods and I for the first time hear the heavy roll of musketry. The enemy are driven from their first line of rifle pits and our troops get possession of the rising ground more than a half way to Missionary ridge—No sooner had our men possession of the woods than our wagons and wood-choppers were busy cutting fire-wood and hauling it into camp. Thy wagons & woodchopers were in the woods when the battle commenced

Several squads of prisoners are brought in—in one lot about a hundred. At the very first of the engagement I heard two bullets whistle by my head. About four oclock we go back to our quarters—the General being well pleased at what had been accomplished. He seems perfectly cool, and one could be with him for hours, and not know that any great movements were going on. Its a mere matter of business with him.

While we are at Dinner this evening the cannon fireing increeses, and the explosions shake the windows. Our mess eat their dinner, and talk, as though they were a thousand miles away from what is likely to be one of the greatest battle fields of the war. The firing continues till dark. I spend the evening with Col Lagow, Capt Hudson, Capt Ross, Maj Rowley, Lt Dunn and others. Cadwallader, the correspondent of the Chicago *Times*, amuses us by relating some hair-breadth escapes he made on the field this after-noon. The ten Gal. is nerely out.

Tuesday Nov. 24. 1863. A damp, drizzly, cold day. I wear my "poncho" most of the morning. After Breakfast—about 7½ oclock—The General sends Cap Ross, Hudson and myself to Fort Wood, with orders to stay there, and report to him any thing of interest. About 2 hours later we see him with Gen Thomas and two or three others riding under the fort to "the front," which is now about a mile from us. We hear that Sherman had succeeded in crossing two thousand troops, by day light, on pontoon bridges made during the night, and we can see his troops taking possession of the north end of Missionary Ridge with but little opposition. During the day one of the most beautiful sights that can be imagined, gives us for a little while some extra excitemt. The beautiful Tenn. river is in view for perhaps 2 miles above us, from Ft. Wood Looking up, a single pontoon boat, filled with men, their bright bayonets bristling in the light, came in sight.—then two or three, then a dosen, then the whole river swarmed with them—all quietly and calmly floating down to-wards us.

About noon as Capts. Parker, Hudson, Ross & myself are standing on the front of the fort talking and wondering why it was so quiet on the left and front—suddenly broke out on the other side of Lookout Mountain, and on either side of the river below us, the fiercest and most tremendeous roars of both cannon and musketry, I ever conceived of. We were fearful that Bragg had precipitated a tremendeous force on Hooker, and was anniheleting him. As the General was to the left and fearing he could not, from his position hear what was going on, we dispatched both Ross and Hudson after him. In about ½ an hour we could see Grant and three or four more riding leisurely to-wards the fort, smoking and appearing more like a farmer out looking at Stock, than a general in a battle. Supposing the General would ride to our right, where this tremendeous attack was being made, I mounted my "Brown" and rode about 5 hundred yards to the bridge over the R.R. to meet him, but looking back at the fort saw him quietly dismounting. So I ride back again and did likewise. The Signal men put their glasses on Lookout, and announced the progress of Hookers forces, as they scaled the mountain, slowly driving the enemy before them. The roar of cannon and the volleys of musketry were made more terrific by the reverberation along the steep, high ridges of the mountains.

As the enemy were driven above the thick mist in which the top of Lookout was enveloped, Grant wrote orders for troops to be sent up the valley to cut off the retreat. As none of the staff, but myself, were about him at the time, I furnshed him the paper and pencil. He wrote on one knee while he knelt, on the ground, with the other. Our successes are reported along the lines of the centre and left, and we hear the loud cheers of the men as they rolled from the right to the left.

At night, from the porch of our quarters, we have a most beautiful view of Lookout. Our camp fires skirt the mountain two thirds of the way up. We stay on the porch most of the evening looking at the beautiful scene—Camp fires and flashes of musketry—till about midnight. The musketry firing, the General says, is extra work—not in the programme. The Gen. says they will evacuate the mountain to night. Many a poor fellow, who this morning, was full of life and health and hope, is, to-night, lying among the crags and bushes of Lookout, cold in death.

> There shall they rot, ambitions honor'd fools
> In these behold the tools—the broken tools
> That Tyrants cast away by myriads

So I went to sleep to dream of the roar of cannon the rattle of musketry and the tramp of charging squadrons

Wednesday, Nov. 25. 63. A beautiful clear cold day. We find the enemy evacuated Lookout during the night and our flag this morning flouts from its top. After breakfast we all go to Fort Wood. (The General gives me his Bay horse today and he rides the Brown) Generals Grant & Hunter and myself were riding to-gether. As we passed a part of the Anderson troop encamped immediately in the rear of Gen Thomases quarter, I remarked to the Gen. that part of the regiment had been recruted in Western Penna. as a body Guard for Anderson and afterwards Buell. Hunter said that Fremont had run the escort or body Guard so much into the ground that it was now looked on as a want of sense to have one, and remarked that if Fremont had had charge of the war, the rebellion would have been a success in 6 months after it started. To which Grant agreed.

After we had been at the Fort some time and as every thing appears to be quiet Lagow and I ride back to quarters for a drink. We stay'd but a few minutes and rode immediately back to the fort but found the General gone. About 11 oclock Sherman became heavely engaged on the extreeme left—every inch of his attempted progress along the ridge being severly contested. About 11 ½ oclock I ride back again, alone, and ordered "Bill," the General's nigger, to get lunch for me and to put up in a haversack enough for the General and five or six others. While "Bill" is getting the lunch ready I bathe myself and put on a clean shirt.

In less than half an hour I was back to Fort Wood, and found General Hunter mounted, and about starting for Orchard Knob, about a mile to the front, where he had sent us word to meet him. Just as we get under the fort one of the big guns is fired over our heads. The sudden and tremendeous report frightens, for a moment, my horse. He gave a sudden spring to one side but I kept my saddle firmly. We pass quite a body of troops in the valley. Suppose them to be Baird's. We go through the woods a little distance, and soon get to the fort of the stony knob on this side of which are a great many officers' horses, and quite a number of troops, ambulances &c I gave my horse to Bradford, one of the General's orderlies, and climbed to the top of the Knob.

We found Grant, Thomas, and several other General Officers and their staffs. The wind blew quite cold, and our overcoats were very comfortable. We are now in the front of the centre. The top of Missionary Ridge is not more than a mile from us by an air line, and the enemy's rifle pits are immediately below or under us, within musket shot. We can see there troops on the road on top of the ridge. Generals and there staffs ride along the top of the ridge and look down on us, as from the third tier of a Theater, and our batteries a mile back of us are throwing shell over our heads at them. I thought it a dangerous place. It is to me astonishing they did not shell us. General Thomas, remarked to Grant, that if the enemy had known who were there, they would have paid us more attention All this time Sherman is attempting to drive them from his end of the ridge and the enemy's whole attention seems to be drawn to him. His troops have been twice repulsed. We can see them advancing across a large open field on the side of the ridge and twice are they driven back with great loss. The cannonaiding and musketry in that quarter is terriffic and is kept up without intermission. All this time the centre and right is quiet. But they are not idle. Heavy bodies of troops, (Gen. Baird's is part of them) are coming up behind and on either side of us, and taking positions. Sherman gets his signal station in sight and the signaling from our quarter to his, commences.

After two oclock Grant asks me if I have anything to eat— and we go down under the hill sit down on a log near a fire and open the lunch which is divided between the General, Gen. Hunter, Dr Kittoe and myself. They were all hungry and enjoyed the lunch. The General tills us he this morning got a dispatch from the President Thanking him for what had been done the two previous days. After smoking and talking pleasantly for half an hour more we go again to the top of the Knoll.

I think it was about half past three when the General gave the orders to fire the six guns which are planted on the Knoll (They were placed here night before last). It was the signal for the storming of the enemies rifle pits along the whole centre. Such an immence roar I never conceived of. All our guns together with those of the enemy all along Missionary Ridge seemed to open up at once. Our stormers moved forward at the rifle pits of the enemy as if they knew they were going to succeed. The roll of musketry from our lines (about two miles in length) and the reply from the enemies rifle pits near the foot of the ridge, was terrific. As our men charged, the Graybacks broke from behind their protection and up the hill, our men following with chear upon chear and the cannon and musketry on top of the hill pouring shot and shell upon them. Regiment after regiment gained the top and planted their colors —most of them gaining it by the many roads that passed from the valley to the top of the ridge.

As the matter is about decided and expecting to have a long

ride in persuit I mount my horse and fly into town,—fill my flask and get back again to near the Knoll, within about a quarter of an hour,—when I catch up to Maj Rowley who is on his way out. We find the General and his party have just left for the Ridge and, we follow. In the valley just under, where we have been standing, we pass many dead & wounded men. Some of the wounded supported by others that are not so badly wounded. It was a horrible sight, but I, expecting it, was not so much shocked as would be supposed.

We got to the top of the ridge by a very rough road, impasable for any thing but horses and men On the top are several captured cannon, and a great many of our troops, resting, drawn up to repell any attempt to retake the heights. The further we get to the north part of the Ridge, the more loud and sharp is the musketry. It seems one continuous roll. Some poor fellows lying on the road, badly wounded—we stop and give some whiskey. We directly meet the General and party, who are returning, as it is now near dark. I ride home with General Hunter The enemy are routed on all hands, and to-morrow, we expect a big ride after them. The General calls to me and says I was very lucky to be here, as "it wasn't in half a dozen life times one could see so much of a battle with comparatively so little danger." He praised General Baird as a "*fine* officer."

We got back in time to have dinner about an hour and a half after dark. Lt. Towner was wounded when only about a hundred yards from the General, on his way back for amunition for some of the captured cannon. The shot knocked him from his horse—but he is not dangerous. The General orders an ambulance to be got ready in the morning with provetions for the staff for three days, and also a suficent guard for it. As Capt. Ross and Maj Rowley are ordered to Sherman for his report, I go over with Col Lagow and spend an hour with Capt. Janes—the Staff Comasserry. As we walk home we see Missionary Ridge illuminated by the camp-fires of our men.

"WILD WITH EXCITEMENT": TENNESSEE,
NOVEMBER 1863

Montgomery C. Meigs: Journal, November 23–25, 1863

Brigadier General Montgomery Meigs had served as quartermaster general of the Union army since May 1861. He had arrived in Chattanooga on September 25 while on an inspection tour of supply depots and remained there for much of the siege, advising Rosecrans and then Grant on logistical matters while sending regular reports to Stanton on the overall situation. Meigs would draw on his journal of the battle in preparing a shorter account that he sent to Stanton on November 26. Widely printed in northern newspapers, it would become famous for reporting that the battle for Lookout Mountain "was fought among the clouds."

JOURNAL OF THE BATTLE OF CHATTANOOGA
Nov. 23d. 24th & 25. 1863.

At noon November 23rd 1863 a demonstration ordered to develope the enemy on Mission Ridge.

Rode to Fort Wood with Grants Head Quarters.

At 2 P.M. skirmishers opened on the rebel pickets all along the line, and drove them in with sharp interchange of musketry.

Our troops advanced steadily in line of battle, and drove the rebels from a long line of rifle-pits, and crowned "Orchard Knob" and the low ridge to the right of it, and formed on that front.

Some two hundred prisoners, I judge, were brought in, some men of course were wounded and some, I fear, killed, though no reports have come in.

Two Alabamians were the first brought in, very much excited and very stupid. Did not know the name of their Brigade Commanders, but said Hindman's Division, to which they belonged were all here.

At 3½ P.M. Gen. Grant was back in his quarters, writing his despatches.

The Artillery firing from Fort Wood continues—shelling, I suppose the rebel Camps and works on Mission Ridge, and endeavoring to prevent any massing against our troops in the advance.

General Thomas reports to night 169 prisoners, Alabamians, our loss not yet reported.

Bridges both broken "Dunbar" ferrying at Chattanooga—Mule Boat at Brown's Ferry—Woods Division still waiting to cross at Brown's Ferry.

> Fort Wood Chattanooga
> 24th November 1863. A.M.

Dropping fire among the pickets in front—Troops resting on their arms since daylight—since I have been here.

Visited the lines and watched the battle from various parts of the field. The principal fighting to day was on the nose of Lookout Mountain which General Hooker carried—He rests to the left of the White House holding the cleared ground.

His Camp fires show to night, and picket firing continues. General Sherman crossed above us, and is established on the south side of the River—expects to carry point of Mission Ridge before he rests for the night.

Howard moved up South Bank of the River and effected a junction with Sherman and returned, leaving him a Brigade and posting another half way. The Dunbar towed up two flats and crossed some 6000 troops during the day. She has been of essential service. Granger, Sheridan and Baird rested in the position seized and fortified yesterday.

The enemy has not to us shown himself in force, except on Lookout, where he resisted Hooker and stood at last checking his advance. His wagons were seen coming down the Summertown Road which looks like abandoning the Mountain.

Letters from my wife and children by Mr. Freas the Carpenter, who arrived during the day.

11 P.M. Point of Lookout Mt. and the N. E. Hill of Mission Ridge are ablaze with Camp fires of Hooker and Sherman. Rest of both Ridges dark. Bright moonlight—clear North

wind—General attack or advance ordered for daybreak. Picket firing seems to have ceased—Rebels have probably evacuated.

And now to bed—I have just returned from Gen. Grant's, Granger will, if the rebels have run, march to-morrow with 20,000 men to relieve Burnside beseiged in Knoxville. Steamer "Paint Rock" will follow him with provisions.

Chattanooga 25th Nov. 1863
Woods Fort 7. A.M.

Sun appeared just above Mission Ridge—Large bodies of troops moving to our left along the summit gaining a position on the high point.

American flag waving from the top of the rock at N. E. end of Lookout Mt. Our troops apparently in possession—no firing.

Clear beautiful morning, smoke and mist hang in the valleys summit clear.

We shall have a battle on Mission Ridge.

Gen. Howard with whom I rode to Woods redoubt parted with me there, and I remained until Mr. C. A. Dana, Asst. Secy. War came up and proposed that we should pay Granger's Head Quarters a visit.

I told him I was waiting for Genl. Grant, near whom I wished to be during the day. But concluding that we could ride to "Orchard Knob" and return by the time any serious movement would be made—I consented to visit Granger.

We found Gen. Wood—Granger was visiting his lines—Gave him the information that the flag waved on Lookout Crest (From wounded prisoner I have since learned that Stevenson evacuated the Mountain about 1 A.M. the night previous.) This was good news to him—Hooker had orders to move to join in a general advance upon the rebel lines.

We rode to the "Orchard Knob" henceforth historical, and there remained 'till Gen. Grant was seen approaching. The first salutation I had on the Knob was from a Rifled piece—a 10 pdr. on the summit of Mission Ridge opposite, which sent a shell whizzing, exploding and sputtering, and dropping its butt into a hole some fifteen feet in front of the group of Gen. W. F. Smith, Major Dana and myself—An officer who saw it fall, I was not looking up being occupied in reading some letters from home, picked it up and handed it to me.

A battery of these 10 pdrs. rifled fired at the "Knob" all day. Head Quarters remained there 'till about 4 P.M., and every few minutes throughout the day, a shell whizzed past the Knob on which stood Generals Grant, Thomas, Granger, Wood, W. F. Smith, Rawlings myself and a crowd of officers of the Staff. No one was hit near us, however, and it was not until Mission Ridge or part of it was carried that any officer of General Grant's Staff was hit. Lt. Towner, when dispatched at my request that some officer should be sent back to bring up artillerists to work against the enemy some of the guns captured on the Heights was shot through the back of the neck and shoulder within a minute after leaving us to execute the order—All others escaped.

The day wore on—cannonade at Sherman's position fortified on the left Knobs of Mission Ridge, and much musketry continued, Orchard Knob replied to the guns on the Ridge, other Batteries to the right joined in the chorus. Woods redoubt with its 30 pdr Parrotts and its $4\frac{1}{2}''$ guns sent shell screaming over us towards the guns on Mission Ridge— Occasionally guns to the right and left of our front on Mission Ridge would open but the only rifled guns seemed to be those directly in front of us, and they alone had range to reach us, and they fired at intervals all day, and we were the conspicuous mark. Occasionally they would drop a shell into our picket, or rather skirmish line, which advanced early in the day, and drove in the rebel pickets.

The day wore away, I was impatient at the delay—night was approaching, and so might be Longstreet, recalled from Burnsides front at Knoxville.

A cannonade at Rossville Gap at last opened, It was of short duration. It was Hooker who had descended the Lookout Mountain and crossed the valley and attacked two Regiments and a section of Artillery guarding the pass. A wagon train loading with flour and the troops and Artillery escaped him and the sound died away.

A line was seen deployed in a cleared field on Sherman's right—a blue line which went steadily up the steep ascent.

Soon another followed in support. How gallant an assault, It is impossible for them to succeed were the exclamations. I watched them with my telescope, an excellent one, saw them pass the fence at the upper edge of the field, enter the oak woods, climb to the edge of the crest of the hill, whose profile is thus: and stop A sputtering musketry fire broke out. The men sought shelter from the deadly fire of the log breast-work above them. I saw the reserve brought up to resist the assault, filling the terrepleine of the entrenchment with a mass of gray. I saw officers leaping into the air and waving their swords urging and calling their rebel soldiers to the front. I saw the reserve fall back again out of fire.

I saw a great body of troops move from a Camp between our front and Sherman and pass steadily along the ride to assist in repelling the assault. I saw the men again urged forward slowly, step, first a few, then more, then the whole body over the breast-works, and advance pouring their fire into our men, who stood fast and returned it.

Then the rebels nearer to us advanced and taking our men crowded under shelter of the hills in flank, poured into them a murderous fire, and the right flank of the group dissolved, and the open field below was filled with men running down the hill. The rebels cast stones from their rifle pits into our men thus wounding some, so near were the two hostile bodies during the half hour or hour that they thus stood in deadly array before the rebel charge.

Our men at last gave way, and fled down the hill and through the field in confusion.

Colonel Putnam, Commanding an Illinois Regiment whom I had noticed, riding a brown horse, leading his men up the slope, difficult for a horse to climb, was shot through the head. A Major who gallantly urged a black charger up the hill, escaped the storm unhurt.

General Grant repeated his order for a general advance, now making it an order that all the troops in sight should advance, drive back the rebel pickets and following them closely, run them into and over their breast-works, which solidly constructed of logs and earth, extended in nearly continuous lines for two miles along the base of the Ridge.

The troops were impatient for work. They were formed; a

strong line of skirmishers, a line of battle deployed behind them:—the signal six cannon shots from "Orchard Knob" was given and forward they sprang with a cheer. With a quick step not a run, they crossed the space between us and the breastworks. The rebels fired a volley, our men fired at will, and the rebels swarming out of the rifle-pits covered the lower slopes behind them turned to look at our advance and firing a few shots, again turned and swarmed up the steep roads, which, by oblique ascents led to the summit.

Mission Ridge is 500 feet high its sides nearly denuded of timber cut for Camp fires but still with many oaks upon the slopes.

The order was to form on our side of the breast-works, and then send a regiment or two to wheel to the right and sweep the rebels out of their works and capture as many as possible.

Every gun on Mission Ridge broke out with shell and shrapnell upon the heads of our gallant troops, who never halted till they reached the breastworks.

Most of them halted there; but the colors of three Regiments pushed on and up the slopes of a projecting spur, too steep to be seen from the summit. Mission Ridge is here five hundred feet in height. Slowly the three red silken flags ascended and the regiments swarmed up after them.

General Grant said it was contrary to orders, it was not his plan—he meant to form the lines and then prepare and launch columns of assault, but, as the men; carried away by their enthusiasm had gone so far, he would not order them back.

Presently he gave the order for the whole line, now well formed to advance and storm the ridge. It extended some two miles in length, and it pressed forward with cheers. Shot and shell and cannister poured into it right and left, our guns, 10 pdr rifles, on "Orchard Knob" responded firing into the batteries, exploding a caisson, and disturbing the gunners.

The line ceased to be a line. The men gathered towards the points of least difficult ascent, for very steep is this hill-side, a horse cannot ascend or descend except by the obliquely graded roads. The three colors approach the summit, another mass, gathered gradually into a confused column or stream, at another point directly, in our front, reaches the summit, the color bearer springs forward and plants his flag upon the crest, a gun gallops wildly to the right, cheer upon cheer rings out from actors and spectators. The men swarm up, color after color reaches the summit, and the rebel line is divided and the confused, astonished and terrified rebels fly this way and that to meet enemies, every way but down the rear slope of the ridge and by this open way they mostly escape.

Bragg whose Head Quarters are in a house in plain sight to the right of our front, astonished at our success leaves the house, passing from the porch through and out the back door, mounts his horse and rides down the hill-side. Our men then crowned the summit, and had they known it, could by a volley, have put an end to this traitors career, as he fled down the road.

Still, between Sherman and Baird, whose division made the left assault, remained a mile of fortified ridge, held by the rebels. Fierce musketry broke out on the summit, for the "unpainted house" guns still blazed each way and Gen. Grant determined to go to the summit, and see that proper order was restored.

I rode with him, soon found three brass pieces, a limber and caisson; but no lanyard and no artillery-men—the cartridges near the piece piled at its wheel were round shot—I directed some of the men lying down behind the rebel breastwork looking to see Bairds line formed across the ridge and hotly engaged give way, while still from the right, at the unpainted house, the cannon blazed,—to bring the limber and caissons behind the breastworks, had the chests examined, found friction tubes and shell, but no lanyard with which to discharge them. An ordnance officer heard me asking for primers and said he had some in his saddle bags. He always carried them and sometimes found them very useful.

The suspension hook from my own and a Captains swordbelt, we wrenched off for hooks, a piece of bed cord, which I found on the ground, completed the Lanyard, and the guns were turned into a battery and ready for use. Gen. Baird spoke to me. I asked Gen. Grant to send back for artillerists and lanyards, and he sent Lt. Towner, who was wounded as he left us.

Gen. Baird requested me to ride with him to the left, now the front, where the musketry roared and raged. We spoke to every officer, many men, wild with excitement—color bearers seeking their Colonels and men their colors—urged the necessity of forming the men at once and that Bragg's army might still by a charge sweep us from the Ridge. Got a line formed across the ridge in the rear of the one so hotly engaged. Set the men to carrying the logs of the rebel-breastworks to the rear edge of the narrow summit, and to forming barricades of timber across the summit. Rode up to the front line and finding that the answer from the part of the hill in rebel possession was dying out, stopped the firing, ordered a breastwork and that the men should lie down behind it, and not fire unless attacked. Ordered a discreet officer and a patrol to be sent out to ascertain what was in front, and finding order being restored and troops regularly organized into bodies which could be handled, marching into position, as it became dark, I, with Gen. Wilson of the Engrs, who had joined me, bade Baird good-night, and rode to my tent.

It was dark as we turned away—the moon just then showed her face above the range, and late I reached my tent—ate a hearty supper and went to Hd Qrs to hear the result.

Hooker came in, reported that we had captured 2000 prisoners on Lookout and 1000 on Mission Ridge, and that Johnson's Division had captured a thousand.

Four thousand to Five thousand prisoners, thirty five guns and many small arms are the trophies. The substantial results are not yet known. Burnside will be relieved at once. Two steam boats arrived at our wharf from Bridgeport during the fight, Hooker having raised the blockade yesterday.

Bragg with a beaten and discontented army in full retreat, burning and destroying behind him. Invasion of Kentucky and Tennessee indefinitely postponed.

The Slave aristocracy broken down. The grandest stroke yet struck for our country.

Our loss is small considering the exploit. The storming of a steep hill five hundred feet high on a front of two miles, every where doubly entrenched by a line of troops which soon lost their formation and streamed upward, aggregating into channels as a sheet of water would have done in descending the same hill. It is unexampled—Another laurel leaf is added to Grant's Crown.

M C MEIGS
Q M Gn
U S A

"THE GRANDEST SIGHT I EVER SAW":
TENNESSEE AND GEORGIA, NOVEMBER 1863

James A. Connolly to Mary Dunn Connolly

Major James A. Connolly of the 123rd Illinois Infantry had fought at Chickamauga, where his brigade, led by Colonel John T. Wilder, had covered the retreat of the Union right wing. Connolly was then assigned to the staff of Brigadier General Absalom Baird, a division commander in the Fourteenth Corps of the Army of the Cumberland. The battle of Chattanooga cost the Union about 5,800 men killed, wounded, or missing, and the Confederates more than 6,600. While Bragg retreated to Dalton, Georgia, twenty-five miles southeast of Chattanooga, Grant sent Sherman to relieve Burnside at Knoxville. As Sherman approached on December 4, Longstreet abandoned his siege and retreated to the east. By then Bragg had resigned as commander of the Army of Tennessee.

Chattanooga, Thursday, Nov. 26, 1863.

Dear wife:

I have just come down off Mission Ridge, up which we fought our way yesterday afternoon. My horse carried me up there without a girth to my saddle, but I can't tell how. We captured quite a good sized army in the way of prisoners and artillery. Right in front of our Division as we climbed the mountain, were massed 42 pieces of artillery, belching away at us, but they couldn't even scare us, as they couldn't depress their guns to reach us, but had to blaze away far over our heads. We captured all these guns. One of the first officers I saw at these guns was old Quartermaster General Meigs, wild with excitement, trying himself, to wheel one of these guns on the rebels, flying down the opposite side of the mountain and furious because he couldn't find a lanyard with which to fire the gun.

Our advance to the base of the Ridge was the grandest sight I ever saw. Our line stretched along the valley for miles, in the open field, in plain view of the rebels on the mountain top, and at a given signal all moved forward as if on parade, through the open valley to the foot of the mountain, then without further orders, slowly, steadily, but broken into irregular groups by the inequalities of the face of the mountain, that long line climbed up the mountain, mostly on hands and knees, amid a terrible storm of shot, shell and bullets; the rebels were driven from their entrenchments on the mountain side, and on our gallant boys went, officers and men mingled together, all rank forgotten, following their old flag away to the mountain top, a struggle for a moment and our flag was planted here and there by scores of color bearers, on the very crest of the Ridge, battery after battery was taken, battle flags and prisoners captured, and the men indeed seemed perfectly frantic—rushing down the opposite side of the mountain after the flying rebels, regardless of officers, orders or anything else.

I slept on the ground on top of the Ridge last night, and when I waked this morning found myself lying within three feet of a dead man who, I thought, was lying there asleep when I laid down there in the dark last night. I have no time to write more; one brigade of our Division started in pursuit this morning, the rest of the Division may be off when I get back to where I left it, so I must hurry.

Thank God I am again unhurt, and in excellent health. Chattanooga is full of prisoners. They are non combatants now, and Grant will remove them to a safe place in accordance with the notice Bragg gave him some days since.

Your husband.

Chattanooga, Dec. 7, 1863.

Dear wife:

I received your letter written Nov. 26, on the 3rd day of this month, and when your letter was brought to my tent I was lying on my cot indulging in some vigorous remarks concerning mules in general, and one mule in particular, which, about two hours before, had given me a hard kick on the leg as I was riding past him, cold and hungry, just returning with my Division from the pursuit of Bragg and his valiant cavaliers whom we so handsomely "cleaned out" as the soldiers say. On

Monday, Nov. 23rd our Division was ordered to move out just in front of the fortifications. We did so, and the rebels, as they looked down on us from Lookout Mountain and Mission Ridge, no doubt thought we had come out for a review. But Sheridan's Division followed us out and formed in line with us. Wonder what the rebels thought then? "Oh, a Yankee review; we'll have some fun shelling them directly." But out came Wood's Division, then Cruft's Division, then Johnson's Division, then Howard's entire Corps of "Potomacs." "What can those Yankee fools mean," Bragg must have thought, as he sat at the door of his tent on Mission Ridge and watched the long lines of blue coats and glistening guns marching around in the valley below him, almost within gun shot of his pickets, and yet not a gun fired. All was peace in Chattanooga valley that day.

The sun shone brightly, the bands played stirring airs; tattered banners that had waved on battle fields from the Potomac to the Mississippi streamed out gaily, as if proud of the battle scars they wore. Generals Grant and Hooker, and Sherman and Thomas and Logan and Reynolds and Sheridan and scores of others, with their staffs, galloped along the lines, and the scene that spread out around me like a vast panorama of war filled my heart with pride that I was a soldier and member of that great army. But what did it all mean? Bragg, from his mountain eyrie, could see what we were doing just as well as Grant who was riding around amongst us. The rebels thought they had us hemmed in so that we dared not move, and so near starved that we could not move. Two o'clock came, and all was yet quiet and peaceful, gay as a holiday review; we could see crowds of rebels watching us from Mission Ridge and Lookout Mountain, but three o'clock came, and a solitary shot away over on our left, among Wood's men, made every fellow think: "Hark"! A few moments and another shot, then a rat-tat-tat-tat made almost every one remark: "Skirmishing going on over there." Wood's line moved forward, a few volleys, still Wood's line moved forward, and Sheridan's started forward, heavy work for a few minutes then all was quiet; two important hills were gained; cheer after cheer rang out in the valley and echoed and reverberated through the gorges of Lookout and Mission Ridge; still it was only 5 o'clock Monday afternoon.

The bands commenced playing and the valley was again peaceful, but we all knew there was "something up," and Bragg must have thought so too. We lay there all night, sleeping on our arms.

Tuesday morning, Nov. 24th, broke bright and beautiful; the sun rose clear; but for whom was it a "sun of Austerlitz"? Grant or Bragg? We talked of Austerlitz and Waterloo at headquarters that morning. During the night the moon was almost totally eclipsed. We talked of that also. It was considered a bad omen among the ancients, on the eve of battle; we concluded also that it was ominous of defeat, but not for us; we concluded that it meant Bragg because he was perched on the mountain top, nearest the moon. Daylight revealed the hills which Wood and Sheridan had won the day before, bristling with cannon of sufficient calibre to reach Bragg's eyrie on Mission Ridge. About 9 o'clock in the morning some 30 heavy guns opened on Mission Ridge. It appeared then that we were to advance right down the valley and attack the rebel centre, but, hark! Away off on our right—3 miles away, on the opposite side of Lookout—we hear firing. What can that mean? Suddenly the cannon, with which we have been pounding away at Mission Ridge, are silent, and all eyes are turned westward toward Lookout Mountain. The sounds of battle increase there but it is on the other side of the mountain from us and we can see nothing, but the word passes around: "Hooker is storming Lookout"! My heart grows faint. Poor Hooker, with his Potomac boys are to be the forlorn hope! What? Storm that mountain peak 2400 feet high, so steep that a squirrel could scarcely climb it, and bristling all over with rebels, bayonets and cannon? Poor boys! far from your quiet New England homes, you have come a long way only to meet defeat on that mountain peak, and find your graves on its rugged sides! Lookout Mountain will only hereafter be known as a monument to a whole Corps of gallant New Englanders who died there for their country! But hold! Some one exclaims: "The firing comes nearer, our boys are getting up"! All eyes are turned toward the Mountain, and the stillness of death reigns among us in the valley, as we listen to the sounds of battle on the other side of the Mountain while all was quiet as a Puritan sabbath on our side of it. How hope and despair alternated in our breasts! How we prayed for their success and longed to assist them, can only be known by those of us who, in that valley, stood watching that afternoon and listening to the swelling diapason of their battle. But the firing actually did grow nearer, manifestly our men were driving them; Oh! now if they only can continue it, but we fear they cannot! I have a long telescope with which I can distinctly see everything on our side of the mountain. I scan the mountain with it closely and continuously, but not a soul can I see. After hours of anxious suspense I see a single rebel winding his way back from the firing and around to our side of the mountain.

I announce to the crowd of Generals standing around: "There goes a straggler"! and in an instant everybody's glass is to his eye, but no more stragglers are seen, still the battle rages, and the little gleam of hope, that solitary straggler raised in our breasts, dies out. Minutes drag like hours, the suspense is awful, but look! look! Here comes a crowd of stragglers! here they come by hundreds, yes by thousands! The mountain is covered with them! They are broken, running! There comes our flag around the point of the mountain! There comes one of our regiments on the double quick! Oh! such a cheer as then went up in the valley! Manly cheeks were wet with tears of joy, our bands played "Hail to the Chief," and 50 brazen throated cannon, in the very wantonness of joy, thundered out from the fortifications of Chattanooga, a salute to the old flag which was then on the mountain top. The work was done. Lookout was ours, never again to be used as a perch by rebel vultures. Didn't we of the old Army of the Cumberland feel proud though? It was one of the regiments that fought at Chickamauga that carried that first flag to the mountain top. It was a brigade of the old Chickamauga army that led the storming party up the mountain. A straggling skirmish fire was kept up along our (the Eastern) side of the mountain, which we could trace by the flashes of the guns, until 11 o'clock at night, but then all became quiet, and again we passed the night in line of battle, sleeping on our arms. Bragg, no doubt, thought Hooker would continue to press forward across the valley from Lookout and attack his left on Mission Ridge in the morning, so he prepared for that during the night, by moving troops from his right to his left, to meet the anticipated attack of the morning, but Sherman, with his Vicksburg veterans, had all this time been lying concealed behind the hills on the North side of the Tenessee river, just North of the northern end of Mission Ridge, where Bragg's right was, awaiting the proper moment to commence his part of the stupendous plan. The time was now come. Lookout was ours; now for Mission Ridge! Before daylight of Wednesday Nov. 25th, Sherman had his pontoons across the river, about 3 miles north of Chattanooga, and under cover of a dense fog, crossed his whole Corps and took possession of the northern extremity of Mission Ridge, finding nothing there but a few pickets, and there he fell to work fortifying. By this time Bragg saw his mistake. The attack of Wednesday was to be on his right, at the North end of Mission Ridge, instead of his left at the South end of the Ridge, so he hurriedly countermarched his troops back from his left to his right. When the fog rose, about ten o'clock in the morning, Sherman attempted to carry the summit of the Ridge but was repulsed; again he tried it but was again repulsed, still again he tried it and was repulsed. This time the fighting was all to the left of where we were instead of to the right, as it had been the day before. Sherman, after terrible fighting, had been repulsed in three successive efforts to crush the enemy's right on the top of the Ridge, and an order came for our Division to move up the river to his support. We started. The enemy could see us from the top of the Ridge, and quickly understood (or thought they did) our design, so they commenced shelling us, as our long line of 20 regiments filed along, but we moved along until we came to where a thin strip of woodland intervened between us and the Ridge. Sheridan's Division followed us and did the same. The enemy supposed of course that we were moving on up the river to the support of Sherman, but we were not; we halted and formed line of battle in that strip of woodland, facing Mission Ridge. This, I confess, staggered me; I couldn't understand it; it looked as though we were going to assault the Ridge, and try to carry it by storm, lined and ribbed as it was with rifle pits, and its topmost verge crowded with rebel lines, and at least 40 cannon in our immediate front frowning down on us; we never could live a moment in the open spaces of 600 yards between the strip of woods in which we were formed, and the line of rifle pits at the base of the mountain, exposed as we would be to the fire of the 40 cannon massed, and from five to eight hundred feet immediately above us, also to the infantry fire from the rifle pits. I rode down along the line of our Division, and there I found Woods Division formed on our right and facing the Ridge just as we were; I rode on and came to Sheridan's Division formed on Woods right and facing the same. Here was a line of veteran troops nearly two miles long, all facing Mission Ridge, and out of sight of the enemy. The purpose at once became plain to me, and I hurried back to my own Division, and on asking Gen. —— he replied: "When 6 guns are fired in quick succession from Fort Wood, the line advances to storm the heights and carry the Ridge if possible. Take that order to Col. ——" (commanding the third brigade of our Division) "and tell him to move forward rapidly when he hears the signal." I communicated the order at once and that was the last I saw of the brigade commander, for he was killed just as he reached the summit of the Ridge. A few moments elapse, it is about half past three o'clock P. M., when suddenly, 6 guns are rapidly fired from Fort Wood. "Forward"! rings out along that long line of men, and forward they go, through the strip of woods, we reach the open space, say 600 yards, between the edge of the woods and the rifle pits at the foot of the Ridge. "Charge"! is shouted wildly from hundreds of throats, and with a yell such as that valley never heard before, the three Divisions (60 regiments) rushed forward; the rebels are silent a moment, but then the batteries on top of the Ridge, open all at once, and the very heavens above us seemed to be rent asunder; shells go screaming over our heads, bursting above and behind us, but they hurt nobody and the men don't notice them; about midway of the open space a shell bursts directly over my head, and so near as to make my horse frantic and almost unmanageable; he plunges and bursts breast strap and girth and off I tumble with the saddle between my legs. My orderly catches my horse at once, throws the blanket and saddle on him, gives me a "leg lift" and I am mounted again, without girth, but I hold on with my knees and catch up with our madcaps at the first rifle pits, over these we go to the second line of pits, over these we go, some of the rebels lying down to be run over, others scrambling up the hill which is becoming too steep for horses, and the General and staff are forced to abandon the direct ascent at about the second line of rifle pits; the long line of men reach the steepest part of the mountain, and they must crawl up the best way they can 150 feet more before they reach the summit, and when they do reach it, can they hold it? The rebels are there in thousands, behind breastworks, ready to hurl our brave boys back as they reach their works. One flag bearer, on hands and knees, is seen away in advance of the whole line; he crawls and climbs toward a rebel flag he sees waving above him, he gets within a few feet of it and hides behind a fallen log while he waves his flag defiantly until it almost touches the rebel flag; his regiment follows him as fast as it can; in a few moments another flag bearer gets just as near the summit at another point, and his regiment soon gets to him, but these two regiments dare not go the next twenty feet or they would be annihilated, so they crouch there and are safe from the rebels above them, who would have to rise up, to fire down at them, and so expose themselves to the fire of our fellows who are climbing up the mountain. The suspense is greater, if possible, than that with which we viewed the storming of Lookout. If we can gain that Ridge; if we can scale those breastworks, the rebel army is routed, everything is lost for them, but if we cannot scale the works few of us will get down this mountain side and back to the shelter of the woods. But a third flag and regiment reaches the other two; all eyes are turned there; the men away above us look like great ants crawling up, crouching on the outside of the rebel breastworks. One of our flags seems to be moving; look! look! look! Up! Up! Up! it goes and is planted on the rebel works; in a twinkling the crouching soldiers are up and over the works; apparently quicker than I can write it the 3 flags and 3 regiments are up, the close fighting is terrific; other flags go up and over at different points along the mountain top—the batteries have ceased, for friend and foe are mixed in a surging mass; in a few moments the flags of 60 Yankee regiments float along Mission Ridge from one end to the other, the enemy are plunging down the Eastern slope of the Ridge and our men in hot pursuit, but darkness comes too soon and the pursuit must cease; we go back to the summit of the Ridge and there behold our trophies—dead and wounded rebels under our feet by hundreds, cannon by scores scattered up and down the Ridge with yelling soldiers astraddle them, rebel flags lying around in profusion, and soldiers and officers completely and frantically drunk with excitement. Four hours more of daylight, after we gained that Ridge would not have left two whole pieces of Bragg's army together.

Our men, stirred by the same memories, shouted "Chickamauga"! as they scaled the works at the summit, and amid the din of battle the cry "Chickamauga"! "Chickamauga"! could be heard. That is not *fancy* it is *fact*. Indeed the plain unvarnished facts of the storming of Mission Ridge are more like romance to me now than any I have ever read in Dumas, Scott or Cooper. On that night I lay down upon the ground without blankets and slept soundly, without inquiring whether my neighbors were dead or alive, but, on waking found I was sleeping among bunches of dead rebels and Federals, and within a few rods of where Bragg slept the night before, if he slept at all.

You must not think that the General and staff remained at the second line of rifle pits on the side of the mountain, where I left them a few pages back, until the fight was over. The steepness of the mountain compelled us to zigzag back and forth, ascending a little with every zigzag until we reached the summit while the hand to hand melee was going on, before the rebels broke away down the Eastern slope.

Early next morning I rode back to my quarters in the city, where I am now writing, got a new saddle girth and wrote you a brief letter, just to let you know I was safe. That was Nov. 26th, Thanksgiving Day in the United States, I believe, and it was the same with me, though my "Thanksgiving Dinner" was hard tack and raw bacon, but it was toothsome as turkey, for hunger makes fine sauce, you know. You wrote me that same day. After writing my hasty letter to you I hurried back to the Ridge and found my Division gone in pursuit of Bragg, but I soon overtook it, and we bivouacked for the night without having overtaken the enemy. On that night (26th) I rolled up in my saddle blanket and slept on the ground soundly. We started at two o'clock, on the morning of the 27th, and reached Chickamauga Creek, the bridge over which the rebels had burned in their retreat, and by daylight we had a bridge over it and marched to Greyville, where we met Davis' Division, which had moved by a different road and had captured a battery and 300 rebels in a fight there that morning. Davis had moved by a shorter road and arrived there ahead of us. I wasn't *very* sorry for it, for by him getting there before us he saved us a fight, and I like to dodge fights, but appear to have poor success at it, and a fellow stands a chance of getting just as badly hurt in a little fight as in a big one. After halting a few moments at Greyville we started in a Southeasterly direction, toward Ringgold, where we heard the sound of a battle going on, and Gen. ——, our Corps Commander, rightly supposed that Hooker, who had taken that road, had come up with the enemy. After marching ten miles very rapidly we reached Hooker and found him hotly engaged with the enemy; our Division was soon in line and ready for the word to "go in" but the rebels withdrew, and fell back to Dalton. We bivouacked at Ringgold on that night (27th) and the next day one brigade of our Division was sent down the railroad toward Dalton to destroy the railroad bridges. I asked leave to accompany this brigade, as I had been over the road with ——'s brigade of mounted infantry, before the battle of Chickamauga, and knew the country and location of the railroad bridges. The General gave me leave to go and direct the expedition, so I went along. We burned 5 railroad bridges, tore up and burned the ties of a mile of the track, took some prisoners, one of them a lieutenant on the staff of Gen. Joe Johnston, and found the houses along the road filled with dead and wounded rebels, whom we left as we found. We got back to Ringgold, in the rain, before dark, and bivouacked for the night, (28th). Gen. Turchin, who had a couple of tents along in a wagon which he had brought with him, loaned us a tent, and we all, General and staff, rolled up in our saddle blankets and slept together under that tent. I enclose a rough pencil sketch, made by one of our staff officers, depicting a portion of our staff that night just before we got any supper. Gen. ——, you see, is making desperate efforts to fry his own supper, consisting entirely of fresh pork. The African, with frying pan is endeavoring to provide something for the rest of us.

No other incidents of note occurred until we returned to Chattanooga, except, as we were returning, I was riding through the woods in company with Gen. ——, our Corps commander, and his staff, when we came across a caisson, loaded with shells, which the rebels had abandoned.

Gen. —— ordered me to find my Division commander and have him bring the caisson in to Chattanooga. I couldn't find my Division commander nor any team that could haul it in, so I went to work with the assistance of my orderly, and knocked some weatherboards off an old church near by, and built a rousing fire under the caisson, but had to hurry away from it after I got my fire well started, and hadn't gone far until the fire reached the powder, and then I had the fun of hearing 90 rebel shells explode together, and I tell you, it made something of a racket in those old Georgia woods. I am glad now that I didn't ask for leave of absence before the fight, for I should have missed it, and should always have regretted it. I shall now get one as soon as I can. Gen. Reynolds has gone to New Orleans to take command there. I should have been glad to go with him, but if I did I wouldn't have got home until the close of the war, and I couldn't think of that. There are many things I intended to write about when I began this, which I have omitted, but this is long enough, and I'll quit. xxxxxxxxx

Your husband.

THE MINE RUN CAMPAIGN: VIRGINIA,
NOVEMBER–DECEMBER 1863

Theodore Lyman: Journal, November 26–December 2, 1863

Aware of Lincoln's mounting frustration over his failure to bring Lee to battle, Meade made plans to turn the Army of Northern Virginia's eastern flank by crossing the Rapidan downriver from the Confederate lines and then marching west through the scrub woods of the Wilderness. One of his aides in the ensuing campaign was Lieutenant Colonel Theodore Lyman, a wealthy Bostonian who had studied natural history at Harvard under Louis Agassiz. While collecting marine specimens in Florida before the war, Lyman had become friends with Meade, who at the time was a first lieutenant in the corps of engineers supervising lighthouse construction projects. After spending the first two years of the war touring Europe, Lyman joined Meade's staff as an (unpaid) volunteer aide in September 1863. In the sketch maps Lyman drew in his notebooks, Union cavalry units are indicated with the letter "C," while corps are indicated by their respective badges: for the First Corps, commanded by Major General John Newton, a disk; for the Second Corps (Major General Gouverneur K. Warren), a three-leaf clover; for the Third Corps (Major General William H. French), a diamond; for the Fifth Corps (Major General George Sykes), a Maltese cross; for the Sixth Corps (Major General John Sedgwick), a Greek cross. The designations "N," "O," "P," and "N' " indicate the order in which the maps appear in Lyman's notebook for the period from August 31, 1863, to March 9, 1864.

———————

November 26, Thursday.
Thanksgiving day, when the fat turkey is served in state. And this was appointed for our flank move on Orange Court House, via our left. At 7¾ A.M. we started. The order of march was 5th followed by 1st Corps to cross by pontoon at Culpeper Mine Ford, advance by a cross road to the Orange C.H. plank road and keep on to "Parker's Store." The 3d followed by the 6th, cross at Jacob's Mills and keep on to form on right of 2d, which crossed at Germanna Mills took a cross

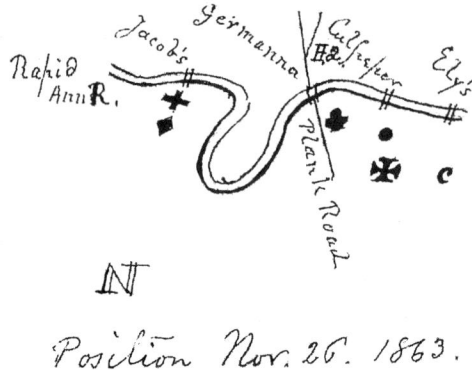

Position Nov. 26. 1863.

road to the Orange Court House turnpike and then keep on to Robertson's Tavern, or, if possible, to Verdiersville.

The 3d Div. of 1st Corps left to guard railroad. Reserve Artillery to follow 1st Corps. Waggon train park at Richardsville, under guard of Merritt's (Buford's) division of cavalry, Custer's division (Kilpatrick's) to hold Raccoon & Morton's Fords. Gregg's Div. to cross at Ely's Ford and cover the advance & left of Sykes. Owing, apparently, to some dullness on part of Gen. Prince, this division did not start till say 7.30, which delayed the rest of the 3d Corps; moreover they had not properly reconnoitred the roads or repaired them, so they took the wrong road, this side of the river, and got their artillery stalled into the bargain! At about 10.30 we got within ½ mile of Germanna Ford & there found the troops massed and the batteries placed, ready to run up and shell the crossing. The Rapidan there runs between high, steep banks whereof the northern dominates the southern, the reverse of what happens at the fords above. Officers were sent to French & Sykes, to find whether they had got up; because it was deemed important to force the river, at the same moment. The communications were difficult, and so the officers did not get back till late, so that our troops (2d Corps) began to cross at about 2 P.M., Sykes having begun at 12, and French not till later. The artillery of the 3d & 6th had finally to come to Germanna and was not over till 5 next morning. We camped at the junction of the plank and dirt roads on the north side of the river. It was quite cold and the water froze in the tent.

November 27, Friday.
We were up before daylight, with a magnificent moon glittering on the hoar frost, but the Staff did not move till 8.45 A.M. Then we crossed on the pontoons and kept down the plank road, to a point some 2 or 3 miles from the river where we struck off, more to the S.W. to make a short cut for the Orange court house turnpike. Before this turn-off we got to the artillery of the 6th Corps, to whom the General gave a good blowing up, for not knowing their precise road. On this side of the river, the country is, for some distance, open farming land; then succeeds dense, scrub-oak wood, penetrated only by farm roads, narrow and intricate, at best, and in wet weather, impossible for artillery. Near the river had been made long rifle-pits, with some entrenched epaulements for guns, but they were quite unoccupied. About midday through the woods we came on the rear of the 2d Corps, moving briskly, and we filed past them, with some difficulty. At 9.30 we heard cannon ahead and, at 10.45 struck the turnpike, along which we advanced to within say 1¼ miles of Robertson's Tavern, and there halted by the roadside, at which time (11) there was brisk skirmishing by Warren, who had gained the ridge of Robertson's Tavern and pushed back the Rebel advance (part of Ewell's Corps.) And now we found ourselves with a weak centre, on the pike and the strong right not heard from, and inexplicably behindhand! Aides were sent to French, under guidance of natives & niggers. Ludlow, sent to Sykes, reported him well up on the left. About 12.45 we heard cannon off on our right, which seemed from the 3d Corps. McBlair came, but he, honest soul, did display his usual muddleheadedness, as to time & place, and could only make out, that French was going along somewhere in the thick woods. At length Cadwalader returned, who had taken an order to French to attack & smash through to Warren, and reported French's left some 2 miles from Warren's right. Meanwhile Gregg, in the left advance, had a sharp fight with the enemy's infantry, in which the cavalry did excellently and, among them, the 1st Mass. Longfellow and Bowditch were

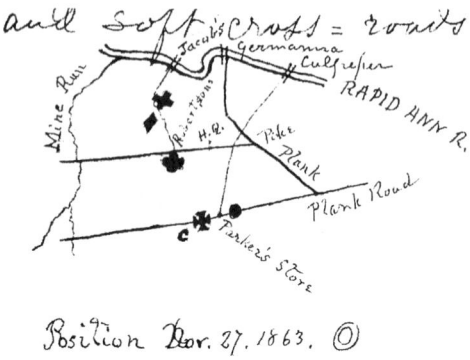

Position Nov. 27. 1863.

here wounded. An aide from Custer stated he had made a good diversion at Raccoon & Morton's Fords, by charging across both, and forcing the enemy to detach a large force to drive him back again. Meanwhile Warren had received orders to attack without French, or not, at his discretion. He concluded it would not be safe; and so we pitched camp where we stood. After dark came a despatch from French that he had had a sharp action, with very heavy musketry (none of which we had heard) and had driven the enemy from the field, taking 900 prisoners (a number which proved greatly exaggerated) and losing some 900 himself in killed, wounded, &c. His fight, also, was with a portion of Ewell's Corps.

November 28, Saturday.
A pretty place to pass my Wedding-day! Twelve months ago we were in Paris, and enjoying the quiets of the Hotel Wagram. And this morning, behold me, with little Wife hundreds of miles away and a cheery prospect of mud and intermittent rain! At 7.45 we rode to Robertson's Tavern 1¼ m. which stands on a ridge along which the 2d Corps was in line of battle and just advancing. The enemy had disappeared from our front, and many thought them in full retreat. After some talk with Gen. Warren, Gen. Meade went to the tavern, and sat by the fire. However, say at 10.15 there was a report that we had come on the enemy in entrenchments; and we all rode to the front, slop, slop in the mud, and amid infantry, artillery &

ambulances going to the front, also. A little behind the crest of the next ridge, and about 1 m. from the tavern the General halted us, and rode alone to reconnoitre. At 11, a battery opened and fired some time, posted just on the left of the pike. They were in entrenchments, sure enough, and we had only to wait for other troops to come along. The rest of the day was occupied by the corps getting into position, a very laborious thing, midst mud and soft cross-roads. The day previous Meade, anxious for his centre, had brought over both Sykes & Newton, from the plank road; and the 5th Corps was now in reserve at Robertson's Tavern, while the First Corps took position in line.

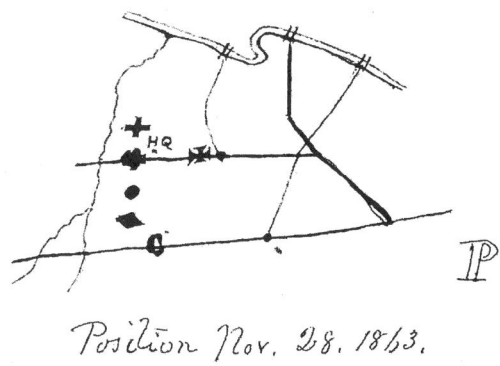

Position Nov. 28. 1863.

November 29, Sunday.
The enemy's position was found to be a very strong one. Along a bold ridge, running nearly north & south across both turnpike and plank road, rising from Mine Run by a steep slope, which in many parts was quite naked, and in others partially wooded, they had thrown up a heavy and continuous breastwork, supported by batteries, for which they had made epaulements. The corresponding high ground east of the Run, and occupied by us, was at least a mile in average distance, so that artillery would be deprived of much of its strong effect, and canister & spherical case pretty much out of the question. Then, at most points the attacking force would be exposed over nearly the whole stretch, to artillery fire, followed by

musketry. It was a bad look out! From our ridge we could see the Rebs in hundreds, standing on top their works, or enlarging some portion of them, with logs and earth. The thing was, if possible, to flank. So Warren, with his own corps & a division of the 6th, marched in the morning and passed towards our left, hoping to get beyond the plank road and attack that afternoon; the rest of the line be ready to support. However, the column was delayed by a report of entrenchments that had no existence, and by some skirmishing, so that they did not get on the enemy's flank till too late for an attack. As it was they created great excitement & a brigade was brought on the double-quick to resist an attack. Major Ludlow came back with fine accounts of the prospect in the morning. The General, much encouraged, made immediate disposition for the attack and put French's two flank (left) divisions under Warren (Prince & Carr) greatly to F's indignation. Sykes had already occupied Warren's vacant position. At 8, or earlier, a general cannonade was to open, for an hour, and then the assault to take place. The grand attack on the left, and others, according to opportunity, along the whole line. One division of the 5th Corps occupied the extreme right. Gregg had continued skirmishing, on the left. The day Sykes & Newton moved along the plank road (27th) the enemy's cavalry performed a feat of extraordinary daring. They dashed on the trains, between the tail of the 5th and head of the 1st Corps, cut out a dozen or more waggons and made off with them. They were chiefly ammunition, but one was a Headquarter waggon, so there was Capt. Barnard, quite without blankets or any comfort, poor man; and his general Bartlett, in a similar fix. A brigade from Merritt was sent to reinforce Gregg.

November 30, Monday.
We were up bright & early, for it was necessary to get the trains out of the way about sunrise, as they would be exposed to shell, when the cannonade opened. All was expectation. Yet such is the force of your surroundings that I felt no particular nervousness—to be sure I did not have to lead an assault—which makes a wide difference. The soldiers of the 2d Corps, that morning pinned bits of paper on their clothes, with their names on them! As for Col. Farnum (he of yacht *Wanderer*

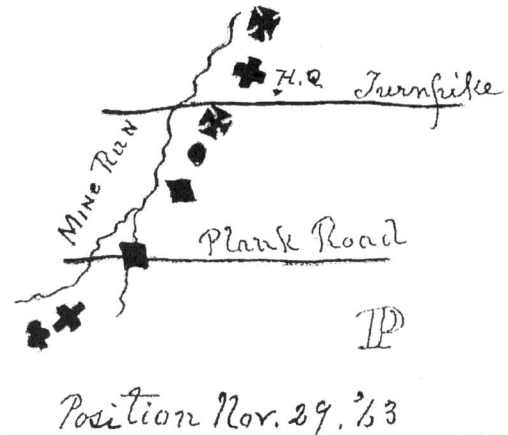

Position Nov. 29, '63

fame) he said he considered himself under sentence of death, that morning, for an hour! A little before 8 General Meade mounted & went a little way in search of Gen. Newton; while we rode, at 8.10, a single gun sounded from the right, and then a cannonade, not very heavy, opened along the line, as far as Newton's part. We returned to Headquarters. At 8.30 came Robling with a note from Gen. Warren, saying the enemy had arrived in great force, during the night, had thrown up more rifle pits, and that, on reexamination of the ground he considered an attack there as hopeless!! The General simply turned to Gen. Humphreys, saying "Read that," and exclaimed to Robling "My God! Gen. Warren has half my army." He then issued orders to cease firing; and soon all was still, save an occasional gun. Disappointment was on every face. For about an hour Gen. Meade remained in consultation with Gens. Sedgwick and Humphreys. Then at 9.45, he rode, with Gen. H, Major Biddle, Mitchell & myself, to Gen. Warren's. We passed along the front, in rear of our batteries, proceeded through a wood and emerged on a bare plateau where was Gen. French's command, then through another pine wood and came out on the plank road. We stopped at a run (a branch of Mine Run) and Gen. Warren rode up and dismounted to talk with the two other Generals; and there they sadly stood, over a fire the orderlies had made them, for it was sharp, and thin ice was on the pools. It was then 10.15. After a very long talk, at noon we rode back, stopping at Gen. French's house. He was very mad and talked loudly. He had pushed his skirmishers to within 300 yards of their works, and his troops had counted on success. Warren's troops were in three lines by the Run; French's were on the plateau, behind earthworks. It was of no use! We came back; the moment had passed, the assault was countermanded and the 2d Corps might unpin their bits of paper. That night was cold; 5 of our men on picket, who had been obliged to wade the stream to get to their places, were frozen to death, and the same fate, it is said, befell some rebels.

December 1, Tuesday.
As I looked out of my tent, at daylight, there were the 4½ inch big guns going to the rear, which argued we were soon to follow. It came out shortly that the generals were unanimous in thinking the moment for the assault had passed; and the order was out to fall back. The 1st Corps would start that afternoon, proceeding to Germanna Ford, and halt, to cover the crossing. The 5th Corps would withdraw at dark and be followed by the 6th, marching for Germanna Ford via the Turnpike & the cross wood-road. The 3d would march at dark, on the plank road, and cross at Culpeper Ford; the 2d following. The pickets would be withdrawn at 3 in the morning and, assembling at Robertson's Tavern, march under Col. Hayes (Joe). Some pickets of the 5th Corps had been 3 days on duty without relief! At sunset, went and took a farewell look at Jonny Reb. They were standing in groups on their parapet, while some were walking about in front. At dark we rode as far as Robertson's Tavern, where we built good fires and kept warm, till the 5th Corps should get past. It was a picturesque sight, so many officers, in their long coats, standing, sitting, or lying on the bare floor. Thereto also enter T. F. Meagher "of the Sword" *ci-devant* commander of the Irish Brigade; was in mufti and very drunk! He talked thickly with the English officers (who, by the by, established themselves in a seemingly safe place this morning, but got shelled for their pains, whereat Stephenson returned with a bit of spherical case, as a trophy). We started immediately in rear of the corps, but could go but at a snail's gain; broken bridge ahead and a slough, which kept

checking the column. Of the many neglected details in the army none are worse than the repair of essential roads. A slight slough, e.g. makes each rank hesitate as it crosses, and almost stops the column. A working party of 10 men would repair such a place in ½ an hour. A whole corps had preceded, but nothing done! We got mightily cold crawling along this way, but at last got past, and then the General broke into a smart trot and we clattered along the most infernal of pikes, in holes and over rocks till we got to the plank road and turned up, to the left, where we found the holes, if possible worse, among the broken boards. We soon came on a train which had missed the way and we set it right. Then we passed the turn-off to Mine Ford (Culpeper) and, immediately after, came on the head of the 5th Corps, debouching from the woods, on the left and striking the plank road for Germanna Ford, which we reached, crossed by the pontoon bridge, and found our camp pitched at the old spot, at juncture of dirt & plank roads; 2 A.M. of *Dec. 2*, Wednesday. Gregg had followed the army, covering both columns. The enemy made no attempt to follow, not even attacking the rear cavalry. In the afternoon we returned to our old camp in the woods, not getting tents pitched till late at night.

All corps returned to their positions, except the 1st & 5th

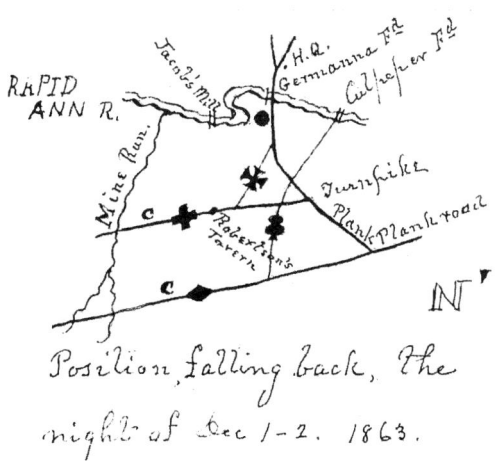

Position, falling back, the night of Dec 1-2. 1863.

which exchanged places. Got a good stock of letters from Deary Mimi and from others. Mrs. Paige is dead. The firm of Paige & Co. is dissolved, which throws out Arthur. It has been very mild north, moving trees as late as the last of November, which is unheard of, almost.

A SOLDIER AT MINE RUN: VIRGINIA,
NOVEMBER–DECEMBER 1863

Wilbur Fisk to The Green Mountain Freeman

Writing to the *Freeman* on November 20, Fisk described a review of the Sixth Corps and presciently observed that "these reviews almost always precede an onward movement." The Mine Run campaign cost the Union about 1,600 men killed, wounded, or missing, and the Confederates about 600.

Second Vermont Regiment
November 29, 1863

This quiet Sabbath morning while the good people of Vermont are attending their accustomed places of worship, we, here in the army, are engaged in a manner widely different. Our regiment is on picket today, close up to the enemy, and picket firing is going on nearly all the time. I have seated myself by our little fire on the support, and as it will be several hours before my turn will come to go on post, perhaps I shall have no better time to acquaint you with our proceedings for the last week or so, than the present.

We are in what I am told is called here, the Owl's Wilderness, and certainly it would be hard to conceive of a name more appropriate. It appears to be one uninterrupted wilderness, extending fifteen or twenty miles either way, without any other inhabitants than owls, buzzards, and such like animals. There may be, once in a while, a small clearing with a log house in the center, and a high fence all around it, and with some signs of the land having been cultivated in modern times, but these places have strayed away so far from all civilization that it will be hardly worth while to take them into account. The land where we are now, is covered with small second-growth pine, and looks as if it had been under cultivation once, but probably worn out and abandoned for more fertile regions. Part of the woods that we have been through is grown up to oak and other solid timber of all sizes, and has probably been forest from time immemorial. The land is level, and has the appearance of being good soil, and if I am any judge I should call it just such land as would tempt the eyes of almost any practical farmer, if it was up in our Northern States, instead of being here in decayed Virginia.

As to the latitude and longitude of our present whereabouts, the man in the moon could tell as well as we. We have marched principally in the night, and in all directions, so it has destroyed all our calculations as to distance and directions, and all we can say about the matter is that we have crossed the Rapidan and are still on the rebels' side of the river. It is cheering to be able, under such circumstances, to put confidence in others, for we should be in a woeful plight if we were obliged to act upon our geographical knowledge at the present time. The sun rises in the southwest, and I noticed that the needle of the compass points almost exactly the wrong way. If anybody was going to desert just now, I should be a poor guide to direct their flight.

One week ago today we had divine services in our regiment, held by Mr. Chandler, from Brattleboro. As we have no Chaplain of our own, and consequently very meagre religious privileges of any kind, it was quite a rarity to hear any one preach. He is connected with the Christian Commission, and in anticipation of a battle, had come out here to act the part of the Good Samaritan to the suffering,—as a great many belonging to that Commission have done, to the everlasting gratitude of those who have been wounded in action,—and to preach the gospel and distribute religious reading where such services are needed. He had a large bundle of papers with him that were eagerly received.

On the morning of the 24th, we had orders to be ready to march at an early hour. Accordingly, at precisely three o'clock in the morning, our quiet dreams were broken up by the rattling of drums all through camp, and forthwith we commenced to break up housekeeping—for the most of us had built us tip top houses—and to prepare for another campaign or for whatever was to be accomplished. The weather was grim and forbidding, and the rain drops as they came pattering on our tent that morning, driven by a regular nor'easter, had a very dismal sound in view of the prospect before us. A rainstorm is a very uninviting auxiliary with which to commence a long campaign at any season of the year, but more especially now when cold weather has come and when wet clothes can hardly be made to suggest anything but discomforts of the least desirable kind. Our tents had become wet and heavy, and to carry these in our knapsacks with all the rest of the clothing that we are obliged to carry at this time of the year, was going to make a pretty heavy draft upon the strength of a fellow's back bone. It is the last straw that breaks the camel's back, and the addition of a few extra pounds of water might have the same effect on us, for our packs have hitherto been as heavy as seemed possible for us to carry. You may judge of our satisfaction then, when we heard that the order to march had been postponed for two days. Some think that other reasons besides unpropitious weather, was the cause of the delay; if not it was rather of an anomaly in our war experience but none the less acceptable for all that. We shall certainly think we have one good reason for respecting Gen. Meade.

Although we had been expecting to move somewhere for a long time, we had but little idea where we were going. There have been all sorts of rumors in camp, and there always are at such times, and almost every man had a rumor of his own. No honest man could believe two of them at the same time. Sometimes it was reported that we were going to New York. Gen. Stannard had command there and wanted us to do service under him. I heard that some officers had offered to bet very extravagantly that such would be the case. It is curious how such rumors will thrive and strengthen themselves in a thousand different ways. It was coolly told in the third brigade, and believed there, that orders had been read to us on dress parade to draw clothing suitable for garrison duty, when no such orders had been read to us at all, and more than all that, our regiment had no dress parade while we stayed in our last camp. Another story was that the army was going to move down to the vicinity of Aquia Creek, and go into winter quarters there again. Going across the Rapidan to attack the enemy once more, seemed to be hardly feasible at this late season. Morever attacking Lee in his old chosen position, we have tried so many times and failed, that a great many think it is high time that that method of maneuvering was played out.

The day, before we did move, I was up in one of the New York regiments, and they were trying to enlist the men over again for another three years. They were managing this matter with a great deal of shrewdness. Every man that put his name down was to have a furlough and go home immediately. As it had become pretty certain that we were to have a long, tedious campaign, cold and stormy it might be in pursuit of the enemy, it was quite a tempting bait for a fellow to write down his name and get rid of it all, and go home and have a jolly time instead. In some of the New York regiments, the enlisting officers have been pretty successful; in others, the boys say they want to breathe free air once more before they enlist again.

Thursday morning, the 26th, we were drummed up again, bright and early, to prepare to march. The air was clear, and there were no signs of rain nor any probability that the movement would be postponed again. Our knapsacks were packed, tents struck, huge bonfires were burning all through the camp, consuming material that had cost us a great deal of pains to collect. The sun was just beginning to melt away the frost, when we fell into line and filed off towards Brandy Station. Camps without number were being deserted, some of which had been fixed up as comfortable as would be needed for winter quarters. The whole army was in motion. Infantry, artillery, and baggage wagons *ad infinitum*, had suddenly waked to life and were crowding along, or halting in a field for it to come their turn to start. It was nearly noon before we got hardly so far as Brandy Station. The marching all day was very slow. Sometimes we would hardly get a half mile from one halting place before we would halt again. As it grew towards night, and we believed that we had got to cross the river before we halted for the night, we began to grow impatient of these vexatious delays, and anxious to get to our journey's end. Before we reached the river we had got a couple of miles of woods to go through, and there was only one little road hardly wide enough for a file of four men to walk in abreast, while on each side was a dense thicket of all sorts of timber that nature ever invented. If we could have marched right straight along in this road it would have been all well enough, but, instead of that, we could only march a few steps at a time, then wait for those ahead of us to clear the way. We would march about a rod, then wait five minutes, when we could march a rod more, and then wait another five minutes, and all this while the weight of our knapsacks was increasing, and our patience steadily diminishing, until the boys began to curse patriots and traitors without much discrimination. Finally, we halted and sat down. An hour passed, and still we didn't move. Some of the boys ventured to make coffee, running the risk of being ordered to fall in just as they were divested of their load, and enjoying their warm drink. By and by orders came that we might make us coffee, and eat our supper, and we all pitched into the business with a will. We had ample time allowed us to finish our meal, and when we were at last ordered to fall in, the road was clear and we could march along as fast as we liked.

We crossed the Rapidan between Germanna and Raccoon Ford, at Jacob's Ferry on a pontoon bridge. The opposite bluff was almost perpendicular and as soon as we had climbed to the top we halted and camped for the night, or for what there was left of it, for it was past midnight when we stopped. Before sunrise we were ordered up, and soon on the march again. There was skirmishing ahead of us and our advance was slow. We gained but three or four miles from the river all day. Towards night firing began to be more rapid and we were ordered forward into line. The third corps were ahead of us. Our line extended into the woods to the extreme right. About quarter before four the firing commenced with terrible earnestness. To us it looked as though there would be a chance for us to have a hand in it. We could not see the fight, for the wood was so dense that we could see but a few rods ahead of us, but from the sound of the firing, and from the number of frightened skedaddlers that were making swift tracks to the rear, we had reason to fear that the battle was going against us. The firing continued till long into the night. Evidently the rebels couldn't break our lines or they would have been on to us. It was difficult to get any exact information of the result of the battle, but the "sum and substance" of what we could get was, that we had been flanked and forced to fall back; that the rebels had charged upon our line and been repulsed; that we in turn charged them, drove them back and gained some ground at the close of the struggle. The Tenth Vermont was in the fight, and there was a report that night that they broke and ran;

other reports contradicted it. I have heard that they bore the test and held their ground like men, although a line ahead of them broke and skedaddled back right through their ranks; and for a Vermont regiment, this is decidedly the most rational story to believe.

After a while the firing ceased and everything was quiet as the grave. We commenced to build fires to warm ourselves and to make coffee by, but an order came to allow no fires on the line. Afterward they concluded to let us have a few small fires, and we eat our suppers and laid down. About midnight we were ordered to pack up and fall in. Our line of march was towards the left. By the number of troops that were in motion, I should judge that all hands left that place during the night. It would be impossible to guess how far we marched before daylight, when we maneuvered around and got into a position here. We didn't march very rapidly, nor very straight, but if I was to make a rough guess at the matter, I should say that we came about a half a dozen miles from where the fight was Friday night, and that now we must be pretty well down towards Chancellorsville. Next time I write, I hope I shall be better informed and be able to write a more intelligent letter.

Second Vermont Regiment
Near Brandy Station
Dec. 8, 1863

Being detailed for fatigue, and out a couple of miles from camp, with but little prospect of returning for at least ten days from the commencement of the detail, I have pulled up my knapsack close to the fire, fully determined to write you another letter by firelight, this evening, unless I am driven from my purpose by the smoke, which persists in drifting directly into my face, let me get on to which side of the fire I will. To be bent down over an outdoor's fire on a cold December night, might have a very inspiring effect for a poetical nature, but for me it is a most uncomfortable position, and sometimes places my patience in great jeopardy. But if I wish to narrate the events of the past few days, I shall probably have no better opportunity to do so than now, and to deprive the public of this important delinquency that I never should have the face to ask forgiveness for.

The last time I wrote, I believe we were on picket away out in the wilderness among the rebels, where we expected every hour to be let against the enemy. We were not let against them while we were there, for reasons known only to the higher authorities, though without doubt it was because we found the enemy much stronger in his position than we expected. Gen. Meade did not wish to inaugurate another Lee's Mill's affair. There was a deep creek between us and the enemy, and the rebels had been busy digging rifle-pits and strengthening their position ever since we came up to them. Both banks were abrupt and steep and difficult to get over, while on the rebel side they had added to these disadvantages by placing every conceivable obstacle in the way of our advance. Trees were felled, abattis made, breastworks were thrown up until they occupied a position that if *we* had occupied we should have considered impregnable against all the rebels in the universe.

Army correspondents, I notice, all have it that "the men" were in the best of spirits, and eager for a dash at the enemy. Now all such statements, though meant, I suppose, to be complimentary, need a slight qualification, and admit of some exceptions. We are in "the best of spirits" almost any time when we can get the best of spirits to put into us, and as for being eager for a dash at the enemy, perhaps it is all true; I can speak for but one, but there was certainly a fellow there about my size that felt no such eagerness at all. I couldn't look over to those gray-coated devils and see their position and the means they were providing for our reception, with any desire to be ordered over there amongst them. If the order had been given to charge, of course I should have charged with the rest, and if I could hurt a rebel so that he would have had to go home and stay with his mother until the war was over, I should have done it; but after all, to tell the plain truth about the matter, and there is no use in lying, in the event of a charge, I know I should have had a strong preference for running the other way and placing as much distance as possible between those rebel minnies and my own precious self. Vermonters are the very best fighters in the world, so everybody says that knows anything about it; but you never see a Vermonter manifest any eagerness to get into a fight, nor any desire to back out after he does get in.

It was expected by some, that a charge would be ordered that Sunday afternoon when we were there on picket, but it was postponed until morning. Early in the morning we were relieved from post, and went back to the reserve. At precisely eight o'clock our artillery opened on the enemy. They commenced with energy, and from two points, pouring in a cross fire and throwing in shot and shell among the rebels with terrible rapidity. The rebels hardly knew what to make of it. From the picket outposts they could be seen hurrying in all directions, some scattering in confusion, and some being collected together for resistance. There seemed to be an endless number of them. We had stirred up their hive, and found a pretty lively swarm, and as large a one as we need wish to contend with. The cannonading was to continue for an hour, and then, hurrah boys for a charge. As we are on picket, we should take the lead, and act as skirmishers. In about half an hour the firing ceased. Pretty soon the order came to pack up and fall in. We did so, and were ordered about to the right of the line, a mile or so further. All the way we kept back from the edge of the woods far enough to prevent the rebels from discovering our movement. We picked our way through a dense and almost impenetrable thicket of small trees and underbrush. We passed by where a storming party of the 5th corps had piled up their knapsacks and haversacks, and were stripped for the charge. After a while we got into our position where we should remain until further orders. It was very cold, but no fires were allowed to be built there. The Johnnies were having their nice comfortable fires, and they appeared to be but a short distance from us. They didn't appear to be at all bashful about showing their position by building fires or coming out in sight. But we must keep back in the woods out of sight and keep warm the best way we could. By scuffling, knocking off hats, and running around a ring that we made a path for in the woods, we managed to keep from freezing. We expected to be ordered into action every minute. The companies to be deployed were selected, but the order to advance did not come. The boys were tired of waiting. If they had got to charge on the enemy, they wanted to do it at once, and have it done with, and not stand there and dread it all day in the cold.

But the sun went down and our line had not moved. Soon the order came to "left face place." It was clear and cold. We got into line after about our usual delay in marching and halting, and as soon as we could collect the material, we had a bright, rousing fire to collect around, and to eat supper by. We made our beds around this fire and slept till morning. Some idea of the weather may be understood from the fact that several of the canteens that I helped fill late in the evening, were frozen solid in the morning, and some had burst open and were spoiled. The next day we had nothing to do but to keep ourselves warm and speculate on the prospects before us. We were on a portion of the plank road that leads from Culpeper to Fredericksburg, and could at any time we chose, move down and take possession of the heights of that place. The enemy were only covering Gordonsville. They were south and west of us, and we were the nearest Fredericksburg. All this looked as if it might be so, but there was an air of mystery and doubt about it that made some of the knowing ones feel incredulous. Our hesitating to attack the day before looked a little as if everything was not so well for us as some pretended to believe. They had a strong position and doubtless were so disposed that they could move down and occupy their old position by Fredericksburg, or they could fight us there; in either case they held us to a disadvantage. It really looked as if Gen. Meade had failed in some brilliant maneuvre by which he had intended to bring Lee out on an open fight, and in this failure, inasmuch as we had declined to fight and give the rebels their advantage, it seemed pretty likely that we should fall back across the river once more. This was rendered certain when night came and we were ordered to pack up and fall in. After marching two or three miles, or such a matter, we halted and formed into line. Skirmishers were thrown out, and we were told that we should remain at least two hours.

It was a certain thing then that we were retreating, and that a part of our brigade was acting as rear-guard. We spread down our blankets, determined to steal a little sleep if we could. The next thing we have any recollection of was of being aroused from a good sweet dream, and ordered to form. We had been there three hours instead of two. We were completely chilled through, and it was quite fortunate that we were awakened when we were, for we were shivering with the cold, and trembling like a man of ninety. We fell into line, and before we had marched far we were warm enough.

It was about daylight when we reached and crossed Germanna Ford the next morning. We noticed as we passed down to the river some well constructed rifle-pits and breastworks, from which the enemy had no doubt intended to dispute our passage across the river, and which we were enabled to dodge through the foresight and generalship of Gen. Meade. We marched about a mile this side of the river before we halted for breakfast. The 5th corps had preceded us, and their men were lying in the bushes on each side of the road, as thickly as they could possibly get together. After breakfast we marched on a little further, and finally in a woods for all day, and the next night. Thursday morning we were ordered to pack up and fall in, which we did, and marched towards our old camp. We marched up to Stevensburg and crossed the Mountain Creek at that place, some distance above the place where we crossed the same stream on our way down a week before. As we came along by the camps of the 5th and 3rd corps we noticed that they were occupying the same houses, and, the same places exactly, that they occupied before we moved. At Brandy Station everything was alive with business. One sutler's wagon was actually unloading from a platform car, just as we passed by. This was an important event, for sutler's goods have heretofore been too scarce to be obtained even by officers, and those who feel that they have a special right to these things. We marched straight back into our old camp. Those that had not burned up their houses before they left had only to put their tent overhead for a roof, and they were as comfortably situated as ever; but some had completely destroyed their houses, and material, and consequently if they built again, had to commence anew. We were told that we had better not make any extensive preparations for comfortable quarters, as our regiment intended to move to a more pleasant locality, which has since been done. Friday night the order came into camp to pack up everything, and be ready to move at a moment's notice. The rebel cavalry had crossed to this side of the Rapidan, and possibly we might be attacked. The officers and men had been given a ration of whiskey that night, and all hands were pretty noisy, though nobody supposed that that had anything to do with the rebel scare. Matters quieted down after a while, and so did the boys, and no enemy disturbed us that night. The next morning we were detailed for this "fatigue," and here we have been ever since. We are building a corduroy road along by the side of the railroad from Rappahannock Station to camp. Our supplies they say have got to be carried over this road. The railroad only carries forage to Brandy Station.

But it is getting to be well on towards midnight, and my fire is nearly gone out. No one would disagree with me, if I should say, it is time this tedious letter was brought to a close, for I am beginning to feel almost as dull as what I have written.

"MY CONSCIENCE IS CLEAR":
VIRGINIA, DECEMBER 1863

George G. Meade to Margaret Meade

Meade wrote to his wife after returning to his headquarters near Brandy Station. In his official report to Halleck on December 7, Meade admitted that the campaign had been "a failure," but insisted the causes of its failure "were beyond my control." He cited French's delays in advancing the Third Corps on November 26–27 as "one of the primary causes of the failure of the whole movement" and criticized Warren's "unfortunate error in judgment" in not attacking on the morning of November 30. The failure at Mine Run caused Lincoln, Stanton, and Halleck to consider replacing Meade with Brigadier General William F. Smith, the chief engineer of the Army of the Cumberland and a former corps commander in the Army of the Potomac, but no decision was made. Meade would remain at his post as his army went into winter quarters.

Head-Quarters, Army of the Potomac,
Decr. 2d.—1863.

Dear Margaret—

I expect your wishes will now soon be gratified;—and that I shall be relieved from the Army of the Potomac. The facts are briefly these.—On the 26th ulto. I crossed the Rapidan intending to turn the right flank of Genl. Lee, and attack him, or compel him to attack me out of his formidable river entrenchments.—I had previously been advised by deserters & others, that he had commenced a line of works running *perpendicular* to the river, but only extending a few miles, by which he designed covering his flank, and permitting him to leave the lower fords unguarded.—I accordingly made my plans to cross in 3 columns, to unite at a common point below his entrenchments, and then to advance rapidly & attack him before he could prepare any defences. The plan was a good one, but owing to the failure of others to whom its execution was necessarily entrusted it failed.—In the first place, one corps was *three* hours behind time in arriving at the river and slow of movement afterwards, which caused a delay of *one day*—enabled the enemy to advance & check my columns before they united, & finally to concentrate his army, in a very formidable position, behind entrenchments almost as strong as those I was making a long detour to avoid. Again after I had come up with the enemy one corps commander reported he had examined a position, where there was not the slightest doubt he could carry the enemys works & on his positive & unhesitating judgement, he was given 28,000 men, and directed to attack the next morning at 8 o'clock. At the same time another attack was to be made by 15,000 men at a point where the enemy evidently was not fully prepared.—On the eventful morning, just as the attack was about being made, I received a despatch from the officer commanding the 28,000 men saying he had changed his opinion, and that the attack on his front was *so hopeless*, that he had assumed the responsibility of suspending it, till further orders were received.—This astounding intelligence reached me just 10 minutes before the hour for attacking, and barely in time to suspend the other attack, which was a secondary one & which even if successful could not be supported with so large a portion of my force away for the main attack.—This lost me another day during which the enemy so strengthened the point threatened by the secondary attack, as to render it nearly as strong as the rest of his line, and to have almost destroyed, the before probable chances of success. Finding no possibility of attacking with hope of success, and power to follow up success, and that the only weak point visible, had been strengthened during the delay caused by the change of opinion of a corps commander—I determined not to attempt an assault.

I could not move any further round the enemys flank, for *want of roads*, and from the danger, at this season of the year of a storm, which could render locomotion, off the *prepared roads* a matter of impossibility.—After reviewing all the circumstances, notwithstanding my most earnest desire to give battle, and in the full consciousness of the fact, that my failure to do so, was certain personal ruin—I having come to the conclusion that an attack could not be successful determined to, & did withdraw the army. I am fully aware it will be said, I did wrong in deciding this question by reasoning, and that I ought to have *tried* & then a *failure* would have been evidence of my good judgement, but I trust I have too much reputation as a General, to be obliged to encounter certain defeat, in order to prove that victory was not possible. Political considerations will however enter largely into the decision, and the failure of the Army of the Potomac to do any thing at this moment will be considered of vital consequence and if *I* can be held responsible for this failure, I will be removed to prove that I am. I therefore consider my fate as settled; but as I have told you before I would rather be ignominiously dismissed, and suffer any thing, than knowingly and willfully have thousands of brave men slaughtered for nothing. It was my deliberate judgement that I ought not to attack. I acted on that judgement, and I am willing to stand or fall by it at all hazards. I shall write to the President giving him a clear statement of the case, and endeavoring to free his action as much as possible, by assuming myself all the responsibility.—I feel of course greatly disappointed—a little more good fortune, and I should have met with brilliant success. As it is my conscience is clear—I did the best I could. If I had thought there was any reasonable degree of probability of success, I would have attacked. I did not think so—on the contrary believed it would result in a useless & criminal slaughter of brave men, and might result in serious disaster to the army—I determined not to attack no other movements were practicable & I withdrew.

There will be a great howl all over the country. Letter writers & politicians will denounce me. It will be proved as clear as the light of day, that an attack was perfectly practicable, and that every one except myself in the army particularly the soldiers, were dying for it and that I had some mysterious object in view either in connection with politics, or stock-jobbing or some thing else about as foreign to my thoughts—and finally the administration will be obliged to yield to popular clamor and discard me. For all this I am prepared justified as I said before by a clear conscience, and the conviction that I have acted from a high sense of duty, to myself as a soldier, to my men as their General, and to my country and its cause, as the agent having its vital interests solemnly entrusted to me, which I have no right to wantonly play with, and to jeopardize either for my own personal benefit, or to satisfy the demands of popular clamor, or interested politicians.—I should like this letter shown confidentially to Cortlandt Parker, Mr. Harding, & other friends, whose good opinion I am anxious to preserve. George was sent with one of the messages to suspend the attack—his horse fell with him—he was a little bruised & cut about the eye, but nothing serious.—I have received your letter of the 30th ulto. Good bye.

Ever yours. *G. G. Meade*

Head-Quarters, Army of the Potomac,
Decr. 7th 1863

Dear Margaret,

I received today your letter of the 5th inst.—I am yet on the anxious bench—not one word has been vouchsafed me from Washington. The papers of course you have seen, but there was one article in the Washington Star, said to have been inspired from high official quarters, which was very severe on me. It was headed "Hesitating Generals"—and referred to my failure at Williamsport—to my running away from Lee with *double* the number of men, and to my recent fiasco, as all combining to show I was not competent to command an army. I should hardly suppose any official, claiming respect would choose as a machine for conveying his ideas to the public such a disreputable sheet as the Star whose drunken editor is the horror of all who know him. Still other indications that have reached me would confirm the report that the article was by authority & is a premonition of my approaching fate. I understand from an officer just returned from Washington, that on meeting a prominent member of the Govt, he was asked if the Army of the Potomac has stopped running yet? and whether there were any fighting men in it among the Generals? To day I sent in my official report in which I have told the plain truth—acknowledged the movement was a failure but claimed the causes were not in my plans, but in the want of support & co-operation on the part of subordinates.—I dont know whether my report will be published, but if it is it will make a sensation, and undoubtedly result in some official investigation. I have received a very kind letter from Cortlandt Parker, (written before he had received yours) in which he sympathizes with me in the failure, but says he is satisfied I have done right, and that I have not lost the confidence of intelligent people, and he hopes I will not resign but hold on to the last.—I have also received a very kind & complimentary letter from Gibbon saying he had as much confidence as ever in my ability to command and that military men would sustain me.—I telegraphed Genl. Halleck that I desired to visit Washn. but his reply was couched in such terms, that tho it gave me permission to go, clearly intimated my presence was not desired, so far as he was concerned. I have in consequence not gone, and now shall not go unless they send for me.—I am only concerned for my reputation as a soldier—if I can preserve that they are at liberty to deprive me of command & even of rank.—

I see the Herald inspired by my *friend* Dan Sickles, is constantly harping on the assertion that Gettysburgh was fought by the *corps commanders* (ie D. S.) and the common soldiers & that no Generalship was displayed. I suppose after a while it will be discovered, I was not at Gettysburgh at all. We have had very cold weather, but George & I continue quite well. I hope Sergie will soon be well again. Love & kisses to all the children. Ever yours

G. G. Meade

"EVERY FREE MAN A VOTER":
PENNSYLVANIA, DECEMBER 1863

Frederick Douglass: Our Work Is Not Done

December 4, 1863

Douglass gave this speech at the thirtieth-anniversary meeting of the American Anti-Slavery Society, held in Philadelphia on December 3–4 and devoted to "a general review and survey of the cause." His remarks were in part a response to the views of William Lloyd Garrison, a founder of the society and its president since 1843, who believed that antislavery societies would no longer be needed once emancipation was complete.

LADIES AND GENTLEMEN: I confess at the outset to have felt a very profound desire to utter a word at some period during the present meeting. As it has been repeatedly said here, it has been a meeting of reminiscences. I shall not attempt to treat you to any of my own in what I have now to say, though I have some in connection with the labors of this Society, and in connection with my experience as an American slave, that I might not inappropriately bring before you on this occasion. I desire to be remembered among those having a word to say at this meeting, because I began my existence as a free man in this country with this association, and because I have some hopes or apprehensions, whichever you please to call them, that we shall never, as a Society, hold another decade meeting.

I well remember the first time I ever listened to the voice of the honored President of this association, and I have some recollection of the feelings of hope inspired by his utterances at that time. Under the inspiration of those hopes, I looked forward to the abolition of slavery as a certain event in the course of a very few years. So clear were his utterances, so simple and truthful, and so adapted, I conceived, to the human heart were the principles and doctrines propounded by him, that I thought five years at any rate would be all that would be required for the abolition of slavery. I thought it was only necessary for the slaves, or their friends, to lift up the hatchway of slavery's infernal hold, to uncover the bloody scenes of American thraldom, and give the nation a peep into its horrors, its deeds of deep damnation, to arouse them to almost phrensied opposition to this foul curse. But I was mistaken. I had not been five years pelted by the mob, insulted by the crowds, shunned by the church, denounced by the ministry, ridiculed by the press, spit upon by the loafers, before I became convinced that I might perhaps live, struggle, and die, and go down to my grave, and the slaves of the South yet remain in their chains.

We live to see a better hope to-night. I participate in the profound thanksgiving expressed by all, that we do live to see this better day. I am one of those who believe that it is the mission of this war to free every slave in the United States. I am one of those who believe that we should consent to no peace which shall not be an abolition peace. I am, moreover, one of those who believe that the work of the American Anti-Slavery Society will not have been completed until the black men of the South, and the black men of the North, shall have been admitted fully and completely into the body politic of America. I look upon slavery as going the way of all the earth. It is the mission of the war to put it down. But a mightier work than the abolition of slavery now looms up before the Abolitionist. This Society was organized, if I remember rightly, for two distinct objects; one was the emancipation of the slave, and the other the elevation of the colored people. When you have taken the chains off the slave, as I believe we shall do, we shall find a harder resistance to the second purpose of this great association than we have found even upon slavery itself.

I am hopeful, but while I am hopeful I am thoughtful withal. If I lean to either side of the controversy to which we have listened to-day, I lean to that side which implies caution, which implies apprehension, which implies a consciousness that our work is not done. Protest, affirm, hope, glorify as we may, it cannot be denied that abolitionism is still unpopular in the United States. It cannot be denied that this war is at present denounced by its opponents as an abolition war; and it is equally clear that it would not be denounced as an abolition war, if abolitionism were not odious. It is equally clear that our friends, Republicans, Unionists, Loyalists, would not spin out elaborate explanations, and denials that this is the character of the war, if abolition were popular. Men accept the term Abolitionist with qualifications. They do not come out square and open-handed, and affirm themselves to be Abolitionists. As a general rule, we are attempting to explain away the charge that this is an abolition war. I hold that it is an abolition war, because slavery has proved itself stronger than the Constitution. It has proved itself stronger than the Union, and has forced upon us the necessity of putting down slavery in order to save the Union, and in order to save the Constitution. (Applause.)

I look at this as an abolition war instead of being a Union war, because I see that the lesser is included in the greater, and that you cannot have the lesser until you have the greater. You cannot have the Union, the Constitution, and republican institutions, until you have stricken down that damning curse, and put it beyond the pale of the Republic. For, while it is in this country, it will make your Union impossible; it will make your Constitution impossible. I therefore call this just what the Democrats have charged it with being, an abolition war. Let us emblazon it on our banners, and declare before the world that this is an abolition war, (applause), that it will prosper precisely in proportion as it takes upon itself this character. (Renewed applause.)

My respected friend, Mr. Purvis, called attention to the existence of prejudice against color in this country. This gives me great cause for apprehension, if not for alarm. I am afraid of this powerful element of prejudice against color. While it exists, I want the voice of the American Anti-Slavery Society to be continually protesting, continually exposing it. While it can be said that in this most anti-slavery city in the Northern States of our Union, in the city of Philadelphia, the city of Brotherly Love, in the city of churches, the city of piety, that the most genteel and respectable colored lady or gentleman may be kicked out of your commonest street car, we are in danger of a compromise. While it can be said that black men, fighting bravely for this country, are asked to take $7 per month, while the government lays down as a rule or criterion of pay a complexional one, we are in danger of a compromise. While to be radical is to be unpopular, we are in danger of a compromise.

While we have a large minority, called Democratic, in every State of the North, we have a powerful nucleus for a most infernal re-action in favor of slavery. I know it is said that we have recently achieved vast political victories. I am glad of it. I value those victories, however, more for what they have prevented than for what they have actually accomplished. I should have been doubly sad at seeing any one of these States wheel into line with the Peace Democracy. But, however it may be in the State of Pennsylvania, I know that you may look for abolition in the creed of any party in New York with a microscope, and you will not find a single line of anti-slavery there. The victories were Union victories, victories to save the Union in such ways as the country may devise to save it. But whatever may have been the meaning of these majorities in regard to the Union, we know one thing, that the minorities, at least, mean slavery. They mean submission. They mean the degradation of the colored man. They mean everything but open rebellion against the Federal government in the South. But the mob, the rioters in the city of New York, convert that city into a hell, and its lower orders into demons, and dash out the brains of little children against the curbstones; and they mean anything and everything that the Devil exacts at their hands. While we had in this State a majority of but 15,000 over this pro-slavery Democratic party, they have a mighty minority, a dangerous minority. Keep in mind when these minorities were gotten. Powerful as they are, they were gotten when slavery, with bloody hands, was stabbing at the very heart of the nation itself. With all that disadvantage, they have piled up these powerful minorities.

We have work to do, friends and fellow-citizens, to look after these minorities. The day that shall see Jeff Davis fling down his Montgomery Constitution, and call home his Generals, will be the most trying day to the virtue of this people that this country has ever seen. When the slaveholders shall give up the contest, and ask for re-admission into the Union, then, as Mr. Wilson has told us, we shall see the trying time in this country. Your Democracy will clamor for peace and for restoring the old order of things, because that old order of things was the life of the Democratic party. "You do take away mine house, when you take away the prop that sustains my house," and the support of the Democratic party we all know to be slavery. The Democratic party is for war for slavery; it is for peace for slavery; it is for the *habeas corpus* for slavery; it is against the *habeas corpus* for slavery; it was for the Florida war for slavery; it was for the Mexican war for slavery; it is for jury trial for traitors for slavery; it is against jury trial for men claimed as fugitive slaves for slavery. It has but one principle, one master; and it is guided, governed and directed by it. I say that with this party among us, flaunting its banners in our faces, with the New York *World* scattered broadcast over the North, with the New York *Express*, with the mother and father and devil of them all, the New York *Herald*, (applause), with those papers flooding our land, and coupling the term Abolitionist with all manner of coarse epithets, in all our hotels, at all our crossings, our highways, and byways, and railways, all over the country, there is work to be done—a good deal of work to be done.

I have said that our work will not be done until the colored man is admitted a full member in good and regular standing into the American body politic. Men have very nice ideas about the body politic where I have travelled; and they don't like the idea of having the negro in the body politic. He may remain in this country, for he will be useful as a laborer, valuable perhaps in time of trouble as a helper; but to make him a full and complete citizen, a legal voter, that would be contaminating the body politic. I was a little curious, some years ago, to find out what sort of a thing this body politic was; and I was very anxious to know especially about what amount of baseness, brutality, coarseness, ignorance, and bestiality, could find its way into the body politic; and I was not long in finding it out. I took my stand near the little hole through which the body politic put its votes. (Laughter.) And first among the mob, I saw Ignorance, unable to read its vote, asking *me* to read it, by the way, (great laughter), depositing its vote in the body politic. Next I saw a man stepping up to the body politic, casting in his vote, having a black eye, and another one ready to be blacked, having been engaged in a street fight. I saw, again, Pat, fresh from the Emerald Isle, with the delightful brogue peculiar to him, stepping up—not walking, but leaning upon the arms of two of his friends, unable to stand, passing into the body politic! I came to the conclusion that this body politic was, after all, not quite so pure a body as the representation of its friends would lead us to believe.

I know it will be said that I ask you to make the black man a voter in the South. Yet you are for having brutality and ignorance introduced into the ballot-box. It is said that the colored man is ignorant, and therefore he shall not vote. In saying this, you lay down a rule for the black man that you apply to no other class of your citizens. I will hear nothing of degradation nor of ignorance against the black man. If he knows enough to be hanged, he knows enough to vote. If he knows an honest man from a thief, he knows much more than some of our white voters. If he knows as much when sober as an Irishman knows when drunk, he knows enough to vote. If he knows enough to take up arms in defence of this government, and bare his breast to the storm of rebel artillery, he knows enough to vote. (Great applause.)

Away with this talk of the want of knowledge on the part of the negro! I am about as big a negro as you will find anywhere about town; and any man that does not believe I know enough to vote, let him try it. I think I can convince him that I do. Let him run for office in my district, and solicit my vote, and I will show him.

All I ask, however, in regard to the blacks, is that whatever rule you adopt, whether of intelligence or wealth, as the condition of voting, you should apply it equally to the black man. Do that, and I am satisfied, and eternal justice is satisfied. Liberty, fraternity, equality, are satisfied; and the country will move on harmoniously.

Mr. President, I have a patriotic argument in favor of insisting upon the immediate enfranchisement of the slaves of the South; and it is this. When this rebellion shall have been put down, when the arms shall have fallen from the guilty hand of traitors, you will need the friendship of the slaves of the South, of those millions there. Four or five million men are not of inconsiderable importance at anytime; but they will be doubly important when you come to reorganize and reestablish republican institutions in the South. Will you mock those bondmen by breaking their chains with one hand, and with the other giving their rebel masters the elective franchise and robbing them of theirs? I tell you the negro is your friend. But you will make him not only your friend in sentiment and heart by enfranchising him, you will thus make him your best defender, your best protector against the traitors and the descendants of those traitors who will inherit the hate, the bitter revenge which shall crystalize all over the South, and seek to circumvent the government that they could not throw off. You will need the black man there as a watchman and patrol; and you may need him as a soldier. You may need him to uphold in peace, as he is now upholding in war, the star-spangled banner. (Applause.) I wish our excellent friend, Senator Wilson, would bend his energies to this point as well as the other—to let the negro have a vote. It will be helping him from the jaws of the wolf. We are surrounded by those who, like the wolf, will use their jaws, if you give the elective franchise to the descendants of the traitors, and keep it from the black man. We ought to be voters there! We ought to be members of Congress! (Applause.) You may as well make up your minds that you have got to see something dark down that way! There is no way to get rid of it. I am a candidate already! (Applause.)

For twenty-five years, Mr. President, you know that when I got as far South as Philadelphia, I felt that I was rubbing against my prison wall, and could not go any further. I dared not go over yonder into Delaware. Twenty years ago, when I attended the first Decade meeting of this Society, as I came along the vales and hills of Gettysburg, my good friends, the anti-slavery people along there, warned me to remain in the house during the daytime and travel in the night, lest I should be kidnapped, and carried over into Maryland. My good friend Dr. Fussell was one of the number who did not think it safe for me to attend an anti-slavery meeting along the borders of this State. I can go down there now. I have been to Washington to see the President; and as you were not there, perhaps you may like to know how the President of the United States received a black man at the White House. I will tell you how he received me—just as you have seen one gentleman receive another! (great applause); with a hand and a voice well-balanced between a kind cordiality and a respectful reserve. I tell you I felt big there. (Laughter.) Let me tell you how I got to him; because every body can't get to him. He has to be a little guarded in admitting spectators. The manner in getting to him gave me an idea that the cause was rolling on. The stairway was crowded with applicants. Some of them looked eager; and I have no doubt some of them had a purpose in being there, and wanted to see the President for the good of the country! They were white, and as I was the only dark spot among them, I expected to have a wait at least half a day; I have heard of men waiting a week; but in two minutes after I sent in my card, the messenger came out, and respectfully invited "Mr. Douglass" in. I could hear, in the eager multitude outside, as they saw me pressing and elbowing my way through, the remark, "Yes, damn it, I knew they would let the nigger through," in a kind of despairing voice—a Peace Democrat, I suppose. (Laughter.) When I went in, the President was sitting in his usual position, I was told, with his feet in different parts of the room, taking it easy. (Laughter.) Don't put this down, Mr. Reporter, I pray you; for I am going down there again to-morrow. (Laughter.) As I came in and approached him, the President began to rise, and he continued to rise until he stood over me (laughter); and he reached out his hand and said, "Mr. Douglass, I know you; I have read about you, and Mr. Seward has told me about you;" putting me quite at ease at once.

Now you will want to know how I was impressed by him. I will tell you that, too. He impressed me as being just what every one of you have been in the habit of calling him—an honest man. (Applause.) I never met with a man, who, on the first blush, impressed me more entirely with his sincerity, with his devotion to his country, and with his determination to save it at all hazards. (Applause.) He told me (I think he did me more honor than I deserve), that I had made a little speech somewhere in New York, and it had got into the papers, and among the things I had said was this: That if I were called upon to state what I regarded as the most sad and most disheartening feature in our present political and military situation, it would not be the various disasters experienced by our armies and our navies, on flood and field, but it would be the tardy, hesitating and vacillating policy of the President of the United States; and the President said to me, "Mr. Douglass, I have been charged with being tardy, and the like;" and he went on, and partly admitted that he might seem slow; but he said,

"I am charged with vacillating; but, Mr. Douglass, I do not think that charge can be sustained; I think it cannot be shown that when I have once taken a position, I have ever retreated from it." (Applause.) That I regarded as the most significant point in what he said during our interview. I told him that he had been somewhat slow in proclaiming equal protection to our colored soldiers and prisoners; and he said that the country needed talking up to that point. He hesitated in regard to it when he felt that the country was not ready for it. He knew that the colored man throughout this country was a despised man, a hated man, and he knew that if he at first came out with such a proclamation, all the hatred which is poured on the head of the negro race would be visited on his Administration. He said that there was preparatory work needed, and that that preparatory work had been done. And he added, "Remember this, Mr. Douglass; remember that Milliken's Bend, Port Hudson, and Fort Wagner are recent events; and that these were necessary to prepare the way for this very proclamation of mine." I thought it was reasonable; but I came to the conclusion that while Abraham Lincoln will not go down to posterity as Abraham the Great, or as Abraham the Wise, or as Abraham the Eloquent, although he is all three, wise, great, and eloquent, he will go down to posterity, if the country is saved, as Honest Abraham, (applause); and going down thus, his name may be written anywhere in this wide world of ours side by side with that of Washington, without disparaging the latter. (Cheers.)

But we are not to be saved by the captain this time, but by the crew. We are not to be saved by Abraham Lincoln, but by that power behind the throne, greater than the throne itself. You and I and all of us have this matter in hand. Men talk about saving the Union, and restoring the Union as it was. They delude themselves with the miserable idea that that old Union can be brought to life again. That old Union, whose canonized bones we so quietly inurned under the shattered walls of Sumter, can never come to life again. It is dead, and you cannot put life into it. The first shot fired at the walls of Sumter caused it to fall as dead as the body of Julius Caesar when stabbed by Brutus. We do not want it. We have outlived the old Union. We had outlived it long before the rebellion came to tell us—

I mean the Union under the old pro-slavery interpretation of it—and had become ashamed of it. The South hated it with our anti-slavery interpretation, and the North hated it with the Southern interpretation of its requirements. We had already come to think with horror of the idea of being called upon here in our churches and literary societies, to take up arms and go down South, and pour the leaden death into the breasts of the slaves, in case they should rise for liberty; and the better part of the people did not mean to do it. They shuddered at the idea of so sacrilegious a crime. They had already become utterly disgusted with the idea of playing the part of bloodhounds for the slave-masters, and watch-dogs for the plantations. They had come to detest the principle upon which the slaveholding States had a larger representation in Congress than the free States. They had come to think that the little finger of dear old John Brown was worth more to the world than all the slaveholders in Virginia put together. (Applause.) What business, then, have we to fight for the old Union? We are not fighting for it. We are fighting for something incomparably better than the old Union. We are fighting for unity; unity of object, unity of institutions, in which there shall be no North, no South, no East, no West, no black, no white, but a solidarity of the nation, making every slave free, and every free man a voter. (Great applause.)

WASHINGTON, D.C., DECEMBER 1863

Abraham Lincoln: Annual Message to Congress

In his annual message and the proclamation accompanying it, President Lincoln outlined a program for the reconstruction of the rebelling states. While some abolitionists criticized his plan for being too lenient to secessionists and for failing to extend the franchise to freed slaves, it was initially well received by a wide range of Republicans. Many Radicals praised it for making emancipation a precondition for the restoration of the Union, while conservatives applauded Lincoln's refusal to endorse the theory, advanced by some Radicals, that the Confederate states had lost their sovereignty and reverted to the status of federal territories.

December 8, 1863

Fellow citizens of the Senate and House of Representatives:

Another year of health, and of sufficiently abundant harvests has passed. For these, and especially for the improved condition of our national affairs, our renewed, and profoundest gratitude to God is due.

We remain in peace and friendship with foreign powers.

The efforts of disloyal citizens of the United States to involve us in foreign wars, to aid an inexcusable insurrection, have been unavailing. Her Britannic Majesty's government, as was justly expected, have exercised their authority to prevent the departure of new hostile expeditions from British ports. The Emperor of France has, by a like proceeding, promptly vindicated the neutrality which he proclaimed at the beginning of the contest. Questions of great intricacy and importance have arisen out of the blockade, and other belligerent operations, between the government and several of the maritime powers, but they have been discussed, and, as far as was possible, accommodated in a spirit of frankness, justice, and mutual good will. It is especially gratifying that our prize courts, by the impartiality of their adjudications, have commanded the respect and confidence of maritime powers.

The supplemental treaty between the United States and Great Britain for the suppression of the African slave trade, made on the 17th. day of February last, has been duly ratified, and carried into execution. It is believed that, so far as American ports and American citizens are concerned, that inhuman and odious traffic has been brought to an end.

I shall submit, for the consideration of the Senate, a convention for the adjustment of possessory claims in Washington Territory, arising out of the treaty of the 15th. June, 1846, between the United States and Great Britain, and which have been the source of some disquiet among the citizens of that now rapidly improving part of the country.

A novel and important question, involving the extent of the maritime jurisdiction of Spain in the waters which surround the island of Cuba, has been debated without reaching an agreement, and it is proposed in an amicable spirit to refer it to the arbitrament of a friendly power. A convention for that purpose will be submitted to the Senate.

I have thought it proper, subject to the approval of the Senate, to concur with the interested commercial powers in an arrangement for the liquidation of the Scheldt dues upon the principles which have been heretofore adopted in regard to the imposts upon navigation in the waters of Denmark.

The long pending controversy between this government and that of Chili touching the seizure at Sitana, in Peru, by Chilian officers, of a large amount in treasure belonging to citizens of the United States, has been brought to a close by the award of His Majesty, the King of the Belgians, to whose arbitration the question was referred by the parties. The subject was thoroughly and patiently examined by that justly respected magistrate, and although the sum awarded to the claimants may not have been as large as they expected, there is no reason to distrust the wisdom of his Majesty's decision. That decision was promptly complied with by Chili, when intelligence in regard to it reached that country.

The joint commission, under the act of the last session, for carrying into effect the convention with Peru on the subject of claims, has been organized at Lima, and is engaged in the business intrusted to it.

Difficulties concerning inter-oceanic transit through Nicaragua are in course of amicable adjustment.

In conformity with principles set forth in my last annual message, I have received a representative from the United States of Colombia, and have accredited a minister to that republic.

Incidents occurring in the progress of our civil war have forced upon my attention the uncertain state of international questions, touching the rights of foreigners in this country and of United States citizens abroad. In regard to some governments these rights are at least partially defined by treaties. In no instance, however, is it expressly stipulated that, in the event of civil war, a foreigner residing in this country, within the lines of the insurgents, is to be exempted from the rule which classes him as a belligerent, in whose behalf the government of his country cannot expect any privileges or immunities distinct from that character. I regret to say, however, that such claims have been put forward, and, in some instances, in behalf of foreigners who have lived in the United States the greater part of their lives.

There is reason to believe that many persons born in foreign countries, who have declared their intention to become citizens, or who have been fully naturalized, have evaded the military duty required of them by denying the fact, and thereby throwing upon the government the burden of proof. It has been found difficult or impracticable to obtain this proof from the want of guides to the proper sources of information. These might be supplied by requiring clerks of courts, where declarations of intention may be made or naturalizations effected, to send, periodically, lists of the names of the persons naturalized, or declaring their intention to become citizens, to the Secretary of the Interior, in whose department those names might be arranged and printed for general information.

There is also reason to believe that foreigners frequently become citizens of the United States for the sole purpose of evading duties imposed by the laws of their native countries, to which, on becoming naturalized here, they at once repair, and though never returning to the United States, they still claim the interposition of this government as citizens. Many altercations and great prejudices have heretofore arisen out of this abuse. It is therefore, submitted to your serious consideration. It might be advisable to fix a limit, beyond which no Citizen of the United States residing abroad may claim the interposition of his government.

The right of suffrage has often been assumed and exercised by aliens, under pretences of naturalization, which they have disavowed when drafted into the military service. I submit the expediency of such an amendment of the law as will make the fact of voting an estoppel against any plea of exemption from military service, or other civil obligation, on the ground of alienage.

In common with other western powers, our relations with Japan have been brought into serious jeopardy, through the perverse opposition of the hereditary aristocracy of the empire, to the enlightened and liberal policy of the Tycoon designed to bring the country into the society of nations. It is hoped, although not with entire confidence, that these difficulties may be peacefully overcome. I ask your attention to the claim of the Minister residing there for the damages he sustained in the destruction by fire of the residence of the legation at Yedo.

Satisfactory arrangements have been made with the Emperor of Russia, which, it is believed, will result in effecting a continuous line of telegraph through that empire from our Pacific coast.

I recommend to your favorable consideration the subject of an international telegraph across the Atlantic ocean; and also of a telegraph between this capital and the national forts along the Atlantic seaboard and the Gulf of Mexico. Such communications, established with any reasonable outlay, would be economical as well as effective aids to the diplomatic, military, and naval service.

The consular system of the United States, under the enactments of the last Congress, begins to be self-sustaining; and there is reason to hope that it may become entirely so, with the increase of trade which will ensue whenever peace is restored. Our ministers abroad have been faithful in defending American rights. In protecting commercial interests, our Consuls have necessarily had to encounter increased labors and responsibilities, growing out of the war. These they have, for the most part, met and discharged with zeal and efficiency. This acknowledgment justly includes those Consuls who, residing in Morocco, Egypt, Turkey, Japan, China, and other oriental countries, are charged with complex functions and extraordinary powers.

The condition of the several organized Territories is generally satisfactory, although Indian disturbances in New Mexico have not been entirely suppressed. The mineral resources of Colorado, Nevada, Idaho, New Mexico, and Arizona are proving far richer than has been heretofore understood. I lay before you a communication on this subject from the governor of New Mexico. I again submit to your consideration the expediency of establishing a system for the encouragement of immigration. Although this source of national wealth and strength is again flowing with greater freedom than for several years before the insurrection occurred, there is still a great deficiency of laborers in every field of industry, especially in agriculture and in our mines, as well of iron and coal as of the precious metals. While the demand for labor is thus increased here, tens of thousands of persons, destitute of remunerative occupation, are thronging our foreign consulates, and offering to emigrate to the United States if essential, but very cheap, assistance can be afforded them. It is easy to see that, under the sharp discipline of civil war, the nation is beginning a new life. This noble effort demands the aid, and ought to receive the attention and support of the government.

Injuries, unforeseen by the government and unintended, may, in some cases, have been inflicted on the subjects or citizens of foreign countries, both at sea and on land, by persons in the service of the United States. As this government expects redress from other powers when similar injuries are inflicted by persons in their service upon citizens of the United States, we must be prepared to do justice to foreigners. If the existing judicial tribunals are inadequate to this purpose, a special court may be authorized, with power to hear and decide such claims of the character referred to as may have arisen under treaties and the public law. Conventions for adjusting the claims by joint commission have been proposed to some governments, but no definitive answer to the proposition has yet been received from any.

In the course of the session I shall probably have occasion to request you to provide indemnification to claimants where decrees of restitution have been rendered, and damages awarded by admiralty courts; and in other cases where this government may be acknowledged to be liable in principle, and where the amount of that liability has been ascertained by an informal arbitration.

The proper officers of the treasury have deemed themselves required, by the law of the United States upon the subject, to demand a tax upon the incomes of foreign consuls in this country. While such a demand may not, in strictness, be in derogation of public law, or perhaps of any existing treaty between the United States and a foreign country, the expediency of so far modifying the act as to exempt from tax the income of such consuls as are not citizens of the United States, derived from the emoluments of their office, or from property not situated in the United States, is submitted to your serious consideration. I make this suggestion upon the ground that a comity which ought to be reciprocated exempts our Consuls, in all other countries, from taxation to the extent thus indicated. The United States, I think, ought not to be exceptionally illiberal to international trade and commerce.

The operations of the treasury during the last year have been successfully conducted. The enactment by Congress of a national banking law has proved a valuable support of the public credit; and the general legislation in relation to loans has fully answered the expectations of its favorers. Some amendments may be required to perfect existing laws; but no change in their principles or general scope is believed to be needed.

Since these measures have been in operation, all demands on the treasury, including the pay of the army and navy, have been promptly met and fully satisfied. No considerable body of troops, it is believed, were ever more amply provided, and more liberally and punctually paid; and it may be added that by no people were the burdens incident to a great war ever more cheerfully borne.

The receipts during the year from all sources, including loans and the balance in the treasury at its commencement, were $901,125,674.86, and the aggregate disbursements $895,796,630.65, leaving a balance on the 1st. July, 1863, of $5,329,044.21. Of the receipts there were derived from customs, $69,059,642.40; from internal revenue, $37,640,787.95; from direct tax, $1,485,103.61; from lands, $167,617.17; from miscellaneous sources, $3,046,615.35; and from loans, $776,682,361.57; making the aggregate, $901,125,674.86. Of the disbursements there were for the civil service, $23,253,922.08; for pensions and Indians, $4,216,520.79; for interest on public debt, $24,729,846.51; for the War Department, $599,298,600.83; for the Navy Department, $63,211,105.27; for payment of funded and temporary debt, $181,086,635.07; making the aggregate, $895,796,630.65, and leaving the balance of $5,329,044.21. But the payment of funded and temporary debt, having been made from moneys borrowed during the year, must be regarded as merely nominal payments, and the moneys borrowed to make them as merely nominal receipts; and their amount, $181,086,635 07, should therefore be deducted both from receipts and disbursements. This being done, there remains as actual receipts $720,039,039.79; and the actual disbursements, $714,709,995.58, leaving the balance as already stated.

The actual receipts and disbursements for the first quarter, and the estimated receipts and disbursements for the remaining three quarters, of the current fiscal year, 1864, will be shown in detail by the report of the Secretary of the Treasury, to which I invite your attention. It is sufficient to say here that it is not believed that actual results will exhibit a state of the finances less favorable to the country than the estimates of that officer heretofore submitted; while it is confidently expected that at the close of the year both disbursements and debt will be found very considerably less than has been anticipated.

The report of the Secretary of War is a document of great interest. It consists of—

1. The military operations of the year, detailed in the report of the general-in-chief.

2. The organization of colored persons into the war service.

3. The exchange of prisoners, fully set forth in the letter of General Hitchcock.

4. The operations under the act for enrolling and calling out the national forces, detailed in the report of the provost marshal general.

5. The organization of the invalid corps; and

6. The operation of the several departments of the quartermaster general, commissary general, paymaster general, chief of engineers, chief of ordnance, and surgeon general.

It has appeared impossible to make a valuable summary of this report except such as would be too extended for this place, and hence I content myself by asking your careful attention to the report itself.

The duties devolving on the naval branch of the service during the year, and throughout the whole of this unhappy contest, have been discharged with fidelity and eminent success. The extensive blockade has been constantly increasing in efficiency, as the navy has expanded; yet on so long a line it has so far been impossible to entirely suppress illicit trade. From returns received at the Navy Department, it appears that more than one thousand vessels have been captured since the blockade was instituted, and that the value of prizes already sent in for adjudication amounts to over thirteen millions of dollars.

The naval force of the United States consists at this time of five hundred and eighty-eight vessels, completed and in the course of completion, and of these seventy-five are iron-clad or armored steamers. The events of the war give an increased interest and importance to the navy which will probably extend beyond the war itself.

The armored vessels in our navy completed and in service, or which are under contract and approaching completion, are believed to exceed in number those of any other power. But while these may be relied upon for harbor defence and coast service, others of greater strength and capacity will be necessary for cruising purposes, and to maintain our rightful position on the ocean.

The change that has taken place in naval vessels and naval warfare, since the introduction of steam as a motive-power for ships-of-war, demands either a corresponding change in some of our existing navy yards, or the establishment of new ones, for the construction and necessary repair of modern naval vessels. No inconsiderable embarrassment, delay, and public injury have been experienced from the want of such governmental establishments. The necessity of such a navy yard, so furnished, at some suitable place upon the Atlantic seaboard, has on repeated occasions been brought to the attention of Congress by the Navy Department, and is again presented in the report of the Secretary which accompanies this communication. I think it my duty to invite your special attention to this subject, and also to that of establishing a yard and depot for naval purposes upon one of the western rivers. A naval force has been created on those interior waters, and under many disadvantages, within little more than two years, exceeding in numbers the whole naval force of the country at the commencement of the present administration. Satisfactory and important as have been the performances of the heroic men of the navy at this interesting period, they are scarcely more wonderful than the success of our mechanics and artisans in the production of war vessels which has created a new form of naval power.

Our country has advantages superior to any other nation in our resources of iron and timber, with inexhaustible quantities of fuel in the immediate vicinity of both, and all available and in close proximity to navigable waters. Without the advantage of public works the resources of the nation have been developed and its power displayed in the construction of a navy of such magnitude which has, at the very period of its creation, rendered signal service to the Union.

The increase of the number of seamen in the public service, from seven thousand five hundred men, in the spring of 1861, to about thirty four thousand at the present time has been accomplished without special legislation, or extraordinary bounties to promote that increase. It has been found, however, that the operation of the draft, with the high bounties paid for army recruits, is beginning to affect injuriously the naval service, and will, if not corrected, be likely to impair its efficiency, by detaching seamen from their proper vocation and inducing them to enter the Army. I therefore respectfully suggest that Congress might aid both the army and naval services by a definite provision on this subject, which would at the same time be equitable to the communities more especially interested.

I commend to your consideration the suggestions of the

Secretary of the Navy in regard to the policy of fostering and training seamen, and also the education of officers and engineers for the naval service. The Naval Academy is rendering signal service in preparing midshipmen for the highly responsible duties which in after life they will be required to perform. In order that the country should not be deprived of the proper quota of educated officers, for which legal provision has been made at the naval school, the vacancies caused by the neglect or omission to make nominations from the States in insurrection have been filled by the Secretary of the Navy.

The school is now more full and complete than at any former period, and in every respect entitled to the favorable consideration of Congress.

During the past fiscal year the financial condition of the Post office Department has been one of increasing prosperity, and I am gratified in being able to state that the actual postal revenue has nearly equalled the entire expenditures; the latter amounting to $11,314,206.84, and the former to $11,163,789 59, leaving a deficiency of but $150,417 25. In 1860, the year immediately preceding the rebellion the deficiency amounted to $5,656,705 49, the postal receipts of that year being $2,645,722 19 less than those of 1863. The decrease since 1860 in the annual amount of transportation has been only about 25 per cent, but the annual expenditure on account of the same has been reduced 35 per cent. It is manifest, therefore, that the Post Office Department may become self-sustaining in a few years, even with the restoration of the whole service.

The international conference of postal delegates from the principal countries of Europe and America, which was called at the suggestion of the Postmaster General, met at Paris on the 11th of May last, and concluded its deliberations on the 8th of June. The principles established by the conference as best adapted to facilitate postal intercourse between nations, and as the basis of future postal conventions, inaugurate a general system of uniform international charges, at reduced rates of postage, and cannot fail to produce beneficial results.

I refer you to the report of the Secretary of the Interior, which is herewith laid before you, for useful and varied information in relation to the public lands, Indian affairs, patents, pensions, and other matters of public concern pertaining to his department.

The quantity of land disposed of during the last and the first quarter of the present fiscal years was three million eight hundred and forty one thousand five hundred and forty nine acres, of which one hundred and sixty one thousand nine hundred and eleven acres were sold for cash, one million four hundred and fifty six thousand five hundred and fourteen acres were taken up under the homestead law, and the residue disposed of under laws granting lands for military bounties, for railroad and other purposes. It also appears that the sale of the public lands is largely on the increase.

It has long been a cherished opinion of some of our wisest statesmen that the people of the United States had a higher and more enduring interest in the early settlement and substantial cultivation of the public lands than in the amount of direct revenue to be derived from the sale of them. This opinion has had a controlling influence in shaping legislation upon the subject of our national domain. I may cite, as evidence of this, the liberal measures adopted in reference to actual settlers; the grant to the States of the overflowed lands within their limits in order to their being reclaimed and rendered fit for cultivation; the grants to railway companies of alternate sections of land upon the contemplated lines of their roads which, when completed, will so largely multiply the facilities for reaching our distant possessions. This policy has received its most signal and beneficent illustration in the recent enactment granting homesteads to actual settlers.

Since the first day of January last the before-mentioned quantity of one million four hundred and fifty-six thousand five hundred and fourteen acres of land have been taken up under its provisions. This fact and the amount of sales furnish gratifying evidence of increasing settlement upon the public lands, notwithstanding the great struggle in which the energies of the nation have been engaged, and which has required so large a withdrawal of our citizens from their accustomed pursuits. I cordially concur in the recommendation of the Secretary of the Interior suggesting a modification of the act in favor of those engaged in the military and naval service of the United States. I doubt not that Congress will cheerfully adopt such measures as will, without essentially changing the general features of the system, secure to the greatest practicable extent, its benefits to those who have left their homes in the defence of the country in this arduous crisis.

I invite your attention to the views of the Secretary as to the propriety of raising by appropriate legislation a revenue from the mineral lands of the United States.

The measures provided at your last session for the removal of certain Indian tribes have been carried into effect. Sundry treaties have been negotiated which will, in due time, be submitted for the constitutional action of the Senate. They contain stipulations for extinguishing the possessory rights of the Indians to large and valuable tracts of land. It is hoped that the effect of these treaties will result in the establishment of permanent friendly relations with such of these tribes as have been brought into frequent and bloody collision with our outlying settlements and emigrants.

Sound policy and our imperative duty to these wards of the government demand our anxious and constant attention to their material well-being, to their progress in the arts of civilization, and, above all, to that moral training which, under the blessing of Divine Providence, will confer upon them the elevated and sanctifying influences, the hopes and consolation of the Christian faith.

I suggested in my last annual message the propriety of remodelling our Indian system. Subsequent events have satisfied me of its necessity. The details set forth in the report of the Secretary evince the urgent need for immediate legislative action.

I commend the benevolent institutions, established or patronized by the government in this District, to your generous and fostering care.

The attention of Congress, during the last session, was engaged to some extent with a proposition for enlarging the water communication between the Mississippi river and the northeastern seaboard, which proposition, however, failed for the time. Since then, upon a call of the greatest respectability a convention has been held at Chicago upon the same subject, a summary of whose views is contained in a memorial addressed to the President and Congress, and which I now have the honor to lay before you. That this interest is one which, ere long, will force its own way, I do not entertain a doubt, while it is submitted entirely to your wisdom as to what can be done now. Augmented interest is given to this subject by the actual commencement of work upon the Pacific railroad, under auspices so favorable to rapid progress and completion. The enlarged navigation becomes a palpable need to the great road.

I transmit the second annual report of the Commissioner of the Department of Agriculture, asking your attention to the developments in that vital interest of the nation.

When Congress assembled a year ago the war had already lasted nearly twenty months, and there had been many conflicts on both land and sea, with varying results.

The rebellion had been pressed back into reduced limits; yet the tone of public feeling and opinion, at home and abroad, was not satisfactory. With other signs, the popular elections, then just past, indicated uneasiness among ourselves, while amid much that was cold and menacing the kindest words coming from Europe were uttered in accents of pity, that we were too blind to surrender a hopeless cause. Our commerce was suffering greatly by a few armed vessels built upon and furnished from foreign shores, and we were threatened with such additions from the same quarter as would sweep our trade from the sea and raise our blockade. We had failed to elicit from European governments anything hopeful upon this subject. The preliminary emancipation proclamation, issued in September, was running its assigned period to the beginning of the new year. A month later the final proclamation came, including the announcement that colored men of suitable condition would be received into the war service. The policy of emancipation, and of employing black soldiers, gave to the future a new aspect, about which hope, and fear, and doubt contended in uncertain conflict. According to our political system, as a matter of civil administration, the general government had no lawful power to effect emancipation in any State, and for a long time it had been hoped that the rebellion could be suppressed without resorting to it as a military measure. It was all the while deemed possible that the necessity for it might come, and that if it should, the crisis of the contest would then be presented. It came, and as was anticipated, it was followed by dark and doubtful days. Eleven months having now passed, we are permitted to take another review. The rebel borders are pressed still further back, and by the complete opening of the Mississippi the country dominated by the rebellion is divided into distinct parts, with no practical communication between them. Tennessee and Arkansas have been substantially cleared of insurgent control, and influential citizens in each, owners of slaves and advocates of slavery at the beginning of the rebellion, now declare openly for emancipation in their respective States. Of those States not included in the emancipation proclamation, Maryland, and Missouri, neither of which three years ago would tolerate any restraint upon the extension of slavery into new territories, only dispute now as to the best mode of removing it within their own limits.

Of those who were slaves at the beginning of the rebellion, full one hundred thousand are now in the United States military service, about one-half of which number actually bear arms in the ranks; thus giving the double advantage of taking so much labor from the insurgent cause, and supplying the places which otherwise must be filled with so many white men. So far as tested, it is difficult to say they are not as good soldiers as any. No servile insurrection, or tendency to violence or cruelty, has marked the measures of emancipation and arming the blacks. These measures have been much discussed in foreign countries, and contemporary with such discussion the tone of public sentiment there is much improved. At home the same measures have been fully discussed, supported, criticised, and denounced, and the annual elections following are highly encouraging to those whose official duty it is to bear the country through this great trial. Thus we have the new reckoning. The crisis which threatened to divide the friends of the Union is past.

Looking now to the present and future, and with reference to a resumption of the national authority within the States wherein that authority has been suspended, I have thought fit to issue a proclamation, a copy of which is herewith transmitted. On examination of this proclamation it will appear, as is believed, that nothing is attempted beyond what is amply justified by the Constitution. True, the form of an oath is given, but no man is coerced to take it. The man is only promised a pardon in case he voluntarily takes the oath. The Constitution authorizes the Executive to grant or withhold the pardon at his own absolute discretion; and this includes the power to grant on terms, as is fully established by judicial and other authorities.

It is also proffered that if, in any of the States named, a State government shall be, in the mode prescribed, set up, such government shall be recognized and guarantied by the United States, and that under it the State shall, on the constitutional conditions, be protected against invasion and domestic violence. The constitutional obligation of the United States to guaranty to every State in the Union a republican form of government, and to protect the State, in the cases stated, is explicit and full. But why tender the benefits of this provision only to a State government set up in this particular way? This section of the Constitution contemplates a case wherein the element within a State, favorable to republican government, in the Union, may be too feeble for an opposite and hostile element external to, or even within the State; and such are precisely the cases with which we are now dealing.

An attempt to guaranty and protect a revived State government, constructed in whole, or in preponderating part, from the very element against whose hostility and violence it is to be protected, is simply absurd. There must be a test by which to separate the opposing elements, so as to build only from the sound; and that test is a sufficiently liberal one, which accepts as sound whoever will make a sworn recantation of his former unsoundness.

But if it be proper to require, as a test of admission to the political body, an oath of allegiance to the Constitution of the United States, and to the Union under it, why also to the laws and proclamations in regard to slavery? Those laws and proclamations were enacted and put forth for the purpose of aiding in the suppression of the rebellion. To give them their fullest effect, there had to be a pledge for their maintenance. In my judgment they have aided, and will further aid, the cause for which they were intended. To now abandon them would be not only to relinquish a lever of power, but would also be a cruel and an astounding breach of faith. I may add at this point, that while I remain in my present position I shall not attempt to retract or modify the emancipation proclamation; nor shall I return to slavery any person who is free by the terms of that proclamation, or by any of the acts of Congress. For these and other reasons it is thought best that support of these measures shall be included in the oath; and it is believed the Executive may lawfully claim it in return for pardon and restoration of forfeited rights, which he has clear constitutional power to withhold altogether, or grant upon the terms which he shall deem wisest for the public interest. It should be observed, also, that this part of the oath is subject to the modifying and abrogating power of legislation and supreme judicial decision.

The proposed acquiescence of the national Executive in any reasonable temporary State arrangement for the freed people is made with the view of possibly modifying the confusion and destitution which must, at best, attend all classes by a total revolution of labor throughout whole States. It is hoped that the already deeply afflicted people in those States may be somewhat more ready to give up the cause of their affliction, if, to this extent, this vital matter be left to themselves; while no power of the national Executive to prevent an abuse is abridged by the proposition.

The suggestion in the proclamation as to maintaining the political framework of the States on what is called reconstruction, is made in the hope that it may do good without danger of harm. It will save labor and avoid great confusion.

But why any proclamation now upon this subject? This question is beset with the conflicting views that the step might be delayed too long or be taken too soon. In some States the elements for resumption seem ready for action, but remain inactive, apparently for want of a rallying point—a plan of action. Why shall A adopt the plan of B, rather than B that of A? And if A and B should agree, how can they know but that the general government here will reject their plan? By the proclamation a plan is presented which may be accepted by them as a rallying point, and which they are assured in advance will not be rejected here. This may bring them to act sooner than they otherwise would.

The objections to a premature presentation of a plan by the national Executive consists in the danger of committals on points which could be more safely left to further developments. Care has been taken to so shape the document as to avoid embarrassments from this source. Saying that, on certain terms, certain classes will be pardoned, with rights restored, it is not said that other classes, or other terms, will never be included. Saying that reconstruction will be accepted if presented in a specified way, it is not said it will never be accepted in any other way.

The movements, by State action, for emancipation in several of the States, not included in the emancipation proclamation, are matters of profound gratulation. And while I do not repeat in detail what I have heretofore so earnestly urged upon this subject, my general views and feelings remain unchanged; and I trust that Congress will omit no fair opportunity of aiding these important steps to a great consummation.

In the midst of other cares, however important, we must not lose sight of the fact that the war power is still our main reliance. To that power alone can we look, yet for a time, to give confidence to the people in the contested regions, that the insurgent power will not again overrun them. Until that confidence shall be established, little can be done anywhere for what is called reconstruction. Hence our chiefest care must still be directed to the army and navy, who have thus far borne their harder part so nobly and well. And it may be esteemed fortunate that in giving the greatest efficiency to these indispensable arms, we do also honorably recognize the gallant men, from commander to sentinel, who compose them, and to whom, more than to others, the world must stand indebted for the home of freedom disenthralled, regenerated, enlarged, and perpetuated. ABRAHAM LINCOLN

Washington, December 8, 1863.

WASHINGTON, D.C., DECEMBER 1863

Abraham Lincoln:
Proclamation of Amnesty and Reconstruction

The proclamation excluded Virginia from the list of states without a loyal government because the Lincoln administration had already recognized the unionist "restored government" of Virginia established in Wheeling in June 1861. When West Virginia was admitted as a state on June 20, 1863, Governor Francis H. Pierpont had relocated the restored government to Alexandria, where it exercised authority over areas occupied by Union forces.

December 8, 1863
By the President of the United States of America:
A Proclamation.

Whereas, in and by the Constitution of the United States, it is provided that the President "shall have power to grant reprieves and pardons for offences against the United States, except in cases of impeachment;" and

Whereas a rebellion now exists whereby the loyal State governments of several States have for a long time been subverted, and many persons have committed and are now guilty of treason against the United States; and

Whereas, with reference to said rebellion and treason, laws have been enacted by Congress declaring forfeitures and confiscation of property and liberation of slaves, all upon terms and conditions therein stated, and also declaring that the President was thereby authorized at any time thereafter, by proclamation, to extend to persons who may have participated in the existing rebellion, in any State or part thereof, pardon and amnesty, with such exceptions and at such times and on such conditions as he may deem expedient for the public welfare; and

Whereas the congressional declaration for limited and conditional pardon accords with well-established judicial exposition of the pardoning power; and

Whereas, with reference to said rebellion, the President of the United States has issued several proclamations, with provisions in regard to the liberation of slaves; and

Whereas it is now desired by some persons heretofore engaged in said rebellion to resume their allegiance to the United States, and to reinaugurate loyal State governments within and for their respective States; therefore,

I, Abraham Lincoln, President of the United States, do proclaim, declare, and make known to all persons who have, directly or by implication, participated in the existing rebellion, except as hereinafter excepted, that a full pardon is hereby granted to them and each of them, with restoration of all rights of property, except as to slaves, and in property cases where rights of third parties shall have intervened, and upon the condition that every such person shall take and subscribe an oath, and thenceforward keep and maintain said oath inviolate; and which oath shall be registered for permanent preservation, and shall be of the tenor and effect following, to wit:

"I, ——, do solemnly swear, in presence of Almighty God, that I will henceforth faithfully support, protect and defend the Constitution of the United States, and the union of the States thereunder; and that I will, in like manner, abide by and faithfully support all acts of Congress passed during the existing rebellion with reference to slaves, so long and so far as not repealed, modified or held void by Congress, or by decision of the Supreme Court; and that I will, in like manner, abide by and faithfully support all proclamations of the President made during the existing rebellion having reference to slaves, so long and so far as not modified or declared void by decision of the Supreme Court. So help me God."

The persons excepted from the benefits of the foregoing provisions are all who are, or shall have been, civil or diplomatic officers or agents of the so-called confederate government; all who have left judicial stations under the United States to aid the rebellion; all who are, or shall have been, military or naval officers of said so-called confederate government above the rank of colonel in the army, or of lieutenant in the navy; all who left seats in the United States Congress to aid the rebellion; all who resigned commissions in the army or navy of the United States, and afterwards aided the rebellion; and all who have engaged in any way in treating colored persons or white persons, in charge of such, otherwise than lawfully as prisoners of war, and which persons may have been found in the United States service, as soldiers, seamen, or in any other capacity.

And I do further proclaim, declare, and make known, that whenever, in any of the States of Arkansas, Texas, Louisiana, Mississippi, Tennessee, Alabama, Georgia, Florida, South Carolina, and North Carolina, a number of persons, not less than one-tenth in number of the votes cast in such State at the Presidential election of the year of our Lord one thousand eight hundred and sixty, each having taken the oath aforesaid and not having since violated it, and being a qualified voter by the election law of the State existing immediately before the so-called act of secession, and excluding all others, shall re-establish a State government which shall be republican, and in no wise contravening said oath, such shall be recognized as the true government of the State, and the State shall receive thereunder the benefits of the constitutional provision which declares that "The United States shall guaranty to every State in this union a republican form of government, and shall protect each of them against invasion; and, on application of the legislature, or the executive, (when the legislature cannot be convened,) against domestic violence."

And I do further proclaim, declare, and make known that any provision which may be adopted by such State government in relation to the freed people of such State, which shall recognize and declare their permanent freedom, provide for their education, and which may yet be consistent, as a temporary arrangement, with their present condition as a laboring, landless, and homeless class, will not be objected to by the national Executive. And it is suggested as not improper, that, in constructing a loyal State government in any State, the name of the State, the boundary, the subdivisions, the constitution, and the general code of laws, as before the rebellion, be maintained, subject only to the modifications made necessary by the conditions hereinbefore stated, and such others, if any, not contravening said conditions, and which may be deemed expedient by those framing the new State government.

To avoid misunderstanding, it may be proper to say that this proclamation, so far as it relates to State governments, has no reference to States wherein loyal State governments have all the while been maintained. And for the same reason, it may be proper to further say that whether members sent to Congress from any State shall be admitted to seats, constitutionally rests exclusively with the respective Houses, and not to any extent with the Executive. And still further, that this proclamation is intended to present the people of the States wherein the national authority has been suspended, and loyal State governments have been subverted, a mode in and by which the national authority and loyal State governments may be reestablished within said States, or in any of them; and, while the mode presented is the best the Executive can suggest, with his present impressions, it must not be understood that no other possible mode would be acceptable.

Given under my hand at the city, of Washington, the 8th. day of December, A.D. one thousand eight hundred and sixty-three, and of the independence of the United States of America the eighty-eighth.

ABRAHAM LINCOLN

By the President:
WILLIAM H. SEWARD, Secretary of State.

SUBDUING THE SOUTH:
NEW YORK, DECEMBER 1863

George Templeton Strong: Diary, December 11–13, 1863

Strong recorded his response to Lincoln's message and proclamation and to a message sent by Jefferson Davis to the Confederate Congress on December 7. The report that Strong noted regarding Alexander H. Stephens, "Vice-President of Rebeldom," turned out to be false.

December 11. Visited by unknown author of *The New Gospel of Peace*, which has been attributed to a score of people, myself among them. The Cincinnati Sanitary Commission Fair people had written to his publisher, Tousey, to ask for the original manuscript that they might make merchandise thereof, whereupon, Mr. X. Y., the evangelist, came to me to say that our Metropolitan Fair could have it for the asking. I closed with the offer, for the manuscript will bring money. Though the squib does not seem to me very particularly clever, it has hit the average popular taste very hard. Seventy thousand copies of the first part and forty thousand of the second have been sold. The author is ———. Who'd have thought it!

President's message and proclamation of conditional amnesty to the rebels, certain classes excepted, finds very general favor. Uncle Abe is the most popular man in America today. The firmness, honesty, and sagacity of the "gorilla despot" may be recognized by the rebels themselves sooner than we expect, and the weight of his personal character may do a great deal toward restoration of our national unity.

Rebeldom has just played us a pretty prank; its audacity is wonderful. Sixteen "passengers" on the peaceful propeller *Chesapeake*, which left New York for Portland last Saturday, took possession of her during her voyage, killed some of her officers and crew, put the rest ashore near St. Johns, and then steamed off with their prize in triumph under Confederate colors. A whole armada has been sent in pursuit, but they won't catch her.

There is almost universal feeling that rebellion has received its death-blow and will not survive through the winter. It is premature, but being coupled with no suggestion that our efforts may safely be slackened, it will do no harm. The *soi-disant* Chivalry shews no sign of disposition to back down and is as rampant, blatant, and blustering as ever. The most truculent and foul-mouthed bravoes and swashbucklers of the South feel a certain amount of discouragement, no doubt, but they generally keep it to themselves. There will be no enduring peace while the class that has hitherto governed the South continues to exist. They are almost universally given over to a reprobate mind and past possibility of repentance. Southern aristocracy must be dealt with as the Clans were after 1745. Parton's life of Butler (a readable book) tells how that general treated their case in New Orleans. Even his remedies were too mild, but they come nearer to what is required than any others yet administered. That book will do much to raise Butler in popular favor. It paints him as of that Jacksonesque type of beauty which we especially appreciate and admire. Parton colors very high and tries to make a demigod of his hero, but I have always thought Butler among the strongest men brought forward by the war.

December 13, SUNDAY. Dr. Peters brings news of a bulletin at Union League Club announcing that A. H. Stephens, Vice-President of Rebeldom, has just presented himself once more at Fortress Monroe with a couple of colleagues as Peace Commissioners, that Butler refused to receive them in any official character, but offered to hear what they had to say as prominent citizens of Secessia, and that they thereupon went back again in a huff, sending a vindictive Parthian shaft behind them in the shape of a notification that they would no longer allow supplies to be sent our starving prisoners at Richmond. If they have done this, it won't much help their cause abroad; but that's a small matter. Government should notify them that inasmuch as they have declared their inability to give their prisoners rations sufficient to sustain life, their refusal to allow us to make up the deficiency will be followed by the execution of the rebel officers in our hands *per diem*, till such refusal is revoked.

Message of Jefferson Davis, "anti-President," to the squad of malefactors now gathered at Richmond and styling themselves members of Congress from Kentucky, Tennessee, Missouri, and other states, is long and doleful and dull—a mélange of lies, sophistry, swagger, lamentation, treason, perjury, and piety. He admits that rebellion has been drifting to leeward during the past year, but refers his gang for consolation to the boundless capacities of the future. He is moral, also, and objects to any action inconsistent with the letter or the spirit of "the constitution we have sworn to obey." This is cool. He and probably the majority of his pals and councillors in Congress assembled had held not less than twenty offices apiece before they concluded to rebel. How many hundred broken oaths to uphold another constitution were represented on the floor while this pious message was being read? Could all these several perjuries have been combined in one colossal act of blasphemy, I think the earth would necessarily have opened and swallowed the perpetrator. Jefferson's act of hypocrisy is (time, place, and presence considered) of like enormity, though less criminal and black. I wonder the assembled peers of Secessia were not startled by a vast resounding guffaw from the Powers of Nature, reverberating from the Chesapeake to the Alleghenies. Jefferson Davis has outbrazened Louis Napoleon himself.

"ONE MISFORTUNE FOLLOWS ANOTHER":
NORTH CAROLINA, DECEMBER 1863

Catherine Edmondston: Diary, December 11, 1863

Catherine Edmondston reflected on the causes of the recent Confederate defeats in Tennessee and the strengths and weaknesses of Jefferson Davis as a leader.

DECEMBER 11, 1863

A fortunate thing it is for us in this Confederacy that it is not 'de rigueur' to testify greif on the receipt of bad news by rending one's clothes! Did that ancient custom prevail the frequency with which one misfortune follows another would tell sadly upon our slender wardrobes! Perhaps, however, the ancients mingled economy in their sorrow and rent their clothes at the seams only. Even that, with thread at 1.75 cts per spool, which I this day paid for one in Clarksville, would be rather hard on us. But to go back to the bad news which has metaphorically rent all the clothes in the country within the past few days. Official dispatches have been received from Gen Longstreet from a point thirty miles from Knoxville in full retreat from that place to Virginia. What he has accomplished the Examiner says may be summed up in a few words —*nothing*. Gild the pill as ye may, Mr Davis, it is a bitter one to swallow. I say Mr Davis for he is, we are told, who detached Longstreet from Bragg's command before the late battle. By his orders, too, was the army of Northern Geo reorganized in the face of the foe & to this cause is the late disaster at Lookout ascribed. Brigades were recast, divisions remoddled, & when the shock of battle came men were led into action by generals who had never led them before. Regiments had lost their old & tried supporters, their fellow regiments in their Brigades, & had to rely on men whom they had never seen before & upon whose support they could not with confidence, *which experience* gives, rely. *Hence* our defeat & hence the small loss we endured, for some Regiments gave way without waiting to see how their new comrades fought. A want of sense it appears to us to reorganize thus in the face of the foe. Mr Davis Message came last night, an able document especially in reference to our *foreign relations*. Lord John Russel, her Majesty's Secretary for foreign affairs, is shown in his true light, petty & deceitful, under the mask of neutrality, claiming credit with the U S. for favouring it. Faugh! If he be a diplomat—I'll none of them! His lies have not the merit of plausibility!

The President's summary of Home affairs is rather gloomy. The currency & the soldiers whose term of enlistment is to expire in the spring are knotty points, but God has led us heretofore & He will lead us still. It is sad to myself to realize how my admiration has lessened for Mr Davis, lessened since the loss of Vicksburg, a calamity brought on us by his obstinacy in retaining Pemberton in command, & now still further diminished by his indomitable pride of opinion in upholding Bragg.

The Examiner says, "It is some comfort we grant to have a President who does not disgrace us by Hoosier English but it is a comfort which is dearly bought at the price of a Memminger & a Bragg." His favourites have cost us much: Mallory, a Navy; Memminger has flooded the land with useless Treasury notes, sapped the fountain head of our prosperity; Huger cost us Roanoke Island & in consequence Norfolk. (He also let McClellan escape at [   ]; Lovel, New Orleans; Pemberton, Vicksburg and the two together the greater part of the Mississippi Valley. Bragg lost us first Kentucky and then Tennessee. His obstinacy in refusing to give Price the command lost Missouri & now the incapable Holmes, also his favourite, is clinching the loss and letting Arkansas slip away likewise. Truly I fear that to him is not given the first element of a ruler—"the discerning of Spirits." He upheld Sidney Johnston when unjustly assailed, however. "No general have I, if indeed great Johnston be not one." Here let us do him justice, but to give such a man as [   ] a Lieut Gen'ship for "auld acquaintance sake" only seems trifling with the interests of the country. But let me "not speak" too much "evil of dignities." Mr Davis whilst he has made many mistakes has presided over our fortunes with dignity & Christian forbearance. Toward a man so harrassed with care as he is, & with such heavy responsibilities resting upon him as he has, requires that we should judge him kindly. Who would have done better if placed in his seat?

Sue, Rachel, & Col Clark dined with us today. Col C gives a melancholly picture of the country late in his command— below Hamilton. The Yankees have destroyed everything & burnt upon a large scale, many plantations being left without a house upon them. They misinterpret our forbearance in Penn last summer, think we abstained from devastating the country through fear, & this is the return they make us. Have been riding on horse back every afternoon latterly & enjoy my rides with Mr E greatly.

"GOD HELP MY COUNTRY": VIRGINIA, JANUARY 1864

Mary Chesnut: Diary, January 1, 1864

Mary Chesnut spent the New Year in Richmond, where her husband Colonel James Chesnut, a former U.S. senator from South Carolina, served as an aide to Jefferson Davis. During the 1860s Mary Chesnut kept a diary that she would later revise and expand between 1881 and 1884. Her diary for the winter of 1863–64 is not known to have survived, and the text printed here is taken from the revised version.

January 1st, 1864. God help my country.

Table talk.

"After the battles around Richmond, hope was strong in me. All that has insensibly drifted away."

"I am like David after the child was dead. Get up, wash my face, have my hair cut, &c&c."

"That's too bad. I think we are more like the sailors who break into the spirits closet when they find out the ship must sink. There seems to be for the first time a resolute feeling to enjoy the brief hour and never look beyond the day."

"I now long, pine, pray, and grieve—and—well, I have no hope. Have you any of old Mr. Chesnut's brandy here still?"

"It is a good thing never to look beyond the hour. Laurence, take this key—look in such a place for a decanter marked &c&c&c."

General Hood's an awful flatterer—I mean an awkward flatterer. I told him to praise my husband to someone else—not to me. He ought to praise me to somebody who would tell J. C., and then praise J. C. to another person who would tell me. Man and wife are too much one person to receive a compliment straight in the face that way—that is, gracefully.

"That"—as an American demonstrative adjective pronoun, or adjective pure and simple—we give it illimitable meaning. Mrs. King, now, we were "weeping and commenting over a stricken deer," one who would say yes but was not asked. "Do you mean to say she is looking to marry him?" Mrs. King, with eyes uplifted and hands clasped: "*That* willing!" Again, of a wounded soldier: "Do you mean to say he is willing to leave the army for so slight an excuse?" Again: "Willing indeed! *That* willing!"

A peculiar intonation, however, must be given to *that* to make it bear its mountain of meaning.

Again, Grundy père was said to be a man of "des absences délicieuses."

"That's Madame Deffand's wit. I made a note of it—fits so many households."

"List of the halfhearted ones—at least we all know they never believed in this thing. Stephens—vice president—No. 1. Ashmore, Keitt, Boyce—of the South Carolina delegation. Orr—he was lugged in, awfully against the grain.

"There now, look at our wisdom. Mr. Mason! We grant you all you are going to say. Who denies it? He is a grand old Virginia gentleman. Straightforward, honest-hearted, blunt, high-headed, and unchangeable in his ways as—as the Rock of Gibraltar. Mr. Hunter, you need not shake your wise head. You know it set all the world a-laughing when we sent Mr. Mason abroad as a *diplomat!*"

"About tobacco, now—the English can't stand chewing—&c&c. They say at the lordliest table Mr. Mason will turn round halfway in his chair and spit in the fire!"

Jack Preston says the parting of high Virginia with its sons at the station is a thing to see—tears streaming from each eye, a crystal drop, from the corner of each mouth a yellow stream of tobacco juice.

"You know yourself, General Lee and General Huger's hearts were nearly rent asunder when they had to leave the old army."

"Oh! Did not Mrs. Johnston tell you of how General Scott thought to save the melancholy, reluctant, slow Joe for the Yankees? But he is a genuine F.F., and he came."

"One more year of Stonewall would have saved us."

"Chickamauga is the only battle we have gained since Stonewall went up!"

"And no results—as usual."

"Stonewall was not so much as killed by a Yankee. He was shot by Mahone's brigade. Now, that is hard."

"General Lee can do no more than keep back Meade."

"One of Meade's armies, you mean. They have only to double on him when he whips one of theirs."

"General Edward Johnson says he got Grant a place. Esprit de corps, you know, would not bear to see an old army man driving a wagon. That was when he found him out west. Put out of the army for habitual drunkenness."

"He is their man, a bullheaded Suwarrow. He don't care a snap if they fall like the leaves fall. He fights to win, that chap. He is not distracted by a thousand side issues. He does not see them. He is narrow and sure, sees only in a straight line."

"Like Louis Napoleon—from a bath in the gutters, he goes straight up."

"Yes, like Lincoln, they have ceased to carp at him because he is a rough clown, no gentleman, &c&c. You never hear now of his nasty fun—only of his wisdom. It don't take much soap and water to wash the hands that the rod of empire sways. They talked of Lincoln's drunkenness, too. Now, since Vicksburg they have not a word to say against Grant's habits."

"He has the disagreeable habit of not retreating before irresistible veterans—or it is reculer pour mieux sauter—&c&c. You need not be afraid of a little dirt on the hands which wield a field marshal's baton, either."

"General Lee and Albert Sidney Johnston, they show blood and breeding. They are of the Bayard, the Philip Sidney order of soldiers."

"Listen, if General Lee had Grant's resources, he would have bagged the last Yankee or had them all safe back, packed up in Massachusetts."

"You mean, if he had not the weight of the negro question on him?"

"No, I mean, if he had Grant's unlimited allowance of the powers of war—men, money, ammunition, arms—[   ].

"His servant had a stray pair of French boots down here,

and he was admiring his small feet and moving one so as to bring his high instep in better line of vision. For an excuse to give him a furlough, they sent some Yankee prisoners down here by him. I said, 'What sort of creatures are they?'"

"Damn splay-footed Yankees, every man jack of them."

"As they steadily tramp this way, I must say, I have ceased to admire their feet myself. How beautiful are the feet &c&c, says the Scriptures."

"Eat, drink, and be merry—tomorrow ye die—they say that, too."

"Why do you call General Preston 'Conscript Father'? On account of those girls?"

"No, indeed. He is at the head of the Conscription Bureau."

"General Young says, 'Give me those daredevil dandies I find in Mrs. C's drawing room. I like fellows who fight and don't care what all the row's about.'"

"Yes, and he sees the same daredevils often enough, stiff and stark, stripped, stone-dead on the battlefield."

"Oh, how can you bring all that to our eyes here!"

"What? Not compliment your drawing-room friends, the fellows who dance and fight with light hearts—who battle fire and famine, nakedness, mud, snow, frost, gunpowder, and—well, no words about it. Take it all as it comes."

"Talking feet—the bluest-blooded American you know, you call him 'the giant foot.'"

"They found that name for him in Bulwer's last. In the last page. A giant foot comes out of the darkness and kicks over the sort of Medea's cauldron of a big pot they were brewing."

Mr. Ould says Mrs. Lincoln found the gardener of the White House so nice she would make him a major general.

Lincoln said to the secretary, "Well! the little woman must have her way—sometimes."

She has the Augean perquisite of cleaning the military stables. She says it pays so well. She need never touch the president's saddle.

"The Roman emperor found all money of good odor."

"We do pitch into our enemies."

"As the English did into the French. And, later, into the Russians."

"They got up in a theater and huzzahed—when they heard the emperor of Russia was dead."

Marriage in high life. Senator Johnson of Arkansas—somewhere out West, I may not "locate" him properly—his friends fondly say "Bob Johnson."

He explained his marriage to Mrs. Davis. He is a devoted friend of the president.

With his foot on the carriage steps, so to speak, he married his deceased wife's sister. He wished to leave her power over his children, to protect them and take care of them while he was away.

Mrs. Davis asked, "Pray, why did you not tell us before?"

"I did not think it a matter worth mentioning. I only proposed it to her the morning I left home, and it was done at once. And now my mind is easy. I can stay here and attend to my business, as a man should. She is quite capable of looking after things at home."

We did not know Mrs. Lawton, and I inquired of Mary P, who did, if she was not unusually clever.

"*That* clever!" said Mary P, imitating the gesture attributed to Mrs. King. "How did you guess it?"

"General Lawton will hear every word I say. No matter how 'superior' the men are who surround us, I knew he was accustomed to hear things worth listening to at home."

Know now why the English, who find out the comfort of life in everything, send off a happy couple to spend the honeymoon out of everybody's way or shut them up at home and leave them. Today the beautiful bride and the happy bridegroom came to see me. They had not one thought to give, except to themselves and their wedding. Or their preliminary love affairs. How it all was, when it was, &c&c&c. She did tell a capital story—if I could write it!

Mrs. Wright of Tennessee came for me to go with her on a calling expedition. Found one cabinet minister's establishment in a state of republican simplicity. Servant who asked us in—out at elbows and knees.

The next a widower, whose house is presided over by a relative.

"Bob Johnson?" whispered Mrs. Wright.

"Not quite," answered another visitor. "Splendid plan, though. Like the waiter in Dickens's book—'Here on suiting—and she suits.'"

"Wigfall's speech—'Our husbandless daughters.'" Said Isabella: "No wonder. Here we are, and our possible husbands and lovers killed before we so much as knew them. Oh! the widows and old maids of this cruel war."

Read *Germaine*—About's. It is only in books that people fall in love with their wives. The arsenic story more probable—science, then, and not theory. After all, is it not as with any other copartnership, say, traveling companions? Their future opinion of each other, "the happiness of the association," depends entirely on what they really are, not what they felt or thought about each other before they had any possible way of acquiring accurate information as to character, habits, &c. Love makes it worse. The pendulum swings back further, the harder it was pulled the other way.

Mrs. Malaprop to the rescue—"Better begin with a little aversion." Not of any weight either way, what we think of people before *we know them*. Did two people ever live together so stupid as to be deceived? What they pretend does not count.

The *Examiner* gives this amount of pleasant information to the enemy.

He tells them we are not ready, and we cannot be before spring. And that now is their time.

Our safeguard, our hope, our trust is in beneficent mud, impassable mud. And so feeling, I hail with delight these long, long rainy days and longer nights. Things are deluging, sloppy, and up to the ankles in water and dirt, enough to satisfy the muddiest-minded croaker of us all.

We have taken prisoner some of Averell's raiders.

Somebody in secret session kicked and cuffed Foote, Foote of Mississippi, in the Senate.

So ends the old year.

The last night of the old year. Gloria Mundi sent me a cup of strong, *good* coffee. I drank two cups, and so I did not sleep a wink.

Like a fool I passed my whole life in review—and bitter memories maddened me quite. Then came a happy thought. I mapped out a story of the war. The plot came to hand, for it was true. Johnny is the hero—light dragoon and heavy swell. I will call it F.F.'s, for it is F.F.'s both of South Carolina and Virginia. It is to be a war story, and the filling out of the skeleton is the pleasantest way to put myself to sleep.

Old Hickory fought for Aunt Rachel of questionable fame. That is, she was married before her other husband died, or before her divorce was settled, or something wrong, but she did not know she was doing wrong. She is said to have been a good woman, but it is all a little confused to my straitlaced ideas. They say when someone asked if old Hickory was a Christian, the answer: "I don't know, but if he wants to go to heaven, the devil can't keep him out of it." And then he stood by Mrs. Eaton in good report and in evil. And now Richmond plays old Hickory with its beautiful Mrs. M.

I can forgive Andrew Jackson the headlong wedding business, but that duel! when he deliberately waited—and after the other man had missed, or failed in some way to shoot at him—slowly and coolly killed him. But the pious North swallowed Andrew Jackson because he put his sword in the balance where we nullifiers were concerned.

England declined Nelson's legacy of Lady Hamilton, but she accepts his glory and his fame as a typical naval hero. English to the core.

There are breaking hearts this beautiful New Year's Day.

Young Frasier, on his way back to Maryland to be married, was shot dead by a Yankee picket.

Read *Volpone* until J. C. emerged for his breakfast. He asked me to make out his list for his New Year's calls.

Mrs. Davis, Mrs. Preston, Mrs. Randolph, Mrs. Elzey, Mrs. Stanard, Mrs. MacFarland, Mrs. Wigfall, Mrs. Miles, Mrs. John Redman Coxe Lewis.

At the president's, J. C. saw L. Q. C. Lamar who, unconfirmed by the Senate, has had to come home from Russia. They must have refused to confirm his nomination simply to annoy and anger Jeff Davis. Everybody knows there is not a cleverer man on either side of the water than Mr. Lamar, or a truer patriot. J. C. said Lamar put his arms round him (he has a warm heart) and said, "*You* are glad to see me, eh?" Lamar is changed so much that at first J. C. did not recognize him. Colonels Browne and Ives there, in full fig, swords and sashes, gentlemen ushers. J. C. was in citizen's dress and stood behind Mrs. Davis all the time, out of the fray. So he enjoyed the fun immensely. No responsibility.

The *Examiner* indulges in a horse laugh. "Is that your idea? England come to the help of a slave power?" Turkey! Why not, O Daniel come to judgment? and India?

But slavery was the sore spot on this continent, and England touched up the Yankees *that they so hated* on the raw when they were shouting hurrah for liberty, hurrah for General Jackson, whom the British turned their backs on, but who did not turn his back on the exconquerors of Waterloo! English writers knew where to flick. They set the Yankees on us by incessant nagging, jeering at the inconsistency. Now the Yankees have the bit in their teeth. After a while they will ascend higher and higher in virtue, until maybe they will even attack Mormonism in its den.

"Little Vick is going to do the best she can for her country. The land of our forefathers is not squeamish but looks out for No. 1," said the irreverent Wigfall. And then he laid sacrilegious hands on the father of his country! He always speaks of him as an old granny, or the mother of his country, because he looked after the butter and cheese on Madam Martha's *Mount Vernon* farm.

"There is one thing that always makes my blood rise hot within me—this good slave-owner who *left* his negroes free when he no longer needed them. He rides his fine horse along the rows where the poor African hoes corn. He takes out his beautiful English hunting watch and times Cuffy. Cuffy, under his great master's eyes, works with a will. With his watch still in hand, Farmer George sees what a man can do in a given time. And by that measure he tasks the others—strong, weak, slow, swift, able-bodied, and unable. There is magnanimity for you! George the 1st of America—the founder of the great U.S. America."

"But Wigfall! You exaggerate. He was not a severe disciplinarian. He was the very kindest of men. Everyone knows that. But you only rave in this manner and say such stuff to be different from other people."

"I get every word of it from his own letters."

"He was no harder on Cuffy than English, French, German landlords are to their white tenants."

"Do you mean to say a poor man must not work for his living, but his rich neighbor must support him in idleness?" &c&c&c.

After he had gone: "You see, we did not expect Wigfall, who shoots white men with so little ceremony, to be so thoughtful, so tender of the poor and helpless—but it is so, it seems. He was in bitter earnest. Did you notice his eyes?" At this moment Dangerfield Lewis and Maria came—and in another second L. Q. Washington was at their heels. J. C. said,

"If walls could speak, what a tale these would have to tell you!"

"How? what?"

"Oh, Louis Wigfall's perversity. He says Lamar is as model a diplomat as Mr. Mason!" I hastily put in, "I really thought the *Washington Lewis* family ought not to hear—well! how aggravating Louis Wigfall can be—so I stopped you. For one thing, he is the very best husband I know and the kindest father."

"AND YET WE MUST GO ON": VIRGINIA, JANUARY 1864

Judith W. McGuire: Diary, January 1, 1864

Judith W. McGuire and her husband, John P. McGuire, the principal of the Episcopal High School of Virginia, had fled their home in Alexandria in May 1861 when the town was occupied by Union troops. In February 1862 the McGuires settled in Richmond, where she later found work as a clerk in the Confederate commissary department. On New Year's Day she wrote in her diary about Lieutenant Colonel Raleigh T. Colston, the son of her sister, Sarah Jane Brockenbrough Colston. The commander of the 2nd Virginia Infantry, Colston had his left leg amputated below the knee after being shot at Payne's Farm on November 27, 1863, during the Mine Run campaign.

January 1, 1864.—A melancholy pause in my diary. After returning from church on the night of the 18th, a telegram was handed me from Professor Minor, of the University of Virginia, saying, "Come at once, Colonel Colston is extremely ill." After the first shock was over, I wrote an explanatory note to Major Brewer, why I could not be at the office next day, packed my trunk, and was in the cars by seven in the morning. That evening I reached the University, and found dear R. desperately ill with pneumonia, which so often follows, as in the case of General Jackson, the amputation of limbs. Surgeons Davis and Cabell were in attendance, and R's uncle, Dr. Brockenbrough, arrived the next day. After ten days of watching and nursing, amid alternate hopes and fears, we saw our friend Dr. Maupin close our darling's eyes, on the morning of the 23d; and on Christmas-day, a military escort laid him among many brother soldiers in the Cemetery of the University of Virginia. He died in the faith of Christ, and with the glorious hope of immortality. His poor mother is heart-stricken, but she, together with his sisters, and one dearer still, had the blessed, and what is now the rare privilege, of soothing and nursing him in his last hours. To them, and to us all, his life seemed as a part of our own. His superior judgment and affectionate temper made him the guide of his whole family. To them his loss can never be supplied. His country has lost one of its earliest and best soldiers. Having been educated at the Virginia Military Institute, he raised and drilled a company in his native County of Berkeley, at the time of the John Brown raid. In 1861 he again led that company to Harper's Ferry. From that time he was never absent more than a week or ten days from his command, and even when wounded at Gaines's Mills, he absented himself but three days, and was again at his post during the several last days of those desperate fights. His fatal wound was received in his nineteenth general engagement, in none of which had he his superior in bravery and devotion to the cause. He was proud of belonging to the glorious Stonewall Brigade, and I have been told by those who knew the circumstances, that he was confided in and trusted by General Jackson to a remarkable degree.

Thus we bury, one by one, the dearest, the brightest, the best of our domestic circles. Now, in our excitement, while we are scattered, and many of us homeless, these separations are poignant, nay, overwhelming; but how can we estimate the sadness of heart which will pervade the South when the war is over, and we are again gathered together around our family hearths and altars, and find the circles broken? One and another gone. Sometimes the father and husband, the beloved head of the household, in whom was centred all that made life dear. Again the eldest son and brother of the widowed home, to whom all looked for guidance and direction; or, perhaps, that bright youth, on whom we had not ceased to look as still a child, whose fair, beardless cheek we had but now been in the habit of smoothing with our hands in fondness—one to whom mother and sisters would always give the good-night kiss, as his peculiar due, and repress the sigh that would arise at the thought that college or business days had almost come to take him from us. And then we will remember the mixed feeling of hope and pride when we first saw this household pet don his jacket of gray and shoulder his musket for the field; how we would be bright and cheerful before him, and turn to our chambers to weep oceans of tears when he is fairly gone. And does he, too, sleep his last sleep? Does our precious one fill a hero's grave? O God! help us, for the wail is in the whole land!

"Rachel weeping for her children, and will not be comforted, because they are not." In all the broad South there will be scarcely a fold without its missing lamb, a fireside without its vacant chair. And yet we must go on. It is our duty to rid our land of invaders; we must destroy the snake which is endeavouring to entwine us in its coils, though it drain our heart's blood. We know that we are right in the sight of God, and that we must

> "With patient mind our course of duty run.
> God nothing does, or suffers to be done,
> But we would do ourselves, if we could see
> The end of all events as well as He."

The Lord reigneth, be the earth never so unquiet.

SACRIFICING SLAVERY: GEORGIA, JANUARY 1864

Patrick R. Cleburne: Memorandum on Emancipation and Enlisting Black Soldiers

January 2, 1864

Born in Cork County, Ireland, Patrick R. Cleburne served as a private in the British army before immigrating to the United States in 1849. He settled in Helena, Arkansas, where he worked as a druggist before passing the bar. Elected colonel of the 1st Arkansas Infantry in 1861, Cleburne later led a brigade at Shiloh and Perryville and a division at Stones River, Chickamauga, and Chattanooga. He read this memorandum at a meeting of the corps and division commanders of the Army of Tennessee held on January 2, 1864, at the Dalton, Georgia, headquarters of Joseph E. Johnston, Bragg's replacement. It was cosigned by thirteen officers, all past or present brigade and regimental commanders in Cleburne's division. Although corps commanders William J. Hardee and Thomas Hindman, a prewar friend of Cleburne's, were sympathetic to his proposal, other generals condemned it in private letters to fellow officers. Alexander P. Stewart wrote that the memorandum was "at war with my social, moral, and political principles," while Patton Anderson described it as a "monstrous proposition" and "revolting to Southern sentiment, Southern pride, and Southern honor." A copy was sent to Jefferson Davis, who told Johnston that the "dissemination or even promulgation of such opinions" could only cause "discouragement, distraction, and dissension." Davis ordered the suppression of the memorandum and of all discussion about it. Cleburne would continue to lead his division until his death in battle at Franklin, Tennessee, on November 30, 1864. His memorandum was first published by the War Department as part of the *Official Records* series in 1898.

COMMANDING GENERAL, THE CORPS, DIVISION,
BRIGADE, AND REGIMENTAL COMMANDERS OF THE
ARMY OF TENNESSEE:

GENERAL: Moved by the exigency in which our country is now placed, we take the liberty of laying before you, unofficially, our views on the present state of affairs. The subject is so grave, and our views so new, we feel it a duty both to you and the cause that before going further we should submit them for your judgment and receive your suggestions in regard to them. We therefore respectfully ask you to give us an expression of your views in the premises. We have now been fighting for nearly three years, have spilled much of our best blood, and lost, consumed, or thrown to the flames an amount of property equal in value to the specie currency of the world. Through some lack in our system the fruits of our struggles and sacrifices have invariably slipped away from us and left us nothing but long lists of dead and mangled. Instead of standing defiantly on the borders of our territory or harassing those of the enemy, we are hemmed in to-day into less than two-thirds of it, and still the enemy menacingly confronts us at every point with superior forces. Our soldiers can see no end to this state of affairs except in our own exhaustion; hence, instead of rising to the occasion, they are sinking into a fatal apathy, growing weary of hardships and slaughters which promise no results. In this state of things it is easy to understand why there is a growing belief that some black catastrophe is not far ahead of us, and that unless some extraordinary change is soon made in our condition we must overtake it. The consequences of this condition are showing themselves more plainly every day; restlessness of morals spreading everywhere, manifesting itself in the army in a growing disregard for private rights; desertion spreading to a class of soldiers it never dared to tamper with before; military commissions sinking in the estimation of the soldier; our supplies failing; our firesides in ruins. If this state continues much longer we must be subjugated. Every man should endeavor to understand the meaning of subjugation before it is too late. We can give but a faint idea when we say it means the loss of all we now hold most sacred—slaves and all other personal property, lands, homesteads, liberty, justice, safety, pride, manhood. It means that the history of this heroic struggle will be written by the enemy; that our youth will be trained by Northern school teachers; will learn from Northern school books their version of the war; will be impressed by all the influences of history and education to regard our gallant dead as traitors, our maimed veterans as fit objects for derision. It means the crushing of Southern manhood, the hatred of our former slaves, who will, on a spy system, be our secret police. The conqueror's policy is to divide the conquered into factions and stir up animosity among them, and in training an army of negroes the North no doubt holds this thought in perspective. We can see three great causes operating to destroy us: First, the inferiority of our armies to those of the enemy in point of numbers; second, the poverty of our single source of supply in comparison with his several sources; third, the fact that slavery, from being one of our chief sources of strength at the commencement of the war, has now become, in a military point of view, one of our chief sources of weakness.

The enemy already opposes us at every point with superior numbers, and is endeavoring to make the preponderance irresistible. President Davis, in his recent message, says the enemy "has recently ordered a large conscription and made a subsequent call for volunteers, to be followed, if ineffectual, by a still further draft." In addition, the President of the United States announces that "he has already in training an army of 100,000 negroes as good as any troops," and every fresh raid he makes and new slice of territory he wrests from us will add to this force. Every soldier in our army already knows and feels our numerical inferiority to the enemy. Want of men in the field has prevented him from reaping the fruits of his victories, and has prevented him from having the furlough he expected after the last reorganization, and when he turns from the wasting armies in the field to look at the source of supply, he finds nothing in the prospect to encourage him. Our single source of supply is that portion of our white men fit for duty and not now in the ranks. The enemy has three sources of supply: First, his own motley population; secondly, our slaves; and thirdly, Europeans whose hearts are fired into a crusade against us by fictitious pictures of the atrocities of slavery, and who meet no hindrance from their Governments in such enterprise, because these Governments are equally antagonistic to the institution. In touching the third cause, the fact that slavery has become a military weakness, we may rouse prejudice and passion, but the time has come when it would be madness not to look at our danger from every point of view, and to probe it to the bottom. Apart from the assistance that home and foreign prejudice against slavery has given to the North, slavery is a source of great strength to the enemy in a purely military point of view, by supplying him with an army from our granaries; but it is our most vulnerable point, a continued embarrassment, and in some respects an insidious weakness. Wherever slavery is once seriously disturbed, whether by the actual presence or the approach of the enemy, or even by a cavalry raid, the whites can no longer with safety to their property openly sympathize with our cause. The fear of their slaves is continually haunting them, and from silence and apprehension many of these soon learn to wish the war stopped on any terms. The next stage is to take the oath to save property, and they become dead to us, if not open enemies. To prevent raids we are forced to scatter our forces, and are not free to move and strike like the enemy; his vulnerable points are carefully selected and fortified depots. Ours are found in every point where there is a slave to set free. All along the lines slavery is comparatively valueless to us for labor, but of great and increasing worth to the enemy for information. It is an omnipresent spy system, pointing out our valuable men to the enemy, revealing our positions, purposes, and resources, and yet acting so safely and secretly that there is no means to guard against it. Even in the heart of our country, where our hold upon this secret espionage is firmest, it waits but the opening fire of the enemy's battle line to wake it, like a torpid serpent, into venomous activity.

In view of the state of affairs what does our country propose to do? In the words of President Davis "no effort must be spared to add largely to our effective force as promptly as possible. The sources of supply are to be found in restoring to the army all who are improperly absent, putting an end to substitution, modifying the exemption law, restricting details, and placing in the ranks such of the able-bodied men now employed as wagoners, nurses, cooks, and other employés, as are doing service for which the negroes may be found competent." Most of the men improperly absent, together with many of the exempts and men having substitutes, are now without the Confederate lines and cannot be calculated on. If all the exempts capable of bearing arms were enrolled, it will give us the boys below eighteen, the men above forty-five, and those persons who are left at home to meet the wants of the country and the army, but this modification of the exemption law will remove from the fields and manufactories most of the skill that directed agricultural and mechanical labor, and, as stated by the President, "details will have to be made to meet the wants of the country," thus sending many of the men to be derived from this source back to their homes again. Independently of this, experience proves that striplings and men above conscript age break down and swell the sick lists more than they do the ranks. The portion now in our lines of the class who have substitutes is not on the whole a hopeful element, for the motives that created it must have been stronger than patriotism, and these motives added to what many of them will call breach of faith, will cause some to be not forthcoming, and others to be unwilling and discontented soldiers. The remaining sources mentioned by the President have been so closely pruned in the Army of Tennessee that they will be found not to yield largely. The supply from all these sources, together with what we now have in the field, will exhaust the white race, and though it should greatly exceed expectations and put us on an equality with the enemy, or even give us temporary advantages, still we have no reserve to meet unexpected disaster or to supply a protracted struggle. Like past years, 1864 will diminish our ranks by the casualties of war, and what source of repair is there left us? We therefore see in the recommendations of the President only a temporary expedient, which at the best will leave us twelve months hence in the same predicament we are in now. The President attempts to meet only one of the depressing causes mentioned; for the other two he has proposed no remedy. They remain to generate lack of confidence in our final success, and to keep us moving down hill as heretofore. Adequately to meet the causes which are now threatening ruin to our country, we propose, in addition to a modification of the President's plans, that we retain in service for the war all troops now in service, and that we immediately commence training a large reserve of the most courageous of our slaves, and further that we guarantee freedom within a reasonable time to every slave in the South who shall remain true to the Confederacy in this war. As between the loss of independence and the loss of slavery, we assume that every patriot will freely give up the latter—give up the negro slave rather than be a slave himself. If we are correct in this assumption it only remains to show how this great national sacrifice is, in all human probabilities, to change the current of success and sweep the invader from our country.

Our country has already some friends in England and France, and there are strong motives to induce these nations to recognize and assist us, but they cannot assist us without helping slavery, and to do this would be in conflict with their policy for the last quarter of a century. England has paid hundreds of millions to emancipate her West India slaves and break up the slave-trade. Could she now consistently spend her treasure to reinstate slavery in this country? But this barrier once removed, the sympathy and the interests of these and other nations will accord with our own, and we may expect from them both moral support and material aid. One thing is certain, as soon as the great sacrifice to independence is made and known in foreign countries there will be a complete change of front in our favor of the sympathies of the world. This measure will deprive the North of the moral and material aid which it now derives from the bitter prejudices with which foreigners view the institution, and its war, if continued, will henceforth be so despicable in their eyes that the source of recruiting will be dried up. It will leave the enemy's negro army no motive to fight for, and will exhaust the source from which it has been recruited. The idea that it is their special mission to war against slavery has held growing sway over the Northern people for many years, and has at length ripened into an armed and bloody crusade against it. This baleful superstition has so far supplied them with a courage and constancy not their own. It is the most powerful and honestly entertained plank in their war platform. Knock this away and what is left? A bloody ambition for more territory, a pretended veneration for the Union, which one of their own most distinguished orators (Doctor Beecher in his Liverpool speech) openly avowed was only used as a stimulus to stir up the anti-slavery crusade, and lastly the poisonous and selfish interests which are the fungus growth of the war itself. Mankind may fancy it a great duty to destroy slavery, but what interest can mankind have in upholding this remainder of the Northern war platform? Their interests and feelings will be diametrically opposed to it. The measure we propose will strike dead all John Brown fanaticism, and will compel the enemy to draw off altogether or in the eyes of the world to swallow the Declaration of Independence without the sauce and disguise of philanthropy. This delusion of fanaticism at an end, thousands of Northern people will have leisure to look at home and to see the gulf of despotism into which they themselves are rushing.

The measure will at one blow strip the enemy of foreign sympathy and assistance, and transfer them to the South; it will dry up two of his three sources of recruiting; it will take from his negro army the only motive it could have to fight against the South, and will probably cause much of it to desert over to us; it will deprive his cause of the powerful stimulus of fanaticism, and will enable him to see the rock on which his so-called friends are now piloting him. The immediate effect of the emancipation and enrollment of negroes on the military strength of the South would be: To enable us to have armies numerically superior to those of the North, and a reserve of any size we might think necessary; to enable us to take the offensive, move forward, and forage on the enemy. It would open to us in prospective another and almost untouched source of supply, and furnish us with the means of preventing temporary disaster, and carrying on a protracted struggle. It would instantly remove all the vulnerability, embarrassment, and inherent weakness which result from slavery. The approach of the enemy would no longer find every household surrounded by spies; the fear that sealed the master's lips and the avarice that has, in so many cases, tempted him practically to desert us would alike be removed. There would be no recruits awaiting the enemy with open arms, no complete history of every neighborhood with ready guides, no fear of insurrection in the rear, or anxieties for the fate of loved ones when our armies moved forward. The chronic irritation of hope deferred would be joyfully ended with the negro, and the sympathies of his whole race would be due to his native South. It would restore confidence in an early termination of the war with all its inspiring consequences, and even if contrary to all expectations the enemy should succeed in overrunning the South, instead of finding a cheap, ready-made means of holding it down, he would find a common hatred and thirst for vengeance, which would break into acts at every favorable opportunity, would prevent him from settling on our lands, and render the South a very unprofitable conquest. It would remove forever all selfish taint from our cause and place independence above every question of property. The very magnitude of the sacrifice itself, such as no nation has ever voluntarily made before, would appal our enemies, destroy his spirit and his finances, and fill our hearts with a pride and singleness of purpose which would clothe us with new strength in battle. Apart from all other aspects of the question, the necessity for more fighting men is upon us. We can only get a sufficiency by making the negro share the danger and hardships of the war. If we arm and train him and make him fight for the country in her hour of dire distress, every consideration of principle and policy demand that we should set him and his whole race who side with us free. It is a first principle with mankind that he who offers his life in defense of the State should receive from her in return his freedom and his happiness, and we believe in acknowledgment of this principle. The Constitution of the Southern States has reserved to their respective governments the power to free slaves for meritorious services to the State. It is politic besides. For many years, ever since the agitation of the subject of slavery commenced, the negro has been dreaming of freedom, and his vivid imagination has surrounded that condition with so many gratifications that it has become the paradise of his hopes. To attain it he will tempt dangers and difficulties not exceeded by the bravest soldier in the field. The hope of freedom is perhaps the only moral incentive that can be applied to him in his present condition. It would be preposterous then to expect him to fight against it with any degree of enthusiasm, therefore we must bind him to our cause by no doubtful bonds; we must leave no possible loop-hole for treachery to creep in. The slaves are dangerous now, but armed, trained, and collected in an army they would be a thousand fold more dangerous; therefore when we make soldiers of them we must make free men of them beyond all question, and thus enlist their sympathies also. We can do this more effectually than the North can now do, for we can give the negro not only his own freedom, but that of his wife and child, and can secure it to him in his old home. To do this, we must immediately make his marriage and parental relations sacred in the eyes of the law and forbid their sale. The past legislation of the South concedes that a large free middle class of negro blood, between the master and slave, must sooner or later destroy the institution. If, then, we touch the institution at all, we would do best to make the most of it, and by emancipating the whole race upon reasonable terms, and within such reasonable time as will prepare both races for the change, secure to ourselves all the advantages, and to our enemies all the disadvantages that can arise, both at home and abroad, from such a sacrifice. Satisfy the negro that if he faithfully adheres to our standard during the war he shall receive his freedom and that of his race. Give him as an earnest of our intentions such immediate immunities as will impress him with our sincerity and be in keeping with his new condition, enroll a portion of his class as soldiers of the Confederacy, and we change the race from a dreaded weakness to a position of strength.

Will the slaves fight? The helots of Sparta stood their masters good stead in battle. In the great sea fight of Lepanto where the Christians checked forever the spread of Mohammedanism over Europe, the galley slaves of portions of the fleet were promised freedom, and called on to fight at a critical moment of the battle. They fought well, and civilization owes much to those brave galley slaves. The negro slaves of Saint Domingo, fighting for freedom, defeated their white masters and the French troops sent against them. The negro slaves of Jamaica revolted, and under the name of Maroons held the mountains against their masters for 150 years; and the experience of this war has been so far that half-trained negroes have fought as bravely as many other half-trained Yankees. If, contrary to the training of a lifetime, they can be made to face and fight bravely against their former masters, how much more probable is it that with the allurement of a higher reward, and led by those masters, they would submit to discipline and face dangers.

We will briefly notice a few arguments against this course. It is said Republicanism cannot exist without the institution. Even were this true, we prefer any form of government of which the Southern people may have the molding, to one forced upon us by a conqueror. It is said the white man cannot perform agricultural labor in the South. The experience of this army during the heat of summer from Bowling Green, Ky., to Tupelo, Miss., is that the white man is healthier when doing reasonable work in the open field than at any other time. It is said an army of negroes cannot be spared from the fields. A sufficient number of slaves is now administering to luxury alone to supply the place of all we need, and we believe it would be better to take half the able-bodied men off a plantation than to take the one master mind that economically regulated its operations. Leave some of the skill at home and take some of the muscle to fight with. It is said slaves will not work after they are freed. We think necessity and a wise legislation will compel them to labor for a living. It is said it will cause terrible excitement and some disaffection from our cause. Excitement is far preferable to the apathy which now exists, and disaffection will not be among the fighting men. It is said slavery is all we are fighting for, and if we give it up we give up all. Even if this were true, which we deny, slavery is not all our enemies are fighting for. It is merely the pretense to establish sectional superiority and a more centralized form of government, and to deprive us of our rights and liberties. We have now briefly proposed a plan which we believe will save our country. It may be imperfect, but in all human probability it would give us our independence. No objection ought to outweigh it which is not weightier than independence. If it is worthy of being put in practice it ought to be mooted quickly before the people, and urged earnestly by every man who believes in its efficacy. Negroes will require much training; training will require time, and there is danger that this concession to common sense may come too late.

P. R. Cleburne, major-general, commanding division; D. C. Govan, brigadier-general; John E. Murray, colonel Fifth Arkansas; G. F. Baucum, colonel Eighth Arkansas; Peter Snyder, lieutenant-colonel, commanding Sixth and Seventh Arkansas; E. Warfield, lieutenant-colonel, Second Arkansas; M. P. Lowrey, brigadier-general; A. B. Hardcastle, colonel Thirty-second and Forty-fifth Mississippi; F. A. Ashford, major Sixteenth Alabama; John W. Colquitt, colonel First Arkansas; Rich. J. Person, major Third and Fifth Confederate; G. S. Deakins, major Thirty-fifth and Eighth Tennessee; J. H. Collett, captain, commanding Seventh Texas; J. H. Kelly, brigadier-general, commanding Cavalry Division.

"THEY HAVE APPEALED TO WAR":
MISSISSIPPI, JANUARY 1864

William T. Sherman to Roswell M. Sawyer

In late December Sherman sent the four divisions he had brought to Chattanooga into winter quarters in southern Tennessee and northern Alabama. He then returned to Vicksburg and began planning a campaign to destroy the railroads in eastern Mississippi around Meridian. Sherman wrote to one of his staff officers in northern Alabama shortly before the start of the Meridian campaign.

Head Qrs. Dept. of the Tenn.
Vicksburg, Jan. 31-1864.

Major R. M. Sawyer
A. A. G. Army of the Tenn., Huntsville, Alabama
Dear Sawyer,

In my former letters I have answered all your questions save one, and that relates to the treatment of inhabitants known or suspected to be hostile or "Secesh." This is in truth the most difficult business of our Army as it advances & occupies the Southern Country. It is almost impossible to lay down Rules and I invariably leave this whole subject to the local commander, but am willing to give them the benefit of my acquired Knowledge and experience.

In Europe whence we derive our principles of war Wars are between Kings or Rulers through hired Armies and not between Peoples. These remain as it were neutral and sell their produce to whatever Army is in possession. Napoleon when at War with Prussia, Austria and Russia bought forage & provisions of the Inhabitants and consequently had an interest to protect the farms and factories which ministered to his wants. In like manner the Allied Armies in France could buy of the French Habitants, whatever they needed, the produce of the soil or manufactures of the Country. Therefore the General Rule was & is that War is confined to the Armies engaged, and should not visit the houses of families or private Interests. But in other examples a different Rule obtained the Sanction of

Historical Authority. I will only instance one when in the reign of William and Mary the English Army occupied Ireland then in a state of revolt. The inhabitants were actualy driven into foreign lands and were dispossessed of their property and a new population introduced. To this day a large part of the North of Ireland is held by the descendants of the Scotch emigrants sent there by Williams order & an Act of Parliament. The War which now prevails in our land is essentially a war of Races. The Southern People entered into a clear Compact of Government with us of the North, but still maintained through State organizations a species of seperate existence with seperate interests, history and prejudices. These latter became stronger and stronger till at last they have led to war, and have developed the fruits of the bitterest Kind. We of the North are beyond all question Right in our Cause but we are not bound to ignore the fact that the people of the South have prejudices which form a part of their nature, and which they cannot throw off without an effort of reason, or by the slower process of natural change. The question then arises Should we treat as absolute enemies all in the South who differ from us in opinion or prejudice, Kill or banish them, or should we give them time to think and gradually change their conduct, so as to conform to the new order of things which is slowly & gradually creeping into their country?

When men take up Arms to resist a Rightful Authority we are compelled to use like force, because all reason and argument cease when arms are resorted to. When the provisions, forage, horses, mules, wagons, &c. are used by our enemy it is clearly our duty & Right to take them also; because otherwise they might be used against us. In like manner all houses left vacant by an inimical people are clearly our Right, and such as are needed as Storehouses, Hospitals & Quarters. But the question arises as to dwellings used by women, children & non-combatants. So long as non-combatants remain in their houses & Keep to their accustomed peaceful business, their opinions and prejudices can in no wise influence the War & therefore should not be noticed; but if any one comes out into the public streets & creates disorder he or she should be punished, restrained or banished, Either to the rear or front as the officer in Command adjudges. If the People or any of them

Keep up a correspondence with parties in hostility they are spies & can be punished according to Law with death or minor punishment. These are well established principles of War & the People of the South having appealed to *War* are barred from appealing for protection to our Constitution which they have practically and publicly defied. They have appealed to War and must abide *its* Rules & Laws. The United States as a belligerent party, claiming Rights in the soil as the ultimate Sovereign, has a right to change the population—and it may be & is both politic and just we should do so in certain districts; When the Inhabitants persist too long in hostility, it may be both politic and right we should banish them and appropriate their lands to a more loyal and useful population. No man could deny but that the United States would be benefited by dispossessing a single prejudiced, hard headed and disloyal planter and substituting in his place a dozen or more patient industrious good families, even if they were of foreign birth. I think it does good to present this view of the case to many Southern Gentlemen, who grew Rich and wealthy, not by virtue *alone* of their personal industry and skill, but in great part by reason of the protection and impetus to prosperity given by our hitherto moderate & magnanimous Government. It is all idle nonsense for these Southern planters to say that they made the South, that they own it, and that they can do as they please, even to break up our Government & shut up the natural avenues of trade, intercourse and Commerce. We Know and they Know if they are inteligent beings, that as compared with the whole World, they are but as 5 millions to one thousand millions—that they did not create the land, that the only title to its use & usufruct is the deed of the U.S. and that if they appeal to War they hold their all by a very insecure tenure. For my part I believe that this War is the result of false Political Doctrine for which we are all as a people more or less responsible, and I would give all a chance to reflect & when in error to recant. I know that Slave owners, finding themselves in possession of a species of property in opposition to the growing sentiment of the whole Civilized World, conceived their property to be in danger and foolishly appealed to War, and that by skilled political handling they involved with themselves the whole South on this Result of error & prejudice. I believe that some of the

Rich & slave holding are prejudiced to an extent that nothing but death & ruin will ever extinguish, but I hope that as the poorer & industrial classes of the South realize their relative weakness, and their dependence upon the fruits of the earth & good will of their fellow men, they will not only discover the error of their ways & repent of their hasty action, but bless those who persistently have maintained a Constitutional Government strong enough to sustain itself, protect its citizens, and promise peaceful homes to millions yet unborn.

In this belief, whilst I assert for our Govt. the highest Military prerogatives, I am willing to bear in patience the political nonsense of Slave Rights, State Rights uncontrolled freedom of conscience, License of the press and such other trash which have deluded the Southern People and carried them into War, Anarchy, & blood shed, and the perpetration of some of the foulest Crimes that have disgraced any time or any people.

I would advise the Commanding officer at Huntsville and such other towns as are occupied by our troops to assemble the Inhabitants & explain to them these plain, selfevident propositions & tell them that it is for them *now* to say whether they and their children shall inherit the beautiful lands which by the accidents of nature have fallen to their share.

The Government of the United States has in North Alabama any and all the rights of Sovereignty which they choose to enforce in War, to take their lives, their homes, their lands, their every thing, because they cannot deny that War does exist by their acts, and War is simply Power unrestrained by Constitution or Compact. If they want Eternal War, well & good. We must accept the issue & will be forced to dispossess them and put our own people who at a simple notice, would come to North Alabama & accept the elegant houses & Plantations now there.

If the People of Huntsville think differently, let them persist in this War three years longer and then they will not be consulted.

Three years ago by a little reflection and patience they could have had a hundred years of Peace & Prosperity, but they *preferred* War. Last year they could have saved their Slaves but now it is too late, all the Powers of Earth cannot restore to them their slaves any more than their dead Grandfathers. Next year in all probability their lands will be taken, for in War we can take them & rightfully too, and in another year they may beg in vain for their lives, for sooner or later there must be an end to strife.

A People who will persevere in a War beyond a certain limit ought to Know the consequences. Many, Many People with less pertinacity than the South has already shown have been wiped out of national Existence.

My own belief, is that even now the non-slaveholding classes of the South are alienating from their associates in War. Already I hear Crimination & recrimination. Those who have property left should take warning in time.

Since I have come down here I have seen many Southern Planters, who now hire their own negroes & acknowledge that they were mistaken and knew not the earthquake they were to make by appealing to secession. They thought that the Politicians had prepared the way, and that they could part the states of this Union in Peace. They now see that we are bound together as one nation by indissoluble ties, and that any interest or any fraction of the people that set themselves up in antagonism to the Nation must perish.

Whilst I would not remit one jot or tittle of our Nations Rights in Peace or War, I do make allowances for past political errors and prejudices.

Our National Congress and the Supreme Court are the proper arenas on which to discuss conflicting opinions & not the Battle field.

You may not hear from me again for some time and if you think it will do any good, Call some of the better people of Huntsville together & explain to them my view. You may even read to them this letter & let them use it, so as to prepare them for my coming.

To those who submit to the Rightful Laws & authority of their State & National Government promise all gentleness and forbearance, but to the petulant and persistant secessionist, why death or banishment is a mercy, and the quicker he or she is disposed of the better. Satan & the rebellious saints of Heaven, were allowed a continuance of existence in Hell, merely to swell their just punishment.

To such as would rebel against a Government so mild and

just as ours was in Peace, a punishment equal would not be unjust.

We are progressing well in this quarter, but I have not changed my opinion that although we may soon make certain the existence of the Power of our National Government yet years must pass before ruffianism, murder & Robbery will cease to afflict this region of our country. Your friend,

W. T. Sherman
Maj. Genl. Comdg.

MEETING "FATHER ABRAHAM":
WASHINGTON, D.C., FEBRUARY 1864

Lois Bryan Adams to the Detroit Advertiser and Tribune

A journalist, schoolteacher, and poet who had edited the literary and household departments of the *Michigan Farmer* for several years, Lois Bryan Adams moved to Washington in the summer of 1863 and began working as a clerk for the recently established Department of Agriculture. Adams contributed regular letters to the *Detroit Advertiser and Tribune* while also serving as a volunteer for the Michigan Soldiers' Relief Association. She wrote about a White House reception and a fund-raising fair held at the Patent Office (where the Department of Agriculture was housed) in letters that appeared in the *Advertiser and Tribune* on February 16 and February 29, 1864.

Life in Washington
A Lady's First Day at the Presidents
Correspondence of the *Advertiser and Tribune*
Washington, February 8, 1864

Saturdays are public reception days at the White House. From 11 till 3 o'clock all who choose can go and pay their respects to the President and his lady, pass through the room and conservatories and go on their way.

One mile west of the Capitol, directly through the heart of the city, stands the Presidential mansion. It is Saturday, the 6th of February, a chilly, cloudy day, with a lowering sky threatening rain; but let us go. Standing at the Seventh street crossing we turn our face to the east, up Pennsylvania Avenue. Look a moment; does it seem possible that we can ever work our way through that thronging, crowding mass, pouring down the broad pavement in one incessant stream? You say no, and look toward the street cars passing each way every two or three minutes, but they are full, too—crowded to suffocation; the sidewalk will be better; there, at least, one may breathe more of Heaven's breath than of their neighbors.

We are on the fashionable, north side of the avenue; but glance across—the other side is nearly as crowded as this and all the broad space between is thronged with double lines of heavy army wagons drawn by four or six mules each, and seemingly endless in each direction; squads and companies of cavalry are passing, some one way and some another; state and private carriages, rattling hacks, omnibuses, street cars and every sort of vehicle imaginable seem mixed up in inextricable confusion; the noise is deafening and the ground trembles; but everybody is hurrying on; let us pass too, if pass we may.

Soldiers are here too, in companies and singly, in every style of uniform, and most uniformly gathered in knots and platoons about the hotel and restaurant doors. There, tearing along through the crowd, come 30 or 40 little negro bootblacks, following the rattling music of a fifer and drummer who are beating up recruits for some low theater tonight; and here are elegantly dressed ladies and gentlemen, and young misses and children, with their jaunty hats and showy scarlet plumes—crowds of everybody, going and coming, and standing at corners gathered about the handsome show windows of the stores and shops. We press on, following close upon the train of those rustling silks that sweep across and dip into the filthy gutters at every crossing, and draw little waving lines of wet dust from every brimming runnel of slop-water running down from back yards and alleys. These silks are going to the President's.

Ah, now, the way is uphill, and growing tiresome. We are passing Willards, and rounding the corner of the Treasury, that immense marble caudle-cup, whose recesses we hope to explore some day, and explain to the public how that wonderful "pap" is made, on which so many Government pets get full. Now the silks have taken themselves into the cars. We go north past the Treasury, and its grounds, and then turn again to the west. All around this square on either side of the avenue the pavement is plastered with sticky mud some inches deep; but passing this we come in front of the President's grounds and find ourselves on broad, dry, granite flagstones clean and white. The avenue here runs east and west again, and the White

House is on the south side some little distance from it. Between the house and the street is a semi-circular park planted with evergreens and other trees, and having a bronze statue of Gen. Lafayette in the center. Around this little park sweeps the broad graveled carriage drive, bordered on the outer side by the wide granite footwalk and passing directly under the deep colored porch of the mansion. The park and drive are surrounded and protected by high iron palings. Iron gates lead into the drive and walk which are nearly always open.

Today guards armed with swords, mounted on handsome black horses, sit facing each other just within the gates at each end of the drive, and two more are stationed directly in front of the house. Between these guards the carriages freighted with their brocades and velvets and plumes make their entrance and exit. Foot guards are at all times pacing up and down the pavement before the house. Let us go up the steps and enter the open doors. Here is a mother plainly dressed, leading her little boy of ten to whom she is telling the story of Abraham Lincoln's youth. In the vestibule a waiter stands, motioning with his hand the way for visitors to go. The mother and child pass on; we follow. There is no crowd, nobody going in just now but us. Just inside the door of the blue room stands the President between two young men, and a plump, round-faced, smiling man stands opposite him. Between these two the mother leads her boy. The President takes her hand in one of his, places the other on the boy's brown curls, says some kindly words to both, and they pass on.

The same hand takes mine, the eyes look down as kindly; he bows low and says, "How do you do?" in a tone that seems to demand a friendly reply. But no reply comes. My heart is on my lips, but there is no shape or sound of words. In one glance at that worn yet kindly face I read a history that crushes all power of speech, and before I am fairly conscious that I have touched the hand and looked into the eyes of our honored Father Abraham, I find myself on the opposite side of the room. Doubtless if he had a thought about me it was, "What a stupid creature! who does not know enough to give a name or answer a civil question!"

Six months had I been in Washington without seeing the President. Six months of anxious waiting for friends whose long-promised "some day" never seemed to draw any nearer, till at last, tired of patience and friends together, I went alone. And that was the way I met him. I, who had honored him from the first moment he put his hand so firmly to the helm of our mighty ship of state, to steer her through the perilous sea of blood and strife; I, who could have knelt to touch the hand that first swept the curse from the nation's capitol, and then proclaimed freedom to all, in the name of God and humanity; I, the child of a State so loyal and true to her very heart's core that her veteran troops, almost to a man, have re-pledged themselves to stand by him till the fiery ordeal is past; I, who had sung for him, knowing he had not time to sing for himself, and had longed for the day to come when I might speak to him as well as for him—that was the way I did it!

It is late, for it has taken at least two hours' walking on the streets, to say nothing of numerous advances and retreats up and down the sweep of the semi-circle, to get resolution up to the point of accomplishing even this. There is but time to glance about us and then retire with the already departing crowd.

The blue room is a circular apartment, papered, draped, and furnished with the color from which it takes its name. In the center, under the massive chandelier, is a white marble table, supporting a vase of rare flowers, and beside it stands Mrs. Lincoln, now in animated conversation with the ladies and gentlemen gathered about her. We need not speak to her—she will never know we have been in the room—many others come in the same way, only to look and go. Another time we shall have confidence to pay her the respect due to her station.

It is a general remark that Mrs. Lincoln, at her receptions and parties, is always dressed with the most perfect taste—always richly and elegantly, and never over-dressed. Today she was robed in purple velvet; she wears a postilion basque, waist or body of the same, made high at the throat, and relieved by an elegant point lace collar, fastened by a knot of some dainty white material, in the center of which glistens a single diamond. The seams of the basque and skirt are corded in white, and the skirt, basque, and full open sleeves all richly trimmed with a heavy fringe of white chenille. The delicate head-dress is of purple and white to match the dress. It is all very becoming, and she is looking exceedingly well, receiving and dismissing her guests with much apparent ease and grace. Mrs. Lincoln is short in stature, plump, and round favored, with a very pleasant countenance.

But the President with his attendants has already left the room; the guests are fast departing; the conservatory doors are closed; we pass out with the rest, and pass a resolution to make better use of the next reception day at the White House.
L.

From Washington
OPENING OF THE GREAT FAIR AT THE PATENT OFFICE
From Our Own Correspondent
Washington, February 23, 1864

Washington celebrated the birthday of its great namesake in a very appropriate manner. The 22nd was the day set apart for the inauguration of the grand Fair got up by the ladies for the benefit of the Christian Commission and the families of the District volunteers. Although quite a little army of soldiers, clerks, and others, officered by the lady managers had been at work on the decorations of the hall, all was not yet quite complete when the hour for admitting the public arrived, but amid the blaze of splendor that everywhere met the eye, these little deficiencies were quite unnoticed.

The hall itself is the grandest place that could have been selected for such an exhibition. It is in the third story of the Patent Office building, on the partially finished and unoccupied north side, and is 300 feet in length by 75 feet wide, and high in proportion. The floor is of marble, and the walls, though yet unplastered, have been so wreathed and draped with evergreens and the national colors, that scarcely a blemish is visible. Down the center and along each side, stands, booths, bowers, and fairy-like arbors are ranged, all brilliant with the "red, white, and blue," draped, festooned, and bound and blended with the twining wreaths of evergreen. These booths and bowers all bear appropriate mottoes, and are all filled with the beautiful and tempting things that Fairs are made of, with pleasant-faced ladies adding still stronger temptations for visitors to invest in the great charity scheme. The hall is warmed by registers, and well lighted with gas, and presents by night a scene of bewildering beauty and dazzling splendor.

At the extreme west of the hall a handsome stage is built up, at the back of which is a large brazen shield, from which spears and lances radiate like sunbeams, bearing on their points small crimson pennons, while behind them flash the everywhere present stars and stripes. The front of this stage is handsomely draped and festooned, like everything else, with red, white and blue, and evergreens fashioned in various symbolic forms. On each side of the front is a splendid stand of arms, surmounted by armor and an ancient plumed helmet, and intertwined with evergreens.

It was expected that Edward Everett would have been here to deliver the opening address, but he did not come, and his place was very happily supplied by the Hon. L. E. Chittenden. The vast hall was crowded almost to suffocation long before the speaker was announced, and the passing time was somewhat enlivened by the martial music of the band present.

A little before eight, a general buzz and clapping of hands went through the crowd, and it was whispered that the President was coming up the hall. Very soon, accompanied by his son Robert, the Rev. Mr. Sunderland, Hon. B. B. French, and other gentlemen, he passed through to the rear of the stage, came upon it and quietly took his seat on a sofa in one corner, with his son beside him. Prayer was offered by Mr. Sunderland in a most fervent and patriotic spirit, after which Mr. Chittenden was introduced. His address was of considerable length, but so earnest, patriotic, and eloquent, that it was listened to throughout with rapt attention, the audience frequently showing their hearty approval by sincere and merited applause. After the address, the Hon. B. B. French, Commissioner of Public Buildings, read an original poem on the occasion of the present gathering and exhibition. It was also radically patriotic and anti-slavery in its tone, and was loudly applauded by the audience.

When Mr. French retired there was a universal clapping of hands for the President to come forward. It continued so long and so earnest that several gentlemen on the stage went to him to persuade him to gratify the general desire; but it was some moments before he would allow himself to be moved at all, and when he did rise and come forward, it was evidently with very great reluctance. He was looking extremely pale and worn, but smiled good-naturedly as he remarked that he thought the Committee who had invited him to be present had practiced a little fraud upon him, as no intimation had been given that he would be expected to say a word. He was unprepared for a speech, and felt that after the eloquent address and poem to which the audience had listened, any attempt of his would be a failure; besides, from the position he occupied everything that he said necessarily went into print, therefore, it was advisable that he should say nothing foolish. (Laughter and applause, and a voice, "Nothing foolish ever comes from our President.") It was very difficult to say sensible things. In speaking without preparation he might make some bad mistake, which, if published, would do both the nation and himself harm. Therefore, he would only say that he thanked the managers of the fair for the persevering manner in which they had prosecuted the enterprise for so good an object, and with this expression of his gratitude, he hoped they would accept his apology and excuse him from speaking.

He then retired to his seat amidst the hearty applause of the multitude. Soon after this the benediction was pronounced, and the President and his party withdrew. There was music by the band, and some singing on the stage afterward, and the hall was filled till midnight and after by the crowds who on this first day of opening came more to see than to buy.

One of the most attractive features among the decorations at this fair, is a miniature representation of Gen. U. S. Grant's headquarters at Chattanooga. Near the center of the hall a space some 14 feet square is inclosed, and within are built up two little mountains of rock work, mosses, and branches of evergreen. On the top of one mountain is a fort, with soldiers, cannon, and everything complete; on the other a lookout; a rustic bridge spans the gorge between them, and at the bottom of the gorge is a small body of water with a boat and ducks on its surface; and along its banks and scattered among the rocks are turtles, cattle, goats, and birds, as like as life. A winding gravel road runs from the fort to the lookout, and heavily laden wagons are ascending the heights of each mountain. On the low ground beneath the foot and protected by it, is a rustic building, with the name "U. S. Grant" over the door. Around the whole enclosure slender columns with evergreens springing up, from the tops of which light arches meet over the center, forming a sort of airy dome. Altogether it is very beautiful and draws crowds of admirers.

As a sort of side scene some enterprising ladies have got up a representation of a New England kitchen a hundred years ago. Here several hoopless dames may be seen in petticoat and short gown, with high-crowned cambric caps and other evidences of antiquity; one is spinning at the big wheel, another at the little one; one winding yarn from old-time swifts, one carding; young girls churning, knitting and paring apples; visitors coming in with their antique calash sunbonnets; the fortune-teller in her red cloak and hood, the circulating snuff-box, strings of dried apples along the wall, the wooden mortar and pestle and iron candlesticks on the chimney-piece, old-fashioned pitchers and pewter dishes on the dresser—all are there, and the identical old fire-place, that some of us may remember, with the pot hanging from the crane, and the fore-stick burned in two. It all seems very well done except the talking. When people here attempt Yankee talk, they slide down at once into the negro slang, which is quite another thing. However, the New England kitchen at the Washington fair promises to be a very attractive and remunerative feature.

L.

SINKING OF THE HOUSATONIC:
SOUTH CAROLINA, FEBRUARY 1864

Francis J. Higginson to John A. Dahlgren

The U.S.S. *Housatonic*, a wooden steam sloop armed with eleven guns, had joined the South Atlantic Blockading Squadron off Charleston in September 1862. Over the next seventeen months she helped capture several blockade runners, fought a gun duel with two Confederate ironclad rams, and supported Union troops during the battle for Charleston Harbor. On February 17, 1864, the *Housatonic* was sunk by an underwater explosive charge. Her executive officer, Lieutenant Francis J. Higginson, reported the loss of his vessel, unaware that the *Housatonic* was the first ship ever to be sunk in combat by a submarine.

———————

U. S. S. CANANDAIGUA.
Off Charleston, S. C., February 18, 1864.

Sir: I have the honor to make the following report of the sinking of the U. S. S. *Housatonic*, by a rebel torpedo off Charleston, S. C., on the evening of the 17th instant:

About 8:45 P. M. the officer of the deck, Acting Master J. K. Crosby, discovered something in the water about 100 yards from and moving toward the ship. It had the appearance of a plank moving in the water. It came directly toward the ship, the time from when it was first seen till it was close alongside being about two minutes.

During this time the chain was slipped, engine backed, and all hands called to quarters.

The torpedo struck the ship forward of the mizzenmast, on the starboard side, in a line with the magazine. Having the after pivot gun pivoted to port we were unable to bring a gun to bear upon her.

About one minute after she was close alongside the explosion took place, the ship sinking stern first and heeling to port as she sank.

Most of the crew saved themselves by going into the rigging, while a boat was dispatched to the *Canandaigua*. This vessel came gallantly to our assistance and succeeded in rescuing all but the following-named officers and men, viz, Ensign E. C. Hazeltine, Captain's Clerk C. O. Muzzey, Quartermaster John Williams, Landsman Theodore Parker, Second-Class Fireman John Walsh.

The above officers and men are missing and are supposed to have been drowned.

Captain Pickering was seriously bruised by the explosion and is at present unable to make a report of the disaster.

Very respectfully, your obedient servant,

F. J. HIGGINSON,
Lieutenant.

Rear-Admiral JOHN A. DAHLGREN,
Commanding South Atlantic Blockading Squadron.

A SUBMARINE TORPEDO BOAT: SOUTH CAROLINA,
OCTOBER 1863–FEBRUARY 1864

James H. Tomb:
Notes on the H. L. Hunley

In 1863 a group of engineers in Mobile designed and built a forty-foot-long submarine that was named for Horace L. Hunley, a Louisiana lawyer and merchant who helped finance the project. Driven by a hand-cranked propeller, the *H. L. Hunley* was equipped with diving planes, hand-pumped ballast tanks, and a primitive snorkel device, and could remain underwater for two hours. Sent to Charleston by rail, the submarine sank during a test on August 29, drowning five of its crew. After being raised from the harbor, she sank again on October 15, killing Hunley and seven other men. The second sinking was witnessed by James H. Tomb, an engineer who served on the *David*, a small steam-driven boat with a low silhouette designed for making night attacks on Union warships. Like the *David*, the *Hunley* was armed with a spar torpedo intended to be rammed into an enemy hull and then detonated from a distance. On February 17, 1864, the *Hunley* disappeared shortly after she sank the *Housatonic*. In 1995 the submarine was located four miles off the coast and one hundred yards from the wreck of her target. The *Hunley* was raised in 2000, and in 2004 the remains of Lieutenant George E. Dixon and his seven crew members were buried in Charleston.

CHARLESTON, S. C., *January, 1865*

There was a submarine torpedo boat, not under the orders of the Navy, and I was ordered to tow her down the harbor three or four times by Flag-Officer Tucker, who also gave me orders to report as to her efficiency as well as safety. In my report to him I stated, "The only way to use a torpedo was on the same plan as the 'David'—that is, a spar torpedo—and to strike with his boat on the surface, the torpedo being lowered to 8 feet. Should she attempt to use a torpedo as Lieutenant Dixon intended, by submerging the boat and striking from below, the level of the torpedo would be above his own boat, and as she had little buoyancy and no power, the chances were the suction caused by the water passing into the sinking ship would prevent her rising to the surface, besides the possibility of his own boat being disabled." Lieutenant Dixon was a very brave and cool-headed man, and had every confidence in his boat, but had great trouble when under the water from lack of air and light. At the time she made the attempt to dive under the receiving ship in Charleston Harbor, Lieutenant Dixon, James A. Eason, and myself stood on the wharf as she passed out and saw her dive, but she did not rise again, and after a week's effort she was brought to the surface and the crew of 7 men were found in a bunch near the manhole. Lieutenant Dixon said they had failed to close the after valve.

The last night the "David" towed him down the harbor his torpedo got foul of us and came near blowing up both boats before we got it clear of the bottom, where it had drifted. I let him go after passing Fort Sumter, and on my making report of this, Flag-Officer Tucker refused to have the "David" tow him again. The power for driving this boat came from 7 or 8 men turning cranks attached to the propeller shaft, and when working at their best would make about 3 knots. She was very slow in turning, but would sink at a moment's notice and at times without it. The understanding was that from the time of her construction at Mobile up to the time when she struck *Housatonic* not less than 33 men had lost their lives in her. She was a veritable coffin to this brave officer and his men.

J. H. TOMB.

A SOLDIER'S WIDOW:
VIRGINIA, FEBRUARY 1864

Judith W. McGuire:
Diary, February 28, 1864

McGuire had noted in her diary on December 12, 1863, that the price of bacon was $2.50 a pound, and then wrote: "How are the poor to live? Though it is said that the *poor genteel* are the real sufferers. Money is laid aside for paupers by every one who can possibly do it, but persons who do not let their wants be known are the really poor." On February 15, 1864, she recorded that bacon was now selling for $8 a pound.

28*th*.—Our hearts ache for the poor. A few days ago, as E. was walking out, she met a wretchedly dressed woman, of miserable appearance, who said she was seeking the Young Men's Christian Association, where she hoped to get assistance and work to do. E. carried her to the door, but it was closed, and the poor woman's wants were pressing. She then brought her home, supplied her with food, and told her to return to see me the following afternoon. She came, and with an honest countenance and manner told me her history. Her name is Brown; her husband had been a workman in Fredericksburg; he joined the army, and was killed at the second battle of Manassas. Many of her acquaintances in Fredericksburg fled last winter during the bombardment; she became alarmed, and with her three little children fled too. She had tried to get work in Richmond; sometimes she succeeded, but could not supply her wants. A kind woman had lent her a room and a part of a garden, but it was outside of the corporation; and although it saved house-rent, it debarred her from the relief of the associations formed for supplying the city poor with meal, wood, etc. She had evidently been in a situation little short of starvation. I asked her if she could get bread enough for her children by her work? She said she could sometimes, and when she could not, she "got turnip-tops from her piece of a garden, which were now putting up smartly, and she boiled them, with a little salt, and fed them on that." "But do they satisfy your hunger," said I? "Well, it is something to go upon for awhile, but it does not stick by us like as bread does, and then we gets hungry again, and I am afraid to let the children eat them too often, lest they should get sick; so I tries to get them to go to sleep; and sometimes the woman in the next room will bring the children her leavings, but she is monstrous poor." When I gave her meat for her children, taken from the bounty of our Essex friends, tears of gratitude ran down her cheeks; she said they "had not seen meat for so long." Poor thing, I promised her that her case should be known, and that she should not suffer so again. A soldier's widow shall not suffer from hunger in Richmond. It must not be, and will not be when her case is known. Others are now interested for her. This evening Mrs. R. and myself went in pursuit of her; but though we went through all the streets and lanes of "Butcher Flat" and other vicinities, we could get no clue to her. We went into many small and squalid-looking houses, yet we saw no such abject poverty as Mrs. Brown's. All who needed it were supplied with meal by the corporation, and many were supporting themselves with Government work. One woman stood at a table cutting out work; we asked her the stereotyped question—"Is there a very poor widow named Brown in this direction?" "No, ladies; I knows two Mrs. Browns, but they ain't so poor, and ain't no widows nuther." As neither of them was our Mrs. B., we turned away; but she suddenly exclaimed, "Ladies, will one of you read my husband's last letter to me? for you see I can't read writing." As Mrs. R. took it, she remarked that it was four weeks old, and asked if no one had read it to her? "Oh yes, a gentleman has read it to me four or five times; but you see I loves to hear it, for may-be I shan't hear from him no more." The tears now poured down her cheeks. "He always writes to me every chance, and it has been so long since he wrote that, and they tell me that they have been fighting, and may-be something has happened to him." We assured her that there had been no fighting—not even a skirmish. This quieted her, and Mrs. R. read the badly written but affectionate letter, in which he expresses his anxiety to see her and his children, and his inability to get a furlough. She then turned to the mantel-piece, and with evident pride took from a nail an old felt hat, through the crown of which were two bullet-holes. It was her husband's hat, through which a bullet had passed in the battle of Chancellorsville, and, as she remarked, must have come "very nigh grazing his head." We remarked upon its being a proof of his bravery, which gratified her very much; she then hung it up carefully, saying that it was just opposite her bed, and she never let it be out of her sight. She said she wanted her husband to fight for his country, and not "to stand back, like some women's husbands, to be drafted; she would have been ashamed of that, but she felt uneasy, because something told her that he would never get back." Poor woman! we felt very much interested in her, and tried to comfort her.

HANGING DESERTERS:
NORTH CAROLINA, FEBRUARY 1864

John Paris: Sermon Preached at Kinston

February 28, 1864

On February 1, 1864, Confederate forces began an unsuccessful attempt to retake New Bern, North Carolina, held by the Union since March 1862. Before withdrawing on February 3, Brigadier General Robert F. Hoke's North Carolina brigade overran several Union outposts and captured more than 300 prisoners. Among them were fifty-three soldiers from the 2nd North Carolina Union Volunteers, one of two white Union regiments recruited in the coastal areas of the state. When Major General George E. Pickett, the commander of the Department of North Carolina, learned that some of the prisoners had deserted from the Confederate army before enlisting in the Union forces, he ordered their court-martial. Between February 5 and February 22, twenty-two men from the 2nd North Carolina Union Volunteers were convicted of desertion and treason and hanged in Kinston, thirty miles northwest of New Bern. The executions were witnessed by Hoke's brigade and, in many cases, by the families of the men who were hanged (most of the condemned were from nearby counties). At least twenty-one of the remaining unionist prisoners would later die from disease in Confederate prison camps. John Paris, a Methodist clergyman who had served as chaplain of the 54th North Carolina Infantry since July 1862, preached a sermon on the executions before Hoke's brigade on February 28 and later published it as a pamphlet.

NOTE

On the morning of the first of February, Brig. Gen. R. F. Hoke forced the passage of Batchelor's Creek, nine miles west from Newbern; the enemy abandoned his works and retreated upon the town. A hot and vigorous pursuit was made, which resulted in the capture of a large number of prisoners, and the surrender to our forces of many others, who were cut off from escape by the celerity of the pursuit, and our troops seizing and holding every avenue leading into the town, near the enemy's batteries.

Among the prisoners taken, were about fifty native North Carolinians, dressed out in Yankee uniform, with muskets upon their shoulders. Twenty-two of these men were recognized as men who had deserted from our ranks, and gone over to the enemy. Fifteen of them belonged to Nethercutt's Battalion. They were arraigned before a court martial, proved guilty of the charges, and condemned to suffer death by hanging.

It became my duty to visit these men in prison before their execution, in a religious capacity. From them I learned that bad and mischievous influences had been used with every one to induce him to desert his flag, and such influences had led to their ruin. From citizens who had known them for many years, I learned that some of them had heretofore borne good names, as honest, harmless, unoffending citizens. After their execution I thought it proper, for the benefit of the living, that I should deliver a discourse before our brigade, upon the death of these men, that the eyes of the living might be opened, to view the horrid and ruinous crime and sin of desertion, which had become so prevalent. A gentleman from Forsyth county, who was present at the delivery of the discourse, solicited a copy for publication, which has been granted.

For the style and arrangement, as it was preached as well as written in the camp, no apology is offered. Having no pecuniary interest in its publication, it is respectfully submitted to all who go for the unqualified independence of the Southern Confederacy.

J. PARIS,

Hoke's Brigade, April 1st, 1864.

SERMON

MATTHEW XXVII CHAPTER 3, 4, AND 5TH VERSES.

3. Then Judas which had betrayed him, when he saw that he was condemned, repented himself, and brought again the thirty pieces of silver to the chief priests and elders,

4. Saying, I have sinned in that I have betrayed the innocent blood. And they said, what is that to us? See thou to that.

5. And he cast down the pieces of silver in the temple, and departed, and went and hanged himself.

You are aware, my friends, that I have given public notice that upon this occasion I would preach a funeral discourse upon the death of the twenty-two unfortunate, yet wicked and deluded men, whom you have witnessed hanged upon the gallows within a few days. I do so, not to eulogize or benefit the dead. But I do so, solely, for the benefit of the living: and in doing so, I shall preach in my own way, and according to my own manner, or rule. What I shall say will either be true or false. I therefore request that you will watch me closely; weigh my arguments in the balance of truth; measure them by the light of candid reason, and compare them by the Standard of Eternal Truth, the Book of God; what is wrong, reject, and what is true, accept, for the sake of the truth, as responsible beings.

Of all deserters and traitors, Judas Iscariot, who figures in our text, is undoubtedly the most infamous, whose names have found a place in history, either sacred or profane. No name has ever been more execrated by mankind: and all this has been justly done. But there was a time and a period when this man wore a different character, and had a better name. A time when he went forth with the eleven Apostles at the command of the Master to preach the gospel, heal the sick and cast out devils. And he, too, returned with this same chosen band, when the grand, and general report was made of what they had done and what they had taught.

But a change came over this man. He was the treasurer of the Apostolic board; an office that warranted the confidence and trust of his compeers. "He bare the bag and kept what was put therein." Possibly this was the grand and successful temptation presented him by the evil One. He contracted an undue love for money, and Holy Writ informs us "the love of money is the root of all evil;" so must it ever be when valued above a good name, truth or honor. Now comes his base and unprincipled desertion of his blessed Master. He goes to the chief priests. His object is selfish, base and sordid,—to get money.

He enters into a contract with them, to lead their armed guards to the place to which the Saviour had retired, that they might arrest him. Thirty pieces of silver is the price agreed upon,— about twenty-two dollars and fifty cents of our money. A poor price, indeed, for any man to accept for his reputation, his life, his soul, his all. When Judas saw that the Saviour was condemned, it is stated in the text that "he repented himself, and brought again the thirty pieces of silver to the chief priests and elders, saying, I have sinned in that I have betrayed the innocent blood." "And he cast down the thirty pieces of silver in the temple, and departed and went and hanged himself." The way of transgressors is truly hard. As sure as there is a God in heaven, justice and judgment will overtake the wicked; though he may flourish as a green bay tree for awhile, yet the eye of God is upon him and retribution must and will overtake him.

Let us now consider what this man gained by his wicked transaction. First, twenty-two dollars and fifty cents. Secondly, a remorse of conscience too intolerable to be borne. An immortality of infamy without a parallel in the family of man. What did he lose? His reputation. His money. His apostleship. His peace of conscience, his life, his soul, his all.

Well may it be said that this man is the most execrable of all whose names stand on the black list of deserters and traitors that the world has furnished from the beginning until now.— Turning to the history of our own country, I find written high on the scroll of infamy the name of Benedict Arnold, who at one time stood high in the confidence of the great and good Washington. What was his crime? Desertion and treason. He too hoped to better his condition by selling his principles for money,to the enemies of his country, betraying his Washington into the hands of his foes, and committing the heaven-insulting crime of perjury before God and man. Verily, he obtained his reward; an immortality of infamy; the scorn and contempt of the good and the loyal of all ages and all countries.

Thus, gentlemen, I have brought before you two grand prototypes of desertion, whose names tower high over all on the scroll of infamy. And I now lay down the Proposition, that every man who has taken up arms in defence of his country, and basely deserts or abandons that service, belongs in principle and practice to the family of Judas and Arnold. But what was the status of those twenty-two deserters whose sad end and just fate you witnessed across the river in the old field? Like you they came as volunteers to fight for the independence of their own country. Like you they received the bounty money offered by their country. Like you they took upon themselves the most solemn obligations of this oath: "I, A. B. do solemnly swear that I will bear true allegiance to the Confederate States of America, and that I will serve them honestly and faithfully against all their enemies or opposers whatsoever, and observe and obey the orders of the Confederate States, and the orders of the officers appointed over me, according to the rules and articles for the government of the Confederate States, so help me God."

With all the responsibilities of this solemn oath upon their souls, and all the ties that bind men to the land that gave them birth, ignoring every principle that pertains to the patriot, disowning that natural as well as lawful allegiance that every man owes to the government of the State which throws around him the ægis of its protection, they went, boldly, Judas and Arnold-like, made an agreement with the enemies of their country, took an oath of fidelity and allegiance to them, and agreed with them for money to take up arms and assist in the unholy and hellish work of the subjugation of the country which was their own, their native land! These men have only met the punishment meted out by all civilized nations for such crimes. To this, all good men, all true men, and all loyal men who love their country, will say, Amen!

But who were those twenty-two men whom you hanged upon the gallows? They were your fellow-beings. They were citizens of our own Carolina. They once marched under the same beautiful flag that waves over our heads; but in an evil hour, they yielded to mischievous influence, and from motives or feelings base and sordid, unmanly and vile, resolved to abandon every principle of patriotism, and sacrifice every impulse of honor; this sealed their ruin and enstamped their lasting disgrace. The question now arises, what are the influences and the circumstances that lead men into the high and damning crimes, of perjury and treason? It will be hard to frame an answer that will fit every case. But as I speak for the benefit of those whom I stand before to-day, I will say I have made the answer to this question a matter of serious inquiry for more than eighteen months. The duties of my office as Chaplain have brought me much in contact with this class of men. I have visited twenty-four of them under sentence of death in their cells of confinement, and with death staring them in the face, and only a few short hours between them and the bar of God. I have warned them to tell the whole truth, confess everything wrong before God and man, and yet I have not been able to obtain the full, fair and frank confession of everything relating to their guilt from even one of them, that I thought circumstances demanded, although I had baptized ten of them in the Name of the Holy Trinity. In confessing their crimes, they would begin at Newbern, where they joined the enemy, saying nothing about perjury and desertion. Every man of the twenty-two, whose execution you witnessed, confessed that bad or mischievous influences had been used with him to influence him to desert. All but two, willingly gave me the names of their seducers. But none of these deluded and ruined men seemed to think he ought to suffer the penalty of death, because he had been persuaded to commit those high crimes by other men.

But gentlemen, I now come to give you my answer to the question just asked. From all that I have learned in the prison, in the guard house, in the camp, and in the country, *I am fully satisfied, that the great amount of desertions from our army are produced by, and are the fruit of a bad, mischievous, restless, and dissatisfied, not to say disloyal influence that is at work in the country at home.* If in this bloody war our country should be overrun, this same mischievous home influence will no doubt be the prime agent in producing such a calamity. Discontentment has, and does exist in various parts of the State. We hear of these malcontents holding public meetings, not for the purpose of supporting the Government in the prosecution of the war, and maintenance of our independence, but for the purpose of finding fault with the Government. Some of these meetings have been dignified with the name of "peace meetings;" some have been ostensibly called for other purposes, but they have invariably been composed of men who talk more about their "rights," than about their duty and loyalty to their country. These malcontents profess to be greatly afflicted in mind about the state of public affairs. In their doleful croakings they are apt to give vent to their melancholy lamentations in such words as these: "The country is ruined!" "We are whipt!" "We might as well give up." "It is useless to attempt to fight any longer!" "This is the rich man's war and the poor man's fight;" &c. Some newspapers have caught the mania and lent their influence to this work of mischief; whilst the pulpit, to the scandal of its character for faith and holiness, has belched forth in some places doctrines and counsels through the ministrations of unworthy occupants, sufficient to cause Christianity to blush under all the circumstances. I would here remark, standing in the relation which I do before you, that the pulpit and the press, when true and loyal to the Government which affords them protection, are mighty engines for good but when they see that Government engaged in a bloody struggle for existence, and show themselves opposed to its efforts to maintain its authority by all constitutional and legal means, such a press, and such pulpits should receive no support for an hour from a people that would be free. The seal of condemnation should consign them to oblivion.

Such sentiments as we have just alluded to, are sent in letters to our young men in the army, by writers professing to be friends; often with an urgent and pressing invitation to come home; and some have even added that execrable and detestable falsehood, the quintescence of treason, "the State is going to secede." Letters coming into our camps on the Rappahannock and Rapidan sustain this position. What are the effects produced upon our young men in the ranks? With the illiterate, they are baleful indeed. The incautious youth takes it for granted that the country is ruined and that the Government is his enemy. The poisonous contagion of treason from home gets hold in his mind and steals into his feelings. This appeal from home has overcome him. The young man of promise and of hope once, now becomes a deserter. Is guilty by one false step of the awful crimes of perjury and desertion. The solemn obligations of his oath are disregarded; he takes to the woods, traverses weary roads by night for days, until he reaches the community in which he claims his home; but for what? To engage in any of the honorable vocations of life? No, gentlemen. But to lie hidden from the face of all good, true and loyal men. But for what purpose? To keep from serving his country as a man and a citizen. To consume the provisions kept in the country for the support of the women and children, families of soldiers who are serving their country, indeed; and lastly, to get his living in part, at least, by stealing and robbing. And here allow me to say, I am not sufficiently skilled in language to command words to express the deep and unutterable detestation I have of the character of a deserter. If my brother were to be guilty of such a high crime, I should certainly make an effort to have his name changed to something else, that I, and my children after me, might not feel the deep and lasting disgrace which his conduct had enstamped upon it.

I hold, gentlemen, that there are few crimes in the sight of either God or man, that are more wicked and detestable than desertion. The first step in it is perjury. Who would ever believe such an one in a court of justice again? The second, is treason. He has abandoned the flag of his country; thus much he has aided the common enemy. Those are startling crimes, indeed, but the third is equally so. He enstamps disgrace upon the name of his family and children.

From amidst the smoke and flames of Sinai God has declared that He "is a jealous God, visiting the iniquities of the fathers upon the children unto the third and fourth generations of them that hate me." The infamy that the act of disloyalty on the part of a father places his children in after him, is a disability they cannot escape: it was his act, not theirs; and to them it has become God's visitation according to the text quoted above. The character of infamy acquired by the tories of the revolution of 1776, is to this day imputed to their descendants, in a genealogical sense. Disloyalty is a crime that mankind never forget and but seldom forgive; the grave cannot cover it.

Many cry out in this the day of our discontent, and say, "we want peace." This is true, we all want peace, the land mourns on account of the absence of peace, and we all pray for peace. You have often heard me pray for peace, but I think you will bear me witness to-day that you have never heard me pray for peace without independence. God forbid that we should have a peace that brought no independence.

But how are we to obtain peace? There are but two modes

known by which to obtain this most desirable boon. First: to lay down our arms, cease to fight, and submit to the terms of our enemy, the tyrant at Washington. Fortunately for us, we already know what those terms are. They stand recorded in his law books, and in his published orders and edicts,—and constitute with our enemies, *the law of the land*, so far as we are concerned.

1. The lands of our citizens are to be sold for the purpose of paying the enormous public debt of the Yankees. This part of the programme has already been put into operation at points held by the enemy, as in Fairfax county, Va., and Beaufort, S. C. In the latter place, the lands have been laid off into thirty acre lots, and bought mostly by negroes.

2. The negroes, everywhere, to be declared free, and placed upon a state of equality with the whites.

3. Every man who has taken any part in the war, denied the right of voting at the polls.

4. Our Governors and Judges appointed by the Federal Government at Washington, and sent to rule over us at his pleasure.

5. Even the men selected to administer to us in holy things at the altars of our God, must be men approved and appointed by his military authorities; as it is now done in Norfolk and Portsmouth, where I am acquainted.

In addition to this, Gentlemen, we of course will have to endure the deep and untold mortification of having bands of negro soldiers stationed in almost every neighborhood, to enforce these laws and regulations.

These things would be some of the "*blessings,*" we would obtain by such a peace. Tell me to-day, sons of Carolina, would not such a peace bring ten-fold more horrors and distress to our country than this war has yet produced? Can any people on the face of this earth, fit to be freemen, ever accept a peace that will place them in such a condition? Never! never! never!

The great and good Stonewall Jackson, a few weeks before his death was talking with a friend about the probable issue of the war; the conversation turned upon the possibility of the Confederate States being brought again under the rule and authority of the United States; when our illustrious chief remarked, that if he could have his choice in view of such a contingency, he would prefer the grave as his refuge. What patriot would not? What soldier would not? What freeman would not? This was the noble sentiment of a man whom we all believed to be fit to live, or fit to die.

The other mode by which to obtain peace, is to fight it out to the bitter end, as our forefathers did in the revolution of 1776, and reduce our enemies, by our manly defence, to the necessity of acknowledging our independence, and "letting us alone." We are involved in this bloody war, and the question before us is, not how did we get into it, but how shall we get out of it?

Many tell us the war cloud looks dark and impenetrable to mortal vision. This is all true. But are we not men? Have we not buckled on the armor, putting our trust in the Lord of hosts, as the arbiter of our destiny as a nation? Shall we then lay down our arms before we are overthrown? God forbid! Sons of Carolina, let your battle-cry be, Onward! Onward! until victory shall crown the beautiful banner that floats over us to-day with such a peace as freemen only love, and brave men only can accept. We are engaged in a mighty work, the establishment of an empire, which we trust by the blessing of God will become the freest, the best and the greatest on the face of the earth. Every man must act his part in this great work. Let us then look to the manner in which we perform the part which duty assigns, that there may be no regrets or heart-burnings hereafter. For just as sure as this cruel war began, it will have an end, and that end is nearer now than when it began. And when the sweet and lovely days of delightful peace return to cheer us, and friend meets with friend, and talk over the trials, the perils and sufferings we have endured in freedom's cause; with what emotions of pleasure shall we speak of the soldier ever true and faithful who stood by us, faithful alike both in the sunshine and storm of war. But what will then be said of the miserable skulker? May God give him a better heart that he may become a better man and a better soldier.

From the position which I occupy, I have been enabled to notice deserters and skulkers closely, and I have made it my business to inquire into their history, and I am happy to say for the credit of Christianity, that among the multitude I have known guilty of desertion, only three of that number professed to be members of any Church, and they had been no credit to the religion they professed, as it lived only upon their lips and was a stranger in their hearts.

The true christian is always a true patriot. Patriotism and Christianity walk hand in hand. When perils and dangers gather around the country that protects him, he then belongs to no party but his country's party; his loyalty must stand unquestioned and unquestionable. As one that fears God, he knows that, *if a man is not for his country, he is against it.* Hence, there is no neutral ground or position for him to occupy; but to stand by his country as its fast, unwavering friend, that its triumph may be his triumph, and its destiny his destiny. There is no toryism in a Christian's heart. The two principles cannot dwell together.

War is the scourge of nations. God is no doubt chastising us for our good. When the ends of His providence are accomplished, He will no doubt remove the rod. But the ways of His providence are generally dark to mortal vision. Yet he is able to bring light out of darkness. We are only drinking now from a cup, from which every nation upon the face of the earth have drank before us. We have walked the bloody road of revolution for three years; and still we face the foe. Our fathers trod it for seven, and in the end were successful.

The pious Dr. Watts tells us in one of his beautiful hymns, that,

> "God moves in a mysterious way,
> His wonders to perform;
> He plants his footsteps in the sea,
> And rides upon the storm."

His ways with the nations of the earth are deeply mysterious to mortal vision and whilst they are the exhibitions of His majesty and power, we should regard them likewise as the evidence of his goodness and mercy towards fallen man. As He deals with individuals, so does He deal with nations. He lifteth up one and putteth down another; but all this is done for the good of the whole. Righteousness exalteth a nation, but sin is a reproach to any people, is the doctrine laid down in Holy Writ. Proud Egypt, the cradle of the arts and sciences, has sadly fallen from her ancient glory and splendor. Ezekiel, speaking as the oracle of God, and accusing her of her sins, declared "she shall become the basest of the kingdoms," and the words of the Seer have become verified to the letter. For transgression, the chosen people of God, the Israelites, were compelled to wander forty years in the Arabian desert, thus suffering the chastisement of the disfavor of offended Deity. And when they were permitted to cross over Jordan into the land of promise, they were required to do a strange and wondrous work; namely, to destroy the nations of this goodly land and possess it for their own inheritance. The sins of these nations had cried unto heaven, and Israel became the instrument in the hand of God by which the judgments of offended Justice was meted out to the guilty nations. Jerusalem, the lovely, queenly Jerusalem, whose beautiful temple was the glory of the whole earth, in which the presence of the Eternal Shekinah was visible annually to mortal eye, and where Solomon in all his glory once reigned—sinned with an high hand against God; she knew not the day of her visitation, the cup of her iniquity was full; the judgment of offended heaven overtook her; her glory departed; the besom of destruction swept over her, and she is now trodden down by the gentiles—a crumbling monument of her departed greatness.

Babylon, once the proud mistress of the East, whose spacious walls, hanging gardens, and lofty temples stood as the wonders of the world, and Daniel, the prophet, robed in the vestments of royal honors, once spake, and wrote by heaven's prompting of things to come has fallen; her greatness is lost; her walls have perished; her palaces have crumbled; her temples are entombed, and the wandering Arab now nightly pitches his tent over the spot where Belshazzar held his impious feast. Where is the Nineveh? The mighty Nineveh? And Tadmor, and Persepolis, and hundred-gated Thebes? They belong only to the past, the silence of death has spread its sepulchral pall over them, and the relics of fallen greatness alone remain to mark the spot where they lie entombed. Sparta has departed from the map of nations, and Athens is but the tomb of the Athens that was. These have all sinned, and "there is a God that judgeth in the earth."

Four years ago, these Confederate States formed an integral part of the U. States. Perhaps no nation of people ever sinned against more light, and abused more privileges than the United States. The Northern pulpits hatched and fostered the spirit that produced this cruel and bloody war: but cruel and bloody as it is, I believe in God, to-day, that great good to us of the South as a people, if we will only depart from our sins and lean upon the Almighty Arm. If He be for us, who can stand successfully against us? He gave to our fathers a Washington, a man who feared God, to guide them through the revolution of 1776. He has given to us a Lee, a man of like faith and of like hopes, to be our leader in these dark days of trial, and we all love to follow where he leads.

He lent to us a Jackson, that bright and shining light of Christianity, whose ardent piety and strong faith always presented the same beauties, in the halls of science, at the altars of God, around the camp-fires, or on the battle-field. Oh, what a model of a Christian soldier! Well do I remember how his presence cheered us as he rode along our line on the morning of the first battle of Fredericksburg, after the artillery began to roar heavily. His very appearance seemed to be the presage of victory. He seemed like one sent by God. But God has seen proper in His providence to take him away, and whatsoever He doeth is right. Let us then bow, to the hand that afflicts in such dispensations as this, take courage and press onward.

Let us then humble ourselves before God as a people, confess our sins, and implore His protecting power to guide us through this mighty struggle to a successful issue. He has certainly done great things for us as a people, whereof we should be glad.

I think you will bear me witness that I have never been hopeful of an early peace in my intercourse among you. But to-day I fancy that I can discover a little cloud, in the political heavens as large as a man's hand at least, that seems to portend peace. Take courage, then, companions in arms. All things around us to-day bid us be of good courage. History fails to tell us of ten millions of freemen being enslaved, who had determined to be free. A braver or more patriotic army than we have, never followed their chief to victory. Their endurance challenges the admiration of the world. When I have seen our brave men in winter's cold and summer's heat, marching from battle-field to battle-field, bare-footed as they were born, and without a murmur, I could not doubt our final success. *Such men as these, were never born to be slaves.* Again when I have turned my eye homeward from the camp, and witnessed the labors of our fair country women, in preparing clothing to meet the wants of the suffering in the field, and witnessed their untiring devotion to the relief of the sick and wounded in the hospitals, I knew that the history of no country, and of no age afforded anything like a parallel, and my faith assured me we never were born to be slaves of the Yankees. Then let your trust to-day be strong in the God of nations.

Surely, then, no man can be found in all our land who owes allegiance to his country, that is so lost to himself, and to all that is noble and patriotic, as to say, "I am for the Union as it was." Such an one could only merit the good man's scorn, and desire the tory's infamy for himself, and disgrace for his children.

Gentlemen, I have followed your fortunes for twenty months, leaving wife and children far behind me. I have rejoiced in your prosperity, and mourned over your adversity. Marches, battles, sufferings are before us still. By the help of God I am with you, and hope still to be with you to share in your triumphs, your sufferings and your joys. If these be the days to try men's souls, for my country's sake I am willing to be tried, by bearing my humble part in this mighty struggle.

For, standing before you to-day, you must permit me to say in the language of a noble patriot, "I am for my country right, yea, for my country wrong." My loyalty to her is unqualified, and without any conditions. Her cause is always my cause. If her cause be right, she shall have my free support; if it be wrong she shall have my unqualified support. Therefore, when I shall sleep in the dust, you must not say to my children, "your father was a conservative, (or any other name,) when his country was engaged in a bloody struggle for existence." Then you would do me wrong, and do them wrong also. I belong only to my country's party. But it may be said, that I can afford to use strong language when I am not required to take position in the front ranks on the battle-field. The duties of my office require me, as you are aware, to take position in the rear, to assist with the wounded, but yet at Fredericksburg, Williamsport, Mine Run, and Batchelor's Creek, I was under the fire of both artillery and musketry, and I will here add that if ever my country calls upon me to fall into ranks in her defence with a musket on my shoulder, my answer shall be, "here am I."

Then, to-day, in the light of this beautiful Sabbath sun, let us take courage, and with renewed trust in God, resolve to do our whole duty as patriots and soldiers, and leave the event to the Arbiter of nations. *Amen!*

BATTLE OF OLUSTEE:
FLORIDA, FEBRUARY 1864

Oliver W. Norton to Elizabeth Norton Poss

Oliver W. Norton had been commissioned as a first lieutenant in the 8th U.S. Colored Infantry in November 1863 and joined the regiment the following month at its training camp near Philadelphia. Recruited mainly in eastern Pennsylvania and Delaware, the regiment sailed to South Carolina in January and was then sent to Florida. On February 7, Union troops occupied Jacksonville, beginning a campaign intended to gain control of northern Florida and, if possible, establish a loyal government in the state. Norton and the 8th U.S. Colored Infantry were among the 5,000 Union troops under Brigadier General Truman B. Seymour who encountered 5,000 Confederate defenders in the pine woods near Olustee Station, about fifty miles west of Jacksonville, on February 20. In the battle that followed, the Confederates lost 964 men killed, wounded, or missing, while Union losses totaled 1,861, including an unknown number of black soldiers who were killed after being captured. The 54th Massachusetts Infantry helped cover the Union retreat, which continued until Seymour's command reached Jacksonville on February 22. "If there is a second lieutenant in our regiment who couldn't plan and execute a better battle, I would vote to dismiss him for incompetency," Norton wrote to his father the day after he had described the fighting in a letter to his sister.

―――――――

Jacksonville, Fla.,
Monday, Feb. 29, 1864.

Dear Sister L.:—

You will probably see accounts of the battle of Olustee, or Ocean Pond, in the papers. I have ordered a copy of the Brookville Republican, containing a letter from Dr. Heichold, descriptive of the battle, sent to you, but I will give you some of my own ideas about it, too; you always express a preference for them, you know.

Well, the morning of Saturday, the 20th, found us at Barber's Ford on the St. Mary's river ready to march and loaded down with ten days' rations. Our force consisted of the One hundred-fifteenth, Forty-seventh and Forty-eighth New York Regiments, Seventh New Hampshire and Seventh Connecticut (repeating rifles), Fifty-fourth Massachusetts (colored) of Fort Wagner memory, the First North Carolina Colored and the Eighth, twenty pieces of artillery, one battalion cavalry and the Fortieth Massachusetts (mounted infantry).

We started marching in three columns, artillery in the road, flanked by the infantry on either side. After marching twelve miles we halted near a few desolate houses called Sanders and while resting heard a few musket shots in advance. We supposed our cavalry had met a few of the enemy's pickets. Their force was supposed to be at Lake City, twelve miles distant, so we moved on up the railroad. The skirmishing increased as we marched, but we paid little attention to it. Pretty soon the boom of a gun startled us a little, but not much, as we knew our flying artillery was ahead, but they boomed again and again and it began to look like a brush. An aide came dashing through the woods to us and the order was—"double quick, march!" We turned into the woods and ran in the direction of the firing for half a mile, when the head of the column reached our batteries. The presiding genius, General Seymour, said: "Put your regiment in, Colonel Fribley," and left.

Military men say it takes veteran troops to maneuver under fire, but our regiment with knapsacks on and unloaded pieces, after a run of half a mile, formed a line under the most destructive fire I ever knew. We were not more than two hundred yards from the enemy, concealed in pits and behind trees, and what did the regiment do? At first they were stunned, bewildered, and knew not what to do. They curled to the ground, and as men fell around them they seemed terribly scared, but gradually they recovered their senses and commenced firing. And here was the great trouble—they could not use their arms to advantage. We have had very little practice in firing, and, though they could stand and be killed, they could not kill a concealed enemy fast enough to satisfy my feelings.

After seeing his men murdered as long as flesh and blood could endure it, Colonel Fribley ordered the regiment to fall back slowly, firing as they went. As the men fell back they gathered in groups like frightened sheep, and it was almost impossible to keep them from doing so. Into these groups the rebels poured the deadliest fire, almost every bullet hitting some one. Color bearer after color bearer was shot down and the colors seized by another. Behind us was a battery that was wretchedly managed. They had but little ammunition, but after firing that, they made no effort to get away with their pieces, but busied themselves in trying to keep us in front of them. Lieutenant Lewis seized the colors and planted them by a gun and tried to rally his men round them, but forgetting them for the moment, they were left there, and the battery was captured and our colors with it.

Colonel Fribley was killed soon after his order to fall back, and Major Burritt had both legs broken. We were without a commander, and every officer was doing his best to do something, he knew not what exactly. There was no leader. Seymour might better have been in his grave than there. Many will blame Lieutenant Lewis that the colors were lost. I do not think he can be blamed. Brave to rashness, he cannot be accused of cowardice, but man cannot think of too many things.

Some things in this story look strange. Officers should know exactly what to do, you may say. Certainly, but it is a damper on that duty when there is a certainty on the mind that the commander does not know. When, with eight or ten regiments ready, you see only two or three fighting, and feel you are getting whipped from your general's incompetency, it is hard to be soldierly.

I saw from the commencement of our retreat that the day was lost, but I confess to you that I was in doubt whether I ought to stay and see my men shot down or take them to the rear. Soldierly feelings triumphed, but at what a cost!

Captain Dickey was shot early in the fight and the command of the company devolved on me. He was not seriously wounded, a ball through the face.

Captain Wagner was standing by me when he fell, pierced by three balls. I seized him and dragged him back a few rods and two of his men then took him to the rear. I carried his sword through the fight. Several times I was on the point of throwing it away, thinking he must be dead, but I saved it and had the pleasure of giving it to him and hearing that he is likely to recover.

Of twenty-two officers that went into the fight, but two escaped without marks. Such accurate firing I never saw before. I was under the impression all the time that an inferior force was whipping us, but the deadly aim of their rifles told the story.

Well, you are wanting to know how I came off, no doubt. With my usual narrow escapes, but escapes. My hat has five bullet holes in it. Don't start very much at that—they were all made by one bullet. You know the dent in the top of it. Well, the ball went through the rim first and then through the top in this way. My hat was cocked up on one side so that it went through in that way and just drew the blood on my scalp. Of course a quarter of an inch lower would have broken my skull, but it was too high. Another ball cut away a corner of my haversack and one struck my scabbard. The only wonder is I was not killed, and the wonder grows with each succeeding fight, and this is the fifteenth or sixteenth, Yorktown, Hanover, Gaines' Mill, Charles City, Malvern, Bull Run, Antietam, Shepherdstown Ford, Fredericksburg, Richards Ford, Chancellorsville, Loudon Valley, Gettysburg, Manassas Gap, Rappahannock Station and Olustee, to say nothing of the shelling at Harrison's Landing or the skirmish at Ely's Ford. Had any one told me when I enlisted that I should have to pass through so many I am afraid it would have daunted me. How many more?

Company K went into the fight with fifty-five enlisted men and two officers. It came out with twenty-three men and one officer. Of these but two men were not marked. That speaks volumes for the bravery of negroes. Several of these twenty-three were quite badly cut, but they are present with the company. Ten were killed and four reported missing, though there is little doubt they are killed, too.*

---

* *Note.*—The regiment went into the battle with five hundred and fifty-four officers and enlisted men. Of these, three hundred and nineteen were killed or disabled by serious wounds. Many others were slightly wounded, but remained on duty.

A flag of truce from the enemy brought the news that prisoners, black and white, were treated alike. I hope it is so, for I have sworn never to take a prisoner if my men left there were murdered.

This is the first letter I have written since the fight, and it is to you, my best beloved sister. It is written in haste, in a press of business, but you will excuse mistakes and my inattention to the matter of your own letter. You may pray for me—I need that, and do write to me as often as you find time.

THE KILPATRICK-DAHLGREN RAID:
VIRGINIA, MARCH 1864

John B. Jones: Diary,
March 1–2 and 5, 1864

The prisoner exchange cartel signed by the opposing sides in July 1862 began to collapse in the summer of 1863 because of the Confederate refusal to treat black soldiers and their officers as prisoners of war. Union officials insisted that black and white prisoners be treated equally under the cartel, and later protested when men paroled at Vicksburg returned to the Confederate ranks without being properly exchanged. By February 1864 some 5,000 Union prisoners were being held in Richmond, where they suffered from hunger, disease, and exposure. Brigadier General Judson Kilpatrick, a division commander in the Army of the Potomac's cavalry corps, gained approval from Lincoln and Stanton for a raid on the Confederate capital aimed at freeing the prisoners. On February 28 Kilpatrick and 3,500 men crossed the Rapidan sixty miles north of Richmond, then split up the next day. The main force under Kilpatrick encountered unexpectedly strong resistance when it reached the northern outskirts of the city on March 1, while a smaller body of 460 men led by Colonel Ulric Dahlgren was unable to cross the James River and attack Richmond from the south. While Kilpatrick and most of his command reached the Union lines on the Peninsula, Dahlgren was killed in an ambush on March 2. In papers found on his body Dahlgren wrote that once the prisoners were released and the city captured, "it must be destroyed and Jeff Davis and Cabinet killed." The papers were given to Davis on March 4 and published in the Richmond press the next day. Kilpatrick would later deny having given or received orders to burn the city or to kill Confederate leaders.

MARCH 1ST.—Dark and raining.

As the morning progressed, the city was a little startled by the sound of artillery in a northern direction, and not very distant. Couriers and horsemen from the country announced the approach of the enemy *within* the outer fortifications; a column of 5000 cavalry. Then Hon. James Lyons came in, reporting that the enemy were shelling his house, one and a half miles from the city. And Gen. Elzey (in command) said, at the department, that a fight was in progress; and that Brig.-Gen. Custis Lee was directing it in person. But an hour or so after the report of artillery ceased, and the excitement died away. Yet the local troops and militia are marching out as I write; and a caisson that came in an hour ago has just passed our door, returning to the field. Of course the city is full of rumors, and no one yet knows what has occurred. I presume it was only distant shelling, as no wounded men have been brought in.

It is reported that the enemy captured Mr. Seddon's family twenty-five miles distant,—also Gen. Wise's. To-morrow we shall know more; but no *uneasiness* is felt as to the result. In a few hours we can muster men enough to defend the city against 25,000.

A letter from Gen. Whiting suggests that martial law be proclaimed in North Carolina, as a Judge Pearson—a traitor, he thinks—is discharging men who have in conscripts as substitutes, on the ground that the act of Congress is unconstitutional. The President suggests a General Order, etc., complying with Gen. W.'s request.

Col. A. C. Myers, late Quartermaster-General, writes again, indignantly resenting the President's indorsement, etc. as unfounded and injurious, etc.

The President indorses this letter as follows: "Unless this letter is designed to ask whether Col. M. is still in the army, or discharged by the appointment of a successor, I find nothing which changes the case since my indorsement referred to, as causing resentment and calling for vindication. Your orders were certainly official communications. Not having seen them, I can express no opinion upon their terms.—JEFFERSON DAVIS."

MARCH 2D.—A slight snow on the ground this morning—but bright and cool. Last night, after I had retired to bed, we heard a brisk cannonading, and volleys of musketry, a few miles distant.

This morning an excitement, but no alarm, pervaded the city. It was certainly a formidable attempt to take the city by surprise. From the number of disgraceful failures heretofore, the last very recently, the enemy must have come to the desperate resolution to storm the city this time at all hazards. And indeed the coming upon it was sudden, and if there had been a column of 15,000 bold men in the assault, they might have penetrated it. But now, twenty-four hours subsequently, 30,000 would fail in the attempt.

The Department Clerks were in action in the evening in five minutes after they were formed in line. Capt. Ellery, Chief Clerk of 2d Auditor, was killed, and several were wounded. It rained fast all the time, and it was very dark. The enemy's cavalry charged upon them, firing as they came; they were ordered to lie flat on the ground. This they did, until the enemy came within fifteen yards of them, when they rose and fired, sending the assailants to the right and left, helter-skelter. How many fell is not yet known.

To-day Gen. Hampton sent in 77 prisoners, taken six miles above town—one lieutenant-colonel among them; and Yankee horses, etc. are coming in every hour.

Gov. Vance writes that inasmuch as Judge Pearson still grants the writ of *habeas corpus*, and discharges all who have put substitutes in the army, on the ground of the unconstitutionality of the act of Congress, he is bound by his oath to sustain the judge, even to the summoning the military force of the State to resist the Confederate States authorities. But to avoid such a fatal collision, he is willing to abide the decision of the Supreme Court, to assemble in June; the substitute men, meantime, to be left unmolested. We shall soon see the President's decision, which will probably be martial law.

Last night, when it was supposed probable that the prisoners of war at the Libby might attempt to break out, Gen. Winder ordered that a large amount of powder be placed under the building, with instructions to blow them up, if the attempt were made. He was persuaded, however, to consult the Secretary of War first, and get his approbation. The Secretary would give no such order, but said the prisoners must not be permitted to escape under any circumstances, which was considered sanction enough. Capt. —— obtained an order for, and procured several hundred pounds of gunpowder, which were placed in readiness. Whether the prisoners were advised of this I know not; but I told Capt. —— it could not be justifiable to spring such a mine in the absence of their knowledge of the fate awaiting them, in the event of their attempt to break out,—because such prisoners are not to be condemned for striving to regain their liberty. Indeed, it is the *duty* of a prisoner of war to escape if he can.

Gen. Winder addressed me in a friendly manner to-day, the first time in two years.

The President was in a bad humor yesterday, when the enemy's guns were heard even in his office.

The last dispatch from Gen. Lee informs us that Meade, who had advanced, had fallen back again. But communications are cut between us and Lee; and we have no intelligence since Monday.

Gen. Wilcox is organizing an impromptu brigade here, formed of the furloughed officers and men found everywhere in the streets and at the hotels. This looks as if the danger were not yet regarded as over.

The Secretary of War was locked up with the Quartermaster and Commissary-Generals and other bureau officers, supposed to be discussing the damage done by the enemy to the railroads, etc. etc. I hope it was not a consultation upon any presumed necessity of the abandonment of the city!

We were paid to-day in $5 bills. I gave $20 for half a cord of wood, and $60 for a bushel of common white cornfield beans. Bacon is yet $8 per pound; but more is coming to the city than usual, and a decline may be looked for, I hope. The farmers above the city, who have been hoarding grain, meat, etc., will lose much by the raiders.

MARCH 5TH.—Clear and pleasant, after a slight shower in the morning.

The raid is considered at an end, and it has ended disastrously for the invaders.

Some extraordinary memoranda were captured from the raiders, showing a diabolical purpose, and creating a profound sensation here. The cabinet have been in consultation many hours in regard to it, and I have reason to believe it is the present purpose to deal summarily with the captives taken with Dahlgren, but the "sober second thought" will prevail, and they will not be executed, notwithstanding the thunders of the press. Retaliation for such outrages committed on others having been declined, the President and cabinet can hardly be expected to begin with such sanguinary punishments when *their own* lives are threatened. It would be an act liable to grave criticism. Nevertheless, Mr. Secretary Seddon has written a letter to-day to Gen. Lee, asking his views on a matter of such importance as the execution of some *ninety* men of Dahlgren's immediate followers, not, as he says, to divide the responsibility, nor to effect a purpose, which has the sanction of the President, the cabinet, and *Gen. Bragg*, but to have his *views*, and information as to what would probably be its effect on the army under his command. We shall soon know, I hope, what Gen. Lee will have to say on the subject, and I am mistaken if he does not oppose it. If these men had been put to death in the heat of passion, on the field, it would have been justified, but it is too late now. Besides, *Gen. Lee's son* is a captive in the hands of the enemy, designated for retaliation whenever we shall execute any of their prisoners in our hands. It is cruelty to Gen. Lee!

It is already rumored that Gen. Butler has been removed, and a flag of truce boat is certainly at City Point, laden with prisoners sent up for exchange.

The Commissary-General has sent in a paper saying that unless the passenger cars on the Southern Road be discontinued, he cannot supply half enough meal for Lee's army. He has abundance in Georgia and South Carolina, but cannot get transportation. He says the last barrel of flour from Lynchburg has gone to the army.

We have news from the West that Morgan and his men will be in the saddle in a few days.

After all, Mr. Lyon's house was not touched by any of the enemy's shells. But one shell struck within 300 yards of one house in Clay Street, and not even the women and children were alarmed.

The price of a turkey to-day is $60.

SUMMONED TO WASHINGTON:
TENNESSEE, MARCH 1864

Ulysses S. Grant to William T. Sherman

On December 14, 1863, Elihu B. Washburne introduced a bill in the House of Representatives reviving the grade of lieutenant general, a rank previously held only by George Washington and, by brevet (honorary) appointment, Winfield Scott. President Lincoln signed the bill on February 29 and nominated Grant for the position. The nomination was confirmed by the Senate on March 2. As he prepared to leave for Washington, Grant acknowledged his debt to Sherman and to Major General James B. McPherson, who had served as Grant's chief engineer at Fort Donelson and Shiloh and commanded a corps in the Army of the Tennessee during the Vicksburg campaign.

Nashville Tennessee,
March 4th 1864.

DEAR SHERMAN,

The bill reviving the grade of Lieut. Gen. in the Army has become a law and my name has been sent to the Senate for the place. I now receive orders to report to Washington, *in person*, immediately, which indicates either a confirmation or a likelyhood of confirmation. I start in the morning to comply with the order but I shall say very distinctly on my arrival there that I accept no appointment which will require me to make that city my Hd Qrs. This however is not what I started out to write about.

Whilst I have been eminently successful in this War, in at least gaining the confidence of the public, no one feels more than me how much of this success is due to the energy, skill, and harmonious puting forth of that energy and skill, of those who it has been my good fortune to have occupying a subordinate position under me. There are many officers to whom these remarks are applicable to a greater or less degree, proportionate to their ability as soldiers, but what I want is to express my thanks to you and McPherson as *the men* to whom, above all others, I feel indebted for whatever I have had of success. How far your advice and suggestions have been of assistance you know. How far your execution of whatever has been given you to do entitles you to the reward I am receiving you cannot know as well as me. I feel all the gratitude this letter would express, giving it the most flattering construction.

The word *you* I use in the plural intending it for Mc. also. I should write to him, and will some day, but starting in the morning I do not know that I will find time just now.

Your friend
U. S. GRANT
Maj. Gen.

"COME OUT WEST":
TENNESSEE, MARCH 1864

William T. Sherman to Ulysses S. Grant

Grant arrived in Washington on March 8 and met Lincoln for the first time that night. He received his commission as lieutenant general the next day and was assigned command of the Union armies on March 10, the same day he went to Virginia to meet with Meade. By the time Grant received Sherman's letter, he had decided on a course different from the one Sherman had recommended. Grant would make his headquarters in the field with the Army of the Potomac while keeping Meade as its commander. Sherman would succeed Grant as commander of the Military Division of the Mississippi, and McPherson would replace Sherman as commander of the Army of the Tennessee.

[private and confidential]

Near Memphis, March 10, 1864

General Grant

Dear General:

I have your more than kind and characteristic letter of the 4th, and will send a copy of it to General McPherson at once.

You do yourself injustice and us too much honor in assigning to us so large a share of the merits which have led to your high advancement. I know you approve the friendship I have ever professed to you, and will permit me to continue as heretofore to manifest it on all proper occasions.

You are now Washington's legitimate successor, and occupy a position of almost dangerous elevation; but if you can continue as heretofore to be yourself, simple, honest, and unpretending, you will enjoy through life the respect and love of friends, and the homage of millions of human beings who will award to you a large share for securing to them and their descendants a government of law and stability.

I repeat, you do General McPherson and myself too much honor. At Belmont you manifested your traits, neither of us being near; at Donelson also you illustrated your whole character. I was not near, and General McPherson in too subordinate a capacity to influence you.

Until you had won Donelson, I confess I was almost cowed by the terrible array of anarchical elements that present themselves at every point; but that victory admitted the ray of light which I have followed ever since.

I believe you are as brave, patriotic, and just, as the great prototype Washington; as unselfish, kind-hearted, and honest, as a man should be; but the chief characteristic in your nature is the simple faith in success you have always manifested, which I can liken to nothing else than the faith a Christian has in his Saviour.

This faith gave you victory at Shiloh and Vicksburg. Also, when you have completed your best preparations, you go into battle without hesitation, as at Chattanooga—no doubts, no reserve; and I tell you that it was this that made us act with confidence. I knew wherever I was that you thought of me, and if I got in a tight place you would come—if alive.

My only points of doubt were as to your knowledge of grand strategy, and of books of science and history; but I confess your common-sense seems to have supplied all this.

Now as to the future. Do not stay in Washington. Halleck is better qualified than you are to stand the buffets of intrigue and policy. Come out West; take to yourself the whole Mississippi Valley; let us make it dead-sure, and I tell you the Atlantic slope and pacific shores will follow its destiny as sure as the limbs of a tree live or die with the main trunk! We have done much; still much remains to be done. Time and time's influences are all with us; we could almost afford to sit still and let these influences work. Even in the seceded States your word *now* would go further than a President's proclamation, or an act of Congress.

For God's sake and for your country's sake, come out of Washington! I foretold to General Halleck, before he left Corinth, the inevitable result to him, and I now exhort you to come out West. Here lies the seat of the coming empire; and from the West, when our task is done, we will make short work of Charleston and Richmond, and the impoverished coast of the Atlantic. Your sincere friend,

W. T. Sherman

CHRONOLOGY

BIOGRAPHICAL NOTES

NOTE ON THE TEXTS

NOTES

INDEX

Chronology
January 1863–March 1864

1863　President Abraham Lincoln issues Emancipation Proclamation, freeing all slaves in enumerated Confederate-held areas on January 1. General William T. Sherman withdraws his troops from the Yazoo River north of Vicksburg, Mississippi, on January 2. (Sherman had unsuccessfully attacked the Confederate positions at Chickasaw Bluffs on December 29, 1862, as part of a failed Union attempt to capture Vicksburg.) After a lull on New Year's Day, General Braxton Bragg resumes attacks on Union forces along Stones River near Murfreesboro, Tennessee, January 2 (battle had begun on December 31). On January 3 Bragg withdraws his Army of Tennessee to Tullahoma, thirty-five miles to the south. Confederates lose approximately 12,000 men killed, wounded, or missing at Stones River, while General William S. Rosecrans's Army of the Cumberland loses about 13,000. General John A. McClernand, a politically influential War Democrat and former Illinois congressman who had been authorized by Lincoln to raise and lead troops against Vicksburg, assumes command of Sherman's forces at Milliken's Bend, Louisiana, January 4. The same day, Lincoln responds to protests by revoking General Ulysses S. Grant's order of December 17, 1862, expelling all Jews from the Department of the Tennessee. Lincoln nominates John P. Usher on January 5 to replace Caleb P. Smith as secretary of the interior. On January 11, Union forces under McClernand capture Fort Hindman and almost 4,800 Confederate prisoners at Arkansas Post, fifty miles up the Arkansas River, at the cost of 1,061 men killed, wounded, or missing. The same day, the Confederate raider *Alabama* sinks the Union gunboat *Hatteras* off Galveston, Texas. Jefferson Davis sends message to new session of the Confederate Congress on January 12 in which he praises recent military successes at Fredericksburg and Vicksburg, criticizes Britain and France for failing to recognize southern independence, and calls the Emancipation Proclamation "the most execrable measure recorded in the history of guilty man," one which makes restoration of the Union "forever impossible." In Virginia General Ambrose Burnside, commander of the Army of the Potomac, begins offensive on January 20 designed to cross the Rappahannock River above Fredericksburg and outflank General Robert E. Lee's Army of Northern Virginia. When heavy rain makes the roads impassable, Burnside abandons the movement, which becomes known as the "Mud March," on January 22. Burnside asks Lincoln on January 24 to either remove several of his generals, including Joseph Hooker, or accept his resignation. The next day, Lincoln replaces Burnside with Hooker as commander of the Army of the Potomac. Union navy bombards Fort McAllister outside of Savannah, Georgia, on January 27 (attack is designed to test effectiveness of modern naval guns against earth fortifications). Grant assumes direct command of operations against Vicksburg on January 30 and assigns McClernand to command of one of four infantry corps in the Army of the Tennessee. On Grant's orders Union troops continue work on canal cutting across peninsula opposite Vicksburg, and begin attempt to open a water route through several Louisiana lakes, rivers, and bayous to the Mississippi below the city. Confederate ironclad rams *Chicora* and *Palmetto State* damage two Union gunboats off Charleston, South Carolina, on January 31, but are unable to break the blockade of the port.

Fort McAllister is bombarded again on February 1. Union ram *Queen of the West* runs past Confederate batteries at Vicksburg, Mississippi, on February 2, and begins capturing ships bringing supplies down the Red River to the Confederate garrison at Port Hudson, Louisiana, the other remaining Confederate stronghold on the Mississippi. On February 3 Union forces cut through Mississippi River levee at Yazoo Pass, beginning attempt to open route through the waterways of the Mississippi Delta to the Yazoo River northeast of Vicksburg. The same day, Secretary of State William H. Seward rejects proposal by French foreign minister Édouard Drouyhn de Lhuys for peace negotiations between the Union and the Confederacy. Queen Victoria declares in address to Parliament on February 5 that her government believes a British attempt to mediate the conflict would be unsuccessful. Union ironclad gunboat *Indianola* runs Vicksburg batteries on

February 13. *Queen of the West* runs aground on the Red River below Alexandria, Louisiana, on February 14 and is abandoned by crew. Cherokee National Council meets at Cowskin Prairie in northeastern Indian Territory, February 17, and votes to revoke its October 1861 treaty of alliance with the Confederacy and to abolish slavery in the Cherokee Nation. (Cherokees remain divided between pro-Union faction led by John Ross and Thomas Pegg and pro-Confederate faction headed by Stand Watie.) Four Confederate vessels, including the captured *Queen of the West*, sink the *Indianola* in shallow water south of Vicksburg on February 24. Lincoln signs legislation creating Arizona Territory, February 24, and establishing national banking system authorized to issue banknotes, February 25. U.S.S. *Vanderbilt* seizes the British merchant vessel *Peterhoff* in the Danish West Indies, February 25, on suspicion that the ship, bound for Matamoros, Mexico, was carrying contraband cargo intended for importation into the Confederacy. British protest removal of official mailbag from the *Peterhoff*, raising Anglo-American tensions. (Incident is resolved in April 1863 when U.S. officials return the mail unopened.) Confederates abandon attempt to salvage the *Indianola* and destroy the ship on February 26 after Union forces float a coal barge disguised as a gunboat downriver.

On March 3 Lincoln signs conscription act making most males between twenty and forty-five eligible for service if voluntary enlistments fail to meet the recruitment quotas for their district. The law allows individuals who are drafted to avoid service by hiring a substitute or paying a $300 commutation fee. Lincoln also signs into law on March 3 a bill adding a tenth justice to the Supreme Court, as well as an act authorizing the president to suspend the writ of habeas corpus during the "present rebellion" while limiting his power to detain persons indefinitely without charge. Union naval force bombards Fort McAllister on March 3 and then withdraws to prepare for attack on Charleston, South Carolina. Jacksonville, Florida, is occupied by Union troops, March 10–29, who gather provisions and recruit freed slaves for service in the 1st and 2nd South Carolina Volunteer regiments. In the *Prize Cases*, decided March 10, the U.S. Supreme Court upholds 5–4 the legality of the blockade proclamations issued by

Lincoln in April 1861. Lincoln issues proclamation on March 10 granting amnesty to soldiers absent without leave who return to duty by April 1. Confederates at Fort Pemberton on the Tallahatchie River repel Union gunboats attempting to reach the Yazoo River by way of Yazoo Pass, March 11. Two ships from Union squadron led by Rear Admiral David G. Farragut run past the Confederate defenses at Port Hudson on night of March 14. Union gunboats make unsuccessful attacks on Fort Pemberton, March 13 and March 16, then withdraw. Grant and Acting Rear Admiral David D. Porter send expedition up Steele's Bayou on March 16 in attempt to open route through the southern Mississippi Delta to the Yazoo northeast of Vicksburg. In Virginia, Union cavalry cross the Rappahannock River at Kelly's Ford on March 17 and skirmish with Confederate cavalry before withdrawing. French banking house Erlanger & Cie floats £3 million loan to the Confederacy financed by sale of cotton bonds, March 19. (Proceeds from loan eventually total about $8.5 million, which Confederate agents use to buy arms and war supplies in Europe.) Porter abandons Steele's Bayou expedition on March 22 when Confederates block passage of Union gunboats up Deer Creek in the southern delta. West Virginia voters overwhelmingly approve amendment to state constitution abolishing slavery through gradual emancipation, March 26. The same day, the Confederate Congress passes law authorizing government agents to impress property, including slaves, in support of military operations. On March 29 Grant orders McClernand's corps to begin marching to New Carthage, Louisiana, in preparation for a possible crossing of the Mississippi south of Vicksburg.

Farragut begins blockading the mouth of the Red River on April 1. Several hundred women riot in Richmond, Virginia, on April 2 to protest food shortages. Nine Union ironclads bombard Fort Sumter and other fortifications guarding Charleston Harbor on April 7, but are repulsed by artillery fire that sinks one ship and seriously damages five others. In southeastern Virginia two divisions detached from the Army of Northern Virginia under General James Longstreet begin siege of Suffolk, April 11, while gathering forage and supplies for Lee's army. Union forces under General Nathaniel P. Banks attack Fort Bisland on

Bayou Teche in southern Louisiana, April 12–13. The Confederates evacuate the fort on April 14, the same day Union gunboats sink the *Queen of the West* on nearby Grand Lake. Ship carrying 453 former slaves sails from Fort Monroe, Virginia, on April 14, beginning colonization project on Île à Vache off Haiti authorized by Lincoln in 1862. Union gunboats and transports run past the batteries at Vicksburg on the night of April 16, providing Grant with the means to cross the Mississippi south of the city. Union cavalry brigade led by Colonel Grierson conducts raid from La Grange, Tennessee, through central Mississippi to Baton Rouge, Louisiana, April 17–May 2, destroying railroads and further confusing Confederate commanders as to Union intentions. Second Union fleet of transport steamers runs past the Vicksburg batteries on April 22 as most of Grant's army moves down the west bank of the Mississippi below the city. Confederate Congress passes its first comprehensive tax law, April 24, laying taxes on income, licenses, and products, and imposing a 10 percent "tax in kind" on agricultural produce for the year. (Law is resented by many small farmers for not taxing the land and slaves of plantation owners.) Union army issues General Orders No. 100, a comprehensive code of the laws of war drafted by jurist Francis Lieber, April 24. In Virginia, Hooker begins offensive on April 27, sending one wing of his army up the Rappahannock to turn Lee's left flank while the other wing prepares to cross the river at Fredericksburg. Union troops cross the Rappahannock and Rapidan rivers west of Fredericksburg, April 29, as cavalry forces begin raid on railroad lines supplying Lee's army. On April 30 Hooker halts Union advance at Chancellorsville, ten miles west of Fredericksburg. Grant has Sherman feint an attack along the Yazoo on April 29, then crosses the Mississippi with more than 20,000 men at Bruinsburg, thirty miles southwest of Vicksburg, on April 30.

On May 1 Grant defeats Confederate forces at Port Gibson, Mississippi. Lee leaves 10,000 men to defend Fredericksburg and sends the rest of his army to face Hooker. Fighting begins on May 1 as Hooker resumes advance toward Fredericksburg, then withdraws to defensive positions around Chancellorsville. On May 2 Lee sends General Thomas J. (Stonewall) Jackson with about

30,000 men on a twelve-mile march to strike Hooker's exposed right flank west of Chancellorsville. Jackson attacks in the late afternoon and routs the Union Eleventh Corps, but is then accidentally shot by his own men while attempting to continue his offensive in darkness. On the morning of May 3 Lee's army drives Union forces from Chancellorsville north toward the Rappahannock after Hooker is concussed by debris from the impact of a Confederate cannonball. The same day, the other wing of Hooker's army captures Marye's Heights at Fredericksburg and advances toward Chancellorsville, but is stopped by Confederate defenders at Salem Church. In Mississippi, Grant captures Grand Gulf on May 3 and learns that General Nathaniel P. Banks's expedition against Port Hudson has been delayed. Grant abandons plan to cooperate with Banks and decides instead to advance into central Mississippi and have his men live off the countryside as they march. Longstreet abandons siege of Suffolk on May 4 and moves north to reinforce Lee. The same day, Lee attacks at Salem Church, and the Union forces there withdraw across the Rappahannock on the night of May 4. Lee plans attack on Hooker's defensive line near the Rappahannock, but the Union troops withdraw north of the river on the night of May 5. Chancellorsville costs the Union about 17,000 men killed, wounded, or missing, and the Confederates about 13,000. In Ohio, former Democratic congressman Clement L. Vallandigham is arrested in Dayton by Union soldiers on May 5 on orders from General Ambrose Burnside, commander of the Department of the Ohio. Vallandigham is convicted by a military commission on May 7 of having expressed "disloyal sentiments and opinions" in a recent speech and is sentenced to imprisonment for the duration of the war. Banks occupies Alexandria, Louisiana, on May 7. The same day, Sherman's corps crosses the Mississippi and joins Grant's army as it advances into central Mississippi. Jackson dies from his wounds at Guiney Station, Virginia, on May 10. Grant's army defeats Confederates at Raymond, Mississippi, May 12, and captures Jackson, May 14, frustrating attempt by General Joseph E. Johnston to assemble reinforcements there. While Sherman's men destroy factories and railroads in Jackson, Grant turns most of his army west toward Vicksburg. Grant's forces defeat General John C. Pemberton's army at Champion Hill, May 16, and capture crossings on the Big Black River, May 17, forcing the Confederates to retreat inside the Vicksburg fortifications. Banks evacuates Alexandria on May 17 and begins advance on Port Hudson. Grant orders assault on Vicksburg that fails, May 19. The same day, Lincoln commutes Vallandigham's sentence to banishment in Confederate-held territory. Banks begins siege of Port Hudson, May 21. Grant orders second assault on Vicksburg, May 22, which also fails, then begins siege operations. Vallandigham is expelled across the lines in Tennessee, May 25. Union troops, including two black Louisiana regiments, make unsuccessful assault on fortifications at Port Hudson on May 27. Lee reorganizes the infantry of the Army of Northern Virginia, previously divided into two corps led by Longstreet and Jackson, into three corps commanded by Longstreet, Richard S. Ewell, and A. P. Hill, May 30.

On June 1 Burnside orders the suppression of the *Chicago Times*, an anti-administration Democratic newspaper, for "repeated expression of disloyal and incendiary sentiments" (Lincoln revokes suppression order on June 4). Army of Northern Virginia begins moving toward Shenandoah Valley of Virginia on June 3 as Lee plans an invasion of the North. French troops occupy Mexico City, June 7, as part of attempt by Napoleon III to install the Hapsburg archduke Maximilian as emperor of Mexico. On June 7, Confederate forces attack Union supply depot at Milliken's Bend, Louisiana, defended by brigade of black troops; after several hours of intense fighting, the Confederates retreat under fire from Union gunboats. In Virginia the largest cavalry battle of the war is fought on June 9 when Union forces cross the Rappahannock and engage Confederate cavalry near Brandy Station before withdrawing. (Although inconclusive, the engagement increases confidence of the Army of the Potomac's cavalry corps.) Ohio Democratic convention nominates Vallandigham for governor, June 11. Grant receives significant reinforcements at Vicksburg, some of which he uses to guard against a possible offensive from central Mississippi by Joseph E. Johnston. Second Union assault at Port Hudson is repulsed on June 14. Ewell defeats Union forces at Winchester, Virginia, June 15, opening the Shenandoah Valley to the remainder of Lee's army. The same day, Confederate

troops cross the Potomac into western Maryland as
Hooker moves north, keeping his army between Lee and
Washington, D.C. Vallandigham sails for Bermuda from
Wilmington, North Carolina, on June 17. (After arriving
in Halifax, Nova Scotia, on July 5, he will campaign for
governor of Ohio from exile in Canada.) As the siege of
Vicksburg continues, Grant relieves McClernand for insubordination on June 18 and replaces him with General
Edward O. C. Ord. West Virginia becomes the thirty-fifth
state on June 20. Advance Confederate forces cross into
Pennsylvania on June 22. William S. Rosecrans's Army of
the Cumberland begins offensive on June 23, advancing
from Murfreesboro toward Tullahoma with objective of
driving the Confederates out of central Tennessee. On
June 25 General J.E.B. Stuart, Lee's cavalry commander,
begins weeklong raid through Virginia, Maryland, and
Pennsylvania. (Stuart's absence will deprive Lee of his
main source of intelligence regarding Union troop movements.) The same day, Hooker's army starts to cross the
Potomac into Maryland. After series of disputes with
General-in-chief Henry W. Halleck, Hooker offers his resignation as commander of the Army of the Potomac on
June 27, and Lincoln replaces him with General George G.
Meade. On June 28 Meade assumes command at Frederick, Maryland, and orders advance north toward Pennsylvania. The same day, Lee learns that the Army of the
Potomac is in Maryland and issues orders reuniting his
three infantry corps in preparation for battle. Union cavalry enters Gettysburg, Pennsylvania, on June 30 and deploys north and west of the small crossroads town.

Fighting begins outside Gettysburg on the morning of
July 1 as Confederate infantry advancing from the west
encounters dismounted Union cavalry. As both sides bring
up reinforcements, the Confederates capture Gettysburg
but are unable to prevent Union troops from establishing
defensive line on the high ground south of the town.
Confederate attacks on both Union flanks on July 2 result
in heavy casualties on both sides but fail to drive the Army
of the Potomac from the high ground. Lee orders assault
against the Union center on July 3 that is repulsed with
heavy Confederate losses. The battle costs the Confederates about 28,000 men killed, wounded, or missing, and
the Union about 23,000. In Mississippi Pemberton opens

negotiations, July 3, and surrenders Vicksburg and its garrison of 30,000 on July 4 after Grant agrees to parole the Confederate prisoners. Confederate attack against Union garrison at Helena, Arkansas, is repulsed the same day. Lee begins retreat from Gettysburg on evening of July 4. Lincoln refuses on July 6 to receive Confederate vice president Alexander H. Stephens, who had requested safe passage to Washington in attempt to open peace negotiations. Bragg retreats with his army to Chattanooga, Tennessee, July 7, after being outmaneuvered by Rosecrans during Union advance from Murfreesboro. Union authorities begin implementing conscription, July 7. General John Hunt Morgan and 2,000 Confederate cavalry cross Ohio River at Brandenburg, Kentucky, July 8, and begin raid through southern Indiana and Ohio. Confederate garrison of 6,000 surrenders at Port Hudson, Louisiana, on July 9, giving the Union control of the entire length of the Mississippi. Union troops land on Morris Island at the southern entrance to Charleston Harbor, July 10, but fail to capture Fort Wagner at the northern end of the island, July 11. Meade plans attack on Lee's army at Williamsport, Maryland, July 12, but then postpones it. Mob in New York City burns draft office on July 13, beginning riots in which blacks and prominent Republicans become targets. Lee's army crosses Potomac River from Williamsport into West Virginia, July 13–14, shortly before planned Union advance on the Confederate lines. Union troops led by Sherman force Joseph E. Johnston to abandon Jackson, Mississippi, on July 16. New York draft riots are suppressed by Union troops on July 17 after at least 105 people are killed. In South Carolina, Union forces led by the 54th Massachusetts Infantry, a black regiment, are repulsed with heavy losses in unsuccessful assault on Fort Wagner, July 18. Union troops and gunboats defeat Morgan at Buffington Island on the Ohio River, July 19, and capture most of his command. Attempt by Meade to cut off Lee's withdrawal through the Shenandoah Valley fails when Union forces are blocked at Manassas Gap, Virginia, on July 23. Morgan is captured in Salineville, Ohio, July 29. Lincoln issues order on July 30 pledging retaliation for the execution or enslavement of black Union prisoners of war on July 30.

On August 1 Jefferson Davis offers amnesty to soldiers absent without leave if they report for duty within twenty days. Horatio Seymour, the Democratic governor of New York, asks Lincoln to suspend conscription in his state on August 3; on August 7 Lincoln refuses. In Virginia, Lee withdraws south of the Rapidan River on August 4. Union forces at Helena, Arkansas, begin advance on Little Rock, August 10. Rosecrans resumes offensive in Tennessee on August 16 with Chattanooga as his objective, while Burnside's Army of the Ohio begins advance from Kentucky toward Knoxville in eastern Tennessee. Union siege artillery on Morris Island engages in intensive bombardment of Fort Sumter, August 17–23, causing heavy damage. Confederate guerrillas from Missouri led by William C. Quantrill raid Lawrence, Kansas, on August 21, killing 180 men. Union artillery shells city of Charleston, August 22–24. In Missouri, Union general Thomas Ewing issues General Orders No. 11 on August 25, expelling almost the entire civilian population of four counties along the Kansas border in an effort to suppress Confederate guerrillas. (Order will result in the expulsion of between 10,000 and 20,000 persons.) Alabama legislature adopts resolution on August 29 asking the Confederate Congress to consider using slaves as soldiers. Rosecrans's Army of the Cumberland crosses the Tennessee River below Chattanooga, August 29–September 4. Union artillery resumes intense bombardment of Fort Sumter, August 30–September 1.

Burnside's army occupies Knoxville on September 2. In response to protests from U.S. minister Charles Francis Adams, on September 3 British foreign secretary Lord Russell orders that two ironclad rams built for the Confederacy by the Laird shipyards in Liverpool be detained in port. On September 5 Adams sends another note to Russell, warning that the United States will go to war with Great Britain if the rams are allowed to sail. Confederates evacuate Fort Wagner on night of September 6 after weeks of bombardment, giving Union forces control of all of Morris Island. Confederate artillery repulses attempt by Union gunboats and troop transports to sail up Sabine Pass on the Texas-Louisiana border, September 8. Attempt by landing party of Union sailors and marines to capture Fort Sumter on night of September 8 is defeated. Rosecrans's army occupies Chattanooga, September 9, as Bragg retreats into northwest Georgia. The same day, Burnside's army captures Confederate garrison at the Cumberland

Gap, a mountain pass at the juncture of Kentucky, Tennessee, and Virginia. Davis sends Longstreet and two divisions from the Army of Northern Virginia by rail to reinforce Bragg, September 9 (Bragg also receives reinforcements from Mississippi and eastern Tennessee). Union forces occupy Little Rock, Arkansas, September 10. Lincoln issues proclamation on September 15 suspending the writ of habeas corpus, including in cases where judges issue writs releasing draftees from the military. In northwest Georgia the opposing armies skirmish on September 18 as Rosecrans concentrates his forces along the western side of Chickamauga Creek. Battle begins on September 19 as Bragg attacks Union positions with limited success. On September 20 Confederate assault splits the Union center. Rosecrans and the Union right wing retreat toward Chattanooga, while General George H. Thomas and the Union left hold defensive position on Snodgrass Hill for several hours before withdrawing at nightfall. Battle costs Confederates about 18,000 men killed, wounded, or missing, and the Union about 16,000. Rosecrans establishes defensive line around Chattanooga on September 22, the same day Grant begins sending reinforcements from Mississippi to Tennessee. Bragg seizes heights overlooking Chattanooga from the south and east on September 23 and begins laying siege to the city. On night of September 23 Lincoln approves proposal by Secretary of War Edwin M. Stanton to send two corps from the Army of the Potomac west under the command of Joseph Hooker. First Union troops leave Virginia on September 25 and arrive in Bridgeport, Alabama, about thirty miles west of Chattanooga, on September 30 after traveling 1,200 miles by train (rail movement of more than 20,000 men is completed on October 8).

Confederate cavalry led by General Joseph Wheeler raids eastern Tennessee, October 1–9, attacking wagon trains and depots used to supply Rosecrans's army at Chattanooga. Confederate attorney general Thomas H. Watts resigns on October 1 after winning election as governor of Alabama. On night of October 5, Confederate steamboat *David* uses a torpedo (underwater explosive charge) mounted on a spar to damage the Union ironclad *New Ironsides* off Charleston. Jefferson Davis leaves Richmond on October 6 to visit Bragg's army. Lord Russell orders seizure of Laird rams on October 8. Lee begins offensive in northern Virginia on October 9 that turns the right flank of the Army of the Potomac and forces Meade to retreat across the Rappahannock and fall back toward Centreville. Davis arrives at headquarters of the Army of Tennessee near Chattanooga on October 9 and tries to resolve conflict between Bragg and his generals, many of whom seek his replacement. On October 13, Republicans win victories in several state elections, including Ohio, where John A. Brough, a War Democrat running for governor on the Union ticket, defeats Vallandigham by more than 100,000 votes, and Pennsylvania, where Republican governor Andrew G. Curtin defeats George W. Woodward, a Peace Democrat. Confederate attack on Union rearguard at Bristoe Station, Virginia, October 14, fails to disrupt Meade's withdrawal to Centreville. The same day, Davis leaves Bragg's headquarters and begins tour through Georgia, Alabama, Mississippi, and the Carolinas in effort to rally public support for the war. Lincoln issues proclamation on October 17 calling for 300,000 new volunteers and ordering draft for January 1864 (draft is postponed). Lee abandons offensive in northern Virginia and begins withdrawal to the Rappahannock, October 18. Secretary of War Edwin M. Stanton meets with Grant at Indianapolis on October 18 and gives Grant order appointing him commander of the newly created Military Division of the Mississippi (division covers the territory between the Alleghenies and the Mississippi, except for Louisiana). Grant replaces Rosecrans with George H. Thomas and makes Sherman the new commander of the Army of the Tennessee. After arriving in Chattanooga on October 23, Grant orders implementation of plan devised by General William F. Smith to open new supply line to the Army of the Cumberland. Union artillery resumes heavy bombardment of Fort Sumter, October 26–December 5. New supply route into Chattanooga is opened, October 27. Attempt by Longstreet to break the new line is repulsed at Wauhatchie, Tennessee, on night of October 28.

Union forces land on Brazos Island at the mouth of the Rio Grande, November 2. During his return to Richmond, Jefferson Davis visits Charleston and inspects its harbor defenses, November 2–4, as bombardment of Fort Sumter continues. On November 4 Bragg sends Longstreet and his two divisions to retake Knoxville. Elections held in the eleven seceding states for the Second Confederate Congress, May 28–November 4, result in increased number of representatives opposed to Davis, although supporters of the administration still hold a majority in the new Congress, which will meet in May 1864. (Confederate soldiers and refugees from Kentucky and Missouri elect representatives, February 10–May 2, 1864.) In Texas, Union forces occupy Brownsville on November 6. Union troops capture Confederate bridgehead at Rappahannock Station, Virginia, on November 7. Lee withdraws across the Rapidan, November 10. Sherman and the first of four divisions from the Army of the Tennessee reach Bridgeport, Alabama, on November 13 as Grant plans offensive against Bragg. In fighting at Campbell's Station, Tennessee, on November 16 Longstreet fails to prevent Burnside from retreating inside the fortifications around Knoxville. Union forces occupy Corpus Christi, Texas, November 16. The same day, Union artillery resumes bombardment of Charleston, South Carolina. Lincoln delivers address at dedication of national cemetery at Gettysburg on November 19. Union offensive at Chattanooga begins on November 23 as Thomas captures advance Confederate position at Orchard Knob. On November 24, Hooker's troops seize Lookout Mountain while Sherman occupies hill near the north end of Missionary Ridge. Sherman's attack on November 25 fails to push back the Confederate right and Hooker's advance against the Confederate left is delayed, but Thomas's men break the Confederate center on Missionary Ridge and force Bragg to retreat into northern Georgia. Meade crosses the Rapidan River on November 26 in attempt to turn Lee's right flank. Attempt by Longstreet to capture Fort Sanders outside of Knoxville is repulsed on November 29. Meade cancels attack against Lee's positions along Mine Run south of the Rapidan on November 30. Davis accepts Bragg's resignation as commander of the Army of Tennessee, November 30.

Meade withdraws the Army of the Potomac across the Rapidan on December 1 and goes into winter quarters. As relief force led by Sherman approaches Knoxville, Longstreet abandons siege on December 4 and withdraws into northeast Tennessee. Davis sends message to the Confederate Congress on December 7, acknowledging defeat at

Chattanooga and grave "reverses" at Vicksburg and Port Hudson while calling for continued resistance. In his annual message to Congress on December 8, Lincoln outlines his plan for restoring loyal governments in the insurrectionary states. The same day, he issues a proclamation of amnesty and reconstruction. Republican congressmen James M. Ashley of Ohio and James F. Wilson of Iowa introduce proposals in the House of Representatives on December 14 to abolish slavery by constitutional amendment. Davis names Joseph E. Johnston as commander of the Army of Tennessee on December 16. Confederate Congress abolishes the hiring of substitutes for military service on December 28. Davis appoints George Davis (no relation) as Confederate attorney general, December 31.

1864 On January 2 General Patrick R. Cleburne proposes to meeting of senior commanders in the Army of Tennessee in Dalton, Georgia, that the Confederacy emancipate slaves and enlist them as soldiers. John B. Henderson, a Unionist from Missouri, introduces proposal in the Senate on January 11 for a constitutional amendment abolishing slavery. Confederate raider *Alabama* burns merchant vessel *Emma Jane* off southern India on January 14, the thirty-seventh American ship it has captured since sinking the *Hatteras* in January 1863. Convention of Arkansas Unionists meeting in Little Rock adopts new state constitution abolishing slavery, January 19. Lincoln writes letter on January 23 approving efforts by plantation owners in Mississippi and Arkansas to hire former slaves as free laborers and resume growing cotton.

On February 1 Lincoln orders draft on March 10 of up to 500,000 men, depending on number of voluntary enlistments (draft is postponed to April 15). The same day, Lincoln orders ship sent to the Île à Vache off Haiti to evacuate those colonists wishing to leave. (Ship returns to the United States on March 20 with all 368 surviving colonists.) In North Carolina, Confederate forces under General George E. Pickett make an unsuccessful attempt to capture Union-held New Bern, February 1–3. Sherman leaves Vicksburg on February 3 with 25,000 men and begins marching across central Mississippi toward Meridian, destroying railroads and war materials and stripping the countryside of food and forage. The same day, Davis sends message to the Confederate Congress warning of increasing "discontent, disaffection, and disloyalty" within the Confederacy and asking that the privilege of the writ of habeas corpus be suspended (previous suspension had expired in February 1863). Union forces occupy Jacksonville, Florida, on February 7. Illinois Republican Lyman Trumbull, chairman of the Senate Judiciary Committee, reports text of proposed constitutional amendment abolishing slavery to the Senate on February 10. General William Sooy Smith and 7,000 Union cavalry leave Collierville, Tennessee, on February 11 with orders to destroy railroads in northern Mississippi before joining Sherman at Meridian. Sherman's troops occupy Meridian, February 14–20, destroying railroads, storehouses, and an arsenal. On February 15 the Confederate Congress suspends writ of habeas corpus through August 1, 1864, including in cases of desertion and draft evasion, and on February 17 it requires all Confederate soldiers to serve for the duration of the war and makes all white males from seventeen to fifty eligible for conscription. Experimental Confederate submarine *H. L. Hunley* uses spar torpedo to sink the Union sloop *Housatonic* off Charleston on the night of February 17; the *Hunley* also sinks, with the loss of all seven crew members. The "Pomeroy Circular," confidential letter sent to influential Republicans by Senator Samuel C. Pomeroy criticizing Lincoln and supporting the nomination of Secretary of the Treasury Salmon P. Chase, is published in the Washington press on February 20. Union advance toward Lake City, Florida, is defeated at Olustee, February 20. Confederate cavalry led by General Nathan Bedford Forrest defeats William Sooy Smith's raiding force at Okolona, Mississippi, February 22. Davis appoints Braxton Bragg as his chief military advisor on February 24. General Judson Kilpatrick crosses Rapidan on February 28 with 3,500 men on cavalry raid aimed at freeing Union prisoners of war held in Richmond. Lincoln signs legislation reestablishing the rank of lieutenant general and nominates Grant for the position, February 29.

On March 1 Kilpatrick abandons attempt to enter Richmond and begins retreat toward Union lines. Senate confirms Grant's nomination on March 2. Embarrassed by the publication of the "Pomeroy Circular," Chase declares on

March 5 that he is not a candidate for president. The same day, the Richmond newspapers publish documents found during the Kilpatrick raid on the body of Union colonel Ulric Dahlgren outlining a plot to kill Jefferson Davis and burn Richmond. Grant arrives in Washington on March 8, and meets Lincoln for the first time that evening at a White House reception. He receives his commission the following day, and on March 10 is named general-in-chief of the armies of the United States.

Biographical Notes

Henry Livermore Abbott (January 21, 1842–May 6, 1864) Born in Lowell, Massachusetts, the son of a lawyer active in Democratic politics. Graduated from Harvard College in 1860 and began studying law in his father's office. Commissioned second lieutenant, 20th Massachusetts Volunteer Infantry Regiment, July 10, 1861. Formed close friendship with his fellow officer Oliver Wendell Holmes Jr. Fought at Ball's Bluff. Promoted to first lieutenant, November 1861. Fought at Fair Oaks and in the Seven Days' Battles, where he was wounded in the arm at Glendale. Older brother Edward killed at Cedar Mountain. Fought at Fredericksburg (December 1862 and May 1863) and Gettysburg; promoted to captain, December 1862, and major, October 1863. Became acting commander of the 20th Massachusetts after all of the regimental officers senior to him were killed or wounded at Gettysburg. Led the regiment at Briscoe Station and fought at Mine Run and at the battle of the Wilderness, where he was fatally wounded on May 6, 1864.

Charles Francis Adams (August 18, 1807–November 21, 1886) Born in Boston, Massachusetts, the son of John Quincy Adams and Louisa Johnson Adams and grandson of John and Abigail Adams. Graduated from Harvard in 1825. Admitted to the bar in 1829. Married Abigail Brown Brooks the same year. Served as a Whig in the Massachusetts house of representatives, 1841–43, and in the state senate, 1844–45. Vice-presidential candidate of the Free Soil Party in 1848. Edited *The Works of John Adams* (1850–56). Served in Congress as a Republican, 1859–61. As U.S. minister to Great Britain, 1861–68, helped maintain British neutrality in the Civil War. Served as the U.S. representative on the international arbitration tribunal that settled American claims against Great Britain for losses caused by Confederate commerce raiders built in British shipyards, 1871–72. Edited the *Memoirs of John Quincy Adams* (1874–77). Died in Boston.

Henry Adams (February 16, 1838–March 27, 1918) Born in Boston, Massachusetts. Brother of Charles Francis Adams Jr., son of lawyer Charles Francis Adams and Abigail Brooks Adams, grandson of John Quincy Adams, great-grandson of John Adams. Graduated Harvard 1858; studied law in Berlin and Dresden until 1860. Served as secretary to father while Charles Francis Adams served in Congress, 1860–61, and as U.S. minister to Great Britain, 1861–68. Reported British reaction to the American Civil War as anonymous London correspondent of *The New York Times*, 1861–62. Returned to Washington, D.C., in 1868 to work as journalist. Appointed assistant professor of history at Harvard (1870–77); assumed editorship of *North American Review* (1870–76). Married Marion Hooper in 1872. Published *The Life of Albert Gallatin* (1879), biography; *Democracy* (1880), a novel that appeared anonymously; *John Randolph* (1882), a biography; *Esther* (1884), a novel that appeared pseudonymously; *History of the United States during the Administrations of Thomas Jefferson and James Madison* (1889–91); *Mont-Saint-Michel and Chartres: A Study of Thirteenth-Century Unity* (1904); *The Education of Henry Adams* (1907). Died in Washington.

Lois Bryan Adams (October 14, 1817–June 28, 1870) Born in Whitestown, New York, the daughter of a carpenter. Family moved in 1823 to Michigan Territory and settled near Ypsilanti, then moved to the Constantine area in 1835. Attended White Pigeon Academy, branch of the University of Michigan, in 1839. Married James R. Adams, a newspaper editor, in 1841. Moved to Kentucky after her husband died of consumption in 1848, and taught school for three years before returning to Michigan in 1851. Began writing for the monthly (later weekly) *Michigan Farmer* and for the *Detroit Advertiser and Tribune*. Moved to Detroit in 1853 to work on the *Michigan Farmer*, and became its copublisher in 1854 and household editor in 1856. Sold her interest in the publication in 1861. Published *Sybelle and Other Poems* (1862). Moved to Washington, D.C., in 1863 to take post as clerk in the recently formed Department of Agriculture and became assistant to the director of the agricultural museum. Volunteered during the war for the Michigan Soldiers' Relief Association while contributing columns to the *Detroit Advertiser and Tribune*. Continued work at the Department of Agriculture after the war. Died in Washington, D.C.

John A. Andrew (May 31, 1818–October 30, 1867) Born in Windham, Maine, the son of a storekeeper and a former schoolteacher. Graduated from Bowdoin College in 1837. Studied law in Boston and began practice there after being admitted to the bar in 1840. An antislavery Whig, Andrew helped organize the Free Soil Party in Massachusetts in 1848. Married Eliza Jane Hersey in 1848. Elected as a Republican in 1857 to one-year term in the state house of representatives. Raised money for John Brown's legal defense after the Harpers Ferry raid in 1859. Elected governor of Massachusetts in 1860 and was reelected four times, serving from January 1861 to January 1866. Began strengthening state militia immediately after taking office in 1861, and became a strong supporter of the Union war effort and of emancipation. Urged enlistment of black soldiers, and organized the 54th and

55th Massachusetts Infantry in 1863, the first black infantry regiments raised by a northern state. Resumed law practice after retiring from office in 1866. Died in Boston.

George Richard Browder (January 11, 1827–September 3, 1886) Born in Logan County, Kentucky, the son of a slave-owning farmer. Attended Male Academy in Clarksville, Tennessee. Licensed as a Methodist preacher in 1846, ordained as a deacon in 1848 and as an elder in 1850. Married Ann Elizabeth Warfield in 1850. Received farm in Logan County as gift from his father in 1853. Preached on Logan circuit, 1861–63, and at Hadensville, 1863–65. Continued preaching after the war despite recurring illness. Appointed presiding elder of the Louisville Conference in 1876 and served until his death in Logan County.

Joshua Lawrence Chamberlain (September 8, 1828–February 24, 1914) Born in Brewer, Maine, the son of a farmer. Graduated from Bowdoin College in 1852 and from Bangor Theological Seminary, a Congregational institution, in 1855. Accepted professorship at Bowdoin, where he taught natural theology, logic, rhetoric, and modern languages. Married Frances (Fanny) Caroline Adams in 1855. Used two-year leave of absence, originally granted by the college to study languages in Europe, to obtain commission as lieutenant colonel in the newly formed 20th Maine Infantry in August 1862. Served in reserve at Antietam and saw action at Shepherdstown and Fredericksburg. Became colonel of the 20th Maine in late May 1863 and led the regiment at Gettysburg, where it helped defend Little Round Top on July 2. Promoted to command the Third Brigade, First Division, Fifth Corps in August 1863, but fell ill with malaria in November. Served on court-martial duty in early 1864 before rejoining the 20th Maine at Spotsylvania in May 1864. Led regiment at the North Anna River and Cold Harbor before becoming commander of the First Brigade, First Division, Fifth Corps. Seriously wounded by gunshot to the pelvis while leading brigade in assault at Petersburg on June 18, 1864. Promoted to brigadier general. Returned to brigade command in November 1864. Wounded in arm and chest at Quaker Road, March 29, 1865. Led brigade at White Oak Road, Five Forks, and in the Appomattox campaign. Received formal surrender of the Army of Northern Virginia on April 12, where he ordered his men to salute the defeated Confederates. Mustered out on January 15, 1866, and returned to professorship at Bowdoin. Served four one-year terms as governor of Maine, 1867–71. President of Bowdoin, 1871–83. Taught moral philosophy, 1874–79, and published *Maine, Her Place in History* (1877). Resigned as college president in 1883 from ill health due to war wounds. Wrote memoir of the final campaign in Virginia,

The Passing of the Armies (published posthumously in 1915). Died in Portland, Maine.

John Hampden Chamberlayne (June 2, 1838–February 18, 1882) Born in Richmond, Virginia, the son of a physician. Attended the University of Virginia, 1855–58, read law in Richmond, and was admitted to Virginia bar in 1860. Enlisted in the 21st Virginia Regiment and served in western Virginia, 1861–62. Became artillery sergeant in the Army of Northern Virginia, February 1862, and was promoted to lieutenant, June 1862. Served at Mechanicsville, Gaines's Mill, Glendale, Cedar Mountain, Second Manassas, Antietam, Fredericksburg, and Chancellorsville. Captured at Millerstown, Pennsylvania, on June 28, 1863. Exchanged in March 1864. Served in Overland campaign and the siege of Petersburg. Promoted to captain, August 1864. Evaded surrender at Appomattox Court House and joined Confederate forces in North Carolina before giving his parole at Atlanta, Georgia, on May 12, 1865. Became journalist at the *Petersburg Index* in 1869. Married Mary Walker Gibson in 1873. Edited the *Norfolk Virginian*, 1873–76. Founded *The State* newspaper in Richmond in 1876 and edited it until his death. Died in Richmond.

Mary Chesnut (March 31, 1823–November 22, 1886) Born Mary Boykin Miller in Statesburg, Sumter County, South Carolina, the daughter of Stephen Miller, a former congressman who later served as governor of South Carolina and in the U.S. Senate, and Mary Boykin Miller. Educated at a French boarding school in Charleston. Married James Chesnut Jr. in 1840 and lived on Mulberry, the Chesnut family plantation near Camden, South Carolina. Lived in Washington, D.C., while husband served in the Senate, 1859–60. Spent much of the Civil War in Richmond, Virginia, where her husband served as an advisor to Jefferson Davis, and formed close friendship with Varina Davis. Wrote three unfinished novels after the war, and extensively revised and expanded her wartime journal from 1881 to 1884. Died in Camden.

William Henry Harrison Clayton (June 1840–December 18, 1917) Born in Pittsburgh, Pennsylvania. Moved with family to Cincinnati, Ohio, in 1842 and to western Van Buren County, Iowa, where his father bought a farm in 1855. Enlisted in Company H, 19th Iowa Infantry, in August 1862, and was made the company clerk. Served in southern Missouri and northern Arkansas, September 1862–May 1863, and fought in the battle of Prairie Grove. Promoted to sergeant in April 1863. Sent with regiment to Vicksburg in mid-June and served in siege until Confederate surrender on July 4, 1863. Remained in Mississippi until late July, when the 19th Iowa was posted to

Louisiana. Captured along with two hundred men from his regiment at Sterling's Plantation near Morganza, Louisiana, on September 29, 1863. Held as prisoner of war at Shreveport, Louisiana, and Marshall and Tyler, Texas, before being exchanged in July 1864. Rejoined regiment and served at Fort Barrancas near Pensacola, Florida, August–December 1864, and at the entrance to Mobile Bay and in southeastern Mississippi, December 1864–March 1865. Saw action in the siege of Spanish Fort near Mobile, March 27–April 8, 1865. Remained at Mobile after Confederate surrender until July 1865, when his regiment was mustered out. Returned to Iowa, then moved in fall 1865 to Pittsburgh, where he worked as a bookkeeper. Married cousin Elizabeth Cooper in 1869; she died in 1876. Moved in 1879 to farm in Orange, California. Married cousin Ora Clayton in 1879. Gave up farming in 1887 to become public notary and sell insurance and real estate. Served as Orange city treasurer, 1888–92 and 1898–1904, and as city councilman, 1894–98. Died in Orange.

Patrick R. Cleburne (March 16, 1828–November 30, 1864) Born in Ovens, County Cork, Ireland, the son of a physician. Apprenticed in 1844 to a physician in Mallow. Applied to study medicine at Apothecaries' Hall in Dublin, but was rejected for failing to meet the Greek and Latin requirements. Enlisted as private in the 41st Regiment of Foot in 1846 and served on garrison duty in Ireland during the Great Famine. Promoted to corporal in 1849. Purchased discharge and emigrated to United States with his sister and two brothers; arrived in New Orleans on December 25, 1849. Settled in 1850 in Helena, Arkansas, where he managed and later co-owned a drugstore. Sold his share in the store in 1854 and read law. Admitted to bar in January 1856 and began successful legal practice. Became close friend of Democratic politician Thomas C. Hindman (later a Confederate general). Feud between Hindman and Know-Nothing leader Dorsey Rice resulted in gunfight in May 1856 in which Cleburne killed Rice's brother-in-law and was himself seriously wounded. Elected captain of Yell Rifles, a local militia company, in summer 1860 and colonel of the 1st Arkansas Infantry in May 1861. Appointed brigade commander in Army of Central Kentucky in October 1861. Promoted to brigadier general in March 1862. Led brigade at Shiloh, Richmond (Kentucky), and Perryville, and was shot in mouth at Richmond. Promoted to major general in December 1862. Commanded division at Stones River, Chickamauga, and Chattanooga. Proposed emancipating and arming slaves in address to generals of the Army of Tennessee, January 2, 1864. Led division in Atlanta campaign and in General John B. Hood's invasion of Tennessee. Killed in battle of Franklin.

Richard Cobden (June 3, 1804–April 2, 1865) Born in Heyshott, near Midhurst, West Sussex, England, the son of a farmer. Attended Bowes Hall School in Yorkshire before entering his uncle's calico trading firm in London in 1819. Formed his own trading partnership in 1828 and opened calico printing works in Sabden, Lancashire, in 1831. Moved to Manchester in 1832. Traveled to the United States, Europe, and the Middle East. Published pamphlets *England, Ireland, and America* (1835) and *Russia* (1836), criticizing military expenditures and advocating free trade. Helped form Anti-Corn-Law League to campaign for repeal of duties on imported grain. Began friendship and political collaboration with orator John Bright. Married Catherine Anne Williams in 1840. Elected to Parliament in 1841. Following the repeal of the Corn Laws in 1846, traveled to France, Spain, Italy, and Russia. Campaigned for free trade, international arbitration, and the reduction of armaments. Opposed the Crimean War and criticized British policy in China. Lost parliamentary seat in 1857 but was elected by another constituency in 1859. Helped negotiate commercial treaty with France in 1860, and organized international peace conferences. Publicly supported the Union and opposed British intervention in the Civil War. Died in London.

James A. Connolly (March 8, 1838–December 15, 1914) Born in Newark, New Jersey, the son of a tanner. Moved with family around 1850 to Chesterville, Ohio. Graduated from Selby Academy in Chesterville and studied law. Admitted to the bar in 1859 and served as assistant clerk of the Ohio state senate, 1859–60. Moved to Charleston, Illinois, in 1860. Mustered into service as major of the newly-formed 123rd Illinois Infantry in September 1862. Fought at Perryville. Married Mary Dunn, sister of the judge with whom he had read law, in February 1863. Fought at Milton (Vaught's Hill) and Chickamauga. Joined staff of the Third Division, Fourteenth Corps, commanded by Brigadier General Absalom Baird. Served at Chattanooga, in the Atlanta campaign, and in Sherman's marches through Georgia and the Carolinas. Helped escort Abraham Lincoln's body to Springfield. Returned to law practice in Charleston before moving to Springfield in 1886. Served in Illinois state house of representatives, 1872–76, as U.S. attorney for the Southern District of Illinois, 1876–85 and 1889–94, and as a Republican congressman, 1895–99. Died in Springfield.

Richard Cordley (September 6, 1829–July 11, 1904) Born in Nottingham, England. Family moved to farm in Livingston County, Michigan Territory, in 1833. Attended Ann Arbor Classical School. Graduated from the University of Michigan in 1854 and Andover Theological Seminary in 1857. Recruited by American Home Missionary Society to settle in Kansas. Became minister of Plymouth Congregational Church in Lawrence in December 1857. Founded quarterly (later monthly) publication *Congregational Record* and married Mary Ann Minta Cox in 1859. Established Sunday and night schools to educate runaway slaves, helped other fugitives flee to Canada, and founded the Second Congregational Church ("Freedman's Church") for freed slaves in 1862. Escaped injury during William Quantrill's raid on Lawrence on August 21, 1863, although his house and office were destroyed. Helped found the University of Kansas in 1866. Resigned position at Plymouth Congregational in 1875. Served as pastor in Flint, Michigan, 1875–78, and Emporia, Kansas, 1878–84. Returned to Lawrence and served as pastor of Plymouth Congregational from 1884 until his death. Published *A History of Lawrence, Kansas* (1895) and *Pioneer Days in Kansas* (1903). Died in Lawrence.

Kate Cumming (December 1826–June 5, 1909). Born Catherine Cumming in Edinburgh, Scotland. Moved with family to Montreal and then to Mobile, Alabama, arriving there by 1845. Volunteered after the battle of Shiloh in April 1862 to help nurse Confederate soldiers in northern Mississippi. Returned to Mobile after two months, then began serving in September 1862 as hospital matron in Chattanooga, where she was officially enrolled as a member of the Confederate army medical department. Following the evacuation of Chattanooga in the summer of 1863, served at several field hospitals in Georgia and Alabama. Returned to Mobile after the war. Published *A Journal of Hospital Life in the Confederate Army of Tennessee* (1866). Moved with father in 1874 to Birmingham, Alabama, where she taught school and gave music lessons. Published *Gleanings from Southland* (1895). Died in Birmingham.

William Parker Cutler (July 12, 1812–April 11, 1889) Born in Warren Township, Washington County, Ohio, the son of a farmer active in local and state politics. Attended Ohio University at Athens, then returned to work on family farm. Elected to Ohio house of representatives as a Whig, 1844–47, and served as speaker, 1846–47. Married Elizabeth P. Voris in 1849. Trustee of Marietta College, 1849–89, and was a delegate to the state constitutional convention in 1850. President of Marietta & Cincinnati Railroad, 1850–54 and 1858–60. Served in U.S. Congress as a Republican, 1861–63; defeated for reelection. President of Marietta & Pittsburgh Railroad, 1868–72, and served as contractor on railroad construction projects in Indiana and Illinois, 1869–73. Died in Marietta, Ohio.

Maria Lydig Daly (September 12, 1824–August 21, 1894) Born Maria Lydig in New York City, the daughter of a wealthy grain merchant and landowner. Married Judge Charles P. Daly of the New York Court of Common Pleas, the son of poor Irish immigrants, in 1856 despite opposition from many members of her family who objected to his Catholicism and family background. Supported the Woman's Central Association of Relief during the Civil War and visited sick and wounded soldiers. Died at her country home in North Haven, New York.

Jefferson Davis (June 3, 1808–December 6, 1889) Born in Christian (now Todd) County, Kentucky, the son of a farmer. Moved with his family to Mississippi. Graduated from West Point in 1828 and served in the Black Hawk War. Resigned his commission in 1835 and married Sarah Knox Taylor, who died later in the year. Became a cotton planter in Warren County, Mississippi. Married Varina Howell in 1845. Elected to Congress as a Democrat and served 1845–46, then resigned to command a Mississippi volunteer regiment in Mexico, 1846–47, where he fought at Monterrey and was wounded at Buena Vista. Elected to the Senate and served from 1847 to 1851, when he resigned to run unsuccessfully for governor. Secretary of war in the cabinet of Franklin Pierce, 1853–57. Elected to the Senate and served from 1857 to January 21, 1861, when he withdrew following the secession of Mississippi. Inaugurated as provisional president of the Confederate States of America on February 18, 1861. Elected without opposition to six-year term in November 1861 and inaugurated on February 22, 1862. Captured by Union cavalry near Irwinville, Georgia, on May 10, 1865. Imprisoned at Fort Monroe, Virginia, and indicted for treason. Released on bail on May 13, 1867; the indictment was dropped in 1869 without trial. Published *The Rise and Fall of the Confederate Government* in 1881. Died in New Orleans.

Theodore A. Dodge (May 28, 1842–October 25, 1909) Born in Pittsfield, Massachusetts, the son of a manufacturer. Educated at Berlin, Heidelberg, and University College, London. Commissioned first lieutenant in Company G, 101st New York Infantry, in February 1862. Led company in the Seven Days' Battles at Oak Grove, Glendale, and Malvern Hill. Became regimental adjutant during the summer of 1862. Fought at Second Bull Run and was wounded in leg at Chantilly. Resigned from 101st New York and became adjutant of the 119th New York Infantry in November 1862. Fought at Chancellorsville. Wounded in ankle at Gettysburg on July 1 and had right leg amputated below the knee five days later. Commissioned as captain in the Veteran Reserve Corps in November 1863. Served in the enrollment and desertion branches of the Provost Marshal General's office in Washington, D.C. Married Jane Marshall Neil in 1865. Attended Columbia Law School and was admitted to the District of Columbia bar in 1866. Commissioned as captain in the regular army and served as superintendent of military buildings in Washington, 1866–70.

Moved to Cambridge, Massachusetts, and became successful manufacturer of tires and other rubber products. Published *The Campaign of Chancellorsville* (1881), *A Bird's-eye View of Our Civil War* (1883), *Patroclus and Penelope* (1886), *Great Captains* (1889), *Alexander* (1890), *Hannibal* (1891), *Caesar* (1892), *Riders of Many Lands* (1894), *Gustavus Adolphus* (1895), *Army and Other Tales* (1899), and *Napoleon* (1904–7). Following the death of his wife, married Clara Isabel Bowden in 1892. Moved to Paris in 1900. Died in Nanteuil-le-Hadouin, Oise, France.

Francis Adams Donaldson (June 7, 1840–May 3, 1928). Born in Philadelphia, where he was raised by his aunt after the death of his parents. Worked as clerk in a shipping company. Enlisted in June 1861 in the 1st California Regiment (later the 71st Pennsylvania Infantry) and became a sergeant in Company H. Captured at Ball's Bluff and was a prisoner in Richmond until his exchange in February 1862. Returned to his regiment and was promoted to second lieutenant. Served in Peninsula campaign and was wounded in the arm at Fair Oaks on May 31, 1862. Commissioned as captain of Company M, 118th Pennsylvania Infantry, in August 1862. Served at Antietam, Shepherdstown, Fredericksburg, Chancellorsville, Gettysburg, and in the Bristoe and Mine Run campaigns. Feuded with his commanding officer, Lieutenant Colonel James Gwyn, who refused to give Donaldson permission to resign from the regiment. In December 1863 Donaldson publicly insulted and threatened Gwyn, resulting in Donaldson's court-martial and dismissal from the army. (Sentence was changed in March 1864 to dismissal without "disability" after Donaldson made a personal appeal to President Lincoln.) Returned to Philadelphia and entered the insurance business. Founded his own company in 1866 and remained at its head until 1917. Married Mary Heyburger Landell in 1872. Died in Philadelphia.

Frederick Douglass (February 1818–February 20, 1895) Born Frederick Bailey in Talbot County, Maryland, the son of a slave mother and an unknown white man. Worked on farms and in Baltimore shipyards. Escaped to Philadelphia in 1838. Married Anna Murray, a free woman from Maryland, and settled in New Bedford, Massachusetts, where he took the name Douglass. Became a lecturer for the American Anti-Slavery Society, led by William Lloyd Garrison, in 1841. Published *Narrative of the Life of Frederick Douglass, An American Slave* (1845). Began publishing *North Star*, first in a series of antislavery newspapers, in Rochester, New York, in 1847. Broke with Garrison and became an ally of Gerrit Smith, who advocated an antislavery interpretation of the Constitution and participation in electoral politics. Published *My Bondage and My Freedom* (1855).

Advocated emancipation and the enlistment of black soldiers at the outbreak of the Civil War. Met with Abraham Lincoln in Washington in August 1863 and August 1864, and wrote public letter supporting his reelection in September 1864. Continued his advocacy of racial equality and women's rights after the Civil War. Served as U.S. marshal for the District of Columbia, 1877–81, and as its recorder of deeds, 1881–86. Published *Life and Times of Frederick Douglass* (1881). After the death of his wife Anna, married Helen Pitts in 1884. Served as minister to Haiti, 1889–91. Died in Washington, D.C.

Lewis Douglass (October 9, 1840–September 19, 1908) Born in New Bedford, Massachusetts, oldest son of abolitionist Frederick Douglass and Anna Murray Douglass. Moved with family in 1848 to Rochester, New York, where he attended public schools and later worked as a printer for *Frederick Douglass' Paper* and *Douglass' Monthly*. Along with his brother Charles, enlisted in the 54th Massachusetts Infantry in March 1863. Promoted to sergeant major in April. Fought at Fort Wagner. Given medical discharge on May 10, 1864, after months of illness. Moved to Denver, Colorado, with brother Frederick in 1866 and worked as secretary for a mining company. Returned east in 1869 to work in the Government Printing Office in Washington, D.C. Married Amelia Loguen in 1869. Assisted father in editing and publishing weekly Washington newspaper *The New National Era*, 1870–74. Served on legislative council for the District of Columbia, 1872–73, and as assistant U.S. marshal for the District, 1877–81. Began successful real estate business. Died in Washington.

Catherine Edmondston (October 10, 1823–January 3, 1875) Born Catherine Ann Devereux in Halifax County, North Carolina, the daughter of a plantation owner. Married Patrick Edmondston in 1846. Lived on Looking Glass plantation in Halifax County. Published pamphlet *The Morte d'Arthur: Its Influence on the Spirit and Manners of the Nineteenth Century* (1872), in which she accused the Union army of barbarism. Died in Raleigh.

Wilbur Fisk (June 7, 1839–March 12, 1914). Born in Sharon, Vermont, the son of a farmer. Family moved to Lowell, Massachusetts, in 1852 to work in woolen mills, then returned to Vermont in 1854 and settled on farm in Tunbridge. Worked as hired farm laborer and taught in local schools. Enlisted in September 1861 in Company E, 2nd Vermont Infantry. Contributed regular letters under the name "Anti-Rebel" to *The Green Mountain Freeman* of Montpelier from December 11, 1861, to July 26, 1865. Saw action in the siege of Yorktown and in the Seven Days' Battles. Hospitalized with severe diarrhea in Washington, D.C., in early September 1862. Recovered in convalescent camp in Fairfax, Virginia, then went absent without leave and married Angelina Drew of Lawrence, Massachusetts, in February 1863. Returned to regiment in March 1863 and served at Chancellorsville, Gettysburg, Rappahannock Station, Mine Run, the Wilderness, Spotsylvania, North Anna, Cold Harbor, and Petersburg. Sent with regiment in July 1864 to help defend the capital against Jubal Early's Washington raid. Served in the Shenandoah Valley at Winchester, Fisher's Hill, and Cedar Creek before returning to Petersburg siege lines in December 1864. Detached for guard duty at Sixth Corps hospital at City Point, Virginia, in January 1865, and served there for remainder of the war. Rejoined family, who had moved to Geneva, Kansas, and worked on farm. Licensed as Congregational preacher in 1874, and the following year became pastor of a church in Freeborn, Minnesota, where he served until his retirement in 1909. Following the death of his first wife in 1898, married Amanda Dickerson Dickey in 1909. Died in Geneva, Kansas.

Samuel W. Fiske (July 23, 1828–May 22, 1864) Born in Shelburne, Massachusetts. Graduated from Amherst College in 1848. Taught school, studied for three years at Andover Theological Seminary, then returned to Amherst in 1853 as a tutor. Traveled in Europe and the Middle East. Published *Dunn Browne's Experiences in Foreign Parts* (1857), travel letters written to the *Springfield Republican* under a nom de plume. Became pastor of the Congregational church in Madison, Connecticut, in 1857. Married Elizabeth Foster in 1858. Became second lieutenant in the 14th Connecticut Infantry in August 1862. Signing himself Dunn Browne, wrote weekly letters to the *Springfield Republican* describing campaigns and camp life (collected in 1866 under the title *Mr. Dunn Browne's Experiences in the Army*). Served at Antietam and Fredericksburg. Promoted to captain in early 1863. Captured at Chancellorsville on May 3, 1863, was paroled in late May and exchanged in June. Served at Gettysburg. Wounded in the battle of the Wilderness on May 6, 1864, and died in Fredericksburg, Virginia.

Charlotte Forten (August 17, 1837–July 22, 1914) Born in Philadelphia, the daughter of Robert Bridges Forten, a sail maker, and Mary Virginia Woods Forten; both parents were members of prominent black Philadelphia families and active abolitionists. Mother died in 1840. Moved to Salem, Massachusetts, in 1853 and lived with family of black abolitionist Charles Lenox Remond while attending Higginson Grammar School and Salem Normal School. Graduated in 1856. Taught school in Salem and Philadelphia and tutored her cousins in Byberry, Pennsylvania, 1856–62, while suffering several bouts of illness. Published poems and essays in *The Liberator*, *Christian Recorder*, and *National Anti-Slavery Standard*. Moved to St. Helena Island, South Carolina, in October 1862 to teach freed slaves, becoming one of the first black schoolteachers in the Sea Islands. Helped nurse wounded soldiers of the 54th Massachusetts after the battle of Fort Wagner in July 1863. Returned to Philadelphia in May 1864. Published essay "Life on the Sea Islands" in the *Atlantic Monthly*, May–June 1864. Moved to Boston in 1865 to work as secretary at the New England Freedmen's Union Commission, an organization that supplied financial and material support to teachers of freed slaves. Published translation of French novel *Madame Thérèse; or, The Volunteers of '92* by Emile Erckman and Alexandre Chatrain in 1869. Taught school in Charleston, South Carolina, 1871–72, and Washington, D.C., 1872–73. Worked as clerk in U.S. Treasury Department, 1873–78. Married the Reverend Francis Grimké, nephew of abolitionists Sarah and Angelina Grimké, in 1878. Lived in Jacksonville, Florida, 1885–89, where her husband pastored the Laura Street Presbyterian Church. Returned to Washington, D.C., in 1889 when Francis Grimké became the pastor of the Fifteenth Street Presbyterian Church. Continued to publish essays and poems. Became a founding member of the National Association of Colored Women in 1896. Died in Washington.

Arthur James Lyon Fremantle (November 11, 1835–September 25, 1901). The son of a major general in the British army, Fremantle graduated from the Royal Military College at Sandhurst and entered the army in 1852. Commissioned in Coldstream Guards in 1853. Promoted to captain in the Coldstream and lieutenant colonel in the army in 1860. Posted the same year to Gibraltar, where he met Confederate naval commander Raphael Semmes in 1862. Became increasingly sympathetic to the Confederate cause and obtained six months' leave to go to North America. Entered Texas from Mexico in April 1863 and traveled through the Confederacy, meeting Sam Houston, Joseph E. Johnston, Braxton Bragg, Pierre G. T. Beauregard, Jefferson Davis, Robert E. Lee, and James Longstreet. Witnessed the battle of Gettysburg, then crossed the lines in western Maryland and sailed from New York in July 1863. Published *Three Months in the Southern States, April–June 1863* in late 1863. Married Mary Hall in 1864. Commanded a battalion in the Coldstream Guards, 1877–80, and served as aide-de-camp to the Duke of Cambridge, commander-in-chief of the army, 1881–82. Promoted to major general in 1882. Served in Sir Garnet Wolseley's expeditionary force in the Sudan as governor of Suakin, 1884–85, commander of the Brigade of Guards, and chief of staff before returning to England in 1886. Served as governor of Malta, 1894–99. Died at Cowes on the Isle of Wight.

Benjamin B. French (September 4, 1800–August 12, 1870) Born in Chester, New Hampshire, the son of a lawyer who later served as the state attorney general. Admitted to the bar in 1825, the same year he married Elizabeth S. Richardson. Served in New Hampshire house of representatives, 1831–33. Assistant clerk of the U.S. House of Representatives, 1833–45; clerk of the House, 1845–47. President of the Magnetic Telegraphic Company, 1847–50. Commissioner of public buildings in Washington, 1853–55. Left Democratic Party and became a Republican. Appointed commissioner of public buildings in 1861. After the death of his wife in 1861, married Mary Ellen Brady, 1862. Oversaw completion of the U.S. Capitol and helped organize Lincoln's funeral. Worked as clerk in the Treasury Department after position of commissioner of public buildings was abolished in 1867 by Radical Republicans angered by his support of President Andrew Johnson. Died in Washington, D.C.

Isaac Funk (November 17, 1797–January 29, 1865) Born in Clark County, Kentucky, the son of a farmer. Family moved to farm in Fayette County, Ohio, in 1807. Attended school for parts of three winters before age thirteen. Spent year working in the Kanawha salt works in western Virginia before returning to Ohio in 1821. Began trading in cattle and hogs with his father and brother Absalom. Moved with Absalom in 1824 to McLean County, Illinois, and settled on farm in area later known as Funk's Grove. Married Cassandra Sharp in 1826. Expanded livestock business, eventually owning 25,000 acres of land on which he raised cattle and hogs for sale in Chicago and other markets. Served as a Whig in the Illinois house of representatives, 1840–42. Helped found Illinois Wesleyan University in 1850. A friend and supporter of Abraham Lincoln, Funk was a delegate to the 1860 Republican convention in Chicago and campaigned for Lincoln in the fall. Served as a Republican in the Illinois state senate from 1862 until his death in Bloomington, Illinois.

James Henry Gooding (August 28, 1838–July 19, 1864). Born into slavery in North Carolina, Gooding had his freedom purchased by James M. Gooding, possibly his father, and was brought to New York City. Enrolled in September 1846 in the New York Colored Orphan Asylum, where he was educated. Indentured in 1850, possibly to a dentist, but left position in 1852. Signed on to whaling ship *Sunbeam* in New Bedford, Massachusetts, claiming to be a freeborn man from Troy, New York, and sailed in July 1856. Worked in galley as ship hunted sperm whales in the Indian and Pacific oceans before returning to New Bedford in April 1860. Made second whaling voyage as steward on *Black Eagle*, May 1860–November 1861, hunting right whales off western Greenland. Sailed for Montevideo as cook and steward on merchant ship *Richard Mitchell* in January 1862. Returned to New Bedford in late summer and married Ellen Louisa Allen in September 1862. Wrote six poems during his voyages that were printed in broadside form. Enlisted in the 54th Massachusetts Infantry on February 14, 1863, and became a private in Company C. Wrote forty-eight letters from the 54th Massachusetts that were printed in the New Bedford *Mercury*, March 1863–February 1864, signed "J.H.G." and "Monitor." Fought at Fort Wagner. Wrote letter to President Lincoln in September 1863 protesting unequal pay for black soldiers. Promoted to corporal in December 1863. Wounded in leg and taken prisoner at battle of Olustee, February 20, 1864. Died in prison camp at Andersonville, Georgia.

Ulysses S. Grant (April 22, 1822–July 23, 1885) Born in Point Pleasant, Ohio, the son of a tanner. Graduated from West Point in 1843. Served in the U.S.-Mexican War, 1846–48, and promoted to first lieutenant in 1847. Married Julia Dent in 1848. Promoted to captain, 1854, and resigned commission. Worked as a farmer, real estate agent, and general store clerk, 1854–61. Commissioned colonel, 21st Illinois Volunteers, June 1861, and brigadier general of volunteers, August 1861. Promoted to major general of volunteers, February 1862, after victories at Forts Henry and Donelson. Defeated Confederates at Shiloh, April 1862, and captured Vicksburg, Mississippi, July 1863. Promoted to major general in the regular army, July 1863, and assigned to command of Military Division of the Mississippi, covering territory between the Alleghenies and the Mississippi, October 1863. Won battle of Chattanooga, November 1863. Promoted to lieutenant general, March 1864, and named general-in-chief of the Union armies. Accepted surrender of Robert E. Lee at Appomattox Court House, April 9, 1865. Promoted to general, July 1866. Served as secretary of war ad interim, August 1867–January 1868. Nominated for president by the Republican Party in 1868. Defeated Democrat Horatio Seymour, and won reelection in 1872 by defeating Liberal Republican Horace Greeley. President of the United States, 1869–77. Made world tour, 1877–79. Failed to win Republican presidential nomination, 1880. Worked on Wall Street, 1881–84, and was financially ruined when private banking firm of Grant & Ward collapsed. Wrote *Personal Memoirs of U.S. Grant*, 1884–85, while suffering from throat cancer, and completed them days before his death at Mount McGregor, New York.

Edward O. Guerrant (February 28, 1838–April 26, 1916). Born in Sharpsburg, Kentucky, the son of a physician. Graduated from Centre College in Danville, Kentucky, in 1860. Briefly attended Danville Seminary and taught school in Flat Creek. Enlisted as private in the Confederate 1st Battalion Kentucky Mounted Rifles at Gladesville,

Virginia, in February 1862. Became clerk on staff of Brigadier General Humphrey Marshall, the Confederate commander in southwestern Virginia, and was commissioned as his assistant adjutant general in December 1862. Continued his staff duties under Marshall's successors William Preston, John S. Williams, and John Hunt Morgan, serving in southwestern Virginia, eastern Kentucky, and northeastern Tennessee and seeing action in several engagements. Surrendered in eastern Kentucky in late April 1865. Studied medicine at Jefferson Medical College, Philadelphia, and Bellevue Hospital, New York. Established medical practice in Mount Sterling, Kentucky, in 1867. Married Mary Jane DeVault in 1868. Entered Union Theological Seminary at Hampden-Sydney College in Virginia in 1873 and was licensed as a Presbyterian preacher in 1875. Served as minister of the First Presbyterian Church in Louisville, 1879–82. Appointed by the Kentucky Synod in 1882 as evangelist to eastern Kentucky. Became minister of churches in Troy and Wilmore in 1885. Contributed two articles to the *Century Magazine* "Battles and Leaders of the Civil War" series. Helped establish several schools in eastern Kentucky. Published *Bloody Breathitt* (1890), *The Soul Winner* (1896), *Forty Years Among the Highlanders* (1905), *The Galax Gatherers: The Gospel among the Highlanders* (1910), and *The Gospel of the Lilies* (1912). Founded the Inland Mission, also known as the Society of Soul Winners, in 1897 to continue evangelical work in Appalachia. Died in Douglas, Georgia.

Henry W. Halleck (January 16, 1814–January 9, 1872) Born in Westernville, New York, the son of a farmer. Educated at Union College. Graduated from West Point in 1839. Published *Elements of Military Art and Science* (1846). Served in California during the U.S.-Mexican War. Resigned from the army in 1854 as captain. Married Elizabeth Hamilton, granddaughter of Alexander Hamilton, in 1855. Practiced law in California. Published *International Law, or, Rules Regulating the Intercourse of States in Peace and War* (1861). Commissioned as a major general in the regular army in August 1861. Commanded the Department of the Missouri, November 1861–March 1862, and the Department of the Mississippi, March–July 1862. General-in-chief of the Union army from July 11, 1862, to March 12, 1864, when he was succeeded by Ulysses S. Grant. Served as chief of staff for the remainder of the war. Commanded Military Division of the Pacific, 1866–69, and the division of the South, 1869–72. Died in Louisville, Kentucky.

Cornelia Hancock (February 8, 1840–December 31, 1927) Born in Hancock's Bridge, near Salem, New Jersey, the daughter of a Quaker fisherman. Educated in Salem schools. Brother and several cousins enlisted in Union army in 1862. Traveled to Gettysburg with her brother-in-law Dr. Henry T. Child in July 1863 and served as volunteer nurse in Second Corps and general army hospitals until September. Volunteered as nurse at the Contraband Hospital for escaped slaves in Washington, D.C., October 1863–February 1864, and at army hospitals in Virginia at Brandy Station, February–April 1864; Fredericksburg and White House, May–June 1864; and City Point, June 1864–May 1865. Founded the Laing School for freed slaves in Pleasantville, South Carolina, in 1866 with funds from the Freedmen's Bureau and donations from the Philadelphia Yearly Meeting of the Society of Friends. Resigned as principal in 1875 and returned to Philadelphia. Visited England and studied efforts to help the poor in London. Helped found the Philadelphia Society for Organizing Charitable Relief in 1878 and the Children's Aid Society of Philadelphia in 1882. Engaged in philanthropic work in the Sixth Ward and in "Wrightsville," a slum neighborhood in South Philadelphia. Retired in 1914 to Atlantic City, New Jersey, where she died.

John Hay (October 8, 1838–July 1, 1905) Born in Salem, Indiana, the son of a doctor. Family moved to Warsaw, Illinois. Graduated from Brown University in 1858. Studied law in office of his uncle in Springfield, Illinois. Traveled to Washington in 1861 as assistant private secretary to Abraham Lincoln, serving until early in 1865. First secretary to American legation in Paris, 1865–67; chargé d'affaires in Vienna, 1867–68; and legation secretary in Madrid, 1868–70. Published *Castilian Days* (1871) and *Pike County Ballads and Other Pieces* (1871). Married Clara Louise Stone in 1874. Served as assistant secretary of state, 1879–81. Political novel *The Bread-Winners*, an attack on labor unions, published anonymously in 1884. In collaboration with John G. Nicolay, wrote *Abraham Lincoln: A History* (10 volumes, 1890) and edited *Complete Works of Abraham Lincoln* (2 volumes, 1894). Ambassador to Great Britain, 1897–98. Served as secretary of state in the administrations of William McKinley and Theodore Roosevelt, 1898–1905. Among first seven members elected to American Academy of Arts and Letters in 1904. Died in Newbury, New Hampshire.

Charles B. Haydon (1834–March 14, 1864) Born in Vermont. Raised in Decatur, Michigan. Graduated from the University of Michigan in 1857, then read law in Kalamazoo. Joined the Kalamazoo Home Guard on April 22, 1861, then enlisted on May 25 for three years' service in the 2nd Michigan Infantry. Fought at Blackburn's Ford during the First Bull Run campaign. Commissioned second lieutenant in September 1861 and promoted to first lieutenant in February 1862. Fought at Williamsburg, Fair Oaks, the Seven Days' Battles, Second Bull Run, and Fredericksburg; promoted to captain in September 1862. Regiment was sent to Kentucky in April 1863 and to Vicksburg in June as part of the Ninth Corps. Wounded in the shoulder while leading his company at Jackson, Mississippi, on July 11, 1863. Returned to active duty in December 1863 and was made lieutenant colonel of the 2nd Michigan. Died of pneumonia in Cincinnati while returning to Michigan on a thirty-day furlough after reenlisting.

William W. Heartsill (October 17, 1839–July 27, 1916) Born in Louisville, Tennessee. Educated at local schools. Began working in a wholesale merchandise firm in Nashville in 1856. Moved to Marshall, Texas, in 1859, where he became a clerk in a dry goods store. Enlisted in W. P. Lane Rangers, a cavalry company, in April 1861. Helped guard Texas frontier against Indian raids until November 1862, when his company was sent to Arkansas. Taken prisoner in the surrender of Fort Hindman at Arkansas Post, January 1863. Exchanged at City Point, Virginia, in April 1863 and sent to central Tennessee, where the enlisted men from the Lane Rangers became part of a consolidated Texas infantry regiment. Fought at Chickamauga and served in siege of Chattanooga. Deserted in early November 1863 along with several other Lane Rangers and returned to Texas, where he resumed service under his former commander in the Rangers. Served as guard at prisoner-of-war camp at Tyler, Texas, in spring 1864. Posted to Louisiana and Arkansas in summer 1864 before returning to Texas, where he served until the Confederate surrender there in May 1865. Returned to Marshall and acquired a grocery and saddle store. Married Judith Elizabeth Stevens. Printed memoir *Fourteen Hundred and 91 Days in the Confederate Army* one page at a time on his personally owned press, 1874–76. Elected mayor, 1876, and member of the board of aldermen, 1881. Died in Waco, Texas.

Francis J. Higginson (July 19, 1843–September 13, 1931) Born in Boston and raised in Deerfield, Massachusetts. Graduated from U.S. Naval Academy in 1861. Assigned to frigate *Colorado* and was wounded during raid in September 1861 that burned schooner *Judah* in Pensacola harbor. Served on gunboat *Cayuga* in passage of Forts Jackson and St. Philip and the capture of New Orleans. Promoted to lieutenant in August 1862. Assigned to South Atlantic Blockading Squadron and served on gunboat *Vixen*, frigate *Powhatan*, and the sloop *Housatonic*. Participated in bombardment of Charleston Harbor and served in the landing party that unsuccessfully attempted to capture Fort Sumter in September 1863. Executive officer of the *Housatonic* when it was sunk by Confederate submarine *H. L. Hunley*, February 17, 1864. Promoted to lieutenant commander, 1866, and commander, 1876. Married Grace Glenwood Haldane in 1878. Promoted to captain in 1891. Commanded battleship *Massachusetts* in Spanish-American War, 1898, taking part in naval blockade of Cuba and invasion of Puerto Rico. Promoted to commodore, 1898, and rear admiral, 1899. Commanded North Atlantic Fleet, 1901–3. Published *Naval Battles of the Century* (1903). Retired from navy in 1905. Died in Kingston, New York.

Thomas Wentworth Higginson (December 22, 1823–May 9, 1911) Born in Cambridge, Massachusetts, the son of the bursar of Harvard College. Graduated from Harvard in 1841. Taught school and tutored in Boston suburbs before entering Harvard Divinity School. Graduated in 1847 and was ordained by the Unitarian First Religious Society in Newburyport, Massachusetts. Married Mary Elizabeth Channing in 1847. Became active in abolitionism, temperance, women's rights, and other reform movements. Resigned pulpit in 1849. Lectured and wrote for newspapers before becoming minister of nondenominational Free Church in Worcester, Massachusetts, in 1852. Helped lead unsuccessful attempt to free fugitive slave Anthony Burns from the Boston courthouse in 1854 in which a guard was killed. Traveled to Kansas in 1856 with group of antislavery settlers he had helped recruit and outfit. Began contributing essays and stories to the *Atlantic Monthly*. Became member of the "Secret Six," group of radical abolitionists who financed and supported John Brown's raid on Harpers Ferry, 1858–59. Began correspondence with Emily Dickinson in 1862. Joined 51st Massachusetts Infantry as captain in September 1862. Accepted colonelcy of 1st South Carolina Volunteers, regiment of freed slaves raised in the Sea Islands, in November 1862. Led series of expeditions that gathered supplies and freed slaves in coastal Georgia, Florida, and South Carolina from January until July 1863, when he was wounded. Fell ill with malaria in October 1863. Wrote letters to newspapers calling for equal pay for black soldiers. Left South Carolina in May 1864 and moved to Newport, Rhode Island. Resigned commission in October 1864. Continued writing for magazines and became advocate for woman suffrage. Published novel *Malbone: An Oldport Romance* (1869), memoir *Army Life in a Black Regiment* (1870), and *Young Folks' History of the United States* (1875). Wife died in 1877. Moved to Cambridge, Massachusetts, in 1878. Married Mary (Minnie) Potter Thatcher, 1879. Served as Republican in the Massachusetts house of representatives, 1879–83. Edited *Poems* (1890) of Emily Dickinson with Mabel Loomis Todd. Published memoirs *Cheerful Yesterdays* (1898) and *Parts of a Man's Life* (1905). Died in Cambridge.

Emma Holmes (December 17, 1838–January 1910) Born in Charleston, South Carolina, the daughter of a physician and plantation owner. Family moved to Camden, South Carolina, in June 1862, where she began teaching. Returned after the war to Charleston, where she continued to teach and tutor. Died in Charleston.

BIOGRAPHICAL NOTES 773

Jedediah Hotchkiss (November 30, 1828–January 17, 1899). Born near Windsor, New York, the son of a farmer. Graduated from Windsor Academy in 1846. Taught school for a year in Lykens Valley, Pennsylvania, then became tutor to family living on Mossy Creek in the Shenandoah Valley of Virginia. Taught himself mapmaking. Became principal of the newly established Mossy Creek Academy in 1852. Married Sara Ann Comfort in 1853. Moved in 1859 to Churchville, Virginia, where he opened the Loch Willow Academy. Closed the academy in June 1861 and offered services to Confederate army. Served as mapmaker for Confederate forces in western Virginia until August 1861, when he contracted typhoid fever. Resumed military service in March 1862 and became topographical engineer on the staff of Thomas J. (Stonewall) Jackson. Performed reconnaissances and made detailed maps during Jackson's Shenandoah Valley campaign in the spring of 1862. Remained in the valley until July 1862, then rejoined Jackson's staff and served in the Second Manassas and Maryland campaigns and at Fredericksburg and Chancellorsville. Following Jackson's death, continued mapmaking and reconnaissance duties under Richard S. Ewell during Gettysburg campaign. Served under Jubal Early in his raid on Washington and in the subsequent campaign in the Shenandoah Valley. Performed reconnaissance duties in western Virginia in the spring of 1865. Kept a school in Staunton, Virginia, 1865–67. Published *The Battlefields of Virginia; Chancellorsville* with William Allan (1867). Continued to work as topographer, and became promoter and investor in mining and land development projects in western Virginia and West Virginia. Published *Virginia: A Geographical and Political Summary* (1876) and, with Joseph A. Waddell, *Historical Atlas of Augusta County* (1885). Contributed maps to the *Atlas of the War of the Rebellion* (1880–1901). Wrote *Virginia*, third volume in twelve-volume series *Confederate Military History* (1899). Died in Staunton, Virginia.

David Hunter (July 21, 1802–February 2, 1886) Born in Princeton, New Jersey, the son of a Presbyterian minister. Graduated from West Point in 1822. Married Maria Indiana Kinzie, 1829. Resigned commission in July 1836, but reentered the army in November 1841 as paymaster. Commissioned as brigadier general of volunteers, May 1861, and promoted to major general, August 1861. Led brigade at First Bull Run, where he was wounded. Commanded Department of Kansas, November 1861–March 1862, and Department of the South, March–September 1862 and January–June 1863. Declared military emancipation of slaves in Department of the South, May 9, 1862; his order was revoked by President Lincoln on May 19. Attempted to recruit black regiments in the spring of 1862 but failed to receive War

Department authorization. Served as president of the court-martial that convicted General Fitz John Porter in January 1863. Commanded the Army of West Virginia in the Shenandoah Valley, May–June 1864. Retreated from the valley following his defeat at Lynchburg, and resigned command in August 1864. President of the military commission that tried the conspirators in the Lincoln assassination, May–June 1865. Resigned commission on July 31, 1866. Died in Washington, D.C.

John S. Jackman (December 1841–December 21, 1912). Born in Carroll County, Kentucky. Worked as carpenter and schoolteacher. Moved to Bardstown. Enlisted in September 1861 at Bowling Green in the Confederate 5th (later the 9th) Kentucky Infantry. Saw action at Shiloh, Stones River, Chickamauga, Chattanooga, and in the Atlanta campaign. Wounded in the head by shell fragment at Pine Mountain, Georgia, on June 14, 1864. Rejoined regiment in December 1864 in Georgia, where he spent the remainder of the war. Studied law in Russellville, Kentucky, after the war and began successful chancery practice in Louisville in 1871. Helped publish the Confederate veterans' journal *Southern Bivouac*, 1882–87. Died in Louisville.

Harriet Ann Jacobs (1813–March 7, 1897) Born in Edenton, North Carolina, the daughter of slaves. After the death of her mother in 1819, she was raised by her grandmother and her white mistress, Margaret Horniblow, who taught her to read, write, and sew. In 1825 Horniblow died, and Jacobs was sent to the household of Dr. James Norcom. At sixteen, to escape Norcom's repeated sexual advances, Jacobs began a relationship with a white lawyer, Samuel Tredwell Sawyer (later a member of the U.S. House of Representatives), with whom she had two children, Joseph (b. 1829) and Louisa Matilda (b. 1833). In 1835, Jacobs ran away and spent the next seven years hiding in a crawl space above her freed grandmother's storeroom. In 1842, she escaped to New York City, where she was reunited with her children. Worked as a nurse for the family of Nathaniel Parker Willis; moved to Boston in 1843 to avoid recapture by Norcom. Moved to Rochester in 1849, where she became part of a circle of abolitionists surrounding Frederick Douglass. In 1852, Cornelia Grinnell Willis, second wife of Nathaniel Parker Willis, purchased Jacobs's manumission. Published *Incidents in the Life of a Slave Girl, Written by Herself* pseudonymously in 1861. From 1862 to 1868 engaged in Quaker-sponsored relief work among former slaves in Washington, D.C.; Alexandria, Virginia; and Savannah, Georgia. She then lived with her daughter in Cambridge, Massachusetts, and in Washington, D.C., where she died.

Hannah Johnson (c. 1820–?) The daughter of a slave who escaped from Louisiana to the North before her birth, Johnson was self-taught and was living in Buffalo, New York, in 1863 when she wrote to President Lincoln about her son, who was serving in the 54th Massachusetts Volunteer Infantry.

Charles C. Jones Jr. (October 28, 1831–July 19, 1893) Born in Savannah, Georgia, the son of minister Charles C. Jones and Mary Jones. Educated at South Carolina College and the College of New Jersey (Princeton). Graduated from Dane Law School at Harvard, 1855. Practiced law in Savannah, where he served as alderman, 1859–60, and mayor, 1860–61. Married Ruth Berrien Whitehead, 1858, and after her death, Eva Berrien Eve, 1863. Commissioned lieutenant in Chatham Artillery, August 1861. Promoted to lieutenant colonel and made chief of artillery for Georgia, October 1862. Practiced law in New York City, 1866–77, then returned to Georgia. Published several historical and archaeological studies, including *Indian Remains in Southern Georgia* (1859), *The Monumental Remains of Georgia* (1861), *Antiquities of the Southern Indians* (1873), and *The History of Georgia* (1883). Died in Augusta, Georgia.

Charles C. Jones Sr. (December 20, 1804–March 16, 1863) Born in Liberty County, Georgia, the son of a plantation owner. Educated at Phillips Andover Academy, Andover Theological Seminary, and Princeton Theological Seminary. Married first cousin Mary Jones in 1830. Pastor of the First Presbyterian Church, Savannah, 1831–32. Returned to Liberty County, where he owned three plantations. Taught at Columbia Theological Seminary, South Carolina, 1837–38 and 1848–50. Published *Catechism of Scripture Doctrine and Practice* (1837) and *The Religious Instruction of the Negroes of the United States* (1842). Lived in Philadelphia, 1850–53, while serving as the corresponding secretary of the board of domestic missions of the Presbyterian Church. Died in Liberty County.

John B. Jones (March 6, 1810–February 4, 1866) Born in Baltimore, Maryland. Lived in Kentucky and Missouri as a boy. Married Frances Custis in 1840. Became editor of the *Saturday Visitor* in Baltimore, 1841. Published several novels, including *Wild Western Scenes* (1841), *The War Path* (1858), and *Wild Southern Scenes* (1859). Established weekly newspaper *Southern Monitor* in Philadelphia, 1857. Fearing arrest as a Confederate sympathizer, Jones moved in 1861 to Richmond, Virginia, where he worked as a clerk in the Confederate War Department. Died in Burlington, New Jersey, shortly before the publication of *A Rebel War Clerk's Diary*.

Elizabeth Blair Lee (June 20, 1818–September 13, 1906) Born in Frankfort, Kentucky, daughter of journalist Francis Preston Blair and

Elizabeth Gist Blair, sister of Montgomery Blair (postmaster general, 1861–64) and Frank Blair (a Union major general, 1862–65). Moved with family in 1830 to Washington, D.C., where her father edited the *Globe* and advised Andrew Jackson. Educated at boarding school in Philadelphia. Married naval officer Samuel Phillips Lee, a cousin of Robert E. Lee, in 1843. Became board member and active patron of the Washington City Orphan Asylum in 1849. Lived in Washington and at the Blair estate in Silver Spring, Maryland. Died in Washington.

Robert E. Lee (January 19, 1807–October 12, 1870) Born in Westmoreland County, Virginia, the son of Revolutionary War hero Henry "Light-Horse Harry" Lee and Ann Carter Lee. Graduated from West Point in 1829. Married Mary Custis, great-granddaughter of Martha Washington, in 1831. Served in the U.S.-Mexican War, and as superintendent of West Point, 1852–55. Promoted to colonel in March 1861. Resigned commission on April 20, 1861, after declining offer of field command of the Federal army. Served as commander of Virginia military forces, April–July 1861; commander in western Virginia, August–October 1861; commander of the southern Atlantic coast, November 1861–March 1862; and military advisor to Jefferson Davis, March–May 1862. Assumed command of the Army of Northern Virginia on June 1, 1862, and led it until April 9, 1865, when he surrendered to Ulysses S. Grant at Appomattox. Named general-in-chief of all Confederate forces, February 1865. Became president of Washington College (now Washington and Lee), September 1865. Died in Lexington, Virginia.

Francis Lieber (March 18, 1798–October 2, 1872) Born Franz Lieber in Berlin, Prussia. Fought in the Prussian army in the Waterloo campaign and was seriously wounded at Namur. Imprisoned for four months for anti-government activities in 1819. Received degree in mathematics from Jena in 1820. Studied at Dresden, then served briefly as volunteer in the Greek War of Independence in 1822. Left Greece and traveled to Rome, where the Prussian ambassador, the historian Barthold Niebuhr, encouraged him to publish a book on his experiences in Greece (it appeared in 1823). Returned to Berlin in 1823 and continued his study of mathematics. Arrested in 1824 and imprisoned for six months for alleged subversion. Fled to England in 1826. Immigrated to Boston in 1827, where he served as director of a newly established gymnasium and swimming school. After the gymnasium venture failed, edited the *Encyclopaedia Americana*, published successfully in thirteen volumes, 1829–33. Married Mathilda Oppenheimer in 1829. Moved to Philadelphia in 1834 and published a constitution and plan of education for Girard College. Accepted a chair in history and political economy at South Carolina College (later University of South Carolina) in Columbia in 1835. Published numerous books and essays on law, government, and politics, including *Legal and Political Hermeneutics* (1837), *Manual of Political Ethics* (1838–39), and *On Civil Liberty and Self-Government* (1853). Resigned position in South Carolina in 1855. Appointed professor of history and political science at Columbia College in New York in 1857. During the Civil War one of his sons was killed fighting for the Confederacy in 1862, while his other two sons fought for the Union, one of them losing an arm at Fort Donelson. Became adviser to Henry W. Halleck on the laws of war. Wrote *A Code for the Government of Armies*, issued in revised form by the Union War Department as General Orders No. 100 in April 1863. Became professor at Columbia Law School in 1865. Helped gather and preserve the records of the Confederate government. Appointed in 1870 to commission settling claims arising from the U.S.-Mexican War. Died in New York City.

Abraham Lincoln (February 12, 1809–April 15, 1865) Born near Hodgenville, Kentucky, the son of a farmer and carpenter. Family moved to Indiana in 1816 and to Illinois in 1830. Settled in New Salem, Illinois, and worked as a storekeeper, surveyor, and postmaster. Served as a Whig in the state legislature, 1834–41. Began law practice in 1836 and moved to Springfield in 1837. Married Mary Todd in 1842. Elected to Congress as a Whig and served from 1847 to 1849. Became a public opponent of the extension of slavery after the passage of the Kansas-Nebraska Act in 1854. Helped found the Republican Party of Illinois in 1856. Campaigned in 1858 for Senate seat held by Stephen A. Douglas and debated him seven times on the slavery issue; although the Illinois legislature reelected Douglas, the campaign brought Lincoln national prominence. Received Republican presidential nomination in 1860 and won election in a four-way contest; his victory led to the secession of seven southern states. Responded to the Confederate bombardment of Fort Sumter by calling up militia, proclaiming the blockade of southern ports, and suspending habeas corpus. Issued preliminary and final emancipation proclamations on September 22, 1862, and January 1, 1863. Appointed Ulysses S. Grant commander of all Union forces in March 1864. Won reelection in 1864 by defeating Democrat George B. McClellan. Died in Washington, D.C., after being shot by John Wilkes Booth.

Theodore Lyman (August 23, 1833–September 9, 1897) Born in Waltham, Massachusetts, the son of a wealthy merchant and textile manufacturer. Graduated from Harvard in 1855. Studied natural history with Louis Agassiz after graduation. Traveled to Florida in 1856 to collect marine specimens for the Harvard Museum of Comparative Zoology. Graduated from Lawrence Scientific School at Harvard in 1858. Married Elizabeth Russell, a cousin of Robert Gould Shaw, in

1858. Traveled in Europe, 1861–63. Joined staff of George G. Meade in September 1863 with rank of lieutenant colonel and served until Lee's surrender. Returned to home in Brookline, Massachusetts, and resumed work at Museum of Comparative Zoology. Served in Congress as an independent, 1883–85. Retired from scientific work in 1887 due to failing health. Died in Brookline.

Judith W. McGuire (March 19, 1813–March 21, 1897) Born Judith White Brockenbrough near Richmond, Virginia, the daughter of a judge. Married John P. McGuire, an Episcopalian rector, in 1846. Moved to Alexandria in 1852 when husband became principal of the Episcopal High School of Virginia. Fled Alexandria in May 1861 and settled in Richmond in February 1862. Worked as a clerk in the Confederate commissary department, November 1863–April 1864. Published *Diary of a Southern Refugee, During the War* (1867). Kept a school with her husband in Essex County in the 1870s. Published *General Robert E. Lee: The Christian Soldier* (1873). Died in Richmond.

Lafayette McLaws (January 15, 1821–July 24, 1897) Born in Augusta, Georgia, the son of a cotton broker. Attended the University of Virginia, 1837–38. Graduated from West Point in 1842 and was commissioned in the infantry. Saw action in the war with Mexico at Fort Brown, Monterrey, and the siege of Veracruz. Married Emily Taylor, niece of Zachary Taylor, in 1849. Served in New Mexico, Indian Territory, and Utah. Resigned commission as captain in March 1861 and joined the Confederacy. Commissioned colonel of the 10th Georgia Infantry in June 1861. Promoted to brigadier general, September 1861, and major general, May 1862. Led division at Williamsburg, Savage's Station, Malvern Hill, Harpers Ferry, Antietam, Fredericksburg, Chancellorsville, Gettysburg, the siege of Chattanooga, and Knoxville, Relieved of his command in December 1863 by his corps commander James Longstreet for failing to capture Fort Sanders during the Knoxville campaign. Assigned to defend Savannah, Georgia, in May 1864. Commanded division in the Carolinas campaign and at Bentonville. Served as court clerk in Richmond County, Georgia, 1866–68. Bought farm in Effingham County, Georgia, in 1870. Appointed postmaster for Savannah by Ulysses S. Grant in 1876 and served until 1885. President of company that sought to build canal from the Atlantic to the Gulf of Mexico, 1876–84. Died in Savannah.

George G. Meade (December 31, 1815–November 6, 1872) Born in Cádiz, Spain, the son of an American merchant. Family returned to Philadelphia in 1816. Graduated from West Point in 1835. Resigned in 1836 to work as engineer and surveyor. Married Margaretta Sergeant in 1840. Reentered army in 1842 as topographical engineer. Served under Zachary Taylor in the U.S.-Mexican War at Palo Alto, Resaca de la Palma, and Monterrey, and under Winfield Scott in the siege of Veracruz. Engaged in engineering and surveying duties in Delaware Bay, Florida, and the northern lakes, 1847–61. Commissioned as brigadier general of volunteers, August 1861. Became brigade commander in the Army of the Potomac, October 1861. Fought at Mechanicsville, Gaines's Mill, and Glendale, where he was wounded. Returned to duty in August 1862. Commanded brigade at Second Bull Run and a division at South Mountain and Antietam, where he temporarily led the First Corps after Joseph Hooker was wounded. Promoted to major general of volunteers, November 1862. Commanded division at Fredericksburg. Appointed commander of the Fifth Corps in December 1862 and led it at Chancellorsville. Replaced Hooker as commander of the Army of the Potomac on June 28, 1863, and led it until the end of the war. Received the thanks of Congress for his victory at Gettysburg. Promoted to major general in the regular army, September 23, 1864. Held postwar commands in the South and in the mid-Atlantic states. Died in Philadelphia.

Montgomery C. Meigs (May 3, 1816–January 2, 1892) Born in Augusta, Georgia, the son of a physician. Moved with family to Philadelphia. Graduated from West Point in 1836 and began service in engineering corps. Married Louisa Rodgers in 1841. Supervised construction of the Washington Aqueduct, 1852–60, and of the wings and dome of the Capitol, 1853–59. Promoted to brigadier general, May 1861, and made army quartermaster general, a post he held throughout the war. Designed the Pension Building in Washington, D.C., after retiring from the army in 1882. Died in Washington.

Herman Melville (August 1, 1819–September 28, 1891) Born in New York City, the son of a merchant. Educated at schools in New York City and in upstate New York. Worked as bank clerk, bookkeeper, and schoolteacher. Sailed for Pacific on whaling ship in 1841 and returned in 1844 on frigate *United States*. Published *Typee* (1846) and *Omoo* (1847), fictionalized accounts of his experiences in the South Seas. Married Elizabeth Shaw in 1847. Published *Mardi* (1849), *Redburn* (1849), *White-Jacket* (1850), *Moby-Dick* (1851), *Pierre; or, The Ambiguities* (1852), *Israel Potter* (1855), *The Piazza Tales* (1856), and *The Confidence-Man* (1857). Visited Union troops in Virginia in spring 1864. Published poetry collection *Battle-Pieces and Aspects of the War* (1866). Worked as customs inspector in New York City, 1866–85. Published long poem *Clarel* (1876) and two small books of poetry, *John Marr and Other Sailors* (1888) and *Timoleon* (1891). Died in New York City, leaving *Billy Budd, Sailor*, in manuscript.

Matthew M. Miller (November 28, 1840–1918) Born in Galena, Illinois. Attended Yale College but left school to enlist as a private in the 45th Illinois Volunteers. Fought at Shiloh. Promoted to first lieutenant, June 1862, and became captain of Company I, 9th Louisiana (African Descent) Infantry, November 1862. Fought at Milliken's Bend. Mustered out in May 1865. Returned to Illinois and practiced law. Married Anna Florence Woodbury in Boston in 1873. Moved to Kansas, where he died.

Sarah Morgan (February 28, 1842–May 5, 1909) Born in New Orleans, the daughter of a lawyer. Family moved in 1850 to Baton Rouge, where father served as a judge. Spent war with widowed mother and sisters in Baton Rouge, in the countryside near Port Hudson, and in Union-occupied New Orleans. Two of her brothers died of illness in January 1864 while serving in the Confederate army. Moved with mother to brother's plantation near Columbia, South Carolina, in 1872. Began writing editorials for the Charleston *News and Courier* in 1873 as "Mr. Fowler." Married Francis Warrington Dawson, editor of the *News and Courier*, in 1874. Husband killed in 1889 by doctor who had been paying unwanted attentions to family's governess. Moved in 1899 to Paris, where her son lived. Published *Les Aventures de Jeannot Lap*, version of Brer Rabbit stories, in 1903. Died in Paris.

Charles F. Morse (September 22, 1839–December 11, 1926) Born in Boston, Massachusetts. Graduated from Harvard in 1858. Commissioned as first lieutenant in Company B of the 2nd Massachusetts Infantry in May 1861. Became friends with fellow officer Robert Gould Shaw. Fought at Front Royal. Promoted to captain in July 1862 and fought at Cedar Mountain and Antietam. Served as provost marshal of the Twelfth Corps during the Chancellorsville campaign. Promoted to major and fought with 2nd Massachusetts at Gettysburg. Sent with regiment to Tennessee in early autumn 1863. Promoted to lieutenant colonel. Served in Atlanta campaign and in Sherman's march across Georgia. Led regiment in the Carolinas campaign until March 16, 1865, when he was wounded at Averasborough, North Carolina. Mustered out in July 1865. After failed attempt at cotton farming in Georgia, became general superintendent of the Atchison, Topeka, and Santa Fe Railroad in 1870. Married Ellen Mary Holdrege in 1874. Appointed general manager of the Kansas City Stockyards Company in 1879 by Charles Francis Adams, Jr., the company president. Successfully increased stockyard business and later served as company president. Published *Letters Written During the Civil War, 1861–1865* (1898). Retired to Falmouth, Massachusetts, in 1913. Wrote memoir *A Sketch of My Life Written for My Children: And a Buffalo*

Hunt in Nebraska in 1871, posthumously published in 1927. Died in Falmouth.

William H. Neblett (March 2, 1826–May 4, 1871) Born in Winchester, Mississippi, the son of a physician. Family moved to Texas in 1839. Attended school in Anderson and studied law. Married Elizabeth Rowan Scott in 1852. Moved in 1855 to Corsicana, where he practiced law and raised cotton and corn on plantation. Edited weekly secessionist newspaper *Navarro Express* in 1860. Moved to Lake Creek in Grimes County in 1861. Enlisted as private in the 20th Texas Infantry in March 1863. Served at Galveston as guard for gunboat *Bayou City* before obtaining position as clerk in brigade headquarters. Transferred to quartermaster department in Houston in July 1864 on grounds of ill health, suffering from rheumatism and neuralgia. Returned to plantation after war. Died in Anderson, Texas.

Oliver W. Norton (December 17, 1839–October 1, 1920) Born in Angelica, New York, the son of a Presbyterian minister. Educated at academy in Montrose, Pennsylvania. Taught school in 1858 in Waites Corner, New York. Family moved to Springfield, Pennsylvania, in 1860, where he taught school and worked on a farm. Enlisted in Company K, 83rd Pennsylvania Infantry, in 1861. Served as brigade bugler under Daniel Butterfield and became first bugler to play "Taps." Saw action in the Seven Days' Battles, Second Bull Run, Fredericksburg, Chancellorsville, and Gettysburg, where he served as Strong Vincent's brigade bugler during the fighting for Little Round Top. Commissioned first lieutenant with the 8th U.S. Colored Troops in November 1863. Fought at Olustee, Petersburg, and Darbytown Road. Mustered out in November 1865. Worked as bank clerk in New York City. Married Lucy Coit Fanning in 1870. Moved to Chicago and established business manufacturing cans and sheet-metal goods with his brother Edwin. Published *Army Letters 1861–1865* (1903), *Strong Vincent and his brigade at Gettysburg, July 2, 1863* (1909), and *The Attack and Defense of Little Round Top* (1913). Died in Chicago.

Frederick Law Olmsted (April 26, 1822–August 23, 1903) Born in Hartford, Connecticut, the son of a merchant. Attended schools in Hartford and boarded with several tutors in Connecticut and Massachusetts. Worked in dry goods importing firm in New York City, 1840–42. Traveled to Canton (Guangzhou), China, 1842–43. Studied farming and moved in 1848 to a farm his father purchased for him on Staten Island, New York, where he experimented with new agricultural and landscaping methods. Visited Europe in 1850. Published *Walks and Talks of an American Farmer in England* (1852). Traveled through the South, 1852–54. Published *A Journey in the Seaboard*

Slave States (1856), later much expanded as *The Cotton Kingdom: A Traveler's Observations on Cotton and Slavery in the American Slave States* (1861). Won contest along with Calvert Vaux to design new Central Park in Manhattan and was named architect-in-chief of the project in 1858. Married Mary Cleveland Olmsted, his brother's widow, in 1859. Became general secretary of the U.S. Sanitary Commission in 1861. Directed operations of hospital ships during the Peninsula campaign, May–July 1862. Made inspection tour of the Midwest and Mississippi valley, February–April 1863. Resigned from Sanitary Commission in September 1863 and became manager of the Mariposa Estate in northern California. Returned to New York in 1865 and established landscape architecture firm with Vaux, working on park and college campus projects across the United States. Moved to Brookline, Massachusetts, in 1881. Retired in 1895. Suffering from senility, became a patient in 1898 at McLean Asylum in Belmont, Massachusetts, where he died.

John Paris (September 1, 1809–October 6, 1883) Born in Orange County, North Carolina. Licensed to preach in the Methodist Protestant Church in 1839. Ordained as a deacon in 1842 and chosen as a church elder in 1844. Married Sally Ann Bellamy in 1845. Following her death, married Maria Yancey in 1849. Published *History of the Methodist Protestant Church* (1849) and *Baptism, Its Mode, Its Design, and Its Subjects* (1852). Moved to Virginia in 1852. Became chaplain of the 54th North Carolina Infantry in July 1862 and served with regiment at Fredericksburg, Chancellorsville, Plymouth, Drewry's Bluff, and in the Shenandoah Valley and Appomattox campaigns. Served as pastor on the Albemarle Circuit in North Carolina after the war. Published "Soldier's History of the War" in periodical *Our Living and Our Dead* (1874–76), "Causes Which Produced the War" in *Southern Historical Monthly* (1876), and *The Methodist Protestant Manual* (1878). Died in Buffalo Springs, Virginia.

Edmund DeWitt Patterson (March 20, 1842–May 22, 1914) Born Lorain County, Ohio, the son of a farmer and a schoolteacher. Raised by his grandfather and uncle after his mother's death in 1852. Attended local schools to age seventeen. Sold books and magazines in Tennessee and Alabama. Taught school and worked as a store clerk in Waterloo, Alabama. Enlisted in May 1861 in Company D, 9th Alabama Infantry. Saw action at Williamsburg and Fair Oaks and was seriously wounded at Glendale. Rejoined regiment in November 1862. Fought at Chancellorsville and Gettysburg, where he was captured on July 2, 1863. Held in prison camp at Johnson's Island, Ohio, until prisoner exchange in March 1865. Studied law after the war. Married Eleanor Mildred McDougal in 1869 and entered law partnership with her father, serving as clerk and master of chancery court for Hardin County, Tennessee, 1870–82. Elected to Tennessee state senate for one term in 1882. Served as circuit court judge, 1886–97. Died in Redlands, California.

Catharine Peirce (March 16, 1828–April 2, 1867) Born Catharine Milner in Pennsylvania, the daughter of a schoolteacher. Married Taylor Peirce in York County, Pennsylvania, in 1846. Joined husband, who had been working as a farm laborer, in Union, Iowa, in 1851. Spent war with children, brother, and sister-in-law in Des Moines, Iowa, helping brother to run boardinghouse for transient soldiers while her husband served in the Union army. Died in Des Moines while giving birth to her daughter Catharine, who survived.

Taylor Peirce (July 20, 1822–November 21, 1901) Born in Chester County, Pennsylvania. Married Catharine Milner in York County, Pennsylvania, in 1846. Traveled to Iowa to trade with Fox and Sac Indians. Became farm laborer in Iowa in 1850. Enlisted in 22nd Iowa Infantry at Newton in August 1862 and became sergeant in Company C. Served in southern Missouri, in the Vicksburg campaign, and in southern Louisiana and coastal Texas. Sent with regiment to the Shenandoah Valley in August 1864 and fought at Winchester and Cedar Creek. Served with regiment on garrison duty at Savannah, Georgia, and Morehead City, North Carolina, in winter and spring of 1865. Returned after the war to Des Moines, Iowa, where his wife died in 1867. Served as city clerk of Des Moines, 1871–79, and city auditor, 1874–77. Married Eliza Ann Van Horn in 1873. After 1879 worked in grain business and in a plow factory. Died in Des Moines.

George Hamilton Perkins (October 20, 1836–October 24, 1899) Born in Hopkinton, New Hampshire, the son of a lawyer. Graduated from the U.S. Naval Academy in 1856. Returned to the United States from West Africa in summer 1861 and was assigned to the gunboat *Cayuga* as first lieutenant in December 1861. Served in passage of Forts Jackson and St. Philip and the capture of New Orleans, April 1862. Patrolled the lower Mississippi River and served on blockade duty off Mobile, Alabama and the Texas coast, 1862–64. Promoted to lieutenant commander, December 1862. Assumed command of the ironclad monitor *Chickasaw* in July 1864. Fought in battle of Mobile Bay, August 5, 1864. Commanded *Chickasaw* on Gulf blockade duty for remainder of the war. Married Anna Minot Weld in 1870. Retired as captain in 1891. Died in Boston.

Samuel Pickens (June 9, 1841–September 9, 1890) Born in Greensboro, Alabama, the son of a wealthy plantation owner. Attended University of Virginia. Helped manage family plantation before the war. Enlisted in Company D, 5th Alabama Infantry, in September 1862. Fought at Chancellorsville and Gettysburg. Wounded at Winchester on September 19, 1864. Captured at Petersburg on April 2, 1865. Returned to family plantation after war.

Whitelaw Reid (October 27, 1837–December 15, 1912). Born near Cedarville, Ohio, the son of a farmer. Graduated from Miami University in 1856. Edited and published the *Xenia News*, 1857–60. Supported Abraham Lincoln in the 1860 presidential election. In 1861 began contributing to the *Cincinnati Times*, *Cleveland Herald*, and *Cincinnati Gazette*. Reported on the 1861 Union offensive in western Virginia and the battle of Shiloh for the *Gazette*. Became the Washington correspondent for the *Gazette* in June 1862, signing his dispatches "Agate," while also contributing reports to the *Chicago Tribune* and newspapers in St. Louis, Cleveland, Detroit, and Pittsburgh. Reported from the field at Gettysburg. Published *After the War* (1866), describing his travels through the South following the Confederate surrender. Unsuccessfully tried to raise cotton in Louisiana and Alabama, 1866–67. Published *Ohio in the War: Her Statesmen, Her Generals, and Soldiers* (1868). Reported on the impeachment trial of President Andrew Johnson and the 1868 political conventions for the *Gazette*. Joined the *New York Tribune* in 1868 and served as its managing editor, 1869–72. Following the death of Horace Greeley, he became the *Tribune*'s editor, 1872–1905, and publisher, 1872–1912. Served as U.S. minister to France, 1889–92. Nominated by the 1892 Republican convention as vice presidential running mate for President Benjamin Harrison (election was won by former president Grover Cleveland). Served as member of the commission that negotiated peace treaty with Spain in 1898 and as U.S. ambassador to Great Britain, 1905–12. Died in London.

John M. Schofield (September 29, 1831–March 4, 1906) Born in Gerry, New York, the son of a Baptist minister. Family moved to Bristol, Illinois, in 1843. Worked as surveyor and teacher before being nominated for West Point. Graduated in 1853 and commissioned in artillery. Taught natural philosophy at West Point, 1855–60. Married Harriet Whitehorn Bartlett in 1857. Obtained leave of absence in 1860 to teach physics at Washington University in St. Louis. Commissioned as major in 1st Missouri Infantry in April 1861. Served as chief of staff to Nathaniel Lyon and saw action at Wilson's Creek, where Lyon was killed. Promoted to brigadier general in November 1861 and held series of positions in Missouri. Commanded Department of the Missouri, May 1863–January 1864. Commanded the Army of the Ohio in the Atlanta campaign. Promoted to major general in May 1864. Commanded Twenty-third Corps at Franklin and Nashville and in

North Carolina, where he joined Sherman's army in March 1865. Served as agent of the State Department in France, 1865–66, negotiating withdrawal of French troops from Mexico. Commanded the Department of the Potomac, August 1866–June 1868, implementing Reconstruction in Virginia. Secretary of War under President Andrew Johnson, June 1868–March 1869. Commanded Department of the Missouri, 1869–70, and the Department of the Pacific, 1870–76. Traveled to Hawaii in 1872 and recommended acquisition of naval base at Pearl Harbor. Superintendent of West Point, 1876–81. Commanding general of United States Army, 1888–95. After death of first wife, married Georgia Kilburne in 1891. Published *Forty-six Years in the Army* (1897). Died in St. Augustine, Florida.

Raphael Semmes (September 27, 1809–August 30, 1877) Born in Charles County, Maryland. Raised by his uncle in Washington, D.C., after being orphaned in early childhood. Appointed midshipman in U.S. Navy in 1826. Served in Mediterranean, West Indies, and in Florida during the Second Seminole War. Promoted to lieutenant in 1837. Married Anne Elizabeth Spencer in 1837, the same year he was promoted to lieutenant. Assigned to blockade duty at the outbreak of the U.S.-Mexican War and took command of the brig *Somers* in October 1846. Exonerated by court of inquiry after *Somers* sank in a sudden squall on December 8, 1846, with the loss of more than half its crew. Served in landing at Veracruz and subsequent march to Mexico City. Practiced law in Mobile, Alabama, after the war while awaiting orders. Published *Service Afloat and Ashore during the Mexican War* (1851). Promoted to commander in 1855. Resigned from U.S. Navy in February 1861. Commissioned as commander in the Confederate navy in March 1861 and given command of commerce raider *Sumter*. Escaped blockade in the Gulf of Mexico in June 1861 and captured or burned eighteen American merchant vessels in the Caribbean and Atlantic before being blockaded in Gibraltar in January 1862. Promoted to captain and assumed command of raider *Alabama* in August 1862. Captured or destroyed sixty-four American ships in the Caribbean, Atlantic Ocean, and Indian Ocean before the *Alabama* was sunk off Cherbourg, France, by the Union sloop *Kearsarge* on June 19, 1864. Escaped to England on a British yacht and returned to Virginia in January 1865. Commanded James River Squadron until the end of the war. Arrested for treason in December 1865 but was released in April 1866. Taught literature and philosophy at Louisiana State Seminary (later Louisiana State University) and edited *Memphis Daily Bulletin* before returning to law practice in Mobile. Published *Memoirs of Service Afloat during the War Between the States* (1869). Died at Point Clear, Alabama.

Robert Gould Shaw (October 10, 1837–July 18, 1863) Born in Boston, the son of a wealthy merchant and lawyer; both parents were active abolitionists. Family moved to West Roxbury, Massachusetts, in 1841 and to Staten Island, New York, in 1847. Traveled with family in Europe, 1851–56, and was educated at boarding school in Switzerland and by private tutors in Hanover, Germany. Attended Harvard, 1856–59. Worked for uncle's mercantile company in New York City, 1859–61. Commissioned as second lieutenant in 2nd Massachusetts Infantry in May 1861 and was later promoted to captain. Fought at Front Royal, Cedar Mountain, and Antietam. Accepted colonelcy of 54th Massachusetts Infantry, the first black regiment to be raised by a northern state, in January 1863. Married Annie Kneeland Haggerty on May 2, 1863, shortly before regiment left for South Carolina. Led regiment in raid on Darien, Georgia, June 11, 1863. Killed while leading assault on Fort Wagner in Charleston Harbor and was buried in mass grave with his soldiers.

William T. Sherman (February 8, 1820–February 14, 1891) Born in Lancaster, Ohio, the son of an attorney. Graduated from West Point in 1840. Served in Florida and California, but did not see action in the U.S.-Mexican War. Married Ellen Ewing in 1850. Promoted to captain; resigned his commission in 1853. Managed bank branch in San Francisco, 1853–57. Moved in 1858 to Leavenworth, Kansas, where he worked in real estate and was admitted to the bar. Named first superintendent of the Louisiana State Seminary of Learning and Military Academy at Alexandria (now Louisiana State University) in 1859. Resigned position when Louisiana seceded in January 1861. Commissioned colonel, 13th U.S. Infantry, May 1861. Commanded brigade at First Bull Run, July 1861. Appointed brigadier general of volunteers, August 1861, and ordered to Kentucky. Assumed command of the Department of the Cumberland, October 1861, but was relieved in November at his own request. Returned to field in March 1862 and commanded division under Ulysses S. Grant at Shiloh. Promoted major general of volunteers, May 1862. Commanded corps under Grant during Vicksburg campaign, and succeeded him as commander of the Army of the Tennessee, October 1863, and as commander of the Military Division of the Mississippi, March 1864. Captured Atlanta, September 1864, and led march through Georgia, November–December 1864. Marched army through the Carolinas and accepted the surrender of Confederate General Joseph E. Johnston at Durham Station, North Carolina, April 26, 1865. Promoted to lieutenant general, 1866, and general, 1869, when he became commander of the army. Published controversial *Memoirs of General W. T. Sherman* (1875, revised 1886). Retired from army in 1884 and moved to New

York City. Rejected possible Republican presidential nomination, 1884. Died in New York City.

William Wrenshall Smith (August 15, 1830–c. 1904) Born in Washington, Pennsylvania, where he graduated from Washington College in 1852. Worked in the family dry goods business and banking office. His mother was the sister of Ellen Wrenshall Dent, Ulysses S. Grant's mother-in-law, and during the Civil War he visited Grant's headquarters several times. Married Emma Willard McKennan in 1867. Founded Trinity Hall, a boys' school, in Washington, Pennsylvania, in 1879.

George E. Stephens (1832–April 24, 1888) Born in Philadelphia, the son of free blacks who had fled from Virginia after the Nat Turner rebellion. Worked as upholsterer and cabinetmaker. An active abolitionist, he helped found the Banneker Institute, a literary society and library for blacks, in Philadelphia in 1853. Served on coastal survey ship *Walker* in 1857–58 and visited Charleston, South Carolina. Became cook and personal servant to Lieutenant Colonel Benjamin Tilghman of the 26th Pennsylvania Infantry in 1861 while serving as war correspondent for the New York *Weekly Anglo-African*, an influential black newspaper. Helped recruit in early 1863 for the 54th Massachusetts Infantry, the first black regiment raised by a northern state, then enlisted in the regiment as a sergeant. Served in siege of Charleston, South Carolina, and fought in the assault on Fort Wagner on July 18, 1863. Continued to write for the *Anglo-African* and protested the failure of black soldiers to receive equal pay. Commissioned as first lieutenant before being mustered out in July 1865. Worked for the Freedman's Bureau in Virginia educating freed slaves, 1866–70. Returned to Philadelphia before moving in 1873 to Brooklyn, where he worked as an upholsterer until his death.

Kate Stone (May 8, 1841–December 28, 1907) Born Sarah Katherine Stone in Hinds County, Mississippi, the daughter of a plantation owner. Family moved to plantation in Madison Parish, Louisiana, thirty miles northwest of Vicksburg. Educated at boarding school in Nashville. Two of her five brothers died while serving in the Confederate army in 1863. Family fled plantation in March 1863 during the Vicksburg campaign and went to eastern Texas. Returned to plantation in November 1865. Married Henry Bry Holmes in 1869. Founded local chapter of the United Daughters of the Confederacy. Died in Tallulah, Louisiana.

George Templeton Strong (January 26, 1820–July 21, 1875) Born in New York City, the son of an attorney. Graduated from Columbia College in 1838. Read law in his father's office and was admitted to the bar in 1841. Joined father's firm. Married Ellen Ruggles in 1848. Served on Columbia board of trustees and as vestryman of Trinity Episcopal Church. Helped found the U.S. Sanitary Commission, June 1861, and served as its treasurer through the end of the war; also helped found the Union League Club of New York in 1863. Died in New York City.

Walter H. Taylor (June 13, 1838–March 1, 1916) Born in Norfolk, Virginia, the son of a commission merchant. Graduated from Norfolk Military Academy. Attended Virginia Military Institute, 1854–55. Worked in Norfolk branch of Bank of Virginia, 1855–61. Joined 6th Virginia Infantry in April 1861. Became assistant adjutant general on staff of Robert E. Lee in May 1861 and served with him in Richmond, western Virginia, and South Carolina. Continued in position when Lee took command of the Army of Northern Virginia in June 1862 and served until Lee's surrender at Appomattox. Promoted to lieutenant colonel in January 1864. Married Elizabeth Selden Saunders in Richmond, Virginia, on night of April 2, 1865. Returned to Norfolk after the war and worked in hardware business before becoming president of the Marine Bank in 1876. Served as director of several insurance and railroad companies. Published *Four Years with General Lee* (1878) and *General Lee: His Campaigns in Virginia, 1861–1865* (1906). Died in Norfolk.

James H. Tomb (March 16, 1839–May 25, 1929) Born in Savannah, Georgia, the son of a painter. Family moved in 1852 to New Berlin, Florida, where father operated a sawmill. Commissioned in Confederate navy in June 1861. Served on the Mississippi as engineer on gunboats *Jackson* and *McRae*. Captured at Forts Jackson and St. Phillip in April 1862. Exchanged in October 1862. Assigned to ironclad ram *Chicora* and served in successful attack on Union fleet blockading Charleston, South Carolina, on January 31, 1863. Worked on design of torpedoes (underwater explosive devices). Became engineer of ironclad ram *David*, which damaged U.S.S. *New Ironsides* in a night attack off Charleston on October 5, 1863. Made unsuccessful attack on the U.S.S. *Memphis* in March 1864. Served at Charleston until its evacuation in February 1865. Surrendered and paroled in Florida in May 1865. Served with Brazilian navy during the Paraguayan War, 1866–67. Opened hotel in St. Louis in 1872. Married Sarah Green in 1880. Retired in 1905 to Jacksonville, Florida, where he died.

Clement L. Vallandigham (July 29, 1820–June 17, 1871) Born in New Lisbon, Ohio, the son of a Presbyterian minister. Attended New Lisbon Academy and Jefferson College in Washington, Pennsylvania. Served as principal of Union Academy in Snow Hill, Maryland,

1838–40. Returned to Ohio in 1840 to study law. Admitted to bar in 1842. Served as a Democrat in the Ohio house of representatives, 1845–46. Married Louisa Anna McMahon in 1846. Moved in 1847 to Dayton, where he practiced law and edited the *Dayton Western Empire*, 1847–49. Served in Congress, 1858–63, and became a leading "Peace Democrat" opposed to emancipation and the continued prosecution of the war. Arrested in Dayton on May 5, 1863, and tried before military commission for expressing "disloyal sentiments and opinions." Expelled across lines into Confederate-held territory in Tennessee. Made his way to Canada in June 1863 after receiving Democratic nomination for governor of Ohio and campaigned from exile, but was defeated in October 1863. Returned to United States in June 1864 and helped draft peace platform adopted by Democratic national convention in August. Resumed law practice. Accidentally shot himself on June 16, 1871, while demonstrating to other attorneys how his client's alleged victim could have accidentally shot himself during an altercation (his client was later acquitted). Died the following day in Lebanon, Ohio.

Charles S. Wainwright (December 31, 1826–September 13, 1907) Born in New York City, the son of a farmer from Dutchess County in the Hudson Valley. Helped manage family estate near Rhinebeck. Served in New York state militia. Commissioned as major in the 1st New York Artillery on October 17, 1861. Served as chief of artillery in Hooker's division, Army of the Potomac, from January 1862. Promoted to lieutenant colonel, April 1862, and colonel, May 1862. Fought at Williamsburg and Fair Oaks before falling ill in early June 1862. Returned from sick leave in August 1862 and became chief of artillery in the First Corps in September 1862; joined his command after the battle of Antietam. Served at Fredericksburg, Chancellorsville, and Gettysburg. Commanded artillery brigade in Fifth Corps, 1864–65, and served in the Overland campaign, the siege of Petersburg, and the Appomattox campaign. Returned to farming in Dutchess County before moving to Washington, D.C., around 1884. Died in Washington.

Henry C. Whelan (January 8, 1835–March 2, 1864) Born in Philadelphia, the son of a merchant. Attended University of Pennsylvania for two years. Worked in shoe store. Commissioned as captain in 6th Pennsylvania Cavalry in September 1861. Promoted to major in March 1863. Fought at Brandy Station and in Mine Run campaign. Returned in December 1863 to Philadelphia, where he died of pulmonary disease.

Walt Whitman (May 31, 1819–March 26, 1892) Born in Huntington

Township, New York, the son of a farmer and carpenter. Moved with family to Brooklyn in 1823. Learned printing trade at Brooklyn newspapers. Taught school on Long Island, 1836–38. Became freelance journalist and printer in New York and Brooklyn. Published first edition of *Leaves of Grass* in 1855 (revised editions appeared in 1856, 1860, 1867, 1870, 1881, and 1891). Traveled to northern Virginia in December 1862 after learning that his brother George had been wounded at Fredericksburg. Became volunteer nurse in Washington, D.C., army hospitals. Published *Drum-Taps* and *Sequel to Drum-Taps* in 1865. Worked as clerk at the Interior Department, 1865, and the office of the attorney general, 1865–73. Published prose recollections of his war experiences in *Memoranda During the War* (1875) and *Specimen Days and Collect* (1882). Died in Camden, New Jersey.

Charles B. Wilder (August 28, 1802–May 7, 1882) Born in Needham, Massachusetts. Married Mary Ann Guild in 1827. Became successful paper merchant. Appointed superintendent of contrabands at Fort Monroe, Virginia, in February 1863 and commissioned as captain. Charged with embezzlement in 1865 after he purchased confiscated land in Virginia with the intent of distributing it to freed slaves, but was acquitted at court-martial. Mustered out in March 1866. Moved to Jacksonville, Florida, where he died.

Alpheus S. Williams (September 20, 1810–December 21, 1878) Born in Deep River, Connecticut, the son of a manufacturer. Graduated from Yale College in 1831. Admitted to the bar in 1834. Moved to Detroit in 1836, where he practiced law and joined the local militia company. Married Jane Hereford Pierson in 1839; she died in 1848. Served as probate judge of Wayne County, 1840–44, and published the *Detroit Daily Advertiser*, 1843–48. Commissioned as brigadier general of volunteers in August 1861. Commanded brigade in the Army of the Potomac, October 1861–March 1862. Led a division in the Shenandoah Valley campaign and at Cedar Mountain and Second Bull Run. Assumed temporary command of Twelfth Corps at Antietam following the death of General Mansfield. Commanded division at Chancellorsville and was temporary commander of the Twelfth Corps at Gettysburg. Sent with his division in September 1863 to Tennessee, where they guarded railroads. Served in the Atlanta campaign and commanded the Twentieth Corps in the march through Georgia and the Carolinas. Mustered out on January 15, 1866. Served as U.S. minister to San Salvador, 1866–69. Returned to Detroit. Married Martha Ann Tillman in 1873. Elected to Congress as a Democrat and served from 1875 until his death in Washington, D.C.

William Winters (1830–April 8, 1864?) Born in Connecticut.

Married Harriet J. Smith in Cincinnati, Ohio, in 1853. Moved to Hawes Creek Township in Bartholomew County, Indiana, where he worked as a saddle and harness maker. Enlisted in Company I, 67th Indiana Infantry, in August 1862. Taken prisoner along with his regiment when the Union garrison at Munfordville, Kentucky, surrendered on September 17, 1862. Returned to Indiana after being paroled the day after his capture. Exchanged in late November 1862. Regiment joined Sherman's expedition against Vicksburg. Saw action at Chickasaw Bayou. Served as hospital attendant during expedition to capture Arkansas Post and in army camps near Vicksburg. Saw action at Port Gibson, Champion Hill, Big Black River, and in the siege of Vicksburg. Sent with regiment to southern Louisiana in August 1863 and to Matagorda Bay, Texas, in December. Returned to southern Louisiana in February 1864 and served in Red River campaign. Missing in action and presumed killed in the battle of Sabine Crossroads.

Jonathan Worth (November 18, 1802–September 5, 1869) Born in Guilford County, North Carolina, the son of a physician. Attended Caldwell Institute in Greensboro. Married Martitia Daniel in 1824, the same year he began practicing law in Asheboro. Served in North Carolina house of commons, 1830–32, where he opposed nullification. Served in state senate, 1840–41 and 1858–61. Opposed secession in 1861. Elected state treasurer in 1862 and served until 1865, when he was elected governor. Reelected in 1866. Opposed ratification of the Fourteenth Amendment and the Reconstruction Act of 1867, which made southern state governments subject to military authority. Declined to run for reelection in 1868 and refused to recognize the election of William W. Holden as his successor. Removed from office by military authority in July 1868. Died in Raleigh.

Note on the Texts

This volume collects nineteenth-century writing about the Civil War, bringing together public and private letters, newspaper and magazine articles, memoranda, speeches, journal and diary entries, proclamations, messages, commission testimony, poems, and sermons written by participants and observers and dealing with events in the period from January 1863 to March 1864. Most of these documents were not written for publication, and most of them existed only in manuscript form during the lifetimes of the persons who wrote them. With ten exceptions, the texts presented in this volume are taken from printed sources. In cases where there is only one printed source for a document, the text offered here comes from that source. Where there is more than one printed source for a document, the text printed in this volume is taken from the source that appears to contain the fewest editorial alterations in the spelling, capitalization, paragraphing, and punctuation of the original. In ten instances where no printed sources (or no complete printed sources) were available, the texts in this volume are printed from manuscripts.

This volume prints texts as they appear in the sources listed below, but with a few alterations in editorial procedure. The bracketed conjectural readings of editors, in cases where original manuscripts or printed texts were damaged or difficult to read, are accepted without brackets in this volume when those readings seem to be the only possible ones; but when they do not, or when the editor made no conjecture, the missing word or words are indicated by a bracketed two-em space, i.e., [   ]. In cases where a typographical error or obvious misspelling in manuscript was marked by earlier editors with "[*sic*]," the present volume omits the "[*sic*]" and corrects the typographical error or slip of the pen. In some cases, obvious errors were not marked by earlier editors with "[*sic*]" but were printed and then followed by a bracketed correction; in these instances, this volume removes the brackets and accepts the editorial emendation. Bracketed editorial insertions used in the source texts to identify persons or places, to expand contractions and abbreviations, or to clarify meaning have been deleted in this volume. In instances where canceled, but still legible, words were printed in the source texts with lines through the deleted material, or where canceled words were printed and indicated with an asterisk, this volume omits the canceled words.

In *The Papers of Jefferson Davis*, material that was written in interlined form in manuscript is printed within diagonal marks; this volume prints the interlined words and omits the diagonals.

The texts of the letters from Matthew M. Miller to his aunt and from George Hamilton Perkins to Susan G. Perkins were presented as quoted material in the sources used in this volume, with quotation marks placed at the beginning of each paragraph and at the end of the text; this volume omits the quotation marks.

Sherman's Civil War: Selected Correspondence of William T. Sherman, 1860–1865 (1999), edited by Brooks D. Simpson and Jean V. Berlin, presents Sherman's letter to Ellen Ewing Sherman of June 27, 1863, in a text in which erased material is indicated by "<erased>," "<sentence erased>," "<remainder of sentence erased>," and "<phrase erased>." In this volume, the erased material is indicated by a bracketed two-em space, i.e., [   ].

Inside Lincoln's White House: The Complete Civil War Diary of John Hay (1997), edited by Michael Burlingame and John R. Turner Ettlinger, prints a paragraph in the July 15, 1863, entry describing Hay's visits to concert saloons with Robert Todd Lincoln (page 376.28–31 in this volume) as canceled material because it was crossed out in the manuscript. This volume prints the paragraph without cancelation marks because it is likely that it was crossed out by someone other than Hay, possibly after his death. Similarly, in the instances in his diary where Hay originally referred to Lincoln as "the Tycoon," the word "Tycoon" was later crossed out in the manuscript and "President" added. These instances are printed in *Inside Lincoln's White House* with "Tycoon" canceled and then followed by "President," but in this volume at pages 376.32 and 563.5 "Tycoon" is printed without cancelation and "President" is omitted.

The text of the journal of Jedediah Hotchkiss presented in *Make Me a Map Of the Valley: The Civil War Journal of Stonewall Jackson's Topographer* (1973), edited by Archie P. McDonald, is based on a typescript prepared under Hotchkiss's personal supervision. In the typescript of the entry for May 2, 1863, there are two blank spaces where the names of a house on the Chancellorsville battlefield and of a Confederate officer were omitted. The text presented in *Make Me a Map Of the Valley* supplies the missing names in brackets. In this volume, these bracketed insertions are deleted, a two-em space is left blank at pages 178.24 and 179.11, and the names are printed in the notes. Similarly, there are three blank spaces in the entry for May 15, 1863, in the diary of Edward O. Guerrant where two dates and the name of a battle were omitted. In the text presented in *Bluegrass Confederate: The Headquarters Diary of Edward O. Guerrant* (1999), edited by William C. Davis and Meredith L. Swentor, the omitted dates and names are supplied in brackets. This volume deletes the bracketed insertions, leaves a two-em space blank at pages 220.37, 221.5, and 221.14, and prints the dates and the name of the battle in the notes.

Two setting errors that appeared in the printed source texts are corrected in this volume: at 465.34, "while it could prevent depredations" becomes "while it could not prevent depredations," and at 593.5, "Tuesday morning, Dec. 24th" becomes "Tuesday morning, Nov. 24th." Eight slips of the pen in documents printed from manuscript sources are also corrected: at 17.13–14, "seemed in in excellent spirits, said they" becomes "seemed in excellent spirits, said they"; at 334.9, "when the skirmisher on both flanks" becomes "when the skirmishers on both flanks"; at 334.11, "only two offices besides myself" becomes "only two officers besides myself"; at 335.23, "before & the the rest as quick" becomes "before & the rest as quick"; at 393.25–26, "have troops enough to built them" becomes "have troops enough to build them"; at 457.24, "privalege" becomes "privilege"; at 458.1, "theory in practice of Government" becomes "theory in practice of the Government"; at 458.14–15, "regret this his bill" becomes "regret that his bill."

The following is a list of the documents included in this volume, in the order of their appearance, giving the source of each text. The most common sources are indicated by these abbreviations:

CWAL   *The Collected Works of Abraham Lincoln*, ed. Roy P. Basler (8 vols., New Brunswick, N.J.: Rutgers University Press, 1953). Copyright © 1953 by the Abraham Lincoln Association. Used by permission.

DCDT   *Dear Catharine, Dear Taylor: The Civil War Letters of a Union Soldier and His Wife*, ed. Richard L. Kiper, letters transcribed by Donna B. Vaughn (Lawrence: University Press of Kansas, 2002). Copyright © 2002 by University Press of Kansas.

Norton   Oliver Willcox Norton, *Army Letters, 1861–1865* (Chicago: O. L. Deming, 1903).

OR   *The War of the Rebellion: A Compilation of the Official Records of the Union and Confederate Armies* (128 vols., Washington, D.C.: Government Printing Office, 1880–1901).

ORN   *Official Records of the Union and Confederate Navies in the War of the Rebellion* (30 vols., Washington, D.C.: Government Printing Office, 1894–1922).

PJD   *The Papers of Jefferson Davis* (13 vols. to date, Baton Rouge: Louisiana State University Press, 1971–2012). Volume 9 (1997), ed. Lynda Lasswell Crist and Mary Seaton Dix, Volume 10 (1999), ed. Lynda Lasswell Crist. Copyright © 1997, 1999 by Louisiana State University Press. Used by permission of the publisher.

PUSG	The Papers of Ulysses S. Grant, ed. John Y. Simon (31 vols. to date, Carbondale: Southern Illinois University Press, 1967–2009). Volume 8 (1979), Volume 9 (1982), Volume 10 (1982). Copyright © 1979, 1982 by The Ulysses S. Grant Association. Published with the permission of The Ulysses S. Grant Association.
SCW	Sherman's Civil War: Selected Correspondence of William T. Sherman, 1860–1865, ed. Brooks D. Simpson and Jean V. Berlin (Chapel Hill: The University of North Carolina Press, 1999). Copyright © 1999 by The University of North Carolina Press, www.uncpress.unc.edu. Used by permission of the publisher.

Edmund DeWitt Patterson: Journal, January 20, 1863. *Yankee Rebel: The Civil War Journal of Edmund DeWitt Patterson*, ed. John G. Barrett (Chapel Hill: The University of North Carolina Press, 1966), 93–94. Copyright © 1966 by The University of North Carolina Press, www.uncpress.unc.edu. Used by permission of the publisher.

Theodore A. Dodge: Journal, January 21–24, 1863. *On Campaign with the Army of the Potomac: The Civil War Journal of Theodore Ayrault Dodge*, ed. Stephen W. Sears (New York: Cooper Square Press, 2001), 150–56. Copyright © 2001 by Stephen W. Sears.

Henry Adams to Charles F. Adams Jr., January 23, 1863. *The Letters of Henry Adams*, vol. I, ed. J. C. Levenson, Ernest Samuels, Charles Vandersee, Viola Hopkins Winner (Cambridge: The Belknap Press of Harvard University Press), 326–27. Copyright © 1982 by the Massachusetts Historical Society. Used by permission of the Adams Family Papers, Massachusetts Historical Society.

George G. Meade to Margaret Meade, January 23, 26, and 28, 1863. Manuscript, George Gordon Meade Papers, Historical Society of Pennsylvania, Philadelphia.

Abraham Lincoln to Joseph Hooker, January 26, 1863. *CWAL*, vol. VI, 78–79.

John A. Andrew to Francis Shaw, January 30, 1863. Manuscript, John A. Andrew Papers, Massachusetts Historical Society, Boston. Used by permission.

William Parker Cutler: Diary, February 2 and 9, 1863. Allan G. Bogue, "William Parker Cutler's Congressional Diary of 1862–63," *Civil War History*, vol. 33, no. 4 (December 1987), 329–330. Copyright © 1987 by Kent State University Press.

George Templeton Strong: Diary, February 3–5, 1863. George Templeton Strong, *Diary of the Civil War, 1860–1865*, ed. Allan Nevins (New York: The Macmillan Publishing Company, 1962), 293–95. Reprinted with permission of Scribner, a Division of Simon &

Schuster, Inc., from *The Diary of George Templeton Strong* by Allan Nevins and Milton Halsey Thomas. Copyright © 1952 by The Macmillan Publishing Company; copyright renewed © 1980 by Milton Halsey Thomas. All rights reserved.

Oliver W. Norton to Edwin Norton, February 6, 1863. *Norton*, 134–37.

Robert E. Lee to Mary Lee, February 8, 1863. *The Wartime Papers of Robert E. Lee*, ed. Clifford Dowdey and Louis H. Manarin (Boston: Little, Brown, 1961), 401–2. Copyright © 1961 by Commonwealth of Virginia.

Robert Gould Shaw to Annie Haggerty, February 8, 1863. *Blue-Eyed Child of Fortune: The Civil War Letters of Colonel Robert Gould Shaw*, ed. Russell Duncan (Athens: The University of Georgia Press, 1992), 285–86. Copyright © 1992 by The University of Georgia Press. Used by permission of The University of Georgia Press.

Richard Cobden to Charles Sumner, February 13, 1863. *American Historical Review*, vol. 2, no. 2 (January 1897), 308–9.

Isaac Funk: Speech in the Illinois State Senate, February 14, 1863. *Copperheads Under the Heel of an Illinois Farmer* (New York: 1863), 1–3.

Taylor Peirce to Catharine Peirce, February 16, 1863. *DCDT*, 79–81.

William T. Sherman to Thomas Ewing Sr., February 17, 1863, and to John Sherman, February 18, 1863. *SCW*, 398–405.

Clement L. Vallandigham: Speech in Congress, Washington, D.C., February 23, 1863. *Congressional Globe Appendix*, 37th Congress, 3rd Session, 172–77.

Samuel W. Fiske to the *Springfield Republican*, February 25, 1863. *Mr. Dunn Browne's Experiences in the Army: The Civil War Letters of Samuel W. Fiske*, ed. Stephen W. Sears (New York: Fordham University Press, 1998), 58–60. Copyright © 1998 by Stephen W. Sears.

Charles C. Jones Jr. to Charles C. Jones Sr. and Mary Jones, March 3, 1863. *The Children of Pride: A True Story of Georgia and the Civil War*, Abridged Edition, ed. Robert Manson Myers (New Haven: Yale University Press, 1984), 351–52. Copyright © 1972, 1984 by Robert Manson Myers.

Charles C. Jones Sr. to Charles C. Jones Jr., March 4, 1863. *The Children of Pride: A True Story of Georgia and the Civil War*, Abridged Edition, ed. Robert Manson Myers (New Haven: Yale University Press, 1984), 352–53. Copyright © 1972, 1984 by Robert Manson Myers. Used by permission of the publisher.

Harriet Jacobs to Lydia Maria Child, March 18, 1863. *The Harriet Jacobs Family Papers*, vol. II, ed. Jean Fagan Yellin (Chapel Hill: The University of North Carolina Press), 468–70. Copyright © 2008 Jean Fagan Yellin. Used by permission of the publisher.

William Henry Harrison Clayton to Nide and Rachel Pugh, March 26, 1863. *A Damned Iowa Greyhound: The Civil War Letters of*

William Henry Harrison Clayton, ed. Donald C. Elder III (Iowa City: University of Iowa Press, 1998), 52–55. Copyright © 1998 by University of Iowa Press. Used by permission of the publisher.

Henry W. Halleck to Ulysses S. Grant, March 31, 1863. *OR*, series 1, vol. XXIV, part 3, 156–57.

Frederick Law Olmsted to John Olmsted, April 1, 1863. *The Papers of Frederick Law Olmsted, Volume IV: Defending the Union, 1861–1863*, ed. Jane Turner Censer (Baltimore: The Johns Hopkins University Press, 1986), 570–76. Copyright © 1986 by The Johns Hopkins University Press.

Frederick Douglass: Why Should a Colored Man Enlist?, *Douglass' Monthly*, April 1863. *The Life and Writings of Frederick Douglass*, vol. III, ed. Philip S. Foner (New York: International Publishers, 1952), 340–44. Copyright © 1952 by International Publishers Co. Inc.

Jefferson Davis to William M. Brooks, April 2, 1863. *PJD*, vol. 9, 122–24. Used by permission of the publisher.

John B. Jones: Diary, April 2–4, 1863. J. B. Jones, *A Rebel War Clerk's Diary at the Confederate States Capital*, vol. I (Philadelphia: J. B. Lippincott & Co., 1866), 284–87.

Whitelaw Reid to the *Cincinnati Gazette*, April 4, 1863. *A Radical View: The "Agate" Dispatches of Whitelaw Reid 1861–1865*, vol. 1, ed. James G. Smart (Memphis, Tenn.: Memphis State University Press), 257–58.

Charles S. Wainwright Diary, April 5–12, 1863. *A Diary of Battle: The Personal Journals of Colonel Charles S. Wainwright*, ed. Allan Nevins (New York: Harcourt, Brace & World, Inc., 1962), 176–79. Copyright © 1962 by Allan Nevins.

Francis Lieber: No Party Now, But All for Our Country, April 11, 1863. Francis Lieber, *No Party Now, But All for Our Country* (New York: C.S. Westcott & Co., 1863), 1–8.

Catharine Peirce to Taylor Peirce, April 12, 1863. *DCDT*, 97–98.

James A. Connolly to Mary Dunn Connolly, April 20, 1863. "Major James Austin Connolly," *Transactions of the Illinois State Historical Society for the Year 1928* (Springfield: Illinois State Historical Library, 1928), 241–43. Used by permission of the Abraham Lincoln Presidential Library.

Ulysses S. Grant to Jesse Root Grant, April 21, 1863. *PUSG*, vol. 8, 109–10.

David Hunter to Jefferson Davis, April 23, 1863. *PJD*, vol. 9, 152.

Kate Stone: Journal, April 25, 1863. *Brokenburn: The Journal of Kate Stone, 1861–1868*, ed. John Q. Anderson (Baton Rouge: Louisiana State University Press, 1955), 194–99. Copyright © 1989 by Louisiana State University Press. Used by permission of the publisher.

Wilbur Fisk to *The Green Mountain Freeman*, April 26, 1863. *Hard Marching Every Day: The Civil War Letters of Private Wilbur Fisk*,

1861–1865, ed. Emil and Ruth Rosenblatt (Lawrence: University Press of Kansas, 1992), 70–74. Copyright © 1983, 1992 by Emil Rosenblatt.

John Hampden Chamberlayne to Martha Burwell Chamberlayne, April 30, 1863. *Ham Chamberlayne—Virginian: Letters and Papers of an Artillery Officer in the War for Southern Independence 1861–1865*, ed. C. G. Chamberlayne (Richmond, Va.: Dietz Printing Co., 1932), 171–72. Copyright © 1932 by C. G. Chamberlayne.

Sarah Morgan: Diary, April 30, 1863. *The Civil War Diary of Sarah Morgan*, ed. Charles East (Athens: The University of Georgia Press, 1991), 489–92. Copyright © 1991 by The University of Georgia Press. Used by permission of The University of Georgia Press.

Samuel Pickens: Diary, May 1–3, 1863. *Voices from Company D: Diaries by the Greensboro Guards, Fifth Alabama Infantry Regiment, Army of Northern Virginia*, ed. G. Ward Hubbs (Athens: The University of Georgia Press, 2003), 159–63. Copyright © 2003 by The University of Georgia Press. Used by permission of the Pickens Family Papers, The Doy Leale McCall Sr. Collection, The Doy Leale McCall Rare Book and Manuscript Library, University of South Alabama, Mobile, AL.

Jedediah Hotchkiss: Journal, May 2–6, 1863. Jedediah Hotchkiss, *Make Me a Map Of the Valley: The Civil War Journal of Stonewall Jackson's Topographer*, ed. Archie P. McDonald (Dallas: Southern Methodist University Press, 1973), 137–42. Copyright © 1973 by Southern Methodist University Press. Used by permission of the publisher.

Taylor Peirce to Catharine Peirce, May 4, 1863. *DCDT*, 105–9.

Catherine Edmondston: Diary, May 5–7, 9, and 11–12, 1863. *"Journal of a Secesh Lady": The Diary of Catherine Ann Devereux Edmondston, 1860–1866*, ed. Beth G. Crabtree and James W. Patton (Raleigh: North Carolina Division of Archives and History, 1979), 387–90, 390–91, 391–92. Copyright © 1979 by the North Carolina Division of Archives and History. Used by permission.

Charles Morse to His Family, May 7, 1863. Charles Fessenden Morse, *Letters Written During the Civil War, 1861–1865* (Boston: T. R. Marvin & Son, 1898), 127–39.

Samuel W. Fiske to the *Springfield Republican*, May 9 and 11, 1863. *Mr. Dunn Browne's Experiences in the Army: The Civil War Letters of Samuel W. Fiske*, ed. Stephen W. Sears (New York: Fordham University Press, 1998), 76–84. Copyright © 1998 by Stephen W. Sears.

Charles B. Wilder: Testimony before the American Freedmen's Inquiry Commission, May 9, 1863. *Freedom: A Documentary History of Emancipation, 1861–1867. Series I, Volume I: The Destruction of Slavery*, ed. Ira Berlin, Barbara J. Fields, Thavolia Glymph, Joseph P. Reidy, Leslie S. Rowland (New York: Cambridge University Press, 1985), 88–90. Copyright © 2010 by Cambridge University Press. Reprinted with permission of Cambridge University Press.

Thomas Wentworth Higginson: Journal, May 10, 1863. *The Complete Civil War Journal and Selected Letters of Thomas Wentworth Higginson*, ed. Christopher Looby (Chicago: The University of Chicago Press, 2000), 143–45. Copyright © 2000 by The University of Chicago. Reprinted with permission of The University of Chicago Press.

Edward O. Guerrant: Diary, May 15, 1863. *Bluegrass Confederate: The Headquarters Diary of Edward O. Guerrant*, ed. William C. Davis and Meredith L. Swentor (Baton Rouge: Louisiana State University Press, 1999), 275–77. Copyright © 1999 by Louisiana State University Press. Used by permission of the publisher.

George Richard Browder: Diary, May 17–26, 1863. *The Heavens Are Weeping: The Diaries of George Richard Browder, 1852–1886*, ed. Richard L. Troutman (Grand Rapids, Mich.: Zondervan Publishing House, 1987). Copyright © 1987 by Richard L. Troutman.

Harper's Weekly: The Arrest of Vallandigham, May 30, 1863. *Harper's Weekly*, May 30, 1863.

Oliver W. Norton to Elizabeth Norton Poss, June 8, 1863. *Norton*, 158–61.

Robert Gould Shaw to Annie Haggerty Shaw, June 9–13, 1863. *Blue-Eyed Child of Fortune: The Civil War Letters of Colonel Robert Gould Shaw*, ed. Russell Duncan (Athens: The University of Georgia Press, 1992), 341–45. Copyright © 1992 by The University of Georgia Press. Used by permission of The University of Georgia Press.

William Winters to Harriet Winters, June 9, 1863. *The Musick of the Mocking Birds, the Roar of the Cannon: The Civil War Diary and Letters of William Winters*, ed. Steven E. Bloodworth (Lincoln: University of Nebraska Press, 1998), 55–57. Copyright © 1998 by University of Nebraska Press.

Matthew M. Miller to His Aunt, June 10, 1863. *OR*, series 3, vol. III, 452–53.

Robert E. Lee to Jefferson Davis, June 10, 1863. *The Wartime Papers of Robert E. Lee*, ed. Clifford Dowdey and Louis H. Manarin (Boston: Little, Brown, 1961), 507–9. Copyright © 1961 by Commonwealth of Virginia.

William T. Sherman to John T. Swayne, June 11, 1863. *SCW*, 479–81.

Henry C. Whelan to Mary Whelan, June 11, 1863. Typescript, Cadwalader Family Collection, Historical Society of Pennsylvania, Philadelphia.

Abraham Lincoln to Erastus Corning and Others, June 12, 1863. *New-York Daily Tribune*, June 15, 1863.

William Henry Harrison Clayton to Amos and Grace Clayton and to George Washington Clayton and John Quincy Adams Clayton,

June 18 and 28, 1863. *A Damned Iowa Greyhound: The Civil War Letters of William Henry Harrison Clayton*, ed. Donald C. Elder III (Iowa City: University of Iowa Press, 1998), 73–77. Copyright © 1998 by University of Iowa Press. Used by permission of the publisher.

Charles B. Haydon: Journal, June 20, 1863. *For Country, Cause & Leader: The Civil War Journal of Charles B. Haydon*, ed. Stephen W. Sears (New York: Ticknor & Fields, 1993), 331–33. Copyright © 1993 by Stephen W. Sears.

William T. Sherman to Ellen Ewing Sherman, June 27, 1863. *SCW*, 489–93.

Edmund DeWitt Patterson: Journal, June 24–30, 1863. *Yankee Rebel: The Civil War Journal of Edmund DeWitt Patterson*, ed. John G. Barrett (Chapel Hill: The University of North Carolina Press, 1966), 109–12. Copyright © 1966 by The University of North Carolina Press, www.uncpress.unc.edu. Used by permission of the publisher.

Lafayette McLaws to Emily McLaws, June 28, 1863. *A Soldier's General: The Civil War Letters of Major General Lafayette McLaws*, ed. John C. Oeffinger (Chapel Hill: The University of North Carolina Press, 2002), 192–94. Copyright © 2002 by The University of North Carolina Press, www.uncpress.unc.edu. Used by permission of the publisher.

Alpheus S. Williams to Irene and Mary Williams, June 29, 1863. *From the Cannon's Mouth: The Civil War Letters of Alpheus S. Williams*, ed. Milo M. Quaife (Detroit: Wayne State University Press, 1959), 220–22.

Samuel W. Fiske to the *Springfield Republican*, June 30, 1863. *Mr. Dunn Browne's Experiences in the Army: The Civil War Letters of Samuel W. Fiske*, ed. Stephen W. Sears (New York: Fordham University Press, 1998), 99–102. Copyright © 1998 by Stephen W. Sears. Reprinted with permission by Stephen W. Sears.

Arthur James Lyon Fremantle: Diary, July 1–4, 1863. Arthur James Lyon Fremantle, *Three Months in the Southern States, April–June 1863* (New York: John Bradburn, 1864), 251–76.

Samuel Pickens: Diary, July 1–3, 1863. *Voices from Company D: Diaries by the Greensboro Guards, Fifth Alabama Infantry Regiment, Army of Northern Virginia*, ed. G. Ward Hubbs (Athens: The University of Georgia Press, 2003), 182–84. Copyright © 2003 by The University of Georgia Press. Used by permission of the Pickens Family Papers, The Doy Leale McCall Sr. Collection, The Doy Leale McCall Rare Book and Manuscript Library, University of South Alabama, Mobile, AL.

Francis Adams Donaldson, Narrative of Gettysburg, July 2–3, 1863. *Inside the Army of the Potomac: The Civil War Experience of Captain Francis Adams Donaldson*, ed. J. Gregory Acken (Mechanicsburg,

Pa.: Stackpole Books, 1998), 298–310. Copyright © 1998 by Stackpole Books. Used by permission of the publisher.

Elizabeth Blair Lee to Samuel Phillips Lee, July 3 and 4–5, 1863. *Wartime Washington: The Civil War Letters of Elizabeth Blair Lee*, ed. Virginia Laas (Urbana: University of Illinois Press, 1990), 281–83. Copyright © 1991 by the Board of Trustees of the University of Illinois. Reprinted from the Blair and Lee Family Papers, Manuscripts Division, Department of Rare Books and Special Collections, Princeton University Library.

Joshua Lawrence Chamberlain to George B. Herendeen, July 6, 1863. Manuscript, Maine State Archives, Augusta.

Henry Livermore Abbott to Josiah Gardner Abbott, July 6, 1863. Manuscripts, Abbott Family Civil War Letters (MS Am 800.26). Houghton Library, Harvard University, series III, folder 19. Used by permission of the Houghton Library, Harvard University, MS Am 800.26.

Lafayette McLaws to Emily McLaws, July 7, 1863. *A Soldier's General: The Civil War Letters of Major General Lafayette McLaws*, ed. John C. Oeffinger (Chapel Hill: The University of North Carolina Press, 2002), 195–97. Copyright © 2002 by The University of North Carolina Press, www.uncpress.unc.edu. Used by permission of the publisher.

Cornelia Hancock to Her Cousin, July 7, 1863, and to Ellen Hancock Child, July 8, 1863. *Letters of a Civil War Nurse: Cornelia Hancock, 1863–1865*, ed. Henrietta Stratton Jaquette (Lincoln: University of Nebraska Press, 1998), 7–12.

Catharine Peirce to Taylor Peirce, July 5, 1863. *DCDT*, 126–27.

William Henry Harrison Clayton to Amos and Grace Clayton, July 5, 1863. Donald C. Elder, ed., *A Damned Iowa Greyhound: The Civil War Letters of William Henry Harrison Clayton* (Iowa City: University of Iowa Press, 1998), 78–81. Copyright © 1998 by University of Iowa Press. Used by permission of the publisher.

William T. Sherman to Ellen Ewing Sherman, July 5, 1863. *SCW*, 499–502.

William Winters to Harriet Winters, July 6, 1863. Stephen E. Woodworth, ed., *The Musick of the Mocking Birds, the Roar of the Cannon* (Lincoln: University of Nebraska Press, 1998), 63–65. Used by permission of the publisher.

Benjamin B. French: Journal, July 8, 1863. Benjamin Brown French, *Witness to the Young Republic: A Yankee's Journal, 1828–1870*, ed. Donald B. Cole and John J. McDonough (Hanover, N.H.: University Press of New England, 1989), 426. Copyright © 1989 by University Press of New England, Lebanon, N.H. Used by permission of the publisher.

Catherine Edmondston: Diary, July 8–11, 1863. *"Journal of a Secesh Lady": The Diary of Catherine Ann Devereux Edmondston, 1860–1866*, ed. Beth G. Crabtree and James W. Patton (Raleigh: North Carolina Division of Archives and History, 1979), 424–29. Copyright © 1979 by the North Carolina Division of Archives and History. Used by permission.

George Hamilton Perkins to Susan G. Perkins, July 29, 1863. *Letters of Capt. Geo. Hamilton Perkins* (Concord, N.H.: Ira C. Evans, 1886), 116–19.

Charles B. Haydon: Journal, July 11, 1863. *For Country, Cause & Leader: The Civil War Journal of Charles B. Haydon*, ed. Stephen W. Sears (New York: Ticknor & Fields, 1993), 337–39. Copyright © 1993 by Stephen W. Sears.

John Hay: Diary, July 11–15, 1863. *Inside Lincoln's White House: The Complete Civil War Diary of John Hay*, ed. Michael Burlingame and John R. Turner Ettlinger (Carbondale and Edwardsville: Southern Illinois University Press, 1997), 61–63. Copyright © 1997 by the Board of Trustees, Southern Illinois University. Used by permission.

Abraham Lincoln to Ulysses S. Grant, July 13, 1863. *CWAL*, vol. VI, 326.

Abraham Lincoln to George Meade, July 14, 1863. *CWAL*, vol. VI, 327–28.

Samuel Pickens: Diary, July 14, 1863. *Voices from Company D: Diaries by the Greensboro Guards, Fifth Alabama Infantry Regiment, Army of Northern Virginia*, ed. G. Ward Hubbs (Athens: The University of Georgia Press, 2003), 186–87. Copyright © 2003 by The University of Georgia Press. Used by permission of the Pickens Family Papers, The Doy Leale McCall Sr. Collection, The Doy Leale McCall Rare Book and Manuscript Library, University of South Alabama, Mobile, AL.

George Templeton Strong: Diary, July 13–17, 1863. George Templeton Strong, *Diary of the Civil War, 1860–1865*, ed. Allan Nevins (New York: The Macmillan Company, 1962), 335–41. Reprinted with permission of Scribner, a Division of Simon & Schuster, Inc., from *The Diary of George Templeton Strong* by Allan Nevins and Milton Halsey Thomas. Copyright © 1952 by Macmillan Publishing Company; copyright renewed © 1980 by Milton Halsey Thomas. All rights reserved.

Emma Holmes: Diary, July 16–19, 1863. Manuscript, South Caroliniana Library, University of South Carolina, Columbia.

Walter H. Taylor to Richard Taylor, July 17, 1863. R. Lockwood Tower, ed., *Lee's Adjutant: The Wartime Letters of Colonel Walter Herron Taylor, 1862–1865* (Columbia: University of South Carolina Press, 1995), 59–63. Copyright © 1995 by University of South Carolina. Used by permission of the publisher.

James Henry Gooding to the *New Bedford Mercury*, July 20, 1863. James Henry Gooding, *On the Altar of Freedom: A Black Soldier's Civil War Letters From the Front*, ed. Virginia M. Adams (Amherst:

The University of Massachusetts Press, 1991), 36–39. Copyright © 1991 by The University of Massachusetts Press. Used by permission of the publisher.

Lewis Douglass to Amelia Loguen, July 20, 1863. *The Mind of the Negro as Reflected in Letters Written During the Crisis, 1800–1860*, ed. Carter G. Woodson (Washington, D.C.: The Association for the Study of Negro Life and History, Inc., 1926), 544. Copyright © 1926 by The Association for the Study of Negro Life and History, Inc.

Charlotte Forten: Journal, July 20–24, 1863. *The Journals of Charlotte Forten Grimké*, ed. Brenda Stevenson (New York: Oxford University Press), 494–98. Copyright © 1988 by Oxford University Press, Inc. Used by permission of Brenda Stevenson.

Maria Lydig Daly: Diary, July 23, 1863. Maria Lydig Daly, *Diary of a Union Lady, 1861–1865*, ed. Harold Earl Hammond (New York: Funk & Wagnalls, 1962), 249–52. Copyright © 1962 by Funk and Wagnalls Company, Inc.

Herman Melville: The House-top. Herman Melville, *Battle-Pieces and Aspects of the War* (New York: Harper & Brothers, 1866), 86–87.

Henry Adams to Charles Francis Adams Jr., July 23, 1863. *The Letters of Henry Adams*, vol. I, ed. J. C. Levenson, Ernest Samuels, Charles Vandersee, Viola Hopkins Winner (Cambridge: The Belknap Press of Harvard University Press), 373–76. Copyright © 1982 by the Massachusetts Historical Society. Reprinted courtesy of the Adams Family Papers, Massachusetts Historical Society. Used by permission.

George G. Meade to Henry W. Halleck, July 31, 1863. *OR*, series 1, vol. XXVII, part 1, 108–10.

Robert E. Lee to Jefferson Davis, July 31, 1863. *The Wartime Papers of Robert E. Lee*, ed. Clifford Dowdey and Louis H. Manarin (Boston: Little, Brown, 1961), 564–65. Copyright © 1961 by Commonwealth of Virginia.

Hannah Johnson to Abraham Lincoln, July 31, 1863. *Freedom: A Documentary History of Emancipation, 1861–1867. Series II: The Black Military Experience*, ed. Ira Berlin (Cambridge and New York: Cambridge University Press, 1982), 582–83. Copyright © 2010 by Cambridge University Press. Reprinted with permission of Cambridge University Press.

Frederick Douglass to George L. Stearns, August 1, 1863. *The Life and Writings of Frederick Douglass*, vol. III, ed. Philip S. Foner (New York: International Publishers, 1952), 367–69. Copyright © 1952 by International Publishers Co. Inc. Used by permission of the publisher.

Frederick Douglass: The Commander-in-Chief and His Black Soldiers. *The Life and Writings of Frederick Douglass*, vol. III, ed. Philip S. Foner (New York: International Publishers, 1952), 369–72. Copyright © 1952 by International Publishers Co. Inc. Used by permission of the publisher.

Walt Whitman to Lewis Kirk Brown, August 1, 11, and 15, 1863. *Walt Whitman and the Civil War: A Collection of Original Articles and Manuscripts*, ed. Charles I. Glicksberg (Philadelphia: University of Pennsylvania Press, 1933), 94–98. Copyright © 1933 by University of Pennsylvania Press.

George E. Stephens to the *Weekly Anglo-African*, August 7, 1863. *A Voice of Thunder: The Civil War Letters of George E. Stephens*, ed. Donald Yacovone (Urbana: University of Illinois Press, 1997), 250–55. Copyright © 1997 by the Board of Trustees of the University of Illinois.

Robert E. Lee to Jefferson Davis, August 8, 1863. *PJD*, vol. 9, 326–27.

Jefferson Davis to Robert E. Lee, August 11, 1863. *PJD*, vol. 9, 337–38.

Wilbur Fisk to *The Green Mountain Freeman*, August 10, 1863. *Hard Marching Every Day: The Civil War Letters of Private Wilbur Fisk, 1861–1865*, ed. Emil and Ruth Rosenblatt (Lawrence: University Press of Kansas, 1992), 129–32. Copyright © 1983, 1992 by Emil Rosenblatt.

Frederick Douglass to George L. Stearns, August 12, 1863. Manuscript, Historical Society of Pennsylvania, Philadelphia.

William H. Neblett to Elizabeth Scott Neblett, August 18, 1863. Erika L. Murr, ed., *A Rebel Wife in Texas: The Diary and Letters of Elizabeth Scott Neblett, 1852–1864* (Baton Rouge: Louisiana State University Press, 2001), 137–40. Copyright © 2001 by Louisiana State University Press. Used by permission of the publisher.

Richard Cordley: Narrative of the Lawrence Massacre. *The Congregational Record*, September and October 1863, vol. V, nos. 9 and 10, 98–115.

Ulysses S. Grant to Abraham Lincoln, August 23, 1863. *PUSG*, vol. 9, 195–97.

Jonathan Worth to Jesse G. Henshaw, August 24, 1863. *The Correspondence of James Worth*, vol. I, ed. J. G. de Roulhac Hamilton (Raleigh: North Carolina Historical Commission, 1909), 257–58.

John M. Schofield to Thomas Ewing Jr., August 25, 1863. *OR*, series 1, vol. XXII, part 2, 471–72.

Abraham Lincoln to James C. Conkling, August 26, 1863. *CWAL*, vol. VI, 406–10.

Ulysses S. Grant to Elihu B. Washburne, August 30, 1863. *PUSG*, vol. 9, 217–18.

Charles Francis Adams to Lord Russell, September 5, 1863. *Papers Relating to Foreign Affairs, Accompanying the Annual Message of the President to the first session of the Thirty-Eighth Congress, 1863*, part I (Washington, D.C.: Government Printing Office, 1864), 367–68.

Charles C. Jones Jr. to Mary Jones, September 6 and 9, 1863. *The Children of Pride: A True Story of Georgia and the Civil War*, Abridged Edition, ed. Robert Manson Myers (New Haven: Yale

University Press, 1984), 397–98. Copyright © 1972, 1984 by Robert Manson Myers. Used by permission of the publisher.

Raphael Semmes: Journal, September 16–24, 1863. *ORN*, series I, vol. II, 765–67.

William T. Sherman to Henry W. Halleck, September 17, 1863. *SCW*, 543–50.

William W. Heartsill: Journal, September 17–28, 1863. W. W. Heartsill, *Fourteen Hundred and 91 Days in the Confederate Army* (Wilmington, N.C.: Broadfoot Publishing Company, 1992), 271–77. Copyright © 1992 by Broadfoot Publishing Company.

John S. Jackman: Diary, September 18–21, 1863. *Diary of a Confederate Soldier: John S. Jackman of the Orphan Brigade*, edited by William C. Davis (Columbia: University of South Carolina Press, 1990), 86–89. Copyright © 1990 by University of South Carolina. Used by permission of the publisher.

Kate Cumming: Journal, September 28–October 1, 1863. Kate Cumming, *A Journal of Hospital Life in the Confederate Army of Tennessee, from the battle of Shiloh to the end of the war* (Louisville, Ky.: 1866), 94–99.

Jefferson Davis: Speech at Missionary Ridge, Tennessee, October 10, 1863. *PJD*, vol. 10, 21–22.

Oliver W. Norton to Elizabeth Norton Poss, October 15, 1863. *Norton*, 183–85.

Jefferson Davis: Speech at Wilmington, North Carolina, November 5, 1863. *PJD*, vol. 10, 49–51.

Walter H. Taylor to Bettie Saunders, November 15, 1863. R. Lockwood Tower, ed., *Lee's Adjutant: The Wartime Letters of Colonel Walter Herron Taylor, 1862–1865* (Columbia: University of South Carolina Press, 1995), 86–89. Copyright © 1995 by University of South Carolina. Used by permission of the publisher.

Cornelia Hancock to an Unknown Correspondent, November 15, 1863. *Letters of a Civil War Nurse: Cornelia Hancock, 1863–1865*, ed. Henrietta Stratton Jaquette (Lincoln: University of Nebraska Press, 1998), 31–32.

John Hay: Diary, November 18–19, 1863. *Inside Lincoln's White House: The Complete Civil War Diary of John Hay*, ed. Michael Burlingame and John R. Turner Ettlinger (Carbondale and Edwardsville: Southern Illinois University Press, 1997), 111–14. Copyright © 1997 by the Board of Trustees, Southern Illinois University. Used with permission.

Abraham Lincoln: Address at Gettysburg, November 19, 1863. *CWAL*, vol. VII, 22–23.

Petition from the Colored Citizens of Beaufort, November 20, 1863. *Freedom: A Documentary History of Emancipation, 1861–1867. Series I, Volume II: The Wartime Genesis of Free Labor: The Upper South*, ed. Ira Berlin, Steven F. Miller, Leslie S. Rowland (New

York: Cambridge University Press, 1993), 166. Copyright © 1993 by Cambridge University Press. Reprinted with the permission of Cambridge University Press.

William W. Smith: Journal, November 13–25, 1863. Smith, William Wrenshall, "Holocaust Holiday: The Journal of a Strange Vacation to the War-torn South and a Visit with U.S. Grant," *Civil War Times Illustrated*, XVIII, 6 (Oct. 1979), 28–40. Copyright © 1979 by Historical Times Inc.

Montgomery C. Meigs: Journal, November 23–25, 1863. "First Impressions of Three Days' Fighting: Quartermaster General Meigs's 'Journal of the Battle of Chattanooga,'" ed. John M. Hoffman, in *Ulysses S. Grant: Essays and Documents*, ed. David L. Wilson and John Y. Simon (Carbondale and Edwardsville: Southern Illinois University Press, 1981), 70–76. Copyright © 1981 by The Ulysses S. Grant Association. Used by permission of The Ulysses S. Grant Association.

James A. Connolly to Mary Dunn Connolly, November 26 and December 7, 1863. "Major James Austin Connolly," *Transactions of the Illinois State Historical Society for the Year 1928* (Springfield: Illinois State Historical Library, 1928), 297–304. Used by permission of the Abraham Lincoln Presidential Library.

Theodore Lyman: Journal, November 26–December 2, 1863. David W. Lowe, ed., *Meade's Army: The Private Notebooks of Lt. Col. Theodore Lyman* (Kent, Ohio: Kent State University Press, 2007), 70–76. Copyright © 2007 by Kent State University Press. Used by permission of the publisher.

Wilbur Fisk to *The Green Mountain Freeman*, November 29 and December 8, 1863. *Hard Marching Every Day: The Civil War Letters of Private Wilbur Fisk, 1861–1865*, ed. Emil and Ruth Rosenblatt (Lawrence: University Press of Kansas, 1992), 166–74. Copyright © 1983, 1992 by Emil Rosenblatt.

George G. Meade to Margaret Meade, December 2 and 7, 1863. Manuscript, George Gordon Meade Papers, Historical Society of Pennsylvania, Philadelphia.

Frederick Douglass: Our Work Is Not Done, December 4, 1863. *The Frederick Douglass Papers, Series One: Speeches, Debates, and Interviews*, vol. 3, ed. John W. Blassingame (New Haven: Yale University Press, 1985), 598–609. Copyright © 1985 by Yale University. Reprinted by permission. Used by permission of the publisher.

Abraham Lincoln: Annual Message to Congress, December 8, 1863. *CWAL*, vol. VII, 36–53.

Abraham Lincoln: Proclamation of Amnesty and Reconstruction, December 8, 1863. *CWAL*, vol. VII, 53–56.

George Templeton Strong: Diary, December 11–13, 1863. George Templeton Strong, *Diary of the Civil War, 1860–1865*, ed. Allan

Nevins (New York: The Macmillan Publishing Company, 1962), 379–80. Reprinted with permission of Scribner, a Division of Simon & Schuster, Inc., from *The Diary of George Templeton Strong* by Allan Nevins and Milton Halsey Thomas. Copyright © 1952 by The Macmillan Publishing Company; copyright renewed © 1980 by Milton Halsey Thomas. All rights reserved.

Catherine Edmondston: Diary, December 11, 1863. *"Journal of a Secesh Lady": The Diary of Catherine Ann Devereux Edmondston, 1860–1866*, ed. Beth G. Crabtree and James W. Patton (Raleigh: North Carolina Division of Archives and History, 1979), 505–6. Copyright © 1979 by the North Carolina Division of Archives and History. Used by permission.

Mary Chesnut: Diary, January 1, 1864. *Mary Chesnut's Civil War*, ed. C. Vann Woodward (New Haven: Yale University Press, 1981), 519–26. Copyright © 1981 by C. Vann Woodward, Sally Bland Meets, Barbara C. Carpenter, Sally Bland Johnson, and Katherine W. Herbert. Used by permission of the publisher.

Judith W. McGuire: Diary, January 1, 1864. Judith W. McGuire, *Diary of a Southern Refugee, during the war*, 3rd edition (Richmond, Va.: J.W. Randolph & English, Publishers, 1889), 248–50.

Patrick R. Cleburne: Memorandum on Emancipation and Enlisting Black Soldiers, January 2, 1864. *OR*, series I, vol. LII, part 2, 586–92.

William T. Sherman to Roswell M. Sawyer, January 31, 1864. *SCW*, 598–602.

Lois Bryan Adams to the *Detroit Advertiser and Tribune*, February 8, 23, 1864. Lois Bryan Adams, *Letter from Washington, 1863–1865*, ed. Evelyn Leasher (Detroit: Wayne State University Press, 1999), 77–80, 83–85. Copyright © 1999 by Wayne State University Press.

Francis J. Higginson to John A. Dahlgren, February 18, 1864. *ORN*, series I, vol. XV, 328.

James H. Tomb: Notes on the *H. L. Hunley*, January 1865. *ORN*, series I, vol. XV, 334–35.

Judith W. McGuire: Diary, February 28, 1864. Judith W. McGuire, *Diary of a Southern Refugee, during the war*, 3rd edition (Richmond, Va.: J.W. Randolph & English, Publishers, 1889), 252–55.

John Paris: Sermon Preached at Kinston, N.C., February 28, 1864. *A Sermon: preached before Brig.-Gen. Hoke's Brigade, at Kinston, N.C., on the 28th of February, 1864, by Rev. John Paris, Chaplain Fifty-Fourth Regiment N.C. Troops, upon the death of twenty-two men, who had been executed in the presence of the brigade for the crime of desertion* (Greensborough, N.C.: A. W. Ingold & Co., 1864).

Oliver W. Norton to Elizabeth Norton Poss, February 29, 1864. *Norton*, 197–201.

John B. Jones: Diary, March 1–2 and 5, 1864. J. B. Jones, *A Rebel War Clerk's Diary at the Confederate States Capital*, vol. II (Philadelphia: J. B. Lippincott & Co., 1866), 162–65, 166–67.

Ulysses S. Grant to William T. Sherman, March 4, 1864. *PUSG*, vol. 10, 186–87.

William T. Sherman to Ulysses S. Grant, March 10, 1864. *SCW*, 602–04.

This volume presents the texts of the printings and manuscripts chosen as sources here but does not attempt to reproduce features of their typographic design or physical layout. In the texts that have been printed from manuscript, dashes at the end of sentences have been changed to periods, the beginnings of sentences have been capitalized, and punctuation at the end of sentences and closing quotation marks have been supplied. The texts are printed without alteration except for the changes previously discussed and the correction of typographical errors. Spelling, punctuation, and capitalization are often expressive features, and they are not altered, even when inconsistent or irregular. The following is a list of typographical errors corrected, cited by page and line number: 1.22, fours.; 26.40, *montem*; 74.8, accused-; 74.9, point.; 74.10, amend,/ments.; 111.18–19, arrangments; 123.37, truy; 126.15, to-dry; 128.9, not be; 136.11, no pursue; 144.10, thal may; 151.32, than any; 170.1, haven; 184.13, lnftry; 213.22, Carolina There; 213.26, A.; 214.15, them One; 219.17, unkindest" stroke of all"; 221.25, 4000000; 221.29, 40000,000; 266.4, sevral; 296.10, right, Our; 365.28, this It; 368.26, 20th; 405.16, 3 killed; 432.12, be; 475.25, burning But; 479.19, head; 482.33, manths; 486.1, consnmed.; 544.6, answred,; 547.16, fulfilled He; 552.1, of government; 554.2–3, degredation; 554.10, shackless; 572.40, decend; 573.37, consecreated; 576.35, movemnts; 579.39, of of; 581.21, doszen; 594.32, mounain; 653.12, hertofore; 674.14, diary After; 696.22, it's name.; 709.32, Chapter,; 729.19, suggest.

Notes

In the notes below, the reference numbers denote page and line of this volume (the line count includes headings, but not rule lines). No note is made for material included in the eleventh edition of *Merriam-Webster's Collegiate Dictionary*. Biblical references are keyed to the King James Version. Quotations from Shakespeare are keyed to *The Riverside Shakespeare*, ed. G. Blakemore Evans (Boston: Houghton Mifflin, 1974). Footnotes and bracketed editorial notes within the text were in the originals. For further historical and biographical background, references to other studies, and more detailed maps, see James McPherson, *Battle Cry of Freedom: The Civil War Era* (New York: Oxford University Press, 1988); *Encyclopedia of the American Civil War: A Political, Social, and Military History*, edited by David S. Heidler and Jeanne T. Heidler (New York: W. W. Norton, 2002); *The Library of Congress Civil War Desk Reference*, edited by Margaret E. Wagner, Gary W. Gallagher, and Paul Finkelman (New York: Simon & Schuster, 2002); and Aaron Sheehan-Dean, *Concise Historical Atlas of the U.S. Civil War* (New York: Oxford University Press, 2008).

4.8 Stahel's Division] The First Division of the Eleventh Corps had been commanded by Brigadier General Julius Stahel (1825–1912) until January 10, 1863, when Stahel was succeeded by Brigadier General Nathaniel C. McLean (1815–1905).

4.23–24 Colonel and Lieutenant Col.] Colonel Elias Peissner (1825–1863), a Bavarian-born professor of German and political economy at Union College in Schenectady, recruited the 119th New York Infantry in the summer of 1862 and commanded the regiment until May 2, 1863, when he was killed at Chancellorsville. Lieutenant Colonel John T. Lockman (1834–1912), a native of New York City, succeeded Peissner and led the regiment for the remainder of the war.

5.12 three letters from you] Theodore A. Dodge mailed portions of his wartime journal to his family in New York.

5.25 Von Steinwehr] Brigadier General Adolph von Steinwehr (1822–1877) commanded the Second Division of the Eleventh Corps.

6.32–33 Grand Divisions . . . Franklin] In November 1862 Burnside had organized the Army of the Potomac into three Grand Divisions: the Right, commanded by Major General Edwin V. Sumner (1797–1863); the Center, commanded by Major General Joseph Hooker (1814–1879); and the Left, commanded by Major General William B. Franklin (1823–1903). Each Grand Division was composed of two infantry corps and was assigned its own cavalry and artillery.

9.18 John] John Quincy Adams II (1833–1894), older brother of Henry Adams and Charles Francis Adams Jr. A lawyer, he served during the war on the staff of Massachusetts governor John A. Andrew.

10.8 Mary] Mary Adams (1845–1928), younger sister of Henry Adams and Charles Francis Adams Jr.

10.17 Lebe wohl.] Farewell.

12.36 Markoe] Captain Francis Markoe Bache (1833–1867), the son of Meade's sister, Maria Del Carmen Meade Bache (1810–1877), and Lieutenant Colonel Hartman Bache (1798–1872), an officer in the Army Corps of Engineers. Francis Markoe Bache joined Meade's staff in the summer of 1863 after the battle of Gettysburg.

12.37 Halleck] Major General Henry W. Halleck (1815–1872), general-in-chief of the Union armies from July 1862 to March 1864.

13.12 George] Lieutenant George Meade (1843–1897), General Meade's son, was serving with the 6th Pennsylvania Cavalry.

13.15 *Doubleday . . . Reserves*] Major General Abner Doubleday (1819–1893) had been assigned to command the Third Division of the First Corps, which Meade had led at South Mountain, Antietam, and Fredericksburg. The division included thirteen infantry regiments that were formerly part of the Pennsylvania Reserve Volunteer Corps, organized by the state authorities in May 1861 when Pennsylvania raised more troops than the federal government had initially called for.

13.18 Mr. Meredith] William M. Meredith (1799–1873) was secretary of the treasury, 1849–50, and attorney general of Pennsylvania, 1861–67.

13.21 my nomination] Meade had been appointed major general of volunteers on November 29, 1862.

14.8 Grand Division organization broken up] Hooker abolished the Grand Divisions on February 5, 1863, and Meade resumed command of the Fifth Corps.

14.27–28 *Dan Butterfield* & *Dan Sickles*] Major General Daniel Butterfield (1831–1901), a former superintendent of the American Express Company, had commanded a brigade in the Peninsula campaign and at Second Bull Run and a corps at Fredericksburg. Hooker appointed Butterfield chief of staff of the Army of the Potomac on January 29, 1863, and he served until July 9, 1863, when Meade replaced him with Major General Andrew A. Humphreys. Brigadier General Daniel E. Sickles (1819–1914) had served as a Democratic congressman from New York, 1857–61. Sickles had commanded a brigade during the Peninsula campaign and a division at Fredericksburg. Appointed commander of the Third Corps by Hooker on February 3, 1863, he served until July 2, 1863, when he was seriously wounded at Gettysburg.

15.18   Gibbons] Brigadier General John Gibbon (1827–1896) commanded a brigade at Second Bull Run, South Mountain, and Antietam, and a division at Fredericksburg.

15.39–40   we go to the James River] A week after the Union defeat at Fredericksburg, Major Generals William B. Franklin and William F. Smith had proposed to President Lincoln that the Army of the Potomac abandon its position on the Rappahannock River and instead advance on Richmond along the north and south banks of the James River.

16.12–13   General . . . Fremont, Hunter] Major Generals John C. Frémont (1813–1890), the Republican presidential nominee in 1856, and David Hunter (1802–1886) were both abolitionists.

16.20–21   Couch . . . Sedgwick] Darius Couch (1822–1897), commander of the Second Corps; Franz Sigel (1824–1902), commander of the recently formed Reserve Grand Division; Henry W. Slocum (1827–1894), commander of the Twelfth Corps; William F. Smith (1824–1903), commander of the Sixth Corps; John Sedgwick (1813–1864), who succeeded William F. Smith as commander of the Sixth Corps in February 1863.

16.23   Reynolds] John Reynolds (1820–1863), commander of the First Corps.

16.26   *Stoneman*] George Stoneman (1822–1894), commander of the Third Corps, who became commander of the Army of the Potomac's newly established Cavalry Corps in February 1863.

16.37   the Regulars.—Humphreys] Two brigades of regular U.S. infantry served in the Second Division of the Fifth Corps. Brigadier General Andrew A. Humphreys (1810–1883) commanded the Third Division in the Fifth Corps.

17.2   Secy.] Edwin M. Stanton (1814–1869), secretary of war, 1862–68.

17.5   *Berry*] Major General Hiram G. Berry (1824–1863) had led a brigade in the Peninsula campaign and at Fredericksburg. He commanded the First Division of the Third Corps from February 1863 to May 3, when he was killed at Chancellorsville. Like Butterfield and Sickles, Berry had not attended West Point.

17.14   en Prince] In a princely manner; lavishly.

17.21   South Mountain] The battle of South Mountain was fought in western Maryland on September 14, 1862.

18.30–32   I have heard, . . . a Dictator.] Henry J. Raymond (1820–1869), the editor of *The New York Times*, was told by his correspondent William Swinton on January 22, 1863, that Hooker had recently denounced Burnside as incompetent, described "the President and Government at Washington as imbecilic and 'played out,'" and called for a dictator. Raymond had repeated these remarks to Lincoln at a White House reception on January 24.

21.9–10   Capt. Hallowell of the 20th Mass. Infantry] Captain Norwood Penrose (Pen) Hallowell (1839–1914), an 1861 graduate of Harvard College, had fought at Ball's Bluff and Fair Oaks and had been wounded at Glendale and Antietam.

22.6   Oliver T. Beard] Lieutenant Colonel Oliver T. Beard of the 48th New York Infantry had led a company of the 1st South Carolina Volunteers, a recently organized black regiment, in successful raids along the Georgia and Florida coasts in November 1862. Beard resigned his commission on December 24, 1862.

23.18   Mr Stevens] Thaddeus Stevens (1792–1868) served in Congress as an antislavery Whig from Pennsylvania, 1849–53, and as a Republican from 1859 until his death.

24.2–3   "*Our God is marching on.*"] Julia Ward Howe (1819–1910), "The Battle Hymn of the Republic" (1862).

24.6   Capt Carpenter . . . Jessie Scouts] Captain Charles C. Carpenter commanded the Jessie Scouts, an irregular intelligence-gathering detachment formed in Missouri in 1861 by John C. Frémont and named in honor of his wife, Jessie Benton Frémont. After Frémont was relieved of his command in November 1861, Carpenter collected intelligence in Missouri, Kentucky, and Tennessee until the spring of 1862, when Major General Ulysses S. Grant ordered him expelled from his military district for horse stealing. Carpenter then rejoined Frémont in western Virginia, where he gave a dramatic account of his alleged exploits behind Confederate lines to the *Philadelphia Inquirer* in June 1862.

24.22   Washburne of Ill.] Elihu B. Washburne (1816–1887) was a Whig, and then Republican, congressman from Illinois, 1853–69. Washburne met Ulysses S. Grant shortly after the outbreak of the war and became his political patron.

24.24–27   the canal . . . the Yazoo] See Chronology, January–March 1863.

24.29–30   the gun boat . . . Vicksburg blockade] The *Queen of the West*. See Chronology, February 1863.

25.11   Joe Kernochan and Aspinwall] Joseph Kernochan (1789–1864) was a retired dry goods merchant. William H. Aspinwall (1807–1875) was a founder and former president of the Pacific Mail Steamship Company who had financed the construction of a railroad across the Isthmus of Panama in the 1850s.

25.13   at 823] 823 Broadway, between 12th and 13th Streets, the headquarters of the U.S. Sanitary Commission.

25.14   Murray Hoffman]   Hoffman (1791–1878) was assistant vice-chancellor of New York, 1839–43, a judge of the New York Superior Court, 1853–61, and the author of several legal treatises.

25.15   Dr. Bellow's]   Henry Bellows (1814–1882), a Unitarian pastor from New York City, helped found the U.S. Sanitary Commission in 1861 and served as its president throughout the war.

25.16   Gibbs and Agnew]   Oliver Wolcott Gibbs (1822–1908) was professor of chemistry at the Free Academy (later City College of New York), 1849–63, and at Harvard, 1863–87. Cornelius Rea Agnew (1830–1888), an ophthalmologist, was surgeon general of New York state, 1859–62. Both men served on the executive committee of the Sanitary Commission.

25.33   Rosecrans]   Major General William S. Rosecrans (1819–1898) commanded the Union Army of the Cumberland, which was deployed around Murfreesboro, Tennessee.

26.20   vibices]   Patches of effused blood beneath the skin.

26.39–40   *fortem . . . mentem*]   Latin: to keep a resolute attitude in difficult circumstances.

27.6   *adynamia*]   Lack of strength.

27.7   Bidwell]   Marshall S. Bidwell (1799–1872), Strong's law partner.

28.14   Wicks]   Sergeant Oscar Wicks had served with Norton in Company K of the 83rd Pennsylvania Infantry. Wicks was medically discharged on January 21, 1863.

28.21   Malvern Hill]   Union troops and artillery repulsed Confederate attacks at Malvern Hill near the James River on July 1, 1862, in the last of the Seven Days' Battles.

28.28   L.]   Norton's sister Elizabeth Norton Poss, known as Libby.

29.9   hog-car]   A railroad freight car used for transporting hogs.

29.19   Hanover Court House . . . Gaines' Mill]   The battle of Hanover Court House, fought north of Richmond on May 27, 1862, was a Union victory. Gaines' Mill, the third of the Seven Days' Battles, was fought on June 27, 1862, and ended with the Confederates driving Union forces south across the Chickahominy River.

33.20   Agnes]   Eleanor Agnes Lee (1841–1873), Lee's daughter.

33.25–27   Mrs. Jones . . . her husband]   Sarah Taylor Jones (1831–1917), a niece of Zachary Taylor, was the widow of Major General David R. Jones, a division commander in Lee's army who died of heart disease in Richmond on January 15, 1863.

33.27–28   Fitzhugh . . . Charlotte]   Brigadier General William Henry

Fitzhugh Lee (1837–1891), Lee's son, who commanded a cavalry brigade in the Army of Northern Virginia; Charlotte Wickham Lee (d. 1863), the wife of W.H.F. Lee.

33.32–33 George . . . Perry] The brothers George and Perry Parks were slaves owned by Lee's father-in-law, George Washington Parke Custis (1781–1857). Under the terms of Custis's will, they were freed on December 29, 1862.

34.3 *Annie Haggerty*] The daughter of a wealthy New York auctioneer, Annie Kneeland Haggerty (1835–1907) met Shaw in 1861 and became engaged to him at the end of 1862.

34.30 Susie's] Sarah Susannah Shaw Minturn (1839–1926), Shaw's sister.

37.3 vast gathering at Exeter Hall] A public meeting held by the London Emancipation Society on January 29, 1863, at Exeter Hall on the Strand, which could hold three thousand people in its main hall and another thousand in a smaller room. Henry Adams attended the event, and wrote to his brother Charles the following day: "Every allusion to the South was followed by groaning, hisses and howls, and the enthusiasm for Lincoln and for everything connected with the North, was immense."

38.4–5 "they who take . . . the sword."] Cf. Matthew 26:52.

38.9–10 when your Senatorial . . . the 4th,] The third session of the 37th Congress ended on March 3, 1863, after which the Senate held a special session, March 4–14.

40.3 Mr. Speaker] Francis Hoffmann (1822–1903), Republican lieutenant governor of Illinois, 1861–65. (Under the 1848 Illinois constitution, the lieutenant governor served as speaker of the senate.)

41.6 Colonel Mack] Alonzo W. Mack (1822–1871), an attorney, served in the Illinois house of representatives, 1858–60, and the state senate, 1860–68. Mack organized the 76th Illinois Infantry in August 1862 and served as its colonel until January 1863, when he resigned his commission in order to return to the state senate.

44.18 Col Stone] William M. Stone (1827–1893) commanded the 22nd Iowa Infantry from August 1862 to August 1863, when he resigned to run for governor on the Republican ticket. He served as governor of Iowa, 1864–68.

44.29 Gen Bentons] Brigadier General William P. Benton (1828–1867) commanded the First Division of the Union Army of Southeast Missouri.

45.33 Lieutenant Murray] Neill Murray (1827–1899) was the first lieutenant of Company C, 22nd Iowa Infantry. Murray was wounded in the assault on Vicksburg on May 22, 1863, and resigned his commission on May 27.

45.36 Cyrus & Mary . . . the babys] Cyrus Milner (1822–1881), brother of Catharine Peirce and husband of Mary Milner (1824–1900), Taylor Peirce's sister. Catharine and Taylor Peirce had three children: Sarah, born 1853; Frank, born 1858; and Ellis, born 1862.

45.34   Capt Ault]   Adam T. Ault (1822–1883) commanded Company C until August 1863, when he resigned due to chronic dysentery.

47.3–4   *Thomas Ewing Sr. . . . John Sherman*]   Thomas Ewing (1789–1871) served as a senator from Ohio, 1831–37 and 1850–51; as secretary of the treasury, 1841; and as secretary of the interior, 1849–50. William T. Sherman had married Ellen Ewing, his eldest daughter, in 1850. John Sherman (1823–1900) served as a Republican congressman from Ohio, 1855–61; as a senator, 1861–77 and 1881–97; as secretary of the treasury, 1877–81; and as secretary of state, 1897–98.

47.29–30   slips . . . Cincinnati Commercial]   Ellen Ewing Sherman (1824–1888) had sent clippings of favorable pieces about Sherman's leadership that appeared on January 24 and February 2, 1863.

48.10   Andre]   Major John André (1750–1780), an aide to Sir Henry Clinton, was captured in civilian disguise by New York militiamen on September 23, 1780, after he secretly met with Benedict Arnold to arrange for the surrender of West Point. André was tried as a spy and hanged on October 2, 1780.

48.32–33   the Manassas movement . . . McDowell]   Brigadier General Irvin McDowell (1818–1885) advanced with 30,000 men into northeastern Virginia on July 16, 1861, with the objective of defeating the 20,000 Confederate troops at Manassas Junction under General Pierre G. T. Beauregard (1818–1893). General Joseph E. Johnston (1807–1891) shifted his command of 11,000 men by rail out of the Shenandoah Valley and reinforced Beauregard at Manassas, leading to the Union defeat at the first battle of Bull Run on July 21.

48.36–37   Beauregard at Corinth]   Beauregard moved his headquarters to Corinth, Mississippi, in late March 1862 and retreated there after the battle of Shiloh, April 6–7. His army remained at Corinth until May 29, when Beauregard ordered its evacuation.

48.40   Halleck . . . Forts Henry & Donaldson]   As commander of the Department of the Missouri, Halleck was Grant's immediate superior in February 1862 when Grant's forces captured the two forts.

49.4   post of Arkansas]   See Chronology, January 1863.

50.13–15   Dr. Hewit . . . Dr. McMillan]   Henry S. Hewit (1825–1873) became the medical director of Grant's army in February 1862. Correspondent Whitelaw Reid, writing as "Agate," published a report in the *Cincinnati Gazette* on April 4 accusing Hewit of incompetence, drunkenness, and disloyalty. Hewit was removed from his post in late April, but was reinstated later in the year. Charles McMillan (c. 1825–1890) was the medical director of Sherman's corps.

50.35   do.]   Ditto.

52.20 Peter Hagner] Hagner (1772–1850) was an accounting clerk in the War Department, 1793–1817, and auditor of the U.S. Treasury, 1817–49.

53.26–27 The Captain . . . badly, cowardly] Frank W. Flanner was dismissed from the service on March 2, 1863.

53.30–31 Island No. 10] An island in the Mississippi near New Madrid, Missouri.

57.22 Mr. SPEAKER] Schuyler Colfax (1823–1885) was presiding as speaker pro tempore. A Republican congressman from Indiana, 1855–69, he was speaker of the house, 1863–69, and vice president of the United States, 1869–73.

57.31 Mr. OLIN] Abram B. Olin (1808–1879) was a Republican congressman from New York, 1857–63.

58.4 Mr. CAMPBELL] James H. Campbell (1820–1895) was a Republican congressman from Pennsylvania, 1859–63.

58.13 His threat] In his speech earlier in the day, Campbell had defended the Lincoln administration for arresting "spies and traitors" in the North and said: "Let me tell gentlemen on the other side that so far from condemning these arrests, it would be better for them if they could read the writing on the wall, and make their peace with liberty and their country while there is yet time. If they cannot see the evidence of a healthy reaction among the masses they are blind to the signs of the times. The error of the Government has been *leniency*. If it had given to traitors a drum-head court-martial and hempen cord, it would have better pleased the loyal men of the United States. [Applause in the galleries.] If I mistake not, the day is not far distant when the people will be so aroused against rebellion that traitors, their aiders and abettors, will call upon the rocks and mountains to cover them."

58.40 Mr. ROBINSON] James Robinson (1823–1886) was a Democratic congressman from Illinois, 1859–65 and 1871–75.

59.4 Mr. COX] Samuel Cox (1824–1889) was a Democratic congressman from Ohio, 1857–65, and from New York, 1869–73, 1873–85, and 1886–89.

59.17 Mr. ROSCOE CONKLING] Conkling (1829–1888) was a Republican congressman from New York, 1859–63 and 1865–67, and a senator, 1867–81.

59.22 Mr. JOHNSON] Philip Johnson (1818–1867) was a Democratic congressman from Pennsylvania, 1861–67.

59.33 Mr. VERREE] John Paul Verree (1817–1889) was a Republican congressman from Pennsylvania, 1859–63.

60.17–21 a gentleman . . . State and city] John Van Buren (1810–1866), son of Martin Van Buren, was a prominent New York Democrat who had supported John C. Breckinridge in the 1860 presidential election. Speaking to a

NOTES 817

Democratic meeting on February 10, 1863, Van Buren had said that "until the South can put down the men who led her into rebellion, the war must go on." In a speech to a Democratic campaign rally on October 13, 1862, Van Buren proposed that McClellan "be authorized" to take Richmond, after which a convention would be held at which "our Southern brethren" would be free to either rejoin the Union "under the Constitution as it is" or to separate.

60.22–23 "wayward sisters depart in peace."] In his October 13, 1862, speech, John Van Buren had read a letter sent by General Winfield Scott to William H. Seward on March 3, 1861, outlining four alternative policies the new administration could adopt toward the seceding states: offer new constitutional concessions, impose a blockade, launch an invasion with an army of 300,000 men, or "Say to the seceded States—wayward sisters, depart in peace."

60.34 the recent election] In the fall 1862 elections, the Democrats won the governorships of New Jersey and New York, legislative majorities in Illinois, Indiana, and New Jersey, and gained thirty-four seats in the House of Representatives, although the Republicans retained control of Congress.

61.29–30 "healthy reaction" . . . Mr. CAMPBELL] See note 58.13.

63.22 Baba] Turkish for "father," sometimes used as an honorific in the Ottoman Empire.

63.25 Turkish bow-string and the sack] Enemies of the Ottoman sultan were sometimes strangled with a bow-string or thrown in sacks into the Bosphorus.

65.3 Mr. WHITE] Chilton White (1826–1900) was a Democratic congressman from Ohio, 1861–65.

65.29 insurrection in Poland] An insurrection against Russian rule began in Poland on January 22, 1863. It was suppressed in 1864.

67.22–23 a single day . . . the king] The prohibition of a political banquet by the government of King Louis-Philippe led to demonstrations in Paris on February 22, 1848, that quickly turned into a popular revolution. Louis-Philippe abdicated on February 24, and the Second Republic was proclaimed that evening.

68.34–37 "inquire into . . . treasonable practices"] This provision was omitted from the seventh section of the final bill, which gave provost marshals the power to arrest deserters and spies.

69.8 act . . . twenty-fifth Edward III] The Treason Act of 1351, passed in the twenty-fifth year of the reign of Edward III.

69.15 act of Henry IV] The Treason Act of 1399, which repealed several laws expanding the crime of high treason enacted during the reign of Richard II (1377–99).

69.19 Lord Hale observes] Sir Matthew Hale (1609–1676), in his posthumously published *Historia Placitorum Coronæ: The History of the Pleas of the Crown* (2 vols., 1736).

69.37 Blackstone remarks,] William Blackstone (1723–1780), *Commentaries on the Laws of England* (4 vols., 1765–69), bk. IV, ch. 6.

70.23–24 Erskine . . . Hardy] Thomas Erskine (1750–1823) successfully defended Thomas Hardy (1752–1832), secretary of the radical London Corresponding Society, against charges of high treason in 1794. The speech quoted by Vallandigham was given by Erskine on February 5, 1781, at the trial of the anti-Catholic agitator Lord George Gordon (1751–1793), who had been charged with high treason for inciting the London "No Popery" riots of 1780. Gordon was acquitted.

70.39–40 declaration of Montesquieu] Charles de Secondat, Baron de Montesquieu (1689–1755), *The Spirit of the Laws* (1748), bk. XII, ch. 7.

71.2 Madison, in the Federalist] *The Federalist* No. 43, January 23, 1788.

71.11–12 Story, . . . declared] Joseph Story (1779–1845), *Commentaries on the Constitution of the United States* (3 vols., 1833), bk. III, ch. 39, sec. 1793. Story was an associate justice of the U.S. Supreme Court, 1811–45.

72.30 Barré] Isaac Barré (1726–1802) was a member of Parliament, 1761–90.

72.35–36 Ohio Senator . . . who said] Thomas Corwin (1794–1865), in a speech in the Senate on February 11, 1847, said: "If I were a Mexican, I would tell you, 'Have you not room in your own country to bury your dead men? If you come into mine, we will greet you with bloody hands, and welcome you to hospitable graves.'" Corwin was a Whig congressman, 1831–40; governor of Ohio, 1840–42; a U.S. senator, 1845–50; and secretary of the treasury, 1850–53. He served in Congress as a Republican, 1859–61, and as U.S. minister to Mexico, 1861–64.

72.40–73.2 Abraham Lincoln . . . this House?] In a speech delivered on January 12, 1848.

74.1 Forts Warren and La Fayette?] Fort Warren, on Georges Island in Boston Harbor, and Fort Lafayette, on the Brooklyn side of the entrance to New York harbor, were used to hold political prisoners during the Civil War.

75.32–33 Hamilton . . . Federalist] Cf. *The Federalist* No. 84, May 28, 1788.

77.7–11 twenty-fifth section . . . confinement indefinitely] Under the twenty-fifth section of the final bill, persons convicted of resisting the draft were subject to a $500 fine and two years' imprisonment.

77.12–13 the draft . . . complete] The Militia Act of July 17, 1862, made all able-bodied male citizens from eighteen to forty-five members of their

NOTES 819

respective state militias and authorized the president to call state militia into federal service for up to nine months. On August 4 the Lincoln administration summoned 300,000 militia into service, subject to the number of voluntary enlistments in each state. Although many states filled their recruiting quotas with volunteers, several states conducted militia drafts.

77.30–32   Keyes . . . Mr. MAY]   John W. Kees, the editor of the *Circleville Watchman*, a Democratic weekly in Ohio, was arrested on June 29, 1862, and held in the Old Capitol prison in Washington, D.C., for seventeen days before being released. Edson B. Olds (1802–1869), a former Democratic congressman from Ohio, was arrested on August 12, 1862, and held in Fort Lafayette until his release on December 12, 1862. During his imprisonment Olds was elected to the Ohio house of representatives. Dennis A. Mahony (1821–1879), editor of the *Dubuque Herald*, was arrested on August 14, 1862, and David Sheward (1825–after 1895), editor of the Fairfield *Constitution and Union*, was detained three days later. The two Iowa Democrats were held in the Old Capitol prison until November 11, 1862, when they were discharged after swearing allegiance to the United States. Mahony wrote about his arrest and detention in his book *The Prisoner of State* (1863). Kees, Olds, Mahony, and Sheward were all arrested on orders from Secretary of War Stanton for disloyalty and discouraging enlistments, although none of the men were ever charged. William J. Allen (1829–1901) was a Democratic congressman from Illinois, 1862–65, who advocated letting southern Illinois decide whether it should join the Confederacy. Allen was arrested on August 14, 1862, two months after winning a special election to Congress, and taken to Washington, where he was paroled to a hotel because of illness. President Lincoln ordered his discharge on September 16, 1862. Henry May (1816–1866) was a Unionist congressman from Maryland, 1861–63. He was arrested on suspicion of disloyalty on September 13, 1861, and imprisoned at Fort Lafayette. May was paroled on October 14 and discharged on December 12, 1861.

78.26   Festus]   See Acts 25:16.

79.2   prisoner of Chillon]   Poem (1816) by Lord Byron.

79.10   Weed]   Thurlow Weed (1797–1882), editor of the *Albany Evening Journal*, 1830–62, and a close political associate of William H. Seward.

79.15–16   minion of Mr. Seward]   Seth C. Hawley (1810–1884), a New York attorney Seward had engaged to examine the cases of political prisoners being held in New York and Boston.

80.37–81.2   lad of fifteen . . . "disloyal practices"]   A similar story, regarding an unnamed thirteen-year-old boy, appeared in the Columbus *Crisis* on December 24, 1862, and was later circulated in Democratic campaign literature in 1864.

81.10–13   hump-back carrier . . . Fort La Fayette]   George A. Hubbell, a news agent on the Naugatuck Railroad who suffered from a spinal deformity, was arrested on September 20, 1861, and imprisoned in Fort Lafayette on the orders of Secretary of War Simon Cameron for selling the *New York Daily News* after its circulation in Connecticut had been banned by U.S. marshal David H. Carr. Nathan Hubbell, a Methodist preacher and Republican, wrote to President Lincoln on September 21 vouching for his brother's loyalty, and Hubbell was released on Seward's orders on September 26, 1861. Benjamin Wood (1820–1900), a Democratic congressman from New York, 1861–65 and 1881–83, was editor and publisher of the *New York Daily News*, 1860–1900. His brother, Fernando Wood (1812–1881), was the Democratic mayor of New York, 1855–57 and 1860–61, and served in Congress, 1841–43, 1863–65, and 1867–81.

81.17 Hamilton declares] In *The Federalist* No. 84, May 28, 1788.

81.19 Blackstone declares] In *Commentaries on the Laws of England* (4 vols., 1765–69), bk. I, ch. 1.

81.26 "the pestilence . . . darkness."] Psalm 91:6.

83.4 Patrick Henry, in the Virginia Convention] Cf. Patrick Henry's speech in the Virginia Ratifying Convention, June 5, 1788.

83.17 Hamilton, in the Federalist] *The Federalist* No. 29, January 9, 1788.

84.7 answer of Hamilton] In *The Federalist* No. 29.

85.6 indemnity and suspension bill] The bill, which became law on March 3, 1863, authorized the president to suspend the privilege of the writ of habeas corpus "during the present rebellion" and indemnified government officials against legal proceedings brought against them for arrests made under presidential authority.

85.9 an Attorney General] Edward Bates (1793–1869) served as attorney general, 1861–64. He submitted an opinion to Congress on July 13, 1861, defending the constitutionality of Lincoln's suspension of the writ of habeas corpus.

85.19–21 Chief Justice . . . supreme court of Wisconsin] While sitting as a U.S. circuit court judge in Baltimore, Chief Justice Roger B. Taney ruled in *Ex parte Merryman* on May 28, 1861, that President Lincoln lacked the constitutional authority to suspend the writ of habeas corpus. The Supreme Court of Wisconsin issued a writ of habeas corpus on December 4, 1862, for Nicholas Kemp, who had been arrested by the military for participating in a riot against the militia draft in Port Washington on November 10. When the army refused to respond, the court ruled 3–0 on January 13, 1863, that Lincoln's suspension of the writ was legally void, but did not attempt to enforce its decision.

85.40 opinion of Story] In *Commentaries on the Constitution of the United States* (3 vols., 1833), bk. III, ch. 32, sec. 1336.

86.24 Mr. SHEFFIELD] William P. Sheffield (1820–1907) was a Union congressman from Rhode Island, 1861–63.

86.29–30   the bill . . . Senate in 1807]   On January 22, 1807, President Thomas Jefferson sent a special message to Congress in which he accused former vice president Aaron Burr of conspiring to foment war with Spain and detach the western states from the Union. William Branch Giles, a Democratic-Republican senator from Virginia, immediately introduced a bill in Congress suspending the writ of habeas corpus in cases of treason for three months. It passed the Senate on January 23 with only one dissenting vote, but was rejected by the House of Representatives, 113–19, on January 26.

87.33–34   the words . . . Job]   Job 2:4.

87.38   Mr. BIDDLE]   Charles J. Biddle (1819–1873) was a Democratic congressman from Pennsylvania, 1861–63.

90.25   Hartford Times]   A Democratic newspaper that supported Thomas H. Seymour's candidacy for governor.

91.3   western Egypt]   "Egypt" was a popular name for southern Illinois.

91.33–34   "winter of our discontent"]   *Richard III* I.i.1.

93.22–23   columbiad]   A large cannon used for coastal defense.

94.21   Genesis Point]   The peninsula on which Fort McAllister was built.

94.38–40   General Walker . . . Taliaferro]   Brigadier General William H. T. Walker (1816–1864), Brigadier General Thomas L. Clingman (1812–1897), Brigadier General William B. Taliaferro (1822–1898).

97.25   Your dear baby]   Mary Ruth Jones (1861–1934) was born on June 25, 1861, seven days before the death of her sister Julia Berrien Jones (1859–1861) from scarlet fever, and twelve days before the death of her mother Ruth Berrien Jones (1837–1861) from puerperal fever.

97.26–27   Daughter, Robert, . . . Stiles]   Mary Sharpe Jones Mallard (1835–1889), daughter of Charles C. Jones Sr. and Mary Jones; her husband, Robert Q. Mallard (1830–1904), a Presbyterian clergyman; Katherine Clay Stiles (1832–1916), a family friend.

98.17   L. M. CHILD]   Lydia Maria Child (1802–1880), a novelist and author of popular advice books, had edited the *National Anti-Slavery Standard* from 1841 to 1843; her antislavery works included *An Appeal in Favor of that Class of Americans Called Africans* (1833) and *Correspondence between Lydia Maria Child and Gov. Wise and Mrs. Mason of Virginia* (1860).

99.27   New York *Evangelist*]   The *Home Evangelist*, a monthly magazine published in New York by the American Baptist Home Mission Society, printed an article, "A Visit to the Freedmen," in its March 1863 number that said: "The three vices that prevail are lying, thieving and licentiousness. Drunkenness is increasing."

99.30   Gen. Saxton]   Brigadier General Rufus Saxton (1824–1908), the Union military governor of coastal South Carolina and Georgia, 1862–65.

102.1 butternuts] A term, derived from the use of butternut dyes in homespun clothing and military uniforms, for upland southerners; for upland southerners who had settled in the southern counties of Illinois, Indiana, and Ohio; and for Confederate soldiers.

102.5 Yellville] Town in northern Arkansas, about forty miles southeast of Forsyth, Missouri.

102.25 Hindman at Prairie Grove] Major General Thomas C. Hindman (1828–1868) unsuccessfully attacked Union forces at Prairie Grove in northwest Arkansas on December 7, 1862, before retreating the next day. The battle engaged about 11,000 Confederate and 9,000 Union soldiers, and cost the Confederates about 1,300 men killed, wounded, or missing, and the Union about 1,250.

102.30 Blunt] Brigadier General James G. Blunt commanded a Union division at Prairie Grove.

104.16 "Nincy" and Ab. Buckles] Absalom Nincehelser (1833–1907) and Abner J. Buckles (1833–1909) served with Clayton in Company H of the 19th Iowa Infantry.

104.21–22 Lt. Ferguson . . . Lt. Sommerville] Walter Ferguson commanded Company H in January 1863 before being sent home due to illness. He was discharged on February 26, 1863. George W. Sommerville (1819–1896) later commanded Company H and published a history of the unit in 1890.

105.29–30 General Banks] Major General Nathaniel P. Banks (1816–1894) commanded the Army of the Gulf, December 1862–May 1864.

106.35–36 "hewers of . . . of water."] Joshua 9:23.

108.27 Gen'l Hurlbert] Major General Stephen A. Hurlbut (1815–1882) commanded the Sixteenth Corps in the Army of the Tennessee.

108.28 Columbus] Columbus, Kentucky.

108.29 Jackson] Jackson, Tennessee.

108.31 Gen'l McPherson] Major General James B. McPherson (1828–1864) commanded the Seventeenth Corps in the Army of the Tennessee.

109.5–6 Col. Bissell's . . . Regiment] Josiah Wolcott Bissell (1818–1891) commanded the "Engineer Regiment of the West," organized in the fall of 1861 with men from Michigan, Illinois, Iowa, and Missouri.

109.14–15 Admiral Porter] Acting Rear Admiral David D. Porter (1813–1891), commander of the Mississippi Squadron.

109.18 Sunflower and Blackwater expeditions] Unsuccessful Union attempts to reach the Yazoo River to the northeast of Vicksburg via Steele's Bayou and the Sunflower River, and by way of Yazoo Pass and the Coldwater River. See Chronology, February–March 1863.

NOTES

109.28 Parrotts] Muzzle-loading rifled cannon, named after the New York ordnance manufacturer Robert R. Parrott (1804–1877).

109.32 Hewit] See note 50.13–15.

110.37 Captain Janney] William L. Jenney (1832–1907) was a civilian engineer who had joined the Union army in 1861.

111.1 Cranch] Christopher Pearse Cranch (1813–1892), a Unitarian minister, poet, and painter who lived in Paris, 1853–63.

111.2 Politechnique and Centrale] The École Polytechnique, scientific school founded in Paris in 1794 to train managers for the French civil service, and the École Centrale des Arts et Manufactures, engineering school founded in Paris in 1829. Janney had studied at the École Centrale.

111.10–11 Farragut's . . . Hartford] Rear Admiral David G. Farragut (1801–1870), commander of the West Gulf Blockading Squadron, had run past the batteries at Port Hudson, Louisiana, on the night of March 14 in his flagship, the steam sloop *Hartford*.

111.12 Dick Taylor's] Major General Richard Taylor (1826–1879), the son of Zachary Taylor, commanded the Confederate District of West Louisiana. Olmsted had visited his sugar plantation near New Orleans in 1853.

111.13–17 McMillan . . . Herald's correspondent.] Charles McMillan had been accused of "criminal oversight" by Thomas W. Knox (1835–1896), correspondent for the *New York Herald*, in a January 18, 1863, dispatch story that led to Knox's court-martial; see headnote on p. 47 in this volume.

111.26 Gen'l Steele] Major General Frederick Steele (1819–1868) commanded the First Division in Sherman's Fifteenth Corps.

111.30 Gen'l Blair's] Brigadier General Frank Blair (1821–1875) commanded a brigade in Sherman's corps. Blair served as a Republican congressman from Missouri, 1857–59, 1861–62, and 1863–64. He was the brother of Montgomery Blair, postmaster general, 1861–64, and the son of Francis Preston Blair, an adviser to President Lincoln.

114.24 Governors of Iowa and Wisconsin] Samuel J. Kirkwood (1813–1894) was the Republican governor of Iowa, 1860–64 and 1876–77; a senator, 1866–67 and 1877–81; and secretary of the interior, 1881–82. Edward Salomon (1828–1909) was the Republican governor of Wisconsin, 1862–64.

114.27 Governor of Illinois] Richard Yates (1815–1873) was the Republican governor of Illinois, 1861–65. Yates served in Congress as a Whig, 1851–55, and in the Senate as a Republican, 1865–71.

115.4–5 Governor of Indiana] Oliver Perry Morton (1823–1877) was the Republican governor of Indiana, 1861–67, and a senator, 1867–77.

115.20–21 his adjutant General] Lieutenant Colonel John A. Rawlins (1831–1869).

115.32 Breese his flag-captain] Lieutenant Commander Kidder Randolph Breese (1831–1881) was the captain of Porter's flagship *Black Hawk*, a converted river steamboat.

118.10 "*A man's . . . a' that.*"] Song (1795) by Robert Burns.

118.11–12 American citizen, . . . highest legal adviser] Attorney General Edward Bates issued an opinion on November 29, 1862, declaring that free black persons born in the United States were American citizens.

120.14 another Detroit] William Faulkner, a Detroit tavern keeper, was arrested on February 26, 1863, for allegedly raping a nine-year-old white girl. Although Faulkner claimed to be of Spanish and American Indian ancestry, he was identified in the newspapers as a "negro." The case was extensively covered in the *Detroit Free Press*, a Democratic newspaper that for months had been warning its readers that the Emancipation Proclamation would result in racial "amalgamation" and the loss of jobs for white labor. Faulkner was convicted of rape on March 6 and sentenced to life imprisonment. After an attempt to lynch him outside the courthouse failed, white mobs began attacking black residents and setting fire to their homes and businesses. Two men, one white and one black, were killed and approximately thirty-five buildings destroyed before troops ended the rioting before midnight. Faulkner was pardoned in 1870 after his accuser recanted her story.

123.2–3 Tallahatchie and at Deer Creek,] See Chronology, March 1863.

123.27 Governor Letcher] John Letcher (1813–1884) was governor of Virginia, 1860–64. He had previously served in Congress as a Democrat, 1851–59.

123.34 Col. I. W. Garrett] Isham W. Garrott (1816–1863) and William M. Brooks had practiced law together in Marion, Alabama, before the war. Garrott became the colonel of the 20th Alabama Infantry in 1861 and led the regiment until June 17, 1863, when he was killed at Vicksburg.

125.10 Judge Campbell] John A. Campbell (1811–1889) was an associate justice of the U.S. Supreme Court, 1853–61, and an assistant secretary in the Confederate War Department, 1862–65.

125.11 Judge Meredith] John A. Meredith (1814–1882) was judge of the Richmond circuit court, 1852–69. Meredith had ruled on February 24, 1863, in a habeas corpus case that every citizen of Maryland, and every foreigner, who had previously enlisted in the Confederate service for any length of time was subject to conscription.

125.14–15 the mayor] Joseph C. Mayo (1795–1872) was mayor of Richmond, 1853–65 and 1866–68.

125.38–39 Gen. Elzey . . . Secretary of War] Major General Arnold Elzey (1816–1871), commander of the Richmond defenses; Brigadier General John H. Winder (1800–1865), the Confederate provost marshal; James A. Seddon (1815–1880), Confederate secretary of war, 1862–65.

126.11   Gen. D. H. Hill] Major General Daniel Harvey Hill (1821–1889), commander of the Confederate Department of North Carolina and Southern Virginia.

126.23–24   the tax bill] See Chronology, April 24, 1863.

126.25–26   Gen. Blanchard . . . Massachusetts] Brigadier General Albert G. Blanchard (1810–1891) had been relieved of his command in northern Louisiana for failing to stop raids by the Union forces camped along the Mississippi near Vicksburg. A West Point graduate, Blanchard had settled in Louisiana after resigning from the army in 1840.

126.31–32   the capture . . . five guns] The Union gunboat *Diana* ran aground in Berwick Bay, Louisiana, on March 28, 1863, after being damaged by Confederate artillery fire and was captured by troops from the 13th Battalion Texas Cavalry and the 28th Louisiana Infantry. On April 14, 1863, the Confederates burned the *Diana* to prevent her from being retaken by Union forces after their victory at Bayou Teche.

126.34–35   Charleston . . . the forts] See Chronology, April 7, 1863.

129.22   Liverpool Point] On the Maryland shore of the lower Potomac, about thirty-five miles south of Washington.

130.5–6   General Hunt] Brigadier General Henry J. Hunt (1819–1889) was chief of artillery of the Army of the Potomac, 1862–65.

130.7–8   Fifth . . . Franklin] Major General Fitz John Porter (1822–1901) commanded the Fifth Corps, May–November 1862. He was cashiered from the army on January 21, 1863, after being convicted at court-martial of disobedience and misconduct at Second Bull Run. Major General William B. Franklin commanded the Sixth Corps from May to November 1862, when he became commander of the Left Grand Division of the Army of the Potomac (see note 6.32–33).

130.12–13   Major DePeyster . . . Howe's division] John Watts De Peyster Jr. (1841–1873) was commissioned in 1862 as a major in the 1st New York Light Artillery, Wainwright's regiment, and later assigned to command the artillery in the Second Division of the Sixth Corps, led by Brigadier General Albion P. Howe (1818–1897).

130.26   Colonel Von Vegesack] Ernst von Vegesack (1820–1903), a Swedish military officer, came to the United States in 1861 to join the Union army. He commanded the 20th New York Infantry at South Mountain, Antietam, Fredericksburg, and Chancellorsville, then returned to Sweden after the regiment mustered out at the end of its two-year enlistment term in June 1863.

131.9   one of his sons] Thomas (Tad) Lincoln (1853–1871).

132.25–26   Sanderson] Lieutenant Colonel James M. Sanderson (1815?–1871), a former New York hotel manager and author of *Camp Fires and Camp*

Cooking; or, Culinary Hints for the Soldier (1862), was the commissary of subsistence of the First Corps.

132.29–30 Dupont's fleet . . . *Keokuk* sunk] Rear Admiral Samuel Francis Du Pont (1803–1865), commander of the South Atlantic Blockading Squadron, 1861–63, led the unsuccessful naval assault on Charleston Harbor. The *Keokuk* was badly damaged by Confederate shore batteries on April 7 and sank the next day.

132.36–37 first report . . . Conduct of the War] The seven-member Joint Committee on the Conduct of the War, made up of three senators and four representatives and dominated by Radical Republicans, was established by Congress on December 10, 1861, in response to the Union defeats at Bull Run and Ball's Bluff. It issued its first report, which focused primarily on the operations of the Army of the Potomac, on April 6, 1863.

133.5–7 War Department order . . . treasonable sentiments] General Orders No. 89, issued by the adjutant general's office in the War Department on April 6, 1863, announced that Lieutenant John M. Garland of the 42nd New York Infantry had been dishonorably discharged for writing that the Emancipation Proclamation was "as unconstitutional as it is unjust" and that the "principles" and "hearts" of the administration were "blacker than the 'nigger' they are fighting for." (Garland's letter, addressed to the Reverend Elliott H. Thompson in Shanghai, was opened by the post office because it carried insufficient postage.)

138.5–6 fair Italy has risen] Victor Emmanuel II of Sardinia-Piedmont was proclaimed king of a united Italy in 1861.

138.27–28 "corner-stone] In a widely reported speech given in Savannah, Georgia, on March 21, 1861, Confederate vice president Alexander H. Stephens (1812–1883) said that the "corner-stone" of the Confederacy "rests upon the great truth, that the negro is not equal to the white man; that slavery—subordination to the superior race—is his natural and normal condition."

139.25 our Crawfords?] Thomas Crawford (1814–1857), American sculptor born and raised in New York City who spent much of his career in Italy. His work included the design for the Statue of Freedom on top of the U.S. Capitol dome.

142.18–19 James Louis Petigru] Petigru (1789–1863) was attorney general of South Carolina, 1822–30, and led the opposition to nullification in the state house of representatives, 1830–32. He later served as the U.S. attorney for South Carolina, 1850–53, and opposed secession in 1860.

142.19–20 Baphomet] A pagan idol allegedly worshipped by the medieval Knights Templar.

145.6–11 foreign minister . . . breach] Henri Mercier (1816–1886), the French minister to the United States from July 1860 to December 1863, was considered by many northerners to be sympathetic to the Confederacy. In January 1863 Mercier had become involved with the Colorado mining promoter William Cornell Jewett (1823–1893), Horace Greeley of the *New York Tribune*, and Congressman Clement L. Vallandigham in an unsuccessful attempt to gain support for European mediation of the war.

148.19 the 19th regulars] The 19th U.S. Infantry.

148.25 my long illness] Connolly had fallen ill with typhoid fever in November 1862.

149.26 Morgan . . . Forrest] Brigadier General John Hunt Morgan (1825–1864), Major General Joseph Wheeler (1836–1906), Brigadier General John Wharton (1828–1865), and Brigadier General Nathan Bedford Forrest (1821–1877). Wheeler was a cavalry corps commander, and Morgan, Wharton, and Forrest were cavalry division commanders, in the Army of Tennessee.

149.34 Burnsides' armies] Major General Ambrose Burnside (1824–1881) had taken command of the Department of the Ohio on March 17, 1863.

152.16 Hains Bluff] Hayne's Bluff, overlooking the Yazoo River about eleven miles northeast of Vicksburg.

153.21 this Department] The Department of the South, which included South Carolina, Georgia, and most of Florida.

154.6 Mr. Jefferson has beautifully said] Cf. Query XVIII, *Notes on the State of Virginia* (1785).

155.17 Van Dorn] Major General Earl Van Dorn (1820–1863) commanded a cavalry corps in the Army of Tennessee. On April 10, 1863, Van Dorn conducted a reconnaissance of the Union positions at Franklin, Tennessee, before withdrawing to Spring Hill.

155.18–19 Brother Coley and Dr. Buckner] Coleman Stone (c. 1844–1863) served with the 28th Mississippi Cavalry. He died on September 22, 1863, from injuries he received by being thrown from his horse. Dr. C. B. Buckner, a druggist and planter who served as a captain with the 28th Mississippi Cavalry, was married to Kate Stone's aunt, Laura Ragan Buckner.

157.3 Little Sister] Amanda Stone (c. 1850–1934).

157.24 Mrs. Alexander] The mother of Mary Hardison.

158.5 Jimmy] Kate Stone's brother, James A. Stone (c. 1847–1905).

158.15 Mamma] Kate Stone's widowed mother, Amanda Ragan Stone (c. 1824–1892).

158.25 Webster] A slave who worked as a dining room servant and coachman on the Stone plantation.

158.29 Beverly] Laura Ragan Buckner's daughter, who was about three years old.

159.29 Johnny's lap] Kate Stone's brother, John B. Stone (c. 1848–1930).

160.9 Charles] A slave who worked with Webster in the dining room of the Stone plantation.

160.17–18 Finish this another day.] In her journal for April 27, 1863, Stone described how her family traveled in two dugouts through bayous and swamps to the plantation of Dr. James G. Carson, where they stayed for nearly three weeks before resuming their westward flight.

163.29 this brigade] The Second Brigade of the Second Division in the Sixth Corps was made up of the 2nd, 3rd, 4th, 5th, and 6th Vermont Infantry and the 26th New Jersey Infantry.

165.20 a disgraceful affair] On the night of April 19, 1863, as many as a dozen soldiers from the 5th Vermont Infantry attacked a black family living in a cabin near their picket line, beating John Frazier and raping his wife and her twelve-year-old niece. When the picket guard was alerted and approached the cabin, they were fired upon and returned fire, wounding one of the assailants. Although the victims were unable to identify most of their attackers, Sergeant Lawson M. Perkins was court-martialed and sentenced to five years in prison on May 22, 1863. Perkins was released on December 16, 1864, and returned to duty with the 5th Vermont before mustering out in June 1865. Private Moses D. Emerson was also convicted and imprisoned, but was released on August 8, 1864, and returned to the 5th Vermont, where he served for the remainder of the war.

167.34 Rhodes'] Brigadier General Robert E. Rodes (1829–1864) commanded a division in the Second Corps of the Army of Northern Virginia, led by Lieutenant General Thomas J. (Stonewall) Jackson.

167.37 A. P. Hill] Major General Ambrose Powell Hill (1825–1865) led a division in Jackson's corps. (A. P. Hill was not related to Major General Daniel Harvey Hill.)

167.38 Trimble & Early] The division in Jackson's corps assigned to Major General Isaac R. Trimble (1802–1888) was led in the Chancellorsville campaign by Brigadier General Raleigh E. Colston (1825–1896) because Trimble was still recovering from being wounded at Second Manassas. Major General Jubal A. Early (1816–1894) led a division in Jackson's corps.

170.5–6 Revocation . . . Nantes] In 1685 Louis XIV revoked the Edict of Nantes, issued by Henry IV in 1598, which had granted religious and political rights to French Protestants.

170.20 Brother's] Philip Hicky Morgan (1825–1900), Sarah Morgan's half brother, was a successful attorney in New Orleans who had remained loyal to the Union.

170.24 Gen. Bowen] Brigadier General James Bowen (1808–1886) was the provost marshal of the Union Department of the Gulf.

171.6   Miriam] Sarah Morgan's older sister, Miriam Morgan (1840–1898), later Miriam Morgan Dupré.

171.17–18   George and Gibbes] Sarah Morgan's brothers George M. Morgan (1838–1864) and Thomas Gibbes Morgan (1835–1864) were serving with the Confederate army in Virginia. George M. Morgan would die of illness at Orange Court House on January 12, 1864; Thomas Gibbes Morgan was captured at Rappahannock Station on November 7, 1863, and died of illness in the prison camp at Johnson's Island, Ohio, on January 21, 1864.

171.19   Banks . . . Attakapas] A region of southern Louisiana that includes Bayou Teche. See Chronology, April 1863.

172.31–32   the river] The Rappahannock.

172.33   Hamilton's Crossing] A railroad depot five miles southeast of Fredericksburg.

173.8   Col. Sam. B. Pickens] Colonel Samuel B. Pickens (1839–1891) commanded the 12th Alabama Infantry, 1862–65.

175.11   Capt. Williams] Captain Jonathan W. Williams (1840–1908) commanded Company D of the 5th Alabama Infantry, in which Pickens served.

175.21–22   Col. Hobson] Lieutenant Colonel Edwin Lafayette Hobson (1835–1901), second in command of the 5th Alabama Infantry.

176.40   Col. Oneil] Colonel Edward A. O'Neal (1818–1890), Pickens's brigade commander.

178.11   The Generals] Jackson and Lee.

178.15   General Stuart] Major General J.E.B. Stuart (1833–1864) commanded the cavalry corps of the Army of Northern Virginia.

178.23   the   house] The Luckett house.

179.11   Smith and   .] Smith and Wilbourn. Lieutenant James Power Smith (1837–1923) was one of Jackson's aides; Captain Richard E. Wilbourn (1838–1875) was the chief signal officer in Jackson's corps.

179.14   Dr. McGuire] Hunter H. McGuire (1835–1900) was the medical director of Jackson's corps.

179.15   Lacey] The Reverend Beverly Tucker Lacy (1819–1900), a Presbyterian minister who served as the chaplain of Jackson's corps.

179.30   Colonel Long] Armistead L. Long (1825–1891), one of Lee's staff officers.

179.34–36   Anderson . . . McLaws] Major General Richard Anderson (1821–1879) and Major General Lafayette McLaws (1821–1897) commanded divisions in the First Corps of the Army of Northern Virginia, led by Lieutenant General James Longstreet. During the Chancellorsville campaign

Anderson and McLaws reported directly to Lee while Longstreet was on detached duty in southeast Virginia.

180.8   the Irish Battalion]   The 1st Virginia Infantry Battalion.

180.11   Major A. S. Pendleton]   Alexander S. Pendleton (1840–1864), Jackson's assistant adjutant general (chief of staff).

180.32   Boswell]   Captain James K. Boswell (1838–1863), a topographical engineer serving on Jackson's staff.

181.3   Major J. Horace Lacey]   Lacy (1823–1906) was the brother of Beverly Tucker Lacy (see note 179.15).

181.7   Brown]   Sergeant Samuel Howell Brown (1831–1905), who had served as surveyor of Jefferson County, Virginia, before the war.

181.22–23   Morrison . . . Mrs. Jackson]   Lieutenant Joseph G. Morrison (1842–1906), one of Jackson's aides, was the brother of Mary Anna Morrison Jackson (1831–1915).

181.25–26   Colonel Crutchfield]   Colonel Stapleton Crutchfield (1835–1865), the chief of artillery in Jackson's corps, had his leg amputated after being wounded on May 2.

181.40   Col. French]   Colonel Samuel Bassett French (1820–1898) served as a military aide to Virginia governor John Letcher.

182.4   Stoneman]   Major General George Stoneman led a cavalry raid against the railroads between Richmond and Fredericksburg, April 29–May 8, that failed to seriously disrupt Lee's supply line.

182.17   United States Ford]   A ford across the Rappahannock.

184.30–32   Genl Carr . . . Genl McClernand]   Brigadier General Eugene A. Carr (1830–1910), Brigadier General Alvin P. Hovey (1821–1891), and Brigadier General Peter J. Osterhaus (1823–1917) commanded divisions in the Thirteenth Corps of the Army of the Tennessee. Major General John A. McClernand (1812–1900), the corps commander, had been a Democratic congressman from Illinois, 1843–51 and 1859–61.

185.37–38   Genl Green . . . Baldwin]   Brigadier General Martin E. Green (1815–1863), Brigadier General Edward D. Tracy (1833–1863), and Brigadier General William E. Baldwin (1827–1864) commanded brigades in the division led by Brigadier General John S. Bowen (1830–1863). Tracy was killed at Port Gibson, Green was killed during the siege of Vicksburg, and Bowen died of dysentery shortly after Vicksburg surrendered.

186.12   about 3,500 of their men]   Confederate losses at Port Gibson were reported as sixty killed, 340 wounded, and 387 missing.

186.35–36   the 23 Iowa . . . the loss]   The regiment's casualties at Port Gibson were reported as nine killed and twenty-six wounded.

187.12 Lt Col Glasgow] Lieutenant Colonel Samuel L. Glasgow (1838–1916) led the 23rd Iowa Infantry at Port Gibson.

187.32 Genl Quinbys brigade] Brigadier General Isaac F. Quinby (1821–1891) commanded a division in the Seventeenth Corps.

187.33 Smiths Divisions] Brigadier General Andrew J. Smith (1815–1897) led a division in the Thirteenth Corps.

190.23 Libby Prison] Prison for Union soldiers in Richmond that was established in a warehouse formerly used by Libby & Sons, a ship provisioning company.

190.26–27 "One blast . . . men."] Cf. Sir Walter Scott, *The Lady of the Lake* (1810), Canto VI, stanza 18.

191.20–21 "With His . . . the victory."] Cf. Psalm 98:1.

191.34–35 His brother in Law] Edmondston confused D. H. Hill, whose wife Isabella was a sister of Mary Anna Morrison Jackson, with A. P. Hill.

192.16–17 Col Duke of Wise's Legion] Colonel Richard T. W. Duke (1822–1898) was the commander of the 46th Virginia Infantry. Organized in 1861 as part of Wise's Legion, a force in northwestern Virginia commanded by Brigadier General Henry A. Wise, the regiment was later posted to Chaffin's Bluff along the James River south of Richmond. Wise (1806–1876) had served as a congressman from Virginia, 1833–44, and as governor, 1856–60.

192.19 Tunstall's] Tunstall Station, about fifteen miles east of Richmond.

193.19–20 Gen Paxton . . . Stonewall Brigade] Brigadier General Elisha F. Paxton (1828–1863) was killed at Chancellorsville on May 3. The Stonewall brigade was recruited from the Shenandoah Valley of Virginia in April 1861 and was commanded by Thomas J. Jackson at the first battle of Manassas, July 21, 1861, where both the brigade and its commander earned the nickname "Stonewall" for their defensive stand on Henry Hill.

193.23–24 Van Dorn is dead] Major General Earl Van Dorn was shot to death in Spring Hill, Tennessee, on May 7, 1863, by Dr. George B. Peters, who claimed Van Dorn was having an affair with his wife.

193.33 Hascosea] Plantation in Halifax County, North Carolina, used as a summer home by the Edmondstons.

194.14–15 "Little children . . . idols."] 1 John 5:21.

194.23–24 Thomas Jones . . . wife] Thomas Devereux Jones (1838–1863) and Martha (Pattie) Ann Skinner (1842–1889) were married on January 1, 1863. A captain in the 27th North Carolina Infantry, Jones was wounded at Bristoe Station, Virginia, on October 14, 1863, and died in Richmond on November 6.

194.27 Hill's repulse at Washington] Major General D. H. Hill unsuccessfully besieged the Union garrison at Washington, North Carolina, March 30–April 15, 1863.

196.18   Colonel McVicars] Lieutenant Colonel Duncan McVicar (1827–1863) of the 6th New York Cavalry.

197.4   General Geary] Brigadier General John W. Geary (1819–1873) commanded the Second Division of the Twelfth Corps.

197.20   General Howard] Major General Oliver Otis Howard (1830–1909), commander of the Eleventh Corps since April 1863.

197.28   General Williams' Division] Brigadier General Alpheus S. Williams (1810–1878) commanded the First Division of the Twelfth Corps.

198.22   Dutchmen] Many of the soldiers in the Eleventh Corps were German-American.

199.5   General Birney's Division] Brigadier General David B. Birney (1825–1864) commanded the First Division of the Third Corps.

201.32   General Patrick] Brigadier General Marsena R. Patrick (1811–1888), provost marshal of the Army of the Potomac.

203.18   The old Second] The 2nd Massachusetts Infantry.

205.26   general of brigade] Colonel Samuel S. Carroll (1832–1893) commanded the First Brigade in the Third Division of the Second Corps.

205.33   French's division] Brigadier General William H. French (1815–1881) commanded the Third Division of the Second Corps.

208.25   "the best army . . . planet,"] At a dinner held on April 8, 1863, during President Lincoln's visit to army headquarters, Hooker had called the Army of the Potomac "the finest army on the planet."

208.34–209.1   Longstreet didn't come up at all] See Chronology, May 4–5, 1863.

214.17   the Merrimack] In 1861, Union forces scuttled and burned the steam frigate U.S.S. *Merrimack* when they evacuated the Norfolk navy yard. The Confederates raised and rebuilt the ship as the ironclad ram C.S.S. *Virginia* and used it to attack the Union fleet in Hampton Roads on March 8, 1862. After fighting its historic duel with the ironclad U.S.S. *Monitor* on March 9, the *Virginia* remained at Norfolk until May 11, 1862, when it was blown up to prevent its capture following the Confederate evacuation of the city.

216.21   Dr Rogers] Dr. Seth Rogers (1823–1893), a friend of Higginson's and the owner of the Worcester Hydropathic Institution, served as surgeon of the 1st South Carolina Volunteers.

217.14–18   Maj Strong . . . Lt. Col. Billings] Lieutenant Colonel Liberty Billings (1823–1877) was dismissed from the army for incompetence by an examining board on July 28, 1863, at which time Major John D. Strong was promoted to lieutenant colonel and became the regiment's second in command. Strong resigned his commission on August 15, 1864.

218.29   The Tribune correspondent]   Clarence A. Page (1838–1873) was a war correspondent for the *New-York Daily Tribune*, 1862–65.

219.11   Col. Hawkins']   Colonel Hiram Hawkins (1826–1914) commanded the Confederate 5th Kentucky Infantry.

219.17   "That is . . . of all"!]   Maria Edgeworth (1767–1849), *The Modern Griselda* (1804).

220.26–27   "*He gave . . . away*".]   Cf. Job 1:21.

220.37   on   at]   On May 10 at.

221.3   Major Hawkes]   Major Wells J. Hawks (1814–1873), the chief commissary officer in Jackson's corps.

221.5   on   where]   On May 11 where.

221.13   Gen Ewell]   Richard S. Ewell (1817–1872) commanded a division under Jackson, March 1862–August 1862, and the Second Corps of the Army of Northern Virginia, May 1863–May 1864.

221.14   the battle of   ]   The battle of Groveton (or Brawner Farm), August 28, 1862, was part of the Second Manassas campaign.

221.18   "fame is . . . brass"]   See Horace, *Odes*, bk. III. xxx.

221.31–32   *Balaams numerical horse*]   See Numbers 22:21–35.

222.19–20   Brig Genl Shackelford]   A native of Lincoln County, Kentucky, James M. Shackelford (1827–1909) commanded a Union brigade with its headquarters in Russellville.

223.3   "submit to . . . that be"]   See Romans 13:1.

223.22–23   Buckner . . . Boone & Burnett]   Camp Boone and Camp Burnett were set up near Clarksville in northwestern Tennessee in the summer of 1861 to recruit and train Kentucky Confederate troops. Brigadier General Simon Bolivar Buckner (1823–1914) took command of the camps in September 1861 and led several regiments into Kentucky in order to occupy Bowling Green.

224.20   Lizzie]   Browder's wife, Ann Elizabeth Warfield Browder (d. 1897).

224.26   Bro Alexander]   William Alexander (1818–1883), a Methodist preacher who shared the Logan County circuit with Browder.

227.17–18   General Burnside . . . Cincinnati Court]   Vallandigham applied for a writ of habeas corpus in the U.S. Circuit Court for the Southern

District of Ohio on May 9, 1863, two days after his conviction by a military commission. On May 11 Burnside submitted a written statement to the court in which he declared that "my duty requires me to stop license and intemperate discussion, which tends to weaken the authority of the Government and army." After hearing arguments from attorneys representing Vallandigham and Burnside, Judge Humphrey H. Leavitt refused to issue a writ and stated that Burnside, as an agent of the president, had the power during time of war to "arrest persons who, by their mischievous acts of disloyalty, impede or endanger the military operations of the government."

228.3 Fernando Wood's party] Fernando Wood (see note 81.10–13) was a leading New York Peace Democrat.

232.23 Colonel Montgomery] James Montgomery (1814–1871) later commanded a brigade of black troops in South Carolina and Florida before resigning his commission in 1864.

233.1 Mr. Butler King's] Thomas Butler King (1800–1864), a lawyer and planter who served in Congress as a Whig, 1839–43 and 1845–50.

234.31 Effie] Shaw's sister, Josephine Shaw (1843–1905), who married Colonel Charles Russell Lowell Jr. (1835–1864) in October 1863. Lowell was fatally wounded at Cedar Creek, Virginia, on October 19, 1864, while leading the 2nd Massachusetts Cavalry.

235.13 "Semmes"] Raphael Semmes (1809–1877), captain of the Confederate commerce raider *Alabama*, 1862–64.

235.33–37 Pierce Butler . . . three hundred slaves] In 1836 Pierce Butler (1810–1867) inherited a half-share in the coastal Georgia rice and cotton plantations of his grandfather Pierce Butler (1744–1822), a South Carolina delegate to the Constitutional Convention who later served in the Senate. Heavily in debt from gambling and financial losses in the panic of 1857, Butler sold 429 men, women, and children at a Savannah race course in March 1859 for $303,850.

236.2 Miss Fanny] English actress and writer Frances Anne (Fanny) Kemble (1809–1893) married Pierce Butler in 1834. They separated in 1845 and were divorced in 1849, in part because of her opposition to slavery. Kemble published an account of her stay on the Butler plantations, *Journal of a Residence on a Georgian Plantation in 1838–1839*, in 1863.

236.25 the young ladies] Sarah Butler Wister (1835–1908) and Frances Butler Leigh (1838–1910), the daughters of Fanny Kemble and Pierce Butler.

237.24 Mr. Ritchie] Lieutenant John Ritchie (1836–1919) served as the quartermaster of the 54th Massachusetts, 1863–65.

241.20 Colonel Page] Lieutenant Colonel Page of the 9th Louisiana Infantry (African Descent), who took command of the regiment after Colonel Hermann Lieb (1826–1908) was wounded.

241.32 enemy cried, "No quarters"] In a report dated June 8, 1863, Colonel Lieb wrote that in the fighting along the levee the Confederates charged "madly on with cries of 'No quarters for white officers, kill the damned Abolitionists, but spare the niggers' &c." Captain Corydon Heath of the 9th Louisiana (African Descent) and Second Lieutenant George Conn of the 11th Louisiana (African Descent) were recorded in Union army records as having been killed after being taken prisoner at Milliken's Bend.

241.34–35 Colonel Allen . . . Brigadier-General Walker] Colonel Robert T. P. Allen (1813–1888), the commander of the 17th Texas Infantry, survived the battle. Major General John G. Walker (1821–1893) commanded the division that attacked the Union lines at Milliken's Bend, but was not present on the battlefield.

246.21–23 General Hurlbut . . . Lawyer] Major General Stephen A. Hurlbut (1815–1882) was born in South Carolina and was admitted to the bar there in 1837. Hurlbut moved to Illinois in 1845 and served as a Republican in the Illinois house of representatives, 1859–61.

249.21 Haseltine] Major James Henry Hazeltine.

249.26–29 Captain Treichel . . . Captain Leiper] William P. C. Treichel was discharged from the army as a major in July 1864; William White (b. 1843) was mustered out as a captain in November 1864; Charles B. Davis was killed at Brandy Station, June 9, 1863; Samuel R. Colladay (1842–1884) was captured at Brandy Station, exchanged in March 1864, and resigned from the army; Charles Lewis Leiper (1842–1899) was promoted to major in September 1864 and served as the last commander of the 6th Pennsylvania Cavalry.

249.31 Major Morris] Robert Morris (1837–1863), the great-grandson of the Revolutionary financier Robert Morris, commanded the 6th Pennsylvania Cavalry at Brandy Station. He was taken prisoner during the battle and died of scurvy in Libby prison at Richmond on August 13, 1863.

251.13 Captain Rodenbaugh] Theophilus F. Rodenbough (1838–1912) of the 2nd U.S. Cavalry.

251.33 Frazier's] Captain William West Frazier (1839–1921), commander of Company B in the 6th Pennsylvania Cavalry.

252.13 5th Cavalry] The 5th U.S. Cavalry.

252.25 Lieut. Lennig] Thompson Lennig (1841–1911) was taken prisoner at Brandy Station and exchanged in March 1864.

252.30 Bulwer's "What will he do with it"] Novel (1858) by Edward Bulwer-Lytton, originally published under the pseudonym Pisistratus Caxton.

252.39 General Buford] Brigadier General John Buford (1826–1863) commanded the First Division of the Cavalry Corps of the Army of the Potomac.

253.17 Rudolph Ellis] Captain Rudolph Ellis (1837–1915) commanded Company B of the 6th Pennsylvania Cavalry.

258.29–30 General John C. Breckinridge] Breckinridge (1821–1875), vice president of the United States, 1857–61, and the southern Democratic candidate for president in 1860, commanded a division in the Army of Tennessee.

258.31 Gen. John B. Magruder, Gen. William B. Preston] Magruder (1807–1871) commanded the Confederate forces in Texas; Preston (1816–1887), the U.S. minister to Spain, 1858–61, commanded a brigade in the Army of Tennessee.

258.32 Commodore Franklin Buchanan] Buchanan (1800–1874) commanded the Confederate squadron at Mobile, Alabama.

261.27–31 the judge . . . President Jackson] Humphrey H. Leavitt (1796–1873) was appointed as federal district judge for Ohio by Andrew Jackson in 1834 and served until 1871.

261.37–38 battle of New-Orleans . . . treaty of peace] The battle of New Orleans was fought on January 8, 1815. News of the Treaty of Ghent, signed on December 24, 1814, reached New Orleans on February 25, but official confirmation did not arrive in the city until March 13.

262.3 Mr. Louiallier] Louis Louaillier, a member of the state senate, published an article in the *Louisiana Courier* on March 3, 1815, criticizing Jackson's continued imposition of martial law. Jackson had Louaillier arrested on March 5 and court-martialed two days later on charges of spying, mutiny, libel, disobedience, and misconduct. Although the court-martial cleared Louaillier of all charges, Jackson refused to release him.

262.5 Judge Hall] Dominic A. Hall (1765–1820), U.S. district judge for New Orleans, 1804–12, and for Louisiana, 1812–20.

262.7 arrested both the lawyer and the judge] Jackson did not order the arrest of Pierre L. Morel, the attorney who obtained the writ of habeas corpus from Judge Hall.

262.21–22 Congress refunded . . . Douglas,] Congress passed a bill indemnifying Jackson for the fine in 1843. Stephen A. Douglas (1813–1861) served as Democratic congressman from Illinois, 1843–47, and as a senator, 1847–61.

266.27 Johnston . . . reinforcements] See Chronology, May–June 1863.

269.6 at Salem.] The 19th Iowa Infantry was camped near Salem in southern Missouri from May 2 to June 3, 1863.

269.9 Chequest boys] Men from the Chequest Valley in southeastern Iowa, where the Clayton family farm was located.

269.17–18 Col. Kent . . . Mrs. Wittemeyer] Lieutenant Colonel Daniel

Kent (1819–1898), commander of the 19th Iowa Infantry at Vicksburg; Annie Turner Wittenmyer (1827–1900), an agent for the Iowa State Army Sanitary Commission (an auxiliary of the U.S. Sanitary Commission) and the Keokuk Ladies' Soldiers' Aid Society.

269.19   Gen. Herron]   The 19th Iowa Infantry was assigned in Missouri and at Vicksburg to the division commanded by Major General Francis J. Herron (1837–1902).

271.5   Lt. Col. May]   Dwight May (1822–1880) had commanded Company I of the 2nd Michigan Infantry, in which Haydon served, until his resignation in December 1861. He was commissioned as lieutenant colonel of the 25th Michigan Infantry in October 1862.

271.20   "Eat drink . . . you die."]   See Ecclesiastes 8:15, Isaiah 22:13, and Luke 12:19.

271.27–28   "Let joy be unconfined."]   Lord Byron, *Childe Harold's Pilgrimage*, Canto III (1816), stanza 23.

274.12–13   Charley . . . Hugh]   Ellen Ewing Sherman's brothers Charles Ewing (1835–1883), a lieutenant colonel who was serving as inspector general of the Fifteenth Corps, and Hugh Boyle Ewing (1826–1905), a brigadier general who commanded a brigade in the Fifteenth Corps.

274.37   Tom Bartley]   Thomas W. Bartley (1812–1885) married Susan Denman Sherman (1825–1876), Sherman's sister, in 1848. A former state legislator, Bartley served on the Ohio supreme court, 1852–59, and was its chief justice, 1853–54 and 1856–59.

275.38–39   the invariable Hill]   John Hill, a black servant hired by Sherman.

276.5   McCoy]   Lieutenant James C. McCoy (d. 1875), who served as one of Sherman's aides, 1862–65.

276.10–11   Genl. Sherman of New Orleans]   Union brigadier general Thomas W. Sherman (1813–1879), a division commander in the Army of the Gulf who lost a leg in the assault on Port Hudson, May 27, 1863.

276.18   Mrs. Wilkinson]   Mary Stark Wilkinson (1809–1901).

276.19–20   her husband . . . Manassas]   Robert A. Wilkinson (1809–1862) was killed in the second battle of Manassas, August 30, 1862, while serving as lieutenant colonel of the 15th Louisiana Infantry.

276.24   General Wilkinson of the old wars]   James Wilkinson (1757–1825), grandfather of Robert A. Wilkinson, served in the Revolution, on the frontier, and in the War of 1812. He was accused of complicity in Aaron Burr's conspiracy to detach the western states from the Union, but was acquitted by a court of inquiry.

276.25–26 the famous Land case of Penrose St. Louis] Thomas Ewing Sr. successfully argued *Bissell v. Penrose*, a case involving conflicting claims to a valuable land tract in St. Louis, before the U.S. Supreme Court in 1850.

276.26 at Alexandria] Sherman was the founding superintendent of the Louisiana State Seminary of Learning and Military Academy at Alexandria, 1859–61.

276.30–31 Vicksburg . . . his fate.] On July 3, 1863, Sherman wrote to Grant, asking him to help Mary Wilkinson see her son once the Vicksburg garrison had surrendered.

277.30–31 Minnie & Willy . . . Tom & Lizzy] Sherman's children Maria Boyle Ewing Sherman (1851–1913), William Tecumseh Sherman Jr. (1854–1863), Thomas Ewing Sherman (1856–1915), and Mary Elizabeth Sherman (1852–1925).

278.17–19 General Wright . . . General's son] Brigadier General Ambrose R. Wright (1826–1872) commanded a brigade in A. P. Hill's Third Corps. Lieutenant William A. Wright (1844–1929), the brigade ordnance officer, was exchanged in May 1864.

278.20 Manassas] Lieutenant Wright was wounded at the second battle of Manassas on August 30, 1862.

279.31 sing "Rally round the flag,"] "The Battle Cry of Freedom" (1862), song with words and music by George F. Root (1820–1895).

279.34 Florence or Athens, Alabama] A Union cavalry brigade commanded by Colonel Florence M. Cornyn (1829–1863) raided Florence, Alabama, on May 28, 1863, and burned seven cotton mills and several other buildings. Union troops from a brigade commanded by Colonel John B. Turchin (1822–1901) pillaged Athens, Alabama, on May 2, 1862.

279.38 "Gaine's Mills,"] See note 29.19.

280.1 "squirrel tail rifles."] The 13th Regiment of the Pennsylvania Reserves (see note 13.15), also known as the 1st Pennsylvania Rifles and the Bucktail Rifles.

280.19 Heath's and Pender's divisions] Major General Henry Heth (1825–1899) and Major General William Dorsey Pender (1834–1863) commanded divisions in A. P. Hill's corps. Pender was wounded at Gettysburg on the afternoon of July 2 and died on July 18 after having his leg amputated.

280.26–27 "The Bonnie Blue Flag,"] A popular Confederate marching song, written in 1861 by the variety performer Harry Macarthy (1834–1888) and sung to the tune of "The Irish Jaunting Car."

280.28 Hood . . . McLaws] Major General John B. Hood (1831–1879) and Major General Lafayette McLaws (1821–1897) commanded divisions in Lieutenant General James Longstreet's First Corps.

NOTES 839

281.35–282.1 Charles J. Faulkner] Faulkner (1806–1884) had served in Congress as a Whig and as a Democrat, 1851–59, and as U.S. minister to France, 1860–61. He resigned his military commission in June 1863.

283.4 Mr Roman] James D. Roman (1809–1867), a lawyer and banker, served in Congress as a Whig, 1847–49.

284.1–2 Thadeus Stevens] See note 23.18.

284.11–13 WmR . . . Laura & Bet.] McLaws's brother, William Raymond McLaws (1818–1880); his sister, Anna Laura McLaws (1816–1894); and his niece, Lillie Huguenin McLaws (b. 1860).

285.3–4 *Irene and Mary Williams*] Irene Williams (1843–1907) and Mary Williams (1846–1935) lived with their father's relatives in Connecticut. Their mother had died in 1849.

285.20 Dr. Steiner] Lewis H. Steiner (1827–1892), a physician and medical writer, was the chief inspector for the U.S. Sanitary Commission with the Army of the Potomac.

287.29–30 "Divinity which shapes . . . as we will."] *Hamlet*, V.ii.10–11.

289.17–19 "chief burgess" . . . surrender the city] David Small (1809–1885), publisher of the *York Gazette* and chief burgess (mayor) of York, went outside of the city on June 28, 1863, to arrange its surrender with Brigadier General John B. Gordon (1832–1904). The Confederates occupied the town until June 30.

291.10–11 "a little more sleep . . . slumber"] See Proverbs 6:10.

292.27 Colonel Walton] James B. Walton (1813–1885), the senior artillery officer in Longstreet's corps, commanded the Washington Artillery, a battalion from New Orleans, 1861–64.

293.2 Johnson's] Major General Edward Johnson (1816–1873).

294.32–33 General Reynolds] Major General John Reynolds (1820–1863), commander of the First Corps, was killed late in the morning of July 1 west of the town of Gettysburg.

295.28 Lawley] Francis Lawley (1825–1901) reported from the Confederacy for *The Times* of London, October 1862–April 1865.

295.30 Major Clark] Major John J. Clarke (1832?–1880), an engineer who served on Longstreet's staff.

295.31–32 the stout Austrian . . . Major Walton] Captain Fitzgerald Ross (b. 1825), an Englishman who joined the Austrian cavalry in 1850, traveled through the Confederacy from May 1863 to April 1864 while on a leave of absence and later wrote *A Visit to the Cities and Camps of the Confederate States* (1865). Major William M. Walton (1832–1915) was one of Longstreet's staff officers.

295.33 *ciréd*] Waxed.

295.35 Colonel Sorrell] Lieutenant Colonel Gilbert Moxley Sorrell (1838–1901), Longstreet's chief of staff, 1862–64.

296.2 Captain Schreibert] Justus Scheibert (1831–1903), a Prussian engineer sent to observe the American Civil War for professional purposes, later wrote *Seven Months in the Rebel States during the North American War, 1863* (1868).

296.32 Pickett] Major General George E. Pickett (1825–1875).

296.34–35 Colonel Manning] Peyton T. Manning (1837–1868), Longstreet's ordnance officer.

298.12 Hill's Florida brigade] The brigade, commanded at Gettysburg by Colonel Daniel Lang (1838–1917), was assigned to the division led by Major General Richard H. Anderson (1821–1879) in A. P. Hill's Third Corps. Previous to Lee's reorganization of the Army of Northern Virginia in late May 1863, Anderson's division had been part of Longstreet's First Corps.

298.20 General Barksdale . . . Semmes] Brigadier General William Barksdale (1821–1863), who had served as a Democratic congressman from Mississippi, 1853–61, died on July 3. Brigadier General Paul J. Semmes (1815–1863), a cousin of Confederate naval officer Raphael Semmes, died on July 10. Both men led brigades assigned to McLaws's division in Longstreet's corps.

298.27 Major Fairfax] Major John W. Fairfax (1828–1908), one of Longstreet's aides.

299.35 Heth and Pettigrew] Brigadier General James J. Pettigrew (1828–1863) led one of the brigades in Heth's division, and had assumed command of the division after Heth was wounded on July 1. Another division from Hill's corps, commanded by Major General Isaac Trimble (1802–1888), also participated in the July 3 assault on the Union center.

299.36–37 absence of two brigades] The brigades had been detached for service in North Carolina.

300.36 Oxford-street] A main shopping street in the West End of London.

301.36–38 Major Latrobe . . . Captain Goree] Osmun Latrobe (1835–1915) and Thomas J. Goree (1835–1905), officers on Longstreet's staff.

302.38 This officer . . . the Potomac.] Pettigrew was mortally wounded in a rearguard action near Williamsport, Maryland, on July 14 and died three days later.

303.9–11 General Willcox . . . state of his brigade.] Brigadier General Cadmus M. Wilcox (1824–1890) commanded a brigade in Anderson's division that had been ordered to advance on Pickett's right flank. In his official report of July 17, 1863, Wilcox wrote that his brigade had lost 577 men killed, wounded, or missing, on July 2 and another suffered another 204 casualties on July 3.

303.30–31   Generals Garnett . . . Kemper] Garnett, Armistead, and Kemper commanded the three brigades in Pickett's division. Brigadier General Richard B. Garnett (1817–1863) was killed during the assault; Brigadier General Lewis A. Armistead (1817–1863) died of his wounds in a Union hospital on July 5; and Brigadier General James L. Kemper (1823–1895), who was left behind when the Confederates retreated on July 4, survived his wound and was exchanged in September 1863.

304.19–21   Johnson's division . . . advantages there.] The Confederates made a series of unsuccessful attacks on Culp's Hill on the morning of July 3.

304.25–27   Yankee cavalry . . . have escaped.] On the afternoon of July 3 a Union cavalry brigade led by Brigadier General Elon J. Farnsworth (1837–1863) unsuccessfully attacked Hood's division on the Confederate right flank. Farnsworth was killed, and his brigade lost another 106 men killed, wounded, or missing.

304.29   Moses's] Major Raphael Moses (1812–1893), Longstreet's chief commissary officer.

305.7   Dr. Barksdale] Randolph Barksdale (1831–1907), the medical inspector of Longstreet's corps, was not related to Brigadier General William Barksdale.

305.25   General Pendleton (the parson)] Brigadier General William N. Pendleton (1809–1883), chief of artillery of the Army of Northern Virginia, 1862–65. A West Point graduate, Pendleton had resigned from the army in 1833 and become an Episcopal clergyman.

307.15   General Milroy] Brigadier General Robert H. Milroy (1816–1890), a division commander in the Eighth Corps, was driven out of Winchester, Virginia, by Ewell, June 14–15, 1863.

308.34   Doles'] Brigadier General George P. Doles (1830–1864) commanded a brigade in the division led by Major General Robert E. Rodes.

309.17   26th Regt.] The 26th Alabama Infantry.

309.18   Mr. Mushat] Dr. John Patrick Mushat (1830–1890), assistant surgeon of the 5th Alabama Infantry.

310.20   Col. Hall] Colonel Josephus M. Hall (1828–1915), commander of the 5th Alabama Infantry.

311.9   Ramseur . . . Iversons] Brigadier General Stephen D. Ramseur (1837–1864) and Brigadier General Alfred Iverson commanded brigades in Rodes's division.

311.11–15 Tom Biscoe . . . 5th La. Regt.] Captain Thomas H. Biscoe (c. 1839–1864) was originally from Greene County, Alabama, but had been living in New Orleans when he joined the 5th Louisiana Infantry. Biscoe assumed command of the regiment after Major Alexander Hart was wounded on July 2 during an attack on Cemetery Hill. The 5th Louisiana was part of a brigade led by Brigadier General Harry T. Hays (1820–1876) in the division commanded by Jubal A. Early.

312.30 our division] The First Division of the Fifth Corps, commanded by Brigadier General James Barnes (1801–1869). Donaldson's regiment, the 118th Pennsylvania Infantry, was part of the division's First Brigade.

313.7 our Colonel] Lieutenant Colonel James Gwyn (1828–1906).

314.35 Capt. John Fassitte . . . General Birney] Captain John B. Fassett (1836–1905), an aide to Brigadier General David B. Birney (1825–1864). Birney commanded the First Division of the Third Corps, which held the north side of the salient formed by Sickles's advance toward the Emmitsburg Road.

314.39 Captain Crocker] Lemuel B. Crocker (1829–1885), commander of Company K of the 118th Pennsylvania Infantry.

315.11 P.V.] Pennsylvania Volunteers.

317.37 Capt. Richd. W. Davids] Davids (1825–1863) was the commander of Company G of the 118th Pennsylvania Infantry.

318.12 Maj. Herring] Major Charles S. Herring (1829–1889), second in command of the 118th Pennsylvania Infantry at Gettysburg.

318.25 Maj. Biddle] James Cornell Biddle (1835–1898).

319.12–14 Pennsylvania Reserves . . . Genl. Crawford] Nine regiments of the Pennsylvania Reserves that had previously been assigned to the Third Division of the First Corps (see note 13.15) fought at Gettysburg as part of the Third Division of the Fifth Corps, commanded by Brigadier General Samuel W. Crawford (1829–1892).

319.23–24 the 2nd and 3rd brigade] The Second Brigade, First Division, Fifth Corps fought alongside the First Brigade in the woods of the Rose Farm, while the Third Brigade fought on Little Round Top.

319.26–28 The 16th Mich. . . . colonel being bayonetted] Lieutenant Colonel Norval E. Welch (1835–1864) commanded the 16th Michigan Infantry, which fought on July 2 on Little Round Top as part of the Third Brigade. Colonel Harrison H. Jeffords (1834–1863), the commander of the 4th Michigan Infantry in the Second Brigade, was bayoneted on July 2 in the wheat field of the Rose Farm and died the following day.

320.8 news of the 22nd Virginia Regt.] Donaldson's brother, John P. Donaldson (1838–1901), moved from Philadelphia to Charleston, Virginia

NOTES   843

(later West Virginia), in 1858. He joined the Confederate army in 1861 and was serving as a captain with the 22nd Virginia Infantry in southern West Virginia during the battle of Gettysburg. John P. Donaldson was captured at Cold Harbor on June 3, 1864, and remained a Union prisoner for the rest of the war.

320.9–10   Bradley Johnson]   Colonel Bradley T. Johnson (1829–1903), a prominent Maryland Confederate.

322.27   Capt. O'Neill]   Captain Henry O'Neill, the commander of Company A of the 118th Pennsylvania Infantry.

325.25   tete monte]   *Tête montée*: swelled head.

325.31–32   Genl McClellands dismissal by Grant]   Grant, who had long been unhappy with John A. McClernand's performance, removed him from command of the Thirteenth Corps on June 18 after Sherman and McPherson strongly protested McClernand's publication of a self-congratulatory order in the newspapers without authorization.

326.13   Blair]   Francis Preston Blair Lee (1857–1944), the only child of Elizabeth Blair Lee and Samuel Phillips Lee.

326.26   Betty]   Elizabeth Blair (1841–1872), daughter of Montgomery Blair.

326.36   Robt]   Robert Leamy Meade (1817–1841), brother of George G. Meade.

327.1   Apo]   Apolline Alexander Blair (1828–1908), the wife of Frank Blair.

327.11–12   Dahlgren son a Capt. . . . Robt. Lee]   Captain Ulric Dahlgren (1842–1864), a Union cavalry officer, was the son of Rear Admiral John A. Dahlgren (1809–1870), commander of the South Atlantic Blockading Squadron. On July 2 Dahlgren captured a courier in Greencastle, Pennsylvania, and seized an unenciphered letter in which Davis told Lee not to expect to receive reinforcements from North Carolina or the Richmond area. Dahlgren lost his right leg in a skirmish in Hagerstown, Maryland, on July 6. Promoted to colonel, he was killed on March 2, 1864, during a failed cavalry raid on Richmond (see pp. 728–32 in this volume).

327.17   Cooper]   Brigadier General Samuel Cooper (1798–1876), adjutant general of the Confederate War Department.

327.18   Beauregard]   Lee had proposed that General Pierre G. T. Beauregard, the Confederate commander at Charleston, South Carolina, be sent to northern Virginia with the purpose of threatening an attack on Washington while Lee's army was in Pennsylvania.

327.21–22   the White House]   White House Landing on the Pamunkey River, twenty-three miles east of Richmond.

328.36–329.1   Col. Vincent commanding the Brigade,]   Colonel Strong

Vincent (1837–1863) commanded the Third Brigade of the First Division in the Fifth Corps.

330.40–331.1   Col. Rice . . . mortally wounded] Colonel James C. Rice (1828–1864), the commander of the 44th New York Infantry, took over the brigade after Vincent was wounded.

331.6   "Wolf Hill"] A hill three miles northeast of Big Round Top.

331.28   Genl. Laws] Brigadier General Evander M. Law (1836–1920) led one of the brigades in Hood's division and took over command of the division when Hood was wounded on the afternoon of July 2.

332.18–21   Lt. W. L. Kendall . . . Lieut. A. N. Linscott] Lieutenant Warren L. Kendall of Company G died on July 5, Captain Charles W. Billings of Company C died on July 15, and Lieutenant Arad N. Linscott of Company I died on July 27.

332.29–31   Capt Woodward . . . Adjt. Gifford] Captain Orpheus S. Woodward (1835–1919) and Lieutenant Martin Van Buren Gifford (1837–1922).

333.18–19   Henry Ropes] First Lieutenant Henry Ropes (1839–1863), the commander of Company K of the 20th Massachusetts Infantry, had joined the regiment in November 1861 and fought at Fair Oaks, the Seven Days' Battles, Antietam, Fredericksburg, and Chancellorsville. He was killed at Gettysburg by the premature explosion of a Union shell on the morning of July 3 while reading a novel by Charles Dickens.

333.24   Col. Hall] Colonel Norman J. Hall (1837–1867) commanded the Third Brigade, Second Division, Second Corps, at Fredericksburg, Chancellorsville, and Gettysburg.

333.31–33   pique against Revere . . . he is regretted] Colonel Paul Joseph Revere (1832–1863), a grandson of the Revolutionary War hero, was appointed major of the 20th Massachusetts in July 1861, but left the regiment in August 1862 to serve on the staff of Major General Edwin V. Sumner. Abbott and several other officers had opposed his appointment as regimental commander in May 1863, believing the colonelcy should have been given to Lieutenant Colonel George N. Macy, who had led the regiment at Fredericksburg and Chancellorsville. Revere was wounded by a shell burst at Gettysburg on the evening of July 2 and died two days later.

334.1–2   Macy . . . Herbert Mason] Lieutenant Colonel George N. Macy (1837–1875) was wounded on July 3 and lost his left hand. He resumed command of the 20th Massachusetts in late October 1863. Captain Herbert Mason, the commander of Company H, was wounded on July 3 and medically discharged in March 1864.

334.7   Patten] Captain Henry Lyman Patten (1836–1864), the commander of Company D, was wounded on July 2. He returned to the regiment later in the year and was mortally wounded at Deep Bottom, Virginia, on August 17, 1864, while serving as acting commander of the 20th Massachusetts.

334.18   Paine]   Second Lieutenant Sumner Paine (1845–1863) was killed on July 3.

335.16–17   Baxter's Pennsylvania men]   Colonel DeWitt C. Baxter commanded the 72nd Pennsylvania Infantry. The gap in the line to the right of the 20th Massachusetts was caused by the retreat of several companies from the 71st Pennsylvania.

335.32   Gen Webb]   Brigadier General Alexander Webb (1835–1911) commanded the Second Brigade, Second Division, Second Corps, which was posted to the right of Hall's brigade on July 3. It was made up of the 71st, 72nd, 69th, and 106th Pennsylvania regiments.

335.35   miserable rowdy named Hays]   Brigadier General Alexander Hays (1819–1864) commanded the Third Division in the Second Corps.

335.38–40   Hays . . . Gibbon]   Brigadier General William Hays (1819–1875) took command of the Second Corps on July 3 after Major General Winfield Scott Hancock was wounded during the Confederate assault on Cemetery Ridge. Hancock (1824–1886) had replaced Major General Darius N. Couch as commander of the Second Corps on May 22, 1863. Brigadier General John Gibbon (1827–1896), commander of the Second Division of the Second Corps, was wounded on July 3.

336.25–26   first day's . . . second day's]   July 2 and July 3, 1863.

337.11   Wm Kelly]   Corporal William P. Kelley (c. 1843–1865) was captured at Spotsylvania on May 12, 1864, and died in a Confederate prison camp at Wilmington, North Carolina, on March 5, 1865.

337.17   Fletcher]   Fletcher Abbott (1843–1925), Henry Livermore Abbott's younger brother, was serving as a Union staff officer in Louisiana. He was medically discharged from the army in December 1863.

337.18–19   George & Mary Welch . . . John]   George B. Perry was commissioned as a first lieutenant in the 20th Massachusetts in July 1861 and served until September 1862, when he was discharged because of illness. Perry became formally engaged to Caroline Abbott (1839–1872), Henry Livermore Abbott's sister, early in 1864. His cousin, John Gardner Perry (1840–1926), who joined the 20th Massachusetts as an assistant surgeon in April 1863, had his leg broken by a horse on June 15, 1863. He returned to the regiment in September 1863 and served until his discharge in August 1864. Mary Ann Welch was a young woman from Lowell, Massachusetts, whom Abbott corresponded with during the war.

339.10–12   Kershaw . . . Wofford]   Brigadier General Joseph B. Kershaw (1822–1894) and Brigadier General William T. Wofford (1824–1884).

339.21–23   Colonel Carter . . . Lt. Col. Fiser]   James W. Carter (c. 1830–1863), Thomas M. Griffin (1816–1878), William D. Holder (1824–1900), William De Saussure (1819–1863), and John C. Fiser (1838–1876).

341.19   Will]   William N. Hancock (1832–1911), Cornelia Hancock's brother.

341.28–29   Mrs. Harris]   Ellen Orbison Harris (1816–1902), field secretary for the Ladies' Aid Society of Philadelphia.

342.20–22   Major General Schenk . . . Miss Dix]   Major General Robert C. Schenck (1809–1890), commander of the Middle Department, which included Baltimore. Dorothea Dix (1802–1887) served as superintendent of female nurses for the Union army, 1861–65. In an account of her Gettysburg experiences written after the war, Hancock recalled that at the Baltimore Depot Dix had "immediately objected to my going farther on the score of my youth and rosy cheeks. I was then just twenty-three years of age." (It was Dix's policy not to use women under the age of thirty as nurses.) Despite Dix's objections, Hancock boarded the train for Gettysburg.

342.24   Doctor Horner's house]   Dr. Robert Horner (1825–1899), who lived on Chambersburg Street.

343.25   E. W. Farnham]   A writer, lecturer, and social reformer who had served as matron of the female prison at Sing Sing, Eliza W. Farnham (1815–1864) helped organize nursing care for the wounded at Gettysburg.

345.3–4   First Minnesota Regiment . . . the late battle.]   During the fighting on Cemetery Ridge on July 2, General Hancock personally ordered the 1st Minnesota Infantry to counterattack an advancing Confederate brigade so as to gain time for other Union reinforcements to arrive. The survivors of the charge then helped defend Cemetery Ridge against the Confederate assault on July 3. The regiment had reported 399 men present for duty on June 30, and lost 233 men killed, wounded, or missing at Gettysburg.

345.9   The Colonel]   Colonel William J. Colvill (1830–1905).

345.29–30   Senator Wilson, Mr. Washburn]   Henry Wilson (1812–1875) was a Republican senator from Massachusetts, 1855–73; for Elihu B. Washburne, see note 24.22.

345.34   Dr. Child]   Henry T. Child (c. 1816–1890), a Quaker physician and philanthropist from Philadelphia and the husband of Hancock's sister Ellen.

346.18   Mr Palmer]   Frank W. Palmer (1827–1907) was the publisher of the *Iowa State Register*, 1861–66, and its editor, 1861–68.

346.25–26   Rachel . . . Aunt Hannah]   Taylor Peirce's sister, Rachel Peirce Gibson (b. 1827), and his aunt, Hannah Kirk Peirce.

NOTES   847

349.19   the National salute] A Fourth of July salute in which one gun was fired for each state in the Union, i.e., in 1863 a thirty-five-gun salute.

349.20   Ormes] Brigadier General William W. Orme (1832–1866) commanded the Second Brigade in the division led by Major General Francis J. Herron.

350.31   Lizzie Cooper] A cousin of Clayton's who lived in Pittsburgh. She married Clayton in 1869 and died in 1876.

352.23   Ords corps . . . Parkes] On June 18 Grant had named Major General Edward O. C. Ord (1818–1883) to replace McClernand as commander of the Thirteenth Corps. Major General John G. Parke (1827–1900) commanded the Ninth Corps, which had reinforced Grant at Vicksburg in June.

354.34–35   reach the same points by Grenada] That is, by advancing on Vicksburg from the north along the Mississippi Central Railroad.

355.15   Dayton] Captain Lewis M. Dayton (1835–1891), one of Sherman's aides.

355.27   Carter] A former slave Sherman had hired to care for his horses.

355.28   Hammond] Captain John H. Hammond (1833–1890), an officer on Sherman's staff.

361.11–12   Sound the loud . . . people are *FREE*!] Opening lines of "Miriam's Song" (1816), also known as "Sound the Loud Timbrel," by Thomas Moore (1779–1852). The poem was inspired by Exodus 15:20.

362.16   Scales] Alfred M. Scales (1827–1892) commanded a brigade in Pender's division in A. P. Hill's corps. Wounded on July 1, Scales returned to duty in August 1863.

362.19–20   Sickles, . . . assassinate no more men] Major General Daniel E. Sickles (see note 14.27–28), the commander of the Third Corps, was wounded on the afternoon of July 2 and had his right leg amputated. In 1859 he had shot and killed Philip Barton Key (1818–1859), U.S. attorney for Washington and the son of Francis Scott Key, because Key was having an affair with his wife, Teresa Bagioli Sickles (1836–1867). Sickles became the first defendant to be acquitted on grounds of temporary insanity in an American murder case.

362.25–29   Gen Lee has issued . . . Pope's and Steinwehr's!] Lee issued General Orders No. 72 on June 21, 1863, forbidding the pillaging of private property but allowing designated officers to requisition supplies and pay for them with Confederate currency and vouchers. Major General John Pope (1822–1892), commander of the Army of Virginia, issued a series of orders from July 18 to July 23, 1862, regarding the treatment of southern civilians. General Orders No. 5 authorized his troops to seize the property of disloyal citizens without compensation; General Orders No. 7 made captured guerrillas subject to execution without civil trial; and General Orders No. 11 allowed Union commanders to expel across the lines male citizens who refused to take the oath of allegiance, to execute persons who violated the oath, and to treat expelled persons who returned, and persons who communicated across the lines, as spies. Brigadier General Adolph von Steinwehr (1822–1877), one of Pope's division commanders, seized five prominent citizens in Luray, Virginia, on July 13, 1862, and declared that one of them would be executed for every Union soldier killed by "bushwhackers." There is no record of civilians being executed or expelled under Pope's orders, and von Steinwehr later released his hostages unharmed.

362.29 A no 20.] Edmondston placed newspaper clippings regarding Lee's orders in another part of her journal.

363.4–5 Brashear city] Renamed Morgan City in 1876.

363.14 the R R at Magnolia] The Wilmington and Weldon Railroad, which ran through Magnolia, North Carolina.

363.16 Gen Martins] Brigadier General James G. Martin (1819–1878) commanded a Confederate brigade in North Carolina.

363.17 Murad the Unlucky] Story by Maria Edgeworth (1768–1849), published in her *Popular Tales* (1804).

363.20 her brother, Col Evans,] Colonel Peter G. Evans (1822–1863), the commander of the 5th North Carolina Cavalry, was wounded and captured at Upperville, Virginia, on June 21, 1863, and died in Washington, D.C., on July 24.

363.24 German Gen Weitzel] Brigadier General Henry W. Wessells (1809–1889), who was born in Connecticut, commanded the Union expedition against Williamstown. Brigadier General Godfey Weitzel (1835–1884), who was born in Ohio, commanded a division in Louisiana in the Port Hudson campaign.

363.26 Rainbow Banks] A bluff on the Roanoke River two miles below Hamilton, North Carolina.

363.28 the Gunboat] The ironclad ram C.S.S. *Albemarle*, which was commissioned on April 17, 1864, and sunk on the night of October 27.

364.5–6 like "Widrington" in "*doleful dumps*,"] A reference to a seventeenth-century version of the medieval "Ballad of Chevy-Chase": "For Withrington needs must I wail / As one in doleful dumps; / For when his legs were smitten off, / He fought upon the stumps."

364.8 Com Barron] Commodore Samuel Barron (1809–1888), a Confederate naval officer.

365.1 Loring] Major General William W. Loring (1818–1886) commanded a division under Johnston in Mississippi.

365.36 Hannah More's ill "*bile*"] In a letter to Sir William Weller Pepys

NOTES 849

of July 1, 1823, the English evangelical writer and philanthropist Hannah More (1745–1833) wrote that there were "but two great evils in the world, sin and bile."

365.38 Petigru again wounded!] James J. Pettigrew (see notes 299.35 and 302.40) was wounded at Fair Oaks (Seven Pines) on May 31, 1862, and at Gettysburg on July 3, 1863, before being mortally wounded near Williamsport, Maryland, on July 14.

366.19 Northern Generals . . . Lovel & New Orleans] Major General Mansfield Lovell (1822–1884), the Confederate commander in Louisiana when New Orleans surrendered to Union naval forces on April 25, 1862, was born in Washington, D.C., to northern parents. An 1842 graduate of West Point who served in the war with Mexico, Lovell resigned from the army in 1854 and worked at an ironworks in Trenton and as deputy street commissioner in New York City before joining the Confederate army in the fall of 1861.

366.26–27 Londonderry . . . Antwerp] Protestants loyal to William of Orange held out in Londonderry (Derry) under siege from Irish and French Jacobite forces, April 18–July 31, 1689. The Dutch held Antwerp against the Spanish from July 1584 to August 1585, when they were forced to surrender.

366.32 court of Inquiry . . . Lovels conduct] At Lovel's request, a court of inquiry examined his conduct at New Orleans. Its findings, published in November 1863, largely exonerated him.

366.40 French] Major General William H. French (1815–1881) commanded the Union garrison at Harpers Ferry during the Gettysburg campaign until July 7, when he became commander of the Third Corps.

367.2–3 "fight him . . . Shrewsbury clock"] Cf. *1 Henry IV*, V.iv.146–148.

367.8 Keyes] Major General Erasmus D. Keyes (1810–1895) commanded a Union division on the Virginia Peninsula.

367.22 "The King does not dine today."] See Henry Wadsworth Longfellow, *Hyperion: A Romance* (1839): "But perhaps you have never heard that, at the court of Naples, when the dead body of a monarch lies in state, his dinner is carried up to him as usual, and the court physician tastes it, to see that it be not poisoned, and then the servants bear it out again, saying, 'The king does not dine today.'"

367.29 Suffolk] Union forces evacuated Suffolk, Virginia, on July 3, 1863.

367.32 Dix] Major General John A. Dix (1798–1879), commander of the Department of Virginia.

371.8 Abner Read] Commander Abner Read (1821–1863) was wounded on July 7 and died July 12.

371.14 Captain Cooke] Lieutenant Commander Augustus P. Cooke (1836–1896), captain of the gunboat *Estrella*.

372.26 Chas. Smith . . . severe shot] Smith later returned to duty with the 2nd Michigan. He was taken prisoner at Peebles' Farm, Virginia, on September 30, 1864, during the siege of Petersburg, and was mustered out in 1865.

373.1 Kearney's] The 2nd Michigan fought in the Peninsula and Second Bull Run campaigns in the division commanded by Brigadier General Philip Kearny (1815–1862), who was killed at Chantilly, Virginia, on September 1, 1862.

373.30 Sergt. Keyser] Sylvester Keyser (1843–1916) was later promoted to captain and commanded Company E of the 2nd Michigan at the end of the war.

374.10 Lt. Montague . . . severe flesh wound] Calvin S. Montague (b. 1838) was commissioned as a captain in the 102nd U.S. Colored Infantry in March 1864 and mustered out as a major in 1865.

375.31 Eckert says Kelly] Major Thomas T. Eckert (1825–1910), superintendent of the War Department telegraph office, and Brigadier General Benjamin Franklin Kelley (1807–1891), commander of the Department of West Virginia.

376.28–31 Went with R.T.L. . . . trinkt and raucht] This paragraph was crossed out in the manuscript of Hay's diary. "R.T.L." refers to Robert Todd Lincoln (1843–1926), Abraham Lincoln's eldest son, then a student at Harvard College. "Where mann sauft and trinkt and raucht": where people drink and drink and smoke.

378.22 Gen. Couch . . . Gen. Smith] Major General Darius N. Couch (1822–1897), commander of the Department of the Susquehanna, and his subordinate Brigadier General William F. Smith (1824–1903) commanded Pennsylvania militia levies during the Gettysburg campaign.

382.15–17 Charley . . . Wall Street] Charles E. Strong (1824–1897), George Templeton Strong's cousin, and Marshall S. Bidwell (1799–1872) were law partners with Strong; their firm had its office at 68 Wall Street.

383.37–38 No. 823 . . . Fifth Avenue] 823 Broadway, between 12th and 13th Streets, the headquarters of the U.S. Sanitary Commission; the Colored Half-Orphan Asylum was located on Fifth Avenue between 43rd and 44th Streets.

383.39 reservoir] The Croton Distributing Reservoir, on the west side of Fifth Avenue between 40th and 42nd Streets.

384.5 Wolcott Gibbs] See note 25.16.

384.6 Maison Dorée] A restaurant on 14th Street between Broadway and Fourth Avenue.

384.18 St. Nicholas Hotel] The hotel was on Broadway between Broome and Spring Streets.

NOTES 851

384.19–21   John Jay . . . John Austin Stevens, Jr.] John Jay (1817–1894), a grandson of the Chief Justice, was a lawyer who had helped organize the New York Republican Party. George W. Blunt (1802–1878) was a publisher of nautical books and maps and a member of the U.S. Coastal Survey and the New York board of harbor pilot commissioners. Frank E. Howe (1829–1883), a merchant originally from Boston, served as Massachusetts state agent in New York, arranging housing and provisions for Massachusetts soldiers in transit through the state and assistance for its sick and wounded men in New York hospitals. John Austin Stevens Jr. (1827–1910) was a New York financier and merchant. All four men were members of the Union League Club, which Strong and other leaders of the Sanitary Commission had helped found in February 1863.

384.25–26   Opdyke . . . Wool] George Opdyke (1805–1880) was the Republican mayor of New York, 1862–63. Major General John E. Wool (1784–1869), a veteran of the War of 1812, commanded the Department of the East.

384.30–31   Colonel Cram] Thomas J. Cram (1804–1883) served as Wool's aide-de-camp, 1861–65.

384.35   Union League Club] The clubhouse was located at 26 East 17th Street.

384.38   We telegraphed] The telegram to President Lincoln was signed by John Jay, George Templeton Strong, Wolcott Gibbs, and James Wadsworth (1819–1891), a lawyer, businessman, and former Democratic mayor of Buffalo who served as chairman of the Loyal League of Union Citizens.

385.13–14   Ellie . . . Johnny] Ellen Caroline Ruggles Strong (1825–1891), George Templeton Strong's wife, and his son, John Ruggles Strong (1851–1941).

385.26   black man hanged] At least eleven African American men were lynched in New York during the draft riots.

385.27   Opdyke's house] At 79 Fifth Avenue, between 15th and 16th Streets.

385.31   *Herald*, *World*, and *News*] Democratic New York newspapers.

385.36   Tiffany's shop, Ball & Blacks] Tiffany & Co. was located at 550 Broadway, between Spring and Prince Streets. Ball, Black & Co., another jewelry store, was located at 565 Broadway at the corner of Prince Street.

386.7   Bellows . . . home] Henry Bellows (see note 25.15). Strong lived at 74 East 21st Street (renumbered 113 East 21st in 1867).

386.10–12   Dudley Field, Jr. . . . his father's] David Dudley Field (1805–1894) was a prominent lawyer who had helped organize the New York Republican Party. His son Dudley Field (1830–1880) was also an attorney.

387.1   "Swinging slow with sullen roar."] John Milton, "Il Penseroso," line 76.

387.15–16 Cisco . . . his establishment] John Jay Cisco (1806–1884), assistant treasurer of the United States, was in charge of the Sub-Treasury building at the corner of Wall and Nassau Streets.

387.18–19 "so cool, so calm, so bright"] See George Herbert, "Virtue," line 1: "Sweet day, so cool, so calm, so bright!"

387.20 Assay Office] Located at 30 Wall Street, next to the Sub-Treasury.

387.21–22 called on Collector Barney] Hiram Barney (1811–1895), collector of customs at New York, 1861–64. The Custom House was located at 55 Wall Street.

387.27 Hoppin] William Jones Hoppin (1813–1895), an attorney and the treasurer of the Union League Club.

387.34 Lieutenant Colonel Jardine] Edward Jardine (1828–1893) had served with the 9th New York Infantry, a two-year regiment, until it was mustered out in May 1863. Jardine was leading a volunteer group of veterans from the 9th New York when his leg was broken by the impact of a homemade bullet. He was sheltered from the mob in a nearby house.

387.39 General Frémont's . . . Craven's] Major General John C. Frémont moved to New York City in 1863. Alfred W. Craven (1810–1879) was chief engineer of the Croton Aqueduct system, 1849–68.

388.27–28 Governor Seymour] Horatio Seymour (1810–1886), the Democratic governor of New York, 1863–64, had repeatedly criticized the draft as unconstitutional. In a speech given at the Academy of Music in New York City on July 4, 1863, Seymour had attacked the Lincoln administration for curtailing civil liberties and warned that "the bloody and treasonable and revolutionary doctrine of public necessity can be proclaimed by a mob as well as by a government."

389.1–2 McCunn . . . the Brookses] John H. McCunn (1825–1872) was a city judge in New York and a prominent Peace Democrat. James Brooks (1810–1873) was a Democratic congressman from New York, 1863–66 and 1867–73, and the editor and part-owner of the *New York Express*. His brother Erastus Brooks (1815–1886) was a co-owner of the *Express*.

390.14–15 James I. . . . negro troops] See headnote, page 402 in this volume.

390.19 some captured to be hung] Several dozen black soldiers captured during the fighting in Charleston Harbor were transferred from a military prison to the city jail in August 1863 to face charges of engaging in slave insurrection. Four men were tried by a South Carolina state tribunal, September 8–10, that ruled it lacked jurisdiction over enemy soldiers in wartime. No further trials were held at Charleston, and in December 1864 the prisoners were returned to military custody.

391.11 Henry Young] Louis Gourdin Young (1833–1922), a Charleston resident, served as Pettigrew's aide; his brother, Henry Edward Young (1831–1918), held several staff positions with the Army of Northern Virginia.

391.32–33   Superintendent Kennedy several wounded]   John A. Kennedy (1803–1873), the superintendent of the New York City Police, 1860–70, was badly beaten by rioters on the morning of July 13.

392.13   the Ironsides]   The U.S.S. *New Ironsides*, an ironclad commissioned in 1862 that carried eighteen guns, had joined the blockading squadron off Charleston in January 1863.

394.21–23   Capt. Ryan . . . Maj. David Ramsey]   Captain William H. Ryan commanded Company C, known as the Irish Volunteers, in the 1st South Carolina Infantry Battalion, known as the Charleston Battalion. Major David Ramsay (1830–1863), the second in command of the Charleston Battalion, died of his wounds on August 4, 1863.

394.31–32   Lieut. Col. Simpkins, commanding the fort]   Lieutenant Colonel John C. Simpkins (1827–1863) of the 1st South Carolina Infantry. The Confederate garrison at Fort Wagner was commanded by Brigadier General William B. Taliaferro.

394.34   Clingman's North Carolinians]   Brigadier General Thomas L. Clingman (1812–1897), a former congressman and U.S. senator from North Carolina, commanded a brigade that included two regiments in the Fort Wagner garrison, the 31st and 51st North Carolina Infantry.

395.1   Lieut. James Powe]   Powe (1835–1898), an officer in the 1st South Carolina Infantry.

395.9–10   Col. Putnam . . . Gen. Israel Putnam]   Colonel Haldimand S. Putnam (1835–1863), commander of the 7th New Hampshire Infantry, led a specially organized brigade in the assault on Fort Wagner. He was the grandson of Israel Putnam (1718–1790), a Connecticut officer in the French and Indian War and the Revolutionary War.

396.7–8   Morgan . . . Indiana]   See Chronology, July 8, July 19–29, 1863.

397.3   *Richard Taylor*]   Taylor (1835–1917) was a Confederate artillery officer who was wounded and captured at Fort Harrison near Richmond in September 1864.

397.11   Mary Lou]   Mary Louisa Taylor (1832–1902), Taylor's sister.

397.15   Rob]   Taylor's brother, Captain Robertson Taylor (1840–1924), assistant adjutant general of the brigade led by Brigadier General William Mahone in A.P. Hill's corps of the Army of Northern Virginia.

397.19   John]   Taylor's brother, Captain John Cowdrey Taylor (b. 1842), an aide to Pemberton who was paroled at the surrender of Vicksburg. He was later captured at Fort Morgan near Mobile on August 23, 1864, and spent the remainder of the war as a prisoner.

401.8 Sally] Sally Louisa Tompkins (1833–1916), a friend of the Taylor family who ran the Robertson Hospital in Richmond, 1861–65.

402.34 Gen. Stevenson] Brigadier General Thomas G. Stevenson (1836–1864) commanded the First Brigade in the First Division of the Department of the South during the siege of Charleston. He was killed at Spotsylvania on May 10, 1864.

403.18 Gen. Terry's brigade] Brigadier General Alfred H. Terry (1827–1890) commanded a division during the Charleston campaign.

404.1–2 Saturday] July 18, 1863.

404.4 Gen. Strong] Brigadier General George C. Strong (1832–1863) commanded the brigade the 54th Massachusetts was assigned to for the assault on Fort Wagner. Strong was wounded during the attack and died on July 30.

404.9 Sebastopol] During the Crimean War the British and French besieged Sevastopol, the main Russian naval base in the Black Sea, from October 1854 until its evacuation by the Russians in September 1855.

404.32 Lieut. Grace] James W. Grace (b. 1833), a merchant from New Bedford, was later promoted to captain and mustered out in August 1865.

405.26–28 DeForrest . . . Chas Creamer] All of the men mentioned by Douglass were from Syracuse, where Helen Amelia Loguen (1843–1936) lived with her father, the Reverend Jermain Loguen, a prominent black abolitionist. Andrew DeForest, Jacob Carter, Charles Whiten, and Charles Creamer were discharged from the 54th Massachusetts in August 1865. George Washington died in a Union military hospital at Beaufort, South Carolina, on August 3, 1863, and Charles Reason died at Beaufort on July 27, 1863.

407.26–27 Mrs. L's . . . Dr. R.] Jean Davenport Lander (1829–1903), an English actress and the widow of Union brigadier general Frederick W. Lander (1821–1862), was the supervisor of nursing at Beaufort, South Carolina; Colonel Thomas Wentworth Higginson (1823–1911), commander of the 1st South Carolina Volunteers; for Dr. Seth Rogers, see note 216.21.

408.6 Mrs. S.] Maltilda Thompson Saxton (1840–1915), a schoolteacher from Philadelphia who had married General Rufus Saxton (see note 99.30) on March 11, 1863.

408.12–13 "Many and low . . . of a friend."] Elizabeth Barrett Browning, "A Court Lady," line 16.

410.6 Mr. P.] Edward L. Pierce (1829–1897), a Boston lawyer and friend of Charles Sumner who had served as a treasury department agent at Port Royal in 1862.

410.10 Major Hallowell] Edward N. Hallowell (1837–1871), a former officer of the 20th Massachusetts, became second in command of the 54th Massachusetts after his brother, Norwood Penrose Hallowell (see note 21.9–10), was commissioned colonel of the black 55th Massachusetts Infantry in June 1863. Edward Hallowell returned to duty in October 1863 and was colonel of the 54th Massachusetts for the remainder of the war.

411.19 Colonel O'Brian] Henry O'Brien (c. 1823–1863), the colonel of the recently formed 11th New York Infantry, was repeatedly beaten and dragged through the streets on the afternoon of July 14 after he failed to disperse a mob at Second Avenue and 34th Street.

411.23–24 Father . . . his house] Philip M. Lydig (1799–1872), a wealthy landowner and retired merchant, owned a house at 84 Laight Street.

411.28 our own block] The Dalys lived at 84 Clinton Place (now West 8th Street).

412.2–3 to see Judge Hilton] Henry Hilton (1824–1899), a Democratic judge on the court of common pleas, lived at 222 Madison Avenue.

412.10 he had $300.] The amount of the commutation fee needed under the 1863 conscription act to avoid being drafted; see the headnote on page 57 in this volume.

412.28 Leonard, the Superintendent of Police] Inspector James Leonard (c. 1820–1869), who helped restore order in several downtown neighborhoods during the riots.

412.38 Mrs. Jarvis and James T. Brady] Maria Louisa Brady Jarvis, the wife of Nathaniel Jarvis, clerk of the court of common pleas; her brother, James T. Brady (1815–1869), a prominent New York lawyer who had successfully defended Daniel E. Sickles (see note 362.18–19) and Lewis Baker, who was charged with murder in the 1855 shooting death of Nativist gang leader William (Bill the Butcher) Poole.

412.39 Susanna Brady] A sister of James T. Brady.

413.19–20 Judge Pierrepont] Edwards Pierrepont (1817–1892), a Democratic former judge of the New York superior court who would support Lincoln's reelection in 1864.

413.23 General Dix] Major General John A. Dix (1798–1879) replaced John E. Wool as commander of the Department of the East on July 18, 1863. Dix had served as a Democratic senator from New York, 1845–49.

415.11 Roman, never to be scourged.] Under Roman law the scourging of citizens was prohibited, and the punishment was reserved for slaves and foreigners.

417.11 Monckton Milnes] Richard Monckton Milnes (1809–1885), a poet, writer, literary patron, biographer of John Keats, and member of Parliament from 1837 to August 1863, when he was made Baron Houghton.

417.15 W. H. Russell] William Howard Russell (1820–1907), British war correspondent who had reported for *The Times* from America on the secession crisis and the war from March 1861 to April 1862.

417.18 Cosmopolitan Club] A club on Berkeley Square in London, founded in 1852, whose members included artists, writers, senior civil servants, and political figures.

417.30 case of the iron-clads] The Laird shipyards in Liverpool were building two ironclad rams for the Confederate navy; see pp. 502–4 in this volume.

418.3–4 Dana, John] Richard Henry Dana, author of *Two Years Before the Mast* (1840), who served as U.S. district attorney for Massachusetts, 1861–66; John Quincy Adams II (see note 9.18).

418.10–11 Judge Goodrich] Aaron Goodrich (1807–1887), secretary to the U.S. legation in Brussels, 1861–69, had previously served as chief justice of the Minnesota territorial supreme court, 1849–51.

418.18 the Trent affair] On November 8, 1861, Captain Charles Wilkes of the U.S.S. *San Jacinto* boarded the British mail packet *Trent* off Cuba and seized the Confederate envoys James M. Mason and John Slidell. The incident caused a major diplomatic crisis that continued until the Lincoln administration decided on December 26 to release the envoys in order to avoid a possible war with Great Britain.

418.30 Pendennis] *The History of Pendennis*, novel (1848–50) by William Makepeace Thackeray.

418.36 Brooks] Brooks Adams (1848–1927), younger brother of Henry Adams and Charles Francis Adams Jr.

418.37–38 Isle of Skye . . . Dr. Johnson] Samuel Johnson and James Boswell traveled through western Scotland together in 1773. Their travels were described by Johnson in *Journey to the Western Islands of Scotland* (1775) and by Boswell in *The Journal of a Tour to the Hebrides, with Samuel Johnson, LL.D.* (1785).

419.20 the Index] A pro-Confederate weekly newspaper published in London, May 1862–August 1865, by Henry Hotze (1833–1887), a Swiss-born journalist from Mobile who was sent to England as a propaganda agent by the Confederate State Department.

421.19 Generals Sedgwick, Wright, Slocum, Hays, Sykes] Major General John Sedgwick commanded the Sixth Corps; Brigadier General Horatio G. Wright (1820–1899) led the First Division of the Sixth Corps; Major General Henry W. Slocum commanded the Twelfth Corps; Brigadier General William Hays was the acting commander of the Second Corps; Major General George Sykes (1822–1880) led the Fifth Corps.

NOTES 857

429.20–21 free men . . . slavery in Texas.] Charles Fairfax Revaleon (1845–1910) and his cousin Charles Gerrish Amos were personal servants to the colonel and staff of the 42nd Massachusetts Infantry. They were captured at Galveston on January 1, 1863, and sold into slavery in Texas. Revaleon and Amos returned to Massachusetts in the summer of 1865.

429.27 slaughtered teamsters at Murfreesboro.] Reports in the northern press claimed that Confederate cavalrymen had killed twenty black teamsters during a raid on the Union supply line during the battle of Stones River (Murfreesboro), December 31, 1862–January 2, 1863. Other reports alleged that the Confederates captured and then killed twenty black teamsters along the Murfreesboro Pike in late January 1863.

430.4 "Hold, enough!"] *Macbeth*, V.8.34.

432.37–40 two white men . . . will retaliate] On July 6, 1863, Confederate authorities selected by lot Henry Sawyer and John Flinn, two Union captains held in Libby Prison in Richmond, and announced that they would be executed in retaliation for the deaths of Captain William Francis Corbin and Lieutenant Thomas Jefferson McGraw, who had been shot as spies on May 15 after being captured within the Union lines in northern Kentucky while secretly recruiting for the Confederate army. President Lincoln responded on July 15 by declaring that if Sawyer and Flinn were executed, the Union would retaliate by hanging Brigadier General William Henry Fitzhugh Lee (see note 33.27–28), who had been captured by Union cavalry in Virginia on June 26. The threatened executions were not carried out, and on March 14, 1864, Sawyer, Flinn, and Brigadier General Neal Dow were exchanged for Lee and another Confederate officer who had been held as a hostage, Captain Robert H. Tyler.

433.26 "shame extremest hell."] John Greenleaf Whittier, "Stanzas for the Times" (1835), line 26.

435.31 Johnny Mahay] Mahay, a soldier in the 101st New York Infantry who was wounded at Second Bull Run by a bullet that perforated his bladder, died in 1864. Whitman later wrote about him in "A Case from Second Bull Run" in *Specimen Days* (1882).

437.29 Dr. Bliss] D. Willard Bliss (1825–1889) was the superintendent of Armory Square Hospital.

442.27 "eternal vigilance . . . liberty."] Cf. the Irish attorney and orator John Philpot Curran, in his speech on the right of election of Lord Mayor of Dublin (1790): "The condition upon which God hath given liberty to man is eternal vigilance; which condition, if he break, servitude is at once the consequence of his crime and the punishment of his guilt."

443.6 Mr. Blair] In a speech to a Union mass meeting in Cleveland on May 20, 1863, Postmaster General Montgomery Blair (1813–1883) had described proposals to colonize freed slaves outside the United States as "a deliverance" from "a war of races which could only end in the extermination of the negro race or amalgamation with it."

443.38   Col. Littlefield] Colonel Milton S. Littlefield (1830–1899) of the 4th South Carolina Volunteers.

444.18–20   Our First Sergeants, . . . $10 a month] The monthly pay for white noncommissioned officers was $17 for a sergeant, $20 for a first sergeant, and $21 for a sergeant major.

445.18–19   anniversary of British West India Emancipation] The Abolition Act of August 28, 1833, went into effect on August 1, 1834.

445.40   decision of Attorney-General Bates] See note 118.11–12.

446.10   day of Jubilee] See Leviticus 25:8–13.

446.25   "Who would be free, . . . the blow."] See Lord Byron, *Childe Harold's Pilgrimage*, Canto II (1812), stanza 76: "Hereditary bondsmen! Know ye not, / Who would be free, themselves must strike the blow?"

447.21   your proclamation] See Chronology, August 1, 1863.

448.17   attack I experienced last spring.] Lee had suffered from chest pains in the spring of 1863.

450.18–20   Sydney Johnston] After he was criticized for a series of Confederate reverses in Kentucky and Tennessee, Confederate general Albert Sidney Johnston (1803–1862) wrote to Davis on March 18, 1862, that "the test of merit in my profession with the people is success."

452.16–17   last Wednesday] August 5, 1863.

457.11   Head Quars 1210 Chesnut St] The headquarters of the Supervisory Committee for Recruiting Colored Regiments.

458.12   the bill drawn up by himself] Stanton presumably refers to the bill regarding black troops introduced in the House of Representatives by Thaddeus Stevens; see pp. 23–24 in this volume.

458.28   Gen Thomas] Brigadier General Lorenzo Thomas (1804–1875), the adjutant general of the U.S. Army, was assigned in March 1863 to recruit black troops.

461.29   Col Lucketts Reg] Colonel Philip N. Luckett (c. 1823–1869) commanded the 3rd Texas Infantry.

461.31   Debray] Colonel Xavier B. DeBray (1818–1895) commanded a brigade at Galveston.

462.4   Cooks Reg] Colonel Joseph J. Cook (1826–1869) commanded the 1st Texas Heavy Artillery.

462.9   Browns Battalion] Lieutenant Colonel Reuben R. Brown (1808–1894) led the 12th Texas Cavalry Battalion.

462.13   Gen Magruder] See note 258.31.

462.36   the capture of Morgan] See Chronology, July 8, July 19–29, 1863.

463.24   Bettie] Elizabeth Neblett (1863–1928), the fifth child of William and Elizabeth Neblett, was born on May 26.

463.27   Mary] Mary Caroline Neblett (1853–1936), their first child.

463.33   Walters] Walter Scott Neblett (1860–1957), their fourth child.

465.30–31   Springfield . . . Lexington] Confederate forces defeated Union troops at Wilson's Creek near Springfield, Missouri, on August 10, 1861, and captured Lexington, Missouri, on September 20, 1861.

466.7–8   Gen. Ewing's staff] Brigadier General Thomas Ewing Jr. (1829–1896) commanded the District of the Border, which covered part of western Missouri and most of Kansas.

466.20–21   "welcomed with bloody hands to hospitable graves."] See note 72.35–36.

467.18   Jim. Lane] James H. Lane (1814–1866) was a Republican senator from Kansas, 1861–66. Lane had commanded an irregular Kansas brigade that looted and burned the town of Osceola, Missouri, on September 23, 1861.

469.15   Kansas Fourteenth] The 14th Kansas Cavalry.

474.12–13   Gov. Robinson] Charles L. Robinson (1818–1894) had served as the Republican governor of Kansas, February 1861–January 1863.

475.16   Gen. Collamore] George W. Collamore (1818–1863), the quartermaster general of the Kansas militia, was elected mayor of Lawrence in the spring of 1863.

477.5–11   His wife . . . wife's sister] Mary Barber Carpenter (1837–1917) and Abigail Barber Morse (1833–1925).

480.14–22   Mr. Rothrock . . . may recover.] Abraham Rothrock (1796–1870) survived, but lost the use of his left arm.

480.22–24   Rev. H. D. Fisher . . . Rev. Mr. Paddock] Hugh Dunn Fisher (1824–1905) and George Washington Paddock (1823–1908) were both Methodist ministers. Fisher had served as the chaplain of the 5th Kansas Cavalry and accompanied it on raids into Missouri during which a number of slaves were freed.

481.27–30   "Uncle Henry" . . . Mr. Ellis] Charles Henry, Benjamin Stonestreet, and Frank Ellis.

482.25   My wife] Elizabeth Acheson Fisher (1826–1901).

485.12 A son of John Speer] John Speer Sr. (1817–1906) was the editor of the *Kansas Weekly Tribune* and the former editor of the *Lawrence Republican*. His nineteen-year-old son John Speer Jr. was killed during the raid, while his fifteen-year-old son William survived. Another son, seventeen-year-old Robert, disappeared during the raid, and may have been burned beyond identification in the fire that destroyed the *Tribune* building.

491.35 the Conservative party] A coalition of former Whigs and conditional unionists that had supported Zebulon B. Vance in the 1862 election for governor.

493.2–4 policy of removing . . . bushwhackers.] Ewing had issued orders on August 18, 1863, authorizing the removal of slaves from rebels and the banishing of the families of "known guerrillas" from Missouri.

500.22 Dana] Charles A. Dana (1819–1897), managing editor of the *New-York Tribune*, 1849–62, served as Secretary of War Stanton's special emissary at Grant's headquarters.

501.4 Col. Chetlain] Augustus L. Chetlain (1824–1914), a merchant from Galena, was the colonel of the 12th Illinois Infantry. Chetlain was promoted to brigadier general in December 1863 and assigned to recruit and organize black troops in Tennessee and western Kentucky.

501.9–10 Vice President Stevens . . . corner stone] See note 138.27–28.

501.22 Rawlins & Maltby] John A. Rawlins (1831–1869) served as Grant's adjutant general, 1861–65. Jasper A. Maltby (1826–1867), the colonel of the 45th Illinois Infantry, commanded a brigade for the remainder of the war.

503.3 the Warrior] H.M.S. *Warrior*, an ironclad steamship commissioned in 1861 that carried forty guns and was considered the most powerful warship of its time.

505.25–26 Battery Haskell] The battery was located on James Island.

506.9 large Blakely gun] A muzzle-loading rifled cannon with a 12.75-inch-diameter bore that could fire a 470-pound shell or a 650-pound solid shot more than five miles. It was named after its designer, the British artillery officer Captain Alexander Blakely.

506.34–35 surrendered by Anderson] Major Robert Anderson (1805–1871) surrendered Fort Sumter to Confederate forces on April 13, 1861.

508.29 *Vanderbilt*] The U.S.S. *Vanderbilt* was a converted sidewheel mail steamer armed with fifteen guns.

509.3–4 the admiral . . . *Narcissus*] Rear Admiral Sir Baldwin Walker (1802–1876) was the commander of the Royal Navy squadron, based at the Cape of Good Hope, that patrolled off West Africa in order to suppress the slave trade. The *Narcissus*, a steam frigate, was the flagship of the West Africa squadron.

509.30   Captain J. H. Coxon]   An officer of the Royal Navy.

510.39   Cape Agulhas and Point Danger]   Cape Agulhas and Point Danger are, respectively, about one hundred miles and sixty miles southeast of Simon's Town.

514.21   Tiers-etat]   Third Estate.

515.16   Jackson]   Brigadier General William H. Jackson (1835–1903) commanded a cavalry division in Mississippi.

515.21–22   Cosby . . . Stephen D. Lee]   Brigadier General George B. Cosby (1830–1909), an 1852 West Point graduate who had resigned from the U.S. Army in May 1861; Brigadier General John W. Whitfield (1818–1879); Major General Stephen D. Lee (1833–1908). Stephen D. Lee was not related to Robert E. Lee.

515.26   Mr. Chase's]   Salmon P. Chase (1808–1873) was secretary of the treasury in the Lincoln administration, 1861–64.

519.24–25   Napoleons design in Mexico]   See Chronology, June 7, 1863.

521.31   Whartons Cavalry]   See note 149.26.

522.12–13   Adams Brigade]   Confederate brigadier general Daniel W. Adams (1821–1872) led a brigade in the division commanded by Major General John C. Breckinridge.

523.32   Gen Hills HcQts]   Daniel H. Hill commanded the corps that Heartsill served in at Chickamauga.

524.17   Col Wilkes]   Colonel Franklin C. Wilkes (c. 1822–1881) commanded a regiment in Deshler's Brigade that had been formed by the consolidation of the dismounted 17th, 18th, 24th, and 25th Texas Cavalry.

524.21   7th Texas]   The 7th Texas Infantry.

524.34–35   Cheathams men]   Major General Benjamin F. Cheatham (1820–1886) commanded a division in the Army of Tennessee.

525.5   Col Mills]   Colonel Roger Q. Mills (1832–1911) commanded Heartsill's regiment, a consolidation of the 6th and 10th Texas Infantry and the dismounted 15th Texas Cavalry.

525.15   W P L Rs]   W. P. Lane Rangers.

525.29   suffered . . . Woods Brigade]   Brigadier General Sterling A. M. Wood (1823–1891) reported that his brigade lost 776 men killed or wounded at Chickamauga.

531.29   Capt. N . . . Dr. S.]   Captain Price C. Newman and First Sergeant James W. Ford of Company C, 9th Kentucky Infantry, and Dr. Preston B. Scott, a surgeon with the 1st Kentucky Brigade. Jackman was a member of Company B of the 9th Kentucky, but served as a regimental clerk during the Chickamauga campaign.

532.4 Cobbs' . . . Slocums'] Captain Robert Cobb (1836–1914) and Captain Culbert H. Slocomb commanded artillery batteries assigned to Breckinridge's division.

532.26 the Col.] Colonel John W. Caldwell (1837–1903), commander of the 9th Kentucky Infantry.

532.36 Napoleon gun] A smoothbore muzzle-loading field artillery gun that fired a twelve-pound projectile with a maximum range of 1,600 yards. It was developed in France under the auspices of Napoleon III.

533.5 Maj. Wilson . . . Gen'l Helm] Major James Wilson, Breckinridge's adjutant; Brigadier General Ben Hardin Helm (1831–1863), who had commanded the 1st Kentucky Brigade since late January 1863.

533.27 J. H.] James Hunter.

533.30 Lt. Col. W.] Lieutenant Colonel John C. Wickliffe.

533.35–36 Col. H. . . . Maj. Hope] Colonel Thomas H. Hunt (1815–1884) commanded the 9th Kentucky Infantry from the fall of 1861 to the spring of 1863. Major John S. Hope was an officer with the 2nd Kentucky Infantry.

535.31 Dr. Heustis] James F. Heustis (1828–1891), a surgeon from Mobile.

536.14 Colonel Colyer] Arthur St. Clair Colyar (1818–1907), a member of the Second Confederate Congress, 1864–65.

537.15 Dr. Ussery] Benjamin W. Ussery (1829–1894), a surgeon with the 42nd Tennessee Infantry.

538.8 Professor Pickett] Joseph Desha Pickett (1822–1900), a minister in the Christian Church (Disciples of Christ), was the chaplain of the 1st Kentucky Brigade and a former professor of rhetoric at Bethany College in Virginia (now West Virginia).

538.27 Colonels Walter] Colonel Harvey W. Walter (1819–1878) served as a judge advocate on Bragg's staff.

539.5 Dr. Stout] Samuel H. Stout (1822–1903) was superintendent of hospitals for the Army of Tennessee.

539.19 Neal Brown] Neill Smith Brown (1810–1886) was the Whig governor of Tennessee, 1847–49, and served as U.S. minister to Russia, 1850–53.

540.36 Hindman's] Major General Thomas C. Hindman (1828–1868) commanded a division in the Army of Tennessee.

541.11 Claiborne's Division] Cleburne's Division.

541.23–24 Managault's Brigade] Brigadier General Arthur M. Manigault (1824–1886) commanded a brigade in Hindman's division.

NOTES 863

542.32 Captain O'Brien] Captain William J. O'Brien of the Alabama 24th Infantry, who had practiced law in Mobile before the war.

543.9 Cowper . . . tea] See William Cowper (1731–1800), *The Task* (1785), Book IV, "A Winter Evening."

544.1–2 Dr. Foard] Andrew J. Foard (c. 1829–1868), the field medical director for the Department of the West.

544.5 Flewellyn] Edward A. Flewellen (1819–1910), the field medical director for the Army of Tennessee.

544.22 Deus's Brigade] Brigadier General Zachariah C. Deas (1819–1882) commanded a brigade in Hindman's division.

545.5–6 like Rachel . . . her children] See Jeremiah 31:15.

545.8–9 "O, what a field . . . Faulkland] See James Montgomery (1771–1854), "Lord Falkland's Dream" (1831): "'Can this,' he sigh'd, 'be virtuous fame and clear? / Ah! what a field of fratricide is here!'" Lucius Cary, second Viscount Falkland (c. 1610–1643), was a royalist member of Parliament who unsuccessfully sought a negotiated end to the English Civil War before being killed at the first battle of Newbury.

548.25–26 Galusha A. Grow] A congressman from Pennsylvania, Grow (1823–1907) served as a Democrat, 1851–57, and as a Republican, 1857–63 and 1894–1903. He was Speaker of the House, 1861–63.

548.34–35 Major General Casey] Silas Casey (1807–1882) headed the board that examined prospective officers for the U.S. Colored Troops.

549.11 Casey's Tactics] Silas Casey, *Infantry Tactics, for the Instruction, Exercise, and Manoeuvres of the Soldier, a Company, Line of Skirmishers, Battalion, Brigade, or Corps D'Armee* (1862).

549.28 rumors of another great battle] See Chronology, October 9–18, 1863.

549.39–40 Curtin . . . Brough] See Chronology, October 13, 1863.

551.10 Mr. Wright] William A. Wright (1807–1878) was a Wilmington banker, lawyer, and railroad investor.

551.21 best soldiers in the Confederate army] Major General William H. C. Whiting (1824–1865) led a division in the Army of Northern Virginia in the Peninsula campaign before being appointed commander of the Wilmington district in November 1862. Whiting was fatally wounded during the Union capture of Fort Fisher, North Carolina, on January 15, 1865.

552.20 President . . . through Wilmington] Davis had spoken in Wilmington on May 28, 1861, while on his way to Richmond.

553.14 great Bethel] Confederate troops repulsed a Union advance at Big Bethel, Virginia, on June 10, 1861.

555.29   George Peterkin] Lieutenant George Peterkin (1841–1916), an aide to Brigadier General William N. Pendleton, chief of artillery of the Army of Northern Virginia.

558.16   Poor Ewell—a cripple—is now laid up]   Lieutenant General Richard S. Ewell had lost his left leg at the battle of Groveton in 1862 and was suffering from an abscess caused by an ill-fitting wooden prosthesis. Ewell was temporarily relieved of command of the Second Corps on November 15 and returned to duty on December 5, 1863, after being fitted with a new leg.

558.23   John H. . . . Pemberton]   John Hobson, Mahew Hobson's brother. Pemberton was a post office village in Goochland County, Virginia.

558.37–39   Venable . . . Col Preston]   Major Charles Venable (1827–1900), a mathematician and astronomer in civilian life, served on Lee's personal staff, 1862–65. Colonel John S. Preston (1809–1881) was chief of the Confederate bureau of conscription, 1863–65.

559.15   Dr. Wright's execution.]   On July 11, 1863, Dr. David M. Wright (1809–1863) shot and killed Lieutenant Anson L. Sanborn (1834–1863), a white officer marching through Norfolk, Virginia, at the head of his company of the 1st U.S. Colored Infantry. Wright was convicted by a military commission and hanged on October 23, 1863.

559.18–21   Mrs. Jack Preston . . . Genl. Hampton]   Celestine Pinckney Huger Preston (1843–1878) was married to Major John S. Preston Jr. (1836–1880), the son of Colonel John S. Preston. Major Preston was an aide to Major General Wade Hampton (1818–1902), who commanded a cavalry division in the Army of Northern Virginia.

562.19–21   Usher & Blair . . . McDougal of Canada]   John P. Usher (1816–1889), secretary of the interior, 1863–65; Montgomery Blair (1813–1883), postmaster general, 1861–64; John G. Nicolay (1832–1901), secretary to Abraham Lincoln, 1860–65; Henri Mercier (1816–1886), the French minister to the United States, 1860–63; Aimé Félix Sainte-Elme Reynaud (1808–1876), the French naval commander in the Gulf of Mexico; Joseph (Giuseppe) Bertinatti (1808–1881), the Italian minister to the United States, 1861–66; Ulissa Isola and Martinez were Italian naval officers whose ships were visiting New York harbor; Cora was the secretary of the Italian legation; Charlotte Brooks Everett Wise (1825–1879), the daughter of Edward Everett; Isaac Wayne MacVeagh (1833–1917), district attorney of Chester County, Pennsylvania, and chairman of the Republican state central committee; William McDougall (1822–1905), commissioner of crown lands in the provincial government of Canada.

562.27   the Edwards case]   Attorney General Edward Bates had removed William W. Edwards as U.S. attorney for the Eastern District of Missouri on November 2, 1863, for "active participation in political enterprises hostile to the known views and wishes of the Executive Government." Edwards had joined other Radicals in an unsuccessful attempt to have John

Schofield replaced as the Union military commander in Missouri with Benjamin F. Butler.

562.32   young Stanton] Edwin L. Stanton (1842–1877), son of Secretary of War Edwin M. Stanton.

562.35   Lamon] Ward Hill Lamon (1828–1893), an Illinois lawyer and friend of Lincoln's who served as U.S. marshal for the District of Columbia, 1861–65. He was the marshal for the dedication ceremony at Gettysburg.

563.1   Forney . . . Mr. Fahnestocks] John W. Forney (1817–1881) was the editor of the *Philadelphia Press* and the *Washington Chronicle*. Harris C. Fahnestock (1835–1914), a banker from Harrisburg, Pennsylvania, was a partner in the Washington branch of Jay Cooke & Company.

563.14   Curtin] Andrew G. Curtin (1815–1894), Republican governor of Pennsylvania, 1861–66.

563.16   the Cameron party] Supporters of Simon Cameron (1799–1889), who served as a Democratic senator from Pennsylvania, 1845–49; Republican senator, 1857–61; secretary of war, 1861–62; and U.S. minister to Russia, 1862–63.

563.24   Harper's] The home of Robert G. Harper (1799–1870), publisher and editor of the *Adams Sentinel*.

563.35   fuglers] A political handler; also, a person who leads crowds in cheering.

564.6   John Young] John Russell Young (1840–1899), managing editor of the *Philadelphia Press* and the *Washington Chronicle*.

564.14–15   in 1860 . . . course he took] Forney had supported Stephen A. Douglas, the northern Democratic candidate, in the 1860 election.

564.26   Judge Shannon] Peter C. Shannon (1821–1899), a Republican member of the Pennsylvania house of representatives, 1862–63, had served as a judge on the Allegheny County district court, 1852–53.

564.34–35   Mr. Everett . . . Mr Stockton] Edward Everett (1794–1865), a Unitarian clergyman, was professor of Greek at Harvard, 1819–25; a Whig congressman from Massachusetts, 1825–35; governor of Massachusetts, 1836–40; U.S. minister to Great Britain, 1841–45; president of Harvard, 1846–49; secretary of state, 1852–53; a senator from Massachusetts, 1853–54; and the vice presidential candidate of the Constitutional Union Party, 1860. Thomas H. Stockton (1808–1868), a Methodist clergyman, was chaplain of the U.S. House of Representatives, 1861–63.

565.3   Genl. Cameron] Simon Cameron, who had served as adjutant general of the Pennsylvania militia, 1829–31.

566.2   *Address at Gettysburg*] The Associated Press report, prepared by

Joseph L. Gilbert, appeared in three major New York newspapers on November 20 as follows:

> Four score and seven years ago our fathers brought forth upon this continent a new Nation, conceived in Liberty, and dedicated to the proposition that all men are created equal. [Applause.] Now we are engaged in a great civil war, testing whether that Nation or any Nation so conceived and so dedicated can long endure. We are met on a great battle-field of that war. We are met to dedicate a portion of it as the final resting-place of those who gave their lives that that nation might live. It is altogether fitting and proper that we should do this. But in a larger sense we cannot dedicate, we cannot consecrate, we cannot hallow this ground. The brave men living and dead who struggled here have consecrated it far above our power to add or detract. [Applause.] The world will little note or long remember what we say here, but it can never forget what they did here. [Applause.] It is for us, the living, rather to be dedicated here to the refinished work that they have thus far so nobly carried on. [Applause.] It is rather for us to be here dedicated to the great task remaining before us, that from these honored dead we take increased devotion to the cause for which they here gave the last full measure of devotion; that we here highly resolve that the dead shall not have died in vain [applause]; that the nation shall, under God, have a new birth of freedom; and that Governments of the people, by the people, and for the people, shall not perish from the earth. [Long-continued applause.]

Subsequent printings of the Associated Press text in other newspapers corrected three likely errors in the New York version: "our power" became "our poor power," "refinished work" became "unfinished work," and "the dead" became "these dead."

569.32–33   Gen Starkweather]   Brigadier General John C. Starkweather (1830–1890) commanded a brigade in the First Division, Fourteenth Corps, in the Army of the Cumberland.

570.1–2   Hookers troops]   See Chronology, September 23, 1863.

570.19   Lagow]   Colonel Clark B. Lagow (1828–1867) had served as an aide to Grant since August 1861.

570.31   Fred Dent]   Frederick Dent (1786–1873), Grant's father-in-law.

570.32   5/20's]   Treasury bonds redeemable after five years and maturing in twenty years that carried 6 percent interest.

570.38–39   Dr. Kittoe . . . Capt Hudson]   Edward D. Kittoe (1814–1887), a surgeon from Galena, Illinois, who served on Grant's staff; Captain Peter D. Hudson (d. 1892), one of Grant's aides.

571.23   General Hunter]   Major General David Hunter (1802–1886); see Biographical Notes.

571.29   Lt. Col. Duff, and Lts. Towner and Dunn] Lieutenant Colonel William L. Duff (1822–1894), Grant's chief of artillery; Lieutenant Horatio N. Towner (1836–1873), assistant chief of artillery; Lieutenant William M. Dunn Jr. (1843–1891), one of Grant's aides.

571.31–33   Lagow . . . his removal.] Lagow submitted his resignation on November 18 and left Grant's headquarters in December 1863.

571.35   Capt. Ross] Captain Orlando H. Ross (1835–1892), a cousin of Grant and one of his aides.

572.5–6   Thomas . . . Branen] Major General George H. Thomas (1816–1870), commander of the Army of the Cumberland; Brigadier General William F. Smith (1824–1903), who was serving as Grant's chief engineer; Major General Joseph J. Reynolds (1822–1899), chief of staff of the Army of the Cumberland; Brigadier General John M. Brannan (1819–1892), chief of artillery of the Army of the Cumberland.

572.32   Col. Hillyer] Colonel William S. Hillyer (1830–1874) served as an aide to Grant, 1861–62, and as provost marshal of the Department of the Tennessee, 1862–63.

573.22   fort Wood] The fort was part of the Union defensive line around Chattanooga.

574.8   very anxious about Burnsides] See Chronology, November 4 and November 16, 1863.

574.20   Gen John E. Smith] Brigadier General John E. Smith (1816–1897) commanded a division in the Seventeenth Corps, Army of the Tennessee.

574.26   Howard] Major General Oliver Otis Howard (1830–1909), commander of the Eleventh Corps, which had been sent west under Hooker's command along with the Twelfth Corps.

574.40   Gen's Meigs, Gen Wilson] Brigadier General Montgomery C. Meigs (1816–1892), quartermaster general of the Union army; Brigadier General James H. Wilson (1837–1925), an engineering officer serving on Grant's staff.

575.13–14   Gen A Baird's . . . Washington man] Brigadier General Absalom Baird (1824–1905), commander of the Third Division, Fourteenth Corps, Army of the Cumberland. Baird and William Wrenshall Smith were both from Washington, Pennsylvania.

575.25   John Acheson] John W. Acheson (1837–1872), a cousin of Baird from Washington, Pennsylvania, was a first lieutenant in the 85th Pennsylvania Infantry who was serving in the Charleston Harbor campaign. He was assigned to Baird's staff in 1864.

577.2   Maj Rowley] Major William R. Rowley (1824–1886) served as an aide to Grant, 1862–64.

577.3–4 Cadwallader . . . Chicago *Times*] Sylvanus Cadwallader (1825–1908).

577.25 Capts. Parker] Captain Ely S. Parker (1828–1895), a Seneca Indian, was an assistant adjutant general on Grant's staff and later served as his military secretary.

578.26–28 There shall . . . by myriads] Lord Byron, *Childe Harold's Pilgrimage*, Canto I (1812), stanza 42.

578.36 the Anderson troop] The 15th Pennsylvania Cavalry, recruited in 1862 by Colonel William J. Palmer (1836–1909). Palmer had earlier raised a troop of cavalry in the autumn of 1861 to serve as a headquarters guard for Brigadier General Robert Anderson, the commander of the Department of the Cumberland and former defender of Fort Sumter.

579.1 Buell] Major General Don Carlos Buell (1818–1898) commanded the Army of the Ohio, November 1861–October 1862.

583.10 Woods Division] Brigadier General Thomas J. Wood (1823–1906) commanded the Third Division, Fourth Corps, Army of the Cumberland.

583.28 Granger, Sheridan] Major General Gordon Granger (1822–1876) commanded the Fourth Corps in the Army of the Cumberland; Major General Philip H. Sheridan (1831–1888) commanded the Second Division in the Fourth Corps.

584.28 Stevenson] Major General Carter L. Stevenson (1817–1888) was a division commander in the Confederate Army of Tennessee.

584.38 Major Dana] Charles A. Dana.

586.29 Colonel Putnam] Colonel Holden Putnam (1820–1863), commander of the 93rd Illinois Infantry, died from his wound.

589.20 Johnson's Division] Brigadier General Richard W. Johnson (1827–1897) commanded the First Division, Fourteenth Corps, Army of the Cumberland.

591.26 notice Bragg gave him] See p. 575.6–8 in this volume.

592.8 Cruft] Brigadier General Charles Cruft (1826–1883) commanded the First Division of the Fourth Corps in the Army of the Cumberland.

592.20 Logan] Major General John A. Logan (1826–1886), a division commander in the Army of the Tennessee, had been named to succeed Sherman as the commander of the Fifteenth Corps, but did not reach Tennessee until December because of his duties in Mississippi. During the battle of Chattanooga the Fifteenth Corps was led by Major General Frank Blair.

593.6 "sun of Austerlitz"] The sun breaking through morning mist on the battlefield became the symbol of Napoleon's victory over the Austrian-Russian army at Austerlitz on December 2, 1805.

NOTES 869

596.11 Gen. ——] General Baird.

596.14 Col. ——"] Colonel Edward H. Phelps (c. 1829–1863), formerly commander of the 38th Ohio Infantry.

599.1 Davis' Division,] Brigadier General Jefferson C. Davis (1828–1879) commanded the Second Division of the Fourteenth Corps in the Army of the Cumberland. (General Davis was not related to the president of the Confederate states.)

599.11 Gen. ——] Major General John M. Palmer (1817–1900) led the Fourteenth Corps.

599.20–21 with —— 's brigade] Colonel John T. Wilder (1830–1917).

599.29–30 Gen. Turchin] Brigadier General John B. Turchin (1822–1901) commanded the First Brigade in Baird's division.

599.33 a rough pencil sketch] The sketch is not reproduced in this volume.

599.35 Gen. ——] General Baird.

600.1–4 Gen. ——, . . . Gen. ——] General Palmer.

602.5–6 Merritt's . . . (Kilpatrick's)] Brigadier General Wesley Merritt (1836–1910) led the First Division of the Cavalry Corps of the Army of the Potomac during the Mine Run campaign after its commander, Brigadier General John Buford (1826–1863), fell ill with typhoid fever (Buford died on December 16). Brigadier General George Armstrong Custer (1839–1876) led the Third Division of the Cavalry Corps during the campaign after Brigadier General Judson Kilpatrick (1836–1881) went on leave following the death of his wife.

602.7 Gregg's Div.] Brigadier General David M. Gregg (1833–1916) commanded the Second Division of the Cavalry Corps.

602.9 Gen. Prince] Brigadier General Henry Prince (1811–1892) commanded the Second Division of the Third Corps.

603.28–30 Ludlow . . . McBlair] Major Benjamin C. Ludlow (1831–1898), an inspector of artillery on Meade's staff; Captain John G. McBlair, one of Meade's aides.

603.33 Cadwalader] Charles Evert Cadwalader (1839–1907), one of Meade's aides.

603.38 Longfellow and Bowditch were here wounded] Second Lieutenant Charles Appleton Longfellow (1844–1893), son of the poet Henry Wadsworth Longfellow, and Captain Henry Pickering Bowditch (1840–1911), grandson of the mathematician and astronomer Nathaniel Bowditch, were both medically discharged from the 1st Massachusetts Cavalry on February 15, 1864. Bowditch was later commissioned as major of the 5th Massachusetts Cavalry, a black regiment.

606.16   Carr]   Brigadier General Joseph B. Carr (1828–1895) commanded the Third Division in the Third Corps.

606.27–29   Capt. Barnard . . . Bartlett]   Captain George M. Barnard (1835–1898) served on the staff of the First Division, Fifth Corps, which was commanded by Brigadier General Joseph J. Bartlett (1834–1893).

606.39–607.1   Col. Farnum (he of yacht *Wanderer* fame)]   Colonel John Egbert Farnum (1824–1870) led the 70th New York Infantry in the Second Division, Third Corps. A veteran of the war with Mexico and of filibustering expeditions in Cuba and Nicaragua, Farnum had served as supercargo on the *Wanderer*, a schooner that illegally landed four hundred African slaves on the Georgia coast in November 1858. His trial on federal piracy charges in Savannah, Georgia, in May 1860 ended in a hung jury.

607.7   Robling]   Lieutenant Washington A. Roebling (1837–1926), an aide to Major General Gouverneur K. Warren. He later served as chief engineer in the construction of the Brooklyn Bridge, 1869–83.

607.11   Gen. Humphreys]   Major General Andrew A. Humphreys (1810–1883), chief of staff of the Army of the Potomac.

608.24–25   Col. Hayes (Joe)]   Colonel Joseph Hayes (1835–1912) commanded the Third Brigade, First Division, Fifth Corps.

608.32–33   T. F. Meagher "of the Sword"]   Thomas F. Meagher (1823–1867), a member of the Young Ireland movement, became known as "Meagher of the Sword" after he declared in a speech in Dublin on July 28, 1846: "Be it in the defense, or be it in the assertion of a people's liberty, I hail the sword as a sacred weapon." Meagher was convicted of high treason in 1848 and exiled the following year to Van Diemen's Land (Tasmania). He escaped to the United States in 1852 and commanded the Irish Brigade in the Second Corps of the Army of the Potomac from November 1861 until May 1863, when he resigned his commission as a brigadier general shortly after the battle of Chancellorsville.

608.34–35   the English officers]   Lieutenant Colonel William Earle (1833–1885) and Lieutenant William Cuffed (1845–1898) of the Grenadier Guards and Captain John Floyd Peel (1827–1910) and Captain Sussex Vane Stephenson (1833–1878) of the Scots Fusilier Guards visited Meade's headquarters, November 14–December 3, 1863.

610.2   Mimi]   Lyman's wife, Elizabeth Russell Lyman (1836–1911).

610.3   Arthur]   Lyman's cousin, Arthur Theodore Lyman (1832–1915).

612.23   the Christian Commission]   Established in 1861 by the Young Men's Christian Association, the United States Christian Commission supplied Union soldiers with food, medical supplies, volunteer nursing care, and religious literature.

613.25   Gen. Standard]   Brigadier General George J. Standard (1820–1886)

NOTES   871

had served as lieutenant colonel of the 2nd Vermont Infantry, June 1861–May 1862. Standard commanded the harbor defenses at New York in late 1863 while recovering from a leg wound he suffered at Gettysburg.

613.29   the third brigade] The Third Brigade, Second Division, Sixth Corps. Fisk served in the Second Brigade of the Second Division.

615.39   The Tenth Vermont] The 10th Vermont Infantry was assigned to the First Brigade, Third Division, Third Corps.

617.9–10   Lee's Mill's affair] On April 16, 1862, the Vermont Brigade (the 2nd, 3rd, 4th, 5th, and 6th Vermont Infantry) made an unsuccessful attack across the Warwick River near Lee's Mill on the Virginia Peninsula. The action cost the brigade 165 men killed, wounded, or missing.

625.2   Cortland Parker, Mr. Harding] Cortland Parker (1818–1907), a prominent New Jersey lawyer who served as public prosecutor of Essex County, 1857–67; George Harding (1827–1902), a leading Philadelphia patent attorney.

625.4   George] Captain George Meade (1843–1897), General Meade's son, was now serving as one of his aides.

625.23   the Star . . . editor] William D. Wallach (1812–1871) was owner and editor of the *Washington Evening Star*, 1855–67.

626.5   Gibbon] Brigadier General John Gibbon (1827–1896), the commander of the Second Division in the Second Corps of the Army of the Potomac, was recovering from a wound suffered at Gettysburg.

626.15   the Herald] The *New York Herald*.

629.25   Mr. Purvis] Robert Purvis (1810–1898), an antislavery activist of mixed racial background, was a founding member of the American Anti-Slavery Society who served as president of the Pennsylvania Anti-Slavery Society, 1845–50. Purvis headed two vigilance committees, 1839–44 and 1852–57, that assisted fugitive slaves in Philadelphia, while also campaigning for the rights of free blacks in Pennsylvania.

630.36   Mr. Wilson] See note 345.29–30.

630.39–631.1   "You do take away . . . my house,"] Cf. *The Merchant of Venice*, IV.i.375–76.

633.30   Dr. Fussell] Dr. Bartholomew Fusel (1794–1871), a Quaker physician and advocate of medical education for women, was a founding member of the American Anti-Slavery Society.

638.24–25   long pending controversy . . . seizure at Sitana] During the Chilean war of independence Chilean forces seized $70,400 in silver in 1821 from an American merchant ship captain in southern Peru, claiming that it was Spanish property. King Leopold I settled the dispute on May 15, 1863, by awarding the American claimants $42,400.

640.16 the Tycoon] Tokugawa Iemochi (1846–1866), shogun of Japan, 1858–66.

640.20–21 the Minister . . . legation at Yedo] Robert H. Pruyn (1815–1882) was U.S. minister to Japan, 1862–65. Most of the American legation at Edo (Tokyo) was destroyed on May 24, 1863, in a fire set by anti-Western samurai.

641.7 Indian disturbances in New Mexico] In the summer of 1863 Colonel Kit Carson (1809–1868) and the 1st New Mexico Cavalry began a campaign designed to end Navaho raiding against settlements in New Mexico and Arizona. The campaign continued until March 1864, when thousands of Navahos were forced by the destruction of their dwellings, crops, and livestock to move onto the reservation at Bosque Redondo in New Mexico.

643.39 General Hitchcock] Major General Ethan Allen Hitchcock (1798–1870) served as the Union commissioner for prisoner exchanges from November 1862 until the end of the war.

649.11–653.8 When Congress assembled . . . any other way.] These eleven paragraphs are in Lincoln's hand in the incomplete preliminary draft, indicating that he himself composed the message from this point on. The preceding parts were probably written by the various members of the cabinet, with the likely exception of the opening paragraph.

658.9–10 *The New Gospel of Peace*] *The New Gospel of Peace According to St. Benjamin*, a pamphlet satirizing Fernando Wood and other prominent Peace Democrats, including his brother Benjamin (see note 81.10–13). The first part ("Book First") was published on July 27, 1863, and the second part on October 24, 1863; subsequent parts appeared on July 22, 1864, and May 19, 1866.

658.12 publisher, Tousey] Sinclair Tousey (1815–1887), a successful New York bookseller and news agent.

658.20 The author is ———.] Richard Grant White (1822–1885), a New York lawyer, literary and music critic, and the editor of a twelve-volume edition of Shakespeare (1857–65).

658.30–31 *Chesapeake* . . . killed] The second engineer of the *Chesapeake* was killed and two other crew members wounded when the ship was seized off Cape Cod on the night of December 7, 1863, by sixteen Confederate sympathizers from the Canadian maritime provinces who planned to refuel in a Canadian port and then sail to Wilmington, North Carolina. A boarding party from the U.S.S. *Ella and Annie* recaptured the *Chesapeake* in Sambro Harbor, Nova Scotia, on December 17 after most of the raiders had fled, and subsequent attempts to prosecute them for piracy in the Canadian courts were unsuccessful.

659.15 the Clans were after 1745] Many Scottish Highland clan leaders were executed or forced into exile after the failed Jacobite uprising of 1745–46. Their estates were confiscated, and parliamentary legislation ended the hereditary power of clan leaders to administer justice in their domains.

659.15–16   Parton's life of Butler] *General Butler in New Orleans* (1863) by James Parton (1822–1891), a New York journalist who had published popular biographies of Horace Greeley, Aaron Burr, and Andrew Jackson.

659.25   Dr. Peters] John Charles Peters (1819–1893), a New York physician and medical writer.

659.26–28   A. H. Stephens, . . . once more at Fortress Monroe] Stephens had approached Fort Monroe on a Confederate flag of truce boat on July 4, 1863, and requested safe passage to Washington in an attempt to open peace negotiations. Lincoln and his cabinet refused to receive him, and Stephens returned to Richmond.

662.19   The Examiner] The *Richmond Examiner*, in an editorial published on December 3, 1863.

662.21–22   Memminger . . . Mallory] Christopher G. Memminger (1803–1888), Confederate secretary of the treasury, February 1861–July 1864; Stephen R. Mallory (c. 1813–1873), Confederate secretary of the navy, February 1861–May 1865.

662.24–26   Huger . . . let McClellan escape] Major General Benjamin Huger (1805–1877), the commander of the Department of Norfolk, May 1861–April 1862, was criticized for not sending sufficient supplies and reinforcements to Roanoke Island in Pamlico Sound before its capture by Union forces on February 8, 1862. Huger later commanded a division in the Army of Northern Virginia during the Seven Days' Battles and was blamed for the Confederate failure to destroy the retreating Union army at Glendale (Frayser's Farm), June 30, and at Malvern Hill, July 1, 1862.

662.26   Lovel, New Orleans] See notes 366.19 and 366.32.

662.29–30   Price . . . Holmes] Sterling Price (1809–1867), the leader of the pro-secession Missouri State Guard, shared command in the state in 1861 with Confederate brigadier general Benjamin McCulloch (1811–1862). In January 1862 both men were placed under Earl Van Dorn, whose defeat at Pea Ridge (Elkhorn Tavern) in northwestern Arkansas, March 7–8, 1862, ended Confederate hopes of gaining control of Missouri. Lieutenant General Theophilus H. Holmes (1804–1880) commanded Confederate forces in Arkansas, September 1863–March 1864.

662.32–33   "the discerning of Spirits."] See 2 Corinthians 12:4–10.

662.38   "not speak" . . . "evil of dignities."] See 2 Peter 2:10.

663.4   Col Clark] Edmondston's brother-in-law, Colonel William J. Clarke (1827–1886), commander of the 24th North Carolina Infantry.

664.14–15　like David . . . my hair cut]　See 2 Samuel 12:19–20.

664.25　General Hood's]　Major General John B. Hood (1831–1875) was recovering from the loss of his right leg at Chickamauga on September 20, 1863.

664.33　Mrs. King,]　Susan Petrigu King (1824–1875), daughter of James L. Petrigru (see note 142.18–19), was a novelist and story writer whose works included *Busy Moments of an Idle Woman* (1854), *Lily* (1855), and *Sylvia's World; and, Crimes Which the Law Does Not Reach* (1859).

665.8　Grundy père]　Thomas Billop Grundy (1827–1879), Chestnut's downstairs neighbor in Richmond.

665.10　Madame Deffand]　Marie Anne de Vichy-Chamrond, Marquise du Deffand (1697–1780), hostess of a Parisian literary salon who corresponded with Voltaire, Montesquieu, Horace Walpole, and Madame de Staël.

665.14–15　Ashmore, . . . Orr]　John D. Ashmore (1819–1871) was a Democratic congressman from South Carolina, 1859–60. Laurence M. Keitt (1824–1864) was a Democratic congressman from South Carolina, 1853–60; a delegate to the Provisional Confederate Congress, 1861–62; and colonel of the 20th South Carolina Infantry, 1862–64. Keitt was mortally wounded at Cold Harbor, Virginia, on June 1, 1864, and died the following day. William W. Boyce (1818–1890) was a Democratic congressman from South Carolina, 1853–60; a delegate to the Provisional Confederate Congress, 1861–62; and a member of the Confederate house of representatives, 1862–65. James L. Orr (1822–1873) was a Democratic congressman from South Carolina, 1849–59, and a Confederate senator, 1862–65.

665.16　Mr. Mason]　James M. Mason (1798–1871) was a Democratic congressman from Virginia, 1837–39, and a senator, 1847–61, who served as Confederate envoy to Great Britain and France, 1861–65.

665.20　Mr. Hunter]　Robert M. T. Hunter (1809–1887) was a congressman from Virginia, 1837–43 and 1845–47, and a senator, 1847–61. A delegate to the Confederate Provisional Congress in 1861 and a Confederate senator, 1862–65, Hunter served as the secretary of state of the Confederacy, July 1861–February 1862.

665.26　Jack Preston]　See note 559.18–21.

665.33　General Scott]　Major General Winfield Scott (1786–1866), a native of Virginia, was general-in-chief of the U.S. Army, 1841–61.

665.35　F.F.]　First Family.

666.4–5　Stonewall . . . Mahone's brigade.]　Brigadier General William Mahone (1826–1895) commanded an infantry brigade composed of five Virginia regiments at Chancellorsville. Jackson was accidentally shot by men of the 18th North Carolina Infantry, one of five North Carolina regiments that made up the brigade commanded by Brigadier General James H. Lane (1833–1907).

666.9 General Edward Johnson] Major General Edward Johnson (1816–1873) commanded a division in the Army of Northern Virginia.

666.13 Suwarrow] Aleksandr Vasilyevich Suvorov (1729–1800), Russian general who successfully commanded troops in the Seven Years' War, 1756–63; in wars with the Turkish Empire, 1768–74 and 1787–91; in suppressing the Polish insurrection of 1794; and in a campaign against the French in Italy and Switzerland in 1799.

666.26 reculer pour mieux sauter] French: step back to make a better jump.

666.30 Bayard . . . Philip Sidney] Pierre Terrail, seigneur de Bayard (1473–1524), French soldier killed at the Sesia River in Italy who became known as "le chevalier sans peur et sans reproche" (the knight without fear and beyond reproach); Sir Philip Sidney (1554–1586), English poet, soldier, and courtier, fatally wounded at the battle of Zutphen in the Netherlands.

667.7 How beautiful are the feet] See Song of Solomon 7:1.

667.11 General Preston] See note 558.37–39.

667.14 General Young] Brigadier General Pierce M. B. Young (1836–1896) led a cavalry brigade in the Army of Northern Virginia.

667.25–26 'the giant foot' . . . Bulwer's last.] A "giant Foot" appears in chapter 87 of Edward Bulwer-Lytton's novel of the occult, *A Strange Story* (1862).

667.29 Mr. Ould] Robert Ould (1820–1882), an attorney from Washington, D.C., was the Confederate commissioner for prisoner exchanges, 1862–65.

667.36 "The Roman emperor . . . good odor."] The Latin saying "pecunia non olet" (money does not smell) is attributed to the emperor Vespasian (9–79 CE).

668.4–5 theater and huzzahed . . . dead."] Theater audiences in London and Manchester cheered the news of the death of Nicholas I in 1855 during the Crimean War.

668.6 Senator Johnson of Arkansas] Robert Ward Johnson (1814–1879) was a Democratic senator from Arkansas, 1853–61, and a Confederate senator, 1862–65.

668.21 Mrs. Lawton, . . . Mary P] Sarah Alexander Lawton (1826–1897); Mary Cantey Preston (1840–1891), daughter of Colonel John S. Preston.

668.25 General Lawton] Brigadier General Alexander R. Lawton (1818–

1896), a former brigade commander in the Army of Northern Virginia who served as Confederate quartermaster general, 1863–65.

668.31–32 beautiful bride . . . happy bridegroom] Probably James Chesnut's cousin John Redman Coxe Lewis (1834–1898) and Maria Freeland Lewis (1838–1920), who were married in December 1863.

669.8 Wigfall] Louis T. Wigfall (1816–1874) was a South Carolina native who moved to Texas in 1846. He served in the Texas house of representatives, 1850–57; in the Texas senate, 1857–59; in the U.S. Senate, 1859–61; and in the Confederate senate, 1862–65.

669.12 *Germaine*] Novel (1857) by Edmond About (1828–1885).

669.22–23 Mrs. Malaprop . . . begin with a little aversion."] See Richard Brinsley Sheridan, *The Rivals* (1775), Act 2, scene 1: "'Tis safest in matrimony to begin with a little aversion."

670.1 Averell's raiders] Brigadier General William W. Averell (1832–1900) led a cavalry brigade that attacked the Virginia & Tennessee Railroad at Salem, Virginia, on December 16, 1863, and then withdrew into West Virginia. Averell reported that 122 of his men were captured during the raid.

670.2–3 Foote of Mississippi] Henry S. Foote (1804–1880) was a Democratic senator from Mississippi, 1847–52, and its governor, 1852–54. He served as representative from Tennessee in the Confederate Congress, 1862–65. During a committee hearing Thomas B. Hanly (1812–1880) of Arkansas brawled with Foote after Foote laughed at him.

670.15 Old Hickory . . . Aunt Rachel] Andrew Jackson and Rachel Donelson Robards (1767–1828) were married in 1791 before her divorce from Lewis Robards was finalized. They were remarried in 1794.

670.23 Mrs. Eaton] Margaret (Peggy) O'Neale Timberlake (1799–1879) married Senator John H. Eaton (1790–1856) of Tennessee, an old friend of Andrew Jackson, on January 1, 1829, less than a year after the death of her first husband. Jackson then named Eaton as secretary of war in his first cabinet despite widespread gossip about Peggy Eaton's character, and defended her reputation after she was snubbed by the wives of the other cabinet members.

670.24 Mrs. M.] Marion Twiggs Myers (c. 1838–1893), wife of Colonel Abraham C. Myers (1811–1889), who served as Confederate quartermaster general, 1861–63. Jefferson Davis's decision to replace Myers with Alexander R. Lawton (see note 668.25) led to a dispute in the Confederate Congress between supporters and opponents of the Davis administration. The conflict was exacerbated by reports that Marion Twiggs Myers had called Varina Howell Davis an "old squaw."

670.25–28 Andrew Jackson . . . coolly killed him.] Jackson shot and killed Charles Dickinson, a young Tennessee lawyer, in a duel in 1806 after being wounded by Dickinson's first shot. Although the duel overtly resulted

NOTES

from a quarrel arising from a horse race bet, it was rumored that Dickinson had insulted Rachel Jackson.

670.31 England declined . . . Lady Hamilton] In a codicil to his will written in 1805 shortly before his death at Trafalgar, Lord Nelson left his mistress, Lady Emma Hamilton (1765–1815), and their daughter Horatia (1801–1881) to the care of the nation. Despite his wishes, the government failed to provide for Lady Hamilton, who died in poverty.

671.1 *Volpone*] Comedy (1606) by Ben Jonson.

671.6 L. Q. C. Lamar] Lucius Quintus Cincinnatus Lamar (1825–1893) was a Democratic congressman from Mississippi, 1857–60, and a member of the Mississippi secession convention. He was appointed as special envoy to Russia by Davis in November 1862 but was recalled in June 1863 after the Confederate senate failed to confirm his nomination. During his time in Europe Lamar visited Paris and London, but did not attempt to go to St. Petersburg because he doubted that the Russian government would receive him.

671.14 Colonels Browne and Ives] William M. Browne and Joseph M. Ives, military aides to Jefferson Davis.

671.20 Daniel comes to judgment] See *The Merchant of Venice*, IV.i.223: "A Daniel come to judgment! yea, a Daniel!"

672.1 "Little Vick] Queen Victoria.

672.29–30 Wigfall, who shoots white men] In 1840 Wigfall became involved in a political feud in South Carolina with Whitfield Brooks, Brooks's son Preston, and their ally, James Carroll. After posting Whitfield Brooks as a scoundrel and coward, Wigfall fatally shot Thomas Bird, Whitfield's nephew, in a gunfight outside the Edgefield District courthouse. He then fought a bloodless duel with Carroll, and a duel with Preston Brooks in which both men were seriously wounded. (While serving in Congress, Preston Brooks would assault Charles Sumner on the Senate floor in 1856.)

672.33–34 Dangerfield Lewis . . . L.Q. Washington] Henry Llewellyn Dangerfield Lewis (1841–1893), a cavalry officer who served as a courier with Stuart's headquarters; his sister-in-law, Maria Freeland Lewis (see note 668.31); Littleton Quinton Washington (1825–1902), chief clerk of the Confederate state department and grandson of Lund Washington, a distant cousin of George Washington.

673.3 *Washington Lewis*] Henry Llewellyn Dangerfield Lewis and his brother, John Redman Coxe Lewis (see note 668.31), were the grandsons of George Washington's nephew, Lawrence Lewis (1767–1839), and of Martha Custis Washington's granddaughter, Eleanor (Nelly) Parke Custis Lewis (1779–1852).

674.16 Professor Minor] John B. Minor (1813–1895) was a professor of law at the University of Virginia, 1845–95.

674.23–25 Surgeons Davis and Cabell . . . Dr. Brockenbrough] Dr. John S. Davis (1824–1885), professor of anatomy at the University of Virginia, 1856–85; Dr. John L. Cabell (1813–1889), professor of anatomy and surgery at the University of Virginia, 1837–89, and superintendent of the Confederate military hospital at Charlottesville; Dr. William Spencer Roane Brockenbrough (1819–1880), Judith W. McGuire's brother, was a physician in Hanover County, Virginia.

674.27 Dr. Maupin] Dr. Socrates Maupin (1808–1871), a physician, was professor of chemistry at the University of Virginia, 1853–71, and dean of the faculty, 1854–70.

675.8 Gaines's Mill] See note 29.19.

676.1–2 "Rachel weeping . . . they are not."] See Jeremiah 31:15.

676.9–12 "With patient mind . . . as well as He."] Cf. John Byrom (1692–1763), *Miscellaneous Poems*, "Miscellaneous Pieces" (1773); "With peaceful Mind thy Race of Duty run; / God Nothing does, or suffers to be done, / But what thou wouldst Thyself, if thou couldst see / Through all Events of Things, as well as He."

676.13 The Lord . . . so unquiet.] Cf. Psalm 99:1, in the 1662 *Book of Common Prayer*.

680.27 words of President Davis] In his message to the Confederate Congress, December 7, 1863.

682.34 Beecher in his Liverpool speech] During a speaking tour of Great Britain, Henry Ward Beecher, the pastor of Plymouth Congregational Church in Brooklyn, New York, addressed a public meeting in Liverpool on October 16, 1863. "It is said that the North is fighting for Union, and not for emancipation. The North is fighting for Union, for that ensures emancipation," Beecher said. "But the motive determines the value; and why are we fighting for the Union? Because we shall never forget the testimony of our enemies. They have gone off declaring that the Union in the hands of the North was fatal to slavery."

685.18 Lepanto] Naval battle fought off western Greece on October 7, 1571, in which Spanish and Venetian naval forces defeated the main Turkish fleet.

685.23–25 slaves of Saint Domingo, . . . French troops] In the Haitian Revolution, 1791–1804.

685.25–26 negro slaves of Jamaica . . . Maroons] The first Maroons were slaves who left Spanish plantations during the English invasion of Jamaica in 1655. Maroon resistance to colonial rule continued until the Second Maroon War in 1795–96.

686.28–38 D. C. Govan, . . . J. H. Kelly] Daniel C. Govan (1829–1911) and Mark P. Lowrey (1828–1885) led brigades in Cleburne's division;

John E. Murray (1843–1864), George F. Baucum (1837–1905), Peter Snyder (1829–1865), Elisha Warfield (1838–1894), Aaron B. Hardcastle (1836–1914), Frederick A. Ashford (1830–1864), John W. Colquitt (1840–1903), Richard J. Person (1843–1909), George S. Deakins (1832–1902), and James H. Collett (1825–1916) commanded regiments in Cleburne's division; John H. Kelly (1840–1864) had commanded the 8th Arkansas Infantry in Cleburne's division at Stones River. Murray was killed at Atlanta on July 22, 1864; Snyder died of typhoid fever at Raleigh, North Carolina, on April 19, 1865; Ashford was killed at Franklin, Tennessee, on November 30, 1864; and Kelly was fatally wounded at Franklin on September 2, 1864.

687.13   A. A. G.] Assistant adjutant general.

694.30   Willards] A popular hotel established in 1847 at the corner of 14th Street and Pennsylvania Avenue.

697.26   Patent Office . . . partially finished] Construction of the building, located at 8th and F Streets N.W., began in 1836 and was not completed until 1868. The building now houses the National Portrait Gallery and the Smithsonian American Art Museum.

698.17   Hon. L. E. Chittenden] A lawyer from Vermont, Lucius E. Chittenden (1824–1900) served as register of the treasury, April 1861–August 1864.

698.24   Rev. Mr. Sunderland, Hon. B. B. French] Byron Sunderland (1819–1901), Presbyterian minister who served as chaplain of the U.S. Senate, 1861–64 and 1873–79. For Benjamin B. French, see Biographical Notes.

703.27   Flag-Officer Tucker] Captain John R. Tucker (1812–1883) commanded the Confederate naval forces at Charleston, 1863–65.

703.32–33   Lieutenant Dixon] George E. Dixon (1837?–1864), a steamboat engineer, had been wounded at Shiloh while serving as a lieutenant with the 21st Alabama Infantry. He became involved with Horace L. Hunley's submarine project after being posted to the Mobile garrison.

704.6–7   attempt to dive . . . receiving ship] On October 15, 1863, the *Hunley* attempted to dive beneath the *Indian Chief*, a schooner used by the Confederate navy as a receiving ship—i.e., a vessel where new recruits were sent to await their permanent assignments.

704.8   James A. Eason] Probably James M. Eason (1819–1887), a Charleston machinist and foundry operator.

704.24   not less than 33 men] A total of twenty-one men died in the *Hunley*; see headnote, p. 703.

709.7   Nethercutt's Battalion] The 8th North Carolina Partisan Rangers, commanded by Major John H. Nethercutt (1824–1867), was a local home guard unit organized in 1862. In August 1863 the battalion became part of the 66th North Carolina Infantry.

710.33–34 "He bare the bag . . . put therein."] Cf. John 12:6.

710.36–37 "the love . . . all evil;"] 1 Timothy 6:10.

711.7–11 "he repented . . . hanged himself."] Matthew 27:3–5.

711.14 flourish as a green bay tree] See Psalm 37:35: "I have seen the wicked in great power, and spreading himself like a green bay tree."

711.26 Benedict Arnold] Major General Benedict Arnold (1741–1801) conspired in 1780 to betray West Point in return for £20,000. He fled to the British lines after his plot was discovered and commanded British and Loyalist troops in Virginia and Connecticut, 1780–81.

713.37–38 "peace meetings"] See pp. 490–91 in this volume.

714.26–27 "the State is going to secede."] Some opponents of the war in North Carolina advocated that the state should secede from the Confederacy and negotiate a separate peace with the Union.

715.23–25 "is a jealous God . . . hate me."] See Deuteronomy 5:9.

717.8–9 "letting us alone."] In his message to the Provisional Confederate Congress of April 29, 1861, Jefferson Davis wrote: "We feel that our cause is just and holy; we protest solemnly in the face of mankind that we desire peace at any sacrifice save that of honor and independence; we seek no conquest, no aggrandizement, no concession of any kind from the States with which we were lately confederated; all we ask is to be let alone; that those who never held power over us shall not now attempt our subjugation by arms."

718.26–29 "God moves . . . rides upon the storm."] From "Light Shining Out of Darkness" (1773) by William Cowper (1731–1800).

719.2 "she shall become . . . kingdoms,"] See Ezekiel 29:15.

719.30 Belshazzar held his impious feast.] See Daniel 5.

719.31 Tadmor] Semitic name for Palmyra.

719.37–38 "there is a God . . . the earth."] See Psalm 58:11.

720.18 first battle of Fredericksburg] The battle of December 13, 1862. The Union capture of Marye's Heights on May 3, 1863, during the Chancellorsville campaign is sometimes called the second battle of Fredericksburg.

723.30 Brookville Republican . . . Dr. Heichold] The *Brookville Republican* was a weekly newspaper published in Jefferson County, Pennsylvania. Alexander P. Heichold, surgeon of the 8th U.S. Colored Infantry, was a resident of Jefferson County.

724.22 Colonel Fribley] Colonel Charles W. Fribley (1835–1864) served as a captain in the 84th Pennsylvania Infantry before being appointed colonel of the 8th U.S. Colored Infantry in November 1863.

NOTES 881

725.12 Major Burritt] Loren Burritt (1837–1889), a former lieutenant in the 56th Pennsylvania Infantry, was promoted to lieutenant colonel and took command of the 8th U.S. Colored Infantry in September 1864, but was unable to continue in the position because of his Olustee wounds. He served on recruiting and court-martial duty for the remainder of the war.

725.16 Lieutenant Lewis] Lieutenant Elijah Lewis (1833–1913) of Company F was mustered out as a captain in 1865.

725.30 Captain Dickey] Captain Alexander G. Dickey (1836–1864), the commander of Company K, was fatally wounded near Richmond in the battle of Darbytown Road on October 13, 1864.

725.33 Captain Wagner] Captain George E. Wagner (1842–1904) was medically discharged in December 1864 because of the wounds he received at Olustee.

726.21 Charles City] Battle fought on June 30, 1862, also known as Glendale, White Oak Swamp, and Frayser's Farm.

726.22 Richards Ford] A ford across the Rappahannock River.

726.25 Harrison's Landing . . . Ely's Ford] A landing on the north bank of the James River, where the Army of the Potomac retreated after the Seven Days' Battles; a ford across the Rapidan River.

728.35 Hon. James Lyons] Lyons (1801–1882) was a Richmond lawyer who served in the Confederate Congress, February 1862–February 1864.

729.1 Gen. Elzey] See note 125.38–39.

729.2–3 Brig.-Gen. Custis Lee] Brigadier General George Washington Custis Lee (1832–1913), son of Robert E. Lee, commanded a brigade in the Richmond defenses.

729.10–11 captured Mr. Seddon's . . . Gen. Wise's] Union cavalry led by Colonel Ulric Dahlgren reached Sabot Hill, the plantation of Confederate secretary of war James A. Seddon (see note 125.38–39), and Eastwood, the nearby home of the daughter and son-in-law of Brigadier General Henry A. Wise (see note 192.16–17), on March 1. Neither family was harmed during the raid.

729.15 Gen. Whiting] See note 551.21.

729.16–19 Judge Pearson . . . unconstitutional.] Richmond M. Pearson (1805–1878) was an associate justice of the North Carolina supreme court, 1848–59, and its chief justice, 1859–78. The conscription act passed by the Confederate Congress on April 16, 1862, had permitted men eligible to be drafted to hire substitutes, but the hiring of substitutes was subsequently abolished on December 28, 1863, and an act passed on January 5, 1864, made persons who had previously provided substitutes eligible for conscription. On February 19 Pearson ruled in *Ex parte Walton* that the act of January 5 violated the contracts clause of the Confederate constitution. Pearson had earlier angered the Davis administration by ruling in April 1863 that the North Carolina militia could not legally be used to apprehend Confederate deserters, and by consistently interpreting the conscription laws in favor of applicants seeking to be discharged from the army.

729.21   Col. A. C. Myers] See note 670.24.

730.16   Gov. Vance] An opponent of the Davis administration, Zebulon B. Vance (1830–1894) was governor of North Carolina, 1862–65. He later served as governor, 1877–79, and in the U.S. Senate, 1879–94.

730.23   Supreme Court, to assemble in June] Pearson had ordered the Walton case to be reargued before the full North Carolina supreme court in June 1864. The court overturned his earlier decision, 2–1, and upheld the act of January 5, 1864. (Although the Confederate constitution provided for a Confederate supreme court, the Confederate Congress never established one, leaving constitutional questions to be decided in various state courts.)

730.27–28   Gen. Winder] Brigadier General John Henry Winder (1800–1865), the Confederate provost marshal, was in charge of the prisoner-of-war camps in the Richmond area.

731.12   Gen. Wilcox] Major General Cadmus M. Wilcox (1824–1890), a division commander in the Army of Northern Virginia who was in Richmond on furlough at the time of the raid.

732.6–7   Mr. Secretary Seddon . . . Gen. Lee] Lee replied to Seddon on March 6 and recommended that none of the Union prisoners captured during the raid be executed.

732.11   *Gen. Bragg*] General Braxton Bragg, who was in Richmond serving as a military advisor to Jefferson Davis.

732.17–18   *Gen. Lee's son* . . . designated for retaliation] See note 432.37–40.

732.21   Gen. Butler has been removed] Major General Benjamin F. Butler had been appointed as the Union agent for prisoner exchanges in December 1863.

732.30   Morgan] Brigadier General John Hunt Morgan escaped from the Ohio state penitentiary in Columbus on November 27, 1863, and reached Confederate-held territory in Tennessee on December 18.

735.33   Belmont] Grant led 3,000 men in a raid against the Confederate camp at Belmont, Missouri, on November 7, 1861.

Index

Abbott, Henry Livermore, 333–37
Abbott, Josiah Gardner, 333
Abolitionism, 20–21, 37, 63, 65, 93, 98, 117, 190, 216, 221–22, 283–84, 360, 407, 427, 459, 480, 501, 627–28, 637, 682–83
Acheson, John, 575
Adams, Brooks, 418
Adams, Charles Francis, 9–10, 417, 502–4
Adams, Charles Francis, Jr., 9, 416
Adams, Henry, 9–10, 416–19
Adams, John, 88
Adams, Lois Bryan, 693–700
Adams, Samuel, 88
Adams, Warren, 394
Adie, Mr., 413
Africa, 218, 270, 508–11, 638
Agassiz, Louis, 601
Agnew, Cornelius R., 25
Agriculture, 127, 462–63
Agriculture Department, U.S., 649, 693
Alabama, 101, 122, 169, 279–80, 354, 363, 551, 582–83, 656, 687, 690–91
Alabama, C.S.S., 502, 508–11
Alabama 4th Regiment, 280
Alabama 5th Regiment, 172–77, 308–11, 380–81
Alabama 9th Regiment, 1, 278
Alabama 12th Regiment, 173, 177
Alabama 15th Regiment, 332
Alabama 16th Regiment, 686
Alabama 23rd Regiment, 186
Alabama 24th Regiment, 541–42
Alabama 26th Regiment, 309
Alabama 36th Regiment, 544
Alabama 47th Regiment, 332
Albany, N.Y., 254, 389, 518
Alexander, Peter W., 447
Alexander the Great, 219
Alexandria, Va., 29, 98, 654, 674
Alford, Joe, 529
Allbranch, Mr., 478
Allegheny Mountains, 569
Allegiance oaths, 169–70, 222–24, 246–47

Allen, A. K., 474–75
Allen, Lieutenant, 529
Allen, Robert T. P., 241
Allen, William J., 77
Altamaha River, 233–34
American Anti-Slavery Society, 627–29, 633
American Freedmen's Inquiry Commission, 213–15, 240
Amnesty, 650–58
Anderson, Alvin, 525
Anderson, Patton, 677
Anderson, Richard, 179–80
Anderson, Robert, 506, 578
André, John, 48
Andrew, John A., 20–22, 34, 427, 444–45
Annapolis, Md., 205, 288, 400
Antietam, battle of, 11, 29–30, 34, 195, 278, 281, 290, 345, 498, 726
Aquia Creek, 3–5, 15, 32, 613
Arago (Union naval vessel), 408
Arcadia plantation, 96
Arizona Territory, 641
Arkansas, 45, 354, 650, 656, 662, 668; reconstruction in, 512–14, 519; unionist refugees from, 101–3
Arkansas 1st Regiment, 677, 686
Arkansas 2nd Regiment, 686
Arkansas 5th Regiment, 686
Arkansas 6th Regiment, 686
Arkansas 7th Regiment, 686
Arkansas 8th Regiment, 686
Arkansas Post, 49, 52–53, 56, 353, 521, 529
Armistead, Lewis A., 303
Armistice proposals, 39, 41, 57, 138
Army, C.S., 127, 134, 169, 427, 490–91, 496, 515, 551, 553, 655; battle of Brandy Station, 249–53; battle of Chancellorsville, 172–83, 189–212, 219–21; battle of Charleston Harbor, 390–96, 402–10; battle of Chattanooga, 569–600; battle of Chickamauga, 521–47; battle of Gettysburg, 292–340, 375–76, 378–79, 397–400, 416–17, 420–24;

883

battle of Milliken's Bend, 240–42; battle of Olustee, 723–27; battle of Port Gibson, 184–88; black soldiers in (proposal), 677–86; conscription, 54, 65, 101–3, 126, 286, 391, 438, 559, 667; defense of Savannah, 93–97; defense of Vicksburg, 108, 122–23, 238–39, 265–68, 273–75, 325, 348–59, 377; deserters, 708–22; in Maryland, 278–79, 281–83, 338, 340, 380–81; Mine Run campaign, 601–26; in Mississippi, 372–74; morale of, 462; in Pennsylvania, 279–81, 283–84, 286; Quantrill's raiders, 465–88; siege of Charleston, 505–7; strategy, 243–45; in Tennessee, 148–50, 521, 526; in Texas, 461–64; in Virginia, 1–3, 32–33, 161, 166–68, 278, 555–59

Army, U.S., 25, 123, 134, 155–56, 169, 260, 496, 500, 560, 643–45, 708; appointment of Burnside, 3; appointment of Hooker, 18–19; appointment of Meade, 285; battle of Brandy Station, 249–53; battle of Chancellorsville, 172–83, 189–212, 219–21; battle of Charleston Harbor, 390–96, 402–10, 425, 429–30; battle of Chattanooga, 569–600; battle of Chickamauga, 521–47; battle of Fredericksburg, 1, 3, 11–12, 17; battle of Gettysburg, 292–345, 375–76, 378–79, 397–400, 416–17, 420–24, 562; battle of Milliken's Bend, 240–42; battle of Olustee, 723–27; battle of Port Gibson, 184–88; black soldiers in, 20–24, 34–35, 99, 105–6, 117–21, 153–54, 171, 216–18, 232–37, 240–42, 271–72, 284, 390, 395, 402–10, 425–34, 441–46, 457–60, 468, 488–89, 497–98, 501, 548, 632, 635, 643, 649–50, 679, 723–26, 728; congressional investigation of, 132, 194; conscription, 54, 57, 60–61, 63–68, 75–78, 82, 85, 347, 382–89, 391, 518, 520; and draft riots, 382, 384, 387–89, 414; effect of newspapers on, 47–56; employment of contrabands, 105–7, 109, 111–13, 213, 568; Grant's command of, 733–36; hospitalized soldiers, 253, 435–40; in Kansas, 465–69, 492; in Kentucky, 222–24; in Maryland, 421; Mine Run campaign, 601–26; in Mississippi, 372–74; in Missouri, 492–94; morale of, 91; officers in, 13–19, 51–52; in Pennsylvania, 286–91; raid on Richmond, 728–32; and reconstruction, 519; recruits from Confederate army, 101–3; reviewed by Lincoln, 129–32; siege of Charleston, 505–7; siege of Vicksburg, 47, 50–51, 108–15, 151–52, 238–40, 264–77, 325, 348–59, 377; in Tennessee, 148–50, 521, 547; in Texas, 461; in Virginia, 1, 3–8, 11–17, 25–28, 28–31, 91, 161–66, 229–31, 235, 270, 278, 286, 289, 452–56, 555–57, 726

Arnold, Benedict, 711
Arrington, Jim, 176
Articles of Confederation, 140–41
Ashford, Frederick A., 686
Ashmore, John D., 665
Aspinwall, William H., 25
Associated Press, 566
Athens, 719
Athens, Ala., 279
Atlanta, Ga., 124, 355, 387, 539
Atlantic City, N.J., 443
Augusta, Ga., 305
Ault, Adam T., 45, 187
Austerlitz, battle of, 593
Austria, 67, 141, 295, 687

Babylon, 719
Baird, Absalom, 575, 579–81, 583, 588–90
Baker, G. W., 475–76
Baldwin, William E., 185
Ball's Bluff, battle of, 312, 333
Baltimore, Md., 32, 285, 287, 306, 327, 342–43, 353, 362, 364, 562, 566
Baltimore and Ohio Railroad, 281, 285
Banks, Alexander, 470
Banks, Nathaniel P., 105, 169, 171, 352, 354, 363–64, 366, 377, 432, 488
Bannes, Charley, 239
Baptists, 481, 538
Barksdale, Randolph, 305
Barksdale, William, 298, 339, 362
Barnard, William, 606

INDEX

Barney, Hiram, 387
Barnum, David, 310, 381
Barquet, Joseph, 445
Barré, Isaac, 72
Bartlett, Joseph J., 606
Batchelor's Creek, battle of, 721
Bates, Edward, 85, 445, 562
Bates County, Mo., 492–94
Baton Rouge, La., 169
Baucum, George F., 686
Baxter, DeWitt C., 335
Baxter Springs, Kans., 492
Bayless, L. R., 526
Beard, Oliver T., 22
Beard (Confederate soldier), 527
Beaufort, N.C., 568
Beaufort, S.C., 232, 407, 410, 716
Beauregard, Pierre G. T., 48, 54, 94–95, 126, 327, 339, 393
Bedell, Charley, 529
Bedell, John, 529
Beecher, Henry Ward, 682
Behan, Mr., 563
Belgium, 638
Bell, G. W., 473
Bellows, Henry W., 25, 386
Belmont, Mo., 735
Bence (Confederate soldier), 527
Benton, William P., 44
Berea, Va., 3–4, 7
Bergen, Mr., 484–85
Bermuda, 395
Berry, Hiram G., 17
Bertinatti, Giuseppe, 562
Best, Clermont L., 198, 200
Bethel, battle of, 553
Bible, 224, 361, 431, 709–11, 715
Biddle, Chapman, 318, 607
Biddle, Charles J., 87
Bidwell, John, 27, 382
Big Black River, 266, 273–7, 352, 356, 365, 377, 512, 529
Big Black River Bridge, battle of, 238, 347
Biggs, George, 387
Bill (Grant's black orderly), 579
Billings, Charles W., 332
Billings, Liberty, 217
Birney, David B., 314
Bissell, Josiah W., 109
Blackstone, William, 69, 81

Blair, Francis Preston, 325, 443
Blair, Frank Preston, Jr., 111, 325–26
Blair, Montgomery, 325, 562–63
Blanchard, Albert G., 126
Blockade, 128, 264, 325, 390, 503, 637, 644, 649, 701–2
Blunt, George W., 384
Bolton, Miss., 352
Bonds, William J., 541
Boonesboro, Md., 278
Border states, 20
Boston, Mass., 20–21, 88, 232, 389, 395, 427, 503
Boston Tea Party, 88
Boswell, James K., 180–81
Bowditch, Nathaniel, 603
Bowen, John S., 170, 184–85
Bowling Green, Ky., 685
Boyce, W. W., 665
Bradfield, Jim, 529
Brady, James T., 412
Brady, Susanna, 412–13
Bragg, Braxton, 292, 325, 363, 387, 396, 398, 516, 521–22, 524, 526–27, 529, 531, 534–35, 538, 540, 544, 546, 553, 569, 575, 577, 588–95, 598, 661–62, 677, 732
Bramhall, Walter M., 131
Brandy Station, Va., 249–53, 614, 616, 620–22
Brannan, John M., 572
Brashear, La., 363
Brattleboro, Vt., 612
Breckinridge, John C., 258, 523, 526, 531, 533
Breese, Kidder R., 115
Bridgeport, Ala., 569, 589
Bright, John, 36
Briscoe, Thomas, 311
Bristoe Station, battle of, 555, 559
Britain, 67, 69–70, 72, 80, 137, 139–40, 255, 262, 292, 462, 519, 608, 637–38, 662, 670–71, 688; and emancipation, 9, 36–38; emancipation of slaves in West Indies, 445, 682; news of Union victories, 416–19; proposed mediation of American conflict, 36; ships for Confederate navy, 417, 502–4, 508
Brokenburn plantation, 155
Brooklyn, N.Y., 435–36

Brooks, William M., 122–23
Brookville Republican, 723
Brough, John, 549
Browder, George Richard, 222–25
Brown, John, 216, 232, 427, 636, 675, 683
Brown, Joseph, 309–10
Brown, Lewis Kirk, 435–40
Brown, Neal, 539
Brown, Samuel Howell, 181
Brown, William Wells, 117
Browne, William M., 671
Buchanan, Franklin, 258
Buckingham, William A., 90
Buckner, Simon B., 258, 546
Buell, Don C., 579
Buffalo, N.Y., 425
Buford, John, 252, 602
Bull Run, 549
Bull Run, battle of (First Bull Run), 48, 54, 290
Bull Run, battle of (Second Bull Run), 3, 11, 28, 270, 290, 529, 705, 726
Bulloch, James D., 502
Burke, Edmund, 72
Burnside, Ambrose, 31, 149, 194, 223, 226–28, 254; appointed commander of Army of the Potomac, 3; after battle of Fredericksburg, 3–6, 8, 11–14, 17; at Chattanooga, 569, 574, 584–85, 589–90; resignation of, 18
Burritt, Loren, 725
Burt, Dr., 539
Burt, George, 478
Burton, James, 310
Butler, Benjamin F., 169, 568, 659, 732
Butler, Pierce M., 235–36
Butterfield, Daniel, 14, 17, 28
Byzantium, 136

Cabinet (Davis administration), 728, 732
Cabinet (Lincoln administration), 133, 254, 564
Cadwalader, George, 603
Cadwallader, Sylvanus, 577
Cairo, Ill., 53, 116, 355, 488
Caledonia, Pa., 284
Calhoun, John C., 142
California, 209
Caloson, Preston, 347
Cameron, Simon, 563, 565

Camp Chase, 80
Campbell, James H., 58, 60–61
Campbell, John A., 125
Canada, 562
Canandaigua, U.S.S., 701–2
Cannon, William J., 1
Cape Colony, 508–11
Cape Town, Cape Colony, 509–10
Carey (Confederate soldier), 174
Carlisle, Pa., 379
Carpenter, Charles C., 24
Carpenter, Louis, 476–77
Carr, Joseph B., 606
Carr, Eugene A., 184–85
Carter, Jacob, 405
Carter, John W., 339
Casey, Silas, 548–49
Cashtown, Pa., 281, 292, 295, 306, 308, 338
Cass County, Mo., 492–94
Catholics, 413, 542
Cedar Mountain, battle of, 34, 195
Centreville, Va., 555
Chamberlain, Captain, 541, 544
Chamberlain, Joshua Lawrence, 328–32
Chamberlayne, John Hampden, 166–68
Chamberlayne, Martha Burwell, 166
Chambersburg, Pa., 279, 281, 283, 308, 338
Champion Hill, battle of, 238, 275
Chancellorsville, Va., 166, 172–83, 189–212, 219–21, 229, 243, 278, 281, 286, 308, 312, 333, 452, 616, 707, 726
Chandler, Reverend, 612
Chandler (Confederate soldier), 1
Chantilly, Va., 3
Charles (freed slave), 156, 160
Charles I, 70
Charleston, S.C., 83, 95–96, 126, 131–32, 170, 270, 327, 387, 423, 439, 446, 516, 552–53, 736; battle of Charleston Harbor, 390–96, 402–10, 425, 429–30, 432–33, 441, 443; siege of, 505–7, 701, 703
Charleston Mercury, 423, 447
Chase, Salmon P., 515, 643
Chattanooga, Tenn., 149, 355, 387, 516, 521, 523, 526, 528, 531, 534–35, 541, 543, 546, 569–600, 677, 687, 699–700, 736

Cheatham, Benjamin F., 524, 546
Chesapeake incident, 658–59
Chesapeake and Ohio Canal, 281
Chesnut, James, 664, 671–72
Chesnut, Mary, 664–73
Chetlain, Augustus L., 501
Chicago, Ill., 239, 648
Chicago Times, 577
Chicago Tribune, 39
Chickahominy River, 181–82, 192, 529
Chickamauga, battle of, 521–47, 552–53, 575, 590, 594, 598–99, 666, 677
Chickasaw Bayou, battle of, 47, 108, 111
Child, Ellen Hancock, 341
Child, Henry T., 341, 345
Child, Lydia Maria, 98
Chile, 638
China, 641
Chittenden, L. E., 698
Choctaw (gunboat), 241
Christian Commission, 693, 697–700
Christianity, 97, 99, 142, 194, 219–20, 222, 224–25, 413, 538, 648, 662, 685, 717–18, 720, 736
Cincinnati, Ohio, 226–27, 239, 658
Cincinnati Commercial, 47, 51, 53
Cincinnati Gazette, 127
Cisco, John J., 387
City Point, Va., 32, 732
Clarke, John J., 295
Clarkson, William, 394
Clayton, Amos and Grace, 264, 348
Clayton, George Washington, 264
Clayton, John Quincy Adams, 264
Clayton, William Henry Harrison, 101–4, 264–69, 348–51
Cleburne, Patrick, 521, 525, 532, 541, 677–86
Clingman, Thomas L., 94, 394
Clinton, Henry, 48
Clinton, Miss., 169, 171, 352, 355
Cobb, Robert, 532
Cobden, Richard, 36–38
Coburn, Carrie, 426
Cochran, Dr., 541
Cogswell, William, 203
Coleman, Cruse, 310
Collamore, George W., 466, 475–76
Collett, James H., 686
Colliday, Samuel R., 249, 253

Colombia, 639
Colorado Territory, 641
Colquitt, John W., 686
Colston, Raleigh T., 674–75
Columbus, Miss., 55, 108
Columbus, Ohio, 61, 80
Colyer, Arthur St. Clair, 536
Comanches, 209
Compensated emancipation, 496–97
Confederacy, 10, 27, 37, 501, 554
Confederate (newspaper), 546
Congregationalists, 465
Congress, C.S., 126, 427, 490, 535, 658, 660, 729–30
Congress, U.S., 13, 39, 56, 71–72, 141, 262, 633, 636, 691, 733, 736; and black soldiers, 20, 23–24, 284, 444, 458; and conscription, 57, 60–61, 63–68, 75–78, 82, 85; investigation of army, 132, 194; Lincoln's message to, 637–53; and proclamation of amnesty and reconstruction, 654–57
Conkling, James C., 495
Conkling, Roscoe, 59
Connecticut, 22, 77, 81, 90–92
Connecticut 4th Regiment, 443–44
Connecticut 6th Regiment, 403
Connecticut 7th Regiment, 724
Connecticut 10th Regiment, 404
Connecticut 14th Regiment, 90
Connolly, James A., 148–50, 590–600
Connolly, Mary Dunn, 148, 590
Conscription, 54, 57, 60–61, 63–68, 75–78, 82, 85, 101–3, 126, 286, 347, 438, 518, 520, 559, 667; and draft riots, 292, 382–89, 391, 411–15
Conscription Act, 57, 60–61, 63–65, 75–77, 82, 85, 144, 382, 391
Constitution, C.S., 630, 684
Constitution, U.S., 26, 54, 58, 62, 69–70, 72–89, 141, 143, 491, 497, 547, 629, 689–90; and amnesty and reconstruction, 650–51, 654–55; and conscription, 60–61, 64–65, 67, 71, 75–77; in wartime, 254–63
Contraband of war, 98–100, 105–7, 109, 111–13, 213–15, 560–61, 568
Cook, Joseph J., 462
Cooke, Augustus P., 371
Cooper, James E., 236
Cooper, James Fenimore, 598

888 INDEX

Cooper, Lieutenant, 541
Cooper, Samuel, 327
Copperheads, 26, 41, 90, 103, 137, 227–28, 280, 344–46, 385, 431, 437, 439, 518, 550
Copperheads under the Heel of an Illinois Farmer, 39
Cordley, Richard, 465–88
Corinth, Miss., 48, 108, 535, 736
Corning, Erastus, 254
Cosby, George B., 515
Cotton, 23, 36, 52, 127, 139, 151, 155, 360, 463
Couch, Darius N., 16, 378–79
Cowin, John, 176
Cox, Samuel S., 59
Coxon, J. H., 509
Cram, Thomas, 384
Craven, Alfred W., 387
Crawford, Samuel W., 319, 331
Creamer, Charles, 405
Crocker, Lemuel L., 314, 318–19
Crosby, Franklin B., 200
Crosby, John K., 701
Crow, James M., 1
Cruft, Charles, 592
Crutchfield, Stapleton, 181, 191
Cuba, 214, 638
Culpeper, Va., 32, 173, 243, 249, 423, 549, 555, 619
Cumberland River, 547
Cumming, Kate, 535–45
Currency, 62
Curtin, Andrew G., 549–50, 562–63
Custer, George Armstrong, 602, 604
Cutler, William Parker, 23–24

Dahlgren, John A., 701–2
Dahlgren, Ulric, 327, 728, 731–32
Dalton, Ga., 590, 599, 677
Daly, Charles P., 411
Daly, Maria Lydig, 411–13
Dana, Charles A., 377, 500, 574, 584
Dapplemyer, Dan, 529
Darien, Ga., 233–35, 237
David (torpedo boat), 703–4
Davids, Richard W., 317–18
Davis, James W., 249, 252–53
Davis, Jefferson, 26, 122–23, 125, 153–54, 165, 192, 243, 292, 327, 352, 360, 366, 384, 388, 391, 423, 427, 429, 432–34, 447, 450–51, 490, 518, 630, 663–64, 671, 677, 679–81, 728–32; message to Confederate Congress (December 1863), 658, 660–63; speech at Missionary Ridge, 546–47; speech at Wilmington, 551–54
Davis, Jefferson C., 599
Davis, Varina Howell, 668, 671
Dayton, Ohio, 226
Deakins, George S., 686
Dearing (Confederate soldier), 537, 539–40
Deas, Zach C., 544
DeBray, Xavier B., 461
Declaration of Independence, 683
Deer Creek, 123
DeForest, Andrew, 405
Delany, Martin, 117
Delaware, 633, 723
Democracy, 60, 90
Democratic Party, 20, 23, 26, 39, 43, 57, 60–61, 73, 81, 88, 90–92, 226, 228, 254, 261, 388, 401, 411, 413, 518, 564, 629–31, 634
Denmark, 638
Dent, Frederick T., 570
De Peyster, John Watts, Jr., 130
Des Moines, Iowa, 146–47, 186, 346
Des Moines River, 147
DeSaussure, William D., 339
Deserters, 102–3, 266, 268, 529, 708–22
Deshler, James, 521, 524–25
Detroit Advertiser and Tribune, 693
Devine, Dr., 539
Dickey, Alexander G., 725
Dickie, Jesse C., 461
Dirt-Eaters, 26
District of Columbia. *See* Washington, D.C.
Dix, Dorothea, 342
Dix, John A., 367, 413
Dix, Ralph C., 470–71
Dixon, George E., 703–4
Dodge, Nathaniel S., 3–5, 7
Dodge, Theodore A., 3–8
Doles, George P., 308, 310–11
Donaldson, Francis Adams, 312–24
Donaldsonville, La., 368–71
Doubleday, Abner, 13, 129
Douglas, Stephen A., 262

INDEX 889

Douglass, Charles, 117
Douglass, Frederick, 20, 117–21, 232, 405, 427–34, 444, 457–60, 627–36
Douglass, Lewis, 117, 405–6, 445
Douglass' Monthly, 117, 427, 431
Draft riots, 292, 382–89, 391, 411–15, 431, 441–42
Du Pont, Samuel F., 93, 132
Duff, William L., 571–72, 575
Duke, Basil, 192
Dumas, Alexandre, 598
Dunbar (Union steamer), 574, 583
Dunleith (store-boat), 108
Dunn, William M., 571, 577
Dykes, Mr., 413

Early, Jubal A., 167, 191
Eason, James E., 704
Eaton, Thomas, 239
Eckert, Thomas T., 375
Edict of Nantes, 170
Edisto River, 402–3
Edmondston, Catherine, 189–94, 362–67, 661–63
Edmondston, Patrick, 194, 364–65, 367, 663
Education, 100
Edward III, 69–70
Edwards, John Newman, 562
Egypt, 641; ancient, 361, 718
Ehles, August, 478
Eldridge, James, 478
Elgin (Confederate soldier), 527
Elkton, Md., 435
Ellery, Captain, 730
Ellis, Frank, 481
Ellis, Mrs., 539
Ellis, Rudolph, 253
Elwood plantation, 181
Elzey, Arnold E., 125, 729
Emancipation, 120, 377, 445, 628; compensated, 496–97; European reaction to, 9, 36–38; federal inquiry concerning, 213–15, 240; and reconstruction, 637, 651–53, 655; southern proposal for, 677–86
Emancipation Proclamation, 9, 20, 36–37, 39, 120, 426, 443, 459, 489, 497–98, 649–50, 652–53, 655
Eminence, Mo., 44–45
Emmitsburg, Md., 297, 338

England, 416–18. *See also* Britain
Espionage, 47–51, 75, 102, 223, 246, 256
Essex, U.S.S., 369–70
Evans, Mrs., 537–38
Everett, Edward, 564, 566, 698
Ewell, Richard S., 221, 281, 292–94, 296, 300, 304, 306–8, 326, 338, 363, 522, 558, 603–4
Ewing, Charles, 274–75
Ewing, Hugh, 274
Ewing, Thomas, Jr., 514
Ewing, Thomas, Sr., 47

Fair Oaks, battle of, 312, 333
Fairfax County, Va., 716
Fairfax, John W., 298
Falling Waters, Va. (later W.Va.), 375, 380–81
Falmouth, Va., 3–6, 11, 13, 15, 90, 201, 337
Farnum, J. Egbert, 606–7
Farragut, David G., 111, 130
Fassitte, John, 314
Faulkner, Charles J., 281–82
Fauquier County, Va., 454
Fayetteville, Ark., 102
Fayetteville, Pa., 280, 338
Federalist, 71, 75, 83
Federalist Party, 72–73
Ferguson, Thomas, 396
Ferguson, Walter C., 104
Festus, Porcius, 78
Field, Dudley, Jr., 386
Fiser, John C., 339
Fisher, Hugh D., 480, 482–83
Fisk, Wilbur, 161–65, 452–56, 611–21
Fiske, Samuel W. (Dunn Browne), 90–92, 205–12, 288–91
Fitch, Edward, 477–78
Fitzgerald, Gerald, 203
Flag, American, 439, 547
Fletcher, Francis H., 445
Flewellyn, Edward A., 544
Florence, Ala., 279
Florida, 2, 122, 216, 293, 298, 441, 601, 631, 656; battle of Olustee, 723–27
Florida, C.S.S., 502
Foard, Andrew J., 544
Food riots, 124–26, 146

Foote, Henry S., 670
Forest Queen (steamboat), 264
Forney, John W., 563–64
Forrest, Nathan B., 149, 189, 193, 515, 528
Forsyth, Mo., 268
Fort Donelson, battle of, 49, 55, 529, 733, 735–36
Fort Henry, 49, 55
Fort Lafayette, 74, 79, 81, 87, 223, 226
Fort Leavenworth, 466
Fort McAllister, 93–97
Fort (Fortress) Monroe, 213, 364, 659
Fort Moultrie, 394, 506
Fort Sumter, 134, 360, 390, 392–94, 505–6, 552, 635
Fort Wagner, 390, 392–93, 395, 402–10, 425, 429–30, 433, 441, 505, 635, 724
Fort Warren, 74, 79
Forten, Charlotte, 407–10
Foster, Charles W., 548
Fowler, Thomas J., 2
Fox, Charles James, 72
France, 37, 67, 110–11, 139, 170, 414, 462, 488, 519, 562, 637, 682, 685, 687
Francis, William A., 445
Franklin, Tenn., 677
Franklin, William B., 7, 14, 16, 130, 336
Frazier, William West, Jr., 251
Frederick, Md., 281, 285, 289, 421
Fredericksburg, Va., 1, 3, 8, 11–12, 17, 28–29, 32, 161, 166, 172–74, 178, 182, 189–92, 197, 201, 222–23, 225, 229, 243, 270, 281, 285, 312, 328, 333, 335, 435, 619, 705, 720–21, 726
Free persons of color, 120, 413, 427, 429
Fremantle, Arthur James Lyon, 292–307
Frémont, John C., 16, 37, 165, 387, 579
French, Benjamin B., 360–61, 698
French, Samuel Bassett, 181–82, 205, 366
French, William H., 205, 366, 601–4, 606–8, 622
French Revolution, 411, 441
Fribley, Charles W., 724–25
Froissart, Jean, 414
Front Royal, Va., 34, 195

Fugitive Slave Law, 120
Fugitive slaves, 425, 442, 561, 631
Funk, Isaac, 39–43
Fussell, Edwin, 633

Gaines's Mill, battle of, 29, 279, 675, 726
Galena, Ill., 501
Galena Advertiser, 240
Galveston, Texas, 461–64
Gambier, Sergeant, 445
Gansevoort, Henry, 414
Garnet, Henry Highland, 117
Garnett, Richard B., 303, 362
Garrison, William Lloyd, 98, 232, 627
Garrott, Isham W., 123
Gates, Levi, 472
Geary, John W., 197
General Orders No. 7, 6
General Orders No. 8, 226
General Orders No. 11, 492
General Orders No. 100, 134
General Orders No. 108, 522
Georgia, 101, 122, 153, 169, 216, 232, 298, 349, 354, 489, 551, 599–600, 656, 732; battle of Chickamauga, 521–47; burning of Darien, 233–35, 237; defense of Savannah, 93–97
Georgia, C.S.S., 502
Georgia 23rd Regiment, 180
Georgia 29th Regiment, 94
Georgia Aid Society, 543
Georgia Relief Committees, 539
German Americans, 130
Germany, 139, 141, 296
Gettysburg, Pa., 280–81, 283, 288, 292–345, 362–67, 375–76, 378–79, 382, 386, 391, 397–400, 416–17, 420–24, 436, 447, 452, 496, 498, 529, 548, 550, 562–67, 626, 633, 726
Gettysburg National Cemetery, 562, 564, 566
Gibbon, John, 335–36
Gibbs, Dr., 541, 544
Gibbs, Oliver Wolcott, 25, 384
Gifford, Martin V., 332
Gilbert, Thomas, 223
Gillmore, Quincy A., 390, 392, 443
Glasgow, Samuel L., 187
Glendale, Va., 1
Godfrey, James, 315–17

Gonzales, Ambrosio J., 393
Gooding, James Henry, 402–4
Gordonsville, Va., 190, 193, 619
Goree, Thomas J., 301
Gourie, Dr., 541, 544
Govan, Daniel C., 686
Grace, James W., 404
Grafton, James I., 203
Grand Gulf, Miss., 353–54, 377
Granger, Gordon, 583–85
Grant, Jesse Root, 151
Grant, Julia Dent, 152, 569
Grant, Ulysses S., 149, 184, 187, 372, 396, 400, 488–89, 495, 500–1, 518–19, 666, 699–700; at Chattanooga, 569–93, 597–99; promotion to lieutenant general, 733–36; at Vicksburg, 24, 47, 50, 105–10, 113–15, 151–52, 238, 266, 273, 325, 348, 352–54, 363–64, 366–67, 377, 397, 416
Greece, ancient, 141, 685, 719
Green, Reverend, 536–37
Green (Union soldier), 347
Green Mountain Freeman, 161, 452, 611
Greencastle, Pa., 279, 283
Greene, George S., 185
Greenwood, Pa., 283, 292, 338
Gregg, David M., 602–3, 606, 609
Grenada, Miss., 354
Grey, Sergeant, 445
Greyville, Ga., 599
Griffin, Thomas, 339
Griffith, Harry, 185–86
Grimes County, Texas, 461–62
Griswold, Jerome F., 475–76
Grow, Galusha A., 548
Guerrant, Edward O., 219–21
Guerrillas, 44, 53, 370, 465, 493–94
Guinea Station, Va., 181–82, 220
Gunboats, 24, 53, 93, 96, 126, 151, 233–34, 236, 240–41, 264–65, 358–59, 363, 368, 370–71, 397, 508, 514

Habeas corpus, writ of, 39, 62, 85–87, 226, 256–58, 261–62, 730
Hadley, Lieutenant, 466–67
Hafner, Charles, 176
Hagerstown, Md., 278–79, 281–84, 306, 340, 364, 367, 379, 381, 399
Hagner, Peter, 52
Haiti, 685

Hale, Matthew, 69
Halifax County, N.C., 189
Hall, Dominick A., 262
Hall, Josephus M., 310
Hall, Norman J., 333–35
Halleck, Henry W., 12–13, 32, 48, 55–56, 105–7, 194, 285, 342, 354, 378, 420, 488, 500, 512, 622, 626, 736
Hallowell, Edward N., 410
Hallowell, Morris L., 21–22
Hallowell, Norwood Penrose, 21–22
Hamilton, Alexander, 75, 81, 83–84
Hamilton, Emma, 670
Hamlett (Confederate soldier), 527
Hampton, Wade, 559, 730
Hancock, Cornelia, 341–45, 560–61
Hancock, John, 88
Hancock, Winfield S., 335, 341, 343
Hanover, Pa., 312
Hanover, Va., 29
Hapgood, Lyman S., 437–38, 440
Hardcastle, Aaron B., 686
Hardee, William J., 677
Hardison, Mr. and Mrs., 155–58
Harpers Ferry, Va. (later W.Va.), 216, 292, 675
Harper's Weekly, 226
Harrisburg, Pa., 283, 327
Harrisburg, Texas, 461
Harrison County, Texas, 529
Harrisonburg, La., 489
Hartford, Conn., 90–91, 116, 389
Hartford, U.S.S., 111
Hartford Times, 90
Hartson, Bill, 104
Haseltine, James Henry, 249, 253
Hausman, Christopher J., 177
Hawkins, Colonel, 219
Hawks, Wells J., 221
Hay, John, 375–76, 562–65
Haydon, Charles B., 270–72, 372–74
Hays, Alexander, 335
Hays, Colonel, 538
Hays, Harry T., 311
Hays, William, 335, 421
Hazeltine, Edward C., 702
Hazlett, Charles, 328
Heartsill, William W., 521–30
Hebrew Military Aid Society, 543
Heichold, Alexander P., 723
Heidlersburg, Pa., 308

Helena, Ark., 51, 108, 151
Helm, Ben Hardin, 531, 533
Henry Charles, 481
Henry, Patrick, 83, 88
Henry IV, 69–70
Henshaw, Jesse G., 490
Herendeen, George B., 328
Hernando, Miss., 55
Herring, Charles R., 318
Herron, Francis J., 269, 350
Heth, Henry, 296, 299, 301, 321, 423, 559
Heustis, James F., 535–36
Hewit, Henry S., 50, 109
Higginson, Francis J., 701–2
Higginson, Thomas Wentworth, 216–18
Hill, Ambrose Powell, 167, 179–80, 182–83, 189, 220–21, 278–79, 281, 294, 297–99, 306, 326, 338, 363, 380–81, 546, 555
Hill, Daniel Harvey, 126, 167, 367, 523–24, 546
Hillyer, William S., 572
Hilton, Henry, 412
Hilton Head, S.C., 402
Hindman, Mrs., 474
Hindman, Thomas C., 102, 540, 582, 677
Hitchcock, Ethan A., 643
Hobson, Edwin L., 175–77
Hobson, John, 558
Hobson, Mayhew, 558
Hoke, Robert F., 708
Holden, William H., 490–91
Holder, William D., 339
Hollander, James, 262
Holly Springs, Miss., 55, 108
Holmes, Emma, 390–96
Holmes, Theophilus H., 662
Homestead Act, 647
Honolulu, Sandwich Islands, 25
Hood, John B., 280, 296, 298, 304, 306, 331–32, 339, 664
Hooker, Joseph, 6, 12–17, 32, 129–32, 161, 165–66, 220, 285–86, 327, 337, 345, 349, 353; appointed commander of Army of the Potomac, 18–19; at Chancellorsville, 172, 180–81, 189–90, 192–96, 198–203, 205, 209, 212; at Chattanooga, 570, 574–75, 577–78, 583–84, 589, 592–93, 599
Hope, John S., 533

Hoppin, William J., 387
Horner, Robert, 342–43
Hospitals, 109, 239, 253, 309–10, 341–45, 353, 357–58, 374, 408–10, 435–40, 535–45, 560–61, 674
Hotchkiss, Jedediah, 178–83
Housatonic, U.S.S., 701–4
House of Representatives, U.S., 23, 39, 57, 141, 262, 458, 637, 733
Houston, Texas, 461, 463
Hovey, Alvin P., 184–85
Howard, Oliver O., 197, 574–75, 584, 592
Howe, Albion P., 130
Howe, Frank, 384, 386
Howe, H. E., 22
Howe, Samuel Gridley, 213
Hudson, Peter T., 570–73, 575, 577
Huger, Benjamin, 662, 665
Huger, Frank, 559
Humphreys, Andrew A., 16–17, 607
Hunley, Horace L., 703
Hunley (Confederate submarine), 701–4
Hunt, Henry J., 130, 132
Hunt family, 540–44
Hunter, David, 16, 132, 153–54, 216, 218, 571–76, 578–80
Huntsville, Ala., 687, 690–91
Hurlbut, Stephen A., 108, 246–47
Husten, Dr., 535
Hutchinson, Edward, 176–77
Hynson, Ringold, 529
Hyslop, Willie, 7–8

Idaho Territory, 641
Illinois, 39–43, 61, 114, 348, 495, 586
Illinois 94th Regiment, 268
Illinois 123rd Regiment, 148, 590–600
Immigrants, 57, 383, 639–40
Index (newspaper), 419
Indiana, 39, 61, 91, 115, 396, 573
Indiana 8th Regiment, 185
Indiana 18th Regiment, 185
Indiana 67th Regiment, 238–39, 357–59
Indianapolis, Ind., 569
Indians, 641, 643, 646, 648
Inquisition, 62
Interior Department, U.S., 646–48
Iowa, 103, 114, 187, 268–69
Iowa 19th Regiment, 101–4, 264–69, 348, 351

INDEX 893

Iowa 21st Regiment, 185
Iowa 22nd Regiment, 44, 146, 184–88, 346
Iowa 23rd Regiment, 185–86, 188, 240–41
Ireland, 688
Irion, James P., 2
Irish Americans, 180, 250–51, 383–86, 389, 394, 412, 608, 631–32
Island No. 10, 53, 108
Isola, Ulissa, 562
Israelites, ancient, 361, 718–19
Italy, 67, 138–39, 562
Iverson, Alfred, 311
Ives, Joseph M., 671

Jackman, John S., 531–34
Jackson, Andrew, 261–62, 325, 670–71
Jackson, Miss., 108, 223, 238, 352–55, 366–67, 372, 396, 529
Jackson, Rachel, 670
Jackson, Samuel B., 177
Jackson, Thomas (Stonewall), 172–74, 178–82, 189–92, 194, 208, 219–22, 282, 286, 293, 558, 665–66, 674–75, 716, 720
Jackson, William H., 515
Jackson County, Mo., 465, 492–94
Jacksonville, Fla., 216, 723
Jacobs, Harriet, 98–100, 232; *Incidents in the Life of a Slave Girl*, 98
Jamaica, 685
James Island, 390, 402–4, 432, 505–7
James River, 15, 728
Janes, Captain, 581
Japan, 640–41
Jardine, Edward, 387
Jay, John, 384
Jayhawkers, 465
Jefferson, Thomas, 154
Jenney, William L., 110–13
Jerusalem, 719
Jesus, 710–11
Joe (former slave), 30–31
John Adams (U.S. naval vessel), 403
Johnson, Alexander H., 445
Johnson, Bradley, 320
Johnson, Edward, 293, 304, 306, 310, 666
Johnson, Felix, 529
Johnson, Hannah, 425–26
Johnson, Philip, 59

Johnson, Richard W., 589, 592
Johnson, Robert, 668
Johnson, Samuel, 418
Johnston, Albert Sidney, 450, 662, 666
Johnston, Joseph E., 48, 54, 238, 258, 266, 273–75, 277, 292, 325, 327, 352, 355, 359, 363–66, 372, 387, 396–97, 599, 665, 677
Jones, Charles C., Jr., 93–97, 505–7
Jones, Charles C., Sr., 93–97
Jones, E. P., 309
Jones, John B., 124–26, 728–32
Jones, Mary, 93, 95, 97, 505
Jones, Matthew, 174, 177
Judas Iscariot, 709–11
Julius Caesar, 16, 635

Kansas, 20, 232, 492–93; Quantrill's raid on Lawrence, 465–88
Kansas 2nd Colored Regiment, 468
Kansas 13th Regiment, 101
Kansas 14th Regiment, 469
Kansas City, Mo., 466–67, 480, 492
Keitt, Laurence M., 665
Kelly, John H., 686
Kelly, William, 337
Kemble, Fanny, 236
Kemper, James L., 303, 362
Kendall, Warren L., 332
Kent, Daniel, 269
Kentucky, 47, 219, 222–24, 270, 537–38, 589, 662
Kentucky 5th Regiment, 531
Kentucky 9th Regiment, 531–34
Keokuk (U.S. warship), 132
Kernochan, Joseph, 25
Kerr, Fanny, 559
Kershaw, Joseph B., 339
Keyes, Erasmus D., 367
Keysburg, Ky., 224
Keyser, Sylvester, 373
Kilpatrick, Judson, 602, 728
Kinston, N.C., 708
Kirkwood, Samuel J., 114
Kittoe, Edward D., 570–71, 580
Knowland, J. T., 172, 310
Knox, Thomas W., 47
Knoxville, Tenn., 569, 584–85, 590, 661

Laborers, 24, 105, 109, 111, 213, 441, 514, 631

Lacey, J. Horace, 181
Lacy, Beverly Tucker, 179–81
Lagow, Clark B., 570–71, 573, 575, 577, 579, 581
Laird, John and Henry H. (shipbuilders), 502, 508
Lamar, Lucius Q. C., 671, 673
Lamon, Ward Hill, 562
Lane, W. P., 521
Lane's Rangers, 521, 525, 527
Latrobe, Osmun, 301
Lavender, Paul, 309–10
Law, Evander, 331
Lawley, Francis, 295, 297–98, 305, 307
Lawrence, Kans., 465–88, 492–93
Lawrence (Confederate soldier), 522, 527
Lawton, Alexander R., 668
Lee, Agnes, 32
Lee, Blair, 326–27
Lee, Sergeant, 445
Lee, Custis, 729
Lee, Elizabeth Blair, 325–27
Lee, Harry, 279
Lee, Mary, 32
Lee, Robert E., 3, 32–33, 161, 166, 258, 278–79, 281, 285, 289, 349, 360–61, 380, 391, 397, 400, 496, 508, 516, 531, 555–59, 601, 613, 619, 622, 625, 665–66, 731–32; at Chancellorsville, 172–73, 178–80, 182–83, 189–90, 192–93; at Fredericksburg, 3; at Gettysburg, 292, 294–300, 302–4, 306, 326–27, 333, 342–43, 362, 364–67, 375–76, 378–79, 386, 416–17, 420–21, 423–24; memoranda for President Davis, 243–45; offer to resign, 447–51
Lee, Samuel Phillips, 325
Lee, Stephen D., 515
Lee, William Henry Fitzhugh, 32, 732
Leesburg, Va., 32, 285, 287
Leiper, Charles, 249, 253
Lenier, William, 174, 310
Lennig, Thompson, 252–53
Leonard, James, 412
Lepanto, battle of, 685
Letcher, John, 123, 125
Lewis, Dangerfield, 672
Lewis, Elijah, 725
Lewis, Howell, 529

Lexington, Mo., 465
Lexington, Va., 221
Libby Prison, 190, 205, 208, 659, 728, 730–31
Liberator, 98
Liberty County, Ga., 96
Lieber, Francis, 134–45
Lincoln, Abraham, 13, 17, 39, 54, 56–57, 62–63, 71–72, 81, 133, 153, 165, 194, 221, 223, 226–27, 271, 276, 283, 285, 325, 327, 354, 360, 367, 384, 391, 411, 425, 495, 499, 512, 568, 580, 601, 622, 624, 633–35, 666–67, 679, 694–99, 716, 728, 735–36; address at Gettysburg, 566–67; appointment of Burnside, 3; appointment of Hooker, 18–19; appointment of Meade, 285; and battle of Gettysburg, 375–76, 378–79, 420–21; and black soldiers, 20, 23–24, 427–34, 457–59, 488, 497–98; on Constitution in wartime, 254–63; and Emancipation Proclamation, 9, 20, 36, 120, 426, 443, 459, 497–98, 649–50, 652–53, 655; message to Congress (December 1863), 637–53, 658; proclamation of amnesty and reconstruction, 650–58; reviews army, 129–32; and siege of Vicksburg, 377; trip to Gettysburg, 562–65
Lincoln, Mary Todd, 131, 531, 667, 696–97
Lincoln, Robert Todd, 376, 698
Linscott, Arad N., 332
Linwood plantation, 169
Lipscombe, Lieutenant, 529
Little Rock, Ark., 354
Littlefield, Milton S., 443–44
Liverpool, England, 502, 508
Logan, John A., 592
Logan County, Ky., 222
Loguen, Amelia, 405
London, England, 36, 292, 416–18
Long, Armistead L., 179, 297
Long Branch, N.J., 443
Longfellow, Charles A., 603
Longley, Otis, 480–81
Longstreet, James, 208, 281, 292–93, 295–302, 304–6, 312, 326, 338–39, 363, 380–81, 522–23, 527–28, 531, 546, 555, 558, 569, 585, 590, 661
Louiallier, Louis, 262

Louis XIV, 170
Louisiana, 20, 108, 111, 126, 169, 184, 193, 276–77, 354, 363–64, 425, 489, 561, 656; battle of Donaldsonville, 368–71; battle of Milliken's Bend, 240–42; reconstruction in, 512–14, 519
Louisiana 5th Regiment, 311
Louisiana 9th (Colored) Regiment, 240–42
Louisiana 11th (Colored) Regiment, 240–41
Louisiana 13th (Colored) Regiment, 240
Louisville, Ky., 25, 223
Lovell, Mansfield, 366, 662
Lowe, Joseph, 475
Lowrey, Mark P., 686
Loyal National League, 134
Luckett, Philip N., 461–62
Ludlow, Benjamin C., 603
Lyman, Theodore, 601–10
Lynchburg, Va., 732
Lyons, James, 728, 732

Macbeth, William, 394
Mack, Alonzo W., 41
Macy, George N., 334–35
Madison, James, 71, 563
Madison Parish, La., 155
Magnolia, Miss., 363
Magnolia (steamboat), 109, 113
Magruder, John B., 258, 363, 365, 462
Mahone, William, 666
Maine 9th Regiment, 404
Maine 20th Regiment, 319, 328–32
Mallory, Stephen, 662
Maltby, Jasper A., 501
Malvern Hill, battle of, 28–29, 726
Manassas, Va., 48, 54, 529
Manigault, Arthur M., 541
Manning, Van H., 296, 299
Marietta, Ga., 546
Marion, Pa., 279
Markoe, John, 12–13
Marshall, Humphrey, 219
Marshall, Texas, 529
Martin, James G., 363–64
Martin, Joseph W., 131
Martin, Oliver P., 115
Martinez, Lieutenant, 562

Martinsburg, Va. (later W.Va.), 281, 367
Mary II, 688
Maryland, 126, 278–79, 281–83, 289, 292, 325, 338, 340, 364, 367, 375–77, 380–81, 399, 421, 633, 650
Mason, Almeda, 223
Mason, Herbert, 334
Mason, James M., 665
Massachusetts, 20–23, 36, 77, 126, 395, 404, 429, 444–45, 666
Massachusetts 1st Regiment, 9, 416, 603
Massachusetts 2nd Regiment, 21, 34, 195
Massachusetts 8th Regiment, 724
Massachusetts 18th Regiment, 315, 318
Massachusetts 20th Regiment, 21, 333–37
Massachusetts 22nd Regiment, 315, 318
Massachusetts 40th Regiment, 724
Massachusetts 51st Regiment, 216
Massachusetts 54th Colored Regiment, 20–22, 34–35, 99, 117–18, 232–37, 402–10, 425, 427, 430, 441, 443–45, 723–24
May, Henry, 77
May, Dwight, 271
Mayflower (Union naval vessel), 403
McBlair, John G., 603
McCain (Confederate soldier), 522, 527
McClellan, George B., 194, 220, 325, 336, 345, 376, 662; attitudes toward, 8, 18, 56; dismissal of, 3
McClernand, John A., 50, 184, 187, 238, 352, 354
McCunn, John H., 389
McDougall, William, 562
McDowell, Irvin, 48, 54
McGuire, Hunter H., 179
McGuire, John, 674
McGuire, Judith W., 674–76, 705–7
McKaye, James, 213
McKelvy, Benjamin F., 2
McLaws, Emily, 281, 338
McLaws, Lafayette, 179, 191, 280–84, 296, 302, 306–7, 312, 331–32, 338–40
McMillan, Charles, 50, 111
McMurray, Joe, 280
McPherson, James B., 108, 110, 264, 353, 518, 733–36
McVeagh, Wayne, 562–65

McVicar, Duncan, 196
Meade, George, 13, 625–26
Meade, George G., 11–17, 199, 439, 496, 549, 555, 557, 666, 731, 735; appointed commander of Army of the Potomac, 285; at Gettysburg, 292, 306, 312, 318, 321, 325–27, 336–37, 345, 362–64, 366, 375–76, 378–79, 386, 391, 420–22; Mine Run campaign, 601, 604–5, 607, 613, 617, 619–20, 622–26
Meade, Margaret, 11, 13, 15, 622
Meagher, Thomas F., 608
Meigs, Montgomery C., 574, 576, 582–90
Melville, Herman: *Battle-Pieces and Aspects of the War*, 414; "The House-top," 414–15
Memminger, Christopher G., 662
Memphis, Tenn., 51, 55, 108, 111–12, 151, 239, 246, 268, 359, 735
Mercier, Henri, 562
Meredith, John A., 125
Meredith, William M., 13
Meridian, Miss., 687
Merrimack, U.S.S., 865
Merritt, Wesley, 602, 606
Merryman, John, 85
Methodists, 222, 224, 486, 708
Mexico, 292, 488, 519
Michigan, 271, 285, 408–9
Michigan 1st Regiment, 315, 318
Michigan 2nd Regiment, 270–72, 372–74
Michigan 16th Regiment, 319
Michigan Soldiers' Relief Association, 693
Middletown, Pa., 308
Militia, 65, 82–84, 129, 285, 383, 385
Militia Act, 23, 441
Miller, Matthew M., 240–42
Milliken's Bend, battle of, 240–42, 429, 432–33, 443, 635
Mills, Henry, 529
Mills, Roger Q., 525
Milnes, Richard Monckton, 417
Milroy, Robert H., 307, 366
Milton, Tenn., 148–50
Mine Run campaign, 601–26, 674, 721
Miner, Mr., 484
Minnesota, 345
Minnesota 1st Regiment, 345

Mississippi, 169, 292, 339, 372–74, 393, 423, 457, 521, 537, 551, 656; battle of Port Gibson, 184–88; reconstruction in, 512–14, 519; siege of Vicksburg, 24–25, 47, 50–51, 54–55, 108–15, 122–23, 151–52, 238–40, 264–77, 325, 348–60, 362–67, 377
Mississippi 1st Colored Regiment, 240
Mississippi 13th Regiment, 339
Mississippi 17th Regiment, 339
Mississippi 18th Regiment, 339
Mississippi 32nd Regiment, 686
Mississippi 45th Regiment, 686
Mississippi River, 24, 26, 47, 50–51, 55, 105, 108–9, 111, 122–23, 130, 151–52, 155, 184, 240–41, 264, 352–55, 359, 368–71, 377, 397, 458, 462, 488, 498, 512–13, 522, 569, 592, 648, 650, 662, 736
Missouri, 44–45, 47, 184, 232, 325, 354, 465, 476, 562, 650, 662; evacuation of western counties, 492–94; unionist refugees in, 101–3
Mitchell, Robert W., 607
Mobile, Ala., 124, 170, 292, 355, 488, 516, 535, 538, 541–44, 703–4
Monocacy River, 285
Monongahela (U.S. warship), 369, 371
Monroe, La., 155, 489
Montague, Calvin S., 271, 374
Montesquieu, baron de (Charles-Louis de Secondat), 70–71
Montgomery, Ala., 630
Montgomery, James, 232–35, 237
Montpelier, Vt., 161
Mooney, Merritt E., 267
Moore, John S., 271
Morel, Pierre, 262
Morgan, Henry, 169–70
Morgan, John Hunt, 149, 189, 193, 224, 396, 462, 515, 732
Morgan, Miriam, 169, 171
Morgan, Sarah, 169–71
Mormons, 671
Morocco, 641
Morris, Robert, Jr., 249–50
Morris, Mrs. Harry, 413
Morris Island, 390, 392–93, 402, 404–5, 407, 441, 443, 505, 507
Morse, Charles F., 195–204
Mount Vernon, Ohio, 226

Murdock, Mrs., 32
Murfreesboro, Tenn., 148, 429, 432, 498, 521–22
Murphy, Mr., 478
Murray, Adjutant, 544
Murray, John E., 686
Murray, Neill, 45
Mushat, John Patrick, 309
Muslims, 685
Muzzey, Charles O., 702
Myers, Abraham C., 729

Napoléon I (Napoléon Bonaparte), 16, 19, 139, 219–20, 687
Napoléon III (Louis Napoléon), 305, 519, 637, 660, 666
Nashville, Tenn., 733
Natchez, Miss., 55, 489
Navy, C.S., 655; action by C.S.S. *Alabama*, 508–11; ships built in Britain, 417, 502–4, 508; sinking of U.S.S. *Housatonic*, 701–4
Navy, U.S., 53, 93, 126, 130, 132, 644–46; battle of Charleston Harbor, 390–96, 403–4; black sailors in, 359; on Mississippi River, 368–71; pursuit of C.S.S. *Alabama*, 508–11; siege of Charleston, 506; siege of Vicksburg, 109, 111, 113, 115, 122, 151, 264–65, 358–59; sinking of U.S.S. *Housatonic*, 701–4
Navy Department, C.S., 662
Navy Department, U.S., 643–46
Neblett, Elizabeth Scott, 461
Neblett, William H., 461–64
Negroes, 224, 716; in Confederate army (proposal), 677–86; as contraband of war, 98–100, 105–7, 109, 111–13, 213–15, 560–61, 568; in Lawrence massacre, 468, 480–81; and New York City draft riots, 383, 385, 389, 391, 411, 413, 431, 441–42; as refugees, 98–100, 105–7, 213–15, 560–61; suffrage for, 632–33, 637; in Union army, 20–24, 34–35, 99, 105–6, 117–21, 153–54, 171, 216–18, 232–37, 240–42, 271–72, 284, 390, 395, 402–10, 425–34, 441–46, 457–60, 468, 488–89, 497–98, 501, 548, 632, 635, 643, 649–50, 679, 723–26, 728; in Union navy, 359

Nelson, Horatio, 670
Neutrality, 503
Nevada Territory, 641
New Bedford, Mass., 402
New Bedford Mercury, 402
New Bern, N.C., 216, 708, 713
New Carthage, La., 152
New Era (gunboat), 53
New Hampshire 7th Regiment, 724
New Jersey, 39, 61, 341
New Jersey 26th Regiment, 163–64
New London, U.S.S., 368–71
New Madrid, Mo., 108
New Mexico Territory, 641
New Orleans, La., 105, 130, 169–71, 256, 261, 275–76, 292, 363–64, 366, 368, 370–71, 561, 600, 659, 662
New Providence, Miss., 108
New York, 22, 39, 60–61, 77, 117, 129, 345, 411, 476, 518, 613–14, 630, 634
New York 6th Regiment, 131
New York 7th Regiment, 389
New York 20th Regiment, 130
New York 47th Regiment, 724
New York 48th Regiment, 22, 404, 724
New York 99th Regiment, 215
New York 100th Regiment, 404
New York 101st Regiment, 3
New York 115th Regiment, 723–24
New York 119th Regiment, 3–8
New York Central Railroad, 254
New York City, 1, 25, 60, 117, 130, 134–35, 326, 395, 441, 503, 630; draft riots in, 292, 382–89, 391, 411–15, 431, 441–42
New York Evangelist, 99
New York Express, 631
New York Herald, 47, 111, 385, 389, 391, 626, 631
New York News, 81, 385
New York Tribune, 218, 383, 391
New York World, 385, 631
Newnan, Ga., 535, 539
Newport, R.I., 443
Newspapers, 47–56, 419
Newton, John, 601, 606–7
Nicaragua, 639
Nice, Eliza Ann, 312
Nicolay, John G., 562–63
Nineveh, 719

Norfolk, Va., 215, 400, 662, 716
North Carolina, 101, 126, 213, 215, 309, 325, 362, 394, 490–91, 551–54, 656, 708, 712, 716–17
North Carolina 1st Colored Regiment, 724
North Carolina 2nd Union Volunteers, 708–9, 712–13
North Carolina 54th Regiment, 708, 721
North Carolina Standard, 490
Norton, Edwin, 28
Norton, Oliver W., 28–31, 229–31, 548–50, 723–27
Nullification, 137
Nurses, 341–45, 435–40, 535–545, 560–61
Nutt, Captain, 522, 526, 529
Nutting, George, 309–10

O'Brien, Henry J., 411
O'Brien, William J., 542
Ogeechee River, 93–93
Ohio, 1, 23, 47, 57, 60–61, 223, 226–27, 254, 353, 549–50
Ohio 63rd Regiment, 404
Ohio River, 53, 80, 547
Okolona, Miss., 535
Oldham, Anthony, 481
Olin, Abraham B., 57
Olmsted, Frederick Law, 108–16
Olmsted, John, 108, 116
Olustee, battle of, 723–27
O'Neal, Edward A., 176, 309
O'Neill, Henry, 322
O'Neill, James, 218
Opdyke, George, 384–85
Orange, Va., 447, 555, 557, 601
Orange and Alexandria Railroad, 555
Ord, Edward O. C., 352
Orme, William W., 349
Ottoman Empire, 136, 641, 671
Ousterhaus, Peter J., 184–87
Owen, Robert Dale, 213
Oxford, Miss., 108, 354
Ozark Mountains, 44–45

Paddock, George, 480
Page, Colonel, 241
Paine, Sumner, 334
Paint Rock (Union steamer), 584

Palmer, Daniel W., 478–79
Palmerston, Viscount (Henry John Temple), 36, 502
Paris, France, 37, 110–11, 441, 604, 646
Paris, John, 708–22
Parke, John G., 352
Parker, Cortlandt, 625–26
Parker, Ely S., 577
Parker, Theodore, 702
Parliament (British), 69–70, 72, 688
Parton, James, 659
Patent Office (Washington), 693, 697–700
Patrick, Marsena R., 201
Patriotism, 53, 60, 97, 119–20, 134–36, 144, 194, 207, 219, 227, 241, 254, 283, 287, 303, 333, 434, 446, 491, 538, 546, 632, 681, 712, 716, 718, 721–22, 736
Patten, Henry Lyman, 334
Patterson, Edmund DeWitt, 1–2, 278–80
Paul Jones (gunboat), 233–34
Pawnee (Union naval vessel), 403, 506–7
Paxton, Elisha F., 193
Pea Ridge, Ark., 44
Peace Democrats, 57, 401, 630, 634
Peace meetings, 490–91
Pearson, Richmond M., 730
Peer, John, 446
Peirce, Catharine, 44, 146–47, 184, 346–47
Peirce, Taylor, 44–46, 146, 184–88, 346
Pemberton, John C., 122–23, 266, 348, 357, 365–67, 398, 662
Pender, William D., 306, 362
Pendleton, Alexander S., 180
Pendleton, William N., 305
Peninsula campaign, 1, 28, 30, 111, 129, 131, 270
Pennsylvania, 23, 61, 130, 243, 268, 278–81, 283–84, 286–91, 445, 496, 549–50, 562–63, 565, 578, 630, 663, 723; battle of Gettysburg, 292–345, 362–67, 375–76, 378–79, 397–400, 416–17, 420–24
Pennsylvania 2nd Regiment, 251
Pennsylvania 5th Regiment, 252, 332

INDEX 899

Pennsylvania 6th Regiment, 249–53
Pennsylvania 10th Regiment, 319
Pennsylvania 12th Regiment, 332
Pennsylvania 29th Regiment, 196
Pennsylvania 79th Regiment, 574
Pennsylvania 83rd Regiment, 28–31, 229, 319, 330–32
Pennsylvania 118th Regiment, 312–24
Perine, James, 478
Perkins, George Hamilton, 368–71
Perkins, Susan G., 368
Perkins, William E., 203
Perryville, Ky., 522, 677
Persepolis, 719
Person, Richard J., 686
Peru, 638
Peterkin, George, 555
Peters, Dr., 389
Petersburg, Va., 124
Petigru, James L., 142
Pettigrew, James Johnston, 299, 301–2, 365, 391
Philadelphia, Pa., 1, 21–22, 98, 117, 122, 327, 335, 353, 407, 441, 457, 627, 629, 633, 723
Pickens, Samuel, 172–77, 308–11, 380–81
Pickens, Samuel B., 173, 177
Pickett, George E., 296, 299, 301, 303–4, 306, 333, 398–99, 708
Pickett, Joseph Desha, 538
Pierpont, Francis H., 654
Pierrepont, Edwards, 413
Pitt, William (Earl of Chatham), 72
Pittsburgh, Pa., 427, 564
Pittsfield, Mass., 414
Poland, 65, 145
Polk, Leonidas, 546
Pomeroy, George, 8
Pomeroy, Samuel C., 457
Pope, John, 362
Port Gibson, Miss., 184–88, 238, 353, 377
Port Hudson, La., 55, 123, 131, 169, 352, 354, 360, 363–66, 387, 397, 400, 432–33, 443, 508, 635
Port Royal, S.C., 153, 216
Port Royal, Va., 32
Porter, David D., 53, 109, 113, 115
Porter, Fitz-John, 130
Portland, Me., 503
Portsmouth, Va., 716

Poss, Elizabeth Norton, 229, 548, 723
Post Office Department, U.S., 646
Potomac River, 132, 219, 278, 285, 289–90, 292, 307, 361, 367, 375, 379–81, 391, 399–400, 424, 500, 508, 529, 592
Powe, James, 395
Powers (Union soldier), 203
Prairie Grove, Ark., 102
Presbyterians, 96, 222
Preston, John S., Jr., 559, 665
Preston, John S., Sr., 558, 667
Preston, William B., 258, 667
Price, Bob, 172, 177
Price, Sterling, 662
Prince, Henry, 602, 606
Princess Royal (gunboat), 370
Prisoners of war, 172, 182–83, 190, 193, 199, 205, 207–8, 268, 293–98, 306, 310, 320–21, 332, 348–50, 352–53, 364, 367, 390, 394–95, 427–34, 459, 524–25, 589, 604, 643, 659–60, 708, 728, 730–31
Prussia, 141, 296, 687
Public land, 646–48
Pugh, Nide and Rachel, 101
Purvis, Robert, 629
Putnam, Haldimand S., 395, 586
Putman, Holden, 586
Putnam, Israel, 395

Quakers, 21, 98, 341
Quantrill, William C., 465–68, 470, 479, 482, 492–93
Quinby, Isaac F., 187

Rabelais, François, 27
Radical Republicans, 23, 36, 127, 133, 457, 637
Railroads, 5–6, 32, 45, 182, 189–90, 192, 281, 283, 327, 352, 512, 528, 530, 555, 599, 647, 649, 687
Rainbow Banks, N.C., 363–64
Raleigh, N.C., 490
Ramseur, Stephen D., 311, 380
Ramsey, David, 394
Ramsey, William, 394–96
Randolph County, N.C., 490–91
Rapidan River, 166, 190, 195–96, 529, 555–56, 601–2, 612–13, 615, 621–22, 714, 728
Rappahannock Railroad, 220

Rappahannock River, 1, 3–5, 11, 28, 32–33, 161, 166, 189–92, 201–2, 209, 219, 229, 249, 285, 398, 435, 439, 452, 454, 529, 555–56, 714
Rawlins, John A., 501, 570–72, 585
Ray, Dr., 541
Ray, J. C., 310
Raymond, Miss., 238, 529
Read, Abner, 371
Readville, Mass., 117, 232, 444
Reason, Charles, 405
Reconstruction, 26, 490–91, 512–20, 637, 650–57
Red River, 514
Refugees, 98–103, 105–7, 155, 169, 213–15, 560–61
Reid, Whitelaw, 127–28
Republican Party, 20, 23, 36, 39, 43, 47, 72, 90, 127, 133, 254, 325, 457, 497, 500, 629, 637
Revere, Paul Joseph, 333
Revolutionary War, 48, 63, 72, 88, 140, 255, 711, 715, 717, 720
Reynaud, Aimé Felix, 562
Reynolds, Charles, 485
Reynolds, John, 16, 132, 294, 362
Reynolds, Joseph J., 572, 592, 600
Reynolds, Mary, 485
Rhett, Robert Barnwell, 423
Rhett, Robert Barnwell, Jr., 423
Rhode Island, 233
Rice, James C., 330–31
Richard II, 69
Richards, George, 155–57
Richmond, Va., 24–26, 33, 60, 64–65, 122–23, 130, 132, 166, 180–82, 190, 192, 195, 212–14, 219, 221, 285–86, 292, 306, 352, 360, 367, 397, 399, 401, 423, 432–33, 447, 450, 529, 558, 660, 664, 674, 705–6, 736; food riot in, 124–26; Libby Prison, 190, 205, 208, 659, 728, 730–31; Union army raid on, 728–32
Richmond Enquirer, 26, 220
Richmond Examiner, 662, 669, 671
Richmond and Fredericksburg Railroad, 32
Riggs, Kate, 483
Riggs, Samuel, 483
Ringgold, Ga., 599
Roberts, Henry, 529

Robertson, Reverend, 237
Robinson, Charles L., 474
Robinson, James C., 59
Rochester, N.Y., 427, 460
Rodenbaugh, Theophilus, 251
Rodes, Robert E., 172, 177, 182, 308–9
Rogers, Seth, 216–17
Rolla, Mo., 44
Roman, James D., 283
Rome, ancient, 78
Ropes, Henry, 333–34, 337
Rose, John, 312
Rosecrans, William S., 25, 193, 353–54, 398, 400, 508, 521, 523, 525–28, 530–31, 546, 549, 555, 569, 582
Ross, Orlando H., 571, 573–75, 577, 581
Rothrock, Abraham, 480
Rowley, William R., 577, 581
Russell, John, 502, 662
Russell, William Howard, 417
Russellville, Ky., 223–24
Russia, 65, 67, 640, 671, 687
Ryan, William H., 394

St. Helena Island, 404, 407
St. Louis, Mo., 55, 116, 239, 269, 368, 492
St. Simons Island, 232–37
Salem, Mo., 269
Salisbury, N.C., 124
Sanders, Lee, 529
Sanderson, James M., 132
Santo Domingo, 685
Sargeant, George H., 478
Saunders, Bettie, 555
Savage, Joseph, 468
Savannah, Ga., 93, 96–97, 146, 170
Savannah Republican, 447
Sawers, Emanuel, 239
Sawyer, Roswell M., 687
Saxton, Rufus, 99, 216, 218
Scales, Alfred M., 362
Scheibert, Justus, 296–97
Schenck, Robert C., 342, 562
Schofield, John M., 492–94
Scotland, 418. *See also* Britain
Scott, Walter, 598
Scott, Winfield, 665, 733
Secession, 44, 137, 222, 229–31, 413, 437–39, 490, 516, 637
Seddon, James A., 125–26, 364, 729, 731–32

Sedgwick, John, 16, 189, 191–92, 201, 203, 336, 421, 601, 607
Sedition, 226–28, 246, 256, 258–60
Semmes, Paul J., 298, 339
Semmes, Raphael, 235, 508–11
Senate, U.S., 13, 17, 23–24, 36, 38, 57, 141, 458, 500, 637–38, 648, 733
Seven Days' Battles, 3, 11, 161, 281, 333
Seward, William H., 79, 445, 562–63, 634, 657
Seymour, Horatio, 388, 411
Seymour, Thomas H., 90–92
Seymour, Truman B., 723–25
Shackelford, James M., 222
Shannon, Peter C., 563–64
Sharpsburg, Md., 278
Shaw, Annie Haggerty, 34–35, 232, 234
Shaw, Francis G., 20, 34
Shaw, Robert Gould, 21, 34–35, 99, 195, 200, 232–37, 395, 402, 404, 407–10, 443
Shaw, Sarah, 34–35
Sheffield, William P., 86
Shenandoah Valley, 219, 221, 243, 278, 292, 397
Shepherdstown, Va. (later W.Va.), 312, 328
Sheridan, Philip H., 583, 592–93, 595–96
Sherman, Ellen Ewing, 47, 273, 352
Sherman, John, 47, 275, 459
Sherman, William T., 47–56, 238, 246–48, 372, 492, 512–20, 733–36; at Chattanooga, 569, 572, 574–77, 580–81, 583, 585–86, 588, 590, 592, 595; rules of war, 687–92; at Vicksburg, 108–11, 115, 151, 273–77, 325, 352–56
Shiloh, battle of, 47, 241, 522, 531, 677, 733, 736
Shreveport, La., 514
Shut, Jacob, 239
Sickles, Daniel E., 14, 17, 131, 193, 197–99, 297, 312, 362, 626
Sigel, Franz, 16
Silver Spring, Md., 325–26
Silver Wave (gunboat), 265
Simon's Town, Cape Colony, 509–10
Simpkins, John C., 394
Sinkler, William, 394
Slave revolts, 685
Slave trade, 638, 682

Slavery, 99, 119–20, 139, 141–44, 513–14; abolition of, 37, 63, 65, 360, 459–60, 496–97, 500–1, 627–29; European attitudes toward, 37; Cleburne's proposal to end, 677–86
Slaves, 127, 224, 271–72, 390, 392–93; armed, 155–59; as contraband of war, 98–100, 105–7, 109, 111–13, 213–15, 560–61, 568; former, capture of, 425–34; fugitive, 425, 442, 561, 631; as refugees, 98–100, 105–7, 213–15, 560–61
Slocomb, Culbert H., 532
Slocum, Henry W., 16, 195–203, 421
Smith, Andrew J., 187
Smith, Charles, 372
Smith, John, 529
Smith, John E., 574
Smith, William F., 16, 18, 378–79, 572, 584–85, 622
Smith, William P., 183
Smith, William Wrenshall, 569–81
Smith (Confederate soldier), 527
Snediker (Confederate soldier), 528
Snyder, Levi, 239
Snyder, Peter, 686
Snyder, Samuel S., 468, 480
Sommerville, George W., 104
Sorrell, Gilbert Moxley, 295, 299, 301
South Carolina, 122, 142, 153, 216, 445, 551, 656, 665, 670, 723, 732; battle of Charleston Harbor, 390–96, 402–10, 425, 429–30, 432–33, 441, 443; siege of Charleston, 505–7, 701, 703
South Carolina 1st Volunteer Colored Regiment, 20, 216–18
South Carolina 2nd Volunteer Colored Regiment, 232–35, 237
South Carolina 15th Regiment, 339
Spain, 67, 141, 638
Sparta, 685, 719
Speer, John, 485
Spotsylvania, Va., 181, 208
Springfield, Ill., 39, 495
Springfield, Mo., 101, 465
Springfield Republican, 90, 205, 288
Stafford, Va., 34, 195, 202, 286
Stahel, Julius H., 4–5
Stannard, George J., 613
Stanton, Edwin L., 562–63

Stanton, Edwin M., 17, 20, 71, 106, 194, 213, 342, 377, 457–59, 569, 582, 622, 643, 728
Stark, Louis, 396
Starkweather, John C., 569–71
Stearns, George L., 427, 430–31, 457–58
Steele, Frederick, 111
Steiner, Lewis H., 285
Steinwehr, Adolph von, 5, 362
Stephens, Alexander H., 501, 658–59, 665
Stephens, George E., 441–46
Stephenson, James, 608
Stevens, John Austin, Jr., 384
Stevens, Thaddeus, 23, 284
Stevensburg, Va., 620
Stevenson, Thomas, 402–3, 584
Stewart, Alexander P., 677
Stockdale, William, 218
Stockton, Thomas H., 564
Stokes, William, 309–10
Stoldt, Gustave, 4
Stone, John, 267
Stone, Kate, 155–60
Stone, William M., 44, 187
Stone, William S., 394
Stoneman, George, 16–17, 111, 131, 182, 189, 193, 215
Stones River, battle of, 148, 521, 531, 677
Stonestreet, Benjamin, 481
Stono River, 506
Story, Joseph, 71, 85–86
Stout, Samuel H., 539
Strong, George C., 404
Strong, Charles, 382, 387, 389
Strong, George Templeton, 25–27, 382–89, 658–60
Strong, James D., 217
Stuart, J.E.B., 178–80, 182, 189–90, 249, 298, 327, 515, 558
Submarines, 701–4
Suffolk, Va., 214–15, 367
Suffrage, 632–33, 637, 640, 716
Sumner, Charles, 36–39
Sumner, Edwin V., 14, 16
Sumter, C.S.S., 508
Sunderland, Byron, 698
Sunflower River, 109, 113
Supreme Court, N.C., 730

Supreme Court, U.S., 85, 655, 691
Susquehanna River, 362
Swails, Stephen A., 445
Swayne, John T., 246
Switzerland (U.S. ram ship), 264
Sykes, George, 421, 601–3, 605–6

Tadmor, 719
Talcott, Thomas, 33
Taliaferro, William B., 94
Tallahatchie River, 123
Talley, Captain, 524
Taneytown, Md., 286
"Taps," 28
Taxation, 62, 126, 497, 642
Taylor, Richard (brother of Walter H. Taylor), 397
Taylor, Richard (Confederate general), 111, 193, 363, 365, 397
Taylor, Walter H., 397–401, 555–59
Tedford, Mr., 540, 543
Telegraph, proposed transatlantic, 640
Tennessee, 49, 55, 101, 108, 222, 292, 352, 363, 423, 489, 521, 526, 539, 547, 650, 656, 661–62, 687; battle of Chattanooga, 569–600; battle of Milton, 148–50
Tennessee 8th Regiment, 686
Tennessee 26th Regiment, 529
Tennessee 35th Regiment, 686
Tennessee River, 48, 521, 529, 569, 583, 589, 595
Territories, 641, 650
Terry, Alfred H., 403
Texas, 103, 155, 292, 298, 304, 429, 461–64, 488–89, 492, 521, 524, 529, 656
Texas 4th Regiment, 332
Texas 5th Regiment, 332
Texas 7th Regiment, 526, 686
Texas 17th Regiment, 240–41
Texas 20th Regiment, 461–64
Thebes, 719
Thomas, George H., 531, 569, 572, 576, 578–80, 583, 585, 592
Thomas, Lorenzo, 105, 458, 488–89, 501
Thompson, George, 203
Thornton, J. W., 479
Thorp, S. M., 475–76
Times (London), 9–10, 416
Tomb, James H., 703–4

Towner, Lieutenant, 571, 575, 581, 585, 588
Tracy, Edward G., 185
Tracy, William G., 203–4
Trask, Josiah C., 475–76
Treasury, U.S., 642–43
Treasury Department, C.S., 662
Treasury Department, U.S., 151, 643
Treichel, William, 249
Trent affair, 418
Trimble, Isaac R., 167
Troy, N.Y., 389
Tucker, John R., 703–4
Tullahoma, Tenn., 148–49, 363, 521, 529
Tupelo, Miss., 685
Turchin, John B., 599
Turks, 136, 641, 671
Tuscumbia (gunboat), 264

U.S. 8th Colored Regiment, 723–26
U.S.-Mexican War, 72–73, 631
U.S. Military Academy (West Point), 122, 281
U.S. Naval Academy (Annapolis), 646
U.S. Sanitary Commission, 25, 108–9, 269, 285, 341, 343, 382, 548, 566, 658
Union Mills, Md., 312
Uniontown, Md., 288
Usher, John P., 562, 646–48
Ussery, Benjamin, 537

Vallandigham, Clement L., 57–89, 223, 226–28, 254, 259–63, 550
Van Dorn, Earl, 155, 189, 192, 222
Van Zandt, Khleber M., 526
Vance, Zebulon B., 490–91, 730
Vanderbilt, U.S.S., 508–11
Vanderson, A. H. M., 527
Vegesack, Ernst von, 130
Venable, Charles S., 559
Vermont, 165, 455, 611, 617
Vermont 2nd Regiment, 161–65, 452–56, 611–21
Vermont 3rd Regiment, 455
Vermont 4th Regiment, 455
Vermont 5th Regiment, 164–65, 455
Vermont 6th Regiment, 455
Vermont 10th Regiment, 615–16
Vernon County, Mo., 492

Verree, John P., 59
Vicksburg, Miss., 24–25, 47–48, 50–51, 54–55, 94, 105, 108–15, 122–23, 131, 147, 151–52, 155, 184, 188, 193, 224–25, 238–40, 246, 264–77, 325, 346, 348–60, 362–67, 377, 387, 397–98, 400, 416, 423, 429, 462, 488–89, 500, 508, 595, 662, 666, 687, 728, 733, 736
Vincent, Strong, 229, 328–31, 548
Virginia, 98, 101, 122–23, 141, 293, 305, 307, 337, 360, 398–99, 516, 521, 636, 654, 661, 665, 670, 735; battle of Brandy Station, 249–53; battle of Chancellorsville, 172–83, 189–212, 219–21; Confederate army in, 1–3, 32–33, 555–59; Mine Run campaign, 601–26; raid on Richmond, 728–32; Union army in, 1, 3–8, 11–17, 25–26, 28–31, 91, 129–32, 229–31, 235, 270, 278, 286, 289, 452–56, 555–57, 726
Virginia 2nd Regiment, 674
Virginia 12th Regiment, 173, 183
Virginia 22nd Regiment, 320
Virginia Central Railroad, 182

Wagner, George E., 725
Wainwright, Charles S., 129–33
Wakarusa, Kans., 473
Walker, John G., 241
Walker, William H. T., 94, 97
Walsh, John, 702
Walter, Harvey W., 538
Walton, James B., 292, 295–96, 299, 301
War, rules of, 687–92
War Department, C.S., 124, 153
War Department, U.S., 17, 129, 133, 328, 429, 441, 457, 518, 548, 643, 677
War of 1812, 261–62
War of the Rebellion, 328
Ward, George, 252
Warfield, Elisha, 686
Warren, Gouverneur K., 328, 601, 603–4, 606–8, 622
Warrenton, Miss., 111, 264–65
Warrenton, Va., 32, 420, 438–39, 452, 454–55
Washburne, Elihu B., 24, 345, 500, 733
Washington, D.C., 11, 13–18, 25, 32, 74, 78, 105, 116, 127, 130, 132, 162, 228,

282, 285, 287, 298, 304, 306, 326–27, 353, 360, 367, 375–78, 413, 428, 454, 457–58, 495, 548, 562, 571, 625–26, 653, 657, 716, 733, 735–36; army hospitals in, 253, 435–40; black refugees in, 98–100, 560–61; contraband hospitals in, 560–61; life in, 693–700
Washington, George (president), 48, 88, 140–41, 672, 697, 711, 720, 733, 735
Washington, George (Union soldier), 405
Washington, Littleton Quinton, 672
Washington, Penn., 569
Washington Star, 625
Washington Territory, 638
Waterloo, battle of, 593, 671
Waterloo, Va., 452, 454–55
Watson (Confederate soldier), 527
Watts, Isaac, 718
Webb, Alexander S., 335
Webb, John, 529
Webb (Confederate soldier), 2
Webster (former slave), 158, 160
Weed, Stephen H., 328
Weekly Anglo-African, 441
Weir, Mrs., 539–40, 543
Weitzel, Godfrey, 363, 369–70
Welles, Gideon, 645–46
West Indies, 445, 682
West Virginia, 375, 380–81, 654
Wharton, Gabriel C., 149, 521
Wheeler, Joseph, 149, 193
Whelan, Henry C., 249–53
Whelan, Mary, 249
Whig Party, 72–73
White, John W., 249, 253
White, Joseph W., 65
White, William, 394–95
White House (Washington), 693–97
White River, 104
Whitfield, John W., 515
Whiting, Charles, 405
Whitman, George, 435
Whitman, Walt, 435–40
Wicks, Oscar, 28–30
Wigfall, Louis T., 669, 672–73
Wilcox, Cadmus M., 303
Wilder, Charles B., 213–15
Wilder, John T., 590

Wilderness, The, 166, 172, 178, 601, 611
Wilderness Run, 182
Wilkes, Franklin C., 524–25
Willard's Hotel (Washington), 694
William III, 688
Williams, Alpheus S., 197–99, 204, 285–87
Williams, Irene, 285
Williams, John, 702
Williams, Jonathan W., 175
Williams, Mary, 285
Williamsburg, Va., 214
Williamsport, Md., 281, 285, 375, 380–81, 386, 421, 625, 721
Williamston, N.C., 363
Wills, David, 562
Wilmington, N.C., 551–52
Wilmington Journal, 551
Wilson, Eli, 403
Wilson, Henry, 23, 345, 500, 630, 633
Wilson, James, 533
Wilson, James H., 574–75, 589
Winchester, Va., 278, 307, 397
Winder, John H., 125, 730–31
Winona (gunboat), 368–69
Winters, Harriet, 238, 357
Winters, William, 238–39, 357–59
Wisconsin, 61, 85, 114
Wisconsin 3rd Regiment, 195
Wisconsin 11th Regiment, 185
Wisconsin 20th Regiment, 268
Wise, Henry A., 192, 729
Wise, Charlotte Everett, 562
Wittemeyer, Annie, 269
Wofford, William T., 339
Wood, Fernando, 228, 389
Wood, Thomas J., 584–85, 592–93, 596
Woodruff, Mr., 17
Woodson, Lieutenant, 529
Woodward, Orpheus S., 332
Wool, John Ellis, 384
Worth, Jonathan, 490–91
Wright, Ambrose R., 278, 421
Wright, David M., 559
Wright, J. L., 310
Wright, Mrs., 668–69

Xerxes, 221

Yates, Richard, 39, 114–15

Yazoo River, 24, 49–50, 55, 108–10, 270, 377, 529
Yellville, Ark., 102
Yonkers, N.Y., 389
York, Pa., 289
Yorktown, Va., 30, 215
Young, Henry, 391
Young, John (northerner), 564
Young, John (southerner), 192
Young, Pierce M. B., 667
Youngblood, J., 177

*This book is set in 10 point ITC Galliard Pro, a
face designed for digital composition by Matthew Carter
and based on the sixteenth-century face Granjon. The paper
is acid-free lightweight opaque and meets the requirements
for permanence of the American National Standards Institute.
The binding material is Brillianta, a woven rayon cloth made
by Van Heek–Scholco Textielfabrieken, Holland.
Composition by Dedicated Book Services. Printing and
binding by Edwards Brothers Malloy, Ann Arbor.
Designed by Bruce Campbell.*

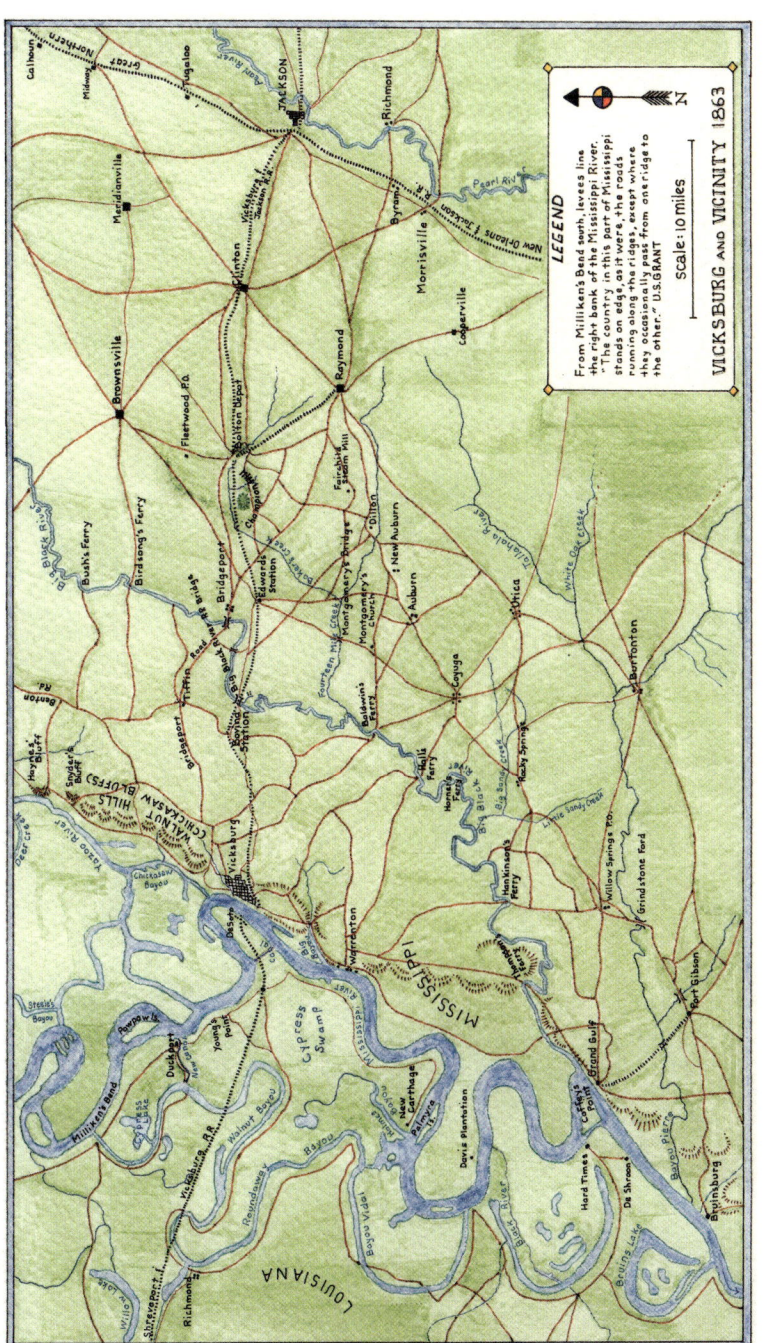

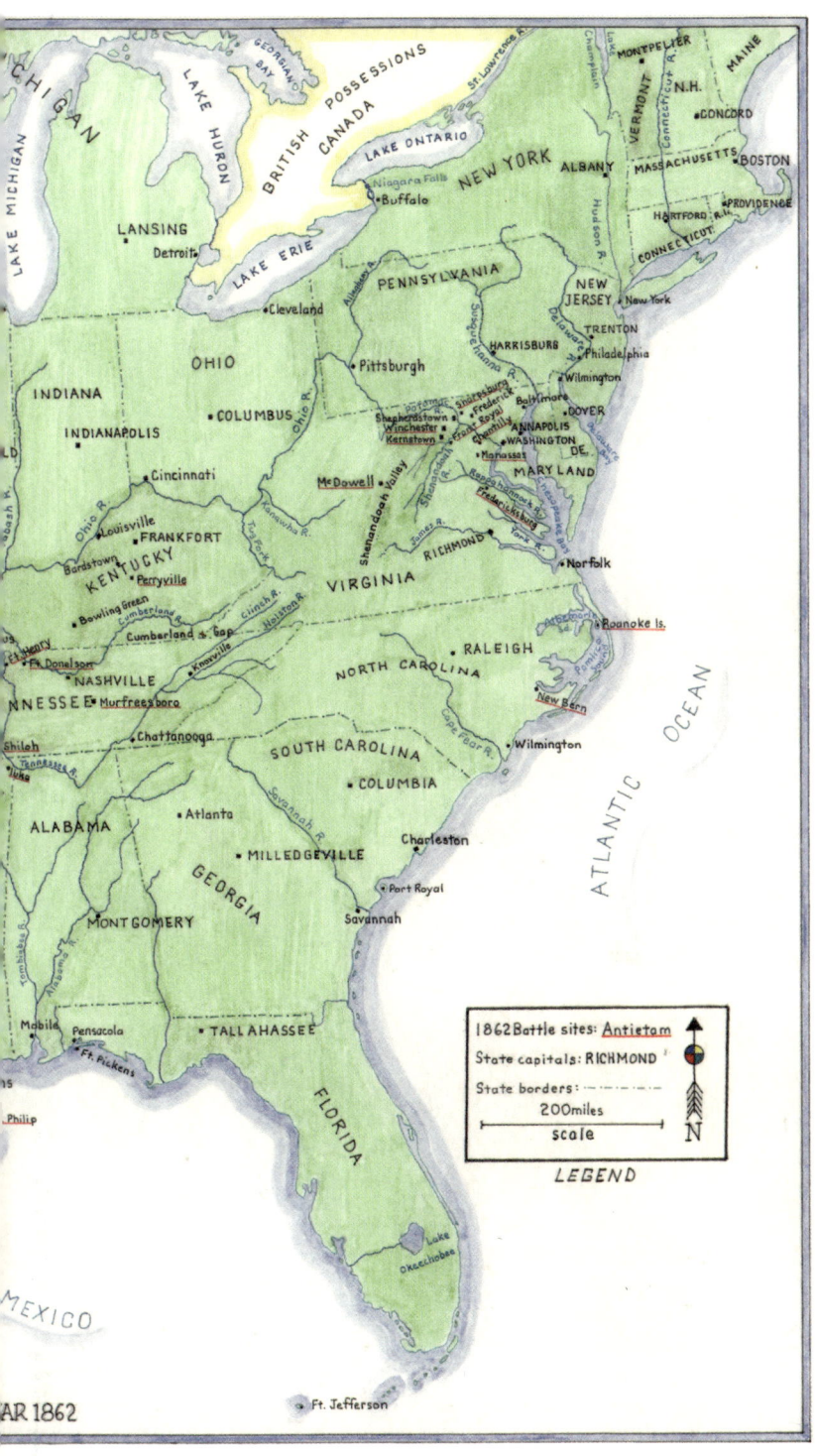

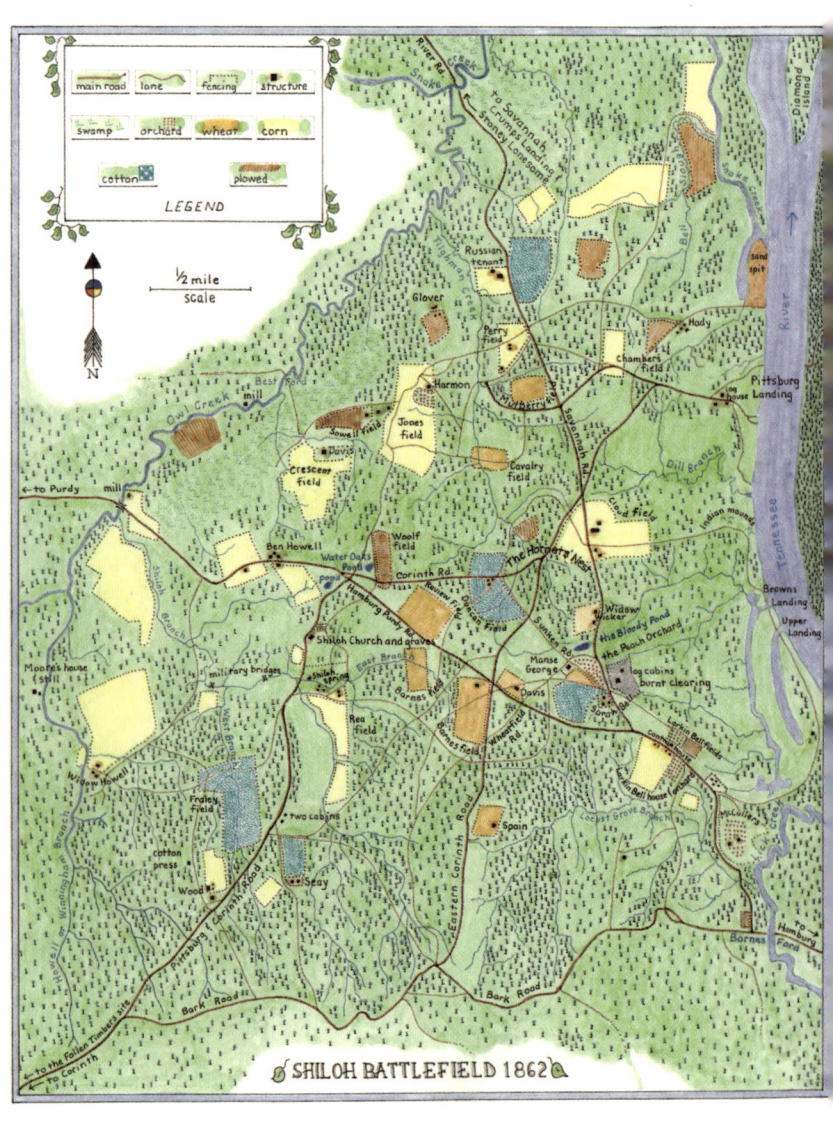

THE CIVIL WAR
THE SECOND YEAR

THE CIVIL WAR

THE SECOND YEAR TOLD BY THOSE WHO LIVED IT

Stephen W. Sears, editor

THE LIBRARY OF AMERICA

Volume compilation, preface, introduction, notes, and
chronology copyright © 2012 by Literary Classics of the
United States, Inc., New York, N.Y.
All rights reserved.
No part of the book may be reproduced commercially
by offset-lithographic or equivalent copying devices without
the permission of the publisher.

Some of the material in this volume is reprinted
by permission of the holders of copyright and publication rights.
See Note on the Texts on page 798 for acknowledgments.

Endpaper maps copyright © 2012 by Earl B. McElfresh,
McElfresh Map Company LLC.

The paper used in this publication meets the
minimum requirements of the American National Standard for
Information Sciences–Permanence of Paper for Printed
Library Materials, ANSI Z39.48–1984.

Distributed to the trade in the United States
by Penguin Random House Inc.
and in Canada by Penguin Random House Canada Ltd.

Library of Congress Control Number: 2011927424
ISBN 978–1–59853–144–2

Second Printing
The Library of America—221

Manufactured in the United States of America

*The Civil War:
The Second Year Told by Those Who Lived It*
is published with support from

THE ANDREW W. MELLON FOUNDATION

and

**THE NATIONAL ENDOWMENT
FOR THE HUMANITIES**

The Civil War: The Second Year Told by Those Who Lived It
is kept in print by a gift from

THE BERKLEY FOUNDATION

to the Guardians of American Letters Fund,
established by The Library of America
to ensure that every volume in the series
will be permanently available.

Contents

Preface.	xxi
Introduction.	xxiii
Frederick Douglass: What Shall Be Done with the Slaves If Emancipated?, January 1862 *"Do nothing with them": January 1862*.	1
John Boston to Elizabeth Boston, January 12, 1862 *A Slave Escapes: Virginia, January 1862*.	6
Salmon P. Chase: Journal, January 6, 1862 *"Vigorous prosecution of the war": Washington, D.C., January 1862*.	8
Abraham Lincoln to Don Carlos Buell and Henry W. Halleck, January 13, 1862 *"My general idea of this war": January 1862*.	10
Abraham Lincoln: President's General War Order No. 1, January 27, 1862; President's Special War Order No. 1, January 31, 1862 *War Orders: January 1862*	12
George B. McClellan to Edwin M. Stanton, February 3, 1862 *A Campaign Against Richmond: February 1862*.	14
Julia Ward Howe: The Battle Hymn of the Republic, February 1862; from *Reminiscences, 1819–1899* *"His terrible swift sword": February 1862*.	24
The New York Times: An Important Arrest, February 11, 1862; The Ball's Bluff Disaster—Gen. McClellan and Gen. Stone, April 12, 1863 *A General is Arrested: Washington, D.C., February 1862*	28

Lew Wallace: from *An Autobiography*
Attack on Fort Donelson: Tennessee, February 1862. 35

John Kennerly Farris to Mary Farris, October 31, 1862
Fort Donelson Surrenders: Tennessee, February 1862 47

Henry Walke: The Western Flotilla at Fort Donelson, Island
   Number Ten, Fort Pillow and Memphis
The River War: February–June 1862 54

Braxton Bragg to Judah P. Benjamin, February 15, 1862
Confederate Strategy: February 1862 77

John B. Jones: Diary, February 8–28, 1862
"These calamities": Virginia, February 1862 80

Jefferson Davis: Message to the Confederate Congress,
   February 25, 1862
Richmond, Virginia, February 1862 84

George E. Stephens to the *Weekly Anglo-African*,
   March 2, 1862
"The boldest feat": Maryland, March 1862 89

Orpheus C. Kerr: from *The Orpheus C. Kerr Papers*
"All quiet on the Potomac": March 1862 93

Dabney H. Maury: Recollections of the Elkhorn Campaign
Battle of Elkhorn Tavern: Arkansas, March 1862. 99

Abraham Lincoln: Message to Congress on Compensated
   Emancipation, March 6, 1862; Abraham Lincoln to
   James A. McDougall, March 14, 1862
Washington, D.C., March 1862 110

Catesby ap Roger Jones: from "Services of the 'Virginia'
   (Merrimac)"
A Naval Revolution: Virginia, March 1862 114

Nathaniel Hawthorne: from "Chiefly About War-Matters"
A Visit to Washington and Virginia: March 1862 121

George B. McClellan to the Army of the Potomac, March 14, 1862,
   and to Samuel L. M. Barlow, March 16, 1862
The "grand campaign" opens: Virginia, March 1862 138

Charles Francis Adams to Charles Francis Adams Jr.,
April 4, 1862
Britain and the Ironclads: London, April 1862   141

Emily Dickinson to Louise and Frances Norcross,
late March 1862
"His big heart shot away": Massachusetts, March 1862   142

Frederick Douglass: The War and How to End It,
March 25, 1862
"The lesson of the hour": March 1862   144

Abraham Lincoln to George B. McClellan, April 9, 1862
"But you must act": Washington, D.C., April 1862.   155

Ulysses S. Grant to Commanding Officer, Advance Forces,
April 6, 1862; to Julia Dent Grant, April 8, 1862; to
Nathaniel H. McLean, April 9, 1862; to Jesse Root
Grant, April 26, 1862; and to Elihu B. Washburne,
May 14, 1862
Battle of Shiloh: Tennessee, April 1862.   157

William T. Sherman to Ellen Ewing Sherman,
April 11, 1862
"We caught the first thunder": Tennessee, April 1862   165

George W. Dawson to Laura Amanda Dawson,
April 26, 1862
"They ran in every direction": Tennessee, April 1862   168

Herman Melville: Shiloh, April 1862
"The church so lone": April 1862   171

Confederate Conscription Acts, April 16 and 21, 1862
Richmond, Virginia, April 1862   172

Abraham Lincoln: Message to Congress, April 16, 1862
Abolishing Slavery in the District of Columbia: April 1862 . .   178

John Russell Bartlett: The "Brooklyn" at the Passage
of the Forts
Running the Gauntlet: Louisiana, April 1862   180

George Hamilton Perkins to Susan G. Perkins,
April 27, 1862
The Fall of New Orleans: Louisiana, April 1862   194

Charles S. Wainwright: Diary, May 5, 1862
Battle of Williamsburg: Virginia, May 1862   199

John B. Jones: Diary, May 14–19, 1862
"*A critical condition*": *Virginia, May 1862* 210

Garland H. White to Edwin M. Stanton, May 7, 1862
"*A black regiment*": *Canada, May 1862* 213

Abraham Lincoln: Proclamation Revoking General Hunter's Emancipation Order, May 19, 1862
Washington, D.C., May 1862 215

Richard Taylor: from *Destruction and Reconstruction*
Meeting Stonewall Jackson: Virginia, May 1862 218

Elizabeth Blair Lee to Samuel Phillips Lee, May 26, 1862
"*The progress of events*": *Washington, D.C., May 1862* 224

Thomas O. Moore: To the People of Louisiana, May 24, 1862
"*No similar instance of infamy*": *Louisiana, May 1862* 227

Lord Palmerston to Charles Francis Adams, June 11, 1862; Benjamin Moran: Journal, June 25, 1862
"*Revolting outrages*": *London, June 1862*. 230

Henry Ropes to William Ropes, June 3–4, 1862
Battle of Fair Oaks: Virginia, May–June 1862 233

Robert E. Lee to Jefferson Davis, June 5, 1862
A Military Assessment: Virginia, June 1862 236

David Hunter to Edwin M. Stanton, June 23, 1862
Arming Freed Slaves: South Carolina, June 1862. 238

Kate Stone: Journal, June 29–July 5, 1862
Fear of the "Yankees": Louisiana, June–July 1862 241

Edward Porter Alexander: from *Fighting for the Confederacy*
The Seven Days Begin: Virginia, June 1862. 246

Charles A. Page: from *Letters of a War Correspondent*
Battle of Gaines's Mill: Virginia, June 1862 258

George B. McClellan to Edwin M. Stanton, June 28, 1862
An Accusation of Betrayal: Virginia, June 1862 265

Abraham Lincoln to William H. Seward, June 28, 1862
"*The present condition of the war*":
Washington, D.C., June 1862. 267

CONTENTS

Charles B. Haydon: Journal, June 25–July 1, 1862
The Union Retreat: Virginia, June–July 1862 269

Asa D. Smith: Narrative of the Seven Days' Battles
Wounded at Glendale: Virginia, June–July 1862 277

Judith W. McGuire: Diary, June 27–30, 1862
"Our beleaguered city": Virginia, June 1862 290

Sallie Brock: from *Richmond During the War*
"Death held a carnival": Virginia, June–July 1862. 294

Sara Agnes Pryor: from *Reminiscences of Peace and War*
A Richmond Hospital: Virginia, June–July 1862. 297

Whitelaw Reid: General Hunter's Negro Soldiers,
July 6, 1862
Debating Black Soldiers: Washington, D.C., July 1862 303

George B. McClellan to Abraham Lincoln, July 7, 1862
"Civil and military policy": Virginia, July 1862 306

Thomas H. Dudley and J. Price Edwards: An Exchange,
July 9, 10, and 16, 1862
Building a Confederate Cruiser: England, July 1862 309

Abraham Lincoln: Appeal to Border State Representatives
for Compensated Emancipation, July 12, 1862
Washington, D.C., July 1862 314

Second Confiscation Act, July 17, 1862
Washington, D.C., July 1862 317

John Pope: Address to the Army of Virginia,
July 14, 1862
"Success and glory": Washington, D.C., July 1862. 323

John Pope: General Orders Nos. 5, 7, 11, July 18,
20, and 23, 1862
A Change in Policy: Washington, D.C., July 1862 325

Fitz John Porter to Joseph C. G. Kennedy,
July 17, 1862
The "idol" of the army: Virginia, July 1862. 329

August Belmont to Thurlow Weed, July 20, 1862
An Appeal for Negotiation: Rhode Island, July 1862. 332

Salmon P. Chase to Richard C. Parsons, July 20, 1862
A "shameful" defeat: Washington, D.C., July 1862 338

Salmon P. Chase: Journal, July 22, 1862
Presidential Emancipation: Washington, D.C., July 1862 . . .   342

Abraham Lincoln: First Draft of the Emancipation
    Proclamation, July 22, 1862
Washington, D.C., July 1862   345

Francis B. Carpenter: from *Six Months at the White House
    with Abraham Lincoln*
Postponing Emancipation: Washington, D.C., July 1862   347

Abraham Lincoln to Cuthbert Bullitt, July 28, 1862
Saving the Government: Washington, D.C., July 1862   349

Charles Sumner to John Bright, August 5, 1862
Cotton and Emancipation: Massachusetts, August 1862   352

Henry W. Halleck to George B. McClellan,
    August 6, 1862
Evacuating the Peninsula: Washington, D.C., August 1862 . .   354

Memorial of a Committee of Citizens of Liberty
    County, Georgia, August 5, 1862
Fleeing Slaves: Georgia, August 1862   358

Confederate War Department: General Orders No. 60,
    August 21, 1862
Retaliation for Arming Slaves: Virginia, August 1862.   364

Abraham Lincoln: Address on Colonization,
    August 14, 1862
Washington, D.C., August 1862.   366

Abraham Lincoln to Horace Greeley, August 22, 1862
*"I would save the Union": Washington, D.C.,
    August 1862.*   372

William T. Sherman to Thomas Hunton,
    August 24, 1862
Slavery and the Laws of War: Tennessee, August 1862   374

John Lothrop Motley to William H. Seward,
    August 26, 1862
Emancipation and Diplomacy: Austria, August 1862   377

Harriet Jacobs to William Lloyd Garrison,
    September 5, 1862
Aiding Contrabands: Washington, D.C., Summer 1862   382

Edward Porter Alexander: from *Fighting for the Confederacy*
The Second Manassas Campaign: Virginia, August 1862 . . . 391

Charles Francis Adams Jr. to Charles Francis Adams,
August 27, 1862
"Treachery": Washington, D.C., August 1862 400

John Hampden Chamberlayne to Martha Burwell
Chamberlayne, September 6, 1862
*"These great operations": Virginia and Maryland,
August–September 1862* 404

John Pope to Henry W. Halleck, September 1, 1862
*"Unsoldierly and dangerous conduct": Virginia,
September 1862* 411

Clara Barton to John Shaver, September 4, 1862
*Aiding the Wounded: Virginia and Washington, D.C.,
August–September 1862* 413

Gideon Welles: Diary, August 31–September 1, 1862
*"McClellan must go down": Washington, D.C.,
August–September 1862* 416

John Hay: Diary, September 1, 1862
"We are whipped again": Washington, D.C., September 1862 . 425

Edward Bates: Remonstrance and Notes on Cabinet
Meeting, September 2, 1862
*"The Prest. was in deep distress": Washington, D.C.,
September 1862* 428

Salmon P. Chase: Journal, September 2, 1862
"A series of failures": Washington, D.C., September 1862 430

George B. McClellan to Mary Ellen McClellan,
September 2, 1862
Restored to Command: Washington, D.C., September 1862. . . 433

Robert E. Lee to Jefferson Davis, September 3, 1862
Invading Maryland: Virginia, September 1862 435

George Templeton Strong: Diary, September 3–4, 1862
"A state of nausea": New York, September 1862 437

William Thompson Lusk to Elizabeth Freeman Lusk,
September 6, 1862
A Demoralized Army: Washington, D.C., September 1862 . . . 439

Abraham Lincoln: Meditation on the Divine Will,
   c. early September 1862
"God wills this contest": Washington, D.C., September 1862 . . 442

Lord Palmerston and Lord Russell: An Exchange,
   September 14, 17, and 23, 1862
Britain Considers Mediation: September 1862 443

Robert E. Lee to Jefferson Davis, September 8, 1862
*"Recognition of our independence": Maryland,
   September 1862* 446

Lewis H. Steiner: Diary, September 5–6, 1862
*A "dirty and repulsive" army: Maryland,
   September 1862* 448

James Richmond Boulware: Diary, September 4–14, 1862
A Confederate in Maryland: September 1862. 454

Alpheus S. Williams to George B. McClellan,
   September 13, 1862; Robert E. Lee: Special Orders
   No. 191, September 9, 1862
The Lost Order: Maryland, September 1862. 459

George W. Smalley: Narrative of Antietam,
   September 17, 1862
Battle of Antietam: Maryland, September 1862. 462

Rufus R. Dawes: from *Service with the Sixth Wisconsin
   Volunteers*
Fight for the Cornfield: Maryland, September 1862. 479

Alpheus S. Williams to Irene and Mary Williams,
   September 22, 1862
"The infernal music": Maryland, September 1862 485

David L. Thompson: With Burnside at Antietam
A Landscape Turned Red: Maryland, September 1862. 496

Samuel W. Fiske to the *Springfield Republican*,
   September 20, 1862
After the Battle: Maryland, September 1862 503

Clifton Johnson: from *Battleground Adventures*
"Our men had won": Maryland, September 1862. 505

Mary Bedinger Mitchell: A Woman's Recollections of
   Antietam
"Noise, confusion, dust": Virginia, September 1862. 511

George B. McClellan to Mary Ellen McClellan, September 20, 1862	
"Our victory was complete": Maryland, September 1862	524
Ephraim Anderson: from *Memoirs: Historical and Personal*	
Battle of Iuka: Mississippi, September 1862	526
Gideon Welles: Diary, September 22, 1862	
"The cause of emancipation": Washington, D.C., September 1862	530
Abraham Lincoln: Preliminary Emancipation Proclamation, September 22, 1862; Proclamation Suspending the Writ of Habeas Corpus, September 24, 1862	
Washington, D.C., September 1862	533
L. A. Whitely to James Gordon Bennett, September 24, 1862	
"The air is thick with revolution": Washington, D.C., September 1862	538
George B. McClellan to William H. Aspinwall, September 26, 1862	
"Servile war" and "despotism": Maryland, September 1862	540
Abraham Lincoln: Record of Dismissal of John J. Key, September 26–27, 1862	
"That is not the game": Washington, D.C., September 1862	541
Fitz John Porter to Manton Marble, September 30, 1862	
"Proclamations of a political coward": Maryland, September 1862	543
Braxton Bragg: To the People of the Northwest, September 26, 1862	
A Confederate Invasion: Kentucky, September 1862	550
Ralph Waldo Emerson: The President's Proclamation, September 1862	
"An event worth the dreadful war": Massachusetts, September 1862	554
Frederick Douglass: Emancipation Proclaimed, October 1862	
"Your deliverance draws nigh!": October 1862	561

Debate in the Confederate Senate on Retaliation for the
  Emancipation Proclamation, September 29 and
  October 1, 1862
Richmond, Virginia, October 1862 567

The Times of London: Editorial on the Emancipation
  Proclamation, October 7, 1862
"This gigantic wickedness": London, October 1862 572

George B. McClellan to Abraham Lincoln,
  October 7, 1862
Obeying Civil Authority: Maryland, October 1862 576

Oscar L. Jackson: from *The Colonel's Diary*
Battle of Corinth: Mississippi, October 1862 578

Charles B. Labruzan: Journal, October 4, 1862
"An awful day": Mississippi, October 1862 585

J. Montgomery Wright: Notes of a Staff-Officer at
  Perryville
Battle of Perryville: Kentucky, October 1862 589

Sam R. Watkins: from *"Co. Aytch," Maury Grays,
  First Tennessee Regiment*
"This grand havoc of battle": Kentucky, October 1862 593

Abraham Lincoln to George B. McClellan,
  October 13, 1862
"Your over-cautiousness": Washington, D.C., October 1862. . . 600

Lord Palmerston to Lord Russell, October 2
  and 22, 1862
Reconsidering Mediation: England, October 1862 603

Charles Sumner to John Bright, October 28, 1862
"The Presdt. is in earnest": Massachusetts, October 1862 606

Francis Preston Blair to Montgomery Blair,
  November 7, 1862
*"An auger too dull to take hold": Washington, D.C.,
  November 1862* 609

George G. Meade to Margaret Meade,
  November 8, 1862
McClellan's Dismissal: Virginia, November 1862 611

Orville H. Browning: Diary, November 29, 1862
Lincoln and McClellan: Washington, D.C., November 1862 . . 614

Abraham Lincoln: Annual Message to Congress,
   December 1, 1862
Washington, D.C., December 1862   617

Edward Porter Alexander: from *Fighting for the Confederacy*
Battle of Fredericksburg: Virginia, December 1862   640

Samuel W. Fiske to the *Springfield Republican*,
   December 15 and 17, 1862
"Murderous butchery": Virginia, December 1862   657

Henry Livermore Abbott to Josiah Gardner Abbott,
   December 14, 1862, and to George B. Perry,
   December 17, 1862
"Thoroughly licked": Virginia, December 1862   660

Clifton Johnson: from *Battleground Adventures*
"An awful day": Virginia, December 1862   664

Walt Whitman: from *Specimen Days*
"Hundreds die every day": Virginia, December 1862   669

Louisa May Alcott: from *Hospital Sketches*
*"Torn and shattered": District of Columbia,
   December 1862*   671

Orville H. Browning: Diary, December 18, 1862
A Cabinet Crisis: Washington, D.C., December 1862   683

Gideon Welles: Diary, December 19–20, 1862
*Lincoln Resolves the Crisis: Washington, D.C.,
   December 1862*   685

Harper's Weekly: The Reverse at Fredericksburg,
   December 27, 1862
"Sickness, disgust, and despair": December 1862   693

George Templeton Strong: Diary, December 27, 1862
Lincoln and Emancipation: New York, December 1862   696

Fitz John Porter to Samuel L. M. Barlow,
   December 29, 1862
*Porter's Court-Martial: Washington, D.C.,
   December 1862*   699

Cyrus F. Boyd: Diary, December 22–25, 1862
Looting in Holly Springs: Mississippi, December 1862   702

Jefferson Davis: Address to the Mississippi Legislature,
    December 26, 1862
Jackson, December 1862 706

William T. Sherman to John Sherman, January 6, 1863
Battle of Chickasaw Bayou: Mississippi, December 1862. 724

Samuel Sawyer, Pearl P. Ingalls, and Jacob G. Forman to
    Samuel R. Curtis, December 29, 1862
Mistreatment of Contrabands: Arkansas, December 1862 . . . 727

Ira S. Owens: from *Greene County in the War*
Battle of Stones River: Tennessee, December 1862–
January 1863 729

Lot D. Young: from *Reminiscences of a Soldier of the*
    Orphan Brigade
"Bloody and useless sacrifice": Tennessee, December 1862–
January 1863 733

Ambrose E. Burnside to Abraham Lincoln,
    January 1, 1863
An Offer to Resign: Washington D.C., January 1863. 739

Abraham Lincoln to Henry W. Halleck, January 1, 1863
"You fail me precisely": Washington, D.C.,
January 1863 741

Abraham Lincoln: Final Emancipation Proclamation,
    January 1, 1863
Washington, D.C., January 1863 742

Benjamin Rush Plumly to Abraham Lincoln,
    January 1, 1863
Celebrating Emancipation: Philadelphia, January 1863 745

Abraham Lincoln to John A. McClernand, January 8, 1863
"Broken eggs can not be mended": Washington, D.C.,
January 1863 748

Chronology 753
Biographical Notes 764
Note on the Texts 798
Notes 816
Index 853

Preface

"Has there ever been another historical crisis of the magnitude of 1861–65 in which so many people were so articulate?"
—Edmund Wilson

THIS Library of America volume is the second in a four-volume series bringing together memorable and significant writing by participants in the American Civil War. Each volume in the series covers approximately one year of the conflict, from the election of Abraham Lincoln in November 1860 to the end of the war in the spring of 1865, and presents a chronological selection of documents from the broadest possible range of authoritative sources—diaries, letters, speeches, military reports, newspaper articles, memoirs, poems, and public papers. Drawing upon an immense and unique body of American writing, the series offers a narrative of the war years that encompasses military and political events and their social and personal reverberations. Created by persons of every class and condition, the writing included here captures the American nation and the American language in the crucial period of their modern formation. Selections have been chosen for their historical significance, their literary quality, and their narrative energy, and are printed from the best available sources. The goal has been to shape a narrative that is both broad and balanced in scope, while at the same time doing justice to the number and diversity of voices and perspectives preserved for us in the writing of the era.

Introduction

PRESIDENT Lincoln began 1862 deeply troubled by the state of the Union, and on January 10 he called a group of advisors and generals to the White House. "The President was greatly disturbed at the state of affairs," wrote one of his listeners, General Irvin McDowell. "Spoke of the exhausted condition of the Treasury; of the loss of public credit; of the Jacobinism in Congress; of the delicate condition of our foreign relations; of the bad news he had received from the West . . . but, more than all, the sickness of General McClellan." The general-in-chief was laid low by typhoid fever, and if something was not done soon, said the President, "the bottom would be out of the whole affair. . . ."

At the other White House, in Richmond, at a cabinet meeting in February, President Davis found the state of the Confederacy equally disturbing. By report, defenses were crumbling east and west, Attorney General Thomas Bragg entered in his diary. "The Pres't said the time had come for diminishing the extent of our lines—that we had not men in the field to hold them and we must fall back." Bragg wondered: "Will the Gov't endure? Can we repel the enemy? Dangers surround us & it commences at our darkest period since the war began."

During the year since the secession of eleven Southern states brought the nation to war with itself, the two presidents had struggled to build, shape, and direct the machinery of war—not a conventional war against a foreign power but a civil war that was by nature peculiarly claustrophobic. Jefferson Davis, for example, felt increasingly hemmed in by enemy incursions wherever he looked.

For Southerners the Union blockade of the Atlantic and Gulf coasts had grown through 1861 from a nuisance to a serious concern, and the Federals' seizure of Port Royal Sound in South Carolina in November gained the blockaders an operational base. Further incursions on both coasts seemed certain in the new year. Confederate efforts in 1861 to wean the border state of Kentucky away from neutrality had resulted in the creation of a thin, largely undermanned defensive line across the state that President Davis discovered he lacked the resources to strengthen. Indeed, Attorney General Bragg's gloomy outlook was brought on by the Yankees breaching this Kentucky line and pressing far up the Tennessee and Cumberland rivers. In the Trans-Mississippi the Rebels' victory at Wilson's Creek in Missouri in August 1861 had not proved decisive enough to secure that border state for the South; certainly the fight would be renewed in 1862, and for Arkansas as well.

Davis's admission that he must draw in his lines applied most immediately to Virginia. The South's stunning victory at Manassas in July 1861, and a second, lesser victory at Ball's Bluff on the upper Potomac in October, had raised hopes for maintaining the Potomac as the Confederacy's northern frontier. The new year dashed such hopes. Keeping Joseph E. Johnston's army at Manassas was no longer tenable in the face of the huge Yankee buildup of forces at Washington. Johnston must fall back to a safer posting. The Confederacy started 1862 on the defensive everywhere.

Lincoln might not feel hemmed in by enemy armies as was Davis, but still he was much constricted by an array of forces, domestic and foreign. His catalog of complaints that January 10 was real. As 1861 turned to 1862, the Union war machine was stalled, making it difficult for the Treasury to find money and credit to support it. The Congress that convened in December was dominated by radical Republicans—to some they raised echoes of the Jacobins of the French Revolution—who challenged the administration's war policies, a challenge given teeth by the investigative Joint Committee on the Conduct of the War. Relations with Great Britain had been badly strained in November when two Confederate envoys were taken off the British steamer *Trent* by U.S.S. *San Jacinto*. The envoys had since been released, but the administration still worried about possible European intervention in the conflict. Lincoln's mention of bad news from the West referred to the continuing reluctance of his generals in the western theater to start moving.

One of the President's more challenging problems was General George B. McClellan. McClellan—dubbed the Young Napoleon by the press—had arrived with fanfare to pick up the pieces after the debacle at Manassas and to resuscitate the

Army of the Potomac. On November 1 McClellan was named general-in-chief of all the Union's armies, replacing Winfield Scott. By the turn of the year, however, McClellan had worn out his welcome through his policy of stubborn inactivity. Confederate cannon closed commerce on the Potomac below Washington, and communications on the upper Potomac were interrupted, leaving the capital to suffer a humiliating partial blockade. McClellan's sole remedial effort ended badly at Ball's Bluff. The typhoid that rendered him hors de combat for some three weeks at the turn of the year brought these problems to a head. Lincoln remarked, according to McDowell, "if General McClellan did not want to use the army, he would like to '*borrow it*,' provided he could see how it could be made to do something."

The Civil War expanded with explosive force in 1862. The rebellion became a war, and by year's end the war became a revolution against slavery. These selections by witnesses to this second year of conflict—their diaries, journals, letters, addresses, essays, memoirs, battle reports, proclamations, newspaper accounts—pick up and develop threads from 1861 and open a number of new ones. The year begins in military stalemate, marks major Union gains in a rush of action, then finds Confederate resistance stiffening. By summer the tide turns, and autumn brings joint Confederate offensives east and west. These invasions crest and fall back. Two Union winter offensives, east and west, end the year as it began, in a military stalemate.

These multiple campaigns took a toll beyond what anyone in that day could have imagined. The tally of the two days at Shiloh on April 6–7 reached 23,700, twice the number of casualties in all the fighting since Fort Sumter. The cost of the Seven Days on the Virginia Peninsula at the end of June came to 36,000. Antietam in Maryland on September 17 was the bloodiest single day of the entire war. The battlefields of 1862 counted at least 208,000 dead, wounded, and captured/missing.

The men who did the fighting on these unprecedented American battlefields have their say in these pages. For many these were the most momentous, unforgettable days of their lives, and whether in letters and diaries or later memoirs, they strove to capture what it had been like. The women who nursed the myriad wounded wanted the world to know their truth as well.

This second year of war marked the first extended test of battlefield commands. Generals rise, flourish, and (some of them) fade away. For the Union, in the western theater, U.S. Grant, William T. Sherman, and William S. Rosecrans show the most gains and the most promise. But their theater commander, Henry W. Halleck, stalls the western war machine. John Pope has his day on the Mississippi; brought east, he comes a cropper in the second battle at Manassas. Don Carlos Buell has *his* day at Perryville in Kentucky, fritters away the victory, and is replaced. In taking New Orleans, Flag Officer David Farragut demonstrates the Union's command of the sea. For the Confederacy, Albert Sidney Johnston seeks at Shiloh to counter Grant's initiative and dies in the attempt. In the autumn Braxton Bragg raises Southern hopes with a drive into Kentucky, then falters and falls back. The western Confederacy ends 1862 where it began, on the defensive, and with that much less to defend.

In the eastern theater, generalship traces a different course. Beginning in April McClellan presses his "grand campaign" on the Peninsula right to the gates of Richmond. His opponent, Joseph E. Johnston, falls wounded on May 31, and afterward remarks, "The shot that struck me down is the very best that has been fired for the Southern cause yet." So it proves. Robert E. Lee takes Johnston's place and alters the course of the war. In less than three months, Lee drives McClellan away from Richmond, whips Pope at Second Manassas, and in September carries the war across the Potomac into Maryland. His invasion is checked by McClellan at Antietam. But McClellan, like Buell in the West, continues to suffer from "the slows" (in Lincoln's phrase) and in due course he too is dismissed. His replacement, Ambrose Burnside, fares ill at Lee's hands at Fredericksburg in December. At year's end only Robert E. Lee is left standing in the eastern theater.

Another, truly revolutionary theme develops in parallel to this landscape of battle in 1862—Abraham Lincoln's sometimes tortuous path to emancipation. Slaves in uncounted numbers cast their votes for emancipation in escaping to Union lines, gaining the status of contraband of war. Congressional confiscation, colonization, plans for compensated emancipation—all have their day before the Emancipation Proclamation is finally promulgated. In his State of the Union message on December 1, Lincoln explains what is at stake for the nation: "In *giving* freedom to the *slave*, we *assure* freedom to the *free*—honorable alike in what we give, and what we preserve. We shall nobly save, or meanly lose, the last best, hope of earth."

Stephen W. Sears

"DO NOTHING WITH THEM": JANUARY 1862

Frederick Douglass: What Shall Be Done with the Slaves If Emancipated?

January 1862

From the beginning of hostilities in April 1861, Frederick Douglass had advocated enlisting black soldiers and had criticized the Lincoln administration for not making the destruction of slavery an essential aim of the war. On January 14, 1862, Douglass warned a Philadelphia audience, "We have attempted to maintain our Union in utter defiance of the moral chemistry of the universe," explaining, "We have sought to bind the chains of slavery on the limbs of the black man, without thinking that at last we should find the other end of that hateful chain about our own necks." That same month, in his journal *Douglass' Monthly*, the nation's leading black abolitionist looked ahead to a time without chains.

IT IS curious to observe, at this juncture, when the existence of slavery is threatened by an aroused nation, when national necessity is combining with an enlightened sense of justice to put away the huge abomination forever, that the enemies of human liberty are resorting to all the old and ten thousand times refuted objections to emancipation with which they confronted the abolition movement twenty-five years ago. Like the one stated above, these pro-slavery objections have their power mainly in the slavery-engendered prejudice, which every where pervades the country. Like all other great transgressions of the law of eternal rectitude, slavery thus produces an element in the popular and depraved moral sentiment favorable to its own existence. These objections are often urged with a show of sincere solicitude for the welfare of the slaves themselves. It is said, what will you do with them? they can't take care of themselves; they would all come to the North; they would not work; they would become a burden upon the State, and a blot upon society; they'd cut their masters' throats; they would cheapen labor, and crowd out the poor white laborer

I

from employment; their former masters would not employ them, and they would necessarily become vagrants, paupers and criminals, overrunning all our alms houses, jails and prisons. The laboring classes among the whites would come in bitter conflict with them in all the avenues of labor, and regarding them as occupying places and filling positions which should be occupied and filled by white men; a fierce war of races would be the inevitable consequence, and the black race would, of course, (being the weaker,) be exterminated. In view of this frightful, though happily somewhat contradictory picture, the question is asked, and pressed with a great show of earnestness at this momentous crisis of our nation's history, What shall be done with the four million slaves if they are emancipated?

This question has been answered, and can be answered in many ways. Primarily, it is a question less for man than for God —less for human intellect than for the laws of nature to solve. It assumes that nature has erred; that the law of liberty is a mistake; that freedom, though a natural want of the human soul, can only be enjoyed at the expense of human welfare, and that men are better off in slavery than they would or could be in freedom; that slavery is the natural order of human relations, and that liberty is an experiment. What shall be done with them?

Our answer is, do nothing with them; mind your business, and let them mind theirs. Your *doing* with them is their greatest misfortune. They have been undone by your doings, and all they now ask, and really have need of at your hands, is just to let them alone. They suffer by every interference, and succeed best by being let alone. The Negro should have been let alone in Africa—let alone when the pirates and robbers offered him for sale in our Christian slave markets—(more cruel and inhuman than the Mohammedan slave markets)—let alone by courts, judges, politicians, legislators and slave-drivers—let alone altogether, and assured that they were thus to be let alone forever, and that they must now make their own way in the world, just the same as any and every other variety of the human family. As colored men, we only ask to be allowed to *do* with ourselves, subject only to the same great laws for the welfare of human society which apply to other men, Jews, Gentiles, Barbarian, Sythian. Let us stand upon our own legs, work with our own hands, and eat bread in the sweat of our own brows. When you, our white fellow-countrymen, have attempted to do anything for us, it has generally been to deprive us of some right, power or privilege which you yourself would die before you would submit to have taken from you. When the planters of the West Indies used to attempt to puzzle the pure-minded Wilberforce with the question, How shall we get rid of slavery? his simple answer was, "quit stealing." In like manner, we answer those who are perpetually puzzling their brains with questions as to what shall be done with the Negro, "let him alone and mind your own business." If you see him plowing in the open field, leveling the forest, at work with a spade, a rake, a hoe, a pick-axe, or a bill—let him alone; he has a right to work. If you see him on his way to school, with spelling book, geography and arithmetic in his hands—let him alone. Don't shut the door in his face, nor bolt your gates against him; he has a right to learn—let him alone. Don't pass laws to degrade him. If he has a ballot in his hand, and is on his way to the ballot-box to deposit his vote for the man whom he thinks will most justly and wisely administer the Government which has the power of life and death over him, as well as others—let him *alone*; his right of choice as much deserves respect and protection as your own. If you see him on his way to the church, exercising religious liberty in accordance with this or that religious persuasion—let him alone.—Don't meddle with him, nor trouble yourselves with any questions as to what shall be done with him.

The great majority of human duties are of this negative character. If men were born in need of crutches, instead of having legs, the fact would be otherwise. We should then be in need of help, and would require outside aid; but according to the wiser and better arrangement of nature, our duty is done better by not hindering than by helping our fellow-men; or, in other words, the best way to help them is just to let them help themselves.

We would not for one moment check the outgrowth of any benevolent concern for the future welfare of the colored race in America or elsewhere; but in the name of reason and religion, we earnestly plead for justice before all else. Benevolence with justice is harmonious and beautiful; but benevolence without justice is a mockery. Let the American people, who have thus far only kept the colored race staggering between partial philanthropy and cruel force, be induced to try what virtue there is in justice. First pure, then peaceable—first just, then generous.—The sum of the black man's misfortunes and calamities are just here: He is everywhere treated as an exception to all the general rules which should operate in the relations of other men. He is literally scourged beyond the beneficent range of truth and justice.—With all the purifying and liberalizing power of the Christian religion, teaching, as it does, meekness, gentleness, brotherly kindness, those who profess it have not yet even approached the position of treating the black man as an equal man and a brother. The few who have thus far risen to this requirement, both of reason and religion, are stigmatized as fanatics and enthusiasts.

What shall be done with the Negro if emancipated? Deal justly with him. He is a human being, capable of judging between good and evil, right and wrong, liberty and slavery, and is as much a subject of law as any other man; therefore, deal justly with him. He is, like other men, sensible of the motives of reward and punishment. Give him wages for his work, and let hunger pinch him if he don't work. He knows the difference between fullness and famine, plenty and scarcity. "But will he work?" Why should he not? He is used to it. His hands are already hardened by toil, and he has no dreams of ever getting a living by any other means than by hard work. But would you turn them all loose? Certainly! We are no better than our Creator. He has turned them loose, and why should not we?

But would you let them all stay here?—Why not? What better is *here* than *there*? Will they occupy more room as freemen than as slaves? Is the presence of a black freeman less agreeable than that of a black slave? Is an object of our injustice and cruelty a more ungrateful sight than one of your justice and benevolence? You have borne the one more than two hundred years—can't you bear the other long enough to try the experiment? "But would it be safe?" No good reason can be given why it would not be. There is much more reason for apprehension from slavery than from freedom. Slavery provokes and justifies incendiarism, murder, robbery, assassination, and all manner of violence.—But why not let them go off by themselves? That is a matter we would leave exclusively to themselves. Besides, when you, the American people, shall once do justice to the enslaved colored people, you will not want to get rid of them. Take away the motive which slavery supplies for getting rid of the free black people of the South, and there is not a single State, from Maryland to Texas, which would desire to be rid of its black people. Even with the obvious disadvantage to slavery, which such contact is, there is scarcely a slave State which could be carried for the unqualified expulsion of the free colored people. Efforts at such expulsion have been made in Maryland, Virginia and South Carolina, and all have failed, just because the black man as a freeman is a useful member of society. To drive him away, and thus deprive the South of his labor, would be as absurd and monstrous as for a man to cut off his right arm, the better to enable himself to work.

There is one cheering aspect of this revival of the old and threadbare objections to emancipation—it implies at least the presence of danger to the slave system. When slavery was assailed twenty-five years ago, the whole land took the alarm, and every species of argument and subterfuge was resorted to by the defenders of slavery. The mental activity was amazing; all sorts of excuses, political, economical, social, theological and ethnological, were coined into barricades against the advancing march of anti-slavery sentiment. The same activity now shows itself, but has added nothing new to the argument for slavery or against emancipation.—When the accursed slave system shall once be abolished, and the Negro, long cast out from the human family, and governed like a beast of burden, shall be gathered under the divine government of justice, liberty and humanity, men will be ashamed to remember that they were ever deluded by the flimsy nonsense which they have allowed themselves to urge against the freedom of the long enslaved millions of our land. That day is not far off.

"O hasten it in mercy, gracious Heaven!"

A SLAVE ESCAPES: VIRGINIA, JANUARY 1862

John Boston to Elizabeth Boston

John Boston wrote to his wife in Owensville, Maryland, from Upton's Hill in Arlington, Virginia. It is not known if Elizabeth Boston ever received his letter, which soon came into the possession of a committee of the Maryland House of Delegates that was attempting to have fugitive slaves excluded from Union army camps. When the committee wrote to Secretary of War Edwin M. Stanton in March 1862 asking that fugitive slaves be expelled from army camps, it received a reply from Assistant Secretary Peter H. Watson stating that "the alleged harboring" of slaves would receive Stanton's attention "as soon as he is relieved from more important and pressing duties."

Upton Hill January the 12 1862
My Dear Wife   it is with grate joy I take this time to let you know Whare I am   i am now in Safety in the 14th Regiment of Brooklyn   this Day i can Adress you thank god as a free man   I had a little truble in giting away But as the lord led the Children of Isrel to the land of Canon So he led me to a land Whare fredom Will rain in spite Of earth and hell   Dear you must make your Self content i am free from al the Slavers Lash   and as you have chose the Wise plan Of Serving the lord i hope you Will pray Much and i Will try by the help of god To Serv him With all my hart   I am With a very nice man and have All that hart Can Wish But My Dear I Cant express my grate desire that i Have to See you   i trust the time Will Come When We Shal meet again   And if We dont met on earth We Will Meet in heven Whare Jesas ranes   Dear Elizabeth tell Mrs Ownees That i trust that She Will Continue Her kindness to you and that god Will Bless her on earth and Save her In grate eternity   My Acomplements To Mrs Owens and her Children   may They Prosper through life   I never Shall forgit her kindness to me   Dear Wife i must Close   rest yourself Contented i am free   i Want you to rite To me Soon as you Can Without Delay   Direct your letter to the 14th Reig-

ment New york State malitia Uptons Hill Virginea In Care of Mr Cranford Comary Write my Dear Soon As you C Your Affectionate Husban Kiss Daniel For me

            John Boston

Give my love to Father and Mother

"VIGOROUS PROSECUTION OF THE WAR":
WASHINGTON, D.C., JANUARY 1862

Salmon P. Chase: Journal, January 6, 1862

In the wake of the Union defeat at Ball's Bluff, Virginia, in October 1861, Congress established the investigative Joint Committee on the Conduct of the War on December 10. The seven-member committee, made up of three senators and four representatives, was dominated by Radical Republicans, including Ohio's Senator Benjamin F. Wade, its chairman. In early January 1862 Major General George B. McClellan, general-in-chief of the Union armies and commander of the Army of the Potomac, fell seriously ill with typhoid fever, leaving the war machine stalled. With a Confederate army camped at Manassas, twenty-five miles southwest of Washington, and Confederate artillery blockading the Potomac River below the city, bellicose committee members initiated a meeting with President Lincoln and his cabinet. As reported by Secretary of the Treasury Salmon P. Chase, they called for a new Army of the Potomac commander, the Radicals' favorite, Irvin McDowell.

MONDAY JANUARY 6TH. Received a note from McClellan's Aid, saying that the General had read the despatch sent him last night, and would take immediate measures to protect the Road; that reinforcements would be immediately sent to Hancock; and that Genl. Banks had been ordered to support Lander.

In fulfillment of engagement with the President of the American Bank Note Company, went to Ulke's, who took a number of Photographs.

Cabinet Meeting held at night to confer with the Joint Committee of the two Houses of Congress on the Conduct of the War. The members of the Committee, especially Messrs. Chandler, Wade, Johnson, Odell and Covode, were very earnest in urging the vigorous prosecution of the War, and in recommending the appointment of Genl. McDowell as Major-General, to command the Army of the Potomac.

A great deal of discussion took place. I expressed my own

views, saying that, in my judgment, Genl. McClellan was the best man for the place he held known to me—that, I believed, if his sickness had not prevented he would by this time have satisfied every body in the country of his efficiency and capacity—that I thought, however, that he tasked himself too severely—that no physical or mental vigor could sustain the strains he imposed on himself, Often on the saddle nearly all day and transacting business at his rooms nearly all night—that, in my judgment, he ought to confer freely with his ablest and most experienced Generals, deriving from them the benefits which their counsels, whether accepted or rejected, would certainly impart, and communicating to them full intelligence of his own plans of action, so that, in the event of sickness or accident to himself, the movements of the army need not necessarily be interrupted or delayed. I added that, in my own opinion, no one person could discharge fitly the special duties of Commander of the Army of the Potomac, and the general duties of Commanding General of the Armies of the United States; and that Genl. McClellan, in undertaking to discharge both, had undertaken what he could not perform.

Much else was said by various gentlemen, and the discussion was concluded by the announcement by the President that he would call on Genl. McClellan, and ascertain his views in respect to the division of the commands.

"MY GENERAL IDEA OF THIS WAR": JANUARY 1862
Abraham Lincoln to Don Carlos Buell and Henry W. Halleck

With General McClellan ill, Lincoln in his role as commander-in-chief sought action from his generals in the western theater. He urged Don Carlos Buell, commander of the Department of the Ohio, to advance into Tennessee, and asked Henry W. Halleck, commander of the Department of Missouri, to support Buell with an attack on the Confederate position at Columbus, Kentucky. When Halleck replied that he was in no condition to support Buell ("I am satisfied that the authorities in Washington do not appreciate the difficulties with which we have to contend here," he wrote), the President endorsed Halleck's response: "It is exceedingly discouraging. As everywhere else, nothing can be done." Lincoln then wrote both his generals with his thoughts on the larger strategic picture, making reference to the Bull Run campaign of July 1861.

COPY—one also sent to Gen. Halleck.
Brig. Genl. Buell.   Executive Mansion,
My dear Sir: Washington, Jan. 13, 1862.
  Your despatch of yesterday is received, in which you say "I have received your letter and Gen. McClellan's; and will, at once devote all my efforts to your views, and his." In the midst of my many cares, I have not seen, or asked to see, Gen. McClellan's letter to you. For my own views, I have not offered, and do not now offer them as orders; and while I am glad to have them respectfully considered, I would blame you to follow them contrary to your own clear judgment—unless I should put them in the form of orders. As to Gen. McClellan's views, you understand your duty in regard to them better than I do. With this preliminary, I state my general idea of this war to be that we have the *greater* numbers, and the enemy has the *greater* facility of concentrating forces upon points of collision; that we must fail, unless we can find some way of making *our* advantage an over-match for *his*; and that this can only be done by menacing him with superior forces at *different* points, at the

same time; so that we can safely attack, one, or both, if he makes no change; and if he *weakens* one to *strengthen* the other, forbear to attack the strengthened one, but seize, and hold the weakened one, gaining so much. To illustrate, suppose last summer, when Winchester ran away to re-inforce Mannassas, we had forborne to attack Mannassas, but had seized and held Winchester. I mention this to illustrate, and not to criticise. I did not lose confidence in McDowell, and I think less harshly of Patterson than some others seem to. In application of the general rule I am suggesting, every particular case will have its modifying circumstances, among which the most constantly present, and most difficult to meet, will be the want of perfect knowledge of the enemies' movements. This had it's part in the Bull-Run case; but worse, in that case, was the expiration of the terms of the three months men. Applying the principle to your case, my idea is that Halleck shall menace Columbus, and "down river" generally; while you menace Bowling-Green, and East Tennessee. If the enemy shall concentrate at Bowling-Green, do not retire from his front; yet do not fight him there, either, but seize Columbus and East Tennessee, one or both, left exposed by the concentration at Bowling Green. It is matter of no small anxiety to me and one which I am sure you will not over-look, that the East Tennessee line, is so long, and over so bad a road. Yours very truly

A. LINCOLN.

WAR ORDERS: JANUARY 1862

Abraham Lincoln: *President's General War Order No. 1 and President's Special War Order No. 1*

Lincoln's efforts to start the Union war effort moving became more specific with these two orders, both of which set Washington's birthday as a target date. Special War Order No. 1, directed at General McClellan and the Army of the Potomac, was intended to execute the President's plan for turning the Confederates' position at Manassas by threatening their communications.

President's General War Order No. 1

Executive Mansion,
President's general } Washington, January 27, 1862.
War Order No. 1

Ordered that the 22nd. day of February 1862, be the day for a general movement of the Land and Naval forces of the United States against the insurgent forces.

That especially—
    The Army at & about, Fortress Monroe.
    The Army of the Potomac.
    The Army of Western Virginia
    The Army near Munfordville, Ky.
    The Army and Flotilla at Cairo.
    And a Naval force in the Gulf of Mexico, be ready for a movement on that day.

That all other forces, both Land and Naval, with their respective commanders, obey existing orders, for the time, and be ready to obey additional orders when duly given.

That the Heads of Departments, and especially the Secretaries of War and of the Navy, with all their subordinates; and the General-in-Chief, with all other commanders and subordinates, of Land and Naval forces, will severally be held to their strict and full responsibilities, for the prompt execution of this order. ABRAHAM LINCOLN

Draft of Order sent to Army & Navy Departments respectively this day. A. LINCOLN

Jan. 27. 1862.

The Secretary of War will enter this Order in his Department, and execute it to the best of his ability. A. LINCOLN
Jan. 27, 1862.

President's Special War Order No. 1

Presidents special War Order, No. 1.
Executive Mansion
Washington January 31, 1862

Ordered that all the disposable force of the Army of the Potomac, after providing safely for the defense of Washington, be formed into an expedition, for the immediate object of siezing and occupying a point upon the Rail Road South Westward of what is known of Manassas Junction, all details to be in the discretion of the general-in-chief, and the expedition to move before, or on, the 22nd. day of February next.

ABRAHAM LINCOLN

A CAMPAIGN AGAINST RICHMOND:
FEBRUARY 1862

George B. McClellan to Edwin M. Stanton

Upon receiving Special War Order No. 1, General McClellan secured Lincoln's permission "to submit in writing my objections to his plan and my reasons for preferring my own." McClellan's plan, addressed to the new secretary of war, Edwin M. Stanton, proposed to strike at the Confederate capital by way of the lower Chesapeake Bay and the Virginia Peninsula. Although his proposal was dated January 31, 1862, McClellan actually submitted it to Stanton on February 3. McClellan's plan, in modified form, would in due course be accepted, reluctantly, by the President.

Hon E M Stanton
Secty of War   Head Quarters of the Army
Sir: Washington January 31st 1862

I ask you indulgence for the following paper, rendered necessary by circumstances.

I assumed command of the troops in the vicinity of Washington on Saturday July 27 1861, 6 days after the battle of Bull Run.

I found no army to command, a mere collection of regiments cowering on the banks of the Potomac, some perfectly raw, others dispirited by their recent defeat.

Nothing of any consequence had then been done to secure the southern approaches to the Capital by means of defensive works; nothing whatever had been undertaken to defend the avenues to the city on the northern side of the Potomac.

The troops were not only undisciplined, undrilled & dispirited—they were not even placed in military positions—the city was almost in a condition to have been taken by a dash of a single regiment of cavalry.

Without one day's delay I undertook the difficult task assigned to me—the task the Hon Secty knows was given to me without my solicitation or foreknowledge. How far I have accomplished it will best be shown by the past & present. The

Capital is secure against attack—the extensive fortifications erected by the labor of our troops enable a small garrison to hold it against a numerous army; the enemy have been held in check; the State of Maryland is securely in our possession; the detached counties of Virginia are again within the pale of our laws, & all apprehension of trouble in Delaware is at an end; the enemy are confined to the positions they occupied before 21 July;—more than all this, I have now under my command a well drilled & reliable Army to which the destinies of the country may be confidently committed. This Army is young, & untried in battle, but it is animated by the highest spirit, & is capable of great deeds. That so much has been accomplished, & such an Army created in so short a time from nothing will hereafter be regarded as one of the highest glories of the Administration & the nation.

Many weeks, I may say many months, ago this Army of the Potomac was fully in condition to repel any attack;—but there is a vast difference between that & the efficiency required to enable troops to attack successfully an Army elated by victory, and entrenched in a position long since selected, studied, & fortified. In the earliest papers I submitted to the Presdt I asked for an effective movable force far exceeding the aggregate now on the banks of the Potomac—I have not the force I asked for. Even when in a subordinate position I always looked beyond the operations of the Army of the Potomac; I was never satisfied in my own mind with a barren victory, but looked to combined & decisive operations.

When I was placed in command of the Armies of the U.S. I immediately turned my attention to the whole field of operations—regarding the Army of the Potomac as only *one*, while the most important, of the masses under my command.

I confess that I did not then appreciate the absence of a general plan which had before existed, nor did I know that utter disorganization & want of preparation pervaded the western armies. I took it for granted that they were nearly, if not quite, in condition to move towards the fulfillment of my plans—I acknowledge that I made a great mistake.

I sent at once, with the approval of the Executive, officers I considered competent to command in Kentucky & Missouri—their instructions looked to prompt movements. I soon found that the labor of creation & organization had to be performed there—transportation, arms, clothing, artillery, discipline—all were wanting; these things required time to procure them; the Generals in command have done their work most creditably—but we are still delayed. I had hoped that a general advance could be made during the good weather of December—I was mistaken.

My wish was to gain possession of the Eastern Tennessee Railroads as a preliminary movement,—then to follow it up immediately by an attack on Nashville & Richmond as nearly at the same time as possible.

I have ever regarded our true policy as being that of fully preparing ourselves & then seeking for the most decisive results;—I do not wish to waste life in useless battles, but prefer to strike at the heart.

Two bases of operations seem to present themselves for the advance of the Army of the Potomac.—

I. That of Washington—its present position—involving a direct attack upon the enemy's entrenched positions at Centreville, Manassas etc, or else a movement to turn one or both flanks of those positions, or a combination of the two plans.

The relative force of the two Armies will not justify an attack on both flanks.

An attack on his left flank alone involves a long line of wagon communication & cannot prevent him from collecting for the decisive battle all the detachments now on his extreme right & left.

Should we attack his right by the line of the Occoquan & a crossing of the Potomac below the Occoquan & near his batteries, we could perhaps prevent the junction of the enemy's extreme right with his centre (we *might* destroy the former), we would remove the obstructions to the navigation of the Potomac, reduce the length of wagon transportation by establishing new depots at the nearest points of the Potomac, & strike more directly his main railway communication.

The fords of the Occoquan below the mouth of Bull Run are watched by the rebels, batteries are said to be placed on the heights in rear (concealed by the woods), & the arrangement of his troops is such that he can oppose some considerable resistance to a passage of the stream. Information has just been received to the effect that the enemy are entrenching a line of heights extending from the vicinity of Sangster's (Union Mills?) towards Evansport. Early in Jany. Sprigg's ford was occupied by Genl Rhodes with 3600 men & 8 guns; there are strong reasons for believing that Davis' Ford is occupied.

These circumstances indicate, or prove, that the enemy anticipate the movement in question & are prepared to resist it.

Assuming for the present that this operation is determined upon, it may be well to examine briefly its probable progress.

In the present state of affairs our columns (for the movement of so large a force must be made in several columns, at least 5 or 6) can reach the Accotinck without danger; during the march thence to the Occoquan our right flank becomes exposed to an attack from Fairfax Station, Sangster's & Union Mills;—this danger must be met by occupying in some force either the two first named places, or, better, the point of junction of the roads leading thence to the village of Occoquan— this occupation must be continued so long as we continue to draw supplies by the roads from this city, or until a battle is won.

The crossing of the Occoquan should be made at all the fords from Wolf's Run to the mouth, the points of crossing not being necessarily confined to the fords themselves.

Should the enemy occupy this line in force we must, with what assistance the flotilla can afford, endeavor to force the passage near the mouth, thus forcing the enemy to abandon the whole line or be taken in flank himself.

Having gained the line of the Occoquan, it would be necesary to throw a column by the shortest route to Dumfries, partly to force the enemy to abandon his batteries on the Potomac, partly to cover our left flank against an attack from the direction of Acquia, & lastly to establish our communication with the river by the best roads, & thus give us new depots.

The enemy would by this time have occupied the line of the Occoquan above Bulls Run, holding Brentsville in force & perhaps extending his lines somewhat further to the S.W.

Our next step would be to prevent the enemy from crossing the Occoquan between Bull Run & Broad Run, to fall upon our right flank while moving on Brentsville; this might be effected by occupying Baconrace Church & the cross roads near the mouth of Bull Run, or still more effectually by moving to the fords themselves & preventing him from debouching on our side. These operations would probably be resisted, & would require some time to effect them. As nearly at the same time as possible we should gain the fords necessary to our purposes above Broad Run.

Having secured our right flank it would become necessary to carry Brentsville at any cost, for we could not leave it between our right flank & main body. The final movement on the Railroad must be determined by circumstances existing at the time.

This brief sketch brings out in bold relief the great advantage possessed by the enemy in the strong central position he occupies, with roads diverging in every direction, & a strong line of defence enabling him to remain on the defensive with a small force on one flank, while he concentrates everything on the other for a decisive action. Should we place a portion of our force in front of Centreville while the rest crosses the Occoquan we commit the error of dividing our Army by a very difficult obstacle & by a distance too great to enable the two portions to support each other, should either be attacked by the masses of the enemy while the other is held in check.

I should perhaps have dwelled more decidedly on the fact that the force left near Sangster's must be allowed to remain somewhere on that side of the Occoquan, until the decisive battle is over, to cover our retreat in the event of disaster, unless it should be decided to select & entrench a new base somewhere near Dumfries—a proceeding involving much time.

After the passage of the Occoquan by the main Army, this covering force could be drawn in to a more central & less exposed position, say Brimstone Hill or nearer the Occoquan.

In this latitude the weather will for a considerable period be very uncertain, & a movement commenced in force on roads in tolerably firm condition will be liable, almost certain, to be much delayed by rains & snow. It will therefore be next to impossible to surprise the enemy, or take him at a disadvantage by rapid manoeuvres;—our slow progress will enable him to divine our purposes & take his measures accordingly.

The probability is, from the best information we possess,

that he has improved the roads leading to his lines of defence, while we must work as we advance.

Bearing in mind what has been said, & the present unprecedented & impassable condition of the roads, it will be evident that no precise period can be fixed upon for the movement on this line, nor can its duration be closely calculated; it seems certain that many weeks *may* elapse before it is possible to commence the march.

Assuming the success of this operation & the defeat of the enemy as certain, the question at once arises as to the importance of the results gained.

I think these results would be confined to the possession of the field of battle, the evacuation of the line of the upper Potomac by the enemy, & the moral effect of the victory—important results it is true, but not decisive of the war, nor securing the destruction of the enemy's main Army; for he could fall back upon other positions, & fight us again & again, should the condition of his troops permit.

If he is in no condition to fight us again out of range of the entrenchments at Richmond we would find it a very difficult & tedious matter to follow him up there—for he would destroy the railroad bridges & otherwise impede our progress through a region where the roads are as bad as they well can be; & we would probably find ourselves forced at last to change the entire theatre of war, or to seek a shorter land route to Richmond with a smaller available force & at an expenditure of much more time than were we to adopt the short line at once.

We would also have forced the enemy to concentrate his forces & perfect his defensive measures at the very points where it is desirable to strike him where least prepared.

II. The second base of operations available for the Army of the Potomac is that of the lower Chesapeake Bay, which affords the shortest possible land routes to Richmond, & strikes directly at the heart of the enemy's power in the East.

The roads in that region are passable at all seasons of the year.

The country now alluded to is much more favorable for offensive operations than that in front of Washington (which is *very* unfavorable)—much more level—more cleared land—the woods less dense—soil more sandy—the spring some two or three weeks earlier.

A movement in force on that line obliges the enemy to abandon his entrenched position at Manassas, in order to hasten to cover Richmond & Norfolk.

He *must* do this, for should he permit us to occupy Richmond his destruction can be averted only by entirely defeating us in a battle in which he must be the assailant.

This movement if successful gives us the Capital, the communications, the supplies of the rebels; Norfolk would fall; all the waters of the Chesapeake would be ours; all Virginia would be in our power; & the enemy forced to abandon Tennessee & North Carolina.

The alternatives presented to the enemy would be to beat us in a position selected by ourselves; disperse;—or pass beneath the Caudine Forks. Should we be beaten in a battle, we have a perfectly secure retreat down the Peninsula upon Fort Monroe, with our flanks perfectly secured by the fleet. During the whole movement our left flank is covered by the water, our right is secure for the reason that the enemy is too distant to reach us in time—he can only oppose us in front; we bring our fleet into full play.

After a successful battle our position would be—Burnside forming our left, Norfolk held securely, our centre connecting Burnside with Buell, both by Raleigh & Lynchburg, Buell in Eastern Tennessee & Northern Alabama, Halleck at Nashville & Memphis.

The next movement would be to connect with Sherman on the left, by reducing Wilmington & Charleston; to advance our centre into South Carolina & Georgia; to push Buell either towards Montgomery, or to unite with the main army in Georgia; to throw Halleck southward to meet the Naval Expedition at New Orleans.

We should then be in a condition to reduce at our leisure all the southern seaports; to occupy all the avenues of communication; to use the great outlet of the Mississippi; to reestablish our Govt & arms in Arkansas, Louisiana & Texas; to force the slaves to labor for our subsistence instead of that of the rebels; —to bid defiance to all foreign interference.

Such is the object I have ever had in view; this is the general plan which I have hoped to accomplish. For many long months I have labored to prepare the Army of the Potomac to play its part in the programme; from the day when I was placed in command of all our armies, I have exerted myself to place all the other armies in such a condition that they too could perform their allotted duties. Should it be determined to operate from the lower Chesapeake, the point of landing which promises the most brilliant results is Urbana on the lower Rappahannock.

This point is easily reached by vessels of heavy draught, it is neither occupied nor observed by the enemy; it is but one long march from West Point, the key to that region, & thence but two marches to Richmond.

A rapid movement from Urbana would probably cut off Magruder in the *Peninsula*, & enable us to occupy Richmond before it could be strongly reinforced. Should we fail in that we could, with the cooperation of the Navy, cross the James & throw ourselves in rear of Richmond, thus forcing the enemy to come out & attack us—for his position would be untenable, with us on the southern bank of the river.

Should circumstances render it not advisable to land at Urbana we can use Mob Jack Bay,—or—the worst coming to the worst—we can take Fort Monroe as a base, & operate with complete security, altho' with less celerity & brilliancy of results, up the Peninsula.

To reach whatever point may be selected as the base, a large amount of cheap water transportation must be collected—consisting mainly of canal boats, barges, wood boats, schooners etc towed by small steamers—all of a very different character from those required for all previous expeditions. This can certainly be accomplished within 30 days from the time the order is given.

I propose, as the best possible plan that can, in my judgment, be adopted, to select Urbana as the landing place of the first detachments. To transport by water four (4) Divisions of Infantry, with their batteries, the Regular Infty, a few wagons, one bridge train & a few squadrons of Cavalry—making the vicinity of Hooker's position the place of embarkation for as many as possible. To move the Regular Cavalry, & Reserve Artillery, the remaining bridge trains, & wagons to a point somewhere near Cape Lookout, then ferry them over the river by means of North River ferry boats, march them over to the Rappahannock (covering the movement by an Infantry force placed near Heathsville), cross the Rappahannock in a similar way.

The expense & difficulty of the movement will thus be much diminished (a saving of transportation of about 10,000 horses!), & the result none the less certain.

The concentration of the Cavalry etc in the lower counties of Maryland can be effected without exciting suspicion, & the movement made without delay from that cause.

This movement, if adopted, will not at all expose the city of Washington to danger.

The total force to be thrown upon the new line would be (according to circumstances) from 110,000 to 140,000. I hope to use the latter number, by bringing fresh troops into Washington, & still leaving it quite safe.

I fully realize that, in all projects offered, time is probably the most valuable consideration—it is my decided opinion that in that point of view the 2nd plan should be adopted. It is possible, nay highly probable, that the weather & state of the roads may be such as to delay the direct movement from Washington, with its unsatisfactory results & great risks, far beyond the time required to complete the second plan. *In the first case*, we can fix no definite time for an advance—the roads have gone from bad to worse—nothing like their present condition has ever been known here before—they are impassable at present, we are entirely at the mercy of the weather. In the second plan, we can calculate almost to a day, & with but little regard to the season.

If at the expense of 30 days delay we can gain a decisive victory which will probably end the war, it is far cheaper than to gain a battle tomorrow that produces no final results, & may require years of warfare & expenditure to follow up.

Such, I think, is precisely the difference between the two plans discussed in this long letter. A battle gained at Manassas will result merely in the possession of the field of combat—at best we can follow it up but slowly, unless we do what I now propose, viz:—change the line of operations.

On the Manassas line the rebels can, if well enough disciplined (& we have every reason to suppose that to be the case) dispute our advance, over bad roads, from position to position.

When we have gained the battle, if we do gain it, the question will at once arise—"What are we to do next?"—

It is by no means certain that we can beat them at Manassas.

On the other line I regard success as certain by all the chances of war.

We demoralize the enemy, by forcing him to abandon his prepared position for one which we have chosen, in which all is in our favor, & where success must produce immense results. My judgment as a General is clearly in favor of this project.

Nothing is *certain* in war—but all the chances are in favor of this movement.

So much am I in favor of the southern line of operations, that I would prefer the move from Fort Monroe as a base, as a certain, tho' less brilliant movement than that from Urbana, to an attack on Manassas.

I know that his Excellency the President, you & I all agree in our wishes—& that our desire is to bring this war to as prompt a close as the means in our possession will permit. I believe that the mass of the people have entire confidence in us—I am sure of it—let us then look only to the great result to be accomplished, & disregard everything else.

In conclusion I would respectfully, but firmly, advise that I may be authorized to undertake at once the movement by Urbana.

I believe that it can be carried into execution so nearly simultaneously with the final advance of Buell & Halleck that the columns will support each other.

I will stake my life, my reputation on the result—more than that, I will stake upon it the success of our cause.

I hope but little from the attack on Manassas;—my judgment is against it. Foreign complications may entirely change the state of affairs, & render very different plans necessary. In that event I will be ready to submit them.

      I am very respectfully your obedient servant
      Geo B McClellan
      Maj Genl Comdg USA

"HIS TERRIBLE SWIFT SWORD": FEBRUARY 1862

Julia Ward Howe: *The Battle Hymn of the Republic;* from Reminiscences, 1819–1899

February 1862

Julia Ward Howe, a poet and the coeditor of the Boston abolitionist newspaper *The Commonwealth*, published "The Battle Hymn of the Republic" in the *Atlantic Monthly* for February 1862. The poem was written during a visit she made to Washington, D.C., in late 1861 with her husband, the social reformer Samuel Gridley Howe, and the Republican governor of Massachusetts, John A. Andrew. Howe later recalled the circumstances of its composition in her 1899 memoir. The music of the song "John Brown's Body" was that of the hymn "Say, brothers, will you meet us?," while its words were collectively composed by the members of a Massachusetts militia battalion in the spring of 1861. Despite its stirring sentiments, the "Battle Hymn" did not replace the singing of the "John Brown" lyrics among all Union soldiers, many of whom were partial to its line "They will hang Jeff. Davis to a tree!"

BATTLE HYMN OF THE REPUBLIC.

Mine eyes have seen the glory of the coming of the
  Lord:
He is trampling out the vintage where the grapes of
  wrath are stored;
He hath loosed the fateful lightning of His terrible swift
  sword:
            His truth is marching on.

I have seen Him in the watch-fires of a hundred circling
  camps;
They have builded Him an altar in the evening dews and
  damps;
I can read His righteous sentence by the dim and flaring
  lamps:
            His day is marching on.

I have read a fiery gospel writ in burnished rows of steel:
"As ye deal with my contemners, so with you my grace shall deal;
Let the Hero, born of woman, crush the serpent with his heel,
    Since God is marching on."

He has sounded forth the trumpet that shall never call retreat;
He is sifting out the hearts of men before His judgment-seat:
Oh, be swift, my soul, to answer Him! be jubilant, my feet!
    Our God is marching on.

In the beauty of the lilies Christ was born across the sea,
With a glory in his bosom that transfigures you and me:
As he died to make men holy, let us die to make men free,
    While God is marching on.

I distinctly remember that a feeling of discouragement came over me as I drew near the city of Washington at the time already mentioned. I thought of the women of my acquaintance whose sons or husbands were fighting our great battle; the women themselves serving in the hospitals, or busying themselves with the work of the Sanitary Commission. My husband, as already said, was beyond the age of military service, my eldest son but a stripling; my youngest was a child of not more than two years. I could not leave my nursery to follow the march of our armies, neither had I the practical deftness which the preparing and packing of sanitary stores demanded. Something seemed to say to me, "You would be glad to serve, but you cannot help any one; you have nothing to give, and there is nothing for you to do." Yet, because of my sincere desire, a word was given me to say, which did strengthen the hearts of those who fought in the field and of those who languished in the prison.

We were invited, one day, to attend a review of troops at

some distance from the town. While we were engaged in watching the manœuvres, a sudden movement of the enemy necessitated immediate action. The review was discontinued, and we saw a detachment of soldiers gallop to the assistance of a small body of our men who were in imminent danger of being surrounded and cut off from retreat. The regiments remaining on the field were ordered to march to their cantonments. We returned to the city very slowly, of necessity, for the troops nearly filled the road. My dear minister was in the carriage with me, as were several other friends. To beguile the rather tedious drive, we sang from time to time snatches of the army songs so popular at that time, concluding, I think, with

"John Brown's body lies a-mouldering in the ground;
His soul is marching on."

The soldiers seemed to like this, and answered back, "Good for you!" Mr. Clarke said, "Mrs. Howe, why do you not write some good words for that stirring tune?" I replied that I had often wished to do this, but had not as yet found in my mind any leading toward it.

I went to bed that night as usual, and slept, according to my wont, quite soundly. I awoke in the gray of the morning twilight; and as I lay waiting for the dawn, the long lines of the desired poem began to twine themselves in my mind. Having thought out all the stanzas, I said to myself, "I must get up and write these verses down, lest I fall asleep again and forget them." So, with a sudden effort, I sprang out of bed, and found in the dimness an old stump of a pen which I remembered to have used the day before. I scrawled the verses almost without looking at the paper. I had learned to do this when, on previous occasions, attacks of versification had visited me in the night, and I feared to have recourse to a light lest I should wake the baby, who slept near me. I was always obliged to decipher my scrawl before another night should intervene, as it was only legible while the matter was fresh in my mind. At this time, having completed my writing, I returned to bed and fell asleep, saying to myself, "I like this better than most things that I have written."

The poem, which was soon after published in the "Atlantic Monthly," was somewhat praised on its appearance, but the vicissitudes of the war so engrossed public attention that small heed was taken of literary matters. I knew, and was content to know, that the poem soon found its way to the camps, as I heard from time to time of its being sung in chorus by the soldiers.

A GENERAL IS ARRESTED:
WASHINGTON, D.C., FEBRUARY 1862

The New York Times: An Important Arrest; The Ball's Bluff Disaster— Gen. McClellan and Gen. Stone

February 11, 1862; April 12, 1863

On October 21, 1861, several Union regiments crossed the Potomac upriver from Washington in a failed attempt to dislodge Confederate troops from Leesburg, Virginia. The battle of Ball's Bluff cost the Union more than 900 men killed, wounded, and missing; among the dead was Colonel Edward D. Baker, a serving Republican senator from Oregon and a friend of President Lincoln. In investigating the defeat, the Joint Committee on the Conduct of the War heard testimony—all of it hearsay and much of it perjured—impugning not the competence but the loyalty to Brigadier General Charles P. Stone, Union commander in the battle. In reporting Stone's arrest, the *Times* correspondent based his story on leaks of supposedly secret testimony supplied him by the committee. The damning testimony against Stone by "officers and men under his command" was in fact a conspiracy, engineered by soldiers whom Stone had charged with "misbehavior before the enemy." Secretary of War Stanton ordered Stone's arrest, and he was held in military prisons, without trial or even charges, for more than six months. He was only released in August 1862. When the committee's Ball's Bluff testimony was published a year later, a *Times* editorial took a new stance on the Stone case. A vindictive Stanton denied Stone important commands and dogged his footsteps until he resigned his commission in 1864.

AN IMPORTANT ARREST.

Gen. Stone Charged with Treason,
and Confined in Fort Lafayette.

NATURE OF THE CHARGES AGAINST HIM.

Misbehavior at the Battle of Ball's Bluff—
Complicity with the Enemy, and Treachery.

WASHINGTON, Monday, Feb. 10.

Gen. STONE was arrested on Sunday morning, at 2 o'clock, by order of the War Department, by a guard under the immediate command of Brig.-Gen. SYKES, of the Provost-Marshal's force, and sent to Fort Lafayette by the afternoon train. The charge against him is understood to be *treasonable complicity with the rebels* in the affair at Ball's Bluff and subsequently. He was lately before the Joint Committee on the Conduct of the War, to answer charges made against him in reference to this, and also to some other later and equally suspicious actions; and it is owing to the revelations made by himself and others before the Committee that he has been deprived of his command and committed to prison.

The following is the substance of the charges under which he was arrested:

1. For misbehavior at the battle of Ball's Bluff.

2. For holding correspondence with the enemy before and since the battle of Ball's Bluff, and receiving visits from rebel officers in his camp.

3. For treacherously suffering the enemy to build a fort or strong work, since the battle of Ball's Bluff, under his guns, without molestation.

4. For a treacherous design to expose his force to capture and destruction by the enemy, under pretence of orders for a movement from the Commanding-General, which had not been given.

A Court-martial will be speedily ordered.

The arrest excites great commotion in public circles here; and certain military functionaries are also greatly perturbed about it. It is rumored that still other arrests will be made immediately. Secretary STANTON has the spirit, the courage, and the determination, to strangle treason, or complicity with treason, wherever and in whomsoever it is discovered.

It is notable that STONE's strongest friends here are Secessionists and Semi-Secessionists of both sexes, and his strongest enemies, or rather those who make the most serious charges against him, are the officers and men under his command. The searching investigation that has been made into his case was owing, in great measure, to the influence brought to bear from a source whence it would seem none could come—his own men. Political influence or personal rivalry have had nothing whatever to do with the case.

Gen. STONE's antecedents are good, bad and dubious. He is a native of Massachusetts, a graduate and afterwards a Professor of Ethics in West Point, served in the Ordnance Corps, was a Lieutenant in command of a battery at the siege of Vera Cruz, was brevetted for gallant conduct at Molino del Rey, and served on the entire line of operations from Vera Cruz to the City of Mexico, under the eye of Gen. SCOTT, who has always expressed the highest confidence in his loyalty and military skill. In 1856 he resigned from the army and went into civil life. He became interested in certain land speculations (known as the Stone-Isham Purchase) in the States of Northern Mexico, Sonora and Chihuahua, but charges of fraud, if not of fillibustering, were made against him by the Mexican officials, and, while engaged with a strong party in surveying his pretended purchase, he was driven from Mexico by the authorities. He tried to raise a sufficient force to hold the land against the Mexicans; but failing, he came here in the early part of the Buchanan *regime*, to try and get the Government to send troops to the Mexican frontier, or otherwise make a demonstration in his favor. It was believed here that he had made, or was going to make, a good deal of money from this Mexican speculation, but not much was known about his operations. It was while staying here, and still engaged in this, as well as other jobs, that the rebellion broke out. On the first of last year, upon the recommendation of Gen. SCOTT, he was appointed to organize the militia of the District of Columbia; and while Washington was yet trembling in fear of the advent of the rebels, his action seemed both loyal and efficient. In May he was appointed

Colonel of the Fourteenth Infantry, and shortly after was made a Brigadier-General, and placed in command of a column under Gen. BANKS, on the Upper Potomac. It was while in this position, and in his command, that the horrible tragedy of Ball's Bluff was enacted. It has been attempted by some to place the responsibility for this affair on the shoulders of the gallant BAKER; but he can no more be held responsible than any of the private soldiers who, like himself, were slaughtered. The rebel General who commanded on that occasion, it will be remembered, attempted to exculpate STONE by giving publicity to certain orders and documents found on the battlefield, but, unfortunately, he did not publish *all* the documents he found. When Senator SUMNER recently referred to STONE in Congress, in connection with this affair, STONE sent the Senator an insulting letter, which has never been published, but in which, it is said, he tried to drag the Senator into a duel. It certainly seems impossible to explain certain circumstances connected with that murderous affair on the Upper Potomac on any other ground than that of treasonable complicity with the rebels in some high quarter.

Col. GORMAN, of the Minnesota First, has been put in temporary command of STONE'S column. He at once proceeded to shell the rebels away from an earthwork they were throwing up on the opposite side of the Potomac, at Edwards' Ferry; he arrested a known rebel spy, whom Gen. STONE had defended, and took other active measures against the rebels in the vicinity of his command. Some of the parties formerly near to Gen. STONE have also been placed under surveillance.

The facts in STONE'S career and his military action for the last six months certainly require explanation, particularly as regards the Ball's Bluff affair, (the facts in which are so familiar to the public,) and also in reference to still later and very suspicious communications with the enemy across the river. His case, it is believed, will speedily pass under the jurisdiction of a military tribunal.

The facts brought to light in Gen. STONE'S case, and the necessary action consequent upon their discovery, have greatly affected Gen. MCCLELLAN, both in body and spirit. Visitors who called upon him on Monday learned that he was confined to his room, with his physician in attendance, and were consequently excluded.

February 11, 1862

THE BALL'S BLUFF DISASTER— GEN. McCLELLAN AND GEN. STONE.

No event in the history of the war has so shocked the public mind as the needless exposure of 1,700 of our soldiers to the murderous onslaught of 4,000 of the enemy at Ball's Bluff, in October of the first year. Nor has any event remained in so much obscurity. All that the people have known of it is that "somebody blundered." But who it was, and why he has never been brought to account, has been a standing puzzle from that day to the present. The dealings with Gen. STONE only complicated the enigma. If he was the man in fault, why should he have been retained in the same command for three months afterward without rebuke, or any diminution of trust? When, afterward, he was so suddenly arrested, why was he suffered to lie in Fort Lafayette nearly a year without trial, or the slightest opportunity of meeting the charges against him? Why was he finally so suddenly released? And why, ever since, has he in vain sought a Court-martial or a Court of Inquiry? These questions have exercised the public mind not a little, but to no purpose. The whole chapter, from beginning to end, has been as impenetrable as the veil of Isis. There was *something* behind, but that was all that could be made out.

The Report of the Committee on the Conduct of the War, as published by us on Friday, has done much toward dispelling the mystery. On some interesting points it is not conclusive, because of conflict of testimony; but it pretty effectually clears up the matters of chief concern. The Committee observe the same impartial course in their report of this affair as in their other reports—confining themselves strictly to a digest of the evidence, avoiding both deductions and comments. But the evidence on the principal points is so specific that it must make the same impression on all fair minds.

It is made apparent that *the prime cause of the disastrous movement was a misconception on the part of Gen. Stone, produced by the default of Gen. McClellan.* The day before the battle (Sunday) Gen. STONE was informed by telegraph from Gen. MCCLELLAN in Washington, that a large force under Gen. MCCALL was at Drainsville, was at that time "sending out heavy reconnoissances in all directions from that point." Gen. STONE was directed in this telegram "to keep a good lookout upon Leesburgh, to see if this movement has the effect to drive them (the rebels) away;" and it was added, "perhaps a slight demonstration on your part would have the effect to move them." Gen. STONE on the same day started a second reconnoitering party toward Leesburgh, and immediately telegraphed the fact to Gen. MCCLELLAN. To that telegram no reply was made; and Gen. STONE was left in entire ignorance of the fact that Gen. MCCALL'S force was ordered by Gen. MCCLELLAN *back* from Drainsville on Monday morning. That fact did not become known to him until Monday night, *after* the battle. The consequence was that Gen. STONE supposed, on the morning of the battle—and had reason to suppose—that Leesburgh was to be threatened on the other side by Gen. MCCALL'S regiments. It was this error, for which he was not responsible, that made the movement across the river, with such insufficient means for retreat, an act of ruinous rashness, instead of being, what it would have been otherwise, a perfectly safe and highly serviceable operation, in full pursuance of the original orders.

It is also made quite apparent that the *movement was approved by McClellan* both at the time and afterward. According to the evidence, Gen. STONE apprised him on the day of the battle that the crossing had been made—received from him a congratulatory dispatch in return, and was directed by him after the battle to hold Edwards' Ferry and "all the ground you now have on the Virginia shore," by intrenching, if necessary, with a promise of reinforcements. This testimony, in conjunction with the fact that Gen. STONE was retained in his full command for three months afterward, would seem to forbid all doubt that he was considered at headquarters to have been not at all in fault.

Again, it is shown that *the primary responsibility of Gen. Stone's arrest and long confinement without trial belongs to Gen. McClellan.* He himself admits, in his own testimony, that Gen.

STONE was arrested and consigned to Fort Lafayette at his instance. Previous to his arrest Gen. STONE was summoned before the War Committee to testify in regard to the Ball's Bluff affair, but his testimony was very indefinite and unsatisfactory. It now appears, from evidence given by him before the Committee six weeks ago, that his reserve at the first examination was owing to instructions which he had received at Gen. MCCLELLAN'S headquarters on the same morning, that "officers giving testimony before the Committee should not state, *without his authority*, anything regarding his plans, his orders for the movements of troops, or his orders concerning the position of troops;" and that this was understood to apply to past orders and transactions as well as future. No authority to make such disclosures was ever accorded by Gen. MCCLELLAN. In consequence, Gen. STONE could not vindicate himself before the Committee. He was sent directly afterwards to Fort Lafayette. His urgent appeal for a military trial, and those of his friends to the same end, were unheeded throughout his incarceration of eleven months; and, to the very last day of Gen. MCCLELLAN'S command, he could get no hearing whatever. We consider the War Department to have been greatly to blame for consenting to this thing. It did so, as was announced at the time, on the ground that the trial could not be had without detriment to the campaigns then in progress, and Gen. MCCLELLAN may have so represented; but this ought not to have been regarded. The complete investigation should have been promptly made, whatever Gen. MCCLELLAN might have thought of it, or however he might have suffered from it. As it is, Gen. STONE has sustained a most flagrant wrong—a wrong which will probably stand as the very worst blot on the National side in the history of the war.

We await with great interest the publication of the entire evidence taken by the Committee relative to the Ball's Bluff calamity, and the subsequent treatment of Gen. STONE. If it shall in any respect present Gen. MCCLELLAN in a less unfavorable light, we shall note the fact with pleasure.

April 12, 1863

ATTACK ON FORT DONELSON:
TENNESSEE, FEBRUARY 1862

Lew Wallace: *from* An Autobiography

It was in the western theater that the Union war machine finally moved. In September 1861 Brigadier General Ulysses S. Grant took command of the Union forces at Cairo, Illinois, at the junction of the Mississippi and Ohio. During the winter he and Flag Officer Andrew H. Foote, commanding the gunboat flotilla based at Cairo, made plans to gain control of the Tennessee and Cumberland rivers, which led into the heart of the Confederacy. Early in February Grant opened the campaign, his targets Forts Henry and Donelson, guarding the two rivers just below the Kentucky-Tennessee border. On February 6 Flag Officer Foote's gunboats bombarded Fort Henry, on the Tennessee, into surrender. Fort Donelson, on the Cumberland, proved a harder nut to crack. On February 15 the Confederates punched a hole in Grant's investing lines. Union division commander Wallace, author of the celebrated novel *Ben-Hur*, described the fighting in his 1906 autobiography.

I HAD long since learned that proud men in the throes of ill-fortune dislike to have the idle and curious make spectacles of them; especially do they hate condolence; wherefore I refrained from going to take a look at the first division reorganizing in my rear. It seemed to me a good time to attend to my own business.

However, as the town clocks in cities of the country endowed with such luxuries were getting ready to strike three, an officer rode up from the rear, and hearing him ask for me, I went to him.

"Are you General Wallace?" he asked.

"I am—at your service."

"Well," he said, "I am—"

Just then a round shot from the fort, aimed lower than usual, passed, it really seemed, not more than a yard above us. We both "ducked" to it, and when I raised my head almost from my horse's neck the stranger was doing himself the same service. We looked at each other, and it was impossible not to laugh.

"I don't know," he said, jocularly, "in what school you were taught to bow, but that one was well done."

"Yes," I retorted, "mine was nearly as low as yours."

To which he added, "They were both behind time"; meaning that they were given after the ball had passed.

Then he took up his fractured remark.

"I was about to say I am General McClernand."

Now I had known General John A. McClernand by reputation as a Democratic politician. His speeches in Congress had been frequent and creditable. My predilections were all on his side, and I ran him over with interest. His face was agreeable, though weather-beaten and unshaven. The snow light gave his eyes a severe squint. His head was covered with one of the abominable regulation wool hats hooked up at one side. Besides being thin and slightly under average height, he was at further disadvantage by sitting too far back in his saddle, and stooping. We shook hands, and he was giving me the details of his battle of the morning, when General Grant joined us, mounted, and attended by a single orderly. I noticed papers in General Grant's right hand which had the appearance of telegrams, and that he seemed irritated and bothered trying to keep some active feeling down. Of course McClernand and I saluted, and gave him instant attention.

From the hollow in front of my position a dropping fire kept ascending.

"Pickets?" General Grant asked.

"My pickets," I replied.

"They will get over that afterwhile," he remarked; then, seriously: "Foote must go to Cairo, taking his iron-clads, some of which are seriously damaged. We will have to await his return; meantime, our line must be retired out of range from the fort."

He stopped. The idea was detestable to him—bitterly so, and, seeing it, I asked to make a suggestion.

He turned to me with a questioning look.

"We have nobody on the right now," I said, "and the road to Clarksville is open. If we retire the line at all, it will be giving the enemy an opportunity to get away to-night with all he has."

Grant's face, already congested with cold, reddened perceptibly, and his lower jaw set upon the other. Without a word, he looked at McClernand, who began to explain. Grant interrupted him.

"Gentlemen," he said, "that road must be recovered before night." Gripping the papers in his hand—I heard them crinkle—he continued: "I will go to Smith now. At the sound of your fire, he will support you with an attack on his side."

Thereupon he turned his horse and rode off at an ordinary trot, while following him with my eyes, wondering at the simplicity of the words in a matter involving so much, I saw Colonel Morgan L. Smith coming up the road beyond him at the head of some troops, and guessed who they were.

General McClernand then spoke. "The road ought to be recovered—Grant is right about that. But, Wallace, you know I am not ready to undertake it."

The significance of the remark was plain. The road in question ran through the position his division had occupied in the morning; and feeling now that General Grant had really been addressing him, General McClernand was asking me to take the proposed task off his hands. I thought rapidly—of my division, by Cruft's return intact, and reinforced—of the Eleventh Indiana and the Eighth Missouri so opportunely arrived—of Colonel Morgan L. Smith—of the order holding me strictly to the defensive now released.

"Did you send to General Charles F. Smith for assistance?" I asked McClernand.

"Yes."

"Well, I see some troops coming, ordered probably to report to you; if they are, and you will direct the officer commanding to report to me, I will try recovery of the road."

At McClernand's request one of my aides—Ross, I think—rode at speed to meet Colonel Morgan L. Smith. Returning, he said, "It is Colonel Smith from General Charles F. Smith, ordered to report to General McClernand."

"Go back, then," said McClernand, "and tell the colonel that I request him to report to General Wallace."

Whereupon I said: "It is getting late, and what is done must be before night. If you will excuse me, I will go at it."

"Certainly," McClernand replied, adding, "I have two or three regiments in order under Colonel Ross, of my division, whom you may find useful."

"All right; send them on."

And as General McClernand left me, I sent to Colonel Smith directing him to halt his regiments behind the battery; with my staff, I then set out to see as much as possible of the ground to be recovered, and decide how best to arrange the attack. My horse objected to the dead men still lying in the road; but getting past them, the hill dipped down into a hollow of width and depth. At the left there was a field; all else appeared thinly covered with scattered trees. The pickets in the hollow were maintaining a lively fusillade, so I turned into the field. I could then see the road ran off diagonally to the right. A bluff rose in front of me partially denuded, and on top of it Confederate soldiers were visible walking about and blanketed. Off to the left the bluff flattened as it went. In that direction I also saw a flag not the stars and stripes, and guessed that the fort lay in studied contraction under it. I saw, too, a little branch winding through the hollow, and thought of my poor horse, then two days without water. The men keeping the thither height caught sight of my party, and interrupted me in the study of their position. Their bullets fell all around us. One cut a lock out of the mane of a horse of one of my orderlies. But I had what we came for, and got away, nobody hurt.

Upon my rejoining them at the battery, the old regiments (Eighth and Eleventh) cheered me; whereat the fort opened, firing harmlessly at the sound. The Eleventh, from their stacked arms, crowded around John—"Old Bailey," they called him—and filling a capful of crumbled crackers, some of them fed him what he would eat. They would have given him drink from their canteens had there been a vessel at hand to hold the water.

While that went on, I got my orders off. Cruft was told, by messenger, to take his brigade down into the hollow, and form line at the foot of the hill held by the Confederates, his left resting on the Wynne's Ferry road. When in position he was to notify me.

Smith was informed of what I have called the bluff, and told that it was to be his point of attack—that he was to conduct the main attack, supported by Cruft on his right and by Ross on the left, and that he was to make the ascent in column of regiments.

Thayer I directed to keep his present position, holding his brigade in reserve with the battery.

By-and-by Colonel Ross—he of Illinois—came up, bringing the Seventeenth and Forty-ninth Illinois regiments that had behaved with distinction in Colonel Morrison's misassault of the 14th. To him I explained that his position would be on the left of the main attack as a support.

I also gave notice to Smith and Ross that I would personally put them in position.

When these preliminaries were disposed of, I looked at the sun and judged that there were at least two hours left me for the operation.

While waiting to hear from Cruft, I chaffed with the old regiments. Of the Eighth Missouri I wanted to know at what hotel they had put up for the night.

"At the Lindell, of course," one of them responded.

"How were the accommodations?"

"Cold, but cheap."

This excited a great laugh.

Halting in front of the Eleventh, I said: "You fellows have been swearing for a long time that I would never get you into a fight. It's here now. What have you to say?"

A spokesman answered: "We're ready. *Let her rip!*"

Very un-Napoleonic, but very American.

Then heavy firing arose out of the hollow, and soon afterwards a man galloped up the hill to tell me that Colonel Cruft was in position, his left on the road.

"It is time to move," I said to Smith.

"Wait until I light a fresh cigar."

That done, and Colonel Ross told to follow, we set off down the road. Hardly had Smith, with whom I was riding, got halfway across the hollow, going straight for the bluff, when a fire ran along the top of it and bullets zipped angrily through the trees, showering us with leaves and twigs. To reply would have required a halt. At the foot of the ascent I left my Missouri friend, saying, "Try the Zouave on them, colonel, and remember to deploy McGinnis when you are nearly up."

Colonel Ross, to whom I rode next, had deployed his command. Going with him until clear of Smith's ground, I asked, "You understand your part, colonel?"

"Yes," he said, "it is to take care of the left of the main attack."

It took me but a moment to get to Cruft, who was exchanging a ragged fire with the enemy above him.

"Colonel Smith is next you on the left," I said to him. "Keep a little behind his line, and when you have cleared the hill, swing left towards the fort, pivoting on him."

I hurried then to the open field spoken of; and by the time I reached it, selected a stand-point for general oversight, and adjusted my field-glass, the advance had become general where Ross and Cruft were ascending slowly, inch by inch, the musketry had risen in measure, and the trees stood half veiled in a smoke momentarily deepening.

Presently my glass settled on Colonel Morgan L. Smith and the climb in his front, which I judged of three hundred short steps. In the patches of snow on the bluffy breast I also noticed some clumps of shrubs and a few trees, and here and there what appeared to be outcropping of rock. The disadvantages were obvious; yet, counting them as odds in the scale of chances, they were not enough to shake my confidence in the outcome, for there were advantages to be taken into the account—among them the Zouave training of both the regiments, meaning that they were nimble on their hands and knees far beyond the ordinary infantrymen, that they could load on their backs and fire with precision on their bellies, and were instinctively observant of order in the midst of disorder. Indeed, *purpose* with them answered all the ends of alignment elbow to elbow.

While making these observations my attention was drawn off by musketry blent with the pounding of artillery in the distance over at the left. It was General Charles F. Smith's supporting attack as promised by General Grant. Then it came to me suddenly that the crisis of the great adventure was on the army, and that as it went the victory would go. A feverish anxiety struck me. My tongue and throat grew dry and parched. I have the feeling now even as I write, such power have incidents at times to stamp themselves on memory.

Returning then to Colonel Smith, I saw skirmishers spring out and cover the front of his column. To my astonishment I also saw the man himself on horseback behind his foremost regiment, bent on riding up the hill—a perilous feat under the most favorable circumstances.*

I would like to describe the ascension of the height by the regiments under Smith, but cannot, for, take it all in all, it was the most extraordinary feat of arms I ever beheld. In the way of suggestion merely, the firing from the top was marked by lulls and furious outbursts. In the outbursts the assailants fell to their hands and knees, and took to crawling, while in the lulls—occasioned by smoke settling so thickly in front of the defenders that they were bothered in taking aim—yards of space were gained by rushes. And these were the spectacles impossible of description. To get an idea of them the reader must think of nearly two thousand vigorous men simultaneously squirming or dashing up the breast of a steep hill slippery with frost, in appearance so many black gnomes burrowing in a cloud of flying leaves and dirty snow. As they climbed on the alignment with which they started became loose and looser until half-way up it seemed utterly lost. There was no firing, of course, except by the skirmishers, and no cheering, not a voice save of officers in exhortation. Occasionally we heard Smith or McGinnis, but most frequently the enemy flinging taunts on the laborers below. "Hi, hi, there, you damned Yanks! Why don't you come up? What are you waiting for?"

They were nearing the top, probably a third of the distance remaining, when the Eleventh, in loose array as it was, rushed by the left flank out of column. They stumbled, and slipped, and fell down, but presently brought up, and faced front, having uncovered the Eighth. To get into line with the latter cost but a moment. About the same time I saw the skirmishers drop and roll out of sight, leaving the line of fire unobstructed. A furious outbreak from the enemy and both regiments sank

---

*I asked Colonel Smith afterwards what he meant by riding. He gave me a characteristic reply. "I thought the sight of me would encourage the boys." In further illustration of the man under fire, a bullet cut his cigar off close to his lips. "Here," he shouted, "one of you fellows bring me a match." The match was brought, and, lighting a fresh cigar, he spurred on and up.

down, and on their bellies half buried in snow delivered their first ragged volley. The next I saw of them they were advancing on their hands and knees. That they would win was no longer a question.

I gave a glance in Cruft's direction and another to Ross. Both were well up in their sections of attack. Just then some one near by broke into a laugh, and called out, "Look there!"

"Where?" I asked, not relishing the diversion.

A party of surgeon's assistants, six or eight in number, seeing us in the field, and thinking it a safe place, started to come across. A shower of bullets overtook them, and when my eyes reached them they were snuggling in the snow behind the kits they carried. And when I remembered how thin the kits were, nothing but oil-cloth, and not more resistant of a minié-ball than tissue-paper, I excused the laugh by joining in it.

Another look towards Cruft, another to Ross, then a brief study of Smith's forlorn hope, by that time nearly to its goal, and I took action.

Regaining the road, I hastened into the hollow, and when about half-way across it noticed a slackening of the enemy's fire; then, hardly a minute elapsing, it ceased entirely. The meaning was unmistakable. We had won! Calling Kneffler, I told him to go to General McClernand and tell him we were on the hill, and that he would oblige me if his artillery did not fire in our direction.

In these moves my horse had answered me readily but with his head down—a thing that had not happened before. The other horses of the company were worse off. There was need for me up on the height, but we stopped by the little brook and broke through the ice. While the poor brutes were drinking greedily, Colonel Webster came to me.

"General Grant sends me," he said, "to tell you to retire your command out of range of the fort and throw up light intrenchments. He thinks it best to wait for reinforcements."

I gave a thought to the position just recovered, with loss unknown, and asked the colonel, "Does the general know that we have retaken the road lost in the morning?"

"I think not," he replied.

"Oh, well! Give him my compliments, colonel, and tell him *I have received the order.*"

Webster gave me a sharp look and left me. I had resolved to disobey the direction, and he saw it, and justified me without saying so—as did General Grant subsequently.

THE SUN was just going down when, with my staff, I rode on to the height just won. To my eager search for what of war and combat it had to offer there was at first nothing which one may not find in any neglected woods pasture; only the air was heavy with the sulphurous smell of powder burned and burning, and through the thin assemblage of trees there went an advancing line of men stretching right and left out of sight. My first point was to catch that line.

The enemy had not waited the coming up of the Yanks. His main body had retired towards his works, and the three commands, Cruft's, Ross's, and Smith's, with just enough resistance before them to keep their blood up, were pushing forward at a pace calling for energetic action if they were to be brought to a halt. That done, however, the three were closed on the centre; then, skirmishers being thrown to the front, we advanced slowly and cautiously.

It was not long until we came on the aftermath of General McClernand's morning struggle. Dead men, not all of them ours, were lying in their beds of blood-stained snow exactly as they had fallen. And the wounded were there also. These, fast as come upon, were given drink and covered with blankets, but left to be picked up later on; and there was no distinction shown between the blue and the gray. The wonder was to find any of them alive.

While following the line I saw a man sitting against a stump in a position natural as life. Besides the Confederate homespun of which his clothes were made, he sported a coon-skin cap with the tail of the animal for plume. His eyes were wide open and there was a broad grin on his face. I would have sworn the look and grin were at me, and, stopping, I spoke to an orderly.

"Find out what that fellow means by grinning that way. If he answers decently, help him."

The orderly dismounted and shook the man, then said, "Why he's dead, sir."

"That can't be. See where he's hit."

The cap when taken off brought away with it a mass that sickened us. A small bullet—from a revolver, probably—had gone through the inner corner of his eye leaving no visible wound, but the whole back of the head was blown off and the skull entirely emptied.

On a little farther we rode over the body of a Confederate lying on his back spread-eagle fashion. A gun clutched in his hand arrested me.

"Get that gun," I said, and one of my men jumped down for it.

It is in my study now, a handsomely mounted, muzzle-loading, old-style squirrel rifle. Sometimes I take it out to try at a mark, when, as a souvenir, it strikes me with one drawback —touching it is to revive the memory of its owner looking up at the sky from his sheet of crimson snow; and that he brought the piece to the field with him intending to kill Yankees as he was in the habit of killing long-tailed rodents does not always suffice to allay the shiver it excites.

It is to be remembered that, in common with my whole command, I was profoundly ignorant of the topography of the locality. That we were moving in the direction of the fort I knew rather as a surmise than a fact. The skirmishers kept up their fire; otherwise the silence impressed me as suspicious. Once I heard the report of a great gun in the distance, and shortly a shell of half-bushel proportions went with a locomotive's scream through the tree-tops; whereupon we knew ourselves in the line of fire from the gun-boats in the river. Disagreeable—yes, vastly so—but there was no help for it. Right after—indeed, as if the unearthly scream of the big shell had been an accepted signal—the holders of the fort awoke, and set their guns to work—how many I had no means of judging.

Through the woods then there sped a peculiar short-stop whistling; nor was there need of one of greater experience in battle to tell us that we were objects of search by cannister and possibly grape-shot. Fragments of the limbs above us rattled down, and occasionally—the thing of greatest impression upon me—a sharp resound, like the cracking of green timber in a zero night, rang through the woods; and that we also instinctively knew to be bullets of iron embedding themselves in some near-by tree-trunks.

Now, as I have no wish to take credit not strictly my due, the effect of this visitation startled me—the more so as it came in the nature of a surprise. I asked myself, however, "Where are we going?" And as the answer did not come readily, I made haste to order another halt.

It happened that my position at the moment was behind Cruft's brigade in what I took to be the road to Charlotte, also the object of anxious solicitude. Making way through the halted line, the situation revealed itself. There, not farther than three hundred yards, a low embankment stretched off on both sides, and behind it, in the background, rose an elaborate earthen pile which a drooping flag on a tall, white staff told me was Fort Donelson proper. Some field-pieces behind the low intrenchment were doing the firing, supported by men lying in the ditch. The heads of these bobbed up and down; and every time one of them bobbed up it was to let loose a streak of brilliant flame, with a keen report and a rising curl of smoke as close attendants. In front of the outwork far extending were our skirmishers behind stumps and logs, and in every depression affording cover, and they, too, were shooting. The interval of separation between the enemies ranged from eighty yards to a hundred and fifty.

The scene was stirring; but it must not be thought it held me long—far from it. While I looked, a sense of responsibility touched me with a distinct shock. What next?

Two things were possible; to continue on or go back out of range. The first meant an assault, and I doubted my authority to go so far. It seemed a step within the province of the commander. Perhaps he was not ready to order it. To be successful, moreover, there was need of support, otherwise the whole garrison could be concentrated against me. So, resolving the skirmishers as they were into a grand guard, Colonel Morgan L. Smith in charge, I retired the line five or six hundred yards.

There was nothing for us then but another night in bivouac without fires, and nothing to eat but crackers; literally suffering from the pinch of hunger added to misery from the pinch of cold. Yet I did not hear a murmur. This, I think, because there was not a soldier there so ignorant as not to know the necessity of keeping a tight grip upon our position.

With the advent of darkness the gun practice ceased, and later even the pickets quit annoying one another. Then silence, and a February night, with stars of pitiless serenity, and a wind not to be better described than as a marrow-searcher.

FORT DONELSON SURRENDERS:
TENNESSEE, FEBRUARY 1862

John Kennerly Farris to Mary Farris

The repulse of the Confederate counterattack on February 15 caused Brigadier General Simon B. Buckner, the commander of the Fort Donelson garrison, to ask Grant for surrender terms, eliciting the soon-to-be-famous reply: "No terms except an unconditional and immediate surrender can be accepted. I propose to move immediately upon your works." Buckner and 12,000 Confederates surrendered on February 16, giving the North its first great victory of the war. The fall of Fort Henry allowed Union gunboats to steam up the Tennessee as far as Muscle Shoals in northern Alabama, while the surrender of Fort Donelson gave Grant control of the Cumberland River and forced the Confederate evacuation of Nashville. Among the Southerners who surrendered at Fort Donelson was John Kennerly Farris, a physician serving with the 41st Tennessee Infantry. He wrote to his wife in the fall of 1862 after being freed in a prisoner exchange. Farris's mention of "Forest Cavalry" near the end of his narrative refers to Lieutenant Colonel Nathan Bedford Forrest, who refused to surrender and slipped away with his men to fight many another day.

───────────

Camp Cold Water near Holly Springs, Misissippi
Friday, October 31, 1862

Well Mary,

I have several times thought I would give you a brief history of my time at Ft. Donnelson and how I hapened to get there.

Thursday, Feb. 13th, 1862. I was in the City of Nashville with some 16 or 20 of our Regt. when I heard the fight had begun at Ft. Donnelson and, knowing our Regt. was there, I was very anxious to be with them—so I went to Lieut. Wilhoit who was in command of the detachment of our Regt., and I believe the detachment of all the Regts. which belonged to Gen. Buckners command, and asked him for an order to rejoin the Regt. He told me he could not give me one without laying himself liable as I was the only Physician with him, or under his command.

This troubled me a good deal and I became anxious to be

with them, and studied about an hour how I would manage to get to the Regt. and the propriety of leaving without an order. Suddenly an idea struck me that I might get an order from the Commander of the Post at Nashville, who I allowed would out rank Lieut. Wilhoit and make me safe in leaving. By enquiring for his quarters, I found him without any difficulty and told him how I was situated there and, further, that I had sent all the sick under my charge to the Hospittle and was there idle and thought my services might be demanded at Ft. Donnelson and I desired to go there. Without returning a word he wrote me a pass down there and told me to take the first boat. I immediately returned to my quarters, took my napsack from my trunk, with a suit of clothes, went down to the River and got abord of a little job boat preparing to leave for Ft. Donnelson.

This was 8 o'clock a.m. The boat was soon ready to start, but was found to be fast upon a pile of iron which the water had covered. They worked to get it off untill two o'clock, apparently to no effect. I grew tired, got off the boat and gave out going, for I was suffering considerably with Rheumatic pains in my shoulders and concluded that I might be more in the way than otherwise. I strolled over town untill nearly sunset when I again concluded that I would go down to the Ft. anyway if I could get off. So I went down to the River again and found the boat off the iron and about ready to start. I got abord, and in a very short time the boat began its move but unfortunately washed down against an old boat which was under repair and lodged against it.

There we remained untill 8 o'clock p.m. when we got clear and started down the River. The little thing was so crowded with passengers that her cabin would not hold over one-fourth of us. So the remainder had to take passage on her decks where we had liked to have frozen during the night; could get neither supper or breakfast Friday morning. Friday about 1 o'clock p.m. we got down to Clarksville. There I got off the uncomfortable little job Boat and got on the *Reunion*, a nice and comfortable boat. We there learned that they were still fighting at Dover. This made all apparently anxious to get on down.

We did not stay there long but went on down the River. When we got in some ten or twelve miles of Dover, we stoped and took on wood enough to pile all round on lower deck to protect the hands from the balls of the enemy, as we did not know but what the boat would be shot into. About dark we landed at Dover. Everything was quiet. The two contending forces were as still as though they had been friends almost. About 10 o'clock in the night I found our Regt. and found the boys nearly worn out with fasting, fatigue and cold. They had not a tent and scarcly a fire. Some were lying on the snow wrapt in their blankets asleep. Some were sitting round a few coals of fire, and some at one thing and some another.

I was very hungry, and asked them for something to eat, as I had eaten but a snack since Thursday morning. They told me they had nothing, nor had had in some time. But one of the boys had a little parched coffee in his pocket, which he gave to me and which I pounded in a tin cup the best I could with an old chunk, and borrowed a coffee pot and made it full of coffee for five of us, who had constructed a little fire barely sufficient to boil a coffee pot of water. We drank the coffee, which seemed to do us a good deal of good, though it was barely fit to drink and would not at all been used under ordinary circumstances.

We five sit around the same little fire untill 3 o'clock a.m. of Saturday talking of the previous and expected fight. All through the night we could once and a while hear the pickets shooting at each other, and some very close to us. At 3 o'clock the Officers came round and gave orders for the men to get in line, for it was thought we might be attacked in a short time. Notwithstanding the ground was covered with snow and the weather very cold, I felt pretty lively and was anxious for the coming conflict, though I knew and told the boys that day would not close without some as hard fightin as had been done dureing the war. Just at day break the Regt. was ordered forward. It was generally known that we were going round on our left wing and engage the enemy, and I never felt more contented in my life.

During the night everything had been quite still, with the exception of an occasional fire by the pickets, and so remained untill we had gone near a half a mile, and by which time the sun had just begun to show itself, peeping as it were over the hills and mountains of the east. At that time we were moving on in line, I keeping with the file closers and watching the appearance of the boys particularly, which I was enabled to do as I had my gun to carry. We struck the foot of a large hill, marched rather across the point, but to my great surprise, just as we got barely on top of the hill, the enemy discovered us & turned loose at us with a cannon—the first that I had ever heard fire in battle. The boys all dropped to the ground, and I followed suit, but we rose in an instant and were ordered to double quick. The ball passed immediate over us.

When I got up, I felt considerably confused & must acknowledge a little fear. The first thing in my mind was that I had got myself voluntarily into a devil of a snap, but at the same moment I thought of you and Sammy & determined not to disgrace you & him if my head was shot off. So I braced myself up & marched strate forward as resolute as death itself, but not without feeling somewhat uncomfortable. I looked at every man in the Regt. to see how they looked. None looked like they were scared, & I argued to myself that it did not look reasonable that God Almighty had so constituted me as to make me more of a coward than any of the Regt.

We had not double quicked over fifty yards untill they cut loose again with a shell. The boys, being used to them, droped to the ground again, and at the same moment I accidently sliped down, hurting my knee on the frozen ground slightly. The shell passed immediately over me, and I think would have cut me into had I not been on the ground. It burst in about 20 yards of us but done us no harm. I rose instantly, and the first thing said to myself, "Well, I will not get hurt today, for providence has saved my life, and God is on my side." We went down the hill at a double quick then followed a hollow something like a quarter or half a mile, the enemy not molesting us. At length we struck the foot of another high hill, at which place a good many of us droped our napsacks and left them on account of fatigue.

It was a good piece to the top, and about half way up a battery had stalled, and the enemy was pouring it to them with ball and shell rapidly. We marched up to it and stoped for it to get out of the way, some of our men assisting in pushing it. At this moment Gen. Floyd rode up and ordered us onward. Our Col. told him we were waiting for the Artillery to get out of the way. He said wait for nothing, but go ahead. We started, the enemy giving us grape, canister and shell heavily. At that point I got used to the things and feared them no more.

We moved on to the top of the Hill, or almost, and was ordered to lie down in a little hollow to the right of the road just behind one of our batterys, which was playing upon the enemy. But was soon ordered to recross the road and lie on the breast of the hill at the termination of a large hollow in the rear of the battery and to the right—also in rear of the 14th Misp. Regt., and a short distance behind them, who were and had been for some time fighting like fury. The enemy endeavored to shell us out of the Hollow, but failed in doing so as their shells passed generally over us. They tried us with grape and canister, but with no effect. We lay there untill eleven o'clock with the exception of 3 companys, which had been ordered off to drive the sharp shooters from some of our batterys and defend them.

Gen. Floyd and our Brigade Surgeon took their position just behind us. About 11 o'clock there came a man running down to us and asked for a Physician to go up to the 14th Misp. Regt. The cries of the wounded at this time was horrorable. The roar of the cannon and the noise of the musketry was deafening. The Brigade surgeon ordered me to go to them. I rose and started as fast as I could to them, having to cross a heavy cannon fire before I reached them, and immediately after crossing that I was in range of the musket balls, which fell all around me and passed over my head so thick that it looked like I could have held up my hat and caught it full.

The Mississippi boys fell fast, but fought like men. I went to work on them, as best I could, and had at length to tear up my havorsack for bandages. I found a fellow with two wounds in the breast and saw he was bleeding from an artery. I carried him down in the hollow to get assistance in dressing his wounds. The brigade surgeon assisted me and ordered me to accompany him to the hospittal and told me to report myself to the medicle director, which I did.

The boats by this time had arrived (I suppose it was 11 1/2 o'clock) to take off the wounded. I was ordered to service in a hospittal, which was in a vacated Hotel, but about the time I got warm, Dr. Clopton sent for me to assist him in the Hospittal he had charge of, which was just across the road. I went over and went to work, but did not work long untill the Yankeys turned loose at the Hospittals and struck ours with several grape loads and passed two cannon balls through.

We went to work to raise the flags higher, and I suppose brought them into notice in about an hour and a half. At about half after one J. K. Buckner was brought in. Poor fellow. I was so sorry for him. I got Dr. Clopton to dress his wound immediately and started him to the boat, telling him never to stop untill he got home. Clopton, myself and another Physician, with occasional help from others, worked on untill 8 o'clock in the night, at which time we got through with all that were sent to our hospittal and got most of them on the boats. The fighting stoped when darkness forbid farther action.

We got our instruments cleaned & sit down to rest at 9 o'clock, & I do not think I was ever tireder in my life. Several Physicians & officers came in, & we talked over some of what we had seen. I told them that we who lived would all be prisoners of war by 3 hours by sun Sunday morning. I felt very much like it. I had seen all day that the enemy had 4 or 5 to one & had us surrounded. I thought we would fight next morning, but knew we would be overpowered. At ten o clock p.m. we lay down on the floor to take a nap for the first in a long time.

At 3 o'clock some fellow came and told us that our forces were going to retreat and ordered us to have the remainder of our wounded put upon the boat and then make our escape if we could and, if not, to surrender as prisoners of war, and we would soon be released. As the order came from the surgeon General, we went to work and after a while got most of them off. I kept asking every one that I would see comeing from our Regt. what had gone with it. At length a gentleman told me that it had cut its way through and was retreating. I ran in and told Dr. Clopton the same and told him I thought we had better go also. So we bundled up and started down to the boats to try to get abord, but could not get nigh them for the guards.

Dr. Clopton asked me what we could do. It was near daylight. I told him we must foot it up the River bank. He did not believe it practable. I insisted on trying; so we put out only taking one blanket. I suppose we went a half mile when we saw, as it was getting a little light, 5 men comeing meeting us, and who we took to be Yankeys. "There," said he, "look yander. What shall we do?" Says I, "March strait forward, for if we run, they will shoot us." We met them. They asked us where we were going. We told them, "Into the Country a little piece". Said they, "The enemy is just before us out here, and you cannot get out." We found that they were our men, who been trying just what we were going to try. It was then proposed that we cross the River on some logs and agreed to, but before we could find any, daylight came upon us, & to our surprise no Regt. but Forest Cavalry had gone, & the white flags were visable upon our works. So we were all prisoners.

THE RIVER WAR: FEBRUARY–JUNE 1862

Henry Walke: *The Western Flotilla at Fort Donelson, Island Number Ten, Fort Pillow and Memphis*

Henry Walke entered the navy in 1827 and served in the Mexican War. In 1862 he commanded the gunboat *Carondelet* at Fort Donelson and later fought in a series of battles on the Mississippi at Island No. Ten (so named because it was the tenth island in the river south of its junction with the Ohio), April 4–7; at Fort Pillow, Tennessee, May 10; and at Memphis, June 6, 1862. He described the campaign in a postwar article written for the *Century* magazine series *Battles and Leaders of the Civil War.*

ON THE 7th of February, the day after the capture of Fort Henry, I received on board the *Carondelet* Colonels Webster, Rawlins, and McPherson, with a company of troops, and under instructions from General Grant proceeded up the Tennessee River, and completed the destruction of the bridge of the Memphis and Bowling Green Railroad.

On returning from that expedition General Grant requested me to hasten to Fort Donelson with the *Carondelet*, *Tyler*, and *Lexington*, and announce my arrival by firing signal guns. The object of this movement was to take possession of the river as soon as possible, to engage the enemy's attention by making formidable demonstrations before the fort, and to prevent it from being reënforced. On February 10th the *Carondelet* alone (towed by the transport *Alps*) proceeded up the Cumberland River, and on the 12th arrived a few miles below the fort.

Fort Donelson occupied one of the best defensive positions on the river. It was built on a bold bluff about 120 feet in height, on the west side of the river, where it makes a slight bend to the eastward. It had 3 batteries, mounting in all 15 guns: the lower, about twenty feet above the water; the second, about fifty feet above the water; the third, on the summit.

When the *Carondelet*, her tow being cast off, came in sight of the fort and proceeded up to within long range of the batteries, not a living creature could be seen. The hills and woods on the west side of the river hid part of the enemy's formidable defenses, which were lightly covered with snow; but the black rows of heavy guns, pointing down on us, reminded me of the dismal-looking sepulchers cut in the rocky cliffs near Jerusalem, but far more repulsive. At 12:50 P.M., to unmask the silent enemy, and to announce my arrival to General Grant, I ordered the bow-guns to be fired at the fort. Only one shell fell short. There was no response except the echo from the hills. The fort appeared to have been evacuated. After firing ten shells into it, the *Carondelet* dropped down the river about three miles and anchored. But the sound of her guns aroused our soldiers on the southern side of the fort into action; one report says that when they heard the guns of the *avant-courrier* of the fleet, they gave cheer upon cheer, and rather than permit the sailors to get ahead of them again, they engaged in skirmishes with the enemy, and began the battle of the three days following. On the *Carondelet* we were isolated and beset with dangers from the enemy's lurking sharp-shooters.

On the 13th a dispatch was received from General Grant, informing me that he had arrived the day before, and had succeeded in getting his army in position, almost entirely investing the enemy's works. "Most of our batteries," he said, "are established, and the remainder soon will be. If you will advance with your gun-boat at 10 o'clock in the morning, we will be ready to take advantage of any diversion in our favor."

I immediately complied with these instructions, and at 9:05, with the *Carondelet* alone and under cover of a heavily wooded point, fired 139 70-pound and 64-pound shells at the fort. We received in return the fire of all the enemy's guns that could be brought to bear on the *Carondelet*, which sustained but little damage, except from two shots. One, a 128-pound solid, at 11:30 struck the corner of our port broadside casemate, passed through it, and in its progress toward the center of our boilers glanced over the temporary barricade in front of the boilers. It then passed over the steam-drum, struck the beams of the upper deck, carried away the railing around the engine-room and burst the steam-heater, and, glancing back into the engine-room, "seemed to bound after the men," as one of the engineers said, "like a wild beast pursuing its prey." I have preserved this ball as a souvenir of the fight at Fort Donelson. When it burst through the side of the *Carondelet*, it knocked down and wounded a dozen men, seven of them severely. An immense quantity of splinters was blown through the vessel. Some of them, as fine as needles, shot through the clothes of the men like arrows. Several of the wounded were so much excited by the suddenness of the event and the sufferings of their comrades, that they were not aware that they themselves had been struck until they felt the blood running into their shoes. Upon receiving this shot we ceased firing for a while.

After dinner we sent the wounded on board the *Alps*, repaired damages, and, not expecting any assistance, at 12:15 we resumed, in accordance with General Grant's request, and bombarded the fort until dusk, when nearly all our 10-inch and 15-inch shells were expended. The firing from the shore having ceased, we retired.

At 11:30 on the night of the 13th Flag-Officer Foote arrived below Fort Donelson with the iron-clads *St. Louis*, *Louisville*, and *Pittsburgh*, and the wooden gun-boats *Tyler* and *Conestoga*. On the 14th all the hard materials in the vessels, such as chains, lumber, and bags of coal, were laid on the upper decks to protect them from the plunging shots of the enemy. At 3 o'clock in the afternoon our fleet advanced to attack the fort, the *Louisville* being on the west side of the river, the *St. Louis* (flag-steamer) next, then the *Pittsburgh* and *Carondelet* on the east side of the river. The wooden gun-boats were about a thousand yards in the rear. When we started in line abreast at a moderate speed, the *Louisville* and *Pittsburgh*, not keeping up to their positions, were hailed from the flag-steamer to "steam up." At 3:30, when about a mile and a half from the fort, two shots were fired at us, both falling short. When within a mile of the fort the *St. Louis* opened fire, and the other iron-clads followed, slowly and deliberately at first, but more rapidly as the fleet advanced. The flag-officer hailed the *Carondelet*, and ordered us not to fire so fast. Some of our shells went over the fort, and almost into our camp beyond. As we drew nearer, the enemy's fire greatly increased in force and effect. But, the officers and crew of the *Carondelet* having recently been long under fire, and having become practiced in fighting, her gunners were as cool and composed as old veterans. We heard the deafening crack of the bursting shells, the crash of the solid shot, and the whizzing of fragments of shell and wood as they sped through the vessel. Soon a 128-pounder struck our anchor, smashed it into flying bolts, and bounded over the vessel, taking away a part of our smoke-stack; then another cut away the iron boat-davits as if they were pipe-stems, whereupon the boat dropped into the water. Another ripped up the iron plating and glanced over; another went through the plating and lodged in the heavy casemate; another struck the pilot-house, knocked the plating to pieces, and sent fragments of iron and splinters into the pilots, one of whom fell mortally wounded, and was taken below; another shot took away the remaining boat-davits and the boat with them; and still they came, harder and faster, taking flag-staffs and smoke-stacks, and tearing off the side armor as lightning tears the bark from a tree. Our men fought desperately, but, under the excitement of the occasion, loaded too hastily, and the port rifled gun exploded. One of the crew, in his account of the explosion soon after it occurred, said: "I was serving the gun with shell. When it exploded it knocked us all down, killing none, but wounding over a dozen men and spreading dismay and confusion among us. For about two minutes I was stunned, and at least five minutes elapsed before I could tell what was the matter. When I found out that I was more scared than hurt, although suffering from the gunpowder which I had inhaled, I looked forward and saw our gun lying on the deck, split in three pieces. Then the cry ran through the boat that we were on fire, and my duty as pumpman called me to the pumps. While I was there, two shots entered our bow-ports and killed four men and wounded several others. They were borne past me, three with their heads off. The sight almost sickened me, and I turned my head away. Our master's mate came soon after and ordered us to our quarters at the gun. I told him the gun had burst, and that we had caught fire on the upper deck from the enemy's shell. He then said: 'Never mind the fire; go to your quarters.' Then I took a station at the starboard tackle of another rifled bow-gun and remained there until the close of the fight." The carpenter and his men extinguished the flames.

When within four hundred yards of the fort, and while the

Confederates were running from their lower battery, our pilothouse was struck again and another pilot wounded, our wheel was broken, and shells from the rear boats were bursting over us. All four of our boats were shot away and dragging in the water. On looking out to bring our broadside guns to bear, we saw that the other gun-boats were rapidly falling back out of line. The *Pittsburgh* in her haste to turn struck the stern of the *Carondelet*, and broke our starboard rudder, so that we were obliged to go ahead to clear the *Pittsburgh* and the point of rocks below. The pilot of the *St. Louis* was killed, and the pilot of the *Louisville* was wounded. Both vessels had their wheel-ropes shot away, and the men were prevented from steering the *Louisville* with the tiller-ropes at the stern by the shells from the rear boats bursting over them. The *St. Louis* and *Louisville*, becoming unmanageable, were compelled to drop out of battle, and the *Pittsburgh* followed; all had suffered severely from the enemy's fire. Flag-Officer Foote was wounded while standing by the pilot of the *St. Louis* when he was killed. We were then about 350 yards from the fort.

There was no alternative for the *Carondelet* in that narrow stream but to keep her head to the enemy and fire into the fort with her two bow-guns, to prevent it, if possible, from returning her fire effectively. The enemy saw that she was in a manner left to his mercy, and concentrated the fire of all his batteries upon her. In return, the *Carondelet's* guns were well served to the last shot. Our new acting gunner, John Hall, was just the man for the occasion. He came forward, offered his services, and with my sanction took charge of the starboard-bow rifled gun. He instructed the men to obey his warnings and follow his motions, and he told them that when he saw a shot coming he would call out "Down" and stoop behind the breech of the gun as he did so; at the same instant the men were to stand away from the bow-ports. Nearly every shot from the fort struck the bows of the *Carondelet*. Most of them were fired on the ricochet level, and could be plainly seen skipping on the water before they struck. The enemy's object was to sink the gun-boat by striking her just below the water-line. They soon succeeded in planting two 32-pound shots in her bow, between wind and water, which made her leak badly, but her compartments kept her from sinking until we could plug up the shot-holes. Three shots struck the starboard casemating; four struck the port casemating forward of the rifle-gun; one struck on the starboard side, between the water-line and plank-sheer, cutting through the planking; six shots struck the pilot-house, shattering one section into pieces and cutting through the iron casing. The smoke-stacks were riddled.

Our gunners kept up a constant firing while we were falling back; and the warning words, "Look out!" "Down!" were often heard, and heeded by nearly all the gun-crews. On one occasion, while the men were at the muzzle of the middle bow-gun, loading it, the warning came just in time for them to jump aside as a 32-pounder struck the lower sill, and glancing up struck the upper sill, then, falling on the inner edge of the lower sill, bounded on deck and spun around like a top, but hurt no one. It was very evident that if the men who were loading had not obeyed the order to drop, several of them would have been killed. So I repeated the instructions and warned the men at the guns and the crew generally to bow or stand off from the ports when a shot was seen coming. But some of the young men, from a spirit of bravado or from a belief in the doctrine of fatalism, disregarded the instructions, saying it was useless to attempt to dodge a cannon-ball, and they would trust to luck. The warning words, "Look out!" "Down!" were again soon heard; down went the gunner and his men, as the whizzing shot glanced on the gun, taking off the gunner's cap and the heads of two of the young men who trusted to luck, and in defiance of the order were standing up or passing behind him. This shot killed another man also, who was at the last gun of the starboard side, and disabled the gun. It came in with a hissing sound; three sharp spats and a heavy bang told the sad fate of three brave comrades. Before the decks were well sanded, there was so much blood on them that our men could not work the guns without slipping.

We kept firing at the enemy so long as he was within range, to prevent him from seeing us through the smoke.

The *Carondelet* was the first in and the last out of the fight, and was more damaged than any of the other gun-boats, as the boat-carpenters who repaired them subsequently informed me. She was much longer under fire than any other vessel of the flotilla; and, according to the report of the Secretary of the Navy, her loss in killed and wounded was nearly twice as great as that of all the other gun-boats together. She fired more shot and shell into Fort Donelson than any other gun-boat, and was struck fifty-four times. These facts are given because a disposition was shown by correspondents and naval historians to ignore the services of the *Carondelet* on this and other occasions.

In the action of the 14th all of the armored vessels were fought with the greatest energy, skill, and courage, until disabled by the enemy's heavy shot. In his official report of the battle the flag-officer said: "The officers and men in this hotly contested but unequal fight behaved with the greatest gallantry and determination."*

Although the gun-boats were repulsed in this action, the

---

*From the report of Captain B. G. Bidwell, "the only officer connected with the heavy batteries of Fort Donelson who was fortunate enough to escape," we take this account of the engagement:

"All was quiet until the evening of the 14th (Friday), when 4 boats came around the point, arranged themselves in line of battle, and advanced slowly, but steadily, up the river to within 200 yards of our battery, and halted, when a most incessant fire was kept up for some time. We were ordered to hold our fire until they got within range of our 32-pounders. We remained perfectly silent, while they came over about one and a half miles, pouring a heavy fire of shot and shell upon us all the time. Two more boats came around the point and threw shell at us. Our gunners were inexperienced and knew very little of the firing of heavy guns. They, however, did some excellent shooting. The rifled gun was disabled by the ramming of a cartridge while the wire was in the vent, it being left in there by a careless gunner,—being bent, it could not be got out,—but the two center boats were both disabled, the left-center (I think) by a ricochet shot entering one of the port-holes, which are tolerably large. The right-center boat was very soon injured by a ball striking her on top, and also a direct shot in the port hole, when she fell back, the two flank boats closing in behind them and protecting them from our fire in retreat. I think these two were not seriously injured. They must have fired near two thousand shot and shell at us. Our Columbiad fired about 27 times, the rifled gun very few times, and the 32-pounders about 45 or 50 rounds each. A great many of our balls took effect, being well aimed. I am confident the efficiency of the gun-boat is in the gun it carries rather than in the boat itself. We can whip them always if our men will only stand to their guns. Not a man of all ours was hurt, notwithstanding they threw grape at us. Their fire was more destructive to our works at 2 miles than at 200 yards. They over-fired us from that distance."

demoralizing effect of their cannonade, and of the heavy and well-sustained fire of the *Carondelet* on the day before, must have been very great, and contributed in no small degree to the successful operations of the army on the following day.

After the battle I called upon the flag-officer, and found him suffering from his wounds. He asked me if I could have run past the fort, something I should not have ventured upon without permission.

The 15th was employed in the burial of our slain comrades. I read the Episcopal service on board the *Carondelet*, under our flag at half-mast; and the sailors bore their late companions to a lonely field within the shadows of the hills. When they were about to lower the first coffin, a Roman Catholic priest appeared, and his services being accepted, he read the prayers for the dead. As the last service was ended, the sound of the battle being waged by General Grant, like the rumbling of distant thunder, was the only requiem for our departed shipmates.

On Sunday, the 16th, at dawn, Fort Donelson surrendered and the gun-boats steamed up to Dover. After religious services the *Carondelet* proceeded back to Cairo, and arrived there on the morning of the 17th, in such a dense fog that she passed below the town unnoticed, and had great difficulty in finding the landing. There had been a report that the enemy was coming from Columbus to attack Cairo during the absence of its defenders; and while the *Carondelet* was cautiously feeling her way back and blowing her whistle, some people imagined she was a Confederate gun-boat about to land, and made hasty preparations to leave the place. Our announcement of the victory at Fort Donelson changed their dejection into joy and exultation. On the following morning an order congratulating the officers and men of the *Carondelet* was received from Flag-Officer Foote.

A few days later the *Carondelet* was taken up on the ways at Mound City, Illinois,—six or seven miles above Cairo on the Ohio River,—for repairs; and a crowd of carpenters worked on her night and day. After the repairs were completed, she was ordered to make the experiment of backing up-stream, which proved a laughable failure. She would sheer from one side of the river to the other, and with two anchors astern she could not be held steady enough to fight her bow-guns down-stream. She dragged both anchors alternately, until they came together, and the experiment failed completely.

On the morning of the 23d the flag-officer made a reconnoissance to Columbus, Kentucky, with four gun-boats and two mortar-boats, accompanied by the wooden gun-boat *Conestoga*, convoying five transports. The fortifications looked more formidable than ever. The enemy fired two guns, and sent up a transport with the pretext, it was said, of effecting an exchange of prisoners. But at that time, as we learned afterward from a credible source, the evacuation of the fort (which General Grant's successes at Forts Henry and Donelson had made necessary) was going on, and the last raft and barge loads of all the movable munitions of war were descending the river, which, with a large quantity previously taken away, could and would have been captured by our fleet if we had received this information in time. On the 4th of March another reconnoissance in force was made with all the gun-boats and four mortar-boats, and the fortress had still a formidable, life-like appearance, though it had been evacuated two days before.

On the 5th of March, while we were descending the Mississippi in a dense fog, the flag-steamer leading, the Confederate gun-boat *Grampus*, or *Dare-devil Jack*, the sauciest little vessel on the river, suddenly appeared across our track and "close aboard." She stopped her engines and struck her colors, and we all thought she was ours at last. But when the captain of the *Grampus* saw how slowly we moved, and as no gun was fired to bring him to, he started off with astonishing speed and was out of danger before the flag-steamer could fire a gun. She ran before us yawing and flirting about, and blowing her alarm-whistle so as to announce our approach to the enemy who had now retired to Island Number Ten, a strong position sixty miles below Columbus (and of the latitude of Forts Henry and Donelson), where General Beauregard, who was now in general command of our opponents, had determined to contest the possession of the river.

On March 15th the flotilla and transports continued on their way to Island Number Ten, arriving in its vicinity about nine in the morning. The strong and muddy current of the river had overflowed its banks and carried away every movable thing.

Houses, trees, fences, and wrecks of all kinds were being swept rapidly down-stream. The twists and turns of the river near Island Number Ten are certainly remarkable. Within a radius of eight miles from the island it crosses the boundary line of Kentucky and Tennessee three times, running on almost every point of the compass. We were greatly surprised when we arrived above Island Number Ten and saw on the bluffs a chain of forts extending for four miles along the crescent-formed shore, with the white tents of the enemy in the rear. And there lay the island in the lower corner of the crescent, with the side fronting the Missouri shore lined with heavy ordnance, so trained that with the artillery on the opposite shore almost every point on the river between the island and the Missouri bank could be reached at once by all the enemy's batteries.

On the 17th an attack was made on the upper battery by all the iron-clads and mortar-boats. The *Benton* (flag-steamer), lashed between the *Cincinnati* and *St. Louis*, was on the east side of the river; the *Mound City*, *Carondelet*, and *Pittsburgh* were on the west side; the last, however, changed her position to the east side of the river before the firing began. We opened fire on the upper fort at 1:20, and by order of the flag-officer fired one gun a minute. The enemy replied promptly, and some of his shot struck the *Benton*, but, owing to the distance from which they were fired, did but little damage. We silenced all the guns in the upper fort except one. During the action one of the rifled guns of the *St. Louis* exploded, killing and wounding several of the gunners,—another proof of the truth of the saying that the guns furnished the Western flotilla were less destructive to the enemy than to ourselves.

From March 17th to April 4th but little progress was made in the reduction of the Confederate works—the gun-boats firing a few shot now and then at long range, but doing little damage. The mortar-boats, however, were daily throwing 13-inch bombs, and so effectively at times that the Confederates were driven from their batteries and compelled to seek refuge in caves and other places of safety. But it was very evident that the great object of the expedition—the reduction of the works and the capture of the Confederate forces—could not be effected by the gun-boats alone, owing to their mode of structure and to the disadvantage under which they were fought in the strong and rapid current of the Mississippi. This was the opinion not only of naval officers, but also of General Pope and other army officers.

On the 23d of March the monotony of the long and tedious investment was unfortunately varied in a very singular manner. The *Carondelet* being moored nearest the enemy's upper fort, under several large cottonwood trees, in order to protect the mortar-boats, suddenly, and without warning, two of the largest of the trees fell across her deck, mortally wounding one of the crew and severely wounding another, and doing great damage to the vessel. This was twelve days before I ran the gauntlet at Island Number Ten with the *Carondelet*.

To understand fully the importance of that adventure, some explanation of the military situation at and below Island Number Ten seems necessary. After the evacuation of New Madrid, which General Pope had forced by blockading the river twelve miles below, at Point Pleasant, the Confederate forces occupied their fortified positions on Island Number Ten and the eastern shore of the Mississippi, where they were cut off by impassable swamps on the land side. They were in a *cul-de-sac*, and the only way open for them to obtain supplies or to effect a retreat was by the river south of Island Number Ten. General Pope, with an army of twenty thousand men, was on the western side of the river below the island. Perceiving the defect in the enemy's position, he proceeded with great promptness and ability to take advantage of it. It was his intention to cross the river and attack the enemy from below, but he could not do this without the aid of a gun-boat to silence the enemy's batteries opposite Point Pleasant and protect his army in crossing. He wrote repeatedly to Flag-Officer Foote, urging him to send down a gun-boat past the enemy's batteries on Island Number Ten, and in one of his letters expressed the belief that a boat could pass down at night under cover of the darkness. But the flag-officer invariably declined, saying in one of his letters to General Pope that the attempt "would result in the sacrifice of the boat, her officers and men, which sacrifice I would not be justified in making."

During this correspondence the bombardment still went on, but was attended with such poor results that it became a subject of ridicule among the officers of Pope's army, one of whom

(Colonel Gilmore, of Chillicothe, Ohio) is reported to have said that often when they met, and inquiry was made respecting the operations of the flotilla, the answer would generally be: "Oh! it is still bombarding the State of Tennessee at long range." And a Confederate officer said that no casualties resulted and no damage was sustained at Island Number Ten from the fire of the gun-boats.

On March 20th Flag-Officer Foote consulted his commanding officers, through Commander Stembel, as to the practicability of taking a gun-boat past the enemy's forts to New Madrid, and all except myself were opposed to the enterprise, believing with Foote that the attempt to pass the batteries would result in the almost certain destruction of the boat. I did not think so, but believed with General Pope that, under the cover of darkness and other favorable circumstances, a gun-boat might be run past the enemy's batteries, formidable as they were with nearly fifty guns. And although fully aware of the hazardous nature of the enterprise, I knew that the aid of a gun-boat was absolutely necessary to enable General Pope to succeed in his operations against the enemy, and thought the importance of this success would justifiy the risk of running the gauntlet of the batteries on Island Number Ten and on the left bank. The army officers were becoming impatient, and it was well known that the Confederates had a number of small gun-boats below, and were engaged in building several large and powerful vessels, of which the renowned *Arkansas* was one. And there was good reason to apprehend that these gun-boats would ascend the river and pass or silence Pope's batteries, and relieve the Confederate forces on Island Number Ten and the eastern shore of the Mississippi. That Pope and Foote apprehended this, appears from the correspondence between them.

The flag-officer now called a formal council of war of all his commanding officers. It was held on board the flag-steamer, on the 28th or 29th of March, and all except myself concurred in the opinion formerly expressed that the attempt to pass the batteries was too hazardous and ought not to be made. When I was asked to give my views, I favored the undertaking, and advised compliance with the requests of General Pope. When asked if I was willing to make the attempt with the *Carondelet*, I replied in the affirmative. Foote accepted my advice, and expressed himself as greatly relieved from a heavy responsibility, as he had determined to send none but volunteers on an expedition which he regarded as perilous and of very doubtful success.

Having received written orders from the flag-officer, under date of March 30th, I at once began to prepare the *Carondelet* for the ordeal. All the loose material at hand was collected, and on the 4th of April the decks were covered with it, to protect them against plunging shot. Hawsers and chain cables were placed around the pilot-house and other vulnerable parts of the vessel, and every precaution was adopted to prevent disaster. A coal-barge laden with hay and coal was lashed to the part of the port side on which there was no iron plating, to protect the magazine. It was truly said that the *Carondelet* at that time resembled a farmer's wagon prepared for market. The engineers led the escape-steam, through the pipes aft, into the wheel-house, to avoid the puffing sound it made when blown through the smoke-stacks.

All the necessary preparations having been made, I informed the flag-officer of my intention to run the gauntlet that night, and received his approval. Colonel N. B. Buford, who commanded the land forces temporarily with the flotilla, assisted me in preparing for the trip, and on the night of the 4th brought on board Captain Hottenstein, of the 42d Illinois, and twenty-three sharp-shooters of his command, who volunteered their services, which were gratefully accepted. Colonel Buford remained on board until the last moment, to encourage us. I informed the officers and crew of the character of the undertaking, and all expressed a readiness to make the venture. In order to resist boarding parties, in case of being disabled, the sailors were well armed, and pistols, cutlasses, muskets, boarding-pikes, and hand-grenades were within reach. Hose was attached to the boilers for throwing scalding water over any who might attempt to board. If it should be found impossible to save the vessel, it was designed to sink rather than burn her. During the afternoon there was a promise of a clear, moonlight night, and it was determined to wait until the moon was down, and then to make the attempt, whatever the chances. Having gone so far, we could not abandon the project without an effect on the men almost as bad as failure.

At 10 o'clock the moon had gone down, and the sky, the earth, and the river were alike hidden in the black shadow of a thunder-storm, which had now spread itself over all the heavens. As the time seemed favorable, I ordered the first master to cast off. Dark clouds now rose rapidly over us and enveloped us in almost total darkness, except when the sky was lighted up by the welcome flashes of vivid lightning, to show us the perilous way we were to take. Now and then the dim outline of the landscape could be seen, and the forest bending under the roaring storm that came rushing up the river.

With our bow pointing to the island, we passed the lowest point of land without being observed, it appears, by the enemy. All speed was given to the vessel to drive her through the tempest. The flashes of lightning continued with frightful brilliancy, and "almost every second," wrote a correspondent, "every brace, post, and outline could be seen with startling distinctness, enshrouded by a bluish white glare of light, and then her form for the next minute would become merged in the intense darkness." When opposite Battery No. 2, on the mainland,* the smoke-stacks blazed up, but the fire was soon subdued. It was caused by the soot becoming dry, as the escape-steam, which usually kept the stacks wet, had been sent into the wheel-house, as already mentioned, to prevent noise. With such vivid lightning as prevailed during the whole passage, there was no prospect of escaping the vigilance of the enemy, but there was good reason to hope that he would be unable to point his guns accurately. Again the smoke-stacks took fire, and were soon put out; and then the roar of the enemy's guns began, and from Batteries Nos. 2, 3, and 4 on the mainland came the continued crack and scream of their rifle-shells, which

---

*During the dark and stormy night of April 1st Colonel George W. Roberts, of the 42d Illinois Regiment, executed a brilliant exploit. Forty picked men, in five barges, with muffled oars, left for Battery No. 1. They proceeded in silence, and were unobserved until within a few rods of the fort, when a flash of lightning discovered them to the sentries, who fired. Our men, who did not reply, were soon climbing up the slippery bank, and in three minutes more the six guns were spiked, Colonel Roberts himself spiking a huge 80-pounder pivot-gun. Some of these guns had been previously dismounted by our fleet, and were now rendered doubly useless.—H. W.

seemed to unite with the electric batteries of the clouds to annihilate us.

While nearing the island or some shoal point, during a few minutes of total darkness, we were startled by the order, "Hard a-port!" from our brave and skillful pilot, First Master William R. Hoel. We almost grazed the island, and it appears were not observed through the storm until we were close in, and the enemy, having no time to point his guns, fired at random. In fact, we ran so near that the enemy did not, probably could not, depress his guns sufficiently. While close under the lee of the island and during a lull in the storm and in the firing, one of our pilots heard a Confederate officer shout, "Elevate your guns!" It is probable that the muzzles of those guns had been depressed to keep the rain out, and that the officers ordered the guns elevated just in time to save us from the direct fire of the enemy's heaviest fort; and this, no doubt, was the cause of our remarkable escape.

Having passed the principal batteries, we were greatly relieved from suspense, patiently endured, however, by the officers and crew. But there was another formidable obstacle in the way—a floating battery, which was the great "war elephant" of the Confederates, built to blockade the Mississippi permanently. As we passed her she fired six or eight shots at us, but without effect. One ball struck the coal-barge, and one was found in a bale of hay; we found also one or two musket-bullets. We arrived at New Madrid about midnight with no one hurt, and were most joyfully received by our army. At the suggestion of Paymaster Nixon, all hands "spliced the main brace."

On Sunday, the 6th, after prayers and thanksgiving, the *Carondelet* with General Gordon Granger, Colonel J. L. Kirby Smith of the 43d Ohio, and Captain Louis H. Marshall of General Pope's staff on board, made a reconnoissance twenty miles down, nearly to Tiptonville, the enemy's forts firing on her all the way down. We returned their fire, and dropped a few shells into their camps beyond. On the way back, we captured and spiked the guns of a battery of one 32-pounder and one 24-pounder, in about twenty-five minutes, opposite Point Pleasant. Before we landed to spike the guns, a tall Confederate soldier, with cool and deliberate courage, posted himself behind a large cottonwood tree, and repeatedly fired upon us, until our Illinois sharp-shooters got to work on him from behind the hammock nettings. He had two rifles, which he soon dropped, fleeing into the woods with his head down. The next day he was captured and brought into camp at Tiptonville, with the tip of his nose shot off. After the capture of this battery, the enemy prepared to evacuate his positions on Island Number Ten and the adjacent shores, and thus, as one of the historians of the civil war says, the *Carondelet* struck the blow that secured that victory.

Returning to New Madrid, we were instructed by General Pope to attack the enemy's batteries of six 64-pounders which protected his rear; and besides, another gun-boat was expected. The *Pittsburgh* (Lieutenant-Commander Thompson) ran the gauntlet without injury, during a thunder-storm, at 2 in the morning of April 7th, and arrived at 5 o'clock; but she was not ready for service, and the *Carondelet* attacked the principal batteries at Watson's Landing alone and had nearly silenced them when the *Pittsburgh* came up astern and fired nearly over the *Carondelet's* upper deck, after she and the Confederates had ceased firing. I reported to General Pope that we had cleared the opposite shores of the enemy, and were ready to cover the crossing of the river and the landing of the army. Seeing themselves cut off, the garrison at Island Number Ten surrendered to Foote on the 7th of April, the day of the Confederate repulse at Shiloh. The other Confederates retreating before Pope's advance, were nearly all overtaken and captured at 4 o'clock on the morning of the 8th; and about the same time the cavalry under Colonel W. L. Elliott took possession of the enemy's deserted works on the Tennessee shore.

The result of General Pope's operations in connection with the services of the *Carondelet* below Island Number Ten was the capture of three generals (including General W. W. Mackall, who ten days before the surrender had succeeded General John P. McCown in the command at Madrid Bend), over 5000 men, 20 pieces of heavy artillery, 7000 stand of arms, and a large quantity of ammunition and provisions, without the loss of a man on our side.

On the 12th the *Benton* (flag-steamer), with the *Cincinnati*, *Mound City*, *Cairo*, and *St. Louis*, passed Tiptonville and signaled the *Carondelet* and *Pittsburgh* to follow. Five Confederate gun-boats came up the next day and offered battle; but after the exchange of a few shots at long range they retired down the river. We followed them all the way to Craighead's Point, where they were under cover of their fortifications at Fort Pillow. I was not aware at the time that we were chasing the squadron of my esteemed shipmate of the U. S. Frigates *Cumberland* and *Merrimac*, Colonel John W. Dunnington, who afterward fought so bravely at Arkansas Post.

On the 14th General Pope's army landed about six miles above Craighead's Point, near Osceola, under the protection of the gun-boats. While he was preparing to attack Fort Pillow, Foote sent his executive officer twice to me on the *Carondelet* to inquire whether I would undertake, with my vessel and two or three other gun-boats, to pass below the fort to coöperate with General Pope, to which inquiries I replied that I was ready at any time to make the attempt. But Pope and his army (with the exception of 1500 men) were ordered away, and the expedition against Fort Pillow was abandoned. Between the 14th of April and the 10th of May two or three of the mortar-boats were towed down the river and moored near Craighead's Point, with a gun-boat to protect them. They were employed in throwing 13-inch bombs across the point into Fort Pillow, two miles distant. The enemy returned our bombardment with vigor, but not with much accuracy or effect. Several of their bombs fell near the gun-boats when we were three miles from the fort.

The Confederate fleet called the "River Defense" having been reënforced, they determined upon capturing the mortar-boats or giving us battle. On the 8th three of their vessels came to the point from which the mortar-boats had thrown their bombs, but, finding none, returned. Foote had given special orders to keep up steam and be ready for battle any moment, day or night. There was so much illness at that time in the flotilla that about a third of the officers and men were under medical treatment, and a great many were unfit for duty. On the 9th of May, at his own request, our distinguished commander-in-chief, Foote, was relieved from his arduous duties. He had become very much enfeebled from the wounds received at Fort Donelson and from illness. He carried with him the sympathy and regrets of all his command. He was succeeded by Flag-Officer Charles Henry Davis, a most excellent officer.

This paper would not be complete without some account of the naval battles fought by the flotilla immediately after the retirement of Flag-Officer Foote, under whose supervision and amid the greatest embarrassments it had been built, organized, and equipped. On the morning of the 10th of May a mortar-boat was towed down the river, as usual, at 5 A. M., to bombard Fort Pillow. The *Cincinnati* soon followed to protect her. At 6:35 eight Confederate rams came up the river at full speed. The *Carondelet* at once prepared for action, and slipped her hawser to the "bare end," ready for orders to "go ahead." No officer was on the deck of the *Benton* (flag-steamer) except the pilot, Mr. Birch, who informed the flag-officer of the situation, and passed the order to the *Carondelet* and *Pittsburgh* to proceed without waiting for the flag-steamer. General signal was also made to the fleet to get under way, but it was not visible on account of the light fog.

The *Carondelet* started immediately after the first verbal order; the others, for want of steam or some other cause, were not ready, except the *Mound City*, which put off soon after we were fairly on our way to the rescue of the *Cincinnati*. We had proceeded about a mile before our other gun-boats left their moorings. The rams were advancing rapidly, and we steered for the leading vessel, *General Bragg*, a brig-rigged, side-wheel steam ram, far in advance of the others, and apparently intent on striking the *Cincinnati*. When about three-quarters of a mile from the *General Bragg*, the *Carondelet* and *Mound City* fired on her with their bow-guns, until she struck the *Cincinnati* on the starboard quarter, making a great hole in the shell-room, through which the water poured with resistless force. The *Cincinnati* then retreated up the river and the *General Bragg* drifted down, evidently disabled. The *General Price*, following the example of her consort, also rammed the *Cincinnati*. We fired our bow-guns into the *General Price*, and she backed off, disabled also. The *Cincinnati* was again struck by one of the enemy's rams, the *General Sumter*. Having pushed on with all speed to the rescue of the *Cincinnati*, the *Carondelet* passed her in a sinking condition, and, rounding to, we fired our bow and starboard broadside guns into the retreating

General Bragg and the advancing rams, *General Jeff. Thompson*, *General Beauregard*, and *General Lovell*. Heading up-stream, close to a shoal, the *Carondelet* brought her port broadside guns to bear on the *Sumter* and *Price*, which were dropping down-stream. At this crisis the *Van Dorn* and *Little Rebel* had run above the *Carondelet*; the *Bragg*, *Jeff. Thompson*, *Beauregard*, and *Lovell* were below her. The last three, coming up, fired into the *Carondelet*; she returned their fire with her stern-guns; and, while in this position, I ordered the port rifled 50-pounder Dahlgren gun to be leveled and fired at the center of the *Sumter*. The shot struck the vessel just forward of her wheel-house, and the steam instantly poured out from her ports and all parts of her casemates, and we saw her men running out of them and falling or lying down on her deck. None of our gun-boats had yet come to the assistance of the *Carondelet*. The *Benton* and *Pittsburgh* had probably gone to aid the *Cincinnati*, and the *St. Louis* to relieve the *Mound City*, which had been badly rammed by the *Van Dorn*. The smoke at this time was so dense that we could hardly distinguish the gun-boats above us. The upper deck of the *Carondelet* was swept with grape-shot and fragments of broken shell; some of the latter were picked up by one of the sharp-shooters, who told me they were obliged to lie down under shelter to save themselves from the grape and other shot of the *Pittsburgh* above us, and from the shot and broken shell of the enemy below us. Why some of our gun-boats did not fire into the *Van Dorn* and *Little Rebel* while they were above the *Carondelet*, and prevent their escape, if possible, I never could make out.

As the smoke rose we saw that the enemy was retreating rapidly and in great confusion. The *Carondelet* dropped down to within half a mile above Craighead's Point, and kept up a continual fire upon their vessels, which were very much huddled together. When they were nearly, if not quite, beyond gunshot, the *Benton*, having raised sufficient steam, came down and passed the *Carondelet*; but the Confederates were under the protection of Fort Pillow before the *Benton* could reach them. Our fleet returned to Plum Point, except the *Carondelet*, which dropped her anchor on the battle-field, two miles or more below the point, and remained there two days on voluntary guard duty. This engagement was sharp, but not decisive.

From the first to the last shot fired by the *Carondelet*, one hour and ten minutes elapsed. After the battle, long-range firing was kept up until the evacuation of Fort Pillow.

On the 25th seven of Colonel Ellet's rams arrived,—a useful acquisition to our fleet. During the afternoon of June 4th heavy clouds of smoke were observed rising from Fort Pillow, followed by explosions, which continued through the night; the last of which, much greater than the others, lit up the heavens and the Chickasaw bluffs with a brilliant light, and convinced us that this was the parting salute of the Confederates before leaving for the lower Mississippi. At dawn next morning the fleet was all astir to take possession of Fort Pillow, the flag-steamer leading. We found the casemates, magazines, and breastworks blown to atoms.

On our way to Memphis the enemy's steamer *Sovereign* was intercepted by one of our tugs. She was run ashore by her crew, who attempted to blow her up, but were foiled in their purpose by a boy of sixteen whom the enemy had pressed into service, who, after the abandonment of the vessel, took the extra weights from the safety-valves, opened the fire-doors and flue-caps, and put water on the fires, and, having procured a sheet, signaled the tug, which came up and took possession. It may be proper to say that on our way down the river we respected private property, and did not assail or molest any except those who were in arms against us.

The morning of the 6th of June we fought the battle of Memphis, which lasted one hour and ten minutes. It was begun by an attack upon our fleet by the enemy, whose vessels were in double line of battle opposite the city. We were then at a distance of a mile and a half or two miles above the city. Their fire continued for a quarter of an hour, when the attack was promptly met by two of our ram squadron, the *Queen of the West* (Colonel Charles Ellet) leading, and the *Monarch* (Lieutenant-Colonel A. W. Ellet, younger brother of the leader). These vessels fearlessly dashed ahead of our gun-boats, ran for the enemy's fleet, and at the first plunge succeeded in sinking one vessel and disabling another. The astonished Confederates received them gallantly and effectively. The *Queen of the West* and *Monarch* were followed in line of battle by the gun-boats, under the lead of Flag-Officer Davis, and all of them opened fire, which was continued from the time we got within good range until the end of the battle—two or three tugs keeping all the while a safe distance astern. The *Queen of the West* was a quarter of a mile in advance of the *Monarch*, and after having rammed one of the enemy's fleet, she was badly rammed by the *Beauregard*, which then, in company with the *General Price*, made a dash at the *Monarch* as she approached them. The *Beauregard*, however, missed the *Monarch* and struck the *General Price* instead on her port side, cutting her down to the water-line, tearing off her wheel instantly, and placing her *hors de combat*. The *Monarch* then rammed the *Beauregard*, which had been several times raked fore and aft by the shot and shell of our iron-clads, and she quickly sank in the river opposite Memphis. The *General Lovell*, after having been badly rammed by the *Queen of the West*, was struck by our shot and shell, and, at about the same time and place as the *Beauregard*, sank to the bottom so suddenly as to take a considerable number of her officers and crew down with her, the others being saved by small boats and our tugs. The *Price*, *Little Rebel* (with a shot-hole through her steam-chest), and our *Queen of the West*, all disabled, were run on the Arkansas shore opposite Memphis; and the *Monarch* afterward ran into the *Little Rebel* just as our fleet was passing her in pursuit of the remainder of the enemy's fleet, then retreating rapidly down the river. The *Jeff. Thompson*, below the point and opposite President's Island, was the next boat disabled by our shot. She was run ashore, burned, and blown up. The Confederate ram *Sumter* was also disabled by our shell and captured. The *Bragg* soon after shared the same fate and was run ashore, where her officers abandoned her and disappeared in the forests of Arkansas. All the Confederate rams which had been run on the Arkansas shore were captured. The *Van Dorn*, having a start, alone escaped down the river. The rams *Monarch* and *Switzerland* were dispatched in pursuit of her and a few transports, but returned without overtaking them, although they captured another steamer.

The scene at this battle was rendered most sublime by the desperate nature of the engagement and the momentous consequences that followed very speedily after the first attack. Thousands of people crowded the high bluffs overlooking the river. The roar of the cannon and shell shook the houses on shore on either side for many miles. First wild yells, shrieks, and clamors, then loud, despairing murmurs, filled the affrighted city. The screaming, plunging shell crashed into the boats, blowing some of them and their crews into fragments, and the rams rushed upon each other like wild beasts in deadly conflict. Blinding smoke hovered about the scene of all this confusion and horror; and, as the battle progressed and the Confederate fleet was destroyed, all the cheering voices on shore were silenced. When the last hope of the Confederates gave way, the lamentations which went up from the spectators were like cries of anguish.

Boats were put off from our vessels to save as many lives as possible. No serious injury was received by any one on board the United States fleet. Colonel Ellet received a pistol-shot in the leg; a shot struck the *Carondelet* in the bow, broke up her anchor and anchor-stock, and fragments were scattered over her deck among her officers and crew, wounding slightly Acting-Master Gibson and two or three others who were standing at the time on the forward deck with me. The heavy timber which was suspended at the water-line, to protect the boats from the Confederate rams, greatly impeded our progress, and it was therefore cut adrift from the *Carondelet* when that vessel was in chase of the *Bragg* and *Sumter*. The latter had just landed a number of her officers and crew, some of whom were emerging from the bushes along the bank of the river, unaware of the *Carondelet's* proximity, when I hailed them through a trumpet, and ordered them to stop or be shot. They obeyed immediately, and by my orders were taken on board a tug and delivered on the *Benton*.

General Jeff. Thompson, noted in partisan or border warfare, having signally failed with those rams at Fort Pillow, now resigned them to their fate. It was said that he stood by his horse watching the struggle, and seeing at last his rams all gone, captured, sunk, or burned, he exclaimed, philosophically, "They are gone, and I am going," mounted his horse, and disappeared.

An enormous amount of property was captured by our squadron; and, in addition to the Confederate fleet, we captured at Memphis six large Mississippi steamers, each marked

"C. S. A." We also seized a large quantity of cotton in steamers and on shore, and the property at the Confederate Navy Yard, and caused the destruction of the *Tennessee*, a large steam-ram, on the stocks, which was to have been a sister ship to the renowned *Arkansas*. About one hundred Confederates were killed and wounded and one hundred and fifty captured. Chief of all results of the work of the flotilla was the opening of the Mississippi River once for all from Cairo to Memphis, and the complete possession of Western Tennessee by the Union forces.

CONFEDERATE STRATEGY: FEBRUARY 1862

Braxton Bragg to Judah P. Benjamin

By mid-February it was evident that the Confederacy's strategy of defending an extended perimeter in the western theater was failing, due especially to the Union's dominance on the western rivers. Braxton Bragg, a West Point graduate who had fought in the Seminole and Mexican wars, was a noted artillery officer in the prewar army who became a Confederate general in 1861. Bragg was commanding troops along the eastern Gulf coast when he suggested a new strategy of concentration in this letter to Confederate Secretary of War Judah P. Benjamin.

HDQRS. DEPARTMENT ALABAMA AND WEST FLORIDA,
Mobile, Ala., February 15, 1862.

Hon. J. P. BENJAMIN,
Secretary of War, Richmond, Va.:

SIR: You will excuse me, at this time of great danger to our cause, for presuming to depart from my usual course and to offer a few suggestions on our future military policy.

1. Our means and resources are too much scattered. The protection of persons and property, as such, should be abandoned, and all our means applied to the Government and the cause. Important strategic points only should be held. All means not necessary to secure these should be concentrated for a heavy blow upon the enemy where we can best assail him. Kentucky is now that point. On the Gulf we should only hold New Orleans, Mobile, and Pensacola; all other points, the whole of Texas and Florida, should be abandoned, and our means there made available for other service. A small loss of property would result from their occupation by the enemy; but our military strength would not be lessened thereby, whilst the enemy would be weakened by dispersion. We could then beat him in detail, instead of the reverse. The same remark applies to our Atlantic seaboard. In Missouri the same rule can be applied to a great extent. Deploring the misfortunes of that

gallant people, I can but think their relief must reach them through Kentucky.

2. The want of success with our artillery everywhere is deplorable; but I believe it can be explained and remedied. This arm requires knowledge, which nothing but study and experience combined can give. Unfortunately, many of our higher officers and a larger proportion of our men consider there is no duty to be done in this contest but to fight. Gallant to a fault, they ignore preparation, and exhaust their energies and time in clamoring for this fight. Calamitous results teach them too late the unfortunate error.

The enemy's light-draught gunboats require of us different defenses for our assailable points. An old-fashioned artillery will not answer. We must have long range guns to reach them, and they must be properly mounted, supplied, and served. Our 8 and 10 inch shell guns have my preference. The rifle gun I consider yet an experiment, not a success, except the light field piece—bronze; still I use them as an auxiliary. Whenever the enemy has brought his shell guns against our lighter metal, we have had to yield. But at Pensacola we crippled and drove off two of his largest and heaviest armed ships with only two 8-inch guns in an open sand battery, served, it is true, by brave men, thoroughly instructed and directed by a competent artillery officer.

We must then oppose the enemy's heavy metal by the same, and put competent men to mount, supply, and serve our own guns. If we have not the guns, it is better to yield the positions than to sacrifice our men and means in a futile attempt at defense. And when you have the guns, it is equally futile if they are handled by incompetent troops. From reports which reach us, it would appear that at least half our guns are rendered useless after the first hour, from different accidents, not attributable to the enemy, but to a want of knowledge, skill, or attention on our own part.

We have the right men, and the crisis upon us demands they should be in the right places. Our little army at Pensacola could furnish you hundreds of instructors competent to build batteries, mount guns, and teach the use of them. Our commanders are learning by bitter experience the necessity of teaching their troops; but a want of instructors is sadly felt.

Pardon me if I have been too free in the expression of my feelings and opinions, and attribute any error to an overzeal in the great cause we all have at heart.

I am, sir, very respectfully, your obedient servant,

BRAXTON BRAGG,
Major-General, Commanding.

"THESE CALAMITIES": VIRGINIA, FEBRUARY 1862

John B. Jones: Diary, February 8–28, 1862

John B. Jones, editor of the *Southern Monitor*, a weekly journal he published in Philadelphia, fled to Richmond shortly before the outbreak of the war and took a job as clerk in the Confederate War Department. That post gave him early notice of a disheartening series of Confederate reverses in February 1862. Jones attended the inauguration of Jefferson Davis on February 22. In his address, Davis was both candid and defiant. "After a series of successes and victories, which covered our arms with glory, we have recently met with serious disasters," he said. "But in the heart of a people resolved to be free these disasters tend but to stimulate to increased resistance."

February 8–20th.—Such astounding events have occurred since the 8th instant, such an excitement has prevailed, and so incessant have been my duties, that I have not kept a regular journal. I give a running account of them.

Roanoke has fallen before superior numbers, although we had 15,000 idle troops at Norfolk within hearing of the battle. The government would not interfere, and Gen. Huger refused to allow the use of a few thousand of his troops.

But Gen. Wise is safe; Providence willed that he should escape the "man-trap." When the enemy were about to open fire on his headquarters at Nag's Head, knowing him to be prostrated with illness (for the island had then been surrendered after a heroic defense), Lieutenants Bagly and Wise bore the general away in a blanket to a distance of ten or fifteen miles. The Yankees would have gladly exchanged all their prisoners for Gen. Wise, who is ever a terror to the North.

Capt. O. Jenning Wise fell, while gallantly cheering his men, in the heat of the battle. A thousand of the enemy fell before a few hundred of our brave soldiers. We lost some 2500 men, for there was no alternative but to surrender.

Capt. Wise told the Yankee officers, who persisted in forcing themselves in his presence during his dying moments, that the South could never be subjugated. They might exterminate us, but every man, woman, and child would prefer death to abject subjugation. And he died with a sweet smile on his lip, eliciting the profound respect of his most embittered enemies.

The enemy paroled our men taken on the island; and we recovered the remains of the heroic Capt. Wise. His funeral here was most impressive, and saddened the countenances of thousands who witnessed the pageant. None of the members of the government were present; but the ladies threw flowers and evergreens upon his bier. He is dead—but history will do him justice; and his example will inspire others with the spirit of true heroism.

And President Tyler is no more on earth. He died after a very brief illness. There was a grand funeral, Mr. Hunter and others delivering orations. They came to me, supposing I had written one of the several biographies of the deceased which have appeared during the last twenty years. But I had written none—and none published were worthy of the subject. I could only refer them to the bound volumes of the MADISONIAN in the State library for his messages and other State papers. The originals are among my papers in the hands of the enemy. His history is yet to be written—and it will be read centuries hence.

Fort Henry has fallen. Would that were all! The catalogue of disasters I feared and foretold, under the policy adopted by the War Department, may be a long and a terrible one.

The mission of the spies to East Tennessee is now apparent. Three of the enemy's gun-boats have ascended the Tennessee River to the very head of navigation, while the women and children on its banks could do nothing more than gaze in mute despair. No batteries, no men were there. The absence of these is what the traitors, running from here to Washington, have been reporting to the enemy. Their boats would no more have ventured up that river without the previous exploration of spies, than Mr. Lincoln would dare to penetrate a cavern without torch-bearers, in which the rattle of venomous snakes could be heard. They have ascended to Florence, and may get footing in Alabama and Mississippi!

And Fort Donelson has been attacked by an immensely superior force. We have 15,000 men there to resist, perhaps, 75,000! Was ever such management known before? Who is responsible for it? If Donelson falls, what becomes of the ten or twelve thousand men at Bowling Green?

February 21st.—All our garrison in Fort Henry, with Gen. Tilghman, surrendered. I think we had only 1500 men there. Guns, ammunition, and stores, all gone.

No news from Donelson—and that is *bad* news. Benjamin says he has no definite information. But prisoners taken say the enemy have been reinforced, and are hurling 80,000 against our 15,000.

February 22d.—Such a day! The heavens weep incessantly. Capitol Square is black with umbrellas; and a shelter has been erected for the President to stand under.

I walked up to the monument and heard the Inaugural read by the President. He read it well, and seemed self-poised in the midst of disasters, which he acknowledged had befallen us. And he admitted that there had been errors in our war policy. We had attempted operations on too extensive a scale, thus diffusing our powers which should have been concentrated. I like these candid confessions. They augur a different policy hereafter, and we may hope for better results in the future. We must all stand up for our country.

Mr. Hunter has resigned, and taken his place in the Senate.

February 23d.—At last we have the astounding tidings that Donelson has fallen, and Buckner, and 9,000 men, arms, stores, everything are in the possession of the enemy! Did the President know it yesterday? Or did the Secretary keep it back till the new government (permanent) was launched into existence? Wherefore? The Southern *people* cannot be daunted by calamity!

Last night it was still raining—and it rained all night. It was a lugubrious reception at the President's mansion. But the President himself was calm, and Mrs. Davis seemed in spirits. For a long time I feared the bad weather would keep the people away; and the thought struck me when I entered, that if there were a Lincoln spy present, we should have more ridicule in the Yankee presses on the paucity of numbers attending the reception. But the crowd came at last, and filled the ample rooms. The permanent government had its birth in storm, but it may yet flourish in sunshine. For my own part, however, I think a provisional government of few men, should have been adopted "for the war."

FEBRUARY 24TH.—Gen. Sydney Johnston has evacuated Bowling Green with his *ten* or *twelve* thousand men! Where is his mighty army now? It never did exist!

FEBRUARY 25TH.—And Nashville must fall—although no one seems to anticipate such calamity. We must run the career of disasters allotted us, and await the turning of the tide.

FEBRUARY 26TH.—Congress, in secret session, has authorized the declaration of martial law in this city, and at some few other places. This might be well under other circumstances; but it will not be well if the old general in command should be clothed with powers which he has no qualifications to wield advantageously. The facile old man will do *anything* the Secretary advises.

Our army is to fall back from Manassas! The Rappahannock is not to be our line of *defense*. Of course the enemy will soon strike at Richmond from some direction. I have given great offense to some of our people by saying the policy of permitting men to go North at will, will bring the enemy to the gates of the city in ninety days. Several have told me that the prediction has been marked in the Secretary's tablets, and that I am marked for destruction if it be not verified. I reply that I would rather be destroyed than that it should be fulfilled.

FEBRUARY 27TH.—Columbus is to be evacuated. Beauregard sees that it is untenable with Forts Henry and Donelson in possession of the enemy. He will not be caught in such a trap as that. But he is erecting a battery at Island No. 10 that will give the Yankees trouble. I hope it may stay the catalogue of disasters.

FEBRUARY 28TH.—These calamities may be a wholesome chastening for us. We shall now go to work and raise troops enough to defend the country. Congress will certainly pass the Conscription Act recommended by the President.

RICHMOND, VIRGINIA, FEBRUARY 1862

Jefferson Davis: Message to the Confederate Congress

The Confederate Provisional Congress adjourned on February 17, 1862, and was succeeded the next day by the First Confederate Congress, which had been elected in November 1861. Three days after being inaugurated for a full six-year term as president, Jefferson Davis submitted a written message to the new Congress on "the State of the Confederacy."

Richmond, February 25, 1862

IN OBEDIENCE to the Constitutional provision requiring the President from time to time to give to the Congress information of the State of the Confederacy, and recommend to their consideration such measures as he shall judge necessary and expedient, I have to communicate that since my message at the last session of the Provisional Congress, events have demonstrated that the Government had attempted more than it had power successfully to achieve.

Hence, in the effort to protect by our arms the whole of the territory of the Confederate States, Sea-board and inland, we have been so exposed as recently to encounter serious disasters. When the Confederacy was formed, the States composing it were, by the peculiar character of their pursuits and a misplaced confidence in their former associates, to a great extent destitute of the means for the prosecution of the war on so gigantic a scale as that which it has attained. The workshops and artisans were mainly to be found in the Northern States, and one of the first duties which devolved upon this Government was to establish the necessary manufactories, and in the meantime, to obtain by purchase from abroad, as far as practicable whatever was required for the public defence. No effort has been spared to effect both these ends, and though the results have not equalled our hopes, it is believed that an impartial judgment will, upon full investigation, award to the various departments of the Government credit for having done all which human power and foresight enabled them to accomplish. The valor and devotion of the people have not only sustained the efforts of the Government, but have gone far to supply its deficiencies.

The active state of military preparation among the nations of Europe in April last, the date when our agents first went abroad, interposed unavoidable delays in the procurement of arms, and the want of a navy has greatly impeded our efforts to import military supplies of all sorts.

I have hoped for several days to receive official reports in relation to our discomfiture at Roanoke Island, and the fall of Fort Donelson. They have not yet reached me, and I am, therefore, unable to communicate to you such information of those events and the consequences resulting from them, as would enable me to make recommendations founded upon the changed condition which they have produced. Enough is known of the surrender at Roanoke Island to make us feel that it was deeply humiliating, however imperfect may have been the preparations for defence. The hope is still entertained that our reported losses at Fort Donelson have been greatly exaggerated, inasmuch as I am not only unwilling but unable to believe that a large army of our people have surrendered without a desperate effort to cut their way through investing forces, whatever may have been their numbers, and to endeavor to make a junction with other divisions of the Army. But in the absence, of that exact information which can only be afforded by official reports, it would be premature to pass judgment, and my own is reserved, as I trust yours will be, until that information is received. In the meantime, Strenuous efforts have been made to throw forward reenforcements to the Armies at the positions threatened, and I cannot doubt that the bitter disappointments we have borne, by nerving the people to still greater exertions, will speedily secure results more accordant with our just expectation, and as favorable to our cause as those which marked the earlier periods of the War.

The reports of the Secretaries of War and the Navy will exhibit the mass of resources for the conduct of the War which we have been enabled to accumulate notwithstanding the very serious difficulties against which we have contended.

They afford the cheering hope that our resources, limited as they were at the beginning of the contest, will, during its progress, become developed to such an extent as fully to meet our future wants.

The policy of enlistment for short terms against which I have steadily contended from the commencement of the war has, in my judgment, contributed in no immaterial degree to the recent reverses which we have suffered, and even now renders it difficult to furnish you an accurate statement of the Army. When the War first broke out many of our people could with difficulty be persuaded that it would be long or serious. It was not deemed possible that anything so insane as a persistent attempt to subjugate these States could be made—still less that the delusion would so far prevail as to give to the war the vast proportions which it has assumed. The people, incredulous of a long War, were naturally averse to long enlistments, and the early legislation of Congress rendered it impracticable to obtain Volunteers for a greater period than twelve months. Now that it has become probable that the war will be continued through a series of years, our high-spirited and gallant soldiers, while generally re-enlisting, are, from the fact of having entered the service for a short term, compelled in many instances to go home to make the necessary arrangements for their families during their prolonged absence.

The quotas of new regiments for the war, called for from the different States, are in rapid progress of organization. The whole body of new levies and re-enlisted men will probably be ready in the ranks within the next thirty days. But, in the meantime, it is exceedingly difficult to give an accurate statement of the number of our forces in the field. They may, in general terms, be stated at 400 regiments of infantry, with a proportionate force of Cavalry and artillery, the details of which will be shown by the report of the Secretary of War. I deem it proper to advert to the fact that the process of furloughs and re-enlistment in progress for the last month had so far disorganized and weakened our forces as to impair our ability for successful defence; but I heartily congratulate you that this evil, which I had foreseen and was powerless to prevent, may now be said to be substantially at an end, and that we shall not again during the war be exposed to seeing our strength diminished by this fruitful cause of disaster—short enlistments.

The people of the Confederate States being principally engaged in agricultural pursuits, were unprovided at the commencement of hostilities with ships, ship-yards, materials for shipbuilding, or skilled mechanics and seamen in sufficient numbers to make the prompt creation of a navy a practicable task even if the required appropriations had been made for the purpose. Notwithstanding our very limited resources, however, the report of the Secretary will exhibit to you a satisfactory progress in preparation, and a certainty of early completion of vessels of a number and class on which we may confidently rely for contesting the vaunted control of the enemy over our waters.

The financial system devised by the wisdom of your predecessors has proved adequate to supplying all the wants of the Government notwithstanding the unexpected and very large increase of expenditures resulting from the great augmentation in the necessary means of defence. The report of the Secretary of the Treasury will exhibit the gratifying fact that we have no floating debt; that the credit of the Government is unimpaired, and that the total expenditure of the Government for the year has been in round numbers one hundred and seventy millions of dollars; less than one-third of the sum wasted by the enemy in his vain effort to conquer us—less than the value of a single article of export—the cotton crop of the year.

The report of the Post Master General will show the condition of that department to be steadily improving—its revenues increasing, and already affording the assurance that it will be selfsustaining at the date required by the Constitution while affording ample mail facilities for the people.

In the Department of Justice, which includes the Patent Office and Public Printing, some legislative provisions will be required, which will be specifically stated in the report of the head of that Department. I invite the attention of Congress to the duty of organizing a Supreme Court of the Confederate States; in accordance with the mandate of the Constitution.

I refer you to my message communicated to the Provisional Congress in November last for such further information touching the condition of public affairs as it might be useful to lay before you; the short interval which has since elapsed not having produced any material changes in that condition other than those to which reference has already been made.

In conclusion, I cordially welcome Representatives who, recently chosen by the people, are fully imbued with their views and feelings, and can so ably advise me as to the needful provisions for the public service. I assure you of my hearty cooperation in all your efforts for the common welfare of the country

JEFFERSON DAVIS

"THE BOLDEST FEAT": MARYLAND, MARCH 1862

George E. Stephens to the Weekly Anglo-African

The son of free blacks who fled to Philadelphia from Virginia after the Nat Turner slave rebellion, George E. Stephens was an abolitionist who worked before the war as a cabinetmaker, upholsterer, and sailor. In October 1861 he became a correspondent for the New York *Weekly Anglo-African*, an influential black newspaper, while serving as a cook and personal servant to Lieutenant Colonel Benjamin Tilghman of the 26th Pennsylvania Infantry Regiment. Stephens spent the winter of 1861–62 along the lower Potomac in Charles County, Maryland, reporting on army camp life and the interactions among soldiers, slaves, and slaveholders. His letter of March 2 appeared in the *Anglo-African* on March 15, 1862.

Head Quarters, Hooker's Division,
Near Budd's Ferry, Md.,
March 2d, 1862.

Mr. Editor.—We have had high winds for the last two or three days, interspersed of course with rain, but if the rain would cease these driving March winds would soon dry up the roads, and the grand army of the Potomac would be able to walk dry shod over into the unhappy land of Canaan, (Dixie's land.)

The rumor has reached us that Gen. Banks has been defeated, and his forces completely routed on the upper Potomac.

Professor Lowe has been unable to make his usual daily balloon reconnaissance on account of the high wind. The wind blew so violently on Tuesday last that he was compelled to disinflate his balloon, but will reinflate it as soon as the winds subside.

We are reliably informed that the rebels immediately in front of us have received large reinforcements; they evidently anticipate an attack.

Brigadier General Naglee, of Pennsylvania, arrived in camp on the 17th ult., and took command of 1st Brigade, in place of

Col. Cowdin, of the 1st Massachusetts regiment, who returns to his command.

Captain Page who has commanded at Liverpool Point, where the contrabands are employed unloading vessels, etc., and where the army supplies are stored, relates that two of these contrabands undertook and accomplished the boldest feat of the war, thus furnishing us with another irrefutable evidence of the courage, daring and skill of the negro, when brought face to face with danger; the strength and permanence of his affections, which is the noblest evidence, too, of a pure, perfect and elevated nature. These men belong to the party Col. Graham brought off when he made his inroad into Virginia. The captain says that one of them came to him and asked permission to recross the river to rescue his wife, declaring that he was almost certain that he could bring her off safely. The captain thought the fellow mad, but he plead so earnestly that he gave him permission, and gave notice of the fact to the commander of the flotilla, to prevent his being fired upon by the gun boats. He left Liverpool Point on a dark night, in a small skiff with muffled oars. His wife lived some six or seven miles up the Occoquan Bay. He reached her, brought her off safe, gathered much valuable information of the strength and position of the enemy, and returned the following night to Liverpool Point with his companion, safe and unharmed. This man is a true type of the negro; jet black, erect and athletic. The other man, a type of the mixed blood, seeing the triumph of his comrade, asked and received permission to secure his wife, and not having as far to go, brought her off triumphantly and returned the same evening that he went upon his errand. When it is remembered that the rebels are very vigilant on account of the expected attack of our forces, and that the beach is lined with sentinels from Martha's Point to Occoquan Bay, whose bivouac fires can be seen every night with common glasses, and also that if they had been detected nothing but instant death would have been meted out to them, we must accord these two of the most daring ventures and successful exploits of the war. If these men and their brethren were allowed to become active instead of passive co-operators with the Union forces, how long would treason be able to so impudently defy the federal powers?

Here is an item I give you for the special benefit of your fair readers. The more susceptible of the sterner sex may also gather whatever satisfaction this little story of love, struggle and triumph, may give. One of the most painful of the revolting sights one sees when sojourning in this land of slavery, is the universal prostitution by their masters of beautiful slave women. There are scarcely any farms or plantations in the south that can boast of no pretty women. They are prized, petted, bartered and sold according to the nature and extent of their charms. Beauties rivaling those of the Caucasian are sold in the slave marts of the U.S. No matter how loathsome to her the purchaser of her charms may be, the hard remorseless necessities of her position compel her to yield. Mary Thomas, a beautiful negress, the slave of a man by the name of Henry Eglon, living near Newport, belonged to this class. Her master had already engaged her to an old lecherous scoundrel. She fell violently in love with an Anglo-African in one of the companies. Longing to be free, and to escape that living martyrdom, the life which her master had marked out for her, and also unite her destiny with that of her lover, she made a bold stroke for life, love and liberty. She did not clothe herself in male apparel, like many of the paler heroines and amazons have done, but maintained a distinction of sex. She had not gone far before Ferrel, a slave master near Port Tobacco, arrested her and locked her up in the jail at that place. Her lover broke the jail open and released her. She had not been released five minutes before Johnny Shackelford, a noted slave hunter, re-arrested her; but the girl fought him bravely. Her lover and the soldiers could not quietly look on such a contest as this; they came to the rescue, and just barely left life in the hunter. And why should she not triumph? Did not she turn her back on slavery and ruin, while the path which she proposed to tread was illuminated with the bright hope of salvation, liberty and love? I rejoice to say that Mary Thomas to-day is free!

There is nothing more galling to a black man than the iteration and reiteration of the foul misrepresentations which the advocate of man-stealing, man-torturing, and man-slaughtering slavery urge against him. There never has been a time in the history of this country, when there was such a scarcity of material to build these heartless lies on. They may oppose us and deny us rights, but our friends and ourselves will soon settle the contest of ideas; but when our enemies add "insult to injury" it incites in us the desire to cut their throats or give them a taste of the horrors of the system they so much love. Although the Government has spurned the loyalty of the negro more pointedly and peremptorily than it has the treason of these slaveholding dogs and their Northern tools and accomplices, they have, as by some unseen power, become active and prominent in this great civil contest, and have impressed the indelible truth upon the minds of the thinking portion of this nation that he is a dreadful power for evil or a grand and noble one for good.

Rum Point and Liverpool Point, as I have often before remarked, are the points where the supplies are landed. Before the contrabands were brought here, details from the various regiments were made to unload the vessels and to store the provisions; these details generally numbered about a hundred men—a whole company. The soldiers were not allowed for this special duty any extra compensation; so the result was, that they skulked out of as much work as they could, upon the principle that it is far more agreeable and much more reasonable to play for nothing than to work for nothing. They were certain to get their $13 per month, and this poor pay and poorer fare formed no incentive to hard manual labor. Since the 30 or 40 muscular blacks have arrived at Liverpool Point it is made the principle depot for stores and Rum Point is made the passenger depot; and these 30 or 40 men do more in the same space of time than a hundred white men—thus reversing the order of things. The black man under the incentives of Free labor, pay, and freedom, goes blithely and gaily to his task; while the white man under the repulsiveness of forced labor and no pay, lounges about and skulks sulkily away. They are also temperate and cleanly; are comfortably housed, clothed and fed by the Government, wives, children, and all; and are to receive ten cents a day pay, which is small—but when the housing, clothing and feeding of a man and his family are considered, his pay is nearly as good as the enlisted soldier; it can all be saved up by them, and will make a small start for them when they shall be released by the authorities.

G.E.S.

"ALL QUIET ON THE POTOMAC": MARCH 1862

Orpheus C. Kerr: from
The Orpheus C. Kerr Papers

The never-changing bulletin "All Quiet on the Potomac," issued by the seemingly immovable Army of the Potomac through the winter of 1861–62, inspired the satirist Robert Henry Newell, writing in the guise of his commentator Orpheus C. Kerr (i.e. "office seeker") to construct a fable. Newell's dispatches, published in the *New York Sunday Mercury*, had many admirers, including President Lincoln, and were published in three wartime volumes under the rubric *The Orpheus C. Kerr Papers*.

WASHINGTON, D. C., March 3d, 1862.

I KNOW a man, my boy, who was driven to lunacy by reliable war news. He was in the prime of life when the war broke out, and took such an interest in the struggle that it soon became nearly equal to the interest on his debts. With all the enthusiasm of vegetable youth he subscribed for all the papers, and commenced to read the reliable war news. In this way he learned that all was quiet on the Potomac, and immediately went to congratulate his friends, and purchase six American flags. On the following morning he wrapt himself in the banner of his country and learned from all the papers that all was quiet on the Potomac. His joy at once became intense; he hoisted a flag on the lightning-rod of his domicil, purchased a national pocket-handkerchief, bought six hand-organs that played the Star-Spangled Banner, and drank nothing but gunpowder tea. In the next six months, however, there was a great change in our military affairs; the backbone of the rebellion was broken, the sound of the thunder came from all parts of the sky, and fifty-three excellent family journals informed the enthusiast that all was quiet on the Potomac. He now became fairly mad with bliss, and volunteered to sit up with a young lady whose brother was a soldier. On the following morning he commenced to read Bancroft's History of the United States, with Hardee's Tactics appended, only pausing long enough to learn from the daily papers that all was quiet on the Potomac. Thus, in a fairy dream of delicious joy, passed the greater part of this devoted patriot's life; and even as his hair turned gray, and his form began to bend with old age, his eye flashed in eternal youth over the still reliable war news. At length there came a great change in the military career of the Republic; the rebellion received its death-wound, and Washington's Birthday boomed upon the United States of America. It was the morning of that glorious day, and the venerable patriot was tottering about the room with his cane, when his great-grandchild, a lad of twenty-five, came thundering into the room with forty-three daily papers under his arm.

"Old man!" says he, in a transport, "there's great news."

"Boy, boy!" says the aged patriot, "do not trifle with me. Can it be that—"

"Bet your life—"

"Is it then a fact that—"

"Yes—"

"Am I to believe that—"

"All is quiet on the Potomac!"

It was too much for the venerable Brutus; he clutched at the air, spun once on his left heel, sang a stave of John Brown's body, and stood transfixed with ecstacy.

"Thank Heving," says he, "for sparing me to see this day!"

After which he became hopelessly insane, my boy, and raved so awfully about all our great generals turning into mud-larks that his afflicted family had to send him to the asylum.

This veracious and touching biography will show you how dangerous to public health is reliable war news, and convince you that the Secretary's order to the press is only a proper insanitary measure.

I am all the more resigned to it, my boy, because it affects me so little that I am even able to give you a strictly reliable account of a great movement that lately took place.

I went down to Accomac early in the week, my boy, having heard that Captain Villiam Brown and the Conic Section of the Mackerel Brigade were about to march upon Fort Muggins, where Jeff Davis, Beauregard, Mason, Slidell, Yancey, and the whole rebel Congress were believed to be intrenched. Mounted on my gothic steed Pegasus, who only blew down once in the whole journey, I repaired to Villiam's department, and was taking notes of the advance, upon a sheet of paper spread on the ground, when the commander of Accomac approached me, and says he:

"What are you doing, my bantam?"

"I'm taking notes," says I, "for a journal which has such an immense circulation among our gallant troops that when they begin to read it in the camps, it looks, from a distance, as though there had just been a heavy snow-storm.'

"Ah!" says Villiam, thoughtfully, "newspapers and snow-storms are somewhat alike; for both make black appear white. But," said Villiam philosophically, "the snow is the more moral; for you can't lie in that with safety, as you can in a newspaper. In the language of General Grant at Donelson," says Villiam, sternly: "I propose to move upon your works immediately."

And with that he planted one of his boots right in the middle of my paper.

"Read that ere Napoleonic dockyment," says Villiam, handing me a scroll. It was as follows:

EDICK.

Having noticed that the press of the United States of America is making a ass of itself, by giving information to the enemy concerning the best methods of carrying on the strategy of war, I do hereby assume control of all special correspondents, forbidding them to transact anything but private business; neither they, nor their wives, nor their children, to the third and fourth generation.

I. It is ordered, that all advice from editors to the War Department, to the general commanding, or the generals commanding the armies in the field, be absolutely forbidden; as such advice is calculated to make the United States of America a idiot.

II. Any newspaper publishing any news whatever, however obtained, shall be excluded from all railroads and steamboats, in order that country journals, which receive the same news during the following year, may not be injured in cirkylation.

III. This control of special correspondents does not include the correspondent of the London Times, who wouldn't be believed if he published all the news of the next Christian era. By order of

VILLIAM BROWN, Eskevire,
Captain Conic Section Mackerel Brigade.

I had remounted Pegasus while reading this able State paper, my boy, and had just finished it, when a nervous member of the advance-guard accidentally touched off a cannon, whose report was almost immediately answered by one from the dense fog before us.

"Ha!" says Captain Villiam Brown, suddenly leaping from his steed, and creeping under it—to examine if the saddle-girth was all right—"the fort is right before us in the fog, and the rebels are awake. Let the Orange County Company advance with their howitzers, and fire to the north-east."

The Orange County Company, my boy, instantly wheeled their howitzers into position, and sent some pounds of grape toward the meridian, the roar of their weapons of death being instantaneously answered by a thundering crash in the fog.

Company 3, Regiment 5, Mackerel Brigade, now went forward six yards at double-quick, and poured in a rattling volley of musketry, dodging fearlessly when exactly the same kind of a volley was heard in the fog, and wishing that they might have a few rebels for supper.

"Ha!" says Captain Villiam Brown, when he noticed that nobody seemed to be killed yet; "Providence is on our side, and this here unnatural rebellion is squelched. Let the Anatomical Cavalry charge into the fog, and demand the surrender of Fort Muggins," continued Villiam, compressing his lips with mad valor, "while I repair to that tree back there, and see if there is not a fiendish secessionist lurking behind it."

The Anatomical Cavalry immediately dismounted from their horses, which were too old to be used in a charge, and gallantly entered the fog, with their sabres between their teeth, and their hands in their pockets—it being a part of their tactics to catch a rebel before cutting his head off.

In the meantime, my boy, the Orange County howitzers and the Mackerel muskets were hurling a continuous fire into the clouds, stirring up the angels, and loosening the smaller planets. Sturdily answered the rebels from the fog-begirt fort; but not one of our men had yet fallen.

Captain Villiam Brown was just coming down from the top of a very tall tree, whither he had gone to search for masked batteries, when the fog commenced lifting, and disclosed the Anatomical Cavalry returning at double-quick.

Instantly our fire ceased, and so did that of the rebels.

"Does the fort surrender to the United States of America?" says Villiam, to the captain of the Anatomicals.

The gallant dragoon, sighed, and says he:

"I used my magnifying glass, but could find no fort."

At this moment, my boy, a sharp sunbeam cleft the fog as a sword does a vail, and the mist rolled away from the scene in two volumes, disclosing to our view a fine cabbage-patch, with a dense wood beyond.

Villiam deliberately raised a bottle to his face, and gazed through it upon the unexpected prospect.

"Ha!" says he sadly, "the garrison has cut its way through the fog and escaped, but Fort Muggins is ours! Let the flag of our Union be planted on the ramparts," says Villiam, with much perspiration, "and I will immediately issue a proclamation to the people of the United States of America."

Believing that Villiam was somewhat too hasty in his conclusions, my boy, I ventured to insinuate that what he had taken for a fort in the fog, was really nothing but a cabbage inclosure, and that the escaped rebels were purely imaginary.

"Imaginary!" says Villiam, hastily placing his canteen in his pocket. "Why, didn't you hear the roar of their artillery?"

"Do you see that thick wood yonder?" says I.

Says he, "It is visible to the undressed eye."

"Well," says I, "what you took for the sound of rebel firing, was only the echo of your own firing in that wood."

Villiam pondered for a few moments, my boy, like one who was considering the propriety of saying nothing in as few words as possible, and then looked angularly at me, and says he:

"My proclamation to the press will cover all this, and the news of this here engagement will keep until the war is over. Ah!" says Villiam, "I wouldn't have the news of this affair published on any account; for if the Government thought I was trying to cabbage in my Department, it would make me Minister to Russia immediately."

As the Conic Section of the Mackerel Brigade returned slowly to head-quarters, my boy, I thought to myself: How often does man, after making something his particular forte, discover at last that it is only a cabbage-patch, and hardly large enough at that for a big hog like himself!

Yours, philanthropically,
Orpheus C. Kerr.

BATTLE OF ELKHORN TAVERN:
ARKANSAS, MARCH 1862

Dabney H. Maury: Recollections of the Elkhorn Campaign

Following their victory at Wilson's Creek in southwestern Missouri in August 1861, the Confederates were pushed back into northwestern Arkansas by Brigadier General Samuel R. Curtis. A counterstroke by Major General Earl Van Dorn, Confederate commander in the Trans-Mississippi, led to the battle of Elkhorn Tavern (or Pea Ridge) on March 7–8, 1862. With 14,000 Confederate and 10,000 Union troops engaged, it was the war's largest battle west of the Mississippi. The Union lost 1,384 men killed, wounded, or missing, while Confederate casualties may have totaled 2,000. Colonel Dabney H. Maury, a West Point graduate, served on Van Dorn's staff and offered a Confederate view of the fighting in an article published by the Southern Historical Society in 1876. The Northern victory at Elkhorn Tavern kept Missouri in the Union and disrupted Confederate plans for the Trans-Mississippi.

———————

MONTGOMERY WHITE SULPHUR SPRINGS, VA.,
June 10th, 1876.

Colonel WM. PRESTON JOHNSTON:

My dear Colonel—In compliance with your request, I will endeavor to write you some recollections of the campaign of Elkhorn. As I am not able to refer to any documents, I can only give you my recollections; and I hope, therefore, that any one who can correct my mistakes of omission will do so, for after a lapse of so long a time, passed in events of such absorbing interest as those of our great war, one's memory loses many facts.

In January, 1862, General Earl Van Dorn was appointed commander of the Trans-Mississippi Department, then a part of the great territorial command of your father, General Sydney Johnston. I was ordered from the Potomac to go with Van Dorn as chief of the staff of his Trans-Mississippi district.

In February we reached Jacksonport, Arkansas, on the White

river, and soon after moved up to Pocahontas, in the northeastern part of Arkansas, and began to organize an expedition against Saint Louis. Van Dorn's plan was to carry Saint Louis by a *coup de main*, and then to throw his forces into Illinois and transfer the war into the enemy's country.

We had been busily occupied in preparing for this operation, when, late in February, Colonel Clay Taylor arrived at headquarters with dispatches from General Price, then in Boston mountains in northwest Arkansas. General Price related that after his victory at Springfield, or Oakhill, he had been forced by the reinforced enemy to retreat through Missouri down into Arkansas; that General McCulloch, commanding the Texans, was near him in Boston mountain; that the enemy, under Generals Curtis and Siegel, were lying only two marches distant, not over 18,000 strong, and might be overcome by a vigorous, combined attack of all the forces of McCulloch and Price,—but that points of difference of opinion and precedence of rank had arisen between them, in consequence of which no co-operation could be efficiently conducted; and he prayed that Van Dorn, as their common superior, would come at once to Boston mountains, combine the forces of the discordant generals, and lead them to attack the enemy's army.

As our designed operations upon Saint Louis depended mainly upon these commands of Price and McCulloch for success, Van Dorn at once set out for Boston mountains, where he knew he would find a battle ready for him, and, should victory crown him, the success of his Saint Louis expedition would be assured.

We took a steamer for Jacksonport, whence on February 23d, we mounted our horses and started upon our ride across the State to Van Buren. Our party consisted of Van Dorn, myself, Lieutenant Sullivan, who was nephew and aid-de-camp to General Van Dorn, my negro boy Jem, and a guide—a stupid, hulking fellow, who did us more harm than service. Leaving Jacksonport in the morning, we rode twelve miles to the spacious and hospitable farm house of a planter named Bryan, I think. I shall be sorry if I have not given his name, for he was very intelligent and very hospitable, and with him and the kind mistress of his house and her daughters, we found the most cordial and comfortable entertainment we ever met with beyond the Mississippi, and in the trials and disappointments which soon after befell us, we often reverted to that night as a "green spot" in our Arkansas experience.

Next morning, February 24th, we set out after a most abundant breakfast, on our ride across the State of Arkansas. Van Dorn on his black mare, a powerful, hardy thoroughbred, led off in a trot which, for the ensuing five days, carried us along at about fifty miles a day.

He wore a very beautiful Turkish cimeter, the gift of a friend. It was the only article of personal belonging in which I ever knew him to evince especial pleasure. When about five miles from the house he missed his sabre from its sheath. Sullivan insisted on riding back to look for it, while we pursued our way in that relentless trot. Something was said about the "bad omen," which jarred on my feelings and was remembered. Sullivan soon rejoined us with the sword, which he found lying in the road a mile or so behind us.

On the second day, February 25th, we crossed Black river. The stream was narrow, but rapid and deep to the banks. The ferryboat was a long "dug out."

Van Dorn entered first, taking with him Jem, and at the moment of leaving the shore the guide also stepped into the boat and capsized it. Van Dorn, being at the further end, was thrown well out into the stream—encumbered with his heavy cavalry cloak, boots, spurs and sabre; but he struck strongly out for the shore, with a countenance as smiling as ever a schoolboy wore in a summer bath.

Seeing he was all right, I directed my interest and efforts to Jem, who, though a stout swimmer and not excessively encumbered by raiment, seemed to realise all the gravity of his position. His round eyes were distended to their utmost, and he blew the water out at every stroke with the snort of a porpoise, and was the picture of a negro who knew he was swimming for his life. I stood ready with my sash to throw out to him, but he soon struck bottom at the very shore, and scrambled out. The day was very bleak; and after crossing over the river we halted for two hours in a very comfortless house, where Van Dorn made an ineffectual effort to dry his clothes, which resulted in the severest attack of chill and fever I ever saw. It clung to him throughout the campaign, and except when in the presence of the enemy, made him quake as Cassius tells us Cæsar did.

I revert to this whole march as peculiarly devoid of interest or pleasure. The country was monotonous and unpicturesque, while some of the people were ignorant of the causes and objects of the war and unsympathetic with us; but there were many honorable exceptions to this, and every night of our five days' trip we received hospitable entertainment in the house of an Arkansas planter; and every night we each slept in a feather bed, which closed about us like a poultice and drew out all the soreness of the sore bones and the saddle-galls which our fifty miles' ride had left with us. After a lifetime of experience in the cavalry service, I then discovered in a feather bed the only panacea for a jaded horseman's ills.

Although I had not made a day's march in the saddle for months prior to our trip across Arkansas, and although every day we trotted from fifty to fifty-five miles, on leaving our feather beds at dawn for our saddles, we found all the stiffness and soreness had been drawn out of us, and we were as fresh and nimble as if we were just setting out.

The United States War Department ought to know about this, and all the cavalry ought to sleep in feather beds: no man can get good rest on the bare ground. And "post traders" would make great profit in feathers if the constituted authorities would only adopt them.

We rode into Van Buren on the evening of February 28th, and next morning, March 1st, left Van Buren for Price's camp in Boston mountains, distant about thirty miles.

The weather was bitter cold, and all day we rode over an ascending mountain road until dark, when we came to the little farm house in which the leader of the Missourians had made his headquarters.

I was much impressed by the grand proportions and the stately air of the man who up to that time had been the foremost figure of the war beyond the Mississippi.

General Price was one of the handsomest men I have ever seen. He was over six feet two inches in stature, of massive proportions, but easy and graceful in his carriage and his gestures; his hands and feet were remarkably small and well shaped; his hair and whiskers, which he wore in the old English fashion, were silver white; his face was ruddy and very benignant, yet firm in its expression; his profile was finely chiseled, and bespoke manhood of the highest type; his voice was clear and ringing, and his accentuation singularly distinct. A braver or a kinder heart beat in no man's bosom; he was wise in counsel and bold in action, and never spared his own blood on any battle field. No man had greater influence over his troops; and as he sat his superb charger with the ease and lightness of one accustomed all his days to "ride a thoroughbred horse," it was impossible to find a more magnificent specimen of manhood in its prime, than Sterling Price presented to the brave Missourians, who loved him with a fervor not less than we Virginians felt for Lee.

On this our first meeting, General Price showed us the hospitality traditional of his native State (Virginia). He took Van Dorn to share his chamber, and sent a staff officer to conduct Sullivan and me to the bivouac of his staff, where we found sumptuous entertainment.

Never before or since have I enjoyed such luxurious accommodations in camp as were at my service that wintry night, in the camp of Price's staff in the Boston mountains.

We were conducted to a beautiful little meadow, where the staff and the band (all through the war he carried with him a fine band) had cast their lines in one of the pleasantest places I have ever been in during campaign. The General's following was very numerous, and it seemed to me they were as thoroughly good fellows as I ever met. We were entertained at a glorious supper and soon after were conducted to our tent. It was a very large wall tent, the central portion of which was occupied by a bed of blankets and buffalo robes near a foot deep. In front of the tent, a huge fire of logs had been burning for more than an hour, heating the ground and the air of the tent, the doors of which were thrown wide open to receive the genial warmth.

We were soon enjoying, in a wearied soldier's slumber, all of these judicious arrangements, and awoke next morning in prime condition for anything before us.

And first came a breakfast, the peer of the supper, and the last breakfast of that quality I ever saw. I can never forget—for it was the first and the last time I enjoyed that dish—the *kidneys stewed in sherry!* which, late in the course of that breakfast, were served to me as a sort of *chasse* by a generous young Missouri colonel, who had brought to that rough field of war this memento of the more refined culinary accomplishments he had acquired in Saint Louis.

The breakfast dispatched, we mounted our horses and were soon on our way over the mountain ridge which divided Price's camp from that of the Texans under General McCulloch.

McCulloch's little army was bivouacked several miles distant from the Missourians. We found the noted Texan ranger occupying a small farm house on the mountain side—comfortless and bare enough it was.

In person, in manner and in character, McCulloch presented a strong contrast with Price. He was near six feet tall, was spare and wirey, and somewhat inclined to a stoop in his shoulders. His deep set gray eyes were shaded by rather heavy eyebrows, which gave an expression of almost suspicious scrutiny to his countenance. In manner, he was undemonstrative, reticent, and, to us, even cautious. He was calm and anxious in view of the enterprise we had undertaken; but avowed his confidence in it, and co-operated heartily for its success.

His whole conduct during these operations impressed us very favorably as to his capacity for war, and but for his untimely death, he would have played an important part in our struggle.

His staff was limited to five or six earnest, working men, and all about him bespoke the stern seriousness of soldiers trained to arms. Frank Armstrong, Lindsay Lomax, Edward Dillon, —— Kimmell, were members of his staff, whom I found with him, all of whom served often and long with me in the stirring events of the great contest we had embarked in.

A full conference with McCulloch, whose remarkable knowledge of roads and country were much relied upon in the operations of that campaign, enabled Van Dorn to organize the corps of Price and of McCulloch into an army of about 16,000 men, and to march at dawn of March 1st to attack the enemy in the valley of Sugar creek at the "Elkhorn tavern."

The night had been bitter cold. We had slept in a sort of barn or stable, and had only a little coffee and hard bread to eat. The snow was falling fast as we rode to the head of the column: and we did not feel very bright, until we were struck with the splendid appearance of a large regiment we were passing. It halted as we came upon its flank, faced to the front and presented arms, and as General Van Dorn reached its centre, three rousing cheers rang out upon the morning air, and made us feel we were with soldiers. It was the ever glorious Third Louisiana which thus cheered us.

That day we crossed over Boston mountain, and encamped near Fayetteville. Our cavalry, under McIntosh, was sent forward to make a demonstration.

Next morning, March 2d, we passed through Fayetteville, and camped for the night at Fulton springs, a few miles this side of Bentonville.

Van Dorn knew the enemy was occupying three detached camps, and the design was to strike the main body at Elkhorn before the divisions of Siegel or of Carr could join it.

He ordered the army to march at 3 A. M. of the third, hoping to reach Bentonville before Siegel, with his 7,000 men, could pass that point and join Curtis in Sugar creek canon. But the enemy was up before we could get the troops to move; and on the march, they would delay at the crossing of every stream (and they were numerous), till they could pass by single file over a log dry shod. And thus it was, that when the head of our column debouched from the timber out upon the open prairie, three miles from Bentonville, we had the mortification to see the head of Siegel's column already entering that village, and marching so rapidly through it, on the Sugar Creek road, that we were unable to intercept or delay his movements.

Even yet McIntosh, with his mounted men, might have thrown himself across his (Siegel's) road, dismounted and formed line in his front, and thus delayed him till we could close in behind and cause his surrender. But his impetuous valor induced him to attempt a sort of charge upon Siegel's veteran infantry, with his wild men on wilder horses. Siegel met the attack with a volley or two, which scattered McIntosh's horsemen in every direction, and then resumed his rapid march.

We pressed on in pursuit, but the road led along a narrow canon shut in by steep rocks and hills, and we could only *follow* Siegel, who, whenever he passed a favorable point, placed a battery in position to check the head of our column as we reached it. Long before dark he had closed up upon Curtis' army, and we halted for the night beyond cannon range.

Our march had been along the main Telegraph road from Bentonville to Springfield, on which, in our front, lay the enemy's army. Van Dorn had learned from McCulloch of a road by which we might turn off to the left from the Telegraph road, make a detour of eight miles, and come into the Telegraph road again in the enemy's rear. We therefore halted, as if for the night, just at the junction of this road; and as soon as it was full dark, the army was moved out upon this road to the left, leaving a force of 1,000 men to cover the movement, and occupy the enemy.

We found the route very bad, and it had been much obstructed by the enemy; so that our march was slow, and it was 8 A. M. when we debouched into the main Telegraph road, about two miles north of Elkhorn tavern and quite in rear of the enemy. We occupied the only route by which he could retire to Missouri.

The game seemed now to be in our own hands; but never was a well conceived plan more completely defeated in its execution than ours was by the remarkable mischances which befell us that day—all of which were plainly traceable to our own want of discipline.

When Price's corps advanced along the Telegraph road, we found only some skirmishers and a battery to oppose us, the whole Federal army having concentrated towards its front, where we were supposed to be; but very soon Curtis discovered he had a heavy force in his rear, and made such quick and efficient changes to meet us that we had plenty to do; but we bore the enemy steadily back, and were pretty warmly engaged, when McCulloch sent to request that instead of closing up and joining in our attack, he should strike the enemy from where he then was. Van Dorn assented, and soon both armies were warmly engaged, McCulloch's position being some three miles distant from ours, and his attack being made upon the enemy's defences in the front.

By two o'clock, Price had forced the enemy back along his whole line, and Van Dorn sent orders to McCulloch to press the enemy vigorously in his front, and he would close in upon him with all his (Price's) force, and end the battle.

Just at this moment a staff officer, Colonel Edward Dillon, galloped up, with disaster on his face. Riding close up to Van Dorn, he said, in a low tone, "McCulloch is killed, McIntosh is killed, Hebert is killed, and the attack on the front has ceased."

The General set his lips, ordered every thing to be urged to the attack, and that the troops of McCulloch's corps should be at once moved up to join us.

Meantime the enemy, finding himself no longer pressed in front, transferred heavy reinforcements to meet us. About sunset we discovered that a new line of battle had been formed 300 yards in our front, in the edge of the timber. The fences had been cleared, so as to form breastworks of the rails, before we knew of this attack, and had the enemy charged us then, we would have been probably beaten.

But he gave us fifteen minutes, in which time Van Dorn brought up some guns in a position to enfilade his line, and quickly dismounted all of the cavalry within reach, to extend our line upon the left, and then we all charged with a yell, and the enemy, delivering a brief fire, broke and fled, and our whole line pursued him quite into his wagon trains.

It was not yet dark, we had every thing on the move, and Van Dorn was urging up all available troops to join in the continued pressure of the enemy, when he found General Price had already stopped the pursuit and ordered the troops to fall back to take up a position for the night.

We made our headquarters for the night at the Elkhorn tavern, where the enemy's had been in the morning.

Price's corps had been hotly engaged from 10 A. M. till after sunset, and had been constantly victorious. We had now won the field, but we had lost very heavily. Generals Slack, McCulloch, McIntosh and Hebert were killed, while General Price and many others were wounded, and our losses told upon us. The ammunition of the troops in action was exhausted, and to our dismay, when the reserve train of ammunition was sought for, it could not be found. The prudent and intelligent ordnance officer in charge of it had sent it off beyond Bentonville, about fifteen miles, and the enemy lay between!

McCulloch's corps was much disorganized, and when it was found there was no fresh supply of ammunition for Price's troops, all idea of resuming the attack next morning was abandoned. Van Dorn decided to await attack on the ground he had won, and meantime to put his wagon trains upon a road towards Van Buren, and to make the best dispositions for a defensive movement in the morning. Our line was formed about 1,200 yards from the Elkhorn tavern, south of it, and was under command of General Henry Little, one of the best and bravest of the Missourians. With him was the brigade of Colonel Rives and Little's own brigade. All of these were staunch troops, veterans of many battles. He had also Bledsoe's battery, Wade's battery, McDonald's battery and the battery of the gallant young Churchill Clarke, already the Pelham of that army. A cannon shot carried off his head that morning while he was working his guns.

This line was held most gallantly till 10 o'clock, when, the trains and the artillery and most of the army being on the road, we withdrew it and ordered it to cover our march. The gallant fellows faced about with cheers, believing they were only changing front to fight in some other position. The enemy was too much crippled to follow, and we marched back to Van Buren.

The battle of Elkhorn was then ended, and many a noble soldier had fallen, but of all who fell that day, I remember none who was more regretted than Colonel Rives. His very presence and manner bespoke a man of lofty nature, worthy of all the love and admiration in which he was held throughout that army. Only a few minutes before he fell he rode out of the line to give some explanation in person to Van Dorn of the condition of affairs, and as he concluded his brief interview, and turned his horse to gallop back to his place, we exclaimed, "What a noble looking fellow he is." Ten minutes after an aid-de-camp reported, "Colonel Rives is down, sir."

The battle of Elkhorn illustrates the danger of co-operative attack. Had Van Dorn adhered to his original plan and fallen on the enemy's rear with all the forces of Price and McCulloch, the disasters of the day would have been averted. We may fairly conclude that it was lost through want of discipline and cohesion in our army. Had we marched at the hour appointed in the order on the morning of the 4th, we would have cut off

Siegel at Bentonville; even had we moved as rapidly as infantry should march, we must have met him there.

The remarkable fatality which befell McCulloch and McIntosh was fairly attributable to the same indiscipline. McCulloch was killed by a sharpshooter while riding alone to reconnoitre the ground in front of his army—where he ought not to have been.

McIntosh, being thus left in command of that wing, yielded to a gallant impulse and placed himself at the head of a regiment of Texas horse, which was moving to charge a Federal battery. He was one of the few killed in the charge, and was entirely out of his proper place when he fell.

The battle might yet have gone in our favor had it been pressed half an hour longer on the evening of the 5th. The cessation of our attack then was a fatal error.

And finally, the inexcusable incompetency of the ordnance officer who sent our ordnance train beyond reach, so that we could not resume the offensive on the morning of the 6th, completed the mischances which caused a well planned, bold and bravely fought battle to go against the Confederate arms, and left no other results than a loss to the enemy in killed and wounded, a few prisoners and two light batteries, which we took with us back to Van Buren, and the moral effect with which our unexpected attack had impressed him by the boldness and energy of our enterprise, so that he did not venture upon any aggressive movement against us.

WASHINGTON, D.C., MARCH 1862

Abraham Lincoln: Message to Congress on Compensated Emancipation; Abraham Lincoln to James A. McDougall

In his annual message of December 3, 1861, President Lincoln recommended that Congress financially support states that adopted measures for gradual emancipation and that it provide for the colonization of freed slaves outside of the United States. Four months later, Lincoln renewed his call for gradual and compensated emancipation in the hopes of ending slavery in the border states of Delaware, Maryland, Kentucky, and Missouri. His letter to Senator James A. McDougall was intended to counter objections to the plan's cost, but the California Democrat opposed it as an unconstitutional use of federal funds. Although Congress passed the resolution Lincoln sought, the border states refused to act and no enabling legislation was introduced.

March 6, 1862

Fellow-citizens of the Senate, and House of Representatives,

I recommend the adoption of a Joint Resolution by your honorable bodies which shall be substantially as follows:

"Resolved that the United States ought to co-operate with any state which may adopt gradual abolishment of slavery, giving to such state pecuniary aid, to be used by such state in it's discretion, to compensate for the inconveniences public and private, produced by such change of system."

If the proposition contained in the resolution does not meet the approval of Congress and the country, there is the end; but if it does command such approval, I deem it of importance that the states and people immediately interested, should be at once distinctly notified of the fact, so that they may begin to consider whether to accept or reject it. The federal government would find it's highest interest in such a measure, as one of the most efficient means of self-preservation. The leaders of the existing insurrection entertain the hope that this government will ultimately be forced to acknowledge the independence of some part of the disaffected region, and that all the slave states North of such part will then say "the Union, for which we have struggled, being already gone, we now choose to go with the Southern section." To deprive them of this hope, substantially ends the rebellion; and the initiation of emancipation completely deprives them of it, as to all the states initiating it. The point is not that *all* the states tolerating slavery would very soon, if at all, initiate emancipation; but that, while the offer is equally made to all, the more Northern shall, by such initiation, make it certain to the more Southern, that in no event, will the former ever join the latter, in their proposed confederacy. I say "initiation" because, in my judgment, gradual, and not sudden emancipation, is better for all. In the mere financial, or pecuniary view, any member of Congress, with the census-tables and Treasury-reports before him, can readily see for himself how very soon the current expenditures of this war would purchase, at fair valuation, all the slaves in any named State. Such a proposition, on the part of the general government, sets up no claim of a right, by federal authority, to interfere with slavery within state limits, referring, as it does, the absolute control of the subject, in each case, to the state and it's people, immediately interested. It is proposed as a matter of perfectly free choice with them.

In the annual message last December, I thought fit to say "The Union must be preserved; and hence all indispensable means must be employed." I said this, not hastily, but deliberately. War has been made, and continues to be, an indispensable means to this end. A practical re-acknowledgement of the national authority would render the war unnecessary, and it would at once cease. If, however, resistance continues, the war must also continue; and it is impossible to foresee all the incidents, which may attend and all the ruin which may follow it. Such as may seem indispensable, or may obviously promise great efficiency towards ending the struggle, must and will come.

The proposition now made, though an offer only, I hope it may be esteemed no offence to ask whether the pecuniary consideration tendered would not be of more value to the States and private persons concerned, than are the institution, and property in it, in the present aspect of affairs.

While it is true that the adoption of the proposed resolution would be merely initiatory, and not within itself a practical measure, it is recommended in the hope that it would soon lead to important practical results. In full view of my great responsibility to my God, and to my country, I earnestly beg the attention of Congress and the people to the subject.

ABRAHAM LINCOLN
March 6. 1862.

Hon. James A. McDougal   Executive Mansion
U.S. Senate   Washington, March 14, 1862

My dear Sir: As to the expensiveness of the plan of gradual emancipation with compensation, proposed in the late Message, please allow me one or two brief suggestions.

Less than one half-day's cost of this war would pay for all the slaves in Delaware at four hundred dollars per head:

Thus, all the slaves in Delaware, by the Census of 1860, are	1798
	400
Cost of the slaves,	$ 719,200.
One day's cost of the war	"2,000,000.

Again, less than eighty seven days cost of this war would, at the same price, pay for all in Delaware, Maryland, District of Columbia, Kentucky, and Missouri.

Thus, slaves in Delaware	1798
" " Maryland	87,188
" " Dis. of Col.	3,181
" " Kentucky	225,490
" " Missouri	114,965
	432,622
	400
Cost of the slaves	$173,048,800
Eightyseven days' cost of the war	"174,000,000.

Do you doubt that taking the initiatory steps on the part of those states and this District, would shorten the war more than eighty-seven days, and thus be an actual saving of expense?

A word as to the *time* and *manner* of incurring the expence. Suppose, for instance, a State devises and adopts a system by which the institution absolutely ceases therein by a named day—say January 1st. 1882. Then, let the sum to be paid to such state by the United States, be ascertained by taking from the Census of 1860, the number of slaves within the state, and multiplying that number by four hundred—the United States to pay such sum to the state in twenty equal annual instalments, in six per cent. bonds of the United States.

The sum thus given, as to *time* and *manner*, I think would not be half as onerous, as would be an equal sum, raised *now*, for the indefinite prossecution of the war; but of this you can judge as well as I.

I inclose a Census-table for your convenience. Yours very truly

A. LINCOLN

A NAVAL REVOLUTION: VIRGINIA, MARCH 1862

Catesby ap Roger Jones: from "Services of the 'Virginia' (Merrimac)"

The outbreak of war found the steam frigate U.S.S. *Merrimack* laid up at the Norfolk navy yard for engine repairs. Scuttled and burned by the Federals when they evacuated the yard, she was raised and rebuilt as the ironclad ram C.S.S. *Virginia*. In an article written for the *Southern Historical Society Papers* in 1883, Catesby ap Roger Jones, *Virginia*'s executive officer, describes the two-day battle with the Union squadron at Hampton Roads on March 8–9. Franklin Buchanan, *Virginia*'s commander, was wounded on March 8 by a sharpshooter ashore, and Jones commanded against U.S.S. *Monitor* in the historic duel of the ironclads the next day.

THE ATTACK was postponed to Saturday, March 8th. The weather was favorable. We left the navy yard at 11 A. M., against the last half of the flood tide, steamed down the river past our batteries, through the obstructions, across Hampton Roads, to the mouth of James river, where off Newports News lay at anchor the frigates Cumberland and Congress, protected by strong batteries and gunboats. The action commenced about 3 P. M. by our firing the bow-gun* at the Cumberland, less than a mile distant. A powerful fire was immediately concentrated upon us from all the batteries afloat and ashore. The frigates Minnesota, Roanoke and St. Lawrence with other vessels, were seen coming from Old Point. We fired at the Congress on passing, but continued to head directly for the Cumberland, which vessel we had determined to run into, and in less than fifteen minutes from the firing of the first gun we rammed her just forward of the starboard fore chains. There were heavy spars about her bows, probably to ward off torpedoes, through which we had to break before reaching the side

---

*It killed and wounded ten men at the after pivot gun of the Cumberland. The second shot from the same gun killed and wounded twelve men at her forward pivot gun. Lieutenant Charles C. Simms pointed and fired the gun.

of the ship. The noise of the crashing timbers was distinctly heard above the din of battle. There was no sign of the hole above water. It must have been large, as the ship soon commenced to careen. The shock to us on striking was slight. We immediately backed the engines. The blow was not repeated. We here lost the prow, and had the stem slightly twisted. The Cumberland* fought her guns gallantly as long as they were above water. She went down bravely, with her colors flying. One of her shells struck the still of the bow-port and exploded; the fragments killed two and wounded a number. Our after nine-inch gun was loaded and ready for firing, when its muzzle was struck by a shell, which broke it off and fired the gun. Another gun also had its muzzle shot off; it was broken so short that at each subsequent discharge its port was set on fire. The damage to the armor was slight. Their fire appeared to have been aimed at our ports. Had it been concentrated at the water-line we would have been seriously hurt, if not sunk. Owing to the ebb tide and our great draft we could not close with the Congress without first going up stream and then turning, which was a tedious operation, besides subjecting us twice to the full fire of the batteries, some of which we silenced.

We were accompanied from the yard by the gunboats Beaufort, Lieutenant-Commander W. H. Parker, and Raleigh, Lieutenant-Commander J. W. Alexander. As soon as the firing was heard up James river, the Patrick Henry, Commander John R Tucker, Jamestown, Lieutenant Commander J. N. Barney, and the gunboat Teaser, Lieutenant-Commander W. A. Webb, under command of Captain John R. Tucker, stood down the river, joining us about four o'clock. All these vessels were gallantly fought and handled, and rendered valuable and effective service.

The prisoners from the Congress stated that when on board that ship it was seen that we were standing up the river, that three cheers were given under the impression that we had quit the fight. They were soon undeceived. When they saw us

---

*She was a sailing frigate of 1,726 tons, mounting two ten-inch pivots and twenty-two nine-inch guns. Her crew numbered 376; her loss in killed and wounded was 121.

heading down stream, fearing the fate of the Cumberland, they slipped their cables, made sail, and ran ashore bows on. We took a position off her quarter, about two cables' length distant, and opened a deliberate fire. Very few of her guns bore on us, and they were soon disabled. The other batteries continued to play on us, as did the Minnesota, then aground about one and one-half miles off. The St. Lawrence also opened on us shortly after. There was great havoc on board the Congress. She was several times on fire. Her gallant commander, Lieutenant Joseph B. Smith,* was struck in the breast by the fragment of a shell and instantly killed. The carnage was frightful. Nothing remained but to strike their colors, which they did. They hoisted the white flag, half-masted, at the main and at the spanker gaff. The Beaufort and Raleigh were ordered to burn her. They went alongside and secured several of her officers and some twenty of her men as prisoners. The officers urgently asked permission to assist their wounded out of the ship. It was granted. They did not return. A sharp fire of musketry from the shore killed some of the prisoners and forced the tugs to leave. A boat was sent from the Virginia to burn her, covered by the Teaser. A fire was opened on them from the shore, and also from the Congress, with both of her white flags flying, wounding Lieutenant Minor and others. We replied to this outrage upon the usages of civilized warfare by reopening on the Congress with hot shot and incendiary shell. Her crew escaped by boats, as did that of the Cumberland. Canister and grape would have prevented it; but in neither case was any attempt made to stop them, though it has been otherwise stated, possibly from our firing on the shore or at the Congress.

We remained near the Congress to prevent her recapture. Had she been retaken, it might have been said that the Flag-Officer permitted it, knowing that his brother† was an officer of that vessel.

A distant and unsatisfactory fire was at times had at the Min-

---

*His sword was sent by flag of truce to his father, Admiral Joseph Smith.

†One of the sad attendants of civil war—divided families—was here illustrated. The Flag-Officer's brother was Paymaster of the Congress. The First and Second Lieutenants had each a brother in the United States army. The father of the Fourth Lieutenant was also in the United States army. The father of one of the Midshipmen was in the United States navy.

nesota. The gunboats also engaged her. We fired canister and grape occasionally in reply to musketry from the shore, which had become annoying.

About this time the Flag Officer was badly wounded by a rifle-ball, and had to be carried below. His bold daring and intrepid conduct won the admiration of all on board. The Executive and Ordnance officer, Lieutenant Catesby Ap R. Jones, succeeded to the command.

The action continued until dusk, when we were forced to seek an anchorage. The Congress was riddled and on fire. A transport steamer was blown up. A schooner was sunk and another captured. We had to leave without making a serious attack on the Minnesota, though we fired at her as we passed on the other side of the Middle Ground, and also at the St. Lawrence.* The latter frigate fired at us by broadsides, not a bad plan for small calibres against iron-clads, if concentrated. It was too dark to aim well. We anchored off our batteries at Sewell Point. The squadron followed.

The Congress† continued to burn; "she illuminated the heavens, and varied the scene by the firing of her own guns and the flight of her balls through the air," until shortly after midnight, "when her magazine exploded, and a column of burning matter appeared high in the air, to be followed by the stillness of death," [extract from report of General Mansfield, U. S. A.] One of the pilots chanced about 11 P. M. to be looking in the direction of the Congress, when there passed a strange looking craft, brought out in bold relief by the brilliant light of the burning ship, which he at once proclaimed to be the Ericsson. We were therefore not surprised in the morning to see the Monitor at anchor near the Minnesota. The latter ship was still aground. Some delay occurred from sending our wounded out of the ship; we had but one serviceable boat left. Admiral Buchanan was landed at Sewell Point.

At eight A. M. we got under way, as did the Patrick Henry, Jamestown and Teaser. We stood towards the Minnesota and opened fire on her. The pilots were to have placed us

---

*A sailing frigate of fifty guns and 1,726 tons.
†A sailing frigate of 1,867 tons, mounting fifty guns. She had a crew of 434, of whom there were 120 killed and missing.

half-a-mile from her, but we were not at any time nearer than a mile. The Monitor* commenced firing when about a third of a mile distant. We soon approached, and were often within a ship's length; once while passing we fired a broadside at her only a few yards distant. She and her turret appeared to be under perfect control. Her light draft enabled her to move about us at pleasure. She once took position for a short time where we could not bring a gun to bear on her. Another of her movements caused us great anxiety; she made for our rudder and propeller, both of which could have been easily disabled. We could only see her guns when they were discharged; immediately afterward the turret revolved rapidly, and the guns were not again seen until they were again fired. We wondered how proper aim could be taken in the very short time the guns were in sight. The Virginia, however, was a large target, and generally so near that the Monitor's shot did not often miss. It did not appear to us that our shell had any effect upon the Monitor. We had no solid shot. Musketry was fired at the lookout holes. In spite of all the care of our pilots we ran ashore, where we remained over fifteen minutes. The Patrick Henry and Jamestown, with great risk to themselves, started to our assistance. The Monitor and Minnesota were in full play on us. A small rifle-gun on board the Minnesota, or on the steamer alongside of her, was fired with remarkable precision.

When we saw that our fire made no impression on the Monitor, we determined to run into her if possible. We found it a very difficult feat to do. Our great length and draft, in a comparatively narrow channel, with but little water to spare, made us sluggish in our movements, and hard to steer and turn. When the opportunity presented all steam was put on; there was not, however, sufficient time to gather full headway before striking. The blow was given with the broad wooden stem, the iron prow having been lost the day before. The Monitor received the blow in such a manner as to weaken its effect, and the damage was to her trifling. Shortly after an

---

*She was 173 feet long and 41 feet wide. She had a revolving circular iron turret eight inches thick, nine feet high and twenty feet inside diameter, in which were two eleven-inch guns. Her draft was ten feet.

alarming leak in the bows was reported. It, however, did not long continue.

Whilst contending with the Monitor, we received the fire of the Minnesota,* which we never failed to return whenever our guns could be brought to bear. We set her on fire and did her serious injury, though much less than we then supposed. Generally the distance was too great for effective firing. We blew up a steamer alongside of her.

The fight had continued over three hours. To us the Monitor appeared unharmed. We were therefore surprised to see her run off into shoal water where our great draft would not permit us to follow, and where our shell could not reach her. The loss of our prow and anchor, and consumption of coal, water, &c., had lightened us so that the lower part of the forward end of the shield was awash.

We for some time awaited the return of the Monitor to the Roads. After consultation it was decided that we should proceed to the navy-yard, in order that the vessel should be brought down in the water and completed. The pilots said if we did not then leave that we could not pass the bar until noon of the next day. We therefore at 12 M. quit the Roads and stood for Norfolk. Had there been any sign of the Monitor's willingness to renew the contest we would have remained to fight her. We left her in the shoal water to which she had withdrawn, and which she did not leave until after we had crossed the bar on our way to Norfolk.

The official report says: "Our loss is two killed and nineteen wounded. The stem is twisted and the ship leaks; we have lost the prow, starboard anchor, and all the boats; the armor is somewhat damaged, the steam-pipe and smoke-stack both riddled, the muzzles of two of the guns shot away. It was not easy to keep a flag flying; the flag-staffs were repeatedly shot away; the colors were hoisted to the smoke-stack, and several times cut down from it." None were killed or wounded in the fight with the Monitor. The only damage she did was to the

---

*She was a screw steam frigate of 3,200 tons, mounting forty-three guns of eight, nine and ten-inch calbre. She fired 145 ten-inch, 349 nine-inch, and 35 eight-inch shot and shell, and 5,567 pounds of powder. Her draft was about the same as the Virginia.

armor. She fired forty-one shots. We were enabled to receive most of them obliquely. The effect of a shot striking obliquely on the shield was to break all the iron, and sometimes to displace several feet of the outside course; the wooden backing would not be broken through. When a shot struck directly at right angles, the wood would also be broken through, but not displaced. Generally the shot were much scattered; in three instances two or more struck near the same place, in each case causing more of the iron to be displaced, and the wood to bulge inside. A few struck near the water-line. The shield was never pierced; though it was evident that two shots striking in the same place would have made a large hole through everything.

A VISIT TO WASHINGTON AND VIRGINIA:
MARCH 1862

Nathaniel Hawthorne: from "Chiefly About War-Matters"

"There is no remoteness of life and thought, no hermetically sealed seclusion, except, possibly, that of the grave, into which the disturbing influences of this war do not penetrate," Nathaniel Hawthorne observed at the beginning of "Chiefly About War-Matters," an essay describing the celebrated writer's March visit to Washington and Virginia that was published in the *Atlantic Monthly* for July 1862. Hawthorne deleted the passage recalling his meeting with Lincoln after *Atlantic* editor James T. Fields objected to his description of the President's "awkwardness & general uncouth aspect." (The suppressed section is restored here, and the differences between Hawthorne's original version and the 1862 magazine text are described in the endnotes in this volume.) The argumentative footnotes supposedly by editor Fields are actually by Hawthorne. His mention in the first paragraph of the President's "private grief" refers to the death of Willie Lincoln, age eleven, who died on February 20.

OF COURSE, there was one other personage, in the class of statesmen, whom I should have been truly mortified to leave Washington without seeing; since (temporarily, at least, and by force of circumstances) he was the man of men. But a private grief had built up a barrier about him, impeding the customary free intercourse of Americans with their chief-magistrate; so that I might have come away without a glimpse of his very remarkable physiognomy, save for a semi-official opportunity of which I was glad to take advantage. The fact is, we were invited to annex ourselves, as supernumeraries, to a deputation that was about to wait upon the President, from a Massachusetts whip-factory, with a present of a splendid whip.

Our immediate party consisted only of four or five, (including Major Ben Perley Poore, with his note-book and pencil,) but we were joined by several other persons, who seemed to have been lounging about the precincts of the White House, under the spacious porch, or within the hall, and who swarmed in with us to take the chances of a presentation. Nine o'clock had been appointed as the time for receiving the deputation, and we were punctual to the moment, but not so the President, who sent us word that he was eating his breakfast, and would come as soon as he could. His appetite, we were glad to think, must have been a pretty fair one; for we waited about half-an-hour, in one of the ante-chambers, and then were ushered into a reception-room, in one corner of which sat the Secretaries of War and of the Treasury, expecting, like ourselves, the termination of the presidential breakfast. During this interval, there were several new additions to our groupe, one or two of whom were in a working-garb; so that we formed a very miscellaneous collection of people, mostly unknown to each other, and without any common sponsor, but all with an equal right to look our head-servant in the face. By-and-by, there was a little stir on the staircase and in the passage-way; and in lounged a tall, loose-jointed figure, of an exaggerated Yankee port and demeanor, whom, (as being about the homeliest man I ever saw, yet by no means repulsive or disagreeable,) it was impossible not to recognize as Uncle Abe.

Unquestionably, Western man though he be, and Kentuckian by birth, President Lincoln is the essential representative of all Yankees, and the veritable specimen, physically, of what the world seems determined to regard as our characteristic qualities. It is the strangest, and yet the fittest thing in the jumble of human vicissitudes, that he, out of so many millions, unlooked-for, unselected by any intelligible process that could be based upon his genuine qualities, unknown to those who chose him, and unsuspected of what endowments may adapt him for his tremendous responsibility, should have found the way open for him to fling his lank personality into the chair of state—where, I presume, it was his first impulse to throw his legs on the council-table, and tell the cabinet-ministers a story. There is no describing his lengthy awkwardness, nor the uncouthness of his movement; and yet it seemed as if I had been in the habit of seeing him daily, and had shaken hands with him a thousand times in some village-street; so true was he to the aspect of the pattern American, though with a certain extravagance which, possibly, I exaggerated still further by the delighted eagerness with which I took it in. If put to guess his calling and livelihood, I should have taken him for a country-schoolmaster, as soon as anything else. He was dressed in a rusty black frock-coat and pantaloons, unbrushed, and worn so faithfully that the suit had adapted itself to the curves and angularities of his figure, and had grown to be an outer skin of the man. He had shabby slippers on his feet. His hair was black, still unmixed with gray, stiff, somewhat bushy, and had apparently been acquainted with neither brush nor comb, that morning, after the disarrangement of the pillow; and as to a night-cap, Uncle Abe probably knows nothing of such effeminacies. His complexion is dark and sallow, betokening, I fear, an insalubrious atmosphere around the White House; he has thick black eyebrows and an impending brow; his nose is large, and the lines about his mouth are very strongly defined.

The whole physiognomy is as coarse a one as you would meet anywhere in the length and breadth of the States; but, withal, it is redeemed, illuminated, softened, and brightened, by a kindly though serious look out of his eyes, and an expression of homely sagacity, that seems weighted with rich results of village-experience. A great deal of native sense; no bookish cultivation, no refinement; honest at heart, and thoroughly so, and yet, in some sort, sly—at least, endowed with a sort of tact and wisdom that are akin to craft, and would impel him, I think, to take an antagonist in flank, rather than to make a bull-run at him right in front. But, on the whole, I liked this sallow, queer, sagacious visage, with the homely human sympathies that warmed it; and, for my small share in the matter, would as lief have Uncle Abe for a ruler as any man whom it would have been practicable to put in his place.

Immediately on his entrance, the President accosted our Member of Congress, who had us in charge, and, with a comical twist of his face, made some jocular remark about the length of his breakfast. He then greeted us all round, not waiting for an introduction, but shaking and squeezing everybody's hand with the utmost cordiality, whether the individual's name was announced to him or not. His manner towards us was wholly without pretence, but yet had a kind of natural dignity, quite sufficient to keep the forwardest of us from clapping him on the shoulder and asking for a story. A mutual acquaintance being established, our leader took the whip out of its case, and began to read the address of presentation. The whip was an exceedingly long one, its handle wrought in ivory, (by some artist in the Massachusetts state-prison, I believe,) and ornamented with a medallion of the President, and other equally beautiful devices; and along its whole length, there was a succession of golden bands and ferules. The address was shorter than the whip, but equally well made, consisting chiefly of an explanatory description of these artistic designs, and closing with a hint that the gift was a suggestive and emblematic one, and that the President would recognize the use to which such an instrument should be put.

This suggestion gave Uncle Abe rather a delicate task in his reply, because, slight as the matter seemed, it apparently called for some declaration, or intimation, or faint foreshadowing of policy in reference to the conduct of the war, and the final treatment of the rebels. But the President's Yankee aptness and not-to-be-caughtness stood him in good stead, and he jerked or wriggled himself out of the dilemma with an uncouth dexterity that was entirely in character; although, without his gesticulation of eye and mouth—and especially the flourish of the whip, with which he imagined himself touching up a pair of fat horses—I doubt whether his words would be worth recording, even if I could remember them. The gist of the reply was, that he accepted the whip as an emblem of peace, not punishment; and this great affair over, we retired out of the presence in high good humor, only regretting that we could not have seen the President sit down and fold up his legs, (which is said to be a most extraordinary spectacle,) or have heard him tell one of those delectable stories for which he is so celebrated. A good many of them are afloat upon the common talk of Washington, and are certainly the aptest, pithiest, and funniest little things imaginable; though, to be sure, they smack of the frontier freedom, and would not always bear repetition in a drawing-room, or on the immaculate page of the Atlantic.

Good Heavens, what liberties have I been taking with one of the potentates of the earth, and the man on whose conduct more important consequencies depend, than on that of any other historical personage of the century! But with whom is an American citizen entitled to take a liberty, if not with his own chief-magistrate? However, lest the above allusions to President Lincoln's little peculiarities (already well-known to the country and to the world) should be mis-interpreted, I deem it proper to say a word or two, in regard to him, of unfeigned respect and measurable confidence. He is evidently a man of keen faculties, and, what is still more to the purpose, of powerful character. As to his integrity, the people have that intuition of it which is never deceived. Before he actually entered upon his great office, and for a considerable time afterwards, there is no reason to suppose that he adequately estimated the gigantic task about to be imposed on him, or, at least, had any distinct idea how it was to be managed; and, I presume, there may have been more than one veteran politician who proposed to himself to take the power out of President Lincoln's hands into his own, leaving our honest friend only the public responsibility for the good or ill-success of the career. The extremely imperfect developement of his statesmanly qualities, at that period, may have justified such designs. But the President is teachable by events, and has now spent a year in a very arduous course of education; he has a flexible mind, capable of much expansion, and convertible towards far loftier studies and activities than those of his early life; and, if he came to Washington as a backwoods humorist, he has already transformed himself into as good a statesman (to speak moderately) as his prime-minister.*

Among other excursions to camps and places of interest in the neighborhood of Washington, we went, one day, to Alexandria. It is a little port on the Potomac, with one or two shabby wharves and docks, resembling those of a fishing vil-

---

*We hesitated to admit the above sketch, and shall probably regret our decision in its favor. It appears to have been written in a benign spirit, and perhaps conveys a not inaccurate impression of its august subject; but it lacks *reverence*, and it pains us to see a gentleman of ripe age, and who has spent years under the corrective influence of foreign institutions, falling into the characteristic and most ominous fault of Young America.

lage in New England, and the respectable old brick town rising gently behind. In peaceful times, it no doubt bore an aspect of decorous quietude and dulness; but it was now thronged with the Northern soldiery, whose stir and bustle contrasted strikingly with the many closed warehouses, the absence of citizens from their customary haunts, and the lack of any symptom of healthy activity; while army-wagons trundled heavily over the pavements, and sentinels paced the sidewalks, and mounted dragoons dashed to-and-fro on military errands. I tried to imagine how very disagreeable the presence of a Southern army would be, in a sober town of Massachusetts; and the thought considerably lessened my wonder at the cold and shy regards that are cast upon our troops, the gloom, the sullen demeanor, the declared or scarcely hidden sympathy with rebellion, which are so frequent here. It is a strange thing in human life, that the greatest errors both of men and women often spring from their sweetest and most generous qualities; and so, undoubtedly, thousands of warm-hearted, sympathetic, and impulsive persons have joined the rebels, not from any real zeal for the cause, but because, between two conflicting loyalties, they chose that which necessarily lay nearest the heart. There never existed any other government, against which treason was so easy, and could defend itself by such plausible arguments, as against that of the United States. The anomaly of two allegiances (of which that of the State comes nearest home to a man's feelings, and includes the altar and the hearth, while the General Government claims his devotion only to an airy mode of law, and has no symbol but a flag) is exceedingly mischievous in this point of view; for it has converted crowds of honest people into traitors, who seem to themselves not merely innocent, but patriotic, and who die for a bad cause with as quiet a conscience as if it were the best. In the vast extent of our country—too vast, by far, to be taken into one small human heart—we inevitably limit to our own State, or, at farthest, to our own Section, that sentiment of physical love for the soil which renders an Englishman, for example, so intensely sensitive to the dignity and well-being of his little island, that one hostile foot, treading anywhere upon it, would make a bruise on each individual breast. If a man loves his own State, therefore, and is content to be ruined with her, let us shoot him if we can, but allow him an honorable burial in the soil he fights for.*

In Alexandria, we visited the tavern in which Colonel Ellsworth was killed, and saw the spot where he fell, and the stairs below, whence Jackson fired the fatal shot, and where he himself was slain a moment afterwards; so that the assassin and his victim must have met on the threshold of the spirit-world, and perhaps came to a better understanding before they had taken many steps on the other side. Ellsworth was too generous to bear an immortal grudge for a deed like that, done in hot blood, and by no skulking enemy. The memorial-hunters have completely cut away the original woodwork around the spot, with their pocket-knives; and the staircase, balustrade, and floor, as well as the adjacent doors and door-frames, have recently been renewed; the walls, moreover, are covered with new paper-hangings, the former having been torn off in tatters; and thus it becomes something like a metaphysical question whether the place of the murder actually exists.

Driving out of Alexandria, we stopt on the edge of the city to inspect an old slave-pen, which is one of the lions of the place, but a very poor one; and a little farther on, we came to a brick church where Washington used sometimes to attend service—a pre-revolutionary edifice, with ivy growing over its walls, though not very luxuriantly. Reaching the open country, we saw forts and camps on all sides; some of the tents being placed immediately on the ground, while others were raised over a basement of logs, laid lengthwise, like those of a log-hut, or driven vertically into the soil in a circle; thus forming a solid wall, the chinks closed up with Virginia mud, and above it the pyramidal shelter of the tent. Here were in progress all the occupations, and all the idleness, of the soldier in the tented field; some were cooking the company-rations in pots hung over fires in the open air; some played at ball, or developed their muscular power by gymnastic exercise; some read newspapers; some smoked cigars or pipes; and many were cleaning their arms and accoutrements, the more carefully, perhaps,

---

*We do not thoroughly comprehend the author's drift in the foregoing paragraph, but are inclined to think its tone reprehensible, and its tendency impolitic in the present stage of our national difficulties.

because their division was to be reviewed by the Commander-in-Chief, that afternoon. Others sat on the ground, while their comrades cut their hair; it being a soldierly fashion (and for excellent reasons) to crop it within an inch of the skull. Others, finally, lay asleep in breast-high tents, with their legs protruding into the open air.

We paid a visit to Fort Ellsworth, and from its ramparts (which have been heaped up out of the muddy soil, within the last few months, and will require still a year or two to make them verdant) we had a beautiful view of the Potomac, a truly majestic river, and the surrounding country. The fortifications, so numerous in all this region, and now so unsightly with their bare, precipitous sides, will remain as historic monuments, grass-grown and picturesque memorials of an epoch of terror and suffering; they will serve to make our country dearer and more interesting to us, and afford fit soil for poetry to root itself in; for this is a plant which thrives best in spots where blood has been spilt long ago, and grows in abundant clusters in old ditches, such as the moat around Fort Ellsworth will be, a century hence. It may seem to be paying dear for what many will reckon but a worthless weed; but the more historical associations we can link with our localities, the richer will be the daily life that feeds upon the past, and the more valuable the things that have been long established; so that our children will be less prodigal than their fathers, in sacrificing good institutions to passionate impulses and impracticable theories. This herb of grace, let us hope, may be found in the old footprints of the war.

Even in an aesthetic point of view, however, the war has done a great deal of enduring mischief by causing the devastation of great tracts of woodland scenery, in which this part of Virginia would appear to have been very rich. Around all the encampments, and everywhere along the road, we saw the bare sites of what had evidently been tracts of hard-wood forest, indicated by the unsightly stumps of well-grown trees, not smoothly felled by regular axe-men, but hacked, haggled, and unevenly amputated, as by a sword or other miserable tool in an unskilful hand. Fifty years will not repair this desolation. An army destroys everything before and around it, even to the very grass; for the sites of the encampments are converted into barren esplanades, like those of the squares in French cities, where not a blade of grass is allowed to grow. As to other symptoms of devastation and obstruction, such as deserted houses, unfenced fields, and a general aspect of nakedness and ruin, I know not how much may be due to a normal lack of neatness in the rural life of Virginia, which puts a squalid face even upon a prosperous state of things; but undoubtedly the war must have spoilt what was good, and made the bad a great deal worse. The carcasses of horses were scattered along the wayside. One very pregnant token of a social system thoroughly disturbed was presented by a party of Contrabands, escaping out of the mysterious depths of Secessia; and its strangeness consisted in the leisurely delay with which they trudged forward, as dreading no pursuer, and encountering nobody to turn them back.

They were unlike the specimens of their race whom we are accustomed to see at the North, and, in my judgment, were far more agreeable. So rudely were they attired—as if their garb had grown upon them spontaneously—so picturesquely natural in manners, and wearing such a crust of primeval simplicity, (which is quite polished away from the northern black man,) that they seemed a kind of creature by themselves, not altogether human, but perhaps quite as good, and akin to the fauns and rustic deities of olden times. I wonder whether I shall excite anybody's wrath by saying this? It is no great matter. At all events, I felt most kindly towards these poor fugitives, but knew not precisely what to wish in their behalf, nor in the least how to help them. For the sake of the manhood which is latent in them, I would not have turned them back, but I should have felt almost as reluctant, on their own account, to hasten them forward to the stranger's land; and, I think, my prevalent idea was, that, whoever may be benefitted by the results of this war, it will not be the present generation of negroes, the childhood of whose race is now gone forever, and who must henceforth fight a hard battle with the world, on very unequal terms. On behalf of my own race, I am glad, and can only hope that an inscrutable Providence means good to both parties.

There is an historical circumstance, known to few, that connects the children of the Puritans with these Africans of Virginia, in a very singular way. They are our brethren, as being lineal descendants from the May Flower, the fated womb of which, in her first voyage, sent forth a brood of Pilgrims upon Plymouth Rock, and, in a subsequent one, spawned Slaves upon the southern soil;—a monstrous birth, but with which we have an instinctive sense of kindred, and so are stirred by an irresistible impulse to attempt their rescue, even at the cost of blood and ruin. The character of our sacred ship, I fear, may suffer a little by this revelation; but we must let her white progeny offset her dark one—and two such portents never sprang from an identical source before!

While we drove onward, a young officer on horseback looked earnestly into the carriage, and recognized some faces that he had seen before; so he rode along by our side, and we pestered him with queries and observations, to which he responded more civilly than they deserved. He was on General McClellan's staff, and a gallant cavalier, high-booted, with a revolver in his belt, and mounted on a noble horse, which trotted hard and high without disturbing the rider in his accustomed seat. His face had a healthy hue of exposure and an expression of careless hardihood; and, as I looked at him, it seemed to me that the war had brought good fortune to the youth of this epoch, if to none beside; since they now make it their daily business to ride a horse and handle a sword, instead of lounging listlessly through the duties, occupations, pleasures —all tedious alike—to which the artificial state of society limits a peaceful generation. The atmosphere of the camp and the smoke of the battle-field are morally invigorating; the hardy virtues flourish in them, the nonsense dies like a wilted weed. The enervating effects of centuries of civilization vanish at once, and leave these young men to enjoy a life of hardship, and the exhilarating sense of danger—to kill men blamelessly, or to be killed gloriously—and to be happy in following out their native instincts of destruction, precisely in the spirit of Homer's heroes, only with some considerable change of mode. One touch of nature makes not only the whole world, but all time akin. Set men face to face, with weapons in their hands, and they are as ready to slaughter one another, now, after playing at peace and good-will for so many years, as in the rudest ages, that never heard of peace-societies, and thought no wine so delicious as what they quaffed from an enemy's skull! Indeed, if the report of a Congressional committee be reliable, that old-fashioned kind of goblet has again come into use, at the expense of our northern head-pieces—a costly drinking-cup to him that furnishes it. Heaven forgive me for seeming to jest upon such a subject;—only, it is so odd, when we measure our advances from barbarism, and find ourselves just here!*

We now approached General McClellan's head-quarters, which, at that time, were established at Fairfax Seminary. The edifice was situated on a gentle elevation, amid very agreeable scenery, and, at a distance, looked like a gentleman's seat. Preparations were going forward for reviewing a division of ten or twelve thousand men, the various regiments composing which had begun to array themselves on an extensive plain, where, methought, there was a more convenient place for a battle than is usually found, in this broken and difficult country. Two thousand cavalry made a portion of the troops to be reviewed. By-and-by, we saw a pretty numerous troop of mounted officers, who were congregated on a distant part of the plain, and whom we finally ascertained to be the Commander-in-Chief's staff, with McClellan himself at their head. Our party managed to establish itself in a position conveniently close to the General, to whom, moreover, we had the honor of an introduction; and he bowed, on his horseback, with a good deal of dignity and martial courtesy, but no airs, nor fuss, nor pretension, beyond what his character and rank inevitably gave him.

Now, at that juncture, and, in fact, up to the present moment, there was, and is, a most fierce and bitter outcry, and detraction loud and low, against General McClellan, accusing him of sloth, imbecility, cowardice, treasonable purposes, and, in short, utterly denying his ability as a soldier, and questioning his integrity as a man. Nor was this to be wondered at; for when, before, in all history, do we find a general in command of half-a-million of men, and in presence of an enemy inferior in numbers and no better disciplined than his own troops, leaving it still debateable, after the better part of a year, whether

---

*We hardly expected this outbreak in favor of War, from the Peaceable Man; but the justice of our cause makes us all soldiers at heart, however quiet in our outward life. We have heard of twenty Quakers in a single company of a Pennsylvania regiment.

he was a soldier or no? The question would seem to answer itself in the very asking. Nevertheless, being most profoundly ignorant of the art of war, like the majority of the General's critics, and, on the other hand, having some considerable impressibility by men's characters, I was glad of the opportunity to look him in the face, and to feel whatever influence might reach me from his sphere. So I stared at him, as the phrase goes, with all the eyes I had; and the reader shall have the benefit of what I saw—to which he is the more welcome, because, in writing this article, I feel disposed to be singularly frank, and can scarcely restrain myself from telling truths, the utterance of which I should get slender thanks for.

The General was dressed in a simple, dark-blue uniform, without epaulets, booted to the knee, and with a cloth cap upon his head; and, at first sight, you might have taken him for a corporal of dragoons, of particularly neat and soldierlike aspect, and in the prime of his age and strength. He is only of middling stature, but his build is very compact and sturdy, with broad shoulders and a look of great physical vigor, which, in fact, he is said to possess; he and Beauregard having been rivals in that particular, and both distinguished above other men. His complexion is dark and sanguine, with dark hair. He has a strong, bold, soldierly face, full of decision; a Roman nose, by no means a thin prominence, but very thick and firm; and if he follows it, (which I should think likely,) it may be pretty confidently trusted to guide him aright. His profile would make a more effective likeness than the full face, which, however, is much better in the real man than in any photograph that I have seen. His forehead is not remarkably large, but comes forward at the eyebrows; it is not the brow nor countenance of a prominently intellectual man, (not a natural student, I mean, or abstract thinker,) but of one whose office it is to handle things practically and to bring about tangible results. His face looked capable of being very stern, but wore, in its repose, when I saw it, an aspect pleasant and dignified; it is not, in its character, an American face, nor an English one. The man, on whom he fixes his eye, is conscious of him. In his natural disposition, he seems calm and self-possessed, sustaining his great responsibilities cheerfully, without shrinking or weariness, or spasmodic effort, or damage to his health, but all with quiet, deep-drawn breaths; just as his broad shoulders would bear up a heavy burthen without aching beneath it.

After we had had sufficient time to peruse the man, (so far as it could be done with one pair of very attentive eyes,) the General rode off, followed by his cavalcade, and was lost to sight among the troops. They received him with loud shouts, by the eager uproar of which—now near, now in the centre, now on the outskirts of the division, and now sweeping back towards us in a great volume of sound—we could trace his progress through the ranks. If he is a coward, or a traitor, or a humbug, or anything less than a brave, true, and able man, that mass of intelligent soldiers, whose lives and honor he had in charge, were utterly deceived, and so was this present writer; for they believed in him, and so did I; and, had I stood in the ranks, I should have shouted with the lustiest of them. Of course, I may be mistaken; my opinion, on such a point, is worth nothing, although my impression may be worth a little more; neither do I consider the General's antecedents as bearing very decided testimony to his practical soldiership. A thorough knowledge of the science of war seems to be conceded to him; he is allowed to be a good military critic; but all this is possible, without his possessing any positive qualities of a great general, just as a literary critic may show the profoundest acquaintance with the principles of epic poetry, without being able to produce a single stanza of an epic poem. Nevertheless, I shall not give up my faith in General McClellan's soldiership until he is defeated, nor in his courage and integrity even then.*

THE WATERS around Fortress Monroe were thronged with a gallant array of ships of war and transports, wearing the Union

---

*Apparently with the idea of balancing his gracious treatment of the Commander-in-chief, the author had here inserted some idle sarcasms about other officers whom he happened to see at the review; one of whom (a distinguished general,) he says, "sat his horse like a meal-bag, and was the stupidest looking man he ever saw." Such license is not creditable to the Peaceable Man, and we do him a kindness in crossing out the passage.

flag—"Old Glory"—as I hear it called in these days. A little withdrawn from our national fleet lay two French frigates, and, in another direction, an English sloop, under that banner which always makes itself visible, like a red portent in the air, wherever there is strife. In pursuance of our official duty, (which had no ascertainable limits,) we went on board the flag-ship, and were shown over every part of her, and down into her depths, inspecting her gallant crew, her powerful armament, her mighty engines, and her furnaces, where the fires are always kept burning, as well at midnight as at noon, so that it would require only five minutes to put the vessel under full steam. This vigilance has been felt necessary, ever since the Merrimac made that terrible dash from Norfolk. Splendid as she is, however, and provided with all but the very latest improvements in naval armament, the Minnesota belongs to a class of vessels that will be built no more, nor ever fight another battle; being as much a thing of the past as any of the ships of Queen Elizabeth's time, which grappled with the galleons of the Spanish Armada.

On her quarter-deck, an elderly flag-officer was pacing to-and-fro, with a self-conscious dignity to which a touch of the gout or rheumatism perhaps contributed a little additional stiffness. He seemed to be a gallant gentleman, but of the old, slow, and pompous school of naval worthies, who have grown up amid rules, forms, and etiquette, which were adopted full-blown from the British navy into ours, and are somewhat too cumbrous for the quick spirit of to-day. This order of nautical heroes will probably go down, along with the ships in which they fought valorously, and strutted most intolerably. How can an Admiral condescend to go to sea in an iron pot? What space and elbow-room can be found for quarter-deck dignity in the cramped look-out of the Monitor, or even in the twenty feet diameter of her cheese-box? All the pomp and splendor of naval warfare are gone by. Henceforth, there must come up a race of engine-men and smoke-blackened cannoniers, who will hammer away at their enemies under the direction of a single pair of eyes; and even heroism—so deadly a gripe is science laying on our noble possibilities—will become a quality of very minor importance, when its possessor cannot break through the iron crust of his own armament and give the world a glimpse of it.

At no great distance from the Minnesota, lay the strangest-looking craft I ever saw. It was a platform of iron, so nearly on a level with the water that the swash of the waves broke over it, under the impulse of a very moderate breeze; and on this platform was raised a circular structure, likewise of iron, and rather broad and capacious, but of no great height. It could not be called a vessel at all; it was a machine, and I have seen one of somewhat similar appearance employed in cleaning out the docks; or, for lack of a better similitude, it looked like a gigantic rat-trap. It was ugly, questionable, suspicious, evidently mischievous; nay, I will allow myself to call it devilish; for this was the new war-fiend, destined, along with others of the same breed, to annihilate whole navies and batter down old supremacies. The wooden walls of Old England cease to exist, and a whole history of naval renown reaches its period, now that the Monitor comes smoking into view; while the billows dash over what seems her deck, and storms bury even her turret in green water, as she burrows and snorts along, oftener under the surface than above. The singularity of the object has betrayed me into a more ambitious vein of description than I often indulge; and, after all, I might as well have contented myself with simply saying that she looked very queer.

Going on board, we were surprised at the extent and convenience of her interior accommodations. There is a spacious ward-room, nine or ten feet in height, besides a private cabin for the commander, and sleeping accommodations on an ample scale; the whole well-lighted and ventilated, though beneath the surface of the water. Forward, or aft, (for it is impossible to tell stem from stern,) the crew are relatively quite as well provided for as the officers. It was like finding a palace, with all its conveniences, under the sea. The inaccessibility, the apparent impregnability, of this submerged iron fortress are most satisfactory; the officers and crew get down through a little hole in the deck, hermetically seal themselves, and go below; and until they see fit to re-appear, there would seem to be no power given to man, whereby they can be brought to light. A storm of cannon-shot damages them no more than a handful of dried peas. We saw the shot-marks made by the great artillery of the Merrimac on the outer casing of the iron tower; they were about the breadth and depth of shallow saucers, almost imperceptible dents; with no corresponding bulge on the interior surface. In fact, the thing looked altogether too safe; though it may not prove quite an agreeable predicament to be thus boxed up in impenetrable iron, with the possibility, one would imagine, of being sent to the bottom of the sea, and, even there, not drowned, but stifled. Nothing, however, can exceed the confidence of the officers in this new craft. It was pleasant to see their benign exultation in her powers of mischief, and the delight with which they exhibited the circumvolutory movement of the tower, the quick thrusting forth of the immense guns to deliver their ponderous missiles, and then the immediate recoil, and the security behind the closed port-holes. Yet even this will not long be the last and most terrible improvement in the science of war. Already we hear of vessels, the armament of which is to act entirely beneath the surface of the water; so that, with no other external symptoms than a great bubbling and foaming, and gush of smoke, and belch of smothered thunder out of the yesty waves, there shall be a deadly fight going on below; and, by-and-by, a sucking whirlpool, as one of the ships goes down.

The Monitor was certainly an object of great interest; but on our way to Newport News, whither we next went, we saw a spectacle that affected us with far profounder emotion. It was the sight of the few sticks that are left of the frigate Congress, stranded near the shore, and still more, the masts of the Cumberland rising midway out of the water, with a tattered rag of a pennant fluttering from one of them. The invisible hull of the latter ship seems to be careened over, so that the three masts stand slantwise; the rigging looks quite uninjured, except that a few ropes dangle loosely from the yards. The flag (which never was struck, thank Heaven!) is entirely hidden under the waters of the bay, but is still doubtless waving in its old place, although it floats to-and-fro with the swell and reflux of the tide, instead of rustling on the breeze. A remnant of the dead crew still man the sunken ship, and sometimes a drowned body floats up to the surface.

That was a noble fight. When was ever a better word spoken

than that of Commodore Smith, the father of the commander of the Congress, when he heard that his son's ship was surrendered?—"Then Joe's dead!" said he; and so it proved. Nor can any warrior be more certain of enduring renown than the gallant Morris, who fought so well the final battle of the old system of naval warfare, and won glory for his country and himself out of inevitable disaster and defeat. That last gun from the Cumberland, when her deck was half-submerged, sounded the requiem of many sinking ships. Then went down all the navies of Europe, and our own, Old Ironsides and all, and Trafalgar and a thousand other fights became only a memory, never to be acted over again; and thus our brave countrymen come last in the long procession of heroic sailors that includes Blake and Nelson, and so many Mariners of England, and other mariners as brave as they, whose renown is our native inheritance. There will be other battles, but no more such tests of seamanship and manhood as the battles of the past; and, moreover, the millennium is certainly approaching, because human strife is to be transferred from the heart and personality of man into cunning contrivances of machinery, which, by-and-by, will fight out our wars with only the clank and smash of iron, strewing the field with broken engines, but damaging nobody's little finger except by accident. Such is obviously the tendency of modern improvement. But, in the meanwhile, so long as manhood retains any part of its pristine value, no country can afford to let gallantry like that of Morris and his crew, any more than that of the brave Worden, pass unhonored and unrewarded. If the Government do nothing, let the people take the matter into their own hands, and cities give him swords, gold boxes, festivals of triumph, and, if he needs it, heaps of gold. Let poets brood upon the theme, and make themselves sensible how much of the past and future is contained within its compass, till its spirit shall flash forth in the lightning of a song!

THE "GRAND CAMPAIGN" OPENS:
VIRGINIA, MARCH 1862

George B. McClellan to the Army of the Potomac and to Samuel L. M. Barlow

On March 8 Joseph E. Johnston's Confederate army at Manassas began withdrawing southward behind the Rappahannock River. This forced McClellan to shift the starting point of his "grand campaign" against Richmond from Urbanna on the Rappahannock to Fort Monroe, at the tip of the Virginia Peninsula. The first troops embarked on March 17. In the close of his address to the army, McClellan drew on an address of Napoleon's to his army during the Italian campaign. With McClellan taking the field with the Army of the Potomac, Lincoln removed him from the general-in-chief's post without appointing a successor. The general told his confidant Samuel L. M. Barlow, a New York lawyer and Democratic political leader, that Lincoln was his strongest friend, but in fact the President was then virtually his only friend in the administration.

SOLDIERS OF THE ARMY OF THE POTOMAC! Headquarters Army of the Potomac, *Fairfax Court House, Va., March 14, 1862.*

For a long time I have kept you inactive, but not without a purpose: you were to be disciplined, armed and instructed; the formidable artillery you now have, had to be created; other armies were to move and accomplish certain results. I have held you back that you might give the death-blow to the rebellion that has distracted our once happy country. The patience you have shown, and your confidence in your General, are worth a dozen victories. These preliminary results are now accomplished. I feel that the patient labors of many months have produced their fruit; the Army of the Potomac is now a real Army,—magnificent in material, admirable in discipline and instruction, excellently equipped and armed;—your commanders are all that I could wish. The moment for action has arrived, and I know that I can trust in you to save our country. As I ride through your ranks, I see in your faces the sure presage of victory; I feel that you will do whatever I ask of you. The period of inaction has passed. I will bring you now face to face with the rebels, and only pray that God may defend the right. In whatever direction you may move, however strange my actions may appear to you, ever bear in mind that my fate is linked with yours, and that all I do is to bring you, where I know you wish to be,—on the decisive battlefield. It is my business to place you there. I am to watch over you as a parent over his children; and you know that your General loves you from the depths of his heart. It shall be my care, as it has ever been, to gain success with the least possible loss; but I know that, if it is necessary, you will willingly follow me to our graves, for our righteous cause. God smiles upon us, victory attends us, yet I would not have you think that our aim is to be attained without a manly struggle. I will not disguise it from you: you have brave foes to encounter, foemen well worthy of the steel that you will use so well. I shall demand of you great, heroic exertions, rapid and long marches, desperate combats, privations, perhaps. We will share all these together; and when this sad war is over we will all return to our homes, and feel that we can ask no higher honor than the proud consciousness that we belonged to the ARMY OF THE POTOMAC.

                              GEO. B. MCCLELLAN
                          Major General Commanding

My dear Barlow   Washington March 16 1862

I am here for a few hours only, my Hd Qtrs being on the other side of the river.

I came back last night from Fairfax C.H.—en route for the decisive battle. My movements gave us Manassas with the loss of one life—a gallant cavalry officer—history will, when I am in my grave, record it as the brightest passage of my life that I accomplished so much at so small a cost. It will appear in the future that my advance from Harper's Ferry, & the preparation for turning their right flank have induced them to give up what Halleck & the newspapers would call "the rebel stronghold of the East."

I shall soon leave here on the wing for Richmond—which you may be sure I will take. The Army is in magnificent spirits, & I think are half glad that I now belong to them alone.

Mrs McC joins me in kindest regards to Mrs B & yourself. Do not mind the abolitionists—all I ask of the papers is that they should defend me from the most malicious attacks—tho' to speak frankly I do not care to pay much attention to my enemies.

My wife received your note & desires her thanks for it.

The President is all right—he is my strongest friend.

In haste sincerely yours
Geo B McClellan

S L M Barlow Esq

BRITAIN AND THE IRONCLADS:
LONDON, APRIL 1862

Charles Francis Adams to Charles Francis Adams Jr.

Charles Francis Adams, the son of John Quincy Adams and grandson of John Adams, had served as U.S. minister to Great Britain since May 1861. He wrote to his son, a lieutenant with the 1st Massachusetts Cavalry stationed at Port Royal, South Carolina, to remark on how the reverberations of the *Virginia-Monitor* battle on March 9 had quieted the British lion.

London, April 4, 1862

THE LATE military successes have given us a season of repose. People are changing their notions of the power of the country to meet such a trial, which is attended with quite favorable consequences to us in our position. Our diplomacy is almost in a state of profound calm. Even the favorite idea of a division into two states is less put forward than it was. Yet the interest with which the struggle is witnessed grows deeper and deeper. The battle between the Merrimack and our vessels has been the main talk of the town ever since the news came, in Parliament, in the clubs, in the city, among the military and naval people. The impression is that it dates the commencement of a new era in warfare, and that Great Britain must consent to begin over again. I think the effect is to diminish the confidence in the result of hostilities with us. In December we were told that we should be swept from the ocean in a moment, and all our ports would be taken. They do not talk so now. So far as this may have an effect to secure peace on both sides it is good. . . .

We are much encouraged now by the series of successes gained, and far more by the marked indications of exhaustion and discouragement in the south. They must be suffering in every way. Never did people pay such a penalty for their madness. And the worst is yet to come. For emancipation is on its way with slow but certain pace. Well for them if it do not take them unaware.

"HIS BIG HEART SHOT AWAY":
MASSACHUSETTS, MARCH 1862

Emily Dickinson to Louise and Frances Norcross

Late March 1862

On March 14, in battle at New Berne, the Union army enlarged its foothold on the North Carolina coast. Lieutenant Colonel William S. Clark, 21st Massachusetts Infantry, wrote in his official report that while leading an attack "the noblest of us all, my brave, efficient, faithful adjutant, First Lieut. F.A. Stearns, Company I, fell mortally wounded. . . ." They brought the body of Frazar Stearns back home to Amherst, where his father was president of the college there, for services and burial. Emily Dickinson was watching.

Dear Children,

You have done more for me—'tis least that I can do, to tell you of brave Frazer—"killed at Newbern," darlings. His big heart shot away by a "minie ball."

I had read of those—I didn't think that Frazer would carry one to Eden with him. Just as he fell, in his soldier's cap, with his sword at his side, Frazer rode through Amherst. Classmates to the right of him, and classmates to the left of him, to guard his narrow face! He fell by the side of Professor Clark, his superior officer—lived ten minutes in a soldier's arms, asked twice for water—murmured just, "My God!" and passed! Sanderson, his classmate, made a box of boards in the night, put the brave boy in, covered with a blanket, rowed six miles to reach the boat,—so poor Frazer came. They tell that Colonel Clark cried like a little child when he missed his pet, and could hardly resume his post. They loved each other very much. Nobody here could look on Frazer—not even his father. The doctors would not allow it.

The bed on which he came was enclosed in a large casket shut entirely, and covered from head to foot with the sweetest flowers. He went to sleep from the village church. Crowds came to tell him goodnight, choirs sang to him, pastors told how brave he was—early-soldier heart. And the family bowed their heads, as the reeds the wind shakes.

So our part in Frazer is done, but you must come next summer, and we will mind ourselves of this young crusader—too brave that he could fear to die. We will play his tunes—maybe he can hear them; we will try to comfort his broken-hearted Ella, who, as the clergyman said, "gave him peculiar confidence." . . . Austin is stunned completely. Let us love better, children, it's most that's left to do.

Love from
Emily.

"THE LESSON OF THE HOUR": MARCH 1862

Frederick Douglass: The War and How to End It

March 25, 1862

In the winter and spring of 1862 abolitionist orators such as William Lloyd Garrison, Wendell Phillips, and Frederick Douglass lectured to audiences increasingly receptive to their call for an immediate end to slavery. Douglass delivered this address in Rochester, New York, where he had made his home since 1848, and printed the text in the April *Douglass' Monthly*.

I STAND here to-night to advocate in my humble way, the unrestricted and complete Emancipation of every slave in the United States, whether claimed by loyal or disloyal masters. This is the lesson of the hour.

Through the certain operation of the *changeless laws of the universe*, Emancipation, which has long been a great and solemn national duty, pressing heavily on the national conscience has at last become a great and all commanding national necessity.

I choose not to insist upon these comprehensive propositions as a colored man to-night nor as one having special reasons for hating slavery, although, upon these grounds I might well base a claim to be heard, but my ground is taken as an American citizen, feeling with all others a deep and living interest in the welfare of the whole country.

In the tremendous conflict through which we are passing, all events steadily conspire, to make the cause of the slave and the cause of the country identical. He who to-day fights for Emancipation, fights for his country and free Institutions, and he who fights for slavery, fights against his country and in favor of a slaveholding oligarchy.

This was always so, though only abolitionists perceived the fact. The difference between them and others is this: They got an earlier glimpse at the black heart of slavery—than others did. They saw in times of seeming peace, for the peace we have had, was only seeming—what we can only see in times of open war. They saw that a nation like ours, containing two such opposite forces as liberty and slavery, could not enjoy permanent peace, and they said so and got mobbed for saying so. But let that pass.

Before I proceed to discuss the subject announced for my lecture this evening, allow me to make a few remarks on the mighty events which have marked and are marking the progress of the war. It requires a large share of wisdom and coolness, to properly weigh and measure the great facts which have already passed into history; but it requires a much larger share of these qualities, to enable man to discriminate between, and to determine the proper relations and bearings of the great living facts, transpiring before our eyes.

The obvious reason is this: important events often succeed each other so rapidly, and take the place of each other so quickly, that it becomes almost impossible to give to any one of them, that measure of reflection, which is necessary to form an intelligent judgement.

We are an intelligent people, apt scholars, but I think that few of us fully appreciate the solemn events that are now passing before our eyes.

It is known that we are at war, at war among ourselves, civil war the worst of all wars, but the real scope and significance of this war is but imperfectly understood by millions of the American people.

The very air is filled with conflicting statements in respect to the cause of this war, and naturally enough, it is also filled with contradictory theories as to the manner of restoring the country to peace.

I shall not stay here to discuss the long train of events, and the certain action of social forces which have finally culminated in this rebellion. The limits of the occasion will not permit any such lengthy discussion. The most that I can do, is to point out a few of the leading features of the contest, and enforce the lesson which I think they plainly teach and the path of duty they mark out for our feet.

The first enquiry which concerned the loyal north upon the

sudden outburst of this stupendous rebellion, naturally related to the strength of the rebels, and the amount of force and skill required for their speedy suppression. Even at this vital point we blundered. We misconceived the real state of the case, and misread the facts then passing before us. We were quite incredulous of the tremendous strength and vigor of the foe against whom we were called upon to battle.

We are a charitable people, and in excess of charity were disposed to put the very best construction upon the strange behavior of our southern brethren. We admitted that South Carolina might secede. It was like her to do so. She had talked extravagantly about going out of the union, and she must do something extravagant and startling to save a show of consistency. Georgia too, we thought might possibly go out, but we were quite sure that these twin rebel States, would stand alone in their infamy, and that they would soon tire of their isolation, repent of their folly, and come back to the union. Traitors fled the Cabinet, the House and the Senate, and hastened away to fan the flames of treason at home. Still we doubted that any thing very serious would come of it. We treated it as a bubble on the wave, a nine day's wonder. Calm and thoughtful men ourselves, we relied on the sober second thought of others. Even a shot at one of our ships, an insult offered to our flag, caused only a momentary feeling of indignation and resentment, such as a mother might feel toward a naughty child who had thrown away his bread and stamped defiance at her authority. It was not until Beauregard opened his slave built batteries upon the starving garrison in Charleston harbor, that the confiding North, like a sleeping lion, was roused from his lair, and shook his thundering mane in wrath. We were slow to wake, but we did awake. Still we were scarcely conscious of the skill, power and resources of the enemy. We still hoped that wiser and better counsels would ultimately prevail. We could not believe but that a powerful union sentiment still existed at the South, and that a strong reaction would yet take place there in favor of the union. To the very last we continued to believe in the border States. We could not believe that those States would plunge madly into the bloody vortex of rebellion. It required the assaults of a blood thirsty mob spilling the blood of loyal soldiers to convince us of Baltimore treason.

I need not tell you, how in all this study of passing events, we have been grossly mistaken. Every hope based upon the sanity, loyalty, and good disposition of the South has been woefully disappointed. While armies were forming, and the most formidable preparations were making, we continued to dream of peace, and even after the war was fairly begun, we thought to put down the rebellion by a show of force rather than by an exercise of force. We showed our teeth but did not wish to use them. We preferred to fight with dollars rather than daggers. The fewer battles the better was the motto, popular at Washington, and peace in sixty days trembled along the wires. We now see what we could not at first comprehend. We are astonished at the strength and vigor of the foe. Treason had shot its poisonous roots deeper, and has spread them farther than our calculations had allowed for. Now I have a reason for calling attention to this unwillingness on our part to know the worst. It has already caused much trouble, and I have reason to apprehend that it will cause us much more. We need warnings a thousand times repeated. A hint to the wise is enough for the wise, and although we are wise and can take a hint, the trouble is we don't heed it unless it comes in the shape of a rifled cannon ball battering against the walls of our forts, or an iron clad ram, sinking our navy and threatening our whole Atlantic Coast. Let me under score this point of weakness and as I think blindness on our part for it still lingers with us.

Even now, you need not go far to find newspapers clinging still to the delusion that there is a strong union sentiment at the South. While the rebels are waging a barbarous war, of unparalleled ferocity, marshalling the savage Indian to the slaughter of your sons, and poisoning the wells in their retreats, we are still speaking of them as our erring brothers, to be won back to the union by fondling, rather than fighting. This has been our great error. We failed to comprehend the vital force of the rebellion. First, because we were dazzled and bewildered by the wild rapidity of the strange events, which burst upon us, and secondly because of our habitual leniency to the South and to slaveholders grimly confronting us at the outset.

I have said that the first question was how to whip the rebels. That was the bitter problem. We were sadly unprepared to fight.

Treason had become the warp and woof of the army and navy. Floyd had stolen all the arms, and Cobb had stolen all the money. The nation was at the mercy of the merciless. How to procure arms, and brave men to use them, was naturally first in order. Like the rod of Moses it swallowed all others. It even hushed the voice of abolitionists and wheeled them into line with its imperative demands.

It was the great physical question. Men of muscle understood it as well as men of mind. But now there is another and a mightier question destined to try men's souls more severely than the first.

For not that which is spiritual is first, but that which is natural; after that, that which is spiritual. The physical part of this tremendous conflict is at last in a hopeful way. The great armies of the North are in motion. Baltimore is at the mercy of McHenry, Western Virginia clings to the union, Kentucky is no longer neutral, Missouri has gone to Arkansas. North Carolina is invaded, Florida has followed the fortunes of Bragg, and Tennessee is under Foote.

Brave hearts and strong hands, have met and disposed of the first question. I knew they would from the first. The slaveholding rebels have fought, and have fought well, and will do so again. They are proud, brave and desperate, but proud, brave and desperate as they are, I tell no secret when I say, they can run as well as fight.

General McClellan in his recent address to his army—takes pains to compliment these traitors. He is "sad" at the thought of striking them. The traitors themselves show no such weakness. The language of their Generals is altogether of another character. There is no epithet too vile for them, by which to characterize our army. But McClellan, is careful to tell us that the Southern army is composed of foemen worthy of our steel. I do not like this. It looks bad. Instead of being foemen worthy of our steel, they are rebels and traitors worthy of our hemp.

I do not wonder that all the haters of Impartial Liberty at the North are especially devoted to this "sad" reluctant General, who instead of portraying the baseness of the traitors takes pains to compliment them. It is seriously doubted if he will ever try his steel upon them. Thus far he has entirely failed to do any thing of the sort. But, whether McClellan ever overtakes the rebels or not, the army of the Potomac has moved, and brave men sweep both the Eastern and Western border of the rebellion. So that I look upon the first question, the question as to how to break down the military power of the rebels as in good hands and the public mind is happily relieved at that point.

But now a higher and more important problem presses for consideration. It is a problem for statesmen rather than Generals. Soldiers can capture a State, but statesmen must govern a State. It is sometimes hard to pull down a house but it is always harder to build one up.

This is the question now to be decided, having broken down the rebel power in the seceded States, how shall we extend the Constitution and the Union over them? We know how to make war, we know how to conquer, but the question is do we know how to make peace? We can whip the South, but can we make the South loyal? Baltimore is in our hands, but her parlors and drawing rooms are full of Traitors. The army is at Nashville but the people have fled. General Sherman writes loving epistles to erring rebels, but no one will carry them to the rebels, nor will the rebels touch them. The fact is the South hates the north. It hates the Union. The feeling is genuine and all-pervading. Whence comes this hate? This is an imperative inquiry for statesmen, who would place the peace of this government on an immovable foundation. You are of the same race, the same language, the same sacred historic memories. Why do they hate you? Certainly not because you have been in any manner ungenerous or unjust to them. Why do they hate you? Is it because they are naturally worse than other men? Not at all. I hold that the slaveholder is just as good as his slave system will allow him to be. If I were a slaveholder, and was determined to remain such, I would equal the worst, both in cruelty to the slave and in hatred to the north. I should hate the declaration of Independence, hate the Constitution, hate the Golden rule, hate free schools, free speech, free press, and every other form of freedom. Because in them all, I should see an enemy to my claim of property in man. I should see that the whole North is a point blank and killing condemnation of all my pretensions. The real root of bitterness, that which has generated this intense Southern hate toward the North, is Slavery. Here is the stone of stumbling and the rock of offence. Once I felt it necessary to argue this point. The time for such argument has past. Slavery stands confessed as the grand cause of the war. It has drilled every rebel soldier, loaded, primed, aimed and fired every rebel cannon since the war began. No other interest, commercial, manufacturing or political, could have wrought such a social earthquake amongst us. It has within itself that which begets a character in all around it favorable to its own continuance. It makes slaves of the negroes, vassals of the poor whites and tyrants of the masters. Pride, injustice, ingratitude, lust of dominion, cruelty, scorn, and contempt are the qualities of this rebellion, and slavery breeds them all. The tyrant wants no law above his own will, no associates but men of his own stamp of baseness. He is willing to administer the laws when he can bend them to his will, but he will break them when he can no longer bend them. Where labor is performed under the lash, justice will be administered under the bowie knife. The south is in this respect just what slavery has made her. She has been breeding thieves, rebels and traitors, and this stupendous conflict is the result. She could not do otherwise and cherish slavery in the midst of her.

Now the great question is what shall be the conditions of peace? What shall be done with slavery? We have gradually drifted to this vital question. Slavery is the pivot on which turns all the machinery of this tremendous war, and upon it will depend the character of the future of our peace or want of it.

It is really wonderful how we have been led along towards this grand issue, and how all efforts to evade, postpone, and prevent its coming, have been mocked and defied by the stupendous sweep of events.

It was oracularly given out from Washington many months ago, that whether this rebellion should succeed or fail, the status of no man in the country would be changed by the result. You know what that meant. Europe knew what that meant. It was an assurance given to the world in general, and the slaveholding states in particular, that no harm should come to slavery in the prosecution of the war for the Union. It was a last bid for a compromise with the rebels. But despite of diplomatic disclaimers, despite border State influence, despite the earlier proclamation of the President himself, the grand question of

Emancipation now compels attention and the most thoughtful consideration of men in high places of the nation.

By the events of this war, Washington has become to the nation what Syracuse was to the State of New York after the rescue of Jerry, the grand centre for abolition meetings. A new Congress has assembled there.

Dr. Cheever, Ralph Waldo Emerson, Gerrit Smith, Wendell Phillips, William Goodell and William Lloyd Garrison may now utter in safety their opinions on slavery in the national capital. Meanwhile Congress has a bill before it for the abolition of slavery in the District of Columbia. Kill slavery at the heart of the nation, and it will certainly die at the extremities. Down with it there, and it is the brick knocked down at the end of the row by which the whole line is prostrate.

More and better, the infernal business of slave catching by our army in Missouri and on the Potomac, is at last peremptorily forbidden under penalty of dismissal from the service. This looks small, but is not so. It is a giant stride toward the grand result.

I thank all the powers of earth and sky, that I am permitted to be a witness to this day's events. That slavery could always live and flourish in this country I have always known to be a foul and guilty heresy. That the vile system must eventually go down I have never doubted, even in the darkest days of my life in slavery. But that I should live to see the President of the United States deliberately advocating Emancipation was more than I ever ventured to hope.

It is true that the President lays down his propositions with many qualifications some of which to my thinking, are unnecessary, unjust and wholly unwise. There are spots on the Sun. A blind man can see where the President's heart is. I read the spaces as well as the lines of that message, I see in them a brave man trying against great odds, to do right. An honest patriot endeavoring to save his country in its day of peril. It is the first utterance, and first utterances are not according to Carlyle the most articulate and perfect. Time and practice will improve the President as they improve other men. He is tall and strong but he is not done growing, he grows as the nation grows. He has managed to say one good word, and to say it so distinctly that all the world may hear. He has dared to say that the highest interest of the country will be promoted by the abolition of slavery. And this, bear in mind, is not said in the bitterness of defeat, but when every morning brought news of glorious victories over the slaveholding rebels. The message comes at the call of no desperation. The time selected for sending it to Congress and the nation must be read with the document itself in order to appreciate its true significance.

Right upon the heels of the message comes the appointment of John C. Frémont, a man whose name thrills the young heart of America with every sentiment of honor, patriotism, and bravery. John C. Frémont carries his department in his name. He goes to free the mountains of rebels and traitors and the good wishes of all but traitors will go with him. Here is a new chapter of the war:

Frémont's proclamation, was revised and modified by the President; Frémont was removed from his post when in the act of striking the foe. Calumny did its worst upon Frémont. But he was brave and calm, with Jessie by his side he could not well be otherwise, and though strong himself without that pride of American women to support him, he must have fallen. I saw them as they passed eastward, after the chief had fallen. One glance at the young General and his noble wife told me that Frémont would rise again. He has risen. The rebels will hear it. His war horse is already pawing on all their mountains! But what shall be the conditions of peace? How shall the Union be reconstructed? To my mind complete Emancipation is the only basis of permanent peace. Any other basis will place us just at the point from which we started. To leave slavery standing in the rebel States, is to leave the eggs of treason in the nest from whence we shall have to meet a larger brood of traitors, and rebels at another time; it is to transmit to posterity the question that ought to be settled to-day. Leave slavery where it is, and you leave the same generator of hate towards the north which has already cost us rivers of blood and millions of treasure. Leave slavery in the south and it will be as dangerous for a Northern man to travel in the south, as for a man to enter a powder magazine with fire. Despots are suspicious, and every slaveholder is an unmitigated despot, a natural foe to every form of freedom. Leave slavery in the south, and you will fill the north with a full fledged breed of servile panderers to slavery, baser than all their predecessors.

Leave slavery where it is and you will hereafter, as heretofore, see in politics a divided, fettered, north, and an united south. You will see the statesmen of the country facing both ways, speaking two languages, assenting to the principles of freedom in the north, and bowing to the malign spirit and practices of slavery at the South. You will see all the pro-slavery elements of the country attracted to the south, giving that section ascendancy again in the counsels of the nation and making them masters of the destinies of the Republic. Restore slavery to its old status in the Union and the same elements of demoralization which have plunged this country into this tremendous war will begin again to dig the grave of free Institutions.

It is the boast of the South that her Institutions are peculiar and homogeneous, and so they are. Her statesmen have had the wit to see that contact with the free North must either make the North like herself, or that she herself must become like the North. They are right. The South must put off the yoke of slavery or the North must prepare her neck for that yoke, provided the union is restored. There is a middle path— We have pursued that middle path. It is *compromise* and by it we have reached the point of civil war with all its horrid consequences. The question is shall we start anew in the same old path?

Who wants a repetition of the same event thro' which we are passing? Who wants to see the nation taxed to keep a standing army in the South to maintain respect for the Federal Government and protect the rights of citizens of the United States? To such a man I say, leave slavery still dominant at the South and you shall have all your wants supplied.

On the other hand abolish slavery and the now disjointed nation like kindred drops would speedily mingle into one. Abolish slavery and the last hinderance to a solid nationality is abolished. Abolish slavery and you give conscience a chance to grow, and you will win the respect and admiration of mankind. Abolish slavery and you put an end to all sectional politics founded upon conflicting sectional interests, and imparting strife and bitterness to all our general elections, and to the debates on the floor of Congress. Abolish slavery and the citizens of each state will be regarded and treated as equal citizens of the United States, and may travel unchallenged and unmolested in all the states of the Union. Abolish slavery and you put an end to sectional religion and morals, and establish free speech and liberty of conscience throughout your common country. Abolish slavery and rational, law abiding Liberty will fill the whole land with peace, joy, and permanent safety now and forever.

"BUT YOU MUST ACT":
WASHINGTON, D.C., APRIL 1862

Abraham Lincoln to George B. McClellan

Departing Washington for Fort Monroe with his army, General McClellan told his wife, "I feel very glad to get away from that sink of iniquity. . . ." In his contempt he left behind a careless, poorly drawn plan for protecting the capital, with the result that Lincoln retained Irvin McDowell's army corps for its defense. On meeting the first Confederate resistance on the Peninsula, at Yorktown, McClellan determined on a siege, and initiated what became the leitmotif of his campaign—the constant (and delusional) complaint that he was greatly outnumbered. In his letter the President sought to reason with the general.

Major General McClellan.   Washington,
My dear Sir.   April 9. 1862

Your despatches complaining that you are not properly sustained, while they do not offend me, do pain me very much.

Blencker's Division was withdrawn from you before you left here; and you knew the pressure under which I did it, and, as I thought, acquiesced in it—certainly not without reluctance.

After you left, I ascertained that less than twenty thousand unorganized men, without a single field battery, were all you designed to be left for the defence of Washington, and Manassas Junction; and part of this even, was to go to Gen. Hooker's old position. Gen. Banks' corps, once designed for Manassas Junction, was diverted, and tied up on the line of Winchester and Strausburg, and could not leave it without again exposing the upper Potomac, and the Baltimore and Ohio Railroad. This presented, (or would present, when McDowell and Sumner should be gone) a great temptation to the enemy to turn back from the Rappahanock, and sack Washington. My explicit order that Washington should, by the judgment of *all* the commanders of Army corps, be left entirely secure, had been neglected. It was precisely this that drove me to detain McDowell.

I do not forget that I was satisfied with your arrangement to leave Banks at Mannassas Junction; but when that arrangement was broken up, and *nothing* was substituted for it, of course I was not satisfied. I was constrained to substitute something for it myself. And now allow me to ask "Do you really think I should permit the line from Richmond, *via* Mannassas Junction, to this city to be entirely open, except what resistance could be presented by less than twenty thousand unorganized troops?" This is a question which the country will not allow me to evade.

There is a curious mystery about the *number* of the troops now with you. When I telegraphed you on the 6th. saying you had over a hundred thousand with you, I had just obtained from the Secretary of War, a statement, taken as he said, from your own returns, making 108,000 then with you, and *en route* to you. You now say you will have but 85,000, when all *en route* to you shall have reached you. How can the discrepancy of 23,000 be accounted for?

As to Gen. Wool's command, I understand it is doing for you precisely what a like number of your own would have to do, if that command was away.

I suppose the whole force which has gone forward for you, is with you by this time; and if so, I think it is the precise time for you to strike a blow. By delay the enemy will relatively gain upon you—that is, he will gain faster, by *fortifications* and *re-inforcements*, than you can by re-inforcements alone.

And, once more let me tell you, it is indispensable to *you* that you strike a blow. *I* am powerless to help this. You will do me the justice to remember I always insisted, that going down the Bay in search of a field, instead of fighting at or near Mannassas, was only shifting, and not surmounting, a difficulty—that we would find the same enemy, and the same, or equal, intrenchments, at either place. The country will not fail to note —is now noting—that the present hesitation to move upon an intrenched enemy, is but the story of Manassas repeated.

I beg to assure you that I have never written you, or spoken to you, in greater kindness of feeling than now, nor with a fuller purpose to sustain you, so far as in my most anxious judgment, I consistently can. *But you must act.* Yours very truly

A. LINCOLN

BATTLE OF SHILOH: TENNESSEE, APRIL 1862

Ulysses S. Grant to Commanding Officer, Advance Forces; to Julia Dent Grant; to Nathaniel H. McLean; to Jesse Root Grant; and to Elihu B. Washburne

With their perimeter defense in tatters, the Confederate commanders in the West, Albert Sidney Johnston and Pierre G. T. Beauregard, turned to concentration, gathering about 40,000 men at Corinth, in northern Mississippi, to try to counter Grant's southward advance along the Tennessee River. Grant's army of 40,000, camped at Pittsburg Landing on the Tennessee, was unprepared for the sudden Confederate attack on April 6; the two-day battle took the name of a country church called Shiloh. This set of Grant's correspondence charts the course of the action and the aftermath. He wrote first to a commander in Don Carlos Buell's army, on the march to join him. In writing to his wife, Grant considerably overcounts the enemy forces. His official report details the arrival of reinforcements that enabled him to counterattack on April 7. In writing his father, Grant defends himself against press reports that he was taken by surprise at Shiloh. Jesse Grant sent the letter to the *Cincinnati Commercial*, which printed it on May 2 as coming from "a personal friend of Gen. Grant." Grant sought further support from his confidant Congressman Elihu B. Washburne, who on May 2 defended the general in a speech to the House.

Pittsburg, April 6th 1862

COMD.G OFFICER
ADVANCE FORCES NEAR PITTSBURG, TEN.
GEN.

The attack on my forces has been very spirited from early this morning. The appearance of fresh troops on the field now would have a powerful effect both by inspiring our men and disheartening the enemy. If you will get upon the field leaving all your baggage on the East bank of the river it will be a move to our advantage and possibly save the day to us.

The rebel forces is estimated at over 100.000 men.

My Hd Qrs. will be in the log building on top of the hill where you will be furnished a staff officer to guide you to your place on the field.

> Respectfully &c
> U. S. GRANT
> Maj. Gen.

> Pittsburg, Ten. April 8th 1862

DEAR JULIA,

Again another terrible battle has occured in which our arms have been victorious. For the number engaged and the tenacity with which both parties held on for two days, during an incessent fire of musketry and artillery, it has no equal on this continent. The best troops of the rebels were engaged to the number of 162 regiments as stated by a deserter from their camp, and their ablest generals. Beaurigard commanded in person aided by A. S. Johnson, Bragg, Breckenridge and hosts of other generals of less note but possibly of quite as much merit. Gen. Johnson was killed and Bragg wounded. The loss on both sides was heavy probably not less than 20,000 killed and wounded altogether. The greatest loss was sustained by the enemy. They suffered immensly by demoralization also many of their men leaving the field who will not again be of value on the field.

I got through all safe having but one shot which struck my sword but did not touch me.

I am detaining a steamer to carry this and must cut it short.

Give my love to all at home. Kiss the children for me. The same for yourself.

Good night dear Julia.

> ULYS.

Head Quarters Disct of West Tenn
Pittsburgh April 9th 1862

Capt N H McLean
A A Genl Dept of the Mississippi
Saint Louis. Mo.
Capt

It becomes my duty again to report another battle fought between two great armies, one contending for the maintainance of the best Government ever devised the other for its destruction. It is pleasant to record the success of the army contending for the former principle.

On Sunday morning our pickets were attacked and driven in by the enemy. Immediately the five Divisions stationed at this place were drawn up in line of battle ready to meet them. The battle soon waxed warm on the left and center, varying at times to all parts of the line.

The most continuous firing of musketry and artillery ever heard on this Continent was kept up until night fall, the enemy having forced the entire line to fall back nearly half way from their Camps to the Landing. At a late hour in the afternoon a desperate effort was made by the enemy to turn our left and get possession of the Landing, transports &c. This point was guarded by the Gun boats Tyler and Lexington, Capt's Gwinn & Shirk U S N commanding Four 20 pounder Parrott guns and a battery of rifled guns. As there is a deep and impassable ravine for artillery or Cavalry and very difficult for Infantry at this point. No troops were stationed here except the neccessary Artillerists and a small Infantry force for their support Just at this moment the advance of Maj Genl Buells Column (a part of the Division under Genl Nelson) arrived, the two Generals named both being present. An advance was immediately made upon the point of attack and the enemy soon driven back.

In this repulse much is due to the presence of the Gun boats Tyler and Lexington and their able Commanders Capt Gwinn and Shirk.

During the night the Divisions under Genl Crittenden and McCook arrived. Genl Lew Wallace, at Crumps Landing six miles below, was ordered at an early hour in the morning to hold his Division in readiness to be moved in any direction to which it might be ordered. At about 11 oClock the order was delivered to move it up to Pittsburgh, but owing to its being led by a circuitous route did not arrive in time to take part in Sundays action.

During the night all was quiet, and feeling that a great moral advantage would be gained by becoming the attacking party, an advance was ordered as soon as day dawned. The result was a gradual repulse of the enemy at all parts of the line from morning until probably 5 oClock in the afternoon when it became evident the enemy was retreating. Before the close of the action the advance of Genl T J Woods Division arrived in time to take part in the action.

My force was too much fatigued from two days hard fighting and exposure in the open air to a drenching rain during the intervening night to pursue immediately.

Night closed in cloudy and with heavy rain making the roads impracticable for artillery by the next morning. Genl Sherman however followed the enemy finding that the main part of the army had retreated in good order.

Hospitals of the enemies wounded were found all along the road as far as pursuit was made. Dead bodies of the enemy and many graves were also found.

I enclose herewith report of Genl Sherman which will explain more fully the result of this pursuit.

Of the part taken by each seperate Command I cannot take special notice in this report, but will do so more fully when reports of Division Commanders are handed in.

Genl Buell, coming on the Field with a distinct army, long under his command, and which did such efficient service, commanded by himself in person on the field, will be much better able to notice those of his command who particularly distinguished themselves than I possibly can.

I feel it a duty however to a gallant and able officer Brig Genl W T Sherman to make special mention. He not only was with his Command during the entire of the two days action, but displayed great judgment and skill in the management of his men. Altho severely wounded in the hand the first day, his place was never vacant. He was again wounded and had three horses killed under him. In making this mention of a gallant officer no disparagement is intended to the other Division Commanders Major Generals John A McClernand and Lew Wallace, and Brig Generals S A Hurlbut, B M. Prentiss and W H L Wallace, all of whom maintained their places with credit to themselves and the cause   Genl Prentiss was taken prisoner in the first days action, and Genl W H L Wallace severely, probably mortally wounded. His Ass Adj Genl Capt William McMichael is missing, probably taken prisoner.

My personal Staff are all deserving of particular mention, they having been engaged during the entire two days in conveying orders to every part of the field. It consists of Col J D Webster, Chief of Staff, Lt Col J B McPherson Chief Engineer, assisted by Lieuts W L B Jenney and William Kossack, Capt J A Rawlins A A Genl Capts W S Hillyer, W R Rowley and C B Lagow aides-de-Camp Col G. G. Pride Volunteer aide and Capt J P Hawkins Chief Commissary who accompanied me upon the field.

The Medical Department under the direction of Surgeon Hewitt Medical Director, showed great energy in providing for the wounded and in getting them from the field regardless of danger.

Col Webster was placed in special charge of all the artillery and was constantly upon the field. He displayed, as always heretofore, both skill and bravery. At least in one instance he was the means of placing an entire Regiment in a position of doing most valuable service, and where it would not have been but for his exertions.

Lt Col McPherson attached to my staff as Chief Engineer deserves more than a passing notice for his activity and courage. All the grounds beyond our Camps for miles have been reconnoitred by him, and plats carefully prepared under his supervision, give accurate information of the nature of approaches to our lines. During the two days battle he was constantly in the saddle leading troops as they arrived to points where their services were required. During the engagement he had one horse shot under him.

The Country will have to mourn the loss of many brave men who fell at the battle of Pittsburgh, or Chilo more properly. The exact loss in killed and wounded will be known in a day or two. At present I can only give it approximately at 1500 killed and 3500 wounded.

The loss of Artillery was great, many pieces being disabled

by the enemies shots and some loosing all their horses and many men. There was probably not less than two hundred horses killed.

The loss of the enemy in killed and left upon the field was greater than ours. In wounded the estimate cannot be made as many of them must have been sent back to Corinth and other points.

The enemy suffered terribly from demorilization and desertion. A flag of Truce was sent in to day from Genl Beaurigard. I enclose herewith a copy of the Correspondence.

> I am. Very Respectfully
> Your Obt Servt
> U. S. GRANT
> Major General Comdg

Pittsburg Landing, Tenn., April 26, 1862.

I will go on, and do my duty to the very best of my ability, without praise, and do all I can to bring this war to a speedy close. I am not an aspirant for any thing at the close of the war.

There is one thing I feel well assured of; that is, that I have the confidence of every brave man in my command. Those who showed the white feather will do all in their power to attract attention from themselves. I had perhaps a dozen officers arrested for cowardice in the first day's fight at this place. These men are necessarily my enemies.

As to the talk about a surprise here, nothing could be more false. If the enemy had sent us word when and where they would attack us, we could not have been better prepared. Skirmishing had been going on for two days between our reconnoitering parties and the enemy's advance. I did not believe, however, that they intended to make a determined attack, but simply that they were making a reconnoisance in force.

My headquarters were in Savannah, though I usually spent the day here. Troops were constantly arriving to be assigned to brigades and divisions, all ordered to report at Savannah, making it necessary to keep an office and some one there. I was also looking for Buell to arrive, and it was important that I should have every arrangement complete for his speedy transit to this side of the river.

U. S. GRANT.

Camp Near Corinth, Miss.
May 14th 1862

HON. E. B. WASHBURN,
DEAR SIR:

The great number of attacks made upon me by the press of the country is my apology for not writing to you oftener, not desiring to give any contradiction to them myself.—You have interested yourself so much as my friend that should I say anything it would probably be made use of in my behalf. I would scorn being my own defender against such attacks except through the record which has been kept of all my official acts and which can be examined at Washington at any time.

To say that I have not been distressed at these attacks upon me would be false, for I have a father, mother, wife & children who read them and are distressed by them and I necessarily share with them in it. Then too all subject to my orders read these charges and it is calculated to weaken their confidance in me and weaken my ability to render efficient service in our present cause. One thing I will assure you of however; I can not be driven from rendering the best service within my ability to suppress the present rebellion, and when it is over retiring to the same quiet it, the rebellion, found me enjoying.

Notoriety has no charms for me and could I render the same services that I hope it has been my fortune to render our just cause, without being known in the matter, it would be infinately prefferable to me.

Those people who expect a field of battle to be maintained, for a whole day, with about 30,000 troops, most of them entirely raw, against 70,000, as was the case at Pittsburg Landing, whilst waiting for reinforcements to come up, without loss of life, know little of War. To have left the field of Pittsburg for the enemy to occupy until our force was sufficient to have gained a bloodless victory would have been to left the Tennessee to become a second Potomac.—There was nothing left for me but to occupy the West bank of the Tennessee and to hold it at all hazards. It would have set this war back six months to have failed and would have caused the necessity of raising, as it were, a new Army.

Looking back at the past I cannot see for the life of me any important point that could be corrected.—Many persons who have visited the different fields of battle may have gone away displeased because they were not permitted to carry off horses, fire arms, or other valuables as trophies. But they are no patriots who would base their enmity on such grounds. Such I assure you are the grounds of many bitter words that have been said against me by persons who at this day would not know me by sight yet profess to speak from a personal acquaintance.

I am sorry to write such a letter, infinately sorry that there should be grounds for it. My own justification does not demand it, but you, a friend, are entitled to know my feelings.

As a friend I would be pleased to give you a record, weekly at furthest, of all that transpires in that portion of the army that I am, or may be, connected with, but not to make public use of.

I am very truly Yours
U. S. GRANT.

"WE CAUGHT THE FIRST THUNDER": TENNESSEE, APRIL 1862

William T. Sherman to Ellen Ewing Sherman

Brigadier General William T. Sherman had taken command of a division under Grant in March. Shermans' division caught the brunt of the Confederates' initial attack at Shiloh on Sunday, April 6, and he was more candid than Grant in admitting that it came as a surprise, and how unprepared were the Union forces. The "old Louisiana cadet" prisoner whom he mentions was from the Louisiana Seminary and Military Academy, where Sherman was superintendent before the war.

———————

Camp Shiloh, Apl. 11, 1862

Dearest Ellen,

Well we have had a big battle where they Shot real bullets and I am safe, except a buckshot wound in the hand and a bruised shoulder from a spent ball—The first horse I rode was one I captured from the Enemy soon after I got here, a beautiful sorrel race mare that was as fleet as a deer, and very easy in her movements to which I had become much attached—She was first wounded and then shot dead under me. This occurred Sunday when the firing on both sides was terrific and I had no time to save saddle, holsters or valise. I took the horse of my aid McCoy till it was shot, when I took my Doctors horse and that was shot—My Camp was in advance of all others and we caught the first thunder, and they captured all our tents and two horses of mine hitched to the trees near my tent were Killed. So I am completely unhorsed—The first man killed in the Battle was my orderly close by my side a young handsome faithful soldier who carried his Carbine ever ready to defend me his name was Holliday and the Shot that killed him was meant for me. After the Battle was over I had him brought to my camp and buried by a tree Scarred with balls and its top carried off by a Cannon ball. These about embrace all the personal events connected with myself—My troops were very raw and Some Regiments broke at the first fire. Others behaved better, and I managed to keep enough all the time to form a Command and was the first to get back to our front Line. The Battle on Sunday was very severe. They drove back our left flank on the River, but I held the Right flank out about a mile & half, giving room for Reinforcements to come in from Crumps landing to our North, and for Buells army to land—Beauregard, Bragg Johnston, Breckinridge and all their Big men were here, with their best soldiers and after the Battle was over I found among the prisoners an old Louisiana Cadet named Barrow who sent for me and told me all about the others, many of whom were here and Knew they were fighting me. I gave him a pair of socks, drawers & Shirt and treated him very kindly. I wont attempt to give an account of the Battle, but they Say that I accomplished some important results, and Gen. Grant makes special mention of me in his Report which he shew me. I have worked hard to Keep down but somehow I am forced into prominence and might as well submit. One thing pleased me well—On Sunday we caught thunder and were beaten back—Buell arrived very opportunely and came out to see me—the place of operations was agreed on, and his fresh Kentucky troops to advance boldly out direct from the Steamboat landing to Shiloh my Head Qrs.—I was on the Right and to advance when he got abreast of me—This was done, and I edged to the Road, and reached it about 500 yards from here, just where the hardest fighting was, and then met the same Kentucky troops I had at Muldrough hill. They all recognized me and such shouting you never heard. I asked to pass their Ranks and they gave me the lead. I have since visited their Camps and never before received such marks of favor—Johns Brigade is also here, indeed we must now have 75,000 men. Figures begin to approximate my standard—Halleck is coming with reinforcements. We have been attacked & beaten off our enemy. Now we must attack him. This would occur at once, but it has been raining so that our Roads are almost impassable. The Enemy expected to crush us before Buell got here. The scenes on this field would have cured anybody of war. Mangled bodies, dead, dying, in every conceivable shape, without heads, legs; and horses! I think we have buried 2000 since the fight our own & the Enemy, and the wounded fill houses, tents, steamboats and Every conceivable place. My division had about 8000 men—at least half ran away, and out of the remaining half, I have 302 soldiers 16 officers killed and over 1200 wounded. All I can say this was a Battle, and you will receive so many graphic accounts that my picture would be tame. I Know you will read all accounts—cut out paragraphs with my name for Willy's future Study—all Slurs you will hide away, and gradually convince yourself that I am a soldier as famous as Gen. Greene. I still feel the horrid nature of this war, and the piles of dead Gentlemen & wounded & maimed makes me more anxious than ever for some hope of an End but I know such a thing cannot be for a long long time. Indeed I never expect it or to survive it. You ask for money—I have none, and now am without horse saddle bridle, bed, or anything—The Rebels, Breckinridge had my Camp and cleaned me out. You must learn to live without money, as that is going to be a scarce commodity—plant a garden & raise your own vegetables—[   ]

"THEY RAN IN EVERY DIRECTION":
TENNESSEE, APRIL 1862

George W. Dawson to Laura Amanda Dawson

Captain Dawson's 1st Missouri Infantry, in John C. Breckinridge's Reserve Corps, pressed the Federal left on the first day of Shiloh. The fighting Dawson describes for his wife, at the so-called Sunken Road, was some of the fiercest of the battle, and at day's end his regiment had pushed close enough to the Tennessee to draw the fire of the Union gunboats. Shiloh cost the Union 13,000 men killed, wounded, or missing, while Confederate casualties totaled about 10,700.

Memphis, Tenn.
April 26th

My dear sweet Wife,

    I wrote you a short note by Mart Dunklin but for fear you didn't get it I send you this by Mr. Robbins. You are no doubt uneasy and anxious to hear what had become of me and others. Well I will give you a kind of history. After I left you I came to Memphis and from thence I went to Murfeestown, Tenn. where I found the Reg. & in a day or so we marched & continued to do so till we arrived ten miles this side of Huntsville, Ala. Here we took Rail for 20 miles and then footed it again to Corinth, Miss. Having marched through 1/4 of Ky. all of Tenn. part of Alabama and 30 miles into Miss. you may be assured that we were some what leg weary. We arrived at Corinth Some time before the fight at Shiloh. So you might guess that we had a hand in the fight—and I must say that it was no tea party—but a hard fought Battle. Yet when ever we pressed the Yanks they gave way and we again charged them but that they ran in every direction. We were held in reserve till about 10 oclock Sunday Morning. We were then ordered forward at the double quick step for 2 1/2 miles and as soon as formed into line the Feds opened on us—at the first fire 3 of my men were wounded slightly but one of them Jim Henley has since died of Lock Jaw.

We immediately charged them and put them to rout, we then changed our direction and soon found another Brigade which poured a heavy fire on us which we returned in good stile. Our Col. Rich was shot off of his horse. Lt. Carrington was badly wounded. Capt. Sprague was here killed. We received reinforcements and charged them when they threw down their guns and scampered off like cowardly dogs. We continued to press them and run them down the river bank immediately to their gun boats if which had not been there we would have captured the last one of them. They shelled us from the Gun Boats for over 1 hour. I never heard such thunder and such shower of shell and C. Yet, these did not damage except to kill one or two men—Night coming one we drew off to one of their Camps where we found every thing a solider could want to which we helped our selves. We ate their grub, and slept in their cots as quietly as if we had no enemy in 100 miles. But they Continued to throw Shell at us all night and shell all burst beyond us—passing over our camp. Monday Morning the Feds having been reinforced with 40,000 men renewed the fight—about sun up. We commenced drawing off our forces before we were Attacked. Our Brigade fought them all day Monday in covering the retreat of our army—which was done in the very best of order Lieut. Joseph T. Hargett was killed Monday. I had 43 men when I went into the fight and on coming out had 21 having lost in killed and wounded 22. Yet most of the wounded are slightly so. The other companies of our Reg. did not suffer so much. I had forgotten to tell you I had been Elected Capt. Cam Riley having been elected Lt. Col. He had Command of our Reg. during the fight and acted bravely.

We are expecting a fight at Corinth which will be the biggest fight that will be on record in the next 100 years. I am satisfied that they will out number us but when we have them out of reach of their Gun Boats we will whip them worse that at Shiloh. The fate of our cause rests on us here. I know we have right on our side God is also with us and we must succeed will do it. War is dangerous and one cannot tell after coming out of one hard fought battle whether there is a chance to get out of the second, but I will hope for the best, knowing that if I am killed that I die fighting for My Country and my rights, also that I have your prayers constantly ascending to Heaven. Just hope you and my dear children if I am not allowed to see you again you must bear up and don't get unhappy I yet may see you again Oh what a pleasure is the thought. If you & children are only with me I could be happy but I am lonely & sad.

I have sold some of my land to Robbins so you may sign the deed. I will invest the money in Texas. Where I only wish you were.

Bob, Will Hunter, Wm. Post, Wm. Watkins and T. I. F. all were uninjured Cam Pinnell died of his wounds. Thos. Emory was slightly wounded—All are improving. Many will be able to go into the next fight.

I wish you to write me a long letter giving a detailed account of every thing that has taken place since I left, also how you are getting along and what prospect you have for something to eat this Summer and Winter. I feel very anxious to hear—and if there is any chance I want you to come down to Memphis and I will try to get you to Texas.

My love to all—but especially to you my sweet wife. Kiss our dear children a thousand times for me. Remember me to my friends if I have any. Hoping to hear from you soon I remain your devoted husband.

       Geo. W. Dawson

Excuse mistakes the gas is so high up that I can't see.

"THE CHURCH SO LONE": APRIL 1862

Herman Melville: Shiloh

Herman Melville remembered the "dying foemen" in a poem that first appeared in *Battle-Pieces and Aspects of the War*, published in August 1866. In his preface to the book, Melville wrote that with "few exceptions, the Pieces in this volume originated in an impulse imparted by the fall of Richmond," suggesting that most of the poems were written after April 1865.

Shiloh

A Requiem
(APRIL, 1862)

Skimming lightly, wheeling still,
   The swallows fly low
Over the field in clouded days,
   The forest-field of Shiloh—
Over the field where April rain
Solaced the parched ones stretched in pain
Through the pause of night
That followed the Sunday fight
   Around the church of Shiloh—
The church so lone, the log-built one,
That echoed to many a parting groan
     And natural prayer
   Of dying foemen mingled there—
Foemen at morn, but friends at eve—
   Fame or country least their care:
(What like a bullet can undeceive!)
   But now they lie low,
While over them the swallows skim,
   And all is hushed at Shiloh.

RICHMOND, VIRGINIA, APRIL 1862

Confederate Conscription Acts

With one-year enlistments in the Confederate army expiring in the spring of 1862, Jefferson Davis saw conscription as the only answer to impending chaos. To Congress on March 28 he proposed that all men between eighteen and thirty-five "should pay their debt of military service to the country, that the burdens should not fall exclusively on the most ardent and patriotic." Congress approved his proposal on April 16, and equally important, extended current enlistments to three years or the duration of the war. Substitutes might be hired, and, under further legislation adopted on April 21, exemptions were made for a variety of occupations. In September 1862 the age of eligibility for conscription was raised to forty-five, and the following month exemptions were extended to cover one white male from every plantation with twenty or more slaves. The Confederate conscription act was the first draft law in American history, and became highly controversial. It was denounced as illegitimate because the Confederate Constitution had not explicitly authorized conscription, while the "twenty slaves" provision was attacked for favoring the rich; its enforcement would provoke widespread evasion and resistance throughout the South, especially in upland regions.

An Act to further provide for the public defence.

In view of the exigencies of the country, and the absolute necessity of keeping in the service our gallant army, and of placing in the field a large additional force to meet the advancing columns of the enemy now invading our soil: Therefore

The Congress of the Confederate States of America do enact, That the President be, and he is hereby authorized to call out and place in the military service of the Confederate States, for three years, unless the war shall have been sooner ended, all white men who are residents of the Confederate States, between the ages of eighteen and thirty-five years at the time the call or calls may be made, who are not legally exempted from military service. All of the persons aforesaid who are now in the armies of the Confederacy, and whose term of service will expire before the end of the war, shall be continued in the service for three years from the date of their original enlistment. unless the war shall have been sooner ended: *Provided, however*, That all such companies, squadrons, battalions, and regiments, whose term of original enlistment was for twelve months, shall have the right, within forty days, on a day to be fixed by the Commander of the Brigade, to re-organize said companies, battalions, and regiments, by electing all their officers, which they had a right heretofore to elect, who shall be commissioned by the President: *Provided, further*, That furloughs not exceeding sixty days, with transportation home and back, shall be granted to all those retained in the service by the provisions of this Act beyond the period of their original enlistment, and who have not heretofore received furloughs under the provisions of an Act entitled "An Act providing for the granting of bounty and furloughs to privates and non-commissioned officers in the Provisional Army," approved eleventh December, eighteen hundred and sixty-one, said furloughs to be granted at such times and in such numbers as the Secretary of War may deem most compatible with the public interest: and *Provided, further*, That in lieu of a furlough the commutation value in money of the transportation herein above granted, shall be paid to each private, musician, or non-commissioned officer who may elect to receive it, at such time as the furlough would otherwise be granted: *Provided, further*, That all persons under the age of eighteen years or over the age of thirty-five years, who are now enrolled in the military service of the Confederate States, in the regiments, squadrons, battalions, and companies hereafter to be re-organized, shall be required to remain in their respective companies, squadrons, battalions and regiments for ninety days, unless their places can be sooner supplied by other recruits not now in the service, who are between the ages of eighteen and thirty-five years; and all laws and parts of laws providing for the re-enlistment of volunteers and the organization thereof into companies, squadrons, battalions, or regiments, shall be and the same are hereby repealed.

SEC. 2. *Be it further enacted*, That such companies, squadrons, battalions, or regiments organized, or in process of organization by authority from the Secretary of War, as may be within thirty days from the passage of this Act, so far completed as to have the whole number of men requisite for organization actually enrolled, not embracing in said organizations any persons now in service, shall be mustered into the service of the Confederate States as part of the land forces of the same, to be received in that arm of the service in which they are authorized to organize, and shall elect their company, battalion, and regimental officers.

SEC. 3. *Be it further enacted*, That for the enrollment of all persons comprehended within the provisions of this Act, who are not already in service in the armies of the Confederate States, it shall be lawful for the President, with the consent of the Governors of the respective States, to employ State officers, and on failure to obtain such consent, he shall employ Confederate officers, charged with the duty of making such enrollment in accordance with rules and regulations to be prescribed by him.

SEC. 4. *Be it further enacted*, That persons enrolled under the provisions of the preceding Section, shall be assigned by the Secretary of War, to the different companies now in the service, until each company is filled to its maximum number, and the persons so enrolled shall be assigned to companies from the States from which they respectively come.

SEC. 5. *Be it further enacted*, That all Seamen and ordinary Seamen in the land forces of the Confederate States, enrolled under the provisions of this Act, may, on application of the Secretary of the Navy, be transferred from the land forces to the Naval service.

SEC. 6. *Be it further enacted*, That in all cases where a State may not have in the army a number of Regiments, Battalions, Squadrons or Companies, sufficient to absorb the number of persons subject to military service under this Act, belonging to such State, then the residue or excess thereof, shall be kept as a reserve, under such regulations as may be established by the Secretary of War, and that at stated periods of not greater than three months, details, determined by lot, shall be made from said reserve, so that each company shall, as nearly as practicable, be kept full: *Provided*, That the persons held in reserve may remain at home until called into service by the President: *Provided, also*, That during their stay at home, they shall not receive pay: *Provided, further*, That the persons comprehended in this Act, shall not be subject to the Rules and Articles of War, until mustered into the actual service of the Confederate States; except that said persons, when enrolled and liable to duty, if they shall wilfully refuse to obey said call, each of them shall be held to be a deserter, and punished as such, under said Articles: *Provided, further*, That whenever, in the opinion of the President, the exigencies of the public service may require it, he shall be authorized to call into actual service the entire reserve, or so much as may be necessary, not previously assigned to different companies in service under provision of section four of this Act; said reserve shall be organized under such rules as the Secretary of War may adopt: *Provided*, The company, battalion and regimental officers shall be elected by the troops composing the same: *Provided*, The troops raised in any one State shall not be combined in regimental, battalion, squadron or company organization with troops raised in any other States.

SEC. 7. *Be it further enacted*, That all soldiers now serving in the army or mustered in the military service of the Confederate States, or enrolled in said service under the authorizations heretofore issued by the Secretary of War, and who are continued in the service by virtue of this Act, who have not received the bounty of fifty dollars allowed by existing laws, shall be entitled to receive said bounty.

SEC. 8. *Be it further enacted*, That each man who may hereafter be mustered into service, and who shall arm himself with a musket, shot-gun, rifle or carbine, accepted as an efficient weapon, shall be paid the value thereof, to be ascertained by the mustering officer under such regulations as may be prescribed by the Secretary of War, if he is willing to sell the same, and if he is not, then he shall be entitled to receive one dollar a month for the use of said received and approved musket, rifle, shot-gun or carbine.

SEC. 9. *Be it further enacted*, That persons not liable for duty may be received as substitutes for those who are, under such regulations as may be prescribed by the Secretary of War.

SEC. 10. *Be it further enacted*, That all vacancies shall be filled by the President from the company, battalion, squadron or regiment in which such vacancies shall occur, by promotion according to seniority, except in case of disability or other incompetency: *Provided, however*, That the President may, when in his opinion, it may be proper, fill such vacancy or vacancies by the promotion of any officer or officers, or private or privates from such company, battalion, squadron or regiment who shall have been distinguished in the service by exhibition of valor and skill; and that whenever a vacancy shall occur in the lowest grade of the commissioned officers of a company, said vacancy shall be filled by election: *Provided*, That all appointments made by the President shall be by and with the advice and consent of the Senate.

SEC. 11. *Be it further enacted*, That the provisions of the first section of this Act, relating to the election of officers, shall apply to those regiments, battalions, and squadrons which are composed of twelve months and war companies combined in the same organization, without regard to the manner in which the officers thereof were originally appointed.

SEC. 12. *Be it further enacted*, That each company of infantry shall consist of one hundred and twenty-five, rank and file; each company of field artillery of one hundred and fifty, rank and file; each of cavalry, of eighty, rank and file.

SEC. 13. *Be it further enacted*, That all persons, subject to enrollment, who are not now in the service, under the provisions of this Act, shall be permitted, previous to such enrollment, to volunteer in companies now in the service.

APPROVED April 16, 1862.

An Act to exempt certain persons from enrollment for service in the Armies of the Confederate States.

The Congress of the Confederate States of America do enact, That all persons who shall be held to be unfit for military services under rules to be prescribed by the Secretary of War; all in the service or employ of the Confederate States; all judicial and executive officers of Confederate or State Governments; the members of both Houses of the Congress and of the Legislatures of the several States and their respective officers; all clerks of the officers of the State and Confederate Governments allowed by law; all engaged in carrying the mails; all ferrymen on post routes; all pilots and persons engaged in the marine service and in actual service on river and railroad routes of transportation; telegraphic operators, and ministers of religion in the regular discharge of ministerial duties; all engaged in working iron mines, furnaces and foundries; all journeymen printers actually employed in printing newspapers; all presidents and professors of colleges and academies, and all teachers having as many as twenty scholars; superintendents of the public hospitals, lunatic asylums and the regular nurses and attendants therein, and the teachers employed in the institution for the deaf and dumb, and blind; in each apothecary store now established and doing business, one apothecary in good standing who is a practical druggist; superintendents and operatives in wool and cotton factories, who may be exempted by the Secretary of War;—shall be and are hereby exempted from military service in the armies of the Confederate States.

APPROVED April 21, 1862.

ABOLISHING SLAVERY IN THE DISTRICT OF
COLUMBIA: APRIL 1862

Abraham Lincoln: Message to Congress

In April Congress abolished slavery in the District of Columbia, providing compensation of up to $300 per slave and appropriating $100,000 for the voluntary colonization of freed slaves outside the United States. The bill received unanimous Republican support, but was opposed by a majority of Democrats and border state unionists. Signed into law by President Lincoln, who privately favored gradual emancipation in the District, the measure freed some 3,200 people. (Congress passed the supplemental legislation Lincoln asked for on July 12.) On June 19 Lincoln would sign a bill abolishing slavery in the federal territories, without compensation or provision for colonization.

April 16, 1862

Fellow citizens of the Senate, and House of Representatives.

The Act entitled "An Act for the release of certain persons held to service, or labor in the District of Columbia" has this day been approved, and signed.

I have never doubted the constitutional authority of congress to abolish slavery in this District; and I have ever desired to see the national capital freed from the institution in some satisfactory way. Hence there has never been, in my mind, any question upon the subject, except the one of expediency, arising in view of all the circumstances. If there be matters within and about this act, which might have taken a course or shape, more satisfactory to my judgment, I do not attempt to specify them. I am gratified that the two principles of compensation, and colonization, are both recognized, and practically applied in the act.

In the matter of compensation, it is provided that claims may be presented within ninety days from the passage of the act "but not thereafter"; and there is no saving for minors, femes-covert, insane, or absent persons. I presume this is an omission by mere over-sight, and I recommend that it be supplied by an amendatory or supplemental act.

ABRAHAM LINCOLN

April 16. 1862.

RUNNING THE GAUNTLET:
LOUISIANA, APRIL 1862

John Russell Bartlett: The "Brooklyn" at the Passage of the Forts

On the night of April 23–24, 1862, Flag Officer David G. Farragut signaled his battle fleet to force the passage between Forts Jackson and St. Philip, which guarded the Mississippi about seventy miles below New Orleans. Four days earlier, two daring gunboat captains had made a breach in the hulks and chains barricading the river just wide enough for Farragut's warships to pass through one at a time and challenge the forts. John Russell Bartlett, then a midshipman aboard the sloop of war *Brooklyn*, described the fighting in *Battles and Leaders of the Civil War*.

From February 2d to March 7th, 1862, the United States steamer *Brooklyn*, Captain Thomas T. Craven, was engaged in blockading Pass à l'Outre, one of the mouths of the Mississippi River. It is impossible to describe the monotony of the life on board ship during this period. Most of the time there was a dense fog, so thick that we could not see the length of the ship. The fog collected in the rigging, and there was a constant dripping from aloft like rain, which kept the decks wet and made things generally uncomfortable. No news was received from the North, and our waiting and watching seemed endless. We had our routine of drill each day, but nothing to talk about. Our only excitement was the lookout at the main-topgallant cross-tree, who was above the fog-bank, shouting "Smoke h-oo!" It was a great relief to shout through the deck-trumpet, "Where away?" but the answer was always the same, —"Up the river, sir!" Days and weeks went by, and the smoke came no nearer. Once only, on February 24th, it came out of the river, and we had an exciting chase of a blockade-runner, following her for miles, with an officer aloft conning the ship by the smoke seen above the fog; we captured the chase, which proved to be the steamer *Magnolia* with 1200 bales of cotton.

At last the spell was broken, for on the 7th of March the *Hartford* and *Pensacola* arrived with Captain D. G. Farragut, then flag-officer commanding the West Gulf Blockading Squadron, and we learned that we were going to open the Mississippi River.

I had never met Farragut, but had heard of him from officers who were with him in the *Brooklyn* on her previous cruise. He had been represented as a man of most determined will and character—a man who would assume any responsibility to accomplish necessary ends. I saw a great deal of him at the Head of the Passes and after we passed the forts. Often, when I came on board the *Hartford* with a message from the captain of the *Brooklyn*, Farragut sent me somewhere to carry an order or to do certain duty. I was much impressed with his energy and activity and his promptness of decision and action. He had a winning smile and a most charming manner and was jovial and talkative. He prided himself on his agility, and I remember his telling me once that he always turned a handspring on his birthday, and should not consider that he was getting old until he was unable to do it. The officers who had the good fortune to be immediately associated with him seemed to worship him. He had determination and dash in execution, but in planning and organizing he appeared to want method. He showed me one day an old envelope containing memoranda, and said that that was all the record or books that he kept. He had, however, the good fortune to have on his staff two of the best organizers and administrators of detail in the service,—Captains Henry H. Bell at New Orleans and Percival Drayton at Mobile.

On the 15th of March we began to congregate at the Head of the Passes, and at this time the energy and activity of the flag-officer made themselves felt. We lay here several weeks preparing our ships for the coming action, drilling the crews, firing at targets, and getting in provisions and coal. Farragut was about the fleet from early dawn until dark, and if any officers or men had not spontaneous enthusiasm he certainly infused it into them. I have been on the morning watch, from 4 to 8, when he would row alongside the ship at 6 o'clock, either hailing to ask how we were getting along, or, perhaps, climbing over the side to see for himself. One of the preparations that we made at the Head of the Passes was to hang the chain-cables along each side, abreast of the engine and boilers. A jack-stay, or iron rod, was fastened by means of eye-bolts to the ship's side about eight feet above the water, and one of the chain-cables in bights was suspended to it and fastened with spun yarn. The links of the cable were of iron an inch and a half in diameter, and each strand, or bight, was lapped over the next, the links fitting between each other so that it made an almost continuous coat of mail. It extended about two feet below the water-line. Around the steam-drum, which rose five feet above the berth-deck, sand-bags were piled, and the sick-bay, in the bow, was filled solid with hawsers and rigging, taken from the hold, which had been cleared to form a hospital for the surgeon. Everything was arranged for the convenience of the surgeon in attending the wounded. At the main hatch a cot-frame was rigged and slung from two davits so that the wounded men could be lowered to the berth-deck and thence carried to the surgeon in the forehold. A howitzer was placed in the foretop and one in the maintop. A large kedge-anchor was hung to the main brace bumkin on each quarter, with a hawser attached, to be used whenever it became necessary to turn the ship suddenly.

There was considerable delay in getting the larger vessels over the bar and in filling up with ammunition and coal. At last, on April 16th, Farragut steamed up with the fleet and anchored just below the point where Porter's mortar-vessels, or, as the sailors used to call them, the "bummers," had taken their position and had made ready to open fire upon the forts. Admiral Porter has described in this work the part taken by these vessels in the opening of the lower Mississippi. I can vouch for the accuracy of their aim, for I used to sit on the cross-trees all day, when not on duty, seeing the shells fall into the fort and witnessing the havoc they made in it.

We had plenty of occupation while anchored below the forts, and as an accompaniment one of the mortars was fired every half minute all day. It was trying work for the poor fellows on the mortar-schooners, for when their mortar was fired, all of them were obliged to go aft and stand on tiptoe with open mouths to receive the concussion. The powder blackened everything, and the men looked like negroes. At intervals fire-rafts came down. The first one caused much alarm, and we prepared to slip our cable and get out of the way. The rafts were immense flat-boats with wood piled loosely twenty feet high and saturated with tar and resin, and the flame from them would rise a hundred feet into the air. They certainly looked dangerous, but they were set adrift only one at a time and otherwise were so badly managed that in a little while they merely served to amuse us. The fleet lay under the point on the right bank, and the rafts would tend to the left bank with the strength of the current, and so pass harmlessly by or ground on the bank. Others caught in the obstructions and failed to come down. Sometimes boats from the ships were sent to help tow them away. If there had been any one man to direct the enemy's operations, and so secure concert of action, we should have fared badly; for half a dozen rafts chained together and pushed into position by their gun-boats would have made havoc with the fleet. One night five rafts were sent down, one of which had been towed over to the right bank and came almost directly into the fleet; the *Westfield* made for it and pushed it out into the stream; but it came so near that even with hose playing on the side and rigging the *Brooklyn's* paint was badly blistered.

The forts kept up a continual fire from their rifle-guns, and now and then a shell would pass uncomfortably near the ship. To keep down this fire as much as possible, and thus protect the mortar-vessels, one of the smaller sloops or two of the gun-boats were kept under way. They would steam up to the west bank under cover of the trees and suddenly shoot out into the stream and open fire with their 11-inch pivots, and then drift down-stream. As they were always in rapid motion, it was difficult for the gunners in the forts to hit them; still, a number of men were wounded.*

On the 23d, after five days of continual firing, Commander Porter informed the flag-officer that his men were worn out from want of sleep and rest, and that his ammunition was

---

*There were none killed in the sloops or gun-boats in the bombardment preceding the battle. Twenty-four men were wounded, including one on board the schooner *Norfolk Packet*. Two deaths are reported April 18th–24th, one of them on board the mortar-schooner *Arletta*, and one by a fall from the mast-head on board the *Katahdin*.—J. R. B.

nearly expended. The obstructions, which had formed an apparently impassable barrier, had now been overcome. The opening of a passage through the hulks was one of the most daring feats of the war, and here again the want of concert among the independent floating commands of the enemy led him to neglect the protection of what was really his main reliance for defense. The only cause for delay was now removed. Councils of war were held on board the *Hartford* every day during the bombardment, and the plan of running by the forts was fully discussed. Some of the captains thought it suicidal and believed that the whole fleet would be annihilated; others, that perhaps one or two vessels might get by, but they would be sunk by the rams. All this time Farragut maintained that it must and should be done, even if half the ships were lost. A final council was called on the afternoon of the 23d, and it was decided to attempt the passage that night.*

The present article is intended merely as a personal narrative of the passage of the forts as seen from the deck of the *Brooklyn*. This vessel was a flush-deck sloop-of-war, carrying 22 9-inch guns, 1 80-pounder Dahlgren rifle, and 1 30-pounder Parrott rifle. A small poop-deck extended about fifteen feet from the taffrail, and under this were the steering-wheel and binnacles. I was a midshipman on board doing lieutenant's duty, having charge of a regular watch and in command of a division of guns. My division consisted of 4 guns (2 guns' crews) at the after end of the ship. The guns were numbered in pairs 10 and 11. The No. 11 gun on the starboard side was shifted over to the port side under the poop-deck, and both the No. 11 guns were manned by the marines. It was expected that our principal work would be with our port battery directed against Fort Jackson on the right bank. My two crews manned the No. 10

---

*In July, 1861, I was on board the steam frigate *Mississippi* when she made a visit to the Southwest Pass, and having been sent to the *Powhatan*, commanded by Lieutenant D. D. Porter, near by, I walked up and down the quarter-deck with the commanding officer. He was very much exasperated that the department at Washington delayed sending vessels of proper draught to enter the river, and said that if he had half a dozen good vessels he would undertake to run by the forts and capture New Orleans. Admiral Porter has already recounted in this work the prominent part that he took in the opening of the Mississippi, and I therefore omit further reference to it.—J. R. B.

gun on each side, and also prepared to man the 30-pounder on the poop if occasion should require. On each side of the poop there was a ladder to the main deck. While steaming up to the hulks and until it was necessary for me to be at my guns, I stood on the port ladder with my head above the rail, where I could watch our approach to the forts, and I mounted this ladder several times to see what was going on as we advanced.

On the poop were Captain Craven, Midshipman John Anderson, who had volunteered a few days before from the *Montgomery*, which did not take part in the action, Captain's Clerk J. G. Swift, afterward a graduate of West Point and a lieutenant in the army, and two quartermasters. There was a small piece of ratline stuff carried around the poop, about waist-high. Captain Craven stood at the forward edge of the poop with his hands on this line, and did not move during the whole passage. I had the good fortune during the war to serve with many brave commanders, but I have never met in the service, or out of it, a man of such consummate coolness, such perfect apparent indifference to danger as Admiral Craven. As I write, I hear the sad news of his death.

At 2 o'clock on the morning of the 24th two red lights were hoisted at the peak of the flag-ship as a signal to get under way. All hands had been on deck since midnight to see that everything about the deck and guns was ready for action, and when the decks were wet down and sanded, it really began to look as if we were going to have some pretty hot business on our hands. The anchor was hove up with as little noise as possible, and at half-past 2 we steamed off, following the *Hartford* toward the entrance to the opening which had been made in the obstructions. The Confederates opened fire about 3 o'clock, when the advance division came in sight and range of the forts, and as we passed ahead of the mortar-vessels we also came in range; but the forts were so far ahead that we could not bring our broadside guns to bear. For twenty minutes we stood silent beside the guns, with the shot and shell from Forts St. Philip and Jackson passing over us and bursting everywhere in the air. As we came to the obstruction the water-battery on the Fort Jackson side opened a most destructive fire, and here the *Brooklyn* received her first shot. We gave the water-battery a broadside of grape. With our own smoke and the smoke from the vessels immediately ahead, it was impossible to direct the ship, so that we missed the opening between the hulks and brought up on the chain. We dropped back and tried again; this time the chain broke, but we swung alongside of one of the hulks, and the stream-anchor, hanging on the starboard quarter, caught, tore along the hulk, and then parted its lashings. The cable secured us just where the Confederates had the range of their guns, but somebody ran up with an axe and cut the hawser, and we began to steam up the river.* A few moments later there was a sudden jar, and the engines stopped. The propeller had no doubt struck some hard object, but no one knew the cause of the stoppage; and as Craven called out, "Stand by the starboard anchor," and a fatal pause under the enemy's fire seemed imminent, a thrill of alarm ran through the ship. The alarm was groundless, however, as no injury was done, and presently the engines started again, and the ship moved on.

There were many fire-rafts, and these and the flashing of the guns and bursting shells made it almost as light as day, but the smoke from the passing fleet was so thick that at times one could see nothing ten feet from the ship. While entangled with the rafts, the *Brooklyn* was hulled a number of times; one shot from Fort Jackson struck the rail just at the break of the poop and went nearly across, plowing out the deck in its course. Another struck Barney Sands, the signal quartermaster, and cut his body almost in two. The first lieutenant, Lowry, coming along at the time, inquired who it was, and understanding the response to be "Bartlett," instead of "Barney," he passed the word that he had sent down "all that was left of poor Bartlett." As he came on deck and was about in all parts of the ship during the fight, he gave the men news of the progress of the fight and of the casualties, and for once I was completely out of existence.

The ship was now clear of the hulks and steamed up the river, throwing shells and shrapnel into Fort Jackson as fast as

---

*I went on the poop to help clear the hawser, and looked around for my classmate Anderson. He must have been knocked overboard by a shot when we first came to the obstructions. The anchor on the port quarter was broken off close to the stock at this point by a shot from Fort Jackson.—J. R. B.

the guns could be loaded and fired. When just abreast of the fort a shot struck the side of the port of No. 9 gun on the port side, and at the same time a shell burst directly over the gun. The first captain's head was cut off and nine of the gun's crew were wounded. I was standing amidships between the two No. 10 guns, and was struck on the back by the splinters and thrown to the deck. I was on my feet in a moment and turned to my port gun. There were only two men standing at it, the first loader and the first sponger, who were leaning against the side of the ship: the others were all flat on deck, one of them directly in the rear of the gun. The gun had just been loaded, and I pulled this man to one side, clear of the recoil, and fired the gun. It was a time when every one felt that he must do something. After the discharge of the gun the men on the deck got up and came to their places. None of them were seriously hurt. The captain of the gun found a piece of shell inside his cap, which did not even scratch his head; another piece went through my coat-sleeve.

Just after passing Fort Jackson we saw a bright glare on the starboard quarter, and a moment after Captain Craven said, in his deep bass voice, "One bell!" (to slow down), and then, "Two bells!" (to stop her). I went up the poop ladder, and there in plain sight on the left bank, just below Fort St. Philip, was the *Hartford*, with a fire-raft alongside and with flames running up the rigging on the tarred rope to the mast-head. The tug *Mosher* was near by, but I did not see the ram *Manassas*. It was evidently Craven's intention when he saw Farragut's trouble to go to his rescue. As the engine stopped, the *Brooklyn* dropped down, her head swinging to starboard, until she was on a line between Fort Jackson and the *Hartford*. The fort immediately opened fire on the *Brooklyn* with renewed energy, and she would have been blown out of the water had not the enemy aimed too high and sent the shot through the rigging, boats, and hammock-nettings, many of them just clearing the rail. The port battery was manned, and shell and shrapnel were fired as fast as the guns could be loaded. The *Brooklyn* remained under the fire of Fort Jackson until Craven saw Farragut free from the fire-raft, and then she steamed ahead. This was one of the coolest and bravest acts that I saw during the war, but it was not mentioned in any official report or newspaper account at the time. In fact, the *Brooklyn's* passage of the forts was hardly noticed by the newspaper correspondents, as Craven had old-fashioned ideas and would allow no reporters on board. I am glad, even at this late date, that I can put on record this act of heroism.

As the *Hartford* lay aground with the fire-raft alongside, her crew were at their work, and I saw the flag-officer distinctly on the port side of the poop looking toward us. From this point the *Brooklyn* steamed ahead, toward Fort St. Philip, and passed close to the fort, firing grape from the starboard battery. When she first came abreast of the fort there was a long blaze of musketry from the parapet, but it soon stopped when she got to work.* We were at this time less than one hundred feet from the bank, and the *Hartford* had passed ahead. The barbette guns of the fort not being depressed sufficiently, we received no damage while passing, but we were so close that the powder scorched the faces and clothes of the men. A bullet entered the port of No. 1 gun and struck Lieutenant James O'Kane, who had charge of the first division, in the leg. He fell to the deck, but would not allow himself to be carried below until he had himself fired two of the broadside guns into Fort St. Philip. But the most uncomfortable position on board the ship, during this part of the engagement, was that of the quartermaster, Thomas Hollins, who stood in the starboard main chains, heaving the lead and calling out the soundings. The outside of the ship near him was completely peppered with bullets, and the flames from the enemy's guns seemed almost to reach him; still he stood coolly at his post, and when abreast of the fort he was heard calling out, "Only thirteen feet, sir."

As we passed clear of Fort St. Philip, Captain Craven gave orders to load the starboard battery with solid shot. He had seen the iron-clad *Louisiana*, moored just above the fort. She gave us one or two shots, but when we came directly abeam of her, she closed her port shutters and received our broadside.

---

*I was afterward in charge of a boat from the *Brooklyn* which landed the paroled Confederate prisoners at New Orleans, and they said that the grape came like rain, but that the worst of all were the "infernal lamp-posts" that we fired; that the fort was full of them. These were the stands that held the grape—cylinders attached to a cast-iron base, around which the grape-shot are secured.—J. R. B.

We could hear our shot strike against her iron sides. We gave but one broadside and then sheered out into the river. A 9-inch shell, fired by the *Louisiana*, struck the *Brooklyn* about a foot above the water-line, on the starboard side of the cutwater, near the wood ends, forced its way for three feet through the dead-wood and timbers, and remained there. At New Orleans this shot was cut out, and it was found that in their hurry the gunners had neglected to remove the lead patch from the fuse, so that the shell did not explode. Had it done so it would have blown the whole bow off, and the *Brooklyn* would have gone to the bottom.

As we swung out into the current and steamed up the river, we began to see the vessels ahead fighting with the Confederate gun-boats, and a few moments later the cry came aft, "A steamer coming down on our port bow." We could see two smoke-stacks and the black smoke from them. I took a look from the poop ladder, and saw a good-sized river steamer coming down on us, crowded with men on her forward deck, as if ready to board. The order had already been given, "Stand by to repel boarders," and to load with shrapnel; the fuses were cut to burn one second. As she approached, Craven gave the vessel a sheer to starboard, and we began with No. 1 gun, the guns aft following in quick succession, the shells bursting almost immediately as they left the guns. There was a rush of steam, shrieks from the people on board the steamer, and, when it came time for my No. 10 gun to fire, the steamer was lost in the smoke. This was the only one of the river flotilla which we encountered or fired into. Just after our engagement with this steamer, a column of black smoke, which came from the dreaded *Manassas*, was seen on the starboard side, and the cry was passed along by men who were looking out of the ports, "The ram, the ram!" Craven called out, "Give her four bells! Put your helm hard-a-starboard!" Then I saw the smoke-stacks of the *Manassas* and the flash from her gun, and the next moment I was nearly thrown on the deck by the concussion, caused by her striking us just amidships. The ram was going full speed but against the current, and, with our helm to starboard, the blow was not at right angles to our keel, though nearly so. I ran to the No. 10 port, the gun being in, and looked out, and saw her almost directly alongside. A man came out of her little hatch aft, and ran forward along the port side of the deck, as far as the smoke-stacks, placed his hand against one, and looked to see what damage the ram had done. I saw him turn, fall over, and tumble into the water, but did not know at the moment what caused his sudden disappearance, until I asked the quartermaster, who was leadsman in the chains, if he had seen him fall.

"Why, yes, sir," said he, "I saw him fall overboard,—in fact, I helped him; for I hit him alongside of the head with my hand-lead."

No guns were fired at the ram from the starboard battery; all the crews a moment before had been at the port guns. As the *Manassas* drifted by I ran up on the poop, calling the gun's crew with me, to see if I could hit her with the 30-pounder Parrott, but we were unable to depress it sufficiently, at its high elevation, to bring it to bear before she was lost to sight in the smoke. The shot which she had fired came through the chain and planking, above the berth-deck, through a pile of rigging placed against the ship's side, and just entered the sand-bags placed to protect the steam-drum.

A few moments after this incident a vessel passed on our starboard side, not ten feet from us, and I could see through the port the men loading a pivot gun. She was directly abreast of No. 10 gun and I took the lock-string to fire, when a cry came from on board the vessel, "Don't fire, it is the *Iroquois!*" At the same moment, Lieutenant Lowry also shouted from near the mainmast, "Don't fire!" Seeing the black smoke pouring from her stack, and noticing that it was abaft the mainmast, I called to Captain Craven, "It can't be the *Iroquois!* It is not one of our vessels, for her smoke-stack is abaft her mainmast!" Captain Craven, however, repeated the order, "Don't fire!" and I obeyed. I was sure it was one of the Confederate gun-boats, but it was my duty to obey orders, and thus the Confederate gun-boat *McRae* escaped being sunk by the *Brooklyn*; for the gun had been depressed, and a 9-inch shell would have gone through her deck and out below the water-line.

Just after leaving Fort St. Philip a shot came in on the starboard quarter and went across the deck, taking off a marine's head and wounding three other men. Lieutenant Lowry came along about this time, and I heard him report to Captain Craven that Lieutenant O'Kane had been wounded. Craven directed him to put me in charge of the First Division, to which Lowry answered:

"I sent poor Bartlett down below half an hour ago cut in two."

"Oh, no, you did not," said Craven; "he is on deck close to you."

Lowry turned and was as much surprised as if he had seen a ghost, and told me to run forward and take charge of the First Division. There had been terrible havoc here. The powder-man of the pivot gun had been struck by a shell, which exploded and blew him literally to atoms, and parts of his body were scattered all over the forecastle. The gun was disabled, a primer having broken off in the vent; but there was nothing to fire at, as all the vessels that we passed had been run on the bank and either set on fire or deserted. It was now almost daylight, and we could see the crews of the deserted boats running for cover to the woods a little way back. Shortly after, the *Brooklyn* came up with the other vessels and anchored near a point where there had been an encampment of troops. They only remained long enough to land and bury the dead. The commanding officers assembled on board the *Hartford* to offer their congratulations to the flag-officer.

About the time that the *Brooklyn* arrived at quarantine the *Manassas* was seen steaming up the river, and Farragut made signal to the *Mississippi* to attack her. She ran down toward her, but the *Manassas* sheered toward the left bank and ran her nose ashore. When the *Mississippi* opened fire upon her, the crew poured out of the little hatch aft, ran along the deck, and jumped on shore and over the levee into the swamp beyond.

The fleet steamed up the river during the afternoon of the 24th until dark, and then came to anchor. Nothing of importance occurred during the passage. Soon after midnight a great blaze of light was seen up the river, and fearing fire-rafts, all the vessels got under way, and remained so until daylight, when they proceeded up the river toward New Orleans. At 6 o'clock we passed a large vessel loaded with cotton on fire, and at 7:30 passed two more in the same condition. Arrived at Chalmette, four miles below the city, we found that batteries had been erected on both banks, armed with field-pieces. A few broadsides made the troops leave their guns and disperse into the country. The *Brooklyn* fired 21 shells from the 80-pound Dahlgren into the battery on the left bank and a couple of broadsides into that on the right.

The fleet steamed on to the city, passing close to the levees, which were swarming with people. They were simply a howling mob. The Confederate flags were flying about the city, and we passed so close—not more than two hundred feet from the bank—that the people called out abusive names and shouted at us in derision. In the French quarter there was apparently some disturbance, and a body of troops was seen firing a volley into the crowd. As the ship arrived abreast of the Customhouse and anchored off Canal street, a pouring rain came down, but even this did not seem to reduce the crowd. Soon after we had anchored, burning steamers, barges, and other vessels loaded with cotton came drifting down on fire. Among the burning vessels was the Confederate iron-clad *Mississippi*. It seemed the purpose of the mob to destroy everything. During the night the city was set on fire in a dozen different places, and there was a continual ringing of fire-alarm bells.

The next day we steamed up the river, as obstructions and batteries had been reported above the city. All the fortifications were deserted, but an immense raft was found lying along the left bank. This was made of four logs lashed together side by side, with a heavy chain extending their whole length. It had been the intention of the Confederates to stretch this boom across the river to prevent Foote and his flotilla from reaching New Orleans. The barrier looked formidable as it lay under the river-bank, but when the Confederates had finished their work they could not get the raft across the river on account of the current. They made the lower end fast to the bank, and with three steamboats took the upper end and endeavored to reach the opposite bank, but the huge structure was more than they could manage, and the current swept it down the river with such force that it broke, drifted from the steamers, and swung around against the bank and so proved a failure.*

On the day after the passage of the forts, it was noticed that

---

*The river, when we arrived at New Orleans, was higher than it ever had been known to be before, and the levees had been added to, to prevent the

the *Brooklyn* leaked more than usual, but not enough to give any alarm, as the steam-pumps were able to keep her free, and in the course of a few days the leak diminished. It was not until the coal in the starboard bunker had been used up and the side of the ship was uncovered that we realized what a blow she had received from the *Manassas*. On the outside the chain had been driven its depth into the planking, and on the inside, for a length of five feet or more, the planking was splintered and crushed in. The only thing that prevented the prow of the *Manassas* from sinking us was the fact that the bunker was full of coal.

The wound gave no trouble so long as we remained in the river, as the mud held in suspension in the river water filled up all the interstices between the fibers of the wood. When we went out to sea and rolled about a little, and the ship began to work, it was found that she leaked very badly, and she was obliged to go to Pensacola, heave down, and bolt on a large patch of plank to cover the spot where the ram had struck.

---

water from overflowing. As we found it, the water was within a few inches of the top of the levee.—J. R. B.

NOTE.—Since writing the above article, I have compared it carefully with letters I wrote to my father from New Orleans. In some instances I do not agree with the official reports in the sequence of events, but I hold to my own account. Craven says he encountered the *Manassas* a few minutes after passing the obstructions. I place this event well above the forts, and this is corroborated by Captain Warley of the *Manassas*. Farragut, in his official report, does not state exactly where he encountered the fire-raft, but says: "The fire was extinguished. In the meantime our battery was never silent, but poured its missiles of death into Fort St. Philip, opposite to which we had got by this time." I place the *Hartford* at this time just below the fort, or abreast of the lower flanking battery, as the iron-clad *Louisiana* was moored to the bank immediately above. When the *Manassas* rammed the *Brooklyn* she had two smoke-stacks, but she lost one before she drifted down the river.—J. R. B.

THE FALL OF NEW ORLEANS:
LOUISIANA, APRIL 1862

George Hamilton Perkins to Susan G. Perkins

Twenty-five-year-old Lieutenant George Hamilton Perkins piloted the gunboat *Cayuga* in the passage of Forts Jackson and St. Philip and afterwards accompanied Captain Theodorus Bailey, Farragut's second in command, to accept the surrender of New Orleans. Their walk to City Hall was witnessed by the writer George Washington Cable, then aged seventeen. "Two officers of the United States Navy were walking abreast, unguarded and alone, looking not to right or left, never frowning, never flinching, while the mob screamed in their ears, shook cocked pistols in their faces, cursed and crowded and gnashed upon them," Cable wrote in 1885. "It was one of the bravest deeds I ever saw done." On April 28 the bypassed Forts Jackson and St. Philip surrendered, and troops led by Major General Benjamin F. Butler occupied the city on May 1 as the Union gained control of both ends of the Mississippi River.

NEW ORLEANS, April 27, 1862.

We arrived here two days ago, after what was 'the most desperate fight and greatest naval achievement on record,' so every one says. Wednesday night, April 23, we were ordered to lead the way, and be ready to run by the forts at two o'clock in the morning; and at two o'clock precisely the signal was made from the Hartford to 'get underweigh.'

Captain Harrison paid me the compliment of letting me pilot the vessel, and though it was a starlight night we were not discovered until we were well under the forts; then they opened a tremendous fire on us. I was very anxious, for the steering of the vessel being under my charge gave me really the whole management of her. The Cayuga received the first fire, and the air was filled with shells and explosions which almost blinded me as I stood on the forecastle trying to see my way, for I had never been up the river before. I soon saw that the guns of the forts were all aimed for the mid-stream, so I steered close under the walls of Fort St. Philip, and although our masts and rigging got badly shot through, our hull was but little damaged.

After passing the last battery and thinking we were clear, I looked back for some of our vessels, and my heart jumped up into my mouth, when I found I could not see a *single one*. I thought they all must have been sunk by the forts. Then looking ahead I saw eleven of the enemy's gunboats coming down upon us, and it seemed as if we were '*gone*' sure. Three of these made a dash to board us, but a heavy charge from our eleven-inch gun settled the Gov. Moore, which was one of them. A ram, the Manasses, in attempting to butt us, just missed our stern, and we soon settled the third fellow's 'hash.' Just then some of our gunboats, which had passed the forts, came up, and then all sorts of things happened. There was the wildest excitement all round. The Varuna fired a broadside into *us*, instead of the enemy. Another of our gunboats attacked one of the Cayuga's prizes,—I shouted out, 'Don't fire into that ship, she has surrendered!' Three of the enemy's ships had surrendered to us before any of our vessels appeared, but when they did come up we all pitched in, and settled the eleven rebel vessels, in about twenty minutes. Our short fight with the Gov. Moore—it used to be the Morgan—was very exciting. We were alongside of each other, and had both fired our guns, and it all depended on which should get reloaded first. The large forward gun on the Gov. Moore was a ten-inch shell, ours an eleven-inch, and we were so near, they were almost muzzle to muzzle.

Ours was fired first, and Beverly Kennon, the Captain of the Gov. Moore, is now a prisoner on board the Cayuga. He tells me our shot was the one that ruined him,—disabled his vessel, capsized his gun, and killed thirteen of the gun's crew. Beverly Kennon used to be an officer in our navy.

The Cayuga still led the way up the river, and at daylight we discovered a regiment of infantry encamped on shore. As we were very close in, I shouted to them to come on board and deliver up their arms, or we would blow them all to pieces. It seemed rather odd for a regiment on shore to be surrendering to a ship! They hauled down their colors, and the Colonel and command came on board and gave themselves up as prisoners of war. The regiment was called the Chalmette Regiment, and has been quite a famous one. The officers we released on parole and allowed them to retain their side-arms, all except one Captain, who I discovered was from New Hampshire. His name is Hickory, and he came from Portsmouth. I took his sword away from him and have kept it.

The next thing that happened was the sinking of the Varuna, which had been disabled by one of the enemy's vessels running into her. Soon after this the Commodore came up in the Hartford and ordered us all to anchor and take a little rest before attacking New Orleans, which was now within twenty miles.

By this time our ship had received forty-two shots in masts and hull, and six of our men had been wounded; one of the boys had to have one of his legs cut off. All this time, night and day, firerafts and ships loaded with burning cotton had been coming down the river and surrounded us everywhere. Besides these, the bombardment was continuous and perfectly awful. I do not believe there ever was anything like it before, and I never expect to see such a sight again. The river and shore were one blaze, and the sounds and explosions were terrific. Nothing I could say would give you any idea of these last twenty-four hours!

The next morning, April 25, we all got underweigh again, the Cayuga still leading, and at about nine o'clock New Orleans hove in sight. We called all hands and gave three cheers and a tiger!

There were two more fortifications still between us and New Orleans, called the Chalmette Batteries, but Captain Bailey thought they could not be of much account, and that we had best push on. When we arrived in sight of these batteries, no flag floated over them, and there was not a man to be seen—nothing but the guns, which seemed abandoned. In fact, though, there were a lot of treacherous rascals concealed in these batteries, and when we had come close enough to make them feel sure they could sink us, they opened a heavy fire. We gave them back as well as we could, but they were too much for one gunboat; so, after getting hit fourteen times, and the shot and shell striking all about us, we decided not to advance any further until some of the ships came up. Soon we had the Hartford on one side and the Pensacola on the other, and then the rebel battery was silenced very quick.

After this, there were no further obstacles between us and the city, and the fleet were soon anchored before it. The Commodore ordered Captain Bailey to go on shore, and demand its surrender, and he asked me to go with him. We took just a boat and a boat's crew, with a flag of truce, and started off. When we reached the wharf there were no officials to be seen; no one received us, although the whole city was watching our movements, and the levee was crowded in spite of a heavy rainstorm. Among the crowd were many women and children, and the women were shaking rebel flags, and being rude and noisy.

They were all shouting and hooting as we stepped on shore, but at last a man, who, I think, was a German, offered to show us the way to the council-room, where we should find the mayor of the city.

As we advanced, the mob followed us in a very excited state. They gave three cheers for Jeff Davis and Beauregard, and three groans for Lincoln. Then they began to throw things at us, and shout, 'Hang them!' 'Hang them!' We both thought we were in a *bad fix*, but there was nothing for us to do, but just go on.

We reached the city hall, though, in safety, and there we found the mayor and council. They seemed in a very solemn state of mind, though I must say, from what they said, they did not impress me as having much *mind* about anything, and certainly not much sense. The mayor said *he* had nothing to do with the city, as it was under martial law, and we were obliged to wait till General Lovell could arrive.

In about half an hour this gentleman appeared. He was very pompous in his manner and silly and airy in his remarks. He had about fifteen thousand troops under his command, and said he would 'never surrender,' but would withdraw his troops from the city as soon as possible, when the city would fall into the hands of the mayor and he could do as he pleased with it.

The mob outside had by this time become perfectly infuriated. They kicked at the doors and swore they would have us out and hang us! Of course Captain Bailey and I *felt perfectly at our ease all this while!* Indeed, every person about us, who had any sense of responsibility, was frightened for our safety. As soon as the mob found out that General Lovell was not going to surrender, they swore they would have us out anyway;

but Pierre Soule and some others went out and made speeches to them, and kept them on one side of the building, while we went out the other, and were driven to the wharf in a close carriage. Finally we got on board ship all right; but of all the blackguarding I ever heard in my life that mob gave us the worst.

The mayor told the flag-officer this morning that the city was in the hands of the mob, and was at our mercy, and that he might blow it up or do with it as he chose. They still fly the state flag on the custom-house, and as we have not yet any forces with which to land and make an attack, we can do nothing at present, unless we blow up the city.

I do not know where General Butler is. So far, only fourteen of our fleet have passed the forts out of all the ships that started. None of us know what has become of them, and the forts have not yet surrendered. Until then, there can be no going up and down the river.

This morning we have been ordered to take Captain Bailey down to a bayou, where he will pass out in a boat, and taking a ship below will proceed home, as bearer of despatches.

We expect to make another attack on the forts to-morrow or next day, if General Butler arrives with the troops. The Southerners say our victory was one of the greatest ever known. They never dreamed of our being able to pass the forts; and if the attempt had been made in the daytime, our fleet must surely all have been sunk. We may be in a bad fix now, if the forts do not fall, and it is not safe for any one to leave our ships and go anywhere in a boat. The mob rule in the city, and they are perfectly reckless. We are still feeling the effects of the excitement which the attack caused. Nothing is settled, and there is danger and risk about every movement.

I have written this letter at railroad speed. I am all right so far, as regards my health. We expect another good fight to-morrow or next day, when we go back to take the forts.

I hope you are all well at home, and you must excuse this letter, for it seems as though I could not stop to form words. Should I ever see you again I can tell it all so much better. I cannot say yet how many men have been lost on our side, but I think the number is quite small.

BATTLE OF WILLIAMSBURG: VIRGINIA, MAY 1862

Charles S. Wainwright: Diary, May 5, 1862

General McClellan required a month to get his siege guns posted to bombard the Yorktown lines. At the last moment, Joseph E. Johnston evacuated the position and withdrew up the Peninsula. On May 5, at Williamsburg, the Confederates fought a rear-guard action against the pursuing Union forces. Major Charles S. Wainwright, commanding the artillery in Joseph Hooker's division, records his first time under fire.

BATTLE OF WILLAMSBURG, MAY 5, 1862, MONDAY. By three o'clock we were again stirring. Leaving orders for Bramhall and Smith to push on so soon as horses and men were fed, I rode on and routed up Osborn and Webber. The men were tired and wet, for it had begun to rain at two o'clock and was now pouring; cold too, the chill striking into one's very bones. The crossroad from the church was very muddy, and when we got into the Warwick Court House road it was so terribly cut up that it was with difficulty we could get along. Starting out the men, and moving the four or five miles, which seemed twenty, I made it after seven o'clock when I got up to where General Hooker had halted the infantry. He said that he was only waiting for me to come up in order to attack, and where would I put my batteries? As of course I had to look about me a little, the General rode up the road with me; but so soon as we emerged from the woods the rebs opened on us so sharp that we got off our horses, and proceeded out on foot and alone.

The rain was coming down in torrents, making all objects at any distance very indistinct. The road by which we had come up lay through a heavy wood for half a mile or more behind us; some hundred yards inside this wood it made a thorough cut of say thirty yards in length, the bank being six to eight feet high on either side. On both sides of the road the rebs had felled a large amount of the timber as it debouches into the plain in front of Williamsburg. Directly up the road, about eight hundred yards from where we stood at the outer edge of the felled timber, was a large redoubt from which they were firing quite lively. To the right and left of this one we could see a number of other earthworks in the distance; on our left there seemed to be a field battery behind the crest of a knoll (have since found that it was in a small redoubt built in a hollow so that the top of the parapet was about on a level with the top of the crest). On our side of the plain I could see nothing but woods on either hand with a heavy slashing of felled trees in front. The road was the only way to get on to the plain, and that would be ugly enough for some five hundred yards; the rebel redoubt, Fort Magruder, having a raging fire down it. Still I thought the open plain the proper place, and told the General so; but he said he could not support the batteries out there, his pickets only being at the outer edge of the slashing. On our left the slashing extended up the road about three hundred yards farther than it did on the right, a large triangular field having been lately cleared there, and planted in corn last year. Not being able to go out on to the plain, I told the General that the only place left one was this fallow lot; but I might get a couple of guns in the road. "Get them in then as quick as you can," were his orders.

Going back to the edge of the woods, where Captain Webber had halted his battery, I directed him to put his first piece out at the farthest corner of the slashing in the road; his second also in the road but some twenty yards to the rear, a slight bend in the road here placing them thus in echelon; and the other two sections in the newly cleared field to the right of the road: leaving his caissons in the wood. He at once moved out himself with the first section, while I directed the posting of the other two. Gaps in the fence were pulled down, and after a great deal of trouble from bad drivers and balky horses I got them all in. Almost before the first piece had turned into the field, Lieutenant Eakin fell at my feet terribly wounded in the shoulder. We were both of us on foot, he standing about four feet in front of me. A shell struck the road half a dozen yards from us and burst as it fell, a piece of it entering his left shoulder just below the collar bone; he fell against me, and at once called out that he was a dead man. I got a couple of men to carry him off, but had full occupation myself driving the horses of the guns up to the pulling point. At last, I had all four guns posted; when looking around what was my horror, on seeing that nearly all the limber had cleared off under shelter of the woods, and that there was not more than one or two men near each gun. This was an awful beginning for one's first battle, and knowing what a wretched battery this was, I reproached myself with having so far yielded to Webber's claims as senior officer as to have given him the advance instead of Bramhall.

Rushing back to the road, where the men had hid themselves behind the large felled trees, I met Webber, without his hat, covered with mud and almost wild. "Major," says he, "Lieutenant Pike and two men have been hit and I cannot get the others up to their guns." Though we slammed at them with our sabres, and poked them out with the point, it was no good; drive two or three to a gun, and by the time you got some more up the first had hid again. Never in my life was I so mortified, never so excited, never so mad. It had at any rate the good effect of making me forget my own danger, and the place was an awful hot one there in the road. There was a certain amount of excuse for the men. Their captain had just joined them; their other officers knew nothing; two of them were shot down at once, as also a couple of the men, and one horse of the leading gun killed; it was a very hot place for men to have their first experience in; and they were a wretched lot of men. Some of them did stick to their guns, but not enough to work them, and the drivers had carried the limbers way to the rear. The first piece had three men keep to it, who got off two or three shots; a wheel horse of their limber being killed, the drivers could not run away with it, so they ran off without it.

General Hooker meantime, it seems, was anxiously waiting for the battery to open. Seeing how things stood, for he was not far to the rear, he sent Captain Dickenson, his adjutant-general, to me to say that he would give me a company of infantry to work the guns. Looking at it coolly now, I have no doubt it was only meant, in good part, to get me out of my trouble; but then it appeared as a slur on the artillery, almost an insult, and made me very mad. "Thank the General," said I, "but I have artillery men that can and will man those guns." Running back to my horse, I rode to Osborn's battery, just in the rear of Webber's caissons; shouted to the men that General

Hooker wanted to send infantry to fight our guns; called upon them for the honour of the First New York Artillery to save me, their own major, from such a disgrace; in short made them a speech, the first speech of my life; and closed by asking who would volunteer to serve the guns of an abandoned regular battery. The men were mounted on the chests, sergeants and officers at their posts. I have no doubt all heard me, for I was very much excited, and don't know now what I said; but almost before I had done, Sergeant Horn of the first or second piece, whom I had often had occasion to praise on drill, standing up in his stirrups, replied, "Every one of us, Sir." The men jumped from the boxes, officers dismounted, detachments were regularly formed, and marched to the abandoned pieces as if on drill. A more beautiful thing it was impossible to see, not a man flinching; the infantry on the roadside gave them three cheers, and wasn't I a proud man?—proud of the First New York Artillery.

Fire once opened, the enemy's shots were not nearly so sure and it became comparatively safe to be about there. It was just about eight o'clock when we opened fire; half an hour later Bramhall came up, and I at once moved his battery into the fallow lot, to the right of Webber's. One of his pieces had been left behind stuck in the mud, and though it came up later in the day, was not put in position. Webber's men kept coming back as they got over their fright, but there were not over five of them to a gun at any time during the day. The rain made all objects at any distance very indistinct. At no time could we see any large body of the enemy; our work was simply to silence and keep silent their artillery. They seemed to have three guns in Fort Magruder and three or more in the sunken redoubt. Occasionally a shot would come from a third work still farther to their right, but their works to our right did not trouble us at all during the day. In an hour we had silenced them totally, at least for a time, and held up our own fire. . . .

Half an hour, perhaps, after we had ceased firing, long rolls of musketry were heard at this point to the left. Every moment I expected to see our men rush into the open, but after a time we found the firing to recede into the woods, as if our men were being beaten instead of gaining ground; so I turned my four left pieces to the left, and opened on the corner of the woods. Infantry officers tell me that shell fell directly in the rebel column, and burst with great effect. It was now my turn to get it hot and heavy from all three of the rebel batteries; the redoubt away to our left opening very strong, which forced me to throw Bramhall's right far forward in echelon. How long this fight lasted I do not know, but it seemed to me all day. At last, however, we got their fire under, and shortly afterward, all being quiet, I spoke to General Hooker about dispositions for the night, thinking it must be near sundown. He thought too it was late, and we were both astonished when Captain Dickenson told us it was twenty minutes passed eleven!—the day not half through. It seemed a good week since I got up.

This time they left us quiet for an hour or more, so that one had a little time to look around. I proposed to General Hooker to get my two twelve-pounder howitzers around to where the infantry were, so as to fire down the ravine by which the enemy's columns came up, if possible, but he said there was no road by which he could get them there that he knew of. Since then I have been sorry that I did not go to look for myself, as there was a small wood road, I find, which led in that direction. General Hooker stayed all the time just where the road came out of the wood, and did not go over to the place where our infantry were engaged at all. On passing around among my guns, I found that two of Bramhall's pieces were disabled by shot wedging in the bore. One of them we replaced with his sixth piece which had been stuck on the road coming up; the other shot, I believe, they got home after a time. One of Webber's howitzers had cracked so badly as to render it unsafe, and was hauled off. This left us ten guns in position, but my men had got the range, and worked admirably. . . .

During this lull General Hooker sent word to Sumner on our right that he was holding the enemy here, and begging him to attack. Captain Benson commanding, "M" of the Second Artillery took the message, passing out on the open ground in front of the wood. He got back safely, and brought his saddle in, but left his horse dead on the plain. Many of our officers said they could hear firing to our right, quite early in the day; though I did not hear any myself. It seems it was Hancock's attack. Had old Sumner followed him up with the whole of Smith's division as he asked, and as Smith himself wanted to do, there is not a doubt in my mind that Williamsburg could have been carried, the heavy losses in our division saved, and probably very many prisoners, and a good part of their train captured. I hear that Wheeler with "E" Company of our regiment was in with Hancock, and that the latter did grandly.

About twelve-thirty o'clock the enemy made a second charge on our infantry, driving them back some distance into the wood at one time; their artillery fired but little, and I could render but little aid for fear of firing into our own men. General Hooker was a good deal worried at one time, and much excited. Taylor's brigade was sent over to reinforce the others, and drove the rebs back again. Whenever there would be a regular succession of volleys the General would rub his hands, and exclaim "That's Dwight, that's Dwight." This fight was doubtless a hard one, but when it was over everything settled down and remained so quiet that I began to hope it was over for the day.

My own men were very tired, some of them completely broken down; they were all unaccustomed to fighting and doubtless worked harder than was necessary. Finally we were getting short of men at some of the guns, so many being required on account of their sinking and the badness of the ground; and as everything was so quiet I asked the General's permission to ride back and look up Smith who had not yet made his appearance, though he had no farther to come than Bramhall and should have started at the same time. Some three hundred to four hundred yards back in the woods I passed our field hospitals where the wounded were receiving their first dressing, and then sent back in ambulances about a mile or so to where the main hospital was established in and around a fine large house occupied by the overseer of "Buck" Allen, who has large plantations around here. Our little Doctor Goddard remained all day at the front, and gave his first care to our wounded almost among the guns where they fell. The road was now awful; my horse sank to his knees at almost every step. Ammunition and hospital waggons were stuck all along. . . . When we got to within a mile of the front, I heard heavy firing for the first time since I had gone back. Pushing on as fast as I could alone, just as I reached the hospital I met the first of a string of ambulances, waggons, and other vehicles, just breaking into a run; the men too were starting, hospital attendants and such like. In fact, the commencement of a stampede. The road was so narrow at this point that but one waggon could pass at a time. One of my limbers was first; all were yelling and hollering to their horses and to those in front to get on. Drawing my sabre, I rode right at the lead driver of the limber, and brought that up short, so stopping the whole concern. The firing at the front was diminishing, and the stampede died out in a few minutes. Just then Chauncey McKeever came galloping back, waving his sword and swearing like a demon, "Shoot the cowards!" In a few minutes a couple of squadrons of cavalry, who had been sent around by a road to our left came back. McKeever insisted they should fire on the waggoners, though I told him that the fright was all over. The man seemed crazy, so fearing the officer in command of the cavalry might be as great a fool as himself and fire, I pushed on to the front out of the way.

There I found a sad change for the worse had taken place during my absence. The enemy, reinforced it is said by Longstreet's whole division, which had come back from six miles beyond Williamsburg, had attacked at the old point, and driven our men entirely back to the road. Colonel Starr had withdrawn his regiment from the slashing on the left of my guns, and gone to help our infantry. The enemy pushed on over the felled timber to our left, and through the woods behind it, until they had possession of the road in rear of the batteries. All was up then at once with the guns, there being no exit, at least that we knew of, for horses; and had there been they could not possibly have hauled the pieces out of the soft ground of the field. Bramhall turned his guns at once towards them and fired canister until they were directly on him, when he withdrew his men over the slashing in his rear into the wood, and so across to the other road where General Sumner was, and reported to him, getting most undeservedly cursed for his pains. Our infantry had fought nobly, Dwight's regiment especially. It lay in the slashing, and held their ground until all their ammunition was gone, Dwight and Farnum both wounded, and the rebs all but surrounding them.

By the time I got up the fighting was over. We had lost possession of all the slashing on the left of the road, but held the woods for some distance in that direction. General Heintzelman was there in consultation with Hooker. Osborn had got a dozen or so of his men together, and manned one piece which he had planted in the road just in front of the little thorough cut. So soon as Smith came up, to hurry whom I sent Lieutenant Ames back, I put two of his Parrotts and his section of six-pounders in position on . . . a little knoll, and comparatively open; they had perfect command of the road but nothing more. We did not have to wait many minutes. It was perhaps half an hour after the other guns were captured when the rebs charged in column down the road; my five pieces were all loaded with canister, but I held fire until the head of the column was well down to within about 150 yards of us, and two whole regiments were plainly in view. Three rounds to a gun then blew the whole thing away, except small parties which got into the slashing on the left of the road, and picked off my cannoneers so badly that after trying two or three rounds of canister on them I was obliged to let the men cover themselves behind the trees. Finding no infantry at all near my guns to reply to these fellows, I went back to General Hooker, and asked him to send some, which he promised to do. After waiting ten minutes or so, and finding that the rascals were working up nearer and nearer to me all the time, I again went back and found General Grover, to whom I made the same request, and from whom I received the same promise. Still no supports came. Four of Smith's men had been hit, and I began to be anxious lest another attack should be made, as I could find no infantry within 100 yards to my rear. Going a third time, I found the head of Kearny's column just come up. To Kearny I put my request. This time, instantly he turned to the First Company of a Michigan regiment: "Captain, you will take your company, and put them wherever Major Wainwright here says"—which was done as promptly as it was ordered, and I saw no more of my friends in the slashing. . . .

Shortly before sunset the whole of our division was withdrawn, Kearny's taking our place, and Thompson's battery of the Second Artillery relieving Smith's on the knoll, which with Osborn's I moved back to an open field about three-fourths of a mile to the rear where we bivouacked for the night.

Thus ended my first fight. In looking back to it, I cannot

but first of all be grateful to Providence that I escaped unhurt. For a good part of ten hours I was exposed to more or less artillery and musketry fire; when we ran the gauntlet with Kearny, and when the canister was fired over our heads, it was almost a miracle that I was not hit. Besides this, I was kicked over by one of "H" Company's horses while trying to force them into the field, his hoof striking me just below the stomach, and throwing me halfway across the road; an inch higher or lower would have ruined me for life if it did not prove fatal. Quite early in the day a minie ball carried off my left stirrup, slitting the wooden side of its whole breadth, but not even cutting the shoe. My good bay was equally fortunate, escaping unhurt, a mere shaving of one hoof only being cut off.

Of my officers, Bramhall and his lieutenants were all that I could have asked of them, cool, quiet, attending closely to their business and taking good care of their men. When they were not actually firing, the large stumps left in the field afforded excellent cover; and to the fact that their officers required them to use this cover, it must be attributed, together with the softness of the ground, which swallowed up the enemy's shot as it were, and the fact that the large part of their fuses were not cut at all, that there was not a single man hit in this battery. Osborn was slow (as I expected), but did capital service. He astonished me, when in the evening I told him to move to the rear, by replying in his drawling way, "Major, I shan't go until I get that gun out." The gun he spoke of was one that lay buried in the mud on the side of the road, just in front of the knoll in a small hollow where at the time the rebel shot and shell were falling so fast, that I told him he might leave it till morning, as there was no fear of Kearny being driven back. He did get the gun, though with the loss of a man; and I learned that there was a good deal more grit in him than I thought. . . .

I saw but two or three cases among the men of the volunteer batteries of any inclination to shirk, while the very admirable behaviour of Sergeant Horn, and of Sergeant Doran with his Irishmen, almost wiped out the disgrace the men of "H" Company brought on themselves at the beginning of the fight. One of these men I found afterward with a musket he had picked up hunting around for cartridges and fighting it out on his own account.

The total loss in our division was 1,576 out of not more than 8,000 actually engaged. I have heard of but one field officer killed, Major L. M. Morris, of the Eighth New Jersey. Seven out of nine captains in this regiment, I hear, were killed or wounded. My own loss was four killed, and twenty wounded, one mortally. It is wonderful that it should have been so small. One man also is missing, but may turn up. At night I was much worried as I did not know what had become of Bramhall's men or Webber's either.

Wet to the skin and very tired, I lay down at night with the officers of Osborn's battery under a paulin, but could not sleep much for the cold, and for thinking. I had often asked myself how I should feel in my first fight, and expected to be a good deal frightened, though I knew pride would keep one up to the mark. The sight of blood often making me feel faint, I was more afraid of the effect the sight of dead and wounded would have on me than of anything else. Whatever may have been the cause, whether it was having so much to do, or whether it was excitement, or both together. I know not, but I cannot recall having felt the least personal fear while under fire. After I got back to the rear after Smith, there was some reluctance to go to the front again, a sort of nervous lassitude, but the instant I heard the heavy firing this was over. The excitement too was different from what I expected; I certainly never was more conscious nor did my mind ever see things more coolly or reason clearer. As to seeing men shot, dead or dying, I had no feeling but one of perfect indifference. When Lieutenant Eakin fell against me, and cried out that he was "a dead man," I had no more feeling for him, than if he had tripped over a stump and fallen; nor do I think it would have been different had he been my brother.

As to my official acts, I see but two that I wish had been different. First, that I did not go over myself on to the ground where our infantry were, and see whether it were not possible to get my howitzers around there; and second, that I should have gone to the rear for Smith's battery. To be sure, it is very doubtful whether he would have got up at all had I not gone; neither can I see that anything more could have been done or saved had I remained; but the guns were lost during my absence, and I confess it, I am a little ashamed to have been to the rear at that time.

General Hooker was in the road just to the rear of my batteries, and under fire all day, as brave as brave could be beyond a doubt. But he seemed to know little of the ground where his infantry were fighting; and I must say did not impress me at all favourably as to his powers as a general. His great idea was to go ahead quick until you ran against the enemy, and then fight him; the spirit of Heintzelman's order of the night before, "not to let Sumner get into Williamsburg first," seemed to be his main rule of action. Kearny on the other hand was calm and deliberate, and would not put a man into position until he had examined his ground, and knew what he had to do. Old Heintzelman did not get there until about one P.M. or later; he may have done a great deal without my knowing it. . . .

Soon after the enemy's second attack, which took all our troops to drive back, say by 12:30 o'clock, General Hooker sent to Heintzelman and Sumner for reinforcements. None came until Kearny arrived, he says at two o'clock; I feel very sure it was nearly if not quite four o'clock. He came up all the way from Yorktown. General Sumner had the whole of Keyes's corps, three divisions, only a mile or two to our right. . . . As early as ten o'clock in the morning Hancock with his brigade attacked the extreme left of the enemy, drove them back, and shortly afterward got possession of one of their works, when he sent back word to General Smith, his division commander, that if he would give him another brigade he could push around to the rear of Williamsburg. Smith at once ordered up the whole division, but was stopped by Sumner who would not let Hancock go any farther; and lay there all day with his 30,000 doing nothing. It is very hard to understand such things. I know there is an awful amount of jealousy among our leading generals, but hardly think it can go so far; at the same time, it is equally hard to suppose they are actual fools.

"A CRITICAL CONDITION": VIRGINIA, MAY 1862

John B. Jones: Diary, May 14–19, 1862

Johnston resumed his retreat after Williamsburg, with McClellan following slowly up the Peninsula until his army was within sight of Richmond. Norfolk was abandoned and the C.S.S. *Virginia* blown up to prevent her capture, opening the James to the Union navy. Confederate War Department clerk Jones speculated on the fate of the capital.

MAY 14TH—Our army has fallen back to within four miles of Richmond. Much anxiety is felt for the fate of the city. Is there no turning point in this long lane of downward progress? Truly it may be said, our affairs at this moment are in a critical condition. I trust in God, and the chivalry and patriotism of the South *in the field*.

The enemy's fleet of gun-boats are ascending James River, and the obstructions are not completed. We have but one or two casemated guns in battery, but we have brave men there.

MAY 15TH.—The enemy's gun-boats, Monitor, Galena, etc. are at Drewry's Bluff, eight miles below the city, shelling our batteries, and our batteries are bravely shelling them. The President rode down to the vicinity this morning, and observed the firing.

The guns are heard distinctly in the city, and yet there is no consternation manifested by the people. If the enemy pass the obstructions, the city will be, it is true, very much at their mercy. They may shell us out of it, and this may occur any hour. South of the city the enemy have no forces, and we can find refuge there. I suppose the government would go to Lynchburg. I shall remain with the army, *and see that the tobacco be burnt, at all hazards, according to law*. I have seen some of our generals, and am convinced that the Baltimore rabble, and those that direct them, will be suppressed, or exterminated, if they attempt to throw impediments in the way of our soldiers in the work of destroying the tobacco, as enjoined by Congress.

Our marksmen will keep up an incessant fire into the port-holes of the gun-boats; and if it be at all practicable, we will board them. So hope is by no means extinct. But it is apprehended, if the enemy gets within shelling distance of the city, there will be an attack along our lines by McClellan. We must beat him there, as we could never save our guns, stores, etc. retreating across the river. And we *will* beat him, for we have 80,000 men, and more are coming.

Joyful tidings! the gun-boats have been repulsed! A heavy shot from one of our batteries ranged through the Galena from stem to stern, making frightful slaughter, and disabling the ship; and the whole fleet turned about and steamed down the river! We have not lost a dozen men. We breathe freely; and the government will lose no time in completing the obstructions and strengthening the batteries.

MAY 16TH.—McClellan is intrenching—that is, at least, significant of a respite, and of apprehension of attack.

MAY 17TH.—Gen. Lee has admonished Major Griswold on the too free granting of passports. Will it do any good?

MAY 18TH.—All quiet to-day except the huzzas as fresh troops arrive.

MAY 19TH.—We await the issue before Richmond. It is still believed by many that it is the intention of the government and the generals to evacuate the city. If the enemy were to appear in force on the south side, and another force were to march on us from Fredericksburg, we should be inevitably taken, in the event of the loss of a battle—an event I don't anticipate. Army, government, and all, might, it is true, be involved in a common ruin. Wrote as strong a letter as I could to the President, stating what I have every reason to believe would be the consequences of the abandonment of Richmond. There would be demoralization and even insubordination in the army. Better die here! With the exception of the business portion of the city, the enemy could not destroy a great many houses by bombardment. But if defeated and driven back, our troops would make a heroic defense in the streets, in the walled grave-yards, and from the windows. Better electrify the world by such scenes of heroism, than surrender the capital and endanger the cause. I besought him by every consideration, not to abandon Richmond to the enemy short of the last extremity.

The legislature has also passed resolutions calling upon the C. S. Government to defend Richmond at all hazards, relieving the Confederate authorities, in advance, of all responsibility for any damage sustained.

This will have its effect. It would be pusillanimous to retire now.

But every preparation had been made to abandon it. The archives had been sent to Columbia, S. C., and to Lynchburg. The tracks over the bridges had been covered with plank, to facilitate the passage of artillery. Mr. Randolph had told his page, and cousin, "you must go with my wife into the country, for to-morrow the enemy will be here." Trunks were packed in readiness—for what? Not one would have been taken on the cars! The Secretary of the Treasury had a special locomotive and cars, constantly with steam up, in readiness to fly with the treasure.

Nevertheless, many of the *old* secessionists have resolved not to leave their homes, for there were no other homes for them to fly to. They say they will never take the oath of allegiance to the despised government of the North, but suffer whatever penalties may be imposed on them. There is a sullen, but generally a calm expression of inflexible determination on the countenances of the people, men, women, and children. But there is no consternation; we have learned to contemplate death with composure. It would be at least an effectual escape from dishonor; and Northern domination is dishonor.

"A BLACK REGIMENT": CANADA, MAY 1862
Garland H. White to Edwin M. Stanton

A minister and personal servant of Senator Robert Toombs of Georgia, Garland H. White escaped from slavery before the Civil War and fled to Canada. Although White received no answer to this letter to the secretary of war, he would later canvass "the intire north & west urging my people to inlist" and in 1864 became the chaplain of the 28th U.S. Colored Infantry, a regiment White helped recruit in Indiana.

London Canada West May 7th 1862
dear sir. please indulg me the liberty of writing you afew lines upon a subject of grave importance to your & my country   It is true I am now stoping in canada for awhile but it is not my home—& before I proceen further I must inform you of your humble correspondent.   My name is G. H. White formerly the Servant of Robert Toombs of Georgia. Mr Wm H Seward knows something about me   I am now a minister, & am called upon By my peopel to tender to your *Hon* thir willingness to serve as soldiers in the southern parts during the summer season or longer if required.   our offer is not for speculation or self interest but for our love for the north & the government at large, & at the same time we pray god that the triumph of the north & restoration of peace if I may call it will prove an eternal overthrow of the institution of slavery which is the cause of all our trouble   if you desire to see me let me hear at an early day.   I am certain of raising a good no. in the west & in the north.   I am aquainted all thro the south for I traveled with Senator Toombs all over it nearly.   I am quite willing to spend my life in preaching against sin & fighting against the same.   Mr Seward & many other of both white & colored know me in Washington   please let me hear from your Hon soon   your most humble servant
Garland H. White
please excuse my bad writing as I never went to School a day in my left.   I learnd what little I know by the hardest.   yet I feel

that the simplist instroment used in the right direction sometimes accomplishs much good. I pray you in gods name to consider the condition of your humble speaker in the distant. A man who are free from all the calumities of your land. yet when he thinks of his sufferring countrymen he can but feel that good might make him instromental in your hands to the accomplishments of some humble good. as simple as this request may seeme to you yet it might prove one of the greatest acts of your life. an act which might redown to your honor to the remotest generation— I want to see my friends at port royal & other places in the South. I now close by saying I hope to hear from you as soon as possible. I shall not be happy till I hear from you on this very important subject & not then if I am denied— So now my chance to do good as I think rest altogether with you. now may the good lord help you to make a faverorabl desition heaven bless you & your dear family is the prayer & your most obedient sirvant G. H. White minister of the gospel London Canada West

A Black regiment headed by the Revd Garland. H. White offers their services in protection of the southern forts during the sickly season

WASHINGTON, D.C., MAY 1862

Abraham Lincoln: Proclamation Revoking General Hunter's Emancipation Order

In March 1862 David Hunter, a general known for his antislavery views, became the commander of the Union-held enclaves along the South Carolina and Georgia coasts. Hunter issued his emancipation order on May 9 without informing the administration, which learned about it from newspaper reports. When Secretary of the Treasury Chase urged Lincoln not to revoke the order, the President replied: "No commanding general shall do such a thing, on *my* responsibility, without consulting me." Lincoln used his proclamation revoking the order to renew his call for gradual compensated emancipation, while asserting that as commander-in-chief he had the power to free slaves if it became "a necessity indispensable to the maintenance of the government."

———————

May 19, 1862
By the President of The United States of America.
A Proclamation.

Whereas there appears in the public prints, what purports to be a proclamation, of Major General Hunter, in the words and figures following, towit:

> *Headquarters Department of the South,*
> Hilton Head, S.C., May 9, 1862.
>
> General Orders No. 11.—The three States of Georgia, Florida and South Carolina, comprising the military department of the south, having deliberately declared themselves no longer under the protection of the United States of America, and having taken up arms against the said United States, it becomes a military necessity to declare them under martial law. This was accordingly done on the 25th day of April, 1862. Slavery and martial law in a free country are altogether incompatible; the persons in these three States—Georgia, Florida and South Carolina—heretofore held as slaves, are therefore declared forever free.
>
> DAVID HUNTER,
> (Official)   Major General Commanding.
> ED. W. SMITH, Acting Assistant Adjutant General.

And whereas the same is producing some excitement, and misunderstanding: therefore

I, Abraham Lincoln, president of the United States, proclaim and declare, that the government of the United States, had no knowledge, information, or belief, of an intention on the part of General Hunter to issue such a proclamation; nor has it yet, any authentic information that the document is genuine. And further, that neither General Hunter, nor any other commander, or person, has been authorized by the Government of the United States, to make proclamations declaring the slaves of any State free; and that the supposed proclamation, now in question, whether genuine or false, is altogether void, so far as respects such declaration.

I further make known that whether it be competent for me, as Commander-in-Chief of the Army and Navy, to declare the Slaves of any state or states, free, and whether at any time, in any case, it shall have become a necessity indispensable to the maintainance of the government, to exercise such supposed power, are questions which, under my responsibility, I reserve to myself, and which I can not feel justified in leaving to the decision of commanders in the field. These are totally different questions from those of police regulations in armies and camps.

On the sixth day of March last, by a special message, I recommended to Congress the adoption of a joint resolution to be substantially as follows:

Resolved, That the United States ought to co-operate with any State which may adopt a gradual abolishment of slavery, giving to such State pecuniary aid, to be used by such State in its discretion to compensate for the inconveniences, public and private, produced by such change of system.

The resolution, in the language above quoted, was adopted by large majorities in both branches of Congress, and now stands an authentic, definite, and solemn proposal of the nation to the States and people most immediately interested in the subject matter. To the people of those states I now earnestly appeal. I do not argue. I beseech you to make the arguments for yourselves. You can not if you would, be blind to the signs of the times. I beg of you a calm and enlarged consideration of them, ranging, if it may be, far above personal and partizan politics. This proposal makes common cause for a common object, casting no reproaches upon any. It acts not the pharisee. The change it contemplates would come gently as the dews of heaven, not rending or wrecking anything. Will you not embrace it? So much good has not been done, by one effort, in all past time, as, in the providence of God, it is now your high previlege to do. May the vast future not have to lament that you have neglected it.

In witness whereof, I have hereunto set my hand, and caused the seal of the United States to be affixed.

Done at the City of Washington this nineteenth day of May, in the year of our Lord one thousand eight hundred and sixty-two, and of the Independence of the United States the eighty-sixth.   ABRAHAM LINCOLN.

By the President:
    WILLIAM H. SEWARD, Secretary of State.

MEETING STONEWALL JACKSON:
VIRGINIA, MAY 1862

Richard Taylor: from Destruction and Reconstruction

Thomas J. Jackson—forever "Stonewall" after his stand at Bull Run in July 1861— initiated a bold campaign in the Shenandoah Valley in the spring of 1862 to distract the Union command and prevent reinforcements from reaching McClellan on the Peninsula. In an 1879 memoir, General Richard Taylor, son of former President Zachary Taylor, recounts joining Jackson with his Louisiana brigade and the action at Front Royal, on May 23, that started the Union flight from the Valley. Taylor affirms that the much-heralded spy Belle Boyd told Stonewall nothing he did not already know.

AT NIGHTFALL of the second day in this camp, an order came from General Jackson to join him at Newmarket, twenty odd miles north; and it was stated that my division commander, Ewell, had been apprised of the order. Our position was near a pike leading south of west to Harrisonburg, whence, to gain Newmarket, the great Valley pike ran due north. All roads near our camp had been examined and sketched, and among them was a road running northwest over the southern foot-hills of Massanutten, and joining the Valley pike some distance to the north of Harrisonburg. It was called the Keazletown road, from a little German village on the flank of Massanutten; and as it was the hypothenuse of the triangle, and reported good except at two points, I decided to take it. That night a pioneer party was sent forward to light fires and repair the road for artillery and trains. Early dawn saw us in motion, with lovely weather, a fairish road, and men in high health and spirits.

Later in the day a mounted officer was dispatched to report our approach and select a camp, which proved to be beyond Jackson's forces, then lying in the fields on both sides of the pike. Over three thousand strong, neat in fresh clothing of gray with white gaiters, bands playing at the head of their regiments, not a straggler, but every man in his place, stepping jauntily as on parade, though it had marched twenty miles and more, in open column with arms at "right shoulder shift," and rays of the declining sun flaming on polished bayonets, the brigade moved down the broad, smooth pike, and wheeled on to its camping ground. Jackson's men, by thousands, had gathered on either side of the road to see us pass. Indeed, it was a martial sight, and no man with a spark of sacred fire in his heart but would have striven hard to prove worthy of such a command.

After attending to necessary camp details, I sought Jackson, whom I had never met. And here it may be remarked that he then by no means held the place in public estimation which he subsequently attained. His Manassas reputation was much impaired by operations in the Valley, to which he had been sent after that action. The winter march on Romney had resulted in little except to freeze and discontent his troops; which discontent was shared and expressed by the authorities at Richmond, and Jackson resigned. The influence of Colonel Alek Boteler, seconded by that of the Governor of Virginia, induced him to withdraw the resignation. At Kernstown, three miles south of Winchester, he was roughly handled by the Federal General Shields, and only saved from serious disaster by the failure of that officer to push his advantage, though Shields was usually energetic.

The mounted officer who had been sent on in advance pointed out a figure perched on the topmost rail of a fence overlooking the road and field, and said it was Jackson. Approaching, I saluted and declared my name and rank, then waited for a response. Before this came I had time to see a pair of cavalry boots covering feet of gigantic size, a mangy cap with visor drawn low, a heavy, dark beard, and weary eyes—eyes I afterward saw filled with intense but never brilliant light. A low, gentle voice inquired the road and distance marched that day. "Keazletown road, six and twenty miles." "You seem to have no stragglers." "Never allow straggling." "You must teach my people; they straggle badly." A bow in reply. Just then my creoles started their band and a waltz. After a contemplative suck at a lemon, "Thoughtless fellows for serious work" came forth. I expressed a hope that the work would not be less well done because of the gayety. A return to the lemon gave me the opportunity to retire. Where Jackson got his lemons "no fellow could find out," but he was rarely without one. To have lived twelve miles from that fruit would have disturbed him as much as it did the witty Dean.

Quite late that night General Jackson came to my camp fire, where he stayed some hours. He said we would move at dawn, asked a few questions about the marching of my men, which seemed to have impressed him, and then remained silent. If silence be golden, he was a "bonanza." He sucked lemons, ate hard-tack, and drank water, and praying and fighting appeared to be his idea of the "whole duty of man."

In the gray of the morning, as I was forming my column on the pike, Jackson appeared and gave the route—north—which, from the situation of its camp, put my brigade in advance of the army. After moving a short distance in this direction, the head of the column was turned to the east and took the road over Massanutten gap to Luray. Scarce a word was spoken on the march, as Jackson rode with me. From time to time a courier would gallop up, report, and return toward Luray. An ungraceful horseman, mounted on a sorry chestnut with a shambling gait, his huge feet with outturned toes thrust into his stirrups, and such parts of his countenance as the low visor of his shocking cap failed to conceal wearing a wooden look, our new commander was not prepossessing. That night we crossed the east branch of the Shenandoah by a bridge, and camped on the stream, near Luray. Here, after three long marches, we were but a short distance below Conrad's store, a point we had let several days before. I began to think that Jackson was an unconscious poet, and, as an ardent lover of nature, desired to give strangers an opportunity to admire the beauties of his Valley. It seemed hard lines to be wandering like sentimental travelers about the country, instead of gaining "kudos" on the Peninsula.

Off the next morning, my command still in advance, and Jackson riding with me. The road led north between the east bank of the river and the western base of the Blue Ridge. Rain had fallen and softened it, so as to delay the wagon trains in rear. Past midday we reached a wood extending from the mountain to the river, when a mounted officer from the rear called Jackson's attention, who rode back with him. A moment later, there rushed out of the wood to meet us a young, rather well-looking woman, afterward widely known as Belle Boyd. Breathless with speed and agitation, some time elapsed before she found her voice. Then, with much volubility, she said we were near Front Royal, beyond the wood; that the town was filled with Federals, whose camp was on the west side of the river, where they had guns in position to cover the wagon bridge, but none bearing on the railway bridge below the former; that they believed Jackson to be west of Massanutten, near Harrisonburg; that General Banks, the Federal commander, was at Winchester, twenty miles northwest of Front Royal, where he was slowly concentrating his widely scattered forces to meet Jackson's advance, which was expected some days later. All this she told with the precision of a staff officer making a report, and it was true to the letter. Jackson was possessed of these facts before he left Newmarket, and based his movements upon them; but, as he never told anything, it was news to me, and gave me an idea of the strategic value of Massanutten—pointed out, indeed, by Washington before the Revolution. There also dawned on me quite another view of our leader than the one from which I had been regarding him for two days past.

Convinced of the correctness of the woman's statements, I hurried forward at "a double," hoping to surprise the enemy's idlers in the town, or swarm over the wagon bridge with them and secure it. Doubtless this was rash, but I felt immensely "cocky" about my brigade, and believed that it would prove equal to any demand. Before we had cleared the wood Jackson came galloping from the rear, followed by a company of horse. He ordered me to deploy my leading regiment as skirmishers on both sides of the road and continue the advance, then passed on. We speedily came in sight of Front Royal, but the enemy had taken the alarm, and his men were scurrying over the bridge to their camp, where troops could be seen forming. The situation of the village is surpassingly beautiful. It lies near the east bank of the Shenandoah, which just below unites all its waters, and looks directly on the northern peaks of Massanutten. The Blue Ridge, with Manassas Gap, through which passes the railway, overhangs it on the east; distant Alleghany bounds the horizon to the west; and down the Shenandoah, the eye ranges over a fertile, well-farmed country. Two bridges spanned the river—a wagon bridge above, a railway bridge some yards lower. A good pike led to Winchester, twenty miles, and another followed the river north, whence many cross-roads united with the Valley pike near Winchester. The river, swollen by rain, was deep and turbulent, with a strong current. The Federals were posted on the west bank, here somewhat higher than the opposite, and a short distance above the junction of waters, with batteries bearing more especially on the upper bridge.

Under instructions, my brigade was drawn up in line, a little retired from the river, but overlooking it—the Federals and their guns in full view. So far, not a shot had been fired. I rode down to the river's brink to get a better look at the enemy through a field-glass, when my horse, heated by the march, stepped into the water to drink. Instantly a brisk fire was opened on me, bullets striking all around and raising a little shower-bath. Like many a foolish fellow, I found it easier to get into than out of a difficulty. I had not yet led my command into action, and, remembering that one must "strut" one's little part to the best advantage, sat my horse with all the composure I could muster. A provident camel, on the eve of a desert journey, would not have laid in a greater supply of water than did my thoughtless beast. At last he raised his head, looked placidly around, turned, and walked up the bank.

This little incident was not without value, for my men welcomed me with a cheer; upon which, as if in response, the enemy's guns opened, and, having the range, inflicted some loss on my line. We had no guns up to reply, and, in advance as has been mentioned, had outmarched the troops behind us. Motionless as a statue, Jackson sat his horse some few yards away, and seemed lost in thought. Perhaps the circumstances mentioned some pages back had obscured his star; but if so, a few short hours swept away the cloud, and it blazed, Sirius-like, over the land. I approached him with the suggestion that the railway bridge might be passed by stepping on the cross-ties, as the enemy's guns bore less directly on it than on the upper bridge. He nodded approval. The 8th regiment was on the right of my line, near at hand; and dismounting, Colonel Kelly led it across under a sharp musketry fire. Several men fell to disappear in the dark water beneath; but the movement continued with great rapidity, considering the difficulty of walking on ties, and Kelly with his leading files gained the opposite shore. Thereupon the enemy fired combustibles previously placed near the center of the wagon bridge. The loss of this structure would have seriously delayed us, as the railway bridge was not floored, and I looked at Jackson, who, near by, was watching Kelly's progress. Again he nodded, and my command rushed at the bridge. Concealed by the cloud of smoke, the suddenness of the movement saved us from much loss; but it was rather a near thing. My horse and clothing were scorched, and many men burned their hands severely while throwing brands into the river. We were soon over, and the enemy in full flight to Winchester, with loss of camp, guns, and prisoners. Just as I emerged from flames and smoke, Jackson was by my side. How he got there was a mystery, as the bridge was thronged with my men going at full speed; but smoke and fire had decidedly freshened up his costume.

"THE PROGRESS OF EVENTS":
WASHINGTON, D.C., MAY 1862
Elizabeth Blair Lee to Samuel Phillips Lee

Elizabeth Blair Lee filled letters to her naval officer husband, serving under Farragut on the Mississippi, with military and domestic news gleaned in part from her well-connected family: father Francis Preston Blair, a longtime Washington political figure and counselor to President Lincoln; brother Montgomery, Lincoln's postmaster general; and brother Frank, Missouri congressman and chairman of the House Committee on Military Affairs. Among her topics were the widespread effects of Jackson's Valley campaign, and the Union navy's attack on Fort Darling, or Drewry's Bluff, on the James River.

Silver Spring May 26, 1862
Dear Phil   I tried to see Capt Fox yesterday to ascertain how get this to Capt Davis but as I failed to see him Minna brought me word today to send it Cairo— so here goes a few lines to meet & welcome you to Memphis whither yr last letter say will be yr destination & many is the anxious hour has it cost me for I had hoped the Iron Navy would *do up* all that part of the work—

We are all very well I am entirely over my attack (Mother says on New Orleans) & have got hearty & sunburnt in my garden over my rejoicings & thanksgivings at your wonderful deliverance from "all of yr enemies— I will never cease to be thankful for so great a mercy miraculous it appears to me the more I think of what you encountered   I lived in terror for weeks about the Forts— but it never occurred to me that they had any naval force of import above them— & I thought the Mortars would demolish them— but alas they were comparatively useless Maigre Fox & Comre Porter   I was proud of your good temper & patriotic desire to have all things done well & peaceably in the Squadron but it cost me some jealous pangs Ill confess—

I wish I could send you some glad tidings & just at this moment— but by a Cabal (a most pertinacious one) against

McClellan Banks was deprived of all his troops but 6,000 & they were sent to McDowell to get him into Richmond via Fredricksburg before McClellan but as Genl fatty did not manage it & McClellan is now in sight of the Steeples of Richmond McDowell is ordered to rescue Banks after he is disgraced by a most disgraceful rout Frémont to was whipped at Franklin by Jackson & then Banks which fact is suppressed by Stanton who is utterly abolitionized & was no doubt the promptor of Hunter's proclamation so say Army people in the City— & Now he is telegraphing all creation & evidently trying to affright the world by his own scare which is described as dreadful— He wanted sink stone ships & block up the Potomac from the Merrimac— but Old Welles put his foot & commission on the proceeding & stopped & the other day when Rogers was repulsed at Fort Darling they say Stanton was all affright but Old Grey beard assured them he was not discouraged & would not be if he lost all of our ships in the James River— I must say I like this calmness— it contrasts handsomely with this fuzzy tricky lawyer's jerks— Who is pretty much divided between his intrigues & jobbing & devotions to the White house where he is ever so prostrate that one can scarce approach old Abe" with giving him a shove to get at him— He and Chase now hunt in couples & both have mounted the Extreme Abolition lacky

I am sorry our friend P King too in his tremors about reelection has joined Wendall Phillips— but our friend Doolittle is still a Republican & so is 9 tenths of the party still loyal to that platform & the Constitution of their Country & to white men rather than the black one— Our fat friend has not been to see us this spring nor to see Frank— but we have been steady in our attentions & will continue them— in spite of his Frémont proclivities for which I say we all ought to be the last to make points upon as to the feelings of other people—

Frank & his family are now staying here with us— & Blair revels in so many juvenile companions & it is refreshing to see them playing with new mown hay on the lawn which never looked as beautiful before & I must add I think the children too were a fine looking set— so sturdy & rosy & joyous the Donkey Cart hauls off the hay & they rake & put it in & it is a lovely hay making to my partial eyes I went to Johns yesterday after church— I did not see who was too vain to let me see his swollen face which gives the poor fellow some pain he took cold when down in the Country a few days since Nelly was jubilant over Banks & Frémonts defeat tho she is very prudent in her talk to everybody but John & me— I have prayed her not to talk to her boys & she has quit it—

I had a long letter from Fanny She is in better health & spirits I sent you a long letter from her to Ship Island— They are all prospering again with the return of trade from Nashville where they are sending bread & meat for cotton & tobacco— in large quantities but secesh does all it can to conceal this revival of trade— they want the money but refuse to see the sources of their prosperity— May God enlighten them is my constant prayer when I think of southern people & the delirious frenzy now upon so many of them—

All of our kindred and friends are well & the papers will post you better than I can as to the progress of events Our whole well doing now seems to hang on the results at Corinth & Richmond— Some think here that the Battle of New Orleans has stopped the Intervention project England hates our progress especially that of the Navy & will hurt whenever she can without ruin to herself & Louis Napoleon only holds off because he hopes the growing enmity between us & England will move to his benefit or that of his Dynasty The people over the waters suffer more from this war than our northern people do who bear its whole expense in every sense & this *strength* is alarming— to all the crowned Heads Goodbye   Ill write another Extra soon   I send my regular bulletins to Ship Island still   Blair sleeps or would join me in love & kisses   Yr devoted Lizzie

"NO SIMILAR INSTANCE OF INFAMY":
LOUISIANA, MAY 1862

Thomas O. Moore: To the People of Louisiana

When the Union soldiers occupying New Orleans were treated with blatant contempt by many of the female inhabitants—from her French Quarter balcony one woman emptied her chamber pot on the head of Flag Officer Farragut—their commander, Major General Benjamin F. Butler, issued General Order No. 28. Butler's "Women's Order" threatened to treat such contempt as the action of "a woman of the town plying her avocation" and subject to arrest (Butler later wrote that his "order executed itself" and no arrests were made). Louisiana's outraged governor, Thomas O. Moore, issued this proclamation in response.

PROCLAMATION.

EXECUTIVE OFFICE,
Opelousas, La., May 24, 1862.
To the People of Louisiana:
The general commanding the troops of the United States now holding possession of New Orleans issued the following order on the 15th instant:

As the officers and soldiers of the United States have been subject to repeated insults from the women (calling themselves ladies) of New Orleans, in return for the most scrupulous non-interference and courtesy on our part, it is ordered that hereafter, when any female shall, by word, gesture, or movement, insult or show contempt for any officer or soldier of the United States, she shall be regarded and held liable to be treated as a woman of the town plying her avocation.
By command of Major-General Butler.

The annals of warfare between civilized nations afford no similar instance of infamy to this order. It is thus proclaimed to the world that the exhibition of any disgust or repulsiveness by the women of New Orleans to the hated invaders of their home and the slayers of their fathers, brothers, and husbands shall constitute a justification to a brutal soldiery for the indulgence of their lust. The commanding general, from his headquarters, announces to his insolent followers that they are at liberty to treat as women of the town the wives, the mothers, the daughters of our citizens, if by word, gesture, or movement any contempt is indicated for their persons or insult offered to their presence. Of the nature of the movement and the meaning of the look these vagabond refuse of the Northern States are to be the judges.

What else than contempt and abhorrence can the women of New Orleans feel or exhibit for these officers and soldiers of the United States? The spontaneous impulse of their hearts must appear involuntary upon their countenances and thus constitute the crime for which the general of those soldiers adjudges the punishment of rape and brutalized passion.

History records instances of cities sacked and inhuman atrocities committed upon the women of a conquered town, but in no instance in modern times, at least without the brutal ravishers suffering condign punishment from the hands of their own commanders. It was reserved for a Federal general to invite his soldiers to the perpetration of outrages at the mention of which the blood recoils in horror—to quicken the impulses of their sensual instincts by the suggestion of transparent excuses for their gratification, and to add to an infamy already well merited these crowning titles of a panderer to lust and a desecrator of virtue.

Maddened by the noble loyalty of our people to the Government of their affections, and at their disgust and execration of their invaders; stung into obliviousness of the world's censure by the grand offering made of our property upon the altar of our liberties; his passions inflamed by the sight of burning cotton illumining the river upon whose waters floats the powerful fleet that effected the downfall of our chief city; disappointed, chafed, and chagrined that our people, unlike his own, do not measure liberty, truth, or honor by a pecuniary standard, he sees the fruits of a victory he did not help to win eluding his grasp, and nothing left upon which to gloat his vengeance but unarmed men and helpless women.

Louisianians! will you suffer such foul conduct of your oppressors to pass unpunished? Will you permit such indignities to remain unavenged? A mind so debased as to be capable of conceiving the alternative presented in this order must be fruitful of inventions wherewith to pollute humanity. Shameless enough to allow their publication in the city, by the countenance of such atrocities they will be multiplied in the country. Its inhabitants must arm and strike, or the insolent victors will offer this outrage to your wives, your sisters, and your daughters. Possessed of New Orleans by means of his superior naval force, he cannot penetrate the interior if you resolve to prevent it. It does not require a force of imposing magnitude to impede his progress. Companies of experienced woodsmen in every exposed locality, with their trusty rifles and shot-guns, will harass his invading columns, deprive him of his pilots, and assure him he is in the country of an enemy. At proper points larger forces will be collected, but every man can be a soldier to guard the approaches to his home. Organize, then, quickly and efficiently. If your enemy attempt to proceed into the interior let his pathway be marked by his blood. It is your homes that you have to defend. It is the jewel of your hearths—the chastity of your women—you have to guard. Let that thought animate your breasts, nerve your arms, quicken your energies, and inspire your resolution. Strike home to the heart of your foe the blow that rids your country of his presence. If need be let his blood moisten your own grave. It will rise up before your children as a perpetual memento of a race whom it will teach to hate now and evermore.

THOS. O. MOORE.

"REVOLTING OUTRAGES": LONDON, JUNE 1862

Lord Palmerston to Charles Francis Adams
Benjamin Moran: Journal, June 25, 1862

Butler's order provoked outrage not only in the Confederacy but in Great Britain as well. Two days after he wrote to envoy Adams, Lord Palmerston told the House of Commons that "an Englishman must blush to think that such an act has been committed by one belonging to the Anglo-Saxon race." Benjamin Moran, a secretary at the American legation, recorded Adams's response to the prime minister.

Confidential.　　　　　　　　　　　BROCKET, 11 June, 1862.

MY DEAR SIR,—I cannot refrain from taking the liberty of saying to you that it is difficult if not impossible to express adequately the disgust which must be excited in the mind of every honorable man by the general order of General Butler given in the inclosed extract from yesterday's *Times*. Even when a town is taken by assault it is the practice of the Commander of the conquering army to protect to his utmost the inhabitants and especially the female part of them, and I will venture to say that no example can be found in the history of civilized nations till the publication of this order, of a general guilty in cold blood of so infamous an act as deliberately to hand over the female inhabitants of a conquered city to the unbridled license of an unrestrained soldiery.

If the Federal Government chuses to be served by men capable of such revolting outrages, they must submit to abide by the deserved opinion which mankind will form of their conduct. My dear Sir, Yours faithfully,

　　　　　　　　　　　　　　　　　　PALMERSTON.

C. F. Adams Esqr.
　　(Address: Private. His Excelcy Chas. F. Adams Esqr.
　　　　　　　　　　　　　　　　Palmerston.)

Wednesday, June 25, 1862. A serious correspondence has just taken place between Lord Palmerston and Mr. Adams which is destined to become historical. His Lordship with that impudence that only an Englishman can be guilty of wrote a private and confidential note to Mr. Adams on the 11th Inst., about Gen'l Butler's late order at New Orleans in which he said he could not "express adequately the disgust which must be excited in the mind of every honorable man" at that regulation "of a General guilty of so infamous an act as to deliberately hand over the female inhabitants of a conquered city to the unbridled license of an unrestrained soldiery."

Mr. Adams replied on the 12th refusing to recognise the note, unless he was assured it was official, and expressing surprise at such an unusual proceeding on the part of the Prime Minister, instead of the Minister of Foreign Affairs,—with whom Foreign Ministers carry on their correspondence on matters connected with the duties of their Mission.

To this Ld. Palmerston rejoined on the 15th by saying his note was official.

In the interview Mr. Adams saw Lord Russell and stated the case to him. He was much offended, & said Ld. Palmerston had exceeded the bounds of good behavior—a thing he had often done of late, and had no business to write such a note.

Mr. Adams renewed the subject on the 16th and after commenting on the nature of his Lordship's letter, said that "the Government he represented would visit with just indignation upon its servants abroad their tame submission to receive under the seal of privacy any indignity which it might be the disposition of the servants of any sovereign however exalted, to offer to it in that form."

Palmerston with his usual insolence answered this in a sophistical strain on the 19th, & on the 20th Mr. Adams closed the affair by a note in which he said he would decline while here to receive such communications from him. This severe reprimand had its intended effect, and his Lordship has remained silent under it.

The incident placed Mr. Adams in a very critical position, and for a few days we considered things so serious as to strongly anticipate a sudden rupture of all intercourse. Fortunately, Mr. Adams' decision saved such a result.

A more impudent proceeding than that of Palmerston in this case cannot be discovered in the whole range of political life. Knowing the brutality of his own officers and soldiers he readily imagined ours of the same stamp, and insolently presumed to lecture Mr. Adams on a thing which was not his business. His ill-manners were properly rebuked. American soldiers, he will find out, are not beasts, altho' English soldiers are; and he will also learn that it is only a debased mind that would construe Gen'l Butler's order as he has done. He has defined it according to English practice. That is all.

This proceeding of Lord Palmerston is one of the most remarkable, and probably without a parallel in Diplomatic history. Mr. Adams was placed in a most awkward predicament & managed the affair with great skill. When the story shall be made public, it will create great astonishment in certain quarters. Had not Palmerston taken the course he did, it was Mr. Adams' intention to have published the correspondence privately and sent it to his colleagues so that they might know what they might at some time or other expect from his Lordship should he remain in office.

BATTLE OF FAIR OAKS: VIRGINIA, MAY–JUNE 1862

Henry Ropes to William Ropes

McClellan's army, as it closed on Richmond, straddled the Chickahominy River, and on May 31–June 1 Joseph E. Johnston struck at the isolated Union left wing south of the river. The brigade of Lieutenant Henry Ropes, 20th Massachusetts Infantry, part of Edwin Sumner's Second Corps, was hurried across the flooding Chickahominy to counter the attack. The battle of Fair Oaks (or Seven Pines) cost the Confederates 6,134 men, killed, wounded, or missing; the Union 5,031; and the fighting ended about where it began. Among the seriously wounded was Johnston, and on June 1 Jefferson Davis replaced him with General Robert E. Lee.

———————

Camp near Fair Oaks Station Va.
1 P.M. Tuesday June 3d 1862.

My dear Father.

I take the first opportunity to inform you of my safety, that a Kind Providence has mercifully preserved me in battle, and above all that I was enabled to do my duty there.

On Saturday last, May 31st, we had not the slightest idea of danger being near till about noon when very heavy firing broke out from the woods West of us and at one time approached very near. We were ordered under arms, but I had no particular expectation of a battle, for we have been often called out in the same way before. The firing ceased, and we heard a report that Casey had been repulsed, but we did not know what to believe. At about 4 O'cl. orders came to fall in with one day's rations and we marched from Camp, and crossed the Chickahominy on the log bridge built by the Mich. Regimt. We came out on a low meadow where our Artillery was stuck in the mud. The 19th Mass. was on picket behind us, the Tammany we left here, and the 7th Mich. and we pushed on alone. After passing the meadow we ascended a small hill and found the country dry and hilly in front. Soon we halted, loaded and primed and then marched on again. In a few moments we heard guns ahead, and we pushed on rapidly, crossed a stream knee deep and took the double quick, for musketry and artillery were now heard in front, rapidly increasing. We drove forward out of breath and very hot, saw the smoke rising over the trees, and soon the road turned from along the edge of the woods, and we saw at the farther end of a large field our Artillery firing with the greatest rapidity, the Infantry forming, all hid in smoke. We again took the double quick step and ran through deep mud and pools of water toward the battle. The whole field in the rear of the line of firing was covered with dead; and wounded men were coming in in great numbers, some walking, some limping, some carried on stretchers and blankets, many with shattered limbs exposed and dripping with blood. In a moment we entered the fire. The noise was terrific, the balls whistled by us and the Shells exploded over us and by our side; the whole scene dark with smoke and lit up by the streams of fire from our battery and from our Infantry in line on each side. We were carried to the left and formed in line, and then marched by the left flank and advanced to the front and opened fire. Our men behaved with the greatest steadiness and stood up and fired and did exactly what they were told. The necessary confusion was very great, and it was as much as all the Officers could do to give the commands and see to the men. We changed position 2 or 3 times under a hot fire. Donnelly and Chase of my company fell not 2 feet from me. The shell and balls seemed all round us, and yet few seemed to fall. We kept up this heavy firing for some time, when the enemy came out of the woods in front and made a grand attack on the battery. They were met by grape and canister and a tremendous fire of the Infantry. They faltered and fell back. Some Regiment charged on them: the whole Rebel line was now in front of us, and Genl. Sumner ordered our whole line to advance. We rushed on with tremendous cheers, the whole together at a charge. The Rebels did not wait for the bayonets but broke and fled. Our Regiment came over a newly ploughed field and sank to the knee. We drove them to the edge of the woods and opened a tremendous fire for a few moments, and then

June 4th 12M. 1862.

I was forced to stop suddenly yesterday for our Company went to occupy a house and yard in advance of our Regiment, and I expected to finish there, but the enemy appeared unexpectedly and opened fire on us and wounded 2 men of Company H, and I was fully occupied till this morning. I will continue my letter where I left it off.

We fired into the woods and then charged and drove them before us. We were then ordered back, and by the left flank and again charged the Rebels in a field on the left where they had rallied. We drove them and halted in the middle of the field and give a few final volleys. It was then dark. We staid there that night. Ground covered with their killed and wounded. We took many prisoners. I will write more fully when I have more time.

On Sunday they attacked us tremendously. We were not in the heat of it and only lost one man.

Fighting more or less all the time till now. No signs of the Rebels today. All Officers well and unhurt. Colonel well, but very busy. He desires me to ask you to send word to his family. I am on picket to-day. The Regiment will probably soon be relieved. Our total loss 30. My Company suffered most in the battle.

Love to Mother and all.

Your affectionate Son
Henry.

A MILITARY ASSESSMENT: VIRGINIA, JUNE 1862

Robert E. Lee to Jefferson Davis

General Lee served as unofficial chief of staff to President Davis for three months before taking command of the Army of Northern Virginia, and as he writes here, he continued supporting Stonewall Jackson's campaign in the Shenandoah. As he organized and reinforced his army, Lee planned his "diversion" against McClellan—this time an assault on the Union right wing north of the Chickahominy River.

Confidential

Hd. Qrs: Near Richmond 5 June '62

After much reflection I think if it was possible to reinforce Jackson strongly it would change the character of the war. This can only be done by the troops in Georgia, S.C. & N.C. Jackson could in that event cross Maryland into Penna. It would call all the enemy from our Southern coast & liberate those states— If these states will give up their troops I think it can be done. McClellan will make this a battle of Posts. He will take position from position, under cover of his heavy guns, & we cannot get at him without storming his works, which with our new troops is extremely hazardous. You witnessed the experiment Saturday. It will require 100,000 men to resist the regular siege of Richmond, which perhaps would only prolong not save it— I am preparing a line that I can hold with part of our forces in front, while with the rest I will endeavour to make a diversion to bring McClellan out. He sticks under his batteries & is working day & night— He is obliged to adhere to the R. R. unless he can reach James river to provision his Army. I am endeavouring to block his progress on the R. R. & have written up to see if I can get made an iron battery on trucks with a heavy gun, to sweep the country in our front. The enemy cannot move his heavy guns except on the R. R. You have seen nothing like the roads in the Chick—bottom. Our people are opposed to work. Our troops, officers, community & press. All ridicule & resist it. It is the very means by which McClellan has

& is advancing. Why should we leave to him the whole advantage of labour. Combined with valour fortitude & boldness, of which we have our fair proportion, it should lead us to success. What carried the Roman soldiers into all countries, but this happy combination. The evidences of their labour last to this day. There is nothing so military as labour, & nothing so important to an army as to save the lives of its soldiers—

I enclose a letter I have recd from Genl D. H. Hill, for your own perusal. Please return it to me. I have taken means to arrest stragglers—I hope he is mistaken about his Brigadiers—I fear not in Rains case. Of Featherston I know nothing. I thought you ought to know it. Our position requires you should know everything & you must excuse my troubling you— The firing in our front has ceased. I believe it was the enemys shell practice. Col Long &c went down early this morg. to keep me advised, but as I hear nothing from them, I assume it is unimportant   very respt & truly

R E L<small>EE</small>

ARMING FREED SLAVES:
SOUTH CAROLINA, JUNE 1862

David Hunter to Edwin M. Stanton

At the same time as he issued his emancipation order in May 1862, General Hunter began organizing a regiment of freed slaves. He wrote to the secretary of war after his actions were challenged by Kentucky congressman Charles A. Wickliffe, a vehement opponent of arming blacks. Denied War Department sanction, Hunter disbanded his slave regiments, but his efforts, and similar efforts by General John W. Phelps on the Gulf coast, marked a first step toward recruiting blacks for the army.

Port Royal So Ca June 23rd 1862

Sir: I have the honor to acknowledge the receipt of a communication from the Adjutant General of the Army, dated June 13th 1862, requesting me to furnish you with information necessary to answer certain resolutions introduced in the House of Representatives, June 9th 1862, on motion of the Hon. Mr. Wickliffe of Kentucky,—their substance being to inquire;

1st Whether I had organized or was organizing a regiment of "Fugitive Slaves" in this Department.

2nd Whether any authority had been given to me from the War Department for such organization;—and

3rd Whether I had been furnished by order of the War Department with clothing, uniforms, arms, equipments and so forth for such a force?

Only having received the letter covering these inquiries at a late hour on Saturday night, I urge forward my answer in time for the Steamer sailing today (Monday),—this haste preventing me from entering as minutely as I could wish upon many points of detail such as the paramount importance of the subject calls for. But in view of the near termination of the present session of Congress, and the wide-spread interest which must have been awakened by Mr Wickliffe's Resolutions, I prefer sending even this imperfect answer to waiting the period necessary for the collection of fuller and more comprehensive data.

To the First Question therefore I reply that no regiment of "Fugitive Slaves" has been, or is being organized in this Department. There is, however, a fine regiment of persons whose late masters are "Fugitive Rebels,"—men who everywhere fly before the appearance of the National Flag, leaving their servants behind them to shift as best they can for themselves.—So far, indeed, are the loyal persons composing this regiment from seeking to avoid the presence of their late owners, that they are now, one and all, working with remarkable industry to place themselves in a position to go in full and effective pursuit of their fugacious and traitorous proprietors.

To the Second Question, I have the honor to answer that the instructions given to Brig. Gen. T. W. Sherman by the Hon. Simon Cameron, late Secretary of War, and turned over to me by succession for my guidance,—do distinctly authorize me to employ all loyal persons offering their services in defence of the Union and for the suppression of this Rebellion in any manner I might see fit, or that the circumstances might call for. There is no restriction as to the character or color of the persons to be employed, or the nature of the employment, whether civil or military, in which their services should be used. I conclude, therefore that I have been authorized to enlist "Fugitive Slaves" as soldiers, could any such be found in this Department.— No such characters, however, have yet appeared within view of our most advanced pickets,—the loyal slaves everywhere remaining on their plantations to welcome us, aid us, and supply us with food, labor and information.— It is the masters who have in every instance been the "Fugitives", running away from loyal slaves as well as loyal soldiers, and whom we have only partially been able to see,—chiefly their heads over ramparts, or, rifle in hand, dodging behind trees,— in the extreme distance.— In the absence of any "Fugitive Master Law", the deserted Slaves would be wholly without remedy, had not the crime of Treason given them the right to pursue, capture and bring back those persons of whose protection they have been thus suddenly bereft.

To the Third Interrogatory, it is my painful duty to reply that I never have received any Specific authority for issues of clothing, uniforms, arms, equipments and so forth to the troops in question,—my general instructions from Mr Cameron to employ them in any manner I might find necessary, and the military exigencies of the Department and the country, being my only, but in my judgment, sufficient justification. Neither have I had any Specific authority for supplying these persons with shovels, spades and pick axes when employing them as laborers, nor with boats and oars when using them as lightermen,—but these are not points included in Mr. Wickliffe's Resolution.— To me it seemed that liberty to employ men in any particular capacity implied with it liberty, also, to supply them with the necessary tools; and acting upon this faith, I have clothed, equipped and armed the only loyal regiment yet raised in South Carolina.

I must say, in vindication of my own conduct, that had it not been for the many other diversified and imperative claims on my time and attention, a much more satisfactory result might have been hoped for; and that in place of only one, as at present, at least five or six well-drilled, brave and thoroughly acclimated regiments should by this time have been added to the loyal forces of the Union.

The experiment of arming the Blacks, so far as I have made it, has been a complete and even marvellous success. They are sober, docile, attentive and enthusiastic, displaying great natural capacities for acquiring the duties of the soldier. They are eager beyond all things to take the field and be led into action; and it is the unanimous opinion of the officers who have had charge of them, that in the peculiarities of this climate and Country they will prove invaluable auxiliaries,—fully equal to the similar regiments so long and successfully used by the British Authorities in the West India Islands.

In conclusion I would say it is my hope,—there appearing no possibility of other reinforcements owing to the exigencies of the Campaign in the Peninsula,—to have organized by the end of next Fall, and to be able to present to the Government, from forty eight to fifty thousand of these hardy and devoted soldiers.— Trusting that this letter may form part of your answer to Mr Wickliffe's Resolutions, I have the honor to be, most respectfully, Your Very Obedt Servt.

FEAR OF THE "YANKEES":
LOUISIANA, JUNE–JULY 1862

Kate Stone: Journal, June 29–July 5, 1862

Brokenburn, a cotton plantation some thirty miles northwest of Vicksburg, Mississippi, in what is now Madison Parish, Louisiana, was home to twenty-one-year-old Kate Stone, who recorded the impressment of slave labor for an early Union effort to bypass the Vicksburg citadel. The rumors she mentions in her July 5 entry refer to the Seven Days' Battles at Richmond.

June 29: Brother Walter brought a letter from My Brother to Mamma. It was sent by Tom Manlove, who is at home on sick leave. In the letter he is despondent and homesick and very anxious about us all now that the enemy is at our very doors. He says that it will kill him to remain idle in Virginia when we are in such danger and that he must come back to see about us and fight with the Mississippi army. He seems so desperate. We fear he will do something rash and get into trouble. He cannot realize that we are safe enough for the present.

We hear today that the Yankees are impressing all the Negro men on the river places and putting them to work on a ditch which they are cutting across the point opposite Vicksburg above DeSoto. They hope to turn the river through there and to leave Vicksburg high and dry, ruining that town and enabling the gunboats to pass down the river without running the gauntlet of the batteries at Vicksburg. They have lately come up as far as Omega, four miles from us, taking the men from Mr. Noland's place down. We hear several have been shot attempting to escape. We were satisfied there would soon be outrages committed on private property. Mamma had all the men on the place called up, and she told them if the Yankees came on the place each Negro must take care of himself and run away and hide. We think they will.

From a late paper we see that Butler is putting his foot down more firmly every day. A late proclamation orders every man in the city to take the oath of allegiance. There will be the most severe penalties in case of refusal. Butler had Mr. Mumford, a gentleman of New Orleans, shot for tearing down the first flag hoisted in New Orleans over the mint. The most infamous order and murder of which only Butler is capable. Is the soul of Nero reincarnated in the form of Butler? Why can he not fall of the scourge of New Orleans, yellow fever?

Gen. Breckinridge started to Vicksburg yesterday in a carriage, and he runs great risk of being captured, as they have pickets across the point. Several of our soldiers have been taken trying to make their way across there. Brother Walter slipped through just in time.

The drought was broken last night by a good rain and the planters are feeling better. This insures a good corn crop and it was beginning to suffer. It is so essential to make good food crops this year. When we heard the cool drops splashing on the roof, "We thanked God and took fresh courage." Such a lovely morning. It is a pleasure to breathe the soft, cool air and look out over the glad, green fields, flashing and waving in the early sunlight.

Mamma had a chill and was in bed all day. How I dread to see her start again having fevers.

Martha, one of Courtney's twins, will die, they think tonight. The poor little creature has suffered a long time.

Mr. Catlin, Mrs. Bledsoe, and my pet aversion, Dr. Slicer, are amusing themselves during all this time of threatened ruin and disaster by getting up fish frys and picnics, aided and abetted by all that set back there calling themselves second-class—and they have named themselves truly.

Sister sent Douglas's hat over to him. Joe Carson's is nearly done, but only Mamma can finish it and she is sick.

June 30: The excitement is very great. The Yankees have taken the Negroes off all the places below Omega, the Negroes generally going most willingly, being promised their freedom by the vandals. The officers coolly go on the places, take the plantation books, and call off the names of all the men they want, carrying them off from their masters without a word of apology. They laugh at the idea of payment and say of course they will never send them back. A good many planters are leaving the river and many are sending their Negroes to the back country. We hope to have ours in a place of greater safety by tomorrow.

Dr. Nutt and Mr. Mallett are said to be already on their way to Texas with the best of their hands. Jimmy and Joe went to the Bend and Richmond today. They saw Julia and Mary Gustine, who sent me word that I was a great coward to run away. Mary had talked to a squad of Yankee soldiers for awhile and found them anything but agreeable.

All on this place, Negroes and whites, are much wrought up. Of course the Negroes do not want to go, and our fear is when the Yankees come and find them gone they will burn the buildings in revenge. They are capable of any horror. We look forward to their raid with great dread. Mrs. Savage sent for her silver today. We have been keeping it since the gunboats came. They will all leave in two days for Bayou Macon. Would like to see them before they get off.

Mamma has been in bed all day. Sister is suffering with a large rising on her leg and Brother Walter from a severe cold. He is spitting blood, all yesterday and today, and tomorrow is compelled to go on a long trip. We have been arranging everything for an early start.

July 5: Another Fourth of July has gone by without any festivities, not even a dinner for the Negroes, but they have holiday. The Yankees told Mr. McRae, while they were holding him prisoner, that they would celebrate the day by a furious attack on Vicksburg. But we have heard few guns since the third. That day we heard them very distinctly, almost a continuous roar. It was said both mortar fleets were firing on Vicksburg. We have not heard the result.

The Yankees are gathering in the Negroes on the river as fast as possible. They have taken all the men able to work from Lake Providence to Pecan Grove and from Omega to Baton Rouge. They are hourly expected at Pecan Grove. Robert is with us to be out of the way when they do come. He is nearly well. The Negroes are eager to go, leaving wife and children and all for freedom promised them, but we hear they are being worked to death on the canal with no shelter at night and not much to eat.

There has been no attempt at resistance. Some of the plantations have been deserted by the owners, some of them burned by the Yankee bands, and some of them not molested. It depends on the temper of the officer in charge. If he feels malicious, he burns the premises. If a good-natured enemy, he takes what he wants and leaves the buildings standing. Most of them are malicious. Mamma will have the Negro men taken to the back country tomorrow, if she can get them to go. Generally when told to run away from the soldiers, they go right to them and I cannot say I blame them.

Mamma has been sick in bed since Sunday and is not yet able to be up all day. We sent for Dr. Devine first, and he gave her a dose of podophyllin that completely exhausted her, since she always suffers dreadfully with nausea, and that nearly killed her. So we sent for Dr. Dancy, and she is improving, but slowly.

Brother Walter went out to Monroe, eighty miles, and got back yesterday. He succeeded in buying enough molasses to last the place the year and some little necessaries at enormous prices. The trading boats are coming down the river again with groceries at ridiculously low prices, but of course no patriot could think of buying from them. Mamma was able to sell her surplus corn and that helped her on wonderfully. She had such quantities of it. And we certainly will have eatables this year, judging from the looks of the great fields of corn, peas, and potatoes. Not much cotton planted.

Mamma so longed for ice while she was ill, but it was impossible to get it, while those wretches on the gunboats could even have ice cream if they wished it.

People going and coming all the week. Mrs. Carson kindly brought Mamma a substitute for lemonade and some crackers. She was out twice.

It is hard for sick people to live on cornbread. We fortunately have a little flour, sent Mamma by Mr. Hardison as a specimen of some home-grown wheat. Joe has been out several times. The last time I was just finishing his hat. I gave it to him and it fitted beautifully. He was so pleased with the gift that it repaid me for the yards of plaiting. Joe is the only "stay-at-home" I would give anything to, but I know so well it is not his fault. Mr. Hornwasher came out with Mrs. Carson, his black eyes sparkling and dancing even more than usual. He still speaks of joining the army.

We hear rumors of a great battle in Virginia and the utter discomfiture of McClellan with Gen. Lee attacking him in front and Stonewall Jackson with 2,800 men in the rear. That was a "stonewall" McClellan found hard to climb. My Brother and Uncle Bo must both have been in the fight, but we have had no news from them for such a long time. It is heart-sickening.

THE SEVEN DAYS BEGIN:
VIRGINIA, JUNE 1862

Edward Porter Alexander:
from Fighting for the Confederacy

In less than a month Lee raised the Army of Northern Virginia to its greatest strength of the war—100,000 men, nearly equal to the Federal army—and determined to break McClellan's impending siege of Richmond. Lieutenant Colonel Edward Porter Alexander, Lee's ordnance chief, records in his personal reminiscences the lead-up to the Seven Days (June 25–July 1) and the fighting on the first three days, through the battle of Gaines's Mill. His memoir, drafted in 1897–99, was published in 1989 as *Fighting for the Confederacy: The Personal Recollections of General Edward Porter Alexander*, edited by Gary W. Gallagher. In his draft Alexander sometimes referred to maps, reports, and figures he intended to add to his manuscript; some of this material is presented in the endnotes to this volume.

THIS BRINGS us to the Seven Days fighting about Richmond. I will give a little map & will outline briefly the principal events & can then in a very small space outline my personal experiences during their occurrence.

Early in June, Gen. Stonewall Jackson, whose reputation up to this time had simply been that of a desperate & stubborn fighter (having only fought so far in the battle of Bull Run), suddenly broke loose up in the Valley of Virginia & not only astonished the weak minds of the enemy almost into paralysis, but dazzled the eyes of military men all over the world by an aggressive campaign which I believe to be unsurpassed in all military history for brilliancy & daring. It seems indeed to me to be only approached by Napoleon's best Italian campaigns. I write away from all books of reference & cannot therefore go into any details, but in general terms what he did was about as follows.

There were two Federal armies out after him in the Valley, one coming up the Valley from the north & one over the mountains from the south west, both superior to him in numbers. Meanwhile, too, McDowell with about 40,000 was at Fredericksburg about 100 miles to his east. But McD. was out not for Jackson, but for Richmond & to co-operate with McClellan against Lee. And he was just about to move too when Jackson began his performances by bouncing upon the army in front of him in the Valley—under Banks I believe—& giving it a complete defeat at Strasburg on _____ & chasing it down the Valley nearly or quite to the Potomac River. This alarmed the Federals for Washington & McDowell was stopped from his proposed advance to Richmond & was ordered to send a strong body of troops to get behind Jackson & unite with the force advancing from the southwest under Frémont. But Jackson hurried back from the Potomac so rapidly as to get between these converging enemies & to defeat each of them separately & to drive each of them back. These battles took place on Jun. 8 & 9th.

Gen. Lee now conceived the plan of bringing Jackson down from the Valley swiftly & secretly & having him surprise & fall upon the Federal right flank. This was posted at Ellison's Mill on Beaver Dam Creek in the same beautiful position—absolutely impregnable to a front attack—which we engineers had selected for our own left-flank had we taken line of battle north of the Chickahominy. Thence the Federal line ran down the Chick. to below the Nine Mile or New Bridge Road, crossing where it crossed & ran over past Seven Pines.

Gen. Lee issued a regular battle order setting forth his whole plan in detail & I cannot explain it better than by simply copying the official copy of it which I received as chief of ordnance. This order & the map will make all clear.

Meanwhile also elaborate efforts were made to deceive the enemy by making him think that our game was to reinforce Jackson strongly up in the Valley, & have him make a vigorous attack on Washington itself. For this purpose Whiting's division (2 brigades, his own & Hood's) was withdrawn from our lines, & sent by rail up to Jackson. Also Lawton's big brigade, arriving from Savannah, was also railroaded up to Jackson. But all was so planned that by railroad & by marching, they would all be back, & all of Jackson's original men with them, concentrated at Ashland on the evening of Wednesday, Jun. 25th. There the battle order took them in hand at 3 A.M. on June 26th,

& started them to march around the enemy's flank at Beaver Dam & to cross the creek above it & to take the enemy in rear, while A. P. & D. H. Hill crossing by Meadow Bridge & Mechanicsville roads threatened its front.

And now I shall have to tell, as my narrative proceeds, of how upon several occasions in the progress of the fighting during the next six days, Gen. Lee's best hopes & plans were upset & miscarried, & how he was prevented from completely destroying & capturing McClellan's whole army & all its stores & artillery by the incredible slackness, & delay & hanging back, which characterized Gen. Jackson's performance of his part of the work.

But little has been said about it in the press. As compared with Longstreet's alleged shortcomings at Gettysburg nothing at all. Gen. Fitzhugh Lee, in his life of Gen. Lee, devotes pages to the latter, & does not remotely refer to the former. But to suppress it robs Gen. Lee of the credit of what seems to me perhaps his greatest achievement. As it was, within a month of taking command he scattered all the tremendous forces concentrated for his destruction & practically deposed McClellan, the "Young Napoleon" of the Federals. But think of the moral effect on the country, & the world had he captured this entire army of 100,000 men with all its stores & arms & artillery. And this he would indoubtedly have done had the Gen. Jackson of those six days been the same Gen. Jackson who had marched & fought in the Valley but a few weeks before, or the same who upon every other battlefield afterward—Cedar Mountain, Second Manassas, Harpers Ferry, Sharpsburg, & Fredericksburg, to his lamented death at Chancellorsville in May '63—made a reputation unequalled in military annals. And just to think—it was practically all done within less than 12 months.

We of Gen. Lee's staff knew at the time that he was deeply, bitterly disappointed, but he made no official report of it & glossed all over as much as possible in his own reports. Indeed, I never thoroughly understood the matter until long after, when all the official reports were published, & I read Gen. Jackson's own statements of times & things, & those of the officers under him & compared them with what I knew of the whole situation.

The question naturally arises, what was the matter with him?

Although the public has heard little of the matter, it has by no means entirely escaped comment and I will give presently some of the things which have been said by Gen. D. H. Hill, his brother in law, & others of his friends.

For myself I think that the one defect in Gen. Jackson's character as a soldier was his religious belief. He believed, with absolute faith, in a personal God, watching all human events with a jealous eye to His own glory—ready to reward those people who made it their chief care, & to punish those who forgot about it. And he specially believed that a particular day had been set aside every week for the praise of this God, & that a personal account was strictly kept with every man as to how he kept this day & that those who disregarded it need expect no favors, but that those who sacrificed all other considerations, however recklessly, to honoring Him by its observance, would be rewarded conspicuously. And I see in Gen. Jackson's whole conduct during the Seven Days a sort of faith that he had God on his side & could trust to Him for victory without overexerting himself & his men.

The only quotation I have at hand concerning Gen. Jackson's conduct during the fighting is from Gen. D. H. Hill, who was Gen. Jackson's brother-in-law & was in his command at the time. In an account of the movements on June 30th & July 1st ending with the Battle of Malvern Hill, published in the Century War Book, Gen. H. says—speaking of the affair at White Oak Swamp on June 30th (which will be more fully explained later):

Our cavalry returned by the lower ford & pronounced it perfectly practicable for infantry. But Jackson did not advance. Why was this? It was the critical day for both commanders, but especially for McClellan. With consummate skill he had crossed his vast train of 5,000 wagons & his immense parks of artillery safely over White Oak Swamp, but he was more exposed now than at any time in his flank march. Three columns of attack were converging upon him, and a strong corps was pressing upon his rear. Escape seemed impossible for him, but he did escape. . . . Gen. Lee through no fault in his plans was to see his splendid prize slip through his hands. Longstreet & A. P. Hill struck the enemy at Frazier's Farm (or Glendale) at 3 P.M., and, both being always ready for a fight, immediately attacked. Magruder, who followed them down the Darbytown Road was ordered to the assistance of Gen. Holmes on the New Market Road, who was not then engaged, & their two divisions took no part in the action. Huger, on the Charles City Road, came upon Franklin's left flank but made no attack. . . . So there were five divisions within sound of the firing, & within supporting distance, but not one of them moved. . . . Maj. Dabney in his life of Jackson thus comments on the inaction of that officer: "On this occasion it would appear, if the vast interests dependent upon Gen. Jackson's co-operation with the proposed attack upon the centre were considered, that he came short of the efficiency in action for which he was everywhere else noted." After showing how the crossing of White Oak might have been effected, Dabney adds: "The list of casualties would have been larger than that presented on the 30th, of one cannoneer wounded, but how much shorter would have been the bloody list filled up the next day at Malvern Hill. This temporary eclipse of Jackson's genius was probably to be explained by physical causes. The labor of the previous days, the sleeplessness, the wear of gigantic cares with the drenching of the comfortless night, had sunk the elasticity of his will, & the quickness of his invention for the nonce below their wonted tension."

And Gen. Hill adds his own solution of the mystery as follows: "I think that an important factor in this inaction was Jackson's pity for his own corps, worn out by long & exhausting marches, & reduced in numbers by its numerous sanguinary battles. He thought that the garrison of Richmond ought now to bear the brunt of the fighting."

This seems to be to me a most remarkable excuse to be tendered by a friend. It was indeed whispered about in the army afterward that Gen. Jackson had said that he did not intend that his corps should do all the fighting, but it was regarded as a slander. I don't think Major Dabney's excuse that his inaction was due to physical exhaustion will at all bear analysis. For three successive nights & two entire days, since the battle of Gaines's Mill, he had been in camp near that battlefield. He had especially done nothing all day Sunday—although every hour then was precious. My own solution of the matter is that he thought that God could & would easily make up for any little shortcomings of his own & give us the victory anyhow.

But in this connection I will quote only one sentence more from Gen. D. H. Hill: "Had all our troops been at Frazer's Farm there would have been no Malvern Hill." And perhaps it is as well to put here also, what Gen. Franklin said about it—who was opposite Jackson on the 30th at White Oak Swamp. It is also from the Century War Book.

And now I can go back to my narrative & outline of the principal events which is to be completed before taking up the story of my small individual experiences.

Gen. Jackson started down to Richmond for a personal conference with Gen. Lee on the approaching event, by rail on Saturday, June 21. The train was due to arrive in Richmond about daylight Sunday morning & the conference might easily have been held on Sunday. But Gen. J. was unwilling to travel on Sunday, at least when such momentous events were in hand. So before midnight he left the train at Louisa C.H., spent the rest of the night with a friend, attended church, two or three times the next day, Sunday, & then, after 12 o'clock Sunday night, mounted his horse & rode the balance of the way to Richmond, about 60 miles—I have not at hand the details of the hour of his arrival, the time of the conference & the time of his return to his command, but all were from 24 to 48 hours later than they need have been, & Gen. Jackson had more over the personal fatigue of a very trying horseback ride of ____ miles. But I believe neither Prest. Davis or Gen. Lee disapproved, & I have no doubt that Gen. Jackson thought that such a conspicuous respect for the Sabbath at such a time would do more to give us a victory than all that his whole army could accomplish without special Divine aid. Wednesday night found himself & his whole command concentrated at Ashland.

He was ordered to march for the enemy's flank at 3 A.M. on Thursday but the official reports which mention the hour of starting all concur that it was after sunrise. The distance he had to go to the enemy's flank was about ____ miles, & early that morning the whole of Gen. Lee's army on the south of the Chickahominy was alert & listening for Jackson's guns & ready to take their respective parts as laid down in the order of battle already given. I remember seeing Mr. Davis & his staff on the hills overlooking the Chickahominy, near the Mechanicsville Road, where Gen. Lee had made his temporary head qrs., & my recollection is that he came as early, at 10 or eleven o'clock, & was on or about the ground all day. For hour after hour passed & nothing was heard of Jackson. At last about 3 P.M., when it was plain that the day was almost gone, our extreme left flank, A. P. Hill's division, crossed the Chick. at Meadow Bridge & started the ball without him, hoping he would still turn up by the time the fight became hot. Hill, on crossing, moved down stream & soon cleared off the small Federal forces about Mechanicsville & opened that road, when D. H. Hill brought over a part of his division & joined him.

They found themselves confronted by the Federal right flank under Fitz John Porter, behind Beaver Dam Creek, near Ellison's Mill. It was the very position told of selected by the engineers & myself for our own flank, had we fought on that side of the river, & they had fortified it with infantry breast works, & pits for guns, & by cutting down all timber in range to give unobstructed fire. The valley of the creek was rendered impassable by the fallen trees & brush, & by the creek on one side of it, & the mill race on the slope of the eastern bank, just in front of the enemy's line. Briefly there was no cover in front within musket range, say 400 yards, & the enemy's line could not be reached by an assaulting force, & his men were quite well sheltered from fire. But there were our people in front of it, & the day was drawing to a close & our major generals were all brash to do something. And the full strength of the position, particularly the inaccessible feature of it, was not apparent to the eye until one had entirely crossed the plain swept by their fire & gotten actually up to the valley of the creek. A. P. Hill's men, advancing confidently were at first allowed by the enemy to approach quite closely, when a sudden & tremendous fire of infantry & artillery at short range drove them back with some loss. We then brought up artillery, & a very severe duel ensued between, perhaps, fifty guns about equally divided between the two sides & there was also some heavy musketry, but at rather long range. A. P. Hill seems now to have recognised the strength of the position—at least he did not again force his infantry close upon it.

But somehow it happened that two regts. of Ripley's brigade of D. H. Hill's division were ordered to charge it. It was a tragic illustration of the absurdities which often happen upon battlefields. Fitz John Porter had about 25,000 men sheltered

& inaccessible & about 1,500 are launched into his fire & told to charge him home. The regiments sent were big green regiments never before under fire but full of the spirit & prestige given to our whole army by our former successes.

Had those green regiments been given anything to do which was within the bounds of possibility it seems reasonable to believe that they would have done it, & in doing it acquired a self confidence which would have made them ever afterward as near invincible as soldiers can get to be. For their charge was indeed a glorious one. Across the level meadows which stretched from Mechanicsville to the edge of the rather deep & narrow Beaver Dam valley, where even every occasional scattered shade tree had been previously cut down by the enemy to give a free field of fire, they swept without a break through all the fire the enemy could throw. And when they finally reached the rather steep descent into the valley, with its swamp & felled timber & creek & race—all within 200 yards of Fitz John Porter's intrenched 20,000—they knew too little of war to turn back but plunged on down & into the entanglement.

There is no wonder that, as the Federal officer wrote, their dead laid "like flies in a bowl of sugar." The following details from the official reports will assist in forming a correct idea of the affair.

Where was General Jackson with his 20,000 men? The official reports show that he went quietly into camp before sundown at Pole Green Church with the noise of the musketry & artillery at Beaver Dam only 3 miles away ringing in his ears. He had marched only 14 miles over good roads & had no opposition except that a single squadron of Federal cavalry had opposed his crossing of Totopotomoy Creek for a little while & then made their escape without loss. A further advance that afternoon of 3 1/2 miles would have completely cut off the retreat of Fitz John Porter's whole corps. Not until the next morning did Fitz John retire safely bag & baggage to the position behind Powhite Creek not far from Gaines's Mill 3 miles below. Comfortably the next morning Gen. Jackson made the 3 1/2 mile march, which closed the trap Gen. Lee had designed for the capture of Porter, & then turning to his right advanced towards where Porter had been the night before. Presently seeing some skirmishers approaching he fired on them with artillery. They were the advance of A. P. Hill's men who had discovered the enemy's retreat & were following. Jackson's fire took the arm off of Capt. Heise of Columbia, S.C., a gentleman I knew well in after years.

Gen. Lee now had 3 divisions, A. P. Hill, D. H. Hill, & Longstreet, across the Chick. & united with Jackson, having his own & Ewell's divisions & the two brigades of Hood & Whiting united under the latter, say 5 1/4 or 6 divisions—& about 50,000 men.

The enemy had excellent engineers & had found a new position nearly as strong as Beaver Dam. I will quote from Gen. Fitz John Porter in the Century War Book:

> The position selected was east of Powhite Creek, about 6 miles from Beaver Dam Creek. The line of battle was semicircular, the extremities being in the Valley of the Chickahominy while the intermediate portion occupied the high grounds along the bank of the creek, & curved around past McGehee's to Elder Swamp. Part of the front was covered by the ravine of the creek. The east bank was lined with trees & underbrush which afforded concealment & protection to our troops, & artillery. . . . Our new line of battle was well selected & strong though long & requiring either more troops to man it than I had, or too great a thinning of my line by the use of the reserves. The east bank of the creek, from the valley of the Chick. to its swampy sources, was elevated sloping & timbered. The bed of the stream was nearly dry, & its west bank gave excellent protection to the first line of infantry, posted under it, to receive the enemy descending the cleared field sloping to it. The swampy grounds along the sources of the creek were open to our view in front for hundreds of yards, & were swept by the fire of infantry & artillery. The roads from Gaines's Mill, & Old Cold Harbor, along which the enemy were compelled to advance, were swept by artillery posted on commanding ground.

In this strong position Porter had about 30,000 men & 75 guns. Slocum reinforced Porter at 4 P.M. with 10,000 & French & Meagher after sundown with 4,000.

Lee's forces crowded the available roads & their advance was slow, but about noon, A. P. Hill got into action with a small advanced force of the enemy at Gaines's Mill, & drove it back upon the main body—& before two o'clock we were up against the enemy's line, A. P. Hill on our right, with Longstreet behind him, Jackson on our left, & all the rest in reserve and in between.

Strong as was Porter's position we had men good enough & enough of them to have beaten him on the very first charge, had one grand simultaneous effort been made. But somehow, God only knows how, every body else seemed to stand still & let A. P. Hill's division, from 2 o'clock until near or quite four, wreck itself in splendid, but vain & bloody, isolated assaults.

But I will again let our adversary, Fitz John Porter tell about it. (He was my old instructor in cavalry drill & tactics at West Point & was one of the best soldiers in all the Federal army.) He first says (in the same article already quoted) about Jackson's strange inactivity opposite his right flank, "The advance column of these troops came a little earlier than those under Longstreet & A. P. Hill, *but were more cautious, and for some hours not so aggressive*" (the italics are mine). Not only was a great deal of useless blood shed caused by the loss of those hours, but the precious daylight was lost, necessary to gather the fruits of victory when finally won. And this is his description of A. P. Hill's fight:

Soon after 2 P.M., A. P. Hill's force, between us & New Cold Harbor again began to show an aggressive disposition, independent of its own troops on its flanks, by advancing from under cover of the woods, in lines well formed & extending, as the contest progressed from in front of Martin's battery to Morell's left. Dashing across the intervening plains, floundering in the swamps, & struggling against the tangled brushwood, brigade after brigade seemed almost to melt away before the concentrated fire of our artillery & infantry; yet others pressed on, followed by supports as dashing & as brave as their predecessors, despite their heavy losses, & the disheartening effect of having to clamber over many of their disabled & dead, & to meet their surviving comrades rushing back in great disorder from the deadly contest. For nearly two hours the battle raged, extending more or less along the whole line to our extreme right. The fierce firing of artillery & infantry, the crash of the shot, the bursting of shells & the whizzing of bullets, heard above the war of artillery & the volleys of musketry, all combined was something fearful.

Regiments quickly replenished their exhausted ammunition by borrowing from more bountifully supplied & generous companions.

Some withdrew, temporarily, for ammunition, & fresh regiments took their places, ready to repulse, sometimes to pursue, their desperate enemy for the purpose of retaking ground from which we had been pressed, & which it was necessary to occupy in order to hold our position.

It was only after A. P. Hill's division was worn out to a frazzle, and when Fitz John Porter had received a reinforcement of a fresh division under Slocum, that the rest of the Confederate divisions began to be put in, & even then attacks were disjointed & partial until near about sundown, when at last Gen. Lee had gradually gotten every thing in, & when a charge by Hood's Texas Brigade finally carried one of the strongest parts of the enemy's line. This break was promptly followed by others at many places, & the bloody victory was ours. But the lateness of the hour, & two fresh brigades sent to him across the Chick., enabled Porter to make an excellent retreat & with wonderfully little loss.

Had Jackson attacked when he first arrived, or during A. P. Hill's attack, we would have had an easy victory—comparatively, & would have captured most of Porter's command. Gen. D. H. Hill wrote in the Century article before quoted, "Porter's weak point at Gaines's Mill was his right flank. A thorough examination of the ground would have disclosed that, & had Jackson's command gone in on the left of the road running by the McGehee house, Porter's whole position would have been turned & the line of retreat cut off."

Had our army been as well organised at this time as it became afterward, & as seasoned to battle, the morning after the battle—Sat., June 28—would doubtless have brought us active movements for new dispositions. For though the enemy had successfully withdrawn his defeated men & guns to the south side of the Chick., we had his whole army cut off from their base of supplies, at the White House on the Pamunkey River, & it was plain that they would have to move, & that immediately. It was a question whether they would go to the James River near City Point, where their fleet & supplies could meet them; or whether they would seek to recross the Chick. lower down & go back to the York.

Ewell's division & Stuart's cavalry were sent down the Chick. on the north side to reconnoitre & see what they were doing.

They were abandoning & burning what they could not move & it was clear that they had adopted the first mentioned alternative. The other divisions all laid in camp or bivouac all of the 28th, recovering from the wear & tear of the battle, caring for wounded, & burying dead of both sides.

BATTLE OF GAINES'S MILL:
VIRGINIA, JUNE 1862

Charles A. Page:
from Letters of a War Correspondent

Correspondent Charles A. Page's account of the battle of Gaines's Mill (June 27) appeared in the *New-York Daily Tribune* on July 4. While Fitz John Porter's Fifth Corps fought for its life north of the Chickahominy, McClellan held his four other army corps south of the river, facing Richmond, expecting to be attacked by Confederate forces he imagined to be 200,000 strong.

SAVAGE'S STATION, Saturday, June 28, 1862.

THE EVENTS of the last two days, recounted in detail, with full lists of the casualties, would require a triple sheet of the "Tribune." Set forth with the ordinary discursiveness of army correspondents, McClellan might push forward to Richmond or be pushed back to Yorktown, before the task were completed by one pen. I shrink from even so much as I mark out for this letter. At no time in the history of the campaign have events so tread upon each other, and at this hour they seem to thicken in a whirl of the immediate future. God grant that these last two days of June, which loom up so portentous, may hasten our advent into Richmond more than the last forty-eight hours seem to have done!

Day before yesterday Porter's corps was strongly attacked in his position at the extreme right, near Mechanicsville, at a late hour in the afternoon. Not being on the ground, I am unable to give a detailed account; but the general features are given me by the brigade commanders.

McCall's Division bore the brunt of the encounter, though Morrell was severely engaged. Our superiority in artillery compensated in a measure for their superiority in numbers.

During long hours of the declining day and through half the night, anxious thousands of brave hearts who fight under Hooker and Keyes and Heintzelman and Sumner listened to that tremendous cannonading, and wondered how it fared with their brethren in arms.

Every attack was magnificently repelled, every inch of ground retained. Our loss was 300 to 400. It was the opinion of our generals that the position could have been maintained yesterday, but authentic information having reached General McClellan that the enemy had been re-enforced by Stonewall Jackson, our whole force was ordered to the Chickahominy, and the movement commenced during the night. The Eighth Illinois Cavalry, Colonel Farnsworth, formed the vigilant rear-guard. The enemy followed closely, took numbers of prisoners, including Company K, of the Pennsylvania Bucktails, and forced our quartermasters to burn at least $100,000 worth of stores. Captain Hooker, one of the best officers of the Eighth Illinois, was mortally wounded and left on the field. But the concentration of forces designed was effected with less loss than was doubtless expected when the order was given. Early in the forenoon of yesterday the pursued columns had taken position on the east bank of the Chickahominy and awaited the pursuers. They had not to wait long.

At this juncture your correspondent reached the field, and henceforth the narrative is that of an eye-witness.

The battle was fought in dense woods. Our forces were posted on the south side of a belt of forest on a line nearly two miles long, the general course of which was nearly parallel with the Chickahominy. The woods vary in depth from forty to one hundred rods; a small stream flows the entire length, and the ascent on either side is quite sharp. Cultivated fields cover the brow and crest of the hills on either side, and in the right rear of our position extend half a mile to the bottom-land of the Chickahominy. On the left the fringe of woods reaches to this bottom-land. At eleven A. M., when I reached the field, our pickets occupied the top of the hill across the ravine along its whole winding length. They reported a battery of the enemy at Gaines House, a mile north in his left rear, and numbers of Rebels in distinct view. This battery soon exchanged shots with guns on our right. Half an hour later they saluted our left with an occasional shell from a position so far westerly as to enfilade our line. Meanwhile an occasional report from a sharpshooter's rifle warned of the enemy's approach. The fire of our batteries on the right gradually grew more rapid, but the day wore away until it was three P. M., and there had been few casualties. *Would the enemy make a serious demonstration?* A volley from one company of a regiment on the left, directed at as many of the enemy who appeared on the crest of the opposite hill, causing them to hurry back, did not answer the question conclusively, for it was followed by dead silence. Twenty minutes later the answer came, and it was unmistakable—it was a tornado of musketry.

Butterfield's Brigade was on our extreme left, Martindale's at his right, Griffin's next, and at our extreme right Sykes' Division of regulars. McCall's Division formed the second line, and were held in reserve.

The ball opened with the centre, but only a moment, and the tornado swept right and left as if one current of electricity had discharged every man's musket. Our men disappeared, sending back cheerful shouts as they rushed into that dense wood where now corpses are thick as the trees. A spatter of Rebel lead lifted little puffs of dust on the hill from which, with straining eyes, I in vain sought to penetrate those dark recesses. A dull, heavy undercurrent of murmur as of the swarming of bees, the sharp ring of a random Minie overhead, the incessant roar of musketry, and now the wounded and the dead being borne out of those jaws of death tell how fierce is the fight. There are cheers and yells, for our men *cheer*, while they, like other savages, *yell*. But we drive them. As yet their superior numbers, enabling them to oppose always with fresh troops, do not tell. The fire slackens from left to right.

A tawny sergeant, whose moustache would vie with a Turkish pasha's tails—I see the fierce light in his eyes now—inquires of me where he shall carry the wounded man he bears on his back, and says, "The sinners are skedaddling!"

The battle had now raged three-fourths of an hour; Slocum's Division, which had already marched to the Chickahominy, was ordered up and McCall had not been engaged. The situation appeared promising. But only a small portion of the enemy's force had been beaten, and he was not disposed to cry quits. For the next hour the terrific firing would break out now at one point, anon at another, indicating that fresh columns were being continually pushed against our decimated lines. During this time every man of McCall's Pennsylvania Reserve was brought into action. Some time earlier his regiments had rushed at double-quick to the supporting positions assigned them, and had thrown themselves flat upon the ground till the order should come, "Up and at them!" At intervals, as some point in the line seemed weak, they went sternly into that wooded valley and shadow of death. Up to this time not a regiment had behaved unseemly. When relieved by new men, to be sure, they would straggle out like a dispersing mob, but they did not fail to "fall in" on the hill at the order. Sometimes a wounded man would be surrounded by a suspicious number of friends, but the skulkers bore no proportion to the true men.

Still at this hour, between half-past five and six, the situation was not hopeful. Beat back as many Rebel regiments as you would, fresh ones were poured into their places. The evidence is conclusive that no repelled assault—and there were a score of such—was renewed by the same column. Our coolest officers began to perceive that the enemy's force was overwhelming— probably 75,000, and 25,000 larger than had been anticipated or provided for.

At this time, Slocum's Division (late Franklin's) was brought into action. There were no more reserves, save cavalry. Every available regiment was fighting or had become exhausted in strength and in cartridges.

I saw Slocum's men go into the fight, and they did it handsomely, the brigades being conducted to their positions amid a murderous fire, by Lieut. Fred. Mead of his staff, who, sick for a month, left his couch for the battle-field. But I confess, from this time on, so great was the confusion that I know nothing circumstantial of the movements and fighting of the several brigades and regiments of any of the divisions, notwithstanding I was coaxed some distance into the woods by Mr. Crountze of "The World," who seemed bent on securing a place among the martyrs.

My note-book says that, at six o'clock, the enemy commenced a determined attack on our extreme left, evidently with a design of flanking us. It was an awful firing that resounded from that smoke-clouded valley,—not heavier than some in the earlier part of the engagement, but more steady and determined. I am told that some men on the other side and farther up the river saw more than a dozen Rebel regiments march in at that point, and, remaining only a few minutes, file out a little distance up the ravine. It was only by overbearing exhausted men with fresh ones that the enemy succeeded in turning that flank, as at length he did succeed, only too well. And he accomplished it in three-quarters of an hour. At the expiration of that time our officers judiciously ordered their men to fall back; the order was not obeyed so judiciously, for they ran back broken, disordered, routed. Simultaneously the wounded and skulkers about the buildings used as hospitals caught a panic, whether from a few riderless horses plunging madly across the field, or from instantaneously scenting the rout, does not appear. A motley mob started pell-mell for the bridges. They were overtaken by many just from the woods, and it seemed as if Bull Run were to be repeated.

As the infantry betook themselves from the point of attack, some twenty guns, fortunately posted in the morning for such an emergency, and which had not yet made a sign, opened a terrific fire of canister at short range. The enemy recoiled. The bridge of Lodi was not half so terrible. Until night set in, until the Valley of the Chickahominy was canopied with sulphur, until their ammunition was exhausted—and many of them went upon the field with over two-hundred rounds—did those guns hold the raging enemy at bay.

Meanwhile, the panic extended. Scores of gallant officers endeavored to rally and re-form the stragglers, but in vain, while many officers forgot the pride of their shoulder-straps and the honor of their manhood, and herded with sneaks and cowards. O that I had known the names of those officers I saw, the brave and the cowardly, that here, now, I might reward and punish by directing upon each individual the respect or the contempt of a whole people!

That scene was not one to be forgotten. Scores of riderless, terrified horses dashing in every direction; thick-flying bullets singing by, admonishing of danger; every minute a man struck down; wagons and ambulances and cannon blockading the way; wounded men limping and groaning and bleeding amid the throng; officers and civilians denouncing and reasoning and entreating, and being insensibly borne along with the mass; the sublime cannonading; the clouds of battle-smoke, and the sun just disappearing, large and blood-red—I cannot picture it, but I see it, and always shall.

Among those most earnest in withstaying the frightened host was ex-Governor Wood of Illinois. A large, handsome old man, with a flowing white beard and the voice of a Stentor. I should not have been astonished had those poor, bewildered men taken him for some old patriarch risen from the dead and calling to them; *had* one risen from the dead they would not have heeded him. I thought, too, of the old regicide who left his concealment to head the simple Puritan villagers against the savages, and then vanished as quickly, leaving his appearance as the tradition of a heavenly visitant.

About this time a new battery and two fresh regiments of Meagher's Brigade were brought up, headed by that officer. The mob parted, and they passed rapidly through, cheering as they went. The answering cheers were sickly.

I do not wish to be harsh with these men. Many of them had fought and marched all the previous day and night. The day was excessively hot. The men were exhausted. I do not think they left the field with an average of two cartridges to the man. If there was a single regiment that did not go into the battle with spirit and maintain it with credit, I do not know it. Besides, he must be a brave and a strong man who whips three of equal training. This much in extenuation. Add to it the statement of several generals that men never fought better. Still, I cannot refrain from expressing the one thought that possessed me at the time,—the fact that 10,000 men were in full retreat.

Some time after the main body had passed on, when that stream had become decently small, in company with Governor Wood, I rode to find the Illinois Cavalry, and came upon them stretched across the plain halting every unwounded man. They had cooped up several thousands, but the task of re-forming them was found impossible by even such officers as their Colonel and Major Clendenning, and they were at length permitted to continue rearward.

I crossed the Chickahominy at eleven P. M., at which time comparative order had been restored. The enemy were in possession of our hospitals and the battle-field, but we still showed a determined front. It was not known by the brigadier-generals whether we should try to hold the position the next day, or cross the river during the night.

At six o'clock this morning I rode to the bridge, with the intention of re-crossing, but was some distance off when I heard the explosion that destroyed it, the force having passed over mainly after midnight. It is impossible at this day to estimate our loss. But few of the dead were brought from the field, and not one-half the wounded. Hundreds of the latter were brought as far as the river, but could not be brought over before the destruction of the bridges. Basing my opinion on the number who were brought over (about 800), and the proportion that number must bear to the remainder, I estimate, the entire wounded at 3500 and the killed at 800. How many prisoners and what amount of stores are lost, it is even still more difficult to estimate. I judge but few stores and several thousand prisoners. The loss in officers is particularly severe.

AN ACCUSATION OF BETRAYAL:
VIRGINIA, JUNE 1862

George B. McClellan to Edwin M. Stanton

Even before the Gaines's Mill defeat, General McClellan determined to give up his campaign and retreat across the Peninsula to the James River and the protection of the navy's gunboats. This telegram to the secretary of war reveals his greatly distorted view of events. The concluding paragraph so shocked the head of the War Department telegraph office that he deleted it before delivering the telegram to Stanton.

Savage Station June 28 12.20 am

I now know the full history of the day. On this side of the river—the right bank—we repulsed several very strong attacks. On the left bank our men did all that men could do, all that soldiers could accomplish—but they were overwhelmed by vastly superior numbers even after I brought my last reserves into action. The loss on both sides is terrible—I believe it will prove to be the most desperate battle of the war. The sad remnants of my men behave as men—those battalions who fought most bravely & suffered most are still in the best order. My regulars were superb & I count upon what are left to turn another battle in company with their gallant comrades of the Volunteers. Had I (20,000) twenty thousand or even (10,000) ten thousand fresh troops to use tomorrow I could take Richmond, but I have not a man in reserve & shall be glad to cover my retreat & save the material & personnel of the Army.

If we have lost the day we have yet preserved our honor & no one need blush for the Army of the Potomac. I have lost this battle because my force was too small. I again repeat that I am not responsible for this & I say it with the earnestness of a General who feels in his heart the loss of every brave man who has been needlessly sacrificed today. I still hope to retrieve our fortunes, but to do this the Govt must view the matter in the same earnest light that I do—you must send me very large reinforcements, & send them at once.

I shall draw back to this side of the Chickahominy & think I can withdraw all our material. Please understand that in this battle we have lost nothing but men & those the best we have.

In addition to what I have already said I only wish to say to the Presdt that I think he is wrong, in regarding me as ungenerous when I said that my force was too weak. I merely reiterated a truth which today has been too plainly proved. I should have gained this battle with (10,000) ten thousand fresh men. If at this instant I could dispose of (10,000) ten thousand fresh men I could gain the victory tomorrow.

I know that a few thousand men more would have changed this battle from a defeat to a victory—as it is the Govt must not & cannot hold me responsible for the result.

I feel too earnestly tonight—I have seen too many dead & wounded comrades to feel otherwise than that the Govt has not sustained this Army. If you do not do so now the game is lost.

If I save this Army now I tell you plainly that I owe no thanks to you or any other persons in Washington—you have done your best to sacrifice this Army.

G B McClellan

Hon E M Stanton

June 28, 1862

"THE PRESENT CONDITION OF THE WAR":
WASHINGTON, D.C., JUNE 1862

Abraham Lincoln to William H. Seward

Secretary of State Seward took this letter with him to New York for a conference with Northern governors, intending to craft a call for new troops. Seward reversed the usual process and persuaded the governors to "respectfully request" of Lincoln "that you at once call upon the several States for such number of men as may be required. . . ." Seward backdated the request to June 28 to avoid any note of panic over McClellan's failings on the Peninsula. Lincoln hastened to "comply" with the governors' call, setting the figure at 300,000. The evacuation of Corinth in northern Mississippi that the President mentions saw the Confederates' western army evade the clutches of General Halleck's hugely superior force.

Hon. W. H. Seward   Executive Mansion
My dear Sir   June 28. 1862.

My view of the present condition of the War is about as follows:

The evacuation of Corinth, and our delay by the flood in the Chicahominy, has enabled the enemy to concentrate too much force in Richmond for McClellan to successfully attack. In fact there soon will be no substantial rebel force any where else. But if we send all the force from here to McClellan, the enemy will, before we can know of it, send a force from Richmond and take Washington. Or, if a large part of the Western Army be brought here to McClellan, they will let us have Richmond, and retake Tennessee, Kentucky, Missouri &c. What should be done is to hold what we have in the West, open the Mississippi, and, take Chatanooga & East Tennessee, without more—a reasonable force should, in every event, be kept about Washington for it's protection. Then let the country give us a hundred thousand new troops in the shortest possible time, which added to McClellan, directly or indirectly, will take Richmond, without endangering any other place which we now hold—and will substantially end the war. I expect to maintain this contest until successful, or till I die, or am conquered, or my term expires, or Congress or the country forsakes me; and I would publicly appeal to the country for this new force, were it not that I fear a general panic and stampede would follow—so hard is it to have a thing understood as it really is. I think the new force should be all, or nearly all infantry, principally because such can be raised most cheaply and quickly. Yours very truly

A. LINCOLN

THE UNION RETREAT:
VIRGINIA, JUNE–JULY 1862

Charles B. Haydon:
Journal, June 25–July 1, 1862

Lieutenant Charles B. Haydon, 2nd Michigan, served in Philip Kearny's division, Army of the Potomac. His journal describes his experiences in the Seven Days. He witnessed the first battle, on June 25 at Oak Grove, a stunted Union advance. Lee's offensive at Mechanicsville and Gaines's Mill north of the Chickahominy was only heard by Haydon. In the retreat across the Peninsula the bitterest fighting he experienced was at Glendale on June 30, where Lee very nearly cut the Potomac army in half. Haydon was not engaged but under fire at the conclusion of the Seven Days, at Malvern Hill on the James. Despite the Union victory at Malvern Hill, McClellan continued his retreat to Harrison's Landing, farther down the James. The Seven Days' Battles cost the Confederates 20,204 men killed, wounded, or missing, while Union losses totaled 15,855.

JUNE 25, 1862 Was a clear cool day. Our Regt. & the 3d Mich. started for picket at 7 A.M. There was a pretty general movement of the troops in our Div. and in Hooker's. It is understood that certain parts of the line are to be advanced. Our left is stationary but a line of skirmishers is thrown forward extending toward the right across our picket front & Hooker's & perhaps farther. The skirmishers advance slowly a short distance when a fire is opened on Hooker's line. It gradually increased to heavy volleys & continued till about 11 A.M. when our men having gained the desired ground ceased to advance.

Everything was quiet till abt 2 P.M. when the enemy opened with field pieces & the musketry was soon after briskly renewed. The musketry soon slackened & the field pieces were reported as taken & retaken by bayonet charges. Four pieces were brought out into the edge of the woods & fired slowly till near night. The trees & bushes rendered them of little service. Abt 5 P.M. the Rebs raised a great shout & charged the battery. Our men lying concealed cut them terribly as they advanced. They gave way unable to stand the fire. For near half an hour there was a continuous & very heavy infantry fire. Several charges were made. The clear, ringing Union cheers & the sharp wild yells of the rebels were every few minutes heard with great distinctness. All we know is that the desired ground was without very great loss gained & held. The battle extended up to the right of our line but our Regt. was not engaged.

JUNE 26   Was a very quiet day till abt 3 P.M. when far to the right was heard the heavy but indistinct roar of musketry. The cannon opened soon after. From that time till 8 P.M. there was the heaviest cannonade I have yet heard. It was continued with great regularity and at the rate of 25 to 40 shots per minute. At dark far along the line toward the right great cheering was heard. It passed rapidly along to our camp. News soon came to us of a great battle & victory at Mechanicsville. The camps were wild with enthusiasm. Our joy was not less lively but we could not give vent to it in the same manner. I got most awfully wet & muddy going up & down the line carrying orders & cautioning the men to unusual vigilance lest the enemy should on some other part of the line attempt to redeem their fortunes. Save the heavy rumble of artillery & baggage wagons along our own lines the stillness of the night was hardly disturbed by a sound.

JUNE 27   We came off picket at 10 A.M. We were called to the rifle pits at one & remained till sundown. The firing on the right was renewed at daylight. It continued till 10 A.M., a part of the time with great rapidity. Towards night there was firing far to the north & much farther to the rear than was agreeable. Troops were seen soon after moving at double quick back along the R.R. This at once suggested that something was wrong but our men were so tired & sleepy that they paid little attention. They seemed to feel a sort of sullen, dogged determination to fight to the last where they were & not to move for anybody. A few more days & nights like the past few & they would as soon die as live. Soon after dark we were called out again & remained till after 10. The picket line is nearly broken up. The 63d Pa. ran like sheep as soon as they were fired on.

JUNE 28   We were called to the rifle pits at 2 1/2 A.M. and remained till 7 when we went in for breakfast but returned immediately after. Before daylight there was fighting far to the right. We could see the explosion of the shells but could not hear the guns. For several reasons I think it best to bring this book (a pocket memorandum) to a close. I cannot send it away & I do not wish it to fall into the hands of the rebels. It is possible it may if it remains with me.

Things just now are checkered. The right wing has fallen back & we are ready for a move of some kind. I dont know what it may be. If a retreat we are the rear guard. If this should be the last news from me good bye all at home. May God bless & prosper you. Arthur will use what money I leave to complete his education. We all realize our situation but everyone is calm, cheerful & determined. We carry 150 rounds of ammunition & intend that the enemy shall have reason to remember Kearney's Div. If I fall it will be in vain for you to attempt to recover my body. Having spoken of the dark side I may say that we by no means acknowledge that we are not to be victorious. I have still great hope of success in the coming battles. I half believe that this retreat is not forced. If it be we are still powerful to hold our own in a new position.

Arthur: my boy, if I should not see you again be of good cheer & console yourself with the thought that I died in a good cause. I would like right well to see you, Father, Eliza & all for a few minutes but it will make little difference in the end. But I have already said too much. We mean to send you news of the greatest victory of the war or at least to make like work for those who shall follow us. All the baggage has been sent away & the road is clear. The most perfect quiet prevails. The men are most of them talking in calm, subdued tones indicative of settled purpose. A few are slowly & silently walking to & fro communing with themselves. The weather is very hot. Ever since the battle of Williamsburgh I have seen some indications of what may happen.

There are many N.Y. & Penn. troops in our army. I have little confidence in them. If they were from Michigan, God bless the state, or from any of the western or New England states there would not be a shadow of doubt as to their conduct. If they run as is quite possible, we may be overwhelmed by numbers in spite of all exertions.

What tries my heart the worst is the disaster to the country if we are beaten. It is awful. Do not however despair. They will lose at least as many men as we & ours will be easier replaced. Wage the war to the last desolate acre of the accursed South. We are sure to conquer in the end. This defeat if it be one can be repaired in 30 days. If they are victorious they cannot live if we hold our ground in other places. I hope soon to see clear day through the clouds & uncertainty which now surround us. I intend to relate the events of this war beneath the shade of the glorious maples where we have passed so many happy hours.

Father: be the result what it may I thank you for having always been to me the kindest & best of parents. Eliza: placed as you were in a peculiar and difficult position as regards me you have always been more than I could have asked. Give my good wishes to all my old acquaintances. Arthur, I advise you to make your education liberal if health will permit but by all means look to that as your help will be needed at home before the other children are old enough to assist. I wish I could see the little ones. I feel a lively interest in them although we are still unacquainted. I have written thus because we all believe that our situation is one of uncommon danger.

JUNE 29   I was kept up all night by a multitude of orders. The tents were struck at 10 P.M. There was a light rain towards morning. We have destroyed everything we cannot carry. At 6 A.M. we moved off by the left flank to our left & rear halting near a sawmill. The rest of the brigade here passed us & went on further to the rear.

Everything is very quiet. There has been no firing since yesterday noon. When everything had passed we retired beyond the second line of rifle pits. We then deployed 5 Co's. across our front abt 1/4 mile off & halted till one P.M. We then fell back abt 3/4 of a mile. At this time Richardson's Div. was sharply engaged near the Williamsburgh road.

At 3 P.M. we retire still farther. The rest of the brigade has gone on & we are only waiting for our skirmishers. Hooker's Div. occupy the road. We have peremptory orders to join the brigade & attempt to pass them. We have to open right & left & a battery passes at full run. We continue retreating through the woods & bushes on each side & some confusion arises. The road becomes narrower & the confusion increases. Some other

Regts. try to crowd through & they make matters still worse. Our Regt. & most of the others are cool & perfectly manageable. The confusion is due entirely to want of efficiency on the part of the officers. The column should at once be halted till order is restored. More artillery passes. A Regt. at double quick cuts ours in two between the 3d & 4th Co's. Three Co's. continue on & 7 Co's. are thrown off to the left on another road. We went abt 1/2 mile when finding that matters were becoming worse the 38th N.Y. and our 3 Co's. filed out of the road & halted till the others passed. When the road is clear we move on again. Gen. Kearney orders us to go slowly as our 3 Co's. are "the rear guard of all God's Creation." This was an encouraging prospect for us with a total of 100 men.

We reach the swamp at Jordan's ford, are ordered to cross, to go to the Charles City road & hold it agt all comers. We cross the first ford, then a second one abt 60 rods wide with water 2 1/2 feet deep. We proceed abt a mile when a Co. of the 3d Maine encounter the enemy. We are deployed through the woods to support them. The force of the enemy is small & soon gives way.

Finding that they were in force nearby Gen. Kearney ordered us to fall back across the fords. Our Co's. were left to cover the retreat. I had hardly any expectation of escaping. The enemy moved down rapidly but our men were soon out of the way & we retired in line with a loss of only 3 men, on the extreme left of the line, who were taken by a party who tried to cut us off from the ford. Several smart volleys & a number of shells followed us but did no harm. We crossed the fords in good time, leaving other troops to guard them & made for another ford 3 miles lower down.

It was now dark. We marched rapidly & notwithstanding their prayers & entreaties we were compelled to leave by the roadside some wounded men of the 3d Maine who had been brought across both fords. We reached the ford abt 9 P.M. & learned that Hooker's Div. & the balance of our Regt. had crossed an hour & a half before. We considered ourselves fortunate to have got thus far though we were apprehensive that we should find the Rebs at the other end of the ford. We plunged in, crossed safely & marched till 11 P.M. The night was very dark

& we did not dare to proceed farther. Nearly choking for want of water we lay down & rested or slept for 3 hours. We were disturbed once by a loose horse which came galloping over us & once by picket firing.

JUNE 30   We were up at 2 A.M. We moved forward a mile & found the rest of the Regt. We move on 1/2 mile farther & halted in a fine open field to rest. We here made coffee, the first we had had in 24 hours. It refreshed us very much. We have nothing but hard crackers to eat. At noon the enemy appeared. We marched 1 1/2 miles at double quick & then formed our line. Our brigade was formed in columns in the woods & remained there an hour.

There is heavy cannonading on our right. We move back 1/2 mile farther. Musketry opens on our left, in front & soon after on our right. We advance to the front where a low, rude breastwork of logs, rails, stones, turf, anything to stop bullets had been hastily thrown up. Two batteries are in position. We are in the edge of woods, before us is an open field 60 rods wide in the wood on the other side of which is the enemy. The 20th Ind. were already at the work & there was no room for us. We move back abt 10 rods & lie flat down waiting for our turn.

The Rebs charge three times in heavy columns determined to break the line. The batteries double shotted with canister played on them at short range, some of the time not more than 10 rods, for an hour & a half. They were at the same time enveloped by the fire of the infantry. I never before saw such slaughter. The head of the column seemed to sink into the ground. Beyond a certain point they could not come. Four Regts. from behind the work kept up an incessant fire which was replied to by the enemy with equal rapidity.

Things remain thus till sundown when the batteries run out of ammunition. We relieve the 20th at the pits & the fire is carried on with renewed vigor. The enemy display a courage & determination known only to Americans. Darkness comes & the full moon shines forth in all its beauty but its mild, peaceful light only serves to render our aim more certain. For an hour after dark there is a steady succession of flashes which are almost blinding. The enemy cease firing. We give tremendous cheers. They send us a terrible volley which we return. Both parties then give three cheers & the day's work is done.

The Rebs were busy till 2 oclock carrying off their wounded. The wounded of 21 different Regts. lay on the field before us, as we learned from the Rebs themselves. Their cries & groans loaded the air, some calling for comrades, some for water, some praying to be killed & others swearing because they were not carried off the field. Our men lay close & the loss in our Regt. is light. The enemy sometimes in looking after their wounded came within a few feet of our picket line but we did not trouble them.

JULY 1, 1862   Gen. Richardson by hard fighting opened the road on which we are to retreat. While we held the enemy in front the army nearly all retreated. At 2 A.M. we withdraw as quietly as possible & commence our retreat. Our dead & all the wounded who could not walk had to be left. It was sad indeed the way the poor fellows begged to be taken along. It could not be done. The most of them will die. The Rebs cannot even take care of their own wounded. Our Regt. was separated by some runaway teams & troops coming in on another road got between the parts.

At sunrise we came to a large, open, undulating field in sight of James River. It was as beautiful a country as my eyes ever beheld. The cultivated field interspersed with belts & clusters of timber & dotted with delightful residences extended several miles. The hills were quite high but the slopes gradual & free from abruptness. Wheat was in the shock, oats were ready for the harvest & corn was abt waist high. All were of most luxuriant growth. The clusters of buildings are almost like villages.

All parts of the field are favorable for Cav. & Arty. There was hard fighting on a part of it yesterday. The country was laid waste, the fences burned, the harvested grain was used by the soldiers for beds & the unharvested was trodden into the ground. The field was covered with troops. I spent two hours in ineffectual search after our lost Co's. They rejoined us soon after I returned. Here we hoped for a little rest but it was not more than an hour before we had to fall in.

We made a circuit of about 2 miles then halted & our brigade was drawn up in a column by battalions on the back side of a gently sloping hill on the crest of which were two batteries. We had been here but a short time when the enemy appeared on the crest of another hill abt a mile off. The inclination of the ground was so slight that our brigade as well as the supports of their batteries could be seen from several points. Both parties opened with shot, shell & shrapnel. We had nothing to do but lie on the ground in the burning sun & take things just as they came.

Their shots were not wild. Almost the first shot (12 lbs. solid) struck among the N.Y. 1st as they lay on the ground killing two & wounding another. One of them was thrown more than 5 ft. into the air. A shell burst in the ground not 4 ft. from Benson's head. One struck abt 10 ft. short of me in the ground & exploded nearly burying me in sand & stubble. I caught a ball from a shrapnel shell before it stopped rolling. Two others struck within reach of me. Three men of our Co. were wounded by one shot. Most of their shell burst abt 150 feet in the air & the fragments scattered over a great space. The wounded were carried to the rear in considerable numbers. The loss of the brigade is 85.

The scene was exciting but I was so exhausted that despite the noise & the bullets I went to sleep. I know not how long I should have slept if the order "Fall in" had not aroused me. The 2d moved off to support another battery. I felt weak & quite used up. When I tried to lead off at double quick I reeled & came near falling. I certainly should have fallen if we had gone far. Presently the fire slackened in our locality. There is a long line of artillery on this range of hills. On a higher one in our rear are a line of heavier pieces which fire over us. From the river in rear of us the gunboats fire by signals over all with 200 lb. shells.

The firing towards night was very heavy, musketry brisk & frequent charges. Our loss is moderate, that of the enemy very severe. With another hour of daylight I believe we could utterly rout them. The cannonading was kept up till long after dark. I went onto a hill in front & saw 50 pieces of artillery playing into a piece of woods where the Rebs had taken shelter. This day's fighting has been the grandest I ever saw. It reminded me of the pictures of great battles in Europe. If our army had been fresh I should have liked all to have been risked on a battle on this field.

WOUNDED AT GLENDALE:
VIRGINIA, JUNE–JULY 1862

Asa D. Smith: Narrative of the Seven Days' Battles

Corporal Smith of the 16th Massachusetts Infantry served in Joseph Hooker's division during the Seven Days. His narrative begins on June 29 as the Army of the Potomac retreated toward the James River. Seriously wounded at Glendale on June 30, Smith eventually reached a hospital at the Naval Academy at Annapolis where he began his recovery. "I guess you can't bite cartridges, nor eat hardtack," said his doctor, who recommended Smith for a discharge that was granted on July 25, 1862.

WE WERE awakened at an early hour, and strange sights met our eyes. We had been told that everything on the right was favorable to our arms, and had no reason to disbelieve it. On this morning the first thing I noticed was that the tents of the officers were cut into ribbons, then that the Quartermaster's stores had been fired. Great piles of bread and meat were on the fire, men were busy banging the stocks of rifles against the trees and throwing the barrels into fires to ruin them. Barrels of sugar and whiskey were being emptied into pools of brackish water, in fact everything was being destroyed that could not be carried. There was an immense amount of property destroyed. We were ordered to tear our overcoats into four pieces and leave them. Then to sling knapsacks and fill our cartridge boxes, haversacks were replenished, and a hearty breakfast eaten.

As soon as possible we were marched into the entrenchments, where we found double the number of troops that usually manned them. I soon discovered that all the artillery had been withdrawn, not a piece being in sight.

It was strange to see the different ideas the men had as to what had happened; so great had been their faith in "Little Mac" that it was almost impossible for some of them to believe it could mean anything but a rapid pursuit of a retreating enemy. We actually thought we had been victorious on the right and were going to move forward. As for myself, as soon as I perceived the destruction going on around me, I felt that things were going wrong, and that it could only mean a withdrawal of our lines.

One thing was noticeable, that no one seemed at all disheartened or worried, everyone said, "We'll make them skedaddle yet." Everyone seemed to think that it was only a temporary affair, and that we might whip them during the movements that were to take place, and that we were fully able to do it.

It was a bit foggy for a while so that one could not see a great distance; but as it came daylight the fog cleared away, and far to the right and left the same conditions appeared.

We were commanded to make no noise, and in a short time the troops began to withdraw, toward the Chickahominy. After falling back some distance, the brigade left the road and filed into a field on the left. As we marched I saw that there were many guns in position on the edge of the wood on our right, and large numbers of men behind them.

Soon we were brought to a front in a place where timber had been cut but not carried away, there being several trees lying on the ground. We were ordered to lie down in position, the brigade being formed left in front, bringing the 16th in the front line.

The ground in our front rose gradually for a short distance, and a railroad cut ran nearly at right angles with our line. On the edge of the cut were three batteries of artillery (eighteen pieces) so placed as to nearly enfilade it, and we were to support them.

About the time we got into position, we heard the rebel yell as they came upon our abandoned works, and knew that they would soon be upon us. Soon artillery and musketry fire began up the line of the railroad, nearer to Richmond, and very quickly came toward us; and shell began to come in our direction. We remained here under this fire for about an hour and a half, and did not see a rebel soldier, as the infantry in the neighborhood were trying to advance down the cut, thus being entirely out of our sight.

The infantry fire became quite heavy, and remained so for at least an hour. Quite a number of unexploded shell and shrapnel came over, but only one did any damage. I saw this one coming straight for us, but it was a little high and struck in the lines of the Pennsylvania 26th, killing a man. As he was lying on the ground it tore off one arm, one leg, and the foot from the remaining leg. The victim gave one shriek and died in a few moments.

After a time the firing ceased, and we were marched to the rear at a lively pace.

The roads were crowded with troops of all arms, making it hard work to move; but we were pushed unmercifully. After some time we reached Savage Station on the railroad, and found troops marching through the village toward the James River. Every road was full, and all were hustling lively.

Great quantities of supplies were being destroyed here, one large warehouse being filled with clothing. All were burned.

On we went toward White Oak Swamp, through the narrow roads, through a growth of tall pine which shut out the breeze, while the sun's rays beat upon us fiercely. The air was full of dust, so that it was impossible to tell the color of anyone's hair or of his uniform. The pace was hurried, and we found ourselves getting short of water and becoming exhausted.

I staggered in the ranks, but did not fall out as did many. At last when it seemed as if I could go but little farther, I was refreshed by a swallow of vinegar kindly given me by a comrade, and struggled along until we reached the swamp, where in company with hundreds of others I got down upon my hands and knees and drank from the rut in the road, where men, horses, mules, guns, etc., had been passing all day.

No time was given us to fill canteens, and we pushed on through the swamp and over White Oak Creek, not coming to a halt till sunset, when we bivouacked in a field on the right of the road, the opposite side being occupied by the 11th U.S. Infantry. Orders were issued to lie behind the stacks, and without tents, just unrolling a blanket, and holding ourselves in readiness to march at two minutes' notice. As soon as relieved, I started after water for my tentmates as well as myself; taking canteens and dippers while they made ready to get supper, gathering wood, etc.

After going some distance I found a well near a house, but was unable to get water as the Headquarters Cavalry Escort had control of it, and no one else could get near it. Hearing of a brook at some distance ahead in a piece of woods I pushed on, and found it; but also found several hundred soldiers washing their feet in it. I followed their example; and after filling my canteens and dippers returned to the regiment just in season to find out that we should have to content ourselves with hardtack and cold water, as General Grover came along and ordered all fires out, saying that they would cause us to be shelled out within a half hour. (As I look back upon this day I do not see how we could have gone through it with so few stragglers. It was a terrible march.)

We lay all night behind the stacks, ready to move at a moment's notice, and at daylight June 30 were aroused and ordered to get breakfast. So I skirmished around and traded some sugar for coffee, and we soon had hot coffee and hardtack for a meal. Shortly after eating, we were ordered to fall in, and were sent through the fields to where the Charles City road was crossed by one leading down from Richmond, and found the road filled with wagons headed for the James River, which were hurrying along as fast as possible. They were in single file, and no wagon was allowed to pass another. If anything broke about wagon or harness, the mules were detached from the wagon and it was pulled out of the line and burned, together with its contents. This procession was passing nearly all day.

The brigade was posted across the Richmond Road, and the division extended to the left with the 1st Division (General Philip Kearny's) beyond that, while the 2nd Corps (General Edwin V. Sumner) joined us on the right. It did not appear that the officers feared an attack here, nevertheless about noon the line was advanced a short distance toward Richmond and posted on higher ground, the 16th being in the advanced line of the division. It was understood that the Pennsylvania Reserves (Generals George G. Meade and George A. McCall) were in our front, and this was probably the reason for not expecting attack. General Hooker and staff rode up an eminence in our rear, and after looking about, the General said, "This would be a good place for a battery; but I guess we won't need it today."

Here we stacked arms, and proceeded to make ourselves as comfortable as possible. There had been considerable fighting about two miles to the right of our position, where Stonewall Jackson was trying to cross White Oak Swamp, and shortly after this the firing grew very heavy in that direction.

In the course of an hour or two, skirmishing commenced in front of McCall, followed very quickly by heavy firing of both artillery and infantry. In a little while it appeared to be nearer, and we were called to arms. We were formed behind a worm fence on a side hill, and in a few minutes a battery came galloping up and took the position previously noted by General Hooker.

Before long the Pennsylvanians began to approach us at a run, and attempted to break to the rear. We gathered in all that we could and reformed them (or part of them) in our rear. Very soon the enemy's artillery opened and quickly got the range, the shells bursting in the air just in front so as to send the pieces directly among us. This continued for some time while the advance forces were being driven. Without any warning there came a sudden, sharp crack followed closely by others, and the screeching of shell from the battery in the rear. The guns were so near that it seemed as though our ear drums would burst; but in a few moments we became somewhat accustomed to the sounds, and minded them very little.

The enemy's shell flew thick and fast, and there were some close calls. One piece came down and grazed the side of my left shoe, partly burying itself in the ground. As I stooped and got hold of it, the Captain saw it, and said, "A miss is as good as a mile, Corporal," and I felt the same way about it.

About this time the enemy got into long rifle range, and began firing. From their position in the bush they could see us, while themselves hidden. The Colonel, wishing to hold his fire and keep the men steady, began to practice them in the manual of arms. (Some years after the war, I heard General Hooker tell the Massachusetts House of Representatives of this, saying that "he had never seen it better done on parade.") The enemy began to climb the rising ground toward our position, and the

Colonel ordered that no man fire until he gave the command, when the front rank was to fire, then the rear rank, after which we were "to load and fire at will."

The men were at the highest pitch of excitement, but so well disciplined were they that this order was obeyed to the letter. Then the men began to cheer (the gray trousers could now be seen below the cloud of smoke, as they steadily approached), when the Colonel said, "Remember the State you come from," whereupon the adjutant called for "three cheers for the old Bay State," which were given with a will.

General Hooker approached the front and said, "Give them hell, boys," and the fight was on.

The ground on the side hill in front was clear of trees for some little distance; but on the right of the road in front of the 2nd Corps the woods came well up to the line. On our left front was an orchard of apple trees (apparently), and sharpshooters were concealed amid the branches and had kept up a steady fire from the first.

The Johnnies climbed the hill with a rush, causing the line to waver for a moment, then it closed up and gave them a murderous fire.

Just as the shock came, I turned my head to the right to speak a word of defiance in the ear of Corporal William E. Eldridge, and before it was turned square to the front something hit me. It felt as though an immense timber had struck me end first, with great force. It was not painful; but seemed to partly daze me. I did not fall, but dropped my rifle and put my hand to my chin, and found that it felt as though torn to pieces. Lieutenant Meserve saw me and told me to go to the rear as soon as possible. From the direction that the ball came, I am of the opinion that it was fired by one of the sharpshooters in the trees.

I started for the 3rd Corps field hospital, which was established in the Willis Church, a small building on the Quaker Road (so called) leading to Malvern Hill. It was but a short distance in the rear, and the nearest way was through the wood and was marked by small hospital flags at intervals. On my way I found two or three small, coarse towels which evidently had been thrown away by some soldier, and used them to try to staunch the hemorrhage, which was quite severe.

On arriving at the field hospital station, I found several surgeons busily at work, with men wounded in apparently about every conceivable manner. The operating tables were made from the seats of the church, placed upon empty beef or pork barrels.

I got a seat beside a young rebel who was shot in one foot and waited for a time, but as nobody came to my assistance I went outside and found D. Harris Clark of Co. B, who was on detail and was an old acquaintance. He found a young New York surgeon and prevailed upon him to attend to my case. Upon his coming (as I could not talk) I made him understand that I wished to know if I would recover, upon which he shook his head and said, "Doubtful." And, after a short interval, "I have seen men recover who were hurt as badly as you are."

This was not very encouraging; but somehow hope was strong and I made up my mind to try for it.

The surgeon took a bandage and, passing it under my chin, pinned the ends together on the top of my head, and said, "This is all I can do for you now." Then he ordered Clark to take my equipment off and get a board and lay me upon it alongside the church, which he did, using my cartridge box and haversack for a pillow.

I lay on the side nearest the field of battle, and so near that very often the bullets would strike the building, but I was not struck.

The fight lasted some two or three hours, during which time I remained in this position, and later got up and sat on a plank placed between two trees near the road.

During the evening the surgeon and assistant surgeon of the regiment (Drs. Jewett and Whiston) found me and looked me over as best they could under the circumstances, and Dr. Jewett told me that he would operate in the morning, saying, "Keep up your courage; we'll make quite a man out of you." I suppose he did not mean to intimate that I previously had not been one. At any rate, it gave me more hope. Then he told Clark to take me into the little schoolhouse where I could sleep on the floor with other wounded.

Then the surgeons started off, and in a moment Dr. Whiston came back and put his fingers into my mouth; then he called Dr. Jewett, saying, "Doctor, his jaw is dislocated on the left side." Dr. Jewett came back, examined it again, and reduced the dislocation. After the dr's. departure, Clark took me to the schoolhouse where I found a great many wounded, among others Lieutenant Colonel Meacham of the regiment.

I lay upon the floor, suffering severely for want of water, and feeling very faint. Someone called Lieutenant Colonel Meacham's attention to me, when he handed me a small flask containing brandy and told me to take a little, but be sparing as it was all he had. After a time I got easier and must have fallen into a doze, from which I was awakened about 2 o'clock A.M. by hearing a call, "Get up and skedaddle; the Johnnies will be here in half an hour."

I got out and met Dr. Jewett, who ordered Comrade Clark and another man to carry me on a stretcher. This they attempted to do; but soon found it was impossible, as the narrow road was filled with columns of infantry and artillery, marching side by side and being pushed to the utmost by their officers.

I got up on my feet, and seeing a Massachusetts regiment (15th) passing I got among the color guard and attempted to keep up with them. As I was very weak I must have bothered them some, and one of them told me to get out, upon which the color sergeant rebuked him, telling him that "he might be wounded some time," and told me to "stay with them as long as I wished."

In the early forenoon we came to open ground, and in front was rising ground, a long slope, with buildings at the top: the now well-known Malvern Hill. On the right as you faced it was a deep ravine through which ran a small stream (Turkey Creek). This hill was about three miles from the James River.

When we came in sight, our forces were marching in every direction about it and forming lines of battle as fast as possible. Under ordinary circumstances it would have been a spectacle well worth seeing. But I was in a terrible condition, and left the 15th regiment and started up the hill by the road toward the river. When I had gotten about one third of the distance, the lieutenant in charge of a battery just swung into position across the road saw me; he came and advised me to get away as soon as possible, as there would be a fight there. So I trudged along, hungry and thirsty, with no canteen or dipper, unable to eat if

I had food and barely able to swallow any drink, if I had been possessed of any.

The day was very warm and my progress was necessarily slow, as I had to stop for rest at short intervals. Quite a number of ambulances passed me; but I was not allowed to occupy one of them.

After some time the fleet in the river opened fire through the creek so as to protect our left flank, and threw a great many 11-inch shells over my head. These shells were known to the soldiers as "dutch ovens," and sometimes were called "blacksmith's shops."

Some time in the afternoon I met Sergeant Matthias Brigham of my company, who was a townsman of mine. He was in charge of a squad of eight men who had been to the river with a wagon train. In the squad were two men of the company (Privates Geo. W. Risley and Perrin H. Benton) and I walked up to them, but none of them knew me. Taking off my forage cap, I showed them the number of the regiment and letter of the company, upon which one of them said, "My God! It's Smith."

After a moment's consultation, these two asked the sergeant if they could go with me to the river, and he said that they were very tired and he was afraid they would not be able to get up with the regiment before night; but they pleaded and he consented, and we started on with one of them on each side holding me up.

After a while we reached a boat landing near a large house, which I was told was Aiken's. The grounds were fenced, so that it was impossible to get to the river, as a guard was set.

My companions inquired for a surgeon, and presently a young man appeared, but did nothing for me, as he was one of a lot of young surgeons sent down to assist in the emergency, and had no instruments as yet, nor any supplies. He thought that it would not be long before some one could attend to me.

As they could do no more and the sound told us that a battle was raging, they left for the front after expressing great sympathy for me. After proceeding a short distance, Benton retraced his steps and offered me his blanket and tin cup. I tried to persuade him to keep them, as I knew that I was unable to carry them, but he threw them down at my feet and departed, with tears streaming down his cheeks.

I remained here for a short time, when I heard that there were a large number of sick and wounded in a ravine some distance above, so I started and was fortunate enough to be directed to the place.

I found there some 1,500 (so I was told), mostly from the 3rd Corps, and began to look about for help. Finally I found Captain James Mason of Co. B, whom I had known before the war. He interested himself, and soon brought Brigadier Surgeon Richard Salter to see me.

Dr. Salter said that he could do nothing for me, telling the captain that I could not live 48 hours. The captain urged him, when he said that he was upon the sick list himself, and was not able for duty; that he had no anesthetics and no instruments with the exception of a small pocket case, and but few bandages, which he felt that he ought to keep as he might save someone's life with them, while they would do me no good.

The captain then asked him as a *personal favor* to do what he could, saying that he had known me before my enlistment; upon which the doctor said he did not think I could survive the operation; but as the captain was persistent the doctor asked me if I thought I could stand it, and knowing that it was my only chance, nodded my head as I was unable to talk.

He then told me to sit down on the ground with my back against a tree, and ordered Sergeant Hugh Boyd of Co. I and another man who (years after) I learned was John Seates of Co. G, Mass. 1st Infantry, to hold my hands and head. My moustache had become matted with blood and was with difficulty cut away, and then before examining the wound he began to dissect out the small pieces of bone, stopping occasionally to ask me if I could "stand it." Although it was terrible to bear, I nodded my head and he went on. After finishing the cutting, he began sewing up the wound in the chin and the holes through my cheeks, after which he moistened a piece of sponge with turpentine and inserted it in the lower part of the wound, which was left open for drainage.

When he had finished, he counted the pieces of bone and said there were eighteen; then after looking at me for a short time he said, "Young man, you have got more nerve than any man I ever saw." He then wanted to know if there was anything in the way of nourishment to be had, and one of the soldiers replied that he had a little honey that I might have, whereupon they stirred some into a little warm water and tried to have me partake of it; but I could not, as it immediately set me to coughing so that I could not swallow anything.

Finally they found a little beef tea (so-called) and I got a very little of it down, the most of it having gone through the opening left for drainage. The surgeon then called for a knapsack, and on one being procured he caused it to be filled with straw, and placed me face down with my forehead resting upon it. Then saying he would dress the wound in the morning, he departed.

Later it began to rain and conditions became very bad, the ground getting muddy, and it being very dark one was liable to be trod upon by others.

Being very much exhausted, I finally got asleep, but was suddenly awakened by a stampede of a large number of mules, who ran over and among us. Fortunately I was not hurt, and had dozed off again when the experience of the previous night was repeated as a squadron of lancers ("Turkey drivers") rode up and ordered us to "skedaddle," as the Johnnies were coming.

Once more I roused myself and started downstream (as we had been directed). It was a very dark night, and the road was narrow, with a column of infantry filling one side of it and artillery the other. The bushes that grew at the side of the road were pushed aside by the passing soldiers, and as they came back into position kept hitting my face, so that I was compelled to take to the fields for the greater part of this distance, which I was told was seven miles. The greater portion of the way it was uncultivated land, some wood; but there were quite a number of large wheat fields through which I made my way; being a great deal of the time halfway to my knees in mud.

Toward daylight the weather cleared, and shortly after sunrise I came upon the bivouac of a regiment of Connecticut infantry who were preparing their breakfast. Some of them took pity upon me and invited me to partake with them; but they had nothing that I could eat, so they gave me what hot coffee I could swallow (which wasn't much) and wished me good luck; and I went on to the river at what I found was Harrison's Landing.

I found a large, square, brick house with outbuildings, overlooking the river, and a long, pile wharf extending to deep water. The river was full of men-of-war, and vessels of every description with supplies for man and beast.

Troops were bivouacked in the mud all about, and were coming in rapidly. After looking about a little, I made my way to the house, as being the place most likely to be used by surgeons. I found two at work in what had been the best room, and wounded men in large numbers anxiously awaiting their turn.

I got into the hall and sat upon the front stairs for a long time, until some officer (if I recollect rightly) took me into the room and told me to sit upon the floor in one corner, so that I should sooner be taken care of.

I passed a terrible day, hungry, thirsty, and faint, watching the surgeons work without anesthetics, and at times seeing a display of brutality by one of them.

I earnestly hoped that I should not fall into his hands, and fortunately I did not. I was not reached until about 4 P.M., when my wound was thoroughly cleaned, and a new piece of sponge moistened with turpentine inserted, a new bandage applied, and a cloth fastened so as to fall over the mouth and keep the flies from it. After this I went to the unfinished attic, where I found several wounded men lying on the floor.

I found a large dictionary, and taking it for a pillow lay down in front of one of the large chimneys, and hoped to get some sleep. After a little time Rev. Arthur B. Fuller, chaplain of the regiment (known by the boys as Glass-eye, owing to some peculiarity of the eyes) appeared, with a kettle of (what he called) beef tea, and inquired if there were any 16th Mass. men there. One of my company was the other side of the chimney and answered. The chaplain gave him some of the tea, whereupon others asked for it, and were told that he had but little and must give it to the wounded of his own regiment. As I could not talk and my companion did not think about me, the chaplain started to go downstairs, so I gave my comrade a pull and made signs that I wished for some, so he called the "Holy Joe" back and I was given a tin cupful; but owing to the conditions of the wound I could swallow but little.

Shortly after, I heard someone say that a boatload of wounded were to go down to the river that night, and knowing that unless I got to a hospital very soon there would be no chance for me, I roused up and went outdoors, where I found some surgeons with four hundred badly wounded men just ready to start for the boat landing.

I immediately attempted to fall in, but was prevented by a surgeon who said the number was already made up; but after looking at me for a moment said, "Follow us down, perhaps we can find room for you." Upon reaching the landing I found a large crowd on the same errand as myself, and was much disappointed; but waited until the four hundred had been taken in boats to a steamer lying in the river. When the last of them were in the boat, the surgeon (who stood at the top of the stairs) looked in my direction and made motions with his hands at the same time saying, "Let that man with the cloth over his face come here." I immediately went forward, and upon my arriving he lifted the cloth that hung over my mouth and chin and said, "Get right into the boat."

"OUR BELEAGUERED CITY":
VIRGINIA, JUNE 1862

Judith W. McGuire: Diary, June 27–30, 1862

Judith W. McGuire and her husband, John, had fled their home in Alexandria, Virginia, in 1861 when the Yankees came. In her diary she narrated the scene in Richmond during the Seven Days, beginning with the battle at Mechanicsville. Her journal was published in 1867 as *Diary of a Southern Refugee, During the War*, with the author identified as "A Lady of Virginia."

June 27th.—Yesterday was a day of intense excitement in the city and its surroundings. Early in the morning it was whispered about that some great movement was on foot. Large numbers of troops were seen under arms, evidently waiting for orders to march against the enemy. A. P. Hill's Division occupied the range of hills near "Strawberry Hill," the cherished home of my childhood, overlooking the old "Meadow Bridges." About three o'clock the order *to move*, so long expected, was given. The Division marched steadily and rapidly to the attack —the Fortieth Regiment, under command of my relative, Colonel J. M. Brockenbrough, in which are so many of our dear boys, leading the advance. The enemy's pickets were just across the river, and the men supposed they were in heavy force of infantry and artillery, and that the passage of the bridge would be hazardous in the extreme; yet their courage did not falter. The gallant Fortieth, followed by Pegram's Battery, rushed across the bridge at double-quick, and with exultant shouts drove the enemy's pickets from their posts. The enemy was driven rapidly down the river to Mechanicsville, where the battle raged long and fiercely. At nine o'clock all was quiet; the bloody struggle over for the day. Our victory is said to be glorious, but not complete. The fighting is even now renewed, for I hear the firing of heavy artillery. Last night our streets were thronged until a late hour to catch the last accounts from couriers and spectators returning from the field. A bulletin from the Assistant Surgeon of the Fortieth, sent to his anxious father, assured me of the safety of some of those most dear to me; but the sickening sight of the ambulances bringing in the wounded met my eye at every turn. The President, and many others, were on the surrounding hills during the fight, deeply interested spectators. The calmness of the people during the progress of the battle was marvellous. The balloons of the enemy hovering over the battle-field could be distinctly seen from the outskirts of the city, and the sound of musketry as distinctly heard. All were anxious, but none alarmed for the safety of the city. From the firing of the first gun till the close of the battle every spot favourable for observation was crowded. The tops of the Exchange, the Ballard House, the Capitol, and almost every other tall house were covered with human beings; and after nightfall the commanding hills from the President's house to the Alms-House were covered, like a vast amphitheatre, with men, women and children, witnessing the grand display of fireworks—beautiful, yet awful—and sending death amid those whom our hearts hold so dear. I am told (for I did not witness it) that it was a scene of unsurpassed magnificence. The brilliant light of bombs bursting in the air and passing to the ground, the innumerable lesser lights, emitted by thousands and thousands of muskets, together with the roar of artillery and the rattling of small-arms, constituted a scene terrifically grand and imposing. What spell has bound our people? Is their trust in God, and in the valour of our troops, so great that they are unmoved by these terrible demonstrations of our powerful foe? It would seem so, for when the battle was over the crowd dispersed and retired to their respective homes with the seeming tranquility of persons who had been witnessing a panorama of transactions in a far-off country, in which they felt no personal interest; though they knew that their countrymen slept on their arms, only awaiting the dawn to renew the deadly conflict, on the success of which depended not only the fate of our capital, but of that splendid army, containing the material on which our happiness depends. Ah! many full, sorrowful hearts were at home, breathing out prayers for our success; or else were busy in the hospitals, administering to the wounded. Those on the hill-sides and house-tops were too nervous and anxious to stay at home—not that they were apprehensive for the city, but for the fate of those who were defending it, and their feeling was too deep for expression. The same feeling, perhaps, which makes me write so much this morning. But I must go to other duties.

Ten o'Clock at Night.—Another day of great excitement in our beleaguered city. From early dawn the cannon has been roaring around us. Our success has been glorious! The citizens—gentlemen as well as ladies—have been fully occupied in the hospitals. Kent, Paine & Co. have thrown open their spacious building for the use of the wounded. General C., of Texas, volunteer aid to General Hood, came in from the field covered with dust, and slightly wounded; he represents the fight as terrible beyond example. The carnage is frightful. General Jackson has joined General Lee, and nearly the whole army on both sides were engaged. The enemy had retired before our troops to their strong works near Gaines's Mill. Brigade after brigade of our brave men were hurled against them, and repulsed in disorder. General Lee was heard to say to General Jackson, "The fighting is desperate; can our men stand it?" Jackson replied, "General, I know our boys—they will never give back." In a short time a large part of our force was brought up in one grand attack, and then the enemy was utterly routed. General C. represents the valour of Hood and his brigade in the liveliest colours, and attributes the grand success at the close of the day greatly to their extraordinary gallantry. The works were the strongest ever seen in this country, and General C. says that the armies of the world could not have driven our men from them.

Another bulletin from the young surgeon of the Fortieth. That noble regiment has lost heavily—several of the "Potomac Rifles" among the slain—sons of old friends and acquaintances. Edward Brockenbrough, dreadfully wounded, has been brought in, and is tenderly nursed. Our own boys are mercifully spared. Visions of the battle-field have haunted me all day. Our loved ones, whether friends or strangers—all Southern soldiers are dear to us—lying dead and dying; the wounded in the hot sun, the dead being hastily buried. McClellan is said to be retreating. "Praise the Lord, O my soul!"

28th.—The casualties among our friends, so far, not very numerous. My dear Raleigh T. Colston is here, slightly wounded; he hopes to return to his command in a few days. Colonel Allen, of the Second Virginia, killed. Major Jones, of the same regiment, desperately wounded. Wood McDonald killed. But what touches me most nearly is the death of my young friend, Clarence Warwick, of this city. Dearly have I loved that warm-hearted, high-minded, brave boy, since his early childhood. To-night I have been indulging sad memories of his earnest manner and affectionate tones, from his boyhood up; and now what must be the shock to his father and brothers, and to those tender sisters, when to-morrow the telegraph shall tell them of their loss! His cousin, Lieutenant-Colonel Warwick, is desperately wounded. Oh, I pray that his life may be spared to his poor father and mother! He is so brave and skilful an officer that we cannot spare him, and how can they? The booming of cannon still heard distinctly, but the sound is more distant.

June 30.—McClellan certainly retreating. We begin to breathe more freely; but he fights as he goes. Oh, that he may be surrounded before he gets to his gun-boats! Rumours are flying about that he is surrounded; but we do not believe it—only hope that he may be before he reaches the river. The city is sad, because of the dead and dying, but our hearts are filled with gratitude and love. The end is not yet—oh that it were!

"DEATH HELD A CARNIVAL":
VIRGINIA, JUNE–JULY 1862

Sallie Brock: from
Richmond During the War

A tutor in prewar Virginia, Sallie Brock spent the war years in Richmond. She described the Seven Days in her memoir, published anonymously "by a Richmond Lady" in 1867.

RICHMOND suffered heavily in the loss of citizens in these battles. There was scarcely a family that had not some one of its numbers in the field. Mothers nervously watched for any who might bring to them news of their boys. Sisters and friends grew pale when a horseman rode up to their doors, and could scarcely nerve themselves to listen to the tidings he brought. Young wives clasped their children to their bosoms, and in agony imagined themselves widows and their little ones orphans. Thoughtful husbands, and sons, and brothers, and lovers, dispatched messengers to report their condition whenever they could, but, alas! the worst fears of many were realized.

Conspicuous amongst the dead of Richmond was the young Colonel of the Fourth Texas regiment. He had won honorable distinction in Italy, under Garibaldi. News arrived of his instant death on the field, and his heart-broken family sat up to receive his body until after the hour of midnight; but when it arrived, and "he lives" was told his mother, the reaction of joy almost deprived her of being. She could not realize it. The revulsion was too great. He spent a few days of mortal agony, and then a sad, mournful procession of heart-broken friends and relatives, and the riderless horse of the young warrior, announced, ah! how sadly, that Richmond's gallant son, Colonel Bradfute Warwick, had fallen!

A horseman rode up to the door of one of our houses on —— street, and cried out to the anxious mother: "Your son, madam, is safe, but Captain —— is killed!" On the opposite side, on the portico of her dwelling, a fair young girl, the betrothed of Captain ——, was said to have been sitting at the moment, and thus heard the terrible announcement!

Every family received the bodies of the wounded or dead of their friends, and every house was a house of mourning or a private hospital.

The clouds were lifted, and the skies brightened upon political prospects, but death held a carnival in our city. The weather was excessively hot. It was midsummer, gangrene and erysipelas attacked the wounded, and those who might have been cured of their wounds were cut down by these diseases.

Our hospitals were loathsome with the bloated, disfigured countenances of the victims of disease, rather than from ghastly wounds. Sickening odors filled the atmosphere, and soldiers' funerals were passing at every moment. Frequently they would be attended by only one or two of the convalescent patients of the hospitals, and sometimes the unknown dead would be borne to the grave, with only the driver of the hearse or cart to attend it.*

The mournful strains of the "Dead March," and the sounds of the muffled drum, betokened an officer *en route* for "the city of the dead," but these honors could not be accorded the poor fellows from the ranks. There were too many of them passing away—the means for costly funerals were not within

---

*One of the grave-diggers at a soldiers' cemetery said to the writer, when speaking of this time, (at a subsequent period,) "We could not dig graves fast enough to bury the soldiers. They were sometimes brought and put out of the hearse or cart, beside an open grave, and we were compelled to bury them in turn. Frequently we were obliged to leave them over night, when, sometimes, the bodies would swell, and burst the coffins in which they were placed, so slightly were they made. Our work was a horrible one! The odor was stifling. On one occasion, one of our grave-diggers contracted disease from a dead body, which he buried, that came to him in this terrible condition, and he died from it in less than twenty-four hours. After that we were almost afraid to continue our business, but then the soldiers must be buried, poor fellows!"

We listened to this horrible account as we stood on the hillside, and saw the hillocks innumerable, that marked the graves of our soldiers. A little girl, who visited the cemetery, on returning to the city said:—"Why, grandma, the soldiers' graves are as thick as potatoe-hills!" And she saw only a moiety of the many which crowded the hillsides around our city, for this was an extension of Hollywood cemetery only. There were several cemeteries especially laid out for the soldiers, and they were soon all filled with the mounds that marked the soldier dead.

our reach—yet were not our hearts less saddened by the less imposing cortege that was borne along with the private nor by the rude coffin in the cart, slowly wending its way unattended by friends, to the soldiers' cemetery. Mothers and sisters, and dear friends came from all parts of the South, to nurse and comfort dear ones in our hospitals, and some, alas! arrived to find a husband, brother, or son already dead or dying, and had the sad companionship of the dead back to their homes.

A RICHMOND HOSPITAL: VIRGINIA,
JUNE–JULY 1862

Sara Agnes Pryor: from Reminiscences of Peace and War

When the Seven Days began Sara Agnes Pryor was nursing her fever-stricken husband Roger, a former U.S. and Confederate congressman now serving as a brigadier general in Lee's army. While her husband rejoined his brigade, Pryor volunteered as a nurse in Richmond, an experience she recalled in a 1904 memoir.

———————

Kent & paine's warehouse was a large, airy building, which had, I understood, been offered by the proprietors for a hospital immediately after the battle of Seven Pines. McClellan's advance upon Richmond had heavily taxed the capacity of the hospitals already established.

When I reached the warehouse, early on the morning after the fight at Mechanicsville, I found cots on the lower floor already occupied, and other cots in process of preparation. An aisle between the rows of narrow beds stretched to the rear of the building. Broad stairs led to a story above, where other cots were being laid.

The volunteer matron was a beautiful Baltimore woman, Mrs. Wilson. When I was presented to her as a candidate for admission, her serene eyes rested doubtfully upon me for a moment. She hesitated. Finally she said: "The work is very exacting. There are so few of us that our nurses must do anything and everything—make beds, wait upon anybody, and often a half a dozen at a time."

"I will engage to do all that," I declared, and she permitted me to go to a desk at the farther end of the room and enter my name.

As I passed by the rows of occupied cots, I saw a nurse kneeling beside one of them, holding a pan for a surgeon. The red stump of an amputated arm was held over it. The next thing I knew I was myself lying on a cot, and a spray of cold water was falling over my face. I had fainted. Opening my eyes, I found the matron standing beside me.

"You see it is as I thought. You are unfit for this work. One of the nurses will conduct you home."

The nurse's assistance was declined, however. I had given trouble enough for one day, and had only interrupted those who were really worth something.

A night's vigil had been poor preparation for hospital work. I resolved I would conquer my culpable weakness. It was all very well,—these heroics in which I indulged, these paroxysms of patriotism, this adoration of the defenders of my fireside. The defender in the field had naught to hope from me in case he should be wounded in my defence.

I took myself well in hand. Why had I fainted? I thought it was because of the sickening, dead odor in the hospital, mingled with that of acids and disinfectants. Of course this would always be there—and worse, as wounded men filled the rooms. I provided myself with sal volatile and spirits of camphor,—we wore pockets in our gowns in those days,—and thus armed I presented myself again to Mrs. Wilson.

She was as kind as she was refined and intelligent. "I will give you a place near the door," she said, "and you must run out into the air at the first hint of faintness. You will get over it, see if you don't."

Ambulances began to come in and unload at the door. I soon had occupation enough, and a few drops of camphor on my handkerchief tided me over the worst. The wounded men crowded in and sat patiently waiting their turn. One fine little fellow of fifteen unrolled a handkerchief from his wrist to show me his wound. "There's a bullet in there," he said proudly. "I'm going to have it cut out, and then go right back to the fight. Isn't it lucky it's my left hand?"

As the day wore on I became more and more absorbed in my work. I had, too, the stimulus of a reproof from Miss Deborah Couch, a brisk, efficient middle-aged lady, who asked no quarter and gave none. She was standing beside me a moment, with a bright tin pan filled with pure water, into which I foolishly dipped a finger to see if it were warm; to learn if I would be expected to provide warm water when I should be called upon to assist the surgeon.

"This water, Madam, was prepared for a raw wound," said Miss Deborah, sternly. "I must now make the surgeon wait until I get more."

Miss Deborah, in advance of her time, was a germ theorist. *My* touch evidently was contaminating.

As she charged down the aisle with a pan of water in her hand, everybody made way. She had known of my "fine-lady faintness," as she termed it, and I could see she despised me for it. She had volunteered, as all the nurses had, and she meant business. She had no patience with nonsense, and truly she was worth more than all the rest of us.

"Where can I get a little ice?" I one day ventured of Miss Deborah.

"Find it," she rejoined, as she rapidly passed on; but find it I never did. Ice was an unknown luxury until brought to us later from private houses.

But I found myself thoroughly reinstated—with surgeons, matron, and Miss Deborah—when I appeared a few days later, accompanied by a man bearing a basket of clean, well-rolled bandages, with promise of more to come. The Petersburg women had gone to work with a will upon my table-cloths, sheets, and dimity counterpanes—and even the chintz furniture covers. My springlike green and white chintz bandages appeared on many a manly arm and leg. My fine linen underwear and napkins were cut, by the sewing circle at the Spotswood, according to the surgeon's directions, into lengths two inches wide, then folded two inches, doubling back and forth in a smaller fold each time, until they formed pointed wedges for compresses.

Such was the sudden and overwhelming demand for such things, that but for my own and similar donations of household linen, the wounded men would have suffered. The war had come upon us suddenly. Many of our ports were already closed, and we had no stores laid up for such an emergency.

The bloody battle of Gaines's Mill soon followed—then Frazier's Farm, within the week, and at once the hospital was filled to overflowing. Every night a courier brought me tidings of my husband. When I saw him at the door my heart would die within me! One morning John came in for certain supplies. After being reassured as to his master's safety, I asked, "Did he have a comfortable night, John?"

"He sholy did! Marse Roger cert'nly was comfortable las' night. He slep' on de field 'twixt two daid horses!"

The women who worked in Kent & Paine's hospital never seemed to weary. After a while the wise matron assigned us hours, and we went on duty with the regularity of trained nurses. My hours were from seven to seven during the day, with the promise of night service should I be needed. Efficient, kindly colored women assisted us. Their motherly manner soothed the prostrate soldier, whom they always addressed as "son."

Many fine young fellows lost their lives for want of prompt attention. They never murmured. They would give way to those who seemed to be more seriously wounded than themselves, and the latter would recover, while from the slighter wounds gangrene would supervene from delay. Very few men ever walked away from that hospital. They died, or friends found quarters for them in the homes in Richmond. None complained! Unless a poor man grew delirious, he never groaned. There was an atmosphere of gentle kindness, a suppression of emotion for the sake of others.

Every morning the Richmond ladies brought for our patients such luxuries as could be procured in that scarce time. The city was in peril, and distant farmers feared to bring in their fruits and vegetables. One day a patient-looking middle-aged man said to me, "What would I not give for a bowl of chicken broth like that my mother used to give me when I was a sick boy!" I perceived one of the angelic matrons of Richmond at a distance, stooping over the cots, and found my way to her and said: "Dear Mrs. Maben, have you a chicken? And could you send some broth to No. 39?" She promised, and I returned with her promise to the poor wounded fellow. He shook his head. "To-morrow will be too late," he said.

I had forgotten the circumstance next day, but at noon I happened to look toward cot No. 39, and there was Mrs. Maben herself. She had brought the chicken broth in a pretty china bowl, with napkin and silver spoon, and was feeding my doubting Thomas, to his great satisfaction.

It was at this hospital, I have reason to believe, that the little story originated, which was deemed good enough to be claimed by other hospitals, of the young girl who approached a sick man with a pan of water in her hand and a towel over her arm.

"Mayn't I wash your face?" said the girl, timidly.

"Well, lady, you may if you want to," said the man, wearily. "It has been washed fourteen times this morning! It can stand another time, I reckon."

I discovered that I had not succeeded, despite many efforts, in winning Miss Deborah. I learned that she was affronted because I had not shared my offerings of jelly and fruit with her, for her special patients. Whenever I ventured to ask a loan from her, of a pan or a glass for water or the little things of which we never had enough, she would reply, "I must keep them for the nurses who understand reciprocity. Reciprocity is a rule *some* persons never seem to comprehend." When this was hammered into my slow perception, I rose to the occasion. I turned over the entire contents of a basket the landlord of the Spotswood had given me to Miss Deborah, and she made my path straight before me ever afterward.

At the end of a week the matron had promoted me! Instead of carving the fat bacon, to be dispensed with corn bread, for the hospital dinner, or standing between two rough men to keep away the flies, or fetching water, or spreading sheets on cots, I was assigned to regular duty with one patient.

The first of these proved to be young Colonel Coppens, of my husband's brigade. I could comfort him very little, for he was wounded past recovery. I spoke little French, and could only try to keep him, as far as possible, from annoyance. To my great relief, place was found for him in a private family. There he soon died—the gallant fellow I had admired on his horse a few months before.

Then I was placed beside the cot of Mr. (or Captain) Boyd of Mecklenburg, and was admonished by the matron not to leave him alone. He was the most patient sufferer in the world, gentle, courteous, always considerate, never complaining. I observed he often closed his eyes and sighed. "Are you in pain, Captain?" "No, no," he would say gently. One day, when I returned from my "rest," I found the matron sitting beside him. Tears were running down her cheeks. She motioned me to take her place, and then added, "No, no, I will not leave him."

The Captain's eyes were closed, and he sighed wearily at intervals. Presently he whispered slowly:—

> "There everlasting spring abides,"

then sighed, and seemed to sleep for a moment.

The matron felt his pulse and raised a warning hand. The sick man's whisper went on:—

> "Bright fields beyond the swelling flood
> Stand—dressed—in living green."

The surgeon stood at the foot of the cot and shook his head. The nurses gathered around with tearful eyes. Presently in clear tones:—

> "Not Jordan's stream—nor death's cold flood
> Shall fright us—from—the shore,"

and in a moment more the Christian soldier had crossed the river and lain down to rest under the trees.

Each of the battles of those seven days brought a harvest of wounded to our hospital. I used to veil myself closely as I walked to and from my hotel, that I might shut out the dreadful sights in the street,—the squads of prisoners, and, worst of all, the open wagons in which the dead were piled. Once I *did* see one of these dreadful wagons! In it a stiff arm was raised, and shook as it was driven down the street, as though the dead owner appealed to Heaven for vengeance; a horrible sight never to be forgotten.

DEBATING BLACK SOLDIERS:
WASHINGTON, D.C., JULY 1862

Whitelaw Reid: General Hunter's Negro Soldiers

Although General Hunter's "experiment" of turning slaves into soldiers did not immediately bear results, his letter on the subject (see Hunter to Stanton, June 23, 1862, in this volume) reached the House of Representatives, where Kentucky conservatives Wickliffe and Mallory opposed printing the letter for the record. The resulting debate was reported in a dispatch by Reid, the Washington correspondent for the *Cincinnati Gazette*. Wickliffe's mention of the "late disaster in South Carolina" referred to the Union defeat at Secessionville at Charleston Harbor on June 16. On August 25 Stanton took a step forward on the matter of black soldiers, authorizing Brigadier General Rufus Saxton, superintendent of contrabands on the South Carolina coast, to enlist "volunteers of African descent." Stanton's order led to the organization of the 1st South Carolina Volunteers in October.

1862, July 6

Gen. David Hunter's letter about his Negro soldiers brought up a lively debate in the House Saturday, in which some very conservative men said some very ultra things, that must prove sadly 'firing for the Southern heart.' Charles A. Wickliffe wanted to reconsider the vote by which Hunter's letter was ordered printed and couldn't contain himself on the insult Hunter had offered to local people. He charged officers of the Government and of the army with having undertaken without law, against order, and in violation of every principle of humanity, to assume the power of enlisting slaves to serve against their masters. General Hunter's letter was in manner and terms unbecoming a General. He held Secretary Stanton responsible for Hunter's conduct and sneeringly said Hunter had better been seeing to his business when the late disaster in South Carolina took place than tinkering with Negroes. Robert Mallory made the usual Kentucky speech against arming the blacks. He ridiculed the idea of making them soldiers; said a single cannon shot would put ten thousand of them to flight; and closed by declaring that arming them was barbarous, inhuman and contrary to the practice of all civilized nations, and that it was most as bad as putting the tomahawk into the hands of the savage. This stirred up Thaddeus Stevens, who inquired, how does it come that they are so dangerous to their masters, when a single cannon shot will put ten thousand to flight? Or how is it they have not courage enough to make soldiers when you call them as savage and dangerous as Indians? But the gentleman was mistaken in his facts. Common history, he repeated, proved them false. It had been the general practise of civilized nations to employ slaves for military purposes, whenever and wherever needed. Owen Lovejoy here begged leave to interrupt, and read from common school history about Jackson's arming slaves in the War of 1812 and his promise to give freedom to all who served. He then read Jackson's General Order, thanking the Negroes for their gallant success, saying that he had not been unaware of their good qualities as soldiers, but that they had far surpassed his highest expectations and reassuring them of emancipation as a reward for their conduct. Lovejoy concluded his demonstration on the Negro-frightened gentlemen by reference to another history, showing that one fourth of the men who helped with Perry's victory on the lakes were Negroes. The effect of all this was sensational. Men who had been denouncing Hunter couldn't have been more astonished if one of Hunter's own bombshells from Port Royal had been dropped among them.

Charles B. Sedgewick heightened the effect by reading an elaborate statement of the New York State Librarian, showing that nearly every civilized Nation had, sometime or other, employed Negroes as soldiers and always with success, and winding up with the example of Brazil, the largest slaveholding empire of the world, using regiments of slaves at this very day as among the best soldiers they have. Alexander S. Diven begged to trespass on Stevens' time, just to say that he had long been profoundly convinced that Congress failed in its imperative duty, just so long as it failed to provide for enlisting Negro troops to serve in unhealthy regions to which they had become acclimated, and he now had a bill to that end prepared and was ready to offer it at the first opportunity. That, resumed Mr.

Stevens, is precisely what I would have done long ago, only I wasn't a conservative, and so they'd have called it an Abolition scheme. Stevens then went on with unusual earnestness and force, to urge the necessity for using Negroes to save white men. He declared that all over his State, households were everywhere desolated today because we hadn't troops enough, and now they wanted to call on them for more, to be sent into unwholesome climates, where exposure was certain death to any white man, and asserting that while such a policy was pursued, the suppression of the rebellion was hopeless. The effect of the discussion was seen when at the close of Stevens' speech, the House laid Wickliffe's motion on the table by a vote of 74 to 29.

There will be no more sneering at Hunter's letter or his Negro brigade.

"CIVIL AND MILITARY POLICY":
VIRGINIA, JULY 1862

George B. McClellan to Abraham Lincoln

The President visited the Army of the Potomac at Harrison's Landing on July 8 to gauge its morale and its prospects, and McClellan took advantage of the opportunity to hand him this letter. McClellan had actually drafted the letter a week or so before the Seven Days, when he was confident of taking Richmond and anticipated resuming the general-in-chief post and advising on war policy. Now, anticipating possible martyrdom on the battlefield, he offered it as a sort of last military will and testament. Lincoln, sharing McClellan's letter with Congressman Frank Blair on the return journey to Washington, remarked that the general's advisory reminded him of a story, the one about "the man who got on a horse, and the horse stuck his hind foot into a stirrup. The man said, 'If you're going to get on I'll get off.'"

(Confidential) Head Quarters, Army of the Potomac
Mr President Camp near Harrison's Landing, Va. July 7th 1862

You have been fully informed, that the Rebel army is in our front, with the purpose of overwhelming us by attacking our positions or reducing us by blocking our river communications. I can not but regard our condition as critical and I earnestly desire, in view of possible contingencies, to lay before your Excellency, for your private consideration, my general views concerning the existing state of the rebellion; although they do not strictly relate to the situation of this Army or strictly come within the scope of my official duties. These views amount to convictions and are deeply impressed upon my mind and heart.

Our cause must never be abandoned; it is the cause of free institutions and self government. The Constitution and the Union must be preserved, whatever may be the cost in time, treasure and blood. If secession is successful, other dissolutions are clearly to be seen in the future. Let neither military disaster, political faction or foreign war shake your settled purpose to enforce the equal operation of the laws of the United States upon the people of every state.

The time has come when the Government must determine upon a civil and military policy, covering the whole ground of our national trouble. The responsibility of determining, declaring and supporting such civil and military policy and of directing the whole course of national affairs in regard to the rebellion, must now be assumed and exercised by you or our cause will be lost. The Constitution gives you power sufficient even for the present terrible exigency.

This rebellion has assumed the character of a War; as such it should be regarded; and it should be conducted upon the highest principles known to Christian Civilization. It should not be a War looking to the subjugation of the people of any state, in any event. It should not be, at all, a War upon population; but against armed forces and political organizations. Neither confiscation of property, political executions of persons, territorial organization of states or forcible abolition of slavery should be contemplated for a moment. In prosecuting the War, all private property and unarmed persons should be strictly protected; subject only to the necessities of military operations. All private property taken for military use should be paid or receipted for; pillage and waste should be treated as high crimes; all unnecessary trespass sternly prohibited; and offensive demeanor by the military towards citizens promptly rebuked. Military arrests should not be tolerated, except in places where active hostilities exist; and oaths not required by enactments—Constitutionally made—should be neither demanded nor received. Military government should be confined to the preservation of public order and the protection of political rights.

Military power should not be allowed to interfere with the relations of servitude, either by supporting or impairing the authority of the master; except for repressing disorder as in other cases. Slaves contraband under the Act of Congress, seeking military protection, should receive it. The right of the Government to appropriate permanently to its own service claims to slave labor should be asserted and the right of the owner to compensation therefor should be recognized. This principle might be extended upon grounds of military necessity and security to all the slaves within a particular state; thus working manumission in such state—and in Missouri, perhaps in Western Virginia also and possibly even in Maryland the expediency of such a military measure is only a question of time. A system of policy thus constitutional and conservative, and pervaded by the influences of Christianity and freedom, would receive the support of almost all truly loyal men, would deeply impress the rebel masses and all foreign nations, and it might be humbly hoped that it would commend itself to the favor of the Almighty. Unless the principles governing the further conduct of our struggle shall be made known and approved, the effort to obtain requisite forces will be almost hopeless. A declaration of radical views, especially upon slavery, will rapidly disintegrate our present Armies.

The policy of the Government must be supported by concentrations of military power. The national forces should not be dispersed in expeditions, posts of occupation and numerous Armies; but should be mainly collected into masses and brought to bear upon the Armies of the Confederate States; those Armies thoroughly defeated, the political structure which they support would soon cease to exist.

In carrying out any system of policy which you may form, you will require a Commander in Chief of the Army; one who possesses your confidence, understands your views and who is competent to execute your orders by directing the military forces of the Nation to the accomplishment of the objects by you proposed. I do not ask that place for myself. I am willing to serve you in such position as you may assign me and I will do so as faithfully as ever subordinate served superior.

I may be on the brink of eternity and as I hope forgiveness from my maker I have written this letter with sincerity towards you and from love for my country.

Very respectfully your obdt svt
Geo B McClellan
Maj Genl Comdg

His Excellency A Lincoln
Presdt U.S.

BUILDING A CONFEDERATE CRUISER:
ENGLAND, JULY 1862

Thomas H. Dudley and
J. Price Edwards: An Exchange

Dudley, the American consul at Liverpool, battled with British authorities over the building of Confederate warships in Great Britain's shipyards, which Dudley charged was in violation of the neutrality laws. His adversary was the Confederate naval agent James D. Bulloch. The vessel that is the subject of this correspondence was labeled by her Laird shipbuilders as "steamer No. 290." To Dudley's frustration, No. 290 set sail from Liverpool on July 29 without hindrance from customs agent Edwards. She took her armament in the Azores and was christened the soon-to-be-notorious C.S.S. *Alabama*.

UNITED STATES CONSULATE,
Liverpool, July 9, 1862.

SIR: In accordance with a suggestion of Earl Russell, in a communication to Mr. Adams, the American minister in London, I beg to lay before you the information and circumstances which have come to my knowledge relative to the gunboat being fitted out by Messrs. Laird, at Birkenhead, for the confederates of the southern United States of America, and intended to be used as a privateer against the United States.

On my arrival and taking charge of the consulate at Liverpool, in November last, my attention was called by the acting consul, and by other persons, to two gunboats being or to be fitted out for the so-called confederate government—the Oreto, fitted out by William C. Miller and Sons and Messrs. Fawcett Preston and Co., and the one now in question. Subsequent events fully proved the suspicion, with regard to the Oreto, to be well founded. She cleared from Liverpool in March last for Palermo and Jamaica, but sailed direct for Nassau, where she now is receiving her armament as a privateer for the so-called confederate government. And my attention was called repeatedly to the gunboat building by Mr. Laird by various persons, who stated that she was also for a confederate privateer, and was being built by Messrs. Laird for that express purpose. In May last two officers of the southern privateer Sumter, named Caddy and Beaufort, passed through Liverpool on their way to Havana or Nassau; while here, stated that there was a gunboat building by Mr. Laird, at Birkenhead, for the southern confederacy, and not long after that a foreman, employed about the vessel in Messrs. Lairds' yard, stated that she was the sister of the Oreto, and intended for the same service; and, when pressed for an explanation, further stated that she was to be a privateer for the southern government in the United States.

When the vessel was first tried, Mr. Wellsman, one of the firm of Fraser, Trenholm and Co., (who are well known as agents for the confederate government) Andrew and Thomas Byrne, and other persons, well known as having been for months actively engaged in sending munitions of war for said government, were present, and have accompanied her on her various trials, as they had accompanied the Oreto on her trial trip and on her departure. In April last the southern screw steamer Annie Childs, which had run the blockade out of Charleston, and the name of which was changed at this port to the Julia Usher, was laden with munitions of war, consisting of a large quantity of powder, rifled cannon, &c., by Messrs. Fraser, Trenholm and Co., for the southern confederacy, and left Liverpool to run the blockade under the command of a Captain Hammer, and having on board several of the crew of the privateer Sumter, to which I have before referred. For some unknown reason this vessel came back, and is now here. Since her return a youth named Robinson, who had gone in her as a passenger, has stated that the gunboat building at Laird's for the southern confederacy was a subject of frequent conversation among the officers while she (Julia Usher) was out, she was all the time spoken of as a confederate vessel, and that Captain Bullock was to command her. That the money for her was advanced by Fraser, Trenholm and Co. That she was not to make any attempt to run the blockade, but would go at once as a privateer. That she was to mount eleven guns. That if the Julia Usher were not going, the six men from the Sumter who were on board the Julia Usher were to join the gunboat. This youth, being a native of New Orleans, was extremely anxious to get taken on board the gunboat, and wished the persons he made the communication to, to assist him and see Captain Bullock on his behalf. He has, I understand, been removed to a school in London. With reference to his statement, I may observe that Captain Hammer referred to is a South Carolinian; has been many years in Fraser, Trenholm and Co.'s employ; is greatly trusted by them, and is also intimate with Captain Bullock, so that he would be likely to be well informed on the subject; and as he had no notion at that time of returning to Liverpool, he would have no hesitation in speaking of the matter to his officers and the persons from the Sumter. I may also state, the Captain Bullock referred to is in Liverpool; that he is an officer of the confederate navy; that he was sent over here for the express purpose of fitting out privateers and sending over munitions of war; that he transacts his business at the office of Fraser, Trenholm and Co.; that he has been all the time in communication with Fawcett, Preston and Co., who fitted out the Oreto, and with Lairds, who are fitting out this vessel; that he goes almost daily on board the gunboat, and seems to be recognized as in authority.

A Mr. Blair, of Paradise street, in this town, who furnished the cabins of the Laird gunboat, has also stated that all the fittings and furniture were selected by Captain Bullock, and were subject to his approval, although paid for by Mr. Laird.

The information on which I have formed an undoubting conviction that this vessel is being fitted out for the so-called confederate government, and is intended to cruise against the commerce of the United States, has come to me from a variety of sources, and I have detailed it to you as far as practicable.

I have given you the names of the persons making the statements; but as the information, in most cases, is given to me by persons out of friendly feeling to the United States and in strict confidence, I cannot state the names of my informants; but what I have stated is of such a character, that little inquiry will confirm its truth. Everything about the vessel shows her to be a war vessel; she has well-constructed magazines; she has a number of canisters of a peculiar and expensive construction, for containing powder; she has already platforms screwed to her decks for the reception of swivel guns. Indeed, the fact she is a war vessel is not denied by Messrs. Laird, but they say she is for the Spanish government. This they stated on the 3d April last, when General Burgoyne visited their yard, and was shown over it and the vessels being built there by Messrs. John Laird, jun., and Henry H. Laird, as was fully reported in the papers at the time. Seeing the statement, and having been already informed from so many respectable sources that she was for the so-called confederate government, I at once wrote to the minister in London to ascertain from the Spanish embassy whether the statement was true. The reply was a positive assurance that she was not for the Spanish government. I am therefore authorized in saying that what was stated on that occasion, as well as statements since made, that she is for the Spanish government, are untrue.

I am satisfied, beyond a doubt, that she is for a confederate war vessel.

If you desire any personal explanation or information, I shall be happy to attend you whenever you may request it.

    Very respectfully, I am your obedient servant,
        THOMAS H. DUDLEY, *Consul*.

J. PRICE EDWARDS, Esq.,
    Collector of Customs, Liverpool.

        CUSTOM-HOUSE,
        Liverpool, July 10, 1862.

SIR: I beg to acknowledge the receipt of your communication of yesterday's date, (received this morning,) and to acquaint you that I shall immediately submit the same for the consideration and direction of the board of customs, under whom I have the honor to serve. I may observe, however, that I am respectfully of opinion that the statement made by you is not such as could be acted upon by the officers of this revenue, unless legally substantiated by evidence.

    I have the honor to be, sir, your obedient servant,
        J. PRICE EDWARDS, *Collector*.

CONSUL FOR THE UNITED STATES OF AMERICA.

CUSTOM-HOUSE,
Liverpool, July 16, 1862.

SIR: With reference to my letter of the 10th instant, acknowledging your communication of the 9th, relative to the vessel built by Messrs. Laird, of Birkenhead, I have to acquaint you, that I am directed by the commissioners of her Majesty's customs to apprise you that their solicitor informs them that the details given by you in regard to the said vessel are not sufficient, in a legal point of view, to justify me in taking upon myself the responsibility of the detention of this ship.

I have the honor to be, sir, your most obedient servant,
J. PRICE EDWARDS, *Collector.*

T. H. DUDLEY, Esq., *&c., &c.*

WASHINGTON, D.C., JULY 1862

Abraham Lincoln: Appeal to Border State Representatives for Compensated Emancipation

The President, in a renewed bid to gain support for compensated emancipation, convened a gathering of border state representatives and senators from Delaware, Maryland, Kentucky, Missouri, Tennessee, and the pending state of West Virginia and read them this appeal. Their response, signed by a majority (twenty out of twenty-eight), rejected the plan on such varied grounds as too costly, unconstitutional, inspiriting to the rebellion, and threatening "rights of property." On July 14 Lincoln sent a draft bill for compensated emancipation to Congress, where it failed of action before adjournment.

July 12, 1862

GENTLEMEN. After the adjournment of Congress, now very near, I shall have no opportunity of seeing you for several months. Believing that you of the border-states hold more power for good than any other equal number of members, I feel it a duty which I can not justifiably waive, to make this appeal to you. I intend no reproach or complaint when I assure you that in my opinion, if you all had voted for the resolution in the gradual emancipation message of last March, the war would now be substantially ended. And the plan therein proposed is yet one of the most potent, and swift means of ending it. Let the states which are in rebellion see, definitely and certainly, that, in no event, will the states you represent ever join their proposed Confederacy, and they can not, much longer maintain the contest. But you can not divest them of their hope to ultimately have you with them so long as you show a determination to perpetuate the institution within your own states. Beat them at elections, as you have overwhelmingly done, and, nothing daunted, they still claim you as their own. You and I know what the lever of their power is. Break that lever before their faces, and they can shake you no more forever.

Most of you have treated me with kindness and consideration; and I trust you will not now think I improperly touch what is exclusively your own, when, for the sake of the whole country I ask "Can you, for your states, do better than to take the course I urge?" Discarding *punctillio*, and maxims adapted to more manageable times, and looking only to the unprecedentedly stern facts of our case, can you do better in any possible event? You prefer that the constitutional relation of the states to the nation shall be practically restored, without disturbance of the institution; and if this were done, my whole duty, in this respect, under the constitution, and my oath of office, would be performed. But it is not done, and we are trying to accomplish it by war. The incidents of the war can not be avoided. If the war continue long, as it must, if the object be not sooner attained, the institution in your states will be extinguished by mere friction and abrasion—by the mere incidents of the war. It will be gone, and you will have nothing valuable in lieu of it. Much of it's value is gone already. How much better for you, and for your people, to take the step which, at once, shortens the war, and secures substantial compensation for that which is sure to be wholly lost in any other event. How much better to thus save the money which else we sink forever in the war. How much better to do it while we can, lest the war ere long render us pecuniarily unable to do it. How much better for you, as seller, and the nation as buyer, to sell out, and buy out, that without which the war could never have been, than to sink both the thing to be sold, and the price of it, in cutting one another's throats.

I do not speak of emancipation *at once*, but of a *decision* at once to emancipate *gradually*. Room in South America for colonization, can be obtained cheaply, and in abundance; and when numbers shall be large enough to be company and encouragement for one another, the freed people will not be so reluctant to go.

I am pressed with a difficulty not yet mentioned—one which threatens division among those who, united are none too strong. An instance of it is known to you. Gen. Hunter is an honest man. He was, and I hope, still is, my friend. I valued him none the less for his agreeing with me in the general wish that all men everywhere, could be free. He proclaimed all men free within certain states, and I repudiated the proclamation. He expected more good, and less harm from the measure, than I could believe would follow. Yet in repudiating it, I gave dissatisfaction, if not offence, to many whose support the country can not afford to lose. And this is not the end of it. The pressure, in this direction, is still upon me, and is increasing. By conceding what I now ask, you can relieve me, and much more, can relieve the country, in this important point. Upon these considerations I have again begged your attention to the message of March last. Before leaving the Capital, consider and discuss it among yourselves. You are patriots and statesmen; and, as such, I pray you, consider this proposition; and, at the least, commend it to the consideration of your states and people. As you would perpetuate popular government for the best people in the world, I beseech you that you do in no wise omit this. Our common country is in great peril, demanding the loftiest views, and boldest action to bring it speedy relief. Once relieved, it's form of government is saved to the world; it's beloved history, and cherished memories, are vindicated; and it's happy future fully assured, and rendered inconceivably grand. To you, more than to any others, the previlege is given, to assure that happiness, and swell that grandeur, and to link your own names therewith forever.

WASHINGTON, D.C., JULY 1862

Second Confiscation Act

On August 6, 1861, Congress passed the First Confiscation Act, authorizing the seizure of slaves used to militarily support the rebellion. After months of contentious debate, Congress adopted a second confiscation measure in July 1862 authorizing the seizure of slaves and other property from persons found by federal courts to be inciting or aiding rebellion. Lincoln found parts of the act legally dubious and prepared a veto message, but when Congress passed a resolution addressing many of his concerns, he signed the act and returned it along with his intended veto message. Although the Second Confiscation Act was seldom enforced, its passage demonstrated the increasing willingness of Congress to act against slavery.

An act to suppress insurrection, to punish treason and rebellion, to seize and confiscate the property of rebels, and for other purposes.

Be it enacted by the Senate and House of Representatives of the United States of America in Congress assembled, That every person who shall hereafter commit the crime of treason against the United States, and shall be adjudged guilty thereof, shall suffer death, and all his slaves, if any, shall be declared and made free; or, at the discretion of the court, he shall be imprisoned for not less than five years and fined not less than $10,000, and all his slaves, if any, shall be declared and made free; said fine shall be levied and collected on any or all of the property, real and personal, excluding slaves, of which the said person so convicted was the owner at the time of committing the said crime, any sale or conveyance to the contrary notwithstanding.

SEC. 2. *And be it further enacted*, That if any person shall hereafter incite, set on foot, assist, or engage in any rebellion or insurrection against the authority of the United States, or the laws thereof, or shall give aid or comfort thereto, or shall engage in, or give aid and comfort to, any such existing rebellion or insurrection, and be convicted thereof, such person shall be punished by imprisonment for a period not exceeding ten years, or by a fine not exceeding ten thousand dollars, and by the liberation of all his slaves, if any he have; or by both of said punishments, at the discretion of the court.

SEC. 3. *And be it further enacted*, That every person guilty of either of the offenses described in this act shall be forever incapable and disqualified to hold any office under the United States.

SEC. 4. *And be it further enacted*, That this act shall not be construed in any way to affect or alter the prosecution, conviction, or punishment of any person or persons guilty of treason against the United States before the passage of this act, unless such person is convicted under this act.

SEC. 5. *And be it further enacted*, That, to insure the speedy termination of the present rebellion, it shall be the duty of the President of the United States to cause the seizure of all the estate and property, money, stocks, credits, and effects of the persons hereinafter named in this section, and to apply and use the same and the proceeds thereof for the support of the Army of the United States—that is to say:

First. Of any person hereafter acting as an officer of the army or navy of the rebels in arms against the Government of the United States.

Secondly. Of any person hereafter acting as President, Vice-President, member of Congress, judge of any court, cabinet officer, foreign minister, commissioner or consul of the so-called Confederate States of America.

Thirdly. Of any person acting as Governor of a State, member of a convention or Legislature, or judge of any court of any of the so-called Confederate States of America.

Fourthly. Of any person who, having held an office of honor, trust, or profit in the United States, shall hereafter hold an office in the so-called Confederate States of America.

Fifthly. Of any person hereafter holding any office or agency under the government of the so-called Confederate States of America, or under any of the several States of the said Confederacy, or the laws thereof, whether such office or agency be national, state, or municipal in its name or character: *Provided*, That the persons thirdly, fourthly, and fifthly above described shall have accepted their appointment or election since the date of the pretended ordinance of secession of the State, or shall have taken an oath of allegiance to, or to support the Constitution of, the so-called Confederate States.

Sixthly. Of any person who, owning property in any loyal State or Territory of the United States, or in the District of Columbia, shall hereafter assist and give aid and comfort to such rebellion; and all sales, transfers, or conveyances of any such property shall be null and void; and it shall be a sufficient bar to any suit brought by such person for the possession or the use of such property, or any of it, to allege and prove that he is one of the persons described in this section.

Sec. 6. *And be it further enacted*, That if any person within any State or Territory of the United States, other than those named, as aforesaid, after the passage of this act, being engaged in armed rebellion against the Government of the United States, or aiding or abetting such rebellion, shall not, within sixty days after public warning and proclamation duly given and made by the President of the United States, cease to aid, countenance, and abet such rebellion, and return to his allegiance to the United States, all the estate and property, money, stocks, and credits of such person shall be liable to seizure, as aforesaid, and it shall be the duty of the President to seize and use them as aforesaid or the proceeds thereof. And all sales, transfers, or conveyances of any such property after the expiration of the said sixty days from the date of such warning and proclamation shall be null and void; and it shall be a sufficient bar to any suit brought by such person for the possession or the use of such property, or any of it, to allege and prove that he is one of the persons described in this section.

Sec. 7. *And be it further enacted*, That to secure the condemnation and sale of any of such property, after the same shall have been seized, so that it may be made available for the purpose aforesaid, proceedings in rem shall be instituted in the name of the United States in any district court thereof, or in any Territorial court or in the United States district court for the District of Columbia, within which the property above described, or any part thereof, may be found, or into which the same, if movable, may first be brought, which proceedings shall conform as nearly as may be to proceedings in admiralty or revenue cases; and if said property, whether real or personal, shall be found to have belonged to a person engaged in rebellion, or who has given aid or comfort thereto, the same shall be condemned as enemies' property and become the property of the United States, and may be disposed of as the court shall decree, and the proceeds thereof paid into the Treasury of the United States for the purposes aforesaid.

SEC. 8. *And be it further enacted*, That the several courts aforesaid shall have power to make such orders, establish such forms of decree and sale, and direct such deeds and conveyances to be executed and delivered by the marshals thereof where real estate shall be the subject of sale, as shall fitly and efficiently effect the purposes of this act, and vest in the purchasers of such property good and valid titles thereto. And the said courts shall have power to allow such fees and charges of their officers as shall be reasonable and proper in the premises.

SEC. 9. *And be it further enacted*, That all slaves of persons who shall hereafter be engaged in rebellion against the Government of the United States, or who shall in any way give aid or comfort thereto, escaping from such persons and taking refuge within the lines of the Army; and all slaves captured from such persons or deserted by them and coming under the control of the Government of the United States, and all slaves of such persons found *on* or being within any place occupied by rebel forces and afterward occupied by the forces of the United States shall be deemed captives of war, and shall be forever free of their servitude, and not again held as slaves.

SEC. 10. *And be it further enacted*, That no slave escaping into any State, Territory, or the District of Columbia, from any other State, shall be delivered up, or in any way impeded or hindered of his liberty, except for crime, or some offense against the laws, unless the person claiming said fugitive shall first make oath that the person to whom the labor or service of such fugitive is alleged to be due is his lawful owner, and has not borne arms against the United States in the present rebellion, nor in any way given aid and comfort thereto; and no person engaged in the military or naval service of the United States shall, under any pretense whatever, assume to decide on the validity of the claim of any person to the service or labor of any other person, or surrender up any such person to the claimant, on pain of being dismissed from the service.

SEC. 11. *And be it further enacted,* That the President of the United States is authorized to employ as many persons of African descent as he may deem necessary and proper for the suppression of this rebellion, and for this purpose he may organize and use them in such manner as he may judge best for the public welfare.

SEC. 12. *And be it further enacted,* That the President of the United States is hereby authorized to make provision for the transportation, colonization, and settlement, in some tropical country beyond the limits of the United States, of such persons of the African race, made free by the provisions of this act, as may be willing to emigrate, having first obtained the consent of the government of said country to their protection and settlement within the same, with all the rights and privileges of freemen.

SEC. 13. *And be it further enacted,* That the President is hereby authorized, at any time hereafter, by proclamation, to extend to persons who may have participated in the existing rebellion in any State or part thereof, pardon and amnesty, with such exceptions and at such time and on such conditions as he may deem expedient for the public welfare.

SEC. 14. *And be it further enacted,* That the courts of the United States shall have full power to institute proceedings, make orders and decrees, issue process, and do all other things necessary to carry this act into effect.

APPROVED July 17, 1862.

JOINT RESOLUTION explanatory of "An act to suppress insurrection, to punish treason and rebellion, to seize and confiscate the property of rebels, and for other purposes."

Resolved by the Senate and House of Representatives of the United States of America in Congress assembled, That the provisions of the third clause of the fifth section of "An act to suppress insurrection, to punish treason and rebellion, to seize and confiscate the property of rebels, and for other purposes," shall be so construed as not to apply to any act or acts done prior to the passage thereof, nor to include any member of a State Legislature or judge of any State court who has not, in accepting or entering upon his office, taken an oath to support the constitution of the so-called "Confederate States of America;" nor shall any punishment or proceedings under said act be so construed as to work a forfeiture of the real estate of the offender beyond his natural life.

APPROVED July 17, 1862.

"SUCCESS AND GLORY":
WASHINGTON, D.C., JULY 1862

John Pope: Address to the Army of Virginia

General Pope was a career soldier who had gained notice for capturing Island No. 10 and New Madrid, Missouri, during the Union operations to open the Mississippi. He had then commanded the Army of Mississippi under Henry Halleck in the nearly bloodless advance on Corinth. Pope issued this address thinking to overcome what he took to be a spiritless and defeatist attitude among the troops of his new command, the Army of Virginia, assembled from the various units that had chased after Stonewall Jackson in the Shenandoah Valley.

HEADQUARTERS ARMY OF VIRGINIA,
Washington, D. C., July 14, 1862.
To the Officers and Soldiers of the Army of Virginia:

By special assignment of the President of the United States I have assumed the command of this army. I have spent two weeks in learning your whereabouts, your condition, and your wants, in preparing you for active operations, and in placing you in positions from which you can act promptly and to the purpose. These labors are nearly completed, and I am about to join you in the field.

Let us understand each other. I have come to you from the West, where we have always seen the backs of our enemies; from an army whose business it has been to seek the adversary and to beat him when he was found; whose policy has been attack and not defense. In but one instance has the enemy been able to place our Western armies in defensive attitude. I presume that I have been called here to pursue the same system and to lead you against the enemy. It is my purpose to do so, and that speedily. I am sure you long for an opportunity to win the distinction you are capable of achieving. That opportunity I shall endeavor to give you. Meantime I desire you to dismiss from your minds certain phrases, which I am sorry to find so much in vogue amongst you. I hear constantly of "taking strong positions and holding them," of "lines of retreat," and of "bases of supplies." Let us discard such ideas. The strongest position a soldier should desire to occupy is one from which he can most easily advance against the enemy. Let us study the probable lines of retreat of our opponents, and leave our own to take care of themselves. Let us look before us, and not behind. Success and glory are in the advance, disaster and shame lurk in the rear. Let us act on this understanding, and it is safe to predict that your banners shall be inscribed with many a glorious deed and that your names will be dear to your countrymen forever.

JNO. POPE,
Major-General, Commanding.

A CHANGE IN POLICY:
WASHINGTON, D.C., JULY 1862

John Pope: General Orders Nos. 5, 7, 11

These general orders, issued "By command of General Pope," marked a hardening of attitudes toward Southern civilians in the war zone. They were prepared at Secretary of War Stanton's direction and approved by the President, but their notoriety clung to Pope. The more draconian measures were not carried out, but the order "to subsist upon the country" was widely followed. "The lawless acts of many of our soldiers are worthy of worse than death," complained an Army of Virginia officer. "The villains urge as authority, 'Gen Pope's order.'" Robert E. Lee, when he saw the orders, termed Pope a "miscreant" and told Stonewall Jackson, "I want Pope to be suppressed."

GENERAL ORDERS, } HEADQUARTERS ARMY OF VIRGINIA,
No. 5. } *Washington, July* 18, 1862.

Hereafter, as far as practicable, the troops of this command will subsist upon the country in which their operations are carried on. In all cases supplies for this purpose will be taken by the officers to whose department they properly belong under the orders of the commanding officer of the troops for whose use they are intended. Vouchers will be given to the owners, stating on their face that they will be payable at the conclusion of the war, upon sufficient testimony being furnished that such owners have been loyal citizens of the United States since the date of the vouchers. Whenever it is known that supplies can be furnished in any district of the country where the troops are to operate the use of trains for carrying subsistence will be dispensed with as far as possible.

By command of Major-General Pope:

GEO. D. RUGGLES,
Colonel, Assistant Adjutant-General, and Chief of Staff.

GENERAL ORDERS, } HEADQUARTERS ARMY OF VIRGINIA,
No. 7. *Washington, July* 20, 1862.

The people of the valley of the Shenandoah and throughout the region of operations of this army living along the lines of railroad and telegraph and along the routes of travel in rear of the United States forces are notified that they will be held responsible for any injury done to the track, line, or road, or for any attacks upon trains or straggling soldiers by bands of guerrillas in their neighborhood. No privileges and immunities of warfare apply to lawless bands of individuals not forming part of the organized forces of the enemy nor wearing the garb of soldiers, who, seeking and obtaining safety on pretext of being peaceful citizens, steal out in rear of the army, attack and murder straggling soldiers, molest trains of supplies, destroy railroads, telegraph lines, and bridges, and commit outrages disgraceful to civilized people and revolting to humanity. Evil-disposed persons in rear of our armies who do not themselves engage directly in these lawless acts encourage them by refusing to interfere or to give any information by which such acts can be prevented or the perpetrators punished.

Safety of life and property of all persons living in rear of our advancing armies depends upon the maintenance of peace and quiet among themselves and upon the unmolested movements through their midst of all pertaining to the military service. They are to understand distinctly that this security of travel is their only warrant of personal safety.

It is therefore ordered that wherever a railroad, wagon road, or telegraph is injured by parties of guerrillas the citizens living within 5 miles of the spot shall be turned out in mass to repair the damage, and shall, beside, pay to the United States in money or in property, to be levied by military force, the full amount of the pay and subsistence of the whole force necessary to coerce the performance of the work during the time occupied in completing it.

If a soldier or legitimate follower of the army be fired upon from any house the house shall be razed to the ground, and the inhabitants sent prisoners to the headquarters of this army. If such an outrage occur at any place distant from settlements, the people within 5 miles around shall be held accountable and made to pay an indemnity sufficient for the case.

Any persons detected in such outrages, either during the act or at any time afterward, shall be shot, without awaiting civil process. No such acts can influence the result of this war, and they can only lead to heavy afflictions to the population to no purpose.

It is therefore enjoined upon all persons, both for the security of their property and the safety of their own persons, that they act vigorously and cordially together to prevent the perpetration of such outrages.

Whilst it is the wish of the general commanding this army that all peaceably disposed persons who remain at their homes and pursue their accustomed avocations shall be subjected to no improper burden of war, yet their own safety must of necessity depend upon the strict preservation of peace and order among themselves; and they are to understand that nothing will deter him from enforcing promptly and to the full extent every provision of this order.

By command of Major-General Pope:

GEO. D. RUGGLES,
Colonel, Assistant Adjutant-General, and Chief-of-Staff.

GENERAL ORDERS, } HEADQUARTERS ARMY OF VIRGINIA,
No. 11. } *Washington, July* 23, 1862.

Commanders of army corps, divisions, brigades, and detached commands will proceed immediately to arrest all disloyal male citizens within their lines or within their reach in rear of their respective stations.

Such as are willing to take the oath of allegiance to the United States and will furnish sufficient security for its observance shall be permitted to remain at their homes and pursue in good faith their accustomed avocations. Those who refuse shall be conducted South beyond the extreme pickets of this army, and be notified that if found again anywhere within our lines or at any point in rear they will be considered spies, and subjected to the extreme rigor of military law.

If any person, having taken the oath of allegiance as above specified, be found to have violated it, he shall be shot, and his property seized and applied to the public use.

All communication with any person whatever living within the lines of the enemy is positively prohibited, except through the military authorities and in the manner specified by military law; and any person concerned in writing or in carrying letters or messages in any other way will be considered and treated as a spy within the lines of the United States Army.

By command of Major-General Pope:

GEO. D. RUGGLES,
Colonel, Assistant Adjutant-General, and Chief of Staff.

THE "IDOL" OF THE ARMY: VIRGINIA, JULY 1862
Fitz John Porter to Joseph C. G. Kennedy

General Porter, Fifth Corps, Army of the Potomac, had commanded in three of the battles in the Seven Days. He was McClellan's closest confidant and purveyor of his views. He wrote to Kennedy, head of the Census Office, thinking him to be influential in the capital. Much to Porter's later discomfort, Kennedy sent the letter to Secretary of State Seward as an example of the "undisguised opinions of men whose convictions are worthy of consideration," and from Seward the letter made its way to Lincoln, Stanton, and even John Pope.

———————

Westover Landing, James River.
July 17" '62

My dear Sir,

Your kind and complimentary letter was recieved last evening. However just & correct my opinions, or of whatever value, I beg of you never to dissiminate them as mine. Where they should have influence they will be unheeded, where they would be received they exist. I have no desire to appear before the public except in my record as military man: in my efforts to crush & speedily this rebellion.

I regret to see that Genl Pope has not improved since his youth and has now written himself down, what the military world has long known, an ass. His address to his troops will make him ridiculous in the eyes of military men abroad as well as at home, and will reflect no credit on Mr. Lincoln who has just promoted him. If the theory he proclaims is practised you may look for disaster.

You say you have reason to believe that an army of 175000 men will soon be ready to march on Richmond. How is it to march? Are fresh, raw troops, to be united with the (acknowledged by him) demoralized troops of Genl Pope, and put in motion from the direction of Washington, Manassas, Warrenton &c? That army will not reach Richmond unless this one clears the way, or it (the former) goes there as prisoners. Or are the troops sufficient to swell this army to 175000 men to be sent to the 75000 now here of well disciplined, well drilled, well officered, veteran troops—who in three days if properly supported can be knocking at the gates of Richmond? Our obstacles lie just in front of that city: The other army has them in every mile of its advance as well as at Richmond, and that very one which Pope scouts—care of communications or attention to the rear—is no trifling one. If opposed Pope's army will be the guard merely for an enormous wagon train—and will not move as a body on an average 20 miles in two weeks. This army sees no reinforcements coming to it, though all feel if there are truly patriotic men of sense at home having influence, they must know that if the ranks of the regiments now in the field were filled up one man would be worth five to service if in new regiments. The confederates know this and have thrown their conscripts into the ranks where they fight like the disciplined troops by their sides. Many lessons in military matters may be taken from them. One is decision, energy, determination and unity in its administration—and in having a policy. I hear the men talk of what they design when they go home. I tell you, the voice is a warning one, and I hear it from the western army, and bodes no good to the present administration, party or to the radicals. I have heard them say among themselves (and officers say it) that the President promised help, but they will put no faith in him, till they see evidences strong as holy writ. They have believed in him as "honest"—but with honesty is expected firmness and decision, and professions alone will not avail. These murmurs bode no good. Our army will soon be getting restless. It is recuperating rapidly, and becoming equipped again, and if we had even 20000 more men Richmond would be looking for us. We must and soon will take the offensive, and we hope for success, but heart must be given our men by support from home. If we could see two or three regiments arriving daily our officers & men would not be afflicted with any other nostalgia than of their home, Richmond.

I have heard that General McClellan has lost favor at Washington: a report which I hope is unfounded and that General Halleck is to be called to Washington as General-in-Chief. I regret both if true. There is no more able commander than McClellan—and no one in whom the army has more confidence. Every army has its idol, and McClellan is the idol of this, and I should deeply regret for the sake of our country anything being done to supercede him. There is no one here in whom the army has more confidence. He is no politician but moves along with the spirit of a true soldier to use to the best advantage the means placed at his disposal to break down this rebellion. But enough of this. All I hope & pray & work for is, a speedy termination of the war by a restoration of union feeling: but many, many lives have to be lost.

The members of my staff are all well and desire remembrance to yourself and family. Butterfield has gone home sick, will return soon if well enough. Excuse this hasty and disconnected letter, written during an hundred interruptions and accept for yourself & family the best & warmest wishes of

       Yours faithfully
       F.J. Porter

J.C.G. Kennedy
Washington, D.C.

AN APPEAL FOR NEGOTIATION:
RHODE ISLAND, JULY 1862

August Belmont to Thurlow Weed

Belmont, the noted financier and national chairman of the Democratic Party, wrote to influential Republican Weed, editor of the *Albany Evening Journal*, in expectation that his letter would find its way to the President, as indeed it did; it is preserved in Lincoln's papers. Belmont's views represented the conservative "War Democrat" wing of his party—supporting the war against secession, but seeking some negotiated path to bring the rebellious states back into a Union "as it was." Lincoln wrote Belmont on July 31, not in direct reply but clearly aware of his views: "Those enemies must understand that they cannot experiment for ten years trying to destroy the government, and if they fail still come back into the Union unhurt."

Copy

New-port. R. I. July 20. 1862.

My dear Mr. Weed.

I have made several attempts to see you during your fleeting visits to New-York, but have not been so fortunate as to find you in.—.

Our National affairs are in a most critical position, more so than they have been at any time since the beginning of this unfortunate war.—.

What frightens me more than the disasters in the field is the apathy and distrust which I grieve to say I meet at every step even from men of standing and hitherto of undoubted loyalty to the Union—

You know my own feelings & convictions on the subject of our national troubles, & I am sure I can speak to you in all candor without the fear of having my thoughts misconstrued, though you may perhaps not share my views.—

My firm conviction is that any other solution to our present difficulties than a reconstruction of but one Government over all the states of our Confederacy would entail upon us & our children an inheritance of the most fearful consequences which must end in the utter disintegration & ruin of the whole country.—.

There are only two modes by which to prevent such a calamity, which is certainly at this moment more threatening than it has ever been before.—.

The one is by an energetic & unrelenting prosecution of the war to crush the rebellion, the other would be to negociate with the leaders of the Rebellion, (to which it would be madness to withold the character of a gigantic revolution) and to see whether it may not yet be possible to reestablish a federal Union—

Both alternatives present difficulties of the gravest nature & which they did not possess in the same degree at the beginning of the contest—

Our army has been decimated by disease & the casualities of war.

I am informed from reliable sources, that McClellan has barely 70.000 men all told & Pope's army, including the corps of McDowell Sigel & Banks is said to number barely 40.000—men. What can we expect to do with such a force against Richmond, which is defended by an enemy having probably double that number under arms, flushed with recent successes, commanded by generals at least equal to our's, directed by *one master spirit* & occupying a central position, in a country hostile to us?—

It is true the President has called out 300/m men, but it would be a *fatal delusion* to beleive, that this number would be sufficient to crush the enemy, even if it was sure that under the present system of volunteers the men would come forward.—. I think I make a liberal estimate, if I put the figure of the federal armies, all told at 400.000 effective men & this number will be reduced to 300/m before the new levies can be brought into the field.—.

When we stopped recruiting in the midst of our successes we dealt a fatal blow to our army, and it is really a wonder to me that our Commanding generals consented to submit to such a measure which crippled them when an overwhelming force became necessary to finish up the good work;— It was a policy hardly less suicidal than if we had stopped sending supplies & amunition to our men in the field. Where we would have found last winter 10 men eager to enlist, anxious to share in our triumphs we will hardly now find one, so deep are the gloom and distrust which have taken hold of our people.—. It would be worse than folly, to shut our eyes to this fact.—. I think ours is the first instance in history where a Government shut off its supplies of men in the midst of a gigantic war.

Look at England her enlistments in the Crimean war, lasted until the very day of the conclusion of peace.—.

There is now only one way to remedy our fatal error, that is for the President to establish a system of conscription by which instead of 300/m *at least 500.000 men are to be called under arms.*—

A straight forward proclamation of the President, setting forth the necessities of the case & appealing to the patriotism of the people will give more confidence than all the ill concealed attempts at palliating our desperate condition.—.

Instead of levying new regiments commanded by inexperienced officers of their own choosing & who for a year to come would barely add anything to our efficiency in the field, the new recruits ought to be collected at camps of instruction in healthy localities East & West, where under the direction of *West point graduates* they should be drilled and disiplined.—.

From thence as fast as they are fit for active duty, they should be forwarded to the army, to be incorporated in the old regiments *without reference to states & only where they are most needed*. This is the only way to create for this war an efficient *United States Army* & will strike a severe blow, to that most fatal of heresies (*States right & States pride*) which lies at the bottom of all our misfortunes. Besides that such a mode would be infinitely more enconomical, and the raw recruits mixed with our old Soldiers, would be of course much more reliable & steady before the enemy's fire, than in seperate regiments, commanded by officers just as inexperienced as themselves.

Simultaneously with these measures which ought to be taken, with the utmost vigor & despatch, we must infuse more life and energie in our naval department. The fact is we have made the great mistake to undertake a war on a gigantic scale by land where our oponnents are at least nearly as strong as we are, instead of throwing our best resources & energies upon that mode of warfare where we had the enemy at our mercy.—.

Had we at the very outset of the rebellion ordered 50 Iron Gunboats, even at the cost of 1 Million of Dollars a piece, we should before last January have been in possession of every southern port. With 200000 men we could have held by land, the line of the Potomac, Missouri & Tennessee and thus hemmed in we would have brought the south to terms, just as Russia had to sue for peace after the fall of Sebastapool.—

I think it is still in our power to accomplish this, though the task has become more difficult since Charleston, Savanah & Mobile have been so strongly fortified during the last six months. No time money & efforts ought to be spared, to build at *least 20* more large iron steamships with which to take & hold every important city on the rebel coast from North Carolina to Texas. If authority for all these measures is not vested in the President, he ought at once to call an extra session of Congress.

I have thus far given you my views of the steps which I consider indispensible if the sword is to be the arbiter of our future destiny, but is there no other way of saving our country, from all the horror & calamities, which even a successful war must entail upon us?

It may appear almost hopeless to attempt to bring the south back to the Union by negociation. Men & women alike in that distracted portion of our country have become frantic & exasperated by the teachings of unprincipled leaders and the miseries of cival war.—. Still I cannot bring myself to the beleif that the door to a reconciliation between the two sections is irrevocably & for ever shut.

The losses & sufferings which have befallen us, have been felt tenfold in the revolted states, and the thinking men of the south must see that a continuation of the war must end, in the utter destruction of their property & institutions.

The frightful carnage of many a battlefield must have convinced each section of the bravery of its opponents and how much better it will be to have them as friends than foes.—.

While I am convinced that the President would be willing to

see the South in the lawful possession of all its constitutional rights. —

—I have not lost all hope, that with these rights guaranteed a reunion of the two sections could not be accomplished. In any event it seems to me that an attempt at negociation should be made & that the time for it has not entirely passed away.—.

If one or two conservative men who without holding any official position possess influence & weight enough with our people and the Government to inspire confidence in their statements to the leading men of the south, could be found to proceed under the authority or at least with the knowledge of the President to Richmond, in order to open negociations I think success might crown their efforts.—.

It is impossible & would be presumptuous in me to point out the conditions of such a compromise, but I think that propositions would prove acceptable to the south, which contained in their general outline an amnesty for all political offences during the war & the calling of a national convention for the purpose of reconstructing the federal compact with such modifications in the constitution as our late sad experience has demonstrated to have become necessary

The war debts of the North & South might either be borne by each respective section or better still be funded & assumed by the general Government.—

The Monroe doctrine to be strictly and uncompromisingly enforced which would require & Justify a larger standing national army & navy than heretofore, thus give us a chance to make provisions for such of their military leaders, who repenting their past errors are willing again to serve that flag, to which as friends & as foes they owe all the distinction which they have ever acheived.

I know that some of these concessions will be very distasteful to our people — they can be to no one more so than to myself.—.

Every sacrifice must however be made at the alter of our country, when we can restore it to peace & prosperity, and with our blood, & with our treasure we must also be ready to yield our prejudices *& even our convictions*

I firmly beleive that the President would find the hearty support of the vast majority of our people in such a policy and he ought not to lose any time in carrying out these views.—. Such men for instance as yourself and Governor H. Seymour would soon be able to find out, whether the men who are guiding the destinies of the South could be brought to listen to the dictates of reason & moderation.

Before we enter upon a new phase in this terrible war, which must carry with it horrors & misery far greater than what we have witnessed yet, I cannot but think that patriotism & humanity alike call for an earnest effort towards reconciliation & peace.

If our efforts should be spurned & rejected we shall stand Justified before God & men and our good cause will have His blessing & the worlds sympathy.

(signed). August Belmont.

A "SHAMEFUL" DEFEAT:
WASHINGTON, D.C., JULY 1862

Salmon P. Chase to Richard C. Parsons

Secretary of the Treasury Chase reviewed the Seven Days' Battles for an old friend who was serving as U.S. consul in Rio de Janeiro. The new general-in-chief, Henry Halleck, was brought from the western theater along with John Pope. Although Chase dated the letter July 20, the cabinet meeting he describes was held on July 21.

Washington July 20, 1862

My dear Parsons

Day before yesterday your friend, Mr. Bond, called bringing pleasant news of you and yours & those winged jewels converted into wingless uses by being cased in gold. Brazilian gold coffining denizens of Brazilian air now made ornaments of Northern dames. Tell Mrs Parsons I am exceedingly obliged by her gift and hope she will not be displeased by my transfer of it to Nettie, who has now almost grown to be a young lady & while delighted with her sisters presents, evidently thought *she* ought not to be passed by. Now a gift to Nettie is a gift to me & Mrs Parsons has thus been made a double giver and has the thanks of us both.

You will have been mortified & grieved by the news of the disasters which have overtaken us. Since the rebellion broke out I have never been so sad.

The defeat of McClellan before Richmond was shameful, and attributable only to gross neglect & incompetency for which he should at once have been dismissed the service in disgrace.

You may think I speak strongly but you may be assured I do not speak one whit too strongly.

Just think of an army of ninety five thousand men, admirably provided, with unequalled artillery—the Commanding General on the south side of the Chicky. with over sixty probably seventy thousand men and a Corps General Porter with some twenty five thousand on the north bank. The enemy has *at most* not over one hundred thousand men inferior to ours in all respects, except perhaps numbers / Of this force two divisions Hugers & Magruder's are on the James or near it below Richmond—the other four or five divisions are in Richmond & in front of it between our army & the city. The whole of these four or five divisions—except perhaps five or ten thousand men left in Richmond—possibly (including Margruders & Hugers) making thirty thousand men left [   ] south side of the Chicky.—the whole of these four or five divisions, I say, march out & attack Porter. Instead of keeping his line of supply open—instead of giving Porter force enough to ensure a victory on the north bank—McClellan orders his base to be abandoned—his supplies withdrawn from the White House—leaves Porter to be beaten by superior numbers—draws him across the Chickahominy to his own force, kept almost wholly inactive thus far, & commences a disgraceful retreat, only saved from becoming a complete rout by the bravery of the men & skill of the Generals of the Corps & their subordinate officers. After five days retreating & fighting he reaches the James River & there has ever since remained & now remains under the protection of the gunboats.

The smallness of our losses in all these movements compared with the numbers of the army & the hardships & confusions incident to such retreats, show how small relatively to the fears of McClellan the enemys strength must have been. The total loss was about 1500 killed, about $\mp$5000 wounded & about 8000 missing.

We ought to won a victory and taken Richmond. We lost a battle & narrowly escaped a capitulation of our entire army.

After the battle & after the retreat & after reaching Harrisons Landing McClellan telegraphed the President that he had not more than 50.000 men by their colors. An actual inspection by the President made a few days afterwards proved that he must have had at that very time over eighty thousand.

Can you conceive anything more disgraceful?

Strange as it may seem the President even yet hesitates about superceding McClellan in the command of the Army of the Potomac. He has however resolved to give him at least a Commander by bringing Gen. Halleck here and giving him the

Command in Chief of all the Armies. Meantime also he has brought Pope here and placed him in command of the Army of Virginia, with all the state east of the Fredericksburgh Railroad to operate it. Already a Cavalry detachment inspired by Pope has cut the Virginia Central Railroad west of Richmond & within thirty or forty miles. By day after tomorrow I hope to hear that another detachment has taken Charlottesville & cleared the road towards Lynchburgh at least for a few miles. It is no secret which need be kept from a man beyond the Equinoctial that Pope hopes to be able to concentrate a force in a few days which will enable him to command all the railway approaches to Richmond from the West. We are calling out more men but we don't need them. What we need is activity in Generals & skill & courage.

The Slavery question perplexes the President almost as much as ever and yet I think he is about to emerge from the obscurities where he has been groping into somewhat clearer light.

Today he has had his Secretaries in Consultation & has read us several orders which he is thinking of promulgating:—one, requiring Generals to subsist their troops as far as may be on the enemy; another, authorizing the employment of negroes as laborers by the Generals; a third in form of a proclamation warning the rebels of the confiscations denounced by Congress and declaring his purpose to enfranchise the slaves of all rebels (unless they return to their allegiance in Sixty days) in all the Gulf States. He has also under consideration the question of authorizing the enlistment or employment of negroes as soldiers by Generals in the Gulf States. So you see the world moves. These measures, if all of them are adopted will decide everything. The three first will go near the same result & must necessarily draw the fourth after them. These measures, & the substitution of an able general for McClellan, & the genius & indefatigable labor of Halleck presiding over all, will I hope soon end this rebellion. I say I hope—but I do not hope so confidently as I did. McClellan is not *yet* superceded—Halleck has not *yet* been tried in this sphere. Room for disappointment certainly—but let me trust that disappointment will not come.

What documents do you receive regularly from the U States? What Newspapers? I take the liberty of sending you a paper from the Wall St Review, which rather shocks my modesty.

Katie and Nettie have both retired or they would send all sorts of good wishes & affectionate remembrances.

We are meditating a little excursion Northward. Best regards to Mrs P and believe me as ever

Most faithfully your friend
S P Chase

Richard Parsons Esq

Don't forget to remember me most cordially to Gen. Webb

PRESIDENTIAL EMANCIPATION:
WASHINGTON, D.C., JULY 1862

Salmon P. Chase: Journal, July 22, 1862

On July 13, the day after his fruitless appeal to border state congressmen to support compensated emancipation, Lincoln revealed privately to Seward and Secretary of the Navy Welles that he had concluded to emancipate the slaves by presidential proclamation. He said, as Welles recorded it, "we must free the slaves or be ourselves subdued." Secretary Chase here reports the President's announcement of his emancipation proclamation to the full cabinet on July 22, drawing on the recent Second Confiscation Act and on his war powers.

TUESDAY, JULY 22D., 1862. This morning, I called on the President with a letter received some time since from Col. Key, in which he stated that he had reason to beleive that if Genl. McClellan found he could not otherwise sustain himself in Virginia, he would declare the liberation of the slaves; and that the President would not dare to interfere with the Order. I urged upon the President the importance of an immediate change in the command of the Army of the Potomac, representing the necessity of having a General in that command who would cordially and efficiently coöperate with the movements of Pope and others; and urging a change before the arrival of Genl. Halleck, in view of the extreme delicacy of his position in this respect, Genl. McClellan being his senior Major-General. I said that I did not regard Genl. McClellan as loyal to the Administration, although I did not question his general loyalty to the country.

I also urged Genl. McClellan's removal upon financial grounds. I told him that, if such a change in the command was made as would insure action to the army and give it power in the ratio of its strength, and if such measures were adopted in respect to slavery as would inspire the country with confidence that no measure would be left untried which promised a speedy and successful result, I would insure that, within ten days, the Bonds of the U.S.—except the 5–20s.—would be so far above par that conversions into the latter stock would take place rapidly and furnish the necessary means for carrying on the Government. If this was not done, it seemed to me impossible to meet necessary expenses. Already there were $10.000.000 of unpaid Requisitions, and this amount must constantly increase.

The President came to no conclusion, but said he would confer with Gen. Halleck on all these matters. I left him, promising to return to Cabinet, when the subject of the Orders discussed yesterday would be resumed.

Went to Cabinet at the appointed hour. It was unanimously agreed that the Order in respect to Colonization should be dropped; and the others were adopted unanimously, except that I wished North Carolina included among the States named in the first order.

The question of arming slaves was then brought up and I advocated it warmly. The President was unwilling to adopt this measure, but proposed to issue a Proclamation, on the basis of the Confiscation Bill, calling upon the States to return to their allegiance—warning the rebels the provisions of the Act would have full force at the expiration of sixty days—adding, on his own part, a declaration of his intention to renew, at the next session of Congress, his recommendation of compensation to States adopting the gradual abolishment of slavery—and proclaiming the emancipation of all slaves within States remaining in insurrection on the first of January, 1863.

I said that I should give to such a measure my cordial support; but I should prefer that no new expression on the subject of compensation should be made, and I thought that the measure of Emancipation could be much better and more quietly accomplished by allowing Generals to organize and arm the slaves (thus avoiding depredation and massacre on the one hand, and support to the insurrection on the other) and by directing the Commanders of Departments to proclaim emancipation within their Districts as soon as practicable; but I regarded this as so much better than inaction on the subject, that I should give it my entire support.

The President determined to publish the first three Orders forthwith, and to leave the other for some further consideration. The impression left upon my mind by the whole discussion was, that while the President thought that the organization, equipment and arming of negroes, like other soldiers, would be productive of more evil than good, he was not unwilling that Commanders should, at their discretion, arm, for purely defensive purposes, slaves coming within their lines.

Mr. Stanton brought forward a proposition to draft 50.000 men. Mr. Seward proposed that the number should be 100.000. The President directed that, whatever number were drafted, should be a part of the 300.000 already called for. No decision was reached, however.

WASHINGTON, D.C., JULY 1862

Abraham Lincoln: First Draft of the Emancipation Proclamation

July 22, 1862

Only the first paragraph of this draft was immediately published, on July 25, in reference to that section of the Second Confiscation Act referring to the potential seizure of property of those in rebellion or abetting rebellion. The following selection explains why the rest of the proclamation—its core—was not immediately made public.

In pursuance of the sixth section of the act of congress entitled "An act to suppress insurrection and to punish treason and rebellion, to seize and confiscate property of rebels, and for other purposes" Approved July 17. 1862, and which act, and the Joint Resolution explanatory thereof, are herewith published, I, Abraham Lincoln, President of the United States, do hereby proclaim to, and warn all persons within the contemplation of said sixth section to cease participating in, aiding, countenancing, or abetting the existing rebellion, or any rebellion against the government of the United States, and to return to their proper allegiance to the United States, on pain of the forfeitures and seizures, as within and by said sixth section provided.

And I hereby make known that it is my purpose, upon the next meeting of congress, to again recommend the adoption of a practical measure for tendering pecuniary aid to the free choice or rejection, of any and all States which may then be recognizing and practically sustaining the authority of the United States, and which may then have voluntarily adopted, or thereafter may voluntarily adopt, gradual abolishment of slavery within such State or States—that the object is to practically restore, thenceforward to be maintained, the constitutional relation between the general government and each, and all the states, wherein that relation is now suspended, or disturbed; and that, for this object, the war, as it has been, will be, prossecuted. And, as a fit and necessary military measure for effecting this object, I, as Commander-in-Chief of the Army and Navy of the United States, do order and declare that on the first day of January in the year of Our Lord one thousand, eight hundred and sixtythree, all persons held as slaves within any state or states, wherein the constitutional authority of the United States shall not then be practically recognized, submitted to, and maintained, shall then, thenceforward, and forever, be free.

> Emancipation Proclamation
> as first sketched and
> shown to the Cabinet in
> July 1862.

POSTPONING EMANCIPATION:
WASHINGTON, D.C., JULY 1862

Francis B. Carpenter: from Six Months at the White House with Abraham Lincoln

An established portrait painter, Carpenter lived at the White House from February to July 1864 while painting his well-known depiction of Lincoln reading the Emancipation Proclamation to the cabinet. In his 1866 memoir Carpenter related a conversation he had with the President on February 6, 1864, in which Lincoln recalled discussing the initial reaction of his cabinet to the proclamation. While it is unlikely that he recorded the President verbatim, the essence of what Carpenter said Lincoln said is supported by other accounts.

"It had got to be," said he, "midsummer, 1862. Things had gone on from bad to worse, until I felt that we had reached the end of our rope on the plan of operations we had been pursuing; that we had about played our last card, and must change our tactics, or lose the game! I now determined upon the adoption of the emancipation policy; and, without consultation with, or the knowledge of the Cabinet, I prepared the original draft of the proclamation, and, after much anxious thought, called a Cabinet meeting upon the subject. This was the last of July, or the first part of the month of August, 1862." (The exact date he did not remember.) "This Cabinet meeting took place, I think, upon a Saturday. All were present, excepting Mr. Blair, the Postmaster-General, who was absent at the opening of the discussion, but came in subsequently. I said to the Cabinet that I had resolved upon this step, and had not called them together to ask their advice, but to lay the subject-matter of a proclamation before them; suggestions as to which would be in order, after they had heard it read. Mr. Lovejoy," said he, "was in error when he informed you that it excited no comment, excepting on the part of Secretary Seward. Various suggestions were offered. Secretary Chase wished the language stronger in reference to the arming of the blacks. Mr. Blair, after he came in, deprecated the policy, on the ground that it would cost the Administration the fall elections. Nothing, however, was offered that I had not already fully anticipated and settled in my own mind, until Secretary Seward spoke. He said in substance: 'Mr. President, I approve of the proclamation, but I question the expediency of its issue at this juncture. The depression of the public mind, consequent upon our repeated reverses, is so great that I fear the effect of so important a step. It may be viewed as the last measure of an exhausted government, a cry for help; the government stretching forth its hands to Ethiopia, instead of Ethiopia stretching forth her hands to the government.' His idea," said the President, "was that it would be considered our last *shriek*, on the retreat." (This was his *precise* expression.) "'Now,' continued Mr. Seward, 'while I approve the measure, I suggest, sir, that you postpone its issue, until you can give it to the country supported by military success, instead of issuing it, as would be the case now, upon the greatest disasters of the war!'" Mr. Lincoln continued: "The wisdom of the view of the Secretary of State struck me with very great force. It was an aspect of the case that, in all my thought upon the subject, I had entirely overlooked. The result was that I put the draft of the proclamation aside, as you do your sketch for a picture, waiting for a victory."

SAVING THE GOVERNMENT:
WASHINGTON, D.C., JULY 1862

Abraham Lincoln to Cuthbert Bullitt

Cuthbert Bullitt and Thomas J. Durant, whose letter Bullitt forwarded to the President, were Louisiana unionists. Lincoln's reply to Bullitt forecast his hardening attitude toward prosecuting the conflict.

PRIVATE
Cuthbert Bullitt Esq Washington D.C.
New Orleans La. July 28. 1862

Sir: The copy of a letter addressed to yourself by Mr. Thomas J. Durant, has been shown to me. The writer appears to be an able, a dispassionate, and an entirely sincere man. The first part of the letter is devoted to an effort to show that the Secession Ordinance of Louisiana was adopted against the will of a majority of the people. This is probably true; and in that fact may be found some instruction. Why did they allow the Ordinance to go into effect? Why did they not assert themselves? Why stand passive and allow themselves to be trodden down by a minority? Why did they not hold popular meetings, and have a convention of their own, to express and enforce the true sentiment of the state? If preorganization was against them *then*, why not do this *now*, that the United States Army is present to protect them? The paralysis—the dead palsy—of the government in this whole struggle is, that this class of men will do nothing for the government, nothing for themselves, except demanding that the government shall not strike its open enemies, lest they be struck by accident!

Mr. Durant complains that in various ways the relation of master and slave is disturbed by the presence of our Army; and he considers it particularly vexatious that this, in part, is done under cover of an act of Congress, while constitutional guaranties are suspended on the plea of military necessity. The truth is, that what is done, and omitted, about slaves, is done and omitted on the same military necessity. It is a military necessity to have men and money; and we can get neither, in sufficient numbers, or amounts, if we keep from, or drive from, our lines, slaves coming to them. Mr. Durant cannot be ignorant of the pressure in this direction; nor of my efforts to hold it within bounds till he, and such as he shall have time to help themselves.

I am not posted to speak understandingly on all the police regulations of which Mr. Durant complains. If experience shows any one of them to be wrong, let them be set right. I think I can perceive, in the freedom of trade, which Mr. Durant urges, that he would relieve both friends and enemies from the pressure of the blockade. By this he would serve the enemy more effectively than the enemy is able to serve himself. I do not say or believe that to serve the enemy is the purpose of Mr. Durant; or that he is conscious of any purpose, other than national and patriotic ones. Still, if there were a class of men who, having no choice of sides in the contest, were anxious only to have quiet and comfort for themselves while it rages, and to fall in with the victorious side at the end of it, without loss to themselves, their advice as to the mode of conducting the contest would be precisely such as his is. He speaks of no duty—apparently thinks of none—resting upon Union men. He even thinks it injurious to the Union cause that they should be restrained in trade and passage without taking sides. They are to touch neither a sail nor a pump, but to be merely passengers,—dead-heads at that—to be carried snug and dry, throughout the storm, and safely landed right side up. Nay, more; even a mutineer is to go untouched lest these sacred passengers receive an accidental wound.

Of course the rebellion will never be suppressed in Louisiana, if the professed Union men there will neither help to do it, nor permit the government to do it without their help.

Now, I think the true remedy is very different from what is suggested by Mr. Durant. It does not lie in rounding the rough angles of the war, but in removing the necessity for the war. The people of Louisiana who wish protection to person and property, have but to reach forth their hands and take it. Let them, in good faith, reinaugurate the national authority, and set up a State Government conforming thereto under the constitution. They know how to do it, and can have the protection of the Army while doing it. The Army will be withdrawn so soon as such State government can dispense with its presence; and the people of the State can then upon the old Constitutional terms, govern themselves to their own liking. This is very simple and easy.

If they will not do this, if they prefer to hazard all for the sake of destroying the government, it is for them to consider whether it is probable I will surrender the government to save them from losing all. If they decline what I suggest, you scarcely need to ask what I will do. What would you do in my position? Would you drop the war where it is? Or, would you prosecute it in future, with elder-stalk squirts, charged with rose water? Would you deal lighter blows rather than heavier ones? Would you give up the contest, leaving any available means unapplied.

I am in no boastful mood. I shall not do *more* than I can, and I shall do *all* I can to save the government, which is my sworn duty as well as my personal inclination. I shall do nothing in malice. What I deal with is too vast for malicious dealing. Yours truly

A. LINCOLN

COTTON AND EMANCIPATION:
MASSACHUSETTS, AUGUST 1862

Charles Sumner to John Bright

Charles Sumner, a Radical Republican senator from Massachusetts who often had the ear of Lincoln on matters of abolition and emancipation, corresponded regularly on the state of the war with the British reformer John Bright, a staunch supporter of the Union cause from his seat in the House of Commons. Bright had written to Sumner on July 14, expressing hopes that the Union capture of New Orleans would allow increased shipments of cotton to English textile mills.

Boston 5th Aug. '62

Dear Mr Bright,

I wish I could sit by the seashore & talk with you again. It is hard to write of events—& of persons, with that fullness & frankness which you require.

The letters which I enclose from Mr Atkinson, a most intelligent & excellent person, will let you see the chance of cotton from the South. *Do not count upon it.* Make yr calculations as if it were beyond reach. His plan of opening Texas reads well on paper, but thus far we have lost by dividing our forces. We must concentrate & crush. The armies of the South must be met & annihilated. If we start an expedition to Texas there will be another diversion. Climate too will be for the present against us.

The correspondence between Genl. Butler & Mr Johnson will shew you that Govt. puts no restraint upon the sale of Cotton. It is the perverseness of the rebels that does it all.

Congress has adjourned. After a few days in Washington, to see the Presdt & cabinet, I have come home—glad of a little rest, but to find new cares here. Our session has been very busy; I doubt if any legislative body ever acted on so many important questions. You who follow our fortunes so kindly, doubtless know what has been done for freedom—for reform generally, &, also in the way of organizing our forces & providing means. There have been differences of opinion on questions of policy—especially on Slavery. This was to be expected. But the Bill of Confiscation & Liberation, which was at last passed, under pressure from our reverses at Richmond, is a practical Act of Emancipation. It was only in this respect that I valued it. The Western men were earnest for reaching the property of the rebels. To this I was indifferent except so far as it was necessary to break up the strongholds of slavery.

I wish that the Cabinet was more harmonious, & that the Presdt. had less *vis inertia*. He is hard to move. He is honest but inexperienced. Thus far he has been influenced by the Border States. I urged him on the 4th July to put forth an edict of Emancipation, telling him he could make the day more sacred & historic than ever. He replied—"I would do it if I were not afraid that half the officers would fling down their arms & three more States would rise." He is plainly mistaken about the officers & I think also with regard to the States. In the cabinet, Chase, who enjoys & deserves public confidence more than any other member, also the Secy of War & Secy of the Navy, are for this policy.—The last call for 300,000 men is recd. by the people with enthusiasm, because it seems to shew a purpose to push the war vigorously.

There is no thought in the cabinet or the Presdt. of abandoning the contest. *Of this be sure*. It will be pushed to the full extent of all the resources of the Republic *including, of course, the slaves*. Strange, it seems to me, that I, who so sincerely accept the principles of Peace, should be mixed up in this terrible war. But I see no way except to go forward; nor do I see any way in which England can get cotton speedily except through our success. England ought to help us with her benedictions; for she is interested next to ourselves. But her adverse sympathies help put off the good day. All here are grateful to you, for yr strong & noble words. God bless you! I say with all my heart.

Ever Yrs,   Charles Sumner

The Army of the Potomac once 160,000 men is reduced by death & casualties to 85,000. Yr Walcheren expedition on a larger scale.

EVACUATING THE PENINSULA:
WASHINGTON, D.C., AUGUST 1862

Henry W. Halleck to George B. McClellan

General Halleck, in his new role of general-in-chief, found a strategic puzzle awaiting him when he reached Washington on July 23. John Pope's Army of Virginia lay in northern Virginia between Washington and Richmond. McClellan's Army of the Potomac lay at Harrison's Landing on the James below Richmond. In between was Lee's Army of Northern Virginia, capable of striking in either direction. As Halleck points out here, his decision to withdraw the Potomac army from the Peninsula stemmed largely from McClellan's claim that the Rebel army, with 200,000 men, outnumbered his own by better than two to one. This was McClellan's fixed delusion; after the carnage of the Seven Days, he comfortably outnumbered Lee.

HEADQUARTERS OF THE ARMY,
Washington, August 6, 1862.

GENERAL: Your telegram of yesterday was received this morning, and I immediately telegraphed you a brief reply, promising to write you more fully by mail.

You, general, certainly could not have been more pained at receiving my order than I was at the necessity of issuing it. I was advised by high officers, in whose judgment I had great confidence, to make the order immediately on my arrival here, but I determined not to do so until I could learn your wishes from a personal interview; and even after that interview I tried every means in my power to avoid withdrawing your army, and delayed my decision as long as I dared to delay it. I assure you, general, it was not a hasty and inconsiderate act, but one that caused me more anxious thoughts than any other of my life; but after full and mature consideration of all the pros and cons, I was reluctantly forced to the conclusion that the order must be issued. There was to my mind no alternative.

Allow me to allude to a few of the facts in the case. You and your officers at one interview estimated the enemy's forces in and around Richmond at 200,000 men. Since then you and others report that they have received and are receiving large re-enforcements from the South. General Pope's army covering Washington is only about 40,000. Your effective force is only about 90,000. You are 30 miles from Richmond, and General Pope 80 or 90, with the enemy directly between you, ready to fall with his superior numbers upon one or the other, as he may elect. Neither can re-enforce the other in case of such an attack.

If General Pope's army be diminished to re-enforce you, Washington, Maryland, and Pennsylvania would be left uncovered and exposed. If your force be reduced to strengthen Pope, you would be too weak to even hold the position you now occupy should the enemy turn round and attack you in full force. In other words, the old Army of the Potomac is split into two parts, with the entire force of the enemy directly between them. They cannot be united by land without exposing both to destruction, and yet they must be united. To send Pope's forces by water to the Peninsula is, under present circumstances, a military impossibility. The only alternative is to send the forces on the Peninsula to some point by water, say Fredericksburg, where the two armies can be united.

Let me now allude to some of the objections which you have urged. You say that the withdrawal from the present position will cause the certain demoralization of the army, "which is now in excellent discipline and condition." I cannot understand why a simple change of position to a new and by no means distant base will demoralize an army in excellent discipline, unless the officers themselves assist in that demoralization, which I am satisfied they will not. Your change of front from your extreme right at Hanover Court-House to your present position was over 30 miles, but I have not heard that it demoralized your troops, notwithstanding the severe losses they sustained in effecting it. A new base on the Rappahannock at Fredericksburg brings you within about 60 miles of Richmond, and secures a re-enforcement of 40,000 or 50,000 fresh and disciplined troops. The change, with such advantages, will, I think, if properly represented to your army, encourage rather than demoralize your troops. Moreover, you yourself suggested that a junction might be effected at Yorktown, but that a flank march across the isthmus would be more hazardous than to retire to Fort Monroe. You will remember that Yorktown is 2 or 3 miles farther than Fredericksburg is. Besides, the latter is between Richmond and Washington, and covers Washington from any attack of the enemy. The political effect of the withdrawal may at first be unfavorable; but I think the public are beginning to understand its necessity, and that they will have much more confidence in a united army than in its separated fragments.

But you will reply, why not re-enforce me here, so that I can strike Richmond from my present position? To do this you said at our interview that you required 30,000 additional troops. I told you that it was impossible to give you so many. You finally thought that you would have "some chance" of success with 20,000. But you afterward telegraphed me that you would require 35,000, as the enemy was being largely re-enforced. If your estimate of the enemy's strength was correct, your requisition was perfectly reasonable, but it was utterly impossible to fill it until new troops could be enlisted and organized, which would require several weeks. To keep your army in its present position until it could be so re-enforced would almost destroy it in that climate. The months of August and September are almost fatal to whites who live on that part of James River, and even after you received the re-enforcements asked for, you admitted that you must reduce Fort Darling and the river batteries before you could advance on Richmond. It is by no means certain that the reduction of these fortifications would not require considerable time, perhaps as much as those at Yorktown. This delay might not only be fatal to the health of your army, but in the mean time General Pope's forces would be exposed to the heavy blows of the enemy without the slightest hope of assistance from you.

In regard to the demoralizing effect of a withdrawal from the Peninsula to the Rappahannock I must remark that a large number of your highest officers, indeed a majority of those whose opinions have been reported to me, are decidedly in favor of the movement. Even several of those who originally advocated the line of the Peninsula now advise its abandonment.

I have not inquired, and do not wish to know, by whose advice or for what reasons the Army of the Potomac was separated into two parts, with the enemy between them. I must take things as I find them. I find the forces divided, and I wish to unite them. Only one feasible plan has been presented for doing this. If you or any one else had presented a better plan I certainly should have adopted it. But all of your plans require re-enforcements, which it is impossible to give you. It is very easy to ask for re-enforcements, but it is not so easy to give them when you have no disposable troops at your command.

I have written very plainly as I understand the case, and I hope you will give me credit for having fully considered the matter, although I may have arrived at very different conclusions from your own.

Very respectfully, your obedient servant,

H. W. HALLECK,
General-in-Chief.

Maj. Gen. GEORGE B. MCCLELLAN,
Commanding, &c., Berkeley, Va.

FLEEING SLAVES: GEORGIA, AUGUST 1862
Memorial of a Committee of Citizens of Liberty County, Georgia

Brigadier General Hugh W. Mercer, Confederate commander at Savannah, received no response from Richmond to his forwarding of this citizens' plea. The memorial suggests the dimensions of the problem of runaway slaves in just this one area of coastal Georgia. In April 1862, Union forces had captured Fort Pulaski and occupied the coastal islands off Savannah, which became a haven for the fleeing slaves.

HEADQUARTERS THIRD DIVISION, DISTRICT OF GEORGIA,
Savannah, August 5, 1862.
Hon. GEORGE W. RANDOLPH,
Secretary of War:
SIR: I have the honor to inclose a memorial presented by a committee of the citizens of Liberty County, in this State, a community noted for their respectability and worth. The subject presented, I would respectfully submit, is one that demands the early notice of the Congress when it shall reassemble, and the instructions of the War Department (in accordance with such legislation as may be adopted) for the government of military commanders. The evil and danger alluded to may grow into frightful proportions unless checked, but the responsibility of life and death, so liable to be abused, is obviously too great to be intrusted to the hand of every officer whose duties may bring him face to face with this question. It is likely to become one of portentous magnitude if the war continues, and I do not see how it can be properly dealt with except by the supreme legislature of the country. I deem the action of Congress in this regard as needful for the protection of military commanders as for their guidance.

I have the honor to be, sir, very respectfully, your obedient servant,

H. W. MERCER,
Brigadier-General, Commanding.

[Inclosure.]

Brigadier-General MERCER,
 Commanding Military District of Georgia, Savannah:

GENERAL: The undersigned, citizens of Liberty County, of the Fifteenth District, would respectfully present for your consideration a subject of grave moment, not to themselves only, but to their fellow-citizens of the Confederate States who occupy not only our territory immediately bordering on that of the old United States, but the whole line of our sea-coast from Virginia to Texas. We allude to the escape of our slaves across the border lines landward, and out to the vessels of the enemy seaward, and to their being also enticed off by those who, having made their escape, return for that purpose, and not infrequently attended by the enemy. The injury inflicted upon the interests of the citizens of the Confederate States by this now constant drain is immense. Independent of the forcible seizure of slaves by the enemy whenever it lies in his power, and to which we now make no allusion, as the indemnity for this loss will in due time occupy the attention of our Government. From ascertained losses on certain parts of our coast, we may set down as a low estimate the number of slaves absconded and enticed off from our sea-board at 20,000, and their value at from $12,000,000 to $15,000,000, to which loss may be added the insecurity of the property along our borders and the demoralization of the negroes that remain, which increases with the continuance of the evil, and may finally result in perfect disorganization and rebellion. The absconding negroes hold the position of traitors, since they go over to the enemy and afford him aid and comfort by revealing the condition of the districts and cities from which they come, and aiding him in creating fortifications and raising provisions for his support, and now that the United States have allowed their introduction into their Army and Navy, aiding the enemy by enlisting under his banners, and increasing his resources in men for our annoyance and destruction. Negroes occupy the position of spies also, since they are employed in secret expeditions for obtaining information by transmission of newspapers and by other modes, and act as guides to expeditions on the land and as pilots to their vessels on the waters of our inlets and rivers.

They have proved of great value thus far to the coast operations of the enemy, and without their assistance he could not have accomplished as much for our injury and annoyance as he has done; and unless some measures shall be adopted to prevent the escape of the negroes to the enemy, the threat of an army of trained Africans for the coming fall and winter campaigns may become a reality.

Meanwhile the counties along the seaboard will become exhausted of the slave population, which should be retained as far as possible for the raising of provisions and supplies for our forces on the coast. In the absence of penalties of such a nature as to insure respect and dread, the temptations which are spread before the negroes are very strong, and when we consider their condition, their ignorance and credulity, and love of change, must prove in too many cases decidedly successful. No effectual check being interposed to their escape, the desire increases among them in proportion to the extent of its successful gratification, and will spread inland until it will draw negroes from counties far in the interior of the State, and negroes will congregate from every quarter in the counties immediately bordering on the sea and become a lawless set of runaways, corrupting the negroes that remain faithful, depredating on property of all kinds, and resorting, it may be, to deeds of violence, which demonstrates that the whole State is interested in the effort to stop this evil; and already have negroes from Middle Georgia made their escape to the sea-board counties, and through Savannah itself to the enemy.

After consulting the laws of the State we can discover none that meet the case and allow of that prompt execution of a befitting penalty which its urgency demands. The infliction of capital punishment is now confined to the superior court, and any indictment before that court would involve incarceration of the negroes for months, with the prospect of postponement of trial, long litigation, large expense, and doubtful conviction; and, moreover, should the negroes be caught escaping in any numbers, there would not be room in all our jails to receive them. The civil law, therefore, as it now stands cannot come to our protection.

Can we find protection under military law? This is the question we submit to the general in command. Under military law the severest penalties are prescribed for furnishing the enemy with aid and comfort and for acting as spies and traitors, all which the negroes can do as effectually as white men, as facts prove, and as we have already suggested. There can be but little doubt that if negroes are detected in the act of exciting their fellow-slaves to escape or of taking them off, or of returning after having gone to the enemy to induce and aid others to escape, they may in each of these cases be summarily punished under military authority. But may not the case of negroes taken in the act of absconding singly or in parties, without being directly incited so to do by one or more others, be also summarily dealt with by military authority? Were our white population to act in the same way, would it not be necessary to make a summary example of them, in order to cure the evil or put it under some salutary control? If it be argued that in case of the negroes it would be hard to mete out a similar punishment under similar circumstances, because of their ignorance, pliability, credulity, desire of change, the absence of the political ties of allegiance, and the peculiar status of the race, it may be replied that the negroes constitute a part of the body politic in fact, and should be made to know their duty; that they are perfectly aware that the act which they commit is one of rebellion against the power and authority of their owners and the Government under which they live. They are perfectly aware that they go over to the protection and aid of the enemy who are on the coast for the purpose of killing their owners and of destroying their property; and they know, further, that if they themselves are found with the enemy that they will be treated as the enemy, namely, shot and destroyed.

To apprehend such transgressors, to confine and punish them privately by owners, or publicly by the citizens of the county by confinement and whipping, and then return them to the plantations, will not abate the evil, for the disaffected will not thereby be reformed, but will remain a leaven of corruption in the mass and stand ready to make any other attempts that may promise success. It is, indeed, a monstrous evil that we suffer. Our negroes are property, the agricultural class of the Confederacy, upon whose order and continuance so much depends—may go off (inflicting a great pecuniary loss, both private and public) to the enemy, convey any amount of valuable information, and aid him by building his fortifications, by raising supplies for his armies, by enlisting as soldiers, by acting as spies and as guides and pilots to his expeditions on land and water, and bringing in the foe upon us to kill and devastate; and yet, if we catch them in the act of going to the enemy we are powerless for the infliction of any punishment adequate to their crime and adequate to fill them with salutary fear of its commission. Surely some remedy should be applied, and that speedily, for the protection of the country aside from all other considerations. A few executions of leading transgressors among them by hanging or shooting would dissipate the ignorance which may be supposed to possess their minds, and which may be pleaded in arrest of judgment.

We do not pray the general in command to issue any order for the government of the citizens in the matter, which, of course, is no part of his duty, but the promulgation of an order to the military for the execution of ringleaders who are detected in stirring up the people to escape, for the execution of all who return, having once escaped, and for the execution of all who are caught in the act of escaping, will speedily be known and understood by the entire slave population, and will do away with all excuses of ignorance, and go very far toward an entire arrest of the evil, while it will enable the citizens to act efficiently in their own sphere whenever circumstances require them to act at all. In an adjoining county, which has lost some 200, since the shooting of two detected in the act of escaping not another attempt has been made, and it has been several weeks since the two were shot.

As law-abiding men we do not desire committees of vigilance clothed with plenary powers, nor meetings of the body of our citizens to take the law into their own hands, however justifiable it may be under the peculiar circumstances, and therefore, in the failure of the civil courts to meet the emergency, we refer the subject to the general in command, believing that he has the power to issue the necessary order to the forces under him covering the whole ground, and knowing that by so doing he will receive the commendation and cordial support of the intelligent and law-abiding citizens inhabiting the military department over which he presides.

All which is respectfully submitted by your friends and fellow-citizens.

R. Q. MALLARD,
T. W. FLEMING,
E. STACY,
Committee of Citizens of the 15th Dist., Liberty County, Ga.

RETALIATION FOR ARMING SLAVES:
VIRGINIA, AUGUST 1862

Confederate War Department: General Orders No. 60

The order outlawing Hunter and Phelps was issued at the direction of Jefferson Davis. Brigadier General John W. Phelps had raised five companies of freed slaves in Louisiana in late July, but was ordered by his superior Benjamin F. Butler to use them as laborers instead. After Phelps resigned in protest, Butler began recruiting troops from among free people of color, and by November had formed three regiments of Louisiana Native Guards. On December 23, 1862, Davis issued a proclamation ordering that Butler be immediately hanged if captured.

GENERAL ORDERS, } WAR DEPT., ADJT. AND INSP. GENERAL'S
No. 60. } OFFICE,
Richmond, August 21, 1862.

I. Whereas, Major-General Hunter, recently in command of the enemy's forces on the coast of South Carolina, and Brigadier-General Phelps, a military commander of the enemy in the State of Louisiana, have organized and armed negro slaves for military service against their masters, citizens of this Confederacy; and whereas, the Government of the United States has refused to answer an inquiry whether said conduct of its officers meets its sanction, and has thus left to this Government no other means of repressing said crimes and outrages than the adoption of such measures of retaliation as shall serve to prevent their repetition:

Ordered, That Major-General Hunter and Brigadier-General Phelps be no longer held and treated as public enemies of the Confederate States, but as outlaws, and that in the event of the capture of either of them, or that of any other commissioned officer employed in drilling, organizing, or instructing slaves with a view to their armed service in this war, he shall not be regarded as a prisoner of war, but held in close confinement for execution as a felon, at such time and place as the President shall order.

By order:

S. COOPER,
Adjutant and Inspector General.

WASHINGTON, D.C., AUGUST 1862

Abraham Lincoln: Address on Colonization

A month after appealing to border state congressmen to adopt compensated emancipation, the President invited a delegation of Washington's black leaders to the White House to promote his plan for colonization. Lincoln's speech to the committee was reported in the *New-York Daily Tribune* on August 15. The Central American site he mentions was the province of Chiriqui, in present-day Panama. Congress had recently appropriated $600,000 to support colonization abroad. The delegation meeting with Lincoln, like the capital's black community in general, was sharply divided on the merits of colonization. Frederick Douglass said it revealed the President's "contempt for Negroes" and "canting hypocrisy." While as many as 500 volunteers did sign up for Chiriqui, the project withered away due to opposition from the surrounding Central American states.

August 14, 1862

This afternoon the President of the United States gave audience to a Committee of colored men at the White House. They were introduced by the Rev. J. Mitchell, Commissioner of Emigration. E. M. Thomas, the Chairman, remarked that they were there by invitation to hear what the Executive had to say to them. Having all been seated, the President, after a few preliminary observations, informed them that a sum of money had been appropriated by Congress, and placed at his disposition for the purpose of aiding the colonization in some country of the people, or a portion of them, of African descent, thereby making it his duty, as it had for a long time been his inclination, to favor that cause; and why, he asked, should the people of your race be colonized, and where? Why should they leave this country? This is, perhaps, the first question for proper consideration. You and we are different races. We have between us a broader difference than exists between almost any other two races. Whether it is right or wrong I need not discuss, but this physical difference is a great disadvantage to us both, as I think your race suffer very greatly, many of them by living among us, while ours suffer from your presence. In a word we suffer on each side. If this is admitted, it affords a reason at least why we should be separated. You here are freemen I suppose.

A VOICE: Yes, sir.

The President—Perhaps you have long been free, or all your lives. Your race are suffering, in my judgment, the greatest wrong inflicted on any people. But even when you cease to be slaves, you are yet far removed from being placed on an equality with the white race. You are cut off from many of the advantages which the other race enjoy. The aspiration of men is to enjoy equality with the best when free, but on this broad continent, not a single man of your race is made the equal of a single man of ours. Go where you are treated the best, and the ban is still upon you.

I do not propose to discuss this, but to present it as a fact with which we have to deal. I cannot alter it if I would. It is a fact, about which we all think and feel alike, I and you. We look to our condition, owing to the existence of the two races on this continent. I need not recount to you the effects upon white men, growing out of the institution of Slavery. I believe in its general evil effects on the white race. See our present condition—the country engaged in war!—our white men cutting one another's throats, none knowing how far it will extend; and then consider what we know to be the truth. But for your race among us there could not be war, although many men engaged on either side do not care for you one way or the other. Nevertheless, I repeat, without the institution of Slavery and the colored race as a basis, the war could not have an existence.

It is better for us both, therefore, to be separated. I know that there are free men among you, who even if they could better their condition are not as much inclined to go out of the country as those, who being slaves could obtain their freedom on this condition. I suppose one of the principal difficulties in the way of colonization is that the free colored man cannot see that his comfort would be advanced by it. You may believe you can live in Washington or elsewhere in the United States the remainder of your life as easily, perhaps more so than you can in any foreign country, and hence you may come to the conclusion that you have nothing to do with the idea of going to a foreign country. This is (I speak in no unkind sense) an extremely selfish view of the case.

But you ought to do something to help those who are not so fortunate as yourselves. There is an unwillingness on the part of our people, harsh as it may be, for you free colored people to remain with us. Now, if you could give a start to white people, you would open a wide door for many to be made free. If we deal with those who are not free at the beginning, and whose intellects are clouded by Slavery, we have very poor materials to start with. If intelligent colored men, such as are before me, would move in this matter, much might be accomplished. It is exceedingly important that we have men at the beginning capable of thinking as white men, and not those who have been systematically oppressed.

There is much to encourage you. For the sake of your race you should sacrifice something of your present comfort for the purpose of being as grand in that respect as the white people. It is a cheering thought throughout life that something can be done to ameliorate the condition of those who have been subject to the hard usage of the world. It is difficult to make a man miserable while he feels he is worthy of himself, and claims kindred to the great God who made him. In the American Revolutionary war sacrifices were made by men engaged in it; but they were cheered by the future. Gen. Washington himself endured greater physical hardships than if he had remained a British subject. Yet he was a happy man, because he was engaged in benefiting his race—something for the children of his neighbors, having none of his own.

The colony of Liberia has been in existence a long time. In a certain sense it is a success. The old President of Liberia, Roberts, has just been with me—the first time I ever saw him. He says they have within the bounds of that colony between 300,000 and 400,000 people, or more than in some of our old States, such as Rhode Island or Delaware, or in some of our newer States, and less than in some of our larger ones. They are not all American colonists, or their descendants. Something less than 12,000 have been sent thither from this country. Many of the original settlers have died, yet, like people elsewhere, their offspring outnumber those deceased.

The question is if the colored people are persuaded to go anywhere, why not there? One reason for an unwillingness to do so is that some of you would rather remain within reach of the country of your nativity. I do not know how much attachment you may have toward our race. It does not strike me that you have the greatest reason to love them. But still you are attached to them at all events.

The place I am thinking about having for a colony is in Central America. It is nearer to us than Liberia—not much more than one-fourth as far as Liberia, and within seven days' run by steamers. Unlike Liberia it is on a great line of travel—it is a highway. The country is a very excellent one for any people, and with great natural resources and advantages, and especially because of the similarity of climate with your native land—thus being suited to your physical condition.

The particular place I have in view is to be a great highway from the Atlantic or Caribbean Sea to the Pacific Ocean, and this particular place has all the advantages for a colony. On both sides there are harbors among the finest in the world. Again, there is evidence of very rich coal mines. A certain amount of coal is valuable in any country, and there may be more than enough for the wants of the country. Why I attach so much importance to coal is, it will afford an opportunity to the inhabitants for immediate employment till they get ready to settle permanently in their homes.

If you take colonists where there is no good landing, there is a bad show; and so where there is nothing to cultivate, and of which to make a farm. But if something is started so that you can get your daily bread as soon as you reach there, it is a great advantage. Coal land is the best thing I know of with which to commence an enterprise.

To return, you have been talked to upon this subject, and told that a speculation is intended by gentlemen, who have an interest in the country, including the coal mines. We have been mistaken all our lives if we do not know whites as well as blacks look to their self-interest. Unless among those deficient of intellect everybody you trade with makes something. You meet with these things here as elsewhere.

If such persons have what will be an advantage to them, the question is whether it cannot be made of advantage to you.

You are intelligent, and know that success does not as much depend on external help as on self-reliance. Much, therefore, depends upon yourselves. As to the coal mines, I think I see the means available for your self-reliance.

I shall, if I get a sufficient number of you engaged, have provisions made that you shall not be wronged. If you will engage in the enterprise I will spend some of the money intrusted to me. I am not sure you will succeed. The Government may lose the money, but we cannot succeed unless we try; but we think, with care, we can succeed.

The political affairs in Central America are not in quite as satisfactory condition as I wish. There are contending factions in that quarter; but it is true all the factions are agreed alike on the subject of colonization, and want it, and are more generous than we are here. To your colored race they have no objection. Besides, I would endeavor to have you made equals, and have the best assurance that you should be the equals of the best.

The practical thing I want to ascertain is whether I can get a number of able-bodied men, with their wives and children, who are willing to go, when I present evidence of encouragement and protection. Could I get a hundred tolerably intelligent men, with their wives and children, to "cut their own fodder," so to speak? Can I have fifty? If I could find twenty-five able-bodied men, with a mixture of women and children, good things in the family relation, I think I could make a successful commencement.

I want you to let me know whether this can be done or not. This is the practical part of my wish to see you. These are subjects of very great importance, worthy of a month's study, instead of a speech delivered in an hour. I ask you then to consider seriously not pertaining to yourselves merely, nor for your race, and ours, for the present time, but as one of the things, if successfully managed, for the good of mankind—not confined to the present generation, but as

> "From age to age descends the lay,
>   To millions yet to be,
> Till far its echoes roll away,
>   Into eternity."

The above is merely given as the substance of the President's remarks.

The Chairman of the delegation briefly replied that "they would hold a consultation and in a short time give an answer." The President said: "Take your full time—no hurry at all."

The delegation then withdrew.

"I WOULD SAVE THE UNION":
WASHINGTON, D.C., AUGUST 1862
Abraham Lincoln to Horace Greeley

Horace Greeley, founder and editor of the *New-York Daily Tribune*, addressed Lincoln in "The Prayer of Twenty Millions," a public letter that appeared on August 20. Greeley expressed disappointment with "the policy you seem to be pursuing with regard to the slaves of Rebels . . ." He charged the President with being unduly influenced by "certain fossil politicians" from the border states and with failing to execute the terms of the Second Confiscation Act. With his reply, published in the *Tribune* on August 25, Lincoln sought to prepare the public for his impending proclamation of emancipation.

Hon. Horace Greely: Executive Mansion,
Dear Sir Washington, August 22, 1862.

I have just read yours of the 19th. addressed to myself through the New-York Tribune. If there be in it any statements, or assumptions of fact, which I may know to be erroneous, I do not, now and here, controvert them. If there be in it any inferences which I may believe to be falsely drawn, I do not now and here, argue against them. If there be perceptable in it an impatient and dictatorial tone, I waive it in deference to an old friend, whose heart I have always supposed to be right.

As to the policy I "seem to be pursuing" as you say, I have not meant to leave any one in doubt.

I would save the Union. I would save it the shortest way under the Constitution. The sooner the national authority can be restored; the nearer the Union will be "the Union as it was." If there be those who would not save the Union, unless they could at the same time *save* slavery, I do not agree with them. If there be those who would not save the Union unless they could at the same time *destroy* slavery, I do not agree with them. My paramount object in this struggle *is* to save the Union, and is *not* either to save or to destroy slavery. If I could save the Union without freeing *any* slave I would do it, and if I could save it by freeing *all* the slaves I would do it; and if I could save it by freeing some and leaving others alone I would also do that. What I do about slavery, and the colored race, I do because I believe it helps to save the Union; and what I forbear, I forbear because I do *not* believe it would help to save the Union. I shall do *less* whenever I shall believe what I am doing hurts the cause, and I shall do *more* whenever I shall believe doing more will help the cause. I shall try to correct errors when shown to be errors; and I shall adopt new views so fast as they shall appear to be true views.

I have here stated my purpose according to my view of *official* duty; and I intend no modification of my oft-expressed *personal* wish that all men every where could be free. Yours,

A. LINCOLN

SLAVERY AND THE LAWS OF WAR:
TENNESSEE, AUGUST 1862

William T. Sherman to Thomas Hunton

In July 1862 Sherman became the Union commander at Memphis. Hunton, a West Point classmate of Sherman and owner of a Mississippi plantation, wrote to him, citing their old school ties, to ask for the return of his slaves who had fled to the Union camps. He told Sherman that he was willing to come to Memphis himself, but only if he did not have to take the oath of allegiance.

Memphis Tenn. Aug. 24th 1862

Thomas Hunton Esq.
Coahoma, Panolo Co. Miss.
My dear Sir,

I freely admit that when you recall the times when we were schoolfellows, when we were younger than now, you touch me on a tender point, and cause me to deeply regret that even you should style yourself a Rebel. I cannot believe that Tom Hunton the Companion of Gaither, Rankin, and Irvin and many others long since dead, and of Halleck, Ord, Stevens and others still living can of his own free will admit the anarchical principle of secession or be vain enough to suppose the present Politicians can frame a Government better than that of Washington, Hamilton & Jefferson. We cannot realize this but delude ourselves into the belief that by some strange but successful jugglery the managers of our Political Machine have raised up the single issue, North or South, which shall prevail in America? or that you like others have been blown up, and cast into the Mississippi of Secession doubtful if by hard fighting you can reach the shore in safety, or drift out to the Ocean of Death, I know it is no use for us now to discuss this War is on us. We are Enemies, still private friends. In the one Capacity I will do you all the harm I can, yet on the other if here you may have as of old my last Cent, my last shirt and pants. You ask of me your negroes, and I will immediately ascertain if they be under my Military Control and I will moreover see that they are one and all told what is true of all—Boys if you want to go to your master, Go—you are free to choose. You must now think for yourselves, Your master has seceded from his Parent Government and you have seceded from him—both wrong by law—but both exercising an undoubted natural Right to rebel. If your boys want to go, I will enable them to go, but I wont advise, persuade or force them—I confess I have yet seen the "Confiscation Act," but I enclose you my own orders defining my position. I also cut out of a paper Grants Orders, and I assert that the Action of all our Leading Military Leaders, Halleck, McClellan, Buell, Grant & myself have been more conservative of slavery than the Acts of your own men. The Constitution of the United States is your only legal title to slavery. You have another title, that of possession, & force, but in Law & Logic your title to your Boys lay in the Constitution of the United States. You may say you are for the Constitution of the United States, as it was—You know it is unchanged, not a word not a syllable, and I can lay my hand on that Constitution and swear to it without one twang. But your party have made *another* and have another in force. How can you say that you would have the old, when you have a new. By the new if successful you inherit the Right of Slavery, but the new is not law till your Revolution is successful. Therefore we who contend for the old existing Law, contend that you by your own act take away your own title to all property save what is restricted by *our* constitution, your slaves included. You know I don't want your slaves, but to bring you to reason I think as a Military Man I have a Right and it is good policy to make *you all* feel that you are but men—that you have all the wants & despondencies of other men, and must eat, be clad &c to which end you must have property & labor, and that by Rebelling you risk both. Even without the Confiscation Act, by the simple laws of War we ought to take your effective slaves, I don't say to free them, but to use their labor & deprive you of it; as Belligerents we ought to seek the hostile Army and fight it and not the people—We went to Corinth but Beaureguard declined Battle, since which time many are dispersed as Guerillas. We are not bound to follow them, but rightfully make war by any means that will tend to bring about an end and restore

Peace. Your people may say it only exasperates, widens the breach and all that, But the longer the war lasts the more you must be convinced that we are no better & no worse than People who have gone before us, and that we are simply reenacting History, and that one of the modes of bringing People to reason is to touch their Interests pecuniary or property.

We never harbor women or children—we give employment to men, under the enclosed order. I find no negroes Registered as belonging to Hunton, some in the name of McGhee of which the Engineer is now making a list—I see McClellan says that negroes once taken shall never again be restored. I say nothing, my opinion is, we execute not make the Law, be it of Congress or War. But it is manifest that if you wont go into a United States District Court and sue for the recovery of your slave property you can never get it, out of adverse hands. No U.S. Court would allow you to sue for the recovery of a slave under the Fugitive Slave Law, unless you acknowledge allegiance. Believing this honestly, so I must act, though personally I feel strong friendship as ever, for very many in the South. With Great Respect Your friend
W. T. Sherman
Maj. Genl.

EMANCIPATION AND DIPLOMACY:
AUSTRIA, AUGUST 1862

John Lothrop Motley to William H. Seward

Motley, a noted historian, served the Lincoln administration as a minister to Austria. He was, as he notes, well versed in European affairs. He offers Secretary of State Seward a shrewd analysis of the ambitions of Louis Napoleon, emperor of the French, and of Great Britain vis-à-vis the American war. Prime Minister Palmerston and Foreign Minister Russell he locates on opposite sides of the slavery question, with their rival John Bright in the wings.

Private & confidential   Vienna Aug 26 1862
My dear Mr Seward,

    I have to express my thanks for your photograph, which Mr F. Seward was so kind as to enclose to me. I have assured my wife & daughter that it gives a rather better idea of the original than photographs usually do.

    I send by this mail a brief despatch, communicating as much in regard to European affairs as you are likely, at this time, to find leisure to read. I have also to acknowledge the receipt of your confidential despatch of July 24. In this you ask me a question, & I esteem it a privilege to answer it very unequivocally. I say, beforehand however, that I dont pretend to offer advice as to home matters. Entertaining a profound conviction that the civil war will never cease, so long as a slave remains in the country, I have refrained from expressing this opinion. To give unsolicited advice on such matters is not within my sphere of duty, & would be almost an impertinence; nor would it be possible for me to say any thing of those belligerent powers of the government in regard to slavery, which slavery, when it drew the sword put into the government's hands, or of the proper time to use those powers with full effect, that is not entirely familiar to you.

    I therefore possess my soul in patience, trusting to the wisdom of the President & yourself & his other counsellors, &

hoping that those fatal words, "too late" which have so often rung the knell of nations are not destined to be the response to a policy which, I feel persuaded, must of necessity be one day announced. You can tell much better than I, how much longer it will be necessary to humour the pro-slavery party of the North, & the requirements of the semi-attached border states. But you have asked me a question in regard to matters concerning which I do claim an opinion. There are not many Americans who have had longer or better opportunities of studying European politics & individual opinions than I have had, & it is my duty to advise the government in regard to them to the best of my ability— It sometimes seems to me, as if there were, at home, an unwillingness to contemplate the great danger which is always impending over us from abroad—

You ask me— "are you sure that to day under the seductions & pressure which could be applied to some European populations they would not rise up & resist our attempt to bestow freedom upon the laborers whose capacity to supply cotton & open a market for European fabrics depends or is thought to depend on their continuance in bondage?" I answer, a thousand times, *No.*

A proclamation of emancipation to the blacks, with compensation to owners thenceforth loyal, even altho' it could not be every where immediately enforced, would strike the sword from England's hands. Moreover, the first enforcement would probably be in Virginia where the principal crop is not cotton but negroes—and there is no population in Europe so depraved as to rise up in favour of breeding fellow creatures to be sold in the market. No public man in England dares confront the anti slavery feeling which is universal in the nation. The French emperor, as you are well aware, & as is perfectly well known to the government here, has been perpetually soliciting the English to join him in armed intervention in our affairs. Of course this is officially denied, & will be so until the blow is resolved upon. Qui nescit dissimulare nescit regnere, & neither England nor France is so ingenuous as to tell *us* their little private schemes for our destruction until they are matured. The time when has perhaps not been settled, but I suppose that nobody is so green as to doubt that Louis Napoleon is ready, & desirous of giving the slaveholders' confederacy a lift with a large auxiliary force by sea & land, if he could only get England to join him; & that thus far, England has restrained him— Of course there are many reasons for her withholding her support. She is getting somewhat sick of her magnanimous ally. He stands too thoroughly exposed before the world as the great conspirator against liberty, civilization & humanity; hostis humani generis, to be reputable company. He is siding with *Russia* now in Eastern questions & against Turkey. He is taking measures for crushing Italy, whose freedom, as England has been telling every body for the last two years, was owing to her "moral support" (whatever that may mean). He is cultivating close relations with Prussia, a power never cordial to England, & he is as much at war with Austria, England's only friend on the continent, as he can be without drawing the sword. He had nearly got England involved in his Mexican villainy, the crowning iniquity of his reign, & he is actively pursuing, in company with her, a gigantic scheme for the dismemberment & conquest of China, which is causing much alarm among the peaceful & liberal portion of the British public—

But all these reasons have comparatively little weight. England is restrained from helping France to set up the slaveholders' confederacy partly because it *is* a slaveholders' confederacy. On the other hand, the anti slavery tendency day by day more manifest & more intense of the American people, & the anti slavery legislation of Congress, have hitherto made it difficult for England to accept the propositions of France. A formal proclamation, in unequivocal & bold language, with compensation to loyal masters, would make it *impossible*. In truth, such a proclamation is what our foreign enemies (and they are Legion) most dread. The aristocratic journalists & stump orators of England have done their best to persuade the world that the North (as they call the U S government) is as much in favor of slavery as the South, and they seize upon what pro-slavery demonstrations in New York or Washington they can find, to exhibit as proofs of their charges. The ignorance of Europe in regard to our politics is so universal & profound that malice may practise upon it to almost any extent. But an authoritative & blunt manifesto could not be lied out of existence. There would be any amount of vituperation as to our motives, but the fact would remain, & England *could* not *fight* to establish a separate slave confederacy against the legitimate U S government which had abolished slavery. And it is doubtful whether France—altho' there is no public opinion, & only one man in France—would fight us without her aid. There are very few among the governing classes of England, who do not sympathize with the South. There are fewer still who do not consider the United States as hopelessly gone. But no man in England or in Europe dares publicly to defend African slavery. It is never attempted. The European world has voted it a nuisance which should be buried out of sight.

I *know* from long & intimate conversations with Lord Russell, that he has always, ever since our troubles began, been strongly opposed to the abolition of slavery by our government. You have had proof enough that he wishes the Union dissolved, for he omits no opportunity of publicly proclaiming that wish. Put the two together, & what do you make of it? Simply that abolition would, in his opinion, prevent dissolution, or certainly that it would prevent an English government's lifting its hands to help the dissolution—

Lord Palmerston, who, the last time I talked with him, knew as much of our politics as I do of those of Japan, is a detester of negro slavery. To oppose it is, I firmly believe, the only serious & earnest purpose that he has ever had in his life, except the still more earnest one to remain the rest of his life prime minister. You see that his recent break with the radicals has rather alarmed him, & he will do his best, in the vacation, to conciliate them.

Bright & his men cant govern England but they can upset a government, for they represent the great unrepresented masses, & feel with those masses. You have seen what Bright's views are on our civil war & on slavery. Suppose our government, in the exercise of its war powers, should abolish slavery now— Do you think Lord Palmerston would dare encounter Bright & the radicals, by levying war upon America in order to destroy our government, just as that government had taken this step? To me it is unimaginable.

I can't close this note, without saying a single word in earnest, & not in merely a political view of the most portentous subject of modern times.

So long as I have been old enough to have opinions, I have

hated slavery, as I have hated all forms of oppression; but until now I have felt that we were bound by law to countenance this mighty wrong to humanity, & that worse evils would flow from an illegal attempt to destroy it. But now the slaveholders have committed the great crime from which we shrank. They have aimed a murderous blow at the heart of the country whose destiny they so long controlled, & they have thus, by levying war, put it in our power, without any violation of law to repair the wrongs done for so many generations to a most deeply injured & unhappy race. If we neglect this golden opportunity of doing justice, I feel that we shall perish as a nation, &, what is even worse, that we shall deserve to perish. I feel that we are *now* as much accountable to God for the existence of slavery as were the slaveholders themselves. A thousand millions spent for abolition are better than this or a greater amount spent in war, without a result, perhaps to white or black, & would be noblest debt ever incurred by a people.

You must pardon me saying thus much in my private capacity. Having the ear of a man so wise & so influential I cannot resist the impulse of opening my mind on this subject.

I remain
my dear Mr Seward
with great respect
Very faithfully & sincerely
J Lothrop Motley

Hon. W.H. Seward
etc etc etc

AIDING CONTRABANDS:
WASHINGTON, D.C., SUMMER 1862

Harriet Jacobs to William Lloyd Garrison

In the summer of 1862 Harriet Jacobs, the author of *Incidents in the Life of a Slave Girl*, went to the District of Columbia and began relief work among the contrabands who had fled there. She wrote about their situation in a letter to the abolitionist leader William Lloyd Garrison that appeared in his newspaper *The Liberator* on September 5, 1862. (The letter was signed "Linda," after "Linda Brent," the pseudonym under which she had published her autobiography in 1861.) Jacobs would continue her relief efforts in Washington and Alexandria, Virginia, until the end of the war.

Dear Mr. Garrison:

I thank you for the request of a line on the condition of the contrabands, and what I have seen while among them. When we parted at that pleasant gathering of the Progressive Friends at Longwood, you to return to the Old Bay State, to battle for freedom and justice to the slave, I to go to the District of Columbia, where the shackles had just fallen, I hoped that the glorious echo from the blow had aroused the spirit of freedom, if a spark slumbered in its bosom. Having purchased my ticket through to Washington at the Philadelphia station, I reached the capital without molestation. Next morning, I went to Duff Green's Row, Government head-quarters for the contrabands here. I found men, women and children all huddled together, without any distinction or regard to age or sex. Some of them were in the most pitiable condition. Many were sick with measles, diptheria, scarlet and typhoid fever. Some had a few filthy rags to lie on; others had nothing but the bare floor for a couch. There seemed to be no established rules among them; they were coming in at all hours, often through the night, in large numbers, and the Superintendent had enough to occupy his time in taking the names of those who came in, and of those who were sent out. His office was thronged through the day by persons who came to hire these poor creatures, who they say will not work and take care of themselves. Single women hire at four dollars a month; a woman with one child, two and a half or three dollars a month. Men's wages are ten dollars per month. Many of them, accustomed as they have been to field labor, and to living almost entirely out of doors, suffer much from the confinement in this crowded building. The little children pine like prison birds for their native element. It is almost impossible to keep the building in a healthy condition. Each day brings its fresh additions of the hungry, naked and sick. In the early part of June, there were, some days, as many as ten deaths reported at this place in twenty-four hours. At this time, there was no matron in the house, and nothing at hand to administer to the comfort of the sick and dying. I felt that their sufferings must be unknown to the people. I did not meet kindly, sympathizing people, trying to soothe the last agonies of death. Those tearful eyes often looked up to me with the language, "Is this freedom?"

A new Superintendent was engaged, Mr. Nichol, who seemed to understand what these people most needed. He laid down rules, went to work in earnest pulling down partitions to enlarge the rooms, that he might establish two hospitals, one for the men and another for the women. This accomplished, cots and mattresses were needed. There is a small society in Washington—the Freedman's Association—who are doing all they can; but remember, Washington is not New England. I often met Rev. W. H. Channing, whose hands and heart are earnestly in the cause of the enslaved of his country. This gentleman was always ready to act in their behalf. Through these friends, an order was obtained from Gen. Wadsworth for cots for the contraband hospitals.

At this time, I met in Duff Green Row, Miss Hannah Stevenson, of Boston, and Miss Kendall. The names of these ladies need no comment. They were the first white females whom I had seen among these poor creatures, except those who had come in to hire them. These noble ladies had come to work, and their names will be lisped in prayer by many a dying slave. Hoping to help a little in the good work they had begun, I wrote to a lady in New York, a true and tried friend of the slave, who from the first moment had responded to every call of humanity. This letter was to ask for such articles as would make comfortable the sick and dying in the hospital. On the Saturday following, the cots were put up. A few hours after, an immense box was received from New York. Before the sun went down, those ladies who have labored so hard for the comfort of these people had the satisfaction of seeing every man, woman and child with clean garments, lying in a clean bed. What a contrast! They seemed different beings. Every countenance beamed with gratitude and satisfied rest. To me, it was a picture of holy peace within. The next day was the first Christian Sabbath they had ever known. One mother passed away as the setting sun threw its last rays across her dying bed, and as I looked upon her, I could but say—"One day of freedom, and gone to her God." Before the dawn, others were laid beside her. It was a comfort to know that some effort had been made to soothe their dying pillows. Still, there were other places in which I felt, if possible, more interest, where the poor creatures seemed so far removed from the immediate sympathy of those who would help them. These were the contrabands in Alexandria. This place is strongly secesh; the inhabitants are kept quiet only at the point of Northern bayonets. In this place, the contrabands are distributed more over the city. In visiting those places, I had the assistance of two kind friends, women. True at heart, they felt the wrongs and degradation of their race. These ladies were always ready to aid me, as far as lay in their power. To Mrs. Brown, of 3d street, Washington, and Mrs. Dagans, of Alexandria, the contrabands owe much gratitude for the kindly aid they gave me in serving them. In this place, the men live in an old foundry, which does not afford protection from the weather. The sick lay on boards on the ground floor; some, through the kindness of the soldiers, have an old blanket. I did not hear a complaint among them. They said it was much better than it had been. All expressed a willingness to work, and were anxious to know what was to be done with them after the work was done. All of them said they had not received pay for their work, and some wanted to know if I thought it would be paid to their masters. One old man said, "I don't kere if dey don't pay, so dey give me freedom. I bin working for ole maas all de time; he nebber gib me five cent. I like de Unions fuss rate. If de Yankee Unions didn't come long, I'd be working tu de ole place now." All said they had plenty to eat, but no clothing, and no money to buy any.

Another place, the old school-house in Alexandria, is the Government head-quarters for the women. This I thought the most wretched of all the places. Any one who can find an apology for slavery should visit this place, and learn its curse. Here you see them from infancy up to a hundred years old. What but the love of freedom could bring these old people hither? One old man, who told me he was a hundred, said he had come to be free with his children. The journey proved too much for him. Each visit, I found him sitting in the same spot, under a shady tree, suffering from rheumatism. Unpacking a barrel, I found a large coat, which I thought would be so nice for the old man, that I carried it to him. I found him sitting in the same spot, with his head on his bosom. I stooped down to speak to him. Raising his head, I found him dying. I called his wife. The old woman, who seems in her second childhood, looked on as quietly as though we were placing him for a night's rest. In this house are scores of women and children, with nothing to do, and nothing to do with. Their husbands are at work for the Government. Here they have food and shelter, but they cannot get work. The slaves who come into Washington from Maryland are sent here to protect them from the Fugitive Slave Law. These people are indebted to Mr. Rufus Leighton, formerly of Boston, for many comforts. But for their Northern friends, God pity them in their wretched and destitute condition! The Superintendent, Mr. Clarke, a Pennsylvanian, seems to feel much interest in them, and is certainly very kind. They told me they had confidence in him as a friend. That is much for a slave to say.

From this place, I went to Birch's slave-pen in Alexandria. This place forms a singular contrast with what it was two years ago. The habitable part of the building is filled with contrabands, the old jail is filled with secesh prisoners—all within speaking distance of each other. Many a compliment is passed between them on the change in their positions. There is another house on Cameron street, which is filled with very destitute people. To these places I distributed large supplies of clothing, given me by the ladies of New York, New Bedford, and Boston. They have made many a desolate heart glad. They have clothed the naked, fed the hungry. To them, God's promise is sufficient.

Let me tell you of another place, to which I always planned my last visit for the day. There was something about this house to make you forget that you came to it with a heavy heart. The little children you meet at this door bring up pleasant memories when you leave it; from the older ones you carry pleasant recollections. These were what the people call the more favored slaves, and would boast of having lived in the first families in Virginia. They certainly had reaped some advantage from the contact. It seemed by a miracle that they had all fallen together. They were intelligent, and some of the young women and children beautiful. One young girl, whose beauty I cannot describe, although its magnetism often drew me to her side, I loved to talk with, and look upon her sweet face, covered with blushes; besides, I wanted to learn her true position, but her gentle shyness I had to respect. One day, while trying to draw her out, a fine-looking woman, with all the pride of a mother, stepped forward, and said—"Madam, this young woman is my son's wife." It was a relief. I thanked God that this young creature had an arm to lean upon for protection. Here I looked upon slavery, and felt the curse of their heritage was what is considered the best blood of Virginia. On one of my visits here, I met a mother who had just arrived from Virginia, bringing with her four daughters. Of course, they belonged to one of the first families. This man's strong attachment to this woman and her children caused her, with her children, to be locked up one month. She made her escape one day while her master had gone to learn the news from the Union army. She fled to the Northern army for freedom and protection. These people had earned for themselves many little comforts. Their houses had an inviting aspect. The clean floors, the clean white spreads on their cots, and the general tidiness throughout the building, convinced me they had done as well as any other race could have done, under the same circumstances.

Let me tell you of another place—Arlington Heights. Every lady has heard of Gen. Lee's beautiful residence, which has been so faithfully guarded by our Northern army. It looks as though the master had given his orders every morning. Not a tree around that house has fallen. About the forts and camps they have been compelled to use the axe. At the quarters, there are many contrabands. The men are employed, and most of the women. Here they have plenty of exercise in the open air, and seem very happy. Many of the regiments are stationed here. It is a delightful place for both the soldier and the contraband. Looking around this place, and remembering what I had heard of the character of the man who owned it before it passed into the hands of its present owner, I was much inclined to say, Although the wicked prosper for a season, the way of the transgressor is hard.

When in Washington for the day, my morning visit would be up at Duff Green's Row. My first business would be to look into a small room on the ground floor. This room was covered with lime. Here I would learn how many deaths had occurred in the last twenty-four hours. Men, women and children lie here together, without a shadow of those rites which we give to our poorest dead. There they lie, in the filthy rags they wore from the plantation. Nobody seems to give it a thought. It is an every-day occurrence, and the scenes have become familiar. One morning, as I looked in, I saw lying there five children. By the side of them lay a young man. He escaped, was taken back to Virginia, whipped nearly to death, escaped again the next night, dragged his body to Washington, and died, literally cut to pieces. Around his feet I saw a rope; I could not see that put into the grave with him. Other cases similar to this came to my knowledge, but this I saw.

Amid all this sadness, we sometimes would hear a shout of joy. Some mother had come in, and found her long-lost child; some husband his wife. Brothers and sisters meet. Some, without knowing it, had lived years within twenty miles of each other.

A word about the schools. It is pleasant to see that eager group of old and young, striving to learn their A, B, C, and Scripture sentences. Their great desire is to learn to read. While in the school-room, I could not but feel how much these young women and children needed female teachers who could do something more than teach them their A, B, C. They need to be taught the right habits of living and the true principles of life.

My last visit intended for Alexandria was on Saturday. I spent the day with them, and received showers of thanks for myself and the good ladies who had sent me; for I had been careful to impress upon them that these kind friends sent me, and that all that was given by me was from them. Just as I was on the point of leaving, I found a young woman, with an infant, who had just been brought in. She lay in a dying condition, with nothing but a piece of an old soldier coat under her head. Must I leave her in this condition? I could not beg in Alexandria. It was time for the last boat to leave for Washington, and I promised to return in the morning. The Superintendent said he would meet me at the landing. Early the next morning, Mrs. Brown and myself went on a begging expedition, and some old quilts were given us. Mr. Clarke met us, and offered the use of his large Government wagon, with the horses and driver, for the day, and said he would accompany us, if agreeable. I was delighted, and felt I should spend a happy Sabbath in exploring Dixie, while the large bundles that I carried with me would help make others happy. After attending to the sick mother and child, we started for Fairfax Seminary. They send many of the convalescent soldiers to this place. The houses are large, and the location is healthy. Many of the contrabands are here. Their condition is much better than that of those kept in the city. They soon gathered around Mr. Clarke, and begged him to come back and be their boss. He said, "Boys, I want you all to go to Hayti." They said, "You gwine wid us, Mr. Clarke?" "No, I must stay here, and take care of the rest of the boys." "Den, if you aint gwine, de Lord knows I aint a gwine." Some of them will tell Uncle Abe the same thing. Mr. Clarke said they would do anything for him—seldom gave him any trouble. They spoke kindly of Mr. Thomas, who is constantly employed in supplying their wants, as far as he can. To the very old people at this place, I gave some clothing, returned to Alexandria, and bade all good bye. Begging me to come back, they promised to do all they could to help themselves. One old woman said— "Honey tink, when all get still, I kin go an fine de old place? Tink de Union 'stroy it? You can't get nothin on dis place. Down on de ole place, you can raise ebery ting. I ain't seen bacca since I bin here. Neber git a libin here, where de peoples eben buy pasly." This poor old woman thought it was nice to live where tobacco grew, but it was dreadful to be compelled to buy a bunch of parsley. Here they have preaching once every Sabbath. They must have a season to sing and pray, and we need true faith in Christ to go among them and do our duty. How beautiful it is to find it among themselves! Do not say the slaves take no interest in each other. Like other people, some of them are designedly selfish, some are ignorantly selfish. With the light and instruction you give them, you will see this selfishness disappear. Trust them, make them free, and give them the responsibility of caring for themselves, and they will soon learn to help each other. Some of them have been so degraded by slavery that they do not know the usages of civilized life; they know little else than the handle of the hoe, the plough, the cotton pad, and the overseer's lash. Have patience with them. You have helped to make them what they are; teach them civilization. You owe it to them, and you will find them as apt to learn as any other people that come to you stupid from oppression. The negroes' strong attachment no one doubts; the only difficulty is, they have cherished it too strongly. Let me tell you of an instance among the contrabands. One day, while in the hospital, a woman came in to ask that she might take a little orphan child. The mother had just died, leaving two children, the eldest three years old. This woman had five children in the house with her. In a few days, the number would be six. I said to this mother, "What can you do with this child, shut up here with your own? They are as many as you can attend to." She looked up with tears in her eyes, and said—"The child's mother was a stranger; none of her friends cum wid her from de ole place. I took one boy down on de plantation; he is a big boy now, working mong de Unions. De Lord help me to bring up dat boy, and he will help me to take care dis child. My husband work for de Unions when dey pay him. I can make home for all. Dis child shall hab part ob de crust." How few white mothers, living in luxury, with six children, could find room in her heart for a seventh, and that child a stranger!

In this house there are scores of children, too young to help themselves, from eight years old down to the little one-day freeman, born at railroad speed, while the young mother was flying from Virginia to save her babe from breathing its tainted air.

I left the contrabands, feeling that the people were becoming more interested in their behalf, and much had been done to make their condition more comfortable. On my way home, I stopped a few days in Philadelphia. I called on a lady who had sent a large supply to the hospital, and told her of the many little orphans who needed a home. This lady advised me to call and see the Lady Managers of an institution for orphan children supported by those ladies. I did so, and they agreed to take the little orphans. They employed a gentleman to investigate the matter, and it was found impossible to bring them through Baltimore. This gentleman went to the captains of the propellers in Philadelphia, and asked if those orphan children could have a passage on their boats. Oh no, it could not be; it would make an unpleasant feeling among the people! Some of those orphans have died since I left, but the number is constantly increasing. Many mothers, on leaving the plantations, pick up the little orphans, and bring them with their own children; but they cannot provide for them; they come very destitute themselves.

To the ladies who have so nobly interested themselves in behalf of my much oppressed race, I feel the deepest debt of gratitude. Let me beg the reader's attention to these orphans. They are the innocent and helpless of God's poor. If you cannot take one, you can do much by contributing your mite to the institution that will open its doors to receive them.

LINDA.

September 5, 1862

THE SECOND MANASSAS CAMPAIGN:
VIRGINIA, AUGUST 1862

Edward Porter Alexander: *from* Fighting for the Confederacy

As soon as he discovered the Federals' intent to evacuate the Peninsula, General Lee moved north with all speed to strike at Pope's Army of Virginia before McClellan's Army of the Potomac could combine with it. In his reminiscences, Alexander, the ordnance chief for Lee's army, traced the complex movements of what would be known as the Second Bull Run (or Second Manassas) campaign.

OUR CAMPAIGN opened early in August. Pope was concentrating east of the Rappahannock the three armies of Frémont, 13,000, Banks, 11,000, & McDowell, 18,000 inf. & 5,000 cavalry. The best return I can find of their numbers would make his whole available force about 47,000.

To Pope came orders from Halleck to make some demonstrations toward our railroad at Gordonsville so as to attract a part of Gen. Lee's troops from Richmond, in order that McClellan might safely weaken his army by beginning to ship it to the Potomac. Nothing could have suited Gen. Lee better. No sooner did Pope send some of his troops across the Rappahannock, than Lee sent Jackson with his own division, Ewell's & A. P. Hill's to look after him. In fact there is a doubt in my mind whether Lee did not himself start Jackson up to Gordonsville before he ever heard of Pope's demonstrations; intending on his part to *force* Halleck to withdraw McClellan in order to defend Washington, & meanwhile, too, intending to take advantage of his interior position & try & crush Pope before McClellan could reach him. Certainly that whole game was formulated in his mind at the very commencement of the campaign & it was executed with a dash & brilliancy equalled by few campaigns in the world, & with as much success as could possibly have been hoped for, considering the odds & all the circumstances, for Pope had the easiest game to play. Lee lost some time by heavy rains & a freshet in the rivers & Pope did get reinforcements of 3 corps from McClellan (3rd, 4th & 5th I believe) & one, the 9th, from No. Ca., but yet Lee cleaned him up, & ran him off the last battle field while two whole corps, Sumner's & Franklin's, were just 1 & 2 days away. It was a beautifully played game on Lee's part anyway.

And now I'll try & outline briefly the different steps. Jackson crossed the Rapidan with his three divisions & on Aug. 9th had a very sharp battle with Banks's corps on the slope of Cedar Mountain. He drove Banks off the field; but he himself suffered sharply, & he recrossed the Rapidan. Among our casualties was Gen. Winder killed—a very promising officer. One of my special friends, Col. Snowden Andrews, of the arty., received here one of the most desperate wounds from which any one ever recovered. A shell exploded by him & a fragment cut open his side so that his liver protruded. But he still lives to tell how he saw it & pushed it back, & got well in spite of all predictions.

On Aug. 13th Gen. Lee himself left Richmond by rail to join Jackson & took with him Longstreet & his division, and Stuart with the cavalry also followed. That still left R. H. Anderson's, D. H. Hill's, McLaws's & Walker's divns. to observe McClellan's diminishing forces, but they were to follow Longstreet as soon as it was apparent that McClellan was gone. I cannot fix the date, exactly, on which I started, but soon after Gen. Lee got to Gordonsville he wired me to come & bring my train with me. So I put Maj. Duffey in motion that very afternoon, & the next day with my light personal wagon I followed. I can remember very little detail about that march. It was a long, stern chase I had, pursuing our men, who were doing wonderful marching around & beyond the enemy, & I only caught up with them after the battle of 2nd Manassas when I was able to replenish all their ammunition & fix them up as well as when they started, & then by sending back empty wagons to Gordonsville, the nearest rail point, I soon got my own train full again.

Gen. Lee of course was very anxious to attack Pope before he could receive all the reinforcements coming to him, & Gen. Longstreet states that he "gave orders that his army should cross the Rapidan on the 18th & make battle. . . . But for some reason not fully explained our movements were delayed, & we did not cross the Rapidan until the 20th. In the meantime a dispatch to Stuart was captured by Pope which gave information of our presence & contemplated advance. This, with information Pope already had, caused him to withdraw to a very strong position, behind the Rappahannock River, & there instead of at Culpeper C.H., where the attack was first meant to be made, Gen. Lee found him."

So far Pope had handled his army very well indeed. It was his policy indeed to avoid a fight except with great advantages of ground, & these the position on the Rappahannock gave him. Gen. Lee came up to the river on Aug. 21st & felt the position strongly in some severe artillery duels across it. But in spite of his pugnacity he thought better of attacking (which would have been pie for Pope like Malvern Hill was for McClellan) & decided to turn him by a long march, striking his communications far in the rear with one half of his army while the other half, protected by the river against an assault, waited for the results. It was a bold & beautiful play. For back at Manassas Junction 24 miles behind Pope's line of battle were enormous stores & depots of Pope's army. But while the game was in progress the two halves of Lee's army would be necessarily far apart & unable to help each other, & only hard fighting & good marching could save them. From Aug. 21st to 24th Lee was reconnoitering & feeling Pope & was held back too by a freshet in the river, but on the 25th Jackson was able to cross at a point, Hinson's Mill, four miles above Pope's right flank. None of his officers were informed where he was going. His men carried 3 days' cooked rations & a few frying pans. A few ambulances & a few wagon loads of ammunition only were taken along. And Munford's 2nd Va. Cavalry picketed all roads leading to the enemy & screened the march. I should have mentioned, by the way, before that Stuart with part of his cavalry had before this gotten in rear of Pope's line, & had given him a little lesson as to the necessity of looking out for his rear, by capturing his own headquarters wagon, with his baggage & valuable correspondence showing the reinforcements which were coming to him; & this had doubtless stimulated Gen. Lee in his earnestness to get at him.

Jackson had with him his own division under Taliaferro,

Ewell's, & A. P. Hill's, say 21,000 infy. men & 2,500 cavalry (14 brig. of infty., 2 brig. of cav., 18 light batteries). His first day's march was from Jeffersonton via Hinson's Mill & Orlean to Salem—over 26 miles. To give an idea of how much of a march this is I will say that Duane & I coming home from Utah in the fall of 1858 tried to make a good march of it, & having empty wagons let the men put their muskets in the wagons so that they marched light, & had perfect roads, & there being only 64 men, they marched without the annoyance of alternate stoppings & hurryings always attendant on long columns. Under these most favorable possible conditions we averaged 22 miles per day, & the one longest march we ever made was 27 miles. So that 26 miles, including the fording of the Rappahannock, & carrying arms, knapsacks, 60 rounds ammunition, & three days' rations over a very uneven country for a column of 25,000 men with ordnance & artillery & ambulances is a very remarkable march. But in this connection it must be said that such heavy marches will always lose some men from the ranks—not quite able to keep up. And another thing I cannot resist thinking & saying—Ah, if only Gen. Jackson had marched like that from Ashland on June 26.

But perhaps his own conscience had had it out with him about the whole Seven Days business for there was never again in him any trace of his Seven Days behavior.

At dawn on the 26th he started again from Salem, & now he turned sharp to his right flank & marched for Manassas Junction, Pope's great depot of supplies. Parallel to his march most the day before, & between him & Pope, were the Bull Run Mountains, a low outlying development of the Blue Ridge chain. These he crossed at Thoro'fare Gap & soon after he was overtaken by Gen. Stuart with 2 brigades of cavalry (Fitz Lee's & Robertson's) who had crossed the Rappahannock that morning & made a forced march to join him. Together they pushed on & during the night reached Manassas, a distance of 25 miles from Salem, & captured a small force there of 8 guns & 300 men.

During this afternoon of the 26th Pope was waked up to the fact that something was going on in his rear, & he began to abandon the line of the Rappahannock & to come back with his whole army by different roads to see what it meant. And when he found it was only Jackson with 3 divisions he was pleased & made sure that Jackson would be destroyed.

So on the morning of the 27th Pope has gone from the Rappahannock to meet Jackson, & Longstreet with the rest of the army, some thirty-thousand men, he says, started to follow Jackson. Gen. Lee gave him his choice to follow on the straight Warrenton Pike after Pope or to follow Jackson's right angled route & he chose the latter, as less apt to be delayed by an enemy's rear guard in strong positions. His marches were not quite up to Jackson's & he reached Thoro'fare Gap late in afternoon of the 3rd day, the 28th, Jackson having passed it in the morning of his second day. We will leave Longstreet there while we bring Jackson up to the same hour.

He devoted the 27th to plundering & burning the Manassas Depot. Ewell's div. was thrown out towards Bristoe Station to look out for Pope's approach, & in the afternoon it was attacked by Hooker & fell back slowly, fighting until dark when it rejoined Jackson.

Early in the morning of the 27th I forgot to say a New Jersey brigade under a Gen. Taylor had arrived near Manassas by train from Washn. City to drive off what the Washn. authorities supposed to be a cavalry raid. Taylor formed & attacked before he found out any better, & he was killed & many of his men captured & also his train, which was burnt, as also the Bull Run R.R. bridge.

Jackson now knew that by morning of the 28th Pope would be concentrating everything on him. So during the night he marched out toward Bull Run & even sent A. P. Hill's divn. across it & as far as Centreville, but it came around & recrossed Bull Run at Stone Bridge & before the afternoon Jackson had, as we may say, ambushed his army south of Bull Run & west of the Warrenton Turnpike nearly parallel to that pike & not more than a mile off in a large wood. Hill's going around by Centreville was probably only intended to mystify the enemy.

It is worth while to pause here for a moment & take note of Jackson's strategy in thus halting his army & taking position to give battle to the whole of Pope's army, in this open country, when he might have gone on a considerable distance towards Thoro'fare Gap, through which Longstreet was coming to meet him. The main object of his flank movement had been to break up Pope's position, behind the Rapidan, which was too strong to be attacked. He had accomplished this & incidentally destroyed vast quantities of stores & now had Pope's entire army racing back to find him & to reopen their communications. Naturally then he might wish to avoid being brought to battle until Longstreet could be near enough to help him, and Longstreet on this day, the 28th, was still far beyond Thoro'fare Gap. He only approached it at sundown on that day, as stated above, & found a division of the enemy there, under Ricketts, opposing his passage. So Jackson with his three divisions had to contemplate standing off Pope's whole army, of about five corps or fifteen divisions, for all of 24 hours, with all the chances that Pope might detain Longstreet longer, or even crush him separately.

But there was a strong reason why he should fight as soon as it was possible to do so. Two additional whole corps of McClellan's veterans from the James, Franklin's & Sumner's, were on the way, but had not yet arrived, to reinforce Pope. If any choice was left to Pope, he might not make the battle until these had arrived. It was worth taking even desperate chances, & the occasion found the man equal to it. Jackson was no longer the Jackson of the Seven Days, but the Jackson of the Valley. Perhaps the experiences of that campaign had awakened him to at least a sub-conscious appreciation that the Lord helps best those who do not trust in Him for even a row of pins, however devoutly they may talk about it, but who appreciate the whole responsibility & hustle for themselves accordingly. However that may be, the Jackson of the Seven Days was never seen on Earth again. In less than nine months he was to lay down his life, shot by mistake by the fire of his own men, but meanwhile here at 2nd Manassas, & at Harpers Ferry, at Sharpsburg, at Fredericksburg, & at Chancellorsville he was to wipe out from men's memories the fact that he had ever been, even temporarily, anything but the Jackson of the Valley.

So now we see him, at midday of the 28th, in line of battle parallel to the Warrenton Pike & in gun shot of it on the west, ready to try conclusions with whatever might seek to pass on that road. He had not very long to wait. In the latter half of the afternoon King's division of McDowell's corps came along hunting for him. Being attacked, they met it half way, & the ground giving their artillery a good chance, they put up an unusually hot fight which lasted until dark & in which our Gen. Ewell lost his leg—leaving Lawton in command of his division. During the night King abandoned his ground & fell back toward Manassas. Late in the evening Jackson's men had been cheered by hearing Longstreet's guns at Thoro'fare Gap, about 20 miles off, & they knew that help was coming. During that night, Longstreet had sent three brigades through another gap, Hopewell, three miles north, & another brigade or two to occupy the heights on each side of the Thoro'fare road, & when the morning dawned Ricketts's division had retreated without a fight & gone towards Bristoe. So Longstreet pushed on with his troops & Gen. Lee went on with him & by noon they had practically connected with Jackson.

Meanwhile Jackson had been doing some of the most desperate fighting ever done. When Pope learned by his attack on King that Jackson had stayed to fight him he thought that he saw victory in his hands. Jackson was almost sandwiched in between Reno's & Heintzelman's corps on the east & McDowell's & Sigel's corps & Reynolds's division on the west, & Porter's corps was close by in front. Pope attacked at dawn with two corps, Sigel's & Heintzelman's. About noon Reno's corps joined in until about 1:30 P.M. From then until about 4:30 there were intermittent calms & squalls. About 5:30 Reno & Heintzelman renewed their attack on his left & McDowell & Reynolds on his right, Sigel having had all the fight taken out of him during the morning.

It will be noted that Porter's corps was not engaged on the Federal side nor Longstreet's on the Confederate. This happened by our cavalry's reporting the advance of a heavy body of Federal infantry soon after Longstreet's arrival on the ground, & he, expecting to be attacked awaited it. Porter either knew or guessed that a much larger force than his own was before him, & he also preferred the defensive & wanted to be attacked. For this he was court-martialed & cashiered. In 1878 however he got a rehearing, & a board of officers on the testimony of Longstreet & other Confederate officers justified & commended his conduct & he was put on the list of retired officers. No one knowing Fitz John Porter personally would believe that he could deliberately fail in his duty as a soldier.

But no one who knew how Pope was regarded by many of the best officers of the old army can doubt that they found some consolation in the fact that it was Pope who was whipped. Gen. Lee had desired to disregard Porter's proximity & to have Longstreet go to support Jackson's battle soon after his arrival, & doubtless that would have been safer play. Later in the evening, however, near sundown, Longstreet did make an assault with a small force, gained some ground & captured a gun, but later abandoned both & fell back to his original position.

This attack cut no figure as help to Jackson's fight, & it is due both to Jackson & his men to say that these three divisions successfully held off four corps & one division (say ten divisions) from dawn till dark of a long summer day. There was said to have been bayonet fighting at some points, & at one place where there was a rocky hill & an old railroad cut & embankment Starke's Louisiana brigade, its ammunition temporarily running low, defended itself partly by throwing stones at the enemy's lines.

Next morning, Aug. 30th, Gen. Pope thought that Lee's army had begun a retreat to the south. Some of his men who had been captured & paroled from within the Confederate lines brought reports to that effect & his reconnoitering officers confirmed it. It was ten o'clock before he found out any better, his whole army, meanwhile, recuperating from the severe fighting of the 29th. And, on his part, Gen. Lee believed for a time that Pope had either begun to retreat or was preparing to do so. He thought Pope's position & force too strong to be immediately assaulted but he was preparing to pursue vigorously at the earliest moment. About noon Pope, realizing that there was still the bulk of Lee's force before him, formed a powerful assaulting force practically comprising the whole of his army of five corps & one extra division & moved upon Jackson's position. The heavy lines & columns made a magnificent sight as they advanced across the open fields, but their direction was such that from some hills in Longstreet's front they were exposed to an oblique, & almost an enfilading fire.

Longstreet saw this, & immediately brought forward all his available artillery, & opened fire on them. Since the experience of the Seven Days, Gen. Lee had begun to throw his isolated batteries together into battalions of artillery. Usually four batteries (three of 4 guns each & one of 6, making 18 guns in all) constituted a battalion, which was commanded by two field officers. But one of Longstreet's battns. was an unusually large one, comprising 5 batteries—22 guns—under Col. Stephen D. Lee and Maj. Del Kemper. Col. Lee was an excellent officer, as may be guessed from his becoming lieut. general within the next two years. And the battalion itself we will hear much more of also, as I succeeded Lee in the command of it on his promotion early in November. Lee's battalion was conspicuous for its brilliant service upon this occasion. It had a beautiful position in easy range & the weight of its fire was very effective in breaking up the enemy's lines & columns. They endeavored to reform again & again, but were again & again broken & confused by the constantly increasing Confederate fire. While in this condition Longstreet's whole force of infantry was at last launched against them, & even Jackson's tired veterans also took the offensive. The enemy was still in superior force & fought well, but they were gradually driven back everywhere & before darkness ended the fighting they had lost from a half to three quarters of a mile of ground.

During the night Pope retreated across Bull Run. The next day he was joined by Sumner's & Franklin's corps near Centreville, but as Lee moved after him in pursuit he fell back toward Washington City. At Ox Hill on Sep. 1st a part of Jackson's forces encountered a strong rear guard & received a temporary check, but Pope made no halt outside of the strong chain of fortifications guarding Washington on the south. The following are the best returns I can find of the forces engaged & the casualties of this campaign.

"TREACHERY": WASHINGTON, D.C.,
AUGUST 1862

Charles Francis Adams Jr. to
Charles Francis Adams

Lieutenant Adams, 1st Massachusetts Cavalry, wrote to his father, the American minister in London, on the eve of Second Bull Run. As Adams discovered, drawing from his insider army sources, it was a time of great mistrust between the armies of McClellan and Pope and great confusion in the War Department, made all the worse as communications were severed between Washington and Pope's army.

Willard's Hotel, Washington
August 27, 1862

Here I am once more in the city of Washington. Since I last wrote the first detachment of our regiment has arrived at Fortress Monroe, and is now in camp at Acquia Creek, while I have come up here to see about this business of Pope's staff. I find the old city much as usual, but still not the same. It was indeed pleasant for me to get here and at least to see something familiar once more, and I looked at all the public buildings and even at Willard's as at old friends. Once more I have really slept in a bed and I really never enjoyed anything in my life, in its kind, more than the delicious little supper which Gautier got up for me. You don't know how much eight months of coarse fare improve one's faculties for gastronomic enjoyment, and last evening I experienced a new sensation.

Here I am though, and what next? Shall I go onto Pope's staff? I think not. This is a very different place from Hilton Head and here I am learning many strange things which make me open my eyes very wide, which make me sorrow over our past and do not encourage me for the future. Here I have access to certain means of information and I think I can give you a little more light than you now have. Do you know that just before leaving the Peninsula McClellan offered to march into Richmond on his own responsibility? Do you know that in the opinion of our leading military men Washington is in more danger than it ever yet has been? Do you know that but for McDowell's jealousy we should have triumphantly marched into Richmond? Do you know that Pope is a humbug and known to be so by those who put him in his present place? Do you know that today he is so completely outgeneraled as to be cut off from Washington? Yet these are not rumors, but facts, doled out to me by members of McClellan's and Halleck's staffs.

Our rulers seem to me to be crazy. The air of this city seems thick with treachery; our army seems in danger of utter demoralization and I have not since the war begun felt such a tug on my nerves as today in Washington. Everything is ripe for a terrible panic, the end of which I cannot see or even imagine. I always mean to be one of the hopeful, but just now I cast about in vain for something on which to hang my hopes. I still believe in McClellan, but I *know* that the nearest advisers of the President —among them Mr. Holt—distrust his earnestness in this war. Stanton is jealous of him and he and Pope are in bitter enmity. All pin their hope on Halleck and we must do as the rest do; but it is hinted to me that Stanton is likely to be a block in Halleck's way, and the jealousies of our generals are more than a new man can manage. We need a head and we must have it; a man who can keep these jealousies under subordination; and we must have him or go to the wall. Is Halleck going to supply our need? I hope he is, but while the question is in doubt we may lose Washington. You will think that I am in a panic and the most frightened man in Washington. I assure you it is not so. I do consider the outside condition of affairs very critical, but it is my glimpse behind the scenes, the conviction that small men with selfish motives control the war without any central power to keep them in bounds, which terrifies and discourages me.

Take the history of the Peninsular campaign. My authorities are one aid of McClellan's and Halleck's Assistant Adjutant General, but the facts speak for themselves, and the inferences any man may draw. Stanton, contrary to the first principle of strategy and for motives not hard to comprehend, divides Virginia into four independent departments. McClellan takes charge of one and a column is taken from him to form another under charge of McDowell. It is solemnly promised McClellan that McDowell shall join him before Richmond, and meanwhile he is retained where he is to protect Washington. Mark the result. McClellan fights the battle of Hanover Court House, with all its loss of life and time, simply to open the road for McDowell to join him and he does open it. McDowell's advance guard hears his cannon on that day, but McDowell does not stir, and McClellan, still looking for him, forms that fatal Chickahominy front of twenty miles. Doubtless McDowell was kept back by orders, but in how far was he instrumental in procuring these orders to suit himself? McClellan's staff do not hesitate to say that he dictated them on pretence of danger to Washington, in reality because his advance would have absorbed his command in that of McClellan. Take the pretence. Jackson makes his raid in the valley of the Shenandoah, and again McDowell's advance hears the sound of his guns. Washington is in danger now. As before he does not move and Jackson escapes and returns to attack McClellan. Had McDowell done his duty either for McClellan or against Jackson, we should now have Richmond and McClellan would now be the conquering hero. He did neither and is now in disgrace, as subordinated to Pope; but McClellan is not the conquering hero. Not half an hour ago Halleck's nephew and private secretary told me that I could not imagine the trouble these jealousies gave his uncle. Said he, "McDowell and Sigel will not fight under Pope. McClellan and Pope are not in sympathy"; and he added an intimation that McClellan was most restive under Halleck.

Under these circumstances what can we expect? What can we hope for? Sigel stands well, but all our army officers are bitter and jealous against him. In Burnside there is indeed hope. He has been true and generous and, what is much, successful. He did not hesitate to award to McClellan the credit of planning his Carolina campaign, and, unlike McDowell, when told to send to McClellan all the troops he could spare, he at once sent him twenty-eight regiments and six batteries, leaving himself and the Major General under him some 3000 men in all. We have some grim old fighters who do their work and do not scheme. Such they tell me are Sumner and Heintzelman; but even of these the last is outspoken against McClellan because he will not fight with more energy. The simple truth is the man has not come and now we mean to supply his place with vast numbers of undrilled recruits. Shall we succeed? You can judge as well as I.

Thus the war is gloomily enough approaching its last and bloodiest stage. Unless Halleck is the man of iron who can rule, it will be discordant numbers against compact strategy. We must face the music, though we do not like the tune. . . .

"THESE GREAT OPERATIONS": VIRGINIA AND
MARYLAND, AUGUST–SEPTEMBER 1862

John Hampden Chamberlayne to Martha Burwell Chamberlayne

Lieutenant "Ham" Chamberlayne's account of Second Bull Run, written to his mother, follows the fortunes of A. P. Hill's division in Stonewall Jackson's wing of the Army of Northern Virginia. In the Ox Hill (or Chantilly) fight Chamberlayne noted the death of two Union generals, Philip Kearny and Isaac Stevens. The campaign cost the Union about 16,000 men killed, wounded, or missing, while Confederate losses totaled about 9,000.

Frederick City, Frederick Co. Maryland
Saturday Sept. 6th 1862

My dear Mother

I am brimful of matter, as an egg of meat. Since my letter, date unknown, from camp in Orange, near Raccoon Ford— there has been no chance to send a letter & therefore I have not written; & now I am at a loss to tell when I can send this.

Let me try to outline our progress, you bearing in mind that I am in Hill's (A. P.) Division in Jackson's Corps, that Corps consisting of Jackson's own Division, in which are Mann, V, Lewis Randolph, & many other friends, Ewells & Hills Divisions; whereby you will not think me egotistical for speaking of Jackson's Corps mostly & of the corps, Hill's Division; for of them I know most & in truth their share was the most memorable even in the almost incredible campaign of the last fortnight. Crossing Rapidan at Somerville, Jackson in front (remember "Jackson," so used, includes Hill Ewell & the Stonewall Division) General Lee without much opposition reached Rappahannock River a few miles above Rappahannock Station, where part of Longstreet's troops had a sharp fight. On friday evening, 22d August, Jackson bivouacked in Culpeper opposite Warrenton Springs, he threw over that evening two Brigades of Ewells; the river rose & destroyed the Bridge;

Saturday the Bridge was rebuilt, that night the two Brigades after some sharp fighting were withdawn.

On Sunday morning the enemy appeared in heavy force & the Batteries of Hills Division were put into position on the hills & shelled their infantry. They retired the infantry & bringing up a large number of Batteries threw a storm of shot & shell at us, we not replying; they must have expended several thousand rounds, & in all, so well sheltered were we, our killed & wounded did not reach 20. That evening Jacksons whole force moved up to Jefferson in Culpeper, Longstreet close to him. The enemy was completely deceived & concluded that we had given the thing up.

Now comes the great wonder. Starting up the bank of the River (on Monday the 25th) we marched through Amosville in Rappahannock Co., still farther up, crossed the Rappahannock within ten miles of the Blue Ridge, marched by strange country paths, across open fields & comfortable homesteads, by a little town called Orleans in Fauquier on & on as if we would never cease—to Salem on the Manassas Gap R. R. reaching it after midnight; up again by day & still on, along the Manassas Gap R. R. meeting crowds along the road, all welcoming, cheering staring with blank amazement, so all day tuesday the 26th through White plains, Haymarket Thoroughfare Gap in Bull Run Mountains, Gainesville to Bristow Station on the Orange & Alexandria R. R., making the distance from Amosville to Bristow (between 45 & 50 miles) within the 48 hours. We burned up at Bristow 2 or three Railway trains & moved on to Manassas Junction on Wednesday taking our prisoners with us. Ewells Division brought up the rear, fighting all the way a force that Pope had sent up from Warrenton supposing us a cavalry party.

Upon reaching the Junction we met a Brigade the 1st New Jersey which had been sent from Alexia on the same supposition, they even were fools enough to send in a flag demanding our surrender; at once & of course we scattered the Brigade, taking several hundred prisoners, killing & wounding many & among them the Brig-Gen. Taylor, who has since died.

At the Junction was a large store depôt, 5 or six pieces of artillery, two trains containing probably 200 large cars loaded down with many millions worth of qr mr. & Commissary stores; beside these there were very large sutlers depôts full of everything; in short there was collected there in a square mile an amount & variety of property such as I had never conceived of (I speak soberly). Twas a curious sight to see our ragged & famished men helping themselves to every imaginable article of luxury or necessity whether of clothing, food or what not; for my part I got a tooth brush, a box of candles, a quantity of lobster salad, a barrel of coffee & other things wh. I forget. But I must hurry on for I have not time to tell the hundredth part & the scene utterly beggars description.

A part of us hunted that Brigade like scattered partridges over the hills just to the right of the Battlefield of the 18th July /61 while the rest were partly plundering partly fighting the forces coming on us from Warrenton. Our men had been living on roasted corn since crossing Rappahannock, & we had brought no wagons so we could carry little away of the riches before us. But the men could eat for one meal at least, so they were marched up and as much of everything eatable served out as they could carry To see a starving man eating lobster salad & drinking rhine wine, barefooted & in tatters was curious; the whole thing is indescribable, I'll tell you sometime may be.

Our situation was now very critical, we were between Alexandria & Warrenton, between the hosts of Mclellan & Pope with our jaded 18000 men, for the Corps had not more then. At nightfall fire was set to the depot, store houses, the loaded trains, several long empty trains, sutler's houses, restaurants & every thing. As the magnificent conflagration began to subside the Stonewall or 1st Division moved off towards the Battlefield of Manassas, the other two to Centreville 6 miles; as day broke we came in sight of Centreville; rested a few hours & towards evening the rear Guard of the Corps crossed Bull Run at Stone Bridge, the scene of the great slaughter of last year, closely pursued by the enemy. A part of their force came up the Warrenton turnpike & in a furious action of two hours, the last two hours of Thursday the 28th August, disputed the possession of a ridge running from Sudley Church Ford to the Warrenton turnpike. We drove them off & on friday morning we held the ridge in front of which runs an incomplete R. R. Cut & embankment. Now we had made a circuit from the Gap in

Bull Run Mt. around to the Junction & Centreville, breaking up the R. R. & destroying their stores, & returned to within six miles of the Gap through which Longstreet *must* come. The enemy disputed his passage & delayed him till late in the day, & meanwhile they threw against our corps all day long vast masses of troops, Sigel, Banks, Pope's own Division; we got out of ammunition, we collected more from cartridge boxes of fallen friend & foe; that gave out, & we charged with the never failing yell & steel.

All day long they threw their masses on us, all day they fell back, shattered & shrieking. When the sun went down their dead were heaped in front of that incomplete Railway, and we sighed with relief for Longstreet could be seen coming into position on our right; the crisis was over, Longstreet never failed yet, but the sun went down *so* slowly. Friday Hill's Division chiefly bore the brunt, on thursday Ewells & Jackson's, tho all were engaged on friday.

On Saturday morning, day even memorable for it broke the back of the great lying nation, our corps still held that ridge & Longstreet formed on our right, obtuse angled to us. So that if they attacked, upon forcing us back, their flank would be exposed to Longstreet, forcing him back, to us. This arrangement was concealed from them, so far that they expected our strength to lie to our left. Skirmishing & distant cannonading lasted till 1 P. M. when the action commenced & soon grew infinitely furious, but they were out generaled & beaten from the start, & at 4 1/2 P. M. or 5 twas plain they were awfully conquered. The fight was by far the most horrible & deadly that I have ever seen. Just at sunset our wings swept round in pursuit; Jackson swinging with his left on the right as a pivot towards the right & Longstreet in the reverse method towards the left. Their dead on the field were in such numbers as to sicken even the veterans of Richmond & the Shenandoah; they left more than 2000 *dead*, rotting clay, & of wounded almost innumerable. Their discipline & the night saved them from a rout. They retreated in tolerable order to Centreville. Twas decisive, their whole army engaged, two corps of ours, & the loss I think was 10 to 1 of ours. Starkes La. Brigade, & the 2nd Brigade of Jackson's 1st Divn., the ammunition partly giving out, fought with the stones from the ground; this *I know* to be fact. Lewis Randolph, it is said, was seen to kill one man with a stone. We lost many valuable men. V. was shot early, in the breast, slightly. I heard of it on Sunday, got leave & found him at the hospital, very dirty in dust & blood but in good hands; I took off my shirt & gave it to him & sent him on his way rejoicing towards Middleburgh where he is now with Tom Dudley. Give him my love & ask him if my outline is not correct. I happened by good luck to have a clean shirt on, having bathed in Bull Run on friday morning & changed my clothing—On Saturday I had the narrowest escape yet, two cannon shot within a minute of each other passed so near to me as almost to take away my breath. The thing was so close that it put me into the wildest spirits.

On Monday our corps moved to Ox Hill between Chantilly and Fairfax C. H. where in the afternoon we had under a driving thunder storm a smart fight, but indecisive, with 3 divisions, in it were killed Generals Kearney & Stephens valuable officers both, worth the battle. Thus this corps fought 6 days out of seven, after enormous marches. On Wednesday the 3rd inst we marched to Drainesville, on thursday, to Leesburg, where we met D. H. Hills Corps, Ripley's Division, & perhaps others. On Yesterday the army crossed the Potomac, D. H. Hill a little earlier in the day than we & at a different ford. We marched till 12 1/2 last night, started today before day & reached this town by 1 P. M. or earlier. It is 24 miles from Leesburg, & within 18 miles of Pennsylvania.

Of the scene at the passage of the Potomac I have not time to speak nor of the battlefield of Leesburg. Saunders, coming on in an independent way captured the telegraph operator, turned him over to Gen. Jackson & heard him send a message to Abe, after which the telegraph was destroyed, the track torn up, B & O. R. R. Stuart yesterday sent a message by another line to Abe. I have seen the Baltimore Sun of today. They are puzzling themselves to guess whether we have really crossed.

I wish, my dear Mother, that I could better tell you of these great matters. But it is easier for you to imagine how tired I am than for me to tell you. In the last 36 hours I have slept two hours & been moving all the rest of the time.

I am proud to have borne even my humble part in these great operations, to have helped, ever so little to consummate the grand plan whose history will be a text book to all young soldiers & whose magnificent, bewildering success places Lee at the side of the Greatest Captains, Hannibal, Caesar, Eugene, Napoleon.

I hope you have preserved my letters in which I have spoken of my faith in Gen. Lee. He & his round table of Generals are worthy of the immortality of Napoleon & his Marshalls. He moves his agencies like a God, secret, complicated, vast, resistless, complete.

John reached me on Sunday the 24th. It was right not to send the horse. I am glad now that he is not here. Give my thanks, with my love to bro. Edward. I hope the colt has recovered. Your letters by John were very grateful. Norborne Starke, I was delighted to see, the day before yesterday. He gave me your most welcome letter. I have never received Sally G's letter nor yours with it. Willy Caskie is in Jackson's 1st Division, but has not been with the army since Cedar Run, August 9th where he was hurt. Please inquire about it. Letters are too scarce & precious to be lost, whether yours or Sally's. I wish I could write better tonight but I am all in a whirl. I write from Maryland, the sickening hope-deferred has at last come to pass.

This part of Md does not welcome us warmly; I have long thought the State was a humbug.

I believe we shall march to Pa tomorrow or next day. John is delighted with the life. Give much love to all my friends. Specially Cousin Harvie & all his house. I think Nannie might write to me a scrap occasionally.

I am truly sorry that the health of Richmond is bad. But the fall weather will improve it. Tell the Grattans that I saw Jimmy this day fortnight. He was well & in fine spirits; anxious to hear from his father about his transfer to a Battery. Norborne Starke wanted me to be Ordnance Officer for his father, but I cant leave this post unless I am offered promotion.

Give no end of love to Hart & bro Edward & Sister. Remember me to the Moores. I hope Dr. Bagby got my letter written from Orange County. Tell Nancy to give my love to Miss Mattie Waller. After what I have seen lately life looks very fleeting & uncertain. If I should never see any of you again, remember that I am in charity with all men, except our enemy whom to hate is lawful, and that many I love very dearly—

Howbeit; care killed a cat. Tell Nancy to sit down when you get this & sing one of her best pieces. So shall I, as I sit here on the banks of Monocacy under the beams of the full, unclouded, moon, fancy that I hear her clear notes welling up in the trills that I remember she used to warble out like a sweet little bird; and straightway from me listening shall flee away all evil thoughts & harsh fancies & the coarse jeer & laughter of camp be hushed leaving only pleasant dreams of home & friends

Your most affectionate son

J. H. C.

Gen. Hill does me the honour always to use me as one of his staff

"UNSOLDIERLY AND DANGEROUS CONDUCT":
VIRGINIA, SEPTEMBER 1862

John Pope to Henry W. Halleck

As the badly beaten Union forces fell back from the Bull Run battlefield toward the defenses of Washington, this dispatch of General Pope's triggered a command crisis. The "commander of a corps" in the Army of the Potomac he mentions was Fitz John Porter, brought to court-martial in December on Pope's charges.

CENTREVILLE, *September* 1—8.50 a.m.
Major-General HALLECK:
All was quiet yesterday and so far this morning. My men are resting; they need it much. Forage for our horses is being brought up. Our cavalry is completely broken down, so that there are not five horses to a company that can raise a trot. The consequence is that I am forced to keep considerable infantry along the roads in my rear to make them secure, and even then it is difficult to keep the enemy's cavalry off the roads. I shall attack again to-morrow if I can; the next day certainly. I think it my duty to call your attention to the unsoldierly and dangerous conduct of many brigade and some division commanders of the forces sent here from the Peninsula. Every word and act and intention is discouraging, and calculated to break down the spirits of the men and produce disaster. One commander of a corps, who was ordered to march from Manassas Junction to join me near Groveton, although he was only 5 miles distant, failed to get up at all, and, worse still, fell back to Manassas without a fight, and in plain hearing, at less than 3 miles' distance, of a furious battle, which raged all day. It was only in consequence of peremptory orders that he joined me next day. One of his brigades, the brigadier-general of which professed to be looking for his division, absolutely remained all day at Centreville, in plain view of the battle, and made no attempt to join. What renders the whole matter worse, these are both officers of the Regular Army, who do not hold back from

ignorance or fear. Their constant talk, indulged in publicly and in promiscuous company, is that the Army of the Potomac will not fight; that they are demoralized by withdrawal from the Peninsula, &c. When such example is set by officers of high rank the influence is very bad amongst those in subordinate stations.

You have hardly an idea of the demoralization among officers of high rank in the Potomac Army, arising in all instances from personal feeling in relation to changes of commander-in-chief and others. These men are mere tools or parasites, but their example is producing, and must necessarily produce, very disastrous results. You should know these things, as you alone can stop it. Its source is beyond my reach, though its effects are very perceptible and very dangerous. I am endeavoring to do all I can, and will most assuredly put them where they shall fight or run away. My advice to you—I give it with freedom, as I know you will not misunderstand it—is that, in view of any satisfactory results, you draw back this army to the intrenchments in front of Washington, and set to work in that secure place to reorganize and rearrange it. You may avoid great disaster by doing so. I do not consider the matter except in a purely military light, and it is bad enough and grave enough to make some action very necessary. When there is no heart in their leaders, and every disposition to hang back, much cannot be expected from the men.

Please hurry forward cavalry horses to me under strong escort. I need them badly—worse than I can tell you.

JNO. POPE,
Major-General.

AIDING THE WOUNDED: VIRGINIA AND
WASHINGTON, D.C., AUGUST–SEPTEMBER 1862

Clara Barton to John Shaver

Overall the treatment and evacuation of the Union wounded from the battlefield at Manassas were chaotic and inept. In a letter to a friend and supporter, nurse Clara Barton describes the heroic efforts of her small band of volunteers. She recorded the deaths of Generals Kearny and Stevens and Colonel Fletcher Webster, son of Daniel Webster. Barton, a clerk in the Patent Office at the outbreak of the war, operated independently to deliver nursing care right to the scene of the fighting, and she became known in the Union army as the "Angel of the Battlefield." In 1881 she founded the American branch of the Red Cross.

Washington, D.C. Sept. 4 / 62

Mr. Shaver,

Dear friend,

Yours awaited me on my return from Fairfax Tuesday evening (or night rather). I left here on Sunday morning in the rain in company with Mr. Wells, Mrs. Morrell, Mr. Haskell, Mr. Alvord, &c. &c., took the train at Morgan Bulleys office, and soon found ourselves at Fairfax. I can not tell you the scenes which awaited our eyes,—the wounded were constantly arriving—but no hospitals this time, only God's great one under the blue canopy. The men were brot down from the field and laid on the ground beside the train and so back up the hill till they covered acres, the bales of hay for forage were broken open and the ground was "littered" like "bedding" for horses,—they came till dark and then it was dark indeed. *One* lantern on the ground made a requisition for candles drew a few, the wind blew just enough to put them out every few minutes, and the men lay so thick we could not take one step in the dark, by midnight there must have been *three thousand* helpless men lying on that hay.

We had *two* water buckets—5 dippers. The stores which we carried to eat, besides hard crackers,— My one *stew pan* which

I remembered to take, and this made coffee for them, all night we made compresses and slings and bound up and wet wounds, when we could get water, fed what we could, travelled miles in the dark over these poor helpless wretches, in terror lest some ones candle fell *into the hay* and consume them all, at length morning came, and we sent up the train with 1250, next 1000, next 1100, next 950, and so on. Still the ambulances came down, and the cars went out and we worked on, took the meat from our own sandwiches & gave it to them and broke the bread into wine and water to feed the poor sinking wretches as they lay in the ambulances.

On Monday the enemies Cavalry appeared in the wood opposite, & a raid was hourly expected. (I neglected to tell you that *Mrs. Fales* sent to me before I started to know *if she could go with me* and I had the train wait, and sent back an ambulance for her and her stores,—and this made three ladies (Mrs Corner is away)) On Monday PM all the wounded then in were sent off, and the danger became so iminent that Mrs Fales thought it best to leave, although she only "*went for stores.*" I begged to be excused from accompanying her, as the ambulances were up to the field for more, and I knew *I* should *never leave a wounded* man there if I knew it, though I were taken prisoner 40 times. At 6 clock it commenced to thunder an lightning, and all at once the artillery began to play joined by the musketry about *two miles distant*, we sat down in our tent, and waited to see them break in but Reno's forces held them back. The *old 21st Mass.* lay between us and the enemy and they couldnt pass. God only knows who is lost. I do not for the next day *all fell* back. Poor Kearney, Stephens & Webster were brought in, and in the PM, Kearney's and Heintzleman's divisions fell back through our camp on their way to Alexandria. We knew this was the last. We put the thousand wounded we had then into the train. I took one car load of them, Mrs M another. The men took to horse, we steam off, and two hours after there was no Fairfax Station, reached Alexandria at 10 oclock at night. And Oh the repast which met those poor men at the train. The people of the Island are the most noble band I ever saw or heard of. I staid in my car and fed the men till they would eat no more. Then the people *would* take us home and feed us, and after this we came home. I had slept 1 1/4 hours since Saturday night but I am well and strong and wait to go again if I have need.

Our forces are all back again in the old places around the city. McClellans army here again and he in command of it all. I am going to search for my friends now. I have told you nothing of the old friends who met me among the wounded and dying on that bloody field. I have no heart to tell it to day but will some time. Can you read this. Oh how I needed stores on that field. To day 2 huge boxes from Jersey have arrived. I dont know when we shall need them next. I will write you a more readable letter in reply to your last to me.

Yours, C.H. Barton

"MCCLELLAN MUST GO DOWN":
WASHINGTON, D.C., AUGUST–SEPTEMBER 1862

Gideon Welles: Diary, August 31–September 1, 1862

Navy secretary Welles spells out the case against McClellan, as made by Secretaries Stanton and Chase in their remonstrance, regarding (among other failings) that general's delay in supporting Pope in the Second Bull Run fighting. The forces held back to defend Washington, under McClellan's orders, were William Franklin's Sixth Corps and Edwin Sumner's Second Corps, some 25,000 men in all.

Sunday 31 *August.* For the last two or three days there has been fighting at the front and army movements of interest. McClellan with most of his army arrived at Alexandria a week or more ago, but inertness, inactivity and sluggishness seem to prevail. Some of the troops have moved forward to join Pope, who has been beyond Manassas where he has encountered Jackson and the Rebel forces for the last three days in a severe struggle.

The energy and rapid movements of the Rebels are in such striking contrast with that of some of our own officers, that the War Department is alarmed and I shall not be seriously surprised at any sudden dash. By request, and in anticipation of the worst, though not expecting it, I have ordered Wilkes and a force of fourteen gunboats, including the five light drafts asked for by Burnside, to come round into the Potomac, and have put W. in command of the flotilla here, disbanding that on the James.

Yesterday, Saturday, P.M. when about leaving the Department, Chase called on me with a protest signed by himself and Stanton, against McClellan and demanding his immediate dismissal. Certain grave offenses were enumerated. He said that Smith had seen and would sign it in turn, but as my name preceded his in order, he desired mine in its place. I told him I was not prepared to sign the document—that I preferred a different method of meeting the question—that if asked by the President, and even if not asked, I was prepared to express my opinion—which, as he knew had long been averse to McClellan and was much aggravated from what I had recently learned at the War Department—that I did not choose to denounce McC. for incapacity, or declare him a traitor but I would say, and it was perhaps my duty to say, that I believed his withdrawal from any command was demanded and that even his dismissal would be a blessing.

Chase said that was not sufficient,—that the time had arrived when the Cabinet must act with energy and promptitude, for either the Government or McClellan must go down. He then proceeded to expose certain acts, some of which were partially known to me, and others, more startling, which were new. I said to C. that he and Stanton were familiar with facts of which I was ignorant, and there might therefore be propriety in their stating what they knew which I could not because I had no knowledge of these facts.

I proposed there should be a general consultation with the President. He objected to this until the document was signed, which should be done at once.

This method of getting signatures without an interchange of views from those who were associated in council was repugnant to my ideas of duty and right. When I asked if the Attorney General and Postmaster General, had seen the paper or been consulted, he replied not yet, their turn had not come. I informed C. that I should desire to advise with them in so important a matter,—that I was disinclined to sign the paper—did not like the proceeding—that I could not, though I wished McClellan removed after what I had heard, and should have no hesitation in saying so at the proper time and place, and, in what I considered the right way.

While we were talking Blair came in. Chase was alarmed, for the paper was in my hand and he evidently feared I should address B. on the subject. This, after witnessing his agitation, I could not do without his consent. Blair remained but a few moments; did not even take a seat. After he left, I asked Chase if we should not consult him. C. said No, not now,—it is best he should know nothing of it. I took a different view—that there was no one of the Cabinet whom I would sooner consult on this subject—that I thought his opinion, often very correct. Chase said this was not the time to bring him in. After he left me, he returned to make a special request that I would make no allusion concerning the paper to Blair or any one else.

Met, by invitation, a few friends last evening at Baron Gerolt's. My call was early and feeling anxious concerning affairs in front, I excused myself to go to the War Department for tidings. Found Stanton and Smith alone in the Secretary's room. The conduct of McClellan was soon taken up,—it had, I inferred, been under discussion before I came in.

Stanton began with a statement of his entrance into the Cabinet in January when he found everything in confusion with unpaid bills to the amount of over $20,000,000 against the Department. His inability to procure any satisfactory information from McClellan, who had no plan and no system. Said this vague, indefinite uncertainty was oppressive. That near the close of January, he pressed this subject on the President, who issued the order to him and myself for an advance on the 22d of February. McClellan began at once to interpose objections— yet did nothing,—but talked always vaguely and indefinitely and of various matters except those immediately in hand. The President insisted on, and ordered a forward movement. Then McClellan informed them he intended a demonstration on the upper waters of the Potomac and boats for a bridge were prepared with great labor and expense. He went up there and telegraphed back that two or three officers had done admirably in preparing the bridge and he wished them to be brevetted. The whole thing eventuated in nothing and he was ordered back.

The President then commanded that the army should proceed to Richmond. McClellan delayed, hesitated, said he must go by way of the Peninsula—would take transports at Annapolis. In order that he should have no excuse, but without any faith in his plan, Stanton said he ordered transports and supplies at Annapolis. The President in the mean time urged and pressed forward a movement towards Manassas—its results— the evacuation by the Rebels who fled before the General came, who did not pursue but came back. The transports were then ordered round to the Potomac where the troops were shipped to Fortress Monroe. The plans,—the number of troops to proceed—the number that was to remain Stanton recounted. These arrangements were somewhat deranged by the sudden raid of Jackson towards Winchester, which withdrew Banks from Manassas, leaving no force between Washington and the Rebel army at Gordonsville. He then ordered McDowell and his division, also Franklin's to remain, to the great grief of McDowell, who believed glory and fighting were all to be with the grand army. McClellan had made the withholding of this necessary force his excuse for not being more rapid and effective,—was constantly complaining. The President wrote him how, by his arrangement, only 18,000 troops, the remnants and odd parcels, were left to protect the Capital. Still McClellan was everlastingly complaining and underrating his forces—said he had but 96,000, when his own returns showed he had 123,000. But to stop his complaints and urge him forward, the President finally, on the 10th of June, sent him McCall and his division, with which he promised to proceed at once to Richmond but did not, until finally attacked.

McClellan's excuse for going by way of the Peninsula was that he might have good roads and dry ground, but his complaints were unceasing, after he got there, of bad roads, and water, and swamps.

When finally ordered to withdraw from James River, he delayed obeying the order for thirteen days, and never did comply until General Burnside was sent to supersede him if he did not move.

Since his arrival at Alexandria Stanton says only delay and embarrassment had governed him. General Halleck had, among other things, ordered General Franklin's division to go forward promptly to support Pope at Manassas. When Franklin got as far as Annandale he was stopped by McClellan, against orders and McClellan's excuse was he thought Franklin might be in danger if he proceeded farther. For twenty four hours that large force remained stationary, hearing the whole time the guns of the battle that was raging in front. In consequence of this delay by command of McClellan, against specific orders, he apprehended our army would be compelled to fall back.

Smith left whilst we were conversing after this detailed narrative, and Stanton dropping his voice, though no one was present, said he understood from Chase that I had declined to sign the protest which he had drawn up against McClellan's continuance in command, and asked if I did not think we ought to get rid of him. I told him I might not differ with him on that point, especially after what I had heard in addition to what I had previously known, but that I disliked the method and manner of proceeding—that it was discourteous and disrespectful to the President were there nothing else. Stanton said he knew of no particular obligations he was under to the President who had called him to a difficult position and imposed upon him labors and responsibilities which no man could carry, and which were greatly increased by fastening upon him a commander who was constantly striving to embarrass him. He could not and would not submit to a continuance of this state of things. I admitted they were bad, severe on him, and he could and stated his case strongly, but I could not indorse it, nor did I like the manner in which it was proposed to bring about a dismissal. He said General Pope telegraphed to McClellan for supplies. The latter informed P. they were at Alexandria, and if P. would send an escort he could have them. A general fighting, on the field of battle, sends to a general in the rear, and in repose, an escort!

Watson Assistant Secretary of War gave me this last fact this morning, and reaffirmed others. He informs me that my course on a certain occasion had offended McClellan and was not approved by others; but that both the President and Stanton had since, and now in their private conversations admitted I was right, and that my letter in answer to a curt and impudent demand of McClellan last spring was proper and correct. Watson says that he always told them I was right, and he complimented me on several subjects which others can speak of and judge better than myself.

We hear, this Sunday morning, that our army has fallen back to Centreville. Pope writes in pretty good spirits we have lost no guns, etc. The Rebels were largely reinforced, while our troops, detained at Annandale by McClellan's orders, did not arrive to support our wearied and exhausted men. McClellan telegraphs that he hears Pope is "badly cut up." Schenck who had a wound in his arm left the battle-field, bringing with him for company an Ohio captain. Both arrived *safe at Willard's.*

They met McCall on the other side of Centreville and Sumner on this. Late! late!

Up to this hour, 1 P.M. no specific intelligence beyond the general facts above stated. There is considerable uneasiness in this city, which is mere panic. I see no cause for alarm. It is impossible to feel otherwise than sorrowful and sad over the waste of life and treasure, and energies of the nation—the misplaced confidence in certain men—the errors of some—perhaps the crimes of others who have been trusted. But my faith in present security and of ultimate success is unshaken. We need better generals but can have no better army. There is much latent disloyal feeling in Washington, which should be expelled. And oh, there is great want of capacity among our military leaders.

I hear that all the churches not heretofore seized are now taken for hospital purposes,—private dwellings are taken to be thus used—among others my neighbor Corcoran's fine house and grounds. There is malice in this. I told General Halleck it was vandalism. He said it would be wrong. Halleck walked over with me from the War Department and is, I perceive quite alarmed for the safety of the city,—it is a fatal error, says that we overrate our own strength and underestimate the Rebels'. This has been the talk of McClellan, which none of us have believed.

Monday 1 *September.* The wounded have been coming in to-day in large numbers. From what I can learn, General Pope's estimate of the killed and wounded greatly exceeds the actual number. He should, however, be best informed, but is greatly given to exaggeration.

Chase tells me that McClellan sends word that there are twenty thousand stragglers on the road between Alexandria and Centreville, which C. says is infamously false and done for infamous purposes. He called on me to-day with a more carefully prepared, and less exceptionable address to the President, stating the signers did not deem it safe that McClellan should be intrusted with an army, etc., and that, if required, they would give their reasons for the protest against continuing him in command. This paper was in the handwriting of Attorney-

General Bates. The former was Stanton's. This was signed by Stanton, Chase, Smith and Bates. A space was left between the two last for Blair and myself. Seward is not in town, and if I am not mistaken is purposely absent to be relieved from participation in this movement, which originates with Stanton who is mad—perhaps with reason. Seward and Stanton act in concert, and Seward has opposed the removal of McClellan until since Halleck has been brought here, and Stanton has become fierce, and determined, when Seward gave way and went away. Then Chase, who is sometimes the victim of intrigue, was taken into Stanton's confidence—made to believe that the opportunity of Seward's absence should be improved to shake off McClellan by a combined Cabinet movement to influence the President, who clung to McClellan. It was not difficult under the prevailing feeling of indignation against McClellan to enlist Smith. I am a little surprised that they got Bates, though he has for some time urged this movement. Chase took upon himself to get my name, and then, if possible, Blair was to come in. In all this, Chase flatters himself that he is attaching Stanton to his interest—not but that he is sincere in his opposition to McClellan, who was once his favorite, but whom he now detests.

I told Chase I thought this paper an improvement on the document of Saturday—that in a conference with the President, I would have no hesitation in saying or agreeing mainly in what was there expressed—substituting "advise" in one place—for I am satisfied the country would not be willing McClellan should have the active command of our forces in the field, though I cannot say what is the feeling of the armies. Reflection had more fully satisfied me that this method of combining to influence or control the President was not right—it was unusual, and would justly be deemed offensive. That the President had called us around him as friends and advisers, to counsel and consult with him on all matters affecting the public welfare, not to enter into combinations against him. Nothing of this kind has hitherto taken place in our intercourse. That we had not been sufficiently formal perhaps, and perhaps not sufficiently explicit and decisive in expressing our views.

Chase disclaimed any movement against the President, and thought the manner respectful and correct. Said it was designed to tell President that the Administration must be broken up, or McC. dismissed. The course he said was unusual, but the case was unusual. We had, it was true, been too informal in our meeting. I had been too reserved in the expression of my views which he did me the compliment to say were sound, etc. Conversation, he said amounted to but little with the President on subjects of this importance. It was like throwing water on a duck's back. A more decisive expression must be made and that in writing.

I was satisfied there was a fixed determination to remove, and if possible disgrace McClellan. Chase frankly stated he desired it, that he deliberately believed McClellan ought to be shot, and should, were he President, be brought to a summary punishment. I told him he was aware my faith in McClellan nine months ago. That as early as last December I had, as he would recollect, expressed my disappointment in the man and stated to him, specially, as the friend and indorser of McClellan, my misgivings, in order to have my doubts removed and confirmed. His indifference, and neglect, his failure in many instances to fulfill his promises, when the Rebels were erecting their batteries on the west bank of the Potomac, to close the navigation of the river, had forfeited my confidence in his efficiency and reliability. But at that time he was a general favorite, and neither he (Chase) nor any one heeded my admonitions.

A few weeks after the navigation of the river was first obstructed by the Rebel batteries, I made known to the President and Cabinet how I was put off by General McClellan with frivolous and unsatisfactory answers, until I ceased conversation with him on the subject. To me it seemed he had no plan or policy of his own, or any realizing sense of the condition of affairs. He was occupied with reviews and dress-parades— perhaps with drills and discipline but was regardless of political aspect of the question, the effect which the closing of the only avenue from the National Capital to the ocean, and the embarrassment which would follow to the Government itself. Though deprecating his course and calling his attention to it, I did not think, as Chase says he does, and as I hear others say, that he was imbecile, a coward, a traitor, but it was notorious that he hesitated, doubted, had not self-reliance—innate moral courage, and was wanting in my opinion in several of the essential requisites of a general in chief command. These are my present convictions. Some statements of Stanton and some recent acts indicate delinquencies of a more serious character. The country is greatly incensed against him.

Chase was disappointed I think a little chagrined, because I would not unite in the written demand to the President. He said he had not yet asked Blair and did not propose to till the others had been consulted. This does not look well. It appears as if there was a combination by two to get their associates committed, *seriatim*, in detail, by a skillful *ex parte* movement without general consultation.

McClellan was first invited to Washington under the auspices of Chase—more than of any one else. Seward soon had greater intimacy with him than any one else. Blair acquiesced in McClellan's selection. In the winter, when Chase began to get alienated from McC. in consequence of his hesitancy and reticence, or both, Blair seemed to confide more in the General, yet I do not think he was a favorite.

"WE ARE WHIPPED AGAIN":
WASHINGTON, D.C., SEPTEMBER 1862

John Hay: Diary, September 1, 1862

The developing command and military crisis and its effects on the President, as recorded by John Hay, one of Lincoln's secretaries. Herman Haupt, whom Lincoln spoke well of, was chief of construction of U.S. military railroads.

———————

Saturday morning, the 30th of August, I rode out into the country and turned in at the "Soldiers home." The President's horse was standing by the door and in a moment the President appeared and we rode into town together.

We talked about the state of things by Bull Run and Pope's prospect. The President was very outspoken in regard to McClellan's present conduct. He said it really seemed to him that McC wanted Pope defeated. He mentioned to me a despatch of McC.s in which he proposed, as one plan of action, to "leave Pope to get out of his own scrape, and devote ourselves to securing Washington." He spoke also of Mcs dreadful panic in the matter of Chain Bridge, which he had ordered blown up the night before, but which order had been countermanded; and also of his incomprehensible interference with Franklin's corps which he recalled once, and then when they had been sent ahead by Halleck's order, begged permission to recall them again & only desisted after Hallecks sharp injunction to push them ahead till they whipped something or got whipped themselves. The President seemed to think him a little crazy. Envy jealousy and spite are probably a better explanation of his present conduct. He is constantly sending despatches to the President and Halleck asking what is his real position and command. He acts as chief alarmist and grand marplot of the Army.

The President, on my asking if Halleck had any prejudices, rejoined "No! Halleck is wholly for the service. He does not care who succeeds or who fails so the service is benefited."

Later in the day we were in Hallecks room. H. was at dinner

& Stanton came in while we were waiting for him and carried us off to dinner. A pleasant little dinner and a pretty wife as white and cold and motionless as marble, whose rare smiles seemed to pain her. Stanton was loud about the McC. business. He was unqualifiedly severe upon McClellan. He said that after these battles, there should be one Court Martial, if never any more. He said that nothing but foul play could lose us this battle & that it rested with McC. and his friends. Stanton seemed to believe very strongly in Pope. So did the President for that matter.

We went back to the Headquarters and found General Halleck. He seemed quiet and somewhat confident. He said the greatest battle of the Century was now being fought. He said he had sent every man that could go, to the field. At the War Department we found that Mr. Stanton had sent a vast army of Volunteer Nurses out to the field, probably utterly useless, over which he gave Genl. Wadsworth command.

Every thing seemed to be going well and hilarious on Saturday & we went to bed expecting glad tidings at sunrise. But about Eight oclock the President came to my room as I was dressing and calling me out said, "Well John we are whipped again, I am afraid. The enemy reinforced on Pope and drove back his left wing and he has retired to Centerville where he says he will be able to hold his men. I dont like that expression. I dont like to hear him admit that his men need holding."

After a while however things began to look better and peoples spirits rose as the heavens cleared. The President was in a singularly defiant tone of mind. He often repeated, "We must hurt this enemy before it gets away." And this Morning, Monday, he said to me when I made a remark in regard to the bad look of things, "No, Mr Hay, we must whip these people now. Pope must fight them, if they are too strong for him he can gradually retire to these fortifications. If this be not so, if we are really whipped and to be whipped we may as well stop fighting."

It is due in great measure to his indomitable will, that army movements have been characterized by such energy and celerity for the last few days. There is one man who seems thoroughly to reflect and satisfy him in everything he undertakes. This is Haupt the Rail Road man at Alexandria. He has as

Chase says a Major General's head on his shoulders. The President is particularly struck with the businesslike character of his despatch, telling in the fewest words the information most sought for, which contrasted so strongly with the weak whining vague and incorrect despatches of the whilom General-in-chief. If heads or shoulder-straps could be exchanged, it would be a good thing, in either case, here. A good railroader would be spoiled but the General gained would compensate. The corps of Haupt starting from Alexandria have acted as Pioneers advance Guard, voltigeurs and every other light infantry arm of the service.

"THE PREST. WAS IN DEEP DISTRESS":
WASHINGTON, D.C., SEPTEMBER 1862

Edward Bates: Remonstrance and Notes on Cabinet Meeting

Attorney General Bates toned down the Stanton-Chase remonstrance against McClellan, and his version gained four signatures from the seven-man cabinet, with Welles promising to support it verbally. The version printed here is Bates's draft of the remonstrance, with the names of the four signers in his handwriting (his fair copy bearing the actual signatures is preserved in Stanton's papers). The attorney general later added his notes on the September 2 cabinet meeting to the draft and wrote an endorsement at the end of the document that suggests the remonstrance was shown or read to the President during the meeting.

The undersigned, who have been honored with your selection, as a part of your confidential advisers, deeply impressed with our great responsibility in the present crisis, do but perform a painful duty in declaring to you our deliberate opinion that, at this time, it is not safe to entrust to Major General McClellan the command of any of the armies of the United States.

And we hold ourselves ready, at any time to explain to you, in detail, the reasons on which this opinion is founded

                            (Signed by) E.M. Stanton, Secy War
                                            S.P. Chase, Secy Treasury
To the President—   C.B. Smith Sec Interior
[Delivered Sept 2d 1862]   Edwd Bates Atty Genl

Note. Mr. Blair p.m.g. declined to sign (no reason given that I heard, but preserving a cautious reticence)

Gideon Welles, Secy Navy, declined to sign, for some reasons of etiquette, but openly declared in Council, his entire want of confidence in the general

W.H. Seward, Sec of State, *absent*

The Prest. was in deep distress. He had already, with, apparently, Gen Halleck's approbation, assigned Genl McClellan to the command of the forts in & around Washington & entrusted him with the defence of the City. At the opening of the Council, he seemed wrung by the bitterest anguish—said he felt almost ready to hang himself—in ansr to something said by Mr Chase, he sd he was far from doubting our sincerity, but that he was so distressed, precisely because he knew we were earnestly sincere.

He was, manifestly alarmed for the safety of the City— He had been talking with Gen Halleck (who, I think is cowed) & had gotten the idea that Pope's army was utterly demoralized—saying that "if Pope's army came within the lines (of the forts) as *a mob*, the City wd be overrun by the enemy in 48 hours!!"

I said that if Halleck doubted his ability to defend the City, he ought to be instantly, broke— 50.000 men were enough to defend it against all the power of the enemy— If the City fell, it would be by treachery in our leaders, & not by lack of power to defend. The shame was that we were reduced to the defensive, instead of the aggressive policy &c— That all the army was not needed to defend the City, & now was the time, above all others, to strike the enemy behind & at a distance &c

Opinion of Stanton, Chase, Smith & Bates, of want of Confidence in Genl. McClellan.
Given to the President Sept. 2d 1862.

"A SERIES OF FAILURES":
WASHINGTON, D.C., SEPTEMBER 1862

Salmon P. Chase: Journal, September 2, 1862

The cabinet meeting of September 2, the most contentious of Lincoln's administration, was recorded in Treasury Secretary Chase's journal. With even Montgomery Blair, a longtime McClellan supporter, admitting that he should no longer be trusted with high command, the cabinet (absent Seward) was unanimous in its condemnation of the general. Lincoln's announcement that he had assigned McClellan to defend Washington, commanding both his army and Pope's, caused Welles to write in his diary, "There was a more disturbed and desponding feeling than I have ever witnessed in council."

TUESDAY, SEPT. 2, 1862. Cabinet met, but neither the President nor Secretary of War were present. Some conversation took place concerning Generals. Mr. F. W. Seward (the Secretary of State being out of town) said nothing. All others agreed that we needed a change in Commander of the Army. Mr. Blair referred to the support he had constantly given McClellan, but confessed that he now thought he could not wisely be trusted with the chief command. Mr. Bates was very decided against his competency, and Mr. Smith equally so. Mr. Welles was of the same judgment, though less positive in expression.

After some time, while the talk was going on, the President came in, saying that not seeing much for a Cabinet Meeting to-day, he had been talking at the Department and Head Quarters about the War. The Secretary of War came in. In answer to some inquiry, the fact was stated, by the President or the Secretary, that McClellan had been placed in command of the forces to defend the Capital—or rather, to use the President's own words, he "had set him to putting these troops into the fortifications about Washington," beleiving that he could do that thing better than any other man. I remarked that this could be done equally well by the Engineer who constructed the Forts; and that putting Genl. McClellan in command for this purpose was equivalent to making him second in command of the entire army. The Secretary of War said that no one was now responsible for the defense of the Capital;—that the Order to McClellan was given by the President direct to McClellan, and that Genl. Halleck considered himself releived from responsibility, although he acquiesced; and approved the Order;—that McClellan could now shield himself, should anything go wrong, under Halleck, while Halleck could and would disclaim all responsibility for the Order given. The President thought Gen. Halleck as much responsible as before; and repeated that the whole scope of the Order was, simply, to direct McClellan to put the troops into the fortifications and command them for the defence of Washington. I remarked that this seemed to me equivalent to making him Commander in Chief for the time being, and that I thought it would prove very difficult to make any substitution hereafter, for active operations;—that I had no feeling whatever against Genl. McClellan;—that he came to the command with my most cordial approbation and support;—that until I became satisfied that his delays would greatly injure our cause, he possessed my full confidence;—that, after I had felt myself compelled to withold that confidence, I had (since the President, notwithstanding my opinion that he should, refrained from putting another in command) given him all possible support in every way, raising means and urging reinforcements;—that his experience as a military commander had been little else than a series of failures;—and that his omission to urge troops forward to the battles of Friday and Saturday, evinced a spirit which rendered him unworthy of trust, and that I could not but feel that giving the command to him was equivalent to giving Washington to the rebels. This and more I said. Other members of the Cabinet expressed a general concurrence, but in no very energetic terms. [Mr. Blair must be excepted, but he did not dissent.]

The President said it distressed him exceedingly to find himself differing on such a point from the Secretary of War and Secretary of the Treasury; that he would gladly resign his place; but he could not see who could do the work wanted as well as McClellan. I named Hooker, or Sumner, or Burnside—either of whom, I thought, would be better.

At length the conversation ended and the meeting broke up, leaving the matter as we found it.

A few Tax Appointments were lying on the table. I asked the President to sign them; which he did, saying he would sign them just as they were and ask no questions. I told him that they had all been prepared in accordance with his directions, and that it was necessary to complete the appointments. They were signed, and I returned to the Department.

RESTORED TO COMMAND:
WASHINGTON, D.C., SEPTEMBER 1862

George B. McClellan to Mary Ellen McClellan

As General McClellan explains in these notes to his wife, his restoration to command was a two-step process—first, command of Washington's defenses, then command of Pope's army as well as his own. The first letter is dated September 2, but it was written in the midnight hours of September 1 and refers to events of that day. While McClellan was never officially removed as head of the Army of the Potomac, he and everyone else understood that he was getting his army back. General Pope was sent to Minnesota to fight the Sioux uprising.

Sept 2 1 am.
. . . Last night I had just finished a very severe application for a leave of absence when I received a dispatch from Halleck begging me to help him out of the scrape & take command here—of course I could not refuse, so I came over this morning, mad as a March hare, & had a pretty plain talk with him & Abe—a still plainer one this evening. The result is that I have reluctantly consented to take command here & try to save the Capital—I don't know whether I can do it or not, for things are far gone—I hope I shall succeed. . . .

I will not work so hard again as I used to—for the next few days I must be at it day & night—once the pressure is over I will make the staff do the work. If when the whole army returns here (if it ever does) I am not placed in command of all I will either insist upon a long leave of absence or resign. . . .

September 2, 1862

Sept 2 12.30 pm.

I was surprised this morning when at bkft by a visit from the Presdt & Halleck—in which the former expressed the opinion that the troubles now impending could be overcome better by me than anyone else. Pope is ordered to fall back upon Washn & as he reenters everything is to come under my command again! A terrible & thankless task—yet I will do my best with God's blessing to perform it. God knows that I need his help. I am too busy to write any more now—Pray that God will help me in the great task now imposed upon me—I assume it reluctantly—with a full knowledge of all its difficulties & of the immensity of the responsibility. I only consent to take it for my country's sake & with the humble hope that God has called me to it—how I pray that he may support me! . . .

Don't be worried—my conscience is clear & I can trust in God.

September 2, 1862

INVADING MARYLAND:
VIRGINIA, SEPTEMBER 1862

Robert E. Lee to Jefferson Davis

In this letter General Lee suggested fairly modest goals in crossing into Maryland, and he started across the Potomac on September 4 without waiting for a response from President Davis. But in suggesting that Braxton Bragg's army, then invading Kentucky, might join him in the eastern campaign, Lee hinted at his greater ambitions.

                      Head Qurs Alex: & Leesburg Road near
                            Drainsville 3d. September 1862
Mr. President—

The present seems to be the most propitious time, since the commencement of the war, for the Confederate Army to enter Maryland. The two grand armies of the U. S. that have been operating in Virginia, though now united, are much weakened and demoralized. Their new levees, of which, I understand, sixty thousand men have already been posted in Washington, are not yet organized, and will take some time to prepare for the field. If it is ever desired to give material aid to Maryland, and afford her an opportunity of throwing off the oppression to which she is now subject, this would seem the most favorable. After the enemy had disappeared from the vicinity of Fairfax C. H. and taken the road to Alexandria & Washington, I did not think it would be advantageous to follow him further. I had no intention of attacking him in his fortifications, and am not prepared to invest them. If I possessed the necessary munitions, I should be unable to supply provisions for the troops. I therefore determined while threatening the approaches to Washington to draw the troops into Loudon, where forage and some provisions can be obtained, menace their possession of the Shenandoah Valley, and if found practicable, to cross into Maryland.

The purpose, if discovered, will have the effect of carrying the enemy north of the Potomac, and if prevented, will not result in much evil. The army is not properly equipped for an invasion of an enemy's territory. It lacks much of the material of war, is feeble in transportation, the animals being much reduced, and the men are poorly provided with clothes, and in thousands of instances, are destitute of shoes. Still we cannot afford to be idle, and though weaker than our opponents in men and military equipments, must endeavor to harass, if we cannot destroy them. I am aware that the movement is attended with much risk, yet I do not consider success impossible, and shall endeavor to guard it from loss. As long as the army of the enemy are employed on this frontier, I have no fears for the safety of Richmond, yet I earnestly recommend that advantage be taken of this period of comparative safety, to place its defence, both by land and water, in the most, perfect condition. A respectable force can be collected to defend its approaches by land, and the steamer Richmond I hope is now ready to clear the river of hostile vessels. Should Genl Bragg find it impracticable to operate to advantage on his present frontier, his army, after leaving sufficient garrisons, could be advantageously employed in opposing the overwhelming numbers which it seems to be the intention of the enemy now to concentrate in Virginia. I have already been told by prisoners that some of Buell's Cavalry have been joined to Gen'l. Pope's Army, and have reason to beleive that the whole of McClellan's, the larger portions of Burnside's & Coxe's, and a portion of Hunter's, are united to it, what occasions me most concern is the fear of getting out of ammunition. I beg you will instruct the Ordnance Dept: to spare no pains in manufacturing a sufficient amount of the best kind, & to be particular in preparing that for the Artillery, to provide three times as much of the long range ammunition, as of that for smooth bore or short range guns.

The points to which I desire the ammunition to be forwarded, will be made known to the Department in time. If the Qur. Master's Department can furnish any shoes, it would be the greatest releif.

We have entered upon September, and the nights are becoming cool.

I have the honor to be with high respect Your Ob't Servant,
R. E. LEE. Gen'l:

"A STATE OF NAUSEA":
NEW YORK, SEPTEMBER 1862

George Templeton Strong: Diary, September 3–4, 1862

Strong was a New York lawyer and treasurer of the U.S. Sanitary Commission, a civilian organization dedicated to improving conditions in army camps and the care of the sick and wounded; Henry W. Bellows was its president. In his diary Strong appraised the gloomy war news in both eastern and western theaters.

September 3. It has been a day of depressing malignant dyspepsia, not only private and physical, but public and moral. *Egomet Ipse*, George T. Strong, to wit, and we the people have been in a state of nausea and irritation all day long. The morning papers and an extra at mid-day turned us livid and blue. Fighting Monday afternoon at Chantilly, the enemy beat back (more or less), and Pope retreating on Alexandria and Washington to our venerable field-worn fortresses of a year ago. Stonewall Jackson (our national bugaboo) about to invade Maryland, 40,000 strong. General advance of the rebel line threatening our hold on Missouri and Kentucky. Cincinnati in danger. A rebel army within forty miles of the Queen City of the West. Martial law proclaimed in her pork shops. On the other hand, we hear that General Stahel and General Kearny have come to life again, or were only "kilt," not killed, after all. Everybody talks down McClellan and McDowell. McDowell *is said* to have lost us the battle of Saturday afternoon by a premature movement to the rear, though his supports were being hurried up. He is an unlucky general.

September 4. It is certain now that the army has fallen back to its old burrows around Washington. It will probably hibernate there. So, after all this waste of life and money and material, we are at best where we were a year ago. McClellan is chief under Halleck. Many grumble at this, but whom can we find that is proved his superior? He is certainly as respectable as any of the mediocrities that make up our long muster roll of generals. The army believes in him, undoubtingly; that is a material fact. And I suppose him very eminently fitted for a campaign of redoubts and redans, though incapable of vigorous offensive operations. There is reason to hope that Stanton is trembling to his fall. May he fall soon, for he is a public calamity. McDowell and Pope are "universally despised"; so writes Bellows. Poor General Kearny is dead and no mistake and will be buried in Trinity Churchyard next Saturday; so says Meurer the sexton. He's a great loss. I don't know whether he understood strategy, but he was a dashing, fearless sabreur who had fought in Mexico, Algeria, and Lombardy, and loved war from his youth up. I remember my father talking thirty years ago about young Kearny, who was studying law in his office, and about this strange, foolish passion for a military life. He was under a very dark cloud six years ago and was cut by many of his friends. But, bad as it was, the lady's family were horribly to blame—most imprudent; and Kearny made all the reparation he could. He married her and treated her with all possible affection and loyalty. Whatever his faults, we shall miss him.

Our Sanitary Commission stores were first on the field after the battle of Saturday and did great service, for all the forty-two wagon loads of the Medical Department were bagged by the rebels at Manassas. Dr. Chamberlain, our inspector in charge, was taken prisoner, but the rebels let him go. Stanton is reported rancorously hostile to the Commission; probably because Bellows has talked to him once or twice like a Dutch uncle, with plainness of speech that was certainly imprudent, though quite justifiable.

A DEMORALIZED ARMY:
WASHINGTON, D.C., SEPTEMBER 1862

William Thompson Lusk to Elizabeth Freeman Lusk

A medical student at Heidelberg and Berlin who had returned home in 1861 to enlist in the 79th New York Infantry, Captain Lusk served on the staff of Major General Isaac Stevens, a division commander in the Ninth Corps who was killed at Chantilly on September 1. The views Lusk expresses to his mother were common among Union soldiers in the aftermath of the Second Bull Run debacle.

HEADQUARTERS 1ST DIVISION,
9th ARMY CORPS,
MERIDIAN HILL, WASHINGTON, D. C.
Sept. 6th, 1862.

My dear Mother:

Now that our General is dead, a Colonel commands the old Division temporarily, and I continue to superintend the office, running the old machine along until different arrangements can be made, when I suppose I shall be set adrift with no pleasant prospects before me. I would resign, were I permitted to do so, and would gladly return to my medical studies this winter, tired as I am of the utter mismanagement which characterizes the conduct of our public affairs. Disheartened by the termination of a disastrous campaign—disasters which every one could and did easily foresee from the course pursued—we find as a consolation, that our good honest old President has told a new story apropos of the occasion, and the land is ringing with the wisdom of the rail-splitting Solomon. Those who were anxious and burning to serve their country, can only view with sullen disgust the vast resources of the land directed not to make our arms victorious, but to give political security to those in power. Men show themselves in a thousand ways incompetent, yet still they receive the support of the Government. Politicians, like Carl Schurz, receive high places in the army without a qualification to recommend them. Stern trusty old soldiers like Stevens are treated with cold neglect. The battle comes—there is no head on the field—the men are handed over to be butchered—to die on inglorious fields. Lying reports are written. Political Generals receive praises where they deserve execration. Old Abe makes a joke. The army finds that nothing has been learned. New preparations are made, with all the old errors retained. New battles are prepared for, to end in new disasters. Alas, my poor country! The army is sadly demoralized. Men feel that there is no honor to be gained by the sword. No military service is recognized unless coupled with political interest. The army is exhausted with suffering—its enthusiasm is dead. Should the enemy attack us here however, we should be victorious. The men would never yield up their Capitol. There is something more though than the draft needed to enable us to march a victorious host to the Gulf of Mexico. Well, I have been writing freely enough to entitle me to accommodations in Fort Lafayette, but I can hardly express the grief and indignation I feel at the past. God grant us better things in future.

I had said my own prospects are somewhat gloomy. When the changes are made in this command, and new hands shall take charge of it, I will have to return to the 79th Regiment—a fate at which I shudder. The Regiment has been in five large battles, and in ten or twelve smaller engagements. While adding on each occasion new luster to its own reputation, it has never taken part in a successful action. The proud body that started from the city over a thousand strong, are now a body of cripples. The handful (230) that remains are foreigners whose patriotism misfortunes have quenched. The *morale* is destroyed—discipline relaxed beyond hope of restoration. The General and all the true friends of the Regiment were of the opinion that it should be mustered out of the service. After performing hard duties in the field for fifteen months I find there is nothing left me, but to sink into disgrace with a Regiment that is demoralized past hope of restoration. This for a reward. I am writing this from the old scene of the mutiny of last year. A strange year it has been. God has marvellously preserved my life through every danger. May he be merciful to my mother in the year to come. My old friend Matteson is dead. He was a Major in Yates' Regiment of Sharpshooters which distinguished itself at Corinth. He died at Rosecrans' Headquarters, of typhoid fever.

We are going to move from here to-morrow, but your safest direction will be Capt. W. T. Lusk, A. A. A. G., 1st Div. 9th Army Corps, Washington (or elsewhere). All the letters sent me since I left Fredericksburg have miscarried, and I am very anxious for news.

Affec'y.,
WILL.

"GOD WILLS THIS CONTEST":
WASHINGTON, D.C., SEPTEMBER 1862

Abraham Lincoln: Meditation on the Divine Will

c. early September 1862

This manuscript is undated. It is thought to have been written in the immediate aftermath of Second Bull Run and the army's command crisis, when the President's fortunes seemed to reach a new low.

The will of God prevails. In great contests each party claims to act in accordance with the will of God. Both *may* be, and one *must* be wrong. God can not be *for*, and *against* the same thing at the same time. In the present civil war it is quite possible that God's purpose is something different from the purpose of either party—and yet the human instrumentalities, working just as they do, are of the best adaptation to effect His purpose. I am almost ready to say this is probably true—that God wills this contest, and wills that it shall not end yet. By his mere quiet power, on the minds of the now contestants, He could have either *saved* or *destroyed* the Union without a human contest. Yet the contest began. And having begun He could give the final victory to either side any day. Yet the contest proceeds.

BRITAIN CONSIDERS MEDIATION:
SEPTEMBER 1862

Lord Palmerston and Lord Russell: An Exchange

When news crossed the Atlantic of the Union defeat at Second Bull Run, following the earlier reports of the collapse of McClellan's Peninsula campaign against Richmond, it raised prospects among Britain's rulers for mediation in the American war—which in turn raised prospects for recognition of the Confederacy. In exploring the possibility, Prime Minister Palmerston and Foreign Secretary Russell thought to bring in the Continental powers to strengthen their hand in the mediation process.

---

94 Piccadilly: September 14, 1862.

My dear Russell,—The detailed accounts given in the 'Observer' to day of the battles of August 29 and 30 between the Confederates and the Federals show that the latter got a very complete smashing; and it seems not altogether unlikely that still greater disasters await them, and that even Washington or Baltimore may fall into the hands of the Confederates.

If this should happen, would it not be time for us to consider whether in such a state of things England and France might not address the contending parties and recommend an arrangement upon the basis of separation? . . . —Yours sincerely,

PALMERSTON.

Lord Russell replied—

Gotha: September 17, 1862.

My dear Palmerston,—Whether the Federal army is destroyed or not, it is clear that it is driven back to Washington, and has made no progress in subduing the insurgent States. Such being the case, I agree with you that the time is come for offering mediation to the United States Government, with a view to the recognition of the independence of the Confederates. I agree further, that, in case of failure, we ought ourselves to recognise the Southern States as an independent State. For the purpose of taking so important a step, I think we must have a meeting of the Cabinet. The 23rd or 30th would suit me for the meeting.

We ought then, if we agree on such a step, to propose it first to France, and then, on the part of England and France, to Russia and other powers, as a measure decided upon by us.

We ought to make ourselves safe in Canada, not by sending more troops there, but by concentrating those we have in a few defensible posts before the winter sets in.

I hope to get home on Sunday, but a letter sent to the Foreign Office is sure to reach me.

If Newcastle has not set off, you might as well speak to him before he goes.

The Queen is, I think, much the better for the new interest which has opened for her.—Yours truly,

J. RUSSELL

Broadlands: September 23, 1862.

My dear Russell,—Your plan of proceedings about the mediation between the Federals and Confederates seems to be excellent. Of course, the offer would be made to both the contending parties at the same time; for, though the offer would be as sure to be accepted by the Southerns as was the proposal of the Prince of Wales by the Danish Princess, yet, in the one case as in the other, there are certain forms which it is decent and proper to go through.

A question would occur whether, if the two parties were to accept the mediation, the fact of our mediating would not of itself be tantamount to an acknowledgment of the Confederates as an independent State.

Might it not be well to ask Russia to join England and France in the offer of mediation? . . .

We should be better without her in the mediation, because she would be too favourable to the North; but on the other hand her participation in the offer might render the North the more willing to accept it.

The after communication to the other European powers

would be quite right, although they would be too many for mediation.

As to the time of making the offer, if France and Russia agree,—and France, we know, is quite ready, and only waiting for our concurrence—events may be taking place which might render it desirable that the offer should be made before the middle of October.

It is evident that a great conflict is taking place to the northwest of Washington, and its issue must have a great effect on the state of affairs. If the Federals sustain a great defeat, they may be at once ready for mediation, and the iron should be struck while it is hot. If, on the other hand, they should have the best of it, we may wait awhile and see what may follow . . .—Yours sincerely,

PALMERSTON.

"RECOGNITION OF OUR INDEPENDENCE": MARYLAND, SEPTEMBER 1862

Robert E. Lee to Jefferson Davis

Writing after his army had crossed the Potomac, Lee revealed to Davis the strategic ambitions behind his invasion of Maryland. The midterm elections in the Northern states Lee sought to influence were due to begin in mid-October.

Headquarters, Near Fredericktown, Maryland
September 8, 1862

Mr. President:

The present posture of affairs, in my opinion, places it in the power of the Government of the Confederate States to propose with propriety to that of the United States the recognition of our independence.

For more than a year both sections of the country have been devastated by hostilities which have brought sorrow and suffering upon thousands of homes, without advancing the objects which our enemies proposed to themselves in beginning the contest.

Such a proposition coming from us at this time, could in no way be regarded as suing for peace, but being made when it is in our power to inflict injury upon our adversary, would show conclusively to the world that our sole object is the establishment of our independence, and the attainment of an honorable peace. The rejection of this offer would prove to the country that the responsibility of the continuance of the war does not rest upon us, but that the party in power in the United States elect to prosecute it for purposes of their own. The proposal of peace would enable the people of the United States to determine at their coming elections whether they will support those who favor a prolongation of the war, or those who wish to bring it to a termination, which can but be productive of good to both parties without affecting the honor of either.

I have the honor to be with high respect, your obt servt
R. E. LEE
Genl Comdg

A "DIRTY AND REPULSIVE" ARMY:
MARYLAND, SEPTEMBER 1862

Lewis H. Steiner: Diary, September 5–6, 1862

Steiner was a physician who served as an inspector for the U.S. Sanitary Commission. His diary of the Confederate occupation of Frederick, Maryland, his native town, was submitted as a report to the commission and then published as a pamphlet. As a Confederate column marched out of town on September 10, Steiner wrote: "The ill-suppressed expressions of delight on the countenances of the citizens could not be interpreted into indications of sympathy with Secession. They manifested only profound delight at the prospect of its speedy departure."

Friday, September 5.—Left Washington at 6 o'clock, under the impression that the Confederate army had crossed the Potomac the preceding evening and were then in Frederick. Anxiety as to the fate of my friends, as well as to the general treatment my native place would receive at rebel hands, made the trip by no means a pleasant one.

Along the road, at different stopping-places, reports reached us as to the numbers of the Confederates that had crossed into Maryland. The passengers began to entertain fears that the train would not be able to reach Frederick. These were, however, quieted by a telegram received at a station near Monrovia, which announced the road open. Arriving at 12 o'clock, M., I found the town full of surmises and rumors. Such information had been received by the Post Quarter Master and the Surgeon in charge of Hospital, that they were busy all the afternoon making arrangements to move off their valuable stores. The citizens were in the greatest trepidation. Invasion by the Southern army was considered equivalent to destruction. Impressment into the ranks as common soldiers, or immurement in a *Southern* prison—these were not attractive prospects for quiet, Union-loving citizens!

Towards nightfall it became pretty certain that a force had crossed somewhere about the mouth of the Monocacy. Telegrams were crowding rapidly on the army officers located here, directing that what stores could not be removed should be burned, and that the sick should as far as possible be sent on to Pennsylvania. Here began a scene of terror seldom witnessed in this region. Lieut. Castle, A. Q. M., burned a large quantity of his stores at the depot. Assist. Surg. Weir fired his storehouse on the Hospital grounds and burned the most valuable of his surplus bedding contained in Kemp Hall, in Church street near Market. Many of our prominent citizens, fearing impressment, left their families and started for Pennsylvania in carriages, on horseback, and on foot. All the convalescents at the Hospital that could bear the fatigue, were started also for Pennsylvania, in charge of Hospital Steward Cox. The citizens removed their trunks containing private papers and other valuables from the bank-vaults, under the firm belief that an attack would be made on these buildings for the sake of the specie contained in them.

About 1 1/2 o'clock, A. M., it was ascertained that Jackson's force—the advance guard of the Southern army—was encamped on Moffat's farm, near Buckeystown, and that this force would enter Frederick after daylight; for what purpose no one knew. Having possession of this amount of information, I retired about two o'clock, being willing to wait the sequel, whatever it might be.

Saturday, September 6.—Found, on visiting the market in the morning, that a very large number of our citizens had "*skedaddled*" (i. e. retired rapidly in good order) last night. Every mouth was full of rumors as to the numbers, whereabouts, and whatabouts of the Confederate force. One old gentleman, whose attachment to McClellan has become proverbial, declared that it was an impossibility for the rebels to cross the Potomac; and another, who looks upon Banks as the greatest of generals, declared that Banks' force had been taken for Confederates, and that the supposed enemies were friends.

At length uncertainty was changed into certainty. About nine o'clock two seedy-looking individuals rode up Market street as fast as their jaded animals could carry them. Their dress was a dirty, faded gray, their arms rusty and seemingly uncared for, their general appearance raffish or vagabondish. They shouted for Jeff. Davis at the intersection of Patrick and

Market street, and then riding to the intersection of Church and Market, repeated the same *strange* jubilant shout. No one expressing an opinion as to the propriety or impropriety of this proceeding, they countermarched and trotted down the street. Then followed some fifty or a hundred horsemen, having among them Bradley T. Johnson, *soi-disant* Colonel C. S. A. These were received with feeble shouts from some secession-sympathizers. They said, "the time of your deliverance has come." It was plain that the deliverance they meant was from the rule of law and order. The sidewalks were filled with Union-loving citizens, who felt keenly that their humiliation was at hand, and that they had no course but submission, at least for a time.

As this force of cavalry entered the town from the south, Capt. Yellot's company retreated west from the town, and disappeared no one knew whither. One ruffian cavalry soldier rode up to Sergt. Crocker (in charge of hospital stores in Kemp Hall) and accosted him with "Sa-ay, are you a Yankee?" "No, I am a Marylander." "What are you doing in the Yankee army?" "I belong to the United States army," said the old man, proudly. "If you don't come along with me, I'll cut your head off." Having waved his sabre over the *unarmed* old man's head, he demanded his keys, and rode off with the sergeant as a prisoner. This display of chivalry did not infuse great admiration of the Southern army into the hearts of the bystanders.

A force of cavalry entered the hospital grounds and took possession of hospital and contents. All the sick were carefully paroled, not excepting one poor fellow then in a moribund condition. After some hours, the medical officers and hospital stewards were allowed to go about town on passes.

At ten o'clock Jackson's advance force, consisting of some five thousand men, marched up Market street and encamped north of the town. They had but little music; what there was gave us "My Maryland" and Dixie in execrable style. Each regiment had a square red flag, with a cross, made of diagonal blue stripes extending from opposite corners: on these blue stripes were placed thirteen white stars. A dirtier, filthier, more unsavory set of human beings never *strolled* through a town—marching it could not be called without doing violence to the word. The distinctions of rank were recognized on the coat collars of officers; but all were alike dirty and repulsive. Their arms were rusty and in an unsoldierly condition. Their uniforms, or rather multiforms, corresponded only in a slight predominance of grey over butternut, and in the prevalence of filth. Faces looked as if they had not been acquainted with water for weeks: hair, shaggy and unkempt, seemed entirely a stranger to the operations of brush or comb. A motlier group was never herded together. But *these* were the chivalry—the deliverers of Maryland from Lincoln's oppressive yoke.

During the afternoon a Provost Marshal was appointed for the town, and he occupied the same office which had been the headquarters of the U. S. Provost Marshal. Guards were posted along our streets, and pickets on the roads leading from Frederick. Our stores were soon thronged with crowds. The shoe stores were most patronized, as many of their men were shoeless and stockingless. The only money most of them had was Confederate scrip, or shinplasters issued by banks, corporations, individuals, etc.—all of equal value. To use the expression of an old citizen "the notes depreciated the paper on which they were printed." The crowded condition of the stores enabled some of the chivalry to *take* what they wanted, (confiscate is the technical expression,) without going through the formality of even handing over Confederate rags in exchange. But guards were placed at the stores wherever requested, and only a few men allowed to enter at a time. Even this arrangement proved inadequate, and the stores were soon necessarily closed. The most intense hatred seems to have been encouraged and fostered in the men's hearts towards Union people, or *Yankees* as they style them; and this word *Yankee* is employed with any and every manner of emphasis possible to indicate contempt and bitterness. The men have been made to believe that "to kill a Yankee" is to do a duty imperatively imposed on them. The following incident will illustrate this: A gentleman was called aside, while talking with some ladies, by an officer who wished information as to shoes. He said he was in want of shoes for his men, that he had United States money if the dealers were so foolish as to prefer it, or he would procure them gold; but if they wouldn't sell he was satisfied to wait until they reached Baltimore, where he had no doubt but that shoes in quantity could be procured. No reply was made. Changing the subject, he inquired how the men were behaving. The answer was *very well*; there was no complaint, although some few had been seen intoxicated on the street. "Who gave them the liquor," said the officer. "Townsmen who sympathize with you and desire to show their love for you." "The only way to do that," said the officer, "is to kill a Yankee: kill a Yankee, sir, if you want to please a Southerner." This was uttered with all imaginable expression of vindictiveness and venom.

Our houses were besieged by hungry soldiers and officers. They ate everything offered them with a greediness that fully sustained the truth of their statement, that their entire subsistence lately had been *green corn, uncooked, and eaten directly from the stalk*. Union families freely gave such food as they had. "If thine enemy hunger, feed him," seemed the principle acted on by our good people. But few of our secession citizens aided them. They seemed ashamed of their Southern brethren. The Union people stood out for their principles, and took care to remind them that they were getting their food from those they had come to destroy. A gentleman relates the following: "In the evening, after having had one of their officers to tea— one whom I had known in former days—two officers came to the door and begged that something might be given them for which they wished to pay. On giving them the last biscuits in the house, one of them offered *pay*. The reply was, 'No sir, whenever you meet a Federal soldier wanting food, recollect that a Union man in Frederick gave you the last morsel of food in his house when *you* were famishing.' The officer's face flushed up, and he replied, 'You are right, sir, I am very, very much obliged to you.' The coals of fire had been heaped on his head."

Outrages were committed on the National flag whenever one fell into the hands of the soldiers. These simply strengthened the Union feeling, and made the men and women of Frederick more attached than ever to the National cause for which their fathers had fought and died. Stauncher, stouter, stronger did Unionism in Frederick grow with each passing hour. We were conquered, not enslaved,—humiliated greatly with the thought that rebel feet were pressing on our soil, but not disposed to bow the knee to Baal.

An attack on the *Examiner* Printing Office being anticipated, a small guard was placed at the door. About nine o'clock, P. M., a rush was made on the guard by some of the Southern soldiers, the door was driven in and the contents of the office thrown into the street. W. G. Ross, Esq., a prominent lawyer of Frederick, called on the Provost Marshal, who soon arrived with a strong force, suppressed the riot, and, having obliged the rioters to return every thing belonging to the office, put them in the guard-house. During the continuance of this disturbance, the oaths and imprecations were terrific. Every one in the neighborhood expected that a general attack would be made on the Union houses. Fortunately, a quiet night ensued.

A CONFEDERATE IN MARYLAND:
SEPTEMBER 1862

James Richmond Boulware: Diary, September 4–14, 1862

Boulware was a surgeon in the 6th South Carolina, Jenkins's Brigade, Longstreet's Corps. In his diary he traces his brigade's march from the crossing of the Potomac through Frederick (where he found a welcome rather warmer than Dr. Steiner suggests) and across South Mountain to Boonsboro and Hagerstown. On September 14 Longstreet backtracked to Boonsboro and the fight at Turner's Gap (or Boonsboro Gap) in South Mountain.

Thursday, 4th:
After eating roast corn for supper last night laid down and slept well. Cooked rations and marched in the direction of Leesburg. Halted a few miles from town and camped for the night.

Friday, 5th:
After cooking rations six days and leaving a number of sick for the hospital at Leesburg, passed through the town. It was a pretty, business looking place. There were quite a number of pretty ladies, they seemed to have on *their finest dresses.* I had not seen so many in such a long time, it was quite a treat. Marched on until 11 o'clock at night and camped about 2 or 3 miles from Potomac River.

Saturday, 6th:
Leaving some sick who were unable to stand long marches (among them was Lt. Brice) we proceeded on towards the river. Came to it, pulled off, for it was nearly waist deep in places, and waded across. I fortunately had my horse and rode over. It was 3/4 of a mile wide—was very clear, could see every rock in the bottom and they were not a few—the bottom was covered with round rocks. We got over and was several hours in getting fixed to move off. Getting ready we moved off in the

hot sun. Travelled until dark, rested and set out again and about 11 o'clock camped at Buckey's Town for the night—at a late hour. I could not get any feed for my horse until late the next day.

Sunday, 7th:

Late in the day we began to march and early in the evening arrived in the vicinity of Frederick City, Maryland. On the road we passed through a rich little valley—crossing the Monocacy River twice—there were some neat little towns—beautifully laid out showing taste as well as superior management. We were pretty well tired when we arrived at Frederick, but when the ranks were broken orders were read that soap would be issued to us and it was required of us to wash both ourselves and clothes. I never was so anxious to get a piece of soap in my remembrance before, for our Hosp. wagon and Ambulance were still behind. I went and washed but would not undertake to wash my clothes for I can not wash clothes. So I put on my dirty clothes thinking my Hosp. wagon would come up in a few days.

Monday, 8th:

I arose this morning having had quite a refreshing sleep, went to the wagon train and found that our hospital wagon and ambulance had arrived during the night very late and Brother Frank and I. D. Gaillord with them. I went to get corn from our Q. M. and received somewhat of a short answer from his Emissary (Blake) or rather his wagonmaster. I proceeded to Col. Steedman and reported no corn for me. Col. went to Q. M. and I soon had corn for my mare for she had been doing without for several days—so I had a fuss on hand. I went to Frederick late in the day—got my mare shod. I happened to meet with some clever Artillerists belonging to Jackson's command and they drove on four shoes for me. They would not take pay but were anxious to get something to drink—so, I being a Surg. managed (by going to Provost Martial) to get at some Jamaica Rum and treated them to two canteens full. We drank out one together and I made a present of the other. I carried one full with me to camp and treated the boys all. It was very good rum too. I took a second wash and putting on a new shirt Bro. Frank brought me, felt a little like myself once more. Capt. Cureton was taken very sick also several others in the Regiment so I could not buy anything in Frederick for the stores were all closed etc.

Tuesday, 9th:

The day was passing away without anything transpiring worth noting. In the afternoon W. E. Boggs and myself walked into the city (for it was a place of considerable importance for an inland town) to get a private house for Capt. Cureton to go to for he was too ill to go any farther with us. So, after making efforts at various houses, we fortunately met with a kind lady—who was an avowed Secessionist—who gave her consent to take him in. In walking about we found other Secessionists—got acquainted with several nice, pretty young ladies, and really had a good time chatting with them. We were doing so well we did not realize the fact that it was dark and yet we had to walk two miles to get to our camp. When we arrived at camp I was told that the Q.M. had refused to give any feed for my horse—without a requisition—So I went to work and made out one according to Army Regulations and presented it. Corn was given me and I refused to take it until I saw it weighed to me. The reply was they had no scales and could not do it. I replied that he had made me come to the Regulations and that I required him to do the same or I would report him again in the morning. I had him. The result was he gave me feed without the requisition. So, after talking for some time as to the cause of our ill feeling, we found out that things were told him and to me that were false, so we quit on good terms.

Wednesday, 10th:

We took up our line of march this morning, passing through Frederick City. Saw a number of pretty ladies and amid waving of Secession flags by the ladies and cheering of the soldiers had a lively time. The ladies bowed gracefully to us and once more I was caught lifting my cap, and not a few times either. After passing the town the march was dull and wearisome. We passed Middletown during the afternoon. It was eight miles distant from Frederick. Marched until near South Mountain Gap and camped for the night.

Thursday, 11th:

I arose, eat my breakfast on sweet milk, apple butter and raised bread—thought it was the best I had eaten in a long time (and without doubt it was). Crossed the mountain and got a splendid view of the valley which had some fine farms on the road. All the people seem to live well and not only *stay there* but *live*. One thing I notice is they every one have a *large fine barn*—finer than the dwelling houses in Virginia—most of them built of hewn stone. Maryland is the finest state I have been in. At one house I noticed a spring—very bold indeed—under a fine dwelling house. The spring house was nicely fixed and in every way betokened a tasty and wealthy citizen. Boonsboro is Union town of the deepest dye—we passed through it without stopping and crossed several streams, having fine bridges over them. Passed Funk's Town—a Union hole. I rode up to a house and asked to purchase some Tomatoes. The lady told me she was Union and could not take our money. I told her I was not surprised to find people Union in sentiment and liked to hear them come out plain and say so. I told them we were not come to pilfer or destroy but to give them a chance to come with if they choosed to do so. Orders not to pillage apple orchards and corn fields were strictly enjoined on us. The lady kindly gave me as many as I wished to carry. The ladies would have buckets of water at their doors and give to the thirsty soldiers as they marched by. One said *"remember a Union lady is giving you water"*. In one instance a *woman*, as we passed through Middletown, came out in her yard and bemeaned our soldiers at a terrible rate. I am glad to say it is the only instance so far. We camped—no name for the place—drew rations and went to sleep, after eating my supper on beef kidney.

Friday, 12th:

We began to march as usual this morning and in the direction of Hagers Town, which was not more than four miles distant. Passed through the town, found it to be a considerable place, yet, like all the others, the stores were closed, and only at a few places would they take Confederate money. We camped two miles from the town. Upon arriving at camp I set out to try my hand at foraging. I bought some apple butter, bread, etc., got as many apples as I could carry, had a long chat with a pretty nice cross-eyed girl—who claimed to be a Secesh. and returned to camp feeling well satisfied as to my excursion besides having something for the boys to eat. I never saw apple butter until I came to Maryland. I am fond of it.

Saturday, 13th:

I went to town this morning but could not buy anything for want of gold or Yankee money (either), yet they tell me Hagers Town is a Secession Town. I believe they (our officers) did get quite a number to enlist in our cause; also at Frederick about 800 joined us. In all so far 1400 joined us since we came into Maryland. I went to the 15th Regt. S.C.V. and to James' Battalion and saw the boys of my acquaintance. Late in the afternoon went back and saw my little cross-eyed girl again, got more apples, etc.

Sunday, 14th:

We began our march this morning and found ourselves retracing our steps towards Boonsboro. Having gone six or eight miles we heard the booming of cannon in the distance and go on met couriers who told us that D. H. Hill was fighting the Yankees at South Mountain near Boonsboro. When we started this morning every one thought we were going into Pennsylvania (for, when at Hagers Town, we were only five miles from the line) but soon saw that were going to engage in battle. About the middle of afternoon we got to Boonsboro, having come sixteen miles, and went on to battle but was near night when we went into battle. We were on the top of high hills and the enemy also on adjacent hills. We merely wished to hold the position and done so. We lost only a few in our (Jenkins) Brigade, yet some of our forces cut up badly. James' Bat. was all killed and taken prisoners with some exceptions. Our Brigade was among the last to leave that night. Our forces were ordered to fall back.

I give a list of killed and wounded at Boonsboro Gap, South Mountain, Md. on 14th September, 1862.

List of Casualties in 6th Regt. S.C.V. on 14th Sept. at Boonsboro Gap, South Mountain, Maryland

Co. C Priv.	Robert Borwick	Killed
" " "	C. C. Stuckey	"
Co. K "	T. S. Chandler	Wounded thigh (broken) severe
Co. I Lt.	Grandison Williams	" elbow slight

Total 4

THE LOST ORDER:
MARYLAND, SEPTEMBER 1862

Alpheus S. Williams to George B. McClellan
Robert E. Lee: Special Orders No. 191

On September 13, in a roadside field, an Indiana soldier found a lost copy of General Lee's instructions for dividing his army to accomplish the capture of the Union garrison at Harpers Ferry. The Lost Order made its way to Alpheus Williams, commanding the Twelfth Corps, who forwarded it, along with a covering note, to General McClellan. "Here is a paper," McClellan told one of his generals, "with which if I cannot whip Bobbie Lee, I will be willing to go home."

Head Qts Banks Corps
Near Fredrick Sept 13/62

General

I enclose a Special order of Genl. Lee Commanding Rebel forces—which was found on the field where my corps is encamped.

It is a document of interest & is no doubt genuine.

I am General
with much respect
Your obt svt
A S Williams
Brig Genl Cdg

The Document was found by a corporal of 27 Ind. Rgt, Col. Colgrove, Gordon's Brigade. AW

(Confidential)

Hd Qrs Army of Northern Va
Sept 9th 1862

Special Orders)
    Nr 191)

III The Army will resume its march to-morrow taking the Hagerstown road. Gen Jacksons Command will form the advance and after passing Middleton with such portion as he may select take the route towards Sharpsburg, cross the Potomac at the most convenient point & by Friday morning take possession of the Baltimore & Ohio RR, capture such of the enemy as may be at Martinsburg and intercept such as may attempt to escape from Harpers Ferry.

IV Gen Longstreets Command will pursue the main road as far as Boonsboro where it will halt, with reserve supply and baggage trains of the Army.

V Gen McLaws with his own division and that of Gen R.H. Anderson will follow Gen Longstreet. On reaching Middleton will take the route to Harpers Ferry and by Friday morning possess himself of the Maryland heights and endeavor to capture the enemy at Harpers Ferry and vacinity.

VI Gen Walker with his division after ac. the object in which he is now engaged will cross the Potomac at Cheeks ford ascend its right bank to Lovettsville take possession of Loudoun Heights if practicable by Friday morning Keys ford on his left and the road between the end of mountain and the Potomac on his right. He will as far as practicable cooperate with Gen McLaws & Genl Jacks in intercepting the retreat of the enemy.

VII Gen D.H. Hill's division will form the rear guard of the Army pursuing the road taken by the main body. The reserve artillery ordnance and supply trains will precede Gen Hill

VIII Gen Stuart will detach a squadron of Cavalry to accompany the Commands of Gen Longstreet Jackson and McLaws and with the main body of the Cavalry will cover the route of the Army & bring up all stragglers that may have been left behind.

IX the commands of Gen Jackson McLaws & Walker after accomplishing the objects for which they have been detached will join the main body of the Army at Boonsboro or Hagerstown.

X   Each Regiment on the march will habitually carry its axes in the Regimental ordnance wagons for use of the men at their encampments to procure wood &c

> By command of Gen R.E. Lee
> R.H. Chilton
> AA General

For
Maj Gen D.H. Hill
Cmdg Division

BATTLE OF ANTIETAM:
MARYLAND, SEPTEMBER 1862

George W. Smalley: Narrative of Antietam

September 19, 1862

With the Lost Order in hand, but setting out some eighteen hours too late to divide and conquer his enemy, McClellan forced his way across South Mountain on September 14. Lee fell back, intending to recross the Potomac. Then Stonewall Jackson reported the capture of the 12,000-man garrison at Harpers Ferry, and Lee took up a defensive position behind Antietam Creek at Sharpsburg and began to reassemble his army. This was neither where nor when he had intended to give battle. He would write after the war, "the loss of the dispatch changed the character of the campaign." After further delays, McClellan elected September 17 as the day of battle. Correspondent George W. Smalley of the *New-York Daily Tribune* witnessed the battle, then rode to Frederick, where he took a train to Baltimore and then New York. His overview of the fighting appeared in the *Tribune* on September 19, and drew a salute from William Cullen Bryant, editor of the rival New York *Evening Post*, as one of "the best battle pieces in literature."

BATTLE-FIELD OF ANTIETAM,
WEDNESDAY EVENING, Sept. 17, 1862.

Fierce and desperate battle between two hundred thousand men has raged since daylight, yet night closes on an uncertain field. It is the greatest fight since Waterloo—all over the field contested with an obstinacy equal even to Waterloo. If not wholly a victory to-night, I believe it is the prelude to a victory to-morrow. But what can be foretold of the future of a fight in which from five in the morning till seven at night the best troops of the continent have fought without decisive result?

I have no time for speculation—no time even to gather details of the battle—only time to state its broadest features, then mount and spur for New-York.

After the brilliant victory near Middletown, Gen. McClellan

pushed forward his army rapidly, and reached Keedysville with three corps on Monday night. That march has already been described. On the day following the two armies faced each other idly until night. Artillery was busy at intervals; once in the morning opening with spirit, and continuing for half an hour with vigor, till the rebel battery, as usual, was silenced.

McClellan was on the hill where Benjamin's battery was stationed, and found himself suddenly under a rather heavy fire. It was still uncertain whether the rebels were retreating or reënforcing. Their batteries would remain in position in either case, and as they had withdrawn nearly all their troops from view, there was only the doubtful indication of columns of dust to the rear.

On the evening of Tuesday, Hooker was ordered to cross the Antietam Creek with his corps, and feeling the left of the enemy, to be ready to attack next morning. During the day of apparent inactivity, McClellan, it may be supposed, had been maturing his plan of battle, of which Hooker's movement was one development.

The position on either side was peculiar. When Richardson advanced on Monday he found the enemy deployed and displayed in force on a crescent-shaped ridge, the outline of which followed more or less exactly the course of Antietam Creek. Their lines were then forming, and the revelation of force in front of the ground which they really intended to hold, was probably meant to delay our attack until their arrangements to receive it were complete.

During that day they kept their troops exposed and did not move them even to avoid the artillery-fire, which must have been occasionally annoying. Next morning the lines and columns which had darkened corn-fields and hill-crests had been withdrawn. Broken and wooded ground behind the sheltering hills concealed the rebel masses. What from our front looked like only a narrow summit fringed with woods was a broad tableland of forest and ravine; cover for troops every where, nowhere easy access for an enemy. The smoothly sloping surface in front and the sweeping crescent of slowly mingling lines was all a delusion. It was all a rebel stronghold beyond.

Under the base of these hills runs the deep stream called Antietam Creek, fordable only at distant points. Three bridges cross it, one on the Hagerstown road, one on the Sharpsburgh pike, one to the left in a deep recess of steeply falling hills. Hooker passed the first to reach the ford by which he crossed, and it was held by Pleasanton with a reserve of cavalry during the battle. The second was close under the rebel centre, and no way important to yesterday's fight. At the third, Burnside attacked and finally crossed. Between the first and third lay most of the battle-lines. They stretched four miles from right to left.

Unaided attack in front was impossible. McClellan's forces lay behind low, disconnected ridges in front of the rebel summits, all or nearly all unwooded. They gave some cover for artillery, and guns were therefore massed on the centre. The enemy had the Shepherdstown road and the Hagerstown and Williamsport road both open to him in rear for retreat. Along one or the other, if beaten, he must fly. This among other reasons determined, perhaps, the plan of battle which McClellan finally resolved on.

The plan was generally as follows: Hooker was to cross on the right, establish himself on the enemy's left if possible, flanking his position, and to open the fight. Sumner, Franklin, and Mansfield were to send their forces also to the right, coöperating with and sustaining Hooker's attack while advancing also nearer the centre. The heavy work in the centre was left mostly to the batteries, Porter massing his infantry supports in the hollows. On the left, Burnside was to carry the bridge already referred to, advancing then by a road which enters the pike at Sharpsburgh, turning at once the rebel flank and destroying his line of retreat. Porter and Sykes were held in reserve. It is obvious that the complete success of a plan contemplating widely divergent movements of separate corps, must largely depend on accurate timing—that the attacks should be simultaneous and not successive.

Hooker moved Tuesday afternoon at four, crossing the creek at a ford above the bridge and well to the right, without opposition. Fronting southwest, his line advanced not quite on the rebel flank but overlapping and threatening it. Turning off from the road after passing the stream, he sent forward cavalry skirmishers straight into the woods and over the fields beyond. Rebel pickets withdrew slowly before them, firing scattering and harmless shots. Turning again to the left, the cavalry went down on the rebel flank, coming suddenly close to a battery which met them with unexpected grape and canister. It being the nature of cavalry to retire before batteries, this company loyally followed the law of its being, and came swiftly back without pursuit.

Artillery was sent to the front, infantry was rapidly deployed, and skirmishers went out in front and on either flank. The corps moved forward compactly, Hooker as usual reconnoitring in person. They came at last to an open grass-sown field inclosed on two sides with woods, protected on the right by a hill, and entered through a corn-field in the rear. Skirmishers penetrating these woods were instantly met by rebel shots, but held their ground, and as soon as supported, advanced and cleared the timber. Beyond, on the left and in front, volleys of musketry opened heavily, and a battle seemed to have begun a little sooner than it was expected.

General Hooker formed his lines with precision and without hesitation. Ricketts's division went into the woods on the left in force. Meade with the Pennsylvania reserves formed in the centre. Doubleday was sent out on the right, planting his guns on the hill, and opening at once on a rebel battery that began to enfilade the central line. It was already dark, and the rebel position could only be discovered by the flashes of their guns. They pushed forward boldly on the right after losing ground on the other flank, but made no attempt to regain their hold on the woods. The fight flashed, and glimmered, and faded, and finally went out in the dark.

Hooker had found out what he wanted to know. When the firing ceased, the hostile lines lay close to each other—their pickets so near that six rebels were captured during the night. It was inevitable that the fight should recommence at daylight. Neither side had suffered considerable loss; it was a skirmish, not a battle. "We are through for to-night, gentlemen," remarked the General, "but to-morrow we fight the battle that will decide the fate of the republic."

Not long after the firing ceased, it sprang up again on the left. General Hooker, who had taken his headquarters in a barn which had been nearly the focus of the rebel artillery, was out at once. First came rapid and unusually frequent picket-shots, then several heavy volleys. The General listened a moment and smiled grimly. "We have no troops there. The rebels are shooting each other. It is Fair Oaks over again." So every body lay down again, but all the night through there were frequent alarms.

McClellan had been informed of the night's work, and of the certainties awaiting the dawn. Sumner was ordered to move his corps at once, and was expected to be on the ground at daylight. From the extent of the rebel lines developed in the evening, it was plain that they had gathered their whole army behind the heights and were waiting for the shock.

The battle began with the dawn. Morning found both armies just as they had slept, almost close enough to look into each other's eyes. The left of Meade's reserves and the right of Ricketts's line became engaged at nearly the same moment, one with artillery, the other with infantry. A battery was almost immediately pushed forward beyond the central woods, over a ploughed field near the top of the slope where the corn-field began. On this open field, in the corn beyond, and in the woods which stretched forward into the broad fields like a promontory into the ocean, were the hardest and deadliest struggles of the day.

For half an hour after the battle had grown to its full strength, the line of fire swayed neither way. Hooker's men were fully up to their work. They saw their General every where in front, never away from the fire, and all the troops believed in their commander, and fought with a will. Two thirds of them were the same men who under McDowell had broken at Manassas.

The half-hour passed, the rebels began to give way a little—only a little, but at the first indication of a receding fire, Forward, was the word, and on went the line with a cheer and a rush. Back across the corn-field, leaving dead and wounded behind them, over the fence, and across the road, and then back again into the dark woods which closed around them went the retreating rebels.

Meade and his Pennsylvanians followed hard and fast—followed till they came within easy range of the woods, among which they saw their beaten enemy disappearing—followed still, with another cheer, and flung themselves against the cover.

But out of those gloomy woods came suddenly and heavily terrible volleys—volleys which smote, and bent, and broke in a moment that eager front, and hurled them swiftly back for half the distance they had won. Not swiftly, nor in panic, any further. Closing up their shattered lines, they came slowly away; a regiment where a brigade had been; hardly a brigade where a whole division had been victorious. They had met at the woods the first volleys of musketry from fresh troops—had met them and returned them till their line had yielded and gone down before the weight of fire, and till their ammunition was exhausted.

In ten minutes the fortune of the day seemed to have changed; it was the rebels now who were advancing, pouring out of the woods in endless lines, sweeping through the cornfield from which their comrades had just fled. Hooker sent in his nearest brigade to meet them, but it could not do the work. He called for another. There was nothing close enough, unless he took it from his right. His right might be in danger if it was weakened, but his centre was already threatened with annihilation. Not hesitating one moment, he sent to Doubleday: "Give me your best brigade instantly."

The best brigade came down the hill to the right on the run, went through the timber in front through a storm of shot and bursting shell and crashing limbs, over the open field beyond and straight into the corn-field, passing as they went the fragments of three brigades shattered by the rebel fire and streaming to the rear. They passed by Hooker, whose eyes lighted as he saw those veteran troops, led by a soldier whom he knew he could trust. "I think they will hold it," he said.

General Hartsuff took his troops very steadily, but, now that they were under fire, not hurriedly, up the hill from which the corn-field begins to descend, and formed them on the crest. Not a man who was not in full view—not one who bent before the storm. Firing at first in volleys, they fired then at will with wonderful rapidity and effect. The whole line crowned the hill and stood out darkly against the sky, but lighted and shrouded ever in flame and smoke. They were the Twelfth and Thirteenth

Massachusetts and another regiment which I cannot remember—old troops all of them.

There for half an hour they held the ridge, unyielding in purpose, exhaustless in courage. There were gaps in the line, but it nowhere bent. Their General was severely wounded early in the fight, but they fought on. Their supports did not come—they determined to win without them. They began to go down the hill and into the corn; they did not stop to think that their ammunition was nearly gone; they were there to win that field, and they won it. The rebel line for the second time fled through the corn and into the woods. I cannot tell how few of Hartsuff's brigade were left when the work was done, but it was done. There was no more gallant, determined, heroic fighting in all this desperate day. General Hartsuff is very severely wounded, but I do not believe he counts his success too dearly purchased.

The crisis of the fight at this point had arrived. Ricketts's division, vainly endeavoring to advance and exhausted by the effort, had fallen back. Part of Mansfield's corps was ordered in to their relief, but Mansfield's troops came back again, and their General was mortally wounded. The left nevertheless was too extended to be turned, and too strong to be broken. Ricketts sent word he could not advance, but could hold his ground. Doubleday had kept his guns at work on the right, and had finally silenced a rebel battery that for half an hour had poured in a galling enfilading fire along Hooker's central line. There were woods in front of Doubleday's hill which the rebels held, but so long as those guns pointed toward them they did not care to attack.

With his left, then, able to take care of itself, with his right impregnable, with two brigades of Mansfield still fresh and coming rapidly up, and with his centre a second time victorious, Gen. Hooker determined to advance. Orders were sent to Crawford and Gordon—the two Mansfield brigades—to move forward at once, the batteries in the centre were ordered to advance, the whole line was called on, and the General himself went forward.

To the right of the corn-field and beyond it was a point of woods. Once carried and firmly held, it was the key of the position. Hooker determined to take it. He rode out in front of his furthest troops on a hill to examine the ground for a battery. At the top he dismounted and went forward on foot, completed his reconnoissance, returned, and remounted. The musketry-fire from the point of woods was all the while extremely hot. As he put his foot in the stirrup a fresh volley of rifle-bullets came whizzing by. The tall, soldierly figure of the General, the white horse which he rode, the elevated place where he was, all made him a most dangerously conspicuous mark. So he had been all day, riding often without a staff-officer or an orderly near him—all sent off on urgent duty—visible every where on the field. The rebel bullets had followed him all day, but they had not hit him, and he would not regard them.

Remounting on this hill, he had not ridden five steps when he was struck in the foot by a ball. Three men were shot down at the same moment by his side. The air was alive with bullets. He kept on his horse a few minutes, though the wound was severe and excessively painful, and would not dismount till he had given his last order to advance. He was himself in the very front. Swaying unsteadily on his horse, he turned in his seat to look about him. "There is a regiment to the right. Order it forward! Crawford and Gordon are coming up. Tell them to carry those woods and hold them—and it is our fight!"

It was found that the bullet had passed completely through his foot. The surgeon who examined it on the spot could give no opinion whether bones were broken, but it was afterward ascertained that though grazed they were not fractured. Of course the severity of the wound made it impossible for him to keep the field, which he believed already won, so far as it belonged to him to win it. It was nine o'clock. The fight had been furious since five. A large part of his command was broken, but with his right still untouched, and with Crawford's and Gordon's brigades just up; above all, with the advance of the whole central line, which the men had heard ordered with cheers, and with a regiment already on the edge of the woods he wanted, he might well leave the field, thinking the battle was won—that *his* battle was won, for I am writing only about the attack on the rebel left.

I see no reason why I should disguise my admiration of Gen. Hooker's bravery and soldierly ability. Remaining nearly all the morning on the right, I could not help seeing the sagacity and promptness of his movements, how completely his troops were kept in hand, how devotedly they trusted him, how keen was his insight into the battle, how every opportunity was seized and every reverse was checked and turned into another success. I say this the more unreservedly, because I have no personal relation whatever with him, never saw him till the day before the fight, and don't like his politics or opinions in general. But what are politics in such a battle?

Sumner arrived just as Hooker was leaving, and assumed command. Crawford and Gordon had gone into the woods, and were holding them stoutly against heavy odds. As I rode over toward the left I met Sumner at the head of his column, advancing rapidly through the timber, opposite where Crawford was fighting. The veteran General was riding alone in the forest, far ahead of his leading brigade, his hat off, his gray hair and beard and moustache strangely contrasting with the fire in his eyes and his martial air, as he hurried on to where the bullets were thickest.

Sedgwick's division was in advance, moving forward to support Crawford and Gordon. Rebel reënforcements were approaching also, and the struggle for the roads was again to be renewed. Sumner sent forward two divisions—Richardson and French—on the left. Sedgwick, moving in column of divisions through the woods in rear, deployed and advanced in line over the corn-field. There was a broad interval between him and the nearest division, and he saw that if the rebel line were complete, his own division was in immediate danger of being flanked. But his orders were to advance, and those are the orders which a soldier—and Sedgwick is every inch a soldier—loves best to hear.

To extend his own front as far as possible, he ordered the Thirty-fourth New-York to move by the left flank. The manœuvre was attempted under a fire of the greatest intensity, and the regiment broke. At the same moment the enemy, perceiving their advantage, came round on that flank. Crawford was obliged to give way on the right, and his troops pouring in confusion through the ranks of Sedgwick's advance brigade, threw it into disorder and back on the second and third lines. The enemy advanced, their fire increasing.

Gen. Sedgwick was three times wounded, in the shoulder, leg, and wrist, but he persisted in remaining on the field so long as there was a chance of saving it. His Adjutant-General, Major Sedgwick, bravely rallying and trying to re-form the troops, was shot through the body, the bullet lodging in the spine, and fell from his horse. Severe as the wound is, it is probably not mortal. Lieut. Howe, of Gen. Sedgwick's staff, endeavored vainly to rally the Thirty-fourth New-York. They were badly cut up and would not stand. Half their officers were killed or wounded, their colors shot to pieces, the color-sergeant killed, every one of the color-guard wounded. Only thirty-two were afterward got together.

The Fifteenth Massachusetts went into action with seventeen officers and nearly six hundred men. Nine officers were killed or wounded, and some of the latter are prisoners. Capt. Simons, Capt. Saunders of the sharp-shooters, Lieut. Derby, and Lieut. Berry are killed. Capt. Bartlett and Capt. Jocelyn, Lieut. Spurr, Lieut. Gale, and Lieut. Bradley are wounded. One hundred and thirty-four men were the only remains that could be collected of this splendid regiment.

Gen. Dana was wounded. Gen. Howard, who took command of the division after Gen. Sedgwick was disabled, exerted himself to restore order; but it could not be done there. Gen. Sumner ordered the line to be re-formed. The test was too severe for volunteer troops under such a fire. Sumner himself attempted to arrest the disorder, but to little purpose. Lieut.-Col. Revere and Capt. Audenried of his staff were wounded severely, but not dangerously. It was impossible to hold the position. Gen. Sumner withdrew the division to the rear, and once more the corn-field was abandoned to the enemy.

French sent word he could hold his ground. Richardson, while gallantly leading a regiment under a heavy fire, was severely wounded in the shoulder. Gen. Meagher was wounded at the head of his brigade. The loss in general officers was becoming frightful.

At one o'clock affairs on the right had a gloomy look. Hooker's troops were greatly exhausted, and their General away from the field. Mansfield's were no better. Sumner's command had lost heavily, but two of his divisions were still comparatively fresh. Artillery was yet playing vigorously in front, though the ammunition of many of the batteries was entirely exhausted, and they had been compelled to retire.

Doubleday held the right inflexibly. Sumner's headquarters were now in the narrow field where the night before Hooker had begun the fight. All that had been gained in front had been lost! The enemy's batteries, which if advanced and served vigorously might have made sad work with the closely-massed troops, were fortunately either partially disabled or short of ammunition. Sumner was confident that he could hold his own, but another advance was out of the question. The enemy, on the other hand, seemed to be too much exhausted to attack.

At this crisis Franklin came up with fresh troops and formed on the left. Slocum, commanding one division of the corps, was sent forward along the slopes lying under the first ranges of the rebel hills, while Smith with the other division was ordered to retake the corn-fields and woods which all day had been so hotly contested. It was done in the handsomest style. His Maine and Vermont regiments and the rest went forward on the run, and cheering as they went, swept like an avalanche through the corn-fields, fell upon the woods, cleared them in ten minutes, and held them. They were not again retaken.

The field and its ghastly harvest which the Reaper had gathered in those fatal hours remained finally with us. Four times it had been lost and won. The dead are strewn so thickly that as you ride over it you cannot guide your horse's steps too carefully. Pale and bloody faces are every where upturned. They are sad and terrible, but there is nothing which makes one's heart beat so quickly as the imploring look of sorely wounded men who beckon wearily for help which you cannot stay to give.

Gen. Smith's attack was so sudden that his success was accomplished with no great loss. He had gained a point, however, which compelled him to expect every moment an attack, and to hold which, if the enemy again brought up reserves, would task his best energies and best troops. But the long strife, the heavy losses, incessant fighting over the same ground repeatedly lost and won inch by inch, and more than all, perhaps, the fear of Burnside on the left and Porter in front, held the enemy in check. For two or three hours there was a lull even in the cannonade on the right, which hitherto had been incessant. McClellan had been over on the field after Sumner's repulse, but had speedily returned to his headquarters. Sumner again sent word that he was able to hold his position, but could not advance with his own corps.

Meantime where was Burnside, and what was he doing? On the right where I had spent the day until two o'clock, little was known of the general fortunes of the field. We had heard Porter's guns in the centre, but nothing from Burnside on the left. The distance was, perhaps, too great to distinguish the sound of his artillery from Porter's. There was no immediate prospect of more fighting on the right, and I left the field which all day long had seen the most obstinate contest of the war, and rode over to McClellan's headquarters. The different battle-fields were shut out from each other's view, but all partially visible from the central hill which Gen. McClellan had occupied during the day. But I was more than ever impressed, on returning, with the completely deceitful appearance of the ground the rebels had chosen, when viewed from the front.

Hooker's and Sumner's struggle had been carried on over an uneven and wooded surface, their own line of battle extending in a semi-circle not less than a mile and a half. Perhaps a better notion of their position can be got by considering their right, centre, and left as forming three sides of a square. So long, therefore, as either wing was driven back, the centre became exposed to a very dangerous enfilading fire, and the further the centre was advanced the worse off it was, unless the lines on its side and rear were firmly held. This formation resulted originally from the efforts of the enemy to turn both flanks. Hooker at the very outset threw his column so far into the heart of the rebel lines that they were compelled to threaten him on the flank to secure their own centre.

Nothing of all this was perceptible from the hills in front. Some directions of the rebel lines had been disclosed by the smoke of their guns, but the whole interior formation of the country beyond the hills was completely concealed. When McClellan arranged his order of battle, it must have been upon information, or have been left to his corps and division commanders to discover for themselves.

Up to three o'clock Burnside had made little progress. His attack on the bridge had been successful, but the delay had been so great that to the observer it appeared as if McClellan's plans must have been seriously disarranged. It is impossible not to suppose that the attacks on right and left were meant in a measure to correspond, for otherwise the enemy had only to repel Hooker on the one hand, then transfer his troops, and push them against Burnside.

Here was the difference between Smith and Burnside. The former did his work at once, and lost all his men at once—that is, all whom he lost at all; Burnside seems to have attacked cautiously in order to save his men, and sending successively insufficient forces against a position of strength, distributed his loss over a greater period of time, but yet lost none the less in the end.

Finally, at four o'clock, McClellan sent simultaneous orders to Burnside and Franklin—to the former to advance and carry the batteries in his front at all hazards and at any cost; to the latter to carry the woods next in front of him to the left, which the rebels still held. The order to Franklin, however, was practically countermanded, in consequence of a message from Gen. Sumner that if Franklin went on and was repulsed, his own corps was not yet sufficiently reörganized to be depended on as a reserve. Franklin, thereupon, was directed to run no risk of losing his present position, and instead of sending his infantry into the woods, contented himself with advancing his batteries over the breadth of the fields in front, supporting them with heavy columns of infantry, and attacking with energy the rebel batteries immediately opposed to him. His movement was a success, so far as it went, the batteries maintaining their new ground, and sensibly affecting the steadiness of the rebel fire. That being once accomplished, and all hazard of the right being again forced back having been dispelled, the movement of Burnside became at once the turning-point of success, and the fate of the day depended on him.

How extraordinary the situation was may be judged from a moment's consideration of the facts. It is understood that from the outset Burnside's attack was expected to be decisive, as it certainly must have been if things went well elsewhere, and if he succeeded in establishing himself on the Sharpsburgh road in the rebel rear. Yet Hooker and Sumner and Franklin and Mansfield were all sent to the right three miles away, while Porter seems to have done double duty with his single corps in front, both supporting the batteries and holding himself in reserve. With all this immense force on the right, but sixteen thousand men were given to Burnside for the decisive movement of the day.

Still more unfortunate in its results was the total failure of these separate attacks on the right and left to sustain, or in any manner coöperate with each other. Burnside hesitated for hours in front of the bridge which should have been carried at once by a *coup de main*. Meantime Hooker had been fighting for four hours with various fortune, but final success. Sumner had come up too late to join in the decisive attack which his earlier arrival would probably have converted into a complete success; and Franklin reached the scene only when Sumner had been repulsed. Probably before his arrival the rebels had transferred a considerable number of troops to their right to meet the attack of Burnside, the direction of which was then suspected or developed.

Attacking first with one regiment, then with two, and delaying both for artillery, Burnside was not over the bridge before two o'clock—perhaps not till three. He advanced slowly up the slopes in his front, his batteries in rear covering, to some extent, the movements of the infantry. A desperate fight was going on in a deep ravine on his right; the rebel batteries were in full play and apparently very annoying and destructive, while heavy columns of rebel troops were plainly visible, advancing, as if careless of concealment, along the road and over the hills in the direction of Burnside's forces. It was at this point of time that McClellan sent him the order above given.

Burnside obeyed it most gallantly. Getting his troops well in hand, and sending a portion of his artillery to the front, he advanced with rapidity and the most determined vigor straight up the hill in front, on top of which the rebels had maintained their most dangerous battery. The movement was in plain view of McClellan's position, and as Franklin on the other side sent his batteries into the field about the same time, the battle seemed to open in all directions with greater activity than ever.

The fight in the ravine was in full progress, the batteries in the centre were firing with new vigor, Franklin was blazing away on the right, and every hill-top, ridge and woods along the whole line was crested and veiled with white clouds of smoke. All day had been clear and bright since the early cloudy morning, and now this whole magnificent, unequalled scene shone with the splendor of an afternoon September sun. Four miles of battle, its glory all visible, its horrors all hidden, the fate of the Republic hanging on the hour—could any one be insensible of its grandeur?

There are two hills on the left of the road, the farthest the lowest. The rebels have batteries on both. Burnside is ordered to carry the nearest to him, which is the farthest from the road. His guns opening first from this new position in front, soon entirely controlled and silenced the enemy's artillery. The infantry came on at once, advancing rapidly and steadily; their long, dark lines and broad masses plainly visible without a glass as they moved over the green hill-side.

The next moment the road in which the rebel battery was planted was canopied with clouds of dust swiftly descending into the valley. Underneath was a tumult of wagons, guns, horses, and men, flying at speed down the road. Blue flashes of smoke burst now and then among them, a horse or a man or half a dozen went down, and then the whirlwind swept on.

The hill was carried, but could it be held? The rebel columns, before seen moving to the left, increase their pace. The guns on the hill above send an angry tempest of shell down among Burnside's guns and men. He has formed his columns apparently in the near angles of two fields bordering the road—high ground about them every where except in rear.

In another moment a rebel battle-line appears on the brow of the ridge above them, moves swiftly down in the most perfect order, and though met by incessant discharges of musketry, of which we plainly see the flashes, does not fire a gun. White spaces show where men are falling, but they close up instantly, and still the line advances. The brigades of Burnside are in heavy column; they will not give way before a bayonet-charge in line, and the rebels think twice before they dash into those hostile masses.

There is a halt, the rebel left gives way and scatters over the field, the rest stand fast and fire. More infantry comes up; Burnside is outnumbered, flanked, compelled to yield the hill he took so bravely. His position is no longer one of attack; he defends himself with unfaltering firmness, but he sends to McClellan for help.

McClellan's glass for the last half-hour has seldom been turned away from the left. He sees clearly enough that Burnside is pressed—needs no messenger to tell him that. His face grows darker with anxious thought. Looking down into the valley where fifteen thousand troops are lying, he turns a half-questioning look on Fitz-John Porter, who stands by his side, gravely scanning the field. They are Porter's troops below, are fresh and only impatient to share in this fight. But Porter slowly shakes his head, and one may believe that the same thought is passing through the minds of both generals. "They are the only reserves of the army; they cannot be spared."

McClellan remounts his horse, and with Porter and a dozen officers of his staff rides away to the left in Burnside's direction. Sykes meets them on the road—a good soldier, whose opinion is worth taking. The three Generals talk briefly together. It is easy to see that the moment has come when every thing may turn on one order given or withheld, when the history of the battle is only to be written in thoughts and purposes and words of the General.

Burnside's messenger rides up. His message is: "I want troops and guns. If you do not send them, I cannot hold my position half an hour." McClellan's only answer for the moment is a glance at the western sky. Then he turns and speaks very slowly: "Tell Gen. Burnside this is the battle of the war. He must hold his ground till dark at any cost. I will send him Miller's battery. I can do nothing more. I have no infantry." Then as the messenger was riding away he called him back. "Tell him if he *cannot* hold his ground, then the bridge, to the last man!—always the bridge! If the bridge is lost, all is lost."

The sun is already down; not half an hour of daylight is left. Till Burnside's message came it had seemed plain to every one that the battle could not be finished to-day. None suspected how near was the peril of defeat, of sudden attack on exhausted forces—how vital to the safety of the army and the nation were those fifteen thousand waiting troops of Fitz-John Porter in the hollow. But the rebels halted instead of pushing on; their vindictive cannonade died away as the light faded. Before it was quite dark the battle was over. Only a solitary gun of Burnside's thundered against the enemy, and presently this also ceased, and the field was still.

The peril came very near, but it has passed, and in spite of the peril, at the close the day was partly a success; not a victory, but an advantage had been gained. Hooker, Sumner, and Franklin held all the ground they had gained, and Burnside still held the bridge and his position beyond. Every thing was favorable for a renewal of the fight in the morning. If the plan of the battle is sound, there is every reason why McClellan should win it.

He may choose to postpone the battle to await his reënforcements. The rebels may choose to retire while it is possible. Fatigue on both sides may delay the deciding battle, yet if the enemy means to fight at all, he cannot afford to delay. His reënforcements may be coming, but where are his supplies? His losses are enormous. His troops have been massed in woods and hollows, where artillery has had its most terrific effect. Ours have been deployed and scattered. From infantry fire there is less difference.

It is hard to estimate losses on a field of such extent, but I think ours cannot be less than six thousand killed and wounded—it may be much greater. Prisoners have been taken from the enemy; I hear of a regiment captured entire, but I doubt it. All the prisoners whom I saw agree in saying that the whole army is there.

FIGHT FOR THE CORNFIELD:
MARYLAND, SEPTEMBER 1862

Rufus R. Dawes: from Service with the Sixth Wisconsin Volunteers

The Battle of Antietam opened at daybreak on September 17 with the advance of Joseph Hooker's First Corps against the Confederate left, on the northern part of the battlefield. Major Dawes was second in command of the 6th Wisconsin Infantry, part of a brigade commanded by John Gibbon. In an 1890 memoir he remembered the struggle for farmer David R. Miller's cornfield.

ABOUT DAYLIGHT, General Doubleday came galloping along the line, and he ordered that our brigade be moved at once out of its position. He said we were in open range of the rebel batteries. The men were in a heavy slumber. After much shaking and kicking and hurrying, they were aroused, and stood up in their places in the lines. Too much noise was probably made, which appears to have aroused the enemy. The column hurriedly changed direction, according to orders, and commenced moving away from the perilous slope which faced the hostile batteries.

We had marched ten rods, when whiz-z-z! bang! burst a shell over our heads; then another; then a percussion shell struck and exploded in the very center of the moving mass of men. It killed two men and wounded eleven. It tore off Captain David K. Noyes's foot, and cut off both arms of a man in his company. This dreadful scene occurred within a few feet of where I was riding, and before my eyes. The column pushed on without a halt, and in another moment had the shelter of a barn. Thus opened the first firing of the great battle of Antietam, in the early morning of September 17th, 1862. The regiment continued moving forward into a strip of woods, where the column was deployed into line of battle. The artillery fire had now increased to the roar of an hundred cannon. Solid shot and shell whistled through the trees above us, cutting off limbs which fell about us. In front of the woods was an open field; beyond this was a house, surrounded by peach and apple trees, a garden, and outhouses.* The rebel skirmishers were in this cover, and they directed upon us a vigorous fire. But company "I" deployed as skirmishers, under command of Captain John A. Kellogg, dashed across the field at a full run and drove them out, and the line of the regiment pushed on over the green open field, the air above our heads filled with the screaming missiles of the contending batteries. The right of the regiment was now on the Sharpsburg and Hagerstown Turnpike. The left wing was obstructed in its advance by the picket fence around the garden before mentioned. As the right wing passed on, I ordered the men of the left wing to take hold all together and pull down the fence. They were unable to do so. I had, therefore, to pass the left wing by the flank through a gate with the utmost haste, and form again in the garden. Here Captain Edwin A. Brown, of company "E," was instantly killed. There is in my mind as I write, the spectacle of a young officer, with uplifted sword, shouting in a loud imperative voice the order I had given him, "Company 'E,' on the right by file into line!" A bullet passes into his open mouth, and the voice is forever silent. I urged the left wing forward with all possible speed. The men scrambled over briars and flower-beds in the garden. Beyond the garden, we entered a peach orchard. I hurried forward to a rail fence skirting the front edge of the orchard, where we overtook the right wing. Before us was a strip of open-field, beyond which on the left-hand side of the turnpike, was rising ground, covered by a large cornfield, the stalks standing thick and high. The rebel skirmishers ran into the corn as we appeared at the fence. Owing to our headlong advance, we were far ahead of the general lines of battle. They were in open fields, and we had the cover of the houses and orchard. Colonel Bragg, however, with his usual battle ardor, ordered the regiment forward. We climbed the fence, moved across the open space, and pushed on into the corn-field. The three right companies of the regiment were crowded into an open field on the right-hand side of the turnpike. Thus we pushed up the hill to the middle of the corn-field.

At this juncture, the companies of the right wing received a

---

*David R. Miller's house.

deadly fire from the woods on their right. To save them, Colonel Bragg, with a quickness and coolness equal to the emergency, caused them to change front and form behind the turnpike fence, from whence they returned the fire of the enemy. Meanwhile, I halted the left wing, and ordered them to lie down on the ground. The bullets began to clip through the corn, and spin through the soft furrows—thick, almost, as hail. Shells burst around us, the fragments tearing up the ground, and canister whistled through the corn above us. Lieutenant Bode of company "F," was instantly killed, and Lieutenant John Ticknor was badly wounded. Sergeant Major Howard J. Huntington now came running to me through the corn. He said: "Major, Colonel Bragg wants to see you, quick, at the turnpike." I ran to the fence in time to hear Bragg say: "Major, I am shot," before he fell upon the ground. I saw a tear in the side of his overcoat which he had on. I feared that he was shot through the body. I called two men from the ranks, who bundled him quickly into a shelter tent, and hurried away with him. Colonel Bragg was shot in the first fire from the woods and his nerve, in standing up under the shock until he had effected the maneuver so necessary for the safety of his men, was wonderful. I felt a great sense of responsibility, when thrown thus suddenly in command of the regiment in the face of a terrible battle. I stood near the fence in the corn-field, overlooking the companies on the turnpike which were firing on the enemy in the woods, and where I could see the left wing also. I noticed a group of mounted rebel officers, whom I took to be a general and staff. I took a rest over the turnpike fence, and fired six shots at the group, the men handing me loaded muskets. They suddenly scattered.

Our lines on the left now came sweeping forward through the corn and the open fields beyond. I ordered my men up to join in the advance, and commanded: "Forward—guide left—march!" We swung away from the turnpike, and I sent the sergeant-major (Howard J. Huntington) to Captain Kellogg, commanding the companies on the turnpike, with this order: "If it is practicable, move forward the right companies, aligning with the left wing." Captain Kellogg said: "Please give Major Dawes my compliments, and say it is impracticable; the fire is murderous."

As we were getting separated, I directed Sergeant Huntington to tell Captain Kellogg that he could get cover in the corn, and to join us, if possible. Huntington was struck by a bullet, but delivered the order. Kellogg ordered his men up, but so many were shot that he ordered them down again at once. While this took place on the turnpike, our companies were marching forward through the thick corn, on the right of a long line of battle. Closely following was a second line. At the front edge of the corn-field was a low Virginia rail fence. Before the corn were open fields, beyond which was a strip of woods surrounding a little church, the Dunkard church. As we appeared at the edge of the corn, a long line of men in butternut and gray rose up from the ground. Simultaneously, the hostile battle lines opened a tremendous fire upon each other. Men, I can not say fell; they were knocked out of the ranks by dozens. But we jumped over the fence, and pushed on, loading, firing, and shouting as we advanced. There was, on the part of the men, great hysterical excitement, eagerness to go forward, and a reckless disregard of life, of every thing but victory. Captain Kellogg brought his companies up abreast of us on the turnpike.

The Fourteenth Brooklyn Regiment, red legged Zouaves, came into our line, closing the awful gaps. Now is the pinch. Men and officers of New York and Wisconsin are fused into a common mass, in the frantic struggle to shoot fast. Every body tears cartridges, loads, passes guns, or shoots. Men are falling in their places or running back into the corn. The soldier who is shooting is furious in his energy. The soldier who is shot looks around for help with an imploring agony of death on his face. After a few rods of advance, the line stopped and, by common impulse, fell back to the edge of the corn and lay down on the ground behind the low rail fence. Another line of our men came up through the corn. We all joined together, jumped over the fence, and again pushed out into the open field. There is a rattling fusilade and loud cheers. "Forward" is the word. The men are loading and firing with demoniacal fury and shouting and laughing hysterically, and the whole field before us is covered with rebels fleeing for life, into the woods. Great numbers of them are shot while climbing over the high post and rail fences along the turnpike. We push on over the open fields half way to the little church. The powder is bad, and the guns have become very dirty. It takes hard pounding to get the bullets down, and our firing is becoming slow. A long and steady line of rebel gray, unbroken by the fugitives who fly before us, comes sweeping down through the woods around the church. *They raise the yell and fire. It is like a scythe running through our line. "Now, save, who can." It is a race for life that each man runs for the cornfield. A sharp cut, as of a switch, stings the calf of my leg as I run. Back to the corn, and back through the corn, the headlong flight continues. At the bottom of the hill, I took the blue color of the state of Wisconsin, and waving it, called a rally of Wisconsin men. Two hundred men gathered around the flag of the Badger state. Across the turnpike just in front of the haystacks, two guns of Battery "B," 4th U. S. artillery were in action. The pursuing rebels were upon them. General John Gibbon, our brigade commander, who in regular service was captain of this battery, grimed and black with powder smoke in himself sighting these guns of his old battery, comes running to me, "Here, major, move your men over, we must save these guns." I commanded "Right face, forward march," and started ahead with the colors in my hand into the open field, the men following. As I entered the field, a report as of a thunderclap in my ear fairly stunned me. This was Gibbon's last shot at the advancing rebels. The cannon was double charged with canister. The rails of the fence flew high in the air. A line of union blue charged swiftly forward from our right across the field in front of the battery, and into the corn-field. They drove back the rebels who were firing upon us. It was our own gallant 19th Indiana, and here fell dead their leader, Lieutenant Colonel A. F. Bachman; but the youngest captain in their line, William W. Dudley, stepped forward and led on the charge. I gathered my men on the turnpike, reorganized them, and reported to General Doubleday, who was himself there. He ordered me to move back to the next woods in the rear, to remain and await instruction. Bullets, shot, and shell, fired by the enemy in the corn-field, were still flying thickly around us, striking the trees in this woods, and cutting off the limbs. I placed my men under

---

*Hood's old Texas brigade, and Law's brigade.

the best shelter I could find, and here we figured up, as nearly as we could, our dreadful losses in the battle. Three hundred and fourteen officers and men had marched with us into battle. There had been killed and wounded, one hundred and fifty-two. Company "C" under Captain Hooe, thirty-five men, was not in the fight in front of the corn-field. That company was on skirmish duty farther to our right. In this service they lost two men. Of two hundred and eighty men who were at the corn-field and turnpike, one hundred and fifty were killed or wounded. This was the most dreadful slaughter to which our regiment was subjected in the war. We were joined in the woods by Captain Ely, who reported to me, as the senior officer present, with the colors and eighteen men of the second Wisconsin. They represented what remained for duty of that gallant regiment.

"THE INFERNAL MUSIC":
MARYLAND, SEPTEMBER 1862

Alpheus S. Williams to Irene and Mary Williams

Brigadier General Williams, a former officer in the Michigan militia, was temporarily commanding the Twelfth Corps as the Maryland campaign opened. On September 15 he turned the corps over to Major General Joseph K. F. Mansfield, a regular officer and West Point graduate; when Mansfield was killed on the 17th, Williams resumed the corps command. In a letter to his daughters, he described the early morning fighting in the East Woods, Miller's Cornfield, and the West Woods.

Camp near Sandy Hook,
Near Harpers Ferry, Sept. 22, 1862.

My Dear Daughters:

I wrote you last from Damascus, I think, on the 11th inst. On the 12th we moved to the neighborhood of Urbana, after a circuitous and tedious march. On the 13th we marched to Frederick expecting an attack all the way. We forded the Monocacy and encamped about a mile east of the city. It was a year ago nearly that we marched through Frederick with flying banners. Alas! of those gallant troops (the old 3rd Brigade) how few remain. On Sunday the 14th we were ordered forward from Frederick crossing the Catoctin Mountain by a very rough road, east of the pike upon which we were encamped a year ago. The road took us very near our old campground at a small hamlet called Shookstown. I found all the people knew me, and I was fairly deluged with peaches, apples, etc. Ascending the mountain, we heard the reports of distant artillery and once on the summit could see that a fierce engagement was going on across the valley and in the gorges of the opposite range of mountains.

We were hurried down and marched over rough roads and finally about sundown I got an order to bivouac the corps.

Before, however, the regiments had filed into the fields a new order came to follow Gen. Sumner's corps over the ploughed fields toward the musketry firing heard in front. I had ordered a supper (after a meal-less day) at a farmhouse and went back to get it and to look after my artillery which had got astray in our field and erratic marches. We had a good meal and I mounted to follow the command when I heard that Capt. Abert, U.S. Topographical Engineers, of my staff had been seriously injured by the fall of his horse. Having directed his removal to the house where Dr. Antisell was, I rode back but met a staff officer on the way with a report that the corps was ordered to Middletown to report to Gen. McClellan. Thither I started in the darkest of nights, but at Middletown could hear nothing of my corps. So I rode from there toward the mountain gap where the fighting had been and got as far as our advanced pickets but could not find my corps.

Back I went to Middletown again, but could get no knowledge of my command. But here I heard with sad heart that Gen. Reno, one of the best officers and bravest fellows, had been killed in the engagement. But one day before he had spent at Damascus half a day with me, full of spirits, full of confidence, and full of good feeling. Of all the major generals he was my *beau ideal* of a soldier. You will remember that he commanded a corps which followed ours along the Rappahannock. I had been thrown much with him. His frankness, absence of pomp and parade, his cheerfulness under all circumstances—that indescribable something in manner, had made me love him at first sight. I could have cried when I heard of his death, but for the thousand cares that oppressed me and for the heavy duties which close up the tender impulses of the heart.

Hearing nothing of my command I again rode to the front and on the pike found a portion of our regiment sleeping calmly with no knowledge of the rest. Soon afterward I found a mounted orderly, who directed me to a by-road leading up through the mountain defiles, and following this I at length at 2 o'clock in the morning found the rear division of my command bivouacking near the column of Hooker, which had been engaged with the enemy. I lodged under the best tree I could find, and at daylight got my whole command under arms and went forward to see what was to be done. On the top of the pass I met almost the first man I knew, Gen. Willcox, who commands a division. The dead lay thick in front, but I could see nothing beyond as the mist hung heavily on the mountain. Our troops, however, were already in motion and skirmishers were firing right and left as they pushed the Rebels forward.

Going back to my command, I met Gen. Mansfield, who had just arrived from Washington to take command of the corps. He is a most veteran-looking officer, with head as white as snow. You may have seen him in Washington. His home is at Middletown, Conn. and he has been inspector general of the army for a long time. With this new commander came an order to march. I went back to my division, rather pleased that I had got rid of an onerous responsibility. We crossed the fields to the Hagerstown pike. Our new commander was very fussy. He had been an engineer officer and never before had commanded large bodies of troops.

Onward we went after being delayed for other columns to pass. Crossing the South Mountain we descended rapidly to Boonsboro where the people, as at Frederick, received us with great rejoicing. I did not tell you that in marching my corps through Frederick we were greatly cheered and ladies brought bouquets to me as commander. The same enthusiasm followed us everywhere. Citizens met us on horseback and the whole population seemed rejoiced that we were chasing the Rebels from the state. At Boonsboro we passed south towards Sharpsburg, taking across lots and in all sorts of out of the ways. We encamped at a crossroads and for the first time for weeks I slept in a house, the home of a Mr. Nicodemus. As I was getting my division into camp I saw other troops arriving and an officer darting up to me put out his hand eagerly to greet me. It was the topographical engineer captain with whom Alph. and Ez. went to New Mexico, now Col. Scammon of an Ohio regiment. I did not feel very kindly, I fear, and yet he looked so changed and so glad to see me that I greeted him in return. He went away and I have not seen him since.

The next morning we were ordered hurriedly to the front, Gen. Mansfield, in an excited and fussy way, announcing that we should be in a general engagement in half an hour. Over we went across lots till we struck a road and after a three-mile march we were *massed* in close column in a small space where the shells of the enemy's guns fell close to us. A high ridge in front did not seem much protection. We lay here all day, and at night fancied we were going to rest. I sought a tent with one of my colonels, who gave me the best bed I had seen for weeks.

During the afternoon, amongst the troops marching up I had seen Col. Stockton and other old friends. It was evident that the Rebels were standing for a fight. Their lines were plainly visible from the elevation in front and one battery had been playing all day with ours. I had got fairly asleep when along came a message to get under arms at once. Oh, how sleepy I was, but there is no help at such times. Up I got and in a few moments the head of my division was moving along an unknown road. We passed a stone bridge over the Antietam and then branched off into the fields. Gen. Mansfield and his escort led the way, but it was so dark and the forests and woods so deep that I could not follow and was obliged to send ahead to stop our leaders repeatedly.

After a weary march we halted in some ploughed ground and I was told to put my division in column in mass. It took a long time as I had five new regiments who knew absolutely nothing of maneuvering. At length about two o'clock in the morning I got under the corner of a rail fence, but the pickets in front of us kept firing and as often as I got asleep Gen. Mansfield would come along and wake me with some new directions. At length I got fairly asleep and for two hours was dead to all sounds or sensations. I shall not, however, soon forget that night; so dark, so obscure, so mysterious, so uncertain; with the occasional rapid volleys of pickets and outposts, the low, solemn sound of the command as troops came into position, and withal so sleepy that there was a half-dreamy sensation about it all; but with a certain impression that the morrow was to be great with the future fate of our country. So much responsibility, so much intense, future anxiety! and yet I slept as soundly as though nothing was before me.

At the first dawn of day the cannon began work. Gen. Hooker's command was about a mile in front of us and it was his corps upon which the attack began. By a common impulse our men stood to arms. They had slept in ranks and the matter of toilet was not tedious, nor did we have time to linger over the breakfast table. My division being in advance, I was ordered to move up in close column of companies—that is a company front to each regiment and the other companies closed up to within six paces. When so formed a regiment looks like a solid mass. We had not moved a dozen rods before the shells and round shot came thick over us and around us. If these had struck our massed regiments dozens of men would have been killed by a single shot.

I had five new regiments without drill or discipline. Gen. Mansfield was greatly excited. Though an officer of acknowledged gallantry, he had a very nervous temperament and a very impatient manner. Feeling that our heavy masses of raw troops were sadly exposed, I begged him to let me deploy them in line of battle, in which the men present but *two* ranks or rows instead of *twenty*, as we were marching, but I could not move him. He was positive that all the new regiments would run away. So on we went over ploughed ground, through cornfields and woods, till the line of infantry fight began to appear.

It was evident that Hooker's troops were giving way. His general officers were hurrying toward us begging for support in every direction. First one would come from the right; then over from the center, and then one urging support for a battery on the left. I had ridden somewhat in advance to get some idea of the field and was standing in the center of a ploughed field, taking directions from Gen. Hooker and amidst a very unpleasant shower of bullets, when up rode a general officer begging for immediate assistance to protect a battery. He was very earnest and absorbed in the subject, as you may well suppose, and began to plead energetically, when he suddenly stopped, extended his hand, and very calmly said, "How are you?" It was Gen. Meade. He darted away, and I saw him no more that day. Hooker's troops were soon withdrawn and I think were not again brought into the field. Was it not a strange encounter?

I had parted with Gen. Mansfield but a moment before this and in five minutes afterward his staff officer reported to me that he was mortally wounded and the command of the corps devolved on me. I began at once to deploy the new regiments. The old ones had already gotten themselves into line. Taking hold of one, I directed Gens. Crawford and Gordon to direct the others. I got mine in line pretty well by having a fence to align it on and having got it in this way I ordered the colonel to go forward and open fire the moment he saw the Rebels. Poor fellow! He was killed within ten minutes. His regiment, advancing in line, was split in two by coming in contact with a barn. One part did very well in the woods but the trouble with this regiment and the others was that in attempting to move them forward or back or to make any maneuver they fell into inextricable confusion and fell to the rear, where they were easily rallied. The men were of an excellent stamp, ready and willing, but neither officers nor men knew anything, and there was an absence of the mutual confidence which drill begets. Standing still, they fought bravely.

When we engaged the enemy he was in a strip of woods, long but narrow. We drove him from this, across a ploughed field and through a cornfield into another woods, which was full of ravines. There the enemy held us in check till 9 1/2 o'clock, when there was a general cessation of musketry. All over the ground we had advanced on, the Rebel dead and wounded lay thick, much more numerous than ours, but ours were painfully mingled in. Our wounded were rapidly carried off and some of the Rebels'. Those we were obliged to leave begged so piteously to be carried away. Hundreds appealed to me and I confess that the rage of battle had not hardened my heart so that I did not feel a pity for them. Our men gave them water and as far as I saw always treated them kindly.

The necessities of the case were so great that I was obliged to put my whole corps into action at once. The roar of the infantry was beyond anything conceivable to the uninitiated. Imagine from 8,000 to 10,000 men on one side, with probably a larger number on the other, all at once discharging their muskets. If all the stone and brick houses of Broadway should tumble at once the roar and rattle could hardly be greater, and amidst this, hundreds of pieces of artillery, right and left, were thundering as a sort of bass to the infernal music.

At 9 1/2 o'clock Gen. Sumner was announced as near at hand with his corps. As soon as his columns began to arrive I withdrew mine by degrees to the shelter of the woods for the purpose of rest, to collect stragglers, and to renew the ammunition. Several of the old regiments had fired nearly forty rounds each man. They had stood up splendidly and had forced back the enemy nearly a mile. The new regiments were badly broken up, but I collected about one-half of them and placed them in support of batteries. The regiments had up to this time suffered comparatively little. The 3rd Wisconsin and the 27th Indiana had lost a good many men, but few officers. I began to hope that we should get off, when Sumner attacked, with but little loss. I rode along where our advanced lines had been. Not an enemy appeared. The woods in front were as quiet as any sylvan shade could be. Presently a single report came and a ball whizzed close to my horse. Two or three others followed all in disagreeable closeness to my person. I did not like to hurry, but I lost as little time as possible in getting out of the range of sharpshooters.

I should have mentioned that soon after I met Gen. Hooker he rode toward the left. In a few minutes I heard he was wounded. While we were talking the dust of the ploughed ground was knocked up in little spurts all around us, marking the spot where musket balls struck. I had to ride repeatedly over this field and every time it seemed that my horse could not possibly escape. It was in the center of the line of fire, slightly elevated, but along which *my* troops were extended. The peculiar singing sound of the bullet becomes a regular whistle and it seems strange that everybody is not hit.

While the battle was raging fiercest with that division the 2nd Division came up and I was requested to support our right with one brigade. I started one over to report to Gen. Doubleday and soon followed to see what became of them. As I entered the narrow lane running to the right and front a battery opened a cross-fire and Pittman and myself had the excitement of riding a mile or so out and back under its severest salutations. We found Gen. Doubleday sheltered in a ravine and apparently in bland ignorance of what was doing on his front or what need he had of my troops, except to relieve his own, but I left the brigade and came back. Finding a battery, I put it in position to meet the flank fire of the Rebel battery and some one else had the good sense to establish another farther in the rear. The two soon silenced this disagreeable customer.

It was soon after my return to the center that Sumner's columns began to arrive. They were received with cheers and went fiercely toward the wood with too much haste, I thought, and too little reconnoitering of the ground and positions held by us. They had not reached the road before a furious fire was opened on them and we had the infernal din over again. The Rebels had been strongly reinforced, and Sumner's troops, being formed in three lines in close proximity, after his favorite idea, we lost a good deal of our fire without any corresponding benefit or advantage. For instance, the second line, within forty paces of the front, suffered almost as much as the front line and yet could not fire without hitting our own men. The colonel of a regiment in the second line told me he lost sixty men and came off without firing a gun.

Sumner's force in the center was soon used up, and I was called upon to bring up my wearied and hungry men. They advanced to the front and opened fire, but the force opposed was enormously superior. Still they held on, under heavy losses, till one o'clock. Some of the old regiments were fairly broken up in this fight and what was left were consolidated and mixed up afterward with the new regiments. The 46th Pennsylvania, Col. Knipe, and the 28th New York, Capt. Mapes, commanding, were especially broken. Col. Knipe has just returned to duty from his wounds. He had but one captain (Brooks) in his regiment present and he was killed early. The 2nd Massachusetts, which had done excellent service in the first engagement, was badly cut up and its lieut. col. (Dwight), mortally wounded. At 1 1/2 o'clock I ordered them back, as reinforcements were at hand.

While this last attack was going on, Gen. Greene, 2nd Division, took possession and held for an hour or more the easterly end of the wood—struggled for so fiercely—where it abuts on the road to Sharpsburg. A small brick school house stands by the road, which I noticed the next day was riddled by our shot and shell. Greene held on till Sumner's men gave way towards the left, when he was drawn out by a rush and his men came scampering to the rear in great confusion. The Rebels followed with a yell but three or four of our batteries being in position they were received with a tornado of canister which made them vanish before the smoke cloud cleared away. I was near one of our brass twelve-pound Napoleon gun batteries and seeing the Rebel colors appearing over the rolling ground I directed the two left pieces charged with canister to be turned on the point. In the moment the Rebel line appeared and both guns were discharged at short range. Each canister contains several hundred balls. They fell in the very front of the line and all along it apparently, stirring up a dust like a thick cloud. When the dust blew away no regiment and not a living man was to be seen.

Just then Gen. Smith (Baldy Smith) who was at Detroit on the light-house duty, came up with a division. They fairly rushed toward the left and front. I hastily called his attention to the woods full of Rebels on his right as he was advancing. He dispatched that way one regiment and the rest advanced to an elevation which overlooked the valley on our left, where the left wing had been fighting for several hours. The regiment sent toward the woods got a tremendous volley and saved itself by rushing over the hillside for shelter. The rest of the brigade got an enfilading fire on a Rebel line and it broke and ran to the rear. One regiment only charged the front, as if on parade, but a second battery sent it scampering.

On this ground the contest was kept up for a long time. The multitude of dead Rebels (I saw them) was proof enough how hotly they contested the ground. It was getting toward night. The artillery took up the fight. We had driven them at all points, save the one woods. It was thought advisable not to attack further. We held the main battlefield and all our wounded, except a few in the woods. My troops slept on their arms well to the front. All the other corps of the center seemed to have vanished, but I found Sumner's the next morning and moved up to it and set to work gathering up our stragglers. The day was passed in comparative quietness on both sides. Our burial parties would exchange the dead and wounded with the Rebels in the woods.

It was understood that we were to attack again at daylight on the 19th, but as our troops moved up it was found the Rebels had departed. Some of the troops followed, but we lay under arms all day, waiting orders. I took the delay to ride over the field of battle. The Rebel dead, even in the woods last occupied by them, was very great. In one place, in front of the position of my corps, apparently a whole regiment had been cut down in line. They lay in two ranks, as straightly aligned as on a dress parade. There must have been a brigade, as part of the line on the left had been buried. I counted what appeared to be a single regiment and found 149 dead in the line and about 70 in front and rear, making over 200 dead in one Rebel regiment. In riding over the field I think I must have seen at least 3,000. In one place for nearly a mile they lay as thick as autumn leaves along a narrow lane cut below the natural surface, into which they seemed to have tumbled. Eighty had been buried in one pit, and yet no impression had apparently been made on the unburied host. The cornfield beyond was dotted all over with those killed in retreat.

The wounded Rebels had been carried away in great numbers and yet every farmyard and haystack seemed a large hospital. The number of dead horses was high. They lay, like the men, in all attitudes. One beautiful milk-white animal had died in so graceful a position that I wished for its photograph. Its legs were doubled under and its arched neck gracefully turned to one side, as if looking back to the ball-hole in its side. Until you got to it, it was hard to believe the horse was dead. Another feature of the field was the mass of army accouterments, clothing, etc. scattered everywhere or lying in heaps where the contest had been severest. I lost but two field officers killed, Col. Croasdale, 128th Pennsylvania and Col. Dwight, 2nd Massachusetts, several men wounded. Gen. Crawford of the 1st Brigade was wounded, not severely. I marvel, not only at my own escape, as I was particularly exposed, on account of raw troops to be handled, but at the escape of any mounted officer.

The newspapers will give you further particulars, but as far as I have seen them, nothing reliable. . . . The "big staff generals" get the first ear and nobody is heard of and no corps mentioned till their voracious maws are filled with puffing. I see it stated that Sumner's corps relieved Hooker's. So far is this from true that my corps was engaged from sunrise till 9 1/2 o'clock before Sumner came up, though he was to be on the ground at daylight. Other statements picked up by reporters from the principal headquarters are equally false and absurd. To me they are laughably *canard*.

On the afternoon of the 18th I received orders to occupy Maryland Heights with my corps. They are opposite Harpers Ferry, and had just been surrendered by Col. Miles. I marched till 2 o'clock in the morning, reaching Brownsvllle. Halted till daylight, men sleeping in the road. I slept on hay in a barn. Started by sunrise up the Heights and marched along a rocky path on the ridge to the Heights overlooking Harpers Ferry. I left my artillery and train at Brownsville. Occupied the Heights without opposition. Found there was no water there; left a strong guard and took the command down the mountain on the east side. Sent a brigade over the river and a regiment to Sandy Hook. This morning (Gen. Sumner's corps having come up) I have sent one division over the river to Loudon Heights and one part way up Maryland Heights in front. The Rebels are in sight in and about and this side Charleston and to the west toward Shepardstown. What is to be done next I know not. It will be my fate, I fear, to go a third time up the valley. Heaven forbid! The valley has been an unfortunate land for me. My friends think I shall get a major generalship. I should if I was of the regular army; but not being such nor a graduated fool I suppose I shall remain a brigadier. Gen. Banks never moves for any of his command, unless solicited personally. Nobody in his corps has received promotion, though he seems to have gathered some newspaper laurels. . . .

It is now nearly six weeks that I have hardly halted a whole day, and when I have it was under orders to be ready to move at a moment. I am so tired and uneasy of this kind of sleepless life. On the march up my command was one day eighteen hours under arms and marching most of the time. But I am well and bear it better than anyone.

Affectionately, my Daughters,
Your Father,
A.S.W.

A LANDSCAPE TURNED RED:
MARYLAND, SEPTEMBER 1862

David L. Thompson: With Burnside at Antietam

As the day wore on, the fighting shifted from the northern sector to the center and finally to the southern end of the battleground. Ambrose Burnside's Ninth Corps forced its way across a stone bridge (known thereafter as Burnside's Bridge) and pushed on to the outskirts of Sharpsburg. A. P. Hill's Confederate division, rushing from Harpers Ferry, caught Burnside's corps in the flank, drove it back to the bridge, and ended the day's fighting. Private Thompson, 9th New York Infantry, narrated his modest role amidst the confusing battle scene for *Battles and Leaders of the Civil War*.

AT ANTIETAM our corps—the Ninth, under Burnside—was on the extreme left, opposite the stone bridge. Our brigade stole into position about half-past 10 o'clock on the night of the 16th. No lights were permitted, and all conversation was carried on in whispers. As the regiment was moving past the 103d New York to get to its place, there occurred, on a small scale and without serious results, one of those unaccountable panics often noticed in crowds, by which each man, however brave individually, merges his individuality for the moment, and surrenders to an utterly causeless fear. When everything was at its darkest and stealthiest one of the 103d stumbled over the regimental dog, and, in trying to avoid treading on it, staggered against a stack of muskets and knocked them over. The giving way of the two or three men upon whom they fell was communicated to others in a sort of wave movement of constantly increasing magnitude, reënforced by the ever-present apprehension of attack, till two regiments were in confusion. In a few seconds order was restored, and we went on to our place in the line—a field of thin corn sloping toward the creek, where we sat down on the plowed ground and watched for a while the dull glare on the sky of the Confederate campfires behind the hills. We were hungry, of course, but, as no fires were allowed, we could only mix our ground coffee and sugar in our hands and eat them dry. I think we were the more easily inclined to this crude disposal of our rations from a feeling that for many of us the need of drawing them would cease forever with the following day.

All through the evening the shifting and placing had gone on, the moving masses being dimly descried in the strange half lights of earth and sky. There was something weirdly impressive yet unreal in the gradual drawing together of those whispering armies under cover of the night—something of awe and dread, as always in the secret preparation for momentous deeds. By 11 o'clock the whole line, four miles or more in length, was sleeping, each corps apprised of its appointed task, each battery in place.

It is astonishing how soon, and by what slight causes, regularity of formation and movement are lost in actual battle. Disintegration begins with the first shot. To the book-soldier all order seems destroyed, months of drill apparently going for nothing in a few minutes. Next after the most powerful factor in this derangement—the enemy—come natural obstacles and the inequalities of the ground. One of the commonest is a patch of trees. An advancing line lags there inevitably, the rest of the line swinging around insensibly, with the view of keeping the alignment, and so losing direction. The struggle for the possession of such a point is sure to be persistent. Wounded men crawl to a wood for shelter, broken troops re-form behind it, a battery planted in its edge will stick there after other parts of the line have given way. Often a slight rise of ground in an open field, not noticeable a thousand yards away, becomes, in the keep of a stubborn regiment, a powerful head-land against which the waves of battle roll and break, requiring new dispositions and much time to clear it. A stronger fortress than a casual railroad embankment often proves, it would be difficult to find; and as for a sunken road, what possibilities of victory or disaster lie in that obstruction, let Waterloo and Fredericksburg bear witness.

At Antietam it was a low, rocky ledge, prefaced by a cornfield. There were woods, too, and knolls, and there were other corn-fields; but the student of that battle knows one corn-field only—*the* corn-field, now historic, lying a quarter of a mile north of Dunker Church, and east of and bordering the Hagerstown road. About it and across it, to and fro, the waves of battle swung almost from the first, till by 10 o'clock in the morning, when the struggle was over, hundreds of men lay dead among its peaceful blades.

While these things were happening on the right, the left was not without its excitement. A Confederate battery discovered our position in our corn-field, as soon as it was light enough to see, and began to shell us. As the range became better we were moved back and ordered to boil coffee in the protection of a hollow. The general plan of battle appears to have been to break through the Confederate left, following up the advantage with a constantly increasing force, sweep him away from the fords, and so crowd his whole army down into the narrow peninsula formed by the Potomac and Antietam Creek. Even the non-military eye, however, can see that the tendency of such a plan would be to bring the two armies upon concentric arcs, the inner and shorter of which must be held by the enemy, affording him the opportunity for reënforcement by interior lines—an immense advantage only to be counteracted by the utmost activity on our part, who must attack vigorously where attacking at all, and where not, imminently threaten. Certainly there was no imminence in the threat of our center or left— none whatever of the left, only a vague consciousness of whose existence even seems to have been in the enemy's mind, for he flouted us all the morning with hardly more than a meager skirmish line, while his coming troops, as fast as they arrived upon the ground, were sent off to the Dunker Church.

So the morning wore away, and the fighting on the right ceased entirely. That was fresh anxiety—the scales were turning perhaps, but which way? About noon the battle began afresh. This must have been Franklin's men of the Sixth Corps, for the firing was nearer, and they came up behind the center. Suddenly a stir beginning far up on the right, and running like a wave along the line, brought the regiment to its feet. A silence fell on every one at once, for each felt that the momentous "now" had come. Just as we started I saw, with a little shock, a line-officer take out his watch to note the hour, as though the affair beyond the creek were a business appointment which he was going to keep.

When we reached the brow of the hill the fringe of trees along the creek screened the fighting entirely, and we were deployed as skirmishers under their cover. We sat there two hours. All that time the rest of the corps had been moving over the stone bridge and going into position on the other side of the creek. Then we were ordered over at a ford which had been found below the bridge, where the water was waist-deep. One man was shot in mid-stream. At the foot of the slope on the opposite side the line was formed and we moved up through the thin woods. Reaching the level we lay down behind a battery which seemed to have been disabled. There, if anywhere, I should have remembered that I was soaking wet from my waist down. So great was the excitement, however, that I have never been able to recall it. Here some of the men, going to the rear for water, discovered in the ashes of some hay-ricks which had been fired by our shells the charred remains of several Confederates. After long waiting it became noised along the line that we were to take a battery that was at work several hundred yards ahead on the top of a hill. This narrowed the field and brought us to consider the work before us more attentively.

Right across our front, two hundred feet or so away, ran a country road bordered on each side by a snake fence. Beyond this road stretched a plowed field several hundred feet in length, sloping up to the battery, which was hidden in a cornfield. A stone fence, breast-high, inclosed the field on the left, and behind it lay a regiment of Confederates, who would be directly on our flank if we should attempt the slope. The prospect was far from encouraging, but the order came to get ready for the attempt.

Our knapsacks were left on the ground behind us. At the word a rush was made for the fences. The line was so disordered by the time the second fence was passed that we hurried forward to a shallow undulation a few feet ahead, and lay down among the furrows to re-form, doing so by crawling up into line. A hundred feet or so ahead was a similar undulation to which we ran for a second shelter. The battery, which at first had not seemed to notice us, now, apprised of its danger, opened fire upon us. We were getting ready now for the charge proper, but were still lying on our faces. Lieutenant-Colonel Kimball was ramping up and down the line. The discreet regiment behind the fence was silent. Now and then a bullet from them cut the air over our heads, but generally they were reserving their fire for that better shot which they knew they would get in a few minutes. The battery, however, whose shots at first went over our heads, had depressed its guns so as to shave the surface of the ground. Its fire was beginning to tell. I remember looking behind and seeing an officer riding diagonally across the field—a most inviting target—instinctively bending his head down over his horse's neck, as though he were riding through driving rain. While my eye was on him I saw, between me and him, a rolled overcoat with its straps on bound into the air and fall among the furrows. One of the enemy's grape-shot had plowed a groove in the skull of a young fellow and had cut his overcoat from his shoulders. He never stirred from his position, but lay there face downward—a dreadful spectacle. A moment after, I heard a man cursing a comrade for lying on him heavily. He was cursing a dying man. As the range grew better, the firing became more rapid, the situation desperate and exasperating to the last degree. Human nature was on the rack, and there burst forth from it the most vehement, terrible swearing I have ever heard. Certainly the joy of conflict was not ours that day. The suspense was only for a moment, however, for the order to charge came just after. Whether the regiment was thrown into disorder or not, I never knew. I only remember that as we rose and started all the fire that had been held back so long was loosed. In a second the air was full of the hiss of bullets and the hurtle of grape-shot. The mental strain was so great that I saw at that moment the singular effect mentioned, I think, in the life of Goethe on a similar occasion—the whole landscape for an instant turned slightly red. I see again, as I saw it then in a flash, a man just in front of me drop his musket and throw up his hands, stung into vigorous swearing by a bullet behind the ear. Many men fell going up the hill, but it seemed to be all over in a moment, and I found myself passing a hollow where a dozen wounded men lay—among them our sergeant-major, who was calling me to come down. He had caught sight of the blanket rolled across my back, and called me to unroll it and help to carry from the field one of our wounded lieutenants.

When I returned from obeying this summons the regiment (?) was not to be seen. It had gone in on the run, what there was left of it, and had disappeared in the corn-field about the battery. There was nothing to do but lie there and await developments. Nearly all the men in the hollow were wounded, one man—a recruit named Devlin, I think—frightfully so, his arm being cut short off. He lived a few minutes only. All were calling for water, of course, but none was to be had. We lay there till dusk,—perhaps an hour, when the fighting ceased. During that hour, while the bullets snipped the leaves from a young locust-tree growing at the edge of the hollow and powdered us with the fragments, we had time to speculate on many things— among others, on the impatience with which men clamor, in dull times, to be led into a fight. We heard all through the war that the army "was eager to be led against the enemy." It must have been so, for truthful correspondents said so, and editors confirmed it. But when you came to hunt for this particular itch, it was always the next regiment that had it. The truth is, when bullets are whacking against tree-trunks and solid shot are cracking skulls like egg-shells, the consuming passion in the breast of the average man is to get out of the way. Between the physical fear of going forward and the moral fear of turning back, there is a predicament of exceptional awkwardness from which a hidden hole in the ground would be a wonderfully welcome outlet.

Night fell, preventing further struggle. Of 600 men of the regiment who crossed the creek at 3 o'clock that afternoon, 45 were killed and 176 wounded. The Confederates held possession of that part of the field over which we had moved, and just after dusk they sent out detachments to collect arms and bring in prisoners. When they came to our hollow all the unwounded and slightly wounded there were marched to the rear—prisoners of the 15th Georgia. We slept on the ground that night without protection of any kind; for, with a recklessness quite common throughout the war, we had thrown away every incumbrance on going into the fight. The weather, however, was warm and pleasant, and there was little discomfort.

The next morning we were marched—about six hundred of us, fragments of a dozen different commands—to the Potomac, passing through Sharpsburg. We crossed the Potomac by the Shepherdstown ford, and bivouacked in the yard of a house near the river, remaining there all day. The next morning (the 19th) shells began to come from over the river, and we were started on the road to Richmond with a mixed guard of cavalry and infantry. When we reached Winchester we were quartered for a night in the court-house yard, where we were beset by a motley crew who were eager to exchange the produce of the region for greenbacks.

On the road between Shepherdstown and Winchester we fell in with the Maryland Battalion—a meeting I have always remembered with pleasure. They were marching to the front by companies, spaced apart about 300 or 400 feet. We were an ungainly, draggled lot, about as far removed as well could be from any claim to ceremonious courtesy; yet each company, as it passed, gave us the military salute of shouldered arms. They were noticeable, at that early stage of the war, as the only organization we saw that wore the regulation Confederate gray, all other troops having assumed a sort of revised regulation uniform of homespun butternut—a significant witness, we thought, to the efficacy of the blockade.

From Winchester we were marched to Staunton, where we were put on board cattle-cars and forwarded at night, by way of Gordonsville, to Richmond, where we entered Libby Prison. We were not treated with special severity, for Libby was not at that time the hissing it afterward became. Our time there, also, was not long. Only nine days after we entered it we were sent away, going by steamer to Camp Parole, at Annapolis. From that place I went home without ceremony, reporting my address to my company officers. Three weeks afterward they advised me that I was exchanged—which meant that I was again, legally and technically, food for powder.

AFTER THE BATTLE:
MARYLAND, SEPTEMBER 1862

Samuel W. Fiske to the Springfield Republican

After defiantly standing his ground on September 18, General Lee fell back across the Potomac into Virginia. McClellan made no serious effort at pursuit. Lieutenant Fiske of the 14th Connecticut Infantry described the aftermath of the struggle in one of his regular letters to the *Springfield* (Massachusetts) *Republican*, writing under his nom de plume Dunn Browne. The combined casualties of the Battle of Antietam reached 22,717 killed, wounded, or missing (Union 12,401, Confederate 10,316), making it the bloodiest single day in American history.

AFTER THE BATTLE

Field of Battle, near Sharpsburg, Md.
Saturday, Sept. 20

The excitement of battle comes in the day of it, but the horrors of it two or three days after. I have just passed over a part of the field, I suppose only a small part of it, and yet I have counted nearly a thousand dead bodies of rebels lying still unburied in groves and corn-fields, on hill sides and in trenches. Three hundred and fifty I was told by one who helped to bury them, were taken this morning from one long rifle pit which lay just in front of where the 14th (among other regiments) made their fight, and were buried in one trench. The air grows terribly offensive from the unburied bodies, and a pestilence will speedily be bred if they are not put under ground. The most of the Union soldiers are now buried, but some of them only slightly. Think now of the horrors of such a scene as lies all around us, for there are hundreds of horses too, all mangled and putrefying, scattered everywhere. Then there are the broken gun carriages, and wagons, the thousands of muskets and all sorts of equipments, the clothing all torn and bloody, and cartridges and cannon shot and pieces of shell, the trees torn with shot and scarred with bullets, the farm houses and barns knocked to pieces and burned down, the crops trampled and wasted, the whole country forlorn and desolate. And yet I saw over all this scene of devastation and horror, yesternight, one of the loveliest double rainbows that ever mortal eyes looked upon. It was as if heaven sat serene over human woes and horrors, and crowned all the earthly evils with the promise of ultimate most glorious good. I took it as an emblem of success to our blessed Union cause, that out of the horrors of battle shall arise the blessings of a more secure freedom and stable system of liberal government.

The enemy has retired in disgrace from his bold invasion of the North with at least 40,000 or 50,000 less men than he entered upon it—and after all our disasters and blunders and waste, let us hope that the successful end is beginning to draw nigh. The waste of this war is tremendous beyond all conception. It would take a long time to reckon that of this one battle. Thousands and thousands and tens of thousands of muskets, stacks of guns, piles of guns like big piles of rails, muskets laid up against rocks and trees and muskets scattered yet over the ground and choking up water courses, muskets rusty and broken and dirty, spoiled and half-spoiled, that a few days ago were bright in the hands of living men, are only one item of the waste. Whole regiments threw away their overcoats and blankets and everything that encumbered them, and they were trampled in the rush of conflicting hosts, and so with equipments and stores and ammunition and everything else. Waste, waste, ruin and destruction. Why, I saw a whole immense stack of unthreshed wheat, big as a barn, scattered in a few minutes over a hundred acre field (the same I think from which it had been reaped) just as bedding for the soldiers for a single night. Much of this waste is unavoidable. Much of it might be helped. Just as it is said that out of the waste of an American kitchen a French family would live comfortably, so it might almost be said that out of the waste of an American war a European war might be carried on. But I must make no more waste of ink now. Yours truly,

DUNN BROWNE

September 20, 1862

"OUR MEN HAD WON":
MARYLAND, SEPTEMBER 1862

Clifton Johnson: from Battleground Adventures

In 1913 Clifton Johnson, a travel writer from Massachusetts, interviewed almost three score civilians about their recollections of the wartime events they had witnessed, publishing his interviews in 1915. This "elderly gentlewoman," as Johnson described her, still lived in her ancestral home in Sharpsburg, and shared her memories of that September day a half-century before.

A Maryland Maiden[1]

WE WERE all up in the Lutheran Church at Sunday-school on the Sunday before the battle when the Rebel cavalry came dashing through the town. The whole assembly flocked out, and there was nothing but excitement from that on. We just imagined something was going to happen, and the children ran home from church in terror. There was no dinner eaten that day. The people were too frightened. We'd go out the front door and stand waiting to see what would be next to come.

I was twenty years old then. My father was a blacksmith, and we lived in this same big stone house on the main street of the town. I suppose the house was built a hundred and fifty or more years ago.

Most of us in this region favored the Union, and the ladies had made a big flag out of material that the townspeople bought. For a while we had it on a pole in the square, but some of the Democratic boys cut the flag rope every night. So we took the flag down and hung it on a rope stretched across from our garret window to that of the house opposite. In

---

[1] We chatted in one of the old-fashioned, wood-panelled rooms of her ancestral village home. She was a slender, elderly gentlewoman, but though the years had left their mark they had in nowise subdued her natural alertness and enthusiasm.

pleasant weather it was out all the time. But when we heard that Lee had crossed the Potomac Pa began to be uneasy, and he says, "Girls, what you goin' to do with that flag? If the Rebels come into town they'll take it sure as the world."

He thought we'd better hide it in the ground somewhere. So a lady friend of mine and I put it in a strong wooden box, and buried it in the ash pile behind the smokehouse in the garden.

When the Rebel cavalry went through that Sunday we had no idea what they were up to, and we could n't help being fearful that we were in danger. We expected trouble that night, but all was quiet until the next day. Then more Rebels came, and they nearly worried us to death asking for something to eat. They were half famished and they looked like tramps—filthy and ragged.

By Tuesday there was enough going on to let us know we were likely to have a battle near by. Early in the day two or three Rebels, who'd been informed by some one that a Union flag was concealed at my father's place, came right to the house, and I met 'em at the door. Their leader said: "We've come to demand that flag you've got here. Give it up at once or we'll search the house."

"I'll not give it up, and I guess you'll not come any farther than you are, sir," I said.

They were impudent fellows, and he responded, "If you don't tell me where that flag is I'll draw my revolver on you."

"It's of no use for you to threaten," I said. "Rather than have you touch a fold of that starry flag I laid it in ashes."

They seemed to be satisfied then and went away without suspecting just how I'd laid it in ashes.

Tuesday afternoon the neighbors began to come in here. Our basement was very large with thick stone walls, and they wanted to take refuge in it if there was danger. There were women and children of all ages and some very old men. Mostly they stood roundabout in the yard listening and looking. The cannonading started late in the day, and when there was a very loud report they scampered to the cellar.

A lot of townspeople run out of the village to a cave about three miles from here near the Potomac. The cave was just an overhanging ledge of rocks, but shells and cannon balls would fly over it and could n't hurt the people under the cliff. I reckon seventy-five went to that cave.

Before day, on Wednesday, a cannon ball tore up the pavement out in front of our house. Oh my soul! we thought we were gone. There was no more sleep, but most of us were awake anyhow. After that, you know, we all flew to the cellar. Very little was stored in there at that time of year. We carried down some seats, and we made board benches around, and quite a number of us got up on the potato bunks and the apple scaffolds. We were as comfortable as we could possibly be in a cellar, but it's a wonder we did n't all take our deaths of colds in that damp place.

We did n't have any breakfast—you bet we did n't—and no dinner was got that day, or supper—no, indeed! We had to live on fear. But a few of the women thought enough to bring some food in their baskets for the children. The battle did n't prevent the children from eating. They did n't understand the danger.

A number of babies were there, and several dogs, and every time the firing began extra hard the babies would cry and the dogs would bark. Often the reports were so loud they shook the walls. Occasionally a woman was quite unnerved and hysterical, and some of those old aged men would break out in prayer.

In the height of the fighting six Rebel soldiers opened the basement door and said, "We're comin' in, but we're not a-goin' to hurt you."

We had a spring in the cellar. The water filled a shallow tank, and that was where our family got what water was used in the house. Those refugee soldiers went back in a little nook right next to the spring. There they stood like sardines in a box, and every once in a while one would slip down into the water.

We had two cows and a horse in our stable, and at dinner time Mother and I went to feed 'em. We climbed up to pull down some hay and found the haymow just full of Rebels a-layin' there hiding.

"Madam, don't be frightened," one of 'em said to Mother. "We're hidin' till the battle is over. We're tired of fightin'. We were pressed into service, and we're goin' to give ourselves up as soon as the Yankees get here."

And that was what they did. When the Yankees rushed into

town these Rebels came through the garden and gave themselves up as prisoners.

There were deserters hid in every conceivable place in the town. We had a lot of sacks of seed wheat on our back porch, and some of the skulkers piled the sacks up on the outside of the porch three or four feet high, as a sort of bulwark, which they lay down behind to shelter themselves. How they did curse their leaders for bringing them into this slaughter pen. They said they hoped the hottest place in hell would be their leaders' portion.

Some of the townsmen in the cellar would come up and venture out under the porch, but they were afraid to stay out; and the danger was n't just fancied either. A shell exploded right out here at our front gate and killed or wounded seven men.

And yet, mind you, on Wednesday afternoon, another girl and myself went up to the attic, and though the bullets were raining on the roof, we threw open the shutter and looked out toward the battleground. We were curious to know what was going on. The bullets could have struck us just as easy, but we did n't seem to fear them. On all the distant hills around were the blue uniforms and shining bayonets of our men, and I thought it was the prettiest sight I ever saw in my life. Yes, there were our men, advancing cautiously, driven back again and again, but persistently returning and pushing nearer. My! it was lovely, and I felt so glad to think that we were going to get them into town shortly. We stayed up there I suppose a couple of hours at that little window, and then old Dr. Kelsey came hunting for us and made us come down. I shall always remember what we saw from that window, and many times I go up to the attic and look out, and the view brings it all back.

In the evening mother and I slipped down to the stable and did the milking. But afterward we went back to the cellar, for the firing kept up till ten o'clock. Then we came up and snatched what little bit we could to eat. We did n't cook anything but took what was prepared, like bread and butter and milk. Our neighbors who had been in the cellar did n't attempt to go home. Some of the older ones we accommodated in beds, others lay on the floors, but the best part of the people sat up all night and watched, for we did n't know what was going to come on us.

About midnight we heard the Rebels retreating. Oh! the cannon just came down the hill bouncing. And the cavalry—my! if they did n't dash through here! The infantry, too, were going on a dead run, and some of the poor, hungry fellows were so weak they were saying to their stronger comrades, "Take hold of my hand, and help me along." A lot of 'em were drownded in going across the Potomac.

We were overjoyed to know that our men had won—yes, we certainly were happy. Well, the next morning everything was quiet. It was an unearthly quiet after all the uproar of the battle. The people who had taken refuge with us saw that the danger was over, and they scattered away to their homes. Father and I went out on the front pavement. We could see only a few citizens moving about, but pretty soon a Federal officer came cautiously around the corner by the church. He asked Father if any one was hurt in the town and said they had tried to avoid shelling it, and he was awful sorry they could n't help dropping an occasional shell among the houses.

I lost no time now in getting our flag from the ash heap so I could have it where it would be seen when our men marched into the town. I draped it on the front of the house, but I declare to goodness! I had to take that flag down. It made the officers think our house was a hotel, and they'd ride up, throw their reins to their orderlies, and come clanking up the steps with their swords and want something to eat. So I hurried to get it swung across the street, and after that, as the officers and men passed under it they all took off their hats. Their reverence for the flag was beautiful, and so was the flag.

I had a little flag in my hand, and while I was waving and waving it and cheering our victorious troops some prisoners marched by, and, bless your soul! among them I saw the very men who had demanded the big flag that was now suspended across the street. They looked at the flag and at me and shouted, "You said it was burned!" and they cursed me till some of our men drew their swords and quieted 'em down. "We'll settle with you when we come through here again," they called back, but they never came.

Our men were much cleaner and better fed than the Rebels, and their clothing was whole. The trains soon arrived with the hardtack, and there were baggage wagons and ambulances and everything. We had our men here with us quite a while camped in the town woods, and so constant was the coming and going of troops and army conveyances on the highways that we did n't get to speak to our neighbors across the street for weeks. Those were exciting times, but we felt safe. Of course there were some common, rough fellows among the soldiers, but as a general thing we found them very nice and we became much attached to them. When they went away it left us decidedly lonely here.

As for the day of the battle, it was tragic, but after the fighting was all over and I just sat and studied everything that had transpired a good deal was really laughable.

Well, the region was dreadfully torn to pieces by the conflict, but now you see no trace of it only the cemeteries.

"NOISE, CONFUSION, DUST":
VIRGINIA, SEPTEMBER 1862

Mary Bedinger Mitchell:
A Woman's Recollections of Antietam

Mary Bedinger was twelve years old at the time of Antietam and lived with her widowed mother and younger brother and sister in Shepherdstown, Virginia. Her reminiscences were published in 1887 in *Battles and Leaders of the Civil War*, having first appeared as "In the Wake of Battle" in the July 1886 *Century Magazine* under the pseudonym Maria Blunt.

September, 1862, was in the skies of the almanac, but August still reigned in ours; it was hot and dusty. The railroads in the Shenandoah Valley had been torn up, the bridges had been destroyed, communication had been made difficult, and Shepherdstown, cornered by the bend of the Potomac, lay as if forgotten in the bottom of somebody's pocket. We were without news or knowledge, except when some chance traveler would repeat the last wild and uncertain rumor that he had heard. We had passed an exciting summer. Winchester had changed hands more than once; we had been "in the Confederacy" and out of it again, and were now waiting, in an exasperating state of ignorance and suspense, for the next move in the great game.

It was a saying with us that Shepherdstown was just nine miles from everywhere. It was, in fact, about that distance from Martinsburg and Harper's Ferry—oft-mentioned names—and from Williamsport, where the armies so often crossed, both to and from Maryland. It was off the direct road between those places and lay, as I said, at the foot of a great sweep in the river, and five miles from the nearest station on the Baltimore and Ohio railroad. As no trains were running now, this was of little consequence; what was more important was that a turnpike road—unusually fine for that region of stiff, red clay—led in almost a straight line for thirty miles to Winchester on the south, and stretched northward, beyond the Potomac, twenty miles to Hagerstown. Two years later it was the scene of "Sheridan's ride." Before the days of steam this had been part of the old posting-road between the Valley towns and Pennsylvania, and we had boasted a very substantial bridge. This had been burned early in the war, and only the massive stone piers remained; but a mile and a half down the Potomac was the ford, and the road that led to it lay partly above and partly along the face of rocky and precipitous cliffs. It was narrow and stony, and especially in one place, around the foot of "Mount Misery," was very steep and difficult for vehicles. It was, moreover, entirely commanded by the hills on the Maryland side, but it was the ford over which some part of the Confederate army passed every year, and in 1863 was used by the main body of infantry on the way to Gettysburg. Beyond the river were the Cumberland Canal and its willow-fringed tow-path, from which rose the soft and rounded outlines of the hills that from their farther slopes looked down upon the battle-field of Antietam. On clear days we could see the fort at Harper's Ferry without a glass, and the flag flying over it, a mere speck against the sky, and we could hear the gun that was fired every evening at sunset.

Shepherdstown's only access to the river was through a narrow gorge, the bed of a small tributary of the Potomac, that was made to do much duty as it slipped cheerily over its rocks and furnished power for several mills and factories, most of them at that time silent. Here were also three or four stone warehouses, huge empty structures, testifying mutely that the town had once had a business. The road to the bridge led through this cleft, down an indescribably steep street skirting the stream's ravine to whose sides the mills and factories clung in most extraordinary fashion; but it was always a marvel how anything heavier than a wheelbarrow could be pulled up its tedious length, or how any vehicle could be driven down without plunging into the water at the bottom.

In this odd little borough, then, we were waiting "developments," hearing first that "our men" were coming, and then that they were not coming, when suddenly, on Saturday, the 13th of September, early in the morning, we found ourselves surrounded by a hungry horde of lean and dusty tatterdemalions, who seemed to rise from the ground at our feet. I did not know where they came from, or to whose command they belonged; I have since been informed that General Jackson recrossed into Virginia at Williamsport, and hastened to Harper's Ferry by the shortest roads. These would take him some four miles south of us, and our haggard apparitions were perhaps a part of his force. They were stragglers, at all events,—professional, some of them, but some worn out by the incessant strain of that summer. When I say that they were hungry, I convey no impression of the gaunt starvation that looked from their cavernous eyes. All day they crowded to the doors of our houses, with always the same drawling complaint: "I've been a-marchin' an' a-fightin' for six weeks stiddy, and I ain't had n-a-r-thin' to eat 'cept green apples an' green cawn, an' I wish you'd please to gimme a bite to eat."

Their looks bore out their statements, and when they told us they had "clean gin out," we believed them, and went to get what we had. They could be seen afterward asleep in every fence corner, and under every tree, but after a night's rest they "pulled themselves together" somehow and disappeared as suddenly as they had come. Possibly they went back to their commands, possibly they only moved on to repeat the same tale elsewhere. I know nothing of numbers, nor what force was or was not engaged in any battle, but I saw the troops march past us every summer for four years, and I know something of the appearance of a marching army, both Union and Southern. There are always stragglers, of course, but never before or after did I see anything comparable to the demoralized state of the Confederates at this time. Never were want and exhaustion more visibly put before my eyes, and that they could march or fight at all seemed incredible.

As I remember, the next morning—it was Sunday, September 14th—we were awakened by heavy firing at two points on the mountains. We were expecting the bombardment of Harper's Ferry, and knew that Jackson was before it. Many of our friends were with him, and our interest there was so intense that we sat watching the bellowing and smoking Heights, for a long time, before we became aware that the same phenomena were to be noticed in the north. From our windows both points could be observed, and we could not tell which to watch more keenly. We knew almost nothing except that there was fighting, that it must be very heavy, and that our friends were surely in it somewhere, but whether at South Mountain or Harper's Ferry we had no means of discovering. I remember how the day wore on, how we staid at the windows until we could not endure the suspense; how we walked about and came back to them; and how finally, when night fell, it seemed cruel and preposterous to go to bed still ignorant of the result.

Monday afternoon, about 2 or 3 o'clock, when we were sitting about in disconsolate fashion, distracted by the contradictory rumors, our negro cook rushed into the room with eyes shining and face working with excitement. She had been down in "de ten-acre lot to pick a few years ob cawn," and she had seen a long train of wagons coming up from the ford, and "dey is full ob wounded men, and de blood runnin' outen dem dat deep," measuring on her outstretched arm to the shoulder. This horrible picture sent us flying to town, where we found the streets already crowded, the people all astir, and the foremost wagons, of what seemed an endless line, discharging their piteous burdens. The scene speedily became ghastly, but fortunately we could not stay to look at it. There were no preparations, no accommodations—the men could not be left in the street—what was to be done?

A Federal soldier once said to me, "I was always sorry for your wounded; they never seemed to get any care." The remark was extreme, but there was much justice in it. There was little mitigation of hardship to our unfortunate armies. We were fond of calling them Spartans, and they were but too truly called upon to endure a Spartan system of neglect and privation. They were generally ill-fed and ill-cared for. It would have been possible at this time, one would think, to send a courier back to inform the town and bespeak what comforts it could provide for the approaching wounded; but here they were, unannounced, on the brick pavements, and the first thing was to find roofs to cover them. Men ran for keys and opened the shops, long empty, and the unused rooms; other people got brooms and stirred up the dust of ages; then swarms of children began to appear with bundles of hay and straw, taken from anybody's stable. These were hastily disposed in heaps, and covered with blankets—the soldiers' own, or blankets begged or borrowed. On these improvised beds the sufferers were placed, and the next question was how properly to dress their wounds. No surgeons were to be seen. A few men, detailed as nurses, had come, but they were incompetent, of course. Our women set bravely to work and washed away the blood or stanched it as well as they could, where the jolting of the long rough ride had disarranged the hasty binding done upon the battle-field. But what did they know of wounds beyond a cut finger, or a boil? Yet they bandaged and bathed, with a devotion that went far to make up for their inexperience. Then there was the hunt for bandages. Every housekeeper ransacked her stores and brought forth things new and old. I saw one girl, in despair for a strip of cloth, look about helplessly, and then rip off the hem of her white petticoat. The doctors came up, by and by, or I suppose they did, for some amputating was done—rough surgery, you may be sure. The women helped, holding the instruments and the basins, and trying to soothe or strengthen. They stood to their work nobly; the emergency brought out all their strength to meet it.

One girl who had been working very hard helping the men on the sidewalks, and dressing wounds afterward in a close, hot room, told me that at one time the sights and smells (these last were fearful) so overcame her that she could only stagger to the staircase, where she hung, half conscious, over the banisters, saying to herself, "Oh, I hope if I faint some one will kick me into a corner and let me lie there!" She did not faint, but went back to her work in a few moments, and through the whole of what followed was one of the most indefatigable and useful. She was one of many; even children did their part.

It became a grave question how to feed so many unexpected guests. The news spread rapidly, and the people from the country neighborhoods came pouring in to help, expecting to stay with friends who had already given up every spare bed and every inch of room where beds could be put up. Virginia houses are very elastic, but ours were strained to their utmost. Fortunately some of the farmers' wives had been thoughtful enough to bring supplies of linen, and some bread and fruit, and when our wants became better known other contributions flowed in; but when all was done it was not enough.

We worked far into the night that Monday, went to bed late,

and rose early next morning. Tuesday brought fresh wagon-loads of wounded, and would have brought despair, except that they were accompanied by an apology for a commissariat. Soon more reliable sources of supply were organized among our country friends. Some doctors also arrived, who—with a few honorable exceptions—might as well have staid away. The remembrance of that worthless body of officials stirs me to wrath. Two or three worked conscientiously and hard, and they did all the medical work, except what was done by our own town physicians. In strong contrast was the conduct of the common men detailed as nurses. They were as gentle as they knew how to be, and very obliging and untiring. Of course they were uncouth and often rough, but with the wounded dying about us every day, and with the necessity that we were under for the first few days, of removing those who died at once that others not yet quite dead might take their places, there was no time to be fastidious; it required all our efforts to be simply decent, and we sometimes failed in that.

We fed our men as well as we could from every available source, and often had some difficulty in feeding ourselves. The townspeople were very hospitable, and we were invited here and there, but could not always go, or hesitated, knowing every house was full. I remember once, that having breakfasted upon a single roll and having worked hard among sickening details, about 4 o'clock I turned wolfishly ravenous and ran to a friend's house down the street. When I got there I was almost too faint to speak, but my friend looked at me and disappeared in silence, coming back in a moment with a plate of hot soup. What luxury! I sat down then and there on the front doorstep and devoured the soup as if I had been without food for a week.

It was known on Tuesday that Harper's Ferry had been taken, but it was growing evident that South Mountain had not been a victory. We had heard from some of our friends, but not from all, and what we did hear was often most unsatisfactory and tantalizing. For instance, we would be told that some one whom we loved had been seen standing with his battery, had left his gun an instant to shake hands and send a message, and had then stepped back to position, while our civilian informant had come away for safety, and the smoke of conflict had hidden battery and all from view. As night drew nearer, whispers of a great battle to be fought the next day grew louder, and we shuddered at the prospect, for battles had come to mean to us, as they never had before, blood, wounds, and death.

On the 17th of September cloudy skies looked down upon the two armies facing each other on the fields of Maryland. It seems to me now that the roar of that day began with the light, and all through its long and dragging hours its thunder formed a background to our pain and terror. If we had been in doubt as to our friends' whereabouts on Sunday, there was no room for doubt now. There was no sitting at the windows now and counting discharges of guns, or watching the curling smoke. We went about our work with pale faces and trembling hands, yet trying to appear composed for the sake of our patients, who were much excited. We could hear the incessant explosions of artillery, the shrieking whistles of the shells, and the sharper, deadlier, more thrilling roll of musketry; while every now and then the echo of some charging cheer would come, borne by the wind, and as the human voice pierced that demoniacal clangor we would catch our breath and listen, and try not to sob, and turn back to the forlorn hospitals, to the suffering at our feet and before our eyes, while imagination fainted at thought of those other scenes hidden from us beyond the Potomac.

On our side of the river there were noise, confusion, dust; throngs of stragglers; horsemen galloping about; wagons blocking each other, and teamsters wrangling; and a continued din of shouting, swearing, and rumbling, in the midst of which men were dying, fresh wounded arriving, surgeons amputating limbs and dressing wounds, women going in and out with bandages, lint, medicines, food. An ever-present sense of anguish, dread, pity, and, I fear, hatred—these are my recollections of Antietam.

When night came we could still hear the sullen guns and hoarse, indefinite murmurs that succeeded the day's turmoil. That night was dark and lowering and the air heavy and dull. Across the river innumerable camp-fires were blazing, and we could but too well imagine the scenes that they were lighting. We sat in silence, looking into each other's tired faces. There were no impatient words, few tears; only silence, and a drawing close together, as if for comfort. We were almost hopeless, yet clung with desperation to the thought that we were hoping. But in our hearts we could not believe that anything human could have escaped from that appalling fire. On Thursday the two armies lay idly facing each other, but we could not be idle. The wounded continued to arrive until the town was quite unable to hold all the disabled and suffering. They filled every building and overflowed into the country round, into farm-houses, barns, corn-cribs, cabins,—wherever four walls and a roof were found together. Those able to travel were sent on to Winchester and other towns back from the river, but their departure seemed to make no appreciable difference. There were six churches, and they were all full; the Odd Fellows' Hall, the Freemasons', the little Town Council room, the barn-like place known as the Drill Room, all the private houses after their capacity, the shops and empty buildings, the school-houses,— every inch of space, and yet the cry was for room.

The unfinished Town Hall had stood in naked ugliness for many a long day. Somebody threw a few rough boards across the beams, placed piles of straw over them, laid down single planks to walk upon, and lo, it was a hospital at once. The stone warehouses down in the ravine and by the river had been passed by, because low and damp and undesirable as sanitariums, but now their doors and windows were thrown wide, and, with barely time allowed to sweep them, they were all occupied,—even the "old blue factory," an antiquated, crazy, dismal building of blue stucco that peeled off in great blotches, which had been shut up for years, and was in the last stages of dilapidation.

On Thursday night we heard more than usual sounds of disturbance and movement, and in the morning we found the Confederate army in full retreat. General Lee crossed the Potomac under cover of the darkness, and when the day broke the greater part of his force—or the more orderly portion of it—had gone on toward Kearneysville and Leetown. General McClellan followed to the river, and without crossing got a battery in position on Douglas's Hill, and began to shell the retreating army and, in consequence, the town. What before was confusion grew worse; the retreat became a stampede. The battery may not have done a very great deal of execution, but it made a fearful noise. It is curious how much louder guns sound when they are pointed at you than when turned the other way! And the shell, with its long-drawn screeching, though no doubt less terrifying than the singing minie-ball, has a way of making one's hair stand on end. Then, too, every one who has had any experience in such things, knows how infectious fear is, how it grows when yielded to, and how, when you once begin to run, it soon seems impossible to run fast enough; whereas, if you can manage to stand your ground, the alarm lessens and sometimes disappears.

Some one suggested that yellow was the hospital color, and immediately everybody who could lay hands upon a yellow rag hoisted it over the house. The whole town was a hospital; there was scarcely a building that could not with truth seek protection under that plea, and the fantastic little strips were soon flaunting their ineffectual remonstrance from every roof-tree and chimney. When this specific failed the excitement became wild and ungovernable. It would have been ludicrous had it not produced so much suffering. The danger was less than it seemed, for McClellan, after all, was not bombarding the town, but the army, and most of the shells flew over us and exploded in the fields; but aim cannot be always sure, and enough shells fell short to convince the terrified citizens that their homes were about to be battered down over their ears. The better people kept some outward coolness, with perhaps a feeling of "*noblesse oblige*"; but the poorer classes acted as if the town were already in a blaze, and rushed from their houses with their families and household goods to make their way into the country. The road was thronged, the streets blocked; men were vociferating, women crying, children screaming; wagons, ambulances, guns, caissons, horsemen, footmen, all mingled— nay, even wedged and jammed together—in one struggling, shouting mass. The negroes were the worst, and with faces of a ghastly ash-color, and staring eyes, they swarmed into the fields, carrying their babies, their clothes, their pots and kettles, fleeing from the wrath behind them. The comparison to a hornet's nest attacked by boys is not a good one, for there was no "fight" shown; but a disturbed ant-hill is altogether inadequate. They fled widely and camped out of range, nor would they venture back for days.

Had this been all, we could afford to laugh now, but there was another side to the picture that lent it an intensely painful aspect. It was the hurrying crowds of wounded. Ah me! those maimed and bleeding fugitives! When the firing commenced the hospitals began to empty. All who were able to pull one foot after another, or could bribe or beg comrades to carry them, left in haste. In vain we implored them to stay; in vain we showed them the folly, the suicide, of the attempt; in vain we argued, cajoled, threatened, ridiculed; pointed out that we were remaining and that there was less danger here than on the road. There is no sense or reason in a panic. The cannon were bellowing upon Douglas's Hill, the shells whistling and shrieking, the air full of shouts and cries; we had to scream to make ourselves heard. The men replied that the "Yankees" were crossing; that the town was to be burned; that *we* could not be made prisoners, but they could; that, anyhow, they were going as far as they could walk, or be carried. And go they did. Men with cloths about their heads went hatless in the sun, men with cloths about their feet limped shoeless on the stony road; men with arms in slings, without arms, with one leg, with bandaged sides and backs; men in ambulances, wagons, carts, wheelbarrows, men carried on stretchers or supported on the shoulder of some self-denying comrade—all who could crawl went, and went to almost certain death. They could not go far, they dropped off into the country houses, where they were received with as much kindness as it was possible to ask for; but their wounds had become inflamed, their frames were weakened by fright and over-exertion: erysipelas, mortification, gangrene set in; and long rows of nameless graves still bear witness to the results.

Our hospitals did not remain empty. It was but a portion who could get off in any manner, and their places were soon taken by others, who had remained nearer the battle-field, had attempted to follow the retreat, but, having reached Shepherdstown, could go no farther. We had plenty to do, but all that day we went about with hearts bursting with rage and shame, and breaking with pity and grief for the needless, needless waste of life. The amateur nurses all stood firm, and managed to be cheerful for the sake of keeping their men quiet, but they could not be without fear. One who had no thought of leaving her post desired to send her sister—a mere child—out of harm's way. She, therefore, told her to go to their home, about half a mile distant, and ask their mother for some yellow cloth that was in the house, thinking, of course, that the mother would never permit the girl to come back into the town. But she miscalculated. The child accepted the commission as a sacred trust, forced her way out over the crowded road, where the danger was more real than in the town itself, reached home, and made her request. The house had its own flag flying, for it was directly in range and full of wounded. Perhaps for this reason the mother was less anxious to keep her daughter with her; perhaps in the hurry and excitement she allowed herself to be persuaded that it was really necessary to get that strip of yellow flannel into Shepherdstown as soon as possible. At all events, she made no difficulty, but with streaming tears kissed the girl, and saw her set out to go alone, half a mile through a panic-stricken rabble, under the fire of a battery and into a town whose escape from conflagration was at best not assured. To come out had been comparatively easy, for she was going with the stream. The return was a different matter. The turbulent tide had now to be stemmed. Yet she managed to work her way along, now in the road, now in the field, slipping between the wagon wheels, and once, at least, crawling under a stretcher. No one had noticed her coming out, she was but one of the crowd; and now most were too busy with their own safety to pay much heed to anything else. Still, as her face seemed alone set toward the town, she attracted some attention. One or two spoke to her. Now it was, "Look-a here, little gal! don't you know you're a-goin' the wrong way?" One man looked at the yellow thing she had slung across her shoulder and said, with an approving nod: "That's right, that's right; save the wounded if ye kin." She meant to do it, and finally reached her sister, breathless but triumphant, with as proud a sense of duty done as if her futile errand had been the deliverance of a city.

I have said that there was less danger than appeared, but it must not be supposed that there was none. A friend who worked chiefly in the old blue factory had asked me to bring her a bowl of gruel that some one had promised to make for one of her patients. I had just taken it to her, and she was walking across the floor with the bowl in her hands, when a shell crashed through a corner of the wall and passed out at the opposite end of the building, shaking the rookery to its foundations, filling the room with dust and plaster, and throwing her upon her knees to the floor. The wounded screamed, and had they not been entirely unable to move, not a man would have been left in the building. But it was found that no one was hurt, and things proceeded as before. I asked her afterward if she was frightened. She said yes, when it was over, but her chief thought at the time was to save the gruel, for the man needed it, and it had been very hard to find any one composed enough to make it. I am glad to be able to say that he got his gruel in spite of bombs. That factory was struck twice. A school-house, full of wounded, and one or two other buildings were hit, but I believe no serious damage was done.

On Saturday morning there was a fight at the ford. The negroes were still encamped in the fields, though some, finding that the town was yet standing, ventured back on various errands during the day. What we feared were the stragglers and hangers-on and nondescripts that circle round an army like the great buzzards we shuddered to see wheeling silently over us. The people were still excited, anticipating the Federal crossing and dreading a repetition of the bombardment or an encounter in the streets. Some parties of Confederate cavalry rode through, and it is possible that a body of infantry remained drawn up in readiness on one of the hills during the morning, but I remember no large force of troops at any time on that day.

About noon, or a little after, we were told that General McClellan's advance had been checked, and that it was not believed he would attempt to cross the river at once—a surmise that proved to be correct. The country grew more composed. General Lee lay near Leetown, some seven miles south of us, and General McClellan rested quietly in Maryland. On Sunday we were able to have some short church services for our wounded, cut still shorter, I regret to say, by reports that the "Yankees" were crossing. Such reports continued to harass us, especially as we feared the capture of our friends, who would often ride down to see us during the day, but who seldom ventured to spend a night so near the river. We presently passed into debatable land, when we were in the Confederacy in the morning, in the Union after dinner, and on neutral ground at night. We lived through a disturbed and eventful autumn, subject to continual "alarms and excursions," but when this Saturday came to an end, the most trying and tempestuous week of the war for Shepherdstown was over.

"OUR VICTORY WAS COMPLETE":
MARYLAND, SEPTEMBER 1862

George B. McClellan to Mary Ellen McClellan

General McClellan expresses to his wife his pride in repelling an enemy he believed greatly outnumbered him. In fact, he overcounted Lee's troops by a factor of three. The meeting of twelve Northern governors at Altoona, Pennsylvania, in late September that McClellan hoped would help rid him of Secretary Stanton and General Halleck had a quite different outcome: it came close to passing a resolution recommending his dismissal.

Sept 20 8 am. Camp near Sharpsburg
. . . Yesterday the enemy completed his evacuation of Maryland —completely beaten—we got many prisoners, muskets, colors, cannon etc—his loss in killed & wounded was very great—so was ours, unfortunately.

Genl Mansfield was killed (or rather died of his wounds)— Genls Sedgwick, Richardson, Dana, Brooks, Hooker, Weber, Rodman—& two others whose names I cannot recall were wounded on Wednesday. Poor Henry Kingsbury died of his wounds the day after the battle.

The battle lasted 14 hours & was without doubt the most severe ever fought on this continent, & few more desperate were ever fought anywhere.

9 am. . . . Am glad to say that I am much better today— for to tell you the truth I have been under the weather since the battle—the want of rest & anxiety brought on my old disease. The battle of Wednesday *was* a terrible one. I presume the loss will prove not less than 10,000 on each side. Our victory was complete & the disorganized rebel army has rapidly returned to Virginia—its dreams of "invading Penna" dissipated for ever. I feel some little pride in having with a beaten and demoralized army defeated Lee so utterly, & saved the North so completely. Well—one of these days history will I

trust do me justice in deciding that it was not my fault that the campaign of the Peninsula was not successful. An opportunity has presented itself through the Governors of some of the states to enable me to take my stand—I have insisted that Stanton shall be removed & that Halleck shall give way to me as Comdr in Chief. I will *not* serve under him—for he is an incompetent fool—in no way fit for the important place he holds. Since I left Washn Stanton has again asserted that *I* not *Pope* lost the battle of Manassas No 2! The only safety for the country & for me is to get rid of both of them—no success is possible with them. I am tired of fighting against such disadvantages & feel that it is now time for the country to come to my help, & remove these difficulties from my path. If my countrymen will not open their eyes & assert themselves they must pardon me if I decline longer to pursue the thankless avocation of serving them. . . .

Thank Heaven for one thing—my military reputation is cleared—I have shown that I can fight battles & *win* them! I think my enemies are pretty effectively killed by this time! May they remain so!!

September 20, 1862

BATTLE OF IUKA: MISSISSIPPI, SEPTEMBER 1862

Ephraim Anderson: from Memoirs: Historical and Personal

After a cautious monthlong advance from the Shiloh battlefield, Union forces occupied Corinth, Mississippi, on May 30, gaining control of a major rail junction. In the hot, dry summer that followed, the Union armies commanded by Ulysses S. Grant and William S. Rosecrans (who succeeded John Pope when Pope went east) occupied northern Mississippi and western Tennessee, repairing and guarding railroads against guerrillas and cavalry raids. Don Carlos Buell, meanwhile, began slowly advancing eastward toward Chattanooga. In September Braxton Bragg began his invasion of Kentucky and ordered Sterling Price, the Confederate commander in northern Mississippi, to prevent Rosecrans from reinforcing Buell. On September 19 Price and 14,000 Confederates fought 9,000 men under Rosecrans south of Iuka, Mississippi, while another Union force under Edward O. C. Ord approached the town from the west. The battle ended on September 20 when Price retreated after losing 1,516 men killed, wounded, or missing; Union losses totaled 782. Corporal Ephraim Anderson of the Confederate 2nd Missouri Infantry recalled the battle in his 1868 memoir.

OUR BRIGADE was soon drawn up about two hundred yards in the rear of the line engaged; our regiment had several men wounded while forming, when we laid down, expecting every moment that our line in front, which had been engaged for some time, and was now fighting almost muzzle to muzzle, would in all probability be overwhelmed by superior numbers, and we would then confront the enemy's lines.

The sun, like a molten ball of fire, hung just above the horizon, and was falling slowly behind a faint streak of crimson clouds low in the west. The fighting on our part was up a gentle slope of thickly timbered land, and extended on into an old field in front, upon the most of which a dense growth of blackjack had sprung up, from seven to fifteen feet high. In the cleared ground upon this field a battery had been charged and taken by our troops at the very muzzles of the pieces; but the infantry gave back step by step, stubbornly clinging to the cover of the bushes, and only leaving their pieces behind after the most desperate struggle to save them.

There was no intermission in the fierceness of the combat until after dark: the Third Louisiana and Third Texas, dismounted cavalry, armed with double-barreled shot-guns, and using buck-shot at close range, assisted by the Seventeenth Arkansas and another regiment, also, I believe, from Arkansas, pressed steadily on and drove the enemy slowly before them. When the fighting ceased for the night, our lines were over two hundred yards in advance of the position occupied by the captured battery, and all the ground that had been fought over was in our possession.

A little after dark our brigade was ordered to the front, to relieve the command that had been fighting: as we advanced up the road we met several detachments rolling down the Federal artillery; among those engaged in this service were some of our acquaintances of the Texas company that had assisted us on provost duty; their regiment had charged in front of the battery and was badly cut to pieces.

The artillery captured was of the best, as fine as is ever found upon the field; the pieces were entirely new and had never been in action before: it was the Tenth Ohio battery from Cincinnati, containing ten guns, and was supported by a division of Ohio troops.

Proceeding to the front, upon the ground where the hardest fighting had been done, the brigade formed, and our company was thrown out at a short distance as pickets and skirmishers, covering the line of the regiment. One of our detachment stepped accidentally upon a wounded soldier, who was lying upon the ground and spoke out—"Don't tread on me." He was asked, "What regiment do you belong to?"

"The Thirty-ninth Ohio."

"How many men has Rosecrans here?"

"Near forty-five thousand."

A little Irishman of our party curtly observed, "Our sixty-five thousand are enough for them."

The moon was nearly full, and threw a strong light upon the pale and ghastly faces of the thickly strewn corpses, while it glanced and sparkled upon the polished gun-barrels and bright sword bayonets of the enemy's guns, which lay scattered around. Everything bore evidence of the bloody character of the action. The dead were so thick, that one could very readily have stepped about upon them, and the bushes were so lapped and twisted together—so tangled up and broken down in every conceivable manner, that the desperate nature of the struggle was unmistakable.

The carnage around the battery was terrible. I do not think a single horse escaped, and most of the men must have shared the same fate. One of the caissons was turned upside down, having fallen back upon a couple of the horses, one of which lay wounded and struggling under it; and immediately behind was a pile of not less than fifteen men, who had been killed and wounded while sheltering themselves there. They were all Federals, and most of them artillery-men. Some of the limbers were standing with one wheel in the air, and strewn thickly around all were the bloody corpses of the dead, while the badly wounded lay weltering in gore. I have been on many battle-fields, but never witnessed so small a space comprise as many dead as were lying immediately around this battery.

That night is well remembered as one marked by many conflicting emotions. Though already much hardened to the rough usages of war and the fearful events which inevitably accompany it—though somewhat accustomed to look upon the faces of the dead and fields of carnage as certain and natural results, yet the groans and cries of the wounded for help and water, the floundering of crippled horses in harness, and the calls of the infirmary corps, as it passed to and fro with litters in search of and bearing off the wounded, rendered the scene very gloomy, sad and impressive. As the night wind rose and fell, swelling with louder, wilder note, or sinking into a gentle, wailing breath, it seemed an invocation from the ghosts of the dead, and a requiem to the departing spirits of the dying.

There were few grey-coats among the dead around, and I gazed upon the blue ones with the feeling that they had come from afar and taken much pains to meet such a fate. It was but little akin to compassion, for war hardens men—especially when their country, their homes and firesides are invaded and laid waste.

Only a few feet from me a groan escaped the lips of a dying man, and I stepped to his side to offer the slight relief that my situation could afford. He was lying almost upon his face, with a thick covering of the bruised bushes twisted over him. Putting them aside, I spoke to him, and turned him in a more comfortable position. He was unable to speak, but looked as though he wanted something, and I placed my canteen to his lips, from which he eagerly drank. After this an effort to speak was made: he could only murmur something inarticulate and unintelligible, and at the same time a look of intense gratitude spread over his countenance. He was a Federal officer, as was easily perceived from his sword, dress and shoulder-straps. Some of the infirmary corps soon passed, and I asked them if they had any brandy or could do anything for him. Their answer was that he was too far gone to lose time with, and their brandy had given out. A few minutes after, he died.

A wounded soldier some distance off, hallooed at intervals until after midnight, repeatedly calling, "Caldwell guards!"—the name of his company, which belonged to the Third Louisiana. The regiment had gone to the rear. I could not leave my post to go to his assistance, and his cries ceased after midnight. Whether he received attention in time or died unnoticed where he had fallen, I never knew.

From our picket lines to those of the Federals it was not more than seventy yards, and at some points even nearer. One of our company unguardedly struck a match to light his pipe, when several shots were immediately fired at him without effect. This was the only firing through the night, and the blaze from the enemy's guns was but a little distance in the brush beyond us.

It seemed certain that a general engagement would take place on the morrow, and our brigade would occupy the post of honor—the front of the line. Though the enemy had a decided advantage in point of numbers, yet our troops were in admirable condition and their spirit was buoyant, fearless, and in every way promising. We were not, however, destined to fight the next morning, and, as the shades of night began to break into faint streaks of approaching day, we were withdrawn slowly from the field.

"THE CAUSE OF EMANCIPATION":
WASHINGTON, D.C., SEPTEMBER 1862

Gideon Welles: Diary, September 22, 1862

Appraising the outcome at Antietam as victory enough for his purposes, Lincoln called together his cabinet to announce he was making the proclamation of emancipation public. Secretary Chase noted in his journal that the President opened the momentous occasion by reading a chapter from humorist Artemus Ward's new book, "and seemed to enjoy it very much—the Heads also (except Stanton) of course. . . . The President then took a graver tone. . . ."

September 22. *Monday* A special Cabinet meeting. The subject was the Proclamation for emancipating the slaves after a certain date, in States that should be in rebellion. For several weeks the subject has been suspended, but never lost sight of. When it was submitted, and in taking up the Proclamation, the President stated that the question was finally decided, the act and the consequences were his, but that he felt it due to us to make us acquainted with the fact and to invite criticism on the paper which he had prepared. There were, he had found, some differences in the Cabinet, but he had, after consulting each and all, individually and collectively, formed his own conclusions and made his own decision. In the course of the discussion which was long, earnest, and on the general principle involved, harmonious, he remarked that he had made a vow, a covenant, that if God gave us the victory in the approaching battle, he would consider it an indication of Divine will, and that it was his duty to move forward in the cause of emancipation. It might be thought strange, he said, that he had in this way submitted the disposal of matters—when the way was not clear to his mind what he should do. God had decided this question in favor of the slaves. He was satisfied it was right, was confirmed and strengthened in his action by the vow and the results. His mind was fixed, his decision made, but he wished his paper announcing his course as correct in terms as it could be made without any change in his determination.

He read the document. One or two unimportant emendations suggested by Seward were approved. It was handed to the Secretary of State to publish to-morrow. After this, Blair remarked that he did not concur in the expediency of the measure at this time, though he approved of the principle, and should therefore wish to file his objections. He stated at some length his views, which were that we ought not to put in greater jeopardy the patriotic element in the Border States, that the results of this Proclamation would be to carry over those States *en masse* to the Secessionists as soon as it was read, and that there was a class of partisans in the Free States endeavoring to revive old parties, who would have a club put into their hands of which they would avail themselves to beat the Administration.

The President said he had considered the danger to be apprehended from the first objection, which was undoubtedly serious, but the objection was certainly as great not to act; as regarded the last, it had not much weight with him. The question of power, authority in the Government was not much discussed at this meeting, but had been canvassed individually by the President in private conversation with the members. Some thought legislation advisable but Congress was clothed with no authority on this subject, nor is the Executive, except under the war power,—military necessity, martial law, when there can be no legislation. This was the view which I took when the President first presented the subject to Seward and myself as we were returning from the funeral of Stanton's child, which we attended—two or three miles beyond Georgetown. Seward was at that time not at all communicative, and I think not willing to advise the movement. It is momentous both in its immediate and remote results, and an exercise of extraordinary power, which cannot be justified on mere humanitarian principles, and would never have been attempted but to preserve the national existence. These were my convictions and this the drift of the discussion.

The effect which the Proclamation will have on the public mind is a matter of some uncertainty. In some respects, it would, I think have been better to have issued it when formerly considered. There is an impression that Seward has opposed and is opposed to the measure. I have not been without that impression chiefly from his hesitation to commit himself, and perhaps because action was suspended but in the final discussion he has as cordially supported the measure as Chase.

For myself the subject has, from its magnitude and its consequences oppressed me, aside from the ethical features of the question. It is a step in the progress of this war which will extend into the distant future. The termination of this terrible conflict seems more remote with every movement, and unless the Rebels hasten to avail themselves of the alternative presented, of which I see little probability, the war can scarcely be other than one of subjugation. There is in the Free States a very general impression that this measure will insure a speedy peace. I cannot say that I so view it. No one in those States dare advocate peace as a means of prolonging slavery if it is his honest opinion, and the pecuniary, industrial and social sacrifice impending will intensify the struggle before us. While however these dark clouds are above and around us, I cannot see how the subject could be avoided. Perhaps it is not desirable it should be.

WASHINGTON, D.C., SEPTEMBER 1862

Abraham Lincoln: Preliminary Emancipation Proclamation; Proclamation Suspending the Writ of Habeas Corpus

While incorporating provisions of the Second Confiscation Act, the Emancipation Proclamation was drawn primarily on the president's war powers, which Lincoln interpreted as not authorizing him to free slaves in loyal states. Thus the proclamation applied only to those states in rebellion, where the Union armies had to be depended upon to free the slaves. The proclamation suspending the writ of habeas corpus nationwide was occasioned in part by resistance to the militia draft instituted in the summer of 1862 to help fill state militia regiments called up for nine months' service. Both proclamations were denounced as unconstitutional exercises of executive power by anti-administration Democrats in the fall elections.

September 22, 1862

By the President of the
United States of America
A Proclamation.

I, Abraham Lincoln, President of the United States of America, and Commander-in-chief of the Army and Navy thereof, do hereby proclaim and declare that hereafter, as heretofore, the war will be prossecuted for the object of practically restoring the constitutional relation between the United States, and each of the states, and the people thereof, in which states that relation is, or may be suspended, or disturbed.

That it is my purpose, upon the next meeting of Congress to again recommend the adoption of a practical measure tendering pecuniary aid to the free acceptance or rejection of all slave-states, so called, the people whereof may not then be in rebellion against the United States, and which states, may then have voluntarily adopted, or thereafter may voluntarily adopt, immediate, or gradual abolishment of slavery within their respective limits; and that the effort to colonize persons of African descent, with their consent, upon this continent, or elsewhere, with the previously obtained consent of the Governments existing there, will be continued.

That on the first day of January in the year of our Lord, one thousand eight hundred and sixty-three, all persons held as slaves within any state, or designated part of a state, the people whereof shall then be in rebellion against the United States shall be then, thenceforward, and forever free; and the executive government of the United States, including the military and naval authority thereof, will recognize and maintain the freedom of such persons, and will do no act or acts to repress such persons, or any of them, in any efforts they may make for their actual freedom.

That the executive will, on the first day of January aforesaid, by proclamation, designate the States, and parts of states, if any, in which the people thereof respectively, shall then be in rebellion against the United States; and the fact that any state, or the people thereof shall, on that day be, in good faith represented in the Congress of the United States, by members chosen thereto, at elections wherein a majority of the qualified voters of such state shall have participated, shall, in the absence of strong countervailing testimony, be deemed conclusive evidence that such state and the people thereof, are not then in rebellion against the United States.

That attention is hereby called to an act of Congress entitled "An act to make an additional Article of War" approved March 13, 1862, and which act is in the words and figure following:

Be it enacted by the Senate and House of Representatives of the United States of America in Congress assembled, That hereafter the following shall be promulgated as an additional article of war for the government of the army of the United States, and shall be obeyed and observed as such:

Article—. All officers or persons in the military or naval service of the United States are prohibited from employing any of the forces under their respective commands for the purpose of returning fugitives from service or labor, who may have escaped from any persons to whom such service or labor is claimed to be due, and any officer who shall be found guilty by a court-martial of violating this article shall be dismissed from the service.

Sec. 2. *And be it further enacted,* That this act shall take effect from and after its passage.

Also to the ninth and tenth sections of an act entitled "An Act to suppress Insurrection, to punish Treason and Rebellion, to seize and confiscate property of rebels, and for other purposes," approved July 17, 1862, and which sections are in the words and figures following:

Sec. 9. *And be it further enacted,* That all slaves of persons who shall hereafter be engaged in rebellion against the government of the United States, or who shall in any way give aid or comfort thereto, escaping from such persons and taking refuge within the lines of the army; and all slaves captured from such persons or deserted by them and coming under the control of the government of the United States; and all slaves of such persons found *on* (or) being within any place occupied by rebel forces and afterwards occupied by the forces of the United States, shall be deemed captives of war, and shall be forever free of their servitude and not again held as slaves.

Sec. 10. *And be it further enacted,* That no slave escaping into any State, Territory, or the District of Columbia, from any other State, shall be delivered up, or in any way impeded or hindered of his liberty, except for crime, or some offence against the laws, unless the person claiming said fugitive shall first make oath that the person to whom the labor or service of such fugitive is alleged to be due is his lawful owner, and has not borne arms against the United States in the present rebellion, nor in any way given aid and comfort thereto; and no person engaged in the military or naval service of the United States shall, under any pretence whatever, assume to decide on the validity of the claim of any person to the service or labor of any other person, or surrender up any such person to the claimant, on pain of being dismissed from the service.

And I do hereby enjoin upon and order all persons engaged in the military and naval service of the United States to observe, obey, and enforce, within their respective spheres of service, the act, and sections above recited.

And the executive will in due time recommend that all citizens of the United States who shall have remained loyal thereto throughout the rebellion, shall (upon the restoration of the constitutional relation between the United States, and their respective states, and people, if that relation shall have been suspended or disturbed) be compensated for all losses by acts of the United States, including the loss of slaves.

In witness whereof, I have hereunto set my hand, and caused the seal of the United States to be affixed.

Done at the City of Washington, this twenty second day of September, in the year of our Lord, one thousand eight hundred and sixty two, and of the Independence of the United States, the eighty seventh.

By the President: ABRAHAM LINCOLN
WILLIAM H. SEWARD, Secretary of State.

September 24 1862

By the President of the United States of America:
A Proclamation.

Whereas, it has become necessary to call into service not only volunteers but also portions of the militia of the States by draft in order to suppress the insurrection existing in the United States, and disloyal persons are not adequately restrained by the ordinary processes of law from hindering this measure and from giving aid and comfort in various ways to the insurrection;

Now, therefore, be it ordered, first, that during the existing insurrection and as a necessary measure for suppressing the same, all Rebels and Insurgents, their aiders and abettors within the United States, and all persons discouraging volunteer enlistments, resisting militia drafts, or guilty of any disloyal practice, affording aid and comfort to Rebels against the authority of the United States, shall be subject to martial law and liable to trial and punishment by Courts Martial or Military Commission:

Second. That the Writ of Habeas Corpus is suspended in respect to all persons arrested, or who are now, or hereafter during the rebellion shall be, imprisoned in any fort, camp, arsenal, military prison, or other place of confinement by any military authority or by the sentence of any Court Martial or Military Commission.

In witness whereof, I have hereunto set my hand, and caused the seal of the United States to be affixed.

Done at the City of Washington this twenty fourth day of September, in the year of our Lord one thousand eight hundred and sixty-two, and of the Independence of the United States the 87th.

By the President: ABRAHAM LINCOLN.
WILLIAM H. SEWARD, Secretary of State.

"THE AIR IS THICK WITH REVOLUTION":
WASHINGTON, D.C., SEPTEMBER 1862

L. A. Whitely to James Gordon Bennett

Whitely was chief Washington correspondent for editor Bennett's *New York Herald*, the nation's largest newspaper, and he, like other reporters (and not a few generals), hastened to evaluate reactions to the President's emancipation decree in the highly politicized Army of the Potomac. The army was in the field, in Maryland, and Whitely wondered if its officers felt the same as the ones he spoke to in the capital.

Confidential

Washington Sep 24" 1862

My dear Sir

A deep and earnest feeling pervades the army, if we are to judge from the Generals, Colonels, Captains and Lieutenants who are here, in reference to the recent proclamation of the President. The army is dissatisfied and the air is thick with revolution. It has been not only thought of but talked of and the question now is where can the man be found. McClellan is idolised but he seems to have no political ambition. The sentiment throughout the whole army seems to be in favor of a change of dynasty. They are unwilling to submit to the control of the faction which has attempted to direct the Government and whose policy is enunciated in the recent proclamation. They demur to this policy and claim that as they are fighting the battles, risking their lives and limbs and really stand as the conservators of all there is in the Government they have a right to dictate its policy. God knows what will be the consequence but at present matters look dark indeed, and there is large promise of a fearful revolution which will sweep before it not only the administration but popular government. As I telegraphed you in one of my despatches, Kentuckians here approve the President's Proclamation. They say that sooner or later it will have to come and I have been strongly importuned by such men as Cassius M. Clay to give, at once, an earnest and hearty support to the policy thus enunciated. I have no doubt that the result will be as Abolitionists desire: Slavery is already practically abolished but the Proclamation is a different affair and if it should not be received more kindly by other Officers of the Army than those whom I have seen it will go far towards producing an expression on the part of the Army that will startle the Country and give us a Military Dictator.

I send this information only as the result of my observations during the last twenty four hours in order that you may know what is to be the condition of affairs here if the expression from the Army of McClellan corresponds to that of the position of the army around Washington. There may be a change in the Government and in the form of Government within a very few days. Your article of a few days ago suggesting that McClellan should dictate to the administration was regarded then as revolutionary, but I have heard a hundred of the same men, who then found fault with it, express today the same opinion.

Very Respectfully
L.A. Whitely

"SERVILE WAR" AND "DESPOTISM":
MARYLAND, SEPTEMBER 1862

George B. McClellan to William H. Aspinwall

Correspondent Whitely thought General McClellan not political enough to consider taking a public stance against the two proclamations, but this letter of McClellan's to one of his home front supporters, New York businessman and prominent Democrat William H. Aspinwall, suggests otherwise.

                      Head-Quarters Army of the Potomac,
                      Sharpsburg Sept 26, 1862

My dear Sir

    I am very anxious to know how you and men like you regard the recent Proclamations of the Presdt inaugurating servile war, emancipating the slaves, & at one stroke of the pen changing our free institutions into a despotism—for such I regard as the natural effect of the last Proclamation suspending the Habeas Corpus throughout the land.

    I shall probably be in this vicinity for some days &, if you regard the matter as gravely as I do, would be glad to communicate with you.

                              In haste I am sincerely yours
                              Geo B McClellan

Wm H Aspinwall esq
New York City

"THAT IS NOT THE GAME":
WASHINGTON, D.C., SEPTEMBER 1862

Abraham Lincoln: Record of Dismissal of John J. Key

In this time of alarming unrest in the Army of the Potomac, Lincoln was told of an allegedly treasonable remark by Major John J. Key, of the War Department staff, and he determined to act on it. The President carefully wrote out this record of the case. Afterward, when Key appealed his dismissal, Lincoln refused to restore him to duty, explaining: "I had been brought to fear that there was a class of officers in the army, not very inconsiderable in numbers, who were playing a game to not beat the enemy when they could. . . . I dismissed you as an example and a warning to that supposed class."

September 26–27, 1862
We have reason to believe that the following is an exact copy of the record upon which Major John J. Key was dismissed from the military service of the United States.

Executive Mansion
Major John J. Key   Washington, Sept. 26. 1862.
   Sir: I am informed that in answer to the question "Why was not the rebel army bagged immediately after the battle near Sharpsburg?" propounded to you by Major Levi C. Turner, Judge Advocate &c. you answered "That is not the game" "The object is that neither army shall get much advantage of the other; that both shall be kept in the field till they are exhausted, when we will make a compromise and save slavery."

   I shall be very happy if you will, within twentyfour hours from the receipt of this, prove to me by Major Turner, that you did not, either litterally, or in substance, make the answer stated. Yours,

A. LINCOLN

(Indorsed as follows)
"Copy delivered to Major Key at 10.25 A.M. September 27th. 1862.

JOHN HAY."

At about 11 o'clock, A.M. Sept. 27. 1862, Major Key and Major Turner appear before me. Major Turner says: "As I remember it, the conversation was, I asked the question why we did not bag them after the battle at Sharpsburg? Major Key's reply was that was not the game, that we should tire the rebels out, and ourselves, that that was the only way the Union could be preserved, we come together fraternally, and slavery be saved"

On cross-examination, Major Turner says he has frequently heard Major Key converse in regard to the present troubles, and never heard him utter a sentiment unfavorable to the maintainance of the Union. He has never uttered anything which he Major T. would call disloyalty. The particular conversation detailed was a private one   A. LINCOLN.
(Indorsed on the above)
In my view it is wholly inadmissable for any gentleman holding a military commission from the United States to utter such sentiments as Major Key is within proved to have done. Therefore let Major John J. Key be forthwith dismissed from the Military service of the United States.   A. LINCOLN.

The foregoing is the whole record, except the simple order of dismissal at the War Department. At the interview of Major Key and Major Turner with the President, Major Key did not attempt to controvert the statement of Major Turner; but simply insisted, and sought to prove, that he was true to the Union. The substance of the President's reply was that if there was a "game" ever among Union men, to have our army not take an advantage of the enemy when it could, it was his object to break up that game.

"PROCLAMATIONS OF A POLITICAL COWARD":
MARYLAND, SEPTEMBER 1862

Fitz John Porter to Manton Marble

General Porter, acting as McClellan's confidant and spokesman, corresponded regularly with *New York World* editor Manton Marble, whose paper was a major Democratic anti-administration voice. Here Porter explains why there was no follow-up to the Antietam battle (falling back on the myth of being outnumbered), and projects his view of the Emancipation Proclamation as the army's view.

(*Excuse brevity* and conciseness)
September 30" '62
My dear friend,
My frequent change of location, together with the irregularity of the mails which I believe are made up in Washington, have deprived me of the pleasures always received for the perusal of your sheets—and kept me in darkness for the past month. I see however from quotations in the Clipper and Phil. Enquirer (the only ones which have reached this benighted region) that you still hammer away at the good cause, relying I presume upon the old simile that the continued dripping of water will wear away stone. But don't you suppose that some of the late orders fulminated at the War Department are aimed at such as you, and fear that some dark morning you will find yourself in Lafayette for being guilty of disloyal practices, of which some ignorant constable is the judge?

I have been expecting daily to hear that the "World" has been upset and eclipsed and no longer permitted to reflect the light of the sun and enlighten the darkened masses of abolitionists, secessionists and other enemies of their country. But you have been spared, no doubt for a good purpose.

You have no doubt been much gratified at our successes, and the rise once more of Genl McClellan. He appreciates the services of the World and the kind sympathy it has extended to him in times of darkness. You have no doubt also been anxious for a continued advance and pursuit of the enemy—and as the radicals say, smite him. T'is easier said than done, but as there *seems* to be a misunderstanding of matters here I will give you (though perhaps unnecessary) our status and the reasons therefor.

First—What was one of the first causes of the rebels having been whipped in Maryland. Because they passed the Potomac and got so far from his base of supplies that starvation had accomplished half the victory.

When he recrossed the Potomac, so difficult was it for us to go and form sufficient head on the opposite bank (having difficult and narrow fords) that he stopped just beyond reach of our guns and yet so close that he could rush upon and annihilate any force before it was half over just as was done at Ball's Bluff, while the other half could render no assistance.

Again we could get insufficient supplies over the river from Frederick and Hagerstown to sustain this army, and of course we would be committing the same blunder as they did, and in two days be half whipped while they, getting nearer their base, would be growing stronger.

They selected a beautiful position behind the Opequon, every foot of which was well swept by them, and every bridge over which was destroyed.

The bridge at Harpers Ferry is not completed and will not be for five or six days. Until then the rail road will be of no use to our one half the army this side of Frederick. When that is completed you may expect a resumption of operations. It will enable supplies to be thrown to Charlestown & towards Martinsburg. But the enemy will not then be at Winchester, or will not be there long. He will try to draw us on. Knowing we would not operate till the R.R. bridge is complete, he leisurely halted at Martinsburg, permitted all his trains to get behind him towards Winchester and has moved off himself in time not to permit us to strike him so soon. Had we crossed in full force at Harpers Ferry or Shepherdstown ford, we would have had to leave Wmport unguarded and Hagerstown and he would have walked into that depot with considerable gusto, and into the B & O. rail road, which is now safe—also the canal.

Now for another material reason. This army is (or was not) in a condition to renew the contest. On Wednesday the 17th Inst. General Sumner who has ever been one of the most anxious to fight declared "his command demoralized and scattered—that he could not risk another attack—but if Genl McClellan was willing to risk a total defeat if he failed, he would advance." So much alarmed was he for his portion of the line, that over one third of my little force (6500) was sent to support him. On Thursday he was opposed to a renewal of the attack and so I believe were other officers. Our artillery ammunition was nearly expended and was not renewed till Friday. A large portion of this army was composed of recruits—new regiments, and Wednesdays fighting had proved they could not be relied upon—and that the loss of General officers and others on whom the troops looked to lead them, had caused want of confidence.

He had then lost about 10000 men in killed and wounded and some 10000 in stragglers. We were much less than the acknowledged strength of the enemy. The battles though apparently easily gained in the first instance were not so, and made many of the troops very cautious, and *slow*, in some cases culpably slow. We are now doing all we can to recover our losses and establish discipline and good drill. One week will do much, but we must re-organize. We must have some good officers—new general officers for those disabled—and confidence must be restored. We want troops to fill up the ranks of our small old regiments. The Governors give us none, and the government has sent no new regiments to us. A promise of 20 new regts is given. How long will it be before fulfilled. Long enough to cause delay and the delay attributed to Genl McClellan.

The fact that no one but political aspirants, and those strongly favoring the party of the administration, can attain favor is producing its effect. The proclamation was ridiculed in the army—caused disgust, discontent, and expressions of disloyalty to the views of the administration, and amounting I have heard, to insubordination. And for this reason. All such bulletins tend only to prolong the war by rousing the bitter feelings of the South—and causing unity of action among them—while the reverse with us. Those who have to fight the battles of the country are tired of the war and wish to see it ended and honorably, by a restoration of the Union. Not merely a suppression of the rebellion—for there is a wide difference, though the President would fain make us think by his working for a "suppression of the rebellion" that they are one & the same. How is this rebellion to be put down except by hard fighting, and who is to do it. We—and who are the sufferers. Look at the number of high officers wounded & killed in the late battles. Without their individual efforts no success would have been attained. As soon as they fell fighting ceased. The army rested on its arms. So it has been in every battle. Every officer of standing and worth must expose himself to an unprecedented degree—without he does so, nothing is accomplished. If he is wounded, all fall with him. He strives to end the contest & finds politicians working to prolong it. All his efforts, all his dangers, are useless. His labor is upset by the absurd proclamation of a political coward, who has not the manliness to sustain opinions expressed but a few days before, and can unblushingly see published side by side, his proclamation and his reasons for not issuing it. What a ruler for us to admire! Yet he holds in his hands the lives of thousands and trifles with them. Surely every father, mother, brother, sister, and friend at home should remember this and when an Election comes exert themselves to hurl such s_____ls from power and restore their relatives to their places. I believe God in his own particular way will punish these wicked rulers and abettors and bring peace to our country in due time. I believe you have full faith in Genl Halleck. I have never known a hypocrite to succeed—nor one who worked for his own ends alone—nor one who professed strong friendship and acted the Enemy—who played the part of Iago. Nor will Halleck. I told you long since he would fall. I expected it earlier, because I expected Stanton to fall, both for the same reason—they deserved it—both have brought all our disasters upon us, in Virginia & Kentucky, and soon I expect to hear of another—that is the crushing of a force which I fear they will throw towards Manassas to interrupt the retreat of the enemy from Winchester. A force they will throw there in the hope the leader will be successful and become prominent over McClellan. I fear they will do this and take from Washington good defensive forces and put in the field to oppose veterans, a raw army—undisciplined, not drilled—and ignorant of their officers and of themselves. If that is done, Lee will suddenly turn his back upon us, as Joe Johnston did on Patterson, and rush to Manassas to wipe out the pride of the north. There will we be—like Patterson—unable to follow, too far to move around by Washington, and accused of treachery to cover the want of skill of those in authority. We suffered once for the mismanagement of Pope and the following such councils as his and Hallecks, and the country was near ruin. Are we to be so again? Watch the movements.

I hope for peace, but I do not see it in the course of the administration or of its supporters the radical elements at the north. I see but one course to "suppress this rebellion and restore the Union." Military matters must be left to the control of him who knows his business and been tried, and politics must not enter therein. We must overcome the armies opposed to us. In doing that we crush or destroy the military, and many of the political, leaders who keep alive the rebellion. We must scatter and break the army, and let the constituent elements (now tired of the war) return to their homes, where by a consistent just and firm policy we can soon make them through the ballot box, express their opinions and assume their rights. We must occupy their seaport towns & cities and by the blockade make them suffer. Hold their cities and counties by military power compel the inhabitants to defray all expenses of the civil functionaries placed over them to execute their own laws as far as applicable and show by a conservative reign, that there is no intention to oppress. In this way I believe the opinion of the people will be softened, the poor enlightened and a new reign established, and before summer returns, peace reign over all the country. But on our part—the part of those at the North—must be done. The monied men, the capitalists (the power now behind the throne) must declare their policy, their demands & they must be a conservative political policy—a military General-in-Chief who is honest and in whom they have confidence—exclusion of politics from the military sphere—support by continued reinforcements when the General-in-Chief shall want them—Energetic prosecution of the task assigned to each commander, and the removal of such men as Mitchell & Butler. In this way the army will penetrate farther into the interior, and one object of the Radicals (professed?) the extinction of slavery more effectually accomplished, for where the army goes slavery disappears. Such men as Stanton Chase and Halleck must be got rid of, and such conservative men—honest and energetic in the prosecution of the war—as Dix & Banks substituted. They can be found.

To day, October 3d I have seen many troops under arms—mine I have been watching and working at for a time, yet I see gross deficiencies. Troops anxious to be instructed are commanded by ignorant men, who have seen no service, and in some cases whole regiments have not one officer who has seen service, because Secretary Stanton published an order that no volunteer would be permitted to leave the Army of the Potomac to assume positions more elevated in the new regiments. At that time the officers would have made many friends for Genl McClellan and proclaimed opinions prejudicial to the Sec of War. Jealousy prevented the promotion of meritorious men, and now the country should thank him for inefficient regiments and inefficient officers. Regiments which have been in service months are as green in all their duties and more innocent of their drill than regiments under experienced officers of three weeks standing. Did Sec Stanton wish an effective army? Did he, and does he, wish to put down this rebellion at an early day, or is he combined with the radical members of the north to prolong it. I should be very loth to go into action with such troops, but if advance now is the order, go I will and we will do our best. I feel we shall be victorious but it will be at great loss. But two weeks will make a wonderful difference. Why dont our governors encourage the filling up the old regiments. The men are discouraged. They get no increase. Every battle reduces their numbers and the men think the next one will be their last. They would not feel so if the regiments were full. They would feel too more could be accomplished. They say the Governors are raising their power to the injury of these men, and when the chance offers they will make the powers that be suffer. There are many causes working in the army to break down the power and influence of the ruling authorities in states. No wonder the radicals wish not for peace. They read the handwriting on the wall and know they are doomed.

The R R bridge over the Potomac is completed. I know not what will be done immediately—if anything. I hope however ere long we can move & will move and that the rebels will be compelled to go south of Richmond, and we be there. A combined movement all over the country by land & sea will crush the rebellion—but it must be done under McClellan's mind—not the present chief—and I think t'will be well done if directed by him. I would like to see Banks in the War Dept, to work with Genl. McC. He is firm, thoughtful, energetic, pure and honest—a patriot. I intended to have given you some interesting items of Popes campaign (or as he declares, the campaign of President & Halleck) but I've been too prolix now. T'will take a week to read this. So good by till you hear of a defeat off yonder or a victory here.

The course of the administration is shaking some of the officers. Sumner has asked for a leave of absence, and is inclined to resign. He is getting old, has been promised command of a department, but does not get it—while such as Mitchell, Curtis & Butler do. Hooker is working for promotion to the General-in-Chief and will turn a somerset to get it. He will soon gone north, or will go. Watch him. He has been a professed friend of Genl McC. He will say what the radicals will state is against McC. or draw inferences which discredit. He is ambitious & unscrupulous. The President is here. His visits have been always followed by injury, so look out. Another proclamation or War Order. Good by till next year—The enemy have only a few men in front of us, and stretch with 8000 men (cvly) from Bunker Hill through Stevensons Station to Berry's.

A CONFEDERATE INVASION:
KENTUCKY, SEPTEMBER 1862

Braxton Bragg:
To the People of the Northwest

In the western theater two Confederate armies, under Edmund Kirby Smith and Braxton Bragg, invaded Kentucky in August. Bragg issued this proclamation four days after occupying Bardstown, thirty miles south of Louisville. He had twin hopes for his proclamation—to split off the northwestern states from the Union through economic arguments; and to rouse Democratic voters in the midterm elections. "A plain, unvarnished argument based on their interests I presumed would have the most effect," Bragg explained to President Davis. But Bragg would find little support and few recruits in the Bluegrass State. "Enthusiasm runs high," he told Davis, "but exhausts itself in words."

HEADQUARTERS C. S. ARMY IN KENTUCKY,
Bardstown, Ky., September 26, 1862.

To the PEOPLE OF THE NORTHWEST:

On approaching your borders at the head of a Confederate army, it is proper to announce to you the motives and the purposes of my presence. I therefore make known to you—

First. That the Confederate Government is waging this war solely for self-defense; that it has no designs of conquest, nor any other purpose than to secure peace and the abandonment by the United States of its pretensions to govern a people who never have been their subjects, and who prefer self-government to a union with them.

Second. That the Confederate Government and people, deprecating civil strife from the beginning and anxious for a peaceful adjustment of all difference growing out of a political separation which they deemed essential to their happiness and well-being, at the moment of its inauguration sent commissioners to Washington to treat for these objects, but that their commissioners were not received or even allowed to communicate the object of their mission; and that on a subsequent occasion a communication from the President of the Confederate States to President Lincoln remained without answer, although a reply was promised by General Scott, into whose hands the communication was delivered.

Third. That among the pretexts urged for the continuance of the war is the assertion that the Confederate Government desires to deprive the United States of the free navigation of the Western rivers, although the truth is that the Confederate Congress, by public act, prior to the commencement of the war, enacted that "the peaceful navigation of the Mississippi River is hereby declared free to the citizens of any of the States upon its borders, or upon the borders of its tributaries," a declaration to which our Government has always been and is still ready to adhere.

From these declarations, people of the Northwest, it is made manifest that, by the invasion of our territories by land and from sea, we have been unwillingly forced into a war for self-defense, and to vindicate a great principle, once dear to all Americans, to wit, that no people can be rightly governed except by their own consent. We desire peace now. We desire to see a stop put to a useless and cruel effusion of blood and that waste of national wealth rapidly leading to, and sure to end in, national bankruptcy. We are, therefore, now, as ever, ready to treat with the United States, or any one or more of them, on terms of mutual justice and liberality. And at this juncture, when our arms have been successful on many hard-fought fields; when our people have exhibited a constancy, a fortitude, and a courage worthy of the boon of self-government, we restrict ourselves to the same moderate demands that we made at the darkest period of our reverses—the demand that the people of the United States cease to war upon us and permit us in peace to pursue our path to happiness, while they in peace pursue theirs. We are, however, debarred from the renewal of former proposals for peace, because the relentless spirit that actuates the Government at Washington leaves us no reason to expect that they would be received with the respect naturally due by nations in their intercourse, whether in peace or war.

It is under these circumstances that we are driven to protect our own country by transferring the seat of war to that of an enemy who pursues us with an implacable and apparently aimless hostility. If the war must continue, its theater must be changed, and with it the policy that has heretofore kept us on the defensive on our own soil. So far, it is only our fields that have been laid waste, our people killed, our homes made desolate, and our frontiers ravaged by rapine and murder. The sacred right of self-defense demands that henceforth some of the consequences of the war shall fall upon those who persist in their refusal to make peace. With the people of the Northwest rests the power to put an end to the invasion of their homes, for, if unable to prevail upon the Government of the United States to conclude a general peace, their own State governments, in the exercise of their sovereignty, can secure immunity from the desolating effects of warfare on their soil by a separate treaty of peace, which our Government will be ready to conclude on the most just and liberal basis.

The responsibility, then, rests with you, the people of the Northwest, of continuing an unjust and aggressive warfare upon the people of the Confederate States. And in the name of reason and humanity I call upon you to pause and reflect what cause of quarrel so bloody have you against these States, and what are you to gain by it. Nature has set her seal upon these States and marked them out to be your friends and allies. She has bound them to you by all the ties of geographical contiguity and conformation and the great mutual interests of commerce and productions. When the passions of this unnatural war shall have subsided and reason resumes her sway, a community of interest will force commercial and social coalition between the great grain and stock growing States of the Northwest and the cotton, tobacco, and sugar regions of the South. The Mississippi River is a grand artery of their mutual national lives which men cannot sever, and which never ought to have been suffered to be disturbed by the antagonisms, the cupidity, and the bigotry of New England and the East. It is from the East that have come the germs of this bloody and most unnatural strife. It is from the meddlesome, grasping, and fanatical disposition of the same people who have imposed upon you and us alike those tariffs, internal-improvement, and fishing-bounty laws whereby we have been taxed for their aggrandizement. It is from the East that will come the tax-gatherer to collect from you the mighty debt which is being amassed mountain high for the purpose of ruining your best customers and natural friends.

When this war ends, the same antagonisms of interest, policy, and feeling which have been pressed upon us by the East, and forced us from a political union where we had ceased to find safety for our interests or respect for our rights, will bear down upon you and separate you from a people whose traditional policy it is to live by their wits upon the labor of their neighbors. Meantime you are being used by them to fight the battle of emancipation, a battle which, if successful, destroys our prosperity, and with it your best markets to buy and sell. Our mutual dependence is the work of the Creator. With our peculiar productions, convertible into gold, we should, in a state of peace, draw from you largely the products of your labor. In us of the South you would find rich and willing customers. In the East you must confront rivals in productions and trade, and the tax-gatherer in all the forms of partial legislation. You are blindly following abolitionism to this end, whilst they are nicely calculating the gain of obtaining your trade on terms that would impoverish your country. You say you are fighting for the free navigation of the Mississippi. It is yours, freely, and has always been, without striking a blow. You say you are fighting to maintain the Union. That Union is a thing of the past. A union of consent was the only union ever worth a drop of blood. When force came to be substituted for consent, the casket was broken and the constitutional jewel of your patriotic adoration was forever gone.

I come, then, to you with the olive branch of peace, and offer it to your acceptance in the name of the memories of the past and the ties of the present and future. With you remains the responsibility and the option of continuing a cruel and wasting war, which can only end, after still greater sacrifices, in such treaty of peace as we now offer, or of preserving the blessings of peace by the simple abandonment of the design of subjugating a people over whom no right of dominion has been conferred on you by God or man.

BRAXTON BRAGG,
General, C. S. Army.

"AN EVENT WORTH THE DREADFUL WAR":
MASSACHUSETTS, SEPTEMBER 1862

Ralph Waldo Emerson: The President's Proclamation

September 1862

In January 1862 the poet-philosopher Ralph Waldo Emerson, a dedicated abolitionist, had given a lecture on the theme "Emancipation is the demand of civilization." He delivered an address on Lincoln's proclamation in Boston in late September and published it in the November 1862 *Atlantic Monthly*.

In so many arid forms which States incrust themselves with, once in a century, if so often, a poetic act and record occur. These are the jets of thought into affairs, when, roused by danger or inspired by genius, the political leaders of the day break the else insurmountable routine of class and local legislation, and take a step forward in the direction of catholic and universal interests. Every step in the history of political liberty is a sally of the human mind into the untried future, and has the interest of genius, and is fruitful in heroic anecdotes. Liberty is a slow fruit. It comes, like religion, for short periods, and in rare conditions, as if awaiting a culture of the race which shall make it organic and permanent. Such moments of expansion in modern history were the Confession of Augsburg, the plantation of America, the English Commonwealth of 1648, the Declaration of American Independence in 1776, the British emancipation of slaves in the West Indies, the passage of the Reform Bill, the repeal of the Corn-Laws, the Magnetic Ocean-Telegraph, though yet imperfect, the passage of the Homestead Bill in the last Congress, and now, eminently, President Lincoln's Proclamation on the twenty-second of September. These are acts of great scope, working on a long future, and on permanent interests, and honoring alike those who initiate and those who receive them. These measures provoke no noisy joy, but are received into a sympathy so deep as to apprise us that mankind are greater and better than we know. At such times it appears as if a new public were created to greet the new event. It is as when an orator, having ended the compliments and pleasantries with which he conciliated attention, and having run over the superficial fitness and commodities of the measure he urges, suddenly, lending himself to some happy inspiration, announces with vibrating voice the grand human principles involved,—the bravoes and wits who greeted him loudly thus far are surprised and overawed: a new audience is found in the heart of the assembly,—an audience hitherto passive and unconcerned, now at last so searched and kindled that they come forward, every one a representative of mankind, standing for all nationalities.

The extreme moderation with which the President advanced to his design,—his long-avowed expectant policy, as if he chose to be strictly the executive of the best public sentiment of the country, waiting only till it should be unmistakably pronounced, —so fair a mind that none ever listened so patiently to such extreme varieties of opinion,—so reticent that his decision has taken all parties by surprise, whilst yet it is the just sequel of his prior acts,—the firm tone in which he announces it, without inflation or surplusage,—all these have bespoken such favor to the act, that, great as the popularity of the President has been, we are beginning to think that we have underestimated the capacity and virtue which the Divine Providence has made an instrument of benefit so vast. He has been permitted to do more for America than any other American man. He is well entitled to the most indulgent construction. Forget all that we thought shortcomings, every mistake, every delay. In the extreme embarrassments of his part, call these endurance, wisdom, magnanimity, illuminated, as they now are, by this dazzling success.

When we consider the immense opposition that has been neutralized or converted by the progress of the war, (for it is not long since the President anticipated the resignation of a large number of officers in the army, and the secession of three States, on the promulgation of this policy,)—when we see how the great stake which foreign nations hold in our affairs has recently brought every European power as a client into this court, and it became every day more apparent what gigantic and what remote interests were to be affected by the decision of the President,—one can hardly say the deliberation was too long. Against all timorous counsels he had the courage to seize the moment; and such was his position, and such the felicity attending the action, that he has replaced Government in the good graces of mankind. "Better is virtue in the sovereign than plenty in the season," say the Chinese. 'T is wonderful what power is, and how ill it is used, and how its ill use makes life mean, and the sunshine dark. Life in America had lost much of its attraction in the later years. The virtues of a good magistrate undo a world of mischief, and, because Nature works with rectitude, seem vastly more potent than the acts of bad governors, which are ever tempered by the good-nature in the people, and the incessant resistance which fraud and violence encounter. The acts of good governors work at a geometrical ratio, as one midsummer day seems to repair the damage of a year of war.

A day which most of us dared not hope to see, an event worth the dreadful war, worth its costs and uncertainties, seems now to be close before us. October, November, December will have passed over beating hearts and plotting brains: then the hour will strike, and all men of African descent who have faculty enough to find their way to our lines are assured of the protection of American law.

It is by no means necessary that this measure should be suddenly marked by any signal results on the negroes or on the Rebel masters. The force of the act is that it commits the country to this justice,—that it compels the innumerable officers, civil, military, naval, of the Republic to range themselves on the line of this equity. It draws the fashion to this side. It is not a measure that admits of being taken back. Done, it cannot be undone by a new Administration. For slavery overpowers the disgust of the moral sentiment only through immemorial usage. It cannot be introduced as an improvement of the nineteenth century. This act makes that the lives of our heroes have not been sacrificed in vain. It makes a victory of our defeats. Our hurts are healed; the health of the nation is repaired. With a victory like this, we can stand many disasters. It does not promise the redemption of the black race: that lies not with us:

but it relieves it of our opposition. The President by this act has paroled all the slaves in America; they will no more fight against us; and it relieves our race once for all of its crime and false position. The first condition of success is secured in putting ourselves right. We have recovered ourselves from our false position, and planted ourselves on a law of Nature.

> "If that fail,
> The pillared firmament is rottenness,
> And earth's base built on stubble."

The Government has assured itself of the best constituency in the world: every spark of intellect, every virtuous feeling, every religious heart, every man of honor, every pest, every philosopher, the generosity of the cities, the health of the country, the strong arms of the mechanics, the endurance of farmers, the passionate conscience of women, the sympathy of distant nations,—all rally to its support.

Of course, we are assuming the firmness of the policy thus declared. It must not be a paper proclamation. We confide that Mr. Lincoln is in earnest, and, as he has been slow in making up his mind, has resisted the importunacy of parties and of events to the latest moment, he will be as absolute in his adhesion. Not only will he repeat and follow up his stroke, but the nation will add its irresistible strength. If the ruler has duties, so has the citizen. In times like these, when the nation is imperilled, what man can, without shame, receive good news from day to day, without giving good news of himself? What right has any one to read in the journals tidings of victories, if he has not bought them by his own valor, treasure, personal sacrifice, or by service as good in his own department? With this blot removed from our national honor, this heavy load lifted off the national heart, we shall not fear henceforward to show our faces among mankind. We shall cease to be hypocrites and pretenders, but what we have styled our free institutions will be such.

In the light of this event the public distress begins to be removed. What if the brokers' quotations show our stocks discredited, and the gold dollar costs one hundred and twenty-seven cents? These tables are fallacious. Every acre in the Free States gained substantial value on the twenty-second of

September. The cause of disunion and war has been reached, and begun to be removed. Every man's house-lot and garden are relieved of the malaria which the purest winds and the strongest sunshine could not penetrate and purge. The territory of the Union shines to-day with a lustre which every European emigrant can discern from far: a sign of inmost security and permanence. Is it feared that taxes will check immigration? That depends on what the taxes are spent for. If they go to fill up this yawning Dismal Swamp, which engulfed armies and populations, and created plague, and neutralized hitherto all the vast capabilities of this continent,—then this taxation, which makes the land wholesome and habitable, and will draw all men unto it, is the best investment in which property-holder ever lodged his earnings.

Whilst we have pointed out the opportuneness of the Proclamation, it remains to be said that the President had no choice. He might look wistfully for what variety of courses lay open to him: every line but one was closed up with fire. This one, too, bristled with danger, but through it was the sole safety. The measure he has adopted was imperative. It is wonderful to see the unseasonable senility of what is called the Peace party, through all its masks, blinding their eyes to the main feature of the war, namely, its inevitableness. The war existed long before the cannonade of Sumter, and could not be postponed. It might have begun otherwise or elsewhere, but war was in the minds and bones of the combatants, it was written on the iron leaf, and you might as easily dodge gravitation. If we had consented to a peaceable secession of the Rebels, the divided sentiment of the Border States made peaceable secession impossible, the insatiable temper of the South made it impossible, and the slaves on the border, wherever the border might be, were an incessant fuel to rekindle the fire. Give the Confederacy New Orleans, Charleston, and Richmond, and they would have demanded St. Louis and Baltimore. Give them these, and they would have insisted on Washington. Give them Washington, and they would have assumed the army and navy, and, through these, Philadelphia, New York, and Boston. It looks as if the battle-field would have been at least as large in that event as it is now. The war was formidable, but could not be avoided. The war was and is an immense mischief, but brought with it the immense benefit of drawing a line, and rallying the Free States to fix it impassably,—preventing the whole force of Southern connection and influence throughout the North from distracting every city with endless confusion, detaching that force and reducing it to handfuls, and, in the progress of hostilities, disinfecting us of our habitual proclivity, through the affection of trade, and the traditions of the Democratic party, to follow Southern leading.

These necessities which have dictated the conduct of the Federal Government are overlooked, especially by our foreign critics. The popular statement of the opponents of the war abroad is the impossibility of our success. "If you could add," say they, "to your strength the whole army of England, of France, and of Austria, you could not coerce eight millions of people to come under this Government against their will." This is an odd thing for an Englishman, a Frenchman, or an Austrian to say, who remembers the Europe of the last seventy years,—the condition of Italy, until 1859,—of Poland, since 1793,—of France, of French Algiers,—of British Ireland, and British India. But, granting the truth, rightly read, of the historical aphorism, that "the people always conquer," it is to be noted, that, in the Southern States, the tenure of land, and the local laws, with slavery, give the social system not a democratic, but an aristocratic complexion; and those States have shown every year a more hostile and aggressive temper, until the instinct of self-preservation forced us into the war. And the aim of the war on our part is indicated by the aim of the President's Proclamation, namely, to break up the false combination of Southern society, to destroy the piratic feature in it which makes it our enemy only as it is the enemy of the human race, and so allow its reconstruction on a just and healthful basis. Then new affinities will act, the old repulsions will cease, and, the cause of war being removed, Nature and trade may be trusted to establish a lasting peace.

We think we cannot overstate the wisdom and benefit of this act of the Government. The malignant cry of the Secession press within the Free States, and the recent action of the Confederate Congress, are decisive as to its efficiency and correctness of aim. Not less so is the silent joy which has greeted it in all generous hearts, and the new hope it has breathed into the world.

It was well to delay the steamers at the wharves, until this edict could be put on board. It will be an insurance to the ship as it goes plunging through the sea with glad tidings to all people. Happy are the young who find the pestilence cleansed out of the earth, leaving open to them an honest career. Happy the old, who see Nature purified before they depart. Do not let the dying die: hold them back to this world, until you have charged their ear and heart with this message to other spiritual societies, announcing the melioration of our planet.

> "Incertainties now crown themselves assured,
> And Peace proclaims olives of endless age."

Meantime that ill-fated, much-injured race which the Proclamation respects will lose somewhat of the dejection sculptured for ages in their bronzed countenance, uttered in the wailing of their plaintive music,—a race naturally benevolent, joyous, docile, industrious, and whose very miseries sprang from their great talent for usefulness, which, in a more moral age, will not only defend their independence, but will give them a rank among nations.

"YOUR DELIVERANCE DRAWS NIGH!":
OCTOBER 1862

Frederick Douglass: Emancipation Proclaimed

October 1862

Douglass believed emancipation long overdue, yet his welcome for Lincoln's action was wholehearted. He published this analysis in his journal *Douglass' Monthly*.

EMANCIPATION PROCLAIMED

Common sense, the necessities of the war, to say nothing of the dictation of justice and humanity have at last prevailed. We shout for joy that we live to record this righteous decree. *Abraham Lincoln*, President of the United States, Commander-in-Chief of the army and navy, in his own peculiar, cautious, forbearing and hesitating way, slow, but we hope sure, has, while the loyal heart was near breaking with despair, proclaimed and declared: "*That on the First of January, in the Year of Our Lord One Thousand, Eight Hundred and Sixty-three, All Persons Held as Slaves Within Any State or Any Designated Part of a State, The People Whereof Shall Then be in Rebellion Against the United States, Shall be Thenceforward and Forever Free.*" "Free forever" oh! long enslaved millions, whose cries have so vexed the air and sky, suffer on a few more days in sorrow, the hour of your deliverance draws nigh! Oh! Ye millions of free and loyal men who have earnestly sought to free your bleeding country from the dreadful ravages of revolution and anarchy, lift up now your voices with joy and thanksgiving for with freedom to the slave will come peace and safety to your country. President Lincoln has embraced in this proclamation the law of Congress passed more than six months ago, prohibiting the employment of any part of the army and naval forces of the United States, to return fugitive slaves to their masters, commanded all officers of the army and navy to respect and obey its provisions. He has still further declared his intention to urge upon the Legislature of all the slave States not in rebellion the immediate or gradual abolishment of slavery. But read the proclamation for it is the most important of any to which the President of the United States has ever signed his name.

Opinions will widely differ as to the practical effect of this measure upon the war. All that class at the North who have not lost their affection for slavery will regard the measure as the very worst that could be devised, and as likely to lead to endless mischief. All their plans for the future have been projected with a view to a reconstruction of the American Government upon the basis of compromise between slaveholding and non-slaveholding States. The thought of a country unified in sentiments, objects and ideas, has not entered into their political calculations, and hence this newly declared policy of the Government, which contemplates one glorious homogeneous people, doing away at a blow with the whole class of compromisers and corrupters, will meet their stern opposition. Will that opposition prevail? Will it lead the President to reconsider and retract? Not a word of it. Abraham Lincoln may be slow, Abraham Lincoln may desire peace even at the price of leaving our terrible national sore untouched, to fester on for generations, but Abraham Lincoln is not the man to reconsider, retract and contradict words and purposes solemnly proclaimed over his official signature.

The careful, and we think, the slothful deliberation which he has observed in reaching this obvious policy, is a guarantee against retraction. But even if the temper and spirit of the President himself were other than what they are, events greater than the President, events which have slowly wrung this proclamation from him may be relied on to carry him forward in the same direction. To look back now would only load him with heavier evils, while diminishing his ability, for overcoming those with which he now has to contend. To recall his proclamation would only increase rebel pride, rebel sense of power and would be hailed as a direct admission of weakness on the part of the Federal Government, while it would cause heaviness of heart and depression of national enthusiasm all over the loyal North and West. No, Abraham Lincoln will take no step backward. His word has gone out over the country and the world, giving joy and gladness to the friends of freedom and progress wherever those words are read, and he will stand by them, and carry them out to the letter. If he has taught us to confide in nothing else, he has taught us to confide in his word. The want of Constitutional power, the want of military power, the tendency of the measure to intensify Southern hate, and to exasperate the rebels, the tendency to drive from him all that class of Democrats at the North, whose loyalty has been conditioned on his restoring the union as it was, slavery and all, have all been considered, and he has taken his ground notwithstanding. The President doubtless saw, as we see, that it is not more absurd to talk about restoring the union, without hurting slavery, than restoring the union without hurting the rebels. As to exasperating the South, there can be no more in the cup than the cup will hold, and that was full already. The whole situation having been carefully scanned, before Mr. Lincoln could be made to budge an inch, he will now stand his ground. Border State influence, and the influence of half-loyal men, have been exerted and have done their worst. The end of these two influences is implied in this proclamation. Hereafter, the inspiration as well as the men and the money for carrying on the war will come from the North, and not from half-loyal border States.

The effect of this paper upon the disposition of Europe will be great and increasing. It changes the character of the war in European eyes and gives it an important principle as an object, instead of national pride and interest. It recognizes and declares the real nature of the contest, and places the North on the side of justice and civilization, and the rebels on the side of robbery and barbarism. It will disarm all purpose on the part of European Government to intervene in favor of the rebels and thus cast off at a blow one source of rebel power. All through the war thus far, the rebel ambassadors in foreign countries have been able to silence all expression of sympathy with the North as to slavery. With much more than a show of truth, they said that the Federal Government, no more than the Confederate Government, contemplated the abolition of slavery.

But will not this measure be frowned upon by our officers and men in the field? We have heard of many thousands who have resolved that they will throw up their commissions and lay down their arms, just so soon as they are required to carry on a war against slavery. Making all allowances for exaggeration there are doubtless far too many of this sort in the loyal army. Putting this kind of loyalty and patriotism to the test, will be one of the best collateral effects of the measure. Any man who leaves the field on such a ground will be an argument in favor of the proclamation, and will prove that his heart has been more with slavery than with his country. Let the army be cleansed from all such proslavery vermin, and its health and strength will be greatly improved. But there can be no reason to fear the loss of many officers or men by resignation or desertion. We have no doubt that the measure was brought to the attention of most of our leading Generals, and blind as some of them have seemed to be in the earlier part of the war, most of them have seen enough to convince them that there can be no end to this war that does not end slavery. At any rate, we may hope that for every pro-slavery man that shall start from the ranks of our loyal army, there will be two anti-slavery men to fill up the vacancy, and in this war one truly devoted to the cause of Emancipation is worth two of the opposite sort.

Whether slavery will be abolished in the manner now proposed by President Lincoln, depends of course upon two conditions, the first specified and the second implied. The first is that the slave States shall be in rebellion on and after the first day of January 1863 and the second is we must have the ability to put down that rebellion. About the first there can be very little doubt. The South is thoroughly in earnest and confident. It has staked everything upon the rebellion. Its experience thus far in the field has rather increased its hopes of final success than diminished them. Its armies now hold us at bay at all points, and the war is confined to the border States slave and free. If Richmond were in our hands and Virginia at our mercy, the vast regions beyond would still remain to be subdued. But the rebels confront us on the Potomac, the Ohio, and the Mississippi. Kentucky, Maryland, Missouri, and Virginia are in debate on the battlefields and their people are divided by the line which separates treason from loyalty. In short we are yet, after eighteen months of war, confined to the outer margin of the rebellion. We have scarcely more than touched the surface of the terrible evil. It has been raising large quantities of food during the past summer. While the masters have been fighting abroad, the slaves have been busy working at home to supply them with the means of continuing the struggle. They will not down at the bidding of this Proclamation, but may be safely relied upon till January and long after January. A month or two will put an end to general fighting for the winter. When the leaves fall we shall hear again of bad roads, winter quarters and spring campaigns. The South which has thus far withstood our arms will not fall at once before our pens. All fears for the abolition of slavery arising from this apprehension may be dismissed. Whoever, therefore, lives to see the first day of next January, should Abraham Lincoln be then alive and President of the United States, may confidently look in the morning papers for the final proclamation, granting freedom, and freedom forever, to all slaves within the rebel States. On the next point nothing need be said. We have full power to put down the rebellion. Unless one man is more than a match for four, unless the South breeds braver and better men than the North, unless slavery is more precious than liberty, unless a just cause kindles a feebler enthusiasm than a wicked and villainous one, the men of the loyal States will put down this rebellion and slavery, and all the sooner will they put down that rebellion by coupling slavery with that object. Tenderness towards slavery has been the loyal weakness during the war. Fighting the slaveholders with one hand and holding the slaves with the other, has been fairly tried and has failed. We have now inaugurated a wiser and better policy, a policy which is better for the loyal cause than an hundred thousand armed men. The Star Spangled Banner is now the harbinger of Liberty and the millions in bondage, inured to hardships, accustomed to toil, ready to suffer, ready to fight, to dare and to die, will rally under that banner wherever they see it gloriously unfolded to the breeze. Now let the Government go forward in its mission of Liberty as the only condition of peace and union, by weeding out the army and navy of all such officers as the late Col. Miles, whose sympathies are now known to have been with the rebels. Let only the men who assent heartily to the wisdom and the justice of the anti-slavery policy of the Government be lifted into command; let the black man have an arm as well as a heart in this war, and the tide of battle which has thus far only waved backward and forward, will steadily set in our favor. The rebellion suppressed, slavery abolished, and America will, higher than ever, sit as a queen among the nations of the earth.

Now for the work. During the interval between now and next January, let every friend of the long enslaved bondman do his utmost in swelling the tide of anti-slavery sentiment, by writing, speaking, money and example. Let our aim be to make the North a unit in favor of the President's policy, and see to it that our voices and votes, shall forever extinguish that latent and malignant sentiment at the North, which has from the first cheered on the rebels in their atrocious crimes against the union, and has systematically sought to paralyze the national arm in striking down the slaveholding rebellion. We are ready for this service or any other, in this, we trust the last struggle with the monster slavery.

RICHMOND, VIRGINIA, SEPTEMBER–OCTOBER 1862

Debate in the Confederate Senate on Retaliation for the Emancipation Proclamation

When the Confederate Senate adjourned on October 13 it adopted a resolution declaring support for whatever retaliatory measures Jefferson Davis chose to adopt. In a proclamation of December 23, 1862, outlawing Union general Benjamin F. Butler, Davis denounced the Emancipation Proclamation as an "effort to excite servile war" and ordered Union officers captured while leading freed slaves to be turned over to state authorities for trial.

SEVERAL propositions under the form of bills, were introduced into the Senate respecting retaliatory measures. These propositions were brought forward in consequence of the proclamation of President Lincoln, issued on the 22d of September, declaring that on the 1st of January ensuing an emancipation proclamation would be issued. The subject came up for the first time on the 29th of Sept., when Mr. Semmes, of Louisiana, offered the following resolution:

Resolved by the Congress of the Confederate States, That the proclamation of Abraham Lincoln, President of the United States of America, issued in the city of Washington, in the year 1862, wherein he declares "that on the first day of January, in the year of our Lord 1863, all persons held as slaves within any State, or designated parts of a State, whereof the people shall be in rebellion against the United States shall be henceforth and forever free," is levelled against the citizens of the Confederate States, and as such is a gross violation of the usuages of civilized warfare, an outrage on the rights of private property, and an invitation to an atrocious servile war, and therefore should be held up to the execration of mankind, and counteracted by such retaliatory measures as in the judgment of the President may be best calculated to secure its withdrawal or arrest its execution.

Mr. Clark, of Missouri, moved that the resolution be referred to the Committee on Foreign Affairs. He was in favor of declaring every citizen of the Southern Confederacy a soldier, authorized to put to death every man caught on our soil in arms against the Government.

Mr. Semmes, of Louisiana, said that the resolution had not been drawn without reflection. The question of retaliation was exclusively an Executive one, to be regulated by circumstances. But it was proper that the legislative department of the Government should express its approval of the retaliation contemplated by the resolution.

Mr. Henry, of Tennessee, said that the resolution did not go far enough. He favored the passage of a law providing that, upon any attempt being made to execute the proclamation of Abraham Lincoln, we immediately hoist the "black flag," and proclaim a war of extermination against all invaders of our soil.

Mr. Phelan, of Mississippi, said that he had always been in favor of conducting the war under the "black flag." If that flag had been raised a year ago the war would be ended now.

Mr. Burnett, of Kentucky, moved that all of said resolutions be referred to the Committee on the Judiciary. This was agreed to.

Subsequently, on the 1st of October, a majority of the Judiciary Committee made a report recommending the passage of the following bill:

Whereas, these States, exercising a right consecrated by the blood of our Revolutionary forefathers, and recognized as fundamental in the American system of government, which is based on the consent of the governed, dissolved the compact which united them to the Northern States, and withdrew from the Union created by the Federal Constitution; and whereas, the Government of the United States, repudiating the principles on which its founders, in their solemn appeal to the civilized world, justified the American Revolution, commenced the present war to subjugate and enslave these States under the pretext of repressing rebellion and restoring the Union; and whereas, in the prosecution of the war for the past seventeen months, the rights accorded to belligerents by the usages of civilized nations have been studiously denied to the citizens of these States, except in cases where the same have been extorted by the apprehension of retaliation, or by the adverse fortune of the war; and whereas, from the commencement of this unholy invasion to the present moment, the invaders have inflicted inhuman miseries on the people of these States, exacting of them treasonable oaths, subjecting unarmed citizens, women, and children to confiscation, banishment and imprisonment; burning their dwelling houses, ravaging the land, plundering private property; murdering men for pretended offences; organizing the abduction of slaves by government officials and at government expense; promoting servile insurrection, by tampering with slaves, and protecting them in resisting their masters; stealing works of art and destroying public libraries; encouraging and inviting a brutal soldiery to commit outrages on women by the unrebuked orders of military commanders, and attempting to ruin cities by filling up the entrances to their harbors with stone: And, whereas, in the same spirit of barbarous ferocity the Government of the United States enacted a law, entitled "An act to suppress insurrection, to prevent treason and rebellion, to seize and confiscate the property of rebels, and for other purposes," and has announced by a proclamation, issued by Abraham Lincoln, the President thereof, that in pursuance of said law, "on the 1st of January, 1863, all persons held as slaves within any State, or designated part of a State, the people whereof shall be in rebellion against the United States, shall be thenceforward and forever free," and has, thereby, made manifest that this conflict has ceased to be a war as recognized among civilized nations, but on the part of the enemy has become an invasion of an organized horde of murderers and plunderers, breathing hatred and revenge for the numerous defeats sustained on legitimate battle fields, and determined, if possible, to exterminate the loyal population of these States, to transfer their property to their enemies, and to emancipate their slaves, with the atrocious design of adding servile insurrection and the massacre of families to the calamities of war; and, whereas, justice and humanity require this Government to endeavor to repress the lawless practices and designs of the enemy by inflicting severe retribution: Therefore, the Confederate States of America do enact,

1. That on and after the 1st of January, 1863, all commissioned and non-commissioned officers of the enemy, except as hereinafter mentioned, when captured, shall be imprisoned at hard labor, or otherwise put at hard labor, until the termination of the war, or until the repeal of the act of the Congress of the United States, herein before recited, or until otherwise determined by the President.

2. Every white person who shall act as a commissioned or non-commissioned officer, commanding negroes or mulattoes against the Confederate States, or who shall arm, organize, train, or prepare negroes or mulattoes for military service, or aid them in any military enterprise against the Confederate States, shall, if captured, suffer death.

3. Every commissioned or non-commissioned officer of the enemy who shall incite slaves to rebellion, or pretend to give them freedom,

under the aforementioned act of Congress and proclamation, by abducting, or causing them to be abducted, or inducing them to abscond, shall, if captured, suffer death.

4. That every person charged with an offence under this act shall be tried by such military courts as the President shall direct; and after conviction, the President may commute the punishment, or pardon unconditionally, or on such terms as he may see fit.

5. That the President is hereby authorized to resort to such other retaliatory measures as in his judgment may be best calculated to repress the atrocities of the enemy.

Mr. Phelan, of Mississippi, submitted a minority report from the same committee, in the form of a lengthy preamble, and the following resolution:

Be it resolved, &c., That from this day forth all rules of civilized warfare should be discarded in the future defence of our country, our liberties and our lives, against the fell design now openly avowed by the Government of the United States to annihilate or enslave us: and that a war of extermination should henceforth be waged against every invader whose hostile foot shall cross the boundaries of these Confederate States.

Mr. Hill, of Georgia: I must be allowed to say for myself that I regard the proclamation of Mr. Lincoln as a mere *brutum fulmen*, and so intended by its author. It is to serve a temporary purpose at the North. I fear we are dignifying it beyond its importance. As the Senate has concluded to notice it, I am in favor of the simplest and most legal action. We must confine our action within the line of right, under the laws of nations. In my opinion we have the right to declare certain acts as crimes, being in conflict with civilized war, and the actors as criminals; and a criminal, though a soldier, is not entitled to be considered a prisoner of war. While, therefore, I approve the general idea to treat persons guilty of certain acts as criminals, contained in the bill reported by the Senator from Louisiana (Mr. Semmes), and agreed to that report as being the one most favored by the majority of the committee, I also, in accordance with the understanding of the committee, propose the following bill, and ask that it be printed for the consideration of the Senate:

1. That if any person singly, or in organized bodies, shall, under pretence of waging war, kill or maim, or in any wise injure the person of any unarmed citizen of the Confederate States, or shall destroy, or seize, or damage the property, or invade the house or domicil, or insult the family of each unarmed citizen; or shall persuade or force any slave to abandon his owner, or shall, by word or act, counsel or incite to servile insurrection within the limits of the Confederate States, all such persons, if captured by the forces of the Confederate States, shall be treated as criminals and not as prisoners of war, and shall be tried by a military court, and, on conviction, suffer death.

2. That every person pretending to be a soldier or officer of the United States, who shall be captured on the soil of the Confederate States, after the 1st day of January, 1863, shall be presumed to have entered the territory of the Confederate States with intent to incite insurrection and abet murder, and unless satisfactory proof be adduced to the contrary, before the military court before which the trial shall be had, shall suffer death. This section shall continue in force until the proclamation issued by Abraham Lincoln, dated at Washington, on the 22d day of September, 1862, shall be rescinded, and the policy therein announced shall be abandoned, and no longer.

Mr. Clark, of Missouri, read a preamble and resolution embracing his views on the subject under consideration. The resolution proposed to recognize the enemy as "savage, relentless, and barbarous," and declares that it "is the duty of the Government of the Confederate States neither to ask quarter for its soldiers nor extend it to the enemy until an awakened or created sense of decency and humanity, or the sting of retaliation, shall have impelled our enemy to adopt or practise the usages of war which prevail among Christian and civilized nations."

On the motion of Mr. Semmes, of Louisiana, the several bills and resolutions were ordered to be printed.

The whole matter was finally disposed of on the last day of the session by the passage of a resolution, declaring that Congress would sustain the President in such retaliatory measures as he might adopt.

"THIS GIGANTIC WICKEDNESS":
LONDON, OCTOBER 1862

The Times of London: Editorial on the Emancipation Proclamation

October 7, 1862

The lordly *Times*, known as "the Thunderer," achieved maximum volume in its condemnation of the Emancipation Proclamation. The *Times* had strongly favored the Confederacy from the beginning of the war, but this editorial marked a new level of ferocity. It appeared as the Palmerston government debated whether Britain should offer to mediate an end to the conflict.

LONDON, TUESDAY, OCTOBER 7, 1862.

It is rarely that a man can be found to balance accurately mischief to another against advantage to himself. President LINCOLN is, as the world says, a good-tempered man, neither better nor worse than the mass of his kind—neither a fool nor a sage, neither a villain nor a saint, but a piece of that common useful clay out of which it delights the American democracy to make great Republican personages. Yet President LINCOLN has declared that from the 1st of January next to come every State that is in rebellion shall be in the eye of Mr. LINCOLN a Free State. After that date Mr. LINCOLN proposes to enact that every slave in a rebel State shall be for ever after free, and he promises that neither he, nor his army, nor his navy will do anything to repress *any* efforts which the negroes in such rebel States may make for the recovery of their freedom. This means, of course, that Mr. LINCOLN will, on the 1st of next January, do his best to excite a servile war in the States which he cannot occupy with his arms. He will run up the rivers in his gunboats; he will seek out the places which are left but slightly guarded, and where the women and children have been trusted to the fidelity of coloured domestics. He will appeal to the black blood of the African; he will whisper of the pleasures of spoil and of the gratification of yet fiercer instincts; and when blood begins to flow and shrieks come piercing through the darkness, Mr. LINCOLN will wait till the rising flames tell that all is consummated, and then he will rub his hands and think that revenge is sweet. This is what Mr. LINCOLN avows before the world that he is about to do. Now, we are in Europe thoroughly convinced that the death of slavery must follow as necessarily upon the success of the Confederates in this war as the dispersion of darkness occurs upon the rising of the sun; but sudden and forcible emancipation resulting from "the efforts the negroes may make for their actual freedom" can only be effected by massacre and utter destruction. Mr. LINCOLN avows, therefore, that he proposes to excite the negroes of the Southern plantations to murder the families of their masters while these are engaged in the war. The conception of such a crime is horrible. The employment of Indians sinks to a level with civilized warfare in comparison with it; the most detestable doctrines of MAZZINI are almost less atrocious; even Mr. LINCOLN'S own recent achievements of burning by gunboats the defenceless villages on the Mississippi are dwarfed by this gigantic wickedness. The single thing to be said for it is that it is a wickedness that holds its head high and scorns hypocrisy. It does not pretend to attack slavery as slavery. It launches this threat of a servile rebellion as a means of war against certain States, and accompanies it with a declaration of general protection to all other slavery.

Where he has no power Mr. LINCOLN will set the negroes free; where he retains power he will consider them as slaves. "Come to me," he cries to the insurgent planters, "and I will preserve your rights as slaveholders; but set me still at defiance, and I will wrap myself in virtue and take the sword of freedom in my hand, and, instead of aiding you to oppress, I will champion the rights of humanity. Here are whips for you who are loyal; go forth and flog or sell your black chattels as you please. Here are torches and knives for employment against you who are disloyal; I will press them into every black hand, and teach their use." Little Delaware, with her 2,000 slaves, shall still be protected in her loyal tyranny. Maryland, with her 90,000 slaves, shall "freely accept or freely reject" any project for either gradual or immediate abolition; but if Mississippi and South Carolina, where the slaves rather outnumber the masters, do not repent, and receive from Mr. LINCOLN a licence to trade in human flesh, that human flesh shall be adopted by Mr. LINCOLN as the agent of his vengeance. The position is peculiar for a mere layman. Mr. LINCOLN, by this proclamation, constitutes himself a sort of moral American Pope. He claims to sell indulgences to own votaries, and he offers them with full hands to all who will fall down and worship him. It is his to bind, and it is his to loose. His decree of emancipation is to go into remote States, where his temporal power cannot be made manifest, and where no stars and stripes are to be seen; and in those distant swamps he is, by a sort of Yankee excommunication, to lay the land under a slavery interdict.

What will the South think of this? The South will answer with a hiss of scorn. But what will the North think of it? What will Pennsylvania say—Pennsylvania, which is already unquiet under the loss of her best customers, and not easy under the absolute despotism of the present Government at Washington? What Boston may say or think is not, perhaps, of much consequence. But what will New York say? It would not answer the purpose of any of these cities to have the South made a howling wilderness. They want the handling of the millions which are produced by the labour of the black man. Pennsylvania desires to sell her manufactures in the South; New York wishes to be again broker, banker, and merchant to the South. This is what the Union means to these cities. They would rather have a live independent State to deal with than a dead dependency where nothing could be earnt. To these practical persons President LINCOLN would be, after his black revolution had succeeded, like a dogstealer who should present the anxious owner with the head of his favourite pointer. They want the useful creature alive. The South without its cotton and its sugar and its tobacco would be of small use to New York, or even to Philadelphia; and the South without the produce of its rice and cotton, and its sugar and tobacco, would be but a sorry gain, even if it could be obtained. If President LINCOLN wants such a conquest as this, the North is, perhaps, yet strong enough to conquer Hayti. A few fanatics, of course, will shout, but we cannot think that, except in utter desperation and vindictiveness, any real party in the North will applaud this nefarious resolution to light up a servile war in the distant homesteads of the South.

As a proof of what the leaders of the North, in their passion and their despair, would do if they could, this is a very sad document. As a proof of the hopelessness and recklessness which prompt their actions, it is a very instructive document. But it is not a formidable document. We gather from it that Mr. Lincoln has lost all hope of preserving the Union, and is now willing to let any quack try his nostrum. As an act of policy it is, if possible, more contemptible than it is wicked. It may possibly produce some partial risings, for let any armed power publish an exhortation to the labouring class of any community to plunder and murder, and there will be some response. It might happen in London, or Paris, or New York. That Mr. Lincoln's emancipation decrees will have any general effect bearing upon the issue of the war we do not, however, believe. The negroes have already abundantly discovered that the tender mercies of the Northerners are cruelties. The freedom which is associated with labour in the trenches, military discipline, and frank avowals of personal abhorrence momentarily repeated does not commend itself to the negro nature. General Butler could, if he pleased, tell strange stories of the ill success of his tamperings with the negroes about New Orleans. We do not think that even now, when Mr. Lincoln plays his last card, it will prove to be a trump. Powerful malignity is a dreadful reality, but impotent malignity is apt to be a very contemptible spectacle. Here is a would-be conqueror and a would-be extirpator who is not quite safe in his seat of government, who is reduced to such straits that he accepts a defeat as a glorious escape, a capitulation of 8,000 men as an unimportant event, a drawn battle as a glorious victory, and the retreat of an invading army which retires laden with plunder and rich in stores as a deliverance. Here is a President who has just, against his will, supplied his antagonists with a hundred and twenty guns and millions of stores, and who is trembling for the very ground on which he stands. Yet, if we judged only by his pompous proclamations, we should believe that he had a garrison in every city of the South. This is more like a Chinaman beating his two swords together to frighten his enemy than like an earnest man pressing on his cause in steadfastness and truth.

OBEYING CIVIL AUTHORITY:
MARYLAND, OCTOBER 1862

George B. McClellan to Abraham Lincoln

General McClellan had second thoughts about taking a public stance against the Emancipation Proclamation after his political advisor William Aspinwall visited him on October 4 and warned him off the idea, suggesting he "quietly continue doing" his "duty as a soldier." Several army officers McClellan consulted gave him the same advice. Still he felt it necessary to address his army on the matter, pointing to the ballot box as "the remedy for political error."

            Hd Quarters Army Potomac
The President, U.S.   7th
 I have issued the following order on your proclamation.
 "Hd Quarters Army Potomac Camp near Sharpsburg Md Oct 7th 1862 Genl Order No. 163. The attention of the officers & soldiers of the Army of the Potomac is called to Genl Order No. 139 War Dept Sept 24th 1862, publishing to the Army the Presidents proclamation of Sept 22d.
 A proclamation of such grave moment to the Nation officially communicated to the Army affords to the Genl Commanding an opportunity of defining specifically to the officers & soldiers under his Command the relation borne by all persons in the Military service of the U.S. towards the Civil Authorities of the Government. The Constitution confides to the Civil Authorities legislative judicial and executive, the power and duty of making expounding & executing the federal laws. Armed forces are raised & supported simply to sustain the Civil Authorities and are to be held in strict subordination thereto in all respects. This fundamental rule of our political system is essential to the security of our Republican Institutions & should be thoroughly understood & observed by every soldier. The principle upon which & the objects for which Armies shall be employed in suppressing Rebellion must be determined & declared by the Civil Authorities and the Chief Executive, who is charged with the administration of the

National affairs, is the proper & only source through which the views & orders of the Government can be made known to the Armies of the Nation. Discussions by officers & soldiers concerning public measures determined upon and declared by the Government when carried at all beyond temperate and respectful expressions of opinion tend greatly to impair & destroy the discipline & efficiency of troops by substituting the spirit of political faction for that firm steady & earnest support of the Authority of the Government which is the highest duty of the American soldier. The remedy for political error if any are committed is to be found only in the action of the people at the polls. In thus calling the attention of this Army to the true relation between the soldiers and the Government the Genl Commanding merely adverts to an evil against which it has been thought advisable during our whole history to guard the Armies of the Republic & in so doing he will not be considered by any right minded person as casting any reflection upon that loyalty & good conduct which has been so fully illustrated upon so many battle fields. In carrying out all measures of public policy this Army will of course be guided by the same rules of mercy and Christianity that have ever controlled its conduct toward the defenceless.

By Command of Maj Genl McClellan. James Hardie Lt Col Aide de Camp Acting Ajt. A Genl."

Geo B McClellan
M.G. Comdg

BATTLE OF CORINTH: MISSISSIPPI,
OCTOBER 1862

Oscar L. Jackson: *from* The Colonel's Diary

After the battle of Iuka, Sterling Price was reinforced by troops from central Mississippi under the command of Earl Van Dorn. On October 3 Van Dorn and Price led 22,000 men in an attack on the 23,000 Union troops at Corinth under William S. Rosecrans and pushed the defenders back to their inner defensive line. When the battle resumed the following morning, some of the fiercest fighting took place around Battery Robinett. Oscar L. Jackson, a company commander in the 63rd Ohio Infantry, recalled the battle in a narrative posthumously published in 1922.

ABOUT TEN o'clock the rebels began pouring out of the timber and forming storming columns. All the firing ceased and everything was silent as the grave. They formed one column of perhaps two thousand men in plain view, then another, and crowding out of the woods another, and so on. I thought they would never stop coming out of the timber. While they were forming, the men were considerable distance from us but in plain sight and as soon as they were ready they started at us with a firm, slow, steady step.

> "Firm paced and slow a fearful front they form,
> Still as the breeze but dreadful as the storm."

So it seemed to us. In my campaigning I had never seen anything so hard to stand as that slow, steady tramp. Not a sound was heard but they looked as if they intended to walk over us. I afterwards stood a bayonet charge when the enemy came at us on the double-quick with a yell and it was not so trying on the nerves as that steady, solemn advance.

I could see that my men were affected by it. They were in line and I knew that they would stand fire but this was a strong test. I noticed one man examining his gun to see if it was clean; another to see if his was primed right; a third would stand a while on one foot then on the other; whilst others were pulling at their blouses, feeling if their cartridge boxes or cap-pouches were all right, and so on, but all the time steadily watching the advancing foe. It is customary in engagements to have some motto or battle cry given by some commander, such as "Fire low," "Stick to your company," "Remember some battle," (naming it). To draw the attention of my company while the charge was advancing I said: "Boys, I guess we are going to have a fight." This is always a doubtful question to an old soldier until he sees it, but they all believed it this time. "I have two things I want you to remember today. One is, we own all the ground behind us. The enemy may go over us but all the rebels yonder can't drive Company H back. The other is, if the butternuts come close enough, remember you have good bayonets on your rifles and use them." And well did they remember what I said.

When the enemy had advanced about one-third of the distance toward us, we got orders to lie down, and then, when the enemy got close enough, we were to fire by companies. The unevenness of the ground now screened us from their view and the second line of infantry, some distance to the rear, appeared to the rebels to be the first they would have to fight, and when they came upon us it was a surprise to them. My company being on the left of the regiment, and our regiment on the left of the brigade, I was among the nearest to the enemy.

The enemy had to come over a bluffish bank a few yards in front of me and as soon as I saw their heads, still coming slowly, I jumped up and said: "Company H, get up." The column was then in full view and only about thirty yards distant. Captain Smith of our regiment thought only about twenty-five yards. Just in front of me was a bush three or four feet high with sear leaves on it. Hitting this with my sword, I said: "Boys, give them a volley just over this. Ready! aim! (and jumping around my company to get from in front of their guns) fire!" In a few seconds the fire was continued along the whole line.

It seems to me that the fire of my company had cut down the head of the column that struck us as deep back as my company was long. As the smoke cleared away, there was apparently ten yards square of a mass of struggling bodies and butternut clothes. Their column appeared to reel like a rope shaken at the end. I had heard this idea advanced and here I saw it plainly. The enemy were stopped, but deploying their column, returned the fire, and, a fine thing for us, fired too low, striking the ground, knocking the dirt and chips all over us, wounding a very few, not one in my company. We got ahead of them with the next volley which we delivered right in their faces. (The guns were all muzzle-loading). At this close distance we fought for perhaps five minutes, when the enemy gave back in confusion. The leafy bush I struck with my sword, on giving the first command to fire, was stripped almost clean. The boys made a fine volley. The enemy came at us in fine order, moving handsomely, but in retreating, every fellow went as suited him, and it appeared to suit all to go fast.

The column that fought us was led by General Rodgers of Texas who fell dead but a few feet from me. When I saw the enemy retreating in such confusion, I remarked to a comrade that we would not have to fight those men any more today, as I thought it would be impossible to rally them again, but strange to say, in some forty minutes I saw them reformed and coming at us again with that slow, steady step, but they made a change in their tactics, for as they came over the bank, or rather out of ravine in front of us, they came at us with a yell on the double-quick. Our men stood firm with loaded guns and fixed bayonets and gave them a volley that threw them somewhat into confusion, slaughtering them fearfully, but pressing on, and firing at us rapidly, they dashed themselves against us like water against a rock and were a second time repulsed and gave back.

Colonel Sprague had all the while been in the thickest of the fight. I think I see him now rush to where the line wavered and with sabre sweeping the air, exclaim, "What does this mean, men? Company —, close up!" He then spoke and said, "Men, it is your time to cheer now," and with a hearty good will did they respond.

Some distance to the left and front of me were a pair of parrot guns, that we called Battery Robinett in distinction from the small fort of the same name a short distance in the rear of them. Captain Brown and his Company A supported these guns immediately, that is, were between me and them. He was almost annihilated by the first two charges and between me and the guns was clear ground. Colonel Sprague gave me this order: "Captain Jackson, move your company up to those guns and hold them." Saluting, I replied, "I will do it," and turning to my command I added, "Left face, forward march." It was like moving into dead men's shoes, for I had seen one company carried away from there on litters, but without a moment's hesitation we moved up.

I had scarce posted my men in rear of the guns when I saw that the enemy were again coming at us, and that a detachment was moving from the main column toward my guns. I knew what they wanted and, as the guns were not for close action, I moved my men in front of them and waited their approach. On they came, formed in their favorite manner, namely, in a solid square or column. I now had but twenty-four men in line formed in two ranks, but even the detachment of the enemy which veered off towards me were formed in a square. As I afterwards learned, they were dismounted Texan rangers and very few of their guns had bayonets. I am told Colonel Sprague asked permission to move up to my support, but permission was denied.

The rebel officer in command of the Texans was marching at the left of his men and when he came nigh us he turned and walked backwards and said to his men, "Boys, when you charge, give a good yell." I heard his command distinctly and it almost made the hair stand up on my head. The next instant the Texans began yelling like savages and rushed at us without firing. The ground in front of us was about like that where we stood previously and at the proper moment I gave them a volley that halted them, cutting down their entire front. I saw they meant to overwhelm us and drive us from the guns, as they out-numbered us. I estimated their force at one hundred men. My men began loading at will and the Texan, by a dexterous movement, was putting his bayonets to the front, doing the thing among and literally over his dead and wounded comrades. I saw that he would strike us before we could get another volley at them and I gave the command, "Don't load, boys; they are too close on you; let them have the bayonet." In a second every bayonet was brought down to a charge. I have never lived through moments of such intense excitement. Events happened quicker than I can record them. The rebels rushed toward us and just before they struck us, I yelled, "Charge!" in order to give my men momentum to meet the shock. My men sprang at the enemy as one man. It reminded me of a man cutting heavy grain, striking at a thick place. The hostile guns clashed. For an instant we parried like boxers, when the enemy gave back, firing at us now for the first as they retired.

Never have I felt so proud of anything as I was of my men. I thought that no such company was in that army. Hand to hand we fought them. A few of the enemy rushed around my left to my rear to get at the guns and two rebels were killed in rear of my line in single-handed combat. Corporal Selby, then a private, killed a rebel with his bayonet there, which is a remarkable thing in a battle and was spoken of in the official report. Selby called on the Texan to surrender, but he replied, "We'll see who surrenders," and made a lunge at Selby with his bayonet. Selby's skill in the bayonet exercise, in which they had been well drilled, gave him the advantage and he parried the stroke and plunged his own bayonet through the body of the Texan, who fell dead with Selby's bayonet sticking in his body. Thomas Lady also killed a man with his bayonet. Lady was mortally wounded. During this time, terrible fighting was being done along the whole line.

My company was fearfully cut up in this last charge. I had but eleven men standing when I thought the enemy was repulsed, but just as they went into the ravine, one of the rebels turned toward us and fired. I was at the head of my command and a little in front. I saw the fire was aimed at me and tried to avoid it but fate willed otherwise and I fell right backwards, indeed "with my back to the field and my feet to the foe." I was struck in the face. I felt as if I had been hit with a piece of timber, so terrible was the concussion and a stunning pain went through my head. I thought I was killed. It was my impression that I would never rise, but I was not alarmed or distressed by the thought that I was dying; it seemed a matter of indifference to me. In a little while I tried to rise and found I could do so. I got up and tried to walk to the rear. There was no one wounded in my company after I fell. Just at that time our supports charged and pursued the retreating foe, and the battle closed. The victory was ours.

When I got on my feet I walked to the rear a few yards till I came to the trunk of a fallen tree. I was too weak to cross it, but I observed Private Frank Ingmire standing on the tree trunk and I said "Ingmire, help me over." "Yes," he replied, "let me help you across," and gave me his left hand. I then noticed that his right arm was dangling at his side, his hand dripping blood. His wrist had been shattered by a ball. He helped me over the log and I took hold of his left arm with both my hands to support myself, saying, "Ingmire, don't leave me," but I only walked a short distance till I felt my hands slipping off his arm, my knees doubling under me, and I sank to the ground unconscious, and knew nothing more until I came to, in the field hospital two days later.

I took into action thirty-three men with myself, an aggregate of thirty-four. The Lieutenants of my company had both resigned and two of my non-commissioned officers were Acting Lieutenants, Sergeant Terry and Corporal Ferris. Acting 1st Sergeant Casey was killed. Acting Lieutenant Sergeant Terry was killed and Acting Lieutenant Corporal Ferris was severely wounded. The Left Guide of the company, Acting Sergeant, Corporal Wilson, was killed. I had six men killed and sixteen wounded, just two-thirds of the company, and myself wounded in addition, making twenty-three killed and wounded out of a company of thirty-four officers and men. Some of the wounded died from their wounds. Nearly all of the remaining eleven had something to show of the fight, such as bullet holes in the clothing, and abrasions of the skin by the balls. I had five bullet holes through my coat, each one of which cut the coat in two places. One that passed through the left breast of the coat, I felt when it went through, but the others I knew nothing about till afterwards. My pistol was knocked out of my hand and I never saw it again. My sword was lost off me in some way after I was wounded. Both Lieutenant Howard of Company G and Corporal Savely of my own company saw me fall when I was hit. They say I fell backwards to the ground and my limbs quivered convulsively, the blood spurted from my face in a stream several inches high. They both thought I was dead, and someone exclaimed, "The Captain is killed!" Both comrades were so intensely occupied in the fight that they could not go to my assistance, but Lieutenant Howard says he saw me when I rose to my feet and started to walk to the rear.

I was struck just below the right eye. It was not a musket ball but something smaller, either a buckshot or a ball from a squirrel rifle, with which some Texan rangers may have been armed. The ball broke through the cheek bone, passing under the inside corner of the eye. The surgeons probed the wound and tried to take the ball out but did not succeed. I was insensible when the wound was dressed. Doctor A. B. Monahan, Assistant Surgeon of our regiment, dressed the wound and he says he quit probing it lest he would entirely destroy my eye. F. M. Green of the 43rd Ohio, who nursed me, says I was unconscious for three days.

I have recollection of almost nothing that happened till I recovered consciousness the second or third day after the battle, when I aroused from my stupor but could scarcely recollect what had happened. Both eyes were swelled completely shut from the wound and although it was day time I supposed it was night, and my first conscious words were, "It is dark." Soon I was able to remember where I had, as it were, quit the world two days before, but I was not really certain whether any of the men of my company were dead. I knew they had nearly all fallen but had no time during the action to examine their wounds. My time was fully occupied with those who could fight.

Corporal Harrison, afterwards Captain, was standing beside me. I hurriedly asked him, "How are my men?" He replied, "The company is badly cut up, Captain." "For God's sake tell me who were killed," I shrieked, and the words are ringing in my ears to this day, every time I think of that fearful question. He replied, "Corporal Wilson is dead, and Sergeant Terry, and Sergeant Casey," and went on with the details. I thought he named the whole company. As soon as I got the news of how terribly my men had suffered, actually a feeling of gladness came over me that I had been wounded and had something to suffer.

"AN AWFUL DAY": MISSISSIPPI, OCTOBER 1862

Charles B. Labruzan:
Journal, October 4, 1862

Lieutenant Labruzan, a company commander in the 42nd Alabama Infantry, fought in the Confederate attack on Battery Robinett. The Confederates failed to break through the inner defenses at Corinth and retreated when the Union counterattacked on the afternoon of October 4. Confederate casualties in the battle were 4,233 men killed, wounded, or missing, while the Union losses totaled 2,520. Labruzan was captured along with his journal, the Corinth section of which found its way into print in 1864 in a regimental history of the 9th Illinois Infantry. Labruzan was paroled and returned to his Alabama regiment, only to become a prisoner again at the surrender of Vicksburg in 1863.

―――――――――

Saturday, Oct. 4th.—An awful day. At 4 o'clock, before day, our Brigade was ordered to the left about one-fourth of a mile, and halted, throwing out lines of skirmishers, which kept up a constant fire. A Battery in front of the right of our Regiment opened briskly, and the enemy replied the same. The cannonading was heavy for an hour and a half. Our Regiment lay down close, and stood it nobly. The shell flew thick and fast, cutting off large limbs and filling the air with fragments. Many burst within 20 feet, and the pieces popped within 2 or 3 feet. It was extremely unpleasant, and I prayed for forgiveness of my sins, and made up my mind to go through. Col. Sawier called for volunteers to assist the 2d Texas skirmishers. I volunteered, and took my company. Captain Perkins and Lieutenant Wumson being taken sick directly after the severe bombardment, I had the Co. all the time. I went skirmishing at 7 1/2, and returned at 9 1/2 o'clock. We got behind trees and logs, and the way the bullets did fly, was unpleasant to see. I think 20 must have passed within a few feet of me, humming prettily. Shells tore off large limbs and splinters. Struck my tree several times. We could only move from tree to tree, and bending low to the ground, while moving. Oh, how anxiously I watched for the bursting of the shells when the heavy roar of the cannon proclaimed their coming. At 9 1/2 o'clock I had my skirmishers relieved, by Captain Rouse's Company. Sent my men to their places, and went behind a log with Major Furges. At 10 o'clock, suddenly the fight fairly opened, with heavy volleys of musketry and the double thundering cannon. This was on the right. In a few minutes the left went into action in splendid style. At 10 1/4 o'clock, Col. Rogers came up by us, only saying "Alabama forces." Our Regiment, with the Brigade rose, unmindful of the shell or shot, and moved forward, marching about 250 yards and rising the crest of a hill. The whole of Corinth, with its enormous fortifications, burst upon our view. The U. S. flag was floating over the forts and in town. We were now met by a perfect storm of grape, cannister, cannon balls and Minnie balls. Oh, God! I have never seen the like! The men fell like grass, even here. Giving one tremendous cheer, we dashed to the bottom of the hill on which the fortifications are situated. Here we found every foot of ground covered with large trees and brush, cut down to impede our progress. Looking to the right and left, I saw several Brigades charging at the same time. What a sight was there. I saw men running at full speed, stop suddenly and fall upon their faces, with their brains scattered all around. Others, with legs and arms cut off, shrieking with agony. They fell behind, beside, and within a few feet of me. I gave myself to God, and got ahead of my company. The ground was literally strewed with mangled corpses. One ball passed through my pants, and they cut twigs right by me. It seemed, by holding out my hand I could have caught a dozen. They buzzed and hissed by me in all directions, but I still pushed forward. I seemed to be moving right in the mouth of cannon, for the air was filled with hurling grape and cannister. Ahead was one continuous blaze. I rushed to the ditch of the fort, right between some large cannon. I grappled into it, and half way up the sloping wall. The enemy were only three or four feet from me on the other side, but could not shoot us for fear of having their heads blown off. Our men were in the same predicament. Only 5 or 6 were on the wall, and 30 or 40 in and around the ditch. Catesby on the wall by my side. A man within two feet of me, put his head cautiously up, to shoot into the fort. But he suddenly dropped his musket, and his brains were dashed in a stream over my fine coat, which I had in my arms, and on my shirt sleeves. Several were killed here, on top one another, and rolled down the embankment in ghastly heaps. This was done by a Regiment of Yankees coming about 40 yards on our left, after finding us entirely cut off, and firing into us. Several of our men cried "put down the flag," and it was lowered, or shot into the ditch. Oh, we were butchered like dogs, as we were not supported. Some one placed a white handkerchief on Sergeant Buck's musket, and he took it to a port hole. But the Yankees snatched it off and took him prisoner. The men fell 10 at a time. The ditch being full, and finding we had no chance, the survivors tried to save themselves as best they could. I was so far up, I could not get off quickly. I do not recollect of seeing Catesby after this, but think he got off before. I trust in God he has. I and Capt. Foster started together, and the air was literally filled with hissing balls. I got about 20 steps, as quick as I could, about a dozen being killed in that distance. I fell down and scrambled behind a large stump. Just then, I saw poor Foster throw up his hands, and saying "Oh, my God!" jumped about two feet from the ground, falling on his face. The top of his head seemed to cave in, and the blood spouted straight up several feet. I could see men fall as they attempted to run, some with their heads to pieces, and others with the blood streaming from their backs. It was horrible. One poor fellow being almost on me, told me his name, and asked me to take his pocket-book if I escaped and give it to his mother, and tell her that he died a brave man. I asked him if he was a Christian, and told him to pray, which he did, with the cannon thundering a deadly accompaniment. Poor fellow. I forgot his request in the excitement. His legs were literally cut to pieces. As our men returned, the enemy poured in their fire, and I was hardly 30 feet from the mouth of the cannon. Minnie balls filled the stump I was behind, and the shells bursted within three feet of me. One was so near it stunned me, and burned my face with powder. The grape-shot hewed large pieces off my stump, gradually wearing it away. I endured the horrors of death here for half an hour, and endeavored to resign myself and prayed. Our troops formed in line in the woods, and advanced a second time to the charge with cheers. They began firing when about half way, and I had to endure it all. I was feigning death. I was right between our own and the enemies fire. In the first charge our men did not fire a gun, but charged across the ditch, and to the very mouth of the cannon, with the bayonet. So also the second charge, but they fired. Thank God, I am unhurt, and I think it was a merciful Providence. Our troops charged by, when I seized a rifle and endeavored to fire it several times, but could not, for the cap was bad. Our boys were shot down like hogs, and could not stand it, and fell back each man for himself. Then the same scene was enacted as before. This time the Yankees charged after them, and as I had no chance at all, and all around we were surrendering, I was compelled to do so, as a rascal threatened to shoot me. I had to give up my sword to him. He demanded my watch also. Took it; but I appealed to an officer, and got it back. I had no means of defending myself for the first time in many years. I cried to see our brave men slaughtered so, and thought where Catesby might be. I have never felt so in all my life. It is now said that our Brigade was never ordered to charge such a place, and that it was a mistake. If so, it was a sad one. Being brought behind the works we found three Regiments drawn up in line, and all of them were fighting our 42d Alabama alone. I helped to carry a wounded man to the Depot, with Lieutenants Marshall, Contra and Preston, they being the only unhurt officers who were prisoners from our Regiment. We and the privates were soon marched to a large house, having a partition for the officers. The men, about 400, in next room. I heard firing again, but I fear we can do nothing. We are treated very politely—more so than I had expected.

BATTLE OF PERRYVILLE:
KENTUCKY, OCTOBER 1862

J. Montgomery Wright: Notes of a Staff-Officer at Perryville

Don Carlos Buell's army reached Louisville on September 25 while Braxton Bragg's Confederate forces were still thirty miles to the south at Bardstown. When Buell began advancing south from Louisville in early October, Bragg tried to unite his army with Edmund Kirby Smith's, which had occupied Frankfort in early September. Before Bragg and Smith could combine forces, Buell brought Bragg to battle at Perryville, some fifty miles southeast of Louisville, on October 8. Major Wright, of Buell's staff, was one of many Union officers surprised by the fighting at Perryville, due to a phenomenon known as acoustic shadow—layers of air of differing densities that muffled sound. Buell was prevented from hearing the battle being fought less than three miles from his headquarters; as a result, most of his army remained unengaged. Union losses in the battle totaled about 4,200 men killed, wounded, or missing, while Confederate casualties were close to 3,400. Wright's account appeared in *Battles and Leaders of the Civil War*.

THE SITUATION at Louisville in the latter part of September, 1862, was not unlike that at Washington after the first battle of Bull Run. The belief was entertained by many that Bragg would capture the city, and not a few had removed their money and valuables across the Ohio River, not over-assured that Bragg might not follow them to the lakes. Nelson had sworn that he would hold the city so long as a house remained standing or a soldier was alive, and he had issued an order that all the women, children, and non-combatants should leave the place and seek safety in Indiana. He had only raw troops and convalescent veterans, and few citizens believed that he could hold out against an attack. His tragic death occurred a few days later.

Buell's arrival changed the situation of affairs. The uncertain defensive suddenly gave way to an aggressive attitude, and speculation turned from whether Bragg would capture Louisville to whether Buell would capture Bragg.

The country through which Buell's army marched is almost destitute of water, but at Perryville a stream flowed between the contending armies, and access to that water was equally important to both armies. Buell accompanied the center corps (Gilbert's), and the advance reached this stream on the evening of October 7th. From that time until the stream was crossed there was constant fighting for access to it, and the only restriction on this fighting was that it should not bring on an engagement until the time for the general attack should arrive. An incident will illustrate the scarcity of water. I obtained a canteenful, and about dark on October 7th, after giving myself a good brushing and a couple of dry rubs without feeling much cleaner, my careless announcement that I was about to take a tin-dipper bath brought General Buell out of his tent with a rather mandatory suggestion that I pour the water back into my canteen and save it for an emergency. The emergency did not come to me, but on the morning of October 9th that water helped to relieve the suffering of some wounded men who lay between the two armies.

At Buell's headquarters, on the 8th, preparations were going on for the intended attack, and the information was eagerly waited for that Crittenden had reached his position on the right. Fighting for water went on in our front, and it was understood that it extended all along the line, but no battle was expected that day. McCook was at Buell's headquarters in the morning, and received, I believe, some oral instructions regarding the contemplated attack. It was understood that care would be taken not to bring on a general engagement, and no importance was attached to the sounds that reached us of artillery-firing at the front of the center. Of course the young officers of the staff, of whom I was one, were not taken into conference by General Buell, but we all knew that the subject of attention that morning was the whereabouts of Crittenden's corps, and the placing it in position on the right for the general engagement that was to be brought on as soon as the army was in line. We all saw McCook going serenely away like a general carrying his orders with him.

In the afternoon we moved out for a position nearer Crittenden, as I inferred from the direction taken. A message came from the line on the left center to General Buell, and in a few moments Colonel James B. Fry, our chief of staff, called me up, and sent me with an order to General Gilbert, commanding the center corps, to send at once two brigades to reënforce General McCook, commanding the left corps. Thus I came to be a witness to some of the curious features of Perryville.

I did not know what was going on at the left, and Colonel Fry did not inform me. He told me what to say to General Gilbert, and to go fast, and taking one of the general's orderlies with me, I started on my errand. I found General Gilbert at the front, and as he had no staff-officer at hand at the moment, he asked me to go to General Schoepf, one of his division commanders, with the order. Schoepf promptly detached two brigades, and he told me I had better go on ahead and find out where they were to go. There was no sound to direct me, and as I tried to take an air line I passed outside the Union lines and was overtaken by a cavalry officer, who gave me the pleasing information that I was riding toward the enemy's pickets. Now up to this time I had heard no sound of battle; I had heard no artillery in front of me, and no heavy infantry-firing. I rode back, and passed behind the cavalry regiment which was deployed in the woods, and started in the direction indicated to me by the officer who called me back. At some distance I overtook an ambulance train, urged to its best speed, and then I knew that something serious was on hand. This was the first intimation I had that one of the fiercest struggles of the war was at that moment raging almost within my sight.

Directed by the officers in charge of the ambulances I made another detour, and pushing on at greater speed I suddenly turned into a road, and there before me, within a few hundred yards, the battle of Perryville burst into view, and the roar of the artillery and the continuous rattle of the musketry first broke upon my ear. It was the finest spectacle I ever saw. It was wholly unexpected, and it fixed me with astonishment. It was like tearing away a curtain from the front of a great picture, or the sudden bursting of a thunder-cloud when the sky in front seems serene and clear. I had seen an unlooked-for storm at sea, with hardly a moment's notice, hurl itself out of the clouds and lash the ocean into a foam of wild rage. But here there was not the warning of an instant. At one bound my horse carried me from stillness into the uproar of battle. One turn from a lonely bridle-path through the woods brought me face to face with the bloody struggle of thousands of men.

Waiting for news to carry back, I saw and heard some of the unhappy occurrences of Perryville. I saw young Forman, with the remnant of his company of the 15th Kentucky regiment, withdrawn to make way for the reënforcements, and as they silently passed me they seemed to stagger and reel like men who had been beating against a great storm. Forman had the colors in his hand, and he and several of his little group of men had their hands upon their chests and their lips apart as though they had difficulty in breathing. They filed into a field, and without thought of shot or shell they lay down on the ground apparently in a state of exhaustion. I joined a mounted group about a young officer, and heard Rumsey Wing, one of Jackson's volunteer aides, telling of that general's death and the scattering of the raw division he commanded. I remembered how I had gone up to Shiloh with Terrill's battery in a small steamer, and how, as the first streak of daylight came, Terrill, sitting on the deck near me, had recited a line about the beauty of the dawn, and had wondered how the day would close upon us all. I asked about Terrill, who now commanded a brigade, and was told that he had been carried to the rear to die. I thought of the accomplished, good, and brave Parsons,—whom I had seen knocked down seven times in a fight with a bigger man at West Point, without ever a thought of quitting so long as he could get up, and who lived to take orders in the church, and die at Memphis of the yellow fever, ministering to the last to the spiritual wants of his parishioners,—and I asked about Parsons's battery. His raw infantry support had broken, and stunned by the disaster that he thought had overtaken the whole army, he stood by his guns until every horse and every man had gone, and the enemy was almost touching him, and had been dragged away at last by one of his men who had come back to the rescue. His battery was a wreck and no one knew then where he was. And so the news came in of men I knew and men with friends about me.

"THIS GRAND HAVOC OF BATTLE":
KENTUCKY, OCTOBER 1862

Sam R. Watkins: from "Co. Aytch," Maury Grays, First Tennessee Regiment

In his 1882 memoir Private Watkins recalls the unrivaled pleasures of the Confederates' march into Kentucky (although overstating the number of new recruits) and the badly led but bloody fighting at Perryville. The battle's results were inconclusive, but Bragg lost his enthusiasm for the offensive and he and Smith withdrew into Tennessee. When Buell failed to pursue the retreating Confederates, Lincoln replaced him with William S. Rosecrans.

———————

WE GO INTO KENTUCKY.

After being thoroughly reorganized at Tupelo, and the troops had recovered their health and spirits, we made an advance into Kentucky. We took the cars at Tupelo and went to Mobile, from thence across Mobile Bay to Montgomery, Alabama, then to Atlanta, from there to Chattanooga, and then over the mountains afoot to the blue-grass regions of Kentucky—the dark and bloody ground. Please remember, patient reader, that I write entirely from memory. I have no data or diary or anything to go by, and memory is a peculiar faculty. I find that I cannot remember towns and battles, and remember only the little things. I remember how gladly the citizens of Kentucky received us. I thought they had the prettiest girls that God ever made. They could not do too much for us. They had heaps and stacks of cooked rations along our route, with wine and cider everywhere, and the glad shouts of "Hurrah for our Southern boys," greeted and welcomed us at every house. Ah, the boys felt like soldiers again. The bands played merrier and livelier tunes. It was the patient convalescing; the fever had left him, he was getting fat and strong; the old fire was seen to illuminate his eyes; his step was buoyant and proud; he felt ashamed that he had ever been "hacked;" he could fight now. It was the same old proud soldier of yore. The bands played "Dixie" and the "Bonnie Blue Flag," the citizens cheered, and the ladies waved their handkerchiefs and threw us bouquets. Ah, those were halcyon days, and your old soldier, kind reader, loves to recall that happy period. Mumfordsville had been captured with five thousand prisoners. New recruits were continually joining our ranks.

Camp Dick Robinson, that immense pile of army stores, had fallen into our hands. We rode upon the summit of the wave of success. The boys had got clean clothes, and had their faces washed. I saw then what I had long since forgotten—a "cockade." The Kentucky girls made cockades for us, and almost every soldier had one pinned on his hat. But stirring events were hastening on, the black cloud of battle and war had begun then to appear much larger than a man's hand, in fact we could see the lightning flash and hear the thunder roar.

We were at Harrodsburg; the Yankees were approaching Perryville under General Buell. The Yankees had been dogging our rear, picking up our stragglers and capturing some of our wagon trains.

This good time that we were having was too good to last. We were in an ecstasy akin to heaven. We were happy; the troops were jubilant; our manhood blood pulsated more warmly; our patriotism was awakened; our pride was renewed and stood ready for any emergency; we felt that one Southern man could whip twenty Yankees. All was lovely and the goose hung high. We went to dances and parties every night.

When General Chalmers marched to Perryville, in flanking and surrounding Mumfordsville, we marched the whole night long. We, the private soldiers, did not know what was going on among the Generals. All that we had to do was march, march, march. It mattered not how tired, hungry, or thirsty we were. All that we had to do was to march that whole night long, and every staff officer who would pass, some fellow would say, "Hey, mister, how far is it to Mumfordsville?" He would answer, "Five miles." It seemed to me we traveled a hundred miles and were always within five miles of Mumfordsville. That night we heard a volley of musketry in our immediate front, and did not know what it meant, but soon we came to where a few soldiers had lighted some candles and were holding them over the body of a dead soldier. It was Captain Allison, if I remember rightly, of General Cheatham's staff. He was very bloody, and had his clothes riddled with balls. I heard that he rode on in front of the advance guard of our army, and had no doubt discovered the Yankee picket, and came galloping back at full speed in the dark, when our advance guard fired on and killed him.

We laid down in a graveyard that night and slept, and when we awoke the sun was high in the heavens, shining in our faces. Mumfordsville had surrendered. The next day Dr. C. T. Quintard let me ride his horse nearly all day, while he walked with the webfeet.

THE BATTLE OF PERRYVILLE.

In giving a description of this most memorable battle, I do not pretend to give you figures, and describe how this General looked and how that one spoke, and the other one charged with drawn sabre, etc. I know nothing of these things—see the history for that. I was simply a soldier of the line, and I only write of the things I saw. I was in every battle, skirmish and march that was made by the First Tennessee Regiment during the war, and I do not remember of a harder contest and more evenly fought battle than that of Perryville. If it had been two men wrestling, it would have been called a "dog fall." Both sides claim the victory—both whipped.

I stood picket in Perryville the night before the battle—a Yankee on one side of the street, and I on the other. We got very friendly during the night, and made a raid upon a citizen's pantry, where we captured a bucket of honey, a pitcher of sweet milk, and three or four biscuit. The old citizen was not at home—he and his whole household had gone visiting, I believe. In fact, I think all of the citizens of Perryville were taken with a sudden notion of promiscuous visiting about this time; at least they were not at home to all callers.

At length the morning dawned. Our line was drawn up on one side of Perryville, the Yankee army on the other. The two enemies that were soon to meet in deadly embrace seemed to be eyeing each other. The blue coats lined the hillside in plain view. You could count the number of their regiments by the number of their flags. We could see the huge war dogs frowning at us, ready at any moment to belch forth their fire and smoke, and hurl their thunderbolts of iron and death in our very midst.

I wondered why the fighting did not begin. Never on earth were our troops more eager for the engagement to open. The Yankees commenced to march toward their left, and we marched almost parallel to our right—both sides watching each other's maneuvers and movements. It was but the lull that precedes the storm. Colonel Field was commanding our brigade, and Lieutenant-Colonel Patterson our regiment. About 12 o'clock, while we were marching through a corn field, in which the corn had been shocked, they opened their war dogs upon us. The beginning of the end had come. Here is where Captain John F. Wheless was wounded, and three others, whose names I have forgotten. The battle now opened in earnest, and from one end of the line to the other seemed to be a solid sheet of blazing smoke and fire. Our regiment crossed a stream, being preceded by Wharton's Texas Rangers, and we were ordered to attack at once with vigor. Here General Maney's horse was shot. From this moment the battle was a mortal struggle. Two lines of battle confronted us. We killed almost every one in the first line, and were soon charging over the second, when right in our immediate front was their third and main line of battle, from which four Napoleon guns poured their deadly fire.

We did not recoil, but our line was fairly hurled back by the leaden hail that was poured into our very faces. Eight color-bearers were killed at one discharge of their cannon. We were right up among the very wheels of their Napoleon guns. It was death to retreat now to either side. Our Lieutenant-Colonel, Patterson, halloed to charge and take their guns, and we were soon in a hand-to-hand fight—every man for himself—using the buts of our guns and bayonets. One side would waver and fall back a few yards, and would rally, when the other side would fall back, leaving the four Napoleon guns; and yet the battle raged. Such obstinate fighting I never had seen before or since. The guns were discharged so rapidly that it seemed the earth itself was in a volcanic uproar. The iron storm passed through our ranks, mangling and tearing men to pieces. The very air seemed full of stifling smoke and fire, which seemed the very pit of hell, peopled by contending demons.

Our men were dead and dying right in the very midst of this grand havoc of battle. It was a life to life and death to death grapple. The sun was poised above us, a great red ball, sinking slowly in the west, yet the scene of battle and carnage continued. I cannot describe it. The mantle of night fell upon the scene. I do not know which side whipped, but I know that I helped bring off those four Napoleon guns that night, though we were mighty easy about it.

They were given to Turner's Battery of our brigade, and had the name of our Lieutenant-Colonel, Patterson, and our color-bearer, Mitchell, both of whom were killed, inscribed on two of the pieces. I have forgotten the names inscribed on the other two pieces. I saw these very four guns surrendered at Missionary Ridge. But of this another time.

The battle of Perryville presented a strange scene. The dead, dying, and wounded of both armies, Confederate and Federal, were blended in inextricable confusion. Now and then a cluster of dead Yankees and close by a cluster of dead Rebels. It was like the Englishman's grog—'alf and 'alf. Now, if you wish, kind reader, to find out how many were killed and wounded, I refer you to the histories.

I remember one little incident that I laughed at while in the very midst of battle. We were charging through an old citizen's yard, when a big yellow cur dog ran out and commenced snapping at the soldiers' legs—they kicking at him to keep him off. The next morning he was lying near the same place, but he was a dead dog.

I helped bring off our wounded that night. We worked the whole night. The next morning about daylight a wounded comrade, Sam Campbell, complained of being cold, and asked me to lie down beside him. I did so, and was soon asleep; when I awoke the poor fellow was stiff and cold in death. His spirit had flown to its home beyond the skies.

After the battle was over, John T. Tucker, Scott Stephens, A. S. Horsley and I were detailed to bring off our wounded that night, and we helped to bring off many a poor dying comrade—Joe Thompson, Billy Bond, Byron Richardson, the two Allen boys—brothers, killed side by side—and Colonel Patterson, who was killed standing right by my side. He was first shot through the hand, and was wrapping his handkerchief around it, when another ball struck and killed him. I saw W. J. Whittorne, then a strippling boy of fifteen years of age, fall, shot through the neck and collar-bone. He fell apparently dead, when I saw him all at once jump up, grab his gun and commence loading and firing, and I heard him say, "D—n 'em, I'll fight 'em as long as I live." Whit thought he was killed, but he is living yet. We helped bring off a man by the name of Hodge, with his under jaw shot off, and his tongue lolling out. We brought off Captain Lute B. Irvine. Lute was shot through the lungs and was vomiting blood all the while, and begging us to lay him down and let him die. But Lute is living yet. Also, Lieutenant Woldridge, with both eyes shot out. I found him rambling in a briar-patch. About fifty members of the Rock City Guards were killed and nearly one hundred wounded. They were led by Captains W. D. Kelley, Wheless, and Steele. Lieutenant Thomas H. Maney was badly wounded. I saw dead on the battle-field a Federal General by the name of Jackson. It was his brigade that fought us so obstinately at this place, and I did hear that they were made up in Kentucky. Colonel Field, then commanding our brigade, and on his fine gray mare, rode up almost face to face with General Jackson, before he was killed, and Colonel Field was shooting all the time with his seven-shooting rifle. I cannot tell the one-half, or even remember at this late date, the scenes of blood and suffering that I witnessed on the battle-field of Perryville. But its history, like all the balance, has gone into the history of the war, and it has been twenty years ago, and I write entirely from memory. I remember Lieutenant Joe P. Lee and Captain W. C. Flournoy standing right at the muzzle of the Napoleon guns, and the next moment seemed to be enveloped in smoke and fire from the discharge of the cannon. When the regiment recoiled under the heavy firing and at the first charge, Billy Webster and I stopped behind a large oak tree and continued to fire at the Yankees until the regiment was again charging upon the four Napoleon guns, heavily supported by infantry. We were not more than twenty paces from them; and here I was shot through the hat and cartridge-box. I remember this, because at that time Billy and I were in advance of our line, and whenever we saw a Yankee rise to shoot, we shot him; and I desire to mention here that a braver or more noble boy was never created on earth than was Billy Webster. Everybody liked him. He was the flower and chivalry of our regiment. His record as a brave and noble boy will ever live in the hearts of his old comrades that served with him in Company H. He is up yonder now, and we shall meet again. In these memoirs I only tell what I saw myself, as every one ought to tell what he saw himself, and in this way the world will know the truth. Now, citizen, let me tell you what you never heard before, and that is this—there were many men with the rank and pay of General, who were not Generals; there were many men with the rank and pay of privates who would have honored and adorned the name of General. Now, I will state further that a private soldier was a private.

It mattered not how ignorant a Corporal might be, he was always right; it mattered not how intelligent the private might be (and so on up); the Sergeant was right over the Corporal, the Sergeant-major over the Sergeant, the Lieutenant over him, and the Captain over him, and the Major over him, and the Colonel over him, and the General over him, and so on up to Jeff Davis. You see, a private had no right to know anything, and that is why Generals did all the fighting, and that is to-day why Generals and Colonels and Captains are great men. They fought the battles of our country. The privates did not. The Generals risked their reputation, the private soldier his life. No one ever saw a private in battle. His history would never be written. It was the Generals that everybody saw charge such and such, with drawn sabre, his eyes flashing fire, his nostrils dilated, and his clarion voice ringing above the din of battle— "in a horn," over the left.

Bill Johns and Marsh Pinkard would have made Generals that would have distinguished themselves and been an honor to the country.

I know to-day many a private who would have made a good General. I know of many a General who was better fitted to be excused from detail and fights, to hang around a camp and draw rations for the company. A private had no way to distinguish himself. He had to keep in ranks, either in a charge or a retreat. But now, as the Generals and Colonels fill all the positions of honor and emoluments, the least I say, the better.

"YOUR OVER-CAUTIOUSNESS":
WASHINGTON, D.C., OCTOBER 1862
Abraham Lincoln to George B. McClellan

When two weeks passed after Antietam and McClellan made no move to resume campaigning, Lincoln traveled to Sharpsburg to confer with him. McClellan wrote to his wife that the president "does feel very kindly towards me personally," while Lincoln told his friend David Davis he sought to make the general understand he would "be a ruined man if he did not move forward, move rapidly & effectively." On his return to Washington, the President issued orders through Halleck on October 6 for the Army of the Potomac to advance. After yet another week passed, this carefully thought-out letter marked Lincoln's final effort to reason with the Young Napoleon.

Major General McClellan   Executive Mansion,
My dear Sir   Washington, Oct. 13, 1862.

You remember my speaking to you of what I called your over-cautiousness. Are you not over-cautious when you assume that you can not do what the enemy is constantly doing? Should you not claim to be at least his equal in prowess, and act upon the claim?

As I understand, you telegraph Gen. Halleck that you can not subsist your army at Winchester unless the Railroad from Harper's Ferry to that point be put in working order. But the enemy does now subsist his army at Winchester at a distance nearly twice as great from railroad transportation as you would have to do without the railroad last named. He now wagons from Culpepper C.H. which is just about twice as far as you would have to do from Harper's Ferry. He is certainly not more than half as well provided with wagons as you are. I certainly should be pleased for you to have the advantage of the Railroad from Harper's Ferry to Winchester, but it wastes all the remainder of autumn to give it to you; and, in fact ignores the question of *time*, which can not, and must not be ignored.

Again, one of the standard maxims of war, as you know, is "to operate upon the enemy's communications as much as possible without exposing your own." You seem to act as if this applies *against* you, but can not apply in your *favor*. Change positions with the enemy, and think you not he would break your communication with Richmond within the next twenty-four hours? You dread his going into Pennsylvania. But if he does so in full force, he gives up his communications to you absolutely, and you have nothing to do but to follow, and ruin him; if he does so with less than full force, fall upon, and beat what is left behind all the easier.

Exclusive of the water line, you are now nearer Richmond than the enemy is by the route that you *can*, and he *must* take. Why can you not reach there before him, unless you admit that he is more than your equal on a march. His route is the arc of a circle, while yours is the chord. The roads are as good on yours as on his.

You know I desired, but did not order, you to cross the Potomac below, instead of above the Shenandoah and Blue Ridge. My idea was that this would at once menace the enemies' communications, which I would seize if he would permit. If he should move Northward I would follow him closely, holding his communications. If he should prevent our seizing his communications, and move towards Richmond, I would press closely to him, fight him if a favorable opportunity should present, and, at least, try to beat him to Richmond on the inside track. I say "try"; if we never try, we shall never succeed. If he make a stand at Winchester, moving neither North or South, I would fight him there, on the idea that if we can not beat him when he bears the wastage of coming to us, we never can when we bear the wastage of going to him. This proposition is a simple truth, and is too important to be lost sight of for a moment. In coming to us, he tenders us an advantage which we should not waive. We should not so operate as to merely drive him away. As we must beat him somewhere, or fail finally, we can do it, if at all, easier near to us, than far away. If we can not beat the enemy where he now is, we never can, he again being within the entrenchments of Richmond.

Recurring to the idea of going to Richmond on the inside track, the facility of supplying from the side away from the enemy is remarkable—as it were, by the different spokes of a wheel extending from the hub towards the rim—and this whether you move directly by the chord, or on the inside arc, hugging the Blue Ridge more closely. The chord-line, as you see, carries you by Aldie, Hay-Market, and Fredericksburg; and you see how turn-pikes, railroads, and finally, the Potomac by Acquia Creek, meet you at all points from Washington. The same, only the lines lengthened a little, if you press closer to the Blue Ridge part of the way. The gaps through the Blue Ridge I understand to be about the following distances from Harper's Ferry, towit: Vestal's five miles; Gregorie's, thirteen, Snicker's eighteen, Ashby's, twenty-eight, Mannassas, thirty-eight, Chester fortyfive, and Thornton's fifty-three. I should think it preferable to take the route nearest the enemy, disabling him to make an important move without your knowledge, and compelling him to keep his forces together, for dread of you. The gaps would enable you to attack if you should wish. For a great part of the way, you would be practically between the enemy and both Washington and Richmond, enabling us to spare you the greatest number of troops from here. When at length, running for Richmond ahead of him enables him to move this way; if he does so, turn and attack him in rear. But I think he should be engaged long before such point is reached. It is all easy if our troops march as well as the enemy; and it is unmanly to say they can not do it.

This letter is in no sense an order.

Yours truly   A. LINCOLN.

RECONSIDERING MEDIATION:
ENGLAND, OCTOBER 1862

Lord Palmerston to Lord Russell

By the date of this first letter, Lord Palmerston was uncertain of the significance of Lee's check in Maryland and still considering the consequences of some form of intervention in the American war. Support from the Continental powers seemed to him essential, but he admitted it was a difficult case. By October 22, however, Palmerston's turnabout was complete. He had scheduled a cabinet meeting for October 23 to set policy for intervening by proposing mediation to the warring sides. But the Emancipation Proclamation, coming on the heels of Antietam, caused a general backing away in Britain from any appearance of supporting a slavery regime. The cabinet was postponed and finally never held, and schemes of intervention faded away.

October 2, 1862.

I return you Granville's letter, which contains much deserving of serious consideration. There is no doubt that the offer of mediation upon the basis of separation would be accepted by the South. Why should it not be accepted? It would give the South in principle the points for which they are fighting. The refusal, if refusal there was, would come from the North, who would be unwilling to give up the principle for which they have been fighting, so long as they had a reasonable expectation that by going on fighting they would carry their point. The condition of things therefore which would be favourable to an offer of mediation would be great success of the South against the North. That state of things seemed ten days ago to be approaching. Its advance has now been lately checked, but we do not yet know the real course of recent events, and still less can we foresee what is about to follow; ten days or a fortnight more may throw a clearer light upon future prospects. As regards possible resentment on the part of the Northerns following upon our acknowledgement of the independence of the South, it is quite true that we should have less to care about that resentment in the spring when communication with

Canada opens, and when our naval force could more easily operate upon the American coast than in winter, when we are cut off from Canada and the American coast is not so safe. But if the acknowledgement were made at one and the same time by England, France and some other Powers, the Yankee would probably not seek a quarrel with us alone, and would not like one against a European Confederation. Such a quarrel would render certain and permanent that southern independence, the acknowledgement of which would have caused it.

The first communication to be made by England and France to the contending parties might be not an absolute offer of mediation but a friendly suggestion whether the time was not come when it might be well for the two parties to consider whether the war, however long continued, would lead to any other result than separation, and whether it might not, therefore, be best to avoid the great evils, which must necessarily flow from a prolongation of hostilities, by at once coming to an agreement to meet upon that principle of separation which must apparently be the inevitable result of the contest, however long it may last. The best thing would be that the two parties should settle details by direct negotiation with each other, though perhaps with the rancorous hatred now existing between them this might be difficult. But their quarrels in negotiation would do us no harm if they did not lead to a renewal of war. An armistice if not accompanied by a cessation of blockades would be all in favour of the North, especially if New Orleans remained in the hands of the North. The whole matter is full of difficulty, and can only be cleared up by some more decided events between the contending armies.

October 22, 1862.

Have just read through your Memorandum on American affairs and Lewis's observations. Your description of the state of things between the two parties is most comprehensive and just. I am, however, much inclined to agree with Lewis that at present we could take no step nor make any communication of a distinct proposition with any advantage. What he says of the effect of an armistice is quite true; unless it is founded upon the acceptance by both parties of some basis of negotiation it is a mere temporary suspension of movements and action, and such suspension would probably be more disadvantageous to one party than to the other. If both parties stood equally in need of a respite they would equally remain quiet; if one party thought its antagonist would gain most by an armistice, that party would refuse it. All that we could possibly do without injury to our position would be to ask the two parties, not whether they would agree to an armistice, but whether they might not lean their thoughts towards an arrangement between themselves. But the answer of each might be written by us beforehand. The Northerners would say that the only condition of arrangement would be the restoration of the Union; the South would say their only condition would be an acknowledgement by the North of Southern independence. We should not be more advanced, and should only have pledged each party more strongly to the object for which they are fighting. I am therefore inclined to change the opinion on which I wrote to you when the Confederates seemed to be carrying all before them, and I am very much come back to our original view of the matter, that we must continue merely to be lookers-on till the war shall have taken a more decided turn.

"THE PRESDT. IS IN EARNEST":
MASSACHUSETTS, OCTOBER 1862

Charles Sumner to John Bright

Senator Sumner wrote to reassure Bright, a member of Parliament and prominent supporter of the Union cause, who had observed that the Emancipation Proclamation "means that you will preserve the Union even tho' it involve a social revolution in the South," and he asked if the government "be thoroughly supported by all the free States in such a policy?" While the Democrats made gains in Congress and governorships and state legislatures in the midterm elections, Republican control of Congress was not at risk.

---

private

Boston 28th Oct. '62

Dear Mr Bright,

I wish that I were at Landudno where for a day I could talk on our affairs, & enjoy a little repose.

The Presdt. is in earnest. He has no thought of any backward step. Of this be assured. Since I last wrote you I have been in Washington, where I saw him daily, & became acquainted precisely with his position at that time. There is nobody in the cabinet who is for "backing-down." It is not talked of or thought of.

The Presdt. was brought slowly to the Proclamation. It was written six weeks before it was put forth, & delayed, waiting for a victory; & the battle of Antietam was so regarded. I protested against the delay, & wished it to be put forth—the sooner the better—without any reference to our military condition. In the cabinet it was at first opposed strenuously by Seward, who, from the beginning has failed to see this war in its true character, & whose contrivances & anticipation have been those merely of a politician, who did not see the elemental forces engaged. But he countersigned the Proclamation, which was written by the Presdt himself, as you may infer from the style.

The old Democracy (more than half of which is now in armed Rebellion) are rallying against the Proclamation. At this moment our chief if not only danger is from the division which they may create at the North. The recent elections have shewn losses for the Administration; but these may be explained by the larger proportion of Republicans who have gone to the war. I regret these losses; but I do not think it possible that we can be without a determined working majority in the House, who will not hearken to any proposition, except the absolute submission of the rebels.

The hesitation of the Administration to adopt the policy of Emancipation led democrats to feel that the President was against it & they have gradually rallied. I think a more determined policy months ago would have prevented them from shewing their heads. The President himself has played the part of the farmer in the fable who warmed the frozen snake at his fire.

But from this time forward our whole policy will be more vigorous, & I should not be astonished to see the whole Rebellion crumble like yr Sepoy Rebellion, which for a while seemed as menacing to yr Indian Empire as ours has been to our Republic. I believe that I have avoided in my letters any very confident predictions. I have never seen our affairs with Mr Seward's eyes. But I have from the beginning seen that our only chance against the Rebellion was by striking Slavery, &, it seemed to me that these mighty armaments on both sides & their terrible shock were intended to insure its destruction. It is time for it to come to an end.

I am grateful to you that you have kept yr faith in us, & I pray you to persevere. I write to you sincerely, as I feel, & I beg you to believe that I would not excite any confidence which I do not believe well-founded.—Of course, we have before us the whole reconstruction of Southern Society. I have seen it so from the beginning. But I have hope that our people will rise to the grandeur of the occasion. The Colonization delusion is from Montgomery Blair, Post-Master Genl. who has made a convert of the President. But thus far I have thought it best to allow it to have a free course & thus to avoid a difference with the Presdt. Our generals are inefficient; but our troops are

excellent. I have loved England, & now deplore her miserable & utterly false position towards my country. God bless you.
Ever Yrs   Charles Sumner

"AN AUGER TOO DULL TO TAKE HOLD":
WASHINGTON, D.C., NOVEMBER 1862

Francis Preston Blair to Montgomery Blair

The wily Washington political veteran explains to his son, the postmaster general, the advice he gave the President regarding the politics of either retaining or dismissing McClellan—politics that bore on the Democrats' presidential nominee for 1864. Should there be a new Army of the Potomac commander, Blair recommends his son Frank, now a general serving in the western theater, to be the new man's chief of staff. The President did not reveal to Blair that he had already reached a decision regarding General McClellan.

I had a long talk with the President last night in his solitude. The torpidity of McClellan, will I fear prove fatal to him & our cause—I urged on the Prest. Mc's late success and the armys devotion to him. The difficulty of finding any other capable of wielding so great a force & to be trusted with working so complicated a machine under increased difficulties impending. His answer was that "he had tried long enough to bore with an auger too dull to take hold"—

I represented to him, the probable effect of superseding Mc & yielding to the pressure which it is known looked to succeed through the fast process of Pope, McDowell &c. Their catastrophe ought to be a warning. Yielding again to the ultras who seek to accomplish our purposes by unusual & extravagant means would give countenance to the charges of late triumph & consequently hold on the public mind—If on the contrary, Mc could be pushed on in the line he has taken & compelled to make a winter campaign, if successful the Democrats in Congress who are in heart on the side of Oligarchy & the South,—would be compelled to make war on him, & he would be compelled to take sides with the President bringing to his support in Congress the real war Democrats, while those who would resuscitate that party to carry the next Presidency, would necessarily take an antiMcClellan man for their candidate—whereas if Mc should fail as a general, he would fail on their conclusive policy and as the chief of that party they would fail with him—

In every aspect in which I can view it, the cause I think would be best served by retaining Mc at least until he makes a failure if that cannot be averted & not change him for an untried man while the Laurels of South Mountain & Antietam are fresh.

I entreated the President to send some common friend to Mc to have an explicit understanding with him—telling him what the President expected him to do & when & telling him that absolute & prompt obedience was the tenure by which alone he held his command. If it be given to Hooker or some others, mere fighting men, who want Brains tell the President I would be glad Frank were appointed Chief of Staff— He could supply strength at least.

Yours afta. F. P. Blair

November 7, 1862

MCCLELLAN'S DISMISSAL:
VIRGINIA, NOVEMBER 1862

George G. Meade to Margaret Meade

On November 5 Lincoln ordered the dismissal of McClellan and his replacement by Ambrose Burnside. Meade, a division commander in the Army of the Potomac—and future commanding general of that army—told his wife of the reaction in the army to McClellan's removal. He found McClellan's situation similar to that of General Zachary Taylor in the Mexican War—and Taylor ended up in the White House.

Camp near Warrenton Va
Nov. 8. 1862

Dear Margaret,

I wrote you yesterday a long and dismal letter founded on a report that Seymour gave me which I have reason to believe to day was founded in mis-apprehension. This morning I found myself accidentally at Reynolds with Gibbons. Some conversation took place about Gibbons position, when Gibbons said that Col. S. Meredith of Indiana, (an old politician utterly incompetent who had been made a Brigadier) had told him he was going to have him made a Major General. Well said Reynolds he has succeeded for I understand *you & I & Meade* are to be promoted. Ah said I I understood yesterday just the reverse. Reynolds observed well but you were told before you would be. The conversation here stopped as I did not wish to let Reynolds know what Seymour had said but I was satisfied Reynolds never told him, it was decided *not* to promote me but may have remained silent, when Seymour referred to my case, thinking he (S) would not like my promotion.

Afterwards in a conversation with Gibbon he told me that McClellan had said to him that he had recommended both of us. I am glad to do McClellan this justice, because altho' I do not think he has treated me altogether as well as I had a right to expect yet I am thankful for what he has done, & wish to give him all the credit that is due particularly as to day the order has been received relieving him from duty with this Army & placing *Burnside* in command.—I must confess I was surprised at this, as I thought the storm had blown over. If he had been relieved immediately after the battle of Antietam, or at any period before he moved, I could have seen some show of reason on *military* grounds. This removal *now* proves conclusively that the cause is political, and the date of the order *Nov. 5* (the day after the N. Yk election) confirms it. I presume they have said—Well if the Democrats choose to come out openly against us & organise a formidable opposition, we will not permit them to have the comd. Genl. of the Army, and as they look on McClellan as the military representative of the Democracy, they have struck a blow at the party thro' him. But they never made a greater mistake in their lives, and like the attempt to put down Taylor in Mexico it will most certainly result in making a martyr of McClellan, and putting him in the White house. Indeed I should not be surprised if it results in bringing about a revolution at the North & in the *people* demanding his restoration.—I understand he takes it very quietly, except that he says all consideration for the administration on his part is now gone, and that it shall be war to the knife between him & them. It is a pity he did not take this stand some time ago, and not have submitted as he has done so long in silence to the outrages perpetrated on him. The army is filled with gloom and their spirit greatly depressed. —Burnside it is said wept like a child, and is the most distressed man in the army—openly says he is not fit for the position, and that McClellan is the only man we have who can handle the large army now collected together, 120,000 men.

It will be a great triumph to the South, will raise & inspirit their army, for McClellan is the only man they respect & fear, and in its moral effect can not but be most injurious to our cause.—I am sick & tired of the whole business, and most heartily wish I could be honorably released. I am sure if I were in McClellans place I would feel most grateful to them for letting me retire without any fault on my part.

I trust this letter will reach you before you have done any action, on my last. Still I would advise the stirring up of our friends, and the interesting personally Gov. Curtin on my behalf, if it can be done quietly without attracting notice—also

Senator Cowan if you can find any mode of approaching him. It is always to one's interest to be identified with a state, and I have at last succeeded in becoming known as a Pennsylvanian.

Every thing has been quiet today, and no indication of the enemy in any force between the Rapidan & Rappahannock. They do not seem disposed to dispute our crossing of the latter river, whatever they may do when we get to the former.—

I understand Porters corps has come up and I will try to see Willie Townsend.—We (the Generals) are going tomorrow in a body to pay our respects & bid farewell to McClellan who leaves in the afternoon. He is ordered to Trenton, N. Jersey to await further orders. I wish I could be with you & remain with you & the dear children. Kiss them all and try & be cheerful.

Ever yours, Geo. G. Meade

LINCOLN AND McCLELLAN:
WASHINGTON, D.C., NOVEMBER 1862

Orville H. Browning: Diary, November 29, 1862

Lincoln unburdened himself on the topic of General McClellan and other matters to his old Illinois friend Senator Browning. His reference to proclamations are those of emancipation and habeas corpus. The allegations the president mentions against General Fitz John Porter at Second Bull Run led to Porter's court-martial in December. By this date Burnside had initiated a winter campaign against the Confederates at Fredericksburg on the Rappahannock.

Saturday Nov 29, 1862 Sheffield arrived this morning before breakfast. At 12 I called on the President. He was apparently very glad to see me, and received me with much cordiality. We had a long familiar talk. When speaking of the result of the recent elections I told him that his proclamations had been disasterous to us. That prior to issuing them all loyal people were united in support of the war and the administration. That the masses of the democratic party were satisfied with him, and warmly supporting him, and that their disloyal leaders could not rally them in opposition—They had no issue without taking ground against the war, and upon that we would annihilate them. But the proclamations had revived old party issues—given them a rallying cry—capitol to operate upon and that we had the results in our defeat. To this he made no reply.

I added that the Republican party could not put down the rebellion—that no party could do it—that it required a union of all loyal men in the free states to give us success, and that without that union we must disasterously fail. To all this he fully assented.

I asked him whether Genl Pope was a failure, or whether he had been sacrificed by the bad faith of his officers. He replied that he knew no reason to suspect any one of bad faith except Fitz John Porter, and that he very much hoped an investigation would relieve him from suspicion, but that at present he believed his disobedience of orders, and his failure to go to Popes aid in the battle of Friday had occasioned our defeat, and deprived us of a victory which would have terminated the war. That all Popes orders, and all his movements had met with the full approval of Genl Halleck and himself with one exception. That during the conflict between Popes and the rebel army, he Pope, had placed a portion of his army in a position, which he pointed out to me on the map, which alarmed him, but that no bad results followed—in fact it had turned out fortunately

That after the last battle fought by Pope the army was much demoralized, and it was feared the enemy would be down on Washington. In this emergency he had called McClellan here to take upon him the defence of the City—That he soon brought order out of chaos, and got the army in good condition. That for such work McClellan had great talents—Indeed for organizing, disciplining and preparing an army for the field and handling it in the field he was superior to any of our Genls That when the rebels crossed into Maryland he sent for Burnsides and told him he must take command of our army, march against the enemy and give him battle. Burnsides declined—said the responsibility was too great—the consequences of defeat too momentous—he was willing to command a Corps under McClellan, but was not willing to take the chief command of the army—hence McClellan was reinstated. The battles of South Mountain and Antietam were fought with ability—as well as any Genl could have fought them, but McClellan was too slow in his movements. He could and ought to have prevented the loss of Harper's Ferry, but was six days marching 40 miles, and it was surrendered. He did not follow up his advantages after Antietam. The army of the enemy should have been annihilated, but it was permitted to recross the Potomac without the loss of a man, and McClellan would not follow. He coaxed, urged & ordered him, but all would not do. At the expiration of two weeks after a peremptory order to that effect he had only 3/4 of his army across the River, and was six days doing that, whereas the rebel army had effected a crossing in one day

He concluded as he has in all the conversations I have had

with him about McClellan by saying that his great defect was his excess of caution I asked him about what Butler told me in Springfield that Fitz John Porter & Genl Griffing had sent a despatch to McClellan to hold on, that they had Pope where they could ruin, and that this despatch was in the Presidents hands—He said there was no shadow of foundation for such a story and no truth in it. I asked him about Burnsides army before Fredericksburg, and whether it was likely soon to accomplish any thing. He answered that Burnsides was now here consulting upon that subject—That he and Halleck had just left the room as I entered. That to get at the enemy he had to cross the Rappanhannock, and that to cross in the face of an opposing army was very hazardous, especially as he did not know its strength, and could not ascertain it. They had just been debating whether to move immediately, or whether to wait a few days till some collateral movement could be made to create a diversion which would render the passage less difficult, and that the question would be decided to day Burnside had then gone with Halleck and would receive his final orders before he left him.

Sheffield arrived this morning, and Cowan at night. Also Giffin and his wife

WASHINGTON, D.C., DECEMBER 1862

Abraham Lincoln:
Annual Message to Congress

Lincoln began his message of December 1 routinely enough, reporting on foreign affairs and financial matters and various domestic concerns, using material supplied by various cabinet officers. But then he elevated both his purpose and his rhetoric, seeking to eliminate the war's root cause, slavery, by means of compensated emancipation and colonization, to be achieved through constitutional amendments. "Mr Lincoln's whole soul is absorbed in his plan of remunerative emancipation," his friend David Davis wrote, "and he thinks if Congress dont fail him that the problem is solved." Congress did fail him, showing little favor for the proposed amendments. Still, Lincoln's closing appeal moved Horace Greeley's *Tribune* to claim, "Sentiments so noble, so forcible, so profoundly true, have very rarely found their way into the manifestoes of rulers and Governments."

December 1, 1862
Fellow-citizens of the Senate and House of Representatives:
Since your last annual assembling another year of health and bountiful harvests has passed. And while it has not pleased the Almighty to bless us with a return of peace, we can but press on, guided by the best light He gives us, trusting that in His own good time, and wise way, all will yet be well.

The correspondence touching foreign affairs which has taken place during the last year is herewith submitted, in virtual compliance with a request to that effect, made by the House of Representatives near the close of the last session of Congress.

If the condition of our relations with other nations is less gratifying than it has usually been at former periods, it is certainly more satisfactory than a nation so unhappily distracted as we are, might reasonably have apprehended. In the month of June last there were some grounds to expect that the maritime powers which, at the beginning of our domestic difficulties, so unwisely and unnecessarily, as we think, recognized the insurgents as a belligerent, would soon recede from that position, which has proved only less injurious to themselves, than to our own country. But the temporary reverses which afterwards befell the national arms, and which were exaggerated by our own disloyal citizens abroad have hitherto delayed that act of simple justice.

The civil war, which has so radically changed for the moment, the occupations and habits of the American people, has necessarily disturbed the social condition, and affected very deeply the prosperity of the nations with which we have carried on a commerce that has been steadily increasing throughout a period of half a century. It has, at the same time, excited political ambitions and apprehensions which have produced a profound agitation throughout the civilized world. In this unusual agitation we have forborne from taking part in any controversy between foreign states, and between parties or factions in such states. We have attempted no propagandism, and acknowledged no revolution. But we have left to every nation the exclusive conduct and management of its own affairs. Our struggle has been, of course, contemplated by foreign nations with reference less to its own merits, than to its supposed, and often exaggerated effects and consequences resulting to those nations themselves. Nevertheless, complaint on the part of this government, even if it were just, would certainly be unwise.

The treaty with Great Britain for the suppression of the slave trade has been put into operation with a good prospect of complete success. It is an occasion of special pleasure to acknowledge that the execution of it, on the part of Her Majesty's government, has been marked with a jealous respect for the authority of the United States, and the rights of their moral and loyal citizens.

The convention with Hanover for the abolition of the stade dues has been carried into full effect, under the act of Congress for that purpose.

A blockade of three thousand miles of sea-coast could not be established, and vigorously enforced, in a season of great commercial activity like the present, without committing occasional mistakes, and inflicting unintentional injuries upon foreign nations and their subjects.

A civil war occurring in a country where foreigners reside

and carry on trade under treaty stipulations, is necessarily fruitful of complaints of the violation of neutral rights. All such collisions tend to excite misapprehensions, and possibly to produce mutual reclamations between nations which have a common interest in preserving peace and friendship. In clear cases of these kinds I have, so far as possible, heard and redressed complaints which have been presented by friendly powers. There is still, however, a large and an augmenting number of doubtful cases upon which the government is unable to agree with the governments whose protection is demanded by the claimants. There are, moreover, many cases in which the United States, or their citizens, suffer wrongs from the naval or military authorities of foreign nations, which the governments of those states are not at once prepared to redress. I have proposed to some of the foreign states, thus interested, mutual conventions to examine and adjust such complaints. This proposition has been made especially to Great Britain, to France, to Spain, and to Prussia. In each case it has been kindly received, but has not yet been formally adopted.

I deem it my duty to recommend an appropriation in behalf of the owners of the Norwegian bark Admiral P. Tordenskiold, which vessel was, in May, 1861, prevented by the commander of the blockading force off Charleston from leaving that port with cargo, notwithstanding a similar privilege had, shortly before, been granted to an English vessel. I have directed the Secretary of State to cause the papers in the case to be communicated to the proper committees.

Applications have been made to me by many free Americans of African descent to favor their emigration, with a view to such colonization as was contemplated in recent acts of Congress. Other parties, at home and abroad—some from interested motives, others upon patriotic considerations, and still others influenced by philanthropic sentiments—have suggested similar measures; while, on the other hand, several of the Spanish-American republics have protested against the sending of such colonies to their respective territories. Under these circumstances, I have declined to move any such colony to any state, without first obtaining the consent of its government, with an agreement on its part to receive and protect such emigrants in all the rights of freemen; and I have, at the same time, offered to the several states situated within the tropics, or having colonies there, to negotiate with them, subject to the advice and consent of the Senate, to favor the voluntary emigration of persons of that class to their respective territories, upon conditions which shall be equal, just, and humane. Liberia and Hayti are, as yet, the only countries to which colonists of African descent from here, could go with certainty of being received and adopted as citizens; and I regret to say such persons, contemplating colonization, do not seem so willing to migrate to those countries, as to some others, nor so willing as I think their interest demands. I believe, however, opinion among them, in this respect, is improving; and that, ere long, there will be an augmented, and considerable migration to both these countries, from the United States.

The new commercial treaty between the United States and the Sultan of Turkey has been carried into execution.

A commercial and consular treaty has been negotiated, subject to the Senate's consent, with Liberia; and a similar negotiation is now pending with the republic of Hayti. A considerable improvement of the national commerce is expected to result from these measures.

Our relations with Great Britain, France, Spain, Portugal, Russia, Prussia, Denmark, Sweden, Austria, the Netherlands, Italy, Rome, and the other European states, remain undisturbed. Very favorable relations also continue to be maintained with Turkey, Morocco, China and Japan.

During the last year there has not only been no change of our previous relations with the independent states of our own continent, but, more friendly sentiments than have heretofore existed, are believed to be entertained by these neighbors, whose safety and progress, are so intimately connected with our own. This statement especially applies to Mexico, Nicaragua, Costa Rica, Honduras, Peru, and Chile.

The commission under the convention with the republic of New Granada closed its session, without having audited and passed upon, all the claims which were submitted to it. A proposition is pending to revive the convention, that it may be able to do more complete justice. The joint commission between the United States and the republic of Costa Rica has completed its labors and submitted its report.

I have favored the project for connecting the United States with Europe by an Atlantic telegraph, and a similar project to extend the telegraph from San Francisco, to connect by a Pacific telegraph with the line which is being extended across the Russian empire.

The Territories of the United States, with unimportant exceptions, have remained undisturbed by the civil war, and they are exhibiting such evidence of prosperity as justifies an expectation that some of them will soon be in a condition to be organized as States, and be constitutionally admitted into the federal Union.

The immense mineral resources of some of those Territories ought to be developed as rapidly as possible. Every step in that direction would have a tendency to improve the revenues of the government, and diminish the burdens of the people. It is worthy of your serious consideration whether some extraordinary measures to promote that end cannot be adopted. The means which suggests itself as most likely to be effective, is a scientific exploration of the mineral regions in those Territories, with a view to the publication of its results at home and in foreign countries—results which cannot fail to be auspicious.

The condition of the finances will claim your most diligent consideration. The vast expenditures incident to the military and naval operations required for the suppression of the rebellion, have hitherto been met with a promptitude, and certainty, unusual in similar circumstances, and the public credit has been fully maintained. The continuance of the war, however, and the increased disbursements made necessary by the augmented forces now in the field, demand your best reflections as to the best modes of providing the necessary revenue, without injury to business and with the least possible burdens upon labor.

The suspension of specie payments by the banks, soon after the commencement of your last session, made large issues of United States notes unavoidable. In no other way could the payment of the troops, and the satisfaction of other just demands, be so economically, or so well provided for. The judicious legislation of Congress, securing the receivability of these notes for loans and internal duties, and making them a legal tender for other debts, has made them an universal currency;

and has satisfied, partially, at least, and for the time, the long felt want of an uniform circulating medium, saving thereby to the people, immense sums in discounts and exchanges.

A return to specie payments, however, at the earliest period compatible with due regard to all interests concerned, should ever be kept in view. Fluctuations in the value of currency are always injurious, and to reduce these fluctuations to the lowest possible point will always be a leading purpose in wise legislation. Convertibility, prompt and certain convertibility into coin, is generally acknowledged to be the best and surest safeguard against them; and it is extremely doubtful whether a circulation of United States notes, payable in coin, and sufficiently large for the wants of the people, can be permanently, usefully and safely maintained.

Is there, then, any other mode in which the necessary provision for the public wants can be made, and the great advantages of a safe and uniform currency secured?

I know of none which promises so certain results, and is, at the same time, so unobjectionable, as the organization of banking associations, under a general act of Congress, well guarded in its provisions. To such associations the government might furnish circulating notes, on the security of United States bonds deposited in the treasury. These notes, prepared under the supervision of proper officers, being uniform in appearance and security, and convertible always into coin, would at once protect labor against the evils of a vicious currency, and facilitate commerce by cheap and safe exchanges.

A moderate reservation from the interest on the bonds would compensate the United States for the preparation and distribution of the notes and a general supervision of the system, and would lighten the burden of that part of the public debt employed as securities. The public credit, moreover, would be greatly improved, and the negotiation of new loans greatly facilitated by the steady market demand for government bonds which the adoption of the proposed system would create.

It is an additional recommendation of the measure, of considerable weight, in my judgment, that it would reconcile, as far as possible, all existing interests, by the opportunity offered to existing institutions to reorganize under the act, substituting only the secured uniform national circulation for the local and various circulation, secured and unsecured, now issued by them.

The receipts into the treasury from all sources, including loans and balance from the preceding year, for the fiscal year ending on the 30th June, 1862, were $583,885,247 06, of which sum $49,056,397 62 were derived from customs; $1,795,331,73 from the direct tax; from public lands $152,203,77; from miscellaneous sources, $931,787 64; from loans in all forms, $529,692,460 50. The remainder, $2,257,065 80, was the balance from last year.

The disbursements during the same period were for congressional, executive, and judicial purposes, $5,939,009 29; for foreign intercourse, $1,339,710,35; for miscellaneous expenses, including the mints, loans, post office deficiencies, collection of revenue, and other like charges, $14,129,771 50; for expenses under the Interior Department, $3,102,985 52; under the War Department, $394,368,407,36; under the Navy Department, $42,674,569 69; for interest on public debt, $13,190,324 45; and for payment of public debt, including reimbursement of temporary loan, and redemptions, $96,096,922 09; making an aggregate of $570,841,700 25; and leaving a balance in the treasury on the first day of July, 1862, of $13,043,546,81.

It should be observed that the sum of $96,096,922 09, expended for reimbursements and redemption of public debt, being included also in the loans made, may be properly deducted, both from receipts and expenditures, leaving the actual receipts for the year $487,788,324 97; and the expenditures, $474,744,778 16.

Other information on the subject of the finances will be found in the report of the Secretary of the Treasury, to whose statements and views I invite your most candid and considerate attention.

The reports of the Secretaries of War, and of the Navy, are herewith transmitted. These reports, though lengthy, are scarcely more than brief abstracts of the very numerous and extensive transactions and operations conducted through those departments. Nor could I give a summary of them here, upon any principle, which would admit of its being much shorter than the reports themselves. I therefore content myself with laying the reports before you, and asking your attention to them.

It gives me pleasure to report a decided improvement in the financial condition of the Post Office Department, as compared with several preceding years. The receipts for the fiscal year 1861 amounted to $8,349,296 40, which embraced the revenue from all the States of the Union for three quarters of that year. Notwithstanding the cessation of revenue from the so-called seceded States during the last fiscal year, the increase of the correspondence of the loyal States has been sufficient to produce a revenue during the same year of $8,299,820 90, being only $50,000 less than was derived from all the States of the Union during the previous year. The expenditures show a still more favorable result. The amount expended in 1861 was $13,606,759 11. For the last year the amount has been reduced to $11,125,364 13, showing a decrease of about $2,481,000 in the expenditures as compared with the preceding year and about $3,750,000 as compared with the fiscal year 1860. The deficiency in the department for the previous year was $4,551,966.98. For the last fiscal year it was reduced to $2,112,814.57. These favorable results are in part owing to the cessation of mail service in the insurrectionary States, and in part to a careful review of all expenditures in that department in the interest of economy. The efficiency of the postal service, it is believed, has also been much improved. The Postmaster General has also opened a correspondence, through the Department of State, with foreign governments, proposing a convention of postal representatives for the purpose of simplifying the rates of foreign postage, and to expedite the foreign mails. This proposition, equally important to our adopted citizens, and to the commercial interests of this country, has been favorably entertained, and agreed to, by all the governments from whom replies have been received.

I ask the attention of Congress to the suggestions of the Postmaster General in his report respecting the further legislation required, in his opinion, for the benefit of the postal service.

The Secretary of the Interior reports as follows in regard to the public lands:

"The public lands have ceased to be a source of revenue.

From the 1st July, 1861, to the 30th September, 1862, the entire cash receipts from the sale of lands were $137,476 26—a sum much less than the expenses of our land system during the same period. The homestead law, which will take effect on the 1st of January next, offers such inducements to settlers, that sales for cash cannot be expected, to an extent sufficient to meet the expenses of the General Land Office, and the cost of surveying and bringing the land into market"

The discrepancy between the sum here stated as arising from the sales of the public lands, and the sum derived from the same source as reported from the Treasury Department arises, as I understand, from the fact that the periods of time, though apparently, were not really, coincident at the beginning point— the Treasury report including a considerable sum now, which had previously been reported from the Interior—sufficiently large to greatly overreach the sum derived from the three months now reported upon by the Interior, and not by the Treasury.

The Indian tribes upon our frontiers have, during the past year, manifested a spirit of insubordination, and, at several points, have engaged in open hostilities against the white settlements in their vicinity. The tribes occupying the Indian country south of Kansas, renounced their allegiance to the United States, and entered into treaties with the insurgents. Those who remained loyal to the United States were driven from the country. The chief of the Cherokees has visited this city for the purpose of restoring the former relations of the tribe with the United States. He alleges that they were constrained, by superior force, to enter into treaties with the insurgents, and that the United States neglected to furnish the protection which their treaty stipulations required.

In the month of August last the Sioux Indians, in Minnesota, attacked the settlements in their vicinity with extreme ferocity, killing, indiscriminately, men, women, and children. This attack was wholly unexpected, and, therefore, no means of defence had been provided. It is estimated that not less than eight hundred persons were killed by the Indians, and a large amount of property was destroyed. How this outbreak was induced is not definitely known, and suspicions, which may be unjust, need not to be stated. Information was received by the

Indian bureau, from different sources, about the time hostilities were commenced, that a simultaneous attack was to be made upon the white settlements by all the tribes between the Mississippi river and the Rocky mountains. The State of Minnesota has suffered great injury from this Indian war. A large portion of her territory has been depopulated, and a severe loss has been sustained by the destruction of property. The people of that State manifest much anxiety for the removal of the tribes beyond the limits of the State as a guarantee against future hostilities. The Commissioner of Indian Affairs will furnish full details. I submit for your especial consideration whether our Indian system shall not be remodelled. Many wise and good men have impressed me with the belief that this can be profitably done.

I submit a statement of the proceedings of commissioners, which shows the progress that has been made in the enterprise of constructing the Pacific railroad. And this suggests the earliest completion of this road, and also the favorable action of Congress upon the projects now pending before them for enlarging the capacities of the great canals in New York and Illinois, as being of vital, and rapidly increasing importance to the whole nation, and especially to the vast interior region hereinafter to be noticed at some greater length. I purpose having prepared and laid before you at an early day some interesting and valuable statistical information upon this subject. The military and commercial importance of enlarging the Illinois and Michigan canal, and improving the Illinois river, is presented in the report of Colonel Webster to the Secretary of War, and now transmitted to Congress. I respectfully ask attention to it.

To carry out the provisions of the act of Congress of the 15th of May last, I have caused the Department of Agriculture of the United States to be organized.

The Commissioner informs me that within the period of a few months this department has established an extensive system of correspondence and exchanges, both at home and abroad, which promises to effect highly beneficial results in the development of a correct knowledge of recent improvements in agriculture, in the introduction of new products, and in the collection of the agricultural statistics of the different States.

Also that it will soon be prepared to distribute largely seeds, cereals, plants and cuttings, and has already published, and liberally diffused, much valuable information in anticipation of a more elaborate report, which will in due time be furnished, embracing some valuable tests in chemical science now in progress in the laboratory.

The creation of this department was for the more immediate benefit of a large class of our most valuable citizens; and I trust that the liberal basis upon which it has been organized will not only meet your approbation, but that it will realize, at no distant day, all the fondest anticipations of its most sanguine friends, and become the fruitful source of advantage to all our people.

On the twenty-second day of September last a proclamation was issued by the Executive, a copy of which is herewith submitted.

In accordance with the purpose expressed in the second paragraph of that paper, I now respectfully recall your attention to what may be called "compensated emancipation."

A nation may be said to consist of its territory, its people, and its laws. The territory is the only part which is of certain durability. "One generation passeth away, and another generation cometh, but the earth abideth forever." It is of the first importance to duly consider, and estimate, this ever-enduring part. That portion of the earth's surface which is owned and inhabited by the people of the United States, is well adapted to be the home of one national family; and it is not well adapted for two, or more. Its vast extent, and its variety of climate and productions, are of advantage, in this age, for one people, whatever they might have been in former ages. Steam, telegraphs, and intelligence, have brought these, to be an advantageous combination, for one united people.

In the inaugural address I briefly pointed out the total inadequacy of disunion, as a remedy for the differences between the people of the two sections. I did so in language which I cannot improve, and which, therefore, I beg to repeat:

"One section of our country believes slavery is *right*, and ought to be extended, while the other believes it is *wrong*, and ought not to be extended. This is the only substantial dispute. The fugitive slave clause of the Constitution, and the law for the suppression of the foreign slave trade, are each as well enforced, perhaps, as any law can ever be in a community where the moral sense of the people imperfectly supports the law itself. The great body of the people abide by the dry legal obligation in both cases, and a few break over in each. This, I think, cannot be perfectly cured; and it would be worse in both cases *after* the separation of the sections, than before. The foreign slave trade, now imperfectly suppressed, would be ultimately revived without restriction in one section; while fugitive slaves, now only partially surrendered, would not be surrendered at all by the other.

"Physically speaking, we cannot separate. We cannot remove our respective sections from each other, nor build an impassable wall between them. A husband and wife may be divorced, and go out of the presence, and beyond the reach of each other; but the different parts of our country cannot do this. They cannot but remain face to face; and intercourse, either amicable or hostile, must continue between them. Is it possible, then, to make that intercourse more advantageous, or more satisfactory, *after* separation than *before*? Can aliens make treaties, easier than friends can make laws? Can treaties be more faithfully enforced between aliens, than laws can among friends? Suppose you go to war, you cannot fight always; and when, after much loss on both sides, and no gain on either, you cease fighting, the identical old questions, as to terms of intercourse, are again upon you."

There is no line, straight or crooked, suitable for a national boundary, upon which to divide. Trace through, from east to west, upon the line between the free and slave country, and we shall find a little more than one-third of its length are rivers, easy to be crossed, and populated, or soon to be populated, thickly upon both sides; while nearly all its remaining length, are merely surveyor's lines, over which people may walk back and forth without any consciousness of their presence. No part of this line can be made any more difficult to pass, by writing it down on paper, or parchment, as a national boundary. The fact of separation, if it comes, gives up, on the part of the seceding section, the fugitive slave clause, along with all other constitutional obligations upon the section seceded from, while

I should expect no treaty stipulation would ever be made to take its place.

But there is another difficulty. The great interior region, bounded east by the Alleghanies, north by the British dominions, west by the Rocky mountains, and south by the line along which the culture of corn and cotton meets, and which includes part of Virginia, part of Tennessee, all of Kentucky, Ohio, Indiana, Michigan, Wisconsin, Illinois, Missouri, Kansas, Iowa, Minnesota and the Territories of Dakota, Nebraska, and part of Colorado, already has above ten millions of people, and will have fifty millions within fifty years, if not prevented by any political folly or mistake. It contains more than one-third of the country owned by the United States—certainly more than one million of square miles. Once half as populous as Massachusetts already is, it would have more than seventy-five millions of people. A glance at the map shows that, territorially speaking, it is the great body of the republic. The other parts are but marginal borders to it, the magnificent region sloping west from the rocky mountains to the Pacific, being the deepest, and also the richest, in undeveloped resources. In the production of provisions, grains, grasses, and all which proceed from them, this great interior region is naturally one of the most important in the world. Ascertain from the statistics the small proportion of the region which has, as yet, been brought into cultivation, and also the large and rapidly increasing amount of its products, and we shall be overwhelmed with the magnitude of the prospect presented. And yet this region has no sea-coast, touches no ocean anywhere. As part of one nation, its people now find, and may forever find, their way to Europe by New York, to South America and Africa by New Orleans, and to Asia by San Francisco. But separate our common country into two nations, as designed by the present rebellion, and every man of this great interior region is thereby cut off from some one or more of these outlets, not, perhaps, by a physical barrier, but by embarrassing and onerous trade regulations.

And this is true, *wherever* a dividing, or boundary line, may be fixed. Place it between the now free and slave country, or place it south of Kentucky, or north of Ohio, and still the truth remains, that none south of it, can trade to any port or place north of it, and none north of it, can trade to any port or place south of it, except upon terms dictated by a government foreign to them. These outlets, east, west, and south, are indispensable to the well-being of the people inhabiting, and to inhabit, this vast interior region. *Which* of the three may be the best, is no proper question. All, are better than either, and all, of right, belong to that people, and to their successors forever. True to themselves, they will not ask *where* a line of separation shall be, but will vow, rather, that there shall be no such line. Nor are the marginal regions less interested in these communications to, and through them, to the great outside world. They too, and each of them, must have access to this Egypt of the West, without paying toll at the crossing of any national boundary.

Our national strife springs not from our permanent part; not from the land we inhabit; not from our national homestead. There is no possible severing of this, but would multiply, and not mitigate, evils among us. In all its adaptations and aptitudes, it demands union, and abhors separation. In fact, it would, ere long, force reunion, however much of blood and treasure the separation might have cost.

Our strife pertains to ourselves—to the passing generations of men; and it can, without convulsion, be hushed forever with the passing of one generation.

In this view, I recommend the adoption of the following resolution and articles amendatory to the Constitution of the United States:

"*Resolved by the Senate and House of Representatives of the United States of America in Congress assembled,* (two thirds of both houses concurring,) That the following articles be proposed to the legislatures (or conventions) of the several States as amendments to the Constitution of the United States, all or any of which articles when ratified by three-fourths of the said legislatures (or conventions) to be valid as part or parts of the said Constitution, viz:

"Article ———.

"Every State, wherein slavery now exists, which shall abolish the same therein, at any time, or times, before the first day of

January, in the year of our Lord one thousand and nine hundred, shall receive compensation from the United States as follows, to wit:

"The President of the United States shall deliver to every such State, bonds of the United States, bearing interest at the rate of —— per cent, per annum, to an amount equal to the aggregate sum of   for each slave shown to have been therein, by the eighth census of the United States, said bonds to be delivered to such State by instalments, or in one parcel, at the completion of the abolishment, accordingly as the same shall have been gradual, or at one time, within such State; and interest shall begin to run upon any such bond, only from the proper time of its delivery as aforesaid. Any State having received bonds as aforesaid, and afterwards reintroducing or tolerating slavery therein, shall refund to the United States the bonds so received, or the value thereof, and all interest paid thereon.

"Article ——.

"All slaves who shall have enjoyed actual freedom by the chances of the war, at any time before the end of the rebellion, shall be forever free; but all owners of such, who shall not have been disloyal, shall be compensated for them, at the same rates as is provided for States adopting abolishment of slavery, but in such way, that no slave shall be twice accounted for.

"Article ——.

"Congress may appropriate money, and otherwise provide, for colonizing free colored persons, with their own consent, at any place or places without the United States."

I beg indulgence to discuss these proposed articles at some length. Without slavery the rebellion could never have existed; without slavery it could not continue.

Among the friends of the Union there is great diversity, of sentiment, and of policy, in regard to slavery, and the African race amongst us. Some would perpetuate slavery; some would abolish it suddenly, and without compensation; some would abolish it gradually, and with compensation; some would remove the freed people from us, and some would retain them with us; and there are yet other minor diversities. Because of these diversities, we waste much strength in struggles among ourselves.

By mutual concession we should harmonize, and act together. This would be compromise; but it would be compromise among the friends, and not with the enemies of the Union. These articles are intended to embody a plan of such mutual concessions. If the plan shall be adopted, it is assumed that emancipation will follow, at least, in several of the States.

As to the first article, the main points are: first, the emancipation; secondly, the length of time for consummating it—thirty-seven years; and thirdly, the compensation.

The emancipation will be unsatisfactory to the advocates of perpetual slavery; but the length of time should greatly mitigate their dissatisfaction. The time spares both races from the evils of sudden derangement—in fact, from the necessity of any derangement—while most of those whose habitual course of thought will be disturbed by the measure will have passed away before its consummation. They will never see it. Another class will hail the prospect of emancipation, but will deprecate the length of time. They will feel that it gives too little to the now living slaves. But it really gives them much. It saves them from the vagrant destitution which must largely attend immediate emancipation in localities where their numbers are very great; and it gives the inspiring assurance that their posterity shall be free forever. The plan leaves to each State, choosing to act under it, to abolish slavery now, or at the end of the century, or at any intermediate time, or by degrees, extending over the whole or any part of the period; and it obliges no two states to proceed alike. It also provides for compensation, and generally the mode of making it. This, it would seem, must further mitigate the dissatisfaction of those who favor perpetual slavery, and especially of those who are to receive the compensation. Doubtless some of those who are to pay, and not to receive will object. Yet the measure is both just and economical. In a certain sense the liberation of slaves is the destruction of property—property acquired by descent, or by purchase, the same as any other property. It is no less true for having been often said, that the people of the south are not more responsible for the original introduction of this property, than are the people of the north; and when it is remembered how unhesitatingly we all use cotton and sugar, and share the profits of dealing in them, it may not be quite safe to say, that the south has been more responsible than the north for its continuance. If then, for a common object, this property is to be sacrificed is it not just that it be done at a common charge?

And if, with less money, or money more easily paid, we can preserve the benefits of the Union by this means, than we can by the war alone, is it not also economical to do it? Let us consider it then. Let us ascertain the sum we have expended in the war since compensated emancipation was proposed last March, and consider whether, if that measure had been promptly accepted, by even some of the slave States, the same sum would not have done more to close the war, than has been otherwise done. If so the measure would save money, and, in that view, would be a prudent and economical measure. Certainly it is not so easy to pay *something* as it is to pay *nothing*; but it is easier to pay a *large* sum than it is to pay a larger one. And it is easier to pay any sum *when* we are able, than it is to pay it *before* we are able. The war requires large sums, and requires them at once. The aggregate sum necessary for compensated emancipation, of course, would be large. But it would require no ready cash; nor the bonds even, any faster than the emancipation progresses. This might not, and probably would not, close before the end of the thirty-seven years. At that time we shall probably have a hundred millions of people to share the burden, instead of thirty one millions, as now. And not only so, but the increase of our population may be expected to continue for a long time after that period, as rapidly as before; because our territory will not have become full. I do not state this inconsiderately. At the same ratio of increase which we have maintained, on an average, from our first national census, in 1790, until that of 1860, we should, in 1900, have a population of 103,208,415. And why may we not continue that ratio far beyond that period? Our abundant room—our broad national homestead—is our ample resource. Were our territory as limited as are the British Isles, very certainly our population could not expand as stated. Instead of receiving the foreign born, as now, we should be compelled to send part of the native born away. But such is not our condition. We have two millions nine hundred and sixty-three thousand square miles.

Europe has three millions and eight hundred thousand, with a population averaging seventy-three and one-third persons to the square mile. Why may not our country, at some time, average as many? Is it less fertile? Has it more waste surface, by mountains, rivers, lakes, deserts, or other causes? Is it inferior to Europe in any natural advantage? If, then, we are, at some time, to be as populous as Europe, how soon? As to when this *may* be, we can judge by the past and the present; as to when it *will* be, if ever, depends much on whether we maintain the Union. Several of our States are already above the average of Europe—seventy three and a third to the square mile. Massachusetts has 157; Rhode Island, 133; Connecticut, 99; New York and New Jersey, each, 80; also two other great States, Pennsylvania and Ohio, are not far below, the former having 63, and the latter 59. The States already above the European average, except New York, have increased in as rapid a ratio, since passing that point, as ever before; while no one of them is equal to some other parts of our country, in natural capacity for sustaining a dense population.

Taking the nation in the aggregate, and we find its population and ratio of increase, for the several decennial periods, to be as follows:—

1790	3,929,827		
1800	5,305,937	35.02 per cent.	ratio of increase
1810	7,239,814	36.45	"
1820	9,638,131	33.13	"
1830	12,866,020	33.49	"
1840	17,069,453	32.67	"
1850	23,191,876	35.87	"
1860	31,443,790	35.58	"

This shows an average decennial increase of 34.60 per cent. in population through the seventy years from our first, to our last census yet taken. It is seen that the ratio of increase, at no one of these seven periods, is either two per cent. below, or two per cent. above, the average; thus showing how inflexible, and, consequently, how reliable, the law of increase, in our case, is. Assuming that it will continue, gives the following results:—

1870	42,323,341	1910	138,918,526
1880	56,967,216	1920	186,984,335
1890	76,677,872	1930	251,680,914
1900	103,208,415		

These figures show that our country *may* be as populous as Europe now is, at some point between 1920 and 1930—say about 1925—our territory, at seventy-three and a third persons to the square mile, being of capacity to contain 217,186,000.

And we *will* reach this, too, if we do not ourselves relinquish the chance, by the folly and evils of disunion, or by long and exhausting war springing from the only great element of national discord among us. While it cannot be foreseen exactly how much one huge example of secession, breeding lesser ones indefinitely, would retard population, civilization, and prosperity, no one can doubt that the extent of it would be very great and injurious.

The proposed emancipation would shorten the war, perpetuate peace, insure this increase of population, and proportionately the wealth of the country. With these, we should pay all the emancipation would cost, together with our other debt, easier than we should pay our other debt, without it. If we had allowed our old national debt to run at six per cent. per annum, simple interest, from the end of our revolutionary struggle until to day, without paying anything on either principal or interest, each man of us would owe less upon that debt now, than each man owed upon it then; and this because our increase of men, through the whole period, has been greater than six per cent.; has run faster than the interest upon the debt. Thus, time alone relieves a debtor nation, so long as its population increases faster than unpaid interest accumulates on its debt.

This fact would be no excuse for delaying payment of what is justly due; but it shows the great importance of time in this connexion—the great advantage of a policy by which we shall not have to pay until we number a hundred millions, what, by a different policy, we would have to pay now, when we number but thirty one millions. In a word, it shows that a dollar will be much harder to pay for the war, than will be a dollar for emancipation on the proposed plan. And then the latter will cost no blood, no precious life. It will be a saving of both.

As to the second article, I think it would be impracticable to return to bondage the class of persons therein contemplated. Some of them, doubtless, in the property sense, belong to loyal owners; and hence, provision is made in this article for compensating such.

The third article relates to the future of the freed people. It does not oblige, but merely authorizes, Congress to aid in colonizing such as may consent. This ought not to be regarded as objectionable, on the one hand, or on the other, in so much as it comes to nothing, unless by the mutual consent of the people to be deported, and the American voters, through their representatives in Congress.

I cannot make it better known than it already is, that I strongly favor colonization. And yet I wish to say there is an objection urged against free colored persons remaining in the country, which is largely imaginary, if not sometimes malicious.

It is insisted that their presence would injure, and displace white labor and white laborers. If there ever could be a proper time for mere catch arguments, that time surely is not now. In times like the present, men should utter nothing for which they would not willingly be responsible through time and in eternity. Is it true, then, that colored people can displace any more white labor, by being free, than by remaining slaves? If they stay in their old places, they jostle no white laborers; if they leave their old places, they leave them open to white laborers. Logically, there is neither more nor less of it. Emancipation, even without deportation, would probably enhance the wages of white labor, and, very surely, would not reduce them. Thus, the customary amount of labor would still have to be performed; the freed people would surely not do more than their old proportion of it, and very probably, for a time, would do less, leaving an increased part to white laborers, bringing their labor into greater demand, and, consequently, enhancing the wages of it. With deportation, even to a limited extent, enhanced wages to white labor is mathematically certain. Labor is like any other commodity in the market—increase the demand for it, and you increase the price of it. Reduce the supply of black labor, by colonizing the black laborer out of the country, and, by precisely so much, you increase the demand for, and wages of, white labor.

But it is dreaded that the freed people will swarm forth, and cover the whole land? Are they not already in the land? Will liberation make them any more numerous? Equally distributed among the whites of the whole country, and there would be but one colored to seven whites. Could the one, in any way, greatly disturb the seven? There are many communities now, having more than one free colored person, to seven whites; and this, without any apparent consciousness of evil from it. The District of Columbia, and the States of Maryland and Delaware, are all in this condition. The District has more than one free colored to six whites; and yet, in its frequent petitions to Congress, I believe it has never presented the presence of free colored persons as one of its grievances. But why should emancipation south, send the free people north? People, of any color, seldom run, unless there be something to run from. *Heretofore* colored people, to some extent, have fled north from bondage; and *now*, perhaps, from both bondage and destitution. But if gradual emancipation and deportation be adopted, they will have neither to flee from. Their old masters will give them wages at least until new laborers can be procured; and the freed men, in turn, will gladly give their labor for the wages, till new homes can be found for them, in congenial climes, and with people of their own blood and race. This proposition can be trusted on the mutual interests involved. And, in any event, cannot the north decide for itself, whether to receive them?

Again, as practice proves more than theory, in any case, has there been any irruption of colored people northward, because of the abolishment of slavery in this District last spring?

What I have said of the proportion of free colored persons to the whites, in the District, is from the census of 1860, having no reference to persons called contrabands, nor to those made free by the act of Congress abolishing slavery here.

The plan consisting of these articles is recommended, not but that a restoration of the national authority would be accepted without its adoption.

Nor will the war, nor proceedings under the proclamation

of September 22, 1862, be stayed because of the *recommendation* of this plan. Its timely *adoption*, I doubt not, would bring restoration and thereby stay both.

And, notwithstanding this plan, the recommendation that Congress provide by law for compensating any State which may adopt emancipation, before this plan shall have been acted upon, is hereby earnestly renewed. Such would be only an advance part of the plan, and the same arguments apply to both.

This plan is recommended as a means, not in exclusion of, but additional to, all others for restoring and preserving the national authority throughout the Union. The subject is presented exclusively in its economical aspect. The plan would, I am confident, secure peace more speedily, and maintain it more permanently, than can be done by force alone; while all it would cost, considering amounts, and manner of payment, and times of payment, would be easier paid than will be the additional cost of the war, if we rely solely upon force. It is much—very much—that it would cost no blood at all.

The plan is proposed as permanent constitutional law. It cannot become such without the concurrence of, first, two-thirds of Congress, and, afterwards, three-fourths of the States. The requisite three-fourths of the States will necessarily include seven of the Slave states. Their concurrence, if obtained, will give assurance of their severally adopting emancipation, at no very distant day, upon the new constitutional terms. This assurance would end the struggle now, and save the Union forever.

I do not forget the gravity which should characterize a paper addressed to the Congress of the nation by the Chief Magistrate of the nation. Nor do I forget that some of you are my seniors, nor that many of you have more experience than I, in the conduct of public affairs. Yet I trust that in view of the great responsibility resting upon me, you will perceive no want of respect to yourselves, in any undue earnestness I may seem to display.

Is it doubted, then, that the plan I propose, if adopted, would shorten the war, and thus lessen its expenditure of money and of blood? Is it doubted that it would restore the national authority and national prosperity, and perpetuate both indefinitely? Is it doubted that we here—Congress and Executive—can secure its adoption? Will not the good people respond to a united, and earnest appeal from us? Can we, can they, by any other means, so certainly, or so speedily, assure these vital objects? We can succeed only by concert. It is not "can *any* of us *imagine* better?" but "can we *all* do better?" Object whatsoever is possible, still the question recurs "can we do better?" The dogmas of the quiet past, are inadequate to the stormy present. The occasion is piled high with difficulty, and we must rise with the occasion. As our case is new, so we must think anew, and act anew. We must disenthrall our selves, and then we shall save our country.

Fellow-citizens, *we* cannot escape history. We of this Congress and this administration, will be remembered in spite of ourselves. No personal significance, or insignificance, can spare one or another of us. The fiery trial through which we pass, will light us down, in honor or dishonor, to the latest generation. We *say* we are for the Union. The world will not forget that we say this. We know how to save the Union. The world knows we do know how to save it. We—even *we here*—hold the power, and bear the responsibility. In *giving* freedom to the *slave*, we *assure* freedom to the *free*—honorable alike in what we give, and what we preserve. We shall nobly save, or meanly lose, the last best, hope of earth. Other means may succeed; this could not fail. The way is plain, peaceful, generous, just—a way which, if followed, the world will forever applaud, and God must forever bless.

December 1, 1862.   ABRAHAM LINCOLN

BATTLE OF FREDERICKSBURG:
VIRGINIA, DECEMBER 1862

Edward Porter Alexander:
from Fighting for the Confederacy

General Burnside took command of the Army of the Potomac on November 7, and in ten days reached the Rappahannock opposite Fredericksburg. He had stolen a march on Lee and Fredericksburg was undefended. A pontoon train for bridging the river was to have been waiting for Burnside, but due to negligence in Washington it did not arrive until well after Lee had assembled his army and readied it to meet an attack. In his memoir, Edward Porter Alexander, now commanding an artillery battalion under James Longstreet's First Corps of the Army of Northern Virginia, spells out the deadly, nearly impregnable defenses awaiting the Union assault.

WITHIN A few days after I had given up my position on Gen. Lee's staff & taken command of my battn. of artillery, news reached us that Gen. McClellan had been deposed from command of the Army of the Potomac & succeeded by Gen. Burnside. No one was surprised then, & still less should anyone be surprised now when McClellan's inability to fight an army stands out so clearly in the light of his whole career, & particularly in his Sharpsburg campaign. Burnside did not want the position, but took it with the advice of his friends, to keep it from being offered to Hooker; of whom the old army influence by no means approved. Burnside was a man almost universally popular, though few thought him, & he did not apparently think himself, any great general. In my mind his name is associated with "Benny Havens's" near West Point, for he was old Benny's greatest admiration of all cadets ever at the Academy. He had graduated long before me, & had left the army but old Benny was always talking, even in my day, of "Ambrose Burnside."

The Federal army gave McClellan immense demonstrations of affection in telling him good-bye, & he devoted a day to receiving them. The men liked him because he had them well cared for, & they believed he would never expose them in action unnecessarily, which was most certainly true. But there was no kick against Burnside. Burnside was understood to have changed McClellan's plan of campaign for one of his own device—McC. had started to operate on a line towards Gordonsville. Burnside changed direction to Fredericksburg. It was certainly a great improvement, giving him a water base & a nearer one, & chances for new water bases, if successful, as he advanced on to Richmond. But he lost his campaign, & his excellent chances, from the miserable slowness & hesitation with which he executed his first step. He had six army corps of infantry, over 100,000 men. Lee was with Longstreet at Culpeper with about 30,000 men, & Jackson was up in the Valley with about the same number. Our pickets held the line of the Rappahannock, & there was a regiment of cavalry, perhaps, and a field battery at Fredericksburg.

On Nov. 17th the leading corps of Burnside's army arrived at Falmouth on the north side of the Rappahannock opposite Fred. but made no serious effort to cross. The news came to Gen. Lee about the _____ & on the 20th Longstreet's columns began to arrive on our side of the river. Burnside could easily with his immense force have crossed & at least occupied the town & a fortified camp on our side of the river. His excuse was the absence of his pontoon trains but he could have torn down houses & made boats or forded plenty of men to have taken the town. And at that time our army was, indeed, dangerously divided; Jackson being still in the Valley. And he did not come down to join us until about Dec. 3rd. Of course my battalion came down with Longstreet's infantry from Culpeper, & I encamped it west of the Plank Road, a mile or so out of town, nearly opposite Mr. Guest's house. I had been dined at that house, & also at Marye's, Stansbury's & Lacy's, when last at Fredbg., with my wife a few weeks after our wedding.

Very soon after my arrival I was directed to assist Gen. Lee's engineer officers in locating & constructing some pits for artillery at various points along the range of hills overlooking the town & valley of the river. The idea was that the enemy was likely to shell the town at any time, & our pits were ordered to be located so as to fire upon their batteries, if they did. But, in selecting the positions, I persuaded the engineers always to advance the guns to the brows of the hills so as to be able to sweep the approaches to the hills if it became necessary. And this brought about a little incident with Gen. Lee which, in the end, I enjoyed immensely. One day when the pits were nearly finished I was with a party working upon one on Marye's Hill, when Captain Sam Johnston, Gen. Lee's engineer in charge of the whole business, came up to tell me that Gen. Lee was inspecting the line man near by, & was blaming him for not having located the pits further back on the hill. He said, "You made me put them here. Now you come along & help me take the cussin." So I rode with him & when I came up Gen. Lee said, "Ah, Col. Alexander, just see what a mistake Captain Johnston has made here in the location of his gun pits, putting them forward at the brow of the hill!" I said, "Gen., I told him to put the pits there, where they could see all this canister & short range ground this side of the town. Back on the hill they can see nothing this side of the river." "But," he says, "you have lost some feet of command you might have had back there." I answered that that was a refinement which would cut no figure in comparison with the increased view, but he rather sat on me & had the last word, though I knew I was right & did not give it up.

Well, when the battle came on, Burnside's most powerful effort was made at that exact point, & the guns there never fired a shot at their distant view, but thousands of rounds into infantry swarming over the canister & short range ground, & contributed greatly to the enemy's bloody repulse. And a few evenings afterward, visiting Gen. Lee's camp, I took the opportunity, when the general was near enough to hear, to say loudly to Johnston, "Sam, it was a mighty good thing those guns about Marye's were located on the brows of the hills when the Yankees charged them!" I was half afraid the general might think me impertinent, though I could not resist the temptation to have one little dig at him. But he took it in silence & never let on that he was listening to us. I was however frequently put at location jobs afterward, &, thence to the close of the war, I never got but one more scolding (Oct. 7th, 1864) which I will tell of when I get to it.

Longstreet's corps at this time consisted of four regular divisions of infantry—Hood's, Pickett's, McLaws's, & Anderson's, & beside these Walker's temporary division of his own & Ransom's brigades was attached to us. Each division had some artillery attached to it, & these division batteries had in the fall gradually been made into battalions, & these battalions marched with the divisions & fought under control of the generals commanding them. Gen. Lee had on his staff a so called chief of artillery, Gen. Pendleton, but at this period his duties consisted principally in commanding a collection of some nine or ten batteries in 3 battalions called the Reserve Artillery, belonging to no corps, but kept ready to reinforce either which should need extra help. Later this command was broken up, & Gen. Pendleton after that was more directly looked on as the official head of all the artillery of the whole army. We made returns to him & drew supplies through him. And, later, each infantry corps had its own chief of artillery who, more & more, took direct command of all the battalions of the corps in battle, as well as on the march & in camp. But, at this time, I am not sure that even the title of "chief of artillery" of a corps was used. At first it was little more than a title given to the ranking battalion commander. But in battle he occupied himself principally with his own battalion. In Longstreet's corps the senior artillery officer was Col. Walton, who commanded the Washington Artillery from New Orleans—three small companies manning only 9 guns. His battalion & my 26 were called Longstreet's reserve artillery, & I made my returns & received orders through Col. Walton.

As I had had so much to do with selecting the line & positions I was practically allowed to choose for myself whether I would take any of the gun-pits on the line, in the approaching battle. But I decided not to take any. I never conceived for a moment that Burnside would make his main attack right where we were the strongest—at Marye's Hill, & I determined to keep most of my guns out in reserve, behind our left flank, expecting the brunt of the attack to fall there; but foot loose & ready to go anywhere. I thought he would try to turn our left flank on the river above Falmouth where his superior artillery, & a cloud of sharpshooters, on the north side could certainly destroy a part of our line near the river bank & enable his storming columns to make a lodgment. The ground is there yet to be looked at, and I submit that Burnside made a great mistake in not directing his attack there. I placed one light battery, Parker's, up that way, in the Stansbury yard & I placed Rhett, who had some heavy 20 pr. Parrott rifles, in pits on a high central hill near the Plank Road which overlooked our whole line & the plateau in rear of it, as a nucleus for a second line in case we were compelled to fall back or change front. The other four batteries I determined to hold in reserve in a little hollow west of the Plank Road whence I had roads in every direction.

Our pickets & the enemy's occupied opposite sides of the river in full view & short range but without firing on each other. It was the first time in the war, I believe, that this had ever happened. Before that they would keep up constant sharpshooting whenever they were within a half mile. But now both sides were willing to postpone killing each other until the grand struggle should be prepared. And, afterward, it became the general custom, to the close of the war, for pickets not to fire when there were no active operations on foot. So we built our batteries on our side & the enemy built a lot on his side, all without disturbance; and, beside our batteries, we very quietly constructed a good many rifle pits, on the edge of the town along the river, preparing to make it warm for them whenever they came to cross. As to the front of Marye's Hill, Gen. Longstreet says that I reported to him that a chicken could not find room to scratch where I could not rake the ground. I don't recall it, but very possibly I said something of the sort. It was exaggeration, but the ground was so thoroughly covered that I never thought Burnside would choose that point for attack.

At this time the enemy got to using his balloons on us again. We had not seen them since the Peninsula campaign. Now he used two of them constantly, endeavoring to locate our roads & encampments.

Jackson had joined us from the Valley about the 3rd. On the afternoon of Dec. 10th I received notice that the enemy intended to move on us the next morning at day break. Stuart had had some scouts within his lines & they had brought the news. Orders had been issued to the whole army that two guns, fired near headquarters, would be a signal upon which all troops must move to their assigned stations. About 4 A.M.

on the 11th, clear, cold, & still, the shots rang out, putting our 60,000 men in motion for their positions, & letting the enemy's 120,000 know that we were ready for them. Fredericksburg was the most dramatic of all our battles; the opposing hills & intermediate plain affording some wonderful & magnificent scenes. And I expect few who heard those two cannon shot, that cold morning, and rose & ate & hastened to their posts by starlight ever forgot the occasion.

The town itself was held by Barksdale's brigade (four Mississippi, & one Florida, regts.) of McLaws's division. McLaws was about the best general in the army for that sort of a job, being very painstaking in details, & having a good eye for ground. He had fixed up his sharpshooters all along the river to the Queen's taste. It was not expected that we could prevent the enemy from crossing but only designed to delay & annoy him as much as possible. Barksdale's men had reported, early in the night, the noise of boats & material being unloaded on the enemy's side, & long before daylight they could hear boats being put in the water & work commenced. But they were ordered to let the enemy get well committed to his work & to wait for good daylight before opening fire. Meanwhile, the guns which served as a signal to us, were also taken as a signal by most of the population of Fredericksburg to abandon the town. By every road there came numbers generally on foot, with carts loaded with bedding, &c. preparing to encamp in the woods back of our lines until the battle was over. The woods were full of them, mostly women & children. A few persons remained in the town, & though it was severely shelled, as will be told presently, no one I think was killed. But Gen. Couch, in the *Century*, speaks of the Federal soldiers looting the houses, & implies that no objection was offered by the officers.

Soon after day there rose from the river the merry popping of Barksdale's rifles. He had waited patiently until the light was good & the enemy getting careless, & he then opened suddenly a deadly fire upon them which ran them all to cover immediately. They deployed a large force of sharpshooters to try & keep down his fire & opened with their artillery & made many fresh attempts to continue their bridge-building, but were invariably driven back with loss. Meanwhile the morning wore on, calm, clear, & cold, but a very heavy smoky mist, something like that of an Indian summer, hung in the river valley in the early hours, gradually disappearing as the sun got power. The troops were all at ease along the line of battle, & looked across at the Federal army grandly displayed on the open slopes & bare hills on the north side; & listened to the fight of the sharpshooters on the river bank, which rose & fell from time to time, & in which from daylight a few Federal guns were taking a hand.

At last, near noon, Burnside out of all patience with the delay, thought to crush out the sharpshooters with one tremendous blow. He already had about 170 guns in position extending from Falmouth, above, to nearly two miles below Fredericksburg. He ordered that every gun within range should be turned upon the town & should throw fifty shells into it as fast as they could do it. Then I think was presented the most impressive exhibition of military force, by all odds, which I ever witnessed. The whole Federal army had broken up their camps, packed their wagons & moved out on the hills, ready to cross the river as soon as the bridges were completed. Over 100,000 infantry were visible, standing apparently in great solid squares upon the hilltops, for a space of three miles, scattered all over the slopes were endless parks of ambulances, ordnance, commissary, quartermaster & regimental whitetopped wagons, also parked in close squares & rectangles, & very impressive in the sense of order & system which they conveyed. And still more impressive to military eyes though less conspicuous & showy were the dark colored parks of batteries of artillery scattered here & there among them. Then, in front, was the three mile line of angry blazing guns firing through white clouds of smoke & almost shaking the earth with their roar. Over & in the town the white winkings of the bursting shells reminded one of a countless swarm of fire-flies. Several buildings were set on fire, & their black smoke rose in remarkably slender, straight, & tall columns for two hundred feet, perhaps, before they began to spread horizontally & unite in a great black canopy. And over the whole scene there hung, high in the air, above the rear of the Federal lines, two immense black, captive balloons, like two great spirits of the air attendant on the coming struggle.

To all this cannonade not one of our guns replied with a single shot! We were saving every single round of ammunition we had for the infantry struggle which we knew would come. I had come forward to Marye's Hill to watch events & I sat there quietly & took it all in. And I could not but laugh out heartily, at times, to catch in the roar of the Federal guns the faint drownded pop of a musket which told that Barksdale's men were still in their rifle pits & still defiant. The contrast in the noises the two parties were making was very ludicrous. In fact the sharpshooters scattered in their pits were very little hurt. The one casualty which was severe was caused by the falling of the chimney of Mr. Roy Mason, Jr.'s, house, which fell upon a Mississippi company held in reserve behind the house, and killed, I was told, seven, who were buried in the yard. But when Burnside advanced his bridge-builders again, on the cessation of the cannonade they were driven back just as promptly as before.

Then the Federals, at last, resorted to what they should have done at first, before daylight in the morning. They ran two or three regiments down into the pontoon boats, & rowed across. They suffered some loss of course but, as the boats drew near our shore, they got under cover of the bank & out of fire. The rest was easy: to form under cover & then take the pits singly and in flank. But Barksdale was now ready to withdraw anyhow. Two or three miles below the town, where there was no cover on our shore, the Federals had already completed a bridge, & were crossing in force. So Barksdale was now ordered to withdraw back out of the town, which he did very succesfully, having however a few isolated men cut off & captured. And so the whole day passed with no more fighting, & at night everything slept on the line of battle. I recall that the night was very cold & indeed the cold spell lasted throughout the battle. I was told that there were one or two cases of pickets without fire being frozen to death (one in the 15th So. Ca.).

The next day was rather uneventful. It was entirely occupied by Burnside in crossing over his army & ours lay quietly on its arms. We could not attack him, for our advance would have been swept by his artillery on the north side, besides which the ground he occupied near the river was also very strong & favorable for defense. Our rifle guns however would fire occasionally at bodies of infantry exposing themselves within range & the enemy's batteries would retaliate at them; & the opposing picket lines in the valley had bullets to spare for any body who would show himself within a thousand yards. Joe Haskell joined me & offered his services as an aid which I gladly availed myself of, & found him exceedingly useful as well as a delightful companion. Our friendship, commenced then, has only grown closer every day since.

Again we slept in position & then dawned Saturday the 13th, which we all knew would bring the struggle. In the early morning all the valley was shrouded in the strange sort of Indian summer mist before referred to. About 9 o'clock the heights on each side became visible & perhaps about ten the plain could be seen from the hills. Infantry pickets & sharpshooters all along the line began firing as soon as they could see, and the Federal heavy batteries from the hills north of the river began to feel for us also. We let them do most of the shooting, but occasionally Rhett's 20 pr. Parrots, or a Whitworth rifle of Lane's battery (the company from Washington, Geo.), from a high hill on our left—or some other rifle gun which got a chance, would try a shot at something offering an attractive target. But we devoted very little fire to their batteries.

Some half mile to the rear and a little to the right of Marye's Hill was a very high & commanding hill called Telegraph Hill (afterwards Lee's Hill) overlooking the entire field down to Hamilton's Crossing—five miles away—where Jackson's right flank rested. Gen. Lee made his headquarters on this hill, & on it were some half a dozen, or more, guns in scattered pits. And among these guns were two 30 pr. Parrot rifles. It was the only time in war that we ever had such heavy guns in the field. They were, however, the right things in the right place here, & filled a great want, until they, unfortunately, both exploded towards the middle of the day, one at the 37th round & one at the 42nd. At one of the explosions Genls. Lee & Longstreet & many staff officers were standing very near, & fragments flew all about them, but none was hurt. And, to finish with these guns, one of these fragments furnished a good story on a green youngster serving on Pickett's staff. He had brought a message to Gen. Lee & he saw the base of one of these large guns, with all in front of the trunnions blown away. He told Gen. P. that "the Yankees had thrown the biggest shell at Gen. Lee that he ever saw. It was about 6 feet long & three feet in diameter with two knobs on one end as thick as his leg & it must weigh over two thousand pounds."

About ten o'clock, the firing in Jackson's front began to indicate serious battle. From Gen. Lee's hill the enemies' lines of battle, preceded by a heavy skirmish line & accompanied with many batteries, could be seen advancing across the plain upon Jackson's position on the wooded hills about Hamilton's Crossing. And there was one very petty little incident. "Sallie" Pelham, as we called him at West Point, major commanding Stuart's horse artillery, was with our cavalry upon the enemy's left flank. When their long lines of infantry advanced & when Pelham found himself almost in their prolongation the temptation to enfilade them was irresistible. With only two guns he galloped forward to where an old gate stood on a small knoll & opened fire on them & soon began to produce a good deal of confusion & delay. They brought up battery after battery to crush him, until he sustained the fire of six 6 gun batteries, when he retired without much damage. Gen. Lee told of the action in a dispatch to Richmond that night in which he spoke of "the gallant Pelham," by which name his memory is still dear to all survivors of the Army of Northern Virginia. Poor fellow, he was killed in the April following, charging with a cavalry squadron, up on the Rapidan, just before Chancellorsville. He was a very young looking, handsome, & attractive fellow, slender, blue eyes, light hair, smooth, red & white complexion, & with such a modest & refined expression that his classmates & friends never spoke of him but as "Sallie" and there never was a Sallie whom a man could love more!

Having started on Jackson's fight I will finish it before I take up Longstreet's, for the two were entirely distinct. As the Federals advanced, in three lines of battle after the little Pelham episode, Jackson's artillery along his whole line opened on them very effectively. They developed a very heavy artillery fire in reply, & their infantry pushed on in very handsome style & making a fine show. But, when they came near enough to receive Jackson's infantry fire, their advance was checked. Several efforts were made to push them on but all failed except at one point upon the line of A. P. Hill's division. I have never known exactly how it came about, but his second brigade from the right, Gregg's, was not in the line between Archer's, the first, & Thomas's, the 3rd, but was back some 200 or 300 yards in the woods, which were quite swampy where the straight line would have been. The error was probably due to the fact that a considerable part of Jackson's force had only arrived that morning from Port Royal, 18 miles below Fredericksburg, where Burnside had been making some demonstrations. So the character of the field was not throughly known to all of his officers.

It happened that Meade's division had the luck to strike that soft spot where it met no infantry fire, & of course it went in. Naturally Archer & Thomas soon began to crumble away on the left flank of Archer & the right of Thomas. Gregg, in the rear, did not seem to know the gap existed, for when the advancing Federals surprised his brigade he thought they were friends & was actually trying to stop his men from firing upon them when he received his mortal wound. Some of the men, & officers too, of Archer's right—finding their left falling back, at first actually fired upon the fugitives, believing that they were deserting their posts without cause. A severe fight now took place in the woods. Gibbon's division, & part of Birney's, reinforced Meade. But Jackson had Early's division in reserve & sent it to repair the breach. They struck like a cyclone & not only whirled the enemy—all of them—out of the woods, but pursued him far out into the plain across the railroad & toward his bridges. That was the end of the battle on the right. After that there was nothing but sharpshooting & some shelling. Gen. Jackson did propose a night attack upon the enemy, & Gen. Lee gave him permission to try it, but after more careful study he decided not to venture it. So now we can take up Longstreet's fight.

About 11 that morning, I had gotten a little uneasy lest all the fighting would go Jackson's way & none of it come ours, for we were practically doing nothing, while the noise Jackson was making now filled the heavens. So I rode over to Gen. Lee's hill to find out what was going on. It took but a few minutes to see that we had no occasion to be jealous of Jackson's luck. The town was evidently already crammed as full of troops as it could hold, &, beside these, dense black columns still pouring into it, or headed for it, were visible coming up the river from below & also moving down to the bridges from the north bank. Evidently more than half of Burnside's whole army was preparing to assault us, & the assault too was not going to be where I had imagined it would be—up along the river bank—but it was going to come right out from the town, & strike where we were strongest. If we couldn't whip it we couldn't whip anything, & had better give up the war at once & go back to our homes. From that moment I felt the elation of a certain & easy victory, & my only care then was to get into it somehow & help do the enemy all the harm I could.

And, very soon, I thought I saw a good chance. I got glimpses of a heavy column of infantry on the north side evidently in motion across a bridge and into the town. My knowledge of the town made me quite sure that they would march up a certain street. Intervening hills, trees, &c. would prevent my seeing even the tops of the houses on the sides of the street, but they would not prevent my cannon shot from a distance flying high over those obstacles & then coming down in the street & bouncing along it where they would meet that advancing column. In fact all three streets must have been full of men anyhow. The only question was whether we could afford to use ammunition in that way, where it could, indeed, worry the enemy & kill some of them, but yet where we could not certainly know what we were doing, & where there was no special issue to be determined.

While I was debating this in my mind I saw a long line of battle advance from the eastern side of the town toward Marye's Hill. A long cut of an unfinished railroad ran obliquely across the open ground they had to cross. They were evidently receiving some long range infantry fire, & also a few shells, & as they came up to this railroad cut, say ten feet deep, the whole brigade of them swarmed into it. They had hardly done so when one of the 30 pr. Parrott guns, right by me, roared out, & I saw the bloodiest shot I ever saw in all my life. The gun exactly enfiladed the cut & it sent its shell right into the heart of the blue mass of men where it exploded. I think it could not have failed to kill or wound as many as 20 men. The sight of that shot excited me so that I felt bound to have some share, so I determined to send forty shot, anyhow, down that street.

So I did not wait to see any more, but started for my battalion to get Moody's Napoleons for the job. After a little reconnoitering I was able to locate them upon the prolongation of the street leading to the bridge & then we fired the forty shots at an elevation to take them nearly to the river. What harm they did, of course, we could not tell, but there were lots of people about where they fell & bounced. The enemy's batteries across the river opened on us & dropped some of their shell very close, but we had no one hurt.

Meanwhile Burnside had ordered his troops in Fredericksburg to carry Marye's Hill. Of his six corps of infantry, two were already in the town, & two more, just below, were brought up during the action which followed. Our line here was held by McLaws's division, with three brigades in line of battle at the foot of the hill: Cobb's Georgians; Kershaw's South Carolinians; & Barksdale's Mississippians, in order from left to right with Semmes's Georgians in reserve. Walker with his own & Ransom's brigade were also in reserve close by in the rear. The Washington Artillery, 9 guns, were in the pits above & also near the Plank Road was Maurin's battery—4 guns of Cabell's battalion. A sunken road, for a part of the way, gave the infantry a beautiful line, &, where that was lacking, McLaws, with his usual painstaking care & study of detail, had utilized ditches & dug trenches & provided for supplies of water & of ammunition & care of the wounded. But there was one feature of the ground which was very favorable to the enemy. There was a little sort of flat ravine running parallel to our position, & about four hundred yards in front of it, in which there was perfect cover from our sight & direct fire, for twenty thousand men or more, & this covered ground could be reached without any serious difficulty.

So the military dimensions of the task were as follows—to charge out of cover, over 400 yards of open ground, broken by a few scattered houses & garden fences, under the direct fire of fourteen guns & three brigades of infantry (say 5,000 muskets)—mostly under cover of pits & walls or trenches. To be sure there were in reserve, behind, three more brigades of infantry & say 22 guns—four of them in pits, but the rest, & the infantry, would have had to fight out in the open. But these reserves were not found necessary to repel the attacks, although toward the last, one brigade of them, Cooke's North Carolina, was brought into action. Had the case been reversed I cannot believe but that the morale of the Army of Northern Virginia would at least have taken them over the guns at the first dash. The difficulties do not begin to compare with what our men went through at either Malvern Hill or Gettysburg, where we went over the guns at the first go, charging those times as far & against five times as many men & guns. I don't wish to seem to brag about our men unduly, but I think that any professional military critic will say that that ravine ought to have enabled the Federals to, at least, have crossed bayonets with us. As it was, none of their lines of battle came within 75 yards, though a few officers & individuals got up nearer—the nearest to about 30 yards.

The first assault was made by a column of 6 brigades who advanced from the ravine above mentioned, each one after the first letting the one in advance get 200 yards' start. Practically every brigade broke up & retreated at or about the 100 yards line: which was where our infantry fire began to get in its full strength. For our men would not fire at long range but would purposely let them get nearer. The fugitives crowded behind the scattered houses, fences and in little depressions here & there, whence they fired back at our guns & line of battle. There were enough of them to keep the air, as it were, swarming with bullets, but the pits & banks enabled us to hold on in spite of them. Meanwhile, too, their siege guns, from the north bank, concentrated & pounded at us, their very best & heaviest, but we just paid no attention to them & let them shoot. One of them however killed Gen. T. R. R. Cobb, with a fragment of shell, smashing his thigh. He was a great loss to us. A man more brave, noble, & lovely in character & disposition, never lived, & he was making his mark as a soldier as rapidly as he had made it in civil & political life before the war.

It is not necessary to go into detail as to the different Federal charges, & how they brought up reinforcements, & made a number of efforts, but none of them any stronger or more serious looking, to us, than the first. A popular impression has seemed to prevail that the Irish Brigade of Thomas Francis Meagher exceeded all others in its dash & gallantry. But while it may be true that his men went as far as the farthest,

Gen. Meagher's official report of the battle shows that personally he was not in the charge, but that as it began he "being lame" started back to town to get his horse & he was soon joined in town by the remnants of his brigade whom he led back to the river bank.

So the battle in front of Marye's Hill would occasionally rise to the intensity of a charge, & decrease to severe sharpshooting & more or less shelling, from about noon till late in the afternoon. About half past three a note came to me from Col. Walton saying that the Washington Artillery was nearly out of ammunition, & calling upon me to relieve it with an equal number of guns from my battalion. Had I not been new to my command, I would have proposed to send in ammunition, & men too, if necessary, but to object to the exposure necessary of both his teams & mine in his gun's being withdrawn & my guns going in. For all the pits were in open ground & some were a little troublesome to get to. But it was my first fight in command of troops, & I was only too glad of the chance to get into those pits, & I determined at once, not only to go, but, once there, to stay to the end of the fight, if it were a week. So I at once selected 9 guns—Woolfolk's 4, Donnell Smith 2, & 3 of Moody's—& started with them for Marye's.

As we came up to the Plank Road, I asked Joe Haskell to ride up to Rhett's battery, which was firing at the time right over the route we had to take, & order it to stop until we passed; as its shells sometimes exploded prematurely. As he spurred ahead we both saw a Parrott shell from the enemy coming which had struck about 100 yards off & ricocheted & was now whirling end over end like a stick. I was just in the line of it as we could both see. Haskell reined up his horse expecting to see me cut down. I merely realized that I had no time to dodge, & wondered where it would hit. It passed under the horse's belly somehow—without touching & struck about fifteen feet beyond her. When we got nearly to Marye's Hill, keeping in low places & under cover as much as possible, the leading driver in trying to avoid the bodies of two dead men in the road got into a narrow deep ditch with both his team & the guns, & made some delay in righting things. Meanwhile the Washington Artillery ran up their teams, limbered up & came out. It was only a few minutes however before we were on hand & went in at a gallop. The sharpshooters & the enemy's guns all went for us, but we were emulating greased lightning just then & we got off very lightly, some 6 men & 12 horses, I think it was, only who were struck. Then we dismounted ammunition chests, & sent running gear & horses back under cover.

Up on Gen. Lee's hill they did not know that Walton had asked me to relieve him, & Gen. Lee, happening to look & see his guns coming out, thought they were retreating. He caught Longstreet's arm & said, "Look there, what does that mean?" Longstreet turned to Maj. Fairfax of his staff & said, "Go & order Walton to go back there and to stay there," but in a few minutes they saw my guns going in, & then they understood.

Meanwhile it happened that the enemy had just brought up a fresh division under command of Gen. Humphreys, of my old corps—the engineers, a splendid old soldier; and they were preparing to make an extra effort. Just as they were getting good & ready for the charge, back in the flat ravine, before mentioned, word was sent back to them that our artillery on the hill had been withdrawn. This raised their hopes, & Humphreys, to diminish the temptation to stop & fire, which is the bane & danger in all charges, ordered that his whole division should go with empty muskets, & rely on the bayonet alone. And so it resulted that we were hardly in our pits & good & ready, when there arose a great hurrah back at the Federal ravine & there swarmed out some three or four long lines of battle and started for us in fine style. That was just what we wanted. Our chests were crammed full of ammunition, & the sun was low; so we set in to improve each shining hour, & get rid of as much as possible of that ammunition before dark. It was for just this sort of chance that we had been saving it up since the beginning. So now we gave them our choicest varieties, canister and shrapnel, just as fast as we could put it in. It was plainly a disagreeable surprise to them, but they faced it very well & came along fairly until our infantry at the foot of the hill opened. There were now six ranks of infantry for a part of the way, & their fire was very heavy.

Then Humphreys broke all up. General Couch, in describing this charge of Humphreys's division, in the Century War Book, writes as follows: "The musketry fire was very heavy &

the artillery fire was simply terrible. I sent word, several times, to our artillery on the right of Falmouth that they were firing into us & tearing our own men to pieces. I thought they had made a mistake in the range. But I learned later that the fire came from the guns of the enemy on their extreme left." This last fire mentioned came from Parker's battery near the Stansbury house. His line got no further than the others had come & his men scattered about, & laid down & fired from behind houses, but the charge was over.

And then, between sundown & dark still one more division, Getty's, was sent in on Humphreys's left. If they had not started with a cheer I don't think that I, at least, would have known they were coming; for I could not see them, but only—when they began to fire—the flashes of their muskets. I was in a pit near the right with one of Jordan's guns, & we had almost ceased to fire for lack of a good target, when this disturbance began, & I ordered them to fire canister at the gun flashes. The gunner, who was a Corporal Logwood, from Bedford Co., Va., aimed & stepped back & ordered fire. But I was watching his aiming, & I thought he had not given quite enough elevation to his gun, so I stopped the man about to pull the lanyard & told Logwood to give the screw another turn or two down. He stepped to the breech to obey, but as he reached out his hand there was a thud, & the poor fellow fell with a bullet through & through the stomach. We had to remove him from under the wheels, & then I aimed the gun myself, & fired until after it got dark when, gradually, the whole field became quiet. Poor Logwood lived for two days, but his case was hopeless from the first.

That was an awful night upon the wounded; especially on the Federal wounded left between the lines, where their friends could give them no relief or assistance. Gen. Couch writes of it, "It was a night of dreadful suffering. Many died of wounds & exposure, and as fast as men died they stiffened in the wintry air, & on the front line were rolled forward for protection to the living. Frozen men were placed for dumb sentries."

"MURDEROUS BUTCHERY":
VIRGINIA, DECEMBER 1862

Samuel W. Fiske to the Springfield Republican

Lieutenant Fiske, ill with typhoid and dysentery, could only watch as his regiment, the 14th Connecticut, lost 120 men in the assault on Marye's Heights behind Fredericksburg. The Army of the Potomac lost more than 12,600 men killed, wounded, or missing in the battle, while Confederate casualties totaled about 5,300.

———————

DUNN BROWNE ON THE BATTLE FIELD

Fredericksburg
December 15

Oh, Republican! My heart is sick and sad. Blood and wounds and death are before my eyes; of those who are my friends, comrades, brothers; of those who have marched into the very mouth of destruction as coolly and cheerfully as to any ordinary duty. Another tremendous, terrible, murderous butchery of brave men has made Saturday, the 13th of December, a memorable day in the annals of this war.

On Friday, Fredericksburg was taken with comparatively little trouble and loss. On Saturday, the grand army corps of Sumner marched up against the heights back of the city, where the enemy lay behind strong fortifications, all bristling with cannon and protected by rifle pits; while our men must cross a wide space of clear, open ground, and then a canal whose every crossing was swept by artillery so perfectly trained beforehand that every discharge mowed down whole ranks of men. Into this grand semi-circle of death our divisions marched with rapid and unflinching step. French's division (to which we belong) behaved splendidly, and the others no less so if we may judge by the losses. Of whole companies and regiments not a man flinched. The grape and canister tore through their ranks, the fearful volleys of musketry from invisible foes decimated their numbers every few moments; the conflict was hopeless; they could inflict scarcely any damage upon the foe; our artillery couldn't cover them, for they would do more damage to friend than to enemy; yet our gallant fellows pressed on, determined to scale those breastworks and take the position of the rebels. But there were none left to do that work. A little handful of a great division approached, and even in a few instances began to climb the works, but only to leave their mangled bodies on the bloody field; a few torn and blackened remnants of the fine regiments sternly retired to the city. The wounded were mainly brought off, though hundreds were killed in the benevolent task. The city is filled with the pieces of brave men who went whole into the conflict. Every basement and floor is covered with pools of blood. Limbs in many houses lie in heaps, and surgeons are exhausted with their trying labors.

But I will not sicken you with a recital of the horrors before us. Why our noble fellows were pushed on into such a hopeless and desperate undertaking I am not military man enough to say. Or why the grand division of Hooker were marching and countermarching all through the day on the other side of the river, and didn't cross over till just at night to help in the bloody business, if it must be undertaken, I do not know either. Indeed I don't know anything hardly save that I am sick at such a destruction of noble human lives, necessary or unnecessary, useful or useless.

Personally, dear Republican, I was not much in the fight except to be under the shell fire a considerable part of the day in my anxiety to reach my regiment, and failing that to get as near as possible, as a spectator of the terrible scene. Sick for two weeks of a fever and diarrhoea, I heard the heavy firing of Thursday from a hospital ten miles distant, got permission from the surgeon in charge to mount a U.S. wagon laden with medical stores and start for the regiment. But the fearful roads of corduroy under a foot or two of mud, and the feeble state of the teams living for weeks on half forage, hindered us, and prevented your correspondent from reaching his post till the day after the battle. And doubtless the sight of the poor remnants of his regiment—one hundred men only reported for duty—and of his brigade, not enough to make half a regiment —and then not having been in the scene where the change was effected, have come over his feelings more powerfully than would otherwise have been the case, and given a sad tinge to what he ever wishes to write cheerfully. For God is over all, and even this thing is right, and shall come out in a result of good, sometime. God grant we may see it!

December 17: Night before last, quietly and without disturbance from the enemy, we evacuated Fredericksburg, and marched back to our respective old camps on this side the Rappahannock. In the darkness and through the deep mud the tired soldiers plodded wearily on their way, and then on their arrival were obliged to lie down on the ground and make the best of a rainy winter's night, before they could proceed to arrange themselves any comfortable quarters. Let us hope that the shattered divisions that bore the brunt of the fatal fight behind Fredericksburg may be left to a little rest before meeting any more of the horrors of a winter's campaign in this terrible country. Oh for a month of that beautiful weather that we wasted in the autumn. We hear rumors of the capture of Fort Darling and of Richmond, but do not credit it. If it only could be so, and that our desperate attack at Fredericksburg could have the excuse of being a part of the preconcerted plan to occupy the attention of the enemy and keep his forces here, it would much relieve many sore and discouraged hearts.

We brought off all our wounded from the city, and have left little that is valuable on the other side, save our unburied heroes on the field of battle. The pontoon bridges too are saved and ready to throw across again, and our heavy artillery command the passage of the river at any time, I suppose.

DUNN BROWNE

December 15 and 17, 1862

"THOROUGHLY LICKED":
VIRGINIA, DECEMBER 1862

Henry Livermore Abbott to Josiah Gardner Abbott and to George B. Perry

Captain Abbott, an 1860 Harvard graduate, commanded Company I in the 20th Massachusetts, Norman J. Hall's brigade, O. O. Howard's division, Darius N. Couch's corps. In these letters to his father and to Perry, a former comrade in the 20th who had been invalided out of service that fall, Abbott is unsparing of the Union generalship at Fredericksburg. Leander F. Alley was a close friend in his company. Abbott's brother Edward had been killed at Cedar Mountain in August, and another soldier brother, Fletcher, was then home on sick leave.

———

Fredericksburg Va
Dec 14 / 62

My dear Papa,

We are still in Fredericksburg (Sunday). The very moment I finished my last letter to mama we were ordered again to the front. Howard, a most conscientious man, but a very poor general, had heard of batteries stormed & rifle pits taken &c, & without stopping to think whether the rifle pits in question were an analogous case, he took the weakest brigade in the army, one which besides was considerably demoralized by the fight of the previous day & the shelling they had suffered, to say nothing of the recollection of their awful loss & defeat at Antietam, he took this brigade & ordered it to advance not altogether, but regt. after regt. The result was that the 19th which first got into position, no sooner reached the brow of the hill than they tumbled right back head over heels into us. Then came our turn. We had about 200 men. We advanced 2 or 3 rods over the brow of the hill under a murderous fire, without the slightest notion of what was intended to be accomplished. Our men however, though they couldn't be got to advance in double-quick against the rifle pits which we soon perceived, didn't on the other hand like the 19th, break & run. They held their position firmly until Col. Hall seeing that the pits could only be carried at the run, & that if carried they were completely enfiladed by a rebel battery on the hill, ordered us to retire, which we did in good order, below the brow of the hill where the whole brigade lay till 2 next morning. Crowds of troops were ordered up, but none found courage even to undertake what the poor little brigade of 1000 men had been unable to accomplish. At 2 oclock, we were relieved by the regulars who were ordered up as a last resort since Hall's brigade had failed to take the pits, which they were to storm this morning. However the generals have changed their minds since & consider the assault impracticable, so nothing has been done to day, except a little shelling—(3 oclock). Hall stoutly condemned the whole attempt by such a weak exhausted brigade, as simply ridiculous. But Howard is so pious that he thought differently. & hinc illae &c. Hooker suffered terribly yesterday & accomplished nothing. The enthusiasm of the soldiers has been all gone for a long time. They only fight from discipline & old associations. McClellan is the only man who can revive it. Macy commanded our regiment as well as it could possibly be commanded. This morning, Gen Howard called him to the front of the regt. & at the same time that he praised the regiment, complimented Macy publicly in the handsomest manner. The regiment during the few minutes they were engaged lost about 60 men & 3 officers. We have now a hundred odd men & 5 company officers with the regiment. I lost only 4 men as all but 10 I had sent out under cover to watch our flanks, which were otherwise entirely unprotected. Alley was killed instantaneously by a bullet through the eye. You will know how I feel about this loss, when I tell you that for a moment I felt the same pang as when I first heard of our great loss. I don't want to say any thing more about him now, for thinking on such a subject makes a man bluer than he ought to be in the presence of the enemy. I have sent his body home by Sergt. Summerhayes with orders to call on you for funds, as I have no money. I will settle it from

Alley's account. For God's sake, don't let Fletcher get on till after Richmond is taken. I couldn't stand the loss of a third brother, for I regard Alley almost as a brother.

I am in excellent health. My scabbard was smashed by a bullet, but I myself was uninjured. Don't you or mama worry yourself about our fighting any more. Howard told us we were so used up that we shouldn't fight again except in direst necessity.

Love to all
Your aff. son
H. L. Abbott

Near Falmouth Va
AM Wednesday

Dear George,

I suppose the letters I have written home, describing the battles have got there. So I will only say as a summing up of them, that we took over 320 men & lost 165 men & 8 officers. However we are getting back the men in the hospitals, the detailed men & that sort of thing, so that we shall soon have a respectable number again. Holmes & Willard will soon return to duty, too. As it is, we have only 5 officers. Macy & our regiment covered itself with glory & have received no end of compliments. The army generally didn't fight well. The new regiments behaved shamefully, as well as many of the old ones. The whole army is demoralized. The 15 Mass was seized with a panic at nothing at all & broke & ran like sheep. They have always been considered one of the most trustworthy regiments in the army. Hooker's troops broke & ran. He is played out. Our loss was 10000. The rebels may have lost 3000. Burnside, who is a noble man, but not a general is going to leave the army entirely. He rode through the town, the last day without a single cheer. That conscientious donkey, Howard, after keeping our brigade shivering & freezing for an hour yesterday afternoon listening to a sermon & benediction from him, proposed (N. B. he may be summed up in the words, devilish *green*) three cheers for Burnside. Several men in a new regiment, the 127th Penn. gave a mockery of 3 cheers. Not a man in the other regiments opened their mouths, except to mutter three cheers for McClellan. We can never win another victory till he comes back, & even then, not till, after 3 months of winter quarters, he has had time to reorganize the army. Financial troubles & foreign intervention may stop the thing before that time expires, but any other course is *certain* destruction. The only two generals left that this brigade believes in are Couch & Hall. We dont know much about the former, except that he protested in the strongest manner against the whole thing. The army went over with the conviction, almost the determination, of getting licked & they have got thoroughly licked. If you people at home, are going to allow us to be butchered any longer by Halleck & Stanton, you will find the enemy at your own doors.

Your aff. friend,
H. L. Abbott

Tell the governor that I have sent an order for $75 on him to pay for embalming the body of Alley. I will pay it from Alley's money, as soon as the funds come.

I was devlish sorry to hear that Fletch met with an accident. Don't let him come back before something new turns up. Old heads like Johnny Sedgwick know too much to come before McClellan.

I forgot to say, that we are in our old quarters, with every prospect of remaining.

December 17, 1862

"AN AWFUL DAY": VIRGINIA, DECEMBER 1862

Clifton Johnson: *from* Battleground Adventures

At the time of the battle, this free black man was a barrel maker in Fredericksburg, and when Clifton Johnson interviewed him in 1913 he was still working at his cooperage there. Johnson referred to him as "The Colored Cooper," but he has since been identified as Joseph Lawson, born in 1831.

THE COLORED COOPER[1]

ME AND my wife was both free born. We could have gone away befo' the battle, but we had a house hyar in Fredericksburg and four small chil'en, and I had work in town makin' barrels. So we stayed all the whole time. There was n't many who did that.

As soon as the Yankees got hyar the slaves began to run away from their mistresses and masters. They went by hundreds. You'd see 'em gittin' out of hyar same as a rabbit chased by a dog. Some carried little bundles tied up, but they could n't tote much. Often one of the women would walk along carrying a child wrapped up in a blanket. Fifteen miles from hyar they got to the Potomac, and the Yankee gunboats would take 'em right to Washington. Then they'd pile in wherever they could git. They never come back this way.

A good many of the Rebel soldiers stole off, too, so they could git into the Yankee lines, and not have to fight.

We had such cold weather that December when the battle was fought that the ice formed quite thick on a pond up hyar in the early days of the month. I promised Mr. Roe, who carried on butchery, that I'd help draw to fill his icehouse. He was to start work on the 13th. The night before was cold—

---

[1] That his years were many was evident in his stooping form and thin white hair, but he was still working. I visited him in the shop where he was making barrels as of yore, and he continued at his task while he told his story.

bitter cold. I wanted to be at the pond early, and when a noise waked me, after I'd been asleep a good long time, I thought it must be near about daybreak. So I got up and went to the barn and fed my horse. But what I'd heard was the Yankees fixin' to come over hyar from the other side of the Rappahannock on pontoon bridges.

Colonel Lang was camped up the lane, and pretty soon he marched right past my door with one thousand Confederate troops. They went down in intrenchments along the river. Then the old signal gun went off, and there was somethin' doin'. I did n't know what it meant—a gun goin' off at that time in the morning. Lang killed about seventy-five men who were makin' the pontoon bridges—swept 'em off clean as a whistle—but later in the day the Yankees come across in their boats and swept him off.

Early in the morning word was sent around that they was goin' to shell the town, and they done it, too. But I did n't git no warning and did n't know a thing of it till I saw people running. Some ran with their nightclothes on. They did n't have any time to play, I tell you. All that could, got out into the country and the woods was full of 'em—white and colored. But I stayed in the town. I think there was two hundred Yankee cannon over the river on the hills. The shelling begun about five o'clock, as near as I can come at it, and the gunners could shoot the bombs and balls just where they wanted to. I know two people was killed dead in bed that morning—an old man and an old woman. We had rough times hyar. I don't want any mo' of that bumbarding in this world. I don't want it in the next world either, if I'm ever able to git there.

Tom Knox who owned the hotel had a narrow escape. He got up when the signal gun fired and put on his clothes as quick as he could and got out of town on foot. He left everything he had behind him, and he was hardly out of the house when a shell come in and split his pillow open. It did n't hurt the bed, but they tell me a knife could n't have cut that pillow into two parts any better than the shell did. The shell was lookin' for Mr. Knox, but it did n't git him. It would have split *him* open if he'd stayed there. Yes, fifteen or twenty minutes longer in his bed would have fixed him.

The neighbors come into my house when the shells begun

to fly. Oh! we had the greatest quantity of women and children there. The house was full. They all wanted to have plenty of company so if any of 'em got hurt the others could help 'em. By and by a solid shot—a twelve-pounder—come right through my house. The Yankees had been firin' a right smart while, and I s'pose the sun was 'bout half an hour high. I was settin' up by the fire with some of the others in my bedroom. The ball cut one of the big house timbers plumb in two, and I never saw so much dirt flyin' around in my life. It took the end off the bureau just as clean as you could with a circular saw, and it left dust and everything else all over the room as if some one had been sowin' seed. Ah, man! I never want to see that pass over no mo'. It was terrible.

I had a splendid cellar under my house, and we all went down into that. We did n't have no breakfast. But I did n't bother my mind at all about that. I was n't hungry a bit. I was already filled up with skeer. The chil'en would have liked breakfast, but 'deed and they did n't git it. They was not so skeered as the grown folks because they did n't know the danger. The older people was just skeered to death, all hands of 'em, and some was mo' uneasy 'bout the chil'en than they was 'bout themselves. We had a tejious time of it with nothin' to do but talk of how the shells was running.

That was an awful day—awful day, but the firin' stopped up some by noon, and we all come up and took a peep. I went out in the back yard where I could look and see the Yankees like bees on them heights across the river. A ball had struck a haystack I had piled up in my lot, and I expected my horse would be killed tied right there in the stable, but he wa'n't hurt a bit. The town seemed to be deserted. I walked up as far as the corner, and looked up and down and could n't see a soul—man or woman, cat or dog. The neighbors stayed at our house until night, and then they went home and give the chil'en something to eat, I reckon.

Next day the place was full of Yankee troops. One of the citizens had a good deal of whiskey in his cellar, and I had helped hide it. The cellar had a brick floor, and we took up a part of it and dug a hole. All the liquor was in jimmy-johns, and we put the whole parcel of 'em down in the ground, covered 'em up with dirt, and laid back the bricks. Nobody would have known anything was buried there if they'd walked over that hyar cellar floor all day. Some one must have told, for the Irish brigade found the whiskey, and the men got so drunk they did n't know what they was doing.

The Rebels was on Marye's Heights. That was a hot place— a hot place! The Yankees never had no chance to win there. They kept chargin' a stone wall at the foot of the Heights. But Lord 'a' mercy! they was all cut to pieces every time. Some got up to the wall so they could put their hands on it, but they couldn't git no further. That wall still stands, and when there comes a rain they say the blood stains show on it even yet.

One of the leading Southern generals in this fight was Stonewall Jackson—you've heard talk of him. He was a plague, he was a honey, old Stonewall was—he was a honey! He wanted his men to take off their pants and just have on drawers so he'd know 'em. They would n't do it, and I don't blame 'em. They did n't have much to take off nohow, I reckon, and it was winter weather. Jackson's men did n't wear no shoes. Instead, they had on each foot a piece of leather tied up behind and before with leather strings. I found one of those foot protectors where they camped. Old Stonewall was a terrible man. He did n't think anything of marching his troops thirty mile in a night. They had the hardest time of any soldiers I heard of in the war. Ha, ha! do you know what kind of food he gave 'em? Three times a day each man got one year of corn—a raw year of corn. They did n't have to stop marching to eat it, but gnawed and chewed it as they tramped along.

I went to the battlefield and took a look around when things got cool, and I can tell you I don't never want to see no mo' war in my day. The battlefield 'peared like somebody had been doin' something—it 'peared awful bad! The dead was scattered around, and some looked like they was fast asleep. When a man had been hit by a shell that exploded it bust him up in such little pieces you would n't 'a' known he was ever the shape of a man. A good many bodies was all laid in a row side of the stone wall with blankets over their faces. I saw some old gray fellers among the dead. They had no business to be in the war at their age. Out in front of the stone wall was the Yankees where they'd fallen one 'pon top of t' other.

The Southern troops took possession of the town after the

battle. Some of 'em was so smoked up I did n't know whether they was white men or black men. They was nasty and dirty, and their clothes was dreadful. If a Rebel wanted a good pair of pants or shoes he had to shoot a Yankee to git 'em. Every Union man that was killed was stripped, and you often could n't tell the Rebels in their borrowed clothing from the Northern soldiers.

A heap of 'em on both sides suffered mightily for food. Some had the rashions but no chance to cook what they had. 'Bout noon one day two Rebel soldiers come up to our house off of the river, and they said to my wife, "Aunty, we've got some fish we want you to fry."

They'd been on picket duty. The Rebel pickets was on this side of the river and the Yankee pickets on the other side layin' there watchin' one another, and these fellers had put in some of their time fishing. They'd caught a mess of herrings, but they did n't have no salt nor nothing to cook 'em with. So my wife took a piece of meat and fried the herrings nicely and gave the men some bread to eat with their fish. Their rashions could n't have been much. Some of the soldiers pulled up wild onions and e't 'em.

"HUNDREDS DIE EVERY DAY":
VIRGINIA, DECEMBER 1862

Walt Whitman: *from* Specimen Days

Walt Whitman was living in Brooklyn and working as a freelance journalist when he learned that his brother George, a captain with the 51st New York Infantry, had been wounded at Fredericksburg. Whitman traveled to Falmouth, across the Rappahannock from the battlefield, and discovered that his brother's wound was slight. After visiting army hospitals and camps around Falmouth, he accompanied a group of wounded soldiers as they were evacuated to Washington by train and steamboat. Whitman would remain in the capital for the next eighteen months, visiting military hospitals while working as a government clerk. He described his time with the Army of the Potomac in *Specimen Days* (1882), drawing on accounts he had previously published in *The New York Times* in 1864; in "'Tis But Ten Years Since," a series of six articles that appeared in the *New York Weekly Graphic* in 1874; and in *Memoranda During the War* (1875).

———————

DOWN AT THE FRONT

FALMOUTH, VA., *opposite Fredericksburgh, December 21, 1862.*—Begin my visits among the camp hospitals in the army of the Potomac. Spend a good part of the day in a large brick mansion on the banks of the Rappahannock, used as a hospital since the battle—seems to have receiv'd only the worst cases. Out doors, at the foot of a tree, within ten yards of the front of the house, I notice a heap of amputated feet, legs, arms, hands, &c., a full load for a one-horse cart. Several dead bodies lie near, each cover'd with its brown woolen blanket. In the door-yard, towards the river, are fresh graves, mostly of officers, their names on pieces of barrel-staves or broken boards, stuck in the dirt. (Most of these bodies were subsequently taken up and transported north to their friends.) The large mansion is quite crowded upstairs and down, everything impromptu, no system, all bad enough, but I have no doubt the best that can be done; all the wounds pretty bad, some frightful, the men in their old clothes, unclean and bloody. Some of the wounded are rebel soldiers and officers, prisoners. One, a Mississippian, a captain, hit badly in leg, I talk'd with some time; he ask'd me for papers, which I gave him. (I saw him three months afterward in Washington, with his leg amputated, doing well.) I went through the rooms, downstairs and up. Some of the men were dying. I had nothing to give at that visit, but wrote a few letters to folks home, mothers, &c. Also talk'd to three or four, who seem'd most susceptible to it, and needing it.

After First Fredericksburg

December 23 to 31.—The results of the late battle are exhibited everywhere about here in thousands of cases, (hundreds die every day,) in the camp, brigade, and division hospitals. These are merely tents, and sometimes very poor ones, the wounded lying on the ground, lucky if their blankets are spread on layers of pine or hemlock twigs, or small leaves. No cots; seldom even a mattress. It is pretty cold. The ground is frozen hard, and there is occasional snow. I go around from one case to another. I do not see that I do much good to these wounded and dying; but I cannot leave them. Once in a while some youngster holds on to me convulsively, and I do what I can for him; at any rate, stop with him and sit near him for hours, if he wishes it.

Besides the hospitals, I also go occasionally on long tours through the camps, talking with the men, &c. Sometimes at night among the groups around the fires, in their shebang enclosures of bushes. These are curious shows, full of characters and groups. I soon get acquainted anywhere in camp, with officers or men, and am always well used. Sometimes I go down on picket with the regiments I know best. As to rations, the army here at present seems to be tolerably well supplied, and the men have enough, such as it is, mainly salt pork and hard tack. Most of the regiments lodge in the flimsy little shelter-tents. A few have built themselves huts of logs and mud, with fire-places.

"TORN AND SHATTERED":
DISTRICT OF COLUMBIA, DECEMBER 1862

Louisa May Alcott: *from* Hospital Sketches

A schoolteacher, writer, and dedicated abolitionist, Louisa May Alcott left her home in Concord, Massachusetts, in December 1862 to volunteer as a nurse at a military hospital in the District of Columbia. Her first experience was with the gravely wounded from Fredericksburg. After a month she contracted typhoid fever, ending her nursing experience. Her book *Hospital Sketches*, in which Alcott appears under the name "Tribulation Periwinkle," was published in August 1863.

———————

CHAPTER III.

A DAY.

"THEY'VE COME! they've come! hurry up, ladies—you're wanted."

"Who have come? the rebels?"

This sudden summons in the gray dawn was somewhat startling to a three days' nurse like myself, and, as the thundering knock came at our door, I sprang up in my bed, prepared

"To gird my woman's form,
And on the ramparts die,"

if necessary, but my room-mate took it more coolly, and, as she began a rapid toilet, answered my bewildered question,—

"Bless you, no child; it's the wounded from Fredericksburg; forty ambulances are at the door, and we shall have our hands full in fifteen minutes."

"What shall we have to do?"

"Wash, dress, feed, warm and nurse them for the next three months, I dare say. Eighty beds are ready, and we were getting impatient for the men to come. Now you will begin to see hospital life in earnest, for you won't probably find time to sit down all day, and may think yourself fortunate if you get to bed by midnight. Come to me in the ball-room when you are ready; the worst cases are always carried there, and I shall need your help."

So saying, the energetic little woman twirled her hair into a button at the back of her head, in a "cleared for action" sort of style, and vanished, wrestling her way into a feminine kind of pea-jacket as she went.

I am free to confess that I had a realizing sense of the fact that my hospital bed was not a bed of roses just then, or the prospect before me one of unmingled rapture. My three days' experiences had begun with a death, and, owing to the defalcation of another nurse, a somewhat abrupt plunge into the superintendence of a ward containing forty beds, where I spent my shining hours washing faces, serving rations, giving medicine, and sitting in a very hard chair, with pneumonia on one side, diptheria on the other, five typhoids on the opposite, and a dozen dilapidated patriots, hopping, lying, and lounging about, all staring more or less at the new "nuss," who suffered untold agonies, but concealed them under as matronly an aspect as a spinster could assume, and blundered through her trying labors with a Spartan firmness, which I hope they appreciated, but am afraid they didn't. Having a taste for "ghastliness," I had rather longed for the wounded to arrive, for rheumatism was n't heroic, neither was liver complaint, or measles; even fever had lost its charms since "bathing burning brows" had been used up in romances, real and ideal; but when I peeped into the dusky street lined with what I at first had innocently called market carts, now unloading their sad freight at our door, I recalled sundry reminiscences I had heard from nurses of longer standing, my ardor experienced a sudden chill, and I indulged in a most unpatriotic wish that I was safe at home again, with a quiet day before me, and no necessity for being hustled up, as if I were a hen and had only to hop off my roost, give my plumage a peck, and be ready for action. A second bang at the door sent this recreant desire to the right about, as a little woolly head popped in, and Joey, (a six years' old contraband,) announced—

"Miss Blank is jes' wild fer ye, and says fly round right away. They's comin' in, I tell yer, heaps on 'em—one was took out dead, and I see him,—ky! warn't he a goner!"

With which cheerful intelligence the imp scuttled away,

singing like a blackbird, and I followed, feeling that Richard was *not* himself again, and wouldn't be for a long time to come.

The first thing I met was a regiment of the vilest odors that ever assaulted the human nose, and took it by storm. Cologne, with its seven and seventy evil savors, was a posy-bed to it; and the worst of this affliction was, every one had assured me that it was a chronic weakness of all hospitals, and I must bear it. I did, armed with lavender water, with which I so besprinkled myself and premises, that, like my friend, Sairy, I was soon known among my patients as "the nurse with the bottle." Having been run over by three excited surgeons, bumped against by migratory coal-hods, water-pails, and small boys; nearly scalded by an avalanche of newly-filled tea-pots, and hopelessly entangled in a knot of colored sisters coming to wash, I progressed by slow stages up stairs and down, till the main hall was reached, and I paused to take breath and a survey. There they were! "our brave boys," as the papers justly call them, for cowards could hardly have been so riddled with shot and shell, so torn and shattered, nor have borne suffering for which we have no name, with an uncomplaining fortitude, which made one glad to cherish each as a brother. In they came, some on stretchers, some in men's arms, some feebly staggering along propped on rude crutches, and one lay stark and still with covered face, as a comrade gave his name to be recorded before they carried him away to the dead house. All was hurry and confusion; the hall was full of these wrecks of humanity, for the most exhausted could not reach a bed till duly ticketed and registered; the walls were lined with rows of such as could sit, the floor covered with the more disabled, the steps and doorways filled with helpers and lookers on; the sound of many feet and voices made that usually quiet hour as noisy as noon; and, in the midst of it all, the matron's motherly face brought more comfort to many a poor soul, than the cordial draughts she administered, or the cheery words that welcomed all, making of the hospital a home.

The sight of several stretchers, each with its legless, armless, or desperately wounded occupant, entering my ward, admonished me that I was there to work, not to wonder or weep; so I corked up my feelings, and returned to the path of duty, which was rather "a hard road to travel" just then. The house had been a hotel before hospitals were needed, and many of the doors still bore their old names; some not so inappropriate as might be imagined, for my ward was in truth a *ball-room*, if gun-shot wounds could christen it. Forty beds were prepared, many already tenanted by tired men who fell down anywhere, and drowsed till the smell of food roused them. Round the great stove was gathered the dreariest group I ever saw— ragged, gaunt and pale, mud to the knees, with bloody bandages untouched since put on days before; many bundled up in blankets, coats being lost or useless; and all wearing that disheartened look which proclaimed defeat, more plainly than any telegram of the Burnside blunder. I pitied them so much, I dared not speak to them, though, remembering all they had been through since the route at Fredericksburg, I yearned to serve the dreariest of them all. Presently, Miss Blank tore me from my refuge behind piles of one-sleeved shirts, odd socks, bandages and lint; put basin, sponge, towels, and a block of brown soap into my hands, with these appalling directions:

"Come, my dear, begin to wash as fast as you can. Tell them to take off socks, coats and shirts, scrub them well, put on clean shirts, and the attendants will finish them off, and lay them in bed."

If she had requested me to shave them all, or dance a hornpipe on the stove funnel, I should have been less staggered; but to scrub some dozen lords of creation at a moment's notice, was really—really——. However, there was no time for nonsense, and, having resolved when I came to do everything I was bid, I drowned my scruples in my washbowl, clutched my soap manfully, and, assuming a business-like air; made a dab at the first dirty specimen I saw, bent on performing my task *vi et armis* if necessary. I chanced to light on a withered old Irishman, wounded in the head, which caused that portion of his frame to be tastefully laid out like a garden, the bandages being the walks, his hair the shrubbery. He was so overpowered by the honor of having a lady wash him as he expressed it, that he did nothing but roll up his eyes, and bless me, in an irresistible style which was too much for my sense of the ludicrous; so we laughed together, and when I knelt down to take off his shoes, he "flopped" also and wouldn't hear of my touching "them dirty craters. May your bed above be aisy darlin', for the day's work ye are doon!—Whoosh! there ye are, and bedad, it's hard tellin' which is the dirtiest, the fut or the shoe." It was; and if he hadn't been to the fore, I should have gone on pulling, under the impression that the "fut" was a boot; for trousers, socks, shoes and legs were a mass of mud. This comical tableau produced a general grin, at which propitious beginning I took heart and scrubbed away like any tidy parent on a Saturday night. Some of them took the performance like sleepy children, leaning their tired heads against me as I worked, others looked grimly scandalized, and several of the roughest colored like bashful girls. One wore a soiled little bag about his neck, and, as I moved it, to bathe his wounded breast, I said,

"Your talisman didn't save you, did it?"

"Well, I reckon it did, marm, for that shot would a gone a couple a inches deeper but for my old mammy's camphor bag," answered the cheerful philosopher.

Another, with a gun-shot wound through the cheek, asked for a looking-glass, and when I brought one, regarded his swollen face with a dolorous expression, as he muttered—

"I vow to gosh, that's too bad! I warn't a bad looking chap before, and now I'm done for; won't there be a thunderin' scar? and what on earth will Josephine Skinner say?"

He looked up at me with his one eye so appealingly, that I controlled my risibles, and assured him that if Josephine was a girl of sense, she would admire the honorable scar, as a lasting proof that he had faced the enemy, for all women thought a wound the best decoration a brave soldier could wear. I hope Miss Skinner verified the good opinion I so rashly expressed of her, but I shall never know.

The next scrubbee was a nice looking lad, with a curly brown mane, and a budding trace of gingerbread over the lip, which he called his beard, and defended stoutly, when the barber jocosely suggested its immolation. He lay on a bed, with one leg gone, and the right arm so shattered that it must evidently follow; yet the little Sergeant was as merry as if his afflictions were not worth lamenting over, and when a drop or two of salt water mingled with my suds at the sight of this strong young body, so marred and maimed, the boy looked up, with a brave smile, though there was a little quiver of the lips, as he said,

"Now don't you fret yourself about me, miss; I'm first rate here, for it's nuts to lie still on this bed, after knocking about in those confounded ambulances, that shake what there is left of a fellow to jelly. I never was in one of these places before, and think this cleaning up a jolly thing for us, though I'm afraid it isn't for you ladies."

"Is this your first battle, Sergeant?"

"No, miss; I've been in six scrimmages, and never got a scratch till this last one; but it's done the business pretty thoroughly for me, I should say. Lord! what a scramble there'll be for arms and legs, when we old boys come out of our graves, on the Judgment Day: wonder if we shall get our own again? If we do, my leg will have to tramp from Fredericksburg, my arm from here, I suppose, and meet my body, wherever it may be."

The fancy seemed to tickle him mightily, for he laughed blithely, and so did I; which, no doubt, caused the new nurse to be regarded as a light-minded sinner by the Chaplain, who roamed vaguely about, informing the men that they were all worms, corrupt of heart, with perishable bodies, and souls only to be saved by a diligent perusal of certain tracts, and other equally cheering bits of spiritual consolation, when spirituous ditto would have been preferred.

"I say, Mrs.!" called a voice behind me; and, turning, I saw a rough Michigander, with an arm blown off at the shoulder, and two or three bullets still in him—as he afterwards mentioned, as carelessly as if gentlemen were in the habit of carrying such trifles about with them. I went to him, and, while administering a dose of soap and water, he whispered, irefully:

"That red-headed devil, over yonder; is a reb, damn him! You'll agree to that, I'll bet? He's got shet of a foot, or he'd a cut like the rest of the lot. Don't you wash him, nor feed him, but jest let him holler till he's tired. It's a blasted shame to fetch them fellers in here, along side of us; and so I'll tell the chap that bosses this concern; cuss me if I don't."

I regret to say that I did not deliver a moral sermon upon the duty of forgiving our enemies, and the sin of profanity, then and there; but, being a red-hot Abolitionist, stared fixedly at the tall rebel, who was a copperhead, in every sense of the word, and privately resolved to put soap in his eyes, rub his nose the wrong way, and excoriate his cuticle generally, if I had the washing of him.

My amiable intentions, however, were frustrated; for, when I approached, with as Christian an expression as my principles would allow, and asked the question—"Shall I try to make you more comfortable, sir?" all I got for my pains was a gruff—

"No; I'll do it myself."

"Here's your Southern chivalry, with a witness," thought I, dumping the basin down before him, thereby quenching a strong desire to give him a summary baptism, in return for his ungraciousness; for my angry passions rose, at this rebuff, in a way that would have scandalized good Dr. Watts. He was a disappointment in all respects, (the rebel, not the blessed Doctor,) for he was neither fiendish, romantic, pathetic, or anything interesting; but a long, fat man, with a head like a burning bush, and a perfectly expressionless face: so I could hate him without the slightest drawback, and ignored his existence from that day forth. One redeeming trait he certainly did possess, as the floor speedily testified; for his ablutions were so vigorously performed, that his bed soon stood like an isolated island, in a sea of soapsuds, and he resembled a dripping merman, suffering from the loss of a fin. If cleanliness is a near neighbor to godliness, then was the big rebel the godliest man in my ward that day.

Having done up our human wash, and laid it out to dry, the second syllable of our version of the word war-fare was enacted with much success. Great trays of bread, meat, soup and coffee appeared; and both nurses and attendants turned waiters, serving bountiful rations to all who could eat. I can call my pinafore to testify to my good will in the work, for in ten minutes it was reduced to a perambulating bill of fare, presenting samples of all the refreshments going or gone. It was a lively scene; the long room lined with rows of beds, each filled by an occupant, whom water, shears, and clean raiment, had transformed from a dismal ragamuffin into a recumbent hero, with a cropped head. To and fro rushed matrons, maids, and convalescent "boys," skirmishing with knives and forks; retreating with empty plates; marching and counter-marching, with unvaried success, while the clash of busy spoons made most inspiring music for the charge of our Light Brigade:

"Beds to the front of them,
  Beds to the right of them,
  Beds to the left of them,
    Nobody blundered.
  Beamed at by hungry souls,
  Screamed at with brimming bowls,
  Steamed at by army rolls,
    Buttered and sundered.
  With coffee not cannon plied,
  Each must be satisfied,
  Whether they lived or died;
    All the men wondered."

Very welcome seemed the generous meal, after a week of suffering, exposure, and short commons; soon the brown faces began to smile, as food, warmth, and rest, did their pleasant work; and the grateful "Thankee's" were followed by more graphic accounts of the battle and retreat, than any paid reporter could have given us. Curious contrasts of the tragic and comic met one everywhere; and some touching as well as ludicrous episodes, might have been recorded that day. A six foot New Hampshire man, with a leg broken and perforated by a piece of shell, so large that, had I not seen the wound, I should have regarded the story as a Munchausenism, beckoned me to come and help him, as he could not sit up, and both his bed and beard were getting plentifully anointed with soup. As I fed my big nestling with corresponding mouthfuls, I asked him how he felt during the battle.

"Well, 'twas my fust, you see, so I aint ashamed to say I was a trifle flustered in the beginnin', there was such an allfired racket; for ef there's anything I do spleen agin, it's noise. But when my mate, Eph Sylvester, caved, with a bullet through his head, I got mad, and pitched in, licketty cut. Our part of the fight didn't last long; so a lot of us larked round Fredericksburg, and give some of them houses a pretty consid'able of a rummage, till we was ordered out of the mess. Some of our fellows cut like time; but I warn't a-goin to run for nobody; and, fust thing I knew, a shell bust, right in front of us, and I keeled over, feelin' as if I was blowed higher'n a kite. I sung out, and the boys come back for me, double quick; but the way they chucked me over them fences was a caution, I tell you. Next day I was most as black as that darkey yonder, lickin' plates on the sly. This is bully coffee, ain't it? Give us another pull at it, and I'll be obleeged to you."

I did; and, as the last gulp subsided, he said, with a rub of his old handkerchief over eyes as well as mouth:

"Look a here; I've got a pair a earbobs and a handkercher pin I'm a goin' to give you, if you'll have them; for you're the very moral o' Lizy Sylvester, poor Eph's wife: that's why I signalled you to come over here. They aint much, I guess, but they'll do to memorize the rebs by."

Burrowing under his pillow, he produced a little bundle of what he called "truck," and gallantly presented me with a pair of earrings, each representing a cluster of corpulent grapes, and the pin a basket of astonishing fruit, the whole large and coppery enough for a small warming-pan. Feeling delicate about depriving him of such valuable relics, I accepted the earrings alone, and was obliged to depart, somewhat abruptly, when my friend stuck the warming-pan in the bosom of his night-gown, viewing it with much complacency, and, perhaps, some tender memory, in that rough heart of his, for the comrade he had lost.

Observing that the man next him had left his meal untouched, I offered the same service I had performed for his neighbor, but he shook his head.

"Thank you, ma'am; I don't think I'll ever eat again, for I'm shot in the stomach. But I'd like a drink of water, if you aint too busy."

I rushed away, but the water-pails were gone to be refilled, and it was some time before they reappeared. I did not forget my patient patient, meanwhile, and, with the first mugful, hurried back to him. He seemed asleep; but something in the tired white face caused me to listen at his lips for a breath. None came. I touched his forehead; it was cold: and then I knew that, while he waited, a better nurse than I had given him a cooler draught, and healed him with a touch. I laid the sheet over the quiet sleeper, whom no noise could now disturb; and, half an hour later, the bed was empty. It seemed a poor requital for all he had sacrificed and suffered,—that hospital bed, lonely even in a crowd; for there was no familiar face for him to look his last upon; no friendly voice to say, Good bye; no hand to lead him gently down into the Valley of the Shadow; and he vanished, like a drop in that red sea upon whose shores so many women stand lamenting. For a moment I felt bitterly indignant at this seeming carelessness of the value of life, the sanctity of death; then consoled myself with the thought that, when the great muster roll was called, these nameless men might be promoted above many whose tall monuments record the barren honors they have won.

All having eaten, drank, and rested, the surgeons began their rounds; and I took my first lesson in the art of dressing wounds. It wasn't a festive scene, by any means; for Dr. P., whose Aid I constituted myself, fell to work with a vigor which soon convinced me that I was a weaker vessel, though nothing would have induced me to confess it then. He had served in the Crimea, and seemed to regard a dilapidated body very much as I should have regarded a damaged garment; and, turning up his cuffs, whipped out a very unpleasant looking housewife, cutting, sawing, patching and piecing, with the enthusiasm of an accomplished surgical seamstress; explaining the process, in scientific terms, to the patient, meantime; which, of course, was immensely cheering and comfortable. There was an uncanny sort of fascination in watching him, as he peered and probed into the mechanism of those wonderful bodies, whose mysteries he understood so well. The more intricate the wound, the better he liked it. A poor private, with both legs off, and shot through the lungs, possessed more attractions for him than a dozen generals, slightly scratched in some "masterly retreat;" and had any one appeared in small pieces, requesting to be put together again, he would have considered it a special dispensation.

The amputations were reserved till the morrow, and the merciful magic of ether was not thought necessary that day, so the poor souls had to bear their pains as best they might. It is all very well to talk of the patience of woman; and far be it from me to pluck that feather from her cap, for, heaven knows, she isn't allowed to wear many; but the patient endurance of these men, under trials of the flesh, was truly wonderful; their fortitude seemed contagious, and scarcely a cry escaped them, though I often longed to groan for them, when pride kept their white lips shut, while great drops stood upon their foreheads, and the bed shook with the irrepressible tremor of their tortured bodies. One or two Irishmen anathematized the doctors with the frankness of their nation, and ordered the Virgin to stand by them, as if she had been the wedded Biddy to whom they could administer the poker, if she didn't; but, as a general thing, the work went on in silence, broken only by some quiet request for roller, instruments, or plaster, a sigh from the patient, or a sympathizing murmur from the nurse.

It was long past noon before these repairs were even partially made; and, having got the bodies of my boys into something like order, the next task was to minister to their minds, by writing letters to the anxious souls at home; answering questions, reading papers, taking possession of money and valuables; for the eighth commandment was reduced to a very fragmentary condition, both by the blacks and whites, who ornamented our hospital with their presence. Pocket books, purses, miniatures, and watches, were sealed up, labelled, and handed over to the matron, till such times as the owners thereof were ready to depart homeward or campward again. The letters dictated to me, and revised by me, that afternoon, would have made an excellent chapter for some future history of the war; for, like that which Thackeray's "Ensign Spooney" wrote his mother just before Waterloo, they were "full of affection, pluck, and bad spelling;" nearly all giving lively accounts of the battle, and ending with a somewhat sudden plunge from patriotism to provender, desiring "Marm," "Mary Ann," or "Aunt Peters," to send along some pies, pickles, sweet stuff, and apples, "to yourn in haste," Joe, Sam, or Ned, as the case might be.

My little Sergeant insisted on trying to scribble something with his left hand, and patiently accomplished some half dozen lines of hieroglyphics, which he gave me to fold and direct, with a boyish blush, that rendered a glimpse of "My Dearest Jane," unnecessary, to assure me that the heroic lad had been more successful in the service of Commander-in-Chief Cupid than that of Gen. Mars; and a charming little romance blossomed instanter in Nurse Periwinkle's romantic fancy, though no further confidences were made that day, for Sergeant fell asleep, and, judging from his tranquil face, visited his absent sweetheart in the pleasant land of dreams.

At five o'clock a great bell rang, and the attendants flew, not to arms, but to their trays, to bring up supper, when a second uproar announced that it was ready. The new comers woke at the sound; and I presently discovered that it took a very bad wound to incapacitate the defenders of the faith for the consumption of their rations; the amount that some of them sequestered was amazing; but when I suggested the probability of a famine hereafter, to the matron, that motherly lady cried out: "Bless their hearts, why shouldn't they eat? It's their only amusement; so fill every one, and, if there's not enough ready to-night, I'll lend my share to the Lord by giving it to the boys." And, whipping up her coffee-pot and plate of toast, she gladdened the eyes and stomachs of two or three dissatisfied heroes, by serving them with a liberal hand; and I haven't the slightest doubt that, having cast her bread upon the waters, it came back buttered, as another large-hearted old lady was wont to say.

Then came the doctor's evening visit; the administration of medicines; washing feverish faces; smoothing tumbled beds; wetting wounds; singing lullabies; and preparations for the night. By eleven, the last labor of love was done; the last "good night" spoken; and, if any needed a reward for that day's work, they surely received it, in the silent eloquence of those long lines of faces, showing pale and peaceful in the shaded rooms, as we quitted them, followed by grateful glances that lighted us to bed, where rest, the sweetest, made our pillows soft, while Night and Nature took our places, filling that great house of pain with the healing miracles of Sleep, and his diviner brother, Death.

A CABINET CRISIS:
WASHINGTON, D.C., DECEMBER 1862

Orville H. Browning: Diary, December 18, 1862

The Fredericksburg debacle fed mounting frustration among Republicans, particularly the radical Republicans, in the Senate over the administration's management of the war. On December 17, meeting in caucus, they passed a resolution calling for "a change in and partial reconstruction of the Cabinet." The caucus's target was Secretary of State Seward, thought to be the frequent architect of bad policies and a malign power behind the throne. These complaints had been fed in backstairs fashion to the radicals by their favorite, Secretary of the Treasury Chase, who hoped to replace Seward's influence with his own. Senator Browning records Lincoln's response to this burgeoning cabinet crisis.

Thursday Decr 18, 1862 With Boone & Head at the Treasury Department in the morning. In the evening went with Mr D W Wise of Boston to the Presidents The Servant at the door reported that he was not in his office—was in the house but had directed them to say that he could not be seen to night.

I told the boy to tell him I wished to see him a moment and went up in to his room. He soon came in. I saw in a moment that he was in distress—that more than usual trouble was pressing upon him. I introduced Mr Wise who wished to get some items for the preparation of a biography, but soon discovered that the President was in no mood to talk upon the subject. We took our leave. When we got to the door the President called to me saying he wished to speak to me a moment. Mr Wise passed into the hall and I returned. He asked me if I was at the caucus yesterday. I told him I was and the day before also. Said he "What do these men want?" I answered "I hardly know Mr President, but they are exceedingly violent towards the administration, and what we did yesterday was the gentlest thing that could be done. We had to do that or worse." Said he "They wish to get rid of me, and I am sometimes half disposed to gratify them." I replied "Some of them do wish to get rid of you, but the fortunes of the Country are bound up with your fortunes, and you stand firmly at your post and hold the helm with a steady hand—To relinquish it now would bring upon us certain and inevitable ruin." Said he "We are now on the brink of destruction. It appears to me the Almighty is against us, and I can hardly see a ray of hope." I answered "Be firm and we will yet save the Country. Do not be driven from your post. You ought to have crushed the ultra, impracticable men last summer. You could then have done it, and escaped these troubles. But we will not talk of the past. Let us be hopeful and take care of the future Mr Seward appears now to be the especial object of their hostility. Still I believe he has managed our foreign affairs as well as any one could have done. Yet they are very bitter upon him, and some of them very bitter upon you." He then said "Why will men believe a lie, an absurd lie, that could not impose upon a child, and cling to it and repeat it in defiance of all evidence to the contrary." I understood this to refer to the charges against Mr Seward.

He then added "the Committee is to be up to see me at 7 O'clock. Since I heard last night of the proceedings of the caucus I have been more distressed than by any event of my life." I bade him good night, and left him

LINCOLN RESOLVES THE CRISIS:
WASHINGTON, D.C., DECEMBER 1862

Gideon Welles: Diary, December 19–20, 1862

Secretary of the Navy Welles picks up the story with the cabinet session the morning of December 19, at which the president reported on his meeting the previous evening with a committee from the Republican caucus, its demands, and reveals that Seward has submitted his resignation. That evening Lincoln arranged a showdown at the White House, with the cabinet (absent Seward) meeting face-to-face with eight Republicans from the caucus. Chase, put on the spot, was forced to side with Lincoln's view of the cabinet's cooperative workings as against the challengers' view. Welles reveals the dénouement on December 20, with the president extracting from Chase his resignation. "Now I can ride," Lincoln told Senator Ira Harris. "I have got a pumpkin in each end of my bag." With both resignations in hand, he announced he would accept neither. To the senators the lessons were clear: to be rid of Seward would cost the cabal its favorite, Chase; and Congress could not dictate to the Executive in such matters as retaining or dismissing cabinet members.

———————

Friday 19 December. Soon after reaching the Department this A.M. I received a note from Nicolay the President's secretary requesting me to attend a special Cabinet meeting at half past ten. All the members were punctually there except Seward.

The President desired that what he had to communicate should not be the subject of conversation elsewhere, and proceeded to inform us that on Wednesday evening, about six o'clock, Senator Preston King and F. W. Seward came into his room each bearing a communication. That which Mr. King presented was the resignation of the Secretary of State, and Mr. F. W. Seward handed in his own.

Mr. King then informed him that at a Republican caucus held that day a pointed and positive opposition had shown itself against the Secretary of State which terminated in a unanimous expression, with one exception, against him and a wish for his removal. The feeling finally shaped itself into resolutions of a general character, and the appointment of a committee of nine to bear them to the President, and to communicate to him the sentiments of the Republican Senators. Mr. King, the former colleague and the friend of Mr. Seward, being also from the same State, felt it to be a duty to inform the Secretary at once of what had occurred. On receiving this information Mr. Seward immediately tendered his resignation. Mr. King suggested it would be well for the committee to wait upon the President at an early moment, and the President agreeing with him, Mr. King on Wednesday morning notified Judge Collamer the chairman, who sent word to the President that they would call at the Executive Mansion at any hour after six that evening, and the President sent word he would receive them at seven.

The committee came at the time specified and the President says the evening was spent in a pretty free discussion and animated conversation. No opposition was manifested towards any other member of the Cabinet than Mr. Seward. Some not very friendly feelings were shown towards one or two others, but no wish that any one should leave but the Secretary of State. Him they charged if not with infidelity with indifference, with want of earnestness in the War, with want of sympathy with the country in this great struggle and with many things objectionable, and especially with a too great ascendency and control of the President. This he said was the point and pith of their complaint.

The President in reply to the committee stated how this movement shocked and grieved him. That the Cabinet he had selected in view of impending difficulties and of all the responsibilities upon him that the members and himself had gone on harmoniously—that there had never been serious disagreements though there had been differences—that in the overwhelming troubles of the country which had borne heavily upon him he had been sustained and consoled by the good feeling and the mutual and unselfish confidence and zeal that pervaded the Cabinet.

He expressed a hope that there would be no combined movement on the part of other members of the Cabinet to resist this assault whatever might be the termination. Said the movement was uncalled for, that there was no such charge, admitting all that was said, as should break up or overthrow a Cabinet, nor was it possible for him to go on with a total abandonment of old friends.

Mr. Bates stated the difference between our system and that of England where a change of ministry involved a new election, dissolution of Parliament, etc.

Three or four members of the Cabinet said they had heard of the resignation: Blair the day preceding, Stanton through the President, on whom he had made a business call. Mr. Bates when coming to the meeting.

The President requested that we should, with him, meet the committee. This did not receive the approval of Mr. Chase, who said he had no knowledge whatever of the movement, or the resignation, until since he had entered the room.

Mr. Bates knew of no good that would come of an interview. I stated that I could see no harm in it, and if the President wished it I thought it a duty. Mr. Blair thought it would be well for us to be present, and finally, all acquiesced. The President named half past seven this evening.

Saturday 20 December. At the meeting last evening there were present of the committee Senators Collamer, Fessenden, Harris, Trumbull, Grimes, Howard, Sumner, and Pomeroy. Wade was absent. The President, and all the Cabinet but Seward were present. The subject was opened by the President, who read the resolutions and stated the substance of his interviews with the committee—their object and purpose. He spoke of the unity of his Cabinet, and how, though they could not be expected to think and speak alike on all subjects, all had acquiesced in measures when once decided. The necessities of the times, he said, had prevented frequent and long sessions of the Cabinet, and the submission of every question at the meetings.

Secretary Chase indorsed the President's statement fully and entirely, but regretted that there was not a more full and thorough consideration and canvass of all important measure in open Cabinet.

Senator Collamer, however, the chairman of the committee succeeded the President, and calmly and fairly presented the views of the committee and of those whom they represented. They wanted united counsels, combined wisdom, and energetic action. If there is truth in the maxim, that in a multitude of counselors there is safety, it might be well that those advisers who were near the President and selected by him, and all of whom were more or less responsible, should be consulted on the great questions which affected the national welfare, and that the ear of the Executive should be open to all and that he should have the minds of all.

Senator Fessenden was skillful but a little tart,—felt, it could be seen, more than he cared to say,—wanted the whole Cabinet to consider and decide great questions, and that no one should absorb the whole Executive. Spoke of a remark which he had heard from J.Q. Adams on the floor of Congress in regard to a measure of his administration. Mr. Adams said the measure was adopted against his wishes and opinion, but he was outvoted by Mr. Clay and others. He wished an administration so conducted.

Grimes, Sumner and Trumbull were pointed, emphatic and unequivocal in their hostility to Mr. Seward, each was unrelenting and unforgiving.

Blair spoke earnestly and well. Sustained the President and dissented most decidedly from the idea of a plural Executive,—claimed that the President was accountable for his administration, might ask opinions or not of either and as many as he pleased, of all or none, of his Cabinet. Mr. Bates took much the same view.

The President managed his own case, speaking freely, and showed great tact and ability provided such a subject were a proper one for such a meeting and discussion. I have no doubt he considered it most judicious to conciliate the Senators with respectful deference, whatever may have been his opinion of their interference. When he closed his remarks, he said it would be a gratification to him if each member of the committee would state whether he now thought it advisable to dismiss Mr. Seward, and whether his exclusion would strengthen or weaken the Administration, and the Union cause in their respective States. Grimes, Trumbull and Sumner, who had expressed themselves decidedly against the continuance of Mr. Seward in the Cabinet indicated no change of opinion. Collamer and Fessenden declined committing themselves on the subject—were not prepared to answer the questions. Senator

Harris felt it a duty to say that while many of the friends of the Administration would be gratified, others would feel deeply wounded, and the effect of Mr. Seward's retirement would, on the whole be calamitous in the State of New York. Pomeroy of Kansas said, personally, he believed the withdrawal of Mr. Seward would be a good movement and he sincerely wished it might take place. Howard of Michigan declined answering the question.

During the discussion the volume of diplomatic correspondence, recently published, was alluded to—some letters denounced as unwise and impolitic were specified, one of which, a confidential dispatch to Mr. Adams, was read. If it was unwise to write, it was certainly injudicious and indiscreet to publish the document. Mr. Seward has genius and talent, no one better knows it than himself, but he is often wanting in true wisdom, sound judgment, and discreet statesmanship. The committee believe that he thinks more of the glorification of Seward than the welfare of the country. He has unwittingly and unwarily begotten a vast amount of distrust and hostility on the part of Senators by his endeavors to impress them and others with the belief that he is the Administration. It is a mistake, they have measured and know him.

It was nearly midnight when we left the President; and it could not be otherwise than that all my wakeful moments should be absorbed with a subject which, time and circumstances considered, was of grave importance to the Administration and the country. A Senatorial combination to dictate to the President in regard to his political family in the height of a civil war which threatens the existence of the Republic cannot be permitted even if the person to whom they object is as obnoxious as they represent. After fully canvassing the subject in all its phases my mind was clear as to the course which it was my duty to pursue, and what I believed was the President's duty also.

My first movement this morning was to call on the President as soon as I supposed he could have breakfasted. Governor Robertson of Kentucky was with him when I went in but soon left. I informed the President I had pondered the events of yesterday and last evening, and felt it incumbent on me to advise him not to accept the resignation of Mr. Seward. That if there were objections, real or imaginary, against Mr. Seward, the time, manner and circumstances—the occasion, and the method of presenting what the Senators considered objections were all inappropriate and wrong. That no party or faction should be permitted to dictate to the President in regard to his Cabinet,—that it would be of evil example and fraught with incalculable injury to the Government and country,—that the legislative department, or the Senate should not be allowed to encroach on the Executive prerogatives,—that it devolved on him, and was his duty to assert and maintain the rights and independence of the Executive,—that he ought not, against his own convictions, to yield one iota of the authority intrusted to him on the demand of either branch of Congress or both combined, or to any party, whatever might be its views and intentions,—that Mr. Seward had his infirmities and errors,— that he and I differed on many things, as did other members of the Cabinet—that he was disposed to step beyond his own legitimate bounds and not duly respect the rights of his associates, but these were matters that did not call for Senatorial interference. In short I considered it for the true interest of the country, now as in the future, that this scheme should be defeated,—that so believing I had, at the earliest moment given him my conclusions.

The President was much gratified—said the whole thing had struck him as it had me, and if carried out as the Senators prescribed the whole Government must cave in. It could not stand. Could not hold water,—the bottom would be out.

I added that, having expressed my wish that he would not accept Mr. Seward's resignation, I thought it equally important that Seward should not press its acceptance. In this he also concurred, and asked if I had seen Seward. I replied I had not, my first duty was with him, and having ascertained that we agreed I would now go over and see him. He earnestly desired me to do so.

I went immediately to Seward's house. Stanton was with him. Seward was excited, talking vehemently to Stanton of the course pursued and the results that must follow if the scheme succeeded,—told Stanton he would be the next victim, that there was a call for a meeting at the Cooper Institute this evening. Stanton said he had seen it. I had not. Seward got the

Herald for me to read but Stanton seized the paper, as Seward and myself then entered into conversation, when he related what the President had already communicated,—how Preston King had come to him, he wrote his resignation at once, and so did Fred, etc., etc. In the mean time Stanton rose and remarking he had much to do and that Governor S. had been over this matter with him, he would leave.

I then stated my interview with the President, my advice that the President must not accept, nor he press, his resignation. Seward was greatly pleased with my views,—said he had but one course before him when the doings of the Senators were communicated, but that if the President and country required from him any duty in this emergency he did not feel at liberty to refuse it. He spoke of his long political experience, dwelt on his own sagacity and his great services, feels deeply this movement which was wholly unexpected,—tries to suppress any exhibition of personal grievance or disappointment, but is painfully wounded, mortified, and chagrined.

I told him I should return and report to the President our interview and that he acquiesced. He said he had no objections, but he thought the subject should be disposed of one way or the other at once. He is disappointed I see that the President did not promptly refuse to consider his resignation, and dismiss, or refuse to parley with the committee.

When I returned to the White House, Chase and Stanton were in the President's office, but he was absent. A few words were interchanged on the great topic in hand. I was very emphatic in my opposition to the acceptance of Seward's resignation. Neither gave me a direct answer or expressed an opinion on the subject, though I think both wished to be understood as acquiescing.

When the President came in, which was in a few moments, his first address was to me, asking if I "had seen the man." I replied that I had, and that he assented to my views. He then turned to Chase and said I sent for you, for this matter is giving me great trouble. At our first interview he rang and directed that a message be sent to Mr. Chase.

Chase said he had been painfully affected by the meeting last evening, which was a total surprise to him, and, after some, not very explicit remarks as to how he was affected, informed the

President he had prepared his resignation. Where is it, said the President quickly, his eye lighting up in a moment. I brought it with me, said Chase, taking it from his pocket—I wrote it this morning. Let me have it, said the President, reaching his long arm and fingers towards C., who held on, seemingly reluctant to part with the letter which was sealed, and which he apparently hesitated to surrender. Something further he wished to say, but the President was eager and did not perceive it, but took the letter.

This said he, looking towards me with a triumphal laugh cuts the Gordian knot. An air of satisfaction spread over his countenance such as I have not seen for some time. I can dispose of this subject now he added, as he turned on his chair and broke the seal. I see my way clear.

Chase sat by Stanton fronting the fire—the President beside the fire his face towards them, Stanton nearest him. I was on the sofa near the east window. While the President was reading the note which was brief, Chase turned round towards me a little perplexed and would, I think have been better satisfied could this interview with the President been without the presence of others, or at least if I was away. The President was delighted and saw not how others were affected.

Mr. President, said Stanton with solemnity, I informed you day before yesterday that I was ready to tender you my resignation. I wish you sir to consider my resignation at this time in your possession.

You may go to your Department said the President, I don't want yours. This, holding out Chase's letter is all I want—this relieves me—my way is clear—the trouble is ended. I will detain neither of you longer. We all rose to leave, but Stanton held back as we reached the door. Chase and myself came downstairs together. He was moody and taciturn. Some one stopped him on the lower stairs and I passed on, but C. was not a minute behind me. Before I reached the Department, Stanton came staving along.

"SICKNESS, DISGUST, AND DESPAIR":
DECEMBER 1862

Harper's Weekly: The Reverse at Fredericksburg

December 27, 1862

The blunder-ridden campaign and battle of Fredericksburg, with its deadly toll of casualties—for the Union, greater even than at Antietam—plunged Northern morale to its lowest point of the war. This *Harper's Weekly* editorial, while thin factually, reflected the national discouragement.

THE REVERSE AT FREDERICKSBURG.

WE HAVE again to report a disastrous reverse to our arms. Defeated with great slaughter in the battle of 13th, General Burnside has now withdrawn the army of the Potomac to the north side of Rappahannock, where the people congratulate themselves that it is at least in safety. And now, who is responsible for this terrible repulse?

General Burnside was appointed to the command of the army of the Potomac on 9th November, and began at once to prepare to shift the base and line of march of his army toward Fredericksburg. In view of such a movement General McClellan had, before his removal, suggested the propriety of rebuilding and occupying the railroad from Aquia Creek to Falmouth; but, for some reason not apparent, the War Department had not acted upon the suggestion. About 12th November General Burnside notified the Department that he would arrive at Fredericksburg in about a week, and that pontoons must be there by that time, in order to enable him to cross and occupy the hills on the south side of the river. On the 21st General Sumner arrived at Fredericksburg, and found that there was not a pontoon there, and the railroad between Aquia Creek and Falmouth being out of order, there was no means of getting any, and no means of procuring supplies. It was absolutely impossible to cross the river, and the enemy were already arriving on the south side and throwing up earth-works.

General Burnside, on discovering this state of things, repaired instantly to Washington to ascertain why he was being sacrificed. What satisfaction he obtained no one knows. But a general officer, one of the most distinguished in the service, not in the army of the Potomac, as early as 23d November, made no secret of his opinion that the movement *via* Fredericksburg "*was a failure*," because Burnside had been unable to occupy the south bank of the Rappahannock in time.

In the course of two weeks pontoons were furnished to the army, the railroad was repaired, and supplies were forthcoming. But, on the other hand, Lee, with 150,000 men, was strongly intrenched on the opposite side of the river, on two ranges of hills which command the slope at the foot of which the Rappahannock runs and Fredericksburg lies. The question was, what was to be done? A council of war was held on the night of 11th. At that council it is understood, that Generals Sumner, Franklin, Hooker, and all the corps commanders who had been invited were decidedly opposed to a movement across the river and up the slope. IT IS RUMORED THAT BURNSIDE THEN SAID THAT HE WAS ORDERED TO CROSS THE RIVER AND ATTACK THE BATTERIES IN FRONT, AND THAT WE WOULD DO IT, NO MATTER WHAT THE COST. This of course closed the discussion, and the Generals made their preparations accordingly. On 12th the river was crossed without serious resistance. On 13th the rebel batteries were attacked in front by the bulk of Burnside's army, and our troops were repulsed with a loss which is now variously estimated at from twelve to seventeen thousand men. The rebel loss is not known, but they can not have lost many score of men. On the night of 15–16th, General Burnside withdrew his army to the north side of the river.

We are indulging in no hyperbole when we say that these events are rapidly filling the heart of the loyal North with sickness, disgust, and despair. Party lines are becoming effaced by such unequivocal evidences of administrative imbecility; it is the men who have given and trusted the most, who now feel most keenly that the Government is unfit for its office, and that the most gallant efforts ever made by a cruelly tried people are being neutralized by the obstinacy and incapacity of their leaders. Where this will all end no one can see. But it must end soon. The people have shown a patience, during the past year, quite unexampled in history. They have borne, silently and grimly, imbecility, treachery, failure, privation, loss of friends and means, almost every suffering which can afflict a brave people. But they can not be expected to suffer that such massacres as this at Fredericksburg shall be repeated. Matters are rapidly ripening for a military dictatorship.

LINCOLN AND EMANCIPATION:
NEW YORK, DECEMBER 1862

George Templeton Strong: Diary, December 27, 1862

As Strong suggests, there were doubters of Lincoln's promise to issue the Emancipation Proclamation. The pamphlet by the lawyer and writer Charles Stillé, titled *How a Free People Conduct a Long War*, would be widely distributed by the U.S. Sanitary Commission, in which both Stillé and Strong were active. The Jefferson Davis proclamation Strong mentions listed a long bill of particulars against General Butler's administration in New Orleans, and declared Butler "a felon, deserving of capital punishment." As for the *brutum fulmen*, back on September 13, replying to a delegation of ministers demanding immediate emancipation, Lincoln said he would not make an empty gesture "inoperative, like the pope's bull against the comet!" (The comet was Halley's, the date 1486, and the tale popular but apocryphal.) On December 30 Strong returned to the subject of the proclamation: "If he come out fair and square, he will do the 'biggest thing' an Illinois jury-lawyer has ever had a chance of doing, and take high place among the men who have controlled the destinies of nations. If he postpone or dilute his action, his name will be a byword and a hissing till the annals of the nineteenth century are forgotten."

December 27. Public affairs unchanged. Will Uncle Abe Lincoln stand firm and issue his promised proclamation on the first of January, 1863? Nobody knows, but I think he will. Charles J. Stillé of Philadelphia has published a clever pamphlet, comparing our general condition as to blunders, imbecility, failures, popular discontent, financial embarrassment, and so on with that of shabby old England during the first years of her Peninsular War. He makes out a strong case in our favor. It is a valuable paper, and we must have it reprinted here, for there are many feeble knees in this community that want to be confirmed and corroborated. It had an excellent effect on Bidwell; a bad case of typhoid despondency in a state of chronic collapse and utter prostration. He rallied a little after reading it, and was heard to remark that "we might possibly come out all right after all."

Jefferson Davis's precious proclamation!! Butler and all Butler's commissioned officers to be hanged, whenever caught. Ditto all armed Negroes, and all white officers commanding them. This is the first great blunder Jeff has committed since the war began. It's evidence not only of barbarism but of weakness, and will disgust his foreign admirers (if anything can) and strengthen the backbone of the North at the same time. If he attempts to carry it out, retaliation becomes a duty, and we can play at extermination quite as well as Jeff Davis.

George Wright, who was here Christmas evening, recounted a talk with some South Carolina woman about the policy of forming nigger regiments. The lady was furious. "Just think how infamous it is that our *gentlemen* should have to go out and fight niggers, and that every nigger they shoot is a thousand dollars out of their own pockets! Was there ever anything so outrageous?" "And then," said Wright, "she was so mad that she just jumped straight up and down a minute or two." No wonder. The liberating proclamation we hope for next Thursday, January 1, 1863, may possibly prove a *brutum fulmen*, "a pope's bull against the comet" (a clever mot of Abe Lincoln's), but the enlisting, arming, and drilling of a few thousand muscular athletic buck niggers, every one of whom knows he will be certainly hanged and probably tortured besides if made prisoner, is a material addition to the national force. How strange that patriotic, loyal people should deny its expediency. This generation is certainly overshadowed by a superstition, not yet quite exploded, that slaveholding rights possess peculiar sanctity and inviolability, that everybody who doubts their justice is an Abolitionist, and that an Abolitionist is a social pariah, a reprobate and caitiff, a leper whom all decent people are bound to avoid and denounce. We shall feel otherwise ten years hence, unless subjugated meanwhile by the pluck and ferocity of the slaveholders' rebellion, and look back on Northern reverence for slavery and slaveholders A.D. 1862, even after the long experience of war with treason arrayed in support of slavery, as we now regard the gross superstitions of ten centuries ago, or the existing superstitions of the Mandingoes and the Zulu Kaffirs. I trust we may not have to remember it as a signal instance of judicial blindness, a paralyzing visitation of divine vengeance on a whole people at the very moment when their national existence depended on their seeing the truth and asserting it.

PORTER'S COURT-MARTIAL:
WASHINGTON, D.C., DECEMBER 1862

Fitz John Porter to Samuel L.M. Barlow

On December 3 a general court-martial was convened in the case of Fitz John Porter, charged with failing to obey orders and misbehavior before the enemy at Second Bull Run. Dispatches and letters were introduced to show Porter's animus toward General Pope, and witnesses testified that at critical points in the first day's fighting he failed to obey Pope's orders. But as Porter points out here, writing to New York lawyer Barlow, the court was neither unbiased nor unaffected by the unrest in the army's high command. Porter's prediction of its verdict was borne out. He was found guilty and cashiered in January 1863. In 1879 an army review board exonerated Porter, yet his conduct at Second Bull Run remains controversial.

Washington.
Dec. 29" 62

My dear Friend.

I missed you the day you left. I caused to be sent you by express, a package of papers, more with a view you might see how biased is the court against me, than for any action. Since then I have seen sufficient of the court—or of the minds of a few of them, the most of them—to know their conclusion is a foregone one, if not determined by order or the wish of those high in power. Within the past two days I have seen sufficient to convince me of their intent and no matter what the record may be, to find a verdict against me. T'is hard that I should be accused of acts so much at variance with my character, and after exposure of life since the dates of these charges, to be accused of these acts, and to be charged with bad faith towards any one. Yet such is the case. Confident of my own innocence I can, not withstanding any decision rendered by the court—(some members of which expect reward either by restoration to command or appointment of relations, or promotion) I can lay my hand on my heart as say there is no guile there or intention to injure our cause or be a defaulter in effort to any one or to my country. God knows I have risked life in too many battles and skirmishes to be criminal now. I intend to make the record plain and honest, and if declared by the court guilty, will show to the world that the court (not I am) is guilty before my maker— I have too many personal enemies & enemies of Genl McClellan on the court.

The army will soon I expect make another effort to turn the enemy's right, lower down the river. If so you may expect to hear that the enemy have flown—and are behind the North Anna—where they cannot be reached—and where the same obstacles will be raised against them as at Fredericksburg—and if the army advances beyond that place—the rail road will not supply their men & animals.—A longer line will have to be guarded and their security diminished. I believe *the policy of the rebels is now* (I judge from their activity.) *to abandon Fredericksburg and induce our army to advance and remain on the line it is now attempting to follow*, the worst line it can take, and to keep it going to James River, and we are fools enough to go where they pull us by the nose. Whatever they wish we have done, and will do as much as if their consils governed.

Banks I have reason to believe is to ascend the Mississippi, and wherever his army may go either Texas or Miss, it is understood freedom to slaves is to be declared, and *insurrection encouraged*. It seems hard to believe Banks has lent himself to such base and inhuman policy, but I believe it is so. You will soon see. I also hear Seward and Chase are as thick as two peas, and their policy the same. So closely connected are they, that the communications between the department buildings are such each can visit the other without being seen. You may rest assured the most intimate relations exist, and that Chase resigned because Seward was to leave, & he was determined to keep him. You may also expect the proclamation to be issued, and commanders of troops directed not to interfere in case of servile insurrections—or the Law of last Congress pointed to—God help us. —Our men & officers are discouraged. The rebels appear to be prospering, and the fear exists that the west may slide from New England and unite with the South. An Effort is being made to solder NYork & the west by the Erie canal being made into a ship canal as an outlet to produce in opposition to the Miss. and thus buy off the west— A game is being played and if the good men of the north dont work. I fear another split will ensue. I do believe if we had one good strong man of influence and character to work the matter through, preliminaries to a settlement might be commenced, and by operating on the fears *of* the chief power, peace might be restored. The wire pullers, by working on the interests of the monied men can effect it. But there must be change—and Butler must not go into the cabinet or be promoted, which he is brought home for—because he is thrown overboard by the Democrats. He will take the bribe unless New York men can bribe higher as soon as he arrives & he should be at once worked upon cautiously. He is to be brought home to work for the radicals. I believe to go into the War Dept, but certainly for no good for *our* party.

I send you these thoughts—to put you in possession of some opinions desired from parties here, & let you see if your own are confirmed. Conservative men are to be pushed to the wall, and radicalism is to rule. Seymour [   ] & Parker & Curtis can check all this.

LOOTING IN HOLLY SPRINGS:
MISSISSIPPI, DECEMBER 1862

Cyrus F. Boyd: Diary, December 22–25, 1862

In November 1862 Ulysses S. Grant began advancing southward along the Mississippi Central Railroad toward the Confederate bastion at Vicksburg. After reaching Oxford, Mississippi, in early December, Grant planned to move against the Confederate army defending Grenada, forty miles to the south, while William T. Sherman led an expedition from Memphis down the Mississippi to Vicksburg. His plans were thwarted on December 20 by Earl Van Dorn, who led 3,500 cavalrymen in a raid on Grant's supply depot at Holly Springs. Sergeant Cyrus F. Boyd of the 15th Iowa Infantry recorded the aftermath of Van Dorn's attack.

Camp at Holly Springs Mississippi
Dec 22d   Weather warm and *roads good* Started at day break toward Holly Springs Had Knapsacks guns and 40 rounds and traveled very fast At noon we ate dinner at the Tallahatchie on our old camp ground. Made a hard march until 7 P M After dark we entered Holly Springs and went through the town and halted on the North side Soon as the men could get their things off they commenced going for things generaly. Every one was gone except those who could not travel from fatigue As for myself I was so far gone that I could not get up to move I could hear hogs squeal and chickens squall in all directions By 11 oclock we had devoured some fresh pig Sergt Gray had secured for our mess a fine Pig. He can hear a hog grunt or a chicken breathe as far as any other man in this Army . . .

Dec 23d   Reveille at 4 A. M. The men were very tired and sore but with about the average amount of groaning and *swearing* they got out. At 8 A M we were told that we should not march to-day The wagons were unloaded and foraging parties sent out Almost all the men left Camp and were soon scattered all over the town in a few hours Soldiers could be seen everywhere Out of the cellar of a large brick residence close to our camp there came a constant stream of men and others kept going in and it resembled a *hive of bees* I went over and found the molasses running about 2 inches deep on the floor of the cellar and the men were wading through and carrying off various articles The occupants of the house were inside and locked up and no one outside except a little Negro boy Around were all the indications of Wealth Beautiful shrubbery and trees and vines and flowers and arbors While I was looking around I heard a *row* inside and soon seen a soldier come through the kitchen window heels first and a boot close to his *rear* and attached to a pair of *shoulder straps* About this time I had *business* toward camp

Going down to the "Clayton House" a large frame building I noticed a great crowd around the front door with their arms full of books and papers. I came around the house and just then a lady raised the window and called to me and asked me if I was an officer I replied that I was not a commissioned officer Said she for Gods sake keep the "soldiers from breaking into my room they have possession of the house and I fear they will *Kill me*" I told her not to fear as no man would disturb her. She was a rather good looking woman and had four little children with her This evening this *same* woman was arrested for *shooting* one of our men who was on guard at the "Clayton House" (2 days ago) She cowardly shot him although he was guarding her property This whole town was literly gutted to-day

Van Dorn was here two days ago with a large force of Cavalry and surprised what few men we had here Then the Rebs blew up several buildings right in the Centre of the town and burned the Depots and all the rolling stock and Warehouses and destroyed more than one million Dollars worth of our supplies and also captured several of our Pay Masters with large amounts of Money. Long trains of cars were burned with all their contents and nothing but the irons and trucks stand on the track for almost a *mile* There has been a fearful destruction of property and many of the citizens were killed by the explosions The 101st Ills Infty and the 2d Ills Cavalry had been left to guard the Post The Cav fought as long as they could and then had to *retreat* The Infantry *surrendered* at the first summons and scarcely fired a gun Col Murphy of the 8th Wisconsin commanded

I found the Court House square filled with horses, cannon

ammunition Women with band-boxes and other traps were leaving in all directions The soldiers were in every house and garret and cellar, store and church, and nook and corner. The streets were white with all kinds of paper and men were running with their arms full of books and ledgers and one lot of soldiers had their arms full of Confederate *bank notes* which were perfect in all except the Presidents signature (I think the President did not have time to sign) The boys said they could do that *themselves* On the east side of the square the large brick buildings which we saw there two weeks ago were now one vast shapeless mass of ruins Some of these buildings had been stored with shell and other ammunition and explosive Material Fully one half the fine buildings on North side of the square were likewise blown to pieces

There had been a Bank in one of them and some gold and silver had been melted among the rubbish and the soldiers wete in digging to their knees in the brick bats Sudden and complete destruction has overtaken this city When we went down through here the women and even the children could insult us in every way and we did not disturb a hair of their heads But it remained for their *own friends* to complete their woe If the Confederates treat their own people thus what would they do with their enemies I came to Genl Grants headquarters and saw him talking to an Officer He stood with his hands in his pockets like a common farmer and looked as unconcerned as if he was selling eggs at 2 cts per dozen Everyone thinks Grant has made another big blunder in allowing the Army thus to be cut off from our base of supplies The Col Murphy who surrendered here is the same man who surrendered about 100,000 000$ worth of supplies at Iuka to Price He is called a *traitor*

I came by a fine large Roman Catholic Church A lot of soldiers were in the building some were taking the organ to pieces and had the pipes out blowing on them and throwing them away Up in the pulpit was a squad playing *cards* and another lot were scattering the library over the floor One daring and reckless soldier climbed to the pinnacle of the temple and took off the little silver image of "Jesus" that stood there. It was at a giddy height but he got it—said to be worth several hundred dollars Every portion of the *fated city* seemed given over to *pillage* and destruction and no hand was raised to save anything from the general *sack and ruin*

Finely dressed ladies were leaving on all the streets and going God knows where Women and children were standing in their houses wailing with the most piteous cries Young girls whose eyes were red with weeping peered from behind the curtains of the windows and gazed listlessly upon the passing throngs that crowded the streets No insults were offered any women or citizen that I saw or heard of

When I had witnessed all this destruction and terror my heart almost ceased to beat when I thought of the sadness and woe that is caused by this inhuman war of brother against brother and how the innocent shall suffer in the cause of treason and Rebellion

Railroad communication is completely broken up and we are about out of provisions and Memphis now our base of supplies which is a long way off Marion Mart one of our Co left here was taken prisoner and parolled by the enemy

Dec 24th From poverty and want we have suddenly become rich and *stuck* up. We have been sleeping on slanting rails and on the cold frosty earth or under a mule wagon or indeed we have slept in all kinds of places with a stone for a pillow But we are above that now We have mahogany bedsteads and the finest lounges that this Market affords The tents are not large enough to hold all the fine furniture now on hands. Dan Embree, Gray, Harv Reid and I are all in one tent We have fine Carpet down, a stove and more stuff than we actually *need*. We are short of provisions but shall *trust* to Gray

Dec 25th Christmas We are not so *merry* as we might be. No demonstration in Camp would indicate this Holiday Have nothing to eat but a little Corn bread and some tough beef Genl Logans Division went North to-day

JACKSON, DECEMBER 1862

Jefferson Davis:
Address to the Mississippi Legislature

The Confederate defeats at Iuka and Corinth, the failure of Bragg's campaign in Kentucky, and the continued Union threat to Vicksburg caused grave concern in Richmond about the war in the western theater. In November Jefferson Davis placed Joseph E. Johnston in overall command of both Bragg's army in Tennessee and the army defending Vicksburg, now led by John C. Pemberton. Davis then decided to appraise the situation in person. After conferring with Bragg in Tennessee, he traveled with Johnston to Mississippi, where they inspected the Vicksburg defenses and met with Pemberton at Grenada. Before returning to Richmond, Davis addressed the Mississippi legislature in Jackson.

December 26, 1862

Friends and Fellow-Citizens, Gentlemen of the House of Representatives and Senate of the State of Mississippi:

After an absence of nearly two years I again find myself among those who, from the days of my childhood, have ever been the trusted objects of my affections, those for whose good I have ever striven, and whose interest I have sometimes hoped I may have contributed to subserve. Whatever fortunes I may have achieved in life have been gained as a representative of Mississippi, and before all, I have labored for the advancement of her glory and honor. I now, for the first time in my career, find myself the representative of a wider circle of interest; but a circle in which the interests of Mississippi are still embraced. Two years ago, nearly, I left you to assume the duties which had devolved on me as the representative of the new Confederacy. The responsibilities of this position have occupied all my time, and have left me no opportunity for mingling with my friends in Mississippi, or for sharing in the dangers which have menaced them. But, wherever duty may have called me, my heart has been with you and the success of the cause in which we are all engaged has been first in my thoughts and in my prayers. I thought when I left Mississippi that the service to which I was called would prove to be but temporary. The last time I had the honor of addressing you from this stand, I was influenced by that idea. I then imagined that it might be my fortune again to lead Mississippians in the field, and to be with them where danger was to be braved and glory won. I thought to find that place which I believed to be suited to my capacity: that of an officer in the service of the State of Mississippi. For, although in the discharge of my duties as President of the Confederate States, I had determined to make no distinction between the various parts of the country—to know no separate State—yet my heart has always beat more warmly for Mississippi, and I have looked on Mississippi soldiers with a pride and emotion such as no others inspired. But it was decided differently. I was called to another sphere of action. How, in that sphere, I have discharged the duties and obligations imposed on me, it does not become me to constitute myself the judge. It is for others to decide that question. But, speaking to you with that frankness and that confidence with which I have always spoken to you, and which partakes of the nature of thinking aloud, I can say with my hand upon my heart, that whatever I have done, has been done with the sincere purpose of promoting the noble cause in which we are engaged. The period which has elapsed since I left you is short; for the time, which may appear long in the life of man, is short in the history of a nation. And in that short period remarkable changes have been wrought in all the circumstances by which we are surrounded. At the time of which I speak, the question presented to our people was "will there be war!" This was the subject of universal speculation. We had chosen to exercise an indisputable right—the right to separate from those with whom we conceived association to be no longer possible, and to establish a government of our own. I was among those who, from the beginning, predicted war as the consequence of secession, although I must admit that the contest has assumed proportions more gigantic than I had anticipated. I predicted war not because our right to secede and to form a government of our own was not indisputable and clearly defined in the spirit of that declaration which rests the right to govern on the consent of the governed, but because I foresaw that the wickedness of the North would precipitate a war upon us. Those who supposed that the exercise of this right of separation could not produce war, have had cause to be convinced that they had credited their recent associates of the North with a moderation, a sagacity, a morality they did not possess. You have been involved in a war waged for the gratification of the lust of power and of aggrandizement, for your conquest and your subjugation, with a malignant ferocity and with a disregard and a contempt of the usages of civilization, entirely unequalled in history. Such, I have ever warned you, were the characteristics of the Northern people—of those with whom our ancestors entered into a Union of consent, and with whom they formed a constitutional compact. And yet, such was the attachment of our people for that Union, such their devotion to it, that those who desired preparation to be made for the inevitable conflict, were denounced as men who only wished to destroy the Union. After what has happened during the last two years, my only wonder is that we consented to live for so long a time in association with such miscreants, and have loved so much a government rotten to the core. Were it ever to be proposed again to enter into a Union with such a people, I could no more consent to do it than to trust myself in a den of thieves.

You in Mississippi, have but little experienced as yet the horrors of the war. You have seen but little of the savage manner in which it is waged by your barbarous enemies. It has been my fortune to witness it in all its terrors; in a part of the country where old men have been torn from their homes, carried into captivity and immured in distant dungeons, and where delicate women have been insulted by a brutal soldiery and forced even to cook for the dirty Yankee invaders; where property has been wantonly destroyed, the country ravaged, and every outrage committed. And it is with these people that our fathers formed a union and a solemn compact. There is indeed a difference between the two peoples. Let no man hug the delusion that there can be renewed association between them. Our enemies are a traditionless and a homeless race; from the time of Cromwell to the present moment they have been disturbers of the peace of the world. Gathered together by Cromwell from the bogs and fens of the North of Ireland and of England, they commenced by disturbing the peace of their own country; they disturbed Holland, to which they fled, and they disturbed England on their return. They persecuted Catholics in England, and they hung Quakers and witches in America. Having been hurried into a war with a people so devoid of every mark of civilization you have no doubt wondered that I have not carried out the policy, which I had intended should be our policy, of fighting our battles on the fields of the enemy instead of suffering him to fight them on ours. This was not the result of my will, but of the power of the enemy. They had at their command all the accumulated wealth of seventy years—the military stores which had been laid up during that time. They had grown rich from the taxes wrung from you for the establishing and supporting their manufacturing institutions. We have entered upon a conflict with a nation contiguous to us in territory, and vastly superior to us in numbers. In the face of these facts the wonder is not that we have done little, but that we have done so much. In the first year of the war our forces were sent into the field poorly armed, and were far inferior in number to the enemy. We were compelled even to arm ourselves by the capture of weapons taken from the foe on the battle-field. Thus in every battle we exchanged our arms for those of the invaders. At the end of twelve months of the war, it was still necessary for us to adopt some expedient to enable us to maintain our ground. The only expedient remaining to us was to call on those brave men who had entered the service of their country at the beginning of the war, supposing that the conflict was to last but a short time, and that they would not be long absent from their homes. The only expedient, I say, was to call on these gallant men; to ask them to maintain their position in front of the enemy, and to surrender for a time their hopes of soon returning to their families and their friends. And nobly did they respond to the call. They answered that they were willing to stay, that they were willing to maintain their position and to breast the tide of invasion. But it was not just that they should stand alone. They asked that the men who had stayed at home—who had thus far been sluggards in the cause—should be forced, likewise, to meet the enemy. From this, resulted the law of Congress, which is known as the conscription act, which declared all men, from the age of eighteen to the age of thirty-five, to be liable to enrolment in the Confederate service. I regret that there has been some prejudice excited against that act, and that it has been subjected to harsher criticism than it deserves. And here I may say that an erroneous impression appears to prevail in regard to this act. It is no disgrace to be brought into the army by conscription. There is no more reason to expect from the citizen voluntary service in the army than to expect voluntary labor on the public roads or the voluntary payment of taxes. But these things we do not expect. We assess the property of the citizen, we appoint tax-gatherers; why should we not likewise distribute equally the labor, and enforce equally the obligation of defending the country from its enemies? I repeat that it is no disgrace to any one to be conscribed, but it is a glory for those who do not wait for the conscription. Thus resulted the conscription act; and thence arose the necessity for the exemption act. That necessity was met; but when it was found that under these acts enough men were not drawn into the ranks of the army to fulfill the purposes intended, it became necessary to pass another exemption act, and another conscription act. It is only of this latter that I desire now to speak. Its policy was to leave at home those men needed to conduct the administration, and those who might be required to support and maintain the industry of the country—in other words, to exempt from military service those whose labor, employed in other avocations, might be more profitable to the country and to the government, than in the ranks of the army.

I am told that this act has excited some discontent and that it has provoked censure, far more severe, I believe, than it deserves. It has been said that it exempts the rich from military service, and forces the poor to fight the battles of the country. The poor do, indeed, fight the battles of the country. It is the poor who save nations and make revolutions. But is it true that in this war the men of property have shrunk from the ordeal of the battle-field? Look through the army; cast your eyes upon the maimed heroes of the war whom you meet in your streets and in the hospitals; remember the martyrs of the conflict; and I am sure you will find among them more than a fair proportion drawn from the ranks of men of property. The object of that portion of the act which exempts those having charge of twenty or more negroes, was not to draw any distinction of classes, but simply to provide a force, in the nature of a police force, sufficient to keep our negroes in control. This was the sole object of the clause. Had it been otherwise, it would never have received my signature. As I have already said, we have no cause to complain of the rich. All of our people have done well; and, while the poor have nobly discharged their duties, most of the wealthiest and most distinguished families of the South have representatives in the ranks. I take, as an example, the case of one of your own representatives in Congress, who was nominated for Congress and elected; but still did a sentinel's duty until Congress met. Nor is this a solitary instance, for men of the largest fortune in Mississippi are now serving in the ranks.

Permit me now to say that I have seen with peculiar pleasure the recommendation of your Governor in his message, to make some provision for the families of the absent soldiers of Mississippi. Let this provision be made for the objects of his affection and his solicitude, and the soldier engaged in fighting the battles of his country will no longer be disturbed in his slumber by dreams of an unprotected and neglected family at home. Let him know that his mother Mississippi has spread her protecting mantle over those he loves, and he will be ready to fight your battles, to protect your honor, and, in your cause, to die. There is another one of the governor's propositions to which I wish to allude. I mean the proposition to call upon those citizens who are not subject to the Confederate conscription law, and to form them into a reserve corps for the purpose of aiding in the defense of the State. Men who are exempted by law from the performance of any duty, do not generally feel the obligation to perform that duty unless called upon by the law. But I am confident that the men of Mississippi have only to know that their soil is invaded, their cities menaced, to rush to meet the enemy, even if they serve only for thirty days. I see no reason why the State may not, in an exigency like that which now presses on her, call on her reserved forces and organize them for service. Such troops could be of material benefit, by serving in intrenchments, and thus relieving the veteran and disciplined soldiers for the duties of the field, where discipline is so much needed. At the end of a short term of service they could return to their homes and to their ordinary avocations, resuming those duties necessary to the public prosperity.

The exemption act, passed by the last Congress, will probably be made the subject of revision and amendment. It seems to me that some provision might be made by which those who are exempt from enrollment now, might, on becoming subject to conscription, be turned over by the State to the Confederate authorities. But let it never be said that there is a conflict between the States and the Confederate government, by which a blow may be inflicted on the common cause. If such a page is to be written on the history of any State, I hope that you, my friends, will say that that State shall not be Mississippi. Let me repeat that there is much that the reserved corps can do. They can build bridges, construct fortifications, act as a sort of police to preserve order and promote the industrial interests of the State and to keep the negroes under control. Being of the people among whom they would act, those misunderstandings would thus be avoided which are apt to arise when strangers are employed in such a service. In this manner the capacity of the army for active operations against the enemy would be materially increased. I hope I shall not be considered intrusive for having entered into these details. The measures I have recommended are placed before you only in the form of suggestions, and, by you, I know I shall not be misinterpreted.

In considering the manner in which the war has been conducted by the enemy, nothing arrests the attention more than the magnitude of the preparations made for our subjugation. Immense navies have been constructed, vast armies have been accumulated, for the purpose of crushing out the rebellion. It has been impossible for us to meet them in equal numbers; nor have we required it. We have often whipped them three to one, and in the eventful battle of Antietam, Lee whipped them four to one. But do not understand me as saying that this will always be the case. When the troops of the enemy become disciplined, and accustomed to the obedience of the camp, they will necessarily approach more nearly to an equality with our own men. We have always whipped them in spite of disparity of numbers, and on any fair field, fighting as man to man, and relying only on those natural qualities with which men are endowed, we should not fear to meet them in the proportion of one to two. But troops must be disciplined in order to develop their efficiency; and in order to keep them at their posts. Above all, to assure this result, we need the support of public opinion. We want public opinion to frown down those who come from the army with sad tales of disaster, and prophecies of evil, and who skulk from the duties they owe their country. We rely on the women of the land to turn back these deserters from the ranks. I thank the Governor for asking the legislature to make the people of the State tributary to this service. In addition to this, it is necessary to fill up those regiments which have for so long a time been serving in the field. They have stood before the foe on many hard fought fields and have proven their courage and devotion on all. They have won the admiration of the army and of the country. And here I may repeat a compliment I have heard which, although it seems to partake of levity, appears an illustration of the esteem in which Mississippians are held. It happened that several persons were conversing of a certain battle, and one of them remarked that the Mississippians did not run. "Oh no!" said another "Mississippians never run." But those who have passed through thirteen pitched battles are not unscathed. Their ranks are thinned, and they look back to Mississippi for aid to augment their diminished numbers. They look back expecting their brothers to fly to their rescue; but it sometimes seems as if the long anticipated relief would never come. A brigade which may consist of only twelve hundred men is expected to do the work of four thousand. Humanity demands that these depleted regiments be filled up. A mere skeleton cannot reasonably be expected to perform the labor of a body with all its flesh and muscle on it. You have many who might assist in revivifying your reduced regiments—enough to fill up the ranks if they would only consent to throw off the shackles of private interest, and devote themselves to the noblest cause in which a man can be engaged. You have now in the field old men and gentle boys who have braved all the terrors and the dangers of war. I remember an instance of one of these, a brave and gallant youth who, I was told, was but sixteen years of age. In one of those bloody battles by which the soil of Virginia has been consecrated to liberty, he was twice wounded, and each time bound up the wound with his own hands, while refusing to leave the field. A third time he was struck, and the life-blood flowed in a crimson stream from his breast. His brother came to him to minister to his wants; but the noble boy said "brother, you cannot do me any good now; go where you can do the Yankees most harm." Even then, while lying on the ground, his young life fast ebbing away, he cocked his rifle and aimed it to take one last shot at the enemy. And so he died, a hero and a martyr. This was one of the boys whose names shed glory on Mississippi, and who, looking back from their distant camps, where they stand prepared to fight your battles, and to turn back the tide of Yankee invasion, ask you now to send them aid in the struggle —to send them men to stand by them in the day of trial, on the right hand and on the left.

When I came to Mississippi I was uncertain in which direction the enemy intended to come, or what point they intended to attack. It had been stated indeed in their public prints, that they would move down upon Mississippi from the North, with the object of taking Vicksburg in the rear, while their navy would attack that place in front. Such was the programme which had been proclaimed for the invasion and subjugation of your State. But when I went to Grenada, I found that the enemy had retired from our front, and that nothing was to be seen of them but their backs. It is probable that they have abandoned that line, with the intention of reinforcing the heavy column now descending the river. Vicksburg and Port Hudson are the real points of attack. Every effort will be made to capture those places with the object of forcing the navigation of the Mississippi, of cutting off our communications with the trans Mississippi department, and of severing the Western from the Eastern portion of the Confederacy. Let, then, all who have at heart the safety of the country, go without delay to Vicksburg and Port Hudson; let them go for such length of time as they can spare—for thirty, for sixty, or for ninety days. Let them assist in preserving the Mississippi river, that great artery of the country, and thus conduce more than in any other way to the perpetuation of the Confederacy and the success of the cause.

I may say here that I did not expect the Confederate enrolling officers to carry on the work of conscription. I relied for this upon the aid of the State authorities. I supposed that State officers would enroll the conscripts within the limits of their respective States, and that Confederate officers would then receive them in camps of instruction. This I believe to be the policy of your Governor's arguments. We cannot too strongly enforce the necessity of harmony between the Confederate Government and the State Governments. They must act together if our cause is to be brought to a successful issue. Of this you may rest assured, whatever the Confederate government can do for the defense of Mississippi will be done. I feel equal confidence that whatever Mississippi can do will likewise be done. It undoubtedly requires legislation to cause men to perform those duties which are purely legal. Men are not apt to feel an obligation to discharge duties from which they may have been exempted. Ours is a representative government, and it is only through the operation of the law that the obligations toward it can be equally distributed. When the last Congress proclaimed that a certain number of men were required to fill up the ranks of the army, that class of men who were already in the field and who were retained in service, would not have been satisfied had there been no conscription of those who had remained at home. I may state also, that I believe this to be the true theory for the military defense of the Confederacy. Cast your eyes forward to that time at the end of the war, when peace shall nominally be proclaimed—for peace between us and our hated enemy will be liable to be broken at short intervals for many years to come—cast your eyes forward to that time, and you will see the necessity for continued preparation and unceasing watchfulness. We have but few men in our country who will be willing to enlist in the army for a soldier's pay. But if every young man shall have served for two or three years in the army, he will be prepared when war comes to go into camp and take his place in the ranks an educated and disciplined soldier. Serving among his equals, his friends and his neighbors, he will find in the army no distinction of class. To such a system I am sure there can be no objection.

The issue before us is one of no ordinary character. We are not engaged in a conflict for conquest, or for agrandizement, or for the settlement of a point of international law. The question for you to decide is, "will you be slaves or will you be independent?" Will you transmit to your children the freedom and equality which your fathers transmitted to you or will you bow down in adoration before an idol baser than ever was worshipped by Eastern idolators? Nothing more is necessary than the mere statement of this issue. Whatever may be the personal sacrifices involved, I am sure that you will not shrink from them whenever the question comes before you. Those men who now assail us, who have been associated with us in a common Union, who have inherited a government which they claim to be the best the world ever saw—these men, when left to themselves, have shown that they are incapable of preserving their own personal liberty. They have destroyed the freedom of the press; they have seized upon and imprisoned members of State Legislatures and of municipal councils, who were suspected of sympathy with the South. Men have been carried off into captivity in distant States without indictment, without a knowledge of the accusations brought against them, in utter defiance of all rights guaranteed by the institutions under which they live. These people, when separated from the South and left entirely to themselves, have, in six months, demonstrated their utter incapacity for self-government. And yet these are the people who claim to be your masters. These are the people who have determined to divide out the South among their Yankee troops. Mississippi they have devoted to the direst vengeance of all. "But vengeance is the Lord's," and beneath his banner you will meet and hurl back these worse than vandal hordes.

The great end and aim of the government is to make our struggle successful. The men who stand highest in this contest would fall the first sacrifice to the vengeance of the enemy in case we should be unsuccessful. You may rest assured then for that reason if for no other that whatever capacity they possess will be devoted to securing the independence of the country. Our government is not like the monarchies of the Old World, resting for support upon armies and navies. It sprang from the people and the confidence of the people is necessary for its success. When misrepresentations of the government have been circulated, when accusations have been brought against it of weakness and inefficiency, often have I felt in my heart the struggle between the desire for justice and the duty not to give information to the enemy—because at such times the correction of error would have been injurious to the safety of the cause. Thus, that great and good man, Gen. A. Sidney Johnston, was contented to rest beneath public contumely and to be pointed at by the finger of scorn, because he did not advance from Bowling Green with the little army under his command. But month after month he maintained his post, keeping the enemy ignorant of the paucity of his numbers, and thus holding the invaders in check. I take this case as one instance; it is not the only one by far.

The issue then being: will you be slaves; will you consent to be robbed of your property; to be reduced to provincial dependence; will you renounce the exercise of those rights with which you were born and which were transmitted to you by your fathers? I feel that in addressing Mississippians the answer will be that their interests, even life itself, should be willingly laid down on the altar of their country.

By the memories of the past; by the glories of the field of Chalmette, where the Mississippians, in a general order of the day, were addressed as the bravest of the brave; by the glorious dead of Mexico; by the still more glorious dead of the battle fields of the Confederacy; by the desolate widows and orphans, whom the martyrs of the war have left behind them; by your maimed and wounded heroes—I invoke you not to delay a moment, but to rush forward and place your services at the disposal of the State. I have been one of those who, from the beginning, looked forward to a long and bloody war; but I must frankly confess that its magnitude has exceeded my expectations. The enemy have displayed more power and energy and resources than I had attributed to them. Their finances have held out far better than I imagined would be the case. But I am also one of those who felt that our final success was certain, and that our people had only to be true to themselves to behold the Confederate flag among those of the recognized nations of the earth. The question is only one of time. It may be remote but it may be nearer than many people suppose. It is not possible that a war of the dimensions that this one has assumed, of proportions so gigantic, can be very long protracted. The combatants must be soon exhausted. But it is impossible, with a cause like ours, we can be the first to cry, "Hold, enough."

The sacrifices which have already been made, have perhaps fallen heavily upon a portion of the people, especially upon the noble little city of Vicksburg. After Memphis and New Orleans had fallen, two points which were considered to be admirably defended, two points which we had no reason to believe would fall, Vicksburg became the object of attack. A few earthworks were thrown up, a few guns were mounted, and Vicksburg received the shock of both fleets; the one which, under Commodore Foote had descended the river, and the one which, under Farragut, had achieved the capture of New Orleans. Nobly did the little city receive the assault, and even the women said, "Rather than surrender let us give them the soil, but with the ashes of our dwellings upon it."

This was the heroic devotion of a people who deserve to be free. Your Governor left his chair, and went himself to the scene of danger. Nothing more profoundly touched me amid my duties in a distant land, than to hear that the chief magistrate of my own State was defending the town which the enemy had made the object of his attack, and that the defense was successful. Now we are far better prepared in that quarter. The works, then weak, have been greatly strengthened; the troops assigned for their defense are better disciplined and better instructed, and that gallant soldier who came with me, has been pouring in his forces to assist in its protection. Himself the son of a Revolutionary hero, he has emulated his father's glorious example upon other fields, and comes to Mississippi to defend, and, as I believe, to protect you.

In the course of this war our eyes have been often turned abroad. We have expected sometimes recognition and sometimes intervention at the hands of foreign nations, and we have had a right to expect it. Never before in the history of the world had a people for so long a time maintained their ground, and showed themselves capable of maintaining their national existence, without securing the recognition of commercial nations. I know not why this has been so, but this I say, "put not your trust in princes," and rest not your hopes in foreign nations. This war is ours; we must fight it out ourselves, and I feel some pride in knowing that so far we have done it without the good will of anybody. It is true that there are now symptoms of a change in public opinion abroad. They give us their admiration—they sometimes even say to us God speed—and in the remarkable book written by Mr. Spence, the question of secession has been discussed with more of ability than it ever has been even in this country. Yet England still holds back, but France, the ally of other days, seems disposed to hold out to us the hand of fellowship. And when France holds out to us her hand, right willingly will we grasp it.

During the last year, the war has been characterized by varied fortunes. New Orleans fell; a sad blow it was to the valley of the Mississippi, and as unexpected to me as to any one. Memphis also fell, and besides these we have lost various points on the Atlantic coast. The invading armies have pressed upon us at some points; at others they have been driven back; but take a view of our condition now and compare it with what it was a year ago—look at the enemy's position as it then was and as it now is; consider their immense power, vast numbers, and great resources; look at all these things and you will be convinced that our condition now will compare favorably with what it was then. Armies are not composed of numbers alone. Officers and men are both to be disciplined and instructed. When the war first began the teacher and the taught were in the condition of the blind leading the blind; now all this is changed for the better. Our troops have become disciplined and instructed. They have stripped the gunboat of its terrors; they have beaten superior numbers in the field; they have discovered that with their short range weapons they can close upon the long range of the enemy and capture them. Thus, in all respects, moral as well as physical, we are better prepared than we were a year ago.

There are now two prominent objects in the programme of the enemy. One is to get possession of the Mississippi river and to open it to navigation in order to appease the clamors of the West and to utilize the capture of New Orleans, which has thus far rendered them no service. The other is to seize upon the capital of the Confederacy, and hold this out as a proof that the Confederacy has no existence. We have recently repulsed them at Fredericksburg, and I believe that under God and by the valor of our troops the capital of the Confederacy will stand safe behind its wall of living breasts. Vicksburg and Port Hudson have been strengthened, and now we can concentrate at either of them a force sufficient for their protection. I have confidence that Vicksburg will stand as before, and I hope that Johnston will find generals to support him if the enemy dare to land. Port Hudson is now strong. Vicksburg will stand, and Port Hudson will stand; but let every man that can be spared from other vocations, hasten to defend them, and thus hold the Mississippi river, that great artery of the Confederacy, preserve our communications with the trans-Mississippi department, and thwart the enemy's scheme of forcing navigation through to New Orleans. By holding that section of the river between Port Hudson and Vicksburg, we shall secure these results, and the people of the West, cut off from New Orleans, will be driven to the East to seek a market for their products, and will be compelled to pay so much in the way of freights that those products will be rendered almost valueless. Thus, I should not be surprised if the first daybreak of peace were to dawn upon us from that quarter.

Some time since, for reasons not necessary to recapitulate, I sent to this State a general unknown to most of you, and, perhaps, even by name, known but to few among you. This was the land of my affections. Here were situated the little of worldly goods I possessed. I selected a general who, in my view, was capable of defending my State and discharging the duties of this important service. I am happy to state, after an attentive, examination, that I have not been mistaken in the general of my choice. I find that, during his administration here everything has been done that could be accomplished with the means at his command. I recommend him to your confidence as you may have confidence in me, who selected him. For the defense of Vicksburg, I selected one from the army of the Potomac, of whom it is but faint praise to say he has no superior. He was sent to Virginia at the beginning of the war, with a little battery of three guns. With these he fought the Yankee gunboats, drove them off, and stripped them of their terrors. He was promoted for distinguished services on various fields. He was finally made a colonel of cavalry, and I have reason to believe that, at the last great conflict on the field of Manassas, he served to turn the tide of battle and consummate the victory.

On succeeding fields he has won equal distinction. Though yet young he has fought more battles than many officers who have lived to an advanced age and died in their beds. I have therefore sent Lee to take charge of the defenses of Vicksburg. I can say then that I have every confidence in the skill and energy of the officers in command. But when I received dispatches and heard rumors of alarm and trepidation and despondency among the people of Mississippi; when I heard even that people were fleeing to Texas in order to save themselves from the enemy; when I saw it stated by the enemy that they had handled other States with gloves, but Mississippi was to be handled without gloves, every impulse of my heart dragged me hither in spite of duties which might have claimed my attention elsewhere. When I heard of the sufferings of my own people, of the danger of their subjugation by a ruthless foe, I felt that if Mississippi were destined for such a fate, I would wish to sleep in her soil. On my way here I stopped at the headquarters of Gen. Johnston. I knew his capacity and his resolution. I imparted to him my own thoughts and asked him to come with me. I found that his ideas were directed in the same channel. He came in the shortest time for preparation; but whatever man can do will be done by him. I have perfect confidence that with your assistance and support he will drive the enemy from the soil of Mississippi. After having visited the army—after having mingled among the people of the State—I shall go away from among you with a lighter heart. I do not think the people of Mississippi are despondent or depressed; those who are so are those on whom the iron tread of the invader has fallen, or those who, skulking from their duty, go home with fearful tales to justify their desertion.

Nor is the army despondent; on the contrary, it is confident of victory. At Grenada I found the only regret to be that the enemy had not come on. At Vicksburg, even without reinforcements, the troops did not dream of defeat. I go, therefore, anxious but hopeful. My attachment to Mississippi, and my esteem for her people, have risen since the war began. I have been proud of her soldiers. I have endeavored to conceal my pride, for I wished to make no distinction between the States of the Confederacy; but I cannot deny that my heart has warmed with a livelier emotion when I have seen those letters upon the boy's cap that have marked him for a Mississippian. Man's affections are not subject to his will; mine are fixed upon Mississippi. And when I return to where I shall find Mississippians fighting for you in a distant State, ween I shall tell them that you are safe here, that you can be defended without calling upon them, and that they are necessary to guard the capital and to prevent the inroads of the enemy in Georgia and Alabama, I shall be proud to say to them for you that they are welcome to stay.

As to the States on the other side of the Mississippi, I can say that their future is bright. The army is organized and disciplined, and it is to be hoped that at no distant day it may be able to advance into that land which has been trodden under the foot of despotism, where old men have been torn from their homes and immured in dugeons, where even the women have been subjected to the insults of the brutal Yankee soldiery—that under the flag of the Confederacy Missouri will again be free.

Kentucky, too, that gallant State whose cause is our cause, the gallantry of whose sons has never been questioned, is still the object of the ardent wishes of Gen. Bragg. I heard him say in an address to his troops, that he hoped again to lead them into Kentucky, and to the banks of the Ohio river.

I can then say with confidence that our condition is in every respect greatly improved over what it was last year. Our armies have been augmented, our troops have been instructed and disciplined. The articles necessary for the support of our troops, and our people, and from which the enemy's blockade has cut us off, are being produced in the Confederacy. Our manufactories have made rapid progress, so much is this the case that I learn with equal surprise and pleasure from the general commanding this department, that Mississippi alone can supply the army which is upon her soil.

Our people have learned to economize and are satisfied to wear home spun. I never see a woman dressed in home spun that I do not feel like taking off my hat to her; and although our women never lose their good looks, I cannot help thinking that they are improved by this garb. I never meet a man dressed in home spun but I feel like saluting him. I cannot avoid remarking with how much pleasure I have noticed the superior morality of our troops, and the contrast which in this respect they present to those of the invader. I can truly say that an army more pious and more moral than that defending our liberties, I do not believe to exist. On their valor and the assistance of God I confidently rely.

BATTLE OF CHICKASAW BAYOU:
MISSISSIPPI, DECEMBER 1862

William T. Sherman to John Sherman

Grant was forced to abandon his advance on Vicksburg by Van Dorn's attack on Holly Springs, but was unable to tell Sherman that he was retreating because Confederate raiders had torn down the telegraph lines. Sherman landed his troops on the Yazoo River north of Vicksburg and on December 29 assaulted the bluffs overlooking Chickasaw Bayou in an attempt to reach high ground. The unsuccessful attack cost the Union forces nearly 1,800 men killed, wounded, or missing, while Confederate casualties totaled about 200. Sherman wrote to his brother John, now a Republican senator from Ohio.

Steamer *Forest Queen*,
January 6, 1863.

Dear Brother,

You will have heard of our attack on Vicksburg and failure to succeed. The place is too Strong, and without the cooperation of a large army coming from the Interior it is impracticable. Innumerable batteries prevent the approach of Gun boats to the city or to the first bluff up the Yazoo, and the only landing between is on an insular space of low boggy ground with innumerable bayous or deep sloughs. I did all that was possible to reach the main Land but was met at every point by Batteries & Rifle pits that we could not pass, and in the absence of Genl. Grants cooperating force I was compelled to reembark my command. My Reports to General Grant a copy of which I send to General Halleck who will let you see it is very full, and more than I could write to you with propriety. Whatever you or the absent may think, not a soldier or officer who was present but will admit I pushed the attack as far as prudence would justify, and that I reembarked my command in the nick of time, for a heavy rain set in which would have swamped us and made it impossible to withdraw artillery & Stores. Up to that time I was acting on the Right Wing of Genl. Grants army, but Gen. McClernand has arrived and we now have a new organization—

McClernand commanding the whole, and our present force divided into two commands or Corps d'Armee one of which is commanded by me and one by Morgan of Cumberland Gap. We are now en route for the Arkansas. Up that River about 50 miles the enemy is entrenched, and has sent down to the Missisipi and captured two steamboats carrying to the fleet supplies. Now it is unwise to leave such a force on our rear and flank and inasmuch as Genl. Grant is not prepared to march down to Vicksburg by Land, we can attack this Post of Arkansas and maybe reach Little Rock. Success in this quarter will have a good Effect on the Main River. But in the end Vicksburg must be reduced, and it is going to be a hard nut to crack—It is the strongest place I ever saw, both by nature and art, and so far as we could observe it is defended by a Competent form of artillery Infantry and Cavalry, besides its Rail Road connections with the interior give them great advantage. I wish you would ask Halleck to allow you to See my Report, and as soon as all the Reports of the Division & Brigade commanders reach Washington from Genl. Grant to where they must first go, you will have a complete picture. Of course newspaper men will first flood the country with their stories and what they will be no one can tell, they having their purposes to Serve and not Knowing my orders or plans. My orders from Grant were to leave Memphis by the 18th and I got off the 20th and I was exactly on time to cooperate with Grant. I did not know that he was delayed by the breaking of his Railroad Communications to his Rear. Indeed I supposed him to be advancing south towards the Yazoo River. My entire force was 30,000, and was every man I could raise at Memphis & Helena, and Grant & Halleck were fully advised of my strength & plans. I suppose you are now fully convinced of the stupendous energy of the South, and their ability to prolong this war indefinitely, but I am further satisfied that if it last thirty years we must fight it out, for the moment the North relaxes its energies, the South will assume the offensive, and it is wonderful how well disciplined and provided they have their men—we found everywhere abundant supplies, even on the Yazoo, and all along the River we found cattle & fat ones feeding quietly. The Country everywhere abounds with corn, and the Soldiers though coarsely are well clad. We hear of the manufacture of all sorts of cloth and munitions of war. The River Plantations are mostly abandoned, and all families negros, stock & cotton removed 25 miles back. All corn has been carried in advance to Vicksburg. We find a few old people along the River but all the Young & middle aged have gone to the war. I see no symptoms of a relaxation of their fierce energy, so that I still regard the war as but fairly begun. Young Henry Sherman was under fire, but is well. He is in Lindseys Brigade of Morgans Division. In time I will move for his promotion.

I think I see at the North & in the discussions in the Senate & Cabinet symptoms of that anarchy which I fear more than war. Stand by the Constituted authorities even if it lead to despotism rather than anarchy which will result if popular clamor is to be the Ruling Power. yrs.

               Sherman

MISTREATMENT OF CONTRABANDS:
ARKANSAS, DECEMBER 1862

Samuel Sawyer, Pearl P. Ingalls, and Jacob G. Forman to Samuel R. Curtis

Slaves who came within the Union lines often suffered from neglect and abuse at the hands of Northern soldiers. Three Union army chaplains sent this appeal to Major General Samuel R. Curtis, the commander of the Department of the Missouri. Sawyer was subsequently appointed superintendent of contrabands at Helena, with Forman serving as his assistant.

———————

Helena Arkansas Dec 29th 1862
General   The undersigned Chaplains and Surgeons of the army of the Eastern Destrict of Arkansas would respectfully call your attention to the Statements & Suggestions following

The Contrabands within our lines are experiencing hardships oppression & neglect the removal of which calls loudly for the intervention of authority. We daily see & deplore the evil and leave it to your wisdom to devise a remedy. In a great degree the contrabands are left entirely to the mercy and rapacity of the unprincipled part of our army (excepting only the limited jurisdiction of capt Richmond) with no person clothed with Specific authority to look after & protect them. Among their list of grievances we mention these:

Some who have been paid by individuals for cotton or for labor have been waylaid by soldiers, robbed, and in several instances fired upon, as well as robbed, and in no case that we can now recal have the plunderers been brought to justice—

The wives of some have been molested by soldiers to gratify thier licentious lust, and thier husbands murdered in endeavering to defend them, and yet the guilty parties, though known, were not arrested. Some who have wives and families are required to work on the Fortifications, or to unload Government Stores, and receive only their meals at the Public table, while their families, whatever provision is intended for them, are, as a matter of fact, left in a helpless & starving condition

Many of the contrabands have been employed, & received in numerous instances, from officers & privates, only counterfeit money or nothing at all for their services. One man was employed as a teamster by the Government & he died in the service (the government indebted to him nearly fifty dollars) leaving an orphan child eight years old, & there is no apparent provision made to draw the money, or to care for the orphan child. The negro hospital here has become notorious for filth, neglect, mortality & brutal whipping, so that the contrabands have lost all hope of kind treatment there, & would almost as soon go to their graves as to their hospital. These grievances reported to us by persons in whom we have confidence, & some of which we know to be true, are but a few of the many wrongs of which they complain— For the sake of humanity, for the sake of christianity, for the good name of our army, for the honor of our country, cannot something be done to prevent this oppression & to stop its demoralizing influences upon the Soldiers themselves? Some have suggested that the matter be laid before the War Department at Washington, in the hope that they will clothe an agent with authority, to register all the names of the contrabands, who will have a benevolent regard for their welfare, though whom all details of fatigue & working parties shall be made though whom rations may be drawn & money paid, & who shall be empowered to organize schools, & to make all needfull Regulations for the comfort & improvement of the condition of the contrabands; whose accounts shall be open at all times for inspection, and who shall make stated reports to the Department— All which is respectfully submitted

	Samuel Sawyer
committee	Pearl P Ingalls
	J. G. Forman

BATTLE OF STONES RIVER:
TENNESSEE, DECEMBER 1862–JANUARY 1863

Ira S. Owens: from Greene County in the War

After replacing Don Carlos Buell in late October, William S. Rosecrans built up supplies and reorganized his command, now named the Army of the Cumberland. On December 26 Rosecrans began advancing from Nashville toward Braxton Bragg's Army of Tennessee at Murfreesboro, thirty miles to the southeast. By December 30 Rosecrans and his army of 42,000 men faced Bragg and 35,000 Confederates along Stones River outside of Murfreesboro. Bragg struck first on December 31 and succeeded in nearly doubling the Union battle line back on itself. Private Ira S. Owens of the 74th Ohio Infantry fought as part of James S. Negley's division in the corps commanded by George H. Thomas. He recalled his first (and only) battle in an 1874 regimental history.

ON THE 26th of December 1862 we received orders to march to Murfreesboro, Tennessee, where the rebels were in strong force. Accordingly we packed up and started, the Army of the Cumberland moving at the same time. We were then going to our first battle. We had not marched far before it began to rain and rained very hard. We marched on through the mud and rain until nearly night, when we halted within two miles of Nashville. We had prepared our suppers and eaten them, and were preparing to spend the night by spreading our blankets on the ground for beds, when the bugle sounded and we were ordered to fall in. Then we marched some two or three miles farther, passing through the town of Nolensville, and halted in the woods. It will be remembered that we had neither shelter tents nor gum blankets, consequently we were exposed to all the rain, which continued nearly all night, so that we had to sit up nearly the whole time. The next day we advanced on toward Murfreesboro, skirmishing in front, as they had been all the day before. Colonel Moody urging us on, telling us if we did not hurry up the battle would be over before we should get there. We marched on until we came to the Nashville pike, some eight or nine miles from Murfreesboro. We halted just at night wet, cold and hungry. It was not long, however, before we had a fire built of rails, and after getting warm and dry we became tolerably comfortable. After getting and eating our suppers we prepared to spend the night. After spreading our blankets down on the ground around the fire we addressed ourselves to sleep. During the night the fire popped out on blankets and burned several large holes in them. Rained some during the night. The next day the being Sunday, we rested and spread out our blankets to dry.

Monday, the 29th, the regiment advanced toward Murfreesboro, except Company C, which was ordered back to Nolensville, to guard some teams which were sent back for part of the baggage, which was left behind, owing to the bad condition of the roads. We arrived at Nolensville, and loaded the teams, and started back. We had left the town but a short time when it was entered by some rebel scouts and plundered of everything. Had we remained an hour longer, in all probability, we should all have been captured. We arrived at the place where we left the regiment, but they had gone on; so we halted and remained all night, and the next morning we advanced toward Murfreesboro, where we found the regiment in line of battle, and skirmishing going on in front. We remained in line through the day and until about 11 o'clock at night, our position being on the center, amid a thick growth of cedars. About 11 o'clock at night we were ordered out to support a battery in front. We remained in line until morning. It was quite cool, and the ground considerably frozen. I had lost my knapsack, putting it in a wagon the day we arrived on the battle ground, and never saw it any more. Consequently I had neither coat nor blanket. I suffered very much during the night with cold. Could not lie down but a few minutes at a time, and dare not go back to the fire, rebels being but a few yards in. I was chilled through and exposed to the enemy, there being no breastworks. It was considered a mark of cowardice to get behind anything to fight. Had the same policy been adopted then as was toward the close of the war, that is, of building works, a great many lives might have been saved. About 6 o'clock on the morning of the 31st of

December, we were relieved by the 37th Indiana Volunteer Infantry. We returned where the regiment lay the day previous, and commenced breakfast, but did not have time to eat it before we were ordered into line. Not having time to drink my coffee, I poured it into my canteen, and swung it around my neck. We marched out to fight, forming double column at half distance. We advanced a short distance, when we formed line and were ordered to lie down. Then it was that the balls and the shrieking shells came whistling over us, and there were to be seen batteries wheeling into position, orderlies riding back and forth, horses without riders, while the yelling of the rebels like so many fiends, and the roar of artillery and musketry, filled the air with horrid din. The battle was raging fiercely. In a short time we were ordered to arise and move forward. We accordingly moved forward in line a few yards, and were then ordered to halt, make ready, aim—fire. Then the Seventy-Fourth opened its first fire on the enemy. For a description of the battle of Stone River, and an account of the same, I refer the reader to "Rosecrans' Campaign with the 14th Army Corps." I was kneeling in a fence corner, loading and firing when we received orders to move to the left to make room for a battery. When I was just in the act of rising, I felt something hit me on the leg, which did not produce much pain at the time, only a smarting sensation. I thought I would say nothing about it. However it began to grow stiff, and I had not proceeded but a short distance before I had to call for help. I was then helped off the field.

We went back the same way we came. But it was getting to be a hot place in the rear. Balls and shells were flying thick and fast around us, striking trees, and cutting off leaves and branches. The rebels were getting around, and we scarcely knew which way to go, for fear of running right into their midst. At last we got out to the pike. On our way we stopped in an old building where several of our wounded boys were. The rebels soon commenced shelling us; so we had to get away as fast as we could. We proceeded about half a mile, when we were overtaken by some ambulances, where I was taken in and taken to the field hospital, five miles distant. Some of the boys who read this will remember the field hospital at the brick house, near Stewart's creek. It was impossible to supply all the wounded with tents. Rails were hauled and thrown in piles similar to farmers when they wish to build fence, and large fires built apart. The wounded were brought and lain by these fires. Men were wounded in every conceivable way, some with their arms shot off, some wounded in the body, some in the head. It was heart-rending to hear their cries and groans. One poor fellow who was near me was wounded in the head. He grew delirious during the night, and would very frequently call his mother. He would say: "Mother, O, Mother, come and help me!" The poor fellow died before morning with no mother near, to soothe him in his dying moments, or wipe the cold sweat from off his brow. I saw the surgeons amputate limbs, then throw the quivering flesh into a pile. Every once in a while a man would stretch himself out and die. Next morning rows of men were laid out side by side ready for the soldier's burial. No weeping friends stood around, no coffin and hearse to bear them away to the grave, no funeral orations delivered; but there, away from home and kindred, they were wrapped in the soldiers' blanket, a trench dug, and their bodies placed side by side, like they fought, a few shovelfulls of earth thrown upon them, when they were left alone.

"BLOODY AND USELESS SACRIFICE":
TENNESSEE, DECEMBER 1862–JANUARY 1863

Lot D. Young: from Reminiscences of a Soldier of the Orphan Brigade

The new Union battle line held on the afternoon of December 31. After a lull on New Year's Day, the battle resumed on the afternoon of January 2 when Bragg attacked the Union positions on the eastern bank of Stones River. Bragg ordered a retreat on January 3, allowing the North to claim victory at Stones River (or Murfreesboro), a battle that cost the Union 12,906 men killed, wounded, or missing and the Confederacy 11,739—about a third of each army. Lieutenant Lot D. Young served in the Confederate 1st Kentucky Brigade, which became known as the "Orphan Brigade" because its members were unable to return to their native state. He remembered the fighting on January 2 in a 1918 memoir.

THE BATTLE progressed steadily and satisfactorily to the Confederates until about four o'clock, when they, in the language of the "bum," "run against a snag." Woods' and Sheridan's divisions, with other of Rosecrans' forces had concentrated upon his extreme left, which was his strongest position for a final and last stand. The conflict here was desperate and bloody, neither party seeming to have much the advantage.

The National cemetery now occupies this identical ground and in which there are more than 6,000 Federal soldiers buried. A beautiful and fit place for the remains of these brave Western soldiers to rest, for here upon this field was displayed a courage that all men must admire.

Both armies slept that night upon the field with the greater part of the field in possession of the Confederates and the advantages and results of the day almost wholly in their favor.

The Orphans spent the night in the rear of and among the artillery they had been supporting. When morning came we found that the enemy was still in our front instead of on the road to Nashville as Bragg believed. Both parties seemed willing that a truce should prevail for the day and scarcely a shot was heard. Bragg believed that Rosecrans' army was "demolished" and would surely retreat to his base (Nashville), and so informed President Davis.

But old "Rosy" had something else in his mind. He was planning and scheming and matured a plan for a trap and Bragg walked right into it with the innocence of a lamb and the ignorance of a man that had never known anything of the art of war, and the butchery of the next day followed as a result of his obstinacy and the lack of military skill. Had he listened to the protestations of General Breckinridge and his officers he might have saved for the time being his military reputation and the lives of several hundred brave and noble men.

The recounting of the steps that led up to this ill-conceived and fatal denouement and the efforts by General Breckinridge to prevent its consummation, by one while not high in rank, but who claims to know something of the facts in the case, may not go amiss even at this late day.

Early on the morning of January 2, Captain Bramblett, commanding Company H, Fourth Kentucky, and who had served with General Breckinridge in Mexico, received orders from him (Breckinridge), to make a thorough reconnaissance of the enemy's position, Company H being at that time on the skirmish line. Captain Bramblett with two of his lieutenants, myself one of them, crawled through the weeds a distance of several hundred yards to a prominent point of observation from which through his field glass and even the naked eye we could see the enemy's concentrated forces near and above the lower ford on the opposite side of the river, his artillery being thrown forward and nearest to the river. His artillery appeared to be close together and covering quite a space of ground; we could not tell how many guns, but there was quite a number. The infantry was seemingly in large force and extended farther down toward the ford. Captain Bramblett was a man of no mean order of military genius and information, and after looking at, and studying the situation in silence for some minutes, he said to us boys, "that he believed Rosecrans was setting a trap for Bragg." Continuing, he said, "If he means to attack us on this side, why does he not reinforce on this side? Why concentrate so much artillery on the bluff yonder? He must be expecting us to attack that force yonder," pointing to Beatty's position on the hill North of us, "and if we do, he will use that artillery on us as we move to the attack." At another time during the afternoon I heard him while discussing the situation with other officers of the regiment use substantially the same argument. I accompanied Captain Bramblett to General Breckinridge's headquarters and heard him make substantially in detail a report containing the facts above recited. Captain Tom Steele was ordered (his company having relieved ours) on the skirmish line to make a reconnaissance also, and made a similar report, and lastly General Breckinridge, to thoroughly and unmistakably understand the situation and satisfy himself, in company with one or two of his staff examined the situation as best he could and I presume reached the same conclusion, and when he (Breckinridge) repaired to Bragg's headquarters and vouchsafed this information and suggested the presumptive plan of the enemy, Bragg said: "Sir, my information is different. I have given the order to attack the enemy in your front and expect it to be obeyed."

What was General Breckinridge to do but attempt to carry out his orders, though in carrying out this unwise and ill-conceived order it should cost in one hour and ten minutes 1,700 of as brave and chivalrous soldiers as the world ever saw. What a terrible blunder, what a bloody and useless sacrifice! And all because General Breckinridge had resented the imputation that the cause of the failure of Bragg's Kentucky campaign was the "disloyalty of her people to the Confederate cause." Could anyone of the thousands of Kentuckians that espoused the cause of the South, complacently acquiesce in this erroneous charge and endorse the spirit that prompted this order and led to the slaughter of so many of her noble boys? This was the view that many of us took of Bragg's course.

How was this wicked and useless sacrifice brought about? "That subordinate must always obey his superior"—is the military law. In furtherance of Bragg's order we were assembled about three o'clock on the afternoon of January 2, 1863 (Friday, a day of ill luck) in a line North of and to the right of Swain's hill, confronting Beatty's and Growes' brigades, with a battery or two of artillery as support. They being intended for the bait that had been thrown across the river at the lower ford, and now occupied an eminence some three-quarters of a mile to the right-front of the Orphan's position on Swain's hill.

This was the force, small as it was that Bragg was so anxious to dislodge. Between the attacking line and federal position was a considerable scope of open ground, fields and pastures, with here and there a clump of bushes or briars, but the entire space was in full view of and covered by the enemy's batteries to the left of the line on the opposite side of the river previously referred to. If the reader will only carry these positions in his eye, he can readily discover the jaws of the trap in this murderous scheme.

A more imposing and thoroughly disciplined line of soldiers never moved to the attack of an enemy than responded to the signal gun stationed immediately in our rear, which was fired exactly at four o'clock. Every man vieing with his fellowman, in steadiness of step and correct alignment, with the officers giving low and cautionary commands, many knowing that it was their last hour on earth, but without hesitating moved forward to their inevitable doom and defeat. We had gotten only fairly started, when the great jaws of the trap on the bluff from the opposite side of the river were sprung, and bursting shells that completely drowned the voice of man were plunging and tearing through our columns, ploughing up the earth at our feet in front and behind, everywhere. But with steadiness of step we moved on. Two companies of the Fourth regiment, my own and adjoining company, encountered a pond, and with a dexterous movement known to the skilled officer and soldier was cleared in a manner that was perfectly charming, obliquing to the right and left into line as soon as passed.

By reason of the shorter line held by the enemy, our line, which was much longer and the colors of each of our battalions being directed against this shorter line, caused our lines to interlap, making it necessary, in order to prevent confusion and crowding, that some of the regiments halt, until the others had passed forward out of the way. When thus halted they would lie down in order to shield themselves from the enemy infantry fire in front, who had by this time opened a lively fusillade from behind their temporary works.

While lying on the ground momentarily a very shocking and disastrous occurrence took place in Company E, immediately on my left and within a few feet of where I lay. A shell exploded right in the middle of the company, almost literally tearing it to pieces. When I recovered from the shock the sight I witnessed was appalling. Some eighteen or twenty men hurled in every direction, including my dear friend, Lieut. George Burnley of Frankfort. But these circumstances were occurring every minute now while the battle was raging all around and about us. Men moved intuitively—the voice being silenced by the whizzing and bursting shells. On we moved, Beatty's and Growes' lines giving way seemingly to allow the jaws of the trap to press with more and ever increasing vigor upon its unfortunate and discomfited victims. But, on we moved, until the survivors of the decoy had passed the river and over the lines stationed on the other side of the river, when their new line of infantry opened on our confused and disordered columns another destructive and ruinous fire.

Coupled with this condition and correlative to it, a battery of Growes and a part of their infantry had been cut off from the ford and seeing our confused condition, rallied, reformed and opened fire on our advanced right now along the river bank. Confronted in front by their infantry, with the river intervening; swept by their artillery from the left and now attacked by both infantry and artillery by an oblique fire from the right, we found ourselves in a helpless condition, from which it looked like an impossibility to escape; and but for the fact that two or three batteries had been ordered into position to check the threatened advance of the enemy and thereby distract their attention, we doubtless would have fared still worse.

We rallied some distance to the right of where we started and found that many, very many, of our noblest, truest and best had fallen. Some of them were left on the field, among whom was my military preceptor, advisor and dear friend, Captain Bramblett, who fell into the hands of the enemy and who died a few days after in Nashville. I shall never forget our parting, a moment or two before, he received his wound—never forget the last quick glance and the circumstances that called it forth. He was a splendid soldier and his loss grieved me very much. Many another gallant Kentuckian, some of our finest line and field officers, were left on the field, a sacrifice to stupidity and revenge. Thirty-seven per cent in one hour and ten minutes—some say one hour—was the frightful summary. Among the first of these was the gallant and illustrious Hanson, whose coolness and bearing was unsurpassed and whose loss was irreparable. He with Breckinridge, understood and was fully sensible of—as indicated by the very seriousness of his countenance—the unwisdom of this move and as shown in their protest to Bragg. What a pity that a strict observance of military rule compelled it to be obeyed against his mature military mind and judgment, causing the loss of such a magnificent soldier and gentleman—uselessly and foolishly.

Comtemplating this awful sacrifice, as he rode by the dead and dying in the rear of our lines, General Breckinridge, with tears falling from his eyes, was heard to say in tones of anguish, "My poor Orphans! My poor Orphans!" little thinking that he was dedicating to them a name that will live throughout the annals of time and crown the history of that dear little band with everlasting immortality.

AN OFFER TO RESIGN:
WASHINGTON, D.C., JANUARY 1863

Ambrose E. Burnside to Abraham Lincoln

Following the Fredericksburg debacle, a cabal of Army of the Potomac general officers conspired against Burnside, going over his head and behind his back to the President to challenge his plans. They succeeded: Burnside's orders for a renewed campaign in the Fredericksburg sector were cancelled on Lincoln's order. On December 31 Burnside met with Lincoln, Stanton, and Halleck to debate the matter but they reached no decision. Believing he had lost the confidence of his lieutenants, Burnside determined to resign his command, and on the morning of January 1 he handed the President this letter ("this morning" in the first line actually refers to the previous day's meeting). Lincoln did not accept the resignation, and when Burnside repeated the offer on January 5, replied that he did "not yet see how I could profit by changing the command." Still, the poisonous matter of the Potomac army command would require resolution in the new year.

WASHINGTON, D.C., *January* 1, 1863.
HIS EXCELLENCY THE PRESIDENT OF THE UNITED STATES:

Since leaving you this morning, I have determined that it is my duty to place on paper the remarks which I made to you, in order that you may use them or not, as you see proper.

I am in command, as you know, of nearly 200,000 men, 120,000 of whom are in the immediate presence of the enemy, and I cannot conscientiously retain the command without making an unreserved statement of my views.

The Secretary of War has not the confidence of the officers and soldiers, and I feel sure that he has not the confidence of the country. In regard to the latter statement, you are probably better informed than I am. The same opinion applies with equal force in regard to General Halleck. It seems to be the universal opinion that the movements of the army have not been planned with a view to co-operation and mutual assistance.

I have attempted a movement upon the enemy, in which I have been repulsed, and I am convinced, after mature deliberation, that the army ought to make another movement in the same direction, not necessarily at the same points on the river; but I am not sustained in this by a single grand division commander in my command. My reasons for having issued the order for making this second movement I have already given you in full, and I can see no reasons for changing my views. Doubtless this difference of opinion between my general officers and myself results from a lack of confidence in me. In this case it is highly necessary that this army should be commanded by some other officer, to whom I will most cheerfully give way.

Will you allow me, Mr. President, to say that it is of the utmost importance that you be surrounded and supported by men who have the confidence of the people and of the army, and who will at all times give you definite and honest opinions in relation to their separate departments, and at the same time give you positive and unswerving support in your public policy, taking at all times their full share of the responsibility for that policy? In no positions held by gentlemen near you are these conditions more requisite than those of the Secretary of War and General-in-Chief and the commanders of your armies. In the struggle now going on, in which the very existence of our Government is at stake, the interests of no one man are worth the value of a grain of sand, and no one should be allowed to stand in the way of accomplishing the greatest amount of public good.

It is my belief that I ought to retire to private life. I hope you will not understand this to savor of anything like dictation. My only desire is to promote the public good. No man is an accurate judge of the confidence in which he is held by the public and the people around him, and the confidence in my management may be entirely destroyed, in which case it would be a great wrong for me to retain this command for a single day; and, as I before said, I will most cheerfully give place to any other officer.

I have the honor to be, very respectfully, your obedient servant,

A. E. BURNSIDE,
Major-General, Commanding Army of the Potomac.

"YOU FAIL ME PRECISELY":
WASHINGTON, D.C., JANUARY 1863
Abraham Lincoln to Henry W. Halleck

Burnside's was not the only high-level command resignation the President received on New Year's Day 1863. After the confrontation with Burnside, Lincoln turned to his general-in-chief to settle the military stalemate on the Rappahannock. Henry Halleck, quailing at the responsibility, replied, "there is a very important difference of opinion in regard to my relations toward generals commanding armies in the field," and submitted his resignation. With no better candidate for general-in-chief, Lincoln withdrew his letter and Halleck remained in his position.

Major Gen. Halleck   Executive Mansion,
My dear Sir: Washington, January 1. 1863.
    Gen. Burnside wishes to cross the Rappahannock with his army, but his Grand Division commanders all oppose the movement. If in such a difficulty as this you do not help, you fail me precisely in the point for which I sought your assistance. You know what Gen. Burnside's plan is; and it is my wish that you go with him to the ground, examine it as far as practicable, confer with the officers, getting their judgment, and ascertaining their temper, in a word, gather all the elements for forming a judgment of your own; and then tell Gen. Burnside that you *do* approve, or that you do *not* approve his plan. Your military skill is useless to me, if you will not do this. Yours very truly
A LINCOLN

Withdrawn, because considered harsh by Gen. Halleck.   A.L. Jan. 1. 1863

WASHINGTON, D.C., JANUARY 1863

Abraham Lincoln:
Final Emancipation Proclamation

Despite his trials with his generals, Lincoln marked January 1, 1863, as memorable—the signing and issuing of the Emancipation Proclamation. He later termed it "the central act of my administration and the great event of the nineteenth century." Mention of compensated emancipation and colonization and the Second Confiscation Act in the September 22 preliminary document was absent in this final version. Added to it were the specific "States and parts of States" in rebellion to which the proclamation applied. And there was a further major addition, made at Secretary Chase's suggestion: beyond an exercise of presidential war powers, the Proclamation was "an act of justice." At the signing Lincoln remarked that at the White House New Year's reception he had been shaking hands for three hours "till my arm is stiff and numb." His signature, he said, would be closely examined, "and if they find my hand trembled, they will say 'he had some compunctions.'" But he did not hesitate, and slowly and firmly he signed in a bold hand. With a smile he said, "That will do."

January 1, 1863
By the President of the United States of America:
A Proclamation.

Whereas, on the twentysecond day of September, in the year of our Lord one thousand eight hundred and sixty two, a proclamation was issued by the President of the United States, containing, among other things, the following, towit:

"That on the first day of January, in the year of our Lord one thousand eight hundred and sixty-three, all persons held as slaves within any State or designated part of a State, the people whereof shall then be in rebellion against the United States, shall be then, thenceforward, and forever free; and the Executive Government of the United States, including the military and naval authority thereof, will recognize and maintain the freedom of such persons, and will do no act or acts to repress such persons, or any of them, in any efforts they may make for their actual freedom.

"That the Executive will, on the first day of January aforesaid, by proclamation, designate the States and parts of States, if any, in which the people thereof, respectively, shall then be in rebellion against the United States; and the fact that any State, or the people thereof, shall on that day be, in good faith, represented in the Congress of the United States by members chosen thereto at elections wherein a majority of the qualified voters of such State shall have participated, shall, in the absence of strong countervailing testimony, be deemed conclusive evidence that such State, and the people thereof, are not then in rebellion against the United States."

Now, therefore I, Abraham Lincoln, President of the United States, by virtue of the power in me vested as Commander-in-Chief, of the Army and Navy of the United States in time of actual armed rebellion against authority and government of the United States, and as a fit and necessary war measure for suppressing said rebellion, do, on this first day of January, in the year of our Lord one thousand eight hundred and sixty three, and in accordance with my purpose so to do publicly proclaimed for the full period of one hundred days, from the day first above mentioned, order and designate as the States and parts of States wherein the people thereof respectively, are this day in rebellion against the United States, the following, towit:

Arkansas, Texas, Louisiana, (except the Parishes of St. Bernard, Plaquemines, Jefferson, St. Johns, St. Charles, St. James, Ascension, Assumption, Terrebonne, Lafourche, St. Mary, St. Martin, and Orleans, including the City of New-Orleans) Mississippi, Alabama, Florida, Georgia, South-Carolina, North-Carolina, and Virginia, (except the fortyeight counties designated as West Virginia, and also the counties of Berkley, Accomac, Northampton, Elizabeth-City, York, Princess Ann, and Norfolk, including the cities of Norfolk & Portsmouth); and which excepted parts are, for the present, left precisely as if this proclamation were not issued.

And by virtue of the power, and for the purpose aforesaid, I do order and declare that all persons held as slaves within said designated States, and parts of States, are, and henceforward shall be free; and that the Executive government of the United States, including the military and naval authorities thereof, will recognize and maintain the freedom of said persons.

And I hereby enjoin upon the people so declared to be free to abstain from all violence, unless in necessary self-defence; and I recommend to them that, in all cases when allowed, they labor faithfully for reasonable wages.

And I further declare and make known, that such persons of suitable condition, will be received into the armed service of the United States to garrison forts, positions, stations, and other places, and to man vessels of all sorts in said service.

And upon this act, sincerely believed to be an act of justice, warranted by the Constitution, upon military necessity, I invoke the considerate judgment of mankind, and the gracious favor of Almighty God.

In witness whereof, I have hereunto set my hand and caused the seal of the United States to be affixed.

Done at the City of Washington, this first day of January, in the year of our Lord one thousand eight hundred and sixty three, and of the Independence of the United States of America the eighty-seventh.

By the President: ABRAHAM LINCOLN
    WILLIAM H. SEWARD, Secretary of State.

CELEBRATING EMANCIPATION:
PHILADELPHIA, JANUARY 1863

Benjamin Rush Plumly to Abraham Lincoln

Plumly, a Quaker abolitionist, wrote to the President about the celebrations greeting the proclamation in Philadelphia. And there were other celebrations that day. In Beaufort, South Carolina, more than five thousand former slaves gathered; in Chicago, Osborne Perry Anderson, the sole black survivor of John Brown's raid on Harpers Ferry, spoke in a church; in Boston, William Wells Brown and Frederick Douglass addressed a crowd of three thousand at Tremont Temple.

Philadelphia,
New Year, 1863,
Midnight.

Mr President
Dear Sir,

I have been, all day, from early morning intil a short time ago, in the Crowded Churches of the Colored People of this City.

During thirty years of active Anti-Slavery life, I have never witnessed, such intense, intelligent and devout "Thanksgiving." It was like unto the solemn joy of an old Jewish Passover.

Occasionally, they sang and shouted and wept and prayed. God knows, I cried, with them.

Your Proclamation not having reached us, I took with me Genl Saxton's, and read it, in some of the Churches. The mention of your name, in *that*, evoked a spontaneous benediction from the whole Congregation. No doubt of the coming of Your Proclamation beset any one of them.

As one of their speakers was explaining the effect of your Act, he was interrupted by a sudden outburst, from four or five hundred voices, singing "The Year of Jubilee."

An old Anti-Slavery song, that commemorates some of our great names, which we sang, stirringly, in the dark days of mobs & outrage, was so changed as to include Your name. It was sung with wonderful effect.

The whole rejoicing took the devotional direction. At the close of the morning Meeting, in one Church, the whole Congregation passed up one aisle to the Communion table, each one receiving a piece of Cake, and depositing a small sum for the Contrabands; all the while singing their moving hymns.

In the Episcopal (Col) Church, the service for the 4th of July, was read.

The places of business, controlled by the Colored people were, generally, closed. In the private houses of the better class, festivals and Love feasts, were held.

There are, in this City, about *30-000*, Colored People.

They have *20* Churches. They all go to Church; for the Black man, like all Oriental or Tropical races, is devout.

To day, all the Churches were open & filled.

They have among them, many men of talent, education and property. There are several excellent orators. All of these,— Ministers and laymen, exhorted the people, to accept the Great Gift, with reverent joy; to make no public demonstration, no procession or parade; To indulge in no resentment for the past, and no impatience for the future, but to "work and wait," trusting in God, for the final triumph of Justice.

Never was demonstration so touching. Many wet eyes of white people, testified to the profound pathos of the occasion.

The Black people all trust *you*. They *beleive* that you desire to do them Justice. They do not beleive that *You*, *wish* to expatriate them, or to enforce upon them, any disability, but—that you *cannot* do *all*, that you would.

The spontaneous outburst of this faith in you, was touching, beyond expression. Some one intimated, that You might be forced into some, form of Colinization. "God wont let him," shouted an old woman. "God's in his *heart*", said another, and the response of the Congregation was emphatic.

Another, thought, there must be some design of God, in having your name "Abraham" that if you were not the "Father" You were to be the "Liberator" of a People. One Minister advised them to thank God, that *He* had raised up an honest man, for the White House, whereupon, they broke forth, five hundred strong, in that ringing hymn, "The Year of Jubilee".

It is a great thing Sir, to be the President of the U. States, even though, thorns are in the Seat of Power. But, it is a greater thing, to be enshrined in the Religious sense of a People, yet in its plastic infancy, but destined to, a distant but grand maturity. I would rather be there, as you are, than be President for Life

> Very truly
> Your ob St
> B. Rush Plumly.

PS. An Editor of the Tribune has just asked me to furnish some account of the matter. I shall take the liberty to use the substance of this letter.

"BROKEN EGGS CAN NOT BE MENDED":
WASHINGTON, D.C., JANUARY 1863

Abraham Lincoln to John A. McClernand

Major General McClernand, a former Democratic congressman from Illinois, wrote to Lincoln from Memphis on December 29 that a "gentleman of the first respectability" had arrived from northern Mississippi, claiming to speak for "officers of high rank in the rebel service, who were formerly my warm personal and political friends." These officers desired "the restoration of peace and are represented to be willing to wheel their columns into the line of that policy," but sought reassurances that the President would not "subvert the institutions of any state," implying that the Emancipation Proclamation stood in the way of peace. On that point Lincoln was unyielding: "it must stand."

Executive Mansion,
Major General McClernand   Washington, January 8. 1863.

My dear Sir Your interesting communication by the hand of Major Scates is received. I never did ask more, nor ever was willing to accept less, than for all the States, and the people thereof, to take and hold their places, and their rights, in the Union, under the Constitution of the United States. For this alone have I felt authorized to struggle; and I seek neither more nor less now. Still, to use a coarse, but an expressive figure, broken eggs can not be mended. I have issued the emancipation proclamation, and I can not retract it.

After the commencement of hostilities I struggled nearly a year and a half to get along without touching the "institution"; and when finally I conditionally determined to touch it, I gave a hundred days fair notice of my purpose, to all the States and people, within which time they could have turned it wholly aside, by simply again becoming good citizens of the United States. They chose to disregard it, and I made the peremptory proclamation on what appeared to me to be a military necessity. And being made, it must stand. As to the States not included in it, of course they can have their rights in the Union as of old. Even the people of the states included, if they choose, need not to be hurt by it. Let them adopt systems of apprenticeship for the colored people, conforming substantially to the most approved plans of gradual emancipation; and, with the aid they can have from the general government, they may be nearly as well off, in this respect, as if the present trouble had not occurred, and much better off than they can possibly be if the contest continues persistently.

As to any dread of my having a "purpose to enslave, or exterminate, the whites of the South," I can scarcely believe that such dread exists. It is too absurd. I believe you can be my personal witness that no man is less to be dreaded for undue severity, in any case.

If the friends you mention really wish to have peace upon the old terms, they should act at once. Every day makes the case more difficult. They can so act, with entire safety, so far as I am concerned.

I think you would better not make this letter public; but you may rely confidently on my standing by whatever I have said in it. Please write me if any thing more comes to light. Yours very truly

A. L<small>INCOLN</small>

CHRONOLOGY

BIOGRAPHICAL NOTES

NOTE ON THE TEXTS

NOTES

INDEX

Chronology
January 1862–January 1863

1862 President Abraham Lincoln and his cabinet meet with the congressional Joint Committee on the Conduct of the War, January 6. Lincoln rejects demand of its chairman, Ohio Republican senator Benjamin F. Wade, that General George B. McClellan be replaced as commander of the Army of the Potomac. (McClellan has served as both commander of the Army of the Potomac and as general-in-chief of the Union army since November 1861.) Appoints Edwin M. Stanton, a Democrat who had served as attorney general in the final months of the Buchanan administration, as secretary of war on January 13, replacing Simon Cameron. The same day, Lincoln meets with McClellan and several cabinet members and military advisers to discuss future operations, but McClellan will not reveal his campaign plans. Union force commanded by General George H. Thomas defeats Confederates at Mill Springs on January 19, breaking the Confederate defensive line in southern Kentucky. Lincoln issues President's General War Order No. 1 on January 27, calling for an advance by Union forces in several war theaters by February 22. President's Special War Order No. 1, issued January 31, directs McClellan and the Army of the Potomac to advance against the Confederate army at Manassas outside Washington.

McClellan responds by submitting a campaign plan on February 3 that would outflank the Confederate army at Manassas and strike at Richmond from lower Chesapeake Bay. General Ulysses S. Grant begins offensive against Forts Henry and Donelson on the Tennessee and Cumberland rivers, just south of the Kentucky-Tennessee border. Fort Henry on the Tennessee surrenders on February 6 after bombardment by Union gunboats. On the Atlantic coast, General Ambrose Burnside captures the Confederate outpost on Roanoke Island in North Carolina's Pamlico Sound, February 7–8. General Charles P. Stone, who had commanded the Union forces defeated at Ball's Bluff, Virginia, in October 1861, is arrested on Stanton's orders in Washington, D.C., on February 9 for alleged treachery.

(Stone is imprisoned without charges for six months before being released.) Grant's army begins siege of Fort Donelson on the Cumberland, February 12. In response to Grant's offensive, Confederates evacuate Bowling Green, Kentucky, on February 14. Confederate counterattack at Fort Donelson is defeated, February 15, and the 12,000-man garrison surrenders on February 16. First Confederate Congress, elected in November 1861, convenes in Richmond on February 18. Confederate force advancing up the Rio Grande Valley from Texas defeats Union troops at Valverde in southern New Mexico Territory, February 21. Jefferson Davis is inaugurated in Richmond on February 22 for a six-year term as president of the Confederacy (Davis had served as provisional president since February 1861). Union troops occupy Nashville, Tennessee's capital, on February 25. The same day, Lincoln signs Legal Tender Act authorizing the U.S. Treasury to issue paper money ("greenbacks") not secured by specie. Confederate Congress gives Davis authority to declare martial law and suspend habeas corpus in areas threatened by Union attack, February 27.

Confederates evacuate Columbus, their last outpost in Kentucky, on March 2. Lincoln sends message to Congress on March 6 calling for federal financial aid to states adopting gradual compensated emancipation. General Samuel R. Curtis defeats Confederates in battle of Elkhorn Tavern (or Pea Ridge) in northwestern Arkansas, March 7–8, securing Missouri for the Union. In Virginia, Confederate General Joseph E. Johnston begins withdrawing his army from Manassas to a new position behind the Rappahannock River on March 8. The same day, the ironclad ram C.S.S. *Virginia* attacks the Union blockading squadron in Hampton Roads, Virginia, destroying two wooden warships and damaging a third. Union ironclad U.S.S. *Monitor* reaches Hampton Roads from New York on evening of March 8. The *Virginia* and *Monitor* fight to a draw on March 9 in the first battle in naval history between ironclad ships. Lincoln removes McClellan as general-in-chief (leaving that post vacant) on March 11, retaining him in command of the Army of the Potomac. In response to the Confederate withdrawal from Manassas, McClellan and his corps commanders meet on March 13 and change the starting point for the campaign against Richmond to Fort Monroe on the Virginia Peninsula. Lincoln signs into law new article of war passed by Congress forbidding Union officers from returning fugitive slaves, March 13. General John Pope captures Confederate outpost at New Madrid,

Missouri, on March 14, initiating a campaign to open the Mississippi River. The same day, Ambrose Burnside expands the Union foothold on the North Carolina coast by defeating the Confederates at New Bern. Peninsula campaign begins on March 17 as the first Union troops embark for Fort Monroe. Grant's army moves up the Tennessee (southward) to Pittsburg Landing, just north of the Mississippi-Tennessee border, where it waits to be joined by General Don Carlos Buell's army before planned advance on Corinth, Mississippi. Davis appoints Judah P. Benjamin to replace Robert M. T. Hunter as Confederate secretary of state, George W. Randolph to succeed Benjamin as secretary of war, and Thomas H. Watts to succeed Thomas Bragg as attorney general. Despite U.S. diplomatic protests, British authorities allow newly built warship *Oreto* to sail from Liverpool on March 22. (Commissioned as C.S.S. *Florida* in the Bahamas, the ship begins raiding Union commerce in January 1863.) General Thomas J. (Stonewall) Jackson, the Confederate commander in the Shenandoah Valley of Virginia, is defeated at Kernstown on March 23. Confederates occupy Santa Fe, New Mexico Territory, March 23, but are then defeated at Glorieta, March 26–28, and forced by lack of supplies to retreat down the Rio Grande to Texas.

In Virginia, McClellan advances from Fort Monroe, April 4, then halts before the Confederate defensive lines extending across the Peninsula from Yorktown on April 5. McClellan decides upon a siege and protests he will be outnumbered after Lincoln withholds General Irvin McDowell's corps to defend Washington. Confederate General Albert Sidney Johnston attacks Union forces at Pittsburg Landing on morning of April 6 and drives them back toward the Tennessee River. General Pierre G. T. Beauregard takes command of Confederate army after Johnston is killed in the afternoon. After being reinforced by Buell's army, Grant counterattacks on April 7 and Confederates retreat toward Corinth. Battle of Shiloh (named after country church on the battlefield) costs the Union about 13,000 men killed, wounded, or missing, the Confederates about 10,700. General John Pope captures Island No. 10 in the Mississippi near New Madrid, April 7. Congress passes resolution approving gradual compensated emancipation on April 10, but plan fails to win support in the border states. Fort Pulaski, guarding the entrance to the Savannah River, surrenders to Union forces on April 11 after a two-day bombardment. Confederate Congress passes conscription act, April 16. The same day, Lincoln signs act abolishing slavery in the District of Columbia. On night of April 24 Union fleet commanded by Flag Officer David Farragut forces passage between Forts Jackson and St. Philip on the lower Mississippi, then sails upriver to New Orleans, which surrenders on April 25. The same day, Union forces continue their gains on the North Carolina coast by capturing Fort Macon at Beaufort. General Jackson begins diversionary campaign in the Shenandoah Valley designed to prevent reinforcements from being sent to McClellan.

On the Virginia Peninsula, General Joseph E. Johnston evacuates Yorktown defenses on May 3, ending month-long siege. The same day, 100,000-man Union army led by General Henry W. Halleck begins slow advance from Pittsburg Landing toward Corinth, Mississippi. Confederates fight rear-guard action at Williamsburg, Virginia, on May 5 against McClellan's pursuing forces. Jackson defeats Union forces at McDowell, Virginia, May 8. President Lincoln visits Fort Monroe and organizes the capture of Norfolk, May 9. The same day, Union General David Hunter orders the military emancipation of slaves in Florida, Georgia, and South Carolina (order is revoked by Lincoln on May 19). In naval battle at Plum Run Bend on the Tennessee shore of the Mississippi, a Confederate flotilla sinks two Union gunboats but suffers heavy damage and is forced to retreat downriver, May 10. Ironclad C.S.S. *Virginia* is blown up on May 11 after Union capture of Norfolk leaves the ship without a port. Union flotilla is repulsed by batteries at Drewry's Bluff on the James River, eight miles below Richmond, on May 15. General Benjamin F. Butler, Union commander in New Orleans, issues controversial "Woman's Order" intended to prevent the city's women from insulting Union soldiers, May 15. Advance division of Farragut's fleet reaches Vicksburg, Mississippi, on May 18, but is unable to compel the garrison to surrender. Lincoln signs Homestead Act, May 20, granting settlers 160 acres of public land. (Absence of Southern representatives and senators from Thirty-seventh Congress will enable Republican majority to pass series of domestic measures, including Pacific Railroad Act and Morrill Act, providing land grants for agricultural colleges, both signed by Lincoln on July 2.) Jackson marches down the Shenandoah Valley (northward) and captures the garrison of Front Royal on May 23. The next day, Lincoln countermands an order sending Irvin McDowell's corps to the Peninsula and orders McDowell and other Union commanders in the

Valley to cut off and capture Jackson. On May 25 Jackson routs Union troops led by General Nathaniel P. Banks at Winchester, then pursues Banks toward Harper's Ferry at the northern end of the Valley. Beauregard evacuates Corinth, Mississippi, May 29–30. After driving Banks from the Valley, Jackson marches south on May 30 and evades Union attempts to trap his command. Joseph E. Johnston attacks the left wing of McClellan's army south of the Chickahominy River near Richmond on May 31, beginning battle of Fair Oaks (or Seven Pines).

Fighting at Fair Oaks ends in draw on June 1 after Confederates lose about 6,100 men killed, wounded, or missing and the Union about 5,000. General Robert E. Lee replaces Johnston, who was badly wounded on May 31, as commander of the Army of Northern Virginia. Confederates begin evacuating Fort Pillow, near Memphis, Tennessee, on June 3. Confederate river flotilla is destroyed by Union gunboats at Memphis on June 6, and the city surrenders. Jackson defeats Union forces in the southern Shenandoah Valley at Cross Keys, June 8, and Port Republic, June 9. Confederate General J.E.B. Stuart leads cavalry reconnaissance that rides completely around McClellan's army on the Peninsula, June 12–15. Union forces attempting to close Charleston Harbor are defeated at Secessionville, South Carolina, on June 16. Jackson leaves the Shenandoah Valley and moves his command to join Lee on the Peninsula. Cumberland Gap, mountain pass in the Appalachians at the juncture of Kentucky, Tennessee, and Virginia, is occupied by Union troops on June 18. Lincoln signs act prohibiting slavery in the territories, June 19. Lee meets with his principal generals on June 23 to plan an offensive against McClellan's army. Lincoln travels to West Point to seek military advice from former general-in-chief Winfield Scott, June 24–25, then returns to Washington and on June 26 names General John Pope to command new Army of Virginia formed from scattered Union commands in the Shenandoah Valley and Northern Virginia. Seven Days' Battles outside of Richmond begin on June 25 with small Union advance at Oak Grove. On June 26 Lee seizes the initiative, attacking McClellan's right wing at Mechanicsville, north of the Chickahominy, and is repulsed. Lee renews his offensive at Gaines's Mill on June 27 and drives the Union forces south across the Chickahominy. McClellan abandons plans for siege of Richmond and orders a retreat across the Peninsula to the James River and the protection of the navy's gunboats. Farragut runs his fleet past the Confederate batteries at Vicksburg on June 28. Union rear guard fights off Confederate pursuers at Savage's Station, June 29, as McClellan's army retreats toward the James. In battle of Glendale (or White Oak Swamp), June 30, Lee narrowly misses his best chance to cut the Army of the Potomac in two.

Seven Days' Battles end on July 1 with Union artillery repelling Lee's attacks at Malvern Hill on the James. Confederates lose 20,204 men killed, wounded, or missing in the Seven Days, while Union casualties total 15,855. Lincoln calls for 300,000 volunteers and signs revenue act establishing federal income tax, July 1. McClellan ends retreat at Harrison's Landing on the James, July 2. Confederate cavalryman John Hunt Morgan conducts extended raid into Kentucky, July 4–28. Lincoln visits Harrison's Landing, July 8–9, to confer with McClellan and his corps commanders. Henry W. Halleck is named general-in-chief on July 11. Union forces occupy Helena, Arkansas, on July 12. Lincoln makes appeal for compensated emancipation to border state representatives, July 12, but the majority of the delegation rejects his plan on July 14. Confederate ironclad C.S.S. *Arkansas* fights its way through Farragut's fleet on the Yazoo River and the Mississippi before reaching protection of the Vicksburg batteries, July 15. Lincoln signs Second Confiscation Act, authorizing the seizure of slaves of persons inciting or supporting rebellion, and Militia Act, authorizing the president to enroll blacks as soldiers or military laborers, on July 17. Pope issues series of orders, July 18–23, permitting the Army of Virginia to live off the land and authorizing the harsh treatment of disloyal civilians. Union General John A. Dix and Confederate General D. H. Hill sign cartel governing prisoner paroles and exchanges (treatment of prisoners had previously been decided mainly by commanders in the field). Lincoln reads draft of preliminary emancipation proclamation to the cabinet on July 22, but after discussion agrees to delay issuing it until there is a Union battlefield victory. British authorities allow another commerce raider built in English shipyards to sail from Liverpool on July 29 despite protests from U.S. diplomats. (Ship is commissioned as C.S.S. *Alabama* in the Azores on August 24, and will capture and burn twenty-two Northern merchant and whaling ships by the end of 1862.) Farragut takes fleet downriver from Vicksburg on July 24, ending Union attempt to capture the city with naval forces alone.

Over McClellan's protests, on August 3 General-in-Chief

Halleck orders the Army of the Potomac to evacuate the Peninsula and combine with Pope's Army of Virginia in northern Virginia. Union garrison at Baton Rouge, Louisiana, repulses Confederate attack on August 5. Confederate ironclad C.S.S. *Arkansas* runs aground near Baton Rouge on August 6 and is burned by her crew. Jackson defeats part of Pope's army at Cedar Mountain on August 9 as new campaign begins in northern Virginia. First detachment of the Army of the Potomac leaves Harrison's Landing, August 14. In White House meeting on August 14 Lincoln urges a delegation of free blacks to embrace colonization project in present-day Panama. Confederates begin fortifying Port Hudson, Louisiana, on August 15, giving them a second bastion on the Mississippi. Confederate General Edmund Kirby Smith begins invasion of eastern Kentucky on August 16. Sioux Indians begin uprising in southwestern Minnesota on August 17 (fighting continues until U.S. victory at Wood Lake on September 23). In response to Horace Greeley's editorial "The Prayer of Twenty Millions," Lincoln writes public letter on slavery and the Union on August 22 (published August 25). Union War Department authorizes recruitment of freed slaves in the coastal islands of Georgia and South Carolina, August 25. Lee sends Jackson's wing of the Army of Northern Virginia on flanking march to the west of Pope's army, August 25. Jackson destroys Pope's supply base at Manassas Junction, August 27. Pope withdraws his army from the northern bank of the Rappahannock River and marches toward Jackson. General Braxton Bragg advances north from Chattanooga, Tennessee, August 28, beginning second Confederate invasion of Kentucky. Second Battle of Bull Run (or Second Manassas) begins August 28 when Jackson attacks a Union column in order to draw Pope into battle. On August 29 Pope unsuccessfully attacks Jackson's position as Lee brings the other wing of his army, commanded by General James Longstreet, onto the field. Longstreet attacks the left wing of Pope's army on August 30 and drives it into retreat. In Kentucky, Kirby Smith defeats a Union force at Richmond, August 29–30. Buell retreats from central Tennessee into Kentucky.

Union forces block flanking move by Jackson at Chantilly, Virginia, on September 1. The Second Bull Run campaign costs the Union about 16,000 men killed, wounded, or missing, the Confederates about 9,200. Despite opposition by his cabinet, on September 2 Lincoln puts McClellan in charge of the Washington defenses, then in command of Pope's army as well as the Army of the Potomac. In Kentucky, Kirby Smith's Confederate forces occupy Lexington, September 2, and Frankfort, September 3. Lee's army begins crossing the Potomac September 4, and occupies Frederick, Maryland, on September 6. Pope is relieved of command and ordered to Minnesota to fight the Sioux uprising, September 5. McClellan starts his army into Maryland in pursuit of the Confederates on September 7. Lee issues order on September 9 dividing his army for an attack on Harper's Ferry, Virginia. A lost copy of Lee's order is found by a Union soldier and given to McClellan on September 13, giving him an opportunity to defeat Lee's divided forces. In London, Prime Minister Lord Palmerston writes to Lord Russell, the foreign secretary, on September 14 that if "greater disasters" befall the Union after Second Bull Run, Britain and France might "address the contending parties and recommend an arrangement upon the basis of separation." In Maryland, McClellan's army fights its way through passes in South Mountain on September 14. Jackson captures 12,000-man Union garrison at Harper's Ferry, September 15. Lee reunites his army behind Antietam Creek near Sharpsburg, Maryland, September 15–16. McClellan attacks Lee's army on September 17. Battle of Antietam ends in a tactical draw; the combined casualties of nearly 23,000 men killed, wounded, or missing make it the bloodiest single day of the war. In Kentucky, Bragg captures the 4,000-man Union garrison at Munfordville, September 17. Lee withdraws his army across the Potomac into Virginia on the night of September 18. Union forces led by General William S. Rosecrans defeat Confederates led by General Sterling Price at Iuka in northern Mississippi on September 19. Lincoln issues preliminary Emancipation Proclamation on September 22, to take effect January 1, 1863, in all territory still in rebellion. Bragg's army occupies Bardstown, Kentucky, September 22. On September 24 Lincoln suspends the writ of habeas corpus nationwide and orders military trials for persons aiding the rebellion. Buell's army reaches Louisville, Kentucky, on September 25.

Buell begins advancing south from Louisville on October 1. Lincoln confers with McClellan at Sharpsburg, October 2–4. Rosecrans successfully defends Corinth, Mississippi, against Confederate attack, October 3–4, ending attempt by General Earl Van Dorn to recapture western Tennessee. Union navy captures Galveston, Texas, October 4 (city is retaken by the Confederates on January 1,

1863). Lincoln orders McClellan to take the offensive, October 6. Buell and Bragg fight inconclusive battle at Perryville, Kentucky, on October 8. J.E.B. Stuart and his cavalry ride around McClellan's army for a second time, reaching as far north as Chambersburg, Pennsylvania, on October 9–12. After uniting his army with Kirby Smith's, Bragg decides on October 12 to abandon his campaign in Kentucky and retreat to Tennessee. British foreign secretary Lord Russell proposes to the cabinet on October 13 that the European powers intervene to arrange an armistice in the American war. Midterm elections are held in Ohio, Indiana, and Pennsylvania, October 14. Prime Minister Lord Palmerston writes to Lord Russell on October 22, expressing doubts about intervention. Buell's failure to pursue the Confederates after Perryville results in his replacement by Rosecrans, October 24. McClellan begins crossing the Potomac into Virginia on October 26. Napoleon III proposes on October 31 that France, Britain, and Russia mediate the American war.

Northern midterm elections conclude on November 4. Democrats win the governorships of New Jersey and New York, legislative majorities in Illinois, Indiana, and New Jersey, and gain thirty-four seats in the House of Representatives, although the Republicans retain control of Congress. Lincoln dismisses McClellan as commander of the Army of the Potomac on November 5 and replaces him with Ambrose Burnside. Nathaniel P. Banks replaces Benjamin F. Butler as commander of the Department of the Gulf on November 8. British cabinet debates and rejects French mediation proposal, November 11–12. Burnside opens winter campaign in Virginia on November 15, advancing from Warrenton toward Fredericksburg. Union troops reach Falmouth, across the Rappahannock from Fredericksburg, on November 17, but then wait for more than a week for pontoon bridges needed to cross the river. Longstreet's corps of Lee's army arrives at Fredericksburg, November 20–23. After George W. Randolph resigns as secretary of war, Jefferson Davis names James A. Seddon as his successor, November 21, and appoints Joseph E. Johnston as overall Confederate commander in the western theater, November 24, with responsibility for Bragg's army in Tennessee and John C. Pemberton's forces in Mississippi. Attorney General Edward Bates issues opinion on November 29 declaring that free black persons born in the United States are American citizens.

In his annual message to Congress on December 1,

Lincoln recommends the adoption of constitutional amendments authorizing gradual, compensated emancipation. Jackson's corps arrives at Fredericksburg, December 1–3, completing the buildup of Lee's army. Grant's army occupies Oxford, Mississippi, December 2, as it prepares to advance down the Mississippi Central Railroad toward Vicksburg. General court-martial of Union General Fitz John Porter begins on December 3 for his alleged misconduct at Second Bull Run (Porter is found guilty on January 10, 1863, and cashiered). Union forces maintain control of northwest Arkansas by defeating Confederate offensive at Prairie Grove, December 7. Jefferson Davis visits Tennessee, December 11–14, and Mississippi, December 19–29, during inspection tour of the western theater. Burnside's engineers bridge the Rappahannock under fire on December 11 as Union troops capture Fredericksburg. On December 13 a series of Union frontal attacks against the Confederate positions on the heights behind Fredericksburg are repulsed, with the Union losing 12,653 men killed, wounded, or missing and the Confederates 5,309. Burnside withdraws his army across the Rappahannock on the night of December 15. Senate Republican caucus votes on December 17 to seek the dismissal of Secretary of State William H. Seward, who submits his resignation after learning of the vote. Lincoln and the cabinet (excluding Seward) meet with a committee from the caucus, December 19. As a result of the meeting, Secretary of the Treasury Salmon P. Chase, Seward's chief cabinet critic, submits his resignation on December 20; Lincoln rejects both resignations, resolving the crisis. Confederate General Nathan Bedford Forrest leads cavalry raid that damages Grant's railroad supply lines in western Tennessee, December 18–20. Van Dorn leads raid that destroys Grant's main supply depot at Holly Springs, Mississippi, on December 20, forcing Grant to retreat. Rosecrans advances from Nashville toward Bragg's army at Murfreesboro, Tennessee, on December 26. Unaware of Grant's retreat, General William T. Sherman leads expedition up the Yazoo River north of Vicksburg on December 26. Sherman attacks Confederate positions on the bluffs above Chickasaw Bayou on December 29 and is repulsed. Bragg attacks Rosecrans's army along Stones River outside of Murfreesboro, December 31. The same day, Lincoln signs statehood bill for West Virginia that provides for gradual emancipation.

1863   Lincoln issues final Emancipation Proclamation on January 1. Sherman withdraws his troops from the Yazoo River to Milliken's Bend, Louisiana, about fifteen miles above Vicksburg, January 2. After lull on New Year's Day, Bragg resumes attacks at Stones River, January 2, then orders retreat on January 3 to Tullahoma, Tennessee, thirty-five miles to the south. Battle costs the Union about 13,000 men killed, wounded, or missing, the Confederates about 12,000. Lincoln nominates John P. Usher on January 5 to succeed Caleb B. Smith as secretary of the interior. On January 8 Lincoln writes to Union General John A. McClernand that "being made," the Emancipation Proclamation "must stand."

Biographical Notes

Henry Livermore Abbott (January 21, 1842–May 6, 1864) Born in Lowell, Massachusetts, the son of a lawyer active in Democratic politics. Graduated from Harvard College in 1860 and began studying law in his father's office. Commissioned second lieutenant, 20th Massachusetts Volunteer Infantry Regiment, July 10, 1861. Formed close friendship with his fellow officer Oliver Wendell Holmes Jr. Fought at Ball's Bluff. Promoted to first lieutenant, November 1861. Fought at Fair Oaks and in the Seven Days' Battles, where he was wounded in the arm at Glendale. Older brother Edward killed at Cedar Mountain. Fought at Fredericksburg (December 1862 and May 1863) and Gettysburg; promoted to captain, December 1862, and major, October 1863. Became acting commander of the 20th Massachusetts after all of the regimental officers senior to him were killed or wounded at Gettysburg. Led the regiment at Briscoe Station and at the battle of the Wilderness, where he was fatally wounded on May 6, 1864.

Charles Francis Adams (August 18, 1807–November 21, 1886) Born in Boston, Massachusetts, the son of John Quincy Adams and Louisa Johnson Adams and grandson of John and Abigail Adams. Graduated from Harvard in 1825. Admitted to the bar in 1829. Married Abigail Brown Brooks the same year. Served as a Whig in the Massachusetts house of representatives, 1841–43, and in the state senate, 1844–45. Vice-presidential candidate of the Free Soil Party in 1848. Edited *The Works of John Adams* (1850–56). Served in Congress as a Republican, 1859–61. As U.S. minister to Great Britain, 1861–68, helped maintain British neutrality in the Civil War. Served as the U.S. representative on the international arbitration tribunal that settled American claims against Great Britain for losses caused by Confederate commerce raiders built in British shipyards, 1871–72. Edited the *Memoirs of John Quincy Adams* (1874–77). Died in Boston.

Charles Francis Adams Jr. (May 27, 1835–March 20, 1915) Born in Boston, Massachusetts, brother of Henry Adams, son of lawyer Charles Francis Adams and Abigail Brooks Adams, grandson of John Quincy Adams, great-grandson of John Adams. Graduated Harvard College, 1856. Read law in Boston and passed bar, 1858. Commissioned first lieutenant, 1st Massachusetts Cavalry, December 1861.

Served at Hilton Head, South Carolina, 1862, and with the Army of the Potomac, 1862–63, including Antietam and Gettysburg campaigns; promoted to captain, October 1862. Commanded detached company on guard service at Army of the Potomac headquarters, spring 1864. Commissioned as lieutenant colonel of the 5th Massachusetts Cavalry, a black regiment, in July 1864, and as its colonel, February 1865; the regiment guarded Confederate prisoners at Point Lookout, Maryland, until March 1865, when it was sent to Virginia. Left army and married Mary Ogden in November 1865. Served on Massachusetts Railroad Commission, 1869–79. President of Union Pacific Railroad, 1884–90. Published series of historical works, including *Three Episodes of Massachusetts History* (1892) and biographies of Richard Henry Dana (1890) and Charles Francis Adams (1900). Died in Washington, D.C.

Louisa May Alcott (November 29, 1832–March 6, 1888) Born in Germantown, Pennsylvania, the daughter of schoolteacher and educational reformer Amos Bronson Alcott. Became a teacher and began publishing poetry and stories in the 1850s. Supported abolitionism, temperance, woman's suffrage, woman's rights, and other reform movements. Traveled to Washington, D.C., in December 1862 to serve as nurse in an army hospital, but soon fell ill with typhoid fever and returned to Massachusetts; described her nursing experiences in *Hospital Sketches* (1863). Her novels include *Little Women* (1868–69), *An Old-Fashioned Girl* (1870), *Little Men* (1871), and *Jo's Boys* (1886). Died in Boston.

Edward Porter Alexander (May 26, 1835–April 28, 1910) Born in Washington, Georgia, the son of a plantation owner. Graduated from West Point in 1857. Married Bettie Mason in 1860. Resigned from U.S. Army in April 1861 and accepted Confederate commission as captain in May 1861. Served as chief of ordnance and chief signal officer of the Army of Northern Virginia, July 1861–November 1862. Promoted to major, April 1862, and lieutenant colonel, July 1862. Assigned command of an artillery battalion in James Longstreet's corps in November 1862, and led it at Fredericksburg. Promoted to colonel in April 1863. Commanded artillery battalion at Chancellorsville, Gettysburg, Chattanooga, and Knoxville. Promoted to brigadier general in February 1864 and became chief of artillery for the corps in March 1864. Served in Overland campaign and was wounded at Petersburg on June 30, 1864. Returned to duty in August 1864 and served until Lee's surrender at Appomattox Court House, April 9, 1865. Professor of mathematics and engineering at the University of South Carolina, 1866–69. Served as president of several Southern railroad companies,

1871–93. Drafted personal reminiscences of the war in 1897–99 (published in 1989 as *Fighting for the Confederacy*) while serving on boundary arbitration commission in Greytown, Nicaragua. Following the death of his wife in 1899, married her niece, Mary Mason, in 1901. Published *Military Memoirs of a Confederate: A Critical Narrative* in 1907. Died in Savannah, Georgia.

Ephraim McDowell Anderson (June 29, 1843–January 10, 1916) Born in Knoxville, Tennessee, the son of a farmer. Family moved in his youth to Monroe County, Missouri. In 1861, became a member of the secessionist Missouri State Guard under General Sterling Price, and participated in the battles of Carthage, Springfield, and Lexington. Joined Company G, 2nd Regiment, 1st Missouri Confederate Brigade, in 1862. Fought at Elkhorn Tavern, Iuka, and Corinth. Surrendered at Vicksburg in July 1863 and was exchanged in September 1863. Served as commissary clerk at Demopolis, Alabama, after illness ended his field service. Invalided out of the Confederate army in late 1864. Returned to farming in Missouri after the war. Published *Memoirs: Historical and Personal; including the campaigns of the First Missouri Confederate Brigade* (1868). Moved in late 1915 to the Confederate Soldiers Home at Higginsville, Missouri, where he died.

John Russell Bartlett (September 26, 1843–November 22, 1904) Born in New York City, the son of a merchant and bookseller. Entered U.S. Naval Academy in 1859. Served as midshipman on the *Mississippi* in the Gulf of Mexico, 1861–62, and on the *Brooklyn* during the passage of Forts Jackson and St. Philip and the capture of New Orleans, April 1862, and the naval attack on Vicksburg, June 1862. Promoted to ensign, September 1863, and lieutenant, February 1864. Served on the *Susquehanna* during the Union attacks on Fort Fisher, North Carolina, December 1864 and January 1865. Promoted to lieutenant commander, 1866, and commander, 1877. Married Jeanie Jenckes in 1872. Retired as a captain in July 1897, then returned to active duty during the Spanish-American War. Died in St. Louis, Missouri.

Clara Barton (December 25, 1821–April 12, 1912) Born Clarissa Howe Barton in North Oxford, Massachusetts, the daughter of a farmer and miller. Taught school in Massachusetts, 1839–50. Attended Clinton Liberal Institute, Oneida County, New York, 1850–51. Taught school at Hightstown, New Jersey, 1851–52, and founded a free public school in nearby Bordentown, New Jersey. Worked as recording clerk and copyist in the U.S. Patent Office in Washington, D.C., 1854–57. Lived in Massachusetts, 1857–60, then returned to Patent Office as copyist in December 1860. Helped care for wounded soldiers in Washington after First Bull Run in July 1861. Operating independently of the army and the U.S. Sanitary Commission, she began furnishing nursing care and supplies directly to the battlefields in August 1862, serving at Cedar Mountain, Second Bull Run, South Mountain, Antietam, and Fredericksburg. Provided assistance to soldiers in coastal South Carolina during the siege of Charleston, April–December 1863. Served as head nurse for field hospital in the Army of the James during the Petersburg campaign, June 1864–January 1865. Established office that traced missing Union soldiers, 1865–69, and spent summer of 1865 identifying graves at the former Confederate prisoner-of-war camp at Andersonville, Georgia. Traveled in Europe, 1869–73, and engaged in relief work during the Franco-Prussian War. Founded the American Red Cross in 1881 and served as its president until 1904. Published *The Red Cross in Peace and War* (1898) and *The Story of My Childhood* (1907). Died in Glen Echo, Maryland.

Edward Bates (September 4, 1793–March 25, 1869) Born in Belmont, Virginia, the son of a planter and merchant. Attended Charlotte Hall Academy in Maryland for three years. Served in militia company in 1813 but did not see action. Moved to St. Louis, Missouri, in 1814. Admitted to the bar, 1816. Delegate to the state constitutional convention in 1820. Attorney general of Missouri, 1820–21. Married Julia Coalter in 1823. Served in state house of representatives, 1822–24 and 1834–36, and state senate, 1830–34. U.S. attorney for Missouri, 1824–26. Served in Congress, 1827–29, but was defeated for reelection. Became leader of Whig Party in Missouri. Candidate for 1860 Republican presidential nomination. Served as attorney general in the Lincoln administration, March 1861–November 1864, before resigning. Opposed Radical Reconstruction in Missouri. Died in St. Louis.

August Belmont (December 8, 1813–November 24, 1890) Born in Alzey in the Rhenish Palatinate, the son of a farmer and trader. Apprenticed to Rothschild banking office in Frankfurt-am-Main, 1828. Arrived in New York City during the Panic of 1837 and founded August Belmont and Company, becoming the Rothschilds' new agent in the United States and soon emerging as one of the leading bankers in the country. Wounded in duel, 1841. Became naturalized citizen in 1844. Married Caroline Slidell Perry, daughter of Commodore Matthew Perry, in 1849. Actively supported Democrat Franklin Pierce in 1852 election. Served as U.S. minister to the Netherlands, 1853–57. Supported Stephen A. Douglas in the 1860 election, and was appointed chairman of the Democratic National Committee, a position he held until 1872. Traveled in Europe, 1861–62, and urged political and financial leaders not to support the Confederacy. Supported

George B. McClellan for the 1864 Democratic presidential nomination. Resigned as party chairman in 1872 when the Democratic convention endorsed Liberal Republican candidate Horace Greeley. Died in New York City.

Francis Preston Blair (April 12, 1791–October 18, 1876) Born in Abingdon, Virginia, the son of a lawyer. Family moved to Kentucky in the early 1790s. Graduated from Transylvania University in 1811. Married Eliza Violet Gist, 1812. Served as Franklin County circuit court clerk, 1812–30. Became editor of the Frankfort *Argus of Western America*. Supported Andrew Jackson in the 1828 presidential election. Moved to Washington, D.C., in 1830 to edit new pro-administration newspaper, *The Globe*. Became a member of Jackson's "Kitchen Cabinet" of unofficial advisers. Cofounded the *Congressional Globe* in 1833 to report debates and proceedings in Congress. Gave up editorship of *The Globe* in 1845 due to differences with the new Polk administration. Moved to estate at Silver Spring, Maryland. Supported Free Soil candidacy of Martin Van Buren in 1848. Helped organize first Republican national convention in 1856. Served as advisor to Abraham Lincoln. Opposed Republican Reconstruction after Lincoln's death and returned to the Democratic Party. Died in Silver Spring, Maryland.

John Boston An escaped slave from Maryland who took refuge with soldiers in the New York State militia who were stationed in Upton Hill, Virginia. It is not known whether his wife, Elizabeth Boston, and his son, Daniel, were free as well.

James Richmond Boulware (May 29, 1835–November 13, 1869) Born and died in Fairfield County, South Carolina. Trained as a doctor, he enlisted at Columbia as an assistant surgeon in the 6th South Carolina Infantry and served in the Army of Northern Virginia until at least the end of 1863. Married Eliza Milling after the war.

Cyrus F. Boyd (May 1837–July 25, 1914) Born in Ohio. Enlisted in Company G, 15th Iowa Infantry, in October 1861 as orderly sergeant. Saw action at Shiloh, April 1862, and Corinth, October 1862, and in the early phases of the Vicksburg campaign. Resigned to become lieutenant in the 34th Iowa Infantry in March 1863, with which he served in the Vicksburg and Red River campaigns. Mustered out in November 1864. Later married and lived in Ainsworth, Nebraska.

Braxton Bragg (March 22, 1817–September 27, 1876) Born in Warrenton, North Carolina, the son of a contractor and builder. Graduated West Point 1837. Served as an artillery officer in the Second Seminole

War and the U.S.-Mexican War. Married Eliza Brooks Ellis, 1849. Resigned from the army in 1856 to become a sugar planter in Louisiana. Joined the Confederate army as a brigadier general, March 1861. Promoted to major general, September 1861, and full general, April 12, 1862. Commanded a corps at Shiloh. Succeeded Pierre G. T. Beauregard as commander of the Army of Mississippi in June 1862. Invaded Kentucky in late August, but withdrew into Tennessee following the battle of Perryville, October 8, 1862. Became commander of the Army of Tennessee in November 1862, and commanded it at battle of Stones River (Murfreesboro), December 31, 1862–January 2, 1863. Won battle of Chickamauga, September 19–20, 1863, but was defeated at Chattanooga, November 23–25, 1863. Resigned from his command, November 29, 1863. Served as military advisor to Jefferson Davis in Richmond until November 1864, then commanded troops in North Carolina. Worked after the war as civil engineer in Mobile, Alabama, and railroad engineer in Galveston, Texas, where he died.

Sallie Brock (March 18, 1831–March 22, 1911) Born Sarah Ann Brock in Madison County, Virginia, the daughter of a hotel owner. Moved with her family to Richmond in 1858. Began working as a tutor in King and Queen County, Virginia, in 1860, but returned to Richmond in 1861 and remained there for the duration of the war. Moved to New York City in 1865. Published *Richmond During the War: Four Years of Personal Observations* (1867). Edited *The Southern Amaranth* (1869), a collection of poetry about the Confederacy and the war, and published a novel, *Kenneth, My King* (1873). Married Richard F. Putnam in 1882. Died in Brooklyn.

Orville H. Browning (February 10, 1806–August 10, 1881) Born in Cynthiana, Kentucky, the son of a farmer and merchant. Studied at Augusta College. Admitted to the bar in 1831 and moved to Quincy, Illinois. Married Eliza Caldwell in 1836. Served as a Whig in the state senate, 1836–40, and in the state house of representatives, 1842–43. Became friends with Abraham Lincoln. Delegate to the convention that founded the Illinois Republican Party in 1856 and to the Republican national convention in 1860. Appointed in June 1861 to U.S. Senate seat left vacant by the death of Stephen A. Douglas and served until January 1863. Practiced law in Washington and served as secretary of the interior in the Andrew Johnson administration, 1866–69. Returned to his law practice in Quincy, Illinois, where he later died.

Ambrose Burnside (May 23, 1824–September 3, 1881) Born in Liberty, Indiana, the son of a court clerk. Graduated from West Point in 1847. Married Mary Richmond Bishop, 1852. Resigned from the army in 1853 to manufacture a breech-loading carbine of his own design at Bristol, Rhode Island. Company failed to win government contract, and Burnside gave up his interest in the venture in 1858. With the aid of his friend George B. McClellan, obtained position with the Illinois Central Railroad and worked in Chicago and New York, 1858–60. Appointed colonel of the 1st Rhode Island Infantry in May 1861. Led a brigade at First Bull Run. Promoted to brigadier general of volunteers, August 1861. Commanded expeditionary force that gained a foothold on the North Carolina coast, winning engagements at Roanoke Island, New Bern, and Beaufort, February–April 1862. Promoted to major general, March 1862. Led a corps at South Mountain and Antietam, September 1862. Refused command of the Army of the Potomac following the Peninsula and Second Bull Run campaigns, but accepted order to replace McClellan on November 7, 1862. Defeated at Fredericksburg on December 13, 1862. Replaced as army commander on January 26, 1863. Commanded the Department of the Ohio, March–December 1863. Occupied Knoxville in September 1863 and withstood Confederate siege, November–December. Commanded the Ninth Corps during the Overland campaign in Virginia, May–June 1864, and during the siege of Petersburg, June–July. After his failure at the battle of the Crater at Petersburg on July 30, 1864, was sent on leave for the remainder of the war. Became president of several railroad companies after the war. Republican governor of Rhode Island, 1866–69, and served as a Republican in the U.S. Senate from 1875 until his death in Bristol, Rhode Island.

Francis Bicknell Carpenter (August 6, 1830–May 23, 1900) Born in Homer, New York, the son of a farmer. Studied with painter Sandford Thayer in Syracuse, New York, for five months before opening studio in Homer in 1846. Moved to New York City at age twenty-one and opened portrait studio. Painted portraits of Millard Fillmore and Franklin Pierce. Married Augusta Prentiss in 1853. Worked in the White House from February to July 1864 on his best-known painting, *First Reading of the Emancipation Proclamation of President Lincoln*, depicting the cabinet meeting held on July 22, 1862. Published *Six Months at the White House with Abraham Lincoln: The Story of a Picture* in 1866. Attended ceremonial donation of the *First Reading* to Congress in 1878. Died in New York City.

John Hampden Chamberlayne (June 2, 1838–February 18, 1882) Born in Richmond, Virginia, the son of a physician. Attended the University of Virginia, 1855–58, read law in Richmond, and was admitted to Virginia bar in 1860. Enlisted in the 21st Virginia Regiment and served in western Virginia, 1861–62. Became artillery sergeant in the

BIOGRAPHICAL NOTES   771

Army of Northern Virginia, February 1862, and was promoted to lieutenant, June 1862. Served at Mechanicsville, Gaines's Mill, Glendale, Cedar Mountain, Second Manassas, Antietam, Fredericksburg, and Chancellorsville. Captured at Millerstown, Pennsylvania, on June 28, 1863. Exchanged in March 1864. Served in Overland campaign and the siege of Petersburg. Promoted to captain, August 1864. Evaded surrender at Appomattox Court House and joined Confederate forces in North Carolina before giving his parole at Atlanta, Georgia, on May 12, 1865. Became journalist at the Petersburg *Index* in 1869. Married Mary Walker Gibson in 1873. Edited the Norfolk *Virginian*, 1873–76. Founded *The State* newspaper in Richmond in 1876 and edited it until his death. Died in Richmond.

Salmon P. Chase (January 13, 1808–May 7, 1873) Born in Cornish, New Hampshire, the son of a farmer. After the death of his father in 1817, he was raised in Worthington, Ohio, by his uncle, Philander Chase, an Episcopal bishop. Graduated from Dartmouth College in 1826. Read law in Washington with Attorney General William Wirt and was admitted to the bar in 1829. Established law practice in Cincinnati, Ohio, in 1830. Married Catherine Jane Garniss, 1834; after her death, Eliza Ann Smith, 1839; and after Smith's death, Sarah Bella Dunlop Ludlow, 1846. Began defending fugitive slaves and those who aided them in 1837. Became a leader in the antislavery Liberty Party and campaigned for the Free Soil ticket in 1848. Served in the U.S. Senate as a Free Soil Democrat, 1849–55. Republican governor of Ohio, 1856–60. Candidate for the Republican presidential nomination in 1860. Won election to the U.S. Senate in 1860, but resigned in March 1861 to become secretary of the treasury. Helped found national banking system and successfully financed Union war effort. Resigned June 29, 1864, after making unsuccessful attempt to challenge Lincoln for the Republican nomination. Appointed chief justice of the U.S. Supreme Court on December 6, 1864, and served until his death. Upheld Radical Reconstruction measures and presided over the 1868 Senate impeachment trial of President Andrew Johnson. Died in New York City.

Jefferson Davis (June 3, 1808–December 6, 1889) Born in Christian (now Todd) County, Kentucky, the son of a farmer. Moved with his family to Mississippi. Graduated from West Point in 1828 and served in the Black Hawk War. Resigned his commission in 1835 and married Sarah Knox Taylor, who died later in the year. Became a cotton planter in Warren County, Mississippi. Married Varina Howell in 1845. Elected to Congress as a Democrat and served 1845–46, then resigned to command a Mississippi volunteer regiment in Mexico,

1846–47, where he fought at Monterrey and was wounded at Buena Vista. Elected to the Senate and served from 1847 to 1851, when he resigned to run unsuccessfully for governor. Secretary of war in the cabinet of Franklin Pierce, 1853–57. Elected to the Senate and served from 1857 to January 21, 1861, when he withdrew following the secession of Mississippi. Inaugurated as provisional president of the Confederate States of America on February 18, 1861. Elected without opposition to six-year term in November 1861 and inaugurated on February 22, 1862. Captured by Union cavalry near Irwinville, Georgia, on May 10, 1865. Imprisoned at Fort Monroe, Virginia, and indicted for treason. Released on bail on May 13, 1867; the indictment was dropped in 1869 without trial. Published *The Rise and Fall of the Confederate Government* in 1881. Died in New Orleans.

Rufus R. Dawes (July 4, 1838–August 1, 1899) Born in Malta, Ohio. Attended the University of Wisconsin; graduated from Marietta College in 1860. Commissioned as captain in 6th Wisconsin Infantry in July 1861. Promoted to major in June 1862 and lieutenant colonel in March 1863. Fought as part of the "Iron Brigade" at Second Bull Run, Antietam, Fredericksburg, Chancellorsville, Gettysburg, the Overland campaign, and Petersburg. Married Mary Beman Gates in January 1864 while on furlough. Mustered out in August 1864 with the rank of colonel. Became a wholesale lumber merchant in Marietta. Served as a Republican congressman, 1881–83. Published *Service with the Sixth Wisconsin Volunteers* in 1890. Died in Marietta, Ohio.

George W. Dawson (July 19, 1831–June 13, 1862) Born in New Madrid, Missouri, the son of a doctor. Became a farmer and married Laura Amanda Lavalle in 1852. Enlisted in June 1861, and was elected second lieutenant in Company I, 1st Missouri Infantry, the state's first Confederate regiment. Elected captain in April 1862 shortly before the battle of Shiloh. Contracted typhoid fever at Corinth, Mississippi, in May 1862 and died in New Madrid.

Emily Dickinson (December 10, 1830–May 15, 1886) Born in Amherst, Massachusetts, the daughter of a lawyer. Attended Mount Holyoke Female Seminary in South Hadley, Massachusetts, 1847–48. Returned to family home and lived there for the remainder of her life, rarely leaving except for trips to Washington, D.C., where her father served in Congress as a Whig, 1853–55, to Philadelphia in 1855, and to Boston and Cambridge in 1864–65. Composed over 1,700 brief lyric poems, most intensively in the years 1859–65; only a few were published during her lifetime, primarily in the *Springfield Daily Republican*, most without her consent and in heavily edited form. Initiated correspondence in April 1862 with writer, reformer, and abolitionist

Thomas Wentworth Higginson, who later commanded the 1st South Carolina Volunteers, the first black regiment in the Union army. They exchanged letters for more than twenty years. In later years she rarely left her house. Fell ill in June 1884, and never fully recovered. Died in Amherst.

Frederick Douglass (February 1818–February 20, 1895) Born Frederick Bailey in Talbot County, Maryland, the son of a slave mother and an unknown white man. Worked on farms and in Baltimore shipyards. Escaped to Philadelphia in 1838. Married Anna Murray, a free woman from Maryland, and settled in New Bedford, Massachusetts, where he took the name Douglass. Became a lecturer for the American Anti-Slavery Society, led by William Lloyd Garrison, in 1841. Published *Narrative of the Life of Frederick Douglass, An American Slave* (1845). Began publishing *North Star*, first in a series of antislavery newspapers, in Rochester, New York, in 1847. Broke with Garrison and became an ally of Gerrit Smith, who advocated an antislavery interpretation of the Constitution and participation in electoral politics. Published *My Bondage and My Freedom* (1855). Advocated emancipation and the enlistment of black soldiers at the outbreak of the Civil War. Met with Abraham Lincoln in Washington in August 1863 and August 1864, and wrote public letter supporting his reelection in September 1864. Continued his advocacy of racial equality and woman's rights after the Civil War. Served as U.S. marshal for the District of Columbia, 1877–81, and as its recorder of deeds, 1881–86. Published *Life and Times of Frederick Douglass* (1881). After the death of his wife Anna, married Helen Pitts in 1884. Served as minister to Haiti, 1889–91. Died in Washington, D.C.

Thomas Haines Dudley (October 9, 1819–April 15, 1893) Born in Burlington County, New Jersey, the son of a farmer. Read law and was admitted to the bar in 1845. Married Emmaline Matlack in 1846. Active in Whig and Republican politics. Attended 1860 Republican national convention and helped swing the New Jersey delegation to Abraham Lincoln on the third ballot. Served as U.S. consul in Liverpool, England, 1861–72. Collected intelligence during the Civil War on Confederate shipbuilding and blockade-running activities, and helped prevent two ironclad rams built for the Confederate navy in the Laird shipyards from sailing in 1863. Provided evidence for the international tribunal arbitrating American claims against Great Britain for losses caused by Confederate commerce raiders built in British shipyards, 1871–72. Resumed law practice and involvement in Republican politics after returning to the United States in 1872. Helped found the American Protective Tariff League. Died in Philadelphia.

Ralph Waldo Emerson (May 25, 1803–April 27, 1882) Born in Boston, Massachusetts, the son of a minister. Graduated from Harvard College in 1821. Studied briefly at Harvard Divinity School in 1825. Ordained pastor of Second Church of Boston in March 1829. Married Ellen Tucker, 1829; she died in 1831. Gave up pastorate in 1832 and sailed for Europe. Settled in Concord, Massachusetts, in 1834. Married Lydia Jackson, 1835. Formed informal discussion group (later called the Transcendental Club), whose members included Margaret Fuller, Bronson Alcott, Orestes Brownson, and Theodore Parker. Published essay *Nature* (1836), *Essays* (1841), and *Essays: Second Series* (1844) while lecturing extensively. Opposed the U.S.-Mexican War and became involved in the abolitionist movement. Published *Representative Men* (1850), *English Traits* (1856), and *The Conduct of Life* (1860). Spoke at meetings held to benefit John Brown's family after his execution. Published verse collection *May-Day and Other Pieces* (1867). Continued to lecture until his health began to fail in 1872. Died in Concord.

John Kennerly Farris (April 18, 1836–August 7, 1910) Born in Franklin County, Tennessee. Studied medicine under a physician in Pleasant Hill, Tennessee. Married Mary Elisabeth Austell in 1857. Practiced in Arkansas before returning to Tennessee in 1860. Enlisted in the 41st Tennessee Infantry on November 26, 1861, and became a hospital steward in January 1862. Captured at Fort Donelson in February 1862, he was exchanged in September 1862. Served with the 41st Tennessee at Port Hudson, Louisiana, and in the Vicksburg campaign. Injured in railroad accident in Georgia in early September 1863. Rejoined regiment in early November and fought in the battle of Chattanooga. Served in Atlanta campaign and in Hood's invasion of Tennessee. Captured at Franklin on December 17, 1864. Escaped and returned to his medical practice in Coffee County, Tennessee. Died in Prairie Plains, Tennessee.

Samuel W. Fiske (July 23, 1828–May 22, 1864) Born in Shelburne, Massachusetts. Graduated from Amherst College in 1848. Taught school, studied for three years at Andover Theological Seminary, then returned to Amherst in 1853 as a tutor. Traveled in Europe and the Middle East. Published *Dunn Browne's Experiences in Foreign Parts* (1857), travel letters written to the *Springfield Republican* under a nom de plume. Became pastor of the Congregational church in Madison, Connecticut, in 1857. Married Elizabeth Foster in 1858. Became second lieutenant in the 14th Connecticut Infantry in August 1862. Signing himself Dunn Browne, wrote weekly letters to the *Springfield Republican* describing campaigns and camp life (collected in 1866 under the title *Mr. Dunn Browne's Experiences in the Army*). Served at Antietam and Fredericksburg. Promoted to captain in early 1863. Captured at Chancellorsville on May 3, 1863, was paroled in late May and exchanged in June. Served at Gettysburg. Wounded in the battle of the Wilderness on May 6, 1864, and died in Fredericksburg, Virginia.

Thomas W. Fleming (September 16, 1815–February 7, 1894) Born in Liberty County, Georgia. Attended Franklin College in Athens (later University of Georgia). Married Susan Eliza Wilson in 1837. Became a plantation owner in Liberty County, and later in Baker County, Georgia.

Jacob Gilbert Forman (January 21, 1820–February 7, 1885) Born in Queensbury, New Brunswick, Canada. Became merchant's clerk in Peekskill, New York, in 1836. Graduated from Transylvania University in Lexington, Kentucky, with law degree in 1843. Married Sarah Elizabeth Carpenter in 1844. Practiced law in Cincinnati before becoming Unitarian minister in Akron, Ohio; later served as pastor in Massachusetts and Illinois. During the Civil War, served as chaplain of the 3rd Missouri Infantry, as acting chaplain of the 1st Missouri Cavalry and the 3rd U.S. Infantry, as superintendent of refugees in St. Louis, and as secretary of the Western Sanitary Commission. Published *The Christian Martyrs: or, The Conditions of Obedience to the Civil Government* (1851) and *The Western Sanitary Commission: A Sketch of Its Origin* (1864). Moved to Lynn, Massachusetts, in 1869 and opened a drugstore. Died in Lynn.

Ulysses S. Grant (April 22, 1822–July 23, 1885) Born in Point Pleasant, Ohio, the son of a tanner. Graduated from West Point in 1843. Served in the U.S.-Mexican War, 1846–48, and promoted to first lieutenant in 1847. Married Julia Dent in 1848. Promoted to captain, 1854, and resigned commission. Worked as a farmer, real estate agent, and general store clerk, 1854–61. Commissioned colonel, 21st Illinois Volunteers, June 1861, and brigadier general of volunteers, August 1861. Promoted to major general of volunteers, February 1862, after victories at Forts Henry and Donelson. Defeated Confederates at Shiloh, April 1862, and captured Vicksburg, Mississippi, July 1863. Promoted to major general in the regular army, July 1863, and assigned to command of Military Division of the Mississippi, covering territory between the Alleghenies and the Mississippi, October 1863. Won battle of Chattanooga, November 1863. Promoted to lieutenant general, March 1864, and named general-in-chief of the Union armies. Accepted surrender of Robert E. Lee at Appomattox Court House, April 9, 1865. Promoted to general, July 1866. Served as secretary of war ad interim,

August 1867–January 1868. Nominated for president by the Republican Party in 1868. Defeated Democrat Horatio Seymour, and won reelection in 1872 by defeating Liberal Republican Horace Greeley. President of the United States, 1869–77. Made world tour, 1877–79. Failed to win Republican presidential nomination, 1880. Worked on Wall Street, 1881–84, and was financially ruined when private banking firm of Grant & Ward collapsed. Wrote *Personal Memoirs of U.S. Grant*, 1884–85, while suffering from throat cancer, and completed them days before his death at Mount McGregor, New York.

Henry W. Halleck (January 16, 1814–January 9, 1872) Born in Westernville, New York, the son of a farmer. Educated at Union College. Graduated from West Point in 1839. Published *Elements of Military Art and Science* (1846). Served in California during the U.S.-Mexican War. Resigned from the army in 1854 as captain. Married Elizabeth Hamilton, granddaughter of Alexander Hamilton, in 1855. Practiced law in California. Published *International Law, or, Rules Regulating the Intercourse of States in Peace and War* (1861). Commissioned as a major general in the regular army in August 1861. Commanded the Department of the Missouri, November 1861–March 1862, and the Department of the Mississippi, March–July 1862. General-in-chief of the Union army from July 11, 1862, to March 12, 1864, when he was succeeded by Ulysses S. Grant. Served as chief of staff for the remainder of the war. Commanded military division of the Pacific, 1866–69, and the division of the South, 1869–72. Died in Louisville, Kentucky.

Nathaniel Hawthorne (July 4, 1804–May 19, 1864) Born in Salem, Massachusetts, the son of a ship's captain. Graduated in 1825 from Bowdoin College, where he formed a lifelong friendship with Franklin Pierce. Began writing short fiction, collected in *Twice-told Tales* (1837), *Mosses from an Old Manse* (1846), and *The Snow-Image, and Other Twice-told Tales* (1851). Worked in customhouses in Boston, 1839–41, and Salem, 1846–49. Married Sophia Peabody in 1842. Published novels *The Scarlet Letter* (1850), *The House of the Seven Gables* (1851), and *The Blithedale Romance* (1852). Wrote campaign biography of Pierce for 1852 election. Served as U.S. consul in Liverpool, England, 1853–57. Published novel *The Marble Faun* (1860). Died in Plymouth, New Hampshire.

John Hay (October 8, 1838–July 1, 1905) Born in Salem, Indiana, the son of a doctor. Family moved to Warsaw, Illinois. Graduated from Brown University in 1858. Studied law in office of his uncle in Springfield, Illinois. Traveled to Washington in 1861 as assistant private secretary to Abraham Lincoln, serving until early in 1865. First secretary to American legation in Paris, 1865–67, chargé d'affaires in Vienna, 1867–68, and legation secretary in Madrid, 1868–70. Published *Castilian Days* (1871) and *Pike County Ballads and Other Pieces* (1871). Married Clara Louise Stone in 1874. Served as assistant secretary of state, 1879–81. Political novel *The Bread-Winners*, an attack on labor unions, published anonymously in 1884. In collaboration with John G. Nicolay, wrote *Abraham Lincoln: A History* (10 volumes, 1890) and edited *Complete Works of Abraham Lincoln* (2 volumes, 1894). Ambassador to Great Britain, 1897–98. Served as secretary of state in the administrations of William McKinley and Theodore Roosevelt, 1898–1905. Among first seven members elected to American Academy of Arts and Letters in 1904. Died in Newbury, New Hampshire.

Charles B. Haydon (1834–March 14, 1864) Born in Vermont. Raised in Decatur, Michigan. Graduated from the University of Michigan in 1857, then read law in Kalamazoo. Joined the Kalamazoo Home Guard on April 22, 1861, then enlisted on May 25 for three years' service in the 2nd Michigan Infantry. Fought at Blackburn's Ford during the First Bull Run campaign. Commissioned second lieutenant in September 1861 and promoted to first lieutenant in February 1862. Fought at Williamsburg, Fair Oaks, the Seven Days' Battles, Second Bull Run, and Fredericksburg; promoted to captain in September 1862. Regiment was sent to Kentucky in April 1863 and to Vicksburg in June as part of the Ninth Corps. Wounded in the shoulder while leading his company at Jackson, Mississippi, on July 11, 1863. Returned to active duty in December 1863 and was made lieutenant colonel of the 2nd Michigan. Died of pneumonia in Cincinnati while returning to Michigan on a thirty-day furlough after reenlisting.

Julia Ward Howe (May 27, 1819–October 17, 1910) Born in New York City, the daughter of a banker. Married the Boston educator and reformer Samuel Gridley Howe in 1843. Edited the antislavery newspaper *Commonwealth* with her husband in the early 1850s, and published poetry collections *Passion Flowers* (1854) and *Words for the Hour* (1857), and travel book *A Trip to Cuba* (1860). Published "The Battle Hymn of the Republic" in the February 1862 *Atlantic Monthly*. Campaigned after the war for woman's suffrage, prison reform, and international peace. Published *Later Lyrics* (1866), *Sex and Education* (1874), *Modern Society* (1881), *Margaret Fuller* (1883), *Reminiscences, 1819–1899* (1899), and a poetry collection, *At Sunset* (1910). In 1907 she became the first woman to be elected to the American Academy of Arts and Sciences. Died in Newport, Rhode Island.

David Hunter (July 21, 1802–February 2, 1886) Born in Princeton, New Jersey, the son of a Presbyterian minister. Graduated from West Point in 1822. Married Maria Indiana Kinzie, 1829. Resigned commission in July 1836, but reentered the army in November 1841 as paymaster. Commissioned as brigadier general of volunteers, May 1861, and promoted to major general, August 1861. Led brigade at First Bull Run, where he was wounded. Commanded Department of Kansas, November 1861–March 1862, and Department of the South, March–September 1862 and January–June 1863. Declared military emancipation of slaves in Department of the South, May 9, 1862; his order was revoked by President Lincoln on May 19. Attempted to recruit black regiments in the spring of 1862 but failed to receive War Department authorization. Served as president of the court-martial that convicted General Fitz John Porter in January 1863. Commanded the Army of West Virginia in the Shenandoah Valley, May–June 1864. Retreated from the valley following his defeat at Lynchburg, and resigned command in August 1864. President of the military commission that tried the conspirators in the Lincoln assassination, May–June 1865. Resigned commission on July 31, 1866. Died in Washington, D.C.

Pearl Parker Ingalls (February 1, 1823–May 18, 1887) Born in Franklin, Ohio, the son of a chair maker. Graduated from Ohio Wesleyan University and became a Methodist minister, holding pastorates for the next forty years in Ohio and Iowa. Became chaplain of the 3rd Iowa Cavalry in 1861. Mustered out in 1863 and returned to Keokuk, Iowa. Helped found the Iowa Soldiers' Orphans' Home in Davenport, serving as secretary, raising donations, and securing financial support from the Iowa legislature. Became editor of the *Iowa State Tribune* in 1879. Died in White City, Kansas.

Oscar Lawrence Jackson (September 2, 1840–February 16, 1920) Born in Shenango Township, Pennsylvania, the son of a storekeeper. Taught school in Shenango Township, 1858–59, and Hocking County, Ohio, 1859–61. Became captain of Company H, 63rd Ohio Infantry, in January 1862. Served at New Madrid, Island No. 10, the siege of Corinth, and the battle of Iuka. Seriously wounded at Corinth, October 4, 1862, and spent seven weeks in the hospital. Rejoined regiment at Corinth in February 1863 and spent remainder of the year on occupation duty in Tennessee and Mississippi. Served in the 1864 Atlanta campaign and the march through Georgia and the Carolinas. Promoted to major in March 1865 and assumed command of the 63rd Ohio. Mustered out on June 30, 1865, as lieutenant colonel. Returned to Pennsylvania and was admitted to the bar in 1866. Served as district attorney of Lawrence County, 1868–71; as county solicitor,

1874–80; and as a Republican member of the U.S. House of Representatives, 1885–89. Died in New Castle, Pennsylvania.

Harriet Ann Jacobs (1813–March 7, 1897) Born in Edenton, North Carolina, the daughter of slaves. After the death of her mother in 1819, she was raised by her grandmother and her white mistress, Margaret Horniblow, who taught her to read, write, and sew. In 1825 Horniblow died, and Jacobs was sent to the household of Dr. James Norcom. At sixteen, to escape Norcom's repeated sexual advances, Jacobs began a relationship with a white lawyer, Samuel Tredwell Sawyer (later a member of the U.S. House of Representatives), with whom she had two children, Joseph (b. 1829) and Louisa Matilda (b. 1833). In 1835, Jacobs ran away and spent the next seven years hiding in a crawl space above her freed grandmother's storeroom. In 1842, she escaped to New York City, where she was reunited with her children. Worked as a nurse for the family of Nathaniel Parker Willis; moved to Boston in 1843 to avoid recapture by Norcom. Moved to Rochester in 1849, where she became part of a circle of abolitionists surrounding Frederick Douglass. In 1852, Cornelia Grinnell Willis, second wife of Nathaniel Parker Willis, purchased Jacobs's manumission. Published *Incidents in the Life of a Slave Girl, Written by Herself*, pseudonymously in 1861. From 1862 to 1868 engaged in Quaker-sponsored relief work among former slaves in Washington, D.C.; Alexandria, Virginia; and Savannah, Georgia. She then lived with her daughter in Cambridge, Massachusetts, and in Washington, D.C., where she died.

Clifton Johnson (January 25, 1865–January 22, 1940) Born in Hadley, Massachusetts. Attended Hopkins Academy, but left in 1880 to work in a book and stationery store to help pay the family mortgage. In the mid-1880s began to write and illustrate for local newspapers and magazines. Attended the Art Students League in New York City in 1887. Johnson wrote, illustrated, or edited 125 books between 1892 and 1938, including biographies of naturalist John Burroughs and inventor Hudson Maxim, a series of travel books, and volumes of children's literature. Interviewed fifty-four civilian witnesses to Civil War battles in 1913 and published their accounts in *Battleground Adventures* (1915). Died in Brattleboro, Vermont.

Catesby ap Roger Jones (April 15, 1821–June 21, 1877) Born at Fairfield, estate in Frederick (now Clarke) County, Virginia, the son of an army officer. Entered U.S. Navy in 1836 as a midshipman. Promoted to lieutenant in 1849. Became specialist in naval ordnance and helped develop the Dahlgren gun. Resigned his commission on April 17, 1861, and entered the Confederate navy in June as a lieutenant. Served as executive officer of the ironclad *Virginia* in battle of Hampton Roads, March 8, 1862, and commanded the ship during its fight with the Union ironclad *Monitor* on March 9. Along with the crew of the now-scuttled *Virginia*, helped defend Drewry's Bluff on the James River against Union naval attack on May 15, 1862. Commanded gunboat *Chattachoochee*, 1862–63. Served as head of the naval foundry and ordnance works at Selma, Alabama, from May 1863 until the end of the war. Married Gertrude Tartt in 1865. Supplied ordnance to South American governments after the war, then returned to Selma, where he was fatally shot in a dispute with a neighbor.

John B. Jones (March 6, 1810–February 4, 1866) Born in Baltimore, Maryland. Lived in Kentucky and Missouri as a boy. Married Frances Custis in 1840. Became editor of the *Saturday Visiter* in Baltimore, 1841. Published several novels, including *Wild Western Scenes* (1841), *The War Path* (1858), and *Wild Southern Scenes* (1859). Established weekly newspaper *Southern Monitor* in Philadelphia, 1857. Fearing arrest as a Confederate sympathizer, Jones moved in 1861 to Richmond, Virginia, where he worked as a clerk in the Confederate war department. Died in Burlington, New Jersey, shortly before the publication of *A Rebel War Clerk's Diary*.

Charles B. Labruzan (February 29, 1840–June 17, 1930) A merchant from Mobile, Alabama, Labruzan became a lieutenant in the 42nd Alabama Infantry. Served as the acting commander of Company F during the battle of Corinth, where he was captured on October 4, 1862. Paroled and exchanged, he became a prisoner again at the surrender of Vicksburg in July 1863. Died in Little River, Alabama.

Elizabeth Blair Lee (June 20, 1818–September 13, 1906) Born in Frankfort, Kentucky, daughter of journalist Francis Preston Blair and Elizabeth Gist Blair, sister of Montgomery Blair (postmaster general, 1861–64) and Frank Blair (a Union major general, 1862–65). Moved with family in 1830 to Washington, D.C., where her father edited the *Globe* and advised Andrew Jackson. Educated at boarding school in Philadelphia. Married naval officer Samuel Phillips Lee, a cousin of Robert E. Lee, in 1843. Became board member and active patron of the Washington City Orphan Asylum in 1849. Lived in Washington and at the Blair estate in Silver Spring, Maryland. Died in Washington.

Robert E. Lee (January 19, 1807–October 12, 1870) Born in Westmoreland County, Virginia, the son of Revolutionary War hero Henry "Light-Horse Harry" Lee and Ann Carter Lee. Graduated from West Point in 1829. Married Mary Custis, great-granddaughter of Martha Washington, in 1831. Served in the U.S.-Mexican War, and as superintendent of West Point, 1852–55. Promoted to colonel in March 1861. Resigned commission on April 20, 1861, after declining offer of field command of the Federal army. Served as commander of Virginia military forces, April–July 1861; commander in western Virginia, August–October 1861; commander of the southern Atlantic coast, November 1861–March 1862; and military advisor to Jefferson Davis, March–May 1862. Assumed command of the Army of Northern Virginia on June 1, 1862, and led it until April 9, 1865, when he surrendered to Ulysses S. Grant at Appomattox. Named general-in-chief of all Confederate forces, February 1865. Became president of Washington College (now Washington and Lee), September 1865. Died in Lexington, Virginia.

Abraham Lincoln (February 12, 1809–April 15, 1865) Born near Hodgenville, Kentucky, the son of a farmer and carpenter. Family moved to Indiana in 1816 and to Illinois in 1830. Settled in New Salem, Illinois, and worked as a storekeeper, surveyor, and postmaster. Served as a Whig in the state legislature, 1834–41. Began law practice in 1836 and moved to Springfield in 1837. Married Mary Todd in 1842. Elected to Congress as a Whig and served from 1847 to 1849. Became a public opponent of the extension of slavery after the passage of the Kansas-Nebraska Act in 1854. Helped found the Republican Party of Illinois in 1856. Campaigned in 1858 for Senate seat held by Stephen A. Douglas and debated him seven times on the slavery issue; although the Illinois legislature reelected Douglas, the campaign brought Lincoln national prominence. Received Republican presidential nomination in 1860 and won election in a four-way contest; his victory led to the secession of seven Southern states. Responded to the Confederate bombardment of Fort Sumter by calling up militia, proclaiming the blockade of Southern ports, and suspending habeas corpus. Issued preliminary and final emancipation proclamations on September 22, 1862, and January 1, 1863. Appointed Ulysses S. Grant commander of all Union forces in March 1864. Won reelection in 1864 by defeating Democrat George B. McClellan. Died in Washington, D.C., after being shot by John Wilkes Booth.

William Thompson Lusk (May 23, 1838–June 12, 1897) Born in Norwich, Connecticut, the son of a merchant. Attended Yale College, 1855–56, then studied medicine in Heidelberg and Berlin, 1858–61. Enlisted as private in the 79th New York Infantry in June 1861. Served at First Bull Run. Commissioned second lieutenant in September 1861. Served in Port Royal expedition, November 1861. Promoted to captain in February 1862. Served at Secessionville, Second Bull Run,

Chantilly, South Mountain, Antietam, and Fredericksburg. Became assistant adjutant general to General Daniel Tyler, commander of Eighth Corps, in 1863. Commanded troops in New York City during the July 1863 draft riots. Resigned commission, September 17, 1863. Married Mary Hartwell Chittenden in 1864. Studied medicine at Edinburgh, Prague, and Vienna, 1864–65. Returned to New York City and began medical career at Bellevue Hospital. Held chair in obstetrics at Bellevue Medical College, 1871–97. Following the death of his wife in 1871, married Matilda Myer Thorn in 1876. Published *The Science and Art of Midwifery* (1882). President of the faculty of Bellevue Medical College, 1889–97. Died in New York City.

Robert Q. Mallard (September 7, 1830–March 3, 1904) Born in Walthourville, Liberty County, Georgia, the son of a plantation owner. Graduated from Franklin College in 1850 and the Columbia Theological College in 1855. Served as pastor of the Walthourville Presbyterian Church, 1856–63. Married Mary Sharpe Jones, the daughter of the Reverend Charles Colcock Jones and Mary Jones of Liberty County, in 1857. Pastor of the Central Presbyterian Church in Atlanta, 1863–66. Moved to New Orleans in 1866, where he continued to serve as a pastor. Published *Plantation Life Before Emancipation* (1892) and *Montevideo-Maybank: Some Memories of a Southern Christian Household in the Olden Times* (1898). After the death of his wife in 1889, married Amarintha Mary Witherspoon. Died in New Orleans.

Dabney H. Maury (May 21, 1822–January 11, 1900) Born in Fredericksburg, Virginia, the son of a naval officer. Graduated from the University of Virginia in 1842 and from West Point in 1846. Wounded at Cerro Gordo in the U.S.-Mexican War. Taught at West Point, 1847–52, and served on the Texas frontier, 1852–56. Published *Skirmish Drill for Mounted Troops* (1859) while serving as superintendent of the cavalry school at Carlisle, Pennsylvania, 1856–60. Resigned from the U.S. Army in May 1861 and joined the Confederacy as a lieutenant colonel of cavalry in July. Served as chief of staff to General Earl Van Dorn at battle of Elkhorn Tavern (Pea Ridge), Arkansas, March 1862. Promoted to brigadier general, March 1862. Fought at Iuka and Corinth, September–October 1862. Promoted to major general, November 4, 1862. Commanded District of the Gulf at Mobile, Alabama, July 1863–April 1865. Taught school in Fredericksburg after the war before becoming an express agent and merchant in New Orleans. Founded Southern Historical Society in Richmond, Virginia, and served as its chairman until 1886. U.S. minister to Colombia, 1886–89.

Published *Recollections of a Virginian in the Mexican, Indian, and Civil Wars* (1894). Died in Peoria, Illinois.

George B. McClellan (December 3, 1826–October 29, 1885) Born in Philadelphia, the son of a surgeon. Graduated from West Point in 1846. Served in the U.S.-Mexican War. Resigned from the army in 1857 to become chief engineer of the Illinois Central Railroad. Became president of the Ohio & Mississippi Railroad in 1860. Married Ellen Marcy, 1860. Appointed major general in the regular army, May 1861. Commanded offensive that drove Confederate troops from western Virginia, July 1861. Assumed command of the Military Division of the Potomac on July 25, 1861, following the Union defeat at First Bull Run. Served as general-in-chief of the Union armies, November 1861–March 1862. Commanded the Army of the Potomac on the Peninsula, in the Second Bull Run campaign, and at Antietam. Relieved of command by President Lincoln on November 7, 1862. Nominated for president by the Democratic Party in 1864, but was defeated by Lincoln. Governor of New Jersey, 1878–81. Died in Orange, New Jersey.

Judith W. McGuire (March 19, 1813–March 21, 1897) Born Judith White Brockenbrough near Richmond, Virginia, the daughter of a judge. Married John P. McGuire, an Episcopalian rector, in 1846. Moved to Alexandria in 1852 when husband became principal of the Episcopal High School of Virginia. Fled Alexandria in May 1861 and settled in Richmond in February 1862. Worked as a clerk in the Confederate commissary department, November 1863–April 1864. Published *Diary of a Southern Refugee, During the War* (1867). Kept a school with her husband in Essex County in the 1870s. Published *General Robert E. Lee: The Christian Soldier* (1873). Died in Richmond.

George G. Meade (December 31, 1815–November 6, 1872) Born in Cádiz, Spain, the son of an American merchant. Family returned to Philadelphia in 1816. Graduated from West Point in 1835. Resigned in 1836 to work as engineer and surveyor. Married Margaretta Sergeant in 1840. Reentered army in 1842 as topographical engineer. Served under Zachary Taylor in the U.S.-Mexican War at Palo Alto, Resaca de la Palma, and Monterrey, and under Winfield Scott in the siege of Veracruz. Engaged in engineering and surveying duties in Delaware Bay, Florida, and the northern lakes, 1847–61. Commissioned as brigadier general of volunteers, August 1861. Became brigade commander in the Army of the Potomac, October 1861. Fought at Mechanicsville, Gaines's Mill, and Glendale, where he was wounded. Returned to duty in August 1862. Commanded brigade at Second Bull Run and a division at South Mountain and Antietam, where he temporarily led the First Corps after Joseph Hooker was wounded. Promoted to major general of volunteers, November 1862. Commanded division at Fredericksburg. Appointed commander of the Fifth Corps in December 1862 and led it at Chancellorsville. Replaced Hooker as commander of the Army of the Potomac on June 28, 1863, and led it until the end of the war. Received the thanks of Congress for his victory at Gettysburg. Promoted to major general in the regular army, September 23, 1864. Held postwar commands in the South and in the mid-Atlantic states. Died in Philadelphia.

Herman Melville (August 1, 1819–September 28, 1891) Born in New York City, the son of a merchant. Educated at schools in New York City and in upstate New York. Worked as bank clerk, bookkeeper, and schoolteacher. Sailed for Pacific on whaling ship in 1841 and returned in 1844 on frigate *United States*. Published *Typee* (1846) and *Omoo* (1847), fictionalized accounts of his experiences in the South Seas. Married Elizabeth Shaw in 1847. Published *Mardi* (1849), *Redburn* (1849), *White-Jacket* (1850), *Moby-Dick* (1851), *Pierre; or, The Ambiguities* (1852), *Israel Potter* (1855), *The Piazza Tales* (1856), and *The Confidence-Man* (1857). Visited Union troops in Virginia in spring 1864. Published poetry collection *Battle-Pieces and Aspects of the War* (1866). Worked as customs inspector in New York City, 1866–85. Published long poem *Clarel* (1876) and two small books of poetry, *John Marr and Other Sailors* (1888) and *Timoleon* (1891). Died in New York City, leaving *Billy Budd, Sailor*, in manuscript.

Hugh W. Mercer (November 27, 1808–June 9, 1877) Born in Fredericksburg, Virginia. Graduated from West Point in 1828. Served as artillery officer until 1835, when he resigned his commission. Married Mary Stites Anderson in 1834. Commissioned as brigadier general, October 1861. Commanded Confederate forces at Savannah, 1862–64. Led a brigade and then a division in the Atlanta campaign, May–July 1864, until poor health caused him to return to Savannah. After the war he was a banker in Savannah, 1866–69, and a commission merchant in Baltimore, 1869–72. Died in Baden Baden, Germany.

Mary Bedinger Mitchell (August 3, 1850–August 17, 1896) Born in Shepherdstown, Virginia (now West Virginia), the daughter of a lawyer and former congressman. Lived in Copenhagen, 1853–56, where father served as U.S. minister to Denmark, and with mother's family in Flushing, New York, 1856–58, before returning to Shepherdstown, where she spent the war. Married John F. B. Mitchell, a former Union officer, in 1871, and moved to Flushing. Published short stories under the name Maria Blunt in *Scribner's, Century,* and other magazines. Died in Flushing.

Thomas O. Moore (April 10, 1804–June 25, 1876) Born near Clinton, North Carolina, the son of a plantation owner. Moved to Rapides Parish, Louisiana, in 1829 to manage uncle's plantation. Married Bethiah Johnston Leonard, 1830. Acquired his own plantation, raising cotton and later sugar. Served as a Democrat in the state house of representatives, 1848–49, and in the state senate, 1856–60. Elected governor of Louisiana in 1859 and served January 1860–January 1864. Strongly supported secession after Lincoln's election. Following the Union occupation of New Orleans in April 1862, moved state capital from Baton Rouge to Opelousas and later Shreveport. Fled to Texas in spring of 1864 to escape Union troops, and to Mexico and Cuba following the Confederate surrender. Returned to Louisiana after being paroled by President Andrew Johnson, and received full pardon on January 15, 1867. Died at his plantation near Alexandria, Louisiana.

Benjamin Moran (August 1, 1820–June 20, 1886) Born in West Marlboro, Pennsylvania, the son of a cotton mill owner. Worked for bookseller and printer John Grigg in Philadelphia. Traveled to England in 1851. Published *The Footpath and Highway: or, Wanderings of an American in Great Britain, in 1851 and '52* (1853). Married Catherine Goulder, an English mill worker. Became private secretary to James Buchanan, then U.S. minister to Great Britain, in 1854. Assistant secretary of the American legation in London, 1857–64, and secretary, 1864–74. Served as minister resident in Portugal, 1874–76, and as chargé d'affaires at Lisbon, 1876–82. Returned to England in 1882 and died at Braintree, Essex.

John Lothrop Motley (April 15, 1814–May 29, 1877) Born in Dorchester, Massachusetts, the son of a merchant. Graduated from Harvard College in 1831. Continued university studies at Göttingen and Berlin, then traveled through Austria, Italy, France, and Britain, 1831–35. Admitted to the bar in 1836. Married Mary Benjamin in 1837. Published novels *Morton's Hope* (1839) and *Merrymount* (1849). Served term in the Massachusetts house of representatives, 1849. Traveled to Europe in 1851 for research on Dutch history. Published *The Rise of the Dutch Republic* (3 vols., 1856) and *History of the United Netherlands* (2 vols., 1860; 2 vols., 1867). Served as U.S. minister to the Austrian Empire, 1861–67, and to Great Britain, 1869–70. Published *The Life and Death of John of Barneveld* (2 vols., 1874). Died near Dorchester, England.

Robert Henry Newell (December 13, 1836–early July 1901) Born in New York City, the son of a lock manufacturer. Assistant editor of the *New York Sunday Mercury*, 1858–62. Began writing satiric letters signed "Orpheus C. Kerr" in March 1861 and continued through April 1865; they were collected in three volumes, published in 1862, 1863, and 1865. Married actress and writer Adah Isaacs Menken in 1862; she divorced him in 1865. Worked at the *New York World*, 1869–74, *New York Daily Graphic*, and *Hearth and Home* before retiring from journalism in 1876. Published poetry collections *The Palace Beautiful* (1865), *Versatilities* (1871), *Studies in Stanzas* (1882); novels *Avery Gliburn* (1867), *The Cloven Foot* (1870), *The Walking Doll* (1872), *There Once Was a Man* (1884); and *Smoked Glass* (1868), a collection of Orpheus C. Kerr letters satirizing Reconstruction politics. Died in Brooklyn, New York.

Ira S. Owens (March 1, 1830–February 19, 1913) Born in Greene County, Ohio. Enlisted in October 1861 from Xenia, Ohio, in the 74th Ohio Infantry as a private. Wounded in the left leg on December 31, 1862, at battle of Stones River (Murfreesboro), his only engagement. Reenlisted in January 1864, promoted to corporal, January 1865, and discharged in July 1865. Resumed farming in Montgomery County, Ohio. Later became a merchant and public notary. Published *Greene County in the War* (1872) and *Greene County Soldiers in the Late War* (1884). Died in Dayton, Ohio.

Charles A. Page (May 22, 1838–May 1873) Born near Dixon, Illinois, the son of a farmer. Graduated from Cornell College in Mount Vernon, Iowa, in 1859. Edited *The Mount Vernon News*, 1859–61. Worked as treasury department clerk in Washington, D.C., 1861, before becoming a correspondent for the *New-York Daily Tribune*, 1862–65, covering campaigns of the Army of the Potomac. Served as U.S. consul in Zurich, Switzerland, 1865–69. Founded successful condensed-milk company. Died in London.

Henry John Temple, third Viscount Palmerston (October 20, 1784–October 18, 1865) Born in Westminster, the son of an Irish peer whose title did not grant him a seat in the House of Lords. Educated at Harrow School, the University of Edinburgh, 1800–3, and St. John's College, Cambridge, 1803–6. Succeeded to his father's peerage in 1802. Entered the House of Commons as a Tory in 1807. Served as secretary at war, 1809–28 (the position made Palmerston responsible for managing the finances of the British army, but did not make him a member of the cabinet). Married Emily, Lady Cowper, a sister of Lord Melbourne, in 1839. Joined the Whigs in 1830 and served as foreign secretary, 1830–34, 1835–41, 1846–51; home secretary, 1852–55;

and prime minister, 1855–58. Became prime minister of the first Liberal government, 1859–65. Died in office at Brocket Hall, Hertfordshire.

George Hamilton Perkins (October 20, 1836–October 24, 1899) Born in Hopkinton, New Hampshire, the son of a lawyer. Graduated from the U.S. Naval Academy in 1856. Returned to the United States from West Africa in summer 1861 and was assigned to the gunboat *Cayuga* as first lieutenant in December 1861. Served in passage of Forts Jackson and St. Philip and the capture of New Orleans, April 1862. Patrolled the lower Mississippi River and served on blockade duty off Mobile and the Texas coast, 1862–64. Promoted to lieutenant commander, December 1862. Assumed command of the ironclad monitor *Chickasaw* in July 1864. Fought in battle of Mobile Bay, August 5, 1864. Commanded *Chickasaw* on Gulf blockade duty for remainder of the war. Married Anna Minot Weld in 1870. Retired as captain in 1891. Died in Boston.

Benjamin Rush Plumly (May 15, 1816–December 29, 1887) Born in Newton, Pennsylvania, the son of a Quaker physician. Worked as a merchant while active in the abolitionist and social reform movements. Married Rebecca Wilson. Served on staff of General John C. Frémont in Missouri, 1861, with rank of major. In 1863 went to New Orleans as an appraiser of abandoned property for the treasury department. Joined the staff of General Nathaniel P. Banks and recruited black soldiers for Banks's Corps d'Afrique. Chairman of the New Orleans Board of Education for Freedmen, 1864–65. Moved to Galveston, Texas, in 1866, where he founded a street railway company. After his wife's death, married Agnes Maria Garland in 1869. Served in the Texas house of representatives, 1870–73, 1881–83, and in 1887. Died in Galveston.

John Pope (March 16, 1822–September 23, 1892) Born in Louisville, Kentucky, the son of a federal district judge. Graduated from West Point in 1842. Joined topographical engineers and conducted surveys in Florida and along the northeastern border. Served in U.S.-Mexican War. Continued survey work in Minnesota, Texas, and New Mexico. Promoted to captain in 1856. Married Clara Pomeroy Horton in 1859. Appointed brigadier general of volunteers in May 1861. Led troops in Missouri, July 1861–February 1862. Became commander of the Army of the Mississippi in February 1862, and captured New Madrid, Missouri, and Island No. 10, March–April 1862. Promoted to major general of volunteers in March 1862. Joined Union advance on Corinth, Mississippi, in May 1862. Named commander of the new Army of Virginia, June 26. Defeated at Second Bull Run, August 28–30, and assigned to the Department of the Northwest on September 6, 1862. After the war he held a series of commands in the West before retiring in 1886. Died in Sandusky, Ohio.

Fitz John Porter (August 31, 1822–May 21, 1901) Born in Portsmouth, New Hampshire, the son of a naval officer. Graduated from West Point in 1845. Served in the U.S.-Mexican War, and as an instructor at West Point, 1849–55. Married Harriet Pierson Cook in 1857. Served as chief of staff of the Union command in the Shenandoah Valley, April–August 1861. Commissioned brigadier general of volunteers, May 1861. Commanded division in the Army of the Potomac, October 1861–May 1862. Appointed commander of the Fifth Corps, Army of the Potomac, May 1862. Served in the Peninsula campaign and in the Seven Days' Battles, where he commanded the Union forces at Mechanicsville, Gaines's Mill, and Malvern Hill. Promoted to major general of volunteers in July 4, 1862. Led Fifth Corps in the Second Bull Run campaign and at Antietam. Relieved of command in November 1862. Convicted by general court-martial of misconduct and disobedience at Second Bull Run and cashiered from the army, January 21, 1863. Worked as mining engineer in Colorado, as merchant in New York City, and as construction engineer and railroad executive in New Jersey. An army board of inquiry exonerated him of all charges in 1879, and in 1886 he was reinstated in the army and placed on the retired list. Served as a New York City police commissioner, 1884–88, and fire commissioner, 1888–89. Died in Morristown, New Jersey.

Sara Agnes Pryor (February 19, 1830–February 15, 1912) Born Sara Agnes Rice in Halifax County, Virginia, the daughter of a Baptist minister. Married Roger Atkinson Pryor in 1848. Lived in Charlottesville, Petersburg, Richmond, and Washington, D.C., while her husband studied law, edited several newspapers, and served in the U.S. Congress, 1859–61. Moved around Virginia, 1861–63, while her husband commanded a regiment and then a brigade the Confederate army. Served as a nurse in Richmond during the Seven Days' Battles. Returned to Petersburg in the autumn of 1863 and remained there during the 1864–65 siege. Moved in 1867 to New York, where her husband was now practicing law, and lived in Brooklyn and later Manhattan. Published *The Mother of Washington and Her Times* (1903), *Reminiscences of Peace and War* (1904), *The Birth of the Nation: Jamestown, 1607* (1907), *My Day: Reminiscences of a Long Life* (1909), and a novel, *The Colonel's Story* (1911). Died in New York City.

Whitelaw Reid (October 27, 1837–December 15, 1912). Born near Cedarville, Ohio, the son of a farmer. Graduated from Miami University in 1856. Edited and published the *Xenia News*, 1857–60. Supported Abraham Lincoln in the 1860 presidential election. In 1861 began contributing to the *Cincinnati Times*, *Cleveland Herald*, and *Cincinnati Gazette*. Reported on the 1861 Union offensive in western Virginia and the battle of Shiloh for the *Gazette*. Became the Washington correspondent for the *Gazette* in June 1862, signing his dispatches "Agate," while also contributing reports to the *Chicago Tribune* and newspapers in St. Louis, Cleveland, Detroit, and Pittsburgh. Reported from the field at Gettysburg. Published *After the War* (1866), describing his travels through the South following the Confederate surrender. Unsuccessfully tried to raise cotton in Louisiana and Alabama, 1866–67. Published *Ohio in the War: Her Statesmen, Her Generals, and Soldiers* (1868). Reported on the impeachment trial of President Andrew Johnson and the 1868 political conventions for the *Gazette*. Joined the *New York Tribune* in 1868 and served as its managing editor, 1869–72. Following the death of Horace Greeley, he became the *Tribune*'s editor, 1872–1905, and publisher, 1872–1912. Served as U.S. minister to France, 1889–92. Nominated by the 1892 Republican convention as vice-presidential running mate for President Benjamin Harrison (election was won by former president Grover Cleveland). Served as member of the commission that negotiated peace treaty with Spain in 1898 and as U.S. ambassador to Great Britain, 1905–12. Died in London.

Henry Ropes (May 16, 1839–July 3, 1863) Born in London, England, the son of an American merchant. Family returned to Boston in 1842. Entered Harvard College in 1858. Commissioned as second lieutenant in Company K, 20th Massachusetts Infantry, on November 25, 1861. Fought in the Peninsula campaign, in the Seven Days' Battles, and at Antietam. Promoted to first lieutenant on October 2, 1862. Fought at Fredericksburg (December 1862 and May 1863) and at Gettysburg, where he was killed by the premature explosion of a Union shell.

Lord John Russell, first Earl Russell (August 18, 1792–May 28, 1878) Born in Westminster, the third son of the future Duke of Bedford. Educated at Westminster School and the University of Edinburgh. Entered the House of Commons as a Whig M. P. in 1813. Published series of historical works, essays, novels, and plays beginning in 1819. Helped draft the Reform Bill of 1832. Married Adelaide, Lady Ribblesdale, in 1835; after her death, married Lady Fannie Elliot in 1841. Served as home secretary, 1835–41; prime minister, 1846–52; foreign secretary, 1852–53; colonial secretary, 1855; foreign secretary in the Palmerston government, 1859–65; and prime minister after Palmerston's death, 1865–66. Created Earl Russell in 1861. Died in Richmond Park, Surrey.

Samuel Sawyer (June 20, 1823–May 23, 1902) Born in Goshen, New York, the son of a farmer. Graduated from the College of New Jersey (Princeton) in 1842. Attended Union Theological Seminary, 1845–48. Ordained as Presbyterian minister in 1849. Held pastorate in Rodgersville, Tennessee, 1848–57. President of the College of Indiana in Marion, 1857–61. Appointed chaplain of the 47th Indiana Infantry in 1861. After the capture of Memphis in 1862, edited a Unionist newspaper in the city until it was closed by General William T. Sherman. Served as superintendent of contrabands at Helena, Arkansas, and St. Louis, 1863. Mustered out in 1864. Held church positions in Knoxville and Maryville, Tennessee, 1864–68; in Chillicothe, Missouri, where he edited a newspaper, 1868–72; and in East St. Louis, Illinois, and Pleasant Grove, New Jersey. Returned to Marion, Indiana, in 1880. Died in Indianapolis.

William T. Sherman (February 8, 1820–February 14, 1891) Born in Lancaster, Ohio, the son of an attorney. Graduated from West Point in 1840. Served in Florida and California, but did not see action in the U.S.-Mexican War. Married Ellen Ewing in 1850. Promoted to captain; resigned his commission in 1853. Managed bank branch in San Francisco, 1853–57. Moved in 1858 to Leavenworth, Kansas, where he worked in real estate and was admitted to the bar. Named first superintendent of the Louisiana State Seminary of Learning and Military Academy at Alexandria (now Louisiana State University) in 1859. Resigned position when Louisiana seceded in January 1861. Commissioned colonel, 13th U.S. Infantry, May 1861. Commanded brigade at First Bull Run, July 1861. Appointed brigadier general of volunteers, August 1861, and ordered to Kentucky. Assumed command of the Department of the Cumberland, October 1861, but was relieved in November at his own request. Returned to field in March 1862 and commanded division under Ulysses S. Grant at Shiloh. Promoted major general of volunteers, May 1862. Commanded corps under Grant during Vicksburg campaign, and succeeded him as commander of the Army of the Tennessee, October 1863, and as commander of the Military Division of the Mississippi, March 1864. Captured Atlanta, September 1864, and led march through Georgia, November–December 1864. Marched army through the Carolinas and accepted the surrender of Confederate General Joseph E. Johnston at Durham Station, North Carolina, April 26, 1865. Promoted to lieutenant general, 1866, and general, 1869, when he became commander of the army. Published controversial memoirs (1875, revised 1886). Retired from army in 1884 and moved to New York City. Rejected possible Republican presidential nomination, 1884. Died in New York City.

George W. Smalley (June 2, 1833–April 4, 1916) Born in Franklin, Massachusetts, the son of a minister. Graduated from Yale in 1853, attended Harvard Law School, and admitted to the bar in 1856. Practiced law in Boston, 1856–61. Reported on the Union capture of Port Royal, South Carolina, the Shenandoah Valley campaign, and the battle of Antietam as a war correspondent for the *New-York Daily Tribune*, November 1861–October 1862. Married Phoebe Garnaut, the adopted daughter of Wendell Phillips, in 1862. Worked in the New York office of the *Tribune*, 1863–65, and helped defend it against draft rioters in July 1863. Reported on the Austro-Prussian War in 1866. Headed London office of the *Tribune*, 1867–95, and directed its reporting of the Franco-Prussian War. American correspondent for *The Times* of London, 1895–1905. Published *London Letters* (1891), *Studies of Men* (1895), and *Anglo-American Memories* (1911). Returned to England in 1905. Died in London.

Asa D. Smith (1836–November 25, 1911) A shoemaker from Natick, Smith enlisted as a corporal in the 16th Massachusetts Infantry on May 7, 1861. Served in the Peninsula campaign with Hooker's Division, Third Corps, Army of the Potomac. Severely wounded at battle of Glendale, June 30, 1862. Hospitalized at the U.S. Naval Academy at Annapolis, Maryland, before being discharged for disability on July 25, 1862. Joined Natick fire department in 1863. Served as deputy state constable from 1865. Married Abbie Louise Newhall in 1866. Graduated from Boston University School of Medicine in 1877. Established medical practice in South Boston from 1878 and in Dorchester from 1901. Died in Dorchester, Massachusetts.

Ezra Stacy (May 31, 1807–December 9, 1878) A plantation owner in Liberty County, Georgia, where he was born and died. Deacon of Midway Church, 1838–66.

Lewis H. Steiner (May 4, 1827–February 18, 1892) Born in Frederick, Maryland, the son of a merchant. Graduated from Marshall College, Mercersburg, Pennsylvania, in 1846. Received M.D. from the University of Pennsylvania in 1849. Practiced in Frederick before moving to Baltimore in 1852. Taught chemistry, physics, natural history, and pharmacy at the Columbian College and the National Medical College in Washington, D.C., 1853–55; at the College of St. James in Hagerstown, Maryland, 1854–59; and at the Maryland College of Pharmacy in Baltimore, 1856–61. Published several pamphlets on medical and scientific subjects and was assistant editor of the *American Medical Monthly*, 1859–61. Returned to Frederick in 1861. Served as chief inspector of the U.S. Sanitary Commission with the Army of the Potomac throughout the war. Married Sarah Spencer Smyth, 1866. Served as a Republican in the Maryland senate, 1871–83. Chief librarian of the Enoch Pratt Free Library in Baltimore, 1884–92. Died in Baltimore.

George E. Stephens (1832–April 24, 1888) Born in Philadelphia, the son of free blacks who had fled from Virginia after the Nat Turner rebellion. Worked as upholsterer and cabinetmaker. An active abolitionist, he helped found the Banneker Institute, a literary society and library for blacks, in Philadelphia in 1853. Served on coastal survey ship *Walker* in 1857–58 and visited Charleston, South Carolina. Became cook and personal servant to Lieutenant Colonel Benjamin Tilghman of the 26th Pennsylvania Infantry in 1861 while serving as war correspondent for the New York *Weekly Anglo-African*, an influential black newspaper. Helped recruit in early 1863 for the 54th Massachusetts Infantry, the first black regiment raised by a northern state, then enlisted in the regiment as a sergeant. Served in siege of Charleston, South Carolina, and fought in the assault on Fort Wagner on July 18, 1863. Continued to write for the *Anglo-African* and protested the failure of black soldiers to receive equal pay. Commissioned as first lieutenant before being mustered out in July 1865. Worked for the Freedman's Bureau in Virginia educating freed slaves, 1866–70. Returned to Philadelphia before moving in 1873 to Brooklyn, where he worked as an upholsterer until his death.

Kate Stone (May 8, 1841–December 28, 1907) Born Sarah Katherine Stone in Hinds County, Mississippi, the daughter of a plantation owner. Family moved to plantation in Madison Parish, Louisiana, thirty miles northwest of Vicksburg. Educated at boarding school in Nashville. Two of her five brothers died while serving in the Confederate army in 1863. Family fled plantation in March 1863 during the Vicksburg campaign and went to eastern Texas. Returned to plantation in November 1865. Married Henry Bry Holmes in 1869. Founded local chapter of the United Daughters of the Confederacy. Died in Tallulah, Louisiana.

George Templeton Strong (January 26, 1820–July 21, 1875) Born in New York City, the son of an attorney. Graduated from Columbia College in 1838. Read law in his father's office and was admitted to the bar in 1841. Joined father's firm. Married Ellen Ruggles in 1848. Served on Columbia board of trustees and as vestryman of Trinity Episcopal Church. Helped found the U.S. Sanitary Commission, June 1861, and served as its treasurer through the end of the war; also helped found the Union League Club of New York in 1863. Died in New York City.

Charles Sumner (January 6, 1811–March 11, 1874) Born in Boston, Massachusetts, the son of a lawyer. Graduated from Harvard College in 1830 and from Harvard Law School in 1833. Practiced law in Boston and became active in social reform movements. Unsuccessful Free Soil candidate for Congress in 1848. Elected to the U.S. Senate as a Free Soiler in 1851. Badly beaten with a cane on the Senate floor by South Carolina congressman Preston Brooks on May 22, 1856, two days after delivering his antislavery speech "The Crime Against Kansas." Reelected as a Republican in 1857, but did not regularly return to his seat in the Senate until December 1859; reelected in 1863 and 1869. Chairman of the Senate Foreign Relations Committee, 1861–71. Supported Radical Reconstruction and the rights of blacks after the war. Married Alice Mason Hooper in 1866. Joined Liberal Republicans in opposing reelection of President Grant in 1872. Died in Washington, D.C.

Richard Taylor (January 27, 1826–April 12, 1879) Born near Louisville, Kentucky, the son of army officer and future president Zachary Taylor. Graduated from Yale College in 1845. Managed father's cotton plantation in Jefferson County, Mississippi, 1848–49. Inherited sugar plantation in St. Charles Parish, Louisiana, after President Taylor's death in 1850. Married Louise Marie Myrthé Bringier, 1851. Served in the Louisiana senate, 1856–61. Commissioned as colonel of the 9th Louisiana Infantry, July 1861. Promoted to brigadier general, October 1861. Commanded the Louisiana Brigade in the Shenandoah Valley campaign of 1862. Promoted to major general, July 1862, and assigned command of the District of Western Louisiana, August 1862. Defeated General Nathaniel P. Banks in the Red River campaign in Louisiana, March–May 1864. Promoted to lieutenant general, May 1864. Commanded the Department of Alabama, Mississippi, and Eastern Louisiana from September 1864 to May 4, 1865, when he surrendered at Citronelle, Alabama. Active in the postwar Democratic Party in Louisiana. *Destruction and Reconstruction: Personal Experiences of the Late War* published posthumously in 1879. Died in New York City.

David L. Thompson (August 28, 1837–March 13, 1926) Born in Windham, Ohio. Taught school before enlisting from Flushing, New York, as private in Company G, 9th New York Infantry, on August 13, 1862. Captured at battle of Antietam, September 17, 1862. Held at Richmond; paroled to Annapolis, Maryland, October 6, 1862, and released from parole, December 1862. After the 9th New York mustered out in May 1863, Thompson joined Company B, 3rd New York Infantry. Served in South Carolina in 1863, in the Bermuda Hundred and Petersburg campaigns in 1864, and in North Carolina, where he was discharged on June 17, 1865, as a lieutenant. Married Mary Ann Wray in 1868. Lived in North Plainfield, New Jersey. Worked as a cashier, then as treasurer of a hardware company. Died in Newark, New Jersey.

Charles S. Wainwright (December 31, 1826–September 13, 1907) Born in New York City, the son of a farmer from Dutchess County in the Hudson Valley. Helped manage family estate near Rhinebeck. Served in New York state militia. Commissioned as major in the 1st New York Artillery on October 17, 1861. Served as chief of artillery in Hooker's division, Army of the Potomac, from January 1862. Promoted to lieutenant colonel, April 1862, and colonel, May 1862. Fought at Williamsburg and Fair Oaks before falling ill in early June 1862. Returned from sick leave in August 1862 and became chief of artillery in the First Corps in September 1862; joined his command after the battle of Antietam. Served at Fredericksburg, Chancellorsville, and Gettysburg. Commanded artillery brigade in Fifth Corps, 1864–65, and served in the Overland campaign, the siege of Petersburg, and the Appomattox campaign. Returned to farming in Dutchess County before moving to Washington, D.C., around 1884. Died in Washington.

Henry Walke (December 24, 1808–March 8, 1896) Born in Princess Anne County, Virginia, the son of a plantation owner. Family moved to Chillicothe, Ohio, in 1811. Entered the U.S. Navy as a midshipman in 1827 and was promoted to lieutenant in 1839. Served on brig *Vesuvius* during the U.S.-Mexican War. Promoted to commander in 1855. Commanded gunboat *Tyler* in support of General Grant's attack on Belmont, Missouri, in November 1861. Assumed command of the ironclad *Carondolet* in January 1862. Saw action at Forts Henry and Donelson, Island No. 10, Plum Run Bend, Memphis, and in battle with the Confederate ironclad *Arkansas* on the Yazoo River, February–July 1862. Promoted to captain in July 1862. Commanded the ironclad ram *Lafayette* during the Vicksburg campaign, February–August 1863, and the steam sloop *Sacramento* on patrol for Confederate raiders in the Atlantic, January 1864–August 1865. Promoted to commodore, 1866, and rear admiral, 1870. Retired in 1871. Published *Naval Scenes and Reminiscences of the Civil War in the United States* (1877). Died in Brooklyn, New York.

Lewis Wallace (April 10, 1827–February 15, 1905) Born in Brookville, Indiana, the son of a lawyer and politician. Reported on Indiana legislature for the *Indianapolis Daily Journal*, 1844–45. Served as second lieutenant with the 1st Indiana Infantry in the U.S.-Mexican War. Admitted to the bar in 1849. Married Susan Arnold Elston in 1852. Served as Democrat in the Indiana state senate, 1856–60. Commissioned colonel of the 11th Indiana Infantry in April 1861. Promoted to brigadier general of volunteers, September 1861. Commanded a division at Forts Henry and Donelson. Promoted to major general in March 1862. Commanded division at Shiloh, where his delay in reaching the battlefield on the first day led to his relief in June 1862. Organized defense of Cincinnati during the Confederate invasion of Kentucky. Appointed commander of Union troops in Maryland in March 1864. Led Union forces in battle of the Monocacy on July 9, 1864, successfully delaying the Confederate advance on Washington, D.C. Served on the military commission that convicted the conspirators in the Lincoln assassination, and was president of the commission that convicted Henry Wirz, the commander of the Andersonville prison camp. Resumed law practice in Indiana. Published *The Fair God* (1873), a novel about the Spanish conquest of Mexico. Served as governor of New Mexico Territory, 1878–81. Published *Ben Hur: A Tale of the Christ* (1880). U.S. minister to the Ottoman Empire, 1881–85. Published *The Boyhood of Christ* (1888) and *The Prince of India* (1893); his autobiography appeared posthumously in 1906. Died in Crawfordsville, Indiana.

Samuel R. Watkins (June 26, 1839–July 20, 1901) Born near Columbia, Tennessee, the son of a farmer. Attended Jackson College in Columbia and worked as a store clerk. Enlisted as a private in Company H, 1st Tennessee Infantry, in May 1861. Fought at Shiloh, Perryville, Murfreesboro (Stones River), Chickamauga, Chattanooga, the Atlanta campaign, Franklin, and Nashville and was wounded three times. Surrendered in North Carolina on April 26, 1865, one of sixty-five men remaining in his regiment and seven in his company. Married Virginia Jane Mayes in 1865. Became farmer and merchant in Columbia, Tennessee. Published memoir *"Co. Aytch," Maury Grays, First Tennessee Regiment, or, A Side Show of the Big Show* (1882). Died near Columbia.

Gideon Welles (July 1, 1802–February 11, 1878) Born in Glastonbury, Connecticut, the son of a merchant. Educated in Vermont at the American Literary, Scientific, and Military Academy (now Norwich University). Editor of the *Hartford Times*, 1826–36. Served as a Democrat in the Connecticut house of representatives, 1827–35. Married Mary Hale in 1835. Postmaster of Hartford, 1836–41. Served as chief of the bureau of provisions and clothing in the navy department, 1846–49. Helped organize Republican Party in Connecticut. Wrote for the *Hartford Evening Press*, the *New York Evening Post*, and other Republican newspapers. Secretary of the navy in the Lincoln and Andrew Johnson administrations, 1861–69. Died in Hartford.

Garland H. White (c. 1829–c. 1894) Born in slavery in Hanover County, Virginia. Sold around 1845 to Robert Toombs of Georgia and became his personal servant. Lived in Washington, D.C., while Toombs served in Congress, 1845–53, and in the Senate, 1853–61. Escaped from the District of Columbia in 1859 and fled to London, Canada West (Ontario), where he became a minister in the African Methodist Episcopal Church. Married Georgiana, a woman from Mississippi, around 1861. Began preaching in Toledo, Ohio, in January 1863. Helped recruit black soldiers in Indiana for the 28th U.S. Colored Infantry. Enlisted in regiment as private in January 1864 and began acting as regimental chaplain. Served with regiment in the Petersburg campaign. Wrote letters describing army life and the war to the *Christian Recorder*, an A.M.E. newspaper. Commissioned as regimental chaplain in October 1864. Reunited with his mother when he entered Richmond with his regiment on April 3, 1865. Served in Texas, July–November 1865, before being mustered out in January 1866. Returned to church in Toledo. Served as minister in Halifax, North Carolina, 1872–82. Lived in Weldon, North Carolina, 1884–89, before moving to Washington, D.C., where he died.

L. A. Whitely (1823–July 20, 1869) Raised in Kentucky. Associate editor of the *Louisville Journal* and later owner of the *Baltimore Clipper*. Accepted offer in 1861 from James Gordon Bennett, publisher of the *New York Herald*, to head its Washington bureau. Worked as clerk in the treasury department from 1861 to June 1863, when he was dismissed by Secretary of the Treasury Chase. Left the *Herald* after the war to become editor of the *National Intelligencer*, a position he held until the newspaper closed in June 1869. Died in Washington, D.C.

Walt Whitman (May 31, 1819–March 26, 1892) Born in Huntington Township, New York, the son of a farmer and carpenter. Moved with family to Brooklyn in 1823. Learned printing trade at Brooklyn newspapers. Taught school on Long Island, 1836–38. Became freelance journalist and printer in New York and Brooklyn. Published first edition of *Leaves of Grass* in 1855 (revised editions appeared in 1856, 1860, 1867, 1870, 1881, and 1891). Traveled to northern Virginia in December 1862 after learning that his brother George had been wounded at Fredericksburg. Became volunteer nurse in Washington, D.C., army hospitals. Published *Drum-Taps* and *Sequel to Drum-Taps* in 1865. Worked as clerk at the interior department, 1865, and the office of the attorney general, 1865–73. Published prose recollections of his war experiences in *Memoranda During the War* (1875) and *Specimen Days and Collect* (1882). Died in Camden, New Jersey.

Alpheus S. Williams (September 20, 1810–December 21, 1878) Born in Deep River, Connecticut, the son of a manufacturer. Graduated from Yale College in 1831. Admitted to the bar in 1834. Moved to Detroit in 1836, where he practiced law and joined the local militia company. Married Jane Hereford Pierson in 1839; she died in 1848. Served as probate judge of Wayne County, 1840–44, and published the *Detroit Daily Advertiser*, 1843–48. Commissioned as brigadier general of volunteers in August 1861. Commanded brigade in the Army of the Potomac, October 1861–March 1862. Led a division in the Shenandoah Valley campaign and at Cedar Mountain and Second Bull Run. Assumed temporary command of Twelfth Corps at Antietam following the death of General Mansfield. Commanded division at Chancellorsville and was temporary commander of the Twelfth Corps at Gettysburg. Sent with his division in September 1863 to Tennessee, where they guarded railroads. Served in the Atlanta campaign and commanded the Twentieth Corps in the march through Georgia and the Carolinas. Mustered out on January 15, 1866. Served as U.S. minister to San Salvador, 1866–69. Returned to Detroit. Married Martha Ann Tillman in 1873. Elected to Congress as a Democrat and served from 1875 until his death in Washington, D.C.

J. Montgomery Wright (February 22, 1839–January 2, 1915) Born John Montgomery Wright in Sackets Harbor, New York, the son of an army officer. Entered West Point in 1859. Commissioned as captain and assistant adjutant general of volunteers, September 1861. Promoted to major in June 1862 and served on the staff of General Don Carlos Buell. Resigned commission in January 1864. Married Nelly Butler Ewing. Served as adjutant general of the Kentucky state militia, 1875–79. Marshal of the U.S. Supreme Court, 1888–1915. Died in Washington, D.C.

Lot D. Young (January 22, 1842–April 2, 1926) Born in Nicholas County, Kentucky. Enlisted in September 1861 in the Confederate 4th Kentucky Infantry. Fought at Shiloh. Promoted to second lieutenant, May 1862, and first lieutenant, March 1863. Fought at Murfreesboro (Stones River), Chickamauga, Missionary Ridge, and in the Atlanta campaign. Severely wounded at Jonesboro, Georgia, on August 31, 1864. Spent six months in hospitals and was unable to rejoin his regiment before the war ended. Published *Reminiscences of a Soldier in the Orphan Brigade* (1918). Died in Lexington, Kentucky.

Note on the Texts

This volume collects nineteenth- and early twentieth-century writing about the Civil War, bringing together public and private letters, newspaper and magazine articles, memoranda, speeches, narratives, journal and diary entries, proclamations, messages, legislative enactments, military orders, poems, songs, and excerpts from memoirs written by participants and observers and dealing with events in the period between January 1862 and January 1863. Most of these documents were not written for publication, and most of them existed only in manuscript form during the lifetimes of the persons who wrote them. With fourteen exceptions, the texts presented in this volume are taken from printed sources. In cases where there is only one printed source for a document, the text offered here comes from that source. Where there is more than one printed source for a document, the text printed in this volume is taken from the source that appears to contain the fewest editorial alterations in the spelling, capitalization, paragraphing, and punctuation of the original. In fourteen instances where no printed sources (or no complete printed sources) were available, the texts in this volume are printed from manuscripts.

This volume prints texts as they appear in the sources listed below, but with a few alterations in editorial procedure. The bracketed conjectural readings of editors, in cases where original manuscripts or printed texts were damaged or difficult to read, are accepted without brackets in this volume when those readings seem to be the only possible ones; but when they do not, or when the editor made no conjecture, the missing word or words are indicated by a bracketed two-em space, i.e., [   ]. In cases where a typographical error or obvious misspelling in manuscript was marked by earlier editors with "[*sic*]," the present volume omits the "[*sic*]" and corrects the typographical error or slip of the pen. In some cases, obvious errors were not marked by earlier editors with "[*sic*]" but were printed and then followed by a bracketed correction; in these instances, this volume removes the brackets and accepts the editorial emendation. Bracketed editorial insertions used in the source texts to identify persons or places, expand contractions and abbreviations, or clarify meaning have been deleted in this volume. In instances where canceled, but still legible, words were printed in the source texts with lines through the deleted material, or where canceled words were printed and indicated with an asterisk, this volume omits the canceled words.

The texts of the letter from George Hamilton Perkins to Susan G. Perkins and of the journal entry by Charles B. Labruzan were presented as quoted material in the sources used in this volume, with quotation marks placed at the beginning of each paragraph and at the end of the text; this volume omits the quotation marks.

In *The Papers of Jefferson Davis*, material that was written in interlined form in manuscript is printed within diagonal marks; this volume prints the interlined words and omits the diagonals. Similarly, interlined material that was presented in footnotes in *Ham Chamberlayne —Virginian: Letters and papers of an artillery officer in the War for Southern Independence 1861–1865* has been incorporated into the text in this volume.

Diary of a Southern Refugee was first published in New York in 1867, with its author identified as "A Lady of Virginia" and with initials substituted for the names of a number of persons referred to in the text. The book was reprinted in 1889 in Richmond by J. W. Randolph & English, with Judith W. McGuire identified as its author, and with an appended list of "Corrections" supplying the omitted names. In the selection from *Diary of a Southern Refugee* presented in this volume, the names supplied in the "Corrections" section of the 1889 printing have been incorporated into the text.

The selections from the diary of Gideon Welles, the secretary of the navy in the Lincoln administration, are taken from *Diary of Gideon Welles* (1960), edited by Howard K. Beale. Welles kept a diary during the Civil War that he extensively revised between 1869 and his death in 1878. The revised text was published in 1911 as *Diary of Gideon Welles*, edited by his son Edgar T. Welles with the assistance of John Morse Jr. and Frederick Bancroft. In the 1960 edition, Beale presented the text of the 1911 edition while printing deleted material from the original diary in the margins and using brackets, italics, strike-through lines, and other editorial markings to indicate the differences between the original version of the diary and the revised text. The texts of the selections from the Welles diary printed in this volume are taken from the 1960 edition and incorporate the changes indicated by Beale in order to present a clear text of the diary as originally written by Welles during the Civil War.

In *The Francis Preston Blair Family in Politics* (1933), William Ernest Smith printed an incomplete text of Francis Preston Blair's letter to Montgomery Blair of November 7, 1862. The text presented in this volume is taken from *The Francis Preston Blair Family in Politics*, with the exception of the first sentence and the closing, which are taken from an unpublished transcription (also incomplete) made by the historian E. B. Long around 1960.

Two errors made in the transcription of documents are corrected in this volume, even though they were not corrected in the printed source texts: at 326.2, "*July 10*" becomes "*July 20*," and at 430.18, "to the report he had" becomes "to the support he had." Five slips of the pen in documents printed from manuscript sources are also corrected: at 414.30–31, "divisions fell back throug" becomes "divisions fell back through"; at 538.21, "to be in in favor" becomes "to be in favor"; at 549.12, "course of the administration is shakin" becomes "course of the administration is shaking"; at 700.13, "supply there men & animals" becomes "supply their men & animals"; at 746.24–25, "to 'work and wait, trusting" becomes "to 'work and wait,' trusting."

The following is a list of the documents included in this volume, in the order of their appearance, giving the source of each text.

Frederick Douglass: What Shall Be Done with the Slaves If Emancipated?, January 1862. *The Life and Writings of Frederick Douglass*, ed. Philip S. Foner, volume 3 (New York: International Publishers Co. Inc., 1952), 188–91. Copyright © 1950. Reprinted from *The Life and Writings of Frederick Douglass*, published by International Publishers, copyright © 1950.

John Boston to Elizabeth Boston, January 12, 1862. *Free at Last: A Documentary History of Slavery, Freedom, and the Civil War*, ed. Ira Berlin, Barbara J. Fields, Steven F. Miller, Joseph P. Reidy, Leslie S. Rowland (New York: The New Press, 1992), 29–30. Copyright © 1992 by The New Press. Reprinted by permission of The New Press.

Salmon P. Chase: Journal, January 6, 1862. *The Salmon P. Chase Papers: Volume I, Journals, 1829–1872*, ed. John Niven (Kent, Ohio: The Kent State University Press, 1993), 321–22. Copyright © 1993 by The Kent State University Press.

Abraham Lincoln to Don Carlos Buell and Henry W. Halleck, January 13, 1862. *The Collected Works of Abraham Lincoln*, volume V, ed. Roy P. Basler (New Brunswick, N.J.: Rutgers University Press, 1953), 98–99. Copyright © 1953 by the Abraham Lincoln Association.

Abraham Lincoln: President's General War Order No. 1, January 27, 1862; President's Special War Order No. 1, January 31, 1862. *The Collected Works of Abraham Lincoln*, volume V, ed. Roy P. Basler (New Brunswick, N.J.: Rutgers University Press, 1953), 111–12, 115. Copyright © 1953 by the Abraham Lincoln Association.

George B. McClellan to Edwin M. Stanton, February 3, 1862. *The Civil War Papers of George B. McClellan: Selected Correspondence, 1860–1865*, ed. Stephen W. Sears (New York: Ticknor & Fields, 1989), 162–70. Copyright © 1989 by Stephen W. Sears. Reprinted with permission by Stephen W. Sears.

Julia Ward Howe: The Battle Hymn of the Republic; from *Reminiscences, 1819–1899*. *Atlantic Monthly*, February 1862; Julia Ward Howe,

Reminiscences, 1819–1899 (Boston: Houghton Mifflin Company, 1899), 273–76.
The New York Times: An Important Arrest; The Ball's Bluff Disaster— Gen. McClellan and Gen. Stone. *The New York Times*, February 11, 1862, April 12, 1863.
Lew Wallace: from *An Autobiography*. Lew Wallace, *An Autobiography*, vol. I (New York: Harper & Brothers, 1906), 410–24.
John Kennerly Farris to Mary Farris, October 31, 1862. "Letters to Mary: The Civil War Diary of John Kennerly Farris," ed. John Abernathy Smith, *Franklin County Historical Review*, volume XXV (1994), 46–52. Copyright © 1994 by The Franklin County Historical Society. Reprinted courtesy of The Franklin County Historical Review.
Henry Walke: The Western Flotilla at Fort Donelson, Island Number Ten, Fort Pillow and Memphis. *Battles and Leaders of the Civil War*, volume I, ed. Robert Underwood Johnson and Clarence Clough Buel (New York: The Century Co., 1887), 430–52.
Braxton Bragg to Judah P. Benjamin, February 15, 1862. *The War of the Rebellion: A Compilation of the Official Records of the Union and Confederate Armies*, series I, volume VI (Washington, D.C.: Government Printing Office, 1882), 826–27.
John B. Jones: Diary, February 8–28, 1862. J. B. Jones, *A Rebel War Clerk's Diary at the Confederate States Capital*, volume I (Philadelphia: J. B. Lippincott & Co., 1866), 109–12.
Jefferson Davis: Message to the Confederate Congress, February 25, 1862. *The Papers of Jefferson Davis*, volume VIII, ed. Lynda Lasswell Crist and Mary Seaton Dix (Baton Rouge: Louisiana State University Press, 1995), 58–62. Copyright © 1995 by Louisiana State University Press.
George E. Stephens to the *Weekly Anglo-African*, March 2, 1862. *A Voice of Thunder: The Civil War Letters of George E. Stephens*, ed. Donald Yacovone (Urbana: University of Illinois Press, 1997), 185–88. Copyright © 1997 by the Board of Trustees of the University of Illinois.
Orpheus C. Kerr: from *The Orpheus C. Kerr Papers*. *The Orpheus C. Kerr Papers* (New York: Blakemon & Mason, 1862), 219–27.
Dabney H. Maury: Recollections of the Elkhorn Campaign. *Southern Historical Society Papers*, volume II (Richmond, Virginia: Southern Historical Society, 1876), 180–92.
Abraham Lincoln: Message to Congress on Compensated Emancipation, March 6, 1862; To James A. McDougall, March 14, 1862. *The Collected Works of Abraham Lincoln*, volume V, ed. Roy P. Basler (New Brunswick, N.J.: Rutgers University Press, 1953), 144–46, 160–61. Copyright © 1953 by the Abraham Lincoln Association.

Catesby ap Roger Jones: from "Services of the 'Virginia' (Merrimac)." *Southern Historical Society Papers*, volume XI, no. 2 (February–March 1883), 67–73.

Nathaniel Hawthorne: from "Chiefly About War-Matters by a Peaceable Man." *The Centenary Edition of the Works of Nathaniel Hawthorne*, volume XXII, *Miscellaneous Prose and Verse*, ed. Thomas Woodson, Claude M. Simpson, and L. Neal Smith (Columbus: The Ohio State University Press, 1994), 410–25, 433–38. Copyright © 1994 by The Ohio State University Press. Reprinted by permission.

George B. McClellan to the Army of the Potomac, March 14, 1862, and to Samuel L. M. Barlow, March 16, 1862. *The Civil War Papers of George B. McClellan: Selected Correspondence, 1860–1865*, ed. Stephen W. Sears (New York: Ticknor & Fields, 1989), 211, 213. Copyright © 1989 by Stephen W. Sears. Reprinted with permission by Stephen W. Sears.

Charles Francis Adams to Charles Francis Adams Jr., April 4, 1862. *A Cycle of Adams Letters, 1861–1865*, volume I, ed. Worthington Chauncey Ford (Boston: Houghton Mifflin Company, 1920), 123–24.

Emily Dickinson to Louise and Frances Norcross, late March 1862. *The Letters of Emily Dickinson*, ed. Thomas H. Johnson (Cambridge: The Belknap Press of Harvard University Press, 1986), 397–98. Reprinted by permission of the publishers from *The Letters of Emily Dickinson*, Thomas H. Johnson, ed., L835, Cambridge, Mass: The Belknap Press of Harvard University Press, Copyright © 1958, 1986, The President and Fellows of Harvard College; 1914, 1924, 1942 by Martha Dickinson Bianchi; 1952 by Alfred Leete Hampson; 1960 by Mary L. Hampson.

Frederick Douglass: The War and How to End It, March 25, 1862. *The Frederick Douglass Papers, Series One: Speeches, Debates, and Interviews*, volume III, ed. John W. Blassingame (New Haven: Yale University Press, 1985), 508–21. Copyright © 1985 by Yale University. Reprinted by permission.

Abraham Lincoln to George B. McClellan, April 9, 1862. *The Collected Works of Abraham Lincoln*, volume V, ed. Roy P. Basler (New Brunswick, N.J.: Rutgers University Press, 1953), 184–85. Copyright © 1953 by the Abraham Lincoln Association.

Ulysses S. Grant to Commanding Officer, Advance Forces, April 6, 1862; to Julia Dent Grant, April 8, 1862; to Captain Nathaniel H. McLean, April 9, 1862; to Jesse Root Grant, April 26, 1862; and to Elihu B. Washburne, May 14, 1862. *The Papers of Ulysses S. Grant*, vol. V, ed. John Y. Simon (Carbondale: Southern Illinois University Press, 1973), 18, 27, 32–36, 78–79, 119–20. Copyright © 1973 by the Ulysses S. Grant Association.

William T. Sherman to Ellen Ewing Sherman, April 11, 1862. *Sherman's*

Civil War: Selected Correspondence of William T. Sherman, 1860–1865, ed. Brooks D. Simpson and Jean V. Berlin (Chapel Hill: The University of North Carolina Press, 1999), 201–2. Copyright © 1999 by The University of North Carolina Press. Used by permission of the publisher.

George W. Dawson to Laura Amanda Dawson, April 26, 1862. "One Year at War: Letters of Capt. Geo. W. Dawson, C.S.A.," ed. H. Riley Bock, *Missouri Historical Review*, volume 73, number 2 (January 1979), 192–95. Copyright © 1979 by The State Historical Society of Missouri. Reprinted with permission of The State Historical Society of Missouri.

Herman Melville: Shiloh: A Requiem. Herman Melville, *Battle-Pieces and Aspects of the War* (New York: Harper & Brothers, 1866), 63.

Confederate Conscription Acts, April 16 and 21, 1862. *Public Laws of the Confederate States of America, Passed at the First Session of the First Congress; 1862. Carefully Collated with the Originals at Richmond*, ed. James M. Matthews (Richmond: R. M. Smith, 1862), 29–32, 51–52.

Abraham Lincoln: Message to Congress, April 16, 1862. *The Collected Works of Abraham Lincoln*, volume V, ed. Roy P. Basler (New Brunswick, N.J.: Rutgers University Press, 1953), 192. Copyright © 1953 by the Abraham Lincoln Association.

John Russell Bartlett: The "Brooklyn" at the Passage of the Forts. *Battles and Leaders of the Civil War*, volume II, ed. Robert Underwood Johnson and Clarence Clough Buel (New York: The Century Co., 1887), 56–69.

George Hamilton Perkins to Susan G. Perkins, April 27, 1862. *Letters of Capt. Geo. Hamilton Perkins* (Concord, N.H.: Ira C. Evans, 1886), 67–72.

Charles S. Wainwright: Diary, May 5, 1862. *A Diary of Battle: The Personal Journals of Colonel Charles S. Wainwright, 1861–1865*, ed. Allan Nevins (New York: Harcourt, Brace & World, Inc., 1962), 47–57. Copyright © 1962 by Allan Nevins.

John B. Jones: Diary, May 14–19, 1862. J. B. Jones, *A Rebel War Clerk's Diary at the Confederate States Capital*, volume I (Philadelphia: J. B. Lippincott & Co., 1866), 125–27.

Garland H. White to Edwin M. Stanton, May 7, 1862. *Freedom: A Documentary History of Emancipation, 1861–1867. Series II: The Black Military Experience*, ed. Ira Berlin (Cambridge and New York: Cambridge University Press, 1982), 82–83. Copyright © 1982, 1995 by Cambridge University Press.

Abraham Lincoln: Proclamation Revoking General Hunter's Emancipation Order, May 19, 1862. *The Collected Works of Abraham Lincoln*, volume V, ed. Roy P. Basler (New Brunswick, N.J.: Rutgers

University Press, 1953), 222–23. Copyright © 1953 by the Abraham Lincoln Association.

Richard Taylor: from *Destruction and Reconstruction*. Richard Taylor, *Destruction and Reconstruction: Personal Experiences of the Late War* (New York: D. Appleton and Company, 1879), 48–53.

Elizabeth Blair Lee to Samuel Phillips Lee, May 26, 1862. *Wartime Washington: The Civil War Letters of Elizabeth Blair Lee*, ed. Virginia Jeans Laas (Urbana: University of Illinois Press, 1991), 151–53. Copyright © 1991 by the Board of Trustees of the University of Illinois. Reprinted from the Blair and Lee Family Papers, Manuscripts Division, Department of Rare Books and Special Collections, Princeton University Library.

Thomas O. Moore: To the People of Louisiana, May 24, 1862. *The War of the Rebellion: A Compilation of the Official Records of the Union and Confederate Armies*, series I, volume XV (Washington, D.C.: Government Printing Office, 1886), 743–44.

Lord Palmerston to Charles Francis Adams, June 11, 1862; Benjamin Moran: Journal, June 25, 1862. Brooks Adams, "The Seizure of the Laird Rams," *Proceedings of the Massachusetts Historical Society*, volume XLV, October 1911–June 1912, 257; *The Journal of Benjamin Moran, 1857–1865*, volume II, ed. Sarah Agnes Wallace and Frances Elma Gillespie (Chicago: The University of Chicago Press, 1949), 1027–29. Copyright © 1949 by The University of Chicago.

Henry Ropes to William Ropes, June 3–4, 1862. Manuscript, Henry Ropes Letters, Boston Public Library.

Robert E. Lee to Jefferson Davis, June 5, 1862. *The Papers of Jefferson Davis*, volume VIII, ed. Lynda Lasswell Crist and Mary Seaton Dix (Baton Rouge: Louisiana State University Press, 1995), 225–26. Copyright © 1995 by Louisiana State University Press.

David Hunter to Edwin M. Stanton, June 23, 1862. *Freedom: A Documentary History of Emancipation, 1861–1867. Series II: The Black Military Experience*, ed. Ira Berlin (Cambridge and New York: Cambridge University Press, 1982), 50–53. Copyright © 1982, 1995 by Cambridge University Press.

Kate Stone: Journal, June 29–July 5, 1862. *Brokenburn: The Journal of Kate Stone, 1861–1868*, ed. John Q. Anderson (Baton Rouge: Louisiana State University Press, 1955), 125–29. Copyright © 1989 by Louisiana State University Press.

Edward Porter Alexander: from *Fighting for the Confederacy*. *Fighting for the Confederacy: The Personal Recollections of General Edward Porter Alexander*, ed. Gary W. Gallagher (Chapel Hill: The University of North Carolina Press, 1989), 94–104. Copyright © 1989 by The University of North Carolina Press.

Charles A. Page: from *Letters of a War Correspondent.* Charles A. Page, *Letters of a War Correspondent*, ed. James R. Gilmore (Boston: L. C. Page, 1899), 3–11.

George B. McClellan to Edwin M. Stanton, June 28, 1862. *The Civil War Papers of George B. McClellan: Selected Correspondence, 1860–1865*, ed. Stephen W. Sears (New York: Ticknor & Fields, 1989), 322–23. Copyright © 1989 by Stephen W. Sears. Reprinted with permission by Stephen W. Sears.

Abraham Lincoln to William H. Seward, June 28, 1862. *The Collected Works of Abraham Lincoln*, volume V, ed. Roy P. Basler (New Brunswick, N.J.: Rutgers University Press, 1953), 291–92. Copyright © 1953 by the Abraham Lincoln Association.

Charles B. Haydon: Journal, June 25–July 1, 1862. *For Country, Cause & Leader: The Civil War Journal of Charles B. Haydon*, ed. Stephen W. Sears (New York: Ticknor & Fields, 1993), 254–62. Copyright © 1993 by Stephen W. Sears. Reprinted with permission by Stephen W. Sears.

Asa D. Smith: Narrative of the Seven Days' Battles. "Asa Smith Leaves the War," ed. Bruce Catton, *American Heritage*, Volume XXII, Number 2 (February 1971), 56–59, 103–4. Copyright © 1971 by American Heritage Publishing Co., Inc. Reprinted by permission of *American Heritage* Magazine.

Judith W. McGuire: Diary, June 27–30, 1862. Judith W. McGuire, *Diary of a Southern Refugee, During the War*, third edition (Richmond, Va.: J. W. Randolph & English, Publishers, 1889), 122–26.

Sallie Brock: from *Richmond During the War.* Sallie Brock Putnam, *Richmond During the War: Four Years of Personal Observation* (New York: G. W. Carleton & Co., 1867), 150–52.

Sara Agnes Pryor: from *Reminiscences of Peace and War.* Sara Agnes Pryor, *Reminiscences of Peace and War* (New York: The Macmillan Company, 1904), 181–88.

Whitelaw Reid: General Hunter's Negro Soldiers, July 6, 1862. *A Radical View: The "Agate" Dispatches of Whitelaw Reid 1861–1865*, volume II, ed. James G. Smart (Memphis, Tennessee: Memphis State University Press), 71–74. Copyright © 1976 Memphis State University Press.

George B. McClellan to Abraham Lincoln, July 7, 1862. *The Civil War Papers of George B. McClellan: Selected Correspondence, 1860–1865*, ed. Stephen W. Sears (New York: Ticknor & Fields, 1989), 344–45. Copyright © 1989 by Stephen W. Sears. Reprinted with permission by Stephen W. Sears.

Thomas H. Dudley and J. Price Edwards: An Exchange, July 9, 10, and 16, 1862. *Correspondence Concerning Claims Against Great Britain,*

Transmitted to the Senate of the United States in Answer to the Resolutions of December 4 and 10, 1867, and of May 27, 1868, volume III (Washington: Philp & Solomons, Booksellers, 1869), 17–19.

Abraham Lincoln: Appeal to Border-State Representatives for Compensated Emancipation, July 12, 1862. *The Collected Works of Abraham Lincoln*, volume V, ed. Roy P. Basler (New Brunswick, N.J.: Rutgers University Press, 1953), 317–19. Copyright © 1953 by the Abraham Lincoln Association.

Confiscation Act, July 17, 1862. *The War of the Rebellion: A Compilation of the Official Records of the Union and Confederate Armies*, series III, volume II (Washington, D.C.: Government Printing Office, 1899), 275–77.

John Pope: Address to the Army of Virginia, July 14, 1862. *The War of the Rebellion: A Compilation of the Official Records of the Union and Confederate Armies*, series I, volume XII, part III (Washington, D.C.: Government Printing Office, 1885), 473–74.

John Pope: General Orders Nos. 5, 7, 11, July 18, 20, and 23, 1862. *The War of the Rebellion: a Compilation of the Official Records of the Union and Confederate Armies*, series I, volume XII, part II (Washington, D.C.: Government Printing Office, 1885), 50–52.

Fitz John Porter to Joseph C. G. Kennedy, July 17, 1862. Manuscript, Fitz-John Porter Papers, Manuscript Division, Library of Congress.

August Belmont to Thurlow Weed, July 20, 1862. Abraham Lincoln Papers at the Library of Congress. Transcribed and annotated by the Lincoln Studies Center, Knox College, Galesburg, Illinois.

Salmon P. Chase to Richard C. Parsons, July 20, 1862. *The Salmon P. Chase Papers: Volume III, Correspondence, 1858–March 1863*, ed. John Niven (Kent, Ohio: The Kent State University Press, 1996), 229–31. Copyright © 1996 by The Kent State University Press.

Salmon P. Chase: Journal, July 22, 1862. *The Salmon P. Chase Papers: Volume I, Journals, 1829–1872*, ed. John Niven (Kent, Ohio: The Kent State University Press, 1993), 350–52. Copyright © 1993 by The Kent State University Press.

Abraham Lincoln: First Draft of the Emancipation Proclamation, July 22, 1862. *The Collected Works of Abraham Lincoln*, volume V, ed. Roy P. Basler (New Brunswick, N.J.: Rutgers University Press, 1953), 336–37. Copyright © 1953 by the Abraham Lincoln Association.

Francis B. Carpenter: from *Six Months at the White House with Abraham Lincoln*. F. B. Carpenter, *Six Months at the White House with Abraham Lincoln: The Story of a Picture* (New York: Hurd and Houghton, 1866), 20–22.

Abraham Lincoln to Cuthbert Bullitt, July 28, 1862. *The Collected Works of Abraham Lincoln*, volume V, ed. Roy P. Basler (New

Brunswick, N.J.: Rutgers University Press, 1953), 344–46. Copyright © 1953 by the Abraham Lincoln Association.

Charles Sumner to John Bright, August 5, 1862. *The Selected Letters of Charles Sumner*, Volume II, ed. Beverly Wilson Palmer (Boston: Northeastern University Press, 1990), 121–22. Copyright © 1990 by Beverly Wilson Palmer; copyright © 1990 by University Press of New England, Lebanon, N.H. Reprinted with permission.

Henry W. Halleck to George B. McClellan, August 6, 1862. *The War of the Rebellion: A Compilation of the Official Records of the Union and Confederate Armies*, series I, volume XI, part I (Washington, D.C.: Government Printing Office, 1884), 82–84.

Memorial of a Committee of Citizens of Liberty County, Georgia, August 5, 1862. *The War of the Rebellion: A Compilation of the Official Records of the Union and Confederate Armies*, series IV, volume II (Washington, D.C.: Government Printing Office, 1900), 35–38.

Confederate War Department: General Orders No. 60, August 21, 1862. *The War of the Rebellion: A Compilation of the Official Records of the Union and Confederate Armies*, series III, volume V (Washington, D.C.: Government Printing Office, 1900), 712.

Abraham Lincoln: Address on Colonization, August 14, 1862. *The Collected Works of Abraham Lincoln*, volume V, ed. Roy P. Basler (New Brunswick, N.J.: Rutgers University Press, 1953), 370–75. Copyright © 1953 by the Abraham Lincoln Association.

Abraham Lincoln to Horace Greeley, August 22, 1862. *The Collected Works of Abraham Lincoln*, volume V, ed. Roy P. Basler (New Brunswick, N.J.: Rutgers University Press, 1953), 388–89. Copyright © 1953 by the Abraham Lincoln Association.

William T. Sherman to Thomas Hunton, August 24, 1862. *Sherman's Civil War: Selected Correspondence of William T. Sherman, 1860–1865*, ed. Brooks D. Simpson and Jean V. Berlin (Chapel Hill: The University of North Carolina Press, 1999), 284–86. Copyright © 1999 by The University of North Carolina Press. Used by permission of the publisher.

John Lothrop Motley to William H. Seward, August 26, 1862. Manuscript, William Henry Seward Papers, University of Rochester.

Harriet Jacobs to William Lloyd Garrison, September 5, 1862. *The Harriet Jacobs Family Papers*, Volume II, ed. Jean Fagan Yellin (Chapel Hill: The University of North Carolina Press, 2008), 399–407. Copyright © 2008 by Jean Fagan Yellin. Used by permission of The University of North Carolina Press.

Edward Porter Alexander: from *Fighting for the Confederacy*. *Fighting for the Confederacy: The Personal Recollections of General Edward Porter Alexander*, ed. Gary W. Gallagher (Chapel Hill: The University of North Carolina Press, 1989), 127–34. Copyright © 1989 The University of North Carolina Press.

Charles Francis Adams Jr. to Charles Francis Adams, August 27, 1862. *A Cycle of Adams Letters, 1861–1865*, volume I, ed. Worthington Chauncey Ford (Boston: Houghton Mifflin Company, 1920), 176–80.

John Hampden Chamberlayne to Martha Burwell Chamberlayne, September 6, 1862. *Ham Chamberlayne—Virginian: Letters and Papers of an Artillery Officer in the War for Southern Independence 1861–1865*, ed. C. G. Chamberlayne (Richmond, Virginia: Dietz Printing Co., 1932), 98–103. Copyright 1932 by C. G. Chamberlayne.

John Pope to Henry W. Halleck, September 1, 1862. *The War of the Rebellion: A Compilation of the Official Records of the Union and Confederate Armies*, series I, volume XII, part II (Washington, D.C.: Government Printing Office, 1884), 82–83.

Clara Barton to John Shaver, September 4, 1862. Manuscript, Clara Barton Papers, Henry E. Huntington Library, San Marino, California.

Gideon Welles: Diary, August 31–September 1, 1862. *Diary of Gideon Welles*, volume I, ed. Howard K. Beale (New York: W. W. Norton & Company, Inc., 1960), 93–104. Copyright © 1960 by W. W. Norton & Company, Inc.

John Hay: Diary, September 1, 1862. *Inside Lincoln's White House: The Complete Civil War Diary of John Hay*, ed. Michael Burlingame and John R. Turner Ettlinger (Carbondale and Edwardsville: Southern Illinois University Press, 1997), 36–38. Copyright © 1997 by the Board of Trustees, Southern Illinois University.

Edward Bates: Remonstrance and Notes on Cabinet Meeting, September 2, 1862. Manuscript, Abraham Lincoln Papers, Library of Congress.

Salmon P. Chase: Journal, September 2, 1862. *The Salmon P. Chase Papers: Volume I, Journals, 1829–1872*, ed. John Niven (Kent, Ohio: The Kent State University Press, 1993), 368–69. Copyright © 1993 by The Kent State University Press.

George B. McClellan to Mary Ellen McClellan, September 2, 1862. *The Civil War Papers of George B. McClellan: Selected Correspondence, 1860–1865*, ed. Stephen W. Sears (New York: Ticknor & Fields, 1989), 428. Copyright © 1989 by Stephen W. Sears. Reprinted with permission by Stephen W. Sears.

Robert E. Lee to Jefferson Davis, September 3, 1862. *The Papers of Jefferson Davis*, volume VIII, ed. Lynda Lasswell Crist and Mary Seaton Dix (Baton Rouge: Louisiana State University Press, 1995), 373–74. Copyright © 1995 by Louisiana State University Press.

George Templeton Strong: Diary, September 3–4, 1862. George

Templeton Strong, *Diary of the Civil War, 1860–1865*, ed. Allan Nevins (New York: The Macmillan Company, 1962), 251–53. Reprinted with permission of Scribner, a Division of Simon & Schuster, Inc., from *The Diary of George Templeton Strong* by Allan Nevins and Milton Halsey Thomas. Copyright © 1952 by Macmillan Publishing Company; copyright renewed © 1980 by Milton Halsey Thomas. All rights reserved.

William Thompson Lusk to Elizabeth Freeman Lusk, September 6, 1862. *War Letters of William Thompson Lusk*, ed. William C. Lusk (New York: [privately printed], 1911), 188–90.

Abraham Lincoln: Meditation on the Divine Will, c. early September 1862. *The Collected Works of Abraham Lincoln*, volume V, ed. Roy P. Basler (New Brunswick, N.J.: Rutgers University Press, 1953), 403–4. Copyright © 1953 by the Abraham Lincoln Association.

Lord Palmerston and Lord Russell: An Exchange, September 14, 17, and 23, 1862. Spencer Walpole, *The Life of Lord John Russell*, volume II (London: Longmans, Green, and Co., 1889), 349–50.

Robert E. Lee to Jefferson Davis, September 8, 1862. *The Wartime Papers of Robert E. Lee*, ed. Clifford Dowdey and Louis H. Manarin (Boston: Little, Brown, 1961), 301. Copyright © 1961 by Commonwealth of Virginia. Reprinted by permission of the National Archives.

Lewis H. Steiner: Diary, September 5–6, 1862. *Report of Lewis H. Steiner, M.D., Inspector of the Sanitary Commission, containing a diary kept during the rebel occupation of Frederick, Md., and an account of the operations of the U.S. Sanitary Commission during the campaign in Maryland, September 1862* (New York: Anson D. F. Randolph, 1862), 5–11.

James Richmond Boulware: Diary, September 4–14, 1862. Typed transcription, Library of Virginia, Richmond.

Alpheus S. Williams to George B. McClellan, September 13, 1862; Robert E. Lee: Special Orders No. 191, September 9, 1862. Manuscript, George B. McClellan Papers, Library of Congress.

George W. Smalley: Narrative of Antietam, September 17, 1862. *The Rebellion Record: A Diary of American Events, with Documents, Narratives, Illustrative Incidents, Poetry, etc.*, volume V, ed. Frank Moore (New York: G. P. Putnam, 1863), 466–72.

Rufus R. Dawes: from *Service with the Sixth Wisconsin Volunteers*. Rufus R. Dawes, *Service with the Sixth Wisconsin Volunteers* (Marietta, Ohio: E. R. Alderman & Sons, 1890), 87–92.

Alpheus S. Williams to Irene and Mary Williams, September 22, 1862. *From the Cannon's Mouth: The Civil War Letters of Alpheus S. Williams*, ed. Milo M. Quaife (Detroit: Wayne State University Press, 1959), 122–32.

David L. Thompson: With Burnside at Antietam. *Battles and Leaders of the Civil War*, volume II, ed. Robert Underwood Johnson and Clarence Clough Buel (New York: The Century Co., 1887), 660–62.

Samuel W. Fiske to the *Springfield Republican*, September 20, 1862. *Mr. Dunn Browne's Experiences in the Army: The Civil War Letters of Samuel W. Fiske*, ed. Stephen W. Sears (New York: Fordham University Press, 1998), 10–12. Copyright © 1998 by Stephen W. Sears. Reprinted with permission by Stephen W. Sears.

Clifton Johnson: from *Battleground Adventures*. Clifton Johnson, *Battleground Adventures: The Stories of Dwellers on the Scenes of Conflict in Some of the Most Notable Battles of the Civil War* (Boston: Houghton Mifflin Company, 1915), 118–24.

Mary Bedinger Mitchell: A Woman's Recollections of Antietam. *Battles and Leaders of the Civil War*, volume II, ed. Robert Underwood Johnson and Clarence Clough Buel (New York: The Century Co., 1887), 686–95.

George B. McClellan to Mary Ellen McClellan, September 20, 1862. *The Civil War Papers of George B. McClellan: Selected Correspondence, 1860–1865*, ed. Stephen W. Sears (New York: Ticknor & Fields, 1989), 473. Copyright © 1989 by Stephen W. Sears. Reprinted with permission by Stephen W. Sears.

Ephraim Anderson: from *Memoirs: Historical and Personal*. Ephraim McD. Anderson, *Memoirs: Historical and Personal; including the campaigns of the First Missouri Confederate Brigade* (St. Louis, Times Printing Co., 1868), 239–44.

Gideon Welles: Diary, September 22, 1862. *Diary of Gideon Welles*, volume I, ed. Howard K. Beale (New York: W. W. Norton & Company, Inc., 1960), 142–45. Copyright © 1960 by W. W. Norton & Company, Inc.

Abraham Lincoln: Preliminary Emancipation Proclamation, September 22, 1862; Proclamation Suspending the Writ of Habeas Corpus, September 24, 1862. *The Collected Works of Abraham Lincoln*, volume V, ed. Roy P. Basler (New Brunswick, N.J.: Rutgers University Press, 1953), 433–36, 436–37. Copyright © 1953 by the Abraham Lincoln Association.

L. A. Whitely to James Gordon Bennett, September 24, 1862. Manuscript, James Gordon Bennett Papers, Library of Congress.

George B. McClellan to William H. Aspinwall, September 26, 1862. *The Civil War Papers of George B. McClellan: Selected Correspondence, 1860–1865*, ed. Stephen W. Sears (New York: Ticknor & Fields, 1989), 482. Copyright © 1989 by Stephen W. Sears. Reprinted with permission by Stephen W. Sears.

Abraham Lincoln: Record of Dismissal of John J. Key, September 26–27, 1862. *The Collected Works of Abraham Lincoln*, volume V, ed. Roy P. Basler (New Brunswick, N.J.: Rutgers University Press, 1953), 442–43. Copyright © 1953 by the Abraham Lincoln Association.

Fitz John Porter to Manton Marble, September 30, 1862. Manuscript, Manton Marble Papers, Library of Congress.

Braxton Bragg: To the People of the Northwest, September 26, 1862. *The War of the Rebellion: A Compilation of the Official Records of the Union and Confederate Armies*, series I, volume LII, part II (Washington, D.C.: Government Printing Office, 1898), 363–65.

Ralph Waldo Emerson: The President's Proclamation, September 1862. *The Atlantic Monthly*, November 1862.

Frederick Douglass: Emancipation Proclaimed, October 1862. *The Life and Writings of Frederick Douglass*, ed. Philip S. Foner, volume III (New York: International Publishers Co. Inc., 1952), 273–77. Copyright © 1950. Reprinted from *The Life and Writings of Frederick Douglass*, published by International Publishers, copyright © 1950.

Appleton's Annual Cyclopedia: Debate in the Confederate Senate on Retaliation for the Emancipation Proclamation, September 29, October 1, 1862. *The American Annual Cyclopedia and Register of Important Events of the Year 1862*, volume II (New York: D. Appleton & Company, 1863), 268–70.

The Times of London: Editorial on the Emancipation Proclamation, October 7, 1862. *The Times*, October 7, 1862.

George B. McClellan to Abraham Lincoln, October 7, 1862. *The Civil War Papers of George B. McClellan: Selected Correspondence, 1860–1865*, ed. Stephen W. Sears (New York: Ticknor & Fields, 1989), 493–94. Copyright © 1989 by Stephen W. Sears. Reprinted with permission by Stephen W. Sears.

Oscar L. Jackson: from *The Colonel's Diary*. *The Colonel's Diary: Journals Kept Before and During the Civil War by the Late Colonel Oscar L. Jackson of New Castle, Pennsylvania, Sometime Commander of the 63rd O.V.I.*, ed. David P. Jackson (Sharon, Pennsylvania: 1922), 71–78.

Charles B. Labruzan: Journal, October 4, 1862. Marion Morrison, *A History of the Ninth Regiment Illinois Volunteer Infantry* (Monmouth, Illinois: John S. Clark, Printer, 1864), 40–43.

J. Montgomery Wright: Notes of a Staff-Officer at Perryville. *Battles and Leaders of the Civil War*, volume III, ed. Robert Underwood Johnson and Clarence Clough Buel (New York: The Century Co., 1888), 60–61.

Sam Watkins: from *"Co. Aytch," Maury Grays, First Tennessee Regiment*. Sam R. Watkins, *"Co. Aytch," Maury Grays, First Tennessee Regiment, or, A Side Show of the Big Show* (Nashville, Tennessee: Cumberland Presbyterian Publishing House, 1882), 50–57.

Abraham Lincoln to George B. McClellan, October 13, 1862. *The Collected Works of Abraham Lincoln*, volume V, ed. Roy P. Basler (New Brunswick, N.J.: Rutgers University Press, 1953), 460–61. Copyright © 1953 by the Abraham Lincoln Association.

Lord Palmerston to Lord Russell, October 2 and 22, 1862. *The Later Correspondence of Lord John Russell, 1840–1878*, ed. G. P. Gooch (London: Longmans, Green and Co., 1925), 326–28.

Charles Sumner to John Bright, October 28, 1862. *The Selected Letters of Charles Sumner*, volume II, ed. Beverly Wilson Palmer (Boston: Northeastern University Press, 1990), 127–28. Copyright © 1990 by Beverly Wilson Palmer; copyright 1990 © University Press of New England, Lebanon, N.H. Reprinted with permission.

Francis Preston Blair to Montgomery Blair, November 7, 1862. William Ernest Smith, *The Francis Preston Blair Family in Politics*, volume II (New York: The Macmillan Company, 1933), 144. Copyright © 1933 by The Macmillan Company.

George G. Meade to Margaret Meade, November 8, 1862. Manuscript, George Gordon Meade Papers, Historical Society of Pennsylvania, Philadelphia.

Orville H. Browning: Diary, November 29, 1862. *The Diary of Orville Hickman Browning*, volume I, ed. Theodore Calvin Pease and James G. Randall (Springfield: Illinois State Historical Library, 1925), 588–90. Copyright © 1927 by the Illinois State Historical Library.

Abraham Lincoln: Annual Message to Congress, December 1, 1862. *The Collected Works of Abraham Lincoln*, volume V, ed. Roy P. Basler (New Brunswick, N.J.: Rutgers University Press, 1953), 518–37. Copyright © 1953 by the Abraham Lincoln Association.

Edward Porter Alexander: from *Fighting for the Confederacy*. *Fighting for the Confederacy: The Personal Recollections of General Edward Porter Alexander*, ed. Gary W. Gallagher (Chapel Hill: The University of North Carolina Press, 1989), 166–79. Copyright © 1989 by The University of North Carolina Press.

Samuel W. Fiske to the *Springfield Republican*, December 15 and 17, 1862. *Mr. Dunn Browne's Experiences in the Army: The Civil War Letters of Samuel W. Fiske*, ed. Stephen W. Sears (New York: Fordham University Press, 1998), 49–51. Copyright © 1998 by Stephen W. Sears. Reprinted with permission by Stephen W. Sears.

Henry Livermore Abbott to Josiah Gardner Abbott, December 14, 1862, and to George Perry, December 17, 1862. Manuscripts, Abbott Family Civil War Letters (MS Am 800.26). Houghton Library, Harvard University, series III, folder 17. Reprinted by permission of the Houghton Library, Harvard University, MS Am 800.26.

Clifton Johnson: from *Battleground Adventures*. Clifton Johnson, *Battleground Adventures: The Stories of Dwellers on the Scenes of Con-*

flict in Some of the Most Notable Battles of the Civil War (Boston: Houghton Mifflin Company, 1915), 143–49.
Walt Whitman: from *Specimen Days. Walt Whitman: Complete Poetry and Collected Prose*, ed. Justin Kaplan (New York: The Library of America, 1982), 712–13.
Louisa May Alcott: from *Hospital Sketches*. L. M. Alcott, *Hospital Sketches* (Boston: James Redpath, 1863), 31–45.
Orville H. Browning: Diary, December 18, 1862. *The Diary of Orville Hickman Browning*, volume I, ed. Theodore Calvin Pease and James G. Randall (Springfield: Illinois State Historical Library, 1925), 599–601. Copyright © 1927 by the Illinois State Historical Library.
Gideon Welles: Diary, December 19–20, 1862. *Diary of Gideon Welles*, volume I, ed. Howard K. Beale (New York: W. W. Norton & Company, Inc., 1960), 194–202. Copyright © 1960 by W. W. Norton & Company, Inc.
Harper's Weekly: The Reverse at Fredericksburg, December 27, 1862. *Harper's Weekly*, December 27, 1862.
George Templeton Strong: Diary, December 27, 1862. George Templeton Strong, *Diary of the Civil War, 1860–1865*, ed. Allan Nevins (New York: The Macmillan Company, 1962), 282–84. Reprinted with permission of Scribner, a Division of Simon & Schuster, Inc., from *The Diary of George Templeton Strong* by Allan Nevins and Milton Halsey Thomas. Copyright © 1952 by Macmillan Publishing Company; copyright renewed © 1980 by Milton Halsey Thomas. All rights reserved.
Fitz John Porter to Samuel L. M. Barlow, December 29, 1862. Manuscript, Samuel L. M. Barlow Papers, Henry E. Huntington Library, San Marino, California.
Cyrus F. Boyd: Diary, December 22–25, 1862. *The Civil War Diary of Cyrus F. Boyd, Fifteenth Iowa Infantry 1861–1863*, ed. Mildred Throne (Baton Rouge: Louisiana State University Press, 1998), 96–99. Copyright © 1953 by the State Historical Society of Iowa.
Jefferson Davis: Address to the Mississippi Legislature, December 26, 1862. *The Papers of Jefferson Davis*, volume VIII, ed. Lynda Lasswell Crist and Mary Seaton Dix (Baton Rouge: Louisiana State University Press, 1995), 565–79. Copyright © 1995 by Louisiana State University Press.
William T. Sherman to John Sherman, January 6, 1863. *Sherman's Civil War: Selected Correspondence of William T. Sherman, 1860–1865*, ed. Brooks D. Simpson and Jean V. Berlin (Chapel Hill: The University of North Carolina Press, 1999), 351–53. Copyright © 1999 by The University of North Carolina Press. Used by permission of the publisher.
Samuel Sawyer et al. to Samuel R. Curtis, December 29, 1862. *Free at*

Last: A Documentary History of Slavery, Freedom, and the Civil War, ed. Ira Berlin, Barbara J. Fields, Steven F. Miller, Joseph P. Reidy, and Leslie S. Rowland (New York: The New Press, 1992), 180–82. Copyright © 1992 by The New Press. Reprinted by permission of The New Press.

Ira S. Owens: from *Greene County in the War*. Ira S. Owens, *Greene County in the War, Being a History of the Seventy Fourth regiment, with sketches of the Twelfth, Ninety Fourth, One Hundred and Tenth, Forty Fourth, and One Hundred and Fifty Fourth Regiments and the Tenth Ohio Battery, embracing anecdotes, incidents and narratives of the camp, march and battlefield, and the author's experiences while in the army* (Xenia, Ohio: Torchlight Job Rooms, 1872), 30–35.

Lot D. Young: from *Reminiscences of a Soldier of the Orphan Brigade*. L. D. Young, *Reminiscences of a Soldier of the Orphan Brigade* (Louisville, Kentucky: Courier-Journal Job Printing Company, 1918), 45–51.

Ambrose E. Burnside to Abraham Lincoln, January 1, 1863. *The War of the Rebellion: A Compilation of the Official Records of the Union and Confederate Armies*, series I, volume XXI (Washington, D.C.: Government Printing Office, 1888), 941–42.

Abraham Lincoln to Henry W. Halleck, January 1, 1863. *The Collected Works of Abraham Lincoln*, volume VI, ed. Roy P. Basler (New Brunswick, N.J.: Rutgers University Press, 1953), 31. Copyright © 1953 by the Abraham Lincoln Association.

Abraham Lincoln: Final Emancipation Proclamation, January 1, 1863. *The Collected Works of Abraham Lincoln*, volume VI, ed. Roy P. Basler (New Brunswick, N.J.: Rutgers University Press, 1953), 28–30. Copyright © 1953 by the Abraham Lincoln Association.

Benjamin Rush Plumly to Abraham Lincoln, January 1, 1863. Manuscript, Abraham Lincoln Papers, Library of Congress.

Abraham Lincoln to John A. McClernand, January 8, 1863. *The Collected Works of Abraham Lincoln*, volume VI, ed. Roy P. Basler (New Brunswick, N.J.: Rutgers University Press, 1953), 48–49. Copyright © 1953 by the Abraham Lincoln Association.

This volume presents the texts of the printings and manuscripts chosen as sources here but does not attempt to reproduce features of their typographic design or physical layout. The texts are printed without alteration except for the changes previously discussed and for the correction of typographical errors. Spelling, punctuation, and capitalization are often expressive features, and they are not altered, even when inconsistent or irregular. The following is a list of typographical errors corrected, cited by page and line number: 8.30–31, Chandler Wade,; 31.40, Mondy; 86.3, wants; 105.33, Seigel's; 115.5, silenced; 116.11, killed; 161.19, danger; 169.17, We are; 170.14, the the next; 286.20, the he; 303.22, heart.; 305.11, Steven's; 335.23, us.?; 359.19–20, Government from; 363.4, P. W.; 406.10, description; 426.25, holding"; 455.8, rick; 526.28, we we would; 567.27, warefare; 568.20, onthe; 584.32, Casey, and; 594.3, solder; 615.28, McLellan; 616.10, Hallack; 680.22, comfortable There; 684.2, replied Some; 684.17, said Why; 708.33, to even; 720.34, he he; 735.1, pointing; 735.2, and; 737.1, lay,.

Notes

In the notes below, the reference numbers denote page and line of this volume (the line count includes headings, but not rule lines). No note is made for material included in the eleventh edition of *Merriam-Webster's Collegiate Dictionary*. Biblical references are keyed to the King James Version. Quotations from Shakespeare are keyed to *The Riverside Shakespeare*, ed. G. Blakemore Evans (Boston: Houghton Mifflin, 1974). Footnotes and bracketed editorial notes within the text were in the originals. For further historical and biographical background, references to other studies, and more detailed maps, see James McPherson, *Battle Cry of Freedom: The Civil War Era* (New York: Oxford University Press, 1988); *Encyclopedia of the American Civil War: A Political, Social, and Military History*, edited by David S. Heidler and Jeanne T. Heidler (New York: W. W. Norton, 2002); and Aaron Sheehan-Dean, *Concise Historical Atlas of the U.S. Civil War* (New York: Oxford University Press, 2008).

5.35 *"O hasten it in mercy, gracious Heaven!"*] Cf. "Universal Emancipation," a poem by William Lloyd Garrison that appeared in the first number of his newspaper *The Liberator*, January 1, 1831: "Oh! hasten it, *in mercy*, righteous Heaven!"

8.21–24 the Road . . . Lander] During a raid on the Baltimore and Ohio Railroad, Confederate troops led by Major General Thomas J. (Stonewall) Jackson shelled Hancock, Maryland, on the upper Potomac River, January 5–6, 1862, before withdrawing. Brigadier General Frederick W. Lander (1821–1862) commanded the troops defending Hancock; Major General Nathaniel P. Banks (1816–1894) commanded a division in the Army of the Potomac.

8.30–31 Chandler Wade . . . Covode] Zachariah Chandler (1813–1879) was a Republican senator from Michigan, 1857–75, and secretary of the interior, 1875–77; Benjamin F. Wade (1800–1878) was a Whig and then a Republican senator from Ohio, 1851–69, and chairman of the Joint Committee on the Conduct of the War, 1861–65; Andrew Johnson (1808–1875) was a Democratic senator from Tennessee, 1857–62, military governor of Tennessee, 1862–64, vice president of the United States, 1864–65, and president, 1865–69; Moses Odell (1818–1866) was a Democratic congressman from New York, 1861–65; John Covode (1808–1871) was a Republican congressman from Pennsylvania, 1855–63 and 1867–71.

11.9 Patterson] Robert Patterson (1792–1881) commanded the Union forces in the Shenandoah Valley in July 1861. His failure to engage General Joseph E. Johnston (1807–1891) allowed Johnston to send most of his troops from Winchester to Manassas Junction, Virginia, in time for them to fight at First Bull Run.

20.16   Caudine Forks]   A valley in southern Italy where the Samnites trapped a Roman army in 321 B.C.E. and forced it to surrender its arms and then march under a yoke of crossed spears.

20.28   Sherman]   Brigadier General Thomas W. Sherman (1813–1879) commanded the Union troops that captured Port Royal, South Carolina, in November 1861.

25.24   Sanitary Commission]   The United States Sanitary Commission, founded in June 1861, was a civilian organization dedicated to improving conditions in Union army camps and caring for sick and wounded soldiers. It was based on the British Sanitary Commission in the Crimean War.

26.9   My dear minister]   James Freeman Clarke (1810–1888), Unitarian minister of the Church of the Disciples in Boston.

29.11   Fort Lafayette]   The fortress, built on an island off Brooklyn at the entrance to New York harbor, was used as a military prison during the Civil War.

31.3   Gen. BANKS]   See note 8.21–24.

32.24   veil of Isis]   The Greek historian Plutarch wrote that the shrine of Isis at Sais in Egypt bore the inscription: "I am all that hath been, and is, and shall be; and my veil no mortal has hitherto raised."

36.10   General John A. McClernand]   Brigadier General John A. McClernand (1812–1900) commanded one of the three Union divisions investing Fort Donelson. McClernand had served in Congress as a Democrat from Illinois, 1843–51 and 1859–61.

37.11–12   Colonel Morgan L. Smith]   Smith (1822–1874) commanded a brigade in the division of Brigadier General Charles F. Smith.

37.22   Cruft's return]   Colonel Charles Cruft (1826–1883) commanded a brigade in Wallace's division.

37.26   General Charles F. Smith]   Brigadier General Charles F. Smith (1807–1862) commanded one of Grant's three divisions investing Fort Donelson.

37.32   Ross]   Lieutenant James R. Ross (1841–1900).

38.2   Colonel Ross]   Colonel Leonard F. Ross (1823–1901), who commanded one of the brigades in McClernand's division.

39.8–9 Colonel Morrison's misassault of the 14th] Colonel William R. Morrison (1824–1909), commanding a brigade in McClernand's division, was wounded in a failed attack on the Fort Donelson lines on February 14.

39.19 the Lindell] A large hotel in St. Louis, Missouri.

39.40 McGinnis] Colonel George F. McGinnis (1826–1910) commanded the 11th Indiana Infantry, Morgan L. Smith's brigade, Charles F. Smith's division.

42.22 Kneffler] Captain Fred Knefler (1833–1901), Wallace's assistant adjutant general.

42.31 Colonel Webster] Colonel Joseph D. Webster (1811–1876), Grant's chief of staff and chief engineer.

49.40 file closers] Soldiers assigned to prevent straggling or fleeing during an advance.

50.38 Gen. Floyd] Brigadier General John B. Floyd (1806–1863) commanded the Confederate garrison at Fort Donelson from February 13 until the early hours of February 16, 1862, when he escaped on a riverboat, leaving Brigadier General Simon Bolivar Buckner to surrender the fort to Grant.

54.15 Rawlins, and McPherson] Captain John A. Rawlins (1831–1869) and Lieutenant Colonel James B. McPherson (1828–1864) of Grant's staff.

55.15 *avant-courrier*] Herald, scout, advance guard.

60.35 Columbiad] A heavy smoothbore cannon.

65.9 Commander Stembel] Commander Roger N. Stembel (1810–1900), captain of the gunboat *Lexington*.

65.26 the renowned *Arkansas*] An ironclad ram laid down at Memphis in October 1861 and completed at Yazoo City, Mississippi, in July 1862. The *Carondelet* was badly damaged in a battle with the *Arkansas* on the Yazoo River on July 15, 1862. After running past the Union fleet at Vicksburg, the *Arkansas* went downriver to Baton Rouge, Louisiana, where it was scuttled on August 6, 1862, after its engines broke down.

68.28 "spliced the main brace."] Received a ration of liquor.

73.4 Colonel Ellet's] A civil engineer known for his work on canals, railroads, and suspension bridges, Charles Ellet (1810–1862) was authorized by Secretary of War Edwin M. Stanton in March 1862 to convert nine Ohio River steamboats into unarmed rams.

75.15–16 Colonel Ellet . . . in the leg] Ellet died from his wounds on June 21, 1862.

75.31 General Jeff. Thompson] Merriwether Jeff Thompson (1826–1876) led Confederate partisans in southeastern Missouri and northeastern Arkansas.

78.20 at Pensacola] The steam frigate U.S.S. *Niagara* and steam sloop U.S.S. *Richmond* bombarded Pensacola, November 22–23, 1861.

80.19 Gen. Huger] Major General Benjamin Huger (1805–1877), the Confederate commander at Norfolk, Virginia.

80.21 Gen. Wise] Brigadier General Henry A. Wise (1806–1876), a former governor of Virginia, 1856–60, and prominent advocate of secession in 1861.

80.29 Capt. O. Jennings Wise] Wise (1831–1862), son of Henry Wise and coeditor of the *Richmond Enquirer*, was mortally wounded at Roanoke Island on February 8, 1862.

80.30 A thousand of the enemy fell] Union casualties in the battle totaled 264 men killed, wounded, or missing.

81.12 President Tyler] John Tyler (1790–1862), president of the United States, 1841–1845, had died on January 18.

81.13 Mr. Hunter] Robert M. T. Hunter (1809–1887) served as the Confederate secretary of state, 1861–62, and in the Confederate Senate, 1862–65. Hunter had earlier been a congressman from Virginia, 1837–43 and 1845–47, and a U.S. senator, 1847–61.

82.6 Benjamin] Judah P. Benjamin (1811–1884) served as the Confederate secretary of war, September 1861–March 1862, and as secretary of state from March 1862 until the end of the war. Benjamin had earlier been a U.S. senator from Louisiana, 1853–61.

82.22 Mr. Hunter has resigned] Hunter resigned as secretary of state to serve in the Confederate Congress.

83.17 the old general in command] Brigadier General John H. Winder (1800–1865), the Confederate provost marshal.

89.25–26 Professor Lowe . . . usual daily balloon reconnaissance] Thaddeus Sobieski Constantine Lowe (1832–1913) was chief of the Union army balloon corps, October 1861–May 1863. His balloon *Constitution* was posted at Budd's Ferry, Maryland, on the lower Potomac.

90.12–13 Colonel Graham . . . inroad into Virginia.] A force of four hundred men led by Colonel Charles K. Graham (1824–1889) of the 74th New York Infantry crossed the Potomac from Maryland on November 9, 1861, and carried out a successful reconnaissance of Mathias Point in Virginia. The Union troops returned with between thirty and forty escaped slaves.

93.34–94.1 Bancroft's History . . . Hardee's Tactics] George Bancroft (1800–1891), *History of the United States* (10 vols., 1834–74; eight volumes had appeared by 1862); William J. Hardee (1815–1873), *Rifle and Light Infantry Tactics* (1855).

94.31 Secretary's order to the press] Secretary of War Edwin M. Stanton issued an order on February 26, 1862, forbidding newspapers that published unauthorized military news from using the telegraph or distributing their publications by railroad.

94.39 Mason, Slidell, Yancey] James M. Mason (1798–1871), Confederate envoy to Great Britain, 1861–1865; John Slidell (1793–1871), Confederate envoy to France, 1861–65; William Lowndes Yancey (1814–1863), Confederate diplomatic commissioner in Britain and France, 1861–62, and a prominent advocate of secession during the 1850s.

95.39 correspondent of the London Times] William Howard Russell (1820–1907) reported on the secession crisis and the Civil War from March 1861 to April 1862, when he returned to England. His description of "the disgraceful conduct" of the Union troops at First Bull Run was denounced in the Northern press.

98.1–2 cabbage . . . Minister to Russia immediately."] Secretary of War Simon Cameron (1799–1889) resigned in January 1862 amid charges of widespread corruption in the War Department and was appointed minister to Russia by President Lincoln.

100.8–10 General Price . . . Springfield, or Oakhill] Major General Sterling Price (1809–1867) led troops of the pro-secession Missouri State Guard in the Confederate victory at Wilson's Creek (also called Oak Hill) in Missouri on August 10, 1861.

100.12 General McCulloch] Brigadier General Benjamin McCulloch (1811–1862) was the Confederate commander at Wilson's Creek.

100.14 Generals Curtis and Siegel] Brigadier General Samuel R. Curtis (1805–1866) and Brigadier General Franz Sigel (1824–1902).

102.1–2 quake as . . . Cæsar did] See *Julius Caesar*, I.ii.119–28.

104.2 *chasse*] Chaser.

108.14 Pelham] John Pelham (1838–1863) was an artillery officer in the Army of Northern Virginia who became known as "the gallant Pelham" after he was praised by Robert E. Lee for his courage at the battle of Fredericksburg. He was killed in action at Kelly's Ford, Virginia, on March 17, 1863.

108.25 Colonel Rives] Colonel Benjamin A. Rives (1822–1862) commanded the 3rd Missouri Infantry in the 1st Brigade of the Missouri State Guard.

110.4 *James A. McDougall*] McDougall (1817–1867) was a Democratic senator from California, 1861–67.

114.30–31 torpedoes] Floating mines.

NOTES 821

116.31–32   Flag-Officer . . . his brother] Franklin Buchanan (1800–1874), the senior officer on board the *Virginia*, was commander of the Chesapeake Bay Squadron. McKean Buchanan (1798–1871) served as paymaster of the U.S.S. *Congress*.

117.29   the Ericsson] The *Monitor* was designed and built by the Swedish-American engineer John Ericsson (1803–1889).

121.29–31   a deputation . . . splendid whip.] Lincoln met with the delegation on March 13, 1862.

121.33   Major Ben Perley Poore] Journalist and writer Benjamin Perley Poore (1820–1887), Washington correspondent of the *Boston Journal*, had served briefly as a major with the 6th Massachusetts Regiment in 1861.

122.17   in the passage-way; and in lounged] In the *Atlantic Monthly* this appeared as "in the passage-way, etc., etc.*" The text that follows from 122.17 ("and in lounged . . .") to 124.38 (". . . immaculate page of the Atlantic") was deleted, and the footnote that appears on 125.33–38 was moved forward to where the passage had been removed.

124.27   he accepted the whip . . . not punishment.] As reported in *The New York Times* on March 22, 1862, Lincoln told the delegation: "let us not think only of whipping rebels, or of those who seem to think only of whipping negroes, but of those pleasant days which it is to be hoped are in store for us, when, seated behind a good pair of horses, we can crack our whips and drive through a peaceful, happy, and prosperous land."

125.33–34   *We hesitated to . . . have been written] In the *Atlantic Monthly* this read: "We are compelled to omit two or three pages, in which the author describes the interview, and gives his idea of the personal appearance and deportment of the President. The sketch appears to have been written . . ."

127.3–4   tavern in which Colonel Ellsworth was killed] During the Union occupation of Alexandria on May 24, 1861, Colonel Elmer Ellsworth (1837–1861), the commander of the 11th New York Infantry, took down a Confederate flag that was flying from the roof of the Marshall House hotel. On his way down the stairs Ellsworth was confronted by James Jackson, the hotel's proprietor, who killed him with a shotgun. Jackson was then shot and bayoneted by a corporal in Ellsworth's regiment. The incident was widely publicized, and both Ellsworth and Jackson were considered martyrs by their respective sides in the conflict.

131.1   report of a Congressional committee] On April 30, 1862, the Joint Committee on the Conduct of the War issued a report on the Confederate treatment of the graves of Union soldiers killed at First Bull Run. It contained the widely reported allegation that a New Orleans artilleryman had taken the skull of a Union soldier for use as a drinking cup on his wedding day.

133.31–36   *Apparently with . . . out the passage.] This footnote was omitted in the *Atlantic Monthly*.

137.1   Commodore Smith] Commodore Joseph Smith (1790–1877), a veteran of the War of 1812, was the father of Lieutenant Joseph Bryant Smith (1826–1862), acting commander of the *Congress*, who was killed on March 8, 1862, during the battle with the *Virginia*.

137.5   the gallant Morris] Lieutenant George U. Morris (1830–1875), executive officer of *Cumberland*, commanded the ship in its fight with the *Virginia*; when called upon to surrender, he replied, "Never! I'll sink alongside!"

137.10   Old Ironsides] The frigate *Constitution*, famous for its service in the War of 1812.

137.27   the brave Worden] Lieutenant John L. Worden (1818–1875) commanded the *Monitor* during its battle with the *Virginia* until he was temporarily blinded by a shell burst.

141.25   In December] On November 8, 1861, Captain Charles Wilkes of the U.S.S. *San Jacinto* boarded the British mail packet *Trent* off Cuba and seized the Confederate envoys James M. Mason and John Slidell (see note 94.39). The incident caused a major diplomatic crisis that continued until the Lincoln administration decided on December 26 to release the envoys in order to avoid a possible war with Great Britain.

142.3–4   *Louise and Frances Norcross*] Louise (1842–1919) and Frances Norcross (1847–1896) were Emily Dickinson's cousins, the daughters of her mother's sister Lavinia Norcross (1812–1860).

142.5   Late March 1862] The funeral of Frazar Stearns (1840–1862) was held on March 22, 1862.

142.22   Professor Clark] Lieutenant Colonel William S. Clark (1826–1886) of the 21st Massachusetts Infantry was professor of chemistry, botany, and zoology at Amherst College, 1852–67, and president of Massachusetts Agricultural College (now University of Massachusetts, Amherst), 1867–79.

142.30   his father.] William A. Stearns (1805–1876), president of Amherst College, 1854–76.

143.9   Austin] William Austin Dickinson (1829–1895), Emily Dickinson's brother.

146.23   a shot at one of our ships] On January 9, 1861, South Carolina batteries opened fire on *Star of the West*, a chartered civilian steamer carrying reinforcements and supplies to Fort Sumter in Charleston Harbor. The ship withdrew without casualties, and the Fort Sumter garrison did not return fire.

NOTES   823

146.39–40   blood thirsty mob . . . Baltimore treason.] A secessionist mob attacked the 6th Massachusetts Regiment as it changed trains in Baltimore on its way to Washington, D.C., on April 19, 1861. Four soldiers and a dozen Baltimore civilians were killed in the fighting, the first fatal casualties of the war.

147.30–31   marshalling the savage Indian . . . your sons] In 1861 the Confederacy formed alliances with the Cherokee, Creek, Choctaw, Chickasaw, and Seminole tribes living in Indian Territory (later Oklahoma), and about eight hundred Cherokees fought with the Confederate army at Elkhorn Tavern (Pea Ridge), Arkansas, March 7–8, 1862. After the battle the Northern press reported that "many of the Federal dead" at Pea Ridge had been scalped and mutilated.

148.2   Floyd . . . Cobb]   John B. Floyd (1806–1863) served as governor of Virginia, 1848–52, before becoming secretary of war in the Buchanan administration in 1857. He resigned on December 29, 1860, after being implicated in a financial scandal, and later served as a Confederate general (see note 50.38). Floyd was accused of treason in the Northern press for transferring 115,000 muskets and rifles from Northern to Southern arsenals in the spring of 1860, and for ordering the shipment of 124 large cannon from Pittsburgh to Mississippi and Texas on December 20, 1860. (The order to transfer the artillery was canceled after his resignation.) Howell Cobb (1815–1868) was a congressman from Georgia, 1843–51 and 1855–57, and its governor, 1851–53. He served as secretary of the treasury in the Buchanan administration from 1857 until his resignation on December 10, 1860, and was subsequently accused of having deliberately undermined the national finances. Cobb supported secession in 1861 and served as a Confederate general, 1862–65.

148.5   the rod of Moses it swallowed all others]   See the description of Aaron's rod in Exodus 7:10–12.

148.26   General McClellan in his recent address]   See pp. 138–39 in this volume.

149.19–20   General Sherman . . . erring rebels]   Following the occupation of Port Royal, Brigadier General Thomas W. Sherman issued a proclamation addressed to "the People of South Carolina" on November 8, 1861, in which he declared that the Union forces "have come amongst you with no feelings of personal animosity; no desire to harm your citizens, destroy your property, or interfere with any of your lawful rights or your social and local institutions, beyond what the causes herein briefly alluded to may render unavoidable."

151.4–5   Syracuse . . . rescue of Jerry]   Jerry McHenry, a fugitive slave from Missouri, was arrested in Syracuse on October 1, 1851. A group of about thirty abolitionists who were attending a Liberty Party convention broke into the police station where he was being held and helped him flee to Canada.

151.7–8 Dr. Cheever . . . William Goodell] George B. Cheever (1807–1890), a Congregationalist minister who helped found the Church Anti-Slavery Society; Gerrit Smith (1797–1874), a philanthropist and social reformer who helped found the Liberty Party in 1840; William Goodell (1792–1878), a social reformer active in the Liberty Party.

151.15–16 slave catching . . . forbidden] A new article of war passed by Congress and signed by President Lincoln on March 13, 1862, prohibited Union officers from returning fugitive slaves.

151.32 that message] Lincoln's message to Congress of March 6, 1862; see pp. 110–12 in this volume.

152.8–9 appointment of John C. Frémont] On March 11, 1862, Major General John C. Frémont (1813–1880) was appointed commander of the Mountain Department, covering western Virginia and eastern Tennessee and Kentucky.

152.15–16 Frémont's proclamation . . . removed] Frémont issued a proclamation on August 30, 1861, declaring martial law in Missouri and emancipating the slaves of secessionists. Lincoln revoked the emancipation provision on September 11 and removed Frémont from command in Missouri on November 2.

152.18 Jessie] Jessie Benton Frémont (1824–1902).

155.18 Blencker's Division] In response to pressure from Radical Republican supporters of Frémont, Lincoln had transferred the division commanded by Brigadier General Louis Blenker (1812–1863) from McClellan's command to Frémont's Mountain Department on March 31, 1862.

155.24–25 Gen. Hooker's old position] The division commanded by Brigadier General Joseph Hooker (1814–1879) had been posted in southern Maryland along the lower Potomac.

156.18 Gen. Wool's command] Brigadier General John E. Wool (1789–1869) commanded the Department of Virginia with headquarters at Fort Monroe.

158.15 162 regiments] There were seventy-six Confederate regiments at Shiloh.

158.16–17 Beaurigard . . . Breckenridge] General Pierre G. T. Beauregard (1818–1893) assumed command of the Confederate army after General Albert Sidney Johnston (1803–1862) was killed on the afternoon of April 6. Major General Braxton Bragg (1817–1876) and Brigadier General John C. Breckinridge (1821–1875) each commanded a corps in the battle. Breckinridge had served as vice president of the United States, 1857–61, and was the Southern Democratic candidate for president in 1860.

158.19 Bragg wounded.] Bragg was not wounded at Shiloh.

159.4   A A GENL]   Assistant adjutant general.

159.24   Parrott guns]   Muzzle-loading rifled cannon, named after the New York ordnance manufacturer Robert R. Parrott (1804–1877).

161.4–5   Genl W H L Wallace . . . wounded.]   Brigadier General W. H. L. Wallace (1821–1862) died on April 10, 1862.

162.9–10   Genl Beaurigard . . . Correspondence]   Beauregard wrote to Grant on April 8, 1862, asking permission to send a mounted party to Shiloh to bury the Confederate dead. Grant replied on April 9 that the warm weather had caused him to have the dead of both sides buried immediately.

162.32   Savannah]   Grant was at Savannah, Tennessee, nine miles downriver from Pittsburg Landing, when the Confederates attacked on April 6.

163.6   E. B. WASHBURN]   Elihu B. Washburne (1816–1887) was a Whig, and then Republican, congressman from Illinois, 1853–69. He served as U.S. minister to France, 1869–77.

166.28   I had at Muldrough hill.]   Sherman occupied Muldraugh Hill, about forty miles south of Louisville, in September 1861.

166.32   Johns Brigade]   A brigade of Ohio troops recruited in the fall of 1861 by Sherman's brother, Ohio Republican senator John Sherman (1823–1900).

167.10   Gen. Greene]   Major General Nathanael Greene (1742–1786), a commander in the Continental Army during the Revolutionary War.

169.14   C.]   Canister.

178.34   femes-covert]   Married women.

180.15   Thomas T. Craven]   Craven (1808–1887) entered the U.S. Navy in 1822 and was promoted to captain in 1861.

181.10–11   Head of the Passes]   The point where the main stem of the Mississippi River divides into three separate channels, or passes: Southwest Pass, South Pass, and Pass a l'Outre ("Pass Beyond").

182.28   Admiral Porter . . . in this work]   David Dixon Porter (1813–1891) contributed "The Opening of the Lower Mississippi" to volume II of *Battles and Leaders of the Civil War* (1887). He was the son of naval officer David Porter (1780–1843), and David G. Farragut (1801–1870) was his adopted brother.

187.9   sponger]   A member of a gun crew who cleaned out the bore of the cannon between firings with a pole-mounted sponge.

191.24   arrived at quarantine]   The quarantine station upriver from Forts Jackson and St. Philip.

197.27   General Lovell]   Major General Mansfield Lovell (1822–1884) commanded the Confederate troops defending New Orleans.

198.1   Pierre Soule]   Pierre Soulé (1801–1870) was the Confederate provost marshal in New Orleans. He had previously served as a U.S. senator, 1849–53, and as U.S. minister to Spain, 1853–55.

199.11–13   Bramhall and Smith . . . Osborn and Webber]   Captain Walter M. Bramhall of the 6th New York Artillery, Captain James E. Smith of the 4th New York Artillery, Captain Thomas W. Osborn of the 1st New York Artillery, and Captain Charles H. Webber of the 1st U.S. Artillery were Wainwright's battery commanders.

203.31   Sumner]   Brigadier General Edwin V. Sumner (1797–1863) was the Union commander at Williamsburg.

203.39–40   Hancock's attack. . . . Smith's division]   Brigadier General Winfield Scott Hancock (1824–1886) attacked on the right of the Union line. He commanded a brigade in the division led by Brigadier General William F. Smith (1824–1903).

204.5   our regiment]   The 1st New York Light Artillery.

204.12   Taylor's brigade]   Colonel Nelson Taylor (1821–1894) commanded the Second Brigade in Hooker's division.

204.15   Dwight]   Colonel William Dwight (1831–1888) commanded the 70th New York Infantry in Taylor's brigade.

205.22–23   Colonel Starr . . . his regiment]   Samuel H. Starr (1810–1891) commanded the 5th New Jersey Infantry.

205.37   Farnum]   Lieutenant Colonel John E. Farnum (1824–1870) was second in command of the 70th New York Infantry.

206.1–2   General Heintzelman]   Brigadier General Samuel P. Heintzelman (1805–1880) commanded the Third Corps of the Army of the Potomac, to which Hooker's division was assigned.

206.24   General Grover]   Brigadier General Cuvier Grover (1828–1885) commanded the First Brigade in Hooker's division.

206.29   Kearny's column]   Brigadier General Philip Kearny (1814–1862) commanded a division in the Third Corps.

210.29–30   *tobacco be burnt . . . law.*]   The Confederate Congress passed a law on March 17, 1862, authorizing military commanders to destroy cotton and tobacco stockpiles in order to prevent them from falling into Union hands.

210.31   the Baltimore rabble]   Former Baltimore policemen and detectives now working for Brigadier General John H. Winder, the Confederate provost marshal. Jones described them in his diary on August 8, 1861, as "petty larceny detectives . . . illiterate men, of low instincts and desperate characters."

211.18   Major Griswold]   A provost marshal serving under General Winder.

212.10   Mr. Randolph]   George W. Randolph (1818–1867) was the Confederate secretary of war, March–November 1862.

213.16   Wm H Seward]   William H. Seward (1801–1872) served in the U.S. Senate, 1849–61, as a Whig and then as a Republican. He was secretary of state in the Lincoln and Andrew Johnson administrations, 1861–69.

218.17   Ewell]   Major General Richard S. Ewell (1817–1872). His division was sent to reinforce Jackson in the Shenandoah Valley in early May 1862.

219.19   Colonel Alek Boteler]   Alexander R. Boteler (1815–1892), a member of Jackson's staff, served in the U.S. Congress, 1859–61, and the Confederate Congress, 1862–64.

219.20   Governor of Virginia]   John Letcher (1813–1884) was governor of Virginia, 1860–64.

219.21   At Kernstown]   The battle was fought on March 23, 1862.

220.4–5   lived twelve miles . . . the witty Dean.]   The essayist and Anglican clergyman Sydney Smith (1771–1845) described his rural parish in Yorkshire as being "so far out of the way that it was actually twelve miles from a lemon."

221.3   Belle Boyd.]   Maria Isabella Boyd (1844–1900), the daughter of a Martinsburg, Virginia, shopkeeper, was living in Front Royal in the spring of 1862. She was subsequently imprisoned twice by the Union authorities for spying. In 1864 she went to England, where she published her memoir *Belle Boyd in Camp and Prison* (1865).

224.14   Capt Fox]   Gustavus Vasa Fox (1821–1883) was assistant secretary of the navy, 1861–65.

224.15   Capt Davis . . . Minna]   Charles Henry Davis (1807–1877), who had succeeded the ailing Andrew H. Foote as commander of the Union gunboat flotilla on the Upper Mississippi on May 9; Mary Elizabeth Woodbury Blair (1821–1887), the wife of Montgomery Blair and sister-in-law of Gustavus Fox.

225.6   Frémont . . . Franklin]   Following their defeat by Jackson at McDowell on May 8, Frémont's troops retreated to Franklin, Virginia (now West Virginia).

225.14–15   when Rogers was repulsed at Fort Darling]   Commander John Rodgers (1812–1882) led the Union flotilla in the attack on Fort Darling (Drewry's Bluff) on the James River on May 15, 1862.

225.15–16   Old Grey beard] Secretary of the Navy Gideon Welles.

225.24–25   P King . . . Doolittle] Preston King (1806–1865), Republican senator from New York, 1857–63; abolitionist Wendell Phillips (1811–1884); James R. Doolittle (1815–1897), Republican senator from Wisconsin, 1857–69.

225.28   Our fat friend] Preston King.

225.33   Blair] Francis Preston Blair Lee, born in 1857, the only child of Elizabeth Blair Lee and Samuel Philips Lee.

225.39   Johns] Captain John F. Lee (1813–1884), Elizabeth Blair Lee's brother-in-law, was judge advocate of the U.S. Army, 1849–62.

226.2   Nelly] Eleanor Anne Hill Lee (d. 1891), John Lee's wife.

226.6   Fanny] Frances Ann Lee Pettit (1816–1889), Elizabeth Blair Lee's sister-in-law.

226.7   Ship Island] An island in the Gulf of Mexico near Biloxi, Mississippi, that served as a Union naval and military base.

230.10   BROCKET] A country house in Hertfordshire.

233.25   Casey] Brigadier General Silas Casey (1807–1882) commanded the Second Division in the Fourth Corps. His division was overrun by the initial Confederate attack at Fair Oaks.

233.30   the Tammany] The 42nd New York Infantry, which had been organized by the Tammany Society in New York City.

235.19   Colonel] Colonel Raymond Lee (1807–1891), commander of the 20th Massachusetts Infantry.

236.26   the R. R.] The Richmond and York River Railroad.

237.8–11   Genl D. H. Hill . . . Featherston] The letter sent to Lee by Major General Daniel Harvey Hill (1821–1889), a division commander in the Army of Northern Virginia, has not been found. At the time, Brigadier General Gabriel J. Rains (1803–1881) and Brigadier General Winfield Scott Featherston (1820–1891) commanded brigades in D. H. Hill's division. Rains was soon relieved of field duty, and Featherston was transferred to James Longstreet's division.

237.15   Col Long] Colonel Armistead L. Long (1825–1891), one of Lee's staff officers.

238.17–18   Mr. Wickliffe of Kentucky] Charles A. Wickliffe (1788–1869) was a congressman, 1823–33 and 1861–63; governor of Kentucky, 1839–40; and postmaster general of the United States, 1841–45.

239.15   Brig. Gen. T. W. Sherman] Brigadier General Thomas W. Sherman commanded the Union forces at Port Royal from November 1861 to March 1862, when he was succeeded by Hunter.

241.10   Brother Walter . . . My Brother]   Walter Stone (c. 1845–1863) enlisted in the Confederate army in September 1862 and died of fever at Clinton, Mississippi, in May 1863; William Stone (c. 1840–c. 1882) was a captain in the Confederate army who was wounded twice fighting in the eastern theater.

241.20–21   a ditch . . . opposite Vicksburg]   Work on the canal began on June 27, 1862, and stopped shortly before Admiral Farragut withdrew his flotilla downriver on July 24.

242.2–3   Mr. Mumford . . . shot]   William B. Mumford (1820–1862) was convicted of treason by a military commission and hanged in New Orleans on June 7, 1862.

243.6   Richmond]   A town in Madison Parish, Louisiana.

246.18   give a little map]   Alexander did not include a map in his manuscript.

247.7   at Strasburg on _____]   Jackson defeated Major General Nathaniel P. Banks at Winchester on May 25, 1862.

248.3   A. P. & D. H. Hill]   Major General Ambrose Powell Hill (1825–1865) and Major General Daniel Harvey Hill were division commanders in the Army of Northern Virginia (the two men were not related).

248.15   Fitzhugh Lee, in his life of Gen. Lee]   Fitzhugh Lee, *General Lee* (1894). A nephew of Robert E. Lee, Fitzhugh Lee (1835–1905) served as a major general in the Confederate army.

249.25   Century War Book]   D. H. Hill, "McClellan's Change of Base and Malvern Hill," in *Battles and Leaders of the Civil War*, volume II (1887).

250.6   Maj. Dabney in his life of Jackson]   Robert Lewis Dabney, *Life and Campaigns of Lieut.-Gen. Thomas J. Jackson, (Stonewall Jackson)* (1866). Dabney (1820–1898), a Presbyterian minister, served as Jackson's adjutant during the Shenandoah Valley campaign and the Seven Days.

251.1–3   Gen. Franklin . . . Century War Book.]   William B. Franklin, "Rear-Guard Fighting During the Change of Base," in *Battles and Leaders of the Civil War*, volume II (1887). Franklin (1823–1903) commanded the Sixth Corps during the Seven Days.

251.32   about ____ miles]   In his book *Military Memoirs of a Confederate: A Critical Narrative* (1907) Alexander wrote that the distance was between fifteen and sixteen miles.

254.13   Fitz John Porter . . . War Book.]   "Hanover Court House and Gaines's Mill," *Battles and Leaders of the Civil War*, volume II (1887).

254.34   Slocum . . . French & Meagher]   Brigadier General Henry W. Slocum (1826–1894) commanded the First Division in the Sixth Corps. Brigadier

General William H. French (1815–1881) and Brigadier General Thomas F. Meagher (1823–1867) commanded brigades in the First Division of the Second Corps.

258.29–30 McCall's Division . . . Morrell] Brigadier General George A. McCall (1802–1868) commanded the Third Division, known as the Pennsylvania Reserves, in the Fifth Corps. Brigadier General George W. Morell (1815–1883) commanded the First Division in the Fifth Corps.

259.12 Pennsylvania Bucktails] The 13th Pennsylvania Reserves.

261.32–33 Mr. Crountze of "The World,"] Lorenzo L. Crounse (1834–1909), a correspondent for the *New York World* who later joined *The New York Times*.

262.20 bridge of Lodi] At the battle of Lodi, fought in Lombardy on May 10, 1796, Napoleon Bonaparte's troops advanced under heavy fire across a bridge over the Adda River and defeated the rear guard of the retreating Austrian army.

263.4 ex-Governor Wood of Illinois] John Wood (1798–1880) served as lieutenant governor of Illinois, 1857–60, and as governor, 1860–61. In May 1861 he was appointed quartermaster-general of Illinois.

263.10–12 the old regicide . . . the savages] According to legend, William Goffe, one of the judges who signed the death warrant for Charles I in 1649, emerged from hiding in Hadley, Massachusetts, in 1675 to defend the town from an Indian attack.

264.13 the entire wounded . . . at 800.] Union losses in the battle of Gaines's Mill were recorded as 894 killed, 3,114 wounded, and 2,829 missing or captured.

265.13 the right bank] The southern bank of the Chickahominy.

271.10 Arthur] Arthur Haydon, Charles Haydon's younger brother.

271.22 Eliza] Eliza Haydon, Charles Haydon's stepmother.

275.12 Gen. Richardson] Brigadier General Israel B. Richardson (1815–1862) commanded the First Division in the Second Corps. Richardson had previously commanded the 2nd Michigan Infantry, Haydon's regiment, May–September 1861.

280.9 General Grover] Smith's brigade commander, Brigadier General Cuvier Grover.

281.34 The Colonel] Colonel Powell T. Wyman (c. 1828–1862), the commander of the 16th Massachusetts Infantry, was killed at Glendale on the afternoon of June 30.

290.19–20 my relative, Colonel J. M. Brockenbrough] John Mercer Brockenbrough (1830–1892) commanded the 40th Virginia Infantry.

291.12 Ballard House] A five-story hotel on Franklin Street in Richmond.

292.9 General C.] Thomas Jefferson Chambers (1802–1865), a lawyer and land speculator who was commissioned as a major general during the Texas Revolution.

292.29–30 "Potomac Rifles"] Company K of the 40th Virginia Infantry.

292.31 Edward Brockenbrough, dreadfully wounded] First Lieutenant Edward Brockenbrough (1835–1862) of the 40th Virginia Infantry died on July 2. John Mercer Brockenbrough (see note 290.19–20) was his older brother.

292.32 Our own boys] Judith McGuire's stepsons, James McGuire (1833–1903) and John P. McGuire Jr. (1836–1906).

292.37 "Praise the Lord, O my soul!"] Psalm 146:1.

292.39 Raleigh T. Colston] Lieutenant Colonel Colston (1834–1863) was the son of Judith McGuire's sister, Sarah Jane Brockenbrough Colston. He was mortally wounded at Mine Run, Virginia, on November 27, 1863.

293.1–2 Major Jones, . . . desperately wounded.] Francis Buckner Jones (1828–1862) died on July 9.

293.10–11 Lieutenant-Colonel Warwick, . . . wounded] Bradfute Warwick (1839–1862) died on July 6.

301.24–29 Colonel Coppens, . . . soon died] Lieutenant Colonel George Gaston Coppens (1836–1862) commanded the 1st Louisiana Zouave Battalion during the Seven Days. He was killed at Antietam on September 17, 1862.

302.3–13 "There everlasting spring . . . the shore,"] Cf. "There is a Land of Pure Delight" (1707), hymn by Isaac Watts (1674–1748).

302.14–15 crossed the river . . . the trees.] Cf. the last words of Lieutenant General Thomas J. (Stonewall) Jackson, May 10, 1863, as reported by his doctor, Hunter McGuire: "Let us cross over the river, and rest under the shade of the trees."

302.20 lively debate . . . Saturday] The debate took place on July 5, 1862.

303.22 Charles A. Wickliffe] See note 238.17–18.

303.33–34 Robert Mallory] Mallory (1815–1885) was a Unionist congressman from Kentucky, 1859–65.

304.5 Thaddeus Stevens] Stevens (1792–1868) served in Congress as an antislavery Whig from Pennsylvania, 1849–53, and as a Republican, 1859–68.

304.13 Owen Lovejoy] Lovejoy (1811–1864) was a Republican congressman from Illinois, 1857–64.

304.16 read Jackson's General Order] As recorded in the *Congressional Globe*, Lovejoy quoted from the address Jackson issued to his black troops on December 18, 1814. Thaddeus Stevens had previously read Jackson's proclamation of September 21, 1814, addressed to "the free colored inhabitants of Louisiana," in which he called upon free men of color to enlist in the war against Great Britain.

304.28 Charles B. Sedgewick] Sedgwick (1815–1883) was a Republican congressman from New York, 1859–63.

304.34 Alexander S. Diven] Diven (1809–1896) was a Republican congressman from New York, 1861–63.

307.35 the Act of Congress] The Confiscation Act of August 6, 1861.

309.16 Earl Russell] Lord Russell, the British foreign secretary, 1859–65; see Biographical Notes.

309.27–32 Oreto . . . privateer] After being commissioned as the C.S.S. *Florida*, the ship began raiding Northern commerce in 1863 and took thirty-three prizes before being captured by the sloop U.S.S. *Wachusett* at Bahia, Brazil, on October 7, 1864.

311.14–15 Captain Bullock . . . confederate navy] James D. Bulloch (1823–1901), a former lieutenant in the U.S. Navy, arrived in Liverpool in June 1861 and began purchasing arms and ships for the Confederacy. Bulloch was commissioned as a commander in the Confederate navy in March 1862.

312.5 General Burgoyne] General John Burgoyne (1782–1871), an officer of the Royal Engineers, had served in the Napoleonic Wars, the War of 1812, and the Crimea. He was the son of General John Burgoyne (1722–1792), who had surrendered his army to the Americans at Saratoga in 1777.

329.2 *Joseph C. G. Kennedy*] Kennedy (1813–1887) was superintendent of the Census, 1850–53 and 1860–65.

329.23 His address to his troops] See pp. 323–24 in this volume.

333.34 we stopped recruiting] On April 3, 1862, Secretary of War Stanton ordered the War Department recruiting service to close its offices.

335.10 Russia . . . Sebastopool.] Sebastopol fell to the British and French on September 9, 1855. Tsar Alexander II accepted peace terms proposed by Austria on January 16, 1856, and the treaty ending the Crimean War was signed in Paris on March 30, 1856.

337.3 Governor H. Seymour] Horatio Seymour (1810–1886) was the Democratic governor of New York, 1853–55 and 1863–65, and the Democratic nominee for president in 1868.

338.17 Nettie] Chase's daughter, Janet Ralston Chase (1847–1925).

339.14 the White House] White House Landing, where the Richmond and York Railroad crossed the Pamunkey River.

340.18 Today] July 21, 1862.

341.1 Katie] Chase's daughter, Catharine Jane Chase (1840–1899).

341.8 Gen. Webb] James Watson Webb (1802–1884) was the editor of the *Morning Courier and New-York Enquirer*, 1829–61, and U.S. minister to Brazil, 1861–69. His military title was honorific.

342.13 Col. Key] Colonel Thomas M. Key (1819–1869) of McClellan's staff.

342.35 5–20s] Bonds redeemable after five years and maturing in twenty years that carried 6 percent interest.

345.10 sixth section of the act of congress] See p. 319.11–28 in this volume.

347.31 Mr. Lovejoy] See note 304.13.

349.3 *Cuthbert Bullitt*] Lincoln later appointed Bullitt (1810–1906) as collector of customs for New Orleans and U.S. marshal for eastern Louisiana.

349.11–12 Mr. Thomas J. Durant] Durant (1817–1882) later served as attorney general of Louisiana, 1863–64.

352.16 Mr Atkinson] Edward Atkinson (1827–1905) was a Boston textile manufacturer.

352.25 Mr Johnson] Reverdy Johnson (1796–1876) served in the U.S. Senate as a Whig from Maryland, 1845–49, and as a Democrat, 1863–68. Secretary of State Seward sent Johnson to New Orleans in July 1862 to investigate complaints made by foreign consuls about the military occupation. In a letter to Johnson, Major General Benjamin F. Butler declared that the military would not confiscate cotton exports, while in another letter Johnson approved permitting an English merchant to export cotton from Confederate-held Mobile in exchange for non-contraband items.

353.9 *vis inertia*] Resistance to motion.

353.36 Yr Walcheren expedition] The British landed an expeditionary force of 39,000 men on the islands of Walcheren and South Beveland in the Scheldt estuary on July 30, 1809. By the time the force was withdrawn on December 9, 1809, nearly 4,000 men had died from malaria, typhus, typhoid, and dysentery, and more than 11,000 of the survivors were still listed as sick in February 1810.

368.31–32 Roberts] Joseph Jenkins Roberts (1809–1876), an immigrant from Virginia, was president of Liberia, 1848–56 and 1872–76.

374.18–19 Gaither . . . Stevens] Edgar B. Gaither (c. 1818–1855), James L. Rankin (c. 1817–1845), William Irvin (c. 1819–1852), Henry W. Halleck (see Biographical Notes), Edward O. C. Ord (1818–1883), and Isaac I. Stevens (1818–1862) had been in the class of 1839 at West Point with Sherman and Hunton.

377.14 F. Seward] Frederick W. Seward (1830–1915), William H. Seward's son, served as assistant secretary of state, 1861–69.

378.35 Qui nescit dissimulare nescit regnare] He who knows not how to dissemble knows not how to rule.

379.6–7 hostis humani generis] Enemy of the human race.

379.15 his Mexican villainy] Spanish, French, and British troops landed in Veracruz, December 1861–January 1862, in an intervention intended to force the Mexican government to pay its foreign debts. In April 1862 the British and Spanish withdrew from the expedition, while the French openly declared their intention to overthrow the government of Benito Juárez and make the Austrian archduke Maximilian (1832–1867) emperor of Mexico.

379.17–18 gigantic scheme . . . conquest of China] Britain and France had defeated the Manchus in the Second Opium War, 1857–60, and forced the Chinese to make a series of military, economic, and political concessions opening the country to European influence. The British and French then defended their interests in China by fighting a series of battles with the Taiping rebels in 1862.

380.28–29 Bright . . . unrepresented masses] A leading Radical member of Parliament, John Bright (1811–1889) advocated an enlarged electoral franchise and the redistribution of seats in the House of Commons in order to increase the representation of the urban population.

382.16–17 Progressive Friends at Longwood] An organization of liberal Quakers founded in Longwood, Pennsylvania, in 1853.

382.23–24 Duff Green's Row] A group of tenements on East Capitol Street.

383.18 Mr. Nichol] Danforth B. Nichols (1812–1907), a Methodist minister.

383.26 Rev. W. H. Channing] William Henry Channing (1810–1884), a Unitarian clergyman and reformer.

383.29 Gen. Wadsworth] Brigadier General James S. Wadsworth (1807–1864) was the military governor of the District of Columbia.

383.31–32 Miss Hannah Stevenson . . . Miss Kendall] Hannah Stevenson (1807–1887) and Julia C. Kendall (1815–1874) were volunteer nurses from Massachusetts at Washington military hospitals.

392.2–3   3rd, . . . 9th]   The Third, Fifth, and Ninth Corps of the Army of the Potomac fought at Second Bull Run.

392.12   Gen. Winder killed]   Brigadier General Charles H. Winder (1829–1862) had commanded a brigade in the Shenandoah Valley campaign and a division in the Seven Days.

394.5   Duane]   James C. Duane (1824–1897) served as an engineering officer with the Army of the Potomac, 1861–62, and as its chief engineer, 1863–65.

399.5–6   Col. Stephen D. Lee]   Lee (1833–1908) later commanded a corps in the Army of Tennessee, 1864–65. He was not related to Robert E. Lee.

401.18   Mr. Holt]   Joseph Holt (1807–1894), a leading Kentucky unionist, had served as postmaster general, March 1859–December 1860, and as secretary of war from January 1861 until the end of the Buchanan administration. Holt was appointed judge advocate general of the U.S. Army by President Lincoln on September 3, 1862, and held the position until 1875.

402.4   battle of Hanover Court House]   On May 27, 1862, McClellan sent 12,000 men to Hanover Court House, fourteen miles north of Richmond, to clear Confederate forces from his right flank. The Union troops defeated 4,000 Confederates and destroyed several railroad bridges before returning to the north bank of the Chickahominy River.

408.28   battlefield of Leesburg]   The battle of Ball's Bluff was fought near Leesburg on October 21, 1861; see p. 28.7–12 in this volume.

409.32   Starke . . . his father]   Brigadier General William E. Starke (1814–1862) commanded a brigade in Jackson's corps at Second Bull Run and Antietam, where he was killed.

413.17–18   Tuesday evening . . . Sunday morning]   September 2 and August 31, 1862.

414.12   On Monday]   September 1.

414.26   Reno's forces]   Major General Jesse Reno (1823–1862) commanded a division in the Ninth Corps of the Army of the Potomac.

414.30   Kearney, Stephens & Webster]   Major General Philip Kearny and Major General Isaac Stevens (1818–1862) were killed at Chantilly on September 1. Colonel Fletcher Webster (1813–1862), a son of Daniel Webster and commander of the 12th Massachusetts Infantry, was killed at Second Bull Run on August 30.

414.37   the Island]   Name for area of southwest Washington bounded by the Potomac River, the Anacostia River, and the Washington Canal.

416.23   Wilkes]   Commodore Charles Wilkes (1798–1877).

416.32   Smith] Caleb P. Smith (1808–1864) was secretary of the interior, 1861–62.

418.5–6   Baron Gerolt's.] Friedrich von Gerolt (1798–1879) was the Prussian minister to the United States, 1844–48 and 1849–71.

420.22   Watson] Peter H. Watson, a patent lawyer and former legal partner of Edwin M. Stanton, was assistant secretary of war, January 1862–July 1864.

420.37   Schenck] Brigadier General Robert C. Schenck (1809–1890) commanded a division in the First Corps of the Army of Virginia at Second Bull Run. Schenck served in Congress from Ohio as a Whig, 1843–51, and as a Republican, 1863–71.

421.17   my neighbor Corcoran's] William Wilson Corcoran (1798–1888) was a Washington banker, philanthropist, and art collector. A Southern sympathizer, Corcoran went to Europe in 1862 and remained abroad for the rest of the war. In his absence both his city home and country estate north of the city were used as military hospitals.

426.39   Haupt] Herman Haupt (1817–1905) served as chief of construction for the U.S. military railroads, April 1862–September 1863.

427.10   voltigeurs] Skirmishers, sharpshooters.

435.29   Loudon] Loudon County, Virginia.

436.24   Coxe's] Brigadier General Jacob D. Cox (1828–1900) commanded the Kanawha Division in western Virginia. During the Maryland campaign the division served with the Ninth Corps of the Army of the Potomac.

437.12   *Egomet Ipse*] I myself.

437.21   Queen City of the West] Cincinnati.

437.23   General Stahel] Brigadier General Julius Stahel (1825–1912) commanded a brigade in the First Corps of the Army of Virginia at Second Bull Run. He assumed command of his division on August 30 after Brigadier General Robert C. Schenck (see note 420.37) was wounded.

438.4   redans] A V-shaped earthwork fortification, with its point projecting toward the enemy.

438.7   Bellows] Henry Bellows (1814–1882), a Unitarian pastor from New York City, helped found the U.S. Sanitary Commission in 1861 and served as its president throughout the war.

438.12   Algeria, and Lombardy] Kearny had fought in Algeria in 1840 while studying French cavalry tactics. In 1859 he fought with the French army against the Austrians at Magenta and Solferino in northern Italy.

NOTES 837

438.16   dark cloud six years ago]   In 1855 Kearny began living openly on his New Jersey estate with Agnes Maxwell, a young woman he had met in Paris, after his wife Diana initially refused him a divorce. Kearny and Maxwell were eventually able to marry in April 1858.

439.34–440.1   Carl Schurz, . . . the army]   Schurz (1829–1906) had campaigned for Lincoln in 1860 among German-American voters. He was commissioned as a brigadier general in April 1862 and commanded a division in the First Corps of the Army of Virginia at Second Bull Run.

440.18   Fort Lafayette]   See note 29.11.

440.37–8   the mutiny of last year.]   The 79th New York Infantry lost 198 men killed, wounded, or captured at First Bull Run, including its commander, Colonel James Cameron. Many in the regiment believed they should be permitted to return to New York to recruit replacements and elect new officers. On August 14, 1861, the regiment refused orders to strike camp at Washington and march into Virginia. The mutiny ended later in the day when the 79th New York was confronted by regular troops and addressed by their new commander Colonel Isaac Stevens (see note 414.30), a regular officer. Twenty-one suspected ringleaders were sent to Fort Jefferson in the Dry Tortugas, where they performed hard labor until February 1862.

443.27   Gotha]   Lord Russell had accompanied Queen Victoria on her visit to the duchy of Saxe-Coburg-Gotha, the home of her consort Prince Albert, who had died on December 14, 1861.

444.14   Newcastle]   Henry Pelham-Clinton, 5th Duke of Newcastle (1811–1864), was secretary of state for the colonies in the Palmerston government, 1859–64.

444.16–17   the new interest . . . for her.]   Edward, the Prince of Wales, had become engaged to Princess Alexandra of Denmark (1844–1925) on September 9, 1862.

444.19   Broadlands]   Palmerston's country estate near Romsey in Hampshire.

450.6   Bradley T. Johnson, *soi-disant* Colonel C.S.A.]   Colonel Johnson (1829–1903) was, like Steiner, a native of Frederick, Maryland.

450.34   "My Maryland"]   "Maryland, My Maryland," song (1861) with words by James Ryder Randall (1839–1908), sung to the German folk tune "Lauriger Horatius" (the same music as "O Tannenbaum!").

452.14   "If thine enemy hunger, feed him,"]   Romans 12:20.

452.29   The coals . . . his head."]   See Romans 12:20.

455.27   Col. Steedman]   Lieutenant Colonel John M. Steedman (d. 1867), commander of the 6th South Carolina Infantry.

460.6   III]   The first two paragraphs of Special Order No. 191 were not included in the copy that was sent to Major General D. H. Hill and subsequently discovered by the Union army. Paragraph I prohibited Confederate soldiers not on official business from visiting Frederick, Maryland, and paragraph II detailed arrangements for evacuating sick soldiers to Virginia.

462.23–24   two hundred thousand men]   The Army of the Potomac had about 75,000 men at Antietam, and the Army of Northern Virginia about 35,000.

462.34   brilliant victory near Middletown]   The battle of South Mountain, fought on September 14, 1862.

463.14–15   Hooker . . . his corps]   Major General Joseph Hooker commanded the First Corps at Antietam.

463.20   Richardson]   Major General Israel B. Richardson commanded a division in the Second Corps.

464.21–22   Sumner, Franklin, and Mansfield]   Major General Edwin V. Sumner commanded the Second Corps, Major General William B. Franklin commanded the Sixth Corps, and Major General Joseph K. F. Mansfield (1803–1862) commanded the Twelfth Corps.

464.25–26   Porter . . . Burnside]   Fitz John Porter commanded the Fifth Corps; Ambrose Burnside commanded the Ninth Corps.

464.29   Sykes]   Brigadier General George Sykes (1822–1880) commanded a division in the Fifth Corps.

465.19–21   Ricketts's . . . Doubleday]   Brigadier General James B. Ricketts (1817–1887), Brigadier General George G. Meade, and Brigadier General Abner Doubleday (1819–1893) commanded the three divisions in Hooker's First Corps.

466.28–29   McDowell . . . Manassas]   Major General Irvin McDowell (1818–1885) had commanded the Third Corps of the Army of Virginia at Second Bull Run. When the Army of Virginia was merged into the Army of the Potomac in September 1862, the Third Corps's troops were assigned to the First Corps.

467.32   General Hartsuff]   Brigadier General George Hartsuff (1830–1874) commanded a brigade in Rickett's division.

471.4–7   Major Sedgwick . . . not mortal.]   William D. Sedgwick (1831–1862), a relative of Major General John Sedgwick (1813–1864), died of his wounds on September 29.

471.17–18   Lieut. Spurr . . . wounded.]   Thomas J. Spurr (1838–1862) died on September 27.

471.21   Gen. Dana was wounded.]   Brigadier General Napoleon J. T. Dana (1822–1905) commanded a brigade in Sedgwick's division.

471.26–27   Lieut.-Col. Revere . . . wounded severely,]   Lieutenant Colonel Paul Joseph Revere (1832–1863) and Captain Joseph C. Audenried (1839–1880) survived their wounds at Antietam. Revere, the grandson of the Revolutionary War hero, was mortally wounded at Gettysburg on July 2, 1863, while commanding the 20th Massachusetts Infantry.

471.30–33   Richardson . . . his brigade.]   Richardson died on November 3, 1862. Brigadier General Thomas F. Meagher (1823–1867) commanded a brigade in Richardson's division.

481.13–14   Lieutenant John Ticknor was badly wounded]   Ticknor (c. 1836–1863) survived his wound, but was killed at Gettysburg on July 1, 1863.

481.16–18   Bragg . . . shot,"]   Lieutenant Colonel Edward S. Bragg (1827–1912) returned to the regiment in November 1862.

482.12   Virginia rail fence.]   A zigzagging rail fence.

483.38–484.1   reported to General Doubleday,]   The 6th Wisconsin was assigned to Doubleday's division.

485.3–4   *Irene and Mary Williams*]   Irene Williams (1843–1907) and Mary Williams (1846–1935) lived with their father's relatives in Connecticut. Their mother had died in 1849.

491.30   Pittman]   Williams's aide, Lieutenant Samuel E. Pittman (1831–1922).

492.39   Napoleon gun]   A smoothbore field artillery gun that fired a twelve-pound projectile with a maximum range of 1,600 yards. It was developed in France under the auspices of Napoleon III.

494.40   just been surrendered]   The Confederates captured Maryland Heights on September 13, 1862.

495.14   third time up the valley.]   Williams had served in the Shenandoah Valley in the winter and spring of 1862.

500.3–4   Lieutenant-Colonel Kimball]   Edgar A. Kimball (1822–1863), commander of the 9th New York Infantry.

500.32–34   singular effect . . . Goethe on a similar occasion]   In August 1792 Johann Wolfgang von Goethe accompanied his patron Karl August, Duke of Saxe-Weimar, in the Austrian-Prussian invasion of revolutionary France. At the battle of Valmy on September 20, Goethe rode out to witness the French artillery bombardment, and later wrote: "In the midst of these circumstances, I was soon able to remark that something unusual was taking place within me: I paid close attention to it, and still the sensation can be described only by similitude. It appeared as if you were in some extremely hot place, and at the same time quite penetrated by the heat of it, so that you feel yourself, as it were, quite one with the element in which you are. The eyes lose nothing of their strength or clearness; but it is as if the world had a kind of brown-red tint, which makes the situation, as well as the surrounding objects, more impressive." (Translation by Robert Farie, 1849.)

503.24 where the 14th . . . made their fight] The 14th Connecticut Infantry attacked the Sunken Road in the center of the Confederate line as part of French's division in Sumner's Second Corps.

505.13 the Sunday before the battle] September 14, 1862.

512.3 "Sheridan's ride."] On October 19, 1864, Confederate troops surprised Union forces at Cedar Creek, Virginia, and drove them from their positions. Major General Philip Henry Sheridan (1831–1888), who was returning to his command from a conference in Washington, learned of the attack in Winchester, Virginia, and rode to the front, rallying stragglers and directing a successful counterattack.

524.19–20 Rodman . . . Kingsbury died] Brigadier Isaac P. Rodman (1822–1862), the commander of a division in the Ninth Corps, died of his wounds on September 30. Colonel Henry W. Kingsbury (1836–1862), commander of the 11th Connecticut Infantry, was mortally wounded in an attack on the Rohrbach (Burnside's) Bridge.

526.22 OUR BRIGADE] The 1st Missouri Confederate Brigade.

531.28–29 when the President . . . funeral of Stanton's child] The funeral was held on July 13, 1862. Welles recorded in his diary Lincoln saying that "he had given it much thought and he had about come to the conclusion that we must free the slaves or be ourselves subdued."

539.1 Cassius M. Clay] Clay (1810–1903), an antislavery Whig from Kentucky who joined the Republican Party in 1856, served as U.S. minister to Russia, 1861–62 and 1863–69.

543.3 *Manton Marble*] Marble (1835–1917) was the editor and owner of the *New York World*, 1862–76.

543.17 the Clipper] The *Baltimore Clipper*, a newspaper published from 1847 to 1865.

543.24 Lafayette] See note 29.11.

547.1 Joe Johnston did on Patterson] See note 11.9.

547.38 Mitchell] Major General Ormsby M. Mitchel (1809–1862) led a division in the Army of the Ohio, December 1861–July 1862. As commander of Union occupation forces in northern Alabama, April–July 1862, Mitchel endorsed harsh reprisals against Confederate guerrilla attacks, and was criticized for the pillaging of Athens, Alabama, by one of his brigades. In September

1862 Mitchel was appointed to command the Department of the South; he died from yellow fever in South Carolina on October 30.

548.4   Dix & Banks] Major General John A. Dix (1798–1879) commanded the Department of Virginia with headquarters at Fort Monroe, June 1862–July 1863. Dix had served as a Democratic senator from New York, 1845–49, and as secretary of the treasury in the Buchanan administration, January–March 1861. Major General Nathaniel P. Banks commanded the defenses of Washington, September–October 1862. Banks had served in Congress, 1853–57, as a Democrat, an American (Know Nothing), and a Republican. He was governor of Massachusetts, 1858–61.

549.15   Curtis] Major General Samuel R. Curtis commanded the Department of the Missouri, September 1862–May 1863.

554.23   Confession of Augsburg] The primary confession of the Lutheran Church (1530), drafted by Philip Melanchthon (1497–1560) and endorsed by Martin Luther.

554.26   emancipation of slaves in the West Indies] The Abolition Act of 1833 resulted in the emancipation of all slaves in the British West Indies in 1838.

554.26–27   passage of the Reform Bill] The Reform Act of 1832 extended the electoral franchise and redistributed seats in the House of Commons.

554.27   repeal of the Corn-Laws] The Corn Laws imposing duties on grain imported into Great Britain were repealed in 1846.

554.27–28   Magnetic Ocean-Telegraph] The first trans-Atlantic telegraph cable was tested in August 1858. It failed the following month, and regular cable service was not established until 1866.

554.28–29   passage of the Homestead Bill] The Homestead Act of 1862 granted 160 acres of public land to settlers in return for making improvements to the claim and residing on it for five years.

557.7–9   "if that fail, . . . on stubble."] John Milton, *Comus* (1637), lines 597–99.

559.19–20   condition of Italy . . . French Algiers] The unification of Italy began with the defeat of Austria by Sardinia-Piedmont and France in 1859; Poland was partitioned among Austria, Prussia, and Russia in 1772, 1793, and 1795; France began its conquest of Algeria in 1830.

560.13–14   "Incertainties . . . endless age."] Shakespeare, Sonnet 107, lines 7–8.

565.36   the late Col. Miles] Colonel Dixon S. Miles (1804–1862), the Union commander at Harper's Ferry, Virginia, was mortally wounded by Confederate artillery fire shortly after he ordered his garrison to surrender on

September 15, 1862. Although a subsequent army inquiry condemned his "incapacity, amounting almost to imbecility," there is no evidence that he had Confederate sympathies.

567.18   Mr. Semmes] Thomas J. Semmes (1824–1899) was a Confederate senator from Louisiana, 1862–65.

567.33   Mr. Clark] John B. Clark (1802–1885) was a Confederate senator from Missouri, 1862–64, and a representative in the Confederate Congress, 1864–65. He served as a Democrat in the U.S. House of Representatives, 1857–61.

568.10   Mr. Henry] Gustavus A. Henry (1804–1880) was a Confederate senator from Tennessee, 1862–65.

568.15   Mr. Phelan] James Phelan (1821–1873) was a Confederate senator from Mississippi, 1862–64.

568.18   Mr. Burnett] Henry C. Burnett (1825–1866) was a Confederate senator from Kentucky, 1862–65. He served as a Democrat in the U.S. House of Representatives, 1855–61.

570.21   Mr. Hill] Benjamin Hill (1823–1882) represented Georgia in the Provisional Confederate Congress, 1861, and in the Confederate Senate, 1862–65.

570.22–23   *brutum fulmen*] Insensible thunderbolt; a futile threat.

573.10–11   "the efforts . . . actual freedom"] Cf. the Preliminary Emancipation Proclamation, p. 534.14–15 in this volume.

573.17   MAZZINI] Italian revolutionary Giuseppe Mazzini (1803–1872), who sought to unite Italy as a democratic republic.

580.14–15   General Rodgers of Texas] Colonel William P. Rogers (1819–1862) commanded the 2nd Texas Infantry.

580.29   Colonel Sprague] Colonel John W. Sprague (1817–1893) commanded the 63rd Ohio Infantry, January 1862–April 1864.

580.36   parrot guns] See note 159.24.

582.30   "with my back . . . to the foe."] From "Lochiel's Warning" (1802), poem by Thomas Campbell (1777–1844).

583.11–12   I sank . . . knew nothing more] David L. Jackson, Oscar L. Jackson's brother, wrote in *The Colonel's Diary* that after he lost consciousness, Jackson was placed among "the supposedly mortally wounded and dying" for several hours until Mose, his black servant, carried him to a field hospital and made the surgeons treat him.

585.25   Col. Sawier] Possibly Lieutenant Colonel Thomas C. Lanier, second in command of the 42nd Alabama Infantry.

NOTES

589.32   His tragic death] Major General William Nelson (1824–1862) was shot to death by Union Brigadier General Jefferson C. Davis (1828–1879) in Louisville on September 29, 1862. The two men had quarreled previously, and when Davis angrily confronted Nelson in the grand hall of the Galt House hotel, Nelson called him a "damned puppy." Davis then flipped a crumpled visiting card into Nelson's face, and Nelson slapped Davis and called him a coward. After Davis borrowed a revolver from a friend in the hotel, he confronted Nelson at the bottom of a stairway and shot him. Davis returned to duty, and was never tried for the killing.

592.16–17   Jackson's . . . death] Union Brigadier General James S. Jackson (1823–1862), a Kentucky lawyer who had served in Congress as a Unionist in 1861 before joining the army.

592.23   Terrill . . . brigade] Brigadier General William R. Terrill (1834–1862) led a brigade in Jackson's division, part of the corps commanded by Major General Alexander McCook.

592.25–29   Parsons] Lieutenant Charles C. Parsons (1838–1878), an 1861 graduate of West Point, resigned from the army in 1870 to become an Episcopal clergyman.

593.34   "Bonnie Blue Flag,"] A popular Confederate marching song, written in 1861 by the variety performer Harry Macarthy (1834–1888) and sung to the tune of "The Irish Jaunting Car."

594.3–4   Mumfordsville] The Union garrison at Munfordville, Kentucky, surrendered on September 17, 1862.

594.6   Camp Dick Robinson] A Union recruiting and training camp established in August 1861 near Danville, Kentucky.

594.26   General Chalmers] Brigadier General James R. Chalmers (1831–1898) commanded a brigade in Bragg's army.

594.40   Cheatham's] Watkins's regiment, the 1st Tennessee Infantry, was assigned to the division commanded by Major General Benjamin F. Cheatham (1820–1886).

596.8–9   Field . . . Patterson] At Perryville, Colonel Hume R. Feild (1834–1921), the commander of the 1st Tennessee Infantry, acted as chief of staff to his brigade commander, Brigadier General George Maney (1826–1901), while Lieutenant Colonel John Patterson led the regiment.

597.14   Missionary Ridge] The ridge was captured by Union troops in the battle of Chattanooga, November 25, 1863.

598.14   Rock City Guards] A Nashville militia battalion whose members formed Companies A, B, and C of the 1st Tennessee Infantry in 1861.

599.1–5   Billy Webster . . . we shall meet again.] William H. Webster (1840–1863) was killed at Chickamauga on September 19, 1863.

603.16 Granville's letter] Granville George Leveson-Gower, 2nd Earl Granville (1815–1891), was the Liberal leader of the House of Lords, 1859–65. He wrote to Russell on September 27 that it was unlikely that both sides in the conflict would accept British mediation, and that if Britain recognized the South, Granville doubted "whether it will be possible for us to avoid drifting into" the war.

604.31–32 Memorandum on . . . Lewis's observations.] In a memorandum sent to the cabinet on October 13, Russell proposed that the Great Powers of Europe should ask both sides to agree to "a suspension of arms for the purpose of weighing calmly the advantages of peace." Sir George Cornewall Lewis (1806–1863), secretary for war, 1861–63, responded on October 17, arguing that an armistice proposal would anger the North and might lead to war with the United States.

606.15 Landudno] Llandudno, a seaside resort in northern Wales.

607.20 Sepoy Rebellion] The Indian rebellion of 1857–58, which began with a series of mutinies by soldiers of the East India Company.

609.25–26 the charges of late . . . the public mind] The text of Blair's letter is taken from *The Francis Preston Blair Family in Politics* (1933) by William Ernest Smith. In an unpublished and incomplete transcription made around 1960 by the historian E. B. Long, this passage reads: "the charges of the Democracy that gave it the late strength & confirmed hold on the public mind."

609.35–610.1 their conclusive policy] In the Long transcription, "their conservative policy."

610.15 supply strength] In the Long transcription, "supply thought."

611.3 *Margaret Meade*] Margaretta Sergeant Meade (1815–1886) was the daughter of a Pennsylvania congressman. She and Meade were married in 1840.

611.15 Seymour] Brigadier General Truman Seymour (1824–1891) commanded a brigade in Meade's division.

611.17 Reynolds] John F. Reynolds (1820–1863) assumed command of the First Corps of the Army of the Potomac in late September 1862 and led it until his death at Gettysburg on July 1, 1863.

611.18 Gibbons position] John Gibbon (1827–1896) had recently been advanced from brigade to division command within the First Corps.

611.19 Col. S. Meredith . . . old politician] Colonel Solomon Meredith (1810–1875) had commanded the 19th Indiana Infantry in Gibbon's brigade until October 1862, when he was promoted to brigadier general. Meredith had served as a county sheriff, state legislator, and U.S. marshal, and was active in Indiana Republican politics.

NOTES 845

611.22–23   *you & I & Meade . . . promoted.*] Reynolds and Meade were promoted to major general effective November 29, 1862; Gibbon was promoted to major general in June 1864.

612.15   attempt to put down Taylor in Mexico] Zachary Taylor became a popular hero after defeating the Mexicans at Palo Alto and Resaca de la Palma, May 8–9, 1846. On September 24 he accepted the surrender of Monterrey under terms that allowed the Mexican garrison to depart peacefully and established an eight-week armistice. The Polk administration subsequently repudiated the armistice, transferred many of Taylor's troops to the Veracruz expedition commanded by Winfield Scott, and ordered Taylor to remain on the defensive. He disregarded his orders, advanced south, and defeated the Mexicans at Buena Vista, February 22–23, 1847. In 1848 Taylor won the Whig nomination and was elected president.

612.39   Gov. Curtin]   Andrew G. Curtin (1817–1894) was the Republican governor of Pennsylvania, 1861–67.

613.1   Senator Cowan]   Edgar Cowan (1815–1885) was a Republican senator from Pennsylvania, 1861–67.

614.12   Sheffield]   William S. Sheffield (1820–1907), a Union congressman from Rhode Island, 1861–63.

615.3   battle of Friday]   August 29, 1862.

616.2–3   Butler . . . Griffing]   Browning recorded his conversation with William Butler (1797–1876), the Republican state treasurer of Illinois, 1859–63, in his diary on November 12, 1862. Brigadier General Charles Griffin (1825–1867) commanded a brigade in the Fifth Corps under Porter at Second Bull Run.

618.25–26   treaty with Great Britain . . . slave trade]   The treaty was signed in Washington by Secretary of State Seward and Lord Lyons, the British minister to the United States, on April 7, 1862, and ratified by the Senate on April 25. Under its terms the Royal Navy was for the first time permitted to stop and search American ships suspected of engaging in the slave trade.

620.34–35   republic of New Granada]   Colombia, which at the time included present-day Panama.

625.26   chief of the Cherokees]   John Ross (1790–1866) was elected principal chief of the Cherokee in 1839.

626.28   Colonel Webster]   See note 42.31.

626.34   The Commissioner]   Isaac Newton (1800–1867), commissioner of agriculture, 1862–67. (The first secretary of agriculture with cabinet rank was appointed in 1889.)

627.22–23   "One generation . . . forever."]   Ecclesiastes 1:4.

640.28 "Benny Havens's"] A tavern in Buttermilk Falls (now Highland Falls), New York, near West Point.

644.24–25 Gen. Longstreet says] In "The Battle of Fredericksburg," published in *Battles and Leaders of the Civil War*, volume III (1888).

645.29–30 Gen. Couch, in the *Century*] Darius N. Couch, "Sumner's 'Grand Right Division,'" *Battles and Leaders of the Civil War*, volume III (1888).

647.11–15 The one casualty . . . in the yard.] Alexander later crossed out this sentence in his manuscript and wrote: "PS I have come to doubt the truth of this incident which was told me at the time by Roy Mason, himself, but I never heard it mentioned again by *any one*. It is inherently exceedingly improbable. Some of the 7 would only have been wounded."

648.18 Whitworth rifle] A rifled artillery gun capable of firing a twelve-pound projectile over four miles.

653.29–33 Gen. T. R. R. Cobb, . . . before the war.] General Thomas R. R. Cobb (1823–1862) commanded a brigade in Longstreet's corps. A prominent lawyer in Georgia, Cobb became an influential advocate of immediate secession following Lincoln's election and served in the Provisional Confederate Congress. He was the younger brother of Howell Cobb (see note 148.2).

657.21 grand army corps of Sumner] In November 1862 Burnside organized the Army of the Potomac into three Grand Divisions: the Right, commanded by Edwin V. Sumner; the Center, commanded by Joseph Hooker and the Left, commanded by William B. Franklin. Each Grand Division was composed of two corps, and was assigned its own cavalry and artillery.

658.30–31 heavy firing of Thursday] December 11, 1862, when Union troops crossed the Rappahannock and captured Fredericksburg.

659.19 Fort Darling] Union name for the fortifications on Drewry's Bluff overlooking the James River eight miles below Richmond.

660.20–21 Howard, . . . poor general] Major General Oliver O. Howard (1830–1909) had commanded a brigade at Fair Oaks, South Mountain, and Antietam, where he assumed command of the Second Division of the Second Corps after Major General John Sedgwick was wounded.

660.24–25 the fight of the previous day] Hall's brigade had been heavily engaged in the street fighting in Fredericksburg on December 11, during which Abbott's company of the 20th Massachusetts had lost ten men killed and twenty-five wounded.

660.28 the 19th] The 19th Massachusetts Infantry.

661.19 hinc illae &c.] *Hinc illae lacrimae*: hence these tears. Terence, *Andria*, line 126.

661.23 Macy] Captain George N. Macy (1837–1875) was the acting commander of the 20th Massachusetts Infantry.

661.32 Alley] Leander F. Alley (c. 1834–1862), a whaler from Nantucket, enlisted in the 20th Massachusetts in July 1861 and was promoted to second lieutenant in August 1862.

661.35 our great loss.] Edward Abbott (1840–1862), a captain in the 2nd Massachusetts Infantry, was killed at Cedar Mountain, Virginia, on August 9, 1862.

662.1 Fletcher] Fletcher Abbott (1843–1925), a second lieutenant in the 2nd Massachusetts Infantry, was suffering from dysentery and on sick leave. He later served as a staff officer in Louisiana before being medically discharged in December 1863.

662.20 Holmes] Captain Oliver Wendell Holmes Jr. (1841–1935) was returning to duty after being wounded at Antietam. Holmes later served as an associate justice of the U.S. Supreme Court, 1902–32.

663.17 the governor] John A. Andrew (1818–1867) was the Republican governor of Massachusetts, 1861–66.

663.22 Johnny Sedgwick] Major General Sedgwick returned to duty on December 22, 1862, after being wounded at Antietam.

665.7 Colonel Lang] Captain David Lang (1838–1917) was the acting commander of the 8th Florida Infantry.

671.19–20 "To gird . . . ramparts die,"] Felicia Dorothea Hemans (1793–1835), "Marguerite of France" (1832).

673.1–2 Richard was *not* himself again] Cf. "Conscience, avaunt, Richard's himself again," line by Colley Cibber (1671–1757) in Act V of his popular adaptation (1700) of Shakespeare's *Richard III*.

674.1 "a hard road to travel"] Cf. "Jordan is a Hard Road to Travel," song (1853) by Daniel Decatur Emmett (1815–1904).

674.32 *vi et armis*] With force and arms.

677.13 Dr. Watts] Isaac Watts (1674–1748), English theologian, logician, and writer of hymns.

678.1–12 "Beds . . . wondered."] Cf. Alfred Tennyson (1809–1892), "The Charge of the Light Brigade" (1854).

678.23 Munchausenism] An exaggerated or untrue story, after Karl Friedrich von Münchhausen (1720–1797), a German soldier and traveler known for his tales of fantastic adventures.

681.23 Thackeray's "Ensign Spooney"] In his novel *Vanity Fair* (1848).

683.17–18 Mr D W Wise] Daniel W. Wise (1813–1898) was an antislavery Methodist clergyman from Massachusetts and editor of the Methodist newspaper *Zion's Herald*.

685.21 Nicolay] John G. Nicolay (1832–1901) was Lincoln's private secretary, 1860–61, and his principal secretary in the White House, 1861–65.

685.27 Preston King and F. W. Seward] For King, see note 225.24–25; for Seward, see note 377.14.

686.10–11 Judge Collamer] Jacob Collamer (1791–1865) served as a judge of the Vermont Superior Court, 1833–42; as a Whig congressman, 1843–49; and as a Republican senator, 1855–65.

687.21–23 Fessenden . . . Wade was absent.] William P. Fessenden (1806–1869), Republican senator from Maine, 1854–64 and 1865–69, and secretary of the treasury, 1864–65; Ira Harris (1802–1875), Republican senator from New York, 1861–67; Lyman Trumbull (1813–1896), Republican senator from Illinois, 1855–73; James W. Grimes (1816–1872), Republican senator from Iowa, 1859–69; Jacob M. Howard (1805–1871), Republican senator from Michigan, 1862–71; Charles Sumner (1811–1874), Free Soil and then Republican senator from Massachusetts, 1851–74; Samuel C. Pomeroy (1816–1891), Republican senator from Kansas, 1861–73. Benjamin F. Wade (see note 8.30–31) was at Burnside's headquarters in Virginia.

688.12 heard from J.Q. Adams . . . Congress] Fessenden had served in Congress as a Whig, 1841–43.

688.15 Mr. Clay] Henry Clay was secretary of state in the administration of John Quincy Adams, 1825–29.

689.12 confidential dispatch to Mr. Adams, was read.] In a dispatch of July 5, 1862, to Charles Francis Adams, the American minister to Great Britain, Seward wrote: "The extreme advocates of African slavery and its most vehement opponents were acting in concert together to precipitate a servile war— the former by making the most desperate attempt to overthrow the federal Union, the latter by demanding an edict of universal emancipation."

689.36–37 Governor Robertson of Kentucky] George Robertson (1790–1874) had served in Congress, 1817–21; in the Kentucky state legislature; and on the Kentucky court of appeals, 1828–43.

NOTES   849

692.35   Stanton came staving along.] In the remainder of his diary entry for December 20, 1862 Welles recorded a conversation with Senator Preston King and speculated about Stanton's involvement in the attempt to oust Seward from the cabinet.

696.29–30   Peninsular War.] Campaign fought on the Iberian peninsula, 1808–14, by Britain and its Portuguese and Spanish allies against the French.

696.33   Bidwell] Marshall S. Bidwell (1799–1872), Strong's law partner.

697.3   Jefferson Davis's precious proclamation!!] Davis issued the proclamation on December 23, 1862.

697.21–22   *brutum fulmen*] See note 570.22–23.

700.21   Banks] Major General Nathaniel P. Banks had recently replaced Benjamin F. Butler as commander of the Department of the Gulf.

701.18   Seymour . . . Curtis] Horatio Seymour (1810–1886), Democratic governor of New York, 1863–65, and Joel Parker (1816–1888), Democratic governor of New Jersey, 1863–66, were both elected in November 1862. George Ticknor Curtis (1812–1894), a conservative Democrat, was a prominent lawyer, legal scholar, and historian; his brother, Benjamin R. Curtis (1809–1874), who served as an associate justice of the U.S. Supreme Court, 1851–57, had recently published *Executive Power*, a pamphlet attacking the constitutionality of the Emancipation Proclamation and the suspension of habeas corpus by the Lincoln administration.

703.39   Col Murphy] Colonel Robert C. Murphy was dismissed from the service on January 10, 1863, for his "cowardly and disgraceful conduct" in failing to defend Holly Springs.

704.28–30   Col Murphy . . . Iuka] Murphy failed to destroy the supply depot at Iuka, Mississippi, when he retreated from the town on September 14, 1862. He was court-martialed and acquitted in October 1862.

710.18–19   conscription act . . . exemption act.] See pp. 172–76 in this volume.

711.18   your Governor] John Pettus (1813–1867) was governor of Mississippi, 1859–63.

714.24   when I went to Grenada] Davis visited the Confederate army at Grenada, Mississippi, December 23–25, 1862.

716.27   "But vengeance is the Lord's,"] Cf. Romans 12:19.

717.5–8   Gen. A. Sidney Johnston . . . Bowling Green] Confederate troops under Johnston's command occupied Bowling Green, Kentucky, from September 18, 1861, to February 14, 1862.

717.20–21   field of Chalmette]   Chalmette Plantation in Louisiana, the site of the battle of New Orleans, January 8, 1815.

718.3   "Hold, enough."]   *Macbeth*, V.viii.34.

718.26   that gallant soldier]   General Joseph E. Johnston.

718.38–39   "put not your trust in princes,"]   Psalm 146:3.

719.5   remarkable book . . . Mr. Spence]   *The American Union: its effect on national character and policy, with an inquiry into secession as a constitutional right, and the causes of the disruption*, published in London in September 1861 by James Spence (1816–1905), a Liverpool businessman who became a prominent English supporter of the Confederacy.

720.22   a general unknown]   Lieutenant General John C. Pemberton (1814–1881), an artillery officer before the war, commanded the Department of South Carolina, Georgia, and Florida, March–September 1862. Davis appointed him to command the Department of Mississippi and Eastern Louisiana in October 1862.

720.33–34   one from the army of the Potomac]   Brigadier General Stephen D. Lee (see note 399.5–6). The Confederate Army of Northern Virginia was known as the Army of the Potomac before June 1862.

721.12–14   stated by the enemy . . . handled without gloves]   Major General Henry W. Halleck wrote to Ulysses S. Grant on August 2, 1862: "It is very desirable that you should clean out West Tennessee and North Mississippi of all organized enemies. If necessary, take up all active sympathizers, and either hold them as prisoners or put them beyond our lines. Handle that class without gloves, and take their property for public use."

724.34–35   Gen. McClernand]   McClernand (see note 36.10), now a major general, had been authorized by Lincoln and Stanton to lead an expedition against Vicksburg.

725.3   Morgan of Cumberland Gap]   Brigadier General George W. Morgan (1820–1893) occupied the Cumberland Gap from June 18 to September 17, 1862, when the Confederate invasion of Kentucky forced him to abandon his position and retreat to the Ohio River.

725.9–10   attack this Post of Arkansas]   Sherman captured Arkansas Post (also known as Fort Hindman) on January 11, 1863.

726.7   Henry Sherman]   Henry S. Sherman (1845–1893), a sergeant major in the 120th Ohio Infantry, was the son of Charles Taylor Sherman (1811–1879), the eldest of Sherman's siblings.

727.21   capt Richmond]   The officer in charge of black military laborers at Helena.

729.34   Colonel Moody] Colonel Granville Moody (1812–1887), a Methodist minister, commanded the 74th Ohio Infantry, December 1861–May 1863.

731.19–20   "Rosecrans' Campaign . . . Army Corps."] *Rosecrans' Campaign with the Fourteenth Army Corps, or the Army of the Cumberland; a narrative of personal observations, with an appendix, consisting of official reports of the battle of Stone River* (1863) by William D. Bickham (1827–1894), a correspondent for the *Cincinnati Commercial* who served as a volunteer aide to Major General William S. Rosecrans (1819–1898) at Stones River.

733.16   THE BATTLE] The fighting on December 31, 1862.

733.23–25   The National cemetery . . . 6,000 Federal soldiers buried.] Established in 1864, the cemetery was used to rebury soldiers disinterred in 1865–66 from wartime graves at several locations in Tennessee. The task of moving and burying the remains was carried out by men of the 111th U.S. Colored Troops.

734.11   General Breckinridge] John C. Breckinridge (see note 158.16–17), now a major general, commanded a division in the Army of Tennessee.

737.5–6   Lieut. George Burnley] Burnley died from his wounds on January 3, 1863.

738.3   Hanson] Brigadier General Roger W. Hanson (1827–1863), commander of the Orphan Brigade, was wounded on January 2 and died on January 4.

740.5–6   single grand division commander] See note 657.21.

745.28   Genl Saxton's] Brigadier General Rufus Saxton (1824–1908), the Union military governor of South Carolina, issued a proclamation on or before December 24, 1862, under the heading "A Happy New-Year's Greeting to the Colored People in the Department of the South." As printed in *The New York Times* on January 9, 1863, it read:

"In accordance, as I believe, with the will of our Heavenly Father, and by direction of your great and good friend, whose name you are all familiar with, ABRAHAM LINCOLN, President of the United States, and Commander-in-Chief of the army and the navy, on the 1st day of January, 1863, you will be declared 'forever free.'

"When, in the course of human events, there comes a day which is destined to be an everlasting beacon-light, marking a joyful era in the progress of a nation and the hopes of a people, it seems to be fitting the occasion that it should not pass unnoticed by those whose hopes it comes to brighten and to bless. Such a day to you is January 1, 1863. I therefore call upon all the colored people in this department to assemble on that day at the headquarters of the First Regiment of South Carolina Volunteers, there to hear the President's proclamation read, and to indulge in such other manifestations of joy as may be called forth by the occasion. It is your duty to carry this good news to your brethren who are still in Slavery. Let all your voices, like merry bells, join loud and clear in the grand chorus of liberty—'We are free,' 'We are free,'—until listening, you hear its echoes coming back from every cabin in the land—'We are free,' 'We are free.'"

745.34   "The Year of Jubilee."]   A slave spiritual.

Index

Abbott, Edward, 660
Abbott, Fletcher, 660, 662–63
Abbott, Henry Livermore, 660–63
Abbott, Josiah Gardner, 660
Abert, William S., 486
Abolitionism, 1, 5, 24, 89, 140, 144, 148, 151, 225, 305, 352, 381–82, 539, 543, 547, 553–54, 562, 671, 676, 697, 745
Accotink Creek, 17
Adams, Charles Francis, 141, 230–32, 309, 400
Adams, Charles Francis, Jr., 141, 400–3
Adams, John, 141
Adams, John Quincy, 141, 688–89
Africa, 2, 368–69, 534
Agriculture Department, U.S., 626–27
Alabama, 20, 47, 77, 81, 168, 722, 743
Alabama (C.S. gunboat), 309–13
Alabama 42nd Regiment, 585–88
Albany Evening Journal, 332
Alcott, Louisa May: *Hospital Sketches*, 671–82
Aldie, Va., 602
Alexander, Edward Porter: *Fighting for the Confederacy*, 246–57, 391–99, 640–56
Alexander, J. W., 115
Alexandria, Va., 125–27, 290, 382, 384–90, 405, 414, 416, 419–21, 426–27, 435, 437
Algiers, 559
Allegheny Mountains, 221–22, 629
Allen, James W., 292–93
Allen brothers (soldiers), 597
Alley, Leander F., 660–63
Allison, Robert D., 594–95
Alps (U.S. transport boat), 54, 56
Altoona, Pa., 524
Alvord, Mr., 413
Ames, Nelson, 206
Amherst, Mass., 142
Amnesty, 336
Amosville, Va., 405
Anderson, Ephraim: *Memoirs*, 526–29

Anderson, John, 185–86
Anderson, Osborne Perry, 745
Anderson, R. H., 392, 460, 643
Andrew, John A., 24
Andrews, Snowden, 392
Annandale, Va., 419–20
Annapolis, Md., 418, 502
Antietam, battle of, 462–525, 530, 541–43, 600, 603, 606, 610, 612, 615, 640, 660, 693, 712
Antietam Creek, 462–64, 488, 498–99
Antisell, Thomas, 486
Aquia, Va., 17
Aquia Creek, 400, 602, 693
Archer, James J., 650
Arkansas, 20, 74, 148, 725–26, 743; battle of Elkhorn Tavern, 99–109; treatment of contrabands in, 727–28
Arkansas (C.S. gunboat), 65, 76
Arkansas River, 725–26
Arkansas 17th Regiment, 527
Arletta (U.S. mortar schooner), 183
Arlington, Va., 6–7, 386
Armstrong, Frank, 104
Army, C.S., 8, 10, 12–13, 85, 148, 210–11, 306, 308, 333–34, 352, 740; battle of Antietam, 462–524; battle of Ball's Bluff, 28–34; battle of Chickasaw Bayou, 724–26; battle of Corinth, 578–88; battle of Elkhorn Tavern, 99–109; battle of Fair Oaks, 233–35; battle of Fort Donelson, 35–63, 81–83; battle of Fredericksburg, 614, 616, 640–83, 693–95; battle of Holly Springs, 702–5; battle of Iuka, 526–29; battle of Perryville, 589–99; battle of Shiloh, 157–71; battle of Stones River, 729–38; battle of Williamsburg, 199–209; conscription, 83, 172–77, 330, 710–12, 715; enlistment, 86, 172; following Antietam, 543–49, 600–2; following Second Bull Run, 420–21, 423, 429, 437; in Kentucky, 550–53; in Maryland, 448–58, 524, 544, 615;

853

along Mississippi River, 62–65, 67–69; President Davis on, 706–7, 709–15, 717–23; Second Bull Run campaign, 391–99, 404–12, 416, 443; Seven Days' Battles, 246–67, 269, 290, 292, 294–302, 338–40; in Shenandoah Valley, 218–23; strategy, 77–79, 236–37, 435–36, 446–47, 460–61; and Union army retreat in Virginia, 269–89, 418–19; in Virginia, 16–23, 80–83, 138, 155, 354–57; war orders for, 459–60

Army, U.S., 24–27, 89, 131, 148–49, 198, 210, 225, 236, 306, 308, 329–31, 333–35, 342, 353, 358–59, 384, 386, 388, 449–50, 460, 555, 607, 621, 706, 708, 712–14, 719, 722; advance on Richmond, 14, 16, 19–21, 83, 138, 140, 210–12, 225–26, 233, 236, 246–47, 250–51, 258, 265, 267, 278, 306, 329–30, 333, 338–40, 353–56, 400–2, 418–19, 443; battle of Antietam, 462–524; battle of Ball's Bluff, 8, 28–34; first battle of Bull Run, 10–11, 14; battle of Chickasaw Bayou, 724–26; battle of Corinth, 578–88; battle of Elkhorn Tavern, 99–100, 105–9; battle of Fair Oaks, 233–35; battle of Fort Donelson, 35–56, 61–62, 81–83; battle of Fredericksburg, 614, 616, 640–83, 693–95; battle of Holly Springs, 702–5; battle of Iuka, 526–29; battle of Perryville, 589–99; battle of Shiloh, 157–71; battle of Stones River, 729–38; battle of Williamsburg, 199–209; black soldiers in, 1, 213–14, 238–40, 303–5, 340, 344, 348, 364, 569, 697; congressional investigation of, 8–9, 28–29, 32, 34, 131; conscription, 533, 536; court-martial of General Porter, 699–701; defense of Washington, 425, 429–31, 433–35, 440; and dismissal of General McClellan, 609–16, 640–41; and Emancipation Proclamation, 537–38, 543, 546, 561–62, 564, 576–77, 742–44; employment of contrabands, 387, 389, 727–28; evacuation from Peninsula, 354–57; factions in, 400–3; following Antietam, 543–49, 600–2; following Second Bull Run, 419–23, 425–26, 435–37, 442; and fugitive slaves, 6–7, 90–92, 151, 534–35; General Hunter's emancipation order, 215–17; General McClellan's command of, 14–16, 23; general orders for, 325–28; General Pope's address to, 323–24; Lincoln as commander-in-chief, 10–11, 216, 346; along Mississippi River, 66–73; morale of, 435, 439–41, 541–42, 615, 693; in New Orleans, 227–29, 349–51; Peninsula campaign, 199–212, 233–35, 400–1; proposed campaign in Virginia, 14, 16–23, 138–40, 155–56; resignation of General Burnside, 739–41; retreat in Virginia, 269–89, 418–19; Second Bull Run campaign, 391–99, 404–16, 437, 439–40, 442–43; Seven Days' Battles, 246–67, 269, 290, 292, 338–40; in Shenandoah Valley, 219, 221–23; strategy, 600–2; war orders for, 12–13, 576–77

Ashby's Gap, Va., 602
Ashland, Va., 247, 251, 394
Aspinwall, William H., 540, 576
Atkinson, Edward, 352
Atlanta, Ga., 593
Atlantic Monthly, 24, 26, 121, 554
Atlantic Ocean, 77, 147, 335, 358–59, 621, 719
Audenried, J. C., 471
Austria-Hungary, 377, 379, 559, 620

Bachman, A. F., 483
Bagly, Lieutenant, 80
Bailey, Thomas, 194, 196–98
Baker, Edward D., 28, 31
Balloon reconnaissance, 89
Ball's Bluff, battle of, 8, 28–34, 544
Baltimore, Md., 146, 148–49, 210, 297, 390, 443, 462, 558
Baltimore and Ohio Railroad, 155, 408, 460, 511, 544
Baltimore Sun, 408
Banks, Nathaniel P., 8, 31, 89, 155–56, 221, 225–26, 247, 333, 391–92, 419, 449, 495, 548–49, 700
Bardstown, Ky., 550
Barksdale, William, 645, 647, 652
Barlow, Samuel L. M., 138–40, 699
Barney, J. N., 115

Bartlett, Amos, 471
Bartlett, John Russell, 180–93
Barton, Clara, 413–15
Bates, Edward, 417, 421–22, 428–30, 687–88
Baton Rouge, La., 243
Beatty, Samuel, 735, 737
Beaufort, S.C., 745
Beaufort (C.S. gunboat), 115–16
Beaufort (naval officer), 310
Beauregard, Pierre G. T., 62, 83, 132, 146, 157–58, 162, 166, 197, 375
Bell, Henry H., 181
Bellows, Henry W., 437–38
Belmont, August, 332–37
Benjamin, Judah P., 77, 82–83, 85–87
Benjamin, Samuel N., 463
Bennett, James Gordon, 537
Benson, Henry C., 203, 276
Benton, Perrin H., 285
Benton (U.S. flag steamer), 63, 69, 72, 75
Bentonville, Ark., 105–7, 109
Berry, William, 471
Bidwell, B. G., 60
Bidwell, John, 696–97
Birkenhead, England, 309–10, 313
Blair, Francis Preston, 224, 609–10
Blair, Frank, 224–25, 306, 609–10
Blair, Montgomery, 224, 347–48, 417–18, 422, 424, 428, 430–31, 531, 607, 609, 624, 687–88
Blair, Mr., 311
Blake, Robert, 137
Blenker, Louis, 155
Blockade, 310, 350, 502, 604, 618–19
Blue Ridge Mountains, 220–21, 394, 405, 601–2
Bode, William F., 481
Boggs, W. E., 456
Bond, Billy, 597
Boonsboro, Md., 454, 457–58, 460–61, 487
Boonsboro Gap, battle of, 454, 458
Border states, 110–13, 146, 314–16, 342, 353, 366, 372, 378, 531, 533, 558, 563–64
Borwick, Robert, 458
Boston, Elizabeth, 6–7
Boston, John, 6–7
Boston, Mass., 352, 383, 385–86, 554, 558, 606, 683, 745

Boteler, Alek, 219
Boulware, Frank, 455
Boulware, James Richmond, 454–58
Bowling Green, Ky., 11, 82–83, 717
Boyd, Belle, 218, 221
Boyd, Carlile, 301–2
Boyd, Cyrus F., 702–5
Boyd, Hugh, 286
Bradley, Lieutenant, 471
Bragg, Braxton, 148, 158, 166, 435–36, 526, 589–90, 593, 706, 722; proclamation to people of Kentucky, 550–53; at Stones River, 729, 733–36, 738; war strategy, 77–79
Bragg, Edward S., 480–81
Bragg, Thomas, 87
Bramblett, William Peter, 734–35, 737
Bramhall, Walter M., 199, 201–5, 207–8
Brazil, 304, 338
Breckinridge, John C., 158, 166–68, 242, 734–35, 738
Brentsville, Va., 17–18
Brice, Lieutenant, 454
Brigham, Matthias, 285
Bright, John, 352, 377, 380, 606
Bristow, Va., 397, 405
Britain, 134, 137, 141, 226, 230–32, 240, 334, 400, 559, 633, 687, 696, 709; building of Confederate ships, 309–13; and emancipation, 377–80, 572–75, 603, 606–8; emancipation of slaves in West Indies, 554; neutrality of, 309; proposed mediation of American conflict, 443–45, 572, 603–5; proposed recognition of Confederacy, 443–44, 719; and Southern cotton, 352–53; suppression of slave trade, 618
Broad Run, 17–18
Brock, Sallie: *Richmond during the War*, 294–96
Brockenbrough, Edward, 292
Brockenbrough, J. M., 290
Brokenburn plantation, 241–45
Brooklyn, N.Y., 6, 482, 669
Brooklyn (U.S. sloop of war), 180–93
Brooks, George A., 492
Brooks, William T., 524
Brown, Charles E., 580
Brown, Edwin A., 480
Brown, John, 745
Brown, Mrs., 384, 388

Brown, William Wells, 745
Browning, Orville H., 614–16, 683–84
Brownsville, Md., 495
Bryan (planter), 100
Bryant, William Cullen, 462
Buchanan, Franklin, 114, 116–17
Buchanan, James, 30
Buckner, J. K., 52
Buckner, Simon B., 47, 82
Buell, Don Carlos, 10–11, 20, 23, 157, 159–60, 166, 375, 436, 526, 589–91, 593–94, 729
Buford, N. B., 66
Bull Run, 16–18, 395, 399, 406, 408
Bull Run, battle of (First Bull Run), 10–11, 14, 218–19, 246, 406, 589
Bull Run, battle of (Second Bull Run), 248, 391–99, 404–16, 425–26, 437, 439–40, 442–43, 466, 525, 614, 699, 721
Bullitt, Cuthbert, 349
Bulloch, James D., 309–11
Burch, Richard, 71
Burgoyne, John F., 312
Burnett, Henry C., 568
Burnley, George, 737
Burnside, Ambrose E., 20, 402, 416, 419, 431, 436; at Antietam, 464, 472–78, 496; appointed commander of Army of the Potomac, 611–12, 615; at Fredericksburg, 614, 616, 640–41, 646–47, 650–52, 662, 693–94; resignation of, 739–41
Butler, Benjamin F., 352, 547, 549, 567, 616, 701; in New Orleans, 194, 198, 227, 230–32, 241–42, 364, 575, 696–97
Butterfield, Daniel, 260, 331
Byrne, Andrew, 310
Byrne, Thomas, 310

Cabell, Henry C., 652
Cabinet (Lincoln administration), 8, 338, 342–43, 346–47, 352–53, 416–24, 426, 428–32, 530–32, 606, 683–92, 726
Cable, George Washington, 194
Caddy (naval officer), 310
Cairo, Ill., 12, 35–36, 61, 76, 224
Cairo (U.S. gunboat), 69
Cameron, Simon, 239–40

Camp Parole, 502
Campbell, Sam, 597
Canada, 213–14, 444, 604, 629
Canals, 626, 700
Cape Lookout, 22
Carlyle, Thomas, 151
Carondelet (U.S. gunboat), 54–61, 63–73, 75
Carpenter, Francis B.: *Six Months at the White House with Abraham Lincoln*, 347–48
Carr, Eugene A., 105
Carrington, Edward, 169
Casey, Eli J., 583–84
Caskie, Willy, 409
Castle, G. T., 449
Catesby (soldier), 586–88
Catholics, 704, 709
Cayuga (U.S. gunboat), 194–96, 198
Cedar Mountain, battle of, 248, 660
Census of 1860, 111–13
Centreville, Va., 16, 18, 395, 399, 406–7, 411, 420–21, 426
Century, 54, 511, 645, 655
Chalmers, James R., 594
Chalmette, La., 717
Chamberlain, John, 438
Chamberlayne, John Hampden, 404–10
Chamberlayne, Martha Russell, 404
Chamberlayne, Nancy, 409–10
Chancellorsville, Va., 248, 396, 649
Chandler, T. S., 458
Channing, William Henry, 383
Chantilly, Va., 408, 437, 439
Charles County, Md., 89–92
Charles Town, Va. (now W.Va.), 495, 544
Charleston, S.C., 20, 146, 303, 310, 335, 558, 619
Charlottesville, Va., 340
Chase, Salmon P., 8–9, 122, 215, 225, 338–44, 347–48, 353, 416–19, 421–24, 427–32, 530, 532, 548, 623, 685, 687, 691–92, 700, 742
Chattanooga, Tenn., 267, 526, 593
Cheatham, Benjamin F., 594
Cheever, George B., 151
Cherokees, 625
Chesapeake Bay, 14, 19–21, 156
Chester Gap, Va., 602
Chicago, Ill., 745

INDEX

Chickahominy River, 233, 236, 247, 251–52, 254, 256, 258–60, 262–64, 266–67, 269, 278, 338–39, 402
Chickasaw Bayou, battle of, 724–26
Chile, 620
Chilton, R. H., 461
China, 379, 620
Chiriquí (Panama), 366, 369–70
Christianity, 2, 4, 307–8, 571, 587
Cincinnati, Ohio, 437, 527
Cincinnati (U.S. gunboat), 63, 69, 71–72
Cincinnati Commercial, 157
Cincinnati Gazette, 303
Civil war, 153, 307, 381, 618–19, 707–8
Clark, Harris, 283–84
Clark, John B., 567, 571
Clark, William S., 142
Clarke, Churchill, 108
Clarke, James Freeman, 26
Clarke (superintendent of contrabands), 385, 388
Clarksville, Tenn., 36, 48
Clay, Cassius M., 539
Clay, Henry, 688
Clendenin, David R., 263
Clipper (newspaper), 543
Clopton, A. G., 51–52
Coahoma County, Miss., 374
Cobb, Howell, 148
Cobb, T. R. R., 652–53
Colgrove, Silas, 459
Collamer, Jacob, 686–88
Colonization, 110, 178, 343, 366–71, 534, 607, 617, 619–20, 636–37, 742, 746
Colorado Territory, 629
Colston, Raleigh T., 292
Columbia, S.C., 212
Columbus, Ky., 10–11, 61–62
Comary, Cranford, 7
Commerce, 618–20
Commonwealth, 24
Compensated emancipation, 110–13, 178–79, 216, 307–8, 314–16, 342–43, 345, 378, 536, 617, 627, 631–33, 635–38, 742
Compromises, 153, 336
Concord, Mass., 671
Conestoga (U.S. gunboat), 56, 62
Confederacy (Confederate States of America), 318–22, 322, 378–80, 443–44, 446, 511, 522, 533, 550–52, 569, 571, 706, 714–15
Confiscation Act (1861), 317
Confiscation Act (1862), 317–22, 340, 342–43, 345, 352, 372, 375, 533, 742
Confiscation of property, 317–22
Congress, C.S., 82–83, 210, 358, 551, 559, 712, 715; Conscription Acts, 83, 172–77, 710–11; Davis's message to, 84–88; response to Emancipation Proclamation, 567–71
Congress, U.S., 31, 36, 157, 216, 224, 238, 268, 307, 335, 349, 352, 366, 376, 379, 531, 533–34, 554, 561, 569–70, 606–7, 609, 685, 688, 690, 700; and black soldiers, 224, 238, 303–5; Confiscation Acts, 317–22, 340, 342–43, 345, 352, 372, 375, 533, 742; investigation of Union army, 8–9, 28–29, 32, 34, 131; Lincoln's messages to, 110–12, 178–79, 617–39; and slavery, 110–12, 151–52, 154, 314
Congress (U.S. frigate), 114–17, 136–37
Connecticut, 634
Connecticut 14th Regiment, 503, 657–59
Conscription, 83, 172–77, 344, 533, 536, 710–12, 715
Conscription Acts (Confederate), 83, 172–77, 710–11
Constitution, C.S., 87, 172, 322
Constitution, U.S., 149, 306–7, 372, 375, 563, 568, 576, 617, 627–28, 630, 638, 744, 748
Contra, Lieutenant, 588
Contraband of war, 90–92, 215–17, 238–40, 364, 382–90, 727–28, 746
Cooke, John R., 653
Cooper, Samuel, 365
Coppens, Gaston, 301
Corcoran, William W., 421
Corinth, Miss., 157, 162–63, 168–69, 226, 267, 323, 375, 441, 526, 578–88, 706
Corner, Mrs., 414
Costa Rica, 620
Cotton, 76, 87, 180, 226, 241, 244, 352–53, 378, 629, 632
Couch, Darius N., 645, 655–56, 660, 663
Couch, Deborah, 298–99, 301
Covode, John, 8

Cowan, Edgar, 613, 616
Cowdin, Robert, 90
Cox, Jacob D., 436
Cox (hospital steward), 449
Craven, Thomas T., 180, 185–91, 193
Crawford, Samuel W., 468–70, 489, 494
Crimean War, 334–35, 680
Crittenden, Thomas L., 159, 590–91
Croasdale, Samuel L., 494
Crocker, Sergeant, 450
Cromwell, Oliver, 708–9
Crounse, Lorenzo L., 261
Cruft, Charles, 38–40, 42–43, 45
Culpeper, Va., 393, 404–5, 600, 641
Cumberland (U.S. frigate), 70, 114–16, 136–37
Cumberland River, 35, 44, 47–48, 52–56
Cureton, James D., 456
Currency, 621–23
Curtin, Andrew G., 612
Curtis, Samuel R., 99–100, 105–6, 549, 701, 727

Dabney, Robert L., 250
Dagans, Mrs., 384
Dakota Territory, 629
Damascus, Va., 485–86
Dana, Napoleon J. T., 471, 524
Davis, Charles H., 71, 73, 224
Davis, David, 600, 617
Davis, Jefferson, 24, 80, 82–83, 172, 197, 210–11, 233, 236, 251, 291, 364–65, 435, 446, 449, 550–51, 567, 570–71, 599, 696–97, 734; address to Mississippi legislature, 706–23; message to Confederate Congress (February 1862), 84–88
Davis, Varina Howell, 82
Dawes, Rufus R.: *Service with the Sixth Wisconsin Volunteers*, 479–84
Dawson, George W., 168–70
Dawson, Laura Amanda, 168
De Soto Parish, La., 241
Declaration of Independence, 554
Delaware, 15, 368, 573, 637; slaves in, 110, 112–13, 314
Democracy, 572
Democratic Party, 36, 110, 138, 178, 332, 505, 533, 540, 543, 550, 559, 563, 606–7, 609, 612, 614, 701, 748
Denmark, 444, 620
Deportation, 636–37
Derby, Richard, 471
Detroit, Mich., 493
Devlin, John, 501
Dickenson, Captain, 201, 203
Dickinson, Emily, 142–43
Dillon, Edward, 104, 107
District of Columbia: contrabands in, 382–84, 387; military hospitals in, 669–82; slavery in, 112–13, 151, 178–79, 637. *See also* Washington, D.C.
Diven, Alexander S., 304
Dix, John A., 548
"Dixie," 450, 593
Doran, Sergeant, 207
Doubleday, Abner, 465, 467–68, 472, 479, 483, 491
Douglass, Frederick, 1–5, 144–54, 366, 561–66, 745
Douglass' Monthly, 1, 144, 561
Dover, Tenn., 48–49
Dranesville, Va., 33, 408
Drayton, Percival, 181
Dudley, Thomas H., 309–13
Dudley, Tom, 408
Dudley, William W., 483
Duffey, George, 392
Dumfries, Va., 17–18
Dunklin, Mart, 168
Dunnington, John W., 70
Durant, Thomas J., 349–50
Dwight, Wilder, 492, 494
Dwight, William, 204–5

Eakin, Chandler P., 200, 208
Early, Jubal A., 650
Education, 3, 387
Edward, Prince of Wales, 444
Edwards, J. Price, 309, 312–13
Eglon, Henry, 91
Eldridge, William E., 282
Elizabeth I, 134
Elkhorn Tavern, battle of, 99–109
Ellet, A. W., 73
Ellet, Charles, 73, 75
Elliott, W. L., 69
Ellsworth, Elmer E., 127
Ely, George B., 484

Emancipation, 1–5, 141, 352–53, 372–73; compensation for, 110–13, 178–79, 216, 307–8, 314–16, 342–43, 345, 378, 536, 617, 627, 631–33, 635–38, 742; European reaction to, 377–81, 555, 563, 572–75, 603, 606–8; General Hunter's order, 215–17, 238–40, 303–5; immediate, 144, 151–52
Emancipation Proclamation, 342–48, 353, 372, 378–79, 530–36, 538–40, 543, 546, 554–77, 603, 606–8, 614, 627, 696–97, 742–45, 748–49
Embree, Dan, 705
Emerson, Ralph Waldo, 151, 554–60
Emory, Thomas, 170
Equality, 4, 154, 367
Erie Canal, 700
Eugène de Savoie-Carignan, 409
Evansport, Va., 17
Ewell, Richard S., 218, 254, 256, 391, 394–95, 397, 404–5, 407

Fair Oaks, battle of, 233–35, 247, 466
Fairfax, J. W., 655
Fairfax, Va., 17, 131, 138–39, 408, 413–14, 435
Fales, Mrs., 414
Falmouth, Va., 641, 643, 647, 656, 662, 669, 693
Farnsworth, John F., 259, 263
Farnum, John E., 205
Farragut, David G., 180–82, 184, 187, 191, 194, 224, 227, 718
Farris, John Kennerly, 47–53
Farris, Mary, 47
Fawcett, Preston & Co. (shipbuilders), 309, 311
Fayetteville, Ark., 105
Featherston, Winfield S., 237
Feild, Hume R., 596, 598
Fergus, W. C., 586
Ferrel (overseer), 91
Ferris, Corporal, 583
Fessenden, William P., 687–88
Fields, James T., 121
Fiske, Samuel W. (Dunn Browne), 503–4, 657–59
Flag, Confederate, 717
Fleming, P. W., 363
Florence, Ala., 81

Florida, 77, 148, 215, 743
Flournoy, W. C., 598
Floyd, John B., 50–51, 148
Foote, Andrew H., 35–36, 56, 58, 61–62, 64–66, 69–71, 148, 192, 718
Forest Queen (U.S. steamer), 724
Forman, Jacob G., 727–28
Forman, James B., 592
Forrest, Nathan B., 47, 53
Fort Darling, 210–11, 224–25, 659
Fort Donelson, battle of, 35–62, 70, 81–83, 85
Fort Ellsworth, 128
Fort Henry, 35, 47, 54, 62, 81–83
Fort Jackson, 180–87, 194–95, 198, 224
Fort Lafayette, 29, 32, 34, 440, 543
Fort Magruder, 200, 202
Fort McHenry, 148
Fort (Fortress) Monroe, 12, 20–21, 23, 133, 138, 155, 356, 400, 418
Fort Pillow, 54, 70–73, 75
Fort Pulaski, 358
Fort St. Philip, 180–85, 187–88, 190, 194–95, 198, 224
Fort Sumter, 146, 558
Foster, George W., 587
Fox, Gustavus Vasa, 224
France, 134, 226, 377–80, 443–45, 504, 559, 604, 619–20, 719
Frankfort, Ky., 589
Franklin, William, 250–51, 261, 392, 396, 399, 416, 419, 425, 464, 472, 474–76, 478, 498, 694
Fraser, Trenholm & Co. (shipbuilders), 310–11
Frederick, Md., 404, 446, 448–56, 458–59, 462, 485, 487, 544
Fredericksburg, Va., 211, 225, 247–48, 355–56, 396, 441, 497, 602, 614, 616, 640–83, 693–95, 700, 719, 739
Fredericksburg Railroad, 340
Free persons of color, 4–5, 364, 636–37, 664
Frémont, Jessie Benton, 152
Frémont, John C., 152, 225, 247, 391
French, William H., 254, 470–71, 657
Frigates, 70, 114–19, 134–37, 184
Front Royal, Va., 218, 221
Fry, James B., 591
Fugitive Slave Law, 376, 385

Fugitive slaves, 6–7, 90–92, 129–30, 151, 239, 258–63, 374–76, 385, 534–35, 561, 627–28
Fuller, Arthur B., 288

Gaillord, I. D., 455
Gaines's Mill, battle of, 246, 250, 254, 256, 258–65, 269, 292, 299
Gainesville, Va., 405
Gale, W., 471
Galena (U.S. gunboat), 210–11
Garibaldi, Giuseppe, 294
Garrison, William Lloyd, 144, 151, 382
General Beauregard (C.S. ram ship), 72, 74
General Bragg (C.S. ram ship), 71–72, 74–75
General Jeff Thompson (C.S. ram ship), 72, 74
General Lovell (C.S. ram ship), 72, 74
General Orders No. 60 (C.S.), 364–65
General Price (C.S. ram ship), 71–72, 74
General Sumter (C.S. ram ship), 71–72, 74–75
General War Order No. 1 (U.S.), 12–13
General War Order No. 139 (U.S.), 576–77
General War Order No. 163 (U.S.), 576–77
Georgetown (District of Columbia), 531
Georgia, 20, 146, 215, 236, 722, 743; slaves in, 358–63
Georgia 15th Regiment, 501
Gerolt, Friedrich von, 418
Getty, George W., 656
Gettysburg, Pa., 248, 512, 653
Gibbon, John, 479, 483, 611, 650
Gibson, Thomas, 75
Gilbert, Charles C., 590–91
Gilmore, William E., 65
Glendale, Va., 269, 277–89
Goddard, Dr., 204
Goethe, Johann Wolfgang von, 500
Goodell, William, 151
Gordon, John B., 459, 468–70, 489
Gordonsville, Va., 391–92, 419, 502, 641
Gorman, Willis A., 31
Governor Moore (C.S. gunboat), 195
Governors, state, 524–25, 545, 548
Graham, Charles K., 90

Grampus (C.S. gunboat), 62
Granger, Gordon, 68
Grant, Jesse Root, 157
Grant, Julia Dent, 157–58
Grant, Ulysses S., 375, 526; at Fort Donelson, 35–37, 40, 43, 47, 54–56, 61–62; in Mississippi, 702, 704, 724–25; at Shiloh, 157–66
Granville, Earl (Granville Leveson-Gower), 603
Gray, Amos H., 702, 705
Greeley, Horace, 372, 617
Green, F. M., 584
Greene, George S., 492
Gregg, Maxcy, 650
Gregory's Gap, Va., 602
Grenada, Miss., 702, 706, 714, 721
Griffin, Charles, 260, 616
Grimes, James W., 687–88
Griswold, Major, 211
Grose, William, 735, 737
Grover, Cuvier, 206, 280
Groveton, Va., 411
Gulf of Mexico, 12, 77, 335, 440
Gunboats, 35–36, 44, 47, 54–76, 78, 81, 115–17, 159, 168–69, 180, 183, 189–90, 194–96, 198, 210–11, 241, 244, 265, 293, 309–12, 335, 339, 416, 664, 720, 724
Gwin, William, 159

Habeas corpus, writ of, 533, 536–37, 540, 614
Hagerstown, Md., 454, 457–58, 461, 464, 480, 487, 512, 544
Haiti, 388, 574, 620
Hall, John, 58
Hall, Norman J., 660–61, 663
Halleck, Henry W., 20, 23, 139, 411, 724–25; attitudes toward, 374–75, 401–3, 433–34, 437, 524–25, 546–49, 663; as general-in-chief, 330, 338–40, 342–43, 354–57, 391, 419, 421–22, 425–26, 429, 431, 437, 524–25, 600, 615–16, 739, 741; in Kentucky, 10–11, 166; in Mississippi, 267, 323
Hamilton, Alexander, 374
Hammer, Captain, 310–11
Hampton Roads, 114–20
Hancock, Winfield S., 8, 203–4, 209
Hannibal, 409

Hanover, Va., 355, 402
Hanover (Germany), 618
Hanson, Roger, 738
Hardie, James, 577
Hargett, Joseph T., 169
Harper's Ferry, Va. (now W.Va.), 139, 248, 396, 459–60, 462, 485, 494–96, 511–23, 544, 600, 602, 615, 745
Harper's Weekly, 693–95
Harris, Ira, 685, 687, 689
Harrison, Charles M., 584
Harrison, Napoleon B., 194
Harrisonburg, Va., 218, 221
Harrodsburg, Ky., 594
Hartford (U.S. warship), 181, 184–85, 187–88, 191, 193–94, 196
Hartsuff, George L., 467–68
Haskell, Joseph, 648, 654
Haskell, Mr., 413
Haupt, Herman, 425–27
Hawkins, J. P., 161
Hawthorne, Nathaniel, 121–37
Hay, John, 425–27, 542
Haydon, Charles B., 269–76
Haymarket, Va., 602
Heathsville, Va., 22
Hebert, Louis, 107
Heintzelman, Samuel, 206, 209, 258, 397, 402, 414
Heise, Henry C., 254
Helena, Ark., 725, 727
Henley, Jim, 169
Henry, Gustavus A., 568
Hewit, Henry S., 161
Hill, Ambrose Powell, 248–49, 252, 254–56, 290, 391, 394–95, 404–5, 407, 410, 496, 649
Hill, Benjamin H., 570
Hill, Daniel Harvey, 237, 248–50, 252, 254, 256, 392, 408, 458, 460–61
Hillyer, W. S., 161
Hilton Head, S.C., 215
Hodge (soldier), 598
Hoel, William R., 68
Hollins, Thomas, 188
Holly Springs, Miss., 702–5, 724
Holmes, Oliver Wendell, Jr., 662
Holmes, Theophilus H., 250
Holt, Joseph, 401
Homestead Act, 554, 625
Honduras, 620

Hood, John B., 247, 254, 256, 292, 483, 643
Hooe, Alexander S., 484
Hooker, Joseph, 21, 89, 155, 431, 549, 610, 640, 694; at Antietam, 463–75, 478–79, 486, 488–89, 491, 494, 524; at Fredericksburg, 658, 661–62; at Second Bull Run, 395; in Seven Days' Battles, 258–59, 269, 272–73, 277, 280–82; at Williamsburg, 199–201, 203–4, 206, 209
Hopewell, Va., 397
Horn, Sergeant, 202, 207
Horsley, A. S., 597
Hospitals, 277, 282–89, 297–302, 383–84, 389, 413, 448–50, 455, 518–20, 657, 662, 669–82, 731–32
Hottenstein, John A., 66
House of Representatives, U.S., 224, 238, 303–5, 607, 617
Howard, Andrew J., 583–84
Howard, Jacob M., 687, 689
Howard, Oliver O., 471, 660–62
Howe, Church, 471
Howe, Julia Ward: "The Battle Hymn of the Republic," 24–27
Howe, Samuel Gridley, 24–25
Huger, Benjamin, 80, 250, 339
Humphreys, Andrew A., 655–56
Hunter, David, 215–16, 225, 238–40, 303–5, 315, 364, 436
Hunter, Robert M., 81–82
Hunter, Will, 170
Huntington, Howard J., 481–82
Hunton, Thomas, 374
Huntsville, Ala., 168
Hurlbut, S. A., 161

Illinois, 614, 626, 629, 748
Illinois 2nd Regiment, 703
Illinois 8th Regiment, 259, 263
Illinois 17th Regiment, 39
Illinois 42nd Regiment, 66–67
Illinois 49th Regiment, 39
Illinois 101st Regiment, 703
Illinois and Michigan Canal, 626
Illinois River, 626
Immigrants, 558, 629
India, 559, 607
Indiana, 589, 611, 629
Indiana 11th Regiment, 37–39, 41
Indiana 19th Regiment, 483

Indiana 27th Regiment, 459, 491
Indiana 37th Regiment, 731
Indians, 304, 433, 625–26
Ingalls, Pearl P., 727–28
Ingmire, Frank, 583
Interior Department, U.S., 624–25
Iowa, 629
Iowa 15th Regiment, 702–5
Ireland, 559, 709
Iroquois (U.S. warship), 190
Irvine, Lute B., 598
Island No. 10, battle of, 54, 62–69, 83, 323
Italy, 294, 379, 559, 620
Iuka, Miss., 526–29, 578, 704, 706

Jackson, Andrew, 304
Jackson, James S., 592, 598
Jackson, James W., 127
Jackson, Miss., 706
Jackson, Oscar L., 578–84
Jackson, Thomas (Stonewall), 236, 292, 325, 437, 449–50, 455, 460; at Antietam, 462, 513; at Fredericksburg, 641, 644, 648–50, 667; at Second Bull Run, 391–92, 394–99, 402, 404–9, 416; in Seven Days' Battles, 245–56, 259; in Shenandoah Valley, 218–25, 323, 402, 419
Jacksonport, Ark., 99–100
Jacobs, Harriet (Linda Brent), 382–90; *Incidents in the Life of a Slave Girl*, 382
James, George S., 458
James River, 21, 114–15, 210–11, 224–25, 236, 256, 265, 269, 275, 277, 279–80, 284, 293, 329, 339, 354, 356, 396, 416, 419, 700
Jamestown (C.S. warship), 115, 117–18
Japan, 380, 620
Jefferson, Thomas, 374
Jeffersonton, Va., 394, 405
Jem (slave), 100–2
Jenkins, Micah, 454, 458
Jenney, W. L. B., 161
Jerry (slave), 151
Jewett, Dr., 283–84
Jews, 2
Jocelyn, Stephen P., 471
John (slave), 299–300
"John Brown's Body," 24, 26
Johns, Bill, 599

Johnson, Andrew, 8
Johnson, Bradley T., 450
Johnson, Clifton: *Battleground Adventures*, 505–10, 664–68
Johnson, Reverdy, 352
Johnston, Albert Sidney, 83, 99, 157–58, 166, 717
Johnston, Joseph E., 138, 199, 210, 233, 547, 706, 720–21
Johnston, Sam, 642
Johnston, William Preston, 99
Joint Committee on the Conduct of the War, 8–9, 28–29, 32, 34, 131
Jones, Catesby ap Roger, 114–20
Jones, John B., 80–83, 210–12
Jones, William M., 293
Jordan, Tyler, C., 656
Julia Usher (C.S. warship), 310–11
Julius Caesar, 409
Justice Department, C.S., 87

Kansas, 625, 629
Katahdin (U.S. warship), 183
Kearneysville, Va. (now W. Va.), 518
Kearny, Philip, 206–7, 209, 269, 271, 273, 280, 404, 408, 413–14, 437–38
Keedysville, Md., 463
Kelley, W. D., 598
Kellogg, John A., 480–82
Kelly, Henry B., 222–23
Kelsey, Dr., 508
Kemper, Del, 399
Kendall, Miss, 383
Kennedy, Joseph C. G., 329
Kennon, Beverly, 195
Kentucky, 10–11, 15, 35, 63, 77–78, 122, 148, 168, 267, 303, 435, 437, 526, 537, 546, 564, 629, 689, 706, 722, 733, 735, 737; battle of Perryville, 589–93; General Bragg's proclamation, 550–53; slaves in, 110, 112–13, 314
Kentucky 15th Regiment, 592
Kernstown, Va., 219
Kerr, Orpheus C. (Robert Henry Newell), 93–98
Kershaw, Joseph B., 652
Key, John J., 541–42
Key, Thomas M., 342
Keyes, E. D., 209, 258
Kimball, John W., 500
Kimmel, Manning M., 104

INDEX

King, Preston, 685–86, 691
King, Rufus, 396–97
Kingsbury, Henry W., 524
Knefler, Fred, 42
Knipe, Joseph F., 492
Knox, Tom, 665
Kossack, William, 161

Laborers, 1–2, 636–37
Labruzan, Charles B., 585–88
Lady, Thomas, 582
Lagow, C. B., 161
Laird, John and Henry H. (shipbuilders), 309–13
Lander, Frederick W., 8
Lane, John, 648
Lang, David, 665
Law, E. M., 483
Lawson, Joseph, 664–68
Lawton, Alexander R., 247, 397
Lee, Blair, 226
Lee, Elizabeth Blair, 224–25
Lee, Fitzhugh, 248, 394
Lee, Joe P., 598
Lee, Robert E., 103, 211, 233, 245, 297, 325, 354, 386; at Antietam, 462, 503, 506, 518, 522, 524, 603, 712; at Fredericksburg, 640–43, 648–50, 655; memoranda for President Davis, 236–37, 435–36, 446–47; Second Bull Run campaign, 391–93, 395, 397–99, 404, 409; in Seven Days' Battles, 246–51, 253–54, 256, 269, 292; Special Orders No. 191, 459–62
Lee, Samuel Philips, 224
Lee, Stephen D., 399, 721
Leesburg, Va., 28, 33, 408, 454
Leetown, Va. (now W.Va.), 518, 522
Leighton, Rufus, 385
Letcher, John, 219
Lewis, George C., 604
Lexington (U.S. gunboat), 54, 159
Libby Prison, 502
Liberator, 382
Liberia, 368–69, 620
Liberty County, Ga., 358–63
Lincoln, Abraham, 1, 15, 23, 28, 81, 83, 93, 197, 224, 266–68, 323, 325, 329–30, 332–36, 377, 388, 401, 408, 432, 439–40, 451, 549, 551, 593; address on colonization, 366–71; cabinet crisis, 683–92; as commander-in-chief, 10–11, 216, 346, 533, 561, 743; dismissal of General McClellan, 609–16; dismissal of Major Key, 541–42; and Emancipation Proclamation, 342–48, 353, 372, 530–36, 538, 540, 546, 554–76, 606–7, 614, 627, 696–97, 742–45, 748–49; and General McClellan, 8–9, 14, 138, 140, 155–56, 306, 339, 417–31, 433–34, 576–77, 600–2, 609–10; General War Order No. 1, 12–13; Hawthorne on, 121–25; meditation on divine will, 442; message to Congress (March 1862), 110–12; message to Congress (April 1862), 178–79; message to Congress (December 1862), 617–39; proclamation suspending writ of habeas corpus, 533, 536–37, 614; resignation of General Burnside, 739–41; revocation of General Hunter's emancipation order, 215–17, 315–16; and slavery, 150–52, 178–79, 314–17, 340, 343, 349–50, 352–53, 367–68, 372–73, 617, 627–38; Special War Order No. 1, 12–13
Lincoln, William Wallace (Willie), 121
Lindsey, Daniel W., 726
Little, Henry, 108
Little Rebel (C.S. ship), 72, 74
Little Rock, Ark., 725
Liverpool, England, 309–10, 312–13
Logan, John A., 705
Logwood, James A., 656
Lomax, Lindsay, 104
London, England, 141, 309, 311–12, 400, 572, 575
London, Ont., 213–14
Long, Armistead L., 237
Longstreet, James, 205, 248–49, 254–55, 392, 395–99, 404–5, 407, 454, 460, 640–44, 648–50, 655
Looting, 702–5
Loudon, Va., 435
Louisiana, 20, 241–45, 364, 743; Union army in, 227–29, 349–51
Louisiana (C.S. warship), 188–89, 193
Louisiana 3rd Regiment, 105, 527, 529
Louisiana Native Guards, 364
Louisiana State Seminary and Military Academy, 165–66

Louisville, Ky., 550, 589–90
Louisville (U.S. gunboat), 56, 58
Lovejoy, Owen, 304, 347
Lovell, Mansfield, 197
Lovettsville, Md., 460
Lowe, Thaddeus, 89
Lowry, Reigert B., 186, 190–91
Luray, Va., 220
Lusk, Elizabeth Freeman, 439
Lusk, William Thompson, 439–41
Lynchburg, Va., 20, 210, 212, 340

Maben, Mrs., 300
Mackall, W. W., 69
Macy, George N., 661
Madison Parish, La., 241
Magnolia (steamer), 180
Magruder, John B., 21, 339
Maine, 472
Maine 3rd Regiment, 273
Mallard, R. Q., 363
Mallory, Robert, 303
Mallory, Stephen, 85
Malvern Hill, battle of, 249–50, 269, 393, 653
Manassas, Va., 8, 11–13, 16, 20, 22–23, 83, 138–39, 155–56, 248, 329, 391, 393, 395, 397, 405–7, 411, 416, 418–19, 438, 546–47, 602
Manassas (C.S. ram ship), 187–91, 193, 195
Manassas Gap Railroad, 405
Maney, George, 596
Maney, Thomas H., 598
Manlove, Thomas, 241
Mansfield, Joseph K., 117, 464, 468, 471, 475, 485, 487–89, 524
Mapes, William, 492
Marble, Manton, 543
Marshall, J. B., 588
Marshall, Louis H., 68
Mart, Marion, 705
Martial law, 83, 327–28, 360–61, 437, 531, 536
Martin, Augustus P., 255
Martindale, John H., 260
Martinsburg, Va. (now W.Va.), 460, 511, 544
Maryland, 5, 15, 22, 236, 355, 385, 409, 435–37, 446, 537, 564, 573, 637; battle of Antietam, 462–524; Confederate Army in, 448–58, 524, 544, 615; slaves in, 6, 110, 112, 308, 314
Mason, James, 286
Mason, Roy, Jr., 647
Massachusetts, 24, 629, 634
Massachusetts 1st Regiment, 90, 141, 286, 400
Massachusetts 2nd Regiment, 492, 494
Massachusetts 12th Regiment, 467–68
Massachusetts 13th Regiment, 467–68
Massachusetts 15th Regiment, 284, 471, 662
Massachusetts 16th Regiment, 277–89
Massachusetts 19th Regiment, 233
Massachusetts 20th Regiment, 233–35, 660–63
Massachusetts 21st Regiment, 142, 414
Matteson, Frederick W., 440–41
Maurin, Victor, 652
Maury, Dabney H., 99–109
Mazzini, Giuseppe, 573
McCall, George A., 33, 258, 260, 280–81, 419, 421
McClellan, George B., 8–10, 12–13, 31–34, 148, 155–56, 329–31, 333, 342, 354, 375–76, 436, 449, 459; at Antietam, 462–64, 466, 473–75, 477–78, 486, 503, 518–19, 522, 524; attitudes toward, 400–2, 437–38, 524–25, 537–38, 543, 545–46, 548–49, 609–10, 661, 663, 700; cabinet opposition to, 416–24, 426, 428–32; dismissal of, 609–16, 640–41, 693; and emancipation, 540, 576–77; Hawthorne on, 130–33; memorandum for Stanton, 14–23; message to Army of the Potomac, 138–39; military policy of, 306–8; Peninsula campaign, 199, 210–11, 218, 225, 233, 236–37, 245, 400–1, 443, 525; political aspirations, 611–12; and President Lincoln, 8–9, 14, 138, 140, 155–56, 306, 339, 417–31, 433–34, 576–77, 600–2, 609–10; Second Bull Run campaign, 391–93, 396, 406, 415, 525; in Seven Days' Battles, 246–49, 258–59, 265–67, 269, 292–93, 297, 338–40, 354
McClellan, Mary Ellen, 140, 155, 433, 524, 600
McClernand, John A., 36–38, 42–43, 160, 724–25, 748

McCook, A. M., 159, 590–91
McCown, John P., 69
McCoy, J. C., 165
McCulloch, Benjamin, 100, 104, 106–9
McDonald, Wood, 293
McDougall, James A., 110, 112
McDowell, Irwin, 8, 11, 155, 225, 247, 333, 391, 396–97, 401–2, 419, 437–38, 466, 609
McGinnis, George F., 39, 41
McGuire, John, 290
McGuire, Judith W., 290–93
McIntosh, James, 105, 107, 109
McKeever, Chauncey, 205
McLaws, Lafayette, 392, 460, 643, 645, 652
McLean, Nathaniel H., 157, 159
McMichael, William, 161
McPherson, J. B., 54, 161
McRae (C.S. gunboat), 190
Meacham, George A., 284
Mead, Frederick, 261
Meade, George G., 280, 465–66, 489, 611–13, 650
Meade, Margaret, 611
Meagher, Thomas F., 254, 471, 653–54
Mechanicsville, Va., 252–53, 258, 269–70, 290–91, 297
Melville, Herman: *Battle-Pieces and Aspects of the War*, 171; "Shiloh," 171
Memminger, Christopher G., 87, 212
Memphis, Tenn., 20, 54, 73–76, 168, 170, 224, 374, 592, 702, 705, 718–19, 725, 748
Memphis and Bowling Green Railroad, 54
Mercer, Hugh W., 358–59
Meredith, J., 611
Merrimack (U.S. frigate), 70, 114. *See also Virginia* (C.S. warship)
Meserve, Stephen E., 282
Mexico, 30, 379, 438, 620
Michigan, 485, 629, 676
Michigan 2nd Regiment, 269–76
Michigan 3rd Regiment, 269
Michigan 7th Regiment, 233
Middleburgh, Va., 408
Middletown, Md., 456–57, 460, 462, 486
Miles, Dixon S., 494, 565
Miller, David R., 479, 485

Miller, William C., 309
Miller, Marcus P., 477
Minnesota, 433, 625–26, 629
Minnesota (U.S. frigate), 114, 116–19, 134–35
Minnesota 1st Regiment, 31
Minor, Robert D., 116
Mississippi, 81, 157, 168, 267, 374, 573, 670, 700, 748; battle of Chickasaw Bayou, 724–26; battle of Corinth, 578–88; battle of Holly Springs, 702–5; battle of Iuka, 526–29; President Davis' address to legislature of, 706–23
Mississippi (U.S. frigate), 184, 191–92
Mississippi 14th Regiment, 51
Mississippi Central Railroad, 702
Mississippi River, 20, 35, 54, 62–76, 180–98, 224, 267, 323, 551–53, 564, 573, 626, 700, 702, 714, 718–20, 725–26
Missouri, 15, 63, 77, 99, 148, 151, 267, 437, 564, 629, 722; slaves in, 110, 112–13, 308, 314
Missouri 1st Regiment, 168–69
Missouri 2nd Regiment, 526–29
Missouri 8th Regiment, 37–39, 41
Missouri River, 335
Mitchel, Ormsby M., 547, 549
Mitchell, A. T., 597
Mitchell, J., 366
Mitchell, Mary Bedinger (Maria Blunt), 511–23
Mobile, Ala., 77, 181, 335, 593
Mobile Bay, 593
Monahan, A. B., 584
Monarch (U.S. ram ship), 73–74
Monitor (U.S. warship), 114, 117–20, 134–36, 141, 210
Monocacy River, 410, 448, 455, 485
Monroe, La., 244
Monroe Doctrine, 336
Montgomery, Ala., 20, 593
Montgomery (U.S. warship), 185
Moody, George V., 652, 654
Moody, Granville, 729
Moore, Thomas O., 227–29
Moran, Benjamin, 230–32
Morell, George W., 255, 258
Morgan, G. W., 725–26
Morocco, 620
Morrell, Mrs., 413

Morris, George U., 137
Morris, L. M., 208
Morrison, William R., 39
Mosher (tug), 187
Motley, John Lothrop, 377–81
Mound City (U.S. gunboat), 63, 69, 71–72
Mumford, Mr., 242
Munford, Thomas T., 393
Munfordville, Ky., 12, 594–95
Murfreesboro, Tenn., 168, 729–30, 733
Murphy, Robert C., 703–4
Muslims, 2

Naglee, Henry M., 89
Napoléon I (Napoléon Bonaparte), 138, 246, 248, 409
Napoléon III (Louis Napoléon), 226, 377–79
Nashville, Tenn., 16, 20, 47–48, 83, 149, 226, 729–30, 733–34, 737
National Freedman's Relief Association, 383
Navy, C.S., 87, 210, 436; *Monitor-Virginia* (*Merrimack*) duel, 114–20, 135–37, 141; at mouth of Mississippi River, 187–93, 195–96; ships built in Britain, 309–13; western river activity, 65, 69–76. *See also* Gunboats
Navy, U.S., 12–13, 20–21, 133–34, 147, 210–11, 216, 224–26, 265, 335, 359, 416, 561–62, 621, 712; and Emancipation Proclamation, 742–44; fall of New Orleans, 194–98; *Monitor-Virginia* (*Merrimack*) duel, 114–20, 135–37, 141; at mouth of Mississippi, 180–93; western river activity, 35–36, 44, 47, 54–76, 78, 81, 159, 168–69. *See also* Gunboats
Navy Department, U.S., 623
Nebraska Territory, 629
Negley, James S., 729
Negotiation, 332–37
Negroes, 381; as Americans, 129–30; colonization of, 110, 178, 343, 366–71; as contraband of war, 382–90, 727–28, 746; and emancipation celebrations, 745–47; free, 4–5, 364, 636–37, 664; in Union army, 1, 213–14, 238–40, 303–5, 340, 344, 348, 364, 569, 697
Nelson, Horatio, 137

Nelson, William, 159, 589
Netherlands, 620, 709
Neutrality, 309, 619
New Bedford, Mass., 385
New Bern, N.C., 142
New Granada (Colombia), 620
New Hampshire, 678
New Jersey, 634
New Jersey 1st Regiment, 405
New Jersey 8th Regiment, 208
New Madrid, Mo., 64–65, 68–69, 323
New Mexico Territory, 487
New Orleans, La., 20, 77, 180–81, 184, 188–89, 191–98, 224, 226–31, 242, 311, 349–52, 558, 575, 604, 629, 643, 696, 718–20, 743
New York, 482, 574, 626, 634, 689, 700–1
New York 1st Regiment, 202, 276
New York 9th Regiment, 496
New York 14th Regiment, 6–7, 482
New York 28th Regiment, 492
New York 34th Regiment, 470–71
New York 38th Regiment, 273
New York 51st Regiment, 669
New York 79th Regiment, 439–41
New York City, 89, 267, 379, 383–85, 437, 462, 540, 558, 574–75, 629, 699
New York Evening Post, 462
New York Herald, 537, 691
New York Sunday Mercury, 93
New York Times, 28–34, 669
New York Tribune, 258, 366, 372, 462, 617, 747
New York World, 543
Newcastle, Duke of (Thomas Pelham-Holles), 444
Newmarket, Va., 218, 221
Newport News, Va., 114, 136
Nicaragua, 620
Nichols, Danforth B., 383
Nicodemus, Mr., 487
Nicolay, John G., 685
Nixon, George, 68
Nolensville, Tenn., 729–30
Norcross, Louise and Frances, 142
Norfolk, Va., 20, 80, 114, 119, 134, 210, 743
Norfolk Packet (schooner), 183
North Carolina, 20, 142, 148, 236, 343, 402, 743
Norway, 619

Noyes, David K., 479
Nurses, 297–302, 413–15, 426, 515–20

Oak Grove, battle of, 269
Observer (London), 443
Occoquan, Va., 17
Occoquan Creek, 16–18
Odell, Moses F., 8
Ohio, 487, 629, 634, 724
Ohio 10th Regiment, 527
Ohio 39th Regiment, 527
Ohio 43rd Regiment, 68, 584
Ohio 63rd Regiment, 578–84
Ohio 74th Regiment, 729–32
Ohio River, 10–11, 35, 54, 61, 564, 589, 722
O'Kane, James, 188, 191
Omega plantation, 241–43
Opelousas, La., 227
Opequon Creek, 544
Orange, Va., 404, 409
Orange and Alexandria Railroad, 405
Ord, E. O. C., 374, 526
Oreto (C.S. warship), 309–11
Orleans, Va., 405
Orphan Brigade, 733–38
Orpheus C. Kerr Papers, 93–98
Osborn, Thomas W., 199, 201, 206–8
Osceola, Miss., 70
Ottoman Empire, 379, 620
Owens, Ira S.: *Greene County in the War*, 729–32
Owensville, Md., 6
Ox Hill, battle of, 399, 404, 408
Oxford, Miss., 702

Pacific Ocean, 621
Page, Captain, 90
Page, Charles A., 258–64
Palmerston, Viscount (Henry John Temple), 230–32, 377, 380, 443–45, 572, 603–5
Panama, 366, 369–72
Panola County, Miss., 374
Paris, France, 575
Parker, William W., 644, 656
Parker, Joel, 701
Parker, W. H., 115
Parliament (British), 141, 230, 352, 606, 687
Parsons, Charles C., 592
Parsons, Richard C., 338

Patrick Henry (C.S. warship), 115, 117–18
Patriotism, 224, 337, 350, 531, 549, 553, 619, 697
Patterson, John, 596–98
Patterson, Robert, 11, 547
Pea Ridge, Ark., 99
Pelham, John, 649
Pemberton, John C., 706
Pendleton, William N., 643
Peninsula campaign, 199–212, 233–35, 400–1, 443, 525, 644
Pennsylvania, 131, 236, 355, 408–9, 449, 465–66, 512, 524, 574, 601, 613, 634
Pennsylvania 26th Regiment, 89, 279
Pennsylvania 46th Regiment, 492
Pennsylvania 63rd Regiment, 270
Pennsylvania 127th Regiment, 662
Pennsylvania 128th Regiment, 494
Pensacola, Fla., 77–78, 193
Pensacola (U.S. warship), 181, 196
Perkins, George Hamilton, 194–98
Perkins, James B., 585
Perkins, Susan, 194
Perry, George B., 660
Perry, Oliver H., 304
Perryville, Ky., 589–99
Peru, 620
Petersburg, Va., 299
Pettus, John J., 711, 715, 718
Phelan, James, 568, 570
Phelps, John W., 238, 364
Philadelphia, Pa., 189, 390, 558, 574, 696; emancipation celebration in, 745–47
Philadelphia Inquirer, 543
Phillips, Wendell, 144, 151, 225
Pickett, George E., 643, 648
Pike, Horace L., 201
Pilgrims, 130, 709
Pinkard, Marsh, 599
Pinnell, Cam, 170
Pittman, Samuel E., 491
Pittsburg Landing, Tenn., 157–71
Pittsburgh (U.S. gunboat), 56, 58, 63, 69, 71–72
Pleasanton, Alfred, 464
Plumly, Benjamin Rush, 745–47
Poland, 559
Pomeroy, Samuel C., 687, 689
Poore, Benjamin Perley, 121
Pope, John, 338, 429, 436–38, 526, 609, 614, 616; address to Army of

Virginia, 323–24; General McClellan's antagonism toward, 416, 420, 425, 433–34, 525, 549; General Orders Nos. 5, 7, and 11, 325–28; at Island No. 10, 64–65, 68–70; at Second Bull Run, 391–402, 405–7, 411–12, 416, 419–21, 426, 525, 547, 615, 699; in Virginia, 323–30, 333, 340, 354–56
Population, 633–35
Port Hudson, Miss., 714, 720
Port Royal, S.C., 141, 238, 304
Port Royal, Va., 650
Porter, David D., 182–84, 196–97, 224
Porter, Fitz John, 338–39, 613, 616; at Antietam, 464, 472–73, 475, 477; court-martial of, 411, 614, 699–701; and General McClellan, 329–31, 543–49, 700; at Second Bull Run, 397–98, 411–12, 614–15; in Seven Days' Battles, 252–56, 258
Portsmouth, Va., 743
Portugal, 620
Post, William, 170
Post Office Department, U.S., 624
Potomac River, 8, 12, 14–16, 19, 28, 31, 33, 89, 93, 99, 125, 128, 151, 155, 164, 225, 247, 335, 391, 408, 416, 418, 423, 435, 446, 448–49, 454, 460, 498, 502–3, 506, 509, 511–12, 517–18, 544, 548, 564, 601–2, 615, 664, 669
Powhatan (U.S. warship), 184
Prentiss, B. M., 161
Preston, Thomas T., 588
Price, Sterling, 100, 102–4, 106–8, 526, 528, 704
Pride, G. G., 161
Prisoners of war, 47, 53, 82, 109, 115–16, 188, 259, 264, 329, 385, 405, 438, 458, 471, 478, 501–2, 585, 588, 705
Property, in slaves, 632–33, 636, 717
Prussia, 379, 619–20
Pryor, Roger, 297
Pryor, Sara Agnes: *Reminiscences of Peace and War*, 297–302
Puritans, 129, 263, 709

Quakers, 131, 709, 745
Queen of the West (U.S. ram ship), 73–74
Quintard, C. T., 595

Race, 2, 367, 381, 390, 556, 572, 637
Railroads, 13, 16, 18–19, 54, 155, 236, 340, 395, 405–8, 413–14, 425–27, 460, 511, 526, 544, 548, 593, 600, 626, 693–94, 702–3, 725
Rains, Gabriel J., 237
Raleigh, N.C., 20
Raleigh (C.S. gunboat), 115–16
Randolph, George W., 212, 358
Randolph, Lewis, 404, 408
Ransom, Robert, 643, 652
Rapidan River, 392–93, 396, 404, 613, 649
Rappahannock River, 21–22, 83, 138, 155, 355–56, 391, 393–95, 404–6, 486, 613–14, 616, 640–43, 645–47, 659, 665, 668–69, 693–94, 740–41
Rawlins, John A., 54, 161
Reconstruction, 607
Reid, Harv, 705
Reid, Whitelaw, 303–5
Reno, Jesse L., 397, 414, 486
Republican Party, 8, 24, 28, 178, 225, 332, 352, 545, 606–7, 614, 683, 685–86, 724
Revere, Paul J., 471
Revolutionary War, 368, 568
Reynolds, Joseph J., 397, 611
Rhett, A. B., 644, 648, 654
Rhode Island, 368, 634
Rhodes, Robert E., 17
Rich, Lucius L., 169
Richardson, Byron, 597
Richardson, Israel B., 272, 275, 463, 470–71, 524
Richmond, Captain, 727
Richmond, Va., 77, 80, 82, 84, 156, 171, 219, 280, 336, 358, 364, 391–92, 407, 409, 436, 502, 549, 558, 564, 601–2, 641, 649, 659, 662, 706, 719–20; life in, 290–302; Union army advance on, 14, 16, 19–21, 83, 138, 140, 210–12, 225–26, 233, 236, 246–47, 250–51, 258, 265, 267, 278, 306, 329–30, 333, 338–40, 353–56, 400–2, 418–19, 443
Richmond (C.S. warship), 436
Ricketts, James B., 396–97, 465–66
Riley, Cam, 169
Rio de Janeiro, Brazil, 338
Ripley, Roswell, 252, 408

Risley, George W., 285
Rives, Benjamin A., 108
Roanoke (U.S. frigate), 114
Roanoke Island, 80, 85
Robbins, James K., 168, 170
Roberts, George W., 67
Roberts, Joseph J., 368
Robertson, Beverly H., 394
Robinson, James F., 689
Rochester, N.Y., 144
Rocky Mountains, 626, 629
Rodgers, John, 225
Rodman, Isaac P., 524
Rogers, William P., 580, 586
Romney, Va. (now W. Va.), 219
Ropes, Henry, 233–35
Ropes, William, 233
Rosecrans, William S., 441, 526–27, 578, 593, 729, 731, 733–34
Ross, James R., 37
Ross, Leonard F., 38–40, 42–43
Ross, W. G., 453
Rouse, Captain, 586
Rowley, W. R., 161
Ruggles, George D., 325, 327–28
Russell, John, 231, 377, 380, 443–45, 603–5
Russia, 335, 379, 444–45, 620–21

St. Lawrence (U.S. frigate), 114, 116–17
St. Louis, Mo., 100, 104, 558
St. Louis (U.S. gunboat), 56, 58, 63, 69, 72
Salem, Va., 394, 405
Salter, Richard, 286–87
San Francisco, Calif., 621, 629
Saunders, John, 471
Saunders (army officer), 408
Savannah, Ga., 247, 335, 358–60
Savannah, Tenn., 162
Savely, James W., 583
Sawier, Colonel, 585
Sawyer, Samuel, 727–28
Saxton, Rufus, 303, 745
Scammon, Eliakim P., 487
Scates, Walter B., 748
Schenk, R. C., 420
Schoepf, Albin F., 591
Schurz, Carl, 439
Scott, Winfield, 30, 551
Seates, John, 286
Secession, 146, 149, 212, 306, 374–75, 448, 456, 531, 543, 555, 559, 628, 707–8, 719
Secessionville, S.C., 303
Sedgwick, Charles B., 304
Sedgwick, John, 470–71, 524, 663
Sedgwick, William D., 471
Selby, Edward M., 582
Semmes, Paul J., 652
Semmes, Thomas J., 567–68, 570–71
Senate, C.S., 567–71
Senate, U.S., 620, 687–91, 726
Sepoy Mutiny, 607
Sevastopol, Russia, 335
Seven Days' Battles, 246–67, 269, 277, 290–93, 297, 306, 329, 338–41, 354, 394, 396, 398
Seward, Frederick W., 377, 430, 685, 691
Seward, William H., 213, 215, 267, 329, 342, 344, 347–48, 377, 422, 424, 428, 430, 531–32, 536–37, 606–7, 619, 683–91, 700, 744
Seymour, Horatio, 337, 701
Seymour, Truman, 611
Shackelford, Johnny, 91
Sharpsburg, Md., 248, 396, 460, 462, 464, 474, 480, 487, 492, 502–3, 505, 524, 541–42, 576, 600, 640
Shaver, John, 413
Shenandoah River, 220
Shenandoah Valley, 218–25, 236, 246–48, 323, 326, 396, 402, 407, 435, 511–12, 601, 641, 644
Shepherdstown, Va. (now W. Va.), 495, 502, 511–23, 544
Sheridan, Philip H., 512, 733
Sherman, Ellen Ewing, 165
Sherman, Henry, 726
Sherman, John, 724
Sherman, Thomas W., 20, 149, 239
Sherman, William T., 160, 165–67, 374–76, 702, 724–26
Sherman, Willie, 167
Shields, James, 219
Shiloh, battle of, 69, 157–71, 526, 592
Ship Island, 226
Shirk, James W., 159
Shookstown, Md., 485
Sigel, Franz, 100, 105, 109, 333, 397, 402
Silver Spring, Md., 224

Simms, Charles C., 114
Simons, James, 471
Sioux, 433, 625
Slack, William Y., 107
Slave revolts, 89, 569, 573
Slave trade, 378, 618, 628
Slavery, 145, 353, 377, 381, 532, 541–42, 556, 573, 603, 697; abolition of, 149–54, 178–79, 213, 216, 308, 343, 345, 539, 547–48, 562, 564, 566, 630–32; benefits/disadvantages of, 1, 4–5; destruction as war aim, 562–66, 606–7, 617; in District of Columbia, 112–13, 151, 178–79, 637; European attitudes toward, 379–81; and Lincoln, 150–52, 178–79, 314–17, 340, 343, 349–50, 352–53, 367–68, 372–73, 617, 627–38; in territories, 178
Slaves, 20, 172, 241–44, 514, 519, 711, 726; colonization of, 110, 178, 343, 366–71, 534, 607, 617, 619–20, 636–37, 742, 746; confiscation of, 317–22, 340, 342–43, 345, 352, 372, 374–76; as contraband of war, 90–92, 215–17, 238–40, 364, 382–90, 727–28, 746; emancipation of, 1–5, 110–13, 144, 151–52, 178–79, 215–17, 238–40, 303–5, 307–8, 314–16, 342–48, 352–53, 372–73, 377–78, 380, 530, 533–36, 540, 554, 556–57, 561–66, 572, 742–44, 749; fugitive, 6–7, 90–92, 129–30, 151, 239, 358–63, 374–76, 385, 534–35, 561, 627–28, 717; property in, 632–33, 636, 717
Slocum, Henry W., 254, 256, 260–61, 472
Smalley, George W., 462–78
Smith, Asa D., 277–89
Smith, Caleb B., 416, 418–19, 422, 428–30, 624
Smith, Charles F., 37, 40
Smith, Christopher E., 579
Smith, Donnell, 654
Smith, Edmund Kirby, 550, 589, 593
Smith, Edward W., 215
Smith, Gerrit, 151
Smith, James E., 199
Smith, J. L. Kirby, 68
Smith, Joseph, 137
Smith, Joseph B., 116, 137
Smith, Morgan L., 37–43, 45

Smith, William F., 203–4, 206, 208–9, 472, 474, 493
Snicker's Gap, Va., 602
Somerville, Va., 404
Soule, Pierre, 198
South Carolina, 5, 20, 146, 215, 236, 240, 303, 311, 364, 573, 697, 743
South Carolina 1st Volunteer (Colored) Regiment, 303
South Carolina 6th Regiment, 454, 458
South Carolina 15th Regiment, 458, 647
Southern Monitor, 80
Sovereign (steamer), 73
Spain, 312, 619–20
Special Orders No. 191, 459–62
Special War Order No. 1, 12–13
Spence, James, 719
Sprague, J. Kemp, 169
Sprague, John W., 580–81
Springfield, Ill., 616
Springfield Republican, 503, 657
Spurr, Thomas J., 471
Stacy, E., 363
Stahel, Julius H., 437
Stansbury, John L., 644
Stanton, Edwin M., 6, 12–14, 28–30, 122, 156, 213, 225, 238, 265, 303, 325, 329, 353, 401, 416–20, 422, 424, 426, 428–31, 438, 524–25, 530–31, 546, 548, 623, 663, 687, 690–92, 739–40
Starke, Norborne, 409
Starke, William E., 398, 407, 409
Starr, Samuel H., 205
State legislature (Maryland), 6
State legislature (Mississippi), 706
State legislatures, 715–16
Staunton, Va., 502
Stearns, Frazar A., 142–43
Steedman, John M., 455
Steele, Bailey P., 598
Steele, Tom, 735
Steiner, Lewis H., 448–54
Stembel, Roger N., 65
Stephens, George E., 89–92
Stephens, Scott, 597
Stevens, Isaac, 404, 408, 413–14, 439–40
Stevens, Thaddeus, 304–5
Stevenson, Hannah, 383

Stillé, Charles J., 696
Stockton, Thomas B. W., 488
Stone, Charles P., 28
Stone, Kate, 241–45
Stone, Walter, 241–44
Stone, William, 241, 245
Stones River, 734
Stones River, battle of, 729–38
Strasburg, Va., 156, 247
Strong, George Templeton, 437–38, 696–98
Stuart, J. E. B., 256, 392–94, 408, 460, 644, 649
Stuckey, C. C., 458
Sullivan, Clement, 100–1, 103
Summerhayes, John W., 661
Sumner, Charles, 31, 352–53, 606–8, 687–88
Sumner, Edwin V., 155, 203, 205, 209, 233–34, 258, 280, 392, 396, 399, 402, 416, 421, 431, 464, 466, 470–75, 478, 486, 490–95, 544–45, 549, 657, 693–94
Sumter (C.S. privateer), 310
Supreme Court, C.S., 87
Sweden, 620
Swift, J. G., 185
Switzerland (U.S. ram ship), 74
Sykes, George, 29, 260, 464, 477
Sylvester, Eph, 678–79
Syracuse, N.Y., 151

Taliaferro, William B., 393
Tallahatchie River, 702
Taxation, 558, 623–25
Taylor, Clay, 100
Taylor, George W., 395, 405
Taylor, Nelson, 204
Taylor, Richard: *Destruction and Reconstruction*, 218–23
Taylor, Zachary, 218, 611–12
Teaser (C.S. gunboat), 115–17
Telegraph, 621, 724
Tennessee, 10–11, 16, 20, 63, 65, 76, 81, 148, 168, 267, 526, 593, 629, 706; battle of Fort Donelson, 35–62, 81–83; battle of Shiloh, 157–71; battle of Stones River, 729–38; slaves in, 314
Tennessee (C.S. gunboat), 76
Tennessee 1st Regiment, 593–99
Tennessee 41st Regiment, 47–53

Tennessee River, 35, 47, 54, 81, 157, 163–64, 166, 168–69, 335
Terrill, William R., 592
Territories, 621, 629; slavery in, 178
Terry, Robert, 583–84
Texas, 20, 77, 170, 352, 581, 700, 721, 743
Texas 2nd Regiment, 585
Texas 3rd Regiment, 527
Texas 4th Regiment, 294
Texas Rangers, 581, 596
Thomas, Edward L., 650
Thomas, E. M., 366
Thomas, George H., 729
Thomas, Mary, 91
Thompson, David L., 496–502
Thompson, Egbert, 69
Thompson, James, 206
Thompson, Joe, 597
Thompson, M. Jeff, 75
Thornton's Gap, Va., 602
Ticknor, John, 481
Tilghman, Benjamin, 89
Tilghman, Lloyd, 82
Times (London), 230, 572–75
Tiptonville, Tenn., 68–69
Tobacco, 210, 226
Toombs, Robert, 213
Townsend, Willie, 613
Treasury Department, U.S., 111, 623, 625
Trenton, N.J., 613
Trumbull, Lyman, 687–88
Tucker, John R., 115
Tucker, John T., 597
Tupelo, Miss., 593
Turner, Levi C., 541–42
Turner, Nat, 89
Turner, William, 597
Tyler, John, 81
Tyler (U.S. gunboat), 54, 56, 159

U.S. 11th Infantry, 279
U.S. 28th Colored Infantry, 213
U.S.-Mexican War, 30, 54, 611–12, 717, 734
U.S. Military Academy (West Point), 255, 374, 485, 592, 640, 649
U.S. Naval Academy (Annapolis), 277
U.S. Sanitary Commission, 25, 437–38, 448, 696
Urbanna, Va., 21, 23, 138, 485

872 INDEX

Van Buren, Ark., 100, 102, 108–9
Van Dorn, Earl, 99–108, 578, 702–3, 724
Van Dorn (C.S. ship), 72
Varuna (U.S. gunboat), 195–96
Vatican, 620
Vermont, 472
Vestal's Gap, Va., 602
Vicksburg, Miss., 241–43, 585, 702, 706, 714, 718, 720–21, 724–26
Victoria, Queen, 444
Vienna, Austria, 377
Virginia, 5, 90, 103, 148, 378, 401, 457, 503, 524, 546, 564, 629, 714, 743; areas under Union control, 15, 125–37, 382, 384–90, 435–36; battle of Ball's Bluff, 8, 28–34; battle of Bull Run, 10–11, 14; battle of Fair Oaks, 233–35; battle of Fredericksburg, 614, 616, 640–83, 693–95; battle of Williamsburg, 199–209; contrabands in, 382, 384–89; fighting at Harper's Ferry, 459–60, 462, 485, 494–96, 511–23; Peninsula campaign, 199–212, 233–35, 400–1; proposed Union army campaign in, 14, 16–23, 138–40, 155–56; Second Bull Run campaign, 391–99, 404–16; Seven Days' Battles, 246–67, 269, 277, 338–40; Shenandoah Valley campaign, 218–33; slaves in, 6–7; Union army advance on Richmond, 14, 16, 19–21, 83, 138, 140, 210–12, 225–26, 233, 236, 246–47, 250–51, 258, 265, 267, 278, 306, 329–30, 333, 338–40, 353–56, 400–2, 418–19, 443; Union army retreat in, 269–89, 339–40; Union army treatment of civilians in, 325–28
Virginia (C.S. warship), 114–20, 136–37, 141, 210, 225
Virginia 2nd Regiment, 393
Virginia Central Railroad, 340
Voting, 3

Wade, Benjamin F., 8
Wadsworth, James, 383, 426
Wainwright, Charles S., 199–209
Walke, Henry, 54–76
Walker, Edward J., 643, 652
Walker, John G., 392, 460
Wallace, Lew, 159; *Autobiography*, 35–46

Wallace, W. H. L., 161
Waller, Mattie, 409
Walton, James B., 643, 654–55
War Department, C.S., 80–81, 358, 364–65
War Department, U.S., 29, 34, 102, 238–40, 265, 400, 416–18, 421, 426, 541–43, 549, 576, 623, 693, 701
War of 1812, 304, 717
War orders, 12–13, 576–77
War powers, 533, 742–43
Ward, Artemus (Charles Farrar Browne), 530
Warrenton, Va., 329, 395–96, 404–6, 611
Warwick, Bradfute, 293–94
Warwick, Clarence, 293
Washburne, Elihu B., 157, 163
Washington, D.C., 8, 10, 12, 24–26, 81, 93, 112, 121, 124, 139, 147, 150–51, 163, 184, 213, 217, 224, 265, 303, 323, 325–27, 329–30, 338, 349, 352, 354, 366–67, 372, 379, 395, 400, 413, 421, 423–24, 437, 439, 445, 448, 487, 525, 536–39, 541, 543, 550, 558, 571, 574, 600, 602, 606, 609, 625, 640, 664, 694, 699, 725, 739, 741, 744, 748; defense of, 13–16, 19, 22, 30, 155, 247, 267, 355–56, 391, 399, 401–2, 411–12, 416, 419, 425, 429–31, 433–35, 440, 443, 546–47, 589, 615. *See also* District of Columbia
Washington, George, 127, 221, 368, 374
Waterloo, battle of, 462, 497, 681
Watkins, Sam R., 593–99
Watkins, William, 170
Watson, Peter H., 6, 420
Watts, Isaac, 677
Webb, W. A., 115
Webber, Charles H., 199–203, 208
Weber, Max, 524
Webster, Billy, 598–99
Webster, Daniel, 413
Webster, Fletcher, 413–14
Webster, Joseph D., 42–43, 54, 161, 626
Weed, Thurlow, 332
Weekly Anglo-African, 89–92
Weir, R. F., 449
Welles, Gideon, 12, 59, 225, 342, 353, 416–24, 428, 430, 530–32, 623, 685–92
Wells, Mr., 413

Wellsman, James T., 310
West Indies, 3, 240, 309–10, 554
West Virginia, 314, 743
Westfield (U.S. warship), 183
Wharton, John A., 596
Wheeler, Charles C., 204
Wheless, John F., 596, 598
Whiston, Edward A., 283
White, Garland H., 213–14
White Sulphur Springs, Va. (now W. Va.), 99
Whitely, L. A., 537–40
Whiting, William H. C., 247, 254
Whitman, George, 669
Whitman, Walt: *Specimen Days*, 669–70
Whittorne, W. J., 598
Wickliffe, Charles A., 238, 240, 303, 305
Wilberforce, William, 3
Wilhoit, Lieutenant, 47–48
Wilkes, Charles, 416
Willard, Sidney, 662
Willard's Hotel (Washington), 400, 420
Willcox, Orlando B., 487
Williams, Alpheus S., 459–61, 485–95
Williams, Grandison, 458
Williams, Irene and Mary, 485
Williamsburg, Va., 199–210, 271
Williamsport, Va. (now W. Va.), 511, 513, 544
Wilmington, N.C., 20
Wilson, John, 583–84
Wilson, Mrs. (nurse), 297–98

Winchester, Va., 11, 156, 219, 221–23, 419, 502, 511, 518, 544, 546, 600–1
Winder, John H., 392
Wing, Rumsey, 592
Wisconsin, 482–83, 629
Wisconsin 2nd Regiment, 484
Wisconsin 3rd Regiment, 491
Wisconsin 6th Regiment, 479–84
Wisconsin 8th Regiment, 703
Wise, D. W., 683
Wise, Henry A., 80
Wise, Lieutenant, 80
Wise, O. Jennings, 80–81
Woldridge, John H., 598
Wolf's Run, 17
Wood, John, 263
Wood, T. J., 160, 733
Wool, John E., 156
Woolfolk, Pichegru, 654
Worden, John L., 137
Wright, George, 697
Wright, J. Montgomery, 589–92
Wumson, Lieutenant, 585

Yates, Richard, 441
Yazoo River, 724–26
Yellot, Captain, 450
Yorktown, Va., 155, 199, 209, 258, 355–56
Young, Lot D.: *Reminiscences of a Soldier of the Orphan Brigade*, 733–38

Zouaves (Brooklyn), 482
Zouaves (St. Louis), 39–40

*This book is set in 10 point Linotron Galliard,
a face designed for photocomposition by Matthew Carter
and based on the sixteenth-century face Granjon. The paper
is acid-free lightweight opaque and meets the requirements
for permanence of the American National Standards Institute.
The binding material is Brillianta, a woven rayon cloth made
by Van Heek-Scholco Textielfabrieken, Holland. Composition
by Dedicated Business Services. Printing and binding
by Edwards Brothers Malloy, Ann Arbor.
Designed by Bruce Campbell.*

THE LIBRARY OF AMERICA SERIES

The Library of America fosters appreciation and pride in America's literary heritage by publishing, and keeping permanently in print, authoritative editions of America's best and most significant writing. An independent nonprofit organization, it was founded in 1979 with seed funding from the National Endowment for the Humanities and the Ford Foundation.

1. Herman Melville: *Typee, Omoo, Mardi*
2. Nathaniel Hawthorne: *Tales and Sketches*
3. Walt Whitman: *Poetry and Prose*
4. Harriet Beecher Stowe: *Three Novels*
5. Mark Twain: *Mississippi Writings*
6. Jack London: *Novels and Stories*
7. Jack London: *Novels and Social Writings*
8. William Dean Howells: *Novels 1875–1886*
9. Herman Melville: *Redburn, White-Jacket, Moby-Dick*
10. Nathaniel Hawthorne: *Collected Novels*
11. Francis Parkman: *France and England in North America*, vol. I
12. Francis Parkman: *France and England in North America*, vol. II
13. Henry James: *Novels 1871–1880*
14. Henry Adams: *Novels, Mont Saint Michel, The Education*
15. Ralph Waldo Emerson: *Essays and Lectures*
16. Washington Irving: *History, Tales and Sketches*
17. Thomas Jefferson: *Writings*
18. Stephen Crane: *Prose and Poetry*
19. Edgar Allan Poe: *Poetry and Tales*
20. Edgar Allan Poe: *Essays and Reviews*
21. Mark Twain: *The Innocents Abroad, Roughing It*
22. Henry James: *Literary Criticism: Essays, American & English Writers*
23. Henry James: *Literary Criticism: European Writers & The Prefaces*
24. Herman Melville: *Pierre, Israel Potter, The Confidence-Man, Tales & Billy Budd*
25. William Faulkner: *Novels 1930–1935*
26. James Fenimore Cooper: *The Leatherstocking Tales*, vol. I
27. James Fenimore Cooper: *The Leatherstocking Tales*, vol. II
28. Henry David Thoreau: *A Week, Walden, The Maine Woods, Cape Cod*
29. Henry James: *Novels 1881–1886*
30. Edith Wharton: *Novels*
31. Henry Adams: *History of the U.S. during the Administrations of Jefferson*
32. Henry Adams: *History of the U.S. during the Administrations of Madison*
33. Frank Norris: *Novels and Essays*
34. W.E.B. Du Bois: *Writings*
35. Willa Cather: *Early Novels and Stories*
36. Theodore Dreiser: *Sister Carrie, Jennie Gerhardt, Twelve Men*
37a. Benjamin Franklin: *Silence Dogood, The Busy-Body, & Early Writings*
37b. Benjamin Franklin: *Autobiography, Poor Richard, & Later Writings*
38. William James: *Writings 1902–1910*
39. Flannery O'Connor: *Collected Works*
40. Eugene O'Neill: *Complete Plays 1913–1920*
41. Eugene O'Neill: *Complete Plays 1920–1931*
42. Eugene O'Neill: *Complete Plays 1932–1943*
43. Henry James: *Novels 1886–1890*
44. William Dean Howells: *Novels 1886–1888*
45. Abraham Lincoln: *Speeches and Writings 1832–1858*
46. Abraham Lincoln: *Speeches and Writings 1859–1865*
47. Edith Wharton: *Novellas and Other Writings*
48. William Faulkner: *Novels 1936–1940*
49. Willa Cather: *Later Novels*
50. Ulysses S. Grant: *Memoirs and Selected Letters*
51. William Tecumseh Sherman: *Memoirs*
52. Washington Irving: *Bracebridge Hall, Tales of a Traveller, The Alhambra*
53. Francis Parkman: *The Oregon Trail, The Conspiracy of Pontiac*
54. James Fenimore Cooper: *Sea Tales: The Pilot, The Red Rover*
55. Richard Wright: *Early Works*
56. Richard Wright: *Later Works*
57. Willa Cather: *Stories, Poems, and Other Writings*
58. William James: *Writings 1878–1899*
59. Sinclair Lewis: *Main Street & Babbitt*
60. Mark Twain: *Collected Tales, Sketches, Speeches, & Essays 1852–1890*
61. Mark Twain: *Collected Tales, Sketches, Speeches, & Essays 1891–1910*
62. *The Debate on the Constitution: Part One*
63. *The Debate on the Constitution: Part Two*
64. Henry James: *Collected Travel Writings: Great Britain & America*
65. Henry James: *Collected Travel Writings: The Continent*

66. *American Poetry: The Nineteenth Century*, Vol. 1
67. *American Poetry: The Nineteenth Century*, Vol. 2
68. Frederick Douglass: *Autobiographies*
69. Sarah Orne Jewett: *Novels and Stories*
70. Ralph Waldo Emerson: *Collected Poems and Translations*
71. Mark Twain: *Historical Romances*
72. John Steinbeck: *Novels and Stories 1932–1937*
73. William Faulkner: *Novels 1942–1954*
74. Zora Neale Hurston: *Novels and Stories*
75. Zora Neale Hurston: *Folklore, Memoirs, and Other Writings*
76. Thomas Paine: *Collected Writings*
77. *Reporting World War II: American Journalism 1938–1944*
78. *Reporting World War II: American Journalism 1944–1946*
79. Raymond Chandler: *Stories and Early Novels*
80. Raymond Chandler: *Later Novels and Other Writings*
81. Robert Frost: *Collected Poems, Prose, & Plays*
82. Henry James: *Complete Stories 1892–1898*
83. Henry James: *Complete Stories 1898–1910*
84. William Bartram: *Travels and Other Writings*
85. John Dos Passos: *U.S.A.*
86. John Steinbeck: *The Grapes of Wrath and Other Writings 1936–1941*
87. Vladimir Nabokov: *Novels and Memoirs 1941–1951*
88. Vladimir Nabokov: *Novels 1955–1962*
89. Vladimir Nabokov: *Novels 1969–1974*
90. James Thurber: *Writings and Drawings*
91. George Washington: *Writings*
92. John Muir: *Nature Writings*
93. Nathanael West: *Novels and Other Writings*
94. *Crime Novels: American Noir of the 1930s and 40s*
95. *Crime Novels: American Noir of the 1950s*
96. Wallace Stevens: *Collected Poetry and Prose*
97. James Baldwin: *Early Novels and Stories*
98. James Baldwin: *Collected Essays*
99. Gertrude Stein: *Writings 1903–1932*
100. Gertrude Stein: *Writings 1932–1946*
101. Eudora Welty: *Complete Novels*
102. Eudora Welty: *Stories, Essays, & Memoir*
103. Charles Brockden Brown: *Three Gothic Novels*
104. *Reporting Vietnam: American Journalism 1959–1969*
105. *Reporting Vietnam: American Journalism 1969–1975*
106. Henry James: *Complete Stories 1874–1884*
107. Henry James: *Complete Stories 1884–1891*
108. *American Sermons: The Pilgrims to Martin Luther King Jr.*
109. James Madison: *Writings*
110. Dashiell Hammett: *Complete Novels*
111. Henry James: *Complete Stories 1864–1874*
112. William Faulkner: *Novels 1957–1962*
113. John James Audubon: *Writings & Drawings*
114. *Slave Narratives*
115. *American Poetry: The Twentieth Century*, Vol. 1
116. *American Poetry: The Twentieth Century*, Vol. 2
117. F. Scott Fitzgerald: *Novels and Stories 1920–1922*
118. Henry Wadsworth Longfellow: *Poems and Other Writings*
119. Tennessee Williams: *Plays 1937–1955*
120. Tennessee Williams: *Plays 1957–1980*
121. Edith Wharton: *Collected Stories 1891–1910*
122. Edith Wharton: *Collected Stories 1911–1937*
123. *The American Revolution: Writings from the War of Independence*
124. Henry David Thoreau: *Collected Essays and Poems*
125. Dashiell Hammett: *Crime Stories and Other Writings*
126. Dawn Powell: *Novels 1930–1942*
127. Dawn Powell: *Novels 1944–1962*
128. Carson McCullers: *Complete Novels*
129. Alexander Hamilton: *Writings*
130. Mark Twain: *The Gilded Age and Later Novels*
131. Charles W. Chesnutt: *Stories, Novels, and Essays*
132. John Steinbeck: *Novels 1942–1952*
133. Sinclair Lewis: *Arrowsmith, Elmer Gantry, Dodsworth*
134. Paul Bowles: *The Sheltering Sky, Let It Come Down, The Spider's House*
135. Paul Bowles: *Collected Stories & Later Writings*
136. Kate Chopin: *Complete Novels & Stories*
137. *Reporting Civil Rights: American Journalism 1941–1963*
138. *Reporting Civil Rights: American Journalism 1963–1973*
139. Henry James: *Novels 1896–1899*
140. Theodore Dreiser: *An American Tragedy*
141. Saul Bellow: *Novels 1944–1953*
142. John Dos Passos: *Novels 1920–1925*

143. John Dos Passos: *Travel Books and Other Writings*
144. Ezra Pound: *Poems and Translations*
145. James Weldon Johnson: *Writings*
146. Washington Irving: *Three Western Narratives*
147. Alexis de Tocqueville: *Democracy in America*
148. James T. Farrell: *Studs Lonigan: A Trilogy*
149. Isaac Bashevis Singer: *Collected Stories I*
150. Isaac Bashevis Singer: *Collected Stories II*
151. Isaac Bashevis Singer: *Collected Stories III*
152. Kaufman & Co.: *Broadway Comedies*
153. Theodore Roosevelt: *The Rough Riders, An Autobiography*
154. Theodore Roosevelt: *Letters and Speeches*
155. H. P. Lovecraft: *Tales*
156. Louisa May Alcott: *Little Women, Little Men, Jo's Boys*
157. Philip Roth: *Novels & Stories 1959–1962*
158. Philip Roth: *Novels 1967–1972*
159. James Agee: *Let Us Now Praise Famous Men, A Death in the Family*
160. James Agee: *Film Writing & Selected Journalism*
161. Richard Henry Dana Jr.: *Two Years Before the Mast & Other Voyages*
162. Henry James: *Novels 1901–1902*
163. Arthur Miller: *Collected Plays 1944–1961*
164. William Faulkner: *Novels 1926–1929*
165. Philip Roth: *Novels 1973–1977*
166. *American Speeches: Part One*
167. *American Speeches: Part Two*
168. Hart Crane: *Complete Poems & Selected Letters*
169. Saul Bellow: *Novels 1956–1964*
170. John Steinbeck: *Travels with Charley and Later Novels*
171. Capt. John Smith: *Writings with Other Narratives*
172. Thornton Wilder: *Collected Plays & Writings on Theater*
173. Philip K. Dick: *Four Novels of the 1960s*
174. Jack Kerouac: *Road Novels 1957–1960*
175. Philip Roth: *Zuckerman Bound*
176. Edmund Wilson: *Literary Essays & Reviews of the 1920s & 30s*
177. Edmund Wilson: *Literary Essays & Reviews of the 1930s & 40s*
178. *American Poetry: The 17th & 18th Centuries*
179. William Maxwell: *Early Novels & Stories*
180. Elizabeth Bishop: *Poems, Prose, & Letters*
181. A. J. Liebling: *World War II Writings*
182s. *American Earth: Environmental Writing Since Thoreau*
183. Philip K. Dick: *Five Novels of the 1960s & 70s*
184. William Maxwell: *Later Novels & Stories*
185. Philip Roth: *Novels & Other Narratives 1986–1991*
186. Katherine Anne Porter: *Collected Stories & Other Writings*
187. John Ashbery: *Collected Poems 1956–1987*
188. John Cheever: *Collected Stories & Other Writings*
189. John Cheever: *Complete Novels*
190. Lafcadio Hearn: *American Writings*
191. A. J. Liebling: *The Sweet Science & Other Writings*
192s. *The Lincoln Anthology: Great Writers on His Life and Legacy from 1860 to Now*
193. Philip K. Dick: *VALIS & Later Novels*
194. Thornton Wilder: *The Bridge of San Luis Rey and Other Novels 1926–1948*
195. Raymond Carver: *Collected Stories*
196. *American Fantastic Tales: Terror and the Uncanny from Poe to the Pulps*
197. *American Fantastic Tales: Terror and the Uncanny from the 1940s to Now*
198. John Marshall: *Writings*
199s. *The Mark Twain Anthology: Great Writers on His Life and Works*
200. Mark Twain: *A Tramp Abroad, Following the Equator, Other Travels*
201. Ralph Waldo Emerson: *Selected Journals 1820–1842*
202. Ralph Waldo Emerson: *Selected Journals 1841–1877*
203. *The American Stage: Writing on Theater from Washington Irving to Tony Kushner*
204. Shirley Jackson: *Novels & Stories*
205. Philip Roth: *Novels 1993–1995*
206. H. L. Mencken: *Prejudices: First, Second, and Third Series*
207. H. L. Mencken: *Prejudices: Fourth, Fifth, and Sixth Series*
208. John Kenneth Galbraith: *The Affluent Society and Other Writings 1952–1967*
209. Saul Bellow: *Novels 1970–1982*
210. Lynd Ward: *Gods' Man, Madman's Drum, Wild Pilgrimage*
211. Lynd Ward: *Prelude to a Million Years, Song Without Words, Vertigo*
212. *The Civil War: The First Year Told by Those Who Lived It*
213. John Adams: *Revolutionary Writings 1755–1775*
214. John Adams: *Revolutionary Writings 1775–1783*
215. Henry James: *Novels 1903–1911*
216. Kurt Vonnegut: *Novels & Stories 1963–1973*

217. *Harlem Renaissance: Five Novels of the 1920s*
218. *Harlem Renaissance: Four Novels of the 1930s*
219. Ambrose Bierce: *The Devil's Dictionary, Tales, & Memoirs*
220. Philip Roth: *The American Trilogy 1997–2000*
221. *The Civil War: The Second Year Told by Those Who Lived It*
222. Barbara W. Tuchman: *The Guns of August & The Proud Tower*
223. Arthur Miller: *Collected Plays 1964–1982*
224. Thornton Wilder: *The Eighth Day, Theophilus North, Autobiographical Writings*
225. David Goodis: *Five Noir Novels of the 1940s & 50s*
226. Kurt Vonnegut: *Novels & Stories 1950–1962*
227. *American Science Fiction: Four Classic Novels 1953–1956*
228. *American Science Fiction: Five Classic Novels 1956–1958*
229. Laura Ingalls Wilder: *The Little House Books, Volume One*
230. Laura Ingalls Wilder: *The Little House Books, Volume Two*
231. Jack Kerouac: *Collected Poems*
232. *The War of 1812: Writings from America's Second War of Independence*
233. *American Antislavery Writings: Colonial Beginnings to Emancipation*
234. *The Civil War: The Third Year Told by Those Who Lived It*
235. Sherwood Anderson: *Collected Stories*
236. Philip Roth: *Novels 2001–2007*
237. Philip Roth: *Nemeses*
238. Aldo Leopold: *A Sand County Almanac & Other Writings on Ecology and Conservation*
239. May Swenson: *Collected Poems*
240. W. S. Merwin: *Collected Poems 1952–1993*
241. W. S. Merwin: *Collected Poems 1996–2011*
242. John Updike: *Collected Early Stories*
243. John Updike: *Collected Later Stories*
244. Ring Lardner: *Stories & Other Writings*
245. Jonathan Edwards: *Writings from the Great Awakening*
246. Susan Sontag: *Essays of the 1960s & 70s*
247. William Wells Brown: *Clotel & Other Writings*
248. Bernard Malamud: *Novels and Stories of the 1940s & 50s*
249. Bernard Malamud: *Novels and Stories of the 1960s*
250. *The Civil War: The Final Year Told by Those Who lived It*
251. *Shakespeare in America: An Anthology from the Revolution to Now*
252. Kurt Vonnegut: *Novels 1976–1985*
253. *American Musicals 1927–1949: The Complete Books & Lyrics of Eight Broadway Classics*
254. *American Musicals 1950–1969: The Complete Books & Lyrics of Eight Broadway Classics*
255. Elmore Leonard: *Four Novels of the 1970s*
256. Louisa May Alcott: *Work, Eight Cousins, Rose in Bloom, Stories & Other Writings*
257. H. L. Mencken: *The Days Trilogy, Expanded Edition*
258. Virgil Thomson: *Music Chronicles 1940–1954*
259. *Art in America 1945–1970: Writings from the Age of Abstract Expressionism, Pop Art, and Minimalism*

To subscribe to the series or to order individual copies, please visit www.loa.org or call (800) 964-5778.

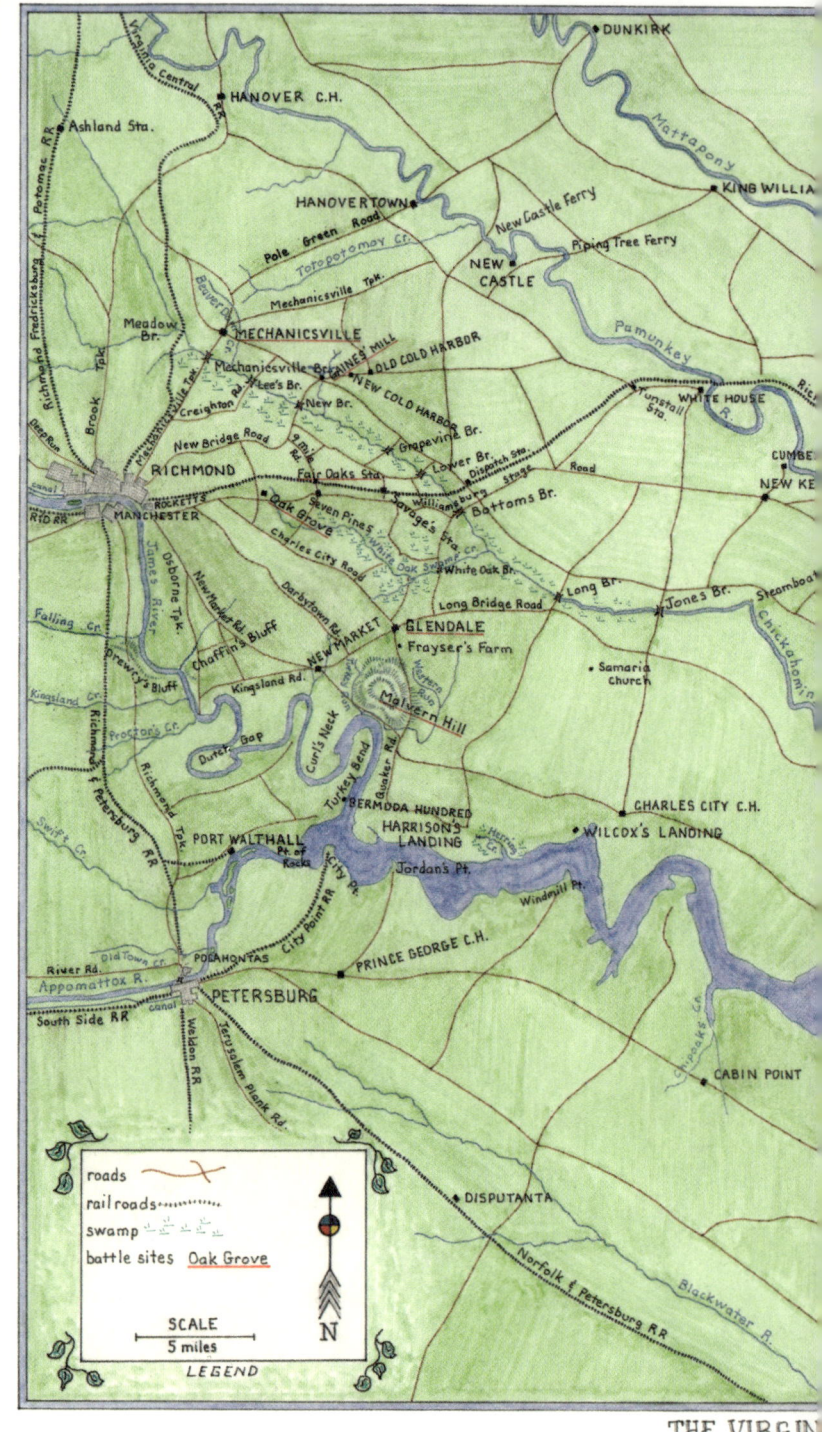

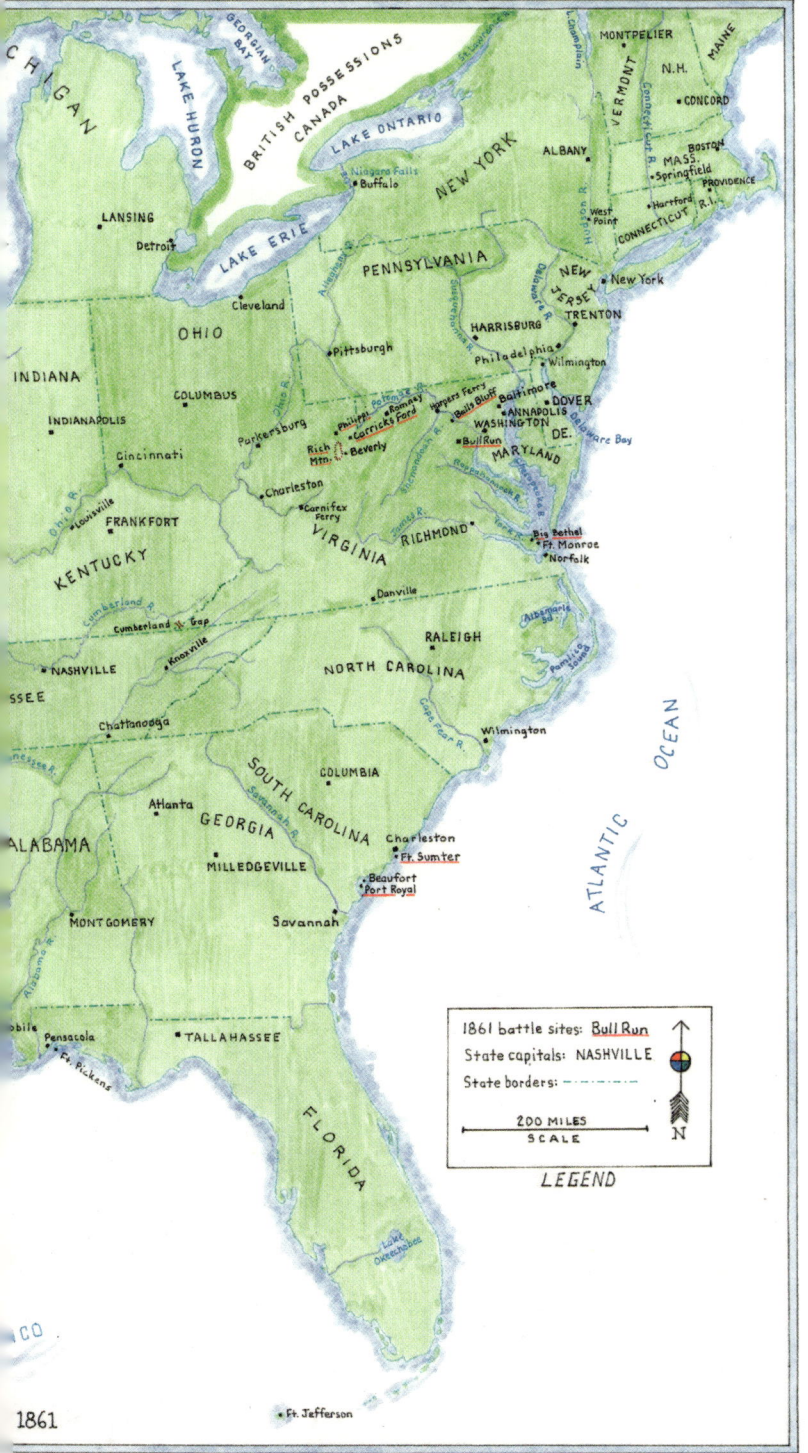

THE CIVIL WAR

THE FIRST YEAR

The Civil War

THE FIRST YEAR TOLD BY THOSE WHO LIVED IT

Edited by
Brooks D. Simpson
Stephen W. Sears
Aaron Sheehan-Dean

THE LIBRARY OF AMERICA

Volume compilation, preface, introduction, notes,
and chronology copyright © 2011 by
Literary Classics of the United States, Inc., New York, N.Y.
All rights reserved.
No part of the book may be reproduced commercially
by offset-lithographic or equivalent copying devices without
the permission of the publisher.

Some of the material in this volume is reprinted
by permission of the holders of copyright and publication rights.
See Note on the Texts on page 729 for acknowledgments.
Endpaper maps copyright © 2011 by Earl B. McElfresh,
McElfresh Map Company LLC.

The paper used in this publication meets the
minimum requirements of the American National Standard for
Information Sciences–Permanence of Paper for Printed
Library Materials, ANSI Z39.48–1984.

Distributed to the trade in the United States
by Penguin Random House Inc.
and in Canada by Penguin Random House Canada Ltd.

Library of Congress Control Number: 2010931718
ISBN 978–1–59853–088–9

Fourth Printing
The Library of America—212

Manufactured in the United States of America

The Civil War:
The First Year Told by Those Who Lived It
is published with support from

THE ANDREW W. MELLON FOUNDATION

and

**THE NATIONAL ENDOWMENT
FOR THE HUMANITIES**

The Civil War: The First Year Told by Those Who Lived It
is kept in print by a gift from

THE BERKLEY FOUNDATION

to the Guardians of American Letters Fund,
established by The Library of America
to ensure that every volume in the series
will be permanently available.

Contents

Preface xix
Introduction xxi

Charleston Mercury: What Shall the South Carolina
  Legislature Do?, November 3, 1860
Calling a Secession Convention: November 1860 1

John G. Nicolay: Memoranda Regarding Abraham Lincoln,
  November 5–6, 1860
"Alarms from the South": Illinois, November 1860 5

New-York Daily Tribune: Going to Go, November 9, 1860
The Threat of Secession: November 1860 8

Jefferson Davis to Robert Barnwell Rhett Jr.,
  November 10, 1860
The Need for Southern Cooperation: November 1860 11

Benjamin Hill: Speech at Milledgeville, November 15, 1860
Debating Secession: Georgia, November 1860 14

New York Daily News: The Right of States to Secede,
  November 16, 1860
"States cannot exist disunited": November 1860 34

Sam Houston to H. M. Watkins and Others,
  November 20, 1860
"I am for the Union as it is": Texas, November 1860 37

George Templeton Strong: Diary, November 20,
  November 26–December 1, 1860
"Our sore national sickness": New York, November 1860 43

Edward Bates: Diary, November 22, 1860
"This dangerous game": Missouri, November 1860 48

William G. Brownlow to R. H. Appleton, November 29, 1860
*The "Wicked Spirit" of Secession: Tennessee,
  November 1860* 49

Frederick Douglass: The Late Election, December 1860
Lincoln and Slavery: December 1860 57

CONTENTS

William T. Sherman to Thomas Ewing Sr. and to
John Sherman, December 1, 1860
Secessionism in Louisiana: December 1860 63

James Buchanan: from the Annual Message to Congress,
December 3, 1860
Washington, D.C., December 1860 67

J.D.B. DeBow: The Non-Slaveholders of the South,
December 5, 1860
The Benefits of Slavery: December 1860 85

Joseph E. Brown to Alfred H. Colquitt and Others,
December 7, 1860
Advocating Secession: Georgia, December 1860 98

Abraham Lincoln to John A. Gilmer, December 15, 1860
Restating Positions on Slavery: December 1860 109

New-York Daily Tribune: The Right of Secession,
December 17, 1860
Rejecting Coercion: December 1860 111

Benjamin F. Wade: Remarks in the U.S. Senate,
December 17, 1860
"I stand by the Union": December 1860 114

John J. Crittenden: Remarks in the U.S. Senate,
December 18, 1860
A Compromise over Slavery: December 1860 128

Henry Adams to Charles Francis Adams Jr.,
December 18–20, 1860
*"Meanness and rascality": Washington, D.C.,
December 1860* 143

John G. Nicolay: Memorandum Regarding Abraham
Lincoln, December 22, 1860
A Confidential Message: Illinois, December 1860 147

South Carolina Declaration of the Causes of Secession,
December 24, 1860
Charleston, December 1860 149

Abner Doubleday: from *Reminiscences of Forts Sumter
and Moultrie in 1860–'61*
Occupying Fort Sumter: South Carolina, December 1860 156

Catherine Edmondston: Diary, December 26–27, 1860
*"A terrible revulsion of feeling": South Carolina,
December 1860* 163

CONTENTS

Stephen F. Hale to Beriah Magoffin, December 27, 1860
Urging Kentucky to Secede: December 1860 165

Herman Melville: Misgivings
"The tempest bursting": 1860 177

Mary Jones to Charles C. Jones Jr., January 3, 1861
"Sad foreboding": Georgia, January 1861 178

Henry Adams to Charles Francis Adams Jr., January 8, 1861
*"All depends on Virginia": Washington, D.C.,
January 1861* 180

Mississippi Declaration of the Causes of Secession,
January 9, 1861
Jackson, January 1861 183

Elizabeth Blair Lee to Samuel Phillips Lee, December 25,
January 9–10, 1861
"A warlike aspect": Washington, D.C., January 1861 186

Catherine Edmondston: Diary, January 9–13, 1861
The "Star of the West": South Carolina, January 1861 189

Jefferson Davis: Farewell Address in the U.S. Senate,
January 21, 1861
Washington, D.C., January 1861 193

Robert E. Lee to George Washington Custis Lee,
January 23, 1861
The Evils of Anarchy and Civil War: January 1861 199

Jefferson Davis: Inaugural Address, February 18, 1861
Montgomery, Alabama, February 1861 201

Frederick Douglass: The New President, March 1861
Hopes for Lincoln's Administration: March 1861 207

Abraham Lincoln: First Inaugural Address, March 4, 1861
Washington, D.C., March 1861 210

Catherine Edmondston: Diary, March 4, 1861
*"That wretch Abraham Lincoln": North Carolina,
March 1861* 220

Alexander H. Stephens: "Corner-Stone" Speech,
March 21, 1861
Vindicating Slavery: Georgia, March 1861 221

Edward Bates: Diary, March 9–April 8, 1861
*Relieving Fort Sumter: Washington, D.C.,
March–April 1861*   237

Gideon Welles: Memoir of Events, March 1861
Seward and Fort Sumter: Washington, D.C., March 1861 . . .   242

William H. Seward: Memorandum for the President,
April 1, 1861
Challenging Lincoln: Washington, D.C., April 1861   248

Abraham Lincoln to William H. Seward, April 1, 1861
"I must do it": Washington, D.C., April 1861   250

Mary Chesnut, Diary, April 7–15, 1861
The War Begins: South Carolina, April 1861   252

Abner Doubleday: from *Reminiscences of Forts Sumter
and Moultrie in 1860–'61*
Bombardment and Surrender: South Carolina, April 1861 . . .   261

George Templeton Strong: Diary, April 13–16, 1861
New Yorkers Respond: April 1861   269

The New York Times: The People and the Issue,
April 15, 1861
Vindicating National Honor: April 1861   275

Pittsburgh Post: The War Begun—The Duty of American
Citizens, April 15, 1861
Fighting "the mad rebellion": April 1861   278

William Howard Russell: from *My Diary North and South*,
April 17, 1861
Celebration in Charleston: South Carolina, April 1861   281

Charles C. Jones Sr. to Charles C. Jones Jr., April 20, 1861
"Infidel" Enemies: Georgia, April 1861   294

John B. Jones: Diary, April 15–22, 1861
Secessionism in Richmond: Virginia, April 1861   297

John W. Hanson: from *Historical Sketch of the Old Sixth
Regiment of Massachusetts Volunteers*
The Baltimore Riot: April 1861   305

Ulysses S. Grant to Frederick Dent, April 19, 1861, and to
Jesse Root Grant, April 21, 1861
"I have but one sentiment now": Illinois, April 1861   310

Jefferson Davis: Message to the Confederate Congress,
   April 29, 1861
Montgomery, Alabama, April 1861 313

Frederick Douglass: How to End the War, May 1861
"Strike down slavery itself": May 1861 333

Walt Whitman: First O Songs for a Prelude
New York, Spring 1861 336

Winfield Scott to George B. McClellan, May 3, 1861
A Strategic Plan: May 1861 339

Charles B. Haydon: Diary, May 3–12, 1861
Life in Army Camp: Michigan, May 1861 341

Ulysses S. Grant to Jesse Root Grant, May 6, 1861
Predicting a Short War: May 1861 347

John Hay: Diary, May 7–10, 1861
*Life in the Executive Mansion: Washington, D.C.,
   May 1861* 350

Judith W. McGuire: Diary, May 10, 1861
Fearing Attack in Alexandria: Virginia, May 1861 355

William T. Sherman to John Sherman, May 11, 1861
Rioting in St. Louis: Missouri, May 1861 358

Benjamin F. Butler to Winfield Scott, May 24, 1861
Slaves Seeking Freedom: Virginia, May 1861 361

The New York Times: General Butler and the Contraband of
   War, June 2, 1861
Defining Runaway Slaves: Virginia, May 1861 364

Kate Stone: Journal, May 15–27, 1861
"Our Cause is just": Louisiana, May 1861 369

George Templeton Strong: Diary, May 29–June 2, 1861
A Visit to Washington: May–June 1861 376

John Brown's Body, May 1861
Massachusetts, May 1861 383

Roger B. Taney: Opinion in *Ex parte Merryman*, June 1, 1861
The Writ of Habeas Corpus: Maryland, May 1861 386

Henry A. Wise: Speech at Richmond, June 1, 1861
"I rejoice in this war": Virginia, June 1861 401

Charles C. Jones Jr. to Charles C. Jones Sr. and Mary Jones,
June 10, 1861
The "blinded, fanatical" North: Georgia, June 1861   404

Henry Adams to Charles Francis Adams Jr., June 10–11, 1861
Anglo-American Relations: London, June 1861   407

John Ross to Benjamin McCulloch, June 17, 1861
Cherokee Neutrality: Indian Territory, June 1861   412

James Russell Lowell: The Pickens-and-Stealin's Rebellion,
June 1861
Emancipating Northern Opinion: June 1861   415

Abraham Lincoln: Message to Congress in Special Session,
July 4, 1861
Washington, D.C., July 1861   427

Kate Stone: Journal, July 4, 1861
An Unobserved Holiday: Louisiana, July 1861   443

Ulysses S. Grant: from *Personal Memoirs of U. S. Grant*
Facing the Enemy: Missouri, July 1861   444

Sallie Brock: from *Richmond During the War*
Defeats in Western Virginia: July 1861   447

Sullivan Ballou to Sarah Ballou, July 14, 1861
A Farewell Letter: July 1861   451

Charles Minor Blackford: from *Letters from Lee's Army*
Battle of Manassas: Virginia, July 1861   454

William Howard Russell: from *My Diary North and South*
The Union Army Retreats: Virginia, July 1861   464

Samuel J. English to his Mother, July 24, 1861
"Death and confusion everywhere": Virginia, July 1861   491

Emma Holmes: Diary, July 22–23, 1861
News of Manassas: South Carolina, July 1861   495

Elizabeth Blair Lee to Samuel Phillips Lee, July 23, 1861
Straggling Soldiers: Washington, D.C., July 1861   498

Walt Whitman: from *Specimen Days*
"A terrible shock": Washington, D.C., July 1861   500

Abraham Lincoln: Memoranda on Military Policy, July 23, 1861
Washington, D.C., July 1861   504

CONTENTS xv

Mary Chesnut: Diary, July 24, 1861
Celebrating Victory: Virginia, July 1861 506

Crittenden-Johnson Resolutions, July 22–25, 1861
Noninterference with Slavery: July 1861 522

George B. McClellan to Mary Ellen McClellan, July 27, 1861
Assuming Command: Washington, D.C., July 1861 524

William T. Sherman to Ellen Ewing Sherman, July 28, 1861
"Our men are not good Soldiers": July 1861 526

Horace Greeley to Abraham Lincoln, July 29, 1861
"Our late awful disaster": July 1861 531

George B. McClellan: Memorandum for the President,
August 2, 1861
Washington, D.C., August 1861 533

Confiscation Act, August 6, 1861
A Measure Against Slavery: August 1861 538

George B. McClellan to Mary Ellen McClellan, August 8, 9,
and 16, 1861
"The Presdt is an idiot": August 1861 540

E. F. Ware: from *The Lyon Campaign in Missouri*
Battle of Wilson's Creek: Missouri, August 1861 543

W. E. Woodruff: from *With the Light Guns in '61–'65*
*Confederate Artillery at Wilson's Creek: Missouri,
August 1861* 554

John C. Frémont: Proclamation, August 30, 1861
Freeing the Slaves of Rebels: Missouri, August 1861 561

Abraham Lincoln to John C. Frémont, September 2, 1861
Modifying a Proclamation: September 1861 563

Frederick Douglass: Fighting Rebels with Only One Hand,
September 1861
The Need for Black Soldiers: September 1861 564

Abraham Lincoln to Orville H. Browning, September 22, 1861
Revoking Frémont's Proclamation: September 1861 568

John Ross: Message to the National Council, October 9, 1861
*A Cherokee-Confederate Alliance: Indian Territory,
October 1861* 571

Henry Livermore Abbott to Josiah Gardner Abbott, October 22, 1861 *Battle of Ball's Bluff: Virginia, October 1861*	576
George B. McClellan to Mary Ellen McClellan, October 25, 26, 30, and 31, 1861 *Replacing Winfield Scott: October 1861*	581
Charles Francis Adams Jr. to Henry Adams, November 5, 1861 *"I am tired of incompetents": November 1861*	585
George B. McClellan to Samuel L. M. Barlow, November 8, 1861 *Preparing for the Next Battle: November 1861*	587
Ulysses S. Grant to Jesse Root Grant, November 8, 1861 *Battle of Belmont: Missouri, November 1861*	590
Lunsford P. Yandell Jr. to Lunsford Yandell Sr., November 10, 1861 *A Doctor at Belmont: Missouri, November 1861*	592
Samuel Francis Du Pont to Sophie Du Pont, November 13–15, 1861 *The Capture of Port Royal: South Carolina, November 1861*	596
Sam Mitchell: Narrative of the capture of the Sea Islands, November 1861 *A Former Slave Remembers: South Carolina, November 1861*	603
Henry Tucker: God in the War, November 15, 1861 *A Confederate Sermon: Georgia, November 1861*	605
Jefferson Davis: Message to the Confederate Congress, November 18, 1861 *Richmond, Virginia, November 1861*	627
Harper's Weekly: The Great Review *The Army of the Potomac: Virginia, November 1861*	636
Ulysses S. Grant to Jesse Root Grant, November 27, 1861 *Slavery and the Press: November 1861*	639
Sallie Brock: from *Richmond During the War* *Shortages and Inflation: Virginia, Autumn 1861*	641
Benjamin Moran, Journal, November 27–December 3, 1861 *The "Trent" Affair: London, November–December 1861*	645

Henry Adams to Charles Francis Adams Jr., November 30, 1861 *War with England: London, November 1861*	651
Abraham Lincoln, Annual Message to Congress, December 3, 1861 *Washington, D.C., December 1861*	653
Charles Francis Adams Jr. to Henry Adams, December 10, 1861 *Preparing to Enlist: Boston, December 1861*	672
Let My People Go *A Song of the Contrabands: Virginia, 1861*	674
Robert E. Lee to George Washington Custis Lee, December 29, 1861 *Not Relying on Foreign Aid: December 1861*	678
Edward Bates: Diary, December 31, 1861 *The President's Duty to Act: Washington, D.C., December 1861*	681
Irvin McDowell: Memorandum, January 10–13, 1862 *Lincoln and McClellan: Washington, D.C., January 1862* . . .	683
Montgomery C. Meigs, Memoir of Meetings with President Lincoln, January 10–13, 1862 *"The bottom is out of the tub": Washington, D.C., January 1862*	691
Edwin M. Stanton to Charles A. Dana, January 24, 1862 *"This army has got to fight": January 1862*	693
Chronology	697
Biographical Notes	707
Note on the Texts	729
Notes	744
Index	793

Preface

"Has there ever been another historical crisis of the magnitude of 1861–65 in which so many people were so articulate?"
—Edmund Wilson

THIS Library of America volume is the first in a four-volume series bringing together memorable and significant writing by participants in the American Civil War. Each volume in the series covers approximately one year of the conflict, from the election of Abraham Lincoln in November 1860 to the end of the war in the spring of 1865, and presents a chronological selection of documents from the broadest possible range of authoritative sources—diaries, letters, speeches, military reports, newspaper articles, memoirs, poems, and public papers. Drawing upon an immense and unique body of American writing, the series offers a narrative of the war years that encompasses military and political events and their social and personal reverberations. Created by persons of every class and condition, the writing included here captures the American nation and the American language in the crucial period of their modern formation. Selections have been chosen for their historical significance, their literary quality, and their narrative energy, and are printed from the best available sources. The goal has been to shape a narrative that is both broad and balanced in scope, while at the same time doing justice to the number and diversity of voices and perspectives preserved for us in the writing of the era.

Introduction

As Abraham Lincoln looked out from the East Portico of the United States Capitol on March 4, 1865, he saw assembled before him a throng of Americans, each of whom had been marked in some way by nearly four long years of war. It had been precisely four years since he had stood in the same place and expressed his hope that somehow war could be avoided. Now he recalled that moment as he delivered his Second Inaugural Address. "All dreaded it—all sought to avert it," he declared. Yet that had not been enough. "Both parties deprecated war; but one of them would *make* war rather than let the nation survive; and the other would *accept* war rather than let it perish. And the war came."

The letters, diaries, speeches, poems, memoirs, and other documents collected in this volume help us understand how and why that war came, and how Americans, North and South, white and black, male and female, experienced secession and armed conflict as it moved across the land. Few of them doubted that slavery was, as Lincoln said in his Second Inaugural, "somehow, the cause of the war." Yet, as the President also recalled, no one "expected for the war, the magnitude, or the duration, which it has already attained." Most Americans "looked for an easier triumph, and a result less fundamental and astounding" than what eventually happened, including the destruction of slavery. It is often difficult for readers today to grasp just how revolutionary and astonishing the Civil War was to those who experienced it, and how events that we may believe to have been practically inevitable were at best barely conceivable to many Americans at the time. By reading what people wrote as history unfolded before them, we can gain a better appreciation for what people thought was at stake, and for what the war was all about.

In the same address Lincoln spoke of "the bond-man's two hundred and fifty years of unrequited toil." The origins of the Civil War can indeed be traced back to 1619 and the beginnings of African slavery in Virginia, and then forward through the compromises regarding slavery adopted by the Constitutional Convention, the spread of cotton cultivation throughout the Deep South, the Missouri Compromise of 1820 that prohibited slavery in most of the Louisiana Purchase territory, and the emergence of the abolitionist movement in the 1830s. With the outbreak of the U.S.-Mexican War in 1846, the pace of events quickened, as the prospect of acquiring new territory revived the sectional controversy over the expansion of slavery. An attempt by Henry Clay—the seventy-three-year-old Kentucky Whig celebrated for his role in passing the Missouri Compromise—to fashion a new compromise in 1850 faltered when his "Omnibus Bill" failed to win Senate approval. It fell to a younger man, the ambitious Illinois Democrat Stephen A. Douglas, to forge two different sectionally-based coalitions, one to pass antislavery measures—the admission of California as a free state, the abolition of the slave trade in the District of Columbia—and another to adopt proslavery ones—a new, stronger fugitive slave law, the organization of New Mexico and Utah as territories where slavery would be permitted. None of these measures were supported by a majority of both Northern and Southern senators and representatives, and what became known as the "Compromise of 1850" was more of an uneasy truce.

In 1854 Stephen A. Douglas ended the truce he had helped fashion four years earlier. Hoping to win Southern support for the construction of a transcontinental railroad along a northern route, Douglas won passage of the Kansas-Nebraska Act, which repealed the Missouri Compromise and allowed the question of whether slavery would be permitted in the two newly-organized territories to be decided by their voters. Over the next two years, the passage of the act led to armed conflict in Kansas, the bloody caning of Charles Sumner on the Senate floor, the formation of the Republican Party, and the resurgence of the political career of Abraham Lincoln.

Any expectation that the sectional controversy would be resolved by the Supreme Court ended with the furor aroused in 1857 by the *Dred Scott* decision, which held that the basic principle of the Republican Party—that Congress could exclude slavery from the territories—was unconstitutional. An attempt later in the year to fraudulently impose a proslavery state constitution on Kansas caused Douglas to break with the Southern wing of his party. By 1859 many Southern Democrats were demanding the adoption of a federal slave code, calling for the reopening of the African slave trade, and contemplating secession if a "Black Republican" won the presidency in 1860. The movement toward disunion was hastened by John Brown's failed raid on the federal armory at Harpers Ferry, Virginia, in October 1859. In the immediate aftermath of the incident, white Southerners were fearful that antislavery agitation would soon lead to even bloodier acts of rebellion. Their fear turned to anger when many prominent Northerners praised Brown—Ralph Waldo Emerson declared that he would "make the gallows as glorious as the cross"—and mourned his execution.

It is hardly surprising that this convulsive political atmosphere produced a presidential campaign with four candidates. The Democrats met in April in Charleston, South Carolina, but became hopelessly deadlocked because of Southern opposition to the candidacy of Stephen A. Douglas. After adjourning for six weeks, they reconvened in Baltimore and split along sectional lines, with Northern delegates nominating Douglas and Southerners choosing Vice President John Breckinridge of Kentucky as their candidate. In May the Constitutional Union Party, founded mainly by conservative Whigs from the border states, met in Baltimore and nominated John Bell, a Unionist slaveholder from Tennessee. Later that month the Republicans gathered in Chicago, where Senator William H. Seward of New York, the presumed front-runner for the nomination, was defeated on the third ballot by Abraham Lincoln, in part because many delegates believed Lincoln would have greater appeal to voters in Pennsylvania and the lower Midwest. While Douglas broke with tradition and actively campaigned throughout the country, Lincoln stayed close to Springfield and made no formal speeches.

The election results on November 6 starkly demonstrated the extent of the sectional divide. Breckinridge carried all of the slave states except for Virginia, Kentucky, and Tennessee, which went for Bell, and Missouri, which was won by Douglas. With the exception of New Jersey, whose electoral votes were split between Lincoln and Douglas, Lincoln carried all of the free states. In the end he won a majority of 180 out of 303 electoral votes while receiving 40 percent of the popular vote. For the first time the United States had elected an openly antislavery president from an avowedly antislavery party.

As news of the Republican victory spread across the land, Americans began wondering what would happen next. Would South Carolina secede, and if it did, would the other states from the Deep South immediately follow, or wait for Lincoln's inauguration? Was another compromise, or truce, still possible? How would the North respond to disunion? By February 1861 seven Southern states had seceded and formed the Confederate States of America. Their actions raised new questions and new uncertainties. What would the border states and the upper South do? Would the new Lincoln administration attempt to resupply Fort Sumter, one of the few federal military installations that had not fallen into the hands of the secessionists? Once the Confederate bombardment of Sumter brought war to the sundered nation, people throughout the land asked how long would the war last, how would it end, and what would be its consequences?

We can recapture the uncertainties and the expectations of the period by reading what people thought and said as they witnessed what was happening around them. Few observers anticipated a long or bloody conflict, although one West Point graduate, who had since fallen on hard times and was now clerking in his father's general store, predicted "the doom of Slavery." At the time he penned those words in April 1861, Ulysses S. Grant had no idea that he might be instrumental in the demise of the "peculiar institution." The first nine months of the war would see relatively few battles compared to the years that followed. Some were Confederate victories—First Manassas, Wilson's Creek, Ball's Bluff—and some were Union ones—Rich Mountain, Belmont, Port Royal. Contrary to many predictions, the war would not be suddenly decided by one or two battles. Both sides needed time to raise, organize, and train troops, and to find regimental officers and generals capable of leading them. By January 1862 the Union had kept the crucial border states of Maryland, Kentucky, and Missouri from joining the Confederacy, but was still searching for a strategy that would successfully carry the war into the South. No one knew how much longer the conflict would last, and given that so few people had expected ever to see what had already happened since the election of November 1860, it would have been foolhardy for anyone to have tried to predict what would happen next.

CALLING A SECESSION CONVENTION:
NOVEMBER 1860

Charleston Mercury: What Shall the South Carolina Legislature Do?

November 3, 1860

Three days before the 1860 presidential election, this editorial appeared in the *Charleston Mercury*, a newspaper owned by Robert Barnwell Rhett and edited by his son, Robert Barnwell Rhett Jr. The elder Rhett had advocated secession during the 1850 sectional crisis, and in a speech delivered on July 4, 1859 declared that the South should secede if a Republican president was elected in 1860. In its editorial anticipating a Republican victory, the *Mercury* addressed a question that divided many secessionists in 1860: should the slaveholding states secede individually by "separate action," or first hold a general convention and then secede together by "co-operative action." Circumstances favored immediate action in South Carolina, where the legislature would meet on November 5 to choose presidential electors (in 1860 South Carolina was the only state that chose electors by this method). After learning of Lincoln's victory, the legislature called for the election of a state convention that would meet on January 15, 1861.

THE ISSUE before the country is the extinction of slavery. No man of common sense, who has observed the progress of events, and who is not prepared to surrender the institution, with the safety and independence of the South, can doubt that the time for action has come—now or never. The Southern States are now in the crisis of their fate; and, if we read aright the signs of the times, nothing is needed for our deliverance, but that the ball of revolution be set in motion. There is sufficient readiness among the people to make it entirely successful. Co-operation will follow the action of any State. The example of a forward movement only is requisite to unite Southern States in a common cause. Under these circumstances, the Legislature of South Carolina is about to meet. It happens to assemble in advance of the Legislature of any other State. Being in session at this momentous juncture—the Legislature of that State which is most united in the policy of freeing the South from Black Republican domination—the eyes of the whole country, and most especially of the resistance party of the Southern States, is intently turned upon the conduct of this body. We have innumerable assurances that the men of action in each and all of the Southern States, earnestly desire South Carolina to exhibit promptitude and decision in this conjuncture. Other States are torn and divided, to a greater or less extent, by old party issues. South Carolina alone is not. Any practical move would enable the people of other States to rise above their past divisions, and lock shields on the broad ground of Southern security. The course of our Legislature will either greatly stimulate and strengthen, or unnerve the resistance elements of the whole South. A Convention is the point to which their attention will be chiefly directed.

The question of calling a Convention by our Legislature, does not necessarily involve the question of separate or co-operative action. That is a question for the Convention when it assembles, under the circumstances which shall exist when it assembles. All desire the action of as many Southern States as possible, for the formation of a Southern Confederacy. But each should not delay and wait on the other. As these States are separate sovereignties, each must act separately; and whether one or the other acts first or last, we suppose is of no sort of consequence. What is really essential is this—that by the action of one or more States, there shall be the *reasonable probability* that a Southern Confederacy will be formed. We say *probability*,—because there is no certainty in the future of human affairs; and in the position in which the South will be placed by the election of an Abolitionist white man as President of the United States, and an Abolitionist colored man as Vice-President of the United States, we should not hesitate, somewhat to venture. The existence of slavery is at stake. The evils of submission are too terrible for us to risk them, from vague fears of failure, or a jealous distrust of our sister Cotton States. We think, therefore, that the approaching Legislature should provide for the assembling of a Convention of the people of South Carolina, as soon as it is ascertained that

Messrs. LINCOLN and HAMLIN will have a majority in the Electoral Colleges for President and Vice-President of the United States. The only point of difficulty is as *to the time when the Convention shall assemble*. In our judgment, it should assemble *at the earliest possible time* consistent with the opportunity for co-operative action of other Southern States, which may, like ourselves, be determined not to submit to Black Republican domination at Washington. Delay is fatal; while our move will retard no willing State from co-operation. South Carolina, as a sovereign State, is bound to protect her people, but she should so act as to give the other Southern States the opportunity of joining in this policy. The Governors of Alabama, Mississippi and Georgia can act simultaneously. With this qualification, *the earliest time is the best*, for the following reasons:

1. Our great agricultural staples are going to market. The sooner we act, the more of these staples we will have on hand, to control the conduct of the people of the North and of foreign nations, to secure a peaceful result for our deliverance. Thousands at the North, and millions in Europe, need our Cotton to keep their looms in operation. Let us act, before we have parted with our agricultural productions for the season.

2. The commercial and financial interests of the South require that we should act speedily in settling our relations towards the North. Suspense is embarrassment and loss. Decision, with separation, will speedily open new sources of wealth and prosperity, and relieve the finances of the South through the establishment of new channels. In all changes of Government, respect should be had to all classes of the people, and the least possible loss be inflicted on any.

3. The moral effect of promptitude will be immense. Delay will dispirit our friends, and inspire confidence in our enemies. The evils against which we are to provide are not the growth of yesterday. They have been gathering head for thirty years. We have tried, again and again, to avert them by compromise and submission. Submission has failed to avert them; and wise, prompt and resolute action is our last and only course for safety.

4. Black Republican rule at Washington will not commence until the 4th of March next—four short months. Before that time all that South Carolina or the other Southern States

intend to do, should be done. The settlement of our relations towards the General Government, in consequence of our measures of protection, should be completed during the existing Administration.

5. It is exceedingly important, also, that our measures should be laid as soon as possible before *the present Congress*. The secession of one or more States from the Union must be communicated to the President of the United States. He has done all he could to arrest the sectional madness of the North. He knows that we are wronged and endangered by Black Republican ascendancy, and he will not, we have a right to suppose, lend himself to carry out their bloody policy.

6. By communication from the President of the United States, as well as by the withdrawal from Congress of the members of the seceding States, the question of the right of a State to secede from the Union, with the question of a Force Bill, must arise in Congress for action. The Representatives from the other Southern States will most probably be forced either to continue members of a body which orders the sword to be drawn against the seceding States, or they must leave it. They will most probably leave it; and thus the South will be brought together by action in Congress, even though they fail to co-operate at once by their State authorities. It will not be wise to pretermit either of these instrumentalities for the union and co-action of the Southern States; but, it is our opinion, that Congress is the best place to unite them. By prompt action, and through the question of secession in Congress, the agitations which must ensue, will not only tend to unite the Southern members of Congress, but to unite and stimulate State action in the States they represent.

We conclude, therefore, by urging the Legislature about to assemble, to provide for the calling a Convention, as soon as it is ascertained that Messrs. LINCOLN and HAMLIN have the majority in the Electoral Colleges for President and Vice-President of the United States; and that this Convention shall assemble at the earliest day practicable, consistent with the knowledge of our course by our sister Southern States. To this end we would respectfully suggest Nov. 22d and 23d as the day of election, and December 15th as the time of assembling the Convention of the people of South Carolina.

"ALARMS FROM THE SOUTH":
ILLINOIS, NOVEMBER 1860

John G. Nicolay: Memoranda Regarding Abraham Lincoln

November 5–6, 1860

The day before the election, Abraham Lincoln met in Springfield, Illinois, with Henry S. Sanford, a Northern diplomat and businessman who sought to warn Lincoln about the growing agitation in the South. Their conversation was recorded in a memorandum written by John G. Nicolay, a former journalist and state government clerk who had become Lincoln's personal secretary earlier in the year. Nicolay also wrote a memorandum describing Lincoln's visit to the polls on election day.

―――――――

SANFORD Called to see—if the alarms of many persons might not by some means be relieved—the alarms from the South are seriously affecting our work—am myself largely interested—get no orders from the South—

—reassure the men honestly alarmed

—Lincoln—"There are no such men." have thought much about it—it is the trick by which the South breaks down every Northern man—I would go to Washington without the support of the men who supported me and were my friends before election. I would be as powerless as a block of buckeye wood—

(The man still insisted.)

L.—The honest man (you are talking of honest men) will look at our platform and what I have said—there they will find everything I could now say or which they would ask me to say. —all I could say would be but repetition. Having told them all these things ten times already would they believe the eleventh declaration?

Let us be practical—there are many general terms afloat such as 'conservatism'—'enforcement of the irrepressible conflict at the point of the bayonet'—'hostility to the South &c'—all of which mean nothing without definition. What then could I say to allay their fears, if they will not define what particular act or acts they fear from me or my friends?

(gentleman hands him letters)

"recognize them as a sett of liars and knaves who signed that statement about Seward last year."

(gentleman insists there are other names on the list.) (Mr. L. although he had talked quite good-naturedly before evidently betrayed a little feeling at this part of the conversation.)

(after reading the letter) "Well after reading it, it is about what I expected to find it. (laughing)

"it annoyed me a little to hear that gang of men called respectable. their conduct a year ago was a disgrace to any civilized man."

(the gentleman suggested that the south were making armed preparations, &c.)

L. The North does not fear invasion from the Sl S— and we of the North certainly have no desire and never had to invade the South.

I am rather pleased at the idea that the South is making some 'preparation.' They have talked about a Black Republican Victory until the——

Gen. Have we backed this time?

L. "That is what I am pressed to do now."

"If I shall begin to yield to these threats—If I begin dallying with them, the men who have elected me, if I shall be elected, would give me up before my inauguration—and the South seeing it, would deliberately kick me out."—

If (my friends) should desire me to repeat anything I have before said, I should have no objection to do so. If they required me to say something I had not yet said, I should either do so *or get out of the way.*

If I should be elected the first duty to the Country would be to stand by the men who elected me.

November 5, 1860

It is Election day—and Hon. A Lincoln has just been over to vote. The Court House steps, (in which building the polls were held,) were thronged with People, who welcomed him with immense cheering, and followed him in dense numbers along the hall and up stairs into the Court room, which was also crowded. Here the applause became absolutely deafening, and from the time he entered the room and until he cast his vote and again left it, there was wild huzzaing, waving of hats, and all sorts of demonstrations of applause,—rendering all other noises insignificant & futile.

November 6, 1860

THE THREAT OF SECESSION: NOVEMBER 1860

New-York Daily Tribune: Going to Go

November 9, 1860

The Tribune, *founded and edited by Horace Greeley, was one of the most widely read and influential Republican newspapers in the country. Greeley wrote this editorial responding to the possibility of secession and published it three days after the election. It appeared at a time when many Northerners were uncertain as to whether the states in the lower South would actually leave the Union, or were merely using the threat of secession to extract new concessions regarding slavery. Greeley's apparent willingness to allow the Cotton States to "go in peace" drew criticism from those who found the prospect of disunion unacceptable.*

THE PEOPLE of the United States have indicated, according to the forms prescribed by the Constitution, their desire that Abraham Lincoln of Illinois shall be their next President, and Hannibal Hamlin of Maine their Vice-President. A very large plurality of the popular vote has been cast for them, and a decided majority of Electors chosen who will undoubtedly vote for and elect them on the first Wednesday in December next. The electoral votes will be formally sealed up and forwarded to Washington, there to be opened and counted, on a given day in February next, in the presence of both Houses of Congress; and it will then be the duty of Mr. John C. Breckinridge, as President of the Senate, to declare Lincoln and Hamlin duly elected President and Vice-President of these United States.

Some people do not like this, as is very natural. Dogberry discovered, a good while ago, that "When two ride a horse, one must ride behind." That is not generally deemed the preferable seat; but the rule remains unaffected by that circumstance. We know how to sympathize with the defeated; for we remember how *we* felt when Adams was defeated; and Clay; and Scott; and Fremont. It is decidedly pleasanter to be on the winning side, especially when—as now—it happens also to be the right side.

We sympathize with the afflicted; but we cannot recommend them to do anything desperate. What is the use? They are beaten now; they may triumph next time: in fact, they have generally had their own way: had they been subjected to the discipline of adversity as often as we have, they would probably bear it with more philosophy, and deport themselves more befittingly. We live to learn: and one of the most difficult acquirements is that of meeting reverses with graceful fortitude.

The telegraph informs us that most of the Cotton States are meditating a withdrawal from the Union because of Lincoln's election. Very well: they have a right to meditate, and meditation is a profitable employment of leisure. We have a chronic, invincible disbelief in Disunion as a remedy for either Northern or Southern grievances. We cannot perceive any necessary relation between the alleged disease and this ultra-heroic remedy: still, we say, if anybody sees fit to meditate Disunion, let them do so unmolested. That was a base and hypocritic row that the House once raised, at Southern dictation, about the ears of John Quincy Adams, because he presented a petition for the dissolution of the Union. The petitioner had a right to make the request; it was the Member's duty to present it. And now, if the Cotton States consider the value of the Union debatable, we maintain their perfect right to discuss it. Nay: we hold with Jefferson to the inalienable right of communities to alter or abolish forms of government that have become oppressive or injurious; and if the Cotton States shall become satisfied that they can do better out of the Union than in it, we insist on letting them go in peace. The right to secede may be a revolutionary one, but it exists nevertheless; and we do not see how one party can have a right to do what another party has a right to prevent. We must ever resist the asserted right of any State to remain in the Union and nullify or defy the laws thereof; to withdraw from the Union is quite another matter. And whenever a considerable section of our Union shall deliberately resolve to go out, we shall resist all coercive measures designed to keep it in. We hope never to live in a republic whereof one section is pinned to the residue by bayonets.

But while we thus uphold the practical liberty if not the

abstract right of secession, we must insist that the step be taken, if it ever shall be, with the deliberation and gravity befitting so momentous an issue. Let ample time be given for reflection; let the subject be fully canvassed before the people; and let a popular vote be taken in every case before secession is decreed. Let the people be told just why they are urged to break up the confederation; let them have both sides of the question fully presented; let them reflect, deliberate, then vote; and let the act of secession be the echo of an unmistakable popular fiat. A judgment thus rendered, a demand for separation so backed, would either be acquiesced in without the effusion of blood, or those who rushed upon carnage to defy and defeat it would place themselves clearly in the wrong.

The measures now being inaugurated in the Cotton States with a view (apparently) to Secession, seem to us destitute of gravity and legitimate force. They bear the unmistakable impress of haste—of passion—of distrust of the popular judgment. They seem clearly intended to precipitate the South into rebellion before the baselessness of the clamors which have misled and excited her can be ascertained by the great body of her people. We trust that they will be confronted with calmness, with dignity, and with unwavering trust in the inherent strength of the Union and the loyalty of the American People.

THE NEED FOR SOUTHERN COOPERATION:
NOVEMBER 1860

Jefferson Davis to Robert Barnwell Rhett Jr.

In a private letter to the editor of the *Charleston Mercury*, Senator Jefferson Davis of Mississippi expressed caution about the prospects for secession by separate state action. On November 10, the day Davis wrote to Rhett, the South Carolina legislature advanced the meeting of its state convention to December 17. This action, taken in response to reports of growing support for secession in Georgia, Alabama, and Mississippi, would affect the course of events throughout the South.

WARREN COUNTY, Missi., Nov. 10, 1860.

DEAR SIR:—I had the honor to receive, last night, yours of the 27th ulto., and hasten to reply to the inquiries propounded. Reports of the election leave little doubt that the event you anticipated has occurred, that electors have been chosen securing the election of Lincoln, and I will answer on that supposition.

My home is so isolated that I have had no intercourse with those who might have aided me in forming an opinion as to the effect produced on the mind of our people by the result of the recent election, and the impressions which I communicate are founded upon antecedent expressions.

1. I doubt not that the Gov'r of Missi. has convoked the Legislature to assemble within the present month, to decide upon the course which the State should adopt in the present emergency. Whether the Legislature will direct the call of a convention, of the State, or appoint delegates to a convention of such Southern States as may be willing to consult together for the adoption of a Southern plan of action, is doubtful.

2. If a convention, of the State, were assembled, the proposition to secede from the Union, independently of support from neighboring States, would probably fail.

3. If South Carolina should first secede, and she alone should take such action, the position of Missi. would not

probably be changed by that fact. A powerful obstacle to the separate action of Missi. is the want of a port; from which follows the consequence that her trade being still conducted through the ports of the Union, her revenue would be diverted from her own support to that of a foreign government; and being geographically unconnected with South Carolina, an alliance with her would not vary that state of case.

4. The propriety of separate secession by So. Ca. depends so much upon collateral questions that I find it difficult to respond to your last enquiry, for the want of knowledge which would enable me to estimate the value of the elements involved in the issue, though exterior to your state. Georgia is necessary to connect you with Alabama and thus to make effectual the coöperation of Missi. If Georgia would be lost by immediate action, but could be gained by delay, it seems clear to me that you should wait. If the secession of So. Ca. should be followed by an attempt to coerce her back into the Union, that act of usurpation, folly and wickedness would enlist every true Southern man for her defence. If it were attempted to blockade her ports and destroy her trade, a like result would be produced, and the commercial world would probably be added to her allies. It is therefore probable that neither of those measures would be adopted by any administration, but that federal ships would be sent to collect the duties on imports outside of the bar; that the commercial nations would feel little interest in that; and the Southern States would have little power to counteract it.

The planting states have a common interest of such magnitude, that their union, sooner or later, for the protection of that interest is certain. United they will have ample power for their own protection, and their exports will make for them allies of all commercial and manufacturing powers.

The new states have a heterogeneous population, and will be slower and less unanimous than those in which there is less of the northern element in the body politic, but interest controls the policy of states, and finally all the planting communities must reach the same conclusion. My opinion is, therefore, as it has been, in favor of seeking to bring those states into cooperation before asking for a popular decision upon a new policy and relation to the nations of the earth. If So. Ca.

should resolve to secede before that cooperation can be obtained, to go out leaving Georgia and Alabama and Louisiana in the Union, and without any reason to suppose they will follow her; there appears to me to be no advantage in waiting until the govt. has passed into hostile hands and men have become familiarized to that injurious and offensive perversion of the general government from the ends for which it was established. I have written with the freedom and carelessness of private correspondence, and regret that I could not give more precise information. Very respectfully, Yrs, etc..

JEFFN DAVIS.

DEBATING SECESSION:
GEORGIA, NOVEMBER 1860

Benjamin Hill: Speech at Milledgeville

November 15, 1860

Several prominent Georgians, including Senator Robert Toombs and former congressman Alexander H. Stephens, gave speeches at the state capital in November 1860 while the legislature debated whether to call a convention to consider secession. A successful lawyer active in Georgia politics, Benjamin Hill was a former Whig who had joined the nativist American (Know Nothing) Party during the 1850s. Like many southern Whig-Americans alarmed by the prospect of secession, Hill had supported John Bell, the Constitutional Union candidate, in the 1860 presidential election. (Bell, who ran on a pledge to "*recognize* no political principle other than *the Constitution of the Country, the Union of the States, and the Enforcement of the Laws*," carried Virginia, Kentucky, and Tennessee, but lost in the remainder of the South to John C. Breckinridge.) Hill would vote against secession at the Georgia convention in January 1861; he then went on to serve in the Provisional Confederate Congress and in the Confederate Senate. His refusal in November 1860 to commit himself to either unconditional unionism or to immediate secession was shared by many southern "conditional unionists" and "conditional secessionists" in 1860–61.

Ladies and Friends: While I am speaking to you to-night I earnestly beg for perfect quietness and order. It seems to be a general idea that public speakers feel highly complimented when their opinions are received with boisterous applause. I do not so feel on any occasion, and certainly would not so regard such a demonstration now. The occasion is a solemn and serious one, and let us treat it in no light or trivial manner. One more request. I have invoked good order. I yet more earnestly invoke your kind and considerate attention. No people ever assembled to deliberate a graver issue. The government is the result of much toil, much blood, much anxiety, and much treasure. For nearly a century we have been accustomed to speak and boast of it as the best on earth. Wrapped up in it are the lives, the happiness, the interests, and the peace of thirty millions of freemen now living, and of unnumbered millions in the future.

Whether we shall now destroy that government or make another effort to preserve it and reform its abuses, is the question before us. Is that question not entitled to all the wisdom, the moderation, and the prudence we can command? Were you ever at sea in a storm? Then you know the sailor often finds it necessary, to enable him to keep his ship above the wave, to throw overboard his freight, even his treasure. But with his chart and his compass he never parts. However dark the heavens or furious the winds, with these he can still point the polar star, and find the port of his safety. Would not that sailor be mad who should throw these overboard?

We are at sea, my friends. The skies are fearfully darkened. The billows roll threateningly. Dangers are on every side. Let us throw overboard our passions, our prejudices, and our party feelings, however long or highly valued. But let us hold on— hold on to reason and moderation. These, and these alone, point always to the fixed star of truth, by whose guidance we may yet safely come to shore.

We must agree. We do agree if we but knew it. Our people must be united to meet this crisis. Divisions now would not only be unfortunate, but exceedingly disastrous. If divisions arise they cannot be based on our interests or our purposes, for these are and must be the same. Divisions must find their origin in our suspicions and jealousies. Let us give these suspicions and jealousies to the winds. Let us assume as the basis of every argument that we are all equally honest, and equally desirous in our various ways of securing one end—our equality and rights. There must be one way better than all others. Let our ambition be to find that way, and unite our people in the advocacy of that way.

I have listened with earnest attention to the eloquent speeches made by all sides, and I believe a common ground of agreement can be found, if not for universal, at least for very general agreement. Those who hold that the Constitution is wrong, and the Union bad *per se*, of course will agree to nothing but immediate disunion, and such I shall not be able to affect.

In the first place what are our grievances. All the speakers, thus far, even the most ultra, have admitted that the mere Constitutional election of any man is no ground for resistance. The mere election of Mr. Lincoln is on all sides admitted not to be grievance. Our State would not be thrown on a false issue on this point.

We complain, in general terms, that the anti-slavery sentiment at the North has been made an element of political power.

In proof of this we make the following specifications:

1. That a large political party has been organized in the Northern States, the great common idea of which is to prohibit the extension of slavery by Congress, and hostility to slavery generally.

2. That this party has succeeded in getting the control of many of the Northern State Legislatures and have procured the passage of acts nullifying the fugitive slave law, encouraging the rescue of fugitives, and seeking to punish as felons citizens of our Southern States who pursue their slaves in the assertion of a plain Constitutional right.

3. That this party has elected governors in Northern States who refuse, some openly and others under frivolous pretexts, to do their plain Constitutional duties, when these involve the recognition of property in slaves.

4. That Northern courts, chosen by the same party, have assumed to declare the fugitive slave law unconstitutional in the teeth of the decisions of the United States courts, and of every department of the United States Government.

5. We complain that the Northern States, thus controlled, are seeking to repudiate every Constitutional duty or provision, in favor or in recognition of slavery—to work the extinction of slavery, and to secure to the negro social and political equality with the white race; and, as far as possible, they disregard and nullify even the laws of the Southern States on these subjects. In proof of this complaint, we show that Northern governors have actually refused to deliver up fugitives from

justice, when the crime charged against such fugitives recognized under State law property in slaves.

Thus, a Northern man married a Southern lady having a separate estate in slaves. He deceived the lady, stole her negroes, sold them, and pocketed the money, and fled to a Northern State. He was charged with larceny under the laws of the State in which the crime was committed. A true bill was obtained and a demand was properly made for his return, and the Governor of the State to which he fled refused to deliver him up on the ground that to commit larceny a man must steal property, and as slaves were not property according to the laws of the Northern State, it could not be property according to the laws of the Southern State; that therefore the Southern court, jury, and governor were all wrong in obeying the laws of their own State, instead of the laws of the Northern State; that the defendant was not guilty and could not be guilty, and should not be delivered up.

The same principle was involved to shield several of the conspirators in the John Brown raid.

The inexorable logic of this party, on such a premise, must array them against the whole Constitution of the United States; because that instrument, in its very frame-work, is a recognition of property in slaves. It was made by slaveholding States. Accordingly we find this party a disunion party, and its leaders—those of them who follow their logic to its practical consequences—disunionists *per se*. I would not quote from the low and the ignorant of that party, but I will quote from the learned and the honored.

One of the most learned disciples of this party, says:

> The Constitution is the cause of every division which this vexed question of slavery has ever occasioned in this country. If (the Constitution) has been the fountain and father of our troubles, by attempting to hold together, as reconciled, two opposing principles, which will not harmonize nor agree, the only hope of the slave is over the ruins of the government. The dissolution of the Union is the abolition of slavery.

One of the ablest, and oldest, and long honored senators of that party—a senator even before the existence of the Republican party—said to the nominating convention of that party:

I believe that this is not so much a convention to change the administration of the government, as to say whether there shall be any government to be administered. You have assembled, not to say whether this Union shall be preserved, but to say whether it shall be a blessing or a scorn and hissing among the nations.

I could quote all night, my friends, to show that the tendency of the Republican party is to disunion. That to be a Republican is to be logically and practically against the Constitution and the Union. And we complain that this party is warring upon us, and at the same time, and in the same way, and by a necessary consequence, warring upon the Constitution and the Union.

6. We complain, in the last place, that this party, having thus acquired the control of every department of government—legislative, executive, and judicial—in several of the Northern States, and having thus used every department of the State government so acquired, in violation of the Constitution of the United States, in disregard of the laws of the Southern States, and in utter denial of the property and even liberty of the citizens of the Southern States—this party, I say, with these principles, and this history, has at last secured the executive department of the Federal Government, and are seeking to secure the other two departments—the legislative and the judicial.

Here, then, is a party seeking to administer the government on principles which must destroy the government—proposing to preserve the Union upon a basis on which the Union, in the very nature of things, cannot stand; and offering peace on terms which must produce civil war.

Now, my friends, the next question is, shall these grievances be resisted? I know of no man who says they ought not to be resisted. For myself, I say, and say with emphasis, they ought to be resisted—resisted effectively and at all hazards.

What lessons have we here? We have seen differences running high—even apparent bitterness engendered. Passion gets up, debates become jeers and gibes and defiance. One man says he will not resist Lincoln. His adversary pronounces that treason to the South and the man a black Republican. Another man says he will resist Lincoln and demand immediate secession. His adversary pronounces that treason to the Constitution and the man a disunionist.

What do you mean by Lincoln? Stop and define. The first means by Lincoln the man elected, the second means by Lincoln the issue on which he is elected. Neither will resist the first, both will resist the latter, and so they agree and did agree all the time they were disputing!

These grievances are our real complaint. They have advanced to a point which makes a crisis: and that point is the election of Lincoln. We dare not, we will not let this crisis pass without a settlement. That settlement must wipe out existing grievances, and arrest threatened ones. We owe it to our Constitution, to our country, to our peace, to our posterity, to our dignity, to our self-respect as Union men and Southern men, to have a cessation of these aggressions and an end to these disturbances. I do not think we should wait for any further violation of the Constitution. The Constitution has already been violated and even defied. These violations are repeated every day. We must resist, and to attempt to resist and not do so effectively—even to the full extent of the evil—will be to bring shame on ourselves, and our State, and our cause.

Having agreed on our complaints, and discovered that all our suspicions of each other are unfounded, and that our disputes on this point had their origin in hasty conclusions and thoughtless mistakes, let us, with an encouraged charity and forbearance, advance to the next step in this argument.

Who shall inaugurate this resistance? Who shall determine the mode, the measure, and the time of this resistance?

My reply is: The people through their delegate convention duly assembled.

It is not necessary for me now to urge this point. Here again we have had disputes without differences.

I have the pleasure of announcing to-night that the prominent leaders, of all shades of opinion on this subject, came together this day, and agreed that it was the right and privilege of the people in convention to pass on these questions. On this point we have disputed for a week, and to-day, acting as Georgians should act, we came together in a spirit of kindness, and in fifteen minutes our hearts were all made glad by the discovery that our differences or disputes were founded on groundless suspicions, and *we are agreed*. We are all for resistance, and we are all for the people in convention to say how and where and by what means we shall resist.

I never beheld a scene which made my heart rejoice more sincerely. Oh, that I could see the same spirit of concord on the only remaining question of difference. With my heart full of kindness I beg you, my friends, accompany me now to question. I do believe we can agree again. My solemn conviction is that we differ as little on this as we did on the other point, in every material view. At least, nearly all the quarrels of the world in all ages have been founded more in form than substance.

Some men are honest, wise, and prudent. Others are equally honest and intelligent, but rash and impetuous. The latter are often to be loved and encouraged; but the first alone are to be relied on in emergencies.

We often appeal to the history of our fathers to urge men to indignation and resentment of wrongs. Let us study all that history. Let me show you from that history, an example of metal and over-confidence on the one hand, and of coolness and wisdom on the other.

During our colonial history, the English government sent General Braddock to America to dislodge and drive back the French and Indians. The general, in arranging the company, assigned to his own command the duty of recovering the Ohio Valley and the great Northwest. It was necessary to capture Fort Duquesne. He never thought of any difficulties in the way of success. He promised Newcastle to be beyond the mountains in a very short period. Duquesne he thought would stop him only three or four days, and there was no obstruction to his march to Niagara. He declared the Indians might frighten the raw American militia, but could make no impression on the British regulars. This was Braddock.

One of that raw American militia who had joined Braddock's command, was the young Washington, then only about twenty-three years old. He became one of Braddock's aids. Hearing his general's boasts, and seeing his thoughtless courage, Washington quietly said to him, "We shall have more to do than to go up the hills and come down." Speaking of

Braddock to another, Washington said, "He was incapable of arguing without warmth, or giving up any point he had asserted, be it ever so incompatible with reason or common sense."

Braddock was considered on all hands to be a brave, gallant, and fearless officer.

Here, then, are two men, both brave, noble, and intelligent, engaged together to accomplish a common enterprise for the good of their country. The one was rash, thoughtless, never calculating difficulties, nor looking forward to and providing against obstructions.

He arranged his express and sent forward the news of his victory beforehand. But the other was cool, calculating, cautious, wise, and moderate. He was a man who thought before he acted and then he acted the hero.

Now, for results: Braddock was surprised before he reached the fort. His British regulars fled before the yelling Indians, and the raw American militia were slain by them. Braddock himself fought bravely and he was borne from the field of his shame, leaving more than half his little army dead, and himself senseless with a mortal wound. After the lapse of a day he came to himself, and his first exclamation was, "Who would have thought it!" Again he roused up and said, "We shall better know how to deal with them another time." Poor general, it was too late, for with that sentence he died! For more than a century he has slept near Fort Necessity, and his only history might be written for his epitaph: "He was brave but rash, gallant but thoughtless, noble but bigoted. He fought hastily, died early, and here he lies."

The young Washington was also brave, and in the thickest of the fight. Horse after horse fell from under him. The bullets of the Indians whistled around him and through his clothes, but Providence spared him. Even the Indians declared some God protected him. So cool, so brave, so wise and thoughtful was the conduct of this young officer, before, during, and after the battle that even then a distinguished man "points him out as a youth raised up by Providence for some noble work." Who does not know the history of Washington; yet who can tell it? Our glorious revolution, that wise Constitution, this happy, widespread, and ever spreading country—struggling millions fired on by the example of his success, are some of the chapters already written in that history. Long chapters of yet unrealized glory, and power, and happiness shall be endlessly added, if the wisdom of him who redeemed our country can be continued to those who inherit it. The last hour of constitutional liberty, perpetuated to the glory of the end, or cut short in the frenzy of anarchy, shall wind up the history of Washington. Behold here the sudden destructon of the rash man and his followers, and the still unfolding success of the cool and thoughtful man, and then let us go to work to meet this crisis that is upon us.

Though there are various modifications of opinions, there are really but two modes of resistance proposed. One method is to make no further effort in the Union, but to assume that the Union either cannot or ought not to be preserved, and secede at once and throw ourselves upon the consequences. The other method is to exhaust certain remedies for these grievances in the Union, with the view of preserving our rights and the Union with them, if possible; looking, however, to and preparing for secession as an ultimate resort, certainly to be had, if those grievances cannot be remedied and completely remedied and ended in the Union.

Irreconcilable as these differences at first view seem to be, I maintain a point of complete reconciliation can be reached.

Now, let us look to the reason urged by the advocates of these two modes of redress.

The advocates of the first mode declare that these grievances are the fruits of an original, innate anti-slavery fanaticism. That the history of the world will show that such fanaticism is never convinced, is never satisfied, never reasons, and never ends but in victory or blood. That accordingly this fanaticism in the Northern States has been constantly progressive, always getting stronger and more impudent, defiant, and aggressive; and that it will never cease except in our subjugation unless we tear loose from it by dissolving the Union. These advocates say they have no faith in any resistance in the Union, because, in the nature of the evil, none can be effectual.

The advocates of the second mode of resistance, of whom I am humbly one, reason after another fashion: We say, in the first place, that while it is true that this anti-slavery sentiment has become fanatical with many, yet it is not necessarily so in its nature, nor was it so in its origin. Slavery has always existed in some form. It is an original institution. Besides, we say the agitation now upon us did not originate in fanaticism or philanthropy but in cupidity.

England owned the West Indies and there she had some slaves. She had possessions in East India which she believed were adapted to the growth of cotton, and which article of produce she desired to monopolize.

The Southern States were her only dangerous competitors. She desired to cripple or break down the cultivation of the cotton plant in the South. The South could not use her own soil and climate in the successful production of cotton without the African slave. England therefore must manage to set free the slave and turn the South over to some inadequate peasantry system, something like the coolie system. To this end England raised a great cry of philanthropy in behalf of the poor negro. As a show of sincerity she abolished slavery in the West Indies near us, thinking thereby to affect the same institutions in her Southern neighbor. She taught her lessons of false philanthropy to our Northern pulpits and Northern papers, and thus to our Northern people.

At this time the Northern politicians saw in this inflammable subject fine material for political agitation, party success, and self-promotion. They leaped upon the wave and rode on it. The Southern politicians raised the counter cry, leaped on the counter wave, and met the Northern politicians—in office. As long as the people answered the politicians called, and the result is what we now see. The subject is interminable in politics, because utterly illegitimate as a political issue. Thus it has never approached, but receded from a political solution, and increasing in excitement as it has progressed; all statesmanship, North and South, is dwarfed to a mere wrangling about African slavery. Slavery will survive, but the Constitution, the Union, and peace may not. The Southern States will continue to raise cotton, but the hoping subject of tyranny in the earth may not continue to point to the beautiful success of the experiment of self-government in America.

While the storm which England raised in America has been going on, England has been trying to raise cotton in India. She has failed. Her factories are at home, but her cotton can't come from India. She must have cotton. Four millions of her people can't live without it. The English throne can't stand without it. It must come from the Southern States. It can't be raised in the South without slave labor. And England has become the defender of slavery in the South.

I will frankly state that this revolution in English sentiment and policy has not yet reached the Northern people. The same causes must slowly produce it.

But while the anti-slavery sentiment has spread in the North, the pro-slavery sentiment has also strengthened in America. In our early history the Southern statesmen were anti-slavery in feeling. So were Washington, Jefferson, Madison, Randolph, and many of that day, who had never studied the argument of the cotton gin, nor heard the eloquent productions of the great Mississippi Valley. Now our people not only see the justice of slavery, but its providence too. The world can never give up slavery until it is ready to give up clothing and food. The South is a magnificent exemplification of the highest Christian excellence. She is feeding the hungry, clothing the naked, blessing them that curse her, and doing good to them that despitefully use and persecute her.

We say again that even the history of the slavery agitation in this country does not justify the very conclusion that Abolitionism has been always progressive. Whenever popular sentiment in politics has condemned the agitation, Abolitionism has declined. Many instances could be given. In 1848 the Abolition candidate for the Presidency received about 300,000 votes. At the end of Mr. Fillmore's administration in 1852, the candidate of that party received about half that vote, and a fugitive slave could be recovered almost without opposition in any Northern State. Even the act of Massachusetts, nullifying the fugitive slave law of 1793, had not been applied to the new fugitive slave law of 1850, and was not so applied until 1855, after the agitation had been revived.

These, and many other similar reasons, we urge for believing that all the enumerated grievances—the results of slavery agitation—are curable by remedies within the Union.

But suppose our reasoning all wrong! How shall we be convinced? Only by the experiment; for in the nature of the case, nothing but a trial can test the virtue of the remedies proposed. Let us try these remedies, and if we fail, this failure will establish the truth of the positions of the advocates of immediate secession, and we shall all join in that remedy.

For let it be understood, we are all agreed that these grievances shall be resisted—shall be remedied—most effectively remedied; and if this cannot be done in the Union, then the Union must go. And we must not let this crisis pass without forever solving this doubt. If the Union and the peace of slavery cannot exist together, then the Union must go; for slavery can never go, the necessities of man and the laws of Heaven will never let it go, and it must have peace. And it has been tantalized and meddled with as long as our self-respect can permit.

But what remedies in the Union do we propose? I will answer:

The grievances enumerated are of two kinds—existing and threatened. The existing actual grievances are all violations of the Federal Constitution and Federal laws, either by Northern citizens or Northern States. Now, what does good statesmanship, good logic, and common sense naturally suggest? Why, that the Federal Government shall enforce its laws. No State can enforce, or punish, for the violation of a Federal law. The power offended must adequately punish the offender. The punishment must be such as to redress the past, and by certainty and terror secure the future. The Federal law is offended. The Northern States and people are the offenders. The South is damaged by the offense. This gives her the right to demand the redress at the hands of the Federal Government, and if that government, for want of will or power, shall not grant the redress, then that government is a demonstrated failure. And when government ends, self-defense begins. We can then take redress in our own way, and to our entire satisfaction.

Let the Georgia Convention meet. Let her not simply demand but command that this war on slavery shall cease—that these unconstitutional acts and proceedings shall be repealed and abandoned by the States, or repudiated and redressed by the Federal Government. Let her invite all the States to join in this demand. If no others will come to their duty and meet with us, let the fifteen Southern States join in this demand, and let the penalty of refusal, even to the demand of one State, be the abandonment of the Union, and any other, even harsher remedy, each State may think her rights and honor require.

We have an instance before us, made by the North. When, in 1833, South Carolina was refusing to obey a Federal law, in the execution of which the Northern States had an interest, Congress passed a force bill, and put it in the hands of a Southern President for enforcement, even with the army and the navy and the militia—if needed.

Let us turn this battery against Northern rebels. The constitutionality of the act which South Carolina resisted was doubted. A Southern State never nullified, nor refused to obey, a plain constitutional law. But here are the Northern States, and people nullifying and setting at defiance the plainest Constitutional provisions, and laws passed in pursuance thereof; and, instead of demanding of the Federal Government the enforcement of its laws for the protection of our rights, we are spending our breath and wasting our strength, in vain boastings of wrath and hurtful divisions of our own people.

Some of our wisest Southern statesmen think we have laws already sufficient for this crisis, if enforced. We have an act in 1795, and one in 1807, and perhaps others, to execute the laws, to suppress insurrections, and repel invasions. If these and other enactments are sufficient, let us have them enforced.

A Voice.—The presidents we have already had won't enforce that law.

Mr. Hill.—Then you ought to have dissolved long ago. If the grievance has been by men of our own choosing, why have we not complained before. Let us begin now. Let us begin with Mr. Buchanan. A few days ago, and perhaps now, a fugitive is standing protected by a Northern mob in a Northern State, in defiance of the United States Marshal. Let us demand now that Mr. Buchanan enforce the law against that rebel and against that State which protects him, or suffers him to be protected on her soil. Let us have out the army and navy, and if they are not sufficient let there be a call for volunteers. Many of us say we are ready to fight, anxious to fight. Here is a chance. Let us tender our services.

If the laws now existing are not sufficient, let us have them sufficient. It is our right. We are entitled to a force bill for every clause in the Constitution necessary to our rights. What have our statesmen been after that these laws are not sufficient? Some of these nullifying grievances have existed since 1843, and is it possible that our statesmen have been all asleep, or lost or forgetful in wrangling about slavery? Let us begin now and perfect our laws for the enforcement of every Constitutional right, and against every rebel enemy. Let the convention add to the contingencies of disruption in the Georgia platform. Let the refusal to enforce the laws granted for our protection and defense be one contingency, and the refusal to grant the laws needed for that protection and defense be another contingency.

A Voice.—How long will you wait?

Mr. Hill.—Until the experiment is tried and both the demands enumerated may be tested and the contingencies may transpire before the fourth of March next. If they do not, if a larger time shall be needed, Mr. Lincoln cannot do us damage. As you heard last night, he cannot even form his Cabinet unless he make it acceptable to a Democratic Senate. And I go further and say that he cannot get even his salary—not a dime to pay for his breakfast—without the consent of Congress.

Nor would I have the Southern States, nor even Georgia, to hesitate to demand the enforcement of those laws at the hands of Mr. Lincoln, if we cannot test it before. The North demanded of a Southern President the execution of the law against a Southern State in 1833. Now let the South compel a Northern President to execute the laws against a Northern people; yea, the very rebels that elected him.

A Voice.—Do you believe Lincoln would issue his proclamation?

Mr. Hill.—We can make him do it. It is his oath. He will be a traitor to refuse, and we shall have the right to hang him. He dare not refuse. He would be on Southern territory, and for his life he dare not refuse.

A Voice.—The "Wide Awakes" will be there.

Mr. Hill.—Very well, if we are afraid of the "Wide Awakes" we had better surrender without further debate. The "Wide Awakes" will be there if we secede, and if they are to be dreaded, our only remedy is to hide. No, my friends, we are not afraid of anybody. Arm us with the laws of our country and the Constitution of our fathers, and we fear no enemy. Let us make war upon that Constitution and against those laws and we will be afraid of every noise in the bushes. He who feels and knows he is right, is afraid of nothing; and he who feels and knows he is wrong, is afraid of nothing, too.

We were told the other night by a gentleman urging immediate secession that we had never had a member in Congress but who was afraid to demand the laws for the enforcement of these Constitutional rights. And this is true, but whose fault is that? Shame upon us that we have been afraid to demand our rights at the hands of our own government, administered to this hour by men of our own choice, and yet insist on our courage to sustain us in seceding from that government in defiance of its power. No, we have a right to go out, but let us know we *must* exercise that right before we go, and how can we know it unless we ask first? The Declaration of Independence, which you invoke for an example, says, a decent respect to the opinions of mankind requires us to declare the causes which impel us to the separation. When we separate and allege our grievances as our causes, and mankind shall ask us if we attempted, even demanded a redress of those grievances and causes before we went out, shall we hang our heads and say no? A people who are afraid to demand respect for their rights, can have no rights worthy to be respected. Our fathers demanded, yea petitioned, warned, and conjured, and not until the government was deaf to the voice of justice and consanguinity, did they acquiesce in the necessity which announced their separation. It is not the cowardice of fear, but the courage of right and duty, to demand redress at the hands of our government.

I confess I am anxious to see the strength of this government now tested. The crisis is on us; not of our seeking, but in spite of our opposition, and now let us meet it.

I believe we can make Lincoln enforce the laws. If fifteen Southern States will take that Constitution and the laws and his oath, and shake them in the face of the President, and demand their observance and enforcement, he cannot refuse. Better make *him* do it than any one else. It will be a magnificent vindication of the power and the majesty of the law, to make the President enforce the law, even to hanging, against the very rebels who have chosen him to trample upon it. It will be a vindication that will strike terror to the hearts of the evil-doers for a century to come. Why, Lincoln is not a monarch. He has no power outside of the law, and none inside of the law except to enforce it. The law is our king over all. From the President to the humblest citizen we are the equal subjects of this only ruler. We have no cause for fear except when we offend this only sovereign of the Republican citizen, and have no occasion for despair until his protection is denied us.

I am also willing, as you heard last night, that our Convention or State should demand of the nullifying States the repeal of their obnoxious laws. I know this idea has been characterized as ridiculous. I cannot see wherein. You would make such demands of any foreign power interfering with your rights, and why do less toward a confederate State?

But in my opinion, the wisest policy, the most natural remedy, and the surest way to vindicate our honor and self-respect, is to demand the unconditional observance of the Constitution by every State and people, and to enforce that demand. And if it be necessary, call out for this purpose the whole power of the government even to war on the rebellious State. And when a State shall allow a fugitive to be rescued in her jurisdiction and carried beyond the reach of the owner, require her to indemnify the owner, and make the government compel that indemnity, even to the seizure of the property of the offending State and her people. One such rigid enforcement of the law will secure universal obedience. Let the law be executed though the heavens fall, for there can be no government without law, and law is but sand, if not enforced. If need be, let the State continuing in rebellion against the Constitution be driven from the Union. Is this Union a good? If so, why should we surrender its blessings because Massachusetts violates the laws of that Union? Punish the guilty. Drive Massachusetts to the duties of the Constitution or from its benefits. Make the general government do this, and abandon the government when it shall take sides with the criminal. It would be a trophy to fanaticism, above all her insolence, to drive the dutiful out of the Union with impunity on its part. Let us defend the Union against its enemies, until that Union shall take sides with the enemy, and then let us defend ourselves against both.

In the next place let us consider the benefits of this policy. First, let us consider its benefits if we succeed; and then its benefits if we fail.

If we succeed we shall have brought about a triumph of law over the fell spirit of mobocracy, never surpassed in the world's history, and the reward of that triumph will be the glorious vindication of our equality and honor, and at the same time the establishment of the Union in its integrity forever. And I tell you, my friends, we owe it to our history, ourselves, and our posterity, yea, to constitutional liberty itself, to make this trial. Can it be possible that we are living under a government that has no power to enforce its laws? We have boasted of our form of government. We have almost canonized its authors as saints, for their patriotism and wisdom. They have reputations world-wide. They have been, for nearly a century, lauded as far above all antiquity, and all previous statesmen. Their faces and their forms have been perpetuated in brass and marble for the admiring gaze of many generations made happy in the enjoyment of their labors. In verse and song, in history and philosophy, in light literature and graver learning, their names are eulogized, and their deeds commemorated, and their wisdom ennobled. The painter has given us the very faces and positions of the great counselors, as they sat together deliberating in the formation of this Constitution. The pulpit has placed their virtues next to the purity and inspiration of the early apostles. The Senate Chamber has invoked their sayings as the test of good policy. The fireside has held up to its juvenile circle their manners as the models of good breeding. The demagogue on the hustings has falsely caught at their mantles to hide his own shame.

All this, because we have been accustomed to believe that they succeeded in framing the best Constitution and in organizing the best government the world ever saw. Is that government, after all, a failure? Who shall give us a better, and how shall we commemorate the worth of such wiser benefactors? But if this government cannot enforce its laws, then it is a failure.

We have professed to feel and realize its blessings. Eloquence has portrayed in magic power its progress in all the elements of power, wealth, greatness, and happiness. Not a people on earth, since we achieved our independence, has shown symptoms of a desire to be free, that we have not encouraged by our sympathies, and as the sufficient evidence of all success in self-government, we have pointed them to our example. There is not a people on earth who do not point to America and sigh for a government like that of the United States. Shall we now say to all these: Stop, you are mistaken. Our reputation is not deserved. Be content with your harsher rule. The people are not capable of self-government. This very government, which you admire, and which we have thought was a model, is unable to protect our own people from the robber, the thief, the murderer, and the fanatic!

Fellow-citizens, before we settle down in such a conclusion, let us make the effort and put this government to the test.

Another advantage to be derived from success is, that we shall thus end the agitation of slavery forever. Its agitation in politics was wrong from the beginning. Debate its morality and justice as much as you please. It will stand the argument. But don't drag it down into a party political issue. Show me the man who agitates slavery as a political party question and I will show you the true enemy of slavery and the Union, I care not whether he lives North or South. The safety and peace of the slaveholder and the Union demand that this agitation should not longer be allowed.

But, in the second place, if we fail, we cannot be damaged, but great benefits will result from the effort.

In the next place we shall have time to get ready for secession. If we secede now, in what condition are we? Our secession will either be peaceable or otherwise. If peaceable, we have no ships to take off our produce. We could not get and would not have those of the government from which we had just seceded. We have no treaties, commercial or otherwise, with any other power. We have no postal system among our own people. Nor are we prepared to meet any one of the hundred inconveniences that must follow, and all of which can be avoided by taking time.

But suppose our secession be not peaceable. In what condition are we for war? No navy, no forts, no arsenals, no arms but bird guns for low trees. Yet a scattered people, with nothing dividing us from our enemy but an imaginary line, and a long sea and gulf coast extending from the Potomac to Galveston Bay, if all should secede. In what condition are we to meet the thousand ills that would beset us, and every one of which can be avoided by taking time. "We have more to do than to go up the hills and come down." Secession is no holiday work.

While we are seeking to redress our wrongs in the Union, we can go forward, making all necessary preparations to go out if it should become necessary. We can have a government system perfect, and prepared, ready for the emergency, when the necessity for separation shall come.

Again, if we fail to get redress in the Union, that very failure will unite the people of our State. The only real ground of difference now is: some of us think we can get redress in the Union, and others think we cannot. Let those of us who still have faith make that effort which has never been made, and if we fail, then we are ready to join you. If you will not help us make that effort, at least do not try to prevent. Let us have a fair trial. Keep cool and keep still. If we cannot save our equality, and rights, and honor in the Union, we shall join you and save them out of it.

Voice.—When you fail to save your rights in the Union, if you refuse to go with us then, what will you do?

Mr. Hill.—But we will go. We allow not *if* to our conduct in that connection. If, when we come to join you, you get stubborn and refuse to go, then we shall go without you.

Now, my secession friends, I have all confidence in your zeal and patriotism, but simply let us take time and get ready. Let us work for the best, and prepare for the worst. Until an experiment is made, I shall always believe that the Constitution has strength enough to conquer all its enemies—even the Northern fanatic. If it proves to have not that strength, I will not trust it another hour.

A third benefit to be derived from the failure of an honest effort to redress our grievances in the Union, is the Union of all the Southern States. Some of the States will not secede now. Some of the States who suffer most from the grievances we have enumerated will not secede now. Because they think these grievances can be redressed in the Union. If this idea be a dream, let us wake up to the reality by an actual experiment.

A further benefit to be desired is, that if all the Southern States get ready and secede together, we shall be allowed to do so peaceably. Certainly, it is our right to go peaceably any way. The government, though having the right to enforce its laws against all the world, has no right to coerce back a seceding State. But the attempt might be made and the peace broken, if only one State should secede, or even a few. But let all the Southern States get ready and go together, and no earthly power would interfere or molest. My own opinion is that every Western and Northwestern State, and the Middle States, and perhaps all but the New England States, would go with us. And the glorious result at last might be that we should hold the government with all its power, and thrust off only those who have been faithless to it.

But the Southern States alone, with the territory naturally falling into our hands, would form the greatest government then on earth. The world must have our products; and after peace was once secured to us, the world would furnish our navies and our army, without the expense to us of a ship or a soldier.

Finally, my friends, we shall have secured, by this policy, the good opinion of all mankind and of ourselves. We shall have done our duty to history, to our children, and to Constitutional liberty, the great experiment of self-government. We shall have also discerned the defects in our present government, and will be prepared to guard against them in another. Above all we shall have found good consciences, and secured that, either in the Union or out of it, which is dearer to us than any Union, and more to be desired than all constitutions however venerated—that which is the end of all our efforts, and the desire of all our hearts, our equality as States, our rights as citizens, and our honor as men.

"STATES CANNOT EXIST DISUNITED":
NOVEMBER 1860

New York Daily News:
The Right of States to Secede

November 16, 1860

The *New York Daily News* was a conservative newspaper that had supported John C. Breckinridge, the proslavery Southern Democratic candidate, in the 1860 election. Despite its stated opposition to the principle of secession, in subsequent editorials the *Daily News* would consistently oppose attempts to "coerce" the seceding states, and in June 1861 it would denounce the Lincoln administration's war measures as illegal and unconstitutional.

THE PEOPLE often act without reflection. Statesmen and politicians, either contracting the sentiment of the populace or influenced by ambitious motives, encourage the action of the people upon an erroneous and often fatal idea. The present agitation at the South is of this nature. If it is not quieted it will bring evils upon this Confederacy, the number and extent of which it is painful to think of, and the termination of which it is impossible to foretell. The Herald and The Tribune both tell us that a State has a right to secede; but can we believe them? Let the reflecting men study the formation of this Government, the only true source of information, and learn for themselves whether a State has such a right or not.

On the Fourth day of July, 1776, thirteen American colonies declared themselves free and independent States. Throwing off their allegiance to the British Crown and the Governments, which at that time consisted of the Provincial, Proprietary and Charter Governments, they established one of their own. In 1774 the first Congress passed the Bill of Rights, which is as dear to us as the Bill of Rights passed during the reign of Charles the First is to Englishmen. The affairs of the Government were conducted by Congress until near the close of the Revolution, without any substantial form of government.

In March, 1781, the last State acceded to the Articles of Confederation, and the Thirteen Independent States became a confederacy called The United States of America. The object of the States in establishing a confederacy under the Articles of Confederation was to form *a permanent union* for the mutual support and protection of each other. The intention of parties in forming a contract should always be considered. Knowing the intention of our forefathers, can we violate their contract? Each State, in accepting the Articles of Confederation, was bound by them. It was a contract and was binding. Secessionists ask who would enforce it? We answer, the majority. The Articles commenced thus: "Articles of Confederation and PERPETUAL UNION, between the States of," &c. Then came the articles defining the powers granted by the States to Congress, and the rights reserved to themselves. In Article 13 it says: "And the Articles of this Confederation shall be *inviolably* observed by *every* State, and the Union shall be *perpetual*." At the close of the last Section in the same Article and immediately preceding the signing of the Articles—that there might be no mistake in the duration of the Union—the language is nearly repeated, viz.: "And that the Articles thereof shall be inviolably observed by the States we respectively represent, and that the Union shall be *perpetual*."

One of the main arguments used by persons believing that States have a right to secede is this, that there is no *definite* time fixed for the duration of the Confederacy. Can anything be more plain than the language used that it is to be *perpetual*, to *endure forever*? They will say to this that under the Constitution, which is substituted for the Articles of Confederation, no such language is used. Not until they had signed the Articles of Confederation did they become United States, and in that contract they declared themselves to be United States, and to remain united forever. They, as United States, adopted the Constitution. It reads thus: "Constitution of the United States of America. We, the people of the United States, in order to form a *more perfect Union*, &c." Not to limit the Union, but to make it more perfect! They became United States, and *forever* under the Articles of Confederation, and neither was abrogated or annulled by the Constitution! In the words of the preamble, both were affirmed. Where does the power lie to alter the compact? In the highest power of the land. In the States themselves and with the Government, as with all corporate bodies, the majority must rule. No decree of a Court can dissolve the States as it can a Corporation. The only power is with the States themselves, and a State once a member of the Confederacy cannot secede without the consent of the others —the majority must rule. If there was any other power to decree the dissolution of the Union, it should be left to that power; but there is none. The General Government cannot coerce a Territory to become a member of the Confederacy. But once having signed the compact and become a member of the Union, it cannot withdraw without the consent of the other members.

If one State has a right to withdraw, all may withdraw; and we should have loss of name, loss of national existence, civil war, servile war, loss of liberty, and, ultimately, the subjugation and overthrow of the most glorious Republic which ever existed. Could Pennsylvania withdraw from the Union if Congress did not impose a high protective tariff on iron, what would be the result? She would have to support a Government at great expense; maintain an army and navy; the tariff she might impose would not benefit her at all; on the contrary, it would prove a detriment; there being no greater comity between her and other countries, the other States would purchase iron where they could buy the cheapest. Bankruptcy of the State would follow, and, consequently, poverty of her citizens. The same rule would apply, in a greater or less degree, to every other State. The whole country, and every individual, would necessarily feel the effects of secession; but it would be most injurious to the seceding States. History tells us that States cannot exist disunited. The compact of these States is binding upon all, and the man who attempts to violate it will be responsible to future generations for the misery which his acts may produce.

"I AM FOR THE UNION AS IT IS":
TEXAS, NOVEMBER 1860

Sam Houston to H. M. Watkins and Others

As the post-election crisis continued, sixty-four Texas citizens sent Governor Sam Houston a public letter from Huntsville requesting his opinion on "the best course to pursue" at a time when "too hasty action may prove deleterious, and to prolong too much an expression of opinion may prove fatal to our best interests." Houston wrote this reply as part of his ultimately unsuccessful campaign to keep Texas from leaving the Union. By refusing to call a special session of the legislature, Houston hoped to prevent the meeting of a state convention, but in January 1861 secessionists held extralegal elections for convention delegates, and on February 1 the convention voted 166–8 to secede. The secession ordinance was then submitted to a popular vote and approved by a 3-to-1 margin on February 23. When Houston refused to swear allegiance to the new Confederate States of America, the hero of Texas independence was removed from office on March 16, 1861.

Austin, Texas, November 20, 1860.
Messrs. H. M. Watkins, P. W. Kittrell, Sanford Gibbs, R. P. Archer, James L. Smither, G. M. Baker, and Others.

Gentlemen: Your letter of the 14th inst., asking my views respecting the present crisis in our political affairs, is at hand. I can reply but briefly; and I shall therefore do so the more frankly, feeling that this is a time when the plain truth should be spoken by every lover of his country.

I recognize among you the names of men of all parties. Some of you are my old and tried friends, and patriotic citizens of Texas. To such, especially, I look with confidence now, when the country is agitated and revolution threatened. In all the troubles of the Republic I found you to be the friends of Constitutional liberty. Having seen the throes of one Revolution, having shared in its vicissitudes, and having borne a part in bringing Texas into the Union, I trust that you, in common with patriots of those times, will ask some more weighty reason for overthrowing the Government, than rash enthusiasts yet have given; and that while others are carried away by the impulse of the moment, the men of experience will be calm and decided.

I had hoped that an opportunity would have been afforded me to rejoice in the triumph of some one of the conservative candidates for the Presidency. Had the candidates for whom the voice of Texas was declared, been elected, I should have had an additional cause of gratification; but such is not the case. On the contrary, I must regret and deplore the election of men whose only claims to the confidence and support of the whole country, must be the official character with which the Constitution invests them.

In remembering the many evidences which a portion of the Northern people have presented of their willingness to disregard their constitutional obligations and infringe upon the rights of their Southern brethren, I am not in the least surprised at the indignant responses now uttered by Southern men. It shows that if the time should come when we can no longer trust to the Constitution for our rights, the people will not hesitate to maintain them. It will be well if those States, which have yielded to a fanatical sentiment, so far as to interpose between the Federal authority and the Constitutional rights of a whole section of the Union, will now, inspired by a spirit of patriotism and nationality, retrace that step. Upon a citizen of their own section and one of their own party, they have now placed a responsibility which he cannot avoid. As the Chief Executive of the nation, he will be sworn to support the Constitution and execute the Laws. His oath will bring him in conflict with the unconstitutional statutes, created by his party in many of the States. Elected by that party, it is but natural that the conservatism of the nation will watch his course with jealous care, and demand at his hands a rigid enforcement of the Federal laws. Should he meet the same resistance, which other Executives have met, it will be his duty to call to his aid the conservative masses of the country, and they will respond to the call.—Should he falter or fail, and by allowing the laws to be subverted, aid in oppressing the people of the South, he must be hurled from power. From the moment of his inauguration, there will commence an "irrepressible conflict" different from that which the party of Mr. Lincoln is based upon. It will be an "irrepressible conflict" between The Constitution, which he has sworn to support, and the unconstitutional enactments and aims of the party which has placed him in power. He had declared that the Fugitive Slave Law is Constitutional. In its enforcement, the conflict is with the North alone. I need not assure you that whenever the time shall come, when we must choose between a loss of our Constitutional rights and revolution, I shall choose the latter; but if I, who have led the people of Texas in stormy times of danger, hesitate to plunge into revolution now, it is not because I am ready to submit to the Black Republican rule, but because I regard the Constitution of my country, and am determined to stand by it. Mr. Lincoln has been constitutionally elected and, much as I deprecate his success, no alternative is left me but to yield to the Constitution. The moment that instrument is violated by him, I will be foremost in demanding redress and the last to abandon my ground.

When I contemplate the horrors of civil war, such as a dissolution of the Union will ultimately force upon me, I cannot believe that the people will rashly take a step fraught with these consequences. They will consider well the blessings of the government we have, and it will only be when the grievances we suffer are of a nature that, as freemen, we can no longer bear them, that we will raise the standard of revolution. Then the civilized world, our own consciences, and posterity, will justify us. If that time should come, then will be the day and hour. If it has not—if our rights are yet secure, we cannot be justified. Has the time come? If it has, the people who have to bear the burthens of revolution must themselves effect the work.

Those who reside in cities and towns, where masses are carried in crowds and influenced by passionate appeals, may be ready for hasty action, but the working men and farmers, whose all is identified with the prosperity and peace of the country, will ask time to reflect.

As all will be alike involved in the horrors which will come after dissolution all have the right to consider whether dissolution shall come. The liberties and securities of all are at stake. It is not a question for politicians to tamper with. The masses must settle it for themselves. They are to consider whether with Congress and the Supreme Court largely in favor of the Constitution, revolution will be justified, because the President, who is constitutionally elected, is inimical to them. It must come to this.

With all these checks and guarantees in our favor, it is urged that we should no longer wait, but at once let go the Constitution. Passion is rash—wisdom considers well her way. When the bone and sinew of the country, after calmly considering the issue in all its bearings, shall feel that a yoke of oppression is upon them, they will rise to shake it off. Then, when their now peaceful homes are the scene of desolation, they will feel no pang of regret. Moved by a common feeling of resistance, they will not ask for the forms of law to justify their action. Nor will they follow the noisy demagogue who will flee at the first show of danger. Men of the people will come forth to lead them, who will be ready to risk the consequences of revolution.

If the Union be dissolved now, will we have additional security for slavery? Will we have our rights better secured? After enduring civil war for years, will there be any promise of a better state of things than we now enjoy? Texas, especially, has these things to consider. Our Treasury is nearly empty. We have near half a million of dollars in the Treasury of the United States. A million of our school fund is invested in U. S. Bonds. We have an extensive frontier to defend. Pecuniary or personal considerations ought to weigh nothing when tyranny is in the scale; but are we justified in sacrificing these, when we have yet the Constitution to protect us and our rights are secured.

Let us not embrace the higher law principle of our enemies and overthrow the Constitution; but when we have to resist, let it be in the name of the Constitution and to uphold it.

Why this military display and call to arms in Texas. Have we enemies at home or is an enemy marching upon us? When was there the time, when the citizens of the country were not ready to flock to its standard in its defense? Are the people to deliberate on this question with a military despotism in their midst, ready to coerce them? We want sober thought and calm reason, not furious harrangues or the argument of bayonets.

If this government is to fall, wisdom must furnish another and a better one, and if patriots yield now to the rash and reckless, who only aspire to military glory, or for anarchy and rapine, they may find that in the wreck of one free government, they have lost the power to rear another.

I trust the gloom which now hangs over the land will soon be dispelled. Now is the time for the patriot to come forth and consider what is to be gained by a change. We are called upon to desert the gallant thousands who for years have been fighting our battles against fanaticism in the North. Heretofore they have aided us to conquer and we have been willing to abide with them. Now, after a struggle more glorious than any yet have been made, they have been driven back. They still offer us the guarantees of the Constitution and are ready to battle with us in its defense. Let true men all over Texas and the South see to it, that we leave them not without a cause.

I cannot believe that we can find at present more safety out of the Union than in it. Yet I believe it due to the people that they should know where they stand. Mr. Lincoln has been elected upon a sectional issue. If he expects to maintain that sectional issue, during his administration, it is well we should know it. If he intends to administer the government with equality and fairness, we should know that. Let us wait and see.

I have left upon record my position, should the rights of Texas be sacrificed by the Federal Government. In reply to Mr. Seward, in the Senate, I used these words; and I pray my friends to consider them calmly, as they were uttered:

"Whenever one section of this country presumes upon its strength for the oppression of the other, then will our Constitution be a mockery, and it would matter not how soon it were severed into a thousand atoms and scattered to the four winds. If the principles are disregarded upon which the annexation of Texas was consummated, there will be for her neither honor nor interest in the Union; if the mighty in the face of written law, can place with impunity an iron yoke upon the neck of the weak, Texas will be at no loss how to act, or where to go before the blow aimed at her vitals is inflicted. In a spirit of good faith she entered the federal fold. By that spirit she will continue to be influenced until it is attempted to make her the victim of federal wrong.

"And she will violate no federal rights, so will she submit to no violation of her rights by federal authority. The covenant she entered into with the Government must be observed, or it will be annulled. Louisiana, was a purchase, California, New Mexico, and Utah a conquest, but Texas was a voluntary annexation. If the condition of her admission is not complied with on the one part, it is not binding on the other. If I know Texas, she will not submit to the threatened degradation foreshadowed in the recent speech of the Senator from New York. She would prefer restoration to that independence which she once enjoyed, to the ignominy ensuing from sectional dictation. Sorrowing for the mistake which she had committed in sacrificing her independence at the altar of her patriotism, she would unfurl again the banner of the "Lone Star" to the breeze, and re-enter upon a national career, where, if no glory awaited her, she would, at least, be free from subjection by might, to wrong and shame."

Here, I take my stand! So long as the Constitution is maintained by the "Federal authority," and Texas is not made the victim of "federal wrong" I am for the Union as it is.

I am now an aged man. My locks have become white in toiling, as I believe, for the liberties of mankind. Were I young, that I might look forward to the future, feeling that whatever danger might come my strong arm would be at hand to defend my family, I should feel less anxiety than I do at present. The years that I will have to endure the misfortunes of civil war, will be but few. If I could feel that with the close of my career would end the miseries of my race, I could share its misfortunes with patience; but to feel that the perils of revolution must continue; that war with its attendant horrors of bloodshed, rapine, and devastation must still be visited upon it, would embitter my last moments, and after living to witness the dissolution of the best government that ever existed, I would sink to the grave without a hope that freedom would be regenerated or our posterity ever enjoy again the blessings with which we have parted. Let us pause and ponder well before we take action outside of the Constitution! Truly thy friend

              Sam Houston.

"OUR SORE NATIONAL SICKNESS":
NEW YORK, NOVEMBER 1860

George Templeton Strong: Diary, November 20, November 26–December 1, 1860

George Templeton Strong was a successful lawyer in New York City who served as a trustee of Columbia College and as a vestryman of Trinity Church. A former Whig turned Republican, Strong recorded his reaction to the growing secessionist movement in the diary he had been keeping for 25 years.

———————

November 20. Wall Street was a shade less disconsolate this morning. Stocks rallied at the First Board but began to waver and fall again at the Second. The banks cannot bring about a decisive reaction; the disease is too deep-seated.

The revolutionary movement in South Carolina and the Gulf States seems, on the whole, to be gaining strength and consistency. No signs yet of any "sober second thought." Conservatism and common-sense (if any be left in the Cotton States), are still intimidated and silent. Probably the Border States, led by Virginia, will try to mediate and pacify. Dissolution of the Union and re-opening of the slave trade would be disastrous to them, so they naturally desire to make peace. But their mediation will probably be upon the basis of recognition by the North of the extremest Southern exactions (slave trade excepted). The North must consent that slavery be introduced into the territories; Massachusetts, Vermont, Wisconsin, and other states must repeal their "personal liberty" laws that interfere with the Fugitive Slave Law. That plan will not work. Those state laws ought to be repealed, but the South has no right to demand their repeal and make their enactment an excuse for treason, because they are utterly unconstitutional and mere nullities, and no one doubts the United States Supreme Court would so adjudge them.

If these traitors succeed in dismembering the country, they

will have a front place in the Historical Gallery of Celebrated Criminals. No political crime was ever committed as disastrous to mankind and with so little to provoke or excuse the wrong as that which these infamous disunionists are conspiring to perpetrate. . . .

November 26. Today's newspapers indicate no new symptom in our sore national sickness. The tide is still rising, I think, in all the Cotton States. Reaction and ebb are sure to follow, but they may come too late. This growing excitement may do irreparable mischief before it dies out and reaction sets in. The country may be overwhelmed by a flood of disaster and disgrace before the tide begins to fall.

November 27. Nothing new in Wall Street, except that stocks are all down again. Secession certainly gains favor at the South, and grows more threatening every day. But there are symptoms of backing down at the North. There are demonstrations toward repeal of the obnoxious "personal liberty bills" of certain Northern states. It seems likely that Republican leaders and wire-pullers have concluded on a policy of concession and conciliation. I hope it may be in time to prevent terrible mischief.

These "personal liberty laws" are unconstitutional and void. They are mere nullities, and do no harm to the South. What one nigger has South Carolina lost by the legislation of Vermont or Wisconsin? The clamor about them is a palpable humbug. Still they ought to be repealed, being wrong in spirit and interest.

November 28. No political news of importance. The progress of events has startled and staggered some of our notables, who were laughing secession to scorn a fortnight ago. John C. Green, for one, "never dreamed these Southerners would go so far." I think, from all indications, that the Republican leaders are frightened and ready to concede everything, to restore the Missouri Compromise line and satisfy the fugitive slave remedies of the South. A movement that way has certainly begun. But it may be too soon for the North and too late for the South. Suppose it prevail. How will it be received in Massachusetts and Western New York? Will Republicans feel that they have been sold by their leaders, and recalcitrate into more intense anti-Southern feeling? I think they will and that many Republicans will enroll themselves as Abolitionists. But if this crisis pass over without disruption and ruin, if our national life endure another year, I think a strong Union party will come into being and control extremists, South and North both.

November 29. Thanksgiving Day. No political news today. Congress meets Monday. Mr. Ruggles's friend, Senator Dixon, is in town on his way to Washington. Horribly frightened. Connecticut expects him to do something in the Senate, and he is anxiously enquiring, "What shall I do to be saved from the humiliation of admitting that I'm unequal to my high place?"

Tom Corwin was in town Tuesday night with the draft of some "Bill of Rights" which he means to propose, affirming the rights which the South pretends to believe endangered.

There's a bad prospect for both sections of the country. Southern ruffianism and brutality are very bad, but the selfishness, baseness, and corruption of the North are not good at all. Universal suffrage has been acquiesced in for many years. It is no longer debated. But it's at the root of our troubles. What we want is a strong government, instead of a "government of opinion." If there be disunion, a strong government will be demanded and will come into being somehow, both North and South. Democracy and equality and various other phantasms will be dispersed and dissipated and will disappear forever when two hostile families of states stand side by side, and a great civil war becomes inevitable. To which party will God give a great general, when that crisis is upon us?

December 1. Sorry to learn that the Vermont legislature refuses to repeal its personal liberty bill.

A money indemnity for run-away niggers might satisfy the South (if it wanted to be satisfied), but I fear no such arrangement is practicable. Every worthless Cuffee and superannuated Dinah south of the Potomac would be somehow exported into the free states within a year and would have to be paid for.

One hears queer talk in these days of excitement. That white-cravatted, conservative, old, quiet Dutchman, Edward Bancker, thinks every man ought to be hanged that voted for Lincoln, and "means to go South and shoulder a musket." So he tells me, but I think fear for the future of his bank stocks and real estate has slightly deranged his mind, for he is said to have experienced some slight aberrations a few years since, when he had a fierce quarrel with a neighbor about a right of way on Staten Island. Willy Cutting talks mysteriously of an organization to revolutionize the city immediately upon the secession of the South. New York and Brooklyn are to be a free port, and with one or two adjoining counties, Westchester and Kings, I suppose, to constitute an independent principality. Mayor and Common Council to be kicked out, if not hanged, and suffrage to be confined to owners of $5,000 worth of property. A promising prospect.

Why *do* the people so furiously rage together just now? What has created our present unquestionable irritation against the South? What has created the Republican party?

Its nucleus was the abolition handful that has been vaporing for thirty years, and which, till about 1850, was among the more insignificant of our *isms*. Our feeling at the North till that time was not hostility to slavery, but indifference to it, and reluctance to discuss it. It was a disagreeable subject with which we had nothing to do. The battles in Congress about the right of petition, and the Giddings business, made little impression on us. But the clamor of the South about the admission of California ten years ago introduced the question of slavery to the North as one in which it had an interest adverse to the South. That controversy taught us that the two systems could not co-exist in the same territory. It opened our eyes to the fact that there were two hostile elements in the country, and that if we allowed slaves to enter any territorial acquisition, our own free labor must be excluded from it. The question was unfortunate for our peace. But we might have forgotten it had not S. A. Douglas undertaken to get Southern votes by repealing the Missouri Compromise. That was the fatal blow. Then came the atrocious effort to force slavery on Kansas by fraud and violence, with the full support of old Buchanan and his Southern counselors, the brutal beating of the eloquent and erudite Sumner with the cordial approbation and applause of the South, the project to revive the slave trade, and (a little earlier) a sentimental romance, *Uncle Tom's Cabin*, that set all Northern women crying and sobbing over the sorrows of

Sambo. The Fugitive Slave Law stimulated sectional feeling by making slavery visible in our own communities, and above all, the intolerable brag and bluster and indecent arrogance of the South has driven us into protest against their pretensions, and into a determination to assert our own rights in spite of their swagger.

"THIS DANGEROUS GAME":
MISSOURI, NOVEMBER 1860

Edward Bates: Diary, November 22, 1860

A successful lawyer and former congressman from St. Louis, Missouri, Edward Bates was a candidate for the Republican presidential nomination in 1860, receiving 48 out of 466 votes on the first ballot. Bates recorded his appraisal of the movement toward secession in his diary.

Wednesday night. Nov 22.

The news from *the South*, as to secession, does not improve. The leaders of the movement, in Alabama, Georgia, and especially S. Carolina, are more urgent than ever, taking every means to get their followers pledged to extreme measures, and to draw in and commit the timid and the doubtful, without allowing time to look to the consequences and reflect upon the bottomless pit that lies before them.

Still I think that (except with a few demented fanatics) it is all brag and bluster, hoping thus to make a better compromise with the timid patriotism of their opponents. In playing this dangerous game, they may go farther than they now intend, and actually commit their states to open rebellion and civil war. If they *will* push it to that dread extremity, the Government, having been as mild and forbearing as possible, up to that point, will no doubt, find it wise policy to make the war as sharp and prompt as possible, in order to shorten it, and prevent its running into social and servile war, and chronic anarchy, such as prevails in Mexico.

The letters and telegrams from *the South*, bear plain evidence of exagiration, and make a false shewing of the unanimity of the people, in support of the traitorous design. A very little time will show.

If we must have civil war, perhaps it is better now, than at a future day.

THE "WICKED SPIRIT" OF SECESSION:
TENNESSEE, NOVEMBER 1860

William G. Brownlow to R. H. Appleton

A Methodist minister and the editor of the *Knoxville Whig*, William G. Brownlow was a leading Unionist in eastern Tennessee. Brownlow wrote this letter in response to a note, dated November 23 from Greenwood, South Carolina, in which R. H. Appleton cancelled his subscription to the *Whig*, proclaiming: "Secession now and forever! So say the Methodists of South Carolina." Brownlow printed his letter to Appleton in his newspaper on December 8 and continued to argue against secession. In a referendum held on February 9, 1861, Tennessee voters rejected holding a state convention by 69,387 to 57,798, with opposition to secession especially strong in eastern Tennessee, a mountainous region where, as in western Virginia, there were relatively few slaveholders. After the outbreak of the war the Tennessee legislature declared its independence from the United States, and on June 8 a second referendum endorsed its decision by 104,913 to 47,238, although 70 percent of the voters in eastern Tennessee continued to oppose secession. Brownlow refused to swear allegiance to the Confederacy and maintained the *Whig* as a Unionist newspaper until its suppression on October 24. Arrested for treason on December 6, the defiant editor was imprisoned without trial and then sent across the lines into Union territory in March 1862.

KNOXVILLE, NOV. 29, 1860.

MR. APPLETON:—

Your note, calling for account and ordering a discontinuance, is before me. You are not indebted to me for subscription, but, on the contrary, there are fifteen weeks of subscription due you. I take no offence whatever at your discontinuance, as *that* is every man's right in this free country. But, before parting with you, you must allow me to give you my views upon your favorite doctrine of "Secession." I am equally opposed to the wicked spirit of *Sectionalism* at the North and of *Secession* at the South. Your motto is, "Secession now and forever!" I offset this with the following patriotic sentiments from General JACKSON'S Message of 1833:—

"THE CONSTITUTION AND THE LAW IS SUPREME, AND THE UNION IS INDISSOLUBLE."

Sir, the political journals, North and South, are discussing the right of a State to secede from the Union. For my part, I deny the right of secession altogether, though I admit the right of *revolution* when circumstances justify it. It must be an *extreme* case of oppression on the part of Government, and of *continued* oppression, that will justify revolution. Such a case was presented when the American Colonies revolted; and in that case revolution was called for and was successful.

But the idea of one of these States at its pleasure claiming and exercising the right to secede from this Union, is a more monstrous and absurd doctrine than has ever been put forth in any republic. If the doctrine be true that the right exists, our Government is a mere rope of sand. Concede the truth of this dogma, and Cuba, after we may have paid *two hundred millions* for her purchase to Old Spain, may take offence, and, as a State, may at once secede, and leave the United States Treasury to whistle! We now have a case in point. Texas speaks of going out of the Union with Carolina, and I presume will do so. Less than twenty years ago, she was admitted into the Union upon her own solicitation, our Government paying millions to discharge her debts, and other millions to go into her coffers. Is she now at liberty to secede with all this booty, and array herself against this Government in all time to come? Certainly not. For, if she is, Louisiana, and all the States carved out of that purchase, for which we paid FIFTEEN MILLIONS, may do likewise, and carry with them the mouth of the Mississippi River, transferring it to any European Power.

So, too, States in which large amounts of Government property may be situated may at any time secede with that property, —just as South Carolina, Georgia, Florida, and Alabama, with their Government fortifications, arsenals, custom-houses, navy-yards, and other property, strung along the coasts from Charleston to Mobile, may at any time do. Construct a Pacific Railroad at an expense of millions paid from the common treasure, and the two or three States through which it passes, and which it so enriches, may take offence at something Maine and

New Hampshire are doing, and decamp with the whole road, its stationary, running stock, and guarantees, taking all the property with them, and forming an alliance with some Government hostile to the very nation which built the road. Now, are Maryland, Virginia, Tennessee, Kentucky, and other States remaining loyal to the Union, to look quietly on, and even approve the exodus of those which have been thus enriched at their expense, and recognize the right of each of them to secede and take the common property of all the remaining States with them? I say most emphatically not!

This question of the right of secession is upon us, and we have to look it in the face, and meet it as it becomes men. Therefore let us reason together upon the subject, divesting ourselves of passion and prejudice. The right of secession, if it exist at all, is an *absolute* one, and a State has as much right to exercise it at one time as another. The Secessionists will concede the correctness of this position. If she may secede at will, she may do so in anticipation of a bloody and protracted war with a foreign Power, so as to avoid any draft upon her for men or money. If she can secede when she chooses, she owes no allegiance to the Government one hour after she decides to secede, but will then be just as independent of the Government as she is of France or England. In the midst of a violent and protracted foreign war, then, it will be the right of any one of the States of this Union, not only to desert our own Government, but at the same time to ally herself to the enemy the remaining States are fighting! Our Government, under such principles, if recognized, could not exist twenty-four hours. Other nations, and our own citizens, could have no faith in the permanence of such a Government. It would lack the vital principle of existence, because it would lack every thing like credit. No capitalist with a thimbleful of sense would lend it a dollar; for no man could feel assured that such a Government would last long enough to pay a six months' loan, to say nothing of loans for a term of years. All who deal with Governments repose upon their *public faith*; and where this is destroyed they feel that all is lacking. Business must be destroyed; for men of sense and means would not embark either their industry or capital, unless it were under the shelter of laws and institutions not liable to change. In support of this, I need only call attention to the great fall in the price of State bonds, negroes, and all other property in the South, in *anticipation* of the rupture with which we are threatened. Things are bad enough with us in the South, and they are even worse at the North, because of what seems to be inevitable. And yet they are to grow worse each day we live in this state of uncertainty. And your good State of South Carolina, Mr. Appleton, is more to blame for these evils which affect the country than any one State in the Union.

I have, myself, no sympathy or respect for the anti-slavery men of the North, who are agitating this question, and enacting their "Personal Liberty Laws," with a view to defeat the operations of the "Fugitive Slave Law." I am a native of Virginia, as also were my parents before me, but for thirty years I have been a citizen of Tennessee, and I expect to end my days within her borders. My wife and children are natives of Tennessee, and all I have is here. I am a Union man in the fullest acceptation of that term, and I shall stand by the ship of state, as long as the storm is howling overhead, and the breakers are roaring on the lee-shore, though we have neither sun, moon, nor stars to light the way! And pardon me, sir, when I ask you, who but cowards would seek to desert the ship? Who but madmen would seek for safety out of it? Who but crazy mutineers would refuse to come to the rescue of the ship, passengers, and crew? South Carolina, at this trying moment, refuses to do duty. The storm affrights her. Her Senators and Representatives in Congress resign their seats, instead of remaining at their posts, and fighting the battle on the floor of Congress, where it ought to be fought and must be lost or won. Their hearts fail before the Northern Abolition *Simoon*, and seeing only death, as they apprehend, staring them in the face, if they abide on board, they take to the boats, abandon the vessel in which we have all sailed together, through many a gale, these eighty years past, and intend, with *poles* and *paddles*, to *scuttle* through their cypress-swamps!

I admit the danger that menaces you all on board; but do you not multiply the peril tenfold by desertion? An overwhelming majority of the people of the Southern States have decided at the ballot-box in favor of the Union, voting for

BELL and DOUGLAS. I regard the Abolitionists as the "mutineers;" and I ask you, I ask all South Carolina, is it manly, is it magnanimous, is it just, to throw yourselves into the sea, and leave these border States to destruction? No, Mr. Appleton, it is not magnanimous, it is not just! I tell you, and your Methodist brethren, in the language of the good Book they so much revere, that "Except ye abide in the ship, ye cannot be saved."

I am sorry to hear you say that the Methodists of South Carolina are now and forever the advocates of Secession! To appeal to them in behalf of the Union, is but beating the air, and wasting one's breath; but I say to them, through you, that I will stand to the Stars and Stripes—I shall cling to the Union! I say to them, however, as a heroic Christian apostle said to an equally panic-stricken generation of bolters, "Except ye abide in the ship, ye cannot be saved." You may leave the vessel,— you may go out in the rickety boats of your little State, and hoist your miserable *cabbage-leaf* of a Palmetto flag; but, depend upon it, men and brethren, you will be dashed to pieces on the rocks!

But the clergy,—the ministers of God, the followers on earth of the Prince of Peace,—at this threatening crisis, are going likewise! I know there are among that class of citizens, in South Carolina, some of the best men, as well as the most fearless and self-sacrificing men, of which the American people can boast. Why, oh, why are these men on the side of civil war, bloodshed, and revolution? They have offered up prayers and supplication, and made appeals to Heaven, but, alas! they have been—not for the preservation but for the destruction of the Union. I hear of no Paul among them, seeking to calm the minds of his companions, and to declare to them, "Except ye abide in the ship, ye cannot be saved." The venerable Dr. PIERCE, of Georgia, is an exception to this rule, and has spoken out like an American citizen and a Christian philosopher. To my mind it is clear that the clergy of South Carolina are wanting in *courage* to do what their "consciences dictate to be done." If they possessed the courage of their Master, they would from a Christian stand-point speak out in thunder tones! Jesus of Nazareth walked the earth thirty odd years, in the midst of millions of Roman Empire slaves, and dared to counsel them against rebellion and insurrection, and to exhort them to be *obedient to their masters.* Here was a courage worthy of God! Would that my South Carolina Methodist brethren would endeavor, humbly and courageously, to follow His example!

I believe the Union is in danger, and in regard to the consequences of its dissolution I shall not lengthen out this epistle in an attempt to portray the consequences. What I have to say to your ministers and church-going people is, that the importance of the times demands the grave and serious reflection and prayerful deliberation of every individual and State, before they proceed to take any action. One false step, such as contemplated by South Carolina, may plunge the people of the United States into unutterable woe! We now need the cool deliberation, the conservatism, and the wisdom of the nation, to "pour oil upon the troubled waters,"—to calm the storm now raging in the political elements, and to save this Union. And to no class of men living have we greater cause to look for help in this good work, than to the ministers and members of the Methodist Church, whose Discipline and Constitution, as well as their Bible, require loyalty to the civil Government, obedience to rulers, and a devotion to a country that forbids their assenting to its overthrow, directly or indirectly! The South should resist unlawful aggressions, but she should do it *in* the Union, *under* the Constitution, and with a scrupulous regard to the *forms* of law. Secession is no remedy for any evils in our Government, real or imaginary, past, present, or to come.

I will go further, if you please, and affirm that the Constitution has, in the clearest terms, recognized the right of property in slaves. That sacred instrument prohibits any State into which a slave may have fled, from passing any law to discharge him from bondage, and declares that he shall be surrendered to his lawful owner by the authorities of any State within whose limits he may be found. More than this, sir, the Constitution makes the existence of slavery our foundation of political power, by giving to the Slave States representatives in Congress not only in proportion to the whole number of free negroes, but also in proportion to the *three-fifths of the number of slaves.* The Northern States, by their "Personal Liberty Laws," have placed themselves in a state of revolution, and unless they repeal these laws, the revolution—a thing that never goes backward—must go on, until these rebellious States are declared out of the Union, and the truly conservative States take the Union in charge!

I have, my dear sir, defined my position, and in such terms as not to be misunderstood. I have already extended my remarks beyond what I intended in the outset. I will therefore close with brief extracts from the pens of three distinguished men, and I ask your attention to what they have said. The two first assisted in framing the Constitution. Mr. JEFFERSON remarked, in a letter to John Taylor, dated June 1, 1798,

> "If on the temporary superiority of the one party the other is to resort to a scission of the Union, no Federal Government can ever exist.
>
> "Who can say what would be the evils of a scission, and when and where they would end? Better keep together as we are; haul off from Europe as soon as we can, and from attachments to all portions; and, if they show their power just sufficiently to hoop us together, it will be the happiest situation in which we can exist. If the game were sometimes against us at home, we must have patience till luck turns, and then we shall have opportunity to win back the principles we have lost."

Mr. MADISON, in a paper he drew up a short time before his death, gives us this advice:—

> "The advice nearest my heart and deepest in my conviction is, that the Union of the States be cherished and perpetuated. Let the open enemy to it be regarded as a Pandora with her box opened, and the disguised one as the serpent creeping with his deadly wiles into Paradise."

Gen. JACKSON, in his message to Congress, January 7, 1833, thus disposes of the question of Secession:—

> "The right of the people of a single State to absolve themselves at will, and without the consent of the other States, from their most solemn obligations, and hazard the liberties and happiness of the millions composing this Union, cannot be acknowledged. Such authority is believed utterly repugnant both to the principles upon which

the General Government is constituted, and to the objects which it was expressly formed to attain."

To these sentiments I subscribe as heartily and as unswervingly as I do to those I have preceded them with.

Very respectfully, &c.,

W. G. BROWNLOW.

LINCOLN AND SLAVERY: DECEMBER 1860

Frederick Douglass: The Late Election

December 1860

In the spring of 1860 Frederick Douglass returned to his home in Rochester, New York, from a lecture tour of Britain. Writing in June in his abolitionist journal *Douglass' Monthly*, he described the recently nominated Abraham Lincoln as "a man of unblemished private character; a lawyer, standing near the front rank at the bar of his own State, has a cool, well balanced head; great firmness of will; is perseveringly industrious; and one of the most frank, honest men in political life." Although Douglass wished the Republican platform had called for "'Death to Slavery,' instead of 'No more Slave States,'" he expressed his hopes for Lincoln's election. (Douglass would himself vote for his longtime friend Gerrit Smith, the Radical Abolition candidate, on whose ticket he served as an elector in New York State.) Following the election he reassessed Lincoln and the Republican Party in an article in the December *Douglass' Monthly*.

———————

OUR LAST monthly paper announced the probable election of Abraham Lincoln and Hannibal Hamlin, the Republican candidates for President and Vice President of the U. S. What was then only speculation and probability, is now an accomplished fact. Pennsylvania, in her State election of October, it is true, had made this result, to a degree, certain; but there were efforts and appliances resorted to by the enemies of the Republican party, which could not fail to cause doubt and anxiety in the minds of the most sanguine.—The deed is, however, now done, and a new order of events connected with the great question of slavery, is now fairly opening upon the country, the end whereof the most sagacious and far-sighted are unable to see and declare. No preceding election resembles this in its issues and parties, and none resembles it in the effects it has already produced, and is still likely to produce. It was a contest between sections, North and South, as to what shall be the principles and policy of the national Government in respect to the slave system of the fifteen Southern States. The broadest assertion of a right of property in man, holding such property equally innocent, sacred and legal under the Constitution, as property in houses, lands, horses, sheep, and horned cattle, and like the latter entitled to Congressional protection in all the Territories, and by parity of reasoning, in all the States of the American Union. The Southern candidate for the Presidency, Mr. Breckinridge, fully represented this broad assertion of what Lord Mansfield well declared to be so opposed to nature, that nothing short of positive law could support it, and Brougham denounced as the "wild and guilty fantasy" of property in man. Mr. Lincoln, the Northern Republican candidate, while admitting the right to hold men as slaves in the States already existing, regards such property as peculiar, exceptional, local, generally an evil, and not to be extended beyond the limits of the States where it is established by what is called positive law. We thus simply state the issue, more for the benefit of our trans-Atlantic friends and readers, than for those at home, who have heard and read little else during the last three or four months. The clamor now raised by the slaveholders about "Northern aggression," "sectional warfare," as a pretext of dissolving the Union, has this basis only: The Northern people have elected, against the opposition of the slaveholding South, a man for President who declared his opposition to the further extension of slavery over the soil belonging to the United States. Such is the head and front, and the full extent of the offense, for which "minute men" are forming, drums are beating, flags are flying, people are arming, "banks are closing," "stocks are falling," and the South generally taking on dreadfully.

By referring to another part of our present monthly, our respected readers will find a few samples of the spirit of the Southern press on the subject. They are full of intrigue, smell of brimstone, and betoken a terrific explosion. Unquestionably, "secession," "disunion," "Southern Confederacy," and the like phrases, are the most popular political watch words of the cotton-growing States of the Union. Nor is this sentiment to be entirely despised. If Mr. Lincoln were really an Abolition President, which he is not; if he were a friend to the Abolition movement, instead of being, as he is, its most powerful enemy, the dissolution of the Union might be the only effective mode of perpetuating slavery in the Southern States—since if it could succeed, it would place slavery beyond the power of the President and his Government. But the South has now no such cause for disunion. The present alarm and perturbation will cease; the Southern fire-eaters will be appeased and will retrace their steps.—There is no sufficient cause for the dissolution of the Union. Whoever lives through the next four years will see Mr. Lincoln and his Administration attacked more bitterly for their pro-slavery truckling, than for doing any anti-slavery work. He and his party will become the best protectors of slavery where it now is, and just such protectors as slaveholders will most need. In order to defeat him, the slaveholders took advantage of the ignorance and stupidity of the masses, and assured them that Lincoln is an Abolitionist. This, Mr. Lincoln and his party will lose no time in scattering to the winds as false and groundless. With the single exception of the question of slavery extension, Mr. Lincoln proposes no measure which can bring him into antagonistic collision with the traffickers in human flesh, either in the States or in the District of Columbia. The Union will, therefore, be saved simply because there is no cause in the election of Mr. Lincoln for its dissolution. Slavery will be as safe, and safer, in the Union under such a President, than it can be under any President of a Southern Confederacy. This is our impression, and we deeply regret the facts from which it is derived.

With an Abolition President we should consider a successful separation of the slave from the free States a calamity, greatly damaging to the prospects of our long enslaved, bruised and mutilated people; but under what may be expected of the Republican party, with its pledges to put down the slaves should they attempt to rise, and to hunt them should they run away, a dissolution of the Union would be highly beneficial to the cause of liberty.—The South would then be a Sicily, and the North a Sardinia. Mr. Lincoln would then be entirely absolved from his slave-hunting, slave-catching and slave-killing pledges, and the South would have to defend slavery with her own guns, and hunt her Negroes with her own dogs. In truth, we really wish those brave, fire-eating, cotton-growing States would just now go at once outside the Union and set up for themselves, where they could be got at without disturbing other people, and got away from without encountering other people. Such a consummation was "one devoutly to be wished." But no, cunning dogs, they will smother their rage, and after all the dust they can raise, they will retire within the Union and claim its advantages.

What, then, has been gained to the anti-slavery cause by the election of Mr. Lincoln? Not much, in itself considered, but very much when viewed in the light of its relations and bearings. For fifty years the country has taken the law from the lips of an exacting, haughty and imperious slave oligarchy. The masters of slaves have been masters of the Republic. Their authority was almost undisputed, and their power irresistible. They were the President makers of the Republic, and no aspirant dared to hope for success against their frown. Lincoln's election has vitiated their authority, and broken their power. It has taught the North its strength, and shown the South its weakness. More important still, it has demonstrated the possibility of electing, if not an Abolitionist, at least an *anti-slavery reputation* to the Presidency of the United States. The years are few since it was thought possible that the Northern people could be wrought up to the exercise of such startling courage. Hitherto the threat of disunion has been as potent over the politicians of the North, as the cat-o'-nine-tails is over the backs of the slaves. Mr. Lincoln's election breaks this enchantment, dispels this terrible nightmare, and awakes the nation to the consciousness of new powers, and the possibility of a higher destiny than the perpetual bondage to an ignoble fear.

Another probable effect will be to extinguish the reviving fires of the accursed foreign slave trade, which for a year or two have been kindled all along the Southern coast of the Union. The Republican party is under no necessity to pass laws on this subject. It has only to enforce and execute the laws already on the statute book. The moral influence of such prompt, complete and unflinching execution of the laws, will be great, not only in arresting the specific evil, but in arresting the tide of popular demoralization with which the successful prosecution of the horrid trade in naked men and women was overspreading the country. To this duty the Republican party will be prompted, not only by the conscience of the North, but by what perhaps will be more controlling party interests.

It may also be conceded that the election of Lincoln and Hamlin, notwithstanding the admission of the former that the South is entitled to an efficient Fugitive Slave Law, will render the practice of recapturing and returning to slavery persons who have heroically succeeded, or may hereafter succeed in reaching the free States, more unpopular and odious than it would have been had either Douglas, Bell or Breckinridge been elected. Slaves may yet be hunted, caught and carried back to slavery, but the number will be greatly diminished, because of the popular disinclination to execute the cruel and merciless Fugitive Slave Law. Had Lincoln been defeated, the fact would have been construed by slave-holders, and their guilty minions of the country, as strong evidence of the soundness of the North in respect to the alleged duty of hounding down and handing over the panting fugitive to the vengeance of his infuriated master. No argument is needed to prove this gain to the side of freedom.

But chief among the benefits of the election, has been the canvass itself. Notwithstanding the many cowardly disclaimers, and miserable concessions to popular prejudice against the colored people, which Republican orators have felt themselves required, by an intense and greedy desire of success, to make, they have been compelled also to recur to first principles of human liberty, expose the baseless claim of property in man, exhibit the hideous features of slavery, and to unveil, for popular execration, the brutal manners and morals of the guilty slave-masters.—The canvass has sent all over the North most learned and eloquent men to utter the great truths which Abolitionists have for twenty years been earnestly, but unsuccessfully endeavoring to get before the public mind and conscience. We may rejoice in the dissemination of the truth by whomsoever proclaimed, for the truth will bear its own weight, and bring forth its own fruit.

Nevertheless, this very victory threatens and may be the death of the modern Abolition movement, and finally bring back the country to the same, or a worse state, than Benj. Lundy and Wm. Lloyd Garrison found it thirty years ago. The Republican party does not propose to abolish slavery anywhere, and is decidedly opposed to Abolition agitation. It is not even, by the confession of its President elect, in favor of the repeal of that thrice-accursed and flagrantly unconstitutional Fugitive Slave Bill of 1850. It is plain to see, that once in power, the policy of the party will be only to seem a little less yielding to the demands of slavery than the Democratic or Fusion party, and thus render ineffective and pointless the whole Abolition movement of the North. The safety of our movement will be found only by a return to all the agencies and appliances, such as writing, publishing, organizing, lecturing, holding meetings, with the earnest aim not to prevent the extension of slavery, but to abolish the system altogether. Congress should be at once memorialized for the abolition of slavery in the District of Columbia, and the slave trade between the States. The same zeal, activity, energy and earnestness should be displayed in circulating petitions, as in the earlier stages of the movement. We have the pen, voice and influence of only one man, and that man of the most limited class; but with few or many, in whatever vicissitudes which may surround the cause, now or hereafter, we shall join in no cry, and unite in no demand less than the complete and universal *abolition* of the whole slave system. Slavery shall be destroyed.

SECESSIONISM IN LOUISIANA: DECEMBER 1860

William T. Sherman to Thomas Ewing Sr. and to John Sherman

William T. Sherman, an 1840 graduate of West Point, had resigned from the army as a captain in 1853 and worked as a banker in San Francisco before accepting a position in 1859 as superintendent of the new State Seminary and Military Academy at Alexandria, Louisiana. Sherman described the political situation in the state after the 1860 election in letters to his father-in-law, Thomas Ewing Sr., and to his brother John, who was then serving as a Republican congressman from Ohio. When the Louisiana convention voted 113–17 in favor of secession on January 26, 1861, Sherman would resign his position and rejoin his wife and children in Lancaster, Ohio.

———————

                      Louisiana State Seminary of Learning
                      and Military Academy
                      Alexandria, Decr. 1, 1860

Hon. Thos. Ewing
Dear Sir

    Since I last wrote you I have observed a marked change in public opinion here—I was in town all day yesterday, with a Dr. Smith, Senator in the State Legislature, who is the Vice President of our Board of Supervisors and who is just from New Orleans—He is originally from Kentucky, but was an active supporter of Breckinridge in this state. He tells me he was surprised at the tone of feeling in New Orleans, which he described, and which I find corroborated by the Editorials of all the leading City papers. All go to the effect that secession is a sure thing, the only questions being the times when and how. Immediate Secession, unqualified and unconditional is the prevailing sentiment, the Bell party going even further than the Breckinridge adherents. Dr. Smith will attend the Session of the Legislature next week, the 10th inst, and says the calling of a convention will be the first and inevitable step—this will be he says unanimous—next the arming of the state, and putting herself in an attitude of defense—to this he says there will be no opposition. The convention will meet in January and the Questions submitted to them will be immediate Secession, or a General convention of all southern states, Louisiana to instruct her Delegates, to demand that the Northern States shall repeal the Laws adverse to slavery, and give pledges of future good behavior—Dr. S. thinks it will be all the Conservative men of this state will attempt, to carry this latter alternative against the adherents of the immediate secession: but I told him that for the South to demand of the North such conditions would be idle. The machinery of a Democratic Government is too slow, to bring about such pledges under a pressure when public feeling cannot be moulded by men—It occurs to me that Texas might withdraw from the Confederation, resuming her status as before the Treaty—It might be that S. Carolina, Georgia Alabama and Florida might also fall out, & arrange by Treaty for the break of our Commercial Sea bond, but the moment Mississipi Arkansas, & Louisiana declare an independence, sovereign & complete, with a right to control, interrupt or tax the Commerce of the Mississipi, justly and fairly a storm would arise in those states bordering on the Territories, that would be fearful as compared with anything heretofore known on this Continent. They argue, however as their policy will be free trade, no possible interruption can occur to the usual navigation: but however they may start, some tax and obstruction will result, and then of course retaliation & war.

Now for myself I have told the Governor & all in Authority that as long as Louisiana is a part of the United States I will serve here in my present sphere, and moreover in case of domestic insurrection or molestation from without, I will head the Cadets under my Command, but that I will do no act inconsistent with my allegiance to the General Government: that as long as the form of Govt. indicated by the Constitution of the U.S. is in existence, that I will stand by it—As I have no other means of existence now save this, I will stay here till the Convention meets and does some act of Treason. Then I shall quit—but when to go is a question I cannot solve, and must trust to the confusion that must result from the dissolution of this Govt. I must therefore change my whole plan, and leave

Ellen where she is, till this storm either subsides, or passes away, or until I can do something else: If I leave here suddenly & unexpectedly, I will fetch up at St. Louis—Clay has been very sick, is so still, but I begin to have hopes. Give Ellen the benefit of your advice as to probabilities &c—I am in good health but must have continuous and active employment. as ever with respect,

W. T. Sherman

Louisiana State Seminary of Learning
and Military Academy.
Alexandria, Decr. 1, 1860.

Dear Brother,

When I last wrote you I had observed what I thought a general quiet, and determination to submit as heretofore to the General Election of Lincoln, and as the House which has been under construction for me was drawing to a completion I gave Ellen notice to hold herself ready to start about the 15 instant with all the family, so as to get out of Ohio before the close of the River, and to take advantage of the present condition of Red River. But the whole case has changed. The quiet which I thought the usual acquiescence of the People was merely the prelude to the storm of opinion that now seems irresistable— Politicians have by hearing the prejudices of the people, and moving with the current have succeeded in destroying the Government—It cannot be stopped now I fear—I was in Alexandria all day yesterday, and had a full and unreserved conversation with Dr. S. A. Smith, State Senator, who is a man of education, property, influence and qualified to Judge—He was during the canvas a Breckinridge man, but though a Southern in opinion is really opposed to a dissolution of our Government. He has returned from New Orleans where he says he was amazed to See evidences of Public sentiment which could not be mistaken—The Legislature meets Dec. 10—at Baton Rouge—the calling a Convention forthwith is to be unanimous—the Bill for arming the State ditto—The Convention will meet in January, and only two questions will be agitated—Immediate dissolution, a declaration of State Independence, a General Convention of Southern States with instructions to demand of the Northern States to repeal all laws hostile to Slavery, and pledges of future good behavior.

Of course this latter demand cannot from the nature of an anarchical Democratic Government ever be entertained & therefore if these things be so, and all the Public prints of New Orleans confirm these views of Dr. Smith, Uncle Sam is already a Sick old man—whether the South or North be benefitted is a question that no man can solve—If Texas would draw off, no great harm would follow—Even if S. Carolina, Georgia, Alabama & Florida would cut away, it might be the rest could get along, but I think the secession of Mississipi, Louisiana and Arkansas will bring war—for though they now say that Free trade is their Policy yet it wont be long before steamboats will be taxed and molested all the way down. Therefore when the Convention meets in January, as they will assuredly do, and resolve to secede, or to elect members to a General Convention with instructions inconsistent with the nature of things I must quit this place for it is neither right for me to Stay nor would the Governor be justified in placing me in this position of Trust for the moment Louisiana assumes a position of hostility then this becomes an arsenal & fort. I wont move however until the last moment for I am at a loss what else to do. I will watch the proceedings of Congress with deep interest, and catch at the first chance of reconciliation —Let me hear the moment you think dissolution is inevitable. What Mississipi and Georgia do, this State will do likewise. Affectionately,

W. T. S.

WASHINGTON, D.C., DECEMBER 1860

James Buchanan: from the Annual Message to Congress

President James Buchanan met with his cabinet on November 9 to discuss the situation in the South and particularly in South Carolina. Buchanan proposed a general convention of the states to address the sectional crisis and on November 10 presented the cabinet with a draft document condemning the doctrine of secession. The draft drew praise from the four Unionist members of the cabinet, but was criticized by its three Southerners—Secretary of the Treasury Howell Cobb, Secretary of War John Floyd, and Secretary of the Interior Jacob Thompson—all of whom would later join the Confederacy. In preparing his annual message to Congress, the President drew upon a legal opinion regarding the constitutionality of secession and coercion submitted by Attorney General Jeremiah Black. Despite his hope that it would reduce sectional tensions, Buchanan's message was criticized by many Southerners for denying the constitutionality of secession, and by many Northerners for concluding that the federal government could not prevent states from seceding.

WASHINGTON CITY, *December 3, 1860*.
Fellow-Citizens of the Senate and House of Representatives:
Throughout the year since our last meeting the country has been eminently prosperous in all its material interests. The general health has been excellent, our harvests have been abundant, and plenty smiles throughout the land. Our commerce and manufactures have been prosecuted with energy and industry, and have yielded fair and ample returns. In short, no nation in the tide of time has ever presented a spectacle of greater material prosperity than we have done until within a very recent period.

Why is it, then, that discontent now so extensively prevails, and the Union of the States, which is the source of all these blessings, is threatened with destruction?

The long-continued and intemperate interference of the

Northern people with the question of slavery in the Southern States has at length produced its natural effects. The different sections of the Union are now arrayed against each other, and the time has arrived, so much dreaded by the Father of his Country, when hostile geographical parties have been formed.

I have long foreseen and often forewarned my countrymen of the now impending danger. This does not proceed solely from the claim on the part of Congress or the Territorial legislatures to exclude slavery from the Territories, nor from the efforts of different States to defeat the execution of the fugitive-slave law. All or any of these evils might have been endured by the South without danger to the Union (as others have been) in the hope that time and reflection might apply the remedy. The immediate peril arises not so much from these causes as from the fact that the incessant and violent agitation of the slavery question throughout the North for the last quarter of a century has at length produced its malign influence on the slaves and inspired them with vague notions of freedom. Hence a sense of security no longer exists around the family altar. This feeling of peace at home has given place to apprehensions of servile insurrections. Many a matron throughout the South retires at night in dread of what may befall herself and children before the morning. Should this apprehension of domestic danger, whether real or imaginary, extend and intensify itself until it shall pervade the masses of the Southern people, then disunion will become inevitable. Self-preservation is the first law of nature, and has been implanted in the heart of man by his Creator for the wisest purpose; and no political union, however fraught with blessings and benefits in all other respects, can long continue if the necessary consequence be to render the homes and the firesides of nearly half the parties to it habitually and hopelessly insecure. Sooner or later the bonds of such a union must be severed. It is my conviction that this fatal period has not yet arrived, and my prayer to God is that He would preserve the Constitution and the Union throughout all generations.

But let us take warning in time and remove the cause of danger. It can not be denied that for five and twenty years the agitation at the North against slavery has been incessant. In 1835 pictorial handbills and inflammatory appeals were circulated extensively throughout the South of a character to excite the passions of the slaves, and, in the language of General Jackson, "to stimulate them to insurrection and produce all the horrors of a servile war." This agitation has ever since been continued by the public press, by the proceedings of State and county conventions and by abolition sermons and lectures. The time of Congress has been occupied in violent speeches on this never-ending subject, and appeals, in pamphlet and other forms, indorsed by distinguished names, have been sent forth from this central point and spread broadcast over the Union.

How easy would it be for the American people to settle the slavery question forever and to restore peace and harmony to this distracted country! They, and they alone, can do it. All that is necessary to accomplish the object, and all for which the slave States have ever contended, is to be let alone and permitted to manage their domestic institutions in their own way. As sovereign States, they, and they alone, are responsible before God and the world for the slavery existing among them. For this the people of the North are not more responsible and have no more right to interfere than with similar institutions in Russia or in Brazil.

Upon their good sense and patriotic forbearance I confess I still greatly rely. Without their aid it is beyond the power of any President, no matter what may be his own political proclivities, to restore peace and harmony among the States. Wisely limited and restrained as is his power under our Constitution and laws, he alone can accomplish but little for good or for evil on such a momentous question.

And this brings me to observe that the election of any one of our fellow-citizens to the office of President does not of itself afford just cause for dissolving the Union. This is more especially true if his election has been effected by a mere plurality, and not a majority of the people, and has resulted from transient and temporary causes, which may probably never again occur. In order to justify a resort to revolutionary resistance, the Federal Government must be guilty of "a deliberate, palpable, and dangerous exercise" of powers not granted by the Constitution. The late Presidential election, however, has been held in strict conformity with its express provisions. How, then, can the result justify a revolution to destroy this very Constitution? Reason, justice, a regard for the Constitution, all require that we shall wait for some overt and dangerous act on the part of the President elect before resorting to such a remedy. It is said, however, that the antecedents of the President elect have been sufficient to justify the fears of the South that he will attempt to invade their constitutional rights. But are such apprehensions of contingent danger in the future sufficient to justify the immediate destruction of the noblest system of government ever devised by mortals? From the very nature of his office and its high responsibilities he must necessarily be conservative. The stern duty of administering the vast and complicated concerns of this Government affords in itself a guaranty that he will not attempt any violation of a clear constitutional right.

After all, he is no more than the chief executive officer of the Government. His province is not to make but to execute the laws. And it is a remarkable fact in our history that, notwithstanding the repeated efforts of the antislavery party, no single act has ever passed Congress, unless we may possibly except the Missouri compromise, impairing in the slightest degree the rights of the South to their property in slaves; and it may also be observed, judging from present indications, that no probability exists of the passage of such an act by a majority of both Houses, either in the present or the next Congress. Surely under these circumstances we ought to be restrained from present action by the precept of Him who spake as man never spoke, that "sufficient unto the day is the evil thereof." The day of evil may never come unless we shall rashly bring it upon ourselves.

It is alleged as one cause for immediate secession that the Southern States are denied equal rights with the other States in the common Territories. But by what authority are these denied? Not by Congress, which has never passed, and I believe never will pass, any act to exclude slavery from these Territories; and certainly not by the Supreme Court, which has solemnly decided that slaves are property, and, like all other property, their owners have a right to take them into the common Territories and hold them there under the protection of the Constitution.

So far then, as Congress is concerned, the objection is not to anything they have already done, but to what they may do hereafter. It will surely be admitted that this apprehension of future danger is no good reason for an immediate dissolution of the Union. It is true that the Territorial legislature of Kansas, on the 23d February, 1860, passed in great haste an act over the veto of the governor declaring that slavery "is and shall be forever prohibited in this Territory." Such an act, however, plainly violating the rights of property secured by the Constitution, will surely be declared void by the judiciary whenever it shall be presented in a legal form.

Only three days after my inauguration the Supreme Court of the United States solemnly adjudged that this power did not exist in a Territorial legislature. Yet such has been the factious temper of the times that the correctness of this decision has been extensively impugned before the people, and the question has given rise to angry political conflicts throughout the country. Those who have appealed from this judgment of our highest constitutional tribunal to popular assemblies would, if they could, invest a Territorial legislature with power to annul the sacred rights of property. This power Congress is expressly forbidden by the Federal Constitution to exercise. Every State legislature in the Union is forbidden by its own constitution to exercise it. It can not be exercised in any State except by the people in their highest sovereign capacity, when framing or amending their State constitution. In like manner it can only be exercised by the people of a Territory represented in a convention of delegates for the purpose of framing a constitution preparatory to admission as a State into the Union. Then, and not until then, are they invested with power to decide the question whether slavery shall or shall not exist within their limits. This is an act of sovereign authority, and not of subordinate Territorial legislation. Were it otherwise, then indeed would the equality of the States in the Territories be destroyed, and the rights of property in slaves would depend not upon the guaranties of the Constitution, but upon the shifting majorities of an irresponsible Territorial legislature. Such a doctrine, from its intrinsic unsoundness, can not long influence any considerable portion of our people, much less can it afford a good reason for a dissolution of the Union.

The most palpable violations of constitutional duty which have yet been committed consist in the acts of different State legislatures to defeat the execution of the fugitive-slave law. It ought to be remembered, however, that for these acts neither Congress nor any President can justly be held responsible. Having been passed in violation of the Federal Constitution, they are therefore null and void. All the courts, both State and national, before whom the question has arisen have from the beginning declared the fugitive-slave law to be constitutional. The single exception is that of a State court in Wisconsin, and this has not only been reversed by the proper appellate tribunal, but has met with such universal reprobation that there can be no danger from it as a precedent. The validity of this law has been established over and over again by the Supreme Court of the United States with perfect unanimity. It is founded upon an express provision of the Constitution, requiring that fugitive slaves who escape from service in one State to another shall be "delivered up" to their masters. Without this provision it is a well-known historical fact that the Constitution itself could never have been adopted by the Convention. In one form or other, under the acts of 1793 and 1850, both being substantially the same, the fugitive-slave law has been the law of the land from the days of Washington until the present moment. Here, then, a clear case is presented in which it will be the duty of the next President, as it has been my own, to act with vigor in executing this supreme law against the conflicting enactments of State legislatures. Should he fail in the performance of this high duty, he will then have manifested a disregard of the Constitution and laws, to the great injury of the people of nearly one-half of the States of the Union. But are we to presume in advance that he will thus violate his duty? This would be at war with every principle of justice and of Christian charity. Let us wait for the overt act. The fugitive-slave law has been carried into execution in every contested case since the commencement of the present Administration, though often, it is to be regretted, with great loss and inconvenience to the master and with considerable expense to the Government. Let us trust that the State legislatures will repeal their unconstitutional and obnoxious enactments. Unless this shall be done without unnecessary delay, it is impossible for any human power to save the Union.

The Southern States, standing on the basis of the Constitution, have a right to demand this act of justice from the States of the North. Should it be refused, then the Constitution, to which all the States are parties, will have been willfully violated by one portion of them in a provision essential to the domestic security and happiness of the remainder. In that event the injured States, after having first used all peaceful and constitutional means to obtain redress, would be justified in revolutionary resistance to the Government of the Union.

I have purposely confined my remarks to revolutionary resistance, because it has been claimed within the last few years that any State, whenever this shall be its sovereign will and pleasure, may secede from the Union in accordance with the Constitution and without any violation of the constitutional rights of the other members of the Confederacy; that as each became parties to the Union by the vote of its own people assembled in convention, so any one of them may retire from the Union in a similar manner by the vote of such a convention.

In order to justify secession as a constitutional remedy, it must be on the principle that the Federal Government is a mere voluntary association of States, to be dissolved at pleasure by any one of the contracting parties. If this be so, the Confederacy is a rope of sand, to be penetrated and dissolved by the first adverse wave of public opinion in any of the States. In this manner our thirty-three States may resolve themselves into as many petty, jarring, and hostile republics, each one retiring from the Union without responsibility whenever any sudden excitement might impel them to such a course. By this process a Union might be entirely broken into fragments in a few weeks which cost our forefathers many years of toil, privation, and blood to establish.

Such a principle is wholly inconsistent with the history as well as the character of the Federal Constitution. After it was framed with the greatest deliberation and care it was submitted to conventions of the people of the several States for ratification. Its provisions were discussed at length in these bodies, composed of the first men of the country. Its opponents contended that it conferred powers upon the Federal Government dangerous to the rights of the States, whilst its advocates maintained that under a fair construction of the instrument there was no foundation for such apprehensions. In that mighty struggle between the first intellects of this or any other country it never occurred to any individual, either among its opponents or advocates, to assert or even to intimate that their efforts were all vain labor, because the moment that any State felt herself aggrieved she might secede from the Union. What a crushing argument would this have proved against those who dreaded that the rights of the States would be endangered by the Constitution! The truth is that it was not until many years after the origin of the Federal Government that such a proposition was first advanced. It was then met and refuted by the conclusive arguments of General Jackson, who in his message of the 16th of January, 1833, transmitting the nullifying ordinance of South Carolina to Congress, employs the following language:

> The right of the people of a single State to absolve themselves at will and without the consent of the other States from their most solemn obligations, and hazard the liberties and happiness of the millions composing this Union, can not be acknowledged. Such authority is believed to be utterly repugnant both to the principles upon which the General Government is constituted and to the objects which it is expressly formed to attain.

It is not pretended that any clause in the Constitution gives countenance to such a theory. It is altogether founded upon inference; not from any language contained in the instrument itself, but from the sovereign character of the several States by which it was ratified. But is it beyond the power of a State, like an individual, to yield a portion of its sovereign rights to secure the remainder? In the language of Mr. Madison, who has been called the father of the Constitution—

> It was formed by the States; that is, by the people in each of the States acting in their highest sovereign capacity, and formed, consequently, by the same authority which formed the State constitutions. * * * Nor is the Government of the United States, created by the Constitution, less a government, in the strict sense of the term, within the sphere of its powers than the governments created by the

constitutions of the States are within their several spheres. It is, like them, organized into legislative, executive, and judiciary departments. It operates, like them, directly on persons and things, and, like them, it has at command a physical force for executing the powers committed to it.

It was intended to be perpetual, and not to be annulled at the pleasure of any one of the contracting parties. The old Articles of Confederation were entitled "Articles of Confederation and Perpetual Union between the States," and by the thirteenth article it is expressly declared that "the articles of this Confederation shall be inviolably observed by every State, and the Union shall be perpetual." The preamble to the Constitution of the United States, having express reference to the Articles of Confederation, recites that it was established "in order to form a more perfect union." And yet it is contended that this "more perfect union" does not include the essential attribute of perpetuity.

But that the Union was designed to be perpetual appears conclusively from the nature and extent of the powers conferred by the Constitution on the Federal Government. These powers embrace the very highest attributes of national sovereignty. They place both the sword and the purse under its control. Congress has power to make war and to make peace, to raise and support armies and navies, and to conclude treaties with foreign governments. It is invested with the power to coin money and to regulate the value thereof, and to regulate commerce with foreign nations and among the several States. It is not necessary to enumerate the other high powers which have been conferred upon the Federal Government. In order to carry the enumerated powers into effect, Congress possesses the exclusive right to lay and collect duties on imports, and, in common with the States, to lay and collect all other taxes.

But the Constitution has not only conferred these high powers upon Congress, but it has adopted effectual means to restrain the States from interfering with their exercise. For that purpose it has in strong prohibitory language expressly declared that—

> No State shall enter into any treaty, alliance, or confederation; grant letters of marque and reprisal; coin money; emit bills of credit;

make anything but gold and silver coin a tender in payment of debts; pass any bill of attainder, ex post facto law, or law impairing the obligation of contracts.

Moreover—

No State shall without the consent of the Congress lay any imposts or duties on imports or exports, except what may be absolutely necessary for executing its inspection laws.

And if they exceed this amount the excess shall belong to the United States. And—

No State shall without the consent of Congress lay any duty of tonnage, keep troops or ships of war in time of peace, enter into any agreement or compact with another State or with a foreign power, or engage in war, unless actually invaded or in such imminent danger as will not admit of delay.

In order still further to secure the uninterrupted exercise of these high powers against State interposition, it is provided that—

This Constitution and the laws of the United States which shall be made in pursuance thereof, and all treaties made or which shall be made under the authority of the United States, shall be the supreme law of the land, and the judges in every State shall be bound thereby, anything in the constitution or laws of any State to the contrary notwithstanding.

The solemn sanction of religion has been superadded to the obligations of official duty, and all Senators and Representatives of the United States, all members of State legislatures, and all executive and judicial officers, "both of the United States and of the several States, shall be bound by oath or affirmation to support this Constitution."

In order to carry into effect these powers, the Constitution has established a perfect Government in all its forms—legislative, executive, and judicial; and this Government to the extent of its powers acts directly upon the individual citizens of every State, and executes its own decrees by the agency of its own officers. In this respect it differs entirely from the Government under the old Confederation, which was confined to making requisitions on the States in their sovereign character. This left it in the discretion of each whether to obey or to refuse, and they often declined to comply with such requisitions. It thus became necessary for the purpose of removing this barrier and "in order to form a more perfect union" to establish a Government which could act directly upon the people and execute its own laws without the intermediate agency of the States. This has been accomplished by the Constitution of the United States. In short, the Government created by the Constitution, and deriving its authority from the sovereign people of each of the several States, has precisely the same right to exercise its power over the people of all these States in the enumerated cases that each one of them possesses over subjects not delegated to the United States, but "reserved to the States respectively or to the people."

To the extent of the delegated powers the Constitution of the United States is as much a part of the constitution of each State and is as binding upon its people as though it had been textually inserted therein.

This Government, therefore, is a great and powerful Government, invested with all the attributes of sovereignty over the special subjects to which its authority extends. Its framers never intended to implant in its bosom the seeds of its own destruction, nor were they at its creation guilty of the absurdity of providing for its own dissolution. It was not intended by its framers to be the baseless fabric of a vision, which at the touch of the enchanter would vanish into thin air, but a substantial and mighty fabric, capable of resisting the slow decay of time and of defying the storms of ages. Indeed, well may the jealous patriots of that day have indulged fears that a Government of such high powers might violate the reserved rights of the States, and wisely did they adopt the rule of a strict construction of these powers to prevent the danger. But they did not fear, nor had they any reason to imagine, that the Constitution would ever be so interpreted as to enable any State by her own act, and without the consent of her sister States, to discharge her people from all or any of their federal obligations.

It may be asked, then, Are the people of the States without redress against the tyranny and oppression of the Federal Government? By no means. The right of resistance on the part of the governed against the oppression of their governments can not be denied. It exists independently of all constitutions, and has been exercised at all periods of the world's history. Under it old governments have been destroyed and new ones have taken their place. It is embodied in strong and express language in our own Declaration of Independence. But the distinction must ever be observed that this is revolution against an established government, and not a voluntary secession from it by virtue of an inherent constitutional right. In short, let us look the danger fairly in the face. Secession is neither more nor less than revolution. It may or it may not be a justifiable revolution, but still it is revolution.

What, in the meantime, is the responsibility and true position of the Executive? He is bound by solemn oath, before God and the country, "to take care that the laws be faithfully executed," and from this obligation he can not be absolved by any human power. But what if the performance of this duty, in whole or in part, has been rendered impracticable by events over which he could have exercised no control? Such at the present moment is the case throughout the State of South Carolina so far as the laws of the United States to secure the administration of justice by means of the Federal judiciary are concerned. All the Federal officers within its limits through whose agency alone these laws can be carried into execution have already resigned. We no longer have a district judge, a district attorney, or a marshal in South Carolina. In fact, the whole machinery of the Federal Government necessary for the distribution of remedial justice among the people has been demolished, and it would be difficult, if not impossible, to replace it.

The only acts of Congress on the statute book bearing upon this subject are those of February 28, 1795, and March 3, 1807. These authorize the President, after he shall have ascertained that the marshal, with his *posse comitatus*, is unable to execute civil or criminal process in any particular case, to call forth the militia and employ the Army and Navy to aid him in performing this service, having first by proclamation commanded the insurgents "to disperse and retire peaceably to their respective abodes within a limited time." This duty can not by possibility be performed in a State where no judicial authority exists to issue process, and where there is no marshal to execute it, and where, even if there were such an officer, the entire population would constitute one solid combination to resist him.

The bare enumeration of these provisions proves how inadequate they are without further legislation to overcome a united opposition in a single State, not to speak of other States who may place themselves in a similar attitude. Congress alone has power to decide whether the present laws can or can not be amended so as to carry out more effectually the objects of the Constitution.

The same insuperable obstacles do not lie in the way of executing the laws for the collection of the customs. The revenue still continues to be collected as heretofore at the customhouse in Charleston, and should the collector unfortunately resign a successor may be appointed to perform this duty.

Then, in regard to the property of the United States in South Carolina. This has been purchased for a fair equivalent, "by the consent of the legislature of the State," "for the erection of forts, magazines, arsenals," etc., and over these the authority "to exercise exclusive legislation" has been expressly granted by the Constitution to Congress. It is not believed that any attempt will be made to expel the United States from this property by force; but if in this I should prove to be mistaken, the officer in command of the forts has received orders to act strictly on the defensive. In such a contingency the responsibility for consequences would rightfully rest upon the heads of the assailants.

Apart from the execution of the laws, so far as this may be practicable, the Executive has no authority to decide what shall be the relations between the Federal Government and South Carolina. He has been invested with no such discretion. He possesses no power to change the relations heretofore existing between them, much less to acknowledge the independence of that State. This would be to invest a mere executive officer with the power of recognizing the dissolution of the confederacy among our thirty-three sovereign States. It bears no resemblance to the recognition of a foreign *de facto* government, involving no such responsibility. Any attempt to do this would, on his part, be a naked act of usurpation. It is therefore my duty to submit to Congress the whole question in all its bearings.

The course of events is so rapidly hastening forward that the emergency may soon arise when you may be called upon to decide the momentous question whether you possess the power by force of arms to compel a State to remain in the Union. I should feel myself recreant to my duty were I not to express an opinion on this important subject.

The question fairly stated is, Has the Constitution delegated to Congress the power to coerce a State into submission which is attempting to withdraw or has actually withdrawn from the Confederacy? If answered in the affirmative, it must be on the principle that the power has been conferred upon Congress to declare and to make war against a State. After much serious reflection I have arrived at the conclusion that no such power has been delegated to Congress or to any other department of the Federal Government. It is manifest upon an inspection of the Constitution that this is not among the specific and enumerated powers granted to Congress, and it is equally apparent that its exercise is not "necessary and proper for carrying into execution" any one of these powers. So far from this power having been delegated to Congress, it was expressly refused by the Convention which framed the Constitution.

It appears from the proceedings of that body that on the 31st May, 1787, the clause "*authorizing an exertion of the force of the whole against a delinquent State*" came up for consideration. Mr. Madison opposed it in a brief but powerful speech, from which I shall extract but a single sentence. He observed:

> The use of force against a State would look more like a declaration of war than an infliction of punishment, and would probably be considered by the party attacked as a dissolution of all previous compacts by which it might be bound.

Upon his motion the clause was unanimously postponed, and was never, I believe, again presented. Soon afterwards, on the 8th June, 1787, when incidentally adverting to the subject, he said: "Any government for the United States formed on the supposed practicability of using force against the unconstitutional proceedings of the States would prove as visionary and fallacious as the government of Congress," evidently meaning the then existing Congress of the old Confederation.

Without descending to particulars, it may be safely asserted that the power to make war against a State is at variance with the whole spirit and intent of the Constitution. Suppose such a war should result in the conquest of a State; how are we to govern it afterwards? Shall we hold it as a province and govern it by despotic power? In the nature of things, we could not by physical force control the will of the people and compel them to elect Senators and Representatives to Congress and to perform all the other duties depending upon their own volition and required from the free citizens of a free State as a constituent member of the Confederacy.

But if we possessed this power, would it be wise to exercise it under existing circumstances? The object would doubtless be to preserve the Union. War would not only present the most effectual means of destroying it, but would vanish all hope of its peaceable reconstruction. Besides, in the fraternal conflict a vast amount of blood and treasure would be expended, rendering future reconciliation between the States impossible. In the meantime, who can foretell what would be the sufferings and privations of the people during its existence?

The fact is that our Union rests upon public opinion, and can never be cemented by the blood of its citizens shed in civil war. If it can not live in the affections of the people, it must one day perish. Congress possesses many means of preserving it by conciliation, but the sword was not placed in their hand to preserve it by force.

But may I be permitted solemnly to invoke my countrymen to pause and deliberate before they determine to destroy this the grandest temple which has ever been dedicated to human freedom since the world began? It has been consecrated by the blood of our fathers, by the glories of the past, and by the hopes of the future. The Union has already made us the most prosperous, and ere long will, if preserved, render us the most powerful, nation on the face of the earth. In every foreign region of the globe the title of American citizen is held in the highest respect, and when pronounced in a foreign land it causes the hearts of our countrymen to swell with honest pride. Surely when we reach the brink of the yawning abyss we shall recoil with horror from the last fatal plunge.

By such a dread catastrophe the hopes of the friends of freedom throughout the world would be destroyed, and a long night of leaden despotism would enshroud the nations. Our example for more than eighty years would not only be lost, but it would be quoted as a conclusive proof that man is unfit for self-government.

It is not every wrong—nay, it is not every grievous wrong—which can justify a resort to such a fearful alternative. This ought to be the last desperate remedy of a despairing people, after every other constitutional means of conciliation had been exhausted. We should reflect that under this free Government there is an incessant ebb and flow in public opinion. The slavery question, like everything human, will have its day. I firmly believe that it has reached and passed the culminating point. But if in the midst of the existing excitement the Union shall perish, the evil may then become irreparable.

Congress can contribute much to avert it by proposing and recommending to the legislatures of the several States the remedy for existing evils which the Constitution has itself provided for its own preservation. This has been tried at different critical periods of our history, and always with eminent success. It is to be found in the fifth article, providing for its own amendment. Under this article amendments have been proposed by two-thirds of both Houses of Congress, and have been "ratified by the legislatures of three-fourths of the several States," and have consequently become parts of the Constitution. To this process the country is indebted for the clause prohibiting Congress from passing any law respecting an establishment of religion or abridging the freedom of speech or of the press or of the right of petition. To this we are also indebted for the bill of rights which secures the people against any abuse of power by the Federal Government. Such were the apprehensions justly entertained by the friends of State rights at that period as to have rendered it extremely doubtful whether the Constitution could have long survived without those amendments.

Again the Constitution was amended by the same process, after the election of President Jefferson by the House of Representatives, in February, 1803. This amendment was rendered necessary to prevent a recurrence of the dangers which had seriously threatened the existence of the Government during the pendency of that election. The article for its own amendment was intended to secure the amicable adjustment of conflicting constitutional questions like the present which might arise between the governments of the States and that of the United States. This appears from contemporaneous history. In this connection I shall merely call attention to a few sentences in Mr. Madison's justly celebrated report, in 1799, to the legislature of Virginia. In this he ably and conclusively defended the resolutions of the preceding legislature against the strictures of several other State legislatures. These were mainly founded upon the protest of the Virginia legislature against the "alien and sedition acts," as "palpable and alarming infractions of the Constitution." In pointing out the peaceful and constitutional remedies—and he referred to none other—to which the States were authorized to resort on such occasions, he concludes by saying that—

> The legislatures of the States might have made a direct representation to Congress with a view to obtain a rescinding of the two offensive acts, or they might have represented to their respective Senators in Congress their wish that two-thirds thereof would propose an explanatory amendment to the Constitution; or two-thirds of themselves, if such had been their option, might by an application to Congress have obtained a convention for the same object.

This is the very course which I earnestly recommend in order to obtain an "explanatory amendment" of the Constitution on the subject of slavery. This might originate with Congress or the State legislatures, as may be deemed most advisable to attain the object. The explanatory amendment might be confined to the final settlement of the true construction of the Constitution on three special points:

1. An express recognition of the right of property in slaves in the States where it now exists or may hereafter exist.

2. The duty of protecting this right in all the common Territories throughout their Territorial existence, and until they shall be admitted as States into the Union, with or without slavery, as their constitutions may prescribe.

3. A like recognition of the right of the master to have his slave who has escaped from one State to another restored and "delivered up" to him, and of the validity of the fugitive-slave law enacted for this purpose, together with a declaration that all State laws impairing or defeating this right are violations of

the Constitution, and are consequently null and void. It may be objected that this construction of the Constitution has already been settled by the Supreme Court of the United States, and what more ought to be required? The answer is that a very large proportion of the people of the United States still contest the correctness of this decision, and never will cease from agitation and admit its binding force until clearly established by the people of the several States in their sovereign character. Such an explanatory amendment would, it is believed, forever terminate the existing dissensions, and restore peace and harmony among the States.

It ought not to be doubted that such an appeal to the arbitrament established by the Constitution itself would be received with favor by all the States of the Confederacy. In any event, it ought to be tried in a spirit of conciliation before any of these States shall separate themselves from the Union.

THE BENEFITS OF SLAVERY: DECEMBER 1860

J.D.B. DeBow:
The Non-Slaveholders of the South

In *The Impending Crisis of the South: How to Meet It* (1857) Hinton Rowan Helper of North Carolina had argued that slavery harmed the interests of nonslaveholding whites. Describing slaveholders as "arrant demagogues," Helper wrote that slavery lay "at the root of all the shame, poverty, ignorance, tyranny, and imbecility of the South." *The Impending Crisis* was widely distributed in abridged form in the North, while its circulation was banned in several southern states. James D. B. DeBow, the secessionist editor of the influential Southern monthly *DeBow's Review*, sought to refute Helper's argument in an article that first appeared as part of a series of pro-secession pamphlets published in Charleston, South Carolina, by Robert Gourdin.

NASHVILLE, Dec. 5, 1860.

My dear Sir:—Whilst in Charleston recently, I adverted, in conversation with you, to some considerations affecting the question of slavery in its application to the several classes of population at the South and especially to the non-slaveholding class, who, I maintained, were even more deeply interested than any other in the maintainance of our institutions, and in the success of the movement now inaugurated, for the entire social, industrial and political independence of the South. At your request, I promised to elaborate and commit to writing the points of that conversation, which I now proceed to do, in the hope that I may thus be enabled to give some feeble aid to a cause which is worthy of the Sydneys, Hampdens and Patrick Henrys, of earlier times.

When in charge of the national census office, several years since, I found that it had been stated by an abolition Senator from his seat, that the number of slaveholders at the South did not exceed 150,000. Convinced that it was a gross misrepresentation of the facts, I caused a careful examination of the returns to be made, which fixed the actual number at 347,255, and communicated the information, by note, to Senator Cass, who read it in the Senate. I first called attention to the fact that the number embraced slaveholding families, and that to arrive at the actual number of slaveholders, it would be necessary to multiply by the proportion of persons, which the census showed to a family. When this was done, the number was swelled to about 2,000,000.

Since these results were made public, I have had reason to think, that the separation of the schedules of the slave and the free, was calculated to lead to omissions of the single properties, and that on this account it would be safe to put the number of families at 375,000, and the number of actual slaveholders at about two million and a quarter.

Assuming the published returns, however, to be correct, it will appear that one-half of the population of South Carolina, Mississippi, and Louisiana, excluding the cities, are slaveholders, and that one-third of the population of the entire South are similarly circumstanced. The average number of slaves is nine to each slave-holding family, and one-half of the whole number of such holders are in possession of less than five slaves.

It will thus appear that the slaveholders of the South, so far from constituting numerically an insignificant portion of its people, as has been malignantly alleged, make up an aggregate, greater in relative proportion than the holders of any other species of property whatever, in any part of the world; and that of no other property can it be said, with equal truthfulness, that it is an interest of the whole community. Whilst every other family in the States I have specially referred to, are slaveholders, but one family in every three and a half families in Maine, New Hampshire, Massachusetts and Connecticut, are holders of agricultural land; and, in European States, the proportion is almost indefinitely less. The proportion which the slaveholders of the South, bear to the entire population is greater than that of the owners of land or houses, agricultural stock, State, bank, or other corporation securities anywhere else. No political economist will deny this. Nor is that all. Even in the States which are among the largest slaveholding, South Carolina, Georgia and Tennessee, the land proprietors outnumber nearly two to one, in relative proportion, the owners of the same property in Maine, Massachusetts and Connecticut, and if the average number of slaves held by each family throughout the South be but nine, and if one-half of the whole number of slaveholders own under five slaves, it will be seen how preposterous is the allegation of our enemies, that the slaveholding class is an organized wealthy aristocracy. *The poor men of the South are the holders of one to five slaves, and it would be equally consistent with truth and justice, to say that they represent, in reality, its slaveholding interest.*

The fact being conceded that there is a very large class of persons in the slaveholding States, who have no direct ownership in slaves; it may be well asked, upon what principle a greater antagonism can be presumed between them and their fellow-citizens, than exists among the larger class of non-landholders in the free States and the landed interest there? If a conflict of interest exists in one instance, it does in the other, and if patriotism and public spirit are to be measured upon so low a standard, the social fabric at the North is in far greater danger of dissolution than it is here.

Though I protest against the false and degrading standard, to which Northern orators and statesmen have reduced the measure of patriotism, which is to be expected from a free and enlightened people, and in the name of the non-slaveholders of the South, fling back the insolent charge that they are only bound to their country by its "loaves and fishes," and would be found derelict in honor and principle and public virtue in proportion as they are needy in circumstances; I think it but easy to show that the interest of the poorest non-slaveholder among us, is to make common cause with, and die in the last trenches in defence of, the slave property of his more favored neighbor.

The non-slaveholders of the South may be classed as either such as desire and are incapable of purchasing slaves, or such as have the means to purchase and do not because of the absence of the motive, preferring to hire or employ cheaper white labor. A class conscientiously objecting to the ownership of slave-property, does not exist at the South, for all such scruples have long since been silenced by the profound and unanswerable arguments to which Yankee controversy has driven our statesmen, popular orators and clergy. Upon the sure testimony of God's Holy Book, and upon the principles of universal polity, they have defended and justified the institution. The exceptions which embrace recent importations into Virginia, and into some of the Southern cities from the free States of the North, and some of the crazy, socialistic Germans in Texas, are too unimportant to affect the truth of the proposition.

The non-slaveholders are either urban or rural, including among the former the merchants, traders, mechanics, laborers and other classes in the towns and cities; and among the latter, the tillers of the soil in sections where slave property either could, or could not be profitably employed.

As the *competition of free labor with slave labor* is the gist of the argument used by the opponents of slavery, and as it is upon this that they rely in support of a future social *conflict* in our midst, it is clear that in cases where the competition cannot possibly exist, the argument, whatever weight it might otherwise have, must fall to the ground.

Now, from what can such competition be argued in our cities? Are not all the interests of the merchant and those whom he employs of necessity upon the side of the slaveholder? The products which he buys, the commodities which he sells, the profits which he realizes, the hopes of future fortune which sustain him; all spring from this source, and from no other. The cities, towns and villages of the South, are but so many agencies for converting the products of slave labor into the products of other labor obtained from abroad, and as in every other agency the interest of the agent is, that the principal shall have as much as possible to sell, and be enabled as much as possible to buy. In the absence of every other source of wealth at the South, its mercantile interests are so interwoven with those of slave labor as to be almost identical. What is true of the merchant is true of the clerk, the drayman, or the laborer whom he employs—the mechanic who builds his houses, the lawyer who argues his causes, the physician who heals, the teacher, the preacher, etc., etc. If the poor mechanic could have ever complained of the competition, in the cities, of slave labor with his, that cause of complaint in the enormous increase of value of slave property has failed, since such increase has been exhausting the cities and towns of slave labor, or making it so valuable that he can work in competition with it and receive a rate of remuneration greatly higher than in any of the non-slaveholding towns or cities at the North. In proof of this, it is only necessary to advert to the example of the City of Charleston, which has a larger proportion of slaves than any other at the South, where the first flag of Southern independence was unfurled, and where the entire people, with one voice, rich and poor, merchant, mechanic and laborer, stand nobly together. Another illustration may be found in the city of New York, almost as dependent upon Southern slavery as Charleston itself, which records a majority of nearly thirty thousand votes against the further progress of abolitionism.

As the competition does not exist in the cities it is equally certain that it does not exist in those sections of the South, which are employed upon the cultivation of commodities, in which slave labor could not be used, and that there exists no conflict there except in the before stated cases of Virginia and Texas, and some of the counties of Missouri, Maryland and Kentucky. These exceptions are, however, too unimportant to affect the great question of slavery in fifteen States of the South, and are so kept in check as to be incapable of effecting any mischief even in the communities referred to. It would be the baldest absurdity to suppose that the poor farmers of South Carolina, North Carolina and Tennessee, who grow corn, wheat, bacon and hogs and horses, are brought into any sort of competition with the slaves of these or other States, who, while they consume these commodities, produce but little or none of them.

The competition and conflict, if such exist at the South, between slave labor and free labor, is reduced to the single case of such labor being employed side by side, in the production of the same commodities and could be felt only in the cane, cotton, tobacco and rice fields, where almost the entire agricultural slave labor is exhausted. Now, any one cognizant of the actual facts, will admit that the free labor which is employed upon these crops, disconnected from and in actual independence of the slave-holder, is a very insignificant item in the account, and whether in accord or in conflict would affect nothing the permanency and security of the institution. It is a competition from which the non-slaveholder cheerfully retires when the occasion offers, his physical organization refusing to endure that exposure to tropical suns and fatal miasmas which alone are the condition of profitable culture and any attempt to reverse the laws which God has ordained, is attended with disease and death. Of this the poor white foreign laborer upon our river swamps and in our southern cities, especially in Mobile and New Orleans, and upon the public works of the South, is a daily witness.

Having then followed out, step by step, and seen to what amounts the so much paraded competition and conflict between the non-slaveholding and slaveholding interests of the South; I will proceed to present several general considerations which must be found powerful enough to influence the non-slaveholders, if the claims of patriotism were inadequate, to resist any attempt to overthrow the institutions and industry of the section to which they belong.

1. *The non-slaveholder of the South is assured that the remuneration afforded by his labor, over and above the expense of living, is larger than that which is afforded by the same labor in the free States.* To be convinced of this he has only to compare the value of labor in the Southern cities with those of the North, and to take note annually of the large number of laborers who are represented to be out of employment there, and who migrate to our shores, as well as to other sections. No white laborer in return has been forced to leave our midst or remain without employment. Such as have left, have immigrated from States where slavery was less productive. Those who come among us are enabled soon to retire to their homes with a handsome competency. The statement is nearly as true for the agricultural as for other interests, as the statistics will show.

The following table was recently compiled by Senator Johnson, of Tennessee, from information received in reply to a circular letter sent to the points indicated.

Daily wages in New Orleans, Charleston and Nashville:

	Bricklayers.	Carpenters.	Laborers
	$2½ to 3½	$2¼ to 2¾	$1 to 1½.

Daily wages in Chicago, Pittsburg and Lowell, Mass.:

	Bricklayers.	Carpenters.	Laborers.
	$1½ to $2	$1½ to 1¾	75¢ to $1.

The rates of board weekly for laborers as given in the census of 1850, were in Louisiana $2 70, South Carolina $1 75, Tennessee $1 32, in Illinois $1 49, Pennsylvania $1 72, Massachusetts $2 12. The wages of the agricultural classes as given in Parliamentary reports are in France $20 to $30 per annum with board. In Italy $12 to $20 per annum. In the United States agricultural labor is highest in the Southwest, and lowest in the Northwest, the South and North differing very little, by the official returns.

2. *The non-slaveholders, as a class, are not reduced by the necessity of our condition, as is the case in the free States, to find employment in crowded cities and come into competition in close and sickly workshops and factories, with remorseless and untiring machinery.* They have but to compare their condition in this particular with the mining and manufacturing operatives of the North and Europe, to be thankful that God has reserved them for a better fate. Tender women, aged men, delicate children, toil and labor there from early dawn until after candle light, from one year to another, for a miserable pittance, scarcely above the starvation point and without hope of amelioration. The records of British free labor have long exhibited this and those of our own manufacturing States are rapidly reaching it and would have reached it long ago, but for the excessive bounties which in the way of tariffs have been paid to it, without an equivalent by the slaveholding and non-slaveholding laborer of the South. Let this tariff cease to be paid for a single year and the truth of what is stated will be abundantly shown.

3. *The non-slaveholder is not subjected to that competition with foreign pauper labor, which has degraded the free labor of the North and demoralized it to an extent which perhaps can never be estimated.* From whatever cause, it has happened, whether from climate, the nature of our products or of our labor, the South has been enabled to maintain a more homogeneous population and show a less admixture of races than the North. This the statistics show.

RATIO OF FOREIGN TO NATIVE POPULATION.

Eastern States	12.65	in every 100
Middle States	19.84	" "
Southern States	1.86	" "
South-western States	5.34	" "
North-western States	12.75	" "

Our people partake of the true American character, and are mainly the descendants of those who fought the battles of the Revolution, and who understand and appreciate the nature and inestimable value of the liberty which it brought. Adhering to the simple truths of the Gospel and the faith of their fathers, they have not run hither and thither in search of all the absurd and degrading isms which have sprung up in the rank soil of infidelity. They are not Mormons or Spiritualists, they are not Owenites, Fourierites, Agrarians, Socialists, Free-lovers or Millerites. They are not for breaking down all the forms of society and of religion and re-constructing them; but prefer law, order and existing institutions to the chaos which radicalism involves. The competition between native and foreign labor in the Northern States, has already begotten rivalry and heart-burning, and riots; and lead to the formation of political parties there which have been marked by a degree of hostility and proscription to which the present age has not afforded another parallel. At the South we have known none of this, except in two or three of the larger cities, where the relations of slavery and freedom scarcely exist at all. The foreigners that are among us at the South are of a select class, and from education and example approximate very nearly to the native standard.

4. *The non-slaveholder of the South preserves the status of the white man, and is not regarded as an inferior or a dependant.* He is not told that the Declaration of Independence, when it says that all men are born free and equal, refers to the negro equally with himself. It is not proposed to him that the free negro's vote shall weigh equally with his own at the ballot-box, and that the little children of both colors shall be mixed in the classes and benches of the school-house, and embrace each other filially in its outside sports. It never occurs to him, that a white man could be degraded enough to boast in a public assembly, as was recently done in New York, of having actually slept with a negro. And his patriotic ire would crush with a blow the free negro who would dare, in his presence, as is done in the free States, to characterize the father of the country as a "scoundrel." No white man at the South serves another as a body servant, to clean his boots, wait on his table, and perform the menial services of his household. His blood

revolts against this, and his necessities never drive him to it. He is a companion and an equal. When in the employ of the slaveholder, or in intercourse with him, he enters his hall, and has a seat at his table. If a distinction exists, it is only that which education and refinement may give, and this is so courteously exhibited as scarcely to strike attention. The poor white laborer at the North is at the bottom of the social ladder, whilst his brother here has ascended several steps and can look down upon those who are beneath him, at an infinite remove.

5. *The non-slaveholder knows that as soon as his savings will admit, he can become a slaveholder, and thus relieve his wife from the necessities of the kitchen and the laundry, and his children from the labors of the field.* This, with ordinary frugality, can, in general, be accomplished in a few years, and is a process continually going on. Perhaps twice the number of poor men at the South own a slave to what owned a slave ten years ago. The universal disposition is to purchase. It is the first use for savings, and the negro purchased is the last possession to be parted with. If a woman, her children become heir-looms and make the nucleus of an estate. It is within my knowledge, that a plantation of fifty or sixty persons has been established, from the descendants of a single female, in the course of the lifetime of the original purchaser.

6. *The large slaveholders and proprietors of the South begin life in great part as non-slaveholders.* It is the nature of property to change hands. Luxury, liberality, extravagance, depreciated land, low prices, debt, distribution among children, are continually breaking up estates. All over the new States of the Southwest enormous estates are in the hands of men who began life as overseers or city clerks, traders or merchants. Often the overseer marries the widow. Cheap lands, abundant harvests, high prices, give the poor man soon a negro. His ten bales of cotton bring him another, a second crop increases his purchases, and so he goes on opening land and adding labor until in a few years his draft for $20,000 upon his merchant becomes a very marketable commodity.

7. *But should such fortune not be in reserve for the non-slaveholder, he will understand that by honesty and industry it may be realized to his children.* More than one generation of poverty in a family is scarcely to be expected at the South, and

is against the general experience. It is more unusual here for poverty than wealth to be preserved through several generations in the same family.

8. *The sons of the non-slaveholder are and have always been among the leading and ruling spirits of the South; in industry as well as in politics.* Every man's experience in his own neighborhood will evince this. He has but to task his memory. In this class are the McDuffies, Langdon Cheves, Andrew Jacksons, Henry Clays, and Rusks, of the past; the Hammonds, Yanceys, Orrs, Memmingers, Benjamins, Stephens, Soules, Browns of Mississippi, Simms, Porters, Magraths, Aikens, Maunsel Whites, and an innumerable host of the present; and what is to be noted, these men have not been made demagogues for that reason, as in other quarters, but are among the most conservative among us. Nowhere else in the world have intelligence and virtue disconnected from ancestral estates, the same opportunities for advancement, and nowhere else is their triumph more speedy and signal.

9. *Without the institution of slavery, the great staple products of the South would cease to be grown, and the immense annual results, which are distributed among every class of the community, and which give life to every branch of industry, would cease.* The world furnishes no instances of these products being grown upon a large scale by free labor. The English now acknowledge their failure in the East Indies. Brazil, whose slave population nearly equals our own, is the only South American State which has prospered. Cuba, by her slave labor, showers wealth upon old Spain, whilst the British West India Colonies have now ceased to be a source of revenue, and from opulence have been, by emancipation, reduced to beggary. St. Domingo shared the same fate, and the poor whites have been massacred equally with the rich.

EXPORTS.

	1789.	1860.
HAYTI, ...	$27,829,000	$5 to 6,000,000

Sugar is no longer exported, and the quantity of Coffee scarcely exceeds one-third, and of Cotton one-tenth, of the exports of 1789. This I give upon Northern authority.

JAMAICA.	1805.	1857.
Sugar	150,352 hhds.	30,459 hhds.
Rum	93,950 "	15,991 "
Coffee	24,137,393 lbs.	7,095,623 lbs.

The value of the present slave production of the South is thus given:

United States Exports for 1859.

Of Southern Origin—	1859.
Cotton	$161,434,923
Tobacco	21,074,038
Rice	2,207,048
Naval Stores	3,694,474
Sugar	196,735
Molasses	75,699
Hemp	9,227
Total	188,693,496
Other from South	8,108,632
Cotton Manufactures	4,989,733
Total from South	198,389,351
From the North	78,217,202
Total Merchandise	278,392,080
Specie	57,502,305

To the Southern credit, however, must be given:

60 per cent. of the cotton manufactured, being, for raw materials	$3,669,106
Breadstuffs (the North having received from the South a value as large in these as the whole foreign export)	40,047,000
	43,716,106
Add	198,389,351
Southern	242,105,457
Northern contributions	34,501,008

10. *If emancipation be brought about as will undoubtedly be the case, unless the encroachments of the fanatical majorities of the North are resisted now the slaveholders, in the main, will escape the degrading equality which must result, by emigration, for which they would have the means, by disposing of their personal*

chattels: whilst the non-slaveholders, without these resources, would be compelled to remain and endure the degradation. This is a startling consideration. In Northern communities, where the free negro is one in a hundred of the total population, he is recognized and acknowledged often as a pest, and in many cases even his presence is prohibited by law. What would be the case in many of our States, where every other inhabitant is a negro, or in many of our communities, as for example the parishes around and about Charleston, and in the vicinity of New Orleans where there are from twenty to one hundred negroes to each white inhabitant? Low as would this class of people sink by emancipation in idleness, superstition and vice, the white man compelled to live among them, would by the power exerted over him, sink even lower, unless as is to be supposed he would prefer to suffer death instead.

In conclusion, my dear sir, I must apologize to the non-slaveholders of the South, of which class, I was myself until very recently a member, for having deigned to notice at all the infamous libels which the common enemies of the South have circulated against them, and which our every-day experience refutes; but the occasion seemed a fitting one to place them truly and rightly before the world. This I have endeavored faithfully to do. They fully understand the momentous questions which now agitate the land in all their relations. They perceive the inevitable drift of Northern aggression, and know that if necessity impel to it, as I verily believe it does at this moment, the establishment of a Southern confederation will be a sure refuge from the storm. *In such a confederation our rights and possessions would be secure, and the wealth being retained at home, to build up our towns and cities, to extend our railroads, and increase our shipping, which now goes in tariffs or other involuntary or voluntary tributes,* to other sections; opu-*

---

*The annual drain in profits which is going on from the South to the North is thus set down by Mr. Kettell, of New York:

Bounties to fisheries, per annum	$1,500,000
Customs, per annum, disbursed at the North	40,000,000
Profits of manufacturers	30,000,000
Profits of importers	16,000,000
Profits of shipping, imports and exports	40,000,000
Profits of travellers	60,000,000

lence would be diffused throughout all classes, and we should become the freest, the happiest and the most prosperous and powerful nation upon earth.

Your obedient servant,

J. D. B. DeBOW.

ROBERT N. GOURDIN, Esq., Charleston, S. C.

Profits of teachers and others at the South, sent North 5,000,000
Profits of agents, brokers, commissions, etc. 10,000,000
Profits of capital drawn from the South 30,000,000

Total from these sources $231,500,000

This, from the beginning of the Government, making all proper deduction from year to year, has given to the North over $2,500,000,000 of Southern wealth. Are her accumulations, then, surprising, and can one be surprised if accumulation should appear to be less in the South!

ADVOCATING SECESSION:
GEORGIA, DECEMBER 1860

Joseph E. Brown to Alfred H. Colquitt and Others

December 7, 1860

Joseph E. Brown had defeated Benjamin Hill in 1857 to become governor of Georgia. In this public letter in support of secession, Brown argued that the poor whites of the Georgia mountains had a vital interest in preserving slavery. On January 19, 1861, the state convention voted, 164–133, not to delay action until after Lincoln took office, and then approved, 208–89, an ordinance of secession.

Gentlemen: Your letter requesting me to give to the people of Georgia my views upon the issues involved in the election of delegates to the State Convention, which is to assemble in January next, has been received.

Such is the extent of my official labors at present, that I can devote but little time to the preparation of a reply. If, however, any importance is attached to my opinions, in the present perilous times, I cheerfully give them to my fellow citizens. I propose to discuss briefly three propositions.

1st. Is the election of Mr. Lincoln to the Presidency, sufficient cause to justify Georgia and the other Southern States in seceeding from the Union?

2d. What will be the results to the institution of slavery which will follow submission to the inauguration and administration of Mr. Lincoln as the President of one section of the Union?

3d. What will be the effect which the abolition of Slavery will have upon the interests and the social position of the large class of nonslaveholders and poor white laborers, who are in the South?

First, is the election of Mr. Lincoln sufficient cause to justify the secession of the Southern States from the Union? In my opinion the election of Mr. Lincoln, viewed only in the light of the triumph of a successful candidate, is not sufficient cause for a dissolution of the Union. This, however, is a very contracted and narrow view of the question. Mr. Lincoln is a mere mote in the great political atmosphere of the country, which, as it floats, only shows the direction in which the wind blows. He is the mere representative of a fanatical abolition sentiment—the mere instrument of a great triumphant political party, the principles of which are deadly hostile to the institution of Slavery, and openly at war with the fundamental doctrines of the Constitution of the United States. The rights of the South, and the institution of slavery, are not endangered by the triumph of Mr. Lincoln, as a man; but they are in imminent danger from the triumph of the powerful party which he represents, and of the fanatical abolition sentiment which brought him into power, as the candidate of the Northern section of the Union, over the united opposition of the Southern section against him. The party embracing that sentiment, has constantly denied, and still denies, our equality in the Union, and our right to hold our slaves as property; and avows its purpose to take from us our property, so soon as it has the power. Its ability to elect Mr. Lincoln as its candidate, shows it now has the power to control the Executive branch of the Government. As the President, with the advice and consent of the Senate, appoints the Judges of the Supreme Court of the United States, when vacancies occur, its control of the Executive power will, in a few years, give it the control of the Judicial Department; while the constant increase of abolition sentiment, in the Northern States, now largely in the majority in Congress, together with the admission of other free States, will very soon, give it the power in the Legislative Department. The whole Government will then be in the hands of our enemies. The election of Mr. Lincoln is the first great step in this programme. It is the triumph of the Northern over the Southern section of the Union: of Northern fanaticism over Southern equality and Southern rights. While, therefore, the election of Mr. Lincoln, as a man, is no sufficient cause to justify secession, the triumph of the Northern section of the Union over the Southern section, upon a platform of avowed hostility to our rights, does, in my opinion, afford ample cause to justify the South in withdrawing from a confederacy where her equality, her honor, and the rights of her people, can no longer be protected.

Second, What will be the result to the institution of slavery, which will follow submission to the inauguration and administration of Mr. Lincoln as the President of one section of the Union? My candid opinion is, that it will be the total abolition of slavery, and the utter ruin of the South, in less than twenty-five years. If we submit now, we satisfy the Northern people that, come what may, we will never resist. If Mr. Lincoln places among us his Judges, District Attorneys, Marshals, Post Masters, Custom House officers, etc., etc., by the end of his administration, with the control of these men, and the distribution of public patronage, he will have succeeded in dividing us to an extent that will destroy all our moral powers, and prepare us to tolerate the running of a Republican ticket, in most of the States of the South, in 1864. If this ticket only secured five or ten thousand votes in each of the Southern States, it would be as large as the abolition party was in the North a few years since. It would hold a balance of power between any two political parties into which the people of the South may hereafter be divided. This would soon give it the control of our elections. We would then be powerless, and the abolitionists would press forward, with a steady step, to the accomplishment of their object. They would refuse to admit any other slave States to the Union. They would abolish slavery in the District of Columbia, and at the Forts, Arsenals and Dock Yards, within the Southern States, which belong to the United States. They would then abolish the internal slave trade between the States, and prohibit a slave owner in Georgia from carrying his slaves into Alabama or South Carolina, and there selling them. These steps would be taken one at a time, cautiously, and our people would submit. Finally, when we were sufficiently humiliated, and sufficiently in their power, they would abolish slavery in the States. It will not be many years before enough of free States may be formed out of the present territories of the United States, and admitted into the Union, to give them sufficient strength to change the Constitution, and remove all Constitutional barriers which now deny to Congress this power. I do not doubt, therefore, that submission to the administration of Mr. Lincoln will result in the final abolition of slavery. If we fail to resist now, we will never again have the strength to resist.

3rd, What effect will the abolition of slavery have upon the interest and social position of the large class of nonslaveholders and poor white laborers in the South? Here would be the scene of the most misery and ruin. Probably no one is so unjust as to say that it would be right to take from the slaveholder his property without paying him for it. What would it cost to do this? There are, in round numbers, 4,500,000 slaves in the Southern States. They are worth, at a low estimate, 500 dollars each. All will agree to this. Multiply the 4,500,000 by 500 and you have twenty-two hundred and fifty millions of dollars, which these slaves are worth. No one would agree that it is right to rob the Southern slaveholders of this vast sum of money without compensation. The Northern States would not agree to pay their proportion of the money, and the people of the South must be taxed to raise the money. If Georgia were only an average Southern State, she would have to pay one fifteenth part of this sum, which would be $150,000,000. Georgia is much more than an average State, and she must therefore pay a larger sum. Her people now pay less than half a million of dollars a year, of tax. Suppose we had ten years within which to raise the $150,000,000, we should then have to raise, in addition to our present tax, $15,000,000 per annum, or over thirty times as much as we now pay.—The poor man, who now pays one dollar, would then have to pay $30.00. But suppose the Northern States agreed to help pay for these slaves, (who believes they would do it?) the share of Georgia would then be about one thirtieth of the twenty-two hundred and fifty millions of dollars, or over seventy-five millions; which, if raised in ten years, would be over fifteen times as much as our present tax. In this calculation, I have counted the slave-holder as taxed upon his own slaves to raise money to pay him for them. This would be great injustice to him. If the sum is to be raised by the tax upon others, the nonslaveholders and poor white men of the South, would have to pay nearly the whole of this enormous sum, out of their labor. This would load them and their children with grievous indebtedness and heavy taxes for a long time to come. But suppose we were rid of this difficulty, what shall be done with these 4,500,000 negroes, when set free? Some of the Northern States have already passed laws prohibiting free negroes from coming into their limits. They will help to harbor our runaway slaves, but will not receive among them our free negroes. They would not permit them to go there and live with them. Then what? One may say, send them to Africa. To such a proposition I might reply, send them to the moon. You may say that is not practicable. It is quite as much so as it is for us to pay for and send this vast number of negroes to Africa, with the means at our command.

No one would be so inhuman as to propose to send them to Africa and set them down upon a wild, naked sea coast, without provisions for at least one year. What will it cost to take them from their present home to Africa, and carry provisions there to keep them a single year? (if left with only one year's supply, many of them would starve to death.) It cannot be done for $250.00 each. At that sum it would amount to eleven hundred and twenty-five millions of dollars. Where will we get the money? Our people must be taxed to raise it. This would be half as large a sum as the above estimate of the value of the negroes. If the Southern States had it to raise Georgia's part would be over $75,000,000, which added to the part of the amount to be paid to owners for the negroes, would amount to $225,000,000; which must be raised by taxing the people, or loading them with a debt which would virtually enslave our whole people for generations to come. It must be remembered that we own no territory in Africa large enough to colonize 4,500,000 people. This too must be bought at a very heavy cost. The Northern people would not consent to be taxed to raise these enormous sums, either to pay for the negroes, or to pay for sending them to Africa, or to pay for land upon which to colonize them; as they do not wish to do either. They wish to take them from their owners without pay, and set them free, and let them remain among us. Many people at the North, say that negroes are our fit associates; that they shall be set free, and remain among us—intermarrying with our children, and enjoying equal privileges with us. But suppose we were over the difficulty of paying the owners for the negroes, and they were taken from their masters without pay, and set free and left among us, (which is the ultimate aim of the Black Republicans,) what would be the effect upon our society? We should still have rich men and poor men. But few of our slave owners have invested all they have in negroes. Take their negroes from them unjustly, and they will many of them still be more wealthy than their neighbors. If all were left for a time with equal wealth, every person who has noticed man and society knows that, in a few years, some would grow rich and others poor. This has always been the case, and always will be. If we had no negroes, the rich would still be in a better condition to take care of themselves than the poor. They would still seek the most profitable and secure investment for their capital. What would this be? The answer suggests itself to every mind: it would be land. The wealthy would soon buy all the lands of the South worth cultivating. Then what? The poor would all become tenants, as they are in England, the New England States, and all old countries where slavery does not exist. But I must not lose sight of the 4,500,000 free negroes to be turned loose among us. They, too, must become tenants, with the poor white people for they would not be able to own lands. A large proportion of them would spend their time in idleness and vice, and would live by stealing, robbing and plundering. Probably one fourth of the whole number would have to be maintained in our penitentiary, prisons, and poor houses. Our people, poor and rich, must be taxed to pay the expense of imprisoning and punishing them for crime. This would be a very heavy burden. But suppose three fourths of the whole number would work for a living. They would have to begin the world miserably poor, with neither land, money nor provisions. They must therefore become day laborers for their old masters, or such others as would employ them. In this capacity they would at once come in competition with the poor white laborers. Men of capital would see this, and fix the price of labor accordingly. The negro has only been accustomed to receive his victuals and clothes for his labor. Few of them, if free, would expect anything more. It would therefore be easy to employ them at a sum sufficient to supply only the actual necessaries of life. The poor white man would then go to the wealthy land-owner and say, I wish employment. Hire me to work. I have a wife and children who must have bread. The land-owner would offer probably twenty cents per day. The laborer would say, I cannot support my family on that sum. The landlord replies, That is not my business. I am sorry for you, but I must look to my own interest. The black man who lives on my land has as strong an arm, and as heavy muscles as you have, and can do as much labor. He works for me at that rate, you must work for the same price, or I cannot employ you. The negro comes into competition with the white man and fixes the price of his labor, and he must take it or get no employment.

Again, the poor white man wishes to rent land from the wealthy landlord—this landlord asks him half the crop of common upland or two thirds or even three fourths, for the best bottom land. The poor man says this seems very hard. I cannot make a decent support for my family at these rates. The landlord replies, here are negroes all around me anxious to take it at these rates; I can let you have it for no less. The negro therefore, comes into competition with the poor white man, when he seeks to rent land on which to make his bread, or a shelter to protect his wife and his little ones, from the cold and from the rain; and when he seeks employment as a day laborer. In every such case if the negro will do the work the cheapest, he must be preferred. It is sickening to contemplate the miseries of our poor white people under these circumstances. They now get higher wages for their labor than the poor of any other country on the globe. Most of them are land owners, and they are now respected. They are in no sense placed down upon a level with the negro. They are a superior race, and they feel and know it. Abolish slavery, and you make the negroes their equals, legally and socially (not naturally, for no human law can change God's law) and you very soon make them all tenants, and reduce their wages for daily labor to the smallest pittance that will sustain life. Then the negro and the white man, and their families, must labor in the field together as equals. Their children must go to the same poor school together, if they are educated at all. They must go to church as equals; enter the Courts of justice as equals, sue and be sued as equals, sit on juries together as equals, have the right to give evidence in Court as equals, stand side by side in our military corps as equals, enter each others' houses in social intercourse as equals; and very soon their children must marry together as equals. May our kind Heavenly Father avert the evil, and deliver the poor from such a fate. So soon as the slaves were at liberty, thousands of them would leave the cotton and rice fields in the lower parts of our State, and make their way to the healthier climate in the mountain region. We should have them plundering and stealing, robbing and killing, in all the lovely vallies of the mountains. This I can never consent to see. The mountains contain the place of my nativity, the home of my manhood, and the theatre of most of the acts of my life; and I can never forget the condition and interest of the people who reside there. It is true, the people there are generally poor; but they are brave, honest, patriotic, and pure hearted. Some who do not know them, have doubted their capacity to understand these questions, and their patriotism and valor to defend their rights when invaded. I know them well, and I know that no greater mistake could be made. They love the Union of our fathers, and would never consent to dissolve it so long as the constitution is not violated, and so long as it protects their rights; but they love liberty and justice more; and they will never consent to submit to abolition rule, and permit the evils to come upon them, which must result from a continuance in the Union when the government is in the hands of our enemies, who will use all its power for our destruction. When it becomes necessary to defend our rights against so foul a domination, I would call upon the mountain boys as well as the people of the lowlands, and they would come down like an avalanche and swarm around the flag of Georgia with a resolution that would strike terror into the ranks of the abolition cohorts of the North. Wealth is timid, and wealthy men may cry for peace, and submit to wrong for fear they may lose their money: but the poor, honest laborers of Georgia, can never consent to see slavery abolished, and submit to all the taxation, vassalage, low wages and downright degradation, which must follow. They will never take the negro's place; God forbid.

I know that some contemptible demagogues have attempted to deceive them by appealing to their prejudices, and asking them what interest they have in maintaining the rights of the wealthy slaveholder. They cannot be deceived in this way. They know that the government of our State protects their lives, their families and their property; and that every dollar the wealthy slaveholder has, may be taken by the government of the State, if need be, to protect the rights and liberties of all. One man, in a large neighborhood, has a mill. Not one in fifty has a mill. What would be thought of the public speaker who would appeal to the fifty, and ask them what interest they have in defending their neighbor's mill, if an abolition mob were trying to burn it down? Another has a store. Not one in fifty has a store. Who would say the fifty should not help the one if an invader is about to burn his store? Another has a blacksmith shop. Not one in fifty has a blacksmith shop. Shall the shop be destroyed by the common enemy and no one protect the owner because no one near, has the same peculiar kind of property? It may be that I have no horse, and you have a horse; or that I have a cow, and you have no cow. In such case, if our rights of property are assailed by a common enemy, shall we not help each other? Or I have a wife and children, and a house, and another has neither wife and children, nor house. Will he, therefore, stand by and see my house burned and my wife and children butchered, because he has none? The slaveholder has honestly invested the money, which it has cost him years of toil to make, in slaves, which are guaranteed to him by the laws of our State. The common enemy of the South seeks to take the property from him. Shall all who do not own slaves, stand by and permit it to be done? If so, they have no right to call on the slaveholder, by taxation, or otherwise, to help protect their property or their liberties. Such a doctrine is monstrous; and he who would advance it, deserves to be rode upon the sharpest edge of one of Lincoln's rails. The doctrine strikes at the very foundation of society, and if carried out, would destroy all property, and all protection to life, liberty and happiness.

The present is a critical time with the people of the South. We all, poor and rich, have a common interest, a common destiny. It is no time to be wrangling about old party strifes. Our common enemy, the Black Republican party, is united and triumphant. Let us all unite. If we cannot all see alike, let us have charity enough towards each other, to admit that all are equally patriotic in their efforts to advance the common cause. My honest convictions are, that we can never again live in peace with the Northern abolitionists, unless we can have new constitutional guarantees, which will secure our equal rights in the Territories, and effectually stop the discussion of the slavery question in Congress, and secure the rendition of fugitive slaves. These guarantees I do not believe the people of the Northern States will ever give, while we remain together in the Union. Their opinion is, that we will always compromise away a portion of our rights, and submit, for the sake of peace. If the Cotton States would all secede from the Union before the inauguration of Mr. Lincoln, this might possibly lead to a Convention of all the States, which might terminate in a reunion with the new constitutional guarantees necessary for our protection. If the Northern States then failed to give these guarantees, there can be no doubt that Virginia, Maryland, North Carolina, Delaware, Kentucky, Missouri, and Tennessee would unite with the Cotton States in a Southern Confederacy and we should form a Republic in which, under the old Constitution of our fathers, our people could live in security and peace. I know that many of our people honestly believe that it would be best to wait for these border slave States to go out with us. If we wait for this, we shall *submit*; for some of those States will not consent to go, and the North will then consent to give us no new guarantees of peace. They will say that we have again blustered and submitted, as we always do.

In my late message to the General Assembly, I recommended the enactment of retaliatory laws against these Northern States which have nullified the fugitive slave law. I think those laws should still be enacted. They would have been equally applicable had either of the other candidates for the Presidency been successful. Now that Mr. Lincoln is successful, they should be upon our statute book, so long as we remain in the Union. There can no longer be a reasonable doubt, that the gallant State of South Carolina will secede from the Union very soon after her Convention meets. The States of Florida, Alabama and Mississippi will follow in quick succession. While our Convention is in session, we shall probably be surrounded on every side but one, with free and independent States out of the Union. With these States, we have a common interest. Thus surrounded, shall Georgia remain under abolition rule, and refuse to unite with her sister States around her? I trust not. If so, we forfeit all claim to our proud title of

Empire State of the South. Why remain? Will the Northern States repeal their personal liberty bills and do us justice? No. The Legislature of one of the nullifying States (Vermont) has just adjourned. A bill has been introduced for the repeal of those unconstitutional and offensive laws. The question has been discussed, and it is reported that the House in which the bill was introduced, has refused to pass the repealing law, by a vote of over two-thirds. This action has been had with full knowledge of the state of things now existing in the South, and shows a deliberate determination not to do us justice. Is further notice to Vermont necessary? I am aware that the fears of some have been appealed to, and they have been told that if we secede, the United States Government will attempt to coerce us back into the Union, and we shall have war.

The President in his late message, while he denies our Constitutional right to secede, admits that the General Government has no Constitutional right to coerce us back into the Union, if we do secede. Secession is not likely, therefore, to involve us in war. Submission may. When the other States around us secede, if we remain in the Union, thousands of our people will leave our State, and it is feared that the standard of revolution and rebellion may be raised among us, which would at once involve us in civil war among ourselves. If we must fight, in the name of all that is sacred, let us fight our common enemy, and not fight each other.

In my opinion, our people should send their wisest and best men to the Convention, without regard to party distinctions, and should intrust much to their good judgment and sound discretion, when they meet. They may, then, have new lights before them, which we do not now have; and they should be left free to act upon them.

My fervent prayer is, that the God of our fathers may inspire the Convention with wisdom, and so direct their counsels as to protect our rights and preserve our liberties to the latest generation.

>I am, gentlemen, with great respect,
> Your fellow citizen,
>   JOSEPH E. BROWN

RESTATING POSITIONS ON SLAVERY:
DECEMBER 1860

Abraham Lincoln to John A. Gilmer

Abraham Lincoln remained in Springfield after the election, where he met with Republican leaders, considered cabinet appointments, and was beset by office-seekers. John A. Gilmer, an American (Know Nothing) congressman from North Carolina, wrote to Lincoln from Washington on December 10. Warning that the "present perilous condition of the Country" threatened the "destruction of the Union," Gilmer asked the president-elect to publicly answer a series of questions regarding his positions on slavery in the hope that a "clear and definite exposition of your views" might "go far to quiet, if not satisfy all reasonable minds." Lincoln replied on December 15.

Strictly confidential.
Hon. John A. Gilmer: Springfield, Ill. Dec 15, 1860.
My dear Sir—Yours of the 10th is received. I am greatly disinclined to write a letter on the subject embraced in yours; and I would not do so, even privately as I do, were it not that I fear you might misconstrue my silence. Is it desired that I shall shift the ground upon which I have been elected? I can not do it. You need only to acquaint yourself with that ground, and press it on the attention of the South. It is all in print and easy of access. May I be pardoned if I ask whether even you have ever attempted to procure the reading of the Republican platform, or my speeches, by the Southern people? If not, what reason have I to expect that any additional production of mine would meet a better fate? It would make me appear as if I repented for the crime of having been elected, and was anxious to apologize and beg forgiveness. To so represent me, would be the principal use made of any letter I might now thrust upon the public. My old record cannot be so used; and that is precisely the reason that some new declaration is so much sought.

Now, my dear sir, be assured, that I am not questioning *your* candor; I am only pointing out, that, while a new letter would hurt the cause which I think a just one, you can quite as well effect every patriotic object with the old record. Carefully read pages 18, 19, 74, 75, 88, 89, & 267 of the volume of Joint Debates between Senator Douglas and myself, with the Republican Platform adopted at Chicago, and all your questions will be substantially answered. I have no thought of recommending the abolition of slavery in the District of Columbia, nor the slave trade among the slave states, even on the conditions indicated; and if I were to make such recommendation, it is quite clear Congress would not follow it.

As to employing slaves in Arsenals and Dockyards, it is a thing I never thought of in my life, to my recollection, till I saw your letter; and I may say of it, precisely as I have said of the two points above.

As to the use of patronage in the slave states, where there are few or no Republicans, I do not expect to inquire for the politics of the appointee, or whether he does or not own slaves. I intend in that matter to accommodate the people in the several localities, if they themselves will allow me to accommodate them. In one word, I never have been, am not now, and probably never shall be, in a mood of harassing the people, either North or South.

On the territorial question, I am inflexible, as you see my position in the book. On that, there is a difference between you and us; and it is the only substantial difference. You think slavery is right and ought to be extended; we think it is wrong and ought to be restricted. For this, neither has any just occasion to be angry with the other.

As to the state laws, mentioned in your sixth question, I really know very little of them. I never have read one. If any of them are in conflict with the fugitive slave clause, or any other part of the constitution, I certainly should be glad of their repeal; but I could hardly be justified, as a citizen of Illinois, or as President of the United States, to recommend the repeal of a statute of Vermont, or South Carolina.

With the assurance of my highest regards I subscribe myself Your obt. Servt.,   A. LINCOLN

P.S. The documents referred to, I suppose you will readily find in Washington.   A. L.

REJECTING COERCION: DECEMBER 1860

New-York Daily Tribune: The Right of Secession

December 17, 1860

Thurlow Weed, the editor of the *Albany Evening Journal* and a powerful figure in the New York Republican party, had criticized Horace Greeley's stance on secession. Greeley responded to his journalistic and political rival in an editorial.

The Albany Evening Journal courteously controverts our views on the subject of Secession. Here is the gist of its argument:

"Seven or eight States" *have* "pretty unanimously made up their minds" to leave the Union. Mr. Buchanan, in reply, says that "ours is a Government of popular opinion," and hence, if States rebel, there is no power residing either with the Executive or in Congress, to resist or punish. Why, then, is not this the end of the controversy? Those "seven or eight States" are going out. The Government remonstrates, but acquiesces. And THE TRIBUNE regards it "*unwise to undertake to resist such Secession by Federal force.*"

If an individual, or "a single State," commits Treason, the same act in two or more individuals, or two or more States, is alike treasonable. And how is Treason against the Federal Government to be resisted, except by "Federal force?"

Precisely the same question was involved in the South Carolina Secession of 1833. But neither President Jackson, nor Congress, nor the People, took this view of it. The President issued a Proclamation declaring Secession Treason. Congress passed a Force Law; and South Carolina, instead of "madly shooting from its sphere," returned, if not to her senses, back into line.

—Does *The Journal* mean to say that if *all* the States and their People should become tired of the Union, it would be treason on their part to seek its dissolution?

—We have repeatedly asked those who dissent from our view of this matter to tell us frankly whether they do or do not assent to Mr. Jefferson's statement in the Declaration of Independence that governments "derive their *just* powers from *the consent of the governed*; and that, whenever any form of government becomes destructive of these ends, *it is the right of the people to alter or abolish it*, and to institute a new government," &c., &c. We *do* heartily accept this doctrine, believing it intrinsically sound, beneficent, and one that, universally accepted, is calculated to prevent the shedding of seas of human blood. And, if it justified the secession from the British Empire of Three Millions of colonists in 1776, we do not see why it would not justify the secession of Five Millions of Southrons from the Federal Union in 1861. If we are mistaken on this point, why does not some one attempt to show wherein and why? For our own part, while we deny the right of slaveholders to hold slaves against the will of the latter, we cannot see how Twenty Millions of people can rightfully hold Ten or even Five in a detested union with them, by military force.

Of course, we understand that the principle of Jefferson, like any other broad generalization, may be pushed to extreme and baleful consequences. We can see why Governor's Island should not be at liberty to secede from the State and Nation and allow herself to be covered with French or British batteries commanding and threatening our City. There is hardly a great principle which may not be thus "run into the ground." But if seven or eight contiguous States shall present themselves authentically at Washington, saying, "We hate the Federal Union; we have withdrawn from it; we give you the choice between acquiescing in our secession and arranging amicably all incidental questions on the one hand, and attempting to subdue us on the other"—we could not stand up for coercion, for subjugation, for we do not think it would be just. We hold the right of Self-Government sacred, even when invoked in behalf of those who deny it to others. So much for the question of Principle.

Now as to the matter of Policy:

South Carolina will certainly secede. Several other Cotton States will probably follow her example. The Border States are evidently reluctant to do likewise. South Carolina has grossly insulted them by her dictatorial, reckless course. What she expects and desires is a clash of arms with the Federal Government, which will at once commend her to the sympathy and coöperation of every Slave State, and to the sympathy (at least) of the Pro-Slavery minority in the Free States. It is not difficult to see that this would speedily work a political revolution, which would restore to Slavery all, and more than all, it has lost by the canvass of 1860. We want to obviate this. We would expose the seceders to odium as disunionists, not commend them to pity as the gallant though mistaken upholders of the rights of their section in an unequal military conflict.

We fully realize that the dilemma of the incoming Administration will be a critical one. It must endeavor to uphold and enforce the laws, as well against rebellious slaveholders as fugitive slaves. The new President must fulfill the obligations assumed in his inauguration oath, no matter how shamefully his predecessor may have defied them. We fear that Southern madness may precipitate a bloody collision that all must deplore. But if ever "seven or eight States" send agents to Washington to say "We want to get out of the Union," we shall feel constrained by our devotion to Human Liberty to say, Let them go! And we do not see how we could take the other side without coming in direct conflict with those Rights of Man which we hold paramount to all political arrangements, however convenient and advantageous.

"I STAND BY THE UNION": DECEMBER 1860

Benjamin F. Wade: Remarks in the U.S. Senate

December 17, 1860

Benjamin Wade of Ohio entered the Senate as a Whig in 1851 and was subsequently elected as a Republican. He made these remarks during a debate over whether the Senate should appoint a special committee to address the sectional crisis. After engaging in an extended exchange with several Southern senators over the enforcement of the fugitive slave law, Wade spoke in defense of the platform adopted by the 1860 Republican convention.

BUT, SIR, I wish to inquire whether the southern people are injured by, or have any just right to complain of, that platform of principles that we put out, and on which we have elected a President and Vice President. I have no concealments to make, and I shall talk to you, my southern friends, precisely as I would talk upon the stump on the subject. I tell you that in that platform we did lay it down that we would, if we had the power, prohibit slavery from another inch of free territory under this Government. I stand on that position to-day. I have argued it probably to half a million people. They stand there, and have commissioned and enjoined me to stand there forever; and, so help me God, I will. I say to you frankly, gentlemen, that while we hold this doctrine, there is no Republican, there is no convention of Republicans, there is no paper that speaks for them, there is no orator that sets forth their doctrines, who ever pretends that they have any right in your States to interfere with your peculiar institution; but, on the other hand, our authoritative platform repudiates the idea that we have any right or any intention ever to invade your peculiar institution in your own States.

Now, what do you complain of? You are going to break up

this Government; you are going to involve us in war and blood, from a mere suspicion that we shall justify that which we stand everywhere pledged not to do. Would you be justified in the eyes of the civilized world in taking so monstrous a position, and predicating it on a bare, groundless suspicion? We do not love slavery. Did you not know that before today? before this session commenced? Have you not a perfect confidence that the civilized world are against you on this subject of loving slavery or believing that it is the best institution in the world? Why, sir, everything remains precisely as it was a year ago. No great catastrophe has occurred. There is no recent occasion to accuse us of anything. But all at once, when we meet here, a kind of gloom pervades the whole community and the Senate Chamber. Gentlemen rise and tell us that they are on the eve of breaking up this Government, that seven or eight States are going to break off their connection with the Government, retire from the Union, and set up a hostile Government of their own, and they look imploringly over to us, and say to us "you can prevent it; we can do nothing to prevent; but it all lies with you." Well, sir, what can we do to prevent it? You have not even condescended to tell us what you want; but I think I see through the speeches that I have heard from gentlemen on the other side. If we would give up the verdict of the people, and take your platform, I do not know but you would be satisfied with it. I think the Senator from Texas rather intimated, and I think the Senator from Georgia more than intimated, that if we would take what is exactly the Charleston platform on which Mr. Breckinridge was placed, and give up that on which we won our victory, you would grumblingly and hesitatingly be satisfied.

Mr. IVERSON. I would prefer that the Senator would look over my remarks before quoting them so confidently. I made no such statement as that. I did not say that I would be satisfied with any such thing. I would not be satisfied with it.

Mr. WADE. I did not say that the Senator said so; but by construction I gathered that from his speech. I do not know that I was right in it.

Mr. IVERSON. The Senator is altogether wrong in his construction.

Mr. WADE. Well, sir, I have now found what the Senator

said on the other point to which he called my attention a little while ago. Here it is:

"Nor do we suppose that there will be any overt acts upon the part of Mr. Lincoln. For one, I do not dread these overt acts. I do not propose to wait for them. Why, sir, the power of this Federal Government could be so exercised against the institution of slavery in the southern States, as that, without an overt act, the institution would not last ten years. We know that, sir; and seeing the storm which is approaching, although it may be seemingly in the distance, we are determined to seek our own safety and security before it shall burst upon us and overwhelm us with its fury, when we are not in a situation to defend ourselves."

That is what the Senator said.
Mr. IVERSON. Yes; that is what I said.
Mr. WADE. Well, then, you did not expect that Mr. Lincoln would commit any overt act against the Constitution—that was not it—you were not going to wait for that, but were going to proceed on your supposition that probably he might; and that is the sense of what I said before.

Well, Mr. President, I have disavowed all intention on the part of the Republican party to harm a hair of your heads anywhere. We hold to no doctrine that can possibly work you an inconvenience. We have been faithful to the execution of all the laws in which you have any interest, as stands confessed on this floor by your own party, and as is known to me without their confessions. It is not, then, that Mr. Lincoln is expected to do any overt act by which you may be injured; you will not wait for any; but anticipating that the Government may work an injury, you say you will put an end to it, which means simply, that you intend either to rule or ruin this Government. That is what your complaint comes to; nothing else. We do not like your institution, you say. Well, we never liked it any better than we do now. You might as well have dissolved the Union at any other period as now, on that account, for we stand in relation to it precisely as we have ever stood: that is, repudiating it among ourselves as a matter of policy and morals, but nevertheless admitting that where it is out of our jurisdiction, we have no hold upon it, and no designs upon it.

Then, sir, as there is nothing in the platform on which Mr.

Lincoln was elected of which you complain, I ask, is there anything in the character of the President elect of which you ought to complain? Has he not lived a blameless life? Did he ever transgress any law? Has he ever committed any violation of duty of which the most scrupulous can complain? Why, then, your suspicions that he will? I have shown that you have had the Government all the time until, by some misfortune or maladministration, you brought it to the very verge of destruction, and the wisdom of the people had discovered that it was high time that the scepter should depart from you, and be placed in more competent hands; I say that this being so, you have no constitutional right to complain; especially when we disavow any intention so to make use of the victory we have won as to injure you at all.

This brings me, sir, to the question of compromises. On the first day of this session, a Senator rose in his place and offered a resolution for the appointment of a committee to inquire into the evils that exist between the different sections, and to ascertain what can be done to settle this great difficulty! That is the proposition, substantially. I tell the Senator that I know of no difficulty; and as to compromises, I had supposed that we were all agreed that the day of compromises was at an end. The most solemn compromises we have ever made have been violated without a whereas. Since I have had a seat in this body, one of considerable antiquity, that had stood for more than thirty years, was swept away from your statute-books. When I stood here in the minority arguing against it; when I asked you to withhold your hand; when I told you it was a sacred compromise between the sections, and that when it was removed we should be brought face to face with all that sectional bitterness that has intervened; when I told you that it was a sacred compromise which no man should touch with his finger, what was your reply? That it was a mere act of Congress—nothing more, nothing less—and that it could be swept away by the same majority that passed it. That was true in point of fact, and true in point of law; but it showed the weakness of compromises. Now, sir, I only speak for myself; and I say that, in view of the manner in which other compromises have been heretofore treated, I should hardly think any two of the Democratic party would look each other in the face and say "compromise" without a smile. [Laughter.] A compromise to be brought about by act of Congress, after the experience we have had, is absolutely ridiculous.

But what have we to compromise? Sir, I am one of those who went forth with zeal to maintain the principles of the great Republican party. In a constitutional way we met, as you met. We nominated our candidates for President and Vice President, and you did the same for yourselves. The issue was made up; and we went to the people upon it. Although we have been usually in the minority; although we have been generally beaten, yet, this time, the justice of our principles, and the maladministration of the Government in your hands, convinced the people that a change ought to be wrought; and after you had tried your utmost, and we had tried our utmost, we beat you; and we beat you upon the plainest and most palpable issue that ever was presented to the American people, and one that they understood the best. There is no mistaking it; and now, when we come to the Capitol, I tell you that our President and our Vice President must be inaugurated, and administer the Government as all their predecessors have done. Sir, it would be humiliating and dishonorable to us if we were to listen to a compromise by which he who has the verdict of the people in his pocket, should make his way to the presidential chair. When it comes to that, you have no Government; anarchy intervenes; civil war may follow it; all the evils that may come to the human imagination may be consequent upon such a course as that. The moment the American people cut loose from the sheet anchor of free government and liberty—that is, whenever it is denied in this Government that a majority fairly given shall rule—the people are unworthy of free government. Sir, I know not what others may do; but I tell you that, with the verdict of the people given in favor of the platform upon which our candidates have been elected, so far as I am concerned, I would suffer anything to come before I would compromise that away. I regard it as a case where I have no right to extend comity or generosity. A right, an absolute right, the most sacred that a free people can ever bestow on any man, is their undisguised, fair verdict, that gives him a title to the office that he is chosen to fill; and he is recreant to the principle of free government who will ask a question beyond the fact whether a man has the verdict of the people, or if he will entertain for a moment a proposition in addition to that. It is all I want. If we cannot stand there, we cannot stand anywhere. Any other principle than that would be as fatal to you, my friends, as to us. On any other principle, anarchy must immediately ensue.

You say that he comes from a particular section of the country. What of that? If he is an honest man, bound by his constitutional duties, has he not as good a right to come from one side as the other? Here, gentlemen, we ought to understand each other's duties a little. I appeal to every candid man upon the other side, and I put this question: if you had elected your candidate, Mr. Breckinridge, although we should have been a good deal disheartened, as everybody is that loses his choice in such a matter as this; although it would have been an overthrow that we should have deplored very much, as we have had occasion almost always to deplore the result of national elections, still do you believe that we would have raised a hand against the Constitution of our country because we were fairly beaten in an election? Sir, I do not believe there is a man on the other side who will not do us more credit than to suppose that if the case were reversed, there would be any complaint on our side. There never has been any from us under similar circumstances, and there would not be now. Sir, I think we have patriotism enough to overcome the pride and the prejudice of the canvass, and submit gracefully to the unmistakable verdict of the people; and as I have shown that you have nothing else to complain of, I take it that this is your complaint. Some of you have said that the election of Mr. Lincoln showed hostility to you and your institution. Sir, it is the common fate of parties to differ, and one does not intend to follow exactly the course of policy of the other; but when you talk of constitutional rights and duties, honest men will observe them alike, no matter to what party they belong.

I say, then, that so far as I am concerned, I will yield to no compromise. I do not come here begging, either. It would be an indignity to the people that I represent if I were to stand here parleying as to the rights of the party to which I belong. We have won our right to the Chief Magistracy of this nation in the way that you have always won your predominance; and if you are as willing to do justice to others as to exact it from them, you would never raise an inquiry as to a committee for compromises. Here I beg, barely for myself, to say one thing more. Many of you stand in an attitude hostile to this Government; that is to say, you occupy an attitude where you threaten that, unless we do so and so, you will go out of this Union and destroy the Government. I say to you, for myself, that, in my private capacity, I never yielded to anything by way of threat, and in my public capacity I have no right to yield to any such thing; and therefore I would not entertain a proposition for any compromise; for, in my judgment, this long, chronic controversy that has existed between us must be met, and met upon the principles of the Constitution and laws, and met now. I hope it may be adjusted to the satisfaction of all; and I know no other way to adjust it, except that way which is laid down by the Constitution of the United States. Whenever we go astray from that, we are sure to plunge ourselves into difficulties. The old Constitution of the United States, although commonly and frequently in direct opposition to what I could wish, nevertheless, in my judgment, is the wisest and best Constitution that ever yet organized a free Government; and by its provisions I am willing, and intend, to stand or fall. Like the Senator from Mississippi, I ask nothing more. I ask no ingrafting upon it. I ask nothing to be taken away from it. Under its provisions a nation has grown faster than any other in the history of the world ever did before in prosperity, in power, and in all that makes a nation great and glorious. It has ministered to the advantages of this people; and now I am unwilling to add or take away anything till I can see much clearer than I can now that it wants either any addition or lopping off.

There is one other subject about which I ought to say something. On that side of the Chamber, you claim the constitutional right, if I understand you, to secede from the Government at pleasure, and set up an adverse Government of your own; that one State, or any number of States, have a perfect constitutional right to do it. Sir, I can find no warrant in the Constitution for any doctrine like that. In my judgment, it would be subversive of all constitutional obligation. If this is so, we really have not now, and never have had, a Government; for that certainly is no Government of which a State can do just as it pleases, any more than it would be of an individual. How can a man be said to be governed by law, if he will obey the law or not just as he sees fit? It puts you out of the pale of Government, and reduces this Union of ours, of which we have all boasted so much, to a mere conglomeration of States, to be held at the will of any capricious member of it. As to South Carolina, I will say that she is a small State; and probably, if she were sunk by an earthquake to-day, we would hardly ever find it out, except by the unwonted harmony that might prevail in this Chamber. [Laughter.] But I think she is unwise. I would be willing that she should go her own gait, provided we could do it without an example fatal to all government; but standing here in the highest council of the nation, my own wishes, if I had any, must be under the control of my constitutional duty.

I do not see how any man can contend that a State can go out of this Union at pleasure, though I do not propose now to argue that question, because that has been done by men infinitely more able to argue it than I am. When it was raised some thirty years ago, and challenged the investigation of the best minds of this nation of all parties, it received a verdict that I supposed had put it at rest forever. General Jackson, with all the eminent men that surrounded him in his Cabinet, and in the councils of the nation, with hardly any exception, except Mr. Calhoun, held that the doctrine was a delusion, not to be found in the Constitution of the United States; and not only so, but utterly destructive of all Governments. Mr. Calhoun held the contrary. Mr. Webster, in his great controversy with Mr. Hayne upon that subject, was supposed to have overthrown him, even upon nullification, so utterly, that it was believed at the time that the doctrine could never arise or sprout up again. But here it is today in full bloom and glory: a State has a right to secede. Mr. Calhoun did not hold so. He held that a State had a right to nullify a law of Congress that they believed to be unconstitutional. He took that distinction between the power of a State to nullify a law of Congress and secession. Grounding herself upon the resolutions of 1798–99, he held that a State, in her sovereign capacity, judging in the last resort as to whether a law was warranted by the Constitution or not, must be the sole judge of the infraction of the

Constitution by the enactment of a law, and also of the mode of remedy. In that, he hardly had a second at that period. But when you come to the doctrine of secession, he himself says that that is not a constitutional remedy. He did not treat it as such. Nay, sir, he goes much further than the President of the United States has gone in his message, in which he declares that the United States has no power to make war upon a seceding State. Mr. Calhoun says we undoubtedly have that power. One remedy he calls peaceable and constitutional, and the other not. I have not the book with me; I intended to have brought it, but forgot it; but you will find this doctrine laid down in his famous letter to Governor Hamilton, taking and working out the distinction between peaceable nullification and secession, that puts an end to all the relationship between the General Government and the State, and enables the General Government, if they see fit, to declare war upon such a State. Therefore I take it that a State has no constitutional right to go out of this Government.

I acknowledge, to the fullest extent, the right of revolution, if you may call it a right, and the destruction of the Government under which we live, if we are discontented with it, and on its ruins to erect another more in accordance with our wishes. I believe nobody at this day denies the right; but they that undertake it, undertake it with this hazard: if they are successful, then all is right, and they are heroes; if they are defeated, they are rebels. That is the character of all revolution: if successful, of course it is well; if unsuccessful, then the Government from which they have rebelled treats them as traitors.

I do not say this because I apprehend that any party intends to make war upon a seceding State. I only assert their right from the nature of the act, if they see fit to do so; but I would not advise nor counsel it. I should be very tender of the rights of a people, if I had full power over them, who are about to destroy a Government which they deliberately come to the conclusion they cannot live under; but I am persuaded that the necessities of our position compel us to take a more austere ground, and hold that if a State secedes, although we will not make war upon her, we cannot recognize her right to be out of the Union, and she is not out until she gains the consent of the Union itself; and that the Chief Magistrate of the nation, be he who he may, will find under the Constitution of the United States that it is his sworn duty to execute the law in every part and parcel of this Government; that he cannot be released from that obligation; for there is nothing in the Constitution of the United States that would warrant him in saying that a single star has fallen from this galaxy of stars in the Confederacy. He is sworn not to know that a State has seceded, or pay the least respect to their resolutions that claim they have. What follows? Not that we would make war upon her, but we should have to exercise every Federal right over her if we had the power; and the most important of these would be the collection of the revenues. There are many rights that the Federal Government exercises over the States for the peculiar benefit of the people there, which, if they did not want, they could dispense with. If they did not want the mails carried there, the President might abolish the offices, and cease to carry their mails. They might forego any such duty peculiarly for the benefit of the people. They might not elect their officers and send them here. It is a privilege they have; but we cannot force them to do it. They have the right under the Constitution to be represented upon equal terms with any other State; but if they see fit to forego that right, and do not claim it, it is not incumbent upon the President to endeavor to force them to do an act of that kind.

But when you come to those duties which impose obligations upon them, in common with the other members of the Confederacy, he cannot be released from his duty. Therefore, it will be incumbent on the Chief Magistrate to proceed to collect the revenue of ships entering their ports, precisely in the same way and to the same extent that he does now in every other State of the Union. We cannot release him from that obligation. The Constitution, in thunder tones, demands that he shall do it alike in the ports of every State. What follows? Why, sir, if he shuts up the ports of entry so that a ship cannot discharge her cargo there or get papers for another voyage, then ships will cease to trade; or, if he undertakes to blockade her, and thus collect it, she has not gained her independence by secession. What must she do? If she is contented to live in this equivocal state all would be well, perhaps; but she could not live there. No people in the world could live in that condition.

What will they do? They must take the initiative and declare war upon the United States; and the moment that they levy war force must be met by force; and they must, therefore, hew out their independence by violence and war. There is no other way under the Constitution, that I know of, whereby a Chief Magistrate of any politics could be released from this duty. If this State, though seceding, should declare war against the United States, I do not suppose there is a lawyer in this body but what would say that the act of levying war is treason against the United States. That is where it results. We might just as well look the matter right in the face.

The Senator from Texas says—it is not exactly his language—we will force you to an ignominious treaty up in Faneuil Hall. Well, sir, you may. We know you are brave; we understand your prowess; we want no fight with you; but, nevertheless, if you drive us to that necessity, we must use all the powers of this Government to maintain it intact in its integrity. If we are overthrown, we but share the fate of a thousand other Governments that have been subverted. If you are the weakest, then you must go to the wall; and that is all there is about it. That is the condition in which we stand, provided a State sets herself up in opposition to the General Government.

I say that is the way it seems to me, as a lawyer. I see no power in the Constitution to release a Senator from this position. Sir, if there was any other, if there was an absolute right of secession in the Constitution of the United States when we stepped up there to take our oath of office, why was there not an exception in that oath? Why did it not run "that we would support the Constitution of the United States unless our State shall secede before our term was out?" Sir, there is no such immunity. There is no way by which this can be done that I can conceive of, except it is standing upon the Constitution of the United States, demanding equal justice for all, and vindicating the old flag of the Union. We must maintain it, unless we are cloven down by superior force.

Well, sir, it may happen that you can make your way out of the Union, and that, by levying war upon the Government, you may vindicate your right to independence. If you should do so, I have a policy in my mind. No man would regret more than myself that any portion of the people of these United

States should think themselves impelled, by grievances or anything else, to depart out of this Union, and raise a foreign flag and a hand against the General Government. If there was any just cause on God's earth that I could see that was within my reach, of honorable release from any such pretended grievance, they should have it; but they set forth none; I can see none. It is all a matter of prejudice, superinduced unfortunately, I believe, as I intimated before, more because you have listened to the enemies of the Republican party and what they said of us, while, from your intolerance, you have shut out all light as to what our real principles are. We have been called and branded in the North and in the South and everywhere else, as John Brown men, as men hostile to your institutions, as meditating an attack upon your institutions in your own States—a thing that no Republican ever dreamed of or ever thought of, but has protested against as often as the question has been up; but your people believe it. No doubt they believe it because of the terrible excitement and reign of terror that prevails there. No doubt they think so, but it arises from false information, or the want of information—that is all. Their prejudices have been appealed to until they have become uncontrolled and uncontrollable.

Well, sir, if it shall be so; if that "glorious Union," as we all call it, under which the Government has so long lived and prospered, is now about to come to a final end, as perhaps it may, I have been looking around to see what policy we should adopt; and through that gloom which has been mentioned on the other side, if you will have it so, I still see a glorious future for those who stand by the old flag of the nation. There lie the fair fields of Mexico all before us. The people there are prejudiced against you. They fear you intend to overrun and enslave them. You are a slavery propaganda, and you are fillibusters. That has raised a violent antagonism between you and them. But, sir, if we were once released from all obligation to this institution, in six months they would invite us to take a protectorate over them. They owe England a large debt, and she has been coaxing and inviting us to take the protectorate of that nation. They will aid us in it; and I say to the commercial men of the North, if you go along with me, and adopt this policy, if we must come to this, you will be seven-fold indemnified by the trade and commerce of that country for what you lose by the secession. Talk about eating ice and granite in the North! Why, sir, Great Britain now carries on a commerce with Mexico to the amount of nearly a hundred million dollars. How much of it do we get? Only about eight million. Why so? Because, by our treatment of Mexico, we have led them to fear and to hate us; and they have been compelled, by our illiberal policy, to place themselves under the shadow of a stronger nation for their own protection.

The Senator from Illinois [Mr. DOUGLAS] and my colleague [Mr. PUGH] have said that we Black Republicans were advocates of negro equality, and that we wanted to build up a black government. Sir, it will be one of the most blessed ideas of the times, if it shall come to this, that we will make inducements for every free black among us to find his home in a more congenial climate in Central America or in Lower Mexico, and we will be divested of every one of them; and then, endowed with the splendid domain that we shall get, we will adopt a homestead policy, and we will invite the poor, the destitute, industrious white man from every clime under heaven, to come in there and make his fortune. So, sir, we will build up a nation, renovated by this process, of white laboring men. You may build yours up on compulsory servile labor, and the two will flourish side by side; and we shall very soon see whether your principles, or that state of society, or ours, is the most prosperous or vigorous. I might say, sir, that, divested of this institution, who doubts that the provinces of Canada would knock at our doors in a day? Therefore, my friends, we have all the elements for building up an empire—a Republic, founded on the great principles of the Declaration of Independence, that shall be more magnificent, more powerful, and more just than this world has ever seen at any other period. I do not know that I should have a single second for this policy; but it is a policy that occurs to me, and it reconciles me in some measure to the threatened loss or secession of these States.

But, sir, I am for maintaining the Union of these States. I will sacrifice everything but honor to maintain it. That glorious old flag of ours, by any act of mine, shall never cease to wave over the integrity of this Union as it is. But if they will not have it so, in this new, renovated Government of which I have spoken, the 4th of July, with all its glorious memories, will never be repealed. The old flag of 1776 will be in our hands, and shall float over this nation forever; and this Capitol, that some gentlemen said would be reserved for the southern republic, shall still be the Capitol. It was laid out by Washington; it was consecrated by him; and the old flag that he vindicated in the Revolution shall still float from the Capitol. [Applause in the galleries.]

The PRESIDING OFFICER. The Sergeant-at-Arms will take proper measures to preserve order in the gallery or clear it.

Mr. WADE. I say, sir, I stand by the Union of these States. Washington and his compatriots fought for that good old flag. It shall never be hauled down, but shall be the glory of the Government to which I belong, as long as my life shall continue. To maintain it, Washington and his compatriots fought for liberty and the rights of man. And here I will add that my own father, although but a humble soldier, fought in the same great cause, and went through hardships and privations sevenfold worse than death, in order to bequeath it to his children. It is my inheritance. It was my protector in infancy, and the pride and glory of my riper years; and, Mr. President, although it may be assailed by traitors on every side, by the grace of God, under its shadow I will die.

A COMPROMISE OVER SLAVERY: DECEMBER 1860

John J. Crittenden:
Remarks in the U.S. Senate

December 18, 1860

A former Whig who helped form the Constitutional Union party in 1860, Senator John J. Crittenden of Kentucky made these remarks while proposing a set of constitutional amendments and congressional resolutions regarding slavery that became known as the Crittenden Compromise. His proposals were referred to a special Committee of Thirteen, whose members included Crittenden, Benjamin Wade, William H. Seward, Stephen A. Douglas, Jefferson Davis, and Robert Toombs. The compromise failed to win committee approval when all five of its Republican members, along with Davis and Toombs, voted against the amendment regarding slavery in the territories. Crittenden brought his proposals before the full Senate in January 1861, but they were again blocked by determined Republican opposition. Lincoln helped defeat the Crittenden proposals by writing several private letters to Republican leaders urging that there be no compromises made on the question of extending slavery.

Mr. CRITTENDEN. I am gratified, Mr. President, to see in the various propositions which have been made, such a universal anxiety to save the country from the dangerous dissensions which now prevail; and I have, under a very serious view and without the least ambitious feeling whatever connected with it, prepared a series of constitutional amendments, which I desire to offer to the Senate, hoping that they may form, in part at least, some basis for measures that may settle the controverted questions which now so much agitate our country. Certainly, sir, I do not propose now any elaborate discussion of the subject. Before presenting these resolutions, however, to the Senate, I desire to make a few remarks explanatory of them, that the Senate may understand their general scope.

The questions of an alarming character are those which have

grown out of the controversy between the northern and southern sections of our country in relation to the rights of the slaveholding States in the Territories of the United States, and in relation to the rights of the citizens of the latter in their slaves. I have endeavored by these resolutions to meet all these questions and causes of discontent, and by amendments to the Constitution of the United States, so that the settlement, if we can happily agree on any, may be permanent, and leave no cause for future controversy. These resolutions propose, then, in the first place, in substance, the restoration of the Missouri compromise, extending the line throughout the Territories of the United States to the eastern border of California, recognizing slavery in all the territory south of that line, and prohibiting slavery in all the territory north of it; with a provision, however, that when any of those Territories, north or south, are formed into States, they shall then be at liberty to exclude or admit slavery as they please; and that, in the one case or the other, it shall be no objection to their admission into the Union. In this way, sir, I propose to settle the question, both as to territory and slavery, so far as it regards the Territories of the United States.

I propose, sir, also, that the Constitution shall be so amended as to declare that Congress shall have no power to abolish slavery in the District of Columbia so long as slavery exists in the States of Maryland and Virginia; and that they shall have no power to abolish slavery in any of the places under their special jurisdiction within the southern States.

These are the constitutional amendments which I propose, and embrace the whole of them in regard to the questions of territory and slavery. There are other propositions in relation to grievances, and in relation to controversies, which I suppose are within the jurisdiction of Congress, and may be removed by the action of Congress. I propose, in regard to legislative action, that the fugitive slave law, as it is commonly called, shall be declared by the Senate to be a constitutional act, in strict pursuance of the Constitution. I propose to declare, that it has been decided by the Supreme Court of the United States to be constitutional, and that the southern States are entitled to a faithful and complete execution of that law, and that no amendment shall be made hereafter to it which will impair its efficiency. But, thinking that it would not impair its efficiency, I have proposed amendments to it in two particulars. I have understood from gentlemen of the North that there is objection to the provision giving a different fee where the commissioner decides to deliver the slave to the claimant, from that which is given where he decides to discharge the alleged slave; the law declares that in the latter case he shall have but five dollars, while in the other he shall have ten dollars—twice the amount in one case than in the other. The reason for this is very obvious. In case he delivers the servant to his claimant, he is required to draw out a lengthy certificate, stating the principal and substantial grounds on which his decision rests, and to return him either to the marshal or to the claimant to remove him to the State from which he escaped. It was for that reason that a larger fee was given to the commissioner, where he had the largest service to perform. But, sir, the act being viewed unfavorably and with great prejudice, in a certain portion of our country, this was regarded as very obnoxious, because it seemed to give an inducement to the commissioner to return the slave to the master, as he thereby obtained the larger fee of ten dollars instead of the smaller one of five dollars. I have said, let the fee be the same in both cases.

I have understood, furthermore, sir, that inasmuch as the fifth section of that law was worded somewhat vaguely, its general terms had admitted of the construction in the northern States that all the citizens were required, upon the summons of the marshal, to go with him to hunt up, as they express it, and arrest the slave; and this is regarded as obnoxious. They have said, "in the southern States you make no such requisition on the citizen;" nor do we, sir. The section, construed according to the intention of the framers of it, I suppose, only intended that the marshal should have the same right in the execution of process for the arrest of a slave that he has in all other cases of process that he is required to execute—to call on the *posse comitatus* for assistance where he is resisted in the execution of his duty, or where, having executed his duty by the arrest, an attempt is made to rescue the slave. I propose such an amendment as will obviate this difficulty and limit the right of the master and the duty of the citizen to cases where, as in regard to all other process, persons may be called upon to assist in resisting opposition to the execution of the laws.

I have provided further, sir, that the amendments to the Constitution which I here propose, and certain other provisions of the Constitution itself, shall be unalterable, thereby forming a permanent and unchangeable basis for peace and tranquillity among the people. Among the provisions in the present Constitution, which I have by amendment proposed to render unalterable, is that provision in the first article of the Constitution which provides the rule for representation, including in the computation three fifths of the slaves. That is to be rendered unchangeable. Another is the provision for the delivery of fugitive slaves. That is to be rendered unchangeable.

And with these provisions, Mr. President, it seems to me we have a solid foundation upon which we may rest our hopes for the restoration of peace and good-will among all the States of this Union, and all the people. I propose, sir, to enter into no particular discussion. I have explained the general scope and object of my proposition. I have provided further, which I ought to mention, that, there having been some difficulties experienced in the courts of the United States in the South in carrying into execution the laws prohibiting the African slave trade, all additions and amendments which may be necessary to those laws to render them effectual should be immediately adopted by Congress, and especially the provisions of those laws which prohibit the importation of African slaves into the United States. I have further provided it as a recommendation to all the States of this Union, that whereas laws have been passed of an unconstitutional character, (and all laws are of that character which either conflict with the constitutional acts of Congress, or which in their operation hinder or delay the proper execution of the acts of Congress,) which laws are null and void, and yet, though null and void, they have been the source of mischief and discontent in the country, under the extraordinary circumstances in which we are placed; I have supposed that it would not be improper or unbecoming in Congress to recommend to the States, both North and South, the repeal of all such acts of theirs as were intended to control, or intended to obstruct the operation of the acts of Congress, or which in their operation and in their application have been made use of for the purpose of such hindrance and opposition, and that they will repeal these laws or make such explanations or corrections of them as to prevent their being used for any such mischievous purpose.

I have endeavored to look with impartiality from one end of our country to the other; I have endeavored to search up what appeared to me to be the causes of discontent pervading the land; and, as far as I am capable of doing so, I have endeavored to propose a remedy for them. I am far from believing that, in the shape in which I present these measures, they will meet with the acceptance of the Senate. It will be sufficiently gratifying if, with all the amendments that the superior knowledge of the Senate may make to them, they shall, to any effectual extent, quiet the country.

Mr. President, great dangers surround us. The Union of these States is dear to the people of the United States. The long experience of its blessings, the mighty hopes of the future, have made it dear to the hearts of the American people. Whatever politicians may say; whatever of dissension may, in the heat of party politics, be created among our people, when you come down to the question of the existence of the Constitution, that is a question beyond all party politics; that is a question of life and death. The Constitution and the Union are the life of this great people—yes, sir, the life of life. We all desire to preserve them, North and South; that is the universal desire. But some of the southern States, smarting under what they conceive to be aggressions of their northern brethren and of the northern States, are not contented to continue this Union, and are taking steps, formidable steps, towards a dissolution of the Union, and towards the anarchy and the bloodshed, I fear, that are to follow. I say, sir, we are in the presence of great events. We must elevate ourselves to the level of the great occasion. No party warfare about mere party questions or party measures ought now to engage our attention. They are left behind; they are as dust in the balance. The life, the existence of our country, of our Union, is the mighty question; and we must elevate ourselves to all those considerations which belong to this high subject.

I hope, therefore, gentlemen will be disposed to bring the

sincerest spirit of conciliation, the sincerest spirit and desire to adjust all these difficulties, and to think nothing of any little concessions of opinions that they may make, if thereby the Constitution and the country can be preserved.

The great difficulty here, sir—I know it; I recognize it as the difficult question, particularly with the gentlemen from the North—is the admission of this line of division for the territory, and the recognition of slavery on the one side, and the prohibition of it on the other. The recognition of slavery on the southern side of that line is the great difficulty, the great question with them. Now, I beseech them to think, and you, Mr. President, and all, to think whether, for such a comparative trifle as that, the Union of this country is to be sacrificed. Have we realized to ourselves the momentous consequences of such an event? When has the world seen such an event? This is a mighty empire. Its existence spreads its influence throughout the civilized world. Its overthrow will be the greatest shock that civilization and free government have received; more extensive in its consequences; more fatal to mankind and to the great principles upon which the liberty of mankind depends, than the French revolution with all its blood, and with all its war and violence. And all for what? Upon questions concerning this line of division between slavery and freedom? Why, Mr. President, suppose this day all the southern States, being refused this right; being refused this partition; being denied this privilege, were to separate from the northern States, and do it peacefully, and then were to come to you peacefully and say, "let there be no war between us; let us divide fairly the Territories of the United States:" could the northern section of the country refuse so just a demand? What would you then give them? What would be the fair proportion? If you allowed them their fair relative proportion, would you not give them as much as is now proposed to be assigned on the southern side of that line, and would they not be at liberty to carry their slaves there, if they pleased? You would give them the whole of that; and then what would be its fate?

Is it upon the general principle of humanity, then, that you [addressing Republican Senators] wish to put an end to slavery, or is it to be urged by you as a mere topic and point of party controversy to sustain party power? Surely I give you credit for looking at it upon broader and more generous principles. Then, in the worst event, after you have encountered disunion, that greatest of all political calamities to the people of this country, and the disunionists come, the separating States come, and demand or take their portion of the Territories, they can take, and will be entitled to take, all that will now lie on the southern side of the line which I have proposed. Then they will have a right to permit slavery to exist in it; and what do you gain for the cause of anti-slavery? Nothing whatever. Suppose you should refuse their demand, and claim the whole for yourselves: that would be a flagrant injustice which you would not be willing that I should suppose would occur. But if you did, what would be the consequence? A State north and a State south, and all the States, north and south, would be attempting to grasp at and seize this territory, and to get all of it that they could. That would be the struggle, and you would have war; and not only disunion, but all these fatal consequences would follow from your refusal now to permit slavery to exist, to recognize it as existing, on the southern side of the proposed line, while you give to the people there the right to exclude it when they come to form a State government, if such should be their will and pleasure.

Now, gentlemen, in view of this subject, in view of the mighty consequences, in view of the great events which are present before you, and of the mighty consequences which are just now to take effect, is it not better to settle the question by a division upon the line of the Missouri compromise? For thirty years we lived quietly and peacefully under it. Our people, North and South, were accustomed to look at it as a proper and just line. Can we not do so again? We did it then to preserve the peace of the country. Now you see this Union in the most imminent danger. I declare to you that it is my solemn conviction that unless something be done, and something equivalent to this proposition, we shall be a separated and divided people in six months from this time. That is my firm conviction. There is no man here who deplores it more than I do; but it is my sad and melancholy conviction that that will be the consequence. I wish you to realize fully the danger. I wish you to realize fully the consequences which are to follow. You can give increased stability to this Union; you can give it an existence, a glorious existence, for great and glorious centuries to come, by now setting it upon a permanent basis, recognizing what the South considers as its rights; and this is the greatest of them all: it is that you should divide the territory by this line and allow the people south of it to have slavery when they are admitted into the Union as States, and to have it during the existence of the territorial government. That is all. Is it not the cheapest price at which such a blessing as this Union was ever purchased? You think, perhaps, or some of you, that there is no danger, that it will but thunder and pass away. Do not entertain such a fatal delusion. I tell you it is not so. I tell you that as sure as we stand here disunion will progress. I fear it may swallow up even old Kentucky in its vortex—as true a State to the Union as yet exists in the whole Confederacy—unless something be done; but that you will have disunion, that anarchy and war will follow it, that all this will take place in six months, I believe as confidently as I believe in your presence. I want to satisfy you of the fact.

Mr. President, I rise to suggest another consideration. I have been surprised to find, upon a little examination, that when the peace of 1783 was made, which recognized the independence of this country by Great Britain, the States north of Mason and Dixon's line had but a territory of one hundred and sixty-four thousand square miles, while the States south of Mason and Dixon's line had more than six hundred thousand square miles. It was so divided. Virginia shortly afterwards ceded to the United States all that noble territory northwest of the Ohio river, and excluded slavery from it. That changed the relative proportion of territory. After that, the North had four hundred and twenty-five thousand square miles, and the South three hundred and eighty-five thousand. Thus, at once, by the concession of Virginia, the North, from one hundred and sixty-four thousand, rose to four hundred and twenty-five thousand square miles, and the South fell from six hundred thousand to three hundred and eighty-five thousand square miles. By that cession the South became smaller in extent than the North. Well, let us look beyond. I intend to take up as little time as possible, and to avoid details; but take all your subsequent acquisitions of Florida, of Louisiana, of Oregon, of Texas, and the acquisitions made from Mexico. They have been so divided and so disposed of that the North has now two millions, two hundred thousand square miles of territory, and the South has less than one million.

Under these circumstances, when you have been so greatly magnified—I do not complain of it, I am stating facts—when your section has been made so mighty by these great acquisitions, and to a great extent with the perfect consent of the South, ought you to hesitate now upon adopting this line which will leave to you on the north side of it nine hundred and odd thousand square miles, and leave to the South only two hundred and eighty-five thousand? It will give you three times as much as it will give her. There is three times as much land in your portion as in hers. The South has already occupied some of it, and it is in States; but altogether the South gets by this division two hundred and eighty-five thousand square miles, and the North nine hundred thousand. The result of the whole of it is, that the North has two million two hundred thousand square miles and the South only one million.

I mention this as no reproach, as no upbraiding, as no complaint—none at all. I do not speak in that spirit; I do not address you in that temper. But these are the facts, and they ought, it seems to me, to have some weight; and when we come to make a peace-offering, are we to count it, are we to measure it nicely in golden scales? You get a price, and the dearest price, for all the concession asked to be made—you have the firmer establishment of your Union; you have the restoration of peace and tranquillity, and the hopes of a mighty future, all secured by this concession. How dearly must one individual, or two individuals, or many individuals, value their private opinions if they think them more important to the world than this mighty interest of the Union and Government of the United States!

Sir, it is a cheap sacrifice. It is a glorious sacrifice. This Union cost a great deal to establish it; it cost the yielding of much of public opinion and much of policy, besides the direct or indirect cost of it in all the war to establish the independence of this country. When it was done, General Washington himself said, Providence has helped us, or we could not have accomplished this thing. And this gift of our wisest men; this great work of their hands; this work in the foundation and the structure of which Providence himself, with his benignant hand, helped—are we to give it all up for such small considerations? The present exasperation; the present feeling of disunion, is the result of a long-continued controversy on the subject of slavery and of territory. I shall not attempt to trace that controversy; it is unnecessary to the occasion, and might be harmful. In relation to such controversies, I will say, though, that all the wrong is never on one side, or all the right on the other. Right and wrong, in this world, and in all such controversies, are mingled together. I forbear now any discussion or any reference to the right or wrong of the controversy, the mere party controversy; but in the progress of party, we now come to a point where party ceases to deserve consideration, and the preservation of the Union demands our highest and our greatest exertions. To preserve the Constitution of the country is the highest duty of the Senate, the highest duty of Congress—to preserve it and to perpetuate it, that we may hand down the glories which we have received to our children and to our posterity, and to generations far beyond us. We are, Senators, in positions where history is to take notice of the course we pursue.

History is to record us. Is it to record that when the destruction of the Union was imminent; when we saw it tottering to its fall; when we saw brothers arming their hands for hostility with one another, we stood quarreling about points of party politics; about questions which we attempted to sanctify and to consecrate by appealing to our conscience as the source of them? Are we to allow such fearful catastrophies to occur while we stand trifling away our time? While we stand thus, showing our inferiority to the great and mighty dead, showing our inferiority to the high positions which we occupy, the country may be destroyed and ruined; and to the amazement of all the world, the great Republic may fall prostrate and in ruins, carrying with it the very hope of that liberty which we have heretofore enjoyed; carrying with it, in place of the peace we have enjoyed, nothing but revolution and havoc and anarchy. Shall it be said that we have allowed all these evils to come upon our country, while we were engaged in the petty and small disputes and debates to which I have referred? Can it be that our name is to rest in history with this everlasting stigma and blot upon it?

Sir, I wish to God it was in my power to preserve this Union by renouncing or agreeing to give up every conscientious and other opinion. I might not be able to discard it from my mind; I am under no obligation to do that. I may retain the opinion, but if I can do so great a good as to preserve my country and give it peace, and its institutions and its Union stability, I will forego any action upon my opinions. Well now my friends, [addressing the Republican Senators,] that is all that is asked of you. Consider it well, and I do not distrust the result. As to the rest of this body, the gentlemen from the South, I would say to them, can you ask more than this? Are you bent on revolution, bent on disunion? God forbid it. I cannot believe that such madness possesses the American people. This gives reasonable satisfaction. I can speak with confidence only of my own State. Old Kentucky will be satisfied with it, and she will stand by the Union and die by the Union if this satisfaction be given. Nothing shall seduce her. The clamor of no revolution, the seductions and temptations of no revolution, will tempt her to move one step. She has stood always by the side of the Constitution; she has always been devoted to it, and is this day. Give her this satisfaction, and I believe all the States of the South that are not desirous of disunion as a better thing than the Union and the Constitution, will be satisfied and will adhere to the Union, and we shall go on again in our great career of national prosperity and national glory.

But, sir, it is not necessary for me to speak to you of the consequences that will follow disunion. Who of us is not proud of the greatness we have achieved? Disunion and separation destroy that greatness. Once disunited, we are no longer great. The nations of the earth who have looked upon you as a formidable Power, a mighty Power, and rising to untold and immeasurable greatness in the future, will scoff at you. Your flag, that now claims the respect of the world, that protects American property in every port and harbor of the world, that protects the rights of your citizens everywhere, what will become of it? What becomes of its glorious influence? It is gone; and with it the protection of American citizens and property. To say nothing of the national honor which it displayed to all the world, the protection of your rights, the protection of your property abroad is gone with that national flag, and we are hereafter to conjure and contrive different flags for our different republics according to the feverish fancies of revolutionary patriots and disturbers of the peace of the world. No, sir; I want to follow no such flag. I want to preserve the union of my country. We have it in our power to do so, and we are responsible if we do not do it.

I do not despair of the Republic. When I see before me Senators of so much intelligence and so much patriotism, who have been so honored by their country, sent here as the guardians of that very union which is now in question, sent here as the guardians of our national rights, and as guardians of that national flag, I cannot despair; I cannot despond. I cannot but believe that they will find some means of reconciling and adjusting the rights of all parties, by concessions, if necessary, so as to preserve and give more stability to the country and to its institutions.

Mr. President, I have occupied more time than I intended. My remarks were designed and contemplated only to reach to an explanation of this resolution.

The PRESIDENT OFFICER, (Mr. FITZPATRICK in the chair.) Does the Senator desire the resolution to be read?

Mr. CRITTENDEN. Yes, sir; I ask that it be read to the Senate.

Mr. GREEN. The hour has arrived for the consideration of the special order.

Mr. CRITTENDEN. I desire to present this resolution now to the Senate; and I ask that it may be read and printed.

The PRESIDENT OFFICER. The Secretary will report the resolution.

The Secretary read it, as follows:

A joint resolution (S. No. 50) proposing certain amendments to the Constitution of the United States.

Whereas serious and alarming dissensions have arisen between the northern and southern States, concerning the rights and security of the rights of the slaveholding States, and especially their rights in the common territory of the United States; and whereas it is eminently desirable and proper that these dissensions, which now threaten the very existence of this Union, should be permanently quieted and settled by constitutional provisions, which shall do equal justice to all sections, and thereby restore to the people that peace and good-will which ought to prevail between all the citizens of the United States: Therefore,

Resolved by the Senate and House of Representatives of the United States of America in Congress assembled, (two thirds of both Houses concurring,) That the following articles be, and are hereby, proposed and submitted as amendments to the Constitution of the United States, which shall be valid to all intents and purposes, as part of said Constitution, when ratified by conventions of three fourths of the several States:

ARTICLE 1. In all the territory of the United States now held, or hereafter acquired, situate north of latitude 36° 30′, slavery or involuntary servitude, except as a punishment for crime, is prohibited while such territory shall remain under territorial government. In all the territory south of said line of latitude, slavery of the African race is hereby recognized as existing, and shall not be interfered with by Congress, but shall be protected as property by all the departments of the territorial government during its continuance. And when any Territory, north or south of said line, within such boundaries as Congress may prescribe, shall contain the population requisite for a member of Congress according to the then Federal ratio of representation of the people of the United States, it shall, if its form of government be republican, be admitted into the Union, on an equal footing with the original States, with or without slavery, as the constitution of such new State may provide.

ART. 2. Congress shall have no power to abolish slavery in places under its exclusive jurisdiction, and situate within the limits of States that permit the holding of slaves.

ART. 3. Congress shall have no power to abolish slavery within the District of Columbia, so long as it exists in the adjoining States of Virginia and Maryland, or either, nor without the consent of the inhabitants, nor without just compensation first made to such owners of slaves as do not consent to such abolishment. Nor shall Congress at any time prohibit officers of the Federal Government, or members of Congress, whose duties require them to be in said District, from bringing with them their slaves, and holding them as such during the time their duties may require them to remain there, and afterwards taking them from the District.

ART. 4. Congress shall have no power to prohibit or hinder the transportation of slaves from one State to another, or to a Territory in which slaves are by law permitted to be held, whether that transportation be by land, navigable rivers, or by the sea.

ART. 5. That in addition to the provisions of the third paragraph of the second section of the fourth article of the Constitution of the United States, Congress shall have power to provide by law, and it shall be its duty so to provide, that the United States shall pay to the owner who shall apply for it, the full value of his fugitive slave in all cases when the marshal or other officer whose duty it was to arrest said fugitive was prevented from so doing by violence or intimidation, or when, after arrest, said fugitive was rescued by force, and the owner thereby prevented and obstructed in the pursuit of his remedy for the recovery of his fugitive slave under the said clause of the Constitution and the laws made in pursuance thereof. And in all such cases, when the United States shall pay for such fugitive, they shall have the right, in their own name, to sue the county in which said violence, intimidation, or rescue was committed, and to recover from it, with interest and damages, the amount paid by them for said fugitive slave. And the said county, after it has paid said amount to the United States, may, for its indemnity, sue and recover from the wrong doers or rescuers by whom the owner was prevented from the recovery of his fugitive slave, in like manner as the owner himself might have sued and recovered.

ART. 6. No future amendment of the Constitution shall affect the five preceding articles; nor the third paragraph of the second section of the first article of the Constitution; nor the third paragraph of the second section of the fourth article of said Constitution; and no amendment shall be made to the Constitution which shall authorize or give to Congress any power to abolish or interfere with slavery in any of the States by whose laws it is, or may be, allowed or permitted.

And whereas, also, besides those causes of dissension embraced in the foregoing amendments proposed to the Constitution of the United States, there are others which come within the jurisdiction of Congress, and may be remedied by its legislative power; and whereas it is the desire of Congress, as far as its power will extend, to remove all just cause for the popular discontent and agitation which now disturb the peace of the country, and threaten the stability of its institutions: Therefore,

1. *Resolved by the Senate and House of Representatives of the United States of America in Congress assembled*, That the laws now in force for the recovery of fugitive slaves are in strict pursuance of the plain and mandatory provisions of the Constitution, and have been sanctioned as valid and constitutional by the judgment of the Supreme Court of the United States; that the slaveholding States are entitled to the faithful observance and execution of those laws, and that they

ought not to be repealed, or so modified or changed as to impair their efficiency; and that laws ought to be made for the punishment of those who attempt by rescue of the slave, or other illegal means, to hinder or defeat the due execution of said laws.

2. That all State laws which conflict with the fugitive slave acts of Congress, or any other constitutional acts of Congress, or which, in their operation, impede, hinder, or delay the free course and due execution of any of said acts, are null and void by the plain provisions of the Constitution of the United States; yet those State laws, void as they are, have given color to practices, and led to consequences, which have obstructed the due administration and execution of acts of Congress, and especially the acts for the delivery of fugitive slaves, and have thereby contributed much to the discord and commotion now prevailing. Congress, therefore, in the present perilous juncture, does not deem it improper, respectfully and earnestly to recommend the repeal of those laws to the several States which have enacted them, or such legislative corrections or explanations of them as may prevent their being used or perverted to such mischievous purposes.

3. That the act of the 18th of September, 1850, commonly called the fugitive slave law, ought to be so amended as to make the fee of the commissioner, mentioned in the eighth section of the act, equal in amount in the cases decided by him, whether his decision be in favor of or against the claimant. And to avoid misconstruction, the last clause of the fifth section of said act, which authorizes the person holding a warrant for the arrest or detention of a fugitive slave, to summon to his aid the *posse comitatus*, and which declares it to be the duty of all good citizens to assist him in its execution, ought to be so amended as to expressly limit the authority and duty to cases in which there shall be resistance or danger of resistance or rescue.

4. That the laws for the suppression of the African slave trade, and especially those prohibiting the importation of slaves in the United States, ought to be made effectual, and ought to be thoroughly executed; and all further enactments necessary to those ends ought to be promptly made.

"MEANNESS AND RASCALITY":
WASHINGTON, D.C., DECEMBER 1860

Henry Adams to Charles Francis Adams Jr.

Charles Francis Adams, the son of John Quincy Adams and the grandson of John Adams, was serving his first term as a Republican representative from Massachusetts when Congress reconvened in December 1860. Adams would play a prominent role on the special Committee of Thirty-Three that was appointed on December 4 to consider proposals for sectional compromise. Five measures were reported from the committee in January 1861, only one of which would be adopted by both the House and Senate: a constitutional amendment forbidding Congress from abolishing or interfering with slavery in the states. The amendment was approved by the House, 133–65, on February 28 (with Adams voting in favor), and by the Senate, 24–12, on March 3, but was ratified by only two states. During the winter of 1860–61 Henry Adams, who had recently returned from two years of travel and study in Europe, served as his father's private secretary. He described events in Washington to his older brother, Charles Francis Adams Jr.

Tuesday. Dec. 18. 1860.

Dear Charles

I'm a confoundedly unenterprising beggar. It's an outrageous bore to make calls and as society is all at odds and ends here, I make no acquaintances except those of the family. Even political matters are slow. There are no fights. Everyone is good-natured except those who are naturally misanthropic and even those who are so frightened that they can't breathe in more than a whisper, still keep their temper.

This makes it almost slow work. Then we dine at five and after that I don't feel as if I wanted to run much, especially as there are no parties nor receptions. The President divides his time between crying and praying; the Cabinet has resigned or else is occupied in committing treason. Some of them have done both. The people of Washington are firmly convinced that there is to be an attack on Washington by the southerners or else a slave insurrection, and in either case or in any contingency they feel sure of being ruined and murdered. There is no money nor much prospect of any and all sources of income are dry, so that no one can entertain. You see from this that there's no great chance for any violent gaiety.

Every one takes to politics for an occupation, but do you know, to me this whole matter is beginning to get stale. It does not rise to the sublime at all. It is merely the last convulsion of the slave-power, and only makes me glad that the beast is so near his end. I have no fear for the result at all. It must come out right. But what a piece of meanness and rascality, of braggadocio and nonsense the whole affair is. What insolence in the South and what cowardice and vileness at the North. The other day in that precious Committee of Thirty Three where our good father is doing his best to do nothing, in stalked the secessionists with Reuben Davis of Miss. at their head, and flung down a paper which was to be their ultimatum. That was to be taken up at once or the South would secede. The Committee declined to take it up till they had discussed the Fugitive Slave law. So out stalked the secessionists but not wholly away. They only seceded into the next room where they sat in dignity, smoking and watching the remaining members through the folding doors, while Davis returned to say that he did not wish to be misunderstood; they seceded only while the other proposition should be under discussion. Is that not a specimen of those men. Their whole game is a bare bluff.

The heroism of this struggle is over. That belonged to us when we were a minority; when Webster was pulled down and afterwards in the Kansas battle and the Sumner troubles. But now these men are struggling for power and they kick so hard that our men hardly dare say they'll take the prize they've won. In Massachusetts all are sound except Rice, but we've some pretty tight screws on him and I think he'll hold. Thayer I count out. Of course he's gone. But Pennsylvania is rotten to the core just as she was in the revolution when John Adams had such a battle with Dickinson. There is some sound principle in the western counties but Philadelphia is all about our ears. Ohio is not all she should be, and Indiana is all she should not be just as that mean state always was. Illinois is tolerably well in some respects and Wisconsin is a new Vermont, but there's too low a tone everywhere. They don't seem to see their way.

Dec. 20. Mr Appleton and Mr Amory have been on here the last four or five days engaged in saving the Union. Mr Appleton has buried himself among his southern friends so as not to encourage much any politeness on our side. After passing two whole days in the senate-chamber with Mason and his other attachments, he tapped Sumner on the shoulder and pretended to be very glad to see him. Sumner had not taken any notice of him of course till then, but on this notice, he turned round and they shook hands. The conversation however was not very brotherly, as Sumner in answer to some remark on the state of affairs, immediately began to haul the Boston Courier and Caleb Cushing over the coals as the great causes of the present misrepresentation, which Appleton of course couldn't quite agree in. However, it was all friendly enough I believe. Appleton called here when he knew that our father must be at the House, without asking for mamma, and never has called on Sumner at all.

Mr Amory dined here to-day. Mr Etheridge was invited to meet him but didn't come. Anthony of R.I. was also invited and did come. We had a very pleasant dinner. Mr Amory was amusing and told us his experiences in saving the country, which don't seem to have been very successful. He had talked with Douglas a long time and Douglas had been moral, demonstrating from the examples of Wellington and Peale, that a change of sentiments in cases of urgency was the duty of good citizens. Mr Amory seemed to think that Douglas was the very dirtiest beast he had yet met. He is, by the way, by his present course, destroying the power he has left. Pugh's speech to-day was disgusting. Those men are trying to build the Democratic party up again.

That blessed committee is still at work all the time and tomorrow a vote will be taken on the territorial question. Our father's course will be such as not to need much active support since Winter Davis is assuming the decided course of breaking with the south and he will bear the brunt of the battle. It seems likely that no minority report of any consequence will be needed. Tomorrow will decide and I have a letter all ready for next Monday's Advertiser in case the vote should go right. As to last Monday's letter which has not appeared, I am not sorry for it, as it was written when everything looked fishy. You can tell Hale this and mark what he says or looks, for I do much mistrust me that he suppressed that letter. One ought to have appeared this morning and I shall look with curiosity tomorrow to see.

I am not sorry that affairs have taken such a turn as to relieve our father. He will be strongly pushed for the Treasury and I don't care to have him expose himself now. Lincoln is all right. You can rely on that. He has exercised a strong influence through several sources on this committee and always right, but as yet there is no lisp of a Cabinet. Not even Seward had been consulted a week ago, though perhaps this visit of his to New York may have something to do with it.

As for my Advertiser letters, it will take a little time for me to make headway enough here to do much. But I do not wish to hurry matters. As yet there has been no great demand; that is, no active fighting, and I doubt if there will be. But these things will arrange themselves so soon as I begin to take a position here.

Johnson's speech yesterday was a great relief to us and it cut the secessionists dreadfully hard. Jeff. Davis was in a fever all through it and they all lost their temper. Sumner dined here yesterday and was grand as usual, full of the diplomatic corps. He told Alley a little while ago that of course if he went into the Cabinet it could be only as Sec. of State, and Alley recommended him to give up all idea of it. I think he'd better.

H.B.A.

A CONFIDENTIAL MESSAGE:
ILLINOIS, DECEMBER 1860

John G. Nicolay: Memorandum Regarding Abraham Lincoln

December 22, 1860

On December 20 South Carolina became the first state to break away from the Union when its convention approved an ordinance of secession, 169–0. The following day a report appeared in *The New York Times* claiming that President Buchanan had ordered Major Robert Anderson, the commander of the federal garrison at Fort Moultrie in Charleston harbor, to surrender if attacked. In fact, Secretary of War John Floyd had sent instructions to Anderson on December 21, ordering him to "exercise a sound military discretion" if his command came under attack, but to avoid "a vain and useless sacrifice" of life "upon a mere point of honor." Abraham Lincoln's response to the *Times* report was recorded in Springfield by his secretary John G. Nicolay.

WHEN Mr. Lincoln came to the office this morning, after the usual salutations, he asked me what the news was. I asked him if he had seen the morning dispatches. He replied "no." "Then," said I, "there is an important rumor you have not seen. The Times correspondent telegraphs that Buchanan has sent instructions to Maj. Anderson to surrender Fort Moultrie if it is attacked."

"If that is true they ought to hang him!" said he with warmth.

After some further conversation he remarked—

"Among the letters you saw me mail yesterday was one to Washburne, (of Ill.) who had written me that he had just had a long conversation with Gen. Scott, and that the General felt considerably outraged that the President would not act as he wished him to in reinforcing the forts &c. I wrote to Washburne to tell Gen. Scott confidentially, that I wished him to be prepared, immediately after my inauguration to make arrangements at once to hold the forts, or if they have been taken, to take them back again."

Afterwards he repeated the substance of the above in another conversation with Wm H Herndon; adding at the close with much emphasis: "There can be no doubt that in *any* event that is good ground to live and to die by."

CHARLESTON, DECEMBER 1860

South Carolina Declaration of the Causes of Secession

December 24, 1860

Four days after voting to secede, the South Carolina convention approved the declaration that follows, as well as an address calling for the formation of a "Confederacy of Slaveholding States."

DECLARATION OF THE IMMEDIATE CAUSES WHICH INDUCE AND JUSTIFY THE SECESSION OF SOUTH CAROLINA FROM THE FEDERAL UNION.

The People of the State of South Carolina, in Convention assembled, on the 26th day of April, A. D., 1852, declared that the frequent violations of the Constitution of the United States, by the Federal Government, and its encroachments upon the reserved rights of the States, fully justified this State in then withdrawing from the Federal Union; but in deference to the opinions and wishes of the other slaveholding States, she forbore at that time to exercise this right. Since that time, these encroachments have continued to increase, and further forbearance ceases to be a virtue.

And now the State of South Carolina having resumed her separate and equal place among nations, deems it due to herself, to the remaining United States of America, and to the nations of the world, that she should declare the immediate causes which have led to this act.

In the year 1765, that portion of the British Empire embracing Great Britain, undertook to make laws for the government of that portion composed of the thirteen American Colonies. A struggle for the right of self-government ensued, which resulted, on the 4th of July, 1776, in a Declaration, by the Colonies, "that they are, and of right ought to be, FREE AND

INDEPENDENT STATES; and that, as free and independent States, they have full power to levy war, conclude peace, contract alliances, establish commerce, and to do all other acts and things which independent States may of right do."

They further solemnly declared that whenever any "form of government becomes destructive of the ends for which it was established, it is the right of the people to alter or abolish it, and to institute a new government." Deeming the Government of Great Britain to have become destructive of these ends, they declared that the Colonies "are absolved from all allegiance to the British Crown, and that all political connection between them and the State of Great Britain is, and ought to be, totally dissolved."

In pursuance of this Declaration of Independence, each of the thirteen States proceeded to exercise its separate sovereignty; adopted for itself a Constitution, and appointed officers for the administration of government in all its departments—Legislative, Executive and Judicial. For purposes of defence, they united their arms and their counsels; and, in 1778, they entered into a League known as the Articles of Confederation, whereby they agreed to entrust the administration of their external relations to a common agent, known as the Congress of the United States, expressly declaring, in the first Article "that each State retains its sovereignty, freedom and independence, and every power, jurisdiction and right which is not, by this Confederation, expressly delegated to the United States in Congress assembled."

Under this Confederation the war of the Revolution was carried on, and on the 8d September, 1783, the contest ended, and a definite Treaty was signed by Great Britain, in which she acknowledged the independence of the Colonies in the following terms:

"ARTICLE I.—His Britannic Majesty acknowledges the said United States, viz: New Hampshire, Massachusetts Bay, Rhode Island and Providence Plantations, Connecticut, New York, New Jersey, Pennsylvania, Delaware, Maryland, Virginia, North Carolina, South Carolina and Georgia, to be FREE, SOVEREIGN AND INDEPENDENT STATES; that he treats with them as such; and for himself, his heirs and successors, relinquishes all claims to the government, propriety and territorial rights of the same and every part thereof."

Thus were established the two great principles asserted by the Colonies, namely: the right of a State to govern itself; and the right of a people to abolish a Government when it becomes destructive of the ends for which it was instituted. And concurrent with the establishment of these principles, was the fact, that each Colony became and was recognized by the mother Country as a FREE, SOVEREIGN AND INDEPENDENT STATE.

In 1787, Deputies were appointed by the States to revise the Articles of Confederation, and on 17th September, 1787, these Deputies recommended, for the adoption of the States, the Articles of Union, known as the Constitution of the United States.

The parties to whom this Constitution was submitted, were the several sovereign States; they were to agree or disagree, and when nine of them agreed the compact was to take effect among those concurring; and the General Government, as the common agent, was then to be invested with their authority.

If only nine of the thirteen States had concurred, the other four would have remained as they then were—separate, sovereign States, independent of any of the provisions of the Constitution. In fact, two of the States did not accede to the Constitution until long after it had gone into operation among the other eleven; and during that interval, they each exercised the functions of an independent nation.

By this Constitution, certain duties were imposed upon the several States, and the exercise of certain of their powers was restrained, which necessarily implied their continued existence as sovereign States. But to remove all doubt, an amendment was added, which declared that the powers not delegated to the United States by the Constitution, nor prohibited by it to the States, are reserved to the States, respectively, or to the people. On 23d May, 1788, South Carolina, by a Convention of her People, passed an Ordinance assenting to this Constitution, and afterwards altered her own Constitution, to conform herself to the obligations she had undertaken.

Thus was established, by compact between the States, a

Government, with defined objects and powers, limited to the express words of the grant. This limitation left the whole remaining mass of power subject to the clause reserving it to the States or to the people, and rendered unnecessary any specification of reserved rights.

We hold that the Government thus established is subject to the two great principles asserted in the Declaration of Independence; and we hold further, that the mode of its formation subjects it to a third fundamental principle, namely: the law of compact. We maintain that in every compact between two or more parties, the obligation is mutual; that the failure of one of the contracting parties to perform a material part of the agreement, entirely releases the obligation of the other; and that where no arbiter is provided, each party is remitted to his own judgment to determine the fact of failure, with all its consequences.

In the present case, that fact is established with certainty. We assert that fourteen of the States have deliberately refused, for years past, to fulfil their constitutional obligations, and we refer to their own Statutes for the proof.

The Constitution of the United States, in its fourth Article, provides as follows:

"No person held to service or labor in one State, under the laws thereof, escaping into another, shall, in consequence of any law or regulation therein, be discharged from such service or labor, but shall be delivered up, on claim of the party to whom such service or labor may be due."

This stipulation was so material to the compact, that without it that compact would not have been made. The great number of the contracting parties held slaves, and they had previously evinced their estimate of the value of such a stipulation by making it a condition in the Ordinance for the government of the territory ceded by Virginia, which now composes the States north of the Ohio River.

The same article of the Constitution stipulates also for rendition by the several States of fugitives from justice from the other States.

The General Government, as the common agent, passed laws to carry into effect these stipulations of the States. For many years these laws were executed. But an increasing hostility on the part of the non-slaveholding States to the institution of slavery, has led to a disregard of their obligations, and the laws of the General Government have ceased to effect the objects of the Constitution. The States of Maine, New Hampshire, Vermont, Massachusetts, Connecticut, Rhode Island, New York, Pennsylvania, Illinois, Indiana, Michigan, Wisconsin and Iowa, have enacted laws which either nullify the Acts of Congress or render useless any attempt to execute them. In many of these States the fugitive is discharged from the service or labor claimed, and in none of them has the State Government complied with the stipulation made in the Constitution. The State of New Jersey, at an early day, passed a law in conformity with her constitutional obligation; but the current of anti-slavery feeling has led her more recently to enact laws which render inoperative the remedies provided by her own law and by the laws of Congress. In the State of New York even the right of transit for a slave has been denied by her tribunals; and the States of Ohio and Iowa have refused to surrender to justice fugitives charged with murder, and with inciting servile insurrection in the State of Virginia. Thus the constituted compact has been deliberately broken and disregarded by the non-slaveholding States, and the consequence follows that South Carolina is released from her obligation.

The ends for which this Constitution was framed are declared by itself to be "to form a more perfect union, establish justice, insure domestic tranquillity, provide for the common defence, promote the general welfare, and secure the blessings of liberty to ourselves and our posterity."

These ends it endeavored to accomplish by a Federal Government, in which each State was recognized as an equal, and had separate control over its own institutions. The right of property in slaves was recognized by giving to free persons distinct political rights, by giving them the right to represent, and burthening them with direct taxes for three-fifths of their slaves; by authorizing the importation of slaves for twenty years; and by stipulating for the rendition of fugitives from labor.

We affirm that these ends for which this Government was instituted have been defeated, and the Government itself has been made destructive of them by the action of the non-slaveholding States. Those States have assumed the right of deciding upon the propriety of our domestic institutions; and have denied the rights of property established in fifteen of the States and recognized by the Constitution; they have denounced as sinful the institution of slavery; they have permitted the open establishment among them of societies, whose avowed object is to disturb the peace and to eloign the property of the citizens of other States. They have encouraged and assisted thousands of our slaves to leave their homes; and those who remain, have been incited by emissaries, books and pictures to servile insurrection.

For twenty-five years this agitation has been steadily increasing, until it has now secured to its aid the power of the common Government. Observing the *forms* of the Constitution, a sectional party has found within that Article establishing the Executive Department, the means of subverting the Constitution itself. A geographical line has been drawn across the Union, and all the States north of that line have united in the election of a man to the high office of President of the United States, whose opinions and purposes are hostile to slavery. He is to be entrusted with the administration of the common Government, because he has declared that that "Government cannot endure permanently half slave, half free," and that the public mind must rest in the belief that slavery is in the course of ultimate extinction.

This sectional combination for the submersion of the Constitution, has been aided in some of the States by elevating to citizenship, persons, who, by the supreme law of the land, are incapable of becoming citizens; and their votes have been used to inaugurate a new policy, hostile to the South, and destructive of its peace and safety.

On the 4th of March next, this party will take possession of the Government. It has announced that the South shall be excluded from the common territory, that the judicial tribunals shall be made sectional, and that a war must be waged against slavery until it shall cease throughout the United States.

The guaranties of the Constitution will then no longer exist; the equal rights of the States will be lost. The slaveholding States will no longer have the power of self-government, or self-protection, and the Federal Government will have become their enemy.

Sectional interest and animosity will deepen the irritation, and all hope of remedy is rendered vain, by the fact that public opinion at the North has invested a great political error with the sanctions of a more erroneous religious belief.

We, therefore, the People of South Carolina, by our delegates in Convention assembled, appealing to the Supreme Judge of the world for the rectitude of our intentions, have solemnly declared that the Union heretofore existing between this State and the other States of North America, is dissolved, and that the State of South Carolina has resumed her position among the nations of the world, as a separate and independent State; with full power to levy war, conclude peace, contract alliances, establish commerce, and to do all other acts and things which independent States may of right do.

OCCUPYING FORT SUMTER:
SOUTH CAROLINA, DECEMBER 1860

Abner Doubleday: from Reminiscences of Forts Sumter and Moultrie in 1860–'61

Captain Abner Doubleday, an 1842 graduate of West Point, had been assigned to Fort Moultrie in Charleston Harbor in 1858, and was commanding an artillery company there when the secession crisis began. In his 1876 memoir, Doubleday described Fort Sumter; Major Robert Anderson's assumption of command at Charleston on November 21, 1860; and Anderson's crucial decision to relocate the garrison from its highly vulnerable position at Fort Moultrie, where it was exposed to an overland attack, to a more secure one inside Fort Sumter.

THE FIRST thing that attracted the eye of the stranger, upon approaching Charleston from the sea, was Fort Sumter. It was built on an artificial island made of large blocks of stone. The walls were of dark brick, and designed for three tiers of guns. The whole structure, as it rose abruptly out of the water, had a gloomy, prison-like appearance. It was situated on the edge of the channel, in the narrowest part of the harbor, between Fort Moultrie and Cummings Point, distant about a mile from the former place, and twelve hundred yards from the latter. The year before, it had been used by us as a temporary place of confinement and security for some negroes that had been brought over from Africa in a slaver captured by one of our naval vessels. The inevitable conflict was very near breaking out at that time; for there was an eager desire on the part of all the people around us to seize these negroes, and distribute them among the plantations; and if the Government had not acted promptly in sending them back to Africa, I think an attempt would have been made to take them from us by force, on the ground that some of them had violated a State law by landing at Moultrieville.

It was now openly proclaimed in Charleston that declarations in favor of the Union would no longer be tolerated; that the time for deliberation had passed, and the time for action had come.

On the 21st our new commander arrived and assumed command. He felt as if he had a hereditary right to be there, for his father had distinguished himself in the Revolutionary War in defense of old Fort Moultrie against the British, and had been confined a long time as a prisoner in Charleston. We had long known Anderson as a gentleman; courteous, honest, intelligent, and thoroughly versed in his profession. He had been twice brevetted for gallantry—once for services against the Seminole Indians in Florida, and once for the battle of Molino del Rey in Mexico, where he was badly wounded. In politics he was a strong pro-slavery man. Nevertheless, he was opposed to secession and Southern extremists. He soon found himself in troubled waters, for the approaching battle of Fort Moultrie was talked of everywhere throughout the State, and the mob in Charleston could hardly be restrained from making an immediate assault. They were kept back once through the exertions of Colonel Benjamin Huger, of the Ordnance Department of the United States Army. As he belonged to one of the most distinguished families in Charleston, he had great influence there. It was said at the time that he threatened if we were attacked, or rather mobbed, in this way, he would join us, and fight by the side of his friend Anderson.* Colonel Memminger, afterward the Confederate Secretary of the Treasury, also exerted himself to prevent any irregular and unauthorized violence.

Anderson had been urged by several of us to remove his command to Fort Sumter, but he had invariably replied that he was specially assigned to Fort Moultrie, and had no right to vacate it without orders. Our affairs, however, were becoming

*He left the United States service soon after the attack on Fort Sumter, and joined the Confederates. He did so reluctantly, for he had gained great renown in our army for his gallantry in Mexico, and he knew he would soon have been promoted to the position of Chief of our Ordnance Department had he remained with us.

critical, and I thought it my duty to speak to him again on the subject. He still apparently adhered to his decision. Nevertheless, he had fully determined to make the change, and was now merely awaiting a favorable opportunity. To deceive the enemy, he still kept at work with unabated zeal on the defenses of Fort Moultrie. This exactly suited the purposes of the rebel leaders, for they knew we could make no effectual defense there, and our preparations would only increase the prestige of their victory. We were not authorized to commence hostilities by burning the adjacent houses, and yet, if they were not leveled, clouds of riflemen could occupy them, and prevent our men from serving the guns. Under any circumstances, it was plain that we must soon succumb from over-exertion and loss of sleep incident to repelling incessant attacks from a host of enemies. The fact that through the provident care of the Secretary of War the guns of Fort Sumter would also be turned upon us, enfilading two sides of Fort Moultrie, and taking another side in reverse, was quite decisive as to the impossibility of our making a lengthened defense.

Up to this time we had hoped, almost against hope, that, even if the Government were base enough to desert us, the loyal spirit of the patriotic North would manifest itself in our favor, inasmuch as our little force represented the supremacy of the Constitution and the laws; but all seemed doubt, apathy, and confusion there. Yancey was delivering lectures in the Northern States, as a representative of the Disunionists, not only without molestation, but with frequent and vociferous applause from the Democratic masses, who could not be made to believe there was any real danger.

In making his arrangements to cross over, Anderson acted with consummate prudence and ability. He only communicated his design to the staff-officers, whose co-operation was indispensable, and he waited until the moment of execution before he informed the others of his intention. No one, of course, would deliberately betray a secret of this kind, but it sometimes happens, under such circumstances, that officers give indications of what is about to take place by sending for their washing, packing their trunks, and making changes in their messing arrangements.

Without knowing positively that any movement had been

projected, two circumstances excited my suspicions. Once, while I was walking with the major on the parapet, he turned to me abruptly, and asked me what would be the best course to take to render the gun-carriages unserviceable. I told him there were several methods, but my plan would be to heap pitch-pine knots around them, and burn them up. The question was too suggestive to escape my attention.

On the day previous to our departure, I requested him to allow me to purchase a large quantity of wire, to make an entanglement in front of the part of the work I was assigned to defend. He said, with a quizzical look, "Certainly; you shall have a mile of wire, if you require it." When I proposed to send for it immediately, he smiled, and objected in such a peculiar way that I at once saw that he was no longer interested in our efforts to strengthen Fort Moultrie.

As a preliminary to the proposed movement, he directed the post quartermaster, Lieutenant Hall, to charter three schooners and some barges, for the ostensible purpose of transporting the soldiers' families to old Fort Johnson, on the opposite side of the harbor, where there were some dilapidated public buildings belonging to the United States. The danger of the approaching conflict was a good pretext for the removal of the non-combatants. All this seemed natural enough to the enemy, and no one offered any opposition. In reality, these vessels were loaded with supplies for all the troops, with reference to a prolonged residence in Fort Sumter. Hall was directed to land every thing there as soon as a signal-gun was fired. In the mean time he sailed for Fort Johnson, and lay off and on, waiting for the signal.

Anderson had broken up his own mess, and on the last evening of our stay (December 26th) I left my room to ask him in to take tea with us. The sun was just setting as I ascended the steps leading to the parapet and approached him. He was in the midst of a group of officers, each of whom seemed silent and distrait. As I passed our assistant-surgeon, I remarked, "It is a fine evening, Crawford." He replied in a hesitating and embarrassed manner, showing that his thoughts were elsewhere. I saw plainly that something unusual had occurred. Anderson approached me as I advanced, and said quietly, "I have determined to evacuate this post immediately, for the purpose of occupying Fort Sumter; I can only allow you twenty minutes to form your company and be in readiness to start." I was surprised at this announcement, and realized the gravity of the situation at a glance. We were watched by spies and vigilance-committees, who would undoubtedly open fire upon us as soon as they saw the object of the movement. I was naturally concerned, too, for the safety of my wife, who was the only lady in the fort at that time, and who would necessarily be exposed to considerable danger. Fortunately, I had little or no property to lose, as, in anticipation of a crisis, I had previously sent every thing of value to New York. Some of the other officers did not fare so well. The doctor, not expecting so sudden a *dénouement*, had necessarily left his medical stores unpacked. Foster, who had taken a house outside for his family, was wholly unprepared, and lost heavily.

I made good use of the twenty minutes allowed me. I first went to the barracks, formed my company, inspected it, and saw that each man was properly armed and equipped. This left me ten minutes to spare. I dashed over to my quarters; told my wife to get ready to leave immediately, and as the fighting would probably commence in a few minutes, I advised her to take refuge with some family outside, and get behind the sand-hills as soon as possible, to avoid the shot. She hastily threw her wearing-apparel into her trunks, and I called two men to put her baggage outside the main gate. I then accompanied her there, and we took a sad and hasty leave of each other, for neither knew when or where we would meet again. As soon as this was accomplished, I strapped on my revolver, tied a blanket across my shoulders, and reported to Major Anderson that my men were in readiness to move.

In the mean time Lieutenant Jefferson C. Davis, of my company, who had been detailed to command the rear guard, aimed the guns, which were already loaded, to bear upon the passage to Fort Sumter, and Captain Foster and Assistant-surgeon Crawford, with two sergeants and three privates, remained with him, and took post at five columbiads, in readiness to carry out Major Anderson's design, which was to sink the guard-boats, should they attempt to fire into us or run us down while *en route*. Certainly the major showed no lack of determination or energy on this occasion.

If we were successful in crossing, Davis was to follow with the remainder of the men. Foster and Mr. Moale agreed to remain behind until morning. They also volunteered to place themselves at the guns, and cover the retreat of the rear guard under Davis, in case an attempt was made to intercept them.

The chaplain, the Rev. Matthias Harris, being a non-combatant, and having his family in the village, was not notified. Neither was Surgeon Simons, of the army, who was living in a house adjoining the fort, and directly in line with our guns. When he saw the movement in progress, he hastened out with his family, to shelter them behind the sand-hills as soon as possible.

Every thing being in readiness, we passed out of the main gates, and silently made our way for about a quarter of a mile to a spot where the boats were hidden behind an irregular pile of rocks, which originally formed part of the sea-wall. There was not a single human being in sight as we marched to the rendezvous, and we had the extraordinary good luck to be wholly unobserved. We found several boats awaiting us, under charge of two engineer officers, Lieutenants Snyder and Meade. They and their crews were crouched down behind the rocks, to escape observation. In a low tone they pointed out to me the boats intended for my company, and then pushed out rapidly to return to the fort. Noticing that one of the guard-boats was approaching, they made a wide circuit to avoid it. I hoped there would be time for my party to cross before the steamer could overhaul us; but as among my men there were a number of unskillful oarsmen, we made but slow progress, and it soon became evident that we would be overtaken in mid-channel. It was after sunset, and the twilight had deepened, so that there was a fair chance for us to escape. While the steamer was yet afar off, I took off my cap, and threw open my coat to conceal the buttons. I also made the men take off their coats, and use them to cover up their muskets, which were lying alongside the rowlocks. I hoped in this way that we might pass for a party of laborers returning to the fort. The paddle-wheels stopped within about a hundred yards of us; but, to our great relief, after a slight scrutiny, the steamer kept on its way. In the mean time our men redoubled their efforts, and we soon arrived at our destination. As we ascended the steps of the wharf, crowds of workmen rushed out to meet us, most of them wearing secession emblems. One or two Union men among them cheered lustily, but the majority called out angrily, "What are these soldiers doing here?" I at once formed my men, charged bayonets, drove the tumultuous mass inside the fort, and seized the guard-room, which commanded the main entrance. I then placed sentinels to prevent the crowd from encroaching on us. As soon as we had disembarked, the boats were sent back for Seymour's company. The major landed soon after in one of the engineer boats, which had coasted along to avoid the steamer. Seymour's men arrived in safety, followed soon after by the remaining detachments, which had been left behind as a rear-guard. The latter, however, ran a good deal of risk, for in the dark it passed almost under the bow of the guard-boat *Niña*. The whole movement was successful beyond our most sanguine expectations, and we were highly elated. The signal-gun was fired, and Hall at once sailed over, and landed the soldiers' families and supplies. As soon as the schooners were unloaded, the disloyal workmen were placed on board and shipped off to the main-land. Only a few of the best and most reliable were retained.

Upon leaving me, my wife took refuge temporarily in the residence of Dan Sinclair, the sutler of the post, a most excellent man, and one to whom we were indebted for many kindnesses. Finding that the people of Moultrieville were not yet aware of the change that had taken place, and that every thing was tranquil, she ventured back to the fort, and finished the removal of all our effects. After this, in company with the chaplain's family, she walked up and down the beach the greater part of the night, looking anxiously toward Fort Sumter to see if there were any indications of trouble or disturbance there. In the morning she took up her residence at the chaplain's house. As for the other ladies, both Mrs. Simons and Mrs. Foster fled to the city at the first intimation of danger, and Mrs. Seymour was already there.

"A TERRIBLE REVULSION OF FEELING":
SOUTH CAROLINA, DECEMBER 1860

Catherine Edmondston: Diary, December 26–27, 1860

Catherine Edmondston lived with her husband, Patrick, on their plantation in Halifax County, North Carolina. While visiting her parents in Aiken, South Carolina, she learned that Anderson had moved his garrison from Fort Moultrie to Fort Sumter. President Buchanan had told a delegation of South Carolina congressmen on December 10 that he did not intend to reinforce the garrison at Fort Moultrie. Many Southerners believed Buchanan had also promised not to change the military situation at Charleston in any way, and thus saw the occupation of Fort Sumter as the violation of his pledge.

DECEMBER 26, 1860

In the morning we had a terrible revulsion of feeling which seemed to plunge us at once from the most profound peace into almost War! Major Anderson, the U S Commander of Forts Moultrie, Sumter, & Pinckney, in the night suddenly evacuated Moultrie & Pinckney after spiking the Guns, burning the carriages, and cutting down the Flag staff, and retreated with his whole command into Sumter! Most remarkable conduct & well calculated to bring on the attack which he seems to dread, but of which, beyond a few idle threats there has as yet been no evidence. We heard it on the morning of the 26th, & it seemed to plunge us into a sea of care after basking in the sunshine of happiness.

DECEMBER 27, 1860

On the 27th the Government of SC took possession of the vacant forts Moultrie & Pinckney & hoisted the Palmetto Flag in defiance as it were to the US. Preparations were hastily made to put them in a defencible position. Troops were ordered from the interior, & batteries commenced on the channel with a view to prevent the re-inforcement of Sumter.

Thus has one ill advised act thrown down the gauntlet as it were, which SC is not slow to accept!

We had a delightful visit in Aiken disturbed only by exciting news from Charleston and the passage of Troops, which was so new to us that it excited the liveliest forebodings. The Ladies of SC displayed an enthusiasm & earnestness in their preparations for War that was almost sublime in its unity & self devotion. They spent their whole time scraping lint, making bandages, & even learned to make Cartridges. One lady in Aiken made 500 with her own hands. Never was known such unanimity of action amongst all classes.

South Carolina having seceeded from the US, amidst the jeers & laughter of the whole country calmly organized her own government & prepared for War singly and alone. It at first made one smile to see the news from Washington put under the head of "Foreign News," but all disposition to it was soon taken away by the sight of the terribly earnest way in which all looked at & spoke of it. I often thought, "Have we indeed come to this?" Pray God that Mr. Buchanan would quietly withdraw the troops from Sumter. Let SC peaceably go her own way. Perhaps after a little, when she sees that Mr Lincoln does not meddle with Slavery, she may return & this threatened dismemberment of our country may be prevented. But God ordained otherwise. Papa entered most keenly into it, regretted that he was not a son of her soil, & was as enthused about the attitude adopted by SC as the youngest man in the State.

On the 3d of Jan Georgia seized Fort Pulaski, & Alabama, the arsenal at Mt Vernon with 20,000 stand of arms.

URGING KENTUCKY TO SECEDE: DECEMBER 1860

Stephen F. Hale to Beriah Magoffin

By the end of November 1860 secession conventions had been called in South Carolina, Georgia, Florida, Alabama, and Mississippi. Anticipating the secession of their states, the governors of Mississippi and Alabama sent commissioners to the other fourteen slaveholding states to encourage their secession and to promote the formation of a southern confederacy. (The state conventions of South Carolina, Georgia, and Louisiana would also appoint commissioners.) Stephen F. Hale, a lawyer and state legislator from Alabama who had been born and educated in Kentucky, returned to his native state in late December 1860. With the legislature not in session, he sent this letter to Beriah Magoffin, the state's governor. Magoffin summoned the legislature into session in January 1861, but it voted not to call a state convention.

FRANKFORT, *December 27, 1860*.
His Excellency B. MAGOFFIN,
Governor of the Commonwealth of Kentucky:
　I have the honor of placing in your hands herewith a commission from the Governor of the State of Alabama, accrediting me as a commissioner from that State to the sovereign State of Kentucky, to consult in reference to the momentous issues now pending between the Northern and Southern States of this confederacy. Although each State, as a sovereign political community, must finally determine these grave issues for itself, yet the identity of interests, sympathy, and institutions, prevailing alike in all of the slave-holding States, in the opinion of Alabama renders it proper that there should be a frank and friendly consultation by each one with her sister Southern States touching their common grievances and the measures necessary to be adopted to protect the interest, honor, and safety of their citizens. I come, then, in a spirit of fraternity, as the commissioner on the part of the State of Alabama, to confer with the authorities of this Commonwealth

in reference to the infraction of our constitutional rights, wrongs done and threatened to be done, as well as the mode and measure of redress proper to be adopted by the sovereign States aggrieved to preserve their sovereignty, vindicate their rights, and protect their citizens. In order to a clear understanding of the appropriate remedy, it may be proper to consider the rights and duties, both of the State and citizen, under the Federal compact, as well as the wrongs done and threatened. I therefore submit for the consideration of Your Excellency the following propositions, which I hope will command your assent and approval:

1. The people are the source of all political power, and the primary object of all good governments is to protect the citizen in the enjoyment of life, liberty, and property; and whenever any form of government becomes destructive of these ends, it is the inalienable right and the duty of the people to alter or abolish it.

2. The equality of all the States of this confederacy, as well as the equality of rights of all the citizens of the respective States under the Federal Constitution, is a fundamental principle in the scheme of the federal government. The union of these States under the Constitution was formed "to establish justice, insure domestic tranquillity, provide for the common defense, promote the general welfare, and secure the blessings of liberty to her citizens and their posterity;" and when it is perverted to the destruction of the equality of the States, or substantially fails to accomplish these ends, it fails to achieve the purposes of its creation, and ought to be dissolved.

3. The Federal Government results from a compact entered into between separate, sovereign, and independent States, called the Constitution of the United States, and amendments thereto, by which these sovereign States delegated certain specific powers to be used by that Government for the common defense and general welfare of all the States and their citizens; and when these powers are abused, or used for the destruction of the rights of any State or its citizens, each State has an equal right to judge for itself as well of the violations and infractions of that instrument as of the mode and measure of redress; and if the interest or safety of her citizens demands it, may resume

the powers she had delegated without let or hindrance from the Federal Government or any other power on earth.

4. Each State is bound in good faith to observe and keep on her part all the stipulations and covenants inserted for the benefit of other States in the constitutional compact (the only bond of union by which the several States are bound together), and when persistently violated by one party to the prejudice of her sister States, ceases to be obligatory on the States so aggrieved, and they may rightfully declare the compact broken, the union thereby formed dissolved, and stand upon their original rights as sovereign and independent political communities; and further, that each citizen owes his primary allegiance to the State in which he resides, and hence it is the imperative duty of the State to protect him in the enjoyment of all his constitutional rights, and see to it that they are not denied or withheld from him with impunity by any other State or government.

If the foregoing propositions correctly indicate the objects of this government, the rights and duties of the citizen, as well as the rights, powers, and duties of the State and Federal Governments under the Constitution, the next inquiry is, what rights have been denied, what wrongs have been done, or threatened to be done, of which the Southern States or the people of the Southern States can complain?

At the time of the adoption of the Federal Constitution African slavery existed in twelve of the thirteen States. Slaves are recognized both as property and as a basis of political power by the Federal compact, and special provisions are made by that instrument for their protection as property. Under the influences of climate and other causes, slavery has been banished from the Northern States; the slaves themselves have been sent to the Southern States and there sold, and their price gone into the pockets of their former owners at the North. And in the meantime African slavery has not only become one of the fixed domestic institutions of the Southern States, but forms an important element of their political power, and constitutes the most valuable species of their property, worth, according to recent estimates, not less than $4,000,000,000; forming, in fact, the basis upon which rests the prosperity and wealth of most of these States, and supplying the commerce of the world with its richest freights, and furnishing the manufactories of two continents with the raw material, and their operatives with bread. It is upon this gigantic interest, this peculiar institution of the South, that the Northern States and their people have been waging an unrelenting and fanatical war for the last quarter of a century; an institution with which is bound up not only the wealth and prosperity of the Southern people, but their very existence as a political community. This war has been waged in every way that human ingenuity, urged on by fanaticism, could suggest. They attack us through their literature, in their schools, from the hustings, in their legislative halls, through the public press, and even their courts of justice forget the purity of their judicial ermine to strike down the rights of the Southern slave-holder and override every barrier which the Constitution has erected for his protection; and the sacred desk is desecrated to this unholy crusade against our lives, our property, and the constitutional rights guaranteed to us by the compact of our fathers. During all this time the Southern States have freely conceded to the Northern States and the people of those States every right secured to them by the Constitution, and an equal interest in the common territories of the Government; protected the lives and property of their citizens of every kind, when brought within Southern jurisdiction; enforced through their courts, when necessary, every law of Congress passed for the protection of Northern property, and submitted ever since the foundation of the Government, with scarcely a murmur, to the protection of their shipping, manufacturing, and commercial interests, by odious bounties, discriminating tariffs, and unjust navigation laws, passed by the Federal Government to the prejudice and injury of their own citizens.

The law of Congress for the rendition of fugitive slaves, passed in pursuance of an express provision of the Constitution, remains almost a dead letter upon the statute book. A majority of the Northern States, through their legislative enactments, have openly nullified it, and impose heavy fines and penalties upon all persons who aid in enforcing this law, and some of those States declare the Southern slave-holder who goes within their jurisdiction to assert his legal rights under the Constitution guilty of a high crime, and affix imprisonment in the penitentiary as the penalty. The Federal officers who attempt to discharge their duties under the law, as well as the owner of the slave, are set upon by mobs, and are fortunate if they escape without serious injury to life or limb; and the State authorities, instead of aiding in the enforcement of this law, refuse the use of their jails, and by every means which unprincipled fanaticism can devise give countenance to the mob and aid the fugitive to escape. Thus there are annually large amounts of property actually stolen away from the Southern States, harbored and protected in Northern States and by their citizens; and when a requisition is made for the thief by the Governor of a Southern State upon the Executive of a Northern State, in pursuance of the express conditions of the Federal Constitution, he is insultingly told that the felon has committed no crime, and thus the criminal escapes, the property of the citizen is lost, the sovereignty of the State is insulted, and there is no redress, for the Federal courts have no jurisdiction to award a mandamus to the Governor of a sovereign State to compel him to do an official executive act, and Congress, if disposed, under the Constitution has no power to afford a remedy. These are wrongs under which the Southern people have long suffered, and to which they have patiently submitted, in the hope that a returning sense of justice would prompt the people of the Northern States to discharge their constitutional obligations and save our common country. Recent events, however, have not justified their hopes. The more daring and restless fanatics have banded themselves together, have put in practice the terrible lessons taught by the timid by making an armed incursion upon the sovereign State of Virginia, slaughtering her citizens, for the purpose of exciting a servile insurrection among her slave population, and arming them for the destruction of their own masters. During the past summer the abolition incendiary has lit up the prairies of Texas, fired the dwellings of the inhabitants, burned down whole towns, and laid poison for her citizens, thus literally executing the terrible denunciations of fanaticism against the slaveholder, "Alarm to their sleep, fire to their dwellings, and poison to their food."

The same fell spirit, like an unchained demon, has for years swept over the plains of Kansas, leaving death, desolation, and ruin in its track. Nor is this the mere ebullition of a few half-crazy fanatics, as is abundantly apparent from the sympathy manifested all over the North, where, in many places, the tragic death of John Brown, the leader of the raid upon Virginia, who died upon the gallows a condemned felon, is celebrated with public honors, and his name canonized as a martyr to liberty; and many, even of the more conservative papers of the Black Republican school, were accustomed to speak of his murderous attack upon the lives of the unsuspecting citizens of Virginia in a half-sneering and half-apologetic tone. And what has the Federal Government done in the meantime to protect slave property upon the common territories of the Union? Whilst a whole squadron of the American Navy is maintained on the coast of Africa at an enormous expense to enforce the execution of the laws against the slave-trade (and properly, too), and the whole Navy is kept afloat to protect the lives and property of American citizens upon the high seas, not a law has been passed by Congress or an arm raised by the Federal Government to protect the slave property of citizens from Southern States upon the soil of Kansas, the common territory and common property of the citizens of all the States, purchased alike by their common treasure, and held by the Federal Government, as declared by the Supreme Court of the United States, as the trustee for all their citizens; but, upon the contrary, a territorial government, created by Congress and supported out of the common treasury, under the influence and control of emigrant-aid societies and abolition emissaries, is permitted to pass laws excluding and destroying all that species of property within her limits, thus ignoring on the part of the Federal Government one of the fundamental principles of all good governments—the duty to protect the property of the citizen—and wholly refusing to maintain the equal rights of the States and the citizens of the States upon their common territories.

As the last and crowning act of insult and outrage upon the people of the South, the citizens of the Northern States, by overwhelming majorities, on the 6th day of November last, elected Abraham Lincoln and Hannibal Hamlin President and Vice-President of the United States. Whilst it may be admitted that the mere election of any man to the Presidency is not *per se* a sufficient cause for a dissolution of the Union, yet when the issues upon and circumstances under which he was elected are properly appreciated and understood, the question arises whether a due regard to the interest, honor, and safety of their citizens, in view of this and all the other antecedent wrongs and outrages, do not render it the imperative duty of the Southern States to resume the powers they have delegated to the Federal Government and interpose their sovereignty for the protection of their citizens.

What, then, are the circumstances under which and the issues upon which he was elected? His own declarations and the current history of the times but too plainly indicate he was elected by a Northern sectional vote, against the most solemn warnings and protestations of the whole South. He stands forth as the representative of the fanaticism of the North, which, for the last quarter of a century, has been making war upon the South, her property, her civilization, her institutions, and her interests; as the representative of that party which overrides all constitutional barriers, ignores the obligation of official oaths, and acknowledges allegiance to a higher law than the Constitution, striking down the sovereignty and equality of the States, and resting its claims to popular favor upon the one dogma—the equality of the races, white and black.

It was upon this acknowledgment of allegiance to a higher law that Mr. Seward rested his claims to the Presidency in a speech made by him in Boston before the election. He is the exponent, if not the author, of the doctrine of the irrepressible conflict between freedom and slavery, and proposes that the opponents of slavery shall arrest its further expansion, and by Congressional legislation exclude it from the common territories of the Federal Government, and place it where the public mind shall rest in the belief that it is in the course of ultimate extinction. He claims for free negroes the right of suffrage and an equal voice in the Government; in a word, all the rights of citizenship, although the Federal Constitution, as construed by the highest judicial tribunal in the world, does not recognize Africans imported into this country as slaves or their descendants—whether free or slaves—as citizens.

These were the issues presented in the last Presidential

canvass, and upon these the American people passed at the ballot box. Upon the principles then announced by Mr. Lincoln and his leading friends we are bound to expect his administration to be conducted. Hence it is that in high places among the Republican party the election of Mr. Lincoln is hailed not simply as a change of administration, but as the inauguration of new principles and a new theory of government, and even as the downfall of slavery. Therefore it is that the election of Mr. Lincoln cannot be regarded otherwise than a solemn declaration, on the part of a great majority of the Northern people, of hostility to the South, her property, and her institutions; nothing less than an open declaration of war, for the triumph of this new theory of government destroys the property of the South, lays waste her fields, and inaugurates all the horrors of a San Domingo servile insurrection, consigning her citizens to assassinations and her wives and daughters to pollution and violation to gratify the lust of half-civilized Africans. Especially is this true in the cotton-growing States, where, in many localities, the slave outnumbers the white population ten to one.

If the policy of the Republicans is carried out according to the programme indicated by the leaders of the party, and the South submits, degradation and ruin must overwhelm alike all classes of citizens in the Southern States. The slave-holder and non-slave-holder must ultimately share the same fate; all be degraded to a position of equality with free negroes, stand side by side with them at the polls, and fraternize in all the social relations of life, or else there will be an eternal war of races, desolating the land with blood, and utterly wasting and destroying all the resources of the country. Who can look upon such a picture without a shudder? What Southern man, be he slave-holder or non-slave-holder, can without indignation and horror contemplate the triumph of negro equality, and see his own sons and daughters in the not distant future associating with free negroes upon terms of political and social equality, and the white man stripped by the heaven-daring hand of fanaticism of that title to superiority over the black race which God himself has bestowed? In the Northern States, where free negroes are so few as to form no appreciable part of the community, in spite of all the legislation for their protection, they still remain a degraded caste, excluded by the ban of society from social association with all but the lowest and most degraded of the white race. But in the South, where in many places the African race largely predominates, and as a consequence the two races would be continually pressing together, amalgamation or the extermination of the one or the other would be inevitable. Can Southern men submit to such degradation and ruin? God forbid that they should.

But it is said there are many constitutional conservative men at the North who sympathize with and battle for us. That is true; but they are utterly powerless, as the late Presidential election unequivocally shows, to breast the tide of fanaticism that threatens to roll over and crush us. With them it is a question of principle, and we award to them all honor for their loyalty to the Constitution of our fathers; but their defeat is not their ruin. With us it is a question of self-preservation. Our lives, our property, the safety of our homes and our hearthstones, all that men hold dear on earth, is involved in the issue. If we triumph, vindicate our rights, and maintain our institutions, a bright and joyous future lies before us. We can clothe the world with our staple, give wings to her commerce, and supply with bread the starving operative in other lands, and at the same time preserve an institution that has done more to civilize and Christianize the heathen than all human agencies besides—an institution alike beneficial to both races, ameliorating the moral, physical, and intellectual condition of the one and giving wealth and happiness to the other. If we fail, the light of our civilization goes down in blood, our wives and our little ones will be driven from their homes by the light of our own dwellings, the dark pall of barbarism must soon gather over our sunny land, and the scenes of West India emancipation, with its attendant horrors and crimes (that monument of British fanaticism and folly), be re-enacted in their own land upon a more gigantic scale.

Then, is it not time we should be up and doing, like men who know their rights and dare maintain them? To whom shall the people of the Southern States look for the protection of their rights, interests, and honor? We answer, to their own sons and their respective States. To the States, as we have seen, under our system of government, is due the primary allegiance of the citizen, and the correlative obligation of protection devolves upon the respective States—a duty from which they cannot escape, and which they dare not neglect without a violation of all the bonds of fealty that hold together the citizen and the sovereign. The Northern States and their citizens have proved recreant to their obligations under the Federal Constitution. They have violated that compact and refused to perform their covenants in that behalf.

The Federal Government has failed to protect the rights and property of the citizens of the South, and is about to pass into the hands of a party pledged for the destruction not only of their rights and their property, but the equality of the States ordained by the Constitution, and the heaven-ordained superiority of the white over the black race. What remains, then, for the Southern States and the people of these States if they are loyal to the great principles of civil and religious liberty, sanctified by the sufferings of a seven-years' war and baptized with the blood of the Revolution? Can they permit the rights of their citizens to be denied and spurned, their property spirited away, their own sovereignty violated, and themselves degraded to the position of mere dependencies instead of sovereign States; or shall each for itself, judging of the infractions of the constitutional compact, as well as the mode and measure of redress, declare that the covenants of that sacred instrument in their behalf, and for the benefit of their citizens, have been willfully, deliberately, continuously, and persistently broken and violated by the other parties to the compact, and that they and their citizens are therefore absolved from all further obligations to keep and perform the covenants thereof; resume the powers delegated to the Federal Government, and, as sovereign States, form other relations for the protection of their citizens and the discharge of the great ends of government? The union of these States was one of fraternity as well as equality; but what fraternity now exists between the citizens of the two sections? Various religious associations, powerful in numbers and influence, have been broken asunder, and the sympathies that bound together the people of the several States at the time of the formation of the Constitution have ceased to exist, and feelings of bitterness and even hostility have sprung up in their place. How can this be reconciled and a spirit of fraternity established? Will the people of the North cease to make war upon the institution of slavery and award to it the protection guaranteed by the Constitution? The accumulated wrongs of many years, the late action of their members in Congress refusing every measure of justice to the South, as well as the experience of all the past, answers, No, never!

Will the South give up the institution of slavery and consent that her citizens be stripped of their property, her civilization destroyed, the whole land laid waste by fire and sword? It is impossible. She cannot; she will not. Then why attempt longer to hold together hostile States under the stipulations of a violated Constitution? It is impossible. Disunion is inevitable. Why, then, wait longer for the consummation of a result that must come? Why waste further time in expostulations and appeals to Northern States and their citizens, only to be met, as we have been for years past, by renewed insults and repeated injuries? Will the South be better prepared to meet the emergency when the North shall be strengthened by the admission of the new Territories of Kansas, Nebraska, Washington, Jefferson, Nevada, Idaho, Chippewa, and Arizona as non-slave-holding States, as we are warned from high sources will be done within the next four years, under the administration of Mr. Lincoln? Can the true men at the North ever make a more powerful or successful rally for the preservation of our rights and the Constitution than they did in the last Presidential contest? There is nothing to inspire a hope that they can.

Shall we wait until our enemies shall possess themselves of all the powers of the Government; until abolition judges are on the Supreme Court bench, abolition collectors at every port, and abolition postmasters in every town; secret mail agents traversing the whole land, and a subsidized press established in our midst to demoralize our people? Will we be stronger then or better prepared to meet the struggle, if a struggle must come? No, verily. When that time shall come, well may our adversaries laugh at our folly and deride our impotence. The deliberate judgment of Alabama, as indicated by the joint resolutions of her General Assembly, approved February 24, 1860, is that prudence, patriotism, and loyalty to all the great principles of civil liberty, incorporated in our Constitution and consecrated by the memories of the past, demand that all the Southern States should now resume their delegated powers, maintain the rights, interests, and honor of their citizens, and vindicate their own sovereignty. And she most earnestly but respectfully invites her sister sovereign State, Kentucky, who so gallantly vindicated the sovereignty of the States in 1798, to the consideration of these grave and vital questions, hoping she may concur with the State of Alabama in the conclusions to which she has been driven by the impending dangers that now surround the Southern States. But if, on mature deliberation, she dissents on any point from the conclusions to which the State of Alabama has arrived, on behalf of that State I most respectfully ask a declaration by this venerable Commonwealth of her conclusions and position on all the issues discussed in this communication; and Alabama most respectfully urges upon the people and authorities of Kentucky the startling truth that submission or acquiescence on the part of the Southern States at this perilous hour will enable Black Republicanism to redeem all its nefarious pledges and accomplish all its flagitious ends; and that hesitation or delay in their action will be misconceived and misconstrued by their adversaries and ascribed not to that elevated patriotism that would sacrifice all but their honor to save the Union of their fathers, but to division and dissension among themselves and their consequent weakness; that prompt, bold, and decided action is demanded alike by prudence, patriotism, and the safety of their citizens.

Permit me, in conclusion, on behalf of the State of Alabama, to express my high gratification at the cordial manner in which I have been received as her commissioner by the authorities of the State of Kentucky, as well as the profound personal gratification which, as a son of Kentucky, born and reared within her borders, I feel at the manner in which I, as the commissioner from the State of my adoption, have been received and treated by the authorities of the State of my birth. Please accept assurances of the high consideration and esteem of,

Your obedient servant, &c.,

S. F. HALE,
Commissioner from the State of Alabama.

"THE TEMPEST BURSTING": 1860
Herman Melville: Misgivings

Herman Melville published *Battle-Pieces and Aspects of the War*, his first book of poetry, in 1866. In his preface, Melville wrote that with "few exceptions, the Pieces in this volume originated in an impulse imparted by the fall of Richmond" in April 1865, and were "composed without reference to collective arrangement, but, being brought together in review, naturally fell into the order assumed." Melville placed "Misgivings" at the beginning of the volume, immediately following a poem about the execution of John Brown.

―――――――

WHEN ocean-clouds over inland hills
    Sweep storming in late autumn brown,
And horror the sodden valley fills,
    And the spire falls crashing in the town,
I muse upon my country's ills—
The tempest bursting from the waste of Time
On the world's fairest hope linked with man's foulest crime.

Nature's dark side is heeded now—
    (Ah! optimist-cheer disheartened flown)—
A child may read the moody brow
    Of yon black mountain lone.
With shouts the torrents down the gorges go,
And storms are formed behind the storm we feel:
The hemlock shakes in the rafter, the oak in the driving keel.

"SAD FOREBODING": GEORGIA, JANUARY 1861
Mary Jones to Charles C. Jones Jr.

Mary Jones lived with her husband Charles, a Presbyterian clergyman, at Montevideo plantation in Liberty County, Georgia. Her eldest child, Charles Jr., was a lawyer in Savannah.

Montevideo, *Thursday*, January 3rd, 1861

My dear Son,

Your affectionate favor was this day received, and from our heart of hearts we respond to your kind wishes—"A Happy New Year!"—although every moment seems fraught with the sad foreboding that it may be only one of trial and suffering. But "God is our refuge and strength, a very present help in trouble. Therefore will not we fear." Read Psalm 46. I trust the Lord of Hosts will be with us!

An indescribable sadness weighs down my soul as I think of our once glorious but now dissolving Union! Our children's children—what will constitute their national pride and glory? *We* have no alternative; and necessity demands that we now protect ourselves from entire destruction at the hands of those who have rent and torn and obliterated every national bond of union, of confidence and affection. When your brother and yourself were very little fellows, we took you into old Independence Hall; and at the foot of Washington's statue I pledged you both to support and defend the Union. *That Union* has passed away, and you are free from your mother's vow.

Your father thinks the occupation of Fort Pulaski will produce more effect than anything that has occurred. How can the South delay united and decided action? . . . The results may be awful unless we are united.

Did your father tell you old Montevideo gave forth her response on the night of the 26th in honor of Carolina and in sympathy with Savannah? Strange to say, as we walked out to view the illumination from the lawn, we discovered that there were thirteen windows on the front of the house, each of which had one brilliant light resembling a star; and without design one of them had been placed far in the ascendant—emblematic, as we hailed it, of the noble and gallant state which must ever be regarded as the polar star of our Southern confederacy.

And now, my dear son, we will look within the home circle. I trust you have regained your accustomed strength, and dear little Julia still improving. Your sister and Robert and the little ones have been with us for two weeks, and left us today. So did your uncle, who spent the day and night with us.

Enclosed I send your brother's letter, with the hope that you may yet help him to obtain the appointment. Would it be possible for you individually, or through Colonel Lawton or anyone else, to see *Governor Brown* whilst he is in Savannah, and if possible to secure the appointment for him? Poor boy, my heart sympathizes very deeply with his disappointments and perplexities. I know you will do all you can to aid him. I believe him worthy of and qualified for the trust, or I would not ask it even for my child.

Your dear father is very unwell from a severe cold. I want to write Ruth a few lines, and my paper is at an end. . . . With love from Father and myself to you both, and kisses for our little darling,

Your affectionate mother,
M. Jones.

"ALL DEPENDS ON VIRGINIA":
WASHINGTON, D.C., JANUARY 1861

Henry Adams to Charles Francis Adams Jr.

Henry Adams wrote to his brother at a time when their father's attempts to frame a sectional compromise made him an increasingly controversial figure in their home state. In late December 1860 Charles Francis Adams sponsored a proposal in the Committee of Thirty-Three for the immediate admission of New Mexico, with the tacit understanding that it would enter the Union as a slave state. Adams hoped the measure would help draw the border states away from the secessionist Deep South, but his support for the proposal was criticized by many Massachusetts Republicans for abandoning the essential party principle of opposition to the expansion of slavery. Although the committee voted 13–11 in favor of admitting New Mexico, the measure was rejected by the House, 115–71, on March 1.

Washington. 8 Jan. 1861.

My dear Boy

Your story temporarily bluffs me, but I'll see if I can't find something to go it better. The account shall be settled immediately. If you see Ben Crowninshield I wish you would ask him whether he has received a letter I wrote him in answer to one of his, and why he has not answered it.

I think we do not feel so confident here as usual. Seward is evidently very low-spirited, though that is owing partly to the labor of preparing his speech. But I have noticed a marked change in the tone of our excellent father, consequent on information which he has received but has not confided in me. Until now he has steadily believed that the border-states would not go, and his measures were intended to influence them. But now I think he gives it up. His theory is that all depends on Virginia and that Virginia is lost. If this turns out to be the case, it increases our difficulties very badly. It makes war inevitable; war before the 4th of March.

God forbid that I should croak, or foresee what is not to

come. You and I, friend, are young enough to be sanguine where others despair. For one, I intend to remain in this city. If there is war I intend to take such part in it as is necessary or useful. It would be a comfort if such times come, to know that the Massachusetts regiments are ready, and if one can be formed on the Cromwell type, I will enrol myself. Of course we can not doubt the result; but I must confess that I had hoped to avoid a real battle. If Virginia and Maryland secede, they will strike at this city, and we shall have to give them such an extermination that it were better we had not been borne. I do not want to fight them. Is thy servant a South Carolinian that he should do this thing. They are mad, mere maniacs, and I want to lock them up till they become sane; not kill them. I want to educate, humanize and refine them, not send fire and sword among them. Let those that will, howl for war. I claim to be sufficiently philanthropic to dread it, and sufficiently Christian to wish to avoid it and to determine to avoid it, except in self-defence. Tell your warlike friends in Massachusetts that we want no bloodthirsty men here. If the time comes when men are wanted, it will be men who fight because there is no other way; not because they are angry; men who will come with their bibles as well as their rifles and who will pray God to forgive them for every life they take.

I am confident that if an actual conflict could be kept off for a few months, there could be none. The South are too weak to sustain such a delay. There would be a reaction among themselves from mere starvation and ruin. But if Virginia goes out, I do not see how it is to be avoided.

This is solemn, but I have enough self-respect to keep me from joining with any body of men who act from mere passion and the sense of wrong. Don't trust yourself to that set, for they will desert you when you need their support. They don't know what they're after. Support any honorable means of conciliation. Our position will be immensely strengthened by it. We cannot be too much in the right. It is time for us, who claim to lead this movement, to become cool and to do nothing without the fear of God before our eyes.

I passed this evening at the Bayards where I saw Florey for the first time. I like the Bayards well. They're ladies, which is more than I can say for most of the young women here. They send all sorts of regards to you and John and Arthur and hope you will come on. Tomorrow evening I shall take tea there with some of their friends.

Loo is here and is amiable as possible. Since New Years day, I have been laid up by a violent cold which completely upset me, but now it's over. I don't hear much that is very novel. Seward dined here yesterday and was for him quite subdued.

My letters have, I think, done some good in sustaining papa at home and it was a relief to see the Advertiser of yesterday declare itself at last. I am convinced that his course is the only true and great one, and that it will ultimately meet the wishes of the whole North. You need not fear a compromise. The worst that is to be feared is, in my opinion a division in the party. No compromise would, I think, call back the South. We are beyond that stage where a compromise can prevent the struggle. Let them pass their measures if they can; the contest is on us and all the rotten twine that ever was spun, can't tie up this breach.

Yrs ever   H.B.A.

JACKSON, JANUARY 1861

Mississippi Declaration of the Causes of Secession

January 9, 1861

On January 9, 1861, Mississippi became the second state to break away from the Union when its convention voted, 85–15, to secede. It was quickly followed by Florida (January 10), Alabama (January 11), Georgia (January 19), Louisiana (January 26), and Texas (February 1). In Alabama the convention approved a secession ordinance that described the Republicans as "a sectional party avowedly hostile to the domestic institutions and to the peace and security of the people of the State," while the Georgia and Texas conventions adopted declarations of causes similar to the ones issued in South Carolina and Mississippi. The Georgia declaration denounced the "avowed purpose" of the Republican party "to subvert our society and subject us not only to the loss of our property but the destruction of ourselves, our wives, and our children, and the desolation of our homes, our altars, and our firesides." In Texas, the convention declared that the Republicans "demand the abolition of negro slavery throughout the confederacy, the recognition of political equality between the white and negro races, and avow their determination to press on their crusade against us, so long as a negro slave remains in these States."

A DECLARATION OF THE IMMEDIATE CAUSES WHICH INDUCE AND JUSTIFY THE SECESSION OF THE STATE OF MISSISSIPPI FROM THE FEDERAL UNION.

In the momentous step which our State has taken of dissolving its connection with the government of which we so long formed a part, it is but just that we should declare the prominent reasons which have induced our course.

Our position is thoroughly identified with the institution of slavery—the greatest material interest of the world. Its labor supplies the product which constitutes by far the largest and most important portions of the commerce of the earth. These products are peculiar to the climate verging on the tropical regions, and by an imperious law of nature, none but the black race can bear exposure to the tropical sun. These products have become necessities of the world, and a blow at slavery is a blow at commerce and civilization. That blow has been long aimed at the institution, and was at the point of reaching its consummation. There was no choice left us but submission to the mandates of abolition, or a dissolution of the Union, whose principles had been subverted to work out our ruin.

That we do not overstate the dangers to our institution, a reference to a few unquestionable facts will sufficiently prove.

The hostility to this institution commenced before the adoption of the Constitution, and was manifested in the well-known Ordinance of 1787, in regard to the Northwestern Territory.

The feeling increased, until, in 1819–20, it deprived the South of more than half the vast territory acquired from France.

The same hostility dismembered Texas and seized upon all the territory acquired from Mexico.

It has grown until it denies the right of property in slaves, and refuses protection to that right on the high seas, in the Territories, and wherever the government of the United States had jurisdiction.

It refuses the admission of new slave States into the Union, and seeks to extinguish it by confining it within its present limits, denying the power of expansion.

It tramples the original equality of the South under foot.

It has nullified the Fugitive Slave Law in almost every free State in the Union, and has utterly broken the compact which our fathers pledged their faith to maintain.

It advocates negro equality, socially and politically, and promotes insurrection and incendiarism in our midst.

It has enlisted its press, its pulpit and its schools against us, until the whole popular mind of the North is excited and inflamed with prejudice.

It has made combinations and formed associations to carry out its schemes of emancipation in the States and wherever else slavery exists.

It seeks not to elevate or to support the slave, but to destroy his present condition without providing a better.

It has invaded a State, and invested with the honors of martyrdom the wretch whose purpose was to apply flames to our dwellings, and the weapons of destruction to our lives.

It has broken every compact into which it has entered for our security.

It has given indubitable evidence of its design to ruin our agriculture, to prostrate our industrial pursuits and to destroy our social system.

It knows no relenting or hesitation in its purposes; it stops not in its march of aggression, and leaves us no room to hope for cessation or for pause.

It has recently obtained control of the Government, by the prosecution of its unhallowed schemes, and destroyed the last expectation of living together in friendship and brotherhood.

Utter subjugation awaits us in the Union, if we should consent longer to remain in it. It is not a matter of choice, but of necessity. We must either submit to degradation, and to the loss of property worth four billions of money, or we must secede from the Union framed by our fathers, to secure this as well as every other species of property. For far less cause than this, our fathers separated from the Crown of England.

Our decision is made. We follow in their footsteps. We embrace the alternative of separation; and for the reasons here stated, we resolve to maintain our rights with the full consciousness of the justice of our course, and the undoubting belief of our ability to maintain it.

"A WARLIKE ASPECT":
WASHINGTON, D.C., JANUARY 1861

Elizabeth Blair Lee to Samuel Phillips Lee

From the Maryland estate of her politically prominent family, Elizabeth Blair Lee wrote about unfolding events to her husband, an American naval officer on his way to join the East India squadron in the China Sea. Her father, Francis Preston Blair, was a former adviser to President Andrew Jackson who had joined the Republican party, her brother Montgomery would serve as postmaster general in the Lincoln administration, and her brother Frank was a Republican congressman from Missouri who would become a general in the Union army.

———————

Silver Spring   December 25, 1860
Dear Phil   It might happen that currents winds & waves might prevent you from stopping at the Cape of Good Hope & on getting to Batavia you would want to know how even these 15 days have passed with us Well your pilot letter alone made me feel you had gone when for a time not even the perpetual talk of civil war around me here reconciled me— however I rally quickly & now I can feel thankful for all the mercies of God on this day of rejoicing— Tho I so miss you aching to share with me the exhuberance of Blair in Xmas gifts & joys

No political event has occurred except that South Carolina ordained herself on the 20th out of the Union whereupon the stocks rise. Patriotism is now above par. The Union Flag streams from nearly every house top— Father returned home from the City last night singing & happier about politics than Ive seen him since the election— Still he & all thinking men are sure that peaceable secession is a fallacy

Our party are in the labors of Cabinet Making & from all I hear it will hardly get through safely for the party— Bates has certainly got a place & L feels obliged to ask Seward & yet he dont want him to accept— but *he will.* so it hangs at present Our Maryland nominee has also got a promise in writing— but *all* are yet held under advisement— Things pecuniary are not any brighter in St Louis   Frank from necessity has gone to work at Law with Bay as a partner

Jany 9th 1861   I concluded to make this letter cover the first month of your absence & it has been a long weary one This year commences with a warlike aspect   Majr Anderson in command at Fort Moultrie denyed reinforcement tho his importunate wife insulted the President when her entreaties failed to move him to send them— But Providence over rules even the most determined— An immense theft to the amount of several Millions of State Bonds lodged in the Interior Dept was discovered or confessed by a Mr. Bailey book keeper— Floyd was implicated in this fraud & he availed himself of Maj Andersons transfer of his forces to Fort Sumter to make a plea for resignation— These changes have produced a change of policy in the administration— Old Buck is now odius to the South because he has concluded not to act any longer in concert with Traitors and to execute the Laws & protect Govt property— Andersons movement was masterly & has made him now the Hero of the day. On yesterday there was nearly as many guns fired in his honor as that of Genl Jackson— whose spirit is now invoked daily for the protection of the Country. Mississippi is to secede to day & tomorrow King Jeff is to make his adieux to the Senate. He will take his wrath out of old Buck— But on this change of policy in the President— Stocks begin to rise again & there is a tone of firmness & hope in the community— that has given at least more fortitude to bear our troubles with—

Jany 10th   Mr. Slidell and Mr. Davis were intense in the bitterness of their denunciations of the President around whom now the Republicans rally as it is a great onus off the Republican party that he devotes to the South & Democracy should begin the War— which I fear was commenced yesterday— A Steamer was sent to Maj Anderson by Scotts orders under Holt— now acting Secy of War with more men & provisions. She was fired at by the South Carolinians from Fort Moultrie & a light house battery when she put back— Anderson sent an officer to Govr Pickens— they say with a threat to destroy Charleston if that attack on the Steamer was repeated to day. Her owners are telegraphed today that she safely unloading at Fort Sumter— it looks like a back down in S.C. & it will be no misfortune to the Country to prove she is unequal to any of

her threats   Anderson says he could hold his position in defiance of the whole South— I see to day that Hartstene has resigned— he is the highest on the list who have done so & there are very few resignations— Comre Shubrick went to Charleston & has returned saying they are all stark mad— *save men of large estates* & it is evident they are to be fleeced The Jews have already quit— The monied men north will not take the U State Loan— whilst the Treasury Department is in the hands of a Secessionist— Our Party are in great distress at the idea of having Cameron in the Treasury it is said to day he declines but that tis thought a ruse— to quiet the protest now being made against this appointment— Even the Sun— the hotest Secession paper in Maryland gives up that Maryland will go out— there is no disunion or secession in the State— Our neighbors are all civil & even when there was talk of attacking Washn we were to be protected. But the Presidents change of front has quieted all *that talk* for it never amounted to anything else— The North rallies unitedly to the Union & for the execution of the Laws & a maintenance of the Constitution— in letter & spirit— Thus your people are on the strongest & safest side of the Contest— Missouri is to go thro the ferment of her democratic Legislature— but she is considered safe & so is Kentucky— North Carolina & Tennesse— but Virginia is shaky— but it will go back to the people there & that will give time— & confidently hoped a happy result
Thompson resigned when reinforcements were sent to Majr Anderson who is a kinsman of Mary Blair & a Kentuckian were at the Brevort with the Jesups this fall

Our home routine has been unaltered & so far this winter we have good health— Blair is rarely kept indoors all day— The winter is very wet so far & tho frequent snow— no ice yet to put up for summer— Mary & Betty in town   I do less reading than ever before. They have got used to doing without me & want to keep the habit— but so far my home here is comfortable— Our boy is sturdy & well & everybodys pet & particularly his Grand Pa's— who is of late struck with his abiding loyal love to my Papa— it was only yesterday he ordered Becky to Pack his clothing— "I am going to Sea to talk to Papa— he would not take either Becky or I with "Papa will take care of me" Yours ever Lizzie

THE "STAR OF THE WEST":
SOUTH CAROLINA, JANUARY 1861

Catherine Edmondston: Diary, January 9–13, 1861

On December 28, 1860, three commissioners from South Carolina met with President Buchanan and demanded the evacuation of Fort Sumter. At the insistence of Jeremiah Black, who had replaced Lewis Cass as secretary of state earlier in the month, the President rejected their demands in a strongly worded reply drafted by Black and Edwin Stanton, the new attorney general. Buchanan then approved a plan to supply and reinforce the fort, and on January 5, 1861, the chartered steamer *Star of the West* sailed from New York with two hundred soldiers on board. The ship reached Charleston on January 9 but safely retreated after being fired upon. Lacking instructions, Major Anderson did not order the guns at Fort Sumter to open fire. Catherine Edmondston and her husband were visiting his brother Lawrence at his house overlooking Charleston harbor when the *Star of the West* arrived.

JANUARY 9, 1861

On the morning of the 9th as we were dressing we suddenly heard the report of a heavy gun! followed by another! and another! A few moments sufficed to collect us all out in the front of the house where we had a fine view of Sumter, Moultrie & the Channel, and there sad to relate, steaming up the channel was a vessel with the US Flag flying at her peak! The expected re-inforcements for Sumter doubtless! Boom! Another cannon from the shore Batteries on Morris Island. "Is she struck?" No! On she comes! Another! and another, whilst Sumter opens her Port Holes and slowly runs out her cannon, prepared for instant action. Now a heavy gun from Fort Moultrie! Will Sumter respond? No! Not yet! Another from Moultrie! How with Sumter now? Still silent! The vessel turns slowly. Is she struck? No one can tell, but slowly, reluctantly as it were, almost with a baffled look, the Steamer retreats down the channel.

Thank God! Every one ejaculates! But what think we of the treacherous Government who whilst pretending to treat, assuring its own Cabinet & the nation that no re-inforcements should be sent, deliberately breaks faith and attempts it? I blush for my country! Would that the North was not our exponent! Eleven guns in all were fired. Good God! Is this true? Is this the beginning of the Civil War of which we have heard so much, was the thought which sprung into my mind. And as I afterwards sat at Lawrence's breakfast table and looked from the luxurious & peaceful family scene in doors, across the still smooth water smiling in the beauty of the crisp morning air, to Sumter, standing stern, silent, sullen, defiant as it were, bristling with cannon, whilst a light smoke stealing up from her Battlements told that they were heating shot, ready for instant action, & thought how in an instant it could all be changed, that horror & ruin might take the place of peace and comfort, never did I feel so vividly the full force & beauty of the Collect for Peace in our Prayer book. Never did I utter it so fervently, never desire it so earnestly!

The same day we went back to the city & found it full of flying rumours. Men in Uniform filling the streets, singly and in squads, all wending their way to East Bay where steamers were firing up & leaving with re-inforcements, munitions of War & supplies for Pinckney, Moultrie & the Batteries below on Morris Island. Left on the same day for Raleigh.

JANUARY 10, 1861

Arrived on the morning of the 10th carrying with us the news of the repulse of the "Star of the West"—for so was the steamer called—& Mr Buchanan's treachery. Every where it was received with surprised dismay, the feeling almost universally being to leave SC to herself, give her her Fort if she required it, but deny her all the benefits of the Government, refuse her all Postal intercourse etc. Predictions were freely made that in that event, in a year at most she would if Mr Lincoln's government should be an impartial one, petition to return into the Union. She met but few sympathizers, but Mr Miller is the only man whom I have yet seen who upholds the action of the Government. Margaret's exclamation when she heard it was "Why Kate, you have been seeing History!"

Found Annie D at home, her Mother having become uneasy at last begged her father to go for her. I am glad of it, as a grave cause of uneasiness is thus removed from their minds. Frank Coffin and John Devereux struck up a friendship to which David's & Jonathan's was but a joke. The other children all well and already inflamed against the Yankees & "old Lincoln." The North is sowing the wind; see that ere the next generation she does not reap the Whirlwind!

JANUARY 13, 1861

Got home safely to Looking Glass on Sunday the 13th. My cough much better, from a practice reccommended me by Dr Coffin of "swabbing out" my throat with a spunge and a weak solution of Caustic. Saw Mrs Mills at Mt Pleasant—told me she had been cured of her Asthma by Iodide of Potassa. Made a note for Dolly's benefit.

Found Father much excited against SC—cannot say enough of the folly of her conduct. It almost frightened me to hear him. I hope he will not say so much to Mr Edmondston. I do not think he does her full justice. For instance he thinks it beneath their pretentions to chivalry, ungenerous & unhandsome in fact, that they fired one shot at the Star of the West after she turned to retreat! I do not agree with him, & tho' this "Gentlemen of the English Guards fire . . . we never fire first!" may be very grand—yet it is too high strung for me! I never before heard of an action in which the firing ceased until the Flag was hauled down.

We went on as usual all the month of Jan. Killed Hogs, attended to house hold matters, Planted garden seed, Rode, walked, went to Hascosea, wrote letters, Read my new books —in short enjoyed ourselves in our usual way, the only draw back being the difference of feeling on Political matters between ourselves & father. As for Mama & Susan they are really bitter in their expressions, & Susan talked more nonsense about her "devotion to the Flag" than I ever thought I should hear a sensible woman like her utter! Altogether it was rather uncomfortable at times being with them.

Brother had a hearty laugh on me. He declared that he thought that the war would begin then & there between Mama & myself, because when I said that SC & Va had both a right to their Forts Sumter & Monro, & that when they reclaimed them the Government ought to restore them, she became personal, called me "Catherine Edmondston!" told me that I had been brought up by honest people, & that she was surprised that I should be guilty of uttering such dishonourable & dishonest sentiments, & more to the same purpose. I made some retort & was going on when fortunately I remembered my Mother's last injunction & checked myself. But I was very indignant! What a pity that politics will intrude into private life!

WASHINGTON, D.C., JANUARY 1861

Jefferson Davis: Farewell Address in the U.S. Senate

January 21, 1861

On the morning of January 21, 1861, five southern senators—David Yulee and Stephen Mallory of Florida, Clement Clay and Benjamin Fitzpatrick of Alabama, and Jefferson Davis of Mississippi—announced on the Senate floor that they were "withdrawing" as a result of the secession of their respective states. (James Hammond and James Chesnut of South Carolina did not return to Washington when Congress reconvened in December 1860, and Robert Toombs of Georgia and Albert Brown of Mississippi had left the Senate earlier in January; Alfred Iverson of Georgia would withdraw on January 28, followed by Judah Benjamin and John Slidell of Louisiana on February 4.) During its special session in March 1861, the Republican-controlled Senate of the new 37th Congress approved a resolution declaring the seats of Mallory, Clay, Davis, Brown, Toombs, and Benjamin to be vacant. (The resolution did not address the seats formerly held by Yulee, Fitzpatrick, Hammond, Iverson, and Slidell, all of whose terms had expired with the end of the 36th Congress.) When the Senate reconvened in July 1861, it expelled nine senators from Arkansas, North Carolina, Tennessee, Texas, and Virginia who had joined the Confederacy, as well as James Chesnut of South Carolina (who had never formally withdrawn), leaving the unionist Andrew Johnson of Tennessee as the sole remaining senator from the eleven Confederate states.

I RISE, Mr. President, for the purpose of announcing to the Senate that I have satisfactory evidence that the State of Mississippi, by a solemn ordinance of her people in convention assembled, has declared her separation from the United States. Under these circumstances, of course my functions are terminated here. It has seemed to me proper, however, that I should appear in the Senate to announce that fact to my associates, and I will say but very little more. The occasion does not invite me to go into argument; and my physical condition would not permit me to do so if it were otherwise; and yet it seems to become me to say something on the part of the State I here represent, on an occasion so solemn as this.

It is known to Senators who have served with me here, that I have for many years advocated, as an essential attribute of State sovereignty, the right of a State to secede from the Union. Therefore, if I had not believed there was justifiable cause; if I had thought that Mississippi was acting without sufficient provocation, or without an existing necessity, I should still, under my theory of the Government, because of my allegiance to the State of which I am a citizen, have been bound by her action. I, however, may be permitted to say that I do think she has justifiable cause, and I approve of her act. I conferred with her people before that act was taken, counseled them then that if the state of things which they apprehended should exist when the convention met, they should take the action which they have now adopted.

I hope none who hear me will confound this expression of mine with the advocacy of the right of a State to remain in the Union, and to disregard its constitutional obligations by the nullification of the law. Such is not my theory. Nullification and secession, so often confounded, are indeed antagonistic principles. Nullification is a remedy which it is sought to apply within the Union, and against the agent of the States. It is only to be justified when the agent has violated his constitutional obligation, and a State, assuming to judge for itself, denies the right of the agent thus to act, and appeals to the other States of the Union for a decision; but when the States themselves, and when the people of the States, have so acted as to convince us that they will not regard our constitutional rights, then, and then for the first time, arises the doctrine of secession in its practical application.

A great man who now reposes with his fathers, and who has been often arraigned for a want of fealty to the Union, advocated the doctrine of nullification, because it preserved the Union. It was because of his deep-seated attachment to the Union, his determination to find some remedy for existing ills short of a severance of the ties which bound South Carolina to the other States, that Mr. Calhoun advocated the doctrine of nullification, which he proclaimed to be peaceful, to be within the limits of State power, not to disturb the Union, but only to be a means of bringing the agent before the tribunal of the States for their judgment.

Secession belongs to a different class of remedies. It is to be justified upon the basis that the States are sovereign. There was a time when none denied it. I hope the time may come again, when a better comprehension of the theory of our Government, and the inalienable rights of the people of the States, will prevent any one from denying that each State is a sovereign, and thus may reclaim the grants which it has made to any agent whomsoever.

I therefore say I concur in the action of the people of Mississippi, believing it to be necessary and proper, and should have been bound by their action if my belief had been otherwise; and this brings me to the important point which I wish on this last occasion to present to the Senate. It is by this confounding of nullification and secession that the name of a great man, whose ashes now mingle with his mother earth, has been invoked to justify coercion against a seceded State. The phrase "to execute the laws," was an expression which General Jackson applied to the case of a State refusing to obey the laws while yet a member of the Union. That is not the case which is now presented. The laws are to be executed over the United States, and upon the people of the United States. They have no relation to any foreign country. It is a perversion of terms, at least it is a great misapprehension of the case, which cites that expression for application to a State which has withdrawn from the Union. You may make war on a foreign State. If it be the purpose of gentlemen, they may make war against a State which has withdrawn from the Union; but there are no laws of the United States to be executed within the limits of a seceded State. A State finding herself in the condition in which Mississippi has judged she is, in which her safety requires that she should provide for the maintenance of her rights out of the Union, surrenders all the benefits, (and they are known to be many,) deprives herself of the advantages, (they are known to be great,) severs all the ties of affection, (and they are close and enduring,) which have bound her to the Union; and thus divesting herself of every benefit, taking upon herself every burden, she claims to be exempt from any power to execute the laws of the United States within her limits.

I well remember an occasion when Massachusetts was arraigned before the bar of the Senate, and when then the doctrine of coercion was rife and to be applied against her because of the rescue of a fugitive slave in Boston. My opinion then was the same that it is now. Not in a spirit of egotism, but to show that I am not influenced in my opinion because the case is my own, I refer to that time and that occasion as containing the opinion which I then entertained, and on which my present conduct is based. I then said, if Massachusetts, following her through a stated line of conduct, chooses to take the last step which separates her from the Union, it is her right to go, and I will neither vote one dollar nor one man to coerce her back; but will say to her, God speed, in memory of the kind associations which once existed between her and the other States.

It has been a conviction of pressing necessity, it has been a belief that we are to be deprived in the Union of the rights which our fathers bequeathed to us, which has brought Mississippi into her present decision. She has heard proclaimed the theory that all men are created free and equal, and this made the basis of an attack upon her social institutions; and the sacred Declaration of Independence has been invoked to maintain the position of the equality of the races. That Declaration of Independence is to be construed by the circumstances and purposes for which it was made. The communities were declaring their independence; the people of those communities were asserting that no man was born—to use the language of Mr. Jefferson—booted and spurred to ride over the rest of mankind; that men were created equal—meaning the men of the political community; that there was no divine right to rule; that no man inherited the right to govern; that there were no classes by which power and place descended to families, but that all stations were equally within the grasp of each member of the body-politic. These were the great principles they announced; these were the purposes for which they made their declaration; these were the ends to which their enunciation was directed. They have no reference to the slave; else, how happened it that among the items of arraignment made against

George III was that he endeavored to do just what the North has been endeavoring of late to do—to stir up insurrection among our slaves? Had the Declaration announced that the negroes were free and equal, how was the Prince to be arraigned for stirring up insurrection among them? And how was this to be enumerated among the high crimes which caused the colonies to sever their connection with the mother country? When our Constitution was formed, the same idea was rendered more palpable, for there we find provision made for that very class of persons as property; they were not put upon the footing of equality with white men—not even upon that of paupers and convicts; but, so far as representation was concerned, were discriminated against as a lower caste, only to be represented in the numerical proportion of three fifths.

Then, Senators, we recur to the compact which binds us together; we recur to the principles upon which our Government was founded; and when you deny them, and when you deny to us the right to withdraw from a Government which thus perverted threatens to be destructive of our rights, we but tread in the path of our fathers when we proclaim our independence, and take the hazard. This is done not in hostility to others, not to injure any section of the country, not even for our own pecuniary benefit; but from the high and solemn motive of defending and protecting the rights we inherited, and which it is our sacred duty to transmit unshorn to our children.

I find in myself, perhaps, a type of the general feeling of my constituents towards yours. I am sure I feel no hostility to you, Senators from the North. I am sure there is not one of you, whatever sharp discussion there may have been between us, to whom I cannot now say, in the presence of my God, I wish you well; and such, I am sure, is the feeling of the people whom I represent towards those whom you represent. I therefore feel that I but express their desire when I say I hope, and they hope, for peaceful relations with you, though we must part. They may be mutually beneficial to us in the future, as they have been in the past, if you so will it. The reverse may bring disaster on every portion of the country; and if you will have it thus, we will invoke the God of our fathers, who delivered them from the power of the lion, to protect us from the ravages of the bear; and thus, putting our trust in God and in our own firm hearts and strong arms, we will vindicate the right as best we may.

In the course of my service here, associated at different times with a great variety of Senators, I see now around me some with whom I have served long; there have been points of collision; but whatever of offense there has been to me, I leave here; I carry with me no hostile remembrance. Whatever offense I have given which has not been redressed, or for which satisfaction has not been demanded, I have, Senators, in this hour of our parting, to offer you my apology for any pain which, in heat of discussion, I have inflicted. I go hence unencumbered of the remembrance of any injury received, and having discharged the duty of making the only reparation in my power for any injury offered.

Mr. President, and Senators, having made the announcement which the occasion seemed to me to require, it only remains to me to bid you a final adieu.

THE EVILS OF ANARCHY AND CIVIL WAR:
JANUARY 1861

Robert E. Lee to George Washington Custis Lee

An 1829 graduate of West Point who had distinguished himself in the U.S.-Mexican War, Lieutenant Colonel Robert E. Lee wrote to his eldest son while serving as the acting commander of the Department of Texas. Lee would return to Washington on March 1 and resign his commission in the U.S. Army on April 20, three days after Virginia voted to secede.

FORT MASON, TEXAS, January 23, 1861.

I received Everett's "Life of Washington" which you sent me, and enjoyed its perusal. How his spirit would be grieved could he see the wreck of his mighty labors! I will not, however, permit myself to believe, until all ground of hope is gone, that the fruit of his noble deeds will be destroyed, and that his precious advice and virtuous example will so soon be forgotten by his countrymen. As far as I can judge by the papers, we are between a state of anarchy and civil war. May God avert both of these evils from us! I fear that mankind will not for years be sufficiently Christianized to bear the absence of restraint and force. I see that four States have declared themselves out of the Union; four more will apparently follow their example. Then, if the Border States are brought into the gulf of revolution, one-half of the country will be arrayed against the other. I must try and be patient and await the end, for I can do nothing to hasten or retard it.

The South, in my opinion, has been aggrieved by the acts of the North, as you say. I feel the aggression, and am willing to take every proper step for redress. It is the principle I contend for, not individual or private benefit. As an American citizen, I take great pride in my country, her prosperity and institutions, and would defend any State if her rights were invaded.

But I can anticipate no greater calamity for the country than a dissolution of the Union. It would be an accumulation of all the evils we complain of, and I am willing to sacrifice everything but honor for its preservation. I hope, therefore, that all constitutional means will be exhausted before there is a resort to force. Secession is nothing but revolution. The framers of our Constitution never exhausted so much labor, wisdom, and forbearance in its formation, and surrounded it with so many guards and securities, if it was intended to be broken by every member of the Confederacy at will. It was intended for "perpetual union," so expressed in the preamble, and for the establishment of a government, not a compact, which can only be dissolved by revolution, or the consent of all the people in convention assembled. It is idle to talk of secession. Anarchy would have been established, and not a government, by Washington, Hamilton, Jefferson, Madison, and the other patriots of the Revolution. . . . . Still, a Union that can only be maintained by swords and bayonets, and in which strife and civil war are to take the place of brotherly love and kindness, has no charm for me. I shall mourn for my country and for the welfare and progress of mankind. If the Union is dissolved, and the Government disrupted, I shall return to my native State and share the miseries of my people, and save in defense will draw my sword on none.

MONTGOMERY, ALABAMA, FEBRUARY 1861

Jefferson Davis: Inaugural Address

February 18, 1861

Delegates from South Carolina, Georgia, Florida, Alabama, Mississippi, and Louisiana met on February 4, 1861, in Montgomery, where they were later joined by representatives from Texas. The delegates adopted a provisional constitution for the Confederate States of America, and on February 9 voted by state delegations for a provisional president and vice-president. Although he had not sought the position, Jefferson Davis received the votes of all six states. A West Point graduate, Davis had commanded a Mississippi volunteer regiment in Mexico and later served as secretary of war in the Pierce administration. He was favored by the delegates because of his military background, and because of reports that his election would be favorably received in Virginia. Davis arrived in Montgomery on February 16 and delivered his inaugural address two days later.

———————

Gentlemen of the Congress of the Confederate States of America, Friends, and Fellow-citizens: Called to the difficult and responsible station of Chief Magistrate of the Provisional Government which you have instituted, I approach the discharge of the duties assigned to me with humble distrust of my abilities, but with a sustaining confidence in the wisdom of those who are to guide and aid me in the administration of public affairs, and an abiding faith in the virtue and patriotism of the people. Looking forward to the speedy establishment of a permanent government to take the place of this, which by its greater moral and physical power will be better able to combat with many difficulties that arise from the conflicting interests of separate nations, I enter upon the duties of the office to which I have been chosen with the hope that the beginning of our career, as a Confederacy, may not be obstructed by hostile opposition to our enjoyment of the separate existence and independence we have asserted, and which, with the blessing of Providence, we intend to maintain.

Our present political position has been achieved in a manner unprecedented in the history of nations. It illustrates the American idea that governments rest on the consent of the governed, and that it is the right of the people to alter or abolish them at will whenever they become destructive of the ends for which they were established. The declared purpose of the compact of the Union from which we have withdrawn was to "establish justice, insure domestic tranquillity, provide for the common defense, promote the general welfare, and secure the blessings of liberty to ourselves and our posterity;" and when, in the judgment of the sovereign States composing this Confederacy, it has been perverted from the purposes for which it was ordained, and ceased to answer the ends for which it was established, a peaceful appeal to the ballot box declared that, so far as they are concerned, the Government created by that compact should cease to exist. In this they merely asserted the right which the Declaration of Independence of July 4, 1776, defined to be "inalienable." Of the time and occasion of its exercise they as sovereigns were the final judges, each for itself. The impartial and enlightened verdict of mankind will vindicate the rectitude of our conduct; and He who knows the hearts of men will judge of the sincerity with which we have labored to preserve the Government of our fathers in its spirit.

The right solemnly proclaimed at the birth of the United States, and which has been solemnly affirmed and reaffirmed in the Bills of Rights of the States subsequently admitted into the Union of 1789, undeniably recognizes in the people the power to resume the authority delegated for the purposes of government. Thus the sovereign States here represented have proceeded to form this Confederacy; and it is by abuse of language that their act has been denominated a revolution. They formed a new alliance, but within each State its government has remained; so that the rights of person and property have not been disturbed. The agent through which they communicated with foreign nations is changed, but this does not necessarily interrupt their international relations. Sustained by the consciousness that the transition from the former Union to the present Confederacy has not proceeded from a disregard on our part of just obligations, or any failure to perform every constitutional duty, moved by no interest or passion to invade the rights of others, anxious to cultivate peace and commerce with all nations, if we may not hope to avoid war, we may at least expect that posterity will acquit us of having needlessly engaged in it. Doubly justified by the absence of wrong on our part, and by wanton aggression on the part of others, there can be no cause to doubt that the courage and patriotism of the people of the Confederate States will be found equal to any measure of defense which their honor and security may require.

An agricultural people, whose chief interest is the export of commodities required in every manufacturing country, our true policy is peace, and the freest trade which our necessities will permit. It is alike our interest and that of all those to whom we would sell, and from whom we would buy, that there should be the fewest practicable restrictions upon the interchange of these commodities. There can, however, be but little rivalry between ours and any manufacturing or navigating community, such as the Northeastern States of the American Union. It must follow, therefore, that mutual interest will invite to good will and kind offices on both parts. If, however, passion or lust of dominion should cloud the judgment or inflame the ambition of those States, we must prepare to meet the emergency and maintain, by the final arbitrament of the sword, the position which we have assumed among the nations of the earth.

We have entered upon the career of independence, and it must be inflexibly pursued. Through many years of controversy with our late associates of the Northern States, we have vainly endeavored to secure tranquillity and obtain respect for the rights to which we were entitled. As a necessity, not a choice, we have resorted to the remedy of separation, and henceforth our energies must be directed to the conduct of our own affairs, and the perpetuity of the Confederacy which we have formed. If a just perception of mutual interest shall permit us peaceably to pursue our separate political career, my most earnest desire will have been fulfilled. But if this be denied to us, and the integrity of our territory and jurisdiction be assailed, it will but remain for us with firm resolve to appeal to arms and invoke the blessing of Providence on a just cause.

As a consequence of our new condition and relations, and with a view to meet anticipated wants, it will be necessary to provide for the speedy and efficient organization of branches of the Executive department having special charge of foreign intercourse, finance, military affairs, and the postal service. For purposes of defense, the Confederate States may, under ordinary circumstances, rely mainly upon the militia; but it is deemed advisable, in the present condition of affairs, that there should be a well-instructed and disciplined army, more numerous than would usually be required on a peace establishment. I also suggest that, for the protection of our harbors and commerce on the high seas, a navy adapted to those objects will be required. But this, as well as other subjects appropriate to our necessities, have doubtless engaged the attention of Congress.

With a Constitution differing only from that of our fathers in so far as it is explanatory of their well-known intent, freed from sectional conflicts, which have interfered with the pursuit of the general welfare, it is not unreasonable to expect that States from which we have recently parted may seek to unite their fortunes to ours under the Government which we have instituted. For this your Constitution makes adequate provision; but beyond this, if I mistake not the judgment and will of the people, a reunion with the States from which we have separated is neither practicable nor desirable. To increase the power, develop the resources, and promote the happiness of the Confederacy, it is requisite that there should be so much of homogeneity that the welfare of every portion shall be the aim of the whole. When this does not exist, antagonisms are engendered which must and should result in separation.

Actuated solely by the desire to preserve our own rights, and promote our own welfare, the separation by the Confederate States has been marked by no aggression upon others, and followed by no domestic convulsion. Our industrial pursuits have received no check, the cultivation of our fields has progressed as heretofore, and, even should we be involved in war, there would be no considerable diminution in the production of the staples which have constituted our exports, and in which the commercial world has an interest scarcely less than our own. This common interest of the producer and consumer can only be interrupted by exterior force which would obstruct the transmission of our staples to foreign markets— a course of conduct which would be as unjust, as it would be detrimental, to manufacturing and commercial interests abroad.

Should reason guide the action of the Government from which we have separated, a policy so detrimental to the civilized world, the Northern States included, could not be dictated by even the strongest desire to inflict injury upon us; but, if the contrary should prove true, a terrible responsibility will rest upon it, and the suffering of millions will bear testimony to the folly and wickedness of our aggressors. In the meantime there will remain to us, besides the ordinary means before suggested, the well-known resources for retaliation upon the commerce of an enemy.

Experience in public stations, of subordinate grade to this which your kindness has conferred, has taught me that toil and care and disappointment are the price of official elevation. You will see many errors to forgive, many deficiencies to tolerate; but you shall not find in me either want of zeal or fidelity to the cause that is to me the highest in hope, and of most enduring affection. Your generosity has bestowed upon me an undeserved distinction, one which I neither sought nor desired. Upon the continuance of that sentiment, and upon your wisdom and patriotism, I rely to direct and support me in the performance of the duties required at my hands.

We have changed the constituent parts, but not the system of government. The Constitution framed by our fathers is that of these Confederate States. In their exposition of it, and in the judicial construction it has received, we have a light which reveals its true meaning.

Thus instructed as to the true meaning and just interpretation of that instrument, and ever remembering that all offices are but trusts held for the people, and that powers delegated are to be strictly construed, I will hope by due diligence in the performance of my duties, though I may disappoint your expectations, yet to retain, when retiring, something of the good will and confidence which welcome my entrance into office.

It is joyous in the midst of perilous times to look around upon a people united in heart, where one purpose of high resolve animates and actuates the whole; where the sacrifices to be made are not weighed in the balance against honor and right and liberty and equality. Obstacles may retard, but they cannot long prevent, the progress of a movement sanctified by its justice and sustained by a virtuous people. Reverently let us invoke the God of our fathers to guide and protect us in our efforts to perpetuate the principles which by his blessing they were able to vindicate, establish, and transmit to their posterity. With the continuance of his favor ever gratefully acknowledged, we may hopefully look forward to success, to peace, and to prosperity.

HOPES FOR LINCOLN'S ADMINISTRATION:
MARCH 1861

Frederick Douglass: The New President

March 1861

On the eve of Lincoln's inauguration, Douglass used his *Monthly* to praise the president-elect for refusing to endorse compromise proposals that would have permitted the extension of slavery.

OF ONE satisfaction, one ray of hope amid the darkness of the passing hour, and the reign of doubt and distraction, we may now safely begin to assure ourselves. Before we can again speak to our respected readers through this channel, the long desired 4th of March will have come, Lincoln will be inaugurated at Washington, and his policy declared. Whatever that policy may be towards the seceded and confederated States; whatever it may be towards Slavery, the ruling cause of our nation's troubles, it will at least be a great relief to know it, to rejoice in and defend it, if right, and to make war upon it if wrong. To know what it is, is now the main thing. If he is going to abandon the principles upon which he was elected, compliment the South for being wrong, and censure himself and friends for being right, court treason and curse loyalty, desert his friends and cleave to his enemies, turn his back on the cause of Freedom and give new guarantees to the system of Slavery—whatever policy, whether of peace or war, or neither, it will be a vast gain at least to know what it is. Much of the present trouble is owing to the doubt and suspense caused by the shuffling, do-nothing policy of Mr. Buchanan.— No man has been able to tell an hour before hand what to expect from that source. However well disposed he may have been, the slaveholding thieves and traitors about him have had him under their thumb from the beginning until now. Every man who wishes well to the country will rejoice at his outgoing, and feel that though he leaves the body politic weakened, and the nation's Constitution shattered, his out going, like the subsidence of some pestilence walking in darkness, is a cause for devout thanksgiving. A month longer in power, and perhaps, the epitaph of the American Republic might, if it may not now, be written, and its death consigned to the mouldy tombs of once great, but now extinct, nations.

While not at all too confident of the incorruptible purity of the new President, (for we remember the atmosphere of Washington, and the subtle devices of the enemies of Liberty, among whom he has now gone,) still we hope something from him. His stately silence during these last tumultuous and stormy three months, his stern refusal thus far to commit himself to any of the much advocated schemes of compromise, his refusal to have concessions extorted from him under the terror instituted by thievish conspirators and traitors, the cool and circumspect character of his replies to the various speeches, some delicate, appropriate, and sensible, and some rudely curious and prying, made to him during his circuitous route to Washington, the modesty with which he has pushed aside the various compliments bestowed upon him, all prove that he has not won deceitfully the title of Honest Old Abe. True, indeed, he has made no immoderate promises to the cause of freedom. His party has made none. But what were small in Chicago, will be found large at Washington, and what were moderate in the canvass, have become much augmented by the frowning difficulties since flung in the way of their accomplishment by the movement for disunion. It was a small thing six months ago to say, as the Republican party did say, that the Union shall be preserved, but events have now transpired, which make this a very solemn matter to reduce to practice. Most things are easier said than done, and this thing belongs to the general rule. That declaration in the Chicago platform implied that those who uttered it, believed that this Government possesses ample power for its own preservation, and that those powers should be in their hands, faithfully wielded for that purpose. This, then, is the first question: Will Mr. Lincoln boldly grapple with the monster of Disunion, and bring down his proud looks?

Will he call upon the haughty slave masters, who have risen

in arms, to break up the Government, to lay down those arms, and return to loyalty, or meet the doom of traitors and rebels? He must do this, or do worse.—He must do this, or consent to be the despised representative of a defied and humbled Government. He must do this, or own that party platforms are the merest devices of scheming politicians to cheat the people, and to enable them to crawl up to place and power. He must do this, or compromise the fundamental principle upon which he was elected, to wit, the right and duty of Congress to prohibit the farther extension of Slavery. Will he compromise? Time and events will soon answer this question. For the present, there is much reason to believe that he will not consent to any compromise which will violate the principle upon which he was elected; and since none which does not utterly trample upon that principle can be accepted by the South, we have a double assurance that there will be no compromise, and that the contest must now be decided, and decided forever, which of the two, Freedom or Slavery, shall give law to this Republic. Let the conflict come, and God speed the Right, must be the wish of every true-hearted American, as well as of that of an onlooking world.

WASHINGTON, D.C., MARCH 1861

Abraham Lincoln: First Inaugural Address

March 4, 1861

Lincoln began drafting his inaugural address in Springfield in January 1861 and completed it after his arrival in Washington on February 23. The final version incorporated revisions suggested by his Illinois friend, Orville H. Browning, and by William H. Seward (some of these changes are presented in the Notes in this volume).

FELLOW CITIZENS of the United States:

In compliance with a custom as old as the government itself, I appear before you to address you briefly, and to take, in your presence, the oath prescribed by the Constitution of the United States, to be taken by the President "before he enters on the execution of his office."

I do not consider it necessary, at present, for me to discuss those matters of administration about which there is no special anxiety, or excitement.

Apprehension seems to exist among the people of the Southern States, that by the accession of a Republican Administration, their property, and their peace, and personal security, are to be endangered. There has never been any reasonable cause for such apprehension. Indeed, the most ample evidence to the contrary has all the while existed, and been open to their inspection. It is found in nearly all the published speeches of him who now addresses you. I do but quote from one of those speeches when I declare that "I have no purpose, directly or indirectly, to interfere with the institution of slavery in the States where it exists. I believe I have no lawful right to do so, and I have no inclination to do so." Those who nominated and elected me did so with full knowledge that I had made this, and many similar declarations, and had never recanted them. And more than this, they placed in the platform, for my acceptance, and as a law to themselves, and to me, the clear and emphatic resolution which I now read:

"*Resolved*, That the maintenance inviolate of the rights of the States, and especially the right of each State to order and control its own domestic institutions according to its own judgment exclusively, is essential to that balance of power on which the perfection and endurance of our political fabric depend; and we denounce the lawless invasion by armed force of the soil of any State or Territory, no matter under what pretext, as among the gravest of crimes."

I now reiterate these sentiments: and in doing so, I only press upon the public attention the most conclusive evidence of which the case is susceptible, that the property, peace and security of no section are to be in anywise endangered by the now incoming Administration. I add too, that all the protection which, consistently with the Constitution and the laws, can be given, will be cheerfully given to all the States when lawfully demanded, for whatever cause—as cheerfully to one section, as to another.

There is much controversy about the delivering up of fugitives from service or labor. The clause I now read is as plainly written in the Constitution as any other of its provisions:

"No person held to service or labor in one State, under the laws thereof, escaping into another, shall, in consequence of any law or regulation therein, be discharged from such service or labor, but shall be delivered up on claim of the party to whom such service or labor may be due."

It is scarcely questioned that this provision was intended by those who made it, for the reclaiming of what we call fugitive slaves; and the intention of the law-giver is the law. All members of Congress swear their support to the whole Constitution—to this provision as much as to any other. To the proposition, then, that slaves whose cases come within the terms of this clause, "shall be delivered up," their oaths are unanimous. Now, if they would make the effort in good temper, could they not, with nearly equal unanimity, frame and pass a law, by means of which to keep good that unanimous oath?

There is some difference of opinion whether this clause should be enforced by national or by state authority; but surely that difference is not a very material one. If the slave is to be surrendered, it can be of but little consequence to him, or to others, by which authority it is done. And should any one, in any case, be content that his oath shall go unkept, on a merely unsubstantial controversy as to *how* it shall be kept?

Again, in any law upon this subject, ought not all the safeguards of liberty known in civilized and humane jurisprudence to be introduced, so that a free man be not, in any case, surrendered as a slave? And might it not be well, at the same time, to provide by law for the enforcement of that clause in the Constitution which guarranties that "The citizens of each State shall be entitled to all previleges and immunities of citizens in the several States?"

I take the official oath to-day, with no mental reservations, and with no purpose to construe the Constitution or laws, by any hypercritical rules. And while I do not choose now to specify particular acts of Congress as proper to be enforced, I do suggest, that it will be much safer for all, both in official and private stations, to conform to, and abide by, all those acts which stand unrepealed, than to violate any of them, trusting to find impunity in having them held to be unconstitutional.

It is seventy-two years since the first inauguration of a President under our national Constitution. During that period fifteen different and greatly distinguished citizens, have, in succession, administered the executive branch of the government. They have conducted it through many perils; and, generally, with great success. Yet, with all this scope for precedent, I now enter upon the same task for the brief constitutional term of four years, under great and peculiar difficulty. A disruption of the Federal Union heretofore only menaced, is now formidably attempted.

I hold, that in contemplation of universal law, and of the Constitution, the Union of these States is perpetual. Perpetuity is implied, if not expressed, in the fundamental law of all national governments. It is safe to assert that no government proper, ever had a provision in its organic law for its own termination. Continue to execute all the express provisions of our national Constitution, and the Union will endure forever—it being impossible to destroy it, except by some action not provided for in the instrument itself.

Again, if the United States be not a government proper, but

an association of States in the nature of contract merely, can it, as a contract, be peaceably unmade, by less than all the parties who made it? One party to a contract may violate it—break it, so to speak; but does it not require all to lawfully rescind it?

Descending from these general principles, we find the proposition that, in legal contemplation, the Union is perpetual, confirmed by the history of the Union itself. The Union is much older than the Constitution. It was formed in fact, by the Articles of Association in 1774. It was matured and continued by the Declaration of Independence in 1776. It was further matured and the faith of all the then thirteen States expressly plighted and engaged that it should be perpetual, by the Articles of Confederation in 1778. And finally, in 1787, one of the declared objects for ordaining and establishing the Constitution, was "*to form a more perfect union.*"

But if destruction of the Union, by one, or by a part only, of the States, be lawfully possible, the Union is *less* perfect than before the Constitution, having lost the vital element of perpetuity.

It follows from these views that no State, upon its own mere motion, can lawfully get out of the Union,—that *resolves* and *ordinances* to that effect are legally void; and that acts of violence, within any State or States, against the authority of the United States, are insurrectionary or revolutionary, according to circumstances.

I therefore consider that, in view of the Constitution and the laws, the Union is unbroken; and, to the extent of my ability, I shall take care, as the Constitution itself expressly enjoins upon me, that the laws of the Union be faithfully executed in all the States. Doing this I deem to be only a simple duty on my part; and I shall perform it, so far as practicable, unless my rightful masters, the American people, shall withhold the requisite means, or, in some authoritative manner, direct the contrary. I trust this will not be regarded as a menace, but only as the declared purpose of the Union that it *will* constitutionally defend, and maintain itself.

In doing this there needs to be no bloodshed or violence; and there shall be none, unless it be forced upon the national authority. The power confided to me, will be used to hold, occupy, and possess the property, and places belonging to the government, and to collect the duties and imposts; but beyond what may be necessary for these objects, there will be no invasion—no using of force against, or among the people anywhere. Where hostility to the United States, in any interior locality, shall be so great and so universal, as to prevent competent resident citizens from holding the Federal offices, there will be no attempt to force obnoxious strangers among the people for that object. While the strict legal right may exist in the government to enforce the exercise of these offices, the attempt to do so would be so irritating, and so nearly impracticable with all, that I deem it better to forego, for the time, the uses of such offices.

The mails, unless repelled, will continue to be furnished in all parts of the Union. So far as possible, the people everywhere shall have that sense of perfect security which is most favorable to calm thought and reflection. The course here indicated will be followed, unless current events, and experience, shall show a modification, or change, to be proper; and in every case and exigency, my best discretion will be exercised, according to circumstances actually existing, and with a view and a hope of a peaceful solution of the national troubles, and the restoration of fraternal sympathies and affections.

That there are persons in one section, or another who seek to destroy the Union at all events, and are glad of any pretext to do it, I will neither affirm or deny; but if there be such, I need address no word to them. To those, however, who really love the Union, may I not speak?

Before entering upon so grave a matter as the destruction of our national fabric, with all its benefits, its memories, and its hopes, would it not be wise to ascertain precisely why we do it? Will you hazard so desperate a step, while there is any possibility that any portion of the ills you fly from, have no real existence? Will you, while the certain ills you fly to, are greater than all the real ones you fly from? Will you risk the commission of so fearful a mistake?

All profess to be content in the Union, if all constitutional rights can be maintained. Is it true, then, that any right, plainly written in the Constitution, has been denied? I think not. Happily the human mind is so constituted, that no party can reach to the audacity of doing this. Think, if you can, of a single instance in which a plainly written provision of the Constitution has ever been denied. If, by the mere force of numbers, a majority should deprive a minority of any clearly written constitutional right, it might, in a moral point of view, justify revolution—certainly would, if such right were a vital one. But such is not our case. All the vital rights of minorities, and of individuals, are so plainly assured to them, by affirmations and negations, guarranties and prohibitions, in the Constitution, that controversies never arise concerning them. But no organic law can ever be framed with a provision specifically applicable to every question which may occur in practical administration. No foresight can anticipate, nor any document of reasonable length contain express provisions for all possible questions. Shall fugitives from labor be surrendered by national or by State authority? The Constitution does not expressly say. *May* Congress prohibit slavery in the territories? The Constitution does not expressly say. *Must* Congress protect slavery in the territories? The Constitution does not expressly say.

From questions of this class spring all our constitutional controversies, and we divide upon them into majorities and minorities. If the minority will not acquiesce, the majority must, or the government must cease. There is no other alternative; for continuing the government, is acquiescence on one side or the other. If a minority, in such case, will secede rather than acquiesce, they make a precedent which, in turn, will divide and ruin them; for a minority of their own will secede from them, whenever a majority refuses to be controlled by such minority. For instance, why may not any portion of a new confederacy, a year or two hence, arbitrarily secede again, precisely as portions of the present Union now claim to secede from it. All who cherish disunion sentiments, are now being educated to the exact temper of doing this. Is there such perfect identity of interests among the States to compose a new Union, as to produce harmony only, and prevent renewed secession?

Plainly, the central idea of secession, is the essence of anarchy. A majority, held in restraint by constitutional checks, and limitations, and always changing easily, with deliberate changes of popular opinions and sentiments, is the only true sovereign of a free people. Whoever rejects it, does, of necessity, fly to anarchy or to despotism. Unanimity is impossible; the rule of a minority, as a permanent arrangement, is wholly inadmissable; so that, rejecting the majority principle, anarchy, or despotism in some form, is all that is left.

I do not forget the position assumed by some, that constitutional questions are to be decided by the Supreme Court; nor do I deny that such decisions must be binding in any case, upon the parties to a suit, as to the object of that suit, while they are also entitled to very high respect and consideration, in all paralel cases, by all other departments of the government. And while it is obviously possible that such decision may be erroneous in any given case, still the evil effect following it, being limited to that particular case, with the chance that it may be over-ruled, and never become a precedent for other cases, can better be borne than could the evils of a different practice. At the same time the candid citizen must confess that if the policy of the government, upon vital questions, affecting the whole people, is to be irrevocably fixed by decisions of the Supreme Court, the instant they are made, in ordinary litigation between parties, in personal actions, the people will have ceased, to be their own rulers, having, to that extent, practically resigned their government, into the hands of that eminent tribunal. Nor is there, in this view, any assault upon the court, or the judges. It is a duty, from which they may not shrink, to decide cases properly brought before them; and it is no fault of theirs, if others seek to turn their decisions to political purposes.

One section of our country believes slavery is *right*, and ought to be extended, while the other believes it is *wrong*, and ought not to be extended. This is the only substantial dispute. The fugitive slave clause of the Constitution, and the law for the suppression of the foreign slave trade, are each as well enforced, perhaps, as any law can ever be in a community where the moral sense of the people imperfectly supports the law itself. The great body of the people abide by the dry legal obligation in both cases, and a few break over in each. This, I think, cannot be perfectly cured; and it would be worse in both cases *after* the separation of the sections, than before. The foreign slave trade, now imperfectly suppressed, would be ultimately revived without restriction, in one section; while fugitive slaves, now only partially surrendered, would not be surrendered at all, by the other.

Physically speaking, we cannot separate. We cannot remove our respective sections from each other, nor build an impassable wall between them. A husband and wife may be divorced, and go out of the presence, and beyond the reach of each other; but the different parts of our country cannot do this. They cannot but remain face to face; and intercourse, either amicable or hostile, must continue between them. Is it possible then to make that intercourse more advantageous, or more satisfactory, *after* separation than *before*? Can aliens make treaties easier than friends can make laws? Can treaties be more faithfully enforced between aliens, than laws can among friends? Suppose you go to war, you cannot fight always; and when, after much loss on both sides, and no gain on either, you cease fighting, the identical old questions, as to terms of intercourse, are again upon you.

This country, with its institutions, belongs to the people who inhabit it. Whenever they shall grow weary of the existing government, they can exercise their *constitutional* right of amending it, or their *revolutionary* right to dismember, or overthrow it. I can not be ignorant of the fact that many worthy, and patriotic citizens are desirous of having the national constitution amended. While I make no recommendation of amendments, I fully recognize the rightful authority of the people over the whole subject, to be exercised in either of the modes prescribed in the instrument itself; and I should, under existing circumstances, favor, rather than oppose, a fair oppertunity being afforded the people to act upon it.

I will venture to add that, to me, the convention mode seems preferable, in that it allows amendments to originate with the people themselves, instead of only permitting them to take, or reject, propositions, originated by others, not especially chosen for the purpose, and which might not be precisely such, as they would wish to either accept or refuse. I understand a proposed amendment to the Constitution—which amendment, however, I have not seen, has passed Congress, to the effect that the federal government, shall never interfere with the domestic institutions of the States, including that of persons held to service. To avoid misconstruction of what I have said, I depart from my purpose not to speak of particular amendments, so far as to say that, holding such a provision to now be implied constitutional law, I have no objection to its being made express, and irrevocable.

The Chief Magistrate derives all his authority from the people, and they have conferred none upon him to fix terms for the separation of the States. The people themselves can do this also if they choose; but the executive, as such, has nothing to do with it. His duty is to administer the present government, as it came to his hands, and to transmit it, unimpaired by him, to his successor.

Why should there not be a patient confidence in the ultimate justice of the people? Is there any better, or equal hope, in the world? In our present differences, is either party without faith of being in the right? If the Almighty Ruler of nations, with his eternal truth and justice, be on your side of the North, or on yours of the South, that truth, and that justice, will surely prevail, by the judgment of this great tribunal, the American people.

By the frame of the government under which we live, this same people have wisely given their public servants but little power for mischief; and have, with equal wisdom, provided for the return of that little to their own hands at very short intervals.

While the people retain their virtue, and vigilence, no administration, by any extreme of wickedness or folly, can very seriously injure the government, in the short space of four years.

My countrymen, one and all, think calmly and *well*, upon this whole subject. Nothing valuable can be lost by taking time. If there be an object to *hurry* any of you, in hot haste, to a step which you would never take *deliberately*, that object will be frustrated by taking time; but no good object can be frustrated by it. Such of you as are now dissatisfied, still have the old Constitution unimpaired, and, on the sensitive point, the laws of your own framing under it; while the new administration will have no immediate power, if it would, to change either. If it were admitted that you who are dissatisfied, hold the right side in the dispute, there still is no single good reason for precipitate action. Intelligence, patriotism, Christianity, and a firm reliance on Him, who has never yet forsaken this favored land, are still competent to adjust, in the best way, all our present difficulty.

In *your* hands, my dissatisfied fellow countrymen, and not in *mine*, is the momentous issue of civil war. The government will not assail *you*. You can have no conflict, without being yourselves the aggressors. *You* have no oath registered in Heaven to destroy the government, while *I* shall have the most solemn one to "preserve, protect and defend" it.

I am loth to close. We are not enemies, but friends. We must not be enemies. Though passion may have strained, it must not break our bonds of affection. The mystic chords of memory, streching from every battle-field, and patriot grave, to every living heart and hearthstone, all over this broad land, will yet swell the chorus of the Union, when again touched, as surely they will be, by the better angels of our nature.

"THAT WRETCH ABRAHAM LINCOLN":
NORTH CAROLINA, MARCH 1861

Catherine Edmondston: Diary, March 4, 1861

On the day of President Lincoln's inauguration Catherine Edmondston was at her home in Halifax County, North Carolina. In her diary she alludes to Lincoln's secret railroad trip from Philadelphia to Washington on the night of February 22–23 after he was warned of a plot to assassinate him in Baltimore. The incident was ridiculed in the opposition press, which claimed (falsely) that Lincoln had disguised himself with a Scottish plaid cap.

MARCH 4, 1861

Today was inaugurated that wretch Abraham Lincoln President of the US. We are told not to speak evil of Dignities, but it is hard to realize he is a Dignity. Ah! would that Jefferson Davis was our President. He is a man to whom a gentleman could look at without mortification as cheif of his nation. "How glorious was the" President elect on his tour, asking at Railway Stations for impudent girls who had written him about his whiskers & rewarding their impudence with a kiss! Faugh! Sweet Republican simplicity how charming thou art, when the future head of a great nation, a man upon whom all eyes are bent measures his august person inch by inch with a visitor whom he fears is taller than himself & chuckles to find himself mistaken. But then Saul was a head & shoulders higher than the multitude—why should not Abraham rest his importance on his stature? How dignified was his entrance in disguise into his future Capital. How grateful should we be to the long cloak & Scotch Cap which saved him from the bloody designs of his Southern enemies. Well, we have a Rail Splitter and a tall man at the head of our affairs! Ned Bartley is both & perhaps excels Mr Lincoln in one or both points, but then he is not of Anglo Saxon blood. Neither is the Vice President Mr Hannibal Hamlin. Gentlemen we can match you on all points to a nicety. Ah my country! God keep you when such hands hold the helm!

VINDICATING SLAVERY: GEORGIA, MARCH 1861

Alexander H. Stephens: "Corner-Stone" Speech

March 21, 1861

A former congressman who had opposed immediate secession in the Georgia convention, Stephens was unanimously elected as the provisional vice-president of the Confederacy in February 1861. The text of his speech at the Savannah Atheneum first appeared in the *Savannah Republican* and was accompanied by a reporter's note stating that it was not "a perfect report, but only such a sketch of the address" that embraced the most important points. Stephens would claim after the war that the printed text of his Savannah speech contained "several glaring errors" and exaggerated the importance of his use of the "corner-stone" image to describe the role of slavery in the Confederacy. In a speech delivered in Atlanta nine days before he spoke at Savannah, Stephens had employed the same metaphor, asserting that the founders of the Confederacy had "solemnly discarded the pestilent heresy of fancy politicians, that all men, all races, were equal, and we had made African *inequality* and subordination, and the *equality* of white men, the chief corner stone of the Southern Republic."

Mr. Mayor, and Gentlemen of the Committee, and Fellow Citizens:—For this reception you will please accept most profound and sincere thanks. The compliment is doubtless intended as much, or more, perhaps, in honor of the occasion, and my public position, in connection with the great events now crowding upon us, than to me personally and individually. It is however none the less appreciated by me on that account. We are in the midst of one of the greatest epochs in our history. The last ninety days will mark one of the most memorable eras in the history of modern civilization.

[There was a general call from the outside of the building for the speaker to go out, that there were more outside than in.]

The Mayor rose and requested silence at the doors, that Mr.

Stephens' health would not permit him to speak in the open air.

Mr. STEPHENS said he would leave it to the audience whether he should proceed indoors or out. There was a general cry indoors, as the ladies, a large number of whom were present, could not hear outside.

Mr. STEPHENS said that the accommodation of the ladies would determine the question, and he would proceed where he was.

[At this point the uproar and clamor outside was greater still for the speaker to go out on the steps. This was quieted by Col. Lawton, Col. Freeman, Judge Jackson, and Mr. J. W. Owens going out and stating the facts of the case to the dense mass of men, women, and children who were outside, and entertaining them in brief speeches—Mr. Stephens all this while quietly sitting down until the furor subsided.]

Mr. STEPHENS rose and said: When perfect quiet is restored, I shall proceed. I cannot speak so long as there is any noise or confusion. I shall take my time—I feel quite prepared to spend the night with you if necessary. [Loud applause.] I very much regret that every one who desires cannot hear what I have to say. Not that I have any display to make, or any thing very entertaining to present, but such views as I have to give, I wish *all*, not only in this city, but in this State, and throughout our Confederate Republic, could hear, who have a desire to hear them.

I was remarking, that we are passing through one of the greatest revolutions in the annals of the world. Seven States have within the last three months thrown off an old government and formed a new. This revolution has been signally marked, up to this time, by the fact of its having been accomplished without the loss of a single drop of blood. [Applause.]

This new constitution, or form of government, constitutes the subject to which your attention will be partly invited. In reference to it, I make this first general remark. It amply secures all our ancient rights, franchises, and liberties. All the great principles of Magna Charta are retained in it. No citizen is deprived of life, liberty, or property, but by the judgment of his peers under the laws of the land. The great principle of religious liberty, which was the honor and pride of the old constitution, is still maintained and secured. All the essentials of the old constitution, which have endeared it to the hearts of the American people, have been preserved and perpetuated. [Applause.] Some changes have been made. Of these I shall speak presently. Some of these I should have preferred not to have seen made; but these, perhaps, meet the cordial approbation of a majority of this audience, if not an overwhelming majority of the people of the Confederacy. Of them, therefore, I will not speak. But other important changes do meet my cordial approbation. They form great improvements upon the old constitution. So, taking the whole new constitution, I have no hesitancy in giving it as my judgment that it is decidedly better than the old. [Applause.]

Allow me briefly to allude to some of these improvements. The question of building up class interests, or fostering one branch of industry to the prejudice of another under the exercise of the revenue power, which gave us so much trouble under the old constitution, is put at rest forever under the new. We allow the imposition of no duty with a view of giving advantage to one class of persons, in any trade or business, over those of another. All, under our system, stand upon the same broad principles of perfect equality. Honest labor and enterprise are left free and unrestricted in whatever pursuit they may be engaged. This subject came well nigh causing a rupture of the old Union, under the lead of the gallant Palmetto State, which lies on our border, in 1833. This old thorn of the tariff, which was the cause of so much irritation in the old body politic, is removed forever from the new. [Applause.]

Again, the subject of internal improvements, under the power of Congress to regulate commerce, is put at rest under our system. The power claimed by construction under the old constitution, was at least a doubtful one—it rested solely upon construction. We of the South, generally apart from considerations of constitutional principles, opposed its exercise upon grounds of its inexpediency and injustice. Notwithstanding this opposition, millions of money, from the common treasury had been drawn for such purposes. Our opposition sprang from no hostility to commerce, or all necessary aids for facilitating it. With us it was simply a question, upon *whom* the burden should fall. In Georgia, for instance, we have done as much for the cause of internal improvements as any other portion of the country according to population and means. We have stretched out lines of railroads from the seaboard to the mountains; dug down the hills, and filled up the valleys at a cost of not less than twenty-five millions of dollars. All this was done to open an outlet for our products of the interior, and those to the west of us, to reach the marts of the world. No State was in greater need of such facilities than Georgia, but we did not ask that these works should be made by appropriations out of the common treasury. The cost of the grading, the superstructure, and equipments of our roads, was borne by those who entered on the enterprise. Nay, more—not only the cost of the iron, no small item in the aggregate cost, was borne in the same way—but we were compelled to pay into the common treasury several millions of dollars for the privilege of importing the iron, after the price was paid for it abroad. What justice was there in taking this money, which our people paid into the common treasury on the importation of our iron, and applying it to the improvement of rivers and harbors elsewhere?

The true principle is to subject the commerce of every locality, to whatever burdens may be necessary to facilitate it. If Charleston harbor needs improvement, let the commerce of Charleston bear the burden. If the mouth of the Savannah river has to be cleared out, let the sea-going navigation which is benefitted by it, bear the burden. So with the mouths of the Alabama and Mississippi river. Just as the products of the interior, our cotton, wheat, corn, and other articles, have to bear the necessary rates of freight over our railroads to reach the seas. This is again the broad principle of perfect equality and justice. [Applause.] And it is especially set forth and established in our new constitution.

Another feature to which I will allude, is that the new constitution provides that cabinet ministers and heads of departments may have the privilege of seats upon the floor of the Senate and House of Representatives—may have the right to participate in the debates and discussions upon the various subjects of administration. I should have preferred that this provision should have gone further, and required the President to select his constitutional advisers from the Senate and

House of Representatives. That would have conformed entirely to the practice in the British Parliament, which, in my judgment, is one of the wisest provisions in the British constitution. It is the only feature that saves that government. It is that which gives it stability in its facility to change its administration. Ours, as it is, is a great approximation to the right principle.

Under the old constitution, a secretary of the treasury for instance, had no opportunity, save by his annual reports, of presenting any scheme or plan of finance or other matter. He had no opportunity of explaining, expounding, inforcing, or defending his views of policy; his only resort was through the medium of an organ. In the British parliament, the premier brings in his budget and stands before the nation responsible for its every item. If it is indefensible, he falls before the attacks upon it, as he ought to. This will now be the case to a limited extent under our system. In the new constitution, provision has been made by which our heads of departments can speak for themselves and the administration, in behalf of its entire policy, without resorting to the indirect and highly objectionable medium of a newspaper. It is to be greatly hoped that under our system we shall never have what is known as a government organ. [Rapturous applause.]

[A noise again arose from the clamor of the crowd outside, who wished to hear Mr. Stephens, and for some moments interrupted him. The mayor rose and called on the police to preserve order. Quiet being restored, Mr. S. proceeded.]

Another change in the constitution relates to the length of the tenure of the presidential office. In the new constitution it is six years instead of four, and the President rendered ineligible for a re-election. This is certainly a decidedly conservative change. It will remove from the incumbent all temptation to use his office or exert the powers confided to him for any objects of personal ambition. The only incentive to that higher ambition which should move and actuate one holding such high trusts in his hands, will be the good of the people, the advancement, prosperity, happiness, safety, honor, and true glory of the confederacy. [Applause.]

But not to be tedious in enumerating the numerous changes for the better, allow me to allude to one other—though last, not least. The new constitution has put at rest, *forever*, all the agitating questions relating to our peculiar institution—African slavery as it exists amongst us—the proper *status* of the negro in our form of civilization. This was the immediate cause of the late rupture and present revolution. Jefferson in his forecast, had anticipated this, as the "rock upon which the old Union would split." He was right. What was conjecture with him, is now a realized fact. But whether he fully comprehended the great truth upon which that rock *stood* and *stands*, may be doubted. The prevailing ideas entertained by him and most of the leading statesmen at the time of the formation of the old constitution, were that the enslavement of the African was in violation of the laws of nature; that it was wrong in *principle*, socially, morally, and politically. It was an evil they knew not well how to deal with, but the general opinion of the men of that day was that, somehow or other in the order of Providence, the institution would be evanescent and pass away. This idea, though not incorporated in the constitution, was the prevailing idea at that time. The constitution, it is true, secured every essential guarantee to the institution while it should last, and hence no argument can be justly urged against the constitutional guarantees thus secured, because of the common sentiment of the day. Those ideas, however, were fundamentally wrong. They rested upon the assumption of the equality of races. This was an error. It was a sandy foundation, and the government built upon it fell when the "storm came and the wind blew."

Our new government is founded upon exactly the opposite idea; its foundations are laid, its corner-stone rests upon the great truth, that the negro is not equal to the white man; that slavery—subordination to the superior race—is his natural and normal condition. [Applause.]

This, our new government, is the first, in the history of the world, based upon this great physical, philosophical, and moral truth. This truth has been slow in the process of its development, like all other truths in the various departments of science. It has been so even amongst us. Many who hear me, perhaps, can recollect well, that this truth was not generally admitted, even within their day. The errors of the past generation still clung to many as late as twenty years ago. Those at the North, who still cling to these errors, with a zeal above knowledge, we justly denominate fanatics. All fanaticism springs from an aberration of the mind—from a defect in reasoning. It is a species of insanity. One of the most striking characteristics of insanity, in many instances, is forming correct conclusions from fancied or erroneous premises; so with the anti-slavery fanatics; their conclusions are right if their premises were. They assume that the negro is equal, and hence conclude that he is entitled to equal privileges and rights with the white man. If their premises were correct, their conclusions would be logical and just—but their premise being wrong, their whole argument fails. I recollect once of having heard a gentleman from one of the northern States, of great power and ability, announce in the House of Representatives, with imposing effect, that we of the South would be compelled, ultimately, to yield upon this subject of slavery, that it was as impossible to war successfully against a principle in politics, as it was in physics or mechanics. That the principle would ultimately prevail. That we, in maintaining slavery as it exists with us, were warring against a principle, a principle founded in nature, the principle of the equality of men. The reply I made to him was, that upon his own grounds, we should, ultimately, succeed, and that he and his associates, in this crusade against our institutions, would ultimately fail. The truth announced, that it was as impossible to war successfully against a principle in politics as it was in physics and mechanics, I admitted; but told him that it was he, and those acting with him, who were warring against a principle. They were attempting to make things equal which the Creator had made unequal.

In the conflict thus far, success has been on our side, complete throughout the length and breadth of the Confederate States. It is upon this, as I have stated, our social fabric is firmly planted; and I cannot permit myself to doubt the ultimate success of a full recognition of this principle throughout the civilized and enlightened world.

As I have stated, the truth of this principle may be slow in development, as all truths are and ever have been, in the various branches of science. It was so with the principles announced by Galileo—it was so with Adam Smith and his principles of political economy. It was so with Harvey, and his theory of the circulation of the blood. It is stated that not a single one of the medical profession, living at the time of the announcement of the truths made by him, admitted them. Now, they are universally acknowledged. May we not, therefore, look with confidence to the ultimate universal acknowledgment of the truths upon which our system rests? It is the first government ever instituted upon the principles in strict conformity to nature, and the ordination of Providence, in furnishing the materials of human society. Many governments have been founded upon the principle of the subordination and serfdom of certain classes of the same race; such were and are in violation of the laws of nature. Our system commits no such violation of nature's laws. With us, all of the white race, however high or low, rich or poor, are equal in the eye of the law. Not so with the negro. Subordination is his place. He, by nature, or by the curse against Canaan, is fitted for that condition which he occupies in our system. The architect, in the construction of buildings, lays the foundation with the proper material—the granite; then comes the brick or the marble. The substratum of our society is made of the material fitted by nature for it, and by experience we know that it is best, not only for the superior, but for the inferior race, that it should be so. It is, indeed, in conformity with the ordinance of the Creator. It is not for us to inquire into the wisdom of his ordinances, or to question them. For his own purposes, he has made one race to differ from another, as he has made "one star to differ from another star in glory."

The great objects of humanity are best attained when there is conformity to his laws and decrees, in the formation of governments as well as in all things else. Our confederacy is founded upon principles in strict conformity with these laws. This stone which was rejected by the first builders "is become the chief of the corner"—the real "corner-stone"—in our new edifice. [Applause.]

I have been asked, what of the future? It has been apprehended by some that we would have arrayed against us the civilized world. I care not who or how many they may be against us, when we stand upon the eternal principles of truth, *if we are true to ourselves and the principles for which we contend*, we are obliged to, and must triumph. [Immense applause.]

Thousands of people who begin to understand these truths are not yet completely out of the shell; they do not see them in their length and breadth. We hear much of the civilization and christianization of the barbarous tribes of Africa. In my judgment, those ends will never be attained, but by first teaching them the lesson taught to Adam, that "in the sweat of his brow he should eat his bread," [applause,] and teaching them to work, and feed, and clothe themselves.

But to pass on: Some have propounded the inquiry whether it is practicable for us to go on with the confederacy without further accessions? Have we the means and ability to maintain nationality among the powers of the earth? On this point I would barely say, that as anxiously as we all have been, and are, for the border States, with institutions similar to ours, to join us, still we are abundantly able to maintain our position, even if they should ultimately make up their minds not to cast their destiny with us. That they ultimately will join us—be compelled to do it—is my confident belief; but we can get on very well without them, even if they should not.

We have all the essential elements of a high national career. The idea has been given out at the North, and even in the border States, that we are too small and too weak to maintain a separate nationality. This is a great mistake. In extent of territory we embrace five hundred and sixty-four thousand square miles and upward. This is upward of two hundred thousand square miles more than was included within the limits of the original thirteen States. It is an area of country more than double the territory of France or the Austrian empire. France, in round numbers, has but two hundred and twelve thousand square miles. Austria, in round numbers, has two hundred and forty-eight thousand square miles. Ours is greater than both combined. It is greater than all France, Spain, Portugal, and Great Britain, including England, Ireland, and Scotland, together. In population we have upward of five millions, according to the census of 1860; this includes white and black. The entire population, including white and black, of the original thirteen States, was less than four millions in 1790, and still less in '76, when the independence of our fathers was achieved.

If they, with a less population, dared maintain their independence against the greatest power on earth, shall we have any apprehension of maintaining ours now?

In point of material wealth and resources, we are greatly in advance of them. The taxable property of the Confederate States cannot be less than twenty-two hundred millions of dollars! This, I think I venture but little in saying, may be considered as five times more than the colonies possessed at the time they achieved their independence. Georgia, alone, possessed last year, according to the report of our comptroller-general, six hundred and seventy-two millions of taxable property. The debts of the seven confederate States sum up in the aggregate less than eighteen millions, while the existing debts of the other of the late United States sum up in the aggregate the enormous amount of one hundred and seventy-four millions of dollars. This is without taking into the account the heavy city debts, corporation debts, and railroad debts, which press, and will continue to press, as a heavy incubus upon the resources of those States. These debts, added to others, make a sum total not much under five hundred millions of dollars. With such an area of territory as we have—with such an amount of population—with a climate and soil unsurpassed by any on the face of the earth—with such resources already at our command—with productions which control the commerce of the world—who can entertain any apprehensions as to our ability to succeed, whether others join us or not?

It is true, I believe I state but the common sentiment, when I declare my earnest desire that the border States should join us. The differences of opinion that existed among us anterior to secession, related more to the policy in securing that result by co-operation than from any difference upon the ultimate security we all looked to in common.

These differences of opinion were more in reference to policy than principle, and as Mr. Jefferson said in his inaugural, in 1801, after the heated contest preceding his election, there might be differences of opinion without differences on principle, and that all, to some extent, had been federalists and all republicans; so it may now be said of us, that whatever differences of opinion as to the best policy in having a co-operation with our border sister slave States, if the worst came to the worst, that as we were all co-operationists, we are now all for independence, whether they come or not. [Continued applause.]

In this connection I take this occasion to state, that I was not without grave and serious apprehensions, that if the worst came to the worst, and cutting loose from the old government should be the only remedy for our safety and security, it would be attended with much more serious ills than it has been as yet. Thus far we have seen none of those incidents which usually attend revolutions. No such material as such convulsions usually throw up has been seen. Wisdom, prudence, and patriotism, have marked every step of our progress thus far. This augurs well for the future, and it is a matter of sincere gratification to me, that I am enabled to make the declaration. Of the men I met in the Congress at Montgomery, I may be pardoned for saying this, an abler, wiser, a more conservative, deliberate, determined, resolute, and patriotic body of men, I never met in my life. [Great applause.] Their works speak for them; the provisional government speaks for them; the constitution of the permanent government will be a lasting monument of their worth, merit, and statesmanship. [Applause.]

But to return to the question of the future. What is to be the result of this revolution?

Will every thing, commenced so well, continue as it has begun? In reply to this anxious inquiry, I can only say it all depends upon ourselves. A young man starting out in life on his majority, with health, talent, and ability, under a favoring Providence, may be said to be the architect of his own fortunes. His destinies are in his own hands. He may make for himself a name, of honor or dishonor, according to his own acts. If he plants himself upon truth, integrity, honor and uprightness, with industry, patience and energy, he cannot fail of success. So it is with us. We are a young republic, just entering upon the arena of nations; we will be the architects of our own fortunes. Our destiny, under Providence, is in our own hands. With wisdom, prudence, and statesmanship on the part of our public men, and intelligence, virtue and patriotism on the part of the people, success, to the full measures of our most sanguine hopes, may be looked for. But if unwise counsels prevail—if we become divided—if schisms arise—if dissensions spring up—if factions are engendered—if party spirit, nourished by unholy personal ambition shall rear its hydra head, I have no good to prophesy for you. Without intelligence, virtue, integrity, and patriotism on the part of the people, no republic or representative government can be durable or stable.

We have intelligence, and virtue, and patriotism. All that is required is to cultivate and perpetuate these. Intelligence will not do without virtue. France was a nation of philosophers. These philosophers became Jacobins. They lacked that virtue, that devotion to moral principle, and that patriotism which is essential to good government. Organized upon principles of perfect justice and right—seeking amity and friendship with all other powers—I see no obstacle in the way of our upward and onward progress. Our growth, by accessions from other States, will depend greatly upon whether we present to the world, as I trust we shall, a better government than that to which neighboring States belong. If we do this, North Carolina, Tennessee, and Arkansas cannot hesitate long; neither can Virginia, Kentucky, and Missouri. They will necessarily gravitate to us by an imperious law. We made ample provision in our constitution for the admission of other States; it is more guarded, and wisely so, I think, than the old constitution on the same subject, but not too guarded to receive them as fast as it may be proper. Looking to the distant future, and, perhaps, not very far distant either, it is not beyond the range of possibility, and even probability, that all the great States of the north-west will gravitate this way, as well as Tennessee, Kentucky, Missouri, Arkansas, etc. Should they do so, our doors are wide enough to receive them, but not until they are ready to assimilate with us in principle.

The process of disintegration in the old Union may be expected to go on with almost absolute certainty if we pursue the right course. We are now the nucleus of a growing power which, if we are true to ourselves, our destiny, and high mission, will become the controlling power on this continent. To what extent accessions will go on in the process of time, or where it will end, the future will determine. So far as it concerns States of the old Union, this process will be upon no such principles of *reconstruction* as now spoken of, but upon *reorganization* and new assimilation. [Loud applause.] Such are some of the glimpses of the future as I catch them.

But at first we must necessarily meet with the inconveniences and difficulties and embarrassments incident to all changes of government. These will be felt in our postal affairs and changes in the channel of trade. These inconveniences, it is to be hoped, will be but temporary, and must be borne with patience and forbearance.

As to whether we shall have war with our late confederates, or whether all matters of differences between us shall be amicably settled, I can only say that the prospect for a peaceful adjustment is better, so far as I am informed, than it has been.

The prospect of war is, at least, not so threatening as it has been. The idea of coercion, shadowed forth in President Lincoln's inaugural, seems not to be followed up thus far so vigorously as was expected. Fort Sumter, it is believed, will soon be evacuated. What course will be pursued toward Fort Pickens, and the other forts on the gulf, is not so well understood. It is to be greatly desired that all of them should be surrendered. Our object is *peace*, not only with the North, but with the world. All matters relating to the public property, public liabilities of the Union when we were members of it, we are ready and willing to adjust and settle upon the principles of right, equity, and good faith. War can be of no more benefit to the North than to us. Whether the intention of evacuating Fort Sumter is to be received as an evidence of a desire for a peaceful solution of our difficulties with the United States, or the result of necessity, I will not undertake to say. I would fain hope the former. Rumors are afloat, however, that it is the result of necessity. All I can say to you, therefore, on that point is, keep your armor bright and your powder dry. [Enthusiastic cheering.]

The surest way to secure peace, is to show your ability to maintain your rights. The principles and position of the present administration of the United States—the republican party —present some puzzling questions. While it is a fixed principle with them never to allow the increase of a foot of slave territory, they seem to be equally determined not to part with an inch "of the accursed soil." Notwithstanding their clamor against the institution, they seemed to be equally opposed to getting more, or letting go what they have got. They were ready to fight on the accession of Texas, and are equally ready to fight now on her secession. Why is this? How can this strange paradox be accounted for? There seems to be but one rational solution—and that is, notwithstanding their professions of humanity, they are disinclined to give up the benefits they derive from slave labor. Their philanthropy yields to their interest. The idea of enforcing the laws, has but one object, and that is a collection of the taxes, raised by slave labor to swell the fund, necessary to meet their heavy appropriations. The spoils is what they are after—though they come from the labor of the slave. [Continued applause.]

Mr. Stephens reviewed at some length, the extravagance and profligacy of appropriations by the Congress of the United States for several years past, and in this connection took occasion to allude to another one of the great improvements in our new constitution, which is a clause prohibiting Congress from appropriating any money from the treasury, except by a two-third vote, unless it be for some object which the executive may say is necessary to carry on the government.

When it is thus asked for, and estimated for, he continued, the majority may appropriate. This was a new feature.

Our fathers had guarded the assessment of taxes by insisting that representation and taxation should go together. This was inherited from the mother country, England. It was one of the principles upon which the revolution had been fought. Our fathers also provided in the old constitution, that all appropriation bills should originate in the representative branch of Congress, but our new constitution went a step further, and guarded not only the pockets of the people, but also the public money, after it was taken from their pockets.

He alluded to the difficulties and embarrassments which seemed to surround the question of a peaceful solution of the controversy with the old government. How can it be done? is perplexing many minds. The President seems to think that he cannot recognize our independence, nor can he, with and by the advice of the Senate, do so. The constitution makes no such provision. A general convention of all the States has been suggested by some.

Without proposing to solve the difficulty, he barely made the following suggestion:

"That as the admission of States by Congress under the constitution was an act of legislation, and in the nature of a contract or compact between the States admitted and the others admitting, why should not this contract or compact be regarded as of like character with all other civil contracts—liable to be rescinded by mutual agreement of both parties? The seceding States have rescinded it on their part, they have resumed their sovereignty. Why cannot the whole question be settled, if the north desire peace, simply by the Congress, in both branches, with the concurrence of the President, giving their consent to the separation, and a recognition of our independence?" This he merely offered as a suggestion, as one of the ways in which it might be done with much less violence by constructions to the constitution than many other acts of that government. [Applause.] The difficulty has to be solved in some way or other—this may be regarded as a fixed fact.

Several other points were alluded to by Mr. Stephens, particularly as to the policy of the new government toward foreign nations, and our commercial relations with them. Free trade, as far as practicable, would be the policy of this government. No higher duties would be imposed on foreign importations than would be necessary to support the government upon the strictest economy.

In olden times the olive branch was considered the emblem of peace; we will send to the nations of the earth another and far more potential emblem of the same, the cotton plant. The present duties were levied with a view of meeting the present necessities and exigencies, in preparation for war, if need be; but if we have peace, and he hoped we might, and trade should resume its proper course, a duty of ten per cent. upon foreign importations it was thought might be sufficient to meet the expenditures of the government. If some articles should be left on the free list, as they now are, such as breadstuffs, etc., then, of course, duties upon others would have to be higher—but in no event to an extent to embarrass trade and commerce. He concluded in an earnest appeal for union and harmony, on part of all the people in support of the common cause, in which we were all enlisted, and upon the issues of which such great consequences depend.

If, said he, we are true to ourselves, true to our cause, true to our destiny, true to our high mission, in presenting to the world the highest type of civilization ever exhibited by man—there will be found in our lexicon no such word as fail.

Mr. Stephens took his seat, amid a burst of enthusiasm and applause, such as the Athenæum has never had displayed within its walls, within "the recollection of the oldest inhabitant."

RELIEVING FORT SUMTER:
WASHINGTON, D.C., MARCH–APRIL 1861

Edward Bates: Diary, March 9–April 8, 1861

On the day after his inauguration President Lincoln was told that the garrison at Fort Sumter would run out of supplies within six weeks. As the new cabinet debated whether to evacuate the fort or attempt to resupply it, their deliberations were recorded by Edward Bates, who had been appointed attorney general by Lincoln.

———————

Mar 9. Saturday night. A Cabinet Council upon the State of the Country. I was astonished to be informed that Fort Sumter, in Charleston harbor *must* be evacuated, and that General Scott, Genl. Totten and Major Anderson concur in opinion, that, as the place has but 28 days provision, it must be relieved, if at all, in that time; and that it will take a force of 20,000 men at least, and a bloody battle, to relieve it!

<For several days after this, consultations were held as to the feasibility of relieving Fort Sumter, at which were present, explaining and aiding, Gen Scott, Gen Totten, Comodore Stringham, and Mr. Fox who seems to be *au fait* in both nautical and military matters. The *army* officers and *navy* officers differ widely about the degree of danger to rapid moving vessels passing under the fire of land batteries—The *army* officers think destruction almost inevitable, where the *navy* officers think the danger but slight. The one believes that Sumter cannot be relieved—not even provisioned—without an army of 20.000 men and a bloody battle: The other (the naval) believes that with light, rapid vessels, they can cross *the bar* at high tide of a dark night, run the enemy's forts (Moultrie and Cummings' Point) and reach Sumter with little risk. They say that the greatest danger will be in landing at Sumter, upon which point there may be a concentrated fire. They do not doubt that the place *can* be and *ought* to be relieved. Mr. Fox is anxious to risk his life in leading the relief, and Comodore Stringham seems equally confident of success.

The naval men have convinced me fully that the thing can be done, and yet, as the doing of it would be almost certain to *begin the war*, and as Charleston is of little importance, as compared with the chief points in the Gulf, I am willing to yield to the *military* counsel. and evacuate Fort Sumter, at the same time strengthening the Forts in the Gulf, so as to *look down* opposition, and guarding the coast, with all our naval power, if need be, so as to close any port at pleasure.

And to this effect, I gave the President my written opinion, on the 16th. of March.>

March 16. The President of the United States has required my opinion, in writing, upon the following question

"Assuming it to be possible to now provision Fort Sumter, under all the circumstances, is it wise to attempt it?"

This is not a question of lawful right nor physical power, but of prudence and patriotism only. The right is in my mind unquestionable, and I have no doubt at all that the Government has the power and means, not only to provision the fort, but also, if the exigency required, to man it, with its war complement of 650 men, so as to make it impregnable to any local force that could be brought against it. Assuming all this we come back to the question "Under all the circumstances is it wise *now* to provision the fort?"

The wisdom of the act must be tested by the value of the object to be gained, and by the hazard to be encountered in the enterprise. The object to be gained by the supply of provision, is not to strengthen the fortress, so as to command the harbor and enforce the laws, but only to prolong the labors and privations of the brave little garrison that has so long held it, with patient courage. The possession of the fort as we now hold it, does not enable us to collect the revenue or enforce the laws of commerce and navigation. It may indeed involve a point of honor or a point of pride, but I do not see any great national interest involved in the bare fact of holding the fort, as we now hold it—and to hold it at all we must supply it with provisions. And it seems to me that we may in humanity and patriotism, safely waive the point of pride, in the consciousness that we have the power and lack nothing but the will, to hold

Fort Sumter in such condition as to command the harbor of Charleston, cut off all its commerce, and even lay the City in ashes.

The hazards to be met are many and obvious. If the attempt be made in rapid boats light enough to pass the bar in safety, still they must pass under the fire of Fort Moultrie and the batteries on Morris Island. They might possibly escape that danger, but they cannot hope to escape the armed guard boats which ply all night from the Fort to the outer edge of the bar. These armed guard boats would be sure to take or destroy our unarmed tugs, unless repelled by force, either from our ships outside the bar, or from Fort Sumter within; and that is war. True, war already exists by the act of South Carolina; but this Government has thus far, magnanimously forborne to retort the outrage. And I am willing to forbear yet longer, in the hope of a peaceful solution of our present difficulties. I am most unwilling to strike—I will not say the first blow, for South Carolina has already struck that—but I am unwilling "*under all the circumstances*" at this moment to do any act which may have the semblance, before the world of beginning a civil war, the terrible consequences of which would, I think, find no parallel in modern times. For I am convinced that flagrant Civil war in the Southern States would soon become a social war, and that could hardly fail to bring on a servile war, the horrors of which need not be dwelt upon. To avoid these evils I would make great sacrifices, and fort Sumter is one; but if war be forced upon us by causeless and pertinacious rebellion, I am for resisting it with all the might of the nation.

I am persuaded moreover, that, in several of the misguided States of the South, a large portion of the people are really lovers of the Union, and anxious to be safely back, under the protection of its flag. A reaction has already begun, and, if encouraged by wise, moderate and firm measures on the part of this government, I persuade myself that the nation will be restored to its integrity without the effusion of blood.

For these reasons, I am willing to evacuate fort Sumter, rather than be an active party in the beginning of civil war. The port of Charleston is comparatively, a small thing. If the present difficulties should continue and grow, I am convinced that the real struggle will be at the Mississippi for it is not politically possible for any foreign power to hold the mouth of that river, against the people of the middle and upper valley.

If fort Sumter must be evacuated, then it is my decided opinion that the more Southern forts Pickens, Key West &c should, with out delay, be put in condition of easy defense against all assailants; and that the whole coast, from South Carolina to Texas, should be as well guarded as the power of the navy will enable us.

Upon the whole, I do not think it *wise now* to attempt to provision Fort Sumter.

On the 29th. of March, in Cabinet Council on these subjects, I suggested that, in the desultory conversations by which we had usually conducted our consultations, it was hard to arrive at definite conclusions, and therefore I proposed that the President should state his questions, and require our opinions *seriatim*. This being agreed to, I immediately wrote and read the following memorandum—

"It is my decided opinion that Fort Pickens and Key West ought to be re inforced and supplied so as to *look down* opposition, at all hazards—And this, whether fort Sumter be or be not evacuated."

"It is also my opinion that there ought to be a *naval* force kept upon the Southern coast, sufficient to *command it*, and, if need be *actually close* any port that, practically, ought to be closed, whatever other Station is left unoccupied."

"It is also my opinion that there ought to be immediately established, a line of light, fast-running vessels, to pass, as rapidly as possible, between N. Y. or Norfolk at the North, and Key West or other point in the gulf at the South."

"As to fort Sumter, I think the time is come when it ought to be either evacuated or relieved."

The President was pleased with this mode of proceeding, and requested the other ministers to do the like—which was done—Mr. Seward gave his advice for the immediate evacuation of fort Sumter.

April 8. Monday. To preserve continuity on this important subject, I skip over several days—

This Admn. has kept its own counsel pretty well, yet, its

general purpose to preserve its authority as far as possible, in the South, seems to be known by the press, though its particular means are still only guessed at. For some days, the public is much excited with rumors of military expeditions to various points, tho' most of the guesses point rather to the Gulf than to Charleston.

In fact, at this moment, the matter stands thus—An expedition to *provision* fort Sumter, well appointed, consisting of light-draft, rapid steamers (drawing only 5 or 6 feet, so as to pass Charleston bar) commanded by Mr. Fox, leaves N. York to day or tomorrow, and will reach Charleston on the 11th., or 12th. at farthest. If Maj: Anderson hold out till then, one of two things will happen—either the fort will be well provisioned, the Southrons forbearing to assail the boats, or a fierce contest will ensue, the result of which cannot be foreseen—The fort may be demolished or the City burned—In either case there will be much slaughter.

The President has sent a private messenger to Govr. Pickens, notifying him that *provisions* only, and not men, arms or ammunition, will be landed, and that no attempt will be made to reinforce the fort, unless the provisions or the fort be fired upon.

From the first, I have insisted that it was a capital error to allow batteries to be built around fort Sumter—the erection of those batteries being an *assault*, equal to the throwing of shells. In answer to my direct question today, the Sec.y. of War (Genl. Cameron) told me that the erection of batteries to assail fort Pickens wd. not be allowed—if attempted the Fort would prevent it with shot and shell.

A large naval force is ordered to the southern coast, and, in 3 or 4 days, either there will be some sharp fighting, or the prestige of the Government will be quietly reëstablished.

SEWARD AND FORT SUMTER:
WASHINGTON, D.C., MARCH 1861

Gideon Welles: Memoir of Events, March 1861

Secretary of State William Seward sought to establish himself as the dominant figure in the new administration during the debate over Fort Sumter. Secretary of the Navy Gideon Welles would recall Seward's role in the deliberations in a short memoir written several years after the war.

MR. SEWARD, who from the first had viewed with no favor any attempt to relieve Sumter, soon became a very decisive and emphatic opponent of any proposition that was made; said he had entertained doubts, and the opinions and arguments of Major Anderson and his officers, confirmed by the distinguished military officers who were consulted, had fully convinced him that it would be abortive and useless. It was a duty to defer to these military gentlemen, whose profession and study made them experts, who had by long and faithful service justly acquired the positions they held, and who possessed the confidence of the country. It was, he was satisfied, impossible to relieve and reinforce the garrison; the attempt would provoke immediate hostilities, and if hostilities could not be avoided, he deemed it important that the Administration should not strike the first blow.

The President, though much distressed with the conclusions of the military officers, and the decisive concurrence of the Secretary of State in those conclusions, appeared to acquiesce in what seemed to be a military necessity, but was not disposed to yield until the last moment, and when there was no hope of accomplishing the work if attempted. In the mean time, he sent Mr. Lamon, his late law-partner, to Charleston and others also to make inquiries, among them Mr. Fox, who, like Commander Ward, had been a volunteer under the late administration to relieve Sumter and who never abandoned the idea of its practicability.

Commander Ward was so fully convinced by the arguments of General Scott and General Totten and the opinions of the officers of the garrison, so dissuaded by the opposition of Mr. Seward and the general current of views which prevailed, that he wholly abandoned the project, stating, however, that he held himself in readiness to obey orders and take charge of an expedition, if the Government should at any time deem it expedient that an effort should be made. On the 11th of March he left Washington, and returned to New York.

A strange state of things existed at that time in Washington. The atmosphere was thick with treason. Party spirit and old party differences prevailed, however, amidst these accumulating dangers. Secession was considered by most persons as a political party question, not as rebellion. Democrats to a large extent sympathized with the Rebels more than with the Administration, which they opposed, not that they wished secession to be successful and the Union divided, but they hoped that President Lincoln and the Republicans would, overwhelmed by obstacles and embarrassments, prove failures. The Republicans, on the other hand, were scarcely less partisan and unreasonable. Crowds of them at this period, when the storm of civil war was about bursting on the country, thronged the anterooms of the President and Secretaries, clamorous for the removal of all Democrats, indiscriminately, from office. Patriotism was with them no test, no shield from party malevolence. They demanded the proscription and exclusion of such Democrats as opposed the Rebel movements and clung to the Union, with the same vehemence that they demanded the removal of the worst Rebels who advocated a dissolution of the Union.

Neither party appeared to be apprehensive of or to realize the gathering storm. There was a general belief, indulged in by most persons, that an adjustment would in some way be brought about, without any extensive resort to extreme measures. It seemed probable there might be some outbreak in South Carolina, and perhaps in one or two other places, but such would, it was believed, be soon and easily suppressed. The threatened violence which the nullifiers had thundered for thirty years in the ears of the people had caused their threats to be considered as the harmless ebullitions of excited demagogues throughout the North, while at the South those utterances had so trained the Southern mind, and fired the Southern heart, as to cause them to be received as truthful. The South were, therefore, more united and earnest at this crisis, more determined on seceding, than either the Democrats or Republicans supposed. But, while the great body of the people and most of their leaders in the Northern States, listening to the ninety-day prophecies of Mr. Seward, were incredulous as to any extensive, serious disturbance, there were not a few whose forebodings were grave and sad. All the calamities which soon befell the country these men anticipated. Yet such as were in positions of responsibility would not permit themselves to despond, or despair of the Republic. Mr. Seward possessed a hopeful and buoyant spirit which did not fail him in that dark period, and at no time were his party feelings more decided than during the spring of 1861. Old Whig associates he clung to and strove to retain. All Democrats he distrusted, unless they became identified with the Republican Party. He had probably overestimated his own power and ability to allay the rising storm, and had not the personal influence he supposed. He had prophesied during the winter peace and harmony, within a very brief period after the change of administration was to be effected. These unfortunate prophecies, which became a matter of mirth with many of his friends and of ridicule among his opponents, were not entirely vain imaginings or without some foundation. In the confident belief that he could, if once in place and power, effect conciliation and peace, it had been an object with him to tide the difficulties past the 4th of March. He therefore had operated to that end, and so had Mr. Buchanan, though for different reasons.

Through Mr. Stanton, after that gentleman entered Mr. Buchanan's Cabinet, Mr. Seward and others were secretly advised in regard to the important measures of the Buchanan Administration, and in the course of the winter Mr. Seward came to an understanding, as was alleged and as events and circumstances indicated, with certain of the leading Secessionists. Among other things it was asserted that an agreement had been entered into that no assault should be made on Fort Sumter, provided the garrison should not be reinforced. Mr. Buchanan was to observe the status thus understood during the short remaining period of his administration, and Mr. Seward, as the coming premier, was, on the change of administration, to carry forward the policy of non-reinforcement of Sumter. If not supplied or reinforced, famine would certainly effect the downfall of the fortress without bloodshed on either side. Until blood was spilled, there was hope of conciliation. In fulfillment of this arrangement, Mr. Seward opposed any and every scheme to reinforce Sumter, and General Scott, who was old and much under his influence, if not a party to the understanding, seconded or took a leading part in that opposition.

On the 5th of March commissioners from the Rebel Government arrived in Washington and soon put themselves in communication with the Secretary of State, but the specific object which they had in view, and the negotiations or understanding between him and the parties were not immediately detailed to the Cabinet. They undoubtedly influenced the mind and course of Mr. Seward, who did not relinquish the hope of a peaceful adjustment of difficulties, and he in conversation continued to allure his friends with the belief that he should be able to effect a reconciliation.

In the many, almost daily, discussions which for a time were held in regard to Sumter, the opposition to forwarding supplies gathered strength. Commodore Stringham, as well as Commander Ward, on a final application which I made to him, by request of the President, and finally by the President himself, said he was compelled to advise against it. The time had gone by. It was too late. The military gentlemen had satisfied him it was impossible, that nothing could be gained by it, were the attempt made, that it would be attended with a useless sacrifice of blood and treasure, and he felt constrained to state his belief of the inability of the Navy to give relief.

Postmaster-General Blair, who had been a close and near observer of what had taken place through the winter and spring, took an opposite view from Mr. Seward and General Scott. To some extent he was aware of the understanding which Mr. Seward had with the members of Buchanan's Administration, or was suspicious of it, and his indignation that any idea of abandoning Sumter should be entertained or thought of was unbounded. With the exception of Mr. Seward, all his colleagues concurred with Mr. Blair at the commencement, but as the subject was discussed, and the impossibility and inutility of the scheme was urged, with assurance from the first military men in the country, whose advice was sought and given, that it was a military necessity to leave Sumter to its fate, the opinions of men changed, or they began at least to waver. Mr. Blair saw these misgivings, in which he did not at all participate, and finally, observing that the President, with the acquiescence of the Cabinet, was about adopting the Seward and Scott policy, he wrote his resignation, determined not to continue in the Cabinet if no attempt were made to relieve Fort Sumter. Before handing in his resignation, a delay was made at the request of his father. The elder Blair sought an interview with the President, to whom he entered his protest against non-action, which he denounced as the offspring of intrigue. His earnestness and indignation aroused and electrified the President; and when, in his zeal, Blair warned the President that the abandonment of Sumter would be justly considered by the people, by the world, by history, as treason to the country, he touched a chord that responded to his invocation. The President decided from that moment that an attempt should be made to convey supplies to Major Anderson, and that he would reinforce Sumter. This determination he communicated to the members of the Cabinet as he saw them, without a general announcement in Cabinet-meeting. The resolve inspired all the members with hope and courage, except Mr. Seward, who was evidently disappointed. He said it was of vastly more importance to turn our attention to Fort Pickens. I told him this had been done and how; that we had a considerable naval force there, almost the whole of the Home Squadron, and we had sent, a fortnight before, orders to land the troops under Captain Vogdes from the Brooklyn. He said that still more should, in his opinion, be done; that it was practicable to save Fort Pickens, but it was confessedly impossible to retain Sumter. One would be a waste of effort and energy and life, would extinguish all hope of peace, and compel the Government to take the initiative in hostile demonstrations, while the other would be an effective and peaceable movement. Although, as already mentioned, stated Cabinet-meetings were not then established, the members were in those early days of the Administration frequently together, and the President had every day more or less interviews with them, individually or collectively. The Secretary of State spent much of each day at the Executive Mansion and was vigilant to possess himself of every act, move, and intention of the President and of each of his associates. Perhaps there was an equal desire on their part to be informed of the proceedings of the Administration in full, but less was known of the transactions of the State Department than of any other.

CHALLENGING LINCOLN:
WASHINGTON, D.C., APRIL 1861

William H. Seward: Memorandum for the President

Seward's attempts to assume the dominant role in the administration culminated in this memorandum. As part of his recommendations for domestic policy, Seward advocated the defense and reinforcement of "all the Forts in the Gulf." By April 1, 1861, the federal government retained only three posts in the Gulf of Mexico: Fort Taylor on Key West, Fort Jefferson in the Dry Tortugas, and Fort Pickens on Santa Rosa Island at the entrance to Pensacola Bay, all of which would remain in Union hands throughout the war.

SOME THOUGHTS for the President's consideration

April 1. 1861.

1st. We are at the end of a month's administration and yet without a policy either domestic or foreign.

2d This, however, is not culpable, and it has been unavoidable. The presence of the Senate, with the need to meet applications for patronage have prevented attention to other and more grave matters.

3d. But further delay to adopt and prosecute our policies for both domestic and foreign affairs would not only bring scandal on the Administration, but danger upon the country.

4th. To do this we must dismiss the applicants for office. But how? I suggest that we make the local appointments forthwith, leaving foreign or general ones for ulterior and occasional action.

5th. The policy—at home. I am aware that my views are singular, and perhaps not sufficiently explained. My system is built upon this *idea* as a ruling one, namely that we must

Change the question before the Public from one upon Slavery, or about Slavery

for a question upon *Union or Disunion*.

In other words, from what would be regarded as a Party question to one of *Patriotism* or *Union*

The occupation or evacuation of Fort Sumter, although not in fact a slavery, or a party question is so *regarded*. Witness, the temper manifested by the Republicans in the Free States, and even by Union men in the South.

I would therefore terminate it as a safe means for changing the issue. I deem it fortunate that the last Administration created the necessity.

For the rest. I would simultaneously defend and reinforce all the Forts in the Gulf, and have the Navy recalled from foreign stations to be prepared for a blockade. Put the Island of Key West under Martial Law

This will raise distinctly the question of *Union* or *Disunion*. I would maintain every fort and possession in the South.

For *Foreign Nations*.

I would demand explanations from *Spain* and France, categorically, at once.

I would seek explanations from Great Britain and Russia, and send agents into *Canada*, *Mexico* and *Central America*, to rouse a vigorous continental *spirit of independence* on this continent against European intervention.

And if satisfactory explanations are not received from Spain and France,

Would convene Congress and declare war against them

But whatever policy we adopt, there must be an energetic prosecution of it.

For this purpose it must be somebody's business to pursue and direct it incessantly.

Either the President must do it himself, and be all the while active in it; or

Devolve it on some member of his Cabinet. Once adopted, debates on it must end, and all agree and abide.

It is not in my especial province.

But I neither seek to evade nor assume responsibility

"I MUST DO IT": WASHINGTON, D.C., APRIL 1861
Abraham Lincoln to William H. Seward

It is likely this letter was never sent and that Lincoln instead responded to Seward's memorandum in a private conversation.

Hon: W. H. Seward: Executive Mansion April 1, 1861

My dear Sir: Since parting with you I have been considering your paper dated this day, and entitled "Some thoughts for the President's consideration." The first proposition in it is, "1st. We are at the end of a month's administration, and yet without a policy, either domestic or foreign."

At the *beginning* of that month, in the inaugeral, I said "The power confided to me will be used to hold, occupy and possess the property and places belonging to the government, and to collect the duties, and imposts." This had your distinct approval at the time; and, taken in connection with the order I immediately gave General Scott, directing him to employ every means in his power to strengthen and hold the forts, comprises the exact domestic policy you now urge, with the single exception, that it does not propose to abandon Fort Sumpter.

Again, I do not perceive how the re-inforcement of Fort Sumpter would be done on a slavery, or party issue, while that of Fort Pickens would be on a more national, and patriotic one.

The news received yesterday in regard to St. Domingo, certainly brings a new item within the range of our foreign policy; but up to that time we have been preparing circulars, and instructions to ministers, and the like, all in perfect harmony, without even a suggestion that we had no foreign policy.

Upon your closing propositions, that "whatever policy we adopt, there must be an energetic prossecution of it"

"For this purpose it must be somebody's business to pursue and direct it incessantly"

"Either the President must do it himself, and be all the while active in it, or"

"Devolve it on some member of his cabinet"

"Once adopted, debates on it must end, and all agree and abide" I remark that if this must be done, *I* must do it. When a general line of policy is adopted, I apprehend there is no danger of its being changed without good reason, or continuing to be a subject of unnecessary debate; still, upon points arising in its progress, I wish, and suppose I am entitled to have the advice of all the cabinet. Your Obt. Servt. A. LINCOLN

THE WAR BEGINS: SOUTH CAROLINA, APRIL 1861

Mary Chesnut, Diary, April 7–15, 1861

On April 6 President Lincoln sent a message to the governor of South Carolina, informing him that an expedition would be sent to supply Fort Sumter "with provisions only; and that, if such attempt be not resisted, no effort to throw in men, arms, ammunition, will be made, without further notice, or in case of an attack on the fort." In response, Jefferson Davis and his cabinet ordered the fort captured before the relief expedition arrived. The outbreak of the war at Charleston was witnessed and later described by Mary Chesnut. Her husband, James Chesnut, helped draft the South Carolina ordinance of secession after leaving the U.S. Senate. A member of the Provisional Confederate Congress, James Chesnut served as an aide to General Pierre G. T. Beauregard during the siege of Fort Sumter. (Mary Chesnut kept a journal during the 1860s that she extensively revised and expanded between 1881 and 1884. Selections from her 1880s manuscript were published posthumously in 1905 as *A Diary from Dixie*, and in a new edition using the same title in 1949. The text presented in this volume is taken from *Mary Chesnut's Civil War* [1981], edited by C. Vann Woodward, which prints the text of the 1880s manuscript, but also includes significant passages from the 1860s journal that Chesnut omitted in her revised version.)

April 7, 1861. Yesterday Mrs. Wigfall and I made a few visits. At the first house they wanted Mrs. Wigfall to settle a dispute. "Was she indeed fifty-five?" Fancy her face—more than ten years bestowed upon her so freely.

Then Mrs. Gibbes asked me if I had ever been in Charleston before.

Says Charlotte Wigfall (to pay me for my snigger when that false fifty was flung in her teeth), "And she thinks this is her native heath and her name is MacGregor."

She said it all came upon us for breaking the Sabbath, for indeed it was Sunday.

Allen Green came up to speak to me at dinner in all of his soldier's toggery. It sent a shiver through me.

Tried to read Margaret Fuller Ossoli. But could not.

The air is too full of war news. And we are all so restless. News so warlike I quake. My husband speaks of joining the artillery. . . . [ ] last night I find he is my all, and I would go mad without him. Mr. Manning read me a letter from his wife last night—very complimentary."

Went to see Miss Pinckney—one of the last of the 18th century Pinckneys. She inquired particularly about a portrait of her father, Charles Cotesworth Pinckney—which she said had been sent by him to my husband's grandfather. I gave a good account of it. It hangs in the place of honor in the drawing room at Mulberry. She wanted to see my husband, for "his grandfather, my father's friend, was one of the handsomest men of his day."

We came home, and soon Mr. Robert Gourdin and Mr. Miles called.

Governor Manning walked in, bowed gravely, and seated himself by me.

Again he bowed low, in mock heroic style and, with a grand wave of his hand, said, "Madame, your country is invaded."

When I had breath to speak, I asked, "What does he mean?"

"He means this. There are six men-of-war outside of the bar. Talbot and Chew have come to say that hostilities are to begin. Governor Pickens and Beauregard are holding a council of war."

Mr. Chesnut then came in. He confirmed the story.

Wigfall next entered in boisterous spirits. He said, "There was a sound of revelry by night, &c&c&c."

In any stir or confusion, my heart is apt to beat so painfully. Now the agony was so stifling—I could hardly see or hear. The men went off almost immediately. And I crept silently to my room, where I sat down to a good cry.

Mrs. Wigfall came in, and we had it out on the subject of civil war. We solaced ourselves with dwelling on all its known horrors, and then we added what we had a right to expect, with Yankees in front and negroes in the rear.

"The slave-owners must expect a servile insurrection, of course," said Mrs. Wigfall, to make sure that we were unhappy enough.

Suddenly loud shouting was heard. We ran out. Cannon

after cannon roared. We met Mrs. Allen Green in the passageway, with blanched cheeks and streaming eyes.

Governor Means rushed out of his room in his dressing gown and begged us to be calm.

"Governor Pickens has ordered, in the plenitude of his wisdom, seven cannon to be fired as a signal to the Seventh Regiment. Anderson will hear as well as the Seventh Regiment. Now you go back and be quiet: fighting in the streets has not begun yet."

So we retired. Dr. Gibbes calls Mrs. Allen Green "Dame Placid." There was no placidity today. Cannons bursting and Allen on the island.

No sleep for anybody last night. The streets were alive with soldiers, men shouting, marching, singing.

Wigfall, the Stormy Petrel, in his glory. The only thoroughly happy person I see.

Today things seem to have settled down a little.

One can but hope still. Lincoln or Seward have made such silly advances and then far sillier drawings back. There may be a chance for peace, after all.

Things are happening so fast.

My husband has been made an aide-de-camp of General Beauregard.

Three hours ago we were quietly packing to go home. The convention has adjourned.

Now he tells me the attack upon Fort Sumter may begin tonight. Depends upon Anderson and the fleet outside. The *Herald* says that this show of war outside of the bar is intended for Texas.

John Manning came in with his sword and red sash. Pleased as a boy to be on Beauregard's staff while the row goes on. He has gone with Wigfall to Captain Hartstene with instructions.

Mr. Chesnut is finishing a report he had to make to the convention.

Mrs. Hayne called. She had, she said, "but one feeling, pity for those who are not here."

Jack Preston, Willie Alston—"the take-life-easys," as they are called—with John Green, "the big brave," have gone down to the island—volunteered as privates.

Seven hundred men were sent over. Ammunition wagons rumbling along the streets all night. Anderson burning blue lights—signs and signals for the fleet outside, I suppose.

Today at dinner there was no allusion to things as they stand in Charleston Harbor. There was an undercurrent of intense excitement. There could not have been a more brilliant circle. In addition to our usual quartet (Judge Withers, Langdon Cheves, and Trescot) our two governors dined with us, Means and Manning.

These men all talked so delightfully. For once in my life I listened.

That over, business began. In earnest, Governor Means rummaged a sword and red sash from somewhere and brought it for Colonel Chesnut, who has gone to demand the surrender of Fort Sumter.

And now, patience—we must wait.

Why did that green goose Anderson go into Fort Sumter? Then everything began to go wrong.

Now they have intercepted a letter from him, urging them to let him surrender. He paints the horrors likely to ensue if they will not.

He ought to have thought of all that before he put his head in the hole.

April 12, 1861. Anderson will not capitulate.

Yesterday was the merriest, maddest dinner we have had yet. Men were more audaciously wise and witty. We had an unspoken foreboding it was to be our last pleasant meeting. Mr. Miles dined with us today. Mrs. Henry King rushed in: "The news, I come for the latest news—all of the men of the King family are on the island"—of which fact she seemed proud.

While she was here, our peace negotiator—or envoy—came in. That is, Mr. Chestnut returned—his interview with

Colonel Anderson had been deeply interesting—but was not inclined to be communicative, wanted his dinner. Felt for Anderson. Had telegraphed to President Davis for instructions.

What answer to give Anderson, &c&c. He has gone back to Fort Sumter, with additional instructions.

When they were about to leave the wharf, A. H. Boykin sprang into the boat, in great excitement; thought himself ill-used. A likelihood of fighting—and he to be left behind!

I do not pretend to go to sleep. How can I? If Anderson does not accept terms—at four—the orders are—he shall be fired upon.

I count four—St. Michael chimes. I begin to hope. At half-past four, the heavy booming of a cannon.

I sprang out of bed. And on my knees—prostrate—I prayed as I never prayed before.

There was a sound of stir all over the house—pattering of feet in the corridor—all seemed hurrying one way. I put on my double gown and a shawl and went, too. It was to the housetop.

The shells were bursting. In the dark I heard a man say "waste of ammunition."

I knew my husband was rowing about in a boat somewhere in that dark bay. And that the shells were roofing it over—bursting toward the fort. If Anderson was obstinate—he was to order the forts on our side to open fire. Certainly fire had begun. The regular roar of the cannon—there it was. And who could tell what each volley accomplished of death and destruction.

The women were wild, there on the housetop. Prayers from the women and imprecations from the men, and then a shell would light up the scene. Tonight, they say, the forces are to attempt to land.

The *Harriet Lane* had her wheelhouse smashed and put back to sea.

We watched up there—everybody wondered. Fort Sumter did not fire a shot.

Today Miles and Manning, colonels now—aides to Beauregard—dined with us. The latter hoped I would keep the peace. I give him only good words, for he was to be under fire all day and night, in the bay carrying orders, &c.

Last night—or this morning truly—up on the housetop I was so weak and weary I sat down on something that looked like a black stool.

"Get up, you foolish woman—your dress is on fire," cried a man. And he put me out. It was a chimney, and the sparks caught my clothes. Susan Preston and Mr. Venable then came up. But my fire had been extinguished before it broke out into a regular blaze.

Do you know, after all that noise and our tears and prayers, nobody has been hurt. Sound and fury, signifying nothing. A delusion and a snare.

Louisa Hamilton comes here now. This is a sort of news center. Jack Hamilton, her handsome young husband, has all the credit of a famous battery which is made of RR iron. Mr. Petigru calls it the boomerang because it throws the balls back the way they came—so Lou Hamilton tells us. She had no children during her first marriage. Hence the value of this lately achieved baby. To divert Louisa from the glories of "the battery," of which she raves, we asked if the baby could talk yet.

"No—not exactly—but he imitates the big gun. When he hears that, he claps his hands and cries 'Boom boom.'" Her mind is distinctly occupied by three things—Lieutenant Hamilton, whom she calls Randolph, the baby, and "the big gun"—and it refuses to hold more.

Pryor of Virginia spoke from the piazza of the Charleston Hotel.

I asked what he said, irreverent woman. "Oh, they all say the same thing, but he made great play with that long hair of his, which he is always tossing aside."

Somebody came in just now and reported Colonel Chesnut asleep on the sofa in General Beauregard's room. After two such nights he must be so tired as to be able to sleep anywhere.

Just bade farewell to Langdon Cheves. He is forced to go home, to leave this interesting place. Says he feels like the man who was not killed at Thermopylae. I think he said that unfortunate had to hang himself when he got home for very shame. Maybe fell on his sword, which was a strictly classic way of ending matters.

I do not wonder at Louisa Hamilton's baby. We hear nothing, can listen to nothing. Boom, boom, goes the cannon—all the time. The nervous strain is awful, alone in this darkened room.

"Richmond and Washington ablaze," say the papers. Blazing with excitement. Why not? To us these last days' events seem frightfully great.

We were all in that iron balcony. Women—men we only see at a distance now. Stark Means, marching under the piazza at the head of his regiment, held his cap in his hand all the time he was in sight.

Mrs. Means leaning over, looking with tearful eyes.

"Why did he take his hat off?" said an unknown creature. Mrs. Means stood straight up.

"He did that in honor of his mother—he saw me." She is a proud mother—and at the same time most unhappy. Her lovely daughter Emma is dying in there, before her eyes—consumption. At that moment I am sure Mrs. Means had a spasm of the heart. At least, she looked as I feel sometimes. She took my arm, and we came in.

April 13, 1861. Nobody hurt, after all. How gay we were last night.

Reaction after the dread of all the slaughter we thought those dreadful cannons were making such a noise in doing.

Not even a battery the worse for wear.

Fort Sumter has been on fire. He has not yet silenced any of our guns. So the aides—still with swords and red sashes by way of uniform—tell us.

But the sound of those guns makes regular meals impossible. None of us go to table. But tea trays pervade the corridors, going everywhere.

Some of the anxious hearts lie on their beds and moan in solitary misery. Mrs. Wigfall and I solace ourselves with tea in my room.

These women have all a satisfying faith. "God is on our side," they cry. When we are shut in, we (Mrs. Wigfall and I) ask, "Why?" We are told: "Of course He hates the Yankees."

"You'll think that well of Him."

Not by one word or look can we detect any change in the demeanor of these negro servants. Laurence sits at our door, as sleepy and as respectful and as profoundly indifferent. So are they all. They carry it too far. You could not tell that they hear even the awful row that is going on in the bay, though it is dinning in their ears night and day. And people talk before them as if they were chairs and tables. And they make no sign. Are they stolidly stupid or wiser than we are, silent and strong, biding their time?

So tea and toast come. Also came Colonel Manning, A.D.C. —red sash and sword—to announce that he has been under fire and didn't mind. He said gaily, "It is one of those things— a fellow never knows how he will come out of it until he is tried. Now I know. I am a worthy descendant of my old Irish hero of an ancestor who held the British officer before him as a shield in the Revolution. And backed out of danger gracefully." Everybody laughs at John Manning's brag. We talked of *St. Valentine's Eve; or, The Maid of Perth* and the drop of the white doe's blood that sometimes spoiled all.

The war steamers are still there, outside the bar. And there were people who thought the Charleston bar "no good" to

Charleston. The bar is our silent partner, sleeping partner, and yet in this fray he is doing us yeoman service.

April 15, 1861. I did not know that one could live such days of excitement.

They called, "Come out—there is a crowd coming."

A mob indeed, but it was headed by Colonels Chesnut and Manning.

The crowd was shouting and showing these two as messengers of good news. They were escorted to Beauregard's headquarters. Fort Sumter had surrendered.

Those up on the housetop shouted to us, "The fort is on fire." That had been the story once or twice before.

When we had calmed down, Colonel Chesnut, who had taken it all quietly enough—if anything, more unruffled than usual in his serenity—told us how the surrender came about.

Wigfall was with them on Morris Island when he saw the fire in the fort, jumped in a little boat and, with his handkerchief as a white flag, rowed over to Fort Sumter. Wigfall went in through a porthole.

When Colonel Chesnut arrived shortly after and was received by the regular entrance, Colonel Anderson told him he had need to pick his way warily, for it was all mined.

As far as I can make out, the fort surrendered to Wigfall.

But it is all confusion. Our flag is flying there. Fire engines have been sent to put out the fire.

Everybody tells you half of something and then rushes off to tell something else or to hear the last news. Manning, Wigfall, John Preston, &c, men without limit, beset us at night.

In the afternoon, Mrs. Preston, Mrs. Joe Heyward, and I drove round the Battery. We were in an open carriage. What a changed scene. The very liveliest crowd I think I ever saw. Everybody talking at once. All glasses still turned on the grim old fort.

BOMBARDMENT AND SURRENDER:
SOUTH CAROLINA, APRIL 1861

Abner Doubleday: *from* Reminiscences of Forts Sumter and Moultrie in 1860–'61

In his 1876 memoir, Abner Doubleday described the bombardment of Fort Sumter and the negotiations leading to its surrender on April 14, 1861.

As SOON as the outline of our fort could be distinguished, the enemy carried out their programme. It had been arranged, as a special compliment to the venerable Edmund Ruffin, who might almost be called the father of secession, that he should fire the first shot against us, from the Stevens battery on Cummings Point, and I think in all the histories it is stated that he did so; but it is attested by Dr. Crawford and others who were on the parapet at the time, that the first shot really came from the mortar battery at Fort Johnson.* Almost immediately afterward a ball from Cummings Point lodged in the magazine wall, and by the sound seemed to bury itself in the masonry about a foot from my head, in very unpleasant proximity to my right ear. This is the one that probably came with Mr. Ruffin's compliments. In a moment the firing burst forth in one continuous roar, and large patches of both the exterior and interior masonry began to crumble and fall in all directions. The place where I was had been used for the manufacture of cartridges, and there was still a good deal of powder there, some packed and some loose. A shell soon struck near the ventilator, and a puff of dense smoke entered the room, giving me a strong impression that there would be an immediate explosion. Fortunately, no sparks had penetrated inside.

Nineteen batteries were now hammering at us, and the balls

---

*I have since learned that the shell from Fort Johnson was not a hostile shot, but was simply intended as a signal for the firing to commence.

and shells from the ten-inch columbiads, accompanied by shells from the thirteen-inch mortars which constantly bombarded us, made us feel as if the war had commenced in earnest.

When it was broad daylight, I went down to breakfast. I found the officers already assembled at one of the long tables in the mess-hall. Our party were calm, and even somewhat merry. We had retained one colored man to wait on us. He was a spruce-looking mulatto from Charleston, very active and efficient on ordinary occasions, but now completely demoralized by the thunder of the guns and crashing of the shot around us. He leaned back against the wall, almost white with fear, his eyes closed, and his whole expression one of perfect despair.* Our meal was not very sumptuous. It consisted of pork and water, but Dr. Crawford triumphantly brought forth a little farina, which he had found in a corner of the hospital.

When this frugal repast was over, my company was told off in three details for firing purposes, to be relieved afterward by Seymour's company. As I was the ranking officer, I took the first detachment, and marched them to the casemates, which looked out upon the powerful iron-clad battery of Cummings Point.

In aiming the first gun fired against the rebellion I had no feeling of self-reproach, for I fully believed that the contest was inevitable, and was not of our seeking. The United States was called upon not only to defend its sovereignty, but its right to exist as a nation. The only alternative was to submit to a powerful oligarchy who were determined to make freedom forever subordinate to slavery. To me it was simply a contest, politically speaking, as to whether virtue or vice should rule.

My first shot bounded off from the sloping roof of the battery opposite without producing any apparent effect. It seemed useless to attempt to silence the guns there; for our metal was not heavy enough to batter the work down, and every ball glanced harmlessly off, except one, which appeared

---

*In this he was an exception to most negroes. Those I have seen in the colored regiments in Texas have shown themselves to be among the best and most reliable men in the service for operations against the Indians. It was a line of negroes that charged over the torpedoes at Mobile.

to enter an embrasure and twist the iron shutter, so as to stop the firing of that particular gun.

I observed that a group of the enemy had ventured out from their intrenchments to watch the effect of their fire, but I sent them flying back to their shelter by the aid of a forty-two-pounder ball, which appeared to strike right in among them.

The firing continued all day, without any special incident of importance, and without our making much impression on the enemy's works. They had a great advantage over us, as their fire was concentrated on the fort, which was in the centre of the circle, while ours was diffused over the circumference. Their missiles were exceedingly destructive to the upper exposed portion of the work, but no essential injury was done to the lower casemates which sheltered us.

Some of these shells, however, set the officers' quarters on fire three times; but the flames were promptly extinguished once or twice through the exertions of Peter Hart, whose activity and gallantry were very conspicuous.

The night was an anxious one for us, for we thought it probable that the launches, filled with armed men from the fleet, might take advantage of the darkness to come in with provisions and supplies. Then, too, it was possible that the enemy might attempt a night attack. We were on the alert, therefore, with men stationed at all the embrasures; but nothing unusual occurred. The batteries fired upon us at stated intervals all night long. We did not return the fire, having no ammunition to waste.

On the morning of the 13th, we took our breakfast—or, rather, our pork and water—at the usual hour, and marched the men to the guns when the meal was over.

From 4 to 6 1/2 A.M. the enemy's fire was very spirited. From 7 to 8 A.M. a rain-storm came on, and there was a lull in the cannonading. About 8 A.M. the officers' quarters were ignited by one of Ripley's incendiary shells, or by shot heated in the furnaces at Fort Moultrie. The fire was put out; but at 10 A.M. a mortar shell passed through the roof, and lodged in the flooring of the second story, where it burst, and started the flames afresh. This, too, was extinguished; but the hot shot soon followed each other so rapidly that it was impossible for us to contend with them any longer. It became evident that the entire block, being built with wooden partitions, floors, and roofing, must be consumed, and that the magazine, containing three hundred barrels of powder, would be endangered; for, even after closing the metallic door, sparks might penetrate through the ventilator. The floor was covered with loose powder, where a detail of men had been at work manufacturing cartridge-bags out of old shirts, woolen blankets, etc.

While the officers exerted themselves with axes to tear down and cut away all the wood-work in the vicinity, the soldiers were rolling barrels of powder out to more sheltered spots, and were covering them with wet blankets. The labor was accelerated by the shells which were bursting around us; for Ripley had redoubled his activity at the first signs of a conflagration. We only succeeded in getting out some ninety-six barrels of powder, and then we were obliged to close the massive copper door, and await the result. A shot soon after passed through the intervening shield, struck the door, and bent the lock in such a way that it could not be opened again. We were thus cut off from our supply of ammunition, but still had some piled up in the vicinity of the guns. Anderson officially reported only four barrels and three cartridges as on hand when we left.

By 11 A.M. the conflagration was terrible and disastrous. One-fifth of the fort was on fire, and the wind drove the smoke in dense masses into the angle where we had all taken refuge. It seemed impossible to escape suffocation. Some lay down close to the ground, with handkerchiefs over their mouths, and others posted themselves near the embrasures, where the smoke was somewhat lessened by the draught of air. Every one suffered severely. I crawled out of one of these openings, and sat on the outer edge; but Ripley made it lively for me there with his case-shot, which spattered all around. Had not a slight change of wind taken place, the result might have been fatal to most of us.

Our firing having ceased, and the enemy being very jubilant, I thought it would be as well to show them that we were not all dead yet, and ordered the gunners to fire a few rounds more. I heard afterward that the enemy loudly cheered Anderson for his persistency under such adverse circumstances.

The scene at this time was really terrific. The roaring and crackling of the flames, the dense masses of whirling smoke, the bursting of the enemy's shells, and our own which were exploding in the burning rooms, the crashing of the shot, and the sound of masonry falling in every direction, made the fort a pandemonium. When at last nothing was left of the building but the blackened walls and smoldering embers, it became painfully evident that an immense amount of damage had been done. There was a tower at each angle of the fort. One of these, containing great quantities of shells, upon which we had relied, was almost completely shattered by successive explosions. The massive wooden gates, studded with iron nails, were burned, and the wall built behind them was now a mere heap of débris, so that the main entrance was wide open for an assaulting party. The sally-ports were in a similar condition, and the numerous windows on the gorge side, which had been planked up, had now become all open entrances.

About 12.48 P.M. the end of the flag-staff was shot down, and the flag fell.* It had been previously hanging by one halliard, the other having been cut by a piece of shell. The exultation of the enemy, however, was short-lived. Peter Hart found a spar in the fort, which answered very well as a temporary flag-staff. He nailed the flag to this, and raised it triumphantly by nailing and tying the pole firmly to a pile of gun-carriages on the parapet. This was gallantly done, without undue haste, under Seymour's supervision, although the enemy concentrated all their fire upon the spot to prevent Hart from carrying out his intention. From the beginning, the rebel gunners had been very ambitious to shoot the flag down, and had wasted an immense number of shots in the attempt.

———

About 2 P.M., Senator Wigfall, in company with W. Gourdin Young, of Charleston, unexpectedly made his appearance at one of the embrasures, having crossed over from Morris Island in a small boat, rowed by negroes. He had seen the flag come down, and supposed that we had surrendered in consequence

---

*It is claimed that this shot was fired by Lieutenant W. C. Preston, of South Carolina.

of the burning of the quarters. This visit was sanctioned by the commander of Morris Island, Brigadier-general James W. Simons. An artillery-man, serving his gun, was very much astonished to see a man's face at the entrance, and asked him what he was doing there. Wigfall replied that he wished to see Major Anderson. The man, however, refused to allow him to enter until he had surrendered himself as a prisoner, and given up his sword. This done, another artillery-man was sent to bring an officer. Lieutenant Davis came almost immediately, but it took some time to find Anderson, who was out examining the condition of the main gates. I was not present during this scene, or at the interview that ensued, as I was engaged in trying to save some shells in the upper story from the effects of the fire. Wigfall, in Beauregard's name, offered Anderson his own terms, which were, the evacuation of the fort, with permission to salute our flag, and to march out with the honors of war, with our arms and private baggage, leaving all other war material behind. As soon as this matter was arranged, Wigfall returned to Cummings Point.

In the mean time, Beauregard having noticed the white flag, sent a boat containing Colonel James Chestnut, and Captain Lee, Colonel Roger A. Pryor, and Colonel William Porcher Miles, to ascertain the meaning of the signal. A second boat soon followed, containing Major D. K. Jones, who was Beauregard's adjutant-general, Ex-Governor J. L. Manning, and Colonel Charles Alston.

Miles and Pryor were exceedingly astonished when they heard that Wigfall had been carrying on negotiations in Beauregard's name, and stated that, to their certain knowledge, he had had no communication with Beauregard. They spoke of the matter with great delicacy, for Wigfall was a parlous man, and quick to settle disputed points with the pistol. Anderson replied with spirit that, under the circumstances, he would run up his flag again, and resume the firing. They begged him, however, not to take action until they had had an opportunity to lay the whole subject before General Beauregard; and Anderson agreed to wait a reasonable time for that purpose. The boat then returned to the city. In due time another boat arrived, containing Colonels Chestnut and Chisholm, and Captain Stephen D. Lee, all aids of Beauregard. They came to notify Major Anderson that the latter was willing to treat with him on the basis proposed. Colonel Charles Alston soon came over with Major Jones (who was chief-of-staff to Beauregard, and adjutant-general of the Provisional Army), to settle the details of the evacuation. There was some difficulty about permitting us to salute our flag; but that, too, was finally conceded. In case we held out for another day, the rebels had made arrangements to storm the fort that night.

———————

All of the preliminaries having been duly adjusted, it was decided that the evacuation should take place the next morning. Our arrangements were few and simple, but the rebels made extensive preparations for the event, in order to give it the greatest *éclat*, and gain from it as much prestige as possible. The population of the surrounding country poured into Charleston in vast multitudes, to witness the humiliation of the United States flag. We slept soundly that night for the first time, after all the fatigue and excitement of the two preceding days.

The next morning, Sunday, the 14th, we were up early, packing our baggage in readiness to go on board the transport. The time having arrived, I made preparations, by order of Major Anderson, to fire a national salute to the flag. It was a dangerous thing to attempt, as sparks of fire were floating around everywhere, and there was no safe place to deposit the ammunition. In that portion of the line commanded by Lieutenant Hall, a pile of cartridges lay under the muzzle of one of the guns. Some fire had probably lodged inside the piece, which the sponging did not extinguish, for, in loading it, it went off prematurely, and blew off the right arm of the gunner, Daniel Hough, who was an excellent soldier. His death was almost instantaneous. He was the first man who lost his life on our side in the war for the Union. The damage did not end here, for some of the fire from the muzzle dropped on the pile of cartridges below, and exploded them all. Several men in the vicinity were blown into the air, and seriously injured. Their names were George Fielding, John Irwin, George Pinchard, and Edwin Galway, and, I think, James Hayes. The first-named being very badly hurt, was left behind, to be cared for by the rebels.

He was sent over to Charleston, where he was well treated, finally cured, and forwarded to us without being exchanged.

The salute being over, the Confederate troops marched in to occupy the fort. The Palmetto Guard, Captain Cuthbert's company, detailed by Colonel De Saussure, and Captain Hollinquist's Company B, of the regulars, detailed by Colonel Ripley, constituted the new garrison under Ripley.* Anderson directed me to form the men on the parade-ground, assume command, and march them on board the transport. I told him I should prefer to leave the fort with the flag flying, and the drums beating Yankee Doodle, and he authorized me to do so. As soon as our tattered flag came down, and the silken banner made by the ladies of Charleston was run up, tremendous shouts of applause were heard from the vast multitude of spectators; and all the vessels and steamers, with one accord, made for the fort. Corporal Bringhurst came running to tell me that many of the approaching crowd were shouting my name, and making threatening demonstrations. The disorder, however, was immediately quelled by the appearance of Hartstein, an ex-officer of our navy, who threw out sentinels in all directions, and prevented the mob from landing.

*Edmund Ruffin entered the fort as a volunteer ensign of the Palmetto Guard; Captain Samuel Ferguson received the keys of Fort Sumter, and raised the Confederate flag over the ramparts; Lieutenant-colonel F. J. Moses raised the State flag. Moses has since figured as the Republican governor of South Carolina.

NEW YORKERS RESPOND: APRIL 1861

George Templeton Strong: Diary, April 13–16, 1861

On April 15, the day after Fort Sumter surrendered, President Lincoln issued a proclamation calling forth 75,000 militia and summoning Congress to meet on July 4 in special session. George Templeton Strong recorded the reaction in New York City to the beginning of hostilities.

April 13. Here begins a new chapter of my journal, entitled WAR—EXSURGAT DEUS *et dissipentere inimici ejus, et fugerunt qui oderunt eum a facie ejus. Amen!*
This morning's papers confirmed last night's news; viz., that the rebels opened fire at Sumter yesterday morning. During the day came successive despatches, *all one way*, of course, for the Charleston telegraphs are under Charleston control, and in addition to the local taste for brag and lying, there are obvious motives for a high-colored picture of damage done the fort. It tends to prevent reinforcement by any supplementary expedition that might be extemporized if the parties appeared to be at all equally matched.

In substance, the despatches say that firing ceased at six P.M. yesterday, but shells continued to be thrown into the fort all night at intervals of twenty minutes. Cannonade resumed this morning with brilliant success. The fort on fire. "Flames bursting from the embrasures." Raft outside and men passing up water. Great havoc among them. Two explosions in the fort. Major Anderson "believed to be gradually (!) blowing it up." Nobody hurt in the rebel batteries. No impression made on that formidable battle-scow "the Floating Battery." Major Anderson has ceased firing. Then came a fourth edition of the *Evening Post*, with a despatch that he has surrendered. This was while I was at the New York Club. On coming home, I find Ellie in possession of a still later *Herald* extra. The ships are engaged with the batteries; (this we had earlier). Two are sunk. The rest are shelling the city, which is on fire. I take this last item to be invented for the sake of stimulating wrath and fury in the Border States.

To shell Charleston, the ships must have worked their way into the harbor and passed Sumter. If so, they must have silenced the batteries and been able to throw supplies into the fort, which is hardly to be hoped. Had they done so, the object of the expedition would have been accomplished. And I doubt whether they would have fired on the city under any circumstances. But that damnable little hornet's nest of treason deserves to be shelled. It's a political Sodom. . . .

So Civil War is inaugurated at last. God defend the Right.

The Northern backbone is much stiffened already. Many who stood up for "Southern rights" and complained of wrongs done the South now say that, since the South has fired the first gun, they are ready to go all lengths in supporting the government. The New York *Herald* is noncommittal this morning. It may well be upholding the Administration and denouncing the Democratic party within a week. It takes naturally to eating dirt and its own words (the same thing). Would I were in Sumter tonight, even with the chance of being forced to surrender (seventy men against seven thousand) and of being lynched thereafter by the Chivalry of Charleston. The seventy will be as memorable as the "four hundred" of the Light Brigade at Balaklava, whatever be their fate.

It is said the President will assume the right to call for volunteers, whether the law give it or not. If he does, there will soon be a new element in the fray; viz., the stern anti-slavery Puritanism that survives in New England and in the Northwest. Ossawattomie John Brown would be worth his weight in gold just now. What a pity he precipitated matters and got himself prematurely hanged!

April 14, SUNDAY. Fine day. Morning *Herald* announces *Surrender of Fort Sumter* and great jubilation in Charleston. To Trinity Church with Ellie and Miss Rosalie and Johnny. On our way back, I made a detour to the *Tribune* office. The whole story discredited there. Lots of private despatches quoted, inconsistent with surrender, and tending to show there had been no serious fight.

Mr. Ruggles dined with us. This evening Dr. Rae and his pretty wife were here by appointment, with their two young friends from England. . . . There is no doubt that Fort Sumter has surrendered. Despatches received by Mrs. Anderson, Cottenet, and others settle that point. But no reliable details of the transactions have reached us. If it be true, as Charleston telegrams assert, that after forty hours' firing "no one is hurt," *Punch* and the *Charivari* have an inviting topic for jokes at our expense. . . .

From all I can learn, the effect of this on Democrats, heretofore Southern and quasi-treasonable in their talk, has fully justified the sacrifice. I hear of F. B. Cutting and Walter Cutting, Hewitt, Lewis Rutherfurd, Judge Vanderpoel, and others of that type denouncing rebellion and declaring themselves ready to go all lengths in upholding government. If this class of men has been secured and converted to loyalty, the gain to the country is worth ten Sumters. CAM, heretofore strongly Southern in his talk, was declaring his readiness this evening to shoulder a musket in defence of Washington. That is the next point to be thought of. "He is the true Pope who lives in the Vatican." It must be defended at any cost.

At Trinity Church today, Vinton read the prayer, "In time of war and tumults," and the Amen of the white-robed choir boys was emphasized by a suggestive trumpet-stop coloring from the organ.

April 15. Events multiply. The President is out with a proclamation calling for 75,000 volunteers and an extra session of Congress July 4. It is said 200,000 more will be called within a few days. Every man of them will be wanted before this game is lost and won. Change in public feeling marked, and a thing to thank God for. We begin to look like a United North. Willy Duncan (!) says it may be necessary to hang Lincoln and Seward and Greeley hereafter, but our present duty is to sustain Government and Law, and give the South a lesson. The New York *Herald* is *in equilibrio* today, just at the turning point. Tomorrow it will denounce Jefferson Davis as it denounced Lincoln a week ago. The *Express* is half traitorous and half in favor of energetic action against traitors. The *Journal of Commerce* and the little *Day-Book* show no signs of reformation yet, but though they are contemptible and without material influence for evil, the growing excitement against their treasonable talk will soon make them more cautious in its utterance. The *Herald* office has already been threatened with an attack.

Mayor Wood out with a "proclamation." He must still be talking. It is brief and commonplace, but winds up with a recommendation to everybody to obey the laws of the land. This is significant. The cunning scoundrel sees which way the cat is jumping and puts himself right on the record in a vague general way, giving the least possible offence to his allies of the Southern Democracy. The *Courier* of this morning devotes its leading article to a ferocious assault on Major Anderson as a traitor beyond Twiggs, and declares that he has been in collusion with the Charleston people all the time. This is wrong and bad. It is premature, at least. . . .

Expedition to Governor's Island this morning; Ellie and I, Charley Strong and wife, Dan Messenger, Christie, Miss Kate Fearing, Tom Meyer, and one or two more. Officer of the day was Lieutenant Webb of Maine, whose guests we were. He treated us most hospitably, and had out the band, playing an hour or two for our delectation. Its programme included that jolliest of tunes, "Dixie Land," and "Hail Columbia." We took off our hats while the latter was played. Everybody's patriotism is rampant and demonstrative now. About three hundred recruits on the Island, mostly quite raw. I discoursed with one of them, an honest-looking, simple-minded boy from somewhere near Rochester, probably some small farmer's son. "He had voted for Abe Lincoln, and as there was going to be trouble, he might as well *fight* for Abe Lincoln," so he enlisted two weeks ago. "Guessed they were going to get some hard knocks when they went down South, but then he had always kind o' wanted to see the world—that was one reason why he 'listed."

Great activity on the Island. Guns and all manner of warlike munitions and apparatus are being shipped, generally for Pensacola.

April 16. A fine storm of wind and rain all day. The conversion of the New York *Herald* is complete. It rejoices that rebellion is to be put down and is delighted with Civil War, because it will so stimulate the business of New York, and all this is what "we" (the *Herald*, to wit) have been vainly preaching for months. This impudence of old J. G. Bennett's is too vast to be appreciated at once. You must look at it and meditate over it for some time (as at Niagara and St. Peter's) before you can take in its immensity. His capitulation is a set-off against the loss of Sumter. He's a discreditable ally for the North, but when you see a rat leaving the enemy's ship for your own, you overlook the offensiveness of the vermin for the sake of what its movement indicates. This brazen old scoundrel was hooted up Fulton Street yesterday afternoon by a mob, and the police interfered to prevent it from sacking his printing office. Though converted, one can hardly call him penitent. St. Paul did not call himself the Chief of the Apostles and brag of having been a Christian from the first.

This and other papers say the new war policy will strangle secession in the Border States. But it seems to me that every indication from Virginia, North Carolina, and elsewhere points the other way. No news from Slave-ownia today, but most gladdening reports from North, West, and East of unanimity and resolution and earnestness. We are aroused at last, and I trust we shall not soon relapse into apathy. Ellie indisposed again. I begin to be seriously uneasy about the constantly recurring attacks of slight illness—headache and the like—that have visited her of late.

Trinity Church Vestry tonight; special meeting on St. George's Chapel and a very long debate. The appropriation required is large ($6,000 per annum, at least), and in moving it, I premised that the whole question turned on the ability of the vestry to spend that sum. If they have it to spare, the Chapel can be maintained, otherwise not; and a smaller appropriation just keeping up the establishment in its present dead-alive condition would do no good and be simply throwing away so much money, besides bringing a certain amount of discredit on Trinity Church. A smaller appropriation was moved as a substitute and carried by a large majority, Swift and I voting in the negative, with three or four others. . . .

Thence to New York Club. Our talk was of war. Subscribed to a fund for equipment of the Twelfth Regiment and put down my name for a projected Rifle Corps, but I fear my near-sightedness is a grave objection to my adopting that arm. I hear that Major Burnside has surrendered his treasurership of the Illinois Central Railroad and posted down to Rhode Island to assume command of volunteers from that state. Telegram that 2,500 Massachusetts volunteers are quartered in Faneuil Hall, awaiting orders.

GOD SAVE THE UNION, AND CONFOUND ITS ENEMIES. AMEN.

VINDICATING NATIONAL HONOR: APRIL 1861

The New York Times: The People and the Issue

April 15, 1861

A former assistant to Horace Greeley, Henry Raymond founded *The New York Times* in 1851. Originally a Free Soil Whig, Raymond became a Republican, and had supported Lincoln in the 1860 election.

THE REVERBERATIONS from Charleston harbor have brought about what months of logic would have been impotent to effect—the rapid condensation of public sentiment in the Free States. The North is now a unit. Party lines have shriveled, as landmarks disappear before the outpouring of volcanic lava. The crucial test of this is New York City—the spot most tainted by the Southern poison. Not the thick insulation which the commercial spirit puts between the conscience and duty—not the obliquity engendered by long years of the most perverse political education—have been able to withstand the electric fire of loyal indignation evoked by the assassin-stroke aimed at the heart of the Republic. There are now no such ardent supporters of the Government as those who have been life-long Democrats. It is a fact full of omen, and one which persons imperfectly acquainted with the impulses that lie at the bottom of the popular heart could never have anticipated, that the very roughs of the City are aroused, and bring their passionate devotion to the cause of their country. One intense, inspiring sentiment of patriotism has fused all other passions in its fiery heat. Let the Administration now know that twenty millions of loyal freemen approve its act, and imperiously demand the vindication of the integrity and majesty of the Republic.

Viewed in the light of these events, the lull that for so many weeks reigned in the public spirit becomes very intelligible. A suspense—a long, dumb, unconscious waiting, very pathetic in its character—held the people's mind. Treason so vile paralyzed thought and will. The way was not clear what to do. It could not at first be believed that the country really held men so insane, so suicidal, as to attempt to transform such threats as theirs into deeds. The sheer demonism which marked the programme of social construction put forth by the Slave Power, caused it rather to assume the aspect of a terrific species of irony. And then, when the designs of the rebels became only too apparent, and it was evident that naught but the exercise of sovereign Might could avail to check those frenzied men, there was honest hesitancy in resorting to the force of arms. Civil war runs counter to the theory of the Republic. The framers of our Government made such provisions as would forever render rebellion unnecessary. All experience has shown how easily this Government can be induced to change its rulers, if any good reason for doing so was presented, and earnestly and persistently forced upon public opinion. Besides this, there was a doubt in many minds as to the degree to which the theory of Democracy allowed of opposition to the avowed and deliberate will of sovereign States. On the whole, it presented itself as a painful, perplexing problem. That problem has at length been solved by the public conscience, and the solution sweeps away forever the sophistries as to State Rights and coercion which entangled the subject. The lull is over—and an equinoctial storm of popular indignation has ensued.

In entering upon this struggle, the great community of Free States does so, prepared to bring to bear on the vindication of its national honor inexhaustible material resources. Her census shows returns which, under other circumstances, would have been the wonder of the world. It has, indeed, been industriously declared by timid croakers that "war is national ruin." There is no more absurd chimera. The Free States are richer and more populous than England was under PITT, when she fought the long fight with NAPOLEON, and vastly stronger than France when she battled triumphantly against all the Continental powers.

As to moral force, it panoplies the Republic as with a wall of fire. She enters the contest with that triple arming which justice gives to a cause. The moral conscience of the world is on her side. It is true that the rebels, lured by the support of that European element whose sympathies are contingent with the rate of duties levied on imported goods by the United States, have hoped for the recognition of the European Powers. That delusion is doomed to be rudely dispelled. The rulers of England and France do not dare to recognize that League. The unmaking of Ministries would hang on the decision, and they know it.

The Administration is not brought face to face with a *Revolution*. This is not the attitude. It has to deal with a plot, a conspiracy. There will be no "fraternal blood" shed, unless it be the blood of men who are willfully and persistently in the position of traitors. The right of revolution is not denied;—changes, prompted by causes material or moral, and effected through legal and constitutional means, are contemplated with calmness. But that Treason should be claimed as a right—that anarchy should rule—it is this which thrills with indignant amazement. How profound has been the humiliation, how hot the indignation, are shown in the tumultuous surgings of passion that are now baptising with one common sentiment of constitutional unity and patriotic devotion every loyal American heart.

FIGHTING "THE MAD REBELLION": APRIL 1861

Pittsburgh Post: The War Begun—The Duty of American Citizens

April 15, 1861

The *Pittsburgh Post* was a Democratic newspaper that had supported Stephen A. Douglas, the Northern Democratic candidate, in 1860.

FOR TWO days the country has been in a condition of the most intense excitement.

The awful catastrophe so long anticipated has at last fallen upon us.

The die is cast. The choice between compromise and battles has been made. Civil war is upon us. "Unto the end of the war desolations are determined."

For two days business has been almost suspended in our streets, and every one, old and young, men and women, have been asking, "What of the battle?"

The telegraph first announced the brief fact that the battle had commenced. Then came statement after statement—contradictory, inconsistent, almost incredible. Fort Sumter was on fire. Its magazines had exploded. Its walls were crumbling. The U. S. vessels were in the offing, not firing a gun. The white flag, the Federal flag, the flag of the Confederate States, were each in turn reported as floating from Fort Sumter. People scarce knew what to believe.

The despatches which we publish this morning leave no doubt that Fort Sumter has unconditionally surrendered to the forces of the Confederate States; that Major Anderson has been driven out by fire within the walls of the fort; that a brisk cannonading from the Charleston batteries has seriously damaged the fort; that Major Anderson and his command have been compelled to yield; that the United States vessels in the harbor of Charleston looked calmly on and made no effort to reinforce or assist the fort, and, most singular of all, that after two thousand balls had been fired the battle had resulted without the loss of a single man on either side.

Thus much for the facts which may be found in this morning's paper.

The war has begun. The first blow has been struck. The aspect of the question is now wholly changed from what it has hitherto been. Before it was a political one, and all the conservative men deprecating the horrors of a civil war, have earnestly urged a fair compromise granting to the South her just rights under the Constitution. But the South has determined not to wait for the adjustment of the difficulty lawfully and Constitutionally, but has decided upon an armed revolution against the Government. The South has struck the first blow, a successful blow, but one which will unite the North as one man for the Union. The authority of the Government of our country must be maintained and supported by every loyal American citizen. The wrongs of the South are now a matter of minor consideration. The integrity of the Government and the authority of those who hold its power, is now the great object of national consideration.

A civil war has actually commenced between the sections of this once glorious Union. The heart of every patriot bleeds at this solemn truth. The true men of the country have now a great duty to perform. The preliminaries are over—revolution has taken arms and proceeded to the last extremity—and now every man who reveres the memory of Washington, must use his efforts and devote his wealth, his personal services and his life if necessary, in defending the integrity of the Government which the patriots of the revolution handed down as a PERPETUAL BLESSING to their posterity.

However much we may deprecate the political causes which have driven the South to this insane madness—this fratricidal war—the time is past for crimination and recrimination as to what might have been done, and what ought to have been done. The Flag of Our Country—the glorious Stars and Stripes must be supported and defended by every American. The fight has now begun. An appeal has been made to the

God of Battles. The past must answer for itself. Those who have caused the war must answer to their country and their God for what they have done.

The American flag—the flag of our Union—and the honored banner of a government which is bound to protect the interests of the whole country, the North as well as the South—has been fired into by American citizens, disloyal to the government of the country. We have appreciated their wrongs—we have advocated the restoration of their rights—we have not spared their enemies.

But now, they have fired upon the flag of their country, and of ours. No American of true heart and brave soul will stand this. No American ought to stand it.

The integrity of a great government must be maintained. Its power to punish, as well as to protect its children must be used. Political partizanship must now cease to govern men on this issue. Pennsylvania and Pennsylvanians are for the Union. The government which the people have appointed, and which is responsible to the people for its every act, would be derelict of its duty as a government, if it did not protect its property, its citizens, its flag, and its granted rights against all usurpers, all rebels, all traitors—external or internal foes, of whatever character.

We were born and bred under the stars and stripes. We have been taught to regard the anniversary of American Independence as a sacred day. For our whole life we have looked upon our national emblems as tokens of safety and prosperity to us and to our children, and no matter what may have been the wrongs of the South, in the Union, we would have resisted them to the extent of our ability; but when the South becomes an enemy to the American system of government; takes an attitude of hostility to it, and fires upon the flag, which she, as well as we, are bound to protect, our influence goes for that flag, no matter whether a Republican or a Democrat holds it, and we will sustain any administration, no matter how distasteful its policy may be to us personally, in proving to the world, that the American eagle,—the proud bird of our banner—fears not to brave the wrath of foreign foes, or the mad rebellion of its own fostered children.

CELEBRATION IN CHARLESTON:
SOUTH CAROLINA, APRIL 1861

William Howard Russell:
from My Diary North and South

An Anglo-Irish correspondent for *The Times* of London, William Howard Russell had become famous for his war reporting from the Crimea and India. He landed at New York on March 16, 1861, to observe the secession crisis firsthand, and would remain in America until April 9, 1862. In *My Diary North and South* (1863), he described his visit to Charleston on April 17, three days after the surrender of Fort Sumter.

April 17th.—The streets of Charleston present some such aspect as those of Paris in the last revolution. Crowds of armed men singing and promenading the streets. The battle-blood running through their veins—that hot oxygen which is called "the flush of victory" on the cheek; restaurants full, revelling in bar rooms, club-rooms crowded, orgies and carousings in tavern or private house, in tap-room, from cabaret—down narrow alleys, in the broad highway. Sumter has set them distraught; never was such a victory; never such brave lads; never such a fight. There are pamphlets already full of the incident. It is a bloodless Waterloo or Solferino.

After breakfast I went down to the quay, with a party of the General's staff, to visit Fort Sumter. The senators and governors turned soldiers wore blue military caps, with "palmetto" trees embroidered thereon; blue frockcoats, with upright collars, and shoulder-straps edged with lace, and marked with two silver bars, to designate their rank of captain; gilt buttons, with the palmetto in relief; blue trowsers, with a gold-lace cord, and brass spurs—no straps. The day was sweltering, but a strong breeze blew in the harbour, and puffed the dust of Charleston, coating our clothes, and filling our eyes with powder. The streets were crowded with lanky lads, clanking spurs, and sabres, with awkward squads marching to and fro, with drummers beating calls, and ruffles, and points of war; around them groups of grinning negroes delighted with the glare and glitter, a holiday, and a new idea for them—secession flags waving out of all the windows—little Irish boys shouting out, "Battle of Fort Sumter! New edishun!"—As we walked down towards the quay, where the steamer was lying, numerous traces of the unsettled state of men's minds broke out in the hurried conversations of the various friends who stopped to speak for a few moments. "Well, governor, the old Union is gone at last!" "Have you heard what Abe is going to do?" "I don't think Beauregard will have much more fighting for it. What do you think?" And so on. Our little Creole friend, by the bye, is popular beyond description. There are all kinds of doggerel rhymes in his honour—one with a refrain—

> "With cannon and musket, with shell and petard,
> We salute the North with our Beau-regard"—

is much in favour.

We passed through the market, where the stalls are kept by fat negresses and old "unkeys." There is a sort of vulture or buzzard here, much encouraged as scavengers, and—but all the world has heard of the Charleston vultures—so we will leave them to their garbage. Near the quay, where the steamer was lying, there is a very fine building in white marble, which attracted our notice. It was unfinished, and immense blocks of the glistening stone destined for its completion, lay on the ground. "What is that?" I inquired. "Why, it's a custom-house Uncle Sam was building for our benefit, but I don't think he'll ever raise a cent for his treasury out of it." "Will you complete it?" "I should think not. We'll lay on few duties; and what we want is free-trade, and no duties at all, except for public purposes. The Yankees have plundered us with their custom-houses and duties long enough." An old gentleman here stopped us. "You will do me the greatest favour," he said to one of our party who knew him, "if you will get me something to do for our glorious cause. Old as I am, I can carry a musket—not far, to be sure, but I can kill a Yankee if he comes near." When he had gone, my friend told me the speaker was a man of fortune, two of whose sons were in camp at Morris' Island, but that he was suspected of Union sentiments, as he had a Northern wife, and hence his extreme vehemence and devotion.

There was a large crowd around the pier staring at the men in uniform on the boat, which was filled with bales of goods, commissariat stores, trusses of hay, and hampers, supplies for the volunteer army on Morris' Island. I was amused by the names of the various corps, "Tigers," "Lions," "Scorpions," "Palmetto Eagles," "Guards," of Pickens, Sumter, Marion, and of various other denominations, painted on the boxes. The original formation of these volunteers is in companies, and they know nothing of battalions or regiments. The tendency in volunteer outbursts is sometimes to gratify the greatest vanity of the greatest number. These companies do not muster more than fifty or sixty strong. Some were "dandies," and "swells," and affected to look down on their neighbours and comrades. Major Whiting told me there was difficulty in getting them to obey orders at first, as each man had an idea that he was as good an engineer as any body else, "and a good deal better, if it came to that." It was easy to perceive it was the old story of volunteer and regular in this little army.

As we got on deck, the major saw a number of rough, long-haired-looking fellows in coarse gray tunics, with pewter buttons and worsted braid lying on the hay-bales smoking their cigars. "Gentlemen," quoth he, very courteously, "You'll oblige me by not smoking over the hay. There's powder below." "I don't believe we're going to burn the hay this time, kernel," was the reply, "and anyway, we'll put it out afore it reaches the 'bustibles," and they went on smoking. The major grumbled, and worse, and drew off.

Among the passengers were some brethren of mine belonging to the New York and local papers. I saw a short time afterwards a description of the trip by one of these gentlemen, in which he described it as an affair got up specially for himself, probably in order to avenge himself on his military persecutors, for he had complained to me the evening before, that the chief of General Beauregard's staff told him to go to ——, when he applied at head-quarters for some information. I found from the tone and looks of my friends, that these literary gentlemen were received with great disfavour, and Major Whiting, who is a bibliomaniac, and has a very great liking for the best English writers, could not conceal his repugnance and antipathy to my unfortunate confrères. "If I had my way, I would fling them into the water; but the General has given them orders to come on board. It is these fellows who have brought all this trouble on our country."

The traces of dislike of the freedom of the press, which I, to my astonishment, discovered in the North, are broader and deeper in the South, and they are not accompanied by the signs of dread of its power which exist in New York, where men speak of the chiefs of the most notorious journals very much as people in Italian cities of past time might have talked of the most infamous bravo or the chief of some band of assassins. Whiting comforted himself by the reflection that they would soon have their fingers in a vice, and then pulling out a ragged little sheet, turned suddenly on the representative thereof, and proceeded to give the most unqualified contradiction to most of the statements contained in "the full and accurate particulars of the Bombardment and Fall of Fort Sumter," in the said journal, which the person in question listened to with becoming meekness and contrition. "If I knew who wrote it," said the major, "I'd make him eat it."

I was presented to many judges, colonels, and others of the mass of society on board, and, "after compliments," as the Orientals say, I was generally asked, in the first place, what I thought of the capture of Sumter, and in the second, what England would do when the news reached the other side. Already the Carolinians regard the Northern States as an alien and detested enemy, and entertain, or profess, an immense affection for Great Britain.

When we had shipped all our passengers, nine-tenths of them in uniform, and a larger proportion engaged in chewing, the whistle blew, and the steamer sidled off from the quay into the yellowish muddy water of the Ashley River, which is a creek from the sea, with a streamlet running into the head waters some distance up.

The shore opposite Charleston is more than a mile distant, and is low and sandy, covered here and there with patches of brilliant vegetation, and long lines of trees. It is cut up with creeks, which divide it into islands, so that passages out to sea exist between some of them for light craft, though the navigation is perplexed and difficult. The city lies on a spur or promontory between the Ashley and the Cooper rivers, and the land behind it is divided in the same manner by similar creeks, and is sandy and light, bearing, nevertheless, very fine crops, and trees of magnificent vegetation. The steeples, the domes of public buildings, the rows of massive warehouses and cotton stores on the wharfs, and the bright colours of the houses, render the appearance of Charleston, as seen from the river front, rather imposing. From the mastheads of the few large vessels in harbour floated the Confederate flag. Looking to our right, the same standard was visible, waving on the low, white parapets of the earthworks which had been engaged in reducing Sumter.

That much-talked-of fortress lay some two miles ahead of us now, rising up out of the water near the middle of the passage out to sea between James' Island and Sullivan's Island. It struck me at first as being like one of the smaller forts off Cronstadt, but a closer inspection very much diminished its importance; the material is brick, not stone, and the size of the place is exaggerated by the low back ground, and by contrast with the sea-line. The land contracts on both sides opposite the fort, a projection of Morris' Island, called "Cumming's point," running out on the left. There is a similar promontory from Sullivan's Island, on which is erected Fort Moultrie, on the right from the sea entrance. Castle Pinckney, which stands on a small island at the exit of the Cooper River, is a place of no importance, and it was too far from Sumter to take any in the bombardment: the same remarks apply to Fort Johnson on James' Island, on the right bank of the Ashley River below Charleston. The works which did the mischief were the batteries of sand on Morris' Island, at Cumming's Point, and Fort Moultrie. The floating battery, covered with railroad-iron, lay a long way off, and could not have contributed much to the result.

As we approached Morris' Island, which is an accumulation of sand covered with mounds of the same material, on which there is a scanty vegetation alternating with salt-water marshes, we could perceive a few tents in the distance among the sand-hills. The sand-bag batteries, and an ugly black parapet, with guns peering through port-holes as if from a ship's side, lay before us. Around them men were swarming like ants, and a crowd in uniform were gathered on the beach to receive us as we landed from the boat of the steamer, all eager for news, and provisions, and newspapers, of which an immense flight immediately fell upon them. A guard with bayonets crossed in a very odd sort of manner, prevented any unauthorised persons from landing. They wore the universal coarse gray jacket and trousers, with worsted braid and yellow facings, uncouth caps, lead buttons stamped with the palmetto-tree. Their unbronzed fire-locks were covered with rust. The soldiers lounging about were mostly tall, well-grown men, young and old, some with the air of gentlemen; others coarse, long-haired fellows, without any semblance of military bearing, but full of fight, and burning with enthusiasm, not unaided, in some instances, by coarser stimulus.

The day was exceedingly warm and unpleasant, the hot wind blew the fine white sand into our faces, and wafted it in minute clouds inside eyelids, nostrils, and clothing; but it was necessary to visit the batteries, so on we trudged into one and out of another, walked up parapets, examined profiles, looked along guns, and did everything that could be required of us. The result of the examination was to establish in my mind the conviction, that if the commander of Sumter had been allowed to open his guns on the island, the first time he saw an indication of throwing up a battery against him, he could have saved his fort. Moultrie, in its original state, on the opposite side, could have been readily demolished by Sumter. The design of the works was better than their execution—the sand-bags were rotten, the sand not properly revetted or banked up, and the traverses imperfectly constructed. The barbette guns of the fort looked into many of the embrasures, and commanded them.

The whole of the island was full of life and excitement. Officers were galloping about as if on a field-day or in action. Commissariat carts were toiling to and fro between the beach and the camps, and sounds of laughter and revelling came from the tents. These were pitched without order, and were of all shapes, hues, and sizes, many being disfigured by rude charcoal drawings outside, and inscriptions such as "The Live Tigers," "Rattlesnake's-hole," "Yankee Smashers," &c. The vicinity of the camps was in an intolerable state, and on calling the attention of the medical officer who was with me, to the danger arising from such a condition of things, he said with a sigh, "I know it all. But we can do nothing. Remember they're all volunteers, and do just as they please."

In every tent was hospitality, and a hearty welcome to all comers. Cases of champagne and claret, French pâtés, and the like, were piled outside the canvas walls, when there was no room for them inside. In the middle of these excited gatherings I felt like a man in the full possession of his senses coming in late to a wine party. "Won't you drink with me, sir, to the— (something awful)—of Lincoln and all Yankees?" "No! if you'll be good enough to excuse me." "Well, I think you're the only Englishman who won't." Our Carolinians are very fine fellows, but a little given to the Bobadil style—hectoring after a cavalier fashion, which they fondly believe to be theirs by hereditary right. They assume that the British crown rests on a cotton bale, as the Lord Chancellor sits on a pack of wool.

In one long tent there was a party of roystering young men, opening claret, and mixing "cup" in large buckets; whilst others were helping the servants to set out a table for a banquet to one of their generals. Such heat, tobacco-smoke, clamour, toasts, drinking, hand-shaking, vows of friendship! Many were the excuses made for the more demonstrative of the Edonian youths by their friends. "Tom is a little cut, sir; but he's a splendid fellow—he's worth half-a-million of dollars." This reference to a money standard of value was not unusual or perhaps unnatural, but it was made repeatedly; and I was told wonderful tales of the riches of men who were lounging round, dressed as privates, some of whom at that season, in years gone by, were looked for at the watering places as the great lions of American fashion. But Secession is the fashion here. Young ladies sing for it; old ladies pray for it; young men are dying to fight for it; old men are ready to demonstrate it. The founder of the school was St. Calhoun. Here his pupils carry out their teaching in thunder and fire. States' Rights are displayed after its legitimate teaching, and the Palmetto flag and the red bars of the Confederacy are its exposition. The utter contempt and loathing for the venerated Stars and Stripes, the abhorrence of the very words United States, the intense hatred of the Yankee on the part of these people, cannot be conceived by anyone who has not seen them. I am more satisfied than ever that the Union can never be restored as it was, and that it has gone to pieces, never to be put together again, in the old shape, at all events by any power on earth.

After a long and tiresome promenade in the dust, heat, and fine sand, through the tents, our party returned to the beach, where we took boat, and pushed off for Fort Sumter. The Confederate flag rose above the walls. On near approach the marks of the shot against the *pain coupé*, and the embrasures near the salient were visible enough; but the damage done to the hard brickwork was trifling, except at the angles: the edges of the parapets were ragged and pock-marked, and the quay wall was rifted here and there by shot; but no injury of a kind to render the work untenable could be made out. The greatest damage inflicted was, no doubt, the burning of the barracks, which were culpably erected inside the fort, close to the flank wall facing Cumming's Point.

As the boat touched the quay of the fort, a tall, powerful-looking man came through the shattered gateway, and with uneven steps strode over the rubbish towards a skiff which was waiting to receive him, and into which he jumped and rowed off. Recognising one of my companions as he passed our boat, he suddenly stood up, and with a leap and a scramble tumbled in among us, to the imminent danger of upsetting the party. Our new friend was dressed in the blue frockcoat of a civilian, round which he had tied a red silk sash—his waistbelt supported a straight sword, something like those worn with Court dress. His muscular neck was surrounded with a loosely-fastened silk handkerchief; and wild masses of black hair, tinged with grey, fell from under a civilian's hat over his collar; his unstrapped trousers were gathered up high on his legs, displaying ample boots, garnished with formidable brass spurs. But his face was one not to be forgotten—a straight, broad brow, from which the hair rose up like the vegetation on a river bank, beetling black eyebrows—a mouth coarse and grim, yet full of power, a square jaw—a thick argumentative nose—a new growth of scrubby beard and moustache—these were relieved by eyes of wonderful depth and light, such as I never saw before but in the head of a wild beast. If you look some day when the sun is not too bright into the eye of the Bengal tiger, in the Regent's Park, as the keeper is coming round, you will form some notion of the expression I mean. It was flashing, fierce, yet calm—with a well of fire burning behind and spouting through it, an eye pitiless in anger, which now and then sought to conceal its expression beneath half-closed lids, and then burst out with an angry glare, as if disdaining concealment.

This was none other than Louis T. Wigfall, Colonel (then of his own creation) in the Confederate army, and Senator from Texas in the United States—a good type of the men whom the institutions of the country produce or throw off—a remarkable man, noted for his ready, natural eloquence; his exceeding ability as a quick, bitter debater; the acerbity of his taunts; and his readiness for personal encounter. To the last he stood in his place in the Senate at Washington, when nearly every other Southernman had seceded, lashing with a venomous and instant tongue, and covering with insults, ridicule, and abuse, such men as Mr. Chandler, of Michigan, and other Republicans: never missing a sitting of the House, and seeking out adversaries in the bar rooms or the gambling tables. The other day, when the fire against Sumter was at its height, and the fort, in flames, was reduced almost to silence, a small boat put off from the shore, and steered through the shot and the splashing waters right for the walls. It bore the colonel and a negro oarsman. Holding up a white handkerchief on the end of his sword, Wigfall landed on the quay, clambered through an embrasure, and presented himself before the astonished Federals with a proposal to surrender, quite unauthorised, and "on his own hook," which led to the final capitulation of Major Anderson.

I am sorry to say, our distinguished friend had just been paying his respects *sans bornes* to Bacchus or Bourbon, for he was decidedly unsteady in his gait and thick in speech; but his head was quite clear, and he was determined I should know all about his exploit. Major Whiting desired to show me round the work, but he had no chance. "Here is where I got in," quoth Colonel Wigfall. "I found a Yankee standing here by the traverse, out of the way of our shot. He was pretty well scared when he saw me, but I told him not to be alarmed, but to take me to the officers. There they were, huddled up in that corner behind the brickwork, for our shells were tumbling into the yard, and bursting like,"—&c. (The Colonel used strong illustrations and strange expletives in narrative.) Major Whiting shook his military head, and said something uncivil to me, in private, in reference to volunteer colonels and the like, which gave him relief; whilst the martial Senator—I forgot to say that he has the name, particularly in the North, of having killed more than half a dozen men in duels—(I had an escape of being another)—conducted me through the casemates with uneven steps, stopping at every traverse to expatiate on some phase of his personal experiences, with his sword dangling between his legs, and spurs involved in rubbish and soldiers' blankets.

In my letter I described the real extent of the damage inflicted, and the state of the fort as I found it. At first the batteries thrown up by the Carolinians were so poor, that the United States' officers in the fort were mightily amused at them, and anticipated easy work in enfilading, ricocheting, and battering them to pieces, if they ever dared to open fire. One morning, however, Capt. Foster, to whom really belongs the credit of putting Sumter into a tolerable condition of defence with the most limited means, was unpleasantly surprised by seeing through his glass a new work in the best possible situation for attacking the place, growing up under the strenuous labours of a band of negroes. "I knew at once," he said, "the rascals had got an engineer at last." In fact, the Carolinians were actually talking of an escalade when the officers of the regular army, who had "seceded," came down and took the direction of affairs, which otherwise might have had very different results.

There was a working party of Volunteers clearing away the rubbish in the place. It was evident they were not accustomed to labour. And on asking why negroes were not employed, I was informed: "The niggers would blow us all up, they're so stupid; and the State would have to pay the owners for any of them who were killed and injured." "In one respect, then, white men are not so valuable as negroes?" "Yes, sir,—that's a fact."

Very few shell craters were visible in the terreplein; the military mischief, such as it was, showed most conspicuously on the parapet platforms, over which shells had been burst as heavily as could be, to prevent the manning of the barbette guns. A very small affair, indeed, that shelling of Fort Sumter. And yet who can tell what may arise from it? "Well, sir," exclaimed one of my companions, "I thank God for it, if it's only because we are beginning to have a history for Europe. The universal Yankee nation swallowed us up."

Never did men plunge into unknown depth of peril and trouble more recklessly than these Carolinians. They fling themselves against the grim, black future, as the cavaliers under Rupert may have rushed against the grim, black Ironsides. Will they carry the image farther? Well! The exploration of Sumter was finished at last, not till we had visited the officers of the garrison, who lived in a windowless, shattered room, reached by a crumbling staircase, and who produced whiskey and crackers, many pleasant stories and boundless welcome. One young fellow grumbled about pay. He said: "I have not received a cent. since I came to Charleston for this business." But Major Whiting, some days afterwards, told me he had not got a dollar on account of his pay, though on leaving the United States' army he had abandoned nearly all his means of subsistence. These gentlemen were quite satisfied it would all be right eventually; and no one questioned the power or inclination of the Government, which had just been inaugurated under such strange auspices, to perpetuate its principles and reward its servants.

After a time our party went down to the boats, in which we were rowed to the steamer that lay waiting for us at Morris' Island. The original intention of the officers was to carry us over to Fort Moultrie, on the opposite side of the Channel, and to examine it and the floating iron battery; but it was too late to do so when we got off, and the steamer only ran across and swept around homewards by the other shore. Below, in the cabin, there was spread a lunch or quasi dinner; and the party of Senators, past and present, aides-de-camp, journalists, and flaneurs, were not indisposed to join it. For me there was only one circumstance which marred the pleasure of that agreeable reunion. Colonel and Senator Wigfall, who had not sobered himself by drinking deeply, in the plenitude of his exultation alluded to the assault on Senator Sumner as a type of the manner in which the Southerners would deal with the Northerners generally, and cited it as a good exemplification of the fashion in which they would bear their "whipping." Thence, by a natural digression, he adverted to the inevitable consequences of the magnificent outburst of Southern indignation against the Yankees on all the nations of the world, and to the immediate action of England in the matter as soon as the news came. Suddenly reverting to Mr. Sumner, whose name he loaded with obloquy, he spoke of Lord Lyons in terms so coarse, that, forgetting the condition of the speaker, I resented the language applied to the English Minister, in a very unmistakeable manner; and then rose and left the cabin. In a moment I was followed on deck by Senator Wigfall: his manner much calmer, his hair brushed back, his eye sparkling. There was nothing left to be desired in his apologies, which were repeated and energetic. We were joined by Mr. Manning, Major Whiting, and Senator Chesnut, and others, to whom I expressed my complete contentment with Mr. Wigfall's explanations. And so we returned to Charleston. The Colonel and Senator, however, did not desist from his attentions to the good—or bad—things below. It was a strange scene—these men, hot and red-handed in rebellion, with their lives on the cast, trifling and jesting, and carousing as if they had no care on earth—all excepting the gentlemen of the local press, who were assiduous in note and food taking. It was near nightfall before we set foot on the quay of Charleston. The city was indicated by the blaze of lights, and by the continual roll of drums, and the noisy music, and the yelling cheers which rose above its streets. As I walked towards the hotel, the evening drove of negroes, male and female, shuffling through the streets in all haste, in order to escape the patrol and the last peal of the curfew bell, swept by me; and as I passed the guard-house of the police, one of my friends pointed out the armed sentries pacing up and down before the porch, and the gleam of arms in the room inside. Further on, a squad of mounted horsemen, heavily armed, turned up a bye-street, and with jingling spurs and sabres disappeared in the dust and darkness. That is the horse patrol. They scour the country around the city, and meet at certain places during the night to see if the niggers are all quiet. Ah, Fuscus! these are signs of trouble.

> "Integer vitæ, scelerisque purus
> Non eget Mauri jaculis neque arcu,
> Nec venenatis gravidâ sagittis,
> Fusce, pharetrâ."

But Fuscus is going to his club; a kindly, pleasant, chatty, card-playing, cocktail-consuming place. He nods proudly to an old white-woolled negro steward or head-waiter—a slave—as a proof which I cannot accept, with the curfew tolling in my ears, of the excellencies of the domestic institution. The club was filled with officers; one of them, Mr. Ransome Calhoun,[*] asked me what was the object which most struck me at Morris' Island; I tell him—as was indeed the case—that it was a letter copying-machine, a case of official stationery, and a box of Red Tape, lying on the beach, just landed and ready to grow with the strength of the young independence.

But listen! There is a great tumult, as of many voices coming up the street, heralded by blasts of music. It is a speech-making from the front of the hotel. Such an agitated, lively multitude! How they cheer the pale, frantic man, limber and dark-haired, with uplifted arms and clenched fists, who is perorating on the balcony! "What did he say?" "Who is he?" "Why it's he again!" "That's Roger Pryor—he says that if them Yankee trash don't listen to reason, and stand from under, we'll march to the North and dictate the terms of peace in Faneuil Hall! Yes, sir—and so we will, certa-i-n su-re!" "No matter, for all that; we have shown we can whip the Yankees whenever we meet them—at Washington or down here." How much I heard of all this to-day—how much more this evening! The hotel as noisy as ever—more men in uniform arriving every few minutes, and the hall and passages crowded with tall, good-looking Carolinians.

[*]Since killed in a duel by Mr. Rhett.

"INFIDEL" ENEMIES: GEORGIA, APRIL 1861
Charles C. Jones Sr. to Charles C. Jones Jr.

Educated at Andover and Princeton, Charles C. Jones was a Presbyterian clergyman and plantation owner in Liberty County, Georgia, known for his evangelical work among slaves. He wrote to his son, the mayor of Savannah, shortly after the outbreak of the war.

Montevideo, *Saturday*, April 20th, 1861

My dear Son,

We are aware of your numerous engagements, and never think anything of your not writing as frequently as usual, for we know that you will always write us whenever you can. Your two last came last night with the papers.

A kind Providence seems to watch over our Confederacy. Whoever read or heard of so important and desperate a battle as that of Fort Sumter without the loss of a man on the side of the victors or on the side of the vanquished? And how remarkable that the only men killed were killed saluting their own flag as it was lowered in defeat! May this battle be an earnest of all others that shall be forced upon us in its merciful and glorious success. All honor to Carolina! I hope our state may emulate her bravery and patriotism—and *her self-sacrificing generosity*, in that she has borne out of her own treasury the entire expense of her army and fortifications and all matériel of war, and has not and will not call upon our government for one cent of it. Georgia is well able to do the like for her own seaport and her own territory, and there must be some movement of our chief men to secure so honorable an act. It will relieve our new government, and enable it to appropriate its funds in other directions for our honor and our defense.

We are favored again, in providence, by the belligerent acts and declarations of Mr. Lincoln, which have precipitated the border states upon a decision in our favor precisely at the moment most favorable to us. I never believed we should have war until after Lincoln's inaugural address—and not altogether then, thinking that there were some preventing considerations of interest and self-preservation, and some residuum of humanity and respect for the opinions of the civilized world in the Black Republican party. But in this I have been mistaken. Christianity with its enlightening and softening influences upon the human soul—at least so far as the great subject dividing our country is concerned—finds no lodgment in the soul of that party, destitute of justice and mercy, without the fear of God, supremely selfish and arrogant, unscrupulous in its acts and measures, intensely malignant and vituperative, and persecuting the innocent even unto blood and utter destruction. That party is essentially *infidel!* And these are our enemies, born and reared in our own political family, for whom we are to pray, and from whom we are to defend ourselves!

The conduct of the government of the old United States towards the Confederate States is an outrage upon Christianity and the civilization of the age, and upon the great and just principles of popular sovereignty which we have contended for and embraced for near an hundred years, and brands it with a deserved and indelible infamy. We have nothing left us but to work out our independence, relying, as our good President instructs us, upon "a just and superintending Providence." The ordering out of such large bodies of men is an easy matter; but to *officer*, to *equip*, to *maintain*, and (*more than all*) to *maneuver and bring these forces into safe action with the enemy*—these are the burdens and the arts and realities of war. And we wait Lincoln's success. He is not training and educating the people up to the point of war gradually and familiarizing them with it, but he plunges them up to their necks in it at once. But enough. What is it all for? Are the people of the free states going to attempt *the subjugation* of our Confederacy under the fanatical and brutal lead of Black Republicans? I agree with you fully in your view of the character and conduct of this party. It would be a sublime spectacle to see the conservative portion of the free states uniting with our Confederacy in overthrowing the present government in Washington and installing a better one in its place—not for us, but for themselves. But I fear that portion of the free states have not the decision and daring and patriotism for the effort. *Douglas* leads off for coercion! A miserable politican and patriot he.

No man can even conjecture where this strife is to end. Yet it is under the control of God. He can "still the tumult of the people," and we can but cast this care upon Him and humbly await His interposition. It may be long delayed; it may be immediate. We must maintain our equanimity, go to our daily duties and by His help faithfully discharge them as in times past, and stand ready for emergencies when they arise, and keep in good heart all around us. The Lord keep you, my dear son, and strengthen you to serve Him and to fear His great and holy name, and to discharge your various and responsible duties to your family and country with cheerfulness and self-possession, with purity and integrity, and with intelligence, decision, and kindness. Seek to do all things well, and everything in its proper time.

Am glad you have consented to deliver the address to your company the 1st of May. You may do good by it, and should like to come and hear you.

The package from Mr. —— was his finish of the copy of the first volume of my church history. Arrived safe. . . .

The news from Baltimore and Washington is out here in the form of rumor. The events of the morning are old by the evening. The scenes succeed almost as rapidly as those of a play. Marvelous if Lincoln, who gave us twenty days to disperse, is in less than ten dispersed himself! As our mails North are stopped, send us what news of interest you can spare. Special prayer should be offered for the *life* of our President; I hope he will not expose his person.

Your affectionate father,
C. C. Jones.

SECESSIONISM IN RICHMOND:
VIRGINIA, APRIL 1861

John B. Jones: Diary, April 15–22, 1861

The editor of the *Southern Monitor*, a weekly journal published in Philadelphia, John B. Jones feared that he would be arrested as a Confederate sympathizer once war began. Anticipating that hostilities would soon break out, Jones left his home in Burlington, New Jersey, on April 9 and arrived in Richmond three days later, where the Virginia convention had been meeting since February. After weeks of debate, on April 4 the convention rejected a motion to secede, 90–45, but remained in session. On April 17, three days after the surrender of Fort Sumter, the convention reversed itself and voted 88–55 to leave the Union—a decision that would be overwhelmingly approved in a referendum held on May 23. Virginia would soon be followed by Arkansas (May 6), North Carolina (May 20), and Tennessee (June 8), resulting in the formation of an eleven-state Confederacy.

———————

APRIL 15TH.—To-day the secession fires assumed a whiter heat. In the Convention the Union men no longer utter denunciations against the disunionists. They merely resort to pretexts and quibbles to stave off the inevitable ordinance. They had sent a deputation to Washington to make a final appeal to Seward and Lincoln to vouchsafe them such guarantees as would enable them to keep Virginia to her moorings. But in vain. They could not obtain even a promise of concession. And now the Union members as they walk the streets, and even Gov. Letcher himself, hear the indignant mutterings of the impassioned storm which threatens every hour to sweep them from existence. Business is generally suspended, and men run together in great crowds to listen to the news from the North, where it is said many outrages are committed on Southern men and those who sympathize with them. Many arrests are made, and the victims thrown into Fort Lafayette. These crowds are addressed by the most inflamed members of the

Convention, and never did I hear more hearty responses from the people.

APRIL 16TH.—This day the Spontaneous People's Convention met and organized in Metropolitan Hall. The doorkeeper stood with a drawn sword in his hand. But the scene was orderly. The assembly was full, nearly every county being represented, and the members were the representatives of the most ancient and respectable families in the State. David Chalmers, of Halifax County, I believe, was the President, and Willoughby Newton, a life-long Whig, among the Vice-Presidents. P. H. Aylett, a grandson of Patrick Henry, was the first speaker. And his eloquence indicated that the spirit of his ancestor survived in him. But he was for moderation and delay, still hoping that the other Convention would yield to the pressure of public sentiment, and place the State in the attitude now manifestly desired by an overwhelming majority of the people. He was answered by the gallant Capt. Wise, who thrilled every breast with his intrepid bearing and electric bursts of oratory. He advocated action, without reference to the other Convention, as the best means of bringing the Unionists to their senses. And the so-called Demosthenean Seddon, and G. W. Randolph (grandson of Thomas Jefferson), Lieut.-Gov. Montague, James Lyons, Judge Robertson, etc., were there. Never, never did I hear more exalted and effective bursts of oratory. And it was apparent that messages were constantly received from the other Convention. What they were, I did not learn at the moment; but it was evident that the Unionists were shaking in their shoes, and they certainly begged one— just one—day's delay, which was accorded them. The People's Convention agreed to adjourn till 10 o'clock A.M. the next day. But before we separated a commotion was observed on the stage, and the next moment a Mr. P., from Gov. Wise's old district, rushed forward and announced that he had just arrived from Norfolk, where, under instructions, and *with the acquiescence of Gov. Letcher*, he had succeeded in blocking the channel of the river; and this would either secure to us, or render useless to the United States, certain ships of the navy, stores, armament, etc., of the value of millions of dollars. This announcement was received with the wildest shouts of joy. Young men threw up their hats, and old men buttoned their coats and clapped their hands most vigorously. It was next hinted by some one who seemed to know something of the matter, that before another day elapsed, Harper's Ferry would fall into the hands of the secessionists.

At night the enthusiasm increases in intensity, and no further opposition is to be apprehended from the influence of Tim Rives, Baldwin, Clemens, etc. etc. It was quite apparent, indeed, that if an ordinance of secession were passed by the new Convention, its validity would be recognized and acted upon by the majority of the people. But this would be a complication of the civil war, now the decree of fate.

Perhaps the occurrence which has attracted most attention is the raising of the Southern flag on the capitol. It was hailed with the most deafening shouts of applause. But at a quiet hour of the night, the governor had it taken down, for the Convention had not yet passed the ordinance of secession. Yet the stars and stripes did not float in its stead; it was replaced by the flag of Virginia.

APRIL 17TH.—This was a memorable day. When we assembled at Metropolitan Hall, it could be easily perceived that we were on the threshold of momentous events. All other subjects, except that of a new political organization of the State, seemed to be momentarily delayed, as if awaiting action elsewhere. And this plan of political organization filled me with alarm, for I apprehended it would result in a new conflict between the old parties—Whig and Democrat. The ingenious discussion of this subject was probably a device of the Unionists, two or three of them having obtained seats in the Revolutionary Convention. I knew the ineradicable instincts of Virginia politicians, and their inveterate habit of public speaking, and knew there were well-grounded fears that we should be launched and lost in an illimitable sea of argument, when the business was Revolution, and death to the coming invader. Besides, I saw no hope of unanimity if the old party distinctions and designations were not submerged forever.

These fears, however, were groundless. The Union had received its *blessure mortelle*, and no power this side of the Potomac could save it. During a pause in the proceedings, one of the leading members arose and announced that he had information that the vote was about being taken in the other

Convention on the ordinance of secession. "Very well!" cried another member, "we will give them another chance to save themselves. But it is the last!" This was concurred in by a vast majority. Not long after, Lieut.-Gov. Montague came in and announced the passage of the ordinance by the other Convention! This was succeeded by a moment too thrilling for utterance, but was followed by tears of gladness and rapturous applause. Soon after, President Tyler and Gov. Wise were conducted arm-in-arm, and bare-headed, down the center aisle amid a din of cheers, while every member rose to his feet. They were led to the platform, and called upon to address the Convention. The venerable ex-President of the United States first rose responsive to the call, but remarked that the exhaustion incident to his recent incessant labors, and the nature of his emotions at such a momentous crisis, superadded to the feebleness of age, rendered him physically unable to utter what he felt and thought on such an occasion. Nevertheless, he seemed to acquire supernatural strength as he proceeded, and he spoke most effectively for the space of fifteen minutes. He gave a brief history of all the struggles of our race for freedom, from *Magna Charta* to the present day; and he concluded with a solemn declaration that at no period of our history were we engaged in a more just and holy effort for the maintenance of liberty and independence than at the present moment. The career of the dominant party at the North was but a series of aggressions, which fully warranted the steps we were taking for resistance and eternal separation; and if we performed our whole duty as Christians and patriots, the same benign Providence which favored the cause of our forefathers in the Revolution of 1776, would again crown our efforts with similar success. He said he might not survive to witness the consummation of the work begun that day; but generations yet unborn would bless those who had the high privilege of being participators in it.

He was succeeded by Gov. Wise, who, for a quarter of an hour, electrified the assembly by a burst of eloquence, perhaps never surpassed by mortal orator. During his pauses a silence reigned, pending which the slightest breathing could be distinctly heard, while every eye was bathed in tears. At times the vast assembly rose involuntarily to their feet, and every emotion and expression of feature seemed responsive to his own. During his speech he alluded to the reports of the press that the oppressors of the North had probably seized one of his children sojourning in their midst. "But," said he, "if they suppose hostages of my own heart's blood will stay my hand in a contest for the maintenance of sacred rights, they are mistaken. Affection for kindred, property, and life itself sink into insignificance in comparison with the overwhelming importance of public duty in such a crisis as this." He lamented the blindness which had prevented Virginia from seizing Washington before the Republican hordes got possession of it—but, said he, we must do our best under the circumstances. It was now Independence or Death—although he had preferred fighting in the Union—and when the mind was made up to die rather than fail, success was certain. For himself, he was eager to meet the ordeal, and he doubted not every Southern heart pulsated in unison with his own.

Hon. J. M. Mason, and many other of Virginia's distinguished sons were called upon, and delivered patriotic speeches. And finally, *Gov. Letcher* appeared upon the stage. He was loudly cheered by the very men who, two days before, would gladly have witnessed his execution. The governor spoke very briefly, merely declaring his concurrence in the important step that had been taken, and his honest purpose, under the circumstances, to discharge his whole duty as Executive of the State, in conformity to the will of the people and the provisions of the Constitution.

Before the *sine die* adjournment, it was suggested that inasmuch as the ordinance had been passed in secret session, and it was desirable that the enemy should not know it before certain preparations could be made to avert sudden injury on the border, etc., that the fact should not be divulged at present.

APRIL 18TH.—In spite of every precaution, it is currently whispered in the streets to-day that Virginia has seceded from the Union; and that the act is to be submitted to the people for ratification a month hence. This is perhaps a blunder. If the Southern States are to adhere to the old distinct sovereignty doctrine, God help them one and all to achieve their independence of the United States. Many are inclined to think the safest plan would be to obliterate State lines, and merge them all into an indivisible nation or empire, else there may be incessant conflicts between the different sovereignties themselves, and between them and the General Government. I doubt our ability to maintain the old cumbrous, complicated, and expensive form of government. A national executive and Congress will be sufficiently burdensome to the people without the additional expense of governors, lieutenant-governors, a dozen secretaries of State, as many legislatures, etc. etc. It is true, State rights gave the States the right to secede. But what is in a name? Secession by any other name would smell as sweet. For my part, I like the name of Revolution, or even Rebellion, better, for they are sanctified by the example of Washington and his compeers. And separations of communities are like the separations of bees when they cannot live in peace in the same hive. The time had come apparently for us to set up for ourselves, and we should have done it if there had been no such thing as State sovereignty. It is true, the Constitution adopted at Montgomery virtually acknowledges the right of any State to secede from the Confederacy; but that was necessary in vindication of the action of its fathers. That Constitution, and the *permanent* one to succeed it, will, perhaps, never do. They too much resemble the governmental organization of the Yankees, to whom we have bid adieu forever in disgust.

APRIL 19TH.—Dispatches from Montgomery indicate that President Davis is as firm a States right man as any other, perfectly content to bear the burdens of government six years, and hence I apprehend he will not budge in the business of guarding Virginia until after the ratification of the secession ordinance. Thus a month's precious time will be lost; and the scene of conflict, instead of being in Pennsylvania, near Philadelphia, will be in Virginia. From the ardor of the volunteers already beginning to pour into the city, I believe 25,000 men could be collected and armed in a week, and in another they might sweep the whole Abolition concern beyond the Susquehanna, and afterward easily keep them there. But this will not be attempted, nor permitted, by the Convention, so recently composed mostly of Union men.

To-night we have rumors of a collision in Baltimore. A regiment of Northern troops has been assailed by the mob. No good can come of mob assaults in a great revolution.

Wrote my wife to make preparations with all expedition to escape into Virginia. Women and children will not be molested for some weeks yet; but I see they have begun to ransack their baggage. Mrs. Semple, daughter of President Tyler, I am informed, had her plate taken from her in an attempt to get it away from New York.

APRIL 20TH.—The news has been confirmed. It was a brickbat "Plug Ugly" fight—the result of animal, and not intellectual or patriotic instincts. Baltimore has better men for the strife than bar-room champions. The absence of dignity in this assault will be productive of evil rather than good. Maryland is probably lost—for her fetters will be riveted before the secession of Virginia will be communicated by the senseless form of ratification a month hence. Woe, woe to the politicians of Virginia who have wrought this delay! It is now understood that the very day before the ordinance was passed, the members were gravely splitting hairs over proposed amendments to the Federal Constitution!

Guns are being fired on Capitol Hill in commemoration of secession, and the Confederate flag now floats unmolested from the summit of the capitol. I think they had better save the powder, etc.

At night. We have a gay illumination. This too is wrong. We had better save the candles.

APRIL 21ST.—Received several letters to-day which had been delayed in their transmission, and were doubtless opened on the way. One was from my wife, informing me of the illness of Custis, my eldest son, and of the equivocal conduct of some of the neighbors. The Rev. Mr. D., son of the late B——p, raised the flag of the Union on his church.

The telegraphic wires are still in operation.

APRIL 22D.—Early a few mornings since, I called on Gov. Wise, and informed him that Lincoln had called out 70,000 men. He opened his eyes very widely and said, emphatically, "I don't believe it." The greatest statesmen of the South have no conception of the real purposes of the men now in power in the United States. They cannot be made to believe that the Government at Washington are going to wage war immediately. But when I placed the President's proclamation in his hand, he read it with deep emotion, and uttered a fierce

"Hah!" Nevertheless, when I told him that these 70,000 were designed to be merely the videttes and outposts of an army of 700,000, he was quite incredulous. He had not witnessed the Wide-Awake gatherings the preceding fall, as I had done, and listened to the pledges they made to subjugate the South, free the negroes, and hang Gov. Wise. I next told him they would blockade our ports, and endeavor to cut off our supplies. To this he uttered a most positive negative. He said it would be contrary to the laws of nations, as had been decided often in the Courts of Admiralty, and would be moreover a violation of the Constitution. Of course I admitted all this; but maintained that such was the intention of the Washington Cabinet. Laws and Courts and Constitutions would not be impediments in the way of Yankees resolved upon our subjugation. Presuming upon their superior numbers, and under the pretext of saving the Union and annihilating slavery, they would invade us like the army-worm, which enters the green fields in countless numbers. The real object was to enjoy our soil and climate by means of confiscation. He poohed me into silence with an indignant frown. He had no idea that the Yankees would *dare* to enter upon such enterprises in the face of an enlightened world. But I know them better. And it will be found that they will learn how to fight, and will not be afraid to fight.

THE BALTIMORE RIOT: APRIL 1861

John W. Hanson: from Historical Sketch of the Old Sixth Regiment of Massachusetts Volunteers

On April 19 the 6th Massachusetts Regiment was attacked by a secessionist mob as it passed through Baltimore on its way to Washington. Four soldiers and a dozen Baltimore citizens were killed in the fighting, the first fatal casualties of the war. In Massachusetts the skirmish would take on special meaning because it fell on the anniversary of the battles of Lexington and Concord. John W. Hanson became the chaplain of the 6th Massachusetts in 1862 and later wrote the regimental history, in which he drew on three first-hand accounts of the riot.

———————

COL. JONES, in his official report to Maj. William H. Clemence, Maj. Gen. B. F. Butler's Adjutant, dated in Washington, 22d April, says:—

* * * After leaving Philadelphia, I received intimation that our passage through the city of Baltimore would be resisted. I caused ammunition to be distributed, and arms loaded; and went personally through the cars, and issued the following order, viz.:—

"The regiment will march through Baltimore in column of sections, arms at will. You will undoubtedly be insulted, abused, and perhaps assaulted, to which you must pay no attention whatever; but march with your faces square to the front, and pay no attention to the mob, even if they throw stones, bricks, or other missiles; but if you are fired upon, and any one of you is hit, your officers will order you to fire. Do not fire into any promiscuous crowds; but select any man whom you see aiming at you, and be sure you drop him."

Reaching Baltimore, horses were attached the instant that the locomotive was detached, and the cars were driven at a rapid pace across the city. After the cars containing seven companies had reached the Washington depot, the track behind them was barricaded, and the cars containing the band and the following companies, viz.: company C, of Lowell, Capt. Follansbee; company D, of Lowell, Capt. Hart;

company I, of Lawrence, Capt. Pickering; and company L, of Stoneham, Capt. Dike, were vacated; and they proceeded to march in accordance with orders, and had proceeded but a short distance before they were furiously attacked by a shower of missiles, which came faster as they advanced. They increased their step to double-quick, which seemed to infuriate the mob, as it evidently impressed them with the idea that the soldiers dared not fire, or had no ammunition; and pistol-shots were numerously fired into the ranks, and one soldier fell dead. The order, "Fire!" was given, and it was executed; in consequence, several of the mob fell, and the soldiers again advanced hastily. The Mayor of Baltimore placed himself at the head of the column, beside Capt. Follansbee, and proceeded with them a short distance, assuring him that he would protect them, and begging him not to let the men fire; but the mayor's patience was soon exhausted, and he seized a musket from the hands of one of the men, and killed a man therewith; and a policeman, who was in advance of the column, also shot a man with a revolver.

They, at last, reached the cars, and they started immediately for Washington. On going through the train, I found there were about one hundred and thirty missing, including the band and field music. Our baggage was seized, and we have not as yet been able to recover any of it. I have found it very difficult to get reliable information in regard to the killed and wounded.

As the men went into the cars, I caused the blinds to be closed, and took every precaution to prevent any shadow of offence to the people of Baltimore; but still the stones flew thick and fast into the train, and it was with the utmost difficulty that I could prevent the troops from leaving the cars, and revenging the death of their comrades.   *   *   *

EDWARD F. JONES,
Col. Sixth Regt., M. V. M., in service of U. S.

WHY THE MOB WAS SO LENIENTLY TREATED.

Those who have since been made familiar with scenes of war, and with the true method of dealing with such men as those who intercepted the march of the Sixth, might, at first thought, be surprised at the gentle treatment the mob received. But the regiment was anxious to reach Washington, then supposed to be in imminent danger; and it was hoped that the demonstration in Baltimore would not be serious. Besides, the people of the North were trying conciliation. No blood had been shed, and it was universally desired to treat Maryland and other border states with all the forbearance possible. The regiment had been drilled in street-firing, and was amply able to strew the streets of Baltimore with traitor dead; and would have done so but for these considerations. Place the same men under the same circumstances to-day, and there would be grief in hundreds of homes where one mourned on the 19th of April, 1861.

CAPT. FOLLANSBEE'S ACCOUNT.

Capt. Follansbee, under date of Washington, April 20, wrote a letter to H. H. Wilder, Esq., of Lowell, which embodies the observations of as cool a head and brave a heart as were among the two hundred heroes of that day. He says:—

We arrived in Baltimore about 10 o'clock, A.M. The cars are drawn through the city by horses. There were about thirty cars in our train; there being, in addition to Col. Jones' command, about 1200 troops from Philadelphia, without uniforms or arms, they intending to get them here. After we arrived, the cars were taken, two at a time, and drawn to the depot at the lower part of the city, a mob assaulting them all the way. The Lowell Mechanic Phalanx car was the ninth; and we waited till after the rest had left, for our turn, till two men came to me and informed me that I had better take my command, and march to the other depot, as the mob had taken up the track to prevent the passage of the cars. I immediately informed Capt. Pickering, of the Lawrence Light Infantry, and we filed out of the cars in regular order. Capt. Hart's company, of Lowell, and Capt. Dike's, of Stoneham, did the same, and formed on the sidewalk. The captains consulted together, and decided that the command should devolve upon me. I immediately took my position upon the right, wheeled into column of sections, and requested them to march in close order. Before we had started, the mob was upon us, with a secession flag, attached to a pole, and told us we could never march through that city. They would kill every "white nigger" of us, before we could reach the other depot. I paid no attention to them, but, after I had wheeled the battalion, gave the order to march.

As soon as the order was given, the brick-bats began to fly into our ranks from the mob. I called a policeman, and requested him to lead the way to the depot. He did so. After we had marched about a hundred yards, we came to a bridge. The rebels had torn up most of the planks. We had to play "Scotch hop," to get over it. As soon as we had crossed the bridge, they commenced to fire upon us from the street and houses. I ordered the men to protect themselves; and then we returned their fire, and laid a great many of them away. I saw four fall on the sidewalk at one time. They followed us up, and we fought our way to the other depot,—about one mile. They kept at us till the cars started. Quite a number of the rascals were shot, after we entered the cars. We went very slow, for we expected the rails were torn up on the road.

I do not know how much damage we did. Report says, about forty were killed, but I think that is exaggerated: still it may be so. There is any quantity of them wounded. Quite a number of horses were killed. The mayor of the city met us almost half way. He said that there would be no trouble, and that we could get through, and kept with me for about a hundred yards; but the stones and balls whistled too near his head, and he left, took a gun from one of my company, fired, and brought his man down. That was the last I saw of him. We fought our way to the cars, and joined Col. Jones, and the seven companies that left us at the other end of the city; and now we are here, every man of the old Phalanx safe and sound, with the exception of a few marks made by brick-bats, and all we want now is a chance to go to Baltimore, and clean out all the roughs there. If Col. Jones would march his command there, we would do it. There are five or six of the regiment missing, and all of the band. I am in hopes that most, if not all of them are alive. Where a man in Baltimore showed his pistol, axe, or palmetto flag, he was about sure to drop.

ANOTHER TESTIMONY.

A. S. Young, a member of the band, after relating that one of the musicians had left the car to consult with Gen. Small, of the unarmed Pennsylvanians, says:—

As he was returning, he was set upon, and driven into the car, followed by a number of the roughs. We fought them off as long as we could; but coming thicker and faster, some crawling from under the cars, others jumping from the tops, they forced their way in, in spite of our utmost exertions. The door was then partly thrown open by the exertions of our men inside, and partly torn open by the mob outside; and we attempted, by leaping from the car, and running in all directions, to escape from the mob. We were obliged to leave everything behind. Music, instruments, coats, caps, knapsacks, and haversacks. On our way we saw squads of police, who took no notice of us, evidently regarding the whole thing as a good joke. The writer of this saw and spoke to two of them, and was told to "run—run like the devil;" and he did. They could do nothing: they would take care of our property, but could do nothing for us. After running in this way for a half mile, as near as we could judge, we were encountered by a party of women, partly Irish, partly German, and some American, who took us into their houses, removed the stripes from our pants, and we were furnished with old clothes of every description for disguise. We were treated here as well as we could have been in our own homes. Everything we wished was furnished, and nothing would be taken therefor; but we were told that it would be an insult to offer it.

Under the protection of four hundred policemen, these unarmed musicians were able to reach the station, and take the cars back to Philadelphia.

"I HAVE BUT ONE SENTIMENT NOW":
ILLINOIS, APRIL 1861

Ulysses S. Grant to Frederick Dent, April 19, 1861, and to Jesse Root Grant, April 21, 1861

An 1843 graduate of West Point, Ulysses S. Grant had served in Mexico before resigning from the army as a captain in 1854. When the war began, he was working as a clerk in his family's leather-goods store in Galena, Illinois. Grant responded to the news of Fort Sumter in letters to his father-in-law and his father.

Galena, April 19th 1861

MR. F. DENT;
DEAR SIR:

I have but very little time to write but as in these exciting times we are very anxious to hear from you, and know of no other way but but by writing first to you, I must make time.— We get but little news, by telegraph, from St. Louis but from most all other points of the Country we are hearing all the time. The times are indeed startling but now is the time, particularly in the border Slave states, for men to prove their love of country. I know it is hard for men to apparently work with the Republican party but now all party distinctions should be lost sight of and evry true patriot be for maintaining the integrity of the glorious old *Stars & Stripes*, the Constitution and the Union. The North is responding to the Presidents call in such a manner that the rebels may truly quaik. I tell you there is no mistaking the feelings of the people. The Government can call into the field not only 75000 troops but ten or twenty times 75000 if it should be necessary and find the means of maintaining them too. It is all a mistake about the Northern pocket being so sensative. In times like the present no people are more ready to give their own time or of their abundant means. No impartial man can conceal from himself the fact that in all these troubles the South have been the aggressors and the Administration has stood purely on the defensive, more on the defensive than she would dared to have done but for her consiousness of strength and the certainty of right prevailing in the end. The news to-day is that Virginia has gone out of the Union. But for the influance she will have on the other border slave states this is not much to be regreted. Her position, or rather that of Eastern Virginia, has been more reprehensible from the begining than that of South Carolina. She should be made to bear a heavy portion of the burthen of the War for her guilt.—In all this I can but see the doom of Slavery. The North do not want, nor will they want, to interfere with the institution. But they will refuse for all time to give it protection unless the South shall return soon to their allegiance, and then too this disturbance will give such an impetus to the production of their staple, cotton, in other parts of the world that they can never recover the controll of the market again for that comodity. This will reduce the value of negroes so much that they will never be worth fighting over again.—I have just rec'd a letter from Fred. He breathes forth the most patriotic sentiments. He is for the old Flag as long as there is a Union of two states fighting under its banner and when they desolve he will go it alone. This is not his language but it is the idea not so well expressed as he expresses it.

Julia and the children are all well and join me in love to you all. I forgot to mention that Fred. has another heir, with some novel name that I have forgotten.

Yours Truly
U. S. GRANT

Get John or Lewis Sheets to write to me.

Galena, April 21st 1861

DEAR FATHER;

We are now in the midst of trying times when evry one must be for or against his country, and show his colors too, by his every act. Having been educated for such an emergency, at the expense of the Government, I feel that it has upon me superior claims, such claims as no ordinary motives of self-interest can surmount. I do not wish to act hastily or unadvisadly in the matter, and as there are more than enough to respond to the first call of the President, I have not yet offered myself. I have promised and am giving all the assistance I can in organizing the Company whose services have been accepted from this place. I have promised further to go with them to the state Capital and if I can be of service to the Governer in organizing his state troops to do so. What I ask now is your approval of the course I am taking, or advice in the matter. A letter written this week will reach me in Springfield. I have not time to write you but a hasty line for though Sunday as it is we are all busy here. In a few minuets I shall be engaged in directing tailors in the style and trim of uniforms for our men.

Whatever may have been my political opinions before I have but one sentiment now. That is we have a Government, and laws and a flag and they must all be sustained. There are but two parties now, Traitors & Patriots and I want hereafter to be ranked with the latter, and I trust, the stronger party.—I do not know but you may be placed in an awkward position, and a dangerous one pecuniarily, but costs can not now be counted. My advice would be to leave where you are if you are not safe with the veiws you entertain. I would never stultify my opinions for the sake of a little security.

I will say nothing about our business. Orvil & Lank will keep you posted as to that.

Write soon and direct as above.

Yours Truly
U. S. GRANT.

MONTGOMERY, ALABAMA, APRIL 1861

Jefferson Davis: Message to the Confederate Congress

Davis called the Provisional Confederate Congress into special session on April 29 and sent a message regarding the outbreak of hostilities.

MONTGOMERY, April 29, 1861.

Gentlemen of the Congress: It is my pleasing duty to announce to you that the Constitution framed for the establishment of a permanent Government for the Confederate States has been ratified by conventions in each of those States to which it was referred. To inaugurate the Government in its full proportions and upon its own substantial basis of the popular will, it only remains that elections should be held for the designation of the officers to administer it. There is every reason to believe that at no distant day other States, identified in political principles and community of interests with those which you represent, will join this Confederacy, giving to its typical constellation increased splendor, to its Government of free, equal, and sovereign States a wider sphere of usefulness, and to the friends of constitutional liberty a greater security for its harmonious and perpetual existence. It was not, however, for the purpose of making this announcement that I have deemed it my duty to convoke you at an earlier day than that fixed by yourselves for your meeting. The declaration of war made against this Confederacy by Abraham Lincoln, the President of the United States, in his proclamation issued on the 15th day of the present month, rendered it necessary, in my judgment, that you should convene at the earliest practicable moment to devise the measures necessary for the defense of the country. The occasion is indeed an extraordinary one. It justifies me in a brief review of the relations heretofore existing between us and the States which now unite in warfare against us and in a succinct statement of the events which have resulted in this warfare, to the end that mankind may pass intelligent and impartial judgment on its motives and objects. During the war waged against Great Britain by her colonies on this continent a common danger impelled them to a close alliance and to the formation of a Confederation, by the terms of which the colonies, styling themselves States, entered "*severally* into a firm league of friendship with each other for their common defense, the security of their liberties, and their mutual and general welfare, binding themselves to assist each other against all force offered to or attacks made upon them, or any of them, on account of religion, sovereignty, trade, or any other pretense whatever." In order to guard against any misconstruction of their compact, the several States made explicit declaration in a distinct article—that "*each* State *retains its* sovereignty, freedom, and independence, and every power, jurisdiction, and right which is not by this Confederation *expressly delegated* to the United States in Congress assembled."

Under this contract of alliance, the war of the Revolution was successfully waged, and resulted in the treaty of peace with Great Britain in 1783, by the terms of which the several States were *each by name* recognized to be independent. The Articles of Confederation contained a clause whereby all alterations were prohibited unless confirmed by the Legislatures of *every State* after being agreed to by the Congress; and in obedience to this provision, under the resolution of Congress of the 21st of February, 1787, the several States appointed delegates who attended a convention "for the *sole and express purpose* of revising the Articles of Confederation and reporting to Congress and the several Legislatures such alterations and provisions therein as shall, when agreed to in Congress *and confirmed by the States*, render the Federal Constitution adequate to the exigencies of Government and the preservation of the Union." It was by the delegates chosen by the *several States* under the resolution just quoted that the Constitution of the United States was framed in 1787 and submitted to the *several States* for ratification, as shown by the seventh article, which is in these words: "The ratification of the *conventions of nine States* shall be sufficient for the establishment of this Constitution *between the States* so ratifying the same." I have italicized certain words in the quotations just made for the purpose of attracting attention to the singular and marked caution with which the States endeavored in every possible form to exclude the idea that the separate and independent sovereignty of each State was merged into one common government and nation, and the earnest desire they evinced to impress on the Constitution its true character—that of a *compact between* independent States. The Constitution of 1787, having, however, omitted the clause already recited from the Articles of Confederation, which provided in explicit terms that each State *retained* its sovereignty and independence, some alarm was felt in the States, when invited to ratify the Constitution, lest this omission should be construed into an abandonment of their cherished principle, and they refused to be satisfied until amendments were added to the Constitution placing beyond any pretense of doubt the reservation by the States of all their sovereign rights and powers not expressly delegated to the United States by the Constitution.

Strange, indeed, must it appear to the impartial observer, but it is none the less true that all these carefully worded clauses proved unavailing to prevent the rise and growth in the Northern States of a political school which has persistently claimed that the government thus formed was not a compact *between* States, but was in effect a national government, set up *above* and *over* the States. An organization created by the States to secure the blessings of liberty and independence against *foreign* aggression, has been gradually perverted into a machine for their control in their *domestic* affairs. The *creature* has been exalted above its *creators*; the *principals* have been made subordinate to the *agent* appointed by themselves. The people of the Southern States, whose almost exclusive occupation was agriculture, early perceived a tendency in the Northern States to render the common government subservient to their own purposes by imposing burdens on commerce as a protection to their manufacturing and shipping interests. Long and angry controversies grew out of these attempts, often successful, to benefit one section of the country at the expense of the other. And the danger of disruption arising from this cause was enhanced by the fact that the Northern population was increasing, by immigration and other causes, in a greater ratio than the population of the South. By degrees, as the Northern

States gained preponderance in the National Congress, self-interest taught their people to yield ready assent to any plausible advocacy of their right as a majority to govern the minority without control. They learned to listen with impatience to the suggestion of any constitutional impediment to the exercise of their will, and so utterly have the principles of the Constitution been corrupted in the Northern mind that, in the inaugural address delivered by President Lincoln in March last, he asserts as an axiom, which he plainly deems to be undeniable, that the theory of the Constitution requires that in all cases the majority shall govern; and in another memorable instance the same Chief Magistrate did not hesitate to liken the relations between a State and the United States to those which exist between a county and the State in which it is situated and by which it was created. This is the lamentable and fundamental error on which rests the policy that has culminated in his declaration of war against these Confederate States. In addition to the long-continued and deep-seated resentment felt by the Southern States at the persistent abuse of the powers they had delegated to the Congress, for the purpose of enriching the manufacturing and shipping classes of the North at the expense of the South, there has existed for nearly half a century another subject of discord, involving interests of such transcendent magnitude as at all times to create the apprehension in the minds of many devoted lovers of the Union that its permanence was impossible. When the several States delegated certain powers to the United States Congress, a large portion of the laboring population consisted of African slaves imported into the colonies by the mother country. In twelve out of the thirteen States negro slavery existed, and the right of property in slaves was protected by law. This property was recognized in the Constitution, and provision was made against its loss by the escape of the slave. The increase in the number of slaves by further importation from Africa was also secured by a clause forbidding Congress to prohibit the slave trade anterior to a certain date, and in no clause can there be found any delegation of power to the Congress authorizing it in any manner to legislate to the prejudice, detriment, or discouragement of the owners of that species of property, or excluding it from the protection of the Government.

The climate and soil of the Northern States soon proved unpropitious to the continuance of slave labor, whilst the converse was the case at the South. Under the unrestricted free intercourse between the two sections, the Northern States consulted their own interests by selling their slaves to the South and prohibiting slavery within their limits. The South were willing purchasers of a property suitable to their wants, and paid the price of the acquisition without harboring a suspicion that their quiet possession was to be disturbed by those who were inhibited not only by want of constitutional authority, but by good faith as vendors, from disquieting a title emanating from themselves. As soon, however, as the Northern States that prohibited African slavery within their limits had reached a number sufficient to give their representation a controlling voice in the Congress, a persistent and organized system of hostile measures against the rights of the owners of slaves in the Southern States was inaugurated and gradually extended. A continuous series of measures was devised and prosecuted for the purpose of rendering insecure the tenure of property in slaves. Fanatical organizations, supplied with money by voluntary subscriptions, were assiduously engaged in exciting amongst the slaves a spirit of discontent and revolt; means were furnished for their escape from their owners, and agents secretly employed to entice them to abscond; the constitutional provision for their rendition to their owners was first evaded, then openly denounced as a violation of conscientious obligation and religious duty; men were taught that it was a merit to elude, disobey, and violently oppose the execution of the laws enacted to secure the performance of the promise contained in the constitutional compact; owners of slaves were mobbed and even murdered in open day solely for applying to a magistrate for the arrest of a fugitive slave; the dogmas of these voluntary organizations soon obtained control of the Legislatures of many of the Northern States, and laws were passed providing for the punishment, by ruinous fines and long-continued imprisonment in jails and penitentiaries, of citizens of the Southern States who should dare to ask aid of the officers of the law for the recovery of their property. Emboldened by success, the theater of agitation and aggression against the clearly expressed constitutional rights of the Southern States was transferred to the Congress; Senators and Representatives were sent to the common councils of the nation, whose chief title to this distinction consisted in the display of a spirit of ultra fanaticism, and whose business was not "to promote the general welfare or insure domestic tranquillity," but to awaken the bitterest hatred against the citizens of sister States by violent denunciation of their institutions; the transaction of public affairs was impeded by repeated efforts to usurp powers not delegated by the Constitution, for the purpose of impairing the security of property in slaves, and reducing those States which held slaves to a condition of inferiority. Finally a great party was organized for the purpose of obtaining the administration of the Government, with the avowed object of using its power for the total exclusion of the slave States from all participation in the benefits of the public domain acquired by all the States in common, whether by conquest or purchase; of surrounding them entirely by States in which slavery should be prohibited; of thus rendering the property in slaves so insecure as to be comparatively worthless, and thereby annihilating in effect property worth thousands of millions of dollars. This party, thus organized, succeeded in the month of November last in the election of its candidate for the Presidency of the United States.

In the meantime, under the mild and genial climate of the Southern States and the increasing care and attention for the well-being and comfort of the laboring class, dictated alike by interest and humanity, the African slaves had augmented in number from about 600,000, at the date of the adoption of the constitutional compact, to upward of 4,000,000. In moral and social condition they had been elevated from brutal savages into docile, intelligent, and civilized agricultural laborers, and supplied not only with bodily comforts but with careful religious instruction. Under the supervision of a superior race their labor had been so directed as not only to allow a gradual and marked amelioration of their own condition, but to convert hundreds of thousands of square miles of the wilderness into cultivated lands covered with a prosperous people; towns and cities had sprung into existence, and had rapidly increased in wealth and population under the social system of the South; the white population of the Southern slaveholding States had augmented from about 1,250,000 at the date of the adoption of the Constitution to more than 8,500,000 in 1860; and the productions of the South in cotton, rice, sugar, and tobacco, for the full development and continuance of which the labor of African slaves was and is indispensable, had swollen to an amount which formed nearly three-fourths of the exports of the whole United States and had become absolutely necessary to the wants of civilized man. With interests of such overwhelming magnitude imperiled, the people of the Southern States were driven by the conduct of the North to the adoption of some course of action to avert the danger with which they were openly menaced. With this view the Legislatures of the several States invited the people to select delegates to conventions to be held for the purpose of determining for themselves what measures were best adapted to meet so alarming a crisis in their history. Here it may be proper to observe that from a period as early as 1798 there had existed in *all* of the States of the Union a party almost uninterruptedly in the majority based upon the creed that each State was, in the last resort, the sole judge as well of its wrongs as of the mode and measure of redress. Indeed, it is obvious that under the law of nations this principle is an axiom as applied to the relations of independent sovereign States, such as those which had united themselves under the constitutional compact. The Democratic party of the United States repeated, in its successful canvass in 1856, the declaration made in numerous previous political contests, that it would "faithfully abide by and uphold the principles laid down in the Kentucky and Virginia resolutions of 1798, and in the report of Mr. Madison to the Virginia Legislature in 1799; and that it adopts those principles as constituting one of the main foundations of its political creed." The principles thus emphatically announced embrace that to which I have already adverted—the right of each State to judge of and redress the wrongs of which it complains. These principles were maintained by overwhelming majorities of the people of all the States of the Union at different elections, especially in the elections of Mr. Jefferson in 1805, Mr. Madison in 1809, and Mr. Pierce in 1852. In the exercise of a right so ancient, so well-established, and so necessary for self-preservation, the people of the Confederate States, in their conventions, determined that the wrongs which they had suffered and the evils with which they were menaced required that they should revoke the delegation of powers to the Federal Government which they had ratified in their several conventions. They consequently passed ordinances resuming all their rights as sovereign and independent States and dissolved their connection with the other States of the Union.

Having done this, they proceeded to form a new compact amongst themselves by new articles of confederation, which have been also ratified by the conventions of the several States with an approach to unanimity far exceeding that of the conventions which adopted the Constitution of 1787. They have organized their new Government in all its departments; the functions of the executive, legislative, and judicial magistrates are performed in accordance with the will of the people, as displayed not merely in a cheerful acquiescence, but in the enthusiastic support of the Government thus established by themselves; and but for the interference of the Government of the United States in this legitimate exercise of the right of a people to self-government, peace, happiness, and prosperity would now smile on our land. That peace is ardently desired by this Government and people has been manifested in every possible form. Scarce had you assembled in February last when, prior even to the inauguration of the Chief Magistrate you had elected, you passed a resolution expressive of your desire for the appointment of commissioners to be sent to the Government of the United States "for the purpose of negotiating friendly relations between that Government and the Confederate States of America, and for the settlement of all questions of disagreement between the two Governments upon principles of right, justice, equity, and good faith." It was my pleasure as well as my duty to coöperate with you in this work of peace. Indeed, in my address to you on taking the oath of office, and before receiving from you the communication of this resolution, I had said "as a necessity, not a choice, we have resorted to the remedy of separation, and henceforth our energies must be directed to the conduct of our own affairs and the perpetuity of the Confederacy which we have formed. If a just perception of mutual interests shall permit us peaceably to pursue our separate political career, my most earnest desire will have been fulfilled." It was in furtherance of these accordant views of the Congress and the Executive that I made choice of three discreet, able, and distinguished citizens, who repaired to Washington. Aided by their cordial cooperation and that of the Secretary of State, every effort compatible with self-respect and the dignity of the Confederacy was exhausted before I allowed myself to yield to the conviction that the Government of the United States was determined to attempt the conquest of this people and that our cherished hopes of peace were unattainable.

On the arrival of our commissioners in Washington on the 5th of March they postponed, at the suggestion of a friendly intermediary, doing more than giving informal notice of their arrival. This was done with a view to afford time to the President, who had just been inaugurated, for the discharge of other pressing official duties in the organization of his Administration before engaging his attention in the object of their mission. It was not until the 12th of the month that they officially addressed the Secretary of State, informing him of the purpose of their arrival, and stating, in the language of their instructions, their wish "to make to the Government of the United States overtures for the opening of negotiations, assuring the Government of the United States that the President, Congress, and people of the Confederate States earnestly desire a peaceful solution of these great questions; that it is neither their interest nor their wish to make any demand which is not founded on strictest justice, nor do any act to injure their late confederates."

To this communication no formal reply was received until the 8th of April. During the interval the commissioners had consented to waive all questions of form. With the firm resolve to avoid war if possible, they went so far even as to hold during that long period unofficial intercourse through an intermediary, whose high position and character inspired the hope of success, and through whom constant assurances were received from the Government of the United States of peaceful intentions; of the determination to evacuate Fort Sumter; and further, that no measure changing the existing status prejudicially to the Confederate States, especially at Fort Pickens, was in contemplation, but that in the event of any change of intention on the subject, notice would be given to the commissioners. The crooked paths of diplomacy can scarcely furnish an example so wanting in courtesy, in candor, and directness as was the course of the United States Government toward our commissioners in Washington. For proof of this I refer to the annexed documents marked ———, taken in connection with further facts, which I now proceed to relate.

Early in April the attention of the whole country, as well as that of our commissioners, was attracted to extraordinary preparations for an extensive military and naval expedition in New York and other Northern ports. These preparations commenced in secrecy, for an expedition whose destination was concealed, only became known when nearly completed, and on the 5th, 6th, and 7th of April transports and vessels of war with troops, munitions, and military supplies sailed from Northern ports bound southward. Alarmed by so extraordinary a demonstration, the commissioners requested the delivery of an answer to their official communication of the 12th of March, and thereupon received on the 8th of April a reply, dated on the 15th of the previous month, from which it appears that during the whole interval, whilst the commissioners were receiving assurances calculated to inspire hope of the success of their mission, the Secretary of State and the President of the United States had already determined to hold no intercourse with them whatever; to refuse even to listen to any proposals they had to make, and had profited by the delay created by their own assurances in order to prepare secretly the means for effective hostile operations. That these assurances were given has been virtually confessed by the Government of the United States by its sending a messenger to Charleston to give notice of its purpose to use force if opposed in its intention of supplying Fort Sumter. No more striking proof of the absence of good faith in the conduct of the Government of the United States toward this Confederacy can be required than is contained in the circumstances which accompanied this notice. According to the usual course of navigation the vessels composing the expedition designed for the relief of Fort Sumter might be expected to reach Charleston Harbor on the 9th of April. Yet, with our commissioners actually in Washington, detained under assurances that notice should be given of any military movement, the notice was not addressed to *them*, but a messenger was sent to Charleston to give the notice to the Governor of South Carolina, and the notice was so given at a late hour on the 8th of April, the eve of the very day on which the fleet might be expected to arrive.

That this maneuver failed in its purpose was not the fault of those who contrived it. A heavy tempest delayed the arrival of the expedition and gave time to the commander of our forces at Charleston to ask and receive the instructions of this Government. Even then, under all the provocation incident to the contemptuous refusal to listen to our commissioners, and the tortuous course of the Government of the United States, I was sincerely anxious to avoid the effusion of blood, and directed a proposal to be made to the commander of Fort Sumter, who had avowed himself to be nearly out of provisions, that we would abstain from directing our fire on Fort Sumter if he would promise not to open fire on our forces unless first attacked. This proposal was refused and the conclusion was reached that the design of the United States was to place the besieging force at Charleston between the simultaneous fire of the fleet and the fort. There remained, therefore, no alternative but to direct that the fort should at once be reduced. This order was executed by General Beauregard with the skill and success which were naturally to be expected from the well-known character of that gallant officer; and although the bombardment lasted but thirty-three hours our flag did not wave over its battered walls until after the appearance of the hostile fleet off Charleston. Fortunately, not a life was lost on our side, and we were gratified in being spared the necessity of a useless effusion of blood, by the prudent caution of the officers who commanded the fleet in abstaining from the evidently futile effort to enter the harbor for the relief of Major Anderson.

I refer to the report of the Secretary of War, and the papers which accompany it, for further details of this brilliant affair. In this connection I cannot refrain from a well-deserved tribute to the noble State, the eminent soldierly qualities of whose people were so conspicuously displayed in the port of Charleston. For months they had been irritated by the spectacle of a fortress held within their principal harbor as a standing menace against their peace and independence. Built in part with their own money, its custody confided with their own consent to an agent who held no power over them other than such as they had themselves delegated for their own benefit, intended to be used by that agent for their own protection against foreign attack, they saw it held with persistent tenacity as a means of offense against them by the very Government which they had established for their protection. They had beleaguered it for months, felt entire confidence in their power to capture it, yet yielded to the requirements of discipline, curbed their impatience, submitted without complaint to the unaccustomed hardships, labors, and privations of a protracted siege; and when at length their patience was rewarded by the signal for attack, and success had crowned their steady and gallant conduct, even in the very moment of triumph they evinced a chivalrous regard for the feelings of the brave but unfortunate officer who had been compelled to lower his flag. All manifestations of exultation were checked in his presence. Their commanding general, with their cordial approval and the consent of his Government, refrained from imposing any terms that could wound the sensibilities of the commander of the fort. He was permitted to retire with the honors of war, to salute his flag, to depart freely with all his command, and was escorted to the vessel in which he embarked with the highest marks of respect from those against whom his guns had been so recently directed.

Not only does every event connected with the siege reflect the highest honor on South Carolina, but the forbearance of her people and of this Government from making any harsh use of a victory obtained under circumstances of such peculiar provocation attest to the fullest extent the absence of any purpose beyond securing their own tranquillity and the sincere desire to avoid the calamities of war. Scarcely had the President of the United States received intelligence of the failure of the scheme which he had devised for the reënforcement of Fort Sumter, when he issued the declaration of war against this Confederacy which has prompted me to convoke you. In this extraordinary production that high functionary affects total ignorance of the existence of an independent Government, which, possessing the entire and enthusiastic devotion of its people, is exercising its functions without question over seven sovereign States, over more than 5,000,000 of people, and over a territory whose area exceeds half a million of square miles. He terms sovereign States "combinations too powerful to be suppressed by the ordinary course of judicial proceedings or by the powers vested in the marshals by law." He calls for an army of 75,000 men to act as a *posse comitatus* in aid of the process of the courts of justice in States where no courts exist whose mandates and decrees are not cheerfully obeyed and respected by a willing people. He avows that "the *first* service to be assigned to the forces called out" will be not to execute the process of courts, but to capture forts and strongholds situated within the admitted limits of this Confederacy and garrisoned by its troops; and declares that "this effort" is intended "to maintain the perpetuity of popular government." He concludes by commanding "the persons composing the combinations aforesaid"—to wit, the 5,000,000 of inhabitants of these States—"to retire peaceably to their respective abodes within twenty days." Apparently contradictory as are the terms of this singular document, one point is unmistakably evident. The President of the United States called for an army of 75,000 men, whose *first* service was to be to capture our forts. It was a plain declaration of war which I was not at liberty to disregard because of my knowledge that under the Constitution of the United States the President was usurping a power granted exclusively to the Congress. He is the sole organ of communication between that country and foreign powers. The law of nations did not permit me to question the authority of the Executive of a foreign nation to declare war against this Confederacy. Although I might have refrained from taking active measures for our defense, if the States of the Union had all imitated the action of Virginia, North Carolina, Arkansas, Kentucky, Tennessee, and Missouri, by denouncing the call for troops as an unconstitutional usurpation of power to which they refused to respond, I was not at liberty to disregard the fact that many of the States seemed quite content to submit to the exercise of the power assumed by the President of the United States, and were actively engaged in levying troops to be used for the purpose indicated in the proclamation. Deprived of the aid of Congress at the moment, I was under the necessity of confining my action to a call on the States for volunteers for the common defense, in accordance with the authority you had confided to me before your adjournment. I deemed it proper, further, to issue proclamation inviting application from persons disposed to aid our defense in private armed vessels on the high seas, to the end that preparations might be made for the immediate issue of letters of marque and reprisal which you alone, under the Constitution, have power to grant. I entertain no doubt you will concur with me in the opinion that in the absence of a fleet of public vessels it will be eminently expedient to supply their place by private armed vessels, so happily styled by the publicists of the United States "the militia of the sea," and so often and justly relied on by them as an efficient and admirable instrument of defensive warfare. I earnestly recommend the immediate passage of a law authorizing me to accept the numerous proposals already received. I cannot close this review of the acts of the Government of the United States without referring to a proclamation issued by their President, under date of the 19th instant, in which, after declaring that an insurrection has broken out in this Confederacy against the Government of the United States, he announces a blockade of all the ports of these States, and threatens to punish as pirates all persons who shall molest any vessel of the United States under letters of marque issued by this Government. Notwithstanding the authenticity of this proclamation you will concur with me that it is hard to believe it could have emanated from a President of the United States. Its announcement of a mere paper blockade is so manifestly a violation of the law of nations that it would seem incredible that it could have been issued by authority; but conceding this to be the case so far as the Executive is concerned, it will be difficult to satisfy the people of these States that their late confederates will sanction its declarations—will determine to ignore the usages of civilized nations, and will inaugurate a war of extermination on both sides by treating as pirates open enemies acting under the authority of commissions issued by an organized government. If such proclamation was issued, it could only have been published under the sudden influence of passion, and we may rest assured mankind will be spared the horrors of the conflict it seems to invite.

For the details of the administration of the different Departments I refer to the reports of the Secretaries, which accompany this message.

The State Department has furnished the necessary instructions for three commissioners who have been sent to England, France, Russia, and Belgium since your adjournment to ask our recognition as a member of the family of nations, and to make with each of those powers treaties of amity and commerce. Further steps will be taken to enter into like negotiations with the other European powers, in pursuance of your resolutions passed at the last session. Sufficient time has not yet elapsed since the departure of these commissioners for the receipt of any intelligence from them. As I deem it desirable that commissioners or other diplomatic agents should also be sent at an early period to the independent American powers south of our Confederacy, with all of whom it is our interest and earnest wish to maintain the most cordial and friendly relations, I suggest the expediency of making the necessary appropriations for that purpose. Having been officially notified by the public authorities of the State of Virginia that she had withdrawn from the Union and desired to maintain the closest political relations with us which it was possible at this time to establish, I commissioned the Hon. Alexander H. Stephens, Vice President of the Confederate States, to represent this Government at Richmond. I am happy to inform you that he has concluded a convention with the State of Virginia by which that honored Commonwealth, so long and justly distinguished among her sister States, and so dear to the hearts of thousands of her children in the Confederate States, has united her power and her fortunes with ours and become one of us. This convention, together with the ordinance of Virginia adopting the Provisional Constitution of the Confederacy, will be laid before you for your constitutional action. I have satisfactory assurances from other of our late confederates that they are on the point of adopting similar measures, and I cannot doubt that ere you shall have been many weeks in session the whole of the slaveholding States of the late Union will respond to the call of honor and affection, and by uniting their fortunes with ours promote our common interests and secure our common safety.

In the Treasury Department regulations have been devised

and put into execution for carrying out the policy indicated in your legislation on the subject of the navigation of the Mississippi River, as well as for the collection of revenue on the frontier. Free transit has been secured for vessels and merchandise passing through the Confederate States; and delay and inconvenience have been avoided as far as possible, in organizing the revenue service for the various railways entering our territory. As fast as experience shall indicate the possibility of improvement in these regulations no effort will be spared to free commerce from all unnecessary embarrassments and obstructions. Under your act authorizing a loan, proposals were issued inviting subscriptions for $5,000,000, and the call was answered by the prompt subscription of more than $8,000,000 by our own citizens, and not a single bid was made under par. The rapid development of the purpose of the President of the United States to invade our soil, capture our forts, blockade our ports, and wage war against us induced me to direct that the entire subscription should be accepted. It will now become necessary to raise means to a much larger amount to defray the expenses of maintaining our independence and repelling invasion. I invite your special attention to this subject, and the financial condition of the Government, with the suggestion of ways and means for the supply of the Treasury, will be presented to you in a separate communication.

To the Department of Justice you have confided not only the organization and supervision of all matters connected with the courts of justice, but also those connected with patents and with the bureau of public printing. Since your adjournment all the courts, with the exception of those of Mississippi and Texas, have been organized by the appointment of marshals and district attorneys and are now prepared for the exercise of their functions. In the two States just named the gentlemen confirmed as judges declined to accept the appointment, and no nominations have yet been made to fill the vacancies. I refer you to the report of the Attorney-General and concur in his recommendation for immediate legislation, especially on the subject of patent rights. Early provision should be made to secure to the subjects of foreign nations the full enjoyment of their property in valuable inventions, and to extend to our own citizens protection, not only for their own inventions, but for such as may have been assigned to them or may hereafter be assigned by persons not alien enemies. The Patent Office business is much more extensive and important than had been anticipated. The applications for patents, although confined under the law exclusively to citizens of our Confederacy, already average seventy per month, showing the necessity for the prompt organization of a bureau of patents.

The Secretary of War in his report and accompanying documents conveys full information concerning the forces—regular, volunteer, and provisional—raised and called for under the several acts of Congress—their organization and distribution; also an account of the expenditures already made, and the further estimates for the fiscal year ending the 18th of February, 1862, rendered necessary by recent events. I refer to his report also for a full history of the occurrences in Charleston Harbor prior to and including the bombardment and reduction of Fort Sumter, and of the measures subsequently taken for the common defense on receiving the intelligence of the declaration of war against us, made by the President of the United States. There are now in the field at Charleston, Pensacola, Forts Morgan, Jackson, Saint Philip, and Pulaski 19,000 men, and 16,000 are now *en route* for Virginia. It is proposed to organize and hold in readiness for instant action, in view of the present exigencies of the country, an army of 100,000 men. If further force should be needed, the wisdom and patriotism of Congress will be confidently appealed to for authority to call into the field additional numbers of our noble-spirited volunteers who are constantly tendering service far in excess of our wants.

The operations of the Navy Department have been necessarily restricted by the fact that sufficient time has not yet elapsed for the purchase or construction of more than a limited number of vessels adapted to the public service. Two vessels purchased have been named the Sumter and McRae, and are now being prepared for sea at New Orleans with all possible dispatch. Contracts have also been made at that city with two different establishments for the casting of ordnance—cannon shot and shell—with the view to encourage the manufacture of these articles, so indispensable for our defense, at as many points within our territory as possible. I call your attention to the recommendation of the Secretary for the establishment of a magazine and laboratory for preparation of ordnance stores and the necessary appropriation for that purpose. Hitherto such stores have usually been prepared at the navy yards, and no appropriation was made at your last session for this object. The Secretary also calls attention to the fact that no provision has been made for the payment of invalid pensions to our own citizens. Many of these persons are advanced in life; they have no means of support, and by the secession of these States have been deprived of their claim against the Government of the United States. I recommend the appropriation of the sum necessary to pay these pensioners, as well as those of the Army, whose claims can scarcely exceed $70,000 per annum.

The Postmaster General has already succeeded in organizing his Department to such an extent as to be in readiness to assume the direction of our postal affairs on the occurrence of the contingency contemplated by the act of March 15, 1861, or even sooner if desired by Congress. The various books and circulars have been prepared and measures taken to secure supplies of blanks, postage stamps, stamped envelopes, mail bags, locks, keys, etc. He presents a detailed classification and arrangement of his clerical force, and asks for its increase. An auditor of the Treasury for this Department is necessary, and a plan is submitted for the organization of his bureau. The great number and magnitude of the accounts of this Department require an increase of the clerical force in the accounting branch in the Treasury. The revenues of this Department are collected and disbursed in modes peculiar to itself, and require a special bureau to secure a proper accountability in the administration of its finances. I call your attention to the additional legislation required for this Department; to the recommendation for changes in the law fixing the rates of postage on newspapers, periodicals, and sealed packages of certain kinds, and specially to the recommendation of the Secretary, in which I concur, that you provide at once for the assumption by him of the control of our entire postal service.

In the military organization of the States provision is made for brigadier and major generals, but in the Army of the Confederate States the highest grade is that of brigadier general. Hence it will no doubt sometimes occur that where troops of the Confederacy do duty with the militia, the general selected for the command and possessed of the views and purposes of this Government will be superseded by an officer of the militia not having the same advantages. To avoid this contingency in the least objectionable manner I recommend that additional rank be given to the general of the Confederate Army, and concurring in the policy of having but one grade of generals in the Army of the Confederacy, I recommend that the law of its organization be amended so that the grade be that of general. To secure a thorough military education it is deemed essential that officers should enter upon the study of their profession at an early period of life and have elementary instruction in a military school. Until such school shall be established it is recommended that cadets be appointed and attached to companies until they shall have attained the age and have acquired the knowledge to fit them for the duties of lieutenants. I also call your attention to an omission in the law organizing the Army, in relation to military chaplains, and recommend that provision be made for their appointment.

In conclusion, I congratulate you on the fact that in every portion of our country there has been exhibited the most patriotic devotion to our common cause. Transportation companies have freely tendered the use of their lines for troops and supplies. The presidents of the railroads of the Confederacy, in company with others who control lines of communication with States that we hope soon to greet as sisters, assembled in convention in this city, and not only reduced largely the rates heretofore demanded for mail service and conveyance of troops and munitions, but voluntarily proffered to receive their compensation, at these reduced rates, in the bonds of the Confederacy, for the purpose of leaving all the resources of the Government at its disposal for the common defense. Requisitions for troops have been met with such alacrity that the numbers tendering their services have in every instance greatly exceeded the demand. Men of the highest official and social position are serving as volunteers in the ranks. The gravity of age and the zeal of youth rival each other in the desire to be foremost for the public defense; and though at no other point than the one heretofore noticed have they been stimulated by the excitement incident to actual engagement and the hope of distinction for individual achievement, they have borne what for new troops is the most severe ordeal—patient toil and constant vigil, and all the exposure and discomfort of active service, with a resolution and fortitude such as to command approbation and justify the highest expectation of their conduct when active valor shall be required in place of steady endurance. A people thus united and resolved cannot shrink from any sacrifice which they may be called on to make, nor can there be a reasonable doubt of their final success, however long and severe may be the test of their determination to maintain their birthright of freedom and equality as a trust which it is their first duty to transmit undiminished to their posterity. A bounteous Providence cheers us with the promise of abundant crops. The fields of grain which will within a few weeks be ready for the sickle give assurance of the amplest supply of food for man; whilst the corn, cotton, and other staple productions of our soil afford abundant proof that up to this period the season has been propitious. We feel that our cause is just and holy; we protest solemnly in the face of mankind that we desire peace at any sacrifice save that of honor and independence; we seek no conquest, no aggrandizement, no concession of any kind from the States with which we were lately confederated; all we ask is to be let alone; that those who never held power over us shall not now attempt our subjugation by arms. This we will, this we must, resist to the direst extremity. The moment that this pretension is abandoned the sword will drop from our grasp, and we shall be ready to enter into treaties of amity and commerce that cannot but be mutually beneficial. So long as this pretension is maintained, with a firm reliance on that Divine Power which covers with its protection the just cause, we will continue to struggle for our inherent right to freedom, independence, and self-government.

JEFFERSON DAVIS.

"STRIKE DOWN SLAVERY ITSELF": MAY 1861
Frederick Douglass: How to End the War

May 1861

Up until the outbreak of hostilities Douglass worried that the North would resolve the secession crisis by offering new concessions regarding slavery. Once the war began he used his *Monthly* to advocate that it be waged radically, by enlisting black soldiers and making the destruction of slavery an essential aim.

To OUR mind, there is but one easy, short and effectual way to suppress and put down the desolating war which the slaveholders and their rebel minions are now waging against the American Government and its loyal citizens. Fire must be met with water, darkness with light, and war for the destruction of liberty must be met with war for the destruction of slavery. *The simple way, then, to put an end to the savage and desolating war now waged by the slaveholders, is to strike down slavery itself*, the primal cause of that war.

Freedom to the slave should now be proclaimed from the Capitol, and should be seen above the smoke and fire of every battle field, waving from every loyal flag! The time for mild measures is past. They are pearls cast before swine, and only increase and aggravate the crime which they would conciliate and repress. The weak point must be found, and when found should be struck with the utmost vigor. Any war is a calamity; but a peace that can only breed war is a far greater calamity. A long and tame war, waged without aim or spirit, paralyzes business, arrests the wheels of civilization, benumbs the national feeling, corrodes the national heart, and diffuses its baleful influence universally. Sharp, quick, wise, strong and sudden, are the elements for the occasion. The sooner this rebellion is put out of its misery, the better for all concerned. A lenient war is a lengthy war, and therefore the worst kind of war. Let us stop it, and stop it effectually—stop it before its evils are diffused throughout the Northern States—stop it on the soil upon which it originated, and among the traitors and rebels who originated the war. This can be done at once, by *"carrying the war into Africa." Let the slaves and free colored people be called into service, and formed into a liberating army*, to march into the South and raise the banner of Emancipation among the slaves. The South having brought revolution and war upon the country, and having elected and consented to play at that fearful game, she has no right to complain if some good as well as calamity shall result from her own act and deed.

The slaveholders have not hesitated to employ the sable arms of the Negroes at the South in erecting the fortifications which silenced the guns of Fort Sumter, and brought the star-spangled banner to the dust. They often boast, and not without cause, that their Negroes will fight for them against the North. They have no scruples against employing the Negroes to exterminate freedom, and in overturning the Government. They work with spade and barrow with them, and they will stand with them on the field of battle, shoulder to shoulder, with guns in their hands, to shoot down the troops of the U. S. Government.—They have neither pride, prejudice nor *pity* to restrain them from employing Negroes *against white men, where slavery is to be protected and made secure.* Oh! that this Government would only now be as true to liberty as the rebels, who are attempting to batter it down, are true to slavery. We have no hesitation in saying that ten thousand black soldiers might be raised in the next thirty days to march upon the South. One black regiment alone would be, in such a war, the full equal of two white ones. The very fact of color in this case would be more terrible than powder and balls. The slaves would learn more as to the nature of the conflict from the presence of one such regiment, than from a thousand preachers. Every consideration of justice, humanity and sound policy confirms the wisdom of calling upon black men just now to take up arms in behalf of their country.

We are often asked by persons in the street as well as by letter, what our people will do in the present solemn crisis in the affairs of the country. Our answer is, would to God you would let us do something! We lack nothing but your consent.

We are ready and would go, counting ourselves happy in being permitted to serve and suffer for the cause of freedom and free institutions. But you won't let us go. Read the heart-rending account we publish elsewhere of the treatment received by the brave fellows, who broke away from their chains and went through marvelous suffering to defend Fort Pickens against the rebels.—They were instantly seized and put in irons and returned to their guilty masters to be whipped to death! Witness Gen. Butler's offer to put down the slave insurrection in the State of Maryland. The colored citizens of Boston have offered their services to the Government, and were refused. There is, even now, while the slaveholders are marshaling armed Negroes against the Government, covering the ocean with pirates, destroying innocent lives, to sweep down the commerce of the country, tearing up railways, burning bridges to prevent the march of Government troops to the defence of its capital, exciting mobs to stone the Yankee soldiers; there is still, we say, weak and contemptible tenderness towards the blood thirsty, slaveholding traitors, by the Government and people of the country. Until the nation shall repent of this weakness and folly, until they shall make the cause of their country the cause of freedom, until they shall strike down slavery, the source and center of this gigantic rebellion, they don't deserve the support of a single sable arm, nor will it succeed in crushing the cause of our present troubles.

NEW YORK, SPRING 1861

Walt Whitman: First O Songs for a Prelude

In the spring of 1861 Walt Whitman was working as a freelance journalist in New York. He watched as a series of newly-formed Union regiments paraded through the city, part of what Whitman would later describe as the "volcanic upheaval of the nation, after that firing on the flag at Charleston, . . . the grandest and most encouraging spectacle yet vouchsafed in any age, old or new, to democracy." This poem was first published in *Drum-Taps* in 1865.

FIRST O songs for a prelude,
Lightly strike on the stretch'd tympanum pride and joy in my city,
How she led the rest to arms, how she gave the cue,
How at once with lithe limbs unwaiting a moment she sprang,
(O superb! O Manhattan, my own, my peerless!
O strongest you in the hour of danger, in crisis! O truer than steel!)
How you sprang—how you threw off the costumes of peace with indifferent hand,
How your soft opera-music changed, and the drum and fife were heard in their stead,
How you led to the war, (that shall serve for our prelude, songs of soldiers,)
How Manhattan drum-taps led.

Forty years had I in my city seen soldiers parading,
Forty years as a pageant, till unawares the lady of this teeming and turbulent city,
Sleepless amid her ships, her houses, her incalculable wealth,
With her million children around her, suddenly,
At dead of night, at news from the south,
Incens'd struck with clinch'd hand the pavement.

SPRING 1861

A shock electric, the night sustain'd it,
Till with ominous hum our hive at daybreak pour'd out its myriads.

From the houses then and the workshops, and through all the doorways,
Leapt they tumultuous, and lo! Manhattan arming.

To the drum-taps prompt,
The young men falling in and arming,
The mechanics arming, (the trowel, the jack-plane, the blacksmith's hammer, tost aside with precipitation,)
The lawyer leaving his office and arming, the judge leaving the court,
The driver deserting his wagon in the street, jumping down, throwing the reins abruptly down on the horses' backs,
The salesman leaving the store, the boss, book-keeper, porter, all leaving;
Squads gather everywhere by common consent and arm,
The new recruits, even boys, the old men show them how to wear their accoutrements, they buckle the straps carefully,
Outdoors arming, indoors arming, the flash of the musket-barrels,
The white tents cluster in camps, the arm'd sentries around, the sunrise cannon and again at sunset,
Arm'd regiments arrive every day, pass through the city, and embark from the wharves,
(How good they look as they tramp down to the river, sweaty, with their guns on their shoulders!
How I love them! how I could hug them, with their brown faces and their clothes and knapsacks cover'd with dust!)
The blood of the city up—arm'd! arm'd! the cry everywhere,
The flags flung out from the steeples of churches and from all the public buildings and stores,
The tearful parting, the mother kisses her son, the son kisses his mother,
(Loth is the mother to part, yet not a word does she speak to detain him,)

The tumultuous escort, the ranks of policemen preceding,
    clearing the way,
The unpent enthusiasm, the wild cheers of the crowd for
    their favorites,
The artillery, the silent cannons bright as gold, drawn along,
    rumble lightly over the stones,
(Silent cannons, soon to cease your silence,
Soon unlimber'd to begin the red business;)
All the mutter of preparation, all the determin'd arming,
The hospital service, the lint, bandages and medicines,
The women volunteering for nurses, the work begun for in
    earnest, no mere parade now;
War! an arm'd race is advancing! the welcome for battle, no
    turning away;
War! be it weeks, months, or years, an arm'd race is advancing
    to welcome it.

Mannahatta a-march—and it's O to sing it well!
It's O for a manly life in the camp.

And the sturdy artillery,
The guns bright as gold, the work for giants, to serve well the
    guns,
Unlimber them! (no more as the past forty years for salutes
    for courtesies merely,
Put in something now besides powder and wadding.)

And you lady of ships, you Mannahatta,
Old matron of this proud, friendly, turbulent city,
Often in peace and wealth you were pensive or covertly
    frown'd amid all your children,
But now you smile with joy exulting old Mannahatta.

A STRATEGIC PLAN: MAY 1861
Winfield Scott to George B. McClellan

A hero of the War of 1812 and the U.S.-Mexican War, Winfield Scott had served as general-in-chief of the army since 1841. He outlined his grand strategy for defeating the Confederacy in a letter to George B. McClellan, who at the time commanded the Ohio militia. When Scott's proposal was made public, it became popularly known as the "Anaconda Plan" because it sought to constrict the Confederacy by blockade.

HEADQUARTERS OF THE ARMY,
Washington, May 3, 1861.
Maj. Gen. GEORGE B. MCCLELLAN,
Commanding Ohio Volunteers, Cincinnati, Ohio:
SIR: I have read and carefully considered your plan for a campaign, and now send you confidentially my own views, supported by certain facts of which you should be advised.

First. It is the design of the Government to raise 25,000 additional regular troops, and 60,000 volunteers for three years. It will be inexpedient either to rely on the three-months' volunteers for extensive operations or to put in their hands the best class of arms we have in store. The term of service would expire by the commencement of a regular campaign, and the arms not lost be returned mostly in a damaged condition. Hence I must strongly urge upon you to confine yourself strictly to the quota of three-months' men called for by the War Department.

Second. We rely greatly on the sure operation of a complete blockade of the Atlantic and Gulf ports soon to commence. In connection with such blockade we propose a powerful movement down the Mississippi to the ocean, with a cordon of posts at proper points, and the capture of Forts Jackson and Saint Philip; the object being to clear out and keep open this great line of communication in connection with the strict blockade of the sea-board, so as to envelop the insurgent

States and bring them to terms with less bloodshed than by any other plan. I suppose there will be needed from twelve to twenty steam gun-boats, and a sufficient number of steam transports (say forty) to carry all the personnel (say 60,000 men) and material of the expedition; most of the gun-boats to be in advance to open the way, and the remainder to follow and protect the rear of the expedition, &c. This army, in which it is not improbable you may be invited to take an important part, should be composed of our best regulars for the advance and of three-years' volunteers, all well officered, and with four months and a half of instruction in camps prior to (say) November 10. In the progress down the river all the enemy's batteries on its banks we of course would turn and capture, leaving a sufficient number of posts with complete garrisons to keep the river open behind the expedition. Finally, it will be necessary that New Orleans should be strongly occupied and securely held until the present difficulties are composed.

Third. A word now as to the greatest obstacle in the way of this plan—the great danger now pressing upon us—the impatience of our patriotic and loyal Union friends. They will urge instant and vigorous action, regardless, I fear, of consequences—that is, unwilling to wait for the slow instruction of (say) twelve or fifteen camps, for the rise of rivers, and the return of frosts to kill the virus of malignant fevers below Memphis. I fear this; but impress right views, on every proper occasion, upon the brave men who are hastening to the support of their Government. Lose no time, while necessary preparations for the great expedition are in progress, in organizing, drilling, and disciplining your three-months' men, many of whom, it is hoped, will be ultimately found enrolled under the call for three-years' volunteers. Should an urgent and immediate occasion arise meantime for their services, they will be the more effective. I commend these views to your consideration, and shall be happy to hear the result.

With great respect, yours, truly,

WINFIELD SCOTT.

LIFE IN ARMY CAMP: MICHIGAN, MAY 1861

Charles B. Haydon: Diary, May 3–12, 1861

A law clerk from Kalamazoo, Charles B. Haydon enlisted in the local militia on April 22, 1861, and soon became a sergeant in Company I, 2nd Michigan Infantry. In his diary he recorded his experiences at an encampment outside Detroit.

MAY 3   Sergt. Ford & self quartered with the men last night. We had a straw bed & each a blanket & a shawl so that we were warm enough & slept well, but Ford complains considerably. Nearly all the men have bad colds & 3 are sick. The duties of the day commenced at 5 by washing at the pump &c. The day like the latter part of yesterday is cold & disagreeable with fair prospect of another storm which would make the parade ground impassable. I acted as second Sergt. this P.M. & was sharply berated by the Col. for not knowing my business. I very soon learned it however & shall not be caught again on that point. We are becoming more accustomed to camp life &c. Still there is some grumbling amg the men. Those who are living better now than they ever lived before grumble most in many cases. Such are always first to complain when they are away from home.

MAY 4   We had to day the first fine day of camp life. The weather was really comfortable. We could lounge in the sun. I could laugh as heartily to day to hear the Col. blow up others as they did yesterday at my berating. I had the satisfaction of seeing Lieut. Dake on the full run several times (a rare sight). The Capt. did not fare much better.

MAY 5   Sunday. Corpl. Ball & self went up to Ft. Wayne after breakfast to see how the other Regt. was faring. We had a fine ride up & back on a steam boat & saw the fort & men &c. We returned to a late dinner. At 3 P.M. we mustered 18 men in our Co. to march to religious services. We march before breakfast for one hour & after church we drilled 2 hrs. They were busy drilling at the Ft.

We are now quite comfortable & used to camp life. I am surprised to see how quick I came into it. Capt. C. S. May says we shall never know anything again except facing, flanking, filing, marching &c &c. I think he is to some extent correct. I can easily see that if we remain here 6 or 8 weeks it will be dull beyond all description. If we are to remain here for three months I shall be very sorry that I enlisted. I came because I thought we were needed & if we are I shall be well content.

We got news yesterday that one man who enlisted in our Co. at Kalamazoo was dead. His name was Henry Carrier—a good stout boy—he was taken sick the day before we started & died soon after. This is the first death in our Co. & I believe the first in the Regt. There are several on the sick list.

MAY 6 Some rain last night, weather fair this morning. If the men pursue the enemy as vigorously as they do the whores they will make very efficient soldiers.

A smart rain P.M. We were to day examined & took the oath of alligiance to the State. The examination was not rigid, & none were rejected on acct of physical incapacity. Abt a doz. spare men had to be thrown out & will very reluctantly (most of them) go. Some will return home & others will enter other companies of this Regt. to supply the place of those who have been thrown out or have deserted. Many enlisted hastily & from some Co's., especially the Adrian Guards, desertions have been frequent. Till to day the stay of all was merely voluntary, henceforth it will be compulsory. An opportunity was given before taking the oath by our Co. for any who desired to withdraw. Only one went & he (Dennis Stockwell) among abundant groans & hisses from the Co. He returned before the oath & would have come in again if he had been permitted.

Camp life is not much different from what I expected. Card playing, profanity & the stealing of provisions are among the most noted characteristics outside of the duties. There are 4 Co's. of us quartered together, 2 from Kalamazoo, the East Saginaw Guards, & Constantine Union Guards. I noticed at one time this P.M. 15 4-hand games of euchre going on at the same time. No gambling is allowed in camp & strong measures are taken to prevent stealing.

I have not as yet regretted that I enlisted. I went from a sense of duty & I expect that to sustain me in the hardships which I may be called to endure. Only one thing troubles me seriously. That is to get up at 5 A.M. & drill at double quick time before breakfast.

MAY 7   Rain A.M. light. I have been on the go pretty briskly for two days, acting as second & sometimes as first Sergt. owing to the sickness or absence of the other. The battalion drill makes busy work for a new guide & for one who is the only file closer for a large part of the time. The rascals steal everything they can put hands on—stole Ford's shawl (an important part of our bed clothes) to day.

It is reported that we cannot go into service unless we enlist for three years or during the war. I should very much dislike 3 years & I also very much dislike to return without doing anything. If it was not for business I would not hesitate for a moment. After all we can do little while the war continues & we should do all we can to aid the vigorous measures which the Administration is taking.

MAY 8   I am to day Sergt. of the Guard & I find it dull business. It will probably be duller yet before 10 A.M. to morrow. We are out in all abt 26 hours—2 hours on & 4 off. This is the first time I have been on. There is something exceeding solitary in the looks of a sentinel placing slowly up & down in stillness of the night. The weather is fine & we shall have a good night.

The morals of camp life are bad & manners likewise. It is doubtful whether the effect which war has upon the morals of a people is not more to be regretted than its more ostensible evils. I believe I have kept on abt as usual. This open air life will be good for me I think. It seems like old times to be out doors all day.

MAY 9   Morning watch 6 A.M. We passed the night, which was a fine one, in comparative quiet. The Corporals Guard was called for but twice during my watches. The first time my Corpl., a very worthy German, ran without the countersign & was himself arrested & sent to the guard house. I laughed heartily at the joke on the Corpl. I slept well abt 3 hours. My head aches a little & I feel dull & tired this morning. This standing guard is the most tiresome service I have. I believe I would rather march all the time. We were finally relieved abt 11 A.M. after abt 27 hours duty. I have not felt quite as well as usual to day. I have a sour stomach & a tendency toward looseness of the bowels. I do nothing for it save to stop eating.

MAY 10 It rains hard this morning & I am not sorry I can assure on any account save the condition of the grounds. I feel better this m'g but am not yet entirely well. Nearly all the men have diarhea & several are in the hospital quite sick. This is caused by the indiscretion of the men & by the quality of the food. Our victuals are cooked & served out by a contractor at one of the Fair buildings. The quantity is ample & the quality before cooking is good enough. There is a good deal of dirt mixed with it when we get it & some of it comes in very bad shape. The butter is bad & I eat very little of it. We have soup for dinner, made I presume from the fragments of breakfast. I think this soup is one of the principal causes of sickness. The potatoes are of poor quality. The bread thank God is good. We have in addition fresh & salt beef & pork. The provisions would be ample if well served. We have also tea, coffee, sugar & sometimes milk.

It is certain that this Regt. will not be recd for 3 months. We must enlist for 3 yrs during the war unless sooner discharged. I have not yet positively decided to do that. The Co. will stand abt half & half. If I had poorer prospects at home or a better place here I would not hesitate.

Our grounds will be all afloat by night. I wish the state could find dry land enough for us to camp. I would rather sleep in the open air than be quartered in the mud. I fear we shall all be sick when warm weather comes. The boys behaved rather bad in some cases yesterday. The guard house was pretty well filled & one came near being flogged.

MAY 11 It rained nearly all day yesterday & we had no drill except a private one for a few who saw fit to take part in it. I went to town once & spent the balance of the day in studying Hardee &c. This m'g is fine but the grounds are very bad. We have drilled but little to day owing to the state of the ground.

There is a good deal of reluctance to enlist for the war or three years. There are all manner of doubts & excuses raised. I can not wonder very much at it. A step which involves the possibility of 3 yrs in the army is a pretty serious one for most men.

I have pretty much decided to go. It seems to me that I cannot honorably do otherwise. I should very much dislike to return to Kalamazoo in this juncture of affairs.

There is a general laxity of discipline in the camp partly because of 2 days idleness & partly because many of the men expect soon to be discharged & having no prospect of fighting before them care very little whether they do anything or not. There was some disturbance last night at the other building. Several were sent to the Guard House & pistols were freely drawn but none fired. A new made acquaintance of mine, 3d Sergt. of the Hudson Guards, is on trial by a Court Martial to day in consequence. We have no uniform as yet & shall soon be a very ragged Regt. if we do not get it.

MAY 12 Sunday. A fine day, no drilling. Dissatisfaction among some Co's. because the uniform has not been furnished. Meetings were held last night & strong indignation expressed & resolutions passed not to drill after Monday noon if they were not supplied. The consequence is that the men who were foremost in them have gone to the Guard House. Capt. C. S. May has trouble with his Co. He will not be well liked.

Our Capt. was found fault with yesterday for the first time. There is a general outcry agt officers. It is without just cause. Many of the men seem to think they should never be spoken to unless the remarks are prefaced by some words of deferential politeness. Will the gentlemen who comprise the first platoon have the kindness to march forward, or will they please to halt, &c is abt what some of them seem to expect. An officer would need 3 yrs under a French dancing master before he could satisfy them.

I wanted to go to town to day to bathe & be shaved but they refuse to let us out. It surprises me to see how quickly I have fallen into this mode of life. I feel little more uneasiness or inconvenience than if I had been bred to it from youth. I have hardly a thought abt law. I eat, drink, sleep, drill & study Hardee's Tactics as much of course as if I knew no other business. I think I must have been intended for a soldier. If I were but Lieut. instead of 3d Sergt. I should be better satisfied than at present. My pay is very small. I have however money enough for the present.

The boys will upset the table before many days I think. The contractor gets over $3.25 per week for our board & might give better. I bought a pie & some cakes of a peddler this m'g & filled up for once.

We succeeded in getting out about 25 men to church to day. Many of them absolutely refused to go. We must have more discipline or we shall have nothing.

PREDICTING A SHORT WAR: MAY 1861

Ulysses S. Grant to Jesse Root Grant

On April 29 Grant became military aide to Illinois governor Richard Yates. He wrote to his father a week later.

Camp Yates, near Springfield
May 6th 1861

DEAR FATHER;

Your second letter, dated the 1st of May has just come to hand. I commenced writing you a letter three or four days ago but was interrupted so often that I did not finish it. I wrote one to Mary which no doubt was duly recieved but do not rember whether it answers your questions or not.

At the time our first Galena company was raised I did not feel at liberty to engage in hot haste, but took an active interest in drilling them and emparting all the instruction I could, and at the request of the members of the company, and of Mr. Washburn, I come here for the purpose of assisting for a short time in camp, and, if necessary, my services for the War. The next two days after my arrival it was rainy and muddy so that the troops could not drill and I concluded to go home. Governer Yates heard it and requested me to remain. Since that I have been acting in that capacity, and for the last few days have been in command of this camp. The last of the six Regiments called for from this state will probably leave by to-morrow, or the day following, and then I shall be relieved from this command.

The Legislature of this state provided for the raising of Eleven additional Regiments and a Battalion of Artillery, and a portion of these the Governer will appoint me to muster into the service of the State, when I presume my services may end. I might have got the Colonelcy of a Regiment possibly, but I was perfectly sickened at the political wire pulling for all these commissions and would not engage in it. I shall be no ways backward in offering my services when and where they are required, but I feel that I have done more now than I could do serving as a Capt. under a green Colonel, and if this thing continues they will want more men at a later day.—

There has been full 30,000 more volunteers offered their services than can be accepted under the present call, without including the call made by the state; but I can go back to Galena and drill the three or four companies there and render them efficient for any future call.—My own opinion is that this War will be but of short duration. The Administration has acted moste prudently and sagaciously so far in not bringing on a conflict before it had its forces fully martialed. When they do strike our thoroughly loyal states will be fully protected and a few decisive victories in some of the southern ports will send the secession army howling and the leaders in the rebelion will flee the country. All the states will then be loyal for a generation to come, negroes will depreciate so rapidly in value that no body will want to own them and their masters will be the loudest in their declaimations against the institution in a political and economic view. The nigger will never disturb this country again. The worst that is to be apprehended from him is now; he may revolt and cause more destruction than any Northern man, except it be the ultra abolitionest, wants to see. A Northern army may be required in the next ninety days to go south to suppress a negro insurrection. As much as the South have vilified the North they would go on such a mission and with the purest motives.

I have just recieved a letter from Julia. All are well. Julia takes a very sensible vue of our present difficulties. She would be sorry to have me go but thinks the circumstances may warrent it and will not through a single obsticle in the way.

(There is no doubt but the *valiant* Pillow has been planning an attac on Cairo, but as he will learn that that point is well Garrisoned and they have their ditch on the out side, filled with watter, he will probably desist. As however he would find it necessary to receive a wound, on the first discharge of fire arms he would not be a formidable enemy. I do not say he would shoot himself, ah no! I am not so uncharitable as many who served under him in Mexico. I think however he might report himself wounded on the receipt of a very slight scratch, recieved hastily in any way and might eritate the sore until he convinced himself that he had been wounded by the enemy.)

Tell Simp. that I hope he will be able to visit us this Summer. I should like very much to have him stay with us and I want him to make my house his home.

Remember me to all.

ULYSSES

LIFE IN THE EXECUTIVE MANSION:
WASHINGTON, D.C., MAY 1861

John Hay: Diary, May 7–10, 1861

Following his election in November 1860, Lincoln hired John Hay, a Brown graduate and nephew of one of his legal colleagues, to assist his secretary John G. Nicolay. In February 1861 Nicolay and Hay accompanied the president-elect from Springfield to Washington, where they lived in the Executive Mansion while serving as Lincoln's principal secretaries.

---

7 MAY 1861, TUESDAY

I went in to give the President some little items of Illinois news, saying among other things that Singleton was behaving very badly. He replied with emphasis that Singleton was a miracle of meanness, calmly looking out of the window at the smoke of the two Navy steamers puffing up the way, resting the end of the telescope on his toes sublime.

I spoke of the proposition of Browning to subjugate the South, establish a black republic in lieu of the exterminated whites, and extend a protectorate over them, while they raised our cotton. He said, Some of our northerners seem bewildered and dazzled by the excitement of the hour. Doolittle seems inclined to think that this war is to result in the entire abolition of Slavery. Old Col. Hamilton a venerable and most respectable gentleman, impresses upon me most earnestly the propriety of enlisting the slaves in our army."

I told him his daily correspondence was thickly interspersed by such suggestions.

"For my own part," he said, "I consider the central idea pervading this struggle is the necessity that is upon us, of proving that popular government is not an absurdity. We must settle this question now, whether in a free government the minority have the right to break up the government whenever they choose. If we fail it will go far to prove the incapability of the people to govern themselves. There may be one consideration used in stay of such final judgement, but that is not for us to use in advance. That is, that there exists in our case, an instance of a vast and far reaching disturbing element, which the history of no other free nation will probably ever present. That however is not for us to say at present. Taking the government as we found it we will see if the majority can preserve it."

He is engaged in constant thought upon his Message: It will be an exhaustive review of the questions of the hour & of the future.

In the Afternoon we went up to see Ellsworth's Zouave Firemen. They are the largest sturdiest and physically the most magnificent men I ever saw collected together. They played over the sward like kittens, lithe and agile in their strength.

Ellsworth has been intensely disgusted at the wild yarns afloat about them which are for the most part, utterly untrue. A few graceless rascals have been caught in various lapses. These are in irons. One horrible story which has been terrifying all the maiden antiques of the city for several days, has the element of horror pretty well eliminated today, by the injured fair, who proves a most yielding seducee, offering to settle the matter for 25 dollars. Other yarns are due to the restless brains of the press-gang.

The youthful Colonel formed his men in a hollow square, and made a great speech at them. There was more commonsense, dramatic power, tact, energy, & that eloquence that naturally flowers into deeds in le petit Colonels fifteen minute harangue, than in all the speeches that stripped the plumes from our unfortunate ensign in the spread eagle days of the Congress that has flitted. He spoke to them as men, made them proud in their good name, spoke bitterly & witheringly of the disgrace of the recreant, contrasted with cutting emphasis which his men delighted in, the enlistment of the dandy regiment for thirty days, with *theirs* for the war—spoke solemnly & impressively of the disgrace of expulsion—roused them to wild enthusiasm by announcing that he had heard of one officer who treated his men with less consideration than himself and that, if on inquiry the rumor proved true, he would strip him & send him home in irons. The men yelled with delight clapped their hands & shouted "Bully for you."
He closed with wonderful tact and dramatic spirit, by saying

"Now laddies, if any one of you wants to go home, he had better sneak around the back alleys, crawl over fences, and get out of sight before we see him." which got them again. He must have run with this crowd some time in his varied career. He knows them and handles them so perfectly.

8 May 1861, Wednesday

Eames called this morning & brought to my notice a singular omission in Jeff. Davis' manifesto, His ignoring all mention of the right of revolution and confining his defense of his position to the reserved constitutional right of a state to secede. By this means he estops his claim upon the recognition of the world. For even those cabinets that acknowledge the necessity of recognizing all governments, which by virtue of revolution have a defacto existence, would most naturally say to a new government basing its claim to nationality on the constitution of the government vs. which it rebels, "We can entertain no such question of legal construction. The contest as stated by you between you and your government is a municipal one. We have no right to interfere or prejudge the issue of such a case of conflicting interpretation." Jeff. Davis seems to have been so anxious to satisfy the restless consciences of the Borderers, that he utterly overlooks the importance of conciliating the good opinion of the outside world. "There is a hole in your best coat Master Davis.

9 May 1861, Thursday

Saw at breakfast this morning a quiet, shrewd looking man with unobtrusive spectacles, doing his devoir to an egg. I was informed that it was Anderson. The North has been strangely generous with that man. The red tape of military duty was all that bound his heart from its traitorous impulses. His Kentucky brigade will be like himself fighting weakly for a Union they scorn.

There was a very fine matinee at the Navy Yard given by some musical members of the 12th New York. They sang well the Band played well and the President listened well. After the programme, the President begged for the Marseillaise. The prime gentleman gave the first verse and then generously repeated it, interpolating nonchalantly "Liberty or Death" in place of "Abreuve nos sillons," which he had forgotten.

Then we went down to the Pensacola and observed the shooting of the great Dahlgren gun Plymouth. Two ricochette shots were sent through the target and one plumper. The splendid course of the 11 inch shell [   ] through 1300 yds of air, the lighting, the quick rebound & flight through the target with wild skips, throwing up a 30 ft column of spray at every jump, the decreasing leaps and the steady roll into the waves were scenes as novel and pleasant to me as to all the rest of the party. The Prest. was delighted. Capt. Gillis was bored at Dahlgren for laughing at the bad firing from the Pocahontas.

This morning Ellsworths Zouaves covered themselves with glory as with a blanket in saving Willard's Hotel and quenching a most ugly looking fire. They are utterly unapproachable in anything they attempt. Their respectful demeanor to their Chief and his anxious solicitude for their comfort & safety are absolutely touching to behold.

10 May 1861, Friday

Carl Schurz loafed into my room this morning & we spoke of the slaves & their ominous discontent. He agreed with me that the Commandants at Pickens & Monroe were unnecessarily squeamish in imprisoning & returning to their masters the fugitives who came to their gates begging to be employed. Their owners are in a state of open rebellion against the government & nothing would bring them to their senses more readily than a gentle reminder that they are dependent upon the good will of the Government for the security of their lives and property. The action would be entirely just and eminently practicable. Schurz says that thousands of Democrats are declaring that now is the time to remove the cause of all our woes. What we could not have done in many lifetimes the madness and folly of the South has accomplished for us. Slavery offers itself more vulnerable to our attack than at any point in any century and the wild malignity of the South is excusing us, before God & the World.

So we talked in the morning.

But tonight I saw a letter from Mrs. Whitman stating that Thomas Earl, T. W. Higginson the essayist of Boston and young John Brown, were "going to free the slaves." What we were dreaming of came over my mind with horrible distinctness and I shrunk from the apparition. This is not the time nor are these the men to do it. They should wait till the government gives some kind of sanction to the work. Otherwise the horrors of the brutal massacre will move the pity of the magnanimous North, and in the suppression of the insurrection the warring sections may fuse and compromise.

FEARING ATTACK IN ALEXANDRIA:
VIRGINIA, MAY 1861

Judith W. McGuire: Diary, May 10, 1861

Judith W. McGuire lived in Alexandria, Virginia, where her husband, John P. McGuire, was rector of the Episcopal High School of Virginia. When Union troops occupied Alexandria on May 24, 1861, the McGuires would flee their home on the school campus and spend the next four years as refugees; the school was turned into a Union army hospital.

May 10.—Since writing last, I have been busy, very busy, arranging and rearranging. We are now hoping that Alexandria will not be a landing-place for the enemy, but that the forts will be attacked. In that case, they would certainly be repulsed, and we could stay quietly at home. To view the progress of events from any point will be sad enough, but it would be more bearable at our own home, and surrounded by our family and friends. With the supposition that we may remain, and that the ladies of the family at least may return to us, I am having the grounds put in order, and they are now so beautiful! Lilacs, crocuses, the lily of the valley, and other spring flowers, are in luxuriant bloom, and the roses in full bud. The greenhouse plants have been removed and grouped on the lawn, verbenas in bright bloom have been transplanted from the *pit* to the borders, and the grass seems unusually green after the late rains; the trees are in full leaf; every thing is so fresh and lovely. "All, save the spirit of man, is divine."

War seems inevitable, and while I am trying to employ the passing hour, a cloud still hangs over us and all that surrounds us. For a long time before our society was so completely broken up, the ladies of Alexandria and all the surrounding country were busily employed sewing for our soldiers. Shirts, pants, jackets, and beds, of the heaviest material, have been made by the most delicate fingers. All ages, all conditions, meet now on one common platform. We must all work for our country.

Our soldiers must be equipped. Our parlor was the rendezvous for our neighborhood, and our sewing-machine was in requisition for weeks. Scissors and needles were plied by all. The daily scene was most animated. The fires of our enthusiasm and patriotism were burning all the while to a degree which might have been consuming, but that our tongues served as safety-valves. Oh, how we worked and talked, and excited each other! One common sentiment animated us all; no doubts, no fears were felt. We all have such entire reliance in the justice of our cause and the valor of our men, and, above all, on the blessing of Heaven! These meetings have necessarily ceased with us, as so few of any age or degree remain at home; but in Alexandria they are still kept up with great interest. We who are left here are trying to give the soldiers who are quartered in town comfort, by carrying them milk, butter, pies, cakes, etc. I went in yesterday to the barracks, with the carriage well filled with such things, and found many young friends quartered there. All are taking up arms; the first young men in the country are the most zealous. Alexandria is doing her duty nobly; so is Fairfax; and so, I hope, is the whole South. We are very weak in resources, but strong in stout hearts, zeal for the cause, and enthusiastic devotion to our beloved South; and while men are making a free-will offering of their life's blood on the altar of their country, women must not be idle. We must do what we can for the comfort of our brave men. We must sew for them, knit for them, nurse the sick, keep up the faint-hearted, give them a word of encouragement in season and out of season. There is much for us to do, and we must do it. The embattled hosts of the North will have the whole world from which to draw their supplies; but if, as it seems but too probable, our ports are blockaded, we shall indeed be dependent on our own exertions, and great must those exertions be.

The Confederate flag waves from several points in Alexandria: from the Marshall House, the Market-house, and the several barracks. The peaceful, quiet old town looks quite warlike. I feel sometimes, when walking on King's street, meeting men in uniform, passing companies of cavalry, hearing martial music, etc., that I must be in a dream. Oh that it were a dream, and that the last ten years of our country's history were blotted out! Some of our old men are a little nervous, look doubtful, and talk of the impotency of the South. Oh, I feel utter scorn for such remarks. We must not admit weakness. Our soldiers do not think of weakness; they know that their hearts are strong, and their hands well skilled in the use of the rifle. Our country boys have been brought up on horseback, and hunting has ever been their holiday sport. Then why shall they feel weak? Their hearts feel strong when they think of the justice of their cause. In that is *our* hope.

Walked down this evening to see Mrs. Johns. The road looked lonely and deserted. Busy life has departed from our midst. We found Mrs. Johns packing up valuables. I have been doing the same; but after they are packed, where are they to be sent? Silver may be buried, but what is to be done with books, pictures, etc.? We have determined, if we are obliged to go from home, to leave every thing in the care of the servants. They have promised to be faithful, and I believe they will be; but my hope becomes stronger and stronger that we may remain here, or may soon return if we go away. Every thing is so sad around us! We went to the Chapel on Sunday as usual, but it was grievous to see the change—the organ mute, the organist gone; the seats of the students of both institutions empty; but one or two members of each family to represent the absentees; the prayer for the President omitted. When Dr. Packard came to it, there was a slight pause, and then he went on to the next prayer—all seemed so strange! Tucker Conrad, one of the few students who is still here, raised the tunes; his voice seemed unusually sweet, because so sad. He was feebly supported by all who were not in tears. There was night service, but it rained, and I was not sorry that I could not go.

RIOTING IN ST. LOUIS: MISSOURI, MAY 1861
William T. Sherman to John Sherman

The outbreak of the war increased tensions between secessionist and unionist factions in Missouri, and Claiborne Jackson, the pro-Confederate governor, began planning the seizure of the federal arsenal in St. Louis. Captain Nathaniel Lyon, the commander of the arsenal garrison, led a force of regular soldiers and German American volunteers against a state militia encampment on the edge of the city on May 10. William T. Sherman, who had become president of a St. Louis street railroad company after he left Louisiana, witnessed the incident.

Office St. Louis R. R. Co.
St. Louis, May 11, 1861

Hon. John Sherman
Dear Brother,
Very imprudently I was a witness of the firing on the People by the U.S. Militia at Camp Jackson yesterday. You will hear all manner of accounts and as these will be brought to bear on the present Legislature to precipitate events, may be secession I will tell you what I saw. My office is up in Bremen the extreme north of the city. The arsenal is at the extreme south. The State camp was in a pretty grove directly west of the City, bounded by Olive Street & Laclede Avenue. I went to my house on Locust between 11 & 12 at 3 P.M. and saw the whole city in commotion and heard that the U.S. troops were marching from the arsenal to capture the State camp. At home I found Hugh & Charley Ewing & John Hunter so excited they would not wait for dinner, but went out to see the expected Battle. I had no such curiosity and staid to dinner, after which I walked out and soon met a man who told me Gen. Frost had surrendered. I went back home & told Ellen—then took Willy to see the soldiers march back I kept on walking and about 5 1/2 P.M. found myself in the grove, with Soldiers all round standing at rest—I went into the Camp till turned aside by sentinels, and

found myself with a promiscuous crowd, men, women & children, inside the Grove, near Olive Street. On that street the disarmed State troops some 800 were in ranks. Soon a heavy column of U.S. Regulars, followed by militia came down Olive, with music & halted abreast of me. I went up and spoke to Some of the officers and fell back to a Knoll where I met Hugh & Charley & John Hunter. Soon the music again started, and as the Regulars got abreast of the Crowd about 60 yards to my front and right I observed them in confusion, using their bayonets to keep the crowd back as I supposed. Still they soon moved on, and as the militia reached the same point a similar confusion began. I heard a couple of shots then half a dozen & observed the militia were firing on the crowd at that point, but the fire kept creeping to the rear along the flank of the column & hearing balls cutting the leaves of trees over my head I fell down on the grass, and crept up to where Charley Ewing had my boy Willy. I also covered his person—probably a hundred shots passed over the ground, but none near us. As soon as the fire slackened, I picked Willy up, and ran with him till behind the rising ground, and continued at my leisure out of harms way, & went home—I saw no one shot—but some dozen were Killed, among them a woman & little girl. There must have been some provocation at the point where the Regulars charged bayonets, and when the militia began their fire—the rest was irregular & unnecessary—for the crowd, was back in the woods, a fence between them and the street—There was some cheering of the U.S. troops, and some halloos for Jeff Davis.

I hear all of Frosts command who would not take the oath of allegiance to the U.S. are prisoners at the arsenal—I suppose they will be held for the orders of the President—They were mostly composed of young men, who doubtless were secessionist—Frost is a New Yorker, was a graduate of West Point—served some years in the army & married a Miss Graham here, a lady of great wealth & large connections. He was encouraged by order of the Governor, and this brings up the old question of State & U.S. authority we cannot have two Kings—one is enough and of the two the U.S. must prevail, but in all the South, and even here there are plenty who think the State is their King. I think of course that both extremes are determined that Missouri should secede, one from Southern feeling and the other for the satisfaction of beating her. When I got back last evening to my house I found Turner. He gave me a letter for you which I mailed addressed to Mansfield as the More certain method of reaching you. Tom Turner has declined his appointment for reasons the Major gives. I enclose you the copy of a letter I wrote some days since to the Secretary of War—If I must embark in this war I prefer Regulars who can be controlled. I have just received your letter of the 9 from Philadelphia—to which point I have already written to you—As ever yours affectionately

W. T. Sherman

SLAVES SEEKING FREEDOM:
VIRGINIA, MAY 1861

Benjamin F. Butler to Winfield Scott

A successful lawyer and Democratic politician from Massachusetts, Benjamin F. Butler was appointed a brigadier general in the state militia at the start of the war. Commissioned as a major general of U.S. volunteers on May 16, he was given command of the Union forces at Fort Monroe in Virginia. (Located at the end of the peninsula between the York and James rivers, and commanding the entrance to Hampton Roads, the post remained in Union hands throughout the war.) Shortly after his arrival at the fort, Butler faced the question of how the Union army should treat runaway slaves.

HEADQUARTERS DEPARTMENT OF VIRGINIA,
Fort Monroe, May 24, 1861.

Lieut. Gen. WINFIELD SCOTT:

*   *   *   *   *   *   *

Saturday, May 25.—I had written thus far when I was called away to meet Major Cary, of the active Virginia volunteers, upon questions which have arisen of very considerable importance both in a military and political aspect and which I beg leave to submit herewith.

On Thursday night three negroes, field hands belonging to Col. Charles K. Mallory now in command of the secession forces in this district, delivered themselves up to my picket guard and as I learned from the report of the officer of the guard in the morning had been detained by him. I immediately gave personal attention to the matter and found satisfactory evidence that these men were about to be taken to Carolina for the purpose of aiding the secession forces there; that two of them left wives and children (one a free woman) here; that the other had left his master from fear that he would be called upon to take part in the rebel armies. Satisfied of these facts from cautious examination of each of the negroes apart from the others I determined for the present and until better advised as these men were very serviceable and I had great need of labor in my quartermaster's department to avail myself of their services, and that I would send a receipt to Colonel Mallory that I had so taken them as I would for any other property of a private citizen which the exigencies of the service seemed to require to be taken by me, and especially property that was designed, adapted and about to be used against the United States.

As this is but an individual instance in a course of policy which may be required to be pursued with regard to this species of property I have detailed to the lieutenant-general this case and ask his direction. I am credibly informed that the negroes in this neighborhood are now being employed in the erection of batteries and other works by the rebels which it would be nearly or quite impossible to construct without their labor. Shall they be allowed the use of this property against the United States and we not be allowed its use in aid of the United States?

*   *   *   *   *   *   *

Major Cary demanded to know with regard to the negroes what course I intended to pursue. I answered him substantially as I have written above when he desired to know if I did not feel myself bound by my constitutional obligations to deliver up fugitives under the fugitive-slave act. To this I replied that the fugitive-slave act did not affect a foreign country which Virginia claimed to be and that she must reckon it one of the infelicities of her position that in so far at least she was taken at her word; that in Maryland, a loyal State, fugitives from service had been returned, and that even now although so much pressed by my necessities for the use of these men of Colonel Mallory's yet if their master would come to the fort and take the oath of allegiance to the Constitution of the United States I would deliver the men up to him and endeavor to hire their services of him if he desired to part with them. To this Major Cary responded that Colonel Mallory was absent.

*   *   *   *   *   *   *

Trusting that these dispositions and movements will meet the approval of the lieutenant-general and begging pardon for the detailed length of this dispatch, I have the honor to be, most respectfully, your obedient servant,

BENJ. F. BUTLER,
Major-General, Commanding.

DEFINING RUNAWAY SLAVES:
VIRGINIA, MAY 1861

The New York Times: General Butler and the Contraband of War

June 2, 1861

Butler's decision not to return slaves who had escaped from Confederate territory was endorsed by the administration, and "contraband" became a common term for slaves who came within the Union lines.

GENERAL BUTLER AND THE
CONTRABAND OF WAR.

The correspondent of the Boston *Journal*, writing from Fortress Monroe on May 26, gives these interesting particulars of recent events at that point:

The "everlasting nigger" hath heretofore lain *perdu* in the wood pile of this Bailiwick, and the appearance of General BUTLER at the post was the signal for his becoming uproarious. Yesterday morning three negroes came to the picket-guard and gave themselves up. Upon a separate examination of these men it satisfactorily appeared that they were field hands, owned by one Colonel MALLORY, a resident of this neighborhood, heretofore a lawyer, and now engaged in the defence of the soil of Virginia—that's what they call it—as the commandant of the active militia of this immediate district; that MALLORY proposed to take them to Carolina, to be employed in military operations there; that one of them had a wife—a free woman—and several children in the neighborhood; and that they all objected to having anything to do with fighting. Under these circumstances, General BUTLER concluded that the property was contraband of war, seized upon it, and turned it over to the Quartermaster's Department, where labor is much wanted. He proposed to receipt to Colonel

MALLORY for the men, if desired, as he would for the same number of beeves coming into this inclosure under like circumstances.

Yesterday afternoon Gen. BUTLER, accompanied by Major FAY and Capt. HAGGERTY of the Staff, went out on the Hampton road to meet one Major CARY, who represents himself to be an officer of the "active Virginia Volunteers," who requested an interview for the purpose of discussing sundry topics. This Maj. CARY, be it remembered, was a member of the Charleston-Baltimore Convention, and in his company Gen. BUTLER seceded from the Front street Theatre concern and went over to the Hard Shells at the Maryland Institute. So this meeting was but a renewal of an old acquaintanceship. CARY first asked if a passage through the blockading fleet would be allowed to the families of citizens desiring to go North or South to a place of safety. To this the General replied that the presence of the families of belligerents was always the best hostage for the good behavior of citizens; that one of the objects of the blockade was to prevent the admission of supplies of provisions into Virginia while she continued in an attitude hostile to the Government; and that the reduction of the number of consumers would manifestly tend to the postponement of the object in view; and that, moreover, the passage of vessels through the blockade would involve an amount of labor, in the way of a surveillance, to prevent abuse, which it would be impossible to perform. The request must therefore be refused. The Major then desired to know whether or not the passage of persons and families wishing to go North by land, from Virginia, would be permitted. To this the General replied that, with the exception of an interruption at Baltimore, which had now been disposed of, the travel of peaceable citizens through the North had not been hindered; that of the internal line of travel through Virginia his friends had, for the present, entire control; and that, finally, the authorities at Washington could judge better than himself upon this subject, and travelers might well pass that way in going North.

The Major then wanted to know what the General proposed to do about his friend MALLORY's "niggers," and in reply Gen. BUTLER stated the circumstances and his reasons for detaining them, as above recited. Maj. CARY asked if the General wasn't mindful of his constitutional obligations to return fugitives, in accordance with the terms of the Fugitive Slave Act? To this query, answer was made that the slave act was not of force, as to a foreign country, which Virginia claimed to be, and she must count it among the infelicities of her position, that so far, at least, she was taken at her word. But that notwithstanding his great need of just such labor as had thus providentially fallen into his hands, if Col. MALLORY would come into the fortress and take the oath of allegiance to the Government, his negroes should be returned, or hired of him, as he chose. The General further suggested, that in Maryland, a loyal State, fugitives from service had been returned. To all this Maj. CARY had no reply to make, other than that Col. MALLORY was absent. So closed the first meeting for the discussion of the Slavery question in this camp.

Under date of May 27, the same correspondent writes:

Yesterday, eight negroes, belonging to various planters in this neighborhood, came into this camp, one of whom had been employed in the erection of the enemy's sand batteries. They all told the story that they had left their masters because they believed they were to be sent South; one objected that he didn't care to be employed in fighting on the secession side, as he had been heretofore; and one stated very frankly that he supposed that the gentlemen in Fortress Monroe were the friends of the colored population. "We had heard it," said he, in the genuine field-hand dialect, "since last Fall, that if LINCOLN was elected, you would come down and set us free. And the white-folks used to say so, but they don't talk so now; the colored people have talked it all over; we heard that if we could get in here we should be free, or, at any rate, we should be among friends." This morning forty seven came in one squad, embracing all ages from three months to 85 years. Most are owned in this neighborhood, but a few came from beyond —one from well up toward Richmond, and one, a woman, came from the other side of Hampton Roads. There were in this lot half a dozen entire families. Another lot of a dozen good field-hands, many from points far in the interior, also came and expressed their willingness to enroll in the new corps of "Virginia Union Volunteers," and they were forthwith accepted.

There is now $60,000 worth of this sort of property in camp, and the stock is hourly increasing. The subject is becoming one of very great moment. As long as only property contraband of war—that is to say, negroes adapted for, and about to be employed in military movement—come into our possession, the question was comparatively simple; it was simply military. But when women and children come, as they have by the score, it became a humanitarian question. And some in Massachusetts, who have been afflicted by the "ANDREW and BUTLER correspondence," will find solace in the fact that the Massachusetts stores have—by order of the General in command—been taken to feed these panting fugitives. For the present, and until better advised by Gen. SCOTT or President LINCOLN, or somebody else, I understand that the General has decided to retain all the negroes who have come. An officer has been appointed to take a general charge of them, taking receipts from all parties who select servants from his gang, and opening an account with the reputed owner of each negro, charging the expense of caring for and supporting the non-laborers, and crediting the services of the men and women employed. So much for the negro question in its present aspect.

To-day, a Prof. RAYMOND, who is the head of a Seminary in Hampton, called upon the General, and they two had a long confabulation. The Professor, it appears, has a son 15 yrs of age. The youth has been, unfortunately, impressed into the service of the rebels at Norfolk. The anxious parent first desired to know whether there was any law by which he could regain the custody of his son; and for answer he was told that traitors who are in armed rebellion against the Government would not be likely to hearken to its laws in this case. In the United States the laws would protect him in his parental rights. Then he wanted to go over to Norfolk to attempt to reclaim his son, but this could not be permitted. He took occasion to make some general observations on politics, and expressed a belief that Republicanism is a failure, and that the only way to govern men is through a limited monarchy. "That is just where we differ," replied the Colonel, "and we have come down here to teach you the Republic is a success!" Whether or not, in the enforced service of his son in the Rebel army, he found any reason for losing his faith in the Republic, the Professor was unable to say. The people of Hampton have nearly all left; indeed the country around is panic-stricken. Virginia is but just beginning to learn that the path of rebellion is not a pleasant one.

The latest news from the outposts is that the rebels have succeeded, after several attempts, in destroying the bridges each side of Hampton, and that Col. DURYEE had retaliated by seizing every boat in town. Who has the bridge now?

"OUR CAUSE IS JUST": LOUISIANA, MAY 1861

Kate Stone: Journal, May 15–27, 1861

At the start of the war, twenty-year-old Kate Stone was living with her family at Brokenburn, a prosperous cotton plantation near the Mississippi River in what is now Madison Parish, Louisiana, about thirty miles northwest of Vicksburg.

———————

May 15: My Brother started at daybreak this morning for New Orleans. He goes as far as Vicksburg on horseback. He is wild to be off to Virginia. He so fears that the fighting will be over before he can get there that he has decided to give up the plan of raising a company and going out as Captain. He has about fifty men on his rolls and they and Uncle Bo have empowered him to sign their names as members of any company he may select. Mamma regrets so that My Brother would not wait and complete his commission. He could get his complement of men in two weeks, and having been educated at a military school gives him a great advantage at this time. And we think there will be fighting for many days yet.

We gave him quite a list of articles to be bought in the City, for it may be some time before we shop in New Orleans again.

May 23: Mamma was busy all the morning having the carpets taken up and matting put down and summer curtains hung. Of course the house was dusty and disagreeable. Mr. Newton and the children were shut up in the schoolroom and so escaped it, but Uncle Bo wandered aimlessly around, seeking rest and finding none. I retired to the fastness of my room with a new novel and a plate of candy and was oblivious to discomfort until Frank came to say dinner was ready and "the house shorely do look sweet and cool."

In the afternoon Mamma lay down to rest as she was tired out. Mr. Newton and Uncle Bo rode out to Omega for the mail and to hear the news. The boys, Little Sister, and I all went down the bayou for a walk with a running accompaniment of leaping, barking hounds, ranging the fields for a scent of deer or maybe a rabbit. The boys are so disgusted if the dogs race off after a rabbit. They think it ruins them for deer dogs. How pleasant to have the smooth, dry ground underfoot again after so many months of mud. It has been such a long, muddy winter and spring. No one knows what mud is until he lives on a buckshot place and travels buckshot roads.

Tonight a little fire was pleasant and we all gathered around it to hear Mr. Newton read the papers. Nothing but "War, War" from the first to the last column. Throughout the length and breadth of the land the trumpet of war is sounding, and from every hamlet and village, from city and country, men are hurrying by thousands, eager to be led to battle against Lincoln's hordes. Bravely, cheerily they go, willing to meet death in defense of the South, the land we love so well, the fairest land and the most gallant men the sun shines on. May God prosper us. Never again can we join hands with the North, the people who hate us so. We take quite a number of papers: *Harper's Weekly* and *Monthly*, the *New York Tribune*, *Journal of Commerce*, *Littell's Living Age*, the *Whig* and *Picayune* of New Orleans, and the Vicksburg and local sheets. What shall we do when Mr. Lincoln stops our mails?

The Northern papers do make us so mad! Even Little Sister, the child of the house, gets angry. Why will they tell such horrible stories about us? Greeley is the worst of the lot; his wishes for the South are infamous and he has the imagination of Poe. What shall we do when our mails are stopped and we are no longer in touch with the world?

We hear that Mr. Peck has raised a company of Irishmen from the levee camp and that the Richmond company has disbanded and re-enlisted for the war. They were twelve-month men.

Wednesday Uncle Bo went out to the river to drill the men and soon returned with the news that the levee at Airlie came very near giving away last night. The river is very high and a break there would put us entirely under. There are great fears of a tremendous overflow. Men are watching and the Negroes are working on the levees day and night.

The Monticello company, 4th La. Regt., has been ordered

up the river and the Lake Providence Cadets are off for New Orleans.

Late this afternoon Mamma and I went down to see the wife of the new overseer. She seems entirely too nice a woman, for her fashion is evidently from the planter class. I wonder why she married him. She does not look like a contented woman.

Uncle Bo, Ashburn, and I walked back and forth on the gallery in the cool moonlight, talking of soldier life and wondering what we who are left behind will do when both of our men folks are off and away.

From Uncle Bo's room floats the soft sound of violin, flute, and guitar. They are enjoying perhaps their last practice together. May God bless and keep them.

May 24: A lovely spring day, as fair as a poet's dream of May. Mamma is busy doing some machine work on Jimmy's shirts and I have been embroidering so enthusiastically that tonight I am tired out. In the afternoon Mamma, Mrs. Hardison, and I called on Mrs. Graves, and Mrs. Hardison and I adjourned to the orchard and feasted on the best plums, our first this spring. Mrs. Graves promised Mamma a bulb of lovely crimson gladiolus.

The boys went over to the schoolhouse to hear Mr. Ewing's scholars "speak a piece." Mr. Ewing is tutor for the Curry and Hardison children. At the supper table they were rather severe in their criticisms of the speeches; of course they think they could have done better. And they were especially emphatic in their remarks on Mrs. Curry and her two youngest hopefuls. Mrs. Curry insisted on bossing the whole thing. As they were mostly her children and her tutor, I could not see why the boys should object.

Dr. Devine came up from the quarters, where he had been to see one of the sick Negroes, in high feather and his new Sunday suit. He did not have as much news as usual but perhaps more truth. It is a lovely moonlight night and Brother Walter is out riding the levee, watching in Mr. Newton's place. Ashburn and I walked a long time on the gallery after supper, he playing the flute and I repeating to myself poems recently learned—the last, "The Jacobite Fiddler," from a recent number of the *Living Age*.

May 25: My Brother returned this evening. He did not succeed in joining the Monticello Guards from Carroll Parish. They had gone up the river, but he joined the Jeff Davis Guards at Vicksburg and was elected 3rd lieutenant. It is an Irish company officered by Americans. It was raised by Dr. Buckner and Capt. Manlove, and if My Brother had seen either of them on his way to New Orleans, they would have given him the captaincy. Tom Manlove is a captain. Uncle Bo cannot join it as a private, as the association would not be pleasant; and he is so disappointed not to be with My Brother. He hopes to get into the Volunteer Southerns, which will leave Vicksburg in a few days.

The Jeff Davis Guards leave for Richmond on Monday, and so My Brother and Uncle Bo get off in the morning as early as possible. My Brother told us much of the soldiers he saw in New Orleans: the Zouaves, with their gay, Turkish trousers and jackets and odd drill; the Tiger Rifles, recruited from the very dregs of the City and commanded by a man who has served a term in the penitentiary; and the Perrit Guards, the gambler's company—to be admitted one must be able to cut, shuffle, and deal on the point of a bayonet.

My Brother is in extravagant spirits. He is so glad to get off, and then he saw Kate and I think they have made it up again. Uncle Bo is very sad for he so wanted for them both to be in the same company. Now they can only hope to be in the same regiment. I can see them go, for I feel I know they will return. The parting will be dreadful for Mamma. She so depends on My Brother, her oldest and best beloved. The boys are disgruntled because they cannot go too.

May 26: Our two loved ones left us this morning, but we cannot think it a last farewell. My heart tells me they will come again. They go to bear all hardships, to brave all dangers, and to face death in every form, while we whom they go to protect are lapped safe in luxurious ease. But oh! the weary days of watching and waiting that stretch before us! We who stay behind may find it harder than they who go. They will have new scenes and constant excitement to buoy them up and the consciousness of duty done.

Mr. Catlin came over to tell them good-bye. My Brother explained everything to him and gave him a letter for the men Brother had been drilling. I hope they will not blame him.

Mamma fitted them out with everything she thought they could need. And their three horses were well loaded down. Wesley went to wait on them and was very proud of the honor of being selected to "go to battle with Marse Will." We hope he will do, though he has not been much about the house. Uncle Bo would not take a man for himself. He says a private has no business with a body servant, but if he changes his mind, a boy can be sent to him at any time.

Both will belong to infantry companies, and they will be fitted out with uniforms in Vicksburg. Brother Coley went with them as far as Vicksburg. They left so quickly that none of their friends knew in time to come over to say good-bye. Mr. Valentine will be sorry. He is such a friend of My Brother's.

They said good-bye in the fairest, brightest of May mornings. Will they come again in the summer's heat, the autumn's grey, or the winter's cold?

Mr. Newton and the boys rode out to the river with them. As they rode away, out of the yard and through the quarters, all the house servants and fieldhands watched them go. And many a heartfelt "Good-bye, Marse William and Marse Bo—God bless you" went with them.

I hope we put up everything they need. We lined their heavy blankets with brown linen and put pockets at the top for soap, combs, brushes, handkerchiefs, etc. The linen is tied to the blankets with strong tapes so that it can be easily taken off and washed. And we impressed it on Wesley that he must keep everything clean and take the best care of both our soldiers as long as they are together. He promised faithfully to do his best. Mamma has been very brave and stood the separation better than I hoped.

May 27: Mamma has been busy all day sewing on Jimmy's shirts and going through the vegetable and flower garden, all in a flourishing state. So many flowers, though our garden is but a new one yet. We must save all sorts of seeds, as we will get no more from the North. Mamma is having quantities of peas, potatoes, and all things eatable planted, as our only chance for anything from this time until the close of the war will be to raise it ourselves. Strict economy is to be the order of the day.

It is probable that meat will be very high, and by advice of Mr. Fellowes Mamma will try to raise enough to do the place. She has put Jeffery to devoting his whole time to the hogs and cattle. We have not a great quantity of either just now, but they will soon grow.

Times are already dreadfully hard. It was difficult for My Brother to raise enough money to fit them out—could only do it by pledging cotton at the bank.

Webster, who went to bring the horses back, came this morning. Wonka is the horse Uncle Bo gave me some time ago. He is such a lovely blood bay, so spirited, with every gait, and fleet as the wind when we start on a race. But I shall give him to Uncle Bo when he gets home. He will deserve a good horse after walking so long.

All Uncle Bo's jewelry, he left with me. He has quite an assortment of pins and rings and watch chains. One makes a lovely bracelet and I have often worn it.

Roanoke, a powerful hunter, will belong to Brother Walter until My Brother gets back. I am glad Dr. Buckner did not keep Roanoke.

Ashburn and Johnny, the youngest of the boys, brought us some mulberries from their ride in the woods, but nobody but children cares to eat mulberries. They report the blackberries as nearly ripe, and we will have a lovely trip for them deep in the green woods in an old clearing. They are the finest, glossy, sweet berries ever seen and with the dew on them—delicious.

We had a warm discussion after tea, Mr. Newton contending that the states had no right to secede immediately on Lincoln's election and that they should have remained quiet for four years and seen what would be the policy of the government. We all bitterly oppose this view of the subject. Why, in four years we would have no rights worth fighting for! He thinks that if the states had been patient there would have been no war for years and that it would have been better to submit to Lincoln's rule no matter how unjust than to have provoked a war. But oh, no! We cannot see it that way. We should make a stand for our rights—and a nation fighting for its own homes and liberty cannot be overwhelmed. Our Cause is just and must prevail.

A VISIT TO WASHINGTON: MAY–JUNE 1861

George Templeton Strong: Diary, May 29–June 2, 1861

George Templeton Strong visited Washington and the Union lines in northern Virginia in the late spring of 1861. Shortly after his return to New York, Strong became the treasurer of the newly-formed United States Sanitary Commission, a civilian organization dedicated to improving conditions in army camps and caring for sick and wounded soldiers.

May 29, WEDNESDAY. Off by early train after very early breakfast. Fine day; Wickham Hoffman joined me at the Jersey City depot. No incidents of travel; Baltimore, that nest of traitors and assassins, was traversed in peace. There were crowds at the corners of the streets watching the trains. They were looking out for the troops that were in a train we passed on a turn-off at Havre de Grace. But the crowd was silent and innocuous, for Fort McHenry is now strongly reinforced and Federal Hill is white with the tents of government troops. At Washington in due season, and to Willard's Hotel; densely crowded. We had to put up with one room, a very good one, however, on the second floor. The corridors downstairs are packed with a mob of civilians, army officers, motley militia men, and loafers of every class. The little reception parlor on the side street is the headquarters of Colonel Somebody (D'Utassy, I believe) of the "Garibaldi Guard," a very promising corps, and that end of the first floor passageway is permanently occupied by a guard of swarthy Italians and Hungarians.

Called on sundry people with letters and cards and lodged our pasteboard successfully with all but Mr. Secretary Blair, who was on his own front "stoop" and could not be escaped. We bored him about twenty minutes, not more. He tends a little to prose, but is courteous and intelligent. His talk is encouraging. He thinks there is little fight, if any, in the blustering fire-eating elements of the South; its bar-room swashbucklers will collapse whenever they are resolutely met. And this element constitutes, he thinks, two-thirds of the secession force. We were presented to Mrs. Blair, a lady-like person from New England.

Met Dick Smith, whilom of West Point, who marched me into General Sandford's parlor, where I had some talk with that chieftain and with Clarence Brown and Aleck Hamilton (not James A.'s Aleck, but John C.'s), who are on his staff. Heard all about the Alexandrian movement, for the execution of which Sandford takes much credit to himself. I hear Scott ranks him high for a "trainband" general, experienced only in marches down Broadway. I called with Hoffman at Scott's quarters. Saw Schuyler Hamilton, one of his aids, but did not disturb the meditations of the wily old Lieutenant-General, who lies there like a great spider in the center of his net, throwing out cords that will entangle his buzzing blue-bottle of an antagonist, if all go well.

Many New Yorkers at Willard's. Clarence Cram, Sam Neill, Willy Cutting, and others are begging for commissions. The honorable F. B. Cutting is diligently backing his son's petition; he has already secured a lieutenancy for Hayward Cutting, his youngest son. The Cuttings begging office from Lincoln, and these offices of all others, are a goodly spectacle to those who remember their extravagant, treasonable talk of sixty days ago and ever since last November. Many Republicans are soured by seeing a share of public patronage given to late-converted ultra-Southern Democrats. But the Administration is right. All party lines are wiped out now.

Dan Messenger, Judge Cowles, and others are after jobs in the Civil Service. The Rev. Dr. Bellows is concerned with the proposed Sanitary Commission. President Felton, Peirce, and Emory Washburn of Harvard, and Leutze are lookers-on.

May 30. Afternoon, parade and review of newly arrived regiments. Garibaldi Guard, Colonel Blenker's Germans (very promising corps both), the New York Ninth in their effective black and red uniform, and a fourth that I've forgotten (the "Brooklyn Zouaves").

May 31. Drove with Hoffman, Dan Messenger, and his

friend Charley Smith of Boston to Long Bridge. Our pass was inspected, and we went on. We invaded and (I suppose) "polluted" the Sacred Soil of Virginia. But it is so lacerated and insulted already by entrenchments, that our intrusion was a trifle. A very formidable *tête-du-pont* is in progress at the Virginia end of the bridge, and swarming with working parties. It is not armed yet, nor near completion, and it will need 2,000 men and upwards to occupy it when completed. Thence drove southwards, passing camps of New Jersey, Massachusetts, and other regiments, challenged every half mile, at least, by sentries and required to show our passes. Michiganders just outside Alexandria (fine looking fellows), and Pennsylvanians in the town. They do not seem to me very promising material. We drove to the famous Marshall House where Colonel Ellsworth was assassinated. It's a second-class hotel. Admitted with difficulty and formality; passes countersigned by the "provost-marshal." Explored the house, which is being carried off by relic hunters in little bits. Flag-staff is nearly cut through; stair-banisters, all gone; pieces of floor and stairs gouged out. Ordered dinner at Mansion House and drove a mile and a half northwest to Shooter's (or Sutter's) Hill, where Ellsworth's regiment (the New York Firemen Zouaves) is encamped and working at entrenchments, covering the extreme right of our line. Unfavorably impressed by the Zouaves. The men "sassed" the officers and the officers seemed loose in their notions of military subordination. One of them, a captain, and a rather scrubby specimen of a fire-company foreman in regimentals, said, "I guess we'll have the Colonel we want" (Ellsworth's successor); "if we don't, we'll let them fellows know we're about. We're firemen, we are." Probably a few of the Zouaves will have to be court-martialled and shot before the regiment can be relied on. With or near them are some Massachusetts soldiers and one of Sherman's light batteries. . . .

Returned from Alexandria by a back road, visiting the camp of the New York Twelfth in a secluded, picturesque place, surrounded by woods and enlivened by a rattling stream. The regiment is quartered partly in bush huts, partly in an old tumbledown cotton factory, built forty years ago and never worked from that day to this. . . .

We then visited all the lines south of Long Bridge. Spirit and temper of the men clearly good. Equipment imperfect in many particulars, but I heard no grumbling. One fact is apparent and unmistakable, that discipline and actual service produce good manners. We were challenged and called on to produce our passes a score of times, and the sentinels (except perhaps certain of the Massachusetts boys) were common men enough, country laborers or city roughs. But we experienced no incivility, even of manner. They scrutinized our passes, asked questions sometimes, but were always respectful and courteous, and generally dismissed us with a sort of apology for our detention and some reference to their orders as leaving them no discretion.

We recrossed the Long Bridge and drove to Colonel Burnside's Rhode Island camp, far away on the outskirts of the City of Distances, somewhere northwest of the Capitol. It's a model of neatness and order, with every provision for health and comfort; by far the most sensibly arranged camp I've seen. The huts are well built and ventilated, with convenient bunks, and a covered porch for the mess table. Talked with Goddard and other Providence millionaires who are serving in the ranks, and saw their evening parade, which was creditable and closed with an evening service by chaplain. Chapter in the Bible and extempore prayer. It suggested a field-preaching in the days of Lauderdale and Claverhouse, and though Puritanism is unlovely, the Rhode Island boys will fight none the worse for this daily inculcation of the truth that they are fighting for the laws of God and not merely for those of Congress. Thence to Burnside's quarters. He seems one of the strongest men I've seen in command.

June 1, SATURDAY. Spent the morning at War Office on business. Visited the Capitol, Smithsonian, and so on, with Hoffman. The Capitol has suffered no damage from its occupation by the Northern hordes. Its beautiful frescos are unscathed by the mudsills who were quartered there. Dined with Wise of the navy; Mrs. Wise is a daughter of Edward Everett. Wise is extravagantly funny. He is now in a prominent and responsible position in the Department. After dinner, walked with the lady and her nice children, and N. P. Willis, in the grounds back of the White House, listening to the Marine

Band. Loungers numerous and the crowd bright with uniforms. Firing heard in direction of Alexandria. Excitement, rumors of battle, and rapid dispersion of the audience. It was probably a salute. Returned to Wise's, and escorted Mrs. Wise to reception at Secretary Blair's. Pleasant enough; Seward, General Mansfield, Hamilton, Trowbridge, and others.

Called on Bache this morning and on Trowbridge. Coast Survey office full of business. Surveys of southern ports not yet published are so far advanced that they can be made useful to the blockading squadrons, and copies are being got up and issued with all possible despatch. At two, I happened to see the prisoners brought in who were taken at the Fairfax Court House skirmish Thursday night. They were in a covered waggon, escorted by dragoons, revolver in hand, on their way to Mansfield's headquarters.

This was a dashing little affair, though General McDowell tells me it was injudicious and might have turned out very badly. Fifty United States dragoons . . . were making a reconnaissance, when they were fired on by a rebel guard of two men. They shot one and captured the other, who was interrogated and said there were about 100 men in the village. Relying on this, the dragoons rode in, and found themselves in presence of from 1,000 to 1,500 men. Their treacherous informant was shot down at once and very properly. This I heard in confidence. They charged and dispersed the rebels, rode through the streets more than once under fire from windows and from behind fences, and came off at last with trifling loss and several prisoners. The rebels fired quite wildly. The prisoners begged and cried and knelt and seemed to expect instant military execution. One of them (a son of Colonel Washington who was lost on the *San Francisco*) was seized by the hair of his head and dragged across the pommel of a saddle and carried through the village with the charging dragoons. He took oath of allegiance very promptly when it was tendered him, declaring he was a Union man, coerced into the rebel service, and was liberated by Mansfield and provided with some cloak or overcoat to cover his rebel uniform. . . .

June 2, SUNDAY. Drove with Hoffman to Arlington House, the hereditary mansion of that fine old fellow, Colonel Lee, now unhappily a traitor. A splendid place amid beautiful grounds, through which we strolled a while. The sentinels refused us admission to the house and we were walking back to our carriage when General McDowell came riding up the road with his tail of staff and orderlies. He hailed me, dismounted, took us through the house, and was very kind and obliging. It's a queer place, an odd mixture of magnificence and meanness, like the castle of some illustrious, shabby, semi-insolvent old Irish family; for example, a grand costly portico with half-rotten wooden steps. Hall decorated with pictures, battle-pieces, by some illustrious Custis or other (fearful to behold); also with abundant stags' skulls and antlers. Thence to the camp of the Sixty-ninth, Colonel Corcoran's regiment. Inspected their battalion drill; rather rough. Then visited the New York Twenty-eighth and Fifth Regiments a little in advance, supported by the United States Dragoons, who charged through the streets of Fairfax Court House. Trained soldiers are easily distinguished from even the best volunteers. There was a little bugler of fifteen perhaps, a Brooklyn boy, whose narrative of the fray was spirited and modest. . . . The officers of the Twenty-eighth would not let us drive to Georgetown by the Chain Bridge. It was too hazardous. Rebel pickets were within a mile or two of the road, so we returned by the rope ferry. Orders were issued tonight by telegraph for a general advance. This I had from Wise. But they were countermanded.

Monday morning Hoffman returned to New York. At two I railroaded to Baltimore with Dan Messenger, Smith, and one Lamson of Boston, who is applying for a commission; a very good fellow he seems to be. We had agreed to visit Old Point Comfort and pay our respects to General Butler and Colonel Duryea. From depot to wharf, where we embarked in the *Adelaide*, heavily laden with stores for Fort Monroe, but built for first-class summer passengers to the fashionable hotel at the Point—the "Hygeia Hotel," a Baltimorean Newport in former days. Only half a dozen passengers with us; one a Virginian who wanted to get to Norfolk to look after some property there, and professed himself, in talk with us Union men, to be a sort of Union-lover, of a cold-blooded, anti-coercion type. A very fat and funny old fellow he was, Jenison by name. He was just from Harper's Ferry, where he had friends to see him through. Reports the rebel force at Harper's Ferry undisciplined and insubordinate, the officers and men "all mixed up together." Says he saw a captain enter a bar-room in great excitement and address himself to his commandant. "Colonel, what in H—— shall I do with the boys? They say they won't drill this morning." Colonel replies, "O, well, get two or three of them to turn out, and then I guess the others will come in by degrees." . . .

MASSACHUSETTS, MAY 1861

John Brown's Body

Union veteran George Kimball wrote in an 1890 magazine article that the words to the "John Brown Song" were collectively composed by members of a Massachusetts militia battalion stationed at Fort Warren in Boston Harbor in the spring of 1861. They were inspired by the presence of "a jovial Scotchman in the battalion, named John Brown. . . . As he happened to bear the identical name of the old hero of Harper's Ferry, he became at once the butt of his comrades." Sung to the music of the hymn "Say, brothers, will you meet us?", the "John Brown Song" was sold as a street ballad in Boston in late May 1861, and would be sung by soldiers of the 12th Massachusetts, which many of the militiamen from Fort Warren had joined, as they marched through Boston and New York in July 1861. "John Brown's Body" soon became one of the most popular songs of the Union army. The "jovial Scotchman" who inspired it drowned in the Shenandoah River in June 1862 while serving with the 12th Massachusetts.

John Brown's body lies a-mouldering in the grave;
John Brown's body lies a-mouldering in the grave;
John Brown's body lies a-mouldering in the grave;
   His soul's marching on!

CHORUS.

Glory, halle—hallelujah! Glory, halle—hallelujah!
  Glory, halle—hallelujah!
   His soul's marching on!

He's gone to be a soldier in the army of the Lord!
He's gone to be a soldier in the army of the Lord!
He's gone to be a soldier in the army of the Lord!
   His soul's marching on!

CHORUS.

Glory, halle—hallelujah! Glory, halle—hallelujah!
  Glory, halle—hallelujah!
    His soul's marching on!

John Brown's knapsack is strapped upon his back!
John Brown's knapsack is strapped upon his back!
John Brown's knapsack is strapped upon his back!
    His soul's marching on!

CHORUS.

Glory, halle—hallelujah! Glory, halle—hallelujah!
  Glory, halle—hallelujah!
    His soul's marching on!

His pet lambs will meet him on the way;
His pet lambs will meet him on the way;
His pet lambs will meet him on the way;
    They go marching on!

CHORUS.

Glory, halle—hallelujah! Glory, halle—hallelujah!
  Glory, halle—hallelujah!
    They go marching on!

They will hang Jeff. Davis to a tree!
They will hang Jeff. Davis to a tree!
They will hang Jeff. Davis to a tree!
    As they march along!

CHORUS.

Glory, halle—hallelujah! Glory, halle—hallelujah!
  Glory, halle—hallelujah!
    As they march along!

Now, three rousing cheers for the Union!
Now, three rousing cheers for the Union!
Now, three rousing cheers for the Union!
    As we are marching on!

CHORUS.

Glory, halle—hallelujah! Glory, halle—hallelujah!
Glory, halle—hallelujah!
Hip, hip, hip, hip, Hurrah!

THE WRIT OF HABEAS CORPUS:
MARYLAND, MAY 1861

Roger B. Taney: Opinion in Ex parte Merryman, June 1, 1861

On April 27, 1861, President Lincoln authorized the military to suspend the writ of habeas corpus along the Philadelphia–Washington railroad line. When John Merryman was arrested by the army in Baltimore County on May 25 and imprisoned at Fort McHenry, his lawyer obtained a writ of habeas corpus from Chief Justice Roger B. Taney, who was sitting as a federal circuit judge for Maryland. General George Cadwalader, the commander at Fort McHenry, refused to respond to the writ, and when Taney ordered him to be attached (arrested) for contempt, the marshal carrying Taney's writ was barred from the fort. On May 28 the Chief Justice told a crowded courtroom in Baltimore that he would excuse the marshal from further attempts to enforce the attachment because "the power refusing obedience was so notoriously superior to any the marshal could command." Taney issued this opinion on June 1 and ordered the proceedings in the case sent to the President. Lincoln did not respond directly to the Chief Justice, but did address his unprecedented suspension of habeas corpus in his message to Congress on July 4 (see pp. 433.27–434.36 in this volume). By the end of 1861 Lincoln had authorized the suspension of habeas corpus along the railroad line from Philadelphia to New York City (July 2), from New York City to Bangor, Maine (October 14), and within the state of Missouri (December 2). John Merryman was indicted for treason on July 10, 1861, and released on bail, but was never tried.

THE APPLICATION in this case for a writ of habeas corpus is made to me under the 14th section of the judiciary act of 1789, which renders effectual for the citizen the constitutional privilege of the writ of habeas corpus. That act gives to the courts of the United States, as well as to each justice of the supreme court, and to every district judge, power to grant writs of habeas corpus for the purpose of an inquiry into the cause of commitment. The petition was presented to me, at Washington, under the impression that I would order the prisoner to be brought before me there, but as he was confined in Fort McHenry, in the city of Baltimore, which is in my circuit, I resolved to hear it in the latter city, as obedience to the writ, under such circumstances, would not withdraw General Cadwalader, who had him in charge, from the limits of his military command.

The petition presents the following case: The petitioner resides in Maryland, in Baltimore county; while peaceably in his own house, with his family, it was at two o'clock on the morning of the 25th of May 1861, entered by an armed force, professing to act under military orders; he was then compelled to rise from his bed, taken into custody, and conveyed to Fort McHenry, where he is imprisoned by the commanding officer, without warrant from any lawful authority.

The commander of the fort, General George Cadwalader, by whom he is detained in confinement, in his return to the writ, does not deny any of the facts alleged in the petition. He states that the prisoner was arrested by order of General Keim, of Pennsylvania, and conducted as aforesaid to Fort McHenry, by his order, and placed in his (General Cadwalader's) custody, to be there detained by him as a prisoner.

A copy of the warrant or order under which the prisoner was arrested was demanded by his counsel, and refused: and it is not alleged in the return, that any specific act, constituting any offence against the laws of the United States, has been charged against him upon oath, but he appears to have been arrested upon general charges of treason and rebellion, without proof, and without giving the names of the witnesses, or specifying the acts which, in the judgment of the military officer, constituted these crimes. Having the prisoner thus in custody upon these vague and unsupported accusations, he refuses to obey the writ of habeas corpus, upon the ground that he is duly authorized by the president to suspend it.

The case, then, is simply this: a military officer, residing in Pennsylvania, issues an order to arrest a citizen of Maryland, upon vague and indefinite charges, without any proof, so far as appears; under this order, his house is entered in the night, he is seized as a prisoner, and conveyed to Fort McHenry, and there kept in close confinement; and when a habeas corpus is served on the commanding officer, requiring him to produce the prisoner before a justice of the supreme court, in order that he may examine into the legality of the imprisonment, the answer of the officer, is that he is authorized by the president to suspend the writ of habeas corpus at his discretion, and in the exercise of that discretion, suspends it in this case, and on that ground refuses obedience to the writ.

As the case comes before me, therefore, I understand that the president not only claims the right to suspend the writ of habeas corpus himself, at his discretion, but to delegate that discretionary power to a military officer, and to leave it to him to determine whether he will or will not obey judicial process that may be served upon him. No official notice has been given to the courts of justice, or to the public, by proclamation or otherwise, that the president claimed this power, and had exercised it in the manner stated in the return. And I certainly listened to it with some surprise, for I had supposed it to be one of those points of constitutional law upon which there was no difference of opinion, and that it was admitted on all hands, that the privilege of the writ could not be suspended, except by act of congress.

When the conspiracy of which Aaron Burr was the head, became so formidable, and was so extensively ramified, as to justify, in Mr. Jefferson's opinion, the suspension of the writ, he claimed, on his part, no power to suspend it, but communicated his opinion to congress, with all the proofs in his possession, in order that congress might exercise its discretion upon the subject, and determine whether the public safety required it. And in the debate which took place upon the subject, no one suggested that Mr. Jefferson might exercise the power himself, if, in his opinion, the public safety demanded it.

Having, therefore, regarded the question as too plain and too well settled to be open to dispute, if the commanding officer had stated that, upon his own responsibility, and in the exercise of his own discretion, he refused obedience to the writ, I should have contented myself with referring to the clause in the constitution, and to the construction it received from every jurist and statesman of that day, when the case of Burr was before them. But being thus officially notified that the privilege of the writ has been suspended, under the orders, and by the authority of the president, and believing, as I do, that the president has exercised a power which he does not possess under the constitution, a proper respect for the high office he fills, requires me to state plainly and fully the grounds of my opinion, in order to show that I have not ventured to question the legality of his act, without a careful and deliberate examination of the whole subject.

The clause of the constitution, which authorizes the suspension of the privilege of the writ of habeas corpus, is in the 9th section of the first article. This article is devoted to the legislative department of the United States, and has not the slightest reference to the executive department. It begins by providing "that all legislative powers therein granted, shall be vested in a congress of the United States, which shall consist of a senate and house of representatives." And after prescribing the manner in which these two branches of the legislative department shall be chosen, it proceeds to enumerate specifically the legislative powers which it thereby grants and legislative powers which it expressly prohibits; and at the conclusion of this specification, a clause is inserted giving congress "the power to make all laws which shall be necessary and proper for carrying into execution the foregoing powers, and all other powers vested by this constitution in the government of the United States, or in any department or officer thereof."

The power of legislation granted by this latter clause is, by its words, carefully confined to the specific objects before enumerated. But as this limitation was unavoidably somewhat indefinite, it was deemed necessary to guard more effectually certain great cardinal principles, essential to the liberty of the citizen, and to the rights and equality of the states, by denying to congress, in express terms, any power of legislation over them. It was apprehended, it seems, that such legislation might be attempted, under the pretext that it was necessary and proper to carry into execution the powers granted; and it was determined, that there should be no room to doubt, where rights of such vital importance were concerned; and accordingly, this clause is immediately followed by an enumeration of certain subjects, to which the powers of legislation shall not extend. The great importance which the framers of the constitution attached to the privilege of the writ of habeas corpus, to protect the liberty of the citizen, is proved by the fact, that its suspension, except in cases of invasion or rebellion, is first in the list of prohibited powers; and even in these cases the power is denied, and its exercise prohibited, unless the public safety shall require it.

It is true, that in the cases mentioned, congress is, of necessity, the judge of whether the public safety does or does not require it; and their judgment is conclusive. But the introduction of these words is a standing admonition to the legislative body of the danger of suspending it, and of the extreme caution they should exercise, before they give the government of the United States such power over the liberty of a citizen.

It is the second article of the constitution that provides for the organization of the executive department, enumerates the powers conferred on it, and prescribes its duties. And if the high power over the liberty of the citizen now claimed, was intended to be conferred on the president, it would undoubtedly be found in plain words in this article; but there is not a word in it that can furnish the slightest ground to justify the exercise of the power.

The article begins by declaring that the executive power shall be vested in a president of the United States of America, to hold his office during the term of four years; and then proceeds to prescribe the mode of election, and to specify, in precise and plain words, the powers delegated to him, and the duties imposed upon him. The short term for which he is elected, and the narrow limits to which his power is confined, show the jealousy and apprehension of future danger which the framers of the constitution felt in relation to that department of the government, and how carefully they withheld from it many of the powers belonging to the executive branch of the English government which were considered as dangerous to the liberty of the subject; and conferred (and that in clear and specific terms) those powers only which were deemed essential to secure the successful operation of the government.

He is elected, as I have already said, for the brief term of four years, and is made personally responsible, by impeachment, for malfeasance in office; he is, from necessity, and the nature of his duties, the commander-in-chief of the army and navy, and of the militia, when called into actual service; but no appropriation for the support of the army can be made by congress for a longer term than two years, so that it is in the power of the succeeding house of representatives to withhold the appropriation for its support, and thus disband it, if, in their judgment, the president used, or designed to use it for improper purposes. And although the militia, when in actual service, is under his command, yet the appointment of the officers is reserved to the states, as a security against the use of the military power for purposes dangerous to the liberties of the people, or the rights of the states.

So too, his powers in relation to the civil duties and authority necessarily conferred on him are carefully restricted, as well as those belonging to his military character. He cannot appoint the ordinary officers of government, nor make a treaty with a foreign nation or Indian tribe, without the advice and consent of the senate, and cannot appoint even inferior officers, unless he is authorized by an act of congress to do so. He is not empowered to arrest any one charged with an offence against the United States, and whom he may, from the evidence before him, believe to be guilty; nor can he authorize any officer, civil or military, to exercise this power, for the fifth article of the amendments to the constitution expressly provides that no person "shall be deprived of life, liberty or property, without due process of law"—that is, judicial process.

Even if the privilege of the writ of habeas corpus were suspended by act of congress, and a party not subject to the rules and articles of war were afterwards arrested and imprisoned by regular judicial process, he could not be detained in prison, or brought to trial before a military tribunal, for the article in the amendments to the constitution immediately following the one above referred to (that is, the sixth article) provides, that "in all criminal prosecutions, the accused shall enjoy the right to a speedy and public trial by an impartial jury of the state and district wherein the crime shall have been committed, which district shall have been previously ascertained by law; and to be informed of the nature and cause of the accusation; to be confronted with the witnesses against him; to have compulsory process for obtaining witnesses in his favor; and to have the assistance of counsel for his defence."

The only power, therefore, which the president possesses,

where the "life, liberty or property" of a private citizen is concerned, is the power and duty prescribed in the third section of the second article, which requires "that he shall take care that the laws shall be faithfully executed." He is not authorized to execute them himself, or through agents or officers, civil or military, appointed by himself, but he is to take care that they be faithfully carried into execution, as they are expounded and adjudged by the co-ordinate branch of the government to which that duty is assigned by the constitution. It is thus made his duty to come in aid of the judicial authority, if it shall be resisted by a force too strong to be overcome without the assistance of the executive arm; but in exercising this power he acts in subordination to judicial authority, assisting it to execute its process and enforce its judgments.

With such provisions in the constitution, expressed in language too clear to be misunderstood by any one, I can see no ground whatever for supposing that the president, in any emergency, or in any state of things, can authorize the suspension of the privileges of the writ of habeas corpus, or the arrest of a citizen, except in aid of the judicial power. He certainly does not faithfully execute the laws, if he takes upon himself legislative power, by suspending the writ of habeas corpus, and the judicial power also, by arresting and imprisoning a person without due process of law.

Nor can any argument be drawn from the nature of sovereignty, or the necessity of government, for self-defence in times of tumult and danger. The government of the United States is one of delegated and limited powers; it derives its existence and authority altogether from the constitution, and neither of its branches, executive, legislative or judicial, can exercise any of the powers of government beyond those specified and granted; for the tenth article of the amendments to the constitution, in express terms, provides that "the powers not delegated to the United States by the constitution, nor prohibited by it to the states, are reserved to the states, respectively, or to the people."

Indeed, the security against imprisonment by executive authority, provided for in the fifth article of the amendments to the constitution, which I have before quoted, is nothing more than a copy of a like provision in the English constitution, which had been firmly established before the declaration of independence. Blackstone states it in the following words: "To make imprisonment lawful, it must be either by process of law from the courts of judicature, or by warrant from some legal officer having authority to commit to prison." 1 Bl. Comm. 137.

The people of the United Colonies, who had themselves lived under its protection, while they were British subjects, were well aware of the necessity of this safeguard for their personal liberty. And no one can believe that, in framing a government intended to guard still more efficiently the rights and liberties of the citizen, against executive encroachment and oppression, they would have conferred on the president a power which the history of England had proved to be dangerous and oppressive in the hands of the crown; and which the people of England had compelled it to surrender, after a long and obstinate struggle on the part of the English executive to usurp and retain it.

The right of the subject to the benefit of the writ of habeas corpus, it must be recollected, was one of the great points in controversy, during the long struggle in England between arbitrary government and free institutions, and must therefore have strongly attracted the attention of the statesmen engaged in framing a new and, as they supposed, a freer government than the one which they had thrown off by the revolution. From the earliest history of the common law, if a person were imprisoned, no matter by what authority, he had a right to the writ of habeas corpus, to bring his case before the king's bench; if no specific offence were charged against him in the warrant of commitment, he was entitled to be forthwith discharged; and if an offence were charged which was bailable in its character, the court was bound to set him at liberty on bail. The most exciting contests between the crown and the people of England, from the time of Magna Charta, were in relation to the privilege of this writ, and they continued until the passage of the statute of 31 Car. II., commonly known as the great habeas corpus act.

This statute put an end to the struggle, and finally and firmly secured the liberty of the subject against the usurpation and oppression of the executive branch of the government. It nevertheless conferred no new right upon the subject, but only secured a right already existing; for, although the right could not justly be denied, there was often no effectual remedy against its violation. Until the statute of 13 Wm. III., the judges held their offices at the pleasure of the king, and the influence which he exercised over timid, time-serving and partisan judges, often induced them, upon some pretext or other, to refuse to discharge the party, although entitled by law to his discharge, or delayed their decision, from time to time, so as to prolong the imprisonment of persons who were obnoxious to the king for their political opinions, or had incurred his resentment in any other way.

The great and inestimable value of the habeas corpus act of the 31 Car. II. is, that it contains provisions which compel courts and judges, and all parties concerned, to perform their duties promptly, in the manner specified in the statute.

A passage in Blackstone's Commentaries, showing the ancient state of the law on this subject, and the abuses which were practised through the power and influence of the crown, and a short extract from Hallam's Constitutional History, stating the circumstances which gave rise to the passage of this statute, explain briefly, but fully, all that is material to this subject.

Blackstone says: "To assert an absolute exemption from imprisonment in all cases is inconsistent with every idea of law and political society, and in the end would destroy all civil liberty by rendering its protection impossible. But the glory of the English law consists in clearly defining the times, the causes and the extent, when, wherefore and to what degree, the imprisonment of the subject may be lawful. This it is which induces the absolute necessity of expressing upon every commitment the reason for which it is made, that the court, upon a habeas corpus, may examine into its validity, and according to the circumstances of the case, may discharge, admit to bail or remand the prisoner. And yet early in the reign of Charles I. the court of kings bench, relying on some arbitrary precedents (and those perhaps misunderstood) determined that they would not, upon a habeas corpus, either bail or deliver a prisoner, though committed without any cause assigned, in case he was committed by the special command of the king or by the lords of the privy council. This drew on a parliamentary inquiry, and produced the 'Petition of Right' (3 Car. I.) which recites this illegal judgment, and enacts that no freeman hereafter shall be so imprisoned or detained. But when, in the following year, Mr. Selden and others were committed by the lords of the council, in pursuance of his majesty's special command, under a general charge of 'notable contempts, and stirring up sedition against the king and the government,' the judges delayed for two terms (including also the long vacation) to deliver an opinion how far such a charge was bailable; and when at length they agreed that it was, they however annexed a condition of finding sureties for their good behavior, which still protracted their imprisonment, the chief justice, Sir Nicholas Hyde, at the same time, declaring that 'if they were again remanded for that cause, perhaps the court would not afterwards grant a habeas corpus, being already made acquainted with the cause of the imprisonment.' But this was heard with indignation and astonishment by every lawyer present, according to Mr. Selden's own account of the matter, whose resentment was not cooled at the distance of four and twenty years." 3 Bl. Comm. 133, 134.

It is worthy of remark, that the offences charged against the prisoner in this case, and relied on as a justification for his arrest and imprisonment, in their nature and character, and in the loose and vague manner in which they are stated, bear a striking resemblance to those assigned in the warrant for the arrest of Mr. Selden. And yet, even at that day, the warrant was regarded as such a flagrant violation of the rights of the subject that the delay of the time-serving judges to set him at liberty, upon the habeas corpus issued in his behalf, excited the universal indignation of the bar.

The extract from Hallam's Constitutional History is equally impressive and equally in point: "It is a very common mistake, and that not only among foreigners, but many from whom some knowledge of our constitutional laws might be expected, to suppose that this statute of Car. II. enlarged in a great degree our liberties, and forms a sort of epoch in their history. But though a very beneficial enactment, and eminently remedial in many cases of illegal imprisonment, it introduced no new principle, nor conferred any right upon the subject. From the earliest records of the English law, no freeman could be detained in prison, except upon a criminal charge or conviction, or for a civil debt. In the former case it was always in his power to demand of the court of king's bench a writ of habeas corpus ad subjiciendum, directed to the person detaining him in custody, by which he was enjoined to bring up the body of the prisoner, with the warrant of commitment, that the court might judge of its sufficiency, and remand the party, admit him to bail, or discharge him, according to the nature of the charge. This writ issued of right, and could not be refused by the court. It was not to bestow an immunity from arbitrary imprisonment, which is abundantly provided for in Magna Charta (if indeed it is not more ancient), that the statute of Car. II. was enacted, but to cut off the abuses by which the government's lust of power, and the servile subtlety of the crown lawyers, had impaired so fundamental a privilege." 3 Hall. Const. Hist. 19.

While the value set upon this writ in England has been so great, that the removal of the abuses which embarrassed its employment has been looked upon as almost a new grant of liberty to the subject, it is not to be wondered at, that the continuance of the writ thus made effective should have been the object of the most jealous care. Accordingly, no power in England short of that of parliament can suspend or authorize the suspension of the writ of habeas corpus. I quote again from Blackstone (1 Bl. Comm. 136): "But the happiness of our constitution is, that it is not left to the executive power to determine when the danger of the state is so great as to render this measure expedient. It is the parliament only or legislative power that, whenever it sees proper, can authorize the crown by suspending the habeas corpus for a short and limited time, to imprison suspected persons without giving any reason for so doing." If the president of the United States may suspend the writ, then the constitution of the United States has conferred upon him more regal and absolute power over the liberty of the citizen, than the people of England have thought it safe to entrust to the crown; a power which the queen of England cannot exercise at this day, and which could not have been lawfully exercised by the sovereign even in the reign of Charles the First.

But I am not left to form my judgment upon this great

question, from analogies between the English government and our own, or the commentaries of English jurists, or the decisions of English courts, although upon this subject they are entitled to the highest respect, and are justly regarded and received as authoritative by our courts of justice. To guide me to a right conclusion, I have the Commentaries on the Constitution of the United States of the late Mr. Justice Story, not only one of the most eminent jurists of the age, but for a long time one of the brightest ornaments of the supreme court of the United States; and also the clear and authoritative decision of that court itself, given more than half a century since, and conclusively establishing the principles I have above stated.

Mr. Justice Story, speaking, in his Commentaries, of the habeas corpus clause in the constitution, says: "It is obvious that cases of a peculiar emergency may arise, which may justify, nay, even require, the temporary suspension of any right to the writ. But as it has frequently happened in foreign countries, and even in England, that the writ has, upon various pretexts and occasions, been suspended, whereby persons apprehended upon suspicion have suffered a long imprisonment, sometimes from design, and sometimes because they were forgotten, the right to suspend it is expressly confined to cases of rebellion or invasion, where the public safety may require it. A very just and wholesome restraint, which cuts down at a blow a fruitful means of oppression, capable of being abused, in bad times, to the worst of purposes. Hitherto, no suspension of the writ has ever been authorized by congress, since the establishment of the constitution. It would seem, as the power is given to congress to suspend the writ of habeas corpus, in cases of rebellion or invasion, that the right to judge whether the exigency had arisen must exclusively belong to that body." 3 Story, Comm. Const. § 1336.

And Chief Justice Marshall, in delivering the opinion of the supreme court in the case of Ex parte Bollman and Swartwout, uses this decisive language, in 4 Cranch [8 U. S.] 95: "It may be worthy of remark, that this act (speaking of the one under which I am proceeding) was passed by the first congress of the United States, sitting under a constitution which had declared 'that the privilege of the writ of habeas corpus should not be suspended, unless when, in cases of rebellion or invasion, the public safety may require it.' Acting under the immediate influence of this injunction, they must have felt, with peculiar force, the obligation of providing efficient means, by which this great constitutional privilege should receive life and activity; for if the means be not in existence, the privilege itself would be lost, although no law for its suspension should be enacted. Under the impression of this obligation, they give to all the courts the power of awarding writs of habeas corpus." And again on page 101: "If at any time, the public safety should require the suspension of the powers vested by this act in the courts of the United States, it is for the legislature to say so. That question depends on political considerations, on which the legislature is to decide; until the legislative will be expressed, this court can only see its duty, and must obey the laws." I can add nothing to these clear and emphatic words of my great predecessor.

But the documents before me show, that the military authority in this case has gone far beyond the mere suspension of the privilege of the writ of habeas corpus. It has, by force of arms, thrust aside the judicial authorities and officers to whom the constitution has confided the power and duty of interpreting and administering the laws, and substituted a military government in its place, to be administered and executed by military officers. For, at the time these proceedings were had against John Merryman, the district judge of Maryland, the commissioner appointed under the act of congress, the district attorney and the marshal, all resided in the city of Baltimore, a few miles only from the home of the prisoner. Up to that time, there had never been the slightest resistance or obstruction to the process of any court or judicial officer of the United States, in Maryland, except by the military authority. And if a military officer, or any other person, had reason to believe that the prisoner had committed any offence against the laws of the United States, it was his duty to give information of the fact and the evidence to support it, to the district attorney; it would then have become the duty of that officer to bring the matter before the district judge or commissioner, and if there was sufficient legal evidence to justify his arrest, the judge or commissioner would have issued his warrant to the marshal to arrest him; and upon the hearing of the case, would have held him to bail, or committed him for trial, according to the character of the offence, as it appeared in the testimony, or would have discharged him immediately, if there was not sufficient evidence to support the accusation. There was no danger of any obstruction or resistance to the action of the civil authorities, and therefore no reason whatever for the interposition of the military.

Yet, under these circumstances, a military officer, stationed in Pennsylvania, without giving any information to the district attorney, and without any application to the judicial authorities, assumes to himself the judicial power in the district of Maryland; undertakes to decide what constitutes the crime of treason or rebellion; what evidence (if indeed he required any) is sufficient to support the accusation and justify the commitment; and commits the party, without a hearing, even before himself, to close custody, in a strongly garrisoned fort, to be there held, it would seem, during the pleasure of those who committed him.

The constitution provides, as I have before said, that "no person shall be deprived of life, liberty or property, without due process of law." It declares that "the right of the people to be secure in their persons, houses, papers and effects, against unreasonable searches and seizures, shall not be violated; and no warrant shall issue, but upon probable cause, supported by oath or affirmation, and particularly describing the place to be searched, and the persons or things to be seized." It provides that the party accused shall be entitled to a speedy trial in a court of justice.

These great and fundamental laws, which congress itself could not suspend, have been disregarded and suspended, like the writ of habeas corpus, by a military order, supported by force of arms. Such is the case now before me, and I can only say that if the authority which the constitution has confided to the judiciary department and judicial officers, may thus, upon any pretext or under any circumstances, be usurped by the military power, at its discretion, the people of the United States are no longer living under a government of laws, but every citizen holds life, liberty and property at the will and pleasure of the army officer in whose military district he may happen to be found.*

In such a case, my duty was too plain to be mistaken. I have exercised all the power which the constitution and laws confer upon me, but that power has been resisted by a force too strong for me to overcome. It is possible that the officer who has incurred this grave responsibility may have misunderstood his instructions, and exceeded the authority intended to be given him; I shall, therefore, order all the proceedings in this case, with my opinion, to be filed and recorded in the circuit court of the United States for the district of Maryland, and direct the clerk to transmit a copy, under seal, to the president of the United States. It will then remain for that high officer, in fulfilment of his constitutional obligation to "take care that the laws be faithfully executed," to determine what measures he will take to cause the civil process of the United States to be respected and enforced.

*The constitution of the United States is founded upon the principles of government set forth and maintained in the Declaration of Independence. In that memorable instrument the people of the several colonies declared, that one of the causes which "impelled" them to "dissolve the political bands" which connected them with the British nation, and justified them in withdrawing their allegiance from the British sovereign, was that "he (the king) had affected to render the military independent of, and superior to, the civil power."

"I REJOICE IN THIS WAR": VIRGINIA, JUNE 1861

Henry A. Wise: Speech at Richmond

June 1, 1861

In late May 1861 the Confederacy moved its capital from Montgomery to Richmond, Virginia, where President Davis addressed a crowd on June 1. He was followed by former Virginia governor Henry A. Wise, who had been one of the leading secessionists in the state convention earlier in the year.

MY FRIENDS:—You all know that I am a civil soldier only, and that in that capacity I was nearly worn down in the siege of the Virginia Convention. Thank God, however, that with a little rest, some help, and some damage from the doctors, I have been enabled to recruit my exhausted energies.

The time of deliberation has given place to the time of action, and I have taken up my bed as an individual, in common with others, to march to Richmond to meet the President of our now separate and independent republic. I am ready to obey his orders, not only with pride, pleasure, and devotion to the cause, and respect to the office he fills, but with respect to the man himself as one who has our fullest confidence.

You have to meet a foe with whom you could not live in peace. Your political powers and rights, which were enthroned in that Capitol when you were united with them under the old constitutional bond of the Confederacy, have been annihilated. They have undertaken to annul laws within your own limits that would render your property unsafe within those limits. They have abolitionized your border, as the disgraced North-west will show. They have invaded your moral strongholds and the rights of your religion, and have undertaken to teach you what should be the moral duties of men.

They have invaded the sanctity of your homes and firesides, and endeavored to play master, father, and husband for you in your households; in a word, they have set themselves up as a petty Providence by which you are in all things to be guided and controlled. But you have always declared that you would not be subject to this invasion of your rights.

Though war was demanded, it was not for you to declare war. But now that the armies of the invader are hovering around the tomb of Washington, where is the Virginian heart that does not beat with a quicker pulsation at this last and boldest desecration of his beloved State? Their hordes are already approaching our metropolis, and extending their folds around our State as does the anaconda around his victim. The call is for action.

I rejoice in this war. Who is there that now dares to put on sanctity to depreciate war, or the "horrid glories of war." None. Why? Because it is a war of purification. You want war, fire, blood, to purify you; and the Lord of Hosts has demanded that you should walk through fire and blood. You are called to the fiery baptism, and I call upon you to come up to the altar. Though your pathway be through fire, or through a river of blood, turn not aside. Be in no hurry—no hurry and flurry.

Collect yourselves, summon yourselves, elevate yourselves to the high and sacred duty of patriotism. The man who dares to pray, the man who dares to wait until some magic arm is put into his hand; the man who will not go unless he have a Minié, or percussion musket, who will not be content with flint and steel, or even a gun without a lock, is worse than a coward—he is a renegade. If he can do no better, go to a blacksmith, take a gun along as a sample, and get him to make you one like it. Get a spear—a lance. Take a lesson from John Brown. Manufacture your blades from old iron, even though it be the tires of your cart-wheels. Get a bit of carriage spring, and grind and burnish it in the shape of a bowie knife, and put it to any sort of a handle, so that it be strong—ash, hickory, oak. But, if possible, get a double-barrelled gun and a dozen rounds of buckshot, and go upon the battle-field with these.

If their guns reach further than yours, reduce the distance; meet them foot to foot, eye to eye, body to body, and when you strike a blow, strike home. Your true-blooded Yankee will never stand still in the face of cold steel. Let your aim, therefore, be to get into close quarters, and with a few decided, vigorous movements, always pushing forward, never back, my word for it, the soil of Virginia will be swept of the Vandals who are now polluting its atmosphere.

The band then struck up "Dixie," which was followed by "We may be Happy yet."

THE "BLINDED, FANATICAL" NORTH:
GEORGIA, JUNE 1861

Charles C. Jones Jr. to Charles C. Jones Sr. and Mary Jones

Educated at the College of New Jersey (Princeton) and the Dane Law School at Harvard, Charles C. Jones Jr. was elected mayor of Savannah in October 1860. Jones wrote to his parents while anticipating that a major battle would soon be fought in Virginia.

Savannah, *Monday*, June 10th, 1861

My dear Father and Mother,

Ruth has returned after her short visit to Amanda looking pretty well. She suffered one day from an acute attack, but was soon relieved.

I presume you have observed the appointment of Judge Jackson as a brigadier general in the Confederate service. It is a position he has long and most ardently desired, and I doubt not when the hour of combat comes he will do the states no little service.

That hour must soon arrive. Sincerely do I trust and believe that the God of Battles will in that day send the victory where it of right belongs. I cannot bring my mind to entertain even the impression that a God of justice and of truth will permit a blinded, fanatical people, who already have set at naught all rules of equality, of right, and of honor; who flagrantly violate the inalienable right of private liberty by an arrogant suspension of the privilege of habeas corpus, a writ of right than which none can be dearer to the citizen—and that in the face of judicial process issued by the Chief Justice Taney, renowned for his profound legal attainments, respected for his many virtues and high position, and venerable for his many useful labors and constitutional learning; who set at defiance the right of private property by seizing Negroes, the personal chattels of others, without offer of remuneration or consent of the owner;

who permit their mercenaries to trifle at will with private virtue; who trample under foot sacred compacts and solemn engagements; who substitute military despotism in the place of constitutional liberty; and who without the fear of either God or man in their eyes recklessly pursue a policy subversive of all that is just and pure and high-minded—to triumph in this unholy war. We have our sins and our shortcomings, and they are many; but without the arrogance of the self-righteous Pharisee we may honestly thank God that we are not as they are. Should they be defeated in this fearful contest, how fearful the retribution! Who can appreciate the terrors of this lifted wave of fanaticism when, broken and dismayed, it recoils in confusion and madness upon itself? Agrarianism in ancient Rome will appear as naught in the contrast.

You will observe that I have issued a proclamation requesting the citizens of Savannah to abstain from their ordinary engagements on Thursday next, the day set apart by the President as a day of fasting and prayer, and with one consent to unite in the due observation of the day. You may also notice an anonymous communication in our city papers signed "Citizen," in which I recommend that the suggestion in reference to the taking up of a collection in all places of public worship on that day for the benefit of our army and of our government should meet with a generous, practical, and patriotic adoption. If this plan be pursued generally on that day throughout these Confederate States, the amount received will be large, and the fund thus realized will prove most acceptable to the present finances of the government. The idea is a good one, and should be everywhere carried into effect. I intend myself conscientiously to observe the day. We should all do so.

We are kept very much in the dark with reference to the true movements of our army in Virginia, and it is proper that this should be so. President Davis' presence inspires great enthusiasm and confidence. He appears to be in every respect the man raised for the emergency. At once soldier and statesman, he everywhere acknowledges our dependence upon and our hope in the guiding influence and the protection of a superintending Providence. I regret to know that his health is feeble. In the event of his death, where would we look for a successor?

The Central Railroad Company have declared a semi-annual

dividend payable on and after the 15th inst. of five percent. Very acceptable to all stockholders at the present. I send by this post a copy of Judge Jackson's recent eulogy upon the life and character of the Hon. Charles J. McDonald. We are all well, and unite, my dearest parents, in warmest love to you both. As ever,

Your affectionate son,
Charles C. Jones, Jr.

What was done at Hinesville last Tuesday?

ANGLO-AMERICAN RELATIONS:
LONDON, JUNE 1861

Henry Adams to Charles Francis Adams Jr.

When Lincoln appointed Charles Francis Adams as the new American minister to Great Britain, his son Henry accompanied him to London, where he would serve as his father's confidential secretary. They arrived on May 13, 1861, just as the British government issued a proclamation of neutrality recognizing the Confederates as belligerents under international law, a measure widely seen as a possible prelude to full diplomatic recognition. Adams wrote to his brother in Boston.

———————

London 10 June 1861.
My dear Charles
 Your letters, to the family in general arrived this morning and gave great satisfaction in so far as they were letters, though they made the M. E. & Amb. Plen. as glum as an English Viscount. At that date you had not received our first letters, and as I have not written since then, I feel as though I ought to answer yours at once. It is a relief to know that you are out of the fort and I hope to the Lord that no unhappy chance will carry you off to the wars, however much you may want to go yourself. Not that I want you or anyone to shirk their duties, but simply because I can't see my way straight to where we shall be a year hence, and I don't like to see a man do his best pace on the first quarter. Talking of duties shirked, it has occurred to me that I am probably not innocent in that way myself, for I do not suppose that my property has been taxed. I am not of that mind which approves of neglecting these duties when most called for, and I therefore desire you to make a just estimate of my manifold possessions and hand it in to the authorities, paying said taxes out of such monies as may be received in the way of dividends or may be in your hands. The expenses in this city are enormous and if the Ambassador's private income fails, we must cut our establishment down to a very low

figure, as one can do little here with less than forty thousand, and nothing with less than twenty five thousand dollars. People must occasionally live on less, but if so, they must have assistance from the public charities. The scale of living and the prices are curious examples of the beauties of a high civilization.

As for myself, I have only the same old story to sing which I have chanted many times, especially in my letters to you. I have done nothing whatever in the way of entering society, nor do I mean to take the plunge until after my presentation on the 19th. (Court suit = upwards of $200.00). Getting into society is a beastly repulsive piece of work here. Supposing you are invited to a ball. You arrive at eleven o'clock. A footman in powder asks your name and announces you. The lady or ladies of the house receive you and shake hands. You pass on and there you are. You know not a soul. No one offers to introduce you. No one even looks at you with curiosity. London society is so vast that the oldest habitués know only their own sets, and never trouble themselves even to look at anyone else. No one knows that you're a stranger. You see numbers of men and women just as silent and just as strange as yourself. You may go from house to house and from rout to rout and never see a face twice. You may labor for weeks at making acquaintances and yet go again and again to balls where you can't discover a face you ever saw before. And supposing you are in society, what does it amount to! The state dinners are dull, heavy, lifeless, affairs. The balls are solemn stupid crushes without a scintilla of the gaiety of our balls. No one enjoys them so far as I can hear. They are matters of necessity, of position. People have to entertain. They were born to it and it is one of the duties of life. My own wish is quietly to slide into the literary set and leave the heavy society, which without dancing is a frightful and irredeemable bore to me, all on one side.

After the 19th I must set to work to get a club and make acquaintances of my own age; no easy work with English. But I do not expect or wish to do a great deal in this way this season. There is time enough for all that.

You want to be posted up politically. If the Times has published my letters without mutilation, you will see what I think about it. We arrived here just as the Queen's Proclamation was issued. Of course the question arose what course to take.

Papa's instructions and especially a later despatch, would have justified him in breaking off at once all diplomatic relations with this Government, and we felt no doubt that, as you say, the Americans would have upheld him. But I must confess such a policy appeared to me to be the extreme of shallowness and folly. In the first place it would have been a tremendous load for the country. In the second place it would have been a mere wanton, mad windmill-hitting, for the sympathies and the policy of England are undoubtedly with us as has been already shown. In the third place it would have been ruin in a merely private point of view. Two such wars would grind us all into rags in America. One is already enough to cut down incomes to a dreadful extent.

Papa took the course that seems to me to have been the correct one. He had an interview with Lord John and told him, without bravado or bragg, how the matter was regarded in America, or was likely to be regarded, and announced plainly what course he should be compelled to take if the Government really entertained any idea of encouraging the insurgents, and demanded a categorical answer as to the course the Government meant to pursue. Lord John promised to send this answer by Lord Lyons, protesting at the same time the unreasonableness of the American feeling, and the perfect good-faith of his Government. Since that time no opportunity has escaped the Government of proving their good-will towards us and unless you in America are run mad, and are determined to run your heads right against a stone wall there need be no more difficulty whatever.

Feeling as I did in the matter, of course I did my best in my letters to the Times to quiet rather than inflame. If you choose you can suggest to the Advertiser a leader developing the view which I take, and pointing out the good sense of our worthy Ambassador in maintaining the dignity of the country and yet avoiding a rupture, as contrasted with those noisy jackasses Clay and Burlingame who have done more harm here than their weak heads were worth a thousand times over. I believe it to be essential to our interests now, that Europe should be held on our side. Our troubles have gone too far to be closed by foreign jealousies. The cotton-states would rather annex themselves to England or Spain than come back to us.

I have tried to get some influence over the press here but as yet have only succeeded in one case which has however been of some use. That is the Morning Herald, whose American editor, a young man named Edge, came to call on the Amb. He is going to America to correspond for his paper; at least he says so. If he brings you a letter, let him be asked out to dine and give him what assistance in the way of introductions he wants. He is withal of passing self-conceit and his large acquaintance is fudge, for he is no more than an adventurer in the press; but his manners are good, and so long as he asks nothing in return, it's better to have him an ally than an enemy.

As to the Article on the last Winter which I left in the drawer of your table at the house, I left with it a note of directions. It was merely to the purport that I had not succeeded in making it fit for publication, and as it stood, it was not to be published, but if on reading it you thought you could make anything of it, you might have it for your pains.

Our life here is not of the gayest, at least to my mind. Not that I care much so far as the outside of the house goes, but the Ambassador is more snappish and sulky than I have known him to be for a long time, and mamma has fits of homesickness that don't make us cheerful while Margaret thinks she's going insane with weeping—damn her, I wish she would,—and Bridget is little better, for Margaret infects her. Mary is of as little count in a house as anyone I ever saw and really is a problem to me, for she seems wholly different from all the rest of us. I'm afraid she won't improve with age. Poor Brooks I took off to boarding school this morning. He's a good boy as ever lived and I've become very fond of him though I treat him like a dog. He was very brave about it and indeed was rather glad to go, for our house is not over-cheerful especially for a boy of his age. His school seems pleasant and clean, and he'll learn to play cricket and be a man.

Tuesday. 11th.   To return to politics, and this in absolute secrecy, for I let you know what I've no business to. A despatch arrived yesterday from Seward, so arrogant in tone and so extraordinary and unparalleled in its demands that it leaves no doubt in my mind that our Government wishes to force a war with all Europe. That is the inevitable result of any attempt to carry out the spirit of the letter of these directions, and such a war is regarded in the despatch itself as the probable result. I have said already that I thought such a policy shallow madness, whether it comes from Seward or from any one else. It is not only a crime; it's a blunder. I have done my best to counteract it; I only wish I could really do anything. I urged papa this morning, as the only man who could by any chance stop the thing, to make an energetic effort and induce the British Government to put us so much in the wrong that we couldn't go further. I think he has made up his mind to some effort of the sort and I hope it will succeed with all my soul.

Does Seward count on the support of France? It is not likely, for this despatch applies as much to her as to England. But if he does he is just as much mistaken as he ever was in his life. Any one who knows Napoleon knows that he means to stick with England. I cannot tell you how I am shocked and horrified by supposing Seward, a man I've admired and respected beyond most men, guilty of what seems to me so wicked and criminal a course as this.

I do not think I exaggerate the danger. I believe that our Government means to have a war with England; I believe that England knows it and is preparing for it; and I believe it will come within two months—if at all. If you have any property liable to be affected by it, change the investment. Don't go into the army yet. Wait for a Canadian campaign and meanwhile live if you can on hay. Our incomes will soon have to go to pay our taxes. There's only one comfort that I see, in the whole matter and that is that within a year we shall all be utterly ruined and our Government broken down; in other words, the war on that scale must be short and we of the commercial interests shall be the first to go under. If I have any marine insurance stock, sell it and invest in Dick Fay's woollen manufacturing arrangement if you can; if not, in anything reasonably safe; Massachusetts or Boston city stocks.

I'm in a panic you see.

H.B.A.

CHEROKEE NEUTRALITY:
INDIAN TERRITORY, JUNE 1861

John Ross to Benjamin McCulloch

Since their forced removal from the eastern United States in the 1830s, the Creek, Choctaw, Cherokee, Chickasaw, and Seminole had lived in the Indian Territory (later Oklahoma), where members of all five tribes owned slaves. At the outbreak of the war the Chickasaw, Choctaw, and Seminole allied with the Confederacy, while the Creek divided into pro-Confederate and pro-Union factions. John Ross, the principal chief of the Cherokee since 1839, sought to keep his nation neutral in the conflict.

EXECUTIVE DEPARTMENT, *Park Hill, June* 17, 1861.
Brig. Gen. BEN. MCCULLOCH,
Commanding Troops of Confederate States, Fort Smith, Ark.:

SIR: I have the honor to acknowledge by the first return mail the receipt of your communication dated at Fort Smith, Ark., the 12th instant, informing me that you have been sent by the Government of the Confederate States of America to take command of the district embracing the Indian Territory and to guard it from invasion by the people of the North.

For the expression of your friendship be pleased to accept my heartfelt thanks and the assurance that I cherish none other than a similar sentiment for yourself and people; am also gratified to be informed that you will not interfere with any of our rights and wishes unless circumstances compel you to do so, nor violate or molest our neutrality without good cause.

In regard to the pending conflict between the United States and the Confederate States I have already signified my purpose to take no part in it whatever, and have admonished the Cherokee people to pursue the same course. The determination to that course was the result of consideration of law and policy, and seeing no reason to doubt its propriety, I shall adhere to it in good faith, and hope that the Cherokee people will not fail to follow my example. I have not been able to see any reason why the Cherokee Nation should take any other course, for it seems to me to be dictated by their treaties and sanctioned by wisdom and humanity. It ought not give ground for complaint to either side, and should cause our rights to be respected by both. Our country and institutions are our own. However small the one or humble the others, they are as sacred and valuable to us as are those of your own populous and wealthy State to yourself and your people. We have done nothing to bring about the conflict in which you are engaged with your own people, and I am unwilling that my people shall become its victims. I am determined to do no act that shall furnish any pretext to either of the contending parties to overrun our country and destroy our rights. If we are destined to be overwhelmed, it shall not be through any agency of mine. The United States are pledged not to disturb us in our rights, nor can we suppose for a moment that your Government will do it, as the avowed principle upon which it is struggling for an acknowledged existence is the rights of the States and freedom from outside interference.

The Cherokee people and Government have given every assurance in their power of their sympathy and friendship for the people of Arkansas and of other Confederate States, unless it be in not voluntarily assuming an attitude of hostility toward the Government of the United States, with whom their treaties exist and from whom they are not experiencing any new burdens or exactions. That I cannot advise them to do, and hope that their good faith in adhering to the requirements of their treaties and of their friendship for all the whites will be manifested by strict observance of the neutrality enjoined.

Your demand that those people of the nation who are in favor of joining the Confederacy be allowed to organize into military companies as home guards for the purpose of defending themselves in case of invasion from the North is most respectfully declined. I cannot give my consent to any such organization for very obvious reasons:

1st. It would be a palpable violation of my position as a neutral.

2d. It will place in our midst organized companies not authorized by our laws, but in violation of treaty, and who would soon become efficient instruments in stirring up domestic strife and creating internal difficulties among the Cherokee people.

As in this connection you have misapprehended a remark which I made in conversation at our interview some eight or ten days ago, I hope you will allow me to repeat what I did say. I informed you that I had taken a neutral position and would maintain it honestly, but that in case of a foreign invasion old as I am I would assist in repelling it. I have not signified any purpose as to an invasion of our soil and interference with our rights from the United or Confederate States, because I have apprehended none and cannot give my consent to any.

I have the honor to be, sir, your obedient servant,

JNO. ROSS,
Principal Chief Cherokee Nation.

EMANCIPATING NORTHERN OPINION: JUNE 1861

James Russell Lowell:
The Pickens-and-Stealin's Rebellion

June 1861

A prominent poet and literary critic, James Russell Lowell was professor of Romance languages at Harvard and the founding editor of *The Atlantic Monthly*, where this article appeared.

———————

HAD ANY one ventured to prophesy on the Fourth of March that the immediate prospect of Civil War would be hailed by the people of the Free States with a unanimous shout of enthusiasm, he would have been thought a madman. Yet the prophecy would have been verified by what we now see and hear in every city, town, and hamlet from Maine to Kansas. With the advantage of three months' active connivance in the cabinet of Mr. Buchanan, with an empty treasury at Washington, and that reluctance to assume responsibility and to inaugurate a decided policy, the common vice of our politicians, who endeavor to divine and to follow popular sentiment rather than to lead it, it seemed as if Disunion were inevitable, and the only open question were the line of separation. So assured seemed the event, that English journalists moralized gravely on the inherent weakness of Democracy. While the leaders of the Southern Rebellion did not dare to expose their treason to the risk of a popular vote in any one of the seceding States, the "Saturday Review," one of the ablest of British journals, solemnly warned its countrymen to learn by our example the dangers of an extended suffrage.

Meanwhile the conduct of the people of the Free States, during all these trying and perilous months, had proved, if it proved anything, the essential conservatism of a population in which every grown man has a direct interest in the stability of the national government. So abstinent are they by habit and principle from any abnormal intervention with the machine of administration, so almost superstitious in adherence to constitutional forms, as to be for a moment staggered by the claim to a *right* of secession set up by all the Cotton States, admitted by the Border Slave-States, which had the effrontery to deliberate between their plain allegiance and their supposed interest, and but feebly denied by the Administration then in power. The usual panacea of palaver was tried; Congress did its best to add to the general confusion of thought; and, as if that were not enough, a Convention of Notables was called simultaneously to thresh the straw of debate anew, and to convince thoughtful persons that men do not grow wiser as they grow older. So in the two Congresses the notables talked,—in the one, those who ought to be shelved, in the other, those who were shelved already,—while those who were too thoroughly shelved for a seat in either addressed Great Union Meetings at home. Not a man of them but had a compromise in his pocket, adhesive as Spalding's glue, warranted to stick the shattered Confederacy together so firmly, that, if it ever broke again, it must be in a new place, which was a great consolation. If these gentlemen gave nothing very valuable to the people of the Free States, they were giving the Secessionists what was of inestimable value to them,—Time. The latter went on seizing forts, navy-yards, and deposits of Federal money, erecting batteries, and raising and arming men at their leisure; above all, they acquired a prestige, and accustomed men's minds to the thought of disunion, not only as possible, but actual. They began to grow insolent, and, while compelling absolute submission to their rebellious usurpation at home, decried any exercise of legitimate authority on the part of the General Government as *Coercion*,—a new term, by which it was sought to be established as a principle of constitutional law, that it is always the Northern bull that has gored the Southern ox.

During all this time, the Border Slave-States, and especially Virginia, were playing a part at once cowardly and selfish. They assumed the right to stand neutral between the Government and rebellion, to contract a kind of morganatic marriage with Treason, by which they could enjoy the pleasant sin without the tedious responsibility, and to be traitors in everything but the vulgar contingency of hemp. Doubtless the aim of the political managers in these States was to keep the North amused with schemes of arbitration, reconstruction, and whatever other fine words would serve the purpose of hiding the real issue, till the new government of Secessia should have so far consolidated itself as to be able to demand with some show of reason a recognition from foreign powers, and to render it politic for the United States to consent to peaceable secession. They counted on the self-interest of England and the supineness of the North. As to the former, they were not wholly without justification,—for nearly all the English discussions of the "American Crisis" which we have seen have shown far more of the shop-keeping spirit than of interest in the maintenance of free institutions; but in regard to the latter they made the fatal mistake of believing our Buchanans, Cushings, and Touceys to be representative men. They were not aware how utterly the Democratic Party had divorced itself from the moral sense of the Free States, nor had they any conception of the tremendous recoil of which the long-repressed convictions, traditions, and instincts of a people are capable.

Never was a nation so in want of a leader; never was it more plain, that, without a head, the people "bluster abroad as beasts," with plenty of the iron of purpose, but purpose without coherence, and with no cunning smith of circumstance to edge it with plan and helve it with direction. What the country was waiting for showed itself in the universal thrill of satisfaction when Major Anderson took the extraordinary responsibility of doing his duty. But such was the general uncertainty, so doubtful seemed the loyalty of the Democratic Party as represented by its spokesmen at the North, so irresolute was the tone of many Republican leaders and journals, that a powerful and wealthy community of twenty millions of people gave a sigh of relief when they had been permitted to install the Chief Magistrate of their choice in their own National Capital. Even after the inauguration of Mr. Lincoln, it was confidently announced that Jefferson Davis, the Burr of the Southern conspiracy, would be in Washington before the month was out; and so great was the Northern despondency, that the chances of such an event were seriously discussed. While the nation was falling to pieces, there were newspapers and "distinguished statesmen" of the party so lately and so long in power base enough to be willing to make political capital out of the common danger, and to lose their country, if they could only find their profit. There was even one man found in Massachusetts, who, measuring the moral standard of his party by his own, had the unhappy audacity to declare publicly that there were friends enough of the South in his native State to prevent the march of any troops thence to sustain that Constitution to which he had sworn fealty in Heaven knows how many offices, the rewards of almost as many turnings of his political coat. There was one journal in New York which had the insolence to speak of *President* Davis and *Mister* Lincoln in the same paragraph. No wonder the "dirt-eaters" of the Carolinas could be taught to despise a race among whom creatures might be found to do that by choice which they themselves were driven to do by misery.

Thus far the Secessionists had the game all their own way, for their dice were loaded with Northern lead. They framed their sham constitution, appointed themselves to their sham offices, issued their sham commissions, endeavored to bribe England with a sham offer of low duties and Virginia with a sham prohibition of the slave-trade, advertised their proposals for a sham loan which was to be taken up under intimidation, and levied real taxes on the people in the name of the people whom they had never allowed to vote directly on their enormous swindle. With money stolen from the Government, they raised troops whom they equipped with stolen arms, and beleaguered national fortresses with cannon stolen from national arsenals. They sent out secret agents to Europe, they had their secret allies in the Free States, their conventions transacted all important business in secret session;—there was but one exception to the shrinking delicacy becoming a maiden government, and that was the openness of the stealing. We had always thought a high sense of personal honor an essential element of chivalry; but among the *Romanic* races, by which, as the wonderful ethnologist of "De Bow's Review" tells us, the Southern States were settled, and from which they derive a close entail of chivalric characteristics, to the exclusion of the vulgar Saxons of the North, such is by no means the case. For the first time in history the deliberate treachery of a general is deemed worthy of a civic ovation, and Virginia has the honor of being the first State claiming to be civilized that has decreed the honors of a triumph to a cabinet officer who had contrived to gild a treason that did not endanger his life with a peculation that could not further damage his reputation. Rebellion, even in a bad cause, may have its romantic side; treason, which had not been such but for being on the losing side, may challenge admiration; but nothing can sweeten larceny or disinfect perjury. A rebellion inaugurated with theft, and which has effected its entry into national fortresses, not over broken walls, but by breaches of trust, should take Jonathan Wild for its patron saint, with the run of Mr. Buchanan's cabinet for a choice of sponsors,—godfathers we should not dare to call them.

Mr. Lincoln's Inaugural Speech was of the kind usually called "firm, but conciliatory,"—a policy doubtful in troublous times, since it commonly argues weakness, and more than doubtful in a crisis like ours, since it left the course which the Administration meant to take ambiguous, and, while it weakened the Government by exciting the distrust of all who wished for vigorous measures, really strengthened the enemy by encouraging the conspirators in the Border States. There might be a question as to whether this or that attitude were expedient for the Republican Party; there could be none as to the only safe and dignified one for the Government of the Nation. Treason was as much treason in the beginning of March as in the middle of April; and it seems certain now, as it seemed probable to many then, that the country would have sooner rallied to the support of the Government, if the Government had shown an earlier confidence in the loyalty of the people. Though the President talked of "repossessing" the stolen forts, arsenals, and customhouses, yet close upon this declaration followed the disheartening intelligence that the Cabinet were discussing the propriety of evacuating not only Fort Sumter, which was of no strategic importance, but Fort Pickens, which was the key to the Gulf of Mexico, and to abandon which was almost to acknowledge the independence of the Rebel States. Thus far the Free States had waited with commendable patience for some symptom of vitality in the new Administration, something that should distinguish it from the piteous helplessness of its predecessor. But now their pride was too deeply outraged for endurance, indignant remonstrances were heard from all quarters, and the Government seemed for the first time fairly to comprehend that it had twenty millions of freemen at its back, and that forts might be taken and held by honest men as well as by knaves and traitors. The nettle had been stroked long enough; it was time to try a firm grip. Still the Administration seemed inclined to temporize, so thoroughly was it possessed by the notion of conciliating the Border States. In point of fact, the side which those States might take in the struggle between Law and Anarchy was of vastly more import to them than to us. They could bring no considerable reinforcement of money, credit, or arms to the rebels; they could at best but add so many mouths to an army whose commissariat was already dangerously embarrassed. They could not even, except temporarily, keep the war away from the territory of the seceding States, every one of which had a sea-door open to the invasion of an enemy who controlled the entire navy and shipping of the country. The position assumed by Eastern Virginia and Maryland was of consequence only so far as it might facilitate a sudden raid on Washington, and the policy of both these States was to amuse the Government by imaginary negotiations till the plans of the conspirators were ripe. In both States men were actively recruited and enrolled to assist in attacking the capital. With them, as with the more openly rebellious States, the new theory of "Coercion" was ingeniously arranged like a valve, yielding at the slightest impulse to the passage of forces for the subversion of legitimate authority, closing imperviously so that no drop of power could ooze through in the opposite direction. Lord de Roos, long suspected of cheating at cards, would never have been convicted but for the resolution of an adversary, who, pinning his hand to the table with a fork, said to him blandly, "My Lord, if the ace of spades is not under your Lordship's hand, why, then, I beg your pardon!" It seems to us that a timely treatment of Governor Letcher in the same energetic way would have saved the disasters of Harper's Ferry and Norfolk,—for disasters they were, though six months of temporizing had so lowered the public sense of what was due to the national dignity, that people were glad to see the Government active at length, even if only in setting fire to its own house.

We are by no means inclined to criticize the Administration, even if this were the proper time for it; but we cannot help thinking that there was great wisdom in Napoleon's recipe for saving life in dealing with a mob,—"First fire grape-shot *into* them; after that, over their heads as much as you like." The position of Mr. Lincoln was already embarrassed when he entered upon office, by what we believe to have been a political blunder in the leaders of the Republican Party. Instead of keeping closely to the real point, and the only point, at issue, namely, the claim of a minority to a right of rebellion when displeased with the result of an election, the bare question of Secession, pure and simple, they allowed their party to become divided, and to waste themselves in discussing terms of compromise and guaranties of slavery which had nothing to do with the business in hand. Unless they were ready to admit that popular government was at an end, those were matters already settled by the Constitution and the last election. Compromise was out of the question with men who had gone through the motions, at least, of establishing a government and electing an anti-president. The way to insure the loyalty of the Border States, as the event has shown, was to convince them that disloyalty was dangerous. That revolutions never go backward is one of those compact generalizations which the world is so ready to accept because they save the trouble of thinking; but, however it may be with revolutions, it is certain that rebellions most commonly go backward with disastrous rapidity, and it was of the gravest moment, as respected its moral influence, that Secession should not have time allowed it to assume the proportions and the dignity of revolution, in other words, of a rebellion too powerful to be crushed. The secret friends of the Secession treason in the Free States have done their best to bewilder the public mind and to give factitious prestige to a conspiracy against free government and civilization by talking about the *right* of revolution, as if it were some acknowledged principle of the Law of Nations. There is a right, and sometimes a duty, of rebellion, as there is also a right and sometimes a duty of hanging men for it; but rebellion continues to be rebellion until it has accomplished its object and secured the acknowledgment of it from the other party to the quarrel, and from the world at large. The Republican Party in the November elections had really effected a peaceful revolution, had emancipated the country from the tyranny of an oligarchy which had abused the functions of the Government almost from the time of its establishment, to the advancement of their own selfish aims and interests; and it was this legitimate change of rulers and of national policy by constitutional means which the Secessionists intended to prevent. To put the matter in plain English, they resolved to treat the people of the United States, in the exercise of their undoubted and lawful authority, as rebels, and resorted to their usual policy of intimidation in order to subdue them. Either this magnificent empire should be their plantation, or it should perish. This was the view even of what were called the moderate slave-holders of the Border States; and all the so-called compromises and plans of reconstruction that were thrown into the caldron where the hell-broth of anarchy was brewing had this extent,—no more,—What terms of *submission* would the people make to their natural masters? Whatever other result may have come of the long debates in Congress and elsewhere, they have at least convinced the people of the Free States that there can be no such thing as a moderate slave-holder,—that moderation and slavery can no more coexist than Floyd and honesty, or Anderson and treason.

We believe, then, that conciliation was from the first impossible,—that to attempt it was unwise, because it put the party of law and loyalty in the wrong,—and that, if it was done as a mere matter of policy in order to gain time, it was a still greater mistake, because it was the rebels only who could profit by it in consolidating their organization, while the seeming gain of a few days or weeks was a loss to the Government, whose great advantage was in an administrative system thoroughly established, and, above all, in the vast power of the national idea, a power weakened by every day's delay. This is so true, that already men began to talk of the rival governments at Montgomery and Washington, and Canadian journals recommend a strict neutrality, as if the independence and legitimacy of the mushroom despotism of New Ashantee were an acknowledged fact, and the name of the United States of America had no more authority than that of Jefferson Davis and Company, dealers in all kinds of repudiation and anarchy. For more than a month after the inauguration of President

Lincoln there seemed to be a kind of interregnum, during which the confusion of ideas in the Border States as to their rights and duties as members of the "old" Union, as it began to be called, became positively chaotic. Virginia, still professing neutrality, prepared to seize the arsenal at Harper's Ferry and the navy-yard at Norfolk; she would prevent the passage of the United States' forces "with a serried phalanx of her gallant sons," two regiments of whom stood looking on while a file of marines took seven wounded men in an engine-house for them; she would do everything but her duty,—the gallant Ancient Pistol of a commonwealth. She "resumed her sovereignty," whatever that meant; her Convention passed an ordinance of secession, concluded a league offensive and defensive with the rebel Confederacy, appointed Jefferson Davis commander-in-chief of her land-forces and somebody else of the fleet she meant to steal at Norfolk, and then coolly referred the whole matter back to the people to vote three weeks afterwards whether they *would* secede three weeks before. Wherever the doctrine of Secession has penetrated, it seems to have obliterated every notion of law and precedent.

The country had come to the conclusion that Mr. Lincoln and his cabinet were mainly employed in packing their trunks to leave Washington, when the "venerable Edward Ruffin of Virginia" fired that first gun at Fort Sumter which brought all the Free States to their feet as one man. That shot is destined to be the most memorable one ever fired on this continent since the Concord fowling-pieces said, "That bridge is ours, and we mean to go across it," eighty-seven Aprils ago. As these began a conflict which gave us independence, so that began another which is to give us nationality. It was certainly a great piece of good-luck for the Government that they had a fort which it was so profitable to lose. The people were weary of a masterly inactivity which seemed to consist mainly in submitting to be kicked. We know very well the difficulties that surrounded the new Administration; we appreciate their reluctance to begin a war the responsibility of which was as great as its consequences seemed doubtful; but we cannot understand how it was hoped to evade war, except by concessions vastly more disastrous than war itself. War has no evil comparable in its effect on national character to that of a craven submission to manifest wrong, the postponement of moral to material interests. There is no prosperity so great as courage. We do not believe that any amount of forbearance would have conciliated the South so long as they thought us pusillanimous. The only way to retain the Border States was by showing that we had the will and the power to do without them. The little Bopeep policy of

> "Let them alone, and they'll all come home
> Wagging their tails behind them"

was certainly tried long enough with conspirators who had shown unmistakably that they desired nothing so much as the continuance of peace, especially when it was all on one side, and who would never have given the Government the great advantage of being attacked in Fort Sumter, had they not supposed they were dealing with men who could not be cuffed into resistance. The lesson we have to teach them now is, that we are thoroughly and terribly in earnest. Mr. Stephens's theories are to be put to a speedier and sterner test than he expected, and we are to prove which is stronger,—an oligarchy built *on* men, or a commonwealth built *of* them. Our structure is alive in every part with defensive and recuperative energies; woe to theirs, if that vaunted corner-stone which they believe patient and enduring as marble should begin to writhe with intelligent life!

We have no doubt of the issue. We believe that the strongest battalions are always on the side of God. The Southern army will be fighting for Jefferson Davis, or at most for the liberty of self-misgovernment, while we go forth for the defence of principles which alone make government august and civil society possible. It is the very life of the nation that is at stake. There is no question here of dynasties, races, religions,—but simply whether we will consent to include in our Bill of Rights—not merely as of equal validity with all other rights, whether natural or acquired, but by its very nature transcending and abrogating them all—the Right of Anarchy. We must convince men that treason against the ballot-box is as dangerous as treason against a throne, and that, if they play so desperate a game, they must stake their lives on the hazard. The one lesson that remained for us to teach the political theorists of the Old

World was, that we are as strong to suppress intestine disorder as foreign aggression, and we must teach it decisively and thoroughly. The economy of war is to be tested by the value of the object to be gained by it. A ten years' war would be cheap that gave us a country to be proud of and a flag that should command the respect of the world because it was the symbol of the enthusiastic unity of a great nation.

The Government, however slow it may have been to accept the war which Mr. Buchanan's supineness left them, is acting now with all energy and determination. What they have a right to claim is the confidence of the people, and that depends in good measure on the discretion of the press. Only let us have no more weakness under the plausible name of Conciliation. We need not discuss the probabilities of an acknowledgment of the Confederated States by England and France; we have only to say, "Acknowledge them at your peril." But there is no chance of the recognition of the Confederacy by any foreign governments, so long as it is without the confidence of the brokers. There is no question on which side the strength lies. The whole tone of the Southern journals, so far as we are able to judge, shows the inherent folly and weakness of the Secession movement. Men who feel strong in the justice of their cause, or confident in their powers, do not waste breath in childish boasts of their own superiority and querulous depreciation of their antagonists. They are weak, and they know it. And not only are they weak in comparison with the Free States, but we believe they are without the moral support of whatever deserves the name of public opinion at home. If not, why does their Congress, as they call it, hold council always with closed doors, like a knot of conspirators? The first tap of the Northern drum dispelled many illusions, and we need no better proof of which ship is sinking than that Mr. Caleb Cushing should have made such haste to come over to the old Constitution with the stars and stripes at her mast-head.

We cannot think that the war we are entering on can end without some radical change in the system of African slavery. Whether it be doomed to a sudden extinction, or to a gradual abolition through economical causes, this war will not leave it where it was before. As a power in the State, its reign is already over. The fiery tongues of the batteries in Charleston harbor accomplished in one day a conversion which the constancy of Garrison and the eloquence of Phillips had failed to bring about in thirty years. And whatever other result this war is destined to produce, it has already won for us a blessing worth everything to us as a nation in emancipating the public opinion of the North.

WASHINGTON, D.C., JULY 1861

Abraham Lincoln:
Message to Congress in Special Session

In his proclamation of April 15, President Lincoln had called the new 37th Congress, which was scheduled to meet in December 1861, into session on July 4.

———————

Fellow-citizens of the Senate and House of Representatives:
Having been convened on an extraordinary occasion, as authorized by the Constitution, your attention is not called to any ordinary subject of legislation.

At the beginning of the present Presidential term, four months ago, the functions of the Federal Government were found to be generally suspended within the several States of South Carolina, Georgia, Alabama, Mississippi, Louisiana, and Florida, excepting only those of the Post Office Department.

Within these States, all the Forts, Arsenals, Dock-yards, Custom-houses, and the like, including the movable and stationary property in, and about them, had been seized, and were held in open hostility to this Government, excepting only Forts Pickens, Taylor, and Jefferson, on, and near the Florida coast, and Fort Sumter, in Charleston harbor, South Carolina. The Forts thus seized had been put in improved condition; new ones had been built; and armed forces had been organized, and were organizing, all avowedly with the same hostile purpose.

The Forts remaining in the possession of the Federal government, in, and near, these States, were either besieged or menaced by warlike preparations; and especially Fort Sumter was nearly surrounded by well-protected hostile batteries, with guns equal in quality to the best of its own, and outnumbering the latter as perhaps ten to one. A disproportionate share, of the Federal muskets and rifles, had somehow found their way into these States, and had been seized, to be used against the government. Accumulations of the public revenue, lying within them, had been seized for the same object. The Navy was scattered in distant seas; leaving but a very small part of it within the immediate reach of the government. Officers of the Federal Army and Navy, had resigned in great numbers; and, of those resigning, a large proportion had taken up arms against the government. Simultaneously, and in connection, with all this, the purpose to sever the Federal Union, was openly avowed. In accordance with this purpose, an ordinance had been adopted in each of these States, declaring the States, respectively, to be separated from the National Union. A formula for instituting a combined government of these states had been promulgated; and this illegal organization, in the character of confederate States was already invoking recognition, aid, and intervention, from Foreign Powers.

Finding this condition of things, and believing it to be an imperative duty upon the incoming Executive, to prevent, if possible, the consummation of such attempt to destroy the Federal Union, a choice of means to that end became indispensable. This choice was made; and was declared in the Inaugural address. The policy chosen looked to the exhaustion of all peaceful measures, before a resort to any stronger ones. It sought only to hold the public places and property, not already wrested from the Government, and to collect the revenue; relying for the rest, on time, discussion, and the ballot-box. It promised a continuance of the mails, at government expense, to the very people who were resisting the government; and it gave repeated pledges against any disturbance to any of the people, or any of their rights. Of all that which a president might constitutionally, and justifiably, do in such a case, everything was foreborne, without which, it was believed possible to keep the government on foot.

On the 5th of March, (the present incumbent's first full day in office) a letter of Major Anderson, commanding at Fort Sumter, written on the 28th of February, and received at the War Department on the 4th of March, was, by that Department, placed in his hands. This letter expressed the professional opinion of the writer, that re-inforcements could not be thrown into that Fort within the time for his relief, rendered necessary by the limited supply of provisions, and with a view of holding possession of the same, with a force of less than twenty thousand good, and well-disciplined men. This opinion was concurred in by all the officers of his command; and their *memoranda* on the subject, were made enclosures of Major Anderson's letter. The whole was immediately laid before Lieutenant General Scott, who at once concurred with Major Anderson in opinion. On reflection, however, he took full time, consulting with other officers, both of the Army and the Navy; and, at the end of four days, came reluctantly, but decidedly, to the same conclusion as before. He also stated at the same time that no such sufficient force was then at the control of the Government, or could be raised, and brought to the ground, within the time when the provisions in the Fort would be exhausted. In a purely military point of view, this reduced the duty of the administration, in the case, to the mere matter of getting the garrison safely out of the Fort.

It was believed, however, that to so abandon that position, under the circumstances, would be utterly ruinous; that the *necessity* under which it was to be done, would not be fully understood—that, by many, it would be construed as a part of a *voluntary* policy—that, at home, it would discourage the friends of the Union, embolden its adversaries, and go far to insure to the latter, a recognition abroad—that, in fact, it would be our national destruction consummated. This could not be allowed. Starvation was not yet upon the garrison; and ere it would be reached, *Fort Pickens* might be reinforced. This last, would be a clear indication of *policy*, and would better enable the country to accept the evacuation of Fort Sumter, as a military *necessity*. An order was at once directed to be sent for the landing of the troops from the Steamship Brooklyn, into Fort Pickens. This order could not go by land, but must take the longer, and slower route by sea. The first return news from the order was received just one week before the fall of Fort Sumter. The news itself was, that the officer commanding the Sabine, to which vessel the troops had been transferred from the Brooklyn, acting upon some *quasi* armistice of the late administration, (and of the existence of which, the present administration, up to the time the order was despatched, had only too vague and uncertain rumors, to fix attention) had refused to land the troops. To now re-inforce Fort Pickens, before a crisis would be reached at Fort Sumter was impossible—rendered so by the near exhaustion of provisions in the latter-named Fort. In precaution against such a conjuncture, the government had, a few days before, commenced preparing an expedition, as well adapted as might be, to relieve Fort Sumter, which expedition was intended to be ultimately used, or not, according to circumstances. The strongest anticipated case, for using it, was now presented; and it was resolved to send it forward. As had been intended, in this contingency, it was also resolved to notify the Governor of South Carolina, that he might expect an attempt would be made to provision the Fort; and that, if the attempt should not be resisted, there would be no effort to throw in men, arms, or ammunition, without further notice, or in case of an attack upon the Fort. This notice was accordingly given; whereupon the Fort was attacked, and bombarded to its fall, without even awaiting the arrival of the provisioning expedition.

It is thus seen that the assault upon, and reduction of, Fort Sumter, was, in no sense, a matter of self defence on the part of the assailants. They well knew that the garrison in the Fort could, by no possibility, commit aggression upon them. They knew—they were expressly notified—that the giving of bread to the few brave and hungry men of the garrison, was all which would on that occasion be attempted, unless themselves, by resisting so much, should provoke more. They knew that this Government desired to keep the garrison in the Fort, not to assail them, but merely to maintain visible possession, and thus to preserve the Union from actual, and immediate dissolution —trusting, as herein-before stated, to time, discussion, and the ballot-box, for final adjustment; and they assailed, and reduced the Fort, for precisely the reverse object—to drive out the visible authority of the Federal Union, and thus force it to immediate dissolution.

That this was their object, the Executive well understood; and having said to them in the inaugural address, "You can have no conflict without being yourselves the aggressors," he took pains, not only to keep this declaration good, but also to keep the case so free from the power of ingenious sophistry, as that the world should not be able to misunderstand it. By the affair at Fort Sumter, with its surrounding circumstances, that point was reached. Then, and thereby, the assailants of the Government, began the conflict of arms, without a gun in sight, or in expectancy, to return their fire, save only the few in the Fort, sent to that harbor, years before, for their own protection, and still ready to give that protection, in whatever was lawful. In this act, discarding all else, they have forced upon the country, the distinct issue: "Immediate dissolution, or blood."

And this issue embraces more than the fate of these United States. It presents to the whole family of man, the question, whether a constitutional republic, or a democracy—a government of the people, by the same people—can, or cannot, maintain its territorial integrity, against its own domestic foes. It presents the question, whether discontented individuals, too few in numbers to control administration, according to organic law, in any case, can always, upon the pretences made in this case, or on any other pretences, or arbitrarily, without any pretence, break up their Government, and thus practically put an end to free government upon the earth. It forces us to ask: "Is there, in all republics, this inherent, and fatal weakness?" "Must a government, of necessity, be too *strong* for the liberties of its own people, or too *weak* to maintain its own existence?"

So viewing the issue, no choice was left but to call out the war power of the Government; and so to resist force, employed for its destruction, by force, for its preservation.

The call was made; and the response of the country was most gratifying; surpassing, in unanimity and spirit, the most sanguine expectation. Yet none of the States commonly called Slave-states, except Delaware, gave a Regiment through regular State organization. A few regiments have been organized within some others of those states, by individual enterprise, and received into the government service. Of course the seceded States, so called, (and to which Texas had been joined about the time of the inauguration,) gave no troops to the cause of the Union. The border States, so called, were not uniform in their actions; some of them being almost *for* the Union, while in others—as Virginia, North Carolina, Tennessee, and Arkansas—the Union sentiment was nearly repressed, and silenced. The course taken in Virginia was the most remarkable—perhaps the most important. A convention, elected by the people of that State, to consider this very question of disrupting the Federal Union, was in session at the capital of Virginia when Fort Sumter fell. To this body the people had chosen a large majority of *professed* Union men. Almost immediately after the fall of Sumter, many members of that majority went over to the original disunion minority, and, with them, adopted an ordinance for withdrawing the State from the Union. Whether this change was wrought by their great approval of the assault upon Sumter, or their great resentment at the government's resistance to that assault, is not definitely known. Although they submitted the ordinance, for ratification, to a vote of the people, to be taken on a day then somewhat more than a month distant, the convention, and the Legislature, (which was also in session at the same time and place) with leading men of the State, not members of either, immediately commenced acting, as if the State were already out of the Union. They pushed military preparations vigorously forward all over the state. They seized the United States Armory at Harper's Ferry, and the Navy-yard at Gosport, near Norfolk. They received—perhaps invited—into their state, large bodies of troops, with their warlike appointments, from the so-called seceded States. They formally entered into a treaty of temporary alliance, and co-operation with the so-called "Confederate States," and sent members to their Congress at Montgomery. And, finally, they permitted the insurrectionary government to be transferred to their capital at Richmond.

The people of Virginia have thus allowed this giant insurrection to make its nest within her borders; and this government has no choice left but to deal with it, *where* it finds it. And it has the less regret, as the loyal citizens have, in due form, claimed its protection. Those loyal citizens, this government is bound to recognize, and protect, as being Virginia.

In the border States, so called—in fact, the middle states—there are those who favor a policy which they call "armed neutrality"—that is, an arming of those states to prevent the Union forces passing one way, or the disunion, the other, over their soil. This would be disunion completed. Figuratively speaking, it would be the building of an impassable wall along the line of separation. And yet, not quite an impassable one;

for, under the guise of neutrality, it would tie the hands of the Union men, and freely pass supplies from among them, to the insurrectionists, which it could not do as an open enemy. At a stroke, it would take all the trouble off the hands of secession, except only what proceeds from the external blockade. It would do for the disunionists that which, of all things, they most desire—feed them well, and give them disunion without a struggle of their own. It recognizes no fidelity to the Constitution, no obligation to maintain the Union; and while very many who have favored it are, doubtless, loyal citizens, it is, nevertheless, treason in effect.

Recurring to the action of the government, it may be stated that, at first, a call was made for seventy-five thousand militia; and rapidly following this, a proclamation was issued for closing the ports of the insurrectionary districts by proceedings in the nature of Blockade. So far all was believed to be strictly legal. At this point the insurrectionists announced their purpose to enter upon the practice of privateering.

Other calls were made for volunteers, to serve three years, unless sooner discharged; and also for large additions to the regular Army and Navy. These measures, whether strictly legal or not, were ventured upon, under what appeared to be a popular demand, and a public necessity; trusting, then as now, that Congress would readily ratify them. It is believed that nothing has been done beyond the constitutional competency of Congress.

Soon after the first call for militia, it was considered a duty to authorize the Commanding General, in proper cases, according to his discretion, to suspend the privilege of the writ of habeas corpus; or, in other words, to arrest, and detain, without resort to the ordinary processes and forms of law, such individuals as he might deem dangerous to the public safety. This authority has purposely been exercised but very sparingly. Nevertheless, the legality and propriety of what has been done under it, are questioned; and the attention of the country has been called to the proposition that one who is sworn to "take care that the laws be faithfully executed," should not himself violate them. Of course some consideration was given to the questions of power, and propriety, before this matter was acted upon. The whole of the laws which were required to be faithfully executed, were being resisted, and failing of execution, in nearly one-third of the States. Must they be allowed to finally fail of execution, even had it been perfectly clear, that by the use of the means necessary to their execution, some single law, made in such extreme tenderness of the citizen's liberty, that practically, it relieves more of the guilty, than of the innocent, should, to a very limited extent, be violated? To state the question more directly, are all the laws, *but one*, to go unexecuted, and the government itself go to pieces, lest that one be violated? Even in such a case, would not the official oath be broken, if the government should be overthrown, when it was believed that disregarding the single law, would tend to preserve it? But it was not believed that this question was presented. It was not believed that any law was violated. The provision of the Constitution that "The privilege of the writ of habeas corpus, shall not be suspended unless when, in cases of rebellion or invasion, the public safety may require it," is equivalent to a provision—is a provision—that such privilege may be suspended when, in cases of rebellion, or invasion, the public safety *does* require it. It was decided that we have a case of rebellion, and that the public safety does require the qualified suspension of the privilege of the writ which was authorized to be made. Now it is insisted that Congress, and not the Executive, is vested with this power. But the Constitution itself, is silent as to which, or who, is to exercise the power; and as the provision was plainly made for a dangerous emergency, it cannot be believed the framers of the instrument intended, that in every case, the danger should run its course, until Congress could be called together; the very assembling of which might be prevented, as was intended in this case, by the rebellion.

No more extended argument is now offered; as an opinion, at some length, will probably be presented by the Attorney General. Whether there shall be any legislation upon the subject, and if any, what, is submitted entirely to the better judgment of Congress.

The forbearance of this government had been so extraordinary, and so long continued, as to lead some foreign nations to shape their action as if they supposed the early destruction of our national Union was probable. While this, on discovery, gave the Executive some concern, he is now happy to say that the sovereignty, and rights of the United States, are now everywhere practically respected by foreign powers; and a general sympathy with the country is manifested throughout the world.

The reports of the Secretaries of the Treasury, War, and the Navy, will give the information in detail deemed necessary, and convenient for your deliberation, and action; while the Executive, and all the Departments, will stand ready to supply omissions, or to communicate new facts, considered important for you to know.

It is now recommended that you give the legal means for making this contest a short, and a decisive one; that you place at the control of the government, for the work, at least four hundred thousand men, and four hundred millions of dollars. That number of men is about one tenth of those of proper ages within the regions where, apparently, *all* are willing to engage; and the sum is less than a twentythird part of the money value owned by the men who seem ready to devote the whole. A debt of six hundred millions of dollars *now*, is a less sum per head, than was the debt of our revolution, when we came out of that struggle; and the money value in the country now, bears even a greater proportion to what it was *then*, than does the population. Surely each man has as strong a motive *now*, to *preserve* our liberties, as each had *then*, to *establish* them.

A right result, at this time, will be worth more to the world, than ten times the men, and ten times the money. The evidence reaching us from the country, leaves no doubt, that the material for the work is abundant; and that it needs only the hand of legislation to give it legal sanction, and the hand of the Executive to give it practical shape and efficiency. One of the greatest perplexities of the government, is to avoid receiving troops faster than it can provide for them. In a word, the people will save their government, if the government itself, will do its part, only indifferently well.

It might seem, at first thought, to be of little difference whether the present movement at the South be called "secession" or "rebellion." The movers, however, well understand the difference. At the beginning, they knew they could never raise their treason to any respectable magnitude, by any name which implies *violation* of law. They knew their people possessed as much of moral sense, as much of devotion to law and order, and as much pride in, and reverence for, the history, and government, of their common country, as any other civilized, and patriotic people. They knew they could make no advancement directly in the teeth of these strong and noble sentiments. Accordingly they commenced by an insidious debauching of the public mind. They invented an ingenious sophism, which, if conceded, was followed by perfectly logical steps, through all the incidents, to the complete destruction of the Union. The sophism itself is, that any state of the Union may, *consistently* with the national Constitution, and therefore *lawfully*, and *peacefully*, withdraw from the Union, without the consent of the Union, or of any other state. The little disguise that the supposed right is to be exercised only for just cause, themselves to be the sole judge of its justice, is too thin to merit any notice.

With rebellion thus sugar-coated, they have been drugging the public mind of their section for more than thirty years; and, until at length, they have brought many good men to a willingness to take up arms against the government the day *after* some assemblage of men have enacted the farcical pretence of taking their State out of the Union, who could have been brought to no such thing the day *before*.

This sophism derives much—perhaps the whole—of its currency, from the assumption, that there is some omnipotent, and sacred supremacy, pertaining to a *State*—to each State of our Federal Union. Our States have neither more, nor less power, than that reserved to them, in the Union, by the Constitution—no one of them ever having been a State *out* of the Union. The original ones passed into the Union even *before* they cast off their British colonial dependence; and the new ones each came into the Union directly from a condition of dependence, excepting Texas. And even Texas, in its temporary independence, was never designated a State. The new ones only took the designation of States, on coming into the Union, while that name was first adopted for the old ones, in, and by, the Declaration of Independence. Therein the "United Colonies" were declared to be "Free and Independent States"; but, even then, the object plainly was not to declare their independence of *one another*, or of the *Union*; but directly the contrary, as their mutual pledge, and their mutual action, before, at the time, and afterwards, abundantly show. The express plighting of faith, by each and all of the original thirteen, in the Articles of Confederation, two years later, that the Union shall be perpetual, is most conclusive. Having never been States, either in substance, or in name, *outside* of the Union, whence this magical omnipotence of "State rights," asserting a claim of power to lawfully destroy the Union itself? Much is said about the "sovereignty" of the States; but the word, even, is not in the national Constitution; nor, as is believed, in any of the State constitutions. What is a "sovereignty," in the political sense of the term? Would it be far wrong to define it "A political community, without a political superior"? Tested by this, no one of our States, except Texas, ever was a sovereignty. And even Texas gave up the character on coming into the Union; by which act, she acknowledged the Constitution of the United States, and the laws and treaties of the United States made in pursuance of the Constitution, to be, for her, the supreme law of the land. The States have their *status* IN the Union, and they have no other *legal status*. If they break from this, they can only do so against law, and by revolution. The Union, and not themselves separately, procured their independence, and their liberty. By conquest, or purchase, the Union gave each of them, whatever of independence, and liberty, it has. The Union is older than any of the States; and, in fact, it created them as States. Originally, some dependent colonies made the Union; and, in turn, the Union threw off their old dependence, for them, and made them States, such as they are. Not one of them ever had a State constitution, independent of the Union. Of course, it is not forgotten that all the new States framed their constitutions, before they entered the Union; nevertheless, dependent upon, and preparatory to, coming into the Union.

Unquestionably the States have the powers, and rights, reserved to them in, and by the National Constitution; but among these, surely, are not included all conceivable powers, however mischievous, or destructive; but, at most, such only, as were known in the world, at the time, as governmental powers; and certainly, a power to destroy the government itself, had never been known as a governmental—as a merely administrative power. This relative matter of National power, and State rights, as a principle, is no other than the principle of *generality*, and *locality*. Whatever concerns the whole, should be confided to the whole—to the general government; while, whatever concerns *only* the State, should be left exclusively, to the State. This is all there is of original principle about it. Whether the National Constitution, in defining boundaries between the two, has applied the principle with exact accuracy, is not to be questioned. We are all bound by that defining, without question.

What is now combatted, is the position that secession is *consistent* with the Constitution—is *lawful*, and *peaceful*. It is not contended that there is any express law for it; and nothing should ever be implied as law, which leads to unjust, or absurd consequences. The nation purchased, with money, the countries out of which several of these States were formed. Is it just that they shall go off without leave, and without refunding? The nation paid very large sums, (in the aggregate, I believe, nearly a hundred millions) to relieve Florida of the aboriginal tribes. Is it just that she shall now be off without consent, or without making any return? The nation is now in debt for money applied to the benefit of these so-called seceding States, in common with the rest. Is it just, either that creditors shall go unpaid, or the remaining States pay the whole? A part of the present national debt was contracted to pay the old debts of Texas. Is it just that she shall leave, and pay no part of this herself?

Again, if one State may secede, so may another; and when all shall have seceded, none is left to pay the debts. Is this quite just to creditors? Did we notify them of this sage view of ours, when we borrowed their money? If we now recognize this doctrine, by allowing the seceders to go in peace, it is difficult to see what we can do, if others choose to go, or to extort terms upon which they will promise to remain.

The seceders insist that our Constitution admits of secession. They have assumed to make a National Constitution of their own, in which, of necessity, they have either *discarded*, or *retained*, the right of secession, as they insist, it exists in ours. If they have discarded it, they thereby admit that, on principle, it ought not to be in ours. If they have retained it, by their own construction of ours they show that to be consistent they must secede from one another, whenever they shall find it the easiest way of settling their debts, or effecting any other selfish, or unjust object. The principle itself is one of disintegration, and upon which no government can possibly endure.

If all the States, save one, should assert the power to *drive* that one out of the Union, it is presumed the whole class of seceder politicians would at once deny the power, and denounce the act as the greatest outrage upon State rights. But suppose that precisely the same act, instead of being called "driving the one out," should be called "the seceding of the others from that one," it would be exactly what the seceders claim to do; unless, indeed, they make the point, that the one, because it is a minority, may rightfully do, what the others, because they are a majority, may not rightfully do. These politicians are subtle, and profound, on the rights of minorities. They are not partial to that power which made the Constitution, and speaks from the preamble, calling itself "We, the People."

It may well be questioned whether there is, to-day, a majority of the legally qualified voters of any State, except perhaps South Carolina, in favor of disunion. There is much reason to believe that the Union men are the majority in many, if not in every other one, of the so-called seceded States. The contrary has not been demonstrated in any one of them. It is ventured to affirm this, even of Virginia and Tennessee; for the result of an election, held in military camps, where the bayonets are all on one side of the question voted upon, can scarcely be considered as demonstrating popular sentiment. At such an election, all that large class who are, at once, *for* the Union, and *against* coercion, would be coerced to vote against the Union.

It may be affirmed, without extravagance, that the free institutions we enjoy, have developed the powers, and improved the condition, of our whole people, beyond any example in the world. Of this we now have a striking, and an impressive illustration. So large an army as the government has now on foot, was never before known, without a soldier in it, but who had taken his place there, of his own free choice. But more than this: there are many single Regiments whose members, one and another, possess full practical knowledge of all the arts, sciences, professions, and whatever else, whether useful or elegant, is known in the world; and there is scarcely one, from which there could not be selected, a President, a Cabinet, a Congress, and perhaps a Court, abundantly competent to administer the government itself. Nor do I say this is not true, also, in the army of our late friends, now adversaries, in this contest; but if it is, so much better the reason why the government, which has conferred such benefits on both them and us, should not be broken up. Whoever, in any section, proposes to abandon such a government, would do well to consider, in deference to what principle it is, that he does it—what better he is likely to get in its stead—whether the substitute will give, or be intended to give, so much of good to the people. There are some foreshadowings on this subject. Our adversaries have adopted some Declarations of Independence; in which, unlike the good old one, penned by Jefferson, they omit the words "all men are created equal." Why? They have adopted a temporary national constitution, in the preamble of which, unlike our good old one, signed by Washington, they omit "We, the People," and substitute "We, the deputies of the sovereign and independent States." Why? Why this deliberate pressing out of view, the rights of men, and the authority of the people?

This is essentially a People's contest. On the side of the Union, it is a struggle for maintaining in the world, that form, and substance of government, whose leading object is, to elevate the condition of men—to lift artificial weights from all shoulders—to clear the paths of laudable pursuit for all—to afford all, an unfettered start, and a fair chance, in the race of life. Yielding to partial, and temporary departures, from necessity, this is the leading object of the government for whose existence we contend.

I am most happy to believe that the plain people understand, and appreciate this. It is worthy of note, that while in this, the government's hour of trial, large numbers of those in the Army and Navy, who have been favored with the offices, have resigned, and proved false to the hand which had pampered them, not one common soldier, or common sailor is known to have deserted his flag.

Great honor is due to those officers who remain true, despite the example of their treacherous associates; but the greatest honor, and most important fact of all, is the unanimous firmness of the common soldiers, and common sailors. To the last man, so far as known, they have successfully resisted the traitorous efforts of those, whose commands, but an hour before, they obeyed as absolute law. This is the patriotic instinct of the plain people. They understand, without an argument, that destroying the government, which was made by Washington, means no good to them.

Our popular government has often been called an experiment. Two points in it, our people have already settled—the successful *establishing*, and the successful *administering* of it. One still remains—its successful *maintenance* against a formidable internal attempt to overthrow it. It is now for them to demonstrate to the world, that those who can fairly carry an election, can also suppress a rebellion—that ballots are the rightful, and peaceful, successors of bullets; and that when ballots have fairly, and constitutionally, decided, there can be no successful appeal, back to bullets; that there can be no successful appeal, except to ballots themselves, at succeeding elections. Such will be a great lesson of peace; teaching men that what they cannot take by an election, neither can they take it by a war—teaching all, the folly of being the beginners of a war.

Lest there be some uneasiness in the minds of candid men, as to what is to be the course of the government, towards the Southern States, *after* the rebellion shall have been suppressed, the Executive deems it proper to say, it will be his purpose then, as ever, to be guided by the Constitution, and the laws; and that he probably will have no different understanding of the powers, and duties of the Federal government, relatively to the rights of the States, and the people, under the Constitution, than that expressed in the inaugural address.

He desires to preserve the government, that it may be administered for all, as it was administered by the men who made it. Loyal citizens everywhere, have the right to claim this of their government; and the government has no right to withhold, or neglect it. It is not perceived that, in giving it, there is any coercion, any conquest, or any subjugation, in any just sense of those terms.

The Constitution provides, and all the States have accepted

the provision, that "The United States shall guarantee to every State in this Union a republican form of government." But, if a State may lawfully go out of the Union, having done so, it may also discard the republican form of government; so that to prevent its going out, is an indispensable *means*, to the *end*, of maintaining the guaranty mentioned; and when an end is lawful and obligatory, the indispensable means to it, are also lawful, and obligatory.

It was with the deepest regret that the Executive found the duty of employing the war-power, in defence of the government, forced upon him. He could but perform this duty, or surrender the existence of the government. No compromise, by public servants, could, in this case, be a cure; not that compromises are not often proper, but that no popular government can long survive a marked precedent, that those who carry an election, can only save the government from immediate destruction, by giving up the main point, upon which the people gave the election. The people themselves, and not their servants, can safely reverse their own deliberate decisions. As a private citizen, the Executive could not have consented that these institutions shall perish; much less could he, in betrayal of so vast, and so sacred a trust, as these free people had confided to him. He felt that he had no moral right to shrink; nor even to count the chances of his own life, in what might follow. In full view of his great responsibility, he has, so far, done what he has deemed his duty. You will now, according to your own judgment, perform yours. He sincerely hopes that your views, and your action, may so accord with his, as to assure all faithful citizens, who have been disturbed in their rights, of a certain, and speedy restoration to them, under the Constitution, and the laws.

And having thus chosen our course, without guile, and with pure purpose, let us renew our trust in God, and go forward without fear, and with manly hearts.

July 4, 1861.

AN UNOBSERVED HOLIDAY:
LOUISIANA, JULY 1861

Kate Stone: Journal, July 4, 1861

On the day that Congress met in Washington, Kate Stone reflected on the changes caused by the war.

July 4: Mamma is still in bed but is better. The boys have holiday in honor of the Fourth but more I think to keep up old customs than for any feeling of respect for the day. This is the first Fourth in our memory to pass without a public merrymaking of some kind, but we do not hear of the day's being celebrated in town or country. There are other and sterner duties before us. It would ill become us as a Nation to be celebrating a day of independence when we are fighting for our very existence.

This July sun has set on a Nation in arms against itself, host against host. Those who have clasped each other's hands in kindest spirits less than one short year ago, as friends, as countrymen, as children of one common Mother, now stand opposing each other in deadliest hate, eager to water Old Mother Earth with the blood of her children. Our Cause is right and God will give us the victory. Will the next July sun rise on a Nation peaceful, prosperous, and happy, or on a land desolate and disgraced? He alone knows.

Congress meets today. The lives of thousands hang on its decision. Will it be for peace or war? We should know by Saturday.

Brother Coley returned tonight. He had gone to Memphis with Aunt Sarah. Mr. Miller is stationed only seven hours from Memphis and can run in quite frequently. He is trying to get the Colonelcy of a regiment and is stirring around in his usual style. He says he spends $2,000 a month and lives delightfully. Hope he will make an equal division with Aunt Sarah. Brother Coley enjoyed the trip greatly.

FACING THE ENEMY: MISSOURI, JULY 1861

Ulysses S. Grant: from Personal Memoirs of U. S. Grant

Grant had been appointed commander of the 21st Illinois Volunteers in June 1861, and in July he was ordered to cross into Missouri with his regiment. He would later recall the experience in *Personal Memoirs of U. S. Grant* (1885).

MY SENSATIONS as we approached what I supposed might be "a field of battle" were anything but agreeable. I had been in all the engagements in Mexico that it was possible for one person to be in; but not in command. If some one else had been colonel and I had been lieutenant-colonel I do not think I would have felt any trepidation. Before we were prepared to cross the Mississippi River at Quincy my anxiety was relieved; for the men of the besieged regiment came straggling into town. I am inclined to think both sides got frightened and ran away.

I took my regiment to Palmyra and remained there for a few days, until relieved by the 19th Illinois infantry. From Palmyra I proceeded to Salt River, the railroad bridge over which had been destroyed by the enemy. Colonel John M. Palmer at that time commanded the 13th Illinois, which was acting as a guard to workmen who were engaged in rebuilding this bridge. Palmer was my senior and commanded the two regiments as long as we remained together. The bridge was finished in about two weeks, and I received orders to move against Colonel Thomas Harris, who was said to be encamped at the little town of Florida, some twenty-five miles south of where we then were.

At the time of which I now write we had no transportation and the country about Salt River was sparsely settled, so that it took some days to collect teams and drivers enough to move the camp and garrison equipage of a regiment nearly a thousand strong, together with a week's supply of provision and some ammunition. While preparations for the move were going on I felt quite comfortable; but when we got on the road and found every house deserted I was anything but easy. In the twenty-five miles we had to march we did not see a person, old or young, male or female, except two horsemen who were on a road that crossed ours. As soon as they saw us they decamped as fast as their horses could carry them. I kept my men in the ranks and forbade their entering any of the deserted houses or taking anything from them. We halted at night on the road and proceeded the next morning at an early hour. Harris had been encamped in a creek bottom for the sake of being near water. The hills on either side of the creek extend to a considerable height, possibly more than a hundred feet. As we approached the brow of the hill from which it was expected we could see Harris' camp, and possibly find his men ready formed to meet us, my heart kept getting higher and higher until it felt to me as though it was in my throat. I would have given anything then to have been back in Illinois, but I had not the moral courage to halt and consider what to do; I kept right on. When we reached a point from which the valley below was in full view I halted. The place where Harris had been encamped a few days before was still there and the marks of a recent encampment were plainly visible, but the troops were gone. My heart resumed its place. It occurred to me at once that Harris had been as much afraid of me as I had been of him. This was a view of the question I had never taken before; but it was one I never forgot afterwards. From that event to the close of the war, I never experienced trepidation upon confronting an enemy, though I always felt more or less anxiety. I never forgot that he had as much reason to fear my forces as I had his. The lesson was valuable.

Inquiries at the village of Florida divulged the fact that Colonel Harris, learning of my intended movement, while my transportation was being collected took time by the forelock and left Florida before I had started from Salt River. He had increased the distance between us by forty miles. The next day I started back to my old camp at Salt River bridge. The citizens living on the line of our march had returned to their houses after we passed, and finding everything in good order, nothing carried away, they were at their front doors ready to greet us now. They had evidently been led to believe that the National troops carried death and devastation with them wherever they went.

DEFEATS IN WESTERN VIRGINIA: JULY 1861

Sallie Brock: from
Richmond During the War

A Virginia native, Sallie Brock was working as a tutor in King and Queen County in 1860. As the war began she returned to Richmond, where her father owned a hotel. In a memoir published in 1867, Brock describes learning of the Confederate defeats in western Virginia at Rich Mountain, July 11, and Carrick's Ford, July 13.

DISASTER IN WESTERN VIRGINIA.

THE SMOKE of battle had scarcely cleared away, and the shouts of victory died upon the ear, after the animating contest at Great Bethel, before the news of disaster to our forces in Western Virginia came to dampen the ardor arising from our recent successes. We were to be blessed no longer with bloodless victories. The trial of soul had begun.

The Confederate camp at Philippi had been surprised and dispersed. This disaster, as stated in the Richmond *Dispatch*, was caused by a sentinel sleeping on his post. Intimations of a contemplated attack upon the Confederate camp had been conveyed to them by two heroic women, who rode thirty miles on horseback in the night to warn them of the approach of the Federals, but too late to prevent the confusion that followed. By this misfortune to the Confederates these valorous women were cut off from their homes, and without a change of apparel were compelled to come on to Richmond, where they remained until they could conveniently return to their former places of abode.

The defeat at Rich Mountain occurred a few days after the dispersion at Philippi, and Colonel John Pegram and his entire command of sixteen hundred men were captured.

Nor with this was the measure of disaster in Western Virginia complete. General Garnett was in command of all the forces in the northwestern section of the State. With only about three thousand men he had intrenched himself at Laurel Hill; but from the well-intentioned blunders of inexperienced officers and men, and from the defeat of Colonel Pegram at Rich Mountain, he was compelled to retreat, which he managed to do in good order. Closely pressed by the enemy until he reached the second ford of Cheat River, being himself in the rear, his riderless horse announced to the vanguard that their brave commander had fallen. At Carrick's Ford, where he was killed, the enemy abandoned the pursuit, and the Confederates succeeded in forming a junction with the force under General Jackson.

Although the numbers in killed, wounded and missing were comparatively so small, this disaster was truly discouraging, as it caused the surrender of a very important portion of Northwestern Virginia, and was keenly felt as the very first check to Southern arms. Our troops had not, however, shown any failure in courage; and the fatigue endured by them in the undertaking, and the success of the retreat had not then a parallel in the history of the war. But the deepest regret was experienced at the untimely end of the gallant General Garnett. He was the first officer of high rank who had fallen in battle in the Confederate army, and his death cast the deepest gloom over the hearts of the many who loved and honored him for his bravery and nobility of spirit. He was a native of Essex County, Virginia, and belonged to an old and highly respectable family, numbering in its connection several men of distinguished talent and position. He had himself received a military education, and was thought to possess the genius which would insure him success in his profession.

There is no denying that these reverses were the cause of much anxiety to the Southern people, and for the first time a gloom spread over the souls of many whose sanguine temperaments precluded the idea of possibility of defeat to Southern arms.

But the Richmond people, although they might for a few days be bowed down by defeat, were generally reassured by the very accommodating press, which conveniently and wisely, doubtless, appropriated the proverb, "What cannot be cured must be endured;" and thus succeeded in allaying the usual discouragement and mistrust arising from petty defeats and disappointments.

We had, however, very little time to devote to the luxury of lamentation over our fallen brave, or to the sad misfortunes to our cause in Western Virginia. The sad strains of mournful music, the dull sounds of the muffled drum, as borne in the procession of the lamented Garnett, were only just lost in the busy hum of every-day life in Richmond, when our attention was called to the condition of things in a different portion of the State. Over the Potomac, and especially in the vicinity of Harper's Ferry, which had been evacuated by the Federals, the war-clouds hung heavily and ominously, and it seemed altogether evident to us that it could not be long ere the dark and sombre masses would burst upon us in the lurid lightnings and hoarse thunders of battle. We knew that somewhere in that section of Virginia would be enacted fierce scenes of sanguinary strife. July, 1861, opened upon us with a knowledge of the fact that two of the largest armies that the continent of America had ever seen were ranged in hostile defiance, and awaited with anxiety the signal to measure the relative strength of the North and South. All hearts were directed to that portion of the State over which the storm must soon break.

Our women for a time suspended the busy operations of the needle, and set aside the more expeditious and labor-saving sewing machine, to apply themselves more industriously to the preparation of lint, the rolling of bandages, and the many other nameless necessaries which the signs of the times made apparent would soon be in requisition for the unfortunates which the chances of battle would send among us mutilated and helpless. No longer the sempstress, every woman of Richmond began to prepare herself for the more difficult and responsible duties of the nurse. What pen can describe in fitting terms the history of the anxious hearts hidden behind the busy exterior, in those labors which patriotism dignified into duty, and which were lightened by cheerfulness and love? What pencil can paint the rainbow tints that glowed in the briny tear as it fell upon the snowy pile of lint which accumulated under the hands of her who had laid her heart's idol upon the altar of her country? What imagination can picture the midnight experiences of the restless, anxious ones from whose eyelids sleep had fled, as day after day and night after night brought nearer and nearer the dreaded day, which might close over in the darkness of death all we held most dear? Who can enumerate the prayers wafted on every breath, which in the humble and simple language of the publican went up continually in the cry, "Lord have mercy?"

A FAREWELL LETTER: JULY 1861

Sullivan Ballou to Sarah Ballou

A lawyer who had served in the Rhode Island legislature and campaigned for Lincoln in 1860, Sullivan Ballou was commissioned as a major in the 2nd Rhode Island Volunteers on June 11, 1861. A week before the battle of Bull Run, he wrote a farewell letter to his wife and left it in his trunk at camp. During the battle a six-pound cannon shot shattered his leg, and Ballou died of his wounds on July 28, 1861.

———————

Head-Quarters, Camp Clark,
Washington, D. C., July 14, 1861.

My Very Dear Wife:

The indications are very strong that we shall move in a few days, perhaps to-morrow. Lest I should not be able to write you again, I feel impelled to write a few lines, that may fall under your eye when I shall be no more.

Our movement may be one of a few days duration and full of pleasure—and it may be one of severe conflict and death to me. Not my will, but thine, O God, be done. If it is necessary that I should fall on the battle-field for my country, I am ready. I have no misgivings about, or lack of confidence in, the cause in which I am engaged, and my courage does not halt or falter. I know how strongly American civilization now leans upon the triumph of the government, and how great a debt we owe to those who went before us through the blood and suffering of the Revolution, and I am willing, perfectly willing to lay down all my joys in this life to help maintain this government, and to pay that debt.

But, my dear wife, when I know, that, with my own joys, I lay down nearly all of yours, and replace them in this life with cares and sorrows,—when, after having eaten for long years the bitter fruit of orphanage myself, I must offer it, as their only sustenance, to my dear little children, is it weak or dishonorable, while the banner of my purpose floats calmly and proudly in the breeze, that my unbounded love for you, my darling wife and children, should struggle in fierce, though useless, contest with my love of country.

I cannot describe to you my feelings on this calm summer night, when two thousand men are sleeping around me, many of them enjoying the last, perhaps, before that of death,—and I, suspicious that Death is creeping behind me with his fatal dart, am communing with God, my country and thee.

I have sought most closely and diligently, and often in my breast, for a wrong motive in thus hazarding the happiness of those I loved, and I could not find one. A pure love of my country, and of the principles I have often advocated before the people, and "the name of honor, that I love more than I fear death," have called upon me, and I have obeyed.

Sarah, my love for you is deathless. It seems to bind me with mighty cables, that nothing but Omnipotence can break; and yet, my love of country comes over me like a strong wind, and bears me irresistibly on with all those chains, to the battle-field. The memories of all the blissful moments I have spent with you, come crowding over me, and I feel most deeply grateful to God and you, that I have enjoyed them so long. And how hard it is for me to give them up, and burn to ashes the hopes of future years, when, God willing, we might still have lived and loved together, and seen our boys grow up to honorable manhood around us.

I know I have but few claims upon Divine Providence, but something whispers to me, perhaps it is the wafted prayer of my little Edgar, that I shall return to my loved ones unharmed. If I do not, my dear Sarah, never forget how much I love you, nor that, when my last breath escapes me on the battle-field, it will whisper your name.

Forgive my many faults, and the many pains I have caused you. How thoughtless, how foolish I have oftentimes been! How gladly would I wash out with my tears, every little spot upon your happiness, and struggle with all the misfortune of this world, to shield you and my children from harm. But I cannot. I must watch you from the spirit land and hover near you, while you buffet the storms with your precious little freight, and wait with sad patience till we meet to part no more.

But, O Sarah, if the dead can come back to this earth, and flit unseen around those they loved, I shall always be near you—in the garish day, and the darkest night—amidst your happiest scenes and gloomiest hours—always, always; and, if the soft breeze fans your cheek, it shall be my breath; or the cool air cools your throbbing temples, it shall be my spirit passing by.

Sarah, do not mourn me dead; think I am gone, and wait for me, for we shall meet again.

As for my little boys, they will grow as I have done, and never know a father's love and care. Little Willie is too young to remember me long, and my blue-eyed Edgar will keep my frolics with him among the dimmest memories of his childhood. Sarah, I have unlimited confidence in your maternal care, and your development of their characters. Tell my two mothers, I call God's blessing upon them. O Sarah, I wait for you *there!* Come to me, and lead thither my children.

SULLIVAN.

BATTLE OF MANASSAS: VIRGINIA, JULY 1861

Charles Minor Blackford: from Letters from Lee's Army

After the Provisional Confederate Congress voted in late May to move the Confederate capital from Montgomery to Richmond, political pressure increased in the North for the army at Washington to take offensive action in Virginia. At a meeting held on June 29 General Irvin McDowell asked for more time to train his troops, but was ordered by Lincoln to move against the Confederate army of 20,000 men under General Pierre G. T. Beauregard defending the key railroad junction at Manassas. McDowell began his advance with 30,000 troops on July 16 and attacked across Bull Run on the morning of July 21. By this time General Joseph Johnston had brought most of his 11,000 men by rail to reinforce Beauregard from the Shenandoah Valley. A lawyer from Lynchburg, Charles Minor Blackford was a first lieutenant in Company B, 30th Virginia Volunteers (later the 2nd Virginia Cavalry) who had previously fought in a skirmish at Vienna, Virginia, in June. He was recovering from an attack of dysentery when the battle began.

July 20th.

This day I spent lying down and taking remedies. By night I was so much better I determined to go back to duty. So, with some pain, I mounted my horse and rode back to my company reaching them about nine o'clock much worn down by my ride. The men welcomed me gladly. They had seen no yankees and very little expected the storm that was to break over our heads so soon. A bed of leaves was made for me and I laid down to rest. My own opinion was that a great battle was going to be fought the next day. The thoughts of a thinking man the day before a battle are necessarily solemn, he may be buoyant and hopeful, yet there is a dread uncertainty that comes over his thoughts both as to himself and those dependent on him which makes him grave and almost sad. I was tired and despite the thoughts of the next day's work I soon dropped off to sleep and never moved until roused by my servant, John Scott, early Sunday morning. He told me to get up, something was going on, he did not know what but I'd better get up and make ready. I soon discovered what was about to happen. All the troops around me were up and cooking their breakfast, though it was scarcely light, and every one seemed to think an attack was about to be made upon our lines, but no one knew where. We supposed it would be made down towards the center where it was made on the 18th.

The bivouac of our squadron was on the extreme left near the Henry house as it was called. Mrs. Henry, who lived in it, and was so very old and infirm she refused to move out of it. She was said to have been a Miss Carter, and to have been one of the family who once owned the Sudley farm nearby. Mrs. Henry's house during the day became a strategic point of great importance and was much torn up by shot and shell, by one of which she was killed. In her yard General Bee was killed and near it Colonel Bartow. Near it also it was that General Jackson formed his heroic brigade and received the baptism of fire during which he received the immortal name of "Stonewall." A few days after the battle I got a piece of cedar post from the ruins of the house, and cut some crosses and other things which I sent home as mementoes, and which I still have.

We were thrown into line about sunrise on the brow of a hill which overlooked Bull Run, with quite a wide valley (two hundred yards at least), below us. On the other side the bluff rose quite steeply, but on the top of it there was an open field. We were placed in that position to support a battery of artillery, whose I did not find out for it was moved very soon after the battle began to rage on our extreme left above the stone bridge.

I was still weak and John Scott brought me out to the line of battle another cup of coffee. He also brought some oats for my horse, which had not finished eating when I mounted him. He got an ammunition box to put the oats in and the horse was eating while I drank the coffee. We could distinctly hear the rumble of the yankee artillery on the pike beyond the run, and there was no doubt they were moving in force towards the stone bridge and the Sudley farm and proposed to turn our left wing and sweep down on our side the run and our line.

While we stood thus listening to the rumbling artillery and watching the dust as it arose from many hostile feet, we noticed a Federal battery of four guns suddenly dash out of the woods and throw itself into battery in the open space on the other side of the run above the bluff. We were much interested in the beauty of the movement, all of which we could see plainly, as it was not more than five hundred yards distant, but in a moment they opened upon our lines. The first shells went high above us, but the second were better aimed, and one of them struck the box out of which my horse was eating and shattered it to fragments, and then went on amongst the infantry behind us. John Scott did not move, or show any signs of fear. Having fired those two rounds they limbered up and left us as quickly as they came, and before our battery had done them any injury. When I noticed the first fire in some way I never dreamed the creatures were firing at us, so I went on drinking my coffee, but I was very rudely awakened from the dream by the second round when my indifference was changed to indignation, that they should actually have the impudence to fire at us on our own ground, and when we were doing them no harm.

After this there was a lull for a half hour while we remained in line of battle, but with no enemy in sight, then we heard the sound of cannon and musketry on our left, towards the stone bridge. We were moved up nearer the fighting, two other companies having joined us, and the whole thing being under the command of Lieut.-Col. Thomas T. Munford, of our regiment. The sounds indicated that the battle was growing fast and furious on our left, and that our lines were slowly being driven back, at which we were not surprised, as we knew we had but a small force on our left, and it was then obvious that the enemy was hurling upon it their whole force. We waited orders with great impatience and anxiety, for we saw our people were giving way and we could not see why we could not be of use. The battery we were supporting had been moved and there were no other troops very near us. I think Colonel Cocke forgot us, at all events we remained in the same position until near three o'clock in the evening.

About nine o'clock Generals Beauregard and Johnston, with their respective staffs, dashed by us, about fifty persons, handsomely dressed and mounted, and making a very grand show, and one which appealed to our enthusiasm very much, though all of us thought that one of the two generals should have been up with Colonel Cocke much earlier. Doubtless, however, they had good cause for the delay. Immediately behind them, at a sweeping gallop, came the "Washington Artillery," a battalion of sixteen guns. This was the most inspiring sight I ever saw, and fills me with emotion whenever I think of it now. One not familiar with artillery can little imagine how grand a sight it was. Each gun had four horses, with outriders and officers on horseback and several men mounted on the gun; then the caisson of each gun with its four horses and the like equipment of men, making thirty-two in all. Their ammunition wagons, forges and ambulances, all at full speed, making a procession, which under the circumstances, was very inspiring. Following the battalion next came "Hampton's Legion" of infantry under Col. Wade Hampton. Then a long and continuous line of infantry came pouring by as our troops were moved from the center and right wing to meet the attack on the left.

It is very easy, of course to criticise the conduct of the battle, and it is very unfair, as the critic does not know the inside causes, but while we stood there in nervous anxiety we all concluded our generals had been out-generaled, and the enemy had gained a great point upon them in transferring so many troops without their knowledge to the left, and forcing that wing back as they did. Our troops were put to a great disadvantage when run directly into a fight after moving at almost double-quick from six to ten miles on a hot July day, yet many of them were put to the test. We wondered also why, after it was discovered how the attack was made and that the enemy had stretched out his column from Centreville parallel to our front in the march towards Sudley, an attack was not made on his column, or upon the rear of the column, cutting him off from his base. Instead large forces, even after sending troops to the left, were idle all day at Mitchell's and Blackburn's Fords. No use was made of the cavalry until late in the day and then it was scattered about in small detachments, each acting under different orders, its attack was of little avail except to increase the panic of the enemy inducing a greater loss to them of the material of war. If when the enemy commenced to break, a column of cavalry had crossed Bull Run half way between Manassas and the stone bridge, and opened fire upon them as they moved back on the Warrenton Pike the victory would have been far more disastrous to the enemy and our gain in material so much the greater.

As these troops were passing towards the enemy another dismal line was moving back in the opposite direction. I shall never forget them. They were the wounded, some walking, some on stretchers, some in ambulances, all seeking the field hospital, which was near us in the woods, and all giving proof of their persons as well as their tongues of the terrible carnage on the left, and many giving discouraging tidings that our line was slowly giving way. Troops, certainly none but veterans, should never, if possible, be taken into action so as to see a field hospital or to meet the wounded or demoralized men. It has a bad effect and renders them unsteady.

The news given by the wounded men made us very impatient. We felt there was certainly something for us to do but no orders came. About eleven o'clock we were moved again further to the left, but though within range of artillery we had no actual fighting. The enemy continued to advance and at last, about mid-morning we saw signs of demoralization on the part of some of our troops; but about that time we saw a long column of troops in the same direction moving towards us, which, at first, we thought was the enemy, but to our infinite relief we found was General Jackson's brigade which had just been put off a train of cars on the Manassas road. They doubled quick into action and met the enemy's line and were soon heavily engaged. I was not near enough to mark the fighting, or rather my view was too much obstructed to get a view, but we could tell by the constant roar of cannon and musketry that the contest was severe. It was soon after this that Jackson won his "Stonewall," as I have stated before. I got permission to ride a little distance from our command to get a closer view, and while out in an open field viewing the contest the best I could a bright-eyed boy of some sixteen years of age came up to me with a wounded hand and arm and spoke to me by name. I did not remember ever having seen him before, but he said he remembered me when I was a student at the University of Virginia and that his name was Everett B. Early, of Charlottesville. He had run away from home and gone into the fight and been wounded. He had dressed his wound and was on his way back to take a hand again. He gave me a very intelligent account of the battle.

I was kept in a state of great excitement all day and found it hard to set on my horse from weakness induced by my recent sickness. We had nothing to eat. About four it became obvious that the advance of the enemy had been stopped. Then there was a sudden pause in the firing on their side, and then we could hear cheers and shouts on our lines. We were told by a wounded man that Sherman's and Ricketts' battery had been captured and that the enemy were slowly retiring. Still we were kept waiting though the sound of firing showed us the enemy was now in full retreat and the time for the cavalry had come. About five o'clock an officer came up and told Col. Munford the enemy were in full retreat across Bull Run, and ordered him to cross the stream and make for the pike to cut them off if possible and that Col. Radford with the rest of the regiment had already gone. Both parts of the regiment crossed about the same time, and we dashed up the hill, but the order had come too late for much good to be done. We were received by a scattering fire from the routed column, but they had generally thrown away their arms, and those who had not done so did so as soon as they saw us. It was a terrible rout and the face of the earth was covered with blankets, haversacks, overcoats, and every species of arms. We joined Col. Radford and the other six companies of the regiment as we reached the pike and followed the fleeing yankees, capturing many prisoners, until we came to a block in the road made by a great number of abandoned wagons, cannon and caissons, ambulances and other material at a bridge over a creek about two miles of Centreville. Further advance was checked, or at all events we went no further. From the other side of the creek and on top of the hill the enemy had been able to halt a battery long enough to fire one or two shots at our column, one of which killed Captain Winston Radford, of Bedford, a most excellent man and citizen and the brother of our Colonel. Beyond this our loss was very small and my company had only one or two wounded slightly.

Just as we crossed Bull Run I saw Edmund Fontaine, of

Hanover, resting on a log by the roadside. I asked him what was the matter, and he said he was wounded and dying. He said it very cheerfully and did not look as if anything was the matter. As we came back we found him dead and some of his comrades about to remove the body. It was a great shock to me, as I had known him from boyhood, and though he was younger than I was we had met during many visits to Hanover when I was younger. We went into bivouac a little after dark, for it had become cloudy and was very dark.

It was a day long to be remembered, and such a Sunday as men seldom spend. To all but a scattered few it was our first battle, and its sights and wonders were things of which we had read but scarcely believed or understood until seen and experienced. The rout of the enemy was complete but our generals showed much want of skill in not making the material advantages greater. The Federal army was equipped with every species of munition and property, while ours was wanting in everything. They were stricken with a panic; wherever the panic was increased by the sight of an armed rebel it discovered itself by the natural impulse to throw away arms and accoutrements and to abandon everything in the shape of cannon, caissons, wagons, ambulances and provisions that might impede their flight, yet they managed, despite their flight, to carry off much. They only lost some thirty-odd cannon for example, while with proper management on our part they would not have reached the Potomac with two whole batteries and so with other properties.

Had there been even a slight demonstration on Centreville that evening the panic would have been so increased that we would have made more captures in cannon, small arms and wagons.

During the evening as I was riding over part of the field where there were many dead yankees lying who had been killed, I thought by some of Stuart's regiment, I noticed an old doll-baby with only one leg lying by the side of a Federal soldier just as it dropped from his pocket when he fell writhing in the agony of death. It was obviously a memento of some little loved one at home which he had brought so far with him and had worn close to his heart on this day of danger and death. It was strange to see that emblem of childhood, that token of a father's love lying there amidst the dead and dying where the storm of war had so fiercely raged and where death had stalked in the might of its terrible majesty. I dismounted, picked it up and stuffed it back into the poor fellow's cold bosom that it might rest with him in the bloody grave which was to be forever unknown to those who loved and mourned him in his distant home.

The actual loss of the enemy I do not know but their dead extended for miles and their wounded filled every house and shed in the neighborhood. The wounded doubtless suffered much. Their own surgeons abandoned their field hospitals and joined the fleeing cohorts of the living, and our surgeons had all they could do to look after their own wounded, who of course were the first served. They received kind treatment however, and as soon as our surgeons were free they rendered all the aid in their power.

The enemy had permitted no doubt of the result to cross their minds, and had not kept it a secret in Washington that the final attack was to be made on Sunday. The day was therefore made a gala day by the people of all classes, and they came in great numbers in every possible conveyance to enjoy the rebel rout and possible share in the rebel spoils. Members of Congress and cabinet ministers, department clerks and idle citizens followed the advancing column in all the confidence of exhorting confidence, and there were not wanting many a hackload of the *demi-monde* with their admirers to complete the motley crew. Along the road and amidst abandoned cannon and wagons we found many a forsaken carriage and hack with half-eaten lunches and half-used baskets of champagne, and we received most laughable accounts from the citizens on the roadside of the scenes they saw and the sharp contrast between the proud and confident advance and the wild panic of the flight. The men of our company got many a spoil not known to the ordnance department or used by those who filled the ranks.

We bivouacked in the field and without tent or any shelter but the oilcloths, a vast supply of which we had laid in from those upon which our foes had slept the night before. They were of the very best material and we gladly abandoned ours or kept them to throw over our saddles in the rain. A battle is not a sanitarium for the sick or the cold ground a good bed for a feverish and chilly man. I was so worn and weary that I had no doubt whatever that when I awoke in the morning I would be very ill. Before I laid down I fortunately found an opportunity to send a telegram to my wife and owing to a fortunate accident it got off the next morning and relieved the minds of my people at home and the friends of all my men.

Despite my gloomy anticipations as to the effect on my health I slept like a top and awoke the next morning after daylight feeling very much better. I was aroused by a hard rain falling on my face. I got up at once and crawled into my wagon, which fortunately had come up during the night, and then I had my breakfast owing to John Scott's thoughtfulness. I had heard nothing about my brothers, Capt. Eugene Blackford of the Fourth Alabamas and Lieut. W. W. Blackford, of Stuart's regiment of Cavalry. Both, I knew, had been engaged but I could not hear anything of them. Of course I was anxious.

About eight o'clock a staff officer from somewhere rode up and delivered an order calling for details to gather up arms and spoils from the field and to carry prisoners to the rear. I was sent with twenty men to report to Colonel Evans on the latter duty. When I reported I found also a small detail of infantry and the Colonel put me in charge of the whole detachment and turned over to me several hundred prisoners, who looked very uncomfortable in the rain, with orders to take them to Manassas, six miles to the rear. Before we started Colonel Evans took me into a house in the yard of which he had his headquarters and introduced me to Colonel O. B. Willcox and Captain Ricketts of the Federal army, both of whom were wounded and prisoners. Willcox and Evans seemed very good friends and called each other Orlando and Shanks respectively —"Shanks" being Evans' nickname at West Point. Willcox was very courteous but Ricketts was surly and bitter and complained of his accommodations, which were very much better than those of his captor in the yard or than those of the vast proportion of our wounded men and officers. He had a comfortable room and bed and two surgeons to attend his wounds. One would suppose he expected the rebels to have a first-class hotel on the battlefield ready to receive him and that they had violated all the rules of civilized warfare in failing to do so.

We carried the two officers, placed under my care, in an ambulance, and made them as comfortable as possible. We made rapid progress and I soon delivered my charge to some officer at General Beauregard's headquarters. I had some pleasant chats with Colonel Willcox.

The sights of this day were terrible and more heartrending than those of the day before. Our preparations for the battle, so far as the care of the wounded was concerned, were very imperfect and we were called on to provide for those of both sides. The result was that many of both sides suffered much, but no difference was shown them save in the matter of priority of service. The surgeons were busy all day but still many wounds remained undressed for full twenty-four hours. Luckily it was not very hot and the rain was a comfort.

THE UNION ARMY RETREATS:
VIRGINIA, JULY 1861

William Howard Russell: from My Diary North and South

The Union attack across Bull Run against the Confederate left flank was initially successful, but was halted by determined resistance on Henry House Hill. When the last Confederate reinforcements from the Shenandoah Valley reached the battlefield in the afternoon, Beauregard launched a successful counterattack. The Union forces began a retreat that soon turned into a rout. William Howard Russell left Washington in a hired carriage shortly after daybreak on July 21, hoping to catch up with the advance of McDowell's army. His subsequent report on the battle for *The Times* of London would be denounced in the Northern press for describing "the disgraceful conduct" of the Union troops as an instance of "miserable, causeless panic."

PUNCTUAL to time, our carriage appeared at the door, with a spare horse, followed by the black quadruped on which the negro boy sat with difficulty, in consequence of its high spirits and excessively hard mouth. I swallowed a cup of tea and a morsel of bread, put the remainder of the tea into a bottle, got a flask of light Bordeaux, a bottle of water, a paper of sandwiches, and having replenished my small flask with brandy, stowed them all away in the bottom of the gig; but my friend, who is not accustomed to rise very early in the morning, did not make his appearance, and I was obliged to send several times to the legation to quicken his movements. Each time I was assured he would be over presently; but it was not till two hours had elapsed, and when I had just resolved to leave him behind, that he appeared in person, quite unprovided with *viaticum*, so that my slender store had now to meet the demands of two instead of one. We are off at last. The amicus and self find contracted space behind the driver. The negro boy, grinning half with pain and "the balance" with pleasure, as the

Americans say, held on his rampant charger, which made continual efforts to leap into the gig, and thus through the deserted city we proceeded towards the Long Bridge, where a sentry examined our papers, and said with a grin, "You'll find plenty of Congressmen on before you." And then our driver whipped his horses through the embankment of Fort Runyon, and dashed off along a country road, much cut up with gun and cart wheels, towards the main turnpike.

The promise of a lovely day, given by the early dawn, was likely to be realised to the fullest, and the placid beauty of the scenery as we drove through the woods below Arlington, and beheld the white buildings shining in the early sunlight, and the Potomac, like a broad silver riband dividing the picture, breathed of peace. The silence close to the city was unbroken. From the time we passed the guard beyond the Long Bridge, for several miles we did not meet a human being, except a few soldiers in the neighbourhood of the deserted camps, and when we passed beyond the range of tents we drove for nearly two hours through a densely-wooded, undulating country; the houses, close to the road-side, shut up and deserted, window-high in the crops of Indian corn, fast ripening for the sickle; alternate field and forest, the latter generally still holding possession of the hollows, and, except when the road, deep and filled with loose stones, passed over the summit of the ridges, the eye caught on either side little but fir-trees and maize, and the deserted wooden houses, standing amidst the slave quarters.

The residences close to the lines gave signs and tokens that the Federals had recently visited them. But at the best of times the inhabitants could not be very well off. Some of the farms were small, the houses tumbling to decay, with unpainted roofs and side walls, and windows where the want of glass was supplemented by panes of wood. As we got further into the country the traces of the debateable land between the two armies vanished, and negroes looked out from their quarters, or sickly-looking women and children were summoned forth by the rattle of the wheels to see who was hurrying to the war. Now and then a white man looked out, with an ugly scowl on his face, but the country seemed drained of the adult male population, and such of the inhabitants as we saw were neither as comfortably dressed nor as healthy looking as the shambling slaves who shuffled about the plantations. The road was so cut up by gun-wheels, ammunition and commissariat waggons, that our horses made but slow way against the continual draft upon the collar; but at last the driver, who had known the country in happier times, announced that we had entered the high road for Fairfax Court-house. Unfortunately my watch had gone down, but I guessed it was then a little before nine o'clock. In a few minutes afterwards I thought I heard, through the eternal clatter and jingle of the old gig, a sound which made me call the driver to stop. He pulled up, and we listened. In a minute or so, the well-known boom of a gun, followed by two or three in rapid succession, but at a considerable distance, reached my ear. "Did you hear that?" The driver heard nothing, nor did my companion, but the black boy on the led horse, with eyes starting out of his head, cried, "I hear them, massa; I hear them, sure enough, like de gun in de navy yard;" and as he spoke the thudding noise, like taps with a gentle hand upon a muffled drum, were repeated, which were heard both by Mr. Warre and the driver. "They are at it! We shall be late! Drive on as fast as you can!" We rattled on still faster, and presently came up to a farm-house, where a man and woman, with some negroes beside them, were standing out by the hedge-row above us, looking up the road in the direction of a cloud of dust, which we could see rising above the tops of the trees. We halted for a moment. "How long have the guns been going, sir?" "Well, ever since early this morning," said he; "they've been having a fight. And I do really believe some of our poor Union chaps have had enough of it already. For here's some of them darned Secessionists marching down to go into Alexandry." The driver did not seem altogether content with this explanation of the dust in front of us, and presently, when a turn of the road brought to view a body of armed men, stretching to an interminable distance, with bayonets glittering in the sunlight through the clouds of dust, seemed inclined to halt or turn back again. A nearer approach satisfied me they were friends, and as soon as we came up with the head of the column I saw that they could not be engaged in the performance of any military duty. The men were marching without any resemblance of order, in twos and threes or larger troops. Some without arms, carrying great bundles on their backs; others with their coats hung from their firelocks; many foot sore. They were all talking, and in haste; many plodding along laughing, so I concluded that they could not belong to a defeated army, and imagined M'Dowell was effecting some flank movement. "Where are you going to, may I ask?"

"If this is the road to Alexandria, we are going there."

"There is an action going on in front, is there not?"

"Well, so we believe, but we have not been fighting."

Although they were in such good spirits, they were not communicative, and we resumed our journey, impeded by the straggling troops and by the country cars containing their baggage and chairs, and tables and domestic furniture, which had never belonged to a regiment in the field. Still they came pouring on. I ordered the driver to stop at a rivulet, where a number of men were seated in the shade, drinking the water and bathing their hands and feet. On getting out I asked an officer, "May I beg to know, sir, where your regiment is going to?" "Well, I reckon, sir, we are going home to Pennsylvania." "This is the 4th Pennsylvania Regiment, is it not, sir?" "It is so, sir; that's the fact." "I should think there is severe fighting going on behind you, judging from the firing" (for every moment the sound of the cannon had been growing more distinct and more heavy)?" "Well, I reckon, sir, there is." I paused for a moment, not knowing what to say, and yet anxious for an explanation; and the epauletted gentleman, after a few seconds' awkward hesitation, added, "We are going home because, as you see, the men's time's up, sir. We have had three months of this sort of work, and that's quite enough of it." The men who were listening to the conversation expressed their assent to the noble and patriotic utterances of the centurion, and, making him a low bow, we resumed our journey.

It was fully three and a half miles before the last of the regiment passed, and then the road presented a more animated scene, for white-covered commissariat waggons were visible, wending towards the front, and one or two hack carriages, laden with civilians, were hastening in the same direction. Before the doors of the wooden farm-houses the coloured people were assembled, listening with outstretched necks to the repeated reports of the guns. At one time, as we were descending the wooded road, a huge blue dome, agitated by some internal convulsion, appeared to bar our progress, and it was only after infinite persuasion of rein and whip that the horses approached the terrific object, which was an inflated balloon, attached to a waggon, and defying the efforts of the men in charge to jockey it safely through the trees.

It must have been about eleven o'clock when we came to the first traces of the Confederate camp, in front of Fairfax Court-house, where they had cut a few trenches and levelled the trees across the road, so as to form a rude abattis; but the works were of a most superficial character, and would scarcely have given cover either to the guns, for which embrasures were left at the flanks to sweep the road, or to the infantry intended to defend them.

The Confederate force stationed here must have consisted, to a considerable extent, of cavalry. The bowers of branches, which they had made to shelter their tents, camp tables, empty boxes, and packing-cases, in the *débris* one usually sees around an encampment, showed they had not been destitute of creature comforts.

Some time before noon the driver, urged continually by adjurations to get on, whipped his horses into Fairfax Court-house, a village which derives its name from a large brick building, in which the sessions of the county are held. Some thirty or forty houses, for the most part detached, with gardens or small strips of land about them, form the main street. The inhabitants who remained had by no means an agreeable expression of countenance, and did not seem on very good terms with the Federal soldiers, who were lounging up and down the streets, or standing in the shade of the trees and doorways. I asked the sergeant of a picket in the street how long the firing had been going on. He replied that it had commenced at half-past seven or eight, and had been increasing ever since. "Some of them will lose their eyes and back teeth," he added, "before it is over." The driver, pulling up at a roadside inn in the town, here made the startling announcement, that both he and his horses must have something to eat, and although we would have been happy to join him, seeing that we had no breakfast, we could not afford the time, and were not displeased when a thin-faced, shrewish woman, in black, came out into the verandah, and said she could not let us have anything unless we liked to wait till the regular dinner hour of the house, which was at one o'clock. The horses got a bucket of water, which they needed in that broiling sun; and the cannonade, which by this time had increased into a respectable tumult that gave evidence of a well-sustained action, added vigour to the driver's arm, and in a mile or two more we dashed in to a village of burnt houses, the charred brick chimney stacks standing amidst the blackened embers being all that remained of what once was German Town. The firing of this village was severely censured by General M'Dowell, who probably does not appreciate the value of such agencies employed "by our glorious Union army to develope loyal sentiments among the people of Virginia."

The driver, passing through the town, drove straight on, but after some time I fancied the sound of the guns seemed dying away towards our left. A big negro came shambling along the roadside—the driver stopped and asked him, "is this the road to Centreville?" "Yes, sir; right on, sir; good road to Centreville, massa," and so we proceeded, till I became satisfied from the appearance of the road that we had altogether left the track of the army. At the first cottage we halted, and inquired of a Virginian, who came out to look at us, whether the road led to Centreville. "You're going to Centreville, are you?" "Yes, by the shortest road we can." "Well, then—you're going wrong—right away! Some people say there's a bend of road leading through the wood a mile further on, but those who have tried it lately have come back to German Town and don't think it leads to Centreville at all." This was very provoking, as the horses were much fatigued and we had driven several miles out of our way. The driver, who was an Englishman, said, "I think it would be best for us to go on and try the road anyhow. There's not likely to be any Seceshers about there, are there, sir?"

"What did you say, sir," inquired the Virginian, with a vacant stare upon his face.

"I merely asked whether you think we are likely to meet with any Secessionists if we go along that road?"

"Secessionists!" repeated the Virginian, slowly pronouncing

each syllable as if pondering on the meaning of the word—
"Secessionists! Oh no, *sir*; I don't believe there's such a thing
as a Secessionist in the whole of this country."

The boldness of this assertion, in the very hearing of Beauregard's cannon, completely shook the faith of our Jehu in any information from that source, and we retraced our steps to German Town, and were directed into the proper road by some negroes, who were engaged exchanging Confederate money at very low rates for Federal copper with a few straggling soldiers. The faithful Muley Moloch, who had been capering in our rear so long, now complained that he was very much burned, but on further inquiry it was ascertained he was merely suffering from the abrading of his skin against an English saddle.

In an hour more we had gained the high road to Centreville, on which were many buggies, commissariat carts, and waggons full of civilians, and a brisk canter brought us in sight of a rising ground, over which the road led directly through a few houses on each side, and dipped out of sight, the slopes of the hill being covered with men, carts, and horses, and the summit crested with spectators, with their backs turned towards us, and gazing on the valley beyond. "There's Centreville," says the driver, and on our poor panting horses were forced, passing directly through the Confederate bivouacs, commissariat parks, folds of oxen, and two German regiments, with a battery of artillery, halting on the rising-ground by the road-side. The heat was intense. Our driver complained of hunger and thirst, to which neither I nor my companion were insensible; and so pulling up on the top of the hill, I sent the boy down to the village which we had passed, to see if he could find shelter for the horses, and a morsel for our breakfastless selves.

It was a strange scene before us. From the hill a densely wooded country, dotted at intervals with green fields and cleared lands, spread five or six miles in front, bounded by a line of blue and purple ridges, terminating abruptly in escarpments towards the left front, and swelling gradually towards the right into the lower spines of an offshoot from the Blue-Ridge Mountains. On our left the view was circumscribed by a forest which clothed the side of the ridge on which we stood, and covered its shoulder far down into the plain. A gap in the nearest chain of the hills in our front was pointed out by the bystanders as the Pass of Manassas, by which the railway from the West is carried into the plain, and still nearer at hand, before us, is the junction of that rail with the line from Alexandria, and with the railway leading southwards to Richmond. The intervening space was not a dead level; undulating lines of forest marked the course of the streams which intersected it, and gave, by their variety of colour and shading, an additional charm to the landscape which, enclosed in a framework of blue and purple hills, softened into violet in the extreme distance, presented one of the most agreeable displays of simple pastoral woodland scenery that could be conceived.

But the sounds which came upon the breeze, and the sights which met our eyes, were in terrible variance with the tranquil character of the landscape. The woods far and near echoed to the roar of cannon, and thin frayed lines of blue smoke marked the spots whence came the muttering sound of rolling musketry; the white puffs of smoke burst high above the treetops, and the gunners' rings from shell and howitzer marked the fire of the artillery.

Clouds of dust shifted and moved through the forest; and through the wavering mists of light blue smoke, and the thicker masses which rose commingling from the feet of men and the mouths of cannon, I could see the gleam of arms and the twinkling of bayonets.

On the hill beside me there was a crowd of civilians on horseback, and in all sorts of vehicles, with a few of the fairer, if not gentler sex. A few officers and some soldiers, who had straggled from the regiments in reserve, moved about among the spectators, and pretended to explain the movements of the troops below, of which they were profoundly ignorant.

The cannonade and musketry had been exaggerated by the distance and by the rolling echoes of the hills; and sweeping the position narrowly with my glass from point to point, I failed to discover any traces of close encounter or very severe fighting. The spectators were all excited, and a lady with an opera-glass who was near me was quite beside herself when an unusually heavy discharge roused the current of her blood—"That is splendid. Oh, my! Is not that first-rate? I guess we will be in Richmond this time to-morrow." These, mingled with coarser exclamations, burst from the politicians who had come out to see the triumph of the Union arms. I was particularly irritated by constant applications for the loan of my glass. One broken-down looking soldier observing my flask, asked me for a drink, and took a startling pull, which left but little between the bottom and utter vacuity.

"Stranger, that's good stuff and no mistake. I have not had such a drink since I come South. I feel now as if I'd like to whip ten Seceshers."

From the line of the smoke it appeared to me that the action was in an oblique line from our left, extending farther outwards towards the right, bisected by a road from Centreville, which descended the hill close at hand and ran right across the undulating plain, its course being marked by the white covers of the baggage and commissariat waggons as far as a turn of the road, where the trees closed in upon them. Beyond the right of the curling smoke clouds of dust appeared from time to time in the distance, as if bodies of cavalry were moving over a sandy plain.

Notwitstanding all the exultation and boastings of the people at Centreville, I was well convinced no advance of any importance or any great success had been achieved, because the ammunition and baggage waggons had never moved, nor had the reserves received any orders to follow in the line of the army.

The clouds of dust on the right were quite inexplicable. As we were looking, my philosophic companion asked me in perfect seriousness, "Are we really seeing a battle now? Are they supposed to be fighting where all that smoke is going on? This is rather interesting, you know."

Up came our black boy. "Not find a bit to eat, sir, in all the place." We had, however, my little paper of sandwiches, and descended the hill to a bye lane off the village, where, seated in the shade of the gig, Mr. Warre and myself, dividing our provision with the driver, wound up a very scanty, but much relished, repast with a bottle of tea and half the bottle of Bordeaux and water, the remainder being prudently reserved at my request for contingent remainders. Leaving orders for the saddle horse, which was eating his first meal, to be brought up the moment he was ready—I went with Mr. Warre to the hill once more and observed that the line had not sensibly altered whilst we were away.

An English gentleman, who came up flushed and heated from the plain, told us that the Federals had been advancing steadily in spite of a stubborn resistance and had behaved most gallantly.

Loud cheers suddenly burst from the spectators, as a man dressed in the uniform of an officer, whom I had seen riding violently across the plain in an open space below, galloped along the front, waving his cap and shouting at the top of his voice. He was brought up by the press of people round his horse close to where I stood. "We've whipped them on all points," he cried. "We have taken all their batteries. They are retreating as fast as they can, and we are after them." Such cheers as rent the welkin! The Congress men shook hands with each other, and cried out, "Bully for us. Bravo, didn't I tell you so." The Germans uttered their martial cheers and the Irish hurrahed wildly. At this moment my horse was brought up the hill, and I mounted and turned towards the road to the front, whilst Mr. Warre and his companion proceeded straight down the hill.

By the time I reached the lane, already mentioned, which was in a few minutes, the string of commissariat waggons was moving onwards pretty briskly, and I was detained until my friends appeared at the road-side. I told Mr. Warre I was going forward to the front as fast as I could, but that I would come back, under any circumstances, about an hour before dusk, and would go straight to the spot where we had put up the gig by the road-side, in order to return to Washington. Then getting into the fields, I pressed my horse, which was quite recovered from his twenty-seven mile's ride and full of spirit and mettle, as fast as I could, making detours here and there to get through the ox fences, and by the small streams which cut up the country. The firing did not increase but rather diminished in volume, though it now sounded close at hand.

I had ridden between three and a half and four miles, as well as I could judge, when I was obliged to turn for the third and fourth time into the road by a considerable stream, which was spanned by a bridge, towards which I was threading my way, when my attention was attracted by loud shouts in advance, and I perceived several waggons coming from the direction of the battle-field, the drivers of which were endeavouring to force their horses past the ammunition carts going in the contrary direction near the bridge; a thick cloud of dust rose behind them, and running by the side of the waggons, were a number of men in uniform whom I supposed to be the guard. My first impression was that the waggons were returning for fresh supplies of ammunition. But every moment the crowd increased, drivers and men cried out with the most vehement gestures, "Turn back! Turn back! We are whipped." They seized the heads of the horses and swore at the opposing drivers. Emerging from the crowd a breathless man in the uniform of an officer with an empty scabbard dangling by his side, was cut off by getting between my horse and a cart for a moment. "What is the matter, sir? What is all this about?" "Why it means we are pretty badly whipped, that's the truth," he gasped, and continued.

By this time the confusion had been communicating itself through the line of waggons towards the rear, and the drivers endeavoured to turn round their vehicles in the narrow road, which caused the usual amount of imprecations from the men and plunging and kicking from the horses.

The crowd from the front continually increased, the heat, the uproar, and the dust were beyond description, and these were augmented when some cavalry soldiers, flourishing their sabres and preceded by an officer, who cried out, "Make way there—make way there for the General," attempted to force a covered waggon in which was seated a man with a bloody handkerchief round his head, through the press.

I had succeeded in getting across the bridge with great difficulty before the waggon came up, and I saw the crowd on the road was still gathering thicker and thicker. Again I asked an officer, who was on foot, with his sword under his arm, "What is all this for?" "We are whipped, sir. We are all in retreat. You are all to go back." "Can you tell me where I can find General M'Dowell?" "No! nor can any one else."

A few shells could be heard bursting not very far off, but there was nothing to account for such an extraordinary scene. A third officer, however, confirmed the report that the whole army was in retreat, and that the Federals were beaten on all points, but there was nothing in this disorder to indicate a general rout. All these things took place in a few seconds. I got up out of the road into a corn-field, through which men were hastily walking or running, their faces streaming with perspiration, and generally without arms, and worked my way for about half a mile or so, as well as I could judge, against an increasing stream of fugitives, the ground being strewed with coats, blankets, fire-locks, cooking tins, caps, belts, bayonets—asking in vain where General M'Dowell was.

Again I was compelled by the condition of the fields to come into the road; and having passed a piece of wood and a regiment which seemed to be moving back in column of march in tolerably good order, I turned once more into an opening close to a white house, not far from the lane, beyond which there was a belt of forest. Two field-pieces unlimbered near the house, with panting horses in the rear, were pointed towards the front, and along the road beside them there swept a tolerably steady column of men mingled with field ambulances and light baggage carts, back to Centreville. I had just stretched out my hand to get a cigar-light from a German gunner, when the dropping shots which had been sounding through the woods in front of us, suddenly swelled into an animated fire. In a few seconds a crowd of men rushed out of the wood down towards the guns, and the artillerymen near me seized the trail of a piece, and were wheeling it round to fire, when an officer or sergeant called out, "Stop! stop! They are our own men;" and in two or three minutes the whole battalion came sweeping past the guns at the double, and in the utmost disorder. Some of the artillerymen dragged the horses out of the tumbrils; and for a moment the confusion was so great I could not understand what had taken place; but a soldier whom I stopped, said, "We are pursued by their cavalry; they have cut us all to pieces."

Murat himself would not have dared to move a squadron on such ground. However, it could not be doubted that something serious was taking place; and at that moment a shell burst in front of the house, scattering the soldiers near it, which was followed by another that bounded along the road; and in a few minutes more out came another regiment from the wood, almost as broken as the first. The scene on the road had now assumed an aspect which has not a parallel in any description I have ever read. Infantry soldiers on mules and draught horses, with the harness clinging to their heels, as much frightened as their riders; negro servants on their masters' chargers; ambulances crowded with unwounded soldiers; waggons swarming with men who threw out the contents in the road to make room, grinding through a shouting, screaming mass of men on foot, who were literally yelling with rage at every halt, and shrieking out, "Here are the cavalry! Will you get on?" This portion of the force was evidently in discord.

There was nothing left for it but to go with the current one could not stem. I turned round my horse from the deserted guns, and endeavoured to find out what had occurred as I rode quietly back on the skirts of the crowd. I talked with those on all sides of me. Some uttered prodigious nonsense, describing batteries tier over tier, and ambuscades, and blood running knee deep. Others described how their boys had carried whole lines of entrenchments, but were beaten back for want of reinforcements. The names of many regiments were mentioned as being utterly destroyed. Cavalry and bayonet charges and masked batteries played prominent parts in all the narrations. Some of the officers seemed to feel the disgrace of defeat; but the strangest thing was the general indifference with which the event seemed to be regarded by those who collected their senses as soon as they got out of fire, and who said they were just going as far as Centreville, and would have a big fight to-morrow.

By this time I was unwillingly approaching Centreville in the midst of heat, dust, confusions, imprecations inconceivable. On arriving at the place where a small rivulet crossed the road, the throng increased still more. The ground over which I had passed going out was now covered with arms, clothing of all kinds, accoutrements thrown off and left to be trampled in the dust under the hoofs of men and horses. The runaways ran alongside the waggons, striving to force themselves in among the occupants, who resisted tooth and nail. The drivers spurred, and whipped, and urged the horses to the utmost of their bent. I felt an inclination to laugh, which was overcome by disgust, and by that vague sense of something extraordinary taking place which is experienced when a man sees a number of people acting as if driven by some unknown terror. As I rode in the crowd, with men clinging to the stirrup-leathers, or holding on by anything they could lay hands on, so that I had some apprehension of being pulled off, I spoke to the men, and asked them over and over again not to be in such a hurry. "There's no enemy to pursue you. All the cavalry in the world could not get at you." But I might as well have talked to the stones.

For my own part, I wanted to get out of the ruck as fast as I could, for the heat and dust were very distressing, particularly to a half-starved man. Many of the fugitives were in the last stages of exhaustion, and some actually sank down by the fences, at the risk of being trampled to death. Above the roar of the flight, which was like the rush of a great river, the guns burst forth from time to time.

The road at last became somewhat clearer; for I had got ahead of some of the ammunition train and waggons, and the others were dashing up the hill towards Centreville. The men's great-coats and blankets had been stowed in the trains; but the fugitives had apparently thrown them out on the road, to make room for themselves. Just beyond the stream I saw a heap of clothing tumble out of a large covered cart, and cried out after the driver, "Stop! stop! All the things are tumbling out of the cart." But my zeal was checked by a scoundrel putting his head out, and shouting with a curse, "If you try to stop the team, I'll blow your —— brains out." My brains advised me to adopt the principle of non-intervention.

It never occurred to me that this was a grand débâcle. All along I believed the mass of the army was not broken, and that all I saw around was the result of confusion created in a crude organisation by a forced retreat; and knowing the reserves were at Centreville and beyond, I said to myself, "Let us see how this will be when we get to the hill." I indulged in a quiet chuckle, too, at the idea of my philosophical friend and his stout companion finding themselves suddenly enveloped in the crowd of fugitives; but knew they could easily have regained their original position on the hill. Trotting along briskly through the fields, I arrived at the foot of the slope on which Centreville stands, and met a German regiment just deploying into line very well and steadily—the men in the rear companies laughing, smoking, singing, and jesting with the fugitives, who were filing past; but no thought of stopping the waggons, as the orders repeated from mouth to mouth were that they were to fall back beyond Centreville.

The air of the men was good. The officers were cheerful, and one big German with a great pipe in his bearded mouth, with spectacles on nose, amused himself by pricking the horses with his sabre point, as he passed, to the sore discomfiture of the riders. Behind the regiment came a battery of brass field-pieces, and another regiment in column of march was following the guns. They were going to form line at the end of the slope, and no fairer position could well be offered for a defensive attitude, although it might be turned. But it was getting too late for the enemy wherever they were to attempt such an extensive operation. Several times I had been asked by officers and men, "Where do you think we will halt? Where are the rest of the army?" I always replied "Centreville," and I had heard hundreds of the fugitives say they were going to Centreville.

I rode up the road, turned into the little street which carries the road on the right-hand side to Fairfax Courthouse and the hill, and went straight to the place where I had left the buggy in a lane on the left of the road beside a small house and shed, expecting to find Mr. Warre ready for a start, as I had faithfully promised Lord Lyons he should be back that night in Washington. The buggy was not there. I pulled open the door of the shed in which the horses had been sheltered out of the sun. They were gone. "Oh," said I, to myself, "of course! What a stupid fellow I am. Warre has had the horses put in and taken the gig to the top of the hill, in order to see the last of it before we go." And so I rode over to the ridge; but arriving there, could see no sign of our vehicle far or near. There were two carriages of some kind or other still remaining on the hill, and a few spectators, civilians and military, gazing on the scene below, which was softened in the golden rays of the declining sun. The smoke wreaths had ceased to curl over the green sheets of billowy forest as sea foam crisping in a gentle breeze breaks the lines of the ocean. But far and near yellow and dun-coloured piles of dust seamed the landscape, leaving behind them long trailing clouds of lighter vapours which were dotted now and then by white puff balls from the bursting of shell.

On the right these clouds were very heavy and seemed to approach rapidly, and it occurred to me they might be caused by an advance of the much spoken-of and little seen cavalry; and remembering the cross road from German Town, it seemed a very fine and very feasible operation for the Confederates to cut right in on the line of retreat and communication, in which case the fate of the army and of Washington could not be dubious. There were now few civilians on the hill, and these were thinning away. Some were gesticulating and explaining to one another the causes of the retreat, looking very hot and red. The confusion among the last portion of the carriages and fugitives on the road, which I had outstripped, had been renewed again, and the crowd there presented a remarkable and ludicrous aspect through the glass; but there were two strong battalions in good order near the foot of the hill, a battery on the slope, another on the top, and a portion of a regiment in and about the houses of the village.

A farewell look at the scene presented no new features. Still the clouds of dust moved onwards denser and higher; flashes of arms lighted them up at times; the fields were dotted by fugitives, among whom many mounted men were marked by their greater speed, and the little flocks of dust rising from the horses' feet.

I put up my glass, and turning from the hill, with difficulty forced my way through the crowd of vehicles which were making their way towards the main road in the direction of the lane, hoping that by some lucky accident I might find the gig in waiting for me. But I sought in vain; a sick soldier who was on a stretcher in front of the house near the corner of the lane, leaning on his elbow and looking at the stream of men and carriages, asked me if I could tell him what they were in such a hurry for, and I said they were merely getting back to their bivouacs. A man dressed in civilian's clothes grinned as I spoke. "I think they'll go farther than that," said he; and then added, "If you're looking for the waggon you came in, it's pretty well back to Washington by this time. I think I saw you down there with a nigger and two men." "Yes. They're all off, gone more than an hour and a-half ago, I think, and a stout man—I thought was you at first—along with them."

Nothing was left for it but to brace up the girths for a ride to the Capitol, for which, hungry and fagged as I was, I felt very little inclination. I was trotting quietly down the hill road beyond Centreville, when suddenly the guns on the other side, or from a battery very near, opened fire, and a fresh outburst of artillery sounded through the woods. In an instant the mass of vehicles and retreating soldiers, teamsters, and civilians, as if agonised by an electric shock, quivered throughout the tortuous line. With dreadful shouts and cursings, the drivers lashed their maddened horses, and leaping from the carts, left them to their fate, and ran on foot. Artillerymen and foot soldiers, and negroes mounted on gun horses, with the chain traces and loose trappings trailing in the dust, spurred and flogged their steeds down the road or by the side paths. The firing continued and seemed to approach the hill, and at every report the agitated body of horsemen and waggons was seized, as it were, with a fresh convulsion.

Once more the dreaded cry, "The cavalry! cavalry are coming!" rang through the crowd, and looking back to Centreville I perceived coming down the hill, between me and the sky, a number of mounted men, who might at a hasty glance be taken for horsemen in the act of sabreing the fugitives. In reality they were soldiers and civilians, with, I regret to say, some officers among them, who were whipping and striking their horses with sticks or whatever else they could lay hands on. I called out to the men who were frantic with terror beside me, "They are not cavalry at all; they're your own men"—but they did not heed me. A fellow who was shouting out, "Run! run!" as loud as he could beside me, seemed to take delight in creating alarm; and as he was perfectly collected as far as I could judge, I said, "What on earth are you running for? What are you afraid of?" He was in the roadside below me, and at once turning on me, and exclaiming, "I'm not afraid of you," presented his piece and pulled the trigger so instantaneously, that had it gone off I could not have swerved from the ball. As the scoundrel deliberately drew up to examine the nipple, I judged it best not to give him another chance, and spurred on through the crowd, where any man could have shot as many as he pleased without interruption. The only conclusion I came to was, that he was mad or drunken. When I was passing by the line of the bivouacs a battalion of men came tumbling down the bank from the field into the road, with fixed bayonets, and as some fell in the road and others tumbled on top of them, there must have been a few ingloriously wounded.

I galloped on for a short distance to head the ruck, for I could not tell whether this body of infantry intended moving back towards Centreville or were coming down the road; but the mounted men galloping furiously past me, with a cry of "Cavalry! cavalry!" on their lips, swept on faster than I did, augmenting the alarm and excitement. I came up with two officers who were riding more leisurely; and touching my hat, said, "I venture to suggest that these men should be stopped, sir. If not, they will alarm the whole of the post and pickets on to Washington. They will fly next, and the consequences will be most disastrous." One of the two, looking at me for a moment, nodded his head without saying a word, spurred his horse to full speed, and dashed on in front along the road. Following more leisurely I observed the fugitives in front were suddenly checked in their speed; and as I turned my horse into the wood by the road-side to get on so as to prevent the chance of another block-up, I passed several private vehicles, in one of which Mr. Raymond, of the *New York Times*, was seated with some friends, looking by no means happy. He says in his report to his paper, "About a mile this side of Centreville a stampedo took place amongst the teamsters and others, which threw everything into the utmost confusion, and inflicted very serious injuries. Mr. Eaton, of Michigan, in trying to arrest the flight of some of these men, was shot by one of them, the ball taking effect in his hand." He asked me, in some anxiety, what I thought would happen. I replied, "No doubt M'Dowell will stand fast at Centreville to-night. These are mere runaways, and unless the enemy's cavalry succeed in getting through at this road, there is nothing to apprehend."

And I continued through the wood till I got a clear space in front on the road, along which a regiment of infantry was advancing towards me. They halted ere I came up, and with levelled firelocks arrested the men on horses and the carts and waggons galloping towards them, and blocked up the road to stop their progress. As I tried to edge by on the right of the column by the left of the road, a soldier presented his firelock at my head from the higher ground on which he stood, for the road had a deep trench cut on the side by which I was endeavouring to pass, and sung out, "Halt! Stop—or I fire!" The officers in front were waving their swords and shouting out, "Don't let a soul pass! Keep back! keep back!" Bowing to the officer who was near me, I said, "I beg to assure you, sir, I am not running away. I am a civilian and a British subject. I have done my best as I came along to stop this disgraceful rout. I am in no hurry; I merely want to get back to Washington to-night. I have been telling them all along there are no cavalry near us." The officer to whom I was speaking, young and somewhat excited kept repeating, "Keep back, sir! keep back! you must keep back." Again I said to him, "I assure you I am not with this crowd; my pulse is as cool as your own." But as he paid no attention to what I said, I suddenly bethought me of General Scott's letter, and addressing another officer, said, "I am a civilian going to Washington; will you be kind enough to look at this pass, specially given to me by General Scott." The officer looked at it, and handed it to a mounted man, either adjutant or colonel, who, having examined it, returned it to me, saying, "Oh, yes! certainly. Pass that man!" And with a cry of "Pass that man!" along the line, I rode down the trench very leisurely, and got out on the road, which was now clear, though some fugitives had stolen through the woods on the flanks of the column and were in front of me.

A little further on there was a cart on the right hand side of the road, surrounded by a group of soldiers. I was trotting past when a respectable-looking man in a semi-military garb, coming out from the group, said, in a tone of much doubt and distress—"Can you tell me, sir, for God's sake, where the 69th New York are? These men tell me they are all cut to pieces." "And so they are," exclaimed one of the fellows, who had the number of the regiment on his cap.

"You hear what they say, sir?" exclaimed the man.

"I do, but I really cannot tell you where the 69th are."

"I'm in charge of these mails, and I'll deliver them if I die for it; but is it safe for me to go on? You are a gentleman, and I can depend on your word."

His assistant and himself were in the greatest perplexity of mind, but all I could say was, "I really can't tell you; I believe the army will halt at Centreville to-night, and I think you may go on there with the greatest safety, if you can get through the crowd." "Faith, then, he can't," exclaimed one of the soldiers.

"Why not?" "Shure, arn't we cut to pieces. Didn't I hear the kurnel himsilf saying we was all of us to cut and run, every man on his own hook, as well as he could. Stop at Cinthreville, indeed!"

I bade the mail agent* good evening and rode on, but even in this short colloquy stragglers on foot and on horseback, who had turned the flanks of the regiment by side paths or through the woods, came pouring along the road once more.

Somewhere about this I was accosted by a stout, elderly man, with the air and appearance of a respectable mechanic, or small tavern-keeper, who introduced himself as having met me at Cairo. He poured out a flood of woes on me, how he had lost his friend and companion, nearly lost his seat several times, was unaccustomed to riding, was suffering much pain from the unusual position and exercise, did not know the road, feared he would never be able to get on, dreaded he might be captured and ill-treated if he was known, and such topics as a selfish man

---

*I have since met the person referred to, an Englishman living in Washington, and well known at the Legation and elsewhere. Mr. Dawson came to tell me that he had seen a letter in an American journal, which was copied extensively all over the Union, in which the writer stated he accompanied me on my return to Fairfax Court-house, and that the incident I related in my account of Bull Run did not occur, but that he was the individual referred to, and could swear with his assistant that every word I wrote was true. I did not need any such corroboration for the satisfaction of any who know me; and I was quite well aware that if one came from the dead to bear testimony in my favour before the American journals and public, the evidence would not countervail the slander of any characterless scribe who sought to gain a moment's notoriety by a flat contradiction of my narrative. I may add, that Dawson begged of me not to bring him before the public, "because I am now sutler to the ——th, over in Virginia, and they would dismiss me." "What! For certifying to the truth?" "You know, sir, it might do me harm." Whilst on this subject, let me remark that some time afterwards I was in Mr. Brady's photographic studio in Pennsylvania Avenue, Washington, when the very intelligent and obliging manager introduced himself to me, and said that he wished to have an opportunity of repeating to me personally what he had frequently told persons in the place, that he could bear the fullest testimony to the complete accuracy of my account of the panic from Centreville down the road at the time I left, and that he and his assistants, who were on the spot trying to get away their photographic van and apparatus, could certify that my description fell far short of the disgraceful spectacle and of the excesses of the flight.

in a good deal of pain or fear is likely to indulge in. I calmed his apprehensions as well as I could, by saying, "I had no doubt M'Dowell would halt and show fight at Centreville, and be able to advance from it in a day or two to renew the fight again; that he couldn't miss the road; whiskey and tallow were good for abrasions;" and as I was riding very slowly, he jogged along, for he was a burr, and would stick, with many "Oh dears! Oh! dear me!" for most part of the way joining me at intervals till I reached Fairfax Court House. A body of infantry were under arms in a grove near the Court House, on the right hand side of the road. The door and windows of the houses presented crowds of faces black and white; and men and women stood out upon the porch, who asked me as I passed, "Have you been at the fight?" "What are they all running for?" "Are the rest of them coming on?" to which I gave the same replies as before.

Arrived at the little inn where I had halted in the morning, I perceived the sharp-faced woman in black, standing in the verandah with an elderly man, a taller and younger one dressed in black, a little girl, and a woman who stood in the passage of the door. I asked if I could get anything to eat. "Not a morsel; there's not a bit left in the house, but you can get something, perhaps, if you like to stay till supper time." "Would you oblige me by telling me where I can get some water for my horse?" "Oh, certainly," said the elder man, and calling to a negro he directed him to bring a bucket from the well or pump, into which the thirsty brute buried his head to the eyes. Whilst the horse was drinking the taller or younger man, leaning over the verandah, asked me quietly "What are all the people coming back for?—what's set them a running towards Alexandria?"

"Oh, it's only a fright the drivers of the commissariat waggons have had; they are afraid of the enemy's cavalry."

"Ah," said the man, and looking at me narrowly he inquired, after a pause, "are you an American?"

"No, I am not, thank God; I'm an Englishman."

"Well, then," said he, nodding his head and speaking slowly through his teeth, "There *will* be cavalry after them soon enough; there is 20,000 of the best horsemen in the world in old Virginny."

Having received full directions from the people at the inn for the road to the Long Bridge, which I was most anxious to reach instead of going to Alexandria or to Georgetown, I bade the Virginian good evening; and seeing that my stout friend, who had also watered his horse by my advice at the inn, was still clinging alongside, I excused myself by saying I must press on to Washington, and galloped on for a mile, until I got into the cover of a wood, where I dismounted to examine the horse's hoofs and shift the saddle for a moment, wipe the sweat off his back, and make him and myself as comfortable as could be for our ride into Washington, which was still seventeen or eighteen miles before me. I passed groups of men, some on horseback, others on foot, going at a more leisurely rate towards the capital; and as I was smoking my last cigar by the side of the wood, I observed the number had rather increased, and that among the retreating stragglers were some men who appeared to be wounded.

The sun had set, but the rising moon was adding every moment to the lightness of the road as I mounted once more and set out at a long trot for the capital. Presently I was overtaken by a waggon with a small escort of cavalry and an officer riding in front. I had seen the same vehicle once or twice along the road, and observed an officer seated in it with his head bound up with a handkerchief, looking very pale and ghastly. The mounted officer leading the escort asked me if I was going into Washington and knew the road. I told him I had never been on it before, but thought I could find my way, "at any rate we'll find plenty to tell us." "That's Colonel Hunter inside the carriage, he's shot through the throat and jaw, and I want to get him to the doctor's in Washington as soon as I can. Have you been to the fight?"

"No, sir."

"A member of Congress, I suppose, sir?"

"No, sir; I'm an Englishman."

"Oh indeed, sir, then I'm glad you did not see it, so mean a fight, sir, I never saw; we whipped the cusses and drove them before us, and took their batteries and spiked their guns, and got right up in among all their dirt works and great batteries and forts, driving them before us like sheep, when up more of them would get, as if out of the ground, then our boys would drive them again till we were fairly worn out; they had nothing to eat since last night and nothing to drink. I myself have not tasted a morsel since two o'clock last night. Well, there we were waiting for reinforcements and expecting M'Dowell and the rest of the army, when whish! they threw open a whole lot of masked batteries on us, and then came down such swarms of horsemen on black horses, all black as you never saw, and slashed our boys over finely. The colonel was hit, and I thought it best to get him off as well as I could, before it was too late; And, my God! when they did take to running they did it first-rate, I can tell you," and so, the officer, who had evidently taken enough to affect his empty stomach and head, chattering about the fight, we trotted on in the moonlight: dipping down into the valleys on the road, which seemed like inky lakes in the shadows of the black trees, then mounting up again along the white road, which shone like a river in the moonlight—the country silent as death, though once as we crossed a small water-course and the noise of the carriage wheels ceased, I called the attention of my companions to a distant sound, as of a great multitude of people mingled with a faint report of cannon. "Do you hear that?" "No, I don't. But it's our chaps, no doubt. They're coming along fine, I can promise you." At last some miles further on we came to a picket, or main guard, on the roadside, who ran forward, crying out "What's the news—anything fresh—are we whipped?—is it a fact?" "Well, gentlemen," exclaimed the Major, reining up for a moment, "we are knocked into a cocked hat—licked to h——l." "Oh, pray don't say that," I exclaimed, "It's not quite so bad, it's only a drawn battle, and the troops will occupy Centreville to-night, and the posts they started from this morning."

A little further on we met a line of commissariat carts, and my excited and rather injudicious military friend appeared to take the greatest pleasure in replying to their anxious queries for news. "We are whipped! Whipped like h——."

At the cross-roads now and then we were perplexed, for no one knew the bearings of Washington, though the stars were bright enough; but good fortune favoured us and kept us straight, and at a deserted little village, with a solitary church on the road-side, I increased my pace, bade good-night and good speed to the officer, and having kept company with two men in a gig for some time, got at length on the guarded road leading towards the capital, and was stopped by the pickets, patrols, and grand rounds, making repeated demands for the last accounts from the field. The houses by the road-side were all closed up and in darkness, I knocked in vain at several for a drink of water, but was answered only by the angry barkings of the watch-dogs from the slave quarters. It was a peculiarity of the road that the people, and soldiers I met, at points several miles apart, always insisted that I was twelve miles from Washington. Up hills, down valleys, with the silent, grim woods for ever by my side, the white roads and the black shadows of men, still I was twelve miles from the Long Bridge, but suddenly I came upon a grand guard under arms, who had quite different ideas, and who said I was only about four miles from the river; they crowded round me. "Well, man, and how is the fight going?" I repeated my tale. "What does he say?" "Oh, begorra, he says we're not bet at all; it's all lies they have been telling us; we're only going back to the ould lines for the greater convaniency of fighting to-morrow again; that's illigant, hooro!"

All by the sides of the old camps the men were standing, lining the road, and I was obliged to evade many a grasp at my bridle by shouting out "Don't stop me; I've important news; it's all well!" and still the good horse, refreshed by the cool night air, went clattering on, till from the top of the road beyond Arlington I caught a sight of the lights of Washington and the white buildings of the Capitol, and of the Executive Mansion, glittering like snow in the moonlight. At the entrance to the Long Bridge the sentry challenged, and asked for the countersign. "I have not got it, but I've a pass from General Scott." An officer advanced from the guard, and on reading the pass permitted me to go on without difficulty. He said, "I have been obliged to let a good many go over to-night before you, Congress men and others. I suppose you did not expect to be coming back so soon. I fear it's a bad business." "Oh, not so bad after all; I expected to have been back to-night before nine o'clock, and crossed over this morning without the countersign." "Well, I guess," said he, "we don't do such quick fighting as that in this country."

As I crossed the Long Bridge there was scarce a sound to dispute the possession of its echoes with my horse's hoofs. The poor beast had carried me nobly and well, and I made up my mind to buy him, as I had no doubt he would answer perfectly to carry me back in a day or two to M'Dowell's army by the time he had organised it for a new attack upon the enemy's position. Little did I conceive the greatness of the defeat, the magnitude of the disasters which it had entailed upon the United States or the interval that would elapse before another army set out from the banks of the Potomac onward to Richmond. Had I sat down that night to write my letter, quite ignorant at the time of the great calamity which had befallen his army, in all probability I would have stated that M'Dowell had received a severe repulse, and had fallen back upon Centreville, that a disgraceful panic and confusion had attended the retreat of a portion of his army, but that the appearance of the reserves would probably prevent the enemy taking any advantage of the disorder; and as I would have merely been able to describe such incidents as fell under my own observation, and would have left the American journals to narrate the actual details, and the despatches of the American Generals the strategical events of the day, I should have led the world at home to believe, as, in fact, I believed myself, that M'Dowell's retrograde movement would be arrested at some point between Centreville and Fairfax Court House.

The letter that I was to write occupied my mind whilst I was crossing the Long Bridge, gazing at the lights reflected in the Potomac from the city. The night had become overcast, and heavy clouds rising up rapidly obscured the moon, forming a most phantastic mass of shapes in the sky.

At the Washington end of the bridge I was challenged again by the men of a whole regiment, who, with piled arms, were halted on the chaussée, smoking, laughing, and singing. "Stranger, have you been to the fight?" "I have been only a little beyond Centreville." But that was quite enough. Soldiers, civilians, and women, who seemed to be out unusually late, crowded round the horse, and again I told my stereotyped story of the unsuccessful attempt to carry the Confederate position, and the retreat to Centreville to await better luck next time. The soldiers alongside me cheered, and those next them took it up till it ran through the whole line, and must have awoke the night owls.

As I passed Willard's hotel a little further on, a clock—I think the only public clock which strikes the hours in Washington—tolled out the hour; and I supposed, from what the sentry told me, though I did not count the strokes, that it was eleven o'clock. All the rooms in the hotel were a blaze of light. The pavement before the door was crowded, and some mounted men and the clattering of sabres on the pavement led me to infer that the escort of the wounded officer had arrived before me. I passed on to the livery-stables, where every one was alive and stirring.

"I'm sure," said the man, "I thought I'd never see you nor the horse back again. The gig and the other gentleman has been back a long time. How did he carry you?"

"Oh, pretty well; what's his price?"

"Well, now that I look at him, and to you, it will be 100 dollars less than I said. I'm in good heart to-night."

"Why so? A number of your horses and carriages have not come back yet, you tell me."

"Oh, well, I'll get paid for them some time or another. Oh, such news! such news!" said he, rubbing his hands. "Twenty thousand of them killed and wounded! May-be they're not having fits in the White House to-night!"

I walked to my lodgings, and just as I turned the key in the door a flash of light made me pause for a moment, in expectation of the report of a gun; for I could not help thinking it quite possible that, somehow or another, the Confederate cavalry would try to beat up the lines, but no sound followed. It must have been lightning. I walked up-stairs, and saw a most welcome supper ready on the table—an enormous piece of cheese, a sausage of unknown components, a knuckle-bone of ham, and a bottle of a very light wine of France; but I would not have exchanged that repast and have waited half an hour for any banquet that Soyer or Careme could have prepared at their best. Then, having pulled off my boots, bathed my head, trimmed candles, and lighted a pipe, I sat down to write. I made some feeble sentences, but the pen went flying about the paper as if the spirits were playing tricks with it. When I screwed up my utmost resolution, the "y's" would still run into long streaks, and the letters combine most curiously, and my eyes closed, and my pen slipped, and just as I was aroused from a nap, and settled into a stern determination to hold my pen straight, I was interrupted by a messenger from Lord Lyons, to inquire whether I had returned and if so, to ask me to go up to the Legation, and get something to eat. I explained, with my thanks, that I was quite safe, and had eaten supper, and learned from the servant that Mr. Warre and his companion had arrived about two hours previously. I resumed my seat once more, haunted by the memory of the Boston mail, which would be closed in a few hours, and I had much to tell, although I had not seen the battle. Again and again I woke up, but at last the greatest conqueror but death overcame me, and with my head on the blotted paper, I fell fast asleep.

"DEATH AND CONFUSION EVERYWHERE":
VIRGINIA, JULY 1861
Samuel J. English to his Mother

In a letter home Corporal Samuel English of the 2nd Rhode Island Volunteers—the regiment Sullivan Ballou served in—described his part in the battle that would be known in the North as Bull Run and in the South as Manassas. The Union army lost about 2,900 men killed, wounded, or missing, the Confederates about 1,900.

Camp Clark, July 24th/61
Dear Mother   Washington, D.C.
I rec'd your letter of the 21st shortly after our return to camp and take the earliest opportunity of writing. Yes, we have been & gone and done it. Last Thursday the 16th our brigade consisting of the two Rhode Island regiments, the New York 71st and the New Hampshire 2nd took up our line of march for Fairfax Court House. We crossed Long Bridge about 3 o'clock and continued on for six miles where we bivouacked for the night. Nothing occurred of importance to disturb our slumbers except the passing of troops bound on the same expedition. We commenced our march early in the morning, the 2nd R.I. regiment taking the lead and acting as skirmishers, Co. A taking the advance on the right; Co. D acting as flankers; Co. F acting as rear advance on the right of the column, Co. K acting as advance on the left. Co. C as flankers and Co. G as rear guard. I cannot state exactly the strength of our forces at the time, but should judge there were seven or eight thousand, including 1500 cavalry and two Batteries of artillery with two howitzers belonging to the New York 71st Regt. When within half a mile of the village of Fairfax, word was sent that the rebels' battery was directly in our line of march. Our artillery was immediately ordered to the front and fired three shots into it, making the sand fly, and showing pretty conclusively that the birds had flown. All the time this was taking place your

humble servant was skirting around in the woods as a skirmisher and arrived in the village ahead of the main column. As our company arrived the streets presented the scene of the wildest confusion: old negroes running around, some laughing, some crying and some swearing at a fearful rate. The streets were strewn with the knapsacks, haversacks, canteens, blankets, shirts and most every article pertaining to camp life. The houses were deserted and in some places the tables were set for dinner and coffee warm on the stove. After strolling around a short time we quartered ourselves in the park of Gen. Lee and made ourselves as comfortable as circumstances would permit. The cavalry in the meantime pursuing the retreating rebels and capturing 30 of their men. What particularly pleased me was that the company that lost the mess was the Palmetto Guards and Brooks Guards of South Carolina, having lost all of their camp equipage and barely escaped with their lives. But to continue, the next day our colors started for Manassas but halted and camped three miles this side of Centreville, waiting for our troops and reinforcements to come up; the second regiment being somewhat in advance of the main army; we stay here for three days and Sunday the 21st about 2 o'clock the drums beat the assembly and in ten minutes we were on our march for Bull Run having heard the enemy were waiting to receive us, our troops then numbering 25 or 30 thousand which were divided into three columns ours under Col Hunter taking the right through a thick woods. About eleven o'clock as our pickets were advancing through the woods a volley was poured in upon them from behind a fence thickly covered with brush; the pickets after returning the shots returned to our regiment and we advanced double quick time yelling like so many devils. On our arrival into the open field I saw I should judge three or four thousand rebels retreating for a dense woods, firing as they retreated, while from another part of the woods a perfect hail storm of bullets, round shot and shell was poured upon us, tearing through our ranks and scattering death and confusion everywhere; but with a yell and a roar we charged upon them driving them again into the woods with fearful loss. In the mean time our battery came up to our support and commenced hurling destruction among the rebels. Next orders were given for us to fall back and protect our battery as the enemy were charging upon it from another quarter, and then we saw with dismay that the second R.I. regiment were the only troops in the fight; the others having lagged so far behind that we had to stand the fight alone for 30 minutes; 1100 against 7 or 8 thousand. It was afterwards ascertained from a prisoner that the rebels thought we numbered 20 or 30 thousand from the noise made by us while making the charge. While preparing to make our final effort to keep our battery out of their hands, the 1st R.I. regiment then came filing over the fence and poured a volley out to them that drove them under cover again; they were followed by the New York 71st and the New Hampshire 2nd regiments; with 2,000 regulars bringing up the rear who pitched into the "Sechers" most beautifully. Our regiments were then ordered off the field and formed a line for a support to rally on in case the rebels over powered our troops. When the line had formed again I started off for the scene of action to see how the fight was progressing. As I emerged from the woods I saw a bomb shell strike a man in the breast and literally tear him to pieces. I passed the farm house which had been appropriated for a hospital and the groans of the wounded and dying were horrible. I then descended the hill to the woods which had been occupied by the rebels at the place where the Elsworth zouaves made their charge; the bodies of the dead and dying were actually three and four deep, while in the woods where the desperate struggle had taken place between the U.S. Marines and the Louisiana zouaves, the trees were spattered with blood and the ground strewn with dead bodies. The shots flying pretty lively round me I thought best to join my regiment; as I gained the top of the hill I heard the shot and shell of our batteries had given out, not having but 130 shots for each gun during the whole engagement. As we had nothing but infantry to fight against their batteries, the command was given to retreat; our cavalry not being of much use, because the rebels would not come out of the woods. The R.I. regiments, the New York 71st and the New Hampshire 2nd were drawn into a line to cover the retreat, but an officer galloped wildly into the column crying the enemy is upon us, and off they started like a flock of sheep every man for himself and the devil take the hindermost; while the rebels' shot and shell fell like rain among our exhausted troops. As we gained the cover of the woods the stampede became even more frightful, for the baggage wagons and ambulances became entangled with the artillery and rendered the scene even more dreadful than the battle, while the plunging of the horses broke the lines of our infantry and prevented any successful formation out of the question. The rebels being so badly cut up supposed we had gone beyond the woods to form on for a fresh attack and shelled the woods for full two hours, supposing we were there, thus saving the greater part of our forces, for if they had begun an immediate attack, nothing in heaven's name could have saved us. As we neared the bridge the rebels opened a very destructive fire upon us, mowing down our men like grass, and caused even greater confusion than before. Our artillery and baggage wagons became fouled with each other, completely blocking the bridge, while the bomb shells bursting on the bridge made it "rather unhealthy" to be around. As I crossed on my hands and knees, Capt. Smith who was crossing by my side at the same time was struck by a round shot at the same time and completely cut in two. After I crossed I started up the hill as fast as my legs could carry and passed through Centreville and continued on to Fairfax where we arrived about 10 o'clock halting about 15 minutes, then kept on to Washington where we arrived about 2 o'clock Monday noon more dead than alive, having been on our feet 36 hours without a mouthful to eat, and traveled a distance of 60 miles without twenty minutes halt. The last five miles of that march was perfect misery, none of us having scarcely strength to put one foot before the other, but I tell you the cheers we rec'd going through the streets of Washington seemed to put new life into the men for they rallied and marched to our camps and every man dropped on the ground and in one moment the greater part of them were asleep. Our loss is estimated at 1,000, but I think it greater, the rebels loss from three to five thousand.

NEWS OF MANASSAS:
SOUTH CAROLINA, JULY 1861

Emma Holmes: Diary, July 22–23, 1861

Emma Holmes, the young daughter of a plantation owner, recorded the reaction in Charleston to news of the Confederate victory in Virginia.

July 22

The telegraph this morning announces a great and glorious victory gained yesterday at Bull's Run after ten hours hard fighting. The enemy were completely routed, with tremendous slaughter; the loss on either side is of course not yet known, but ours is light compared to theirs. They have besides lost the whole of the celebrated Sherman Battery, two or three others, and a quantity of ammunition, baggage, etc. Their whole force amounted to about 80,000 while ours was only 35,000; only our left wing, however, commanded by Genl. Johnson, 15,000 in number against 35,000 of the enemy, were mostly engaged. The centre commanded by the President, who arrived on the field about noon, & the right wing, led by Beauregard, were only partially engaged. The Georgia Regiment commanded by Col. Francis S. Bartow seems to have suffered very severely, the Ogelthorpe Light I. from Savannah especially. Col. Bartow was killed as was also Gen. Barnard Bee and Col. B. F. Johnson of the Hampton Legion. The latter arrived only three hours before the battle and seem to have taken a conspicuous part in it. In Gen. Bee the Confederate Army has lost an officer whose place cannot readily be supplied. He stood so high in his profession that, immediately after his arrival quite late from the distant western frontiers, a captain, he was raised to the rank of Brigadier General; he was one of Carolina's noblest sons, and, though we glory in the victory won by the prowess of our gallant men, tears for the honored dead mingle with our rejoicings. Col. Bartow was one of the most talented and prominent men in Savannah and very much beloved; he left Congress to go to Va. with the O. L. I. as their captain, but was made Col. & was acting Brigadier Gen. during the battle. Col. Johnson's loss will also be much felt; he leaves a wife & eight children. A great many Charlestonians are wounded but only three of Kershaw's R. which must have been in the right wing. . . . Rumors are, of course, flying in every direction, none of which are to be relied on, but Willie Heyward went on tonight to see after some of his friends, whom he hears are wounded.

July 23

The telegraph today only confirms what we heard yesterday without additional information, as the wires from Manassas to Richmond were down for some hours. Several gentlemen went on last night with servants & nurses to attend our wounded, and societies for their relief are being organized in the city. The *northern* account of the battle & the dreadful panic which seized their troops, followed by complete demoralization, is most graphic. They admit that the carnage was fearful. The "brag" regiment of N.Y., the 69th, was cut to pieces; the *infamous* Fire Zouaves went into battle 1100 strong and came out 206. The New Orleans Zouaves were let loose on them & most amply were the murder of Jackson & the outrages on women avenged on these fiends; 60 pieces of artillery were taken including Sherman's which was celebrated as Ringgold's during the Mexican War. Carlisle's, Griffin's, the West Point Batteries, & the 8 siege 32-pounder rifle cannon, with which Scott was marching upon Richmond. The Federal Army left Washington commanded by Scott in all the pomp & pageantry of the panoply of war—all so grand and impressive in their own eyes that they did not dream that we would strike a blow but would lay down our arms in terror. They carried 550 pair of handcuffs & invited immense numbers of ladies to follow and see Beauregard and Lee put into irons, expecting to march directly on to Richmond. The contrast of the picture may be imagined—gloom and terror reign in Washington, and they are multiplying fortifications and reinforcing the city.

Today, by Col. Anderson's order, a salute was fired of twenty-one guns, from Forts Moultrie & Sumter, at 12 o'clock, in honor of the victory, & tomorrow their flags will be placed at half-mast and guns fired hourly from 6:00 A.M. till sunset in honor of the illustrious dead. Preparations are being made to receive the bodies in state; the City Hall is draped in mourning as when Calhoun lay in state, & now his statue gleams intensely white through the funeral hangings surrounding the three biers. I have not yet visited the hall but those who have say the impression is awfully solemn. It seems really the "Chamber of the Dead." The bodies were expected today, but a delay occurred & they may not come till Friday. This afternoon the Ladies Charleston Volunteer Aid Society held a meeting at the S.C. Hall, 192 ladies were there and nearly $1000 collected from subscriptions and donations. Miss Hesse Drayton was appointed Superintendent, & Hesse, Assistant, Emily Rutledge, Secy. & Treasurer, & 12 Managers to cut out the work and distribute it. We are to have monthly as well as quarterly meetings. The ladies all seemed to enjoy seeing their friends as well as the purpose for which they came. Mrs. Geo. Robertson & Mrs. Amy Snowden have got up another called Soldiers' Relief Assn. not only for sending clothes, but comforts & necessaries for the sick and wounded, while the ladies interested in the Y.M.C.A. have got up another & already sent on supplies for the hospitals. All are most liberally supported. . . .

STRAGGLING SOLDIERS:
WASHINGTON, D.C., JULY 1861

Elizabeth Blair Lee to Samuel Phillips Lee

Elizabeth Blair Lee related the aftermath of the Union defeat to her husband, who had returned to the United States and was now on blockade duty off Charleston.

———————

Philadelphia   July 23, 1861
Dear Phil   The most comfortable sensation I have about this move from my home is that it will be a relief to you & that after this you will never have an anxious thought about us— feeling we have the most cautious care taken of us—

News from Washington indicates a revival of energy in Washn   They are sad & the secessionist too are equally busy over their dead & wounded   Mr. Pryor a brother of the M.C. says their loss was awful even before he was taken prisoner early in the day— It must have been or they would have followed up their Victory more vigorously which they had not done at 2 olk today Patterson's men are ready to mob him so one of them told me today They say he is as more of an ally to the South than even Genl Jo Johnston The rumors about our loss is all uncertain for the rolls were not called at midday to day & I saw many of the soldiers straggling in late last night & early the morning— One of them sat in the rain on the stone foundation of brother's front fence— I asked if he was hungry? No! Thirsty? no, sick? no,— wounded no no only mad— we are beat & badly because we have no generals— no competent officers He was almost heart broken from his tone & manner— a very respectable looking man— The Citizens treated them well— fed & sheltered them from the storm— Maryland seems *steady*— All was quiet in Balt— as we came thro it— & I saw 50 flags where I saw ten in June—

I shall still stay here a few days & then go to Bethlehem for Mary Blairs party without Dr Hodge advises me to go to the

Sea shore for these headaches which I think comes from the same cause that makes specs comfortable— & if he advises me to go to the sea— Ill go with Mira & Mr. Dick to the Atlantic City— across New Jersey & just 2 hours from here & until this is settled I'll home here under Aunt Becky's care— Blair & Becky are my best protection in my wanderings— & our dear child is certainly a great comfort— He was joyous today in the Cars with hope of going to see Papa   I do hope you will soon come into port— tho this Rhode Island provision looks like keeping you all out but the rest have had their turn & you ought to have yours-Ever yr devoted Lizzie

Betty & Apo go to New York tomorrow— Betty to Martins & Apo to Connecticut

"A TERRIBLE SHOCK":
WASHINGTON, D.C., JULY 1861

Walt Whitman: *from* Specimen Days

Walt Whitman was at his home in Brooklyn when he learned of Bull Run from the New York newspapers. In 1863 Whitman moved to Washington, and it is likely that he spoke there with witnesses to the aftermath of the battle. He described the return of the defeated army to the capital in *Specimen Days* (1882), drawing on accounts he had previously published in "'Tis But Ten Years Since," a series of six articles that appeared in the *New York Weekly Graphic* in 1874, and in *Memoranda During the War* (1875).

CONTEMPTUOUS FEELING

Even after the bombardment of Sumter, however, the gravity of the revolt, and the power and will of the slave States for a strong and continued military resistance to national authority, were not at all realized at the North, except by a few. Nine-tenths of the people of the free States look'd upon the rebellion, as started in South Carolina, from a feeling one-half of contempt, and the other half composed of anger and incredulity. It was not thought it would be join'd in by Virginia, North Carolina, or Georgia. A great and cautious national official predicted that it would blow over "in sixty days," and folks generally believ'd the prediction. I remember talking about it on a Fulton ferry-boat with the Brooklyn mayor, who said he only "hoped the Southern fire-eaters would commit some overt act of resistance, as they would then be at once so effectually squelch'd, we would never hear of secession again —but he was afraid they never would have the pluck to really do anything." I remember, too, that a couple of companies of the Thirteenth Brooklyn, who rendezvou'd at the city armory, and started thence as thirty days' men, were all provided with pieces of rope, conspicuously tied to their musket-barrels, with which to bring back each man a prisoner from the audacious

South, to be led in a noose, on our men's early and triumphant return!

BATTLE OF BULL RUN, JULY, 1861

All this sort of feeling was destin'd to be arrested and revers'd by a terrible shock—the battle of first Bull Run—certainly, as we now know it, one of the most singular fights on record. (All battles, and their results, are far more matters of accident than is generally thought; but this was throughout a casualty, a chance. Each side supposed it had won, till the last moment. One had, in point of fact, just the same right to be routed as the other. By a fiction, or series of fictions, the national forces at the last moment exploded in a panic and fled from the field.) The defeated troops commenced pouring into Washington over the Long Bridge at daylight on Monday, 22d—day drizzling all through with rain. The Saturday and Sunday of the battle (20th, 21st,) had been parch'd and hot to an extreme—the dust, the grime and smoke, in layers, sweated in, follow'd by other layers again sweated in, absorb'd by those excited souls—their clothes all saturated with the clay-powder filling the air—stirr'd up everywhere on the dry roads and trodden fields by the regiments, swarming wagons, artillery, &c.—all the men with this coating of murk and sweat and rain, now recoiling back, pouring over the Long Bridge—a horrible march of twenty miles, returning to Washington baffled, humiliated, panic-struck. Where are the vaunts, and the proud boasts with which you went forth? Where are your banners, and your bands of music, and your ropes to bring back your prisoners? Well, there isn't a band playing—and there isn't a flag but clings ashamed and lank to its staff.

The sun rises, but shines not. The men appear, at first sparsely and shame-faced enough, then thicker, in the streets of Washington—appear in Pennsylvania avenue, and on the steps and basement entrances. They come along in disorderly mobs, some in squads, stragglers, companies. Occasionally, a rare regiment, in perfect order, with its officers (some gaps, dead, the true braves,) marching in silence, with lowering faces, stern, weary to sinking, all black and dirty, but every man with his musket, and stepping alive; but these are the exceptions. Sidewalks of

Pennsylvania avenue, Fourteenth street, &c., crowded, jamm'd with citizens, darkies, clerks, everybody, lookers-on; women in the windows, curious expressions from faces, as those swarms of dirt-cover'd return'd soldiers there (will they never end?) move by; but nothing said, no comments; (half our lookers-on secesh of the most venomous kind—they say nothing; but the devil snickers in their faces.) During the forenoon Washington gets all over motley with these defeated soldiers—queer-looking objects, strange eyes and faces, drench'd (the steady rain drizzles on all day) and fearfully worn, hungry, haggard, blister'd in the feet. Good people (but not over-many of them either,) hurry up something for their grub. They put wash-kettles on the fire, for soup, for coffee. They set tables on the side-walks—wagon-loads of bread are purchas'd, swiftly cut in stout chunks. Here are two aged ladies, beautiful, the first in the city for culture and charm, they stand with store of eating and drink at an improvis'd table of rough plank, and give food, and have the store replenish'd from their house every half-hour all that day; and there in the rain they stand, active, silent, white-hair'd, and give food, though the tears stream down their cheeks, almost without intermission, the whole time. Amid the deep excitement, crowds and motion, and desperate eagerness, it seems strange to see many, very many, of the soldiers sleeping—in the midst of all, sleeping sound. They drop down anywhere, on the steps of houses, up close by the basements or fences, on the sidewalk, aside on some vacant lot, and deeply sleep. A poor seventeen or eighteen year old boy lies there, on the stoop of a grand house; he sleeps so calmly, so profoundly. Some clutch their muskets firmly even in sleep. Some in squads; comrades, brothers, close together—and on them, as they lay, sulkily drips the rain.

As afternoon pass'd, and evening came, the streets, the bar-rooms, knots everywhere, listeners, questioners, terrible yarns, bugaboo, mask'd batteries, our regiment all cut up, &c.—stories and story-tellers, windy, bragging, vain centres of street-crowds. Resolution, manliness, seem to have abandon'd Washington. The principal hotel, Willard's, is full of shoulder-straps—thick, crush'd, creeping with shoulder-straps. (I see them, and must have a word with them. There you are, shoulder-straps!—but where are your companies? where are your men? Incompetents! never tell me of chances of battle, of getting stray'd, and the like. I think this is your work, this retreat, after all. Sneak, blow, put on airs there in Willard's sumptuous parlors and bar-rooms, or anywhere—no explanation shall save you. Bull Run is your work; had you been half or one-tenth worthy your men, this would never have happen'd.)

Meantime, in Washington, among the great persons and their entourage, a mixture of awful consternation, uncertainty, rage, shame, helplessness, and stupefying disappointment. The worst is not only imminent, but already here. In a few hours—perhaps before the next meal—the secesh generals, with their victorious hordes, will be upon us. The dream of humanity, the vaunted Union we thought so strong, so impregnable—lo! it seems already smash'd like a china plate. One bitter, bitter hour—perhaps proud America will never again know such an hour. She must pack and fly—no time to spare. Those white palaces—the dome-crown'd capitol there on the hill, so stately over the trees—shall they be left—or destroy'd first? For it is certain that the talk among certain of the magnates and officers and clerks and officials everywhere, for twenty-four hours in and around Washington after Bull Run, was loud and undisguised for yielding out and out, and substituting the southern rule, and Lincoln promptly abdicating and departing. If the secesh officers and forces had immediately follow'd, and by a bold Napoleonic movement had enter'd Washington the first day, (or even the second,) they could have had things their own way, and a powerful faction north to back them. One of our returning colonels express'd in public that night, amid a swarm of officers and gentlemen in a crowded room, the opinion that it was useless to fight, that the southerners had made their title clear, and that the best course for the national government to pursue was to desist from any further attempt at stopping them, and admit them again to the lead, on the best terms they were willing to grant. Not a voice was rais'd against this judgment, amid that large crowd of officers and gentlemen. (The fact is, the hour was one of the three or four of those crises we had then and afterward, during the fluctuations of four years, when human eyes appear'd at least just as likely to see the last breath of the Union as to see it continue.)

WASHINGTON, D.C., JULY 1861

Abraham Lincoln:
Memoranda on Military Policy

On the afternoon of July 21 President Lincoln followed the fighting from the War Department, where he read telegrams sent every fifteen minutes from Fairfax Station, about four miles east of the Bull Run battlefield. Between 4 P.M. and 6 P.M. a series of messages reported that the Confederate lines had been driven back. After the President went out for his evening ride, Secretary of State Seward arrived at the Executive Mansion and told John Nicolay and John Hay: "The battle is lost. The telegraph says that McDowell is in full retreat, and calls on General Scott to save the Capitol." When Lincoln learned of the defeat he went to confer with General Scott, and then spent the night hearing the accounts of senators and congressmen who had gone out to watch the battle. In the week following Bull Run he would write two memoranda on future military actions.

July 23. 1861.

1 Let the plan for making the Blockade effective be pushed forward with all possible despatch.

2 Let the volunteer forces at Fort-Monroe & vicinity—under Genl. Butler—be constantly drilled, disciplined, and instructed without more for the present.

3. Let Baltimore be held, as now, with a gentle, but firm, and certain hand.

4 Let the force now under Patterson, or Banks, be strengthened, and made secure in it's possition.

5. Let the forces in Western Virginia act, till further orders, according to instructions, or orders from Gen. McClellan.

6. Gen. Fremont push forward his organization, and opperations in the West as rapidly as possible, giving rather special attention to Missouri.

7 Let the forces late before Manassas, except the three months men, be reorganized as rapidly as possible, in their camps here and about Arlington

8. Let the three months forces, who decline to enter the longer service, be discharged as rapidly as circumstances will permit.

9 Let the new volunteer forces be brought forward as fast as possible; and especially into the camps on the two sides of the river here.

July 27, 1861

When the foregoing shall have been substantially attended to—

1. Let Manassas junction, (or some point on one or other of the railroads near it;); and Strasburg, be seized, and permanently held, with an open line from Washington to Manassas; and an open line from Harper's Ferry to Strasburg—the military men to find the way of doing these.

2. This done, a joint movement from Cairo on Memphis; and from Cincinnati on East Tennessee.

CELEBRATING VICTORY: VIRGINIA, JULY 1861
Mary Chesnut: Diary, July 24, 1861

Mary Chesnut was in Richmond during the battle of Manassas, and witnessed the reaction in the Confederate capital to the victory.

July 24, 1861. Here Mr. Chesnut opened my door—and walked in. Of the fullness of the heart the mouth speaketh. I had to ask no questions. He gave me an account of the battle as he saw it (walking up and down my room, occasionally seating himself on a window sill, but too restless to remain still many moments). Told what regiments he was sent to bring up. He took orders to Colonel Jackson—whose regiment stood so stock-still under fire they were called a stone wall. Also, they call Beauregard "Eugene" and Johnston "Marlboro" (s'en va— en guerre). Mr. C rode with Lay's cavalry after the retreating enemy, in the pursuit, they following them until midnight. There then came such a rain—rain such as is only known in semitropical lands.

In the drawing room Colonel Chesnut was the "belle of the ball"—they crowded him so for news. He was the first arrival that they could get at, from the field of battle—handle, so to speak. But the women had to give way to the dignitaries of the land, who were as filled with curiosity as themselves—Mr. Barnwell, Mr. Hunter, the Cobbs, Captain Ingraham, &c&c.

Wilmot DeSaussure says Wilson of Massachusetts, senator U.S.A., came to Manassas en route to Richmond, with his dancing shoes ready for the festive scene which was to celebrate a triumph.

The *Tribune* said: "In a few days" they would have Richmond, Memphis, New Orleans. "They must be taken and at once." For "a few days" maybe now they will modestly substitute "in a few years."

They brought me a Yankee soldier's portfolio from the battlefield. The letters were franked by Senator Harlan. One might shed a few tears over some of his letters. Women—wives and mothers—are the same everywhere.

What a comfort the spelling was. We were willing to admit their universal free school education put their rank and file ahead of us *literarily*. Now, these letters do not attest that fact. The spelling is comically bad.

Not so bad as Wigfall's man, however, who spelt "fi-ar" à la mode de "li-ar."

Mrs. Davis's drawing room last night was brilliant, and she was in great force. Outside a mob collected and called for the president. He did speak. He is an old war-horse—and scents the battlefields from afar. His enthusiasm was contagious. The president took all the credit to himself for the victory—said the wounded roused and shouted for Jeff Davis and the men rallied at the sight of him and rushed on and routed the enemy. The truth is, Jeff Davis was not two miles from the battlefield, but he is greedy for military fame. They called for Colonel Chesnut, and he gave them a capital speech, too. As the public speakers say sometimes, "It was the proudest moment of my life." My life—the woman who writes here, now. I did not hear a great deal of it, for always when anything happens of any moment, my heart beats up in my ears. But the distinguished Carolinians that crowded round me told me how good a speech he made. I was dazed. He gave the glory of the victory to Beauregard and said if the president had not said so much for himself, he would have praised him.

Mrs. McLean was very angry with Joe Davis: he forgot her presence and wished all Yankees were dead.

Somebody said he did remember ladies' presence, for the habit of our men was to call them "Damn Yankees." Mrs. Davis was at her wits' end what to do with Joe Davis, for she is devoted to Mrs. McLean. And when she consults anyone, they only grin, the sentiment being one which meets with almost universal sympathy just now.

There goes the Dead March for some poor soul.

Mrs. Wigfall said when her children were small, she broke them of ever using bad words by washing their mouths with soap and water to cleanse them. Joe Davis is not small, alas! And then somebody told a story—a little girl came running to tell on her brother: "Oh, mama, Charlie is using bad language—curse words."

"What is it?"

"He says 'Damn Yankees' are here prisoners."

"Well, mama, is not that their name? I never hear them called anything else."

Today the president told us at dinner that Mr. Chesnut's eulogy of Bartow in the Congress was highly praised. Men liked it. Two eminently satisfactory speeches in twenty-four hours is doing pretty well. And now I would be happy, but this cabinet of ours are in such bitter quarrels among themselves. Everybody abusing everybody.

Last night, while those splendid descriptions of the battles were being given to the crowd below, from our windows I said, "Then why do we not go on to Washington?"

"You mean, why did they not. The time has passed—the opportunity is lost." Mr. Barnwell said to me: "Silence. We want to listen to the speaker." And Mr. Hunter smiled compassionately: "Don't ask awkward questions."

Mr. C said: "They were lapping round Hampton, and I saw they would flank us. Then that fine fellow Elzey came in view—when I saw it was our flag! At first we thought it was the enemy! And we had our hands full before. They were pushing us hard. Almost at the moment that joyful sight of our flag had relieved my mind. I saw confusion in the enemy's wagon train. Then their panic began."

Kirby Smith came down on the turnpike at the very nick of time. Still, the heroes who fought all day and held the Yankees in check deserve credit beyond words. *Or* it would all have been over before the Joe Johnston contingent came. It is another case of the *eleventh-hour* scrape. The eleventh-hour men claim all the credit, and they who bore the heat and brunt and burden of the day do not like that.

Mrs. Wigfall busy as a bee, making a flag for her Texians. Louis is colonel of the regiment.

Everybody said at first: "Pshaw! There will be no war." Those who foresaw evil were called "Ravens"—ill foreboders. Now the same sanguine people all cry "the war is over"—the very same who were packing to leave Richmond a few days ago. Many were ready to move on at a moment's warning, when the good news came.

There are such owls everywhere. But to revert to the other kind—the sage and circumspect, those who say very little, but that little shows they think the war barely begun. Mr. Rives and Mr. Seddon have just called. Arnoldus VanderHorst came to see me at the same time. He said there was no great show of victory on our side until two o'clock, but when we began to win, we did it in double-quick time. I mean, of course, the battle last Saturday.

I was talking with Hon. Mr. Clingman and the friendly Brewster—when a U.S. surgeon on parole came to see Mrs. McLean. A terrible Confederate female of ardent patriotism and a very large damp mouth said, "How I would like to scalp that creature."

"A descendant of Pocahontas, evidently," said Brewster, with a faint snigger. "She must mean Mrs. McLean, who has a beautiful head of hair. The man is shorn to the quick—no hair to get a purchase, to tear his scalp off."

Mr. Clingman could not look more disgusted than he always does.

Arnold Harris told Mr. Wigfall the news from Washington last Saturday. For hours the telegrams reported at rapid intervals: "great victory," "defeating them at all points."

About three o'clock the telegrams began to come in on horseback—at least, after two or three o'clock there was a sudden cessation of all news. About nine, bulletins came on foot or on horseback, wounded, weary, draggled, footsore, panic-stricken, spreading in their path on every hand terror and dismay.

That was our opportunity. Wigfall can see nothing to stop

us. And when they explain why we did not go, I understand it all less than ever.

Yes, here we will dillydally and Congress orate and generals parade, until they get up an army three times as large as McDowell's that we have just defeated.

Trescot says this victory will be our ruin. It lulls us into a fool's paradise of conceit at our superior valor.

And the shameful farce of their flight will wake every inch of their manhood. It was the very fillip they needed.

There are a quieter sort here who know their Yankees well. They say if the thing begins to pay—government contracts and all that—we will never hear the end of it. At least, until they get their pay out of us. They will not lose money by us. Of that we may be sure. Trust Yankee shrewdness and vim for that.

There seems to be a battle raging at Bethel, but no mortal here can be got to think of anything but Manassas.

Mrs. McLean says she does not see that it was such a great victory, and if it be so great, how can one defeat hurt a nation like the North. What a villain that woman is.

John Waties fought the whole battle over for me. Now I understand it. Before this, nobody could take time to tell the thing consecutively, rationally, and in order.

Again the crowd came, to get Mr. Davis to speak to them. They wanted to hear all about it again.

Afterward they called for Chesnut of South Carolina—who could not be found. He had retired into Mrs. Preston's room.

Mr. Venable said he did not see a braver thing done than the cool performance of a Columbia negro. He brought his master a bucket of ham and rice which he had cooked for him, and he cried, "You must be so tired and hungry, Marster—make haste and eat." This was in the thickest of the fight, under the heaviest of the enemies' guns.

The Federal congressmen were making a picnic of it. Their luggage was all ticketed to Richmond.

"It is a far cry to Lochow"—as the clansmen say.

Cameron has issued a proclamation. They are making ready to come after us on a magnificent scale. They acknowledge us at last—foemen worthy of their steel.

The Lord help us, since England and France won't—or don't. If we could only get a friend outside and open a port.

Mr. Mason came and would march me in state on his arm into Mrs. Davis's drawing room (Maxcy Gregg and Mr. Miles were with me when Mr. Mason and Mr. Seddon called. Mr. Miles and Co. meekly followed). I looked back and wished I was with the unobserved rear guard.

Mr. Mason is a high and mighty Virginian. He brooks no opposition to his will.

They say it is Douglas Ramsay who was killed, and not our friend Wadsworth.

One of these men told me he had seen a Yankee prisoner who asked him what sort of a diggins Richmond was for trade. He was tired of the old concern and would like to take the oath and settle here.

They brought us handcuffs found in the debacle of the Yankee army.

For whom were they? Jeff Davis, no doubt. And the ringleaders.

Tell that to the Marines. We have outgrown the handcuff business on this side of the water.

———

Russell, the Englishman, was in Alexandria. Why did we not follow them there? That's the question.

———

After the little unpleasantness &c&c between Mrs. Davis and Mrs. Wigfall, there was a complete reconciliation, and Mrs. Wigfall in all amity presented Mrs. Davis with the most hideous Chinese monster I ever saw. A Mandarin, I meant to say.

———

All day I was in bed. The night before, sat up too late hearing Mrs. Davis abuse and disabuse Mrs. McLean. Mrs. Joe Johnston and Mrs. McLean have gone to Orange Court House. I am truly glad they did not get to Manassas. Mrs. Davis, Wigfall, &c&c sat with me and told me unutterable stories of the war, but I forget after so much opium. Mr. Chesnut would not go to bed but sat up and gave me such a scolding. . . . Jeff Davis offers Mr. Chesnut anything he wants—and is going to give Mr. Preston a commission. . . .

Dr. Gibbes says he was at a country house near Manassas when a Federal soldier who had lost his way came in, exhausted. He asked for brandy, which the lady of the house gave him. Upon second thought he declined it. She brought it to him so promptly, he said he thought it might be poisoned. His mind was.

She was enraged.

"Sir, I am a Virginia woman. Do you think I could be as base as that? Here—Bill, Tom, disarm this man. He is our prisoner." The negroes came running, and the man surrendered without more ado. Another Federal was drinking at the well. A negro girl said, "You go in and see Missis." The man went in, and she followed crying triumphantly, "Look here—Missis, I got a prisoner too!"

They were not ripe for John Brown, you see.

This lady sent in her two prisoners, and Beauregard complimented her on her pluck and patriotism and presence of mind.

These negroes were rewarded by their owners. Now if slavery is as disagreeable as we think it, why don't they all march over the border, where they would be received with open arms? It amazes me. I am always studying these creatures. They are to me inscrutable in their ways and past finding out.

Dr. Gibbes says the faces of the dead grow as black as charcoal on the battlefield, and they shine in the sun.

Now this horrible vision of the dead on the battlefield haunts me.

Old Ruffin has promised me a John Brown pike—and Dr. Gibbes a handcuff—for my very own, trophies for future generations—more especially, as they see I do not believe any stories of pikes or handcuffs or a cage for Jeff Davis.

Hon. Mr. Hammond is here. Our world collects here—gravitates to Richmond, as it did to Charleston and Montgomery.

These young men say the war is doing them good. Hugh Rose, who has a room in this hotel, offered to share it with his father. It was that or the street for the old gentleman—so great is the crowd. They seem to think it an act of superhuman virtue "to have your father in your room." At least they know it was on Hugh Rose's part.

Camden DeLeon is sure to lose his place as surgeon general. Dr. Gibbes wants it. Dr. Nott is looked upon by many as a fit person for it. DeLeon is always drunk.

Somebody sent me a caricature of Jeff Davis trying to throw sand in John Bull's eyes and stuff wool in his ears.

There are so many wonderful tales here about everybody. That strange-looking man Clingman—I thought the first story funny enough. Dancing is a serious business with him. Some young lady spoke to him while he was dancing with her. "Pray withhold all remarks. It puts me out. I cannot do two things at once. If you will talk, I shall have to stop dancing."

Then, when he was presented to Miss Lane, he bowed low and immediately held his nose. Holding it firmly, he said: "Pardon me. I will retire now. I may come back and make a few remarks." He had bowed so low his nose began to bleed, and he had to hold it with all his might.

Fancy Miss Lane's face. The very queen of the proprieties. I cannot imagine her laughing in the wrong place or at the wrong time.

And yet she must have laughed then. Stories of Clingman abound. He cut his throat because he was not as clever as Mr. Calhoun. Made a failure then, too, for it was sewed up—and he lives still.

One of Mr. Chesnut's anecdotes of Manassas:
He had in his pocket a small paper of morphine. He put it

there to alleviate pain. Ever since Tom Withers's frightful fractured leg, when the doctors would not give him anodyne enough to put him to sleep and quiet his agony for a time, at least, Mr. C always carried morphine powders in his pocket. These he gave Tom in the night, in spite of the faculty, and the soothing of that poor boy's anguish he considered one of the good deeds of his life.

Now a man was howling with pain on the outskirts of the battlefield—by the way, the only one that made any outcry, at least, that he heard that day, be their wounds as grievous as they might. This man proved to be only a case of pain in the stomach. Him he relieved with the opiate and passed on rapidly where he was sent. Later in the day he saw a man lying under a tree who begged for water. He wore the Federal uniform.

As Mr. C carried him the water, he asked him where he was from. The man refused to answer.

"Poor fellow—you have no cause to care about all that now—you can't hurt me. And God knows I would not harm you. What else do you want?"

"Straighten my legs—they are doubled up under me." The legs were smashed. He gave him some morphine to let him at least know a few moments of peace. He says: "This is my first battle. I hope my heart will not grow harder."

Clingman said he credited the statement that they wanted water, for he remembered the avidity with which he drank water himself from dirty pools.

Captain Ingraham told Captain Smith Lee: "Don't be so conceited about your looks. Mrs. Chesnut thinks your brother Robert a handsomer man than you."

I did not contradict the statement, as Clingman would say, and yet it was false.

This is how I saw Robert E. Lee for the first time. I had heard of him, strange to say, in this wise. Though his family, who then lived at Arlington, called to see me in Washington (I thought because of Mrs. Chesnut's intimacy with Nelly Custis in the old Philadelphia days—and Mrs. Lee was Nelly Custis's niece), I had not known the head of the Lee family. He was somewhere with the army then.

Last summer at the White Sulphur, Roony Lee and his wife, that sweet little Charlotte Wickham, was there, and I spoke of Roony with great praise.

Mrs. Izard said: "Don't waste your admiration on him. Wait till you see his father. He is the nearest to a perfect man I ever saw." "How?" "Every way—handsome, clever, agreeable, highbred, &c&c."

Mrs. Stanard came for Mrs. Preston and me, to drive to the camp. She was in an open carriage. A man riding a beautiful horse joined us. He wore a hat with somehow a military look to it. He sat his horse gracefully, and he was so distinguished at all points that I very much regretted not catching the name as Mrs. Stanard gave it to us. He, however, heard ours and bowed as gracefully as he rode, and the few remarks he made to each of us showed he knew all about us.

But Mrs. Stanard was in ecstasies of pleasurable excitement. I felt she had bagged a big fish. Just then they abounded in Richmond. Mrs. Stanard accused him of being ambitious &c. He remonstrated—said his tastes were of the simplest. He "only wanted a Virginia farm—no end of cream and fresh butter—and fried chicken. Not one fried chicken or two—but unlimited fried chicken."

To all this light chat did we seriously incline because the man and horse and everything about him was so fine looking. Perfection—no fault to be found if you hunted for one. As he left us, I said, "Who is it?" eagerly.

"You did not know! Why, it is Robert E. Lee, son of Light Horse Harry Lee, the first man in Virginia"—raising her voice as she enumerated his glories.

All the same, I like Smith Lee better, and I like his looks, too. I know Smith Lee well. Can anybody say they know his brother? I doubt it. He looks so cold and quiet and grand.

And so Dr. Moore was made surgeon general. Dr. Gibbes has the sulks.

Reading the *Herald*—filled with excuses for their disaster. Excuses don't count. We must accept facts.

It is wonderful. Kirby Smith, our Blücher, who came on the field in the nick of time—as at Waterloo. And now we are as the British, who do not remember Blücher. It is all Wellington. So every individual man I see fought and won the battle. From Kershaw up and down—all the eleventh-hour men won the battle, turned the tide—the Marylanders. Elzey & Co. one never hears of—as little as one hears of Blücher in the English Waterloo stories.

Had a painful adventure, in a small way. The poor soul who was debarred the pleasure of rushing to Mrs. Bartow with the news of her husband's death—they call her "bad accident maker to the evening news"—today she came into my room. Adèle Auzé said, "That woman Cousin Mary calls 'bad accident'"—and there was a look of consternation—for she was among us. Mrs. Davis applauded my adroitness: "Is it true your son has met with a bad accident? We are so sorry to hear it."

"Oh, yes—it is a dreadful wound. He was punched in the side by the butt end of a musket."

The deep and absorbing interest I evinced in that wound and the frowns that I gave Adèle when I could turn my head and Adèle's reckless making of comic faces over her blunder—it was overheating, at this state of the thermometer.

Letter from Columbia, S.C.

Home
July 28, 1861

Many thanks to you, my dear Mrs. C, for your kind letter, which I have vainly hoped would have been followed by many more.

Letters from Virginia are like water to the thirsty, fainting body. We look for tidings with that aching of the heart that seems almost beyond endurance. Such tidings as we have had! Exultingly singing and praising God with one voice and the next moment finding us low at His footstool in weeping and prayer and deep humility. His mercies abound and we will not sully the bright glories of the 21st by more than *natural* tears, in grieving over our brave soldiers. I think every man on that battlefield *on our side* was a hero. And we must admit that a *portion* of the "bad cause" fought as bravely as *ours*, but the heart and principle were wanting, and so God gave us the victory. Our brave and noble men! May the merciful God of battles shield them every moment. I feel that they may be again in conflict—this very hour! When Beauregard puts the seal of secrecy upon his doings and prohibits all intercourse, I look for some great achievement to follow.

That was a *dear-bought*, but such a grand, victory. It seems incredible.

I think Havelock's great movement in the East the only recorded event that outstrips it. God help and keep our brave soldiers! This opens the way to a request from John Means to you. He begs you will oblige him by discovering the whereabouts of a young soldier, John Means Thompson (a nephew of Gen. Waddy Thompson), who was wounded slightly. He belongs to the Washington Light Infantry, Captain Conner, from Charleston. His friends apprehend increased dangers in his case from a delicate constitution with pulmonary tendencies. If not in Richmond, would you get a line to Mrs. Singleton at her post, or Mrs. Carrington in Charlottesville? The arrangements for our soldiers we do not exactly take in—are they scattered in the different hospitals or principally in Richmond and Charlottesville? Stark Means, belonging to the Sixth Regiment S.C.V. Colonel Winder is in Virginia. His mother is here and says I must beg you and Mrs. Singleton or any and all of our friends to remember *her*, if anything happens to her son. She is here now with her daughter Emma—very, very ill, and we fear her case will end in consumption, if not already that. John is down today just to see his child and will return tomorrow. Their hearts are torn between these only darling ones—God help them. How little all these things make me feel.

Old Scott! I only wish every disaster on that battlefield could be photographed on his heart and brain—stereotyped on his *vision*—that mortification, remorse, and shame might balance in some degree the horrors he has brought on our country.

Please say to Mrs. Preston, too, to bear in mind our boys. Oh! If you could realize all we dread and yet long to hear, I am sure you ladies would write. There is no detail that is not precious to us—nothing from the seat of war that has not its value to our anxious hearts, worn with suspense, and taking "*all*" our brave ones into the circle of love and care.

Tell Mrs. Preston her dear old mother turned out today for

the national thanksgiving. But our ministers were all absent, and she had to go back home without joining in the *public* praise, but God has heard her hosannas and prayers.

Tell Mrs. Preston I am glad to hear "she is such a charming old lady." Mrs. Taylor says the next thing, you will be calling her an old lady! She joins me, as well as my sisters, in much love to you—to Mrs. P—and *any* and *all* of our dear Columbia friends. You do not know how grieved and mortified I feel that South Carolina and Virginia should feel their "identities" at such a time as this. I cannot realize *individual feeling, personal* sensitiveness. Each man is a modicum of his *country*, and must aim to be the best portion without reference to his neighbors. It is a grand and glorious cause and should not be sullied by petty envyings and jealousies and strife.

All friends here are quite well, or as well as we can be. John Means begs to be most 'specially remembered to you.

If Theo was here he would send you a message of thanks for your successful effort in John West's behalf. Tell me of our ladies, their whereabouts and doings. Let us know what we can do for the hospitals.

I was delighted at the appropriation from Congress, consecrated as it was by prayer, fasting, and tears. God bless you all.

Most truly yours,

Mary Stark

Copy of a letter I wrote to Harriet—

July 25

Dear H,

Mrs. Carrington from Charlottesville writes that there is a great deal needed there for the South Carolina wounded. Today Mrs. George Randolph, who is president of the Ladies' Association here, tells me she wants arrowroot and tamarinds, and there are none to be found. Tomorrow I am going the rounds of the hospitals with her.

Whatever you have to send, direct to Mrs. G. Randolph, Franklin St., Richmond. Always send by express. She is the head and distributes to Winchester, Culpeper, &c&c, and every other place where things are needed.

Ask Kate Williams to get us arrowroot from Florida.

I feel somewhat easy in mind, now Mr. C is once more with

the Congress here. But they will try again. It is not all over. We will have a death struggle.

Everyone who comes from Manassas brings a fresh budget of news. We are still finding batteries—at any rate, rifles and muskets. We had eighteen cannons on our side and we captured 63 (pretty good for beginners), mostly rifled cannon.

The negroes come in loaded like mules.

One man brought four overcoats and, when they cheered him, said, "You never mind—I done give the best one to Marster."

There is no end to the stories and talk. Write to Mary Witherspoon to send her things to Mrs. Randolph's care.

Yours, etc.

M. B. C.

Kept a copy, in case anything goes wrong. Camden is cranky.

A note from Mrs. Randolph:

My dear Mrs. C,

I am much obliged to you for the money sent by the Camden ladies and will hand it to the treasure on Monday. We have received two boxes from South Carolina and sent them to Charlottesville, with other articles purchased here. I am in doubt what it is best to do at this time but will call upon the ladies, if they can be of service at any time. I am as yet sending nothing to Culpeper, expecting orders from the ladies and surgeons there, having told them to call on us when they have need.

I think many comforts were captured. I know 52 barrels of white sugar were taken.

I will see you in a few days and tell you what we are about.

Yours truly,

M. G. Randolph

Franklin St.
July 27

Mr. Venable was praising Hugh Garden and Kershaw's regiment generally. This was delightful. They are my friends and neighbors from home. Showed him Miss Mary Stark's letter—

and we agreed with her. At the bottom of our hearts we believe every Confederate soldier to be a hero. Sans peur, sans reproche.

Hope for the best today. Things must be on a pleasanter footing all over the world. Why? Met the president in the corridor. He took me by both hands. "Have you breakfasted? Come in and breakfast with me?"

Alas, I had had my breakfast. And he said, laughing at his own French, "J'en suis fâché—de tout mon coeur."

When he jokes it is a good sign. "Moi! malheureux! Or is it 'que je suis malheureux?' " he said.

At the public dining room, where I had taken my breakfast with Mr. Chesnut, Mrs. Davis came to him while we were at table. She said she had been to our rooms. She wanted Wigfall hunted up. Mr. Davis thought Chesnut would be apt to know his whereabouts. I ran to Mrs. Wigfall's room, who tells me she was sure he could be found with his regiment in camp. But Mr. C had not to go to the camp, for Wigfall came to his wife's room while I was there. Mr. Davis and Wigfall would be friends, if—if—

We have sent the captured white sugar to Charlottesville hospital.

The Northern papers say we hung and quartered a Zouave—cut him in 4 pieces—and that we tie prisoners to a tree and bayonet them. In other words, we are savages. It ought to teach us not to credit what our papers say of them. It is so absurd an imagination of evil.

We are absolutely treating their prisoners as well as our own men. It is complained of here. I am going to the hospitals here for the enemy's sick and wounded to see for myself.

Mr. C is devoted to Mrs. Long and Mrs. McLean. They do not seem to take his compliments to Sumner l'oncle, or cousin—I do not know which he is—in bad part.

Trescot says Keitt, Boyce, Hammond, and many others hate Jeff Davis. He says disintegration has already begun. Sat up until twelve—he abusing Davis and Mrs. Davis. . . .

Like Martin Luther, he had a right to protest and free himself from the thralldom of Roman Catholic church, but when everybody began to protest against Luther—as it seemed good to them—freely exercising their right of private interpretation—!

Seceding can go on indefinitely with the dissatisfied seceders. Why did we not follow the flying foe across the Potomac? That is the question of the hour in the drawing room—those of us who are not contending as to "who took Ricketts's Battery?" Allen Green—for one—took it. Allen told us that finding a portmanteau with nice clean shirts, he was so hot and dusty he stepped behind a tree and put on a clean Yankee shirt. And was more comfortable.

I was made to do an awfully rude thing. Trescot wanted to see Mr. C on particular business. I left him on the stairs, telling him to wait for me there, I would be back in an instant.

Mr. C listened until I had finished my story—then locked the door and put the key in his pocket. Said I should not be running up and down stairs on Trescot's errands. Today saw Trescot. He waited on the stairs an hour, he said. He was very angry, you may be sure.

The *Tribune* soothes the Yankee self-conceit, which has received a shock—the national vanity, you know—by saying we had 100,000 men on the field at Manassas. We had about 15,000 effective men in all.

And then the *Tribune* tries to inflame and envenom them against us by telling lies as to our treatment of prisoners.

They say when they come against us next, it will be in overwhelming force.

Lord Lyons, who is not our friend, says to them gravely, "Now, perhaps we may be allowed to call them belligerents."

I long to see Russell's letter to the *Times* about Bulls Run and Manassas. It will be rich and rare.

In Washington it is crimination and recrimination. Well—let them abuse one another to their hearts' content.

Mr. Chesnut met his old flame Miss Lizzie Dallas, now Mrs. Tucker. Found her, he *said, old* but very agreeable. Did not mention it to me for several days.

NONINTERFERENCE WITH SLAVERY: JULY 1861

Crittenden-Johnson Resolutions, July 22–25, 1861

These resolutions were introduced in the House of Representatives by John J. Crittenden of Kentucky, who had been elected to Congress in June after completing his Senate term in March 1861, and in the Senate by Andrew Johnson of Tennessee, a unionist who had kept his seat after his state seceded. They were adopted by the House on July 22 and by the Senate on July 25.

Resolved by the House of Representatives of the Congress of the United States, That the present deplorable civil war has been forced upon the country by the disunionists of the southern States, now in arms against the constitutional Government, and in arms around the capital; that in this national emergency, Congress, banishing all feelings of mere passion or resentment, will recollect only its duty to the whole country; that this war is not waged on their part in any spirit of oppression, or for any purpose of conquest or subjugation, or purpose of overthrowing or interfering with the rights or established institutions of those States, but to defend and maintain the *supremacy* of the Constitution, and to preserve the Union with all the dignity, equality, and rights of the several States unimpaired; and that as soon as these objects are accomplished the war ought to cease.

Resolved, That the present deplorable civil war has been forced upon the country by the disunionists of the southern States now in revolt against the constitutional Government and in arms around the capital; that in this national emergency Congress, banishing all feeling of mere passion or resentment, will recollect only its duty to the whole country; that this war is not prosecuted upon our part in any spirit of oppression, nor for any purpose of conquest or subjugation, nor for the purpose of overthrowing or interfering with the rights or established institutions of those States, but to defend and maintain the supremacy of the Constitution and all laws made in pursuance thereof, and to preserve the Union, with all the dignity, equality, and rights of the several States unimpaired; that as soon as these objects are accomplished the war ought to cease.

ASSUMING COMMAND:
WASHINGTON, D.C., JULY 1861

George B. McClellan to Mary Ellen McClellan

An 1846 graduate of West Point who served in Mexico before resigning from the army as a captain in 1857, George B. McClellan was the president of the eastern division of the Ohio and Mississippi Railroad when the war began. Commissioned as a major general in May 1861, McClellan commanded the successful Union offensive in western Virginia in early July, and he was summoned to Washington the day after Bull Run to take command of the defeated army. The texts of the letters McClellan wrote to his wife printed in this volume are taken from partial copies he made in the 1870s while assembling material for his memoirs; the original letters are not known to have survived.

July 27/61 Washington D.C. Saturday
I have been assigned to the command of a Division—composed of Depts of N.E. Va (that under McDowell) & that of Washington (now under Mansfield)—neither of them like it much—especially Mansfield, but I think they must ere long become accustomed to it, as there is no help for it. . . .

I find myself in a new & strange position here—Presdt, Cabinet, Genl Scott & all deferring to me—by some strange operation of magic I seem to have become *the* power of the land. I almost think that were I to win some small success now I could become Dictator or anything else that might please me—but nothing of that kind would please me—*therefore* I *won't* be Dictator. Admirable self denial! I see already the main causes of our recent failure—I am *sure* that I can remedy these & am confident that I can lead these armies of men to victory once more. I start tomorrow very early on a tour through the lines on the other side of the river—it will occupy me all day long & a rather fatiguing ride it will be—but I will be able to make up my mind as to the state of things. Refused invitations to dine today from Genl Scott & four Secy's—had too many things to attend to. . . .

I will endeavor to enclose with this the "thanks of Congress" which please preserve. I feel very proud of it. Genl Scott objected to it on the ground that it ought to be accompanied by a gold medal. I cheerfully acquiesce in the Thanks by themselves, hoping to win the medal by some other action, & the sword by some other fait d'éclat.

"OUR MEN ARE NOT GOOD SOLDIERS": JULY 1861
William T. Sherman to
Ellen Ewing Sherman

Sherman had been commissioned as the colonel of the new 13th U.S. Infantry on May 14 and was given command of the Third Brigade, First Division in June 30. He led his brigade at Bull Run and later wrote to his wife Ellen from Arlington, Virginia, about his first experience of combat.

Fort Corcoran July 28,
Saturday—
Dearest Ellen,
I have already written to you since my return from the Unfortunate defeat at Bulls Run—I had previously conveyed to you the doubts that oppressed my mind on the Score of discipline. Four large columns of poorly disciplined militia left this place—the Long bridge and Alexandria—all concentrating at a place called Centreville 27 miles from Washington. We were the first column to reach Centreville the Enemy abandoning all defenses en route. The first day of our arrival our Commander Genl. Tyler advanced on Bulls Run, about 2 1/2 miles distant, and against orders engaged their Batteries. He sent back to Centreville and I advanced with our Brigade, where we lay for half an hour, amidst descending shots killing a few of our men—The Batteries were full a mile distant and I confess I, nor any person in my Brigade saw an enemy.

Towards evening we returned to Centreville.

That occurred on Thursday. We lay in camp till Saturday night by which the whole army was assembled in and about Centreville. We got orders for march at 2 1/2 Sunday morning. Our column of 3 Brigades—Schenck, Sherman & Keyes—to move straight along a Road to Bulls Run—another of about 10,000 men to make a circuit by the Right (Hunters) and come upon the enemy in front of us—Heintzelmans column of about similar strength also to make a wide circuit to sustain Hunter—We took the road first and about 6 A.M. came in sight of Bull Run—we saw in the grey light of morning men moving about—but no signs of batteries: I rode well down to the Stone Bridge which crosses the Stream, saw plenty of trees cut down—some brush huts such as soldiers use on picket Guard, but none of the Evidences of Strong fortification we had been led to believe. Our business was simply to threaten, and give time for Hunter & Heintzelman to make their circuit. We arranged our troops to this end. Schenck to the left of the Road, & I to the right—Keyes behind in reserve. We had with us two six gun batteries, and a 30 pd. Gun—This was fired several times, but no answer—we shifted positions several times, firing wherever we had reason to suppose there were any troops. About 10 or 11 o.c. we saw the clouds of dust in the direction of Hunters approach. Saw one or more Regiments of the Enemy leave their cover, and move in that direction—soon the firing of musketry, and guns showing the engagement had commenced—early in the morning I saw a flag flying behind some trees. Some of the Soldiers seeing it Called out—Colonel, there's a flag—a flag of truce—a man in the Field with his dog & gun—called out—No it is no flag of truce, but a flag of defiance—I was at the time studying the Ground and paid no attention to him—about 9 oclock I was well down to the River—with some skirmishes and observed two men on horseback ride along a hill, descend, cross the stream and ride out towards us—he had a gun in his hand which he waved over his head, and called out to us, You D——d black abolitionists, come on &c.—I permitted some of the men to fire on him—but no damage was done he remained some time thus waiting the action which had begun on the other side of Bulls Run—we could See nothing, but heard the firing and could judge that Hunters column steadily advanced: about 2 P.M. they came to a stand, the firing was severe and stationary—Gen. Tyler rode up to me and remarked that he might have to Send the N.Y. 69th to the relief of Hunter—a short while after he came up and ordered me with my whole Brigade, some 3400 men to cross over to Hunter. I ordered the movement, led off—found a place where the men could cross, but the Battery could not follow. We crossed the stream, and ascended the Bluff Bank, moving slowly to permit the Ranks to close up—When about half a mile back from the Stream I saw the parties in the fight, and the first danger was that we might be mistaken for Secessionists & fired on—One of my Regiments had on the grey uniform of the Virginia troops—We first fired on some retreating Secessionists, our Lt. Col. Haggerty was killed, and my bugler by my side had his horse shot dead—I moved on and Joined Hunters column. They had had a pretty severe fight—Hunter was wounded, and the unexpected arrival of my brigade seemed a great relief to all. I joined them on a high field with a house—and as we effected the junction the secessionists took to the woods and were *seemingly* retreating and Gen. McDowell who had accompanied Hunter's column ordered me to join in the pursuit—I will not attempt to describe you the scene—their Batteries were on all the high hills overlooking the ground which we had to cross, and they fired with great vigor—our horse batteries pursued from point to point returning the fire, whilst we moved on, with shot shells, and cannister over and all round us. I kept to my horse and head of the Brigade, and moving slowly, came upon their heavy masses of men, behind all kinds of obstacles. They knew the ground perfectly, and at every turn we found new ground, over which they poured their fire. At last we came to a stand, and with my Regiments in succession we crossed a Ridge and were exposed to a very heavy fire, first one Regiment & then another and another were forced back—not by the bayonet but by a musketry & rifle fire, which it seemed impossible to push our men through. After an hour of close contest our men began to fall into confusion. 111 had been killed some 250 wounded and the Soldiers began to fall back in disorder—My horse was shot through the foreleg—my knee was cut round by a ball, and another had hit my Coat collar and did not penetrate an aid Lt. Bagley was missing, and spite of all exertions the confusion increased, and the men would not reform—Similar confusion had already occurred among other Regiments & I saw we were gone. Had they kept their Ranks we were the gainers up to that point—only our field Batteries exposed had been severely cut up, by theirs partially covered. Then for the first time I saw the Carnage of battle—men lying in every conceivable shape, and mangled in a horrible way—but this did not make a particle of impression on me—but horses running about riderless with blood streaming from their nostrils—lying on the ground hitched to guns, gnawing their sides in death—I sat on my horse on the ground where Ricketts Battery had been shattered to fragments, and saw the havoc done. I kept my Regiments under cover as much as possible, till the last moment, when it became necessary to cross boldly a Ridge and attack the enemy by that time gathered in great strength behind all sorts of cover—The Volunteers up to that time had done well, but they were repulsed regiment by Regiment, and I do think it was impossible to stand long in that fire. I did not find fault with them but they fell into disorder—an incessant clamor of tongues, one saying that they were not properly supported, another that they could not tell friend from foe—but I observed the gradual retreat going on and did all I could to stop it. At last it became manifest we were falling back, and as soon as I perceived it, I gave it direction by the way we came, and thus we fell back to Centreville some four miles—we had with our Brigade no wagons, they had not crossed the River. At Centreville came pouring in the confused masses of men, without order or system. Here I supposed we should assemble in some order the confused masses and try to Stem the tide—Indeed I saw but little evidence of being pursued, though once or twice their cavalry interposed themselves between us and our Rear. I had read of retreats before—have seen the noise and confusion of crowds of men at fires and Shipwrecks but nothing like this. It was as disgraceful as words can portray, but I doubt if volunteers from any quarter could do better. Each private thinks for himself—If he wants to go for water, he asks leave of no one. If he thinks right he takes the oats & corn, and even burns the house of his enemy. As we could not prevent these disorders on the way out—I always feared the result—for everywhere we found the People against us—no curse could be greater than invasion by a Volunteer Army. No goths or vandals ever had less respect for the lives & property of friends and foes, and henceforth we ought never to hope for any friends in Virginia—McDowell & all the Generals tried their best to stop these disorders, but for us to say we commanded that army is no such thing—they did as they pleased. Democracy has worked out one result, and the next step is to be seen—Beauregard & Johnston were enabled to effect a Junction, by the failure of Patterson to press the latter, and they had such accurate accounts of our numbers & movements that they had all the men they wanted—We had never more than 18,000 engaged, though Some 10 or 12,000 were within a few miles. After our Retreat here, I did my best to stop the flying masses, and partially succeeded, so that we once more present a front: but Beauregard has committed a sad mistake in not pursuing us promptly. Had he done so, he could have stampeded us again, and gone into Washington. As it is I suppose their plan is to produce Riot in Baltimore, cross over above Leesburg, and come upon Washington through Maryland. Our Rulers think more of who shall get office, than who can save the Country. No body—no one man can save the country. The difficulty is with the masses—our men are not good Soldiers—They brag, but dont perform—complain sadly if they dont get everything they want—and a march of a few miles uses them up. It will take a long time to overcome these things, and what is in store for us in the future I know not. I propose trying to defend this place if Beauregard approaches Washington by this Route, but he has now deferred it Some days and I rather think he will give it up.

The newspapers will tell ten thousand things none of which are true. I have had no time to read them, but I know no one now has the moral courage to tell the truth. Public opinion is a more terrible tyrant than Napoleon—My own hope is now in the Regulars, and if I can escape this Volunteer command I will do so, and stick by my Regular Regiment. Gen. McClellan arrived today with Van Vliet—Stoneman, Benham—Biddle—and many others of my acquaintance. Affecy. &c.

W. T. Sherman

July 28, 1861

"OUR LATE AWFUL DISASTER": JULY 1861
Horace Greeley to Abraham Lincoln

Beginning on June 26, Horace Greeley ran a daily "On to Richmond!" editorial in the New York *Tribune*, calling for the capture of the city before the opening on July 20 of the next session of the Confederate Congress. In the aftermath of Bull Run, Greeley sent this letter to President Lincoln. There is no record that Lincoln ever replied to it, but in April 1864 he would retrieve the letter and show it to his secretaries John Hay and John G. Nicolay. Hay, who called the letter "the most insane specimen of pusillanimity that I have ever read," wrote in his diary that when Nicolay suggested Greeley's rival James Bennett of the New York *Herald* would willingly pay $10,000 for a copy, Lincoln replied: "I need $10,000 very much but he could not have it for many times that."

New York, Monday, July 29, 1861.
Midnight.

Dear Sir:

This is my seventh sleepless night—yours too, doubtless—yet I think I shall not die, because I have no right to die. I must struggle to live, however, bitterly. But to business.

You are not considered a great man, and I am a hopelessly broken one. You are now undergoing a terrible ordeal, and God has thrown the gravest responsibility upon you. Do not fear to meet them.

Can the Rebels be beaten after all that has occurred, and in view of the actual state of feeling caused by our late awful disaster? If they can—and it is your business to ascertain and decide—write me that such is your judgment, so that I may know and do my duty.

And if they *cannot* be beaten—if our recent disaster is fatal—do not fear to sacrifice yourself to your country. If the Rebels are not to be beaten—if that is your judgment in view of all the light you can get—then every drop of blood henceforth shed in this quarrel will be wantonly, wickedly shed, and the guilt will rest heavily on the soul of every promoter of the crime. I pray you to decide quickly, and let me know my duty.

If the Union is irrevocably gone, an Armistice for thirty, sixty, ninety, 120 days—better still, for a year—ought at once to be proposed with a view to a peaceful adjustment. Then Congress should call a National convention to meet at the earliest possible day. And there should be an immediate and mutual exchange or release of prisoners and a disbandment of forces.

I do not consider myself at present a judge of any thing but the public sentiment. That seems to me every where gathering and deepening against a prosecution of the war. The gloom in this city is funereal for our dead at Bull Run were many, and they lie unburied yet. On every brow sits sullen, scowling, black despair.

It would be easy to have Mr. Crittenden move any proposition that ought to be adopted, or to have it come from any proper quarter. The first point is to ascertain what is best that can be done—which is the measure of our duty—and do that very thing at the earliest moment.

This letter is written in the strictest confidence, and is for your eye alone. But you are at liberty to say to members of your Cabinet that you *know* I will second any move you may see fit to make. But do nothing timidly nor by halves.

Send me word what to do. I will live till I can hear it at all events. If it is best for the country and for mankind that we make peace with the Rebels at once and on their own terms, do not shrink even from that. But bear in mind the greatest truth—"Whoso would lose his life for my sake shall save it," do the thing that is the highest right, and tell me how I am to second you.

Yours, in the depths of bitterness,
Horace Greeley

WASHINGTON, D.C., AUGUST 1861

George B. McClellan:
Memorandum for the President

In response to a presidential request, McClellan offered his strategy for prosecuting the war, including recommendations for operations far outside the area of his command.

Memorandum for the Consideration
of His Excellency the President,
submitted at his request.

The object of the present war differs from those in which nations are usually engaged, mainly in this; that the purpose of ordinary war is to conquer a peace and make a treaty on advantageous terms; in this contest it has become necessary to crush a population sufficiently numerous, intelligent and warlike to constitute a nation; we have not only to defeat their armed and organized forces in the field but to display such an overwhelming strength, as will convince all our antagonists, especially those of the governing aristocratic class, of the utter impossibility of resistance. Our late reverses make this course imperative; had we been successful in the recent battle it is possible that we might have been spared the labor and expense of a great effort; now we have no alternative; their success will enable the political leaders of the rebels to convince the mass of their people that we are inferior to them in force and courage, and to command all their resources. The contest began with a class; now it is with a people. Our military success can alone restore the former issue. By thoroughly defeating their armies, taking their strong places, and pursuing a rigidly protective policy as to private property and unarmed persons, and a lenient course as to common soldiers, we may well hope for the permanent restoration of peaceful Union; but in the first instance the authority of the Government must be supported by overwhelming physical force. Our foreign relations and financial credit also imperatively demand that the military action of the Government should be prompt and irresistible.

The rebels have chosen Virginia as their battle-field—and it seems proper for us to make the first great struggle there; but while thus directing our main efforts, it is necessary to diminish the resistance there offered us, by movements on other points, both by land and water. Without entering at present into details, I would advise that a strong movement be made on the Mississippi, and that the rebels be driven out of Missouri. As soon as it becomes perfectly clear that Kentucky is cordially united with us, I would advise a movement through that state into Eastern Tennessee, for the purpose of assisting the Union men of that region, and of seizing the Railroads leading from Memphis to the East. The possession of those roads by us, in connection with the movement on the Mississippi, would go far towards determining the evacuation of Virginia by the rebels. In the mean time all the passes into Western Virginia from the East should be securely guarded; but I would make no movement from that quarter towards Richmond unless the political condition of Kentucky renders it impossible or inexpedient for us to make the movement upon Eastern Tennessee through that state; every effort should however be made to organize, equip, and arm as many troops as possible in Western Virginia, in order to render the Ohio and Indiana regiments available for other operations.

At as early a day as practicable it would be well to protect and reopen the Baltimore & Ohio Railroad. Baltimore & Fort Monroe should be occupied by *garrisons* sufficient to retain them in our possession.

The importance of Harper's Ferry and the line of the Potomac in the direction of Leesburg will be very materially diminished as soon as our force in this vicinity becomes organized, strong and efficient; because no capable general will cross the river north of this city, when we have a strong army here ready to cut off his retreat.

To revert to the West. It is probable that no very large additions to the troops now in Missouri will be necessary to secure that state. I presume that the force required for the movement down the Mississippi will be determined by its commander and the President.

If Kentucky assumes the right position, not more than 20,000 troops will be needed, together with those that can be raised in that state and Eastern Tennessee, to secure the latter region and its railroads; as well as ultimately to occupy Nashville. The Western Virginia troops with not more than from 5 to 10,000 from Ohio and Indiana should under proper management, suffice for its protection. When we have reorganized our main army here, 10,000 men ought to be enough to protect the Balt. & Ohio R.R. and the Potomac—5000 will *garrison* Baltimore—3000 Fort Monroe; and not more than 20,000 will be necessary, at the utmost, for the defence of Washington.

For the main Army of Operations I urge the following composition.

250	Regt's Infantry—say	225,000 men
100	Field Batteries—600 guns	15,000 "
28	Regts. Cavalry	25,500 "
5	" Engineer troops	7,500 "
	Total	273,000 "

This force must be supplied with the necessary engineer and ponton trains, and with transportation for everything save tents. Its general line of operations should be directed that water transportation can be availed of from point to point, by means of the ocean and the rivers emptying into it.

An essential feature of the plan of operations will be the employment of a strong naval force, to protect the movement of a fleet of transports, intended to convoy a considerable body of troops from point to point of the enemy's seacoast; thus either creating diversions and rendering it necessary for them to detach largely from their main body in order to protect such of their cities as may be threatened; or else landing and forming establishments on their coast at any favorable places that opportunity might offer. This naval force should also cooperate with the main army in its efforts to seize the important seaboard towns of the rebels.

It cannot be ignored that the construction of railroads has introduced a new and very important element into war, by the great facilities thus given for concentrating at particular positions large masses of troops from remote sections, and by creating new strategic points and lines of operations. It is intended to overcome this difficulty by the partial operations suggested, and such others as the particular case may require; we must endeavor to seize places on the railways in the rear of the enemy's points of concentration; and we must threaten their seaboard cities in order that each state may be forced by the necessity of its own defence to diminish its contingent to the Confederate Army.

The proposed movement down the Mississippi will produce important results in this connection. That advance and the progress of the main army at the East will materially assist each other by diminishing the resistance to be encountered by each. The tendency of the Mississippi movement upon all questions connected with cotton are too well understood by the President and Cabinet to need any illustration from me.

There is another independent movement which has often been suggested and which has always recommended itself to my judgment. I refer to a movement from Kansas and Nebraska through the Indian Territory upon Red river and Western Texas, for the purpose of protecting and developing the latent Union and free state sentiment well known to predominate in Western Texas, and which like a similar sentiment in Western Virginia, will, if protected, ultimately organize that section into a free state. How far it will be possible to support this movement by an advance through New Mexico from California is a matter which I have not sufficiently examined to be able to express a decided opinion; if at all practicable, it is eminently desirable as bringing into play the resources and warlike qualities of the Pacific States, as well as identifying them with our cause and cementing the bond of Union between them and the General Government. If it is not departing too far from my province I will venture to suggest the policy of an intimate alliance and cordial understanding with Mexico; their sympathies and interests are with us; their antipathies exclusively against our enemies and their institutions. I think it would not be difficult to obtain from the Mexican Government the right to use, at least during the present contest, the road from Guaymas to New Mexico; this concession would very materially reduce the obstacles of the column moving from the Pacific; a similar permission to use their territory for the passage of troops between the Panuco and the Rio Grande would enable us to throw a column by a good road from Tampico or some of the small harbors north of it upon and across the Rio Grande into the country of our friends, and without risk, and scarcely firing a shot. To what extent if any it would be desirable to take into service, and employ Mexican soldiers is a question entirely political, on which I do not venture to offer any opinion.

The force I have recommended is large—the expense is great. It is possible that a smaller force might accomplish the object in view, but I understand it to be the purpose of this great Nation to reestablish the power of the Government, and to restore peace to its citizens, in the shortest possible time. The question to be decided is simply this; shall we crush the rebellion at one blow, terminate the war in one campaign, or shall we leave it as a legacy for our descendants? When the extent of the possible line of operations is considered, the force asked for, for the main army under my command, cannot be regarded as unduly large. Every mile we advance carries us further from our base of operations and renders detachments necessary to cover our communications; while the enemy will be constantly concentrating as he falls back. I propose with the force which I have requested, not only to drive the enemy out of Virginia and occupy Richmond, but to occupy Charleston, Savannah, Montgomery, Pensacola, Mobile, and New Orleans; in other words to move into the heart of the enemy's country, and crush out this rebellion in its very heart. By seizing and repairing the railroads as we advance, the difficulties of transportation will be materially diminished.

It is perhaps unnecessary to state that in addition to the forces named in this memorandum strong reserves should be formed, ready to supply any losses that may occur. In conclusion, I would submit that the exigencies of the treasury may be lessened by making only partial payments to our troops when in the enemy's country and by giving the obligations of the United States for such supplies as may there be obtainable.

Geo B McClellan
Maj Genl USA

Washington D.C. Aug 2 1861

A MEASURE AGAINST SLAVERY: AUGUST 1861

Confiscation Act, August 6, 1861

Two weeks after declaring in the Crittenden-Johnson resolutions that it had no intention of "overthrowing or interfering" with slavery in the Southern states, Congress passed the Confiscation Act, authorizing the seizure of slaves being used to militarily aid the rebellion. The act gave legislative endorsement to the "contraband" policy originated at Fort Monroe in May by General Benjamin Butler.

CHAP. LX—An Act to confiscate Property used for Insurrectionary Purposes.

Be it enacted by the Senate and House of Representatives of the United States of America in Congress assembled, That if, during the present or any future insurrection against the Government of the United States, after the President of the United States shall have declared, by proclamation, that the laws of the United States are opposed, and the execution thereof obstructed, by combinations too powerful to be suppressed by the ordinary course of judical proceedings, or by the power vested in the marshals by law, any person or persons, his, her, or their agent, attorney, or employé, shall purchase or acquire, sell or give, any property of whatsoever kind or description, with intent to use or employ the same, or suffer the same to be used or employed, in aiding, abetting, or promoting such insurrection or resistance to the laws, or any person or persons engaged therein; or if any person or persons, being the owner or owners of any such property, shall knowingly use or employ, or consent to the use or employment of the same as aforesaid, all such property is hereby declared to be lawful subject of prize and capture wherever found; and it shall be the duty of the President of the United States to cause the same to be seized, confiscated, and condemned.

SEC. 2. *And be it further enacted,* That such prizes and capture shall be condemned in the district or circuit court of the

United States having jurisdiction of the amount, or in admiralty in any district in which the same may be seized, or into which they may be taken and proceedings first instituted.

SEC. 3. *And be it further enacted*, That the Attorney General, or any district attorney of the United States in which said property may at the time be, may institute the proceedings of condemnation, and in such case they shall be wholly for the benefit of the United States; or any person may file an information with such attorney, in which case the proceedings shall be for the use of such informer and the United States in equal parts.

SEC. 4. *And be it further enacted*, That whenever hereafter, during the present insurrection against the Government of the United States, any person claimed to be held to labor or service under the law of any State, shall be required or permitted by the person to whom such labor or service is claimed to be due, or by the lawful agent of such person, to take up arms against the United States, or shall be required or permitted by the person to whom such labor or service is claimed to be due, or his lawful agent, to work or to be employed in or upon any fort, navy-yard, dock, armory, ship, intrenchment, or in any military or naval service whatsoever, against the Government and lawful authority of the United States, then, and in every such case, the person to whom such labor or service is claimed to be due shall forfeit his claim to such labor, any law of the State or of the United States to the contrary notwithstanding. And whenever thereafter the person claiming such labor or service shall seek to enforce his claim, it shall be a full and sufficient answer to such claim that the person whose service or labor is claimed had been employed in hostile service against the Government of the United States, contrary to the provisions of this act.

APPROVED, August 6, 1861.

"THE PRESDT IS AN IDIOT": AUGUST 1861

George B. McClellan to Mary Ellen McClellan

General McClellan expressed his increasing frustration with General Scott and President Lincoln in a series of letters to his wife. The "'pronunciamento'" McClellan refers to in the first letter was a memorandum he sent to Lincoln and Scott on August 8, warning that Washington was in "*imminent danger*" of being attacked by "at least 100,000 men"; at the time the Confederates had about 40,000 men in northern Virginia.

Aug 8

. . . Rose early today (having retired at 3 am) & was pestered to death with Senators etc & a row with Genl Scott until about 4 o'clock, then crossed the river & rode beyond & along the line of pickets for some distance—came back & had a long interview with Seward about my "pronunciamento" against Genl Scott's policy. . . .

How does he think that I can save this country when stopped by Genl Scott—I do not know whether he is a *dotard* or a *traitor!* I can't tell which. He *cannot* or *will* not comprehend the condition in which we are placed & is entirely unequal to the emergency. If he cannot be taken out of my path I will not retain my position, but will resign & let the admn take care of itself. I have hardly slept one moment for the last three nights, knowing well that the enemy intend some movement & fully recognizing our own weakness. If Beauregard does not attack tonight I shall look upon it as a dispensation of Providence—he *ought* to do it. Every day strengthens me—I am leaving nothing undone to increase our force—but that confounded old Genl always comes in the way—he is a perfect imbecile. He understands nothing, appreciates nothing & is ever in my way.

Washington Aug 9 1861 1 am.
I have had a busy day—started from here at 7 in the morning & was in the saddle until about 9 this evening—rode over the advanced positions on the other side of the river, was soundly drenched in a hard rain & have been busy ever since my return. Things are improving daily—I received 3 new rgts today—fitted out one new battery yesterday, another today—two tomorrow—about five day after. Within four days I hope to have at least 21 batteries—say 124 field guns—18 co's. of cavalry & some 70 rgts of infantry. Genl Scott is the great obstacle—he will not comprehend the danger & is either a traitor or an incompetent. I have to fight my way against him & have thrown a bombshell that has created a perfect stampede in the Cabinet—tomorrow the question will probably be decided by giving me absolute control independently of him. I suppose it will result in a mortal enmity on his part against me, but I have no choice—the people call upon me to save the country—I *must* save it & cannot respect anything that is in the way.

I receive letter after letter—have conversation after conversation calling on me to save the nation—alluding to the Presidency, Dictatorship &c. As I hope one day to be united with you forever in heaven, I have no such aspirations—I will never accept the Presidency—I will cheerfully take the Dictatorship & agree to lay down my life when the country is saved. I am *not* spoiled by my unexpected & new position—I feel sure that God will give me the strength & wisdom to preserve this great nation—but I tell *you*, who share all my thoughts, that I have no selfish feeling in the matter. I feel that God has placed a great work in my hands—I have not sought it—I know how weak I am—but I know that I mean to do right & I believe that God will help me & give me the wisdom I do not possess. Pray for me, darling, that I may be able to accomplish my task —the greatest, perhaps, that any poor weak mortal ever had to do. . . .

God grant that I may bring this war to an end & be permitted to spend the rest of my days quietly with you. . . .

I met the Prince at Alexandria today & came up with him. He says that Beauregard's head is turned & that he acts like a fool. That Joe Johnston is quiet & sad, & that he spoke to him in very kind terms of me.

16th

. . . I am here in a terrible place—the enemy have from 3 to 4 times my force—the Presdt is an idiot, the old General in his dotage—they cannot or will not see the true state of affairs. Most of my troops are demoralized by the defeat at Bull Run, some rgts even mutinous—I have probably stopped that—but you see my position is not pleasant. . . .

I have, I believe, made the best possible disposition of the few men under my command—will quietly await events & if the enemy attacks will try to make my movements as rapid & desperate as may be—if my men will only fight I think I can thrash him notwithstanding the disparity of numbers. As it is I trust to God to give success to our arms—tho' he is not wont to aid those who refuse to aid themselves. . . .

I am weary of all this. I have no ambition in the present affairs—only wish to save my country—& find the incapables around me will not permit it! They sit on the verge of the precipice & cannot realize what they see—their reply to everything is "Impossible! Impossible!" They think nothing possible which is against their wishes.

6 p.m.— . . . Gen. Scott is at last opening his eyes to the fact that I am right & that we are in imminent danger. Providence is aiding me by heavy rains, which are swelling the Potomac, which may be impassable for a week—if so we are saved. If Beauregard comes down upon us soon I have everything ready to make a manoeuvre which will be decisive. Give me two weeks & I will defy Beauregard—in a week the chances will be at least even.

August 16, 1861

BATTLE OF WILSON'S CREEK:
MISSOURI, AUGUST 1861

E. F. Ware: from
The Lyon Campaign in Missouri

Nathaniel Lyon was commissioned as a brigadier general after his successful defense of the St. Louis arsenal and given command of the Union forces in Missouri. By the beginning of August he had gained control of most of the state, but now faced a force of 11,000 Confederates advancing from the southwest on his headquarters in Springfield. Despite his numerical inferiority, Lyon decided to attack the enemy encampment along Wilson's Creek. Dividing his force of 5,400 men, Lyon led the main body attacking from the north, while 1,200 men under Colonel Franz Sigel advanced from the south on the early morning of August 10. E. F. Ware, at the time a young harness-maker from Burlington serving as a private in Company E, 1st Iowa Infantry, described the battle in a memoir published in 1907.

———————

ON AUGUST 9th shortly before sundown the bugle was blown and we were commanded to "fall in." There were no tents to mark our regimental line. We were sleeping in the open air; the position of the companies was marked by the ashes where the company camp-kettles and mess-pans were standing. Each company of our regiment fell in, making an irregular line which was quite long, owing to the distances between the companies. After standing in line for some minutes General Lyon was seen approaching on his large dapple-gray horse; this was the horse he generally used. Lyon, as he rode by the companies, made a brief speech to each. We could not hear what he said to the companies on each side of us, owing to the distance apart of the companies and the low tones of his voice. When he came to our company his words were:

"Men, we are going to have a fight. We will march out in a short time. Don't shoot until you get orders. Fire low—don't aim higher than their knees; wait until they get close; don't get scared; it's no part of a soldier's duty to get scared."

This is all he said, and is, I believe, a verbatim report, for we often talked it over, and compared notes, practically committing it to memory. He said the same to the other companies, stopping about a minute at each. It was a tactless and chilling speech; there was nothing in it of dash, vim, or encouragement. It was spoken in a low tone and with a solemn look, and apparently with a feeling of exhaustion. He was dressed in uniform, buttoned up to the chin, as if he were cold, although the weather was dry and roasting. We boys considered the speech as a very poor effort and entirely wanting in enthusiasm. He had better not have made it. The absurdity of the last expression struck every one of us,—that it was "no part of a soldier's duty to get scared." It had no sense to it. As Bill Huestis said, "How is a man to help being skeered when he is skeered?" But the speech represented Lyon. His idea was duty; every soldier was to him a mere machine; it was not the "duty" of a soldier to think, and hence he was not to get scared until his superior officer told him so. Lyon might have spoken a few sentences that would have raised his men up to the top notch and endeared himself in their memory for all time; but that was not Lyon; he did not care to endear himself to anybody. This speech of his seemed to me just the kind of speech he would make. On the other hand, dear old Irish General Sweeney, who did not get killed, made a speech to his cavalry, of which I have no notes except that he said (so his boys told) among other things, "Stay together, boys, and we'll saber hell out of them." This had enthusiasm to it.

Among the men Lyon had bitter enemies for his occasional severity and want of consideration. The boys thought, as they had agreed to stay with him voluntarily, that he ought to act better. He seemed to go upon the theory that he did not want his men to think kindly of him; that what he wanted of them was to have them understand that he was not to be fooled with, and that as they were in the employ of the Government it was his duty to see that the Government got everything out of them that could be got for the time being. On the other hand, the boys felt that strange confidence which soldiers always feel in an officer who they believe understands his business. So that speech which General Lyon made produced no particular effect one way or another, and had he not been killed would have been entirely forgotten. In fact, the boys did not like Lyon. They wanted a fight so that they could go home creditably, to themselves and their sweethearts; they knew just exactly how to fire a musket, and they did not intend to be scared, whether it was part of their duty or not, if they could help it.

About sundown we were all marched into the city of Springfield; only about 70 of our company were in line; the balance of our company had broken down and were things of the past. We soon found that we were going southwest. The city was in frightful disorder. Every available means of transportation was being used by the merchants on the city square to load up and haul off their goods. We had brought nothing along with us but fighting material, and had left behind, where we had camped, our blankets and cooking utensils. Storekeepers brought us out, during our very brief stop of a few minutes, tobacco, sugar, and things of that kind. Starting west, it was twilight. When we got out of town we marched along past cornfields. The day had been hot, and as the night began to grow cool, life became more endurable, and the marching was anything but a funeral procession. The boys gave each other elaborate instructions as to the material out of which they wanted their coffins made, and how they wanted them decorated. Bill Huestis said he wanted his coffin made out of sycamore boards, with his last words put on with brass tacks, which were: "I am a-going to be a great big he-angel." (Bill still lives.*) After going several miles in the night, the path we were following became a dim timber road leading tortuously around among the rocks and trees and brush among the hills, and we were ordered to keep still and to make no noise. About that time a cavalryman passed us from the front, and we noticed that he was going slowly, and that his horse's feet had cloths tied around them, banded at the fetlock. During the

*At Ferndale, Calif.

stoppage there was a passing to and fro along the line, and some one said that blankets had been tied around the artillery wheels. We moved short distances from twenty to a hundred yards at a time, and kept halting and closing up, and making very slow progress. Finally we were practically involved in the timber and among the side-hills of a watercourse. There were some little light clouds, but it was light enough to see a short distance around us, by starlight; it was in the dark of the moon. Finally word was passed along the line that we were inside the enemy's pickets, but were two or three miles from their camps. Rumor magnified the number of the enemy to twenty-five thousand. We could see the sheen in the sky of vast camp-fires beyond the hills, but could not see the lights. We also heard at times choruses of braying mules.

About this time, while we were moving along we passed around the brow of a low, rocky hill, and the line stopped at a place where our company stood on a broad ledge of rock. It must have been about 11 o'clock. I never did know the hour; I had traded my watch for ammunition. We all laid down on this rock to get rested. The cool, dewy night air made me feel chilly in the "linings" which I was wearing; but the radiating heat which the rock during the day had absorbed, was peculiarly comfortable. I went to sleep in from five to ten seconds and slept deliciously. I had made up my mind that if we were going to have a battle I certainly would not get killed, but might need all my strength and ability in getting away from the enemy's cavalry. The anxiety which novelists describe, and the wakefulness on the eve of battle, are creatures I presume of the imagination of the novelists respectively, who were never there. I do not know what took place, until, early in the morning, just as there was a slight flush of dawn in the east, somebody came along and woke us all up, and told us to keep still and fall into line. We marched a short distance and struck an open piece of ground where we could see all who were marching, those in our front and those in our rear. The cavalry, artillery and infantry were marching in companies, abreast, and in close order. In a short time as it began to grow a little light we heard a gun fire. In a short time two or three more. Then some regular troops were detailed as skirmishers, and circled around to our left. In a short time we found that the enemy were alive and active. Our regiment was ordered to go in a direction to the left, and to take a position on a low ridge; the enemy in straggling numbers were shooting at us from the ridge. The skirmishers fell back. As we marched up the hill, it came in my way to step over one of the skirmishers who was shot right in front of us. He was a blue-eyed, blonde, fine-looking young man, with a light mustache, who writhed around upon the ground in agony. While I was walking past, I asked him where he was shot, but he seemed unable to comprehend or answer, and perhaps in the noise heard nothing. As we started up the ridge a yell broke from our lines that was kept up with more or less accent and with slight intermissions for six hours. We took a position on the ridge, and the country seemed alive on both our right and left. Wilson's creek was in our front, with an easy descending hillside and a broad meadow before us, in which about five acres of Confederate wagons were parked, axle to axle. The hills bore some scattering oaks, and an occasional bush, but we could see clearly, because the fires had kept the undergrowth eaten out, and the soil was flinty and poor. Since that time a large portion of the country has been covered with a very dense thicket of small oaks. But in those days the few trees were rather large, scrawling, and straggling, and everything could be distinctly seen under them all around. Across the creek, which was not very far, perhaps about a third of a mile, a battery of artillery made a specialty of our ranks, opening out thunderously. We all lay down on the ground, and for some time the shells, round shot and canister were playing closely over our heads. Some few of the canister fell into our ranks. They were coarse cast-iron balls, about an inch to an inch and a half in diameter. Where they struck in the ground the boys hunted for them with their hands. The shells were shrapnels, being filled with leaden balls run together with sulphur. Our company did not have much to do for a while in the way of shooting; we simply laid down on the ridge and watched the battery in front of us, or sat up or kneeled down. When we saw the puff of the artillery we dodged and went down flat, and in the course of fifteen minutes gained so much confidence that we felt no hesitation in walking around and seeing what we could see, knowing that we could dodge the artillery ammunition. This battery was making a specialty of us, but we could evade their missiles; we could see the shells in the air when they were coming toward us, and could calculate their routes.

In a little while two pieces of artillery were run up on the ridge between our company and the company on the right. These were Totten's, and were afterwards increased. They started in to silence the enemy's artillery, and a concentration of fire began in our neighborhood near the cannon. The duel was very interesting, and our boys stayed close to the earth. Considerable damage was done to our artillery, but they were not silenced. One of the large roan artillery horses was standing back of the gun and over the crest of the hill. A shell from the battery in front of us struck this horse somehow and tore off its left shoulder. Then began the most horrible screams and neighing I ever heard. I have since that time seen wounded horses, and heard their frantic shrieks, and so have all other soldiers, but the voice of this roan horse was the limit; it was so absolutely blood-curdling that it had to be put to an end immediately. One of the soldiers shot the horse through the heart.

In a little while, in front of us, appeared, advancing in the meadow, a body of men that we estimated at about one thousand. They seemed to be going to attack somebody on our left. Our artillery stopped firing over their heads at the enemy's battery, and turned upon the meadow; in a short time the enemy were in confusion.

On the edge of the meadow toward us, and between us, was a low rail fence; the enemy rallied under the shelter of it, and, as if by some inspiration or some immediate change of orders, they broke it down in places and started for our artillery. As they got nearer to us, their own artillery ceased to fire, because it endangered them. When they got close the firing began on both sides. How long it lasted I do not know. It might have been an hour; it seemed like a week; it was probably twenty minutes. Every man was shooting as fast, on our side, as he could load, and yelling as loud as his breath would permit. Most were on the ground, some on one knee. The enemy stopped advancing. We had paper cartridges, and in loading we had to bite off the end, and every man had a big quid of paper in his mouth, from which down his chin ran the dissolved gunpowder. The other side were yelling, and if any orders were given nobody heard them. Every man assumed the responsibility of doing as much shooting as he could.

Finally, the field was so covered with smoke that not much could be known as to what was going on. The day was clear and hot. As the smoke grew denser, we stood up and kept inching forward, as we fired, and probably went forward in this way twenty-five yards. We noticed less noise in front of us, and only heard the occasional boom of a gun. The wind, a very light breeze, was in our favor, blowing very gently over us upon the enemy.

Our firing lulled, and as the smoke cleared away, sitting on the fence in front of us, on the edge of the meadow, was a standard-bearer, waving a hostile flag. I do not know its description, but it was not a Union flag. The firing having ceased, we were ordered back and told to lie down, but the boys would not do it until the Rebel artillery opened on us again. Several wanted to shoot at the man on the fence, but the officers went along the line threatening to kill the first man that raised a musket, which was all right, that being the way the game is played. In the mean time, however, a little Irish sergeant, who appeared to stand about five feet high, and sported a large fiery mustache, turned a twelve-pounder on the man who was waving the flag on the fence in such a foolhardy way. The gun went off, the Rebel flag pitched up in the air, and the man fell to pieces gradually over the fence; and at least a thousand men on our side, who saw it, cheered in such loud unison that it could have been heard as far as the report of the twelve-pounder.

I am not able to give, in any moderate limits, the history of the charges and counter-charges on the slope of that hill, but they kept coming. In one of them the Rebel infantry, in its charge, worn down to a point, with its apex touched the twelve-pounder, and one man with his bayonet tried to get the Irish sergeant, who, fencing with his non-commissioned officer's sword, parried the thrusts of the bayonet. I fired at this "apex" at a distance of not over 30 feet. Other secesh were around the guns, but none of them got away. The main body were started back down the slope; the twelve-pounder was then loaded, and assisted their flight.

At one time we were charged by a large detachment of Louisiana troops. They made the most stubborn fight of the day. They had nice new rifled muskets from the armory at Baton Rouge, which armory had by the secession leaders been judiciously filled, before the war, from Northern arsenals. We were borne back by the charge of the Louisiana regiment, slowly in the course of the firing, as much as fifty feet. Squads of Rebel cavalry had been seen in our right rear, and while the enemy were safe in running, we were not. No man deserted the ranks. During that fight Corporal Bill* received a minie ball on the crest of the forehead. The ball went over his head, tearing the scalp, sinking the skull at the point of impact about one-eighth of an inch. He bled with a sickening profusion all over his face, neck, and clothing; and as if half-unconscious and half-crazed, he wandered down the line, asking for me; he was my blanket-mate. He said, "Link, have you got any water in your canteen?" I handed him my canteen and sat him down by the side of a tree that stood near our line, but he got up and wandered around with that canteen, perfectly oblivious; going now in one direction and then in another. From that depression in the skull, wasted to a skeleton, he, an athlete, died shortly after his muster-out, with consumption. How could it be?

We succeeded in repulsing the Louisiana troops, although we were not numerically superior. Our former victory had given us great confidence, and no man broke ranks or ran. As the Louisiana troops yielded back we followed them some little distance down the slope, and when they were gone we put in about fifteen or twenty minutes gathering up fine shotguns and fine rifled muskets, and looking over the poor fellows that were killed and wounded on the hill in front of us.

I was afraid I would run out of ammunition, and I helped myself to the cartridges in the box of a dead soldier who was labeled as a "Pelican Ranger." He had the same kind of gun that I had, and used the same kind of ammunition. I now have two bullets left that I took from that cartridge-box, my only mementoes of the battle. The Louisiana boys showed lots of grit.

After a few minutes another attack was made, but it was

---

*William J. Fuller.

weak and feeble; it must have been a sort of "Butternut Militia" gang. One of them behind a tree, perhaps 50 yards in front of us, after his associates had retired, rose up and deliberately, fired a double-barrel shotgun, both barrels, at us. He injured no one that we knew of, but some one dropped him suddenly, and Seeger of our company ran forward and got his shotgun, kept it, and took it back home to Iowa, a splendid stub-and-twist gun. I saw it all done—in fact I fired at the man behind the tree while he was reloading his shotgun, but don't think I hit him.

About this time we heard yelling in the rear, and we saw a crowd of cavalry coming on a grand gallop, very disorderly, with their apex pointing steadily at our pieces of artillery. We were ordered to face about and step forward to meet them. We advanced down the hill toward them about forty yards to where our view was better, and rallied in round squads of fifteen or twenty men as we had been drilled to do, to repel a cavalry charge. We kept firing, and awaited their approach with fixed bayonets. Our firing was very deadly, and the killing of horses and riders in the front rank piled the horses and men together as they tumbled over one another, from the advancing rear. The charge, so far as its force was concerned, was checked before it got within fifty yards of us. There were 800 of them. This cavalry charge was led by a man named Laswell, formerly from our State,—Ottumwa, Iowa,—who had gone to Texas; we got him.

In the mean time, over our heads our artillery took up the fight; then the cavalry scattered through the woods, leaving the wounded horses and men strewn around. We captured several dismounted men by ordering them in under cover of a gun. A flag was seen lying on the ground about 150 yards in front of us, but no one was ordered or cared to undertake to go and bring it in. In a few minutes a solitary horseman was seen coming towards us, as if to surrender, and the cry therefore rose from us, "Don't shoot!" When within about twenty yards of that flag the horseman spurred his horse, and, leaning from his saddle, picked the flag from the grass, and off he went with it a-flying. The flag bore the "Lone Star" of Texas, and we didn't shoot at the horseman because we liked his display of nerve.

In a few minutes a riderless horse came dashing over the ground, and as he passed a bush, a man with a white shirt, covered with blood, rose from the ground, stopped the horse, slowly and painfully mounted, and rode off. The cry passed, "Don't shoot!" and the man escaped. In the mean time artillery fire concentrated on us, and the Irish sergeant yelled, "They are shooting Sigel's ammunition at us!" Sigel had been whipped. We resumed our place on the ridge.

Some few spasmodic efforts were made to dislodge us, all of which we repulsed. Finally the hostile artillery in front ceased firing, and there came a lull; finally the last charge of the day was made, which we easily repulsed, and the field was ours.

This last charge was not very much of a charge. It was a mixed, heterogeneous charge. I remember one very funny thing that happened in it. We were down on one knee, firing and loading as fast as possible, expecting to rise soon and repel them, for the enemy had slacked up and almost stopped advancing; along came a man in a Union lieutenant's uniform, inquiring for his regiment,—he was lost; we of course did not know where his regiment was; I was near the end of our company line; he pulled out a long plug of chewing-tobacco, thin and black; I grabbed it and bit off a chew; the man next to me wanted a chew; I handed it to him; then it went to the next, and so on down the line; the lieutenant followed it for a while and then gave up and passed on, leaving the remnant of the plug with the company. Every man that took a chew first blew out a big wad of cartridge-paper blackened with gunpowder, which he had bitten off in loading.

Word had been passed along the line that Lyon was killed. A big regular army cavalry soldier on a magnificent horse rode down alongside of the rear of our company, and along the line; he appeared to have been sent for the purpose of bracing us up. He shouted and swore in a manner that was attractive even on the battle-field, and wound up with a great big oath and the expression, "Life ain't long enough for them to lick us in." After this last repulse the field was ours, and we sat down on the ground and began to tell the funny incidents that had happened. We looked after boys who were hurt, sent details off to fill the canteens, and we ate our dinners, saving what we did not want of our big crusts and hanging them over our shoulders again on our gun-slings. We regretted very much the death of General Lyon, but we felt sanguine over our success, and thought the war was about ended.

Our drill had given us more than one advantage: in the *first* place, not much of us could be seen by an advancing regiment while we lay on the ground; we were sort of an unknown quantity, and could only be guessed at. *Second*, we could take a rest and deadly aim and pour in a terrific volley while lying on the ground; this would shock the advancing line if it indeed did not bring them to a dead halt. It embarrassed their alignment and reduced their momentum. *Third*, when they began to fire we rose on one knee; the air was soon full of smoke, and while they always shot over our heads we could see them under the cloud of smoke. The smoke was inclined to rise, but if they were advancing they were on foot and could not see under the smoke. If they advanced they were soon enveloped in their own smoke, their officers could not see their own men, and the men became bewildered at their situation and by their losses in killed and wounded. On the other hand, the air was clear behind us and our officers could manage their men, and we were not staggered by losses. *Fourth*, our men could not break to the rear and run, because they could be seen; while the ranks of the enemy could dissolve and the skulkers get to the rear in the smoke practically unseen. Hence by reason of our drill and situation we could not be dislodged by anything but a very strong force. And we were comparatively safe in comparison with an attacking column. Above all other factors of safety was our drill.

CONFEDERATE ARTILLERY AT WILSON'S CREEK:
MISSOURI, AUGUST 1861

W. E. Woodruff: from
With the Light Guns in '61–'65

Following Lyon's death, the Union forces retreated to Springfield and then to Rolla, 100 miles to the north. The battle cost the Union about 1,300 men killed, wounded, or missing, the Confederates about 1,200. Woodruff, a lawyer from Little Rock, Arkansas, serving as an artillery officer, recorded his experiences during the battle in a memoir published in 1903.

IN AN old package of papers, yellow with age, is found a substantial copy of the report of the Pulaski battery's participation in the battle of the 10th of August. It has never been published within the knowledge of this writer, and it appears now, as having been made when matters were fresh in mind:

"Camp on Wilson's Creek, Mo., Aug. 11, 1861.
"Col. Joseph Hebert, Commanding Advance:—
"Sir:—My battery having been asigned to your command, it becomes my duty to report its participation in the action of yesterday on the ground it occupies. If I am in error, please forward to proper headquarters.

"On the morning of the 9th inst., I was ordered to be in readiness to move promptly against the enemy, at 9 p. m. Later, in consequence of the rain, I was ordered to be 'ready to move at a moment's notice.' My officers and men were ordered to remain at and near their posts, with teams harnessed and hitched, parked at full distance, and remained so all night.

"About 6 a. m. on the 10th, just as my men had finished breakfast, a great commotion was observed on the Springfield road, in a direction northwesterly (as I take it) from my camp. Men, horses and other animals, with and without wagons, carriages, etc., were seen rushing hurriedly and confusedly in great numbers down the roads and to the fords on the west and south. It seemed to be a repetition of the affair at Crane Creek a few days ago, and we were not greatly disturbed. Nevertheless, I ordered officers and men to posts and mounted drivers while awaiting orders. A minute or two later, on the hill five or six hundred yards northwest a rush of teams was observed, which rapidly developed into a light battery, that quickly unlimbered and commenced firing, seemingly in the direction of General McCulloch's headquarters, or of the crowd flying down the main road towards Sharp's house. Almost simultaneously a second battery or section rushed forward to the right and in front of the first, about 200 yards, unlimbered and commenced firing, apparently in the direction of McRae's battalion, or Third Louisiana regiment.* My men had been held a minute or two in expectation of orders, but satisfied the situation was grave, I passed my caissons to the rear and ordered "in battery," at the appearance of the first mentioned force. The second battery or section of the enemy observed my movement, and opened fire on us. We were able to answer the enemy's third or fourth †shot. Generals Pearce and McCulloch were soon on the ground and approved the action taken. Within a few minutes after the enemy opened, the report of a few shots of artillery to the southwest was heard, or at both extremities of our camp. Feeling the importance of staying the assault until our infantry lines were established, the cannonade with the hostile battery was continued half an hour or more, with the double purpose of checking it and for effect on his infantry lines behind.‡

"Early in the action, the Missouri cavalry regiment of Colonel Graves reported, in support of the battery. The colonel was requested to take position on our flanks and rear, if he approved. A considerable force of the enemy was observed in the cornfield near one-half mile immediately north of our position. Foreseeing that it was intended to attack our

---

*Curiously, the tactics outlined in Exodus 4-4 flashed in mind at this time.

†Gen. Price "was greatly aided from the beginning by Woodruff, who had, with true soldierly instinct, thrown his pieces into battery, on the bluff east of the ford, at the sound of Totten's guns, and opened on Lyon a fire which checked his advance and gave the Missourians time to reach Cawthon's position and form a line of battle there."—Snead's Fight for Missouri, p. 274.

‡See p. 277; Snead Ib.

position and dislodge us, the appearance and position of this force, regulars, infantry, cavalry and a battery, was quickly reported to General McCulloch,* who speedily opposed it with McRae's battalion, part of the Third Louisiana, and, I think, Flanagin's regiment, all under Colonel McIntosh. They had to pass under the fire of our guns, stationed at a higher level, to reach the enemy. With the rest of the Third Louisiana regiment, General McCulloch, in a little while, moved rapidly to the west or southwest. Our infantry line being formed, and the threatened attack from the hill north checked, our fire was thereafter directed where it could be advantageously used without injury to our own troops, sometimes at the opposing battery, at others against the assaults of the enemy on the hill to the northwest, in support of Colonel McIntosh, and after in support of our infantry line on the enemy, when the latter was uncovered. About 9 a. m., Colonel Gratiot's Third Arkansas reported in support, and was requested to take the position vacated by Graves' Missouri cavalry. An hour later the Third Arkansas, Colonel Gratiot, passed down the hill to the left of our position, directed by General Pearce, and crossed the creek, and in a little while went into action. Observing a Federal regiment, uniformed in gray, advancing in fine order to meet Gratiot, and having an excellent opportunity to enfilade it while Gratiot was uncovered, we opened on it with the effect of breaking its beautiful line and scattering it its full length, to the depth of a company front or more, when Gratiot met and dispersed it gallantly. The enemy commenced falling back about noon, to the northwest, in good order, their rear covered by artillery and cavalry. We opened on the retreating force, which gave our artillery antagonists opportunity to send a few spiteful shots at us in return.

"CASUALTIES.

"I have to report a loss of four officers and men, killed, wounded and missing. First Lieutenant Omer R. Weaver and Private Hugh Byler were killed by cannon shot; Private Richard C. Byrd, Jr., was wounded in the leg by a minnie ball, sufficiently to disable him from service for some time; two

---

*See last paragraph of Note 1 to appendix.

horses were also killed. The death of Weaver is an irreparable loss to the battery and the cause. Byler was a brave and useful and exemplary soldier. Their loss is all the more deplorable, because if a surgeon had been attached, their valuable lives might possibly have been saved. The missing man had gone to the corral without permission at dawn, and was cut off from return by position of the enemy and his line of fire.

"During a lull in the action, by General Pearce's order, the battery was limbered up and moved to more elevated ground some one hundred yards to the right and rear of the first position.

"Very respectfully, etc.,
"W. E. WOODRUFF, Jr.,
"Captain Pulaski (Arkansas) Light Battery."

The average excellence of behavior of the company was very high. There was only one absentee, and he, a boy, caught away from camp when the battle opened, had no exemplar to point the way to duty. His name is not mentioned. The army roll is challenged for superiors or peers of Tom Cavanaugh, Pat Connolly, Higgins, Cook, Lowe and Quinn, as cannoneers. They were all artists in the service of the piece. The names of a few others are given alphabetically, special mention of whom will excite no jealousy: Blocher, Brodie, Button, Campbell, Curry, Davis, W. R. Douglass George, Halliburton, Hugh Hardy, Jennings, Kimbell, Lewis, Marshall, Mears, Merrick, Mills, Osborne, the two Parks brothers, Pollock, Visart, Watkins, Williams and Woodard, as deserving of commendation. Judgment forbids extending the list, lest the heart run away with the pen and cause it to copy the roll. Ten or more were boys between 15 and 17, and their youth alone prevented some from being placed as sergeants and corporals. All seemed to vie as if each member felt desirous of averting from the State of Arkansas, the odium of an overwhelming disgrace, responsibility for which might be settled upon each.

Many of the incidents of the fight are recalled. It had been arranged between the company officers long before, that in our first engagement each should take the post of gunner at designated pieces. Weaver to take No. 1, I to take No. 2 (to be near the center) Reyburn No. 3, and Brown No. 4, assisted and rested by the proper gunner of the respective pieces. From the shape of the gun, the tendency is to "over-shoot" the mark, the outer surface of the gun being much thicker at the breech than at the muzzle. The difference is more than an inch according to calibre, and in a distance of several hundred yards the overshot is considerable. Only experience can qualify a gunner to determine what elevation to give his piece, to strike with certainty a particular object. It was a fortunate incident that our overshots were effective on the Federal lines and reserve behind. I fired the first shot and the others followed. Weaver was struck within the first hour. He had just been relieved by his gunner, Sergeant Blocher, I believe, and, was struck a moment after with a solid shot, which broke his right arm and crushed his breast. Some one told me Weaver was wounded and wanted to see me. I went to him immediately, and he said, lying on the ground, his wounded arm across his breast: "I am done for; can't you have me moved?" I said, "Yes, immediately, and I will try to get a surgeon." He said, "All right; you had better go back to your gun or post." I called Sergeant Button and told him to detail men to move Weaver, and to get a surgeon if he could. The fight was going on all the time. A little later Byler was struck by a solid shot above the knee. He was removed also. Within an hour Byrd was shot in the leg with a minnie ball and was also removed. Button managed to find Dr. Dunlap, of Fort Smith, who ministered to all while there was life. A wheel horse of the limber of Weaver's gun, one of the "overland" white team, was also killed. All the casualties happened at the same gun and its caisson—a piece of shell splintered the latter and fell inside the chest—except another horse which was killed near us to the left—a sergeant's horse hitched to a small tree.

During the "cornfield fight," a battery, I think Bledsoe's Missouri Battery, opened at a point considerably to the left, west and south of us, and fired apparently at the Federal regulars in the cornfield four or five shots. At the time I thought it was Reed. It may be, however, that it was Guibor's Missouri Battery,* which was camped over a mile to the left and rear of

---

*It was Guibor, as learned from Snead's book long after Woodruff's official report was made. See note to appendix. Guibor had to "move more than a

us as we fired. Neither Reed, Bledsoe or Guibor was in sight. This was the only participation in the fight by the Missouri batteries that I am aware of. It occurred to me at the time, that the missiles of this battery were as dangerous to McIntosh as to the enemy. I had partially discontinued firing in that direction for that reason. The guns sounded beautifully and inspiringly, however. Reed fired a few shots at Sigel's battery, which we heard only, as he was out of sight. All the reports of the Pulaski battery "whipping Totten" are foundationless. He manifested himself a courageous and capable officer. He was in the fight from "end to end" and in the very forefront. He fired, I think, his last shot at us on the retreat, as stated in my report—though there was another regular battery, Du Bois',* in the close vicinity of the Federal force that made the cornfield fight. Totten's guns were abandoned at one stage. Colonel De Rosey Carroll's regiment (he told me) went over his, Totten's ground, and found them abandoned. They were recovered, however and drawn away. I freely say that while our post was dangerous enough, I am glad the conditions were not reversed. He was afterwards dismissed from the army on account of dissipation, a weakness which President Grant might well have overlooked, as Totten suggested to him, when notified of that President's approval of his dismissal. The unkindest thing I ever heard of Captain Totten was a remark of Captain C. C. Danley, in '60 or '61, who remarked: "T. was always a bosom friend of the man he drank with last." Certainly a testimonial to his generous nature, and I can testify to his soldierly qualities.

Generals McCulloch, Price, Pearce and Colonel McIntosh visited our position several times during the day; also President David Walker of the State convention. The demeanor of all was fearless. It is recalled that Price wore throughout the fight a black "plug" hat, which ranged over the field like an oriflamme, to the Missourians.

The bearing of General Lyon was in plain view, and was very gallant. There was another Federal officer, a one-armed Irish man, named Sweeny, as afterwards learned, whose actions were

---

mile" to reach his post in Price's line, which he could not have done at the time Totten opened fire with his battery, and for a half hour after that time.

*It was DuBois. See note to appendix, next to last paragraph.

most gallant in bringing up and encouraging his infantry as his battallions were put into the fight successively. He was always in the thick of it. We did not know the names of either until later. One factor aided the Federals greatly; all their infantry had long range guns; our men had very few; the Federals could pick their distance out of range of our old muskets, squirrel rifles and shot guns, when the two lines clashed. This was signally manifested when Gratiot's minnie rifles were pitted against the last regiment put in the fight, which was arrested long before a return fire was expected. The difference in arms explains the heavy loss of the Confederates.

Next day after the battle the captain went to take a look at the "dutch" prisoners. As we passed a group of Price's Missourians, one of them spoke out so that he could be heard: "There goes the little captain of the battery that saved us yesterday." Then it was assured our boys had done well.

FREEING THE SLAVES OF REBELS:
MISSOURI, AUGUST 1861

John C. Frémont: Proclamation

A former army officer who had gained fame for his western explorations and his service in California during the U.S.-Mexican War, John C. Frémont became the first Republican presidential nominee in 1856. Commissioned as a major general in May 1861, Frémont arrived in St. Louis on July 25 and assumed command of the Union forces in Missouri. As Confederate guerrilla activity increased following the Union defeat at Wilson's Creek, the new commander issued a proclamation.

HEADQUARTERS WESTERN DEPARTMENT,
Saint Louis, August 30, 1861.

Circumstances, in my judgment, of sufficient urgency render it necessary that the commanding general of this department should assume the administrative powers of the State. Its disorganized condition, the helplessness of the civil authority, the total insecurity of life, and the devastation of property by bands of murderers and marauders, who infest nearly every county of the State, and avail themselves of the public misfortunes and the vicinity of a hostile force to gratify private and neighborhood vengeance, and who find an enemy wherever they find plunder, finally demand the severest measures to repress the daily increasing crimes and outrages which are driving off the inhabitants and ruining the State.

In this condition the public safety and the success of our arms require unity of purpose, without let or hinderance to the prompt administration of affairs. In order, therefore, to suppress disorder, to maintain as far as now practicable the public peace, and to give security and protection to the persons and property of loyal citizens, I do hereby extend and declare established martial law throughout the State of Missouri.

The lines of the army of occupation in this State are for the present declared to extend from Leavenworth, by way of the posts of Jefferson City, Rolla, and Ironton, to Cape Girardeau, on the Mississippi River.

All persons who shall be taken with arms in their hands within these lines shall be tried by court-martial, and if found guilty will be shot.

The property, real and personal, of all persons in the State of Missouri who shall take up arms against the United States, or who shall be directly proven to have taken an active part with their enemies in the field, is declared to be confiscated to the public use, and their slaves, if any they have, are hereby declared freemen.

All persons who shall be proven to have destroyed, after the publication of this order, railroad tracks, bridges, or telegraphs shall suffer the extreme penalty of the law.

All persons engaged in treasonable correspondence, in giving or procuring aid to the enemies of the United States, in fomenting tumults, in disturbing the public tranquillity by creating and circulating false reports or incendiary documents, are in their own interests warned that they are exposing themselves to sudden and severe punishment.

All persons who have been led away from their allegiance are required to return to their homes forthwith. Any such absence, without sufficient cause, will be held to be presumptive evidence against them.

The object of this declaration is to place in the hands of the military authorities the power to give instantaneous effect to existing laws, and to supply such deficiencies as the conditions of war demand. But this is not intended to suspend the ordinary tribunals of the country, where the law will be administered by the civil officers in the usual manner, and with their customary authority, while the same can be peaceably exercised.

The commanding general will labor vigilantly for the public welfare, and in his efforts for their safety hopes to obtain not only the acquiescence but the active support of the loyal people of the country.

J. C. FRÉMONT,
Major-General, Commanding.

MODIFYING A PROCLAMATION: SEPTEMBER 1861

Abraham Lincoln to John C. Frémont

John G. Nicolay recorded that when Frémont's proclamation reached Washington, it "at once troubled the Prest and Gen. Scott exceedingly," causing both men to worry that the provision for emancipating slaves would have "an exceedingly discouraging effect" on unionists in Kentucky. Although Lincoln hoped to keep his modification of the proclamation private, Frémont would respond to his letter of September 2 by refusing to modify the proclamation unless he was publicly ordered to do so, a request the President "very cheerfully" granted in a subsequent communication.

Private and confidential.
Major General Fremont: Washington D.C. Sept. 2, 1861.
My dear Sir: Two points in your proclamation of August 30th give me some anxiety. First, should you shoot a man, according to the proclamation, the Confederates would very certainly shoot our best man in their hands in retaliation; and so, man for man, indefinitely. It is therefore my order that you allow no man to be shot, under the proclamation, without first having my approbation or consent.

Secondly, I think there is great danger that the closing paragraph, in relation to the confiscation of property, and the liberating slaves of traiterous owners, will alarm our Southern Union friends, and turn them against us—perhaps ruin our rather fair prospect for Kentucky. Allow me therefore to ask, that you will as of your own motion, modify that paragraph so as to conform to the *first* and *fourth* sections of the act of Congress, entitled, "An act to confiscate property used for insurrectionary purposes," approved August, 6th, 1861, and a copy of which act I herewith send you. This letter is written in a spirit of caution and not of censure.

I send it by a special messenger, in order that it may certainly and speedily reach you. Yours very truly   A. LINCOLN

Copy of letter sent to Gen. Fremont, by special messenger leaving Washington Sep. 3. 1861.

THE NEED FOR BLACK SOLDIERS:
SEPTEMBER 1861

Frederick Douglass: Fighting Rebels with Only One Hand

September 1861

The disillusionment and frustration Douglass expressed at the administration's policy in his *Monthly* increased after Lincoln revoked Frémont's proclamation.

WHAT UPON EARTH is the matter with the American Government and people? Do they really covet the world's ridicule as well as their own social and political ruin? What are they thinking about, or don't they condescend to think at all? So, indeed, it would seem from their blindness in dealing with the tremendous issue now upon them. Was there ever any thing like it before? They are sorely pressed on every hand by a vast army of slaveholding rebels, flushed with success, and infuriated by the darkest inspirations of a deadly hate, bound to rule or ruin. Washington, the seat of Government, after ten thousand assurances to the contrary, is now positively in danger of falling before the rebel army. Maryland, a little while ago considered safe for the Union, is now admitted to be studded with the materials for insurrection, and which may flame forth at any moment.—Every resource of the nation, whether of men or money, whether of wisdom or strength, could be well employed to avert the impending ruin. Yet most evidently the demands of the hour are not comprehended by the Cabinet or the crowd. Our Presidents, Governors, Generals and Secretaries are calling, with almost frantic vehemence, for men.— "Men! men! send us men!" they scream, or the cause of the Union is gone, the life of a great nation is ruthlessly sacrificed, and the hopes of a great nation go out in darkness; and yet these very officers, representing the people and Government, steadily and persistently refuse to receive the very class of men which have a deeper interest in the defeat and humiliation of the rebels, than all others.—Men are wanted in Missouri—wanted in Western Virginia, to hold and defend what has been already gained; they are wanted in Texas, and all along the sea coast, and though the Government has at its command a class in the country deeply interested in suppressing the insurrection, it sternly refuses to summon from among the vast multitude a single man, and degrades and insults the whole class by refusing to allow any of their number to defend with their strong arms and brave hearts the national cause. What a spectacle of blind, unreasoning prejudice and pusillanimity is this! The national edifice is on fire. Every man who can carry a bucket of water, or remove a brick, is wanted; but those who have the care of the building, having a profound respect for the feeling of the national burglars who set the building on fire, are determined that the flames shall only be extinguished by Indo-Caucasian hands, and to have the building burnt rather than save it by means of any other. Such is the pride, the stupid prejudice and folly that rules the hour.

Why does the Government reject the Negro? Is he not a man? Can he not wield a sword, fire a gun, march and countermarch, and obey orders like any other? Is there the least reason to believe that a regiment of well-drilled Negroes would deport themselves less soldier-like on the battle field than the raw troops gathered up generally from the towns and cities of the State of New York? We do believe that such soldiers, if allowed now to take up arms in defence of the Government, and made to feel that they are hereafter to be recognized as persons having rights, would set the highest example of order and general good behavior to their fellow soldiers, and in every way add to the national power.

If persons so humble as we can be allowed to speak to the President of the United States, we should ask him if this dark and terrible hour of the nation's extremity is a time for consulting a mere vulgar and unnatural prejudice? We should ask him if national preservation and necessity were not better guides in this emergency than either the tastes of the rebels, or the pride and prejudices of the vulgar? We would tell him that General Jackson in a slave State fought side by side with

Negroes at New Orleans, and like a true man, despising meanness, he bore testimony to their bravery at the close of the war. We would tell him that colored men in Rhode Island and Connecticut performed their full share in the war of the Revolution, and that men of the same color, such as the noble Shields Green, Nathaniel Turner and Denmark Vesey stand ready to peril every thing at the command of the Government. We would tell him that this is no time to fight with one hand, when both are needed; that this is no time to fight only with your white hand, and allow your black hand to remain tied.

Whatever may be the folly and absurdity of the North, the South at least is true and wise. The Southern papers no longer indulge in the vulgar expression, "free n—rs." That class of bipeds are now called "colored residents." The Charleston papers say:

> "The colored residents of this city can challenge comparison with their class, in any city or town, in loyalty or devotion to the cause of the South. Many of them individually, and without ostentation, have been contributing liberally, and on Wednesday evening, the 7th inst., a very large meeting was held by them, and a Committee appointed to provide for more efficient aid. The proceedings of the meeting will appear in results hereinafter to be reported."

It is now pretty well established, that there are at the present moment many colored men in the Confederate army doing duty not only as cooks, servants and laborers, but as real soldiers, having muskets on their shoulders, and bullets in their pockets, ready to shoot down loyal troops, and do all that soldiers may to destroy the Federal Government and build up that of the traitors and rebels. There were such soldiers at Manassas, and they are probably there still. There is a Negro in the army as well as in the fence, and our Government is likely to find it out before the war comes to an end. That the Negroes are numerous in the rebel army, and do for that army its heaviest work, is beyond question. They have been the chief laborers upon those temporary defences in which the rebels have been able to mow down our men. Negroes helped to build the batteries at Charleston. They relieve their gentlemanly and military masters from the stiffening drudgery of the camp, and devote them to the nimble and dexterous use of arms. Rising above vulgar prejudice, the slaveholding rebel accepts the aid of the black man as readily as that of any other. If a bad cause can do this, why should a good cause be less wisely conducted? We insist upon it, that one black regiment in such a war as this is, without being any more brave and orderly, would be worth to the Government more than two of any other; and that, while the Government continues to refuse the aid of colored men, thus alienating them from the national cause, and giving the rebels the advantage of them, it will not deserve better fortunes than it has thus far experienced.—Men in earnest don't fight with one hand, when they might fight with two, and a man drowning would not refuse to be saved even by a colored hand.

REVOKING FRÉMONT'S PROCLAMATION:
SEPTEMBER 1861

Abraham Lincoln to Orville H. Browning

Lincoln explained his decision to revoke Frémont's proclamation to his friend Orville H. Browning, who had recently been appointed to fill the Senate seat left vacant by the death of Stephen A. Douglas.

Private & confidential.
Hon. O. H. Browning   Executive Mansion
My dear Sir   Washington Sept 22d 1861.
Yours of the 17th is just received; and coming from you, I confess it astonishes me. That you should object to my adhering to a law, which you had assisted in making, and presenting to me, less than a month before, is odd enough. But this is a very small part. Genl. Fremont's proclamation, as to confiscation of property, and the liberation of slaves, is *purely political*, and not within the range of *military* law, or necessity. If a commanding General finds a necessity to seize the farm of a private owner, for a pasture, an encampment, or a fortification, he has the right to do so, and to so hold it, as long as the necessity lasts; and this is within military law, because within military necessity. But to say the farm shall no longer belong to the owner, or his heirs forever; and this as well when the farm is not needed for military purposes as when it is, is purely political, without the savor of military law about it. And the same is true of slaves. If the General needs them, he can seize them, and use them; but when the need is past, it is not for him to fix their permanent future condition. That must be settled according to laws made by law-makers, and not by military proclamations. The proclamation in the point in question, is simply "dictatorship." It assumes that the general may do *anything* he pleases—confiscate the lands and free the slaves of *loyal* people, as well as of disloyal ones. And going the whole figure I have no doubt would be more popular with some

thoughtless people, than that which has been done! But I cannot assume this reckless position; nor allow others to assume it on my responsibility. You speak of it as being the only means of *saving* the government. On the contrary it is itself the surrender of the government. Can it be pretended that it is any longer the government of the U.S.—any government of Constitution and laws,—wherein a General, or a President, may make permanent rules of property by proclamation?

I do not say Congress might not with propriety pass a law, on the point, just such as General Fremont proclaimed. I do not say I might not, as a member of Congress, vote for it. What I object to, is, that I as President, shall expressly or impliedly seize and exercise the permanent legislative functions of the government.

So much as to principle. Now as to policy. No doubt the thing was popular in some quarters, and would have been more so if it had been a general declaration of emancipation. The Kentucky Legislature would not budge till that proclamation was modified; and Gen. Anderson telegraphed me that on the news of Gen. Fremont having actually issued deeds of manumission, a whole company of our Volunteers threw down their arms and disbanded. I was so assured, as to think it probable, that the very arms we had furnished Kentucky would be turned against us. I think to lose Kentucky is nearly the same as to lose the whole game. Kentucky gone, we can not hold Missouri, nor, as I think, Maryland. These all against us, and the job on our hands is too large for us. We would as well consent to separation at once, including the surrender of this capitol. On the contrary, if you will give up your restlessness for new positions, and back me manfully on the grounds upon which you and other kind friends gave me the election, and have approved in my public documents, we shall go through triumphantly.

You must not understand I took my course on the proclamation *because* of Kentucky. I took the same ground in a private letter to General Fremont before I heard from Kentucky.

You think I am inconsistent because I did not also forbid Gen. Fremont to shoot men under the proclamation. I understand that part to be within military law; but I also think, and so privately wrote Gen. Fremont, that it is impolitic in this, that our adversaries have the power, and will certainly exercise it, to shoot as many of our men as we shoot of theirs. I did not say this in the public letter, because it is a subject I prefer not to discuss in the hearing of our enemies.

There has been no thought of removing Gen. Fremont on any ground connected with his proclamation; and if there has been any wish for his removal on any ground, our mutual friend Sam. Glover can probably tell you what it was. I hope no real necessity for it exists on any ground.

Suppose you write to Hurlbut and get him to resign. Your friend as ever   A. LINCOLN

A CHEROKEE-CONFEDERATE ALLIANCE:
INDIAN TERRITORY, OCTOBER 1861

John Ross: Message to the National Council

During the summer of 1861 John Ross became concerned that the Confederacy would seek an alliance with his rival Stand Watie, the leader of a powerful tribal faction. Seeking to avoid a split in the Cherokee Nation, Ross announced on August 21 his intention to negotiate a treaty with the Confederacy. The alliance was concluded on October 7, and two days later Ross successfully argued for its ratification.

———————

Message of the Principal Chief of the Cherokee Nation.

To the National Committee and Council in National Council convened:

FRIENDS AND FELLOW-CITIZENS: Since the last meeting of the National Council events have occurred that will occupy a prominent place in the history of the world. The United States have been dissolved and two governments now exist. Twelve of the States composing the late Union have erected themselves into a government under the style of the Confederate States of America, and, as you know, are now engaged in a war for their independence. The contest thus far has been attended with success almost uninterrupted on their side and marked by brilliant victories. Of its final result there seems to be no ground for a reasonable doubt. The unanimity and devotion of the people of the Confederate States must sooner or later secure their success over all opposition and result in the establishment of their independence and a recognition of it by the other nations of the earth.

At the beginning of the conflict I felt that the interests of the Cherokee people would be best maintained by remaining quiet and not involving themselves in it prematurely. Our relations had long existed with the United States Government and bound us to observe amity and peace alike with all the States. Neutrality was proper and wise so long as there remained a reasonable probability that the difficulty between the two sections of the Union would be settled, as a different course would have placed all our rights in jeopardy and might have led to the sacrifice of the people. But when there was no longer any reason to believe that the Union of the States would be continued there was no cause to hesitate as to the course the Cherokee Nation should pursue. Our geographical position and domestic institutions allied us to the South, while the developments daily made in our vicinity and as to the purposes of the war waged against the Confederate States clearly pointed out the path of interest.

These considerations produced a unanimity of sentiment among the people as to the policy to be adopted by the Cherokee Nation, which was clearly expressed in their general meeting held at Tahlequah on the 21st of August last. A copy of the proceedings of that meeting is submitted for your information.

In accordance with the declarations embodied in the resolutions then adopted the Executive Council deemed it proper to exercise the authority conferred upon them by the people there assembled. Messengers were dispatched to General Albert Pike, the distinguished Indian Commissioner of the Confederate States, who, having negotiated treaties with the neighboring Indian nations, was then establishing relations between his Government and the Comanches and other Indians in the Southwest, who bore a copy of the proceedings of the meeting referred to, and a letter from the executive authorities, proposing on behalf of the nation to enter into a treaty of alliance, defensive and offensive, with the Confederate States.

In the exercise of the same general authority, and to be ready as far as practicable to meet any emergency that might spring up on our northern border, it was thought proper to raise a regiment of mounted men and tender its services to General McCulloch. The people responded with alacrity to the call, and it is believed the regiment will be found as efficient as any other like number of men. It is now in the service of the Confederate States for the purpose of aiding in defending their homes and the common rights of the Indian nations about us. This regiment is composed of ten full companies, with two reserve companies, and, in addition to the force previously authorized to be raised to operate outside of the nation by General McCulloch, will show that the Cherokee people are ready to do all in their power in defense of the Confederate cause, which has now become their own. And it is to be hoped that our people will spare no means to sustain them, but contribute liberally to supply any want of comfortable clothing for the approaching season.

In years long since past our ancestors met undaunted those who would invade their mountain homes beyond the Mississippi. Let not their descendants of the present day be found unworthy of them, or unable to stand by the chivalrous men of the South by whose side they may be called to fight in self-defense. The Cherokee people do not desire to be involved in war, but self-preservation fully justifies them in the course they have adopted, and they will be recreant to themselves if they should not sustain it to the utmost of their humble abilities.

A treaty with the Confederate States has been entered into and is now submitted for your ratification. In view of the circumstances by which we are surrounded and the provisions of the treaty it will be found to be the most important ever negotiated on behalf of the Cherokee Nation, and will mark a new era in its history. Without attempting a recapitulation of all its provisions, some of its distinguishing features may be briefly enumerated.

The relations of the Cherokee Nation are changed from the United to the Confederate States, with guarantees of protection and a recognition in future negotiations only of its constitutional authorities. The metes and boundaries, as defined by patent from the United States, are continued, and a guarantee given for the neutral land or a fair consideration in case it should be lost by war or negotiation, and an advance thereon to pay the national debt and to meet other contingencies. The payment of all our annuities and the security of all our investments are provided for. The jurisdiction of the Cherokee courts over all members of the nation, whether by birth, marriage, or adoption, is recognized.

Our title to our lands is placed beyond dispute. Our relations with the Confederate States is that of a ward; theirs to us that of a protectorate, with powers restricted. The district court, with a limited civil and criminal jurisdiction, is admitted into the country instead of being located in Van Buren, as was the United States court. This is perhaps one of the most important provisions of the treaty, and secures to our own citizens the great constitutional right of trial by a jury of their vicinage, and releases them from the petty abuses and vexations of the old system, before a foreign jury and in a foreign country. It gives us a Delegate in Congress on the same footing with Delegates from the Territories, by which our interests can be represented; a right which has long been withheld from the nation and which has imposed upon it a large expense and great injustice. It also contains reasonable stipulation in regard to the appointing powers of the agent and in regard to licensed traders. The Cherokee Nation may be called upon to furnish troops for the defense of the Indian country, but is never to be taxed for the support of any war in which the States may be engaged.

The Cherokee people stand upon new ground. Let us hope that the clouds which overspread the land will be dispersed and that we shall prosper as we have never before done. New avenues to usefulness and distinction will be opened to the ingenuous youth of the country. Our rights of self-government will be more fully recognized, and our citizens be no longer dragged off upon flimsy pretexts, to be imprisoned and tried before distant tribunals. No just cause exists for domestic difficulties. Let them be buried with the past and only mutual friendship and harmony be cherished.

Our relations with the neighboring tribes are of the most friendly character. Let us see that the white path which leads from our country to theirs be obstructed by no act of ours, and that it be open to all those with whom we may be brought into intercourse.

Amid the excitement of the times it is to be hoped that the interests of education will not be allowed to suffer and that no interruption be brought into the usual operations of the government. Let all its officers continue to discharge their appropriate duties.

As the services of some of your members may be required

elsewhere and all unnecessary expense should be avoided, I respectfully recommend that the business of the session be promptly discharged.

JNO. ROSS.,

Executive Department,
Tahlequah, C. N., October 9, 1861.

BATTLE OF BALL'S BLUFF:
VIRGINIA, OCTOBER 1861

Henry Livermore Abbott to Josiah Gardner Abbott

Several Union regiments crossed the Potomac upriver from Washington on October 21 in an attempt to dislodge Confederate troops from Leesburg, Virginia. Henry Livermore Abbott was a nineteen-year-old Harvard graduate serving as a second lieutenant in Company I, 20th Massachusetts Volunteers. He wrote to his father from an army camp near Poolesville, Maryland, and described his regiment's baptism of fire in the Battle of Ball's Bluff.

———————

Camp Benton
Oct 22nd

Dear Papa,

I suppose you have by this got my telegraphic dispatch & know that we are all safe. I will give you a brief description of the affair, only brief because I am rather played out by 2 days hard work.

It seems that upon Sunday the quartermaster of the 15th Mass. had got across & discovered that there were no pickets on the other side; accordingly to them was given the honor of crossing to attack a rebel camp about 2 miles off from the shore. One company of a hundred men from the 20th was ordered to follow the 15th & take possession of the opposite height as a reserve. Co. I & 57 of Caspar's men with Caspar & George were the reserve.

Sunday night the passage was made by the 15th. We followed, getting over about 5 o'clock & taking the heights. Now look at the absurdity of the thing. To cross the river we had two little row boats that together carried over 30 men at a time. We landed on the hill almost perpendicular & very thickly wooded. When we get on the top, we are drawn up on the only open space there is, about wide enough for a front of two regiments, & about a short rifle shot in length, surrounded on every side by large, unexplored woods. It was in fact one of the most complete slaughter pens ever devised. Here we were kept, while the 15th marched off to surprise the rebel camp.

In the meantime we sent off scouts which resulted in our first sergeant, Riddle, being shot in the arm. The Fifteenth, of course, lose their way, are attacked & send word they are surrounded & we must cover their retreat. It was rather an uncomfortable thing. A hundred men in an unknown country, surrounded by the hidden enemy & cut off virtually, by the badness of transport, from reinforcement. The col. told us there was no doubt it was all up with us.

The 15th, however, held their ground nobly till now, when they fell back on us & shortly after we were reinforced by the rest of our regiment on hand (making only 300) & by Baker's brigade & a couple of howitzers, who came in by boatloads of 30. After a while, however, they got a boat which carried 60, so that the reinforcements came in faster.

Now to begin with the order of battle. I have no right to criticize it in terms. It will be enough to describe it. The uncovered space I have spoken of was the battle ground. Part of Baker's brigade was drawn up on the right flank, on the edge of the wood, with the 15th. The rest was drawn across the opening, back towards the river, 30 feet from the top of the bank. 15 feet behind them the 318 men of our regiment were drawn up in a second, parallel line, under command of Col. Lee. The whole was the command of Gen. Baker. The two howitzers in front entirely unprotected. The enemy in the woods. Here is a rough sketch:

[ ]

You can see from the sketch that 2 of the regts. on our side were left in open view, when they might just as well have been in the woods, while the rebels were conveniently posted in the woods, just at good rifle shot, from which they didn't venture out till the conclusion of the fight.

In the first half hour, the gunners & horses of the howitzers were all killed; the line in front of our regiment was broken & fled so that we were the only force in the open field & from 2 to 6, we kept that field under a heavy fire of rifles & musketry. It seemed as if every square inch of air within six feet of the ground was traversed by bullets as they whistled by us. Tremblet's company got the worst of it. The col. tried to save ours as a reserve. But we foolishly hung all our company's great coats on the trees just behind us. Their red lining was so conspicuous as to draw the enemy's fire at a great rate. Though we were lying down, our men were shot on every side of us. And yet Capt. Bartlett, though standing up nearly all the time, wasn't so much as scratched.

The fight was made up of charges. You would see our capts. rush out in front & cry forward & their companies would follow them at full speed under a tremendous fire till they were obliged to fall back. And this was repeated over & over during the 4 hours fight.

Our company made the last charge. The general was killed, shot by 5 balls; nobody knew who was the senior in command & Col. Lee ordered a retreat. But we were determined to have one more shot. So Frank ordered a charge & we rushed along, followed by all our men without an exception, & by Lieut. Hallowell with 20 men, making about 60 in all. So we charged across the field about half way, when we saw the enemy in full sight. They had just come out of the wood & had halted at our advance. There they were in their dirty gray clothes, their banner waving, cavalry on the flank. For a moment there was a pause. And then, simultaneously, we fired & there came a murderous discharge from the full rebel force. Of course we retreated, but not a man went faster than a walk.

When we got back to the wood, we found the whole regiment cut to pieces & broken up, all the other forces gone & Col. Lee sitting under a tree, swearing he wouldn't go another step, but had rather be taken prisoner. However, we got him to go & we all started down the bank, every body knowing, however, that there was no chance of an escape. The col. ordered a surrender & had a white flag raised but the rebels fired on us & we were obliged to retreat to the river's edge, the rebels pouring down a murderous fire.

When we got down we had lost the col., but heard that the adjutant & major had got him into a boat & carried him across. After that, of course, we had only to look to our own safety. We rallied our men & then proposed to swim across in case they could all do it. We found there were four that couldn't swim, so we were obliged to stay with them, and we sent the rest over. It was hard work to make them leave us, but we insisted upon it, & most of them reached the opposite shore in safety, notwithstanding a heavy fire opened on the swimmers immediately.

With the rest of our men & with Capt. Tremblet & his men, we marched along the shore, picking up about 50 men of Baker's, meaning to surrender ourselves, if we could only get a chance. After we got a mile & a half we found an old nigger who got us a boat & in this we sent across by fives the 70 men with us & then went over ourselves. And so we escaped.

The col., major & adjutant are prisoners, it seems by later intelligence. Capt. Dreher is nearly dead, shot through the head. Capt. Putnam's arm is amputated close to the shoulder. Capt. Babo is killed. Capt. Schmidt has 3 bullets in the legs. Capt. Crowninshield a slight flesh wound. Lieut. Putnam will probably die, shot through the stomach. Lieut. Holmes shot through the breast, will recover, as will Lieut. Lowell, shot in the thigh. Lieut. Wessleheft is dead.

We are now at camp trying to rally enough men to form a company, so as to join it to the two companies that were not engaged & make a battalion of 3 under the command of Col. Palfrey, who was not in the fight, but has since crossed the river with the two unengaged companies.

Gen. Lander has just got back from Washington & is in a horrible rage, swearing that the thing is nothing less than murder. Gen. Banks' column crosses here tomorrow & there will probably be a retreat of the rebels. The little midnight adventure of ours has started the whole thing; now we shall have our revenge.

The good of the action is this. It shows the pluck of our men. They followed their commanders admirably, except in the last charge that we made. Cas wanted to go with us but his men, who had been pretty well cut up, refused to follow. He swore & raved awfully, but it was no go.

The men of our company couldn't possibly have behaved better. They never fired once without an order. They never advanced without an order, as all the rest did. They never retreated without an order, as some of the others did. In short, they never once lost their presence of mind, & behaved as well as if on the parade ground.

Give my love to mamma & the rest.

Your aff. son,
H. L. Abbott
October 22, 1861

REPLACING WINFIELD SCOTT: OCTOBER 1861

George B. McClellan to
Mary Ellen McClellan

The battle of Ball's Bluff cost the Union more than 900 men killed, wounded, or missing, six times the Confederate losses. Its political impact was magnified by the death of Colonel Edward D. Baker, a Republican senator from Oregon, former congressman from Illinois, and friend of President Lincoln. McClellan escaped blame for the defeat, and when Winfield Scott retired on November 1, McClellan replaced him as general-in-chief while retaining command of the Army of the Potomac.

Oct 25

. . . How weary I am of all this business—case after case—blunder after blunder—trick upon trick—I am well nigh tired of the world, & were it not for you would be fully so.

That affair of Leesburg on Monday last was a terrible butchery—the men fought nobly, but were penned up by a vastly superior force in a place where they had no retreat. The whole thing took place some 40 miles from here without my orders or knowledge—it was entirely unauthorized by me & I am in no manner responsible for it.

The man *directly* to blame for the affair was Col Baker who was killed—he was in command, disregarded entirely the instructions he had received from Stone, & violated all military rules & precautions. Instead of meeting the enemy with double their force & a good ferry behind him, he was outnumbered three to one, & had no means of retreat. Cogswell is a prisoner—he behaved very handsomely. Raymond Lee is also taken. We lost 79 killed, 141 wounded & probably 400 wounded & prisoners—stragglers are constantly coming in however, so that the number of missing is gradually being decreased & may not go beyond 300. I found things in great confusion when I arrived there—Genl Banks having assumed command &

having done *nothing*. In a very short time order & confidence were restored. During the night I withdrew everything & everybody to this side of the river—which in truth they should never have left.

Oct 26

For the last 3 hours I have been at Montgomery Blair's talking with Senators Wade, Trumbull & Chandler about war matters—they will make a desperate effort tomorrow to have Genl Scott retired at once. Until that is accomplished I can effect but little good—he is ever in my way & I am sure does not desire effective action—I want to get thro' with the war as rapidly as possible. . . .

I go out soon after bkft to review Porter's Divn, about 5 miles from here.

. . . You remember my wounded friend Col Kelley, whom we met at Wheeling? He has just done a very pretty thing at Romney—thrashed the enemy severely, taken all their guns etc. I am very glad to hear it. You may have heard from the papers etc of the small row that is going on just now between Genl Scott & myself—in which the vox populi is coming out strongly on my side. The affair had got among the soldiers, & I hear that offs & men all declare that they will fight under no one but "our George," as the scamps have taken it into their heads to call me. I ought to take good care of these men, for I believe they love me from the bottom of their hearts. I can see it in their faces when I pass among them. I presume the Scott war will culminate this week—& as it is now very clear that the people will not permit me to be passed over it seems easy to predict the result.

Whatever it may be I will try to do my duty to the army & to the country—with God's help & a single eye to the right I hope that I may succeed. I appreciate all the difficulties in my path—the impatience of the people, the venality & bad faith of the politicians, the gross neglect that has occurred in obtaining arms clothing etc—& also I feel in my innermost soul how small is my ability in comparison with the gigantic dimensions of the task, & that, even if I had the greatest intellect that was ever given to man, the result remains in the hands of God. I do not feel that I am an instrument worthy of the great task, but I *do* feel that I did not seek it—it was thrust upon me. I was called to it, my previous life seems to have been unwittingly directed to this great end, & I know that God can accomplish the greatest results with the weakest instruments— therein lies my hope. I feel too that, much as we in the North have erred, the rebels have been far worse than we—they seem to have deserted from the great cardinal virtues.

October 30, 1861

. . . I have been at work all day nearly on a letter to the Secy of War in regard to future military operations.

I have not been home for some 3 hrs, but am "concealed" at Stanton's to dodge all enemies in shape of "browsing" Presdt etc. . . .

I have been very busy today writing & am pretty thoroughly tired out. The paper is a very important one—as it is intended to place on record the fact that I have left nothing undone to make this army what it ought to be & that the necessity for delay has not been my fault. I have a set of scamps to deal with— unscrupulous & false—if possible they will throw whatever blame there is on my shoulders, & I do not intend to be sacrificed by such people. It is perfectly sickening to have to work with such people & to see the fate of the nation in such hands. I still trust that the all wise Creator does not intend our destruction, & that in his own good time he will free the nation from the imbeciles who curse it & will restore us to his favor. I know that as a nation we have grieviously sinned, but I trust that there is a limit to his wrath & that ere long we will begin to experience his mercy. But it is terrible to stand by & see the cowardice of the Presdt, the vileness of Seward, & the rascality of Cameron—Welles is an old woman—Bates an old fool. The only man of courage & sense in the Cabinet is Blair, & I do not altogether fancy him!

I cannot guess at my movements for they are not within my

own control. I cannot move without more means & I do not possess the power to control those means. The people think me all powerful. Never was there a greater mistake—I am thwarted & deceived by these incapables at every turn. I am doing all I can to get ready to move before winter sets in—but it now begins to look as if we are condemned to a winter of inactivity. If it is so the fault will not be mine—there will be that consolation for my conscience, even if the world at large never knows it. . . .

I have one great comfort in all this—that is that I did not seek this position, as you well know, & I still trust that God will support me & bear me out—he could not have placed me here for nothing. . . .

I am. I have just returned from a ride over the river where I went pretty late, to seek refuge in Fitz Porter's camp. You would have laughed if you could have seen me dodge off. I quietly told the little duke (Chartres) to get our horses saddled, & then we slipped off without escort or orderlies & trotted away for Fitz John's camp where we had a quiet talk over the camp fire.

I saw yesterday Genl Scott's letter asking to be placed on the Retired List & saying nothing about Halleck. The offer was to be accepted last night & they propose to make me at once Commander in Chief of the Army. I cannot get up any especial feeling about it—I feel the vast responsibility it imposes upon me. I feel a sense of relief at the prospect of having my own way untrammelled, but I cannot discover in my own heart one symptom of gratified vanity or ambition.

October 31, 1861

"I AM TIRED OF INCOMPETENTS":
NOVEMBER 1861

Charles Francis Adams Jr. to Henry Adams

Charles Francis Adams Jr. expressed his unhappiness with the Lincoln administration in a letter written from Boston to his brother in London.

———————

Boston, November 5, 1861

By the last mail I got a letter from you intended for the press. I have not however used it as intended. . . . The great facts of the case stand out. Six months of this war have gone and in them we have done much; and by we I mean our rulers. But if we have done much with our means, the rebels have performed miracles with theirs. At the end of six months have we a policy? Are traitors weeded out of our departments? Is our blockade effective? Is the war prosecuted honestly and vigorously? To all these questions there is but one answer. The President is not equal to the crisis; that we cannot now help. The Secretary of War is corrupt and the Secretary of the Navy is incompetent; that we can help and ought to. With the rebels showing us what we can do, we ought to be ashamed not to do more. But for me I despair of doing more without a purification of the Cabinet. With Seward I am satisfied, and so is the country at bottom, for our foreign affairs are creditable. Chase will do and to Blair I make no objection. But all the rest I wish the people would drive from power. Your historical examples are not good. When was England greatest? Was it not when an angry people drove the drivellers from office and forced on an unwilling King the elder Pitt, who reversed at once the whole current of a war? I want to see Holt in the War Department and a New York shipowner in that of the Navy, or else Mr. Dana. I am tired of incompetents and I want to see Lincoln forced to adopt a manly line of policy which all men may comprehend. The people here call for energy, not change, and if

Lincoln were only a wise man he could unite them in spite of party cries, and with an eye solely to the public good.

Herewith you will receive three Independents, in each of which you will find an article by me for your delectation. They answer at some length your suggestion that I am an "abolitionist." I am also assured that they met with favor in the eyes of Wendell Phillips, which indeed I do not understand. I imagine they will not meet your and my father's views, but on the whole I am not dissatisfied with the two last in general and the last in particular. . . .

Please notice the leader in the Independent of the 24th. I did more than I expected in influencing the editorials of the Independent.

PREPARING FOR THE NEXT BATTLE:
NOVEMBER 1861

George B. McClellan to Samuel L. M. Barlow

McClellan discussed his plans in a letter to his friend Samuel Barlow, a New York lawyer and railroad executive active in Democratic politics.

My dear Samuel L. F. X. Q. Q.   Washington Nov 8 1861

Better late than never is a pretty good adage—& never better applied in this instance. I am pretty well fagged out, for it is 1 am, & as I have still more work to do, it suggested itself to me that I would refresh myself by an interlude in the way of a few words to an old friend whom I have treated shamefully. First let me thank you for that "carpet bag" which has been the companion of my woes in Western Va & here—I never shave without thinking of you, & religiously determining to write to you before the close of the day—you can therefore judge how little my promises are to be relied upon! Next let me say that that fine blanket you sent me by Van Vliet (our revered & venerable friend) shall comfort me when we advance. Speaking of an advance let me beg of you not to be impatient (I do not know that you are)—do you & all your friends trust implicitly in me—I am more anxious to advance than any other person in this country—there is no one whose interests would be so much subserved by prompt success as myself.

I feel however that the issue of this struggle is to be decided by the next great battle, & that I owe it to my country & myself not to advance until I have reasonable chances in my favor. The strength of the Army of the Potomac has been vastly overrated in the public opinion. It is now strong enough & well disciplined enough to hold Washington against *any* attack—I care not in what numbers. But, leaving the necessary garrisons here, at Baltimore etc—I cannot yet move in force equal to that which the enemy probably has in my front. We are rapidly increasing in numbers & efficiency. My intention is simply this—I will pay no attention to popular clamor—quietly, & quickly as possible, make this Army strong enough & effective enough to give me a reasonable certainty that, if I am able to handle the form, I will win the first battle. I expect to fight a terrible battle—I know full well the capacity of the Generals opposed to me, for by a singular chance they were once my most intimate friends—tho' we can never meet except as mortal foes hereafter—I appreciate too the courage & discipline of the rebel troops—I believe I know the obstacles in our path. I will first be sure that I have an Army strong enough & well enough instructed to fight with reasonable chances of success—I do not ask for perfect certainty. When I am ready I will move without regard to season or weather—I can overcome *these* difficulties. I think that the interests of the country demand the "festina lente" policy. But of one thing you can rest assured—when the blow *is* struck it will be heavy, rapid, & decisive. Help me to dodge the nigger—we want nothing to do with him. *I* am fighting to preserve the integrity of the Union & the power of the Govt—on no other issue. To gain that end we cannot afford to raise up the negro question—it must be incidental & subsidiary. The Presdt is perfectly honest & is really sound on the nigger question—I will answer for it now that things go right with him. As far as you can, keep the papers & the politicians from running over me—that speech that some rascal made the other day that I did *not dare* to advance, & had said so, was a lie—I have always said, when it was necessary to say anything, that I was not yet strong enough—but, did the public service require it, I would *dare* to advance with 10,000 men & throw my life in the balance.

I have said enough for tonight—& must go back to my work. I hope some time next week to have a review of from 30,000 to 50,000 good troops—can you not bring Madame on to it? If you come alone I can certainly accommodate you in my new house (that once occupied by Bayard Smith, corner of H & 15th)—I *think* I will have my ménage so arranged within two days that I shall be glad to have *her* come too. Telegraph me whether she can accompany you, & I will frankly reply whether my *cook* is ready—I *think* I can have everything ready for it. Do write to me often, & don't get mad if I delay replies—for I am rather busy.

Ever your sincere friend
Geo B McClellan

All this is confidential.

I think that it is now best to resign the Presidency of the O & M—Qu'en pensez vous? Do come on here & see me.

BATTLE OF BELMONT:
MISSOURI, NOVEMBER 1861

Ulysses S. Grant to Jesse Root Grant

Ulysses S. Grant assumed command in early September of the Union forces at Cairo, Illinois, at the junction of the Ohio and Mississippi rivers. On November 7 he led 3,000 men in a raid on the Confederate camp at Belmont, Missouri.

Cairo, November 8th 1861

Dear Father,

It is late at night and I want to get a letter into the Mail for you before it closes. As I have just finished a very hasty letter to Julia that contains about what I would write, and having something els to do myself, I will have my clerk copy it on to this.

Day before yesterday, I left here with about 3000 men in five steamers, convoyed by two Gun Boats, and proceeded down the river, to within about twelve miles of Columbus. The next morning the Boats were dropped down just out of range of the enemies Batteries, and the troops debarked—

During this operation our Gun-Boats exercised the rebels by throwing shells into their Camps and Batteries—

When all ready we proceeded about one mile towards Belmont opposite Columbus: where I formed the troops into lines, and ordered two Companies from each Regiment to deploy as skirmishers, and push on through the woods and discover the position of the enemy. They had gone but a little way when they were fired upon and the *Ball* may be said to have fairly opened.

The whole command with the exception of a small reserve, were then deployed in like manner with the first, and ordered forward. The order was obeyed with great alacrity, the men all showing great courage. I can say with gratification that every Colonel without a single exception, set an example to their commands that inspired a confidence that will always insure victory when there is the slightest possibility of gaining one. I feel truly proud to command such men. From here we fought our way from tree to tree through the woods to Belmont, about 2 1/2 miles, the enemy contesting every foot of ground. Here the enemy had strengthened their position by felling the trees for two or three hundred yards, and sharpening the limbs making a sort of Abattis. Our men charged through making the victory complete, giving us possession of their Camp and Garrison Equipage Artillery and every thing else.

We got a great many prisoners, the majority however succeeded in getting aboard their Steamers, and pushing across the river We burned every thing possible and started back having accomplished all that we went for, and even more. Belmont is entirely covered by the Batteries from Columbus and is worth nothing as a Military Position. Cannot be held without Columbus

The object of the expedition was to prevent the enemy from sending a force into Missouri to cut off troops I had sent there for a special purpose, and to prevent reinforcing Price

Besides being well fortified at Columbus their numbers far exceed ours, and it would have been folly to have attacked them. We found the Confederates well armed and brave. On our return stragglers that had been left in our rear, *now front*, fired into us and more recrossed the river and gave us Battle for full a mile and afterwards at the Boats when we were embarking. There was no hasty retreating or running away. Taking into account the object of the expedition the victory was most complete. It has given me a confidence in the Officers and men of this command, that will enable me to lead them in any future engagement without fear of the result. Genl. McClernand, (who by the way acted with great coolness and courage throughout, and proved that he is a soldier as well as statesman) and my self each had our Horses shot under us. Most of the Field Officers met with the same loss, besides nearly one third of them being Killed or wounded themselves. As near as I can ascertain our loss was about 250 Killed wounded and missing   I write in great haste to get this in the Office tonight

U. S. GRANT

A DOCTOR AT BELMONT:
MISSOURI, NOVEMBER 1861

Lunsford P. Yandell Jr. to Lunsford Yandell Sr.

The fighting at Belmont cost each side more than 600 men killed, wounded, or missing. A surgeon from Kentucky serving with the Confederate army, Lunsford Yandell Jr. wrote about the battle to his father, a prominent Louisville physician.

COLUMBUS, November 10.

MY DEAR FATHER: I know you have been impatient to hear from me since news reached you of the battle, but I have not had time till this morning. Thursday morning two gunboats, with five steamboats, landed six or eight miles above us on the Missouri shore, and were seen to disembark infantry, artillery, and cavalry in large numbers. Troops were thrown across from our side of the river about eight or nine o'clock, and about eleven o'clock the battle commenced and raged till three or four o'clock P.M. The gunboats came down within range of our camp and commenced throwing shot and shell about eight o'clock. One or two shots fell inside our line—one piece near my tent. Hamilton's artillery replied to the boats, and they soon moved out of range, when Captain Stewart, with his Parrott guns, went two miles up the bluff and opened on the boats. Most of his guns threw over the boats, and the enemy's balls did not reach us. Adjutant Hammond and I were with Captain Stewart, and helped the men to place the guns in position a number of times. They were just going to fire one of the guns, when Hammond and I retired some ten or twelve yards. The gun was fired—the explosion was terrific—and some one yelled out "Two men killed!" I rushed up immediately and saw at once that they were killed. The gun had exploded into a thousand atoms. One of the men had his right arm torn to pieces, and the ribs on that side pulpified, though the skin was not broken. He breathed half an hour. The other poor fellow received a piece of iron under the chin, which passed up into the brain—the blood gushing from his nose and ears. He never breathed afterward. A third man received a slight wound of the arm. The fragments of the gun flew in every direction, and I can only wonder that more of us were not killed. A horse hitched near mine received a glancing wound from a piece of the gun.

Our brigade was ordered under arms about noon—or rather, it was kept under arms all the morning, but I was ordered across the river about noon. Our men were previously anxious to be led over soon in the morning; but Gen. Polk would not allow it, as he expected an attack from this side of the river—which was certainly the plan of the enemy, but it was not carried out.

We did not get on the ground till the enemy were in full retreat, and we never got near them; in fact, only one regiment of our brigade pursued them at all, and they only for a mile or two. I went with Col. Scott's regiment, belonging to Col. Neeley's brigade. When about two miles out we were ordered back, as the enemy had reached his boats. I had fifty or eighty men detailed from Scott's regiment to scour the woods with me to pick up the wounded. We found none but Federals, but they were in such numbers we could only take back a few and return for the others. In one cornfield they were lying, dead and wounded, as thick as stumps in a new field. I saw sixty or seventy, and others report as many as two hundred in this field. They were mostly of the Sixth Iowa regiment, and some of the Twenty-seventh Illinois. The Lieutenant-Colonel and three captains I know to have been killed, or wounded and taken prisoners. The Seventh Iowa was almost annihilated. The scene upon the battle-field was awful.

The wounded men groaned and moaned, yelled and shrieked with pain. I had opium, brandy, and water, with which I alleviated their torture, and, poor creatures, they were exceedingly grateful. I was out until two o'clock that night with Col. Neeley and a battalion of the Fourth regiment picking up the wounded. In the woods and in the field the dead were so thick that it required careful riding to keep from tramping their bodies. The only means I had of knowing the road that night was by the corpses I had noticed in the afternoon. In one place there were eleven bodies lying side by side; further on were five; in another place were fifteen near together. These were the only groups that I noticed, but I sometimes found six or eight within a space of twenty yards. Some of the poor creatures had crawled to the foot of trees, and laid their heads upon the roots and crossed their arms; others lay upon their backs with arms and legs outstretched; some were doubled up, and, in fact, they were in every imaginable position. As to the variety of expression depicted upon the faces of the corpses, of which I heard so much, I saw nothing of it. They all looked pretty much alike—as much alike as dead men from any other cause. Some had their eyes open, some closed; some had their mouths open, and others had them closed. There is a terrible sameness in the appearance of all the dead men I have ever seen. The only faces which were disfigured were those that were burned, or shot, or blackened with powder.

There were not many wounds from cannon balls or shells, but I saw almost every variety of wounds from musket and rifle balls. I saw almost all the battle from our camp, which is on top of the high bluff. The Missouri side is low and flat, and much of the battle-ground is open. The battle swayed back and forth many times. Once our men were driven clear under the river bank, having got out of cartridges. For several hours General Pillow held the enemy in check with two thousand men, the enemy having seven thousand infantry, four hundred and fifty cavalry, and I don't recollect their artillery. Pillow acted with great bravery. So did Polk and Cheatham, but they were not in the fight for several hours after Pillow. Pillow's escape is miraculous. Every one of his staff officers had his horse shot under him. One of them, Gus. Henry, had two shot under him. One of his aids was shot through the hip, and his horse was riddled with balls. Pillow wore a splendid uniform, very conspicuous, and rode the handsomest gray mare in the army. As we watched the fighting from the bluff, and saw our men advance and retreat, waver and fall back, and then saw the Arkansas troops' tents on fire, and the Stars and Stripes advancing toward the river, and some of our men crowding down to the very water's edge, I tell you my feelings were indescribable. The scene was grand, but it was terrible, and when I closed my eyes about four o'clock next morning, I could see regiments charging and retreating—men falling and yelling—horses and men torn and mangled—and myriads of horrid spectacles. It was a bloody enjoyment, but we do not know the loss on either side yet.

It is roughly estimated that we lost two hundred and fifty in killed, wounded, and missing, and the enemy five hundred in killed and wounded. An immense number of horses were killed. I rode over the battle-field yesterday. For several miles the trees are torn and barked by balls, and many horses lie upon the ground, some torn open by shells and others riddled by balls. You can see innumerable stains of blood upon the ground. Where poor, gallant Armstrong was killed, there were eleven dead bodies. At the time of his death, he had a cap upon his sword waving it, rallying his men. My friend Captain Billy Jackson was shot in the hip while leading a portion of Russell's brigade. I think he will recover. I am afraid Jimmy Walker (James' son) will not recover. I think he is shot through the rectum.

The day before the battle, Jackson, Major Butler, of the Eleventh Louisiana regiment, Wilson, of Watson's battery, Lieut. Ball, of same regiment, and Major Gus. Henry, and myself dined at Gen. Pillow's. Butler was shot through and died yesterday. Lieut. Ball was dangerously injured, and Henry had two horses shot under him. Jackson I have spoken of. I have given you but a poor account of what I saw, but I have not time to go more into details now, and I am out of kelter besides. You will see a full account in the papers of the fight. I wish the war would close. Such scenes as that of Thursday are sickening; and this destruction of life is so useless. I believe we shall have some terrible fighting very soon on the coast, in Virginia and in Kentucky. Much love to mother and sister when you see them. Mr. Law gave me the letter.

I am your devoted son,

LUNSFORD P. YANDELL.

November 10, 1861

THE CAPTURE OF PORT ROYAL:
SOUTH CAROLINA, NOVEMBER 1861

Samuel Francis Du Pont to Sophie Du Pont

A career naval officer who had served in the U.S.-Mexican War, Captain Samuel Francis Du Pont commanded the fleet that captured the forts guarding Port Royal Sound on November 7. His victory gave the Union possession of an excellent natural harbor that served as a base for the squadron blockading the coast from South Carolina to Florida. In a letter to his wife Du Pont described the abandoned plantations of the region, now occupied by troops under the command of General Thomas W. Sherman (no relation to William T. Sherman).

———————

Wabash, Port Royal, 13 Nov. 1861

My precious Sophie,

I sent a letter by that hard-named steamer, the *Coatzacoalcos* —in a very bad condition, by the way.

Yesterday I made an excursion in the *Seneca* to Beaufort, seventeen miles from this anchorage up the Beaufort River. The scenery, owing to the cabbage palm, is tropical; the mansions of the planters and the Negro quarters, more or less prominent or embowered in the trees, gave a good deal of picturesqueness to the scene. The day was lovely, though warm. General Sherman was with me; my staff, Captains Comstock and Eldridge of the *Baltic* and *Atlantic* I also invited. Ammen, the commander of the *Seneca*, is a kindly and hospitable person as well as a good officer—and had found oysters, boasting he was the only officer who had had the prévoyance to bring oyster tongs for taking them.

You approach Beaufort on its full seaward façade; the houses are two and three stories, with verandas, large, and have a beautiful effect; the streets are wide, the gardens and shrubbery in the yards show the refinements of educated people but without the order of Northern towns of this description.

And now comes, my dear, the saddest picture that you can well conceive of, an *inside* view of this nefarious secession. We landed, three gunboats covering, but in addition the armed launches of this ship we towed up, and the crews went on shore with their howitzers, and we placed pickets, to provide against a treacherous foe, or a cavalry rush, [ ] astern, not that we believed in such a thing, for the terror still continues.

Before our gunboats got up, the Negroes had commenced plundering—the stores were all rifled and looked like a sacked town; by this time our officers stopped the robbery of the private houses, though much had been carried off, in hopes the whites would return. On my asking an old blacky of Mr. Nat Heyward's, as he is called, a millionaire gentleman, why the remainder of the furniture in his handsome mansion was not carried off, he replied, "Massa, because Yankee tell 'em they shoot 'em."

A sadder picture of desolation from the *desertion* of the population cannot be imagined; and the inhabitants fled not from fear of *us* but from the dread of their own Negroes; a few household servants followed their masters, but the field hands they dare not attempt to control, and the overseers had run with the masters. There are fifteen slaves to one white in this part; the latter threatened to shoot if they did not follow them into the interior, but I believe dare not attempt to execute this threat. The Negroes, anxious to show everything, said to Captain Collins, *Unadilla*, "Massa, they more afraid us, than you"—this was often repeated. Yet these are people whose very slaves were to drive us into the sea, fleeing from the institution with terror in their hearts, not taking a thing with them—the center tables with lamps upon them, books and writing cards, safes *unopened* which had defied the strength and ingenuity of the Negroes. The latter, for want of means of carrying things, cut open all the bedding to get the ticking with which to tie up things. Such a mess. Outside the beautiful oleanders and chrysanthemums smiled on this scene of robbery and confusion.

We took all the *public* property, a fine Fresnel lens, and buoys for the channels; and General Sherman having declined holding it as a military point, and as it only absorbs my force from what is more necessary, and exposing it, when the rebels recover from their panic, to devices of fire vessels and masked batteries too far from my support, I have withdrawn the force. I regret to leave the place to the Negroes, but why should I expose my people to save the property of those who are planning their destruction and who disregard the ordinary rules of war?

Mr. *Rhett*'s house was visited, and General Drayton's headquarters—all the same aspect. On our way down we stopped at the ruins of an old Huguenot fort, built by Mons. de Ribaudiere, said to have sustained successfully an assault from a Spanish force from St. Augustine, under Philip the 2d. The outline is left—but we were rejoiced more than anything at seeing such a live-oak grove as I never saw in Florida. We walked through it, touched by the hanging moss—and came up to a large open space covered with sea-island cotton, ungathered and dropping from the pods. The Negroes were all there, their quarters were curious; two were grinding corn between two stones, the earliest form of such a process known. Some fifty bales of cotton, unginned, lay in a building. The Negroes were filthy but friendly, with scarcely any modification of the pure African feature. I had been carrying in my pocket ever since I had left New York some quarters and dimes, and I got a basket of eggs from them—the Negroes running about and gathering them in all directions; others got turkeys. All was paid for, and during the visit of the gunboats and their five days at Beaufort not an article was taken by our men, though things were laying about in all directions. *One* thing we did take, we rescued Mr. Pope's large quarto family Bible from some rubbish and furniture going into a boat. Mr. Dorrance took it to return to its owner at some future day. General Drayton's wife was a Miss Pope.

On our return we found *two* arrivals, water vessels, bringing dates to the 7th. John Goldsborough put back and seems to have *injured himself* much by so doing—he was halfway and could have come here as well as return.

I see the gale was stronger in New York than with us, and causing anxiety for us at home. I saw an absurd general order from Sherman in the *Herald* of the 6th regulating the order of sailing of his transports, etc.—after he knew we had arranged the thing, established the signals, and instructed the transport captains. Then his orders about *landing*; not one item of either could they execute.

Captains Comstock and Eldridge spoke in the warmest

terms of the battle; the gallantry and lead of this ship they dwelt on with earnestness, saying more to others than they did to me, but neither did *other* matters escape them; one of them said to Davis, "The *Susquehanna* stuck to you like wax and was a true supporter, why was the line broken off after her?" Of course this inquiry was turned off. There was no want of courage anywhere, but *entre nous*, a want of head. I think Godon was hurt at something I said, not in reference to the above but to his preventing me from using my port broadside by being in the way during a certain part of the engagement. My remark involved a compliment, by saying he wanted a fight on his *own hook*—but he connected this with the other affair, but I hope he will get over it soon.

Have you heard today of our doings? Davis and Rodgers and myself are always speculating about this, and how much of our doings reached you by the Southern papers. I forgot to tell you to get the *Herald* for the accounts. It will be more full and more friendly.

We are busy tinkering up the engines—some of them are very worthless. Firing off the harbor this morning; I have sent out *Seneca* to see what it means. Probably *Augusta* chasing a vessel off Savannah.

Our Marine battalion was established on Bay Point—they behaved well during the gale on the *Governor*, for which they deserve credit, for it showed *moral* courage, so rare with that class of people; the people of the *Governor* behaved very badly.

8 o'clock. My dearest Sophie, the *Florida* is in and I have your dear letter by her—it was a great treat; though another whole week you will have to have passed before you were relieved by the news from us, except what will have oozed out from the Southern account. Your account of the intensity of interest in the expedition also struck me much and I read some paragraphs of it to Davis and Rodgers. A letter of great interest from Turner conveys the same thing from Philadelphia. But my! What would this have produced if we had not been successful? Drayton thinks the blow was the severest that could have been struck in the whole South—and, in my judgment, far beyond the capture of Charleston or Savannah, for in neither could we have got ships of all sizes. Strange that more vessels are here now than ever entered before in all time!—to

say nothing of the size. One of the finest harbors in the world, it possesses, besides, what we call the roadstead.

I send in the morning the gunboats up to Beaufort, General Sherman writing to a clergyman who has asked protection and wants to send an officer to Port Royal Ferry, three or four miles from Beaufort, and I do not think it prudent to send one boat alone.

I got newspapers in abundance up to the 9th but have not time scarcely to read them. I was sorry for Goldsborough but he bore his disappointment like a man—he was boarded from the *San Jacinto* and told of Mason and Slidell being on board!

15 Nov. 1861 Friday. My dearest Sophie, we are overwhelmed here by events. Yesterday the *Rhode Island*, Trenchard, from the Gulf and now today the *Connecticut*, Woodhull, from New York and Hampton Roads—passed the *Bienville* going into latter place on Tuesday morning a few hours earlier than I thought. I have three letters from you and two notes, Nos. 11, 12, and 13, and though they came this morning I have only read one of them—so great is the pressure upon me of the official correspondence. I only got up on deck once today, for ten minutes after tea, to breathe the fresh air, and yet nothing I like so well as to go there and look at the ships in the harbor and dwell on the wonderful change a few days have wrought in one of the finest harbors in the known world.

The *Atlantic* goes at daylight and McKinley is copying the last of my *detailed* account of our battle—it has given me great labor, but it is accomplished and I feel relieved from its incubus. Davis, who has been on shore on Hilton Head side for the first time, thinks our achievement much greater than he did before seeing the fort and does not wonder that Generals Drayton and Ripley felt sure of destroying us.

I have received all you sent me—the pants, tablecloths, books, and before that the map by Goldsborough's ship. How kind you are—all these things are very acceptable to me and they make me to think of your devotion. I received the *North American* with the notice of the expedition and of myself, and I am free to confess that it is the first time in my life that a newspaper panegyric gratified me. I don't mean of course that I felt that I deserved it all, but its taste and sentiment were so much above those notices generally, and so free from vulgar puffing that it touched me sensibly. The portrait in *Harper's Weekly* is the most miserable of all likenesses I ever saw. But, my dear Sophie, I agree with you—we are not chastened yet by this war as we should be; it is fearful to think how God might chastise us and yet fall short of what we deserve.

This vaingloriousness is bad, and when I see what a reverse would have been to us, however unavoidable, under such absurd expectations, it makes me shrink from men and turn to God with a thankful heart.

In your last you express very properly one of the dangers I am liable to, viz., yielding my own judgment to pressure from without, or to meet exaggerated expectations—but I have had the moral courage to resist this already. Had I engaged Wednesday afternoon when the wind subsided, we should have been discomfited for that day certainly. But I said to myself, as I wrote you I think, if no troops were present, I never should put the thing in question; it would be so wrong—and I determined to do what was right. I knew a success would wipe away all the misgivings of the class who doubt everybody, and these were loudest afterwards in my praise.

Thank Eleu for her pincushion. Write to Peter Kemble I have the shirts and thank him much. I have not time to write to him by this mail. Please also ask Peter to do me the favor to purchase an opera nautical spyglass, the best he can find in New York, to go as high as $25 or $30—perhaps Pike's would be a good place—and to send it to me by Captain Eldridge on the return of the steamer *Atlantic*; and apologize for my troubling him, though from his kind letter I am sure it will give him pleasure. Mr. George W. Blunt also knows about such glasses.

I was glad to see Henry had been to Washington. I will begin soon another letter and note things in yours. I have to write a report about Beaufort. Sherman's flag of truce ended in nothing but being received with hauteur. I think he ought not to have issued a proclamation without showing it to me. I like him, but I think he has one or two intrigants with him who are jealous of us. I hope Sherman will come up to a commander in chief's requirements.

If we were to withdraw the moral effect and physical force of this squadron, I think he and his army would be prisoners of war in one month from this time.

Love to all; I long to hear how our work is received. I see the New York *Times* of 10 November, in his Washington correspondent, says the public will be disappointed in the place.

Every day convinces me it was the point of all others to strike, not *at all* excepting Savannah or Charleston.

Please get me some nice paper of the best quality when you go to Philadelphia, and note and letter, and stubbedy pen—envelopes of all sizes except the long official ones.

Good night and love to all, dearest. Ever your own devoted,
F.

Missroon came in today, not his ship, and I posted him up about Savannah; he looks very well and happy.

A FORMER SLAVE REMEMBERS:
SOUTH CAROLINA, NOVEMBER 1861

Sam Mitchell: Narrative of the capture of the Sea Islands

Sam Mitchell, an eleven-year-old boy tending cows on a plantation on Lady's Island, was one of the thousands of slaves liberated by the Union victory at Port Royal. In a 1937 interview with the Federal Writers' Project of the Works Progress Administration, Mitchell, now eighty-seven, recalled the arrival of Du Pont's ships and the sudden flight of his owner, John Chaplin.

Maussa had nine chillen, six boy been in Rebel army. Dat Wednesday in November w'en gun fust shoot to Bay Pint (Point) I t'ought it been t'under rolling, but dey ain't no cloud. My mother say, 'son, dat ain't no t'under, dat Yankee come to gib you Freedom.' I been so glad, I jump up and down and run. My father been splitting rail and Maussa come from Beaufort in de carriage and tear by him yelling for de driver. He told de driver to git his eight-oar boat name Tarrify and carry him to Charleston. My father he run to his house and tell my mother w'at Maussa say. My mother say, 'You ain't gonna row no boat to Charleston, you go out dat back door and keep a-going. So my father he did so and w'en dey git 'nuf nigger to row boat and Maussa and his family go right away to Charleston.

After Freedom come everybody do as he please. De Yankee open school for nigger and teacher lib in Maussa house to Brickyaa'd. My father git job as carpenter wid Yankee and buy ten acre ob land on Ladies Island.

Did I ebber hear ob Abraham Lincoln? I got his history right here in my house. He was de president of de United

States that freed four million slave. He come to Beaufort befo' de war and et dinner to Col. Paul Hamilton house at de Oaks. He left his gold-headed walking cane dere and ain't nobody know de president of de United States been to Beaufort 'till he write back and tell um to look behind de door and send um his gold-headed walking cane.

A CONFEDERATE SERMON:
GEORGIA, NOVEMBER 1861

Henry Tucker: God in the War

November 15, 1861

Tucker, a Baptist minister, delivered this sermon before the Georgia legislature in the state capitol at Milledgeville.

SERMON.

"Come behold the works of the Lord, what desolations He hath made in the earth.

He maketh wars to cease unto the end of the earth; He breaketh the bow, and cutteth the spear in sunder; He burneth the chariot in the fire."

PSALMS XLVI, 8:9.

Desolation! Desolation! Thousands of our young men have been murdered. Thousands of fathers and mothers among us have been bereaved of their sons. Thousands of widows are left disconsolate and heart-broken, to struggle through life alone. The wail of thousands of orphans is heard through the land, the Ægis of a father's protection being removed from over their defenceless heads. Thousands of brave men are at this moment lying on beds of languishing, some prostrated by the diseases incident to the army and camp, and some by cruel wounds. Every house within reach of the seat of war is a hospital, and every hospital is crowded. Huge warehouses emptied of their merchandize, and churches, and great barns, are filled with long rows of pallets beside each other, containing each a sufferer, pale, emaciated and ghastly. Some writhe with pain; some rage with delirium; some waste with fever; some speak of *home*, and drop bitter tears at the recollection of wives soon to be widows, and babes soon to be fatherless. The nurse hurries with noiseless step, ministering from bedside to bedside. The pious chaplain whispers of Jesus to the dying. The surgeon is in frightful practice, bloody though beneficent; and as his knife glides through the quivering flesh and his saw grates through the bone and tears through the marrow, the suppressed groan bears witness to the anguish. A father stands by perhaps, to see his son mutilated. Mother and wife and sisters at home witness the scene by a dreadful clairvoyance, and with them the operation lasts not for moments but for weeks. Every groan in the hospital or tent, or on the bloody field, wakes echoes at home. There is not a city, nor village, nor hamlet, nor neighborhood that has not its representatives in the army, and scarcely a heart in our whole Confederacy that is not either bruised by strokes already fallen, or pained by a solicitude scarcely less dreadful than the reality. Desolation! Desolation! Hearts desolate, homes desolate, the whole land desolate! Our young men, our brave young men, our future statesmen, and scholars and divines, to whom we should bequeath this great though youthful empire with all its destinies; the flower of our society,—contributions from that genuine and proper aristocracy which consists of intelligence and virtue,—thousands, thousands of them laid upon the altar! And alas! the end is not yet. Another six months may more than double the desolation. Relentless winter may aid the enemy in his work of death. The youth accustomed at home to shelter, and bed, and fire, and all the comforts of high civilization, standing guard on wintry night, exposed to freezing rain and pealing blasts, and having completed his doleful task, retiring to his tent, to lie upon the bare ground, in clothes encrusted with ice, may not falter in *spirit* in view of his hardships; the fires of patriotism may still keep up the warmth at his heart; when he remembers that he is fighting for the honor of his father, and for the purity of his mother and sisters, and for all that is worth having in the world, he may cheerfully brave the terrors of a winter campaign; but though his soul be undaunted, his body will fail. Next spring when the daisies begin to blow, thousands of little hillocks dotted all over the country on mountain side and in valley, marked at each end with a rough memorial stone, and a brief and rude inscription made perhaps with the point of a bayonet, will silently but ah! how impressively, confirm the sad prophecy of this hour. Thus the work of desolation may go on winter after winter, until the malice of our foes is satiated, and until our young men are all gone. But let us not anticipate. The present alone presents subjects of contemplation, enough to fill the imagination and to break the heart.

These are the desolations of war. Do you ask why I present this sad, this melancholy picture? Why I make this heart-rending recital of woes enough to make heaven weep? In so doing I am but following the example of the Psalmist when he says, "Come behold the works of the Lord, what *desolations* He hath made in the earth!" If in the midst of victory when the God of Israel had given success to the arms of his people, their leader and king called upon them to forget their successes and meditate on the desolations of war, it must be right for the man of God now, to call upon his countrymen in the midst of a series of victories such as perhaps were never won in a war before, to forget their triumphs, and contemplate for a little the expense of life and of sorrow which those triumphs have cost.

Come then my countrymen, and behold the desolation. What emotion does it excite? What passion does it stimulate? To what action does it prompt? Indignation at the fanaticism, folly and sin of those who brought it all about. Rage at the authors of our ruin. Retaliation! To arms! To arms! Let us kill! Let us destroy! Let us exterminate the miscreants from the earth! Up with the black flag! They deserve no quarter! They alone are to blame for this horror of horrors. We had no hand in bringing it on. We asked for nothing but our rights. Our desire was for peace. They tormented us without cause while we were with them. What we cherish as a heaven-ordained institution they denounce as the "sum of all villainies." They regarded us as worse than heathen and pirates; they degraded us from all equality; they spurned us from all fellowship; they taught their children to hate us; their ministers of religion chased us like bloodhounds, actually putting weapons of death in the hands of their agents with instructions to murder us. They made a hero and a martyr of him, who at Harper's Ferry openly avowed his design, to enact over in all our land the horrid scenes of St. Domingo,—thus by the popular voice dooming us to death and our wives and daughters to worse than death; and when after these outrages, we sought no retaliation but besought them to let us go in peace, they still clutched us with frantic grasp, in order to filch away our substance, and reduce us to a bondage more degrading than that which they affect to pity in the negro.

I will not continue to give expression to thoughts which alas! have already taken too deep hold on us all. But in the midst of all the rage, resentment, and fury, which a contemplation of these facts of history is calculated to engender, let me repeat to you the words of the text, with an emphasis which perhaps will lift your minds above the consideration of second causes. "Come behold the works of the *Lord*, what desolations *He* hath made in the earth!" If it be important to regard the desolations of war, it is still more so, to be mindful of the source whence they come. This perhaps was the chief object of the Psalmist. If he pointed to the rod, it was that all hearts should be turned towards Him who held it. And this my countrymen it is all important for *us* to remember,—that GOD is in the war. *He* brought it upon us. The wickedness and folly of our enemies may have been the *occasion* of it, but these could not in any proper sense be the *cause*. That is but a shallow philosophy which sees a cause in anything outside of God. The idea of cause involves by necessity the idea of power, and what power is there independent of God? Aside from the will of God, what nexus can there be, between an effect and the antecedent which by a sad misnomer we denominate the cause? Satisfied with a slovenly nomenclature, we apply the term cause to that in which there resides no power. That profounder wisdom which we learn from the inspired oracles demands a better vocabulary; it calls for a word to designate the cause of so-called causes. In want of this, it disallows to earthly antecedents even if invariable, a name which describes that which is to be found only in the Almighty. The guilt of our enemies is what we term a *second* cause, that is to say, it is no cause at all, but only the occasion of a chastisement inflicted by an Almighty arm. God is in the war. God is in everything; in the doings of earth, for "He knoweth our downsitting and our uprising;" in the raptures of paradise, in the flames of perdition. Yea saith the Psalmist, "If I ascend up into heaven Thou art there. If I make my bed in hell, behold Thou art there!" *Psalms* cxxxix, 8.

In the economy of God the wicked are often used as instruments for the accomplishment of divine ends. Satan, when he introduced sin into the world, was the instrument of preparing the way for a brighter display of God's goodness than ever yet had amazed the universe, and was as really the herald of Jesus of Nazareth as was John the Baptist. Those who cried out "Crucify him! crucify him! his blood be upon us and upon our children!" all guilty as they were;—in piercing the veins of a Savior opened the fountain of eternal life to the millions of them who shall be redeemed unto God by his blood, out of every kindred and tongue and people and nation.*

Thus does God cause the wrath of man to praise him. If there be any possible wrath, such as could not by divine almightiness, be so perverted from its wicked end as to promote the glory and exhibit the goodness of God, that remainder of wrath is restrained. In other words, sin is allowed only in so far as God brings good out of it. Thus every evil is the precursor of blessing. The greatest calamities that ever befel the Universe were but the harbingers of glory.

A christian poet has said

> We should suspect some danger nigh
> When we possess delight.

Thank God it is also true, that whenever evil comes, we may know there is good at hand. In national or in individual experience, when the godless soul sees only a dark cloud, fraught with terror and with wrath, to the christian the cloud resolves itself into a blazing star that guides to the best of blessings. When God says to his children "All things work together for good to them that love God," the heart of the believer makes no exceptions, and thus "rejoices in tribulations, also."

It is also a part of the divine economy to use the wicked as instruments for the chastisement of each other.—Two individuals indulge in mutual animosity. Each is wrong; and each by a series of unkindnesses, or acts that deserve a harsher name, inflicts upon the other a well deserved penalty. Neighborhoods give way to ill-will.—Nothing short of a miracle could prevent

---

*Many parallel cases might be referred to; for an interesting one see Gen. 45. 6.

them from distressing each other; and Providence works no such miracle. Nations burn with hate against nations, and as an appropriate punishment for their crimes God turns them loose upon each other, and their perpetual wars result in mutual ruin. History, profane as well as sacred, is full of examples where "Nation was destroyed of nation, and city of city; for God did vex them with all adversity." 2 Chron. xv. 5.

Even in the control of his own children God makes use of the wicked as his instruments of discipline. When Israel did evil in the sight of the Lord, the inspired record declares that "The Lord delivered them into the hand of Midian; and the hand of Midian prevailed against Israel; and Israel was impoverished because of the Midianites." Judges vi. 6. Individual experience too, may often make appropriate the prayer of David when he says "Deliver my soul from the wicked, *which is thy sword*; from men *which are thy hand*." Ps. xvii. 13.

The sin of the wicked is not diminished by the fact that it is over-ruled for good by a superior power. There can be no interference with the personal responsibility of moral creatures. Thus the guilt of those who wage this diabolical war on the unoffending people of these Confederate States, finds no apology in the providence of God. "It must needs be that offences come but woe unto him by whom they come." Luke xvii. 1. Our aggressors must answer for their awful account before the bar of God.—There let us leave them. Our text which was written when the death-smell was fresh on the field of battle, makes no reference to the outrages of the enemy, but points only to God, as the author of the desolation. The Psalmist does not confound the cause of trouble with the occasion of it. He is engrossed, not with the doings of earth, but with those of heaven. He has no eyes to see the wickedness of his foes. He forgets he ever had a foe, and sees only God in the war. Let his example be for our imitation. Surely it is as contrary to religion as it is to a sound philosophy to banish God from the most striking act of his Providence that has occurred within the memory of living man. If it be true then that the hand of God is in this thing (and who can doubt it?) and if we lose sight of that fact, surely a worse evil will come upon us. Among other evils, we may expect to receive in our own souls the consequences of our sin. Resentment, rage, and hate, will be so developed as to take entire possession of us. We shall become blood-thirsty as tigers, cruel as death, and malicious as fiends. All that we expect to accomplish by the war, if bought at such expense to our own character, would cost more than it is worth. If we cannot be free without transforming ourselves into devils, it were better not to be free; for any thraldom is to be preferred before slavery to sin. But if we exclude God from our thoughts, and regard the desolations around us as coming only from the enemy, how is it possible to keep from violating the injunction "avenge not yourselves!" Whose blood would not be set on fire, whose soul would not be carried away with fiercest passions, by contemplation of the frightful evils we sustain, if they be traced to no cause outside the wicked hearts of our enemies! Alas, all of us are too prone to confine our attention to second causes. Methinks I see the apparition of the spirit of David rising from the sleep of centuries, as that of Samuel did under the incantations of the witch of Endor. His form is venerable, his beard is flowing, and on his brow rests the crown of Israel. He touches the harp of solemn sound, and peals forth the notes of the sublime ode whence our text is taken. He waves his hand to the scenes of sorrow wrought by the war now upon us, and making no allusion to our foes, says "Come behold the works of the Lord, what desolations He hath made in the earth!"

When we regard the evils we suffer as the chastisement of the Almighty, there arises within us no spirit of resentment. The fiercer elements of our nature all subside.—We humbly submit to the judgments of the Almighty. Our eyes instead of flashing fire, are melted to tears; our tongues instead of curses and defiance, utter words of penitence and contrition. Whatever comes from God we can bear. We acknowledge his authority. We know that at *his* hands we deserve nothing but indignation and wrath, tribulation and anguish. We know that he is a gracious Father as well as a righteous judge; and we recognise his benevolence even in his chastisements; for "whom the Lord loveth he chasteneth." We only say "It is the Lord, let him do as seemeth him good." Surely this is a better spirit than results from a view of second causes. Surely this is more likely to secure the divine approbation and the divine aid; and if God be for us who can be against us? This is the very spirit which his chastisements are intended to excite; and when the end is accomplished the means will be laid aside. Thus shall war afflict us no more, and God will not allow "the wicked which is his sword" to harm us further. But that other spirit which instead of forgetting the enemy and looking to God, reverses the order and forgetting God looks to the enemy, and which stimulates to frenzy the worst passions known to human nature, tends only to make us more wicked than we were before, and therefore to perpetuate the very causes which made these chastisements necessary. If instead of profiting by the afflictions which God sends upon us, we make them the occasions of additional guilt, what can we expect but that billow after billow of his wrath will overtake us until we shall be utterly destroyed.

The sweet singer of Israel having depicted the desolations which God sends by war, devotes the next strain of his inspired verse to the announcement of the truth that "He maketh wars to *cease* unto the end of the earth." It is He who brings these evils upon us and it is He who takes them away. Nor is it needless for the Psalmist to remind us of what we might have known, that the blessings of peace are from the hand of the Almighty. Here too as in the former case, we are prone to be satisfied with second causes. We are anxious for wise legislation and for skillful generalship. We congratulate ourselves on having such able statesmen as Davis and Stephens, such able generals as Johnston and Beauregard. We glory in the belief that our troops are as brave as the bravest in the world, and that our enemies though outnumbering us four to one as they did at Leesburg, cannot stand before Southern valor in the open field for one moment. We exult (alas! our exultation is not unmixed with sin) when we see the terror-stricken fugitives leaping by hundreds over the steep embankment, and like devil-possessed swine plunging headlong into the Potomac. We are making abundant arrangements to supply ourselves with all the munitions of war. We are casting cannon, manufacturing arms, and fortifying our coasts. Hundreds of thousand of us are already under arms, and hundreds of thousands more are ready and anxious to step into the ranks. We feel safe when we remember that we are so many and so strong, and so brave, and so well prepared to re-enact the scenes of Sumter, and Bethel, and Manassas, and Springfield, and Lexington, and Leesburg, and Columbus. We feel sure that if the enemy will only give us battle once more on the Potomac, our brave boys will again send them shrieking and screaming back to their Northern homes. We doubt not that we shall whip them whenever we come in conflict with them. We shall whip them, and whip them, and whip them again. We shall whip them again and again. We shall whip them until they are satisfied to their hearts' content, that the only safety for themselves is in letting us alone.

My countrymen! it is right for us to resort to all the means of defence which Providence has placed within our reach. It is proper to call into action our best civil and military talent, to strain every energy to the utmost in supplying the material of war. As for that sublime faith which we have in the unconquerable valor of our troops, I admire it, I partake in it. But we are here on dangerous ground. We must not step over the line where God says "Thus far shalt thou go, and no farther." Let us not lean on an arm of flesh. Saith the prophet, "Cease ye from man whose breath is in his nostrils, for wherein is he to be accounted of." Isa. ii. 22. Is our confidence in our success based on the wisdom of our statesmen and generals? That Providence which sustains the flight of the sparrow and numbers the hairs of our head might direct the death-bringing bullet to the vitals of our greatest chieftain. Instead of the horse, the rider might have been slain. "It is better to trust in the Lord than to put confidence in man. It is better to trust in the Lord than to put confidence in Princes." Ps. cxviii. 8–9. Is our trust in the valor of our troops? The same God who struck terror into the hearts of the Midianites when they heard the cry "The sword of the Lord and of Gideon!" the same God who sent confusion and dismay into the ranks of our enemies when the sword of the Lord and of the South prevailed at Manassas, might send a panic among *us* which would scatter us like chaff before the wind. He might send his angels in armies to descend upon us, and filling the air with their unseen presence, every heart might quiver with undefinable dread from unknown cause, and they might smite us with invisible weapons, the very touch of which would curdle our blood. Oh! there is no bravery that can stand before the hosts of the living God. The outward appliances of war, the chieftains and captains, the arms and munitions, the shot and shell, the rifles, infantry, artillery, cavalry, all these are useful in their proper places. But let us not put our confidence in them. They are not to be trusted.—They all may fail. They never yet have made a war to cease. This is the very sentiment of the scripture which says "There is no King saved by the multitude of an host; a mighty man is not delivered by much strength. An horse is a vain thing for safety, neither shall he deliver any by his great strength. Behold the eye of the Lord is upon them that *fear* him!" Ps. xxxiii. 16. "Battle is the Lord's." 2 Chron. xx. 15. "He shall cut off the spirit of princes; he is terrible to the kings of the earth. At thy rebuke O God of Jacob both the chariot and the horse are cast into a dead sleep." Ps. lxxvi. 6–12. "He maketh wars to cease unto the end of the earth!" So earnest is the Psalmists in declaring that the ending of the war as well as the beginning of it is from God, that he reiterates the sentiment four times in the text. First in literal terms, "he maketh wars to cease;" then in figure of speech "he breaketh the bow;" again in similar figure, "he cutteth the spear in sunder;" and for the fourth time he enunciates the same idea in another figure when he says, "he burneth the chariot in the fire." The destruction of the bow, the spear, and the chariot, ancient instruments of war, was a symbolical way of describing peace. The figurative expressions then, mean the same as that which is literal; and if this portion of the ode were stripped of its poetic dress and expressed in plainest terms, it would be simply a fourfold declaration of a single truth. "He maketh wars to cease! *He maketh wars to cease*! HE MAKETH WARS TO CEASE! HE MAKETH WARS TO CEASE unto the end of the earth!" Let this tremendous energy of quadruple emphasis, be for the rebuke, and discomfiture and silencing of those who look to earthly sources for the power to stop this awful war. Ye worshippers of human Deities, who by supposing that the efforts of mortals can terminate the bloody strife, exalt the creature to a level with omnipotence, listen to the voice of the Almighty! "Be still and know that *I* am God! I will be exalted among the heathen, I will be exalted in the earth!"

While it is true that we need constant admonition to wean us from trust in human resources and lift our thoughts to a higher Power, yet it is also a fact, and one most gratifying to the christian, that thus far in the war, there has been a wonderful turning of the hearts of the people to God.—When Col. Hill wrote to the Governor of North Carolina that the Lord of Hosts had given us the victory at Bethel, he spoke the sentiment of the whole army. Our soldiers, from the highest officer to the humblest private in the ranks, habitually ascribe our victories to God. Even the irreligious seem to pause for a moment when they speak of Bethel or Manassas, and reverently acknowledge God in the battle. So universally does this feeling pervade our troops that it excites the wonder of all who have had an opportunity of observing it. When Mr. Memminger introduced into the Confederate Congress the ever-memorable and sublime resolutions ascribing the victory of the 21st of July to the King of kings and Lord of lords, a thrill of acquiescence and hearty appreciation flashed over the whole Confederacy, and the hearts of all the people were melted together. When the news reached this Legislative Hall only day before yesterday, that the Providence of God had brought across the ocean to our shores a ship laden with weapons of defence, and shoes for our feet, and other articles of necessity and comfort, the Representatives of the people here assembled, almost unanimously and simultaneously fell to their knees, and while tears of gratitude streamed from many a cheek, and amid a wide spread murmur of scarcely suppressed sobs, their presiding officer as the spokesman of the Assembly, offered up to God a tribute of prayer and thanksgiving!—Oh! that was a thrilling spectacle, and on which doubtless angels looked with beaming eyes and a new delight. Surely such a scene never occurred before. The record has been entered on the Journal and is now a chronicle of the times. Posterity will read it centuries hence with moistening eyes. Heartstrings will quiver and bosoms will heave with emotion all over the world on perusing this sublimest page in history. It is cheering to believe that the record is copied in heaven, and that this outburst of gratitude which thrilled the breasts of men and angels with such sweet and strange emotion, was not unacceptable to Him, to whom the tribute was paid and whose goodness was the cause of it. And now that His Excellency the President of the Confederate States has set apart this 15th day of November as a day of fasting, humiliation and prayer, calling on all the people to flock to a throne of grace, as a father calls on his children to surround the family altar, the whole people respond; all business has ceased, and the nation is prostrate before God.

The scoffer and the infidel may question the sincerity of the christian, or if not, they will perhaps be surprised to learn that to *his* mind the most cheering evidence of our success in this war is this acknowledgment of God so wide spread in the hearts of the people. This pious and reverent feeling is not the natural offspring of the human heart. If it comes to us from external sources it comes from none that are bad. Satan never turns the heart to God. None but God himself could have inspired this confidence in himself: and he never inspires confidence merely to betray it.—This then is the chief reliance of the christian patriot in this emergency. It is gratifying to see that this devout and proper spirit so generally prevails, and it should be the great aim of all who love God to cultivate and cherish it. The very best of us though we acknowledge God with one breath, are prone to forget him at the next; and while we ascribe the victories of the past to him, we are apt to trust for future victories to our own strong arms and stout hearts, and abundant preparations. No greater calamity could possibly overtake us than to yield to this disposition to forget God. If I were to say that it would be the certain precursor of overwhelming defeat, I should be only repeating what the prophet Isaiah said three thousand years ago, but which like all other truth is not impaired by time:—"Woe to them that stay on horses and trust in chariots because they are many, and in horsemen because they are very strong, but they look not unto the Holy One of Israel, neither seek the Lord."—Is. xxi.i. Woe to you then ye people of Georgia! Woe to you all ye people of these Confederate States! if you are engrossed with outward preparations for battle, and seek not the Lord nor put your trust in the Holy One of Israel, and in the King of glory! Who is this King of glory? "The Lord strong and mighty, the Lord mighty in *battle!*"—Ps. xxiv.8.

Many of the ways of God are past finding out, for "his thoughts are very deep," but in regard to the matter before us, it is not surprising that high and unfaltering faith in God should be the precursor of success. On the contrary it can be shown to be in keeping with all the dealings of his providence with us.

Of course when faith is spoken of, reference is had to real faith, not to counterfeits. Real faith either in God or in anything else is never an inert and unproductive principle. There is in its nature an element which prompts to action. Faith in God prompts to obedience, and if to obedience then to repentance, to reformation and to every virtue. The apostle not without reason places faith first, and hope and charity afterwards. For though charity be the greatest of the three, yet faith is the seed-virtue from which the others spring, certainly without which the others could not exist.

Now let us remember the point already made, that God is in the war. Let us further remember that he has not brought these calamities upon us without a purpose. Without presuming to know any of the secrets of Infinite wisdom, the Almighty has revealed himself to us sufficiently to warrant us in saying, that these afflictions must have been brought upon us either as a punishment for sins that are past, or as a means of making us better in future, or for both these ends. Suppose the object be the first of these. Then such faith in him as prompts to repentance and reformation while it might not logically remove the chastisement, would at least prevent further occasion for it from accruing; and there is reason to hope, that the divine benevolence would not be bound by so strict a logic as not to remove the penalty when the sin that occasioned it is repented of and abandoned. Suppose the object be to make us a better people. When the object is accomplished, there will be no further use for the instrumentality which brought it about. Suppose the object be both retrospective and prospective. The same reasoning that applied to the cases separately will apply to both together; except that the former case being coupled with the latter would receive strength by the connexion, and we should have still better reason to hope that if we cease to sin our Heavenly Parent would cease to chastise.

It is not irreverent to suppose that the divine procedure would be governed by the same principles which control us in the discipline of our children. What father ever continues to use the rod when he is convinced that his child is so heartily sorry for his fault that he will never commit it again? What master would chastise his servant if he knew the servant's grief for his fault to be sincere and profound enough to prevent him from repeating the offence? We are God's children. He is chastising us. Let us acknowledge him; and say "though he slay me yet will I trust in him." Let us confess the sins that brought these evils upon us. Let us repent of them, and so repent as to abandon. Let us do all this, and this war will come to an end. "He maketh wars to cease." He will make *this* war to cease. When we become what we ought to be there can be no motive in the divine mind to continue the chastisement, and the war will cease. The skeptic may ridicule this conclusion. Let him ridicule. "A brutish man knoweth not neither doth a fool understand this."—Ps. xcii.6. He who is enlightened from above, without stopping to ask the opinions of politicians, soldiers or philosophers, and preferring higher authority, goes straight to the oracles of God for a solution of the problem, and is satisfied when he reads: "He maketh wars to cease unto the end of the earth; he breaketh the bow and cutteth the spear in sunder; he burneth the chariot in the fire." The caviller may object, and talk about military and political necessities, and physical and moral impossibilities, and philosophic difficulties. But while he is prating, the providences of God will go right on, and will say to him in due time, "Be still and know that I am God." How strange that we should ask men to predict what the end will be, without asking God who knows all things from the beginning. How strange that we should rely on our puny efforts to bring this dreadful strife to a close, when we know that God only can stop it. For is it not *He* who makes wars to cease? We have been trusting in horses and in chariots. Let us rather remember the name of the Lord our God. Let us pay our vows unto him, and we shall have no further use for these dread instruments of war.—Here then is great good news for the people of these Confederate States! These desolations may be stopped! The red tide of life that flows from the veins of your sons may be staunched! Prosperity may again be established!—"What," exclaims one, "can we entice the enemy from their entrenchments into open field? Then indeed we shall soon destroy them and the remainder will sue for peace!" No my friend, there is no certainty that that would close the war. "What then? shall we cross the Potomac, deliver Maryland, push on to Philadelphia and still farther North until we conquer a peace?" No, no. There can be no assurance of success in such an enterprise. "Shall we then court the friendship of foreign powers, and thus reinforce our army, and re-supply our wasting resources?" Yes! Let us court the friendship, not indeed of a foreign power, for the God of our fathers is not foreign to us, but let us court the favor of heaven, and verily an alliance with the Almighty will make *us* omnipotent!

My countrymen, before God! in my heart and from my soul, I do believe that if the people of this Confederacy were to turn with one heart and one mind to the Lord and walk in his ways, he would drive the invader from our territories and restore to us the blessings of peace. I wish I could express myself with more plainness and with more force. Let me say again, I believe that the quickest and easiest way to terminate this war, and that favorably to ourselves, is for us all to *be good*. We imagine that the only way to get out of our difficulties is to fight out. There is a more excellent way. Let us by faith, obedience and love, so engage the Lord of Hosts on our side that he will fight for us; and when he undertakes our case we are safe, for "he maketh wars to cease," and he will break the bow of the enemy, and cut his spear in sunder, and burn his chariot in the fire, and say unto him, "Be still and know that I am God!" Call it superstition if you please ye men of the world. Say that we are deluded by a religious enthusiasm. But know ye that faith in Israel's God is not superstition, and that confidence in an over ruling providence is no delusion. Enthusiasm there may be, there is, there ought to be, we avow it, we glory in it. The heathen may rage and the people imagine a vain thing, but we rejoice when we can say,—"God is our refuge and strength, a very present help in trouble. Therefore will not we fear though the earth be removed, and though the mountains be carried into the midst of the sea, though the mountains shake with the swelling thereof, Selah! The Lord of Hosts is with us, the God of Jacob is our refuge, Selah!"

Lay what plans you will, and set what schemes you please in operation, and at the summing up of all things at the end of the world, it will be found that God ruled and overruled all things according to the working of his power; and that the great statesmen and great captains who figure so largely in history, were but the unwitting instruments of accomplishing his purposes. We look back over the past and see God in history. We look forward and see him bringing generation after generation upon the earth to work out his designs and not theirs, for before they existed they could have had no designs. Why should the present be an exception? Let us then do justly, and love mercy and walk humbly before God, and by thus falling in with his plans, we shall be on his side and he will be on ours, and those who make war upon us will either see their folly and cease, or if they continue will do nothing more than work out their own ruin. They have no power to harm us. We have no power to make ourselves safe. "Once hath God spoken, yea twice have I heard this, that *power* belongeth unto *God*."—Ps. lxii.ii. Let us fly to that Power and engage it in our behalf, and he who smote great nations and slew mighty kings, Sihon king of Amorites, and Og king of Bashan for his people's sake, will smite the hypocritical nation that wars against us, and will give to us and to our children the heritage of our fathers forever.

I have said that the way to enlist this almightiness on our side is to make the law of God the law of every man's life. Perhaps these terms are too general to convey the idea with power. What then more particularly is to be done. What specific duties must we discharge? What special evils must we forsake? All, all! The whole head is sick, the whole heart is faint, the whole body is corrupt. How small a proportion of our population are disciples of Jesus!—Counting out avowed unbelievers and false professors, how few are left! Here is the place to begin. A pure Gospel is our only hope—I repeat it, a pure Gospel is our only hope. If the Kingdom of Christ be not set up in the hearts of the people no government can exist except by force. All you then who have no personal experience of the grace of the Gospel are so far, in the way of your country's prosperity. The first step for you to take is to believe in the Lord Jesus Christ, confessing your sins and giving him your heart. But aside from this, let us look at our public morals. Passing by profanity, for we are a nation of swearers; passing by drunkenness, for we are a nation of drunkards; passing by Sabbath-breaking, for our cars thunder along the track on the Sabbath as on any other day, and our convivial gatherings are too often on the day of the Lord; passing by covetousness and lying, for too many of our citizens alas! will for the sake of defrauding the public out of a few dollars make false oath in giving in their tax returns; passing by neglect of our children, for too few of them receive that religious instruction and training which is their due; passing by injustice to servants, for while their physical wants are in some cases unsupplied their moral wants are too generally neglected; passing by all these things, and each of the sins of private life which ought to be exchanged for its opposite virtue; let me call especial attention to three things of more public nature, and which are fairer samples of the average of public morals.

In the first place, how is it that in the State of Georgia it is almost impossible to convict a culprit of crime? The most atrocious murders and other outrages are committed with impunity, in the very face of our so-called Courts of Justice. Is the Bench prostituted? Is the Bar prostituted? Or is it the Jury box? In either case it is clear that public virtue is at fault; otherwise these evils would not be tolerated. So notoriously defective is the administration of justice, that in many cases fresh within the memory of us all, citizens have felt it necessary in self-defence to execute criminals without the forms of law. Is not this a step towards barbarism? The example of disregarding the law being set by reputable citizens, will be followed by others not so reputable. When this system is inaugurated where will it stop? Whose life will be safe? This reign of the mob, this lawless execution of men which is little short of murder, will become the rule and not the exception, unless a more healthy public opinion shall correct the evils in our Courts of Justice.

The second evil is kindred to the first. How is it that in all the history of this Legislative body pardon has been granted to every criminal, almost without exception who has ever applied for it? Can it be that all who have been pardoned were innocent? If so there must have been horrid injustice in the Courts which convicted them. The bloodthirsty Jeffreys would scarcely have sent so many innocent men to the gallows. No; under the loose administration of justice already referred to, none but the most glaring cases (with possibly a rare exception) could ever be convicted.—How comes it then that our Legislators turn loose these culprits upon society? It is because they are more anxious to secure a re-election than to promote the good of the State. How comes it that a vote adverse to pardon would endanger their re-election? It is because public opinion is rotten. The fault lies in the low standard of public morals.

But for the third item. Without meaning to indulge in wholesale denunciation of any class of my fellow citizens, it may yet be pertinent to inquire, how is it that so few of our public men are *good* men? Is it to be supposed that all the talent, and all the learning, and all the wisdom, have been vouchsafed to the bad rather than to the good? Does Satan claim a monopoly of all the intellectual power and administrative ability in the world? Perhaps it is not surprising that he should; for he once offered to give to their rightful owner "all the Kingdoms of this world and the glory of them" on condition of receiving his homage in return. But it is preposterous to suppose that there are no good men to be found capable of discharging the highest public trusts.—Why then are they not oftener found in eminent position? It is because the public in estimating a man's fitness for office, throw his morals out of the account; and because popularity can be obtained by means which bad men freely resort to, but which good men eschew. How sad a comment on public virtue! Every voter who allows personal interests, or preferences, or prejudices, or party zeal or anything to influence his suffrage in favor of a bad man in preference to a good one, if the latter be capable, is doing what he can to banish virtue from our councils and God from our support. It might be a fair subject of inquiry, whether he or the outbreaking felon whose place is in the Penitentiary inflicts the greatest injury upon society.

It is time that the preachers of the Gospel, who ought to be if they are not, the great conservators of public morals, had made way upon these monster evils; and I rejoice that I have the opportunity on this public day, before this Legislative body, and before the people of the whole State, to bear my testimony against them.

The three evils just specified are only outward manifestations of an internal distemper, the mere efflorescence of evil deep seated in the public heart. The disappearance of these would indicate a radical change. Suppose public justice to be rightly administered, suppose the influence of virtue in our councils to be predominant; and this is to suppose that thousands upon thousands of individual men have grown wiser and better, that myriads of private faults have been exchanged for corresponding virtues, that the whole complexion of society is changed, and its whole nature improved. Suppose that the Gospel of Christ *which alone can work these changes*, should continue thus to elevate, refine, ennoble and sanctify, until every heart were brought under its sacred influence. How much like heaven our earth would be! Can any one suppose that in such a state of society as this, the heavenly tranquility would ever be disturbed by the clangor of war! Let our whole people at once renounce their evil works and ways with grief, and follow hard after God, and I confidently declare that he would with a mighty hand and an outstretched arm deliver us from our enemies and restore peace and prosperity.—Think you that I ought to modify this positive declaration into a mere expression of opinion? I reiterate the same sentiment in words which no man will dare to question:—"When a man's ways please the Lord he maketh even his enemies to be at peace with him."—Prov. xvi.7. And again. "Let the wicked forsake his way and the unrighteous man his thoughts, and let him turn unto the Lord, and he will have mercy upon him, and unto our God for he will abundantly pardon."—Is. lv.7. Is it said that these words refer to individuals and are not applicable to States? The same conditions of mercy that would suffice for one man would suffice for two, and if for two then for any number, for nations and for all.

From these teachings of Holy Writ, it appears my countrymen, that in carrying on this war which the providence of God has brought upon us, we ought to use a new set of instrumentalities; instrumentalities the object of which shall be not to injure our enemies but to benefit ourselves; to benefit us not in things visible and tangible but in the inner man. Thus shall those faults in our character which made these chastisements necessary be removed, and as matter of moral certainty the sad consequences which we suffer would cease.

Here then is joyful news to thousands of Christian patriots

who burn with desire to aid their country's cause, but who know not what to do. All you have to do is to be good, and in *being* good you are *doing* good; and in doing good you are securing the favor of God and contributing your share towards enlisting Him on the side of our armies. Joy to our venerable fathers, who bowing beneath the weight of years, are unable to gratify their intense desire to fly to arms! Fathers, learn from the word of God; the sins peculiar to old age. Struggle against them. Fixed as your habits may be, try to improve your hearts and lives; and be sure that every success you meet with in the improvement of your graces will tell upon our enemies with more power than the missile from the musket. Joy to our mothers and wives and sisters and daughters! While with busy fingers you ply the needle and the loom for the benefit of our brave defenders, remember that you can render aid far more efficient. Cultivate the graces and practice the virtues enjoined in the Gospel; and though no famous report will be made to the world, God will observe it; though no influence be seen going out from it, yet its influence will be felt in heaven and will descend to earth again. God yearns towards them who seek Him; and when His affections are drawn out towards us, He will be more ready to defend and deliver us. Joy to the invalid, to the blind, and deaf and dumb, and maimed, and poor, and all who by afflictive dispensations are seemingly helpless and apparently a burden to their country in these times of peril. You too can help us in the war. Bear your sorrows with patience, receive the attentions of your friends with gratitude, copy the spirit of Jesus, and as little as the world may think of it, you too will help to drive the invaders from our soil. Scoff sceptic if you please, but we rejoice in the assurance that whatever brings God nigh to us will drive our enemies far away; and what brings God so nigh as the exercise of the spirit and the practice of the duties which His word enjoins? Joy, Joy to you ye preachers of the Gospel! Know ye that whatever makes the people better makes them stronger; that in spreading truth and virtue you are supplying the true sinews of war. Your mission is one of love and peace, and yet in more senses than one you are warriors. Your profession may be thought valueless in these times of bloody strife, but in truth yours is the most efficient branch of the service. The influence of the Gospel is a wall of defence against enemies carnal no less than spiritual. Every pulpit is a battlement whence great moral Columbiads hurl huge thunders against all who would harm us. Joy, joy! ye ministers of the Gospel of peace, for you can fight for your country and yet keep your hands unstained with blood.

See what an accession there is here to our forces in the field. We thought we had an army of some two hundred thousand. Here we have added the whole army of the saints, male and female, of every age, and color, and condition;—a motley band whose uneven ranks excite the sneers of men and devils. But on their banner is inscribed, "Not by might nor by power but by my Spirit saith the Lord." Zech. iv. 6. By that sign they will conquer. Each in his sphere moves quietly along, and men of the world think they are doing nothing, but they are the best soldiers in the war. Their spiritual weapons make no loud report; no blood is seen to follow their stroke; the stroke itself is not seen. The still closet is remote from the scene of battle. But when our enemies rush on a praying people, they rush on their own destruction. Every closet is a masked battery, from whose mysterious depths there goes forth an influence unseen and unheard, but carrying swift disaster to the ranks of our foes. Terror seizes upon them; they feel the dread influence but know not whence it comes, and bewildered and confounded by these assaults on their spiritual nature while yet their bodies are unhurt, they fly, they fly, supposing that they fly not from men but from devils. They know not that they are flying from before the saints of God, from before the armies of the Most High.

My countrymen, we are certain of success in this war if we but use the right means. But those means which are the last that men think of, and the last that they adopt, are the first in order and the first in importance in the Divine estimation. The first and last and only thing that men are apt to do, is to gather together the implements of war and prepare for battle. God forbids not the use of these things; nay, to lay them aside would be but to tempt His Providence. But paramount to this is the purifying of the heart. Let us "seek first the kingdom of God and his righteousness," and trust that all other things will be added. Mat. vi. 33. Let our people forsake their sins and practice goodness, so that it can be said of our land, "thy people shall all be righteous," and the sweet prophecy will be fulfilled in us, which declares, "Violence shall no more be heard in thy land, wasting nor destruction within thy borders; but thou shall call thy walls Salvation and thy gates Praise. A little one shall become a thousand and a small one a strong nation. I the Lord will hasten it in his time." Is. xvi. 18. Yes! when this happy day comes it will be of God, for "He maketh wars to cease unto the end of the earth; He breaketh the bow, and cutteth the spear in sunder; He burneth the chariot in the fire." Suppose every nation were thus to turn to the Lord. Then every nation would secure his blessing. Nation would rise up against nation no more, nor would men longer learn the arts of war. The spears would be beaten into pruning hooks and the swords into ploughshares; the days of Millenial glory would come, and the whole world would be subject to the gentle reign of the Prince of Peace!

RICHMOND, VIRGINIA, NOVEMBER 1861

Jefferson Davis: Message to the Confederate Congress

The Confederacy held elections for congress, president, and vice-president on November 6. Running unopposed, Jefferson Davis and Alexander Stephens were elected to six-year terms that would begin in February 1862. Twelve days after the election Davis sent a message to the Provisional Confederate Congress as it began its fifth session.

RICHMOND, November 18, 1861.
THE CONGRESS of the Confederate States.

The few weeks which have elapsed since your adjournment have brought us so near the close of the year that we are now able to sum up its general results. The retrospect is such as should fill the hearts of our people with gratitude to Providence for his kind interposition in their behalf. Abundant yields have rewarded the labor of the agriculturist, whilst the manufacturing industry of the Confederate States was never so prosperous as now. The necessities of the times have called into existence new branches of manufactures and given a fresh impulse to the activity of those heretofore in operation. The means of the Confederate States for manufacturing the necessaries and comforts of life within themselves increase as the conflict continues, and we are gradually becoming independent of the rest of the world for the supply of such military stores and munitions as are indispensable for war.

The operations of the Army, soon to be partially interrupted by the approaching winter, have afforded a protection to the country and shed a luster upon its arms through the trying vicissitudes of more than one arduous campaign which entitle our brave volunteers to our praise and our gratitude. From its commencement to the present period the war has been enlarging its proportions and expanding its boundaries so as to include new fields. The conflict now extends from the shores of the Chesapeake to the confines of Missouri and Arizona; yet sudden calls from the remotest points for military aid have been met with promptness enough not only to avert disaster in the face of superior numbers, but also to roll back the tide of invasion from the border.

When the war commenced the enemy were possessed of certain strategic points and strong places within the Confederate States. They greatly exceeded us in numbers, in available resources, and in the supplies necessary for war. Military establishments had been long organized and were complete; the Navy, and for the most part the Army, once common to both, were in their possession. To meet all this we had to create not only an Army in the face of war itself, but also the military establishments necessary to equip and place it in the field. It ought indeed to be a subject of gratulation that the spirit of the volunteers and the patriotism of the people have enabled us, under Providence, to grapple successfully with these difficulties. A succession of glorious victories at Bethel, Bull Run, Manassas, Springfield, Lexington, Leesburg, and Belmont has checked the wicked invasion which greed of gain and the unhallowed lust of power brought upon our soil, and has proved that numbers cease to avail when directed against a people fighting for the sacred right of self-government and the privileges of freemen. After more than seven months of war the enemy have not only failed to extend their occupancy of our soil, but new States and Territories have been added to our Confederacy, while, instead of their threatened march of unchecked conquest, they have been driven, at more than one point, to assume the defensive, and, upon a fair comparison between the two belligerents as to men, military means, and financial condition, the Confederate States are relatively much stronger now than when the struggle commenced.

Since your adjournment the people of Missouri have conducted the war in the face of almost unparalleled difficulties with a spirit and success alike worthy of themselves and of the great cause in which they are struggling. Since that time Kentucky, too, has become the theater of active hostilities. The Federal forces have not only refused to acknowledge her right to be neutral, and have insisted upon making her a party to the war, but have invaded her for the purpose of attacking the

Confederate States. Outrages of the most despotic character have been perpetrated upon her people; some of her most eminent citizens have been seized and borne away to languish in foreign prisons, without knowing who were their accusers or the specific charges made against them, while others have been forced to abandon their homes, families, and property, and seek a refuge in distant lands.

Finding that the Confederate States were about to be invaded through Kentucky, and that her people, after being deceived into a mistaken security, were unarmed and in danger of being subjugated by the Federal forces, our armies were marched into that State to repel the enemy and prevent their occupation of certain strategic points which would have given them great advantages in the contest—a step which was justified not only by the necessities of self-defense on the part of the Confederate States, but also by a desire to aid the people of Kentucky. It was never intended by the Confederate Government to conquer or coerce the people of that State; but, on the contrary, it was declared by our generals that they would withdraw their troops if the Federal Government would do likewise. Proclamation was also made of the desire to respect the neutrality of Kentucky and the intention to abide by the wishes of her people as soon as they were free to express their opinions. These declarations were approved by me, and I should regard it as one of the best effects of the march of our troops into Kentucky if it should end in giving to her people liberty of choice and a free opportunity to decide their own destiny according to their own will.

The Army has been chiefly instrumental in prosecuting the great contest in which we are engaged, but the Navy has also been effective in full proportion to its means. The naval officers, deprived to a great extent of an opportunity to make their professional skill available at sea, have served with commendable zeal and gallantry on shore and upon inland waters, further detail of which will be found in the reports of the Secretaries of the Navy and War. In the transportation of the mails many difficulties have arisen, which will be found fully developed in the report of the Postmaster General. The absorption of the ordinary means of transportation for the movements of troops and military supplies; the insufficiency of the rolling stock of railroads for the accumulation of business resulting both from military operations and the obstruction of water communication by the presence of the enemy's fleet; the failure, and even refusal, of contractors to comply with the terms of their agreements; the difficulties inherent in inaugurating so vast and complicated a system as that which requires postal facilities for every town and village in a territory so extended as ours, have all combined to impede the best-directed efforts of the Postmaster General, whose zeal, industry, and ability have been taxed to the utmost extent. Some of these difficulties can only be overcome by time and an improved condition of the country upon the restoration of peace, but others may be remedied by legislation, and your attention is invited to the recommendations contained in the report of the head of that Department.

The condition of the Treasury will doubtless be a subject of anxious inquiry on your part. I am happy to say that the financial system already adopted has worked well so far, and promises good results for the future. To the extent that Treasury notes may be issued the Government is enabled to borrow money without interest, and thus facilitate the conduct of the war. This extent is measured by the portion of the field of circulation which these notes can be made to occupy. The proportion of the field thus occupied depends again upon the amount of the debts for which they are receivable; and when dues, not only to the Confederate and State governments, but also to corporations and individuals, are payable in this medium, a large amount of it may be circulated at par. There is every reason to believe that the Confederate Treasury note is fast becoming such a medium. The provision that these notes shall be convertible into Confederate stock bearing 8 per cent interest, at the pleasure of the holder, insures them against a depreciation below the value of that stock, and no considerable fall in that value need be feared so long as the interest shall be punctually paid. The punctual payment of this interest has been secured by the act passed by you at the last session, imposing such a rate of taxation as must provide sufficient means for that purpose.

For the successful prosecution of this war it is indispensable that the means of transporting troops and military supplies be furnished, as far as possible, in such manner as not to interrupt the commercial intercourse between our people nor place a check on their productive energies. To this end the means of transportation from one section of our country to the other must be carefully guarded and improved. And this should be the object of anxious care on the part of State and Confederate governments, so far as they may have power over the subject.

We have already two main systems of through transportation from the north to the south—one from Richmond along the seaboard; the other through Western Virginia to New Orleans. A third might be secured by completing a link of about forty miles between Danville, in Virginia, and Greensboro, in North Carolina. The construction of this comparatively short line would give us a through route from north to south in the interior of the Confederate States and give us access to a population and to military resources from which we are now in great measure debarred. We should increase greatly the safety and capacity of our means for transporting men and military supplies. If the construction of this road should, in the judgment of Congress as it is in mine, be indispensable for the most successful prosecution of the war, the action of the Government will not be restrained by the constitutional objection which would attach to a work for commercial purposes, and attention is invited to the practicability of securing its early completion by giving the needful aid to the company organized for its construction and administration.

If we husband our means and make a judicious use of our resources, it would be difficult to fix a limit to the period during which we could conduct a war against the adversary whom we now encounter. The very efforts which he makes to isolate and invade us must exhaust his means, whilst they serve to complete the circle and diversify the productions of our industrial system. The reconstruction which he seeks to effect by arms becomes daily more and more palpably impossible. Not only do the causes which induced us to separate still exist in full force, but they have been strengthened, and whatever doubt may have lingered in the minds of any must have been completely dispelled by subsequent events. If instead of being a dissolution of a league it were indeed a rebellion in which we are engaged, we might find ample vindication for the course we have adopted in the scenes which are now being enacted in the United States. Our people now look with contemptuous astonishment on those with whom they had been so recently associated. They shrink with aversion from the bare idea of renewing such a connection. When they see a President making war without the assent of Congress; when they behold judges threatened because they maintain the writ of *habeas corpus* so sacred to freemen; when they see justice and law trampled under the armed heel of military authority, and upright men and innocent women dragged to distant dungeons upon the mere edict of a despot; when they find all this tolerated and applauded by a people who had been in the full enjoyment of freedom but a few months ago—they believe that there must be some radical incompatibility between such a people and themselves. With such a people we may be content to live at peace, but the separation is final, and for the independence we have asserted we will accept no alternative.

The nature of the hostilities which they have waged against us must be characterized as barbarous wherever it is understood. They have bombarded undefended villages without giving notice to women and children to enable them to escape, and in one instance selected the night as the period when they might surprise them most effectually whilst asleep and unsuspicious of danger. Arson and rapine, the destruction of private houses and property, and injuries of the most wanton character, even upon noncombatants, have marked their forays along our borders and upon our territory. Although we ought to have been admonished by these things that they were disposed to make war upon us in the most cruel and relentless spirit, yet we were not prepared to see them fit out a large naval expedition, with the confessed purpose not only to pillage, but to incite a servile insurrection in our midst. If they convert their soldiers into incendiaries and robbers, and involve us in a species of war which claims noncombatants, women, and children as its victims, they must expect to be treated as outlaws and enemies of mankind. There are certain rights of humanity which are entitled to respect even in war, and he who refuses to regard them forfeits his claims, if captured, to be considered as a prisoner of war, but must expect to be dealt with as an offender against all law, human and divine.

But not content with violating our rights under the law of nations at home, they have extended these injuries to us within other jurisdictions. The distinguished gentlemen whom, with your approval at the last session, I commissioned to represent the Confederacy at certain foreign courts, have been recently seized by the captain of a U. S. ship of war on board a British steamer on their voyage from the neutral Spanish port of Havana to England. The United States have thus claimed a general jurisdiction over the high seas, and entering a British ship, sailing under its country's flag, violated the rights of embassy, for the most part held sacred even amongst barbarians, by seizing our ministers whilst under the protection and within the dominions of a neutral nation. These gentlemen were as much under the jurisdiction of the British Government upon that ship and beneath its flag as if they had been on its soil, and a claim on the part of the United States to seize them in the streets of London would have been as well founded as that to apprehend them where they were taken. Had they been malefactors and citizens even of the United States they could not have been arrested on a British ship or on British soil, unless under the express provisions of a treaty and according to the forms therein provided for the extradition of criminals.

But rights the most sacred seem to have lost all respect in their eyes. When Mr. Faulkner, a former minister of the United States to France, commissioned before the secession of Virginia, his native State, returned in good faith to Washington to settle his accounts and fulfill all the obligations into which he had entered, he was perfidiously arrested and imprisoned in New York, where he now is. The unsuspecting confidence with which he reported to his Government was abused, and his desire to fulfill his trust to them was used to his injury. In conducting this war we have sought no aid and proposed no alliances offensive and defensive abroad. We have asked for a recognized place in the great family of nations, but in doing so we have demanded nothing for which we did not offer a fair equivalent. The advantages of intercourse are mutual amongst nations, and in seeking to establish diplomatic relations we were only endeavoring to place that intercourse under the regulation of public law. Perhaps we had the right, if we had chosen to exercise it, to ask to know whether the principle that "blockades to be binding must be effectual," so solemnly announced by the great powers of Europe at Paris, is to be generally enforced or applied only to particular parties. When the Confederate States, at your last session, became a party to the declaration reaffirming this principle of international law, which has been recognized so long by publicists and governments, we certainly supposed that it was to be universally enforced. The customary law of nations is made up of their practice rather than their declarations; and if such declarations are only to be enforced in particular instances at the pleasure of those who make them, then the commerce of the world, so far from being placed under the regulation of a general law, will become subject to the caprice of those who execute or suspend it at will. If such is to be the course of nations in regard to this law, it is plain that it will thus become a rule for the weak and not for the strong.

Feeling that such views must be taken by the neutral nations of the earth, I have caused the evidence to be collected which proves completely the utter inefficiency of the proclaimed blockade of our coast, and shall direct it to be laid before such governments as shall afford us the means of being heard. But, although we should be benefited by the enforcement of this law so solemnly declared by the great powers of Europe, we are not dependent on that enforcement for the successful prosecution of the war. As long as hostilities continue the Confederate States will exhibit a steadily increasing capacity to furnish their troops with food, clothing, and arms. If they should be forced to forego many of the luxuries and some of the comforts of life, they will at least have the consolation of knowing that they are thus daily becoming more and more independent of the rest of the world. If in this process labor in the Confederate States should be gradually diverted from those great Southern staples which have given life to so much of the commerce of mankind into other channels, so as to make them rival producers instead of profitable customers, they will not be the only or even the chief losers by this change in the direction of their industry. Although it is true that the cotton supply from the Southern States could only be totally cut off by the subversion of our social system, yet it is plain that a long continuance of this blockade might, by a diversion of labor and an investment of capital in other employments, so diminish the supply as to bring ruin upon all those interests of foreign countries which are dependent on that staple. For every laborer who is diverted from the culture of cotton in the South, perhaps four times as many elsewhere, who have found subsistence in the various employments growing out of its use, will be forced also to change their occupation.

While the war which is waged to take from us the right of self-government can never attain that end, it remains to be seen how far it may work a revolution in the industrial system of the world, which may carry suffering to other lands as well as to our own. In the meantime we shall continue this struggle in humble dependence upon Providence, from whose searching scrutiny we cannot conceal the secrets of our hearts, and to whose rule we confidently submit our destinies. For the rest we shall depend upon ourselves. Liberty is always won where there exists the unconquerable will to be free, and we have reason to know the strength that is given by a conscious sense not only of the magnitude but of the righteousness of our cause.

JEFF'N DAVIS.

THE ARMY OF THE POTOMAC:
VIRGINIA, NOVEMBER 1861

Harper's Weekly: The Great Review

December 7, 1861

On November 20 General McClellan staged a grand review of the Army of the Potomac at Bailey's Crossroads in Fairfax County, Virginia. The military spectacle demonstrated the progress made during the fall in organizing, equipping, and drilling the main Union fighting force in the eastern theater.

IN THE upper and lower divisions, General M'Call's and General Heintzelman's, from which a march of some eight or ten miles had to be made, the troops were astir at from two to three o'clock in the morning, and were on the march long before daylight. All of the seven divisions on the Virginia side of the Potomac were represented in the review, but enough were left in each to supply double the usual picket force to guard the camps, and a reserve in addition strong enough to repel any attack in force the enemy could make.

As early as nine o'clock the head of the column of General Blenker's division, the head-quarters of which are nearest to Bailey's, began to arrive at the grounds from the Washington road. Soon after General M'Dowell's advance-guard appeared on the road, entering the grounds from the same direction, but further to the west. Next came the head of General Franklin's column, approaching from the Alexandria road; and soon after the division of General Smith began to enter the grounds from the direction of Fall's Church. General Fitz John Porter was next on the ground, bringing his forces by still another road. The troops now poured in from all directions, those under General Heintzelman following General Franklin's division, and the column of General McCall succeeding that of General Smith, and continued without cessation until half past eleven o'clock.

For the last hour the scene was enlivening and brilliant beyond description. The whole immense area of the review grounds was covered with moving masses of men. More than twenty generals, commanding divisions and brigades, with five times the number of staff officers, mounted upon high mottled and richly caparisoned horses, were dashing through the grounds in every direction, superintending the placing in position of the various divisions, brigades, and regiments. Brigades are marching toward every possible point of the compass—some slowly, some in double-quick time, some wheeling into line, others standing in position. Here comes a regiment of cavalry, moving toward its designated station, wheeling to the right at this point and to the left at that, to avoid coming in contact with the moving masses of infantry. There goes a column of artillery, a mile in length, pursuing its way to its destination through bodies of infantry and cavalry.

And so the movements go on, seemingly in confusion, and yet, under the admirable management of General McDowell, who directs every thing, in most perfect order, until there have arrived and taken the various positions assigned not less than seventy thousand men, including seven regiments of cavalry, numbering some eight thousand men, and twenty batteries of artillery, numbering a hundred and twenty pieces.

After the arrival of the President and Cabinet and Commander-in-Chief, preparation was made for marching the troops in review. The honor of leading the column was assigned to the First Rifle Regiment of Pennsylvania Reserve, familiarly known as the "Bucktail Regiment." This regiment was with General M'Clellan in Western Virginia, and was particularly admired for the steadiness and regularity of its movements, and the soldierlike bearing of the men. Some three hours were occupied by the troops in passing. The divisions passed in the following order:

First. General M'Call's division, composed of the brigades of Generals Meade, Reynolds, and Ord.

Second. General Heintzelman's division, composed of the brigades of Generals Sedgwick, Jamison, and Richardson.

Third. General Smith's division, composed of the brigades of Generals Hancock, Brooks, and Benham.

Fourth. General Franklin's division, composed of the brigades of Generals Slocum, Newton, and Kearney.

Fifth. The division of General Blenker, composed of the brigade of General Stahl, and of two brigades commanded by senior Colonels.

Sixth. The division of General Fitz John Porter, composed of the brigades of Generals Morell, Martindale, and Butterfield.

Seventh. The division of General M'Dowell, composed of the brigades of Generals King and Wadsworth, and a brigade now commanded by Colonel Frisbie.

The passage of this large army of volunteers elicited the strongest praise from the very formidable body of old army officers who sat in review. General Sumner, who now for the first time since his return from the Pacific witnessed an exhibition of the progress in drill of the volunteers, expressed much surprise that men coming from civil life should, in so short a period, have been able to compete in soldierly appearance with the veterans of the regular army.

SLAVERY AND THE PRESS: NOVEMBER 1861

Ulysses S. Grant to Jesse Root Grant

Grant would write in his memoirs that from the battle of Belmont to early February 1862 "the troops under my command did little except prepare for the long struggle which proved to be before them." During this period he wrote to his father about the expectations created by the Northern press.

.

Cairo, Illinois,
November 27th, 1861.

DEAR FATHER:
Your letter enclosed with a shawl to Julia is just received.

In regard to your stricture about my not writing I think that you have no cause of complaint. My time is all taken up with public duties.

Your statement of prices at which you proposed furnishing harness was forwarded to Maj. Allen as soon as received and I directed Lagow, who received the letter enclosing it, to inform you of the fact. He did so at once.

I cannot take an active part in securing contracts. If I were not in the army I should do so, but situated as I am it is necessary both to my efficiency for the public good and my own reputation that I should keep clear of Government contracts.

I do not write you about plans, or the necessity of what has been done or what is doing because I am opposed to publicity in these matters. Then too you are very much disposed to criticise unfavorably from information received through the public press, a portion of which I am sorry to see can look at nothing favorably that does not look to a war upon slavery. My inclination is to whip the rebellion into submission, preserving all constitutional rights. If it cannot be whipped in any other way than through a war against slavery, let it come to that legitimately. If it is necessary that slavery should fall that the Republic may continue its existence, let slavery go. But that portion of the press that advocates the beginning of such a war now, are as great enemies to their country as if they were open and avowed secessionists.

There is a desire upon the part of people who stay securely at home to read in the morning papers, at their breakfast, startling reports of battles fought. They cannot understand why troops are kept inactive for weeks or even months. They do not understand that men have to be disciplined, arms made, transportation and provisions provided. I am very tired of the course pursued by a portion of the Union press.

Julia left last Saturday for St. Louis where she will probably spend a couple of weeks and return here should I still remain. It costs nothing for her to go there, and it may be the last opportunity she will have of visiting her father. From here she will go to Covington, and spend a week or two before going back to Galena.

It was my bay horse (cost me $140) that was shot. I also lost the little pony, my fine saddle and bridle, and the common one. What I lost cost about $250. My saddle cloth which was about half the cost of the whole, I left at home.

I try to write home about once in two weeks and think I keep it up pretty well. I wrote to you directly after the battle of Belmont, and Lagow and Julia have each written since.

Give my love to all at home. I am very glad to get letters from home and will write as often as I can. I am somewhat troubled lest I lose my command here, though I believe my administration has given general satisfaction not only to those over me but to all concerned. This is the most important command within the department however, and will probably be given to the senior officer next to General Halleck himself.

There are not so many brigadier generals in the army as there are brigades, and as to divisions they are nearly all commanded by brigadiers.

Yours,
ULYSSES.

SHORTAGES AND INFLATION:
VIRGINIA, AUTUMN 1861

Sallie Brock: from Richmond During the War

In her memoir Sallie Brock described conditions in Richmond in the first autumn of the war.

RICHMOND A CITY OF REFUGE-EXTORTIONS.

RICHMOND had already become a "city of refuge." Flying before the face of the invader, thousands sought within its hospitable walls that security they could not hope to receive in exposed and isolated places. Tales of suffering were even then the theme of thousands of tongues, as the homeless and destitute crowded into our city for safety and support. The usual hotel and boarding-house accommodations were found altogether insufficient to supply comfortable places of sojourn for the great numbers demanding sympathy and shelter. From the first day that war was declared against the South, Richmond was taxed to the utmost extent of her capacity to take care of the surplus population that accumulated within her limits.

Many of the citizens received and entertained these wanderers; but many, by the suspension of the ordinary business pursuits of the city, were so reduced in income that it became an impossibility for them to extend to such numbers the assistance which a native kindness and generosity prompted.

From the extraordinary influx of population, and the existence of the blockade, which prevented the importation of supplies in proportion to the demand, we were compelled to submit to the vilest extortions by which any people were ever oppressed. It was first observed in the increased prices placed upon goods of domestic manufacture. Cotton and woolen fabrics soon brought double prices, even before there was a general circulation of the money issued by the Confederate

Treasury. The wisest laid in supplies sufficient to stock a small shop, and had enough to last during the entire war; but an overwhelming majority, unsupplied with means to use providently, waited for each day to provide for the peculiar wants of the day, and at length suffered for the simplest necessaries of life.

A lady in conversation with a friend, as early as May, 1861, said, "If you need calico, you had better purchase at once, for our ninepence goods have gone up to sixteen cents, and very soon we shall have to pay twenty-five cents. Our ten cent cotton domestics are now retailing at sixteen cents, and before the end of June it is said to be doubtful whether there will be any left in Richmond, and if any, we shall have to pay three prices." Could she have foreseen the time when for a yard of the goods in question she would have to pay as many dollars, and later still twice the amount in dollars, she would indeed have urged her friend, who was incredulous to the truth, to purchase supplies sufficient for a number of years.

The same fact was observable in regard to imported articles of food. The extraordinary increase in price was first noticeable in that demanded for coffee. An old lady, one of the most famous of the many distinguished housewives of Virginia, in great astonishment, said in August, 1861: "Only think! coffee is now thirty cents per pound, and my grocer tells me I must buy at once, or very soon we shall have to pay double that price. Shameful! Why, even in the war of 1812 we had not to pay higher than sixty cents. And now, so soon! We must do without it, except when needed for the sick. If we can't make some of the various proposed substitutes appetizing, why, we can use water. Thank God, no blockade can restrict the supply of that. That, at least, is abundant, and given without money and without price."

Could this conscientious economist then have foreseen the cost of the berry for her favorite beverage at fifty dollars per pound, she would not grudgingly have paid the grocer his exorbitant demand of fifty cents.

During the existence of the war, coffee was a luxury in which only the most wealthy could constantly indulge; and when used at all, it was commonly adulterated with other things which passed for the genuine article, but was often so nauseous that it was next to impossible to force it upon the stomach. Rye, wheat, corn, sweet potatoes, beans, ground-nuts, chestnuts, chiccory, ochre, sorghum-seed, and other grains and seeds, roasted and ground, were all brought into use as substitutes for the bean of Araby; but after every experiment to make coffee of what was not coffee, we were driven to decide that there was nothing coffee but coffee, and if disposed to indulge in extravagance at all, the people showed it only by occasional and costly indulgence in the luxurious beverage.

Tea, sugar, wines, and all imported liquors, increased rapidly in expense as the supply grew scarce, but not in the same ratio as coffee, which had been in universal use at the South—the low price at which it had been purchased, and its stimulating and pleasant effects making it agreeable, necessary and possible for even the poorest to indulge in its use.

The leaves of the currant, blackberry, willow, sage, and other vegetables, were dried and used as substitutes for tea by those who could not or did not feel justified in encouraging the exorbitant demands of successful blockade runners and dealers in the article. When sugar grew scarce, and so expensive that many were compelled to abandon its use altogether, there were substituted honey, and the syrup from sorghum, or the Chinese sugar cane, for all ordinary culinary purposes. The cultivation of the latter has become a very important consideration with the agriculturists of the more northern of the Southern States, being peculiarly adapted to the soil and climate, and furnishing a cheap and excellent substitute for the syrup of the sugar cane of the Gulf States and the West Indies.

With an admirable adaptation to the disagreeable and inconvenient circumstances entailed upon us by the blockade, the necessary self denial practiced by the people was in a spirit of cheerful acquiescence, and with a philosophical satisfaction and contentment that forgot the present in a hopeful looking for better and brighter days in the future.

Cheerfully submitting to inconveniences, and deprived from the first of the usual luxuries and many of the necessaries of life, the people were buoyed up with the hope and belief that their sufferings would be of short duration, and that an honorable independence and exemption from the evils which surrounded them, would soon compensate amply for the self denial they were called upon to practice. The remembrance then would be rather glorious than disagreeable in the reflection that they, too, had shared the travail which wrought the freedom of their country.

If there were any who sighed after the flesh-pots of Egypt, the sighs were breathed in the silence of retirement, and not where the ardor of the more hopeful could be chilled by such signs of discontent.

There was, however, a class in Richmond who very ill endured the severe simplicity and the rigid self-denial to which they were compelled to conform in the Confederate Capital. Gradually and insidiously innovations were permitted, until at last the license tolerated in fashionable society elsewhere grew to be tolerated somewhat in Richmond, and in the course of time prosy Richmond was acknowledged "fast" enough for the fastest.

THE TRENT AFFAIR:
LONDON, NOVEMBER–DECEMBER 1861

Benjamin Moran: *Journal,* *November 27–December 3, 1861*

Acting on his own initiative, Captain Charles Wilkes of the U.S.S. *San Jacinto* stopped the British steamer *Trent* off Cuba on November 8 and seized James Mason and John Slidell, Confederate diplomats on missions to Great Britain and France. His action was widely hailed in the North, but soon provoked an international crisis. Benjamin Moran, a secretary at the American legation in London, recorded the reaction in England to the *Trent* incident.

———————

Wed. 27 Nov. '61. We have received a long note from Earl Russell, dated yesterday, in reply to Mr. Adams' letter of last Friday, announcing the revocation of Mr. Bunch's Exequatur. It is to me a hostile document. His Lordship defends Bunch, and boastfully states that his negotiations with the rebels on the last three articles of the Paris Declaration were authorized, and that Her Majesty's Gov't will continue to make such like communications to both the State Gov'ts & Central Govt. of the South whenever it sees fit to do so, & it will not regard such proceedings with the rebels as inconsistent with its obligations as a friendly power to the Federal Govt. This is an affront these people would not have dared commit, were we not in a crippled state. It seems to me that Lord Palmerston has deliberately determined to force us into a war with England, and I believe this has been his purpose from the beginning. All his movements point to that end. With a malicious wickedness his worst enemy could hardly think of charging him with, he has been playing into the hands of the rebels from the first: and with the aid of the *Times* he has been disseminating falsehoods about our enmity to England, until he has succeeded in making the people of these realms believe that enormous lie that we are doing all we can to involve them in a war. He is a foe to freedom: and if he succeeds in his satanic object of hostilities between the Federal Gov't & Great Britain he will deserve the execrations of mankind. His hatred of us is a boyish passion, strengthened by accumulated years. As he was Secretary at War in 1812 he feels that his life and name will not be free from tarnish unless he can expunge us from the earth, and to do so he must be quick. Age will soon lead him to the grave, and he must glut his ire before he goes. In case he succeeds in this mad scheme, he will have the whole English people with him, and they will religiously believe his monstrous imposition that we picked the quarrel. He is one of their idols, and being a Lord, all he has to do is to put adroitly forth a shameful misrepresentation, bearing the semblance of truth, and with the backing of The Times, it will take such firm hold of the public mind that ages will not eradicate it in case of war.

That such a result will follow I much fear, for it seems as if the demons of darkness were against us. At about 1/2 past 12 this morning we received a telegram from Capt. Britton at Southampton announcing that the West India steamer at that port brought news in there this morning that Capt. Wilkes, of the U.S. Ship of War San Jacinto, had stopped the British mail steamer Trent in the Bahama Channel, not far from St. Thomas, on the 9th Inst, & had forcibly taken Mason, Slidell, Eustis, & Macfarlane out of her: and at 1 o'clk a telegram from Reuter confirmed the statement. That the capture of these arch-rebels gave us great satisfaction at the first blush, was natural: & we gave free vent to our exultation. But on reflection I am satisfied that the act will do more for the Southerners than ten victories, for it touches John Bull's honor, and the honor of his flag. At present the people have hardly recovered from the paralysing effect of the news; but they are beginning to see that their flag has been insulted, and if that devil *The Times*, feeds their ire to-morrow, as it assuredly will, nothing but a miracle can prevent their sympathies running to the South, and Palmerston getting up a war. We have no particulars, but from what we hear, it would seem that Capt. Wilkes acted on his own responsibility, and not on that of the Govt.

I telegraphed the news at once to Mr. Adams, and fear it has not added to his enjoyment of rural retirement. It is odd that he never goes out of town that some thing serious don't arise to call him home.

Thursday, 28 Nov. '61. This morning I went to a Mass at the French Chapel in King St., Portman Square, for the repose of the soul of Dom Pedro the 5th, late King of Portugal. I went directly from the house, & wore my Levee Dress, with crape on the arm, sword hilt, &c. I was the first there of the Diplomatic Corps, not belonging to the Portuguese Mission. Others soon came in, & shortly after 11 o'clock there were about 50 Ambassadors, Secretaries & Attachés, their rich uniforms presenting a gay appearance, as contrasted with the sable hangings on the catafalque and altar. Mass was performed by Cardinal Wiseman, a burly butcher looking man, assisted by some 20 other priests of various grades, & notwithstanding the stupidities of some of the ceremonies, the whole affair was impressive, and had the edifice been even ordinarily respectable, would have been solemn and overpowering. There were several splendid male voices among the singers, and the music was grand. The audience was large, & among them were Queen Amelie, widow of Louis Phillippe, an aristocratic and pensive old lady.

I was addressed by a number of the Diplomatic Corps & asked if we were going to have war with England about Mason & Slidell; but I thought it prudent to be quiet. On leaving, I drove to the Legation in my uniform, where I found Mr. Bright, M.P. deploring Capt. Wilkes act. There was a note from Earl Russell, asking an interview of Mr. Adams at 2 o'ck to-day, and as no answer had been made to it, I drove at once to the F. Office, and told Mr. Layard of Mr. A.'s absence. He told me that he sent the request up at 12 last night.

The newspapers are violent in the extreme, and yet seem in a mist. In all this there is still an ugly look of war. We have had a great deal to do to-day, and many American visitors in a great state of excitement. Wilson and Henry Adams seem to me very indiscreet in some of their remarks about the business to strangers.

Friday, 29 Nov. 61. Mr. Adams returned to town last night. It appears he got my telegram promptly. He regards the Trent affair as serious, and is very grave about it. To-day he has been writing home concerning it, and I have had a vast deal of hard work. Earl Russell fixed quarter to two for an interview, but beyond asking a few questions about the orders of the Capt. of the James Adger, his Lordship said nothing. It is quite evident that Ministers consider the question as serious, and many of them feel very sore and hostile about it. As I was detained late, I remained to dinner. Mr. Adams expressed apprehensions that we would not be here a month and from this I suspect he has reason to believe that the people at the head of the Gov't are not altogether capable of dealing wisely with so delicate a question. We shall certainly be in an unpleasant state of mind concerning this affair for a month, or until we hear from Washington. We ought to hear something next Monday, but of this there is no certainty. Things now are by no means agreeable, and Mrs. Adams assured me that she was miserable at Moncton Milnes after the receipt of my telegram. She felt that they were provoked at what had occurred, friendly as they were, and she couldn't enjoy herself knowing how uncomfortable her presence must necessarily make them after such news. In future she will not go on such visits, for it seems something painful is sure to occur while Mr. Adams is away on such pleasure.

There has been a great crowd of anxious visitors to-day, mostly Americans, to know if war will result, but we can't tell.

Sat. 30 Nov. '61. I got down early, and have been at hard work through the whole of this duly day. Joseph L. Spofford, a youth from New York, whose father is half owner of the Nashville, was the only person I noticed particularly. He is a well-behaved, sensible young man.

Monday, 2 Dec. '61. There is no time for rest now. I was here nearly all day yesterday recording, and putting our accumulated documents to rights. During the morning Mr. Adams called our attention to a curious statement in the *Observer* about American *espionage* in England, in which there are some facts strangely mingled up with a great deal of speculation. From this it is quite clear to me that some person either in the

Foreign Office, or Lord Palmerston's confidence, communicates facts to this *Observer*, and does the work very clumsily.

After having finished my work I dined at Horatio Ward's, and then returned to the Legation for news. There was an ambiguous telegram from Reuter, showing that Capt. Wilkes had acted on his own responsibility, & in that there was some consolation. But I confess I went home sick at heart at the news of the safe arrival of the Fingal at Savannah with her cargo of war material. Her escape from capture is a disgrace to our Navy, & I fear treason in the Squadron is the cause.

This state of feeling was not improved on finding this morning that no despatches had arrived. All the evil spirits are at work against us, and the Despatch bag is shuffling about somewhere between this and Cork.

I went over to see Van de Weyer, the Belgian Minister, & enquire about a Baron de Reiffenberg, who has offered his services to our Govt. The result was damaging to the Baron, who instead of being a military man, is a *litterateur*, and never smelt powder, so far as Van de Weyer knows. I found His Ex.y suffering from illness, and very grumpy.

Col. Jos. L. Chester was here to-day, & presented me with a copy of his "John Rogers, the Martyr." The volume looks well & is finely gotten up. As Chester owes me over £80, I hope the book will not be the only return I shall get therefore.

We have had some forty people here to-day—all anxious, and all gloomy. Among them were A. S. Goodall & Lammot Dupont.

Mr. Adams continues to entertain very gloomy apprehensions of the future, but I don't know what he founds his fears upon. He probably has private advices of which I know nothing.

Tuesday 3 Dec. '61. I stayed here at work until 7.30 last evening, and had to go away without hearing of the arrival of the bag. On my return this morning, I was sick at heart to hear there was nothing from Washington on this trouble. Our despatches, which only arrived this morning, are silent. This is what may be called the extreme of cruel folly. And on all such momentous questions, the Department at Washington, no matter what may be its political cast, has, in all my time here, been equally indifferent about supplying the Minister at an early moment with its views. He, of all men, ought to be advised at once of intentions at Head Quarters, whereas he is generally the last to receive information as to their nature.

At present the excitement in England is truly terrific. The Europa was detained at Cork or Queenstown, until last night, or this morning, to carry out an Ultimatum, and the purport of that is indicated by the London papers of yesterday and to-day. It is alleged that the Law Officers of the Crown have decided that Wilkes did not insult England enough, and the result is a demand for an apology, and the restoration of the men. By harping on this, and asserting that Capt. Wilkes' act was an authorized and deliberate insult of our Gov't, the journals have lashed the nation into a most indecent rage, and the consequence is that mob rule reigns supreme, and the natural English hatred of the American people, which is ordinarily concealed, has been allowed to gush up in its full bitterness from all hearts, high and low. This polite and calm nation is in the throes of a vulgar and coarse excitement such as one might naturally look for among a crowd of the London Fancy, but the like of which no one, not even their worst enemy, would ever expect to seize upon the inoffensive and harmless upper classes of the realm. That pink of modesty and refinement, *The Times*, is filled with such slatternly abuse of us and ours, that it is fair to conclude that all the Fishwifes of Billingsgate have been transferred to Printing House Square to fill the ears of the writers there with their choicest phraseology. There is something positively infernal in the way these assassins are goading the nation on to a war. They daily feed the public mind with the most palpable lies, & stick at nothing. If a war should follow this wicked conduct, reflecting Englishmen will blush in after years at the bigotry and blindness which hurried them into the struggle.

WAR WITH ENGLAND: LONDON, NOVEMBER 1861
Henry Adams to Charles Francis Adams Jr.

Henry Adams expressed his apprehension that an Anglo-American war would break out over the *Trent* affair to his brother in Boston. On December 19 Lord Lyons, the British minister in Washington, formally demanded the release of the Confederate envoys. The crisis was resolved on December 25, when Lincoln and his cabinet decided to release Mason and Slidell. In his reply to Lyons, Secretary of State Seward asserted that Wilkes had rightfully considered the envoys to be "contraband of war," but had erred by not bringing the *Trent* into an American port so that the matter could be tried in a prize court.

———————

London 30 Nov. 1861.
My dear Boy
    If I thought the state of things bad last week you may imagine what I think of them now. In fact I consider that we are dished, and that our position is hopeless. If the Administration ordered the capture of those men, I am satisfied that our present authorities are very unsuitable persons to conduct a war like this or to remain in the direction of our affairs. It is our ruin. Do not deceive yourself about the position of England. We might have preserved our dignity in many ways without going to war with her, and our party in the Cabinet was always strong enough to maintain peace here and keep down the anti-blockaders. But now all the fat's in the fire, and I feel like going off and taking up my old German life again as a permanency. It is devilish disagreeable to act the part of Sisyphus especially when it is our own friends who are trying to crush us under the rock.
    What part it is reserved to us to play in this very tragical comedy I am utterly unable to tell. The Government has left us in the most awkward and unfair position. They have given no warning that such an act was thought of, and seem almost to have purposely encouraged us to waste our strength in trying to maintain the relations which it was itself intending to destroy. I am half-mad with vexation and despair. If papa is

ordered home I shall do as Fairfax did, and go into the war with 'peace' on my mind and lips.

Our position here is of course very unpleasant just now. We were to have gone to Lord Hatherton's on Monday, but now our visit is put off, and I am not without expectations that a very few weeks may see us either on our way home or on the continent. I think that the New Year will see the end.

This nation means to make war. Do not doubt it. What Seward means is more than I can guess. But if he means war also, or to run as close as he can without touching, then I say that Mr Seward is the greatest criminal we've had yet.

We have friends here still, but very few. Bright dined with us last night, and is with us, but is evidently hopeless of seeing anything good. Besides, his assistance at such a time as this is evidently a disadvantage to us, for he is now wholly out of power and influence. Our friends are all very much cast down and my friends of the Spectator sent up to me in a dreadful state and asked me to come down to see them, which I did, and they complained bitterly of the position we were now in. I had of course the pleasure of returning the complaint to any extent, but after all this is poor consolation.

Our good father is cool but evidently of the same mind as I am. He has seen Lord Russell but could give him no information, and my Lord did not volunteer any on his side. You will know very soon what you are to expect.

The house is not cheerful, and our good mother is in a state that does not tend to raise our spirits. Still we manage to worry along and I reserve my complaints for paper. Our minds have been so kept on the stretch for the last week that I feel a sort of permanent lowness and wretchedness which does not prevent laughing and gossiping though it does not give them much zest. Theodore writes me from Paris. No news of importance has yet reached my ears, but you will see my views as usual in the Times. We are preparing for a departure, though as yet we have taken no positive steps towards making future arrangements.

Beaufort was good. It gave me one glorious day worth a large share of all the anxiety and trouble that preceded and have followed it. Our cry now must be emancipation and arming the slaves.

Ever Yrs   HB.A.

WASHINGTON, D.C., DECEMBER 1861

Abraham Lincoln: Annual Message to Congress

In his first annual message to Congress Lincoln reviewed the progress of the conflict and recommended a series of war-related measures, including a program for the emancipation and colonization of slaves confiscated from Confederate owners.

Annual Message to Congress

FELLOW CITIZENS of the Senate and House of Representatives:

In the midst of unprecedented political troubles, we have cause of great gratitude to God for unusual good health, and most abundant harvests.

You will not be surprised to learn that, in the peculiar exigencies of the times, our intercourse with foreign nations has been attended with profound solicitude, chiefly turning upon our own domestic affairs.

A disloyal portion of the American people have, during the whole year, been engaged in an attempt to divide and destroy the Union. A nation which endures factious domestic division, is exposed to disrespect abroad; and one party, if not both, is sure, sooner or later, to invoke foreign intervention.

Nations, thus tempted to interfere, are not always able to resist the counsels of seeming expediency, and ungenerous ambition, although measures adopted under such influences seldom fail to be unfortunate and injurious to those adopting them.

The disloyal citizens of the United States who have offered the ruin of our country, in return for the aid and comfort which they have invoked abroad, have received less patronage and encouragement than they probably expected. If it were just to suppose, as the insurgents have seemed to assume, that foreign nations, in this case, discarding all moral, social, and treaty obligations, would act solely, and selfishly, for the most speedy restoration of commerce, including, especially, the acquisition of cotton, those nations appear, as yet, not to have seen their way to their object more directly, or clearly, through the destruction, than through the preservation, of the Union. If we could dare to believe that foreign nations are actuated by no higher principle than this, I am quite sure a sound argument could be made to show them that they can reach their aim more readily, and easily, by aiding to crush this rebellion, than by giving encouragement to it.

The principal lever relied on by the insurgents for exciting foreign nations to hostility against us, as already intimated, is the embarrassment of commerce. Those nations, however, not improbably, saw from the first, that it was the Union which made as well our foreign, as our domestic, commerce. They can scarcely have failed to perceive that the effort for disunion produces the existing difficulty; and that one strong nation promises more durable peace, and a more extensive, valuable and reliable commerce, than can the same nation broken into hostile fragments.

It is not my purpose to review our discussions with foreign states, because whatever might be their wishes, or dispositions, the integrity of our country, and the stability of our government, mainly depend, not upon them, but on the loyalty, virtue, patriotism, and intelligence of the American people. The correspondence itself, with the usual reservations, is herewith submitted.

I venture to hope it will appear that we have practiced prudence, and liberality towards foreign powers, averting causes of irritation; and, with firmness, maintaining our own rights and honor.

Since, however, it is apparent that here, as in every other state, foreign dangers necessarily attend domestic difficulties, I recommend that adequate and ample measures be adopted for maintaining the public defences on every side. While, under this general recommendation, provision for defending our seacoast line readily occurs to the mind, I also, in the same connexion, ask the attention of Congress to our great lakes and rivers. It is believed that some fortifications and depots of arms and munitions, with harbor and navigation improvements, all at well selected points upon these, would be of great importance to the national defence and preservation. I ask attention to the views of the Secretary of War, expressed in his report, upon the same general subject.

I deem it of importance that the loyal regions of East Tennessee and western North Carolina should be connected with Kentucky, and other faithful parts of the Union, by railroad. I therefore recommend, as a military measure, that Congress provide for the construction of such road, as speedily as possible. Kentucky, no doubt, will co-operate, and, through her legislature, make the most judicious selection of a line. The northern terminus must connect with some existing railroad; and whether the route shall be from Lexington, or Nicholasville, to the Cumberland Gap; or from Lebanon to the Tennessee line, in the direction of Knoxville; or on some still different line, can easily be determined. Kentucky and the general government co-operating, the work can be completed in a very short time; and when done, it will be not only of vast present usefulness, but also a valuable permanent improvement, worth its cost in all the future.

Some treaties, designed chiefly for the interests of commerce, and having no grave political importance, have been negotiated, and will be submitted to the Senate for their consideration.

Although we have failed to induce some of the commercial powers to adopt a desirable melioration of the rigor of maritime war, we have removed all obstructions from the way of this humane reform, except such as are merely of temporary and accidental occurrence.

I invite your attention to the correspondence between her Britannic Majesty's minister accredited to this government, and the Secretary of State, relative to the detention of the British ship Perthshire in June last, by the United States steamer Massachusetts, for a supposed breach of the blockade. As this detention was occasioned by an obvious misapprehension of the facts, and as justice requires that we should commit no belligerent act not founded in strict right, as sanctioned by public law, I recommend that an appropriation be made to satisfy the reasonable demand of the owners of the vessel for her detention.

I repeat the recommendation of my predecessor, in his annual message to Congress in December last, in regard to the disposition of the surplus which will probably remain after satisfying the claims of American citizens against China, pursuant to the awards of the commissioners under the act of the 3rd of March, 1859. If, however, it should not be deemed advisable to carry that recommendation into effect, I would suggest that authority be given for investing the principal, over the proceeds of the surplus referred to, in good securities, with a view to the satisfaction of such other just claims of our citizens against China as are not unlikely to arise hereafter in the course of our extensive trade with that Empire.

By the act of the 5th of August last, Congress authorized the President to instruct the commanders of suitable vessels to defend themselves against, and to capture pirates. This authority has been exercised in a single instance only. For the more effectual protection of our extensive and valuable commerce, in the eastern seas especially, it seems to me that it would also be advisable to authorize the commanders of sailing vessels to re-capture any prizes which pirates might make of United States vessels and their cargoes, and the consular courts, now established by law in eastern countries, to adjudicate the cases, in the event that this should not be objected to by the local authorities.

If any good reason exists why we should persevere longer in withholding our recognition of the independence and sovereignty of Hayti and Liberia, I am unable to discern it. Unwilling, however, to inaugurate a novel policy in regard to them without the approbation of Congress, I submit for your consideration the expediency of an appropriation for maintaining a chargé d'affaires near each of those new states. It does not admit of doubt that important commercial advantages might be secured by favorable commercial treaties with them.

The operations of the treasury during the period which has elapsed since your adjournment have been conducted with signal success. The patriotism of the people has placed at the disposal of the government the large means demanded by the public exigencies. Much of the national loan has been taken by citizens of the industrial classes, whose confidence in their country's faith, and zeal for their country's deliverance from present peril, have induced them to contribute to the support of the government the whole of their limited acquisitions. This fact imposes peculiar obligations to economy in disbursement and energy in action.

The revenue from all sources, including loans, for the financial year ending on the 30th June, 1861, was eighty six million, eight hundred and thirty five thousand, nine hundred dollars, and twenty seven cents, ($86,835,900.27,) and the expenditures for the same period, including payments on account of the public debt, were eighty four million, five hundred and seventy eight thousand, eight hundred and thirty four dollars and forty seven cents, ($84,578,834.47;) leaving a balance in the treasury, on the 1st July, of two million, two hundred and fifty seven thousand, sixty five dollars and eighty cents, ($2,257,065.80.) For the first quarter of the financial year, ending on the 30th September, 1861, the receipts from all sources, including the balance of first of July, were $102,532,509.27, and the expenses $98,239,733.09; leaving a balance on the 1st of October, 1861, of $4,292,776.18.

Estimates for the remaining three quarters of the year, and for the financial year 1863, together with his views of ways and means for meeting the demands contemplated by them, will be submitted to Congress by the Secretary of the Treasury. It is gratifying to know that the expenditures made necessary by the rebellion are not beyond the resources of the loyal people, and to believe that the same patriotism which has thus far sustained the government will continue to sustain it till Peace and Union shall again bless the land.

I respectfully refer to the report of the Secretary of War for information respecting the numerical strength of the army, and for recommendations having in view an increase of its efficiency and the well being of the various branches of the service intrusted to his care. It is gratifying to know that the patriotism of the people has proved equal to the occasion, and that the number of troops tendered greatly exceeds the force which Congress authorized me to call into the field.

I refer with pleasure to those portions of his report which make allusion to the creditable degree of discipline already attained by our troops, and to the excellent sanitary condition of the entire army.

The recommendation of the Secretary for an organization of the militia upon a uniform basis, is a subject of vital importance to the future safety of the country, and is commended to the serious attention of Congress.

The large addition to the regular army, in connexion with the defection that has so considerably diminished the number of its officers, gives peculiar importance to his recommendation for increasing the corps of cadets to the greatest capacity of the Military Academy.

By mere omission, I presume, Congress has failed to provide chaplains for hospitals occupied by volunteers. This subject was brought to my notice, and I was induced to draw up the form of a letter, one copy of which, properly addressed, has been delivered to each of the persons, and at the dates respectively named and stated, in a schedule, containing also the form of the letter, marked A, and herewith transmitted.

These gentlemen, I understand, entered upon the duties designated, at the times respectively stated in the schedule, and have labored faithfully therein ever since. I therefore recommend that they be compensated at the same rate as chaplains in the army. I further suggest that general provision be made for chaplains to serve at hospitals, as well as with regiments.

The report of the Secretary of the Navy presents in detail the operations of that branch of the service, the activity and energy which have characterized its administration, and the results of measures to increase its efficiency and power. Such have been the additions, by construction and purchase, that it may almost be said a navy has been created and brought into service since our difficulties commenced.

Besides blockading our extensive coast, squadrons larger than ever before assembled under our flag have been put afloat and performed deeds which have increased our naval renown.

I would invite special attention to the recommendation of the Secretary for a more perfect organization of the navy by introducing additional grades in the service.

The present organization is defective and unsatisfactory, and the suggestions submitted by the department will, it is believed, if adopted, obviate the difficulties alluded to, promote harmony, and increase the efficiency of the navy.

There are three vacancies on the bench of the Supreme Court—two by the decease of Justices Daniel and McLean, and one by the resignation of Justice Campbell. I have so far forborne making nominations to fill these vacancies for reasons which I will now state. Two of the outgoing judges resided within the States now overrun by revolt; so that if successors were appointed in the same localities, they could not now serve upon their circuits; and many of the most competent men there, probably would not take the personal hazard of accepting to serve, even here, upon the supreme bench. I have been unwilling to throw all the appointments northward, thus disabling myself from doing justice to the south on the return of peace; although I may remark that to transfer to the north one which has heretofore been in the south, would not, with reference to territory and population, be unjust.

During the long and brilliant judicial career of Judge McLean his circuit grew into an empire—altogether too large for any one judge to give the courts therein more than a nominal attendance—rising in population from one million four hundred and seventy-thousand and eighteen, in 1830, to six million one hundred and fifty-one thousand four hundred and five, in 1860.

Besides this, the country generally has outgrown our present judicial system. If uniformity was at all intended, the system requires that all the States shall be accommodated with circuit courts, attended by supreme judges, while, in fact, Wisconsin, Minnesota, Iowa, Kansas, Florida, Texas, California, and Oregon, have never had any such courts. Nor can this well be remedied without a change of the system; because the adding of judges to the Supreme Court, enough for the accommodation of all parts of the country, with circuit courts, would create a court altogether too numerous for a judicial body of any sort. And the evil, if it be one, will increase as new States come into the Union. Circuit courts are useful, or they are not useful. If useful, no State should be denied them; if not useful, no State should have them. Let them be provided for all, or abolished as to all.

Three modifications occur to me, either of which, I think, would be an improvement upon our present system. Let the Supreme Court be of convenient number in every event. Then, first, let the whole country be divided into circuits of convenient size, the supreme judges to serve in a number of them corresponding to their own number, and independent circuit judges be provided for all the rest. Or, secondly, let the supreme judges be relieved from circuit duties, and circuit judges provided for all the circuits. Or, thirdly, dispense with circuit courts altogether, leaving the judicial functions wholly to the district courts and an independent Supreme Court.

I respectfully recommend to the consideration of Congress the present condition of the statute laws, with the hope that Congress will be able to find an easy remedy for many of the inconveniences and evils which constantly embarrass those engaged in the practical administration of them. Since the organization of the government, Congress has enacted some five thousand acts and joint resolutions, which fill more than six thousand closely printed pages, and are scattered through many volumes. Many of these acts have been drawn in haste and without sufficient caution, so that their provisions are often obscure in themselves, or in conflict with each other, or at least so doubtful as to render it very difficult for even the best informed persons to ascertain precisely what the statute law really is.

It seems to me very important that the statute laws should be made as plain and intelligible as possible, and be reduced to as small a compass as may consist with the fullness and precision of the will of the legislature and the perspicuity of its language. This, well done, would, I think, greatly facilitate the labors of those whose duty it is to assist in the administration of the laws, and would be a lasting benefit to the people, by placing before them, in a more accessible and intelligible form, the laws which so deeply concern their interests and their duties.

I am informed by some whose opinions I respect, that all the acts of Congress now in force, and of a permanent and general nature, might be revised and re-written, so as to be embraced in one volume (or at most, two volumes) of ordinary and convenient size. And I respectfully recommend to Congress to consider of the subject, and, if my suggestion be approved, to devise such plan as to their wisdom shall seem most proper for the attainment of the end proposed.

One of the unavoidable consequences of the present insurrection is the entire suppression, in many places, of all the ordinary means of administering civil justice by the officers and in the forms of existing law. This is the case, in whole or in part, in all the insurgent States; and as our armies advance upon and take possession of parts of those States, the practical evil becomes more apparent. There are no courts nor officers to whom the citizens of other States may apply for the enforcement of their lawful claims against citizens of the insurgent States; and there is a vast amount of debt constituting such claims. Some have estimated it as high as two hundred million dollars, due, in large part, from insurgents, in open rebellion, to loyal citizens who are, even now, making great sacrifices in the discharge of their patriotic duty to support the government.

Under these circumstances, I have been urgently solicited to establish, by military power, courts to administer summary justice in such cases. I have thus far declined to do it, not because I had any doubt that the end proposed—the collection of the debts—was just and right in itself, but because I have been unwilling to go beyond the pressure of necessity in the unusual exercise of power. But the powers of Congress I suppose are equal to the anomalous occasion, and therefore I refer the whole matter to Congress, with the hope that a plan may be devised for the administration of justice in all such parts of the insurgent States and Territories as may be under the control of this government, whether by a voluntary return to allegiance and order or by the power of our arms. This, however, not to be a permanent institution, but a temporary substitute, and to cease as soon as the ordinary courts can be re-established in peace.

It is important that some more convenient means should be provided, if possible, for the adjustment of claims against the government, especially in view of their increased number by reason of the war. It is as much the duty of government to render prompt justice against itself, in favor of citizens, as it is to administer the same, between private individuals. The investigation and adjudication of claims, in their nature belong to the judicial department; besides it is apparent that the attention of Congress, will be more than usually engaged, for some time to come, with great national questions. It was intended, by the organization of the court of claims, mainly to remove this branch of business from the halls of Congress; but while the court has proved to be an effective, and valuable means of investigation, it in great degree fails to effect the object of its creation, for want of power to make its judgments final.

Fully aware of the delicacy, not to say the danger, of the subject, I commend to your careful consideration whether this power of making judgments final, may not properly be given to the court, reserving the right of appeal on questions of law to the Supreme Court, with such other provisions as experience may have shown to be necessary.

I ask attention to the report of the Postmaster General, the following being a summary statement of the condition of the department:

The revenue from all sources during the fiscal year ending June 30. 1861, including the annual permanent appropriation of seven hundred thousand dollars ($700,000) for the transportation of "free mail matter," was nine million, forty nine thousand, two hundred and ninety six dollars and forty cents ($9,049,296.40) being about two per cent. less than the revenue for 1860.

The expenditures were thirteen million, six hundred and six thousand, seven hundred and fifty nine dollars and eleven cents. ($13,606,759.11) showing a decrease of more than eight per cent. as compared with those of the previous year, and leaving an excess of expenditure over the revenue for the last fiscal year of four million, five hundred and fifty seven thousand, four hundred and sixty two dollars and seventy one cents ($4,557,462.71.)

The gross revenue for the year ending June 30, 1863, is estimated at an increase of four per cent. on that of 1861, making eight million, six hundred and eighty three thousand dollars ($8,683,000) to which should be added the earnings of the department in carrying free matter, viz: seven hundred thousand dollars ($700,000.) making nine million, three hundred and eighty three thousand dollars, ($9,383,000.)

The total expenditures for 1863 are estimated at $12,528,000, leaving an estimated deficiency of $3,145,000, to be supplied from the treasury, in addition to the permanent appropriation.

The present insurrection shows, I think, that the extension of this District across the Potomac river, at the time of establishing the capital here, was eminently wise, and consequently that the relinquishment of that portion of it which lies within the State of Virginia was unwise and dangerous. I submit for your consideration the expediency of regaining that part of the District, and the restoration of the original boundaries thereof, through negotiations with the State of Virginia.

The report of the Secretary of the Interior, with the accompanying documents, exhibits the condition of the several branches of the public business pertaining to that department. The depressing influences of the insurrection have been especially felt in the operations of the Patent and General Land Offices. The cash receipts from the sales of public lands during the past year have exceeded the expenses of our land system only about $200,000. The sales have been entirely suspended in the southern States, while the interruptions to the business of the country, and the diversion of large numbers of men from labor to military service, have obstructed settlements in the new States and Territories of the northwest.

The receipts of the Patent Office have declined in nine months about $100,000, rendering a large reduction of the force employed necessary to make it self sustaining.

The demands upon the Pension Office will be largely increased by the insurrection. Numerous applications for pensions, based upon the casualties of the existing war, have already been made. There is reason to believe that many who are now upon the pension rolls and in receipt of the bounty of the government, are in the ranks of the insurgent army, or giving them aid and comfort. The Secretary of the Interior has directed a suspension of the payment of the pensions of such persons upon proof of their disloyalty. I recommend that Congress authorize that officer to cause the names of such persons to be stricken from the pension rolls.

The relations of the government with the Indian tribes have been greatly disturbed by the insurrection, especially in the southern superintendency and in that of New Mexico. The Indian country south of Kansas is in the possession of insurgents from Texas and Arkansas. The agents of the United States appointed since the 4th. of March for this superintendency have been unable to reach their posts, while the most of those who were in office before that time have espoused the insurrectionary cause, and assume to exercise the powers of agents by virtue of commissions from the insurrectionists. It has been stated in the public press that a portion of those Indians have been organized as a military force, and are attached to the army of the insurgents. Although the government has no official information upon this subject, letters have been written to the Commissioner of Indian Affairs by several prominent chiefs, giving assurance of their loyalty to the United States, and expressing a wish for the presence of federal troops to protect them. It is believed that upon the repossession of the country by the federal forces the Indians will readily cease all hostile demonstrations, and resume their former relations to the government.

Agriculture, confessedly the largest interest of the nation, has, not a department, nor a bureau, but a clerkship only, assigned to it in the government. While it is fortunate that this great interest is so independent in its nature as to not have demanded and extorted more from the government, I respectfully ask Congress to consider whether something more cannot be given voluntarily with general advantage.

Annual reports exhibiting the condition of our agriculture, commerce, and manufactures would present a fund of information of great practical value to the country. While I make no suggestion as to details, I venture the opinion that an agricultural and statistical bureau might profitably be organized.

The execution of the laws for the suppression of the African slave trade, has been confided to the Department of the Interior. It is a subject of gratulation that the efforts which have been made for the suppression of this inhuman traffic, have been recently attended with unusual success. Five vessels being fitted out for the slave trade have been seized and condemned. Two mates of vessels engaged in the trade, and one person in equipping a vessel as a slaver, have been convicted and subjected to the penalty of fine and imprisonment, and one captain, taken with a cargo of Africans on board his vessel, has been convicted of the highest grade of offence under our laws, the punishment of which is death.

The Territories of Colorado, Dakotah and Nevada, created by the last Congress, have been organized, and civil administration has been inaugurated therein under auspices especially gratifying, when it is considered that the leaven of treason was found existing in some of these new countries when the federal officers arrived there.

The abundant natural resources of these Territories, with the security and protection afforded by organized government, will doubtless invite to them a large immigration when peace shall restore the business of the country to its accustomed channels. I submit the resolutions of the legislature of Colorado, which evidence the patriotic spirit of the people of the Territory. So far the authority of the United States has been upheld in all the Territories, as it is hoped it will be in the future. I commend their interests and defence to the enlightened and generous care of Congress.

I recommend to the favorable consideration of Congress the interests of the District of Columbia. The insurrection has been the cause of much suffering and sacrifice to its inhabitants, and as they have no representative in Congress, that body should not overlook their just claims upon the government.

At your late session a joint resolution was adopted authorizing the President to take measures for facilitating a proper representation of the industrial interests of the United States at the exhibition of the industry of all nations to be holden at London in the year 1862. I regret to say I have been unable to give personal attention to this subject,—a subject at once so interesting in itself, and so extensively and intimately connected with the material prosperity of the world. Through the Secretaries of State and of the Interior a plan, or system, has been devised, and partly matured, and which will be laid before you.

Under and by virtue of the act of Congress entitled "An act to confiscate property used for insurrectionary purposes," approved August, 6, 1861, the legal claims of certain persons to the labor and service of certain other persons have become forfeited; and numbers of the latter, thus liberated, are already dependent on the United States, and must be provided for in some way. Besides this, it is not impossible that some of the States will pass similar enactments for their own benefit respectively, and by operation of which persons of the same class will be thrown upon them for disposal. In such case I recommend that Congress provide for accepting such persons from such States, according to some mode of valuation, in lieu, *pro tanto*, of direct taxes, or upon some other plan to be agreed on with such States respectively; that such persons, on such acceptance by the general government, be at once deemed free; and that, in any event, steps be taken for colonizing both classes, (or the one first mentioned, if the other shall not be brought into existence,) at some place, or places, in a climate congenial to them. It might be well to consider, too,—whether the free colored people already in the United States could not, so far as individuals may desire, be included in such colonization.

To carry out the plan of colonization may involve the acquiring of territory, and also the appropriation of money beyond that to be expended in the territorial acquisition. Having practiced the acquisition of territory for nearly sixty years, the question of constitutional power to do so is no longer an open one with us. The power was questioned at first by Mr. Jefferson, who, however, in the purchase of Louisiana, yielded his scruples on the plea of great expediency. If it be said that the only legitimate object of acquiring territory is to furnish homes for white men, this measure effects that object; for the emigration of colored men leaves additional room for white men remaining or coming here. Mr. Jefferson, however, placed the importance of procuring Louisiana more on political and commercial grounds than on providing room for population.

On this whole proposition,—including the appropriation of money with the acquisition of territory, does not the expediency amount to absolute necessity—that, without which the government itself cannot be perpetuated? The war continues. In considering the policy to be adopted for suppressing the insurrection, I have been anxious and careful that the inevitable conflict for this purpose shall not degenerate into a violent and remorseless revolutionary struggle. I have, therefore, in every case, thought it proper to keep the integrity of the Union prominent as the primary object of the contest on our part, leaving all questions which are not of vital military importance to the more deliberate action of the legislature.

In the exercise of my best discretion I have adhered to the blockade of the ports held by the insurgents, instead of putting in force, by proclamation, the law of Congress enacted at the late session, for closing those ports.

So, also, obeying the dictates of prudence, as well as the obligations of law, instead of transcending, I have adhered to the act of Congress to confiscate property used for insurrectionary purposes. If a new law upon the same subject shall be proposed, its propriety will be duly considered.

The Union must be preserved, and hence, all indispensable means must be employed. We should not be in haste to determine that radical and extreme measures, which may reach the loyal as well as the disloyal, are indispensable.

The inaugural address at the beginning of the Administration, and the message to Congress at the late special session, were both mainly devoted to the domestic controversy out of which the insurrection and consequent war have sprung. Nothing now occurs to add or subtract, to or from, the principles or general purposes stated and expressed in those documents.

The last ray of hope for preserving the Union peaceably, expired at the assault upon Fort Sumter; and a general review of what has occurred since may not be unprofitable. What was painfully uncertain then, is much better defined and more distinct now; and the progress of events is plainly in the right direction. The insurgents confidently claimed a strong support from north of Mason and Dixon's line; and the friends of the Union were not free from apprehension on the point. This, however, was soon settled definitely and on the right side. South of the line, noble little Delaware led off right from the first. Maryland was made to *seem* against the Union. Our soldiers were assaulted, bridges were burned, and railroads torn up, within her limits; and we were many days, at one time, without the ability to bring a single regiment over her soil to the capital. Now, her bridges and railroads are repaired and open to the government; she already gives seven regiments to the cause of the Union and none to the enemy; and her people, at a regular election, have sustained the Union, by a larger majority, and a larger aggregate vote than they ever before gave to any candidate, or any question. Kentucky, too, for some time in doubt, is now decidedly, and, I think, unchangeably, ranged on the side of the Union. Missouri is comparatively quiet; and I believe cannot again be overrun by the insurrectionists. These three States of Maryland, Kentucky, and Missouri, neither of which would promise a single soldier at first, have now an aggregate of not less than forty thousand in the field, for the Union; while, of their citizens, certainly not more than a third of that number, and they of doubtful whereabouts, and doubtful existence, are in arms against it. After a somewhat bloody struggle of months, winter closes on the Union people of western Virginia, leaving them masters of their own country.

An insurgent force of about fifteen hundred, for months dominating the narrow peninsular region, constituting the counties of Accomac and Northampton, and known as eastern shore of Virginia, together with some contiguous parts of Maryland, have laid down their arms; and the people there have renewed their allegiance to, and accepted the protection of, the old flag. This leaves no armed insurrectionist north of the Potomac, or east of the Chesapeake.

Also we have obtained a footing at each of the isolated points, on the southern coast, of Hatteras, Port Royal, Tybee Island, near Savannah, and Ship Island; and we likewise have some general accounts of popular movements, in behalf of the Union, in North Carolina and Tennessee.

These things demonstrate that the cause of the Union is advancing steadily and certainly southward.

Since your last adjournment, Lieutenant General Scott has retired from the head of the army. During his long life, the nation has not been unmindful of his merit; yet, on calling to mind how faithfully, ably and brilliantly he has served the country, from a time far back in our history, when few of the now living had been born, and thenceforward continually, I cannot but think we are still his debtors. I submit, therefore, for your consideration, what further mark of recognition is due to him, and to ourselves, as a grateful people.

With the retirement of General Scott came the executive duty of appointing, in his stead, a general-in-chief of the army. It is a fortunate circumstance that neither in council nor country was there, so far as I know, any difference of opinion as to the proper person to be selected. The retiring chief repeatedly expressed his judgment in favor of General McClellan for the position; and in this the nation seemed to give a unanimous concurrence. The designation of General McClellan is therefore in considerable degree, the selection of the Country as well as of the Executive; and hence there is better reason to hope there will be given him, the confidence, and cordial support thus, by fair implication, promised, and without which, he cannot, with so full efficiency, serve the country.

It has been said that one bad general is better than two good ones; and the saying is true, if taken to mean no more than that an army is better directed by a single mind, though inferior, than by two superior ones, at variance, and cross-purposes with each other.

And the same is true, in all joint operations wherein those engaged, *can* have none but a common end in view, and *can* differ only as to the choice of means. In a storm at sea, no one on board *can* wish the ship to sink; and yet, not unfrequently, all go down together, because too many will direct, and no single mind can be allowed to control.

It continues to develop that the insurrection is largely, if not exclusively, a war upon the first principle of popular government —the rights of the people. Conclusive evidence of this is found in the most grave and maturely considered public documents, as well as in the general tone of the insurgents. In those documents we find the abridgement of the existing right of suffrage and the denial to the people of all right to participate in the selection of public officers, except the legislative boldly advocated, with labored arguments to prove that large control of the people in government, is the source of all political evil. Monarchy itself is sometimes hinted at as a possible refuge from the power of the people.

In my present position, I could scarcely be justified were I to omit raising a warning voice against this approach of returning despotism.

It is not needed, nor fitting here, that a general argument should be made in favor of popular institutions; but there is one point, with its connexions, not so hackneyed as most others, to which I ask a brief attention. It is the effort to place *capital* on an equal footing with, if not above *labor*, in the structure of government. It is assumed that labor is available only in connexion with capital; that nobody labors unless somebody else, owning capital, somehow by the use of it, induces him to labor. This assumed, it is next considered whether it is best that capital shall *hire* laborers, and thus induce them to work by their own consent, or *buy* them, and drive them to it without their consent. Having proceeded so far, it is naturally concluded that all laborers are either *hired* laborers, or what we call slaves. And further it is assumed that whoever is once a hired laborer, is fixed in that condition for life.

Now, there is no such relation between capital and labor as assumed; nor is there any such thing as a free man being fixed for life in the condition of a hired laborer. Both these assumptions are false, and all inferences from them are groundless.

Labor is prior to, and independent of, capital. Capital is only the fruit of labor, and could never have existed if labor had not first existed. Labor is the superior of capital, and deserves much the higher consideration. Capital has its rights, which are as worthy of protection as any other rights. Nor is it denied that there is, and probably always will be, a relation between labor and capital, producing mutual benefits. The error is in assuming that the whole labor of community exists within that relation. A few men own capital, and that few avoid labor themselves, and, with their capital, hire or buy another few to labor for them. A large majority belong to neither class—neither work for others, nor have others working for them. In most of the southern States, a majority of the whole people of all colors are neither slaves nor masters; while in the northern a large majority are neither hirers nor hired. Men with their families—wives, sons, and daughters—work for themselves, on their farms, in their houses, and in their shops, taking the whole product to themselves, and asking no favors of capital on the one hand, nor of hired laborers or slaves on the other. It is not forgotten that a considerable number of persons mingle their own labor with capital—that is, they labor with their own hands, and also buy or hire others to labor for them; but this is only a mixed, and not a distinct class. No principle stated is disturbed by the existence of this mixed class.

Again: as has already been said, there is not, of necessity, any such thing as the free hired laborer being fixed to that condition for life. Many independent men everywhere in these States, a few years back in their lives, were hired laborers. The prudent, penniless beginner in the world, labors for wages awhile, saves a surplus with which to buy tools or land for himself; then labors on his own account another while, and at length hires another new beginner to help him. This is the just, and generous, and prosperous system, which opens the way to all—gives hope to all, and consequent energy, and progress, and improvement of condition to all. No men living are more worthy to be trusted than those who toil up from poverty—none less inclined to take, or touch, aught which they have not honestly earned. Let them beware of surrendering a political power which they already possess, and which, if surrendered, will surely be used to close the door of advancement against such as they, and to fix new disabilities and burdens upon them, till all of liberty shall be lost.

From the first taking of our national census to the last are seventy years; and we find our population at the end of the period eight times as great as it was at the beginning. The increase of those other things which men deem desirable has been even greater. We thus have at one view, what the popular principle applied to government, through the machinery of the States and the Union, has produced in a given time; and also what, if firmly maintained, it promises for the future. There are already among us those, who, if the Union be preserved, will live to see it contain two hundred and fifty millions. The struggle of today, is not altogether for today—it is for a vast future also. With a reliance on Providence, all the more firm and earnest, let us proceed in the great task which events have devolved upon us.

December 3, 1861

PREPARING TO ENLIST:
BOSTON, DECEMBER 1861

Charles Francis Adams Jr. to Henry Adams

Shortly after writing to his brother, Charles Francis Adams Jr. was commissioned as a first lieutenant in the 1st Massachusetts Cavalry. He would sail with his regiment for Port Royal, South Carolina, at the end of the year.

———————

Boston, December 10, 1861

Yours of the 23d of last month reached me yesterday. . . . If we are going to have such a storm as you intimate, I should have to go, so anyhow, and if indeed "all that remains is to drop gracefully," it will not do me or any one else any good for me to anxiously hang on here a few days longer. Yet it does make me feel terribly. We have blundered all summer long and now we have capstoned our blunders by blundering into a war with England. So be it. While there's life there's hope; but I go into the army with a bitter feeling against those under whose lead we have come to this pass, and amid all the shattered idols of my whole life I don't feel as if I cared much when my turn came. I suppose now I shall go into the field against a foreign enemy and I ought to rejoice at that. Still, I don't. Against the rebels I could fight with a will and in earnest. They are traitors, they war for a lie, they are the enemies of morals, of government, and of man. In them we fight against a great wrong—but against England, we shall have forced her into war when she only asked for peace; we shall have made that a cause of quarrel which a few soft words might have turned away. It will be a wicked and causeless war wantonly brought about by us and one in which I most unwillingly would go to my death.

As for Seward I cannot comprehend his policy and so I cannot judge of it, and most slowly and reluctantly will I surrender my faith in him. His policy has been to keep a firm front, and in this it was wise; but I think he might have made himself less offensive to foreign powers in doing it, and I somewhat doubt the expediency of bragging yourself out of the game, as you tell me he has done. Still we have made our bed and now we must lie on it.

I shall probably have joined my regiment this week or early next. You will be surprised to hear that I shall probably regularly enlist and make my début as a simple sergeant in Caspar Crowninshield's company. The truth is they have so backed and filled, and hesitated and delayed, that, having determined to go, I have lost my patience, and have signified to them that I am ready to wait in the ranks until they are ready to give me a commission. Caspar got his company as a promotion for his behavior at Balls Bluff, and I shall get mine, I suppose, at some indefinite future period, when Sargent ceases to be a gas-bag and Williams feels the regiment under his thumb. Meanwhile I shall rough and fight it out with the rest, sleep fifteen in a tent with stable-boys, groom horses, feed like a hog and never wash, and such is my future! Well, it is better than my present, for I shall at least, by going into the army, get rid of the war.

Your last letter, and your statement that there was nothing left but a suspension of relations with England, came peculiarly unpleasantly just now. I had again begun to hope. Our blockade has become so effective and we are developing such enormous strength, that in spite of blunders, the confederates seemed likely to be crushed by brute force and starved to death, while we are really more prosperous than we have been for a year, and our poor more comfortable than they have been for four years. The confederates already, before winter begins, are regulating by law the profit on "articles of prime necessity," and what would it have been before spring? I had begun to hope yet to see this rebellion collapse. Of course a war with England exactly reverses positions. It will be short and desperate, and end in the establishment of a confederate government, I suppose. However, a glorious indifference is coming over me. I can live on my pay, the world will not come to an end this time, and if I do, I shall doubtless be very comfortable in my grave. But I do hate to be blundered out of existence and, before a foreign war just as we were getting the whip-hand. Even Balls Bluff will hide a diminished head; it will stand forth in all history as the Koh-i-noor of blunders. . . .

A SONG OF THE CONTRABANDS: VIRGINIA, 1861

Let My People Go

The Reverend Lewis Lockwood was sent by the American Missionary Association to Fort Monroe, Virginia, in September 1861 to assist the former slaves living within the Union lines. While he was at the fort Lockwood recorded the words to the song from the dictation of Carl Hollosay and other "contrabands," who told him that it had been sung in Virginia and Maryland for at least fifteen or twenty years. Lockwood sent his transcription to Harwood Vernon of the YMCA, who published it in the *New-York Daily Tribune* on December 2, 1861. The transcription also appeared in the *National Anti-Slavery Standard* on December 21.

———————

Let My People Go

A Song of the "Contrabands"

When Israel was in Egypt's land,
   O let my people go!
Oppressed so hard they could not stand,
   O let my people go!

> *O go down, Moses*
> *Away down to Egypt's land,*
> *And tell King Pharaoh,*
> *To let my people go!*

Thus saith the Lord, bold Moses said,
   O let my people go!
If not, I'll smite your first born dead,
   O let my people go!

No more shall they in bondage toil,
   O let my people go!
Let them come out with Egypt's spoil,

O let my people go!

Then Israel out of Egypt came,
  O let my people go!
And left the proud oppressive land,
  O let my people go!

O 'twas a dark and dismal night,
  O let my people go!
When Moses led the Israelites,
  O let my people go!

'Twas good old Moses, and Aaron, too,
  O let my people go!
'Twas they that led the armies through,
  O let my people go!

The Lord told Moses what to do,
  O let my people go!
To lead the children of Israel through,
  O let my people go!

O come along Moses, you'll not get lost,
  O let my people go!
Stretch out your rod and come across,
  O let my people go!

As Israel stood by the water side,
  O let my people go!
At the command of God it did divide,
  O let my people go!

When they had reached the other shore,
  O let my people go!
They sang a song of triumph o'er,
  O let my people go!

Pharaoh said he would go across,
    O let my people go!
But Pharaoh and his host were lost,
    O let my people go!

O Moses, the cloud shall cleave the way,
    O let my people go!
A fire by night, a shade by day,
    O let my people go!

You'll not get lost in the wilderness,
    O let my people go!
With a lighted candle in your breast,
    O let my people go!

Jordan shall stand up like a wall,
    O let my people go!
And the walls of Jericho shall fall,
    O let my people go!

Your foe shall not before you stand,
    O let my people go!
And you'll possess fair Canaan's land,
    O let my people go!

'Twas just about in harvest time,
    O let my people go!
When Joshua led his host Divine,
    O let my people go!

O let us all from bondage flee,
    O let my people go!
And let us all in Christ be free,
    O let my people go!

We need not always weep and mourn,
    O let my people go!
And wear these Slavery chains forlorn,
    O let my people go!

This world's a wilderness of woe,
  O let my people go!
O let us on to Canaan go,
  O let my people go!

What a beautiful morning that will be!
  O let my people go!
When time breaks up in eternity,
  O let my people go!

NOT RELYING ON FOREIGN AID: DECEMBER 1861
Robert E. Lee to George Washington Custis Lee

Robert E. Lee spent the first three months of the war organizing troops and building fortifications in Virginia. Lee was then sent to western Virginia, where he unsuccessfully tried to regain territory lost to the Union during the summer. On November 5 he was given command of the coastal defenses of South Carolina, Georgia, and east Florida, a position Lee would hold until March 1862, when he was recalled to Richmond to serve as military adviser to Jefferson Davis. He wrote to his son while inspecting coastal defenses in South Carolina.

                              Coosawhatchie, South Carolina
                                          December 29, 1861
I have received my dear son your letter of the 21 & am happy that you have arranged with Mr. Stewart about his house. I feel badly about not having paid rent for it all this time as I fear now I ought to have done. But was misled by what was told me at the time. I am willing to do it now if it can be arranged with propriety & if you can do so let me know. Not having had to pay for my quarters in Richmond I never charged for any or fuel either, & thought that the State would gain by Mr. Stewart's liberality if I did not. I find it would have been better for me & him too now, to have done so. If you can get pleasant people to join in taking the house, it would certainly be more agreable for you to live there than at a hotel, but I know how expensive a bachelor's mess is &c., unless there is someone who will attend to it & conduct it economically. If you can make the arrangement, however, do so, & I will pay my share. I feel extremely obliged to Mr. Stewart for his considerate kindness & for his more than kind sentiments & I hope when you see him you will make my acknowledgements. I heard recently from your mother & hope that you were able to get to spend Xmas with them all at the W H. Mary, she thought,

would be there, & if she gets to Richmond it will be a good opportunity for her to pay a visit to her Uncle Carter. I hope C will get into a good regiment & get promoted too. His friend Long is with me as Chief of Ordnance & Arthur Shaaff reported to me a few days since. I sent him to Savannah to organize & instruct some regiments coming into the service there. I wish indeed I could have you with me if it was best for you, but that no man can say & I am content to leave it to him who orders all for the best. I have two officers of the old service as my aids now, but may have to part with them as soon as I can do better for them. I suppose it is in vain for me to expect to keep an instructed officer, there is such demand for their services with troops. I have wished to get one of our young relatives with me if I could find one to whom it would be agreable & useful to me at the same time, for I have so much to attend to, that I must have those with me who can be of service. I have thought of Johnny Lee or Henry, Bev. Turner &c., &c., for there are a host of our relatives in the army. Who can you recommend to me? I have had numerous applications for the post of aid from citizens, but do not want a retinue around me who seek nominal duty or an excuse to get off of real service elsewhere. I have a great deal of work to do & want men able & willing to do it. I received not long since, a letter from Lewis Conrad applying for the appointment of aid to me. I was unable to grant it, for as I have said I have two now. I should like you to tell me, however, what sort of a youth he is & also your opinion of other youths of our house. All that I have said I of course wish you keep profoundly secret. If I had one of them in service with me I could soon see whether they would suit me, or I them. I should dislike to invite them & then for us to be obliged to part. The news from Europe is indeed good, but I think the United States government, notwithstanding their moral & political commitment to Wilkes' act, if it finds that England is in earnest & that it will have to fight or retract, will retract. We must make up our minds to fight our battles ourselves. Expect to receive aid from no one. Make every necessary sacrifice of comfort, money & labour to bring the war to a successful issue & then we will succeed. The cry is too much for help. I am mortified to hear it. We want no aid. We want to be true to ourselves, to be prudent, just, fair, & bold. I am dreadfully disappointed at the spirit here. They have all of a sudden realized the asperities of war, in what they must encounter, & do not seem to be prepared for it. If I only had some veteran troops to take the brunt, they would soon rally & be inspired with the great principle for which we are contending. The enemy is quiet & safe in his big boats. He is threatening every avenue. Pillaging, burning & robbing where he can venture with impunity & alarming women & children. Every day I have reports of landing in force, marching &c. which turns out to be some marauding party. The last was the North Edisto. I yesterday went over the whole line in that region from the Ashepro to the Wadalaw & found everything quiet & could only see their big black ships lying down the Edisto where the water is too broad for anything we have to reach them. They will not venture as yet in the narrow waters. I went yesterday 115 miles but only 35 on horseback. I did not get back till 11 p.m. I took Greenbrier the whole distance. Take good care of Richmond. Draw his forage on my account. Send him to me if opportunity offers, if you do not want him. I have two horses now with me.

> Good bye my dear son
> R. E. LEE

THE PRESIDENT'S DUTY TO ACT:
WASHINGTON, D.C., DECEMBER 1861

Edward Bates: Diary, December 31, 1861

Attorney General Edward Bates records the uncertainty caused at the end of 1861 by General McClellan's illness and by what Bates saw as President Lincoln's unwillingness to assert himself.

———————

Dec 31. Since last date the weather has been and is remarkably fine. Mr. Eads has been here, bringing his wife, Miss Genevieve and little Mattie—He has returned, by way of N. Y. to St Louis (leaving Genevieve with us, untill his return again in a few weeks). He was sadly disappointed about gitting money, and went away in no good humor with Q. M. G Meigs. I hope it will be all right soon.

I think he has made a very favorable impression upon the Navy Dept, especially with Mr. Fox, asst. Sect: He will probably contract for the building of 4 of the 20 *iron ships* ordered for the Navy, at $500.000 a piece—perhaps a little more.

Mr. Gibson shewed me to day a letter from Gov Gamble in very low spirits—Genl Halleck rules out the militia. The goods sent from here—those clothes and blanketts—expressly for Gambles militia are taken and transfered to other troops, this is too bad.

<*Note*. Jany 3 Mr. Gibson read me another letter from Gov Gamble in much better spirits. He thinks, in the main that Halleck is doing very well.>

Genl McClellan and his chief of staff, Genl Marcey, are both very sick—Said to be typhoid fever—and this is making much difficulty.

The Genl: it seems, is very reticent. Nobody knows his plans. The Sec of war and the President himself are kept in ignorance of the actual condition of the army and the intended movements of the General—if indeed they intend to move at all—In fact the whole administration is lamentably deficient in the lack of unity and co-action. There is no quarrell among us, but an absalute want of community of intelligence, purpose and action.

In truth, it is not *an* administration but the separate and disjointed action of seven independent officers, each one ignorant of what his colleagues are doing.

To day in council, Mr. Chase stated the condition of things in sorrowful plainness; and then, as usual, we had a "bald, disjointed chat" about it, coming to no conclusion.

It seemed as if all military operations were to stop, just because Genl McClellan is sick! Some proposed that there should be a council of war composed of Maj: Genls, in order that somebody besides the Genl in chief, may know something about the army; and be able to take command in case Genl McC should die or continue sick.

I differed, and told the President that *he* was commander in chief, and that it was not his *privilege* but his *duty* to command; and *that* implied the necessity to *know* the true condition of things.

That if I was in his place, I *would know*; and if things were not done to my liking, I would order them otherwise. That I believed he could get along easier and much better by the free use of his power, than by this injurious deference to his subordinates.

I said, the Sec of War is but the Adjutant Genl. and the Sec of the Navy the Admiral of the commander in chief, and through them, he ought to know all that is necessary to be known about the army and Navy. And I urged upon him (as often heretofore) the propriety of detailing at least two active and skillful officers to act as his aids, to write and carry his orders, collect his information, keep his military books and papers, and do his bidding generally in military affairs.

But I fear that I spoke in vain. The Prest. is an excellent man, and, in the main wise; but he lacks *will* and *purpose*, and, I greatly fear he, has not *the power to command*.

LINCOLN AND MCCLELLAN:
WASHINGTON, D.C., JANUARY 1862

Irvin McDowell: Memorandum, January 10–13, 1862

This selection is taken from a memorandum written by General Irvin McDowell and first printed in *The Life and Public Services of Abraham Lincoln* (1865), a biography published by Henry J. Raymond of the *New York Times* after Lincoln's assassination. Raymond wrote that he submitted a copy of McDowell's memorandum to the President in 1864, and that Lincoln returned it to him in October with an endorsement: "I well remember the meetings herein narrated. See nothing for me to object to in the narrative as being made by General McDowell, except the phrase attributed to me '*of the Jacobinism of Congress*,' which phrase I do not remember using literally or in substance, and which I wish not to be published in any event."

January 10, 1862.—At dinner at Arlington, Virginia. Received a note from the Assistant Secretary of War, saying the President wished to see me that evening at eight o'clock, if I could safely leave my post. Soon after, I received a note from Quartermaster-General Meigs, marked "Private and confidential," saying the President wished to see me. Note herewith.

Repaired to the President's house at eight o'clock P. M. Found the President alone. Was taken into the small room in the northeast corner. Soon after, we were joined by Brigadier-General Franklin, the Secretary of State, Governor Seward, the Secretary of the Treasury, and the Assistant Secretary of War. The President was greatly disturbed at the state of affairs. Spoke of the exhausted condition of the Treasury; of the loss of public credit; of the Jacobinism in Congress; of the delicate condition of our foreign relations; of the bad news he had received from the West, particularly as contained in a letter from General Halleck on the state of affairs in Missouri; of the want of co-operation between General Halleck and General Buell; but, more than all, the sickness of General McClellan.

The President said he was in great distress, and, as he had been to General McClellan's house, and the General did not ask to see him, and as he must talk to somebody, he had sent for General Franklin and myself, to obtain our opinion as to the possibility of soon commencing active operations with the Army of the Potomac.

To use his own expression, if something was not soon done, the bottom would be out of the whole affair; and, if General McClellan did not want to use the army, he would like to "*borrow it*," provided he could see how it could be made to do something.

The Secretary of State stated the substance of some information he considered reliable, as to the strength of the forces on the other side, which he had obtained from an Englishman from Fortress Monroe, Richmond, Manassas, and Centreville, which was to the effect that the enemy had twenty thousand men under Huger at Norfolk, thirty thousand at Centreville, and, in all, in our front an effective force, capable of being brought up at short notice, of about one hundred and three thousand men—men not suffering, but well shod, clothed, and fed. In answer to the question from the President, what could soon be done with the army, I replied that the question as to the *when* must be preceded by the one as to the *how* and the *where*. That, substantially, I would organize the army into four army corps, placing the five divisions on the Washington side on the right bank. Place three of these corps to the front, the right at Vienna or its vicinity, the left beyond Fairfax Station, the centre beyond Fairfax Court-House, and connect the latter place with the Orange and Alexandria Railroad by a railroad now partially thrown up. This would enable us to supply these corps without the use of horses, except to distribute what was brought up by rail, and to act upon the enemy without reference to the bad state of country roads.

The railroads all lead to the enemy's position. By acting upon them in force, besieging his strongholds, if necessary, or getting between them, if possible, or making the attempt to do so, and pressing his left, I thought we should, in the first place, cause him to bring up all his forces, and mass them on the flank mostly pressed—the left—and, possibly, I thought probably, we should again get them out of their works, and bring on a general engagement on favorable terms to us, at all events keeping him fully occupied and harassed. The fourth corps, in connection with a force of heavy guns afloat, would operate on his right flank, beyond the Occoquan, get behind the batteries on the Potomac, take Aquia, which, being supported by the Third Corps over the Occoquan, it could safely attempt, and then move on the railroad from Manassas to the Rappahannock. Having a large cavalry force to destroy bridges, I thought by the use of one hundred and thirty thousand men thus employed, and the great facilities which the railroads gave us, and the compact position we should occupy, we must succeed by repeated blows in crushing out the force in our front, even if it were equal in numbers and strength. The road by the Fairfax Court-House to Centreville would give us the means to bring up siege mortars and siege materials, and even if we could not accomplish the object immediately, by making the campaign one of positions instead of one of manœuvres, to do so eventually, and without risk. That this saving of wagon transportation should be effected at once, by connecting the Baltimore and Ohio Railroad with the Alexandria roads by running a road over the Long Bridge. That when all this could be commenced, I could better tell when I knew something more definite as to the general condition of the army.

General Franklin being asked, said he was in ignorance of many things necessary to an opinion on the subject, knowing only as to his own division, which was ready for the field. As to the plan of operations, on being asked by the President if he had ever thought what he would do with this army if he had it, he replied that he had, and that it was his judgment that it should be taken—what could be spared from the duty of protecting the capital—*to York River to operate on Richmond*. The question then came up as to the means at hand of transporting a large part of the army by water. The Assistant Secretary of War said the means had been fully taxed to provide transportation for twelve thousand men. After some further conversation, and in reference to our ignorance of the actual condition of the army, the President wished we should come together the next night at eight o'clock, and that General Franklin and I should meet in the mean time, obtain such further information as we might need, and to do so from the staff of the head-quarters of the Army of the Potomac. Immediate orders were to be given to make the railroad over Long Bridge.

January 11.—Held a meeting with General Franklin in the morning at the Treasury building, and discussed the question of the operations which in our judgment were best under existing circumstances of season, present position of the forces, present condition of the country, to be undertaken before going into the matter as to when those operations could be set on foot. I urged that we should now find fortifications in York River, which would require a movement in that direction to be preceded by a naval force of heavy guns to clear them out, as well as the works at West Point. That Richmond was now fortified, that we could not hope to carry it by a simple march after a successful engagement, that we should be obliged to take a siege train with us. That all this would take time, which would be improved by the enemy to mass his forces in our front, and we should find that we had not escaped any of the difficulties we have now before this position, but simply lost time and money to find those difficulties where we should not have so strong a base to operate from, nor so many facilities, nor so large a force as we have here, nor, in proportion, so small a one to overcome. That the war now had got to be one of positions till we should penetrate the line of the enemy. That to overcome him in front, or cut his communication with the South, would, by its moral as well as physical effect, prostrate the enemy, and enable us to undertake any future operations with ease and certainty of success; but that, in order of time as of importance, the first thing to be done was to overcome this army in our front, which is beleaguering our capital, blockading the river, and covering us day by day with the reproach of impotence, and lowering us in the eyes of foreign nations and of our people, both North and South, and that nothing but what is not necessary for this purpose should go elsewhere.

General Franklin suggested whether Governor Chase, in view of what we were charged to do, might not be at liberty to tell us where General Burnside's expedition had gone. I went and asked him. He told me that under the circumstances he felt he ought to do so, and said he was destined for Newbern, North Carolina, by way of Hatteras Inlet and Pamlico Sound, to operate on Raleigh and Beaufort, or either of them. That General McClellan had, by direction of the President, acquainted him with his plan, which was to go with a large part of this Army of the Potomac to Urbana or Toppahannock, on the Rappahannock, and then with his bridge train move directly on Richmond. On further consultation with General Franklin, it was agreed that our inquiries were to be directed to both cases, of going from our present position, and of removing the large part of the force to another base further South.

A question was raised by General Franklin, whether, in deference to General McClellan, we should not inform him of the duty we were ordered to perform. I said the order I received was marked "private and confidential," and as they came from the President, our Commander-in-Chief, I conceived, as a common superior to General McClellan and both of us, it was for the President to say, and not us, and that I would consult the Secretary of the Treasury, who was at hand, and could tell us what was the rule in the Cabinet in such matters. The Secretary was of opinion that the matter lay entirely with the President. We went to Colonel Kingsbury, Chief of Ordnance of the Army of the Potomac, Brigadier-General Van Vliet, Chief Quartermaster, and Major Shivers, Commissary of Subsistence, and obtained all the information desired.

Met at the President's in the evening at eight o'clock. Present the same as on the first day, with the addition of the Postmaster-General, Judge Blair, who came in after the meeting had begun the discussion. I read the annexed paper, marked (A), as containing both General Franklin's and my own views, General Franklin agreeing with me, in view of time, &c., required to take this army to another base, that the operation could best *now* be undertaken from the present base, substantially as proposed. The Postmaster-General opposed the plan, and was for having the army, or as much of it as could be spared, go to York River or Fortress Monroe, either to operate against Richmond, or to Suffolk and cut off Norfolk, that being in his judgment the point (Fortress Monroe or York) from which to make a decisive blow; that the plan of going to the front from this position was Bull Run over again, that it was strategically defective as was the effort last July, as then we would have the operations upon exterior lines, and that it involved too much risk; that there was not as much difficulty as had been supposed in removing the army down the Chesapeake; that only from the Lower Chesapeake could any thing decisive result against the army at Manassas; that to drive them from their present position by operating from our present base would only force them to another behind the one they now occupy, and we should have all our work to do over again. Mr. Seward thought if we only had a victory over them, it would answer, whether obtained at Manassas, or further South. Governor Chase replied, in general terms, to Judge Blair, to the effect that the moral power of a victory over the enemy in his present position would be as great as one elsewhere, all else equal; and the danger lay in the probability that we should find, after losing time and millions, that we should have as many difficulties to overcome below as we now have above.

The President wished to have General Meigs in consultation on the subject of providing water transportation, and desired General Franklin and myself to see him in the morning, and meet again at three o'clock P. M. the next day.

January 12.—Met General Franklin at General Meigs's. Conversed with him on the subject of our mission at his own house. I expressed my views to General Meigs, who agreed with me in the main as to concentrating our efforts against the enemy in front by moving against him from our present position. As to the time in which he could assemble water transportation for thirty thousand men, he thought in about from four to six weeks.

Met at the President's. General Meigs mentioned the time in which he could assemble transports as a month to six weeks. The general subject of operations from the present base was again discussed, General Meigs agreeing that it was best to do so, and to concentrate our forces for the purpose. The President and Mr. Seward said that General McClellan had been out to see the President, and was looking quite well; and that now, as he was able to assume the charge of the army, the President would drop any further proceedings with us. The general drift of the conversation was as to the propriety of moving the army further South, and as to the destination of Burnside's expedition. The Postmaster-General said that if it was the intention to fight out here (Manassas), then we ought to *concentrate.* It was suggested and urged somewhat on the President to countermand, or to have General McClellan countermand, General Burnside's expedition, and bring it up to Acquia. The President was, however, exceedingly averse from interfering, saying he disliked exceedingly to stop a thing long since planned, just as it was ready to strike. Nothing was done but to appoint another meeting the next day at 11 o'clock, when we were to meet General McClellan, and again discuss the question of the movement to be made, &c., &c.

January 13, Monday.—Went to the President's with the Secretary of the Treasury. Present, the President, Governor Chase, Governor Seward, Postmaster-General, General McClellan, General Meigs, General Franklin, and myself, and I think the Assistant Secretary of War. The President, pointing to a map, asked me to go over the plan I had before spoken to him of. He, at the same time, made a brief explanation of how he came to bring General Franklin and General McDowell before him. I mentioned, in as brief terms as possible, what General Franklin and I had done under the President's order, what our investigations had been directed upon, and what were our conclusions, giving as nearly as I could the substance of the paper hereto annexed, marked (B), referring to going to the front from our present base in the way I have hereinbefore stated, referring also to a transfer of a part of the army to another base further south; that we had been informed that the latter movement could not be commenced under a month to six weeks, and that a movement to the front could be undertaken in all of the present week. General Franklin dissented only as to the time I mentioned for beginning operations in the front, not thinking we could get the roads in order by that time. I added, *commence* operations in all of the week, to which he assented.

I concluded my remarks by saying something apologetic in explanation of the position in which we were, to which General McClellan replied somewhat coldly, if not curtly: "You are entitled to have any opinion you please!" No discussion was entered into by him whatever, the above being the only remark he made.

General Franklin said, that, in giving his opinion as to going to York River, he did it knowing it was in the direction of General McClellan's plans.

I said that I had acted entirely in the dark.

General Meigs spoke of his agency in having us called in by the President.

The President then asked what and when any thing could be done, again going over somewhat the same ground he had done with General Franklin and myself.

General McClellan said the case was so clear a blind man could see it, and then spoke of the difficulty of ascertaining what force he could count upon; that he did not know whether he could let General Butler go to Ship Island, or whether he could re-enforce General Burnside. Much conversation ensued, of rather a general character, as to the discrepancy between the number of men paid for and the number effective.

The Secretary of the Treasury then put a direct question to General McClellan, to the effect as to what he intended doing with his army, and when he intended doing it. After a long silence, General McClellan answered that the movement in Kentucky was to precede any one from this place, and that that movement might now be *forced*. That he had directed General Buell, if he could not hire wagons for his transportation, that he must take them. After another pause, he said he must say he was very unwilling to develop his plans, always believing that in military matters the fewer persons who were knowing to them the better; that he would tell them if he was *ordered* to do so. The President then asked him if he had counted upon any particular time; he did not ask what that time was, but had he in his own mind any particular time fixed, when a movement could be commenced. He replied he had. "Then," rejoined the President, "I will adjourn this meeting."

"THE BOTTOM IS OUT OF THE TUB":
WASHINGTON, D.C., JANUARY 1862

Montgomery C. Meigs:
Memoir of Meetings with President Lincoln

Montgomery C. Meigs served as quartermaster-general of the Union army from May 1861 to the end of the war. His account of events in January 1862 is taken from a manuscript Meigs submitted to *The Century Magazine* in 1888, "The Relations of President Lincoln and Secretary Stanton to the Military Commanders in the Civil War," that was first published in 1921.

ON FRIDAY, January 10th, 1862, the President, in great distress, entered my office. He took a chair in front of the open fire and said, "General, what shall I do? The people are impatient; Chase has no money and he tells me he can raise no more; the General of the Army has typhoid fever. The bottom is out of the tub. What shall I do?"

I said, "If General McClellan has typhoid fever, that is an affair of six weeks at least; he will not be able sooner to command. In the meantime, if the enemy in our front is as strong as he believes, they may attack on any day, and I think you should see some of those upon whom in such case, or in case any forward movement becomes necessary, the control must fall. Send for them to meet you soon and consult with them; perhaps you may select the responsible commander for such an event."

The council was called. On Sunday, January 12th, McDowell and Franklin called on me with a summons to the White House for one P.M. These officers, and Messrs. Seward, Chase and Blair of the Cabinet attended. The President announced that he had called this meeting in consequence of the sickness of General McClellan, but he had that morning heard from him that he was better, and would be able to be present the next day; and that, on this promise, he adjourned the discussion for twenty four hours.

The next day, Jany. 13th, the same persons and General McClellan appeared at the rendezvous. The President opened the proceedings by making a statement of the cause of his calling the Council. Mr. Chase, and Mr. Blair, if memory is accurate, both spoke. All looked to McClellan, who sat still with his head hanging down, and mute. The situation grew awkward. The President spoke again a few words. One of the Generals said something; McClellan said something which evidently did not please the speaker, and again was mute.

I moved my chair to the side of McClellan's and urged him, saying, "The President evidently expects you to speak; can you not promise some movement towards Manassas? You are strong." He replied, "I cannot move on them with as great a force as they have." "Why, you have near 200,000 men, how many have they?" "Not less than 175,000 according to my advices." I said, "Do you think so?" and "the President expects something from you." He replied, "If I tell him my plans they will be in the New York Herald tomorrow morning. He can't keep a secret, he will tell them to Tadd." I said: "That is a pity, but he is the President,—the Commander-in-Chief; he has a right to know; it is not respectful to sit mute when he so clearly requires you to speak. He is superior to all."

After some further urging, McClellan moved, and seemed to prepare to speak. He declined to give his plans in detail, but thought it best to press the movement of Buell's troops in the central line of operation. After a few words that brought out nothing more, Mr. Lincoln said, "Well, on this assurance of the General that he will press the advance in Kentucky, I will be satisfied, and will adjourn this Council."

"THIS ARMY HAS GOT TO FIGHT": JANUARY 1862

Edwin M. Stanton to Charles A. Dana

Former attorney general Edwin M. Stanton replaced Simon Cameron in the cabinet on January 15, 1862, amid charges of widespread incompetence and corruption in the War Department. The new Secretary of War stated his intentions in a letter to Charles A. Dana of the *New-York Daily Tribune*.

WASHINGTON, *January 24, 1862.*

MY DEAR SIR: Yours of the 22d only reached me this evening. The facts you mention were new to me, but there is too much reason to fear they are true. But that matter will, I think, be corrected *very speedily.*

You can not tell how much obligation I feel myself under for your kindness. Every man who wishes the country to pass through this trying hour should stand on watch, and aid me. Bad passions and little passions and mean passions gather around and hem in the great movements that should deliver this nation.

Two days ago I wrote you a long letter—a three pager—expressing my thanks for your admirable article of the 21st, stating my position and purposes; and in that letter I mentioned some of the circumstances of my unexpected appointment. But, interrupted before it was completed, I will not inflict, or afflict, you with it.

I know the task that is before us—I say *us*, because the Tribune has its mission as plainly as I have mine, and they tend to the same end. But I am not in the smallest degree dismayed or disheartened. By God's blessing we shall prevail. I feel a deep, *earnest* feeling growing up around me. We have no jokes or trivialities, but all with whom I act show that they are now in dead earnest.

I know you will rejoice to know this.

As soon as I can get the machinery of the office working, the rats cleared out, and the rat holes stopped we shall *move*. This army has got to fight or run away; and while men are striving nobly in the West, the champagne and oysters on the Potomac must be stopped. But patience for a short while only is all I ask, if you and others like you will rally around me.

Yours truly,
EDWIN M. STANTON.

CHRONOLOGY

BIOGRAPHICAL NOTES

NOTE ON THE TEXTS

NOTES

INDEX

Chronology
April 1860 – January 1862

1860　Democratic Party national convention meets in Charleston, South Carolina, on April 23. Convention rejects platform plank calling for congressional legislation protecting slavery in the federal territories, endorsing instead the right of each territorial legislature to permit or prohibit slavery. Vote causes some fifty delegates, including most of six delegations from the Deep South, to bolt the convention on April 30. Senator Stephen A. Douglas of Illinois, the leading Democratic presidential candidate, is unable to secure the two-thirds majority needed for the nomination through fifty-seven ballots, and the deadlocked convention adjourns for six weeks on May 3.

Constitutional Union Party, made up of former members of the Whig and American (Know-Nothing) parties, meets in Baltimore on May 9. The convention nominates John Bell of Tennessee for president and Edward Everett of Massachusetts for vice president, but does not adopt a platform beyond a pledge to support the Constitution, the Union, and the enforcement of the laws. Republican Party national convention meets in Chicago on May 16 with Senator William H. Seward of New York as the leading candidate for the nomination. Seward is unable to gain a majority of the delegates during the first two ballots, and on May 18 Abraham Lincoln of Illinois is nominated on the third ballot. Convention chooses Senator Hannibal Hamlin of Maine as his running mate and adopts a platform opposing the extension of slavery.

Democratic Party reconvenes in Baltimore on June 18. Dispute over seating of rival delegations from the Deep South results in walkout by delegates from the Upper South and border states. Douglas is nominated for president on the second ballot, and former governor of Georgia Herschel V. Johnson becomes the vice-presidential candidate after Senator Benjamin Fitzpatrick of Alabama declines nomination. Southern Democrats meet in Baltimore on June 28 and nominate Vice President John C. Breckinridge of Kentucky for president and Senator Joseph Lane of Oregon for vice president. While Lincoln, Breckinridge, and Bell follow precedent and do not actively campaign, Douglas makes series of speaking tours through the North and South, warning against disunion. Election of Republican governors in key states of Indiana and Pennsylvania on October 9 indicate likelihood of Republican victory in the presidential contest.

Lincoln wins election on November 6, gaining 1,866,452 popular and 180 electoral votes and carrying every free state except New Jersey, whose electoral votes are divided between Lincoln and Douglas. Douglas receives 1,376,957 popular votes, mostly in the free states and the Upper South, but secures only twelve electoral votes in New Jersey and Missouri. Breckinridge wins 849,781 popular and seventy-two electoral votes, carrying eleven slave states, while Bell receives 588,879 popular and thirty-nine electoral votes, winning Kentucky, Tennessee, and Virginia. While Lincoln wins some votes in the border states and Virginia, he does not appear on the ballot in nine Southern states. (There is no popular vote for president in South Carolina, where electors are chosen by the state legislature.)

Election of Lincoln begins movement for immediate secession in South Carolina. President James Buchanan meets with his cabinet to discuss secession and the situation of the federal garrison at Charleston, November 9–10. Cabinet divides along sectional lines, and Buchanan decides to address the crisis in his annual message to Congress on December 3. South Carolina legislature calls for a convention to meet at Columbia on December 17 to consider secession. By the end of November, conventions have been called for January 1861 in Alabama, Mississippi, Florida, and Georgia.

Second session of the 36th Congress meets on December 3. In his message, Buchanan declares secession to be unconstitutional while asserting that the federal government has no right to "coerce" a state attempting to secede. House of Representatives forms a select Committee of Thirty-Three on December 4 to consider responses to the crisis. Presidential electors cast their ballots on December 5. South Carolina convention meets in Columbia on December 17, then adjourns to Charleston due to smallpox epidemic. Senator John J. Crittenden of Kentucky proposes series of constitutional amendments on December 18 that would restore the Missouri Compromise line while offering new protections for slavery; his measures are referred to a select Committee of Thirteen. (The "Crittenden Compromise" is opposed by Lincoln, who writes a series of letters to Republican leaders from Springfield, Illinois, urging them not to permit any further extension of slavery.) South Carolina convention adopts ordinance of secession, 169–0, on December 20. Major Robert Anderson transfers federal garrison at Charleston from Fort Moultrie to Fort Sumter on December 26.

1861   Georgia state troops occupy Fort Pulaski on January 3; by the end of January, state forces seize federal forts and arsenals without bloodshed in Alabama, Florida, Mississippi, Louisiana, and North Carolina. South Carolina batteries open fire on the chartered civilian steamer *Star of the West*, which is carrying supplies and reinforcements for the Fort Sumter garrison, January 9. The ship withdraws without casualties, and Major Anderson does not return fire from Fort Sumter. Mississippi convention votes in favor of secession, 85–15, January 9. Florida convention votes to secede, 62–7, January 10. Alabama convention approves secession, 61–39, January 11. Kentucky legislature meets in special session on January 17 and rejects recommendation by Governor Beriah Magoffin that it call a secession convention. Georgia convention votes to secede from the Union, 208–39, on January 19. Virginia legislature proposes holding a peace convention attended by representatives of all the states, January 19. Louisiana convention approves secession, 113–17, on January 26. Congress admits Kansas as the thirty-fourth state under a constitution prohibiting slavery, January 29.

Convention in Texas votes to secede, 166–8, on February 1. Representatives from South Carolina, Mississippi, Florida, Alabama, Georgia, and Louisiana meet in Montgomery, Alabama, on February 4 to form the Confederate States of America. Peace convention meets in Washington, February 4, with only twenty-one of thirty-four states represented. Montgomery convention adopts a provisional constitution, February 8, and unanimously elects Jefferson Davis of Mississippi as the provisional president and Alexander H. Stephens of Georgia as the provisional vice president of the Confederacy, February 9. Tennessee voters reject holding a secession convention, 69,387–57,798, on February 9. Abraham Lincoln leaves Springfield, Illinois, by train on February 11; during his trip to Washington, D.C., he will make short speeches and appearances in Indiana, Ohio, Pennsylvania, New York, and New Jersey. Jefferson Davis leaves his plantation in Warren County, Mississippi, on February 11 for his inauguration at Montgomery, Alabama. Electoral votes are counted in Congress, February 13, and Lincoln is formally declared president-elect. Davis is inaugurated as provisional president of the Confederacy at Montgomery on February 18. His cabinet includes Robert Toombs (secretary of state), Christopher Memminger (secretary of the treasury), Leroy Walker (secretary of war), Stephen Mallory (secretary of the navy), Judah Benjamin (attorney general), and John Reagan (postmaster general).

In San Antonio, General David E. Twiggs surrenders U.S. army installations in Texas to the state authorities, February 18. Warned in Philadelphia that he might be assassinated in Baltimore, Lincoln travels secretly to Washington on night of February 22–23. Texas voters approve secession, 46,153–14,747, on February 23. Washington peace conference presents plan to Congress similar to the Crittenden Compromise. North Carolina voters reject holding a secession convention, 47,323–46,672, on February 28. Republican opposition prevents adoption of compromise measures permitting the extension of slavery, but on March 3 Congress proposes a Thirteenth Amendment to the Constitution that would prohibit the federal government from abolishing or interfering with slavery in the states (amendment will be ratified by only two states).

Abraham Lincoln is inaugurated as the sixteenth president of the United States on March 4. His cabinet includes the other major contenders for the 1860 Republican nomination: William H. Seward (secretary of state), Salmon P. Chase (secretary of the treasury), Simon Cameron (secretary of war), and Edward Bates (attorney general), as well as Gideon Welles (secretary of the navy), Montgomery Blair (postmaster general), and Caleb B. Smith (secretary of the interior). Lincoln learns on March 5 that the garrison at Fort Sumter will run out of supplies by mid-April, forcing its evacuation. Confederate Provisional Congress adopts permanent constitution on March 11 and submits it to the states for ratification. In a meeting on March 15, Lincoln requests the formal advice of his cabinet on whether to resupply Fort Sumter; five of the seven secretaries recommend evacuating the fort. Arkansas convention votes against secession, 39–35, March 18, and Missouri convention rejects secession, 98–1, March 21. Lincoln decides on March 29 to attempt to reprovision Fort Sumter and to hold Fort Pickens, in Pensacola Bay, Florida; his decision is supported by a majority of the cabinet.

On April 1 Secretary of State Seward sends Lincoln a memorandum recommending that Fort Sumter be evacuated; that the administration should confront a European power as a way of reestablishing national unity; and that the president consider giving the authority to execute both domestic and foreign policy to a member of the cabinet. Lincoln responds by reminding Seward that it is the president who decides which policies to pursue. Virginia convention votes against secession, 90–45, on April 4, but remains in session. Lincoln sends message on April 6 to Francis Pickens, the governor of South Carolina, informing him of the attempt to resupply Fort Sumter. On April 8 the Davis administration authorizes Braxton Bragg, the Confederate commander at Pensacola, to engage any force resupplying or reinforcing Fort Pickens. Union resupply expedition sails for Charleston on April 9. Davis and his cabinet meet on April 9 and order General Pierre G. T. Beauregard to demand the surrender of Fort Sumter. Major Anderson refuses to surrender, April 11. Confederates begin bombardment of the fort at 4:30 A.M. on April 12; the garrison begins to return fire at 7 A.M. Reinforcements land at Fort Pickens, April 12 (the fort will remain in Union hands throughout the war). Anderson surrenders, April 13, and the Confederates occupy Fort Sumter on April 14. (Although there are no fatalities during the bombardment, two members of the garrison are killed by an accidental explosion during the surrender ceremony.)

President Lincoln issues proclamation on April 15 calling forth 75,000 militia and summoning Congress to meet in special session on July 4. Virginia convention votes to secede, 88–55, on April 17. Missouri Governor Claiborne Jackson denounces Lincoln's call for troops and begins planning seizure of the federal arsenal at St. Louis. Federal garrison evacuates U.S. arsenal at Harpers

Ferry, Virginia, April 18. Pro-secessionist mob attacks the 6th Massachusetts Volunteers as it changes trains in Baltimore on April 19. Lincoln declares a blockade of the original seven Confederate states, April 19 (blockade is later extended to Virginia and North Carolina). Federal forces evacuate navy yard at Norfolk, Virginia, April 20. In response to the destruction of railroad bridges and telegraph lines in Maryland, Lincoln suspends the writ of habeas corpus along the rail corridor from Washington to Philadelphia on April 27. Maryland assembly rejects secession, 53–13, on April 29.

Lincoln issues a call for 42,034 volunteers to serve for three years and expands the authorized size of the regular army, May 3. Arkansas convention reassembles and votes to secede, 65–5, May 6; on the same day, the Tennessee legislature declares independence from the United States and schedules referendum on secession. Secessionists riot in St. Louis after Captain Nathaniel Lyon, commander of the garrison guarding the arsenal, captures pro-secessionist militia encampment near the city on May 10. Union troops occupy Baltimore on May 13, securing the movement of supplies and men into Washington. Great Britain declares neutrality in the conflict, May 13, while recognizing both the Union and the Confederacy as belligerent powers under international law. North Carolina convention votes unanimously for secession on May 20, creating an eleven-state Confederacy. Governor Beriah Magoffin proclaims Kentucky's neutrality, May 20. Provisional Congress votes on May 20 to relocate the Confederate capital to Richmond, Virginia. Secession referendum is approved in Virginia, 128,884–32,134, on May 23, although it is opposed by most voters in the western part of the state. Union troops cross the Potomac River and occupy Alexandria, Virginia, on May 24. The same day, at Fort Monroe, Virginia, General Benjamin F. Butler refuses to return escaped slaves who had worked on Confederate fortifications, declaring them contraband of war. While sitting as a U.S. circuit court judge in Baltimore, Chief Justice Roger B. Taney rules on May 28 in *Ex parte Merryman* that President Lincoln lacks the constitutional authority to suspend the writ of habeas corpus. (The administration ignores Taney's opinion, and Lincoln extends the suspension of the writ along the northeastern rail line to New York City, July 2, and to Bangor, Maine,

October 14.) Nathaniel Lyon replaces General William Harney as the Union commander in Missouri on May 31, ending a truce arranged between Harney and Sterling Price, the commander of the pro-secession state militia.

Union troops rout Confederates at Philippi, Virginia, on June 3, marking the start of the Union offensive into northwestern Virginia. Stephen A. Douglas dies in Chicago, June 3. Secession referendum is passed in Tennessee, 104,471–47,183, on June 8, although it is opposed by voters in eastern Tennessee. Attack by 4,400 Union troops against outpost at Big Bethel, Virginia, on June 10 is repulsed by 1,100 defenders, encouraging Confederate belief in the superiority of its soldiers. Unionist delegates meet in Wheeling on June 11 and organize a new Virginia state government that is recognized by Congress and the Lincoln administration. Union force under command of Nathaniel Lyon occupies Jefferson City, Missouri, on June 15 and defeats secessionist forces at Boonville on June 17, securing control of the Missouri River for the Union.

Congress meets in special session in Washington on July 4. Confederates halt Union advance into southwestern Missouri at Carthage on July 5. Union forces under the overall command of General George B. McClellan defeat Confederates at Rich Mountain, Virginia, on July 11, and overrun Confederate rear guard at Carrick's Ford on July 13, ending campaign that gives the Union control of northwestern Virginia. On July 16 Union army of 30,000 men under General Irvin McDowell advances into northeastern Virginia with the aim of defeating the 20,000 Confederate troops under Pierre G. T. Beauregard that are defending Manassas Junction. As Union advance elements skirmish with Confederates at Blackburn's Ford on July 18, General Joseph E. Johnston shifts his command of 11,000 men by rail out of the Shenandoah Valley to reinforce Beauregard at Manassas. Confederate Congress meets for the first time at Richmond, July 20. Union army attacks across Bull Run on morning of July 21, beginning the first major battle of the war. Confederate counterattack in the afternoon sends Union army into retreat; the Union loses about 2,900 men killed, wounded, or missing, the Confederates about 1,900.

Convention of Missouri Unionists meets in Jefferson City on July 22 and chooses new governor to replace Claiborne Jackson. Congress adopts Johnson-Crittenden resolutions on July 25, declaring that the purpose of the war is to preserve the Union and not to overthrow or interfere with "established institutions" (slavery) in the Southern states. Robert M. T. Hunter replaces Robert Toombs as Confederate secretary of state. General George B. McClellan assumes command of the forces around Washington on July 27 (command will later become the Army of the Potomac).

Congress passes revenue act, August 5, establishing the first national income tax, and confiscation act, August 6, authorizing the seizure of slaves being used to militarily aid the rebellion. Nathaniel Lyon is killed on August 10 at Wilson's Creek while leading 5,400 men in an unsuccessful attack against 11,000 Confederates under the command of Benjamin McCulloch and Sterling Price. Victory gives Confederates control of southwestern Missouri. Union naval expedition captures Fort Hatteras, North Carolina, August 29. General John C. Frémont, the Union commander in Missouri, issues proclamation on August 30 declaring martial law throughout the state and emancipating the slaves of secessionists.

Lincoln asks Frémont to withdraw his proclamation, September 2. Concerned by increasing political strength of Kentucky Unionists, Confederates send troops under General Gideon Pillow into the state on September 3 with orders to seize Columbus on the east bank of the Mississippi. Union forces under General Ulysses S. Grant occupy Paducah, Kentucky, at the junction of the Ohio and Tennessee rivers, on September 6. (By the end of the year Confederates will have established a defensive line across southern Kentucky.) When Frémont fails to comply with the president's request, Lincoln orders him to rescind the provisions of his proclamation concerning emancipation, September 11. General Robert E. Lee launches unsuccessful offensive against Union forces at Cheat Mountain in western Virginia, September 11–15. Confederates begin siege of Lexington, Missouri, September 12. Leroy Walker resigns as Confederate secretary of war and is succeeded by Judah Benjamin, who continues to serve as attorney general until November. Lincoln orders the arrest of thirty-one members of the Maryland legislature suspected of disloyalty. Union garrison of 3,600 men surrenders at Lexington, Missouri, on September 20, strengthening the Confederate position in the state.

Union attack across the Potomac at Ball's Bluff, near Leesburg, Virginia, on October 21 is repulsed with the loss of 900 men killed, wounded, or missing; among the dead is Colonel Edward D. Baker, a Republican senator from Oregon and friend of President Lincoln. Secessionist members of the Missouri legislature meet in Neosho on October 31 and vote to join the Confederacy.

George B. McClellan replaces the retiring Winfield Scott as general-in-chief of the Union army on November 1. John C. Frémont is removed from command in Missouri, November 2. Running unopposed, Jefferson Davis is elected to a six-year term as president of the Confederacy on November 6. Union naval expedition led by Commodore Samuel Du Pont captures Port Royal Sound, South Carolina, on November 7, securing a base between Savannah and Charleston for use by the blockade. Ulysses S. Grant leads raid against Confederate camp at Belmont, Missouri, across the Mississippi from Columbus, Kentucky, on November 7. Captain Charles Wilkes, commanding the U.S.S. *San Jacinto*, boards the British mail packet *Trent* off Cuba on November 8 and seizes James M. Mason, the Confederate commissioner to Great Britain, and John Slidell, the Confederate commissioner to France. Unionists in eastern Tennessee launch an unsuccessful uprising against the Confederate authorities on November 8. Port Royal expedition captures Beaufort, South Carolina, on November 9 (victory at Port Royal brings 10,000 former slaves in the Sea Islands under Union control). On November 9 General Henry W. Halleck is placed in command of the new Union Department of the Missouri, with responsibility for operations in Missouri and Kentucky west of the Cumberland River, while General Don C. Buell is given command of the Department of the Ohio, with responsibility for Kentucky east of the Cumberland. Thomas Bragg succeeds Judah Benjamin as Confederate attorney general. Unionist convention at Wheeling adopts constitution on November 26 for proposed new state of West Virginia.

President Lincoln sends his first annual message to Congress on December 3, calling for the gradual abolition of slavery with compensation for slaveowners and the voluntary colonization of former slaves outside the United States. Congress forms the Joint Committee on the Conduct of the War, December 9. Lincoln administration decides on December 26 to release Mason and Slidell to British authorities in order to avoid a possible war between the United States and Great Britain.

1862   Amid charges of widespread corruption and incompetence in the War Department, Lincoln replaces Simon Cameron with Edwin M. Stanton, a Democrat who had served as attorney general in the final months of the Buchanan administration. Stanton takes office as the new secretary of war on January 20.

Biographical Notes

Henry Livermore Abbott (January 21, 1842–May 6, 1864) Born in Lowell, Massachusetts, the son of a lawyer active in Democratic politics. Graduated from Harvard College in 1860 and began studying law in his father's office. Commissioned second lieutenant, 20th Massachusetts Volunteer Infantry Regiment, July 10, 1861. Formed close friendship with his fellow officer Oliver Wendell Holmes Jr. Fought at Ball's Bluff. Promoted to first lieutenant, November 1861. Fought at Fair Oaks and in the Seven Days' Battles, where he was wounded in the arm at Glendale. Older brother Edward killed at Cedar Mountain. Fought at Fredericksburg (December 1862 and May 1863) and Gettysburg; promoted to captain, December 1862, and major, October 1863. Became acting commander of the 20th Massachusetts after all of the regimental officers senior to him were killed or wounded at Gettysburg. Led the regiment at Briscoe Station and at the Battle of the Wilderness, where he was fatally wounded on May 6, 1864.

Charles Francis Adams Jr. (May 27, 1835–March 20, 1915) Born in Boston, Massachusetts, brother of Henry Adams, son of lawyer Charles Francis Adams and Abigail Brooks Adams, grandson of John Quincy Adams, great-grandson of John Adams. Graduated Harvard College, 1856. Read law in Boston and passed bar, 1858. Commissioned first lieutenant, 1st Massachusetts Cavalry, December 1861. Served at Hilton Head, South Carolina, 1862, and with the Army of the Potomac, 1862–63, including Antietam and Gettysburg campaigns; promoted to captain, October 1862. Commanded detached company on guard service at Army of the Potomac headquarters, spring 1864. Commissioned as lieutenant colonel of the 5th Massachusetts Cavalry, a black regiment, in July 1864, and as its colonel, February 1865; the regiment guarded Confederate prisoners at Point Lookout, Maryland, until March 1865, when it was sent to Virginia. Left army and married Mary Ogden in November 1865. Served on Massachusetts Railroad Commission, 1869–79. President of Union Pacific Railroad, 1884–90. Published series of historical works, including *Three Episodes of Massachusetts History* (1892) and biographies of Richard Henry Dana (1890) and Charles Francis Adams (1900). Died in Washington, D.C.

Henry Adams (February 16, 1838–March 27, 1918) Born in Boston, Massachusetts. Brother of Charles Francis Adams Jr., son of lawyer Charles Francis Adams and Abigail Brooks Adams, grandson of John Quincy Adams, great-grandson of John Adams. Graduated Harvard 1858; studied law in Berlin and Dresden until 1860. Served as secretary to father while Charles Francis Adams served in Congress, 1860–61, and as U.S. minister to Great Britain, 1861–68. Reported British reaction to the American Civil War as anonymous London correspondent of *The New York Times*, 1861–62. Returned to Washington, D.C., in 1868 to work as journalist. Appointed assistant professor of history at Harvard (1870–77); assumed editorship of *North American Review* (1870–76). Married Marion Hooper in 1872. Published *The Life of Albert Gallatin* (1879), biography; *Democracy* (1880), a novel that appeared anonymously; *John Randolph* (1882), a biography; *Esther* (1884) a novel that appeared pseudonymously; *History of the United States during the Administrations of Thomas Jefferson and James Madison* (1889–91); *Mont-Saint-Michel and Chartres: A Study of Thirteenth-Century Unity* (1904); *The Education of Henry Adams* (1907). Died in Washington.

Sullivan Ballou (March 28, 1827–July 28, 1861) Born in Smithfield, Rhode Island, the son of a merchant tailor. Educated at Brown University and the National Law School in Ballston Spa, New York. Admitted to Rhode Island bar in 1853 and began practice in Woonsocket. Served as clerk of the Rhode Island house of representatives, 1854–56. Married Sarah Hart Shumway in 1855. Served in the Rhode Island house of representatives, 1857–59. Unsuccessful Republican candidate for state attorney general, April 1861. Commissioned as major of 2nd Rhode Island Infantry, June 11, 1861. Hit by cannon shot at First Battle of Bull Run, July 21, 1861, and had leg amputated. Died of wounds at Sudley, Virginia, a week after the battle.

Edward Bates (September 4, 1793–March 25, 1869) Born Belmont, Virginia, the son of a planter and merchant. Attended Charlotte Hall Academy in Maryland for three years. Served in militia company in 1813 but did not see action. Moved to St. Louis, Missouri, in 1814. Admitted to the bar, 1816. Delegate to the state constitutional convention in 1820. Attorney general of Missouri, 1820–21. Married Julia Coalter in 1823. Served in state house of representatives, 1822–24 and 1834–36, and state senate, 1830–34. U.S. attorney for Missouri, 1824–26. Served in Congress, 1827–29, but was defeated for reelection. Became leader of Whig Party in Missouri. Candidate for 1860 Republican presidential nomination. Served as attorney general in the Lincoln administration, March 1861–November 1864, before resigning. Opposed Radical Reconstruction in Missouri. Died in St. Louis.

Charles Minor Blackford (October 17, 1833–March 10, 1903) Born in Fredericksburg, Virginia, the son of a newspaper editor. Graduated from University of Virginia law school in 1855 and began practice in Lynchburg. Married Susan Leigh Colston in 1856. Commissioned lieutenant in 2nd Virginia Cavalry in May 1861 and saw action at First Manassas. Elected captain of his company in May 1862. Appointed judge advocate of the Confederate First Corps, commanded by General James Longstreet, in December 1862 and held this position for the remainder of the war. Served with the corps in the Gettysburg campaign, in northern Georgia and eastern Tennessee (September 1863–April 1864), and in Virginia, 1864–65. Returned to law practice in Lynchburg after the war. Worked with his wife on editing their wartime letters and had them privately printed, along with writings by his father and brother William, as *Memoirs of Life In and Out of the Army in Virginia during the War between the States* (1894). Published *Campaign and Battle of Lynchburg, Virginia* (1901). Died in Lynchburg.

Sallie Brock (March 18, 1831–March 22, 1911) Born Sarah Ann Brock in Madison County, Virginia, the daughter of a hotel owner. Moved with her family to Richmond in 1858. Began working as a tutor in King and Queen County, Virginia, in 1860, but returned to Richmond in 1861 and remained there for the duration of the war. Moved to New York City in 1865. Published *Richmond During the War: Four Years of Personal Observations* (1867). Edited *The Southern Amaranth* (1869), a collection of poetry about the Confederacy and the war, and published a novel, *Kenneth, My King* (1873). Married Richard F. Putnam in 1882. Died in Brooklyn.

Joseph E. Brown (April 15, 1821–November 30, 1894) Born in Pickens District, South Carolina, son of a farmer. Family moved to Union County, Georgia. Attended Calhoun Academy in Anderson District, South Carolina. Taught school and studied law in Canton, Georgia. Admitted to the Georgia bar, 1845. Attended Yale Law School, 1845–46. Married Elizabeth Grisham in 1847. Served in state senate, 1850, and as circuit judge, 1855–57. Won Democratic nomination for governor and defeated American (Know-Nothing) candidate Benjamin Hill in 1857. Governor of Georgia, 1857–65. Supported secession; came into conflict with Jefferson Davis over assertion of state sovereignty and opposition to conscription. Chief justice of the Georgia Supreme Court, 1868–70. President of the Western and Atlanta Railroad, 1870–90. Served as a Democrat in the U.S. Senate, 1880–91. Died in Atlanta.

William G. Brownlow (August 29, 1805–April 29, 1877) Born in Wythe County, Virginia, the son of a farmer. Moved with family to eastern Tennessee. Learned carpentry before entering the Methodist ministry in 1826. Spent ten years as an itinerant minister. Married Eliza O'Brien in 1837. Founded the *Tennessee Whig* in Elizabethton, 1839. Moved the newspaper to Jonesboro, 1840, and to Knoxville, 1849. Opposed secession in the *Whig* until it was suppressed in October 1861. Arrested by Confederate authorities in December 1861 and expelled into Union territory in March 1862. Went on Northern lecture tour and published *Sketches of the Rise, Progress, and Decline of Secession* (1862). Returned to Knoxville after its capture by the Union army in November 1863. Governor of Tennessee, 1865–69. Republican senator from Tennessee, 1869–75. Died in Knoxville.

James Buchanan (April 23, 1791–June 1, 1868) Born near Mercersburg in Franklin County, Pennsylvania, son of a storekeeper and landowner. Graduated from Dickinson College, 1809, and admitted to the bar, 1812. Served in the Pennsylvania house of representatives, 1814–15, and in Congress, 1821–31. U.S. minister to Russia, 1832–34. Served in the U.S. Senate as a Democrat, 1834–45. Secretary of State in the Polk administration, 1845–49. U.S. minister to Great Britain, 1853–56. Won Democratic nomination in 1856 and defeated Republican John C. Frémont and American (Know-Nothing) Millard Fillmore in the presidential election. President of the United States, 1857–61. Died at his home near Lancaster, Pennsylvania.

Benjamin F. Butler (November 5, 1818–January 11, 1893) Born in Deerfield, New Hampshire, the son of a merchant. Graduated from Waterville (now Colby) College in 1838. Admitted to the bar in 1840 and began practicing law in Lowell, Massachusetts. Married Sarah Hildreth in 1844. Served as a Democrat in the Massachusetts house of representatives, 1853, and in the Massachusetts senate, 1859. Commissioned as brigadier general of Massachusetts militia in April 1861 and as major general of U.S. volunteers in May 1861. Led occupation of Baltimore in May 1861 before becoming commander at Fort Monroe, Virginia. Commanded troops that captured Fort Hatteras, North Carolina, in August 1861. Military governor of New Orleans, May–December 1862. Commanded the Army of the James in Virginia, 1864. Relieved of command by Ulysses S. Grant after his failed assault on Fort Fisher, North Carolina, in December 1864. Served in Congress as a Republican, 1867–75 and 1877–79, and was one of the House managers at the impeachment trial of Andrew Johnson in 1868. Elected governor of Massachusetts as a Democrat and served one-year term in 1883. Presidential candidate of the Greenback and Anti-Monopolist parties in 1884. Died in Washington, D.C.

Mary Chesnut (March 31, 1823–November 22, 1886) Born Mary Boykin Miller in Statesburg, Sumter County, South Carolina, the daughter of Stephen Miller, a former congressman who later served as governor of South Carolina and in the U.S. Senate, and Mary Boykin Miller. Educated at a French boarding school in Charleston. Married James Chesnut Jr. in 1840 and lived on Mulberry, the Chesnut family plantation near Camden, South Carolina. Lived in Washington, D.C., while husband served in the Senate, 1859–60. Spent much of the Civil War in Richmond, Virginia, where her husband served as an advisor to Jefferson Davis, and formed close friendship with Varina Davis. Wrote three unfinished novels after the war, and extensively revised and expanded her wartime journal between 1881 and 1884. Died in Camden.

John J. Crittenden (September 10, 1786–July 26, 1863) Born near Versailles, Woodford County, Kentucky, the son of a farmer. Graduated from the College of William and Mary in 1807 and was admitted to the Kentucky bar. Twice widowed, he married Sarah Lee, 1811, Maria Todd, 1826, and Elizabeth Ashley, 1853. Served in the Kentucky house of representatives, 1811–17, and as an aide-de-camp on the frontier, 1812–13. U.S. senator from Kentucky, 1817–19, 1835–41, 1842–48, and 1855–61. Served as attorney general of the United States, 1841 and 1850–53. Governor of Kentucky, 1848–50. Elected to Congress after leaving the Senate in 1861 and served until his death at Frankfort, Kentucky.

Jefferson Davis (June 3, 1808–December 6, 1889) Born in Christian (now Todd) County, Kentucky, the son of a farmer. Moved with his family to Mississippi. Graduated from West Point in 1828 and served in the Black Hawk War. Resigned his commission in 1835 and married Sarah Knox Taylor, who died later in the year. Became a cotton planter in Warren County, Mississippi. Married Varina Howell in 1845. Elected to Congress as a Democrat and served 1845–46, then resigned to command a Mississippi volunteer regiment in Mexico, 1846–47, where he fought at Monterrey and was wounded at Buena Vista. Elected to the Senate and served from 1847 to 1851, when he resigned to run unsuccessfully for governor. Secretary of war in the cabinet of Franklin Pierce, 1853–57. Elected to the Senate and served from 1857 to January 21, 1861, when he withdrew following the secession of Mississippi. Inaugurated as provisional president of the Confederate States of America on February 18, 1861. Elected without opposition to six-year term in November 1861 and inaugurated on February 22, 1862. Captured by Union cavalry near Irwinville, Georgia, on May 10, 1865. Imprisoned at Fort Monroe, Virginia, and indicted for treason. Released on bail on May 13, 1867; the indictment was dropped in 1869 without trial. Published *The Rise and Fall of the Confederate Government* in 1881. Died in New Orleans.

J.D.B. DeBow (July 10, 1820–February 27, 1867) Born James Dunwoody Bronson DeBow in Charleston, South Carolina, the son of a merchant. Graduated from the College of Charleston, 1843. Admitted to the bar. Became associate editor of the *Southern Quarterly Review* in 1844. Moved to New Orleans, where he founded the political and economic journal *Commercial Review of the South and West*, popularly known as *DeBow's Review*, 1846–62. Appointed professor of political economy and statistics at the University of Louisiana, 1849. Served as superintendent of the U.S. Census, 1853–55, and published *Statistical View of the United States* (1854). Married Caroline Poe in 1854, and after her death, Martha Johns in 1860. Served as cotton purchasing agent for the Confederacy. Revived the *Review* in 1866. Died in Elizabeth, New Jersey.

Abner Doubleday (June 26, 1819–January 26, 1893) Born in Ballston Spa, New York, the son of a newspaper editor. Attended school at Cooperstown (his supposed role in inventing baseball is now discounted). Graduated from West Point in 1842 and served as an artillery officer in the U.S.-Mexican War and the Third Seminole War. Married Mary Hewitt in 1852. Fired the first shot in defense of Fort Sumter in April 1861. Appointed brigadier general of volunteers, February 1862, and major general of volunteers, November 1862. Commanded a brigade at Second Bull Run and a division at South Mountain, Antietam, Fredericksburg, Chancellorsville, and Gettysburg; served as acting corps commander on the first day of the Battle of Gettysburg after the death of Major General John Reynolds. Held no further field commands after Gettysburg. Retired from the army in 1873. Published *Reminiscences of Forts Sumter and Moultrie in 1860–'61* (1876) and *Chancellorsville and Gettysburg* (1882). Died in Mendham, New Jersey.

Frederick Douglass (February 1818–February 20, 1895) Born Frederick Bailey in Talbot County, Maryland, the son of a slave mother and an unknown white man. Worked on farms and in Baltimore shipyards. Escaped to Philadelphia in 1838. Married Anna Murray, a free woman from Maryland, and settled in New Bedford, Massachusetts, where he took the name Douglass. Became a lecturer for the American Anti-Slavery Society, led by William Lloyd Garrison, in 1841. Published *Narrative of the Life of Frederick Douglass, An American Slave* (1845). Began publishing *North Star*, first in a series of antislavery newspapers, in Rochester, New York, in 1847. Broke with Garrison and became an ally of Gerrit Smith, who advocated an antislavery interpretation of the Constitution and participation in electoral politics. Published *My Bondage and My Freedom* (1855). Advocated emancipation and the enlistment of black soldiers at the outbreak of the Civil War. Met with Abraham Lincoln in Washington in August 1863 and August 1864, and wrote public letter supporting his reelection in September 1864. Continued his advocacy of racial equality and woman's rights after the Civil War. Served as U.S. marshal for the District of Columbia, 1877–81, and as its recorder of deeds, 1881–86. Published *Life and Times of Frederick Douglass* (1881). After the death of his wife Anna, married Helen Pitts in 1884. Served as minister to Haiti, 1889–91. Died in Washington, D.C.

Samuel Francis Du Pont (September 27, 1803–June 23, 1865) Born in Bergen Point, New Jersey, the son of a former French diplomat. Moved with family to Delaware, where his uncle had founded the Du Pont gunpowder works. Appointed a midshipman in the U.S. Navy in 1815. Promoted to lieutenant, 1826. Married first cousin Sophie Madeleine du Pont in 1833. Promoted to commander, 1842. Commanded sloop *Cyane* along the Pacific coast during the Mexican War. Promoted to captain, 1855, and flag officer, September 1861. Led South Atlantic blockading squadron in capture of Port Royal, South Carolina, in November 1861. Appointed rear admiral, 1862. Failed to capture Charleston in April 1863 while leading fleet of seven ironclad monitors. Relieved of command in July 1863 at his request. Died in Philadelphia.

Catherine Edmondston (October 10, 1823–January 3, 1875) Born Catherine Ann Devereux in Halifax County, North Carolina, the daughter of a plantation owner. Married Patrick Edmondston in 1846. Lived on Looking Glass plantation in Halifax County. Published pamphlet *The Morte d'Arthur: Its Influence on the Spirit and Manners of the Nineteenth Century* (1872), in which she accused the Union army of barbarism. Died in Raleigh.

Samuel J. English (March 7, 1839–July 31, 1886) Enlisted for three years in the 2nd Rhode Island Infantry at Providence in June 1861. Fought at First Bull Run in July 1861. Promoted to second lieutenant, November 1861, first lieutenant, July 1862, and captain, February 1863. Served as company commander before mustering out in June 1864.

John C. Frémont (January 21, 1813–July 13, 1890) Born in Savannah, Georgia, the son of a school teacher. Educated at College of Charleston. Mathematics instructor in the U.S. Navy, 1833–35. Appointed second lieutenant in the U.S. Army corps of topographical engineers, 1838. Conducted series of western explorations and surveys, 1838–46. Married Jessie Benton, daughter of Senator Thomas

Hart Benton, 1841. Appointed lieutenant colonel, 1846, and helped seize California for the United States, 1846–47. Served as U.S. senator from California, 1850–51. Nominated for president by the Republican Party in 1856 and finished second in three-way race with Democrat James Buchanan and American (Know-Nothing) Millard Fillmore. Commissioned major general in the U.S. Army, May 1861, and given command of Missouri, July 1861. Relieved of command, November 1861. Commanded troops in the Shenandoah Valley, March–June 1862. Again relieved of command, and spent remainder of war awaiting further orders. Nominated for president by faction of Radical Republicans in May 1864, but withdrew from race in September in exchange for the resignation of Montgomery Blair from the Lincoln administration. Governor of Arizona Territory, 1878–81. Died in New York City.

Ulysses S. Grant (April 22, 1822–July 23, 1885) Born in Point Pleasant, Ohio, the son of a tanner. Graduated from West Point in 1843. Served in the U.S.-Mexican War, 1846–48, and promoted to first lieutenant in 1847. Married Julia Dent in 1848. Promoted to captain, 1854, and resigned commission. Worked as a farmer, real estate agent, and general store clerk, 1854–61. Commissioned colonel, 21st Illinois Volunteers, June 1861, and brigadier general of volunteers, August 1861. Promoted major general of volunteers, February 1862, after victories at Forts Henry and Donelson. Defeated Confederates at Shiloh, April 1862, and captured Vicksburg, Mississippi, July 1863. Promoted to major general in the regular army, July 1863, and assigned to command of Military Division of the Mississippi, covering territory between the Alleghenies and the Mississippi, October 1863. Won Battle of Chattanooga, November 1863. Promoted lieutenant general, March 1864, and named general-in-chief of the Union armies. Accepted surrender of Robert E. Lee at Appomattox Court House, April 9, 1865. Promoted to general, July 1866. Served as secretary of war ad interim, August 1867–January 1868. Nominated for president by the Republican Party in 1868. Defeated Democrat Horatio Seymour, and won reelection in 1872 by defeating Liberal Republican Horace Greeley. President of the United States, 1869–77. Made world tour, 1877–79. Failed to win Republican presidential nomination, 1880. Worked on Wall Street, 1881–84, and was financially ruined when private banking firm of Grant & Ward collapsed. Wrote *Personal Memoirs of U.S. Grant*, 1884–85, while suffering from throat cancer, and completed them days before his death at Mount McGregor, New York.

Horace Greeley (February 3, 1811–November 29, 1872) Born in Amherst, New Hampshire, the son of a farmer. Learned printing trade in Vermont, upstate New York, and Pennsylvania. Moved to

New York City in 1831. Founded and edited weekly *New Yorker*, 1834–41. Married Mary Cheney in 1836. Edited Whig campaign newspapers *Jeffersonian*, 1838, and *Log Cabin*, 1840. Founded *New York Tribune*, 1841, and used it to advocate for social reforms and antislavery positions. Served in Congress, 1848–49. Active in Whig and Republican politics. Nominated for president by the Liberal Republicans and the Democrats in 1872, but was defeated by Ulysses S. Grant. Died in New York City.

Stephen F. Hale (January 31, 1816–July 18, 1862) Born in Crittenden County, Kentucky, the son of a Baptist minister. Educated at Cumberland University and the law school of Transylvania University. Moved to Greene County, Alabama, where he practiced law. Married Mary Kirksey in 1844. Served as a lieutenant in the Mexican War, 1846–48. Elected to the Alabama legislature as a Whig, 1843, 1857, and 1859. Traveled to Kentucky in December 1860 as an Alabama commissioner advocating secession. Served in the Provisional Confederate Congress, 1861. Became lieutenant colonel of the 11th Alabama Infantry. Wounded in the Battle of Gaines' Mill, June 27, 1862, and died in Richmond.

John W. Hanson (May 12, 1823–December 14, 1901) Born in Boston, Massachusetts. Ordained as Universalist minister at Wentworth, New Hampshire, in 1845. Married Eliza Holbrook in 1846. Served as pastor in Danvers, Massachusetts, Gardiner, Maine, and Haverhill, Massachusetts. Edited the *Gospel Banner*, 1854–60. Served as chaplain of the 6th Massachusetts Volunteers, 1862–64, and published history of the regiment in 1865. Helped found the Soldiers' Mission, a Universalist organization for aiding Union troops. Edited the *New Covenant*, 1869–84, and wrote more than thirty works on theology. Died in Flagstaff, Arizona.

John Hay (October 8, 1838–July 1, 1905) Born Salem, Indiana, the son of a doctor. Family moved to Warsaw, Illinois. Graduated from Brown University in 1858. Studied law in office of his uncle in Springfield, Illinois. Traveled to Washington in 1861 as assistant private secretary to Abraham Lincoln, serving until early in 1865. First secretary to American legation in Paris, 1865–67, chargé d'affaires in Vienna, 1867–68, and legation secretary in Madrid, 1868–70. Published *Castilian Days* (1871) and *Pike County Ballads and Other Pieces* (1871). Married Clara Louise Stone in 1874. Served as assistant secretary of state 1879–81. Political novel *The Bread-Winners*, an attack on labor unions, published anonymously in 1884. In collaboration with John G. Nicolay, wrote *Abraham Lincoln: A History* (10 volumes, 1890) and edited *Complete Works of Abraham Lincoln* (2 volumes,

1894). Ambassador to Great Britain, 1897–98. Served as Secretary of State in the administrations of William McKinley and Theodore Roosevelt, 1898–1905. Among first seven members elected to American Academy of Arts and Letters in 1904. Died in Newbury, New Hampshire.

Charles B. Haydon (1834–March 14, 1864) Born in Vermont. Raised in Decatur, Michigan. Graduated from the University of Michigan in 1857, then read law in Kalamazoo. Joined the Kalamazoo Home Guard on April 22, 1861, then enlisted on May 25 for three years' service in the 2nd Michigan Infantry. Fought at Blackburn's Ford during the First Bull Run campaign. Commissioned second lieutenant in September 1861 and promoted to first lieutenant in February 1862. Fought at Williamsburg, Fair Oaks, the Seven Days' Battles, Second Bull Run, and Fredericksburg; promoted to captain in September 1862. Regiment was sent to Kentucky in April 1863 and to Vicksburg in June as part of the Ninth Corps. Wounded in the shoulder while leading his company at Jackson, Mississippi, on July 11, 1863. Returned to active duty in December 1863 and was made lieutenant colonel of the 2nd Michigan. Died of pneumonia in Cincinnati while returning to Michigan on a thirty-day furlough after reenlisting.

Benjamin Hill (September 14, 1823–August 16, 1882) Born in Jasper County, Georgia, the son of a farmer. Moved with family to Troup County. Graduated from the University of Georgia in 1844. Studied law and began practice in La Grange. Married Caroline Holt in 1845. Served as a Whig in the state house of representatives, 1851. Unsuccessful American (Know-Nothing) candidate for governor in 1857. Served in the state senate, 1859–60. Opposed immediate secession at the 1861 state convention. Served in the Provisional Confederate Congress, 1861, and in the Confederate Senate, 1862–65. Resumed law practice after the war. Served as a Democrat in Congress, 1875–77, and in the U.S. Senate from 1877 until his death in Atlanta.

Emma Holmes (December 17, 1838–January 1910) Born in Charleston, South Carolina, the daughter of a physician and plantation owner. Family moved to Camden, South Carolina, in June 1862, where she began teaching. Returned after the war to Charleston, where she continued to teach and tutor. Died in Charleston.

Sam Houston (March 2, 1793–July 26, 1863) Born near Lexington, Rockbridge County, Virginia, the son of an army officer. Family moved to Blount County, Tennessee, around 1808. Enlisted in army in 1813 and fought under Andrew Jackson against the Creeks. Resigned commission in 1818 and began to practice law in Lebanon, Tennessee. Served in Congress, 1823–27, and as governor of Tennessee, 1827–29. Moved in 1829 to Indian Territory, where he became a successful trader and a member of the Cherokee Nation. Settled in Texas, 1835, and commanded the army that defeated and captured General Santa Anna at San Jacinto, 1836. President of the Republic of Texas, 1836–38 and 1841–44; served in the Texas congress, 1838–40. Married Margaret Lea in 1840. Served in the U.S. Senate as a Democrat, 1846–59. Governor of Texas, 1859–61. Opposed secession, and was removed from office when he refused to swear allegiance to the Confederacy. Died in Huntsville.

Andrew Johnson (December 29, 1808–July 31, 1875) Born in Raleigh, North Carolina, the son of a bank porter. Learned tailoring and moved to Greenville, Tennessee, in 1826. Married Eliza McArdle, 1827. Elected alderman, 1829–33, and mayor of Greenville, 1834–35 and 1837–38. Served in the Tennessee house of representatives, 1835–37 and 1839–41, in the state senate, 1841–43, and in Congress as a Democrat, 1843–53. Governor of Tennessee, 1853–57. Served in the U.S. Senate, 1857–62. Candidate for Democratic presidential nomination in 1860. Served as military governor of Tennessee, 1862–64, with rank of brigadier general. Nominated for vice president by the National Union (Republican) convention in 1864. Became president following the assassination of Abraham Lincoln in April 1865. Conflict with Republicans in Congress over Reconstruction led to his impeachment in 1868. Acquitted at trial in the U.S. Senate. Failed to win presidential nomination of the Democratic Party in 1868. Returned to the U.S. Senate in March 1875 and served until his death near Elizabethton, Tennessee.

Charles C. Jones Sr. (December 20, 1804–March 16, 1863) Born in Liberty County, Georgia, the son of a plantation owner. Educated at Phillips Andover Academy, Andover Theological Seminary, and Princeton Theological Seminary. Married first cousin Mary Jones in 1830. Pastor of the First Presbyterian Church, Savannah, 1831–32. Returned to Liberty County, where he owned three plantations. Taught at Columbia Theological Seminary, South Carolina, 1837–38 and 1848–50. Published *Catechism of Scripture Doctrine and Practice* (1837) and *The Religious Instruction of the Negroes of the United States* (1842). Lived in Philadelphia, 1850–53, while serving as the corresponding secretary of the board of domestic missions of the Presbyterian Church. Died in Liberty County.

Charles C. Jones Jr. (October 28, 1831–July 19, 1893) Born in Savannah, Georgia, the son of minister Charles C. Jones and Mary Jones. Educated at South Carolina College and the College of New Jersey (Princeton). Graduated from Dane Law School at Harvard,

1855. Practiced law in Savannah, where he served as alderman, 1859–60, and mayor, 1860–61. Married Ruth Berrien Whitehead, 1858, and after her death, Eva Berrien Eve, 1863. Commissioned lieutenant in Chatham Artillery, August 1861. Promoted to lieutenant colonel and made chief of artillery for Georgia, October 1862. Practiced law in New York City, 1866–77, then returned to Georgia. Published several historical and archaeological studies, including *Indian Remains in Southern Georgia* (1859), *The Monumental Remains of Georgia* (1861), *Antiquities of the Southern Indians* (1873), and *The History of Georgia* (1883). Died in Augusta.

John B. Jones (March 6, 1810–February 4, 1866) Born in Baltimore, Maryland. Lived in Kentucky and Missouri as a boy. Married Frances Custis in 1840. Became editor of the *Saturday Visiter* in Baltimore, 1841. Published several novels, including *Wild Western Scenes* (1841), *The War Path* (1858), and *Wild Southern Scenes* (1859). Established weekly newspaper *Southern Monitor* in Philadelphia, 1857. Fearing arrest as a Confederate sympathizer, Jones moved in 1861 to Richmond, Virginia, where he worked as a clerk in the Confederate war department. Died in Burlington, New Jersey, shortly before the publication of *A Rebel War Clerk's Diary*.

Mary Jones (September 24, 1808–April 23, 1869) Born in Liberty County, Georgia, the daughter of a plantation owner. Educated at Carter Academy in Savannah, 1823–27. Married first cousin Charles C. Jones in 1830. Moved to New Orleans in 1868 to live with her daughter. Died in New Orleans.

Elizabeth Blair Lee (June 20, 1818–September 13, 1906) Born Frankfort, Kentucky, daughter of journalist Francis Preston Blair and Elizabeth Gist Blair, sister of Montgomery Blair (postmaster general, 1861–64) and Frank Blair (a Union major general, 1862–65). Moved with family in 1830 to Washington, D.C., where her father edited the *Globe* and advised Andrew Jackson. Educated at boarding school in Philadelphia. Married naval officer Samuel Phillips Lee, a cousin of Robert E. Lee, in 1843. Became board member and active patron of the Washington City Orphan Asylum in 1849. Lived in Washington and at the Blair estate in Silver Spring, Maryland. Died in Washington.

Robert E. Lee (January 19, 1807–October 12, 1870) Born in Westmoreland County, Virginia, the son of Revolutionary War hero Henry "Light-Horse Harry" Lee and Ann Carter Lee. Graduated from West Point in 1829. Married Mary Custis, great-granddaughter of Martha Washington, in 1831. Served in the U.S.-Mexican War, and as superintendent of West Point, 1852–55. Promoted to colonel in March 1861. Resigned commission on April 20, 1861, after declining offer of field command of the Federal army. Served as commander of Virginia military forces, April–July 1861; commander in western Virginia, August–October 1861; commander of the southern Atlantic coast, November 1861–March 1862; and military advisor to Jefferson Davis, March–May 1862. Assumed command of the Army of Northern Virginia on June 1, 1862, and led it until April 9, 1865, when he surrendered to Ulysses S. Grant at Appomattox. Named general-in-chief of all Confederate forces, February 1865. Became president of Washington College (now Washington and Lee), September 1865. Died in Lexington, Virginia.

Abraham Lincoln (February 12, 1809–April 15, 1865) Born near Hodgenville, Kentucky, the son of a farmer and carpenter. Family moved to Indiana in 1816 and to Illinois in 1830. Settled in New Salem, Illinois, and worked as a storekeeper, surveyor, and postmaster. Served as a Whig in the state legislature, 1834–41. Began law practice in 1836 and moved to Springfield in 1837. Married Mary Todd in 1842. Elected to Congress as a Whig and served from 1847 to 1849. Became a public opponent of the extension of slavery after the passage of the Kansas-Nebraska Act in 1854. Helped found the Republican Party of Illinois in 1856. Campaigned in 1858 for Senate seat held by Stephen A. Douglas and debated him seven times on the slavery issue; although the Illinois legislature reelected Douglas, the campaign brought Lincoln national prominence. Received Republican presidential nomination in 1860 and won election in a four-way contest; his victory led to the secession of seven Southern states. Responded to the Confederate bombardment of Fort Sumter by calling up militia, proclaiming the blockade of Southern ports, and suspending habeas corpus. Issued preliminary and final emancipation proclamations on September 22, 1862, and January 1, 1863. Appointed Ulysses S. Grant commander of all Union forces in March 1864. Won reelection in 1864 by defeating Democrat George B. McClellan. Died in Washington, D.C., after being shot by John Wilkes Booth.

James Russell Lowell (February 22, 1819–August 12, 1891) Born in Cambridge, Massachusetts, the son of a Unitarian minister. Graduated Harvard College, 1838, and Harvard Law School, 1840. Published first collection of poetry, *A Year's Life* (1841), followed by *Poems* (1844). Married Maria White in 1844; after her death, married Frances Dunlap in 1857. Became contributing editor to *National Anti-Slavery Standard*. Published *Poems: Second Series*, *A Fable for Critics*, *The Biglow Papers*, and *The Vision of Sir Launfal*, all in 1848. Professor of French and Spanish languages and literatures at Harvard, 1855–86. Became founding editor of *The Atlantic Monthly*, 1857–61.

Co-edited *The North American Review*, 1864–72. Three of his nephews died serving in the Union army. Delivered widely acclaimed "Ode" at Harvard Commemoration of July 21, 1865, in honor of Harvard men killed in the Civil War. Continued to publish poetry and essays. Served as U.S. minister to Spain, 1877–80, and Great Britain, 1880–85. Died in Cambridge, Massachusetts.

George B. McClellan (December 3, 1826–October 29, 1885) Born in Philadelphia, the son of a surgeon. Graduated from West Point in 1846. Served in the U.S.-Mexican War. Resigned from the army in 1857 to become chief engineer of the Illinois Central Railroad. Became president of the Ohio & Mississippi Railroad in 1860. Married Ellen Marcy, 1860. Appointed major general in the regular army, May 1861. Commanded offensive that drove Confederate troops from western Virginia, July 1861. Assumed command of the Military Division of the Potomac on July 25, 1861, following the Union defeat at First Bull Run. Served as general-in-chief of the Union armies, November 1861–March 1862. Commanded the Army of the Potomac on the Peninsula, in the Second Bull Run campaign, and at Antietam. Relieved of command by President Lincoln on November 7, 1862. Nominated for president by the Democratic Party in 1864, but was defeated by Lincoln. Governor of New Jersey, 1878–81. Died in Orange, New Jersey.

Irvin McDowell (October 15, 1818–May 4, 1885) Born in Columbus, Ohio. Graduated from West Point in 1839. Served in U.S.-Mexican War. Married Helen Burden in 1849. Promoted to major in 1856. Named brigadier general and commander of Union forces at Washington through patronage of Secretary of the Treasury Salmon P. Chase, May 1861. Defeated at First Bull Run, July 1861. Commanded division, October 1861–March 1862, and corps, March–September 1862. Criticized for his performance during the Second Bull Run campaign and relieved of command; held no further field assignments during the war. Retired from the army in 1882. Died in San Francisco.

Judith W. McGuire (March 19, 1813–March 21, 1897) Born Judith White Brockenbrough near Richmond, Virginia, the daughter of a judge. Married John P. McGuire, an Episcopalian rector, in 1846. Moved to Alexandria in 1852 when husband became principal of the Episcopal High School of Virginia. Fled Alexandria in May 1861 and settled in Richmond in February 1862. Worked as a clerk in the Confederate commissary department, November 1863–April 1864. Published *Diary of a Southern Refugee, during the war* (1867). Kept a school with her husband in Essex County in the 1870s. Published *General Robert E. Lee, The Christian Soldier* (1873). Died in Richmond.

Montgomery C. Meigs (May 3, 1816–January 2, 1892) Born Augusta, Georgia, the son of a physician. Moved with family to Philadelphia. Graduated from West Point in 1836 and began service in engineering corps. Married Louisa Rodgers in 1841. Supervised construction of the Washington Aqueduct, 1852–60, and of the wings and dome of the Capitol, 1853–59. Promoted to brigadier general, May 1861, and made army quartermaster general, a post he held throughout the war. Designed the Pension Building in Washington, D.C., after retiring from the army in 1882. Died in Washington.

Herman Melville (August 1, 1819–September 28, 1891) Born in New York City, the son of a merchant. Educated at schools in New York City and in upstate New York. Worked as bank clerk, bookkeeper, and schoolteacher. Sailed for Pacific on whaling ship in 1841 and returned in 1844 on frigate *United States*. Published *Typee* (1846) and *Omoo* (1847), fictionalized accounts of his experiences in the South Seas. Married Elizabeth Shaw in 1847. Published *Mardi* (1849), *Redburn* (1849), *White-Jacket* (1850), *Moby-Dick* (1851), *Pierre; or, The Ambiguities* (1852), *Israel Potter* (1855), *The Piazza Tales* (1856), and *The Confidence-Man* (1857). Visited Union troops in Virginia in spring 1864. Published poetry collection *Battle-Pieces and Aspects of the War* (1866). Worked as customs inspector in New York City, 1866–85. Published long poem *Clarel* (1876) and two small books of poetry, *John Marr and Other Sailors* (1888) and *Timoleon* (1891). Died in New York City, leaving *Billy Budd, Sailor* in manuscript.

Sam Mitchell (c. 1848–after 1937) Born on plantation of John Chaplin on Ladies Island, Beaufort, South Carolina, the son of slave parents. Remained with his family in Beaufort after Union occupation in November 1861. Educated in a school established in the plantation house during the war. Lived in Beaufort after the war and was married twice.

Benjamin Moran (August 1, 1820–June 20, 1886) Born West Marlboro, Pennsylvania, the son of a cotton mill owner. Worked for bookseller and printer John Grigg in Philadelphia. Traveled to England in 1851. Published *The Footpath and Highway: or, Wanderings of an American in Great Britain, in 1851 and '52* (1853). Married Catherine Goulder, an English mill worker. Became private secretary to James Buchanan, then U.S. minister to Great Britain, in 1854. Assistant secretary of the American legation in London, 1857–64, and secretary, 1864–74. Served as minister resident in Portugal, 1874–76, and as chargé d'affaires at Lisbon, 1876–82. Returned to England in 1882 and died at Braintree, Essex.

John G. Nicolay (February 26, 1832–September 26, 1901) Born in Essingen, Rhineland-Palatinate, Bavaria. Family emigrated to the United States in 1838 and eventually settled in Pike County, Illinois. Worked for the *Pike County Free Press* in Pittsfield and as a clerk in the office of the Illinois secretary of state. Became private secretary to Abraham Lincoln in 1860. With his friend John Hay, accompanied Lincoln to Washington, D.C., where Nicolay and Hay served as the president's principal secretaries. Married Therena Bates in 1865. Served as consul in Paris, 1865–69, and as marshal of the U.S. Supreme Court, 1872–87. Collaborated with Hay in writing *Abraham Lincoln: A History* (10 volumes, 1890) and editing *Complete Works of Abraham Lincoln* (2 volumes, 1894). Died in Washington.

John Ross (October 3, 1790–August 1, 1866) Born in Turkeytown, Alabama, the son of a trader; by ancestry, seven-eighths Scottish and one-eighth Cherokee. Family moved to Cherokee lands in southern Tennessee, where father owned a store. Educated at academy in Kingston, Tennessee. Married Elizabeth Henley in 1813; after her death, married Mary Stapler in 1844. Joined Cherokee volunteers who served under Andrew Jackson in the Creek War, 1813–14, and fought at Battle of Horsehoe Bend in Alabama. Helped negotiate treaties between Cherokee Nation and the United States in 1816 and 1819. President of the Cherokee National Committee, 1818–26. Became slaveholding landowner in western Georgia, 1827. Elected principal chief of the eastern Cherokee, 1828. Resisted attempts to relocate Cherokee to Indian Territory, but was unable to prevent rival faction from signing treaty in 1835 ceding Cherokee lands and agreeing to removal. Helped organize movement of Cherokees to Indian Territory along "Trail of Tears," 1838–39. Elected principal chief of the united Cherokee in 1839. Advocated neutrality at the outbreak of the Civil War, but signed treaty of alliance with the Confederacy in October 1861 in unsuccessful effort to avoid factional split within the Cherokee Nation. Fled Indian Territory in August 1862 and spent remainder of the war in Washington, D.C., where he sought to restore Cherokee relations with the United States. Died in Washington during post-war treaty negotiations.

William Howard Russell (March 28, 1820–February 10, 1907) Born in Tallaght, Ireland, the son of a businessman. Educated at Trinity College, Dublin. Became journalist for *The Times* of London in 1843. Married Mary Burrowes in 1846; after her death, married the Countess Antoinette Malvezzi in 1884. Reported on the Crimean War,

1854–56, and the Indian Rebellion, 1858–59. Sent to the United States by *The Times* to cover the secession crisis and arrived in March 1861. Traveled through the South until June, when he returned to Washington, D.C. Reported on the Union retreat from Bull Run in July 1861. Remained in the United States until April 1862, when he returned to England after failing to secure a pass to travel with the Union army in Virginia. Published *My Diary North and South* (1863). Reported on the Austro-Prussian War, 1866, and the Franco-Prussian war, 1870–71, for *The Times* and the Anglo-Zulu war, 1879, for *The Daily Telegraph*. Knighted in 1895. Died in London.

Winfield Scott (June 13, 1786–May 29, 1866) Born in Dinwiddie County, Virginia, the son of a farmer. Studied at the College of William and Mary. Practiced law and served in the Virginia militia, 1807, before being commissioned as captain in the U.S. Army in 1808. Served with distinction in the War of 1812, and was promoted to brigadier general in 1814. Married Mary Mayo in 1817. Commanded troops in South Carolina during the nullification crisis, 1832–33. Organized removal of Cherokees from the southeastern United States, 1838. Helped settle Anglo-American dispute over Maine border with Canada, 1838–39. Commissioned major general, 1841, and named general-in-chief of the U.S. Army. Commanded expedition that landed at Vera Cruz and captured Mexico City, 1847. Nominated for president by the Whig Party in 1852, but was defeated by Democrat Franklin Pierce. Helped settle Anglo-American border dispute over Puget Sound, 1859. Retired from army on November 1, 1861. Died at West Point, New York.

William H. Seward (May 16, 1801–October 10, 1872) Born in Florida, New York, the son of a doctor. Graduated from Union College in 1820 and was admitted to the bar in 1822. Married Frances Miller in 1824. Elected to the New York senate as an Anti-Masonic candidate and served until 1834. Unsuccessful Whig candidate for governor in 1834. Elected governor in 1838 and served until 1842. Elected to the U.S. Senate as a Whig and reelected as a Republican, serving from 1849 to 1861. Unsuccessful candidate for the Republican presidential nomination in 1860. Secretary of state in the cabinet of Abraham Lincoln, 1861–65. Wounded by a co-conspirator of John Wilkes Booth on April 14, 1865, but recovered and served as secretary of state under Andrew Johnson, 1865–69. Negotiated the purchase of Alaska in 1867. Died in Auburn, New York.

William T. Sherman (February 8, 1820–February 14, 1891) Born in Lancaster, Ohio, the son of an attorney. Graduated from West Point in 1840. Served in Florida and California, but did not see action in the U.S.-Mexican War. Married Ellen Ewing in 1850. Promoted to captain; resigned his commission in 1853. Managed bank branch in San Francisco, 1853–57. Moved in 1858 to Leavenworth, Kansas, where he worked in real estate and was admitted to the bar. Named first superintendent of the Louisiana State Seminary of Learning and Military Academy at Alexandria (now Louisiana State University) in 1859. Resigned position when Louisiana seceded in January 1861. Commissioned colonel, 13th U.S. Infantry, May 1861. Commanded brigade at First Bull Run, July 1861. Appointed brigadier general of volunteers, August 1861, and ordered to Kentucky. Assumed command of the Department of the Cumberland, October 1861, but was relieved in November at his own request. Returned to field in March 1862 and commanded division under Ulysses S. Grant at Shiloh. Promoted major general of volunteers, May 1862. Commanded corps under Grant during Vicksburg campaign, and succeeded him as commander of the Army of the Tennessee, October 1863, and as commander of the Military Division of the Mississippi, March 1864. Captured Atlanta, September 1864, and led march through Georgia, November–December 1864. Marched army through the Carolinas and accepted the surrender of Confederate General Joseph E. Johnston at Durham Station, North Carolina, April 26, 1865. Promoted to lieutenant general, 1866, and general, 1869, when he became commander of the army. Published controversial memoirs (1875, revised 1886). Retired from army in 1884 and moved to New York City. Rejected possible Republican presidential nomination, 1884. Died in New York City.

Edwin M. Stanton (December 19, 1814–December 24, 1869) Born in Steubenville, Ohio, the son of a physician. Attended Kenyon College. Admitted to bar in 1836. Married Mary Lamson in 1844; after her death, married Ellen Hutchinson in 1856. Practiced law in Cadiz, Ohio, and Steubenville before moving to Pittsburgh, Pennsylvania, in 1847 and Washington, D.C., in 1856. Served as attorney general of the United States, December 1860–March 1861; advised President Buchanan not to evacuate Fort Sumter. Appointed secretary of war in January 1862 by President Lincoln. Continued in office under President Andrew Johnson until August 1867, when Johnson attempted to remove him because of Stanton's support for congressional Reconstruction measures. Restored to office by the Senate in January 1868 under the Tenure of Office Act, but resigned in May 1868 after Johnson was acquitted at his impeachment trial. Appointed to the Supreme Court by Ulysses S. Grant and confirmed by the Senate, but died in Washington before he could be sworn in.

Alexander H. Stephens (February 11, 1812–March 4, 1883) Born in Taliaferro County, Georgia, the son of a farmer. Graduated from the

University of Georgia in 1832. Admitted to the bar in 1834. Served in the Georgia house of representatives, 1836–41, and the Georgia senate, 1842. Elected to Congress as a Whig and then as a Democrat and served from 1843 to 1859. Opposed immediate secession at the Georgia convention in January 1861. Elected provisional vice president of the Confederate States of America in February 1861 and vice president in November 1861. Opposed conscription, the suspension of habeas corpus, and other measures of the Davis administration, and spent much of the war in Georgia. Held unsuccessful peace conference with Abraham Lincoln and William H. Seward at Hampton Roads, Virginia, on February 3, 1865. Arrested by Union troops on May 11, 1865, and imprisoned for five months in Boston. Published *A Constitutional View of the Late War Between the States* (1868–70). Elected to Congress as a Democrat and served from 1873 to 1882. Governor of Georgia from 1882 until his death in Atlanta.

Kate Stone (May 8, 1841–December 28, 1907) Born Sarah Katherine Stone in Hinds County, Mississippi, the daughter of a plantation owner. Family moved to plantation in Madison Parish, Louisiana, thirty miles northwest of Vicksburg. Educated at boarding school in Nashville. Two of her five brothers died while serving in the Confederate army in 1863. Family fled plantation in March 1863 during the Vicksburg campaign and went to eastern Texas. Returned to plantation in November 1865. Married Henry Bry Holmes in 1869. Founded local chapter of the United Daughters of the Confederacy. Died in Tallulah, Louisiana.

George Templeton Strong (January 26, 1820–July 21, 1875) Born in New York City, the son of an attorney. Graduated from Columbia College in 1838. Read law in his father's office and was admitted to the bar in 1841. Joined father's firm. Married Ellen Ruggles in 1848. Served on Columbia board of trustees and as vestryman of Trinity Episcopal Church. Helped found the U.S. Sanitary Commission, June 1861, and served as its treasurer through the end of the war; also helped found the Union League Club of New York in 1863. Died in New York City.

Roger B. Taney (March 17, 1777–October 12, 1864) Born in Calvert County, Maryland, son of a plantation owner. Graduated from Dickinson College in 1795. Read law in Annapolis and began practicing in 1799. Served as Federalist in the Maryland house of delegates, 1799–1800, and in the Maryland senate, 1816–21. Married Anne Key in 1806. Began manumitting his slaves in 1818. Attorney general of Maryland, 1827–31. Served in the Jackson administration as attorney general, 1831–33, and as secretary of the treasury, 1833–34. Appointed chief justice of the U.S. Supreme Court by Jackson; served 1836–64. Wrote opinion of the court in the *Dred Scott* case, 1857. While sitting as a circuit judge in Maryland, ruled in *Ex parte Merryman* (1861) that President Lincoln lacked the authority to suspend the writ of habeas corpus. Dissented in the *Prize Cases* (1863), in which the Court upheld the legality of the blockade proclamation issued by Lincoln in April 1861. Died in Washington, D.C.

Henry Tucker (May 10, 1819–September 9, 1889) Born in Warren County, Georgia. Educated at the University of Pennsylvania and Columbian College (George Washington University). Admitted to the Georgia bar in 1846. Married Mary Catherine West in 1848; after her death, married Sarah O. Stevens in 1853. Ordained as a Baptist minister in 1851 and became pastor of a Baptist church in Alexandria, Virginia, 1854. Professor of literature and metaphysics at Mercer University in Penfield, Georgia, 1856–62. Opposed secession initially, but supported the Confederacy during the war; organized the Georgia Relief and Hospital Association to care for sick and wounded soldiers. Served as president of Mercer University, 1866–71, and as chancellor of the University of Georgia, 1874–78. Editor of the *Christian Index*, 1878–89. Died in Atlanta.

Benjamin F. Wade (October 27, 1800–March 2, 1878) Born in Feeding Hills, Massachusetts, the son of a farmer. Moved with family to Andover, Ohio, in 1821. Worked as a laborer on the Erie Canal, taught school, and studied medicine in Albany, New York, before being admitted to the Ohio bar in 1828. Served in Ohio senate as a Whig, 1837–38 and 1841–42. Married Caroline Rosekrans, 1841. Judge of circuit court of common pleas, 1847–51. Served in the U.S. Senate as a Whig and then as a Republican, 1851–69. Chairman of the Joint Committee on the Conduct of the War, 1861–65. Co-sponsored the Wade-Davis Bill on Reconstruction, 1864, which was pocket-vetoed by President Lincoln. Elected president pro tempore of the Senate in 1867, he would have succeeded Andrew Johnson as president had Johnson been convicted during his impeachment trial. Unsuccessful candidate for Republican vice-presidential nomination in 1868. Died in Jefferson, Ohio.

E. F. Ware (May 29, 1841–July 1, 1911) Born Eugene Fitch Ware in Hartford, Connecticut, the son of a leather worker. Moved with family to Burlington, Iowa, in 1844. Apprenticed in father's harness-making shop. Served in 1st Iowa Infantry, April–August 1861, and fought in the Battle of Wilson's Creek. Enlisted in 4th Iowa Cavalry, November 1861, and saw action in Missouri and Arkansas before mustering out in October 1862. Joined Iowa 7th Cavalry in February

1863 and served with the regiment on the Nebraska frontier. Mustered out as captain in 1866. Settled in Kansas in 1867. Worked on farm and as harness maker before becoming editor of the *Fort Scott Monitor*. Admitted to the bar in 1871. Married Jeanette Huntington in 1874. Served as a Republican in the Kansas senate, 1879–83. U.S. Pension Commissioner, 1902–5. Published a popular collection of poetry, *The Rhymes of Ironquill* (1885); a legal handbook, *From Court to Court* (1901); a collection of essays on psychology, *The Autobiography of Ithuriel* (1909); and two memoirs, *The Lyon Campaign in Missouri* (1907) and *The Indian War of 1864* (1911). Died in Cascade, Colorado.

Gideon Welles (July 1, 1802–February 11, 1878) Born in Glastonbury, Connecticut, the son of a merchant. Educated in Vermont at the American Literary, Scientific, and Military Academy (now Norwich University). Editor of the *Hartford Times*, 1826–36. Served as a Democrat in the Connecticut house of representatives, 1827–35. Married Mary Hale in 1835. Postmaster of Hartford, 1836–41. Served as chief of the bureau of provisions and clothing in the navy department, 1846–49. Helped organize Republican Party in Connecticut. Wrote for the *Hartford Evening Press*, the *New York Evening Post*, and other Republican newspapers. Secretary of the navy in the Lincoln and Andrew Johnson administrations, 1861–69. Died in Hartford.

Walt Whitman (May 31, 1819–March 26, 1892) Born in Huntington Township, New York, the son of a farmer and carpenter. Moved with family to Brooklyn in 1823. Learned printing trade at Brooklyn newspapers. Taught school on Long Island, 1836–38. Became freelance journalist and printer in New York and Brooklyn. Published first edition of *Leaves of Grass* in 1855 (revised editions appeared in 1856, 1860, 1867, 1870, 1881, and 1891). Traveled to northern Virginia in December 1862 after learning that his brother George had been wounded at Fredericksburg. Became volunteer nurse in Washington, D.C., army hospitals. Published *Drum-Taps* and *Sequel to Drum-Taps* in 1865. Worked as clerk at the interior department, 1865, and the office of the attorney general, 1865–73. Published prose recollections of his war experiences in *Memoranda During the War* (1875) and *Specimen Days and Collect* (1882). Died in Camden, New Jersey.

Henry A. Wise (December 3, 1806–September 12, 1876) Born in Drummondtown, Accomack County, Virginia, the son of a lawyer. Graduated from Washington College in Pennsylvania, 1825. Married Ann Jennings in 1828; after her death, he married Sarah Sergeant in 1840. Began legal practice in Accomack County, 1830. Served in Congress, 1833–44, and as U.S. minister to Brazil, 1844–47. Governor of

Virginia, 1856–60. Supported secession in the Virginia convention, 1861. Appointed brigadier general in the Confederate army, 1861, and served until the end of the war in Virginia and the Carolinas. Resumed legal career. Died in Richmond.

W. E. Woodruff (June 8, 1831–July 8, 1907) Born William Edward Woodruff Jr. in Little Rock, Arkansas, the son of the founder of the *Arkansas Gazette*. Graduated from the Western Military Institute in Georgetown, Kentucky, in 1852. Worked for father's land agency before beginning legal practice in Little Rock, 1859. Served as Confederate artillery officer in Missouri, Arkansas, and Indian Territory, and as commissary officer in Texas. Wounded at Battle of Prairie Grove in Arkansas, December 1862, and suffered major hearing loss from artillery service. Ended war as major. Publisher and editor of the *Arkansas Gazette*, 1866–76. Married Ruth Blocher in 1868. Served as state treasurer of Arkansas, 1881–91. Convicted of stealing state funds, but verdict was overturned on appeal. Published *With the Light Guns '61–'65* (1903). Died in Little Rock.

Lunsford P. Yandell (June 6, 1837–March 12, 1884) Born in Rutherford County, Tennessee, the son of a physician. Graduated from the University of Louisville medical school in 1857. Began practicing medicine in Memphis, 1858, and taught at the Memphis Medical College. Served as a surgeon with the Confederate army in the western theater, 1861–65. Married Louise Elliston in 1867. Taught medicine at the University of Louisville from 1869 until his death. Died in Louisville from an overdose of chloral hydrate.

Note on the Texts

This volume collects nineteenth- and early twentieth-century writing about secession and the Civil War, bringing together public and private letters, newspaper and magazine articles, memoranda, speeches, narratives, journal and diary entries, proclamations and declarations, messages, judicial opinions, legislative enactments, poems, songs, sermons, and excerpts from memoirs written by participants and observers and dealing with events in the period between November 1860 and January 1862. Most of these documents were not written for publication, and most of them existed only in manuscript form during the lifetimes of the persons who wrote them. The texts presented in this volume are taken from the best printed sources available. In cases where there is only one printed source for a document, the text offered here comes from that source. Where there is more than one printed source for a document, the text printed in this volume is taken from the source that contains the fewest editorial alterations in the spelling, capitalization, paragraphing, and punctuation of the document.

The present volume prints texts as they appear in the sources listed below, but with a few alterations in editorial procedure. The bracketed conjectural readings of editors, in cases where original manuscripts or printed texts were damaged or difficult to read, are accepted without brackets in this volume when those readings seem to be the only possible ones; but when they do not, or when the editor made no conjecture, the missing word or words are indicated by a bracketed two-em space, i.e., [   ]. In cases where a typographical error or obvious misspelling in a manuscript was marked by earlier editors with "[*sic*]," the present volume omits the "[*sic*]" and corrects the typographical error or slip of the pen. In some cases, obvious errors were not marked by earlier editors with "[*sic*]" but were printed and then followed by a bracketed correction; in these instances, this volume removes the brackets and accepts the editorial emendation. Bracketed editorial insertions used in the source texts to identify persons or places, to expand contractions and abbreviations, or to clarify meaning, have been deleted in this volume. In instances where canceled, but still legible, words were printed in the source texts with lines through the deleted material, this volume omits the canceled words. The texts of the memorandum sent by William H. Seward to President Lincoln and of the letter from Sullivan Ballou to Sarah Ballou were presented as quoted material in the sources used in this volume, with quotation marks placed at the beginning of each paragraph and at the end of the text; this volume omits the quotation marks.

Mary Chesnut's Civil War (1981), edited by C. Vann Woodward, prints the text of the narrative Chesnut prepared between 1881 and 1884, using her journal from the 1860s as a source, but also inserted significant passages from the 1860s journal that Chesnut omitted from her 1880s manuscript, and in some cases restored sensitive material that Chesnut had canceled in her journal. In the selections from *Mary Chesnut's Civil War* included in this volume, the inserted and restored material from the 1860s journal is printed without the single and double angle brackets used to indicate it in the Woodward edition. The inserted material appears at 253.3–4, "News so warlike . . . joining the artillery"; at 253.5–6, "Mr. Manning read . . . very complimentary."; at 259.33, "Everybody laughs at John Manning's brag."; at 260.27–28, "Manning, Wigfall, . . . us at night."; at 507.14–19, "The president took all . . . greedy for military fame."; at 507.26–28, "He gave the glory . . . have praised him."; at 510.19, "What a villain that woman is."; at 511.32–512.3, "All day I was . . . Mr. Preston a commission."; at 513.12, "DeLeon is always drunk."; at 520.35–36, "Sat up until . . . and Mrs. Davis."; at 521.35–37, "Mr. Chesnut met his . . . for several days." At 253.4–5, "last night I find he is my all, and I would go mad without him" was canceled by Chesnut in the manuscript.

Inside Lincoln's White House: The Complete Civil War Diary of John Hay (1997), edited Michael Burlingame and John R. Turner Ettlinger, prints a paragraph criticizing Major Robert Anderson in the May 9, 1861, entry (page 352.26–32 in this volume) as canceled material because it was crossed out in the manuscript. This volume prints the paragraph without cancellation marks because it is likely that it was crossed out by someone other than Hay, possibly after his death.

Diary of a Southern Refugee was first published in New York in 1867, with its author identified as "A Lady of Virginia" and with dashes substituted for the names of a number of persons referred to in the text. The book was reprinted in 1889 in Richmond by J. W. Randolph & English, with Judith McGuire identified as its author, and with an appended list of "Corrections" supplying the omitted names. In the selection from *Diary of a Southern Refugee* presented in this volume, the names supplied in the "Corrections" section of the 1889 printing have been incorporated into the text. The text of the judicial opinion *Ex parte Merryman* presented in this volume is taken from *The Federal Cases, Comprising Cases Argued and Determined in the Circuit and District Courts of the United States* (1895), which used as its source the reports of Chief Justice Roger B. Taney's circuit cases prepared by James Mason Campbell, but which also inserted in brackets a passage taken from the *American Law Register* that is omitted from the Campbell report. This volume prints the inserted passage without brackets.

The text of the letter sent by Henry Livermore Abbott to Josiah Gardner Abbott on October 22, 1861, is taken from *Fallen Leaves: The Civil War Letters of Major Henry Livermore Abbott* (1991), edited by Robert Garth Scott, but with several errors of transcription corrected by referring to the original manuscript in the Houghton Library, Harvard University, MS Am 800.26 (37). At 576.19, "on" becomes "upon"; at 576.30, "two row boats" becomes "two little row boats"; at 576.31, "perpendicular & thickly" becomes "perpendicular & very thickly"; at 577.6, "15th" becomes "Fifteenth"; at 577.15, "regiment . . . (making" becomes "regiment on hand (making"; at 577.20, "criticize it. . . . It will" becomes "criticize it in terms. It will"; at 577.26–27, "under command of Gen. Baker" becomes "under command of Col. Lee. The whole was the command of Gen. Baker"; at 577.27–29, "in front. . . . The rebels had 2 inf[antry] & one cavalry regt.; how full is not known" becomes "in front entirely unprotected. The enemy in the woods. Here is a rough sketch"; at 577.30, ". . . 2 of the regts." becomes "You can see from the sketch that 2 of the regts."; at 577.37–38, "2 [P.M.] to 6" becomes "2 till 6"; at 578.19, "with about 20 men" becomes "with 20 men"; at 578.39–579.1, "across [if] they could" becomes "across in case they could"; at 579.13–14, "it seems . . . Capt. Dreher" becomes "it seems by later intelligence. Capt. Dreher"; at 579.21, "are now in camp" becomes "We are now at camp."

The following is a list of the documents included in this volume, in the order of their appearance, giving the source of each text.

Charleston Mercury: What Shall the South Carolina Legislature Do? *Charleston Mercury*, November 3, 1860.

John G. Nicolay: Memoranda Regarding Abraham Lincoln, November 5–6, 1860. *With Lincoln in the White House: Letters, Memoranda, and other Writings of John G. Nicolay, 1860–1865*, ed. Michael Burlingame (Carbondale and Edwardsville: Southern Illinois University Press, 2000), 7–8. Copyright © 2000 by the Board of Trustees, Southern Illinois University.

New-York Daily Tribune: Going to Go. *New-York Daily Tribune*, November 9, 1860.

Jefferson Davis to Robert Barnwell Rhett Jr., November 10, 1860. *The Papers of Jefferson Davis*, Volume 6, ed. Lynda Laswell Crist and Mary Seaton Dix (Baton Rouge: Louisiana State University Press, 1989), 368–69. Copyright © 1989 by the Louisiana State University Press.

Benjamin Hill: Speech at Milledgeville, November 15, 1860. Benjamin H. Hill, Jr., *Senator Benjamin H. Hill of Georgia: His Life, Speeches and Writings* (Atlanta: T.H.P. Bloodworth, 1893), 238–50.

New York Daily News: The Right of States to Secede. *New York Daily News*, November 16, 1860.

Sam Houston to H. M. Watkins and Others, November 20, 1860. *The Writings of Sam Houston*, Volume VIII, ed. Amelia W. Williams and Eugene C. Barker (Austin: The University of Texas Press, 1943), 192–97.

George Templeton Strong: Diary, November 20, November 26–December 1, 1860. George Templeton Strong, *Diary of the Civil War, 1860–1865*, ed. Allan Nevins (New York: The Macmillan Company, 1962), 64, 65–68. Reprinted with permission of Scribner, a Division of Simon & Schuster, Inc., from *The Diary of George Templeton Strong* by Allan Nevins and Milton Halsey Thomas. Copyright © 1952 by Macmillan Publishing Company; copyright renewed © 1980 by Milton Halsey Thomas. All rights reserved.

Edward Bates: Diary, November 22, 1860. *The Diary of Edward Bates*, ed. Howard K. Beale (Washington: United States Government Printing Office, 1933), 157–58.

William G. Brownlow to R. H. Appleton, November 29, 1860. W. G. Brownlow, *Sketches of the Rise, Progress, and Decline of Secession; with a Narrative of Personal Adventures among the Rebels* (Philadelphia: George W. Childs, 1862), 38–48.

Frederick Douglass: The Late Election, December 1860. Philip S. Foner, *The Life and Writings of Frederick Douglass*, volume 2 (New York: International Publishers Co. Inc., 1950), 526–30. Reprinted from *The Life and Writings of Frederick Douglass*, published by International Publishers, copyright © 1950.

William T. Sherman to Thomas Ewing Sr. and to John Sherman, December 1, 1860. *Sherman's Civil War: Selected Correspondence of William T. Sherman, 1860–1865*, ed. Brooks D. Simpson and Jean V. Berlin (Chapel Hill: The University of North Carolina Press, 1999), 13–15. Copyright © 1999 The University of North Carolina Press.

James Buchanan: from the Annual Message to Congress, December 3, 1860. *A Compilation of the Messages and Papers of the Presidents*, vol. VII, ed. James Richardson (New York: Bureau of National Literature, Inc., 1897), 3157–70.

J.D.B. DeBow: The Non-Slaveholders of the South, December 5, 1860. *The Interest in Slavery of the Southern Non-Slaveholder; The*

Right of Peaceful Secession; Slavery in the Bible (Charleston, S.C.: Evans & Cogswell, 1860), 3–12.
Joseph E. Brown to Alfred H. Colquitt and Others, December 7, 1860. *Secession Debated: Georgia's Showdown in 1860*, ed. William W. Freehling and Craig M. Simpson (New York: Oxford University Press, 1992), 145–59. Copyright © 1992 by William W. Freehling, Craig M. Simpson. By permission of Oxford University Press, Inc.
Abraham Lincoln to John A. Gilmer, December 15, 1860. *The Collected Works of Abraham Lincoln*, Volume IV, ed. Roy P. Basler (New Brunswick, N.J.: Rutgers University Press, 1953), 151–53. Copyright © 1953 by the Abraham Lincoln Association.
New-York Daily Tribune: The Right of Secession, December 17, 1860. *Northern Editorials on Secession*, volume I, ed. Howard Cecil Perkins (New York: D. Appleton-Century, 1942), 199–201. Copyright 1942 by the American Historical Association.
Benjamin F. Wade: Remarks in the U.S. Senate, December 17, 1860. *Congressional Globe*, 36th Congress, 2nd session, 102–04.
John J. Crittenden: Remarks in the U.S. Senate, December 18, 1860. *Congressional Globe*, 36th Congress, 2nd session, 112–14.
Henry Adams to Charles Francis Adams Jr., December 18–20, 1860. *The Letters of Henry Adams*, volume I, ed. J. C. Levenson, Ernest Samuels, Charles Vandersee, Viola Hopkins Winner (Cambridge: The Belknap Press of Harvard University Press, 1982), 208–10. Copyright © 1982 by the Massachusetts Historical Society. Reprinted courtesy of the Adams Family Papers, Massachusetts Historical Society.
John G. Nicolay: Memorandum Regarding Abraham Lincoln, December 22, 1860. *With Lincoln in the White House: Letters, Memoranda, and other Writings of John G. Nicolay, 1860–1865*, ed. Michael Burlingame (Carbondale and Edwardsville: Southern Illinois University Press, 2000), 21. Copyright © 2000 by the Board of Trustees, Southern Illinois University.
South Carolina Declaration of the Causes of Secession, December 24, 1860. *Journal of the Convention of the People of South Carolina, Held in 1860, 1861, and 1862, together with the Ordinances, Reports, Resolutions, etc.* (Columbia, S.C.: R. W. Gibbes, 1862), 461–66.
Abner Doubleday: from *Reminiscences of Forts Sumter and Moultrie in 1860–'61*. Abner Doubleday, *Reminiscences of Forts Sumter and Moultrie in 1860–'61* (New York: Harper & Brothers, 1876), 34–35, 41–43, 58–67.
Catherine Edmondston: Diary, December 26–27, 1860. *"Journal of a Secesh Lady": The Diary of Catherine Ann Devereux Edmondston,*

1860–1866, ed. Beth G. Crabtree and James W. Patton (Raleigh: North Carolina Division of Archives and History, 1979), 29–30. Copyright © 1979 by the North Carolina Division of Archives and History.

Stephen F. Hale to Beriah Magoffin, December 27, 1860. *The War of the Rebellion: a Compilation of the Official Records of the Union and Confederate Armies*, series 4, volume I (Washington, D.C.: Government Printing Office, 1900), 4–11.

Herman Melville: Misgivings. Herman Melville, *Battle-Pieces and Aspects of the War* (New York: Harper & Brothers, 1866), 13.

Mary Jones to Charles C. Jones Jr., January 3, 1861. *The Children of Pride: A True Story of Georgia and the Civil War*, Abridged Edition, ed. Robert Manson Myers (New Haven: Yale University Press, 1984), 38–39. Copyright © 1972 by Robert Manson Myers.

Henry Adams to Charles Francis Adams Jr., January 8, 1861. *The Letters of Henry Adams*, volume I, ed. J. C. Levenson, Ernest Samuels, Charles Vandersee, Viola Hopkins Winner (Cambridge: The Belknap Press of Harvard University Press, 1982), 218–20. Copyright © 1982 by the Massachusetts Historical Society. Reprinted courtesy of the Adams Family Papers, Massachusetts Historical Society.

Mississippi Declaration of the Causes of Secession, January 9, 1861. *Journal of the State Convention and Ordinances and Resolutions Adopted in January, 1861* (Jackson, Miss.: E. Barksdale, 1861), 86–88.

Elizabeth Blair Lee to Samuel Phillips Lee, December 25, January 9–10, 1861. *Wartime Washington: The Civil War Letters of Elizabeth Blair Lee*, ed. Virginia Jeans Laas (Urbana: University of Illinois Press, 1991), 19–21. Copyright © 1991 by the Board of Trustees of the University of Illinois.

Catherine Edmondston: Diary, January 9–13, 1861. *"Journal of a Secesh Lady": The Diary of Catherine Ann Devereux Edmondston, 1860–1866*, ed. Beth G. Crabtree and James W. Patton (Raleigh: North Carolina Division of Archives and History, 1979), 32–34. Copyright © 1979 by the North Carolina Division of Archives and History.

Jefferson Davis: Farewell Address in the U.S. Senate, January 21, 1861. *The Papers of Jefferson Davis*, Volume 7, ed. Lynda Laswell Crist and Mary Seaton Dix (Baton Rouge: Louisiana State University Press, 1992), 18–23. Copyright © 1992 by Louisiana State University Press.

Robert E. Lee to George Washington Custis Lee, January 23, 1861. J. William Jones, *Life and Letters of Robert Edward Lee, Soldier and Man* (New York: Neale Publishing Company, 1906), 120–21.

Jefferson Davis: Inaugural Address, February 18, 1861. *A Compilation of the Messages and Papers of the Confederacy, including the diplomatic correspondence, 1861–1865*, Volume I, ed. James D. Richardson (Nashville: United States Publishing Company, 1905), 32–36.

Frederick Douglass: The New President, March 1861. Philip S. Foner, *The Life and Writings of Frederick Douglass*, volume 3 (New York: International Publishers Co. Inc., 1952), 66–67. Reprinted from *The Life and Writings of Frederick Douglass*, published by International Publishers, copyright © 1950.

Abraham Lincoln: First Inaugural Address, March 4, 1861. *The Collected Works of Abraham Lincoln*, Volume IV, ed. Roy P. Basler (New Brunswick, N.J.: Rutgers University Press, 1953), 262–71. Copyright © 1953 by the Abraham Lincoln Association.

Catherine Edmondston: Diary, March 4, 1861. *"Journal of a Secesh Lady": The Diary of Catherine Ann Devereux Edmondston, 1860–1866*, ed. Beth G. Crabtree and James W. Patton (Raleigh: North Carolina Division of Archives and History, 1979), 39–40. Copyright © 1979 by the North Carolina Division of Archives and History.

Alexander H. Stephens: "Corner-Stone" Speech, March 21, 1861. Henry Cleveland, *Alexander H. Stephens in Public and Private* (Philadelphia: National Publishing Company, 1866), 717–29.

Edward Bates: Diary, March 9–April 8, 1861. *The Diary of Edward Bates*, ed. Howard K. Beale (Washington: United States Government Printing Office, 1933), 177–81.

Gideon Welles: Memoir of Events, March 1861. *Diary of Gideon Welles*, volume I (Boston: Houghton Mifflin Company, 1911), 9–14.

William H. Seward: Memorandum for the President, April 1, 1861. *The Collected Works of Abraham Lincoln*, Volume IV, ed. Roy P. Basler (New Brunswick, N.J.: Rutgers University Press, 1953), 317–18. Copyright © 1953 by the Abraham Lincoln Association.

Abraham Lincoln to William H. Seward, April 1, 1861. *The Collected Works of Abraham Lincoln*, Volume IV, ed. Roy P. Basler (New Brunswick, N.J.: Rutgers University Press, 1953), 316–17. Copyright © 1953 by the Abraham Lincoln Association.

Mary Chesnut: Diary, April 7–15, 1861. *Mary Chesnut's Civil War*, ed. C. Vann Woodward (New Haven: Yale University Press, 1981), 42–50. Copyright © 1981 by C. Vann Woodward, Sally Bland Meets, Barbara C. Carpenter, Sally Bland Johnson, and Katherine W. Herbert.

Abner Doubleday: from *Reminiscences of Forts Sumter and Moultrie in 1860–'61*. Abner Doubleday, *Reminiscences of Forts Sumter and Moultrie in 1860–'61* (New York: Harper & Brothers, 1876), 143–46, 154–59, 162–65, 170–73.

George Templeton Strong: Diary, April 13–16, 1861. George Templeton Strong, *Diary of the Civil War, 1860–1865*, ed. Allan Nevins

(New York: The Macmillan Company, 1962), 118–21. Reprinted with permission of Scribner, a Division of Simon & Schuster, Inc., from *The Diary of George Templeton Strong* by Allan Nevins and Milton Halsey Thomas. Copyright © 1952 by Macmillan Publishing Company; copyright renewed © 1980 by Milton Halsey Thomas. All rights reserved.

The New York Times: The People and the Issue. *The New York Times*, April 15, 1861.

Pittsburgh Post: The War Begun—The Duty of American Citizens. *Pittsburgh Post*, April 15, 1861.

William Howard Russell: from *My Diary North and South*. *My Diary North and South*, vol. I (London: Bradbury and Evans, 1863), 143–61.

Charles C. Jones Sr. to Charles C. Jones Jr., April 20, 1861. *The Children of Pride: A True Story of Georgia and the Civil War*, Abridged Edition, ed. Robert Manson Myers (New Haven: Yale University Press, 1984), 52–54. Copyright © 1972, 1984 by Robert Manson Myers.

John B. Jones: Diary, April 15–22, 1861. J. B. Jones, *A Rebel War Clerk's Diary at the Confederate States Capital*, volume I (Philadelphia: J. B. Lippincott & Co., 1866), 19–26.

John W. Hanson: from *Historical Sketch of the Old Sixth Regiment of Massachusetts Volunteers*. John W. Hanson, *Historical Sketch of the Old Sixth Regiment of Massachusetts Volunteers* (Boston: Lee and Shepard, 1866), 37–42.

Ulysses S. Grant to Frederick Dent, April 19, 1861, and to Jesse Root Grant, April 21, 1861. *The Papers of Ulysses S. Grant*, Volume 2, ed. John Y. Simon (Carbondale and Edwardsville: Southern Illinois University Press, 1969), 3–4, 6–7. Published with the permission of the Ulysses S. Grant Association from *The Papers of Ulysses S. Grant*.

Jefferson Davis: Message to the Confederate Congress, April 29, 1861. *A Compilation of the Messages and Papers of the Confederacy, including the diplomatic correspondence, 1861–1865*, Volume I, ed. James D. Richardson (Nashville: United States Publishing Company, 1905), 63–82.

Frederick Douglass: How to End the War, May 1861. Philip S. Foner, *The Life and Writings of Frederick Douglass*, volume 3 (New York: International Publishers Co. Inc., 1952), 94–96. Reprinted from *The Life and Writings of Frederick Douglass*, published by International Publishers, copyright © 1950.

Walt Whitman: First O Songs for a Prelude. Walt Whitman, *Complete Poetry and Collected Prose*, ed. Justin Kaplan (New York: The Library of America, 1982), 416–18.

Winfield Scott to George B. McClellan, May 3, 1861. *The War of the Rebellion: a Compilation of the Official Records of the Union and*

Confederate Armies, series 1, volume LI, part 1 (Washington, D.C.: Government Printing Office, 1897), 369–70.

Charles B. Haydon: Diary, May 3–12, 1861. *For Country, Cause & Leader: The Civil War Journal of Charles B. Haydon*, ed. Stephen W. Sears (New York: Ticknor & Fields, 1993), 3–7. Copyright © 1993 by Stephen W. Sears. Reprinted by permission of Stephen W. Sears.

Ulysses S. Grant to Jesse Root Grant, May 6, 1861. *The Papers of Ulysses S. Grant*, Volume 2, ed. John Y. Simon (Carbondale and Edwardsville: Southern Illinois University Press, 1969), 20–22. Copyright © 1969 by the Ulysses S. Grant Association. Published with the permission of the Ulysses S. Grant Association from *The Papers of Ulysses S. Grant*.

John Hay: Diary, May 7–10, 1861. *Inside Lincoln's White House: The Complete Civil War Diary of John Hay*, ed. Michael Burlingame and John R. Turner Ettlinger (Carbondale and Edwardsville: Southern Illinois University Press, 1997), 19–23. Copyright © 1997 by the Board of Trustees, Southern Illinois University.

Judith W. McGuire: Diary, May 10, 1861. Judith W. McGuire, *Diary of a Southern Refugee, during the war*, 3rd edition (Richmond, Va.: J.W. Randolph & English, Publishers, 1889), 11–15.

William T. Sherman to John Sherman, May 11, 1861. *Sherman's Civil War: Selected Correspondence of William T. Sherman, 1860–1865*, ed. Brooks D. Simpson and Jean V. Berlin (Chapel Hill: The University of North Carolina Press, 1999), 81–82. Copyright © 1999 The University of North Carolina Press.

Benjamin F. Butler to Winfield Scott, May 24, 1861. *The War of the Rebellion: a Compilation of the Official Records of the Union and Confederate Armies*, series 2, volume I (Washington, D.C.: Government Printing Office, 1894), 752.

The New York Times: General Butler and the Contraband of War. *The New York Times*, June 2, 1861.

Kate Stone: Journal, May 15–27, 1861. *Brokenburn: The Journal of Kate Stone, 1861–1868*, ed. John Q. Anderson (Baton Rouge: Louisiana State University Press, 1955), 13–19. Copyright © 1989 by the Louisiana State University Press.

George Templeton Strong: Diary, May 29–June 2, 1861. George Templeton Strong, *Diary of the Civil War, 1860–1865*, ed. Allan Nevins (New York: The Macmillan Company, 1962), 150–55. Reprinted with permission of Scribner, a Division of Simon & Schuster, Inc., from *The Diary of George Templeton Strong* by Allan Nevins and Milton Halsey Thomas. Copyright © 1952 by Macmillan Publishing Company; copyright renewed © 1980 by Milton Halsey Thomas. All rights reserved.

John Brown's Body, May 1861. *The Rebellion Record: A Diary of American Events, with documents, narratives, illustrative incidents, poetry etc.*, volume II, ed. Frank Moore (New York: G. P. Putnam, 1862), poetry section, 105–06.

Roger B. Taney: Opinion in *Ex parte Merryman*, June 1, 1861. *The Federal Cases, Comprising Cases Argued and Determined in the Circuit and District Courts of the United States*, Book 17 (St. Paul: West Publishing Company, 1895), 147–53.

Henry A. Wise, Speech at Richmond, June 1, 1861. *The Rebellion Record: A Diary of American Events, with documents, narratives, illustrative incidents, poetry, etc.*, volume I, ed. Frank Moore (New York: G.P. Putnam, 1861), documents section, 323–24.

Charles C. Jones Jr. to Charles C. Jones Sr. and Mary Jones, June 10, 1861. *The Children of Pride: A True Story of Georgia and the Civil War*, ed. Robert Manson Myers (New Haven: Yale University Press, 1972), 694–96. Copyright © 1972 by Robert Manson Myers.

Henry Adams to Charles Francis Adams Jr., June 10–11, 1861. *The Letters of Henry Adams*, volume I, ed. J. C. Levenson, Ernest Samuels, Charles Vandersee, Viola Hopkins Winner (Cambridge: The Belknap Press of Harvard University Press, 1982), 237–40. Copyright © 1982 by the Massachusetts Historical Society. Reprinted courtesy of the Adams Family Papers, Massachusetts Historical Society.

John Ross to Benjamin McCulloch, June 17, 1861. *The War of the Rebellion: a Compilation of the Official Records of the Union and Confederate Armies*, series 1, volume XIII (Washington, D.C.: Government Printing Office, 1885), 495–97.

James Russell Lowell: The Pickens-and-Stealin's Rebellion. *The Atlantic Monthly*, June 1861.

Abraham Lincoln: Message to Congress in Special Session, July 4, 1861. *The Collected Works of Abraham Lincoln*, Volume IV, ed. Roy P. Basler (New Brunswick, N.J.: Rutgers University Press, 1953), 421–41. Copyright © 1953 by the Abraham Lincoln Association.

Kate Stone: Journal, July 4, 1861. *Brokenburn: The Journal of Kate Stone, 1861–1868*, ed. John Q. Anderson (Baton Rouge: Louisiana State University Press, 1955), 13–19. Copyright © 1989 by the Louisiana State University Press.

Ulysses S. Grant: from *Personal Memoirs of U. S. Grant*. Ulysses S. Grant, *Memoirs and Selected Letters*, ed. Mary Drake McFeely and William S. McFeely (New York: The Library of America, 1990), 163–65.

Sallie Brock: from *Richmond During the War*. Sallie Putnam, *Richmond During the War; Four Years of Personal Observation* (New York: G. W. Carleton & Co., 1867), 56–59.

Sullivan Ballou to Sarah Ballou, July 14, 1861. *Brown University in the Civil War. A Memorial*, ed. Henry Sweetser Burrage (Providence, R.I.: Providence Press Company, 1868), 105–08.

Charles Minor Blackford: from *Letters from Lee's Army. Letters from Lee's Army, or Memoirs of Life In and Out of the Army in Virginia During the War Between the States*, compiled by Susan Leigh Blackford, annotated by Charles Minor Blackford, edited and abridged for publication by Charles Minor Blackford III (New York: Charles Scribner's Sons, 1947), 26–36. Reprinted with permission of Scribner, a Division of Simon & Schuster, Inc., from *Letters from Lee's Army*, compiled by Susan L. Blackford. Copyright 1947 by Charles Scribner's Sons. All rights reserved.

William Howard Russell: from *My Diary North and South. My Diary North and South*, vol. II (London: Bradbury and Evans, 1863), 214–49.

Samuel J. English to his Mother, July 24, 1861. *All for the Union: A History of the 2nd Rhode Island Volunteer Infantry in the War of the Great Rebellion*, ed. Robert Hunt Rhodes (Lincoln, R.I.: Andrew Mowbray Inc., 1985), 24–31. Copyright © 1985 by Robert Hunt Rhodes.

Emma Holmes: Diary, July 22–23, 1861. *The Diary of Miss Emma Holmes*, ed. John F. Marszalek (Baton Rouge: Louisiana State University Press, 1979), 65–68. © 1979 by Louisana State University Press.

Elizabeth Blair Lee to Samuel Phillips Lee, July 23, 1861. *Wartime Washington: The Civil War Letters of Elizabeth Blair Lee*, ed. Virginia Jeans Laas (Urbana: University of Illinois Press, 1991), 68–69. Copyright © 1991 by the Board of Trustees of the University of Illinois.

Walt Whitman: from *Specimen Days. Walt Whitman: Complete Poetry and Collected Prose*, ed. Justin Kaplan (New York: The Library of America, 1982), 707–11.

Abraham Lincoln: Memoranda on Military Policy, July 23, 1861. *The Collected Works of Abraham Lincoln*, Volume IV, ed. Roy P. Basler (New Brunswick, N.J.: Rutgers University Press, 1953), 457–58. Copyright © 1953 by the Abraham Lincoln Association.

Mary Chesnut: Diary, July 24, 1861. *Mary Chesnut's Civil War*, ed. C. Vann Woodward (New Haven: Yale University Press, 1981), 108–22. Copyright © 1981 by C. Vann Woodward, Sally Bland Meets, Barbara C. Carpenter, Sally Bland Johnson, and Katherine W. Herbert.

Crittenden-Johnson Resolutions, July 22–25, 1861. *Congressional Globe*, 37th Congress, 1st session, 222, 257.

George B. McClellan to Mary Ellen McClellan, July 27, 1861. The

Civil War Papers of George B. McClellan: Selected Correspondence, 1860–1865, ed. Stephen W. Sears (New York: Ticknor & Fields, 1989), 70. Copyright © 1989 by Stephen W. Sears. Reprinted by permission of Stephen W. Sears.

William T. Sherman to Ellen Ewing Sherman, July 28, 1861. *Sherman's Civil War: Selected Correspondence of William T. Sherman, 1860–1865*, ed. Brooks D. Simpson and Jean V. Berlin (Chapel Hill: The University of North Carolina Press, 1999), 122–25. Copyright © 1999 The University of North Carolina Press.

Horace Greeley to Abraham Lincoln, July 29, 1861. Abraham Lincoln Papers at the Library of Congress. Transcribed and annotated by the Lincoln Studies Center, Knox College, Galesburg, Illinois.

George B. McClellan: Memorandum for the President, August 2, 1861. *The Civil War Papers of George B. McClellan: Selected Correspondence, 1860–1865*, ed. Stephen W. Sears (New York: Ticknor & Fields, 1989), 71–75. Copyright © 1989 by Stephen W. Sears. Reprinted by permission of Stephen W. Sears.

Confiscation Act, August 6, 1861. *Congressional Globe* Appendix, 37th Congress, 1st session, 42.

George B. McClellan to Mary Ellen McClellan, August 8, 10, and 16, 1861. *The Civil War Papers of George B. McClellan: Selected Correspondence, 1860–1865*, ed. Stephen W. Sears (New York: Ticknor & Fields, 1989), 81–82, 85. Copyright © 1989 by Stephen W. Sears. Reprinted by permission of Stephen W. Sears.

E. F. Ware: from *The Lyon Campaign in Missouri*. E. F. Ware, *The Lyon Campaign in Missouri* (Topeka, Kansas: Crane & Company, 1907), 310–12, 313–26.

W. E. Woodruff: from *With the Light Guns in '61–'65*. W. E. Woodruff, *With the Light Guns in '61–'65* (Little Rock, Ark.: Central Printing Company, 1903), 39–48.

John C. Frémont: Proclamation, August 30, 1861. *The War of the Rebellion: a Compilation of the Official Records of the Union and Confederate Armies*, series 1, volume III (Washington, D.C.: Government Printing Office, 1881), 466–67.

Abraham Lincoln to John C. Frémont, September 2, 1861. *The Collected Works of Abraham Lincoln*, Volume IV, ed. Roy P. Basler (New Brunswick, N.J.: Rutgers University Press, 1953), 506. Copyright © 1953 by the Abraham Lincoln Association.

Frederick Douglass: Fighting Rebels with Only One Hand, September 1861. Philip S. Foner, *The Life and Writings of Frederick Douglass*, volume 3 (New York: International Publishers Co. Inc., 1952), 151–54. Reprinted from *The Life and Writings of Frederick Douglass*, published by International Publishers, copyright © 1950.

Abraham Lincoln to Orville H. Browning, September 22, 1861. *The*

Collected Works of Abraham Lincoln, Volume IV, ed. Roy P. Basler (New Brunswick, N.J.: Rutgers University Press, 1953), 531–33. Copyright © 1953 by the Abraham Lincoln Association.

John Ross: Message to the National Council, October 9, 1861. *The War of the Rebellion: a Compilation of the Official Records of the Union and Confederate Armies*, series 1, volume XIII (Washington, D.C.: Government Printing Office, 1881), 500–02.

Henry Livermore Abbott to Josiah Gardner Abbott, October 22, 1861. *Fallen Leaves: The Civil War Letters of Major Henry Livermore Abbott*, ed. Robert Garth Scott (Kent, Ohio: The Kent State University Press, 1991), 60–66.

George B. McClellan to Mary Ellen McClellan, October 25, 26, 30, and 31, 1861. *The Civil War Papers of George B. McClellan: Selected Correspondence, 1860–1865*, ed. Stephen W. Sears (New York: Ticknor & Fields, 1989), 111–14. Copyright © 1989 by Stephen W. Sears. Reprinted by permission of Stephen W. Sears.

Charles Francis Adams Jr. to Henry Adams, November 5, 1861. *A Cycle of Adams Letters, 1861–1865*, volume I, ed. Worthington Chauncey Ford (Boston: Houghton Mifflin Company, 1920), 63–64.

George B. McClellan to Samuel L. M. Barlow, November 8, 1861. *The Civil War Papers of George B. McClellan: Selected Correspondence, 1860–1865*, ed. Stephen W. Sears (New York: Ticknor & Fields, 1989), 127–28. Copyright © 1989 by Stephen W. Sears. Reprinted by permission of Stephen W. Sears.

Ulysses S. Grant to Jesse Root Grant, November 8, 1861. *The Papers of Ulysses S. Grant*, Volume 3, ed. John Y. Simon (Carbondale and Edwardsville: Southern Illinois University Press, 1970), 136–38. Copyright © 1970 by the Ulysses S. Grant Association. Published with the permission of the Ulysses S. Grant Association from *The Papers of Ulysses S. Grant*.

Lunsford P. Yandell Jr. to Lunsford Yandell Sr., November 10, 1861. *The Rebellion Record: A Diary of American Events, with documents, narratives, illustrative incidents, poetry, etc.*, volume III, ed. Frank Moore (New York: G. P. Putnam, 1862), document pages 298–99.

Samuel Francis Du Pont to Sophie Du Pont, November 13–15, 1861. Samuel Francis DuPont, *A Selection From His Civil War Letters*, volume I, ed. John D. Hayes (Ithaca, New York: Cornell University Press, 1969), 235–42. Copyright © 1969 by Eleutherian Mills-Hagley Foundation. Reprinted courtesy of Hagley Museum and Library.

Sam Mitchell: Narrative of the capture of the Sea Islands, November 1861. *The American Slave: A Composite Autobiography*, volume III, ed. George P. Rawick (Westport, Conn.: Greenwood Press, 1972), 202–03.

Henry Tucker: God in the War, November 15, 1861. Electronic text provided by The University of North Carolina at Chapel Hill: http://docsouth.unc.edu/imls/tuckerh/tuckerh.html.

Jefferson Davis: Message to the Confederate Congress, November 18, 1861. *A Compilation of the Messages and Papers of the Confederacy, including the diplomatic correspondence, 1861–1865*, Volume I, ed. James D. Richardson (Nashville: United States Publishing Company, 1905), 136–44.

Harper's Weekly: The Great Review. *Harper's Weekly*, December 7, 1861.

Ulysses S. Grant to Jesse Root Grant, November 27, 1861. *The Papers of Ulysses S. Grant*, Volume 3, ed. John Y. Simon (Carbondale and Edwardsville: Southern Illinois University Press, 1970), 226–28. Copyright © 1970 by the Ulysses S. Grant Association. Published with the permission of the Ulysses S. Grant Association from *The Papers of Ulysses S. Grant*.

Sallie Brock: from *Richmond During the War*. Sallie Putnam, *Richmond During the War; Four Years of Personal Observation* (New York: G. W. Carleton & Co., 1867), 78–81.

Benjamin Moran, Journal, November 27–December 3, 1861. *The Journal of Benjamin Moran, 1857–1865*, volume II, ed. Sarah Agnes Wallace and Frances Elma Gillespie (Chicago: The University of Chicago Press, 1949), 912–17. Copyright © 1949 by The University of Chicago.

Henry Adams to Charles Francis Adams Jr., November 30, 1861. *The Letters of Henry Adams*, volume I, ed. J. C. Levenson, Ernest Samuels, Charles Vandersee, Viola Hopkins Winner (Cambridge: The Belknap Press of Harvard University Press, 1982), 263–64. Copyright © 1982 by the Massachusetts Historical Society. Reprinted courtesy of the Adams Family Papers, Massachusetts Historical Society.

Abraham Lincoln, Annual Message to Congress, December 3, 1861. *The Collected Works of Abraham Lincoln*, Volume V, ed. Roy P. Basler (New Brunswick, N.J.: Rutgers University Press, 1953), 35–53. Copyright © 1953 by the Abraham Lincoln Association.

Charles Francis Adams Jr. to Henry Adams, December 10, 1861. *A Cycle of Adams Letters, 1861–1865*, volume I, ed. Worthington Chauncey Ford (Boston: Houghton Mifflin Company, 1920), 79–81.

Let My People Go. *American Poetry: The Nineteenth Century*, volume II, ed. John Hollander (New York: The Library of America, 1993), 786–88.

Robert E. Lee to George Washington Custis Lee, December 29, 1861. *The Wartime Papers of Robert E. Lee*, ed. Clifford Dowdey and Louis H. Manarin (Boston: Little, Brown, 1961), 97–99. Reprinted by permission of the National Archives.

Edward Bates: Diary, December 31, 1861. *The Diary of Edward Bates*, ed. Howard K. Beale (Washington: United States Government Printing Office, 1933), 219–20.

Irvin McDowell: Memorandum, January 10–13, 1862. Henry J. Raymond, *The Life and Public Services of Abraham Lincoln, Sixteenth President of the United States* (New York: Derby and Miller, 1865), 772–77.

Montgomery C. Meigs, Memoir of Meetings with President Lincoln, January 10–13, 1862. "General M. C. Meigs on the Conduct of the Civil War," *The American Historical Review*, vol. 26, no. 2 (January 1921), 292–93.

Edwin M. Stanton to Charles A. Dana, January 24, 1862. Charles A. Dana, *Recollections of the Civil War* (New York: D. Appleton and Company, 1899), 4–5.

This volume presents the texts of the printings chosen as sources here but does not attempt to reproduce features of their typographic design. The texts are printed without alteration except for the changes previously discussed and for the correction of typographical errors. All ellipses in the texts appeared in the printings chosen as sources. Spelling, punctuation, and capitalization are often expressive features, and they are not altered, even when inconsistent or irregular. The following is a list of typographical errors corrected, cited by page and line number: 2.3, unitedin; 24.32, 1703,; 26.33, State; 39.3, "irrespresible; 48.30, of of; 49.24, 1880.; 61.8, odious.; 75.3, them directly; 86.26, truthfulnes,; 90.39–91.1, Massachussetts,; 93.37–38, nonslave. holder,; 99.14, imininent; 100.20, ballance; 107.25, retalitory; 107.30, staute; 108.3, nullifing; 166.27, subtantially; 232.11, become; 275.13, New York, City; 276.11, soveign; 279.19, citizens.; 280.19, direlect; 285.9, imposing; 293.32, Rhelt.; 352.24, Davis.; 364.15, Balliwick; 372.21, penitenitary;; 387.16, General, George; 470.15, commssiariat; 473.33, steams; 474.21, from he; 476.31, inrceased; 477.10, could.; 479.37, theere; 484.5, and and; 531.29, you; 558.6, considerable..; 559.10, couragous; 605.10–11, to bow,; 606.30, when be; 607.30, villanies."; 608.39, ray bed; 608.39, there!; 611.2, Alt that; 616.27, — Woe; 617.37, proceedure; 618.20, he;; 619.33, —God; 621.3, two; 625.15, lond; 625.40, call be; 633.3, gentleman; 641.15, comfortaple; 642.13, have have.

Notes

In the notes below, the reference numbers denote page and line of this volume (the line count includes headings, but not rule lines). No note is made for material included in the eleventh edition of *Merriam-Webster's Collegiate Dictionary*. Biblical references are keyed to the King James Version. Quotations from Shakespeare are keyed to *The Riverside Shakespeare*, ed. G. Blakemore Evans (Boston: Houghton, Mifflin, 1974). Footnotes and bracketed editorial notes within the text were in the originals. For further historical and biographical background, references to other studies, and more detailed maps, see James McPherson, *Battle Cry of Freedom: The Civil War Era* (New York: Oxford University Press, 1988); *Encyclopedia of the American Civil War: A Political, Social, and Military History*, edited by David S. Heidler and Jeanne T. Heidler (New York: W. W. Norton, 2002); and Aaron Sheehan-Dean, *Concise Historical Atlas of the U.S. Civil War* (New York: Oxford University Press, 2008).

2.33 Abolitionist colored man] In a speech given at Charleston on July 9, 1860, Robert Barnwell Rhett, the secessionist publisher of the *Mercury*, alleged that Maine Senator Hannibal Hamlin (1809–1891), the Republican candidate for vice president, was a mulatto. His claim was repeated by Southern newspapers and orators during the campaign, although there was no evidence to support it.

4.16–17 Force Bill] A South Carolina state convention passed a nullification ordinance on November 24, 1832, prohibiting the collection of the federal tariffs authorized in 1828 and 1832 and threatening secession if the federal government responded with force. At the urging of President Andrew Jackson, Congress passed a Force Bill, signed by Jackson on March 2, 1833, authorizing the president to use the military to enforce federal revenue laws; at the same time, Congress also passed a compromise tariff law lowering rates. The South Carolina convention met on March 11 and rescinded the nullification ordinance, ending the crisis.

5.14 SANFORD] Henry Sanford (1823–1891) was a secretary in the American legation in Paris, 1849–54, then began representing American business interests in Central and South America. He served as the U.S. minister to Belgium, 1861–69, and later founded the town of Sanford in Florida.

5.33 irrepressible conflict] In a speech delivered at Rochester, New York, on October 25, 1858, Senator William H. Seward described the "collision" between slavery and free labor as "an irrepressible conflict" that would result in the United States becoming "either entirely a slaveholding nation, or entirely a free-labor nation."

6.7 statement about Seward last year."] The New York Democratic Vigilant Association, a group of wealthy businessmen also known as the Fifth Avenue Hotel Committee, issued an address on October 27, 1859, denouncing John Brown's recent raid on the federal arsenal at Harpers Ferry, Virginia. Signed by thirty-one members of the Association's executive committee, the address quoted extensively from Seward's "irrepressible conflict" speech, asserting that "John Brown has only practiced what William H. Seward preaches," and accusing "republican Senators" of concealing knowledge of Brown's plans from the authorities.

8.27–29 Dogberry . . . must ride behind."] Cf. *Much Ado About Nothing*, III.v.36–37.

9.21–22 John Quincy Adams . . . dissolution of the Union.] As part of his campaign to overturn the rule forbidding the House of Representatives from considering antislavery petitions, congressman and former president John Quincy Adams (1767–1848) presented a petition on January 25, 1842, signed by forty-six residents of Haverhill, Massachusetts, seeking the peaceful dissolution of the Union because of a sectional imbalance in political power. Thomas Marshall (1801–1864), a Kentucky Whig, introduced a resolution censuring Adams for propositioning the House to commit perjury and high treason. After prolonged debate, the motion was defeated 106–93 on February 7, 1842.

16.21 acts nullifying the fugitive slave law] In response to the Fugitive Slave Act of 1850, Ohio, Michigan, Wisconsin, and the New England states passed personal liberty laws guaranteeing various due process protections to persons accused of being escaped slaves.

16.29–30 Northern courts, . . . unconstitutional] In 1854 the Supreme Court of Wisconsin ruled the Fugitive Slave Act of 1850 unconstitutional. Its decision was overturned by the U.S. Supreme Court in *Ableman v. Booth* (1859).

17.3–9 a Northern man . . . Governor of the State] William Dennison (1815–1882), the Republican governor of Ohio from 1860 to 1862, refused to extradite a man named Kennedy who had been indicted for taking slaves from Tennessee and selling them in Virginia.

17.18–19 to shield several . . . John Brown raid.] Seven of the twenty-one men who accompanied John Brown in his raid on Harpers Ferry, October 16–18, 1859, were able to flee the scene. Two of them were captured in Pennsylvania and extradited to Virginia, where they were tried and hanged, while the remaining five were able to escape arrest. When Virginia governor John Letcher sought the extradition of Barclay Coppoc from Iowa in January 1860, Governor Samuel Kirkwood, a Republican, rejected the request as improperly made out. Kirkwood accepted a second set of extradition papers in February, by which time Coppoc had gone into hiding. Letcher also sought the extradition of Owen Brown and Francis Merriam from Ohio, but Governor William Dennison rejected the request on the grounds that there was no proof that Brown and Merriam had fled from Virginia. In April 1860 federal authorities arrested Franklin B. Sanborn, one of the radical abolitionists who had financially supported Brown, for refusing to appear before the Senate committee investigating the Harpers Ferry raid. Sanborn was released on a state writ of habeas corpus, and the warrant for his arrest was rejected by the Massachusetts supreme judicial court as technically invalid.

17.29 most learned disciples of this party] Congregational minister Henry Ward Beecher (1813–1887), in a speech given at North Church, New Haven, Connecticut, on March 16, 1856. Beecher spoke at a meeting held to raise funds for the purchase of Sharps rifles for free-state settlers in Kansas.

17.37–39 honored senators . . . that party] John P. Hale (1806–1873) served in Congress as a Democrat from New Hampshire, 1843–45, and in the Senate as a Free-Soiler, 1847–53, and as a Republican, 1855–65. He spoke on June 17, 1856, at the Republican national convention that nominated John C. Frémont for president.

20.24 General Braddock] Major General Edward Braddock (1695–1755), the commander of British forces in North America, was fatally wounded on July 9, 1755, when his force was ambushed by the French and Indians near the Monongahela River in western Pennsylvania.

20.29 Newcastle] Thomas Pelham-Holles (1693–1768), Duke of Newcastle, was prime minister of Great Britain, 1754–56 and 1757–62.

23.17 abolished slavery in the West Indies] The Abolition Act, passed by Parliament in 1833, resulted in the emancipation of all slaves in the British West Indies in 1838.

24.26–27 In 1848 the Abolitionist . . . the Presidency] In 1848 former president Martin Van Buren (1782–1862) ran on the Free Soil Party ticket.

24.28–29 in 1852, . . . that party] New Hampshire senator John P. Hale headed the Free Soil ticket in 1852.

24.31–33 act of Massachusetts, . . . until 1855] The Massachusetts legislature passed a personal liberty law in 1843 prohibiting the participation of state officials and the use of state courtrooms and jails in the rendition of fugitive slaves. (Similar laws were adopted during the 1840s in Vermont, Connecticut, New Hampshire, Rhode Island, and Pennsylvania.) The personal liberty law passed in Massachusetts in 1855 authorized state judges to issue writs of habeas corpus in fugitive slave cases, releasing prisoners from federal custody and allowing their cases to be heard in state court, where they would be guaranteed the right to counsel and to trial by jury.

NOTES 747

26.31–32 a fugitive is standing protected by a Northern mob] Possibly a reference to Eliza Grayson, a fugitive slave from Nebraska Territory who was arrested by a deputy U.S. marshal in Chicago on November 12, 1860. When a group of African Americans confronted the marshal, he turned Grayson over to the city police, who detained her in the city armory as the crowd outside vowed to prevent her removal from the city. The next morning Calvin DeWolf, an antislavery justice of the peace, issued a warrant charging her with breach of the peace. Grayson was then freed by the crowd and taken to safety while she was being brought to DeWolf's office by a deputy sheriff.

27.36 "Wide Awakes"] The Wide-Awake marching clubs, first organized by the Republicans during the 1856 campaign and revived in 1860, staged mass torchlight parades and other events in support of Lincoln's election.

34.30 first Congress passed the Bill of Rights] The Declaration and Resolves adopted by the First Continental Congress on October 14, 1774.

34.31–32 Bill of Rights . . . Charles the First] The Petition of Right adopted by Parliament in 1628.

38.8–9 candidates . . . Texas was declared] The Southern Democratic ticket of John C. Breckinridge for president and Joseph Lane for vice president.

40.29 the higher law principle] In a speech in the Senate on March 11, 1850, William H. Seward argued that the Constitution permitted the prohibition of slavery in the federal territories and that slavery was unjust under "a higher law than the Constitution."

41.24–25 In reply to Mr. Seward, . . . these words] Houston quotes from a speech he gave on April 20, 1858, advocating establishing an American protectorate over Mexico. In a speech in the Senate on March 3, 1858, opposing the admission of Kansas as a slave state, Seward had described the annexation of Texas as "a bold measure, of doubtful constitutionality, distinctly adopted as an act of intervention in favor of slave labor," and went on to say that the nation "has advanced another stage; it has reached the point where intervention by the Government for slavery and slave labor will no longer be tolerated. Free labor has at last apprehended its rights, its interests, its power, and its destiny; and is organizing itself to assume the government of the Republic."

43.11–12 First Board . . . the Second.] The First Board was the morning trading session, held between 10:30 A.M. and noon, and the Second Board was the afternoon session, held between 2:30 and 3:00 P.M.

43.31 mere nullities] Under the fugitive slave act of 1850, rendition cases were heard and decided by federal commissioners, not in state courts.

44.30–31 John C. Green] John C. Green (1800–1875), a New York merchant, railroad financier, and philanthropist.

45.8 Mr. Ruggles's friend, Senator Dixon] Samuel B. Ruggles (1800–1881), a lawyer and real estate developer, created Gramercy Park in 1831 and later served as a Whig member of the New York assembly, 1838–39, and as a state canal commissioner. Strong had married his daughter Ellen in 1848. James Dixon (1814–1873) was a Whig congressman from Connecticut, 1845–49, and a Republican senator, 1857–69.

45.13 Tom Corwin] Thomas Corwin (1794–1865) of Ohio was a Whig congressman, 1831–40, governor of Ohio, 1840–42, a U.S. senator, 1845–50, and secretary of the treasury, 1850–53. He served in Congress as a Republican, 1859–61, and was U.S. minister to Mexico, 1861–64. In December 1860 he became chairman of the House Committee of Thirty-Three that considered proposals for sectional compromise.

46.4 Willy Cutting] William Cutting (1832–1897) was a New York lawyer who later became a major in the Union army and served as an aide-de-camp to Major General Ambrose Burnside.

46.21 the right of petition, and the Giddings business] In response to an increasing number of petitions calling for the abolition of slavery in Washington, D.C., the House of Representatives adopted a rule on May 26, 1836, requiring that all petitions regarding slavery be tabled without being read or printed. After a prolonged struggle over the right to petition, the rule was revoked on December 3, 1844. Joshua R. Giddings (1795–1864) of Ohio was an antislavery Whig, and later Republican, who served in congress from 1838 to 1859. On March 21, 1842, he introduced nine resolutions in the House regarding the *Creole*, an American brig carrying slaves from Virginia to New Orleans that was seized by slave mutineers in November 1841 and taken to Nassau in the Bahamas, where British authorities freed the slaves who had not participated in the revolt (the mutineers were released in April 1842). Drafted by the abolitionist Theodore Weld, the resolutions declared that the slaves onboard the *Creole* had "violated no law of the United States, incurred no legal penalty, and are justly liable to no punishment" for "resuming their natural rights of personal liberty," and that attempts to reenslave them would be "unauthorized by the Constitution" and "incompatible with our national honor." The next day the House voted 125–69 to censure Giddings. He immediately resigned his seat and was returned to the House after winning a special election, 7,469–393.

46.22–23 the admission of California] In a special message to Congress in January 1850 President Zachary Taylor recommended the immediate admission of California as a free state. His proposal aroused intense Southern opposition both in and out of Congress, including threats of disunion. In September 1850 Congress passed several separate acts that later became known as "the compromise of 1850." The legislation admitted California into the Union as a free state, organized territorial governments for New Mexico and Utah without a congressional prohibition of slavery in those territories, settled the Texas–New Mexico boundary dispute, assumed $10 million of the debt of the Texas republic, abolished the slave trade in the District of Columbia, and replaced the 1793 fugitive slave act with a stronger law.

46.31–32   S. A. Douglas . . . the Missouri Compromise.] In 1819 northern opposition prevented the admission of Missouri as a slave state. The following year Congress passed legislation admitting Missouri as a slave state and Maine as a free state while excluding slavery from the remainder of the Louisiana Purchase territory north of 36° 30′ latitude. In 1854 Democratic senator Stephen A. Douglas of Illinois secured passage of the Kansas-Nebraska Act, which repealed the Missouri Compromise line and allowed the question of whether slavery would be permitted in the newly-organized territories to be decided by their legislatures.

46.33   effort to force slavery on Kansas] In November 1857 a convention held at Lecompton in Kansas Territory approved a proslavery constitution, and in December it was approved in a referendum boycotted by free-state settlers, in which voters were denied the choice of rejecting the document outright. President James Buchanan asked Congress in February 1858 to approve the constitution and admit Kansas as a slave state. Despite the opposition of Senator Stephen A. Douglas, who denounced the Lecompton constitution as a violation of the principle of popular sovereignty, the admission of Kansas was approved by the Senate, 33–25, but was rejected by the House, 120–112. Both the House and the Senate then approved a bill resubmitting the Lecompton constitution under the guise of a land-grant referendum, and on August 2, 1858, it was rejected by the voters of Kansas, 11,300–1,788.

46.35–36   brutal beating . . . Sumner] In his antislavery speech, "The Crime Against Kansas," delivered in the Senate May 19–20, 1856, Charles Sumner (1811–1874) of Massachusetts described Senator Andrew Butler of South Carolina as having chosen "the harlot, Slavery" as his "mistress." On May 22 South Carolina congressman Preston Brooks (1819–1857), a cousin of Senator Butler, approached Sumner as he sat at his desk in the Senate chamber, accused him of libeling South Carolina and Butler, and beat him unconscious with a cane. After a measure to expel him from the House failed to win the necessary two-thirds majority, Brooks resigned his seat and was reelected by his district. Sumner did not return regularly to the Senate until December 1859.

46.37   the project to revive the slave trade] During the 1850s several prominent Southern proslavery advocates, including William Yancey, J.D.B. DeBow, and Leonidas Spratt, began calling for the reopening of the African slave trade, in part as a way of making slaveholding more affordable for Southern farmers. Their proposal failed to win the support of most Southerners, who opposed reopening the trade on moral, political, and economic grounds. (Many slaveholders in the Upper South profited from selling slaves to the cotton states and did not wish to see the price of slaves decline.)

50.1–2   General JACKSON's Message of 1833] President Andrew Jackson submitted a message to Congress on January 16, 1833, requesting the passage of a Force Bill in response to the South Carolina nullification ordinance of November 24, 1832; see note 4.16–17.

50.18–19   Cuba, . . . *two hundred millions*]   In 1854 the Pierce administration authorized the U.S. minister to Spain to offer as much as $130 million for the purchase of Cuba. Although Spain rejected the bid, proslavery expansionists continued to advocate the acquisition of the island.

53.7–8   "Except ye abide in the ship, ye cannot be saved."]   Acts 27:31.

53.32–33   Dr. PIERCE]   Lovick Pierce (1785–1879), a Methodist minister from Georgia.

55.31   message to Congress, January 7, 1833]   The message was sent on January 16, 1833.

58.10   Lord Mansfield]   William Murray, Lord Mansfield (1705–1793), was Lord Chief Justice of the King's Bench, 1756–88. In December 1771 he issued a writ of habeas corpus for James Somerset, a slave brought to England from North America in 1769 who had run away, been recaptured, and was about to be sent by his owner to Jamaica for sale. After hearing several pleadings, Lord Mansfield ruled on June 22, 1772, that slavery could exist only when supported by positive law, and that because no positive law in England authorized the forcible removal of slaves, Somerset should be set free.

58.12   Brougham denounced as the "wild and guilty fantasy"]   A leading British abolitionist, Henry Brougham (1778–1868) spoke in a debate in the House of Commons on July 13, 1830, of "the law written by the finger of God on the heart of man; and by that law, unchangeable and eternal, while men despise fraud, and loathe rapine, and abhor blood, they shall reject with indignation the wild and guilty fantasy that man can hold property in man." Brougham later served as Lord Chancellor, 1830–34, and was a member of the government, headed by Earl Grey, that passed an act in 1833 abolishing slavery in the West Indies.

59.35–36   The South . . . a Sardinia.]   At the beginning of 1860 Sicily and Naples were ruled by an absolutist branch of the Bourbon dynasty, while Sardinia and Piedmont were ruled by the more liberal House of Savoy. In May 1860 Giuseppe Garibaldi (1807–1882) landed in Sicily and led a campaign that succeeded in overthrowing Bourbon rule, and in October a plebiscite approved the union of Sicily with Sardinia-Piedmont.

60.4–5   consummation . . . to be wished."]   Cf. *Hamlet*, III.i.62–63.

60.30–31   reviving fires . . . slave trade]   In November 1858 the schooner *Wanderer* illegally landed about 400 slaves on the Georgia coast. After the ship was seized by federal authorities, press reports and rumors circulated of other attempts to smuggle slaves into the South.

61.38–39   Benj. Lundy and Wm. Lloyd Garrison]   Benjamin Lundy

(1789–1839) was a Quaker abolitionist who published and edited the *Genius of Universal Emancipation*, 1821–35, and the *National Enquirer and Constitutional Advocate of Universal Liberty*, 1836–38. An advocate of gradual emancipation, Lundy supported efforts to colonize free blacks outside the United States. William Lloyd Garrison (1805–1879) met Lundy in 1828 and was the co-editor of *The Genius of Universal Emancipation*, 1829–30. An advocate of immediate abolition who opposed colonization, Garrison edited *The Liberator*, 1831–65. He helped found the American Anti-Slavery Society in 1833 and served as its president, 1843–65.

62.6   Fusion party] In the 1860 presidential election supporters of Stephen A. Douglas (Northern Democratic), John C. Breckinridge (Southern Democratic), and John Bell (Constitutional Union) combined to run anti-Lincoln fusion tickets in New York, New Jersey, and Rhode Island; there was also a Douglas-Breckinridge ticket in Pennsylvania and a Douglas-Bell ticket in Texas.

63.2–3   *Thomas Ewing Sr. . . . John Sherman*] Thomas Ewing (1789–1871) served as a senator from Ohio, 1831–37 and 1850–51, as secretary of the treasury, 1841, and as secretary of the interior, 1849–50. William T. Sherman had married Ellen Ewing, his eldest daughter, in 1850. John Sherman (1823–1900) served as a Republican congressman from Ohio, 1855–61, as a senator, 1861–77 and 1881–97, as secretary of the treasury, 1877–81, and as secretary of state, 1897–98.

65.3   Clay] Sherman's horse, who was ill with glanders. He did not recover, and in early January 1861 Sherman had him shot.

68.39–40   In 1835 . . . inflammatory appeals] In 1835 the American Anti-Slavery Society began mailing thousands of abolitionist pamphlets to prominent Southerners. At the direction of Postmaster General Amos Kendall, Southern postmasters stopped delivering antislavery materials.

69.3–4   "to stimulate them . . . servile war."] From President Jackson's annual message to Congress, December 7, 1835, in which Jackson asked Congress to pass a law prohibiting the circulation through the mail of "incendiary" antislavery publications. The post office bill eventually passed by Congress in 1836 did not include a ban on antislavery mailings.

69.37–38   "a deliberate, . . . exercise"] From the Virginia resolutions, drafted by James Madison and adopted by the Virginia assembly on December 24, 1798. The resolutions condemned the Alien and Sedition Acts as unconstitutional and called upon the states to resist them.

70.28   "sufficient unto the day is the evil thereof."] Matthew 6:34.

70.36–37   the Supreme Court, . . . decided] In *Dred Scott v. Sandford* (1857).

72.10   a State court in Wisconsin] See note 16.29–30.

74.34–75.5 It was formed . . . committed to it.] From a public letter written by James Madison to Edward Everett on August 28, 1830, and published in the October 1830 *North American Review*.

78.33 *posse comitatus*] Literally, "power of the county"; a group of citizens summoned by a sheriff or federal marshal to keep the peace and enforce the law.

83.5 Mr. Madison's . . . in 1799] In December 1799 James Madison began writing an extensive report on the response by other states to the Virginia resolutions of 1798. The report was adopted by the Virginia house of delegates on January 7, 1800.

85.27 Sydneys, Hampdens] Algernon Sydney (1622–1683) was an English republican and opponent of Charles II who was executed for allegedly plotting his assassination. John Hampden (1594–1643) was a leader of the parliamentary opposition to Charles I. He was killed in battle during the English Civil War.

86.1 Senator Cass] Lewis Cass (1782–1866) was a Democratic senator from Michigan, 1845–48 and 1849–57, and the Democratic presidential nominee in 1848. He served as secretary of state, 1857–60.

90.28–29 Senator Johnson, of Tennessee] See Biographical Notes.

92.9 Owenites, Fourierites] Followers of the British social reformer Robert Owen (1771–1858) and the French social theorist Charles Fourier (1772–1837). Several Owenite and Fourierist communal settlements were established in the northern United States in the early nineteenth century.

92.10 Millerites] Followers of the American preacher William Miller (1782–1849) who had predicted that Christ would return to earth between March 1843 and March 1844.

94.8 the McDuffies, Langdon Cheves] George McDuffie (1790–1851) served as a congressman from South Carolina, 1821–34, as governor, 1834–36, and as a senator, 1842–46. Langdon Cheves (1776–1857) was a congressman from South Carolina, 1810–15, and served as Speaker of the House, 1814–15.

94.9–11 Rusks, . . . Maunsel Whites] Thomas J. Rusk (1803–1857) was a Democratic senator from Texas, 1846–57; James Henry Hammond (1807–1864) was governor of South Carolina, 1842–44, and a Democratic senator, 1857–60; William Lowndes Yancey (1814–1863) was a Democratic congressman from Alabama, 1844–46, and a prominent advocate of secession during the 1850s; James L. Orr (1822–1873) was a Democratic congressman from South Carolina, 1849–59, who served as Speaker of the House, 1857–59; Christopher G. Memminger (1803–1888) was a state legislator from South Carolina who later served as the Confederate secretary of the treasury, 1861–64; Judah P. Benjamin (1811–1884) was a Whig, and later Democratic, senator from Louisiana, 1853–61, and later served as the Confederate secretary of state,

1862–65; for Alexander H. Stephens, see Biographical Notes; Pierre Soulé (1801–1870) was a Democratic senator from Louisiana, 1849–53, and U.S. minister to Spain, 1853–55; Albert G. Brown (1813–1880) served as a Democratic congressman from Mississippi, 1839–41 and 1847–53, as governor, 1844–48, and as a senator, 1854–61; William E. Simms (1822–1898) was a Democratic congressman from Kentucky, 1859–61, who later served in the Confederate Senate, 1862–65; William D. Porter (1810–1883) was a South Carolina state senator, 1848–64, served as president of the state senate, 1858–64, and was also the president of the secessionist 1860 Association; Andrew G. Magrath (1813–1893) was U.S. district judge for South Carolina, 1856–60, and later served as governor, 1864–65; William Aiken (1806–1887) was governor of South Carolina, 1844–46, and a Democratic congressman, 1851–57; Maunsel White (1783–1863) was a Louisiana merchant and plantation owner who served in the state senate.

96.34 Mr. Kettell, of New York] Thomas Prentice Kettell (b. 1811), an editor of the *Democratic Review, United States Economist,* and *Hunt's Merchants' Magazine,* published *Southern Wealth and Northern Profits* in 1860.

101.10–11 4,500,000 slaves in the Southern States.] The 1860 census recorded 3,949,557 slaves living in the fifteen slave states.

107.24 my late message . . . Assembly] Brown sent a special message to the legislature on November 7, 1860.

109.3 *John A. Gilmer*] Gilmer (1805–1868) was an American (Know-Nothing) congressman from North Carolina, 1857–61. An opponent of secession in 1860–61, he later served in the Confederate Congress, 1864–65.

111.29–30 "madly shooting from its sphere,"] Cf. *A Midsummer Night's Dream,* II.i.106.

115.25 the Senator from Texas] Louis T. Wigfall (1816–1874) was a South Carolina native who moved to Texas in 1846. He served in the Texas house of representatives, 1850–57, in the Texas senate, 1857–59, in the U.S. Senate, 1859–61, and in the Confederate Senate, 1862–1865.

115.26 the Senator from Georgia] Alfred Iverson Sr. (1798–1873) was a Democratic congressman from Georgia, 1847–49, and a senator, 1855–61.

117.16–17 a Senator . . . a resolution] Lazarus W. Powell (1812–1867) was the Democratic governor of Kentucky, 1851–55, and a senator, 1859–65.

120.23 Senator from Mississippi] Albert G. Brown; see note 94.9–11.

121.28–29 Mr. Webster . . . Mr. Hayne] Robert Hayne (1791–1839) was a senator from South Carolina, 1823–32. In a speech delivered in the Senate on January 19, 1830, Hayne attacked federal land and tariff policies as an attempt by the eastern states to dominate the South and West and called for federal lands to be distributed to the states. Massachusetts Senator Daniel

Webster replied on January 20, defending federal land policies and praising the prohibition of slavery contained in the Northwest Ordinance of 1787. Hayne then responded with a lengthy speech, delivered on January 21 and 25, in which he defended slavery. On January 26–27 Webster gave his second reply to Hayne, which concluded with the phrase "Liberty *and* Union, now and for ever, one and inseparable!" More than 40,000 pamphlet copies of the "Second Reply" were printed within three months of its issue.

121.37 resolutions of 1798–99] The Virginia resolutions of 1798, drafted by James Madison (see note 69.37–38), and the resolutions protesting the Alien and Sedition Acts, drafted by Thomas Jefferson, that were adopted by the Kentucky legislature on November 10, 1798, and November 14, 1799.

122.12 letter to Governor Hamilton] Dated August 28, 1832, Calhoun's public letter was addressed to James Hamilton Jr. (1786–1857), governor of South Carolina, 1830–32.

124.13–14 Faneuil Hall.] A public meeting place in Boston, Massachusetts.

126.10–11 Mr. DOUGLASS . . . Mr. PUGH] Stephen A. Douglas (1813–1861) was a Democratic congressman from Illinois, 1843–47, and a senator, 1847–61. George Pugh (1822–1876) was a Democratic senator from Ohio, 1855–61.

129.10–11 the Missouri compromise] See note 46.31–32.

130.35 *posse comitatus*] See note 78.33

139.21 Mr. FITZPATRICK] Benjamin Fitzpatrick (1802–1869) was the Democratic governor of Alabama, 1841–45, and a senator, 1848–49, 1853–55, and 1855–61.

139.25 Mr. GREEN] James Green (1817–1870) was a Democratic congressman from Missouri, 1847–51, and a senator, 1857–61.

144.16 Reuben Davis of Miss.] Reuben Davis (1813–1890) was a Democratic congressman from Mississippi, 1857–61. He withdrew from Congress in January 1861 and later served as a brigadier general in the Confederate army.

144.29 when Webster was pulled down] In a Senate speech delivered on March 7, 1850, Daniel Webster endorsed a series of compromise measures regarding slavery introduced by Henry Clay, including the passage of a new fugitive slave law. His position was denounced by many antislavery Whigs in Massachusetts, who accused him of betraying his earlier antislavery principles. After Webster resigned from the Senate on July 22, 1850, to become secretary of state under Millard Fillmore, a Free Soil-Democratic coalition succeeded in electing Charles Sumner, an antislavery Whig, to his seat in April 1851.

144.33–34 Rice . . . Thayer] Alexander H. Rice (1818–1895) was mayor of Boston, 1856–57, and a Republican congressman from Massachusetts,

1859–67. Eli Thayer (1819–1899) was a Republican congressman from Massachusetts, 1857–61.

144.36–37   John Adams . . . Dickinson.]   In 1775–76 John Adams was a leading advocate of American independence in the Second Continental Congress, while John Dickinson (1732–1808) of Pennsylvania opposed declaring independence and sought reconciliation with Great Britain.

145.4   Mr. Appleton and Mr. Amory]   William Appleton (1786–1862) was a Whig congressman from Massachusetts, 1851–55, who won election to the House of Representatives in 1860 as a Constitutional Unionist. William Amory (1804–1888) was a cotton manufacturer from Boston.

145.8   Mason]   James Mason (1798–1871) was a Democratic congressman from Virginia, 1837–39, and a senator, 1847–61. He later served as Confederate envoy to Great Britain and France, 1861–1865.

145.15   Boston Courier and Caleb Cushing]   The Boston *Courier* was a conservative newspaper hostile to Sumner. Caleb Cushing (1800–1879) was a Whig congressman from Massachusetts, 1835–43, who became a Democrat and served as attorney general under Franklin Pierce, 1853–57. Cushing supported John C. Breckinridge in the 1860 election, but became a Republican during the Civil War.

145.21–22   Mr Etheridge . . . Anthony]   Emerson Etheridge (1819–1902) was a Whig, and then an American (Know-Nothing) congressman from Tennessee, 1853–57 and 1859–61. He remained loyal to the Union and served as the clerk of the House of Representatives, 1861–63. Henry B. Anthony (1815–1884) was the Whig governor of Rhode Island, 1849–51, and a Republican senator, 1859–84.

145.27   examples of Wellington and Peale]   Arthur Wellesley, Duke of Wellington (1769–1852) was the prime minister of a Tory government, 1828–30, in which Sir Robert Peel (1788–1850) served as home secretary and leader of the House of Commons. In 1829 Wellington and Peel secured the passage of an act allowing Catholics to sit in Parliament and hold public office, believing it was necessary to avoid civil strife in Ireland. The measure was opposed by many in their own party.

145.31–32   Pugh's speech]   Ohio Democrat George E. Pugh (1822–1876) had addressed the Senate on December 20, 1860, urging the adoption of the Crittenden compromise proposals and criticizing Republicans for their opposition to slavery.

145.37   Winter Davis]   Henry Winter Davis (1817–1865) was an American (Know Nothing) congressman from Maryland, 1855–61. He later won election as an Unconditional Unionist and served from 1863 to 1865.

146.5   Hale]   Charles Hale (1831–1882) was the editor and owner of the Boston *Daily Advertiser*. Henry Adams wrote seventeen unsigned letters from Washington, dated December 7, 1860–February 11, 1861, which were published in the *Daily Advertiser*.

146.23 Johnson's speech yesterday] In his speech in the Senate on December 19, 1860, Andrew Johnson of Tennessee called for the preservation of the Union, denounced secession as unconstitutional, and said that the federal government had the power to enforce the laws within states attempting to secede.

146.27 Alley] John B. Alley (1817–1896) was a Republican congressman from Massachusetts, 1859–67.

147.29 Washburne] Elihu Washburne (1816–1887) was a Whig, and then Republican, congressman from Illinois, 1853–69. He served as U.S. minister to France, 1869–77.

147.30 Gen. Scott] Winfield Scott (1786–1866) was general-in-chief of the U.S. Army from 1841 until his retirement on November 1, 1861.

148.5 Wm H Herndon] Herndon (1818–1891) had been Lincoln's law partner in Springfield since 1844.

151.25–26 two of the States . . . into operation] A quorum was achieved by both houses of the First Federal Congress on April 6, 1789, and George Washington was inaugurated on April 30. The Constitution was ratified by North Carolina on November 21, 1789, and by Rhode Island on May 29, 1790.

153.18–20 States of Ohio . . . State of Virginia.] See note 17.18–19.

154.21–22 "Government . . . half slave, half free,"] A paraphrase of a passage from the "House Divided" speech given by Abraham Lincoln at Springfield, Illinois, on June 16, 1858.

154.27–28 citizenship, persons, . . . becoming citizens] The Supreme Court had ruled in *Dred Scott v. Sandford* (1857) that free blacks were not citizens of the United States.

157.10 Anderson] Major Robert Anderson (1805–1871), a native of Kentucky, graduated from West Point in 1825 and was commissioned as an artillery officer. He was appointed brigadier general in May 1861 and commanded Union troops in Kentucky until early October 1861, when he resigned because of failing health. Anderson retired from the army in 1863.

157.13–14 Seminole Indians . . . Molino del Rey] Anderson served in Florida, 1837–38, during the Second Seminole War (1835–42). The Battle of Molino del Rey, fought outside of Mexico City on September 8, 1847, ended in an American victory.

158.25 Yancey] See note 94.9–11.

160.36 columbiads] Large cannons used for coastal defense.

165.2 *Beriah Magoffin*] Magoffin (1815–1885) was the Democratic governor of Kentucky, 1859–62.

169.34 abolition incendiary . . . Texas] On July 8, 1860, fires in north Texas destroyed much of the downtown areas of Dallas and Denton as well as a store in Pilot Point. Although the fires were initially attributed to the spontaneous combustion of volatile phosphorus matches during a period of exceptionally hot weather, on July 12 Charles A. Pryor, the editor of the *Dallas Herald*, wrote the first in a series of letters claiming that they were part of an abolitionist plot to stage a slave insurrection in Texas. Alarmed by reports of further fires and the alleged discovery of stockpiles of poison, vigilance committees were formed throughout northern and eastern Texas, and by September 1860 at least ten whites and twenty blacks were hanged without trial because of their suspected involvement in the purported conspiracy.

169.38–39 "Alarm to their sleep, . . . their food."] In his message to the Virginia general assembly on December 5, 1859, Governor Henry A. Wise asserted that this was the "motto" of "secret societies for mischief" formed by the abolitionists responsible for the underground railroad.

172.14–15 San Domingo servile insurrection] A slave revolt began in Saint-Domingue (Haiti) on August 22, 1791, that eventually resulted in the establishment of an independent republic in 1804.

173.30–32 West India emancipation . . . folly)] Sugarcane production in the West Indies declined sharply after emancipation was completed in 1838 as many former slaves stopped working on plantations.

175.19–20 Jefferson . . . Chippewa] In October 1859 settlers in present-day Colorado created the extralegal Territory of Jefferson, which included parts of the territories of Nebraska, Kansas, New Mexico, Utah, and Washington. The territory was never recognized by the federal government, and its administration disbanded after Congress organized Colorado Territory in February 1861. "Chippewa" probably refers to the unattached territory east of the Missouri River and west of Minnesota that became part of the new Dakota Territory in 1861.

180.20 Ben Crowninshield] Benjamin William Crowninshield (1837–1892), a Harvard classmate of Henry Adams who later served with Charles Francis Adams Jr. as an officer in the 1st Massachusetts Cavalry.

180.23–25 Seward . . . his speech.] Seward gave a conciliatory speech in the Senate on January 12, 1861, in which he stated his willingness to vote for a constitutional amendment protecting slavery in the states from interference by Congress.

181.11–12 Is thy servant . . . this thing.] Cf. 2 Kings 8:13: "is thy servant a dog, that he should do this great thing?"

181.38 the Bayards . . . Florey] James A. Bayard (1799–1880),

Democratic senator from Delaware, 1851–64 and 1867–69; his wife, Ann Willing Francis Bayard; and their daughter Florence Bayard (1842–1898).

182.4   Loo] Louisa Catherine Adams Kuhn (1831–1870), older sister of Henry Adams.

184.15   Ordinance of 1787] The Northwest Ordinance, adopted by the Confederation Congress on July 13, 1787, prohibited slavery in the territory north of the Ohio and east of the Mississippi.

184.20   dismembered Texas] In 1850 Texas ceded to the United States land in present-day Kansas, Oklahoma, New Mexico, Colorado, and Wyoming in return for $10 million.

186.22   exhuberance of Blair] Francis Preston Blair Lee, born in 1857, was the only child of Elizabeth Blair Lee and Samuel Phillips Lee.

186.31   Bates] Edward Bates, who became attorney general. See Biographical Notes.

186.34   Our Maryland nominee] Montgomery Blair (1813–1883) served as postmaster general from March 1861 until his resignation in September 1864.

187.1   Frank] Francis Preston Blair Jr. (1821–1875) was a Republican congressman from Missouri, 1857–59, 1861–62, and 1863–64, and served as a general in the Union army, 1862–63 and 1864–65. An opponent of Radical Reconstruction, he was the Democratic candidate for vice president in 1868.

187.11   Mr. Bailey . . . Floyd] Godard Bailey, a clerk in the Department of the Interior who was married to a cousin of Secretary of War John B. Floyd, had given $870,000 in Indian trust fund bonds to William Russell, a heavily indebted army contractor, in return for promissory notes endorsed by Floyd. Bailey confessed his role in the scheme to President Buchanan on December 22, 1860. Floyd (1806–1863) served as governor of Virginia, 1848–52, before becoming secretary of war in 1857. At a cabinet meeting held on December 27, 1860, he unsuccessfully sought to persuade Buchanan that the garrison at Fort Sumter should be ordered to return to Fort Moultrie. Floyd resigned on December 29 and was succeeded by Postmaster General Joseph Holt, a Kentucky unionist. He later became a brigadier general in the Confederate army, but was relieved of duty after the surrender of Fort Donelson in February 1862.

187.27   Mr. Slidell] John Slidell (1793–1871) was a Democratic congressman from Louisiana, 1843–45, and a senator, 1853–61. He later served as a Confederate envoy to France, 1861–65.

188.2   Hartstene] Henry J. Hartstene (d. 1868) was commissioned in the U.S. Navy in 1828 and served in expeditions to the Pacific, Antarctic, and Arctic. He joined the Confederate navy in 1861.

188.10   Cameron] Simon Cameron (1799–1889) of Pennsylvania served in the Senate as a Democrat, 1845–49, and as a Republican, 1857–61 and 1867–77. An unsuccessful candidate for the Republican presidential nomination in 1860, Cameron became secretary of war in the Lincoln administration and served until January 1862, when he was forced to resign amid charges of widespread corruption and incompetence in the war department.

188.26   Thompson] Jacob Thompson (1810–1885) was a Democratic congressman from Mississippi, 1839–51, before becoming secretary of the interior in 1857. Thompson resigned from the cabinet on January 8, 1861, and later served as a Confederate commissioner in Canada, 1864–65.

191.23–24   "Gentlemen of the . . . fire first!"] In *Historie de Guerre de 1741* (1755), Voltaire wrote that when opposing lines of British and French Guards faced each other at the Battle of Fontenoy in 1745, Lord Charles Hay, a captain of the First Foot Guards, called out, "Gentlemen of the French Guards, fire." The Count d'Antroche, a lieutenant of Grenadiers, replied: "Gentlemen, we never fire first; fire yourselves."

196.3–6   Massachusetts was arraigned . . . fugitive slave in Boston.] Frederick "Shadrach" Minkins was rescued from the Boston federal courthouse by a group of African Americans on February 15, 1851, and later escaped to Canada. Davis spoke in the Senate on February 18, 1851, during a debate over a resolution asking President Millard Fillmore for information about the incident.

196.29–30   language of Mr. Jefferson] Jefferson wrote to Roger C. Weightman on June 24, 1826: "The general spread of the light of science has already laid open the palpable truth, that the mass of mankind has not been born with saddles on their backs, nor a favored few booted and spurred, ready to ride them legitimately, by the grace of God."

199.12   Everett's "Life of Washington"] Edward Everett, *The Life of George Washington* (1860).

210.25–26   one of those speeches] Lincoln's reply to Stephen A. Douglas at Ottawa, Illinois, on August 21, 1858, during the first of their seven debates.

213.9   Articles of Association in 1774.] The articles were adopted by the First Continental Congress.

213.39–214.1   The power confided . . . the government] In the first draft, written in Springfield in January 1861, this passage read: "All the power at my disposal will be used to reclaim the public property and places which have fallen; to hold, occupy and possess these, and all other property and places belonging to the government . . ." Lincoln followed the advice of his friend Orville H. Browning in revising this passage for the final version.

217.36   proposed amendment to the Constitution] A proposed Thirteenth Amendment to the Constitution forbidding Congress from abolishing or interfering with slavery in the states was approved by the House of

Representatives, 133–65, on February 28, and by the Senate, 24–12, on March 3. It was ratified by only two states.

219.10–16   I am loth . . . our nature.] This paragraph was proposed and drafted by William H. Seward as follows: "I close. We are not we must not be aliens or enemies but ~~countrm~~ fellow countrymen and brethren. Although passion has strained our bonds of affection too hardly they must not ~~be broken they will not,~~ I am sure they will not be broken. The mystic chords which proceeding from ~~every ba~~ so many battle fields and ~~patriot~~ so many patriot graves ~~bind~~ pass through all the hearts and ~~hearths~~ all the hearths in this broad continent of ours will yet ~~harmon~~ again harmonize in their ancient music when ~~touched as they surely~~ breathed upon ~~again~~ by the ~~better angel~~ guardian angel of the nation."

220.24–25   Saul . . . multitude] See 1 Samuel 9:2.

223.25–26   Palmetto State, . . . in 1833.] A South Carolina state convention passed a nullification ordinance on November 24, 1832, prohibiting the collection of the federal tariffs authorized in 1828 and 1832 and threatening secession if the federal government responded with force. President Andrew Jackson responded by issuing a proclamation on December 10 asserting federal supremacy and denouncing nullification as illegal. On March 2, 1833, he signed a Force Bill authorizing the military to enforce the revenue laws, as well as a compromise tariff law lowering rates. The South Carolina convention met on March 11 and rescinded the nullification ordinance, ending the crisis.

228.18   curse against Canaan] See Genesis 9:20–27. The passage was sometimes used to justify African slavery.

228.28–29   "one star . . . in glory"] Cf. 1 Corinthians 15:41.

228.34–35   This stone . . . corner."] Cf. Psalm 118:22

229.8–9   "in . . . bread,"] Genesis 3:19.

237.12   General Scott, Genl. Totten] Winfield Scott (1786–1866), general-in-chief of the U.S. Army from 1841 until his retirement on November 1, 1861; Joseph Totten (1788–1864), chief engineer of the U.S. Army from 1838 until his death.

237.18–19   Comodore Stringham, and Mr. Fox] Silas Stringham (1798–1876) was a veteran of the War of 1812, the Algerine War, and the U.S.-Mexican War. He would command the North Atlantic blockading squadron, which patrolled the coasts of Virginia and North Carolina, until his retirement from active duty in December 1861. Gustavus Fox (1821–1883) served in the navy, 1838–56, before becoming a woolen manufacturer in Massachusetts. Fox served as an informal advisor on naval matters to Winfield Scott before becoming chief clerk of the navy department in May 1861. He was appointed

241.18   Govr. Pickens]   Francis Pickens (1805–1869), governor of South Carolina, 1860–1862.

242.30   sent Mr. Lamon . . . Charleston]   Ward Hill Lamon (1828–1893) was Abraham Lincoln's law partner in Danville, Illinois, from 1852 to 1857. He spoke with Major Anderson and Governor Pickens during his visit to Charleston, March 24–25, 1861. Appointed the U.S. marshal for the District of Columbia in 1861, Lamon served as an unofficial presidential bodyguard during the war (he was not present when Lincoln was assassinated).

242.31–32   Commander Ward]   James Harmon Ward (1806–1861) served in the U.S.-Mexican War and wrote books on naval tactics, ordnance, and steam engineering. He was killed during fighting at Mathias Point on the Potomac River on June 27, 1861, the first Union naval officer to die in the Civil War.

244.31–32   Mr. Stanton . . . Mr. Buchanan's Cabinet]   Edwin M. Stanton became attorney general of the United States on December 22, 1860.

246.13   The elder Blair]   Francis Preston Blair (1791–1876), the father of Postmaster General Montgomery Blair, had edited the *Washington Globe*, 1830–45, and advised Andrew Jackson and Martin Van Buren. An opponent of the extension of slavery, Blair helped organize the 1856 Republican convention, and would serve as an adviser to President Lincoln.

246.31–32   orders . . . Captain Vogdes]   An army artillery officer, Captain Israel Vogdes (1816–1889) sailed with reinforcements for Fort Pickens onboard the sloop *Brooklyn* on January 24, 1861, but then received orders from the Buchanan administration not to land his troops unless the fort came under attack. On March 12 General Winfield Scott ordered him to land his men, but when Vogdes received his new instructions on March 31, Captain Henry A. Adams, the naval commander at Pensacola, refused to comply, believing himself still guided by the orders he had received from Buchanan's navy secretary, Isaac Toucey. On April 12 Adams received new orders from Secretary of the Navy Gideon Welles, and Vogdes began landing his troops at Fort Pickens.

249.18–20   explanations from *Spain* . . . Russia]   Spain was reannexing Santo Domingo, and it was rumored that France was planning to recolonize Haiti. Great Britain and France were threatening to send troops to Mexico to force the payment of debts owed to their citizens, and there were reports that Russia was considering recognizing the Confederacy.

252.23   Mrs. Wigfall]   Charlotte Maria Cross Wigfall (born 1818) had married Louis T. Wigfall in 1841.

252.30–31   "And she thinks . . . MacGregor."]   Cf. Sir Walter Scott, *Rob Roy* (1817): "my foot is on my native heath, and my name is MacGregor."

253.1 Margaret Fuller Ossoli] Chesnut's journal from the 1860s indicates that she was reading an essay by Samuel Smiles in *Brief Biographies* (1860) about the American essayist and journalist Margaret Fuller Ossoli (1810–1850).

253.9 Charles Cotesworth Pinckney] An officer in the Continental Army during the Revolutionary War, Pinckney (1746–1825) was a delegate to the Constitutional Convention and later served as a special envoy to France, 1797–98. He was the Federalist candidate for vice president, 1800, and for president, 1804 and 1808.

253.17 Governor Manning] A wealthy plantation owner, John Lawrence Manning (1816–1889) served in the South Carolina house of representatives, 1842–46 and 1865–67, in the state senate, 1846–52 and 1861–65, and as governor, 1852–54. He was a member of the South Carolina secession convention in 1860.

253.23 Talbot and Chew] Captain Theodore Talbot, an army officer, and Robert Chew, a clerk in the State Department, left Washington, D.C., on April 6 and arrived in Charleston on April 8. Chew delivered a message from President Lincoln to Governor Pickens, informing him that an attempt would be made to provision Fort Sumter, while Talbot was prevented from going to Fort Sumter and telling Major Anderson that a relief expedition was being sent to Charleston.

253.27 Wigfall] See note 115.25.

253.27–28 "There was a . . . by night,] Lord Byron, *Childe Harold's Pilgrimage*, Canto III (1816), stanza 21, describing a ball held in Brussels on the eve of the Battle of Waterloo.

254.3 Governor Means] John Hugh Means (1812–1862) was governor of South Carolina, 1850–52. In 1862 he became the colonel of the 17th South Carolina Infantry, and was fatally wounded at the Second Battle of Manassas on August 30, 1862.

254.10–11 "Dame Placid"] A character in *Everyone Has His Faults* (1793), play by Elizabeth Inchbald (1753–1821).

256.33 The *Harriet Lane* . . . smashed] A Coast Guard revenue cutter requisitioned by the navy for the Fort Sumter expedition, the *Harriet Lane* was not damaged during the bombardment.

257.14 Sound and fury, signifying nothing.] *Macbeth*, V.v.27–28.

257.30 Pryor of Virginia] A leading secessionist, Roger A. Pryor (1828–1919) served in the House of Representatives, 1859–61.

259.34 *St. Valentine's* . . . *Perth*] Novel (1828) by Sir Walter Scott, in which Conachar, a Highland chieftain who was suckled as an infant by a white doe, fulfills a prophecy by showing cowardice in combat.

261.10 Edmund Ruffin] A Virginia planter, journalist, and influential writer on agriculture and soil replenishment, Ruffin (1794–1865) became a prominent defender of slavery and advocate of secession in the 1850s. Frustrated by Virginia's failure to secede in early 1861, he went to South Carolina and enlisted as a private in the Palmetto Guards. On June 17, 1865, Ruffin shot himself in Virginia after writing in his diary of his "unmitigated hatred" for the "perfidious, malignant, & vile Yankee race."

262.1   columbiads]   See note 160.36.

262.39   line of negroes . . . torpedoes at Mobile.]   The 1st Division, U.S. Colored Troops, participated in the successful Union assault on Fort Blakeley at Mobile, Alabama, on April 9, 1865, attacking through defensive obstacles that included torpedoes (land mines).

263.34   Ripley's incendiary shells]   Roswell Sabine Ripley (1823–1887), a former U.S. Army artillery officer serving in the South Carolina militia. Ripley later became a Confederate brigadier general.

264.33   case-shot]   Shrapnel shells.

266.31–32   Wigfall . . . the pistol.]   In 1840 Wigfall became involved in a political feud in South Carolina with Whitfield Brooks, Brooks's son Preston, and their ally, James Carroll. After posting Whitfield Brooks as a scoundrel and coward, Wigfall fatally shot Thomas Bird, Whitfield's nephew, in a gunfight outside the Edgefield District courthouse. He then fought a bloodless duel with Carroll, and a duel with Preston Brooks in which both men were seriously wounded. (While serving in Congress, Preston Brooks would assault Charles Sumner on the Senate floor in 1856.)

267.4   the Provisional Army]   Established on February 28, 1861, the Provisional Army of the Confederate States was made up of volunteers who enlisted for twelve months' service (later extended to three years, or for the duration of the war). A much smaller force, the Army of the Confederate States of America, was established on March 6, 1861, and was intended to serve as the regular standing army of the Confederacy.

268.17   shouting my name]   In an earlier passage in *Reminiscences of Forts Sumter and Moultrie in 1860–'61*, Doubleday wrote: "While the battle was going on, a correspondent of the *New York Tribune*, who was in Charleston, wrote that the populace was calling for my head. Fortunately I was not there to gratify them. My relations with the gentlemen of Charleston had always been friendly. The enmity of the mob was simply political, and was founded on the belief that I was the only 'Black Republican,' as they termed it, in the fort."

268.25   Moses . . . governor]   Franklin J. Moses (1838–1906) was Republican governor of South Carolina, 1872–74.

269.10–11   EXSURGAT DEUS . . . *facie ejus*]   Psalm 67:2 in the Latin Vulgate, translated in the Douay-Rheims Bible as: "Let God arise, and let his enemies be scattered: and let them that hate him flee from before his face." (In the King James Version, this is Psalm 68:1.)

270.25–26 "four . . . Balaklava] During the Crimean War Battle of Balaklava, October 25, 1854, confusing orders sent by Lord Raglan, the British commander-in-chief, led the Light Brigade of British cavalry to attack down a valley to their front instead of moving onto the ridge to their right. Of the 673 men in the brigade, 109 were killed and 159 were wounded in the battle. An eyewitness account by correspondent William Howard Russell inspired Alfred Tennyson to write his poem "The Charge of the Light Brigade," which was published on December 9, 1854.

270.31 Ossawattomie John Brown] Brown settled near the town of Osawatomie, Kansas, in 1855, and unsuccessfully defended it against an attack by a large force of proslavery Missouri "Border Ruffians" on August 30, 1856.

271.1 Mr. Ruggles] See note 45.8.

271.8 *Punch* and the *Charivari*] *Punch, or The London Charivari*, a British illustrated weekly magazine founded in 1841 and known for its satiric articles and cartoons.

272.5 Mayor Wood] Fernando Wood (1812–1881), a Democrat, served in Congress, 1841–43, 1863–65, and 1867–81, and as mayor of New York, 1855–57 and 1860–61. In January 1861 he suggested to the aldermen that New York protect its trade with the South by seceding and becoming a free city.

273.1 J. G. Bennett] James Gordon Bennett (1795–1872), a Scottish immigrant, was the founder, publisher, and editor of the highly popular and influential *New York Herald*.

273.40 Major Burnside] Ambrose Burnside (1824–1881) was appointed a major general of volunteers in March 1862. He succeeded George B. McClellan as commander of the Army of the Potomac in November 1862, but was relieved in January 1863 in the aftermath of the Union defeat at Fredericksburg, Virginia. Burnside subsequently commanded the Department of the Ohio in 1863 and a corps in Virginia in 1864. After the war he served as governor of Rhode Island, 1866–68, and in the U.S. Senate, 1875–81.

278.12–13 "Unto . . . determined."] Daniel 9:26.

281.22 Solferino.] On June 24, 1859, a French and Piedmontese-Sardinian army of approximately 130,000 defeated about 120,000 Austrians at Solferino in northern Italy during the Second War of Italian Independence. Almost 40,000 men were killed, wounded, or captured in the battle.

283.16 Major Whiting] William H. C. Whiting (1824–1865), a West Point graduate, served in the U.S. Army engineers until his resignation in February 1861. He was appointed as a brigadier general in the Confederate army, August 1861, and as a major general, February 1863. Whiting was fatally wounded at Fort Fisher, North Carolina, on January 15, 1865, and died a prisoner on Governor's Island in New York harbor on March 10, 1865.

287.15   Bobadil] A braggart soldier in *Every Man in his Humour* (1598, revised 1616) by Ben Jonson.

287.25   Edonian] An ancient Thracian people known in Greek mythology for their love of wine.

287.35   St. Calhoun.] John C. Calhoun (1782–1850) represented South Carolina in Congress, 1811–17, and in the Senate, 1832–43 and 1845–50, and served as secretary of war, 1817–25, as secretary of state, 1844–45, and as vice president of the United States, 1825–32. He became famous for his defense of states' rights and slavery.

288.10   *pain coupé*]   Literally, cut bread.

289.33   *sans bornes*]   Without limits.

290.15   In my letter] Russell's dispatch, dated April 21, was printed in *The Times* of London on May 14, 1861.

291.11   Ironsides.] Name given to the cavalry commanded by Oliver Cromwell in the English Civil War.

291.40   assault on Senator Sumner]   See note 46.35–36.

292.9   Lord Lyons] Richard Bickerton Pemell Lyons, Lord Lyons (1817–1887) was the British minister to the United States, 1858–65.

293.1–4   "Integer . . . pharetrâ."] Horace, *Odes* 22.1: "The man of upright life and pure from wickedness, O Fuscus, has no need of the Moorish javelins or bow, or quiver loaded with poisoned darts."

293.10   Mr. Ransome Calhoun] A nephew of John C. Calhoun, Ransom Calhoun (1827–1865) was a West Point graduate who became colonel of the 1st South Carolina Artillery. In August 1862 Calhoun challenged his subordinate Major Alfred Rhett (1829–1889), the son of Robert Barnwell Rhett, after learning that Rhett had called him a "damned puppy." In the resulting duel, fought on September 5, 1862, Rhett killed Calhoun.

293.12–13   letter copying-machine]   A letterpress machine.

296.5–6   "still the tumult . . . people,"]   Cf. Psalm 65:7.

296.26–27   Lincoln, . . . twenty days to disperse] In his proclamation of April 15, 1861, calling forth 75,000 militia, President Lincoln commanded the "combinations" opposing federal authority in the South to disperse within twenty days.

297.26   Gov. Letcher] John Letcher (1813–1884) served in Congress, 1851–59, and as governor of Virginia, 1860–64.

298.17 the gallant Capt. Wise] Jennings Wise (1831–1862), son of former governor Henry Wise and co-editor of the *Richmond Enquirer.* Wise was fatally wounded at the Battle of Roanoke Island in North Carolina, February 8, 1862.

298.21 Seddon] James Seddon (1815–1880) was a congressman from Virginia, 1845–47 and 1849–51, and served as the Confederate secretary of war, November 1862–February 1865.

299.37 *blessure mortelle*] Mortal wound.

300.8 President Tyler . . . Gov. Wise] John Tyler (1790–1862) served as a congressman from Virginia, 1816–21, as governor, 1825–27, as a U.S. senator, 1827–36, as vice president of the United States, 1841, and as president of the United States, 1841–45. For Henry Wise, see Biographical Notes.

300.14 recent incessant labors] Tyler had presided over the unsuccessful peace conference held in Washington, D.C., February 4–27, 1861. Attended by delegates from twenty-one states, the conference recommended a series of compromise measures that failed to win approval from Congress.

301.18 Hon. J. M. Mason] James M. Mason (1798–1871) was a congressman from Virginia, 1837–39, and a U.S. senator, 1847–61. He served as Confederate envoy to Great Britain and France, 1861–65.

303.8 "Plug Ugly"] The Plug Uglies were a nativist Baltimore street gang of the 1850s.

304.4 Wide-Awake gatherings] See note 27.36.

306.11 Mayor of Baltimore] George William Brown (1812–1890) was mayor of Baltimore from November 1860 to September 1861, when he was arrested by the Union army on suspicion of disloyalty. He was held without charge until November 1862, when he was released shortly after the expiration of his mayoral term.

306.14–17 the mayor's patience . . . with a revolver.] In his memoir *Baltimore and the Nineteenth of April, 1861* (1887), George Brown quoted from Colonel Jones's report, and then wrote: "The statement that I begged Captain Follansbee not to let the men fire is incorrect, although on this occasion I did say, 'Don't shoot.' It then seemed to me that I was in the wrong place, for my presence did not avail to protect either the soldiers or the citizens, and I stepped out from the column. Just at this moment a boy ran forward and handed to me a discharged musket which had fallen from one of the soldiers." After relating how he gave the musket to a shopkeeper, Brown continued: "The statement in Colonel Jones's report that I seized a musket and killed one of the rioters is entirely incorrect. The smoking musket seen in my hands was no doubt the foundation for it. There is no foundation for the other statement that one of the police shot a man with a revolver."

306.30   M. V. M.]   Massachusetts Volunteer Militia.

310.3–4   *Frederick Dent . . . Jesse Root Grant*]   Dent (1786–1873), Grant's father-in-law, owned a farm in St. Louis County, Missouri. Jesse Root Grant (1794–1873) was living in Covington, Kentucky.

311.20   Fred.]   Frederick Tracy Dent (1820–1892), Grant's brother-in-law, was a career army officer who graduated from West Point in 1843. He later served as an aide-de-camp to Grant, 1864–65.

321.3   three . . . citizens]   John Forsyth (1812–1877), editor of the *Mobile Daily Commercial Register*, who had served as U.S. minister to Mexico, 1856–58; Martin Crawford (1820–1883), a Democratic congressman from Georgia, 1855–61; Andre B. Roman (1795–1866), governor of Louisiana, 1831–35 and 1839–43.

321.33–34   an intermediary, . . . character]   John A. Campbell (1811–1889), an associate justice of the U.S. Supreme Court from 1853 until his resignation on April 30, 1861, served as an intermediary between the Confederate commissioners and Secretary of State Seward. Campbell was an assistant secretary of war in the Confederate government, 1862–65, and part of a Southern delegation that unsuccessfully negotiated with Lincoln and Seward at Hampton Roads, Virginia, on February 3, 1865.

322.19   received on the 8th of April a reply]   The memorandum stated the Secretary of State had no authority to recognize the commissioners as diplomatic agents, or to correspond or communicate with them.

325.6   *posse comitatus*]   See note 78.33.

335.5–10   brave fellows . . . State of Maryland.]   Eight runaway slaves sought protection at Fort Pickens on March 12, 1861. They were turned over to the city marshal of Pensacola by Lieutenant Adam J. Slemmer, the commander of the federal garrison at the fort. After receiving false reports of an imminent slave insurrection, Brigadier General Benjamin F. Butler, the Union commander at Annapolis, wrote to Governor Thomas Hicks on April 23, 1861, offering to help suppress any uprising.

339.14–15   your plan for a campaign]   In his letter of April 27, 1861, McClellan proposed forming an army of 80,000 men in Ohio and then advancing either through western Virginia on Richmond, or through Kentucky on Nashville.

339.31–32   Forts Jackson and Saint Philip]   Forts on opposite banks of the Mississippi River southeast of New Orleans.

341.15   the Col.]   Israel B. Richardson (1815–1862), an 1841 graduate of West Point who had retired from the army in 1855. Richardson later served as a brigade and division commander in the Army of the Potomac, and was fatally wounded at Antietam.

344.34–35 studying Hardee] *Rifle and Light Infantry Tactics* (1855) by William J. Hardee (1815–1873), the most widely used training manual of the Civil War era. A veteran of the U.S.-Mexican War and instructor at West Point, Hardee became a Confederate general and served as a corps commander in the western theater.

347.16–17 Mr. Washburn] Congressman Elihu Washburne; see note 147.29.

347.20–21 Governer Yates] Richard Yates (1815–1873) was the Republican governor of Illinois, 1861–65, and served in congress as a Whig, 1851–55, and in the Senate as a Republican, 1865–71.

348.32 *valiant* Pillow] Gideon Pillow (1806–1878), a former law partner of President James Polk, had served as a major general of volunteers in the U.S.-Mexican War. Pillow became a Confederate brigadier general in 1861, but was relieved of duty following his defeat by Grant at Fort Donelson in February 1862.

350.12 Singleton] James W. Singleton (1811–1892) was a Democratic attorney and railroad president in Illinois.

350.17 Browning] Orville Hickman Browning (1806–1881), a longtime friend of Lincoln's who served as a Republican senator from Illinois, June 1861–January 1863, and as secretary of the interior, 1866–69.

350.21 Doolittle] James R. Doolittle (1815–1897) was a Republican senator from Wisconsin, 1857–69.

350.23 Col. Hamilton] James A. Hamilton (1788–1878), a son of Alexander Hamilton, was a New York attorney active in Republican politics.

351.10–11 Ellsworth's Zouave Firemen.] The 11th New York Infantry was made up of volunteer firemen from New York City. Elmer Ellsworth (1837–1861), the regimental commander, had read law in Lincoln's office in Springfield before the war.

351.32–33 the dandy regiment] The 7th New York militia regiment.

352.8 Jeff. Davis' manifesto] Davis's address to the Confederate Congress of April 29, 1861; see pp. 313–32 in this volume.

352.26–32 Saw at breakfast . . . Union they scorn.] This paragraph was crossed out in the manuscript of Hay's diary.

353.3 "Abreuve nos sillons,"] From the "Marseillaise": "Qu'un sang impur / Abreuve nos sillons" ("Let impure blood / soak our fields").

353.5 Dahlgren gun] A muzzle-loading naval gun designed by John A. Dahlgren (1809–1870), a U.S. Navy ordnance officer.

353.21 Carl Schurz] Schurz (1829–1906) was a German émigré who had campaigned for Lincoln among both German- and English-speaking voters. He served as U.S. minister to Spain, 1861–62; as a general in the Union army, 1862–65; as a Republican senator from Missouri, 1869–75; and as secretary of the interior, 1877–81.

354.1–3 Mrs. Whitman . . . young John Brown] Sarah Helen Whitman (1803–1878) was a poet and social reformer who had become friends with John Hay while he was attending Brown University. Thomas Earle, a friend of Thomas Wentworth Higginson, served with the 25th Massachusetts Regiment. Thomas Wentworth Higginson (1823–1911) was a Massachusetts minister, writer, and abolitionist who had helped finance John Brown's raid on Harpers Ferry. Higginson would later command the 1st South Carolina Volunteers, 1862–64, one of the first black regiments to be officially recognized by the U.S. government. John Brown Jr. (1821–1895), John Brown's eldest child, helped his father with preparations for the Harpers Ferry raid, but did not participate in it.

355.26 "All . . . divine."] Lord Byron, *The Bride of Abydos* (1813), canto I, stanza 1.

358.26–27 Hugh & Charley Ewing & John Hunter] Hugh Ewing (1826–1905) and Charles Ewing (1835–1883), Sherman's brothers-in-law, were both attorneys. John Hunter was Charles Ewing's law partner.

358.30 Gen. Frost] Daniel M. Frost (1823–1900) commanded the Missouri militia at Camp Jackson. Frost, a West Point graduate who had served in the U.S.-Mexican War, later became a Confederate general.

358.31 Willy] William T. Sherman Jr. (1854–1863).

360.5–6 Tom Turner . . . his appointment] Sherman had sought his brother's help in obtaining an army commission for Thomas Turner, the son of Sherman's army friend and former banking partner Henry S. Turner (1811–1881). Thomas Turner later joined the Confederate army.

361.18 Major Cary] John B. Cary (1819–1898) had founded the Hampton Military Academy in 1852. He later served as lieutenant colonel of the 32nd Virginia Regiment and was seriously wounded during the Seven Days' Battles in 1862.

365.10 Charleston-Baltimore Convention] See Chronology, April–June 1860.

365.11–12 Front street . . . Maryland Institute.] The Northern Democrats who nominated Stephen A. Douglas met at the Front Street Theater in Baltimore, while the Southern Democrats who nominated John C. Breckinridge met at the Maryland Institute. "Hard Shells" were Northern Democrats who gave strong support to proslavery candidates and policies.

367.11–12 "Andrew and Butler correspondence,"] While serving as a brigadier general of the Massachusetts militia, Benjamin F. Butler offered to suppress a rumored slave insurrection in Maryland (see note 335.5–10). John A. Andrew (1818–1867), the Republican governor of Massachusetts, wrote to Butler on April 25, 1861, criticizing his offer as "unnecessary" and arguing that Union troops should not protect disloyal communities. Butler replied on May 9, defending his action on moral and political grounds and describing the prospect of a slave insurrection as "letting loose four millions of worse than savages upon the homes and hearths of the South."

369.7   My Brother]   William Stone (c. 1840–c. 1882) became a captain in the Confederate army and was wounded twice fighting in the eastern theater.

369.12   Uncle Bo]   Bohanan Ragan, a younger brother of Kate Stone's mother. He joined the Confederate army in 1861 and survived the war.

369.32   Little Sister]   Amanda Stone (c. 1850–1934).

370.9   Mr. Newton]   Albert Newton, who tutored the younger children in the Stone family.

370.31   Richmond]   A town in Madison Parish, Louisiana.

371.8   Ashburn]   Ashburn Ragan, Mrs. Stone's youngest brother, who died of a fever in 1861 at age eighteen.

372.1   "The Jacobite Fiddler,"]   Poem by the English writer George Walter Thornbury (1828–1876).

372.19   Tiger Rifles]   Name originally given to Company B of the 1st Louisiana Special Battalion and later used for the battalion as a whole. The company was mainly recruited from among Irish immigrant dock workers; its commander, Captain Alexander White, had served a prison sentence for pistol-whipping a man.

372.21   Perrit Guards]   The Perrit (or Perret) Guards became Company H of the 5th Louisiana Infantry.

376.11   Wickham Hoffman]   Hoffman (1821–1900), a lawyer in New York City, was an aide-de-camp to Governor Edwin Morgan. He later served as an assistant adjutant general in the Union army, 1862–65, and as a diplomat in France, Britain, Russia, and Denmark.

376.25   (D'Utassy . . . "Garibaldi Guard,"]   The 39th New York Volunteers was recruited in New York City and contained companies made up of Hungarian, German, Swiss, Italian, French, Spanish and Portuguese immigrants. Colonel Frederick George D'Utassy (1827–1892) commanded the regiment until 1863, when he was cashiered and sentenced to one year at hard labor after being court-martialed for fraud and embezzlement.

377.8   General Sandford's parlor]   Charles W. Sandford (1796–1878) served as a major general in the New York state militia throughout the war and commanded troops during the 1863 draft riots in New York City.

377.10 (not James A.'s Aleck, but John C.'s)] James A. Hamilton (see note 350.23) and John C. Hamilton (1792–1882) were both sons of Alexander Hamilton.

377.11 Alexandrian movement] On May 24, 1861, U.S. forces occupied Alexandria, Virginia.

377.15 Schuyler Hamilton] The son of John C. Hamilton, Schuyler Hamilton (1822–1903) graduated from West Point in 1841. He was wounded twice in Mexico and served as an aide-de-camp to General Winfield Scott before resigning from the army in 1855. Hamilton served as Scott's military secretary in 1861 and as a brigadier general in the western theater in 1862 before leaving the army because of poor health.

377.33 President Felton] Cornelius Felton (1807–1862) was president of Harvard, 1860–62.

377.36 Colonel Blenker's Germans] Louis Blenker (1812–1863), a German émigré, organized the 8th New York Infantry Regiment. He later became a brigade and division commander in the Army of the Potomac and served until June 1862, when he was relieved of duty.

377.39 "Brooklyn Zouaves"] The 14th New York militia regiment, also known as the 14th Brooklyn.

378.5 *tête-du-pont*] Bridgehead.

378.14–15 Colonel Ellsworth] During the Union occupation of Alexandria on May 24, 1861, Colonel Elmer Ellsworth (see note 351.10–11) took down a Confederate flag that was flying from the roof of the Marshall House hotel. On his way down the stairs Ellsworth was confronted by James Jackson, the hotel's proprietor, who killed him with a shotgun. Jackson was then shot and bayoneted by a corporal in Ellsworth's regiment. The incident was widely publicized, and both Ellsworth and Jackson were considered martyrs by their respective sides in the conflict.

379.14–15 Colonel Burnside's] See note 273.40.

379.20 Goddard] Robert Hales Ives Goddard (1837–1916) was a partner in Goddard Brothers, a successful textile manufacturing firm in Rhode Island. He enlisted as a private in the Rhode Island militia in 1861 and later served as an officer on the staff of General Ambrose Burnside.

379.24–25 field-preaching . . . Lauderdale and Claverhouse] Following the restoration of episcopacy in Scotland by Charles II in 1662, Presbyterian Covenanters began holding their services in the open air. John Maitland, Duke of Lauderdale (1616–1682), secretary of state for Scotland, 1660–80, and John Graham of Claverhouse (1648–1689), who commanded royal troops in Scotland from 1678 until his death at the Battle of Killiecrankie in 1689, became notorious for their persecution of Covenanters.

379.36   Wise . . . Edward Everett]   A cousin of the Virginia secessionist Henry Wise (see Biographical Notes), Lieutenant Henry Wise (1819–1869) was a naval officer, currently serving in the ordnance bureau, who also wrote popular travel books and adventure novels under the name "Harry Gringo." A Unitarian clergyman and professor of Greek at Harvard who served as president of the college, 1846–49, Everett (1794–1865) was also a congressman from Massachusetts, 1825–35, governor of Massachusetts, 1836–40, U.S. minister to Great Britain, 1841–45, secretary of state, 1852–53, a senator from Massachusetts, 1853–54, and the vice presidential candidate on the 1860 Constitutional Union ticket.

379.39   N. P. Willis]   Nathaniel Parker Willis (1806–1867) was a journalist, poet, and writer of short stories and travel sketches.

380.6   General Mansfield]   Brigadier General Joseph King Fenno Mansfield (1803–1862) commanded the Washington defenses in the spring of 1861. He later led a division in Virginia and a corps at Antietam, where he was fatally wounded.

380.7   Bache . . . Trowbridge.]   Alexander Dallas Bache (1806–1867) was superintendent of the U.S. Coast Survey from 1843 until his death. William P. Trowbridge (1828–1892) was assistant superintendant of the survey.

380.38–40   Arlington House . . . Colonel Lee]   The house had been built by George Washington Parke Custis (1781–1857), grandson of Martha Custis Washington and the adopted son of George Washington. His will gave a life interest in the property to his only child, Mary Custis Lee (1807/8–1873), who had married Robert E. Lee in 1831.

388.22–24   the conspiracy . . . suspension of the writ]   On January 22, 1807, President Thomas Jefferson sent a special message to Congress in which he accused former vice president Aaron Burr of conspiring to foment war with Spain and detach the western states from the Union. William Branch Giles, a Democratic-Republican senator from Virginia, immediately introduced a bill in Congress suspending the writ of habeas corpus in cases of treason for three months. It passed the Senate on January 23 with only one dissenting vote, but was rejected by the House of Representatives, 113–19, on January 26.

393.2   Blackstone]   William Blackstone (1723–1780), *Commentaries on the Laws of England* (4 vols., 1765–69).

393.36   statute of 31 Car. II.]   The Habeas Corpus Act of 1679, passed in the thirty-first year of the reign of Charles II (the beginning of his reign was dated from the execution of Charles I in 1649).

394.4   the statute of 13 Wm. III.]   The Act of Settlement of 1701.

394.20   Hallam's Constitutional History]   Henry Hallam (1777–1859), *The Constitutional History of England, from the accession of Henry VII to the death of George II* (3 vols., 1827).

NOTES

395.1 'Petition of Right' (3 Car. I.)] The Petition of Right passed Parliament and received the royal assent in 1628.

397.6–7 Commentaries . . . Story] *Commentaries on the Constitution of the United States* (3 vols., 1833) by Joseph Story (1779–1845), who served as an associate justice of the U.S. Supreme Court, 1811–45.

397.34 Ex . . . Swartwout] Erick Bollman and Samuel Swartwout were associates of Aaron Burr who were arrested in the lower Mississippi Valley and brought to Washington, D.C., under military guard. After being committed to trial for treason by the circuit court for the District of Columbia, they applied to the U.S. Supreme Court for writs of habeas corpus. On February 13, 1807, Chief Justice John Marshall ruled that under the 14th section of the judiciary act of 1789, the Supreme Court had the power to issue a writ of habeas corpus. In a second opinion delivered on February 21, Marshall ordered Bollman and Swartwout to be discharged, ruling that the evidence presented failed to support charges of treason.

403.6 "We may be Happy yet."] Song from the opera *The Daughter of St. Mark* (1844), with music by Michael William Balfe (1808–1870) and words by Alfred Baum (1796–1860).

404.14–15 Judge Jackson] Henry R. Jackson (1820–1898), an attorney from Savannah who had served as a judge on the Georgia superior court, 1849–53.

405.13–14 Agrarianism in ancient Rome] The movement for redistributing public land led by the tribunes Tiberius Gracchus (163–133 B.C.E.) and Caius Gracchus (153–121 B.C.E.) resulted in violent political and social conflict, and was seen by some as contributing to the eventual decline and fall of the Roman republic.

407.16 M. E. & Amb. Plen.] Minister Extraordinaire and Ambassador Plenipoteniary.

408.37–38 the Times . . . my letters] Henry Adams wrote thirty-one unsigned letters that were printed in *The New York Times*, June 7, 1861–January 21, 1862.

409.15 Lord John] Lord John Russell (1792–1878) was foreign secretary in the Liberal government led by Lord Palmerston, 1859–65. Russell had held unofficial meetings on May 3 and May 9, 1861, with Confederate diplomatic commissioners William Yancey, Pierre Rost, and Ambrose Mann, but refused to discuss British recognition of the Confederacy with them.

409.22 Lord Lyons] See note 292.9.

409.35 Clay and Burlingame] Cassius Clay (1810–1903) was U.S. minister to Russia, 1861–62 and 1863–69. Anson Burlingame (1820–1870) served as a congressman from Massachusetts, 1855–61. He was appointed as U.S. minister to Austria in 1861, but was not accepted by the Austrian government because of his support for Hungarian independence. While traveling to their posts, both Clay and Burlingame made public statements criticizing Britain for granting belligerent rights to the Confederacy.

410.12 the Article on the last Winter] The article was eventually published as "The Great Secession Winter of 1860–1861" in *Proceedings of the Massachusetts Historical Society*, 1909–10.

410.22–24 Margaret . . . Bridget] Family servants.

410.24–27 Mary . . . Brooks] Henry Adams's younger siblings Mary Adams, later Mary Adams Quincy (1846–1928), and Brooks Adams (1848–1927).

410.35–36 despatch . . . Seward] Charles Francis Adams received a dispatch on June 10 from Secretary of State Seward, dated May 21, 1861, instructing him to break off relations with the British government if it held any further meetings with Confederate envoys and to warn Lord Russell that recognition of the Confederacy would result in Anglo-American war. Adams chose not to convey the full force of his instructions, and was assured by Lord Russell that the British government did not intend to recognize the Confederacy or hold further meetings with the Confederate commissioners.

411.4–5 It . . . blunder.] The remark "c'est pire qu'un crime, c'est un faute" ("it was worse than a crime, it was a blunder"), made regarding Napoleon's summary execution of the duc d'Enghien in 1804, has been variously attributed to the French diplomat Charles Maurice de Talleyrand (1754–1838), to Napoleon's minister of police Joseph Fouché (1759–1820), and to the French politician Antoine Boulay de la Meurthe (1761–1840).

412.3 *Benjamin McCulloch*] McCulloch (1811–1862) had fought in the Texas War of Independence, the U.S.-Mexican War, and with the Texas Rangers against the Comanches. He was appointed a brigadier general in the Confederate army in May 1861 and served until March 7, 1862, when he was killed at the Battle of Pea Ridge in Arkansas.

416.10 Convention of Notables] See note 300.14.

417.14–15 Cushings, and Touceys] For Caleb Cushing, see note 145.15. Isaac Toucey (1792–1869), a Democrat from Connecticut, served in congress, 1835–39, as governor, 1846–47, as attorney general of the United States, 1848–49, as a senator, 1852–57, and as secretary of the navy, 1857–61.

418.34–35 wonderful ethnologist . . . Review"] In an article in the February 1861 *De Bow's Review*, George Fitzhugh (1806–1881) wrote: "The Cavaliers, Jacobites, and Huguenots who settled the South, naturally hate, contemn, and despise the Puritans who settled the North. The former are master races, the latter, a slave race, the descendants of the Saxon serfs. The former are Mediterranean races, descendants of the Romans; for Cavaliers and

Jacobites are of Norman descent, and the Normans were of Roman descent, and so were the Huguenots. The Saxons and Angles, the ancestors of the Yankees, came from the cold and marshy regions of the North; where man is little more than a cold-blooded, amphibious biped." A journalist and lawyer from Front Royal, Virginia, Fitzhugh was the author of *Sociology for the South, or the Failure of Free Society* (1854) and *Cannibals All! or, Slaves Without Masters* (1857).

419.2–3 cabinet officer . . . peculation] Secretary of War John Floyd (see note 187.11). Floyd was accused of treason in the Northern press for transferring 115,000 muskets and rifles from Northern to Southern arsenals in the spring of 1860, and for ordering the shipment of 124 large cannon from Pittsburgh to coastal forts in Mississippi and Texas on December 20, 1860. (The order to transfer the artillery was rescinded by Joseph Holt, Floyd's successor as secretary of war.)

419.10 Jonathan Wild] A receiver of stolen goods in London, Wild (c. 1682–1725) became notorious for selling stolen merchandise back to its owners under the guise of helping them to recover their property. He also organized a "corporation" of thieves and informed on those who refused to work for him, becoming known as the "Thief-taker General" for his success in apprehending criminals. Wild was eventually convicted of robbery and hanged at Tyburn.

420.28–33 Lord de Roos . . . your pardon!"] Henry William Fitzgerald de Ros, Baron de Ros (1793–1839) sued John Cumming for libel in 1836 after Cumming accused him of repeatedly cheating at cards. In February 1837 a jury in London determined the accusation to be truthful and delivered a verdict for the defendant. The story of de Ros having his hand pinned with a fork is considered apocryphal.

420.34 Governor Letcher] See note 297.26.

420.35 disasters . . . Norfolk] Federal forces burned the arsenal at Harpers Ferry on April 18, 1861, and the navy yard at Norfolk on April 19 before they were occupied by Virginia militia. The Confederates were able to salvage significant amounts of war matériel from both locations.

423.8–9 two regiments . . . engine-house] John Brown's raid on the Harpers Ferry arsenal ended on October 18, 1859, when a detachment of Marines sent from Washington, D.C., under the command of Lieutenant Colonel Robert E. Lee stormed the fire engine house where Brown and his remaining men were holding several hostages. Twelve companies of Virginia and Maryland militia were at Harpers Ferry by the end of the siege.

423.11 Ancient Pistol] Pistol, a soldier who serves as an ancient (standard bearer) for Sir John Falstaff, is a character in *2 Henry VI, Henry V,* and *The Merry Wives of Windsor.*

426.2 Garrison . . . Phillips] William Lloyd Garrison (see note 61.38–39) and Wendell Phillips (1811–1884), a lawyer, orator, and radical abolitionist allied with Garrison.

444.15 the besieged regiment] Grant had been told that an Illinois regiment was surrounded by rebels along the railroad west of Palmyra, Missouri.

447.12 Great Bethel] On June 10, 1861, about 4,000 Union troops were repulsed when they attacked a Confederate outpost defended by 1,100 men at Great Bethel, Virginia, between Hampton and Yorktown. Less than a hundred men on both sides were killed or wounded in the engagement, also known as Big Bethel or Bethel Church.

447.16–17 camp at Philippi . . . dispersed.] Union troops overran the Confederate camp at Philippi in northwestern Virginia (now West Virginia) on June 3, 1861.

448.21 gallant General Garnett] Confederate Brigadier General Robert S. Garnett (1819–1861) was an 1841 graduate of West Point who fought in the U.S.-Mexican War. Garnet was serving as a major in the U.S. Army when he resigned his commission in April 1861.

452.13–14 "the name . . . fear death,"] Cf. *Julius Caesar*, I.ii.88–89: "I love / The name of honour more than I fear death."

452.27 my little Edgar] Edgar Ballou was born in 1856.

453.9 Little Willie] William Ballou was born in 1859.

455.1–2 my servant, John Scott] Scott was a free black man who had been an officer's servant in the U.S.-Mexican War.

455.9 made on the 18th.] Union and Confederate troops had skirmished on July 18, 1861, near Blackburn's Ford.

456.36–37 Colonel Cocke] Philip St. George Cocke commanded a Confederate brigade during the battle.

457.6 "Washington Artillery"] A New Orleans artillery battalion organized in 1838. Four of its companies served throughout the war with the Army of Northern Virginia, while a fifth company served with the Army of Tennessee.

457.16–17 "Hampton Legion" . . . Wade Hampton.] Hampton (1818–1902) was a wealthy South Carolina plantation owner who raised six infantry companies, four cavalry companies, and an artillery battery in early 1861. The Legion was broken up in 1862 as part of a general reorganization of the Army of Northern Virginia, and its elements were reassigned to different infantry, cavalry, and artillery units. Hampton was successively appointed as a brigadier general (1862), major general (1863), and lieutenant general (1865), and later served as governor of South Carolina, 1876–79, and as a senator, 1879–91.

NOTES

459.11 Sherman's . . . battery] Company E, 3rd U.S. Artillery, was famous for its role in the American victory at Buena Vista in 1847 while under the command of Thomas W. Sherman (1813–1879). Battery I, 1st U.S. Artillery was commanded at Bull Run by Captain James B. Ricketts (1817–1887), who later became a division commander in the Union army.

460.34 Stuart's regiment] The 1st Virginia Cavalry commanded by J.E.B. Stuart (1833–1864), who became the cavalry commander of the Army of Northern Virginia in July 1862.

464.23 my friend] Frederick Warre, an attaché at the British legation in Washington.

464.30 *viaticum*] Provisions for the journey.

480.35 the nipple] The part of the gun's firing mechanism onto which the percussion cap was fitted.

481.21 Mr. Raymond] Henry J. Raymond (1820–1869) was the cofounder and editor of *The New York Times*, 1851–69.

483.14 Cairo] Russell had visited Cairo, Illinois, in late June 1861.

485.28 Colonel Hunter] David Hunter (1802–1886) commanded a division at Bull Run and was later appointed a major general of volunteers.

488.33 chaussée] Causeway, highway.

489.35 Soyer or Careme] Alexis Benoit Soyer (1809–1858) and Marie-Antoine Carême (1784–1833), noted French chefs and writers on cooking.

496.2 left Congress] The Provisional Confederate Congress.

496.23 murder of Jackson] See note 378.14–15.

498.18–20 Patterson's men . . . Genl Jo Johnston] Robert Patterson (1792–1881), a veteran of the War of 1812 and the U.S.-Mexican War, commanded the Union forces in the Shenandoah Valley. His failure to engage Joseph E. Johnston (1807–1891) allowed Johnston to send most of his troops to Manassas Junction in time for them to fight at Bull Run.

498.24 brother's front fence] The front fence of Blair House on Pennsylvania Avenue in Washington, D.C.

504.25 Patterson, or Banks] Robert Patterson was relieved on July 25, 1861, and succeeded as commander of Union forces in the Shenandoah Valley by Major General Nathaniel P. Banks (1816–1894).

506.13–14 "Eugene" . . . en guerre] During the War of the Spanish Succession, Austrian commander Prince Eugène of Savoy (1663–1736) and John Churchill, Duke of Marlborough (1650–1722) won victories together over the French at Blenheim (1704), Oudenarde (1708), and Malplaquet

(1709). "Malbrough s'en va-t-en guerre" ("Marlborough goes off to war") was a popular French folk song of the eighteenth century.

506.24 Wilson of Massachusetts] Henry Wilson (1812–1875) was a Republican senator from Massachusetts, 1855–73, and vice president of the United States, 1873–75.

507.2 Senator Harlan.] James Harlan (1820–1899) served as a Republican senator from Iowa, 1855–65 and 1867–73, and as secretary of the interior, 1865–66.

507.11 Mrs. Davis's drawing room] Varina Howell Davis (1826–1906), wife of Jefferson Davis.

507.29 Mrs. McLean . . . Joe Davis] Margaret Sumner McLean (1828–1905) was married to Eugene McLean, a West Point graduate from Maryland who had resigned his commission and joined the Confederate army. Her father, Edwin Sumner (1797–1863), was a Union general, and her brothers Edwin Jr. and Samuel also served as Union officers. Joseph Robert Davis (1825–1896), a nephew of Jefferson Davis, was serving as an aide to his uncle.

508.19–20 Mr. Barnwell . . . Mr. Hunter] Robert Barnwell (1801–1882) was a congressman from South Carolina, 1829–33, and served in the Senate in 1850. He was a member of the Confederate Provisional Congress, 1861–62, and of the Confederate Senate, 1862–65. Robert M. T. Hunter (1809–1887) was a congressman from Virginia, 1837–43 and 1845–47, and a senator, 1847–61. A member of the Confederate provisional congress in 1861 and of the Confederate Senate, 1862–65, Hunter was appointed as the secretary of state of the Confederacy on July 25, 1861, and served until February 1862.

508.29 Kirby Smith . . . turnpike] Edmund Kirby Smith (1824–1893) commanded a brigade that arrived at Manassas Junction by train from the Shenandoah Valley at midday on July 21 and reached the battlefield in the late afternoon. When Smith was wounded, Colonel Arnold Elzey assumed command of the brigade and joined the counterattack that drove the Union army from the field.

509.11–12 Mr. Rives . . . Arnoldus VanderHorst] William Cabell Rives (1793–1868) served as a congressman from Virginia, 1823–29, as U.S. minister to France, 1829–32 and 1849–53, and as a senator, 1832–34, 1836–39, and 1841–45. Rives was a member of the Confederate Provisional Congress, 1861–62, and of the Confederate House of Representatives, 1864–65. James A. Seddon (1815–1880) was a congressman from Virginia, 1845–47 and 1849–51, a member of the Confederate Provisional Congress, 1861–62, and Confederate secretary of war, 1862–65. Arnoldus VanderHorst (1835–1881) was a plantation owner from South Carolina and an officer in the Confederate army.

509.17–18 Hon. Mr. Clingman . . . Brewster] Thomas Clingman (1812–1897) was a congressman from North Carolina, 1843–45 and 1847–58, and a senator, 1858–61. Clingman later became a brigadier general in the Confederate army. Henry Brewster (1816–1884) was a lawyer from Texas who had practiced in Washington, D.C., before the war, and who later served as a staff officer in the Confederate army.

509.28   Arnold Harris] Harris (c. 1810–1866) was a shipping agent and co-founder of the *States and Union*, an anti-Republican newspaper published in Washington, D.C., from the fall of 1859 until the spring of 1861. On July 22 he left Washington in an attempt to recover the body of Colonel James Cameron, the brother of Secretary of War Simon Cameron, from the Bull Run battlefield, and was arrested the following day by Confederate troops for crossing the lines without a flag of truce. Harris was held in the Richmond county jail until September 30, 1861, when he was released.

510.6   Trescot] William Henry Trescot (1822–1898) was a lawyer from South Carolina who served as secretary of the U.S. legation in London, 1852–54, and as assistant secretary of state, June–December 1860.

510.20   John Waties] A lawyer from Charleston, South Carolina, Waties (1828–1873) fought at Bull Run with Hampton's Legion.

510.26   Mrs. Preston's room.] Caroline and John Preston were friends of the Chesnuts' from Columbia, South Carolina.

510.27   Mr. Venable] Charles Scott Venable (1827–1900), a professor of mathematics and astronomy at South Carolina College, fought at Bull Run as a private in the 2nd South Carolina Infantry. He later served as an aide-de-camp to General Robert E. Lee, 1862–65.

510.35   "It is a far cry to Lochow"] In *The Legend of Montrose* (1819) by Sir Walter Scott, a proverbial expression used by the Campbell clan to express the difficulty of an invading army reaching Loch Awe, their ancestral domain in the Scottish Highlands.

511.6   Mr. Mason] See note 145.8.

512.4   Dr. Gibbes] Robert Wilson Gibbes (1809–1866) was a physician, naturalist, and publisher of the Columbia *Daily South Carolinian*.

513.1   Mr. Hammond] James Henry Hammond (1807–1864) was governor of South Carolina, 1842–44, and a Democratic senator, 1857–60.

513.10   Camden DeLeon . . . surgeon general] David Camden DeLeon (1816–1872) was a surgeon in the U.S. Army, 1838–61. He was appointed as surgeon general of the Confederate army on May 12, 1861, and served until July 30, 1861, when he was succeeded by Samuel Preston Moore (1813–1889), who held the position for the remainder of the war.

513.29–30   Clingman . . . cut his throat] Thomas Clingman (see note 509.17–18) may have attempted suicide in 1834 while suffering from a painful inflammation of the eyes that made him temporarily blind.

515.1 White Sulphur, Roony Lee] White Sulphur Springs, a resort in western Virginia (now West Virginia). William Henry Fitzhugh (Rooney) Lee (1837–1891) was Robert E. Lee's second son and the third of his seven children. He served as a Confederate cavalry officer during the war, rising in rank from captain to major general.

515.30 Smith Lee] Sydney Smith Lee (1802–1869) was an officer in the U.S. Navy, 1820–61. Lee served in the U.S.-Mexican War, commanded Matthew Perry's flagship in the squadron that visited Japan in 1853, and was superintendant of the Philadelphia navy yard before resigning his commission in April 1861. During the Civil War he held a series of shore commands in the Confederate navy.

515.37 Blücher] Field Marshal Gebhard Leberecht von Blücher (1742–1819) led the Prussian army that reached the Waterloo battlefield on the evening of June 18, 1815, as Napoleon was making his final attacks against the Duke of Wellington's positions.

517.7 Havelock's . . . the East] Sir Henry Havelock (1795–1857) led a relief column during the Indian Rebellion that left Allahabad on July 7, 1857, and captured Cawnpore on July 17. His troops fought their way through to the besieged residency at Lucknow on September 25, and reinforced its garrison until the siege was ended by Sir Colin Campbell on November 17. Havelock died of dysentery at Lucknow on November 24, 1857.

518.25 Harriet] Harriet Grant was a niece of Mary Chesnut.

520.2–3 Sans peur, sans reproche] Without peer, without reproach.

520.9 "J'en suis . . . coeur."] I am angry, with all my heart.

520.10–11 "Moi! malheureux . . . malheureux?'] Me! Unhappy! Or is it 'How unhappy I am?'

520.31–33 Mrs. Long . . . or cousin] Mary Sumner Long was the wife of Armistead Long, a Confederate officer, and the sister of Margaret Sumner McLean (see note 507.29). The sisters were distant cousins of Massachusetts Senator Charles Sumner.

520.34 Keitt, Boyce] Lawrence Keitt (1824–1864) was a Democratic congressman from South Carolina, 1853–60, and a member of the Confederate provisional congress, 1861. He became colonel of the 20th South Carolina Regiment in 1862 and was fatally wounded at the Battle of Cold Harbor in 1864. William Boyce (1818–1890) served as a Democrat in congress, 1853–60, and was a member of the Confederate Provisional Congress, 1861–62, and the Confederate House of Representatives, 1862–64.

525.3–4 "thanks of Congress"] McClellan was voted the "thanks of Congress" on July 16, 1861, for his successful campaign in western Virginia.

525.8 fait d'éclat] Glorious deed.

526.19–20   Commander Gen. Tyler] Brigadier General Andrew Tyler (1799–1882) commanded the First Division at Bull Run.

532.29   "Whoso would . . . save it,"] Cf. Matthew 16:25: "whosoever will lose his life for my sake shall find it."

541.37   the Prince] Napoleon Joseph Charles Paul Bonaparte (1822–1891), known as Prince Napoleon, was the first cousin of Napoleon III. He made a private visit to the United States and Canada, July 27–September 26, 1861, and crossed the lines to meet with Beauregard and Joseph Johnston at Manassas, August 8–9.

550.33   "Pelican Ranger."] A member of either Company G or Company D of the 3rd Louisiana Infantry.

551.7–8   stub-and-twist gun] A gun with barrels made from high quality scrap iron.

555.1–2   affair at Crane Creek] On August 2, 1861, Lyon's command skirmished with the Confederate advance guard at Dug Springs, near present-day Clever, Missouri, several miles from Crane Creek. In *With the Light Guns in '61–'65*, Woodruff described the aftermath of the skirmish: "General Rains' unattached Missourians in seeming hordes, came rushing south across the ford at Crane Creek, with any imaginable number and style of vehicles and people, mounted and on foot. Our advance had feigned a retreat on overtaking the enemy, and fallen back in expectation of bringing on an attack at the ford. The disorder was terrifying and had well nigh panicked the unattached and unarmed Missourians."

555.34   Exodus 4-4] Possibly a setting error for Exodus 14:24.

555.39   Snead's Fight for Missouri] Thomas Snead (1828–1890), *The Fight for Missouri, from the election of Lincoln to the death of Lyon* (1886). Snead served at Wilson's Creek as an aide to Sterling Price.

556.38   appendix] The appendix to *With the Light Guns in '61–'65* is not printed in this volume.

559.9   Totten] James Totten (c. 1818–1871), a career artillery officer who graduated from West Point in 1841, surrendered the federal arsenal at Little Rock to Arkansas state authorities on February 8, 1861. After serving in the western theater throughout the Civil War, Totten was dismissed from the army in 1870 after a court-martial convicted him of "neglect of duty" and "conduct to the prejudice of good order and military discipline."

559.29–30   President David Walker] Walker (1806–1879) was president of the Arkansas state convention that rejected, and then approved, secession in 1861. He was an associate justice of the Arkansas supreme court, 1848–57 and 1874–78, and served as its chief justice, 1866–68.

559.35–36   one-armed . . . Sweeny] Thomas Sweeny (1820–1892) came to the United States from Ireland in 1832 and lost his right arm at the Battle of Churubusco in 1847 while serving in a New York volunteer regiment during the U.S.-Mexican War. He later commanded a brigade at the Battle of Shiloh and a division during the 1864 Atlanta campaign.

560.13 "dutch"] German.

566.5–6 Shields Green, . . . Denmark Vesey] Shields Green (1836?–1859), a fugitive slave from Charleston, South Carolina, met John Brown in 1858 while Brown was staying with Frederick Douglass at his home in Rochester, New York. Green joined Brown's raid on Harpers Ferry and was captured, tried for murder, and hanged on December 16, 1859. Nat Turner (1800–1831) led a slave insurrection in Southampton County, Virginia, August 22–24, 1831, during which more than fifty white men, women, and children were killed. More than one hundred African Americans were killed without trial during the suppression of the revolt, and Turner and twenty others were executed. Denmark Vesey (1767?–1822) was a personal servant to slave-trader Joseph Vesey before winning a lottery in 1800 that allowed him to buy his freedom. In 1821–22 he planned a slave uprising in South Carolina set for July 14, 1822. Charleston authorities learned of the plot, and Vesey was executed along with thirty-four other black men.

569.19 Gen. Anderson] See note 157.10.

570.8 Sam. Glover] Samuel T. Glover (1813–1884) was an attorney in St. Louis.

570.10 Hurlbut] Brigadier General Stephen A. Hurlbut (1815–1882), an attorney active in Illinois Republican politics who was serving under Frémont in Missouri, was accused of habitual drunkenness. Hurlbut did not resign and served in the Union army through the war.

574.3 located in Van Buren] The U.S. district court for western Arkansas, which also had jurisdiction over Indian Territory, was located in Van Buren, Arkansas. In 1871 the court was moved to nearby Fort Smith.

576.25–26 Caspar's . . . George] Captain Caspar Crowninshield (1837–1897), an 1860 graduate of Harvard College, commanded Company D of the 20th Massachusetts Infantry. He transferred to the 1st Massachusetts Cavalry in December 1861 and later served with the 2nd Massachusetts Cavalry, becoming its colonel in November 1864. Caspar Crowninshield was a cousin of Benjamin Crowninshield (see note 180.20). First Lieutenant George B. Perry was second-in-command of Company D.

577.6 Riddle . . . arm] First Sergeant William Riddle had his right arm amputated above the elbow.

577.15–16 Baker's brigade] Colonel Edward D. Baker (1811–1861) commanded the Third Brigade of Stone's Division. It was composed of four infantry regiments, only one of which, the 71st Pennsylvania (also known as the

1st California), fought at Ball's Bluff. Baker, a longtime friend of Abraham Lincoln, had served as a Whig congressman from Illinois, 1845–47 and 1849–51. He later moved to the Pacific coast and was a Republican senator from Oregon, 1860–61.

577.26 Col. Lee] Colonel William Raymond Lee (1807–1891), commander of the 20th Massachusetts.

577.27 Gen. Baker] Edward D. Baker had been appointed as a major general of U.S. volunteers, but had not decided whether he would accept the commission, which would require him to resign from the Senate.

577.29 rough sketch:] The sketch is not reproduced in this volume. It depicts the deployment of Baker's troops and the 20th Massachusetts in a rectangular-shaped field with woods on either side, with "Rebels / Hill" written at the top and "Wooded banks / River" at the bottom. A note to the right of the sketch reads: "The Rebels had 2 inf & one cavalry regt. how full is not known," and a note to the left reads: "Engaged on our side 3 regs. consisting 700 of 15th Mass 300 of Mass 20th 700 men of Bakers brig."

578.1–2 Tremblet's company] Captain Henry M. Tremlett (1833–1865) commanded Company A of the 20th Massachusetts. He later became the lieutenant colonel of the 39th Massachusetts Infantry and was fatally wounded at Gravelly Run, Virginia, on March 31, 1865.

578.7 Bartlett] Captain William Francis Bartlett (1840–1876) was the commander of Company I, in which Henry Livermore Abbott served as second lieutenant. Bartlett lost a leg in the Peninsula Campaign in 1862, but continued to serve and was wounded again at Port Hudson in Louisiana, in the Battle of the Wilderness, and in the Petersburg mine assault, where he was captured. He inspired the poem "The College Colonel" by Herman Melville, published in *Battle-Pieces and Aspects of the War* (1866).

578.14 The general] Edward D. Baker.

578.17 Frank] Captain Bartlett.

578.38 adjutant & major] First Lieutenant Charles Lawrence Peirson (1834–1920) was the adjutant of the 20th Massachusetts. He later served as lieutenant colonel of the 39th Massachusetts Infantry. Major Paul Joseph Revere (1832–1863), a grandson of the Revolutionary War hero, became the commander of the 20th Massachusetts in April 1863 and was fatally wounded at Gettysburg on July 2.

579.13 col., major & adjutant are prisoners] Lieutenant Peirson was exchanged on January 27, 1862, and Colonel Lee and Major Revere were paroled on February 23 and exchanged on April 30. Lee resumed command of the regiment during the Peninsula Campaign and led it until after the Battle of Antietam, when he suffered a breakdown and resigned his commission.

579.14 Capt. Dreher is nearly dead] Ferdinand Dreher (c. 1831–1863), a German émigré who commanded Company C, survived his wound. He returned to the regiment in 1862 and was fatally wounded at Fredericksburg.

579.15 Capt. Putnam's arm is amputated] John C. Putnam, the commander of Company H, survived his surgery.

579.17 Lieut. Putnam] Second Lieutenant William Lowell Putnam (1840–1861), the son of the writer Mary Lowell Putnam (1810–1898) and a nephew of James Russell Lowell (see Biographical Notes), died on October 22.

579.18 Lieut. Holmes] Oliver Wendell Holmes Jr. (1841–1935) was later wounded in the neck at Antietam and in the foot at the Second Battle of Fredericksburg, and served with the 20th Massachusetts until his three-year enlistment expired in July 1864. Holmes later served as an associate justice of the Massachusetts supreme judicial court, 1883–99, as its chief justice, 1899–1902, and as an associate justice of the U.S. Supreme Court, 1902–32.

579.19 Lieut. Lowell] First Lieutenant James Jackson Lowell (1837–1862), a nephew of James Russell Lowell, returned to the regiment in February 1862 and was fatally wounded at the Battle of Glendale on June 30.

579.23–24 Col. Palfrey] Lieutenant Colonel Francis Winthrop Palfrey (1831–1889) had remained at Camp Benton. Palfrey served with the 20th Massachusetts until Antietam, where he was disabled by a severe shoulder wound.

579.26 Gen. Lander] Brigadier General Frederick W. Lander (1821–1862) commanded the Second Brigade of Stone's Division, to which the 20th Massachusetts was assigned.

581.24 Stone] Brigadier General Charles Stone (1824–1887) commanded a division in the Army of the Potomac and was Colonel Edward Baker's immediate superior. Stone was later blamed for the defeat at Ball's Bluff by the congressional Joint Committee on the Conduct of the War and fell under suspicion of disloyalty. He was arrested on February 9, 1862, and imprisoned without charge for 189 days. After his release Stone served in various staff and command assignments before resigning from the army in September 1864.

581.27–28 Cogswell is a prisoner] Colonel Milton Cogswell (1825–1882), the commander of the 42nd New York Infantry, crossed the Potomac with a company of his regiment on the afternoon of October 21, 1861, and assumed command of the Union forces at Ball's Bluff after Edward Baker was killed. Cogswell was paroled in March 1862 and exchanged six months later.

582.7 Wade, Trumbull & Chandler] Benjamin Wade (see Biographical Notes); Lyman Trumbull (1813–1896) was a Republican senator from Illinois, 1855–73; Zachariah Chandler (1813–1879) was a Republican senator from Michigan, 1857–75, and secretary of the interior, 1875–77.

582.15   wounded friend Col Kelley] Benjamin F. Kelley (1807–1891) had been wounded during the Union victory at Philippi in western Virginia on June 3, 1861.

582.17   Romney] A town on the South Branch of the Potomac River in northern Virginia (now West Virginia).

584.17   the little duke (Chartres)] Robert Philippe d'Orléans, duc de Chartres (1840–1910), grandson of the deposed French monarch Louis-Philippe, and his brother Louis-Philippe d'Orléans, comte de Paris (1838–1894), served as aides to McClellan from September 1861 to July 1862.

584.22   saying nothing about Halleck.] Scott had wanted Major General Henry W. Halleck (1815–1872) to replace him as general-in-chief.

585.25   Your historical examples] In a letter to Charles Francis Adams Jr. dated October 15, 1861, Henry Adams cited the popular support shown for the ministry led by William Pitt the younger (1759–1806) in 1795 despite a series of defeats in the war with revolutionary France, and then wrote: "The English have the true bull-dogs grip, and that is what we must have if we expect to do anything either in victory or in defeat."

585.28   unwilling King the elder Pitt] William Pitt the elder (1708–1778) became leader of the House of Commons and secretary of state for the southern department in December 1756 despite the opposition of George II. Pitt used his offices to successfully direct British foreign and military policy in the Seven Years' War and presided over a series of victories in Canada, the West Indies, and India before resigning in 1761.

585.29   Holt in the War Department] Joseph Holt (1807–1894), a leading Kentucky unionist, had served as postmaster general, March 1859–December 1860, and as secretary of war from January 1861 until the end of the Buchanan administration. Holt was appointed judge advocate general of the U.S. Army in September 1862 and held the position until 1875.

585.30–31   Mr. Dana] Richard Henry Dana (1815–1882), the author of *Two Years Before the Mast* (1840) and a prominent Boston attorney active in Massachusetts Republican politics. Dana, a friend of Charles Francis Adams Sr., served as U.S. attorney for Massachusetts, 1861–66.

586.3   Independents] *The Independent*, a weekly journal published in New York.

587.17   Van Vliet] Brigadier General Stewart Van Vliet (1815–1901) was chief quartermaster of the Army of the Potomac, August 1861–July 1862.

588.16   "festina lente"] Make haste slowly.

588.36   Bayard Smith] Margaret Bayard Smith (1778–1844), a leading figure in early nineteenth-century Washington society and author of the novels *A Winter in Washington* (1824) and *What Is Gentility?* (1828).

589.6–7 the O & M] The Ohio and Mississippi Railroad.

591.31–32 Genl. McClernand] Brigadier General John A. McClernand (1812–1900) had served as a Democratic congressman from Illinois, 1843–51 and 1859–61. In the spring and summer of 1861 McClernand helped rally southern Illinois to the Union cause.

592.21–22 Parrott guns] Muzzle-loading rifled cannon, named after the New York ordnance manufacturer Robert R. Parrott (1804–1877).

593.11 Gen. Polk] Major General Leonidas Polk (1806–1864) commanded the Confederate forces at Columbus, Kentucky.

593.18 Col. Scott's regiment] The 12th Louisiana Infantry, commanded by Thomas L. Scott (1829–1876).

593.27–30 Sixth Iowa . . . Seventh Iowa] The 7th Iowa Infantry fought at Belmont, the 6th Iowa Infantry did not.

593.36 the Fourth regiment] The 4th Tennessee Infantry, commanded by Rufus P. Neely (1808–1901).

594.24–27 General Pillow . . . Cheatham] Gideon Pillow (see note 348.32) and Brigadier General Benjamin F. Cheatham (1820–1886) were Polk's principal subordinate commanders at Belmont.

595.12 poor, gallant Armstrong] Captain J. Welby Armstrong, a Memphis schoolmaster serving with the 2nd Tennessee Infantry, was killed by artillery fire.

595.14–15 Captain Billy Jackson] William H. Jackson (1835–1903) later commanded a Confederate cavalry division in the western theater.

595.16–17 Jimmy Walker . . . not recover] Walker died of his wounds.

596.14–15 steamer, . . . very bad condition] The *Coatzacoalcos* had been damaged in the gale that scattered the Port Royal expedition on November 1, 1861, three days after it sailed from Hampton Roads, Virginia.

597.34 fine Fresnel lens] A compound lens used in lighthouses, developed by Augustin-Jean Fresnel (1788–1827).

598.4–5 Mr. *Rhett*'s house . . . General Drayton's headquarters] Robert Barnwell Rhett (1800–1876) was a leading South Carolina secessionist and publisher of the *Charleston Mercury*. Brigadier General Thomas F. Drayton (1808–1891) commanded the Confederate defenses at Port Royal.

598.6–7 Mons. de Ribaudiere] Jean Ribault (c. 1520–1565) established a fort at Port Royal in 1562. The fort was abandoned in the spring of 1563 when the garrison built a small boat and sailed for France.

600.11 *San Jacinto* and told of Mason and Slidell being on board!] The U.S.S. *San Jacinto* intercepted the British mail packet *Trent* off Cuba on

November 8, 1861, and seized Confederate envoys James Mason (see note 145.8) and John Slidell (see note 187.27).

600.31 Ripley] Brigadier General Roswell S. Ripley (1823–1887) commanded the defenses at Charleston, South Carolina.

600.35–36 the *North American*] The *Philadelphia North American*.

601.36 a proclamation] Sherman issued a proclamation addressed to "the People of South Carolina" on November 8, 1861. The proclamation concluded: "The obligation of suppressing armed combinations against the constitutional authorities is paramount to all others. If in the performance of this duty other minor but important obligations should be in any way neglected, it must be attributed to necessities of the case, because rights dependent on the laws of the State must be necessarily subordinate to military exigencies created by insurrection and rebellion."

604.1 He come to Beaufort] Similar stories of Lincoln visiting the South before the war, often without being recognized, were recorded in the 1920s and 1930s in the oral histories of former slaves from Missouri, Arkansas, Tennessee, Mississippi, and North Carolina.

604.2 Col. Paul Hamilton] Hamilton (1762–1816) was governor of South Carolina, 1804–6, and secretary of the navy, 1809–12.

607.30 "sum of all villainies."] John Wesley (1703–1791) described the slave trade as "that execrable sum of all villainies" in a 1772 journal entry. The phrase was later used by American abolitionists to describe slavery in the United States.

607.37–38 horrid scenes of St. Domingo] See note 172.14–15.

608.36–37 "He knoweth . . . our uprising;"] Cf. Psalm 139:2.

609.7–8 his blood . . . our children!"] Matthew 27:25.

609.21–22 We should . . . delight] From the hymn "How vain are all things here below" by Isaac Watts (1674–1748).

609.28–29 "All things . . . love God,"] Romans 8:28.

609.30 "rejoices in tribulations, also."] Romans 5:3.

611.10 "avenge not yourselves!"] Romans 12:19.

611.17 Samuel . . . witch of Endor.] See 1 Samuel 28:7–20.

611.36 "whom the Lord . . . chasteneth."] Hebrews 12:6.

611.36–37 "It is the . . . him good."] 1 Samuel 3:18.

612.3–4 "the wicked which is his sword"] Psalm 17:13.

612.29 at Leesburg] Leesburg, Virginia, near the site of the Battle of Ball's Bluff, October 21, 1861.

613.1 Springfield, and Lexington] Springfield was a Confederate name for the Battle of Wilson's Creek, August 10, 1861. Confederate troops commanded by Sterling Price captured Lexington, Missouri, on September 20, 1861.

613.2 Columbus.] The Battle of Belmont, November 7, 1861, was fought across the river from Columbus, Kentucky.

613.18 "Thus far shalt thou go, and no farther."] Cf. Job 38:11.

613.31 "The sword . . . of Gideon!"] Judges 7:20.

614.37–38 "Be still . . . in the earth!"] Psalm 46:10.

615.12 Mr. Memminger] See note 94.9–11.

615.20 ship laden with weapons] The steamer *Fingal* reached Savannah, Georgia, on November 12, 1861, carrying fifteen thousand rifles and two million rounds of ammunition purchased by Confederate agents in Britain.

616.38–39 "his thoughts are very deep,"] Cf. Psalm 92:5.

618.6–7 "though he slay me yet will I trust in him."] Job 13:15.

619.33–37 God is our . . . thereof, Selah!] Psalm 46:1–3.

619.37–38 The Lord . . . refuge, Selah!"] Psalm 46:7.

620.10 love mercy . . . before God] Micah 6:8.

620.18–19 Sihon . . . king of Bashan] See Numbers 21:21–26 and Numbers 21:33–35.

620.27 whole head . . . is faint] Isaiah 1:5.

621.38 The bloodthirsty Jeffreys] George Jeffreys (1648–1689), lord chief justice of England, 1683–85, conducted the notorious "Bloody Assizes" following Monmouth's Rebellion in 1685 that resulted in approximately 200 executions.

622.16–17 "all the Kingdoms . . . glory of them"] Matthew 4:8.

625.40–626.1 "thy people shall all be righteous,"] Isaiah 60:21.

626.11–14 Nation would . . . ploughshares] Isaiah 2:4.

628.18 Bull Run] The Confederate name for the skirmish at Blackburn's Ford, July 18, 1861.

631.11–13 a link of . . . Greensboro] The 48-mile-long Piedmont Railroad linking Danville and Greensboro was completed in late May 1864.

633.3 The distinguished gentlemen] James Mason and John Slidell.

633.24 Mr. Faulkner] Charles J. Faulkner (1806–1884) was a Whig, and then Democratic, congressman from Virginia, 1851–59. He was appointed

U.S. minister to France in January 1860 by President Buchanan, but was replaced by the Lincoln administration in March 1861. On August 12, 1861, Faulkner was arrested in Washington, D.C., where he had gone to settle his accounts. Although he was never formally charged, press reports alleged that he had purchased arms for the Confederacy while serving in France. Faulkner was exchanged on December 25, 1861, for Alfred Ely (1815–1892), a Republican congressman from upstate New York who had been captured by the Confederates at Bull Run.

634.1–2 "blockades to be . . . at Paris] The Declaration of Paris on the maritime laws of war was signed on April 16, 1856, by Great Britain, France, Austria, Sardinia, Russia, and Turkey.

639.17 Lagow] First Lieutenant Clark Lagow (1828–1867), Grant's aide-de-camp.

645.12–13 Earl Russell] See note 409.15.

645.14 revocation of Mr. Bunch's Exequatur] The Lincoln administration revoked the exequatur (official recognition of consular credentials) of Robert Bunch, the British consul at Charleston, South Carolina, after learning that he had held diplomatic conversations with Confederate authorities. Bunch remained in Charleston until February 1863, but had his vice-consul assume responsibility for signing official documents.

645.17 last three articles of the Paris Declaration] The Declaration of Paris (see note 634.1–2) contained four articles. The first article abolished privateering; the second and third articles made both enemy goods carried on neutral ships and neutral goods carried on enemy ships free from capture, unless contraband of war; the fourth article required that to be legally binding, blockades "must be effective; that is to say maintained by a force sufficient really to prevent access to the enemy's coastline."

645.24 Lord Palmerston] Henry John Temple, third Viscount Palmerston (1784–1865) served as foreign secretary, 1830–34, 1835–41, and 1846–51, as home secretary, 1852–55, and as prime minister, 1855–58 and 1859–65.

646.5 Secretary at War] A civilian official responsible for managing the finances of the British army. Palmerston held the position from 1809 to 1828.

646.21 Capt. Wilkes] Charles Wilkes (1798–1877) was commissioned as a midshipman in 1818 and had commanded an expedition that explored Antarctica and the Pacific Northwest, 1838–42.

646.24–25 Eustis, & Macfarlane] George Eustis (1828–1872), secretary to John Slidell, and James Edward MacFarland (1829–1897), secretary to James Mason.

647.25 Mr. Bright] A prominent orator and reformer who served in the House of Commons, 1843–88, John Bright (1811–1889) was a leading British supporter of the Union cause.

647.29 Mr. Layard] Sir Austen Layard (1817–1894) was undersecretary for foreign affairs, 1861–66.

647.34 Wilson] Charles L. Wilson (1818–1878), owner of the *Chicago Daily Journal*, was first secretary of the London legation, 1861–64.

648.4–5 orders . . . James Adger] Commander John B. Marchand (1808–1875), the captain of the U.S.S. *James Adger*, sailed from New York on October 16, 1861, with orders to intercept the Confederate warship *Nashville*, which was believed to be carrying Mason and Slidell to England. The British government had received reports that Marchand while drunk had admitted to having been ordered to remove the Confederate envoys from a British mail steamer.

648.16–17 Moncton Milnes] Richard Monckton Milnes (1809–1885), a poet, writer, literary patron, biographer of John Keats, and a member of parliament from 1837 to 1863, when he was made Baron Houghton.

648.28–29 the Nashville] A side-wheel steamer that sailed between New York and Charleston, the *Nashville* was seized by the Confederates and refitted as a commerce raider. She was destroyed by the Union navy in the Ogeechee River, Georgia, in February 1863.

649.3 Horatio Ward's] Ward (1810–1868) was an American banker living in London.

649.8 arrival of the Fingal] See note 615.20.

649.21–22 Chester . . . the Martyr."] *John Rogers: the Compiler of the First Authorised English Bible; the Pioneer of the English Reformation; and Its First Martyr* (1861) by the American genealogist Joseph Lemuel Chester (1821–1882).

650.20 Fancy] Boxing fans.

652.1 Fairfax] Thomas Fairfax (1612–1671) was a commander of parliamentary forces during the English Civil War, 1642–45, and their commander in chief, 1645–50.

659.13–14 Judge McLean his circuit] John McLean (1785–1861) was appointed to the Supreme Court by President Jackson in 1829 and served until his death on April 4, 1861. His circuit included Michigan, Ohio, Indiana, and Illinois.

665.40 *pro tanto*] To that extent.

673.7–8 Caspar Crowninshield's] See note 576.25–26.

673.14–15 Sargent . . . Williams] Horace Binney Sargent (1821–1908) was the lieutenant-colonel, and Robert Williams (1829–1901) the colonel, of the 1st Massachusetts Cavalry.

NOTES 791

673.40 Koh-i-noor] "Mountain of light," an Indian diamond weighing 191 carats (later recut to 108 carats) that became part of the British crown jewels after the annexation of Punjab in 1849.

678.3 *George Washington Custis Lee*] Lee (1832–1913) was serving as an aide to Jefferson Davis.

678.33 W H. Mary] White House, the Custis family plantation on the Pamunkey River in New Kent County, Virginia. Mary Custis Lee (1835–1918) was Robert E. Lee's second child and oldest daughter.

680.18 Greenbrier . . . Richmond.] Greenbrier was later renamed Traveller, and became the most famous of Robert E. Lee's wartime horses. Richmond died in the summer of 1862.

681.8 Mr. Eads] James B. Eads (1820–1887) was a leading engineer in St. Louis.

681.18 Mr. Gibson . . . Gov Gamble] Charles Gibson (1825–1899) acted as an agent in Washington, D.C., for the Unionist government of Missouri while serving as solicitor general of the U.S. court of claims, 1861–64. Hamilton Gamble (1798–1864), a former judge of the state supreme court, was elected provisional governor of Missouri by Unionist members of the state convention on July 31, 1861, and served until his death.

681.19 Genl Halleck] Major General Henry W. Halleck assumed command of the Department of Missouri on November 19, 1861.

681.26 chief of staff, Genl Marcey] Brigadier General Randolph Marcy (1812–1887), who was McClellan's father-in-law.

683.17 Assistant Secretary of War] Thomas A. Scott (1823–1881), a vice president of the Pennsylvania Railroad, served as assistant secretary of war, August 1861–June 1862.

683.24–25 Brigadier-General Franklin] William B. Franklin (1823–1903) commanded a division in the Army of the Potomac.

683.26 Secretary of the Treasury] Salmon P. Chase (1808–1873) was a Free Soil senator from Ohio, 1849–55, Republican governor of Ohio, 1856–60, secretary of the treasury, 1861–64, and chief justice of the U.S. Supreme Court, 1864–73.

683.33 General Buell] Brigadier General Don C. Buell (1818–1898) commanded the Army of the Ohio.

686.12 West Point.] West Point, Virginia, at the head of the York River.

686.37–39 General Burnside's expedition . . . Newbern] The expedition commanded by Brigadier General Ambrose Burnside sailed for North Carolina from Hampton Roads, Virginia, on January 11, 1862. Burnside captured Roanoke Island at the northern end of Pamlico Sound on February 8 and New Bern on March 14.

687.1   Beaufort]   Burnside captured Beaufort, North Carolina, on April 26, 1862.

687.27–28   annexed paper, marked (A)]   This paper is not included in this volume.

689.21–22   paper hereto annexed, marked (B)]   This paper is not included in this volume.

690.10   Ship Island]   An island in the Gulf of Mexico near Biloxi, Mississippi, that had been occupied by Union forces on September 17, 1861, and made into a base for future operations against New Orleans.

692.21   Tadd."]   Thomas (Tad) Lincoln (1853–1871), President Lincoln's youngest son.

693.2   *Charles A. Dana*]   Dana (1819–1897) was the managing editor of the *New York Tribune*, 1849–62, and the editor of the *New York Sun*, 1868–97. He served as a special commissioner for the War Department, 1862–63, and as assistant secretary of war, 1864–65.

Index

Abbott, Henry Livermore, 576–80
Abbott, Josiah Gardner, 576
Abolitionism, 2, 17, 22–24, 32, 45–46, 52–53, 57–62, 69, 85, 89, 98–101, 104–7, 110, 154, 169–70, 175, 183–84, 227, 270, 302, 317–18, 348, 350, 401, 426, 586
Accomack County, Va., 668
Adams, Abigail Brown Brooks, 145, 410, 648
Adams, Charles Francis, 143–46, 180, 182, 407–11, 586, 645–52
Adams, Charles Francis, Jr., 143, 180, 407, 585–86, 651, 672–73
Adams, Henry, 143–46, 180–82, 407–11, 585, 647, 651–52, 672
Adams, John, 143–44
Adams, John Quincy, 8–9, 143
Adelaide, U.S.S., 381
Adrian, Mich., 342
Africa, 23, 102, 131, 140, 142, 156, 167, 170–73, 221, 226, 229, 316–19, 334, 425, 598, 664
Agriculture, 67; in North, 664; in South, 3, 23, 86, 89–91, 94–95, 103–5, 184, 203–5, 315, 318–19, 332, 627
Aiken, S.C., 163–64
Aiken, William, 94
Alabama, 3, 50, 100, 164, 462; secessionism in, 11–13, 48, 64, 66, 107, 165, 175–76, 183, 193, 201, 427
Alabama River, 224
Alabama 4th Regiment, 462
Albany Evening Journal, 111–12
Alexandria, La., 63, 65
Alexandria, Va., 355–57, 377–80, 466–67, 471, 484–85, 511, 526, 541, 636, 684–85
Alien and Sedition Acts (1798), 83
Allen, A. P., 639
Alley, John B., 146
Alston, Charles, 266–67
Alston, William A., 254
Amendments, constitutional, 82–84, 128–32, 139–43, 217, 303, 391–92
American Missionary Association, 674

American (Know-Nothing) Party, 14, 109
Amory, William, 145
Anaconda Plan, 339–40
Anderson, Eba, 187, 271
Anderson, Robert, 147, 156–60, 163, 187–89, 237, 241–42, 246, 254–56, 260, 264, 266–69, 272, 278, 289, 323–24, 352, 417, 422, 428–29, 496, 569
Anthony, Henry B., 145
Appleton, R. H., 49, 52–53
Appleton, William, 145
Aquia, Va., 685, 689
Archer, R. P., 37
Arizona Territory, 175, 628
Arkansas, 325, 413, 556–57, 594, 663; possible loyalty to Union, 431; secessionism in, 64, 66, 193, 232, 297
Arkansas 3rd Regiment, 556
Arlington, Va., 380–81, 487, 492, 504, 514, 526, 683
Armstrong, J. Welby, 595
Army, C.S., 355–56, 368–73, 377, 380–82, 404–5, 418, 423–24, 447–49, 503, 517, 564, 566, 606, 615, 678–79; battle of Ball's Bluff, 576–81; battle of Belmont, 590–95; battle of Bull Run, 454–96, 506, 519–21, 526–30; battle of Wilson's Creek, 543–60; Davis on, 204, 326, 329–32, 627–30; and Indians, 412, 572–73; Lincoln on, 432, 440, 504, 668; seizure of Fort Sumter, 267–68, 278, 283, 288–70; Union generals' assessment of, 348, 361–62, 536, 540, 591, 684
Army, U.S., 26, 50, 63, 79, 100, 181, 186, 199, 273–74, 336–38, 341–46, 355, 376–83, 402, 447, 449, 498, 500–3, 507, 672–73, 694; and Baltimore riot, 305–9; battle of Ball's Bluff, 576–81; battle of Belmont, 590–95; battle of Bull Run, 454–96, 509–12, 520–21, 526–30; battle of Wilson's Creek, 543–60; black soldiers in, 262, 333–35, 350, 366–67, 565–67, 652; confiscation of property by, 364–68, 538–39, 562–63, 568, 667; Davis on, 322, 325, 329,

793

628–29, 632; and Lincoln, 110, 147–48, 237–38, 240–42, 245–47, 269–70, 303, 310, 312, 324–26, 427–33, 440–41, 504–5, 568–70, 637, 657–58, 661, 664, 667–68, 681–85, 687–92; review of troops, 636–38; and seizure of Fort Sumter, 147–48, 156–62, 237, 261–68, 278; and suspension of habeas corpus, 386, 390–91, 398–400; Union generals' assessment of, 237, 310, 312, 339–40, 347–48, 358–61, 444–46, 524, 526–30, 533–37, 540–42, 581–84, 587–88, 639–40, 681–92

Articles of Association, 213
Articles of Confederation, 35–36, 75, 77, 81, 150–51, 213, 314–15, 437
Ashley River, 284–85
Atlanta, Ga., 14, 221
Atlantic (steamer), 596, 600–1
Atlantic City, N.J., 499
Atlantic Monthly, 415
Atlantic Ocean, 339
Augusta, U.S.S., 599
Austin, Texas, 37
Austria, 229
Auzé, Adèle, 516
Aylett, P. H., 298

Babo, Alois, 579
Bache, Alexander D., 380
Bagley, John, 528
Bahama Channel, 645–46
Bailey, Godard, 187
Baker, Edward D., 577–79, 581
Baker, G. M., 37
Balaklava, battle of, 270
Baldwin, Mr., 299
Ball, C. P., 595
Ball, Corporal, 341
Ballou, Sarah, 451–53
Ballou, Sullivan, 451–53, 491
Ball's Bluff, battle of, 576–81, 612, 673
Baltic (steamer), 596
Baltimore, Md., 220, 296, 302–3, 305–9, 365, 376, 381, 386–87, 398, 498, 504, 530, 534–35, 587
Baltimore County, Md., 386–87
Baltimore and Ohio Railroad, 543–35, 685
Bancker, Edward, 45–46

Bangor, Me., 386
Banks, Nathaniel P., 504, 579, 581–82
Baptists, 605
Barlow, Samuel L. M., 587
Barnwell, Robert W., 506, 508
Bartlett, William F., 578
Bartley, Edward, 220
Bartow, Francis S., 455, 495–96, 508, 516
Bartow, Louisa, 516
Bates, Edward, 48, 186, 237–41, 583, 681–82
Baton Rouge, La., 65, 550
Bayard, James A., 181
Beaufort, S.C., 596–601, 603–4, 652, 687
Beaufort River, 596
Beauregard, Pierre G. T., 252–54, 257–58, 260, 266–67, 281–84, 323, 454, 456, 463–64, 470, 495–96, 506–7, 512, 517, 530, 540–42, 612
Bedford, Va., 459
Bee, Barnard, 455, 495
Belgium, 327, 649
Bell, John, 14, 53, 61, 63
Bellows, Henry W., 377
Belmont, battle of, 590–95, 628, 639–40
Benham, Henry W., 530, 638
Benjamin, Judah, 193
Benjamin, Judah P., 94
Bennett, James Gordon, 273, 531
Bethel, battle of, 447, 510, 612, 615, 628
Bible, 54, 87, 92, 178, 181, 379, 605–26, 674–77
Biddle, James, 530
Bienville, U.S.S., 600
Bill of Rights, U.S., 82, 202, 391–92, 424
Bill of Rights (English), 34
Bill of Rights (1774), 34
Black, Jeremiah, 67, 189
Black Republicans, 3–4, 18, 39, 103, 106, 126, 170, 176, 295
Blackford, Charles Minor: *Letters from Lee's Army*, 454–63
Blackford, Eugene, 462
Blackford, William W., 462
Blackstone, William: *Commentaries on the Laws of England*, 393–96
Blair, Francis Preston, 186, 188, 246

Blair, Frank, 186–87
Blair, Mary, 188, 498
Blair, Montgomery, 186, 245–46, 376–77, 380, 582–83, 585, 687–89, 691–92
Bledsoe, Hiram, 558–59
Blenker, Louis, 377, 636, 638
Blockade, 249, 326, 328, 339–40, 356, 365, 433, 498, 504, 634, 641–43, 651, 655, 658, 666, 673
Blocker, William D., 557–58
Blücher, Gebhard von, 515–16
Blue Ridge Mountains, 470
Blunt, George W., 601
Border States, 43, 53, 107, 113, 180, 199, 229–32, 270, 273, 294, 310–11, 352, 416–17, 419–24, 431–43, 569
Boston, Mass., 171, 196, 335, 354, 378, 381, 383, 407, 411, 490, 585, 651, 672
Boston Courier, 145, 272
Boston Daily Advertiser, 146, 182, 409
Boston Journal, 364
Boyce, William W., 520
Boykin, A. H., 256
Braddock, Edward, 20–21
Brady, Mathew, 483
Brazil, 69, 94
Breckinridge, John C., 8, 14, 34, 58, 61, 63, 65, 115, 119
Brewster, Henry P., 509
Bright, John, 647, 652
Bringhurst, Charles, 268
Britain, 51, 57–58, 112, 225, 229, 249, 271, 276, 284, 292, 411, 415, 417, 482, 484–85, 490, 511, 513, 516, 585, 655, 672–73; and American colonies, 20–21, 149; Confederate commissioners sent to, 327; commerce of, 125–26, 418, 654; and cotton, 23–24, 287, 654; labor in, 91, 103; law in, 390, 392–97, 400; neutrality of, 407–9; recognition of Confederacy, 277, 407, 425; and Revolutionary War, 34, 135, 150, 157, 185, 234, 259, 314, 436; and slavery, 23, 94, 173, 197; and *Trent* affair, 633, 645–52, 679
Britton, Captain, 646
Brock, Sallie: *Richmond during the War*, 447–50, 641–44
Brodie, J. K., 557
Brokenburn plantation, 369–75

Brooklyn, N.Y., 46, 377, 381, 500
Brooklyn, U.S.S., 246, 429
Brooks, William T., 638
Brooks Guard, 492
Brougham, Henry Peter, 58
Brown, Albert G., 94, 193
Brown, Clarence, 377
Brown, George W., 306, 308
Brown, John, 17, 125, 170, 177, 185, 270, 383–85, 402, 512, 607
Brown, John, Jr., 354
Brown, Joseph E., 98–108, 179
Brown, William C., 557
Browning, Orville H., 210, 350, 568
Brownslow, William G., 49–56
Buchanan, James, 26, 46, 108, 111, 113, 143, 147, 163–64, 187–90, 207, 244–45, 415, 417, 419, 425, 655; message to Congress (December 1860), 67–84
Buckner, Dr., 372, 374
Buell, Don C., 683, 690, 692
Bull Run, battle of (First Bull Run), 451, 454–96, 500–7, 509–14, 516, 519, 521, 524, 526–32, 542, 566, 612–13, 615, 628, 687
Bunch, Robert, 645
Burlingame, Anson, 409
Burlington, Iowa, 543
Burlington, N.J., 297
Burnside, Ambrose, 273–74, 379, 684, 688–90
Burr, Aaron, 388, 417
Butler, Benjamin F., 305, 335, 361–67, 381, 504, 538, 690
Butler, Edward, 595
Butterfield, Daniel, 638
Button, C. E., 557–58
Byler, Hugh, 556–58
Byrd, Richard C., 556, 558

Cabinet (Buchanan administration), 67, 244, 419
Cabinet (Davis administration), 224–25, 252
Cabinet (Lincoln administration), 27, 109, 146, 186, 237, 240, 245–47, 249, 251, 304, 419, 423, 435, 524, 532, 536, 541, 564, 583, 585, 637, 651, 687, 691
Cadwalader, George, 386–87
Cairo, Ill., 348, 505, 590, 639

Calhoun, John C., 121–22, 194, 287, 497, 513
Calhoun, Ransome, 293
California, 42, 46, 129, 536, 561, 659
Camden, S.C., 519
Cameron, Simon, 188, 241, 511, 583, 585, 681–82, 693
Camp Benton, 576
Camp Clark, 451, 491
Camp Jackson, 358
Camp Yates, 347
Campbell, J. D., 557
Campbell, John A., 658
Canada, 126, 249, 411, 422
Cape Girardeau, Mo., 562
Cape Hatteras, 668, 686
Carême, Antoine, 489
Carrick's Ford, battle of, 447–48
Carrier, Henry, 342
Carrington, Mrs., 517–18
Carroll, De Rosey, 559
Cary, John B., 361–62, 365–66
Cass, Lewis, 86, 189
Catholicism, 521
Cavanaugh, Tom, 557
Cawthon, James, 555
Central America, 126, 249
Central Railroad, 405–6
Centreville, Va., 457, 459–60, 469–70, 472, 475–78, 480–84, 486, 488, 492, 494, 526, 529, 684–85
Century, 691
Chalmers, David, 298
Chandler, Zachariah, 289, 582
Chaplains, army, 658
Chaplin, John, 603
Charivari, 271
Charles I, 34, 394–96
Charles II, 394–96
Charleston, S.C., 50, 79, 85, 89–90, 96–97, 115, 147, 149, 188, 191, 224, 253, 292–93, 336, 365, 425, 495, 498, 513, 517, 537, 566, 599, 602–3; during seizure of Fort Sumter, 156–64, 187, 189–90, 192, 237–39, 241–42, 252, 254–72, 275, 278–79, 281–91, 322–24, 329, 427, 496–97
Charleston Mercury, 1–4, 11
Charleston Volunteer Aid Society, 497
Charlottesville, Va., 458–59, 517–20
Chase, Salmon P., 585, 682–83, 686–92

Cheat River, 448
Cheatham, Benjamin F., 594
Cherokees, 412–14, 571–75
Chesapeake Bay, 628, 668, 688
Chesnut, James, 193, 252–56, 258, 260, 266, 292, 506–8, 510–14, 520–21
Chesnut, Mary, 252–60, 506–21
Chester, Joseph L., 649
Cheves, Langdon, 94, 255, 258
Chicago, Ill., 90, 110, 208
Chickasaws, 412
China, 656
Chippewa Territory, 175
Chisholm, A. R., 266
Choctaws, 412
Christianity, 24, 53–54, 72, 92, 173, 181, 199, 218, 229, 273, 295, 300, 615–16, 623
Cincinnati, Ohio, 505
Circuit courts, 659–60
Citizenship, 154
Civil war, 31, 66, 80–81, 113, 115, 124, 132, 135, 154, 180, 207, 233, 238–39, 242, 280, 295, 302, 311, 313–14, 316, 324–26, 328, 333–34, 348, 402, 423, 425–26, 442, 449, 509, 523, 532–33, 537, 610, 617, 632, 639–40; use of term, 18, 36, 39–40, 48, 108, 118, 186, 190, 199, 219, 253, 270, 272, 276, 278–79, 299, 415, 522
Claims courts, 661–62
Clay, Clement, 193
Clay, Henry, 8, 94, 409
Clemence, William H., 305
Clemens, Mr., 299
Clingman, Thomas L., 509, 513–14
Coatzacoalcos (steamer), 596
Cobb, Howell, 67, 506
Cobbs, Thomas R., 506
Cocke, Philip St. George, 456–57
Coercion, 67, 80–81, 108, 111–13, 122–23, 195–96, 233, 296, 381, 416, 420, 439, 441
Coffee, 94–95, 642–43
Coffin, Frank, 191
Cogswell, Milton, 581
Collins, Napoleon, 597
Colonization, 102, 126, 653, 666
Colorado Territory, 664–65
Columbia, S.C., 510, 516–18
Columbus, Ky., 590–92, 613

Comanches, 572
Commerce, 64, 67; in North, 125–26, 272, 275, 654–56; in South, 3, 12, 66, 88, 94–97, 167–68, 173, 184, 203–5, 223–24, 230, 235, 315–16, 319, 328, 627, 634–35
Committee of Thirteen, 128
Committee of Thirty-Three, 143–45, 180, 182
Competition, 88–92, 104
Compromises, 8, 107, 117–18, 120, 128, 139, 143, 180, 182, 207–9, 279, 333, 416, 421, 423, 442
Comstock, Jesse, 596, 598
Concord, battle of, 305, 423
Conditional secessionism, 14
Conditional unionism, 14
Confederacy (Confederate States of America), 37, 49, 58–59, 67, 120, 193, 207, 245, 294–95, 302, 339, 401, 405, 417, 423, 428, 454; Davis's inaugural address to, 201–6; Davis's messages in Congress on, 313–32, 627–35; Indian policy of, 412–14, 571–75; Lincoln's reference to, 432; movement to create, 2, 12, 64, 96, 107, 149, 165, 201, 297; recognition by Britain, 277, 407, 425; Stephens' "corner-stone" speech on, 221–36. *See also* Army, C.S.; Congress, C.S.; Constitution, C.S.; Navy, C.S.
Confiscation Act (1861), 538–39
Confiscation of property, 364–68, 538–39, 562–63, 568, 597–98, 665, 667
Congress, under Articles of Confederation, 81, 150, 314
Congress, C.S., 14, 204, 223–25, 231, 234, 252, 425, 432, 454, 473, 496, 508, 510, 518–19, 531, 574, 615; Davis's messages to, 313–32, 627–35
Congress, Continental, 34–35
Congress, U.S., 4, 8, 28, 36, 40, 45–46, 52, 55, 66, 99–100, 114–15, 117–18, 132, 137, 163, 175, 186–87, 227, 234–35, 289, 325, 351, 379, 416, 422, 443, 461, 465, 485, 487, 510, 525, 532, 581, 683; Buchanan's message to, 67–84; Confiscation Act, 538–39, 563, 568–69; Crittenden Compromise, 128, 139–42; Crittenden-Johnson Resolutions, 522–23; Davis's farewell address to, 193–98; and habeas corpus, 386, 388–91, 397–99; Lincoln's messages to, 427–42, 653–71; Lincoln's relationship with, 27, 110, 128, 211–12, 215, 632; and nullification, 26, 121, 131; powers of, 75–76, 79–82; and secession, 80–81, 111; and slavery, 16, 54, 58, 62, 68, 70–72, 107, 129, 143, 153, 168–71, 209, 211, 215, 316–18
Connecticut, 45, 86, 150, 499, 566
Connecticut, U.S.S., 600
Conner, James, 517
Connolly, Pat, 557
Conrad, Lewis, 679
Conrad, Tucker, 357
Constantine, Mich., 342
Constitution, C.S., 201, 204–5, 222–26, 232, 234, 302, 313, 320, 326–27, 418, 438–40
Constitution, U.S., 14, 18–19, 21, 23, 25, 27–30, 32–33, 37, 41–42, 64, 68, 105, 107, 116, 119, 133, 137–38, 149, 153, 158, 166, 184, 188, 205, 208, 223, 225, 234–35, 277, 279, 304, 310, 320, 325, 352, 362, 366, 404–5, 416, 418, 421–22, 425, 522–23, 639; amendments to, 82–84, 128–32, 139–43, 217, 303, 391–92; framing of, 73–81, 151–52, 213, 314–15; and habeas corpus, 388–92, 396–400, 434; and Lincoln, 116, 212–18, 316, 427, 433–34, 436–39, 441–42, 569, 666; and nullification, 26, 43–44, 72, 194; and presidential elections, 8, 16, 38, 40, 69–70, 154; and secession, 35–36, 54–55, 67, 78, 108, 120–24, 217, 436–39, 441–42; and slavery, 16–17, 39, 43, 58, 62, 70–72, 99–100, 110, 152, 167–69, 171, 173–75, 197, 215–16, 226, 317–19; and territories, 70–71, 100, 666
Constitution (British), 225, 392–93
Constitution (South Carolina), 150–51
Constitution (Virginia), 301
Constitutional Convention (1787), 72, 314
Constitutional Union Party, 14, 63, 128
Continental Congress, 34–35
Contraband, 364–68, 538, 651, 673
Cook (Confederate soldier), 557
Cooper River, 285

Coosawhatchie, S.C., 678
Corcoran, Michael, 381
Cork, Ireland, 649–50
Corwin, Thomas, 45
Cottenet, Annie, 271
Cotton, 3, 23–24, 58–59, 89, 93–95, 105, 172, 235, 287, 311, 319, 332, 350, 369, 536, 635, 654
Cotton States, 2, 8–10, 43–44, 58–59, 107, 113, 172, 409, 416
Courts, 16, 18, 72, 78, 99–100, 104, 131, 154, 169, 175, 216, 325, 328, 386, 538–39, 573–74, 621–22, 651, 656, 658–62
Covington, Ky., 640
Cowles, Edward P., 377
Cram, Clarence, 377
Crawford, Martin J., 321–23
Crawford, S. W., 159–60, 261–62
Creeks, 412
Crime, 96, 103, 105, 169
Crimean War, 270
Crittenden, John J., 522, 532; remarks in Senate, 128–42
Crittenden Compromise, 128, 139–42
Crittenden-Johnson Resolutions, 522–23, 538
Cromwell, Oliver, 181, 291
Crowninshield, Benjamin, 180
Crowninshield, Caspar, 576, 579, 673
Cuba, 50, 94, 633, 645
Culpeper, Va., 518–19
Cumberland Gap, 655
Curry, A. M., 557
Cushing, Caleb, 145, 417, 425
Custis, Eleanor (Nelly), 514
Cuthbert, George B., 268
Cutting, F. B., 271, 377
Cutting, Hayward, 377
Cutting, Walter, 271
Cutting, William, 46, 377

Dahlgren, John, 353
Dake, Lieutenant, 341
Dakota Territory, 664
Dana, Charles A., 585, 693
Daniel, Peter V., 658
Danley, C. C., 559
Danville, Va., 631
Davis, Charles H., 599–600
Davis, Henry Winter, 145

Davis, Jefferson, 11–13, 120, 128, 146, 187, 220, 252, 256, 271, 295–96, 302, 352, 359, 384, 401, 405, 417–18, 422–24, 495, 507–8, 510–13, 520, 612, 615, 678; farewell address in U.S. Senate, 193–98; Inaugural Address, 201–6; message to Confederate Congress (April 1861), 313–32; message to Confederate Congress (November 1861), 627–35
Davis, Jefferson C. (lieutenant), 160–61, 266
Davis, Joseph R., 507–8
Davis, Reuben, 144
Davis, Varina Howell, 507, 511, 516, 520
Davis, W. R., 557
Dawson, Mr., 483
Day-Book, 271
DeBow, James D. B., 85–97
DeBow's Review, 85, 418
Declaration of Independence, 28, 34, 78, 92, 112, 126, 149–50, 152, 196–97, 202, 213, 436–37, 440
Delaware, 107, 150, 431, 667
DeLeon, Camden, 513
Democracy, 45, 64, 66, 276, 336, 415, 431, 529
Democratic Party, 27, 34, 58, 62–63, 115, 117, 128, 145, 187, 243–44, 270–72, 275, 278, 280, 299, 319, 353, 361, 377, 417, 587
Dent, Frederick F., 310–11, 640
DeSaussure, Wilmot G., 268, 506
Detroit, Mich., 341
Devereux, John, 191
Devine, Dr., 371
Dickinson, John, 144
Dike, J. H., 306–7
District of Columbia, 59, 662–63, 665; slavery in, 62, 100, 110, 129, 140. *See also* Washington, D.C.
"Dixie," 272, 403
Dixon, James, 45
Doolittle, James R., 350
Dorrance, Mr., 598
Doubleday, Abner: *Reminiscences of Forts Sumter and Moultrie*, 156–62, 261–68
Doubleday, Mary, 162
Douglas, Stephen A., 46, 53, 61, 110, 126, 128, 145, 278, 296, 568

Douglass, Frederick, 57–62, 207–9, 333–35, 564–67
Douglass, W. R., 557
Douglass' Monthly, 57, 207, 333, 564
Drayton, Thomas, 598–600
Drayton, Hesse, 497
Dreher, Ferdinand, 579
Dry Tortugas, 248
Du Bois, John V., 559
Du Pont, Samuel Francis, 596–603
Du Pont, Sophie, 596
Due process of law, 391–92
Duncan, Wiliam B., 271
Dunlap, M. A., 558
DuPont, Lammot, 649
Duryée, Abram, 368, 381
D'Utassy, Frederick, 376

Eads, Genevieve, 681
Eads, James B., 681
Eames, Charles, 352
Earl, Thomas, 354
Early, Everett B., 458–59
East Carroll Parish, La., 372
East Indies, 23, 94, 186
East Saginaw, Mich., 342
Eaton, Mr., 481
Edge (editor), 410
Edisto River, 680
Edmondston, Catherine, 163–64, 189–92, 220
Edmondston, Lawrence, 189–90
Edmondston, Patrick, 163, 189, 191
Education, 92, 104, 507
Eldridge, Oliver, 596, 598, 601
Election of 1800, 230
Election of 1804, 319
Election of 1808, 319
Election of 1852, 319
Election of 1856, 319
Election of 1860, 1–9, 11, 14, 16, 19, 38, 41, 57–63, 65, 69–70, 98–99, 109, 113–14, 118–19, 154, 170–73, 175, 185, 207, 209, 275, 318, 366, 374, 421, 442, 569
Electoral College, 3–4, 8, 11, 57
Ellsworth, Elmer E., 351–53, 378, 493
Elzey, Arnold, 508, 516
Emancipation, 94–96, 102, 104, 173, 184, 333–35, 652–53, 666
England, 229. *See also* Britain

English, Samuel J., 491–94
Equality, 16, 92–93, 95, 99–100, 104–5, 126, 171–73, 183–84, 196–97, 221, 226–27
Essex County, Va., 448
Etheridge, Emerson, 145
Europa (British steamer), 650
Eustis, George, 646
Evans, Nathan G., 462
Everett, Edward, 379; *The Life of George Washington*, 199
Ewing, Charles, 358–59
Ewing, Hugh, 358–59
Ewing, Thomas, 63
Ewing (tutor), 371
Ex parte Bollman (1807), 397–98
Ex parte Merryman (1861), 386–400
Ex parte Swartwout (1807), 397–98
Explanatory amendments, 83–84
Exports/imports, 94–96, 319

Fairfax, Thomas, 652
Fairfax, Va., 356, 380–81, 466, 468, 478, 483–84, 488, 491, 494, 504, 684–85
Fairfax County, Va., 636
Falls Church, Va., 636
Faneuil Hall, 124, 274, 293
Faulkner, Charles J., 633
Fay, Major, 365
Fay, Richard, 411
Fearing, Kate, 272
Felton, Cornelius C., 377
Ferguson, Samuel, 268
Fielding, George, 267–68
Fillmore, Millard, 24
Fingal (British steamer), 649
Fisheries, 96
Fitzpatrick, Benjamin, 139, 193
Flag, American, 126–27, 139, 186, 189, 191, 239, 267–68, 278–80, 287, 299, 303, 310–12, 324, 333, 336, 425, 549, 594, 668
Flag, Confederate, 260, 268, 278, 282, 285, 287–88, 299, 303, 323, 356, 508, 549
Flanagin, Harris, 556
Florida, 50, 135, 157, 438, 518, 596, 598, 659, 678; secessionism in, 64, 66, 107, 165, 183, 193, 201, 427
Florida, Mo., 444–45
Florida, U.S.S., 599

Floyd, John B., 67, 147, 158, 187, 422
Follansbee, Albert S., 305–8
Fontaine, Edmund, 459–60
Forsyth, John, 321–23
Ford, Sergeant, 341
Fort Corcoran, 526
Fort Duquesne, 20
Fort Jackson, 329, 339
Fort Jefferson, 248, 427
Fort Johnson, 159, 261, 285
Fort Lafayette, 297
Fort Mason, 199
Fort McHenry, 376, 386–87, 399
Fort (Fortress) Monroe, 192, 353, 361, 364, 366, 381, 504, 534–35, 538, 674, 684, 687
Fort Morgan, 329
Fort Moultrie, 147, 156–59, 163, 187, 189–90, 237, 239, 263, 285–86, 291, 496–97
Fort Necessity, 21
Fort Pickens, 233, 240, 246, 248, 250, 321, 335, 353, 419, 427, 429
Fort Pinckney, 163, 190, 285
Fort Pulaski, 164, 178, 329
Fort Runyon, 465
Fort St. Philip, 329, 339
Fort Smith, Ark., 412, 558
Fort Sumter, 156–64, 187, 189–90, 192, 233, 237–46, 249–50, 252, 254–73, 275, 278–79, 281–91, 294, 297, 310, 321–24, 329, 334, 419, 423–24, 427–32, 496–97, 500, 612, 667
Fort Taylor, 240, 248, 427
Fort Warren, 383
Fort Wayne, 341–42
Foster, John G., 160–61, 290
Foster, Mrs. John G., 162
Fourierists, 92
Fox, Gustavus Vasa, 237, 241–42, 681
France, 20, 51, 91, 112, 184, 229, 232, 249, 276–77, 327, 411, 425, 511, 633, 645, 654
Frankfort, Ky., 165
Franklin, William B., 636, 638, 683–91
Free labor, 88–96, 103, 126, 669–71
Free love advocates, 92
Free Negroes, 54, 92, 96, 102–5, 126, 154, 171–73, 666

Freeman, Colonel, 222
Frémont, John C., 8, 504, 563–64, 568–70; proclamation, 561–62
French and Indian War, 20–21
French Revolution, 133, 281
Frisbie, Henry N., 638
Frost, Daniel M., 358–59
Fugitive slave laws (1793, 1850), 16, 24, 26, 39, 43–44, 47, 52, 61–62, 68, 72, 84, 107–8, 110, 114, 129–31, 141–42, 144, 152–53, 168–69, 184, 211–12, 216, 316, 362, 366
Fugitive slaves, 16–17, 24, 26, 29, 45, 59, 61, 68, 72, 102, 107, 130–31, 141–42, 152–54, 168–69, 196, 211–12, 216–17, 316–17, 353, 361–68
Fuller, Margaret, 253
Fuller, William J., 550

Galena, Ill., 310–11, 347–48, 640
Galileo Galilei, 228
Galveston Bay, 32
Galway, Edwin, 267
Gamble, Hamilton R., 681
Garden, Hugh, 519
Garibaldi Guard, 376–77
Garnett, Richard B., 447–49
Garrison, William Lloyd, 61, 426
George (Union soldier), 576
George III, 197, 585
Georgetown (District of Columbia), 381, 485
Georgia, 3, 14, 19, 50, 53, 86, 115, 150, 164, 223–24, 230, 495, 616, 621–22, 678; possible loyalty to Union, 500; secessionism in, 11–13, 48, 64, 66, 98–108, 165, 183, 193, 201, 427
Georgia 21st Regiment, 495–96
German immigrants, 88, 308, 358, 377, 470, 473, 475, 477–78
Germantown, Va., 469–70, 479
Gibbes, Caroline, 252
Gibbes, Robert W., 254, 512–13, 515
Gibbs, Sanford, 37
Gibson, Charles, 681
Giddings, Joshua Reed, 46
Gillis, John P., 353
Gilmer, John A., 109–10
Glover, Samuel T., 570
Goddard, Robert H. I., 379

Goldsborough, John, 598, 600
Goodall, A. S., 649
Gourdin, Robert N., 85, 97, 253
Governor (steamer), 599
Governor's Island (New York City), 112, 272
Graham of Claverhouse, John, 379
Grant, Frederick Dent, 311
Grant, Harriet, 518
Grant, Jesse Root, 310–12, 347–49, 590, 639
Grant, Julia Dent, 311, 348, 590, 639–40
Grant, Orvil Lynch, 312
Grant, Samuel Simpson, 349
Grant, Ulysses S., 310–12, 347–49, 559, 590–91, 639–40; *Personal Memoirs*, 444–46
Gratiot, John R., 556, 560
Graves, John R., 555–56
Greeley, Horace, 8–10, 111–13, 271, 275, 370, 531–32
Green, Allen, 252, 521
Green, James S., 139
Green, John, 254
Green, John C., 44
Green, Mrs. Allen, 254
Green, Shields, 566
Greensboro, N.C., 631
Greenwood, S.C., 49
Gregg, Maxcy, 511
Guaymas, Mexico, 536
Guibor, Henry, 558–59
Gulf of Mexico, 233, 238, 240–41, 248–49, 339, 419, 600

Habeas corpus, writ of, 386–400, 404, 433–34, 632
Haggerty, Captain, 365
Haggerty, James, 528
"Hail, Columbia," 272
Haiti, 94, 172, 250, 607, 656
Hale, Charles, 146
Hale, Stephen F., 165–76
Halifax County, N.C., 163, 220
Halifax County, Va., 298
Hall, Norman J., 159, 162, 267
Hallam, Henry: *Constitutional History of England*, 394–96
Halleck, Henry W., 584, 640, 681, 683
Halliburton, Henry, 557

Hallowell, Norwood P., 578
Hamilton, Alexander (1755–1804), 200
Hamilton, Alexander (1815–1907), 377, 380
Hamilton, Jack, 257
Hamilton, James, 122
Hamilton, James A., 350
Hamilton, Louisa, 257–58
Hamilton, Paul, 604
Hamilton, S. D. H., 592
Hamilton, Schuyler, 377
Hamlin, Hannibal, 2–4, 8, 57, 61, 118, 170, 220
Hammond, James H., 94, 193, 513, 520
Hammond, William A., 592
Hampden, John, 85
Hampton, Va., 367–68, 508
Hampton, Wade, 457
Hampton Legion, 457, 495
Hampton Roads, 361, 365–66, 600
Hancock, Winfield S., 638
Hanover, Va., 460
Hanson, John W.: *Historical Sketch of the Old Sixth Regiment of Massachusetts Volunteers*, 305–9
Hardee, William J.: *Rifle and Light Infantry Tactics*, 344–45
Hardy, Hugh F., 557
Harlan, James, 507
Harpers Ferry, Va. (now W.Va.), 381–82, 449, 505, 534
Harpers Ferry arsenal, 170, 299, 383, 420, 423, 432, 607
Harper's Monthly, 370
Harper's Weekly, 370, 601, 636–38
Harris, Arnold, 509
Harris, Matthias, 161
Harris, Thomas, 444–45
Hart, James W., 305, 307
Hart, Peter, 263, 265
Hartstene, Henry J., 188, 254, 268
Harvard University, 377, 404, 415
Harvey, William, 228
Hatherton, Baron (Edward John Littleton), 652
Havana, Cuba, 633
Havelock, Henry, 517
Hay, John, 350–54, 504, 531
Haydon, Charles B., 341–46

Hayes, James, 267
Hayne, Alicia, 254
Hayne, Robert Y., 121
Heintzelman, Samuel P., 526–27, 636–37
Helper, Hinton Rowan: *The Impending Crisis of the South*, 85
Hemp, 95
Henry, Judith, 455
Henry, Gus, 594–95
Henry, Patrick, 85, 298
Herbert, Joseph, 554
Herndon, William H., 148
Hewitt, Abram S., 271
Heyward, Maria, 260
Heyward, Nat, 597
Heyward, Willie, 496
Higgins (Confederate soldier), 557
Higginson, Thomas Wentworth, 354
Hill, Benjamin, 98; speech at Milledgeville, 14–33
Hill, Colonel, 615
Hilton Head, 600
Hinesville, Ga., 406
Hodge, Dr., 498
Hoffman, Wickham, 376–81
Hollinquist, Captain, 268
Hollosay, Carl, 674
Holmes, Oliver Wendell, Jr., 579
Holmes, Emma, 495–97
Holt, Joseph, 187, 585
Hospitals, 449, 458, 461, 497, 517–18, 520, 658
Hough, Daniel, 267
House of Representatives, C.S., 224–25
House of Representatives, U.S., 9, 67, 70, 81–83, 140–41, 143, 145, 180, 227, 289, 318, 391, 427, 522, 538, 653. *See also* Congress, U.S.
Houston, Sam, 37–42
Hudson, Mich., 345
Huestis, Bill, 544–45
Huger, Benjamin, 157, 684
Huguenots, 598
Hungarian immigrants, 376
Hunter, David, 485, 492, 526–28
Hunter, John, 358–59
Hunter, Robert M., 506, 508
Huntsville, Texas, 37
Hurlbut, Stephen A., 570
Hyde, Nicholas, 395

Idaho Territory, 175
Illinois, 5, 8, 90, 110, 144–45, 147, 153, 210, 312, 347–48, 350, 444–45, 581, 593
Illinois Central Railroad, 274
Illinois 13th Regiment, 444
Illinois 21st Regiment, 444–46
Illinois 27th Regiment, 593
Immigrants, 88, 90–92, 126, 308, 315, 358, 370, 372, 376–77, 470, 473, 475, 477–78, 665
Imports/exports, 94–96, 319
Independence Hall, 178
India, 23–24
Indian Territory, 412, 536, 571
Indiana, 144, 153, 534–35
Indians, 157, 262, 412–14, 438, 571–75, 663–64
Inflation, 641–43
Ingraham, Duncan N., 506, 514
Interior Department, U.S., 187, 663–65
Iowa, 153, 543, 551, 593, 659
Iowa 1st Regiment, 543–53
Iowa 6th Regiment, 593
Iowa 7th Regiment, 593
Ireland, 229
Irish immigrants, 308, 370, 372, 473
Ironton, Mo., 562
Irwin, John, 267
Italian immigrants, 376–77
Italy, 59, 91, 284
Iverson, Alfred, 115–16, 193
Izard, Rosetta, 515

Jackson, Andrew, 26, 50, 55–56, 69, 74, 94, 111, 121, 186–87, 195, 565
Jackson, William H., 595
Jackson, Claiborne, 358–59
Jackson, James, 222, 404, 406
Jackson, Thomas (Stonewall), 448, 455, 488, 506
Jackson (Confederate soldier), 496
Jamaica, 95
James River, 361
Jameson, Charles D., 637
Jefferson, Thomas, 9, 24, 55, 83, 112, 196, 200, 226, 230, 298, 319, 388, 440, 666
Jefferson City, Mo., 562
Jefferson Territory, 175
Jeffreys, George, 621

Jenison, Mr., 381–82
Jersey City, N.J., 376
Jesus, 53–54, 606, 609, 620, 624
Jews, 188
"John Brown's Body," 383–85
Johns, Mrs., 357
Johnson, Andrew, 90, 146, 193, 522
Johnson, B. F., 495–96
Johnston, Joseph E., 454, 456, 495, 498, 506, 508, 530, 542, 612
Johnston, Lydia, 511
Jones, Charles C., 178–179, 294–96, 404
Jones, Charles C., Jr., 178–79, 294–96, 404–406
Jones, Custis, 303
Jones, D. K., 266–67
Jones, Edward F., 305–8
Jones, John B., 297–304
Jones, Mary, 178–79, 404
Jones, Mrs. John B., 303
Journal of Commerce, 271, 370
Judiciary Act (1789), 386
Justice Department, C.S., 328–29

Kalamazoo, Mich., 341–42, 345
Kansas, 415, 536, 659, 663
Kansas Territory, 46, 71, 144, 170
Kearney, Philip, 638
Keim, William H., 387
Keitt, Lawrence M., 520
Kelley, Benjamin F., 582
Kemble, Peter, 601
Kentucky, 14, 63, 89, 128, 135, 138, 325, 522, 592, 595, 655, 690, 692; remains in Union, 51, 188, 534–35, 628–29, 667; secessionism in, 107, 165, 188, 232, 563, 569
Kentucky Resolves (1798), 319
Kershaw, Joseph B., 496, 516, 519
Kettell, Thomas P., 96
Key West, Fla., 240, 248–49
Keyes, E. D., 526–27
Kimball, George, 383
Kimball, J. D., 557
King, Rufus, 638
King, Susan, 255
Kings County, N.Y., 46
Kingsbury, Henry D., 687

Kittrell, P. W., 37
Know-Nothing (American) Party, 14, 109
Knoxville, Tenn., 49, 655
Knoxville Whig, 49

Laborers, 88–96, 103–4, 126, 669–71
Lagow, Clark B., 639–40
Lake Providence, La., 371
Lamon, Ward Hill, 242
Lamson, Mr., 381
Lancaster, Ohio, 63
Land ownership, 86–87, 93, 103–4
Lander, Frederick W., 579
Lane, Harriet, 513
Laswell, George S., 551
Lauderdale, Earl of (John Maitland), 379
Laurence (slave), 259
Law, Mr., 595
Law of nations, 325–26, 407, 421, 633–34
Lawrence, Mass., 306–7
Laws, 14, 18, 25–30, 33, 38, 54, 60, 69–70, 72, 76, 78–79, 104, 117, 120, 131–32, 141–42, 158, 188, 194–95, 212, 304, 312, 316, 399–400, 433–34, 436–37, 569, 660
Lawton, Alexander, 179, 222
Lay, George W., 506
Layard, Austen Henry, 647
Leavenworth, Kans., 561
Lebanon, Tenn., 655
Lee, Blair, 186, 188, 499
Lee, Charlotte Wickham, 515
Lee, Elizabeth Blair, 186–88, 498–99
Lee, George Washington Custis, 199, 678
Lee, Henry (Light-Horse Harry), 515
Lee, Mary Custis, 514, 678–79
Lee, Robert E., 199–200, 380, 492, 496, 514–15, 678–80
Lee, Samuel Phillips, 186, 188, 498
Lee, Smith, 514–15
Lee, Stephen D., 266
Lee, William H. (Rooney), 515
Lee, William R., 577–78, 581
Lee family, 514–15
Leesburg, Va., 530, 534, 576, 581, 612–13, 628

"Let My People Go," 674–77
Letcher, John, 297–98, 301, 420
Leutze, Emanuel, 377
Lewis, Didimus, 557
Lexington, battle of (1775), 305
Lexington, Ky., 655
Lexington, Mo., 613, 628
Liberia, 656, 666
Liberty County, Ga., 178, 294
Lincoln, Abraham, 18, 28–29, 34, 45, 106, 117, 146, 186, 190–91, 220, 252, 254, 271–72, 282, 287, 294, 296, 350, 352–53, 357, 359, 367, 370, 375, 377, 407, 418, 451, 503, 524, 531, 533, 536, 540, 565, 581, 583, 585–86; and colonization, 653, 666; on Confederate Army, 432, 440, 504, 668; and confiscation of property, 538, 563–64, 568–70, 653, 665–66; and Constitution, 116, 212–18, 316, 427, 433–34, 436–39, 441–42, 569, 666; and court reform, 658–62; Davis on, 313, 316, 318, 321–22, 324–26, 328–29, 632; election of 1860, 1–9, 11, 14, 16, 19, 38, 41, 57–63, 65, 69–70, 98–99, 109, 113–14, 118–19, 154, 170–73, 175, 185, 207, 209, 275, 318, 366, 374, 421, 442, 569; and emancipation, 653, 666; First Inaugural Address, 210–19; and foreign affairs, 248–51, 651, 654–56; and habeas corpus, 386, 433–34, 632; inauguration of, 98, 101, 107, 113, 118, 207, 210–19, 233, 237, 295, 316, 321, 417, 419, 422–23, 431, 667; memoranda on military policy, 504–5; message to Congress (July 1861), 427–42; message to Congress (December 1861), 653–71; reference to Confederacy, 432; relationship with Congress, 27, 110, 128, 211–12, 215, 632; and Republican Party, 39, 58, 99–100, 109–10, 172, 208, 210, 421; and secession, 1, 4, 99, 107, 208, 213, 215, 217, 234–35, 297, 321–22, 427–28, 432–33, 435–36, 438–39, 442; and slavery, 58–62, 101, 110, 164, 207–11, 215–17, 563, 568, 603–4, 653, 664, 666; and Union army, 110, 147–48, 237–38, 240–42, 245–47, 269–70, 303, 310, 312, 324–26, 427–33, 440–41, 505–5, 568–70, 637, 657–58, 661, 664, 667–68, 681–85, 687–92; and Union Navy, 110, 427–29, 432–33, 440–41, 658
Lincoln, Thomas (Tad), 692
Littell's Living Age, 370, 372
Little Rock, Ark., 554
Living expenses, 90–91
Lockwood, Lewis, 674
London, England, 281, 407–11, 464, 585, 633, 645–52, 665
Long, Armistead L., 679
Long, Mary, 520
Louisiana, 50, 86, 90, 358, 369, 493, 550, 555–56, 565, 595; secessionism in, 13, 63–66, 165, 183, 193, 201, 427
Louisiana Purchase, 42, 50, 135, 184, 666
Louisiana State Seminary and Military Academy, 63–66
Louisiana 3rd Regiment, 556
Louisiana 4th Regiment, 370
Louisiana 11th Regiment, 595
Louisiana 12th Regiment, 593
Louisville, Ky., 592
Lowe (Confederate soldier), 557
Lowell, James Jackson, 579
Lowell, James Russell: "The Pickens-and-Stealin's Rebellion," 415–26
Lowell, Mass., 90, 305, 307
Lynchburg, Va., 454
Lundy, Benjamin, 61
Luther, Martin, 521
Lyon, Nathaniel, 358, 543–45, 552–55, 559
Lyons, James, 298
Lyons, Richard (Lord Lyons), 292, 409, 478, 490, 521, 651, 655

Macfarland, James E., 646
Madison, James, 24, 55, 74–75, 80–81, 83, 200, 319
Madison Parish, La., 369
Magna Carta, 222, 300, 393, 396
Magoffin, Beriah, 165
Magrath, Andrew G., 94
Maine, 8, 50, 86, 153, 272, 415
Mallory, Charles K., 361–62, 364–66
Mallory, Stephen, 193
Manassas, battle of. *See* Bull Run, battle of

INDEX

Manassas, Va., 454, 458, 462, 504–5, 684–85, 687–88, 692
Manlove, Thomas, 372
Manning, John L., 253–55, 257, 259–60, 266, 292
Mansfield, Earl of (William Murray), 58
Mansfield, Joseph K., 380, 524
Mansfield, Ohio, 360
Manufacturing, 23, 67, 91; in North, 168, 665; in South, 95–96, 203–5, 315–16, 627
Marcy, Randolph B., 681
Marines, U.S., 379–80, 493, 599
Marshall, John, 397–98
Marshall, John G., 557
Martial law, 249, 561–62, 568–70
Martindale, John H., 638
Maryland, 89, 129, 140, 150, 186, 335, 420, 516, 530, 619, 674; Baltimore riot, 305–9; remains in Union, 51, 188, 362, 366, 498, 564, 667–68; secessionism in, 107, 181, 188, 303, 564, 569, 667–68; and suspension of habeas corpus, 386–87, 398–400
Mason, James M., 145, 301, 511, 600, 633, 645–47, 651
Mason-Dixon Line, 135, 667
Massachusetts, 24, 29, 43–44, 86, 90–91, 143–44, 150, 153, 180–81, 196, 274, 305–9, 361, 367, 378–79, 383, 411, 418, 506, 576, 672
Massachusetts, U.S.S., 655
Massachusetts 1st Regiment, 672
Massachusetts 6th Regiment, 305–9
Massachusetts 20th Regiment, 576–80
May, C. S., 342, 345
McCall, George A., 636–37
McClellan, George B., 339–40, 504, 524–25, 530, 540–42, 581–84, 587–89, 636–37, 668–69, 681–84, 687–92; memorandum for President, 533–37
McClellan, Mary Ellen, 524, 540–42, 581
McClernand, John A., 591
McCulloch, Benjamin, 412, 555–56, 559, 572–73
McDonald, Charles J., 406
McDowell, Irvin, 380–81, 454, 464, 467, 469, 474–75, 481, 484, 486, 488, 504, 510, 524, 528–29, 636–38; memorandum, 683–91

McDuffie, George, 94
McGuire, John P., 355
McGuire, Judith, 355–57
McIntosh, James, 556, 559
McKinley (Union soldier), 600
McLean, John, 658–59
McLean, Margaret, 507, 509–11, 520
McRae, C.S.S., 329
McRae, Dandridge, 555–56
Meade, George G., 637
Meade, Richard K., 161
Means, Emma, 258
Means, John H., 254–55, 517–18
Means, Robert Stark, 258, 517
Meigs, Montgomery C., 681, 683, 688–92
Melville, Herman: *Battle-Pieces and Aspects of the War*, 177; "Misgivings," 177
Memminger, Christopher G., 94, 157, 615
Memphis, Tenn., 340, 443, 505, 506, 534
Merryman, John, 386, 398
Messenger, Daniel, 272, 377, 381
Methodists, 49, 53–54
Mexican Cession, 135, 184
Mexico, 48, 125–26, 157, 249, 536–37
Meyer, Tom, 272
Michigan, 153, 289, 341–46, 378, 481
Michigan 2nd Regiment, 341–46
Miles, William P., 253, 255, 257, 266, 511
Military courts, 661
Militia, 20–21, 26, 79, 204, 269, 271, 331, 339, 358–59, 383, 390–91, 433, 657–58, 681
Milledgeville, Ga., 14, 605
Miller, Mr., 190
Millerites, 92
Mills, Anderson, 557
Milnes, Richard Monckton, 648
Mining, 91
Minnesota, 659
Mississippi, 3, 86, 94, 120, 328; secessionism in, 11–12, 64, 66, 107, 165, 183–85, 187, 193–95, 201, 427
Mississippi River, 24, 50, 64–65, 224, 240, 328, 339–40, 369–71, 444, 534, 536, 562, 573, 590

Missouri, 48, 89, 186, 325, 386, 504, 534, 562, 565, 628, 683; battle of Belmont, 590–95; battle of Wilson's Creek, 543–61; remains in Union, 188, 667; St. Louis riot, 358–60; Salt River raid, 444–46; secessionism in, 107, 188, 232, 569, 667
Missouri Compromise, 44, 46, 70, 129, 134
Missouri 2nd Regiment, 555
Missroon, John S., 602
Mitchell, Sam, 603–4
Moale, Edward, 161
Mobile, Ala., 50, 90, 262, 537
Molasses, 95
Molino del Rey, battle of, 157
Montague, Robert L., 298, 300
Montevideo plantation, 178, 294
Montgomery, Ala., 201, 231, 302, 313, 401, 422, 432, 454, 513, 537
Monticello, La., 370, 372
Moore, Andrew B., 165
Moore, Samuel P., 515
Moore, Thomas O., 64, 66
Moran, Benjamin, 645–50
Morell, George W., 638
Mormons, 92
Morning Herald (London), 410
Moses, Franklin J., 268
Moultrieville, S.C., 156, 162
Mount Vernon arsenal, 164
Munford, Thomas T., 456, 459
Murat, Joachim, 475

Napoléon I (Napoléon Bonaparte), 276, 421, 503, 530
Napoléon III (Louis Napoléon), 411
Nashville, Tenn., 85, 90, 535
National Anti-Slavery Standard, 674
National debt, 435, 438, 656–57
Naval stores, 95, 298
Navy, C.S., 204, 326, 329–30, 629
Navy, U.S., 26, 50, 79, 100, 170, 186, 298, 322, 350, 390, 423, 535, 539, 585, 628, 632, 681–82; blockade of southern ports, 249, 326, 328, 339–40, 365, 433, 498, 504, 634, 641–43, 651, 655, 658, 666, 673; capture of Port Royal Sound, 596–602; and Lincoln, 110, 427–29, 432–33, 440–41, 658; relief of Fort Sumter, 237–41, 245, 278–79, 429; and *Trent* affair, 633, 645–52, 679
Navy Department, C.S., 329–30, 629
Navy Department, U.S., 379, 435, 658, 681–82
Nebraska Territory, 175, 536
Neely, Rufus P., 593
Negroes, 44, 156, 253, 290, 348, 464, 588, 608; claimed inferiority of, 172, 174, 197, 221, 226–28, 318; and colonization, 102, 126, 653, 666; and equality, 16, 92–93, 95, 99–100, 104–5, 126, 171–73, 183–84, 196–97, 221, 226–27; free, 54, 92, 96, 102–5, 126, 154, 171–73, 666; in Union army, 262, 333–35, 350, 366–67, 565–67, 652. *See also* Slaves
Neill, Samuel, 377
Nevada Territory, 175, 664
New Hampshire, 51, 86, 150, 153, 491, 493
New Hampshire 2nd Regiment, 493
New Jersey, 150, 153, 378, 499
New Mexico Territory, 42, 180, 536, 663
New Orleans, battle of, 565–66
New Orleans, La., 63, 65–66, 90, 96, 329, 340, 369, 371–72, 496, 506, 537, 631
New Orleans Picayune, 370
New Orleans Whig, 370
New York, 42, 44, 46, 57, 96, 146, 150, 153, 359, 378, 381, 482, 491, 493, 496, 499, 527, 565, 648
New York City, 43, 46, 89, 92, 112, 160, 189, 240–41, 243, 269–75, 281, 283–84, 303, 322, 336–38, 376–78, 381, 383, 386, 418, 496, 500, 531–32, 585, 587, 598, 600–1, 633, 681
New York Club, 269, 273
New York Daily News, 34–36
New York Daily Tribune, 8–10, 111–13, 673, 693
New York Evening Post, 269
New York Express, 271
New York Herald, 34, 254, 269–72, 515, 531, 598–99, 692
New York Independent, 586
New York Times, 147, 275–77, 364–68, 481, 602, 683

New York Tribune, 34, 270, 370, 531, 506, 521
New York Weekly Graphic, 500
New York 5th Regiment, 381
New York 9th Regiment, 377
New York 12th Regiment, 381
New York 13th Regiment, 500
New York 28th Regiment, 381
New York 69th Regiment, 496, 527
New York 71st Regiment, 491, 493
Newbern, N.C., 686
Newcastle, Duke of (Thomas Pelham-Holles), 20
Newport, R.I., 381
Newton, Albert, 369–71, 373–74
Newton, John, 638
Newton, Willoughby, 298
Niagara Falls, 20
Nicholasville, Ky., 655
Nicolay, John G., 5–7, 147–48, 350, 504, 531, 563
Norfolk, Va., 240, 298, 367, 381, 420, 423, 432, 684, 687
North American Review, 600
North Carolina, 85, 89, 109, 150, 325, 418, 615, 631, 655, 686–87; possible loyalty to Union, 188, 273, 431, 500, 668; secessionism in, 107, 188, 193, 232, 297
Northampton County, Va., 668
Northwest Ordinance, 135, 152, 184
Nott, Josiah C., 513
Nullification, 9, 194–95; of fugitive slave laws, 16, 24, 26, 29, 43–44, 52, 55, 72, 107–8, 153, 168–69, 184, 317; South Carolina crisis (1833), 26, 50, 55–56, 74, 111, 121–22

Observer (London), 648–49
Occoquan, Va., 685
Oglethorpe Light Infantry, 495–96
Ohio, 63, 65, 114, 144, 153, 339, 534–35
Ohio and Mississippi Railroad, 524, 589
Ohio River, 20, 135, 152, 590
Old Point Comfort. *See* Fort (Fortress) Monroe
Orange, Va., 511, 682
Ord, E.O.C., 637
Oregon, 135, 581, 659
Orr, James L., 94
Osborne, Vincent B, 557

Ottumwa, Iowa, 551
Owenites, 92
Owens, J. W., 222

Palfrey, Francis W., 579
Palmer, John M., 444
Palmerston, Viscount (Henry John Temple), 645–46, 649
Palmetto Guard, 268, 492
Palmyra, Mo., 444
Pamlico Sound, 686
Pánuco River, 536
Paris, France, 281, 634, 645, 652
Parks, J. D., 557
Parliament (British), 91, 225, 394
Patents, 328–29, 663
Patriotism, 30, 32, 38, 40–42, 50, 87, 90, 92, 105–6, 110, 119, 139, 158, 176, 186, 200, 203, 205, 218–19, 231–32, 238, 249–50, 272, 277, 279–80, 294, 296, 300–1, 303, 312, 329, 340, 402, 405, 436, 449, 509, 606, 616, 623, 628, 656–57, 661, 665
Patronage, 110, 377
Patterson, Robert, 498, 504, 530
Paul (apostle), 53, 273
Pearce, N. B., 555–57, 559
Peck, Mr., 370
Pedro V, 647
Peel, Robert, 145
Pegram, John, 447–48
Peirce, Benjamin, 377
Pennsylvania, 36, 57, 90, 144, 150, 153, 280, 302, 308, 378, 387, 399, 467, 637
Pennsylvania 1st Regiment, 637
Pennsylvania 4th Regiment, 467
Pensacola, Fla., 272, 329, 537
Pensacola, U.S.S., 353
Pensacola Bay, 248
Pensions, 663
Personal liberty laws, 43, 52, 55, 108, 153
Perthshire (British steamer), 655
Petigru, James L., 257
Pettus, John J., 165
Philadelphia, Pa., 144, 178, 220, 297, 302, 305, 307, 309, 360, 386, 498, 514, 599, 602, 619
Philip II, 598
Philippi, Va., 447
Phillips, Wendell, 426, 586

Pickens, Francis W., 187, 241, 252–54, 323, 430
Pickering, John, 306–7
Pierce, Franklin, 201, 319
Pierce, Lovick, 53
Pike, Albert, 572
Pillow, Gideon J., 348–49, 594–95
Pinchard, George, 267
Pinckney, Charles Cotesworth, 253
Pinckney, Miss, 253
Pirates, 656
Pitt, William, 276, 585
Pittsburgh, Pa., 90
Pittsburgh Post, 278–80
Plantations, 93, 466
Plymouth, U.S.S., 353
Pocahontas, 509
Pocahontas, U.S.S., 353
Poe, Edgar Allan, 370
Polk, Leonidas, 593–94
Pollock (Confederate soldier), 557
Poolesville, Md., 576
Pope, Miss, 598
Population, 85–87, 96, 101, 172–73, 229–30, 315, 318–19, 325
Port Royal Sound, 596–604, 668, 672
Porter, Fitz-John, 584, 636, 638
Porter, William D., 94
Portugal, 229, 647
Post Office Department, C.S., 330, 629–30
Post Office Department, U.S., 427, 662–63
Potomac River, 32, 45, 299, 378–79, 449, 460, 465, 488, 491, 494, 505, 521, 526, 530, 534–35, 540–42, 576, 581–82, 587, 612–13, 619, 636, 662, 668, 684–87, 694
Poverty, 87, 90–91, 93–94, 98, 101, 103–6
Presbyterians, 178, 294
Presidency (Confederacy), 225
Presidency (United States), 389–92, 396, 442
Preston, Caroline, 510, 515, 517–18
Preston, John S., 512
Preston, John S., Jr., 254, 260
Preston, Susan, 257, 260
Preston, W. C., 265
Price, Sterling, 555, 559–60, 591
Princeton University, 404

Prisoners of war, 359, 380, 462–63, 511–12, 520–21, 532, 581, 632
Proclamation of Neutrality (Britain), 407–9
Property, 52, 105, 171, 174, 210, 222; confiscation of, 364–68, 538–39, 562–63, 568, 597–98, 665, 667; government, 50–51, 79, 187, 213–14, 233, 419, 427–28; in slaves, 16–18, 52, 54, 58, 70–71, 83, 87–88, 93, 99, 101, 106, 153–54, 167–70, 183–85, 311, 316–18, 348, 362, 364, 367, 404
Providence, R.I., 379
Pryor, Roger A., 266, 293, 498
Public lands, 663
Pugh, James L., 126
Punch, 271
Puritans, 270
Putnam, William L., 579

Quincy, Ill., 444
Quinn (Confederate soldier), 557

Race, 140, 171–74, 183, 196, 221, 226–29
Radford, Winston, 459
Radical Abolition Party, 57
Rae, John, 271
Railroads, 50–51, 224, 331, 386, 454, 505, 534–37, 629–31, 655, 667, 684–85
Raleigh, N.C., 190, 687
Ramsay, Douglas, 511
Randolph, G. W., 298
Randolph, John, 24
Randolph, Mary, 518–19
Rappahannock River, 685, 687
Raymond, Henry J., 275, 481; *The Life and Public Services of Abraham Lincoln*, 683
Raymond (professor), 367–68
Red River, 65, 536
Reed (Confederate soldier), 558–59
Reiffenberg, Baron de, 649
Representation, 54–55, 131, 153, 197
Republican Party, 1–2, 6, 8, 16–17, 38, 43–46, 48, 57, 59–61, 63, 111, 114, 116, 118, 125, 128, 133, 138, 143, 180, 183, 186–88, 193, 220, 233, 243–44, 249, 268, 275, 280, 289, 301, 310, 318, 377, 417, 419, 561, 581; Black Republicans, 3–4, 18, 39, 103, 106, 126, 170, 176,

295; and Lincoln, 39, 58, 99–100, 109–10, 172, 208, 210, 421
Republicanism, 431, 442
Reuter, Paul von, 646, 648
Revolution, right to, 78, 112, 122, 166, 277, 352, 421
Revolutionary War, 21, 34–35, 37, 50, 92, 112, 127, 135–36, 139, 144, 149–50, 157, 174, 200, 234, 259, 300, 314, 393, 423, 435, 451, 566
Reyburn, William W., 557
Reynolds, Joseph J., 637
Rhett, Alfred, 293
Rhett, Robert Barnwell, 1, 598
Rhett, Robert Barnwell, Jr., 1, 11
Rhode Island, 145, 150, 153, 274, 379, 451, 491, 493, 499, 566
Rhode Island, U.S.S., 600
Rhode Island 1st Regiment, 493
Rhode Island 2nd Regiment, 451, 491–94
Ribault, Jean, 598
Rice, 89, 95, 105, 319
Rice, Alexander H., 144
Rich Mountain, battle of, 447–48
Richardson, Israel B., 637
Richmond, La., 370, 372
Richmond, Va., 177, 258, 297–304, 327, 366, 401–2, 432, 447–49, 454, 471, 488, 496, 506–21, 531, 534, 537, 627, 631, 641–44, 678–80, 684–87
Richmond Dispatch, 447
Ricketts, James B., 459, 462–63, 521, 529
Riddle, William, 577
Ringgold, Samuel, 496
Rio Grande, 536–37
Ripley, Roswell S., 264, 268, 600
Rives, Tim, 299
Rives, William C., 509
Robertson, Judge, 298
Robertson, Mrs. George, 497
Rochester, N.Y., 57, 272
Rodgers, John, 599
Rolla, Mo., 554, 562
Rome, ancient, 54, 405
Romney, Va. (now W.Va.), 582
Ros, Baron de (Henry Fitzgerald), 420
Rose, Hugh, 513
Ross, John, 412–14; message to Cherokee National Council, 571–75

Ruffin, Edmund, 261, 268, 423, 512
Ruggles, Samuel B., 45, 271
Rum, 95
Rupert, Prince, 291
Rusk, Thomas J., 94
Russell, John, 409, 645, 647–48, 652
Russell, Robert M., 595
Russell, William Howard, 511, 521; *My Diary North and South*, 281–93, 464–90
Russia, 69, 249, 327
Rutherfurd, Lewis, 271
Rutledge, Emily, 497

Sabine, U.S.S., 429
St. Augustine, Fla., 598
St. Louis, Mo., 48, 65, 187, 310, 358–60, 543, 561, 640, 681
Salt River raid, 444–46
San Francisco (steamer), 380
San Jacinto, U.S.S., 600, 633, 645–46
Sandford, Charles W., 377
Sanford, Henry S., 5
Santo Domingo, 250
Sardinia, 59
Sargent, Horace Binney, 673
Saturday Review, 415
Savannah, Ga., 178–79, 221, 294, 404–5, 495–96, 537, 599, 602, 649, 668, 679
Savannah River, 224
Savannah Republican, 221
Schenck, R. C., 526–27
Schmidt, William H., 579
Schurz, Carl, 353
Scotland, 229. *See also* Britain
Scott, John, 455–56, 462
Scott, Robert W., 593
Scott, Winfield, 8, 147, 187, 237, 243, 245–46, 250, 339–40, 361–63, 367, 377, 429, 482, 487, 496, 504, 517, 524–25, 540–42, 563, 581–82, 584, 668
Secession, 8–10, 14, 22, 25, 27–28, 31–34, 43–44, 46, 51, 56, 58–60, 70–71, 73, 85, 112, 125–26, 138, 144, 146, 156–57, 164, 186, 200, 207, 243–44, 261, 281–82, 287, 333, 348, 352, 358–61, 366, 374, 377, 417–18, 420–22, 466, 469–70, 472, 493, 503, 521, 528, 640; Alabama, 11–13, 48, 64, 66, 107, 165, 175–76, 183, 193, 201, 427; Arkansas, 64, 66, 193, 232, 297; and

Constitution, 35–36, 54–55, 67, 78, 108, 120–24, 217, 436–39, 441–42; Davis on, 194–95, 320, 327, 633; Florida, 64, 66, 107, 165, 183, 193, 201, 427; Georgia, 11–13, 48, 64, 66, 98–108, 165, 183, 193, 201, 427; and Lincoln, 1, 4, 99, 107, 208, 213, 215, 217, 234–35, 297, 321–22, 427–28, 432–33, 435–36, 438–39, 442; Louisiana, 13, 63–66, 165, 183, 193, 201, 427; Mississippi, 11–12, 64, 66, 107, 165, 183–85, 187, 193–95, 201, 427; North Carolina, 107, 188, 193, 232, 297; sentiment in Kentucky, 107, 165, 188, 232, 563, 569; sentiment in Maryland, 107, 181, 188, 303, 564, 569, 667–68; sentiment in Missouri, 107, 188, 232, 569, 667; South Carolina, 1–4, 11–13, 43, 48–50, 52–54, 64, 66–67, 74, 107, 113, 121–22, 147, 149–55, 193–94, 201, 223, 252, 427, 500; Tennessee, 49, 107, 188, 193, 232, 297, 522; Texas, 37, 50, 64, 66, 183, 193, 201, 431; and U.S. Congress, 80–81, 111; Virginia, 107, 180–81, 188, 193, 199, 201, 232, 297–304, 311, 327, 362, 401–3, 416, 423, 432, 633

Secession Convention (Alabama), 165, 183
Secession Convention (Florida), 165
Secession Convention (Georgia), 14, 19–20, 25, 27, 29, 98, 107–8, 165, 183, 221
Secession Convention (Louisiana), 63–66, 165
Secession Convention (Mississippi), 11, 165, 183–85, 194
Secession Convention (Missouri), 559
Secession Convention (South Carolina), 1–4, 11, 107, 149–55, 165, 183
Secession Convention (Tennessee), 49
Secession Convention (Texas), 37, 183
Secession Convention (Virginia), 297–302, 401, 423, 432
Sectionalism, 49, 114, 117, 154–55, 171
Seddon, James A., 298, 509, 511
Sedgwick, John, 637
Seeger, John G., 551
Selden, John, 395
Seminoles, 157, 412
Semple, Mrs., 303
Senate, C.S., 14, 224
Senate, U.S., 8, 27, 30, 41, 45, 67, 70, 81–83, 99, 114–15, 121, 128–29, 132, 137, 140–41, 143, 187, 193–98, 234, 248, 252, 289, 318, 427, 522, 538, 568, 581, 653, 655. *See also* Congress, U.S.
Seneca, U.S.S., 596, 599
Seward, William H., 6, 41–42, 128, 146, 171, 180, 186, 210, 240, 243–51, 254, 271, 297, 321–22, 380, 410–11, 504, 540, 583, 585, 651–52, 672–73, 683–84, 688–89, 691
Seymour, Mrs. Truman, 162
Seymour, Truman, 162, 262, 265
Shaaff, Arthur, 679
Shenandoah Valley, 454, 464
Sherman, Ellen Ewing, 65, 358, 526
Sherman, John, 63, 358
Sherman, Thomas W., 596–98, 600–1
Sherman, William T., 63–66, 358–60, 378, 459, 495–96, 526–30
Sherman, Willie, 358–59
Ship Island, 668, 690
Shivers, Major, 687
Shubrick, William B., 188
Sicily, 59
Sidney, Algernon, 85
Sigel, Franz, 543, 552, 559
Silver Spring, Md., 186
Simms, William E., 94
Simons, Dr., 161
Simons, James W., 266
Simons, Mrs., 162
Sinclair, Dan, 162
Singleton, Emma, 517
Singleton, James W., 350
Singleton, Mary, 517
Slave labor, 88–89, 95, 126, 234, 317
Slave revolts, 68–69, 144, 153, 169–70, 172, 184, 197, 253, 335, 348, 607
Slave trade, 43, 46, 60, 62, 100, 110, 131, 140, 142, 153, 156, 170, 216, 316, 418, 664
Slaveholders, 85–93, 95, 101, 105–6, 169, 172, 333–35
Slavery, 1–2, 8, 22, 25, 27, 31, 34, 40, 57, 64, 69, 98, 103–5, 113, 115, 125, 149, 157, 165, 231, 233–34, 248–50, 262, 270, 273, 276, 292, 304, 310, 327, 333–35, 350, 354, 421–22, 425, 431, 465–66,

INDEX   811

500, 522–23, 565–67, 639–40, 675–77; benefits of, 85–97; and Britain, 23, 94, 173, 197; and Congress, 16, 54, 58, 62, 68, 70–72, 107, 129, 143, 153, 168–71, 209, 211, 215, 316–18; and Constitution, 16–17, 39, 43, 58, 62, 70–72, 99–100, 110, 152, 167–69, 171, 173–75, 197, 215–16, 226, 317–19; as "cornerstone" of Confederacy, 221, 226–29, 424; in District of Columbia, 62, 100, 110, 129, 140; and Lincoln, 58–62, 101, 109–10, 164, 207–11, 215–17, 563, 568, 588, 603–4, 653, 664, 666; and representation, 54–55, 131, 153, 197; in territories, 16, 43, 46, 57–59, 62, 68, 70, 83–84, 107, 110, 114, 128–29, 133–35, 137, 139–40, 145, 152, 168, 170, 180, 184, 207, 209, 215–16

Slaves: and Christianity, 24, 229; colonization of, 653, 666; confiscation of, 364–68, 538–39, 563, 568, 653, 665, 667, 674; emancipation of, 562–63, 568–70, 603, 652–53; fugitive, 16–17, 24, 26, 29, 45, 59, 61, 68, 72, 102, 107, 130–31, 141–42, 152–54, 168–69, 196, 211–12, 216–17, 316–17, 353, 361–68; owned by Indians, 412; population of, 86–87, 96, 101, 172–73, 318–19; property in, 16–18, 52, 54, 58, 70–71, 83, 87–88, 93, 99, 101, 106, 153–54, 167–70, 183–85, 311, 316–18, 348, 362, 364, 367, 404; in *Uncle Tom's Cabin*, 46–47; wartime lives of, 259, 265, 282, 293, 370–71, 373, 469–70, 492, 510, 512, 519, 596–98, 603–4. *See also* Negroes

Slidell, John, 187, 193, 600, 633, 645–47, 651
Slocum, Henry W., 638
Small, William P., 308
Smith, Adam, 228
Smith, Bayard, 588
Smith, Captain, 494
Smith, Charles, 378, 381
Smith, Gerrit, 57
Smith, Kirby, 508, 515
Smith, Richard, 377
Smith, S. A., 63–66
Smith, William F., 636–38
Smither, James L., 37

Snead, Thomas L.: *Fight for Missouri*, 555, 558
Snowden, Amy, 497
Snyder, George, 161
Socialism, 88, 92
Solferino, battle of, 281
Soulé, Pierre, 94
South America, 69, 94
South Carolina, 44, 78–79, 86, 89–90, 100, 110, 178, 181, 243, 284, 287, 294, 311, 364, 418, 439, 492, 495, 507, 510, 516–19, 668, 672, 678; capture of Port Royal Sound, 596–602; nullification crisis (1833), 26, 50, 55–56, 74, 111, 121–22; secessionism in, 1–4, 11–13, 43, 48–50, 52–54, 64, 66–67, 74, 107, 113, 121–22, 147, 149–55, 193–94, 201, 223, 252, 427, 500; seizure of Fort Sumter, 156–64, 187, 189–92, 239–41, 261–68, 323–24, 430
South Carolina 6th Regiment, 517
South Carolina 7th Regiment, 254
Southern Monitor, 297
Soyer, Alexis, 489
Spain, 50, 94, 229, 249, 409, 598, 633
Spectator (London), 652
Spiritualism, 92
Spofford, Joseph L., 648
Springfield, Ill., 5–7, 109, 147, 201, 312, 347, 350
Springfield, Mo., 545, 554, 612, 628
Stahel, Julius H., 638
Stanard, Martha, 515
Stanton, Edwin M., 189, 244, 583, 691, 693–94
Star of the West (military transport), 189–91
Stark, Mary, 516–20
State constitutions, 75, 84, 437
State Department, C.S., 327
State Department, U.S., 146, 247, 649–50, 665
State governors, 16, 18
State laws, 77–79, 84, 107–8, 110, 131–32, 142, 153, 156, 168, 317
State legislature (Alabama), 175
State legislature (Georgia), 14, 107, 605, 621–22
State legislature (Illinois), 347
State legislature (Kentucky), 165, 569, 655
State legislature (Louisiana), 63

State legislature (Mississippi), 11
State legislature (Missouri), 188
State legislature (Rhode Island), 451
State legislature (South Carolina), 1, 11, 79
State legislature (Tennessee), 49
State legislature (Texas), 37
State legislature (Vermont), 45, 108
State legislature (Virginia), 83, 319, 432
State legislatures, 16, 18, 71–72, 76, 82–83, 314, 317, 319
States' rights, 4, 9–10, 29, 34–36, 42, 45, 50–51, 77, 99–100, 152, 174, 211, 276, 302, 315, 319–20, 439
Stephens, Alexander H., 14, 94, 327, 424, 612, 627; "Corner-Stone" speech, 221–36
Stewart, Mr., 678
Stewart, R. A., 592
Stockwell, Dennis, 342
Stone, Charles P., 581
Stone, Kate, 369–75, 443
Stone, William, 369, 372–74
Stone family, 369–75, 443
Stoneham, Mass., 306
Stoneman, George, 530
Story, Joseph: *Commentaries on the Constitution of the United States*, 397
Stowe, Harriet Beecher: *Uncle Tom's Cabin*, 46
Strasburg, Va., 505
Stringham, Silas, 237, 245
Strong, Charles, 272
Strong, Ellen Ruggles, 269–70, 272–73
Strong, George Templeton, 43–47, 269–74, 376–82
Strong, John Ruggles, 270
Stuart, J.E.B., 460, 462
Sudley, Va., 457
Suffolk, Va., 687
Sugar, 89, 94–95, 319
Sumner, Charles, 46, 144–46, 291–92, 520
Sumner, Edwin V., 638
Sumter, C.S.S., 329
Supreme Court, U.S., 40, 43, 70–72, 84, 99, 129, 170, 175, 216, 386, 388, 397, 658–60, 662
Susquehanna, U.S.S., 599
Susquehanna River, 302

Sweeny, Thomas W., 544, 559–60

Tahlequah, Indian Territory, 573
Tampico, Mexico, 537
Taney, Roger B., 404; opinion in *Ex parte Merryman*, 386–400
Tappahannock, Va., 687
Tariffs, 36, 91, 96, 168, 223
Taxation, 101–3, 105–6, 123, 153, 230, 234–35, 328, 418, 630
Taylor, John, 55
Taylor, Sally, 518
Tenant farmers, 103–4
Tennessee, 14, 52, 86, 89–90, 325, 439, 505, 534–35, 655; possible loyalty to Union, 51, 188, 431, 522, 668; secessionism in, 49, 107, 188, 193, 232, 297, 522
Tennessee 4th Regiment, 593
Territorial legislature (Colorado Territory), 665
Territorial legislature (Kansas Territory), 71
Territorial legislatures, 68, 71
Territories: for colonization of Negroes, 666; Confederate, 574, 628; establishment of, 135–36, 663–66; new states from, 99–100, 134–35, 175, 180, 184, 235; slavery in, 16, 43, 46, 57–59, 62, 68, 83–84, 107, 110, 114, 128–29, 133–35, 137, 139–40, 145, 152, 168, 170, 180, 184, 207, 209, 215–16
Texas, 88–89, 115, 124, 135, 169, 184, 199, 234, 240, 254, 262, 289, 328, 436–38, 551, 565, 659, 663; possible loyalty to Union, 37–42, 536; secessionism in, 37, 50, 64, 66, 183, 193, 201, 431
Texas 1st Regiment, 509
Thayer, Eli, 144
Thermopylae, battle of, 258
Thompson, Jacob, 67, 188
Thompson, John Means, 517
Thompson, Waddy, 517
Times (London), 281, 408–9, 464, 521, 645–46, 650, 652
Tobacco, 89, 95, 319
Toombs, Robert, 14, 128, 193
Totten, James, 548, 555, 559
Totten, Joseph G., 237, 243
Toucey, Isaac, 417
Treasury, C.S., 225, 330, 630, 641

Treasury, U.S., 40, 50, 170, 656–57, 683
Treasury Department, C.S., 327–28
Treasury Department, U.S., 146, 188, 435, 657
Treaty of Paris (1783), 135, 150–51
Tremblet, Henry M., 578–79
Trenchard, Stephen D., 600
Trent (British steamer), 633, 645–46
Trent affair, 633, 645–52, 679
Trescot, William H., 255, 510, 520–21
Trinity Church (New York City), 270, 273
Trowbridge, William P., 380
Trumbull, Lyman, 582
Tucker, Elizabeth Dallas, 521
Tucker, Henry, 605–26
Turner, Nat, 566
Turner, Thomas, 360, 599
Tybee Island, 668
Tyler, Daniel, 526–27
Tyler, John, 300, 303

U.S. Bonds, 40, 188
U.S. Coast Survey, 380
U.S.–Mexican War, 126, 157, 199, 201, 310–12, 339, 348, 444, 496, 524, 561, 596
U.S. Military Academy (West Point), 63, 156, 199, 201, 310, 359, 377, 462, 466, 524, 658
U.S. Sanitary Commission, 376–77
U.S. 13th Regiment, 526, 530
Unadilla, U.S.S., 597
Unionism, 14, 45, 49, 52, 67, 193, 298, 358, 522, 563
University of Virginia, 458
Urbana, Va., 687
Utah Territory, 42

Van Buren, Martin, 24
Van Vliet, Stewart, 530, 587, 687
Van de Weyer, Jean-Sylvain, 649
VanderHorst, Arnoldus, 509
Vanderpoel, Aaron, 271
Venable, Charles S., 257, 510, 519
Vermont, 43–45, 108, 110, 145, 153
Vernon, Harwood, 674
Vesey, Denmark, 566
Vicksburg, Miss., 369–70, 372–73
Victoria, Queen, 408
Vienna, Va., 454, 684

Vinton, Francis, 271
Virginia, 14, 52, 83, 88–89, 129, 135, 140, 150, 152–53, 169–70, 191–92, 200, 257, 319, 325, 329, 356, 361, 364–69, 376–82, 404–5, 418–20, 439, 447–50, 504–5, 511–12, 515–18, 524, 534–37, 540, 565, 587, 595, 631, 636–37, 642–43, 663, 674, 678, 683–88; battle of Ball's Bluff, 576–81; battle of Bull Run, 454–96, 526–30; possible loyalty to Union, 43, 49, 51, 188, 273, 416, 431, 500, 668; secessionism in, 107, 180–81, 188, 193, 199, 201, 232, 297–304, 311, 327, 362, 401–3, 416, 423, 432, 633
Virginia Resolves (1798), 319
Virginia 1st Regiment, 462
Virginia 2nd Regiment, 454
Virginia 30th Regiment, 454
Visart (Confederate soldier), 557
Vogdes, Israel, 246
Voting, 57, 92, 100, 154, 171–72

Wabash, U.S.S., 595
Wade, Benjamin F., 128, 582; remarks in Senate, 114–27
Wadsworth, James, 511, 638
Wages, 90–91, 103–5
Walker, David, 559
Walker, Jimmy, 595
Wall Street, 43–44
War Department, C.S., 329, 629
War Department, U.S., 339, 379, 428, 435, 504, 585, 655, 657–58, 682, 693
War of 1812, 339, 565–66, 642, 646
Ward, Horatio, 649
Ward, James H., 242–43, 245
Ware, E. F.: *The Lyon Campaign in Missouri*, 543–53
Warre, Fredrick R., 466, 472–73, 478, 490
Warren County, Miss., 11
Washburn, Cadwallader C., 347
Washburn, Emory, 377
Washburne, Elihu B., 147
Washington, D.C., 3, 5, 8, 45, 67, 109–10, 112–13, 164, 180, 186, 193, 199, 207–8, 210, 220, 243, 245, 289, 293, 295–97, 303–5, 307, 321–22, 339, 350, 376–79, 381, 386–87, 415, 417, 422–23, 451, 454, 461, 464–65, 473, 478–83, 485–89, 494, 498, 500–3, 505, 509,

514, 521, 524, 526, 537, 541, 563, 568, 576, 579, 601–2, 633, 636, 648–49, 651, 693; as military target, 143–44, 181, 258, 271, 301, 306, 420, 496, 504, 508, 522, 530, 535, 540, 564, 569, 587, 684. *See also* District of Columbia
Washington, George, 20–22, 24, 68, 72, 92, 127, 136, 178, 199–200, 279, 302, 402, 440–41
Washington, George Marshall, 380
Washington Territory, 175
Waterloo, battle of, 281, 515–16
Watie, Stand, 571
Waties, John, 510
Watkins, H. M., 37
Watkins, Robert R., 557
Weaver, Omer R., 556–58
Webb, William A., 272
Webster, Daniel, 121, 144
Weed, Thurlow, 111
Welles, Gideon, 242–47, 583, 585, 682
Wellington, Duke of (Arthur Wellesley), 145, 516
Wesley (slave), 373
Wesselhoeft, Reinhold, 579
West, John, 518
West Indies, 23, 94, 173, 643, 646
Westchester County, N.Y., 46
Wheeling, Va. (now W.Va.), 582
Whig Party, 14, 43, 114, 128, 244, 275, 298–99
White, Maunsel, 94
White Sulphur Springs, Va. (now W.Va.), 515
White supremacy, 172, 174, 197, 221, 226–28, 318
Whiting, William H. C., 283–84, 289–92
Whitman, Sarah Helen, 354
Whitman, Walt: *Drum-Taps*, 336; "First O Songs for a Prelude," 336–38; *Memoranda during the War*, 500; *Specimen Days*, 500–3
Wide-Awakes, 27, 304
Wigfall, Charlotte, 252–53, 259, 507–9, 511, 520
Wigfall, Louis T., 115, 124, 253–54, 260, 265–66, 289–92, 507, 509, 520
Wilder, H. H., 307
Wilderness, 318
Wilkes, Charles, 633, 645–47, 649–51, 679

Willard's Hotel (Washington), 353, 376–77, 489, 502–3
Willcox, O. B., 462–63
William III, 394
Williams, F. S., 557
Williams, Kate, 518
Williams (Union soldier), 673
Willis, Nathaniel Parker, 379
Wilson, Charles, 647
Wilson, Henry, 506
Wilson (Confederate soldier), 595
Wilson's Creek, battle of, 543–61
Winchester, Va., 518
Winder, John H., 517
Wisconsin, 43–44, 72, 145, 153, 659
Wise, Charlotte, 379–80
Wise, Henry A. (U.S. Navy), 379–81
Wise, Henry A. (Virginia secessionist), 298, 300–1, 303–4; speech at Richmond, 401–3
Wise, O. Jennings, 298
Wiseman, Nicholas, 647
Withers, Thomas Jefferson, 255
Withers, Tom, 514
Witherspoon, Mary, 519
Women, 93, 355–56, 449–50, 496–97, 507, 509
Wood, Fernando, 272
Woodard (Confederate soldier), 557
Woodhull, Maxwell, 600
Woodruff, W. E.: *With the Light Guns in '61–'65*, 554–60
Wounded soldiers, 267–68, 458, 461–63, 497, 514, 528–29, 579, 592–95

Yancey, William Lowndes, 94, 158
Yandell, Lunsford P., 592
Yandell, Lunsford, Jr., 592–95
Yates, Richard, 312, 347
York River, 361, 685–87, 689
Young, A. S., 308–9
Young, W. Gourdin, 265
Young Men's Christian Association, 497, 674
Yulee, David, 193

Zouaves (Brooklyn), 377
Zouaves (New Orleans), 372, 496
Zouaves (New York C...), 493, 496

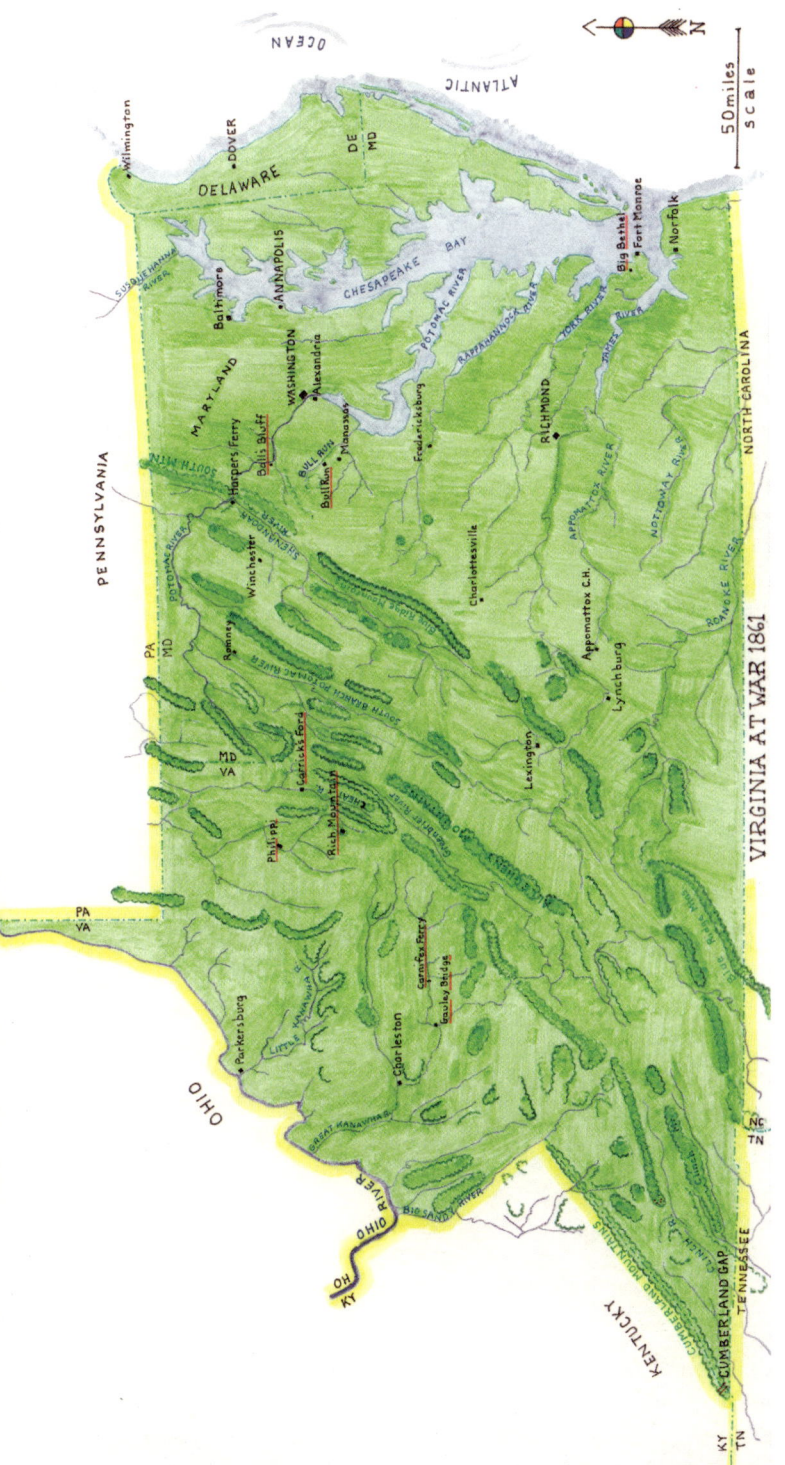